Lecture Notes in Artificial Intelligence 4114

Edited by J. G. Carbonell and J. Siekmann

Subseries of Lecture Notes in Computer Science

De-Shuang Huang
Kang Li
George William Irwin (Eds.)

Computational Intelligence

International Conference on
Intelligent Computing, ICIC 2006
Kunming, China, August 16-19, 2006
Proceedings, Part II

Springer

Series Editors

Jaime G. Carbonell, Carnegie Mellon University, Pittsburgh, PA, USA
Jörg Siekmann, University of Saarland, Saarbrücken, Germany

Volume Editors

De-Shuang Huang
Chinese Academy of Sciences
Institute of Intelligent Machines
Hefei, Anhui, China
E-mail: dshuang@iim.ac.cn

Kang Li
George William Irwin
Queen's University
Belfast, UK
E-mail: {K.Li,G.Irwin}@qub.ac.uk

Library of Congress Control Number: 2006930737

CR Subject Classification (1998): I.2.3, I.2, F.4.1, F.1, I.5, F.2, G.2, I.4

LNCS Sublibrary: SL 7 – Artificial Intelligence

ISSN 0302-9743
ISBN-10 3-540-37274-1 Springer Berlin Heidelberg New York
ISBN-13 978-3-540-37274-5 Springer Berlin Heidelberg New York

Springer is a part of Springer Science+Business Media

springer.com

Printed in Germany

Typesetting: Camera-ready by author, data conversion by Scientific Publishing Services, Chennai, India
Printed on acid-free paper SPIN: 11816171 06/3142 5 4 3 2 1 0

Preface

The International Conference on Intelligent Computing (ICIC) was formed to provide an annual forum dedicated to the emerging and challenging topics in artificial intelligence, machine learning, bioinformatics, and computational biology, etc. It aims to bring together researchers and practitioners from both academia and industry to share ideas, problems and solutions related to the multifaceted aspects of intelligent computing.

ICIC 2006 held in Kunming, Yunnan, China, August 16-19, 2006, was the second International Conference on Intelligent Computing, built upon the success of ICIC 2005 held in Hefei, China, 2005.

This year, the conference concentrated mainly on the theories and methodologies as well as the emerging applications of intelligent computing. It intended to unify the contemporary intelligent computing techniques within an integral framework that highlights the trends in advanced computational intelligence and bridges theoretical research with applications. In particular, bio-inspired computing emerged as having a key role in pursuing for novel technology in recent years. The resulting techniques vitalize life science engineering and daily life applications. In light of this trend, the theme for this conference was **"Emerging Intelligent Computing Technology and Applications"**. Papers related to this theme were especially solicited, including theories, methodologies, and applications in science and technology.

ICIC 2006 received over 3000 submissions from 36 countries and regions. All papers went through a rigorous peer review procedure and each paper received at least three review reports. Based on the review reports, the Program Committee finally selected 703 high-quality papers for presentation at ICIC 2006. These papers cover 29 topics and 16 special sessions, and are included in five volumes of proceedings published by Springer, including one volume of *Lecture Notes in Computer Science* (LNCS), one volume of *Lecture Notes in Artificial Intelligence* (LNAI), one volume of *Lecture Notes in Bioinformatics* (LNBI), and two volumes of *Lecture Notes in Control and Information Sciences* (LNCIS).

This volume of *Lecture Notes in Artificial Intelligence* (LNAI) includes 165 papers covering 7 relevant topics and 9 special session topics.

The organizers of ICIC 2006, including Yunan University, the Institute of Intelligent Machines of the Chinese Academy of Science, and Queen's University Belfast, have made enormous effort to ensure the success of ICIC 2006. We hereby would like to thank the members of the ICIC 2006 Advisory Committee for their guidance and advice, the members of the Program Committee and the referees for their collective effort in reviewing and soliciting the papers, and the members of the Publication Committee for their significant editorial work. We would like to thank Alfred Hofmann, executive editor from Springer, for his frank and helpful advice and guidance throughout and for his support in publishing the proceedings in the Lecture Notes series. In particular, we would like to thank all the authors for contributing their papers. Without the high-quality submissions from the authors, the success of the conference would not have been possible. Finally, we are especially grateful to the

IEEE Computational Intelligence Society, The International Neural Network Society and the National Science Foundation of China for the their sponsorship.

June 2006

De-Shuang Huang
Institute of Intelligent Machines, Chinese Academy of Sciences, China
Kang Li
Queen's University Belfast, UK
George William Irwin
Queen's University Belfast, UK

ICIC 2006 Organization

General Chairs:

De-Shuang Huang, China
Song Wu, China
George W. Irwin, UK

International Advisory Committee

Aike Guo, China
Alfred Hofmann, Germany
DeLiang Wang, USA
Erke Mao, China
Fuchu He, China
George W. Irwin, UK
Guangjun Yang, China
Guanrong Chen, Hong Kong
Guoliang Chen, China
Harold Szu, USA
John L. Casti, USA
Marios M. Polycarpou, USA
Mengchu Zhou, USA
Michael R. Lyu, Hong Kong
MuDer Jeng, Taiwan
Nanning Zheng, China
Okyay Knynak, Turkey
Paul Werbos, USA
Qingshi Zhu, China
Ruwei Dai, China
Sam Shuzhi GE, Singapore
Sheng Zhang, China
Shoujue Wang, China
Songde Ma, China
Stephen Thompson, UK
Tom Heskes, Netherlands
Xiangfan He, China
Xingui He, China
Xueren Wang, China
Yanda Li, China
Yixin Zhong, China
Youshou Wu, China
Yuanyan Tang, Hong Kong
Yunyu Shi, China
Zheng Bao, China

Program Committee Chairs:

Kang Li, UK
Prashan Premaratne, Australia

Steering Committee Chairs:

Sheng Chen, UK
Xiaoyi Jiang, Germany
Xiao-Ping Zhang, Canada

Organizing Committee Chairs:

Yongkun Li, China
Hanchun Yang, China
Guanghua Hu, China

Special Session Chair:

Wen Yu, Mexico

Tutorial Chair:

Sudharman K. Jayaweera, USA

Publication Chair: Xiaoou Li, Mexico

International Liasion Chair: C. De Silva, Liyanage, New Zealand

Publicity Chairs: Simon X.Yang, Canada
Jun Zhang, China

Exhibition Chair: Cheng Peng, China

Program Committee

Aili Han, China
Arit Thammano, Thailand
Baogang Hu, China
Bin Luo, China
Bin Zhu, China
Bing Wang, China
Bo Yan, USA
Byoung-Tak Zhang, Korea
Caoan Wang, Canada
Chao Hai Zhang, Japan
Chao-Xue Wang, China
Cheng-Xiang Wang, UK
Cheol-Hong Moon, Korea
Chi-Cheng Cheng, Taiwan
Clement Leung, Australia
Daniel Coca, UK
Daqi Zhu, China
David Stirling, Australia
Dechang Chen, USA
Derong Liu, USA
Dewen Hu, China
Dianhui Wang, Australia
Dimitri Androutsos, Canada
Donald C. Wunsch, USA
Dong Chun Lee, Korea
Du-Wu Cui, China
Fengling Han, Australia
Fuchun Sun, China
Girijesh Prasad, UK
Guang-Bin Huang, Singapore
Guangrong Ji, China
Hairong Qi, USA
Hong Qiao, China
Hong Wang, China
Hongtao Lu, China
Hongyong Zhao, China
Huaguang Zhang, China
Hui Wang, China
Jiangtao Xi, Australia
Jianguo Zhu, Australia
Jianhua Xu, China
Jiankun Hu, Australia
Jian-Xun Peng, UK
Jiatao Song, China
Jie Tian, China
Jie Yang, China
Jin Li, UK
Jin Wu, UK
Jinde Cao, China
Jinwen Ma, China
Jochen Till, Germany
John Q. Gan, UK
Ju Liu, China
K. R. McMenemy, UK
Key-Sun Choi, Korea
Liangmin Li, UK
Luigi Piroddi, Italy
Maolin Tang, Australia
Marko Hočevar, Slovenia
Mehdi Shafiei, Canada
Mei-Ching Chen, Taiwan
Mian Muhammad Awais, Pakistan
Michael Granitzer, Austria
Michael J.Watts, New Zealand
Michiharu Maeda, Japan
Minrui Fei, China
Muhammad Jamil Anwas, Pakistan
Muhammad Khurram Khan, China
Naiqin Feng, China
Nuanwan Soonthornphisaj, Thailand
Paolo Lino, Italy
Peihua Li, China
Ping Guo, China
Qianchuan Zhao, China
Qiangfu Zhao, Japan
Qing Zhao, Canada
Roberto Tagliaferri, Italy
Rong-Chang Chen, Taiwan
RuiXiang Sun, China
Saeed Hashemi, Canada
Sanjay Sharma, UK
Seán McLoone, Ireland
Seong G. Kong, USA
Shaoning Pang, New Zealand
Shaoyuan Li, China
Shuang-Hua Yang, UK
Shunren Xia, China
Stefanie Lindstaedt, Austria
Sylvia Encheva, Norway
Tai-hoon Kim, Korea

Reviewers

Francesco Pappalardo, Chuleerat Charasskulchai, Siyao Fu, Wenpeng Ding, Fuzhen Huang, Amal Punchihewa, Geoffrey Macintyre, Xue Feng He, Gang Leng, Lijuan Gao, Ray Gao, Andrey Gaynulin, Gabriella Dellino, D.W. Ggenetic, Geoffrey Wang, YuRong Ge, Guohui He, Gwang Hyun Kim, Gianluca Cena, Giancarlo Raiconi, Ashutosh Goyal, Guan Luo, Guido Maione, Guido Maione, Grigorios Dimitriadis, Haijing Wang, Kayhan Gulez, Tiantai Guo, Chun-Hung Hsieh, Xuan Guo, Yuantao Gu, Huanhuan Chen, Hongwei Zhang, Jurgen Hahn, Qing Han, Aili Han, Dianfei Han, Fei Hao, Qing-Hua Ling, Hang-kon Kim, Han-Lin He, Yunjun Han, Li Zhang, Hathai Tanta-ngai, Hang-Bong Kang, Hsin-Chang Yang, Hongtao Du, Hazem Elbakry, Hao Mei, Zhao L, Yang Yun, Michael Hild, Heajo Kang, Hongjie Xing, Hailli Wang, Hoh In, Peng Bai, Hong-Ming Wang, Hongxing Bai, Hongyu Liu, Weiyan Hou, Huaping Liu, H.Q. Wang, Hyungsuck Cho, Hsun-Li Chang, Hua Zhang, Xia Huang, Hui Chen, Huiqing Liu, Heeun Park, Hong-Wei Ji, Haixian Wang, Hoyeal Kwon, H.Y. Shen, Jonghyuk Park, Turgay Ibrikci, Mary Martin, Pei-Chann Chang, Shouyi Yang, Xiaomin Mu, Melanie Ashley, Ismail Altas, Muhammad Usman Ilyas, Indrani Kar, Jinghui Zhong, Ian Mack, Il-Young Moon, J.X. Peng , Jochen Till, Jian Wang, Quan Xue, James Govindhasamy, José Andrés Moreno Pérez, Jorge Tavares, S. K. Jayaweera, Su Jay, Jeanne Chen, Jim Harkin, Yongji Jia, Li Jia, Zhao-Hui Jiang, Gangyi Jiang, Zhenran Jiang, Jianjun Ran, Jiankun Hu, Qing-Shan Jia, Hong Guo, Jin Liu, Jinling Liang, Jin Wu, Jing Jie, Jinkyung Ryeu, Jing Liu, Jiming Chen, Jiann-Ming Wu, James Niblock, Jianguo Zhu, Joel Pitt, Joe Zhu, John Thompson, Mingguang Shi, Joaquin Peralta, Si Bao Chen, Tinglong Pan, Juan Ramón González González, JingRu Zhang, Jianliang Tang, Joaquin Torres, Junaid Akhtar, Ratthachat Chatpatanasiri, Junpeng Yuan, Jun Zhang, Jianyong Sun, Junying Gan, Jyh-Tyng Yau, Junying Zhang, Jiayin Zhou, Karen Rosemary McMenemy, Kai Yu, Akimoto Kamiya, Xin Kang, Ya-Li Ji, Guo-Shiang Lin, Muhammad Khurram, Kevin Curran, Karl Neuhold, Kyongnam Jeon, Kunikazu Kobayashi, Nagahisa Kogawa, Fanwei Kong, Kyu-Sik Park, Lily D. Li, Lara Giordano, Laxmidhar Behera, Luca Cernuzzi, Luis Almeida, Agostino Lecci, Yan Zuo, Lei Li, Alberto Leva, Feng Liang, Bin Li, Jinmei Liao, Liang Tang, Bo Lee, Chuandong Li, Lidija Janezic, Jian Li, Jiang-Hai Li, Jianxun Li, Limei Song, Ping Li, Jie Liu, Fei Liu, Jianfeng Liu, Jianwei Liu, Jihong Liu, Lin Liu, Manxi Liu, Yi Liu, Xiaoou Li, Zhu Li, Kun-hong Liu, Li Min Cui, Lidan Miao, Long Cheng , Huaizhong Zhang, Marco Lovera, Liam Maguire, Liping Liu, Liping Zhang, Feng Lu, Luo Xiaobin, Xin-ping Xie, Wanlong Li, Liwei Yang, Xinrui Liu, Xiao Wei Li, Ying Li, Yongquan Liang, Yang Bai, Margherita Bresco, Mingxing Hu, Ming Li, Runnian Ma, Meta-Montero Manrique, Zheng Gao, Mingyi Mao, Mario Vigliar, Marios Savvides, Masahiro Takatsuka, Matevz Dular, Mathias Lux, Mutlu Avci, Zhifeng Hao, Zhifeng Hao, Ming-Bin Li, Tao Mei, Carlo Meloni, Gennaro Miele, Mike Watts, Ming Yang, Jia Ma, Myong K. Jeong, Michael Watts, Markus Koch, Markus Koch, Mario Koeppen, Mark Kröll, Hui Wang, Haigeng Luo, Malrey Lee, Tiedong Ma, Mingqiang Yang, Yang Ming, Rick Chang, Nihat Adar, Natalie Schellenberg, Naveed Iqbal, Nur Bekiroglu, Jinsong Hu, Nesan Aluha, Nesan K Aluha, Natascha Esau, Yanhong Luo, N.H. Siddique, Rui Nian, Kai Nickel, Nihat Adar, Ben Niu, Yifeng Niu, Nizar Tayem, Nanlin Jin, Hong-Wei Ji, Dongjun Yu, Norton Abrew, Ronghua Yao, Marco Moreno-Armendariz, Osman Kaan Erol, Oh Kyu Kwon, Ahmet Onat, Pawel Herman,

Peter Hung, Ping Sun, Parag Kulkarni, Patrick Connally, Paul Gillard, Yehu Shen, Paul Conilione, Pi-Chung Wang, Panfeng Huang, Peter Hung, Massimo Pica Ciamarra, Ping Fang, Pingkang Li, Peiming Bao, Pedro Melo-Pinto, Maria Prandini, Serguei Primak, Peter Scheir, Shaoning Pang, Qian Chen, Qinghao Rong, QingXiang Wu, Quanbing Zhang, Qifu Fan, Qian Liu, Qinglai Wei, Shiqun Yin, Jianlong Qiu, Qingshan Liu, Quang Ha, SangWoon Lee , Huaijing Qu, Quanxiong Zhou , Qingxian Gong, Qingyuan He, M.K.M. Rahman, Fengyuan Ren, Guang Ren, Qingsheng Ren, Wei Zhang, Rasoul Milasi, Rasoul Milasi, Roberto Amato, Roberto Marmo, P. Chen, Roderick Bloem, Hai-Jun Rong, Ron Von Schyndel, Robin Ferguson, Runhe Huang, Rui Zhang, Robin Ferguson, Simon Johnston, Sina Rezvani, Siang Yew Chong, Cristiano Cucco, Dar-Ying Jan, Sonya Coleman, Samuel Rodman, Sancho Salcedo-Sanz, Sangyiel Baik, Sangmin Lee, Savitri Bevinakoppa, Chengyi Sun, Hua Li, Seamus McLoone, Sean McLoone, Shafayat Abrar, Aamir Shahzad, Shangmin Luan, Xiaowei Shao, Shen Yanxia, Zhen Shen, Seung Ho Hong, Hayaru Shouno, Shujuan Li, Si Eng Ling, Anonymous, Shiliang Guo, Guiyu Feng, Serafin Martinez Jaramillo, Sangwoo Moon, Xuefeng Liu, Yinglei Song, Songul Albayrak, Shwu-Ping Guo, Chunyan Zhang, Sheng Chen, Qiankun Song, Seok-soo Kim, Antonino Staiano, Steven Su, Sitao Wu, Lei Huang, Feng Su, Jie Su, Sukree Sinthupinyo, Sulan Zhai, Jin Sun, Limin Sun, Zengshun Zhao, Tao Sun, Wenhong Sun, Yonghui Sun, Supakpong Jinarat, Srinivas Rao Vadali, Sven Meyer zu Eissen, Xiaohong Su , Xinghua Sun, Zongying Shi, Tony Abou-Assaleh, Youngsu Park, Tai Yang, Yeongtak Jo, Chunming Tang, Jiufei Tang, Taizhe Tan, Tao Xu, Liang Tao, Xiaofeng Tao, Weidong Xu, Yueh-Tsun Chang, Fang Wang, Timo Lindemann, Tina Yu, Ting Hu, Tung-Kuan Liu, Tianming Liu, Tin Lay Nwe, Thomas Neidhart, Tony Chan, Toon Calders, Yi Wang, Thao Tran, Kyungjin Hong, Tariq Qureshi, Tung-Shou Chen, Tsz Kin Tsui, Tiantian Sun, Guoyu Tu, Tulay Yildirim, Dandan Zhang, Xuqing Tang, Yuangang Tang, Uday Chakraborty, Luciana Cariello, Vasily Aristarkhov, Jose-Luis Verdegay, Vijanth Sagayan Asirvadam, Vincent Lee, Markus Vincze, Duo Chen, Viktoria Pammer, Vedran Sabol, Wajeeha Akram, Cao Wang , Xutao Wang, Winlen Wang, Zhuang Znuang, Feng Wang, Haifeng Wang, Le Wang, Wang Linkun, Meng Wang, Rongbo Wang, Xin Wang, Xue Wang, Yan-Feng Wang, Yong Wang, Yongcai Wang, Yongquan Wang, Xu-Qin Li, Wenbin Liu, Wudai Liao, Weidong Zhou, Wei Li, Wei Zhang, Wei Liang, Weiwei Zhang, Wen Xu, Wenbing Yao, Xiaojun Ban, Fengge Wu, Weihua Mao, Shaoming Li, Qing Wu, Jie Wang, Wei Jiang, W Jiang, Wolfgang Kienreich, Linshan Wang, Wasif Naeem, Worasait Suwannik, Wolfgang Slany, Shijun Wang , Wooyoung Soh, Teng Wang, Takashi Kuremoto, Hanguang Wu, Licheng Wu, Xugang Wang, Xiaopei Wu, ZhengDao Zhang, Wei Yen, Yan-Guo Wang, Daoud Ait-Kadi, Xiaolin Hu, Xiaoli Li, Xun Wang, Xingqi Wang, Yong Feng, Xiucui Guan, Xiao-Dong Li, Xingfa Shen, Xuemin Hong, Xiaodi Huang, Xi Yang, Li Xia, Zhiyu Xiang, Xiaodong Li, Xiaoguang Zhao, Xiaoling Wang, Min Xiao, Xiaonan Wu, Xiaosi Zhan, Lei Xie, Guangming Xie, Xiuqing Wang, Xiwen Zhang, XueJun Li, Xiaojun Zong, Xie Linbo, Xiaolin Li, Xin Ma, Xiangqian Wu, Xiangrong Liu, Fei Xing, Xu Shuzheng, Xudong Xie, Bindang Xue, Xuelong Li, Zhanao Xue, Xun Kruger, Xunxian Wang, Xusheng Wei, Yi Xu, Xiaowei Yang, Xiaoying Wang, Xiaoyan Sun, YingLiang Ma, Yong Xu, Jongpil Yang, Lei Yang, Yang Tian, Zhi Yang, Yao Qian, Chao-bo Yan,

Shiren Ye, Yong Fang, Yanfei Wang, Young-Gun Jang, Yuehui Chen, Yuh-Jyh Hu, Yingsong Hu, Zuoyou Yin, Yipan Deng, Yugang Jiang, Jianwei Yang, Yujie Zheng, Ykung Chen, Yan-Kwang Chen, Ye Mei, Yongki Min, Yongqing Yang, Yong Wu, Yongzheng Zhang, Yiping Cheng, Yongpan Liu, Yanqiu Bi, Shengbao Yao, Yongsheng Ding, Haodi Yuan, Liang Yuan, Qingyuan He, Mei Yu, Yunchu Zhang, Yu Shi, Wenwu Yu, Yu Wen, Younghwan Lee, Ming Kong, Yingyue Xu, Xin Yuan, Xing Yang, Yan Zhou, Yizhong Wang, Zanchao Zhang, Ji Zhicheng, Zheng Du, Hai Ying Zhang, An Zhang, Qiang Zhang, Shanwen Zhang, Shanwen Zhang, Zhang Tao, Yue Zhao, R.J. Zhao, Li Zhao, Ming Zhao, Yan Zhao, Bojin Zheng, Haiyong Zheng, Hong Zheng, Zhengyou Wang, Zhongjie Zhu, Shangping Zhong, Xiaobo Zhou, Lijian Zhou, Lei Zhu, Lin Zhu, Weihua Zhu, Wumei Zhu, Zhihong Yao, Yumin Zhang, Ziyuan Huang, Chengqing Li, Z. Liu, Zaiqing Nie, Jiebin Zong, Zunshui Cheng, Zhongsheng Wang, Yin Zhixiang, Zhenyu He, Yisheng Zhong, Tso-Chung Lee, Takashi Kuremoto, Tao Jianhua, Liu Wenjue, Pan Cunhong, Li Shi, Xing Hongjie, Yang Shuanghong, Wang Yong, Zhang Hua, Ma Jianchun, Li Xiaocui, Peng Changping, Qi Rui, Guozheng Li, Hui Liu, Yongsheng Ding, Xiaojun Liu, Qinhua Huang.

Table of Contents

Fuzzy Systems

Fuzzy-Neuro-Evolutionary Hybrids

Supervised, Unsupervised and Reinforcement Learning

Intelligent Agent and Web Applications

Intelligent Fault Diagnosis

Natural Language Processing and Expert Systems

Intelligent Financial Engineering

Special Session on Intelligent Algorithms for Game Theory

Special Session on Intelligent Computing for Information Perception and Integration in Intelligent Control System

Special Session on Language Processing for Affective Computing

Special Session on Intelligent Computing for Software Reliability Engineering

Special Session on Credibility Theory with Applications

Special Session on Intelligent Computing for Agile Manufacturing Systems

Special Session on Networked Control Systems

Special Session on Intelligence Computation and Its Application

Special Session on Intelligent Ad Hoc Networks and Wireless Sensor Networks

A GA Optimization for FLC with Its Rule Base and Scaling Factors Adjustment

Pingkang Li and Xiuxia Du

Beijing Jiaotong University, Beijing, 100044, China
pkli@center.njtu.edu.cn

Abstract. This paper introduces a Genetic Algorithm (GA) based optimization for rule base and scaling factors adjustment to enhance the performance of fuzzy logic controllers. First a recursive rule base adjustment algorithm is developed, which has the benefit that it is computationally more efficient for the generation of a decision table. Then utilizing the advantage of GA optimization, a novel approach that each random combination of the optimized parameters (including the membership function selection for the rule base and controller scaling factors) is coded into a Real Coded string and treated as a chromosome in genetic algorithms is given. The optimization for rule base with the correspondent membership function and scaling factors using GA is easy to be realization in engineering. Simulation results are presented to support this thesis.

1 Introduction

For many practical control problems it is difficult to produce a descriptive process model, yet there are experienced human operators who can provide heuristics and rules for successfully controlling the process [1]. It is common practice that the operator intuitively regulates the actuator to control the process by monitoring the error and its rate changer relative to a pre-determined set-point value. This expertise can be translated into a set of IF-THEN rules referred to as the rule base on which basis a Fuzzy Logic Controller (FLC) can be designed.

Over the last decade, the FLC design has been augmented to address the fact that the FLC may not satisfy certain design criteria, such as set-point error or unwanted oscillatory behavior. Gürocak [2] argued that this deficiency is related to the fact that no standard methods is available to transform human knowledge and experience into rule-bases. Apart from its function as a controller, fuzzy logic applications in control engineering are also proposed to tune the parameters of conventional PID controller [3].

Today the literature contains many attempts to automatically tune a FLC, using various techniques including reinforced learning [4], neural networks [5], nonlinear optimization techniques and genetic algorithms [6]. These changes collectively incorporate changes for example with respect to individual membership functions or factors for weighting the fuzzy variables.

D.-S. Huang, K. Li, and G.W. Irwin (Eds.): ICIC 2006, LNAI 4114, pp. 1–10, 2006.

This paper introduces an alternative design for improving the performance of a FLC. The improvement relates to changes in the fuzzy rule-base that by augmenting the relation matrix with optimized scaling factors. It is shown that the introduced technique is computationally very efficient compared to the other improvements given above. This makes the introduced technique viable for on-line implementation, if high sampling rates are experienced. Note that an optimization implementation of an adaptive FLC has not yet been presented. Note that the computation time for the FLC decision table is time consuming. Thus the recursive algorithm for rule changing is useful, especially for the situation of optimization of the performance. We also show that the relation matrix may not always be symmetric for a satisfactory controller performance, particulary if the process is nonlinear. However, most of the published work relates to symmetric or asymmetric matrices. The benefits of the introduced technique and the application of non-symmetric relation matrices are demonstrated on the basis of a simulation study.

2 The Recursive Algorithm for Fuzzy Control

As shown in Figure 1, the standard optimization FLC architecture includes two basic levels: the first level B is a simple fuzzy controller, whereas the second level A consists of the optimization mechanism, acting as a monitor and evaluator of the low-level controller performance. The optimization part A consists of three main blocks: a performance measure, a state estimator, and an optimization rule modification. The measure of system performance is represents a critical step in producing a successful optimized controller. Usually, two physical features, including the system output Error (E) and the Error Change (CE) are measured to establish a performance decision table. The state estimation block is used to find the relationship between the system output performance and the control input. The performance measure is then employed to calculate the correction value relating to each fuzzy rule based on the estimation model. As far as the rules modification procedure is concerned, the new rules with a new antecedent

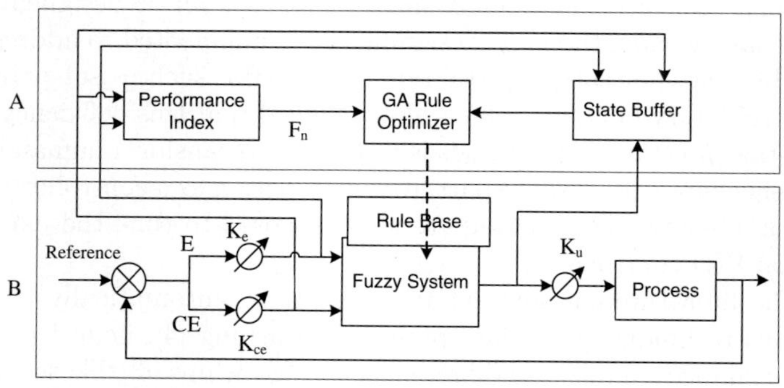

Fig. 1. The Architecture of the Standard FLC Optimization Algorithm

will be added into the fuzzy rule bank, while rules with a similar antecedent and a different consequent would be used to modify the existing rules in the rule bank. However, the computation time for the FLC decision table is time consuming. Thus the recursive algorithm for rule changing is useful, especially for the situation of optimization of the performance. The main purpose of the GA in the proposed algorithm is to generate a suitable Performance decision table output at each sampling instant with only one chromosome from a population being evaluated at that instant. The other chromosomes in the population are then estimated based on the relationships between the GA individuals. Since many of the processes involved have a stochastic influence from external as well as internal mechanisms, such imprecise fitness estimation can however be deemed very reasonable[7][8].

2.1 Look-Up Table Algorithm for a Fuzzy Controller

Fuzzy controllers are usually constructed as a set of heuristic control rules, and the control signals are directly induced from the knowledge base and the fuzzy inference. The control value that corresponds to the centroid of the inferred output fuzzy set could be obtained from the Decision Table (DT). The relation matrix of the fuzzy controller is connected with control rules. Thus, the effect that one rule will have on the relation matrix R can be reconstructed accordingly. The component in the relation matrix R can then be computed on the Cartesian product space according to the fuzzy control rule U_{Rij} and the input variables E_i,CE_j by

$$R = R^{vq} = \bigcup_{i=1,j=1}^{n,m} R_{ij}^{vq} \underline{\underline{\Delta}} \max_{i\in[1,n],j\in[1,m]} \{R_{ij}^{vq}\} \tag{1}$$

and

$$R_{ij}^{vq} = (E_i^k \times CE_j^p) \times U_{Rij} \underline{\underline{\Delta}} \min\left\{[\min\left(E_i^k, CE_j^p\right)]_v, U_{Rij}^q\right\} \tag{2}$$

where $v\underline{\underline{\Delta}}(k-1)s+p$, $q \in [1,t]$, and the other subindexes are: $i \in [1,n]$, $j \in [1,m]$, $k \in [1,r]$, $p \in [1,s]$. The notation $[.]_v$ stands for column index such that $dim[.]_v = v \times 1$.

The elements in the decision table for fuzzy inference decision making can be expressed as:

$$DT_{ij} = \sum_{q=1}^{t} \left(\mu\left(u_{ij}^q\right) \cdot u_{ij}^q\right) \Big/ \sum_{q=1}^{t} \mu\left(u_{ij}^q\right) \tag{3}$$

where

$$u_{ij}^q = \min\left(E_{ik}, CE_{jp}\right)_v \circ R^{vq} \tag{4}$$

The algorithm for creating the rule-based decision table can be now summarized as follows:

Algorithm 1

(1) Obtain the E and CE values: E^k and CE^p for $k = p = 1$;

(2) Compute the values of all membership functions E_i and CE_j for all $i \in [1,n], j \in [1,m]$;

(3) Compute the premise $RF_{ij} = E_i^k \times CE_j^p = min(E_i^k, CE_j^p)$ for all i, j, where RF_{ij} is defined as

$$R_{ij}^{kp} = (E_i^k \times CE_j^p) \times U_{Rij} = RF^{kp} \times U_{Rij} \tag{5}$$

(4) Compute $R_{ij}^{vq} = U_{Rij} \times RF_{ij}$ for all i, j, then form R using Equation (1);

(5) Cycle through all areas until $k = r$ and $p = s$ to determine the COG and store the result in the Decision Table using Equation (3).

For online control output calculation, the algorithm is used by taking $E \times CE$ as index to look up the decision table, and then to output the required crisp value u for control.

Remark 1. The algorithm above provides the simple method for FLC design and application. It differs from rule deletion and addition algorithms such as proposed in ([9] and [10]). Here the elements in the relation matrix R are accurately located. After the input variables are defined and the rule base relation matrix R (and hence the decision table) are formed, the fuzzy control output can be obtained by look up within the DT table.

If the input universe of discourse in a controller is discrete, it is always possible to calculate all possible combinations of the inputs before putting the controller into operation. In a table-based controller the relation between all input combinations and their corresponding outputs are arranged in a look-up table. This table implementation improves execution speed, as the run-time inference is reduced to a table look-up which is faster, at least when the correct entry can be found without too much searching. The sensitivity of the FLC with respect to variations in the rule decision tables has been tested by changing the original decision table values in a limited range. It is pointed out in [11] that, in certain situations, small variations in the rule decision tables do not cause any instability in the proposed fuzzy logic controller.

2.2 Recursive Algorithm

In the fuzzy control application, the rule change position (v, q) cannot be determined in advance. In order to obtain the matrix R_0 from the original relation matrix R^{vq0}, we have the following result.

PROPOSITION[14]
The Initial Fuzzy Rule Base Matrix R_0, defined as

$$R_0 = sub \max_{v,q} \left\{ \underset{ij}{\cup} R_{ij}^{vq} \right\} = sub \max_{ij0} \{R^{vq}\} \tag{6}$$

can be calculated by

$$R_0 = \begin{cases} R_0' & \text{for} \quad R^{vq0} = R^{vq} \\ R^{vq} & \text{otherwise} \end{cases} \tag{7}$$

where $R_0^{'}$ is the companion matrix of R^{vq} in Equation (1), defined as

$$R_0^{'} \triangleq Sub\max\{R^{vq}\} \tag{8}$$

The prove of the Proposition is given in [14].

Remark 2. From the *PROPOSITION* above, the matrix $R_0^{'}$ can be obtained from the matrix R^{vq0} as follows: Assume that an element R_{ij}^{vq0} of R^{vq0} is derived from Equation (1) in the point (i, j). If the max operator value is obtained from multiple location, rather than a single one, then at this (i, j) location $R_0^{'} = R^{vq0}$. On the other hand, if this max operator value is determined by a unique point, then $R_0^{'}$ should be a second large number (sub-maximum function) of the value of this point. Since this $R_0^{'}$ is defined for all matrix indices (v, q), then $R_0^{'}$ can be calculated off line and in advance.

The recursive rule base adjustment algorithm then follows.

Algorithm 2

The recursive fuzzy logic controller design algorithm, obtained by modifying the correspondent fuzzy control rule base u_{Rij} is :

Step 1: For a given rule base FLC, initialize R at $R = R_{ij}^{vq}$ and $R_0 = R_{ij}^{vq}$ using Equation (2);

Step 2: Calculate the matrix R^{vq} (using Equation (1)) according to the fuzzy rules given for all $i \in [1, n]$,$j \in [1, m]$, using algorithm 1, then obtain the new companion matrix $R_0^{'}$ using Equation (8). Apply to controller;

Step 3: For a new fuzzy control rule, calculate the matrices R_{ij}^{vq0} and R_{ij}^{vq1} corresponding to the rules u_{ij0} and u_{ij1} respectively using Equation (1), use Equation (7) to derive R_0, and then obtain the modified matrix R^{vq1};

Step 4: Generate the fuzzy control output by constructing the controller look-up decision table according to Equation (3) from the modified matrix R^{vq1}.

Step 5: Update the matrix $R_0^{'} = R^{vq1}$ if $R^{vq1} \leq R_{ij}^{vq1}$ from Equation (8);

Step 6: Check the control performance. If it is not satisfactory return to step 3, and repeat until all the rules are adjusted properly.

Remark 3. Note that the special case for above recursive algorithm when only the original (or modified) rule base is set to zero. The recursive algorithm will realize the adding rule function by set the original rule to zero, and deleting a rule by set the modified rule to zero. This is an alternative approach for deduction fuzzy control rules as discussed in paper [12][13]. In fact, one can use this algorithm from the very beginning of FLC design to add (or delete) rules individually. In the adding case, the matrix R_0 and $R_0^{'}$ in step 1 will be zero. This is useful when the rules for the controlled process are not all clearly defined.

Remark 4. The effect of a modified fuzzy rule on the control system can be improved according to some system performance algorithm. In a real-time control situation, if the matrices $R_0^{'}$ and R^{vq} are stored in controller memory, then the controller output can be obtained quickly. The proposed algorithm reduces the calculation involved from $n \times m$ operations to only two (the operation of replacing R_{ij}^{vq0} by R_{ij}^{vq1}). The modified Relation Matrix or Decision Table can be copied to the real controller memory in a very short time. The effectiveness of this new algorithm will now be illustrated in the following simulation examples.

3 Fuzzy Logic Controller Optimization Using GA

The design parameters of a FLC can be summarized within two groups: (a) structural parameters, (b) tuning parameters. Basically, the structural parameters include the input/output (I/O) variables to fuzzy inference, fuzzy linguistic sets, membership functions, fuzzy rules, inference mechanism and defuzzification mechanism. The tuning parameters include I/O scaling factors (SF) and parameters of the membership functions (MF). Usually, the structural parameters are determined during off-line design, while the tuning parameters can be calculated during on-line adjustments of the controller to enhance the process performance, as well as to accommodate its adaptive capability to system uncertainty and process disturbance. Figure 2 is the example of the proposed FLC with GA optimization structure. The optimized parameters are Ke,Kce,Ku and $xpid(4)$ with the rule base code parameter. The optimized fuzzy logic controller

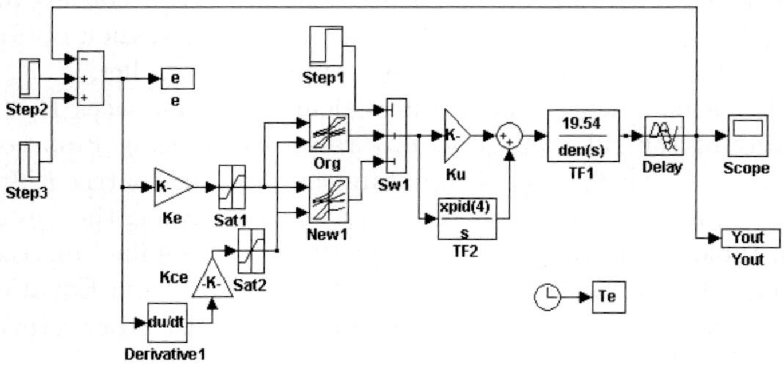

Fig. 2. The Simulation Structure of the FLC Optimization System

(OFLC) is a FLC with its rule-base is optimized by the GA. The rule-base may be arbitrary initialized if there is no a priori knowledge or initialized with a known sub-optimal one. The GA task is to search for the optimal rules. Simple genetic algorithms (SGA), within MATLAB toolbox, is generally the most efficient optimization algorithm on many application domain. Therefore, only a bit of modifications are made in the proposed algorithm to improve its performance.

(1) Coding. In GA, the parameters to be optimized are encoded into strings, and each string is a solution candidate. The encoding scheme depends on the nature of parameters to be optimized. Traditionally, binary coding is used for its simplicity. The shortcoming is the effect of Hamming cliffs on mutation. Real Codes are suggested to alleviate this problem. Each random combination of the

optimized parameters (including the membership function selection for the rule base and controller scaling factors) is coded into a Real Coded string and treated as a chromosome in genetic algorithms. We define the strings as arrays of integers instead of binary coding strings for easier understanding and manipulation. For example, a fuzzy variable with 5 fuzzy sub-sets, NB, NS, ZE, PS, PB is coded as 1;2;3;4;5 respectively. The length of the string is equal to the number of rules needed to be learnt; where each bit of the string represents one rule.

(2) Initialization. OFLC initializes the population using a random generator and(or) a stored rule set. The designed controller can be partially filled up with expert knowledge, previously trained rule set or any initial guess (e.g. common sense). Proper engineering judgement, intuitions and physical properties of the systems can speed up the design cycle and enhance the performance of the FLC. The inclusion of stored rule tables establishes foundations upon which GA explores over a wide territory search space. Intuitively, changes (by mutation and crossover) for these rules may provide useful candidates for the problem. As good initial parameters dramatically speed up convergence, we constructed a population based on the available information. If only random generate and-test is used, there may be less genetic material generated in the population pool. On the other hand, using an initial stored rule set can cover a pre-defined diversity. However, the algorithm can also optimize the controller with an empty rule-base[14].

(3) Performance criteria. Both heuristics and quantitative measures are considered in order to make a decision. For instance, the user specifications about transient accuracy, usually given in terms of required overshoot, rise time and settling time can give a good measure about which control algorithm will give the best performance as compared with the others. In order to make a decision among various controllers after tuning them based on the user specifications, a performance criteria has been defined. For instance, the performance of each controller is evaluated based on a number of factors. The following variance criterion, $J\left(GA_n\right)$, was used as a performance measure:

$$J\left(GA_n\right) = \left(1 - \frac{\sum_{i=1}^{n_y} var\{y_{set} - y_{out}\left(GA_n\right)\}}{\sum_{i=1}^{n_y} var\{y_{out} \longleftarrow\}}\right) \cdot 100\%. \tag{9}$$

Here $var\{.\}$ represents variance, while $y_{set} - y_{out} = e$ was the residual of the GA_n^{th} runs of GA for the system simulation.

4 Simulation Examples

For the FLC shown in Figure 2, suppose that the original Decision Table is calculated as in Table 1: where the elements are created from the normal distribution function, such as

$$\mu_{VS}(x) = \exp[-(\frac{x - a_1}{\sigma_1})^2]$$

and

$$\mu_S(x) = \exp[-(\frac{x - a_2}{\sigma_2})^2]$$

The a_i and σ_i ($i = 1, 2, 3, 4, 5$) are parameters for the optimization.

The random combination of the optimized parameters (including the membership function selection for the rule base and controller scaling factors) is coded into a Real Coded string and treated as a chromosome in genetic algorithms. Figure 3 and Figure 4 are the membership function curves before and after the optimization.

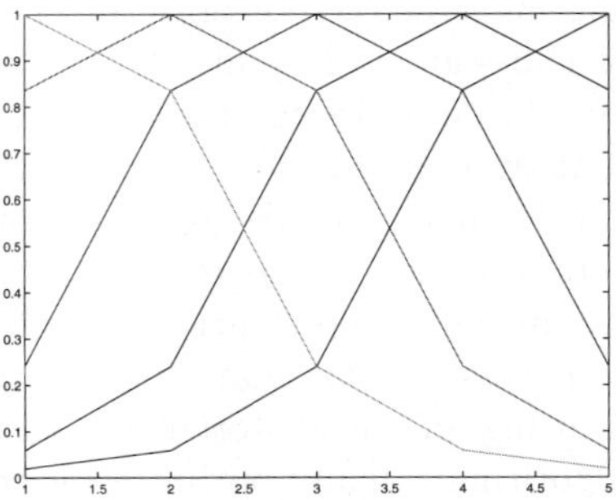

Fig. 3. Membership function before optimization

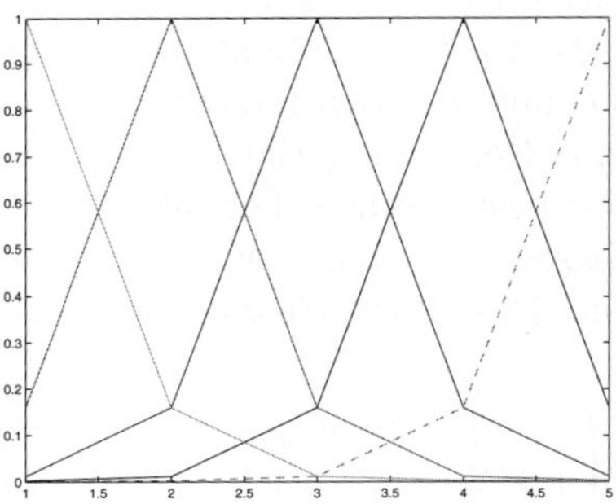

Fig. 4. Membership function after optimization

The control performance for this rule base optimization with GA is now simulated as follows.

Example1. (A damped oscillation time-delay system). The controlled system is a second-order time-delay system modelled as

$$G(s) = \frac{19.54}{s^2 + 0.4s + 0.54} e^{-0.2s}$$

Table 1. The Decision Table Example for 25 Rule Base

$CE\backslash E$	-2	-1	0	1	2
-2	-0.7586	-0.7586	-0.2571	-0.0769	0.0000
-1	-0.7586	-0.4412	-0.0789	-0.0000	0.0769
0	-0.2571	-0.0789	0.0000	0.0789	0.2571
1	-0.0769	-0.0000	0.0789	0.4412	0.7586
2	0.0000	0.0769	0.2571	0.6897	0.7586

Table 2. The Decision Table Example After GA Optimization

$CE\backslash E$	-2	-1	0	1	2
-2	-0.7828	-0.7828	-0.4076	-0.0949	0
-1	-0.7828	-0.4076	-0.4076	0	0.0949
0	-0.4076	-0.4076	0	0	0.4076
1	-0.4076	0	0	0.4076	0.5167
2	-0.2986	0	0.4076	0.4076	0.7828

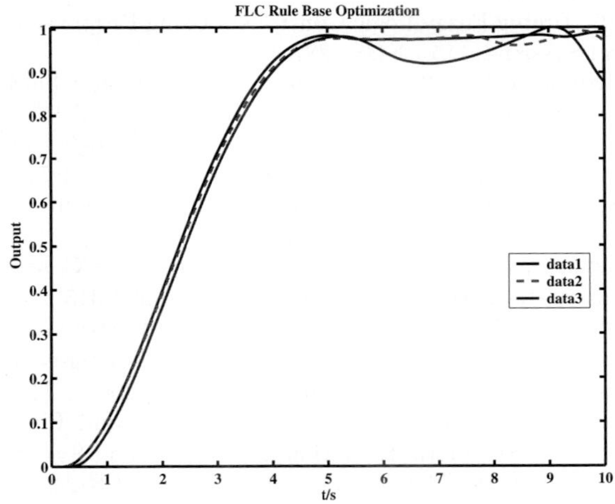

Fig. 5. Comparison of a damped oscillation system with time delay

This is a variation of a vehicle speed control system with a potential disorder [15]. The optimization of GA for closed loop step response before, and after, the rule base optimized from Table 1 to Table 2 is shown in Figure 5. There three GA optimization runs are outlined. Note the performance for data1 is smoother compared with other runs data. The proposed approach works satisfied.

The recursive FLC algorithm has been successfully applied to an Electric Vortex Ergo-graph. However, because of a confidentiality agreement, associated results cannot be included in the paper.

5 Conclusions

This paper studied recent developments in adaptive fuzzy logic control, particularly with respect to optimization implementation. It was shown that if the controller performance is not satisfactory, the rule base should be altered by combined tuning of membership functions and controller scaling factors. The proposed recursive rule base adjustment algorithm, which combining Genetic Algorithm optimization for membership functions and controller scaling factors, has the benefit that it is computationally more efficient for the generation of a decision table, and thus makes it is easier to optimize the system performance. It was further shown that the novel approach that each random combination of the optimized parameters (including the membership function selection for the rule base and controller scaling factors) is coded into a Real Coded string and treated as a chromosome in genetic algorithms is successful.

References

1. Wang, L. X.: A Course in Fuzzy Systems and Control, Prentice-Hall, Upper Saddle River, New York, 1997
2. Gurocak, H. B.: Tuning Fuzzy Logic Controllers Using Response Envelope Method, Fuzzy Sets and Systems, 115 (2000), 287-304
3. Wu, Z. Q., Mizumoto, M.: PID Type Fuzzy Controller and Parameters Adaptive Method. Fuzzy Sets and Systems, 78 (1996) 23-36
4. Berenji, H. R., Khedkar, P.: Learning and Tuning Fuzzy Logic Controllers Through Reinforcements, IEEE Trans. Neural Networks, 3 (1992) 724-740
5. Chao, C., Teng, C. : A PD-like Self-tuning Controller without Steady-state Error, Fuzzy Sets and Systems, 87 (1997), 141-154
6. Herrera, F., Lozano, M., Verdegay, J. L. : Tuning Fuzzy Controllers by Genetic Algorithms, Internat. J. Approx. Reason., 12 (1995) 299-315
7. Mahfouf, M., Linkens, D. A. , Abbod, M. F.: Muti-objective Genetic Optimization of GPC and SOFLC Tuning Parameters Using a Fuzzy-based Ranking Method, IEE Proceedings on Control Theory Application, 147(2000), 344-354
8. Jame, M. , Mahfouf, M., Linkens, D. A.: Elicitation and Fine-tuning of Fuzzy Control Rules Using Symbiotic Evolution, Fuzzy Sets and Systems,2004
9. Eminoglu, I. , Altas, I. H.: The Effects of the Number of Rules on the Output of a Fuzzy Logic Controller Employed to a PM D.C. Motor, Computers and Electrical Engineering, 24 (1998), 245-261
10. Hong, T. P., Chen, J. B.: Processing Individual Fuzzy Attributes for Fuzzy Rule Induction, Fuzzy Sets and Systems, 112 (2000), 127-140
11. Hong, T. P. , Lee, C. Y.: Induction of Fuzzy Rules and Membership Functions from Training Examples, Fuzzy Sets and Systems, 84 (1996) 33-47
12. Tsang, K. M.: Auto-tuning of Fuzzy Logic Controller for Self-regulating Processes, Fuzzy sets and systems, 120 (2001), 169-179
13. Xiong, N. , Litz, L.: Reduction of Fuzzy Control Rules by Means of Premise Learning - method and case study, Fuzzy Sets and Systems, 132 (2002), 217-231
14. Li, P., Irwin, G. W., Kruger, U.: A Recursive Rule Base Adjustment Algorithm for a Fuzzy Logic Controller, Fuzzy Sets and Systems 156 (2005) 267–284
15. Maeda, M. , Murakami, S.: A Self-tuning Fuzzy Controller, Fuzzy Sets and Systems, 51 (1992), 29-40

Chance Constrained Maximum Flow Problem with Fuzzy Arc Capacities

Xiaoyu Ji[1], Lixing Yang[2], and Zhen Shao[3]

[1] School of Business, Renmin University of China, Beijing, 100872, China
xyji@orsc.edu.cn
[2] School of Traffic and Transportation, Beijing Jiaotong University, Beijing, 100044
lxyang@orsc.edu.cn
[3] School of Management, Graduate School of the Chinese Academy of Sciences, Beijing, 100080, China
shaozhen03@gmial.com

Abstract. This paper considers a generalized fuzzy version of maximum flow problem in which arc capacities are fuzzy variables. The problem is to find a maximum flow under some chance constraints with respect to credibility measure of arc flow of network. Some crisp equivalents of fuzzy chance constraints are presented when the fuzzy capacities are characterized by trapezoidal fuzzy numbers and general fuzzy numbers respectively. Furthermore, a genetic algorithm is used to solve the maximum flow with these crisp equivalents. Finally, a numerical example is provided for the effectiveness of the model and algorithm.

1 Introduction

The maximum flow problem (MFP) is one of basic problems for combinatorial optimization in weighted directed graphs. It provides very useful models in a number of practical contexts including communication networks, oil pipeline systems and power systems. The maximum flow problem and its variations have a wide range of applications and have been studied extensively. The MFP was proposed by Fulkerson and Dantzig [3] originally and solved by specializing the simplex method for the linear programming, and Ford and Fulkerson [2] solved it by augmenting path algorithm. In the following years, a number of algorithms have been proposed, the comprehensive survey and bibliography are given in the literatures [1][25]. In many practical applications, however, different kinds of uncertainties must be taken into account. Probability theory has been used to attack randomness in stochastic flow networks. About the stochastic flow networks, many researchers have done lots of work. Fishman [9][10] considered the case of continuous arc capacities that deteriorate randomly with time and showed that how to use the Monte Carlo sampling method for the upper bound. Exact algorithms for computing the distribution of feasible flow had been given in the papers [4][5] . However, our ideas and conceptions of the real world are often vague and subjective in nature. In particular, imprecise observations or possible perturbations mean that capacities of arcs in a network may be better represented by fuzzy numbers than crisp quantities. The MFP with fuzzy capacities

D.-S. Huang, K. Li, and G.W. Irwin (Eds.): ICIC 2006, LNAI 4114, pp. 11–19, 2006.

has been studied in papers [6][7][8]. In their papers, they assumed the membership functions of fuzzy capacities and whole network flow were known, the decision makers were interested in the flow value at least some given flow, then to find such a flow which had a possibly large value and which simultaneously in the possibly best way satisfied the capacity constraints. In real world, the memberships of each arc capacities can been given by experts, but the membership of the whole network flow is hard to acquire for the decision makers, especially for a new network. So it is very necessary and useful to find the network flow value with only knowing the membership functions of arc capacities.

This paper proposes a generalized version of MFP, i.e., fuzzy maximum flow problem (FMFP), which is to find a maximum flow under chance constraints with respect to credibility measure of arc flow of network. Section 2 formulates the FMFP by chance constrained programming. Section 3 presents the crisp equivalents of chance constraints for some special cases. Section 4 gives a genetic algorithm for the maximum flow with crisp equivalents. Finally, a numerical example is provided for illustrating the effectiveness of the proposed model and algorithm.

2 Chance-Constrained Programming for FMFP

Consider a directed flow network $\mathcal{G} = (\mathcal{V}, \mathcal{A}, \mathcal{C})$, where $\mathcal{V}$ means the finite set of nodes, numbered $\{1, 2, \cdots, n\}$. $\mathcal{A}$ means the set of arcs, each arc is denoted by an ordered pair (i, j), where $(i, j) \in \mathcal{A}$. $\mathcal{C}$ means the set of arc capacities. In the fuzzy maximum flow problem (FMFP), every arc (i, j) has a fuzzy, nonnegative, independent flow capacity ξ_{ij} with the membership functions μ_{ij}.

Now, we use the following flow representation

$$\boldsymbol{x} = \{x_{ij} | (i, j) \in \mathcal{A}\}$$

where x_{ij} means that the flow of arc (i, j). The flow is called a feasible flow if the following two conditions are satisfied:

(1) At each node, the incoming flow and outgoing flow must satisfied the following balance conditions.

$$\begin{cases} \sum\limits_{(1,j)\in\mathcal{A}} \boldsymbol{x}_{1j} - \sum\limits_{(j,1)\in\mathcal{A}} \boldsymbol{x}_{j1} = f \\ \sum\limits_{(i,j)\in\mathcal{A}} \boldsymbol{x}_{ij} - \sum\limits_{(j,i)\in\mathcal{A}} \boldsymbol{x}_{ji} = 0, \quad 2 \le i \le n-1 \\ \sum\limits_{(n,j)\in\mathcal{A}} \boldsymbol{x}_{nj} - \sum\limits_{(j,n)\in\mathcal{A}} \boldsymbol{x}_{jn} = -f \\ \forall (i,j) \in \mathcal{A}, \end{cases} \tag{1}$$

in which f means the flow of the network $\mathcal{G}$.

(2) The flow at each arc must be satisfied by the capacity constraint.

In many practical applications, however, different kinds of uncertainties must be taken into account. In this paper, we employ the fuzzy set theory to cope with the fuzziness, which was introduced by Zadeh in 1965 and has been well developed and applied in a wide variety of real problems. In fuzzy set theory, there are three types of measures including possibility, necessary and credibility measure[13][14]. As we all know, a fuzzy event may fail even though its possibility achieves 1, and hold even though its necessity is 0. But the fuzzy event must hold if its credibility is 1 and fail if its credibility is 0. In this paper, we apply credibility measure to model FMFP.

Definition 1. *Let ξ be a fuzzy variable with the membership function $\mu(x)$. Then the possibility measure (*Pos*), necessity measure (*Nec*), credibility measure (*Cr*) of the fuzzy event $\{\xi \geq r\}$ can be represented respectively by*

$$\begin{aligned} \mathrm{Pos}\{\xi \geq r\} &= \sup_{u \geq r} \mu(u), \\ \mathrm{Nec}\{\xi \geq r\} &= 1 - \sup_{u < r} \mu(u), \\ \mathrm{Cr}\{\xi \geq r\} &= \frac{1}{2}[\mathrm{Pos}\{\xi \geq r\} + \mathrm{Nec}\{\xi \geq r\}]. \end{aligned}$$

Sometimes, the decision-maker is interested in the flow which satisfies some chance constraints with at least some given confidence level α. So we have the following definition,

Definition 2. *A flow $\boldsymbol{x}$ is called the α-optimistic maximum flow (α-OMF) from nodes 1 to n if*

$$\max\{f \mid \mathrm{Cr}\{\xi \geq \boldsymbol{x}\} \geq \alpha\} \geq \max\{f' \mid \mathrm{Cr}\{\xi \geq \boldsymbol{x}'\} \geq \alpha\}$$

for any flow $\boldsymbol{x}'$ from nodes 1 to n, where α is a predetermined confidence level.

Chance-constrained programming offers us a powerful means for modelling fuzzy decision systems [15][16][17]. The essential idea of chance-constrained programming of FMFP is to optimize the flow value of network with certain confidence level subject to some chance constraints. In order to find the α-OMF, we propose the following model.

$$\begin{cases} \max f \\ \text{subject to :} \\ \sum\limits_{(1,j)\in\mathcal{A}} \boldsymbol{x}_{1j} - \sum\limits_{(j,1)\in\mathcal{A}} \boldsymbol{x}_{j1} = f \\ \sum\limits_{(i,j)\in\mathcal{A}} \boldsymbol{x}_{ij} - \sum\limits_{(j,i)\in\mathcal{A}} \boldsymbol{x}_{ji} = 0, \quad 2 \leq i \leq n-1 \\ \sum\limits_{(n,j)\in\mathcal{A}} \boldsymbol{x}_{nj} - \sum\limits_{(j,n)\in\mathcal{A}} \boldsymbol{x}_{jn} = -f \\ \mathrm{Cr}\{\xi_{ij} \geq \boldsymbol{x}_{ij}\} \geq \alpha, \\ f \geq 0 \end{cases} \tag{2}$$

where α is a predetermined confidence level provided as an appropriate margin by the decision-maker.

3 Crisp Equivalents

One way of solving fuzzy chance-constrained programming model is to convert the chance constraint

$$\mathrm{Cr}\{\xi \geq \boldsymbol{x}\} \geq \alpha \tag{3}$$

into its crisp equivalent and then solve the equivalent crisp model in deterministic environment. In paper [23], assume that ξ are general fuzzy variables with membership functions $\mu_\xi(x)$, then have
$\mathrm{Cr}\{\xi \geq \boldsymbol{x}\} \geq \alpha$ if and only if $\boldsymbol{x} \leq K_\alpha$, where

$$K_\alpha = \begin{cases} \sup\left\{K \mid K = \mu^{-1}(2\alpha)\right\}, & \textit{if } \alpha < 1/2 \\ \inf\left\{K \mid K = \mu^{-1}(2(1-\alpha))\right\}, & \textit{if } \alpha \geq 1/2. \end{cases} \tag{4}$$

Assume that ξ_{ij} are general fuzzy variables with membership functions $\mu_{\xi_{ij}}(x)$ respectively. Then the model (2) can be reformulated as follows:

$$\begin{cases} \max f \\ \text{subject to :} \\ \quad \sum\limits_{(1,j)\in\mathcal{A}} \boldsymbol{x}_{1j} - \sum\limits_{(j,1)\in\mathcal{A}} \boldsymbol{x}_{j1} = f \\ \quad \sum\limits_{(i,j)\in\mathcal{A}} \boldsymbol{x}_{ij} - \sum\limits_{(j,i)\in\mathcal{A}} \boldsymbol{x}_{ji} = 0, \quad 2 \leq i \leq n-1 \\ \quad \sum\limits_{(n,j)\in\mathcal{A}} \boldsymbol{x}_{nj} - \sum\limits_{(j,n)\in\mathcal{A}} \boldsymbol{x}_{jn} = -f \\ \qquad \boldsymbol{x} \leq K_{\alpha_{ij}} \\ \qquad f \geq 0. \end{cases} \tag{5}$$

Where

$$K_{\alpha_{ij}} = \begin{cases} \sup\left\{K \mid K = \mu^{-1}(2\alpha_{ij})\right\}, & \textit{if } \alpha_{ij} < 1/2 \\ \inf\left\{K \mid K = \mu^{-1}(2(1-\alpha_{ij}))\right\}, & \textit{if } \alpha_{ij} \geq 1/2. \end{cases}$$

When the arc capacities of a network are independent trapezoidal fuzzy variables defined as $\xi_{ij} = (a_{ij}, b_{ij}, c_{ij}, d_{ij})$, respectively. Then when $\alpha > 0.5$, the model (2) can be converted to the following model,

$$\begin{cases} \max f \\ \text{subject to :} \\ \quad \sum\limits_{(1,j)\in\mathcal{A}} \boldsymbol{x}_{1j} - \sum\limits_{(j,1)\in\mathcal{A}} \boldsymbol{x}_{j1} = f \\ \quad \sum\limits_{(i,j)\in\mathcal{A}} \boldsymbol{x}_{ij} - \sum\limits_{(j,i)\in\mathcal{A}} \boldsymbol{x}_{ji} = 0, \quad 2 \leq i \leq n-1 \\ \quad \sum\limits_{(n,j)\in\mathcal{A}} \boldsymbol{x}_{nj} - \sum\limits_{(j,n)\in\mathcal{A}} \boldsymbol{x}_{jn} = -f \\ \qquad x_{ij} < (2\alpha - 1)a_{ij} + 2(1-\alpha)b_{ij} \\ \qquad f \geq 0. \end{cases} \tag{6}$$

4 Genetic Algorithm

Ever since the genetic algorithm was introduced by Holland [12] to tackle combinatorial problems, it has emerged as one of the most efficient stochastic solution search procedures for solving various application problem [11]. But for the characteristic of the MFP, it is more challenging in applying genetic algorithms than many other common graph problems. For example, a flow at each arc can be any value between zero and its flow capacity, rather than a fixed value. Also, the total inflow and outflow must be balance at each vertex. In this section, the argument path approach is used to find the maximum flow in genetic algorithm, each solution is represented by a chromosome. Starting with a population of randomized solutions, better and better solutions are sought through the genetic algorithm. Optimal or near optimal solutions are determined with a reasonable number or iterations. The representation structure, initialization, crossover and mutation operations of chromosomes are given as follows.

4.1 Encoding

In the maximum flow problem, we use the priority-based encoding method[11]. We encode a chromosome by giving each node a distinct priority number from 1 to n, where n is the number of nodes in the network, an example is given in Figure 1. The path from 1 to n is developed by continuously adding the available vertex with the highest priority into the path until the path reaches the terminal node. And we decode it into a flow in the network by path algorithm by the following decoding method.

position: node ID	1	2	3	4	5	6	7	8	9	10
value: priority	7	3	10	4	2	5	9	6	1	8

Fig. 1. Encoding operation

4.2 Decoding

In order to find the flow of network, we give the following procedure, in which, l means the number of paths, p_l means the lth path from node 1 to n, f_l means the flow on this path, c_{ij} means the capacity of arc ij, N_i means the set of nodes with all nodes adjacent to node i.

Step 0. Set number of paths $l \leftarrow 0$.
Step 1. If N_1 is not an empty set, then $l \leftarrow l + 1$; otherwise, go to step 7.
Step 2. The path p_l is developed by adding the available vertex with the highest priority into the path until the path reaches the terminal node. Select the sink node a of path p_l.

Step 3. If the sink node $a = n$, continue; otherwise, update the set of nodes N_i by $N_i = N_i - \{a\}$, return to step 1.
Step 4. Find the flow f_l of the path p_l by $f_l \leftarrow f_{l-1} + \min\{c_{ij} \mid (i,j) \in p_l\}$.
Step 5. Perform the flow capacity c_{ij} of each arc update. Make a new flow capacity $\bar{c_{ij}}$ as follows: $\bar{c_{ij}} = c_{ij} - \min\{c_{ij} \mid (i,j) \in p_l\}$.
Step 6. If the flow capacity $c_{ij} = 0$, perform the set of nodes N_i update which the node j adjacent to node i, $N_i = N_i - j$, $(i,j) \in p_l$ and $c_{ij} = 0$.
Step 7. Output the flow f_l of this chromosome.

4.3 Crossover and Mutation Operator

The position-based crossover operator is used. Generally speaking, the position-based crossover takes some genes from one parent randomly and fills the vacuum position with the genes of the other parent by a left-to-right scan, which is proposed by [24]. In Figure 2, an example with 10 nodes is given. The mutation

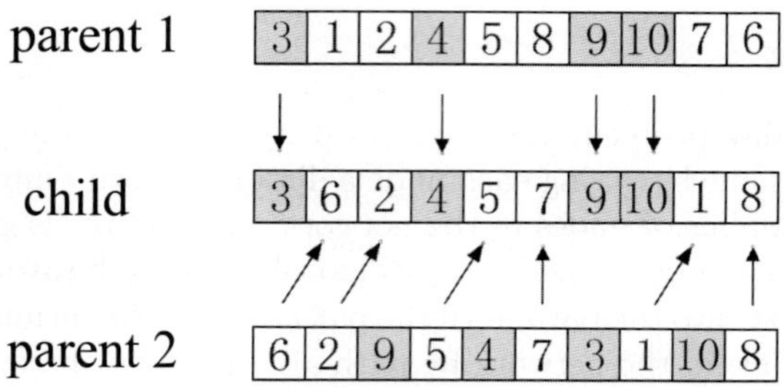

Fig. 2. Crossover operation

operation is done by exchanging the priority values of two randomly generalized nodes.The mutation procedure is shown in Figure 3.

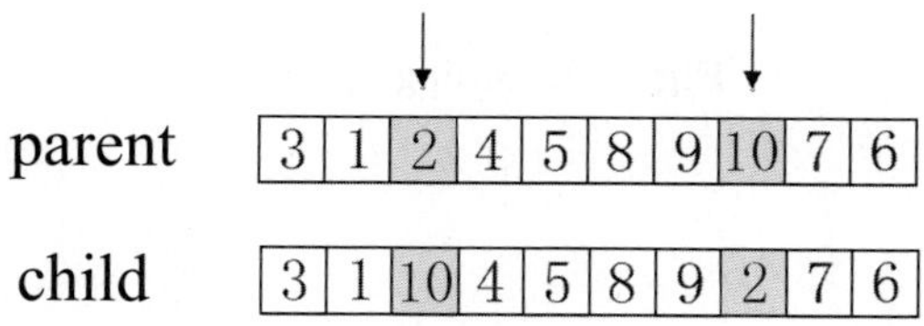

Fig. 3. Mutation operator

4.4 Procedure of Genetic Algorithm

we employ above procedure and genetic operators to find the maximum flow, the procedure can be described as follows,

Step 0. Set genetic parameters.
Step 1. Initialize *pop_size* chromosomes P_k, $k = 1, 2, \cdots, pop\_size$.

Step 2. Find the flow for all chromosomes by above procedure, respectively.

Step 3. Compute the fitness of each chromosome. The rank-based evaluation function is defined as

$$Eval(P_i) = a(1-a)^{i-1},\ i = 1, 2, \cdots, pop\_size,$$

where the chromosomes are assumed to have been rearranged from good to bad according to their objective values and $a \in (0,1)$ is a parameter in the genetic system.

Step 4. Select the chromosomes for a new population.

Step 5. Update the chromosomes P_k, $k = 1, 2, \cdots, pop\_size$ by crossover operation and mutation operation mentioned in the last subsection.

Step 6. Repeat the third to fifth steps for a given number of cycles.

Step 7. Repeat the maximum flow of this network.

5 A Numerical Example

We now illustrate the practical case with a numerical example to explore the importance of our model. Consider a power supply network with fuzzy independent capacities, whose transmission lines are numbered (i,j). Assumed that the capacities of line (i,j) are independent fuzzy trapezoidal variables.

We may associate with each arc of this power network a fuzzy capacity from a known possibility distribution. We would like to find the maximum flow with chance constraints from node 1 to node 8.

Now we find the maximum flow according above algorithm, the parameters of GA are as follows: *pop_size* is 30, the number of generations is 800, the probability of crossover is 0.2, the probability of mutation is 0.2. A run of the genetic algorithm shows that the maximum flow is 74, and the α-OMF are shown in the Table 1, in which $x_{ij}^{0.8}$ means the flow at arc (i,j) when α is 0.8.

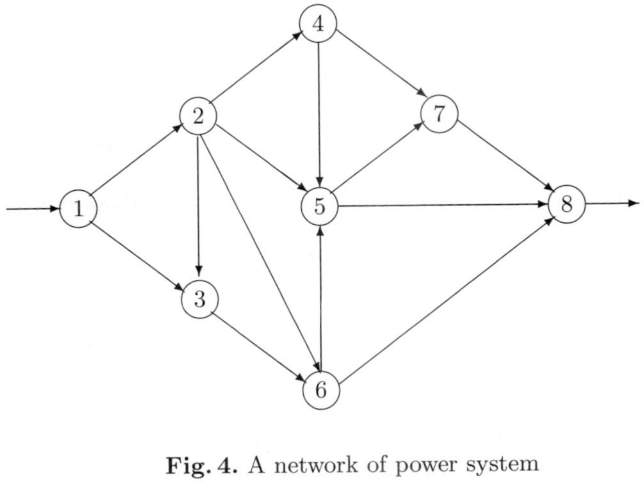

Fig. 4. A network of power system

Table 1. The data of example network

Arc	Fuzzy Capacity	$x_{ij}^{0.8}$	Arc	Fuzzy Capacity	$x_{ij}^{0.8}$
(1,2)	(40,50,70,80)	44	(1,3)	(60,70,90,100)	30
(2,3)	(5,25,40,50)	0	(2,4)	(30,40,60,70)	13
(2,5)	(20,30,50,60)	24	(2,6)	(5,10,25,40)	7
(3,6)	(70,85,95,110)	30	(4,5)	(10,20,40,50)	0
(4,7)	(20,50,60,70)	13	(5,7)	(10,15,25,30)	12
(5,8)	(15,20,35,45)	17	(6,5)	(15,25,35,50)	5
(6,8)	(30,35,40,55)	32	(7,8)	(50,60,70,100)	25

6 Conclusion

In this paper, a generalized fuzzy version of maximum flow problem is considered, in which arc capacities are fuzzy variables. The aim is to find the maximum flow under some chance constraints with respect to credibility measure of arc flow of network. In this paper, the chance-constrained programming model for FMFP is formulated and some crisp equivalents of fuzzy chance constraints are presented. We also solve crisp equivalents by genetic algorithm for α-OMF. To show the applicability of the model and algorithm given in this paper, an example for power network are considered.

Acknowledgments

This work was supported by National Natural Science Foundation of China (No. 60174049), and Specialized Research Fund for the Doctoral Program of Higher Education (No.20020003009).

References

1. Aronson, J.E.: A Survey of Dynamic Network Flows. Ann. Oper. Res. 20 (1989) 1-66
2. Ford, L.R., Fulkerson, D.R.: Maximal Flow Through A Network. Canadian Journal of Mathematics, 8 (1956) 399-404
3. Fulkerson, D.R., Dantzig, G.B.: Computation of Maximum Flow In Network. Naval Research Logisics Quarterly, 2 (1955) 277-283
4. Evans, J.R.: Maximum Flow In Probabilistic Graphs-The Discrete Case. Networks, 6 (1976) 161-183
5. Doulliez, P., Jamoulle, E.: Transportation Networks With Random Arc Capacities. R.A.I.R.O. 3 (1972) 45-60
6. Chanas, S., Kolodziejczyk, W.: Maximum Flow In A Network With Fuzzy Arc Capacities. Fuzzy Sets and Systems, 8 (1982) 165-173
7. Chanas, S., Kolodziejczyk, W.: Real-Valued Flows In A Network With Fuzzy Arc Capacities. Fuzzy Sets and Systems, 13 (1984) 131-139

8. Diamond, Phil: A Fuzzy Max-Flow Min-Cut Theorem. Fuzzy Sets and Systems, 119 (2001) 139-148
9. Fishman, G.S.: The Distribution of Maximum Flow With Application To Multi-State Reliability Systems. Operarions Research, 35 (1987) 607-618
10. Fishman, G.S.: Maximum Flow and Critical Cutset As Descript Multi-State Aystems With Randomly Capacitated Components. Computer Operarions Research, 14 (1987) 507-520
11. Gen, M., Cheng, R.: Genetic Algorithms and Engineer Optimization. John Wiley and Sons, Inc., New York(2000)
12. Holland, J.: Adaptatin In Natural and Artificial System. University of Michigan Press, Ann Arbor. MI. 1975
13. Liu, B.: Theory and Practice of Uncertain Programming. Physica-Verlag, Heidelberg (2002)
14. Liu, B.: Uncertainty Theory: An Introduction To Its Axiomatic Foundations. Springer-Verlag, Berlin (2004)
15. Liu, B.: Iwamura,K.: Chance Constrained Programming With Fuzzy Parameters. Fuzzy Sets and Systems, 94(1998) 227-237
16. Liu, B., Iwamura, K.: A Note On Chance Constrained Programming With Fuzzy Coefficients. Fuzzy Sets and Systems, 100 (1998) 229-233
17. Liu, B.: Minimax Chance Constrained Programming Models For Fuzzy Decision Systems. Information Sciences, 112 (1998) 25-38
18. Liu, B.: Toward Fuzzy Optimization Without Mathematical Ambiguity. Fuzzy Optimization and Decision Making, 1(1) (2002) 43-63
19. Liu, B., Liu, Y.K.: Expected Value of Fuzzy Variable and Fuzzy Expected Value Model. IEEE Transcations on Fuzzy Systems, 10 (2002) 445-450
20. Liu, B., Iwamura, K.: Chance Constrained Programming With Fuzzy Parameters. Fuzzy Sets and Systems, 94 (2) (1998) 227-237
21. Liu, B., Iwamura, K.: A Note On Chance Constrained Programming With Fuzzy Coefficients. Fuzzy Sets and Systems, 100 (1-3) (1998) 229-233
22. Liu, B.: Dependent-Chance Programming In Fuzzy Environments. Fuzzy Sets and Systems, 109 (1) (2000) 97-106
23. Lu, M.: On Crisp Equivalents and Solutions of Fuzzy Programming With Different Chance Measures. Information, 6(2)(2003) 125-134
24. Syswerda, G.: Scheduling Optimization Using Genetic Algorithms. Handbook of Genetic Algorithms, (1991) 332-349
25. Takao, A., Yasuhito, A.: Recent Developments In Maximum Flow Algorithms. Journal of the Operations Research Society of Japan, 43 (1) (2000) 2-31

Delay-Dependent Stability of a Class of Nonlinear Systems with Time Delays Based on Fuzzy Hyperbolic Model

Huaguang Zhang and Jun Yang

School of Information Science and Engineering,
Northeastern University, Shenyang, Liaoning, China 110004
hgzhang@ieee.org, yjneu@126.com

Abstract. This paper concerns a problem of delay-dependent stability of a class of nonlinear continuous-time systems with time delays, based on the fuzzy hyperbolic model (FHM). FHM is a universal approximator, and can be used to establish the model for unknown complex systems. Moreover, the main advantage of using FHM over T-S fuzzy model is that no premise structure identification is need and no completeness design of premise variables space is need. Also an FHM is a kind of valid global description and nonlinear model inherently. The proposed method is addressed by solving a set of linear matrix inequalities (LMIs). A general Lyapunov-Krasovskii functional are used and some additional free-weighting matrices, which bring much flexibility in solving LMIs, are introduced during the proof. The results then have easily been extended to a system with either polytopic-type or norm-bounded uncertainties. A simulation example is given to validate the proposed results.

1 Introduction

It is well known that time delays appear in many complex systems such as chemical systems, electrical systems, biological systems, etc. [1, 2, 3]. Generally speaking, the dynamic behavior of systems with time delays is more complicated than that of systems without any time delays. The existing stability results for time-delay systems can be classified into two categories: (i) delay-independent stability and (ii) delay-dependent stability. The delay-independent stability criteria are not affected by the size of the delay (i.e., the time delays are allowed to be arbitrarily large). On the other hand, the delay-dependent stability criteria are concerned with the size of the delay and usually provides an upper bound of the delay such that the system is stable for any delay less than the upper bound. The delay-independent criteria are considered more conservative in general than the delay-dependent ones, especially when the size of delays is actually small. However, delay-independent criteria are more feasible than delay-dependent ones when the size of time delays is uncertain, unknown or very large [4].

In mathematics, the *complexity* of systems mostly attributes to their nonlinear behaviors. Over the past decades, fuzzy control technique based on Takagi-Sugeno (T–S) model [5] becomes more and more popular to approximate nonlinear time delay systems and the Lyapunov-Krasovskii method and the

D.-S. Huang, K. Li, and G.W. Irwin (Eds.): ICIC 2006, LNAI 4114, pp. 20–31, 2006.

Lyapunov-Razumikhin method, have been used to study the stability of delayed fuzzy systems, where the majority of results are formulated as convex optimization techniques with linear matrix inequality (LMI) constraints, see [8,6,7,9] for example.

Parallel to the T-S model, a new continuous-time fuzzy model, called the generalized fuzzy hyperbolic model (FHM), has recently been proposed in [10] and [11]. Both T-S fuzzy model and FHM are universal approximators, and can be used to establish the model for unknown complex systems. The advantage of using FHM over T-S model is that no premise structure identification is need and no completeness design of premise variables space is need. Furthermore, an FHM is a kind of valid global description and nonlinear model inherently. FHM can be obtained without knowing much information about the real plant, and it can easily derived from a set of fuzzy rules. Also the FHM can be seen as a neural network model, so we can learn the model parameters by back-propagation (BP) algorithm. In general, since the variable of real physical systems are always bounded, it seems more reasonable, and probably more correct in practice by using FHM.

In this paper, firstly, an FHM is proposed to represent a class of nonlinear systems with time delays. Secondly, as literature [12] and [13], stability results are presented by using a general Lyapunov-Krasovskii functional and some free-weighting matrices, which bring much flexibility in solving LMIs. Thirdly, the results are then extended to a system with either polytopic-type or norm-bounded uncertainties. All results are converted into a feasible problem of a set of LMIs, which can be efficiently solved by the convex optimization techniques with global convergence, such as the interior point algorithm [14].

Notation: Throughout this paper, the superscript T stands for matrix transposition, $\mathbb{R}^n$ denotes the n-dimensional Euclidean space, $\mathbb{R}^{n\times r}$ is the set of all $n \times r$ real matrices, and the notation $X > 0$, for $X \in \mathbb{R}^{n\times n}$, means that X is symmetric and positive definite. Identity and zero matrices, of apprppriate dimensions, will be denoted by I and 0, respectively, and $\|\cdot\|$ is Euclidean norm.

2 Preliminaries

In this section we review some necessary preliminaries for the FHM.

Definition 1. ([10,11]) *Given a plant with n input variables $x=(x_1(t),\cdots,x_n(t))^T$ and n output variables $\dot{x} = (\dot{x}_1(t),\cdots,\dot{x}_n(t))^T$. If each output variable corresponds to a group of fuzzy rules which satisfies the following conditions:*

(i) For each output variable $\dot{x}_l$, $l = 1, 2, \cdots, n$, the corresponding group of fuzzy rules has the following form:

$$\begin{aligned} R^j:&\ \text{IF } x_1 \text{ is } F_{x_1} \text{ and } x_2 \text{ is } F_{x_2}, \cdots, \text{ and } x_m \text{ is } F_{x_m} \\ &\ \text{THEN } \dot{x}_l = c^{\pm}_{F_{x_1}} + c^{\pm}_{F_{x_2}} + \cdots + c^{\pm}_{F_{x_m}}, \quad \text{for } j = 1, \cdots, 2^m, \end{aligned} \tag{1}$$

where $m \le n$ and F_{x_i} $(i = 1, \cdots, m)$ are fuzzy sets of x_i, which include P_{x_i} (positive) and N_{x_i} (negative), and $c^{\pm}_{F_{x_i}}$ $(i = 1, \cdots, m)$ are $2m$ real constants corresponding to F_{x_i};

(ii) The constant terms $c^{\pm}_{F_{x_i}}$ in the THEN-part correspond to F_{x_i} in the IF-part; that is, if the language value of F_{x_i} term in the IF-part is P_{x_i}, $c^{+}_{F_{x_i}}$ must appear in the THEN-part; if the language value of F_{x_i} term in the IF-part is N_{x_i}, $c^{-}_{F_{x_i}}$ must appear in the THEN-part; if there is no F_{x_i} in the IF-part, $c^{\pm}_{F_{x_i}}$ does not appear in the THEN-part;

(iii) There are 2^m fuzzy rules in each rule base; that is, there are a total of 2^m input variable combinations of all the possible P_{x_i} and N_{x_i} in the IF-part.

We call this group of fuzzy rules *hyperbolic type fuzzy rule base* (HFRB). To describe a plant with n output variables, we will need n HFRBs.

Lemma 1. ([10,11]) *Given n HFRBs, if we define the membership function of P_{x_i} and N_{x_i} as:*

$$\mu_{P_{x_i}}(x_i) = e^{-\frac{1}{2}(x_i - k_i)^2}, \ \mu_{N_{x_i}}(x_i) = e^{-\frac{1}{2}(x_i + k_i)^2}, \tag{2}$$

where $i = 1, \cdots, n$ and k_i are positive constants. Denoting $c^{+}_{F_{x_i}}$ by $c_{P_{x_i}}$ and $c^{-}_{F_{x_i}}$ by $c_{N_{x_i}}$ and applying singleton fuzzifier, product inference, and the center-average defuzzifier, we can derive:

$$\begin{aligned} \dot{x}_l &= \sum_{i=1}^{m} \frac{c_{P_{x_i}} e^{k_i x_i} + c_{N_{x_i}} e^{-k_i x_i}}{e^{k_i x_i} + e^{-k_i x_i}} = \sum_{i=1}^{m} p_i + \sum_{i=1}^{m} q_i \frac{e^{k_i x_i} - e^{-k_i x_i}}{e^{k_i x_i} + e^{-k_i x_i}} \\ &= \sum_{i=1}^{m} p_i + \sum_{i=1}^{m} q_i \tanh(k_i x_i), \end{aligned} \tag{3}$$

where $p_i = \frac{c_{P_{x_i}} + c_{N_{x_i}}}{2}$ and $q_i = \frac{c_{P_{x_i}} - c_{N_{x_i}}}{2}$. Therefore, the whole system has the following form:

$$\dot{x} = P + A \tanh(kx) \tag{4}$$

where P is a constant vector, A is a constant matrix, $k = diag(k_1, \cdots, k_n)$, and $\tanh(kx) = [\tanh(k_1 x_1), \ \tanh(k_2 x_2), \cdots, \tanh(k_n x_n)]^T$.

We will call (4) a generalized fuzzy hyperbolic model (FHM).

Let $\mathbb{F}$ be the space composed of all functions having the form of the right-hand side of (3). We then have the following lemma.

Lemma 2. ([11]) *For any given real continuous $g(x)$ on the compact set $\mathbb{U} \subset \mathbb{R}^n$ and any $\varepsilon > 0$, there exists an $f(x) \in \mathbb{F}$ such that*

$$\sup_{x \in \mathbb{U}} |g(x) - f(x)| < \varepsilon. \tag{5}$$

Lemma 2 indicates that FHM is a universal approximator.

From Definition 1, if we set $c_{P_{x_i}}$ and $c_{N_{x_i}}$ negative to each other, we can obtain a homogeneous FHM

$$\dot{x} = A\tanh(kx). \tag{6}$$

Since the difference between (4) and (6) is only the constant vector term in (4), there is no essentially difference between the control of (4) and (6).

Considering time-delay systems, for each output variable $\dot{x}_l$, $l = 1, 2, \cdots, n$, the corresponding group of fuzzy rules has changed as follows:

$$\begin{aligned} R^j: &\text{ IF } x_1 \text{ is } F_{x_1} \text{ and } x_2 \text{ is } F_{x_2}, \cdots, \text{ and } x_m \text{ is } F_{x_m}, \text{ and} \\ &\quad x_{d1} \text{ is } F_{x_{d1}} \text{ and } x_{d2} \text{ is } F_{x_{d2}}, \cdots, \text{ and } x_{dm} \text{ is } F_{x_{dm}} \\ &\text{THEN } \dot{x}_l = c^{\pm}_{F_{x_1}} + \cdots + c^{\pm}_{F_{xm}} + c^{\pm}_{F_{x_{d1}}} + \cdots + c^{\pm}_{F_{x_{dm}}}, \quad \text{for } j = 1, \cdots, 2^{2m}, \end{aligned}$$

where $x_{di} = x_i(t-d)$, $d > 0$ denotes a constant time delay, and $F_{x_{di}}$ are fuzzy sets of x_{di} $(i = 1, \cdots, m)$. By using similar derivation, we can obtain a homogeneous FHM as:

$$\dot{x} = A\tanh(kx) + B\tanh(kx(t-d)), \tag{7}$$

where A, B are constant matrices.

3 Main Results

3.1 Stability of a Nominal System

The FHM for the nonlinear system with time delays is proposed as the followings form:

$$\begin{aligned} (\Sigma_o) : \dot{x}(t) &= A\tanh(kx(t)) + B\tanh(kx(t-d)) \\ x(s) &= \phi(s), \qquad s \in [-\bar{d}, 0] \end{aligned} \tag{8}$$

where $x(t) = [x_1(t), x_2(t), \cdots, x_n(t)]^T \in \mathbb{R}^n$, is state vector, d is a constant but unknown time delay satisfying $0 < d \leq \bar{d}$, A, B are constant $n \times n$ matrices and ϕ is a continuously differentiable initial function.

For simplicity, the following notations are used:

$$x = x(t),\ x_d = x(t-d),\ \dot{x} = \dot{x}(t),\ \dot{x}_d = \dot{x}(t-d).$$

Before moving on, we introduce the following lemma, which is essential for the development of our results.

Lemma 3. *For any $x \in \mathbb{R}^n$, matrix $X > 0$ with appropriate dimensions, the following inequalities hold:*

$$\begin{aligned} \dot{\tanh}^T(kx) X \dot{\tanh}(kx) &\leq \dot{x}^T kXk\dot{x} \\ \tanh^T(kx) X \dot{\tanh}(kx) &\leq \tanh^T(kx) Xk\dot{x}, \end{aligned} \tag{9}$$

where $k = diag(k_1, \cdots, k_n)$.

Proof. For any $t \in \mathbb{R}$, there exists function $\mathrm{sech}(t)$ such that $0 < \mathrm{sech}(t) \le 1$. Since $k_i > 0$ is the ith diagonal element of k, $k = k^T$, and $\dot{\tanh}^T(kx) = [\mathrm{sech}^2(k_1x_1)k_1\dot{x}_1, \cdots, \mathrm{sech}^2(k_nx_n)k_n\dot{x}_n]^T$, we have (9) obviously.

Theorem 1. *Given a constant delay upper bound $\bar{d}$, the nominal system Σ_o is asymptotically stable for any $0 < d \le \bar{d}$ if there exist a diagonal matrix $\bar{P} > 0$, matrices $Q > 0$, $R > 0$, $S > 0$, $W > 0$, $Z > 0$, U, N_g $(g = 1, \cdots, 4)$, and T_h $(h = 1, \cdots, 5)$, such that the following LMIs hold:*

$$\Phi := \begin{bmatrix} \Phi_{11} & \Phi_{12} & \Phi_{13} & \Phi_{14} & \bar{d}A^TT_5^T & \bar{d}N_1 \\ * & \Phi_{22} & \Phi_{23} & \Phi_{24} & \bar{d}B^TT_5^T & \bar{d}N_2 \\ * & * & \Phi_{33} & \Phi_{34} & -\bar{d}T_5^T & \bar{d}N_3 \\ * & * & * & \Phi_{44} & 0 & \bar{d}N_4 \\ * & * & * & * & -\bar{d}S & -\bar{d}W \\ * & * & * & * & * & -\bar{d}Z \end{bmatrix} < 0 \tag{10}$$

$$\begin{bmatrix} Q & U \\ * & R \end{bmatrix} > 0, \tag{11}$$

where

$$\begin{aligned}
\Phi_{11} &= Q + \bar{d}S + N_1 + N_1^T - T_1A - A^TT_1^T \\
\Phi_{12} &= -N_1 + N_2^T - T_1B - A^TT_2^T \\
\Phi_{13} &= \bar{P} + U + \bar{d}Wk + N_3^T + T_1 - A^TT_3^T \\
\Phi_{14} &= N_4^T - A^TT_4^T \\
\Phi_{22} &= -Q - N_2 - N_2^T - T_2B - B^TT_2^T \\
\Phi_{23} &= -N_3^T + T_2 - B^TT_3^T \\
\Phi_{24} &= -U - N_4^T - B^TT_4^T \\
\Phi_{33} &= R + T_3 + T_3^T + \bar{d}kZk \\
\Phi_{34} &= T_4^T, \; \Phi_{44} = -R,
\end{aligned}$$

and $*$ denotes the terms that are introduced by symmetry.

Proof. We choose a general Lyapunov-Krasovskii functional for system (8) as:

$$\begin{aligned}
V(t) &= V_1 + V_2 + V_3, \\
V_1 &= 2\sum_{i=1}^{n} \frac{\bar{p}_i}{k_i} \ln(\cosh k_ix_i), \\
V_2 &= \int_{t-d}^{t} \begin{bmatrix} \tanh(kx(s)) \\ \dot{x}(s) \end{bmatrix}^T \begin{bmatrix} Q & U \\ U^T & R \end{bmatrix} \begin{bmatrix} \tanh(kx(s)) \\ \dot{x}(s) \end{bmatrix} ds, \\
V_3 &= \int_{-d}^{0}\int_{t+\theta}^{t} \begin{bmatrix} \tanh(kx(s)) \\ \dot{\tanh}(kx(s)) \end{bmatrix}^T \begin{bmatrix} S & W \\ W^T & Z \end{bmatrix} \begin{bmatrix} \tanh(kx(s)) \\ \dot{\tanh}(kx(s)) \end{bmatrix} dsd\theta,
\end{aligned} \tag{12}$$

where x_i is the ith element of $x(t)$, and k_i is the ith diagonal element of k. Here, $k_i > 0$ and $\bar{p}_i > 0$. Since

$$\cosh(k_i x_i) = \frac{e^{k_i x_i} + e^{-k_i x_i}}{2} \geq (e^{k_i x_i})^{\frac{1}{2}} (e^{-k_i x_i})^{\frac{1}{2}} = 1, \tag{13}$$

and $k_i > 0$, $\bar{p}_i > 0$, we know that $V_1 > 0$ for all $x(t)$ and $V_1 \to \infty$ as $\|x\| \to \infty$. Moreover, since (10) implies that $\begin{bmatrix} S & W \\ W^T & Z \end{bmatrix} > 0$, together with (11), we know the proposed Lyapunov-Krasovskii functional is legitimate.

For any matrices N_g $(g = 1, \cdots, 4)$ of appropriate dimensions, it can been seen that, from Newton-Leibniz formula,

$$\begin{aligned} 2&\left[\tanh^T(kx)N_1 + \tanh^T(kx_d)N_2 + \dot{x}^T N_3 + \dot{x}_d^T N_4\right] \\ &\times \left[\tanh(kx) - \tanh(kx_d) - \int_{t-d}^{t} \dot{\tanh}(kx(s))ds\right] = 0. \end{aligned} \tag{14}$$

Moreover, from the system equation in (8), we have

$$\begin{aligned} 2&\left[\tanh^T(kx)T_1 + \tanh^T(kx_d)T_2 + \dot{x}^T T_3 + \dot{x}_d^T T_4 + \int_{t-d}^{t} \tanh(kx(s))dsT_5\right] \\ &\times [-A\tanh(kx) - B\tanh(kx_d) + \dot{x}] = 0, \end{aligned} \tag{15}$$

for any matrices T_h $(h = 1, \cdots, 5)$ of appropriate dimensions.

Along the trajectories of system Σ_o, together with (14) and (15), the corresponding time derivative of $V(t)$ is given by:

$$\begin{aligned} \dot{V}(t) &= \dot{V_1} + \dot{V_2} + \dot{V_3} \\ &\quad + 2\left[\tanh^T(kx)N_1 + \tanh^T(kx_d)N_2 + \dot{x}^T N_3 + \dot{x}_d^T N_4\right] \\ &\qquad \times \left[\tanh(kx) - \tanh(kx_d) - \int_{t-d}^{t} \dot{\tanh}(kx(s))ds\right] \\ &\quad + 2\left[\tanh^T(kx)T_1 + \tanh^T(kx_d)T_2 + \dot{x}^T T_3 + \dot{x}_d^T T_4 \right. \\ &\qquad \left. + \int_{t-d}^{t} \tanh(kx(s))dsT_5\right] \times [-A\tanh(kx) - B\tanh(kx_d) + \dot{x}] \\ &\quad + d\eta^T(t)\tilde{T}\tilde{Z}^{-1}\tilde{T}^T\eta(t) - \int_{t-d}^{t} \eta^T(t)\tilde{T}\tilde{Z}^{-1}\tilde{T}^T\eta(t)ds \\ &\leq \eta^T(t)(\tilde{\Phi} + \bar{d}\tilde{T}\tilde{Z}^{-1}\tilde{T}^T)\eta(t) \\ &\quad - \int_{t-d}^{t} \left[\eta^T(t)\tilde{T} + \xi^T(s)\tilde{Z}\right]\tilde{Z}^{-1}\left[\eta^T(t)\tilde{T} + \xi^T(s)\tilde{Z}\right]^T ds, \end{aligned} \tag{16}$$

where

$$\eta^T(t) = \left[\tanh^T(kx),\ \tanh^T(kx_d),\ \dot{x}^T,\ \dot{x}_d^T\right]$$

$$\xi^T(s) = \left[\tanh^T(kx(s)),\ \dot{\tanh}^T(kx(s))\right]$$

$$\tilde{\Phi} = \begin{bmatrix} \Phi_{11} & \Phi_{12} & \Phi_{13} & \Phi_{14} \\ * & \Phi_{22} & \Phi_{23} & \Phi_{24} \\ * & * & \Phi_{33} & \Phi_{34} \\ * & * & * & \Phi_{44} \end{bmatrix} \tilde{T} = \begin{bmatrix} A^T T_5^T & N_1 \\ B^T T_5^T & N_2 \\ -T_5^T & N_3 \\ 0 & N_4 \end{bmatrix}, \ \tilde{Z} = \begin{bmatrix} S & W \\ W^T & Z \end{bmatrix}, \tag{17}$$

and $\bar{P} = \ \mathrm{diag}(\bar{p}_1, \bar{p}_2, \cdots, \bar{p}_n) \in \mathbb{R}^{n\times n}$.

Using the Schur complement [14], we know (10) is equivalent to $\tilde{\Phi} + \bar{d}\tilde{T}\tilde{Z}^{-1}\tilde{T}^T < 0$, which guarantees $\dot{V}(t) < 0$. Therefore, the nominal system Σ_o is asymptotically stable [2].

Remark 1. Lemma 3 was utilized in deriving the bound of the first term of $\dot{V}_3$. Except for Lemma 3, no inequalities are needed for the bounds on cross-terms products, such as $-2a^Tb \le a^TXa + b^TX^{-1}b,\ a, b \in \mathbb{R}^n,\ X > 0$ and so on. The conservatism of the delay-dependent criterion stems from the method for evaluating the bounds on some cross-terms product arising in the analysis of the delay-dependent stability problem [15]. Hence, our result has less conservatism for the system Σ_o.

Remark 2. It is clear from the proof of Theorem 1 that the free-weighting matrices N_g $(g = 1, \cdots, 4)$ in (14), and T_h $(h = 1, \cdots, 5)$ in (15) are used to express the relationship among the system variables, and some additional terms, which brings much flexibility in solving LMIs and avoids applying some inequalities for the bounds on cross-terms products. Also the LMIs (10) and (11) in Theorem 1 does not include any terms containing the product of the Lyapunov matrix $\bar{P}$ and the system matrices A, B. The result can readily be extended to a parameter-dependent Lyapunov-Krasovskii functional for a system with polytopic-type uncertainties.

3.2 Stability of a System with Polytopic-Type Uncertainties

Suppose the system matrix A, B are not precisely known, but subject to polytopic-type uncertain domain Ω. In this way, any mated matrices inside the domain Ω can be written as a convex combination of vertices (A_l, B_l) of the uncertainty ploytope, i.e.

$$\Omega := \left\{(A, B) : (A, B) = \sum_{l=1}^{N} \zeta_l(A_l, B_l), \zeta_l > 0, \sum_{l=1}^{N} \zeta_l = 1\right\}, \tag{18}$$

where $A_l \in \mathbb{R}^{n\times n}$, $B_l \in \mathbb{R}^{n\times n}$, $(l = 1, \cdots, N)$.

Now let Σ_p to denote the system Σ_o with polytopic-type uncertainties (18). According to Theorem 1 and Remark 2, we can obtain the following theorem.

Theorem 2. *Given a constant delay upper bound $\bar{d}$, the system Σ_p is asymptotically stable for any $0 < d \leq \bar{d}$ if there exist diagonal matrices $\bar{P}_l > 0$, matrices $Q_l > 0$, $R_l > 0$, $S_l > 0$, $W_l > 0$, $Z_l > 0$, U_l, N_{gl} $(g = 1, \cdots, 4, l = 1, \cdots, N)$, and T_h $(h = 1, \cdots, 5)$, such that the following LMIs hold:*

$$\Phi^{(l)} := \begin{bmatrix} \Phi_{11}^{(l)} & \Phi_{12}^{(l)} & \Phi_{13}^{(l)} & \Phi_{14}^{(l)} & \bar{d}A_l^T T_5^T & \bar{d}N_{1l} \\ * & \Phi_{22}^{(l)} & \Phi_{23}^{(l)} & \Phi_{24}^{(l)} & \bar{d}B_l^T T_5^T & \bar{d}N_{2l} \\ * & * & \Phi_{33}^{(l)} & \Phi_{34}^{(l)} & -\bar{d}T_5^T & \bar{d}N_{3l} \\ * & * & * & \Phi_{44}^{(l)} & 0 & \bar{d}N_{4l} \\ * & * & * & * & -\bar{d}S_l & -\bar{d}W_l \\ * & * & * & * & * & -\bar{d}Z_l \end{bmatrix} < 0 \tag{19}$$

$$\begin{bmatrix} Q_l & U_l \\ * & R_l \end{bmatrix} > 0, \tag{20}$$

where

$$\begin{aligned}
\Phi_{11}^{(l)} &= Q_l + \bar{d}S_l + N_{1l} + N_{1l}^T - T_1 A_l - A_l^T T_1^T \\
\Phi_{12}^{(l)} &= -N_{1l} + N_{2l}^T - T_1 B_l - A_l^T T_2^T \\
\Phi_{13}^{(l)} &= \bar{P}_l + U_l + \bar{d}W_l k + N_{3l}^T + T_1 - A_l^T T_3^T \\
\Phi_{14}^{(l)} &= N_{4l}^T - A_l^T T_4^T \\
\Phi_{22}^{(l)} &= -Q_l - N_{2l} - N_{2l}^T - T_2 B_l - B_l^T T_2^T \\
\Phi_{23}^{(l)} &= -N_{3l}^T + T_2 - B_l^T T_3^T \\
\Phi_{24}^{(l)} &= -U_l - N_{4l}^T - B_l^T T_4^T \\
\Phi_{33}^{(l)} &= R_l + T_3 + T_3^T + \bar{d}kZ_l k \\
\Phi_{34}^{(l)} &= T_4^T, \quad \Phi_{44}^{(l)} = -R_l.
\end{aligned}$$

Proof. Let the parameter-dependent matrices $P(\zeta)$, $Q(\zeta)$, $R(\zeta)$, $S(\zeta)$, $Z(\zeta)$, $U(\zeta)$, $W(\zeta)$ and $N_g(\zeta)$,$(g = 1, \cdots, 4)$, be

$$X(\zeta) = \sum_{l=1}^{N} \zeta_l X_l, \tag{21}$$

where X stands for P, Q, R, S, Z, U, W and N_g. Replacing (21) and (18) with (10) and (11), then the result follows immediately from Theorem 1.

3.3 Stability of a System with Norm-Bounded Uncertainties

The result of previous subsection were derived for the case where the system matrices of Σ_p lie in a given polytope. An alternative way of dealing with uncertain systems is to assume that the system matrices are with norm-bounded uncertainties [16, 17].

Consider the following system

$$\begin{aligned}(\Sigma_n): \dot{x} &= (A+\Delta A)\tanh(kx) + (B+\Delta B)\tanh(kx_d)\\ x(s) &= \phi(s), \qquad s \in [-\bar{d}, 0]\end{aligned} \tag{22}$$

where ϕ, A, B are defined in previous subsection. The matrices ΔA and ΔB denote the norm-bounded uncertainties in system and they are of the form

$$[\Delta A, \Delta B] = MF(t)\,[E_a, E_b] \tag{23}$$

where M, E_a, E_b are known constant matrices of appropriate dimensions and $F(t)$ is a time-varying matrix with Lebesgue-measurable elements satisfying $F^T(t)F(t) \leq I$.

The following lemma is used to deal with a system with norm-bounded uncertainties [18].

Lemma 4. *Given matrices $Q = Q^T$, M, E, and $Y > 0$ with appropriate dimensions*

$$Q + MF(t)E + E^T F^T(t) M^T < 0, \tag{24}$$

for all $F(t)$ satisfying $F^T(t)F(t) \leq Y$, if and only if there exists a scalar $\varepsilon > 0$ such that

$$Q + \varepsilon M M^T + \varepsilon^{-1} E^T Y E < 0. \tag{25}$$

Theorem 3. *Given a constant delay upper bound $\bar{d}$, the system Σ_n is asymptotically stable for any $0 < d \leq \bar{d}$ if there exist a diagonal matrix $\bar{P} > 0$, matrices $Q > 0$, $R > 0$, $S > 0$, $W > 0$, $Z > 0$, U, N_g $(g = 1, \cdots, 4)$, and T_h $(h = 1, \cdots, 5)$, such that the following LMIs hold,*

$$\begin{bmatrix} \Phi_{11} + E_a^T E_a & \Phi_{12} + E_a^T E_b & \Phi_{13} & \Phi_{14} & \bar{d}A^T T_5^T & \bar{d}N_1 & -T_1 M \\ * & \Phi_{22} + E_b^T E_b & \Phi_{23} & \Phi_{24} & \bar{d}B^T T_5^T & \bar{d}N_2 & -T_2 M \\ * & * & \Phi_{33} & \Phi_{34} & -\bar{d}T_5^T & \bar{d}N_3 & -T_3 M \\ * & * & * & \Phi_{44} & 0 & \bar{d}N_4 & -T_4 M \\ * & * & * & * & -\bar{d}S & -\bar{d}W & \bar{d}T_5 M \\ * & * & * & * & * & -\bar{d}Z & 0 \\ * & * & * & * & * & * & -I \end{bmatrix} < 0 \tag{26}$$

$$\begin{bmatrix} Q & U \\ * & R \end{bmatrix} > 0, \tag{27}$$

where $\Phi_{i'j'}$ $(i' = 1, \cdots, 4, i' \leq j' \leq 4)$ are defined in (10).

Proof. Substituting A and B in (10) for $A + MF(t)E_a$ and $B + MF(t)E_b$, respectively, we can obtain

$$\Phi + \Gamma_M^T F(t) \Gamma_E + \Gamma_E^T F(t) \Gamma_M < 0, \tag{28}$$

where

$$\Gamma_M = \left[-M^T T_1^T, -M^T T_2^T, -M^T T_3^T, -M^T T_4^T, \bar{d} M^T T_5^T, 0\right]$$
$$\Gamma_E = \left[E_a, E_b, 0, 0, 0, 0\right].$$

Utilizing Lemma 4, we know that (28) holds means there exists a scalar $\varepsilon > 0$ such that

$$\Phi + \varepsilon \Gamma_M^T \Gamma_M + \varepsilon^{-1} \Gamma_E^T \Gamma_E < 0. \quad (29)$$

That is

$$\varepsilon \Phi + \varepsilon^2 \Gamma_M^T \Gamma_M + \Gamma_E^T \Gamma_E < 0. \quad (30)$$

Replacing $\varepsilon \bar{P}$, εQ, εR, εS, εW, εZ, εU, εN_g $(g = 1, \cdots, 4)$, and εT_h $(h = 1, \cdots, 5)$ with $\bar{P}$, Q, R, S, W, Z, U, N_g $(g = 1, \cdots, 4)$, and T_h $(h = 1, \cdots, 5)$, respectively, and applying the Schur complement, we know that (30) is equivalent to (26) and (27) holds obviously.

4 Simulation Example

Consider the following continuous-time nonlinear system with time delays:

$$\begin{aligned} \dot{x}_1 &= -0.4 \sin x_1 + x_2 - 0.1 x_{d1} \\ \dot{x}_2 &= -1.2 \sin x_1 - 0.1 x_{d2} + 0.37 x_1^3. \end{aligned} \quad (31)$$

Suppose that we have the following HFRBs:

If x_1 is P_{x1} and x_2 is P_{x2} and x_{d1} is $P_{x_{d1}}$, then $\dot{x}_1 = C_{x1}^1 + C_{x2} + C_{x_{d2}}$,
If x_1 is N_{x1} and x_2 is P_{x2} and x_{d1} is $P_{x_{d1}}$, then $\dot{x}_1 = -C_{x1}^1 + C_{x2} + C_{x_{d2}}$,
...
If x_1 is N_{x1} and x_2 is N_{x2} and x_{d1} is $N_{x_{d1}}$, then $\dot{x}_1 = -C_{x1}^1 - C_{x2} - C_{x_{d2}}$,
If x_1 is P_{x1} and x_{d2} is $P_{x_{d2}}$, then $\dot{x}_2 = C_{x1}^2 + C_{x_{d2}}$,
...
If x_1 is N_{x1} and x_{d2} is $N_{x_{d2}}$, then $\dot{x}_2 = -C_{x1}^2 - C_{x_{d2}}$,

Here, we choose membership functions of P_{xi}, N_{xi}, $P_{x_{di}}$ and $N_{x_{di}}$ $(i = 1, 2)$, as follows:

$$\begin{aligned} \mu_{P_{x_i}}(x) &= e^{-\frac{1}{2}(x_i - k_i)^2}, \mu_{N_{x_i}}(x) = e^{-\frac{1}{2}(x_i + k_i)^2} \\ \mu_{P_{x_{di}}}(x) &= e^{-\frac{1}{2}(x_{di} - k_i)^2}, \mu_{N_{x_{di}}}(x) = e^{-\frac{1}{2}(x_{di} + k_i)^2}. \end{aligned} \quad (32)$$

Then, we have the following model:

$$\dot{x} = A \tanh(kx) + B \tanh(kx_d), \quad (33)$$

where $k = diag(k_1, k_2)$, $A = \begin{bmatrix} C_{x1}^1 & C_{x2} \\ C_{x1}^2 & 0 \end{bmatrix}$, $B = \begin{bmatrix} C_{x_{d1}} & 0 \\ 0 & C_{x_{d2}} \end{bmatrix}$.

We construct the FHM as (33) for the nonlinear system in (31) by neural network BP algorithm [10]. So the system matrices A, B, and parameter matrix k can be obtained as:

$$A = \begin{bmatrix} -0.3588 & 3.7569 \\ -0.7549 & 0 \end{bmatrix}, \ B = \begin{bmatrix} -0.0379 & 0 \\ 0 & -0.3275 \end{bmatrix}, k = \begin{bmatrix} 1.6512 & 0 \\ 0 & 0.2704 \end{bmatrix}. \quad (34)$$

In order to validate the proposed results, we add the uncertainties as follows:
i)

$$A = \begin{bmatrix} -0.3588 & 3.7569 + \delta \\ -0.7549 & 0 \end{bmatrix},$$

where $-0.5 \leq \delta \leq 0.5$.

Thus, vertices (A_l, B_l) of the uncertainty ploytope in (18) are given, where

$$A_1 = \begin{bmatrix} -0.3588 & 4.2569 \\ -0.7549 & 0 \end{bmatrix}, A_2 = \begin{bmatrix} -0.3588 & 3.2569 \\ -0.7549 & 0 \end{bmatrix}, B_1 = B_2 = B.$$

ii) $M = I, E_a = \begin{bmatrix} 0.02 & 0.04 \\ 0.04 & 0.02 \end{bmatrix}, E_b = 0.02I$, as the form of (23).

In case i), the maximum value of $\bar{d} = 3.9852$ is obtained by using Theorem 2; In case ii), the maximum value of $\bar{d} = 3.5634$ is obtained by using Theorem 3.

5 Conclusion

In this paper, based on the FHM, the delay-dependent criteria for a class of nonlinear continuous-time systems are presented. A general Lyapunov-Krasovskii functional are used and some additional free-weighting matrices, which bring much flexibility in solving LMIs, are introduced during the proof. The results then easily have been extended to a system with either polytopic-type or norm-bounded uncertainties. A numerical example is given to validate the proposed results.

Acknowledgment

The research is partially supported by the National Natural Science Foundation of China (60325311, 60534010, 60572070) and the Program for Changjiang Scholars and Innovative Research Team in University.

References

1. Hale, J.K., Lunel, S.M.V.: Introduction to Functional Differential Equations. New York: Springer-Verlag (1993)
2. Kolmanovskii, V.B., Myshkis, A.D.: Applied Theory of Functional Differential Equations. Norwell, MA: Kluwer (1992)

3. Niculescu, S.-I., Verriest, E.I., Dugard, L., Dion, J.-D.: Stability and Robust Stability of Time-delay Systems: A Guided Tour. Stability and Control of Time-Delay Systems. Dugard, L., and Verriest, E.I., Eds. London, U.K.: Springer-Verlag **228** (1997) 1–71
4. Luo, J.S., Van, P.P.J., Bosch D.: Independent of Delay Stability Criteria for Uncertain Linear State Space Models. Automatica. **39** (1997) 171–179
5. Takagi, T., Sugeno, M.: Fuzzy Identification of Systems and its Applications to Modeling and Control. IEEE Trans. Syst. Man Cybern. **15** (1985) 116–132
6. Cao, Y.Y., Frank, P.M.: Analysis and Synthesis of Nonlinear Time Delay Systems via Fuzzy Control Approach. IEEE Trans. Fuzzy Syst. **8** (2000) 200–211
7. —— Stability Analysis and Synthesis of Nonlinear Time-delay Systems via Linear Takagi–Sugeno Fuzzy Models. Fuzzy Sets Syst. **124** (2001) 213–219
8. Guan, X.P., Chen,C.L.: Delay-dependent Guaranteed Cost Control for T–S Fuzzy Systems with Time Delays. IEEE Trans. Fuzzy Syst. **12** (2004) 236–249
9. Chen, B., Liu, X.: Delay-dependent Robust H_∞ Control for T–S Fuzzy Systems with Time Delay. IEEE Trans. Fuzzy Syst. **13** (2005) 544–556
10. Zhang, H., Quan, Y.: Modeling, Identification and Control of a Class of Nonlinear System. IEEE Trans. Fuzzy Syst. **9** (2001) 349–354
11. Quan, Y.: Studies on Fuzzy Modeling and Control Methods of Nonlinear Systems. Ph.D. Dissertation. Northeastern University, Shenyang, China (2001)
12. Lin, C., Wang, Q.-G., Lee T.: A Less Conservative Robust Stability Test for Linear Uncertain Time-delay Systems. IEEE Trans. Automat. Contr. **51** (2006) 87–91
13. He, Y., Wu, M., She, J.-H., Liu, G.-P.: Parameter-Dependent Lyapunov Function for Stability of Time-delay Systems with Polytopic-type Uncertainties. IEEE Trans. Automat. Contr. **49** (2004) 828–832
14. Boyd, S., Ghaoui, L.E., Feron, E., Balakrishan, V.: Linear Matrix Inequalities in System and Control Theory. Philadelphia, PA: SIAM (1994)
15. Xu, S., Lam, J.: Improved Delay-dependent Stability Criteria for Timedelay Systems. IEEE Trans. Automat. Contr. **50** (2005) 384–387
16. Fridman, E., Shaked, U.: An Improved Stabilization Method for Linear Time-delay Systems. IEEE Trans. Automat. Contr. **47** (2002) 1931–1937
17. Wu, M., He, Y., She, J.-H.: New Delay-dependent Stability Criteria and Stabilizing Method for Neutral Systems. IEEE Trans. Automat. Contr. **49** (2004) 2266–2271
18. Xie, L.: Output Feedback H_∞ Control of Systems with Parameter Uncertainty. Int. J. Contr. **63** (1996) 741–750
19. Lun, S., Zhang, H., Liu, D.: Fuzzy Hyperbolic H_∞ Filter Design for a Class of Nonlinear Continous-time Dynamic Systems. Proc. of the 43th IEEE Int. Conf. on Decision and Contr. Atlantis, Paradise Island, Bahamas. (2004) 225–230
20. Yang, J., Liu, D., Feng, J., Zhang, H.: Controller Design for a Class of Nonlinear Systems Based on Fuzzy Hyperbolic Model. WCICA06. Dalian, China (to appear)

Evaluation of the Aquaculture Pond Water Quality Based on Fuzzy Mathematics Model

Ruimei Wang[1], Xiaoshuan Zhang[2], Wengui Cai[3], Jinhuan Wu[2], and Zetian Fu[1,*]

[1] College of Economics & Management, China Agricultural University, P.O. Box 129#, Beijing, 100083, People's Republic of china
wangrm73@cau.edu.cn
[2] China Agriculture University, P.O. Box 209#, Beijing, 100083, People's Republic of china
[3] Key Laboratory for Fishery Ecology Environment, Ministry of Agriculture, P.R. China
wangrm73@cau.edu.cn

Abstract. Water quality management plays a very important role in fish life and aquatic product quality. The paper firstly selects the index system and confirm the weight of each of the water quality factors dependent on the fish tolerance to the factors of water quality integrated with the result of the expert questionnaire by the Delphi method with the Water Quality Standard, then constructs the fuzzy evaluation model of the multiplex water quality parameter and classifies the standard of water quality into five classes of standard. At last the paper give an experimental model based on the monitored datum in North China. It shows that it can evaluate the water quality integrative and provide the degree of membership that the water quality belongs to all the standards.

1 Introduction

In the recent years, many fish, the shrimp and the shellfish death and the frequent emerging of all kinds of disease had reduced the fishermen income and brought out the quality unsafety due that the serious aging and eutrophicated aquaculture ponds and the unbalance of ecosystem of aquaculture water [4]. So water quality management has becoming the most important element for constraining the output of the fish. Water quality evaluation is the first step for water quality management, which can justify the current pond water quality situation and provide the water quality management with scientific proof. It is inevitable to construct the complete, rational and scientific index system to achieve better evaluation result of pond water quality. Thus, this paper puts forward the pond water quality model, which consists of evaluation index system and evaluation standards combined the fuzzy theory with expert questionnaire.

2 Confirming the Pond Water Quality Evaluation Indices

There are many factors that influence the pond water quality. An evaluation system can not include all the factors, and for a single factor its influence on the pond water

[*] Corresponding author. Tel.:+86-10-62736323; Fax:+86-10-62736717.

D.-S. Huang, K. Li, and G.W. Irwin (Eds.): ICIC 2006, LNAI 4114, pp. 32–43, 2006.

quality is different. The influencing factors of the fresh breeding pond water quality include physical factors, chemical factors and biological factors. The physical factors include the macro environmental factors and the pond water quality factors. The chemical factors include some basic chemicals and some microelements such as DO (dissolved oxygen), pH, and the biological factors include plankton and other benthic organism and microbes.

Production proves that in the process of the pond water quality evaluation, some factors such as the microelements and toxicants are negligible. Different experts give different values on these factors. That is, experts hold different ideas on selecting which factors to evaluate generally the pond water quality. Because of this, we confirm the pond water quality evaluation indices by the expert questionnaire. Under the instruction of the experts, we choose 14 factors, and ask the experts to give importance on each of the 14 factors. The determination of the factors' importance degree coefficients is the main step of comprehensive judgment. Whether the subset of factor A is appropriately determined or not, will influence the comprehensive judgment directly. We choose the Delphi method to choose the factors' importance degree, and confirm the evaluation indices system.

Suppose that the pond water quality evaluation will choose the appropriate factors to evaluate from the following m factors, such as DO, pH value, transparency, and let the factor set be U, The importance degree fuzziness subset of the factor U is A

$$U = \{u_1, u_2, \cdots, u_m\}, \quad \underset{\sim}{A} = \{a_1, a_2, \cdots, a_m\}. \tag{1}$$

We determine the factors' importance degree coefficients $a_i (i = 1,2,\cdots,m)$ by the Delphi method, the Delphi method is also called expert evaluation method, which combines the experts' intelligence and is one of the effective ways to determine the factors' importance coefficients in the process of problem solving. The work of calculating the factors' importance degree coefficient must be done by the experts, requiring the experts' profound knowledge and the whole situation of the problem needed to be solved.

2.1 Determination of Importance Rank of the Pond Water Quality Factor

According to the concrete situation of the Tianjin fresh water pond water breeding, when choosing the evaluation indices, we must delete the irrelevant and unimportant influential factors.

The factors' importance ranking values F_i by the experts are statistic as follows:

When $\frac{F_{j-k}}{F_{i-k}} \le 1$, *Denote* $A_{ij-k} = 1$ When $\frac{F_{j-k}}{F_{i-k}} > 1$, *Denote* $A_{ij-k} = 0$

Suppose that there are n experts in total. Sum up all the A_{ij-k} value of all the experts. That is,

$$A_{ij} = \sum_{k=1}^{n} A_{ij-k}, i = 1,2,\cdots,m, \quad j = 1,2,\cdots,m \,. \tag{2}$$

Thus, m×m statistic A_{ij} consists of the priority.

It can be give from the result of A_{ij} in every line of the above table.

$\sum A_i$ shows the accumulated value of A_{ij} in the line I, order that

$$\sum A_{\max} = \max\left\{\sum A_1, \sum A_2, \cdots, \sum A_m\right\}, \sum A_{\min} = \min\left\{\sum A_1, \sum A_2, \cdots, \sum A_m\right\}. \tag{3}$$

In evidence, the degree of importance of element is highest which is corresponding with $\sum A_{\min}$, moreover, it is the lowest that comparing with other elements which is corresponding with $\sum A_{\max}$.

2.2 Grading 'd' of Important Degree Between Elements

$a_{\max} = 1, a_{\min} = 0.1(a_{\max}, a_{\min})$ was determined, they can be in [0, 1], then

$$d = \frac{\sum A_{\max} - \sum A_{\min}}{a_{\max} - a_{\min}}. \tag{4}$$

According to equation (4) , it can be given the value of "d".

2.3 Coefficient for Important Degree of Every Elements in Water Quality

$$a_i = \frac{\sum A_i - \sum A_{\min}}{d} + 0.1 \qquad (i = 1, 2, \cdots, m). \tag{5}$$

The fuzzy subset can be given which is planed to determine. According to the above equation, fuzzy subset (Zhang Yue, 1992) of element important degree for aquaculture water quality.

$$\underset{\sim}{A} = (a_1, a_2, \cdots, a_m) = (1.004, 0.866, 0.812, 0.691, 0.74, 0.333, 0.239, 0.737, 0.248, 0.454, 0.449, 0.458, 0.337, 0.1)$$

Evaluation index was give, u_1, u_2, u_3, u_5, u_8. That is DO, pH, Phytoplankton (mg/l,) SD and N.

3 The Confirmation of the Evaluation Standard

3.1 The Confirmation of the Grade of Water Quality

The fish has its adaptability to each biological index, which is due to the fish's physiology. Different fish may have different adaptability for the same index, and the same fish may has different adaptability to deferent indexes. This paper put its emphasis on the adult carp, so the evaluation standard was designed for carp.

The adaptability for fish to element affected on water quality is decided by the distributing of the water element. For the majority of the index, both a high density and a low density will violate fishes' living environment. Further, it can cause fish to get disease or die. According to this principle of normal distribution and the suggestions from the experts, we grade the water quality as the following. Based on the fish's duration to the inspect index, five grades are established, showed in table 1:

Table 1. Fuzzy classification for the pond water quality [7]

Classification	Description
Excellent	All evaluated indexes are in the best scope that fish can live with
Good	Some of the indexes have approached or reached upper limit or lower limit of the best survival region that the fish can live with
Ordinary	Some of the elements have approached or reached upper limit or lower limit of the fish duration; if the water quality keeps on deteriorating, the fish will fall sick or even die.
Bad	Some of the indexes have reached or exceeded upper limit or lower limit of the fish duration, if the water quality keeps on deteriorating, the fish will die substantively.
Very bad	Most of indexes have exceeded upper limit or lower limit of the fish duration, if the water quality keeps on deteriorating; it is difficult for fish to live.

According to the information above, the evaluation standard of the pond water quality can be confirmed by using the questionnaires.

3.2 Dividing of the Evaluation Index of Water Quality

3.2.1 The Distribution of the Evaluation Data

First, we divide the data into several segments in terms of the value of the data from small value to big one, then we get a pillar figure by calculating the ratio of certain evaluation experts to the whole experts. Now, we take a expert questionnaire based on excellent PH as an example. It is shown as the left-side pillar in the figure 1(1-5).

It can be known from left-side pillar in the figure 1(1-5) that the percents of the experts considered that the water quality is excellent to very bad.

3.2.2 Value Determinate of the Standard for Evaluation

The authority of the expert is reflected by the particular expert's familiarity to the degree to which a certain index can affect the water quality. We multiply every evaluation by the authority coefficient. That is to say, we select the expert authority value that lies in the same evaluation interval and add them up, and then we calculate the percentage of the authority coefficient of a particular interval in the gross authority coefficient (Chen Yongsen, 1999). We still take an expert questionnaire based on excellent DO etc. as an example. It is shown as the right-side pillar in the figure 1(1-5).

By the same method, the grade of other five indexes can be determined; it was shown as table 3.

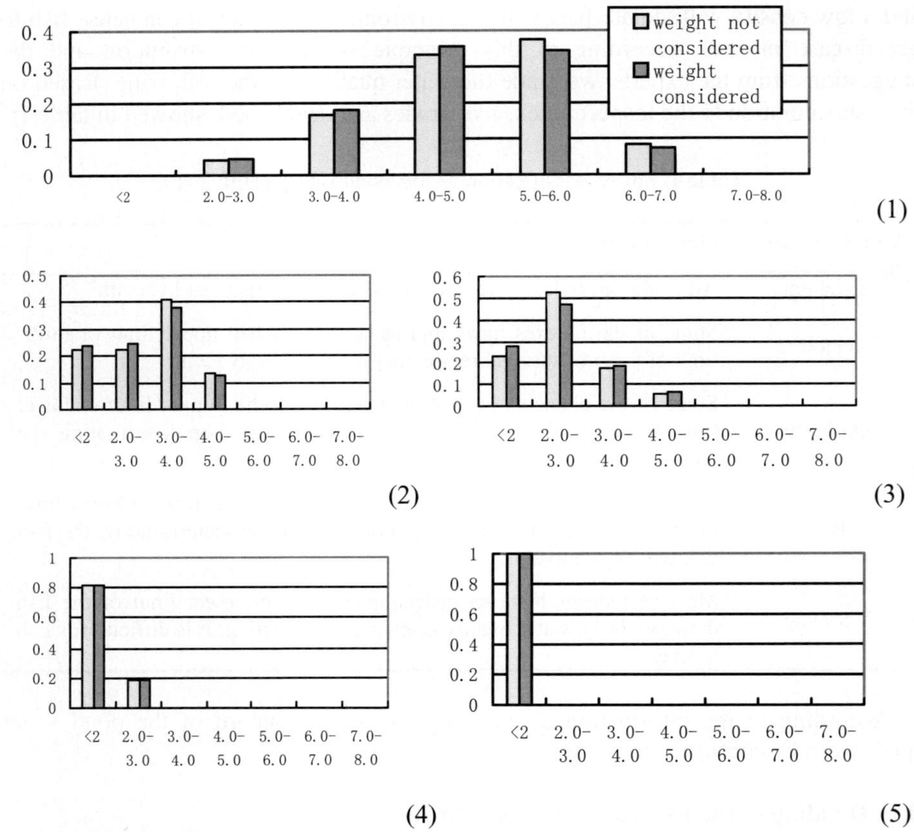

Fig. 1. (1) The condition is that DO is excellent by the expert;figure ; (2) The condition is that DO is good by the expert;figure 1 (3) The condition is that DO is middling by the expertfigure; (4) The condition is that DO is bad by the expert; The condition is that DO is very bad by the expert

Table 2. The scope of standard value of the index system

Index	Excellent	Good	Middling	Bad	Very bad
PH	(7.5,8.5)	(6.5,7.5)or (8.5,9.0]	(6.0,6.5]or (9.0,9.5]	(5.5,6.0] or (9.5,14]	(0,5.5] or (9.5,14]
SD (cm)	(25,40]	(15,25]or (40,60]	(10,15]or (60,80]	(5,10]or (80,100]	(0,5]or (100,150]
TN (mg/l)	(1.5,2.5]	(2.5,4.0]	(4.0,7.0]	(7.0,10]	(10,20]
DO at 8 AM	(4.0,6.0]	(3.0,4.0]	(2.0,3.0]	(0,2]	(0,2]
Phytoplankton (mg/l)	(35,60]	(20,35]or (60,90]	(15,20]or (90,120]	(5,15] or (120,150]	(0,5] or (150,300)

3.2.3 Evaluation Standard

According to the above methods, the evaluation standard can be given as it is showed in the table 2.

4 Fuzzy Synthetically Evaluation of Multinomial Water Quality Element

The same as other phenomenon in the nature, fuzzy phenomenon and fuzzy concept (S.Tamura, et al, 1971) exist in the pond water environment. About the water quality, it makes the changes of the water quality in people's mind be fuzzy, because besides the parameter is multi-changeable that can reflect the water quality, the definition of water quality is fuzzy itself. For example, when people say that the water quality is getting better or worse in recent years, or say that the water quality in one region is better than the one in another region, there is no clear conceptual boundaries between the 'good' and 'bad'. Therefore, a discussion on using the fuzzy theory to study and deal with the water quality is worthwhile.

There belong to both one level and the other level in bad water or good water carving up, which is the called as fuzzy. So the task of the evaluation of the pond water quality is to confirm the sample's the grade of membership in the sample set X to the fuzzy subclass $\tilde{A}$ (D.dubois and H.Prade, 1980).

Suppose that there are several elements (or indexes) to describe the water quality. The element set is $U = \{u_1, u_2, u_3, \cdots, u_n\}$. Again, we suppose the possible comment is m, and comment set is.

$$\tilde{A} = (a_1, a_2, a_3, \cdots, a_m)\,. \tag{6}$$

4.1 The Quantitative Disposal of the Evaluation Index

As a result for the quantitative disposal [1] of the evaluation index of table 3, the standard value of the index system is given in table 3.

Table 3. The standard value after quantitative disposal of the evaluation index

	Excellen t	Good	Middling	Bad	Very bad
PH value	8	7 or 8.75	6.25 or 9.25	55.75 or 9.75	5.25 or 10
SD (cm)	30	10 or 50	10 or 70	10 or 90	10 or 110
TN (mg/l)	2	3.25	5.5	8.5	11
Do at 8 AM	5	3.5	2.5	1	1
Phytoplankton (mg/l)	47.5	25or 75	7.5 or 105	7.5 or 135	160

4.2 The Integrated Weighted Matrix of the Graded Evaluation Index of the Pond Water Quality

According to the water quality standard and the local experts' experiences, the grade C of water quality and m evaluation index can be confirmed. We sample water from n ponds or testing place. In each sample, there are m-inspected values of graded evaluation index. The degree of good or bad for water quality is divided into c classification. It is the value y that the standard for the density of the evaluation index. Therefore, we can get the standard density matrix $y_{m\times c}$ of the c classification water quality and the inspected density matrix $x_{m\times n}$ of the pond water quality.

In pattern recognition, the value in the standard of the evaluation index is confirmed according to the inspected sample value.

$$y_{m\times c} = \begin{bmatrix} y_{11} & y_{12} & \cdots & y_{1c} \\ y_{21} & y_{22} & \cdots & y_{2c} \\ \vdots & \vdots & \vdots & \vdots \\ y_{m1} & y_{m2} & \cdots & y_{mc} \end{bmatrix}. \tag{7}$$

$$x_{m\times n} = \begin{bmatrix} x_{11} & x_{12} & \cdots & x_{1n} \\ x_{21} & x_{22} & \cdots & x_{2n} \\ \vdots & \vdots & \vdots & \vdots \\ x_{m1} & x_{m2} & \cdots & x_{mn} \end{bmatrix}. \tag{8}$$

We divided the index into a descending part and an increasing part. (1) The standard value is decreasing from 1 classification to C classification; (2) the standard value is increasing from 1 classification to C classification. But due to the fish's demand, the majority indexes are the combination of the above two types.

A good or bad concept of pond water quality is very fuzzy. So it can be described by the grade of membership in the fuzzy set. It is regulated in this paper that the element value 1 in the fuzzy matrix correspond to the standard density of 1 classification water quality, 0 in the fuzzy matrix correspond to the standard density of c classification water quality, and the interval [0,1] correspond to the water quality standard density that is between 1 and C classification. To the (1) type index, let corresponding grade of membership be 0 (left apices) if the it is less than or equal to the c classification value; let corresponding grade of membership be 1 (right apices) if the it is larger than or equal to the 1 classification value. The corresponding grade of membership can be confirmed according to the linear transformation when the standard value is between c classification and 1. The corresponding grade of membership of (1) type can be confirmed as in formula (9).

$$r_{ij} = \begin{cases} 0 & x_{ij} \le y_{ic} \\ \dfrac{x_{ij} - y_{ic}}{y_{ic} - y_{i1}} & y_{ic} < x_{ij} < y_{i1} \\ 1 & x_{ij} \ge y_{i1} \end{cases}. \tag{9}$$

The corresponding grade of membership of the h classification can be confirmed according to the linear equation as following (10).

$$s_{ih} = \begin{cases} 0 & , y_{ih} = y_{ic} \\ \dfrac{y_{ih} - y_{ic}}{y_{i1} - y_{ic}} & , y_{ic} < y_{ih} < y_{i1} \\ 1 & , y_{ih} = y_{i1} \end{cases} . \tag{10}$$

To the (2) type index, let corresponding grade of membership be 1 (left apices) if the it is less than or equal to the 1 classification value; let corresponding grade of membership be 0 (right apices) if the it is larger than or equal to the c classification value. The corresponding grade of membership can be confirmed according to the linear transformation when the standard value is between c classification and 1.

According to the linear transformation as formula (12).

$$r_{ij} = \begin{cases} 0 & x_{ij} \geq y_{ic} \\ \dfrac{y_{ic} - x_{ij}}{y_{ic} - y_{i1}} & y_{i1} < x_{ij} < y_{ic} \\ 1 & x_{ij} \leq y_{i1} \end{cases} . \tag{11}$$

$$s_{ih} = \begin{cases} 0 & y_{ih} = y_{ic} \\ \dfrac{y_{ic} - y_{ih}}{y_{ic} - y_{i1}} & y_{i1} < y_{ih} < y_{ic} \\ 1 & y_{ih} = y_{i1} \end{cases} . \tag{12}$$

In the formula, y_{i1}, y_{ih}, and y_{ic} separately stand for grade one, grade h, and grade of standard density of water quality index. r_{ij} is the corresponding grade of membership of density i of sample j , s_{ih} is the corresponding grade of membership of density i of classification h .

We can transform the matrix (1) to a fuzzy matrix of the pond water quality standard by using the equation (8). It is shown in the matrix (13).

$$s_{m \times c} = \begin{bmatrix} s_{11} & s_{12} & \cdots & s_{1c} \\ s_{21} & s_{22} & \cdots & s_{2c} \\ \vdots & \vdots & \vdots & \vdots \\ s_{m1} & s_{m2} & \cdots & s_{mc} \end{bmatrix} . \tag{13}$$

In the same way, transforming the inspected density of the water quality evaluation index can get the inspected density matrix. It is shown in the matrix (14).

$$R_{m \times n} = \begin{bmatrix} r_{11} & r_{12} & \cdots & r_{1n} \\ r_{21} & r_{22} & \cdots & r_{2n} \\ \vdots & \vdots & \vdots & \vdots \\ r_{m1} & r_{m2} & \cdots & r_{mn} \end{bmatrix} . \tag{14}$$

The equation 10 describes the indexes' entire grade of membership in n samples to the fuzzy subset. According to the fuzzy set theory that the grade of membership can be defined as weighted one, we can take the inspected density of the water quality evaluation (14) as the weighted matrix in different element density. And by considering the different indexes' effects on the water quality, we weight the m evaluation indexes' effect on the water quality classification (According to the result of the questionnaire, we can get each index's weight by adding up the optimized value of the 5 indexes of the evaluation index system and then get the result of summation be divided by each index.) $\vec{v} = (v_1, v_2, \cdots v_m)$, ($\sum_{i=1}^{m} vi = 1$), from the above calculations, then $\vec{v} = (0.240\ .21, 0.19, 0.18, 0.18)$.

$$A_{m\times n} = \vec{v} \times R_{m\times n}. \tag{15}$$

The element in matrix $A_{m\times n}$ was normalized in term of arrangement, and then the matrix $W_{m\times n}$ can be gained.

$$W = \begin{Bmatrix} w_{11} & w_{12} & \cdots & w_{1n} \\ w_{21} & w_{22} & \cdots & w_{2n} \\ \cdots & \cdots & \cdots & \cdots \\ w_{31} & w_{32} & \cdots & w_{3n} \end{Bmatrix}. \tag{16}$$

4 3 Fuzzy Pattern Recognition of the Pond Water Quality Evaluation

The weighted matrix of the item m can be described by vector in formula (17):

$$\overline{W} = (W_1, W_2, \cdots, W_M)^T. \tag{17}$$

We use the vector (3-13) to describe the water quality standard (13) of grade H.

$$\overline{s}_h = (s_{1h}, s_{2h}, \cdots, s_{mh})^T. \tag{18}$$

We use the vector in formula (19) to describe the Jth water sample's equation of degree of membership (formula (14)) to the water quality standard.

$$\vec{r}_j = (r_{1j}, r_{2j}, \cdots, r_{mj})^T. \tag{19}$$

So we can consider using the generalized distance of W_i to describe the difference of water quality standard between the jth sample and the grade h.

$$\bar{W}\left|s_h - r_j\right| = \sqrt[p]{\sum_{i=1}^{m} (W_i\left|s_{ih} - r_{ij}\right|)^p}. \tag{20}$$

In the formula (20), p is the distance parameter.

According to the fuzziness of the pond water quality classification, the sample lives under each grade water quality standard with different grades of membership. It can be described by fuzzy matrix $U_{c\times n}$.

$$U_{c\times n} = \begin{bmatrix} u_{11}, & u_{12}, & \cdots, & u_{1n} \\ u_{21}, & u_{22}, & \cdots, & u_{2n} \\ \vdots & \vdots & \vdots & \vdots \\ u_{c1}, & u_{c2}, & \cdots, & u_{cn} \end{bmatrix} = u_{hj}. \tag{21}$$

The constraining condition is:

$$\sum_{h=1}^{c} u_{hj} - 1 = 0 \qquad \sum_{j=1}^{n} u_{hj} > 0. \tag{22}$$

The weighted-generalized distance is:

$$d[\vec{s}_h, \vec{r}_j] = u_{hj} \sqrt[p]{\sum_{i=1}^{m} (W_i\left|s_{ih} - r_{ij}\right|)^p}. \tag{23}$$

We use the least square method to establish a function to express the difference of water quality standard between Sample j and grade h.

$$\min \{F(u_{ij})\} = \sum_{j=1}^{n} \min \left[\sum_{h=1}^{c} u_{hj}^{2} \left[\sum_{i=1}^{m} \left[w_{ij} \left| r_{ij} - s_{ih} \right| \right]^{p} \right]^{2/p} \right] . \tag{24}$$

Then the LaGrange function is constructed as equation 25.

$$L(u_{hj}, \lambda) = \sum_{h=1}^{c} u_{hj}^{2} \left[\sum_{i=1}^{m} \left[w_{ij} (r_{ij} - s_{ih}) \right]^{p} \right]^{2/p} - \lambda \left(\sum_{h=1}^{c} u_{hj} - 1 \right) . \tag{25}$$

The partial derivative is gained by differentiating the λ and u_{hj} of the , and then $L(u_{hj}, \lambda)$ let the partial derivative be zero, so the best expression of element of classification matrix can gained.

When P is equal to 2, it is called Euclidean distance. The researches have proved that it is obvious that the advantages of the distance grade of membership. In practice, the Euclidean distance is to adopt to calculate the grade of membership. Shown in formula (26):

$$u_{hj} = \frac{1}{\sum_{k=1}^{c} \dfrac{\sum_{i=1}^{m} \left[w_{ij} (r_{ij} - s_{ih}) \right]^{2}}{\sum_{i=1}^{m} \left[w_{ij} (r_{ij} - s_{ik}) \right]^{2}}} \tag{26}$$

According to the above formula (3-21), each element in the best classification matrix can be calculated, and then the sample set's grade of membership to each classification can be gained. As a result, a reasonable evaluation for the pond water quality can be made.

5 An Evaluation of a Real Example

In order to test the reliability of the above method, we now evaluate the data collected from NanHe JingWu Co. Fresh Water Aiquiculture Pond in TianJin on the 3rd July and 15th August 2002. Then we compare it with the real situation and analyze the result.

Table 4. Inspected data of the pond water quality

	Number of pond	SD (cm)	PH	TN (mg/l)	DO at 8:00	Phytoplankton (mg/l)
3rd July	1	14	8.6	2.098304	8.46872	73.85
15th July	1	12	8.92	4.74	5.04	51.466
3rd July	2	13	8.4	0.949864	6.20568	58.76
15th July	2	11	9.10	5.05	5.85	69.625
3rd July	3	16.5	8.8	1.184573	7.19576	67.45
15th July	3	14	8.90	5.10	6.08	51.747
3rd July	4	24	8.8	1.087137	7.03664	123.58
15th July	4	16	8.81	5.70	7.51	50.069

The data in table 4 is collected from the pond 1 to pond 4 of Fresh Water Aquiculture Pond in TianJin in NanHe JingWu Co. on the 3rd July and 15th August 2002. By using Fuzzy synthetically evaluation to evaluate the water quality of the four ponds, we get the result that is shown in the following matrix of the grade of membership:

Table 5. The evaluation result for water quality on 3rd July

Grade of water	Degree of dependence			
	Pond number 1	Pond number 2	Pond number 3	Pond number 4
1	0.2333	0.390	0.218	0.473
2	0.530	0.438	0.584	0.350
3	0.153	0.109	0.130	0.095
4	0.050	0.038	0.042	0.048
5	0.336	0.034	0.026	0.034

Table 6. The evaluation result for water quality on 15th July

Grade of water	Degree of dependence			
	Pond number 1	Pond number 2	Pond number 3	Pond number 4
1	0.041	0.018	0.019	0.020
2	0.250	0.097	0.185	0.109
3	0.390	0.410	0.505	0.486
4	0.230	0.377	0.207	0.261
5	0.090	0.098	0.083	0.123

According to principle of the maximal grade of membership and the above matrix, we found that the water quality is good on 3rd July. The water quality of 1st, 2nd and 3rd pond are in grade 2, and the water quality of the 4th pond is excellent and in grade1. The fish lives normally. But compared with the situation on 3rd July, the water quality has been deteriorated on 15$^{th.}$ August. On 15th August, the water quality is all at normal classification. That is to say, some of the indexes have approached or reached the upper limit or lower limit of the fish endurance. If the water quality keeps on deteriorating, the fish will fall sick or will even die. So it is necessary to improve the pond's water quality. On 8th August, the fisherman took some measures to improve the pond's water quality. For several times, the fish has been floating head, and a few fishes died. It is proved by the practice that the result by this classification is accord to the practical situation. So it is a feasible evaluation method.

6 Conclusion

The evaluation indices standard density in the text means bi-directional density method, we establish the pond water quality evaluation model; bring up the optimal ranking mode of the water quality fuzziness evaluation. This method combines together the experts' experience and the method and theory of the evaluation, and it had reflected the fuzziness of the water quality and increase the objectivity of the evaluation, it is a complement to the existed theory of the water quality evaluation.

We evaluate the supervision data from the four ponds separately, and the evaluation results correspond with the basic situation of the pond water quality, indicating that the evaluation method can really reflect the real situation in the pond.

Acknowledgments

This program was supported by Open Fund (fellowship) from both Key Laboratory of Fishery Ecology Environment, Ministry of Agriculture, P. R China (No.2004-5) and Key Laboratory for computer information management technology, Jiangsu Province.

References

1. Bezdek, J.C.: Pattern Recognition with Fuzzy Objective Function Algorithms. Pleaum Press. New York, (1981)
2. Dubois, D., Prade, H.: Fuzzy Sets and Systems-Theory and Application, New York, (1980)
3. Hu, H.Y.: Aquaculture Survey. Beijing: China Agricultural Press. (1995)
4. Hushon, J.M.: Expert system for Environmental Applications. Washington, D.C. American Chemical Society, (1990)
5. Tamura, S., et.: Pattern Classifice Based on Fuzzy Relations IEEE Trans, Smc-1, (1971) 44-54
6. Zhang, Y., Zuo, S.P., Su, F.: The Method and Application of Fuzzy Mathematics, Chapter 4, (1992)
7. Wang, R.M., Fu, Z.T., Fu, L.Z.: Evaluation of the Aquaculture Pond Water Quality, Poster Session 203（Hydrology and Water Quality） at 2003 ASAE Meeting, (2003)

Fuzzy Reasoning Application in Redundant Manipulator Movement Regulation

Jianmin Jiao[1], Huan Li[2], and Hongfu Zuo[1]

[1] Civil Aviation College, Nanjing University of Aeronautics and Astronautics, Yudao Street, Nanjing 210016, China
jjmlh@163.com

[2] Software College, Dahongying Education Group, Ningbo 315175, China
jjmlh@163.com

Abstract. To study the joint velocity vector trajectory regulation and control method of a redundant space manipulator. A novel multi-restriction manipulator joint velocity vector control algorithm, based on fuzzy reasoning theory, is presented. The task executed by the redundant manipulator is broken into a series of sub-tasks expressed with vectors. The subordinate task is executed in the redundancy space of executing the primary task. The conventional joint velocity vector algorithm is combined with fuzzy reasoning theory so that every subordinate task is best optimized. Singular gesture and arithmetic singularity are avoided. The multi-restriction redundant manipulator joint velocity vector control problem is solved. The algorithm validity is proved by the numerical simulation results.

1 Introduction

A space robot (manipulator) is an important part of a space laboratory and space shuttle. It plays important roles in satellite deployment and retrieval, berthing the shuttle to a space station, as well as space shuttle inspection and maintenance[1-2]. As a kind of long-term, large scale, space equipment, it is an important feature needed to work highly reliably with multiple degrees of freedom. In order to improve its reliability, the space manipulator kinematics design should be redundant. We must regulate and control the manipulator in its joint velocity vector trajectory space, so that it can use its redundant degrees of freedom, fulfill its tasks regardless of broken-down joints and singular gestures, and coordinate the motions of the shuttle and manipulator. All these are necessary functions of the space manipulator system.

In regulating and controlling the trajectory of the manipulator's joint velocity vector, we must work out the joint velocity vector trajectory from the manipulator end effector velocity vector trajectory. The restrictions must also be considered, such as the direction and dexterity of the end effector, the range of each joint, and the distance of the manipulator to obstacles. Consequently, the process of executing a task is also the process of fulfilling a task under all the restrictions. The basic method to work out the joint velocity vector is to acquire the minimum module by pseudoinverses Jacobin

D.-S. Huang, K. Li, and G.W. Irwin (Eds.): ICIC 2006, LNAI 4114, pp. 44 – 52, 2006.

matrix in the joint velocity vector space. Then the redundant space of the manipulator is used, a certain target is optimized, such as dexterity, and the joint velocity vector is ultimately acquired.

In this basic method, only one restriction target can be executed optimally. On this basis, the task space expansion method was presented [3], which is used in special manipulator. The larger main manipulator is specified to do lower frequency movement, while the smaller manipulator on the end of large manipulator is specified to do higher frequency movement. They use similar methods, such as Jacobin matrix expansion method, multi restriction Lagrange method [4-5]. In these methods, the restriction equations are combined with the kinematics equations, so that a set of new kinematics equations is formed, and a new Jacobin matrix is produced. The order of the new Jacobin matrix is one lager than the old Jacobin matrix. A common defect of these methods is that arithmetic singularity occurs frequently. Although these methods solve some problems, they don't possess commonality. They are calculation complex and heavy. They also can't meet multiple restrictions in real time control. When multi-restrictions are to be fulfilled, and the multi-restrictions conflict with each other, how can we detect the degree of confliction, and how can we avoid confliction? These problems are difficult to be solved by conventional mathematics. And this can't be runaround in space manipulator control.

Fuzzy reasoning techniques can solve many difficult problems for conventional mathematics [6-9]. For the above mentioned problems, a novel new task-priority singularity robust fuzzy theory based manipulator joint velocity vector solution method is presented, on the basis of conventional method analysis. From the numerical simulation outcome, we can find that the presented method is effective. The multi-tasks are coordinated effectively; the possible singular gestures are avoided.

The conventional manipulator joint velocity vector solution method is introduced in the second section. The new fuzzy reasoning based method is presented in the third section; and this method is singularity robust. In the forth section, three planar cases are simulated; the defects of the old method and the excellence of the new method are validated. The conclusion is given in the fifth section.

2 Task Priority Based Joint Velocity Vector Solution

For a given manipulator, define vector X_E, $X_E \in R^{m_1}$ as the vector of the most important primary task that the manipulator must execute. The series of subordinate tasks are 2, 3… Corresponding subordinate task vectors are $X_2 \in R^{m_2}$, $X_3 \in R^{m_3}$,….. Manipulator joints vector is $\theta \in R^n$. The kinematics equations of the tasks are expressed generally in the form:

$$X_E = f(\theta) \ . \tag{1}$$

$$X_i = f_i(\theta) \ . \tag{2}$$

Subscript i expresses the subordinate task number. Then the differential kinematics equations are deduced:

$$\dot{X}_E = J_E(\theta)\dot{\theta} \ . \tag{3}$$

$$\dot{X}_i = J_i(\theta)\dot{\theta} \ . \tag{4}$$

$$J_i(\theta) = (\partial f_i / \partial \theta) \in R^{m_i \times n} \ .$$

Solution of primary task equation (3) can be written in the general form:

$$\dot{\theta} = J_E^+ \dot{X}_E + (I - J_E^+ J_E) y \ . \tag{5}$$

In equation (5), the second item on the right side of the equal mark is the null-space vector of $J_E(\theta)$. $y \in R^n$ is an arbitrary vector. We can't solve out joint velocity vector just from primary task equation (5). By replacing primary task solution (5) into the second task differential kinematics equation (4), we obtain another equation:

$$\dot{\theta} = J_E^+ \dot{X}_E + [I - J_E^+ J_E] \tilde{J}_2^+ [\dot{X}_2 - J_2 J_E^+ \dot{X}_E] + [I - J_E^+ J_E][I - \tilde{J}_2^+ \tilde{J}_2] Z \ . \tag{6}$$

$$\tilde{J}_2 = J_2(\theta)[I - J_E^+(\theta) J_E(\theta)] \ .$$

This is the manipulator joint velocity vector solution when the second subordinate task is fulfilled in the redundant space of the primary task. If there is still redundancy when the first two tasks are fulfilled, then the value of 'z' in (6) can be solved out by the following tasks. Otherwise, $Z=0$. This is the redundant manipulator joint velocity vector solution when the manipulator must fulfill multi-tasks.

Now suppose $Z=0$, that is to say that the redundancy of the primary task is used fully to fulfill the second subordinate task. From (6) we can derivate:

$$\dot{\theta} = J_E^+ \dot{X}_E + [I - J_E^+ J_E] \tilde{J}_2^+ [\dot{X}_2 - J_2 J_E^+ X_E] \ . \tag{7}$$

Because the above basic solution method can't avoid singularity, so in the singularity the joint actuator can't meet the demand. Therefore the manipulator joint velocity vector solution must be singularity robust. If the singularity can't be avoided, the degree of approaching to singularity must be detected, so as to limit the occurrence of singular values. Gianluca proposed to decompose the singularity of the Jacobin matrix in (7). A different solution to avoid singularity which is instead robust to the occurrence of kinematic singularities is based on the use of the damped least-squares inverse of the end-effector Jacobian matrix [10]. It can be recognized that singular gestures are avoided, and the solution is singularity robust, but there exists some error. It's a compromise between accuracy and continuity. However, arithmetic singularity isn't avoided. That is to say, when the primary task conflicts with the subordinate tasks, the solution goes into singular. From the numerical simulation outcome, we find that the conflicts between primary task and subordinate tasks are avoided, but at the same time the subordinate task is hardly ever executed. And this method can be used with only one restriction task. When the number of restriction tasks increase, the calculation is too complex and heavy. The probability of real time control is uncertain.

3 Fuzzy Theory Based Joint Velocity Vector Solution

The above mentioned task-priority redundancy inverse kinematics algorithms have many defects. When the task number is large, the data operation time becomes longer. In order to solve the problem of multi-restrictions manipulator joint velocity vector regulation and control, the fuzzy reasoning technique is introduced so that the multi-restrictions are coordinated; every restriction task is executed furthest. The calculation time is then cut down. The algorithm is as follow.

First, the null space vector in (7) is multiplied by a coefficient. We can obtain:

$$\dot{\theta}=J_E^+\dot{X}_E+\alpha[I-J_E^+J_E]\tilde{J}_2^+[\dot{X}_2-J_2J_E^+X_E] \; . \tag{8}$$

Through numerical simulation we can find that the null space vector coefficient α in (8) expresses the gain of a null space vector. The bigger the α is, the larger the subordinate task executed. The value of α affects the precision of solution directly. When the primary task conflicts with a subordinate task, the value of α decreases and the subordinate task is less fulfilled, so that the primary task won't be affected. When the primary task doesn't conflict with the subordinate task, the value of α can be increased. The confliction extent between primary task and subordinate task is reflected by the minimum singularity value of $\tilde{J}_2=J_2(\theta)[I-J_E^+(\theta)J_E(\theta)]$. The smaller the minimum singularity value is, the bigger the conflict extent between the primary task and a subordinate task is. So we can evaluate α by the minimum singularity value. The subordinate task is done maximally at the precondition that the primary task is fulfilled. The primary task and subordinate task are coordinated harmoniously.

Second, the task of the manipulator can be decomposed into a series of sub-tasks according to some criterion. The weightiness of these sub-tasks is different. For example, the position of the end-effector is more important in the tasks containing position and gestures, such as welding and cutting. In the other circumstances, the gesture of the end-effector is more important, such as spraying and photographing. To use the redundancy of the manipulator more efficiently, the sub-tasks should be ranked according to their weightiness. The subordinate tasks should be done in the redundant space under the condition that the primary task is executed.

In equation (8), only one subordinate task is optimized. If there are more subordinate tasks, equation (8) can be written in the form:

$$\dot{\theta}=J_E^+\dot{X}_E+\sum\alpha_i[I-J_E^+J_E]\tilde{J}_i^+[\dot{X}_i-J_iJ_E^+X_E] \; . \tag{9}$$

Only one parameter in $\alpha_0,\alpha_1,\ldots\alpha_i$ is non-zero, so that at every moment only one subordinate restriction task X_i is optimized. Other subordinate tasks are ignored. Which subordinate task is optimized should be determined according to some criterions.

In order to solve this problem, fuzzy system theory may be used. So that at every moment only one subordinate task is optimized, and other subordinate tasks are ignored.

Only when the parameters corresponding to one subordinate task exceed a certain limit, is that subordinate task activated and optimized, so that the parameter returns back to the perfect range. The activating limit of different parameters should be decided dynamically by fuzzy reasoning from all the concerned performance indexes. Therefore all the subordinate tasks are best optimized. The fuzzy machine is as figure 1.

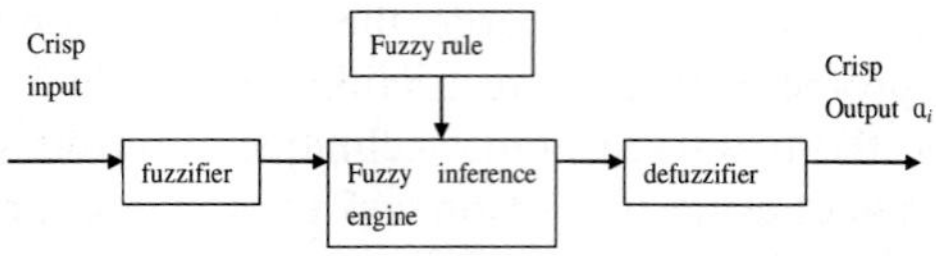

Fig. 1. Mamdani fuzzy reference system

The definite output α_i of fuzzy machine is the coefficient of subordinate task in (9). α_i is calculated according to the state of the system and the given behavioral rules. The inputs of the fuzzy operation system depend on the interesting variables of the specific mission. As an example, the end-effector error, the system's dexterity, the distance to obstacles, and the force sensor readings, can be easily taken into account by setting up a suitable set of fuzzy rules. To avoid the exponential growth of the fuzzy rules to be implemented as the number of tasks increases, the secondary tasks are suitably organized in a hierarchy. Also, the rules have to guarantee that only one α_i is nonzero at any time to avoid confliction between the secondary tasks. The value of α_i is set suitably to acquire perfect control effect, and the subordinate task doesn't conflict with the primary task, i.e. no singularity occurrences. The arithmetic is as follow.

(a) Find initial joint angle vector value θ_0, so that all the restriction subordinate tasks X_i are satisfied best.

(b) Decide α_i by fuzzy machine.

(c) Calculate $\dot{\theta}$ by equation (9), $\dot{\theta}=J_E^+\dot{X}_E+\sum\alpha_i[I-J_E^+J_E]\tilde{J}_i^+[\dot{X}_i-J_iJ_E^+X_E]$. Then the value of θ_{k+1} can be obtained.

(d) Estimate if all the restrictions X_i are satisfied. If the answer is yes, then θ_{k+1} is the reasonable solution, set *k=k+1*, return to (b); if some restrictions aren't satisfied, then give up θ_{k+1}, return to (b).

4 Numerical Simulation

4.1 Case 1

The purpose of this case is to prove the effectivity of the presented fuzzy theory based task-priority manipulator joint velocity vector algorithm. The reason of selecting planar manipulator in this case is that its outcome is more intuitive and easy to understand. This is the same in the following cases. The effects of an algorithm are the same for a planar manipulator and space manipulator. The difference is just different calculation quantum. The parameters of three arms of three degree of freedom planar manipulator are arm length $a_1 = 3.00$, $a_2 = 2.50$, $a_3 = 2.10$, their units are meters; The initial joint angles of the manipulator are: $\theta_1 = -1.52$, $\theta_2 = 1.95$, $\theta_3 = 1.35$, their units are radian. The running range of the joints is 2π. The task of the manipulator is to make the end-effector follow a circle track uniformly, where the center is (2.98, 0.099), and its semi-diameter is one meter. At the same time the distance of the third joint to the circle remains non-zero, the centre of the circle is (4.30,-3.00), the smi-diameter of the circle is 1.41 meter, the circle is used as barrier. That is to say the manipulator can evade barriers, and the dexterity of the manipulator remains bigger. The manipulator executes main task, at the same time executes two other subordinate restriction tasks, they are dexterity and evading barriers. The fuzzy theory based task-priority manipulator movement regulation algorithm (9) is used to solve the inverse kinematics. The numerical outcome is shown in figure 2.

It can be seen that this method is effective, the manipulator fulfilled the task perfectly, the tracking error is very small in figure 3, the barrier is evaded, the gesture of the manipulator is better, that means the dexterity of the manipulator is bigger, no singularity is produced.

4.2 Case 2

The purpose of this case is to prove the effectivity of the presented fuzzy theory based manipulator joint velocity vector algorithm when main task and subordinate restriction conflicts. The parameters of the manipulator are the same as the last case. The parameters of three arms of the three degree-of-freedom planar manipulator are:

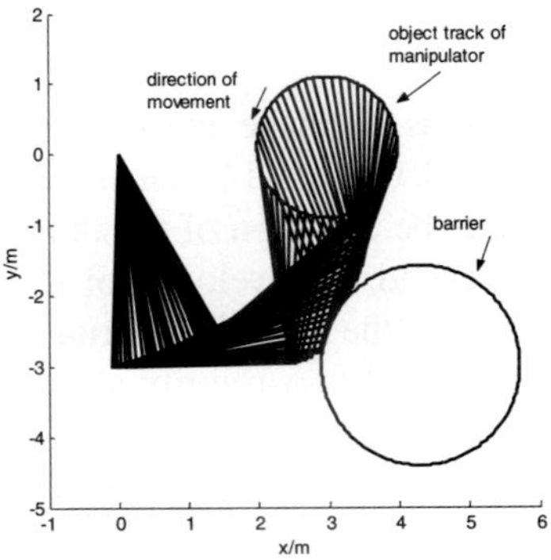

Fig. 2. The manipulator gestures in working process

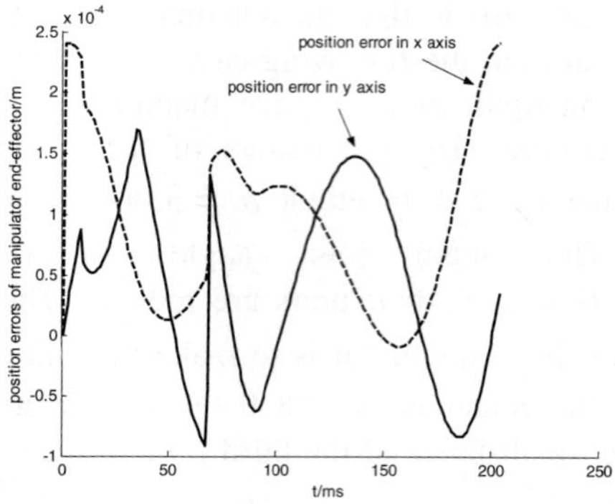

Fig. 3. The end-effector position errors

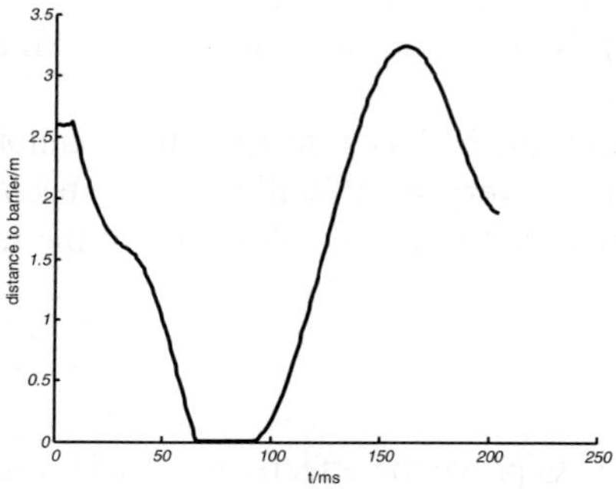

Fig. 4. The distance of manipulator to barrier

$a_1 = 1.95$, $a_2 = 1.61$, $a_3 = 0.70$, their units are meter; The initial joint angles of the manipulator are: $\theta_1 = -0.90$, $\theta_2 = 1.50$, $\theta_3 = 1.00$, their units are radian. The running range of the joints is 2π.

The task of the manipulator is to make the end-effector follow a circle track uniformly, where the center is （3.00，−0.14）, and the semi-diameter is one meter. The subordinate task is to make the direction of the third arm increases uniformly at the speed of 0.001radian per second. The velocity of the end-effector is stable. We can divide the track evenly; making the end-effector run the same journey in the same time interval. The fuzzy theory based task-priority algorithm (9) is used to solve the inverse kinematics. The simulation outcome is as fig 5. It can be seen that this method is effective, the manipulator fulfilled the task perfectly, the tracking error is very small in figure 6, and the direction of the third arm remains running evenly when the subordinate task doesn't conflict with primary task; the subordinate task is given up and the primary task is executed to the utmost when they conflicts. This algorithm is effective.

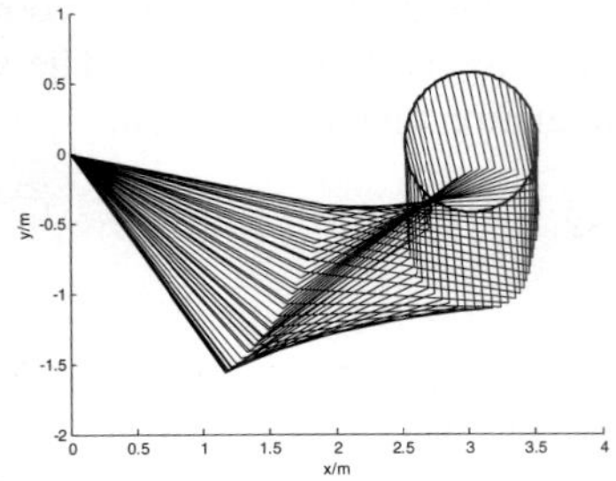

Fig. 5. The manipulator gestures in working process

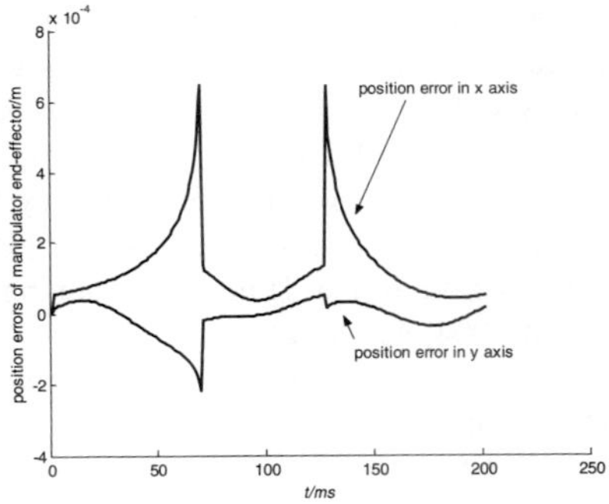

Fig. 6. The end-effector position errors

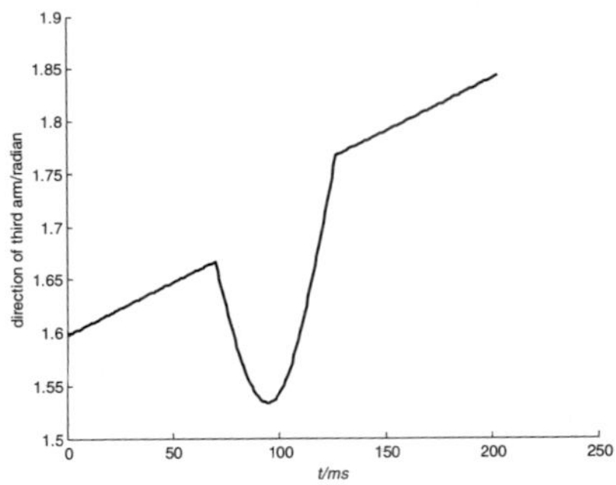

Fig. 7. The direction of the third arm

5 Conclusion

Redundant manipulator fuzzy theory based task-priority singularity-robust inverse kinematics joint velocity vector solution is studied in this article, where the restriction terms are expressed with vectors. From the numerical simulation results we can find that the fuzzy theory based algorithm is effective. It can coordinate a primary task and subordinate tasks. Kinematical singularity is avoided. The algorithm is universal and calculation is simple. The calculation quantum is small.

References

1. Cai, Z.X.: Developing Trends of Robot Technology in 21st Century. Journal of Nanjing University of chemical technology. vol.22. (2000) 73-79
2. Adrian, A.: The Special Purpose Dexterous Manipulator (SPDM) Systems Engineering Report. Journal of Reducing Space Mission Cost. 1(1998) 177-200
3. Olav, E.: Task-Space Tracking With Redundant Manipulators. IEEE Journal of Robotics and Automation. Vol.RA-3. 5(1987) 471-475
4. Homayoun Seraji.: Configuration Control of Redundant Manipulators: Theory and Implementation. IEEE transactions on robots and automation. vol.5. 4(1989) 472-490
5. John, B.: A Constraints-Based Method of The Inverse Kinematics for Redundant Manipulators. Proceedings of the 1987 IEEE. 531-538
6. Gianluca, A., Stefano, C.: A Fuzzy Approach to Redundancy Resolution for Underwater Vehicle-Manipulator Systems. Control Engineering Practice. 11(2003) 445-452
7. Tian, L.F., Curtis C.: An Effective Robot Trajectory Planning Method Using A Genetic Algorithm. Mechatronics. 14(2004) 455-470
8. Gianluca, A., Stefano C.: Fuzzy Redundancy Resolution and Motion Coordination for Underwater Vehicle-Manipulator Systems. IEEE TRANSACTIONS ON FUZZY SYSTEMS. VOL.11. 1(2003) 109-120
9. Shen, Y.S., Knut H¨uper.: Optimal Trajectory Planning of Manipulators Subject to Motion Constraints. IEEE. (2005 0-7803-9177-2/05) 9-16
10. Gianluca A., Stefano C..: Task-priority Redundancy Resolution for Underwater Vehicle-Manipulator Systems. Proceedings of the 1998 IEEE International Conference on Robotics and Automation. (1998) 768-773

GFHM Model and Control for Uncertain Chaotic System

Dongsheng Yang, Huaguang Zhang, Zhiliang Wang, and Yingchun Wang

School of Information Science and Engineering
Northeastern University, Shenyang, Liaoning 110004, P.R. China
ydsyds@tom.com and hgzhang@ieee.org

Abstract. This paper develops a fuzzy hyperbolic control method for chaotic continuous-time systems with uncertainties. First, the generalized fuzzy hyperbolic model (GFHM) is used to model unknown part of a chaotic system. Second, based on Lyapunov functional approach, a sufficient condition for a fuzzy hyperbolic controller and a state feedback controller is given such that the closed-loop system is asymptotic stable. Moreover, considering the influence of both approximation error and external disturbance, fuzzy hyperbolic H_∞ control scheme is addressed . All the results are given in terms of LMI forms, the effectiveness of the proposed method is shown by a simulation example.

1 Introduction

For the latest thirty years , chaos being a ubiquitous phenomenon has drawn more and more attentions. How to utilize the chaos and how to control chaos has being a hot research point in recent years [1]. Since Ott, Grebogi and Yorke proposed their famous OGY method [2], the problem of control chaotic system has been studied by many researchers, but much of the research work makes an assumption that the chaotic system can be modelled [3-4]. In practice, when one designs controller for a plant, there always exist effections of some undetermined factors such as noise, modelling uncertainties, etc. As a result, fuzzy control methods were employed in some applications [7-8].

Recently, Zhang and his co-authers proposed the fuzzy hyperbolic model (FHM) and the generalized fuzzy hyperbolic model (GFHM) [9-11]. It was proved that the generalized fuzzy hyperbolic model is a universal approximator. Compared with the T-S fuzzy model, the GFHM has many merits. For example, there is no need to identify premise structure when modeling a plant by GFHM, therefore, there is much less computation expense than that of using T-S fuzzy model, especially when a lot of fuzzy rules are needed to approximate nonlinear complex systems. In this paper, a GFHM is used to represent the nonlinear part of chaotic systems, then a fuzzy hyperbolic controller is designed. The presented method can also be extended to a wide class of nonlinear systems.

The rest of the paper is organized as follows: In Sec. 2, the preliminary of the GFHM is first revisited. In Sec. 3, the GFHM is used to model a chaotic system, and a controller including a fuzzy controller and a state feedback controller is designed to stabilize the system. Considering the influence of both approximation error and external disturbance, fuzzy hyperbolic H_∞ control scheme is addressed. In Sec. 4, a simulation example is

D.-S. Huang, K. Li, and G.W. Irwin (Eds.): ICIC 2006, LNAI 4114, pp. 53–62, 2006.

demonstrated the effectiveness of the proposed method. Finally, conclusions are made in Sec. 5.

2 Preliminaries

In this section we review some necessary preliminaries for the GFHM[10].

Definition 1 : Given a plant with n input variables $x = [x_1(t), ..., x_n(t)]^T$ and one output variable $y(t)$. we define the generalized input variables as $\bar{x}_i = x_i - d_{ij}(j = 1,\ldots,r_i)$, $m=\sum_{i=1}^{n} r_i$ are the numbers of generalized input variables, $r_i(i = 1,\ldots,n)$ are the numbers to be transformed about x_i, d_{ij} are constants where x_i are transformed. We define the fuzzy rule based on the generalized fuzzy hyperbolic rule base if the following conditions are satisfied:

The fuzzy rules have the following form:

1. IF $(x_1 - d_{11})$ is $F_{x_{11}}$ and ...and $(x_1 - d_{1r_1})$ is $F_{x_{1r_1}}$ and $(x_2 - d_{21})$ is $F_{x_{21}}$ and ...and $(x_n - d_{n1})$ is $F_{x_{n1}}$ and ...and $(x_n - d_{nr_n})$ is $F_{x_{nr_n}}$ THEN
$$y = c_{F_{11}} + \cdots + c_{F_{1r_1}} + c_{F_{21}} + \cdots + c_{F_{n1}} + \cdots + c_{F_{nr_n}} \tag{1}$$
where $F_{x_{ij}}$ are fuzzy sets of $x_i - d_{ij}$, which include P_x (Positive) and N_x (Negative) subsets.
2. The constant $c_{F_{ij}}$ $(i=1,...,n, j=1,...,r_i)$ in the "THEN" part correspond to $F_{x_{zi}}$ in the "IF" part, that is, if there is $F_{x_{ij}}$ in the "IF" part, $c_{F_{ij}}$ must appear in the "THEN" part. Otherwise, $c_{F_{ij}}$ does not appear in the "THEN" part. Denoting $c^{+}_{F_{ij}}$ by c_{P_i} and $c^{-}_{F_{ij}}$ by c_{N_i}.
3. There are $2^m(m = \sum_{i=1}^{n} r_i)$ fuzzy rules for the output variable in the rule base, that is, all the possible P_x and N_x combinations of input variables in the "IF" part and all the linear combinations of constants in the "THEN" part.

In the FHM, there are two types of fuzzy sets, including Positive (P_x) and Negative (N_x). The membership functions of P_x and N_x are defined as :

$$\mu_{P_x}(x_z) = e^{-\frac{1}{2}(x_z - k_z)^2}, \quad \mu_{N_x}(x_z) = e^{-\frac{1}{2}(x_z + k_z)^2} \tag{2}$$

where $k_z > 0$. We can see that only two fuzzy sets are used to represent the input variables. If we transform the input variable x_z, the fuzzy sets may cover the whole input space if w is large enough.

Lemma 1 : For a plant with n input variables and an output variable $y(t)$, if we define the generalized fuzzy hyperbolic rule base and generalized input variables as definition 1, and define the membership functions of the generalized input variables P_x and N_x as (2), then we can derive the following model:

$$y=\sum_{i=1}^{m} \frac{c_{P_i}e^{k_i\bar{x}_i} + c_{N_i}e^{-k_i\bar{x}_i}}{e^{k_i\bar{x}_i}+e^{-k_i\bar{x}_i}} = \sum_{i=1}^{m} a_i + \sum_{i=1}^{m} b_i \frac{e^{k_i\bar{x}_i} - e^{-k_i\bar{x}_i}}{e^{k_i\bar{x}_i} + e^{-k_i\bar{x}_i}} = A + B^T \tanh(K\bar{x}), \tag{3}$$

where $a_i = \frac{c_{P_i}+c_{N_i}}{2}$, $b_i = \frac{c_{P_i}-c_{N_i}}{2}$, $A = \sum_{i=1}^{m} a_i$, $B = [b_1, \cdots, b_m]^T$, $\tanh(K\bar{x})$ is defined by $\tanh(K\bar{x}) = [\tanh(k_1 x_1), \cdots, \tanh(k_m x_m)]^T$, $K = \mathrm{diag}\,[k_1, ..., k_m]$. We call (3) the generalized fuzzy hyperbolic model (GFHM).

Lemma 2 : For any given real continuous $g(x)$ on the compact set $U \subset R^n$ and arbitrary $\varepsilon > 0$, there exists $F(x) \in Y$ such that

$$\sup_{x \in U} |g(x) - F(x)| < \varepsilon. \tag{4}$$

From Definition 1, if we set P_x and N_x negative to each other, we can obtain a homogeneous GFHM:

$$\dot{x} = B^T \tanh(K\bar{x}). \tag{5}$$

Here, we will model chaotic system and design a fuzzy control scheme based on the GFHM.

3 Fuzzy Control of the Chaotic System Via GHFM

Consider a nonlinear system in the following form:

$$\dot{x}(t) = \psi(x(t)) \tag{6}$$

where $x = (x_1, x_2, ..., x_n)$ is the state. $\psi : R^n \to R^n$ is an unknown smooth nonlinear mapping. According to Lemma 1, the system (6) can be represented by a GFHM as follows, which is a kind of global description.

$$\dot{\bar{x}}(t) = \breve{A} \tanh(K\bar{x}) \; + \; \Delta f \tag{7}$$

where $\bar{x} = [x_1, x_2, \cdots, x_n, \cdots, x_m]^T \in R^m$, $\breve{A} \in R^{m\times m}$ is constant matrix. $K = \mathrm{diag}\,[k_1, ..., k_m]$. Δf represents the error between the real plant and the model represented by GFHM.

Assumption 1: there exists a positive definite diagonal matrix Φ_f to satisfy following inequality for any $\bar{x}(t)$.

$$\Delta f^T \Delta f \leq \bar{x}^T(t) \Phi_f \bar{x}(t). \tag{8}$$

In this paper, the idea is to design a controller $u(t)$ which composes of a fuzzy controller and a state feedback controller such that chaotic systems can be stabilized to the equilibrium point.

Consider the following chaotic system :

$$\dot{x}(t) = f(x(t)) \tag{9}$$

Suppose that the linear part of the system is known, then the system can be represented as following

$$\dot{x} = Ax + \psi(x) \tag{10}$$

where $\psi(x)$ is unknown nonlinear part of the system. $A \in R^{n\times n}$ is known constant matrix. According to (7) the nonlinear part of the dynamical system (10) can be expressed as a fuzzy hyperbolic model in the form :

$$\psi(\bar{x}) = \tilde{A}\tanh(K\bar{x}) + \Delta f \tag{11}$$

where Δf is modeling error. $\tilde{A} \in R^{m\times m}$is a constant matrix to be estimated.

For system (10), if the controller $u(t)$ is chosen as follows :

$$u(t) = K_{1u}\tanh(K\bar{x}) + K_{2u}\bar{x} \tag{12}$$

where $K_{1u} \in R^{m\times m}$, $K_{2u} \in R^{m\times m}$ are undetermined parameters matrices with appropriate dimensions.

Now combining (11) and (12), the system (10) can be expressed as follows:

$$\dot{\bar{x}}(t) = \Lambda\tanh(K\bar{x}) + \bar{A}\bar{x} + \Delta f \tag{13}$$

where $\Lambda = \tilde{A} + K_{1u}$, $\bar{A} = \hat{A} + K_{2u}$. $\hat{A}$ is the following augmented form of the matrix A.

$$\hat{A}^T = \begin{bmatrix} A_1^T & ... & A_n^T & A_{11}^T & ... & A_{1r_1}^T & ... & A_{n1}^T & ... & A_{nr_n}^T \\ 0 & ... & 0 & 0 & ... & 0 & ... & 0 & ... & 0 \end{bmatrix}^T$$

where $A_{i1}...A_{ij}$, $(j = 1, \ldots, r_i)$ are same to A_i, $r_i(i = 1, \ldots, n)$ is the number of transformed x_i.

Remark 1: The function $\tanh(K\xi) = [\tanh(k_1\xi_1), \cdots, \tanh(k_m\xi_m)]^T$ always satisfies the following condition

$$0 \le \frac{\tanh(k_j\xi_j)}{k_j\xi_j} \le \delta_j \tag{14}$$

For arbitrary $\xi_i \neq 0$ and some position constant $\delta_j > 0, j = 1, 2, ..., n$. Let $\Gamma =$ diag $(\delta_1, \delta_2, ..., \delta_n)$.

By Remark 1 we have

$$2\tanh^T(Kx)x(t) \le 2x^T(t)K^T\Gamma x(t). \tag{15}$$

Theorem 1: Consider the uncertain chaotic system (10) with a controller of form (12). Suppose that for a constant $\Upsilon > 0$, if there exist matrices $Q > 0$, Π and Ξ such that the following LMI holds, then the chaotic system is asymptotic stable.

$$\begin{bmatrix} \Omega & Q \\ Q & -\Upsilon I \end{bmatrix} < 0 \tag{16}$$

where $\Phi = \Phi_f$. $\Omega = QA + \Pi + A^TQ + \Pi^T + Q\tilde{A}\Gamma K + \Xi\Gamma K + K^T\Gamma\tilde{A}Q + K^T\Gamma\Xi^T + \Upsilon\Phi$.

Proof: Choose the following Lyapunov functional candidate for system (13)

$$V(t) = \bar{x}^TQ\bar{x}, \tag{17}$$

we know that when $\bar{x}_i = 0$, $V(t)|_{t=0} = 0$, otherwise $V(t) > 0$.

$$\begin{aligned}
\dot{V}(t) =& 2\bar{x}^T Q\dot{\bar{x}} \\
=& 2\bar{x}^T Q[\bar{A}\bar{x} + \Lambda\tanh(K\bar{x}) + \Delta f(t)] \\
=& 2\bar{x}^T Q\bar{A}\bar{x} + 2\bar{x}^T Q\Lambda\tanh(K\bar{x}) + 2\bar{x}^T Q\Delta f(t) \\
=& 2\bar{x}^T Q\bar{A}\bar{x} + 2\bar{x}^T Q\Lambda\tanh(K\bar{x}) + 2\bar{x}^T Q\Delta f(t) + \Upsilon\Delta f^T\Delta f - \Upsilon\Delta f^T\Delta f \\
\leq & \bar{x}^T(Q\bar{A} + \bar{A}^T Q + \Upsilon\Phi)\bar{x} + 2\bar{x}^T Q\Lambda\tanh(K\bar{x}) + 2\bar{x}^T Q\Delta f(t) - \Upsilon\Delta f^T\Delta f \\
\leq & \bar{x}^T(Q\bar{A} + \bar{A}^T Q + \Upsilon\Phi)\bar{x} + 2\bar{x}^T Q\Lambda\Gamma K\bar{x} + 2\bar{x}^T Q\Delta f(t) - \Upsilon\Delta f^T\Delta f \\
=& \bar{x}^T(Q\bar{A} + \bar{A}^T Q + Q\Lambda\Gamma K + K^T\Gamma\Lambda^T Q + \Upsilon\Phi)\bar{x} + 2\bar{x}^T Q\Delta f(t) - \Upsilon\Delta f^T\Delta f \\
=& \begin{bmatrix} \bar{x} \\ \Delta f \end{bmatrix}^T \begin{bmatrix} Q\bar{A} + \bar{A}^T Q + Q\Lambda\Gamma K + K^T\Gamma\Lambda^T Q + \Upsilon\Phi & Q \\ Q & -\Upsilon I \end{bmatrix} \begin{bmatrix} \bar{x} \\ \Delta f \end{bmatrix} \\
=& \eta^T\Sigma\eta
\end{aligned} \tag{18}$$

where $\eta = [\ \bar{x}^T \quad \Delta f^T]^T$,$\Sigma = \begin{bmatrix} Q\bar{A} + \bar{A}^T Q + Q\Lambda\Gamma K + K^T\Gamma\Lambda^T Q + \Upsilon\Phi & Q \\ Q & -\Upsilon I \end{bmatrix}$.

If $\Sigma < 0$, $\dot{V}(t) < 0$ for $\eta \neq 0$. we have

$$\begin{bmatrix} \Psi & Q \\ Q & -\Upsilon I \end{bmatrix} < 0 \tag{19}$$

where $\Psi = Q(\hat{A}+K_{2u})+(\hat{A}+K_{2u})^T Q+Q(\tilde{A}+K_{1u})\Gamma K+K^T\Gamma(\tilde{A}+K_{1u})^T Q+\Upsilon\Phi$.

Denote

$$\Pi = QK_{2u}\,, \Xi = QK_{1u}.$$

From (19) we have

$$\begin{bmatrix} \Omega & Q \\ Q & -\Upsilon I \end{bmatrix} < 0. \tag{20}$$

Moreover, the control parameter is given by:

$$\begin{aligned} K_{1u} &= Q^{-1}\Xi \\ K_{2u} &= Q^{-1}\Pi. \end{aligned}$$

This completes the proof.

Consider an uncontrolled chaotic system in the following form with external disturbance :

$$\begin{aligned} \dot{x}(t) &= f(x(t)) + \omega(t) \\ z(t) &= Cx(t) \end{aligned} \tag{21}$$

where $x = (x_1, x_2, ..., x_n)$ is the state.$f \in: R^n \to R^n$ is a smooth nonlinear function vector dependent on $x(t)$. $\omega(t)$ is a bounded external disturbance vector . z is control output vector , C is a matrix with compatible dimension. Now the system (21) can be expressed as follows:

$$\begin{aligned} \dot{\bar{x}}(t) &= \tilde{A}\tanh(K\bar{x}) + \bar{A}\bar{x} + B\bar{\omega}(t) + \Delta f \\ \bar{z}(t) &= \bar{C}\bar{x}(t) \end{aligned} \tag{22}$$

where B and $\bar{C}$ are matrices with compatible dimension.

The design of controller is the same to the controller for the chaotic system without external disturbance.

$$u(t) = K_{1u}\tanh(k\bar{x}) + K_{2u}\bar{x} \tag{23}$$

Theorem 2: Consider the system (21) with a controller of form (23). Suppose that for some constant $\Upsilon > 0$ and $\rho > 0$, there exist some matrices $Q > 0$, Π and Ξ such that the following LMI holds, then the chaotic system is asymptotic stable with disturbance attenuate performance.

$$\begin{bmatrix} \Theta & QB & Q \\ B^T Q & -\Upsilon I & 0 \\ Q & 0 & -\rho^2 I \end{bmatrix} < 0 \tag{24}$$

where $\Theta = Q\hat{A} + \Pi + \hat{A}^T Q + \Pi^T + Q\tilde{A}\Gamma K + \Xi\Gamma K + K^T\Gamma\tilde{A}^T Q + K^T\Gamma\Xi^T + \Upsilon\Phi + \bar{C}^T\bar{C}$.

Consider the system in (24) with the following H_∞ performance , for $\forall\omega(t) = L_2[0, +\infty)$

$$\begin{aligned} J &= \int_0^\infty [\bar{z}^T(t)\bar{z}(t) - \rho^2\bar{\omega}^T(t)\bar{\omega}(t)]dt \\ &= \int_0^\infty [\bar{z}^T(t)\bar{z}(t) - \rho^2\bar{\omega}^T(t)\bar{\omega}(t) + \dot{V}]dt + V(0) - V(t)\mid_{t\to\infty} \end{aligned} \tag{25}$$

Proof : Choose the following Lyapunov functional candidate for system (24)

$$V(t) = \bar{x}^T Q\bar{x}. \tag{26}$$

Consider $V(0) = 0$, we have

$$\begin{aligned} J &= \int_0^\infty [\bar{z}^T(t)\bar{z}(t) - \rho^2\bar{\omega}^T(t)\bar{\omega}(t)]dt \\ &\le \int_0^\infty [\bar{x}^T(t)\bar{C}^T\bar{C}\bar{x}(t) - \rho^2\bar{\omega}^T(t)\bar{\omega}(t) + \dot{V}]dt \\ &= \int_0^\infty [\bar{x}^T(t)\bar{C}^T\bar{C}\bar{x}(t) - \rho^2\bar{\omega}^T(t)\bar{\omega}(t) + 2\bar{x}^T Q[\bar{A}\bar{x} + \Lambda\tanh(K\bar{x}) \\ &\quad + B\bar{\omega}(t) + \Delta f(t)]]dt \\ &\le \int_0^\infty [\bar{x}^T(t)\bar{C}^T\bar{C}\bar{x}(t) - \rho^2\bar{\omega}^T(t)\bar{\omega}(t) + 2\bar{x}^T Q\bar{A}\bar{x} + 2\bar{x}^T Q\Lambda\Gamma\bar{x} + 2\bar{x}^T QB\bar{\omega}(t) \\ &\quad + 2\bar{x}^T Q\Delta f(t) + \Upsilon\Delta f^T\Delta f - \Upsilon\Delta f^T\Delta f]dt \\ &= \int_0^\infty \begin{bmatrix} \bar{x}(t) \\ \Delta f \\ \bar{\omega}(t) \end{bmatrix}^T \begin{bmatrix} \Theta & QB & Q \\ B^T Q & -\Upsilon I & 0 \\ Q & 0 & -\rho^2 I \end{bmatrix} \begin{bmatrix} \bar{x}(t) \\ \Delta f \\ \bar{\omega}(t) \end{bmatrix} dt \end{aligned} \tag{27}$$

If

$$\begin{bmatrix} \Theta & QB & Q \\ B^T Q & -\Upsilon I & 0 \\ Q & 0 & -\rho^2 I \end{bmatrix} < 0, \tag{28}$$

then $J < 0$. Denote

$$\Pi = QK_{2u}, \Xi = QK_{1u}$$

we have (28) is equality to (24).

Then, the controller parameter is given by:

$$K_{1u} = Q^{-1}\Xi$$
$$K_{2u} = Q^{-1}\Pi.$$

This completes the proof.

4 Simulation Study

In this section, we shall present an example to demonstrate the effectiveness and applicability of the proposed method.

Consider the Van der Pol oscillator with parameters as follows [17]:

$$\begin{bmatrix} \dot{x}_1 \\ \dot{x}_2 \\ \dot{x}_3 \end{bmatrix} = \begin{bmatrix} a & m & 0 \\ 1 & -1 & -1 \\ 0 & b & -c \end{bmatrix} \begin{bmatrix} x_1 \\ x_2 \\ x_3 \end{bmatrix} + \psi(x)$$

where $a = 35, b = 300, c = 0.3, m = 100$,the system has two chaotic attractors.

Suppose that we have the following fuzzy rule base:

R1: IF x_1 is P_{x10} and x_2 is P_{x20} and $(x_1 - 1)$ is $P_{x_{11}}$ and $(x_1 + 1)$ is P_{x12}
Then $\dot{x}_1 - \hat{A}x_1 = c_{x_1} + c_{x_2} + c_{x_{11}} + c_{x12}$
R2: IF x_1 is P_{x10} and x_2 is P_{x20} and $(x_1 - 1)$ is $P_{x_{11}}$ and $(x_1 + 1)$ is N_{x12}
Then $\dot{x}_1 - \hat{A}x_1 = c_{x_1} + c_{x_2} + c_{x_{11}} - c_{x12}$
R3: IF x_1 is P_{x10} and x_2 is P_{x20} and $(x_1 - 1)$ is $N_{x_{11}}$ and $(x_1 + 1)$ is N_{x12}
Then $\dot{x}_1 - \hat{A}x_1 = c_{x_1} + c_{x_2} - c_{x_{11}} - c_{x12}$
....
R2^5: IF x_1 is N_{x10} and x_2 is N_{x20} and $(x_1 - 1)$ is $N_{x_{11}}$ and $(x_1 + 1)$ is N_{x12}
Then $\dot{x}_1 - \hat{A}x_1 = -c_{x_1} - c_{x_2} - c_{x_{11}} - c_{x12}$

where

$$\hat{A} = \begin{bmatrix} a & m & 0 & 0 & 0 \\ 1 & -1 & -1 & 0 & 0 \\ 0 & b & -c & 0 & 0 \\ a & m & 0 & 0 & 0 \\ a & m & 0 & 0 & 0 \end{bmatrix}.$$

Here, we choose membership functions of P_{xi} and N_{xi} as follows:

$$\mu_{P_x}(x_z) = e^{-\frac{1}{2}(x_z - k_z)^2}, \quad \mu_{N_x}(x_z) = e^{-\frac{1}{2}(x_z + k_z)^2}$$

GFHM can be seen as a neural network model, so we can learn the model parameters by back-propagation (BP) algorithm. According to Lemma 1 the dynamical nonlinear part of system can be expressed as a fuzzy hyperbolic model in the form

$$\psi(\bar{x}) = -99.914\tanh(2.683 \times (x_1 - 1)) - 99.914\tanh(2.683 \times (x_1 + 1)) + \Delta f$$

$\Phi_f = 0.1I, \quad \Gamma =$ diag (1,1,1,1,1). Under the (0.3, - 0.029329 , - 0.59) initial condition, using Matlab LMI Control Toolbox to solve the LMI (16), we can obtain the solution as follows:

$$Q = \begin{bmatrix} 1.29 & -0.01 & -0.21 & 0 & 0 \\ -0.01 & 1.40 & 0 & 0 & 0 \\ -0.21 & 0 & 0.75 & 0 & 0 \\ 0 & 0 & 0 & 1.40 & 0 \\ 0 & 0 & 0 & 0 & 1.40 \end{bmatrix}$$

$$K_{1u} = \begin{bmatrix} -35.16 & -48.31 & 2.21 & 9.54 & 9.54 \\ -22.90 & 0.56 & -69.4 & -0.08 & -0.08 \\ -5.06 & -143.3 & 0.48 & -0.01 & -0.01 \\ 8.87 & -0.07 & -1.45 & -0.34 & 0.03 \\ 8.87 & -0.07 & -1.45 & 0.03 & -0.34 \end{bmatrix} \quad K_{2u} = \begin{bmatrix} -7.03 & -9.66 & 0.44 & 1.90 & 1.90 \\ -4.58 & 0.11 & -13.8 & -0.01 & -0.01 \\ -1.01 & -28.67 & 0.09 & 0 & 0 \\ 1.77 & -0.01 & -0.29 & -0.06 & -0.06 \\ 1.77 & -0.01 & -0.29 & -0.06 & -0.06 \end{bmatrix}$$

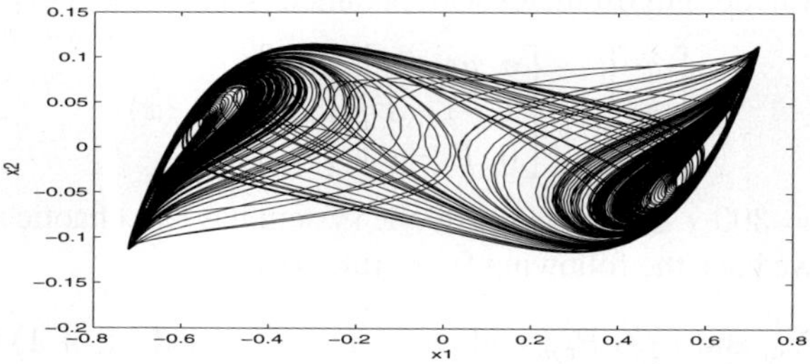

Fig. 1. The phase figure of x1 and x2 based on GFHM

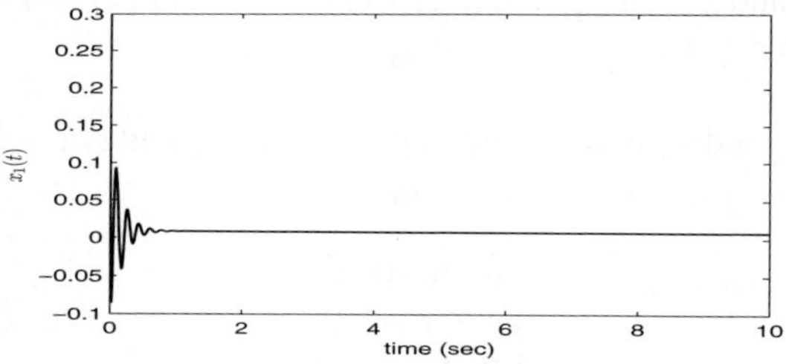

Fig. 2. The state figure of x_1

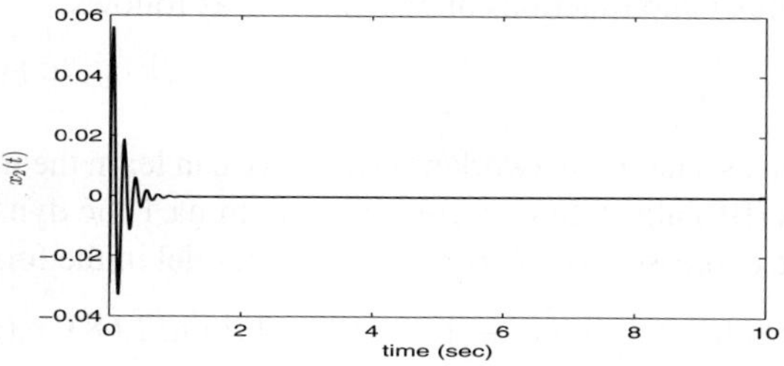

Fig. 3. The state figure of x_2

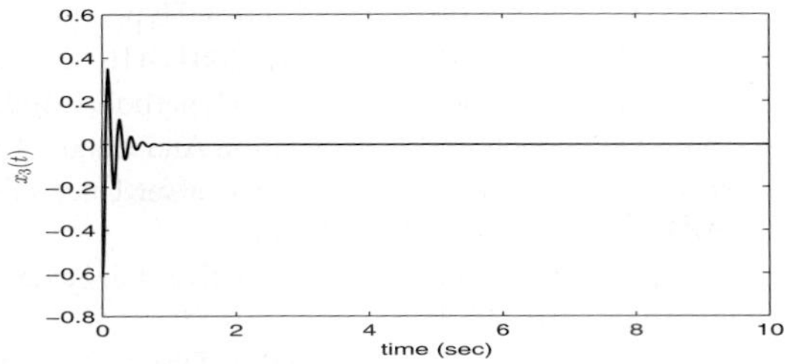

Fig. 4. The state figure of x_3

5 Conclusions

In this paper, we propose the fuzzy hyperbolic control scheme for uncertain nonlinear chaotic systems. The design procedure of the controller is in terms of linear matrix inequalities. The designed controller achieves closed-loop asymptotic stability. Moreover, considering the influence of both approximation error and external disturbance, fuzzy hyperbolic H_∞ control scheme is addressed too. Simulation example is provided to illustrate the design procedure of the proposed method.

Acknowledgment

This work was supported by the National Natural Science Foundation of China 60534010, 60572070, 60521003, 60325311and the Program for Changjiang Scholars and Innovative Research Team in University.

References

1. Chen, G., Fan, J.-Q., Hong, Y. and Qin, H. S. Introduction to chaos control and anti-control.in Advanced Topics in Nonlinear Control Systems,eds. Leung, T. P. & Qin, H.-S. (World scientific,Singapore), Chap. 6 (2001) 193–245
2. E. Ott, C. Grebogi, J. A. Yorke. Controlling chaos, Phys. Rev. Lett. 64 (1990) 1196–1199
3. Sanchez E N, PerezJP, MartinezM, Chen G. Chaos stablilization: An inverse optimal control approach,Latin Amer.Appl.Res.: Int.J.,32 (2002) 111-114
4. Redev R. Control of non-linear system, described by Loren'z model. J. Automatica and Informatics,vol XXXIV (2000) 29-32
5. Chen. G. and Lai. D. Making a dynamical system chaotic: Feedback control of Lyapunov exponents for discrete-time dynamical systems, IEEE Trans. Circuits Syst.-I: Fund. Th. Appl. 44 (1997) 250–253
6. Chen. G. and Lai. D. Feedback anticontrol of discrete chaos, Int. J. Bifurcation and Chaos. 8 (1998) 1585–1590
7. Chen. L. and Chen. G. Fuzzy predictive control of uncertain chaotic systems using time series, Int. J. Bifurcation and Chaos. 9 (1999) 757–767
8. Hun,J., K. C. ark, E. K., Mignon Park.: Fuzzy adaptive synchronization of uncertain chaotic systems. Physics Letters, A. 334 (2005) 295–305
9. H. G. Zhang, Y. B. Quan.: Modelling, Identification and Control of a Class of Non-linear System. IEEE Trans. on Fuzzy Systems. 9(2) (2001) 349-354

10. Zhang,H. G.,Wang, Z. L., M. Li, et al.: Generalized Fuzzy Hyperbolic Model: A Universal Approximator. ACTA AUTOMATIC ASINICA.30 (3) (2004) 416-422
11. Zhang,H. G., Wang,Z. L., D.R.Liu.: Chaotifying Fuzzy Hyperbolic Model Based On Adaptive Inverse Optimal Control Approach. Int. J. Bifurcation And Chaos. 12 (2003) 32-43
12. Corless M.: Guaranteed Rates of Exponential Convergence for Uncertain Systems. Journal of Optimization and Application. 64(3) (1990) 481 - 494
13. Ordones,R., Passino.K. M.: Stable Multi-Output Adaptive Fuzzy/neural Control. IEEE Trans. on Fuzzy Systems. 7, (1999), 345-353
14. Lun,S., Zhang,H.,D. Liu.: Fuzzy Hyperbolic H_∞ Filter Design for a Class of Nonlinear Continuous-time Dynamic Systems. Proc. of the 43th IEEE Int. Conf. on Decision and Control, Atlantis, Paradise Island, Bahamas. (2004), 225–230
15. Margaliot, M., Langholz,G.: Hyperbolic Optimal Control and Fuzzy Control. IEEE Transactions on Systems, Man, and Cybernetics. 29, (1999), 1-9
16. Boyd,S., Ghaoui,L. E., Feron,E., V. Balakrishan.:Linear Matrix Inequalities in System and Control Theory, Philadelphia. PA: SIAM, (1994)
17. Fotsin, H. B., Woafo.P.: Adaptive Synchronization of a Modified and Uncertain Chaotic Van der Pol-Duffing Oscillator Based on Parameter Identification Chaos. Solitons and Fractals. 24, (2005), 1363–1371

Using Fuzzy Decision Tree to Handle Uncertainty in Context Deduction

Donghai Guan, Weiwei Yuan, A. Gavrilov, Sungyoung Lee*, Youngkoo Lee, and Sangman Han

Department of Computer Engineering, Kyung Hee University, Korea
{donghai, weiwei, avg, sylee}@oslab.khu.ac.kr,
yklee@khu.ac.kr, i30000@oslab.khu.ac.kr

Abstract. In context-aware systems, one of the main challenges is how to tackle context uncertainty well, since perceived context always yields uncertainty and ambiguity with consequential effect on the performance of context-aware systems. We argue that uncertainty is mainly generated by two sources. One is sensor's inherent inaccuracy and unreliability. The other source is deduction process from low-level context to high-level context. Decision tree is an appropriate candidate for reasoning. Its distinct merit is that once a decision tree has been constructed, it is simple to convert it into a set of human-understandable rules. So human can easily improve these rules. However, one inherent disadvantage of decision tree is that the use of crisp points makes the decision trees sensitive to noise. To overcome this problem, we propose an alternative method, fuzzy decision tree, based on fuzzy set theory.

1 Introduction

Since first been proposed by Weiser in the early 1990s, ubiquitous computing has been one of the predominant trends in computing over last ten years. In a ubiquitous computing environment, computers will be everywhere around us without our awareness. In other words, computers will have moved into background.

Usually, ubiquitous system makes intelligent decisions by analyzing context information. Context refers to any information that can be used to characterize the situation of an entity. Here, an entity is a person, place, or object that is considered relevant to the interaction between a user and an application, including the user and application themselves [1].

Context is characterized at different levels of abstraction: low-level and high-level. Low-level context (such as temperature, light, voice level) is gathered directly from physical sensors. While high-level context is abstract and inferred from low-level context. For example, User's activity is a kind of high-level context. It can be inferred through some low-level context.

Context is important for system to sense, in turn, think and act. However, one potential problem for context is that it is uncertain. The ability to handle context

* Corresponding author.

D.-S. Huang, K. Li, and G.W. Irwin (Eds.): ICIC 2006, LNAI 4114, pp. 63–72, 2006.

uncertainty has become one of the main challenges in context-aware computing [2] [3] [4] [5].

Context uncertainty comes from many sources. Firstly, sensors are usually not fully reliable. For instance, a motion detector may not be able to detect people in one hundred percent of cases. On the other hand, some sensors may be more prone to cause false alarms, e.g., a face detector claims it has recognized a particular person while it has not [6]. Inherent inaccuracy and unreliability of many sensors makes low-level context uncertain. High-level context uncertainty comes from deduction process itself. Any deduction (inferring) process is uncertain.

Some methods have been proposed to deal with high-level context uncertainty. Bayesian networks is supposed to handle this problem well [6], [7], especially when there are causal relationships between various events. Also, probabilistic logic and fuzzy logic are used to handle uncertainty in [7]. Above methods can solve uncertainty to some extent. However, we argue that all of them are not perfect. The main function of ubiquitous system is to read users' mind and provide appropriate service to them. One distinct requirement is that user need to understand system's reasoning process so that if system acts unreasonably, user can correct it. Another requirement is reasoning algorithm should be powerful enough so that it still can work well in some complicated cases.

All of the above methods cannot fully meet the two requirements. As for Bayesian networks, although its reasoning ability is powerful, it cannot be easily converted into rules. As for probabilistic and fuzzy logic, their reasoning process is expressed by a set of rules. However, it is hard for users to make rules for complicated situations. Decision tree seems to be an appropriate choice. It can be simply to convert into a set of rules. Also, it works well even in some complicated cases. However, one inherent disadvantage is the use of crisp cut points makes the induced decision tree sensitive to noise. To overcome this problem, we propose an alternative method, called fuzzy decision tree, based on fuzzy set theory. This method has been successfully applied to an industrial problem to monitor a typical machining process.

2 High-Level Context Reasoning

High-level context is derived through low-level context fusion, aggregation or generalization. The advantage of high-level context is that it provides more explicit and useful result for application, which is always implicit from the point of low-level context. High-level context is more effective when predicting user's need and delivering appropriate service to user. In a smart office scenario, "five persons in room now" and "projector is working" are low-level context. And from them, we may deduce a high-level context—"they are having meeting now".

Many machine learning techniques are able to achieve this kind of reasoning task. Such as decision tree, neural network, Bayesian networks. Here, we choose decision tree, not for its more powerful reasoning ability than others, but for its result is easily transformed to rules. This is important because users can directly see the rules and they also can change the rules if these deduced rules are explicitly unreasonable.

However, if we select neural network or Bayesian networks, the results are not readable. Sometimes the system's prediction will confuse us and the worst thing is that we have no any idea why system does like this and how to solve it.

To clearly illustrate our method, we devise a scenario. In this scenario, the ubiquitous computing environment is a smart office. The low-level context includes: time, temperature, humidity, light and so on, which could be directly got from sensors. The high-level context is "deducing whether or not some specified devices should be automated selected and work". To easily understand this scenario, the devices here are only referred to heater and humidifier.

Although decision tree learning is able to generate readable results, before using it, we should know whether it is suitable to solve the problem in our scenario. Actually, decision tree learning is generally best suited to problems with the following characteristics [8]:

1) Instances are represented by attribute-value pairs.
2) Instances are described by a fixed set of attributes (e.g., temperature) and their values (e.g., hot).
3) The easiest situation for decision tree learning occurs when each attribute takes on a small number of disjoint possible values (e.g., hot, mild, cold).
4) Extensions to the basic algorithm allow handling real-valued attributes as well (e.g., a floating point temperature).
5) The target function has discrete output values. A decision tree assigns a classification to each example. Simplest case exists when there are only two possible classes (Boolean classification). Decision tree methods can also be easily extended to learning functions with more than two possible output values.
6) A more substantial extension allows learning target functions with real-valued outputs, although the application of decision trees in this setting is less common.
7) The training data may contain errors. Decision tree learning methods are robust to errors - both errors in classifications of the training examples and errors in the attribute values that describe these examples.
8) The training data may contain missing attribute values. Decision tree methods can be used even when some training examples have unknown values (e.g., humidity is known for only a fraction of the examples).

When we use decision tree method in our devised scenario, the input might include time, temperature, light, humidity or other more context information that can be acquired directly from sensors, and the output is Boolean functions, which is the result whether user will operate on some devices (heater, humidifier).

Here, we just use classical decision tree method, so we should transform real-valued attributes to disjoint values. Our experiment data is shown in Table 1. In that table "on" means user turns on the device and "off" means user turns off that device. We have mentioned that the attribute value form should be changed from real to disjoint. The method that transform context from real-valued to disjoint values is shown in Table 2. In the next table (Table 3), we show the transformed training data.

Table 1. Training data for decision tree

Low-level context					High-level context		
Time	Temp	Humidity	Light	Others	Heater	Humidifier	Others
9:00	25	0.2	50		off	on	
9:05	26	0.3	51		off	off	
9:10	27	0.4	52		on	on	
9:15	28	0.5	53		on	off	
9:20	27	0.6	53		off	off	
9:25	27	0.5	52		off	on	
9:30	26	0.4	50		off	on	
9:35	22	0.3	48		on	on	
9:40	23	0.2	49		on	on	
9:45	22	0.2	50		on	off	
9:50	21	0.3	48		off	off	
9:55	19	0.3	49		off	on	
10:00	18	0.5	48		on	off	
10:05	17	0.6	47		on	off	

Table 2. Real value to disjoint value transformation

Temp	Humidity	Light	
$14 \leq T < 20$	$0.2 \leq H < 0.4$	$30 \leq L < 45$	Low
$20 \leq T < 25$	$0.4 \leq H < 0.5$	$45 \leq L < 60$	Middle
$25 \leq T \leq 28$	$0.5 \leq H \leq 0.6$	$60 \leq L \leq 75$	High

After we get Table 3 by applying the crisp cut model, we apply decision tree on that data. The first step in building a decision tree is finding the root node. For this purpose, the information gain for each low-level context must be calculated. In the following calculation, S refers to the whole set of training data and the base of the logarithm is 2. The formulas for the calculation of entropy and information gain for "heater" are shown in equation 1 and equation 2 as follows:

$$E(h) = -\frac{m_{on}}{m_{heater}} \log \frac{m_{on}}{m_{heater}} - \frac{m_{off}}{m_{heater}} \log \frac{m_{off}}{m_{heater}} \qquad (1)$$

Where,

m_{on} is number of tuples, in which Heater= "on"

m_{off} is number of tuples, in which Heater= "off"

$m_{heater} = m_{on} + m_{off}$

Table 3. Transformed training data for decision tree

Low-level context					High-level context		
Time	Temp	Humidity	Light	Others	Heater	Humidifier	Others
9:00	Mid	Low	Mid		off	on	
9:05	High	Low	Mid		off	off	
9:10	High	Mid	Mid		on	on	
9:15	High	High	Mid		on	off	
9:20	High	High	Mid		off	off	
9:25	High	High	Mid		off	on	
9:30	High	Mid	Mid		off	on	
9:35	Mid	Low	Mid		on	on	
9:40	Mid	Low	Mid		on	on	
9:45	Mid	Low	Mid		on	off	
9:50	Mid	Low	Mid		off	off	
9:55	Low	Low	Mid		off	on	
10:00	Low	High	Mid		on	off	
10:05	Low	High	Mid		on	off	

$$G(h,lc) = E(h) - \frac{m_x}{m_{lcm}} E(h,lc = x) - \frac{m_y}{m_{lcm}} E(h,lc = y) - \frac{m_z}{m_{lcm}} E(h,lc = z) \quad (2)$$

Where,

m_x is number of tuples, in which low-level context lcm=x

m_y is number of tuples, in which low-level context lcm=y

m_z is number of tuples, in which low-level context lcm=z

$m_{lcm}=m_x+m_y+m_z$

Therefore, the entropy of the whole set and the information gain for Temp can be calculated as follows:

$$E(h) = -\frac{6}{14} log \frac{6}{14} - \frac{8}{14} log \frac{8}{14} = 0.985$$

$$G(h,temp) = E(h) - \frac{m_{high}}{m_{Temp}} E(h,T = high) - \frac{m_{mid}}{m_{Temp}} E(h,T = mid) - \frac{m_{low}}{m_{Temp}} E(h,T = low)$$

$$= 0.985 - \frac{6}{14} E(h,T = high) - \frac{5}{14} E(h,T = mid) - \frac{3}{14} E(h, = low)$$

$$G(h,T) = 0.048 = -\frac{2}{6} log \frac{2}{6} - \frac{4}{6} log \frac{4}{6} = 0.918$$

$$E(h,T=mid) = -\frac{3}{5}log\frac{3}{5} - \frac{2}{5}log\frac{2}{5} = 0.971$$

$$E(h,T=low) = -\frac{2}{3}log\frac{2}{3} - \frac{1}{3}log\frac{1}{3} = 0.918$$

Therefore,
$G(h,T) = 0.048$

Accordingly, the formulas for the calculation of entropy and information gain for "humidifier" are as follows:

$$E(hu) = -\frac{m_{on}}{m_{humi}}\log\frac{m_{on}}{m_{humi}} - \frac{m_{off}}{m_{humi}}\log\frac{m_{off}}{m_{humi}} \tag{3}$$

$$G(hu,lc) = E(hu) - \frac{m_x}{m_{lc}}E(hu,lc=x) - \frac{m_y}{m_{lc}}E(hu,lc=y) - \frac{m_z}{m_{lc}}E(hu,lc=z) \tag{4}$$

Using the formulas in equation 3 and equation 4 above, the information gain of each low-level context could be calculated. Then, the context with highest information gain would be selected as root node of decision tree.

3 Fuzzy Logic and Fuzzy Decision Tree

Using decision tree method, we could deduce the high-level context. However, still one main problem exists. For example, if the temperature is 14^oC or 20^oC, using the method shown in Table 2, both of them belong to "Low" category. However, the "Low degree" of 14 and 20 are same? Also 19^oC and 20^oC belong to different category based on Table 2, so the deduction result might be totally different. The difference between 19 and 20 is only 1. From this example, it is easily to see the method in table 2 is unreasonable.

The main reason is crisp cut points are used in classical decision trees. In fact, crisp cut model does not match human thing and is not reasonable. This makes decision trees sensitive to noise. To overcome this problem, we incorporate fuzzy theory in decision trees. Instead of crisp boundaries between categories, fuzzy logic introduces a membership function, which reflects how well a given value falls into a category. For example, we can define membership for Temperature as follows:

In Figurel, 0 represents complete non-membership and 1 represents complete membership, while other values representing the degree of membership, or the degree to which the low-context is represented by the linguistic indicator, such as "high", "middle" and "low".

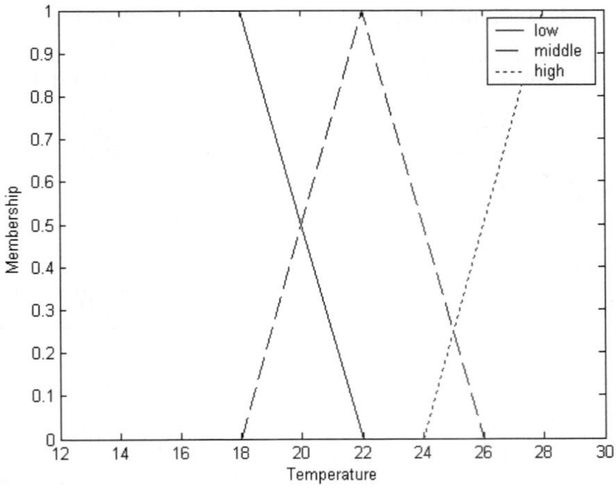

Fig. 1. Membership function for temperature

Using the example partitions shown in Figure 1, the temperature $20\,^{o}C$ would be discretised into the categorical value 'middle' with the membership value 0.5, and the temperature $22\,^{o}C$ would be discretised into the same categorical value but with the membership value 1. Consequently, even though the two temperatures $20\,^{o}C$ and $22\,^{o}C$ have the same categorical value 'middle', they have different membership values.

Also, other low-level context can be defined using the same method like Figure 1. After all the low-level context have their own membership functions, a corresponding high-level context's membership functions can be derived using the following formulas:

$$mf_{hc} = mf_{lc1} mf_{lc2} mf_{lc3} ... mf_{lcn} \tag{5}$$

Where,

mf_{hc} refers to membership function of high-level context

mf_{lcn} refers to membership function of low-level context to a given category

For example, if we only consider three low-level context: Temperature, Light, Humidity.

Temperature is middle with membership 0.8
Humidity is low with membership 0.7
Light is middle with membership 0.6
Then, the corresponding high-level context membership is
$mf_{hc} = 0.8*0.7*0.6 = 0.336$

For illustration, we use the following context information given in Table 4 below.

Table 4. Transformed training data for fuzzy decision tree

Low-level context					High-level context	
Item	Temp	Humi	Light	Others	Humidifier	Membership
1	Mid	Low	Mid		on	0.5
2	High	Low	Mid		on	0.3
3	High	Mid	Mid		on	0.55
4	High	High	Mid		off	0.4
5	High	High	Mid		off	0.3
6	High	High	Mid		on	0.2
7	High	Mid	Mid		off	0.25
8	Mid	Low	Mid		on	0.45
9	Mid	Low	Mid		on	0.6
10	Mid	Low	Mid		on	0.6
11	Mid	Low	Mid		off	0.5
12	Low	Low	Mid		on	0.7
13	Low	High	Mid		off	0.45
14	Low	High	Mid		off	0.5

The first step in building a fuzzy decision tree is also finding the root node. So the information gain for each low-level context must be calculated. The formulas for the calculation of entropy and information gain are essential the same as those for building a conventional decision tree. However, in the case of fuzzy decision tree, the membership values of the high-level context should be used in the calculation. The corresponding formulas for the entropy and information gain G are as follows in equation 6 and equation 7. Here the high-context is humidifier operation prediction.

$$E(hu) = -\frac{m_{on}}{m_{hu}} \log \frac{m_{on}}{m_{hu}} - -\frac{m_{off}}{m_{hu}} \log \frac{m_{off}}{m_{hu}} \tag{6}$$

Where,

$m_{on} = \sum mf_{humidifier}(on)$ sum of all membership values for humidifier=on

$m_{off} = \sum mf_{humidifier}(off)$ sum of all membership values for humidifier=off

$m_{hu} = m_{on} + m_{off}$

$$G(hu, lc) = E(hu) - -\frac{mf_x}{m_{lc}} E(hu, A = x) - \frac{mf_y}{m_{lc}} E(hu, A = y) - \frac{mf_z}{m_{lc}} E(hu, A = z) \tag{7}$$

Where

mf_x sum of all membership values for A=x

mf_y sum of all membership values for A=y

mf_z sum of all membership values for A=z

$m_{lcm}=mf_x+mf_y+mf_z$

Therefore, the entropy of the whole training set and the information gain for Humidity can be calculated as given below. In the case of attributes Light, Temperature, information gains calculation is same with Humidity.

$$m_{on}=0.5+0.3+0.55+0.2+0.45+0.6+0.6+0.7=3.9$$

$$m_{off}=0.4+0.3+0.25+0.5+0.45+0.5=2.4$$

$$E(hu)=-\frac{3.9}{6.3}\log\frac{3.9}{6.3}-\frac{2.4}{6.3}\log\frac{2.4}{6.3}=0.96$$

$$E(hu,hu=high)=-\frac{1.65}{1.85}\log\frac{1.65}{1.85}-\frac{0.2}{1.85}\log\frac{0.2}{1.85}=0.49$$

$$E(hu,hu=middle)=-\frac{0.55}{0.8}\log\frac{0.55}{0.8}-\frac{0.25}{0.8}\log\frac{0.25}{0.8}=0.90$$

$$E(hu,hu=low)=-\frac{3.15}{3.65}\log\frac{3.15}{3.65}-\frac{0.5}{3.65}\log\frac{0.5}{3.65}=0.58$$

$$G(hu,hu)=E(hu)--\frac{1.85}{6.3}E(hu,hu=high)-\frac{0.8}{6.3}E(hu,hu=mid)-\frac{3.65}{6.3}E(hu,hu=low)$$

=0.96-0.14-0.11-0.34
=0.37

Then, the context with highest information gain would be selected as root node of fuzzy decision tree. After the root node is found, we can use the similar way to find the other leaf nodes.

4 Conclusions

In this paper, firstly, we discuss the main sources of context uncertainty. In addition to sensor's inherent inaccuracy and unreliability, high-level context reasoning is also a main source of uncertainty. Furthermore, we propose to use fuzzy decision tree based algorithm to reason high-level context. Fuzzy decision tree is the extension of classical decision tree by incorporating fuzzy set based approach.

There are two main merits to use this approach. First, uncertainty is reduced so that system reliability is improved. What's more, fuzzy decision tree can be easily converted into human readable rules, which makes it possible for users understand system response and improve system performance by directly changing those rules.

Acknowledgement

The research was supported by the Driving Force Project for the Next Generation of Gyeonggi Provincial Government in Republic of Korea.

References

1. Dey, A.K.: A Conceptual Framework and a Toolkit for Supporting the Rapid Prototyping of Context-Aware Applications. In J. of Human-Computer Interaction (HCI). 16 (2001) 97-166
2. Bardram, J. E.: Applications of Context-Aware Computing in Hospital Work – Examples and Design Principles. In Proc. of ACM Symposium on Applied Computing (ACM SAC). (2004) 1574-1579
3. Dey, A.K., Jennifer, M., Gregory, D.A., Scott, C.: Distributed Mediation of Ambiguous Context in Aware Environments. In Proc. of the 15th Annual Symposium on User Interface Software and Technology (UIST 2002), Paris. (2002) 121-130
4. Satyanarayanan, M.: Pervasive Computing: Vision and Challenges. In IEEE PCM. (2001) 10-17
5. Satyanarayan, M.: Coping with Uncertainty. In IEEE CS Pervasive computing Journal. (2001) 2-3
6. Michal: Data Mining Techniques in Ubiquitous Computing, IWCIT03 (2003)
7. Anand, R., Jalal, A.M., Roy, H.C.: Reasoning about Uncertain Contexts in Pervasive Computing Environments, In J. IEEE Pervasive Computing. 3 (2004) 62-70
8. Mitchell, T.: Decision Tree Learning, in T. Mitchell, Machine Learning, The McGraw-Hill Companies, Inc. (1997)

Variable Universe Adaptive Fuzzy Sliding Mode Controller for a Class of Nonlinear System

Yunfeng Liu, Dong Miao, Yunhui Peng, and Xiaogang Yang

303 Branch, Xi'an Research Inst. Of High-tech, Hongqing Town, 710025, China
footballliu@163.com

Abstract. Based on integrating the property of sliding mode control (SMC) with the thought of variable universe in adaptive fuzzy control, a design method of variable universe adaptive fuzzy sliding mode control (FSMC) is proposed. There are two sets of control rule bases. The first set is utilized to approach the equivalent control of SMC. By adjusting the universes of input variables and the membership fuzzy controller of conclusion part in rules on-line, a variable universe adaptive fuzzy control is developed to estimate the equivalent control of SMC control system. The derived adaptive law is applied to adjust the rule parameter for changing the control rules to meet system dynamic. Another set is used to attenuate the switching control of SMC in the sense of heuristic, which ensure the requirement of system stability. Four heuristic control rules are employed to smooth the control law based on the concepts of SMC. We apply the control method to the missile electro-hydraulic servo mechanism. Simulation results verify the validity of the proposed approach.

1 Introduction

Variable structure systems with a sliding mode have been widely developed in recent years [1-3]. The salient advantage of sliding mode control (SMC) derives from the property of robustness to structured and unstructured uncertainties once the system enters the sliding mode. However, system robustness is not assured until the sliding mode is reached. The main drawback of SMC is chattering phenomenon which can excite undesirable high-frequency dynamics [4]. Fuzzy control using linguistic information possesses several advantages such as model-free, robustness, universal approximation theorem and rule-based algorithm. However, the huge amount of fuzzy rules for high-order systems makes the analysis complex [5]. Therefore, some researchers proposed fuzzy sliding mode controllers (FSMC), which integrated fuzzy set theory and SMC into controller design to acquire stability and consistent performance [6]. To guarantee the stability of FSMC, Kim and Lee [7] used some fuzzy control rules to construct the switching control under the assumption that the equivalent control has already exist. The method has the problem that is difficult to guarantee the stability of fuzzy control system as well as to obtain a suitable equivalent control if the nominal mathematics model is unknown in advance.

To overcome the problem, a method of variable universe adaptive FSMC is proposed in this paper. Firstly a variable universe adaptive fuzzy control [8] is

D.-S. Huang, K. Li, and G.W. Irwin (Eds.): ICIC 2006, LNAI 4114, pp. 73–84, 2006.

developed to approximate the equivalent control. Based on the conventional SMC, a variable universe adaptive fuzzy control is introduced. It has the ability of adjusting the universes of input variables and the membership fuzzy controller of conclusion part in rules on-line. Then the switching control is appended to guarantee the stability of the proposed FSMC. Moreover, a set of heuristic control rules is constructed to attenuate the chattering phenomenon of the switching control signal. In this paper, we apply the control method to the missile electro-hydraulic servo mechanism. Simulation results show the advantages of the proposed approach.

2 Problem Statement

Consider a class of uncertain SISO nonlinear system

$$x^{(n)} = f(\boldsymbol{X}) + g(\boldsymbol{X})u + d(\boldsymbol{X}) \ . \tag{1}$$

where state vector $\boldsymbol{X} = (x, \dot{x}, \cdots, x^{(n-1)})^T \in R^n$, $x \in R$; $u \in R$ is the control input; $f(\boldsymbol{X})$ is an unknown nonlinear continuous function whose upper bound is known as $|f(\boldsymbol{X})| \le f_{\max}$; $g(\boldsymbol{X})$ is an unknown gain function with lower bound g_l ; $d(\boldsymbol{X})$ is an unknown disturbance whose upper bound is known as $|d(\boldsymbol{X})| \le D(\boldsymbol{X})$. It is also assumed that x_r is the desired trajectory, and $x_r \in R$ has up to the nth derivative. The objective is to let the state vector $\boldsymbol{X}$ track $\boldsymbol{X}_r$, where $\boldsymbol{X}_r = (x_r, \dot{x}_r, \cdots, x_r^{(n-1)})^T \in R^n$. Let us define the tracking error $e_1 = x_r - x$, and the error vector

$$\boldsymbol{e} = (e_1, e_2, \cdots, e_n)^T = (x_r - x, \dot{x}_r - \dot{x}, \cdots, x_r^{(n-1)} - x^{(n-1)})^T \in R^n \ . \tag{2}$$

Thus, (1) can be rewritten as

$$\begin{cases} \dot{e}_1 = e_2 \\ \vdots \\ \dot{e}_{n-1} = e_n \\ \dot{e}_n = -f(\boldsymbol{X}) - g(\boldsymbol{X})u - d(\boldsymbol{X}) + x_r^{(n)} \end{cases} . \tag{3}$$

The sliding surface is

$$s(\boldsymbol{e}) = \sum_{i=1}^{n-1} c_i e_i + e_n = 0 \ . \tag{4}$$

where $c_i > 0$ are constants. In the design of SMC, an equivalent control is first given so that the states can stay on sliding surface [2]. The equivalent control can be obtained by letting $\dot{s}(e)$ and d equal to zero. That is

$$u_{eq} = \frac{1}{g(\boldsymbol{X})} \left(\sum_{i=1}^{n-1} c_i e_{i+1} - f(\boldsymbol{X}) + x_r^{(n)} \right) \ . \tag{5}$$

The coefficient $c_i > 0$ can be properly chosen such that all the roots of (4) are in the open left-half of the complex plane. That is, if the state trajectory can be forced to slide on sliding surface, a stable equivalent control system is achieved. Based on the principle of SMC, the control law consists of the following two parts. One is the sliding mode equivalent control u_{eq}. Another is the switching control u_h that drives the states toward the sliding surface.

According to (3), (5), so the control law is taken as

$$u = u_{eq} + u_h \ . \tag{6}$$

where $u_h = \frac{1}{g(X)} K_1 \operatorname{sgn}(s)$, $K_1 = D + \eta$, $\operatorname{sgn}(s) = \begin{cases} 1, s > 0 \\ 0, s = 0 \\ -1, s < 0 \end{cases}$

From the analysis above, we get $s\dot{s} \le -\eta|s| < 0$, where $\eta > 0$. So under the control law (6), the sliding surface exists and is reachable. However, since the functions $f(X)$ and $g(X)$ are uncertain, the accurate equivalent control u_{eq} is difficult to reach. Here, the variable universe adaptive fuzzy control is employed to approximate u_{eq}. So the control law consists of the following two parts. One is the estimated equivalent control $\hat{u}_{eq}$ that is constructed by an adaptive mechanism. The function of this term is to force the system state to slide on the sliding surface. Another is the switching control u_h that drives the states toward the sliding surface. Thus, the control law can be represented as

$$u = \hat{u}_{eq} + u_h \ . \tag{7}$$

3 Design of the Adaptive FSMC

3.1 Structure of Variable Universe Adaptive Fuzzy Control

Let $X_i = [-E_i, E_i]$ ($i = 1, 2, \cdots, n$) be the universe of input variable x_i ($i = 1, 2, \cdots, n$), $j = 1, 2, \cdots, m$, and $Y = [-U, U]$ be the universe of output y . $\psi_i = \{A_{ij}\}$ ($1 \le j \le m$) defines a fuzzy partition on X_i ($i = 1, 2, \cdots, n$) and $\Phi_i = \{B_j\}$ ($1 \le j \le m$) stands for a fuzzy partition on Y. ψ_i and Φ_i are regarded as linguistic variables so that a group of fuzzy inference rules is formed as follows:

$$\text{if } x_1 \text{ is } A_{1j} \text{ and } x_2 \text{ is } A_{2j}, \cdots, \text{and } x_n \text{ is } A_{nj} \text{ then } y \text{ is } B_j \ (j = 1, 2, \cdots, m). \tag{8}$$

Let x_{ij} be the peak points of A_{ij}, and y_j be the peak points of B_j ($i = 1, 2, \cdots, n$). By using the results in [9], the fuzzy logic system (i.e. a fuzzy controller) based on (8) can be represented as an n-ary piecewise interpolation function y

$$y(x_1, x_2, \cdots, x_n) = \sum_{j=1}^{m} \prod_{i=1}^{n} A_{ij}(x_i) y_j \ . \tag{9}$$

The so-called variable universe means that some universes, such as X_i and Y, can change with changing variables x_i and y, denoted by

$$\begin{cases} X_i(x_i) = [-\alpha_i(x_i)E_i, \alpha_i(x_i)E_i] \\ Y(y) = [-\beta(y)U, \beta(y)U] \end{cases} . \tag{10}$$

where $\alpha_i(x_i)$ ($i=1,2,\cdots,n$)and $\beta(y)$ are contraction-expansion factors of the universe X_i and Y . In general, a practical contraction-expansion factor is given as follows:

$$\alpha(x)=1-\lambda\exp(-kx^2) \quad \lambda\in(0,1)\,,\quad k>0\ . \tag{11}$$

By means of the conclusions in [9], a variable universe adaptive fuzzy controller based on (10) can be represented by n-ary piecewise dynamic interpolation function:

$$y(\underline{x}(t))=\beta(y(\underline{x}(t)))\sum_{j=1}^{m}\prod_{i=1}^{n}A_{ij}\left(\frac{x_i(t)}{\alpha_i(x_i(t))}\right)y_j\ . \tag{12}$$

where $\underline{x}(t)=(x_1(t),x_2(t),\cdots,x_n(t))^T$. It is obvious that $\alpha(x)$, $\beta(y)$ affect the dynamic function of system. So how to determine a contraction-expansion factor $\beta(y)$ is an important problem. In the paper it is acquired by adaptive law. In order to design the adaptive law of $\beta(t)$, we introduce fuzzy basic function denoted by w_j :

$$w_j(\underline{x})=\prod_{i=1}^{n}A_{ij}\left(\frac{x_i(t)}{\alpha_i(x_i(t))}\right)\ . \tag{13}$$

Then (12) can be simplified into

$$y(\underline{x}(t))=\beta(y)\sum_{j=1}^{m}w_j(x)y_j=\sum_{j=1}^{m}w_j(\underline{x})(\beta(y)\cdot y_j)=\sum_{j=1}^{m}w_j(\underline{x})p_j\ . \tag{14}$$

where $p_j(\underline{x})$ is modified by contraction-expansion factor $\alpha(x)$, and β is modified by p_j through adaptive law.

3.2 The Equivalent Control

In this section, we first construct the FSMC, and then show how to develop an adaptive FSMC controller for obtaining the equivalent control through rules adaptation. Then, we construct the switching control to guarantee system's stability. In this paper, the variable universe adaptive fuzzy control is employed to approximate the equivalent control. The input variables used in FSMC are integrated into two variables (s and $\dot{s}$) [10,11]so that the number of control rules could be minimized than those that use state variables. The jth fuzzy rule is constructed as

$$R^j:\text{if } s \text{ is } A_1^j \text{ and } \dot{s} \text{ is } A_2^j\,,\quad \text{then } \hat{u}_{eq}=p_j \quad (j=1,2,\cdots,N)\ . \tag{15}$$

where A_1^j and A_2^j represent the fuzzy set of input variables s and $\dot{s}$. The rule parameters p_j are on-line adjusted. The output of the adaptive fuzzy controller is

$$\hat{u}_{eq}=\boldsymbol{W}^{\mathrm{T}}(s,\dot{s})\boldsymbol{P}\ . \tag{16}$$

where $\boldsymbol{W}(s,\dot{s})=[w_1(s,\dot{s}),\cdots,w_N(s,\dot{s})]^{\mathrm{T}}$, $w_j(s,\dot{s})=\prod_{i=1}^{2}A_{ij}\left(\frac{s_i(t)}{\alpha_i s_i(t)}\right)$, $\boldsymbol{P}=[p_1,\cdots,p_N]^{\mathrm{T}}$

The main task of this section is to derive an adaptive law to adjust the rule parameter vector $\boldsymbol{P}$ such that the estimated equivalent control $\hat{u}_{eq}$ can be optimally approximated to the equivalent control of the SMC. Suppose there exists the optimal parameter vector $\boldsymbol{P}^* = [p_1^*, p_2^*, \cdots, p_N^*]^{\mathrm{T}}$ such that $\hat{u}_{eq}$ has minimum approximation error $\varepsilon(s,\dot{s}) = u_{eq}^*(s,\dot{s}) - u_{eq}(s,\dot{s})$. Thus,

$$u_{eq}^*(s,\dot{s}) - u_{eq}(s,\dot{s}) = \boldsymbol{W}^{\mathrm{T}}(s,\dot{s})(\boldsymbol{P}^* - \boldsymbol{P}) \ . \tag{17}$$

Define a Lyapunov function candidate:

$$V = (1/2)s^2 + (1/2r)g(\boldsymbol{X})\tilde{\boldsymbol{P}}^{\mathrm{T}}\tilde{\boldsymbol{P}} \ . \tag{18}$$

where $\tilde{\boldsymbol{P}} = \boldsymbol{P} - \boldsymbol{P}^*$ and r is a positive constant. Differentiating (18), we can have

$$\dot{V} = s\dot{s} + (1/r)g(\boldsymbol{X})\dot{\tilde{\boldsymbol{P}}}^{\mathrm{T}}\tilde{\boldsymbol{P}} \ . \tag{19}$$

Differentiating (4) and substituting (7) into (19), then

$$\dot{V} = s\{c_1e_2 + c_2e_3 + \dddot{x}_d - f(\boldsymbol{X}) - g(\boldsymbol{X})[\hat{u}_{eq} + u_h] + d\} + \frac{1}{r}g(\boldsymbol{X})\dot{\tilde{\boldsymbol{P}}}^{\mathrm{T}}\tilde{\boldsymbol{P}} \ . \tag{20}$$

Since (5), (20) can be written as

$$\dot{V} = s[-g(\boldsymbol{X})(\hat{u}_{eq} - u_{eq} + u_h)] + \frac{1}{r}g(\boldsymbol{X})\dot{\tilde{\boldsymbol{P}}}^{\mathrm{T}}\tilde{\boldsymbol{P}} \ . \tag{21}$$

Substituting (17) into (21), then

$$\begin{aligned}\dot{V} &= s\{-g(\boldsymbol{X})[\boldsymbol{W}^{\mathrm{T}}(s,\dot{s})\boldsymbol{P} - \boldsymbol{W}^{\mathrm{T}}(s,\dot{s})\boldsymbol{P}^* + \boldsymbol{W}^{\mathrm{T}}(s,\dot{s})\boldsymbol{P}^* - u_{eq} + u_h]\} + \frac{1}{r}g(\boldsymbol{X})\dot{\tilde{\boldsymbol{P}}}^{\mathrm{T}}\tilde{\boldsymbol{P}} \\ &= s\{-g(\boldsymbol{X})[\varepsilon(s,\dot{s}) + u_h]\} - sg(\boldsymbol{X})\boldsymbol{W}^{\mathrm{T}}(s,\dot{s})\tilde{\boldsymbol{P}} + \frac{1}{r}g(\boldsymbol{X})\dot{\tilde{\boldsymbol{P}}}^{\mathrm{T}}\tilde{\boldsymbol{P}} \\ &.\end{aligned} \tag{22}$$

Choosing the adaptive law

$$\dot{\boldsymbol{P}} = rs\boldsymbol{W}(s,\dot{s}) \ . \tag{23}$$

Since (23), (22) becomes

$$\dot{V} = -g(\boldsymbol{X})s\varepsilon(s,\dot{s}) - g(\boldsymbol{X})su_h \le 0 \ . \tag{24}$$

u_h has the same sign as s (refer to (27)). So In order to complete the adaptive FSMC controller design, the switching control is taken into account to ensure state trajectory moves toward the sliding surface as well as to guarantee the stability of the control system. Achieving this goal, a Lyapunov function candidate is given as

$$V = 0.5s^2 \ . \tag{25}$$

Then differentiate V with respect to time. Substituting (4) and (7) into (25)

$$\begin{aligned}\dot{V} &= s\{c_1e_2 + c_2e_3 + \dddot{x}_d - f(\boldsymbol{X}) - g(\boldsymbol{X})[\hat{u}_{eq} + u_h] + d\} \\ &\le |s|\{|c_1e_2 + c_2e_3 + \dddot{x}_d| + |f(\boldsymbol{X})| + g(\boldsymbol{X})|\hat{u}_{eq}| + |d|\} - sg(\boldsymbol{X})u_h \ .\end{aligned} \tag{26}$$

Choosing the switching control

$$u_h = \text{sgn}(s)K \ . \tag{27}$$

where $K = g_l^{-1}(|c_1e_2 + c_2e_3 + \ddot{x}_d| + f_{\max} + D) + |\hat{u}_{eq}|$. Thus, $\dot{V} \le 0$. i.e., the switching control actually achieves a stable FSMC system.

3.3 The FSMC Law

From (27) it can be seen that the undesirable control input chattering is caused by the discontinuous sign term $\text{sgn}(s)$. The switching control law u_h which guarantees the reachability and existence of the sliding mode is proportional to the uncertainty bound including $f_{\max}$ and D. However, the exact value of the parameter variations and the external load disturbance are difficult to know in advance for practical applications. Therefore, usually a conservative control law with large control gain K is selected. However, it will cause a large amount of chattering phenomenon, which causes high-frequency unmodelled dynamics [12, 13].

Therefore, a fuzzy control law is proposed here, in which a fuzzy inference mechanism is used to facilitate switching control adjustment for minimizing the chattering. The input of the fuzzy controller is s, and the output is u_f to replace the discontinuous sliding switching control u_h. The following rule base is proposed:

(1) if s is positive large (PL) , then u_f is negative large(NL); (2)if s is positive small(PS), then u_f is negative small (NS); (3) if s is negative large(NL), then u_f is positive large(PL); (4)if s is negative small(NS), then u_f is positive small(PS).

Choosing sigmoidal membership functions for s and singletons for u_f, we have

$$\mu_{s\_\text{PL}} = \tanh(\frac{s}{\sigma_s}) \, , \mu_{s\_\text{PS}} = 1 - \mu_{s\_\text{PL}} \, , \mu_{s\_\text{NL}} = -\tanh(\frac{s}{\sigma_s}) \, , \mu_{s\_\text{NS}} = 1 - \mu_{s\_\text{NL}} \, . \tag{28}$$

$$\begin{gathered} \mu_{u_f\_\text{NL}} = \begin{cases} 1 & u_f = -\gamma_m \\ 0 & u_f \ne -\gamma_m \end{cases}, \mu_{u_f\_\text{PL}} = \begin{cases} 1 & u_f = \gamma_m \\ 0 & u_f \ne \gamma_m \end{cases}, \\ \mu_{u_f\_\text{NS}} = \mu_{u_f\_\text{PS}} = \begin{cases} 1 & u_f = 0 \\ 0 & \mu_f \ne 0 \end{cases}. \end{gathered} \tag{29}$$

and using rules (1)-(4), we obtain

$$u_f = \begin{cases} \dfrac{\mu_{s\_\text{PL}} \cdot (-\gamma_m) + \mu_{s\_\text{PS}} \cdot 0}{\mu_{s\_\text{PL}} + \mu_{s\_\text{PS}}} & s > 0 \\ \dfrac{\mu_{s\_\text{NL}} \cdot (\gamma_m) + \mu_{s\_\text{NS}} \cdot 0}{\mu_{s\_\text{NL}} + \mu_{s\_\text{NS}}} & s < 0 \end{cases} . \tag{30}$$

In summary, the fuzzy control u_f can be written as follows:

$$u_f = -\gamma_m \tanh(s / \sigma_s) \ . \tag{31}$$

where $\gamma_m = K$, σ_s is a designed parameter.

As discussed above, a variable universe adaptive FSMC has been developed to estimate the equivalent control of SMC system. The adaptive law is applied to adjust the rule parameter vector $\boldsymbol{P}$. In addition, the switching control has also been derived to ensure the requirement of system stability. Finally, four constructed heuristic control rules are employed to smooth the control law based on the concepts of SMC.

4 Simulation Results and Discussion

To assess the proposed variable universe adaptive FSMC that developed in this paper, a simulation example is applied. We apply the method to a kind of missile electro-hydraulic servo mechanism, which is a typical electro-hydraulic position servo system [14]. Fig.1 shows a structure diagram of missile electro-hydraulic servo mechanism.

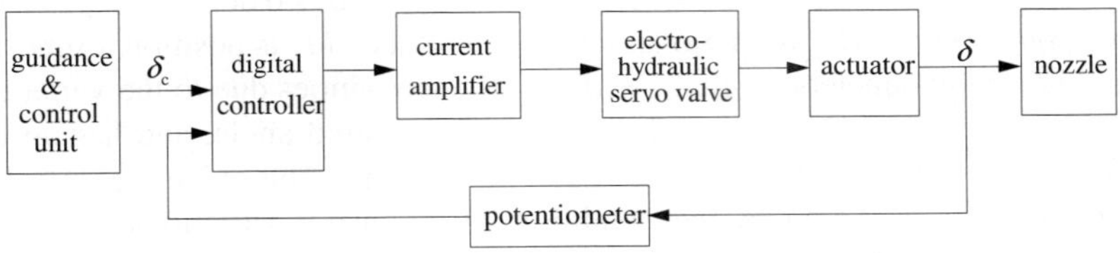

Fig. 1. Structure diagram of missile electro-hydraulic servo mechanism

The closed loop of control system is composed of a digital controller [15], a current amplifier, an electro-hydraulic servo valve, an actuator, and a potentiometer. The objective of the control is to generate the input current such that the angular position of the nozzle is regulated to the desired position. The piston position of the actuator is controlled as follows: Once the voltage input corresponding to the position input δ_c is transmitted to the digital controller, the input current is generated in proportion to the error between the voltage input and the voltage output from the potentiometer. Then the valve spool position is controlled according to the input current applied to the torque motor of the servo valve. Depending on the spool position and the load conditions of the piston, the rate as well as the direction of the flows supplied to each cylinder chamber is determined. The motion of the piston then is controlled by these flows, and then swing angle δ of the nozzle is achieved. At the same time, the piston is influenced by an external disturbance generated from the nozzle. Choose system state: $\boldsymbol{X} = [x_1 \quad x_2 \quad x_3]^T = [\delta \quad \dot{\delta} \quad \ddot{\delta}]^T$, the whole system dynamics model is given by the following derivation equations

$$\begin{cases} \dot{x}_1 = x_2 \\ \dot{x}_2 = x_3 \\ \dot{x}_3 = f(\boldsymbol{X}) + gu - d \end{cases} . \qquad (32)$$

where $a_1 = \frac{4BK_\delta K_{ce}}{IV_T}$, $a_2 = \frac{4B(AR)^2 + 4BK_{ce}n + K_\delta V_T}{IV_T}$, $a_3 = \frac{n}{I} + \frac{4BK_{ce}}{V_T}$, $f(\boldsymbol{X}) = -a_1x_1 - a_2x_2 - a_3x_3$, $g = \frac{4BAR}{IV_T}K_Q K_V K_{ui}$, $d = \frac{4BK_{ce}}{IV_T}M + \frac{1}{I}\cdot\frac{dM}{dt}$

where K_{ui} — servo amplifier gain, K_V — servo valve gain, P_L — load pressure, K_Q — valve flow gain; A — pressure area in the actuator, R — effective torque arm of the linkage, V_T — effective system oil volume, $K_{ce} = C_e + K_c$ (C_e — leakage coefficient of cylinder, K_c — valve pressure gain), B — oil effective bulk modulus, n — coefficient of viscous friction, I — moment of inertia, M — load torque, K_δ — coefficient of position torque, u — input voltage, δ — swing angle of the nozzle.

In the SMC design we usually assume $a_i = a_{i0} + \Delta a_i$ ($i = 1,2,3$), $g = g_0 + \Delta g$, where a_{i0} , g_0 are the nominal parameters of a_i and g , and Δa_i , Δg is the model uncertainty. The nominal value [14]of some parameters are assumed as $k_{ui} = 5mA/V$, $A = 10cm^2$, $K_Q = 12cm^3/(s\cdot mA)$, $R = 17cm$. Substituting the values into (32), we can get $a_{10} = 0$, $a_{20} = 8873.64$, $a_{30} = 37.68$, $g_0 = 179425$, $d = 0.86\dot{M} + 9.73M$, where $M = M_{f0}Sgn\dot{\delta} + M_d$, M_{f0} is frictional torque amplitude, M_d is position torque.

From (32) the parameters a_1, a_2, a_3, g, d are all uncertainties due to the variations of K_Q , B , C_e , K_{ui} and M . It is assumed that δ_d is the desired angle, and has up to 3rd derivative. All state variables are measurable and bound. The objective is to let the state vector $\boldsymbol{X}$ track $\boldsymbol{X}_d$ under the condition of parameter variations and external disturbances, where $\boldsymbol{X}_d = (\delta_d, \dot{\delta}_d, \ddot{\delta}_d)$. Assume the range of the system in (32): $\Delta a_i = 0.5\sin(2\pi t)a_{i0}$, so $f_{\max} = |1.5\times a_{20}x_2 + 1.5\times a_{30}x_3|$, $\Delta g = 0.2\sin(2\pi t)g_0$, so $g_l = 0.8\times g_0$, $M_{f0} = 3000 + 1000\sin 2\pi t$, $M_d = 500 + 100\sin 2\pi t$.

In this study, the Gaussian-typed and singletons are, respectively, used to define the membership functions of IF-part and THEN-part. The quantitative factor of s and $\dot{s}$ is, respectively, $k_1 = 1/3000$, $k_2 = 1/3000000$. The proportional factor of $\hat{u}_{eq}$ is $k_3 = 1.5$. The fuzzy partition of s is $A_1 = NB$, $A_2 = NS$, $A_3 = ZO$, $A_4 = PS$, $A_5 = PB$. The mean of NB , NS , ZO , PS , PB is, respectively, -1 , -0.5 , 0 , 0.5 , 1 . The corresponding variance is 0.3 . The fuzzy partition of $\dot{s}$ is $B_1 = NB$, $B_2 = NS$, $B_3 = ZO$, $B_4 = PS$, $B_5 = PB$. The mean of NB , NS , ZO , PS , PB is, respectively, -1 , -0.5 , 0 , 0.5 , 1 .The corresponding variance is 0.3 .

The contraction-expansions factors $\alpha_1(s)$ and $\alpha_2(\dot{s})$ are defined respectively as $\alpha_1(s) = 1 - 0.9\exp(-0.99s^2)$, $\alpha_2(\dot{s}) = 1 - 0.45\exp(-0.95\dot{s}^2)$.

Table 1. The initial fuzzy rules

s	$\dot{s}$				
	NB	*NS*	*ZO*	*PS*	*PB*
NB	1	0.75	0.5	0.25	0
NS	0.75	0.5	0.25	0	-0.25
ZO	0.5	0.25	0	-0.25	-0.5
PS	0.25	0	-0.25	-0.5	-0.75
PB	0	-0.25	-0.5	-0.75	-1

The parameter vector $\boldsymbol{P}$ is initialized as a linear PD controller with an acceptable performance. The initial fuzzy rules are given in Table 1. The simulation condition and design parameters of variable universe adaptive FSMC controller are specified as follows: (a) initial values of system state variables $\boldsymbol{X}(0)=[1 \quad 0 \quad 0]^T$; (b) sampling time interval $t=0.001s$; (c) Choose the poles of the system as described by (6) at $-60,-60$, we can obtain $c_1=3600$, $c_2=120$; (d) Desired output $\delta_d(t)=\sin 2\pi t$; (e) the adaptive law parameter $r=0.5$; (f) $\sigma_s=500$.

We do simulation research and compare results with that of conventional SMC under the same condition of parameter variations and external disturbances. Simulation results are indicated in Fig. 2—Fig. 7. Fig. 2 and Fig. 3 show the tracking response of the system. Fig. 4 and Fig. 5 show the tracking error. Fig. 6 and Fig. 7 show the control input where the controller is taken as variable universe adaptive FSMC or the conventional SMC.

Simulation analysis: From the simulation results, we can conclude that:

1) If the controller is the conventional SMC, the tracking error is small and there are serious high frequency chattering in the control input due to the sign function in the switching control.

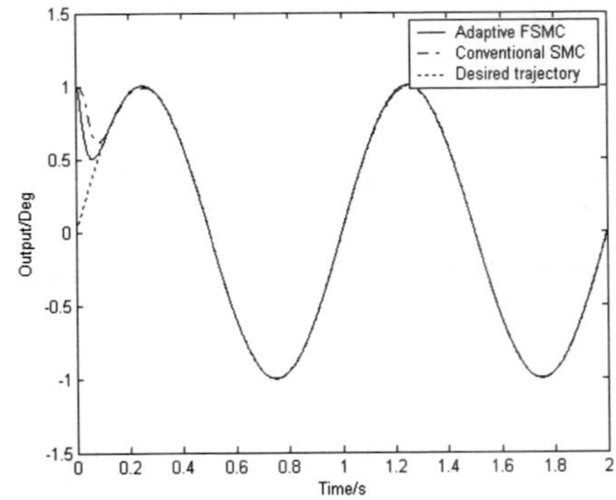

Fig. 2. Tracking response of system

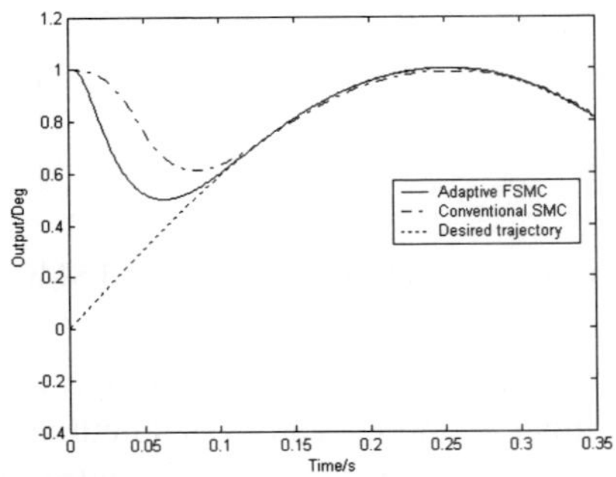

Fig. 3. Magnifying figure of tracking response

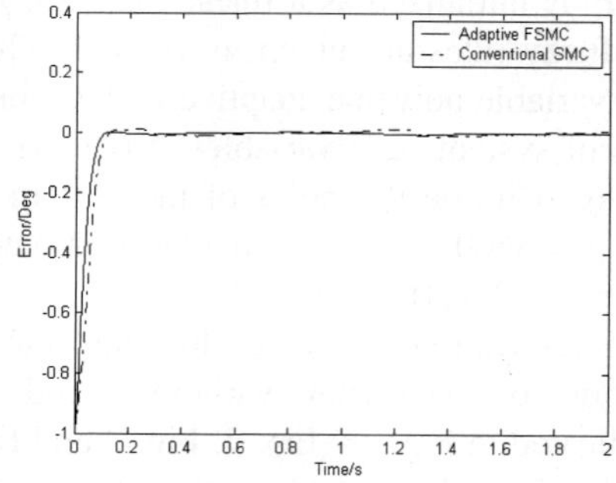

Fig. 4. Tracking error of system

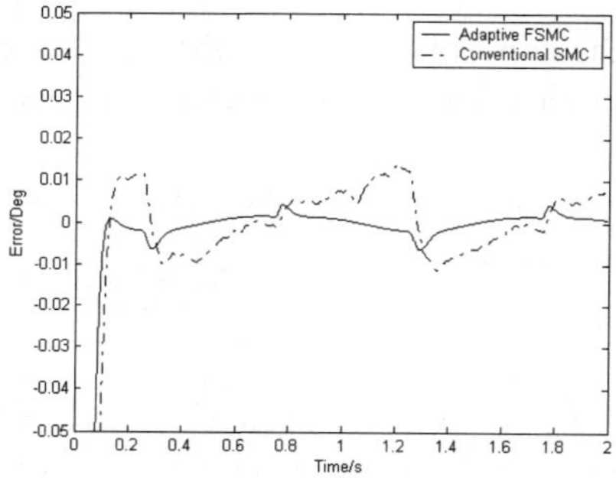

Fig. 5. Magnifying figure of tracking error

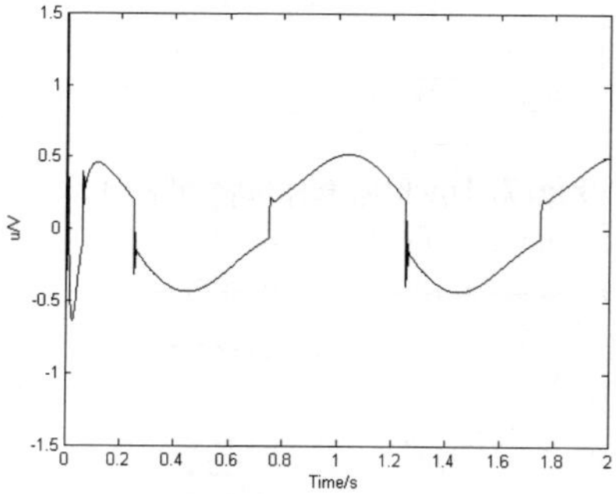

Fig. 6. Control input with adaptive FSMC

2) If the controller is the variable universe adaptive FSMC, chattering phenomenon is attenuated. The control input is smooth, and the strength of the control signal can be significantly reduced too. The transient deviation of control input, which is depicted in Fig.6, is induced owing to the initialization of the value of $\boldsymbol{P}$ especially under the occurrence of uncertainties. The tracking error is smaller than that with conventional

SMC because adjusting the universes of input variables and the membership fuzzy controller of conclusion part in rules on-line can effectively deal with the parametric uncertainty and external disturbances of the system. Good tracking result is obtained. It is robust to the uncertainties and the external disturbance in the missile electro-hydraulic servo mechanism.

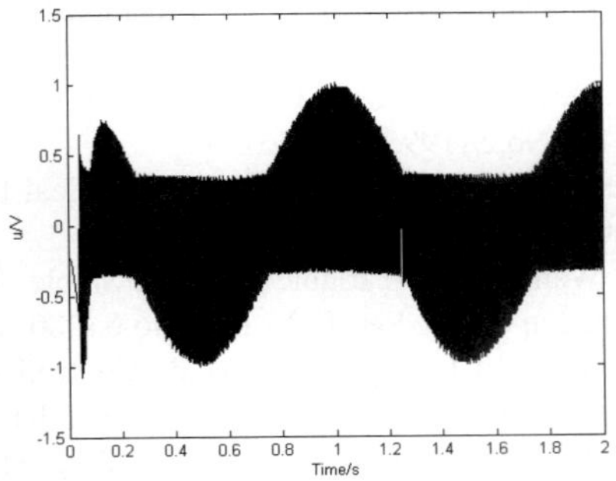

Fig. 7. Control input with Conventional SMC

5 Conclusions

In this paper, a variable universe adaptive control technique is applied to design a fuzzy sliding mode controller to achieve a stable control system. The input variables used in FSMC are integrated into two variables (s and $\dot{s}$) so that the number of control rules could be minimized than those that use state variables. By adjusting the universes of input variables and the membership fuzzy controller of conclusion part in rules on-line, a variable universe adaptive control is developed to estimate the equivalent control of SMC control system. The variable universe adaptive FSMC is stable in the sense of Lyapunov under a given common Lyapunov function. The derived adaptive law is applied to adjust the rule parameter for changing the control rules to meet system dynamic. In general, the switching control depends on the bounds of system and it is usually chosen to be large to ensure the stability of the fuzzy control system, which induces chattering phenomenon. Therefore, four constructed heuristic control rules are employed to smooth the control law based on the concepts of SMC. Simulation results from a kind of missile electro-hydraulic servo mechanism are given to demonstrate the applicability and the effectiveness of the proposed approach.

References

1. Wang, Y. N.: Intelligent Control Engineering for Robots, Beijing, Science Press (2004)
2. Efe, M. O., Kaynak, O., Yu, X. H.: Variable Structure Systems Theory in Computational Intelligence. Variable Structure Control Systems Towards the 21st Century, New York, Springer-Verlag, Vol. 27, No.2 (2002) 364-390

3. Chen, H. M., Su, J. P., Renn, J. C.: A Novel Sliding Mode Control of an Electro-hydraulic Position Servo System. IEEE Trans. Ind. Electron., Vol.85, No.4 (2002) 1928-1936
4. Liu, Y. F., Miao, D.: Research on Variable Structure Robust Control for Electro-hydraulic Servo System. Journal of the Second Artillery Engineering Institute, Vol.18, No.4 (2005) 12-14
5. Gao, W. B., Hung, J. C.: Variable Structure Control of Nonlinear Systems: A New Approach. IEEE Trans. Ind. Electron., Vol.40, No.1 (1993) 45-55
6. Van, A. J., Wal, D.: Application of Fuzzy Control in Industry. Fuzzy Sets and Systems, Vol. 74, No.3 (1995) 33-41
7. Kim, S. W., Lee, J. J.: Design of a Fuzzy Controller with Fuzzy Sliding Surface. Fuzzy Sets and Systems, Vol. 71, No.2 (1995) 359-367
8. Li, H. X.: To See Success of Fuzzy Logic from Mathematical Essence of Fuzzy Control. Fuzzy Systems and Mathematics, Vol.9, No.2 (1995) 1-14
9. Li, H. X., Miao, Z. H., Wang, J. Y.: Variable Universe Stable Adaptive Fuzzy Control of Nonlinear System. Science in China, Ser. E, Vol.45, No.6 (2002) 225-240
10. Chen, J. Y.: Rule Regulation of Fuzzy Sliding Mode Controller Design Direct Adaptive Approach. Fuzzy Sets and Systems, Vol.120, No.6 (2001) 159-168
11. Guan, P., Liu, X. J., Liu, J. Z.: Adaptive Fuzzy Sliding Mode Control for Flexible Satellite. Engineering Application of Artificial Intelligence, Vol.18, No.6 (2005) 451-459
12. Raksoglu, K. A., Sundreeshan, M. K.: A Recurrent Neural Network-based Adaptive Variable Structure Model Following Control of Robotic Manipulators. Automatica, Vol.31, No.2 (1995) 1495-1507
13. Ha, Q. P., Nguyen, Q. H.: Fuzzy Sliding Mode Controllers with Applications. IEEE Transactions on industrial electronics, Vol.48, No.1 (2001) 38-46
14. Zhu, Z. H.: Thrust Vector Control Servo System. Beijing, Astronautics press (1995)
15. Liu, Y. F., Miao, D.: 1553B BUS and Its Application in Electro-hydraulic Servo System. Machine Tool & Hydraulics, Vol.38, No.9 (2004) 106-108

A Dynamic Decision Method Based on Triangular and Pillared Fuzzy Numbers

Dar-Ying Jan and Ziping Chiang

Department of Logistics Management, Leader University, 709, Tainan, Taiwan, ROC
{dyj, ziping}@mail.leader.edu.tw

Abstract. This paper presents a simple and useful decision method for making estimates in uncertain and dynamic environments. We extend traditionally triangular fuzzy numbers to pillared and triangular fuzzy numbers formats that are defined by X-Y-Z axes. The α-cut and the defuzzy method of the proposed fuzzy number type are also defined. Finally, a numerical example based on a multiple attribute decision making method is used to illustrate the proposed method.

1 Introduction

Fuzzy set theory has been used to define linguistic variables in human judgement for a long time [1]. Traditionally, triangular fuzzy numbers are used to define simple and common membership functions on an x-y axis. The y axis is defined as a function of x (f(x)). Considering the trend of global business integrations, enterprises have to evaluate not only uncertain but also dynamic environments. In recent literature, Odanaka Liu et al. explain how fuzzy numbers can be used in dynamic decision environments [2-3]. Moreover, fuzzy dynamic programming methods are used in much research (see [4]-[6]). But there are few examples of literature which consider modifying the formation of fuzzy numbers. For solving the uncertainty and dynamic decision problem, this paper proposes a new type of fuzzy number that can be described by X-Y-Z axes.

2 The Definition of Triangular and Pillared Fuzzy Numbers and Fundamental Operations of Arithmetic

Fig.1 and Fig.2 illustrate two triangular and pillared fuzzy membership functions. Fig.1 can be described as the f(x,t) which does not change in regard to the time axis. Thus, the fuzzy number's mapping of the X-Y plane is the same at different t. This means that the decision maker judges the constant fuzzy membership function. Fig.2 shows the decision maker judging the variable fuzzy membership function. To simplify the problem, we define the triangular and pillared fuzzy number as linear at different $t \in R$.

In this section, we define the proposed fuzzy numbers, fuzzy membership function and fundamental operations of arithmetic.

D.-S. Huang, K. Li, and G.W. Irwin (Eds.): ICIC 2006, LNAI 4114, pp. 85 – 89, 2006.

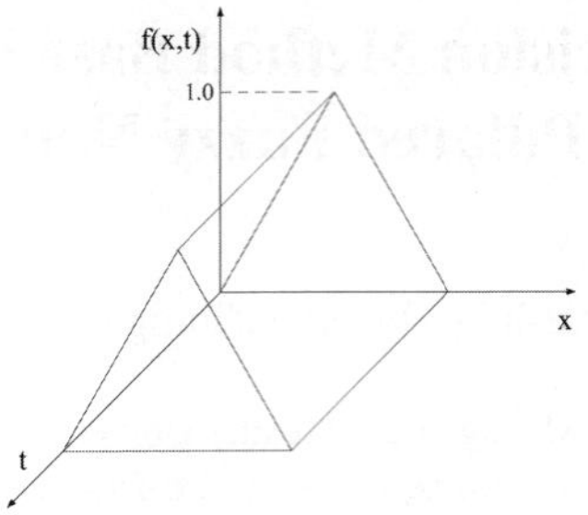

Fig. 1. The example of the constant triangular and pillared fuzzy membership function

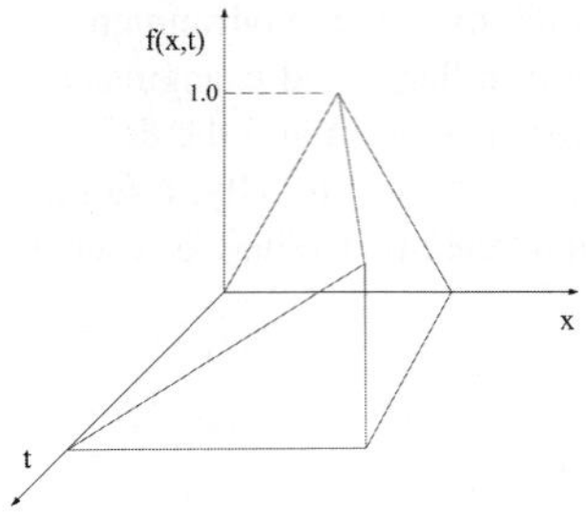

Fig. 2. The example of the variable triangular and pillared fuzzy membership function

Definition 1. Based on [7], we extend the definition of real fuzzy number A as any fuzzy subset of the real line R with membership function f_A which possesses the following properties:

1. f_A is a continuous mapping from R to the closed interval [0, 1].
2. $f_A(x,t) = 0$, for all $x \in (-\infty, a]$ at different t.
3. f_A is strictly increasing on $[a,b]$.
4. $f_A(x,t) = 1$, for all $x \in (b,c]$ at different t.
5. f_A is strictly decreasing on $[c,d]$.
6. $f_A(x,t) = 0$, for all $x \in [d,\infty)$ at different t.
7. f_A is linear on $[p,q]$

where a, b, c, d, p and q are real numbers.

The membership function f_A of the fuzzy number A can also be expressed as:

$$f_A(x,t) = \begin{cases} f_A^L(x,t), & \text{if } a \le x \le b \\ 1, & \text{if } b \le x \le c \\ f_A^R(x,t), & \text{if } c \le x \le d \\ 0, & \textit{otherwise} \end{cases} \tag{1}$$

where $f_A^L(x,t)$ and $f_A^R(x,t)$ are the left and right membership functions of fuzzy number A.

We use triangular fuzzy numbers to define fuzzy membership function f_A based on:

$$f_A(x,t)=\begin{cases}(x-a)/(b-a), \text{if } a\le x\le b\\ (x-c)/(b-c), \text{if } b\le x\le c\\ 0 \quad , \textit{otherwise}\end{cases} \tag{2}$$

where a, b and c are real numbers.

Definition 2. The α-cut of fuzzy number A can be defined as:

$$A^{\alpha}=\{x \mid f_A(x,t)\ge\alpha\} \tag{3}$$

where $x\in R$, $\alpha\in[0,1]$.

A^{α} is a non-empty bounded closed interval contained in R and it can be denoted by $A^{\alpha}=[A_l^{\alpha},A_u^{\alpha}]$, where A_l^{α} and A_u^{α} are the lower and upper bounds of the closed interval. For example, if a triangular fuzzy number $A = (a, b, c)$, then the α-cut of A can be expressed as:

$$A^{\alpha}=[A_l^{\alpha},A_u^{\alpha}]=[(b-a)\alpha+a,(b-c)\alpha+c] \tag{4}$$

Given fuzzy numbers A and B, $A,B\in R^{+}$, the α-cuts of A and B are $A^{\alpha}=[A_l^{\alpha},A_u^{\alpha}]$ and $B^{\alpha}=[B_l^{\alpha},B_u^{\alpha}]$, respectively. By interval arithmetic, some main operations of A and B can be expressed as follows [1]:

$$(A\oplus B)^{\alpha}=[A_l^{\alpha}+B_l^{\alpha}, A_u^{\alpha}+B_u^{\alpha}] \tag{5}$$

$$(A\ominus B)^{\alpha}=[A_l^{\alpha}-B_u^{\alpha}, A_u^{\alpha}-B_l^{\alpha}] \tag{6}$$

$$(A\otimes B)^{\alpha}=[A_l^{\alpha}\, B_l^{\alpha}, A_u^{\alpha}\, B_u^{\alpha}] \tag{7}$$

$$(A\oslash B)=[A_l^{\alpha}/B_u^{\alpha}, A_u^{\alpha}/B_l^{\alpha}] \tag{8}$$

$$(A\otimes r)^{\alpha}=[A_l^{\alpha}\, r, A_u^{\alpha}\, r],\ r\in R^{+}. \tag{9}$$

3 Numerical Example

For illustrating the proposed fuzzy number type, we used fuzzy the simple additive weighting method (FSAW) which is a simple method among the fuzzy multiple attribute decision making methods. Assume decision maker structures a problem with 4 attributes, 3 alternatives, and t=[0,2]. The FSAW method can be described by two steps as [8]:

1. For each alternative, compute a score by multiplying the scale rating of each attribute by its importance weight and summing these products over all attributes.
2. Select the alternative with the highest score. Mathematically the most preferred alternative, U^*, is selected as follows:

$$U^* = \left\{ U_j \,\middle|\, \max_j \left(\sum_{i=1}^{n} (w_i \otimes r_{ij}) / \sum_{i=1}^{n} w_i \right) \right\} \tag{10}$$

The normalized estimative matrix (r_{ij}) and weight matrix (w_i) are shown in Table 1 and Table 2.

Table 1. The normalized estimative matrix (r_{ij})

r_{ij}	Attributes 1	Attributes 2	Attributes 3	Attributes 4
Alternative 1	(0,0.7,1) at t=0 (0,0.8,1) at t=2	(0,0.3,1) at t=0 (0,0.4,1) at t=2	(0,0.7,1) at t=0 (0,0.8,1) at t=2	(0,0.6,1) at t=0 (0,0.6,1) at t=2
Alternative 2	(0,0.2,1) at t=0 (0,0.3,1) at t=2	(0,0.4,1) at t=0 (0,0.5,1) at t=2	(0,0.8,1) at t=0 (0,0.7,1) at t=2	(0,0.9,1) at t=0 (0,0.8,1) at t=2
Alternative 3	(0,0.5,1) at t=0 (0,0.8,1) at t=2	(0,0.5,1) at t=0 (0,0.8,1) at t=2	(0,0.7,1) at t=0 (0,0.9,1) at t=2	(0,0.4,1) at t=0 (0,0.9,1) at t=2

Table 2. The weight matrix (w_i)

w_i	Attributes 1	Attributes 2	Attributes 3	Attributes 4
t=0	(0,0.3,1)	(0,0.2,1)	(0,0.2,1)	(0,0.3,1)
t=2	(0,0.4,1)	(0,0.1,1)	(0,0.3,1)	(0,0.2,1)

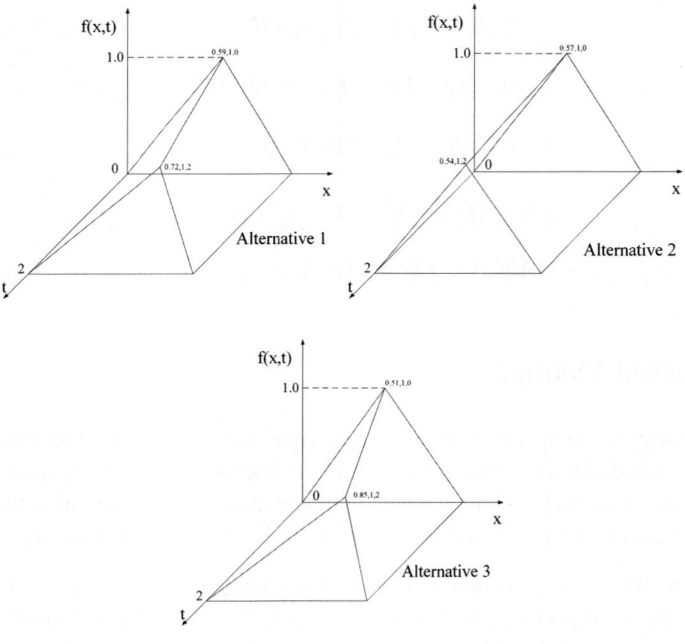

Fig. 3. The total utility fuzzy numbers with 3 alternatives

Based on Eq. (10), we use FSAW to estimate the total utility of each alternative. The total score fuzzy numbers of 3 alternatives are shown in Fig.4.

After α-cut (α=1), the final scores of 3 alternatives are [0.59,0.72], [0.57,0.54], and [0.51,0.85]. Based on the highest of the scores on the time axie, alternative 3 is the suitable solution for this dynamic and uncertain decision problem.

4 Conclusion

This paper proposes a simple and useful fuzzy number type for making estimates in uncertain and dynamic environments. We extend traditional triangular fuzzy numbers to three dimensions. The α-cut and defuzzy method of the proposed fuzzy numbers are also defined. To simplify the problem, we define the triangular and pillared fuzzy number as linear at different $t \in R$. In different time positions, we suggest using a superposition principle for combining the total utility.

References

1. Kaufmann, A., Gupta, M.M.: Introduction to Fuzzy Arithmetic: Theory and Application. New York, VanNostrand Reinhold (1991)
2. Odanaka, T.: Environment System and Dynamic Management Decision. Applied Mathematics and Computation 120 (2001) 255-263
3. Liu, B., Odanaka, T.: Dynamic Fuzzy Criterion Model for Reservoir Operations and a Case Study. Computers & Mathematics with Applications 37 (1999) 65-75
4. Chin, H.-C.: Optimal Shunt Capacitor Allocation by Fuzzy Dynamic Programming. Electric Power Systems Research 35 (1995) 133-139
5. Kacprzyk, J., Esogbue, A.O.: Fuzzy Dynamic Programming: Main Developments and Applications. Fuzzy Sets and Systems 81 (1996) 31-45
6. Yoshida, Y.: Dynamical Aspects in Fuzzy Decision Making. Physica-Verlag (2001)
7. Dubois, D., Prade, H.: Operations on Fuzzy Numbers. International Journal of Systems Science 9 (1978) 613-626
8. Chen, S.J., Hwang, C.L.: Fuzzy Multiple Attribute Decision Making. Springer-Verlag (1992)

A Fuzzy PID Controller for Controlling Flotation De-inking Column

Jinxing Liu[1,2], Huanbin Liu[1], Wenhao Shen[1],
Yonggen Xu[1], and Shuangchun Yang[1]

[1] State Key Laboratory of Pulp and Paper Engineering,
South China University of Technology,
510640, Guangzhou, Guangdong, China
[2] Qufu Normal University
sdcavell@126.com

Abstract. A novel Fuzzy PID controller is proposed in this paper, which is used for treating the control of pulp level and brightness in flotation de-inking column. The essential part of fuzzy PID controller is the fuzzy logic control, which is a multi-input-multi-output controller. A design method of the fuzzy PID controller is presented. The simulation results show that the proposed Fuzzy PID controller has preferable performance and significant advantages over the traditional PID controller.

1 Introduction

Recycling waste paper is an important component of a clean pulp and paper industry. Flotation de-inking plays an important role in this art. The flotation is the process of separating different materials, according as differential wetting of the suspended particles causes unwetted particles to be carried by air bubbles to the surface. The flotation de-inking column shows in Fig.1. According to the expertise, the brightness of pulp is controlled by the flow of pulp output and flow of air bubble. If the flow of air bubble is uncharged, while increasing the flow of pulp output, the brightness of pulp is decreasing, and vice versa. However, increasing the flow of pulp output causes the pulp level low and increasing the flow of pulp input causes the pulp level high. So it is must be considered that the pulp level and the brightness are coupled.

Because the traditional PID controller has its drawbacks, it is difficult to solve the controlling problem of Multi-Input-Multi-Output (MIMO) with coupled variable using traditional PID controller. During the past several years, fuzzy control has emerged as one of the most active and fruitful areas for research in the application of fuzzy sets theory [1], [5], [6]. Many structures of the fuzzy logic controller are given in [2], [3], and [4]. But only one controlled variable was used in Huang's Fuzzy PID Controller [3]. The structure of the MIMO Fuzzy PID controller and its performance was not proposed in Huang's paper. So a novel MIMO Fuzzy PID controller is proposed in this paper for controlling flotation de-inking column.

D.-S. Huang, K. Li, and G.W. Irwin (Eds.): ICIC 2006, LNAI 4114, pp. 90–95, 2006.

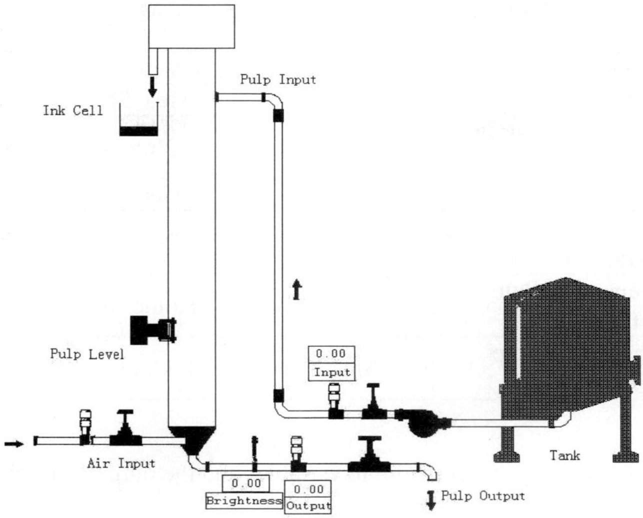

Fig. 1. Flotation de-inking column

2 Design Procedure of MIMO Fuzzy PID Controller

The Fuzzy PID controller proposed in this paper is shown in Fig.2. In this controller, the block of flotation FLC (Fuzzy Logic Control) is the core of our design, which is a four-input-two-output controller. The input variables are error (i.e. the difference between the setpoint and the measured value) of pulp level, derivative of the error, error of brightness and derivative of the error. Outputs of the controller are increment of pulp output and increment of pulp input.

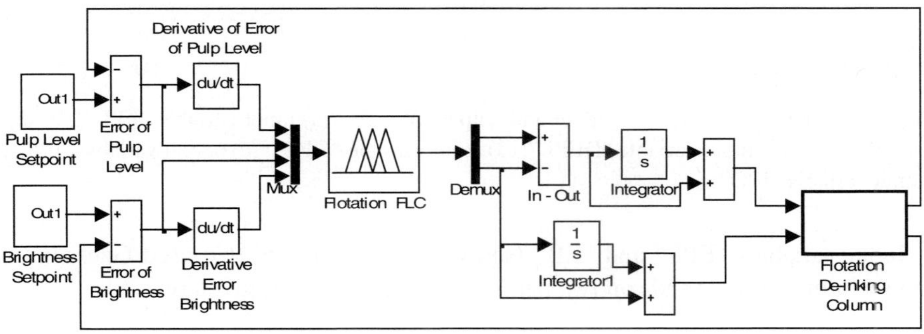

Fig. 2. The flow-sheet of the Fuzzy PID Controller for flotation de-inking column

The linguistic variables necessary to each input variables and output variables are shown in Table 1.

Table 1. Values of Input and Output Variables

Linguistic Variables	Values		
Error of Pulp Level (EPL)	LowPL	MeanPL	HighPL
Derivative of error of Pulp Level (DEPL)	NegtivePL	None	PositivePL
Error of Brightness(EB)	LowB	MeanB	HighB
Derivative of error of Brightness(DEB)	NegtiveB	None	PositiveB
Increment of Pulp Input(IPI)	SmallIn	HoldonIn	LargeIn
Increment of Pulp Output(IPO)	SmallOut	HoldonOut	LargeOut

The membership functions of the input variables and the output variables are shown in Fig.3.

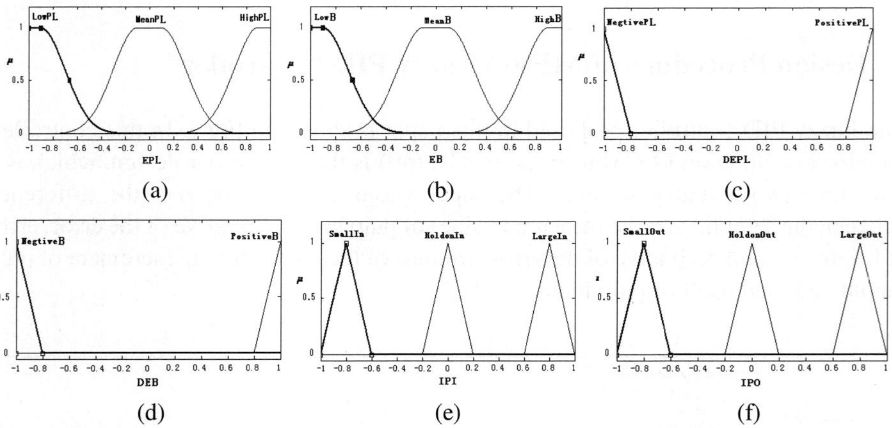

Fig. 3. Membership functions of input and output variables: (a) input variable "EPL"; (b) input variable "EB"; (c) input variable "DEPL"; (d) input variable "DEB"; (e) output variable "IPI"; (f) output variable "IPO"

Input variables "EPL" and "EB" (shown in Fig.3 (a) and (b)) used Gauss2mf. A Gaussian function depends on two parameters sigma and c as given by

$$f(x;\sigma,c) = e^{\frac{-(x-c)^2}{2\sigma^2}} . \tag{1}$$

The function Gauss2mf is a combination of two of these two parameters. The first function, specified by σ1 and c1, determines the shape of the leftmost curve. The second function specified by σ2 and c2 determines the shape of the right-most curve. Whenever c1 < c2, the Gauss2mf function reaches a maximum value of 1. Otherwise, the maximum value is less than one. The parameters are listed in the order: [σ1, c1, σ2, c2].

Input variables "DEPL" and "DEB" (shown in Fig.3 (c) and (d)) used TriMF. Output variables "IPI" and "IPO" (shown in Fig.3 (e) and (f)) used TriMF.

A triangular MF (TriMF) is specified by three parameters {a, b, c}, which determine the x coordinates of three corners:

$$Trimf\,(x;a,b,c) = \max(\min(\frac{x-a}{b-a},\frac{c-x}{c-b}),0)\,. \tag{2}$$

The parameters a and c locate the "feet" of the triangle, and the parameter b locates the peak.

The fuzzy rules are implemented as four inputs and two outputs fuzzy controller with each rule in the following form:

If (EPL is LowPL) and (DEPL is NegtivePL) and (EB is LowB) and (DEB is NegtiveW) then (IPO is SmallOut) and (IPI is LargeIn).

To simplify the design of the rules base, the following strategy is used. The surfaces of two inputs and one output are given while keeping the other inputs constant. The surfaces of the rules are shown in Fig.4. From Fig.4, we can clearly see that our strategy of the rules designed as Fig.2 is implemented well.

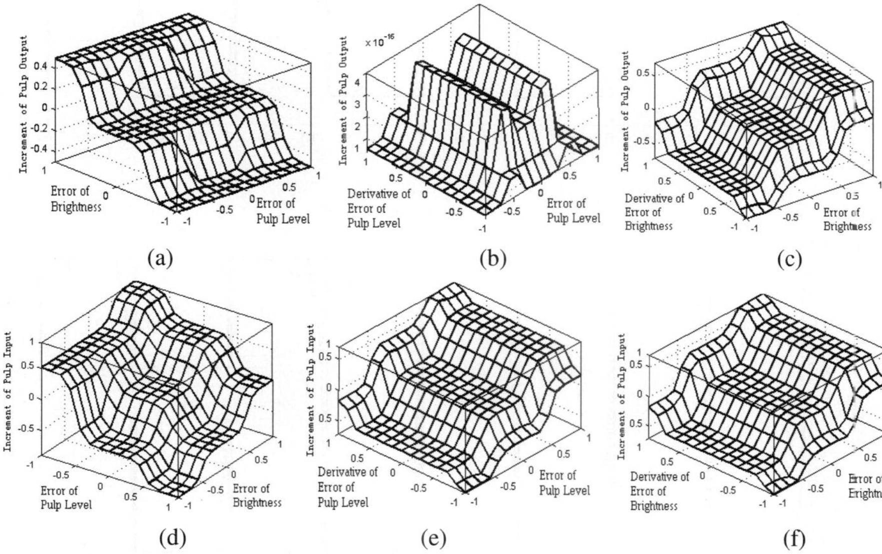

Fig. 4. Surfaces of the rules: (a) error of pulp level and error of brightness control increment of pulp output; (b) error of pulp level and derivative of error of pulp level control increment of pulp output; (c) error of brightness and derivative of error of brightness control increment of pulp output; (d) error of pulp level and error of brightness control increment of pulp input; (e) error of pulp level and derivative of error of pulp level control increment of pulp input; (f) error of brightness and derivative of error of brightness control increment of pulp input

Defuzzification is the way from which a crisp value is extracted from a fuzzy set as a representative value. At present, the commonly used methods may be described as the max criterion and the center of area, which can be referred to [2].

3 Experimental Results

To observe the efficiency of the novel Fuzzy PID controller, the traditional PID controller and Fuzzy PID controller are simultaneously simulated. Results of these experiments are shown in Fig.5.The solid line is the square wave signal to be tracked. The dash line is the tracking line of the Fuzzy PID controller and the dot line represents the performance of the traditional PID controller. Two horizontal dash-dot lines indicate the degree of 95% fitting in the figure.

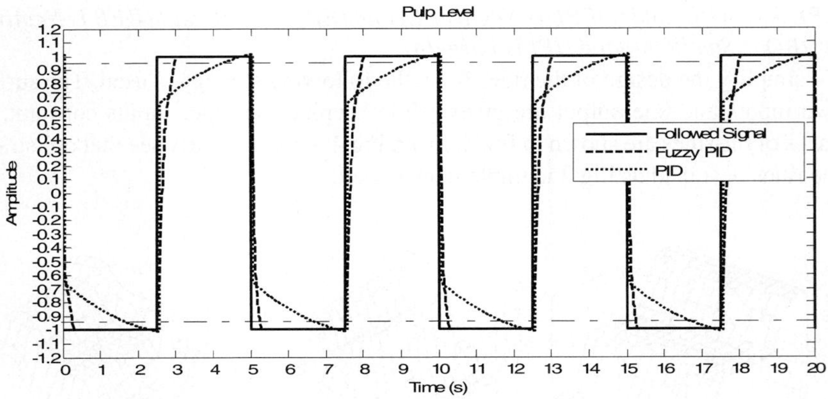

(a)

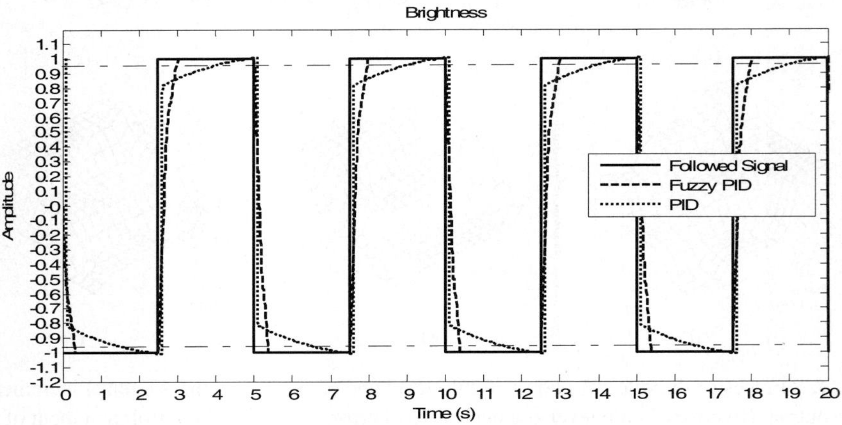

(b)

Fig. 5. The performance of Fuzzy PID controller and comparison with traditional PID controller: (a) result of control pulp level; (b) result of control brightness

The result of the controlling pulp level is shown in Fig.5 (a). The Fuzzy PID controller spends only 0.4 second or less to the degree of 95% fitting, to which the traditional PID controller spends about 2 seconds. Second, the Fuzzy PID has better steady-state characteristic than the traditional PID which has the over-fitting phenomena. A coin has two sides. While the attitude of pulp level varies in [-0.7, 0.7], the traditional PID controller is slightly prior to Fuzzy PID controller in tracking speed. The result of the controlling brightness is shown in Fig.5 (b). From Fig.5 (b), we can make the same conclusion as above-mentioned from the Fig.5 (a).

4 Conclusions

The multi-input-multi-output Fuzzy PID controller is designed for treating the control of pulp level and brightness in flotation de-inking column. The simulation results show that the proposed Fuzzy PID controller has preferable performance and significant advantages over the traditional PID controller.

With the number of the controlled variables increasing, the number of fuzzy rules becomes large rapidly and the efficiency of fuzzy inference system is debased accordingly. So under the condition of satisfying the control need, how to improve the efficiency of fuzzy inference system and how to reduce the number of the fuzzy rules are currently under investigation.

References

1. Zadeh, L. A.: Fuzzy Sets. Information and Control, 8 (1965) 338-353
2. Lee, C. C.: Fuzzy Logic in Control Systems: Fuzzy Logic Controller. IEEE Transaction on Systems, Man, and Cybernetics, 20 (2) (1990) 404-435
3. Huang, T. T.: A Fuzzy PID Controller Being Like Parameter Varying PID. IEEE International Fuzzy Systems Conference Proceedings, Seoul, Korea (1999) 269-276
4. Jang, J. R., Sun, C. T.: Neuro-Fuzzy Modeling and Control. Proceedings of the IEEE, 83 (3) (1995) 378-406
5. Chen, J. X., Li, W.: Application Of Fuzzy Control PID Algorithm In Temperature Controlling Systems. Proceedings of the Second International Conference on Machine Learning and Cybernetics, Xi'an (2003) 2601-2604
6. Yang, J. Q., Huang, J.: Direct Torque Control System For Induction Motors With Fuzzy Speed PI Regular. Proceedings of the 4th International Conference on Machine Learning and Cybernetics, Guangzhou (2005) 778-783

A New Uniform OR Operation Model Based on Generalized S-Norm

Zhicheng Chen[1], Mingyi Mao[2], Weikang Yang[1], and Huacan He[2]

[1] Operating System & Middleware Technology Research Center, Tsinghua University, 100084 Beijing, P.R. China
Chen-zc@mail.tsinghua.edu.cn

[2] Department of Computer Science and Engineering, Northwestern Polytechnical University, 710072 Xi'an, P.R. China
Maomingyi@163.com

Abstract. In universal logic, S-norm is the mathematical model of "OR" operation. S-norm and S-generator were defined on interval [0, 1] in previous work. In the related work, authors put forward a kind of logic based on generalized interval [a, b]. This paper studied the S-norm and S-generator on any interval [a, b], discussed the two kinds of generalized S-generators: "Automorphic increase S-generator" and "Infinite decrease S-generator", and proved the important generating theorem of generalized S-norm. Based on the conceptions of integrated cluster of generalized S-norm and S-generator, authors put forward a new uniform "OR" operation model. The simulation shows that it is not only flexible but controllable. It enlarged the study domain of universal logic, and offered important theory for uncertainties reasoning of complex system.

1 Introduction

Universal logic [1] is a kind of flexibly logic, which is used in uncertainties reasoning of complex systems [2]. Based on fuzzy logic [3,4], it put up two important coefficients: *generalized correlation coefficient "h"* and *generalized self-correlation coefficient "k"* [1]. "*h*" and "*k*" were reflected by N-norm, T-norm and S-norm. This paper mainly studied S-norm and the "OR" operation model.

In triangle-norm theory [5,6], S-norm was defined on interval [0, 1]. Under the basic thought of S-norm and the research achievement on uncertainties reasoning, universal logic defined S-norm, which was a function with several special properties. But it is also on interval [0,1]. There are some problems in the actual application, which discussed in 5th section.

In the real complex problem, it is a fact that the values of many parameters is not in interval [0, 1], and it is not easy to find its ambiguity function. This makes the conversion from real [a, b] to ideal [0, 1] difficult. So It is necessary for us to build up the corresponding model on [a, b] directly. In this paper, we studied the generalized S-norm and generalized S-generator, and put forward a new uniform "OR" operation model on any interval [a, b].

D.-S. Huang, K. Li, and G.W. Irwin (Eds.): ICIC 2006, LNAI 4114, pp. 96 – 101, 2006.

2 Generalized S-Norm and S-Generator

In characteristic space E, for set X,Y∈E, when the fuzzy measure $u(X)=x$, $u(Y)=y$ are precise, which means no any error, the generalized correlation coefficient "*h*" and the generalized self-correlation coefficient "*k*" of universal logic are zero. In this case, we can get the ideal S-norm on any interval [a, b].

$$S(x, y)=\min(b, x+y-a) \tag{1}$$

If $k\neq 0$, it has some influence on logic operation. We need a function $g(x)$, which is continuous and strict monotone on interval [a, b], to revise the logic value:

$$g(S(x, y))=\min(b, g(x)+g(y)-a) \tag{2}$$

$$S(x, y)=g^{-1}(\min(b, g(x)+g(y)-a)) \tag{3}$$

Definition 1
In equation (3), let $S(x, y)$ defined as binary operation by $[a, b]^2\rightarrow[a, b]$, $x, y, z\in[a, b]$, consider these conditions:

S1 (*Boundary condition*): $S(a, y)=y$, $S(b, y)=b$;
S2 (*Monotony property*): $S(x, y)$ is monotone increase on x, y;
S3 (*Continuous property*): $S(x, y)$ is continuous on x, y;
S4 (*Combination law*): $S(S(x, y), z)=S(x, S(y, z))$;
S5 (*Exchange law*): $S(x, y)=S(y, x)$;
S6 (*Big-power property*): $x\in(a, b)$, $S(x, x)>x$.

If $S(x, y)$ satisfies conditions: S1, S2, S4, S5, it is called *generalized S-norm*. If $S(x, y)$ satisfies S1-S5, it is called *generalized continuous S-norm*. If $S(x, y)$ satisfies S1-S6, it is called *generalized Archimedes S-norm*.

Definition 2
In equation (3), if $S(x, y)$ is generalized Archimedes S-norm on [a, b], $g(x)$ is called "*generalized S-generator*". For generalized S-generator $g(x)$, if $g(a)\rightarrow\pm\infty$, it is called "*generalized strict S-generator*"; if $g(a)$ is finite, it is called "*generalized zero-power S-generator*".

This research shows that there are two types of generalized S-generator: "*Automorphic increase S-generator*" and "*Infinite decrease S-generator*". Fig.1(a) shows the automorphic increase S-generator, and Fig.1(b) shows the infinite decrease S-generator.

3 Generating Theorem of Generalized S-Norm

Theorem 1(*Generating theorem of generalized S-norm*)
For $g(x)$, which is continuous and strict monotone function on [a, b], if $g(a)=a$, and satisfies one of the following two conditions:

(1) $g(x)$ is increase function, and $g(b)=b$,
(2) $g(x)$ is decrease function, when x runs to b from b_-, $g(b)\rightarrow-\infty$.

Then $g(x)$ can be taken as generalized S-generator, which means the following operator generated by $g(x)$:

$$S(x, y)=g^{-1}(\min(b, g(x)+g(y)-a)) \tag{4}$$

ie (3) is generalized Archimedes S-norm on [a, b].

Proof
Here proof the theorem according to the properties S1-S6 of definition 1.

(1) From g(x)'s properties, g-1(x) exists.

S1: From $g(a)=a$, $g(b)=b$, we have $a \le f(y)$, $f(y) \le b$, so

$S(a, y) = g^{-1}(\min(b, g(a)+g(y)-a)) = g^{-1}(g(y)) = y$

$S(b, y) = g^{-1}(\min(b, g(b)+g(y)-a)) = g^{-1}(g(b)) = b$

S2: $g(x)$ is monotone, so $S(x, y)$ satisfies S2.

S3: $g(x)$ is continuous, so $S(x, y)$ satisfies S3.

S4: $g(x)$ is monotony increase, so $b \le b+g(x)-a$. There are

$$S(S(x,y),z) = g^{-1}(\min(b, \min(b,g(x)+g(y)a)+g(z)-a))$$
$$= g^{-1}(\min(b, g(x)+g(y)+g(z)-2a))$$
$$S(x,S(y,z)) = g^{-1}(\min(b, g(x)+\min(b, g(y)+g(z)-a)-a))$$
$$= g^{-1}(\min(b, g(x)+g(y)+g(z)-2a)))$$

So $S(S(x, y), z)=S(x, S(y, z))$, it satisfies S4.

S5: From the exchange law of addition, $S(x, y)=S(y, x)$, so it satisfies S5.

S6: Since $g(x)$ is strict monotone increase, let $x \in (a, b)$, $b>g(x)>a$, then $S(x, x)=g^{-1}(\min(b, g(x)+g(x)-a))>g^{-1}(g(x))=x$. So $S(x, y)$ satisfies S6.

(2) $g(x)$ is strict monotone decrease function, the proof is similar to the (1) case.

In (1) case, $g(x)$ is automorphic increase S-generator. In (2) case, g(x) is infinite decrease S-generator. Both of them can generate generalized Archimedes S-norm, which satisfies all the properties S1-S6. We call this theorem "*Generating theorem of generalized S-norm*".

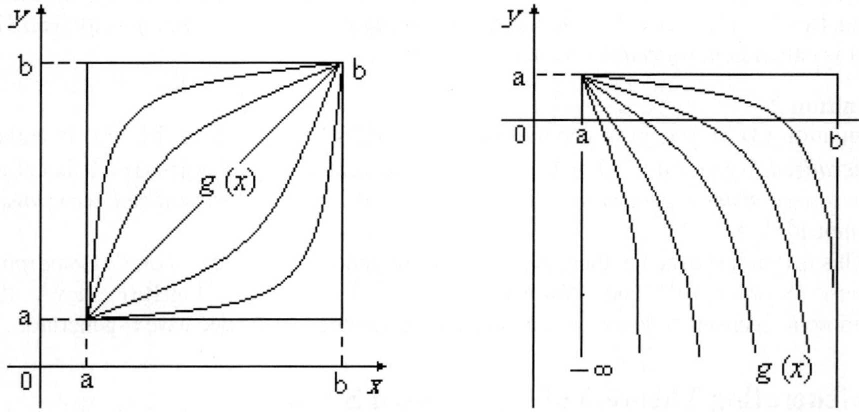

(a) Automorphic Increase S-generator (b) Infinite Decrease S-generator

Fig. 1. The Two Types of S-generators

4 A New Uniform "OR" Operation Model on [a, b]

Here we import the generalized correlation coefficient "*h*" and generalized self-correlation coefficient "*k*" into generalized S-norm and S-generator, and build up the uniform "OR" operation model on any interval [a, b].

4.1 The Conception of Integrated Cluster

Definition 3

Suppose $g(x)$ is generalized S-generator, if $g(x)$ is continuous function on [a, b], we write it as $g(x, h)$, which is called "*Integrated cluster of generalized S-generator*".

Suppose $S(x, y)$ is generalized S-norm, if $S(x, y)$ is continuous function on [a, b], we write it as $S(x, y, h)$, which is called "*Integrated cluster of generalized S-norm*".

For $g(x, h)$, when k=0, there is no error, be called "*0-level Integrated cluster of generalized S-generator*". When $k \neq 0$, there is some error. It is written as $g(x, h, k)$, and is called "*1-level Integrated cluster of generalized S-generator*".

For $S(x, y, h)$, when k=0, there is no error, be called "*0-level Integrated cluster of generalized S-norm*". When $k \neq 0$, there is some error, It is written as $S(x, y, h, k)$, and is called "*1-level Integrated cluster of generalized S-norm*".

Theorem 2

For power function on [a, b]:

$$g(x)=G(x, h)=\mathrm{b}-(\mathrm{b}-\mathrm{a})[(\mathrm{b}-x)/(\mathrm{b}-\mathrm{a})]^m \quad (5)$$

it is *Integrated cluster of generalized S-generator.*

Where $m=(1-2h)/(1-h^2)$, $m \in R$, $h \in [-1,1]$.

Proof

When $m>0$, $g(x)$ is increase, and g(a)=a, g(b)=b, so $g(x)$ is automorphic increase S-generator. When $m<0$, $g(x)$ is decrease, and g(a)=a, $g(\mathrm{b})=-\infty$, so $g(x)$ is infinite decrease S-generator.

Since $m=(1-2h)/(1-h^2)$, "h" continuously changes with m. So power function $g(x)$ is *integrated cluster of generalized S-generator.*

4.2 The Uniform "OR" Operation Model

For deducing "OR operation model", the generalized N-norm and T-norm based on generalized interval [a, b] are used, you can get more detail about generalized N-norm and T-norm from [7,8]. Here give the related expressions.

0-level integrated cluster of generalized N-norm: $N(x)=\mathrm{b}+\mathrm{a}-x$ (6)

1-level integrated cluster of generalized N-norm: $N(x, k)=[(\mathrm{b}-\mathrm{a})^n-(x-\mathrm{a})^n]^{1/n}+\mathrm{a}$ (7)

Generalized T-generator on [a, b]: $f(x)=F(x,h)=(\mathrm{b}-\mathrm{a})[(x-\mathrm{a})/(\mathrm{b}-\mathrm{a})]^m+\mathrm{a}$ (8)

Generating theorem of generalized T-norm: $T(x,y)=f^{-1}(\max(\mathrm{a}, f(x)+f(y)+\mathrm{b}))$ (9)

Definition 4

The uniform OR operation model on [a, b] is defined as the following expressions

0-level OR operation model on [a, b]: $S(x,y,h)=N(T(N(x),N(y),h))$ (10)

1-level OR operation model on [a, b]: $S(x,y,h,k)=N(T(N(x,k),N(y,k),h,k),k)$ (11)

Put (4)-(9) into (10) and (11), we can have the concrete expressions.

$$S(x,y,h)=N(T(N(x),N(y),h))$$
$$=N(F^{-1}(\max(\mathrm{a}, F(N(x),h)+F(N(y),h)-\mathrm{b}),h))$$

$$=b+a-\{(b-a)[(\max(a, ((b-x)^{m}+(b-y)^{m})/(b-a)^{m-1}+2a-b)-a)/(b-a)]^{1/m}+a\}. \quad (12)$$

$$S(x, y, h, k)=N(T(N(x, k),N(y, k), h, k),k)$$
$$=N(F^{-1}(\max(a, F(N(x, k), h, k)+F(N(y, k), h, k)-b), h, k), k). \quad (13)$$

Where $m=(1-2h)/(1-h^2)$, $n=\ln 2/[\ln 2-\ln(k+1)]$, $n\in R_+$, $m\in R$, $h, k\in[-1,1]$.

4.3 The Continuous Change of "OR" Operation Model

According to above $S(x, y, h)$ and $S(x, y, h, k)$, we make simulation of the "OR" operation model on [a, b]. Fig.2 displays the continuous change of "OR" operation with "h" (when k=0). There are the following meanings:

(1) The "OR" operation reflects the degree of truth for both flexible proposition at the same time. If any one proposition runs to true, the $S(x, y, h)$ runs to true.

(2) In the three-dimensional graph, there are four unchangeable eigenvector:

$S(x, a, h, k)=x$, $S(a, y, h, k)=y$, $S(x, b, h, k)=b$, $S(b, y, h, k)=b$.

(3) The truth-value is continuously changeable by adjusting the value of h. when h=1, the truth-value is minimum. With the change of h from 1 to -1, the degree of truth is more and more true. The maximum is b.

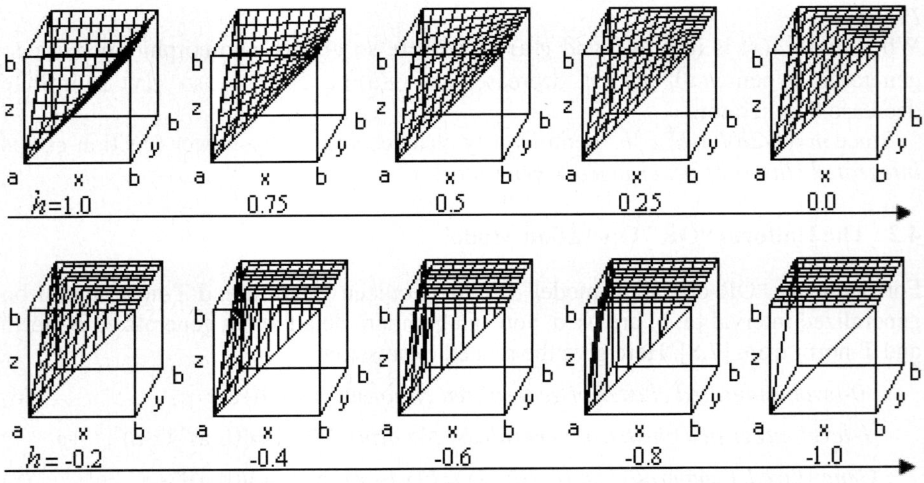

Fig. 2. The Continuous Change of the Uniform "OR" Operation Model

5 Discussions

In universal logic and triangle-norm theories, S-norm was defined as:

$$S(x, y)=g^{-1}(\min(g(1), g(x)+g(y))). \quad (14)$$

There are some problems, which can't be resolved.

(1) $T(x, y)$ is not on any interval [a, b] but only on [0,1], it can't be used in real complex system. We can't simply convert interval [0,1] to [a, b] because there are

many "nonzero coefficients", which can't be displayed on [0, 1]. So the good way is to build up the corresponding theories on interval [a, b] directly.

(2) The expression (14) can't unify the two kinds of S-generator (*Automorphic increase S-generator and Infinite decrease S-generator*). When m changes from $+\infty$ to $-\infty$, h changes from -1 to 1. There exists a broken point on changing curve of the logic operator when m (h) equals to zero.

(3) After analyzing the above $S(x, y)$ deeply, authors define it as expression (4), that is $S(x, y)=g^{-1}(\min(b, g(x)+g(y)-a))$. Here $S(x, y)$ is defined on any interval [a, b]. It gives the uniform expression of the two kinds of S-generator, and is also continuous changeable on [a, b] with h and k. So this OR operation model is more applicable than previous model in the real complex system.

6 Summarization

S-norm is very important conception in universal logic operation. Because it is not easy for us to convert real [a, b] to ideal [0, 1] in complex system, it is necessary for us to study the relative theories on any interval [a, b] directly. This paper mainly studied the generalized S-norm and generalized S-generator, discussed the two kinds of generalized S-generator, gave out the important generating theorem of generalized S-norm. Based on the related integrated cluster, authors put forward a new uniform "OR" operation model on generalized interval [a, b].

This work offered important theory for universal logic in uncertainties reasoning of complex systems, enlarged the study domain, and made it more applicable, flexible and controllable. This uniform OR model is already used to uncertainties reasoning and flexible control now.

References

1. He, H.C., Wang, H., Liu, Y.H. (eds.): Universal Logics Principle, China Science Publishing House, Beijing (2001)
2. Chen, Z.C., He, H.C., Mao, M.Y.: Correlation Reasoning of Complex System Based on Universal Logic, IEEE International Conference on Machine Learning and Cybernetics, 3/5 (2003) 1831-1835
3. Zadeh, L.A.: Fuzzy sets, Information and Control 8 (1965) 338-357
4. Hacck, S.: Deviant Logic and Fuzzy Logic, Beyond the Formalism, 2nd edition, The University of Chicago Press, Chicago (1996)
5. Rovatti, R., Fantuzzi, C.: S-norm aggregation of infinite collections, Fuzzy sets and system, 84 (3) (1996) 255-269
6. Jenei, S.: New Family of Triangular Norms via Contrapositive Symmetrization of Residuated Implications, Fuzzy Sets and Systems 110 (2000) 157-174
7. Chen, Z.C.: Studies on Correlation Reasoning of Fractal, Chaos, and Logic in Complex System, Doctor's Degree paper of Northwestern Polytechnical University, Xi'an (2004)
8. Mao, M.Y., Chen, Z.C, He, H.C.: A New Uniform Neuron Model of Generalized Logic Operators Based on [a, b], International Journal of Pattern Recognition and Artificial Intelligence, 20(2) (2006) 159-171

A Study of Product Development Time Based on Fuzzy Timed Workflow Net

Xianfeng Fan[1,2], Hong-Zhong Huang[1], Jun Hu[1], Xu Zu[1], and Ping Yang[1]

[1] School of Mechatronics Engineering, University of Electronic Science and Technology of China, Chengdu, Sichuan, 610054, China
hzhuang@uestc.edu.cn
[2] Department of Mechanical Engineering, University of Ottawa, Ottawa, Ontario, K1N 6N5, Canada
fanxf@yahoo.com

Abstract. It is necessary to find the relationship between product information and development process for saving product development time. Design information constraint tree (DICT) is proposed to describe the constraint relationships among multi-task information. Fuzzy timed workflow net (FTWN) is introduced to analyze product development time. An algorithm is proposed to map DICT onto FTWN. Task execution time and completion possibility are analyzed. The effectiveness of the proposed method to simulate product development time is validated by an example.

1 Introduction

Shorter product life cycles, more rapid product obsolescence, and increasing global competition intensity have driven companies to strive for a more rapid introduction of new products [1, 2, 3, 4]. Product development process modeling, as a critical step of product development, is usually constrained by resource and time. The primary mission of modeling is to assign an appropriate process in order to save development time and cost.

In order to improve product development quality and efficiency, the relationship between product and development process should be established. Aalst et al proposed a technique to generate a workflow process using Petri Nets [5, 6, 7, 8, 9]. Because of the assumed one-to-one relationship between task and component, it is unable to describe information restrictions and simulate development time. To overcome the disadvantage, design information constraint tree (DICT) is introduced in this paper. The workflow model based on the DICT is established. Fuzzy timed workflow net (FTWN) is introduced as the extension of the workflow model. Development time can be exactly simulated by the proposed method.

This paper is organized as follows. DICT is proposed in Section 2. FTWN is introduced in Section 3. The mapping from DICT onto FTWN is studied in Section 4. Task execution time and completion possibility are analyzed in Section 5. In Section 6, case study is conducted for validation purpose. Conclusions are obtained at last.

D.-S. Huang, K. Li, and G.W. Irwin (Eds.): ICIC 2006, LNAI 4114, pp. 102 – 107, 2006.

2 Design Information Constraint Tree

Various constraints exist in design information. Taking a reducer's development as an example, we need bearing information for the designing of body, shafts information for bearing selection, and gears information related to shafts.

Supposing the execution of task *a* needs the information of both tasks *b* and *d*, probably that of task *c*. Before performing task *a*, tasks *b* and *d* should be completed. Task *c* could be inexistence or uncompleted. Figure 1 describes the constraints, called DICT. An arrowhead with a solid circle means a relationship that must be selected. An arrowhead without a solid circle means a relationship that could be selected. The performance of task *b* needs the information of tasks *e* and *f*. The performance of task *d* needs the information of task *i*, task *f*, and one of tasks *g* and *h*. A hollow circle with two or more arrowheads means a selection relationship. Because the result of task *f* used many times, it could be executed only once. The dashed line with a solid circle means foreword relationship, which means the information of task *f* already exists before the execution of task *d*. Results of task *b* should be checked. Then, we mark *c* on task *b*. The check result determines the next execution of task. Two feedback modes, "and" and "or" are used. Consumed time of each task will be labeled and the DICT of task *a* may be established based on the above relationships.

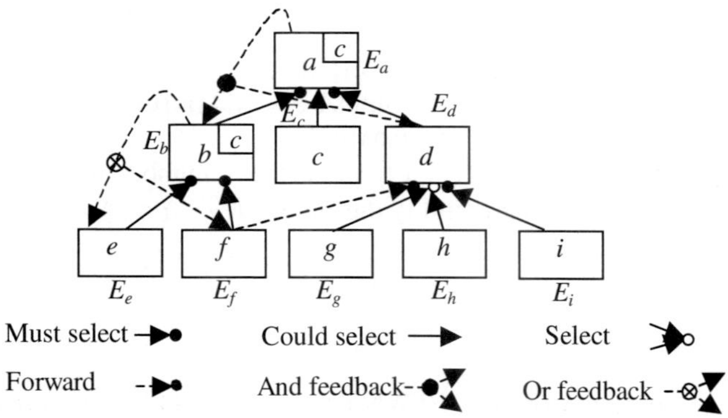

Fig. 1. Design information constraint tree of task *a*

Definition 1. DICT=(V, Rv, E).

(1) Let V={v_1,v_2,…,v_n} be the node set of a tree. (v_i, v_j) means the information flow from v_j to v_i. The constraint set of (v_i, v_j) is represented by Rv.

(2) R={*mand*, *opt*, *cho*, *pre*, *AndFb*, *OrFb*} represent relationships as must select, could select, select, foreword, "and" feedback, and "or" feedback.

(3) E is task-consuming time, obtained by a triangle fuzzy number [EF, MF, LF]. EF, MF, and LF are the shortest, general, and the longest consuming time, respectively.

Definition 2. $R(v_i)$ is the set of nodes directing any node v_i and has relationship R. *mand*(c) is the set of nodes that must be selected by node c.

Definition 3. R means a relationship in DICT. For any node $v \in V$, we have $\hat{v} = \{x \in V \mid (v,x) \in V\}$ and $\hat{v} = \{x \in V \mid (x,v) \in V\}$.

According to the definitions in DICT, we have the following conclusions. There is no isolated node in DICT. $\forall v_i \in V$, $\exists v_j \in V$, $st\ v_i \in R(v_j)$. There is no node only belonged to foreword node. Foreword node must have a father node owning the must select relationship. $\forall v_i, v_j \in V$, if $v_i \in pre(v_j)$, then $\exists v_k \in V$, $v_i \in mand(v_k) \cup cho(v_k)$. Therefore, the DICT is able to represent the information constraint.

3 Fuzzy Timed Workflow Net

A Petri net $PN = (P,T,F)$ is a workflow net (WN) if and only if $(i \in P \wedge {}^{\cdot}i = \Phi) \wedge (o \in P \wedge o^{\cdot} = \Phi)$ and $\overline{PN} = (P, T \cup \{t\}, F \cup \{(o,t),(t,i)\})$ is connected. $t \in \overline{PN} \setminus T$. *i* and *o* represent the input and output places of WN [3].

Definition 4. Fuzzy timed workflow net is $FTWN = \{P,T,F,D,M_0\}$. Where, $WN = \{P,T,F,M_0\}$ is a workflow net. *D* is a triangle fuzzy number [*a*, *b*, *c*], which represents transition firing consuming time: the shortest, general, and the longest.

Assume triangle fuzzy numbers $A=[a_i,b_i,c_i]$, $i=1,2,\ldots,n$. The operation rules are:

(1) Addition: if $A=[a_1,b_1,c_1]$, $B=[a_2,b_2,c_2]$, then $A+B=[a_1+a_2, b_1+b_2, c_1+c_2,]$.

(2) Minimum and Maximum: $\min(A_1,A_2,\ldots,A_n)=[\min(a_i), \min(b_i), \min(c_i)]$, $\max(A_1,A_2,\ldots,A_n)=[\max(a_i), \max(b_i), \max(c_i)]$.

(3) Completion possibility: $\tilde{T}$ is a triangle fuzzy number with membership function $\mu_{\tilde{T}}(x)$. The completion possibility during the $d(a \le d \le c)$ is

$$\pi(d) = \frac{\int_a^d \mu_{\tilde{T}}(x)\mathrm{d}x}{\int_a^c \mu_{\tilde{T}}(x)\mathrm{d}x}. \tag{1}$$

Besides the properties of WN, FTWN possesses the following properties [3]. Each transition position between start place *i* and finish place *o* is considered. The task execution process could be completed without tokens in places except out place *o*.

4 Mapping the DICT onto FTWN

Let node v_0 be the root of the tree representing a product development. According to the following procedures, we obtain the workflow model (See Fig. 2).

(1). Construct a FTWN={*P*, *T*, *F*, *D*, M_0}. Where, $P=\{start_{v0}, end_{v0}\}$, $T=\{v_0\}$, $F=\{(start_{v0}, v_0), (end_{v0}, v_0)\}$, and $V=V-v_0$.

(2). Select a sub-net *N*=(*P*, *T*, *F*, *D*). If $V = \varnothing$, then go to step 4. Select a node $v \in V$ in the tree. If $\breve{v} = \varnothing$, then *v* is marked as $perf_v$. Back to step 2, else go to step 3.

(3). Add transitions $prep_v$ and $perf_v$ before transition *v*, and substitute transition *v* with sub-net where express places and transitions according to *R*. If $x \in \breve{c}$ and

$R(x,c) = mand$, then P_{end}=end_x, P_{start}=$start_x$, $F = (start_x, x) \cup (x, end_x)$, and T=x. If $x, y \in \breve{c}$ and $R(x,c) = cho$, $R(y,c) = cho$, then P_{end}=$end(x,y)$, P_{start}=$start(x,y)$, $T = \{x, y\}$, and $F = (start_{(x,y)}, x) \cup (x, end_{(x,y)}) \cup (start_{(x,y)}, y) \cup (y, end_{(x,y)})$. If $x \in \breve{c}$ and $R(x,c) = opt$, then $F = (start_x, x) \cup (x, end_x) \cup (start_x, skip_x)$, $P_{end} = end_x$, $P_{start} = start_x$, and $T = \{x, skip_x\}$. If $x \in \breve{c}$ and $R(x,c) = pre$, then $F = (perf_x, prep_{(x,y)}) \cup (prep_{(x,y)}, perf_c)$, $T = \phi$, and P=$prep_{(x,y)}$. After dealing with each node of c, go back to step 2.

(4). For any node v that needs checkout feedback line, $R(v, x_1)$= $R(v, x_2)$=*AndFb* or *OrFb*, adding place $submit_v$ and transition $check_v$ before place end_v, and adding place $iterate_v$ and logical transition t after place $check_v$, we construct a new net. P=$P \cup \{submit_v, iterate_v\}$. T=$T \cup \{check_v, t\}$. F=$F \cup \{(perf_v, submit_v), (submit_v, check_v), (perf_v, iterate_v), (check_v, end_v), (iterate_v, t), (t, startx_1), (t, startx_2)\} \backslash (perf_v, end_v)$. If logical feedback is *AndFb*, then it is AND-split transition; if logical feedback is *OrFb*, then it is OR-split transition. We deal with each node with feedback in the tree.

(5). Delete transition *prep* with only one input and output place. Coordinate the workflow model. Add fuzzy timed parameter before transition *prep*, D_i=E_i.

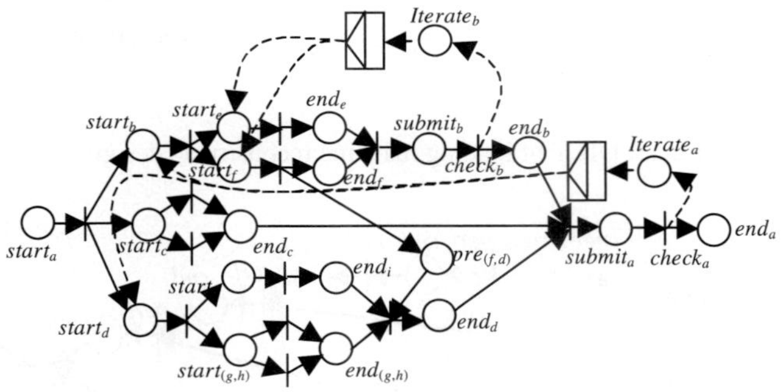

Fig. 2. The FTWN model mapped from DICT as showed in Fig. 1

5 Task Execution Time and Completion Possibility

We take task execution time and task completion possibility with the restricted product development time as criteria to evaluate the performance of transform process. First, from the FTWN, we get the associate matrix C that starts from initial marking M_{start} and ends at marking M_{end}. Then, compute all S-invariant. From the S-invariant, compute the minimum subset of S-invariant, and get the corresponding transitions firing sequence. Last, we compute the fuzzy time of routes, and find out the longest time route and its completion possibility based on the transitions firing sequence.

DICT is able to use for a component level model and for product development consuming time simulation. First, considering effective process management methods established by enterprises, we adopt parallel operation to shorten execution time.

Second, during the initial period of product development, the detailed model of process is not required or sometimes un-existent.

6 A Case Study

In order to verify the effectiveness of the proposed method, a case is studied. The DICT in Fig. 3 is constructed according to the relationships among loader design tasks. Its FTWN is presented in Fig. 3.

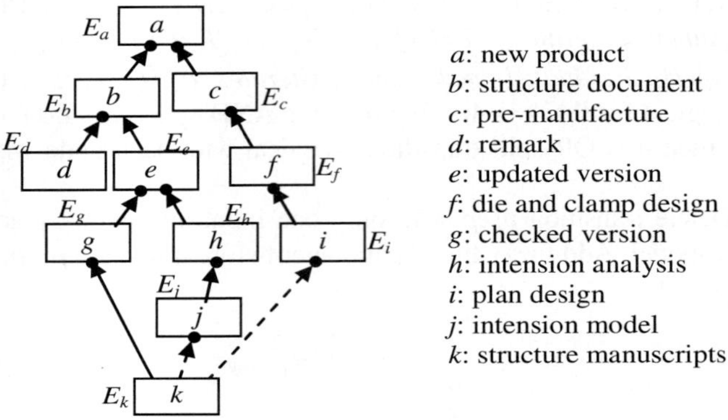

Fig. 3. DICT of loading machine reconstructs design

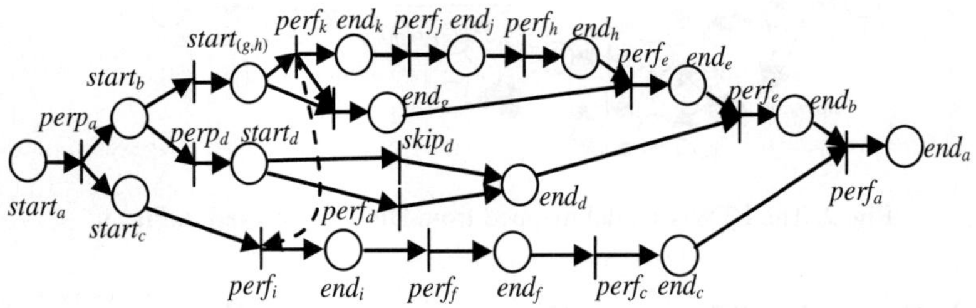

Fig. 4. FTWN model mapped from the DICT in Fig. 3

Assume task execution time are: E_a=[2.5, 3, 3.5], E_b=[3.5, 4, 4.5], E_c=[4, 5, 6], E_d=[0.5, 1, 1.5], E_e=[1, 1.5, 2], E_f=[1.5, 2, 2.5], E_g=[0.5, 1, 1.5], E_h=[2.5, 3, 3.5], E_i=[2.5, 3, 3.5], E_j=[0.5, 1, 1.5], and E_k=[4, 5, 6], respectively. Each transition period in FTWN is known. From $start_a$ to end_a, we may have seven paths. For example, *path*: $prep_a$-$prep_{(g,h)}$-$perf_k$-$perf_j$-$perf_h$-$perf_e$-$perf_b$-$perf_a$. Fuzzy periods of the seven routes are L_1=[14, 17.5, 21], L_2=[11.5, 14.5, 17.5], L_3=[7.5, 9.5, 11.5], L_4=[6, 7, 8], L_5=[6.5, 8, 9.5], L_6=[8, 10, 12], and L_7=[14.5, 18, 21.5], respectively, obtained by fuzzy number operation rules. Hence, the path: $prep_a$- $prep_{(g,h)}$-$perf_k$-$perf_i$-$perf_f$-$perf_c$-$perf_a$, that has the highest completion possibility 90.82% can be obtained according to Eq. (1). Therefore, optimal product development path is able to obtain through time simulation using the proposed method.

7 Conclusions

The DICT is introduced in this paper to represent the constraints existing in product development. FTWN mapped from DICT is constructed to simulate product development processes. Task execution time and task completion possibility are used for evaluation. The advantages such as time simulation can be achieved by the proposed method, which provides a way to select the optimal product development path. A case study is used to verify the effectiveness of the proposed method.

Acknowledgements

This research was supported by the National Natural Science Foundation of China under contract number 50175010, the Excellent Young Teachers Program of the Ministry of Education of China under contract number 1766, and the National Excellent Doctoral Dissertation Special Foundation of China under contract number 200232.

References

1. Carrillo, J.E., Franza, R.M.: Investing in Product Development and Production Capabilities: The Crucial Linkage Between Time-to-Market and Ramp-up Time. Eur. J. Operational Res. 2(2006) 536–556
2. Huang, H.Z., Tian, Z.G., Zuo, M.J.: Intelligent Interactive Multiobjective Optimization Method and Its Application to Reliability Optimization. IIE Transactions. 37(11) (2005) 983-993
3. Huang, H.Z., Bo, R.F., Chen, W.: An Integrated Computational Intelligence Approach to Product Concept Generation and Evaluation. Mechanism and Machine Theory. 41(5) (2006) 567-583
4. Huang, H.Z., Gu Y.K.: Development Mode Based on Integration of Product Models and Process Models. Concurrent Engineering: Research and Applications. 14(1) (2006) 27-34
5. Aalst, W. M. P. van der: On the Automatic Generation of Workflow Processes Based on Product Structures. Computers in Industry. 2(1999) 97–111
6. Aalst, W. M. P. van der: The Application of Petri Nets to Workflow Management. J. Circ., Syst. and Computers. 1(1998) 21–66
7. Huang, H.Z., Zhou, F., Zu, X.: Petri Nets Based Coordination Component for CSCW Environments. Journal of Mechanical Science and Technology. 19(5) (2005) 1123-1130
8. Huang, H.Z., Zu, X.: Hierarchical Timed Colored Petri Nets Based Product Development Process Modeling. Lecture Notes in Computer Science. 3168(2004) 378-387
9. Huang, H.Z., Zuo, M.J., Sun, Z.Q.: Bayesian Reliability Analysis for Fuzzy Lifetime Data. Fuzzy Sets and Systems. 157(12) (2006) 1674-1686

An AHP-Fuzzy Synthetic Evaluation Model Based on Evidence Theory

Xiaoyi Wang[1,2], Chaozhen Hou[1], Jumei Yuan[1], and Zaiwen Liu[2]

[1] Department of Automatic Control, Beijing Institute of Technology
Beijing 100081, P.R. China
[2] College of Information Engineering,
Journal of Beijing Technology and Business University
Beijing 100037, P.R. china
bitwxy2003@bit.edu.cn

Abstract. Considering the indefinite and fuzzy characters existing in index weighs of complex system, a method confirming index weights based on evidence theory was put forward. On the basis of it, an efficiency evaluation model for complex system integrating Analytical Hierarchy Process (AHP) with fuzzy synthetic evaluation method has been set up, which can obtain more reasonable and objective evaluation result for complex system. Through analyzing an example of the system fighting efficiency for missile and gun integration weapon, the result shows the validity and feasibility of this method.

1 Instruction

Reasonable evaluation model is the basic of evaluating complex system accurately, and index weighs in evaluation model are the key factor to decide the ultimate evaluation result. Nowadays, there exist many kinds of methods of confirming index weighs [1-3]. Because of indefinite and fuzzy factors existing in index weighs of complex system, to confirm index weights is one kind of synthetic evaluation process with subjectivity and objectivity, which belongs to a multi-attribute decision making problem in fact. The foregone methods didn't consider those factors adequately, and neglected the limitation and imprecision of expert experience knowledge in evaluation process, which would lead to be short of reliability and veracity to confirm index weights. Considering the stabile math theory basis of evidence theory, which can deal with the uncertainty and un-integrated synthesis problem preferably, therefore it can be applied in multi-attribute decision making problem. Evidence theory method is used to confirm index weights for complex system in this paper, every expert is considered as one-evidence sources, and fuzzy membership function having different expert's authority is set put as the index sustaining function. In order to avoid invalidation problem of evidence information brought by expert's experience knowledge conflicts, one modified evidence combination rule is adopt to synthesize expert knowledge to improve reliability and rationality of confirming index weights. Combining AHP method and fuzzy synthetic evaluation method, a new model using to evaluate complex

D.-S. Huang, K. Li, and G.W. Irwin (Eds.): ICIC 2006, LNAI 4114, pp. 108 – 113, 2006.

system has been put forward. Through analyzing and comparing this method with AHP method in fighting efficiency evaluation for Missile and gun integration weapon, the results show that this method is feasible and viable.

2 The AHP-Fuzzy Evaluation Based on Evidence Theory

2.1 AHP-Fuzzy Evaluation Model

The AHP method having multi-attributes and complex hierarchy structures is a synthesized method of integrating quantitative with qualitative analysis [4], which is always adopted to evaluate complex system. In order to predigest the complication of problem, a three-lever evaluation model based on AHP method was set up as follows.

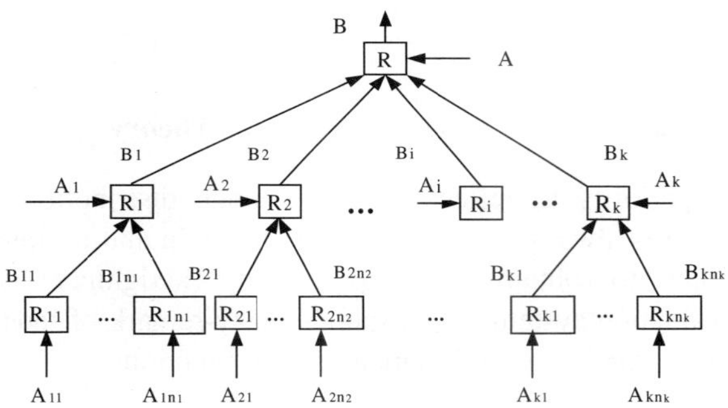

Fig. 1. The three-level synthesis-evaluation model based on AHP method

According to index attribute characters, the goal factor set can be divided into some primary factor sets, namely, $R=\{R_1,R_2,\cdots,R_k\}$, herein $\bigcup R_i = R$, $R_i \bigcap R_j = \phi, i \neq j$, and the weights of factor set R is $A_i = \{A_1, A_2, \cdots, A_k\}$. The primary factor sets still can be divided into secondary level factor sets, namely, $R_i = \{R_{i1}, R_{i2}, \cdots, R_{in_i}\}$, herein $\bigcup R_{ij} = R_i, R_{ij} \bigcap R_{il} = \phi, j \neq l$, and A_{in_i} is its index weight set.

For different factor sets having different effect to the evaluation result of system efficiency, the paper adopts "adding-weight average " algorithm operator (•,+) to synthesize factor sets of each level.

Because there exists many qualitative and quantitative indexes in the system, it is necessary to be normalized to (0,1) before evaluating system. Wherein quantitative indexes have different characters, to the indexes having positive effect to the ultimate results, formula (1) can be adopt to dispose it. To the indexes having negative effect to the ultimate evaluation result, formula (2) can be used to normalize it.

$$g_{ij} = \begin{cases} 1, & t_{ik} \geq M_{ik} \\ \dfrac{t_{ik} - m_{ik}}{M_{ik} - m_{ik}}, & m_{ik} < t_{ik} < M_{ik} \\ 0. & m_{ik} \geq t_{ik} \end{cases} \tag{1}$$

$$g_{ij} = \begin{cases} 0, & t_{ij} \geq m_{ik} \\ \dfrac{M_{ik} - t_{ik}}{M_{ik} - m_{ik}}. & m_{ik} < t_{ik} < M_{ik} \end{cases} \tag{2}$$

For all $i = 1,2,\cdots,n, k = 1,2,\cdots,l$. Index t_{ik} is quantitative index in secondary certain factor sets, g_{ik} is normalized result corresponding to t_{ik}, and M_{ik}, m_{ik} are the maximal and the minimum expectation value of t_{ik}.

Expert-grading method was adopted as normalization method to dispose qualitative indexes. Setting up fuzzy-evaluation remark fuzzy set C={0.9,0.7,0.5,0.3,0.1}, and the remark set is $V = \{V_1, V_2, V_3, V_4, V_5\} = \{very\ good, good, general, bad, very bad\}$. The qualitative indexes can be transferred to fuzzy value in term of formula $W_i = \left(\sum_{j=1}^{5} W_{ij}^2 \bullet C_j\right) \Big/ \left(\sum_{j=1}^{5} W_{ij}^2\right)$.

Herein, C_j is the data corresponding to grade parameters V_j.

2.2 Confirming Index Weights Based on Evidence Theory

For having the superiority to reflect uncertain mode distribution objectively, the membership function is always used to appraise uncertain and un-integrate factors of expert's knowledge to obtain basic probability assignment function [5] in multi-objective evaluation system. The expert's fuzzy-remark of index was set up as Fig.2. The Gauss function is selected as membership function.

$$F(x) = \exp\{-\frac{1}{2\sigma^2}(x-\mu)^T(x-\mu)\} \tag{3}$$

Herein, μ is clustering center, and the set membership function can be obtained through calculating the distance between it's center and variable x.

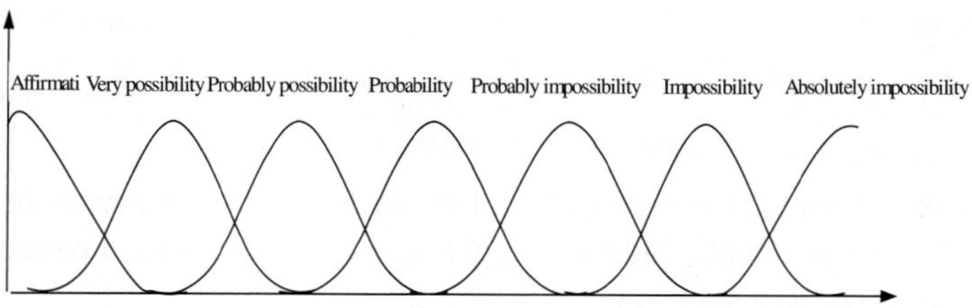

Fig. 2. Fuzzy-remark set of the index

Fuzzy-membership function of index t_{ik} evaluated by expert j is

$$\mu_j(t_{ik}) = F_j(t_{ik}), \quad j = 1,2,\cdots,m \quad k = 1,2,\cdots,l. \tag{4}$$

Herein, m is expert total amount, and n,l is the amount of primary factor sets and secondary factor sets separately. Normalization membership function is

$$\mu'_j(t_{ik}) = \mu_j(t_{ik}) \Big/ \sum_{i=1}^{n} \mu_j(t_{ik}) \tag{5}$$

For different experts having different authorities, the reliability of expert experience knowledge of index t_{ik} is $\beta_j^{t_{1k}}$ $(0 \le \beta_j^{t_{1k}} \le 1)$, which can be obtained in term of the model of FHW. The relative reliability of expert experience knowledge can be obtained by calculating the following formula.

$$\beta_j'^{t_{ik}} = \beta_j^{t_{ik}} \Big/ \sum_{i=1}^{n} \beta_j^{t_{ik}} \tag{6}$$

Definition: Evaluation probability of index t_{ik} evaluated by expert j is the result of multiplying normalized index membership function by relative reliability of expert experience knowledge.

$$P_j(t_{ik}) = \beta_j^{t_{1k}} * \mu_j(t_{ik}) \tag{7}$$

Herein, $\sum_{i=1}^{n} P_j(t_{ik}) \le 1$, and $1 - \sum_{i=1}^{n} P_j(t_{ik})$ is unknown information of expert evaluation. The reliability function of index t_{ik} evaluated by expert j is

$$m_j(t_{ik}) = P_j(t_{ik}), \quad m(\Theta) = 1 - \sum_{i=i}^{n} P_j(t_{ik}). \tag{8}$$

Sometimes, there exist experience knowledge conflicts among individual experts in the process of evaluating index weights, so the modified evidence combination rule [6] was applied in this paper.

$$m(t_{ik}) = \sum_{\cap t_i = t} \prod_{1 \le j \le m} m_j(t_{ik}) + Q * m(\varphi), \quad Q = \frac{1}{n} \sum_{i=1}^{n} m_i(t_{ik}), \quad m(\varphi) = \sum_{\cap t_i = \phi} \prod_{1 \le j \le m} m_j(t_{ik}). \tag{9}$$

The modified evidence theory can convert multi-expert uncertain and un-integrate information to definitude conclusion as index weights allocation, so can improve rationality and objectivity of conforming index weights.

2.3 AHP-Fuzzy Synthetic Evaluation Method Based on Evidence Theory

The method steps are as follows:

Step 1. Setting up reasonable evaluation index system for complex system based on AHP method

Step 2. Normalizing every level index value.

Step 3. Obtaining different level index weights using evidence theory:

Step 3.1. Setting up multi-expert uncertain fuzzy remark sets, such as $V = \{v_1, v_2, \cdots, v_p\}$.

Step 3.2. Confirming fuzzy membership function $\mu_j(t_{ik})$ $(i = 1, 2, \cdots, n \;\; j = 1, 2, \cdots, m)$ of index t_{ik} evaluated by expert j according to formula (4).

Step 3.3. Obtaining reliability function of index t_{ik} evaluated by expert j in term of formula (7).

Step 3.4. Calculating reliability function $m(t_{ik})$ of different index according to formula (9), and make its different index as weight ω_{ik}.

Step 4. Applying formula $D=\sum_{i=1}^{n}\sum_{k=1}^{l}\omega_{ik} * t_{ik}$ to set up mapping relationship between indexes and evaluation result.

3 Efficiency Evaluations for Missile and Gun Integration Weapon

The principle of setting up the index system for complex system should be comprehensive, rational and scientific. After analyzing the characters of Missile and gun integration weapon adequately, using the AHP method to set up the efficiency index system as table 1.

Table 1. Index system for missile and gun integration weapon

	Primary level indexes	Secondary level indexes
The fighting efficiency of Missile and gun integration weapon	The ability of detection and track B1	The perfect detect distance of radar B11
		The detecting distance in interferential circumstanceB12
		Low altitude detecting capacity B13
		Tracking distance of radar B14
		The tracking number of radar B15
	The fighting ability of weapon system B2	Cannon fighting capacity B21
		Photo electricity antagonizing capacity B22
		Missile antagonizing capacity B23
	The ability of system communication B3	Communication security B31
		Communication quality B32
		Communication expedite ratio B33
	The survival ability of weapon system B4	Ant-damage ability B41
		System reliability B42
		System Anti-jamming ability B43

Table 2. The evaluation results of fighting efficiency for weapon system using two methods

	Primary level indexes	Weights(1)	Weights(2)	Secondary level indexes	Weights(1)	Weights(2)	Method (1)、method (2) fuzzy value
The fighting efficiency of Missile and gun integration weapon				B_{11}	0.12	0.09	0.857
	B_1	0.16	0.08	B_{12}	0.44	0.49	0.915
				B_{13}	0.24	0.21	0.789
				B_{14}	0.15	0.11	0.823
				B_{15}	0.05	0.10	0.934
				B_{21}	0.35	0.30	0.948
	B_2	0.52	0.43	B_{22}	0.20	0.21	0.698
				B_{23}	0.45	0.49	0.902
				B_{31}	0.33	0.27	0.805
	B_3	0.18	0.27	B_{32}	0.46	0.50	0.947
				B_{33}	0.21	0.23	0.652
				B_{41}	0.30	0.22	0.754
	B_4	0.14	0.22	B_{42}	0.42	0.48	0.916
				B_{43}	0.28	0.30	0.852
	The ultimate evaluation result of fighting efficiency for weapon system						0.8644 0.8614

Table 2 shows the evaluation process and ultimate evaluation result of fighting efficiency for Missile and gun integration weapon by using the method proposed in this paper (method (1) in table 2) and AHP method (method (2) in table 2) respectively, and evaluation results are 0.8644 and 0.8614. In this example, these two methods have the same evaluation result, namely, the fighting efficiency of the missile and gun integration weapon belongs to "very good".

4 Conclusions

One AHP-fuzzy synthetic evaluation model based on evidence theory has been put forward in this paper, which has several characters.

1) Considering the importance effect of multi-expert experience knowledge in the process of confirming index weights sufficiently. With the increase of expert's authority, the index weights allocation become more accurate, and the final evaluation result become more reliability.
2) The modified evidence method was applied to combine un-integrity and uncertain expert experience knowledge to confirm index weights. In the condition of occurring invalidation knowledge of individual experts, the index weights allocation is still reasonable, so this method has better adaptability and reliability of confirming index weights.
3) In aspect of confirming index weights, this method can not only resolve the problem having more random existing in subjective method, but also avoid the deficiency to set up accurate math model. Moreover, it Combines the merits of fuzzy synthetic evaluation, and makes the system evaluation result become more comprehensive, objective and reliability.

References

1. Zhang, Hui-ying, Dong, Yi, Li, Min-qing: Research for Application of Group Decision Method on Appraisement System of Science Research Schema. IEEE Proceedings of 4th world congress on intelligence control and automation, Shanghai, P.R China (2002) 602-606
2. Huang, De-cai, Shen, Liang-zhong:New Method for Constructing Comparison Matrix Based on the Proportion Scales in the AHP. Journal of System Engineering and Electronics.14 (2003) 8-13
3. Michael, A., Greiner, John W., Fowler, Dan, L. Shunk: A Hybrid Approach Using the Analytic Hierarchy Process and Integer Programming to Screen Weapon Systems Projects. IEEE Transactions on Engineering Management.50 (2003) 192-203
4. Saaty, T. L.: The Analytic Hierarchy Process. New York:McGarw-Hill (1980)
5. Hu,Yong, Gao, Jun, Hu,Liang-mei, Dong,Hou-ming: A New Method of Determining the Basic Belief Assignment in D-S Evidence Theory. IEEE Processing of 2003 International Conference and Machine Learning and Cybemetic (2003) 208-211
6. LI, Bi-cheng, WANG, Bo, WEI, Jun etc: An Efficient Combination Rule of Evidence Theory (in Chinese). Journal of Data Acquisition &Processing.17 (2002) 33-36

Direction Fuzzy Sets

Jixing Wang

Department of Mathematics, Yunnan University, Kunming, China

Abstract. In this paper, several kinds of non-classical fuzzy problems–direction fuzzy problems are presented, which classical fuzzy sets do not deal with well. In order to solve them, direction fuzzy sets are introduced by breaking through the limitations of the definitions of classical fuzzy sets. And the union and intersection of direction fuzzy sets are discussed. Especially, an application example (Escape Model) is dug up to show the significance of the direction fuzzy set theory.

1 Introduction

In 1965, Zadeh firstly presented the concept of fuzzy set in his classic paper[1]. Since then, fuzzy sets have been widely researched and applied [2]. And many significant results have been obtained in almost every field, such as in automation control, in artificial intelligence and so on.

Though it is quite successful, there are still some defects in application. For a simple example, assume a, b, c and d are four factories which produce the same two kinds of product A and B. Suppose that they earned about 20, 40, 50 and 70 million dollars respectively for product A last year. For product B, suppose factory a and b earned about 30 and 60 million dollars respectively, but factory c and d lost about 30 and 80 million dollars. According to classical fuzzy set theory, if we consider the approximate earning ability of the four factories for the two kinds of product A and B respectively, two fuzzy sets $\tilde{A} = 0.2/a + 0.4/b+0.5/c+0.7/d$ and $\tilde{B} = 0.3/a+0.6/b+0/c+0/d$ can be obtained (Here, the presentation of fuzzy set like $\tilde{A}$ is adopted as shown in the above form instead of the form $\tilde{A} = \{(a, 0.2), (b, 0.4), (c, 0.5), (d, 0.7)\}$, given a finite universe, for ease of notation and computation. And the membership degrees of $\tilde{A}$ and $\tilde{B}$ are obtained by $\begin{cases} \min\{\frac{m}{100}, 1\}, & m \geq 0 \\ 0, & m < 0 \end{cases}$, where m (≥ 0) represents earned money, otherwise lost). From fuzzy set theory, $\tilde{A}\cup\tilde{B} = 0.3/a+0.6/b+0.5/c+0.7/d$ should present the potential ability of making money of four factories last year. There is an evident mistake, that is, factory d lost about 10 million dollars overall, but its potential ability of earning money shown in $\tilde{A}\cup\tilde{B}$ is still given as 0.7. Where does this problem come from? The problem comes from the limitation of the value set [0, 1] of membership function of fuzzy set definition itself: "$\tilde{A}$ is said to be a fuzzy set of X if it is characterized by the membership function $\mu_{\tilde{A}}(x)$ from X to [0, 1]."

In fact, people's social practice presents a great number of fuzzy contradictory pairs such as $< tall, small >$, $< fat, thin >$, $< left, right >$, $< earned, lost >$

D.-S. Huang, K. Li, and G.W. Irwin (Eds.): ICIC 2006, LNAI 4114, pp. 114–119, 2006.

and so on (A fuzzy contradictory pair is called a *direction fuzzy problem* if its two components can mutually transform). If such fuzzy contradictory pairs appear together in the same system, and we have to cope with them at the same time, it will result in something discordant if the value sets of the membership functions of fuzzy sets are interval [0, 1]s (seeing the application example). Only nonnegative numbers cannot describe clearly the inner transforming relationships of these fuzzy contradictory pairs. Then, how do we do?

2 Main Conceptions

In order to solve such direction fuzzy problems mentioned in the introduction section, firstly, we should break through the limitations of classical fuzzy sets by introducing direction fuzzy sets as follows.

Definition 1. *Let X be a universe. $\tilde{A}$ is said to be a direction (or state) fuzzy set of X if it is characterized by a function $\mu_{\tilde{A}}$ from X to $[-1, 1]$. $\mu_{\tilde{A}}$ is called the direction (or state) membership function of $\tilde{A}$. The value $\mu_{\tilde{A}}(x)$ of function $\mu_{\tilde{A}}$ at x represents the direction level (or state, degree) of x belonging to (or existing in) the direction fuzzy set $\tilde{A}$. The closer it is to 1 or -1, the clearer its direction (or state) tendency is.*

When X is finite, the direction fuzzy set $\tilde{A}$ is often represented by

$$\tilde{A} = \mu_{\tilde{A}}(x_1)/x_1 + \mu_{\tilde{A}}(x_2)/x_2 + \cdots + \mu_{\tilde{A}}(x_n)/x_n$$

or $\tilde{A}=\{(x_1,\mu_{\tilde{A}}(x_1)),(x_2,\mu_{\tilde{A}}(x_2)),\cdots,(x_n,\mu_{\tilde{A}}(x_n))\}$, where $X = \{x_1, x_2, \cdots, x_n\}$. When not finite, $\tilde{A} = \int_X \mu_{\tilde{A}}(x)/x$.

In this paper, for convenience, we always let X be a universe, and $\tilde{A}, \tilde{B}, \tilde{C}, \cdots$ stand for direction fuzzy sets; $\mu_{\tilde{A}}(x)$ is simply written as $\tilde{A}(x)$.

Definition 2. *The absolute value $|\tilde{A}|$ of direction fuzzy set $\tilde{A}$ is characterized by $|\tilde{A}|(x) = |\tilde{A}(x)|$ for each $x \in X$, which is a classical fuzzy set relative to direction fuzzy set $\tilde{A}$.*

Definition 3. *A direction fuzzy set is said to be empty (or nondirective) iff its membership function is identically equal to zero, denoted by ϕ. A direction fuzzy set $\tilde{A}$ is said to be a subset of direction fuzzy set $\tilde{B}$ (or $\tilde{A}$ is contained in $\tilde{B}$), iff $\tilde{A}(x) \leq \tilde{B}(x)$ for each $x \in X$, denoted by $\tilde{A} \subset \tilde{B}$ or $\tilde{B} \supset \tilde{A}$. A direction fuzzy set $\tilde{A}$ is said to be equal to another $\tilde{B}$ if and only if $\tilde{A}(x) = \tilde{B}(x)$ for each $x \in X$, denoted by $\tilde{A} = \tilde{B}$.*

The notions of union and intersection of two direction fuzzy sets are two basic concepts in our theory. Before dealing with them, we need to extend Zadeh minimum and maximum fuzzy operators $\vee$ and $\wedge$ to $\dot{\vee}$ and $\dot{\wedge}$ as follows.

Definition 4. *$\dot{\vee}$ and $\dot{\wedge}$ are defined by the two mappings from $[-1, 1]^2$ into $[-1, 1]$ such that for any $a, b \in [-1, 1]$*

$$a\dot{\vee}b = \begin{cases} \max(a,b), & a,\, b \geq 0 \\ -\max(-a,-b), & a,\, b \leq 0 \\ a+b, & a \times b < 0 \end{cases}$$

and

$$a\dot{\wedge}b = \begin{cases} \min(a,b), & a,\, b \geq 0 \\ -\min(-a,-b), & a,\, b \leq 0 \\ 0, & a \times b < 0 \end{cases},$$

called direction maximum and minimum operators, respectively. Sometimes $a\dot{\wedge}b$ *and* $a\dot{\wedge}b$ *are denoted by* $\dot{\vee}(a,b)$ *and* $\dot{\wedge}(a,b)$*, respectively.*

Definition 5. *Let* $\tilde{A}$ *and* $\tilde{B}$ *be two direction fuzzy sets of* X*. The union and intersection of* $\tilde{A}$ *and* $\tilde{B}$*, denoted by* $\tilde{A} \cup \tilde{B}$ *and* $\tilde{A} \cap \tilde{B}$*, are characterized by*

$$(\tilde{A} \cup \tilde{B})(x) = \tilde{A}(x)\dot{\vee}\tilde{B}(x) \text{ and } (\tilde{A} \cap \tilde{B})(x) = \tilde{A}(x)\dot{\wedge}\tilde{B}(x)$$

for all $x \in X$*, respectively.*

Example 1. In the example mentioned in the introduction section, let $X = \{a,b,c,d\}$. According to the direction fuzzy set theory, we can define $\tilde{A}$ as $0.2/a + 0.4/b + 0.5/c + 0.7/d$, and $\tilde{B}$ as $0.3/a + 0.6/b - 0.3/c - 0.8/d$ by mapping $\min\{\frac{m}{100}, 1\}$ and $-\min\{\frac{n}{100}, 1\}$, where m and n represent earned and lost money, respectively. Thus, $\tilde{A} \cup \tilde{B} = (0.2\dot{\vee}0.3)/a + (0.4\dot{\vee}0.6)/b + (0.5\dot{\vee}(-0.3))/c + (0.7\dot{\vee}(-0.8))/d = (0.2\vee 0.3)/a + (0.4\vee 0.6)/b + (0.5 + (-0.3))/c + (0.7 + (-0.8))/d = 0.3/a + 0.6/b + 0.2/c - 0.1/d$ which fits the fact.

Remark 1. In order to fit real applications, $\dot{\vee}$ and $\dot{\wedge}$ are often replaced by other direction fuzzy operators (see my other papers), such as $\dot{\oplus}$ and $\dot{\odot}$, defined by,

$$\dot{\oplus}(a,b) \triangleq a\dot{\oplus}b = \begin{cases} \min(1, a+b), & a,\, b \geq 0 \\ -\min(1, -a-b), & a,\, b \leq 0 \\ a+b, & a \times b < 0 \end{cases}$$

and

$$\dot{\odot}(a,b) \triangleq a\dot{\odot}b = \begin{cases} \max(0, a+b-1), & a,\, b \geq 0 \\ -\max(0, -a-b-1), & a,\, b \leq 0 \\ 0, & a \times b < 0 \end{cases}$$

for all $a,\ b \in [-1, 1]$.

3 One Application Example

Example (Escape Test in a Flaming Building–Escape Model)
Situation Setting: There are 7 volunteers, denoted by a, b, c, d, e, f and g, who are taking part in escape test in a flaming building. They are working in a central room in some floor of one building. There are two exits at the left and right ends of the floor. Both two exits are 20 meters away from the center room

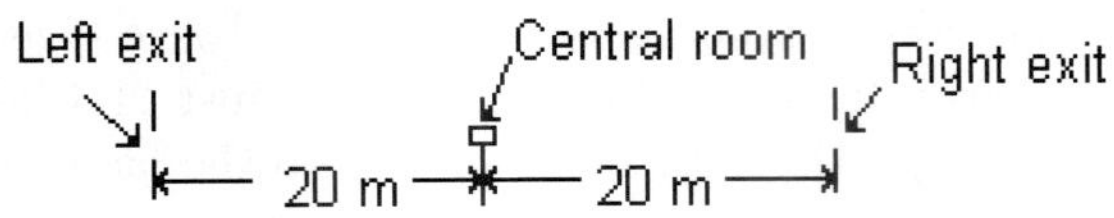

Fig. 1. Escape situation

where they are working in. They should escape to one of the two exits as soon as they can after warning of flaming. But in their some escape ways, they may be blocked by the flaming things (see Fig.1.).

Prize Principle: "One can win some prize if one is one of the three volunteers who are closest to the left or right exits after 5 seconds."

Tested Data: After previous 3 seconds, volunteer a moved 10 meters to the left; b 14.4 meters to the left; c 12 meters to the left; d 15 meters to the right; e 14.8 meters to the right; f 14 meters to the right; g 13 meters to the right.

And after later 2 seconds, volunteer a moved 5 meters to the left; b 3 meters to the right; c 2.2 meters to the left; d 5 meters to the left; e 5.2 meters to the right; f 3 meters to the left; g 3 meters to the right.

In order to study expediently, data are put into the following table.

Table 1. Tested data

Vol.	Prev. 3 Sec. Dir., Dis.	Later 2 Sec. Dir., Dis.	After 5 Sec. Dir., Dis.	After 5 Sec. Dir., Dis. to Exits	Place
a	left, 10	left, 5	left, 15	left, 5	3
b	left, 14.4	right, 3	left, 11.4	left, 8.6	5
c	left, 12	left, 2.2	left, 14.2	left, 5.8	4
d	right, 15	left, 5	right, 10	right, 10	7
e	right, 14.8	right, 5.2	right, 20	right, 0	1
f	right, 14	left, 3	right, 11	right, 9	6
g	right, 13	right, 3	right, 16	right, 4	2

"Volunteers closest to the exits after previous 3 seconds" is a fuzzy set, denoted by $\tilde{A}$. "Volunteers closest to the exits after later 2 seconds" is also a fuzzy set, denoted by $\tilde{B}$. "Volunteers closest to the exits after 5 seconds" is a fuzzy set, denoted by $\tilde{C}$. Then, according to meaning, $\tilde{C}$ should be equal to $\tilde{A} \cup \tilde{B}$.

1. Using classical fuzzy sets

Method (1): If the membership degrees of $\tilde{A}$ and $\tilde{B}$ are calculated by $\min(\frac{d}{20}, 1)$ where d represents moved distance, and the moving directions are ignored, then, we have

$\tilde{A} = 0.5/a + 0.72/b + 0.6/c + 0.75/d + 0.74/e + 0.7/f + 0.65/g,$

$\tilde{B} = 0.25/a + 0.15/b + 0.11/c + 0.25/d + 0.26/e + 0.15/f + 0.15/g.$

If we use $x \oplus y = \min(x + y, 1)$ to calculate the membership degrees of fuzzy set $\tilde{A} \cup \tilde{B}$, we have $\tilde{A} \cup \tilde{B} = 0.75/a + 0.87/b + 0.71/c + 1/d + 1/e + 0.85/f + 0.8/g$.

Since the three degrees of volunteers d and e and b are biggest, these 3 volunteers should get prises. In fact, volunteer b moved just 11.4 meters to the left, that is, 8.6 meters away to the left exit. Contrary to the facts. This tells us, the result is obviously wrong if we ignore the moving direction.

Method (2): If the moving directions are concerned and the membership degrees of $\tilde{A}$ and $\tilde{B}$ are calculated by $\max(\frac{20-d_1}{40}, 0)$ and $\min(\frac{20+d_2}{40}, 1)$, where d_1 represents moved distance in the left direction, and d_2 represents moved distance in the right direction, then, we have the following table

Table 2. Classical fuzzy sets $\tilde{A}$ and $\tilde{B}$ considering directions

Vol.	Prev. 3 Sec. Dir., Dis.	$\tilde{A}(x)$	Later 2 Sec. Dir., Dis.	$\tilde{B}(x)$
a	left, 10.0	0.25	left, 5.0	0.375
b	left, 14.4	0.14	right, 3.0	0.575
c	left, 12.0	0.2	left, 2.2	0.445
d	right, 15.0	0.875	left, 5.0	0.375
e	right, 14.8	0.87	right, 5.2	0.63
f	right, 14.0	0.85	left, 3.0	0.425
g	right, 13.0	0.825	right, 3.0	0.575

At this time, if we use the following method to calculate the membership degrees of the union of $\tilde{A}$ and $\tilde{B}$,

$$g(x,y) = \begin{cases} x \vee y, & x, y \geq \frac{1}{2} \\ x \wedge y, & x, y \leq \frac{1}{2} \\ x + y - \frac{1}{2}, & Others \end{cases},$$

then we have

$\tilde{A} \cup \tilde{B} = 0.25/a + 0.215/b + 0.2/c + 0.75/d + 0.87/e + 0.775/f + 0.825/g.$

From the setting of membership degrees, we know that the volunteers with smallest or biggest degrees can escape. Therefore, the volunteers c and e and g will get prises. This is contrary to the facts.

Remark 2. If we use other methods to calculate the membership degrees of the union, the results are always contrary to the facts.

2. **Using direction fuzzy sets:** In direction fuzzy theory, if we let the right direction be the positive direction, then we have direction membership levels calculated by $\max(\frac{-d_1}{20}, -1)$ and $\min(\frac{d_2}{20}, 1)$, where d_1 represents moved distance in the left direction, and d_2 represents moved distance in the right direction. As a result, we have the following table

That is, $\tilde{A} = -0.5/a - 0.72/b - 0.6/c + 0.75/d + 0.74/e + 0.7/f + 0.65/g$ and $\tilde{B} = -0.25/a + 0.15/b - 0.11/c - 0.25/d + 0.26/e - 0.15/f + 0.15/g$.

If we get the membership levels of $\tilde{A} \cup \tilde{B}$ by $\dot{\oplus}$, then we have $\tilde{A} \cup \tilde{B} = -0.75/a - 0.57/b - 0.71/c + 0.5/d + 1/e + 0.55/f + 0.8/g$. $|\tilde{A} \cup \tilde{B}| = 0.75/a + 0.57/b + 0.71/c + 0.5/d + 1/e + 0.55/f + 0.8/g$.

Table 3. Direction fuzzy sets $\tilde{A}$ and $\tilde{B}$

Vol.	Prev. 3 Sec. Dir., Dis.	Levels of $\tilde{A}$	Later 2 Sec. Dir., Dis.	Levels of $\tilde{B}$
a	left, 10.0	- 0.50	left, 5.0	- 0.25
b	left, 14.4	- 0.72	right, 3.0	0.15
c	left, 12.0	- 0.60	left, 2.2	- 0.11
d	right, 15.0	0.75	left, 5.0	- 0.25
e	right, 14.8	0.74	right, 5.2	0.26
f	right, 14.0	0.70	left, 3.0	- 0.15
g	right, 13.0	0.65	right, 3.0	0.15

According to the theory of direction fuzzy sets, the three volunteers with biggest levels of the absolute value direction fuzzy set $|\tilde{A} \cup \tilde{B}|$ should get prises. Therefore, we have that the first prize winner is volunteer e, the second is g, and the third is a, which completely fits the facts. Moreover, we even have $\tilde{C} = \tilde{A} \cup \tilde{B}$, which can not be obtained in classical fuzzy sets.

General Remark: Since the limitation of paper length, we have to omit many important conceptions, properties, evidences, references etc..

4 Conclusion

In this paper, we have presented several kinds of direction fuzzy problems in the introduction section. For the kind of direction fuzzy problem $< left, right >$, we dug up an application example (Escape Model), which can not be solved by classical fuzzy sets, but can be solved by the direction fuzzy sets. This shows that the introduction of direction fuzzy sets is significant.

References

1. Zadeh, L. A.: Fuzzy sets. Inform. and Control **8** (1965) 338-353
2. Yang, L. B., Gao, Y. Y.: Fuzzy set–theory and applicaiton (Chinese). Huanan Science and Engineering University Press, Second Version, 1995

Fuzzy Compensator Using RGA for TRMS Control

Jih-Gau Juang* and Wen-Kai Liu

Department of Communications and Guidance Engineering
National Taiwan Ocean University, Keelung, Taiwan 20224, ROC
jgjuang@mail.ntou.edu.tw*

Abstract. This paper presents a new approach using fuzzy compensator and PID controller to an experimental propeller setup which is called the twin rotor multi-input multi-output system (TRMS). Some previous works ignored the interactions between two axes and the controller being designed in horizontal or vertical direction separately. The goal of this study is to stabilize the TRMS in significant cross coupling conditions and to experiment with trajectory tracking. The fuzzy compensator and PID controller design is performed by a real-valued GA (RGA) with system performance index as fitness function. We apply the integral of time multiplied by the square error criterion to form a suitable fitness function in the RGA. Simulation results show that the proposed design can successfully adapt system nonlinearity and complex coupling conditions.

1 Introduction

Controller design of the TRMS has been studied for years. Huang and Juang [1]-[2] investigated the effect of the binary genetic algorithm (BGA) on controller tuning for improving system performance. The gains of the PID controller are tuned by the BGA with a nonlinear control design scheme. The controllers are better than the Gauss-Seidel Minimization Procedure. Tsai, Huang, and Juang [3] applied a real-valued genetic algorithm (RGA) on PID tuning to the TRMS control both in the vertical and horizontal axes separately. The system was decoupled into two parts, which are the vertical and horizontal, in order to design a one-degree-of-freedom PID controller. They restricted the connect beam between the main rotor and tail rotor to move only on the vertical or horizontal planes. The impact on the two rotors was ignored. The parameters of the PID controller are tuned by the RGA to reduce the total error and control energy. Fan and Juang [4] compared different kinds of fitness functions in the RGA via trial and error for tuning an optimal PID controller on the TRMS. The computer simulations showed that whether the fitness function suited the objective or was not significantly related to the result. In the conclusion of these papers [3]-[4], they constructed four PID controllers for the TRMS (both in the vertical and horizontal spherical surfaces simultaneously). Although these PID controllers could work in two degrees of freedom (2-DOF), they were still weak in tracking a desired trajectory and in reaching a specific attitude. It is difficult to stabilize the influence between two axes and a non-minimum phase in a vertical plane. Liu, Fan, and Juang [5], quoted the system performance index as a part of the fitness function in the RGA.

D.-S. Huang, K. Li, and G.W. Irwin (Eds.): ICIC 2006, LNAI 4114, pp. 120 – 126, 2006.

The system performance index deals with a modification of the known integral of time multiplied by square error criterion (ITSE). It is more efficient in finding the parameters of four PID controllers. Although these controllers could reduce control force and total error better than before, trajectory tracking of a desired path in 2-DOF oscillates for several seconds.

The main purpose in the control of the TRMS focuses on designing controllers to stabilize the impact between two rotors and to track a desired path and specific attitude in 2-DOF efficiently. In this paper, a fuzzy controller is used as a compensator and is combined with a traditional PID controller. It is a cross-coupled multi-variables controller. In order to make the TRMS follow a desired trajectory, a modified ITSE is implemented in the RGA and is utilized to optimize the gain factors of the fuzzy compensator and PID controller. There are 28 parameters for four controllers and four compensators in vertical and horizontal planes of the TRMS control system. These 28 parameters are tuned individually by the RGA. Simulation results indicate that the new approach has better performance than previous works.

2 System Description

The Two Rotor MIMO System (TRMS) is a laboratory set-up deigned for control experiments. In certain aspects, its behavior resembles that of a helicopter. From the control point of view it exemplifies a high order nonlinear system with significant cross-couplings. The approach to control problems connected with the TRMS proposed in this paper involves some theoretical knowledge of laws of physics and some heuristic dependencies difficult to express in analytical form. A schematic diagram of the laboratory set-up is shown in Fig. 1. The TRMS consists of a beam pivoted on its base in such a way that it can rotate freely both in the horizontal and vertical planes. At both ends of the beam, the rotors (the main and tail rotors) are driven by DC motors. A counterbalance arm with a weight at its end is fixed to the beam at the pivot. The state of the beam is described by four process variables: horizontal and vertical angles measured by position sensors fitted at the pivot and two corresponding angular velocities. Two additional states variables are the angular velocity of the rotors measured by tachogenerators coupled with the driving DC motors. In a normal helicopter, the aerodynamic force is controlled by changing the angle of attack. The laboratory set-up from Fig. 1 is so constructed that the angle of attack is fixed. The aero dynamic force is controlled by varying the speed of the rotors. Therefore, the control inputs are supply voltage of DC motors. A change in the voltage value results in a change of the rotation speed of the propeller which results in a change of the corresponding position of the beam.

A system performance index is used for fitness function in the RGA. It is an optimization criterion for parameters tuning of control system, which is suitable for the RGA. It deals with a modification of the known integral of time multiplied by squared error criterion (ITSE). In order to influence a characteristic value of a signal, it is not necessary to add a special term to the ITSE which may increase the selection pressure in the RGA. An evident possibility is to divide the integral criterion in a special error section for each characteristic value. The general form and most used performance index is shown below.

$$I = \int_0^T f\left(r(t)\ ,e(t)\ ,u(t)\ ,y(t)\ ,t\right) dt \tag{1}$$

$$f = f_{ITSE}\left(e(t),u(t),t\right) = t^n\left(e^2(t) + \alpha \cdot u^2(t)\right) \quad n > 1\ ,\ \alpha > 0 \tag{2}$$

where y is the output response, e is the output error, u is the control input, and r is the reference signal.

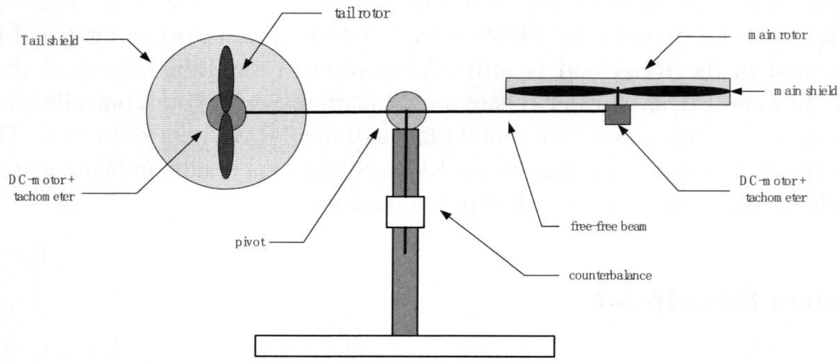

Fig. 1. The laboratory set-up TRMS

3 Control Scheme

The fuzzy controller can be further classified into three types : the direct action (DA) type, the gain scheduling (GS) type and a combination of DA and GS type. In this work, the fuzzy PID application belongs to the DA type with three inputs and one output. The fuzzy PID compensator is placed within the feedback control loop and is used to compute the PID action through fuzzy inference. The structure of the fuzzy compensator is shown in Fig. 2. In order to minimize the output error, the gain factors S_e, S_{ce}, S_{se} and S_u will be tuned by EC, where $e(n) = y_d(n) - y(n)$, $\Delta e(n) = e(n) - e(n-1)$, $\sum e$ is the sum of errors, $\hat{e} = S_e e$, $\Delta\hat{e} = S_{ce} e$, $\sum \hat{e} = S_{se} \sum e$ and $\hat{u}_{PID} = S_u u_{PID}$. Define the linguistic variables that correspond to the input scaled variables $\hat{e}$, $\Delta\hat{e}$ and $\sum \hat{e}$ as $E_i, \Delta E_j, \sum E_k$. The indices *i*, *j* and *k* represent the linguistic values or fuzzy states of the input fuzzy variables and their ranges are *i*=0, 1, 2.., N1-1; *j*=0, 1, 2.., N2-1; *k*=0, 1, 2.., N3-1; where N1, N2 and N3 denote the total numbers of fuzzy states assigned for each fuzzy variables. The total number of rules required for a complete description of the normalized space is $\mathrm{N1} \times \mathrm{N2} \times \mathrm{N3}$. The fuzzy PID structure can be expressed by

$$If\ \hat{e}\ is\ E_i\ AND\ \Delta\hat{e}\ is\ \Delta E_j\ AND\ \sum\hat{e}\ is \sum E_k\ THEN\ \Delta\hat{u}_{PID}\ is\ \Delta U_{m,PID} \tag{3}$$

The final compensator output can be expressed by

$$u_{PID} = S_u \sum_{q=0}^{n} \Delta \hat{u}_{PID}(q) \tag{4}$$

For this work, we apply the Gaussian function for each control variable. The universe of discourse of each input and output variables are defined to be within the range [-1,1] and uniformly portioned in 7 membership functions and are placed with 50% overlap. The number of linguistic variables used for each $\hat{e}_1$, $\hat{e}_2$ and $\hat{e}_3$ is 7. The total number of fuzzy rules is 343. The fuzzy rules are shown in Fig. 3 and is defined as

$$If\ \hat{e}\ is\ PL\ AND\ \Delta\hat{e}\ is\ PL\ AND\ \sum\hat{e}\ isPL\ THEN\ \Delta\hat{u}_{PID}\ is\ PL_{m,PID} \tag{5}$$

The cross-coupled controllers and compensators are presented in Fig. 4.

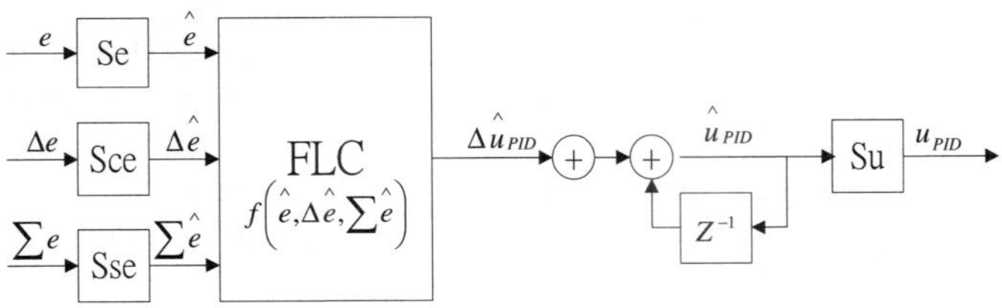

Fig. 2. Structure of fuzzy compensator

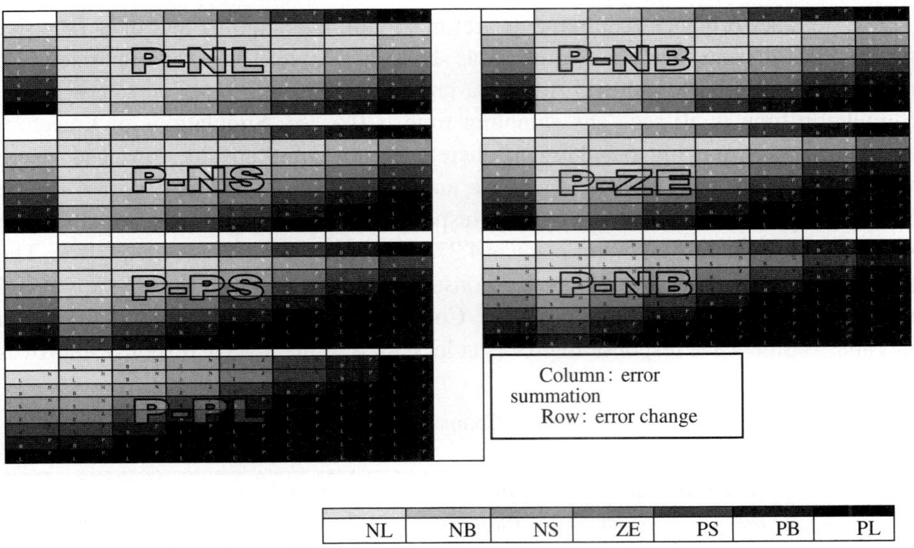

Fig. 3. The fuzzy rules of fuzzy compensator

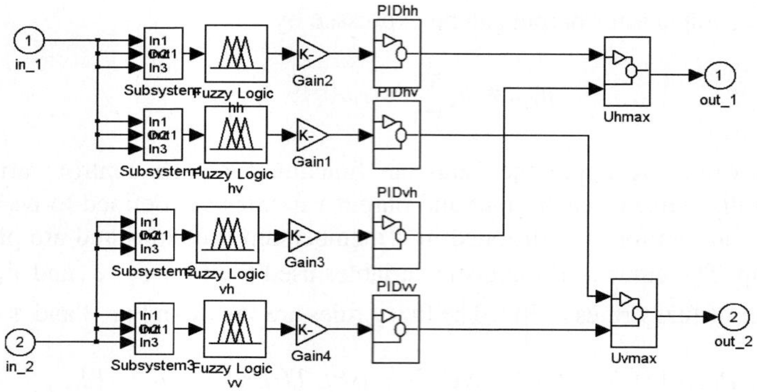

Fig. 4. Cross-coupling fuzzy compensator and PID controller

Four PID controllers and four fuzzy compensators for TRMS are: PID_{vv}, PID_{vh}, PID_{hv}, PID_{hh}, FLC_{vv}, FLC_{vh}, FLC_{hv}, FLC_{hh}, where h denotes horizontal and v denotes vertical. The TRMS control in horizontal and vertical planes requires setting 28 subsystems' parameters. The evolutionary computations use the roulette wheel selection and the Adewuya crossover method [6]. The mutation operator creates one new offspring individual for the new population by randomly mutating a randomly chosen gene of the selected individual.

4 Simulations

The system performance requirements are: maximum overshoot is less than 1%; rise time, delay time and steady state time are as short as possible. The population size is 40, crossover rate is 80% with the Adewuya crossover law, and mutation rate is 2.5%. Simulation time is 50 sec. The sampling time is 0.5 sec. Simulations of trajectory tracking are shown in Fig. 5 and Fig. 6, where reference inputs are sine wave and square wave. The frequency is 1/40 Hz and the amplitudes are 0.5 rad and 0.2 rad on the horizontal plane and the vertical plane, respectively. The total sum of errors of sine wave response on the horizontal plane is 4.377 and is 40.196 on the vertical plane. The total sums of errors of square wave response on the horizontal plane and the vertical plane are 34.906 and 73.246, respectively. Comparisons of this work and [5] are shown in Table 1. Sine wave response improves at least 44%. Square wave response improves at least 26%.

Table 1. Comparisons with [5]

	Error of sine wave response			*Error of square wave response*		
	hor	*ver*	*improve*	*hor*	*ver*	*improve*
[5]	14.0243	72.2283	44.3%	125.3977	99.3753	26.3%
this	4.377	40.196		34.906	73.246	

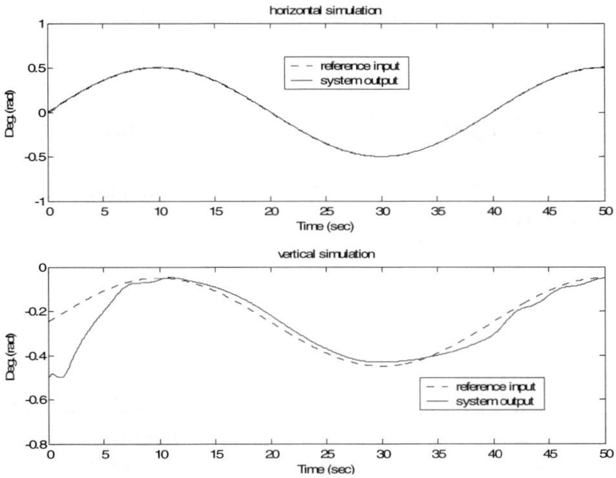

Fig. 5. Sine wave response of TRMS

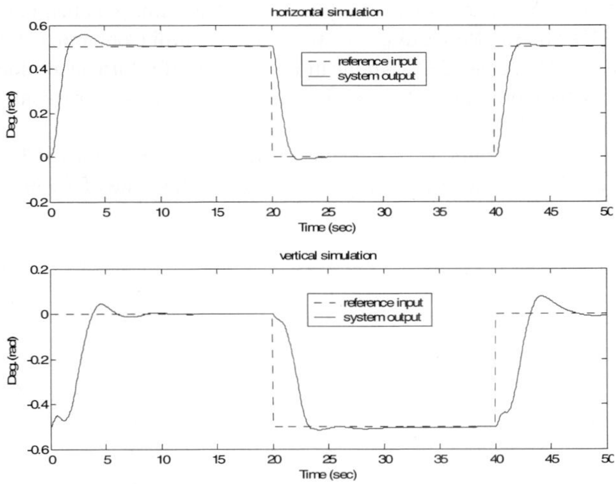

Fig. 6. Square wave response of TRMS

5 Conclusion

In this paper, the control problem of the TRMS is solved. The proposed control scheme utilizes a RGA with a specified system performance index to tune the parameters of the fuzzy compensator and PID controller, which can stabilize the cross-coupling nonlinear system. This approach has successfully overcome the influence of cross-coupling between two axes. In trajectory tracking control, it reduces maximum overshoot, rise time, steady state time and delay time. Compared to previous works, the simulation results show that the new approach can reduce the total error and improve system performance.

Acknowledgement

This work was supported by the National Science Council, Taiwan, ROC, under Grant NSC 93-2213-E-019 -007.

References

1. Huang, M.D., Juang, J.G.: Application of GA and PID Control to Nonlinear TRMS. Proceedings of Conference on Artificial Intelligence and Applications. (2002) 734-739
2. Tsai, C.Y., Huang, M.D., Juang, J.G.: Application of Real-type GA to TRMS Position Control. Proceedings of Automatic Control Conference. (2003) 1267-1273
3. Fang, J.H., Juang, J.G.: Analysis of Optimal fitness Function for TRMS Parameter Searching and Its Implementation on FPGA. Proceedings of Conference on Artificial Intelligence and Applications. (2004) FP4-1
4. Fang, J.H., Tsai, C.Y., Juang, J.G.: Analysis of Optimal Fitness Function on TRMS 1-DOF and 2–DOF PID Control. Proceedings of Automatic Control Conference. (2004) I02-05
5. Liu, W.K., Fan, J.H., Juang, J.G.: Application of System-Performance-Index based Genetic Algorithm to PID Controller. Proceedings of Conference on Artificial Intelligence and Applications. (2004) FP4-3
6. Adewuya, A.A.: New Methods in Genetic Search with Real-valued Chromosomes. M.S. thesis, Dept. of Mechanical Engineering, Massachusetts Institute of Technology. (1996)

Fuzzy-Neural Network Adaptive Sliding Mode Tracking Control for Interconnected System*

Yan-xin Zhang[1,2] and Hai-rong Dong[1,2]

[1] Institute of Automatic control, School of Electronics and Information Engineering, Beijing Jiaotong University, Beijing, 100044, P.R. China
[2] The Key Laboratory of Complex Systems and Intelligence Science, Chinese Academy of Sciences, Beijing, 100044, P.R. China
zyxhyq@yahoo.com.cn,
dhr@telecom.njtu.edu.cn

Abstract. Fuzzy neural network adaptive tracking controller is designed to realize the tracking control for a class of unknown nonlinear interconnected systems. No constraint or matching conditions of the uncertain terms are required. For the low dimensions unknown dynamic of the subsystems and the high one of the interconnected terms, two classes of fuzzy rules are adopted respectively to approximate the unknowns. The neural network is used to counteract the extra gains of the controller. The fuzzy sliding mode control is developed to compensate for the exterior disturb and the fuzzy neural network approximation errors. By the Simultaneity, based on Lyapunov method, the parameters of the systems are regulated on line by the adaptive laws. Global asymptotic stability is assured with the tracking errors converging to a neighborhood of zero.

1 Introduction

Recently years, people applied fuzzy logic system to control the nonlinear unknown dynamic systems [1-4]. There are many results about the stability, robustness and control performance, but most approaches are limited to assume that the uncertainty is known or parameterizable, which are not suitable to deal with the large-scale systems with unknown nonlinear subsystems. In 1994, Wang opened a new area to deal with the ill-defined and complex systems [6]. He firstly designed a fuzzy adaptive controller. But the adaptive laws were limited to nonlinear systems with constant control gain, square-integrable tracking error and the disturbances cannot be eliminated. Tong [3] and [7] improved wang's scheme and presented a globally stable fuzzy indirect controller for a class of interconnected systems with unknown terms. Zhang [8] proposed a kind of fuzzy indirect adaptive tracking controller, in which For the low dimensions unknown dynamic of the subsystems and the high one of the interconnected terms, two classes of fuzzy rules are adopted respectively to approximate the unknowns. But there are a constraint supposes that the gain functions of the controller

* This paper was supported in part by NJTU Paper Foundation of China.

D.-S. Huang, K. Li, and G.W. Irwin (Eds.): ICIC 2006, LNAI 4114, pp. 127 – 133, 2006.

are invertible, which may not be satisfied in the engineering. Based on [8], this paper considers a class of large-scale systems. For the cases that the gain functions of the controller are invertible, a neural network is used to counteract the extra gains of the controller. The fuzzy-neural network adaptive controller guarantees the boundary of all variables of the large-scale systems and the convergence of the tracking errors to a neighbourhood of zero.

2 Model Description and Problem Statement

Consider the nonlinear interconnected large-scale system, which is composed of N interconnected subsystems:

$$y_i^{(n_i)} = f_i(x_i) + g_i(x_i)u_i + H_i(t, x_1, \cdots, x_N) + d_i(t) \quad i = 1,2,\cdots,N \tag{1}$$

Where $x_i \in R^n$ is the state vector of subsystem $\sum_i$. u_i is the input and y_i is the output. $f_i(x_i)$, $g_i(x_i) \in R^{n_i}$ are the unknown dynamics of $\sum_i$ (unknown functions), and $g_i(x_i)$ is non-invertible. $H_i \in R$ represents the interconnected term between the subsystems, they are all smooth functions. $d_i(t)$ are the exterior disturbances. Let $X = (x_1, \cdots, x_N)$.

Control objective: Design adaptive controllers $u_i(x_i \mid \theta_i)$ in the presence of the unknown dynamics of $\sum_i$, the interconnections, and disturbances $d_i(t)$ such that:

(1) The system is stable in Lyapunov sense, i.e., all of variables are bounded.
(2) The tracking errors of each subsystem converge to a neighborhood of zero asymptotically.

3 Assumptions and Controllers Design

Assumption 1: $|d_i(t)| \le c_i^*$, c_i^* is the unknown bounded constant.

Given reference output y_{im}, we assume that the desired output and its derivatives $y_{im}, \dot{y}_{im}, \cdots, y_{im}^{(n_i)}$ are measurable and bounded. Define the tracking errors as $e_{i0} = y_{im} - y_i$. Let $e_i = (e_{i0}, \dot{e}_{i0}, \cdots, e_{i0}^{(n_i-1)})^T$, $K_i = (k_{i(n_i-1)}, \cdots, k_{i0})^T$ and select K_i such that all the roots of the polynomial are in the left half-plane, $\hat{L}_i(s) = s^{(n_i)} + k_{i(n_i-1)} s^{(n_i-1)} + \cdots + k_{i0}$ i.e., $\hat{L}_i(s)$ are Hurwitz polynomial.

In the case of $d_i = H_i \neq 0$, utilize the fuzzy logic system to approximate the unknown functions $f_i(x_i)$, $g_i(x_i)$ and $h_i(X)$. Their membership functions adopt Gaussian's form, and construct the fuzzy logic systems as follows:

$$\begin{aligned}
\hat{f}_i(x_i \mid \theta_{1i}) &= \sum_{j=1}^{p} \theta_{1ij}\xi_{ij}(x_i) = \theta_{1i}^T \xi_i(x_i) \\
\hat{g}_i(x_i \mid \theta_{2i}) &= \sum_{j=1}^{p} \theta_{2ij}\xi_{ij}(x_i) = \theta_{2i}^T \xi_i(x_i) \\
\hat{H}_i(X \mid \theta_{3i}) &= \sum_{k=1}^{q} \theta_{3ik}\gamma_{ik}(X) = \theta_{3i}^T \gamma_i(X)
\end{aligned} \tag{2}$$

Where $\theta_{1i}, \theta_{2i}, \theta_{3i}$ represent the set of the adjustable parameters $\bar{y}_i^l, \bar{\bar{y}}_i^l, \bar{x}_{i,j}^l$ and $\sigma_{i,j}^l$.

Design an indirect fuzzy controller as

$$\begin{aligned}
u_i = {} & \hat{g}_i^T(x_i \mid \theta_{2i})[I + \hat{g}_i(x_i \mid \theta_{2i})\hat{g}_i^T(x_i \mid \theta_{2i})]^{-1}[-\hat{f}_i(x_i \mid \theta_{1i}) - \hat{H}_i(X \mid \theta_{3i}) \\
& + K_i^T e_i + y_{im}^{(n_i)} - c_i u_{fsi} + \frac{1}{2}\eta_i s_i + u_{i2} + L_i u_{fsi}]
\end{aligned} \tag{3}$$

Where $c_i u_{fsi}$ are used to attenuate the exterior disturbances, and $L_i u_{fsi}$ are used to counteract the fuzzy approximation errors. u_{fsi} can be consulted reference [3]. s_i are the linear combinations of the error and their derivatives before $n_i - 1$, u_{i2} is used to counteract the extra gains in the controller.

By substituting (3) into (1), we have the error equation:

$$\begin{aligned}
\dot{e}_{i0}^{(n_i)} = {} & -K_i^T e_i + (\hat{f}_i(x_i \mid \theta_{1i}) - f_i(x_i)) + (\hat{g}_i(x_i \mid \theta_{2i}) - g_i(x_i))u_i + (\hat{H}_i(X \mid \theta_{3i}) - H_i) \\
& + c_i u_{fsi} - \frac{1}{2}\eta_i s_i - d_i(t) - u_{i2} - L_i u_{fsi} - [I + \hat{g}_i(x_i \mid \theta_{2i})\hat{g}_i^T(x_i \mid \theta_{2i})]^{-1} u_{ci}
\end{aligned} \tag{4}$$

Where

$$u_{ci} = -\hat{f}_i(x_i \mid \theta_{1i}) - \hat{H}_i(X \mid \theta_{3i}) + K_i^T e_i + y_{im}^{(n_i)} - c_i u_{fsi} + \frac{1}{2}\eta_i s_i + u_{i2} + L_i u_{fsi} \tag{5}$$

Equivalently,

$$\begin{aligned}
\dot{e}_i = {} & A_i e_i + B[(\hat{f}_i(x_i \mid \theta_{1i}) - f_i(x_i)) + (\hat{g}_i(x_i \mid \theta_{2i}) - g_i(x_i))u_i + (\hat{H}_i(X \mid \theta_{3i}) - H_i)] \\
& + B[c_i u_{fsi} - d_i(t) - \frac{1}{2}\eta_i s_i] + B\{-u_{i2} - L_i u_{fsi} - [I + \hat{g}_i(x_i \mid \theta_{2i})\hat{g}_i^T(x_i \mid \theta_{2i})]^{-1} u_{ci}\}
\end{aligned} \tag{6}$$

Where

$$A_i = \begin{bmatrix} 0 & 1 & 0 & \cdots & 0 \\ 0 & 0 & 1 & \cdots & 0 \\ \vdots & \vdots & \vdots & \ddots & \vdots \\ -k_{i(n_i-1)} & -k_{i(n_i-2)} & -k_{i(n_i-3)} & \cdots & -k_{i0} \end{bmatrix} \qquad B = [0 \;\; 0 \;\; \cdots \;\; 1]^T$$

Suppose $\theta_{1i}^*, \theta_{2i}^*, \theta_{3i}^*$ are the optimal parameters vectors of $\theta_{1i}, \theta_{2i}, \theta_{3i}$, Therefore, for the unknown dynamics of the subsystems and the interconnections, we adopt different approach to realize the approximation, i.e., [8]
Let

$$w_i = (\hat{f}_i(x_i \mid \theta_{1i}^*) - f_i(x_i)) + (\hat{g}_i(x_i \mid \theta_{2i}^*) - g_i(x_i))u_{ci} + (\hat{H}_i(X \mid \theta_{3i}^*) - H_i(X))] \tag{7}$$

Here, denote $v_i = w_i + O(\left|\Phi_{3i}\right|^2)$ as the "minimum approximation error".

Assumption 2: Suppose that the fuzzy logic approximation errors satisfy the following inequalities:

$$\left|v_i\right| < M_e^i \tag{8}$$

On the other hand, there is a redundant term $[I + \hat{g}_i(x_i \mid \theta_{2i})\hat{g}_i^T(x_i \mid \theta_{2i})]^{-1}u_{ci}$ in the error equation, which is caused by the controller gains. Then we design a neural network controller u_{i2} to counteract it.

$$u_{i2} = -\hat{W}_i^T G_i + \hat{\varphi}_i(t)u_{fsi} \tag{9}$$

where $\hat{\varphi}_i(t)$ is the estimated value of the approximation error of the neural network. Rewrite (6) as

$$\begin{aligned} \dot{e}_i = {} & A_i e_i + B\Phi_{1i}^T \xi_i(x_i) + B\Phi_{2i}^T \xi_i(x_i)u_{ci} + B\Phi_{3i}^T \left(\frac{\partial \hat{H}_i(X \mid \theta_{3i})}{\partial \theta_{3i}}\right) + B\Phi_{\eta_i}\frac{s_i}{2} \\ & - B\Phi_{ci}u_{fsi} + B[c_i^* u_{fsi} - d_i(t) - \frac{\eta_i^*}{2}s_i] + B[v_i + L_i u_{fsi}] - B\{\tilde{W}_i^T G_i - \hat{\varphi}_i(t)u_{fsi}\} \end{aligned} \tag{10}$$

Where $\Phi_{ci} = c_i^* - c_i$, $\Phi_\eta = \eta_i^* - \eta_i$, $\tilde{W}_i = W_i - \hat{W}_i$, $\Phi_{1i} = \theta_{1i} - \theta_{1i}^*$, $\Phi_{2i} = \theta_{2i} - \theta_{2i}^*$, $\Phi_{3i} = \theta_{3i} - \theta_{3i}^*$ are parameter matched error vectors.

The designing process of the controller is similar to the one in [3].

Adopt the parameters and control-gains adaptive laws as:

$$\dot{\theta}_{1i} = \begin{cases} -\eta_{i1} e_i^T P_i B \xi_i(x_i) \cdots if \left|\theta_{1i}\right| < M_a, or \left|\theta_{1i}\right| = M_a and\ e_i^T P_i B \theta_{1i}^T \xi_i(x_i) \ge 0 \\ P_1\{-\eta_{i1} e_i^T P_i B \xi_i(x_i)\} \cdots\cdots\cdots\cdots if \left|\theta_{1i}\right| = M_a and\ e_i^T P_i B \theta_{1i}^T \xi_i(x_i) < 0 \end{cases} \tag{11}$$

Where the projection operator $P_1\{*\}$ are defined as:

$$P_1\{-\eta_{1i} e_i^T P_i B \xi_i(x_i)\} = -\eta_{i1} e_i^T P_i B \xi_i(x_i) + \eta_{i1} e_i^T P_i B \frac{\theta_{1i}\theta_{1i}^T \xi_i(x_i)}{\left|\theta_{1i}\right|^2}$$

$$\dot{\theta}_{2i} = \begin{cases} -\eta_{i2} e_i^T P_i B \xi_i(x_i)u_{ci} \cdots if \left|\theta_{2i}\right| < M_b, or \left|\theta_{2i}\right| = M_b and\ e_i^T P_i B \theta_{2i}^T \xi_i(x_i)u_{ci} \ge 0 \\ P_2\{-\eta_{i2} e_i^T P_i B \xi_i(x_i)u_{ci}\} \cdots\cdots\cdots\cdots if \left|\theta_{2i}\right| = M_b and\ e_i^T P_i B \theta_{2i}^T \xi_i(x_i)u_{ci} < 0 \end{cases} \tag{12}$$

Where the projection operators are define as:

$$P_2\{-\eta_{i2}e_i^T P_i B\xi_i(x_i)u_{ci}\} = -\eta_{i2}e_i^T P_i B\xi_i(x_i)u_{ci} + \eta_{i2}e_i^T P_i B\frac{\theta_{2i}\theta_{2i}^T\xi_i(x_i)u_{ci}}{|\theta_{2i}|^2}$$

$$\dot{\theta}_{3i} = \begin{cases} -\eta_{i3}e_i^T P_i B(\frac{\partial\hat{H}_i(X\mid\theta_{3i})}{\partial\theta_{3i}}), & if\,|\theta_{3i}| < M_c, or\,|\theta_{3i}| = M_c and\; e_i^T P_i B\theta_{3i}^T(\frac{\partial\hat{H}_i(X\mid\theta_{3i})}{\partial\theta_{3i}}) \ge 0 \\ P_3\{-\eta_{i3}e_i^T P_i B(\frac{\partial\hat{H}_i(X\mid\theta_{3i})}{\partial\theta_{3i}})\} & if\,|\theta_{3i}| = M_c\; and\; e_i^T P_i B\theta_{3i}^T(\frac{\partial\hat{H}_i(X\mid\theta_{3i})}{\partial\theta_{3i}}) < 0 \end{cases} \quad (13)$$

Where the projection operators $P_3\{*\}$ are define as:

$$P_3\{-\eta_{i3}e_i^T P_i B(\frac{\partial\hat{H}_i}{\partial\theta_{3i}})\} = -\eta_{i3}e_i^T P_i B(\frac{\partial\hat{H}_i}{\partial\theta_{3i}}) + \eta_{i3}e_i^T P_i B\frac{\theta_{3i}\theta_{3i}^T(\frac{\partial\hat{H}_i}{\partial\theta_{3i}})}{|\theta_{3i}|^2} \quad (14)$$

$$\dot{c}_i = \eta_{i4}\left|e_i^T P_i B\right|,\; \dot{\eta}_{i5} = \frac{\eta_{i5}}{2}(e_i^T P_i B)^2,\; \dot{\hat{W}} = \gamma_i G_i e_i^T P_i B,\; \dot{\varphi}_i = \frac{\eta_{i6}}{2}\left|e_i^T P_i B\right|$$

Where P_i is a positive definite matrix, Q_i is arbitrary given positive matrix, which satisfies $P_i A_i + A_i^T P_i = -Q_i$

Theorem 1. For nonlinear system (1), which satisfies assumption 1-2, if adopting control law (3), (9) and the parameters adaptive laws (11)-(14), and selecting $S_i = e_i^T P_i B$, $L_i = M_e^i$, then the control objectives (1) and (2) are achieved.
Proof: (the detail is omitted for saving space)

4 Emulation

Example: Apply the designing method of this article to the following system, which denotes two interconnected handstand cycloid [10].

The dynamic equation is

$$\begin{cases} \dot{x}_1 = x_2 \\ \dot{x}_2 = f_1x_1 + f_3u_1 + f_2x_3 - (\beta_1x_2^2 + f_4) \end{cases}$$
$$\begin{cases} \dot{x}_3 = x_4 \\ \dot{x}_4 = f_1x_3 + f_3u_2 + f_2x_1 - (\beta_2x_4^2 - f_4) \end{cases}$$

Here, f_1, f_2, f_3, f_4, β_1, β_2, g, M, m, L, l, z_1, z_2 is choose the same as Jiang, B, et. al., [10]. Give the tracking reference output as $y_{1m} = \sin(2t)$, $y_{2m} = 2 + \sin(3t)$.

Choose $\eta_1 = 100$, $\eta_2 = 100$, $\eta_{11} = 0.1$, $\eta_{21} = 0.1$, $\eta_{11} = 0.1$, $\eta_{13} = 0.002$, $\gamma_1 = 0.01$, $\gamma_2 = 0.01$, $s_1 = 5\dot{e}_1 + 5e_1$, $s_2 = 5\dot{e}_2 + 5e_2$, $\phi_i = 0.05$, $\sigma(x) = 1/(1+e^{-0.51x})$

By using theorem 1, the controllers are designed as:

$$u_1 = 2[-\theta_{11}\xi_1(X_1) - \theta_{13}\gamma_1(X) + 2\dot{e}_1 + e_1 - 4\sin(2t) - 2u_{fs1} + 50s_1 + (0.01 + \left|-\theta_{11}\xi_1(X_1) - \theta_{13}\gamma_1(X) + 2\dot{e}_1 + e_1 - 4\sin(2t) - 2u_{fs1} + 50s_1\right|)u_{fs1} + \hat{W}_1^T G_1]$$

$$u_2 = 2[-\theta_{21}\xi_2(X_2) - \theta_{23}\gamma_2(X) + 2\dot{e}_2 + e_2 - 9\sin(3t) - 2u_{fs2} + 50s_2 + (0.01 + \left|-\theta_{21}\xi_2(X_2) - \theta_{23}\gamma_2(X) + 2\dot{e}_2 + e_2 - 9\sin(3t) - 2u_{fs2} + 50s_2\right|)u_{fs2} + \hat{W}_2^T G_2]$$

$$\dot{\theta}_{11} = -0.5(\dot{e}_1 + e_1)\xi_1(X_1),\ \dot{\theta}_{21} = -0.5(\dot{e}_2 + e_2)\xi_2(X_2),\ \dot{W}_1 = 0.01(\dot{e}_1 + e_1)\sigma(x_1)\sigma(x_2)$$

$$\dot{\theta}_{13} = -0.01(\dot{e}_1 + e_1)\gamma_1(X),\ \dot{\theta}_{23} = -0.01(\dot{e}_2 + e_2)\gamma_2(X),\ \dot{W}_2 = 0.01(\dot{e}_2 + e_2)\sigma(x_3)\sigma(x_4)$$

By using Matlab, the result is as Fig.1 (on the next page).

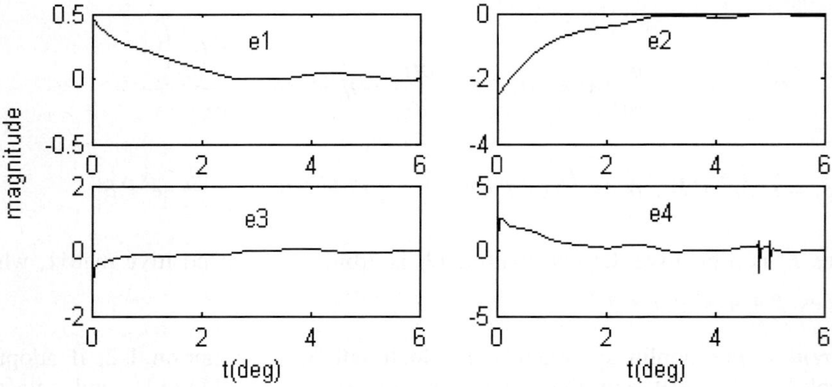

Fig. 1. The curve of the state errors (e_1 is the first state error of subsystem 1, e_2 is the second state error of subsystem 1, e_3 is the first state error of subsystem 2, e_4 is the second state error of subsystem 2)

5 Conclusion

In this paper, the problem of output tracking is discussed for a class of interconnected unknown dynamic systems. We make some primary research about the unknown interconnections of the large-scale systems. The proposed scheme combines the fuzzy logic approximation method, the neural network approximation method, the fuzzy sliding mode control and the adaptive control algorithm. Thus, the constraint condition of the interconnections [7] and the control gain functions [8] can be reduced. The fuzzy-neural network controller realize the tracking goal and assure the close-loop system asymptotically stable in the Lyapunov sense.

References

1. Wang, T: Fuzzy Indirect Adaptive Output Feedback Control for a Class of Nonlinear System, Control and Decision, Vol.15(2), (2000) 161-164
2. Tong, S. C: Fuzzy Indirect Adaptive Output Feedback Control for a Class of Nonlinear System, ACTA AUTOMATICA SINICA, Vol.25(4), (1999) 553-559

3. Tong, S. C., Chai, M., Zhou, J: Fuzzy Adaptive Output Tracking Control of Nonlinear System, Proceedings of IEEE International Fuzzy Systems, Seoul, Korea, Vol.1, (1999) 562-567
4. Buckley, J. J : Fuzzy Input-output Controllers are Universal Approximators, Fuzzy Sets and Systems, Vol.58(3), (1993) 273-278
5. Chang, Y. C: Robust Tracking Control for Nonlinear MIMO Systems Via Fuzzy Approaches, Automatica, Vol.36, (2000) 1535-1545
6. Wang, L. X : Adaptive Fuzzy Systems and Control-Design and Stability Analysis. Englewood Cliffs, NJ:Prentice-Hall, (1994)
7. Tong, S. C., Chai, T. Y., Li, Q. G: Fuzzy Direct Adaptive Control for a Class of Large-scale Nonlinear Systems, International Jounal of Cybernatics and Systems, (1997)
8. Zhang, Y.X., Jing Y.W., Zhang S.Y. Output Tracking Control Problem Based on Fuzzy Logic System, Control and Decision, Vol.18(1), (2003) 13-18
9. Hajjaji, A.E., Rachid, A: Explicit Formulas for Fuzzy Controller, Fuzzy sets and systems, Vol.62(2), (1995) 135-141
10. Jiang, B., Liu, X P., Zhang, S Y: The Output Tracking of Nonlinear Composite System with Similar Structure. Information and Control, Vol.24(2), (1995) 65-69

Measure of Certainty with Fuzzy Entropy Function

Sang-Hyuk Lee, Seong-Pyo Cheon, and Jinho Kim

School of Electrical and Computer Engineering, Pusan National University,
Changjeon-dong, Geumjeong-gu, Busan 609-735, Korea
{leehyuk, buzz74, jinhkim}@pusan.ac.kr

Abstract. To measure the certainty, we use the meaning of entropy. For the selection of reliable data, fuzzy entropy through distance measure is proposed. The appropriateness of the proposed entropy is verified by the definition of entropy measure. To measure the fuzziness of 3-phase stator currents, membership functions are obtained by the Bootstrap method. Finally, the proposed entropy is applied to the membership function of 3-phase currents, and the fuzzy entropy values of phase current each are illustrated.

1 Introduction

Characterization and quantification of fuzziness are important issues that affect the management of uncertainty in many system models and designs. The fact that the entropy of a fuzzy set is a measure of the fuzziness of that fuzzy set has been established by previous researchers [1-7]. Liu proposed the axiomatic definitions of entropy, distance measure, and similarity measure, and discussed the relations between these three concepts. Kosko considered the relation between distance measure and fuzzy entropy. Bhandari and Pal provided a fuzzy information measure for discrimination of a fuzzy set relative to some other fuzzy set. Pal and Pal analyzed classical Shannon information entropy. Also, Ghosh used fuzzy entropy in neural networks. However, that was an uncommon application of proposed entropy, unrelated to the object in this study. Hence, we apply fuzzy entropy to the membership function of the faulty motor stator current.

In this paper, we propose fuzzy entropy with a distance measure. The proposed fuzzy entropy, which has a simple structure compared to the previously proposed entropy, is derived using the well-known Hamming distance measure. With the proposed entropy, we represent another similar entropy. The usefulness of these two entropies is verified by a measure of the fuzziness of 3-phase faulty induction motor stator current. In previous studies just one phase current has been used. Hence, we carry out the measure of the fuzziness of phase current each. For the determination of a faulty motor, the phase stator current is transformed via Wavelet decomposition [14][15], and among the obtained coefficients, the 4th coefficient of the 6th detail is used to decide which fault take place. From the 20 coefficients of the 4th coefficient of the 6th detail, we process the Bootstrap method [16], and we also obtain the membership function via the Central Limit Theorem [16]. Using the proposed fuzzy entropy, we measure the

D.-S. Huang, K. Li, and G.W. Irwin (Eds.): ICIC 2006, LNAI 4114, pp. 134 – 139, 2006.

entropies of each phase current. In the next section, axiomatic definitions of the entropy of fuzzy sets are introduced. In Section 3, entropy is induced by distance measure. In Section 4, fault signals are measured by the proposed entropy measure. Conclusions follow in Section 5. Throughout this paper, terminologies are used in the reference of Fan and Xie[6].

2 Fuzzy Entropy

In this section, we introduce some preliminary results. Liu suggested axiomatic definition of fuzzy entropy, distance measure [4].

Definition 2.1 (Liu, 1992) A real function, $e : F(X) \rightarrow R^+$ is called the entropy on $F(X)$, if has the following properties:

$(E1) : e(D) = 0, \forall D \in P(X);$

$(E2) : e([1/2]) = max_{A \in F(X)} e(A);$

$(E3) : e(A^*) \leq e(A), \textit{ for any sharpening } A^* \textit{ of } A; \textit{ and}$

$(E4) : e(A) = e(A^C), \forall A \in F(X),$

where $[1/2]$ is the fuzzy set in which the value of the membership function is $1/2$.

If we divide a universal set X into two parts D and D^C in $P(X)$, then the fuzziness of fuzzy set A is the sum of the fuzziness of $A \cap D$ and $A \cap D^C$. From this idea, the following definition follows.

Definition 2.2 (Fan and Xie, 1999) Let e be the entropy on $F(X)$. Then, for any $A \in F(X)$,

$$e(A) = e(A \cap D) + e(A \cap D^C) \tag{1}$$

is the σ-entropy on $F(X)$.

From Definitions 2.2, we can focus on an interesting area of universal set and extend the theory of the entropy of fuzzy sets. Fan and Xie derived new entropy via defined entropy, introducd by $e' = e/(2-e)$, where e is an entropy on $F(X)$.

We propose entropy that is induced by distance measure. Among distance measures, Hamming distance commonly uses the σ-distance measure between fuzzy sets A and B,

$$d(A,B) = \frac{1}{n}\sum_{i=1}^{n}|\mu_A(x_i) - \mu_B(x_i)| \tag{2}$$

where $X = \{x_1, x_2, \cdots, x_n\}$, $|k|$ is the absolute value of k. The next proposition shows the distance relation between fuzzy sets and crisp sets.

Proposition 2.1 (Fan and Xie, 1999) Let d be a σ - distance measure on $F(X)$; then

(i) $d(A, A_{near}) \geq d(A^*, A_{near})$

(ii) $d(A, A_{far}) \leq d(A^*, A_{far})$

Fan, Ma and Xie proposed the following theorem [7].

Now we propose another fuzzy entropy induced by distance measure which is different from Fan, Ma and Xie's [7]. The proposed entropy needs only the A_{near} crisp set, and it has an advantage in computation of entropy.

Theorem 2.1. Let d be the σ -distance measure on $F(X)$; if d satisfies $d(A^C, B^C) = d(A, B)$, $A, B \in F(X)$, then

$$e(A) = 2d((A \cap A_{near}),[1]) + 2d((A \cup A_{near},[0]) - 2 \tag{3}$$

is a fuzzy entropy.

Proof. The proposed equation in (3) becomes the entropy for the fuzzy set A if it satisfies Definition 2.1. Hence, we start from $(E1)$. For $(E1)$, $\forall D \in P(X)$, $D_{near} = D$; therefore,

$$\begin{aligned} e(D) &= 2d((D \cap D_{near}),[1]) + 2d((D \cup D_{near}),[0]) - 2 \\ &= 2d(D,[1]) + 2d(D,[0]) - 2 = 0. \end{aligned} \tag{4}$$

$(E2)$ represents that crisp set $1/2$ has the maximum entropy 1. Therefore, the entropy $e([1/2])$ satisfies

$$\begin{aligned} e([1/2]) &= 2d(([1/2] \cap [1/2]_{near}),[1]) + 2d(([1/2] \cup [1/2]_{near}),[0]) - 2 \\ &= 2d(([1/2] \cap [1]),[1]) + 2d(([1/2] \cup [1]),[0]) - 2 \\ &= 2 \cdot 1/2 + 2 \cdot 1 - 2 = 1. \end{aligned}$$

In the above equation, $[1/2]_{near} = [1]$ is satisfied.

$(E3)$ shows that the entropy of the sharpened version of fuzzy set A, $e(A^*)$, is less than or equal to $e(A)$. For the proof, $A^*_{near} = A_{near}$ is also used:

$$\begin{aligned} e(A^*) &= 2d((A^* \cap A^*_{near}),[1]) + 2d((A^* \cup A^*_{near}),[0]) - 2 \\ &= 2d((A^* \cap A_{near}),[1]) + 2d((A^* \cup A_{near}),[0]) - 2 \\ &\leq 2d((A \cap A_{near}),[1]) + 2d((A \cup A_{near}),[0]) - 2 \\ &= e(A). \end{aligned}$$

The inequality in the above equation is satisfied because $d(A, A_{near}) \geq d(A^*, A_{near})$ in Proposition 2.1(i).

Finally, $(E4)$ is proved using the assumption $d(A^C, B^C) = d(A, B)$; hence we have

$$\begin{aligned} e(A) &= 2d((A \cap A_{near}),[1]) + 2d((A \cup A_{near}),[0]) - 2 \\ &= 2d((A \cap A_{near}),[1]) + 2d((A \cup A_{near}),[0]) - 2 \\ &\le 2d((A^C \cup A^C_{near}),[0]) + 2d((A^C \cup A^C_{near}),[1]) - 2 \\ &= e(A^C). \end{aligned}$$

Theorem 2.1 uses only the A_{near} crisp set; hence, we can consider another entropy the considers only A_{far} , and it has a more compact form than Theorem 2.1.

Theorem 2.2. Let d be the σ -distance measure on $F(X)$; if d satisfies

$$d(A^C, B^C) = d(A, B),\ A, B \in F(X),$$

then

$$e(A) = 2d((A \cap A_{far}),[0]) + 2d((A \cup A_{far}),[1]) \tag{5}$$

is a fuzzy entropy.

Proof. In a similar way, we prove that (5) satisfies from $(E1)$ to $(E4)$ in reference [8].

The proposed entropies Theorem 2.1 and 2.2 have the advantage over Liu's that they do not need assumption (i) of Theorem 3.1 to prove (1) and (2). Furthermore, (1) and (2) use only one crisp set, A_{near} and A_{far} , respectively.

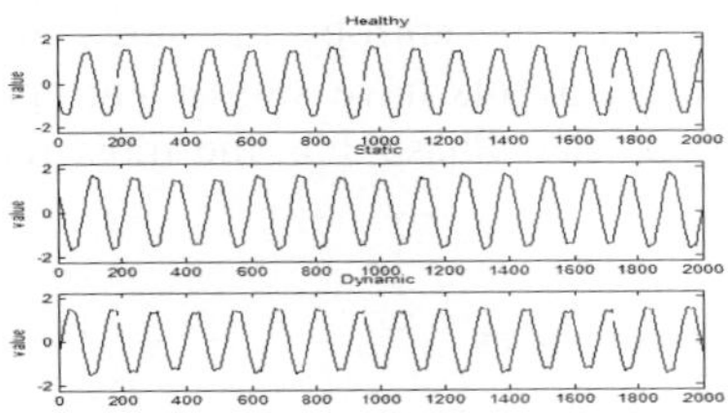

Fig. 1. Stator currents of healthy and family case

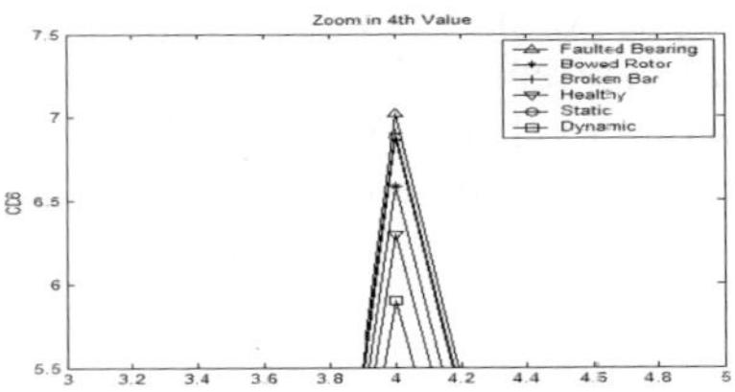

Fig. 2. 4th coefficient of the 6th detail

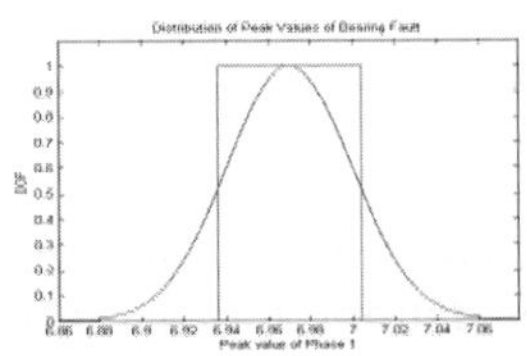

Fig. 3. Membership function of Phase-1 current

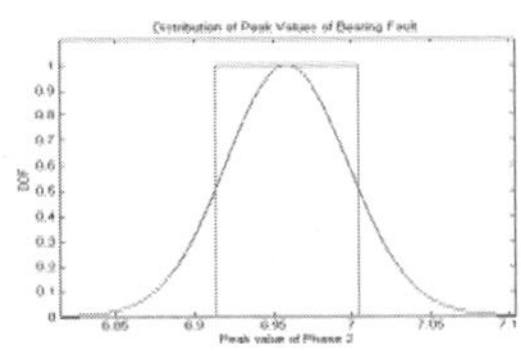

Fig. 4. Membership function of Phase-2 current

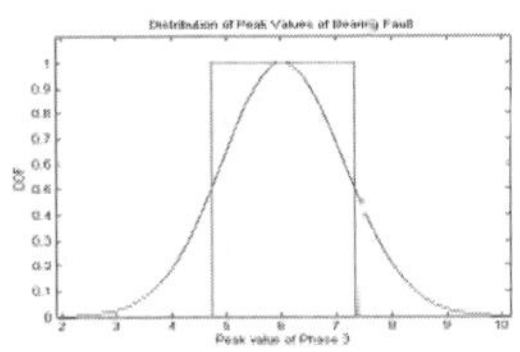

Fig. 5. Membership function of Phase-3 current

3 Illustrative Example

For the fault decision for the faulty motor 3-phase stator currents are given. The stator current is the only information that includes the characteristics of the faults that take place. Data from the induction machine, 220V, 3450 rpm, 4 poles, 24 bars, 0.5 HP motor, were used to verify the results experimentally. Six cases, bearing fault, bowed rotor, broken rotor bar, static eccentricity, dynamic eccentricity, and healthy conditions, are given. The one-phase current for the healthy and faulty signals under the full load are illustrated in Fig. 1. Input signals have 16,384 data points, respectively. The maximum frequency is 3 kHz, and data duration is 2.1333 s. As shown in Fig. 1, the differences of the various signals are not easy to discriminate. Hence, we proceed with Wavelet transformation to detect the characteristics of the 6 signals. Among the 12 details, the 4th coefficient of the 6th detail shown in Fig. 2 has good characteristics for discriminate various faults. To obtain the most reliable information from the 3-phase stator currents, now we have to investigate other phase currents. Proceeding with Wavelet transformation for the other two phase currents, we obtain 20 data for the 4th coefficient of the 6th detail, respectively. To measure the entropies of each phase, we need to construct membership functions. With the 20 data of each phase, we generate 50 data, which are the means of randomly chosen 10 data from the original 20 data, using the Bootstrap method. Then 50 data for Phase 1 from 6.0 to 7.1, 50 data for Phase 2 from 5.0~7.16, and 50 data for Phase 3 from 3.5~9.0 are obtained, respectively.

Now we construct a Gaussian distribution with the 50 data, respectively (by the Central Limit Theorem). After normalizing, we consider three Gaussian functions as membership functions for the 3-phase currents, which are illustrated in Fig.s 3, 4, and 5. For the computation of entropy, we assign the center rectangle to membership function. By Theorems 2.1 and 2.2, we apply fuzzy entropy as shown in Fig.s 3-5. With these membership functions, we can calculate the entropy measures of each phase current. Table 1 indicates that the 3-phase currents have similar entropies in Theorem 2.1 and Theorem 2.2. We can conclude that Phase 1 is the most reliable among the 3-phase currents.

Table 1. Entropies of three phases

	Phase 1	Phase 2	Phase 3
Theorem 2.1	0.62396	0.62504	0.62432
Theorem 2.2	0.62396	0.62504	0.62432

4 Conclusions

We investigated the relations of entropy, distance measure, and similarity measure. From the definition and results of Liu, we proposed a new entropy formula using distance measure. For the faulty induction motor current signals, Wavelet transform was carried out. Through the Wavelet transform, we found that the 4th value of the 6th detail resulting from the 12 scales of wavelet decomposition is useful in analyzing the features of fault signals. Also, the membership function of the 3-phase current signals was formulated using the Bootstrap method and the Central Limit Theorem. Furthermore, the proposed entropy computation was obtained for the faulty induction motor, and the values of the entropies were illustrated.

References

1. Bhandari, D., Pal, N. R.: Some New Information Measure of Fuzzy Sets. Inform. Sci. Vol. 67 (1993) 209-228
2. Ghosh, A.:Use of Fuzziness Measure in Layered Networks for Object Extraction: A Generalization. Fuzzy Sets and Systems Vol. 72 (1995) 331-348
3. Kosko, B.:Neural Networks and Fuzzy Systems. Prentice-Hall, Englewood Cliffs, NJ (1992)
4. Liu Xuecheng: Entropy, Distance Measure and Similarity Measure of Fuzzy Sets and Their Relations. Fuzzy Sets and Systems, Vol. 52 (1992) 305-318
5. Pal, N. R., Pal, S. K.:Object-background Segmentation Using New Definitions of Entropy. IEEE Proc. Vol. 36 (1989) 284-295
6. Fan, J. L., Xie, W. X.:Distance Measure and Induced Fuzzy Entropy. Fuzzy Set and Systems, Vol. 104 (1999) 305-314
7. Fan, J. L., Ma, Y. L., Xie, W. X.: On some properties of distance measures. Fuzzy Set and Systems, Vol. 117 (2001) 355-361
8. Lee, Sang-Hyuk., Kim, Youn-Tae., Cheon, Seong-Pyo., Kim, Sungshin: Reliable Data Selection with Fuzzy Entropy. Lecture Notes in Computer Science, Vol. 3613 (2005) 203 - 212
9. Vas, P.: Parameter Estimation, Condition Monitoring and Diagnosis of Electrical Machines. Clarendron Press, Oxford (1993)
10. Kliman, G. B., Stein, J.: Induction Motor Fault Detection via Passive Current Monitoring. International Conference in Electrical Machines, Cambridge, MA (1990) 13-17
11. Abbaszadeh, K., Milimonfared, J., Haji, M., Toliyat, H. A.: Broken Bar Detection In Induction Motor via Wavelet Transformation. IECON'01: The 27th Annual Conference of the IEEE Industrial Electronics Society, (2001) 95-99
12. Masoud Haji , Hamid, A., Toliyat: Patern Recognition-A Technique for Induction Machines Rotor Fault Detection Eccentricity and Broken Bar Fault. Conference Record of the 2001 IEEE Industry Applications Conference, Vol. 3 (2001) 1572-1578
13. Nandi, S., Toliyat, H. A.: Condition Monitoring and Fault Diagnosis of Electrical Machines A Review. IEEE Industry Applications Conference, Vol. 1 (1999) 197-204
14. Daubechies: Ten Lectures on Wavelets. The Society for Industrial and Applied Mathematics (1992)
15. Mallat, S.: A Wavelet tour of signal processing. Academic Press, CA (1999)
16. Martinez, W. L., Martinez, A.R.: Computational Statistics Handbook with MATLAB. Chapman & Hall/CRC (2002).
17. Development of fault detection algorithm using the stator current. Poscon (2003)

Motion Planning of Redundant Robots with Singularities Using Transputer Based Fuzzy Inverse Kinematic Method

Chih-Jer Lin[1] and Chieh-Li Chen[2]

[1] Department of Mechanical and Automation Engineering, Da-yeh University, 112 Shan-Jau Rd., Da-Tusen, Chang-Hwa,Taiwan, R.O.C.
cjlin414@mail.dyu.edu.tw

[2] Department of Aeronautics and Astronautics, National Cheng-Kung University, 1 University Rd., Tainan, Taiwan, R.O.C.
chiehli@mail.ncku.edu.tw

Abstract. The Fuzzy Inverse Kinematic Mapping Method (FIKM) is used to solve the inverse kinematics for the redundant robots with singularities. This method has some advantage due to the less computation load and robustness to the singularity. The method has also been implemented on a transputer-based parallel processing system to solve the motion planning problem of the redundant robots with singularity.

1 Introduction

The Robots have become increasingly important for industrial automation in recent years. Along with the development of robot arm control theory, there has been increasing demand for more efficient control schemes. Inverse kinematic computation, which maps the Cartesian space specification to the joint space, is usually the computational bottleneck in the robot path planning. On the other hand, it may not have an exact solution and thus a numerical method is required. This problem becomes more complicated when the robot manipulator has redundant degrees of freedom to perform some optimization specification, and the computational load may induce difficulties in real time application of redundant robots. For this reasons, the transputer based parallel processing is applied to deal this problem.

Redundancies in mechanisms have historically been solved through Moore-Penrose pseudo-inverse kinematic method (PIKM), also called the generalized inverse method. This method is first used in the robot control by Whitney in [1]. Let $\underline{\dot{x}}$ be the m-dimensional velocity vector of the hand and $\underline{\dot{\theta}}$ be the n-dimensinal vector of joint angles.

$$\dot{x}_{m\times 1} = J_{m\times n}\dot{\theta}_{n\times 1} \tag{1}$$

D.-S. Huang, K. Li, and G.W. Irwin (Eds.): ICIC 2006, LNAI 4114, pp. 140 – 145, 2006.

$$\text{Then } \dot{\theta} = J^{+}\dot{x} + (I - J^{+}J)z \tag{2}$$

$$\text{where } J^{+} = J^{T}(JJ^{T})^{-1} \tag{3}$$

Since the system is redundant, therefore, n>m .

But the pseudo inverse cannot be used when the J^{+} is singular, that is, the robot pass through a singular position. In the singular cases, the inverse matrix of JJ^{T} can not be obtained; the other methods like the solution together with homogeneous solution or singular decomposition methods should be used to solve this problem.[2] However, the solution of $\underline{z}$ through some optimal problem is very complicated. Therefore, the fuzzy inverse kinematic method (FIKM) is used to solve the redundant inverse kinematics. This method is proposed first by Schacherbauer and Xu in 1993 [3] and it takes advantage of human intuition and experience to avoid exact inverse kinematic mapping; however, they did not discuss the singular problems. In this paper, this method is further studied and modified for the motion planning of redundant robots with singular problems.

2 Problem Formulation

The fussy logic method for the inverse kinematic problem can work with a simple rule-base. The concept of this rule-base can be illustrated by the following example. Considering a planar robot with one link, the end-effector position can be described as

$$\begin{aligned} x &= l \cos \theta \\ y &= l \sin \theta \end{aligned} \tag{4}$$

Linearization around a given joint angle θ yields the following forward kinematic equations:

$$\begin{aligned} dx &= c_x\, d\theta \\ dy &= c_y\, d\theta \end{aligned} \quad \text{or} \quad \begin{aligned} \dot{x} &= c_x\, \dot{\theta} \\ \dot{y} &= c_y\, \dot{\theta} \end{aligned} \text{, where } \begin{aligned} c_x &= -l \sin\theta \\ c_y &= \ \ l \cos\theta \end{aligned} \tag{5}$$

Intuitively, a simple rule for the inverse kinematic may be formulated as

If dx **is PM and** c_x **is NL then** $d\theta$ **is NS.**

However, if an n-link serial robot is considered as composed of n links similar to the presented one, the rule-base can also apply to each of these links. Because the rule-base has been derived using a linearized model, the end-effector position change dx or dy can be the superposition of each results from each link. Let the coefficient c_{ij} be the element of the Jacobian matrix in the ith row and jth column as the following.

$$[dx_i]_{m\times 1} = \lfloor c_{ij} \rfloor_{m\times n} \cdot \lfloor d\theta_j \rfloor_{n\times 1} \tag{6}$$

The membership function c_{ij} and dx_i are defined in Fig. 1. The rule-table through homan ituitivity and experience is given in Table 1. Through the experiment we choose the fuzyy membership function of $d\theta_j$ as Fig. 2.

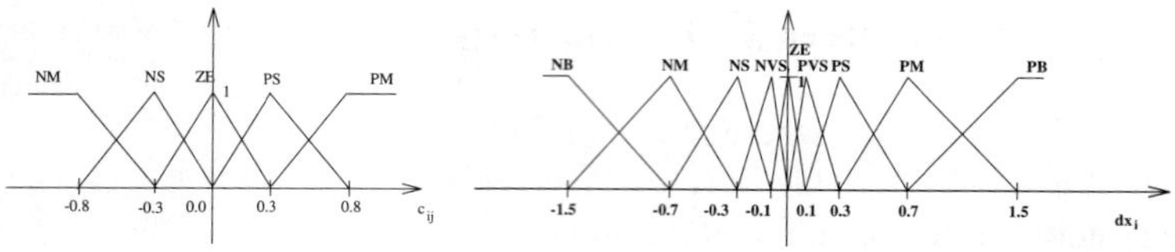

(a) (b)

Fig. 1. Membership functions for c_{ij} and dx_i

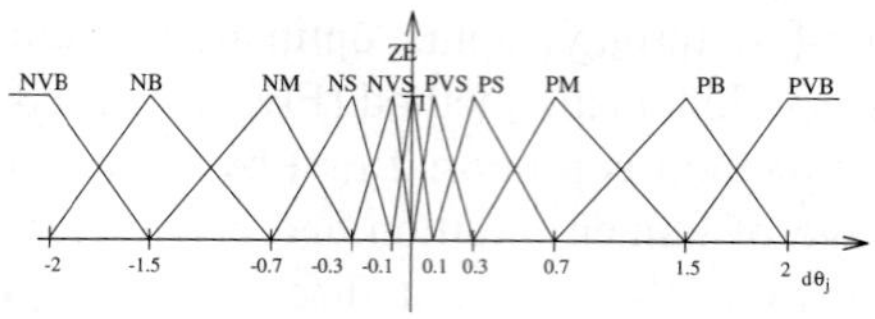

Fig. 2. Membership functions for $d\theta_j$

Table 1. The rule-base for fuzzy inverse kinematic mapping

c_{ij}	dx_i								
	NB	NM	NS	NVS	ZE	PVS	PS	PM	PB
NM	PB	PM	PS	PVS	ZE	NVS	NS	NM	NB
NS	PVB	PB	PM	PS	ZE	NS	NM	NB	NVB
ZE					ZE				
PS	NVB	NB	NM	NS	ZE	PS	PM	PB	PVB
PM	NB	NM	NS	NVS	ZE	PVS	PS	PM	PB

2.1 Determination of $d\theta_j$

Now we discuss in detail how to weight the fuzzy mapping result $d\theta_j$ to the obtained $d\theta_j$ through column and row weighting . Using the fuzzy mapping for each combination of dx_i and c_{ij}, we can determine $d\theta_j$,denoted $d\theta_{ij}{}^{+}$:

$$d\theta_{ij}{}^{+} = \mathrm{FM}(c_{ij}, dx_i) \tag{7}$$

where FM stands for the fuzzy mapping using the membership functions defined in Figs. 2, and 3 and the rule-base of Table 1. Since the application of each $d\theta_{ij}^{+}$ yields dx_i approximately, that is,

$$c_{ij}\, d\theta_{ij}^{+} \approx dx_i \tag{8}$$

The contributions of each $d\theta_{ij}^{+}$ to dx_i should be weighted by some factor, such that the sum of the contributions is close to dx_i:

$$\sum_{j=1}^{n} a_{ij} c_{ij} d\theta_{ij}^{+} \approx dx_i \quad , where\ a_{ij} = \frac{|c_{ij}|}{\sum_{j=1\cdots n} |c_{ij}|} \tag{9}$$

The effective joint angle change after row weighting is accordingly to

$$d\hat{\theta}_{ij} = a_{ij} \cdot d\theta_{ij}^{+} \tag{10}$$

For the jth joint of the robot, there are m $d\hat{\theta}_{ij}$ obtained. These values should be summed to the final solution $d\theta_j$ with column weights b_{ij}.

$$d\theta_j = \sum_{i=1}^{m} b_{ij} \cdot d\hat{\theta}_{ij} \text{ , where } b_{ij} = \frac{|c_{ij}|}{\sum_{i=1\cdots m} |c_{ij}|} \tag{11}$$

The weights b_{ij} are chosen under the following assumption: starting from a particular $d\theta_j$ and considering $d\theta_j + \delta$, the change in dx_i is the highest for the dx_i where the W_{ij} is the largest. To keep errors small, the averaged $d\theta_j$ should be closest to those $d\hat{\theta}_{ij}$ whose corresponding W_{ij} is large. To summarize the weighting scheme, we find that the results of the fuzzy mapping can be weighted through row-weighting and column-weighting to obtain the effective joint angle change $d\theta_j$.

3 Main Results

In order to implement the fuzzy mapping scheme onto the robot path planning, a planar robot with 3 d.o.f. is used to discuss the robustness of singularity for these two methods, PIKM and FIKM. On the other hand, a compromise between these two methods is proposed. The position of the end-effector (x,y) of the robot is derived as follows:

$$\begin{bmatrix} x \\ y \end{bmatrix} = \begin{bmatrix} l_1C_1 + l_2C_{12} + l_3C_{123} \\ l_1S_1 + l_2S_{12} + l_3S_{123} \end{bmatrix} \tag{12}$$

where $S_1 = \sin \theta_1$, $S_{12} = \sin(\theta_1+\theta_2)$, $S_{123} = \sin(\theta_1+\theta_2+\theta_3)$, $C_1 = \cos\theta_1$, $C_{12} = \cos(\theta_1+\theta_2)$, $C_{123} = \cos(\theta_1+\theta_2+\theta_3)$. Derive the equation (12), we obtain:

$$\begin{bmatrix} dx \\ dy \end{bmatrix} = \begin{bmatrix} -l_1S_1 - l_2S_{12} - l_3S_{123} & -l_2S_{12} - l_3S_{123} & -l_3S_{123} \\ l_1C_1 + l_2C_{12} + l_3C_{123} & l_2C_{12} + l_3C_{123} & l_3C_{123} \end{bmatrix} \begin{bmatrix} d\theta_1 \\ d\theta_2 \\ d\theta_3 \end{bmatrix} \tag{13}$$

Define $dx_1 = dx$, $dx_2 = dy$ and denote the element of Jacobian matrix as follows:

$$\begin{bmatrix} dx_1 \\ dx_2 \end{bmatrix} = J \cdot \begin{bmatrix} d\theta_1 \\ d\theta_2 \\ d\theta_3 \end{bmatrix} = \begin{bmatrix} c_{11} & c_{12} & c_{13} \\ c_{21} & c_{22} & c_{23} \end{bmatrix} \begin{bmatrix} d\theta_1 \\ d\theta_2 \\ d\theta_3 \end{bmatrix} \tag{14}$$

For the FIKM, apply the fuzzy mapping relation between dx_i and c_{ij} and use Fig.1-2 and Table 1 to obtain each $d\theta_{ij}^{+}$; then, each $d\theta_j$ can be obtain through row and column weighting. However, the weighting method in Eq. should be modified when the robot is located at the singular positions, then the row weights should be all designed as zeros, that is, $a_{i1} = a_{i2} = a_{i3} = 0$ to avoid singular problems.

4 Case Study

In this section, first, the motion planning task with singularity is use to evaluate these two methods, PIKM and FIKM; second, FIKM is implemented by the transputer-based parallel processing and the efficiencies of parallel processes for four architectures will be discussed. Consider the 3R planar manipulator shown and the parameters of the redundant robot are described as the following: $l_1 = 5, l_2 = 5, l_3 = 1$. The singular task is designed as follows: the initial position of the robot is located near the singular position, that is, $\theta_1 = -0.001^o, \theta_2 = 0.001^o, \theta_3 = 0^o$; the middle position is not singular and the final position is singular, $\theta_1 = 180^o, \theta_2 = 0^o, \theta_3 = 0^o$. The motion planning results of PIKM and FIKM are described in Fig. 3.

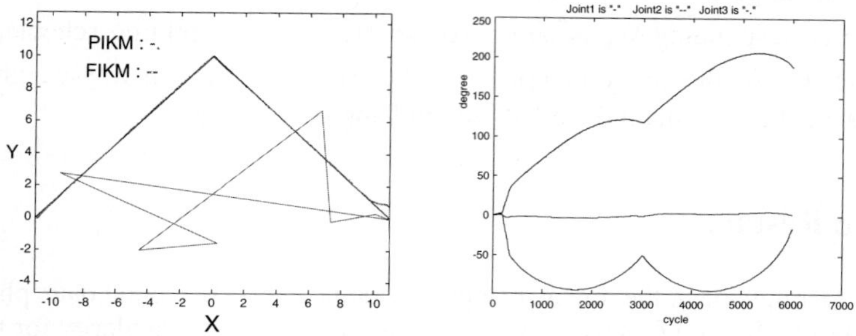

Fig. 3. The motion planning results for the task with singularity

Because the initial position is very near the singularity position, Jacobian matrix is singular so that the initial solution of PIKM will be divergent. However, the proposed FIKM can compute the solutions at the initial position because it uses the fuzzy mapping instead of obtaining the inverse matrix; the resulting data shows that FIKM is more robust than PIKM for singularities. Fig. 3 shows the resulting angular positions by the proposed method and the inverse kinematics solutions by the FIKM are very smooth and singularity robust.

The parallel processing architectures and Occam language are used to realize the FIKM using transputers. The four architectures are applied to compare the computing efficiency of parallel processing and Fig. 4 describes the scheme and computation time. The proposed approaches are implemented by three ***procedures*** as follows.

inout( ) : This procedure handles the communication between the transputer network and the personal computer. ***xwork***( ): It receives the data c_{1j} and dx_1 from the procedure ***inout*** and processes the fuzzy mapping of the X-axis, ***ywork( )***: It does the same work like the procedure ***xwork***, but computes the fuzzy mapping of the Y-axis. The first architecture uses only one transputer to deal with the motion planning task of FIKM and it spends 18 seconds for 3000 cycles. To improve the computing efficiency, Architecture 2 uses parallel processing of two transputers; however, the efficiency is not good because the work loads are not be balanced among the processors. The work loads of the procedures ***xwork*** and ***ywork*** are almost the same and the work load of procedure ***inout*** is less than the former. Therefore, Architecture

3 puts the procedures ***inout*** and ***xwork*** at the same transputer and the procedure ***ywork*** at the other, and then the efficiency is better than the one of Architecture 2. At last, Architecture 4 uses three transputer to perform the parallel processing and the processing time is almost 7 seconds; the lost time should be due to communication overhead. For maximum efficiency in a processor farm, every processor should do the same amount of work; that is, the work load should be evenly balanced among the processors and this can be validated by the former illustration.

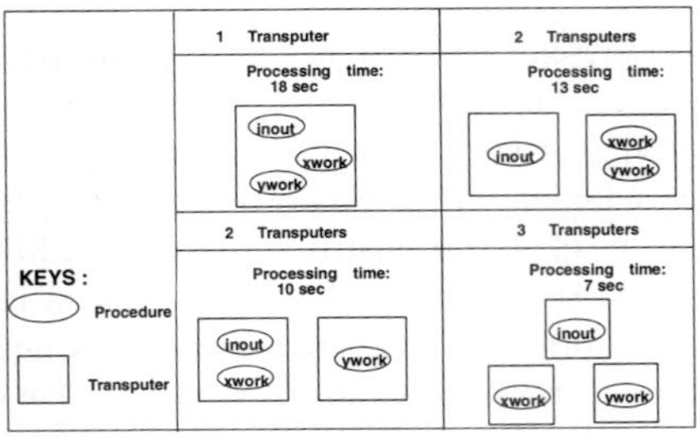

Fig. 4. The parallel processing scheme of the four architectures

5 Conclusion

In this study, a fuzzy inverse kinematic method based on transputer network is proposed to solve the motion problem of redundant manipulators with singularity. It has been shown that the pseudo-inverse kinematic method has some problems at the singular positions; however, the fuzzy inverse kinematic method has robustness to singularity. Further, the four parallel architectures are proposed and used to compare the different efficiencies due the load balanced problems. Results validate the approach.

References

1. Whitney, D. E.: Resolved Motion Rate Control of Manipulators and Human Prostheses. IEEE Trans.Man-Machine Syst. 10 (1969) 45-53
2. Maciejewski, A., Klein, Ch.: The Singular-value Decomposition: Computation and Application to Robots. Int. J. of Rob. Res. 8 (1989) 63-79
3. Schacherbauer, A., Xu, Y. S.: Fuzzy Inverse Kinematic Mapping for a Redundant Robot. Computers in Industry, 12 (1993) 159-168

Robust Passive Control for T-S Fuzzy Systems*

Yanjiang Li, Yanming Fu, and Guangren Duan

Center for Control Theory and Guidance Technology
Harbin Institute of Technology, P.O. Box 416, Harbin, 150001, P.R. China
liyanjiang@hit.edu.cn

Abstract. This paper presents a design method of robust passive controllers for continuous-time Takagi-Sugenon (T-S) fuzzy systems. The parametric uncertainty is assumed to be norm bounded. By applying the Lyapunov stability theory, a sufficient condition on the existence of robust passive controllers is given. With the help of linear matrix inequality (LMI), robust passive controllers are designed such that the closed-loop system is robust stable and satisfies the passive performance. Furthermore, a convex optimization problem with LMI constraints is formulated to design robust passive controller with the maximum dissipation rate. A numerical example demonstrates the validity of this method.

Keywords: T-S fuzzy systems, robust control, passive performance, linear matrix inequalities.

1 Introduction

Most physical systems in real world are characterized by nonlinear differential equations, the stability analysis and stabilizing controller design of nonlinear systems are very important. A typical approach for the analysis and synthesis of nonlinear control systems is to take advantage of local linearization. Takagi-Sugeno (T-S) fuzzy systems can provide an effective representation of complex nonlinear systems in terms of fuzzy sets, described by a set of IF-THEN rules, which can locally represent linear input-output relations of nonlinear systems [1]. It has been proved that T-S fuzzy system can approach any continuous functions in R^n at any precision [2, 3]. There has been an increasing interest in fuzzy control in recent years, yet there have been a lot of useful results on fuzzy systems, mainly focus on stability analysis and controller design [1, 4, 5, 6, 7, 8].

One of the most fundamental results of the stability of feedback systems is the theory of dissipative system. It has played an important role in the system analysis and synthesis. It is well known that dissipativeness is very important in systems, circuit, network and control engineering and theory. The notion of dissipativeness was first introduced in the stability analysis for dynamical systems by Willems [9, 10]. On the other hand, passive theory plays an important role in dissipation theory. There are many important results have been done [11, 12].

In this paper, passive control of uncertain T-S fuzzy systems is investigated. By analyzing Lyapunov stability, a sufficient condition on the existence of robust passive

* This work was supported by Program for Changjiang Scholars and Innovative Research Team in University.

D.-S. Huang, K. Li, and G.W. Irwin (Eds.): ICIC 2006, LNAI 4114, pp. 146 – 151, 2006.

controllers is derived. Robust passive controllers are designed in terms of linear matrix inequalities.

2 Problem Description

Consider the uncertain T-S fuzzy system in which the i th rule is formulated in the following form:

Plant Rule i :

IF $\theta_1(t)$ is N_{i1} and $\cdots$ and $\theta_p(t)$ is N_{ip}, then

$$\begin{cases} \dot{x}(t) = A_i(t)x(t) + B_i(t)u(t) + D_i(t)w(t) \\ z(t) = C_i(t)x(t) + B_{i1}(t)u(t) + D_{i1}(t)w(t) \\ x(t) = \phi(t), \quad t < 0, \ i = 1, 2, \cdots, r, \end{cases} \tag{1}$$

where N_{ij} is a fuzzy set, $x(t) \in R^n$ is the state, $z(t) \in R^q$ is the output, $u(t) \in R^m$ is the control, $w(t) \in R^q$ is the disturbance input which belongs to $L_2[0,\infty)$. r is the number of rules of this T-S fuzzy model. $\theta_1(t)$, $\theta_2(t)$, $\cdots$ $\theta_p(t)$ are the premise variables, let $\theta(t) = (\theta_1(t), \theta_2(t), \cdots \theta_p(t))$. It is assumed that the premise variables do not depend on the input $u(t)$ and the disturbance $w(t)$. $\phi(t)$ is the initial condition of the system. $A_i(t)$, $B_i(t)$, $D_i(t)$, $C_i(t)$, $B_{i1}(t)$, and $D_{i1}(t)$ are uncertain time-variant system matrices with appropriate dimensions which can be described as follow: $A_i(t) = A_i + \Delta A_i(t)$, $B_i(t) = B_i + \Delta B_i(t)$, $D_i(t) = D_i + \Delta D_i(t)$, $C_i(t) = C_i + \Delta C_i(t)$, $B_{i1}(t) = B_{i1} + \Delta B_{i1}(t)$, $D_{i1}(t) = D_{i1} + \Delta D_{i1}(t)$, where A_i , B_i , D_i , C_i , B_{i1} and D_{i1} are constant real matrices with appropriate dimensions, and uncertain matrices satisfy

$$\begin{bmatrix} \Delta A_i(t) & \Delta B_i(t) & \Delta D_i(t) \\ \Delta C_i(t) & \Delta B_{i1}(t) & \Delta D_{i1}(t) \end{bmatrix} = \begin{bmatrix} M_{i1} \\ M_{i2} \end{bmatrix} F_i(t) \begin{bmatrix} N_{i1} & N_{i2} & N_{i3} \end{bmatrix} . \tag{2}$$

where M_{ij} and N_{ik} $(j = 1, 2; k = 1, 2, 3)$ are known constant real matrices that represent the structure of uncertainties, and $F_i(t)$ is an unknown matrix function with Lebesgue measurable elements and satisfies $F_i^T(t)F_i(t) \le I$.

Then the state equation and the output are defined as follows:

$$\begin{cases} \dot{x}(t) = \sum_{i=1}^{r} h_i(\theta(t))(A_i(t)x(t) + B_i(t)u(t) + D_i(t)w(t)) \\ z(t) = \sum_{i=1}^{r} h_i(\theta(t))(C_i(t)x(t) + B_{i1}(t)u(t) + D_{i1}(t)w(t)), \end{cases} \tag{3}$$

where $h_i(\theta(t)) = \frac{\mu_i(\theta(t))}{\sum_{i=1}^{r} \mu_i(\theta(t))}$, $\mu_i(\theta(t)) = \prod_{j=1}^{p} N_{ij}(\theta_j(t))$, in which $N_{ij}(\theta_j(t))$ is the degree of the membership of $\theta_j(t)$ in N_{ij}.

In this paper, we assume that: $\mu_i(\theta(t)) \ge 0$, $\sum_{i=1}^{r} \mu_i(\theta(t)) > 0$, $i = 1, 2, \cdots, r$, for all t . It is clear that $h_i(\theta(t)) \ge 0$, $\sum_{i=1}^{r} h_i(\theta(t)) = 1$, $i = 1, 2, \cdots, r$.

Next, a fuzzy model of a state-feedback controller for the T-S fuzzy model is formulated as follows:

Controller Rule i :

IF $\theta_1(t)$ is N_{i1} and $\cdots$ and $\theta_p(t)$ is N_{ip}, then

$$u(t) = K_i x(t), \quad i = 1, 2, \cdots, r. \tag{4}$$

Hence, the overall fuzzy control law is represented by

$$u(t) = \sum_{i=1}^{r} h_i(\theta(t)) K_i x(t) , \tag{5}$$

where $K_i \in R^{m\times n}, i = 1, 2, \cdots, r$, are constant control gains to be determined.

With the control law (5), the overall closed-loop system can be written as

$$\begin{cases} \dot{x}(t) = \sum_{i=1}^{r}\sum_{j=1}^{r} h_i(\theta(t)) h_j(\theta(t))[(A_i(t) + B_i(t)K_j)x(t) + D_i(t)w(t)] \\ z(t) = \sum_{i=1}^{r}\sum_{j=1}^{r} h_i(\theta(t)) h_j(\theta(t))[(C_i(t) + B_{i1}(t)K_j)x(t) + D_{i1}(t)w(t)] \end{cases} . \tag{6}$$

Definition 1. The dynamic system (3) with $u(t) = 0$ is strictly robust passive and its dissipation rate is ε , if for any $T > 0$, $w(t) \in L_2[0,T]$, and all uncertainties, under zero initial state condition, there exists a scalar $\varepsilon > 0$ such that the following condition is satisfied:

$$\int_0^T w^T(t) z(t) dt \geq \int_0^T \varepsilon w^T(t) w(t) dt . \tag{7}$$

Problem 1. Consider the T-S fuzzy system (3), design state feedback control law (5) such that:

(1) When $w(t) = 0$, the closed-loop system (6) is robust stable;

(2) The closed-loop system (6) is strictly passive, its dissipation rate is ε .

3 Main Results

Theorem 1. Consider system (6), under zero initial state condition, if there exist matrices K_i, $1 \le i \le r$, and K_j, $1 \le i < j \le r$, and symmetric positive definite matrix P , such that the following matrix inequalities hold:

$$\begin{bmatrix} M(i,i) & PD_i(t) - (C_i(t) + B_{i1}(t)K_i)^T \\ * & -D_{i1} - D_{i1}^T + 2\varepsilon I \end{bmatrix} < 0 \;\; 1 \le i \le r , \tag{8}$$

$$\begin{bmatrix} M(i,j) + M(j,i) & \phi_1 \\ * & \phi_2 \end{bmatrix} < 0, \;\; 1 \le i < j \le r , \tag{9}$$

where $M(i,j) = PA_i(t) + A_i^T(t)P + PB_i(t)K_j + K_j^T B_i^T(t)P$, $\phi_2 = -D_{i1}(t) - D_{i1}^T(t) - D_{j1}(t) - D_{j1}^T(t) + 4\varepsilon I$, $\phi_1 = P(D_i(t) + D_j(t)) - [C_i(t) + C_j(t) + B_{i1}(t)K_j + B_{j1}(t)K_i]^T$, then the proposed problem is solvable.

Proof: Consider the following positive definite function as a Lyapunov function of the system (6)

$$V(x(t),t) = x^T(t)Px(t)\ , \tag{10}$$

where P is positive definite matrix. In the following, we let $h_i = h_i(\theta(t))$, $h_j = h_j(\theta(t))$.

Differentiate (10), we can obtain

$$\begin{aligned}\dot V(x(t),t) &= \sum_{i=1}^{r}\sum_{j=1}^{r} h_i h_j \{x^T(t)[PA_i(t) + A_i^T(t)P + PB_i(t)K_j + K_j^T B_i(t)P]x(t) \\ &+ \sum_{i=1}^{r}\sum_{j=1}^{r} h_i h_j [x^T(t)PD_i(t)w(t) + w^T(t)D_i^T(t)Px(t)]\}\end{aligned}\ . \tag{11}$$

From (11), we can get

$$\dot V(x(t),t) \le \sum_{i=1}^{r}\sum_{j=1}^{r} h_i h_j \left\{\begin{bmatrix} x(t) \\ w(t)\end{bmatrix}^T \begin{bmatrix} M(i,j) & PD_i(t) \\ * & 0\end{bmatrix}\begin{bmatrix} x(t) \\ w(t)\end{bmatrix}\right\}, \tag{12}$$

it follows from (13) that

$$\begin{aligned}\dot V(x(t),t) \le \sum_{i=1}^{r} h_i^2 &\left\{\begin{bmatrix} x(t) \\ w(t)\end{bmatrix}^T \begin{bmatrix} M(i,i) & PD_i(t) \\ * & 0\end{bmatrix}\begin{bmatrix} x(t) \\ w(t)\end{bmatrix} + \right. \\ \sum_{i=1}^{r}\sum_{i<j}^{r} h_i h_j &\left.\begin{bmatrix} x(t) \\ w(t)\end{bmatrix}^T \begin{bmatrix} M(i,j)+M(j,i) & P(D_i(t)+D_j(t)) \\ * & 0\end{bmatrix}\begin{bmatrix} x(t) \\ w(t)\end{bmatrix}\right\}.\end{aligned} \tag{13}$$

When $w(t) = 0,$, it is easy to obtain from (8), (9) and (13) that $\dot V(x(t),t) < 0$ thus system (6) is robust stable under the control law (5).

On the other hand, consider the following cost function of system (6)

$$J = \int_0^T \{-2[w^T(t)z(t) - \varepsilon w^T(t)w(t)]\}dt\ . \tag{14}$$

Under zero initial condition, it follows from (11) and (14) that $J = \int_0^T \{-2[w^T(t)z(t) - \varepsilon w^T(t)w(t)] + \dot V(t)\}dt - V(x(T)) \le \int_0^T \{-2[w^T(t)z(t) - \varepsilon w^T(t)w(t)] + \dot V(t)\}dt$.

Let $J_r = \int_0^T \{-2[w^T(t)z(t) - \varepsilon w^T(t)w(t)] + \dot V(t)\}dt$. From (8) and (9), we can obtain

$$\begin{aligned}J_r = \int_0^T &\left\{\sum_{i=1}^{r} h_i^2 \left(\begin{bmatrix} x(t) \\ w(t)\end{bmatrix}^T \begin{bmatrix} M(i,i) & PD_i(t) - (C_i(t) + B_{i1}(t)K_i)^T \\ * & -D_{i1} - D_{i1}^T + 2\varepsilon I\end{bmatrix}\begin{bmatrix} x(t) \\ w(t)\end{bmatrix}\right)\right. \\ &\left. + \sum_{i=1}^{r}\sum_{i<j}^{r} h_i h_j \left(\begin{bmatrix} x(t) \\ w(t)\end{bmatrix}^T \begin{bmatrix} M(i,j)+M(j,i) & \phi_1 \\ * & \phi_2\end{bmatrix}\begin{bmatrix} x(t) \\ w(t)\end{bmatrix}\right)\right\}dt < 0,\end{aligned}$$

then (7) holds for all $T > 0$, namely, the closed-loop system (6) is strictly robust passive.

Based on the well-known Schur complement formula and Theorem 1, design problem of robust passive controller is turned into the following feasible problem of linear matrix inequalities.

Theorem 2. Under zero initial state condition, the closed-loop system (6) is robust stable and strictly robust passive if there exist matrices Y_i, $1 \le i \le r$, and Y_j, $1 \le i < j \le r$, symmetric positive definite matrix X, and some scalars $\delta_i > 0,\ 1 \le i \le r,\ \alpha_{ij} > 0,\ \gamma_{ij} > 0,$ $1 \le i < j \le r$, satisfying the following linear matrix inequalities:

$$\begin{bmatrix} \Psi_i & D_i - (C_i X + B_{i1} Y_i)^T & \delta_i M_{i1} & (N_{i1} X + N_{i2} Y_i)^T \\ * & -D_{i1} - D_{i1}^T + 2\varepsilon I & -\delta_i M_{i2} & N_{i3}^T \\ * & * & -\delta_i I & 0 \\ * & * & * & -\delta_i I \end{bmatrix} < 0,\ 1 \le i \le r, \tag{15}$$

$$\begin{bmatrix} \psi_{ij} & \varphi_1 & \alpha_{ij} M_{i1} & \varphi_3 & \gamma_{ij} M_{j1} & \varphi_4 \\ * & \varphi_2 & -\alpha_{ij} M_{i2} & N_{i3}^T & -\gamma_{ij} M_{j2} & N_{j3}^T \\ * & * & -\alpha_{ij} I & 0 & 0 & 0 \\ * & * & * & -\alpha_{ij} I & 0 & 0 \\ * & * & * & * & -\gamma_{ij} I & 0 \\ * & * & * & * & * & -\gamma_{ij} I \end{bmatrix} < 0,\ 1 \le i < j \le r, \tag{16}$$

where $\varphi_1 = (D_i + D_j) - [C_i X + C_j X + B_{i1} Y_j + B_{j1} Y_i]^T$, $\varphi_4 = (N_{j1} X + N_{j2} Y_i)^T$, $\varphi_3 = (N_{i1} X + N_{i2} Y_j)^T$, $\Psi_{ij} = X^T A_i^T + Y_j^T B_i^T + A_i X + B_i Y_j + X^T A_j^T + Y_i^T B_j^T + A_j X + B_j Y_i$, $\Psi_i = X^T A_i^T + Y_i^T B_i^T + A_i X + B_i Y_i$, $\varphi_2 = -D_{i1} - D_{i1}^T - D_{j1} - D_{j1}^T + 4\varepsilon I$, in this case, the robust passive control law of system (1) is given as follows:

$$u(t) = \sum_{i=1}^{r} h_i(\theta(t)) Y_i X^{-1} x(t). \tag{17}$$

Proof: The proof is omitted for the limitation of length.

Remark 1. The solutions in Theorem 2 parameterize the set of robust passive controllers. The maximum of dissipation rate ε can be solved by solving following convex optimization problem: $\min\limits_{X, Y_i, Y_j, \delta_i, \alpha_{ij}, \gamma_{ij}, \varepsilon} \varepsilon$ s.t. LMI (15-16).

4 A Numerical Example

To illustrate the proposed results, consider a control system, the system matrices and other matrices are given below:

$$A_1 = \begin{bmatrix} -5 & 0 \\ 0 & 4 \end{bmatrix},\ A_2 = \begin{bmatrix} -2 & 0 \\ 0 & -6 \end{bmatrix},\ B_1 = \begin{bmatrix} 1 & 1 \\ 1 & 2 \end{bmatrix},\ D_1 = \begin{bmatrix} 0.2 & 0 \\ 0 & 0.2 \end{bmatrix},\ C_1 = \begin{bmatrix} 0.1 & 0 \\ 0 & 0.2 \end{bmatrix},\ B_{11} = \begin{bmatrix} 0.1 & 0.1 \\ 0.1 & 0.5 \end{bmatrix},$$

$$D_{11} = \begin{bmatrix} 2 & 0 \\ 0 & 1 \end{bmatrix},\ B_2 = \begin{bmatrix} 2 & 1 \\ 1 & 2 \end{bmatrix},\ D_2 = \begin{bmatrix} 0.3 & 0 \\ 0 & 0.3 \end{bmatrix},\ C_2 = \begin{bmatrix} 0.5 & 0 \\ 0 & 0.1 \end{bmatrix},\ B_{21} = \begin{bmatrix} 0.1 & 0.1 \\ 0.1 & 0.4 \end{bmatrix},\ D_{21} = \begin{bmatrix} 1 & 0 \\ 0 & 3 \end{bmatrix},$$

and the uncertainties are given as below:

$$M_{11} = M_{12} = \begin{bmatrix} 0.1 & 0 \\ 0 & 0.1 \end{bmatrix},\ M_{21} = M_{22} = 0,\ N_{11} = N_{13} = \begin{bmatrix} 1 & 0 \\ 0 & 1 \end{bmatrix},\ N_{12} = N_{21} = N_{22} = N_{23} = 0.$$

By the LMI Toolbox in MATLAB and Theorem 2, we can obtain the following state feedback gains matrices:

$$K_1 = \begin{bmatrix} -0.2104 & -3.2550 \\ 0.0768 & -1.6478 \end{bmatrix},\ K_2 = \begin{bmatrix} -4.7169 & 0.3045 \\ 0.1794 & -12.0566 \end{bmatrix}.$$

5 Conclusions

This paper studies the passive analysis and control synthesis of uncertain T-S fuzzy systems by LMI approach together with Lyapunov function method. The sufficient conditions on the existence of robust passive controller are given. The passive controller is designed in terms of LMI. A set of LMIs have been presented guaranteeing that a closed-loop system is stable with a passive performance. Furthermore, passive controller design problem is turned into a convex optimization problem with LMI constraints.

References

1. Chen, B., Liu, X. P.: Fuzzy Guaranteed Cost Control for Nonlinear Systems with Time-Varying Delay. IEEE Trans. on Fuzzy Systems, 13(2) (2005) 238-249
2. Feng, G., Cao, S. G., Rees N.W., Chak C. K.: Design of Fuzzy Control Systems with Guaranteed Stability. Fuzzy Sets systems, 85 (1997) 1–10
3. Cao, G. S., Rees N.W., Feng, G.: Analysis and Design for A Class of Complex Control Systems: Parts I and II. Automatica, 33(6) (1997) 1017–1028
4. Chen, B., Liu, X. P.: Fuzzy Guaranteed Cost Control for Nonlinear Systems with Time-Varying Delay. IEEE Trans. on Fuzzy Systems, 13(2) (2005) 238-249
5. Cao, Y. Y., Frank P. M.: Robust H_∞ Disturbance for A Class of Uncertain Discrete-Time Fuzzy Systems. IEEE Trans. on Fuzzy Systems, 8(4) (2000) 406-415
6. Chang, W. J., Sun, C. C.: Constrained Fuzzy Controller Design of Discrete Takagi-Sugeno Fuzzy Models. Fuzzy sets and systems, 133(1) (2003) 37-55
7. Lun, S. X., Zhang, H. G.: Fuzzy H_∞ Filter Design for A Class of Nonlinear Discrete-Time System with Time Delays. Proceedings of the 5th World Congress on Intelligent Control and Automation, (2004) 1588-1592
8. Zhang, Z., Wu, A. G., Fang, L. H.: Stability Analysis of T-S Fuzzy Systems. Proceedings of the 5th World Congress on Intelligent Control and Automation, (2004) 2579-2583
9. Willems J. C.: Dissipative Dynamical Systems, Part I: General Theory. Arch. Rational Mechanics and Analysis, 45 (1972) 321-351
10. Willems J. C.: Dissipative Dynamical Systems, Part II: Linear Systems with Quadratic Supply Rates. Arch. Rational Mechanics and Analysis, 45 (1972) 352-393
11. Abe N.: Passive and Active Switching Vibration Control with Pendulum Type Damper. Proceedings of the 2004 IEEE International Conference on Control Applications, 2 (2004) 1037-1042
12. Mahmoud M. S., Zribi M.: Passive Control Syntheses for Uncertain Systems with Multiple-State Delays. Computers and Electrical Engineering, 28 (2002) 195-216

Robust Stabilization of Takagi-Sugeno Fuzzy Systems with Parametric Uncertainties Using Fuzzy Region Concept*

Zhicheng Ji, Yinghuan Zhou, and Yanxia Shen

Control Science and Engineering Research Center, Southern Yangtze University, Jiangsu Wuxi 214122, China
zhouyinghuan@163.com

Abstract. A robust controller design method based on the concept of fuzzy region is presented for Takagi-Sugeno (T-S) fuzzy systems with parametric uncertainties. The uncertain T-S fuzzy model is converted into uncertain T-S fuzzy region model. A relaxed sufficient condition is derived for robust stabilization by using Lyapunov function approach in the form of linear matrix inequalities (LMIs). Comparing with other similar conditions, the difficulty of solving LMIs is greatly reduced in this method. The efficiency of the method is illustrated through the simulation of a numerical uncertain fuzzy system.

1 Introduction

Stability analysis of Takagi-Sugeno (T-S) [1] fuzzy control systems has been considered extensively [2,3,4,5,7]. Most researchers have presented the quadratic Lyapunov function approaches to find a common positive definite matrix to satisfy the stability conditions for all subsystems. With the concept of parallel distributed compensation (PDC) [4], the common matrix can be derived by the linear matrix inequality (LMI) technique. However, this method may fail when increasing the controller rules, total number of LMIs and premise variables.

In order to find more relaxed stability conditions, some researchers made good use of the structural information in rule base and proposed the concept of fuzzy region to obtain relaxed stability conditions for a class of fuzzy systems [2,5]. And Sun et al. [6] proposed T-S fuzzy region model by using the concept of fuzzy region then the amount of LMIs can be reduced greatly.

On the other hand, the issue of robust fuzzy controller design for uncertain nonlinear systems has received considerable interest [7,8,9], for uncertainties are frequently the main factor of instability.

Motivated by the aforementioned concerns, this paper expands the T-S fuzzy region model [6] to uncertain T-S fuzzy region model with parametric uncertainties. PDC is employed to design the fuzzy controller and a relaxed sufficient robust stability condition is derived in LMI form.

* This work was supported by Jiangsu Province Hi-tech Plans(Projects) BG2005014.

D.-S. Huang, K. Li, and G.W. Irwin (Eds.): ICIC 2006, LNAI 4114, pp. 152–158, 2006.

This paper is organized as follows. The concepts of fuzzy region are introduced and the uncertain T-S fuzzy region model is derived in Section 2. The controller design method is presented in Section 3. Section 4 shows a numerical example. Finally a conclusion is given in Section 5.

2 Problem Formulation and Preliminaries

Sun et al. [6] proposed the concept of fuzzy region that any premise vector within each fuzzy region fires the same 2^n rules. And these same rules are called a fuzzy rule group. Only one region is fired at any instant. Hence, the common matrix only needs to satisfy the corresponding 2^n LMIs at any instant.

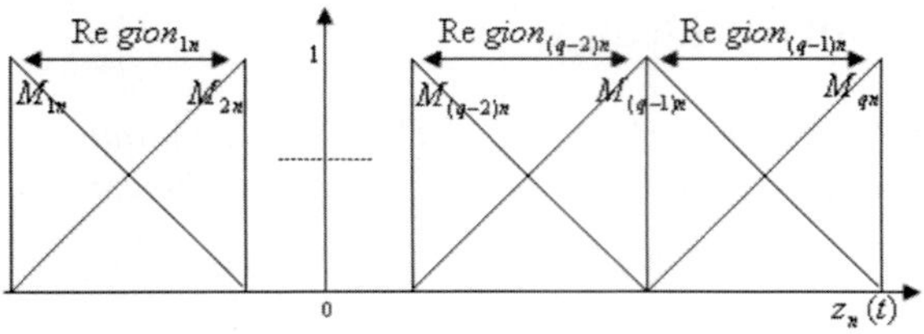

Fig. 1. Structure of the rule premise

Let r, G, f be the number of system rules, fuzzy regions and rules of each fuzzy group respectively, and g is the number of premise variables, q is the number of fuzzy sets of a variable. For general T-S fuzzy models, we have [4]:

$$r = q^g, G = (q-1)^g, f = 2^g \tag{1}$$

Here, we expand T-S fuzzy region model to uncertain T-S fuzzy region model and the uncertain T-S fuzzy system in [9] can be changed into:

$$RR^i\text{: If } z_1(t) \text{ is } Region_{i1} \text{ and } \dots \text{ and } z_n(t) \text{ is } Region_{in}$$

$$\text{Then } \dot{x}(t) = \textstyle\sum_{l=1}^{f} \alpha_l\{A^R_{l[i]}x(t) + B^R_{l[i]}u(t)\} + \sum_{l=1}^{f} \alpha_l\{\Delta A^R_{l[i]}x(t) + \Delta B^R_{l[i]}u(t)\}$$

According to [6], RR^i is the ith rule of region model; $\sum_{l=1}^{f} \alpha_l = 1$, and $\alpha_l = \alpha_l(z(t))$ corresponds to $w_i(z(t))$ of general T-S fuzzy model; $Region_{in}$ denotes the ith fuzzy region of $z_n(t)$, the membership function of fuzzy region is shown in Figure 1; $1 \le i \le G$; $(A^R_{l[i]}, B^R_{l[i]})$ denotes the lth subsystem of the ith fuzzy region, which are suitable values of (A_i, B_i) in [9]. The derivation of subscript l is based on the order of subscript of (A_i, B_i) in a fuzzy region. For example, if the ith fuzzy region contains (A_2, B_2), (A_5, B_5), the relevant matrices expression of fuzzy region model are $(A_{1[i]}, B_{1[i]})$, $(A_{2[i]}, B_{2[i]})$. The whole state output is:

$$\dot{x}(t) = \sum_{i=1}^{G} h^R_i(z(t)) \sum_{l=1}^{f} \alpha_l(A^R_{l[i]}x(t) + B^R_{l[i]}u(t) + \Delta A^R_{l[i]}x(t) + \Delta B^R_{l[i]}u(t)) \tag{2}$$

where $h_i^R(z(t)) = w_i^R(z(t))/\sum_{i=1}^G w_i^R(z(t))$, $w_i^R(z(t)) = \prod_{j=1}^n Region_{ij}(z_j(t))$, $Region_{ij}(z_j(t))$ is the grade of membership of $z_j(t)$ in fuzzy region $Region_{ij}$.

Assumption 1. The parametric uncertainties $(\Delta A_{l[i]}^R, \Delta B_{l[i]}^R)$ considered here are norm-bounded, in the form:

$$[\Delta A_{l[i]}^R, \Delta B_{l[i]}^R] = D_{l[i]}^R F_{l[i]}^R(t)[E_{1l[i]}^R, E_{2l[i]}^R]$$

where $D_{l[i]}^R$, $E_{1l[i]}^R$, $E_{2l[i]}^R$ are known real constant matrices of appropriate dimensions, and $F_{l[i]}^R(t)$ is an unknown matrix function with Lebesgue-measurable elements and satisfies $(F_{l[i]}^R(t))^T F_{l[i]}^R(t) \leq I$, in which I is the identity matrix of appropriate dimension.

3 Robust Control Design

Lemma 1. *[10] Given constant matrices D, E and a symmetric constant matrix S of appropriate dimensions, the following inequality holds:*

$$S + DFE + E^T F^T D^T < 0$$

where F satisfies $F^T F \leq I$, if only if for some $\varepsilon > 0$

$$S + [\varepsilon^{-1}E^T, \varepsilon D] \begin{bmatrix} R & 0 \\ 0 & I \end{bmatrix} \begin{bmatrix} \varepsilon^{-1}E \\ \varepsilon D^T \end{bmatrix} < 0$$

Design the fuzzy controller using the concept of fuzzy region too:

$$u(t) = \sum_{i=1}^{G} h_i^R(z(t)) K_{[i]}^R x(t) \tag{3}$$

For simplicity, we omit $z(t)$ in $h_i^R(z(t))$. By taking advantage of the property that $\sum_{i=1}^G \sum_{j=1}^G h_i^R h_j^R = \sum_{i=1}^G (h_i^R)^2 + 2\sum_{i<j}^G h_i^R h_j^R$ and $h_i^R h_j^R \equiv 0$ for T-S fuzzy region model when $i \neq j$ [6], subsisting (3) into (2), we get:

$$\dot{x}(t) = \sum_{i=1}^{G} (h_i^R)^2 \sum_{l=1}^{f} \alpha_l \{A_{l[i]}^R + \Delta A_{l[i]}^R + (B_{l[i]}^R + \Delta B_{l[i]}^R) K_{[i]}^R\} x(t) \tag{4}$$

Theorem 1. *If there exists a symmetric and positive definite matrix P, some matrices $K_{[i]}^R$ and positive scalar ε_{ii} such that the following LMIs are satisfied, then the continuous time T-S fuzzy region system (2) is asymptotically stabilizable via the T-S fuzzy region model based state feedback controller:*

$$\begin{bmatrix} \Phi_{ii} & (E_{1l[i]}^R Q + E_{2l[i]}^R M_{[i]}^R)^T & D_{l[i]}^R \\ E_{1l[i]}^R Q + E_{2l[i]}^R M_{[i]}^R & -\varepsilon_{ii} I & 0 \\ (D_{l[i]}^R)^T & 0 & -\varepsilon_{ii}^{-1} I \end{bmatrix} < 0$$

$$1 \leq i \leq G, 1 \leq l \leq f$$

where $\Phi_{ii} = Q(A^R_{l[i]})^T + A^R_{l[i]}Q + (M^R_{[i]})^T(B^R_{l[i]})^T + B^R_{l[i]}M^R_{[i]}$,
$Q = P^{-1}$, $M^R_{[i]} = K^R_{[i]}P^{-1}$.

Proof. Define Lyapuov function $V(x(t)) = x(t)^T Px(t)$
so the time derivative of $V(x(t))$ is

$$\begin{aligned}\dot{V}(x(t)) &= \dot{x}(t)^T Px(t) + x^T(t)P\dot{x}(t)\\ &= \sum_{i=1}^{G}(h_i^R)^2\sum_{l=1}^{f}\alpha_l x^T(t)\{[A^R_{l[i]} + \Delta A^R_{l[i]} + (B^R_{l[i]} + \Delta B^R_{l[i]})K^R_{[i]}]^T P\\ &\quad +P[A^R_{l[i]} + \Delta A^R_{l[i]} + (B^R_{l[i]} + \Delta B^R_{l[i]})K^R_{[i]}]\}x(t)\end{aligned}$$

Evidently, $\dot{V}(x(t)) < 0$ can be guaranteed by letting

$$(A^R_{l[i]} + \Delta A^R_{l[i]} + (B^R_{l[i]} + \Delta B^R_{l[i]})K^R_{[i]})^T P + P(A^R_{l[i]} + \Delta A^R_{l[i]} + (B^R_{l[i]} + \Delta B^R_{l[i]})K^R_{[i]}) < 0 \tag{5}$$

Applying Assumption 1 into (5), we can get:

$$\Gamma_{ii} + PD^R_{l[i]}F^R_{l[i]}(t)(E^R_{1l[i]} + E^R_{2l[i]}K^R_{[i]}) + (E^R_{1l[i]} + E^R_{2l[i]}K^R_{[i]})^T(F^R_{l[i]}(t))^T(D^R_{l[i]})^T P < 0 \tag{6}$$

$$\Gamma_{ii} = (A^R_{l[i]} + B^R_{l[i]}K^R_{[i]})^T P + P(A^R_{l[i]} + B^R_{l[i]}K^R_{[i]})$$

According to Lemma 1 and applying Schur complement, the matrix inequalities (6) holds for all $F^R_{l[i]}(t)$ satisfying $(F^R_{l[i]}(t))^T F^R_{l[i]}(t) \leq I$, if and only if there exists a constant $\varepsilon_{ii}^{1/2} > 0$ such that:

$$\begin{bmatrix} \Gamma_{ii} & (E^R_{1l[i]} + E^R_{2l[i]}K^R_{[i]})^T & PD^R_{l[i]} \\ E^R_{1l[i]} + E^R_{2l[i]}K^R_{[i]} & -\varepsilon_{ii}I & 0 \\ (D^R_{l[i]})^T P & 0 & -\varepsilon_{ii}^{-1}I \end{bmatrix} < 0 \tag{7}$$

The matrix inequality (7) is not an LMI and in order to use the convex optimization technique, define the following transformation matrix as $diag[P^{-1}, I, I]$ and take a congruence transformation to change QMI into LMI, we can get:

$$\begin{bmatrix} P^{-1}\Gamma_{ii}P^{-1} & (E^R_{1l[i]}P^{-1} + E^R_{2l[i]}K^R_{[i]}P^{-1})^T & D^R_{l[i]} \\ E^R_{1l[i]}P^{-1} + E^R_{2l[i]}K^R_{[i]}P^{-1} & -\varepsilon_{ii}I & 0 \\ (D^R_{l[i]})^T & 0 & -\varepsilon_{ii}^{-1}I \end{bmatrix} < 0$$

Letting $Q = P^{-1}$, $M^R_{[i]} = K^R_{[i]}P^{-1}$ results in Theorem 1. The proof is completed.

4 Example

In this section, to show the effectiveness of the proposed system controller design technique, we simulate the example used in [6] with parametric uncertainties.The structure of rules of this T-S fuzzy system is shown in Figure 2. $g = 2$, $q = 3$, $r = 9$, $G = 4$, $f = 4$. The system parameters are shown as follows:

$$A_1 = \begin{bmatrix} 0 & \sigma & 0 \\ \upsilon & -0.5 & -3.5 \\ 6 & -2 & \omega \end{bmatrix}, A_2 = \begin{bmatrix} 0 & \sigma & 0 \\ \upsilon & -0.5 & -3 \\ 6 & -2 & \omega \end{bmatrix}, A_3 = \begin{bmatrix} 0 & \sigma & 0 \\ \upsilon & -0.5 & -2.5 \\ 6 & -2 & \omega \end{bmatrix}$$

$$A_4 = \begin{bmatrix} 0 & \sigma & 0 \\ \upsilon & -0.5 & -3.5 \\ 7 & -2 & \omega \end{bmatrix}, A_5 = \begin{bmatrix} 0 & \sigma & 0 \\ \upsilon & -0.5 & -3 \\ 7 & -2 & \omega \end{bmatrix}, A_6 = \begin{bmatrix} 0 & \sigma & 0 \\ \upsilon & -0.5 & -3.5 \\ 7 & -2 & \omega \end{bmatrix}$$

$$A_7 = \begin{bmatrix} 0 & \sigma & 0 \\ \upsilon & -0.5 & -2.5 \\ 8 & -2 & \omega \end{bmatrix}, A_8 = \begin{bmatrix} 0 & \sigma & 0 \\ \upsilon & -0.5 & -3 \\ 8 & -2 & \omega \end{bmatrix}, A_9 = \begin{bmatrix} 0 & \sigma & 0 \\ \upsilon & -0.5 & -3.5 \\ 8 & -2 & \omega \end{bmatrix}$$

$B_1 = B_4 = B_7 = [0; 0; 0.6]^T$, $B_2 = B_5 = B_8 = [0; 0; 0.8]^T$, $B_3 = B_6 = B_9 = [0; 0; 1]^T$.The nominal values of $(\sigma, \upsilon, \omega)$ are $(1, 1, 5)$. We assume that all system parameters are uncertain but bounded within 30% of their nominal values.

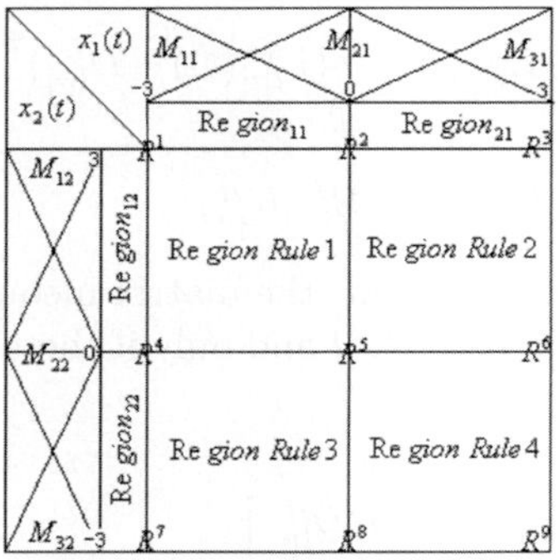

Fig. 2. The structure of premise rules

$i \backslash l$	$l=1$	$l=2$	$l=3$	$l=4$
$i=1$	(A_1, B_1)	(A_2, B_2)	(A_4, B_4)	(A_5, B_5)
$i=2$	(A_2, B_2)	(A_3, B_3)	(A_5, B_5)	(A_6, B_6)
$i=3$	(A_4, B_4)	(A_5, B_5)	(A_7, B_7)	(A_8, B_8)
$i=4$	(A_5, B_5)	(A_6, B_6)	(A_8, B_8)	(A_9, B_9)

Fig. 3. The relationships between matrices

According to the structure of the fuzzy system shown in Figure 2, we obtain the relationship between $(A^R_{l[i]}, B^R_{l[i]})$ and (A_i, B_i) in Figure 3. Based on Assumption 1, we define

$$D^R_{1[1]} = \cdots = D^R_{4[4]} = \begin{bmatrix} 0.3 & 0 & 0 \\ 0 & 0.3 & 0 \\ 0 & 0 & 0.3 \end{bmatrix}, E^R_{11[1]} = \cdots = E^R_{14[4]} = \begin{bmatrix} 0 & \sigma & 0 \\ \upsilon & 0 & 0 \\ 0 & 0 & \omega \end{bmatrix}$$

$$E^R_{21[1]} = \cdots = E^R_{24[4]} = \begin{bmatrix} 0 & 0 & 0 \end{bmatrix}^T$$

By applying Theorem 1 and solving the corresponding LMIs, we obtain the following controller matrices:

$$K^R_{[1]} = \begin{bmatrix} 120.3712 & 100.2569 & -77.9954 \end{bmatrix}, K^R_{[2]} = \begin{bmatrix} 82.7684 & 69.7524 & -55.0280 \end{bmatrix}$$
$$K^R_{[3]} = \begin{bmatrix} 110.0283 & 93.4613 & -74.3929 \end{bmatrix}, K^R_{[4]} = \begin{bmatrix} 84.8027 & 72.1239 & -56.7064 \end{bmatrix}$$

And the common positive definite matrix P to be

$$P = \begin{bmatrix} 9.4568 & 6.8961 & -4.3597 \\ 6.8961 & 5.2235 & -3.2199 \\ -4.3597 & -3.2199 & 2.4833 \end{bmatrix}$$

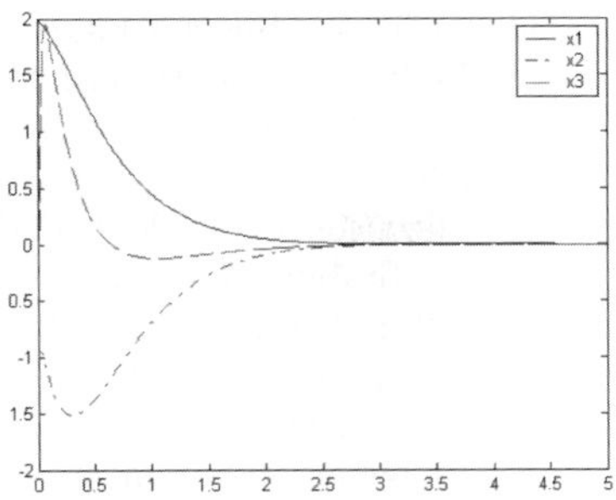

Fig. 4. Response with uncertainties

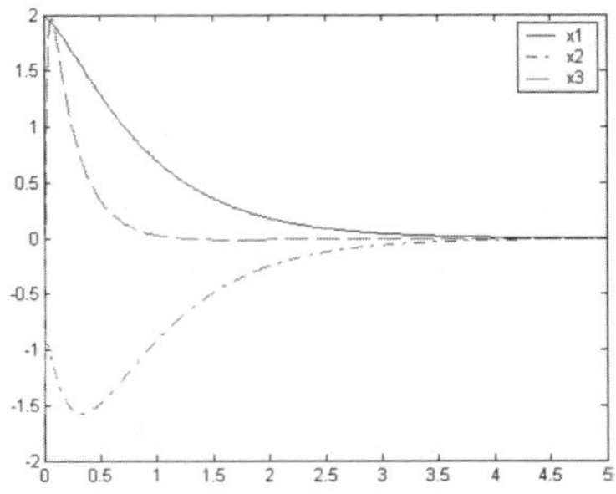

Fig. 5. Response without uncertainties

The system parameters are randomly varied within 30% of their nominal values. The initial values of states are $x(0) = [2; -1; -0.5\pi]^T$.

Figure 4 is the simulation result for the fuzzy T-S system when the system parameter σ changes from 1 to 1.3. Figure 5 shows the simulation result without parametric uncertainties. Two simulation results show that the T-S fuzzy region model based controller, designed by using Theorem 1, is robust against norm-bounded parametric uncertainties. Theorem 1 only needs to solve $G \times f = 16$ LMIs comparing to 29 in [9]. As shown in (1), we can easily find that $G \times f$ will be far smaller than the amount of LMIs to be solved in [9] as the pemise variable g becomes large. Therefor, the proposed condition has much less conservative.

5 Conclusion

This paper has proposed a novel robust controller design method based on fuzzy region concept of the fuzzy system with parametric uncertainties. A relaxed sufficient condition for robust stabilization is derived in the format of LMIs. And the amount of LMIs is reduced greatly. A numerical example of a uncertain fuzzy system demonstrates the advantage of the method.

References

1. Takagi, T., Sugeno, M.: Fuzzy Identification of Systems and Its Applications to Modeling and Control. IEEE Trans. Systems, Man and Cybernetics. **2** (1985) 116–132
2. Xiu, Z. H., Ren, G.: Stability Analysis and Systematic Design of Takagi-Sugeno Fuzzy Control Systems. Fuzzy Sets and Systems. **151** (2005) 119–138
3. Tanaka, K., Sugeno, M.: Stability Analysis and Design of Fuzzy Control System. Fuzzy Sets and Systems. **45** (1992) 135–156
4. Wang, H. O., Tanaka, K., Griffin, M.: An Approach to Fuzzy Control of Nonlinear Systems: Stability and Design Issues. IEEE Trans. Fuzzy Systems. **4** (1996) 14–23
5. Wang, W.-J., Sun, C.-H.: Relaxed Stability and Stabilization Conditions for a T-S Fuzzy Discrete System. Fuzzy Sets and Systems. **156** (2005) 208–225

6. Sun, C.-C., Chung, W.-J., Chang, W.-J.: Design of Takagi-Sugeno Fuzzy-region Controller Based on Fuzzy-region Concept, Rule Reduction and Robust Control Technique, in: Proceeding of the 2004 IEEE International Conference on Networking, Sensing & Control, Taipei, Taiwan, (2004) 914–919
7. Tanaka, T., Ikeda, T., Wang, H. O.: Robust Stabilization of a Class of Uncertain Nonlinear Systems via Fuzzy Control: Quadratic Stabilizability, H^∞ Control Theory, and Linear Matrix Inequalities. IEEE Trans. Fuzzy Systems **4** (1996) 1–13
8. Lo, J.-C., Lin, M.-L.: Robust H^∞ Nonlinear Modeling and Control via Uncertain Fuzzy Systems. Fuzzy Sets and Systems **143** (2004) 189–209
9. Lee, H. J., Park, J. B., Chen, G. R.: Robust Fuzzy Control of Nonlinear Systems with Parametric Uncertainties. IEEE Trans. Fuzzy Systems **9** (2001) 369–379
10. Xie, L.: Output Feedback H^∞ Control of Systems with Parameter Uncertainties. International Journal of Control **63** (1996) 741–750

Quantitative Measurement for Fuzzy System to Input and Rule Perturbations

Dong-Jun Yu[1], Xiao-Jun Wu[2], and Jing-Yu Yang[1]

[1] School of Computer Science and Technology, Nanjing University of Science and Technology, Nanjing, China, 210094
njyudongjun@yahoo.com.cn
[2] School of Computer Science and Technology, Jiangsu University of Science and Technology, Zhenjiang, China, 212003
wu_xiaojun@yahoo.com.cn

Abstract. In practice, input and rule perturbation are two important factors that will heavily influence the performance of fuzzy system. Quantitatively measure the influence of these two kinds of perturbation on the input/output mapping relationship of fuzzy system has great significance, theoretically and practically. In this paper, a statistical-based quantitative measurement for input and rule perturbation is proposed. By using the proposed approach, influence of perturbations on fuzzy system can be computed quantitatively, analytically and efficiently. Simulation results demonstrate the effectiveness of the proposed approach.

1 Introduction

Fuzzy systems have been successfully used in many fields [1][2], such as nonlinear system identification, pattern recognition, machine learning, etc. When applying fuzzy systems, two kinds of perturbation must be carefully considered, the one is *input perturbation* and the other is *rule perturbation*.

In real-life applications, the inputs of a fuzzy system are measured by physical device. Whatever the accuracy of the physical device has, the measurements are never 100% accurate, thus importing input perturbation. In addition, noise is also an important factor that causing input perturbation.

Fuzzy systems are generally implemented by hardware. More specifically, the parameters of fuzzy rules in a fuzzy system are stored in hardware. However, the hardware imprecision- the intrinsic characteristic of hardware- will definitely import rule perturbation [3].

Both input and rule perturbation will influence the performance of fuzzy system. Quantitatively analysis the influence of these two kinds of perturbation on fuzzy system has significant importance.

Statistical- and differential-based approaches are the two key frameworks for the quantitative perturbation analysis of neural, fuzzy and Neuro-Fuzzy systems [4] [5] [6] [7] [8] [9]. In our recent work, a statistical-based measurement for fuzzy system to

D.-S. Huang, K. Li, and G.W. Irwin (Eds.): ICIC 2006, LNAI 4114, pp. 159 – 164, 2006.

input perturbation is proposed. This paper focuses on both input and rule perturbation simultaneously. A statistical-based quantitative perturbation measurement and the corresponding analytical computation method for fuzzy system are presented.

2 Proposed Measurement

MISO (Multi-Input-Single-Output) fuzzy system is considered in this paper. A MISO fuzzy system can be expressed by a set of fuzzy IF-THEN rules [2]:

Rule l : if x_1 is A_1^l ...and x_n is A_n^l, then y is y^l

Let $\mathbf{x}=(x_1,x_2,\cdots,x_n)$ be the input vector, $\mu_{A_i^l}(x_i)$ be the membership function of fuzzy subset A_1^l, y^l be fuzzy singleton, The simplified fuzzy inference system [2] taking the following form is also universal approximator:

$$\hat{y}=f(\mathbf{x})=\sum_{j=1}^{M} y^l\theta_l(\mathbf{x}) \tag{1}$$

Where

$$\theta_l(\mathbf{x})=\prod_{i=1}^{n}\mu_{A_i^l}(x_i) \tag{2}$$

Suppose Guassian membership function is utilized, i.e.,

$$\mu_{A_i^l}(x_i)=\exp(x_i,m_i^l,\sigma_i^l) \tag{3}$$

For a trained fuzzy system, $\mathbf{m}$ and $\boldsymbol{\sigma}$ are determinate ($\mathbf{m}=(\mathbf{m}^1,\cdots,\mathbf{m}^l,\cdots,\mathbf{m}^M)$, $\mathbf{m}^l=(m_1^l,m_2^l,\cdots,m_n^l)$, $\boldsymbol{\sigma}=(\boldsymbol{\sigma}^1,\cdots,\boldsymbol{\sigma}^l,\cdots,\boldsymbol{\sigma}^M)$, $\boldsymbol{\sigma}^l=(\sigma_1^l,\sigma_2^l,\cdots,\sigma_n^l)$). It will be very convenient to compute the output deviation of the fuzzy system when $\mathbf{x}$, $\Delta\mathbf{x}$, $\Delta\mathbf{m}$ and $\Delta\boldsymbol{\sigma}$ ($\Delta\mathbf{m}=(\Delta\mathbf{m}^1,\cdots,\Delta\mathbf{m}^l,\cdots,\Delta\mathbf{m}^M)$, $\Delta\mathbf{m}^l=(\Delta m_1^l,\Delta m_2^l,\cdots,\Delta m_n^l)^T$, $\Delta\boldsymbol{\sigma}=(\Delta\boldsymbol{\sigma}^1,\cdots, \Delta\boldsymbol{\sigma}^l,\cdots,\Delta\boldsymbol{\sigma}^M)$, $\Delta\boldsymbol{\sigma}^l=(\Delta\sigma_1^l,\Delta\sigma_2^l,\cdots,\Delta\sigma_n^l)^T$) are known. However, it is meaningless and unnecessary to compute the output deviation for every possible $\mathbf{x}$, $\Delta\mathbf{x}$, $\Delta\mathbf{m}$ and $\Delta\boldsymbol{\sigma}$, more attention should be paid to finding a common relationship between the input and the output of the fuzzy system under input and rule perturbations. As stated in paper [6], one can treat $\mathbf{x}$ as random variable, and then when the expected rule perturbation ($E(\Delta\mathbf{m})$ and $E(\Delta\boldsymbol{\sigma})$) and the expected input perturbation ($E(\Delta\mathbf{x})$) are known, it will be possible to compute the expected output deviation of the fuzzy system, i.e.,

$$S^{out}=E(f(\mathbf{x}+E(\Delta\mathbf{x}),\mathbf{m}+E(\Delta\mathbf{m}),\boldsymbol{\sigma}+E(\Delta\boldsymbol{\sigma}))-f(\mathbf{x},\mathbf{m},\boldsymbol{\sigma})) \tag{4}$$

However, directly compute formula (4) is relatively complicated and difficult. We propose an approximated computation by defining the following two definitions.

Definition 1: Let M be the number of fuzzy rules, $\mathbf{x} = (x_1, x_2, \cdots, x_n)$ be the input vector, then the expected deviation of the inference node corresponding to the l-th $(1 \le l \le M)$ rule is:

$$s^l = E(\theta_l(\mathbf{x} + E(\Delta\mathbf{x}), \mathbf{m}^l + E(\Delta\mathbf{m}^l), \boldsymbol{\sigma}^l + E(\Delta\boldsymbol{\sigma}^l)) - \theta_l(\mathbf{x}, \mathbf{m}^l, \boldsymbol{\sigma}^l)) \tag{5}$$

Let $\mathbf{r} = (r^1, r^2, \cdots, r^M)^T$ represent the output vector of inference layer in a fuzzy system, which has M rules. r^l $(1 \le l \le M)$ be the output of the l-th inference node. Then formula (1) can be rewritten as

$$\hat{y} = f(\mathbf{x}) = g(\mathbf{r}) = \sum_{l=1}^{M} y^l r^l \tag{6}$$

Definition 2: The expected output deviation of a fuzzy system is defined as

$$\begin{aligned} S^{out} &= E(f(\mathbf{x} + E(\Delta\mathbf{x}), \mathbf{m} + E(\Delta\mathbf{m}), \boldsymbol{\sigma} + E(\Delta\boldsymbol{\sigma})) - f(\mathbf{x}, \mathbf{m}, \boldsymbol{\sigma})) \\ &\overset{def}{=} E(g(\mathbf{r} + E(\Delta\mathbf{r})) - g(\mathbf{r})) \end{aligned} \tag{7}$$

3 Analytical Computation

Let $\rho(\mathbf{x})$ be the density function of $\mathbf{x}$. Suppose $\mathbf{x}$ is uniformly distributed in space $[\gamma_1, \beta_1] \times [\gamma_2, \beta_2] \times \cdots \times [\gamma_n, \beta_n]$, we can obtain s^l defined in definition 1 as:

$$\begin{aligned} s^l &= (\sqrt{2\pi})^n \cdot (\prod_{i=1}^{n} \tfrac{1}{\beta_i - \gamma_i}) \cdot [\\ &\prod_{i=1}^{n} \{[\sigma_i^l + E(\Delta\sigma_i^l)] \cdot (\Phi(\frac{\beta_i - m_i^l - E(\Delta m_i^l) + E(\Delta x_i)}{\sigma_i^l + E(\Delta\sigma_i^l)}) - \Phi(\frac{\gamma_i - m_i^l - E(\Delta m_i^l) + E(\Delta x_i)}{\sigma_i^l + E(\Delta\sigma_i^l)}))\} \\ &- \prod_{i=1}^{n} \{\sigma_i^l \cdot (\Phi(\frac{\beta_i - m_i^l}{\sigma_i^l}) - \Phi(\frac{\gamma_i - m_i^l}{\sigma_i^l}))\}] \end{aligned} \tag{8}$$

According to definition 2, we have

$$S^{out} = E(g(\mathbf{r} + E(\Delta\mathbf{r})) - g(\mathbf{r})) \tag{9}$$

For the convenience of computation, suppose $\mathbf{r}$ uniformly distribute in space $(0,1]^M$. As $r^l \in (0,1]$, $1 \le l \le M$, thus $\rho(\mathbf{r}) = 1$. $E(\Delta\mathbf{r}) = S^r = (s^1, s^2, ..., s^M)^T$, we have

$$\begin{aligned} S^{out} &= E(g(\mathbf{r} + E(\Delta\mathbf{r})) - g(\mathbf{r})) = \int_0^1 \cdots \int_0^1 \rho(\mathbf{r}) \cdot [\sum_{l=1}^{M} y^l (r^l + s^l) - \sum_{j=1}^{M} y^l r^l] dr^1 \cdots dr^M \\ &= \int_0^1 \cdots \int_0^1 (\sum_{l=1}^{M} y^l s^l) dr^1 \cdots dr^M = \sum_{l=1}^{M} y^l s^l \end{aligned} \tag{10}$$

Note, here $\Phi(\cdot)$ is defined as:

$$\Phi(x) = \frac{1}{\sqrt{2\pi}} \int_{-\infty}^{x} e^{-\frac{t^2}{2}} dt, -\infty < x < +\infty \tag{11}$$

According to paper [10], $\Phi(x)$ can be approximated with high accuracy by the following polynomial:

$$\Phi(x) = \begin{cases} 1 - \phi(x)(a_1 k + a_2 k^2 + a_3 k^3) & x \ge 0 \\ 1 - \Phi(-x) & x < 0 \end{cases} \tag{12}$$

Where

$$\phi(x) = \frac{1}{\sqrt{2\pi}} e^{-\frac{x^2}{2}}, -\infty < x < +\infty . \tag{13}$$

4 Experimental Results

Numerical simulations are presented in this section to demonstrate the effectiveness of the proposed algorithm. In the simulation, a 3-input-1-output fuzzy system is utilized. Let $\mathbf{x} = (x_1, x_2, x_3) \in [0,5] \times [0,5] \times [0,5]$ be the input vector. Two fuzzy sets, N (Negative) and P (Positive), are defined on each input dimension. By using complete combination method, we obtain 2^3=8 rules. Rules and the corresponding parameters of the trained fuzzy system are listed in Table 1.

Table 1. Rules and the corresponding parameters of a trained fuzzy system

R	x_1	Parameters		x_2	Parameters		x_3	Parameters		y^l
		m	σ		m	σ		m	σ	
1	N	-0.103	2.341	N	-1.437	3.147	N	-0.532	3.308	3.234
2	N	-0.103	2.341	N	-1.437	3.147	P	6.013	2.103	6.381
3	N	-0.103	2.341	P	6.801	3.011	N	-0.532	3.308	-0.236
4	N	-0.103	2.341	P	6.801	3.011	P	6.013	2.103	-4.235
5	P	5.673	3.142	N	-1.437	3.147	N	-0.532	3.308	3.957
6	P	5.673	3.142	N	-1.437	3.147	P	6.013	2.103	2.346
7	P	5.673	3.142	P	6.801	3.011	N	-0.532	3.308	5.327
8	P	5.673	3.142	P	6.801	3.011	P	6.013	2.103	3.246

Simulation 1: In the first kind of simulation, we fix the input perturbation ($E(\Delta\mathbf{x})$), and range rule perturbation. More specifically, we set $E(\Delta\mathbf{m})$ ranging from –1 to 1 with a fixed step size of 0.2 and $E(\Delta\boldsymbol{\sigma})$) ranging from –2 to 2 with a fixed step size of 0.4, respectively. Then, for the given input perturbation and rule perturbation (e.g. $E(\Delta\mathbf{x}) = (0.2, 0.2, 0.2)$, $E(\Delta\mathbf{m}) = (0.5, 0.5, 0.5)$, $E(\Delta\boldsymbol{\sigma}) = (0.3, 0.3, 0.3)$), we first use the algorithm proposed in section 5 to compute the expected output

deviation of the fuzzy system as the *theoretical result*. *Simulation result* of the expected output deviation of the fuzzy system are obtained as follows: (1) Randomly select N inputs from space [0,5]×[0,5]×[0,5];(2) Compute real output deviation of fuzzy system for each of N inputs under the given input and rule perturbation;(3) Simulation result of the expected output deviation of the fuzzy system is the average of the N real output deviations. From now on, otherwise mentioned, N is set to be 20000. Results are shown in Fig.1.

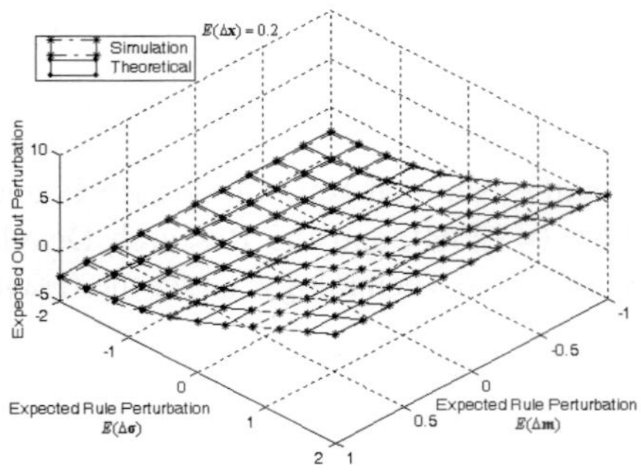

Fig. 1. Results of Simulation 1

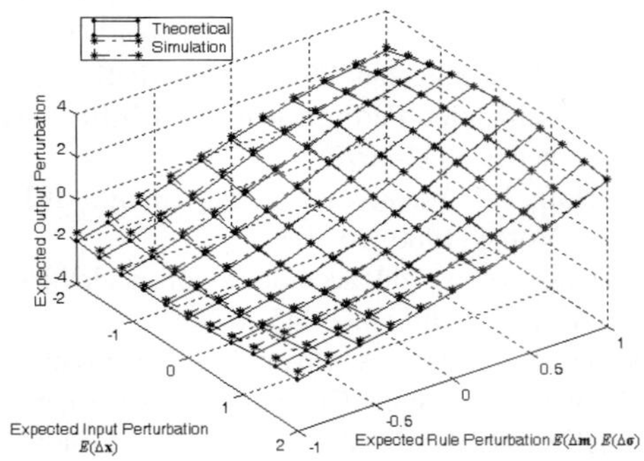

Fig. 2. Results of Simulation 2

Simulation 2: In this simulation, $E(\Delta\mathbf{m})$ and $E(\Delta\boldsymbol{\sigma})$) are set to be equal and ranging from –1 to 1 with a fixed step size of 0.2. Set $E(\Delta\mathbf{x})$ ranging from –2 to 2 with a fixed step size of 0.4. *Theoretical* and *Simulation results* are obtained as described in *Simulation 1*. Results are shown in Fig.2.

By observing experimental results from Fig.1 to Fig.2, it is easy to conclude that the theoretical results obtained by the proposed algorithm are well consistent with the simulation results, thus demonstrating the effectiveness and correctness of the proposed approach.

5 Conclusions

Input and rule perturbations are two import aspects when applying fuzzy systems. How to measure these perturbations quantitatively is very important. This paper presents a statistical-based quantitative measurement, which will do great help to the rapid performance evaluation, robust analysis and sensitivity analysis of fuzzy systems. Simulation results demonstrate the correctness and effectiveness of the proposed algorithm.

Acknowledgments

This work is supported byïthe National Natural Science Foundation of China, under the Grant No. 60572034&60472060, and the Research Development Foundation of Nanjing University of Science and Technology, under the Grant No. AB96125.

References

1. R. R. Yager and D. P. Filev: Essentials of Fuzzy Modeling and Control. New York: Wiley (1994)
2. Wang Shitong: Theory and application of fuzzy system theory, Shanghai Science and Technology Press, China (1997)
3. Wing W. Y, Ng Daniel S, Yeung Ian Cloete: Quantitative Study on Effect of Center Selection to RBFNN Classification Performance, 2004 IEEE International Conference on Systems, Man and Cybernetics 3692-3697
4. B.Widrow and M.E. Hoff, Jr.: Adaptive switching circuits, IRE Western Electric Show and Convention Record, Vol. 4 (1960) 96-104
5. Piche, S.W: The selection of weight accuracies for madalines. IEEE Transactions on Neural Networks, Vol.6, No. 2 (1995) 432-445
6. Xiao-Qin Zeng, Daniel S. Yeung: A Quantified Sensitivity Measure for Multilayer Perceptron to Input Perturbation, Neural Computation, Vol.15, No.1 (2003) 183-212
7. Xiao-Qin Zeng, Daniel S. Yeung: Sensitivity analysis of multilayer perceptron to input and weight perturbations. IEEE Transactions on Neural Networks, Vol.12, No. 6 (2001) 1358-1366
8. Kashif Rashid, Jaime A. Ramirez, and Ernest M. Freeman: A General Approach for Extracting Sensitivity Analysis from a Neuro-Fuzzy Model, IEEE Transaction on Magnetics, Vol. 36, No. 4 (2000):1066-1070
9. J.Y. Choi and C-H Choi: Sensitivity Analysis of Multilayer Perceptron with Differentiable Activation Functions, IEEE Trans. on Neural Networks, Vo1.3, N.o.1 (1992)101 - 107
10. John C.Hull, Options: Futures and Other Derivative Securities. 3rd edn. Prentice Hall Press (1998)

Modeling of Distributed Intrusion Detection Using Fuzzy System

Heesuk Seo[1], Taekyung Kim[2], and Hyungjong Kim[3]

[1] School of Internet Media Engineering, Korea University of Technology and Education, Chunanan, South Korea
histone@kut.ac.kr

[2] Department of Information Electronics, Seoil College, Seoul, South Korea
tkkim@seoil.ac.kr

[3] Korea Information Security Agency, Seoul, South Korea
hykim@kisa.or.kr

Abstract. Application of agent technology in Intrusion Detection Systems (IDSs) has been developed. Intrusion Detection (ID) agent technology can bring IDS flexibility and enhanced distributed detection capability. The security of the ID agent and methods of collaboration among ID agents are important problems noted by many researchers. This paper applies fuzzy logic to reduce the false positives that represent one of the core problems of IDS. ID is a complicated decision-making process, generally involving enormous factors regarding the monitored system. A fuzzy logic evaluation component, which represents a decision agent model of in distributed IDSs, considers various factors based on fuzzy logic when an intrusion behavior is analyzed. The performance obtained from the coordination of an ID agent with fuzzy logic is compared with the corresponding non-fuzzy type ID agent.

1 Introduction

IDSs have greatly evolved over the past few years [1]. Artificial intelligence can be applied to the field of ID research. Fuzzy rule-based inference can be understood from several viewpoints. Conceptually it can be understood using the metaphor of drawing a conclusion using a panel of experts. Mathematically, it can be viewed as an interpolation scheme. Formally, it is a generalization of a logic inference called mo-dus ponens. Dickerson proposed the development an IDS based on fuzzy logic, with a core technique of substituting fuzzy rules for ordinary rules so as to more accurately map knowledge represented in natural languages to that represented in computer languages. Christopher proposed to employ artificial intelligent methods in intrusion detection system in order to recognize the attackers' plans [3].

2 Intrusion Detection and Response

2.1 ID Using BBA

The BB hierarchy is set according to Joseph Barrus & Neil C. Rowe as shown in Figure. 1. They proposed Danger values to be divided into five different levels. These

D.-S. Huang, K. Li, and G.W. Irwin (Eds.): ICIC 2006, LNAI 4114, pp. 165 – 170, 2006.

five BB levels are Minimal, Cautionary, Noticeable, Serious and Catastrophic. The levels of the blackboard are divided by the threshold values. Threshold values are selected according to the following contents.

1) the policies of the network administrator and system security level : the administrator can enforce the system security configuration to protect the network system. In this case threshold values can be a little low.

2) network speed and configuration environment : threshold values can be varied ac-cording to the network speed and configuration environment. Namely threshold values of network, support the high speed network environment, can be a little higher than relatively low speed. And a case of having many internal processes in a local host is a little higher than many networking processes.

3) system performance (CPU, memory) : threshold values of system, have a fast CPU speed, can be a little higher than relatively low. A memory isn't different from a CPU.

4) operating system types : threshold values, OS enforce the security level, can be a little higher than those not.

5) attack types : threshold values can be varied according to the attack types.

A network attack is defined where hosts in an external network attack the host network. In this case the attacked hosts insert related intrusion information in the Network-Attack area of the blackboard. During a host attack, the blackboard level is transmitted to the Host-Attack area of the BB. When the BB state is at the Host-Attack level and any other host is attacked, the BB state changes to Network-Attack. The Minimal, Cautionary, Noticeable, Serious and Catastrophic levels of Network-Attack represent the case when multiple hosts are attacked. A host at the Cautionary level of the Host-Attack and host, which detects the beginning of an attack, transmits a Minimal level to a Cautionary. Then the whole network is at the Cautionary level of the Network-Attack area. The message transmission mechanism of the Network-Attack area on the BB is basically similar to that of the Host-Attack area. When the BB level is at a Noticeable level of the Network-Attack area in the composed simulation environment, then an attacker's packets coming from the attack point are blocked to protect the network. An attacker continuing the attack when the BB level is at the Serious level of the Network-Attack area, all packets coming from the external network are prevented from the damaging the host network.

This case is for the detection of attacks to a single host within the network presented. In this case the attacked host inserts intrusion related information to the Host-Attack area of the blackboard. Each agent must request permission by transmitting a BB_update_request message to the controller, in order to manage consistency and contention problems. The controller transmits an BB_update_permit message to the agent capable of handling the current problem. The agent receiving this message writes (BB_update_action) the intrusion related information to the BB. After updating is completed, the agent transmits the BB_update_completion message to the controller. Controller transmits a BB_broadcasting_of_action_request message for reporting this event to other IDSs. IDSs, receiving the necessary information from the BB, transmit the BB_information_acquisition_completion message to the controller. The BB levels are transmitted according to these steps. When the BB level is at the

Serious level, the agent adds the source IP address to the blacklist of the Firewall model using the network management policy, then all subsequent packets from these sources are blocked.

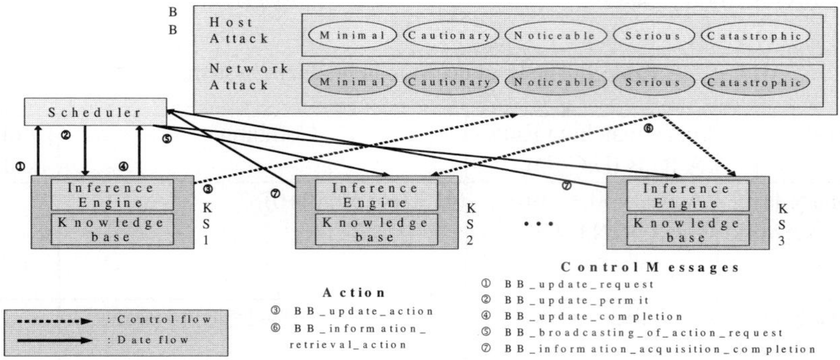

Fig. 1. Messages of IDS and BBA

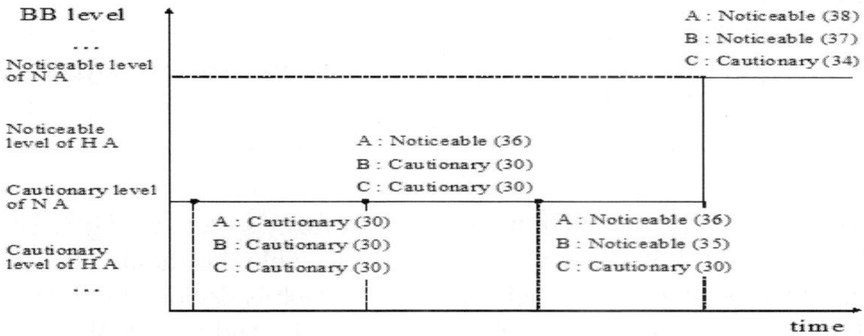

Fig. 2. The blackboard level transition of fuzzy system

2.2 Intrusion Evaluation Using Fuzzy Logic

The fuzzy evaluation component, which is a model of a decision-making agent in distributed IDSs, considers various factors for fuzzy logic calculation when an intrusion behavior is analyzed.

The BB level selection in the previous system is performed according to the agent with the highest BB level among the participating agents [4]. Namely, if an ID agent A is at the Noticeable level and other agents are at the Cautionary level, then the level of the overall system is decided as the Noticeable level, representing the highest level. When the threshold value of Cautionary level is between 31 and 40 and that of Noticeable level is between 41 and 50, it is paramount that the threshold changes. The threshold change from 38 to 39 is not very important, but from 40 to 41 is very important. Since a difference of 1 changes the level of the agent. Therefore, fuzzy logic has been applied for finding a solution to the problem.

Figure 2 presents the membership function of each agent. Fuzzy inference is used in scaling for fast computation. The Standard Additive Model (SAM) has been applied for combining fuzzy logic. The structure of fuzzy rules in the SAM is identical to that of the Mandani model. This is achieved by analyzing the outputs of the individual fuzzy rules and then defuzzifying the combined outcome to obtain a crisp value is the standard procedure. The defuzzification value is calculated by Center of Area (CoA) method.

Table 1. The level decision in the fuzzy system

BB Level	Fuzzy matching Rule (A ID:B ID:C ID)	Combing	Defuzzification
Cautionary level of Network Attack	(A:36 ,B:30 ,C:30) (C,C,C) (N,C,C)	(4*30+6*30)/(4+6)	30
Noticeable level of Network Attack	(A:36 ,B:35 ,C:30) (C,C,C) (C,N,C) (N,C,C) (N,N,C)	(4*30+4*30+5*30+5*40)/(4+4+5+5)	33
Serious level of Host Attack	(A:38 ,B:37 ,C:34) (C,C,C) (N,C,C) (C,C,N) (N,C,N) (C,N,C) (N,N,C) (C,N,N) (N,N,N)	(2*30+2*30+2*30+2*40)/(2+2+2+2) + (3*30+3*40+6*40+4*40)/(3+3+6+4)	36

The level transition is presented in the proposed fuzzy system as Fig 3. Though the threshold of ID agent A is changed at 36 (the Noticeable threshold value of the non fuzzy system) by the attack, the blackboard level which is decided by the fuzzy logic calculation is still Cautionary level of Network Attack. And though ID agent A is at the Noticeable level (threshold value is at 36), ID agent B is at the Noticeable level (threshold value is at 35), ID agent C is at the Cautionary level (threshold value is at 30), the BB level is still Cautionary level of Network Attack. If threshold value of ID agent A reaches 38, that of B reaches 37, that of C reaches 34, then BB level is transit to the Noticeable level of Network Attack. False positive error ratio and false negative error ratio are lessened by this difference in the fuzzy system. The BB level transition of the fuzzy system is smoother than that of non fuzzy system. As a result, we assume that FPER of IDS which has many false positive is lessened.

3 Simulation Result

Simulation is demonstrated for two cases. The first case shows when only the BB detects the intrusion, the second uses the BB and fuzzy logic to detect the intrusion. The jolt and mailbomb attacks are used for simulation in both cases. The False Positive Error Ratio (FPER) and False Negative Error Ratio (FNER) are measured as performance indexes in the simulation. This is presented in previous studies where the ID agents using the BB for coordination are superior in ID to those not using a blackboard.

Figures 3 and 4 presents the false positive error ratio of the system using the BB levels and the system using the BB and fuzzy logic for the mailbomb and jolt attack. A false positive represents an incorrect alarm from acceptable behavior. Fig. 3,4 present an increasing false positive error ratio by strengthening the security level. This increase in the error ratio is due to the fact that the higher the security level, the more error IDSs make in both cases. The FPER of the system using fuzzy logic is lower than the system using only the BB. The simulation results present the ID agent using fuzzy logic more accurately detects the intrusion using overall network information. Nowa-days one of the main problems of an IDS is the high false positive rate. The number of alerts that IDS launches is clearly higher than the number of real attacks. The pro-posed system lessens the false positive error ratio by using fuzzy logic.

Figures 5 and 6 presents the false negative error ratio of the system using BB levels and the system using BB and fuzzy logic for the mailbomb and jolt attacks. A false nega-tive represents a missed alarm condition. Fig. 5,6 presents a decrease in the false positive error ratio as the security level is increased. For all cases, the error ratio of the proposed system is lower than that of the previous system, since intrusions that are detected are based on shared information. The fuzzy logic evaluation component, which is a model of a decision agent in the distributed IDS, considers various factors

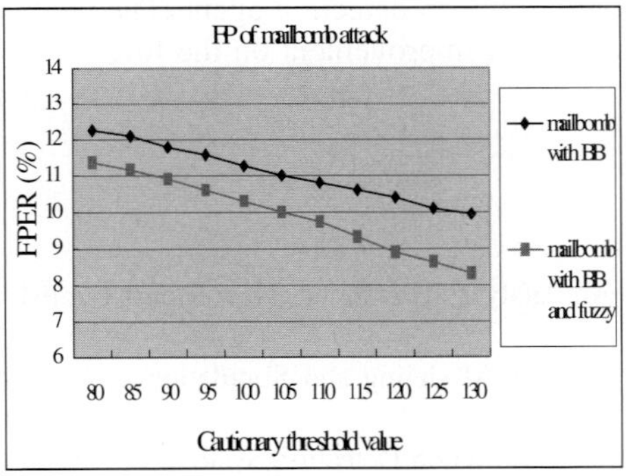

Fig. 3. FPER of mailbomb attack

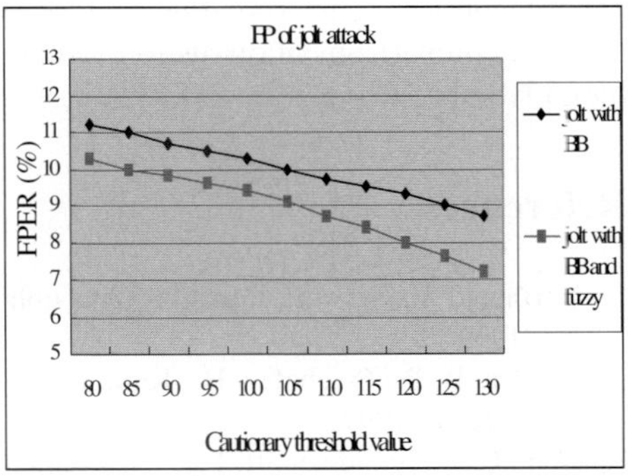

Fig. 4. FPER of jolt attack

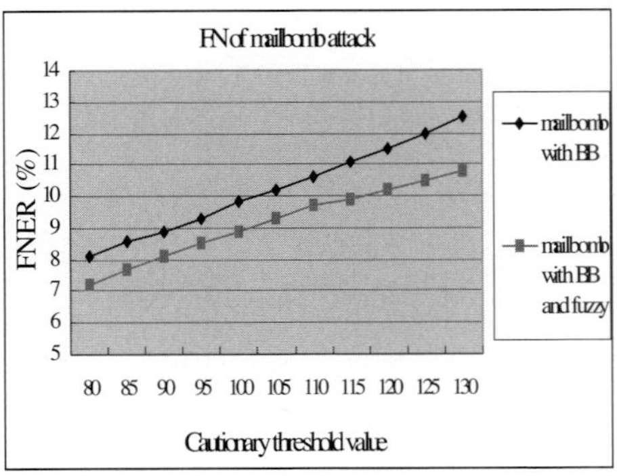

Fig. 5. FNER of mailbomb attack

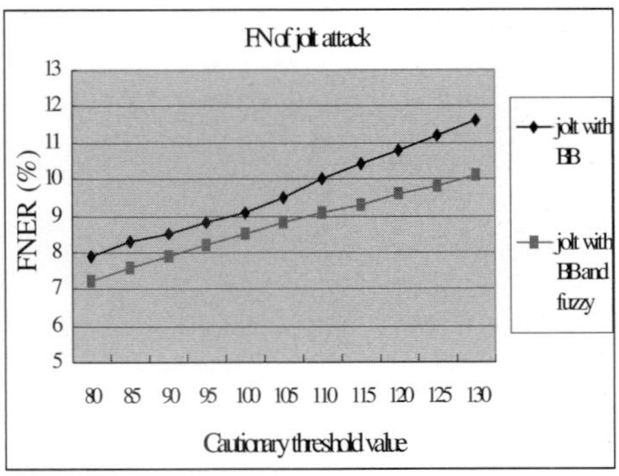

Fig. 6. FNER of jolt attack

based on fuzzy logic when intrusion behavior is judged. The performance obtained from the coordination of intrusion detection agent with fuzzy logic is compared with the corresponding intrusion detection agent. The results of these comparisons demonstrate a relevant improvement when fuzzy logic is involved.

4 Conclusion and Future Work

We can save the time and effort through the proposed simulation environment since the analysis of the network security using the real system is usually not feasible and the construction of the real experimental environment requires unrealistic amount of budget as well as time. The results of simulation on this research will be influenced to standardize for security system and to evaluate performance of security system. If multiple intrusion detection agents share intrusion related information with one another, detection capability can be greatly enhanced. A system using BB architecture for information sharing can easily be expanded by adding new agents, and by increasing the number of BB levels. Collaboration between the firewall component and the IDS will provide the added efficiency in protecting the network. The performance obtained from the coordination of intrusion detection agent with fuzzy logic is compared against the corresponding non fuzzy type intrusion detection agent. The results of these comparisons allow us to evaluate a relevant improvement on the fuzzy logic based BBA.

References

1. Northcutt, S.: Network Intrusion Detection –An Analyst's Handbook. New Riders Publishing, 1999
2. Zeigler, B. P., Praehofer, H., Kim, T. G.: Theory of Modeling and Simulation 2ed. Academic Press, 1999
3. Geib, C. W., Goldman, R. P.: Plan Recongnition in Intrusion Detection System. In DARPA Information Survivability Conference & Exposition 2 (2001) 46-55
4. Seo, H. S., Cho, T. H.: Simulation Model Design of Security System based on Policy-Based Framework. Simulation Transactions of The Society for Modeling and Simulation International, 79 (9) (2003) 515-527

Temporal Error Concealment Algorithm Using Fuzzy Metric

Changcai Lai[1], Chongyang Hao[1], and Xiangyu Shen[2]

[1] College of Electronic and Information Engineering, Northwestern Polytechnical University Xi'an, Shaanxi, 710072, China
pipidang@mail.nwpu.edu.cn, cyhao@nwpu.edu.cn
[2] College of Computer Science, Northwestern Polytechnical University Xi'an, Shaanxi, 710072, China
lai_software@sina.com

Abstract. To efficiently recover the lost motion vectors of corrupt macroblocks, we introduce a new fuzzy metric based on Sugeno fuzzy integral as distortion metric in temporal error concealment. The proposed fuzzy metric can suit the HVS (human visual system) fairly well. Also, we integrate the proposed algorithm into H.264/AVC decoder. Experimental results from decoding several types of video sequences have shown that our scheme can considerably improve the visual quality of reconstructed images and achieve the PSNR gain at different frame.

1 Introduction

To achieve robust transmission of compressed video data over noisy channels, error concealment techniques are important and attract more attentions recently [1],[2]. Generally, spatial error concealment (SEC) method and temporal error concealment (TEC) are two groups of error concealment techniques [3]. In [4], the authors describe the main SEC method used in H.264/AVC reference decoder. Several TEC methods based on boundary matching algorithm (BMA) have been proposed in [5],]6] to recover the corrupt macroblocks coded in H.264/AVC. However, these BMAs use the SAD (sum of absolute difference) as the base of boundary matching criterion. As well known, SAD has the drawback that it dose not consider of the character of human visual system. In this paper, we make the matching criterion more consistent with the human visual system and use it into temporal error concealment.

2 Definition of Fuzzy Metric and Its Fast Calculation

Image quality assessment is an important issue in various image applications such as image or video compression. The most widely used measures are Peak Signal to Noise Ratio (PSNR), SAD etc. But the limitations of above distortion metrics have led to many efforts to develop more sophisticated measures that approximate the response of real human observers. Although many efforts have been made to establish some computational models for the human visual perception, the knowledge of this

D.-S. Huang, K. Li, and G.W. Irwin (Eds.): ICIC 2006, LNAI 4114, pp. 171–176, 2006.

subject is still quite primitive. Some perceptional image quality metrics based on HVS models are too complicated to be used in real time video applications. Here, we present a real time computational image distortion metric that is more consistent with the HVS.

Definition 1: Let σ be a σ algebra on nonempty set $\mathbf{X}$, μ is a fuzzy measure as defined in [7] from σ to [0, 1], $\boldsymbol{A} \in \sigma$, h is a measurable nonnegative real valued function on σ, denotes that $\boldsymbol{H}_{\alpha} = \{x \mid h(x) \geqslant \alpha\}$. The Sugeno's fuzzy integral of h over $\boldsymbol{A}$ is defined as

$$\int_A h(x)\mathrm{d}\mu = \sup_{\alpha\in[0,1]} \min(\alpha, \mu(A \cap H_{\alpha})). \tag{1}$$

Definition 2: Let $\mathbf{S} = \{s_1, s_2, \cdots s_k\}$, $\mathbf{C}\ \{c_1, c_2, \cdots c_k\}$ be the pixel set on blocks or on their borders, where s_i, c_i are pixel intensities. Then the difference between $\mathbf{S}$ and $\mathbf{C}$ is defined as:

$$|\mathbf{S} - \mathbf{C}| = (|s_1 - c_1|, |s_2 - c_2|, \cdots, |s_k - c_k|). \tag{2}$$

where K is the number of pixels in the set $\mathbf{S}$ and $\mathbf{C}$, $\alpha_i = |s_i - c_i|$ is the ith pixel difference in $\mathbf{S}$ and $\mathbf{C}$, $i = 1,2,3 \cdots k$. $\boldsymbol{H}_{\alpha_i} = \{|s - c| \mid |s - c| \geq |s_i - c_i|\}$ is the set of all differences, the absolute value of which is larger than α_i, μ is the number of elements in set H_{α_i}. Then

$$FM(s,c) = \max_{0 \le i \le K} \min(\alpha_i, \mu(H_{\alpha_i})). \tag{3}$$

FM is the fuzzy metric between two blocks or borders of block. Compared to the conventional image metrics such as SAD or PSNR, FM not only takes into account the difference between the corresponding pixels, but also the proportion of the pixels whose corresponding differences are larger than a given value. Therefore, it is the ideal evaluation of blocks or borders difference. The following steps are used to speed up the calculation of FM :

Step 1: create an array with 256 elements to count every pixel difference.

Step 2: compute the absolute difference value a_i between two pixels in the same position in different blocks or block borders. The value of a_i ranges from 0 to 255, then add 1 to the element of array with subscript a_i.

Step 3: repeat Step 2 for every pixel and get the maximum absolute difference value $a_{\max}$ between two pixels.

Step 4: for every pixel difference a_i from 1 to $a_{\max}$, count for the number of pixel difference that is more than a_i, then the fuzzy measure $\mu(H_{\alpha_i})$ that is corresponding to every pixel difference is achieved.

Step 5: compute the fuzzy metric in equation (2) with the achieved $\mu(H_{\alpha_i})$.

For a $m \times m$ block, only $2m^2$ times subtract, add and compare operation are needed in the fast algorithm, $(m-1)^2 - 2$ times similar computation is reduced compared with the original formula which need $m^2 \times (m-1)^2$ similar computation.

3 Fuzzy Metric Based Temporal Error Concealment

When motion vectors are lost, the algorithm firstly investigates the motion activity of correctly received macroblocks of current image. If the motion activity is smaller than a predefined threshold, the corrupt macroblocks are concealed by the copy of blocks in spatially corresponding positions in reference frame. Otherwise, the missing motion vector of the corrupt macroblock is estimated from one of its neighbor macroblocks to recover the corrupt macroblock. As shown in Fig.1, the missing motion vector is selected from a set of candidates with fuzzy metric based boundary matching algorithm (FBMA), by minimize the luminance fuzzy distortion calculated as formula (4).

$$D_{FM} = FM(\hat{Y}, Y). \tag{4}$$

Where FM is the fuzzy metric defined as (3), $\hat{\mathbf{Y}}$ and $\mathbf{Y}$ represent the pixel values of the previous and current frame, respectively defined as $\hat{\mathbf{Y}} = \{\hat{Y}(mvp)_i^{IN}\}$ and $\mathbf{Y} = \{Y_i^{OUT}\}$, in which $\hat{Y}(mvp)_i^{IN}$ is the ith reconstructed boundary luminance value in the predicted block pointed to by $\mathbf{mvp}$, here $\mathbf{mvp}$ is the predicted motion vector. Y_i^{OUT} is the ith boundary luminance value in the neighboring blocks, and N is the total number of calculated boundary pixels.

In H.264/AVC reference software, as shown in Fig.2, $\mathbf{mvp}$ is selected from the following motion vector candidates $\{\mathbf{ZV}, \mathbf{V1}, \mathbf{V2}, \mathbf{V3}, \mathbf{V4}, \mathbf{V5}, \mathbf{V6}, \mathbf{V7}, \mathbf{V8}\}$, $\mathbf{ZV}$ means (0,0,0). For the purpose of reducing the complexity of error concealment, we restrict the number of candidates and choose the $\mathbf{mvp}$ on the basis of different block sizes. Fist, estimate the mode of the lost macroblock as [8] based on the modes of its neighboring macroblocks, according to the estimation of mode, there are four types of motion vector candidates as described in Fig.3.

If the lost macroblock is estimated as (a), the candidates to be used for concealing the macroblock are as H.264/AVC reference software. For (b), the candidates of Blk0 are $\{\mathbf{ZV}, \mathbf{V1}, \mathbf{V2}, \mathbf{V3}, \mathbf{V7}\}$ and candidates of Blk1 are $\{\mathbf{ZV}, \mathbf{V4}, \mathbf{V5}, \mathbf{V6}, \mathbf{V8}\}$. In case (c), the candidates of Blk0 are $\{\mathbf{ZV}, \mathbf{V1}, \mathbf{V3}, \mathbf{V4}, \mathbf{V5}\}$ and the candidates

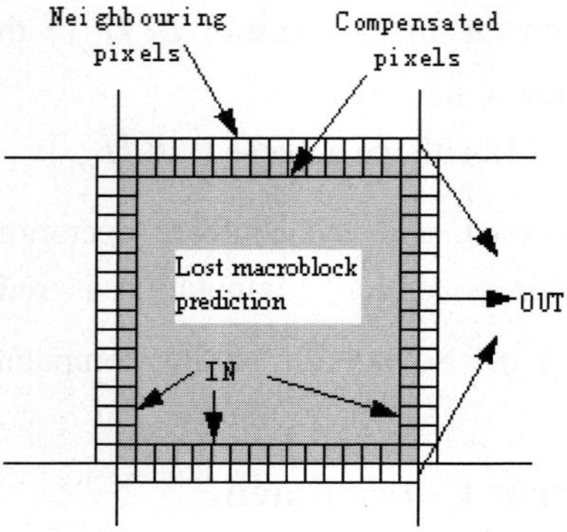

Fig. 1. Boundary matching

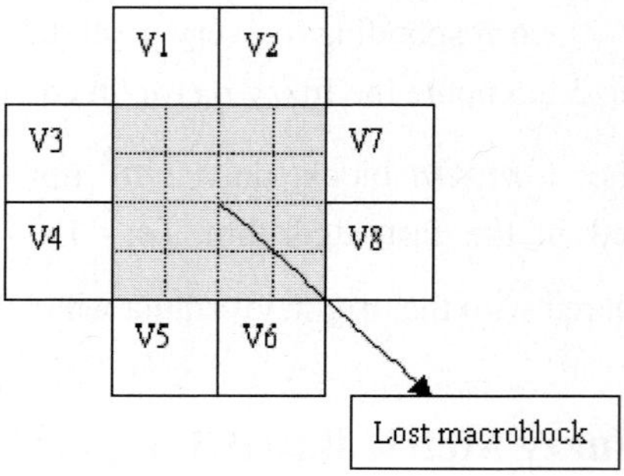

Fig. 2. Motion vector candidates

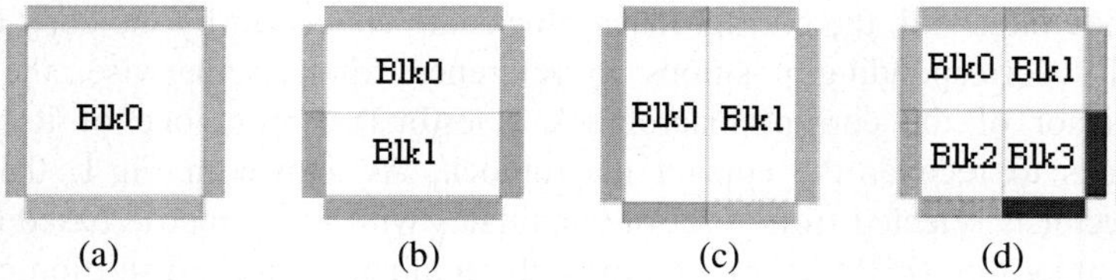

Fig. 3. Estimated mode of lost macroblock

of Blk1 are $\{\mathbf{ZV}, \mathbf{V2}, \mathbf{V6}, \mathbf{V7}, \mathbf{V8}\}$. If the lost macroblock is estimated as (d), the candidates are as follows: Blk0: $\{\mathbf{ZV}, \mathbf{V1}, \mathbf{V3}\}$, Blk1: $\{\mathbf{ZV}, \mathbf{V2}, \mathbf{V7}\}$, Blk2: $\{\mathbf{ZV}, \mathbf{V4}, \mathbf{V5}\}$ and Blk3: $\{\mathbf{ZV}, \mathbf{V6}, \mathbf{V8}\}$. Among all candidates, the one with the minimum fuzzy distortion value in (4) is selected for concealing the lost macroblock. By reducing the number of motion vector candidates, the proposed method has lower complexity than the reference software.

4 Experiments

JM8.4 reference software is selected as platform to simulate our algorithm. Some macroblocks in the video sequence are randomly dropped with 25% block loss rate, which are supposed to be caused by transmission errors. Fig.4 is the result of JM and proposed FBMA at frame 6 of the children sequence. As shown by (b) and (c), the visual quality of (c) is much better than (b), especially in the region marked with black circle line. The similar result with Fig. 4 is achieved in Fig. 5. The PSNR performance at different frame of tennis is shown in Fig.6. As shown by the experimental results, our fuzzy metric based temporal error concealment significantly outperforms the method of H.264/AVC reference software both in visual quality and PSNR. In addition, the proposed algorithm does not lead to any increase of decoding time.

(a) Original frame (b) concealed by JM (c) concealed by FBMA

Fig. 4. Results of different concealment methods at frame 6 of children sequence

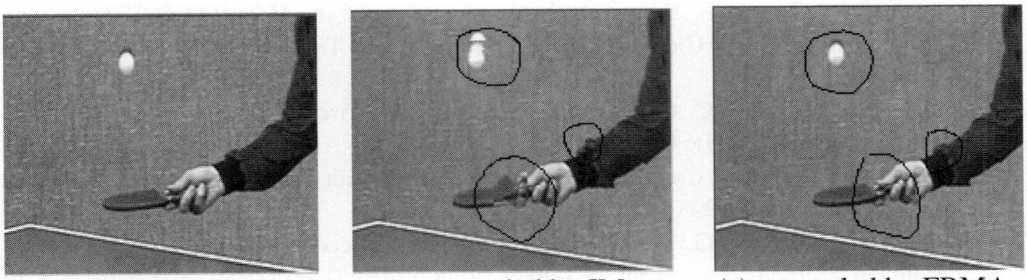

(a) Original frame (b) concealed by JM (c) concealed by FBMA

Fig. 5. Results of different concealment methods at frame 6 of tennis sequence

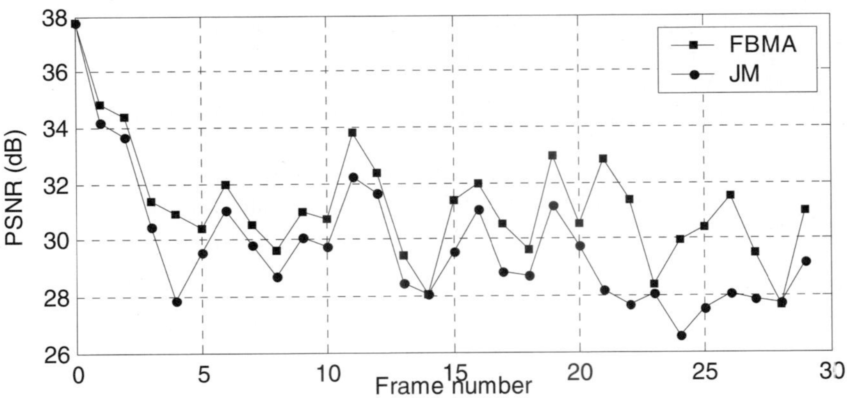

Fig. 6. PSNR performance at different frame of tennis

5 Conclusions

Unlike the common used boundary matching algorithm based on SAD, this paper uses the fuzzy metric based on Sugeno fuzzy integral as the criterion to recover the lost motion vectors of corrupt macroblocks. The present fuzzy metric is more consistent with the human visual system. Simulation results demonstrate the better performance of the proposed method both in visual quality and PSNR. The proposed fuzzy metric is also may be used in encoder to select the prediction mode of macroblock, which can improve the efficiency of encoder.

Acknowledgements

This work is supported by the Doctoral Foundation of National Education Ministry of China（20040699015）.

References

1. Wiegand, T., Sullivan, G., Bjøntegaard, G.: Overview of the H.264/AVC Video Coding Standard. IEEE Trans on Circuits and Systems for Video Technology, Vol.13 (2003)560–576
2. Stephan, W.: H.264/AVC Over IP. IEEE Trans on Circuits and Systems for Video Technology, Vol.13 (2003)645–656
3. Wang, Y., Zhu, Q.: Error Control and Concealment for Video Communication: A Review. In Proc. IEEE, Vol. 86 (1998)974–997
4. Wiegand, T., Sullivan, G.: Joint Model Reference Encoding Methods and Decoding Concealment Methods. Document JVT-I049, Joint Video Team (JVT) of ISO/IEC MPEG and ITU-T VCEG, San Diego, USA (2003)
5. Bongsoo, J., Byeungwoo J.: Selective Temporal Error Concealment Algorithm for H.264/AVC. 2004 IEEE international Conference on Multimedia and Expo (ICME), Taipei China (2004)411–414
6. Jinghong, Z., Lappui, C.: A Temporal Error Concealment Algorithm for H.264 Using Lagrange Interpolation. 2004 IEEE International Symposium on Circuits and Systems Proceedings, Vancouver, BC, Canada (2004)
7. Junli, L., Gang, C.: A Fuzzy Image Metric With Application to Fractal Coding. IEEE Trans on Image Process Vol.11 No.6 (2002) 636–643
8. Donghyung, K., Siyoung, Y.: A New Temporal Error Concealment Method for H.264 using Adaptive Block Sizes. ICIP 2005 IEEE International Conference on Image Processing, Vol.3 (2005) 928–931

Universal Approximation of Binary-Tree Hierarchical Fuzzy Systems with Typical FLUs

Xiangyan Zhang and Naiyao Zhang

Department of Automation, Tsinghua University
Beijing 100084, China
Zhangxiangyan03@mails.tsinghua.edu.cn

Abstract. The universal approximation property of binary-tree hierarchical fuzzy systems (HFS) is examined in this paper. A binary-tree hierarchical fuzzy system with typical FLUs (fuzzy logic units) is defined. The analytical expression of HFS is derived, and the system is shown to preserve universal approximation property. A simple example is also given to show the theory.

1 Introduction

Fuzzy control theories have been successfully applied to a variety of areas. However, the applications are usually restricted to systems with limited input variables due to curse of dimension. The problem of "curse of dimension" is defined from two aspects: first, the system's fuzzy rules increase exponentially with the input variables; second, the system's parameters to be designed will also increase exponentially with the input variables. Therefore, if the number of input variables is very large, the fuzzy systems become unimplemetable due to the overload of memory. To tackle this difficulty, Raju [1] proposed hierarchical fuzzy systems in 1991.Through years of development, various achievements have been accomplished in the field of hierarchical fuzzy systems[2]. In addition, the International Journal of Intelligent Systems presented a special issue on hierarchical fuzzy systems in 2002[3]. Although many theories on hierarchical fuzzy systems have been achieved, a lot of problems are still unsolved and need future research [3].

Universal approximation property, the main and base property of the hierarchical fuzzy systems, has drawn the attention of the community. Wang [4] [5] proved that the series-hierarchical fuzzy systems had the universal approximation property, but the designed systems' parameters would increase exponentially with the number of inputs. Then, Waratt [6], Huwendiek [7] and Liu [8] proved that the hierarchical fuzzy systems with different structures all had the universal approximation property. To date, the binary-tree hierarchical fuzzy systems have not been well studied. Therefore, this paper focuses on the binary-tree hierarchical fuzzy systems and their universal approximation property. To make our theory of the hierarchical fuzzy systems more simply and more applicable, the universal approximation of the hierarchical fuzzy systems with typical FLUs is analyzed herein.

This paper is organized as follows. First, the ordinary binary-tree hierarchical fuzzy systems with typical FLUs are defined in Section 2. Then, in Section 3, the analytical expression is derived and the systems are shown to preserve approximation property.

D.-S. Huang, K. Li, and G.W. Irwin (Eds.): ICIC 2006, LNAI 4114, pp. 177 – 182, 2006.

2 Definition of Binary-Tree Hierarchical Fuzzy Systems with Typical Fuzzy Logic Units (FLUs)

The structure of proposed HFS with $L(L \geq 2)$ layer hierarchy is shown in Fig.1. $x = (x_1, \ldots, x_n)^T \in R^n$ is a collection of input variables for HFS; $y_{k1}, y_{k2}, \ldots, y_{k\lceil n/2^k \rceil}$ are the outputs of the FLUs at the kth layer; and y_{L1} is the output of the HFS. The configuration of the hierarchical fuzzy system is the superposition of the FLUs, and to make the conclusions more useful and succinct, the typical FLUs are used. And each typical FLU is concretely defined from four aspects as following:

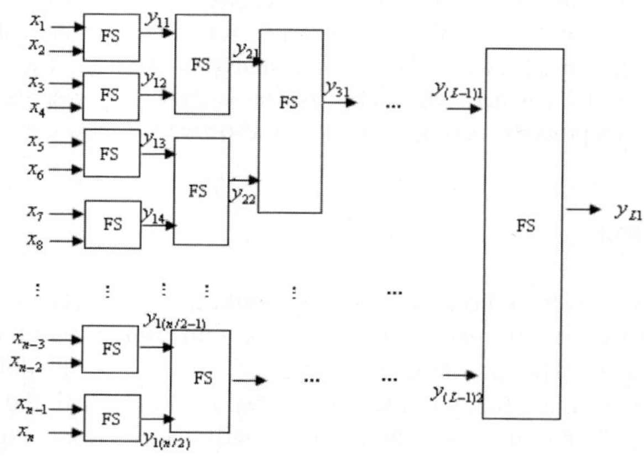

Fig. 1. the structure of the hierarchical fuzzy systems

1) The Membership functions of input and output variables

Without loss of generality, it is supposed that all the input and output variables fall in [-1, 1] (this can be easily achieved by scaling the variables). There are 2m+1 continuous fuzzy sets A_{ij} ($j \in \{-m, -m+1, \ldots, m-1, m\}$) defined over [-1, 1] for i-th input variable x_i ($i \in \{1, \ldots, n\}$). The centers of the fuzzy set A_{ij} locates at λ_i^j, where $\lambda_i^{-m} = -1, \lambda_i^0 = 0, \lambda_i^m = 1$. The fuzzy sets of each input variable adopt the triangular-shaped, full-overlapped, symmetrical about vertical axis, but not uniformly spaced membership functions as shown in Fig.2. For the intermediate variable and the output variable, $(2mn+1)$ fuzzy sets should be defined in order to satisfy the linear control rules. $y_{kt}(k = 1, \ldots, L)$ represents the output of the t-th fuzzy system in the k-th level. The fuzzy sets of y_{kt} are denoted by $B_{kt}^{q_{kt}}(q_{kt} = -mn, \cdots, mn)$ with singleton, equally spaced membership function as shown in Fig.3. The fuzzy set $B_{kt}^{q_{kt}}$ locates at $\delta^{q_{kt}}$, where $\delta^{-mn} = -1, \delta^0 = 0, \delta^{mn} = 1$. Since the output's membership function is equally spaced, $\delta^{q_{kt}} = q_{kt} / (mn) = q_{kt} \cdot V$.

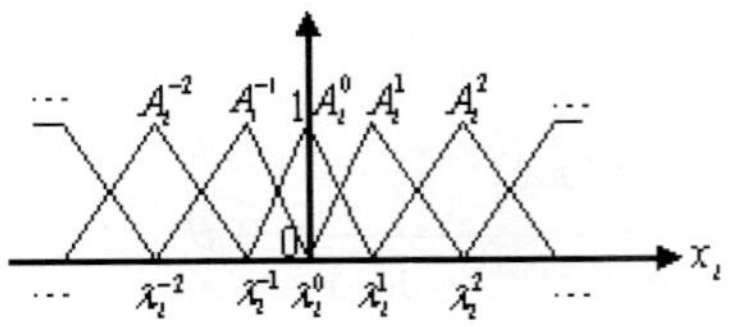

Fig. 2. The membership function of x_i

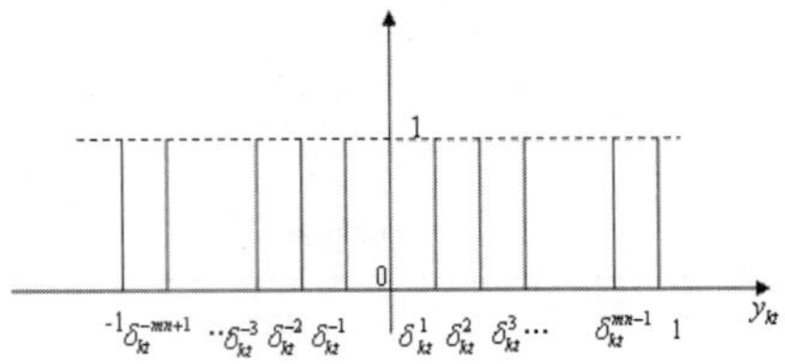

Fig. 3. The membership function of y_{kt}

2) Fuzzy inference rules

The t-th($s=2t-1$) fuzzy system of the k-th level is also a typical fuzzy system which is constructed from the following rules:

$$\text{if } y_{(k-1)s} \text{ is } B_{(k-1)s}^{q_{(k-1)s}} \; and \; y_{(k-1)(s+1)} \text{ is } B_{s+1}^{q_{(k-1)(s+1)}}, \quad \text{then } y_{k\lceil (s+1)/2\rceil} = \delta_{k\lceil (s+1)/2\rceil}^{q_{(k-1)s}+q_{(k-1)(s+1)}}$$

3) Fuzzy inference method

The Sum-Product inference method is used, in which the fuzzy operators are defined as follows:

Sum (Bounded Sum): $a_1 \oplus a_2 \oplus \ldots \oplus a_m = \min\{1, a_1 + a_2 + \ldots + a_m\}$

Product: $a_1 a_2 \ldots a_m = a_1 \times a_2 \times \ldots \times a_m$, $\forall\ a_1, a_2, \cdots, a_m \in [0,1]$

4) Defuzzification algorithm

The center of area (COA) algorithm is adopted for defuzzification. Because the singleton-shaped membership function is defined for output variable, the COA algorithm can be replaced by the weighted mean method.

3 Universal Approximation of Binary-Tree Hierarchical Fuzzy System with Typical Fuzzy Subsystems

Lemma 1 [9]. For the HFS defined as before, let the input variable $x_i \in [\lambda_i^{p_i}, \lambda_i^{p_i+1}]$, $i=1,2,\ldots,n$, $-m \le k_i \le m-1$ the output of the HFS is then:

$$y_{L1} = \frac{1}{nm}(h_n + \frac{n}{2}) + \frac{1}{nm}\sum_{i=1}^{n} \frac{x_i - \dfrac{\lambda_i^{p_i+1} + \lambda_i^{p_i}}{2}}{\lambda_i^{p_i+1} - \lambda_i^{p_i}}, \text{ where } h_n = \sum_{i=1}^{n} p_i \,.$$

Theorem 1. Any HFS is equivalent to a piecewise linear function

Proof of Theorem 1. From lemma 1, we know

$$y_{L1} = \frac{1}{nm}(h_n + \frac{n}{2}) + \frac{1}{nm}\sum_{i=1}^{n} \frac{x_i - \dfrac{\lambda_i^{p_i+1} + \lambda_i^{p_i}}{2}}{\lambda_i^{p_i+1} - \lambda_i^{p_i}}, \; h_n = \sum_{i=1}^{n} p_i \,. \tag{1}$$

Let $p = (p_1, p_2, \ldots, p_n)$ *and* $-m \le p_i \le m$

$$y_{L1}=\frac{1}{nm}(h_n+\frac{n}{2})+\frac{1}{nm}\sum_{i=1}^{n}\frac{x_i-\dfrac{\lambda_i^{p_i+1}+\lambda_i^{p_i}}{2}}{\lambda_i^{p_i+1}-\lambda_i^{p_i}}$$
$$=\frac{1}{nm(\lambda_1^{p_1+1}-\lambda_1^{p_1})}x_1+\frac{1}{nm(\lambda_1^{p_2+1}-\lambda_1^{p_2})}x_2+\ldots+\frac{1}{nm(\lambda_1^{p_n+1}-\lambda_1^{p_n})}x_n+\theta \quad . \tag{2}$$

Let

$$\begin{cases}\dfrac{1}{nm(\lambda_1^{p_1+1}-\lambda_1^{p_1})}=a_{p1}\\ \cdots \\ \dfrac{1}{nm(\lambda_n^{p_n+1}-\lambda_n^{p_n})}=a_{pn}\\ \theta=\dfrac{1}{nm}(h_n+\dfrac{n}{2})-\dfrac{1}{2nm}\left[\dfrac{\lambda_1^{p_1+1}+\lambda_1^{p_1}}{\lambda_1^{p_1+1}-\lambda_1^{p_1}}+\dfrac{\lambda_2^{p_2+1}+\lambda_2^{p_2}}{\lambda_2^{p_2+1}-\lambda_2^{p_2}}+\cdots+\dfrac{\lambda_n^{p_n+1}+\lambda_n^{p_n}}{\lambda_n^{p_n+1}-\lambda_n^{p_n}}\right]=a_{p0}.\end{cases} \quad . \tag{3}$$

Then, one concludes

$$y_{L1}=\sum_{i=1}^{n}a_{pi}x_i, \quad where \ \ p=(p_1,p_2,\ldots,p_n) \ and \ -m\le p_i\le m \, . \tag{4}$$

Therefore, the output of HFS is a linear function of the input variables in the definite region.

Now one can define the piecewise line functions:

$$S=\sum_{i=1}^{n}a_{pi}x_i, \quad where \ \ p=(p_1,p_2,\ldots,p_n) \ and \ -m\le p_i\le m. \tag{5}$$

Let the coefficients to be same, then the HFS and the piecewise function is equivalent. Consequently,

$$y_{L1}(p_1,p_2,\ldots,p_n)=S(p_1,p_2,\ldots,p_n)\, . \tag{6}$$

Therefore, the analytical expression of the hierarchical fuzzy systems with typical fuzzy systems is a piecewise linear function in nature. Theorem 1 is proved.

Lemma 2 [8]**.** Let f: $R^n \to R$($x\in U=[-1,1]^n$) be a continuous function, then for arbitrary $\varepsilon>0$, there is a piecewise linear function $S: R^n\to R$, satisfying supp $(s)\subset[-1,1]^n$,further $\|f-S\|_{\infty,U}<\varepsilon$.

According to Lemma 2, for any given continuous function f, there is a piecewise line function that can approximate f for any small $\varepsilon>0$. Moreover, from Theorem 1, any piecewise linear function is equivalent to a HFS. Therefore, the defined hierarchical fuzzy systems with typical FLUs have the universal approximation property.

Theorem 2. The defined HFS with typical FLUs has the universal approximation property. Let f: $R^n \rightarrow R(x \in U = [-1,1]^n)$ be a continuous function. Then for any arbitrary $\varepsilon > 0$, there exists a binary-tree hierarchical fuzzy system, which satisfies $\left\| y_{L1} - f \right\|_{\infty,[-1,1]^n} < \varepsilon$.

Proof of Theorem 2. From Lemma 2, we know for any continuous function f, we can find a piecewise linear function S that satisfies:

$$\left\| S - f \right\|_{\infty,[-1,1]^n} < \varepsilon . \tag{7}$$

Form Theorem 1, it is concluded that for any piecewise function S there is a hierarchical fuzzy system with typical FLUs corresponding to it. That is:

$$y_{L1} = S . \tag{8}$$

Hence,

$$\begin{aligned} \left\| y_{L1} - f \right\|_{\infty,[-1,1]^n} &= \left\| y_{L1} - S + S - f \right\|_{\infty,[-1,1]^n} = \left\| S - f \right\|_{\infty,[-1,1]^n} + \left\| y_{L1} - S \right\|_{\infty,[-1,1]^n} \\ &= \left\| S - f \right\|_{\infty,[-1,1]^n} < \varepsilon. \end{aligned} \tag{9}$$

Therefore, for any continuous functions, there is a hierarchical fuzzy system which can approximate it with any desirable precision. This conclusion is very useful for the wide application of the hierarchical fuzzy systems, that is, the hierarchical fuzzy systems can be used in any case if necessary.

4 Simulation

Consider the function f on $U=[-1,1]^4$.

$$f(x_1, x_2, x_3, x_4) = \frac{1}{1 + \sin^2(\pi x_1) + \sin^2(\pi x_2) + \sin^2(\pi x_3) + \sin^2(\pi x_4)} . \tag{10}$$

Assume that f is unknown, but we know the values of f at some regular points in U. Our task is to design a hierarchical fuzzy system to approximate f for any small $\varepsilon = 0.1$.

First, find a piecewise linear function which approximates f. Second, find the HFS by Theory 1 which is equal to the above piecewise function. The detailed process is not listed here. From above calculating, We get the minimum m=3.The number of rules of the hierarchical fuzzy systems is $2 \times 3^2 = 18$. While the number of rules of the ordinary fuzzy system is $4^3 = 64$, So, the hierarchical systems solve the problem of curse of dimension in some sense.

5 Conclusions

In this paper, it is shown that the binary-tree hierarchical fuzzy system is equivalent to a piecewise linear function and the systems have the universal approximation property as well. A simulation example simply shows the importance of the theory to solve curse of dimension. The universal approximation property provides the basic theory for the application of the hierarchical fuzzy systems. However, for further practical use, the sufficient and necessary conditions of the universal approximation property and the design methods of corresponding binary-tree hierarchical systems need to be studied in the future.

Acknowledgements

This work is supported by National Natural Science Foundation of China (60474024) and Doctoral Fund of Ministry of Education of China (20040003106).

References

1. Raju, G.V.S., Zhou, J., Kisner R.A.: Hierarchical Fuzzy Control. International Journal of Control 54(1991)1201-1216.
2. Zhang, X.Y., et al.: A Review of Hierarchical Fuzzy Systems and Hierarchical Fuzzy Control. Journal of centeral south university (science and technology) 36(2005)25-31
3. Torra, V.: Special Issue on Hierarchical Fuzzy Systems. International Journal of Intelligent Systems 17(2002)447.
4. Wang, L.X.: Universal Approximation by Hierarchical Fuzzy Systems. Fuzzy Sets and Systems 93(1998) 223-230.
5. Chen, W., Wang, L.X.: A Note on Universal Approximation by Hierarchical Fuzzy Systems. Information Sciences 123(2000) 241-248.
6. Rattasirim, W., Halgamuge S.K.: Computationally Advantageous and Stable Hierarchical Fuzzy Systems for Active Suspension. IEEE Transactions on Industrial Electronics 50(2003)48-61
7. Huwendiek, O., Brockman W.: Function Approximation with Decomposed Fuzzy Systems. Fuzzy Sets and Systems (1999) 273-286
8. Liu, P.Y., Li, H.X.: Hierarchical TS Fuzzy System and Its Universal Approximation. Information Sciences 169(2005) 279-303
9. Du, X.Y., Zhang, N.Y.: Equivalence Analysis of Binary-tree-type Hierarchical Fuzzy Systems. Journal of Tsinghua University 44(2004) 993-996

A New Fuzzy Membership Function with Applications in Interpretability Improvement of Neurofuzzy Models

John Q. Gan and Shang-Ming Zhou

Department of Computer Science, University of Essex
Colchester CO4 3SQ, United Kingdom
jqgan@essex.ac.uk

Abstract. Local model interpretability is a very important issue in neurofuzzy local linear models applied to nonlinear state estimation, process modelling and control. This paper proposes a new fuzzy membership function with desirable properties for improving the interpretability of neurofuzzy models. A learning algorithm for constructing neurofuzzy models based on this new membership function and a hybrid objective function is derived as well, which aims to achieve optimal balance between global model accuracy and local model interpretability. Experimental results have shown that the proposed approach is simple and effective in improving the interpretability of Takagi-Sugeno fuzzy models while preserving the model accuracy at a satisfactory level.

1 Introduction

Fuzzy models have been widely and successfully used in many areas such as system modeling and control, data analysis, and pattern recognition. Traditionally, fuzzy rules are generated from human expert knowledge or heuristics, which brings about good high-level semantic generalization capability. On the other hand, some researchers have made efforts to build fuzzy models from observational data, leading to many successful applications 1-5. Compared to heuristic fuzzy rules, the fuzzy rules generated from data are able to model unknown complex systems or processes more accurately at the price of losing model interpretability. Recently, more and more efforts have been made to approach the problem of interpretability of data-driven fuzzy models 6-15.

Although Takagi-Sugeno (TS) fuzzy model 1 has been very successful in system modeling and control, one problem is that its local models often exhibit eccentric behaviors which are hard to be interpreted and thus bring about difficulties in its applications. One type of fuzzy model interpretability is about distinguishable and physically reasonable input space partitioning. For a TS fuzzy model, the interpretability of its local linear models, *e.g.*, the reflection of real local linearity of the system to be modeled in the TS local models, is essential to the success of its applications to areas such as nonlinear state estimation and process control 4561215. A heuristic criterion for fuzzy clustering inspires us to develop appropriate membership functions (MFs) for constructing interpretable TS fuzzy models. This criterion states that "good" clusters are actually not very fuzzy 16. The requirements directly related to this type of interpretability in TS fuzzy models are that under the

D.-S. Huang, K. Li, and G.W. Irwin (Eds.): ICIC 2006, LNAI 4114, pp. 183 – 194, 2006.

condition of preserving global model accuracy at a satisfactory level, fuzzy sets should have large core regions, and that adjacent fuzzy sets should be less overlapped. These requirements cannot be met by traditional MFs such as triangular MFs and Gaussian MFs. Trapezoidal MFs can meet these requirements to some extent, but they are not suitable for tuning by automatic learning. In order to generate distinguishable fuzzy sets with the above desirable properties, Zhou and Gan 15 suggested a linguistic modifier that can enlarge the ε-insensitive core of a fuzzy set and at the same time lessen the overlapping with adjacent MFs. This paper proposes a new fuzzy membership function, which is much simpler than the one suggested in 15 but possesses the same desirable properties, and develops a corresponding learning scheme for constructing interpretable TS fuzzy models.

In the next section, the new fuzzy membership function is proposed based on the ideas from linguistic modifiers. A learning scheme for constructing interpretable TS fuzzy models based on this new membership function and a hybrid objective function is developed in Section 3. Experimental results are given in Section 4, which demonstrate the effectiveness of the new approach in comparison with other two interpretability-oriented methods.

2 A New Fuzzy Membership Function

The ε-insensitive core of a fuzzy set is important in evaluating the modification of a membership function, which is defined as

$$VCore_{\varepsilon}(A) = \{x \mid 1 \geq \mu(x) \geq 1 - \varepsilon\} \quad (1)$$

where ε is a small positive real number, and $\mu(x)$ is the MF of the fuzzy set A.

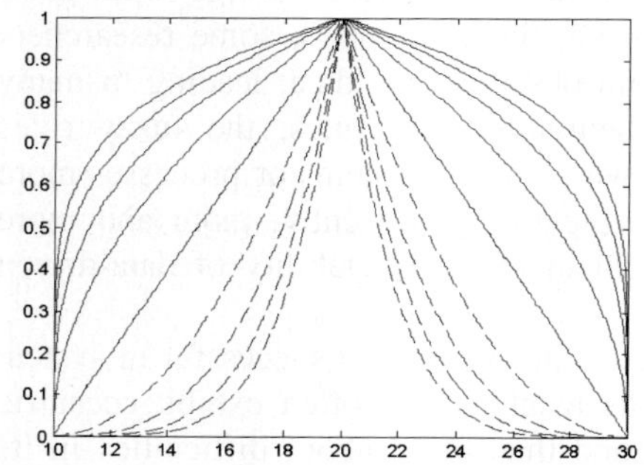

Fig. 1. Linguistic hedges $\mu(x) = (\mu^{o}(x))^{\alpha}$

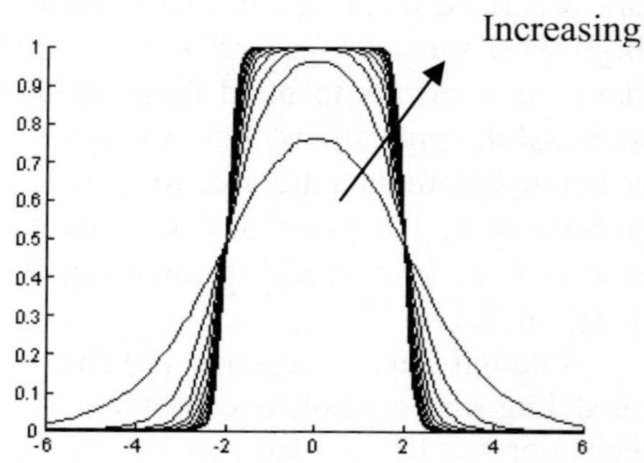

Fig. 2. The new membership function: $\beta_1 = -2, \beta_2 = 2$

The traditional linguistic hedge $\mu(x) = (\mu^{o}(x))^{\alpha}$ 17 has been suggested to adjust the overlapping of adjacent MFs for flexibility and interpretability improvement 18. Liu *et al.* 19 proposed a linguistic hedge fuzzy logic controller by combining linguistic hedges and genetic algorithms, in which the linguistic hedges are used to modify the shapes of MFs whilst the genetic algorithms to find the optimal linguistic hedge combination. Casillas *et al.* 13 introduced a genetic tuning process for automatically obtaining good balance between interpretability and accuracy of fuzzy models, in which linguistic hedges are used to perform MF modifications. One problem in this type of linguistic hedges is that reducing overlapping of adjacent fuzzy sets will greatly shrink the ε -insensitive core, as shown in Fig. 1, which usually degrades the model accuracy considerably.

What is desirable in improving model interpretability and preserving model accuracy at the same time is that reducing overlapping will not much affect the ε -insensitive core or that reducing overlapping and enlarging the ε -insensitive core both occur at the same time. To obtain such a desirable property, Zhou and Gan 15 proposed the following linguistic modifier:

$$\mu(x; C_1, \beta, C_2, p, q) = \begin{cases} \frac{1}{(\mu_{C_1})^{pq-1}} \left(\mu^o(x)\right)^{pq} & x < C_1 \\ 1 - \frac{1}{\left(1-\mu_{C_1}\right)^{p-1}} \left(1-\mu^o(x)\right)^p & C_1 \le x < \beta \\ 1 - \frac{1}{\left(1-\mu_{C_2}\right)^{p-1}} \left(1-\mu^o(x)\right)^p & \beta \le x < C_2 \\ \frac{1}{(\mu_{C_2})^{pq-1}} \left(\mu^o(x)\right)^{pq} & C_2 \le x \end{cases} \tag{2}$$

where $\mu^o(x)$ is an initial MF, parameters C_1, C_2, β, p, q are for controlling the ε -insensitive core and overlapping in a desirable manner, $\mu_{C_1} = \mu^o(C_1)$ and $\mu_{C_2} = \mu^o(C_2)$. Compared to the linguistic hedge $\mu(x) = (\mu^o(x))^\alpha$, the linguistic modifier defined by (2) is much more complex, with piece-wise functions and too many tuning parameters, and makes MFs tuning a complicated process. Aiming to overcome this disadvantage, this paper proposes a new fuzzy membership function, which is very simple but can also enlarge the ε -insensitive core and at the same time lessen the overlapping with adjacent MFs, as shown in Fig. 2. It should be noted that a partition of unity and a maximum membership value of 1 can be obtained by normalization. These issues have no side effect on model accuracy and local model interpretability and thus will not be addressed in this paper.

This new membership function is defined by the combination of two sigmoid functions as follows:

$$\mu(x; \beta_1, \beta_2, \rho) = \frac{1}{1 + e^{-\rho(x-\beta_1)}} - \frac{1}{1 + e^{-\rho(x-\beta_2)}} \tag{3}$$

where β_1, β_2, ρ are parameters for adjusting the position and shape of the defined MF. Fig. 2 shows the desirable property of this membership function for balancing fuzzy model accuracy and interpretability. This will be further explored in the following sections by applying it in constructing interpretable TS fuzzy models.

3 Constructing Interpretable TS Fuzzy Models Using the New Membership Function

3.1 TS Model Based on the New Membership Function

In this paper, TS models with the following fuzzy rules will be addressed:

$$R_i : \text{if } x_1 \text{ is } A_{i_1,1} \text{ and } \ldots \text{ and } x_n \text{ is } A_{i_n,n},$$
$$\text{then } y_i = a_{i0} + a_{i1}x_1 + \cdots + a_{in}x_n \tag{4}$$

where R_i is the ith rule of the TS system, x_j are input variables, y_i is the output variable of the ith local model, $A_{i_j,j}$ are fuzzy sets about x_j, a_{ij} are the consequent parameters that have to be identified from given data sets, and $1 \le i_1 \le L_1$, …, $1 \le i_n \le L_n$, $1 \le i \le L = \prod_{j=1}^{n} L_j$, with L_j being the number of fuzzy sets about x_j. The global output of a TS model is calculated by

$$y = \sum_{i=1}^{L} w_i y_i \tag{5}$$

where w_i is the normalized firing strength of rule R_i:

$$w_i = \frac{\tau_i}{\sum_{i=1}^{L} \tau_i} \tag{6}$$

and τ_i is called the firing strength of rule R_i, which is computed as follows:

$$\tau_i = \prod_{j=1}^{n} A_{i_j,j}(x_j) \tag{7}$$

It can be seen that in this TS model, given the fuzzy sets about every variable on its domain of discourse, the rule base includes all the possible combinations of these fuzzy sets to cover the whole input space. For the sake of representing the rules clearly, the rules are sorted as follows: corresponding to a combination of fuzzy sets $A_{i_1,1}$, …, $A_{i_n,n}$, the rule is indexed as

$$i = \sum_{j=1}^{n-1} [(i_j - 1) \cdot \prod_{l=j+1}^{n} L_l] + i_n \tag{8}$$

In this paper, membership functions $A_{i_j,j}(x_j)$ are defined by the newly proposed membership function as follows:

$$A_{i_j,j}(x_j) = \frac{1}{1+e^{-\rho_{i_j,j}\left(x_j-\beta_{i_j,j}^{(1)}\right)}} - \frac{1}{1+e^{-\rho_{i_j,j}\left(x_j-\beta_{i_j,j}^{(2)}\right)}} \tag{9}$$

where $\rho_{i_j,j}$ are MF modification parameters, $\beta_{i_j,j}^{(1)}$ and $\beta_{i_j,j}^{(2)}$, satisfying $\beta_{i_j,j}^{(1)} < \beta_{i_j,j}^{(2)}$, are two parameters that control the position of $A_{i_j,j}(x_j)$ and can be determined by a clustering algorithm. The core center of $A_{i_j,j}(x_j)$ can be calculated as $\left(\beta_{i_j,j}^{(1)}+\beta_{i_j,j}^{(2)}\right)/2$. Next, a learning scheme is developed for constructing TS fuzzy models based on the new membership function and a hybrid objective function.

3.2 Learning Objective Function and Algorithm

In order to improve the TS local model interpretability while preserving its global model accuracy at a satisfactory level, the following hybrid objective function is used to guide the learning process:

$$J = J_G + \lambda J_F \tag{10}$$

where λ is a regularization coefficient, J_G is the global accuracy measure defined as

$$J_G = \frac{1}{2}\sum_{k=1}^{N}\left\| d(k) - y(k)\right\|^2 \tag{11}$$

where $d(k)$ is the desired output, and J_F is the index of fuzziness of the TS fuzzy model, defined by

$$J_F = \sum_{i_1=1}^{L_1}\cdots\sum_{i_n=1}^{L_n}\sum_{j=1}^{n} F(A_{i_j,j}) \tag{12}$$

where $F(A_{i_j,j})$ is the *index of fuzziness* of $A_{i_j,j}$, defined by 2021

$$F_q(A_{i_j,j}) = \frac{2}{\sqrt{N}}\sqrt{\sum_{k=1}^{N}\left(A_{i_j,j}(x(k)) - \underline{A}_{i_j,j}(x(k))\right)^2} \tag{13}$$

and

$$\underline{A}_{i_j,j}(x) = \begin{cases} 1 & if\ \beta_{i_j,j}^{(1)} \le x \le \beta_{i_j,j}^{(2)} \\ 0 & otherwise \end{cases} \tag{14}$$

Least-square estimation of consequent parameters. In order to identify the consequent parameters in the TS model, a base matrix M can be defined as follows:

$$M = \begin{bmatrix} M_1^T(1) & \cdots & M_L^T(1) \\ & & \\ M_1^T(N) & & M_L^T(N) \end{bmatrix}_{N \times L(n+1)} \tag{15}$$

where $M_i^T = (w_i \; w_i x_1 \; \cdots \; w_i x_n)$. By representing the consequent parameters by a column vector $\mathbf{a} = (a_{10} \; a_{11} \cdots a_{1n} \; a_{20} \; a_{21} \cdots a_{2n} \cdots\cdots a_{L0} \; a_{L1} \cdots a_{Ln})^T$, the TS model can be reformulated as follows:

$$M \cdot \mathbf{a} = \mathbf{d} \tag{16}$$

where $\mathbf{d} = (d(1) \cdots d(N))^T$ is the desired output vector. The least-squares estimate of $\mathbf{a}$ can be obtained by

$$\mathbf{a}^* = M^+ \mathbf{d} \tag{17}$$

where M^+ is the Moore-Penrose inverse of matrix M.

Gradient-descent algorithm for updating premise parameters. For the sake of simplicity, the premise parameters $\beta_{i_j,j}^{(1)}$ and $\beta_{i_j,j}^{(2)}$ can be determined by a clustering algorithm in the initialization stage. However, the premise parameters $\{\rho_{i_j,j}\}$ are updated in terms of the hybrid objective function defined in (10), which aims at achieving a good trade-off between the global approximation ability and the interpretability of local models. The equation for updating parameters $\{\rho_{i_j,j}\}$ is as follows:

$$\rho_{s,j}(t+1) = \rho_{s,j}(t) - \gamma \frac{\partial J}{\partial \rho_{s,j}} \tag{18}$$

where t is the iteration step, γ is the learning rate. From (10) we have

$$\frac{\partial J}{\partial \rho_{s,j}} = \frac{\partial J_G}{\partial \rho_{s,j}} + \lambda \frac{\partial J_F}{\partial \rho_{s,j}} \tag{19}$$

where

$$\frac{\partial J_G}{\partial \rho_{s,j}} = -\sum_{k=1}^{N} \sum_{i=1}^{L} (d(k) - y(k)) y_i(k) \frac{\partial w_i(k)}{\partial \rho_{s,j}} \tag{20}$$

$$\frac{\partial w_i(k)}{\partial \rho_{s,j}} = \frac{\sum_{l=1}^{L} \tau_l(k) \frac{\partial \tau_i(k)}{\partial \rho_{s,j}} - \tau_i \sum_{l=1}^{L} \frac{\partial \tau_l(k)}{\partial \rho_{s,j}}}{\left(\sum_{l=1}^{L} \tau_l(k) \right)^2} \tag{21}$$

$$\frac{\partial \tau_i(k)}{\partial \rho_{s,j}} = \prod_{q \neq j} A_{i_q,q}(x_q(k)) \frac{\partial A_{i_j,j}(x_j(k))}{\partial \rho_{s,j}} \tag{22}$$

and

$$\frac{\partial J_F}{\partial \rho_{s,j}} = \sum_{1 \leq i_j \leq L_j} \frac{\partial F(A_{i_j,j})}{\partial \rho_{s,j}} \tag{23}$$

$$\frac{\partial F(A_{i_j,j})}{\partial \rho_{s,j}} = \frac{2}{\sqrt{N}} \cdot \frac{\sum_{k=1}^{N} [A_{i_j,j}(x_j(k)) - \underline{A}_{i_j,j}(x_j(k))] \frac{\partial A_{i_j,j}(x_j(k))}{\partial \rho_{s,j}}}{\sqrt{\sum_{k=1}^{N} [A_{i_j,j}(x_j(k)) - \underline{A}_{i_j,j}(x_j(k))]^2}} \tag{24}$$

$$\frac{\partial A_{i_j,j}(x_j(k))}{\partial \rho_{s,j}} = \begin{cases} \frac{\partial A_{s,j}(x_j(k))}{\partial \rho_{s,j}} & i_j = s \\ 0 & i_j \neq s \end{cases} \tag{25}$$

$$\frac{\partial A_{s,j}(x_j(k))}{\partial \rho_{s,j}} = \frac{\left(x_j(k) - \beta_{s,j}^{(1)}\right) e^{-\rho_{s,j}(x_j(k) - \beta_{s,j}^{(1)})}}{\left(1 + e^{-\rho_{s,j}(x_j(k) - \beta_{s,j}^{(1)})}\right)^2} - \frac{\left(x_j(k) - \beta_{s,j}^{(2)}\right) e^{-\rho_{s,j}(x_j(k) - \beta_{s,j}^{(2)})}}{\left(1 + e^{-\rho_{s,j}(x_j(k) - \beta_{s,j}^{(2)})}\right)^2} \tag{26}$$

The above-defined least-square estimation and gradient-descent updating are carried out alternatively in two-stages. At each stage either the premise parameters are updated with the consequent parameters fixed or vice versa.

4 Experimental Results

In this section, the proposed new membership function and learning algorithm for constructing interpretable TS fuzzy models are evaluated in terms of global model accuracy and local model interpretability, which are measured respectively by root mean squared error (*RMSE*):

$$RMSE = \sqrt{\frac{1}{N} \sum_{k=1}^{N} \left(d^{(k)} - y^{(k)}\right)^2} \tag{27}$$

and local model interpretability evaluation value (*LMIEV*) 22:

$$LMIEV = \sqrt{\sum_{i=1}^{L} \sum_{x^{(k)} \in N^{(i)}} \tau_i \left(y_i(k) - y^{(k)} \right)^2} \tag{28}$$

where $N^{(i)}$ is the neighborhood of the core centre of the MF defined by (7). From (28), it can be seen that a smaller *LMIEV* value indicates better local model interpretability.

Due to the page limit, this section presents one example only, but with numerical and graphical comparison of three interpretability-oriented TS model construction methods. The data set used in the experiment was generated as follows, with high-level noise:

$$z = \tilde{z} + \hat{n} \tag{29}$$

$$\tilde{z} = \frac{3\sin(\pi x)}{1 + x^2} \tag{30}$$

where $\tilde{z}$ is the original signal, and $\hat{n}$ is a Gaussian noise with zero mean and variance of 0.1. The task here is to recover the original signal from the noisy data by constructing a TS model. The data set used in the experiment consists of 600 samples $\{(x(k), d(k))\}_{k=1}^{N}$ (*N*=600), which were randomly collected for the purpose of parameter identification with $x(k) \in [-4, 2]$. For the purpose of comparison, two other schemes for interpretability-oriented TS model construction were also tested, which are the TS model construction method based on linguistic modifier (2) and developed by Zhou and Gan 15, and the combination of global and local learning method suggested by Yen *et al.* 6.

For a fair comparison, in all the three methods the initial input space partitioning was done by using the GK fuzzy clustering algorithm 23 with Xie-Berni clustering validity index 24. 8 clusters were generated from the given data samples, which were used as the values of the β parameters in (9) to determine the MF positions (used for the same purpose in the other two methods). By using (9) and initializing the modification parameter values as 5, the 8 initial MFs are obtained, as shown in Fig. 3. The TS model and its local models constructed by using these initial MFs are illustrated in Fig. 4, with *RMSE*=0.4519. It can be seen that although the global model accuracy is very good, its local models have poor interpretability in the sense that its local models do not well reflect the real local behavior (linearity) of the real signal in corresponding local regions. The proposed method is then used to improve the local model interpretability without serious sacrifice of its global model accuracy. Fig. 5 shows the 8 MFs generated by the method proposed in this paper by setting λ=6 and stopping the learning process at a preset *RMSE* value. The corresponding modification parameter values are $[\rho_1\, \rho_2\, \rho_3\, \rho_4\, \rho_5\, \rho_6\, \rho_7\, \rho_8] = [21.88\;\; 20.63\;\; 20.49\;\; 14.11\;\; 9.92\;\; 11.17\;\; 14.64\;\; 21.27]$. The TS model and its local models constructed by using these learnt MFs are illustrated in Fig. 6, with *RMSE*=0.4637 and *LMIEV=0.5444*. Using the linguistic modifier based TS model construction method developed in 15, the 8 MFs generated are shown in Fig. 7, and the corresponding TS model and its local models are illustrated in Fig. 8, with *RMSE*=0.4600 and *LMIEV*=0.5652. Furthermore, the interpretability-oriented learning scheme suggested by Yen *et al.* 6 was also applied to the same data set to construct a TS model. This scheme combines global learning and local learning by a global influence factor α and a local influence factor β with $\alpha + \beta = 1$. In this scheme, a larger β leads to local models with better interpretability but degrades global model accuracy. The TS model and its local models constructed with β=0.2, which generated a TS model with a similar global model accuracy as by the other two methods, are shown in Fig. 9, with *RMSE*=0.4643 and *LMIEV*=0.6637.

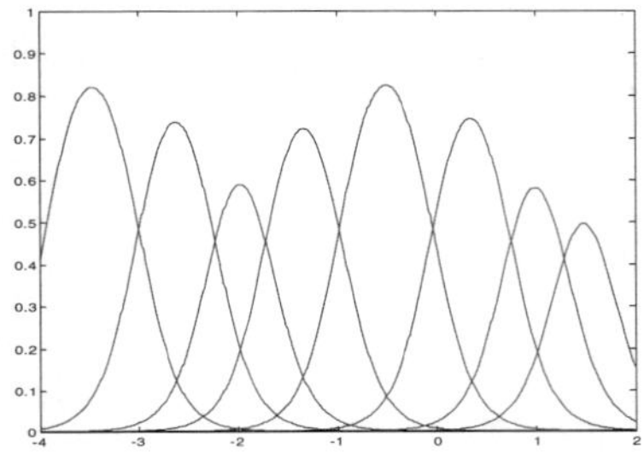

Fig. 3. Initial MFs generated by setting initial modification parameter values as 5 in (9)

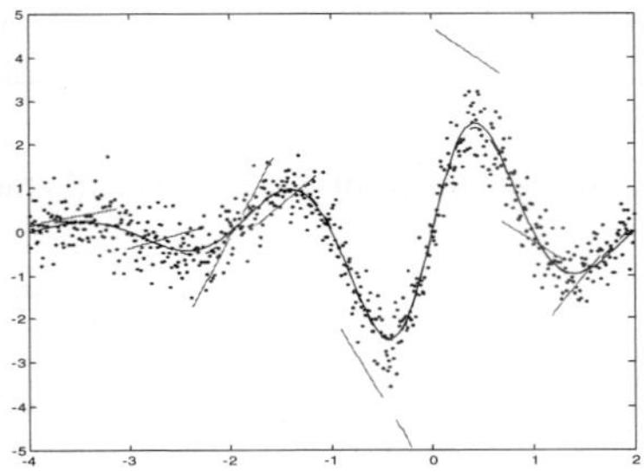

Fig. 4. TS model and local models produced by the initial MFs: solid line for true signal; dotted line for signal recovered; dashed lines for local models

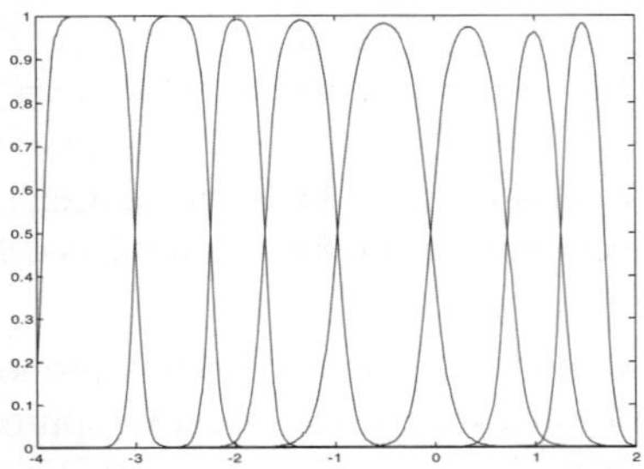

Fig. 5. MFs generated by the proposed method

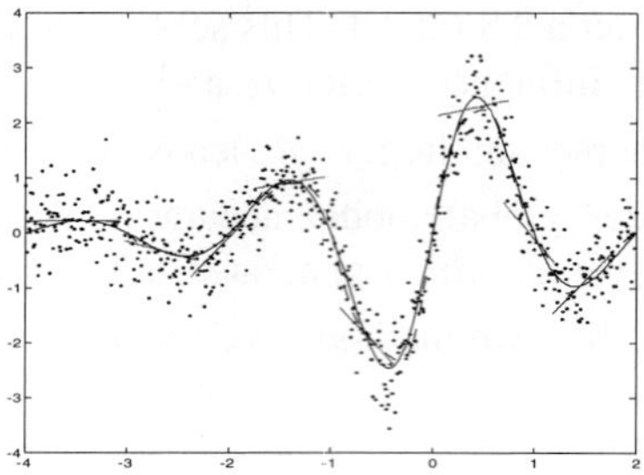

Fig. 6. TS model and local models produced by the learnt MFs: solid line for true signal; dotted line for signal recovered; dashed lines for local models

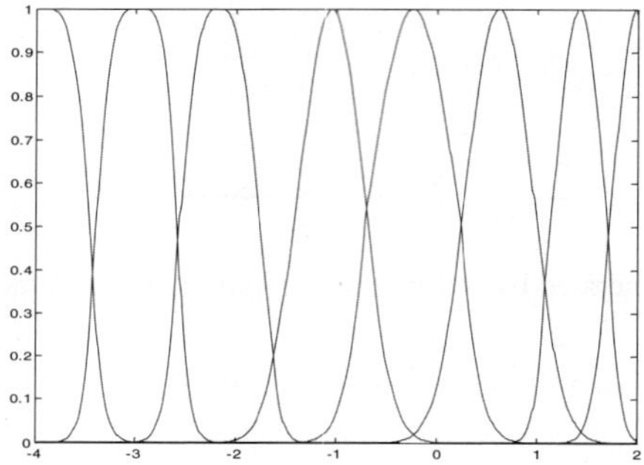

Fig. 7. MFs generated by Zhou and Gan's method

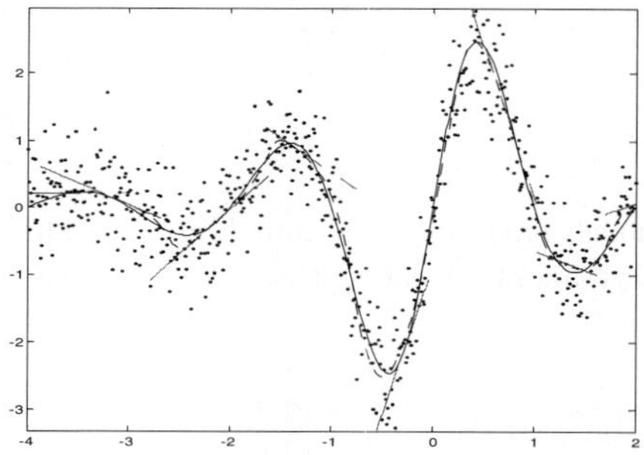

Fig. 8. TS model and local models produced by Zhou and Gan's method: solid line for true signal; dotted line for signal recovered; dashed lines for local models

From Figs. 6, 8, and 9, it can be seen that the newly proposed membership function and the learning algorithm form a simple and effective approach to the construction of interpretable TS fuzzy models. The *RMSEs* and *LMIEVs* of the three methods are summarized in Table 1, which shows that the newly developed method is capable of achieving better local model interpretability with comparable global model accuracy, with an extra advantage of simplicity that is the main motivation of this work.

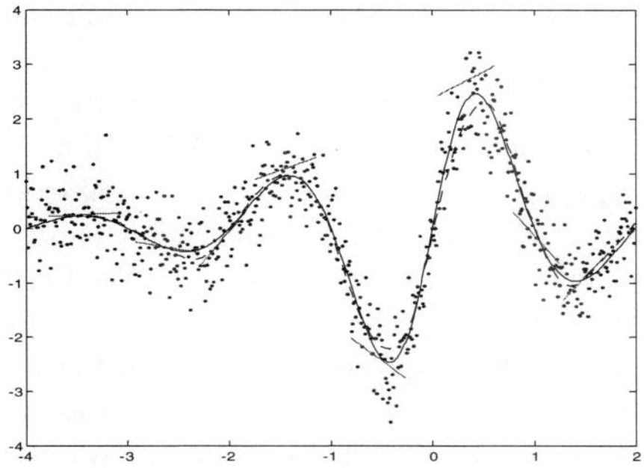

Fig. 9. TS model and local models produced by the Yen *et al.*'s method with β=0.2: solid line for true signal; dotted line for signal recovered; dashed lines for local models

Table 1. Comparison of *RMSEs* and *LMIEVs* of Three Methods

	RMSE	*LMIEV*
Newly proposed method	0.4637	0.5444
Zhou and Gan's method	0.4600	0.5652
Yen *et al.*'s method	0.4643	0.6637

5 Conclusions

A new membership function is proposed in this paper, which is simple and has desirable properties for constructing interpretable neurofuzzy models. A learning scheme based on this new membership function is developed as well for achieving optimal balance between global model accuracy and local model interpretability. Experimental results, in comparison with other two interpretability-oriented methods for constructing TS fuzzy models, have provided favorable evidence to support the new approach. In our future research, the models constructed by the new method will be expected to find successful applications in nonlinear state estimation, process modeling and control.

References

1. Takagi, T., Sugeno, M.: Fuzzy Identification of Systems and Its Applications to Modeling and Control, IEEE Trans. on Systems, Man and Cybernetics, Vol. 15, No. 1, (1985) 116-132
2. J.-S.R, Jang.: ANFIS: Adaptive-Network-Based Fuzzy Inference System, IEEE Trans. on Systems, Man and Cybernetics, Vol. 23, No. 3, (1993) 665-685
3. Wang, L-X.: Adaptive Fuzzy Systems and Control, Englewood Cliffs, NJ: Prentice-Hall, 1994
4. Gan, Q., Harris, C.J.: Fuzzy Llocal Linearization and Local Basis Function Expansion in Nonlinear System Modeling, IEEE Trans. on Systems, Man and Cybernetics - Part B, Vol. 29, No. 4, (1999) 559-565

5. Harris, C.J, Hong, X., Gan,Q.:Adaptive Modeling, Estimation and Fusion from Data - A Neurofuzzy Approach, Springer (2002)
6. J. Yen, L. Wang, C.W. Gillespie.: Improving the Interpretability of TSK Fuzzy Models by Combining Gglobal Learning and Local Learning," IEEE Trans. on Fuzzy Systems, Vol. 6, No. 4, (1998) 530-537
7. Oliveira, J.V. de.: Semantic Constraints for Membership Function Optimization, IEEE Trans. on Systems, Man and Cybernetics-Part A, Vol. 29, No. 1,(1999) 128-138
8. Jin, Y.: Fuzzy Modeling of High-Dimensional Systems: Complexity Reduction and Iinterpretability Iimprovement, IEEE Trans. on Fuzzy Systems, Vol. 8, No. 2, (2000) 212-221
9. Hoppner, F., Klawonn, F.: Obtaining Interpretable Fuzzy Models From Fuzzy Clustering and Fuzzy Regression, Proc. of the 4th Int. Conf. on Knowledge-based Intelligent Eng. Syst. and Allied Tech (KES), Brighton, UK, (2000)162-165
10. Roubos,H., Setnes, M.: Compact and Transparent Fuzzy Models and Classifiers Through iterative complexity reduction, IEEE Trans. on Fuzzy Systems, Vol. 9, No. 4, (2001) 516-524
11. Guillaume, S.: Designing Fuzzy Inference Systems from Data: An Interpretability-oriented Review, IEEE Trans. on Fuzzy Systems, Vol. 9, No. 3,(2001) 426-443
12. Johansen, T.A., Babuska, R.: Multi-objective Identification of Takagi-Sugeno Fuzzy Models, IEEE Trans. on Fuzzy Systems, Vol. 11, No. 6, (2003)847-860
13. Casillas, J., Cordon, O. , Herrera,F., L. Magdalena.: Interpretability Improvements to Find the Balance Between Interpretability-accuracy in Fuzzy Modeling: An Overview, in J. Casillas, O. Cordon, F. Herrera, and L. Magdalena (Eds.), Interpretability Issues in Fuzzy Modeling, Vol. 128 of Studies in Fuzziness and Soft Computing, Springer, (2003) 3-24
14. Zhou, S.-M., Gan, J.Q.: Interpretability Improvement of Input Space Partitioning by Merging Fuzzy Sets Based on An Entropy Measure, Proc. of IEEE Int. Conference on Fuzzy Systems (FUZZ-IEEE2004), Budapest, Hungary, July (2004) 287-292
15. Zhou, S.-M., Gan.,J.Q.: Improving the Interpretability of Takagi-Sugeno Fuzzy Model by Using Linguistic Modifiers and A Multiple Objective Learning Scheme, Proc. of the Int. Joint Conf. on Neural Networks (IJCNN2004), Budapest, (2004) 2385-2390
16. Bezdek,J.C.: Pattern Recognition with Fuzzy Objective Function Algorithms. New York: Plenum, (1981)
17. Zadeh., L.A.: A Fuzzy-set Theoretic Interpretation of Linguistic Hedges, Journal of Cybernetics, Vol. 2, No. 2, (1972) 4-34
18. Jakel, J., Groll,L.,R. Mikut, Tree-oriented Hypothesis Generation for Interpretable Fuzzy rules, Proc. of 7th European Congress on Intelligent Techniques and Soft Computing, Aachen, Germany, (1999) 279-280
19. Liu, B.-D., Chen, C.-Y., Tsao, J.-Y.: Design of Aadaptive Fuzzy Logic Controller Based on Linguistic-hedge Concepts and Genetic Algorithms, IEEE Trans. on Systems, Man and Cybernetics - Part B, Vol. 31, No. 1,(2001) 32-53
20. Kaufmann.: Introduction to the Theory of Fuzzy Subsets, Academic Press: New York, (1975)
21. Yager, R.R.: On the Measure of Fuzziness and Negation Part I: Membership in the Unit Interval, Int. Journal of Gen. Syst., Vol. 5, (1979) 221–229
22. Zhou, S.-M.: Machine Learning and Intelligent Data Analysis for Interpretable Neurofuzzy System Modelling, Ph.D. Thesis, Department of Computer Science, University of Essex, UK,(2006)
23. Gustafson ,D.E., Kessel,W.: Fuzzy Clustering With a Fuzzy Covariance Matrix," Proc. of IEEE-CDC, Voll.2 K.S. Fu (ed.), IEEE Press, Piscataway, New Jersey, (1979)761-766
24. Xie, X.L., Berni.,G.A.:Validity Measure for Fuzzy Clustering, IEEE Trans. Pattern Analysis and Machine Intelligence, Vol.3, No.3, (1991)841–846

Fuzzy Data Clustering Using Artificial Immune Network

Li Liu and Wenbo Xu

School of Information Technology , Southern Yangtze University
Wuxi, Jiangsu, 214122, China
yxhll@pub.wx.jsinfo.net

Abstract. This paper presents a novel fuzzy clustering method named as AINFCM, which solves the traditional fuzzy clustering problems by searching for the optimal centroids of clusters using artificial immune network technology. Based on the clone and affinity mutation principals of biological immunity mechanism, containing memory cells, the AINFCM is capability of maintaining local optima solutions and exploring the global optima defined as minimum of the objective function. The algorithm is described theoretically and compared with classical K-means, K-medoid, FCM and GK Clustering methods using PC, CE, SC, S, ADI and DI validity indexes. Parameter setting was also discussed to analyze how sensitive the AINFCM is to user-defined parameters.

1 Introduction

Cluster analysis divides data into groups (clusters) such that similar data objects belong to the same cluster and dissimilar data objects to different clusters. In real-world applications, there is very often no sharp boundary between clusters so that fuzzy clustering is often much more suited for the data. Applications of fuzzy cluster analysis include data analysis, pattern recognition, and image segmentation.

Membership degrees between zero and one are used in fuzzy clustering instead of crisp assignments of the data to clusters. The terminologies to denominate the representatives of clusters are centers, centroids or prototypes. The family of objective function-based fuzzy clustering algorithms includes fuzzy c-means algorithm (FCM)[1], Gustafson-Kessel algorithm (GK)[2], Gath-Geva algorithm (GG)[3] and many others.

FCM, the most prominent fuzzy clustering algorithm is a local optimization algorithm, a random selection of initial value may lead to crisp premise fuzzy set. In order to present a global optimization version of FCM, some biological inspired evolutionary algorithm was used. A genetic algorithm was proposed to evolve step FCM and shown good results [4]. However, the degeneration of genetic algorithm may increase iteration times and decrease veracity.

The vertebrate immune system has several useful theories from the viewpoint of information processing. The immune network theory imitates the activities of the immune cells, the emergence of memory and the discrimination between our

D.-S. Huang, K. Li, and G.W. Irwin (Eds.): ICIC 2006, LNAI 4114, pp. 195–205, 2006.

own cells (known as self) and external invaders (known as non-self). There are several immune network models presented in the literature. The aiNet immune network model proposed by Leandro N. de Castro can be used for data compression and hierarchical data clustering [5]. An adaptive version of aiNet named as opt-aiNet is able to implement function optimization [6].

In this paper, AINFCM algorithm working as an artificial immune network was proposed to perform fuzzy data clustering, according to the view that data clustering is essentially centroids optimization problem. The objective function of FCM algorithm was adopted as optimal function. So, based on the clone and affinity mutation principals of biological immunity mechanism, containing memory cells, the AINFCM is capability of maintaining local optima solutions and exploring the global optima.

The outline of this paper was as follows. In section 2, the AINFCM algorithm was described. In section 3, AINFCM was tested for Iris and wine data set and compared with K-means, K-medoid, FCM and GK clustering algorithms according to 6 validity indexes. The setting of immune network parameters was also discussed. Finally, we draw some conclusions and looked at future research.

2 Fuzzy C-Means Algorithm (FCM)

Fuzzy c-means (FCM) is a method of clustering which allows one piece of data to belong to two or more clusters. This method can be seen as a strategy for minimizing the following objective function:

$$J(U, c_1, \ldots, c_c) = \sum_{i=1}^{c} J_i = \sum_{i=1}^{c} \sum_{j}^{n} u_{ij}^m d_{ij}^2, \tag{1}$$

under the constraints:

$$\sum_{i=1}^{c} u_{ij} = 1, \forall j = 1, \ldots, n \quad . \tag{2}$$

where $u_{ij} \in [0, 1]$ indicates the membership of data vector x_i assigned to clusteri^{th}. $c_j$is the jth centroid of C and d_{ij} is the Euclidean distance between data vectorx_i and centroidc_j. Parameter $m \in [1, \infty)$ is so-called fuzzifier, which is used to control how much clusters are allowed to overlap [7].

FCM is carried out through an iterative optimization of the objective function shown as equation (1). Taken the constraints (2) into account by Lagrange function, the new objective function is constructed as following:

$$\begin{aligned} J(U, c_1, \ldots, c_c, \lambda_1, \ldots, \lambda_n) &= J(U, c_1, \ldots, c_c) + \sum_{j=1}^{n} \lambda_j \left(\sum_{i=1}^{c} u_{ij} - 1\right) \\ &= \sum_{i=1}^{c} \sum_{j}^{n} u_{ij}^m d_{ij}^2 + \sum_{j=1}^{n} \lambda_j \left(\sum_{i=1}^{c} u_{ij} - 1\right), \end{aligned} \tag{3}$$

with the update of membership u_{ij} and the cluster centers c_j by:

$$c_j = \frac{\sum_{j=1}^{n} u_{ij}^m x_j}{\sum_{j=1}^{n} u_{ij}^m} \quad , \tag{4}$$

$$u_{ij} = \frac{1}{\sum_{k=1}^{c} \left(\frac{d_{ij}}{d_{kj}}\right)^{\frac{2}{m-1}}} \quad . \tag{5}$$

3 AINFCM Algorithm

3.1 Artificial Immune Network Theory

The immune network theory, as originally proposed by Jerne [8], hypothesized a novel viewpoint of lymphocyte activities, natural antibody (Ab) production, pre-immune repertoire selection, tolerance, self/nonself discrimination, memory and the evolution of the immune system[9]. The immune system was formally defined as an enormous and complex network of paratopes, which recognize sets of idiotopes, and of idiotopes(Ag), that are recognized by sets of paratopes. The relevant events in the immune system are not only the molecules, but alsc their interactions. The immune cells can respond either positively or negatively to the recognition signal. A positive response would result in cell proliferation, activation and antibody secretion, while a negative response would lead to tolerance and suppression. In general terms, the structure of most network models can be represented as

$$\begin{aligned} RPV = InfluxofNnewCells - DeathofUnstimulatedCells \\ +ReproductionofStimulatedCells, \end{aligned} \tag{6}$$

where RPV is the rate of population variation, and the last term includes Ab–Ab recognition and Ag–Ab stimulation.

3.2 Problem Description

The artificial immune network is an edge-weighted graph, not necessarily fully connected, composed of a set of nodes, called antibodies, and sets of node pairs called edges with an assigned number called weight, or connection strength. To fuzzy data clustering problem:

Antigens (Ag) represent data set for data clustering.$Ag_{N\times P} \subset \Re^P$ Euclidean Shape-space.N is the number of data and P is the dimension degree.

Antibodies(Ab) are evolved centroids of clusters. $Ab_{M\times CP} \subset \Re^{CP}$,where $CP = P \times ClusterNumber$,M is the number of network cells.

From objective function equation (1) we can see that the goal of FCM is to obtain the optimal centroids set C and membership matrix U. Since there is relationship between C and U, it is feasible to encode either C or U. We encode C into antibodies of immune network accounting for calculation scle.

Fitness (f) evaluates a set of given centroids, which is inversely proportional to objective function J. The smaller FCM objective function J is, the better output centroids C are. f can be calculated as:

$$f = \frac{1}{J\left(Ab_i, Ag\right) + 1}, \qquad f \in [0, 1] \quad . \tag{7}$$

Similarity of Ab_i to Ab_j describes the recognition level within antibodies.

$$Similarity\left(Ab_i, Ab_k\right) = D\left(Ab_i, Ab_k\right) = \sqrt{\sum_{i=1}^{P}\left(Ab_{j_i}, Ab_{k_i}\right)^2} \quad . \tag{8}$$

Clone and Mutation: Through clone process,offspring cells are identical copies of their parent cell as a certain clone rate. Then offspring will suffer a somatic mutation so that they become variations of their parent. Clone rate N and mutation rate β are proportional to the fitness of Ab, which determine the next generation of antibodies.

$$Ab^* = Ab + \beta N(0, 1), \tag{9}$$

where $N(0,1)$is a Gaussian random variable of zero mean and standard deviation $\sigma = 1$.
Stop criterion can be set as a fixed iteration number of step FCM, combined with following:

$$\|f^{(n+1)} - f^{(n)}\| < \varepsilon \quad . \tag{10}$$

3.3 Process of AINFCM

Set the parameters and initialize immune network.
While stopping criterion is not met *do*
Calculate the fitness value of network cells and normalize the vector of fitness.
Select best antibodies to lone and mutate proportionally to their fitness values.
Calculate fitness vector of new generation.
Reselect highest fitness cells with $\varsigma\%$ from new generation.
Suffer network suppression and remove cells with lower fitness value and higher similarity value.
Random add $d\%$ new cells.
Calculate the highest fitness value of network cells.
Determine the clusters and membership function.

4 Experiments

The AINFCM algorithm was applied to several fuzzy data clustering problems in order to assess its performance. In this paper, Iris data set and Wine data set were selected to illustrated the process of AINFCM algorithm.

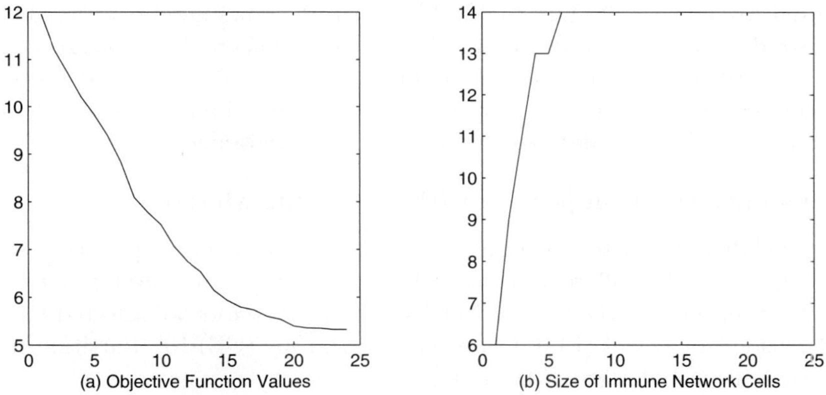

Fig. 1. Iris data set (a) Objective function value in each iteration (b) Size of immune network cells in each iteration

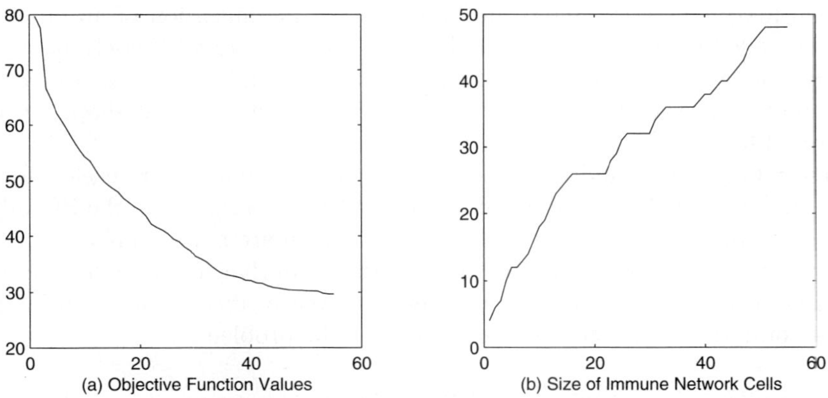

Fig. 2. Wine data set (a) Objective function value in each iteration (b) Size of immune network cells in each iteration

Iris data set
The data set contains 3 classes of 50 instances with 5 attributes. One class is linearly separable from the other two classes; the latter are nonlinear separated from each other.
Wine data set
The Wine data contains the chemical analysis of 178 wines grown in the same region in Italy but derived from three different cultivars. The problem is to distinguish the three different types based on 13 continuous attributes derived from chemical analysis.

Fig.1 showed that after 10 times iteration, the immune network for Iris data set became stable containing 16 memory cells, and the value of objective function decreased from 20 to 5. In fig.2, after 40 times iteration, the immune network became stable containing 45 memory cells, and the value of objective function decreased from 75 to 30. The AINFCM algorithm shows good convergence for these two data set.The number of attributes mainly affects the convergence rate and size of immune network of the AINFCM algorithm. Noticed that the value of objective function is a relative value, which can only be used as a evaluation for the results of a fixed data set running with different algorithms.

4.1 Validity and Comparison with Clustering Methods

Cluster validity refers to the problem whether a given fuzzy partition result fits to the data all. Different scalar validity measures have been proposed in the literature, none of them is perfect by oneself, therefore we selected 6 criteria: Partition Coefficient (PC), Classification Entropy (CE)[10], Partition Index (SC), Separation Index (S), ADI and DI [11].

There were four clustering methods compared with AINFCM: K-means, K-medoid, FCM and GK [12]. K-means and K-medoid are hard partitioning methods, which are simple and popular, although these algorithms have some numerical problems. The FCM (Fuzzy C-means) clustering algorithm is a classical fuzzy clustering algorithm based on the minimization of an objective function called C-means functional. The GK (Gustafson and Kessel) algorithm extends the standard fuzzy c-means algorithm by employing an adaptive distance norm, in order to detect clusters of different geometrical shapes in one data set [14].

Firstly, from table1 and table2 we can see that PC and CE are useless for K-means and K-medoid, while they are hard clustering methods. So the PC values of K-means and K-medoid are 1, CE values of them are not a number.

Secondly, the values in the table1 were better than that in the table2, because the numerical values of all validity indexes were greatly affected by the attributes number of data set, which represented scale of the problem.

Table 1. The values of PC, CE, SC, S, DI, ADI validity indexes for Iris data set

	PC	CE	SC	S	DI	ADI
AINFCM	0.74671	0.47642	0.26236	0.0027312	0.070093	0.011067
K-means	1	NaN	0.49752	0.0049515	0.016397	0.0095903
K-medoid	1	NaN	0.49295	0.0048583	0.089868	0.0091068
FCM	0.74252	0.46721	0.62591	0.0063462	0.034696	0.0090153
GK	0.72774	0.46631	0.51275	0.0048623	0.043001	0.01935

Table 2. The values of PC, CE, SC, S, DI, ADI validity indexes for Wine data set

	PC	CE	SC	S	DI	ADI
AINFCM	0.53128	0.88701	1.21505	0.00891	0.13170	0.00120
K-means	1	NaN	0.97091	0.00673	0.13511	0.00222
K-medoid	1	NaN	0.84543	0.00500	0.14236	0.00697
FCM	0.50338	0.85461	1.62950	0.01200	0.14232	0.00452
GK	0.35420	1.06823	8.69256	0.06058	0.10961	0.00201

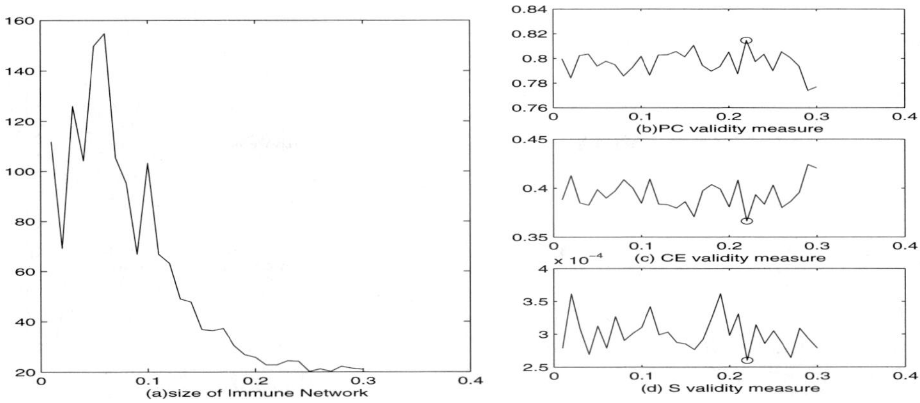

Fig. 3. AINFCM sensitivity to ts. (a) Relationship between and size of immune network. (b) Validity measure values of PC,CE and S in consideration of $ts \in [0.1, 0.3]$.

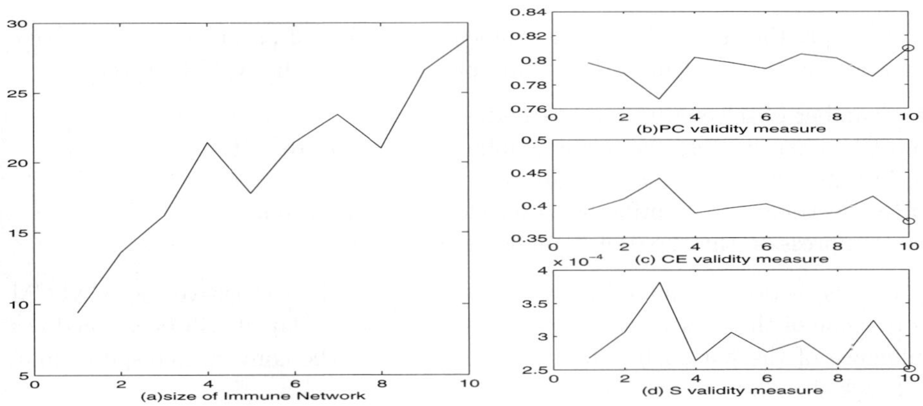

Fig. 4. AINFCM sensitivity to n. (a) Relationship between n and size of immune network. (b) Validity measure values of PC,CE and S in consideration of $n \in [1, 10]$.

Thirdly, the table1 illustrated that the value of PC index for AINFCM algorithm was greater than the value for FCM and GK algorithm, at the same time, the values of S, SC indexes for AINFCM algorithm were smaller than the values for FCM and GK algorithm. Table2 illustrated that the AINFCM algorithm was good than K-means, K-medoid and GK algorithms according to all five indexes and good than FCM algorithm according to S, DI and ADI indexes.

In short, the results partly depend from the structure of the data, and no validity index is perfect by itself for a clustering problem.

4.2 Network Parameter Setting

During the process, number of clusters, parameters of immune network were fixed as $m = 2$,$\varepsilon = 1e - 3$.

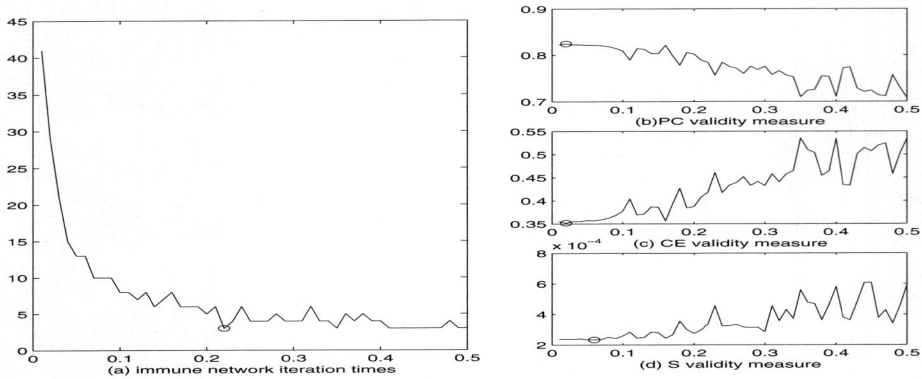

Fig. 5. AINFCM sensitivity to β. (a) Relationship between β and size of immune network. (b) Validity measure values of PC,CE and S in consideration of $\beta \in [0, 0.5]$.

To apply the AINFCM to any problem, a number of parameters for immune network have to be defined. The main parameters for the AINFCM were:

n : Number of selected n best antibodies;
N : Clone parameter, max clone number of each selected Ab;
β: Mutate parameter, max mutate rate;
ς: Reselection rate of antibodies after clone and mutation;
ts : Suppression threshold of immune network cells;

In this section, we intend to discuss and analyze how sensitive the AINFCM is to some of these user-defined parameters. In particular, it will be studied the influence of the parameters ts , n ,N ,β and ς in the convergence speed, final network size and validity index values.

Figure 3 (a) illustrates that the suppression threshold ts , which leads to the deletion of similar network memory cells with lower fitness, controls the final network size and is responsible for the network plasticity. Too large value for ts indicates small network size, while too small value results in larger immune network . The value of ts at minimum position of CE and S validity measure is same as that of maximum value of PC validity measure, which indicates the optimal $ts = 0.22$.

In each iteration, n best Ab with the highest fitness will be selected to undergo mutation. The clone rate and mutation rate are proportional to the fitness of each selected antibody. Figure 4 (a) demonstrates this suspicion. Figure 4 (b) shows that larger value of n will improve the validity of AINFCM, but for PC and CE measures, it shows little influence. To acquire a balance between network size and validity, $n = 4$ or$n = 8$ can be set.

Figure 5 illustrates that the mutate parameter β is critical to control the iteration times of AINFCM final network size and is responsible for the convergence of the network. Too small value for β leads to large iteration times. The value of β at minimum position of CE and S validity measure and at that of maximum

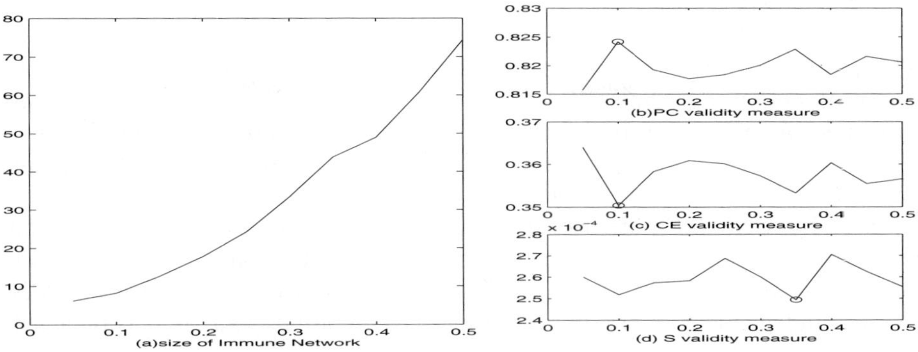

Fig. 6. AINFCM sensitivity to ς. (a) Relationship between ς and size of immune network. (b) Validity measure values of PC,CE and S in consideration of $\varsigma \in [0, 0.5]$.

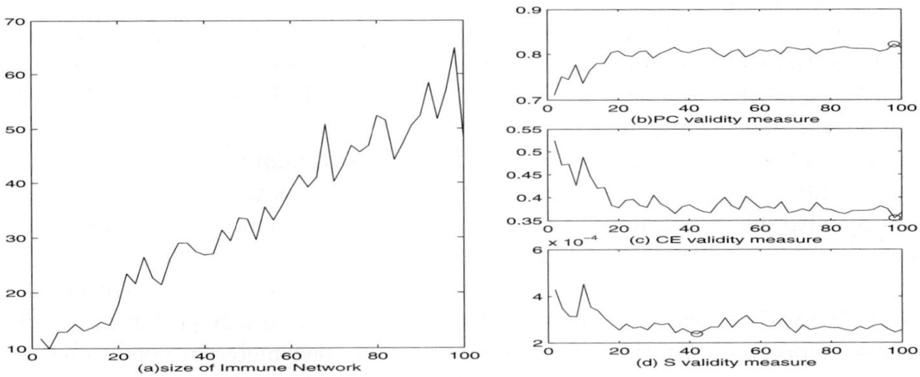

Fig. 7. AINFCM sensitivity to N. (a) Relationship between N and size of immune network. (b) Validity measure values of PC,CE and S in consideration of $N \in [1, 100]$.

value of PC validity measure indicate the optimal β value. To acquire a balance between convergence time and validity, $\beta = 0.05$ can be set.

Figure 6 illustrates that the reselection rate of antibodies after clone and mutation ς is critical to control the iteration times of AINFCM final network size and is responsible for the convergence of the network. Too small value for ς leads to large iteration times. The value ofς at minimum position of CE and S validity measure and at that of maximum value of PC validity measure indicate the optimalς value. To acquire a balance between convergence time and validity,$\varsigma = 0.1$ can be set.

Figure 7 illustrates that the clone parameter, maximum clone number of each selected antibody.N controls the iteration times of AINFCM final network size and is responsible for the convergence of the network. Too small value for$N$ leads to low value of validity measures. To acquire a balance between convergence time and validity, $N = 20$ can be set.

5 Summary and Conclusions

This paper presented an immune network AINFCM for fuzzy clustering. Firstly, the results of our experiments clearly show that the AINFCM algorithm is able to keep local optimal centroids of clusters as memory network cells and to explore global optimum through clone and mutation and renew processes of the immune network.

Secondly,AINFCM outperforms K-means, K-medoid, and GK algorithm according to Partition Coefficient, Classification Entropy, Partition Index, Separation Index, ADI and DI criteria. Compared with FCM algorithm, AINFCM is independent of the initially random individuals and show comparable performance.

Thirdly, parameter setting is an important and heavy task for biological based algorithms. In this paper, the parameters of the AINFCM immune network were set according to a balance between convergence time and validity. The suppression threshold ts , which leads to the deletion of similar network memory cells with lower fitness, controls the final network size and is responsible for the network plasticity. The mutate parameter β is critical to control the iteration times and is responsible for the convergence of the network. In most cases, $\beta = 0.05$ can be set.

Noticed that AINFCM and other algorithms use random initialization, so different running issues different partition results, such as values of the centroids and membership function matrix. To minimize the influence of random initialization, average value of partition results for each algorithm should be used.

With regards to future research we are focus on several topics. We plan to exert AINFCM to various structure data set in order to test performance and adapt to special applications. Since there are many parameters needed to be set, we are going to do further study for self-adjusting parameters.

References

1. Dunn, J. C.: A Fuzzy Relative of the ISODATA Process and Its Use in Detecting Compact Well-Separated Clusters. Journal of Cybernetics, **3** (1973) 32–57
2. Ska, R. B., Van Der Veen, P. J., Kaymak, U. : Improved Covariance Estimation for Gustafson-Kessel Clustering. IEEE International Conference on Fuzzy Systems, (2002) 1081–1085
3. Gath, I., Geva, A. B.: Unsupervised Optimal Fuzzy Clustering. IEEE Transactions on Pattern Analysis and Machine Intelligence, 7 (1989) 773-781
4. Velasco, J. R. , Opez, S. L , Magdalena, L.: Genetic Fuzzy Clustering for The Definition of Fuzzy Sets. Proc. Sixth IEEE International Conference on Fuzzy Systems, Barcelona (1997) 1665-1670
5. Castro, D., Zuben, V. L. N.: AiNet: An Artificial Immune Network for Data Analysis. Idea Group Publishing, USA (2001) 231–259
6. Leandro, N. D. C., Jon, T.: An Artificial Immune Network for Multimodal Function Optimization. Proceedings of IEEE Congress on Evolutionary Computation (CEC'02), Hawaii, **1** (2002) 699–674

7. Klawonn, F., Hoppner, F. : What Is Fuzzy about Fuzzy Clustering? Understanding and Improving The Concept of The Fuzzifier. In: MR Berthold: Advances in Intelligent Data Analysis, Springer, Berlin (2003) 254–264
8. Jerne, N. K.: Towards A Network Theory of the Immune System. Ann. Immuno, 125C (1974) 373–389
9. Perelsen, A. S. , Oster, G. F. : Theoretical Studies of Clonal Selection: Minimal Antibody Repertoire Size and Reliability of Self-Nonself Discrimination. J. Theor. Biol. 81(1979) 645–670
10. Bezdek, J. C.: Pattern Recognition with Fuzzy Objective Function Algorithms. Plenum Press, Harris (1981)
11. Bensaid, A. M., Hall, L. O., Bezdek, J. C., Clarke, L. P., Silbiger, M. L. Arrington, J. A., Murtagh, R. F. V.: Validity-guided Clustering with Applications to Imige Segmentation. IEEE Transactions on Fuzzy Systems, 4 (1996) 112–123
12. Balazs, B., Janos, A., Balazs, F.: Fuzzy Clustering and Data Analysis Toolbox For Use with Matlab. http://www.fmt.vein.hu/softcomp/

RAOGA-Based Fuzzy Neural Network Model of Design Evaluation

Li-Hua Xue[1,2], Hong-Zhong Huang[1], Jun Hu[1], Qiang Miao[1], and Dan Ling[1]

[1] School of Mechatronics Eng., University of Electronic Science and Technology of China, Chengdu, Sichuan 610054, China
hzhuang@uestc.edu.cn
[2] School of Mechanical Eng., Dalian University of Technology, Dalian, Liaoning 116023, China
xuelih@hotmail.com

Abstract. This paper presents a new Fuzzy Neural Network (FNN) model to evaluate design alternatives in conceptual design. In the proposed method, a fuzzy reasoning based on feedforward neural network is used to evaluate concepts, and a learning algorithm based on ranking-based adaptive evolutionary operator genetic algorithm (RAOGA) is utilized to adjust fuzzy weights and thresholds with fuzzy inputs and outputs in FNN.

1 Introduction

The evaluation and decision of conceptual design is very important, which is the key to total design of products. The process of conceptual design is very complicated and the information in this stage is incomplete, uncertain and imprecise [1-2]. Conventional methods, such as weighted objectives method, are not flexible to deal with fuzzy information [3]. The recent advances of fuzzy set theory provide new tools for managing incomplete and imprecise information. Thurston and Carnaban proposed the Fuzzy Weighted Average (FWA) to multi-criteria design evaluation [4]. However, Vanegas and Labib pointed that the normalized weights were not used in the conventional FWA method to avoid the extended division, which increased the imprecision [5]. Identification of the importance of each criterion is another important task in conceptual design evaluation. The analytical hierarchy process (AHP) is the commonly used method to determine the relative importance of each alternative or criterion. But some subjective problems are inevitable when AHP is adopted.

This paper proposed a FNN model to evaluate design alternatives in conceptual design. In the proposed method, a feedforward neural network-based fuzzy reasoning was used to evaluate concepts and a RAOGA-based learning algorithm was adopted to adjust fuzzy weights and thresholds with fuzzy inputs and outputs of FNN.

The paper is organized as follows: Section 2 proposes the FNN model with a RAOGA-based fuzzy learning algorithm. Section 3 presents application of FNN model to evaluate and identify design alternatives in conceptual design. Section 4 concludes this paper.

D.-S. Huang, K. Li, and G.W. Irwin (Eds.): ICIC 2006, LNAI 4114, pp. 206–211, 2006.

2 RAOGA-Based FNN Model

FNN is an evaluation method based on knowledge, which simulates the logic thinking of human brain and has strong approaching capability of nonlinear function. In this paper, a FNN model with fuzzy inputs and fuzzy weights will be used to conceptual design evaluation.

2.1 Structure of Evaluation Model

According to the features of conceptual design evaluation, the FNN model presented in this research is shown in Fig. 1, where n_{I}, n_{H} and n_{O} are the numbers of neurons in input layer, hidden layer and output layer respectively.

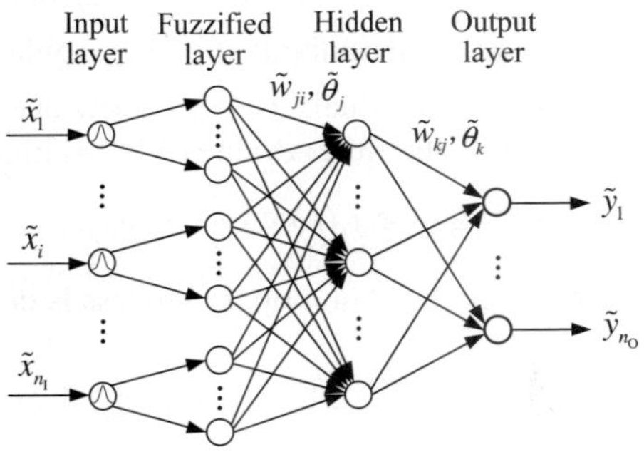

Fig. 1. FNN model of conceptual design evaluation

The input and output relation of each unit of the FNN can be seen in [6].

In engineering application, triangular or trapezoidal functions are usually used to depict fuzzy variables. But Kuo and Xue pointed that the assumption of triangular or trapezoidal distribution is not similar to human beings' thinking [7]. In this paper, to simplify the problem, symmetric normal function denoted with two-tuple (μ, σ) is used to represent membership function of fuzzy numbers. Normal distribution of fuzzy numbers is shown in Fig. 2.

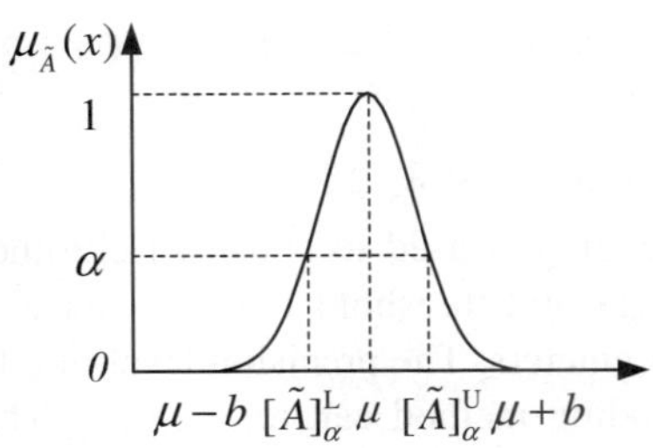

Fig. 2. Normal distribution fuzzy number

Normal function-shaped fuzzy numbers can be elaborated with two-tuple (μ, σ), where μ is the centre of normal function. According to the "3σ rule", we can let $\sigma = b/3$. As shown in Fig. 2, b is the half span length of normal function.

2.2 RAOGA

To avoid the deficiencies of simple genetic algorithm, in this research, a ranking based adaptive evolutionary operator genetic algorithm is adopted to train fuzzy weights and thresholds of FNN.

The evolutionary process of RAOGA can be described with Markov chain. Let state space be $S = B^{l*n}$, where l represents the binary length of every individual and n is the population size of GA. Every element in state space can be viewed as an integer expressed with binary codes. Let $\pi_i(k)$ represent the kth binary segment of the ith element in state space, i.e. $\pi_i(k)$ is kth individual in the population of state i.

In RAOGA, the ranking of individuals is performed according to their fitness values. In the state i after ranking, the fitness value of left is bigger than that of right.

$$f_i(1) \geq f_i(2) \geq \cdots \geq f_i(k) \geq \cdots \geq f_i(n) \ . \tag{1}$$

The selection ratio of $\pi_i(k)$ in the evolutionary process is defined as

$$s(\pi_i(k)) = \frac{1}{n} + \alpha(t) \cdot \frac{n+1-2k}{n(n+1)} \qquad (k = 1, 2, \cdots, n) \ . \tag{2}$$

Where $\alpha(t)$ is adaptive coefficient of selection operator, $0 < \alpha(t) < 1$.

The action of crossover is to combine useful genetic information in the individuals to be swapped to generate offspring. The crossover ratio of RAOGA is defined as

$$p_c(\pi_i(k)) = \lambda_c \cdot [1 - \exp(-\frac{\beta_c(k-1)}{n})] \qquad (k = 1, 2, \cdots, n) \ . \tag{3}$$

Where λ_c and β_c are constants, $0 < \lambda_c \leq 1$.

Mutation simulates the change of gene mode caused by accidental factors in natural evolutionary environment. The mutation ratio of RAOGA is defined as

$$p_m(\pi_i(k)) = \lambda_m \cdot [1 - \exp(-\frac{\beta_m(k-1)}{n})] \qquad (k = 1, 2, \cdots, n) \ . \tag{4}$$

Where λ_m and β_m are constants, $0 < \lambda_m \leq 1$.

In RAOGA, binary encoding is used to construct chromosomes of fuzzy weights and thresholds, Each weight and threshold is expressed as normal function-shaped fuzzy number with two parameters. The precision level of a fuzzy weight is 8 bits per parameter. The detailed coding method can refer to [8]. The construction of fitness function in RAOGA can be seen in [6].

2.3 RAOGA-Based Learning Mechanism of FNN

The learning of FNN is to construct the nonlinear mapping between fuzzy inputs and fuzzy outputs and make FNN have the capability of association and judgment. The learning process of FNN based on RAOGA is summarized as follows:

Step 1. Map solution space into genetic search space represented with binary code, set values of λ_c, λ_m, β_c and β_m, determine the population size, the function $\alpha(t)$ and termination conditions of RAOGA, and construct fitness function.

Step 2. Initialize the fuzzy weights and fuzzy thresholds.

Step 3. Repeat Step 4 for $p = 1, 2, \cdots, m$, where *p* is the number of samples.

Step 4. Repeat the following procedures for $\alpha = \{\alpha_1, \alpha_2, \cdots, \alpha_n\}$.

Calculate α -cuts of fuzzy output and the total squared error;

Step 5. Evaluate each individual in the population of RAOGA.

Step 6. If termination conditions are met, go to Step 10.

Step 7. Rank individuals and calculate selection ratio of each individual.

Step 8. Compute crossover ratio according to Eq. (4), create new individuals by crossover and replace poor parent individuals with the newly generated ones.

Step 9. Compute mutation ratio according to Eq. (5) and mutate at randomly selected point. Return to Step 5.

Step 10. Stop search and translate into the fuzzy weights and thresholds of FNN.

After training, the FNN model can be used to the evaluation of conceptual design.

3 Case Study: Evaluation and Selection of Tank Engines

FNN will be capable of associating and reasoning after learning fuzzy rules. In this section, the conceptual design evaluation of tank engines is used as an example to illustrate and verify the proposed RAOGA-based FNN evaluation model.

Evaluation is an important task in the design process of tank engines. In this section, we use the RAOGA-based FNN model to perform the design evaluation of tank engines. Consider the example described with linguistic values shown in table 1, in which the seven evaluation criteria are strengthening coefficient, specific density, volume power, oil consumption, reliability, maintainability and life cycle cost.

Table 1. Linguistic description of tank engines

Evaluation criteria	Linguistic variables			
	Design 1	Design 2	Design 3	Design 4
Strengthening coefficient	Medium	Very Good	Good	Very Good
Specific density	Good	Medium	Medium	Good
Volume power	Poor	Good	Very Good	Medium
Oil consumption	Good	Medium	Poor	Good
Reliability	Medium	Good	Good	Very good
Maintainability	Poor	Good	Medium	Good
Life cycle cost	Good	Poor	Medium	Poor

As shown in Fig. 3, the normal function-shaped fuzzy numbers are defined to elaborate the linguistic values of "very poor (VP)", "poor (P)", "medium (M)", "good (G)" and "very good (VG)".

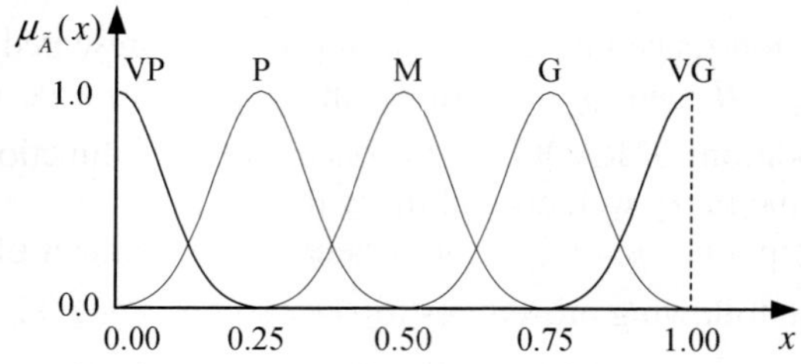

Fig. 3. Membership function of linguistic variables

In the learning algorithm of FNN, parameters are specified as follows:

(1) The number of input neurons is seven, inputs of which are fuzzy numbers corresponding to the seven evaluation criteria respectively. The number of hidden neurons is twenty. The number of output neurons is one, the output of which is the fuzzy number of evaluation value.

(2) Values of α : $\alpha = 0.2, 0.4, 0.6, 0.8, 1.0$;

(3) Population size of RAOGA is 50, $\lambda_c = 1$, $\lambda_m = 0.2$, $\beta_c = 5$, $\beta_m = 10$. $\alpha(t)$ is defined as the following piecewise function:

$$\alpha(t) = 0.2 + \frac{t}{400} \qquad (t \geq 300) \ . \tag{5}$$

(4) Termination condition is that the iterative number reaches 20000.

100 samples are used to train the FNN model. Fig. 4 is the error curve of fuzzy neural network training.

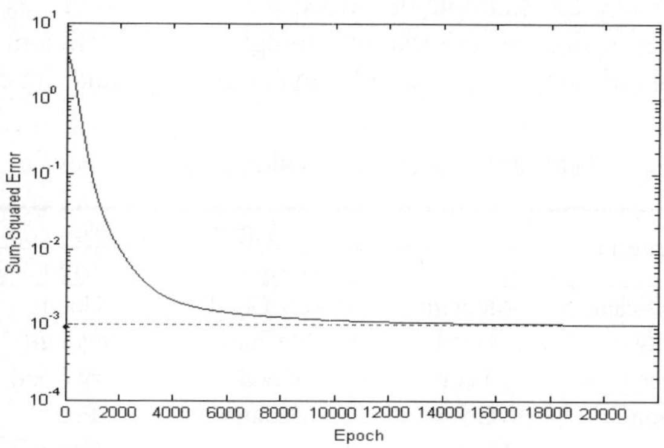

Fig. 4. Error curve of fuzzy neural network training

The four tank engine designs in Table 1 are evaluated with the trained FNN model. Table 2 is the output of the RAOGA-based FNN corresponding to the serial values of α. The ranking of design candidates is performed by fuzzy centroid method.

Table 2. Evaluation results of tank engine designs

	$\alpha=0.2$		$\alpha=0.4$		$\alpha=0.6$		$\alpha=0.8$		$\alpha=1.0$		Centroid	Rating
	$[\tilde{O}]^L_{0.2}$	$[\tilde{O}]^U_{0.2}$	$[\tilde{O}]^L_{0.4}$	$[\tilde{O}]^U_{0.4}$	$[\tilde{O}]^L_{0.6}$	$[\tilde{O}]^U_{0.6}$	$[\tilde{O}]^L_{0.8}$	$[\tilde{O}]^U_{0.8}$	$[\tilde{O}]^L_{1.0}$	$[\tilde{O}]^U_{1.0}$	$\overline{x}$	
Design 1	0.24	0.55	0.29	0.50	0.33	0.49	0.36	0.44	0.39	0.40	0.3993	4
Design 2	0.39	0.69	0.42	0.66	0.46	0.62	0.49	0.60	0.54	0.55	0.5430	2
Design 3	0.38	0.67	0.41	0.64	0.44	0.61	0.46	0.58	0.52	0.52	0.5211	3
Design 4	0.45	0.76	0.49	0.70	0.52	0.69	0.55	0.65	0.60	0.61	0.6023	1

From the Table 2, it is easy to see that Design 4 is the best scheme of tank engine.

4 Conclusions

The evaluation and selection of conceptual design alternatives is a challenging task. This paper introduced a RAOGA-based FNN model to evaluate design alternatives. Applying RAOGA to adjusting fuzzy weights and thresholds of FNN avoids the differentiable information being used and simplifies the calculating process. A case study of tank engines evaluation was given to show the effectiveness of the introduced method.

References

1. Huang, H.Z., Bo, R.F., Chen, W.: An Integrated Computational Intelligence Approach to Product Concept Generation and Evaluation. Mechanism and Machine Theory. 41(5) (2006) 567-583
2. Gu, Y.K., Huang, H.Z.: Fuzzy Mapping between Physical Domain and Function Domain in Design Process. International Journal of Uncertainty, Fuzziness and Knowledge-Based Systems. 12(1) (2004) 7-20
3. Huang, H.Z., Zu, X.: Hierarchical Timed Colored Petri Nets Based Product Development Process Modeling. Lecture Notes in Computer Science. 3168 (2004) 378-387
4. Thurston, D.L., Carnahan, J.V.: Fuzzy Ratings and Utility Analysis in Preliminary Design Evaluation of Multiple Attributes. ASME Journal of Mechanical Design. 114 (1992) 648-658
5. Vanegas, L.V., Labib, A.W.: Application of New Fuzzy-Weighted Average (NFWA) Method to Engineering Design Evaluation. International Journal of Production Research. 39 (2001) 1147-1162
6. Ishibuchi, H., Kwon, K., Tanaka, H.: A Learning Algorithm of Fuzzy Neural Networks with Triangular Fuzzy Weights. Fuzzy Sets and Systems. 71 (1995) 277-293
7. Kuo, R.J., Xue, K.C.: An Intelligent Sales Forecasting System through Integration of Artificial Neural Network and Fuzzy Neural Network. Computers in Industry. 37 (1998) 1-15
8. Aliev, R. A., Fazlollahi, B., Vahidov, R. M.: Genetic Based Learning of Fuzzy Neural Networks. Part I: feed-forward fuzzy neural networks. Fuzzy Sets and Systems. 118 (2001) 351-358

The Development of a Weighted Evolving Fuzzy Neural Network

Pei-Chann Chang[1], Chen-Hao Liu[1], Chia-Hsuan Yeh[2], and Shih-Hsin Chen[1]

[1] Department of Industrial Engineering and Management, Yuan-Ze University, 135 Yuan-Dong Rd., Taoyuan 32026, Taiwan, R.O.C.
iepchang@saturn.yzu.edu.tw,
{s929510, s939506}@mail.yzu.edu.tw

[2] Department of Information Management, Yuan-Ze University, 135 Yuan-Dong Rd., Taoyuan 32026, Taiwan, R.O.C.
imcyeh@saturn.yzu.edu.tw

Abstract. This study modifies the Evolving Fuzzy Neural Network Framework (EFuNN framework) proposed by Kasabov (1998) and adopts a weighted factor to calculate the importance of each factor among these different rules. In addition, an exponential transfer function (exp (-D)) is employed to transfer the distance of any two factors into the value of similarity among different rules, thus a different rule clustering method is developed accordingly. The intensive experimental results show that the WEFuNN performs very well when applied in the PCB sales forecasting.

1 Introduction

The field of Artificial Intelligence (AI), such as Neural Network (NN), Fuzzy Theory, Expert System (ES), Genetic Algorithms (GA), and Rule Induction has been rapidly developed in recent years. Each algorithm has their own strengths but there are still some limitations of them. In order to reduce these limitations, the hybrid algorithm was developed from combining two or three different A.I. approaches and then draws on the strength of each to offset the weakness of the others. Thus, the main ideal of this research is to develop a better weighted evolving fuzzy neural network for various applications.

This study modifies the Evolving Fuzzy Neural Network Framework (EFuNN framework) proposed by Kasabov [14] and adopts a weighted factor to calculate the value of similarity of different rules.

2 Literature Review

Soft computing algorithm which combined fuzzy theory with neural network has found a variety of applications in various fields ranging from industrial environment control system, process parameters, semi-conductor machine capacity forecasting, business environment forecasting, financial analysis, stock index fluctuation forecasting, consumer loan, medical diagnosis and electricity demand forecasting.

The study by Lin and Lee [19] is the most earliest study to combines the fuzzy theory with neural network. They proposed a hybrid model which combines the idea

D.-S. Huang, K. Li, and G.W. Irwin (Eds.): ICIC 2006, LNAI 4114, pp. 212 – 221, 2006.

of fuzzy logic controller, neural network structure and learning abilities into an integrated neural-network-based fuzzy logic control and decision system. Subsequently, several researchers also investigate some related studies with regard to the application of this combined approach and then continually developed several kinds of approaches [4, 5, 6, 7, 8, 12, 16, 17, 18, 20, 21, 22, and 23]. The commonly used methods are as follows:

1. Fuzzy Adaptive Learning Control Systems (FALCON) [Zhong, 1999]
2. Fuzzy Back-Propagation Network (FBPN)
3. Adaptive Neuro-Fuzzy Inference Systems (ANFIS)
4. Fuzzy Hyper Rectangular Composite Neural Networks (FHRCNNs)
5. Fuzzy Neural Network (FuNN)

Some of the previous studies concerning the application of fuzzy neural network in the forecast aspect will be presented as follows:

Kasabov [15] modified fuzzy neural network and then proposed the method of FuNN/2. Under the framework of FuNN, the author employed the function of Genetic Algorithms which has the ability to search quickly in large spaces and then offset the insufficiency of neural network's parameters setting. The EFuNN combined unsupervised learning and supervised learning was proposed by Kasabov [14]. The first stage: in order to achieve the objective of connecting fuzzy rules, Kasabov employed unsupervised learning to adjust the connection weights of fuzzy input and fuzzy rule. The second stage: the supervised learning of BPN was used to adjust the connection weights of fuzzy rule and fuzzy output so as to achieve the goal of inner rule of incoming vectors and outgoing vectors.

Abraham and Baikunth [1] proposed a method of Fuzzy Neural Network that employed hybrid supervised and unsupervised learning to forecast short-term electricity demand in the State of Victoria. The authors regarded "the maximum and minimum temperatures of the day", "previous day's electricity demand", "season" and "the day of week" as input factors and used EFuNN to develop a forecasting model of electricity demand. The EFuNN forecasting technique is also compared with Conjugate Gradient Algorithm (CGA), Back-propagation Network (BPN) and Box-Jenkins. Abraham et al. [2] utilized Fuzzy Neural to forecast the long-term rainfall in Kerala state. The rainfall was affected by global warming, season, storms and butterfly effect and so on. Under the BPN framework, the authors made explicit values to be fuzzy and then proceeded with fuzzy rule aggregation, clustering and extraction. Moreover, employed a process of training via BPN algorithms and adjusted the weights of concealment to output through each time of training. Abraham et al. [3] applied Fuzzy Neural Network to analyze the strategic decision-making of stock market. Firstly, the researchers choose six stock indices from the listing companies in the Nasdaq Stock Market and used conjugate gradient algorithm to forecast these stocks. Kasabov [13] investigated the short-term forecasting of the Gross Domestic Product (GDP) for totally 15 countries which are EU countries, USA and so on. The related factors considered in this study are Consumer Product Index (CPI), Interest Rate (IR), Unemployment Rate and GDP per capita. The results of this study revealed that the MSE of the 15 countries performed well after fuzzy rule re-aggregation, rule adaptation and rule extraction. It also reveled that the results of EFuNN forecasting are highly accurate in various kinds of environments.

3 Development of WEFuNN

The main ideal of this research is to modified the EFuNN [13], generate better weight combination so as to improve the forecasting accuracy. The WEFuNN will be used to forecast the demand of PCB product and it is a five-layer network (Figure. 1) where nodes and connections are created/connected as data examples are presented.

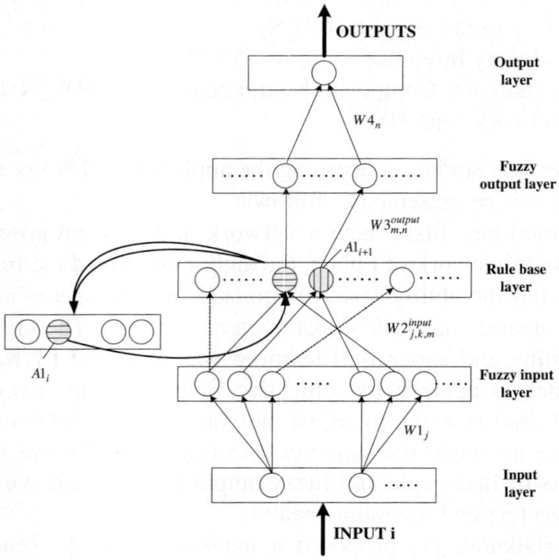

Fig. 1. Architecture of WEFuNN

3.1 Feed-Forward Learning Phase

For each training case, there are four characteristics to be processed by using the following steps:

3.1.1 Data Fuzzification Step

Triangular membership function is used to transfer the input characteristics to the fuzzy membership function $\tilde{\mu}_x$ (Figure. 2 & Eq. 1).

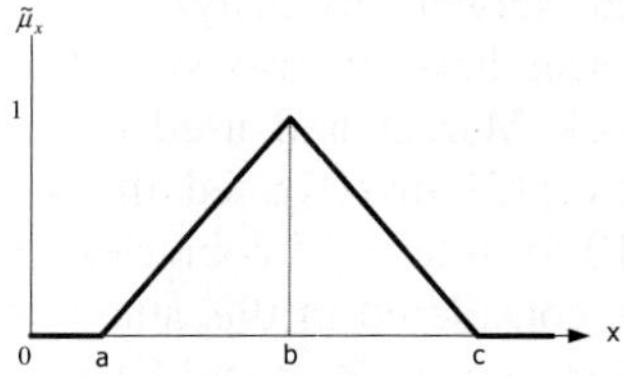

Fig. 2. The triangular membership function

$$\tilde{\mu}_x = \begin{cases} 0, x < a \\ \dfrac{x-a}{b-a}, a \le x < b \\ \dfrac{c-x}{c-b}, b \le x < c \\ 0, x \ge c \end{cases} \tag{1}$$

In this research, we added the dynamic weight ($W1_j$) for character j between the 1st layer and the 2nd layer. This process can derive better forecasting result because the triangular membership function will become a non-isosceles one.

For the first data, $MF^{input}_{j,k}(1)$ is its input fuzzy membership function for the j-th characters and the k-th region. $MF^{output}_n(1)$ is its output fuzzy membership function for the n-th fuzzy region.

3.1.2 Initial Network Setting Step

In the beginning, there is no fuzzy rule in the network. Thus, the first rule should be built by the first data input. The connection weights between the 2nd layer and the 3rd layer are $W2^{input}_{j,k,m}$; between the 3rd layer and the 4th layer are $W3^{output}_{m,n}$; between the 4th layer and the output layer are $W4_n$. m is the rule number.

3.1.3 Network Constructing Step

In order to construct the fuzzy rule and weights of the network, all of the training data must process the following sub-steps:

Step 1. Similarity Computing

Instead of Kasabov's fuzzy distance function, weighted Euclidean distance $D_{i,m}$ is used to generate the distance between the i-th case and the m-th rule, which have been determined.

$$D_{i,m} = \sqrt{\sum_j \sum_k W2^{input}_{j,k,m} \times [MF^{input}_{j,k}(i) - R_{j,k}(m)]^2} \tag{2}$$

In this weighted distance function, the direct distance between case i and rule m is computed to represent the difference of them. This study further takes the weights into account in an effort to express the degree of importance between each factor. Moreover, to present the relation between distance and similarity, an exponential transfer function is used to transfer the distance to the similarity. Which,

$$A_{i,m} = \exp(-D_{i,m}) \tag{3}$$

Comparing with the linear transfer function, we will get much larger similarity in the close distance and much smaller similarity in the large distance from this function.

Step 2. Rule Determining

Find the most similar rule of case i, where $A1_i = \max(A_{i,m})$. If $A1_i > S$, here S is the similarity threshold, it presents that the case has to merge in this rule. Thus, go to *Step 3*. Otherwise, create a new fuzzy rule and compute its connection weights, $W2_{j,k,m}^{input}$ and $W3_{m,n}^{output}$, then go to *Network Generating Step*.

Step 3. Output Computing

In this sub-step, saturating linear transfer function will be used to transfer the fuzzy membership function of case i to the fuzzy forecast output,

$$A2_{i,m} = Satlin(W3_{m,n}^{output} \times A1_i) \tag{4}$$

The figure of Saturating linear transfer function will be shown as follows:

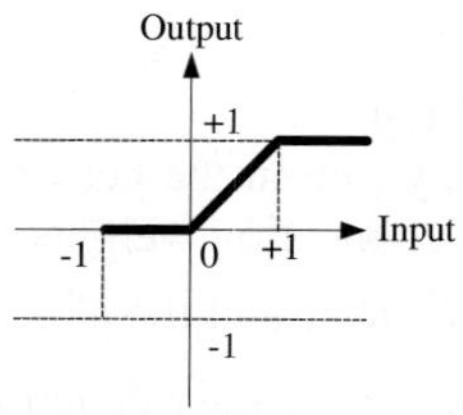

Fig. 3. Saturating linear transfer function

Step 4. Error Computing

Compute the error between fuzzy forecast of the case i and its actual fuzzy demand A_i,

$$Err_i = | A2_{i,m} - A_i | \tag{5}$$

If $Err_i < E_{thr}$ retain this forecasting result, where E_{thr} is the error threshold. Otherwise, create a new fuzzy rule and compute its connection weights, $W2_{j,k,m}^{input}$ and $W3_{m,n}^{output}$, then go to *Network Generating Step*.

Step 5. Defuzzification

Each fuzzy forecast output has been defuzzified to the real forecast output. where,

$$O_i = W4_n \times A2_{i,m} \tag{6}$$

Step 6. Weights Updating

For the occurrence of each merging process, the connection weights $W2_{j,k,m}^{input}$ and $W3_{m,n}^{output}$ should be updated as follows,

$$dist = [MF_{j,k}^{input}(i) - R_{j,k}(m)_{old}] \quad (7)$$

$$R_{j,k}(m)_{new} = R_{j,k}(m)_{old} + \alpha_1 \times dist \quad (8)$$

$$MF_n^{output}(i)_{new} = MF_n^{output}(i)_{old} + \alpha_2 \times (Err) \times (A1_i) \quad (9)$$

where, α_1 is the learning rate of $R_{j,k}(m)$ and α_2 is the learning rate of $MF_n^{output}(i)$. The diagram of weights updating process will be presented below.

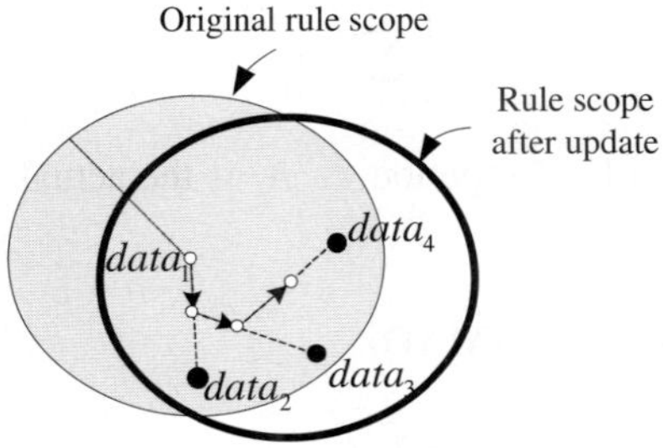

Fig. 4. The diagram of rule scope before/after update

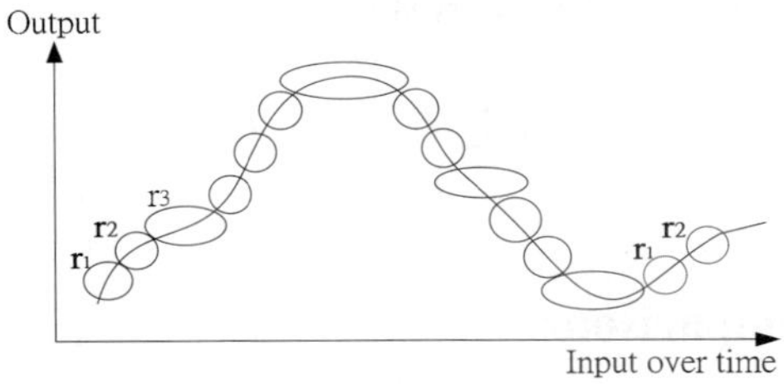

Fig. 5. The Diagram of fuzzy rule generating

3.1.4 Network Generating Step

For each training data, go to *Network Constructing Step* to generate our network which includes the connection weights and fuzzy rules.

After network feed-forward training phase, we can get the fuzzy rules of these training data. And these fuzzy rules will be used to forecast in recall forecast phase. The original concept of fuzzy rule after generating will be similar as Figure 5.

3.2 Recall Forecast Phase

In general, the most similar rule can be retrieved from the rule base for each testing data according to the similarity $D_{i,m}$. In addition, the fuzzy output from this similar rule will be treated as the fuzzy forecast of this testing data. After defuzzification, we can get the forecast demand. However, the concept of K-NN (k-nearest neighbor method, Gordon, 1997) is utilized to find the forecast in this research.

The most similar k rules of each testing data will be considered, the distances between the k-nearest rules and the testing data present the ratios in summarizing the forecasts of k rules. Thus, we can get the combined result from many different rules. To sum up, we expect that we can get more accurate forecasting results.

3.3 Evaluating Indices

The forecasting methods of evaluating indices are presented as follows:

3.3.1 Mean Absolute Percentage Error (MAPE)

$$MAPE = \frac{1}{n}\sum_{t=1}^{n}\frac{|F_t - A_t|}{A_t} \tag{10}$$

where F_t is the expected value for period t, A_t is the actual value for period t, n is the total number of periods.

3.3.2 Mean Absolute Deviation (MAD)

$$MAD = \frac{1}{n}\sum_{t=1}^{n}|F_t - A_t| \tag{11}$$

3.3.3 Root of Mean Squared Error (RMSE)

$$RMSE = \sqrt{\sum_{t=1}^{n}(F_t - A_t)^2 \Big/ n} \tag{12}$$

4 Integrated Comparisons

The best parameter combination of WEFuNN was collected from the Taguchi experimental design, and the result is shown as Table 1:

Table 1. Detail parameter setting of WEFuNN

Factors	The best parameters
The no. of fuzzy region in X_1	9
The no. of fuzzy region in X_4	9
Weight of X_1	0.26
Weight of X_2	0.2
Weight of X_4	0.35

In this section, it will focus on the comparisons between WEFuNN and other forecasting models. As shown in Table 2, this study employed MAPE and MAD to evaluate the degree of accuracy. Among these five forecasting models, WEFuNN is the most accurate forecasting model since the value of MAPE and MAD is 2.11% and

16445 square foot respectively. In addition, RMSE is used as an evaluating index for the degree of precise. The value of RMSE is 24909 square foot. The results show that WEFuNN has the best degree of precise among these five forecasting models. Accordingly, it could be concluded that the WEFuNN forecasting model proposed in this study has considerably accurate forecasting ability.

Table 2. The comparison of each forecasting methods

	WEFuNN	EFuNN	BPN	MRA	GANN
MAPE	2.11%	6.44%	8.76%	9.88%	3.06%
MAD	16445	47072	72494	82673	23991
RMSE	24909	59081	114785	131115	33497

According to the experimental results above, it could draw some conclusions:

1. The model taken other domains into consideration rather than just focus on the trend factors and seasonal factors will get a better result no matter in the average or the standard deviation of error. Therefore, to take other domains into account can reduce the error and standard deviation effectively and then increase the accuracy and stability of the model.
2. The forecasting model taken all input factors into account and offered these factors different weight value will derive more accurate results than the forecasting model with the same weight value between each factor.
3. Considering the accuracy and the precise of the forecasting model, the WEFuNN is superior to other forecasting models since it has the minimum value of MAPE and RMSE.
4. As for the cost variance caused by the forecasting errors, WEFuNN has the minimum error cost when compared with other forecasting models.
5. The WEFuNN usually takes one epoch to get the results. It is faster than other forecasting models such as BPN.
6. The forecasting ability of Multiple Regression Analysis is the worst one among the five forecasting models as it is only suitable for the linear question and its forecasting ability for the non-linear question is comparatively poor and weak.

5 Discussions

According to the experimental results shown in the previous section, it could be concluded that the forecasting model proposed in this study is superior to the others. The possible reasons might be as follows:

1. WEFuNN utilized weight which is allocated according to the degree of importance in each factor to calculate the similarity. This approach is much better than EFuNN with the same weight in each factor.
2. The original WEFuNN used Fuzzy Distance Function to calculate the value of similarity. Thus, the value of similarity is 1-D when the distance between the two factors is D. However, in this study, exponential transfer function (exp(-D)) is

employed to transfer the distance to the value of similarity, and the result shows that the outcome is better after using the exponential transfer function.

3. At the recall stage, the method of combining WEFuNN with K-Nearest-Neighbor to get the fuzzy rule is much accurate than the method of WEFuNN which only find out the most similar fuzzy rule. It is because that K-Nearest-Neighbor can modify the accuracy of the forecasting results and relatively adapt to the complicated environmental change.
4. As can been seen from the experimental results, the forecasting results of WEFuNN, EFuNN and GANN are better than that of BPN which employed the Gradient Steepest Descent Method. According to Chang (2005), this result is in line with the previous finding that the performance of the Gradient Steepest Descent Method is not good.

References

1. Abraham, A., Baikunth, N.: A Neuro-Fuzzy Approach for Modeling Electricity Demand in Victoria. Applied Soft Computing. (2001) 127–138
2. Abraham, A., Steinberg, D., Philip, N.S.: Rainfall Forecasting Using Soft Computing Models and Multivariate Adaptive Regression Splines. IEEE SMC Transactions, Special Issue on Fusion of Soft Computing and Hard Computing in Industrial Applications (2001)
3. Abraham, A., Baikunth, N., Mahanti, P.K.: Hybrid Intelligent Systems for Stock Market Analysis. Lecture Notes in Computer Science, Vol. 2074. Springer-Verlag, Berlin Heidelberg New York (2001) 337–345
4. Arifovic, J., Gencay, R.: Using Genetic Algorithms to Select Architecture of a Feedback Artificial Neural Network. Physica A. (2001) 574–594
5. Chang, P.C., Hsieh, J.C.: A Neural Network Approach for Due-Date Assignment in a Wafer Fabrication Factory. Int. J. Industrial Engineering. 10 (2003) 55–61
6. Chang, P.C., Wang, Y.W., Tsai, C.Y.: Evolving Neural Network for Printed Circuit Board Sales. Expert Systems with Applications. 29 (2005) 83–92
7. Chang, P.C., Lai, C.Y.: A Hybrid System Combining Self-Organizing Maps with Case-Based Reasoning in Wholesaler's New-release Book Forecasting. Expert Systems with Applications. 29 (2005) 183–192.
8. Chang, P.C., Wang, Y.W., Liu C.H.: Fuzzy Back-Propagation Network for PCB sales forecasting. Lecture Notes in Computer Science, Vol. 3610. Springer-Verlag, Berlin Heidelberg New York (2005) 364–373
9. Chang, T.C., Lin, S.J.: Grey Relation Analysis of Carbon Dioxide Emissions from Industrial Production and Energy Uses in Taiwan. Journal of Environmental Management. 56 (1999) 247–257
10. Chung, I.F.: Reinforcement Neural Fuzzy Inference Networks and its Applications. PHD thesis, Department of electronic and control engineering, National Chaio-Tung University, Taiwan (1999)
11. Elalfi, A.E., Haque, R., Elalami, M.E.: Extracting Rules from Trained Neural Network Using GA for Managing E-businesss. Applied Soft Computing. 4 (2004) 65–77
12. Kasabov, N.: Evolving Fuzzy Neural Networks for On-line Knowledge Discovery. The Information Science Discussion Paper Series (2001)
13. Kasabov, N.: Evolving Fuzzy Neural Networks-Algorithms, Applications and Biological Motivation. In Proc. of Iizuka'98, Iizuka, Japan (1998)

14. Kasabov, N., Kim, J., Watts, M.J.: Funn/2-A Fuzzy Neural Network Architecture for Adaptive Learning and Knowledge Acquistion. Information Sciences. 101 (1997) 155–175
15. Kim, K.J., Han, I.: Genetic Algorithms Approach to Feature Discretization in Artificial Neural Networks for the Prediction of Stock Price Index. Expert Systems with Application. 19 (2000) 125–132
16. Kuo, R.J., Chen, J.A.: A Decision Support System for Order Selection in Electronic Commerce Based on Fuzzy Neural Network Supported by Real-coded Genetic Algorithm. Expert Systems with Application. 26 (2004) 141–154
17. Liang, R.H.: Application of Grey Relation Analysis to Hydroelectric Generation Scheduling. Int. J. Electrical Power & Energy Systems. 21 (1999) 357–364
18. Lin, C.T., Lee, C.G.: Neural-Network-Based Fuzzy Inference System. IEEE Transactions on Computer. 40 (1991) 1320–1336
19. Liu, Z., Liu, A., Wang, C., Niu, Z.: Evolving Neural Network Using Real Coded Genetic Algorithm for Multispectral Image Classification. Future Generation Computer System. 20 (2004) 1119–1129
20. Montana, D., Davis, L.: Training Feed Forward Neural Networks Using Genetic Algorithms. Proceedings of 11th International Joint Conference on Artificial Intelligence, San Mateo, CA, Morgan Kaufmanns. (1989) 762–767
21. Sexton, R.S., Gupta, J.N.D.: Comparative Evaluation of Genetic Algorithm and Backpropagation for Training Neural Networks. Information Sciences. 129 (2000) 45–59
22. Srinivasan, D.: Evolving Artificial Neural Networks for Short Term Load Forecasting. Neural computing. 23 (1998) 265–276
23. Yao, X.: Evolving Artificial Neural Networks. Proceedings of the IEEE. 87 (1999) 1423–1447

Fuzzy Neural Classifier for Transformer Fault Diagnosis Based on EM Learning

Hongsheng Su and Qunzhan Li

School of Electrical Engineering, Southwest Jiaotong University,
Chengdu 610031, China
shsen@163.com

Abstract. A novel fuzzy neural classifier and learning algorithm are proposed based on EM learning in this paper. The method firstly applies rough set of its information measurement ability to evaluate system parameters importance. Then, based on EM learning the unknown parameters of fuzzy member functions are estimated. Then a fuzzy neural classifier based on EM algorithm is generated. The research indicates that the proposed network possesses higher diagnosis precision and speed as well as excellent anti-interference abilities, and is an ideal pattern classifier. In the end, a practical application in transformer fault diagnosis shows the availability of the method.

1 Introduction

In recent years, with the fast advancement of artificial neural networks (ANN), it has already been in a broad application in diverse fields such as artificial intelligence (AI), patter recognition (PR), expert systems (ES), image processing and other related fields. Due to its prominent characteristics of self-learning and non-linearity as well as parallel distributed processing, ANN is considered very suitable to facility fault diagnosis[1], and has been successful application in power systems[2],[3], mechanical engineering[4],[5], chemical engineering[6],[7] and medical systems[8],[9], etc. Clearly, to achieve parallel algorithm and nonlinear mapping are the most excellent properties of neural networks.

However, ANN can't distinguish those knowledge is redundant and those knowledge is useless in knowledge base, and also, it is difficult to evaluate importance of system parameters. Another one flaw of ANN is disposal of ill data, that is, if one input datum belongs to several classes simultaneously, ANN can't implement effective processing. To tackle the problems, in the paper rough set and fuzzy set are respectively applied to measure importance of system parameters so as to simplify networks structure and process fuzzy imprecise information so as to improve anti-interference abilities. Thus the constructed networks can possess stronger fault tolerance and information processing abilities, and more adaptive to dynamic indeterminate environment.

In addition, while constructing fuzzy membership functions, the related parameters can't be confirmed correctly. In generic methods, these parameters are subjectively set by man, the error is unavoidable. Hence, EM learning is applied to estimate the

D.-S. Huang, K. Li, and G.W. Irwin (Eds.): ICIC 2006, LNAI 4114, pp. 222 – 229, 2006.

unknown parameters in the paper. Since it can overcome the subjectivity in identifying the hidden parameters, the error therefore is reduced.

The following contents include parameter evaluation technique; fuzzy neural network and EM algorithm; example analysis and conclusions, etc.

2 Importance of System Parameters

While *R* is used to express a group of system parameters or only is a parameter of system, *R* can be applied to define or describe the correct degree of the investigated object or ability of classifying object or denoting system, and can be measured using system parameter importance factor.

Definition 1. Set *X* is characteristic vector set of input objects, and x_i represents the ith characteristic in *X*, for output pattern *Y*, the importance factor of characteristic x_i is defined as follows[10].

$$\gamma_{xi}(Y)=card(pos_X(Y)-pos_{X-xi}(Y))/card(U) \quad (1)$$

In equation (1), *U* expresses universe. Clearly, for output pattern *Y*, if character variable x_i has larger importance factor $\gamma_{xi}(Y)$, then its classification role is large, inversely, and small. If $\gamma_{xi}(Y)=0$, then the variable x_i can be ignored, reduction of the redundant attributes therefore is accomplished.

3 EM Algorithm

EM algorithm is developed by Dempster in 1977[11], and is a broadly applied learning algorithm while the hidden variables exist. EM algorithm may be used to deal with the situation that the values of some variables can't be directly observed all along but the probabilistic distributions followed by them are known. EM algorithm has already been used to train Bayesian networks and radial basis function, etc. In addition, it is still a basis for hidden Markov models.

3.1 Basic EM Algorithm

Set data $\boldsymbol{Y}=\boldsymbol{X}\cup\boldsymbol{Z}$, $\boldsymbol{X}$ is the observed data, and $\boldsymbol{Z}$ is the hidden data. Noting that the unobserved $\boldsymbol{Z}$ may be viewed as a random variable, whose probabilistic distributions relay on parameter $\boldsymbol{\theta}$ and data $\boldsymbol{X}$. Clearly, *Y* is also for that a random variable. Set $\boldsymbol{h}$ is the initial assumption value of $\boldsymbol{\theta}$ and $\boldsymbol{h}'$ is the revised value of $\boldsymbol{h}$ in process of iteration each time. EM algorithm seeks the maximum likelihood hypothesis $\boldsymbol{h}'$ by letting $E[lnP(\boldsymbol{Y}/\boldsymbol{h}')]$ up to the maximum. In general, the probabilistic distribution followed by $\boldsymbol{Y}$ is unknown because it is confirmed by the estimated parameter $\boldsymbol{\theta}$. However, EM algorithm may estimate the distribution of $\boldsymbol{Y}$ by the use of the current hypothesis $\boldsymbol{h}$ to replace $\boldsymbol{\theta}$. Now we can define a function $Q(\boldsymbol{h}'|\boldsymbol{h})$ as follows.

$$Q(\boldsymbol{h}^1 | \boldsymbol{h}) = E[ln\, P(Y / \boldsymbol{h}') | \boldsymbol{h}, X) . \quad (2)$$

Then EM algorithm may be described as follows.

Step1. (*Estimation step or E step*). The probabilistic distribution in ***Y*** is worked out according to the observed data ***X*** and hypothesis ***h*** of the current $\boldsymbol{\theta}$ so as to further calculate *Q*(***h***'|***h***), that is

$$Q(\boldsymbol{h}^{1} \mid \boldsymbol{h}) \leftarrow E[\ln P(Y / \boldsymbol{h}') \mid \boldsymbol{h}, X)\,. \tag{3}$$

Step 2. (*Maximization step or M step*). Using ***h***' that can make *Q*(***h***'|***h***) up to the maximum to replace ***h***, that is

$$\boldsymbol{h}' \leftarrow \underset{h'}{\operatorname{argmax}}\, \boldsymbol{Q}(\boldsymbol{h}^{1} \mid \boldsymbol{h})\,. \tag{4}$$

3.2 Estimation of the Means of *k* Gauss Distributions

Set $\boldsymbol{\theta}$=<u_1, u_2 ,…, u_k> is the average value of *k* Gauss distributions, the observed data is ***X***=|<x_i>|, the hidden variable ***Z***=|<z_{i1},z_{i2},…,z_{ik}>|. For convenient analysis, Set the variances of *k* Gauss distributions are equal and also known beforehand, that is, $\sigma_1 = \sigma_2 = \ldots = \sigma_k = \sigma$. With respect to each x_i , then we have

$$P(y_i \mid \boldsymbol{h}') = p(x_i, z_{i1}, z_{i2}, \ldots, z_{ik} \mid \boldsymbol{h}') = \frac{1}{\sqrt{2\pi\sigma^2}} e^{-\frac{1}{2\sigma^2}\sum_{j=1}^{k} z_{ij}(x_i - u_j')^2}\,. \tag{5}$$

In (5), only one of all z_{ij} equals one while other z_{ij}=0. The distribution of single example x_i is $p(y_i|\boldsymbol{h}')$, then *lnP*(***Y***|***h***') of all *m* examples therefore is represented by

$$\begin{aligned} \ln P(Y \mid h') &= \ln \prod_{i=1}^{m} p(y_i \mid h') = \sum_{i=1}^{m} \ln p(y_i \mid h')\,. \\ &= \sum_{i=1}^{m} (\ln \frac{1}{\sqrt{2\pi\sigma^2}} - \frac{1}{2\sigma^2} \sum_{j=1}^{k} z_{ij}(x_i - u_j')^2) \end{aligned} \tag{6}$$

In general, to the linear function *f*(*x*), *E*[*f*(*x*)]=*f*[*E*(*x*)]. Therefore, from (**6**) we have

$$E[\ln P(Y \mid h')] = \sum_{i=1}^{m} (\ln \frac{1}{\sqrt{2\pi\sigma^2}} - \frac{1}{2\sigma^2} \sum_{j=1}^{k} E(z_{ij})(x_i - u_j')^2) \tag{7}$$

Then

$$Q(h' \mid h) = \sum_{i=1}^{m} (\ln \frac{1}{\sqrt{2\pi\sigma^2}} - \frac{1}{2\sigma^2} \sum_{j=1}^{k} E(z_{ij})(x_i - u_j)^2) \tag{8}$$

Where

$$E\,(z_{ij}) = \frac{e^{-\frac{1}{2\sigma^2}(x_i - u_j)^2}}{\sum_{in=1}^{k} e^{-\frac{1}{2\sigma^2}(x_i - u_n)^2}} \tag{9}$$

According to (4) and (8)

$$\begin{aligned} \arg\max_{h'}(h' \mid h) &= \arg\max_{h'} \sum_{i=1}^{m}(ln\frac{1}{\sqrt{2\pi\sigma^2}} - \frac{1}{2\sigma^2}\sum_{j=1}^{k} E(z_{ij})(x_i - u_j^{'})^2) \\ &= \underset{h'}{\operatorname{argmin}} \sum_{i=1}^{m}\sum_{j=1}^{k} E(z_{ij})(x_i - u_j^{'})^2 \end{aligned} \tag{10}$$

From (10), we have

$$u_j \leftarrow \frac{\sum_{i=1}^{m} E(z_{ij})x_i}{\sum_{i=1}^{m} E(z_{ij})} \tag{11}$$

3.3 Practical EM Algorithm

In practical algorithm, the variance σ is unknown, σ therefore requires to be estimated, that is $\boldsymbol{\theta}$=< u_1, u_2 ,…, u_k ; σ>=< $\boldsymbol{h}$, σ>. Wherefore, we use method below to replace M-step in EM learning

1) Firstly, set hypothesis σ' meets

$$Q(\boldsymbol{h},\sigma' \mid \boldsymbol{h},\sigma) \leftarrow \underset{\sigma'}{\operatorname{argmax}}\, Q(h,\sigma' \mid h,\sigma) \cdot \tag{12}$$

2) Then, $\boldsymbol{h}'$ meets

$$Q(\boldsymbol{h}',\sigma' \mid \boldsymbol{h},\sigma') \leftarrow \underset{h'}{\operatorname{argmax}}\, Q(\boldsymbol{h}',\sigma' \mid h,\sigma') \cdot \tag{13}$$

Alternately applying the formula (12) and (13), the conditional maximum may be achieved, eventually. The method therefore is called ECM algorithm.

4 Fuzzy Neural Classifier with ECM Learning-Based

During fault diagnosis, to dispose incomplete and imprecise information Gauss subjection degree function is often used as fuzzy membership function, and defined as

$$u_A(x) = \exp(-\frac{1}{2}(\frac{x - C_i}{\sigma_i})^2) \ . \tag{14}$$

In (14), Gauss function is confirmed by $\{C_i,\sigma_i\}$. The parameter $\{C_i, \sigma_i\}$ can be learned through ECM algorithm. Assume that objects set of class is composed of N input vectors, and every input vector consists of n-dimensional variables, s- dimensional variables are abstracted from n-dimensional space, after fuzzification, $C\times s$-dimension input vector is gained. For convenience analysis, let C=3, then

$$\boldsymbol{u}(\boldsymbol{X}_j) = [u_H(x_{1j}), u_M(x_{1j}), u_L(x_{1j}),\ldots,\ u_H(x_{sj}), u_M(x_{sj}), u_L(x_{sj})] \tag{15}$$

In (15), $\boldsymbol{X}_j$ expresses input vector, u_H, u_M and u_L represent Gauss membership function defined by (14), respectively. From (15), the dimension of fuzzy input information should be 3×*s*, 3×*s* neurons for that are required in input layer of neural classifier. Set drill samples has *N* objects, they are divided as *Q* classes, according to every classification, set n_k input objects are mapped to output class *l*, then we have.

$$\sum_{l=1}^{Q} n_{lk} = N \,. \tag{16}$$

Thus input objects and output *l* establish a relationship. While characteristic attribute *i* of n_k input objects is mapped to *l*, we define centre of *l* regarding *i* as follows.

$$u_{il} = \frac{\sum_{j=1}^{n_k} f_l(\boldsymbol{X}_j) x_{ij}}{\sum_{j=1}^{n_k} f_l(\boldsymbol{X}_j)}, \quad i=1,2,\ldots s;\ l=1,2,\ldots,Q. \tag{17}$$

Similarly, fuzzy variable vector of U_l may be expressed by

$$\boldsymbol{u}(\boldsymbol{U}_l) = [\boldsymbol{u}_H(u_{1l}), \boldsymbol{u}_M(u_{1l}), \boldsymbol{u}_L(u_{1l}), \ldots,\ \boldsymbol{u}_H(x_{sl}), \boldsymbol{u}_M(x_{sl}), \boldsymbol{u}_L(x_{sl})] \,. \tag{18}$$

Distance between $\boldsymbol{X}_j$ and class *l* is defined by

$$D_{jl} = \frac{\| \boldsymbol{u}(\boldsymbol{X}_j) - \boldsymbol{u}(\boldsymbol{U}_l) \|}{\sum_{i=1}^{s} \gamma_{x_i} x_{ij}} = \frac{\sum_{i=1}^{s} \sum_{p=1}^{3} [\boldsymbol{u}_p(x_{ij}) - \boldsymbol{u}_p(u_{il})]^2}{\sum_{i=1}^{s} \sum_{p=1}^{3} \gamma_{x_i} \boldsymbol{u}_p(x_{ij})} \,. \tag{19}$$

where subscript *P*=1,2, 3 expresses *H,M,L*, γ_{xi} is an importance factor of x_i to output class. Noting that defuzzification is done, therefore, output results may be exactly expressed out. $f_l(\boldsymbol{X}_j)$ is used to express a level that input $\boldsymbol{X}_j$ belons to *l* , and defined as

$$f_l(\boldsymbol{X}_j) = (1 + D_{lj})^{-1} = \frac{\sum_{i=1}^{s} \gamma_{x_i} x_{ij}}{\sum_{i=1}^{s} \gamma_{x_i} x_{ij} + \| \boldsymbol{u}(\boldsymbol{X}_j) - \boldsymbol{u}(\boldsymbol{X}_l) \|} \,. \tag{20}$$

In learning algorithm of networks, the aim function of classifier is defined as

$$\boldsymbol{E} = \frac{1}{2} \sum_{l=1}^{Q} \sum_{j=1}^{n_k} f_l(\boldsymbol{X}_j) \| \boldsymbol{X}_j - \boldsymbol{U}_l \| \,. \tag{21}$$

where

$$\| \boldsymbol{X}_j - \boldsymbol{U}_l \| = \sum_{i=1}^{s} (x_{ij} - u_{il})^2 = \sum_{i=1}^{s} \sum_{p=1}^{3} [\boldsymbol{u}_p(x_{ij}) - \boldsymbol{u}_p(x_{il})]^2. \tag{22}$$

The center of the network output class is acquired by minimizing aim function (21). Each classification center is attained through the following algorithm.

$$\frac{\partial \boldsymbol{E}}{\partial u_{il}} = \frac{1}{2} f_l(\boldsymbol{X}_j)(\| \boldsymbol{X}_j - \boldsymbol{U}_l \|) + \frac{1}{2} \| \boldsymbol{X}_j - \boldsymbol{U}_l \| f_l^{'}(\boldsymbol{X}_j) \,. \tag{23}$$

From (19) to (23), we have

$$\frac{\partial \boldsymbol{E}}{\partial u_{il}} = -(x_{ij} - u_{il}) f_l^{\,2}(\boldsymbol{X}_j) \,. \tag{24}$$

$$\frac{du_{il}}{dt} = -\eta(t) \frac{\partial \boldsymbol{E}}{\partial u_{il}} \,. \tag{25}$$

According to gradient drop principle, each center of l is updated by

$$u_{il}(t+1) = u_{il}(t) + \eta(t)(x_{ij} - u_{il}) f_l^{\,2}(\boldsymbol{X}_j) \,. \tag{26}$$

where $\eta(t)$ =1/|*t*| is a learning decline factor.

In light of (26), update u_{il}, till $|u_{il}(t+1)-u_{il}|<\varepsilon$, where ε is a very small positive number. After networks learning, a group of certain classification centre u_{il} is achieved, then according to (19), D_{jl} may be calculated. Based on (20), $f_l(\boldsymbol{X}_j)=(1+D_{jl})^{-1}$ that expresses an extent $\boldsymbol{X}$ belongs to l can be work out. Input vector $\boldsymbol{X}$ is believed to belong to l since max$\{f_i(\boldsymbol{X}), i=1,2,\ldots\ldots,Q\}=f_l(\boldsymbol{X})$.

5 Example Analysis

In light of Rogers ratio diagnosis table and data of the transformer DGA, history data library of transformer fault diagnosis is established as shown Table 1. The condition attributes *a*, *b*, *c* and *d* respectively express CH_4/H_2, C_2H_6/CH_4, C_2H_4/C_2H_6 and C_2H_2/C_2H_4, the decision attribute *D* express diagnosis result. Where *D*=1 represents normal aging; *D*=2 is local discharge; *D*=3 is overheating, but temperature is no more than 150 °C; *D*=4 is overheating, but temperature is between 150°C and 200 °C; *D*=5 is also overheating, but temperature is between 200°C and 300°C; *D*=6 is naked metal overheating; *D*=7 expresses circumfluence in winding; *D*=8 is iron-heart/hull circumfluence or tie-in overload; *D*=9 is electric arc discharge, and is non perfoliate discharge; *D*=10 is electric arc discharge, but is perfoliate; *D*=11 is continuous discharge accident; *D*=12 is local discharge with creepage electricity trace. In Table 1, *U* expresses universe, *n* expresses is sample frequency.

According to equation (1), the important factor of each attribute is worked out as γ_a= 9/12, γ_b= 6/12, γ_c= 9/12, γ_d= 6/12. It is easy to see from Table 1 that samples 8 and 16 are noise, they therefore may be eliminated. According to (14) and (15), order *C*=3 for *a*,*c*,*d* and *C*=2 for *b*, the initial parameter $\boldsymbol{h}=\boldsymbol{\theta}=(<u_{aH}, u_{aM}, u_{aL}>, <u_{bH}, u_{bL}>, <u_{cH}, u_{cM}, u_{cL}>, <u_{dH}, u_{dM}, u_{dL}>, \sigma)$ = (<0.2,1.2,2.5>, <0.5,0.5>, <0.2,0.5,1.8>, <0.5,0.3,0.6>,σ=0.5). After ECM learning, we get $\boldsymbol{h}$=(<0,1.5,3>,<0,1>,<0,1,2>, <0,1,2>,σ=0.75). Below an diagnosis example then is given out.

The gas volume capacities in transformer oil are tested as $\varphi(CH_4)=74\times10^{-6}$, $\varphi(H_2)=60\times10^{-6}$, $\varphi(C_2H_2)=103\times10^{-6}$, $\varphi(C_2H_6)=58\times10^{-6}$, $\varphi(C_2H_4)=187\times10^{-6}$. Rogers ratio code is (1,0,2,1), and fuzzy characteristic vector is $\boldsymbol{X}$=(0.03,0.8,1,0.14,1, 0.14,1, 0.14,0.14,1,0.14), the output result of fuzzy neural classifier is described by (0.53,0.5,0.57,0.52,0.49,0.55,0.60,0.79,0.46,0.54,0.56,0.55), since max$\{f_i(\boldsymbol{X}), i=1,$

Table 1. The history data library

U	*n*	*a*	*b*	*c*	*d*	*D*
1	60	0	0	0	0	1
2	38	3	0	0	0	2
3	35	1	0	0	0	3
4	30	2	0	0	0	3
5	35	1	1	0	0	4
6	40	2	1	0	0	4
7	43	0	1	0	0	5
8	5	0	1	1	0	5
9	35	0	0	1	0	6
10	3	1	0	1	0	6
11	42	1	0	1	0	7
12	35	1	0	2	0	8
13	50	0	0	0	1	9
14	35	0	0	1	2	10
15	35	0	0	2	2	11
16	5	1	0	2	0	11
17	45	3	0	0	1	12
18	25	3	0	0	2	12

2,…,12} =0.79= $f_8(X)$, diagnosis result is D=8, that is, iron-heart/hull circumfluence or tie-in overload, fielded inspection proves the diagnosis result is correct.

6 Conclusions

Rough set is applied to evaluate system parameters importance and implement attribute reduction, effectively drop the scale of solution and system space dimensions, and simplify the neural networks architecture, improve real-time properties of fault diagnosis. Meanwhile, ECM algorithm is applied to automatically acquire the relevant parameters hidden in samples, which makes the algorithm possess stronger robustness. Fuzzy characteristic vector makes fault-tolerance of system dramatically improved, fuzzy outputs can interpret single and multi-fault phenomenon. Hence, The learning algorithm of the proposed network is ubiquitous, training time is also shorter, and is an ideal pattern classifier.

References

1. Yu, H.J.: Intelligent Diagnosis Based on Neural Networks. 1st edn. Metallurgy Industry Publication House, BJ (2000)
2. Su, H.S., Li, Q.Z.: Substation Fault Diagnosis Method Based on Rough Set Theory and Neural Network Model. Power System Technology. 16 (2005) 66-70
3. Zhang, Y.: An Artificial New Network Approach to Transformer Fault Diagnosis. IEEE Trans. on Power Delivery. 11 (1996) 1836-1841

4. Sunan, H., Wei, R.: Use of Neural Fuzzy Networks with Mixed Genetic/Gradient Algorithm in Automated Vehicle Control. IEEE Trans. on Industrial Electronics. 11 (1999) 1090-1016
5. Yang, J., Fen, Z.S., Huang, K.L. (ed.): Intelligent Fault Diagnosis Technology for Equipment. 1st edn. National Defence Industry Press, BJ (2004)
6. Hoskins, J.C., Kaliyur, K.M., Himmelblau, D.M.: Fault Diagnosis in Complex Chemical Plants Using Artificial Neural Networks. AIChE Journal. 11 (1991) 137-141
7. Li, H.Q., Wan, B.W.: Application of Modular Wavelet Neural Networks in Industries Product Quality Control. Control and Decision. 19 (2004) 195-298
8. Narendra, K.S., Mukhopadhyay, S.: Adaptive Control of Nonlinear Multivariable Systems Using Neural Networks. Neural Networks. 7 (1994) 737-742
9. Hunt, K.J., Sbarbaro, D., Zbkowski, R., Gawthrop, P.J.: Neural Networks for Control Systems – ASurvey. Automatica. 28 (1992) 1083-1112
10. Zeng, H.: Intelligent Calculating. 1st edn. Chongqing University Press, Chongqing (2004)
11. Dempster, A.P., Larid, N.M., Rubin, D.B.: Maximum Likelihood from Incomplete Data via the EM Algorithm. Journal of the Royal Statistical Society, Series B, 39 (1997)1-38

System Identification Using Hierarchical Fuzzy CMAC Neural Networks

Floriberto Ortiz Rodriguez[1], Wen Yu[1], and Marco A. Moreno-Armendariz[2]

[1] Departamento de Control Automático, CINVESTAV-IPN
A.P. 14-740, Av.IPN 2508, México D.F., 07360, México
yuw@ctrl.cinvestav.mx
[2] Centro de Investigación en Computación-IPN
AV. Juan de Dios Bátiz S/N,
Unidad Profesional "Adolfo López Mateos"
México, D.F.C.P. 07738, México

Abstract. The conventional fuzzy CMAC can be viewed as a basis function network with supervised learning, and performs well in terms of its fast learning speed and local generalization capability for approximating nonlinear functions. However,it requires an enormous memory and the dimension increase exponentially with the input number. Hierarchical fuzzy CMAC (HFCMAC) can use less memory to model nonlinear system with high accuracy. But the structure is very complex, the normal training for hierarchical fuzzy CMAC is difficult to realize. In this paper a new learning scheme is employed to HFCMAC. A time-varying learning rate assures the learning algorithm is stable. The calculation of the learning rate does not need any prior information such as estimation of the modeling error bounds. The new algorithms are very simple, we can even train each sub-block of the hierarchical fuzzy neural networks independently.

1 Introduction

The Cerebellar Model Articulation Controller (CMAC) presented by Albus [1] is an auto-associative memory feedforward neural network, which is a simple mathematics mode of the cerebellar based on the neurophysiological theory. Because of the simple structure and fast learning speed of CMAC, it has been successfully used in many areas especially in control and robot where the real-time capabilities of the network are of the particular importance. In CMAC the data for a quantized state are constant and the derivative information is not preserved. To overcome this problem a new structure of CMAC called Fuzzy CMAC (FCMAC) [3], [7], uses fuzzy set (fuzzy label) as the input clusters instead of crisp set. Compared to normal CMAC which associates with numeric values, FCMAC can model a problem using linguistic variables based a set of If-Then fuzzy rules which are determined by fuzzy membership functions. Thus, the FCMAC network becomes more robust, highly intuitive and easily comprehended.

In the design of the fuzzy CMAC is common to use a table look-up approach, which is a time-consuming task. Especially when the number of inputs is huge,

D.-S. Huang, K. Li, and G.W. Irwin (Eds.): ICIC 2006, LNAI 4114, pp. 230–235, 2006.

the memory of fuzzy CMAC increase exponentially. This would be overload the memory and make the fuzzy system very hard to implement. Generally n input variables with m quantization, has $n-$dimension space and m^n memory. This phenomenon is called "curse of dimensionality". In order to deal with the memory explosion problem. A number of low-dimensional fuzzy CMAC in a hierarchical form are consisted, instead of a single high-dimensional fuzzy CMAC. This is main idea of hierarchical fuzzy CMAC (HFCMAC) [2] [5]. But they did not give learning algorithms.

Both neural networks and fuzzy logic are universal estimators. Resent results show that the fusion procedure of these two different technologies seems to be very effective for nonlinear systems identification. Gradient descent and backpropagation are always used to adjust the parameters of membership functions (fuzzy sets) and the weights of defuzzification (neural networks) for fuzzy neural networks.

The stability problem of fuzzy neural identification is very important in applications. It is well known that normal identification algorithms (for example, gradient descent and least square) are stable in ideal conditions. In the presence of unmodeled dynamics, they might become unstable. Some robust modifications must be applied to assure stability with respect to uncertainties. Projection operator is an effective tool to guarantee fuzzy modeling bounded . It was also used by many fuzzy-neural systems [7]. Another general approach is to use robust adaptive techniques [4] in fuzzy neural modeling. For example, [9] applied a switch $\sigma-$modification to prevent parameters drift. By using passivity theory, we successfully proved that for continuous-time recurrent neural networks, gradient descent algorithms without robust modification were stable and robust to any bounded uncertainties [10], and for continuous-time identification they were also robustly stable [11]. Nevertheless, do hierarchical fuzzy CMAC has the similar characteristics?

In this paper backpropagation-like approach is applied to system identification via hierarchical fuzzy CMAC neural networks (FCMAC), which is capable of resolving high-dimensional classification problems well. The new algorithms are very simple, we can even train the parameters of each sub-block independently. Time-varying learning rates is used to hierarchical FCMAC neural networks. One example is given to illustrate the effectiveness of the suggested algorithms.

2 Hierarchical Fuzzy CMAC for System Identification

Consider following discrete-time nonlinear system to be identified

$$\begin{aligned} y(t) &= h\left[x\left(t\right)\right] = \Psi\left[X\left(t\right)\right] \\ &= \Psi\left[y\left(t-1\right), y\left(t-2\right), \cdots u\left(t-1\right), u\left(t-2\right), \cdots\right] \end{aligned} \cdot \tag{1}$$

where $X\left(t\right) = \left[y\left(t-1\right), y\left(t-2\right), \cdots u\left(t\right), u\left(t-1\right), \cdots\right]^T$.

This network can be divided into five layers: Input Layer (L_1), Fuzzified Layer (L_2), Fuzzy Association Layer (L_3), Fuzzy Post-association Layer (L_4) and Output Layer (L_5). The input Layer transfers input $x = (x_1, x_2..x_n)^T$ to the next layer $mf_i = x_i, i = 1, ...n$, n is the number of input variables. Each node at Fuzzified Layer corresponds to a linguistics variable which are expressed by membership functions $\mu_{A^i_j}$, there are m quantizations (membership functions) for each input. The number of the nodes in this layer is n^m. Fuzzified Layer accomplishes the fuzzification of input variables. And it corresponds to both sensor layer of CMAC and fuzzifier of fuzzy logic controller. Fuzzy Association Layer connects fuzzified layer and accomplishes the matching of precondition of fuzzy logic rule. Each node at this layer completes fuzzy implication operation (flo) to obtain firing strength $\alpha_j = \pi(x) \, flo\{mf_i(x_1), ..., mf_n(x_n)\}$. If we use product rule for flo, $\alpha_k = \prod_{i=1}^{n} \lambda_k \left(\mu_{A^i_j}\right)$, where k is association times, $k = 1 \cdots l$, l is association number, λ is the selection vector of association memory which is defined as $\lambda_k \left(\mu_{A^i_j}\right) = \mu_{A^i_{j,k}} = [0, 0 \cdots 1, 0 \cdots] \begin{bmatrix} \mu_{A^i_1}, \\ \vdots \\ \mu_{A^i_m} \end{bmatrix}$, $i = 1 \cdots n$. Fuzzy post-association layer will calculate the normalization of firing strength and prepare for fuzzy inference, $\bar{\alpha}_k = \alpha_k / \sum_{k=1}^{l} \alpha_k == \left(\prod_{i=1}^{N_i} \mu_{A^i_j}, \right) / \left(\sum_{j=1}^{N_A} \prod_{i=1}^{N_i} \mu_{A^i_j}, \right)$. In the output layer, Takagi fuzzy inference will be used, that is, consequence of each fuzzy rule is defined as a function of input variables R^j :IF x_1 is A^1_j $\cdots$ and x_n is A^n_j THEN y is $f(x_1, x_2, ..., x_n)$. The output of the CMAC can be expressed in a vector notation as

$$y = \sum_{k=1}^{l} w_k \varphi_k, \quad y(x) = W^T \varphi(x) \tag{2}$$

where w_k plays the role of connective weight, W is adjustable weight values, $\varphi(x)$ is base function defined as $\varphi_k = \prod_{i=1}^{n} \lambda_k \left(\mu_{A^i_j},\right) / \sum_{k=1}^{l} \prod_{i=1}^{n} \lambda_k \left(\mu_{A^i_j},\right)$. We use l ($k = 1 \cdots l$) times to perform association from an input vector $X = [x_1, \cdots, x_n] \in \Re^n$ to an output linguistic y. Each input variable x_i $(i = 1 \ldots n)$ has m quantizations. So the memory space is $l \times m^n$. The number of memory has to increase exponentially with the number of input variables. A serious problem facing fuzzy CMAC applications is how to deal with this memory explosion problem. One approach to deal with this difficulty is use hierarchical fuzzy CMAC. This kind of systems have the nice property that the number of memory needed to construct the fuzzy system increases only *linearly* with the number of variables. For example each sub-block has two input, the memory space is $l \times m^2 \times b$, b is number of sub-block.

We use the following example to explain how to use the backpropagation technique for hierarchical fuzzy CMAC neural networks. The output of each hierarchical block of fuzzy CMAC is given by $\hat{y}_r = \sum_{k=1}^{l} w_{r,k} \varphi_{r,k}$, $r = 1, 2, 3$. The outputs of each hierarchical block fuzzy CMAC in the previous layer are used as the input linguistic variables of the next layer. The intermediate outputs, however, are artificial in nature in many cases and do not possess physical meaning. Thus if they are used as the input variables of the next layer, then the involved fuzzy rules in the middle of the hierarchical structure have little physical meaning and consequently is hard to design. This phenomenon becomes prominent as the number of layers grows larger in an hierarchical system. The performance index is defined as $J = \frac{1}{2}e_3^2$, $e_3 = \widehat{y}_3 - y$. For FCMAC$_3$, the learning algorithm is

$$w_{3,k}(t+1) = w_{3,k}(t) - \eta\varphi_{3,k}(t)\, e_3(t) \tag{3}$$

where $\eta > 0$ is learning rate. For subsystem FCMAC$_2$, if we want to update $w_{2,k}$, we should calculate $\frac{\partial J}{\partial w_{2,k}} = \frac{\partial J}{\partial \widehat{y}_3}\frac{\partial \widehat{y}_3}{\partial \widehat{y}_2}\frac{\partial \widehat{y}_2}{\partial w_{2,k}}$. We know $\frac{\partial \widehat{y}_3}{\partial \widehat{y}_2}$ corresponds to $x_{3,2}(k)$, so

$$\begin{aligned} &\frac{\partial J}{\partial \widehat{y}_3} = \widehat{y}_3 - y = e_3(t) \\ &\frac{\partial \widehat{y}_3}{\partial \widehat{y}_2} = \frac{\partial \widehat{y}_3}{\partial z_{3,k}}\frac{\partial z_{3,k}}{\partial \widehat{y}_2} = \left[\frac{a_3}{b_3^2} - \frac{w_{3,k}}{b_3}\right] z_{3,k}\left[2\frac{\widehat{y}_2 - c_{3,2}^i}{\left(\sigma_{3,2}^i\right)^2}\right] \\ &\frac{\partial \widehat{y}_2}{\partial w_{2,k}} = \varphi_{2,k} = \frac{z_{2,k}}{b_2} \end{aligned} \tag{4}$$

where $z_{3,k} = \prod_{i=1}^{n}\lambda_k\left(\mu_{A_j^i},\right)$, $a_3 = \sum_{k=1}^{l} w_{3,k} z_{3,k}$, $b_3 = \sum_{k=1}^{l} z_{3,k}$. The gradient learning for $w_{2,k}$ is

$$\begin{aligned} &w_{2,k}(t+1) = w_{2,k}(t) - \eta\varphi_{2,k}(t)\frac{z_{2,k}}{b_2} 2\frac{\widehat{y}_3 - w_{3,k}}{b_3} z_{3,k}\frac{\widehat{y}_2 - c_{3,2}^i}{\left(\sigma_{3,2}^i\right)^2} e_3(t) \\ &= w_{2,k}(t) - \eta\varphi_{2,k}(t)\, e_2(t) \end{aligned} \tag{5}$$

where

$$e_2(t) = 2\frac{\widehat{y}_3 - w_{3,k}}{b_3} z_{3,k}\frac{\widehat{y}_2 - c_{3,2}^i}{\left(\sigma_{3,2}^i\right)^2} e_3(t) = \frac{\partial \widehat{y}_3}{\partial \widehat{y}_2} e_3(t)$$

So (5) has the same form as (3). Similar we can obtain with

$$\begin{aligned} &e_1(t) = \frac{\partial \widehat{y}_3}{\partial \widehat{y}_1} e_3(t), \quad \frac{\partial \widehat{y}_3}{\partial \widehat{y}_1} = 2\frac{\widehat{y}_3 - w_3^i}{b_3} z_{3,k}\frac{y_2 - c_{3,1}^i}{\left(\sigma_{3,1}^i\right)^2} \\ &w_{1,k}(t+1) = w_{1,k}(t) - \eta\varphi_{1,k}(t)\, e_1(t) \end{aligned}$$

In general , the training procedures are as follows:

1) According to the structure of the hierarchical fuzzy CMAC neural networks, we calculate the output of each sub-fuzzy CMAC neural networks by (2). Some outputs of fuzzy CMAC neural networks should be the inputs of the next level.
2) Calculate the error for each block. We start from the last block, the identification error is $e_o(t) = \widehat{y}_o(t) - y(t)$, where $e_o(k)$ is identification error, $\widehat{y}_o(k)$ is the output of the whole hierarchical fuzzy CMAC neural networks, $y(k)$ is the output the plant. Then we back propagate the error form the structure of the hierarchical fuzzy CMAC neural networks.We can calculate

the error for the block p (defined as e_p) form its former block q (defined as e_q). By the chain rule discussed above

$$e_p(k) = 2\frac{\widehat{y}_q - w_q^i}{b_q} z_{q,k} \frac{\widehat{y}_p - c_{q,p}^i}{\left(\sigma_{q,p}^i\right)^2} e_q(k) \tag{6}$$

3) Train the Gaussian function (membership functions in the premise and the consequent parts) for each block independently, for p_th block backpro pagation-like algorithm is

$$w_{p,k}(k+1) = w_{p,k}(k) - \eta\varphi_{p,k}(t)\, e_p(k). \tag{7}$$

3 Stable Learning

Since we assume the base function $\varphi_{r,k}$ of CMAC for each block is known, only the weights need to be updated for system identification. We will design a stable learning algorithm such that the output $\widehat{y}(t)$ of fuzzy CMAC neural networks (2) can follow the output $y(t)$ of nonlinear plant (1). Let us define identification error vector $e(t)$ as $e(t) = \widehat{y}(t) - y(t)$. By (6) $e(t)$ can be propagated to each sub-block, named $e_p(t)$. We define the virtual output of the plant as $y_p(t)$, which is corresponding to the output of the sub-block $\widehat{y}_p(t)$, so $e_p(t) = \widehat{y}_p(t) - y_p(t)$. For p_th block, we assume the nonlinear plant can be expressed. According to function approximation theories of fuzzy logic [9] and neural networks [11], the identified nonlinear process (1) can be represented as $y_p(t) = W^*\varphi[X(t)] - \mu(t)$, where W^* is unknown weights which can minimize the unmodeled dynamic $\mu(t)$. The identification error can be represented by $e_p(t) = \widetilde{W}(t)\varphi[X(t)] + \mu(t)$, where $\widetilde{W}(t) = W(t) - W^*$. In this paper we are only interested in open-loop identification, we assume that the plant (1) is bounded-input and bounded-output (BIBO) stable, *i.e.*, $y(t)$ and $u(t)$ in (1) are bounded. By the bound of the base function φ, $\mu(t)$ is bounded. The following theorem gives a stable gradient descent algorithm for fuzzy neural modeling.

Theorem 1. *If we use the hierarchical fuzzy CMAC neural networks to identify nonlinear plant (1), the gradient descent algorithm (7) with a time-varying learning rate as the following, can make identification error* $e(t)$ *bounded*

$$W(t+1) = W(t) - \eta_t e(t)\varphi^T[X(t)] \tag{8}$$

where the scalar $\eta_t = \dfrac{\eta}{1 + \|\varphi[X(t)]\|^2}$, $0 < \eta \leq 1$. *The normalized identification error* $e_N(t) = \frac{e(t)}{1+\max_t\left(\|\varphi[X(t)]\|^2\right)}$ *satisfies the following average performance*

$$\limsup_{T\to\infty} \frac{1}{T}\sum_{t=1}^{T} \|e_N(t)\|^2 \leq \overline{\mu} \tag{9}$$

where $\overline{\mu} = \max_t \left[\|\mu(t)\|^2\right]$.

4 Conclusions

In this paper we propose a simple training algorithm for hierarchical fuzzy CMAC neural networks. The modelling process can be realized in each sub-block independently. The new stable algorithms with time-varying learning rates are applied to hierarchical fuzzy CMAC neural networks. Further works will be done on structure training and adaptive control.

References

1. Albus, J.S.: A New Approach to Manipulator Control: The Cerebellar Model Articulation Controller (CMAC). Journal of Dynamic Systems, Measurement, and Control, Transactions of ASME (1975) 220-227
2. Lee, H., Chen, C.M., Lu, Y.F.: A Self-organizing HCMAC Neural Network Classifier. IEEE Transaction on Neural Networks Vol.14(1) (2003) 15-27
3. Chiang, C.T., Lin, C.S.: CMAC with General Basis Functions Neural Networks. Vol.9(7) (1996) 1199-1211
4. Ioannou, P.A., Sun, J.: Robust Adaptive Control. Prentice Hall (1996)
5. Hu, J.S., Hu, G.W., Wang, J.B., Liu, B.: FCMAC Based On Minesweeping Strateg Proceedings of the Fourth International Conference on Machine Learning and Cybernetics, Guangzhou (2005) 18-21
6. Commuri, S., Jagannathan, S., Lewis, F.L.: CMAC Neural Network Control of Robot Manipulators. Journal of Robotic Systems (1997)
7. Kim, Y.H., Lewis, F.L.: Optimal Design of CMAC Neural-Network Controller for Robot Manipulators. IEEE Transactions On Systems, Man, And Cybernetics—Part C: Applications And Reviews. Vol.30(1) (2000)
8. Sastry, P. S., Santharam, G.: Unnikrishnan, K.P., Memory Neural Networks for Identification and Control of Dynamic Systems IEEE Trans. Neural Networks Vol.5 (1994) 306-319
9. Wang, L. X.: Analysis and Design of Hierarchical Fuzzy Systems. IEEE Transactions on Fuzzy Systems. Vol. 7(3) (1999) 617-624
10. Yu, W., Li, X.: Some Stability Properties of Dynamic Neural Networks. IEEE Trans. Circuits and Systems, Part I. Vol.48(1) (2001) 256-259
11. Yu, W., Li, X.: Some New Results on Dystem Identification With Dynamic Neural Networks, IEEE Trans. Neural Networks. Vol.12(2) (2001) 412-417

A Reliable Resilient Backpropagation Method with Gradient Ascent

Xugang Wang[1], Hongan Wang[1], Guozhong Dai[1], and Zheng Tang[2]

[1] Intelligence Engineering Laboratory, Institute of Software, The Chinese Academy of Sciences, Beijing 100080, China
{wxg, wha, gzd}@iel.iscas.ac.cn
[2] Faculty of Engineering, Toyama University, Toyama-shi, Japan, 930-8555
tang@iis.toyama-u.ac.jp

Abstract. While the Resilient Backpropagation (RPROP) method can be extremely fast in converging to a solution, it suffers from the local minima problem. In this paper, a fast and reliable learning algorithm for multi-layer artificial neural networks is proposed. The learning model has two phases: the RPROP phase and the gradient ascent phase. The repetition of two phases can help the network get out of local minima. The proposed algorithm is tested on some benchmark problems. For all the above problems, the systems are shown to be capable of escaping from the local minima and converge faster than the Backpropagation with momentum algorithm and the simulated annealing techniques.

1 Introduction

Since the introduction of Backpropagation algorithm (BP) [1], there have been a number of refinements made to the Backpropagation algorithm [2][3][4][5]. Up to now, the Resilient RPROP method has been proven to be one of the best first-order learning methods for neural networks [6]. While the RPROP method can be extremely fast in converging to a solution, it suffers from the same problem faced by all gradient decent based methods: it may often converge to local minima. Numerous approaches those added some noise during the learning process or used the simulated annealing to modify the gradient decent based learning model have been proposed in order to help the network escape from local minima [7][8][9][10]. However, these methods were usually very slow and failed to converge to a global minimum within a reasonable number of iterations [11] [12]. A similar gain parameter adaptive method has been applied to the traditional backpropagation algorithm in our previous work [21]. But it has not been used in the fast gradient descent method yet.

This paper proposes a novel approach using both the RPROP method and gradient ascent to supervised learning for multi-layer artificial neural networks. Instead of adding any noise to the learning process, we design a deterministic algorithm that is expected to be more effective than the noise-adding algorithms to solve the local minima problem. The systems are shown to be capable of escaping from local minima and converge more reliably than the RPROP method by simulations.

D.-S. Huang, K. Li, and G.W. Irwin (Eds.): ICIC 2006, LNAI 4114, pp. 236 – 244, 2006.

2 Algorithm

Usually, the activation function of the feed-forward neural network is given by a sigmoid function with the "gain" parameter g:

$$f(x) = \frac{1}{1 + e^{-gx}}. \tag{1}$$

In general, the gain parameter of the sigmoid function is set to a positive constant [13] and not changed by the learning rule. However, there is evidence suggesting that the nervous system has mechanisms that modulate the neural response function in a manner similar to the "gain" parameter [14]. There is also evidence that these amines play an important role in the modulation of learning [15]. Some improved learning algorithms modifying gain parameters have been proposed [16][17] to speed up the learning.

2.1 RPROP Phase

In this phase, we modify the weights and thresholds using the RPROP method to decease the overall error measure *E*. In iteration *t*, the weights is updated as follows:

$$w_{ij}(t+1) = w_{ij}(t) + \Delta w_{ij}(t), \tag{2}$$

where w_{ij} denotes the weight in neural network from neuron *j* to neuron *i*. Δw_{ij} is the weight-update of w_{ij}.

The main difference of the RPROP method to other techniques is that the sizes of weight-update are independent of the absolute value of the partial derivatives. The weight-updates are computed as:

$$\Delta w_{ij}(t) = -sign(\frac{\partial E}{\partial w_{ij}}(t))\Delta_{ij}(t), \tag{3}$$

where the sign (.) operator return +1 if its argument is positive, -1 if the argument is negative, and 0 otherwise. The Δ_{ij} is initialized to a constant Δ_0 and adapted for each weight individually using the following rule: If the partial derivative $\frac{\partial E}{\partial w_{ij}}$ possesses the same sign for consecutive steps, the update value is increased, whereas if it changes sign, the update value is decreased. The update values are bounded by the parameters $\Delta\min$ and $\Delta\max$. The detailed explanation could be referred from [5].

The RPROP rule causes each iteration to modify weights and thresholds to approximate a minimum very rapidly. But, if the network descends into a minimum that achieves insufficient accuracy, it fails to learn. To help the network escape from the local minima, we add a gradient ascent phase in the gain space.

2.2 Gradient Ascent Phase

First, we must consider when a gradient ascent phase should be started. In the RPROP phase, the absolute value of the change of the error measure is accumulated for every n-correction. Here one correction corresponds to the modification to weights and thresholds for all patterns. If the accumulation is less than a very small pre-selected constant ρ, the network is considered to converge to a global or local minimum, then the RPROP phase stops. If the resulting error measure is smaller than an error criterion or a pre-selected maximal number of learning epochs is reached, terminate the learning procedure. Otherwise, go to the gradient ascent phase.

Here suppose that a vector $\{\mathbf{g}\}$ corresponds to the gain parameters of neurons. We can modify the vector $\{\mathbf{g}\}$ iteratively in a way that is similar to the weights and thresholds but to increase the error measure. At iteration t+1, the updated gain parameter g_j of neuron j are given by

$$g_j(t+1) = g_j(t) + \Delta g_j(t). \tag{4}$$

For the gain vector $\{g\}$, the modification requires the change of the gain to be in the positive gradient direction. Then the gain-updates are computed as

$$\Delta g_j(t) = sign(\frac{\partial E}{\partial g_j}(t))\Delta_j(t), \tag{5}$$

where $\Delta_j(t)$ is the update value of gain parameter g_j in iteration t, $\frac{\partial E}{\partial g_j}(t)$ is the derivative of the error measure with respect to the gain parameter (g_j) of neuron j. Similarly, $\Delta_j(t)$ is updated . For each neuron j an individual update value Δ_j is adjusted as follows:

$$\Delta_j(t) = \begin{cases} \min(\Delta_j(t-1) * \lambda^+, \Delta_{\max}) & \text{if } \frac{\partial E}{\partial g_j}(t-1) \cdot \frac{\partial E}{\partial g_j}(t) > 0 \\ \max(\Delta_j(t-1) * \lambda^-, \Delta_{\min}) & \text{if } \frac{\partial E}{\partial g_j}(t-1) \cdot \frac{\partial E}{\partial g_j}(t) < 0 \\ \Delta_j(t-1) & \text{otherwise} \end{cases} \tag{6}$$

In the gradient ascent phase, the absolute change value of the error measure E is also accumulated for every gain correction. If the accumulated value of the error measure E is larger than a pre-selected small constant return to the RPROP phase again. In the RPROP phase, using the new gains, the RPROP method is performed right along. In this way, the two phases are repeated until the error measure is less than the error criteria or when the number of epochs reached an upper limit.

3 Simulations

In our simulations, the Backpropagation algorithm used is its improved form – the Backpropagation with momentum algorithm [1]. The learning rate η is set to 0.5 and momentum term parameter α is set to 0.8 in all experiments. The only exception is the ionosphere data problem where η is set to 1.0 and α is set to 0. The process of the simulated annealing method is based on [10] and the same parameters as in [10] are used in our simulations. Since the proposed algorithm and the RPROP method have a number of parameters in common and the gain parameters are modified in a manner analogous to the weights and thresholds, these parameters are set to the same value as those used in RPROP [5]. The increase factor η^+=1.01 and decrease factor η^-=0.99 are set for the update of weights and thresholds. The choice of increase factor λ^+ and decrease factor λ^- used in gradient ascent phase is also very important. In order to investigate the sensitivity of the gain parameter to these factors, we have performed our proposed algorithms with different pairs of increase factor λ^+ and decrease factor λ^-.

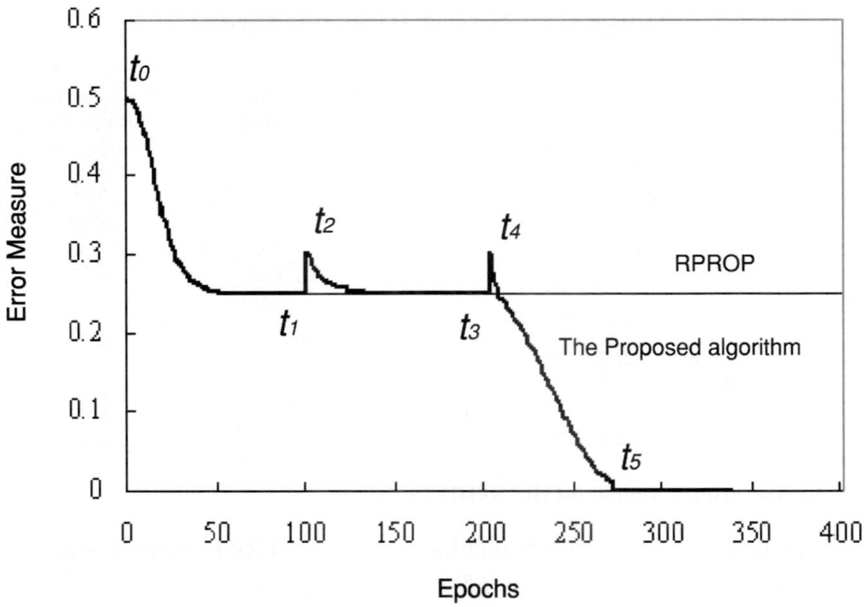

Fig. 1. Learning curve for the *exclusive-or* problem

3.1 Exclusive-OR (XOR) Problem

It is useful to begin with the *exclusive-or* problem since it is the classic problem requiring hidden units and since many other difficult problems involve an *exclusive-or* as a subproblem [1]. A simple architecture (2-2-1 network) with one hidden layer containing two hidden neurons and no direct connections from input to output is used.

Figure 1 shows the typical learning curves of the proposed algorithm and the RPROP method for the *exclusive-or* problem. In this figure, we can see that while the there is a local minimum for the Backpropagation algorithm converged into a local minimum, the proposed algorithm avoided the local minimum and trained the network successfully with two gradient ascent phases (t_2 and t_4).

Furthermore, to see how well the method is being made of escape from local minima, we generate 100 initial weights vectors randomly for the *exclusive-or* problem and performed the learning with the proposed algorithm, the original RPROP method, the Backpropagation with momentum term algorithm and the simulated annealing method respectively. The weights and thresholds are initialized randomly from –1.0 to 1.0 and the gains of all neurons are set to 1.0 initially.

The results of the simulation are shown in Table 1. Note that this problem exhibits over 94% global convergence when the proposed algorithms are utilized, while only 68% convergence for the original RPROP method and 78% for the Backpropagation with momentum algorithm. Although the average epoch of the proposed algorithm is slightly larger than that of the original RPROP method, it is much less than the Backpropagation with momentum algorithm and the simulated annealing method.

Table 1. Simulation results for the XOR problem

Algorithms	Success Rate (100 trials)	Avg. Number of Epochs
RPROP	68%	257
Backpropagation algorithm	78%	427
SA method	97%	3896
The proposed algorithm (λ^+ =1.1, λ^- =0.9)	97%	269
The proposed algorithm (λ^+ =1.2, λ^- =0.5)	96%	295
The proposed algorithm (λ^+ =2.0, λ^- =0.1)	94%	296

3.2 The Modified Exclusive-OR (XOR) Problem

The modified XOR problem is different form the classical XOR problem because one more pattern is included, that's $x_1 = 0.5, x_2 = 0.5$ and $output = 1.0$, such that several local minima exist simultaneously and a unique global minimum exits [18, 19]. We use a 2-2-1 neural network to solve this problem.

To explain how the network escapes from local minima more clearly, it is useful to plot a map of the function approximated by the network in the multi-dimensional space spanned by the input variables. Figure 2 shows the simulation results that illustrate the relationship between the output and two inputs (X1 and X2) of network

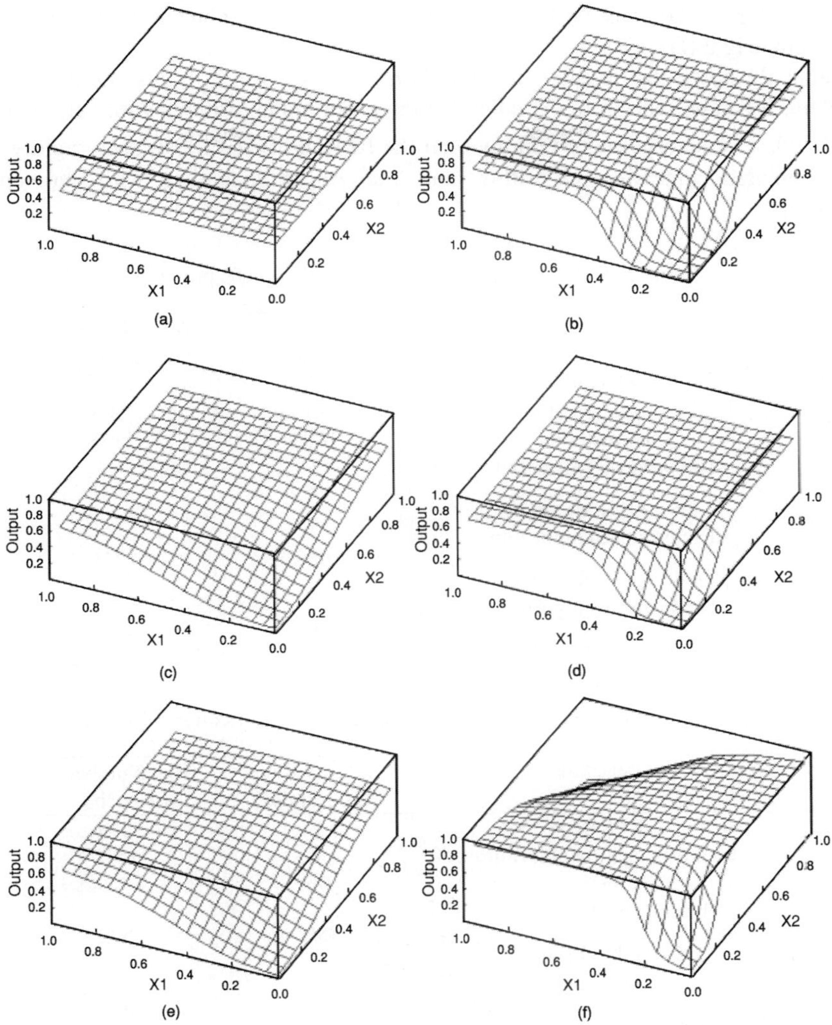

Fig. 2. The relationship between the output and two inputs (*X1* and *X2*) for modified XOR problem during the RPROP phase and the gradient ascent phase: (a) the network starts with initial weights; (b) the network got stuck into the first local minimum; (c) the first gradient ascent learning was performed; (d) the network reached the second local minimum; (e) the second gradient ascent learning was performed; (f) the network finally converged to the global minimum

during the RPROP phase and the gradient ascent phase for the modified XOR problem. The two horizontal axes correspond to the two inputs to the network, and the vertical axis is the output of the network. As can been seen, from an initial state (Fig.2 (a)), the network got stuck into the first local minimum (Fig.2 (b)). After the first gradient ascent learning (Fig.2 (c)) the network returned to RPROP phase and reached the second local minimum (Fig.2 (d)). Then the second gradient ascent learning (Fig.2 (e)) was performed, the network finally converged to the global minimum (Fig.2 (f)).

Table 2 shows the results of simulations for 100 run for this modified XOR problem. It can be seen from the table that the proposed algorithms with various value of λ^+ and λ^- converge more reliably than the RPROP method and more rapidly than the simulated annealing algorithm and the Backpropagation with momentum algorithm.

Table 2. Simulation results for the modified XOR problem

Algorithms	SuccessRate (100 trials)	Avg. Number of Epochs
RPROP	72%	128
Backpropagation algorithm	70%	503
SA method	100%	3178
The proposed algorithm (λ^+ =1.1, λ^- =0.9)	93%	347
The proposed algorithm (λ^+ =1.2, λ^- =0.5)	96%	221
The proposed algorithm (λ^+ =2.0, λ^- =0.1)	96%	323

Table 3. Simulation results for ionosphere data classification problem

Algorithms	Success Rate (100 trials)	Avg. Number of Epochs
RPROP	72%	249
Backpropagation algorithm	13%	1510
SA method	0%	------
The proposed algorithm (λ^+ =1.1, λ^- =0.9)	88%	572
The proposed algorithm (λ^+ =1.2, λ^- =0.5)	82%	301
The proposed algorithm (λ^+ =2.0, λ^- =0.1)	82%	514

3.3 Ionosphere Data

Furthermore, we apply our method to a 'real-world' problem: classification of radar returns from the ionosphere. The data set was created by Johns Hopkins University and obtained from the databases [20]. There are 34 attributes used to represent the pattern. Each pattern belongs to two classes: "Good" or "Bad" that were free electrons in the ionosphere. "Good" radar returns that were represented by 0 in the experiment are those showing evidence of some type of structure in the ionosphere. "Bad" returns that were represented by 1 are those that do not.

The database consists of 351 data patterns. We use the first 200 instances for training, which were carefully split almost 50% "Good" and 50% "Bad". A 34-3-1 neural network model was used to solve this problem. We set the error criteria =0.01 and performed 100 trails for the proposed algorithm, the RPROP method, the Backpropagation with momentum algorithm, and the simulated annealing method. For the Backpropagation with momentum algorithm, we set $\eta=1.0, \alpha=0$.

The simulation results are shown in Table 3. They demonstrate that the proposed algorithm is superior to the RPROP method and the Backpropagation with momentum algorithm in network training. The data of the simulated annealing method are the results obtained from performing simulated annealing learning on computers for 24 hours.

4 Conclusion

In this paper we have presented a fast and reliable algorithm for multi-layer artificial neural networks. The proposed method updates weights and thresholds by RPROP rule to minimize the error measure. Once a local minimum is found, it increases the error measure intentionally and temporarily by modifying the gain parameters in a gradient ascent direction of the error measure to help the network escape from the local minimum. Finally, the learning method is applied to several benchmark problems and a realistic "real-world" problem, indicating that the proposed learning algorithm significantly outperforms the RPROP method in global optimization and the simulated annealing method and the Backpropagation with momentum algorithm in convergence speed.

Acknowledgments

The work was supported in part by the grant-in-aid for National Fundamental Research Project of China (973 Project) (2002CB312103), the National Natural Science Foundation of China under Grant No. 60503054, the Key Innovation Project from Institute of Software, Chinese Academy of Sciences and Science Research of the Ministry of Education, Science and Culture of Japan under Grant (c)(2)12680392.

References

1. Rumelhart, D. E., Hinton, G. E., Williams, R. J.: Learning Internal Representations by Back-propagating Errors. in D.E. Rumelhart and J.L. McClelland (Eds.), Parallel Distributed Processing: Explorations in the Microstructure of Cognition, Vol.1 (MIT Press, Cambridge, MA, 1986) 318–362
2. Fahlman, S. E.: An Empirical Study of Learning Speed in Back-propagation Networks. Technical Report, Department of Computer Science, Carnegie Mellon University, Pittsburgh, PA (1988)
3. Jacobs, R.A.: Increased Rates of Convergence through Learning Rate Adaptation. Neural networks, Vol. 1, No.4 (1988) 295–307

4. Tollenaere, T.: SuperSAB: Fast Adaptive Backpropagation with Good Scaling Properties, Neural Networks, Vol. 3, No.5 (1990) 561–573
5. Riedmiller, M., Braun, H.: A Direct Adaptive Method for Faster Backpropagation Learning: The RPROP algorithm. in: Ruspini, H., (Ed.) Proc. of the ICNN 93, San Francisco, (IEEE Service Center, Piscataway, NJ, 1993) 586–591
6. Igel, C., Husken, M.: Empirical Evaluation of the Improved Rprop Learning Algorithm. Neurocomputing, Vol.50(C) (2003) 105–123
7. Wang, C., Principe, J.C.: Training Neural Networks with Additive Noise in the Desired Signal. IEEE Trans. Neural Networks, Vol. 10, No. 6 (1999) 1511–1517
8. Hanson, S. J.: Behavioral Diversity, Search and Stochastic Connectionist Systems. in Quantitative Analysis of Behavior: Neural Network Models of Conditioning and Action, Cambridge, MA: Harvard Press (1990) 295–344
9. Amato, S., Apolloni, B., Caporali, G., Madesani, U., Zanaboni, A.: Simulated Annealing Approach in Backpropagation. Neurocomputing, Vol.3, No.5/6 (1991) 207–220
10. Owen C. B., Abunawass, A. M.: Application of Simulated Annealing to the Backpropagation Model Improves Convergence, SPIE Proceedings, Vol.1966 (1993) 269–276
11. Ingman, D., Merlis,Y.: Local Minimization Escape Using Thermodynamic Properties of Neural Networks. Neural Networks, Vol. 4, No. 3 (1991) 395–404
12. Hassoun, M.: Fundamentals of Artificial Neural Networks. Cambridge, MA: MIT Press (1995)
13. Zurada, J.M.: Introduction to Artificial Neural Systems, West Publishing Company (1992)
14. Servan-Schreiber, C., Printz, H., Cohen, J.D.: A Network Model of Neuromodulatory Effects: Gain, Signal-to-Noise Ratio, and Behavior. Science, Vol.249 (1990) 892–895.
15. Kamatsu, T., Pettigrew, J. D.: Depletion of Brain Cathecolamines: Failure of Ocular Dominance Shift After Neurocular Occlusion in Kittens. Science, Vol.194 (1976) 206–208
16. Kruschke, J.K., Movellan, J.R.: Benefits of the Gain: Speeded Learning and Minimal Hidden Layers in Back Propagation Networks. IEEE Trans. on Systems, Man and Cybernetics, Vol. 21, No. 1 (1991) 273–280
17. Engelbrecht, A.P., Cloete, I., Geldenhuys, J., Zurada, J.M.: Automatic Scaling using Gamma Learning for Feedforward Neural Networks. in J. Mira, F. Sandoval (eds), in Lecture Notes in Computer Science, Vol. 930, Springer-Verlag, Berlin Heidelberg New York (1995) 374–381
18. Gori, M. and Tesi, A.: On the Problem of Local Minima in Backpropagation. IEEE Trans. Pattern Anal. Machine Intelligence, Vol.14, No.1 (1992) 76–85
19. Lee, H.M., Chen, C.M., Huang, T.C.: Leaning Efficiency Improvement of Backpropagation Algorithm by Error Saturation Prevention Method. Neurocomputing, Vol. 41 (2001) 125–143
20. Sigillito, V. G., Wing, S. P., Hutton, L. V., Baker, K. B.: Classification of Radar Returns from the Ionosphere Using Neural Networks. Johns Hopkins APL Technical Digest 10 (1989) 262-266
21. Tang, Z., Wang, X.G., Tamura, H., Ishii M.: An Algorithm of Supervised Learning for Multilayer Neural Networks. Neural Computation Vol.15, No.5 (2003) 1125-1142

Face Recognition Using Null Space-Based Local Discriminant Embedding

Yanmin Niu[1] and Xuchu Wang[2]

[1] College of Physics and Information Techniques, Chongqing Normal University, Chongqing 400047, China
niuym@cqnu.edu.cn

[2] Key Lab on Opto-Electronic Technique and Systems, Ministry of Education, Chongqing University, Chongqing 400044, China
seadrift.wang@gmail.com

Abstract. The manifold learning methods can discover the varying intrinsic features in face image space. However, in order to efficiently solve face image recognition problem with an image database, the extraction of discriminative features should be firstly considered. This paper proposes a new discriminative manifold learning method for face recognition. Besides like the recently proposed local perserving projectioin and local discriminative embedding algorithms which can preserve the local structure similarity in the face submanifold, our method emphasizes the discriminative property of embedding much more by a proposed Fisher Manifold Discriminant Embedding (Fisher MDE) criterion to build an object function and achieve the maximum. Experimental results on three open face datasets indicate the proposed method achieves lower error rates and provides a promising performance.

1 Introduction

Face recognition is an attracting and challengeable task both in human perception research and real-world applications. Since last decade, subspace-based methods, originated from Turk's Eigenface based on the Principal Components Analysis (PCA) [1] and improved by Belhumeur's Fisherface based on Fisher Linear Discriminant Analysis (LDA) [2], have dominated the approaches in face recognition for good performance and computational feasibility. Both of them try to transform a given set of face images into a smaller set of basis images using matrix decomposition techniques. While the unsupervised Eigenface intends to maximize the covariance and the supervised Fisherface intends to maximize the discriminability. Although Martinez explained that LDA doesn't always outperform than PCA [3], LDA is still widely accepted in face recognition and more effective than PCA.

Recently, human faces are thought of varying intrinsic features such as illumination, pose and expression, but both PCA and LDA effectively discover only the global linear structure. Kernel methods are introduced to mapping this nonlinear structure due to their success in Support Vector Machine (SVM). So there appear many nonlinear face recognition methods such as Kernel PCA (KPCA) [4],

D.-S. Huang, K. Li, and G.W. Irwin (Eds.): ICIC 2006, LNAI 4114, pp. 245–255, 2006.

Kernel LDA (KDA) [5] and etc. However, most of these methods are not only computationally expensive, but also too implicit for choosing parameters.

More recently, Faces are also thought of data points possibly residing close to a nonlinear submanifold embedded in a high-dimensional observation space. Some nonlinear techniques i.e. Isomap [6], LLE [7] and Laplacian Eigenmaps [8], have been proposed to discover the nonlinear structure of the manifold. These nonlinear methods do yield impressive results on some benchmark artificial datasets. However, they are developed based on reconstruction and perhaps are not optimal for classification viewpoint [9][10][11]. Moreover, they are difficult for new-come data which is essential for face or digital number recognition. In order to cope with this problem, Yang proposed an extended Isomap method [9] that utilized LDA to replace Multidimensional Scaling (MDS) during the low-dimensional embedding process. He and Niyogi proposed a Local Preserving Projections (LPP) method [10][11], which is an optimal linear approximation to Laplacian Beltrami operator on the face manifold, and very flexible in connection with both PCA/LDA versus clustering/classification. However, LPP shares local preserving character to LLE, which still goes against in face recognition in some sense. Chen and Chang proposed Local Discriminant Embedding (LDE) [12] and extension versions which seek to dissociate the submanifold of each class from one another, and outperform than many classical methods.

Our proposed method in this paper focuses on the supervised classification and is mainly motivated by LDE, moreover, it owns more discriminative ability essentially to different face classes. We introduce a Fisher Manifold Discriminant Embedding (MDE) criterion to build an object function. According to this criterion, the discriminant embedding can be divided in LDE and null space LDE two cases, and the later can get a better performance in many cases. The experimental results on three open datasets show the effectiveness and superiority of our method.

The rest of this paper is organized as follows: in Section 2, the proposed MDE criterion and null space-based LDE (NLDE) method is described from the start of ill-pose problem in LDA. Experimental results and discussions are presented in Section 3 and some main interests for future work are concluded in Section 4.

2 Null Space-Based Local Discriminant Embedding (NLDE)

2.1 Null Space-Based Methods for LDA

Suppose $\{\omega_i\}_{i=1}^{c}$ are c known pattern classes, $\{x_i\}_{i=1}^{N}$ are N h-dimensional samples, n_i is the number of samples in the subset ω_i. Let m be the mean sample of all samples and be the mean for the i-th class, then we can calculate the between-class scatter matrix S_b, the within-class scatter matrix S_w and the total scatter matrix S_t. As a linear statistic classification method, Fisher LDA tries to find a linear transform W so that after its application the scatter of sample vectors is minimized within each class and the scatter of mean vectors around the total mean vector is maximized simultaneously. By using between-class scatter matrix S_b and within-class scatter matrix S_w, Fisher LDA can be formulated as an optimization problem, and the objective function is highlighted as follows:

$$\arg\max J_F(W) = \frac{|W^T S_b W|}{|W^T S_w W|} \tag{1}$$

In many practical applications, there are not enough samples to make the within-class scatter matrix nonsingular (i.e. small sample size problem, SSSP) and S_w is ill-posed. In order to cope with this problem, Belhumeur [2] use PCA to reduce dimensionality. Yang [13] proposed a direct LDA method to diagonalize the S_b and S_w. Chen [14] regarded the null space of S_w was particularly useful in discriminability and proposed a way to makes use of it. Huang [15] followed this basic idea by firstly removing the common null space of both S_b and S_w, which means the null space of total-scatter matrix S_t is also removed since $S_t = S_b + S_w$. In our earlier research [16], the null space-based methods show more promising results on some face datasets, too.

2.2 Null Space-Based Local Discriminant Embedding

From viewpoint of manifold learning, $\mathcal{M}$ is supposed as a manifold embedded in $\mathbb{R}^h$ and $\{x_i \in \mathbb{R}^h\}_{i=1}^N$, any subset of data points that belong to the same class is assumed to lie in a submanifold of $\mathcal{M}$. We want to discover the most of a discriminative submanifold for classification, data visualization, dimensionality reduction and etc, so the object becomes the discovery of a most preserving or discriminative submanifold. Just like the basic idea of LPP, we intend to respect this fact: if two data points are close, we hope them still keep close in submanifold and vice versa. Of course, when class information is labeled, there are some points are close in different class and are far away in same class because of the noisy point and the outliers. According to the basic manifold assumptions, similarities can be locally measured, and in order to emphasis the similarity and dissimilarity among the neighborhoods of a point, we use two neighborhood graphs to measure this locality under the constraint of class information. They are defined as similar in [12]:

Let $Nb = \{x_j\}_{j=1}^b$ is a subset of b nearest neighbors of a data point x_i , G and $\overline{G}$ denote two undirected graphs both over all points. We consider each pair of points x_i, x_c and $x_c \in Nb$, when they are from same class an edge is added to between x_i, x_c (The ε -ball implementation way also can be considered). When they are from different classes, an edge is added to $\overline{G}$ between x_i, x_c.

According to neighborhood graphs G and $\overline{G}$, the affinity matrix S and $\overline{S}$ can be specified, where each element s_{ij} refers to the weight of the edge between x_i, x_j in S ,and refers $\overline{s}_{ij}$ to $\overline{S}$. The weight can be given by the way of "heat kernel", "cosine kernel" or "simple-minded". For example, a heat kernel is a Guassian-like function as follows:

$$s_{ij} = \begin{cases} exp(-\frac{\|x_i - x_j\|^2}{2\sigma^2}); \sigma \in \mathbb{R} & \text{if } x_i, x_j \text{ are connected in G} \\ 0 & \text{else} \end{cases} \tag{2}$$

and a cosine kernel is a similarity distance measure as follows:

$$s_{ij} = \begin{cases} \frac{<x_i,x_j>^2}{<x_i,x_i><x_j,x_j>} & \text{if } x_i, x_j \text{ are connected in G} \\ 0 & \text{else} \end{cases} \tag{3}$$

where $< \cdot, \cdot >$ means a kind of inner product operation. An advantage of cosine kernel is it doesn't need to adjust parameter. In the following, we propose a Fisher Manifold Discrimiant Embedding (MDE) criterion $\overline{J}_M(W)$ for classification purpose:

$$\arg\max \overline{J}_M(W) = \frac{\sum_{i,j} \|y_i - y_j\|^2 \overline{s}_{ij}}{\sum_{i,j} \|y_i - y_j\|^2 s_{ij}} \tag{4}$$

where y_i is the shape of x_i after manifold embedding, $y_i = W^T x_i$, and $\|y_i - y_j\|^2$ is the difference measure of y_i and y_j in a difference matrix. Apparently the $\overline{J}_M(W)$ is formally like Fisher criterion in Eq.1. Both of them want to find a transform which can minimize the within-class difference and maximize the between-class difference simultaneously. The optimization can be solved as follows. Let $J_M(W) = \sum_{i,j} \|W^T x_i - W^T x_j\|^2 s_{ij}$, so

$$\begin{aligned} J_M(W) &= \sum\nolimits_{i,j} (W^T x_i - W^T x_j)^T (W^T x_i - W^T x_j) s_{ij} \\ &= 2 \sum\nolimits_{i,j} W^T (x_i s_{ij} x_i^T - x_i s_{ij} x_j^T) W \\ &= 2(W^T X D X^T W - W^T X S X^T W) \\ &= 2 W^T X (D - S) X^T W \end{aligned} \tag{5}$$

Let Laplacian matrix $L = D - S$, the fact that L is symmetric and positive semidefinite causes XLX^T is symmetric and positive semidefinite. So $J_W(W) \geq 0$, and the Fisher MDE criterion can be analyzed from the following two aspects:

(1) $J_W(M) > 0$. This case happens when L is non-singular.The solving method is same as Local Discriminant Embedding (LDE), and the embedding matrix $W = [w_1, w_2, ..., w_k]$ can be obtained by solving the following generalized eigenvector problem:

$$X\overline{L}X^T w = \lambda X L X^T w \tag{6}$$

where $\overline{L} = \overline{D} - \overline{S}$ and $\overline{J}_M(W)$ is a max finite real number in $\mathbb{R}$.

(2) $J_W(M) = 0$. In this case, consider the property of symmetric and positive semidefinite matrix:

$$\begin{aligned} J_M(W) = 2W^T X(D - S)X^T W &= 0 \\ \Leftrightarrow X(D - S)X^T W &= 0 \\ \Leftrightarrow X(D - S)X^T &= 0 \\ \Leftrightarrow (D - S)X^T &= 0 \end{aligned} \tag{7}$$

It means that mapping the data points to the null space of L can make $J_M(W) = 0$. $L \in \mathbb{R}^{n \times n}$, the rank of L is $n - c$ [11]. so the dimensionality of the null space of

L is $c-1$. Let $W_{null} = \{v_i\}_{i=1}^{c-1}$ is the basis set which spans the null space of L, so firstly after consideration of using PCA as preprocessing for noise reduction(note that the reconstruction is without any loss. For simplicity, we still use X to represent the original data points after PCA dimensionality reduction). We then project the data $X \to \tilde{X}, \tilde{X} = W_{null}^T X$, and change the Fisher MDE criterion as follows:

$$\arg\max \tilde{\overline{J}}_M(W) = \sum_{i,j} \|\tilde{y}_i - \tilde{y}_j\|^2 \overline{s}_{ij} \tag{8}$$

where $\tilde{y}_i = W^T \tilde{x}_i$, and apparently, $\tilde{\overline{J}}_M(W) = W^T W_{null}^T X \overline{L} X^T W_{null} W$, where $\overline{L} = \overline{D} - \overline{S}$. Since $W_{null}^T X \overline{L} X^T W_{null}$ is a full rank matrix, we can solve the optimization problem by finding the generalized eigenvectors $\{w_i\}_{i=1}^k$ corresponding to the k largest eigenvalues of $W_{null}^T X \overline{L} X^T W_{null}$ and $W = \{w_i\}_{i=1}^k$. So the embedding matrix is $W_{null} W$ after PCA process. Theoretically speaking, it is notable that $\overline{J}_M(W) \to +\infty$ and the discriminability is the best one.

3 Experimental Results and Discussion

Here we compared our proposed method with the several other face recognition methods (Eigenface, Fisherface, Null-space LDA, LPP and LDE) using the publicly available Yale, AT&T and CMU PIE database. Our intension is to discover different characteristics among these methods.

The AT&T database [17] contains 400 images of 40 persons where the variations are mainly due to the facial contours, scale and pose of a person in the image. The Yale database [18] contains 165 images of 15 individuals where the images demonstrate variations in lighting condition, face expression, and with/without glasses. The CMU PIE database [19] contains 41368 face images of 68 subjects under varying pose, illumination and expression. Some processes during the experiment are marked as follows:

- For each image in Yale database, we manually crop the face to size of 92×112 (same as the resolution in AT&T). For computational efficiency, each image in both two databases is down-sampled to 1/4 of the original size. For PIE database, we use the dataset collected by He [11]. Which means each face image is cropped to 32×32 sizes and one individual holds 170 images. We lastly normalize them to be zero-mean and unit-variance vectors.
- The parameters, such as the number of principle components for dimensionality reduction in Eigenface, LPP and LDE methods, are empirically determined to achieve the lowest error rate by each method. So at last, the dimensionality of projection is different among these methods. The neighbor number for each test is same as the training number of per subject. For Fisherface and our proposed NLDE method, the projection dimensionality are both $c-1$.
- The recognition is performed using nearest-neighbor (1-NN) classifier for its simplicity. And the number for training/test is changeable for different purpose.

The experimental details is discussed as follows:

(1) Experiment on the AT&T Database: We firstly use a case to compare the performance of different methods where first 5 images of each individual for training and the rest for testing. For those methods need PCA to reduce dimensionality firstly, the number of principal components is decided by remaining 95% energy. The heat kernel with same parameter is designed to measure the affinity matrix. The recognition results are shown in Fig.1 and the best recognition rates are shown in Table1.

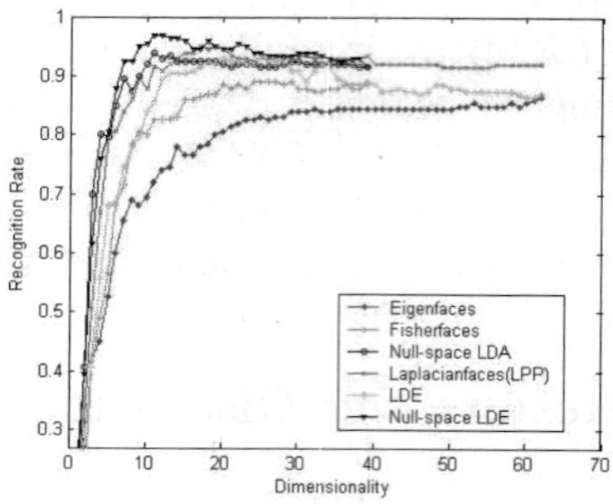

Fig. 1. A case of recognition accuracy versus dimensionality on AT&T database (first 5 images of each individual for training and the other for testing)

Table 1. Best recognition rate versus dimension reduction on AT&T database,data are from Fig.1

Approach	Rate(%)	Max Dim.(Reduced)
Eigenfaces(PCA)	86.5	62(62)
Fisherfaces(PCA+LDA)	89.0	39(24)
Null-space LDA (LDA)	94.0	39(11)
Laplacianfaces (PCA+LPP)	95.0	62(17)
LDE (PCA+LDE)	93.0	62(20)
Null-space LDE	97.0	39(11)

From Fig.1 we can find that the performance of Null-space LDA is better than Eigenfaces and Fisherfaces because it considers the most discriminative vector in the null space of the within-class scatter matrix S_w. Among the manifold-based methods, Null-space LDE method outperforms the others. We also find two interesting things:

- The recognition curve of Eigenfaces and Laplacianfaces is similar;
- The recognition curve of Null-space LDA and Null-space LDE is similar;

We further repeat 10 times to get the average values of the best recognition rate of each method under different training samples. The result is reported in Table 2. Here we preserve the number of principal components for 98% energy.

(2) Experiment on the Yale database: The subjects in this database is much less than AT&T dataset, while the illumination condition is more complex. For

Table 2. Performance comparison on AT&T database, each method is gotten from the average best recognition rate of 10 times under different training samples by random selection

Racog.Rate(%)	2	3	5	7	9
Eigenfaces(PCA)	72.19(60)	78.75(75)	84.89(108)	82.62(80)	82.57(33)
Fisherfaces(PCA+LDA)	76.25(25)	83.21(39)	93.44(33)	95.83(32)	90.00(17)
Null-space LDA (LDA)	82.18(39)	88.93(39)	96.00(37)	97.46(38)	97.50(36)
Laplacianfaces (PCA+LPP)	81.16(48)	87.50(36)	96.02(31)	95.83(37)	99.78(12)
LDE (PCA+LDE)	75.94(63)	84.29(43)	93.52(51)	95.92(24)	99.78(13)
Null-space LDE	83.13(35)	90.97(39)	97.01(33)	97.68(37)	99.84(13)

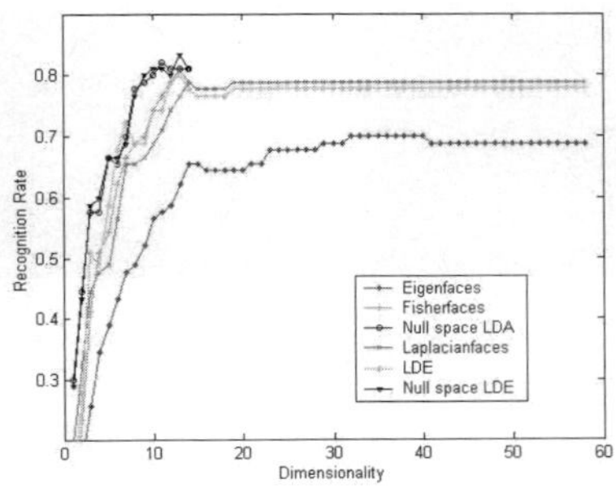

Fig. 2. A case of recognition accuracy versus dimensionality on Yale database (first 5 images of each individual for training and the other for testing)

Table 3. Best recognition rate versus dimension reduction on AT&T database,data are from Fig.2

Approach	Rate(%)	Max Dim.(Reduced)
Eigenfaces(PCA)	70.0	58(32)
Fisherfaces(PCA+LDA)	81.11	14(13)
Null-space LDA (LDA)	82.22	14(11)
Laplacianfaces (PCA+LPP)	78.89	58(14)
LDE (PCA+LDE)	80.0	58(13)
Null-space LDE	83.33	14(13)

those methods use PCA to reduce dimensionality, we preserve 95% energy, Fig.2 shows a case of recognition curves of different methods and Table3 gives the best recognition ration versus reduced dimensionality, where we still can find the two distinctive characters mentioned above. Table 4 reports the average best performance of different methods by 10 times experiments.

(3) Experiment on the CMU PIE database: This selected dataset only contains five near frontal poses (C05, C07, C09, C27, C29) and all the images under different illuminations and expressions. So, there are 170 images for each individual. In the stage of case study, we use five images of each subject for training and the other five images of each subject for testing. Fig.3 depicts twenty images

Table 4. Performance comparison on Yale database, each method is gotten from the average best recognition rate of 10 times under different training samples by random selection

Racog.Rate(%)	2	3	5	7	9
Eigenfaces(PCA)	54.07(22)	55.56(29)	59.17(59)	76.67(27)	93.33(44)
Fisherfaces(PCA+LDA)	48.89(11)	76.67(13)	78.89(10)	86.67(14)	90.00(14))
Null-space LDA (LDA)	57.04(14)	78.33(14)	81.10(9)	88.33(11)	93.33(9)
Laplacianfaces (PCA+LPP)	61.00(12)	79.17(15)	77.78(10)	88.33 (14)	98.88(14)
LDE (PCA+LDE)	758.52(26)	74.17(18)	78.89(10)	88.33(13)	98.93(13)
Null-space LDE	61.96(14)	78.50(14)	82.22(13)	90.00 (9)	98.96(10)

Fig. 3. The samples of cropped face images of two subjects on PIE database, the upper row is for training and the down for testing

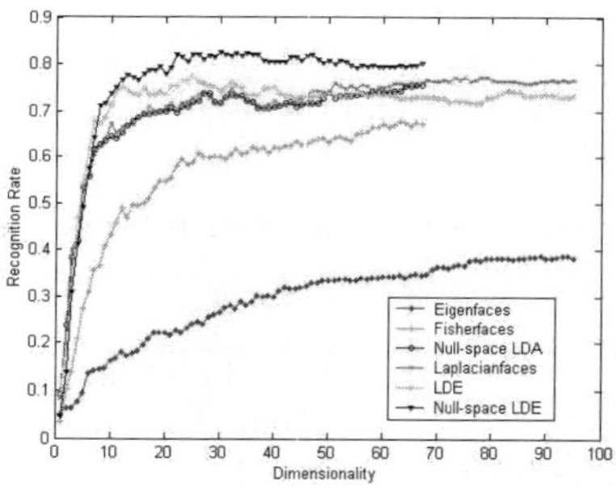

Fig. 4. A Case of Recognition Accuracy versus Dimensionality on PIE Database (the 5 images of each individual for training are 1,4,7,10,13 and the images for testing are 2, 5, 8, 11, 14)

Table 5. Best recognition rate versus dimension reduction on PIE database, data come from Fig.4

Approach	Rate(%)	Max Dim.(Reduced)
Eigenfaces(PCA)	38.82	95(89)
Fisherfaces(PCA+LDA)	67.84	67(63)
Null-space LDA (LDA)	75.59	67(66)
Laplacianfaces (PCA+LPP)	77.66	95(73)
LDE (PCA+LDE)	77.35	95(25)
Null-space LDE	82.65	67(30)

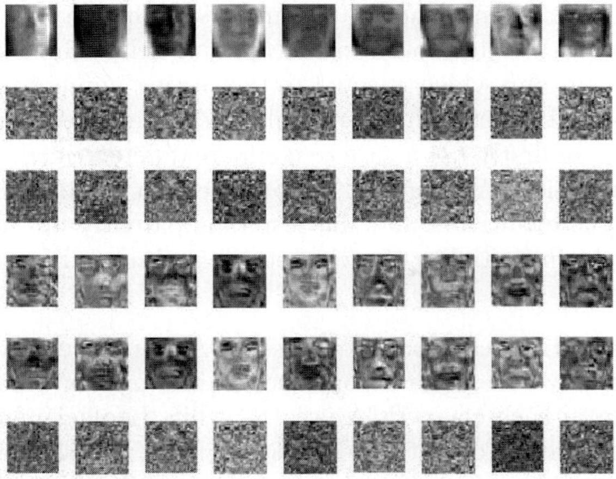

Fig. 5. The first 9 basis images of different methods calculated from PIE database, where each row represents a method from up to low: Eigenfaces,Fisherfaces, Null-space LDA, Laplacianfaces, LDE, Null-space LDE. Visually, the basis image of methods considering similarity are more like face, while those considering discriminability are more like dissimilarity in face. Some remarkable features still exist in the base face images.

Table 6. Performance comparison on PIE database, each method is gotten from the average best recognition rate of 10 times under different training samples by random selection

Racog.Rate(%)	5	10	15
Eigenfaces(PCA)	39.17(90)	56.33(118)	61.14(123)
Fisherfaces(PCA+LDA)	67.89(61)	77.28(62)	83.46(65)
Null-space LDA (LDA)	75.21(64)	78.68(65)	84.20(58)
Laplacianfaces (PCA+LPP)	78.30(75)	79.31(89)	86.92(115)
LDE (PCA+LDE)	78.83(26)	80.26(32)	87.27(60)
Null-space LDE	81.07(28)	82.35(33)	87.43(61)

of two individual, for each subject, the upper row is for training and the down row is for testing.

For those methods need PCA to dimensionality reduction firstly, we decide the number of principal components by remaining the 95% energy. The affine matrix is based on heat kernel. Fig.4 shows the recognition curves of various methods. And the first 10 basis images are shown in Fig.5, where each row represents a method, from up to down there are methods of Eigenfaces, Fisherfaces, Null-space LDA, Laplacianfaces, LDE and Null-space LDE.

Table 6 reports the average best performance of different methods by 10 times experiments. For those methods need PCA to dimensionality reduction firstly, we decide the number of principal components by preserving the 95% energy. Considering the computational cost, we choose the cosine kernel-based affine matrix because it doesn't need adjust parameters. Although the training number of each individual can be improved to 169, we only select three kinds (5, 10 and 15) for experiment, and which is equal to the testing number per class.

(4) Discussion: Three experiments on three datasets have been carried out. On each dataset, we firstly use a case to compare different methods and prepare for parameter selection. Although it is not sure that we have chosen the best parameter for each evaluation and the results apparently are not the best, we still try to keep the impartiality of each method, and some discussions are drawn as follows:

- Eigenfaces and Laplacianfaces both use PCA to reduce dimensionality and preserve the very vectors for reconstruction in a matrix which describes the assimilability in each class. PCA uses S_t, while Laplacianfaces uses S_t and L. The optimization objects of Null-space LDA and Null-space LDE are similar; both of them want to get a set of most discriminative vectors in a null space of a matrix which describes the assimilability in each class. Null-space LDA consider the null space of S_w, while Null-space LDE consider the null space of L , and add the dissimilarity to the $\overline{L}$. So it can get the promising performance among all the methods.
- The performance of methods considering face submanifold is better than those not considering this local structure. However, when the training number of each individual is not very large, null-space methods, even not considering face submanifold, give more effective results and vice versa. So combining the advantage of null-space and local discriminant embedding can yield impressive results.
- In the manifold consideration, although their basis images are visually different in detail (see Fig.5), the difference of the methods based on discriminant embedding and the methods based on preserving embedding is not very large as called. Both of them preserve the local structure which is more important than global structure for classification. But when the idea of null space is introduced, the advantage of discriminant embedding is remarkably improved.
- From the viewpoint of dimensionality reduction, all the methods based on manifold learning can achieve the presetting object more quickly. While some methods such as PCA are not so effective. Moreover, PCA-based method is always regarded without consideration of discriminability, however, in some case, it actually outperforms than LDA-based methods as discussed by Martinez.

4 Conclusion and Future Work

In this paper, a new face recognition method based on most discriminative manifold learning is proposed. Our method is similar as the LDE algorithm while gives it a remarkable extension from different start point. The basic idea of our method can be modeled by a Fisher Manifold Discriminant Embedding (MDE) criterion. The implementation of our method is similar with LPP, LDE, but it is simpler, faster and more powerful in face recognition. From the combined viewpoint of disrciminant analysis and manifold learning, our proposed method can discover the most discriminative nonlinear structure of the face images and is an optimal solution for face recognition. Of course, it can be extended by kernel methods, 2D representation and etc, which is our next main research interests.

References

1. Turk, M., Pentland, A.: Eigenfaces for recognition. Journal of Cognitive Neuroscience, 3(1) (1991) 71–86
2. Belhumeur, P.N., Hespanha, J.P., Kriegman, D.J.: Eigenfaces vs.fisherfaces: recognition using class specific linear projection. IEEE Trans. Pattern Anal. Mach. Intell.,19 (7) (1997) 711–720
3. Martinez, A.M., Kak, A.C.: Pca versus lda. IEEE Trans. Pattern Anal. Mach. Intell., 23(2) (2001) 228–233
4. Schölkopf, B., Smola, A.J., Müller, K.R.: Nonlinear component analysis as a kernel eigenvalue problem. Neural Computation, 10(5) (1998) 1299–1319
5. S. Mika, G. Ratsch, J.e.a.: Fisher discriminant analysis with kernels. In: Proc. IEEE Neural Networks for Signal Processing, USA (1999) 41–48
6. Tenenbaum, J.B., de Silva, V., Langford, J.C.: A global geometric framework for nonlinear dimensional reduction. Science, 290(5500) (2000) 2319–2323
7. Roweis, S., L.K.Saul: Nonlinear dimensional reduction by locally linear embedding. Science, 290 (5500) (2000) 2323–2326
8. Belkin, M., Niyogi, P.: Laplacian eigenmaps and spectral techniques for embedding and clustering. In Dietterich, T.G., Becker, S., Ghahramani, Z., eds.: Advances in Neural Information Processing Systems(NIPS), MIT Press (2001) 585–591
9. Yang, M.H.: Face recognition using extended isomap. In: ICIP, (2) (2002) 117–120
10. He, X., Niyogi, P.: Locality preserving projections. In Thrun, S., Saul, L.K., Schölkopf, B., eds.: Advances in Neural Information Processing Systems(NIPS), MIT Press (2003)
11. He, X., Yan, S., Hu, Y., Niyogi, P., Zhang, H.J.: Face recognition using Laplacianfaces. IEEE Trans. Pattern Anal. Mach. Intell., 27(3) (2005) 328–340
12. Chen, H.T., Chang, H.W., Liu, T.L.: Local discriminant embedding and its variants. In: CVPR (2), IEEE Computer Society (2005) 846–853
13. Yang, J., Yu, H., Kunz, W.: An efficient lda algorithm for face recognition. In: 6th International Conference on Control, Automation, Robotics and Vision (ICARCV2000), Singapore (2000)
14. Chen, L.F., Liao, H.Y.M., Ko, M.T., Lin, J.C., Yu, G.J.: A new LDA-based face recognition system which can solve the small sample size problem. Pattern Recognition, 33(10) (2000) 1713–1726
15. Huang, R., Liu, Q., Lu, H., Ma, S.: Solving the small sample size problem of LDA. In: ICPR, (3) (2002) 29–32
16. X.Wang, J.Li, Y.Niu: Face recognition using linear- and kernel-based FDA in modified null space. Submitted to Neurocomputing (2005)
17. AT&T Lab: AT&T face database (2002) http://www.uk.research.att.com/facedatabase/.
18. Yale Univ.: Face database (2002) http://cvc.yale.edu/projects/yalefaces/.
19. Sim, T., Baker, S., Bsat, M.: The CMU database. IEEE Trans. Pattern Anal. Mach. Intell., 25 (2003) 1615–1618

Reformulated Parametric Learning Based on Ordinary Differential Equations

Shuang-Hong Yang[1,2] and Bao-Gang Hu[1,2]

[1] National Laboratory of Pattern Recognition, Institute of Automation
[2] Beijing Graduate School, Chinese Academy of Sciences
P.O. Box 2728, Beijing, 100080, China
{shyang, hubg}@nlpr.ia.ac.cn

Abstract. This paper presents a new parametric learning scheme, namely, *Reformulated Parametric Learning* (*RPL*). Instead of learning the parameters directly on the original model, this scheme reformulates the model into a simpler yet equivalent one, and all parameters are estimated on the reformulated model. While a set of simpler equivalent models can be obtained from deriving *Equivalent Decomposition Models* (*EDM*) through their associated ordinary differential equations, to achieve the simplest EDM is a combination optimization problem. For a preliminary study, we apply the RPL to a simple class of models, named '*Additive Pseudo-Exponential Models*' (*APEM*). While conventional approaches have to adopt nonlinear programming to learn APEM, the proposed RPL can obtain equivalent solutions through *Linear Least -Square* (*LLS*) method. Numeric work confirms the better performance of the proposed scheme in comparing with conventional learning scheme.

1 Introduction

Machine learning is a technique of acquiring inherent rules or hidden patterns according to information suggested by past experiences and available evidences. Usually it is impossible to identify the patterns exactly and completely, thus one has to construct good and useful approximations, which are usually done by determining a pre-designed approximator, also called learning machine, to optimize performance criterion based on a collection of observed data ([1], [2], [11], [12]).

A parametric learning machine is in general a function with a set of parameters which needs to be learned, and therefore the learning problem is reduced to a parameter identification task formularized as below (also see Fig.1, [13]):

$$\boldsymbol{\theta} = \arg\max J(f(\boldsymbol{x}), g(\boldsymbol{x};\boldsymbol{\theta})) \tag{1}$$

where $f(\boldsymbol{x})$ is the target system to be approximated, $g(\boldsymbol{x}, \boldsymbol{\theta})$ is a parametric learning machine which is usually designed according to prior knowledge, $\boldsymbol{\theta}$ stands for the parameter vector of $g(\boldsymbol{x}, \boldsymbol{\theta})$, $\boldsymbol{x}$ stands for the input vector, the object function $J(\cdot)$ stands for the performance criterion.

In order to get an approximation of $f(\boldsymbol{x})$, one needs to identify all the parameters of the learning machine, that is, to solve $\boldsymbol{\theta}$ from formula (1) to finally determine $g(\boldsymbol{x}, \boldsymbol{\theta})$.

D.-S. Huang, K. Li, and G.W. Irwin (Eds.): ICIC 2006, LNAI 4114, pp. 256–267, 2006.

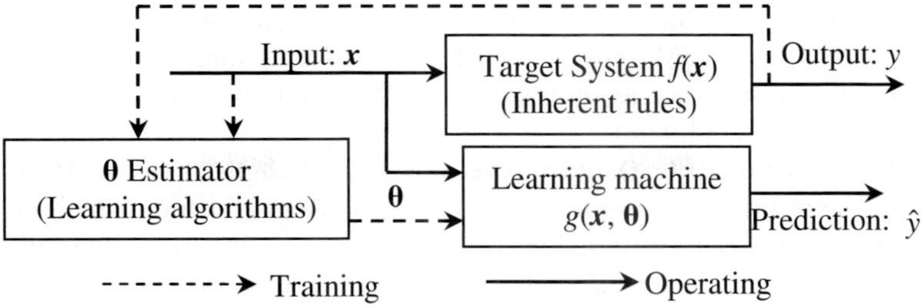

Fig. 1. Schematic diagram of a typical parametrical learning task: the structure of the learning machine is pre-designed, in the training phase, the parameters are estimated to finally determine the learning machine, which is then applied to make prediction of the system outputs in the operating phase

However, this is usually not an easy job because most popular learning machines, such as neural network (RBF NN, sigmoid NN, etc., [2], [6]), Generalized Linear Models ([4]) and so on, are, typically, nonlinear functions of $\boldsymbol{\theta}$. Thus, to obtain a solution, nonlinear programming or other optimization tools are adopted to solve (1). This leads to many drawbacks in reality: firstly, due to the slow learning algorithm which is usually based on gradient, the learning speed is far lower than required especially when it is getting close to convergence, thus the computation cost can be unacceptably high, which make it impossible to apply the algorithm to large scale problems or tasks involve huge amount of data (e.g., data mining); secondly, it is prone to be trapped into a local minimum and produce a non-optimal solution, which may have very poor generalization performance; etc.

In this paper, we first indicate that the conventional direct learning scheme, or learning directly on the original model, is not the only option we can choose in order to learn the parameters, since the learning machine may have many equivalent models. Then we propose a novel learning scheme of learning indirectly and equivalently on a much simpler model which is derived from the original learning machine (this scheme is called Reformulated Parametric Learning, *RPL*). One way to obtain such simpler equivalent model is to decompose the learning machine into several sub-models, the combination of which is equivalent to the original learning machine (such sub-models are called equivalent decomposition models, *EDM*).

For *SISO* (single-input-single-output) tasks, it is very easy to derive EDM by the associated ordinary differential equations (*ODE*) of the learning machine. Usually, a learning machine may have many EDMs, and the learning process will become much easier if we learn the all the parameters by using the simplest EDM. However, in most situations, to obtain the simplest EDM is a combination optimization problem, which is not easy, either. Fortunately, we don't need to derive the simplest EDM frequently since most popularly used learning machines share several structures, we just need to derive the simplest EDM for each structure. We also find that for a quite simple type of learning machines, which we called *APEM* (Additive Pseudo-Exponential Models), the result is quite simple: the simplest EDM of APEM is linear for all the parameters and thus they can be determined analytically. Note that the APEM itself is nonlinear, yet its EDM is totally linear, the result is quite interesting and enlightening. Numerical studies on APEM shows that RPL outperforms direct learning in many aspects, such as much higher learning speed, better generalization performance and ease to reach the global optimum.

Although the idea of RPL has been revealed much strength, it suffers from some weaknesses. The reformulated model is usually a generalized function which involves unordinary operations (e.g., differential operation), thus it may introduce ill-posed problems. In this paper, since the EDMs are derived based on the associated ODE of the learning machine, the reformulated model involves numerical differential of observed data, which is a typical ill-posed problem. Thus a major bottleneck is that the illposedness of numerical differentiation makes the solutions, or learning results, extremely susceptible to data noise. As an alternative, the Tikhonov regularization methods are introduced to relieve this problem.

The rest of this paper is organized as follows. Equivalent learning machines, equivalent decomposition models (EDM) and the overview idea of RPL are introduced in Section 2. In Section 3, as a case study, we apply RPL to APEM and provide some simple numerical experiments on APEM. Section 4 summarizes the main results of this paper.

2 Reformulated Parametric Learning

From the previous section, we can see that the learning task in parametric learning is equivalent to identify all the parameters of the learning machine. From this point of view, one can define learning machines on which one will almost always obtain the same estimations of parameters to be equivalent.

Definition 1: Equivalent Learning Models. Given two learning models $y=g(\boldsymbol{x}, \boldsymbol{\theta})$ and $y=h(\boldsymbol{x}, \boldsymbol{\beta})$, they are defined to be equivalent if there exists mappings $\boldsymbol{u}:\mathbf{R}(\boldsymbol{\theta})\rightarrow\mathbf{R}(\boldsymbol{\beta})$ and $\boldsymbol{v}:\mathbf{R}(\boldsymbol{\theta})\rightarrow\mathbf{R}(\boldsymbol{\beta})$, such that for any given $\boldsymbol{\theta}\in\mathbf{R}(\boldsymbol{\theta})$, $g(\boldsymbol{x}, \boldsymbol{\theta}) \equiv h(\boldsymbol{x}, \boldsymbol{\beta} \mid \boldsymbol{\beta}=\boldsymbol{u}(\boldsymbol{\theta}))$ always holds, and for any given $\boldsymbol{\beta}\in \mathbf{R}(\boldsymbol{\beta})$, $h(\boldsymbol{x}, \boldsymbol{\beta}) \equiv h(\boldsymbol{x}, \boldsymbol{\theta} \mid \boldsymbol{\theta}=\boldsymbol{v}(\boldsymbol{\beta}))$ always holds. Where $\boldsymbol{\theta}=(\theta_1, \theta_2, \ldots, \theta_m)$ and $\boldsymbol{\beta}=(\beta_1, \beta_2, \ldots, \beta_n)$ are the parameter vectors of the two learning models, $\mathbf{R}(\boldsymbol{\theta})$ and $\mathbf{R}(\boldsymbol{\beta})$ stand for the admissible spaces of $\boldsymbol{\theta}$ and $\boldsymbol{\beta}$ respectively, $\equiv$ denotes the identical-equal relationship and $\mid$ means "in the condition of".

It should be noted that the equivalent learning models we defined above are equivalent in that they can approximate the same input-output relationships such that the learning process based on them will produce equivalent estimations of parameters. From this point of view, $y=g(\boldsymbol{x}, \boldsymbol{\theta})$ and $y=h(\boldsymbol{x}, \boldsymbol{\beta})$ are equivalent because if we can learn $\boldsymbol{\theta}$ on a given training set by using $y=g(\boldsymbol{x}, \boldsymbol{\theta})$ as the learning model, we can also learn the almost same $\boldsymbol{\theta}$ from the same training set by using $y=h(\boldsymbol{x}, \boldsymbol{\beta})$ as the learning model and then applying the mapping $\boldsymbol{\theta}=\boldsymbol{v}(\boldsymbol{\beta})$. This means that learning directly on the learning machine is not the unique option one can choose in order to learn the parameters, if the learning machine has equivalent learning models. Compared with direct learning, we call the learning based on its equivalent models as RPL. It is to say, if a learning machine is too hard to be learned but the learning process based on one of its equivalent models is much easier, we prefer to learn indirectly and equivalently on the latter.

Obviously, the relationship between the two models, $y=g(\boldsymbol{x}, \boldsymbol{\theta})$ and $y=h(\boldsymbol{x}, \boldsymbol{\beta})$, is an equivalence relationship if they are equivalent learning models, that is, the relationship is reflexive, transitive and symmetric ([14]). Thus, the learning machine itself is one of its equivalent learning models, that is, the conventional direct learning process, or learning directly on the original model, is just a special case of RPL.

However, for a given learning machine, is there any equivalent learning models on which the learning is much easier and more probable to obtain good solutions? It is a common idea that we usually try to divide a problem into several sub-problems if it is too complicated to solve directly. By dividing a problem and solving the sub-problems separately, we can reduce the solution space and obtain the optimal solution much more easily.

Definition 2: Equivalent Decomposition Model (EDM). A model $y=h(\boldsymbol{x}, \boldsymbol{\beta})$ is defined as an *EDM* of the given learning machine $y=g(\boldsymbol{x}, \boldsymbol{\theta})$, if it is equivalent to $y=g(\boldsymbol{x}, \boldsymbol{\theta})$ and can be reformulated as below.

$$\begin{cases} h_1(\boldsymbol{x}, y, \boldsymbol{\beta}_1) = 0 \\ h_2(\boldsymbol{x}, y, \boldsymbol{\beta}_2) = 0 \end{cases} \tag{2}$$

where $\boldsymbol{\beta}_1=(\beta_1, \beta_2, \ldots, \beta_k)$, $\boldsymbol{\beta}_2=(\beta_{k+1}, \beta_{k+2}, \ldots, \beta_m)$, $k<m$, $\boldsymbol{\beta}=\boldsymbol{\beta}_1\oplus\boldsymbol{\beta}_2$,and $\oplus$ denotes the direct sum operator of two vectors.

It is obvious that if $y=h(\boldsymbol{x}, \boldsymbol{\beta})$ can be rewritten as (2), we can learn $\boldsymbol{\beta}_1$ and $\boldsymbol{\beta}_2$ separately. However, dose there always exist EDM for any given learning machine and how can we get EDM for a given learning machine? According to the differential equation theory we know that the general solution of a given n-th order ordinary differential equation (*ODE*) is a function with n independent free parameters, and that for any analytic function with n independent parameters there always exists an n-th order ODE whose general solution can be formularized as a function with n free parameters ([5]). It enlightens us that we can derive the EDM of a given SISO learning machine by using ODE.

Suppose we have a learning machine $y=g(x, \boldsymbol{\theta})=g(x, \theta_1, \theta_2, \ldots, \theta_k, \ldots, \theta_m)$, and we want to derive a EDM such that we can learn $\boldsymbol{\theta}_1=(\theta_1, \theta_2, \ldots, \theta_k)$ and $\boldsymbol{\theta}_2=(\theta_{k+1}, \theta_{k+2}, \ldots, \theta_m)$ separately. One feasible way is to derive derivative of $y=g(x, \boldsymbol{\theta})$ till the k-th order (see formula (3)). Then eliminated $\boldsymbol{\theta}_1$ from equations (3), we will get an equation which is formularized as formula (4). Combine formula (4) and the original model, we have finally got a EDM of $y=g(x, \boldsymbol{\theta})$ which can be formularized as equations (5), where $\tilde{\theta}_{k+1}, \tilde{\theta}_{k+2}, \ldots, \tilde{\theta}_m$ stand for the optimal solutions of $\theta_{k+1}, \theta_{k+2}, \ldots, \theta_m$, which is learned by using the equation (5-a) as the learning model. That is to say, in order to learn the parameters of $y=g(x, \boldsymbol{\theta})$, we can first learn $\theta_{k+1}, \theta_{k+2}, \ldots, \theta_m$ by using the equation (5-a) as the learning model, and then learn the rest parameters by using the equation (5-b) as the learning model under the condition that $\theta_{k+1}, \theta_{k+2}, \ldots, \theta_m$ take the values of the optimal solution we have obtained.

$$\begin{cases} y = g(x;\theta_1,\theta_2,...,\theta_m) \\ \dfrac{dy}{dx} = g'(x;\theta_1,\theta_2,...,\theta_m) \\ \cdots \quad \cdots \quad \cdots \quad \cdots \\ \dfrac{d^k y}{dx^k} = g^{(k)}(x;\theta_1,\theta_2,...,\theta_m) \end{cases} , \tag{3}$$

$$\varphi(x, y, \frac{dy}{dx}, \frac{d^2y}{dx^2},..., \frac{d^k y}{dx^k}; \theta_{k+1}, \theta_{k+2},...,\theta_m) = 0 , \tag{4}$$

$$\begin{cases} \varphi(x, y, \dfrac{dy}{dx}, \dfrac{d^2y}{dx^2},..., \dfrac{d^k y}{dx^k}; \theta_{k+1}, \theta_{k+2},...,\theta_m) = 0 & \text{(5-a)} \\ y = g(x;\theta_1,\theta_2,...,\theta_k \mid \theta_{k+1} = \tilde{\theta}_{k+1}, \theta_{k+2} = \tilde{\theta}_{k+2},...,\theta_m = \tilde{\theta}_m) & \text{(5-b)} \end{cases} ,$$

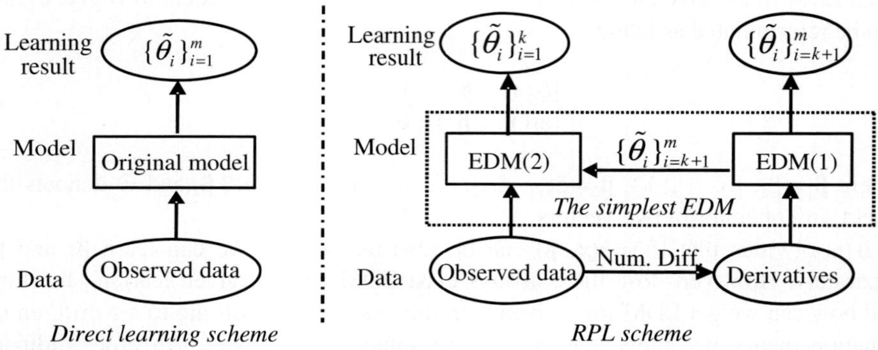

Fig. 2. While in conventional learning scheme, all the parameters are learned by using the original model directly as the learning model, in RPL scheme, the derivative information is first obtained through numerical differentiation, then a subset of parameters, θ_{k+1}, θ_{k+2}, …, θ_m, are learned by using EDM(1), i.e. equation(5-a), as the learning model, and the rest parameters are learned by using EDM(2), or equation(5-b), as learning model under the condition that θ_{k+1}, θ_{k+2}, …, θ_m take the values of the optimal solution we have obtained

The EDM of a model is not unique, actually if derived by ODE, there are at least 2^m EDMs for a given machine with m parameters, which means that it is a combination problem to get the simplest EDM of a given learning machine. But fortunately, we needn't do this frequently, because most learning machines shared a few structures, and once when we get the simplest EDM for a given structure, anytime afterwards when we employ a learning machine with that structure in application we can learn the parameters immediately by using the simplest EDM of that structure without bothering to derive it again. The basic principal of RPL is demonstrated in Fig.2.

By ODE, we have provided not only an existence proof of RPL scheme, but also a feasible way to do so. However, it should be noted that the EDM has become a generalized function since it involves differentiation operations. In fact, the nature of RPL is to extract as much as possible information of the learning machine and observed data to make the learning process easier. And by ODE, we are in fact adding the derivative information to make the learning process easier.

3 Case Study: Applying RPL to APEM

In this section we apply RPL to a class of learning models called APEM. Some computation issues are discussed in the second subsection and numerical studies are provided in the final subsection.

3.1 Learning APEM

We call a simple type of learning models formularized as (6), *Additive Exponential Models* (*AEM*), and any model that can be rewritten as AEM (see (7)) is called *Additive Pseudo-Exponential Models* (*APEM*).

$$y=\sum_{i=1}^{m} P_i(x,\boldsymbol{\beta}_i) f(x,\theta_i)=\sum_{i=1}^{m}\sum_{j=0}^{p_i-1} \beta_{ij} x^j \exp\{\theta_i x\} \quad (6)$$

$$t(y)=\sum_{i=1}^{m} P_i(s(x),\boldsymbol{\beta}_i) f(s(x),\theta_i) \quad (7)$$

where $P_i(x,\boldsymbol{\beta}_i)$ is a polynomial and $f(x,\theta_i)$ is an exponential function, $t(\cdot)$ and $s(\cdot)$ stands for two specific transformation.

Obviously, AEM can be seen as the general solution of the ODE below.

$$y^{(M)}+a_{M-1}y^{(M-1)}+\ldots+a_1 y'+a_0 y=0 \quad (8)$$

where $M=\sum_{i=1}^{m} p_i$,and $\{a_i\}$ are the coefficients of the characteristic polynomial of ODE(8), which can be formularized as (9) :

$$\varphi(\lambda)=\prod_{i=1}^{m}(\lambda-\theta_i)^{p_i}=\lambda^M+a_{M-1}\lambda^{M-1}+\ldots+a_1\lambda+a_0 . \quad (9)$$

In other words, the characteristic equation of ODE (8) is: $\varphi(\lambda)$=0.

Note that the parameters $\{a_i\}$ in equation (8) are all independent of $\{\beta_{ij}\}$, in fact, each a_i is a function of $\{\theta_i\}$, thus, actually we now have got a EDM for AEM, which can be formularized as below.

$$\begin{cases} y^{(M)}+a_{M-1}y^{(M-1)}+\ldots+a_1 y'+a_0 y=0 & (10\text{-a}) \\ y=\sum_{i=1}^{m} P_i(x,\boldsymbol{\beta}_i) f(x,\theta_i \mid \theta_i=\tilde{\theta}_i) & (10\text{-b}) \end{cases}$$

where $\{\tilde{\theta}_i\}$ are the roots of the algebraic equation $\varphi(\lambda)$=0 under the condition that $\{a_j\}$ take values of the optimal solution learned by using equation (10-a) as the learning model.

It is amazing that we have got a totally linear EDM (see (10)) for the nonlinear AEM (see (7)). Based on (10) we can establish an algorithm of learning all the parameters of AEM linearly, which is described as Algorithm (I).

Algorithm (I)

Step1: Learn $\{a_j\}$ by using (10-a) as the learning model;
Step2: Solve the algebraic equation: $\varphi(\lambda)=0$;
Step3: Learn $\{\boldsymbol{\beta}_i\}$ by using (10-b) as the learning model..

In fact, both equations in (10) can be written compactly as linear vector equations: $X\alpha=\boldsymbol{b}$, thus the solutions of Step 1 and Step 3 in Algorithm (I) can be determined analytically (usually realized by linear least-square, *LLS*). Fig. 3 shows the flow chart of Algorithm (I).

The parameters of the more generalized APEM model can also be learned by Algorithm (I), but we need to apply the transformation $t(\cdot)$ and $s(\cdot)$ to the data set at first, then it is quite natural to adopt Algorithm (I) to learn APEM since the relation between $u= t(y)$ and $v= s(x)$ can be described as AEM.

Finally, it's worth mentioning that Algorithm (I) is also possible to be extended for *MISO* (multi-input-single-output) tasks, but in that case, it should be described in tensor representation.

3.2 Several Computation Issues

3.2.1 Over-Determined Linear Equations

Finding the vector $\boldsymbol{\alpha}$ that satisfying equation $\boldsymbol{X\alpha=b}$, given the data matrix $\boldsymbol{X}$ and supervisor vector $\boldsymbol{b}$, is the linear inverse problem associated to $\boldsymbol{X\alpha=b}$ ([3], [8]). In general, it is ill-posed, i.e., the solution either not exists, is not unique or stable. Usually, the existence and uniqueness of the solution can be restored by introducing the Moore-Penrose generalized inverse of $\boldsymbol{X}$, which is denoted as $\boldsymbol{X}^\dagger$ and defined by Penrose equations ([3], [8]). And the solution of $\boldsymbol{X\alpha=b}$ can be formularized as $\boldsymbol{\alpha}= \boldsymbol{X}^\dagger\boldsymbol{b}$. However, this solution is usually not stable, or, it doesn't depend continuously on the training data. So, it is still an ill-posed problem. One possible way to get a stable solution is to replace $\boldsymbol{X\alpha=b}$ with the following convex problem ([3][7][8][9]).

$$\boldsymbol{\alpha} = \arg\min\left(\|\boldsymbol{X\alpha}-\boldsymbol{b}\|^2 + \mu\|\boldsymbol{\alpha}\|^2\right) \tag{11}$$

And for $\mu>0$, we can get a unique stable solution given by

$$\boldsymbol{\alpha}_\lambda = \left(\boldsymbol{X}^T\boldsymbol{X} + \mu\boldsymbol{I}\right)^{-1}\boldsymbol{X}^T\boldsymbol{b} \tag{12}$$

Formula (12) is well known as the Tikhonov regularization method of linear inverse problem, in regression analysis it is similar to the ridge regression methods. However, another problem of how to choose the regularization parameter μ arises.

It should be noted that: 1). in learning tasks, the number of training examples is usually larger than the dimensionality of an example, so $\boldsymbol{X\alpha=b}$ is often over-determined; and 2). the Moore-Penrose generalized solution $\boldsymbol{\alpha}= \boldsymbol{X}^\dagger$b is the unique minimum-norm least-squares solution of $\boldsymbol{X\alpha=b}$, that is, it can minimize the training error, and it has the minimum norm among all the least-square solutions, and it is unique. According to computation learning theory, the norm of the weights is usually associated with the confidence interval, thus, the smallest norm least-square solution may also mean a solution having the best generalization performance ([13]).

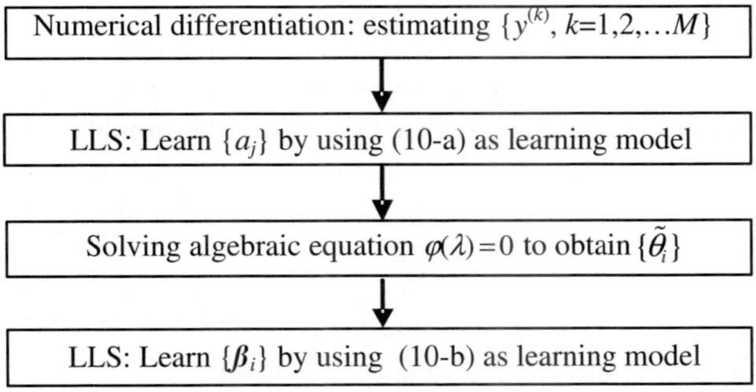

Fig. 3. Flowchart of Algorithm (I)

3.2.2 Differentiation of Noisy Data

To implement the Step1 of Algorithm (I), we need to obtain $\{y^{(k)}\}$ first. In general, the only way of getting the derivative of y is numerical differentiation of observed data since the exact $y=f(\boldsymbol{x})$ is unknown. Again this is an ill-posed problem due to the noise in the observed data ([3], [8], [9]), i.e., instead of the exact $f(\boldsymbol{x})$ we only observed a noisy one, $f_\sigma(\boldsymbol{x})$. In the worst case, the noise is not differentiable so that one cannot even compute a derivative. Or if it is possible to get a derivative, the error can be arbitrarily large even when the noise is arbitrarily small.

One way to solve this problem is again the famous Tikhonov regularization methods, which in this case is equivalent to the following functional minimization problem:

$$\min\left(\int (f - f_\sigma)^2 dx + \mu \int (df\,')^2 dx\right). \tag{13}$$

In a very simple case, the error bound of the derivative is of order $\sqrt{\sigma}$ ([3],[9]), where σ (usually σ<<1) is the norm of the data error. This means the noise in derivative is much larger than that in the data, and, the higher the order of the derivative is, the larger the noise will be. Besides, in this paper, in order to get a reasonable estimation of $\{y^{(k)}\}$, we need to further assume that the observed data is neither too sparse nor too skew.

3.3 Numerical Studies of Learning APEM by RPL

In this subsection, numerical experiments on APEM are demonstrated to evaluate the proposed RPL methods in comparing with the conventional Gradient-Decent (*GD*) based methods. All the simulations are carried out in MATLAB7.0 environment running on a Pentium 4 2.4GHz CPU. Note that all the experiments are just simple demos of RPL since APEM is neither popular nor powerful as a learning machine, further numeric studies will be available when we finish deriving the simplest EDM of other learning machine structures, such as sigmoid, Gaussian RBF and so on, which will be included in our future work. For simplicity, the APEM we used in our experiments is in the following expression, which we called an 'APEM (*m*, *p*) model':

$$t(y)=\sum_{i=1}^{m}\sum_{j=0}^{p-1}\beta_{ij}[s(x)]^{j}\exp\{\theta_i s(x)\} \tag{14}$$

Example 1: Identifying second-order Linear Control Systems
The unit step response of a second-order linear control system, whose transfer function is $G(s)=\omega^2/(s^2+2\zeta\omega s+\omega^2)$ (where $0<\zeta<1$) ,can be formularized as below:

$$y(t)=1-e^{-\varsigma\omega t}\frac{1}{\sqrt{1-\varsigma^2}}\sin(\omega_d t+\alpha), \tag{15}$$

where $\alpha=\tan^{-1}(\sqrt{1-\varsigma^2}/\varsigma), \omega_d=\omega\sin\alpha=\omega\sqrt{1-\varsigma^2}$, and we set the damping ratio $\zeta=0.35$ and the nature frequency $\omega=1$ in our experiments.

To fit the step response, or to identify ω and ζ based on the step response, is a very important problem in control engineering. In this example we apply RPL to such a task and investigate the performance of RPL in compared with GD based learning.

Note that equation (15) can be rewritten as an APEM(2,1):

$$1-y(t)=\beta_1\exp(\theta_1 t)+\beta_2\exp(\theta_2 t) , \tag{16}$$

where $\beta_1=0.5+0.5i\bullet\tan^{-1}(\alpha)$, $\theta_1=-\omega\cos(\alpha)+i\bullet\omega\sin(\alpha)$, $\beta_2=\mathrm{conj}(\beta_1)$, $\theta_2=\mathrm{conj}(\theta_1)$, i denotes the imaginary unit, and conj is the conjugate operator. Thus, Algorithm (I) can be employed to estimated β_1 and θ_1, and ω and ζ are obtained by the following equations:

$$\zeta=|\mathrm{imag}(\beta_1)|/|\beta_1| , \omega=-\mathrm{real}(\theta_1)/\zeta , \tag{17}$$

where imag(*z*) and real(*z*) denote the imaginary part and real part of the complex variable *z* respectively.

The effective of RPL is evaluated in compared with GD-based method on the data set sampled with Δt=0.1. In the first simulation, the data is pure, i.e., no data noise is involved, while a additive sine noise is considered in the second simulation. The results of the simulations are demonstrated in Table 1 and Fig 4, from which we can get the following conclusions:

— The GD-based method is dependent on the initialization of the simulation, occasionally it can be trapped into a local minima and get a very bad solution; in contrast, the solution of RPL is far more stable, in fact, the RPL method is totally deterministic, i.e., it will always obtain the unique optimum solution from its sight.
— The computation cost of RPL is much lower than that of GD-based method, since its solution can be analytically determined.
— The estimation error of RPL solution is much smaller than that of GD-based method when the data is pure.
— The RPL method is extremely susceptible to data noise.

Table 1. Comparison of RPL and GD based learning in identifying a sencond-order linear control system

Setup	Methods	RMSE	Time (sec)	Parameter Estimation Error(relative)
No noise, and μ=0	GD based	0.0066	0.92	Err_ζ=6.4%, Err_ω=7.4%
	RPL (m=2,p=1)	0.000081	0.0016	Err_ζ=0.15%, Err_ω=0.19%
With noise 0.05sin(πt), and μ=0.001	GD based	0.010	1.2	Err_ζ=17%, Err_ω=19%
	RPL (m=2,p=1)	0.017	0.0015	Err_ζ=20%, Err_ω=25%

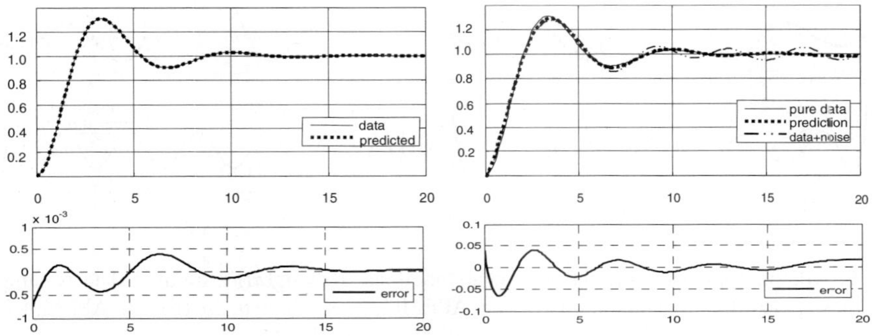

(a) (b)

Fig. 4. RPL in identifying a second-order linear control system: (a) the observed data is pure, i.e., no noise is involved in. (b) The observed data is polluted by an additive sine noise $n(t)$=0.05sin(πt/2). In both simulations, the RPL prediction (dots) is almost coincident with the true function (pure data).

Example 2: Approximation Nonlinear Functions
In this example, we investigate the performance of RPL in approximating nonlinear functions and the function below is taken as an example:

$$x(t)=\sin(\pi t)/t, \text{ where } t\in[-4,4]\,. \tag{18}$$

Note that the above function $x(t)$ cannot be rewritten as an APEM with finite m, since its Fourier expansion has infinite exponential terms. For this example, we employ an APEM(2, 3)(m=2, p=3, see equation(14)), an APEM(4, 1), an APEM(4, 2) and an APEM(4, 3) in four simulations respectively, and demonstrate the results in Fig. 5, from which we can get the following conclusions:

— Though APEM model is not a good enough learning machine, it is still possible to get reasonable solutions through RPL scheme when APEM is adopted to learning tasks.

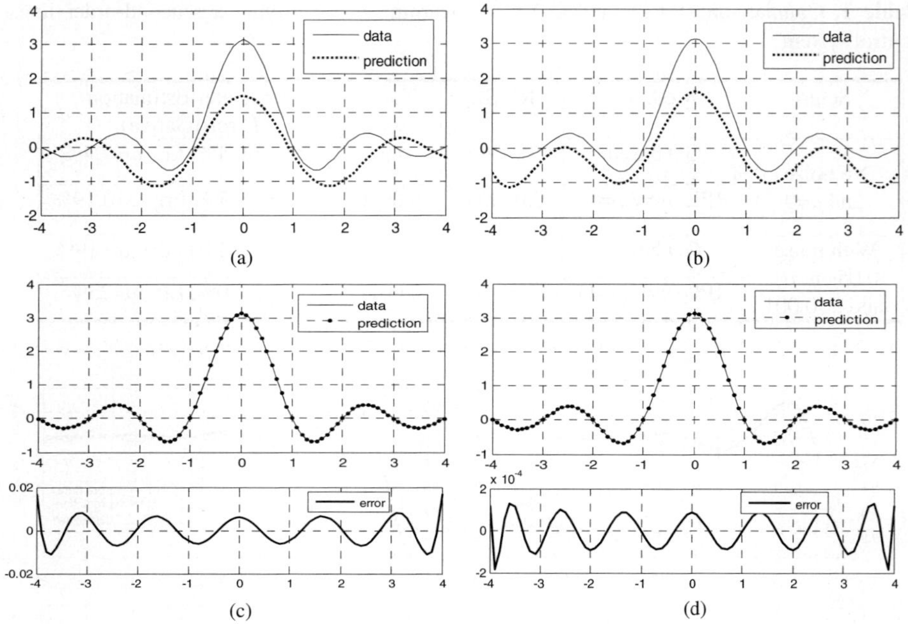

Fig. 5. RPL in approximating the nonlinear functions, $x(t)=\sin(\pi t)/t$, training data is sampled with a step $\Delta t=0.1$. In simulation (a), an APEM(2,3) is adopted, in (b), an APEM(4,1) is adopted, in (c) an APEM(4,2) and in (d),an APEM(4,3) is adopted.

— Like other machine learning method, RPL method can get a good solution only when a proper learning machine is designed. In other words, RPL is just a method to learning parameters, it has nothing to do with model selection, thus, to get a reasonable learning result, one should choose a suitable learning machine first.

4 Conclusion

The main goal of learning is to infer a function from a finite set of examples, which is equivalent to parameter identification when the structure of the learning machine has been designed. In conventional learning, the parameters are usually learned directly on the learning models, and nonlinear programming or other optimization tools are therefore adopted to obtain a solution, which leads to many demerits. Different from the conventional scheme, the proposed RPL scheme learn all the parameters on an equivalent reformulated model, and the former is only a special case of RPL, but is probably not the optimal one because the original learning machine is probably not the simplest model in its equivalence class. The EDMs of APEM is totally linear and thus all the parameters can be analytically determined. EDM of other learning machine may be nonlinear, but there exists a simplest one among all those EDM's, thus learning on the simplest EDM may be always a better choice. Our future work will mainly focus on exploring the robustness of RPL to data noise and deriving simplest EDMs for other learning machines such as sigmoid models Gaussian models and so on.

Acknowledgements

This work is supported partially by National Science Foundation of China (#60275025, #60121302). The authors would also like to thank the other members of NLPR machine learning Group, Yu-Jiu Yang, Hong-Jie Xing, Han-Bing Qu and Yong Wang, for their helpful comments and suggestions.

References

1. Mitchell, T.M.: Machine Learning. The McGraw-Hill Companies, Inc. (1997)
2. Duda, R.O., Hart, P.E., Stork, D.G.: Pattern Classification (2nd Ed). John Wiley & Sons Inc. (2001)
3. Kirsch, A.: An Introduction to the Mathematical Theory of Inverse Problems. Springer-Verlag, Berlin Heidelberg New York. (1996)
4. McCullagh, P., Nelder, J.: Generalized Linear Models. (2nd Ed). Chapman & Hall. (1989)
5. Edwards, C.H., Penney, D.E.: Differential Equations and Boundary Value Problems, Computing and Modeling. (3rd Ed), Prentice Hall. (2004)
6. Haykin, S: Neural Networks, a Comprehensive Foundation.(2nd Ed), Printice Hall, New York. (1999)
7. Vito, E., Rosasco, L., Caponnetto, A., Giovannini, U., Odone, F.: Learning from Examples as an Inverse Problem. Journal of Machine Learning Research. 6. (2005) 883-904
8. Tarantola, A.: Inverse Problem Theory: Methods for Data Fitting and Model Parameter Estimation. Elsevier, New York. (1987)
9. Anger, G.: Inverse Problems in Differential Equations. Plenum Press, New York. (1990)
10. Bertero, M., Mol, C., Pike, E.R.: Linear Inverse Problems with Discrete Data. I. General Formulation and Singular System Analysis. Inverse Problems. 1 (1985) 301-330
11. Alpaydin, E.: Introduction to Machine Learning. MIT Press. (2004)
12. Jain, A. K., Duin, R., Mao, J.: Statistical Pattern Recognition: A Review. IEEE Transactions on Pattern Analysis and Machine Intelligence, 22 (2000) 4-38
13. Vapnik, V.N.: The Nature of Statistical Learning Theory. Springer-Verlag, Berlin Heidelberg New York. (1999)
14. Mendelson, E.: Introduction to Mathematical Logic (4th Ed). Chapman & Hall/ CRC, (1997)

Supervised Feature Extraction Algorithm Based on Continuous Divergence Criterion

Shifei Ding[1,2], Zhongzhi Shi[2], and Fengxiang Jin[3]

[1] College of Information Science and Engineering,
Shandong Agricultural University, Taian 271018 P.R. China
[2] Key Laboratory of Intelligent Information Processing, Institute of Computing Technology,
Chinese Academy of Sciences, Beijing 100080 P.R. China
[3] College of Geo-Information Science and Engineering,
Shandong University of Science and Technology, Qingdao 266510 P.R. China
sfding@sdau.edu.cn, shizz@ics.ict.ac.cn, fxjin@sdust.edu.cn

Abstract. Feature extraction plays an important part in pattern recognition (PR), data mining, machine learning et al. In this paper, a novel supervised feature extraction algorithm based on continuous divergence criterion (CDC) is set up. Firstly, the concept of the CDC is given, and some properties of the CDC are studied, and proved that CDC here is a kind of distance measure, i.e. it satisfies three requests of distance axiomatization, which can be used to measure the difference degree of a two-class problem. Secondly, based on CDC, the basic principle of supervised feature extraction are studied, a new concept of accumulated information rate (AIR) is given, which can be used to measure the degree of feature compression for two-class, and a new supervised feature extraction algorithm is constructed. At last, the experimental results demonstrate that the algorithm here is valid and reliable.

1 Introduction

Pattern recognition (PR) is the scientific discipline whose goal is the classification of objects into a number of categories or classes. We know that the procedure of a PR system includes four stsges, that is information acquisition, feature extraction and selection, classifier design and system evaluation [1, 2]. In all 4 stages, the feature extraction or selection plays an important part in the PR system. A major problem associated with the PR is the so called curse of dimensionality. The number of features at the disposal of the designer of a PR system is usually very large. There is more than one reason for the necessity to reduce the number of features to a sufficient minimum. Computational complexity is the obvious one. A related reason is that although two features may carry good classification information when treated separately, there is little gain if they are combined together in a feature vector, because of a high mutual correlation. Thus, complexity increases without much gain. Another major reason is that imposed by the required generalization properties of the classifier. Generally speaking, the higher the ratio of the number of training patterns N to the number of free classifier parameters, the better the generalization properties of the resulting classifier. A large number of features is directly translated into a large

D.-S. Huang, K. Li, and G.W. Irwin (Eds.): ICIC 2006, LNAI 4114, pp. 268 – 277, 2006.

number of classifier parameters, e.g., synaptic weights in a neural network, weights in a linear classifier. Thus, for a finite and usually limited number N of training patterns, keeping the number features as small as possible is in line with our desire to design classifiers with good generalization capabilities. One might expect that the inclusion of increasing numbers of features would increase the likelihood of including enough information to separate the class volumes. Unfortunately, this is not true if the size of the training data set does not also increase rapidly with each additional feature included[3,4]. In order to choose a subset of the original features by reducing irrelevant and redundant, many feature selection algorithms have been studied. The literature contains several studies on feature selection for unsupervised learning in which the objective is to search for a subset of features that best uncovers "natural" groupings (clusters) from data according to some criterion. For example, principal components analysis (PCA) is an unsupervised feature extraction method that has been successfully applied in the area of face recognition, feature extraction and feature analysis. But PCA method is effective to deal with the small size and high-dimensional problems, and gets the extensive application in Eigenface and feature extraction. In high-dimensional cases, it is very difficult to compute the principal components directly. Fortunately, the algorithm of Eigenfaces artfully avoids this difficulty by virtue of the singular decomposition technique. Thus, the problem of calculating the eigenvectors of the total covariance matrix, a high-dimensional matrix, is transformed into a problem of calculating the eigenvectors of a much lower dimensional matrix[5-7]. Partial least squares (PLS) regession is introduced for information feature compression, which is proven to be more advantages than principal component analysis (PCA), in its simplicity, robustness,and clearly qualitative explanation. It is powerful for multicollinearity, particularly when the number of predictor variables is large and the sample size is small. Meanwhile the information of data matrix X is compressed while considering maximum correlation with objctive matrix Y[8,9]. Some authors make use of the concept of Shannon information theory[10], and propose two new concepts of possibility information function (PIF) and possibility information entropy (PIE), and improve the algorithm of PCA called IPCA. Comparing PCA with IPCA, we find that IPCA is efficient, and the principal components by IPCA contain more information than that by PCA.

In this paper, the authors are going on studying supervised feature extraction problem based on continuous divergence criterion (CDC). In second 2, we study and discuss the continuous divergence criterion (CDC), including some new concepts and some properties. In section 3, we give some principles of supervised feature extraction based on CDC, and a new supervised feature extraction algorithm is designed.

2 Continuous Divergence Criterion

Given two classes ω_1, ω_2, and a feature vector x, we select ω_1 if

$$P(\omega_1 \mid x) > P(\omega_2 \mid x) \tag{1}$$

The classification error probability depends on the difference between $P(\omega_1 \mid x)$ and $P(\omega_2 \mid x)$. Hence, the ratio $P(\omega_1 \mid x)/P(\omega_2 \mid x)$ can convey useful information concerning the discriminatory capabilities associated with an adopted feature vector x, with respect to the two classes ω_1, ω_2. In the sequel, we assume that the priori probabilities, $P(\omega_1), P(\omega_2)$, are known. This is a very reasonable assumption, because even if they are not known, they can easily be estimated from the available training feature vectors. Indeed, if N is the total number of available training patterns, and N_1, N_2 of them belong to ω_1 and ω_2, respectively, then $P(\omega_1) \approx N_1/N$, $P(\omega_2) \approx N_2/N$. The other statistical quantities assumed to be known are the class-conditional probability density functions $p(x \mid \omega_1), p(x \mid \omega_2)$, describing the distribution of the feature vectors in each of the classes. Then the log-likelihood function is defined as

$$D_{12}(x) = \log \frac{p(x \mid \omega_1)}{p(x \mid \omega_2)} \tag{2}$$

This can be used as a measure of the separability information of class ω_1 with respect to ω_2. Clearly, for completely overlapped classes we get $D_{12}(x) = 0$. Since x takes different values, it is natural to consider the average value over class ω_1, the average separability information (ASI) is defined as follows.

Definition 1. Let X be a continuous random variable with two probability density functions $p(x \mid \omega_1), p(x \mid \omega_2)$, the ASI is defined by

$$D_{12} = E[D_{12}(x)] = \int_x p(x \mid \omega_1) D_{12}(x) dx = \int_x p(x \mid \omega_1) \log \frac{p(x \mid \omega_1)}{p(x \mid \omega_2)} dx \tag{3}$$

where E denotes mathematical expectation.

It is not difficult to see that D_{12}, i.e. ASI is always non-negative and is zero if and only if $p(x \mid \omega_1) = p(x \mid \omega_2)$. However, it is not a true distance distribution, since it is not symmetric and does not satisfy the triangle inequality. Nonetheless, it is often useful to think of ASI as a separability measure for class ω_1. Similar arguments hold for class ω_2 and we define

$$D_{21} = E[D_{21}(x)] = \int_x p(x \mid \omega_2) D_{21}(x) dx = \int_x p(x \mid \omega_2) \log \frac{p(x \mid \omega_2)}{p(x \mid \omega_1)} dx \tag{4}$$

In order to make ASI true distance measure between distributions for the classes ω_1 and ω_2, with respect to the adopted feature vector x, the definition of ASI is improved as follows.

Definition 2. Suppose that D_{12}, D_{21} are defined by the formulae (3) and (4), then the sum

$$S(1,2) = D_{12} + D_{21} = \int_x [p(x \mid \omega_1) - p(x \mid \omega_2)] \log \frac{p(x \mid \omega_1)}{p(x \mid \omega_2)} dx \tag{5}$$

is known as continuous divergence criterion (CDC).

The value of CDC can be used as a separability measure for the classes ω_1, ω_2 with probability density functions $p(x \mid \omega_1), p(x \mid \omega_2)$, with respect to the adopted feature vector x. About the CDC, we give the following Theorem.

Theorem 1. The CDC, i.e. $S(1,2)$ satisfies the following basic properties:

(Ⅰ) Non-negativity: $S(1,2) \geq 0$, $S(1,2) = 0$ if and only if $p(x \mid \omega_1) = p(x \mid \omega_2)$;

(Ⅱ) Symmetry: $S(1,2) = S(2,1)$;

(Ⅲ) Triangle inequation: Suppose that class ω_3 is another class with the class-conditional probability density function $p(x \mid \omega_3)$, with respect to the adopted feature vector x, describing the distribution of the feature vectors in class ω_3, then

$$S(1,2) \leq S(1,3) + S(3,2) \tag{6}$$

Proof. according to the definition of ASI, the properties (Ⅰ) and (Ⅱ) are right obviously. Now we prove the property (Ⅲ) as follows.

Based on the formulae (2), (3) and (4), we have

$$S(1,3) + S(3,2) - S(1,2) = \int_x [p(x \mid \omega_1) - p(x \mid \omega_3)] \log \frac{p(x \mid \omega_1)}{p(x \mid \omega_3)} dx$$

$$+ \int_x [p(x \mid \omega_3) - p(x \mid \omega_2)] \log \frac{p(x \mid \omega_3)}{p(x \mid \omega_2)} dx - \int_x [p(x \mid \omega_1) - p(x \mid \omega_2)] \log \frac{p(x \mid \omega_1)}{p(x \mid \omega_2)} dx$$

$$= \int_x p(x \mid \omega_1) \log \frac{p(x \mid \omega_2)}{p(x \mid \omega_3)} dx + \int_x p(x \mid \omega_3) \log \frac{p(x \mid \omega_3)}{p(x \mid \omega_2)} dx$$

$$+ \int_x p(x \mid \omega_2) \log \frac{p(x \mid \omega_2)}{p(x \mid \omega_3)} dx + \int_x p(x \mid \omega_3) \log \frac{p(x \mid \omega_3)}{p(x \mid \omega_1)} dx$$

$$\geq \int_x p(x \mid \omega_1) \log \frac{p(x \mid \omega_2)}{p(x \mid \omega_3)} dx \geq 0 .$$

which is the triangle inequation.

Therefore, the CDC is a true distance measure, which can be used to measure the degree of variation between two random variables. We think of CDC as separability criterion of the classes for information feature extraction. We can see that the smaller the value of CDC, the smaller the difference of two groups of data. In particular, when the value of CDC is zero, the two groups of data are same completely, namely there is no difference at this time. For information feature extraction, under the condition of the given reduction dimensionality denoted by d, we should select d characteristics, and make the value of CDC incline toward biggest.

For a multi-class problem, the value of CDC is computed for every class pair ω_i, ω_j as follows

$$S(i,j) = D_{ij} + D_{ji} = \int_x [p(x \mid \omega_i) - p(x \mid \omega_j)] \log \frac{p(x \mid \omega_i)}{p(x \mid \omega_j)} dx \tag{7}$$

and the average CDC can be computed by

$$d = \sum_i \sum_j P(\omega_i)P(\omega_j)S(i,j) \tag{8}$$

It can be used to be separability criterion of the multi-class problem for information feature extraction.

Assume now that the density functions are Gaussians $N(\mu_i, \Sigma_i)$ and $N(\mu_j, \Sigma_j)$, respectively, the computation of the ASI is simplified as follows.

As

$$D_{ij} = \int_{-\infty}^{+\infty} p(x \mid \omega_i) \log \frac{p(x \mid \omega_i)}{p(x \mid \omega_j)} dx$$

$$= \int_{-\infty}^{+\infty} \left\{ \frac{1}{2} \log \left| \frac{\Sigma_j}{\Sigma_i} \right| - \frac{1}{2} tr\left[\Sigma_i^{-1}(x-\mu_i)(x-\mu_i)'\right] + \frac{1}{2} tr\left[\Sigma_j^{-1}(x-\mu_j)(x-\mu_j)'\right] \right\} p(x \mid \omega_i) dx$$

$$= \frac{1}{2} \log \left| \frac{\Sigma_j}{\Sigma_i} \right| - \frac{1}{2} tr\left[\Sigma_i^{-1}\right] \int_{-\infty}^{+\infty} \left[(x-\mu_i)(x-\mu_i)'\right] p(x \mid \omega_i) dx$$

$$+ \frac{1}{2} tr\left[\Sigma_j^{-1}\right] \int_{-\infty}^{+\infty} \left[(x-\mu_j)(x-\mu_j)'\right] p(x \mid \omega_i) dx$$

$$= \frac{1}{2} \log \left| \frac{\Sigma_j}{\Sigma_i} \right| - \frac{1}{2} tr\left[\Sigma_i^{-1} \Sigma_i\right] + \frac{1}{2} tr\left[\Sigma_j^{-1}\right] \int_{-\infty}^{+\infty} \left[(x-\mu_i)(x-\mu_i)'\right] p(x \mid \omega_i) dx$$

$$= \frac{1}{2} \log \left| \frac{\Sigma_j}{\Sigma_i} \right| - \frac{1}{2} tr\left[\Sigma_i(\Sigma_j^{-1} - \Sigma_i^{-1})\right] + \frac{1}{2} tr\left[\Sigma_j^{-1}(\mu_i-\mu_j)(\mu_i-\mu_j)'\right] \tag{9}$$

So, the value of CDC for two-class is

$$S(i,j) = D_{ij} + D_{ji} = \int_{-\infty}^{+\infty} [p(x \mid \omega_i) - p(x \mid \omega_j)] \log \frac{p(x \mid \omega_i)}{p(x \mid \omega_j)} dx$$

$$= \frac{1}{2} tr\left[(\Sigma_i - \Sigma_j)(\Sigma_j^{-1} - \Sigma_i^{-1})\right] + \frac{1}{2} tr\left[(\Sigma_i^{-1} + \Sigma_j^{-1})(\mu_i-\mu_j)(\mu_i-\mu_j)'\right]$$

$$= \frac{1}{2} tr\left[(\Sigma_i^{-1} \Sigma_j + \Sigma_j^{-1} \Sigma_i - 2I)\right] + \frac{1}{2} (\mu_i-\mu_j)'(\Sigma_i^{-1} + \Sigma_j^{-1})(\mu_i-\mu_j) \tag{10}$$

According to formula (9), if the covariance matrices of the two Gaussian distributions are equal, i.e. $\Sigma_i = \Sigma_j = \Sigma$, then the value of CDC is simplified to

$$D_{ij} = \frac{1}{2} tr\left[\Sigma^{-1}(\mu_i-\mu_j)(\mu_i-\mu_j)'\right] = \frac{1}{2} (\mu_i-\mu_j)'\Sigma^{-1}(\mu_i-\mu_j) \tag{11}$$

Put the formula (11) into the formula (10), we get

$$S(i,j) = (\mu_i-\mu_j)'\Sigma^{-1}(\mu_i-\mu_j) \tag{12}$$

For one-dimension case, the value of CDC is further simplified to

$$S(i,j)=\frac{(\mu_i-\mu_j)^2}{\sigma^2}. \tag{13}$$

3 Supervised Feature Extraction Algorithm Based on CDC

3.1 Principle

Suppose the relation of n -dimensionality original feature vector x and d -dimensionality transform vector, 2nd feature vector, y is

$$y=W'x \tag{14}$$

where W being $n\times d$ transform matrix, and $d\le n$, so W being $n\times d$ compression matrix. Assume now that the density functions are Gaussians $N(\mu_i,\Sigma_i)$ and $N(\mu_j,\Sigma_j)$, respectively, then after transform (14), the CDC can express as follows.

$$J_D(W)=\frac{1}{2}Tr\{W'MW[(W'\Sigma_1 W)^{-1}+(W'\Sigma_2 W)^{-1}]\}$$

$$+\frac{1}{2}Tr[(W'\Sigma_1 W)^{-1}W'\Sigma_2 W+(W'\Sigma_2 W)'W'\Sigma_1 W-2E] \tag{15}$$

where $M=(\mu_1-\mu_2)(\mu_1-\mu_2)'$.

(1) When $\Sigma_1=\Sigma_2=\Sigma$, $\mu_1\ne\mu_2$, the formula (15) can be changed as

$$J_D(W)=Tr[(W'\Sigma W)^{-1}W'MW] \tag{16}$$

let $\partial J_D(W)/\partial W=0$, we can get

$$MW-\Sigma W(W'\Sigma W)^{-1}W'MW=0 \tag{17}$$

Suppose eigenvalue matrix and eigenvector matrix of the matrix $(W'\Sigma W)^{-1}W'MW$ are Λ and U respectively, that is $(W'\Sigma W)^{-1}W'MWU=U\Lambda$, so the formula (17) is

$$\Sigma^{-1}MWU=WU\Lambda \tag{18}$$

let $V=WU$, i.e. $W=VU^{-1}$, then we can get a conclusion that V is an eigenvector matrix of $\Sigma^{-1}M$, and Λ is a digonal eigenvalue matrix of $\Sigma^{-1}M$. According to the formula (18), $J_D(W)$ is simplified as

$$J_D(W)=Tr(\Sigma^{-1}M)=Tr(\Lambda) \tag{19}$$

so the optimal feature extraction matrix, W, is composed of eigenvectors of $\Sigma^{-1}M$. As the rank of M is one, i.e. $R(M)=1$, so the matrix $\Sigma^{-1}M$ has only one nonzero eigenvalue λ, therefore optimum transform W is an eigenvector ξ of $\Sigma^{-1}M$ corresponding to the nonzero eigenvalue λ, i.e.

$$\Sigma^{-1}(\mu_1-\mu_2)(\mu_1-\mu_2)'\xi=\lambda\xi \tag{20}$$

let $\lambda=(\mu_1-\mu_2)'\xi$, then

$$W=\xi=\Sigma^{-1}(\mu_1-\mu_2) \tag{21}$$

(2) When $\Sigma_1\neq\Sigma_2$, $\mu_1=\mu_2$, the formula (15) can be simplified as

$$J_D(W)=\frac{1}{2}Tr[(W'\Sigma_1 W)^{-1}(W'\Sigma_2 W)+(W'\Sigma_2 W)^{-1}(W'\Sigma_1 W)-2E] \tag{22}$$

let $\partial J_D(W)/\partial W=0$, we can get

$$\begin{aligned}&[\Sigma_1 W-\Sigma_2 W(W'\Sigma_2 W)^{-1}(W'\Sigma_1 W)][(W'\Sigma_2 W)^{-1}(W'\Sigma_1 W)\\&-(W'\Sigma_1 W)^{-1}(W'\Sigma_2 W)]\cdot(W'\Sigma_1 W)^{-1}=0\end{aligned} \tag{23}$$

so

$$\Sigma_2^{-1}\Sigma_1 W-W(W'\Sigma_2 W)^{-1}(W'\Sigma_1 W)=0 \tag{24}$$

suppose the digonal eigenvalue matrix of $(W'\Sigma_2 W)^{-1}(W'\Sigma_1 W)$ is Λ, and eigenvector matrix is U, i.e.

$$(W'\Sigma_2 W)^{-1}(W'\Sigma_1 W)U=U\Lambda \tag{25}$$

put the formula (25) into the formula (24), we can get

$$\Sigma_2^{-1}\Sigma_1 WU=WU\Lambda \tag{26}$$

This shows that $V=WU$ is an eigenvector matrix of $\Sigma_2^{-1}\Sigma_1$, and Λ is a digonal eigenvalue matrix of $\Sigma_2^{-1}\Sigma_1$. So the formula (22) is simplified as

$$\begin{aligned}J_D(W)&=\frac{1}{2}Tr[(U\Lambda U^{-1})^{-1}+U\Lambda U^{-1}-2E]\\&=\frac{1}{2}Tr[\Lambda+\Lambda^{-1}-2E]=\frac{1}{2}\sum_{i=1}^{d}(\lambda_i+\lambda_i^{-1}-2)\end{aligned} \tag{27}$$

where λ_i is eigenvalues of matrix $\Sigma_2^{-1}\Sigma_1$.

So for given $d\leq n$, in order to make $J_D(W)\rightarrow\max$, the transform matrix W is composed of d eigenvectors of matrix $\Sigma_2^{-1}\Sigma_1$, which is corresponded to d eigenvalues, satisfied following inequality.

$$\lambda_1 + \lambda_1^{-1} \geq \lambda_2 + \lambda_2^{-1} \geq \cdots \geq \lambda_d + \lambda_d^{-1} \geq \cdots \geq \lambda_n + \lambda_n^{-1} \tag{28}$$

the total sum of eigenvalues above is denoted by $V_n = \sum_{k=1}^{n} (\lambda_k + \lambda_k^{-1})$, and so $V_d = \sum_{k=1}^{d} (\lambda_k + \lambda_k^{-1})$, and then the accumulated information rale (AIR) is defined as

$$\text{AIR}=\frac{V_d}{V_n} \tag{29}$$

the value of AIR can be used to measure the degree of information compression. Generally speaking, so long as AIR$\geq 80\%$ or bigger, we can reach the purpose of feature extraction.

If $V_i \geq 80\%$, we may select d eigenvectors $u_1, u_2, \cdots, u_d$ corresponding to the first d eigenvalues satisfied with the formula (28), and then we may construct the information extraction matrix $W = (u_1, u_2, \cdots, u_d)$.

3.2 Algorithm

According to the basic principle above, a new supervised feature extraction algorithm based on CDC is derived as follows.

Step 1: Compute covariance matrixes Σ_1, Σ_2 for two-class known samples. suppose there are two-class samples denoted by $X^{(1)}, X^{(2)}$.

Step 2: Compute eigenvalues of matrix $\Sigma_2^{-1}\Sigma_1$ and corresponding eigenvectors according to Jacobi method.

Step 3: Construct feature extraction matrix W based on the formule (28) and (29).

Step 4: Make transformation $Y^{(i)} = T'X^{(i)}$ $(i = 1,2)$, and the purpose to compress the data information is attained.

4 Example Analysis

Suppose that there are data vector $x = (x_1, x_2, \cdots, x_6)'$ composed of 6 features, and the original measured data is listed in table 1 and table 2.

Applied DPS data processing system, we can get all eigenvalues and corresponding to eigenvectors of matrix $\Sigma_1^{-1}\Sigma_2$, according to algorithm set up above, the optimum feature extraction matrix $W_{6\times 2}$ is attained, and so the results of $X^{(1)}, X^{(2)}$ are

$$Y^{(1)} = \begin{pmatrix} 2.029 & 0.588 & 1.374 & 1.518 & 1.657 & 0.875 & 1.988 & 1.324 & 1.594 & 0.233 \\ 1.329 & 1.335 & 1.408 & 1.380 & 1.443 & 1.419 & 1.431 & 1.408 & 1.408 & 1.421 \end{pmatrix}$$

$$Y^{(2)} = \begin{pmatrix} 1.2139 & 1.2575 & 1.2765 & 1.2693 & 1.2249 & 1.1833 & 1.3111 \\ 1.2902 & 1.2442 & 1.5465 & 1.5051 & 1.4562 & 1.5146 & 1.4006 \end{pmatrix}$$

while AIR=93.8504%, that is to say, when $d = 2$, the information content contained by Y can reach 93.8504% of the total information content of X after being compression.

Table 1. The 1st class data $X^{(1)}$

No.	features					
	x_1	x_2	x_3	x_4	x_5	x_6
1	1.170	0.060	5.000	163	6.50	8.10
2	0.680	0.078	7.000	93	8.10	8.10
3	1.010	0.071	11.000	83	7.70	8.10
4	1.090	0.073	17.000	115	6.90	8.10
5	0.964	0.057	7.750	112	4.43	8.40
6	0.415	0.038	4.400	101	4.30	8.50
7	1.346	0.079	9.000	133	9.10	8.45
8	1.108	0.081	8.200	99	14.80	8.40
9	0.995	0.059	4.800	77	6.70	8.00
10	0.842	0.120	11.500	66.5	3.42	8.35

Table 2. The 2nd class data $X^{(2)}$

No.	features					
	x_1	x_2	x_3	x_4	x_5	x_6
1	0.740	0.056	6	165	6.50	8.20
2	0.660	0.037	5	138	10.70	7.80
3	0.770	0.055	3	95	8.80	9.10
4	0.820	0.057	18	72	4.80	8.50
5	0.496	0.030	4.8	107	2.77	8.60
6	0.650	0.045	6	52	4.30	8.50
10	0.842	0.120	11.5	66.5	3.42	8.35

5 Conclusions

From information theory, we study and discuss the supervised feature extraction problem in this paper, and come to a conclusion that the concept of CDC has given and proved that it is a kind of distance measure, based on CDC, we have studied the principle of supervised feature extraction, and constructed a new feature extraction algorithm.

Acknowledgements

This study is supported by the National Natural Science Foundation of China under grant no.60435010 and no.40574001, the China Postdoctor Science Foundation under grant no.2005037439, the Key Laboratory Opening Foundation of the Crop-Biology of Shandong Province under grant no.20040010, and the Doctoral Science Foundation of Shandong Agricultural University under grant no. 23241.

References

1. Duda, R.O., Hart, P.E. (eds.): Pattern Classification and Scene Analysis. Wiley, New York (1973)
2. Theodoridis, S., Koutroumbas, K. (eds.): Pattern Recognition, Second Edition. Academic Press, New York (2003)
3. Fukunaga, K. (ed.): Introduction to Statistical Pattern Recognition. Academic Press, 2nd ed., New York (1990)
4. Hand, D.J. (ed.): Discrimination and Classification. Wiley, New York (1981)
5. Turk, M., Pentland, A.: Eigenfaces for recognition. Journal Cognitive Neuroscience. 3 (1) (1991) 71-86
6. Turk, M., Pentland, A.: Face recognition using Eigenfaces. In: Proceedings IEEE Conference on Computer Vision and Pattern Recognition. (1991) 586-591
7. Yang, J., Yang, J.Y.: A Generalized K-L Expansion Method That Can Deal with Small Sample Size and High-dimensional Problems. Pattern Analysis Applications. 6(6) (2003) 47-54
8. Wang H.W. (ed.): Partial Least Squares Regression and Applications. National Defence Industry Press, Beijing (2000)
9. Ding, S.F., Jin, F.X., Shi, Z.Z.: Information Feature Compression Algorithm Based on Partial Least Squares. Journal of Computer-aided Design & Computer Graphics 17 (2) (2005) 368-371
10. Shannon, C.E.: A Mathematical Theory of Communication. Bell Syst. Tech. J. 27 (1948) 379-423
11. Cover, T.M., Thomas, J.A. (eds.): Elements of Information Theory. Wiley. New York (1991)
12. Ding, S.F., Shi, Z.Z.: Symmetric Cross Entropy and Information Feature Compression Algorithm. Journal of Computational Information Systems. 1(2) (2005) 247-252
13. Chen, S.H., Lu, C.L.: An Entropic Approach to Dimensionality Reduction in the Representation Space on Discrete Processes. Journal of Nanjing Institute of Meteorology. 24 (1) (2001) 74-82

A New Binary Classifier: Clustering-Launched Classification

Tung-Shou Chen[1], Chih-Chiang Lin[1], Yung-Hsing Chiu[1], Hsin-Lan Lin[2], and Rong-Chang Chen[3,*]

[1] Graduate School of Computer Science and Information Technology
[2] Graduate School of Business Administration
[3] Department of Logistics Engineering and Management
National Taichung Institute of Technology
{tschen, s18933102, s18943108, s18941113, rcchens}@ntit.edu.tw

Abstract. One of the powerful classifiers is Support Vector Machine (SVM), which has been successfully applied to many fields. Despite its remarkable achievement, SVM is time-consuming in many situations where the data distribution is unknown, causing it to spend much time on selecting a suitable kernel and setting parameters. Previous studies proposed understanding the data distribution before classification would assist the classification. In this paper, we exquisitely combined with clustering and classification to develop a novel classifier, Clustering-Launched Classification (CLC), which only needs one parameter. CLC employs clustering to group data to characterize the features of the data and then adopts the one-against-the-rest and nearest-neighbor to find the support vectors. In our experiments, CLC is compared with two well-known SVM tools: LIBSVM and mySVM. The accuracy of CLC is comparable to LIBSVM and mySVM. Furthermore, CLC is insensitive to parameter, while the SVM is sensitive, showing CLC is easier to use.

1 Introduction

Classification is one of the most fundamental data mining tasks [1-3]. Examples of classification applications include pattern recognition, bio-informatics, and fault detection in industry applications and so on [4-6]. Some useful tools have been employed for classification. Among them, one of the tools with the most potential for classification is the Support Vector Machine (SVM) [7], which has already been successfully applied to a wide variety of fields such as signal de-noising [8], bio-informatics [9], intrusion detection [10], face recognition [11], credit card fraud detection [12, 13] and more.

SVM developed by V.N. Vapnik [7] is a supervised machine learning technique based on the generalized portrait algorithm. SVM can generate classification function from a set of training data with complex distribution. SVM can precisely map the non-separable data into a higher-dimensional feature space and define a separating hyper-plane, called the optimal hyper-plane that maximizes the margin. Based on the data, SVM can find some parts of the training set as the support vectors and then

* Corresponding author.

D.-S. Huang, K. Li, and G.W. Irwin (Eds.): ICIC 2006, LNAI 4114, pp. 278 – 283, 2006.

assign the data into well-defined classes [7]. SVM has high accuracy of classified results; however, SVM is time-consuming in many situations where the distribution of the data is unknown [5, 6]. This is because that one might spend much time on finding a suitable kernel and setting its related parameters for good classification accuracy [9, 10, 19]. In addition, SVM is difficult to understand for those without good background of mathematics or machine learning, resulting in poor interpretation in the results and failure to make the best use of SVM.

As previous literature proposed [1, 2, 13], understanding the distribution of the data prior to classifying and then using or developing suitable classifiers would help increase the accuracy of classification. To improve the problems described in the last paragraph, in this paper, we develop an integrated classifier which combines clustering with classification. This novel classifier is called Clustering-Launched Classification (CLC), which possesses of high accuracy, is easy to use and only needs one parameter. We firstly employ Divisive Hierarchical K-means algorithm (DHK) [14] to cluster the data into several groups to characterize the features of the data. Clustering techniques can group a set of data to many clusters in line with different features. The data which are grouped into the same cluster have maximum similarity [14-16]. Hence, the distribution of the data in each group can be clarified. Sequentially, in order to classify the data, we adopt the concept of the SVM to find the support vectors by using one-against-the-rest algorithm [17] and nearest-neighbor methods [18]. The data are substituted by support vectors; therefore, the performance of this method is effective. In the testing phase, we also adopt the nearest-neighbor to predict the class of a new instance. The results obtained by the proposed approach in this paper show that CLC can classify the data with high accuracy.

2 Proposed Classifier: Clustering-Launched Classification (CLC)

Consider a training vector set $V= \{v_1, v_2, v_3, ..., v_i,\}$ and a training set $R=\{< v_1, t_1>, < v_2, t_2>, < v_3, t_3>, \ldots, < v_i, t_i>\}$, where t_i, i=1, 2, 3, …, n, is the class of each instance. Each training vector v_i is k dimensional. The value of t_i symbolizes the class of the corresponding vector. CLC is a two-class classifier; thus, the value of t_i is set to be either -1 or +1, $t_i \in \{-1,+1\}$.

The training set R is divided into two subsets, a negative subset R^- and a positive subset R^+, where $R^- = \{<v_i,t_i>| t_i = -1$ and $i = 1, 2, 3, \ldots, n^-\}$, $R^+ = \{<v_i,t_i>| t_i = +1$ and $i = 1, 2, 3, \ldots, n^+\}$, and $R^- \cup R^+ = R$. Likewise, we define V^- and V^+ in R^- and R^+. Give two vectors v_i and v_j. Let $sim(v_i,v_j)$ represent the similarity value between v_i and v_j. The larger the similarity value, the more similar the two vectors.

The proposed classifier contains two phases: the training and the testing phases. The two phases are separately described as follows.

2.1 The Training Phase of CLC

2.1.1 Clustering

The original DHK regards the training set R as a group, which will be divided into smaller groups until the total number of groups set by user.

In this phase, CLC uses DHK to divide the training set R into a number of groups, $G= \{g_1, g_2, g_3, ..., g_i\}$, where i=1, 2, 3, ..., n. The groups G is divided into two subsets, a negative subset g^- and a positive subset g^+, where $g^-_i \cup g^+_i = g_i$, $g^-_i \in R^-$, and $g^+_i \in R^+$. CLC terminates clustering when $\max(\|g^+_i\|/\|g_i\|, \|g^-_i\|/\|g_i\|) \geq d$. d is the parameter set by user. In our experiments, a suitable value of d is 0.9.

After clustering, g_i consists of majority and minority. CLC eliminate the minority, because we regard the minority as noises. It means that the class t_i of g_i is the same.

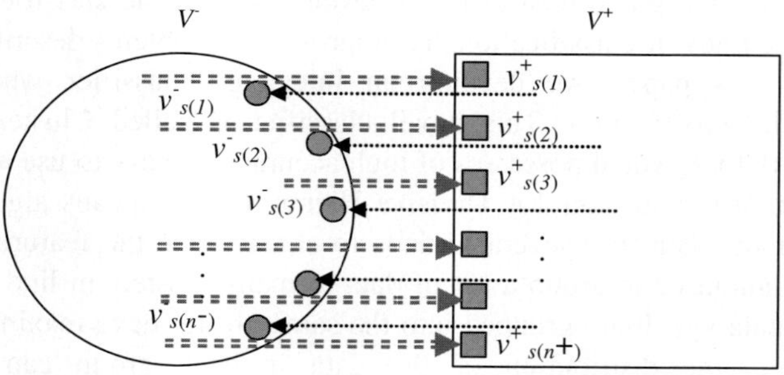

Fig. 1. The concept of support vectors

2.1.2 Collection of Support Vectors

CLC employs one-against-the-rest and nearest-neighbor to decide which support vector is. CLC selects a group g_i as V^+ and see the rest as V^-. Then, CLC tries to identify the support vector from the training vector set V. When consider a vector $v^+_i \in V^+$, for example, as Figure 1 shows, is an example of the support vectors in a two-dimensional feature space. In this figure, gray circles and squares are support vectors. we can define the corresponding support vector $v^+_{s(i)}$ of v^+_i as follows: $v^+_{s(i)}$ is the support vector of v^+_i if and only if $v^-_{s(i)}$ belongs to V^- and $sim(v^+_i,v^-_{s(i)})$ is the maximum of $sim(v^+_i, v^-_j)$ for each $v^-_j \in V^-$.

If we let V^-_s be the support vector set in V^-, then $V^-_s = \{v^-_{s(1)}, v^-_{s(2)}, v^-_{s(3)},..., v^-_{s(n-)}\}$, where n^- is the size of the negative training set.If there are two vectors v^+_i and v^+_p whose support vectors are the same, some overlap must exist in $\{v^-_{s(1)}, v^-_{s(2)}, v^-_{s(3)},..., v^-_{s(n-)}\}$. $V^-_s = \{v^-_{s1}, v^-_{s2}, v^-_{s3},..., v^-_{sn-}\}$ after deleting the overlap. Here sn^- means the number of support vectors in V^-. In the same way, CLC can find the support vector set V^+_s in V^+, with $V^+_s = \{v^+_{s1}, v^+_{s2}, v^+_{s3},..., v^+_{sn+}\}$, sn^+ denoting the number of support vector in V^+. The class t_i of the training set R which in each group g_i are the same, hence V^+_s and V^-_s are easy to obtain.

2.2 The Testing Phase of CLC

In the testing phase, consider an input vector u. Let $max\_sim^-(u)$ stand for the maximum similarity value of $sim(u,sv^-_i)$ for all sv^-_i in V^-_s, and $max\_sim^+(u)$ stand for the maximum similarity value of $sim(v_i,sv^+_i)$ for all sv^+_i in V^+_s. If $max\_sim^-(u) > max\_sim^+(u)$, u will belong to class -1; otherwise, u will belong to class +1.

3 Experimental Results and Discussion

All experimental results in this paper were obtained from an IBM PC with an Intel Pentium IV 3.0 GHz CPU and 768 Mbytes RAM. We used Microsoft Visual C++ to develop the proposed classifier. To demonstrate the effectiveness of CLC, we performed experiments by using the published template datasets and compared the results with LIBSVM [19] and mySVM [20]. The comparison is based on 5-fold and 10-fold cross validations. The experimental results are listed by accuracy rate, as shown in Table 1. In these experiments, parameter d is set to be 0.9. We define the accuracy rate as follows:

$$accuracy\ rate\ (\%) = (the\ number\ of\ correct\ separation\ in\ V) / \|R\| \tag{1}$$

Four template datasets were tested in our experiments. The first is WDBC dataset which has 30 attributes and the size of instances is 569. The second is Diabetes dataset with 8 attributes and 768 instances. The third is Ionosphere dataset consisting of 34 attributes and 351 instances. The fourth is Sonar dataset which contains 60 attributes and the size of instances is 208. All of the datasets can be found in UCI machine learning database [21].

Table 1. The accuracy rate comparison of CLC, LIBSVM and mySVM

Datasets / Classifiers	Diabetes		Ionosphere		WDBC		Sonar	
	5 fold	10 fold	5 fold	10 fold	5 fold	10 fold	5 fold	10 fold
CLC	**84.7%**	**85.7%**	**88.0%**	**89.4%**	**94.0 %**	**94.5%**	**88.8%**	**91.0%**
LIBSVM	**77.3%**	**77.2%**	**91.5%**	**92.0%**	**96.1%**	**96.5%**	**79.8%**	**79.3%**
MySVM	**76.8%**	**77.5%**	**94.9%**	**94.9%**	**98.1%**	**98.1%**	**85.1%**	**86.0%**

We tried to find the best accuracy rates of LIBSVM and mySVM in the same experiment environment as would be used in CLC. We have tried linear, polynomial and radial kernel functions. The best results for both mySVM and LIBSVM were obtained using RBF kernel function, whose related parameter gamma was set from 0.0001 to 100 and parameter C ranged from 0.01 to 10000. In each step, the next parameter value was set be 10 times larger than the previous one. In Table 1, we can find that the accuracy of CLC is comparable to LIBSVM and mySVM. For WDBC datasets, the accuracy of CLC is slightly less than LIBSVM and mySVM. Moreover, the accuracy of CLC was found to be better than that of LIBSVM and mySVM in Diabetes and Sonar datasets. Note also that while the accuracy of mySVM and LIBSVM were better than that of CLC in some situations, their accuracy could be worse than CLC's if one chooses unsuitable parameters.

CLC is insensitive to parameter setting. This is because the parameter d only influences on the clustering results but not on selecting support vectors and prediction. On the other hand, as has been shown in some previous studies, SVM is sensitive to parameter setting. Especially, the result is unacceptable when using some inappropriate parameters. In our experiments, the range of parameter d is varied from 0.6 to 0.9, but the accuracy rate does not change dramatically.

4 Conclusions

Previous scholars suggested that knowing the distribution of the data before classifying and then using or developing suitable classifiers would help improve the classification accuracy. Hence, we present a new integrated classifier: Clustering-Launched Classification (CLC), which combines clustering with classification, to classify data conveniently and efficiently. The concept of CLC is much easier to be understood than SVM, which was derived from a complex statistical learning theory. CLC is also simpler to use, while SVM generally requires some kernels and their related parameters to be selected for getting better performance. Contrast to SVM, CLC needs only one parameter. Because the basic concept of CLC can be realized intuitively, it is not only much easier to use than SVM, but also can easy to redo.

To demonstrate the effectiveness of CLC, we performed experiments by using four published template datasets and compared the results with LIBSVM and mySVM. Four template datasets, WDBC, Diabetes, Ionosphere, and Sonar, are applied in our experiments. All of the datasets can be found in UCI machine learning database. Our experimental results indicate that the accuracy of CLC is as good as LIBSVM and mySVM. Additionally, CLC is insensitive to parameter setting, but the others are sensitive, indicating CLC is a more easy-to-use tool for classification. This tool is freely available at http://163.17.136.185/CLC/CLC.htm.

References

1. Dunham, M.H.: Data Ming: Introductory and Advanced Topics. Prentice Hall (2003)
2. Roiger, R.J., Geatz, M.W.: Data Mining: A Tutorial-Based Primer. Addison Wesley (2003)
3. Han, J., Kamber, M.: Data Mining: Concepts and Techniques. Morgan Kaufmann (2000)
4. Liang, X.: Mathematical Analysis of Classifying Convex Clusters Based on Support Functionals. Lecture Notes in Computer Science (LNCS) 3584 (2005) 761-768
5. Chen, T.S., Chen, R.C., Lin, C.C., Tsai, T.H., Li, S.Y., Liang, X.: Classification of Microarray Gene Expression Data Using a New Binary Support Vector System. Proceedings of IEEE International Conference on Neural Networks and Brain (ICNN&B) (2005) 485-489
6. Chen, R.C., Chen, T.S., Lin, C.C.: A New Binary Support Vector Approach for Increasing Detection Rate of Credit Card Fraud. International Journal of Pattern Recognition and Artificial Intelligence 20 (2) (2006) 227-239
7. Vapnik, V.N.: The Nature of Statistical Learning Theory. Springer (1995)
8. Sun, B.Y., Huang D.S., Fang, H.T.: Lidar Signal De-noising Using Least Squares Support Vector Machine. IEEE Signal Processing Letter, 12 (2005) 101-104
9. Zhao, X. M., Huang, D. S., Cheung, Y. M., Wang, H. Q., Huang, X.: A Novel Hybrid GA/SVM System for Protein Sequences Classification. Lecture Notes in Computer Science (LNCS) (2004) 11–16
10. Chen, R.C., Chen, J., Chen, T.S., Hsieh, C.H., Chen, T.Y., Wu, K.Y.: Building an Intrusion Detection System Based on Support Vector Machine and Genetic Algorithm. Lecture Notes in Computer Science (LNCS) (2005) 409-414
11. Qiao, H., Zhang, S., Zhang, B., Keane, J.: Intelligent Robots and Systems. Proceedings of 2004 IEEE/RSJ International Conference (IROS) 2 (2004) 2015-2020

12. Chen, R.C., Chen, T.S., Chien, Y.E., Yang, Y.R.: Novel Questionnaire-Responded Transaction Approach with SVM for Credit Card Fraud Detection. Lecture Notes in Computer Science (LNCS) (2005) 916-921
13. Chen, R.C., Chiu, M.L., Huang, Y.L., Chen, L.T.: Detecting Credit Card Fraud by Using Questionnaire-Responded Transaction Model Based on Support Vector Machines. Lecture Notes in Computer Science (LNCS) (2004) 800-806
14. Chen, T.S., Chen, Y.T., Lin, C.C., Chen, R.C.: A Combined K-Means and Hierarchical Clustering Method for Improving the Clustering Efficiency of Microarrary. Proceedings of International Symposium on Intelligent Signal Processing and Communications Systems (ISPACS), (2005) 405-408
15. Chen, T.S., Tu, B.J., Li, S.C.: A Distance-between-clusters Based Gene Selection Technique on Microarray. Proceedings of International Conference on Informatics, Cybernetics, and Systems (ICICS), (2003) 1532-1537
16. Cover, T. M., Hart, P.E.: Nearest Neighbor Pattern Classification. IEEE Transactions on Information Theory, (1967) 21-27
17. Chang, C.C., Lin, C.J.: LIBSVM: A Library for Support Vector Machines, Software available at http://www.csie.ntu.edu.tw/~cjlin/libsvm (2001)
18. Cover, T. M., and Hart, P. E.: Nearest Neighbor Pattern Classification, IEEE Transactions on Information Theory (1967) 21-2719.
19. Chang, C.C. and Lin, C.J.: LIBSVM: A Library for Support Vector Machines,Software available at http://www.csie.ntu.edu.tw/~cjlin/libsvm (2001) 20.
20. Ruping, S.: mySVM-Manual, University of Dortmund, Lehrstuhl Informatik, 8 (2000) 21.
21. Newman, D.J., Hettich, S., Blake, C.L., and Merz, C.J.: UCI Repository ofMachine Learning Databases, http://www.ics.uci.edu/~mlearn/MLRepository.html (1998)

A Novel Clustering Algorithm Based on Variable Precision Rough-Fuzzy Sets*

Zhiqiang Bao[1], Bing Han[2], and Shunjun Wu[1]

[1] Key Lab of Radar Signal Processing, Xidian University, Xi'an 710071, China
[2] School of Electronic Engineering, Xidian Univ., Xi'an 710071, China
bzq1978@tom.com, hanbing@lab202.xidian.edu.cn,
sjwu@xidian.edu.cn

Abstract. In the field of cluster analysis and data mining, fuzzy c-means algorithm is one of effective methods, which has widely used in unsupervised pattern classification. However, the above algorithm assumes that each feature of the samples plays a uniform contribution for cluster analysis. To consider the different contribution of each dimensional feature of the given samples to be classified, this paper presents a novel fuzzy c-means clustering algorithm based on feature weighted, in which the Variable Precision Rough-Fuzzy Sets is used to assign the weights to each feature. Due to the advantages of Rough Sets for feature reduction, we can obtain the better results than the traditional one, which enriches the theory of FCM-type algorithms. Then, we apply the proposed method into video data to detect shot boundary in video indexing and browsing. The test experiment with UCI data and the video data from CCTV demonstrate the effectiveness of the novel algorithm.

1 Introduction

Cluster analysis is one of multivariate statistical analysis methods and one of important branches of unsupervised pattern recognition [1], whose basic task is to partition an unlabelled sample set into several subsets so that the homogenous samples can be classified into same subset and inhomogenous samples can be classified into another subsets. So, cluster analysis can be used to quantificationally determine the relationship of closeness among objects under studying and to realize the reasonable and valid classification and analysis.

Fuzzy c-means algorithm [2] is one of effective and typical methods for fuzzy cluster analysis of the categorical data, which has widely applied to various fields such as unsupervised pattern classification, computer vision and fuzzy intelligent control. In the traditional fuzzy c-means algorithm, it is implied that each dimensional feature of the given samples to be analyzed has the same contribution for classification. However, in practice, the contribution of each feature is different from others, since the features come from different sensors with different dimension, precision and reliability. In the other hand, not all the extracted features are suitable and effective for

* This work was supported by National Natural Science Foundation of China (No. 60102005) and National Key Lab. Foundation (J14203220033).

D.-S. Huang, K. Li, and G.W. Irwin (Eds.): ICIC 2006, LNAI 4114, pp. 284 – 289, 2006.

pattern classification. So, the practical application of existing fuzzy *c*-means algorithm is limited to some extend.

Variable selection and feature weighting have been important research topics in cluster analysis, even in the fields of data mining, image processing and pattern recognition, which is often used to assign a weight to each feature according to its contribution and find the most effective features. The Rough Sets (RS) theory introduced by Pawlak in the early 1980s [3] is an effective mathematical analysis tool to deal with vagueness and uncertainty in the areas of machine learning, knowledge acquisition, and pattern recognition *etc.*. The limitation of Pawlak Rough Sets model is the fact that the class proposed is absolutely determinate. The classification by Rough Sets model is precise because classification is processed according to the equivalence relation strictly. That is, there not exists 'inclusion' to some extent. Generally, when samples may be polluted by noises, even include error examples, the Pawlak Rough Sets is not suitable to deal with them. So, the variable precision rough set model is introduced, which is the extension of Pawlak Rough Sets model. The variable precision rough set model introduces the parameter β. That is to say, this model admits the existence of a certain error rate. In addition, due to the effectiveness and good performance of dealing with the fuzzy data(or numerical data) using Rough-Fuzzy Sets(FRS)[4] by considering the continuous data as the membership, we introduce the variable precision Rough-Fuzzy Sets into the fuzzy *c*-means clustering to assign the weights to each feature.

2 Variable Precision Rough-Fuzzy Sets

The rough sets theory introduced by Pawlak in the early 1980s[3] is an effective mathematical analysis tool to deal with vagueness and uncertainty in the areas of machine learning, knowledge discovery, expert systems, and pattern recognition *etc.*.

Definition 1[4]: Let X be a set, R be an equivalence relation defined on X and the output class A be a fuzzy set. A rough-fuzzy set is a tuple $(\underline{A}_\alpha, \overline{A}_\beta)$ where the lower approximation $\underline{A}_\alpha$ and the upper approximation $\overline{A}_\beta$ of A are fuzzy sets of X/R depending coefficients $0 \le \beta \le \alpha \le 1$, with membership functions defined by

$$\underline{A_\alpha} = \{x \in U \mid \underline{A}(x) \ge \alpha\}; \quad \overline{A}_\beta = \{x \in U \mid \underline{A}(x) \ge \beta\}. \tag{1}$$

The lower approximation $\underline{A}_\alpha$ and the upper approximation $\overline{A}_\beta$ can be expressed as the elements whose the membership affirmatively belonging to fussy set A in the U no less than the coefficient α and those elements whose the membership possibly belonging to fussy set A in the U no less than the coefficient β.

Definition 2: Let X be a set, R be an equivalence relation defined on X, $A \in F(U)$, the definition of class accuracy $\eta_R(A)$ of A is

$$\eta_R(A) = {|\underline{A}_\alpha|} \big/ {|\overline{A}_\beta|}. \tag{2}$$

where $|\overline{A}_\beta| = 0$, then $\eta_R(A) = 0$.

3 Feature Weighted Clustering Algorithm Based on VPFRS

As an effective unsupervised analysis tool, the FCM algorithm has been widely used in many fields. Recently, It has been introduced into content based video indexing and browsing by more and more researchers [5].

In the case of using FCM-means algorithms to perform cluster analysis, it is always assumed that features are extracted perfectly and are mutually independent. So, one seldom considers the influence of feature quality on the classification. It thus arises a problem whether or not each entity of feature vector contribution uniformly for the classification. Obviously, it is impossible. However, all the existing FCM-means algorithms make a positive default. To overcome this drawback, a novel feature-weighted FCM algorithm based on the Variable Precision Rough-Fuzzy Sets (VPFRS-FWCM) is proposed in the section, which considers the different contribution of every entity in feature vector for the classification. Hence, it obtain more effective in the cluster analysis.

Let $X=\{x_1,x_2,\cdots,x_n\}$ be a given set of objects to be clustering processed, and x_i denotes the m features of the i-th object (sample), Let $P=\{p_1,p_2,\cdots,p_l\}$ ($l=1,2,\cdots,c$), represent the means of the i-th class. The crisp c-partition is extended to fuzzy c-partition. For the fuzzy c-means clustering, the objective function is modified as

$$J(W,P)=\sum_{l=1}^{c}(\sum_{i=1}^{n}\mu_{li}^{2}\sum_{j=1}^{m}\omega_l^2\,|\,x_{jl}-p_{jl}\,|^2)\,. \tag{3}$$

In which $\mu_{li}\in[0,1]$ indicates the membership degree of sample x_j to the l-th cluster. Note that we weight an exponential 2 for μ_{li} to guarantee the extension from crisp partition to fuzzy partition not trivial.

By minimizing the objective function $J(W,P)$, the optimal clustering result can be achieved. The weights will be calculated by Variable Precision Rough Sets as Eq.(4) according to the Eq.(2).

$$\omega=\eta_R(Q)=|\underline{Q}_\alpha| \Big/ |\overline{Q}_\beta| \tag{4}$$

where R and Q are conditional attributes and decision attribute respectively, n is the number of samples. $\underline{Q}_\beta$ is the β ($0\le\beta\le1$)lower approximation of R depending on Q.

Due to the advantage of our algorithm to deal with continuous data, the proposed method is applied into video data to detect shot boundary in video indexing and browsing.

4 Shot Boundary Detection Scheme Based on VPFRS-WFCM

4.1 The Feature Extraction of Video Data

To detect the video shot boundaries, 12 candidate features are usually extracted for common use [5-7]. The component in RGB model and in HSV model respectively(*R,G,B;H,S,V*), Gray-histogram(*G-H*), Color-histogram (the color histogram of

RGB model and the color histogram of HSV model respectively: *RGB-H* and *HSV-H*) and Statistic features(mean, variance and skewness: *M*, *St*, *P*)[5].

4.2 The Detection Scheme

According to the characteristics of news scenes, shot transition can be divided into three types: *cut transition*, *gradual transition* and *no transition*. Due to the great capacity of video data, the computer cannot deal with a lot of data once. So, the video is partitioned into several clips. During a mount of observation and experiments, a little news unit often lasts less than 150 seconds and the shot transition is no more than 5 seconds. Therefore, we select 150 frames in length and deal with 300 units video clips to select optimal feature for shot boundary detection and generate general rules for different shot transition types firstly. That is to say, the 300 units with each of including 150 frames are selected to perform feature selection. Therefore, the number of condition attributes, the number of samples and the number of decisions in proposed method are 12, 300 and 3 respectively, where the original decisions of VPFRS is made by Twin Comparison method [7]. The scheme of shot boundary detection is shown in the Fig.1. Then, the detail procedure can be referred as the Ref. [5].

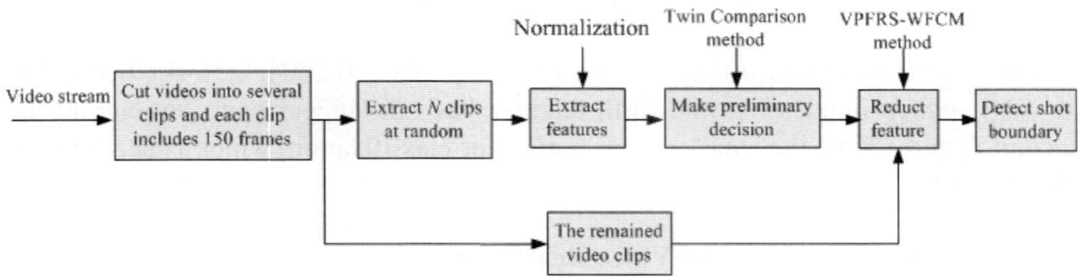

Fig. 1. The scheme of shot boundary detection

5 Experimental Results

There are two coefficient α and β in Rough-Fuzzy Sets. According to the need of this paper, we set β is one. Then, during the variation of WCN and WCR with the coefficient α ,The optimal α can be obtained. That is, the best performance of clustering is in $\alpha = 0.7$.

5.1 Experiments on the UCI Real Data

We employ the real data set of *Iris* as tested data [8] to verify the effectiveness and robustness of our proposed algorithm. The *Iris* data set contains 150 samples in 4-dimensional feature space, and the 4 components of each sample represent the petal length, petal width, sepal length and sepal width of *Iris*. The whole data set is often divided into 3 categories, i.e., Setosa, Versicolor and Virginica, each of which is composed of 50 samples. In feature space, the samples of the Setosa are separated from the other 2 categories, while there exists overlapping between the Versicolor and the

Virginica. We employ the traditional fuzzy *c*-means algorithm (FCM) and the proposed algorithm to classify the *Iris* data set. And the wrong classified number (WCN) of samples and the wrong classification rate (WCR) are used as criteria for comparing the performance of the 2 clustering algorithms. For the data set of *Iris*, Hathaway provided the real cluster centers of the above 3 categories in 1995 [9]: $p1$ = (5.00, 3.42, 1.46, 0.24), $p2$ = (5.93, 2.77, 4.26, 1.32), $p3$ = (6.58, 2.97, 5.55, 2.02). So, the sum of the squared error (SSE) between the obtained cluster centers by the algorithm and the real centers can also be used as evaluation criteria. The comparison of performance between the FCM and our algorithms is shown in the Table 1.

Table 1. The comparison of performance between the FCM and our algorithms

Algorithms	WCN	WCR	The obtained cluster centers	SSE
FCM	16	10.67%	P_1=(5.0042,3.4262,1.4692,0.2484) P_2=(5.8946,2.7460,4.4154,1.4273) P_3=(6.8484,3.0750,5.7283,2.0741)	0.155
Our method	4	2.67%	P_1=(5.0044,3.4089,1.4761,0.2461) P_2=(5.9454,2.7623,4.3393,1.3499) P_3=(6.6808,3.0356,5.6039,2.0889)	0.03

In addition, the obtained feature weight is ω = [0.3002, 0.2804, 0.2844, 0.7185] in $\alpha = 0.7$, which implies that the forth features have the bigger contribution and the second features have the smaller contribution for classification, which is accord with the real data.

5.2 Experiments on the News Video Real Data

To verify the proposed method on large data sets, The method described above is applied into 7 news from CCTV lasting over 3*h*, whose frame size is 352×240 and frame rate is 30 frames per second, which include cut, fade and dissolve, as well as zoom, pan and other camera motions and object motions, including 2112 shots, where

Table 2. The comparison of our method with the histogram method

Program	Proposed method					Twin Comparison[7]method				
video	H	M	F	R	P	H	M	F	R	P
News 1	372	12	10	96.8%	97.3%	380	30	36	92.0%	90.5%
News 2	322	9	8	97.2%	97.5%	350	15	42	95.4%	88.0%
News 3	400	16	20	96.0%	95.0%	400	46	50	88.4%	87.5%
News 4	245	13	11	94.7%	95.5%	250	22	25	91.1%	90.0%
News 5	187	10	10	94.7%	94.7%	190	17	20	90.9%	89.5%
News 6	246	7	8	97.1%	96.8%	255	18	28	92.7%	89.0%
News 7	338	14	12	95.9%	96.4%	358	22	40	93.5%	88.9%
Total	2110	81	79	96.2%	96.3%	2183	170	241	92.0%	89.0%

there are 1999cuts and 113 gradual transitions. We conduct an experiment with Twin Comparison method [7] on the same video clips. The experimental results are summarized in Table 2. We use the standard *recall* and *precision* criteria, shown in reference[6].H,M,F,R and P are denoted Hits, Misses, False alarms, Recall, Precision respectively. And the number of right hits is hits minus false alarms.

6 Conclusions

This paper present a novel feature weighted fuzzy *c*-means algorithm based on Variable Precision Rough Sets. The experimental results on UCI data sets demonstrate the effectiveness of the proposed feature weighted clustering algorithm. In real application, the proposed algorithm is complemented into shot transition detection in video indexing and browsing.The experimental results with real news totaled over 190 minutes in length video from CCTV show that our method is reasonable and effective.

References

1. He Q.: Advance of the Theory and Application of Fuzzy Clustering Analysis, Fuzzy System and Fuzzy Mathematics, 12 (2) (1998) 89–94 (In Chinese)
2. Huang, Z. X., Michael, K. N.: A Fuzzy K-modes Algorithm for Clustering Categorical Data, IEEE Transactions on Fuzzy Systems, 7 (4) (1999) 446-452
3. Pawlak, Z.: Rough Set. International Journal of Computer and Information Science. 11 (5) (1982) 341-356
4. Dubois, D., Prade, H.: Rough fuzzy Sets and Fuzzy Rough Sets. International Journal of General Systems, (17) (1990) 191-209
5. Gao, X. B., Han, B., Ji, H. G.: Shot Boundary Detection Method for News Video Based on Rough Sets and Fuzzy Clustering. Lecture Notes in Computer Sciences, 3656 (2005) 231-238
6. Xiao, X. B., Tang, O.: Unsupervised Model-free News Video Segmentation. IEEE Trans. on Circuits and Systems for Video Technology, 12(9) (2002) 765-776
7. Zhang, H. J.: Automatic Partitioning of Full Motion Video. Multimedia Systems, 1 (1) (1993) 10-28
8. Duda, R. O., Hart, P. E.: Pattern Classification and Scene Analysis, New York, (1973)
9. Bezdek, J. C.: Pattern Recognition with Fuzzy Object Function Algorithms, Plenum. New York (1981)

Applying Bayesian Approach to Decision Tree

Yatong Zhou, Taiyi Zhang, and Zhigang Chen

Dept. Information and Communication Engineering,
Xi'an Jiaotong University, 710049 Xi'an, P.R. China
{zytong, tyzhang, chenzig}@mailst.xjtu.edu.cn

Abstract. Applying Bayesian approach to decision tree (DT) model, and then a Bayesian-inference-based decision tree (BDT) model is proposed. For BDT we assign prior to the model parameters. Together with observed samples, prior are converted to posterior through Bayesian inference. When making inference we resort to simulation methods using reversible jump Markov chain Monte Carlo (RJMCMC) since the dimension of posterior distribution is varying. Compared with DT, BDT enjoys the following three advantages. Firstly, the model's learning procedure is implemented with sampling instead of a series of splitting and pruning operations. Secondly, the model provides output that gives insight into different tree structures and recursive partition of the decision space, resulting in better classification accuracy. And thirdly, the model can indicate confidence that the sample belongs to a particular class in classification. The experiments on music style classification demonstrate the efficiency of BDT.

1 Introduction

The Bayesian approach is attractive in being logically consistent, simple, adaptive, and flexible. When applied to a machine learning model, it can treat uncertainty uniformly at all levels of the modeling process. Thus not only builds the ability to infer the parameters of the model in Bayesian framework but also provides confidence that the sample belongs to a particular class in classification.

In recent years, various researchers have been devoting themselves to applying Bayesian approach to learning models. For example, Sollich applied Bayesian approach to support vector machine (SVM) and interpreted it as maximum a posteriori solutions to inference problems with Gaussian processes priors [1]. Holmes proposed a Bayesian approach to multivariate linear splines (MLS) fitting [2]. In literature [3], a Bayesian version of the multivariate adaptive regression spline (MARS) model was illustrated. Additionally, Denson presented a Bayesian version of the classification and regression tree (CART), resulting in BCART model [4].

Decision tree (DT) model has received a great deal of attention over recent years in the fields of machine learning and data mining because of its simplicity and effectiveness [5]. Motivated by the works from Sollich, Holmes and Denson *etc.*, we apply Bayesian approach to DT and seek to incorporate the Bayesian inference into the learning procedure of the model. As a result, a Bayesian-inference-based decision tree (BDT) model is built in this paper.

D.-S. Huang, K. Li, and G.W. Irwin (Eds.): ICIC 2006, LNAI 4114, pp. 290 – 295, 2006.

2 A Review on Decision Tree Model

The DT model addresses a classification problem by building a binary tree. The tree consisting of nodes and branches is a recursive structure for expressing classification rules. For each tree structure, there is a corresponding recursive partition of the decision space. In partitioning, the decision space is partitioned into a set of non-overlapping subregions, which have clear boundaries with each other.

The DT model are usually constructed beginning with the root of the tree and proceeding down to its leaf nodes according to a series of splitting and pruning operations [5]. The classification boundary obtained by DT can be represented as

$$f(\mathbf{x}) = \sum_{i=1}^{k} \beta_i B_i(\mathbf{x}), \tag{1}$$

where β_i are the coefficients of the basis functions $B_i(\mathbf{x})$ and k is the number of leaf nodes. The basis functions is the product of J_i Heavisine functions defined as

$$B_i(\mathbf{x}) = \prod_{j=1}^{J_i} H\left[S_{ji}\left(x^{v(ji)} - r_{ji} \right) \right], \tag{2}$$

where the sign indicators S_{ji} is equal ± 1. The knot points r_{ji} give the positions of the splits and $v(ji)$ give the index of the variable which is being split on the r_{ji}.

In the DT model, the parameters k, J_i, S_{ji}, r_{ji}, $v(ji)$ and β_i ($j = 1, 2, \cdots, J_i$, $i = 1, 2, \cdots, k$) are set to single optimal values. This optimization is achieved gradually in the model's learning procedure that includes a series of splitting and pruning operations. For convenience, we take these parameters the vector $\boldsymbol{\theta}^{(k)}$ as a whole.

3 Proposed Bayesian-Inference-Based Decision Tree

3.1 Implemental Process of BDT Model

The BDT model is proposed when applying Bayesian approach to DT model. In general, the Bayesian approach consists of the following steps when it is applied to a learning model. Firstly, prior distributions are assigned to the parameters of the model. Together with observed samples, prior is converted to posterior through Bayesian inference. Finally, posterior is calculated by some approximation techniques such as MCMC, mean field method and soon on. BDT also follows above-mentioned steps.

The BDT model's prior is places on all unknown parameters. It is useful to write it in factorized form that highlights conditional dependencies

$$P\left(k, \boldsymbol{\theta}^{(k)}\right) = P(k) P\left(\boldsymbol{\theta}^{(k)} \mid k\right) \quad . \tag{3}$$

Similar with BCART [4], a Poisson distribution with parameter λ is used to specify the prior for the number of leaf nodes k, giving

$$P(k) = \lambda^k / (e^\lambda - 1) k! \ . \tag{4}$$

The conditional distribution $P(\boldsymbol{\theta}^{(k)} \mid k)$ can be factorized as the product of the probability over each element of the vector $\boldsymbol{\theta}^{(k)}$. On the other hand, we assume the likelihood with the form of

$$P(D \mid k, \boldsymbol{\theta}^{(k)}) = \prod_{n=1}^{N} \left(\frac{1}{1 + \exp\left(-f\left(\mathbf{x}_n, k, \boldsymbol{\theta}^{(k)}\right)\right)} \right)^{t_n} \left(1 - \frac{1}{1 + \exp\left(-f\left(\mathbf{x}_n, k, \boldsymbol{\theta}^{(k)}\right)\right)} \right)^{1-t_n} . \tag{5}$$

where D is the learning samples set. Finally, the posterior $P(k, \boldsymbol{\theta}^{(k)} \mid D)$ can be obtained with the prior and the likelihood according to Bayesian inference

$$P(k, \boldsymbol{\theta}^{(k)} \mid D) = P(\boldsymbol{\theta}^{(k)}, k) P(D \mid k, \boldsymbol{\theta}^{(k)}) / P(D) . \tag{6}$$

Similarly with DT, the classification boundary obtained by BDT can also be represented as

$$f\left(\mathbf{x}, k, \boldsymbol{\theta}^{(k)}\right) = \sum_{i=1}^{k} \beta_i B_i(\mathbf{x}) . \tag{7}$$

After that, the parameterized output of BDT can be represented as

$$P\left(t \mid \mathbf{x}, k, \boldsymbol{\theta}^{(\mathbf{k})}\right) = \frac{1}{1 + \exp\left(-f\left(\mathbf{x}, k, \boldsymbol{\theta}^{(k)}\right)\right)} . \tag{8}$$

By marginalization which integrates the vector $\boldsymbol{\theta}^{(k)}$ out from the Eq. (8), we obtain the output of BDT, the confidence that the sample $\mathbf{x}$ belongs to a particular class t

$$P(t \mid \mathbf{x}) = \sum_k \int P\left(t \mid \mathbf{x}, k, \boldsymbol{\theta}^{(\mathbf{k})}\right) P\left(k, \boldsymbol{\theta}^{(k)} \mid D\right) d\boldsymbol{\theta}^{(k)} . \tag{9}$$

Clearly the integral in Eq. (9) is analytical intractable and some approximation method is required. An elegant solution is provided by MCMC simulation which allows one to draw N_c samples $\left(k_n, \boldsymbol{\theta}_n^{(k_n)}\right)$, $n = 1, 2, \cdots, N_c$, from the posterior distribution $P\left(k, \boldsymbol{\theta}^{(k)} \mid D\right)$ and then approximate Eq. (9) by

$$P(t \mid \mathbf{x}) \approx \frac{1}{N_c} \sum_{n=1}^{N_c} P\left(t \mid \mathbf{x}, k_n, \boldsymbol{\theta}_n^{(k_n)}\right) . \tag{10}$$

3.2 Sampling Via RJMCMC

Now the key to BDT is how to draw N_c samples from $P\left(k, \boldsymbol{\theta}^{(k)} \mid D\right)$. In the BDT, the parameter k is unknown and the dimension of the posterior distribution is varying. Therefore we will generate samples from the posterior by RJMCMC [6]. For the BDT model, supposing the current number of leaf nodes equals to k_m, i.e. $k = k_m$, the corresponding model posterior is $P\left(k_m,\boldsymbol{\theta}^{(k_m)} \mid D\right)$. We construct ergodic Markov chains admitting $P\left(k_m,\boldsymbol{\theta}^{(k_m)} \mid D\right)$ as the invariant distribution. However, the Markov chains would admit $P\left(k_n,\boldsymbol{\theta}^{(k_n)} \mid D\right)$ as the invariant distribution when the number of leaf nodes changes to k_n. The parameters $\boldsymbol{\theta}^{(k_m)} \in R^{N_m}$ and $\boldsymbol{\theta}^{(k_n)} \in R^{N_n}$ are model dependent and the dimension of subspaces R^{N_m} and R^{N_n} are different.

RJMCMC allows the sampler to jump between the different subspaces. To ensure a common measure, it requires the extension of each pair of communicating subspaces, R^{N_m} and R^{N_n}. It also requires the definition of deterministic, differential, invertible dimension matching functions $\varphi_{n\to m}$ and $\varphi_{m\to n}$ between the extended subspaces.

$$\left(\boldsymbol{\theta}^{(k_m)},\mathbf{u}_{m,n}\right)=\varphi_{n\to m}\left(\boldsymbol{\theta}^{(k_n)},\mathbf{u}_{n,m}\right),\quad \left(\boldsymbol{\theta}^{(k_n)},\mathbf{u}_{n,m}\right)=\varphi_{m\to n}\left(\boldsymbol{\theta}^{(k_m)},\mathbf{u}_{m,n}\right) \tag{11}$$

where $\mathbf{u}_{m,n}$ and $\mathbf{u}_{n,m}$ are auxiliary variables. If the current state of the chain is $\left(k_n,\boldsymbol{\theta}^{(k_n)}\right)$, we jump to $\left(k_m,\boldsymbol{\theta}^{(k_m)}\right)$ by generating $\mathbf{u}_{n,m} \sim q_{n\to m}\left(\cdot \mid n,\boldsymbol{\theta}^{(k_n)}\right)$, ensuring that Eq. (11) holds, and accepting the jump according to some probability ratio. The RJMCMC sampler is iterated until enough samples have been collected. An initial portion is discarded to allow time for the chain to converge sufficiently closely to its invariant distribution. In the end N_c samples can be obtained.

According to above theoretical depiction, we can infer that BDT enjoys the following three advantages. Firstly, unlike DT making inference about $\boldsymbol{\theta}^{(k)}$ in the learning procedure that includes a series of splitting and pruning operations, BDT mimics partitioning and pruning by regarding $\boldsymbol{\theta}^{(k)}$ as additional parameters and makes inference about them during the sampling. So the model is more intuitive and flexible. Secondly, the output of BDT is approximated by Eq. (10), where the parameter k could take N_c different values. Since k is the number of leaf nodes of BDT, we change the structure of the tree when we change k. Hence, BDT provides output that gives insight into N_c kinds of tree structures. Moreover, for each tree structure there is a corresponding recursive partition of the decision space. Thus BDT provides output that also gives insight into N_c kinds of recursive partition schemes. Compared with the DT model considering only one tree structure and one recursive partition scheme, it is anticipated that BDT can obtain better performance. Thirdly, BDT can output posterior class probability $P(t \mid \mathbf{x})$.

4 Experiments

Music style classification has been receiving an increasing attention in recent years. To verify the efficiency of the BDT model, we employ it as the classifiers to automatically classify music into the pre-defined classes----pleasurable music and sorrowful music. Usually, in music style classification one takes MIDI as sample source, and the other takes audio as source [7]. However, our work will take music staff as source since it is quite general. We collected 320 music staffs to construct a staff database. These staffs include pianos, symphonies, popular songs, and Chinese folk songs downloading from CDs and the Internet. Based on the pre-defined staff conversion rule, a segment of music staff given in Fig.1 could be converted into the text file as following

1. 6#_ 3. 2__ 3__| 2-- 3| 7#_ 5#_ 3__ 2__ 7#_ 3_ 2__ 3__ 5#_|1_ 6#. 6#-| 1^_ 6. 6-|1^_ 2^. 1^_ 2^_ 1^__ 2^__ 6| 1^_ 6. 6-| 6---||$

It is a challenge to extract the most common and salient features to characterize the music style from unstructured text files. People usually define the commonness by some high-level perceptive features, such as melody and rhythm. However it is difficult to give a determinate description for these high-level features. Fortunately, the high-level features can be reflected through some low-level features. The first low-level feature we extracted is the number of sharp octave (NSO) that reflects the music's melody. The second feature, the number of simple meters (NSM), is extracted to reflect the music's rhythm. The third feature we used is the music playing speed (MPS). After extraction, three features are sent into the classifier.

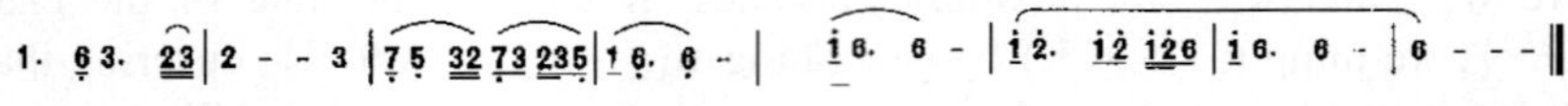

Fig. 1. Example of staff segmentation for a piece of music

The experiment is simulated in Matlab circumstance. The computer used is Celeron (2.8GHZ) PC with 256 RAM. In the experiment, 10 pleasurable and sorrowful music samples are selected respectively from the database to form the training set. The remaining samples are put into the test set. That means we will use totally 20 samples for the training and 300 samples for the testing. A comparative evaluation between DT and BDT is carried out and the results shown in Fig. 2 and Table 1 are promising.

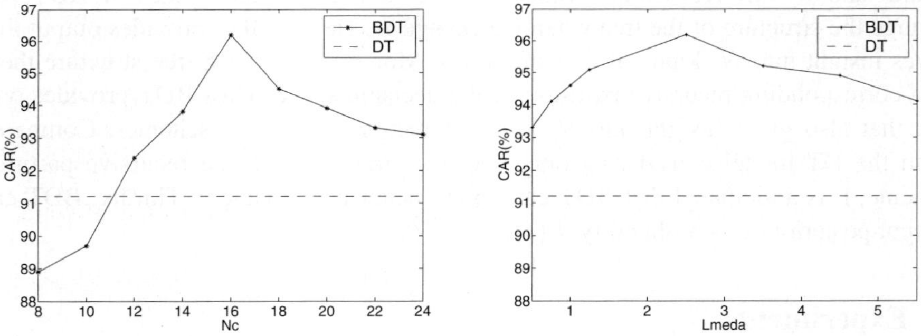

Fig. 2. Classification accuracy rate (CAR) comparison between BDT and DT. The left graph shows the dependence of CAR on the parameter N_c with the fixed value of $\lambda = 2.5$. The right graph shows the dependence of CAR on the parameter λ with $N_c = 16$.

The BDT model has two main user set parameters N_c and λ. Fig. 2 illustrates the variation of classification accuracy rate (CAR) with two parameters. From the left graph we can see that BDT outperforms DT in all the cases except for $N_c = 8$ and $N_c = 10$. In Fig.2, the curve in right graph is quite different from that of left graph. It's found that the BDT outperforms DT in all the cases no matter what value of the parameter λ taken. Furthermore, the CAR curve with the parameter λ is relatively flat. This implies that λ has little influence on the performance of BDT.

To give a further investigation on model's computational efficiency, we compare the CPU time in seconds consumed for learning between BDT and DT. With view of Table.1, the CPU time for BDT is little longer than DT, whereas CAR improves a lot if the parameter N_c selected appropriately (such as $N_c = 15$ or $N_c = 20$). In other words, BDT takes little longer time and yields quite better performance.

Table 1. Classification results on music database with the fixed value of $\lambda = 2.5$. Time denotes the CPU time in seconds consumed for learning.

Items	DT	BDT					
N_c	---	5	10	15	20	40	100
Time	10.1	10.5	12.5	15.2	19.7	31.6	68.9
CAR	91.2%	86.3%	89.7%	95.0%	93.9%	93.0%	92.8%

5 Conclusions

In this paper, Bayesian approach is applied to the DT model, and then a Bayesian-inference-based BDT model is proposed. Based on theoretical analysis, BDT enjoys some advantages. As anticipated, experimental results on music style classification exhibit the performance of BDT far superior to existing DT model. The results also show the performance of BDT relying heavily on the parameter N_c. Future investigation needs to be done into whether the better likelihood function exists.

References

1. Sollich, P.: Bayesian Methods for Support Vector Machines: Evidence and Predictive Class Probabilities. Machine learning. 46(2002) 21-52
2. Homes, C. C., Mallick, B. K.: Bayesian Piecewise Linear Regression using Multivariate Linear Splines. J Roy Statist Soc Series B. 63(2001) 3-18
3. Denson, D. G. T., Mallick, B. K., Smith A. F.: Bayesian MARS. Statistics and Computing. 8(1998) 337-346
4. Denson D. G. T.: Simulation Based Bayesian Nonparametric Regression Methods. Ph. D Dissertation. Imperial College, London University (2001)
5. Duda R. O., Hart P. E., Stork D. G.: Pattern Classification. Wiley, New York (2002)
6. Green P. J.: Reversible Jump Markov Chain Monte Carlo Computation and Bayesian Model Determination. Biometrika. 82(1995) 711-732
7. Zhang Y. B., Zhou J.: A Study on Content-based Music Classification. In: Jordan (eds.): Proc. 7th Int. Sym. Signal Processing and Its Applications, Paris, France. 2(2003) 113-116

Approximation Algorithms for *K*-Modes Clustering

Zengyou He, Shengchun Deng, and Xiaofei Xu

Department of Computer Science and Engineering,
Harbin Institute of Technology, China
zengyouhe@yahoo.com, dsc@hit.edu.cn, xiaofei@hit.edu.cn

Abstract. In this paper, we study clustering with respect to the *k*-modes objective function, a natural formulation of clustering for categorical data. One of the main contributions of this paper is to establish the connection between *k*-modes and *k*-median, i.e., the optimum of *k*-median is at most the twice the optimum of *k*-modes for the same categorical data clustering problem. Based on this observation, we derive a deterministic algorithm that achieves an approximation factor of 2. Furthermore, we prove that the distance measure in *k*-modes defines a metric. Hence, we are able to extend existing approximation algorithms for metric *k*-median to *k*-modes. Empirical results verify the superiority of our method.

1 Introduction

Clustering categorical data is an important research topic in data mining. The *k*-modes algorithm [1] extends the *k*-means paradigm to cluster categorical data. Because the *k*-modes algorithm uses the same clustering process as *k*-means, it preserves the efficiency of the *k*-means algorithm. Recently, some *k*-modes based clustering algorithms have been proposed [2-5].

Although the *k*-modes algorithm is very efficient, it suffers two well-known problems as *k*-means algorithm: the solutions are only locally optimal and their qualities are sensitive to the initial conditions. To overcome locally optimal in *k*-modes clustering, some techniques such as tabu search [4] and genetic algorithm [5] have been investigated to find the globally optimal solution. However, they cannot provide approximation guarantees. Thus, effective approximation algorithms should be designed for *k*-modes clustering. To the best of our knowledge, such kinds of approximation algorithms are still not available to date and this paper is the first attempt to this problem.

In this paper, we study clustering with respect to the *k*-modes objective function. We first establish the connection between the *k*-modes problem and the well-known *k*-median problem by proving that the optimum of *k*-median is at most the twice the optimum of *k*-modes for the same categorical data clustering problem. Based on this observation, we derive a deterministic algorithm that achieves an approximation factor of 2. Furthermore, we prove that the distance measure in *k*-modes defines a metric. Hence, we are able to extend existing approximation algorithms for metric *k*-median (e.g., [6], [7]) to *k*-modes.

D.-S. Huang, K. Li, and G.W. Irwin (Eds.): ICIC 2006, LNAI 4114, pp. 296 – 302, 2006.

2 *K*-Modes Clustering

Let *X, Y* be two categorical objects described by *m* categorical attributes. The simple distance measure between *X* and *Y* is defined by the total mismatches of the corresponding attribute values of the two objects. The smaller the number of mismatches is, the more similar the two objects. Formally,

$$d(X,Y)=\sum_{j=1}^{m}\delta(x_j,y_j)\cdot \tag{1}$$

where

$$\delta(x_j,y_j)=\begin{cases}0 & (x_j=y_j)\\ 1 & (x_j\neq y_j)\end{cases}. \tag{2}$$

Let ***S*** be a set of categorical objects described by *m* categorical attributes A_1, ..., A_m. A mode of ***S*** $=\{X_1, X_2, \ldots, X_n\}$ is a vector $Q=[q_1, q_2,\ldots, q_m]$ that minimizes

$$D(S,Q)=\sum_{i=1}^{n}d(X_i,Q)\cdot \tag{3}$$

Here, *Q* is not necessarily an object of ***S***.

Let $n_{c_{k,r}}$ be the number of objects having the *k*th category $c_{k,r}$ in attribute A_r and $f(A_r=c_{k,r})=n_{c_{k,r}}/n$ be the relative frequency of category $n_{c_{k,r}}$ in ***S***. The function $D(S,Q)$ is minimized iff $f(A_r=q_r)\geq f(A_r=c_{k,r})$ for $q_r\neq c_{k,r}$ and all $r = 1, \ldots, m$.

The optimization problem for partitioning a set of *n* objects described by *m* categorical attributes into *k* clusters $S_1, S_2, \ldots S_k$ becomes to minimize

$$\sum_{i=1}^{k}\sum_{X\in S_i}d(X,Q_i)\cdot \tag{4}$$

where Q_i is the mode of cluster S_i.

In the above *k*-modes clustering problem, the representative point of each cluster S_i, i.e., the mode Q_i, is not necessarily contained in S_i. If we restrict the representative point to be in S_i, it becomes the well-known *k*-median problem. In the next section, we will show that the optimum of *k*-median is at most the twice the optimum of *k*-modes for the same categorical data clustering problem. Hence, the loss is modest even restricting representatives to be points contained in original set.

3 Approximation Algorithms

Lemma 1: Let ***S*** be a set of *n* categorical objects described by *m* categorical attributes and *Q* be the mode of ***S***. Then, there exists a $X_i\in S$ such that

$$\sum_{j=1}^{n}d(X_j,X_i)\leq 2\sum_{j=1}^{n}d(X_j,Q)\cdot \tag{5}$$

Proof: To prove the lemma, we only need to show the following inequality holds.

$$\sum_{i=1}^{n}\sum_{j=1}^{n} d(X_j, X_i) \le 2n\sum_{j=1}^{n} d(X_j, Q) \cdot \quad (6)$$

Recalling that $n_{c_{k,r}}$ is the number of objects having the kth category $c_{k,r}$ in attribute A_r and $f(A_r = c_{k,r}) = n_{c_{k,r}} / n$ is the relative frequency of category $n_{c_{k,r}}$ in ***S***. Without loss of generality, we can assume that $q_r = c_{1,r}$ in attribute A_r, i.e., the first category $c_{1,r}$ in attribute A_r has largest relative frequency in ***S*** for all r = 1, …, m.

Considering the left-hand side of (6), the contribution of the rth attribute is $n^2 \sum_k f(A_r = c_{k,r})(1 - f(A_r = c_{k,r}))$; On the other hand, the contribution of the rth attribute to the right-hand side is $n^2(1 - f(A_r = c_{1,r}))$. Hence, we have

$$\frac{n^2 \sum_k f(A_r = c_{k,r})(1 - f(A_r = c_{k,r}))}{n^2(1 - f(A_r = c_{1,r}))} = \frac{\sum_k f(A_r = c_{k,r})(1 - f(A_r = c_{k,r}))}{1 - f(A_r = c_{1,r})}$$

$$= \frac{\sum_k f(A_r = c_{k,r}) - \sum_k f^2(A_r = c_{k,r})}{1 - f(A_r = c_{1,r})} = \frac{1 - \sum_k f^2(A_r = c_{k,r})}{1 - f(A_r = c_{1,r})} = \frac{1 - f^2(A_r = c_{1,r}) - \sum_{k \ne 1} f^2(A_r = c_{k,r})}{1 - f(A_r = c_{1,r})}$$

$$= 1 + f(A_r = c_{1,r}) - \frac{\sum_{k \ne 1} f^2(A_r = c_{k,r})}{1 - f(A_r = c_{1,r})} \le 1 + f(A_r = c_{1,r}) \le 2$$

Summing over r, we can verify inequality (6).

Lemma 2: The optimum of k-median is at most the twice the optimum of k-modes for the same categorical data clustering problem.

Proof: Let $OPT^O = \{(S_1^O, Q_1), (S_2^O, Q_2), \ldots, (S_k^O, Q_k)\}$ be the optimal solution of k-modes clustering, and $OPT^E = \{(S_1^E, Y_1), (S_2^E, Y_2), \ldots, (S_k^E, Y_k)\}$ be the optimal solution of k-median clustering. According to Lemma 1, we can find a solution $P^E = \{(S_1^O, W_1), (S_2^O, W_2), \ldots, (S_k^O, W_k)\}$ for k-median clustering such that $\sum_{X \in S_i^O} d(X, W_i) \le 2 \sum_{X \in S_i^O} d(X, Q_i)$ for all i = 1, …, k. When considering all partitions, we have $\sum_{i=1}^{k} \sum_{X \in S_i^O} d(X, W_i) \le 2 \sum_{i=1}^{k} \sum_{X \in S_i^O} d(X, Q_i) \cdot$

Furthermore, since OPT^E is the optimal solution of k-median clustering, we have $\sum_{i=1}^{k} \sum_{X \in S_i^E} d(X, Y_i) \le \sum_{i=1}^{k} \sum_{X \in S_i^O} d(X, W_i) \cdot$

Thus, we obtain $\sum_{i=1}^{k} \sum_{X \in S_i^E} d(X, Y_i) \le 2 \sum_{i=1}^{k} \sum_{X \in S_i^O} d(X, Q_i)$, i.e., the optimum of k-median is at most the twice the optimum of k-modes for the same categorical data clustering problem.

By enumerating all k-subsets of ***S***, we could find the optimal solution of k-median problem. Therefore, by Lemma 2, we can solve the k-modes clustering deterministically in time $O(kn^{k1})$, for a 2-approximation to the optimal solution. That is, we can derive a deterministic algorithm that achieves an approximation factor of 2.

The above deterministic algorithm is feasible for small *k*; for larger *k*, we can use existing efficient approximation algorithms for metric *k*-median (e.g., [6], [7]) since the distance measure in *k*-modes defines a metric (as shown in Lemma 3). That is, the distance is nonnegative, symmetric, satisfy the triangle inequality, and the distance between points *X* and *Y* is zero if and only if *X* = *Y*.

Lemma 3: The distance measure *d* in *k*-modes is a valid distance metric, such that: (1) $d(X,Y) > 0, \forall X \neq Y$, (2) $d(X,Y) = 0, \forall X = Y$, (3) $d(X,Y) = d(Y,X)$ and (4) $d(X,Y) + d(Y,Z) \geq d(X,Z), \forall X,Y,Z$

Proof: It is easy to verify that the first three properties are true. We prove the fourth statement is true. To simplify the presentation, we view the points *X* ,*Y* and *Z* as sets of elements. Thus, we have $d(X,Y) = m - |X \cap Y|$, $d(Y,Z) = m - |Y \cap Z|$, and $d(X,Z) = m - |X \cap Z|$. To prove the lemma, we only need to show the following inequality holds:

$2m - |X \cap Y| - |Y \cap Z| \geq m - |X \cap Z|$, i.e., $|X \cap Y| - |X \cap Z| + |Y \cap Z| \leq m$

We have $|X \cap Y| - |X \cap Z| + |Y \cap Z| \leq |X \cap (Y - Z)| + |Y \cap Z| \leq |Y - Z| + |Y \cap Z| = |Y| = m$

Thus, the fourth statement is true.

By Lemma 3, we know that the *k*-median problem with distance measure *d* in *k*-modes is a metric *k*-median problem. Therefore, one obvious idea for designing approximation algorithms for *k*-modes clustering is the direct adaptation and use of existing approximation algorithms for metric *k*-median. More precisely, as shown in Theorem 1, one α-approximation algorithm for metric *k*-median is a 2α-approximation algorithm for *k*-modes clustering by Lemma 2 and Lemma 3.

Theorem 1: For the same categorical data clustering problem with respect to the *k*-modes objective function, any α-approximation algorithm for metric *k*-median will be a 2α-approximation algorithm for *k*-modes clustering, where α is the approximation ratio guaranteed.

Proof: Trivial.

According to Theorem 1, we are able to select effective α-approximation algorithm in metric *k*-median literature such as algorithms in [6] and [7] to approximate *k*-modes clustering with approximation ratio 2α guaranteed.

4 Empirical Studies

We experimented with two real-life datasets: the Congressional Votes dataset and Mushroom dataset, which were obtained from the UCI Repository [8].

Congressional Votes Dataset: It is the United States Congressional Voting Records in 1984. Each record represents one Congressman's votes on 16 issues. All attributes are Boolean with Yes (denoted as *y*) and No (denoted as *n*) values. A classification label of Republican or Democrat is provided with each record. The dataset contains 435 records with 168 Republicans and 267 Democrats.

The Mushroom Dataset: It has 22 attributes and 8124 records. Each record represents physical characteristics of a single mushroom. A classification label of poisonous or edible is provided with each record. The numbers of edible and poisonous mushrooms in the dataset are 4208 and 3916, respectively.

Validating clustering results is a non-trivial task. In the presence of true labels, as in the case of the data sets we used, the clustering accuracy for measuring the clustering results was computed as follows. Given the final number of clusters, k, clustering accuracy r was defined as: $r = (\sum_{i=1}^{k} a_i) / n$, where n is the number of objects in the dataset and a_i is the number of objects with the class label that dominates cluster S_i. Consequently, the clustering error is defined as $e = 1-r$.

Furthermore, we also compare the objective function values produced by both algorithms since such measure is non-subjective and provides hints on the goodness of approximation.

We studied the clusterings found by our algorithm and the original *k*-modes algorithm [1]. For the *k*-modes algorithm, we use the first *k* distinct records from the data set to construct initial *k* modes. That is, we use one run to get the clustering outputs for *k*-modes.

On the congressional voting dataset, we let the algorithms produce two clusters, i.e., *k*=2. Table 1 shows the clusters, class distribution, clustering errors and objective function values produced by two algorithms. As Table 1 shows, *k*-modes algorithm and our algorithm have similar performance. In particular, the objective function value of our algorithm is only a little lower than that of *k*-modes. It provides us hints that local search heuristics based *k*-modes algorithm could find good solutions in some cases. However, as shown in the next experiment, such algorithm does not provide a performance guarantee and can produce very poor clustering output.

Table 1. Clustering results on the congressional votes dataset

k-modes (Clustering Error: 0.136, Objective Function Value: 1706)		
Cluster NO	No of Republicans	No of Democrats
1	154	45
2	14	222
Our 2-Approximation Algorithm (Clustering Error: 0.149, Objective Function Value: 1701)		
Cluster NO	No of Democrats	No of Democrats
1	158	55
2	10	212

Table 2. Clustering results on the mushroom dataset

k-modes (Clustering Error: 0.435, Objective Function Value: 63015)		
Cluster NO	No of Edible	No of Poisonous
1	1470	1856
2	2738	2060
Our 2-Approximation Algorithm (Clustering Error: 0.121, Objective Function Value: 62512)		
Cluster NO	No of Edible	No of Poisonous
1	4182	960
2	26	2956

Table 2 contrasts the clustering results on mushroom dataset. The number of clusters is still set to be 2 since there are two natural clusters in this dataset. As shown in Table 2, our algorithm performed much better than *k*-modes algorithm with respect to both clustering accuracy and objective function values. It further empirically confirms the fact that our algorithm deserves good performance guarantee.

5 Conclusions

This paper reveals an interesting fact that the optimum of *k*-median is at most the twice the optimum of *k*-modes for the same categorical data clustering problem. This observation makes possible the study of *k*-modes clustering problem from a metric *k*-median perspective. From this viewpoint, effective approximation algorithms are designed and empirically studied.

Furthermore, it is already known that the optimum of *k*-median is also at most the twice the optimum of *k*-means for a numeric data clustering problem [6]. Hence, it is straightforward to show that optimum of *k*-median is at most the twice the optimum of *k*-prototypes [1] for a mixed data clustering problem. Based on this fact, we can get a similar deterministic algorithm that achieves an approximation factor of two for *k*-prototypes clustering. Further investigating such kinds of approximation algorithms for *k*-prototypes clustering would be a promising future research direction.

To date, local search algorithm [9] provides the smallest approximation ratio for metric *k*-median problem. A natural question one may ask is "Does the local search heuristics based *k*-modes algorithm provide a bounded performance guarantee?" The general problem is open and provides promising future research directions.

Acknowledgements

This work was supported by the High Technology Research and Development Program of China (No. 2004AA413010, No. 2004AA413030) .

References

1. Huang, Z.: Extensions To The K-means Algorithm for Clustering Large Data Sets with Categorical Values. Data Mining and Knowledge Discovery, 2 (1998) 283-304
2. He, Z., Deng, S., Xu, X.: Improving K-modes Algorithm Considering Frequencies of Attribute Values in Mode. Lecture Notes in Artificial Intelligence, 3801, (2005) 157-162
3. Huang, Z., Ng., M. K.: A Fuzzy K-modes Algorithm for Clustering Categorical Data. IEEE Transactions on Fuzzy Systems, 7 (4) (1999) 446-452
4. Ng, M. K., Wong, J. C.: Clustering Categorical Data Sets Using Tabu Search Techniques. Pattern Recognition, 35 (12) (2002) 2783-2790
5. Gan, G., Yang, Z., Wu, J.: A Genetic *k*-Modes Algorithm for Clustering Categorical Data. Lecture Notes in Artificial Intelligence, 3584 (2005) 195-202
6. Mettu, R. R., Plaxton, C. G.: Optimal Time Bounds for Approximate Clustering. Machine Learning, 56 (1-3) (2004) 35-60

7. Meyerson, A., O'Callaghan, L., Plotkin, S. A.: A *k*-Median Algorithm with Running Time Independent of Data Size. Machine Learning, 56(1-3) (2004) 61-87
8. Merz, C. J., Merphy, P.: UCI Repository of Machine Learning Databases. http://www.ics.uci.edu/~mlearn/MLRRepository.html, (1996)
9. Arya, V., Garg, N., Khandekar, R., Meyerson, A., Munagala, K., Pandit, V.: Local Search Heuristics for k-Median and Facility Location Problems. SIAM Journal on Computing, 33 (3) (2004) 544-562

Convergence of a New Decomposition Algorithm for Support Vector Machines

Yan-Guo Wang[1], Hong Qiao[1], and Bo Zhang[2]

[1] Institute of Automation, Chinese Academy of Sciences,
100080 Beijing, China
hong.qiao@mail.ia.ac.cn

[2] Institute of Applied Mathematics, Chinese Academy of Sciences,
100080 Beijing, China
b.zhang@amt.ac.cn

Abstract. Decomposition methods is the main way for solving support vector machines (SVMs) with large data sets. In this paper a new decomposition algorithm is proposed, and its convergence is also proved.

1 Introduction

Support vector machines (SVMs) introduced by Vapnik and co-workers [2],[3],[4] are a new classification method (see [1]). The problem arising in SVMs is as follows:

$$\begin{cases} \min\ f(\alpha) = \frac{1}{2}\alpha^{\mathsf{T}} Q\alpha - e^{\mathsf{T}}\alpha \\ \text{s.t. } \ 0 \le \alpha_i \le C, \quad \forall i \\ \qquad \sum_i y_i\alpha_i = 0 \end{cases} \tag{1}$$

Q is a symmetric and positive semi-definite matrix with $Q_{ij} = y_i y_j K(x_i, x_j)$.

It is difficult to solve (1) directly due to the large amount of training samples in real world problems. Up to now, the major method to conquer this difficulty is decomposition methods (see, e.g. [5],[6],[7],[8]) with essential idea as follows:

1) Let α^0 be the initial solution which satisfies constrains of (1) and set $k = 0$.
2) If α^k is an optimal solution of (1), stop. Otherwise, select the working set B from the samples, with the remaining part being the non-working set N.
3) Solve the sub-optimization problem with the same objective function and constrains as in (1), while with a different and lower-dimensional variable α_B.
4) Set α_B^{k+1} be the solution in step 3), $\alpha_N^{k+1} = \alpha_N^k$, set $k \leftarrow k+1$, go to step 2).

The difference among various decomposition algorithms lies in working set selection (WSS). Platt's SMO [5] selects one pair which violates KKT-conditions most. In [9], a generalized SMO algorithm is proposed based on the concept of τ-violating pair and its convergence is also proved. However, $|B|$ is limited to 2 in the above algorithms. SVM^{light} [6] chooses $q/2$ most KKT-violating pairs with convergence proved in [11] under condition $\min_I(\min(eig(Q_{II}))) > 0$, Q_{II} is any $|I| \times |I|$ submatrix of Q with $|I| \le q$. Note that this condition is removed in [12] for the modified SMO proposed in [10] (i.e., in the case $q = 2$).

D.-S. Huang, K. Li, and G.W. Irwin (Eds.): ICIC 2006, LNAI 4114, pp. 303–308, 2006.

2 A New Decomposition Algorithm

As showed in [9], KKT-conditions of (1) can be simplified as

$$F_i(\alpha) \geq F_j(\alpha), \forall i \in I_{up}(\alpha) \cup I_{mid}(\alpha), j \in I_{low}(\alpha) \cup I_{mid}(\alpha) \tag{2}$$

where $I_{up}(\alpha) = \{i : y_i = 1, \alpha_i = 0\} \cup \{i : y_i = -1, \alpha_i = C\}$, $I_{mid}(\alpha) = \{i : 0 < \alpha_i < C\}$, and $I_{low}(\alpha) = \{i : y_i = 1, \alpha_i = C\} \cup \{i : y_i = -1, \alpha_i = 0\}$. Here $F_i(\alpha) = \frac{[Q\alpha]_i - 1}{y_i} = y_i[\nabla f(\alpha)]_i$ and $[Q\alpha]_i$ denotes the i-th element of vector $Q\alpha$.

Definition 1. *(τ-violating pair). (i,j) is called a τ-violating pair at α for (1) iff $F_i(\alpha) < F_j(\alpha) - \tau$, where $i \in I_{up}(\alpha) \cup I_{mid}(\alpha)$ and $j \in I_{low}(\alpha) \cup I_{mid}(\alpha)$.*

WSS of the New Decomposition Algorithm

Let τ be a given positive parameter and q_m be an even number. Choose a τ-violating set as $|B|$, which consists of $q/2$ independently-selected τ-violating pairs, where q is an even number satisfying $2 \leq q \leq q_m$.

3 Convergence Proof

First we consider the k-th iteration in the new algorithm. Let us denote the initial point as α, $\mathbf{H}$ be the $q-1$ dimensional hyper-plane in which the minimization takes place and $\alpha(\boldsymbol{t})$ be any point in $\mathbf{H}$. Then $\alpha(\boldsymbol{t})$ can be expressed as

$$\alpha(\boldsymbol{t}) = \alpha + \mathbf{A}\boldsymbol{t}, \tag{3}$$

where $\boldsymbol{t}$ is a vector parameter in $\mathbb{R}^{q-1}$ and $\mathbf{A}$ is a $q \times (q-1)$ matrix defined by

$$\mathbf{A} = \begin{pmatrix} \frac{-(q-1)}{y_1} & \cdots & \frac{1}{y_1} \\ \vdots & \ddots & \vdots \\ \frac{1}{y_{q-1}} & \cdots & \frac{-(q-1)}{y_{q-1}} \\ \frac{1}{y_q} & \cdots & \frac{1}{y_q} \end{pmatrix} \tag{4}$$

Then the objective is to minimize $\psi(\boldsymbol{t}) = f(\alpha(\boldsymbol{t}))$.

Since $\psi(\boldsymbol{t}) = f(\alpha(\boldsymbol{t}))$ is a quadratic function of the variable $\boldsymbol{t}$, we have

$$\psi(\boldsymbol{t}) = \psi(\mathbf{0}) + \sum_{i=1}^{q-1} \frac{\partial \psi(\mathbf{0})}{\partial t_i} t_i + \frac{1}{2} \sum_{i,j=1}^{q-1} \frac{\partial^2 \psi(\mathbf{0})}{\partial t_i \partial t_j} t_i t_j, \tag{5}$$

$$\frac{\partial \psi(\boldsymbol{t})}{\partial t_i} = \sum_{j=1}^{q} \frac{\partial f(\alpha(\boldsymbol{t}))}{\partial \alpha_j} \frac{\partial \alpha_j}{\partial t_i} = \sum_{j=1}^{q} F_j(\alpha(\boldsymbol{t})) - q \cdot F_i(\alpha(\boldsymbol{t})), \quad i = 1, \cdots, q-1, \tag{6}$$

Theorem 1. *Suppose $\alpha_{new} = \alpha(\boldsymbol{t}^*)$ is the optimal value obtained in the k-th iteration, with α be the initial value, then $f(\alpha) - f(\alpha_{new}) \geq \frac{\tau}{4\sqrt{q-1}} \cdot \|\alpha - \alpha_{new}\|$.*

Proof. We first consider the case that the coefficient of $t_i t_j$ in expanding expression of $\psi(\boldsymbol{t})$ equals to zero for all $i \neq j$ and equals to 1 or 0 for all $i = j$. In this case, the shape of function $\psi(\boldsymbol{t})$ is a regular hyper-paraboloid in $\mathbb{R}^q$. Let us introduce a series of intermediate points between $\mathbf{0}$ and $\boldsymbol{t}^*$ with definition as

$$\begin{cases} t_j^{(i)} = t_j^{(i-1)} + t_j^* \text{ if } & j = i \\ t_j^{(i)} = t_j^{(i-1)} & \forall \ \ j \neq i \end{cases}$$

From $\boldsymbol{t}^{(i-1)}$ to $\boldsymbol{t}^{(i)}$, only t_i changes, so in the single direction along t_i-axis

$$\psi(\boldsymbol{t}) = \psi(\boldsymbol{t}^{(i-1)}) + \frac{\partial \psi(\boldsymbol{t}^{(i-1)})}{\partial t_i} \cdot (t_i - t_i^{(i-1)}) + \frac{1}{2} \frac{\partial^2 \psi(\boldsymbol{t}^{(i-1)})}{\partial t_i^2} \cdot (t_i - t_i^{(i-1)})^2. \quad (7)$$

Suppose the optimal point in this direction with no constraints is $\boldsymbol{t}^{(i')}$, then

$$\frac{\partial \psi(\boldsymbol{t}^{(i')})}{\partial t_i} = \frac{\partial \psi(\boldsymbol{t}^{(i-1)})}{\partial t_i} + \frac{\partial^2 \psi(\boldsymbol{t}^{(i-1)})}{\partial t_i^2} (t_i^{(i')} - t_i^{(i-1)}) = 0. \quad (8)$$

Thus it follows from(7) and (8) that

$$\psi(\boldsymbol{t}^{(i')}) = \psi(\boldsymbol{t}^{(i-1)}) + \frac{1}{2} \frac{\partial \psi(\boldsymbol{t}^{(i-1)})}{\partial t_i} (t_i^{(i')} - t_i^{(i-1)}). \quad (9)$$

Since $t_i^* = t_i^{(i)} - t_i^{(i-1)}$ is the actual increment in the t_i-axis direction from $\mathbf{0}$ to $\boldsymbol{t}^*$ and $\psi(\boldsymbol{t})$ is a convex function of $\boldsymbol{t}$, there is

$$t_i^{(i)} - t_i^{(i-1)} = \lambda_i [t_i^{(i')} - t_i^{(i-1)}], \quad 0 \leq \lambda_i \leq 1. \quad (10)$$

From the convexity of $\psi(\boldsymbol{t})$, addition with equations (9) and (10), we have

$$\begin{aligned} \psi(\boldsymbol{t}^{(i)}) &\leq \psi(\boldsymbol{t}^{(i-1)}) + \lambda_i [\psi(\boldsymbol{t}^{(i')}) - \psi(\boldsymbol{t}^{(i-1)})] \\ &= \psi(\boldsymbol{t}^{(i-1)}) + \tfrac{1}{2} t_i^* \tfrac{\partial \psi(\boldsymbol{t}^{(i-1)})}{\partial t_i} \qquad \forall i = 1, \ldots, q-1. \end{aligned} \quad (11)$$

It follows that

$$\psi(\boldsymbol{t}^{(0)}) - \psi(\boldsymbol{t}^{(q-1)}) = \sum_{i=1}^{q-1} \left[\psi(\boldsymbol{t}^{(i-1)}) - \psi(\boldsymbol{t}^{(i)}) \right] \geq - \sum_{i=1}^{q-1} \frac{1}{2} t_i^* \frac{\partial \psi(\boldsymbol{t}^{(i-1)})}{\partial t_i}. \quad (12)$$

Since $\frac{\partial \psi(\boldsymbol{t})}{\partial t_i}$ only depends on t_i, and noting that $t_i^{(i-1)} = t_i^{(0)} = 0$, $t_i^* = t_i^{(q-1)}$, then we have $\frac{\partial \psi(\boldsymbol{t}^{(i-1)})}{\partial t_i} = \frac{\partial \psi(\mathbf{0})}{\partial t_i}$, $\forall i = 1, \ldots, q-1$. Thus (12) becomes

$$\psi(\mathbf{0}) - \psi(\boldsymbol{t}^*) \geq - \sum_{i=1}^{q-1} \frac{1}{2} t_i^* \frac{\partial \psi(\mathbf{0})}{\partial t_i} \quad (13)$$

We now examine $\frac{\partial \psi(\mathbf{0})}{\partial t_i}$. From (6) it is clear that the largest value of $|\frac{\partial \psi(\mathbf{0})}{\partial t_i}|$ and $|F_i(\alpha(\mathbf{0}))|$ occur at the same index. Suppose $\max_{i=1,\ldots,q-1}\{|\frac{\partial \psi(\mathbf{0})}{\partial t_i}|\} =$

$|\frac{\partial\psi(\mathbf{0})}{\partial t_{i0}}|$[1], where $F_{i_0}(\alpha(\mathbf{0})) = \min_{i=1,\ldots,q}\{F_i(\alpha(\mathbf{0}))\}$. For the working set $\{(i_1, j_1), \ldots, (i_{\frac{q}{2}}, j_{\frac{q}{2}})\}$, we have $F_{i_s}(\alpha(\mathbf{0})) < F_{j_s}(\alpha(\mathbf{0})) - \tau, \quad \forall s = 1, \ldots, q/2$. Thus from (6) we obtain that

$$\frac{\partial\psi(\mathbf{0})}{\partial t_{i0}} = \sum_{s=1}^{q/2}[F_{i_s}(\alpha(\mathbf{0})) - F_{i_0}(\alpha(\mathbf{0}))] + \sum_{s=1}^{q/2}[F_{j_s}(\alpha(\mathbf{0})) - F_{i_0}(\alpha(\mathbf{0}))] > \frac{q}{2}\cdot\tau$$

Consequently,

$$\max_{i=1,\ldots,q-1}\{|\frac{\partial\psi(\mathbf{0})}{\partial t_i}|\} > \frac{q}{2}\cdot\tau. \tag{14}$$

Next we examine the value of t_i^*. Note the assumption we made in the beginning, we'll know that variables t_i $(i = 1, ..., q-1)$ all move along exactly the same shape of parabola in the optimization, the only difference being their initial and end locations. It can be seen that if $\left|\frac{\partial\psi(\mathbf{0})}{\partial t_{i0}}\right| = max_{i=1,\ldots,q-1}\left\{\left|\frac{\partial\psi(\mathbf{0})}{\partial t_i}\right|\right\}$, i.e. variable t_{i_0} stands at the highest initial location on the parabola among these variables, then it also changes most while reaching its end location, which means

$$|t_{i_0}^*| = \max_{i=1,\ldots,q-1}\{|t_i^*|\}. \tag{15}$$

We now consider the sign of $\frac{\partial\psi(\mathbf{0})}{\partial t_i}$. Note that the objective of optimization is to minimize $\psi(\boldsymbol{t})$, therefore, $t_i^* \le 0$ if $\frac{\partial\psi(\mathbf{0})}{\partial t_i} \ge 0$, and $t_i^* \ge 0$ if $\frac{\partial\psi(\mathbf{0})}{\partial t_i} \le 0$. So $-\frac{1}{2}t_i^*\cdot\frac{\partial\psi(\mathbf{0})}{\partial t_i} \ge 0, \quad \forall i = 1, \ldots, q-1$, which together with (13) implies that

$$\psi(\mathbf{0}) - \psi(\boldsymbol{t}^*) \ge \sum_{i=1}^{q-1}\frac{1}{2}|t_i^*|\cdot|\frac{\partial\psi(\mathbf{0})}{\partial t_i}| \ge \frac{1}{2}|t_{i_0}^*|\cdot|\frac{\partial\psi(\mathbf{0})}{\partial t_{i_0}}| \ge \frac{1}{2}|t_{i_0}^*|\cdot\frac{q}{2}\tau,$$

that is,

$$f(\alpha) - f(\alpha_{new}) \ge \frac{1}{4}q\tau\cdot|t_{i_0}^*|. \tag{16}$$

Now let us evaluate $\|\alpha - \alpha_{new}\|$. From (3) and (4) it follows that

$$\|\alpha(0) - \alpha(\boldsymbol{t}^*)\|^2 = \|\mathbf{A}\boldsymbol{t}^*\|^2 = q^2\left(\sum_{i=1}^{q-1}(t_i^*)^2\right) - q\left(\sum_{i=1}^{q-1}t_i^*\right)^2 \le q^2\|\boldsymbol{t}^*\|^2,$$

then from this and (15) it is easy to see that

$$q\cdot\sqrt{q-1}\cdot|t_{i_0}^*| \ge q\cdot\sqrt{\sum_{i=1}^{q-1}t_i^{*2}} = q\cdot\|\boldsymbol{t}^*\| \ge \|\mathbf{A}\boldsymbol{t}^*\| = \|\alpha - \alpha_{new}\|. \tag{17}$$

Combining (16) and (17) gives

$$f(\alpha) - f(\alpha_{new}) \ge \frac{\tau}{4\sqrt{q-1}}\cdot\|\alpha - \alpha_{new}\|. \tag{18}$$

[1] For the case that $\max_{i=1,\ldots,q-1}\{|\frac{\partial\psi(\mathbf{0})}{\partial t_i}|\} = |\frac{\partial\psi(\mathbf{0})}{\partial t_{j0}}|$, a similar result holds as $\frac{\partial\psi(\mathbf{0})}{\partial t_{j0}} < -\frac{q}{2}\cdot\tau$.

Finally, we consider the case that the assumption about expanding expression of $\psi(\boldsymbol{t})$ does not hold. In this case there exists a transformation matrix $\mathbf{P}$ from current basis to a canonical basis of $\mathbf{A}^\top Q\mathbf{A}$, so that $\mathbf{P}^\top(\mathbf{A}^\top Q\mathbf{A})\mathbf{P}$ is a canonical form. Furthermore, since Q is positive semi-definite, then there exists a matrix $\mathbf{D}$ that transforms the canonical matrix above into a diagonal matrix $\mathbf{I}'$ with the diagonal elements 1 or 0. Thus, if we change the definition of vector $\boldsymbol{t}$ into $\alpha(\boldsymbol{t}) = \alpha + (\mathbf{APD}) \cdot \boldsymbol{t}$, then the quadratic terms of $\psi(\boldsymbol{t})$ becomes

$$\frac{1}{2}(\mathbf{APD}\boldsymbol{t})^\top \cdot Q \cdot (\mathbf{APD}\boldsymbol{t}) = \frac{1}{2}\boldsymbol{t}^\top \cdot \mathbf{D}^\top[\mathbf{P}^\top(\mathbf{A}^\top Q\mathbf{A})\mathbf{P}]\mathbf{D} \cdot \boldsymbol{t} = \frac{1}{2}\boldsymbol{t}^\top \cdot \mathbf{I}' \cdot \boldsymbol{t}.$$

From this it is found that the coefficients of all the new $t_i t_j$ terms are equal to zero for all $i \neq j$, and equal to 1 or 0 for all $i = j$. Thus this case is reduced to the first case discussed above. The proof of the theorem is thus complete. ■

We now give the convergence proof of our new decomposition algorithm.

Theorem 2. *The sequence $\{\alpha(k)\}$ obtained from the new decomposition algorithm converges for a given positive parameter τ and an even number q_m.*

Proof. From (18) it follows that for $k \geq 0$

$$\begin{aligned} f(\alpha(k)) - f(\alpha(k+1)) &\geq \frac{\tau}{4\sqrt{q-1}} \cdot \|\alpha(k) - \alpha(k+1)\| \\ &\geq \frac{\tau}{4\sqrt{q_m - 1}} \cdot \|\alpha(k) - \alpha(k+1)\|. \end{aligned}$$

By repeated application of the above inequality, together with the use of triangle inequality, we get

$$f(\alpha(k)) - f(\alpha(k+l)) \geq \frac{\tau}{4\sqrt{q_m - 1}} \cdot \|\alpha(k) - \alpha(k+l)\|, \quad \forall k, l \geq 0. \tag{19}$$

Since $\{f(\alpha(k))\}$ is decreasing and bounded from below, there exists an f_τ such that $f(\alpha(k)) \to f_\tau$. This together with (19) implies that $\{\alpha(k)\}$ is a Cauchy sequence, thus the sequence $\{\alpha(k)\}$ converges to some value α_τ. ■

4 Conclusions

In this paper we proposed a new decomposition algorithm for SVMs based on the concept of τ-violating set. Moreover, the convergence of the new algorithm is also proved. Experiments have also show its convergence, and tightness of bound of $\alpha(k)$'s movement given by (18). (In fact, the two sides of (18) are almost equal in some iterations.) It should be remarked that the mathematical skills used in this paper should be inspiring for further theoretical research of the SVMs decomposition methods.

The concept of τ-violating pairs was first introduced in [9], where a generalized SMO algorithm was proposed which chooses a τ-violating pair as the working set. The size of the working set selected in [9] is restricted to be $q = 2$, so no optimization procedure is needed. There are other decomposition algorithms which use different strategies to select the working set (e.g. Joachims' SVM^{light} algorithm [6] and Platt's SMO algorithm [5]). In Table I below we compare our algorithm with some of the existing decomposition algorithms.

Table 1. Comparison among some decomposition algorithms

Algorithms	working set size q	working set selection	convergence	condition
SVM^{light} [6]	$q \geq 2$	most KKT-violating pairs	convergence	$\min_I(\min(eig(Q_{II}))) > 0$
SMO [5]	$q = 2$	most KKT-violating pair	convergence	no
Generalized SMO [9]	$q = 2$	τ-violating pair	convergence	no
Our New Algorithm	$q \geq 2$	τ-violating set	convergence	no

References

1. Burges, C.J.C.: A Tutorial on Support Vector Machines for Pattern Recognition. Data Mining and Knowledge Discovery, VOL. 2, (1998) 121–167
2. Scholkopf, B., Burges, C.J.C., Smola, A.J. (eds.): Advances in Kernel Methods-Support Vector Learning. MA: MIT Press, Cambridge. (1998)
3. Vapnik, V.: The Nature of Statistical Learning Theory. Springer, New York. (1995)
4. Vapnik, V.: Statistical Learning Theory. Wiley, New York. (1998)
5. Platt, J.C.: Fast Training of Support Vector Machines Using Sequential Minimal Optimization. Advances in Kernel Methods-Support Vector Learning. Scholkopf, B., Burges, C.J.C., Smola, A.J. (eds.) MA: MIT Press, Cambridge. (1998)
6. Joachims, T.: Making Large-scale SVM Learning Practical. Advances in Kernel Methods-Support Vector Learning. Scholkopf, B., Burges, C.J.C., Smola, A.J. (eds.) MA: MIT Press, Cambridge. (1998)
7. Osuna, E., Freund, R., Girosi, F.: Trainig Support Vector Machines: An Application to Face Detection. Proceedings of CVPR'97, (1997)
8. Saunders, C., Stitson, M.O., Weston, J., Bottou, L., Scholkopf, B., Smola, A.J.: Support Vector Machines Reference Manual. Royal Holloway, University of London, U.K., Tech. Rep. CSD-TR-98-03. (1998)
9. Keerthi, S., Gilbert, E.: Convergence of a Generalized SMO Algorithm for SVM Classifier Design. Machine Learning, VOL. 46, (2002) 351–360
10. Keerthi, S., Shevade, S., Bhattacharyya, C., Murthy, K.: Improvements to Platt's SMO Algorithm for SVM Classifier Design. Neural Computation, VOL. 13, (2001) 637–649
11. Lin, C.J.: On the Convergence of the Decomposition Method for Support Vector Machines. IEEE Transactions on Neural Networks, VOL. 12, (2001) 1288–1298
12. Lin, C.J.: Asymptotic Convergence of an SMO Algorithm without Any Assumptions. IEEE Transactions on Neural Networks, VOL. 13, (2002) 248–250
13. Lin, C.J.: A Formal Analysis of Stopping Criteria of Decomposition Methods for Support Vector Machines. IEEE Transactions on Neural Networks, VOL. 13, (2002) 1045–1052

Online Learning of Bayesian Network Parameters with Incomplete Data

Sungsoo Lim and Sung-Bae Cho

Dept. of Computer Science, Yonsei University
Shinchon-dong, Seodaemun-ku,
Seoul 120-749, Korea
lss@sclab.yonsei.ac.kr, sbcho@cs.yonsei.ac.kr

Abstract. Learning Bayesian network is a problem to obtain a network that is the most appropriate to training dataset based on the evaluation measures given. It is studied to decrease time and effort for designing Bayesian networks. In this paper, we propose a novel online learning method of Bayesian network parameters. It provides high flexibility through learning from incomplete data and provides high adaptability on environments through online learning. We have confirmed the performance of the proposed method through the comparison with Voting EM algorithm, which is an online parameter learning method proposed by Cohen, *et al.*

1 Introduction

The parameters of a Bayesian network (BN) are determined by the use of expert opinion or by learning from data [1]. The former has the advantage of reflecting experts' knowledge, but it is a difficult and time-consuming process. Moreover, it is not clear whether the network designed by the experts is really the most appropriate model for the domain. Although the latter, learning from data, can overcome the problems of the former, it is not always available because the data cannot be ready at all the time the BN is constructed. Furthermore, it cannot consider the change of environments.

To overcome these limitations, online learning methods are discussed [2], [3]. Online learning of BN parameters is a method that learns parameters of BN using the given data and parameters at time t. Cohen, *et al.* proposed Voting EM algorithm which adopts EM(η) algorithm to online learning [4], [5]. Zhang, *et al.* verified the usefulness of Voting EM algorithm by utilizing it to flood decision-supporting system [6].

Although, in the case of complete data, Voting EM algorithm can quickly converge to the proper parameters, in the case of incomplete data, it adapts parameters partially and incorrectly. It is because Voting EM algorithm is based on EM algorithm. EM algorithm can estimate the missing data by using many data, but Voting EM algorithm, which uses only one data, cannot do well. In this paper, we propose a novel method for online BN parameter learning which can overcome the limitation of Voting EM algorithm.

D.-S. Huang, K. Li, and G.W. Irwin (Eds.): ICIC 2006, LNAI 4114, pp. 309 – 314, 2006.

2 Voting EM Algorithm

Let x_i be a node in the network that takes any value from the set $\{x_i^1, x_i^2, \cdots, x_i^p\}$ and π_i be the set of parents of in the network that takes one of the configurations denoted by $\{\pi_i^1, \pi_i^2, \ldots, \pi_i^p\}$ then we can define an entry in the CPT (Conditional Probability Table) of the variable x_i as $\theta_{ijk} = P(x_i = x_i^k \mid \pi_i = \pi_i^j)$. Online learning of BN parameters is to get the new set of parameters Θ_{t+1} from the given set of parameters Θ_t and the observed data d_t at time t as follows:

$$\Theta_{t+1} = \arg\max_{\Theta}[\eta L(\Theta \mid D) - d(\Theta, \Theta_t)]\cdot \tag{1}$$

Where $L(\Theta|D)$ denotes log likelihood and $d(\Theta, \Theta_t)$ denotes the distance between the sets of parameters, Θ and Θ_t. Therefore, Θ_{t+1} is the new set of parameters which has high log likelihood with given data set D and the character of the set of parameter Θ_t. η, which is the importance of log likelihood comparing with distance factor, denotes learning rate. Bauer, *et al.* solve the maximization problem of Eq. (1) with constrains that $\Sigma_k\, \theta_{ijk} = 1$ for all i and j, called EM(η) algorithm [3]. Cohen, *et al.* proposed Voting EM algorithm which adapted EM(η) algorithm to online learning [4], [5].

$$\theta_{ijk}^{t+1} = \begin{cases} (1-\eta)\theta_{ijk}^t + \eta, & \text{if } x_i = x_i^k \text{ at } d_t \text{ and } P(\pi_i^j \mid d_t, \theta_t) \neq 0 \\ (1-\eta)\theta_{ijk}^t, & \text{if } x_i \neq x_i^k \text{ at } d_t \text{ and } P(\pi_i^j \mid d_t, \theta_t) \neq 0 \\ \theta_{ijk}^t, & \text{otherwise} \end{cases} \cdot \tag{2}$$

As shown in the Eq. (2), Voting EM algorithm only learns the parameter θ_{ijk}^{t+1} when the node x_i is observed. Moreover, even though the node x_i is observed, if all of the parent nodes of x_i are not observed, it does not learn correctly because it does not consider the relation between the node x_i and unobserved parent nodes.

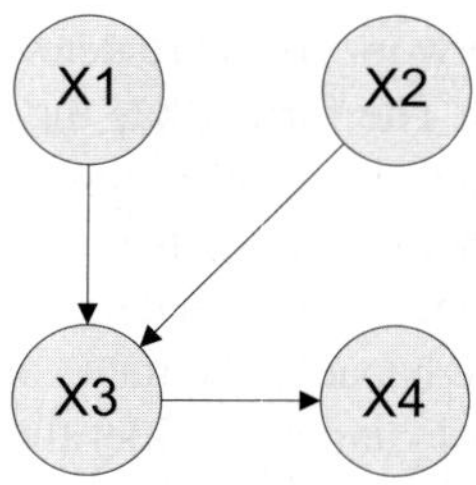

Fig. 1. Simple Bayesian network

For example, if there exists Bayesian network like Fig. 1 and if the node x_3 is unobserved node ($d_t = \{x_1^a, x_2^b, x_3^?, x_4^d\}$), the parameters at the node x_3 are not learned and the parameters at the node x_4 are learned without considering the effect of the node x_3 as follows: In the case of $P(x_3^j \mid d_t, \Theta_t) \neq 0$, if $x_4^k \neq x_4^d$ then $\theta_{4jk}^{t+1} = (1-\eta)\, \theta_{4jk}^t$ and if $x_4^k = x_4^d$ then $\theta_{4jk}^{t+1} = (1-\eta)\, \theta_{4jk}^t + \eta$. Otherwise, $\theta_{4jk}^{t+1} = \theta_{4jk}^t$. In other words, if the node x_3 is unobserved, the node x_4 only learns the probability $P(x_4 = x_4^d \mid d_t, \Theta_t)$ and it cannot correctly learn the relation between x_3 and x_4 which means $P(x_4 = x_4^d \mid \pi_4^j, d_t, \Theta_t)$. In this paper, we propose a novel method to overcome such limitations of Voting EM algorithm which can learn BN parameters with incomplete data.

3 Proposed Learning Method

The data used for learning BN parameters online are the observed value $\hat{x}_i^k$, which denotes the value of observed state of each node x_i, and the predicted value $P(x_i = x_i^k \mid d_t - \{x_i\}, \Theta_t)$, which shows how well the set of parameters Θ_t can predict the situation d_t. The value of $\hat{x}_i^k$ is 1 when the state of node x_i is k; otherwise, it becomes 0. Using these data, we first find the set of parameters $\overline{\Theta}$ well fit for the data d_t, and get the next set of parameters Θ_{t+1} by exponential smoothing method as following equation:

$$\forall\, ijk,\ \theta_{ijk}^{t+1} = (1-\eta)\theta_{ijk}^{t} + \eta\overline{\theta}_{ijk}\,. \tag{3}$$

where η denotes the rate of convergence.

Now let us find out how we get the set of parameters $\overline{\Theta}$. If we have the Bayesian network structure that consists of n nodes, let $O = \{x_{O_1}, x_{O_2}, \cdots, x_{O_a}\}$ be the set of observed nodes except x_i and $U = \{x_{U_1}, x_{U_2}, \cdots, x_{U_{n-a-1}}\}$ be the set of unobserved nodes except x_i. Then we can get the predicted value $P(x_i = x_i^k \mid d_t - \{x_i\}, \Theta_t)$ by Eq. (4) and it can be rewritten as Eq. (5), which consists of CPT variables, by using the independent assumption and chain rules.

$$P(x_i = x_i^k \mid d_t - \{x_i\}, \Theta_t) = \frac{\sum_{\text{for all state of } x \in U} P(x_{o_1} = x_{o_1}^{s_1}, \cdots, x_{o_a} = x_{o_a}^{s_a}, x_i = x_i^k, x_{u_1}, \cdots, x_{u_{n-a-1}})}{\sum_{\text{for all state of } x \in U \cup \{x_i\}} P(x_{o_1} = x_{o_1}^{s_1}, \cdots, x_{o_a} = x_{o_a}^{s_a}, x_i, x_{u_1} \cdots, x_{u_{n-a-1}})}\,. \tag{4}$$

$$\frac{\sum_{\text{for all state of } x \in U} P(x_{o_1} = s_1 \mid \pi_{o_1}) \times \cdots \times P(x_{o_a} = s_a \mid \pi_{o_a}) \times P(x_i \mid \pi_i) \times P(x_{u_1} \mid \pi_{u_1}) \times \cdots \times P(x_{u_{n-a-1}} \mid \pi_{u_{n-a-1}})}{\sum_{\text{for all state of } x \in U \cup \{x_i\}} P(x_{o_1} = s_1 \mid \pi_{o_1}) \times \cdots \times P(x_{o_a} = s_a \mid \pi_{o_a}) \times P(x_i \mid \pi_i) \times P(x_{u_1} \mid \pi_{u_1}) \times \cdots \times P(x_{u_{n-a-1}} \mid \pi_{u_{n-a-1}})}\,. \tag{5}$$

Through canceling, we can simplify Eq. (5) to $A / (A + B)$, where A and B consist of the sum of multiplication of CPT variables. Therefore, we can update the parameters as the following. If the observed value $\hat{x}_i^k$ is 1, it increases A and decreases B; if the value is 0, it decreases A and increases B. However, there are too many factors consisting of A and B, and so it requires much computational time to apply for all i and k. We assume that only the parent nodes of x_i affect the node x_i and the affected parent nodes are independent. With these assumptions, we can rewrite Eq. (5) as Eq. (6).

We update the parameters, which are related with the predicted value $P(x_i = x_i^k \mid d_t - \{x_i\}, \Theta_t)$ by using Eq. (6) and the value of observed node $\hat{x}_i^k$ according to the weight to the predicted value.

$$\begin{aligned} P(x_i = x_i^k \mid d_t - \{x_i\}, \Theta_t) &= \sum_{\text{for all } j} P(x_i = x_i^k \mid \pi_i^j, d_t - \{x_i\}, \Theta_t) P(\pi_i^j \mid d_t - \{x_i\}, \Theta_t) \\ &= \sum_{j \in P(\pi_i^j \mid d_t - \{x_i\}, \theta^t) \neq 0} \theta_{ijk}^t \prod_{x_a^b \in \pi_i^j} P(x_a^b \mid d_t - \{x_i\}, \Theta_t) \end{aligned} \tag{6}$$

The following pseudo code shows the whole process of the proposed method.

Pseudo code of proposed method

```
procedure OnlineLearning(d_t)
begin
  for all x_i∈S    //S is the structure of BN
    for k:=0 to p_i
      if x̂_i^k :=1 then Update(i,k,1.0);
      else if x̂_i^k :=0 then Update(i,k,-1.0);
  for all ω_ijk ∈ Ω   //Ω is a set of weights for updating _t
    if ω_ijk > 0 then θ̄_ijk := (1- ω_ijk) + _ijk^t + ω_ijk;
    else θ̄_ijk := (1- ω_ijk) + _ijk^t;
  for all i, j ∈ Θ̄
    normalize to Σ_∀k θ̄_ijk=1;
  for all θ̄_ijk ∈ Θ̄
    _ijk^t+1 := (1-η) _ijk^t + η θ̄_ijk;
end

procedure Update(i,j,w)
begin
  if w<threshold then return;
  for all π_i^j ∈ S
    ω_ijk := ω_ijk + wP( _i^j | d_t-{x_i}, _t);
  for all π_i^j ∈ S
    if P( _i^j | d_t-{x_i}, _t) ≠0 then
      for all x_a^b ∈ _i^j and x_a at d_t=null
        Update(a, b, w _ijk^t ∏_{x_c^d ∈ π_i^j -{x_a^b}} P(x_c^d | d_t-{x_i}, _t));
end
```

4 Experiments

We have conducted a comparison test with Voting EM algorithm at Asia network to manifest the performance of the proposed method. We have collected 10,000 data as the samples of learning data: To test the adaptability, we get the first 5,000 of the data from the real network and the last 5,000 of the data from the modified network where the probability of the attack of tubercle when he or she visits Asia to 40%.

The comparison test has been conducted by changing the missing rate of data and the learning rate. The missing rate that is unobserved value at the tuberculosis node is changed from 0% to 100% with 10% intervals and the learning rate is changed from 1% to 50% with 1% intervals. We evaluate the learned parameters using the distance between the learned parameter and real parameter as follows:

$$D(\theta,\theta') = \sum_{\text{for all } i,j,k} |\, \theta_{ijk} - \theta'_{ijk} \,| \cdot \tag{7}$$

Fig. 2 shows the distance of Voting EM algorithm and the proposed method from the real parameters in terms of missing rate and learning rate. As shown in Fig. 3(a), when the given data is complete, both algorithms manifest the same performance:

When the data is complete, the proposed method is the same as the Voting EM algorithm. However, when the data is incomplete, Voting EM algorithm shows great difference when compared with the result of the complete data. It shows that Voting EM algorithm is weak when the incomplete data is used. Especially, when the missing rate is 100% (no data at tuberculosis node), it has learned nothing. On the other hand, the proposed method is robust at incomplete data. In the case of learning rate, Fig. 2(b) shows that the proposed method performs better than Voting EM algorithm. Moreover, it shows that the learning 2% provides the best performance.

Fig. 3 shows the convergence of the proposed method and Voting EM algorithm to real value according to the missing rate at tuberculosis node. As shown in Fig. 3(a), the proposed method provides better performance than Voting EM algorithm and Fig. 3(b) shows that the proposed method can acknowledge the change of environments though Voting EM algorithm learns nothing when the missing rate is 100%. Although it seems that the proposed method shows worse performance than Voting EM algorithm after time 9000 in Fig. 3(b), if we compare it with all the other parameters, the proposed method performs better than Voting EM algorithm as shown Fig. 2(a).

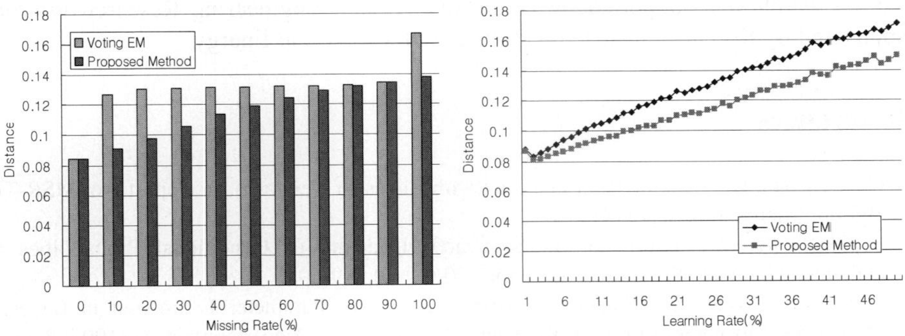

(a) Result through the missing rate (b) Result through the learning rate

Fig. 2. Result of comparison test

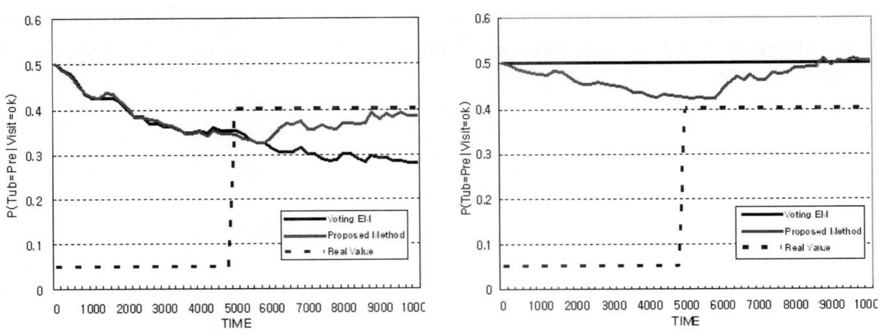

(a) Missing Rate 50% (b) Missing Rate 100%

Fig. 3. Convergence to real value at node *tuberculosis* using $\eta = 0.02$

5 Concluding Remarks

Online BN learning is needed for modeling the variable environment or the change of user's preference. Voting EM algorithm is one of good methods to learn BN parameters online. However, there are limits to its capability in learning with the incomplete data. In this paper, we have proposed an online learning method of BN parameters which works well with incomplete data. We have confirmed the performance of the proposed method through the comparison with Voting EM algorithm.

For the future works, it is required to analyze the convergence of the proposed method and conduct more experiments in realistic domains. In addition, by adding a mechanism in order to automatically adjust the learning rate η, we can obtain an enhanced version of the online learning method that learns more quickly than the present method.

Acknowledgments

This research was supported by Brain Science and Engineering Research Program sponsored by Korean Ministry of Commerce, Industry and Energy.

References

1. Heckerman, D.: A Tutorial on Learning with Bayesian Networks. In Report No. MSR-TR-95-06, Microsoft Research (1995)
2. Spiegelhalter, D., Lauritzen, S.: Sequential Updating of Conditional Probabilities on Directed Graphical Structures. Networks, 20 (1990) 579-605
3. Bauer, E., Koller, D., Singer, Y.: Update Rules for Parameter Estimation in Bayesian Networks. Proceedings of the 13th. Annual Conference on Uncertainty in AI (1997) 3-13
4. Cohen, I., Bronstein, A., Cozman, F. G.: Online Learning of Bayesian Network Parameters. In Report No. HPL-2001-55, HP Labs (2001)
5. Cohen, I., Bronstein, A., Cozman, F. G.: Adaptive Online Learning of Bayesian Network Parameters. In Report No. HPL-2001-156, HP Labs (2001)
6. Zhang, S. Z., Yu, H., Ding, H., Yang, N. H., Wang, X. K.: An Application of Online Learning Algorithm for Bayesian Network Parameter. Machine Learning and Cybernetics, 1 (2003) 153-156

A Genetic Algorithm for Optimization of Bandwidth Assignment in Hose-Modeled VPN*

Yuanping Zou, Zhengkun Mi, and Xudong Meng

College of Communications & Information Engineering,
Nanjing University of Posts & Telecommunications
zyuanp@vip.sina.com, mizk@njupt.edu.cn

Abstract. Quality of Service (QoS) and Traffic Engineering (TE) capabilities are two important techniques in IP networks to support real-time applications. Multi Protocol Label Switching (MPLS) plays an important role in terms of QoS and TE provisioning. The paper investigates the optimal resource allocation in MPLS-based VPN. Firstly the hose model is introduced; then, the traffic engineering using hose model to provide multi-VPN services in MPLS network is formulated. A genetic algorithm (GA) for the optimization of the bandwidth assignment in hose-modeled VPN to provide multi services is presented. The optimal model and instances of the algorithm are given too. The results of the instances show that the proposed method can balance the network load and is simple to be implemented.

1 Introduction

Nowadays, VPN based on MPLS is becoming prevalent. How to allocate the LSP bandwidth plays an important role in the ensuring of the VPN's QoS. The basic requirement of VPN is to improve the utilization of network resource while satisfying the user's profiled-traffic demand, that is to say, the bandwidth reserved for VPN shall be as little as possible while the QoS of VPN service is satisfied.

Another requirement is to avoid over-utilizing of some network resources while other resources are under-utilized, which is the problem that TE must resolve. The main object of TE is to optimize the routing of network traffic and to balance the network load while improving the utilization of network resources and ensuring the traffic performance. Differentiated Services (DiffServ) and MPLS proposed by IETF are promising technologies to implement the TE [1,2].

Generally, the pipe model is used in the optimization of bandwidth allocation in MPLS network. In the pipe model the VPN customers have to specify QoS requirements and the traffic load between each pair of endpoints for each type of traffic. But the traffic is stochastic in VPN application and the users are normally unable to predict the traffic load between each pair of endpoints. What

* The research is funded by the Chinese National Science Foundation under grant number 60472105 and in part by NUPT Research Foundation (NY 2005-002) and Jiangsu Provincial Education Bureau Doctoral Program Foundation (JS 2002-10).

D.-S. Huang, K. Li, and G.W. Irwin (Eds.): ICIC 2006, LNAI 4114, pp. 315–323, 2006.

the user can give is the bandwidth that shall be provided for each site. Two values are given for each site: B_{in}, the capacity required for aggregate outgoing traffic from the endpoint into the network (to other endpoints of the VPN) and B_{out}, the capacity required for aggregate incoming traffic from the network into the endpoints (from other endpoints of the VPN), the network provider should guarantee the QoS of the service among all sites of the VPN when the injecting traffic of each site is no more than its B_{in} and receiving traffic of each site is no more than its B_{out}. Since the traditional pipe model is not suitable for VPN services, Duffield gave a hose model. As mentioned in [3,4], the hose model provides customers with the following advantages over the pipe model: (1) only B_{in} and B_{out} per hose endpoint need to be specified, as compared to the bandwidth for each pipe between pairs of hose endpoints in pipe model; (2) flexibility-traffic load from and to a hose endpoint can be distributed arbitrarily among other endpoints if the bandwidth of each endpoint is not violated; and (3) multiplexing gain among the same VPN users.

Tequila task group of IETF presented a heuristic approach for bandwidth allocation in multi-service networks in [5]. The approach uses the traditional gradient projection method. In the method not only the initial bandwidth assignment needs to be given but also the first and second derivatives of objective function have to be computed. So the objective function must be continuous, differentiable and convex. Practically, sometimes the objective function does not possess the"nice" properties. Kumar in [6] proposed an algorithm using optimal VPN tree for provisioning VPN, but the algorithm assumes that the link capacity is infinite. The algorithm is not applicable when the link capacity is finite. This paper gives a GA for the optimization of bandwidth assignment in hose-modeled VPN. Neither the initial bandwidth assignment nor the objective function needs to be continuous, differentiable and convex in the algorithm. Furthermore it is able to balance the traffic load effectively.

2 Notations and Definitions

Notation	Description
$TT^k_{d,i}$	Hose traffic trunk of the class k service of VPN d rooted at i, where $i \in \{VPNd\}$
$D^k_{d,i}$	The max traffic load can be injected to the networks from hose traffic trunk $TT^k_{d,i}$
H	The set of hose traffic trunks
s	Hose traffic trunk tree corresponding to $TT^k_{d,i}$
S	The set of hose traffic trunks trees
$x^k_{d,s}$	Bandwidth allocated to the tree $s \in S$

Definition 1. *Hose traffic trunk: A hose traffic trunk is the aggregation of a set of traffic flows with similar QoS requirements. Each traffic trunk is associated with an ingress and a set of egress nodes. In this paper, a hose is also identical with a traffic trunk.*

Definition 2. *QoS hop-count constraint:Assume that a link has a worst delay and loss probability bounds for each type of PHB corresponding to the max transmit delay and the max loss probability of the link. We can accumulate the max delay and the max loss probability of links in a path, thus the constraints of end-to-end delay and end-to-end loss probability is converted to QoS hop-count constraints. Finally, the more severe hop-count constraint is selected as QoS hop-count constraint.*

Definition 3. *Hose traffic trunk tree: Trees that root at the ingress site of a hose and termite at egress sites of a hose and the only path in the tree from the source endpoint to other destination endpoint satisfies QoS hop-count constraint of the hose. Generally, there are several trees of hose traffic trunk corresponding to a hose.*

Definition 4. *Bandwidth of a tree: Same bandwidth is allocated to all links in a tree, the bandwidth is called bandwidth of a tree.*

3 Problem Statement and Modeling

3.1 Hose Model

A hose is the interface for customers (sites) to access a network. A customer of a VPN can send traffic to the network without knowledge of the point to point demand. Using the hose model, the amount of bandwidth allocated to access links and core links can be decreased.

As shown in Fig. 1, the VPN is composed of three sites. Assume the maximum sending rate and receiving rate for each site is 1Mbps. For the hose rooted at site 1, if we reserve the bandwidth using pipe model, we require two pipes, allocate bandwidth of 6Mbps to core links and 4Mbps to access links. However if hose model is used, only one hose is needed, bandwidth of 4Mbps is allocated to core links and 3Mbps is allocated to access links.

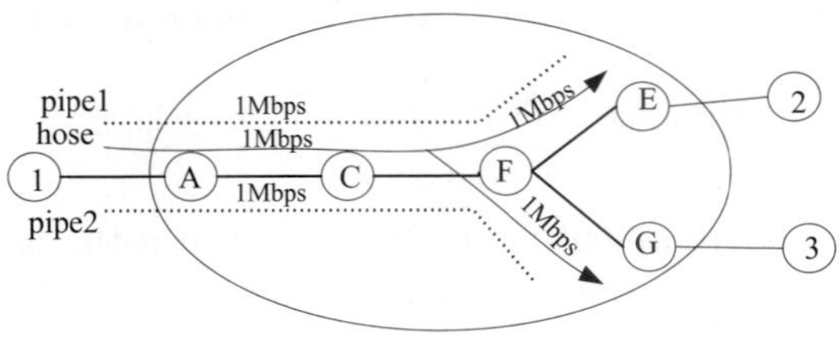

Fig. 1. Efficiency implications of the hose trunk model

Parameters of service level subscriber for a hose model include: VPN member, ingress, egresses, the maximum traffic load that an ingress is able to inject to the network, the maximum traffic load from the network to the ingress of the hose and the associated QoS.

3.2 Problem Statement

The network can be expressed as $G = (V, E)$, where V is the set of network nodes and E is the set of links between adjacent nodes. Assume that there are N nodes and L links. For each link $(m, n) \in E$, the following parameters need to be allocated: link capacity $b_{(m,n)}$, percent of bandwidth allocated to $k \in K$ type service, h^k , the set of PHB classes K supported by the link, maximum delay $D^k_{(m,n)}$ and maximum loss probability $L^k_{(m,n)}$ for each type of services. When implementing traffic engineering in multi service environment, we can carry out different bandwidth constraints for different type of services[7], thus transforming traffic engineering in multi service environment into several independent traffic engineering in single service environment. In this paper, firstly, the traffic is classified as different hoses according to the QoS of the traffic and different types of hose traffic trunks are mapped to different class of hoses respectively, then traffic load is balanced by several trees of hose traffic trunk for each hose.

3.3 Objectives of TE

One of the primary objectives of TE is to avoid over-loading of some network resources while other network resources are under-loaded; the other objective is to minimize the overall network cost while satisfying the QoS requirements of all trunks as long as their traffic is within the trunk's bandwidth limit. If a function $F_{(m,n)}$ associated to a link (m, n) is used, the above objectives can be associated with the following optimization criteria[5]:

$$\text{Minimize}\left(\max_{(m,n)\in E} F_{(m,n)}\right). \tag{1}$$

$$\text{Minimize}\left(\sum_{(m,n)\in E)} F_{(m,n)}\right). \tag{2}$$

The first criterion attempts to minimize the maximum utilization among all the links, hence avoid over-utilizing parts of the network. The other criterion tries to keep up a low overall network cost. We define a compromise between them as follows:

$$\text{Minimize} \sum_{(m,n)\in E} (F_{(m,n)})^n, n \geq 1. \tag{3}$$

Where n is a parameter representing a tradeoff between the maximum utilization among all the links and overall network cost.
When $n = 1$, only overall network cost is considered, if $n = \infty$, only the maximum utilization is considered.

3.4 GA Formulation

Let $z^k_{(m,n)}$ be traffic load in the link(m, n) after all k class of traffic demands are allocated to the trees. Let $f(z^k_{(m,n)})$ be:

$$f(z^k_{(m,n)}) = \begin{cases} (\frac{z^k_{(m,n)}}{b_{(m,n)} - z^k_{(m,n)}})^n & \text{if } z^k_{(m,n)} \leq h^k b_{(m,n)} \\ pent * (\frac{h^k b_{(m,n)}}{b_{(m,n)} - h^k b_{(m,n)}})^n & \text{if } z^k_{(m,n)} > h^k b_{(m,n)} \end{cases} . \quad (4)$$

Where *pent* is penalty coefficient.

Let $z = [z^k_{(m,n)}]$, $x = [x^k_{d,s}]$ be a vector of size 1-by-L and a vector of size 1-by-M (M is the number of all trees for class k service) respectively.

We have:

$$\mathbf{z} = \mathbf{x}' * Q. \quad (5)$$

Where, Q is a $L * M$ matrix called tree–link incidence matrix.

Each row in the matrix corresponds to a tree and each column in the matrix associates with one link.

If tree i uses link j, the element Q_{ij} in the matrix is 1, otherwise, it is 0.

The problem of bandwidth assignment in Hose-modeled VPN for class k service is formulated by the following form in a GA:

$$\text{Minimize} \sum_{(m,n)\in E} f(z^k_{(m,n)}). \quad (6)$$

$$\text{s.t.} \sum_{s\in S} x^k_{d,s} \leq D^k_{d,i} \text{ For all } TT^k_{d,i} \in H. \quad (7)$$

$$0 \leq x^k_{d,s} \leq D^k_{d,i}. \quad (8)$$

For each hose, $TT^k_{d,i}$ is the sum of bandwidth allocated to independent trees of a hose that must satisfy constraint (7).

Constraint (8) is lower and upper bounds of independent variables respectively.

In above problem, the network topology, link capacity, $D^k_{d,i}$, the max traffic load can be injected to the networks from hose traffic trunk $TT^k_{d,i}$ and trees of each hose are given and $x^k_{d,s}$ is decision variable. So the number of independent decision variable, w is:

$$w = u * (v - 1). \quad (9)$$

Where u, v are the number of hoses of class service and the number of trees associated to each hose.

4 Optimal Algorithm Based on GA for Bandwidth Assignment

4.1 Solution Representation

A string of bandwidth allocated to trees is represented by a chromosome and each gene represents bandwidth allocated to a tree. Real-valued code technique is used .A real-valued code representation moves the original problem closer to the problem representation which offers higher precision with more consistent results across replications.

4.2 Fitness Function

Fitness function must give a high fitness for chromosomes with lower objective function values. The fitness function is defined as:

$$F(z^k_{(m,n)}) = const - \sum_{(m,n)\in E} f(z^k_{(m,n)}). \tag{10}$$

In the formulation, *const* is a large constant.

4.3 Genetic Operators

Genetic operators are as following:

- Population size is ten times of the number of independent variable
- Roulette wheel selection together with elite children maintained parent
- Intermediate crossover, with crossover fraction 0.85 [8]
- Using adaptive and feasible mutation, mutation step size and direction are adaptive and the solution after each mutation must be feasible [8].

5 Numerical Experiments and Results

We evaluate our algorithms by simulation using Matlab genetic algorithm toolbox in a network which has 10 nodes and 9 bidirectional core links.

The network topology, as well as the labels of nodes and links is shown in Fig. 2. The number above the link is the link capacity and links without capacity label is with infinite capacity.

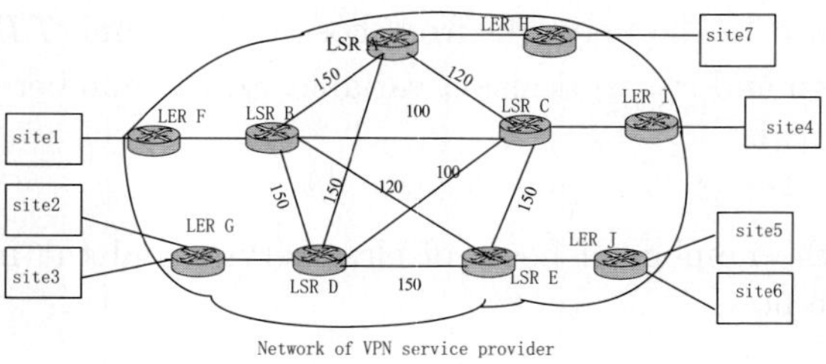

Fig. 2. Network topology

There are three VPNs that have subscribed SLS from provider. VPN1 consists of site1, site3 and site5, VPN2 consists of site2, site4 and site6, VPN3 consists of site3, site4 and site7. There are three types of services: EF, AF and BE. The values of simulation parameters are shown in table 1.

Since an edge node only accesses to a core node, only links between core nodes are considered. In order to balance the load, the links superposed among trees corresponding to a hose is as little as possible.

Table 1. The values of simulation parameters

Traffic type	Max. bandwidth constraint	Hop-count constraint	The number. of trees of a hose	Total trees of hoses	The number of independent variable
EF	10%	4	2	18	9
AF	80%	5	3	27	18

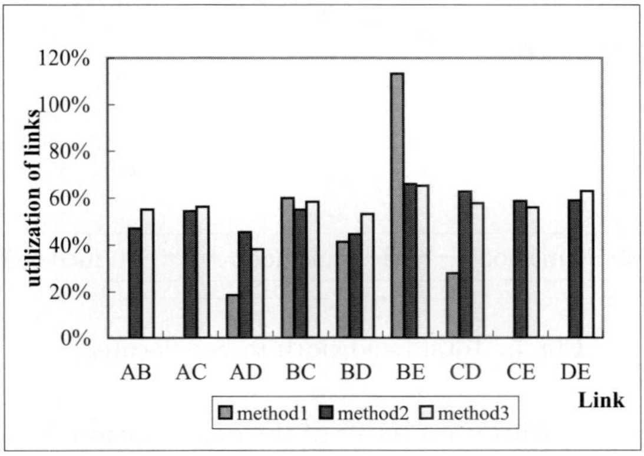

Fig. 3. Utilization rate of links

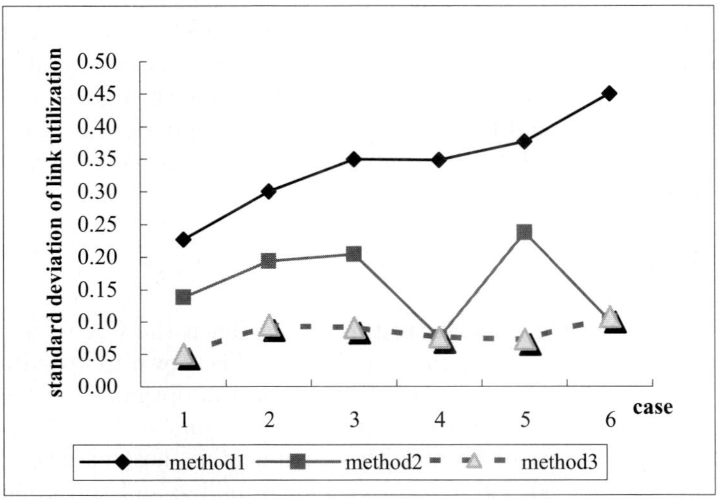

Fig. 4. Standard deviation of link utilization

6 groups of data are used in optimization and the result is compared with the method proposed in [5] and the method given by Kumar. In the following figures these methods is represented by method 3, method 2, method 1 respectively.

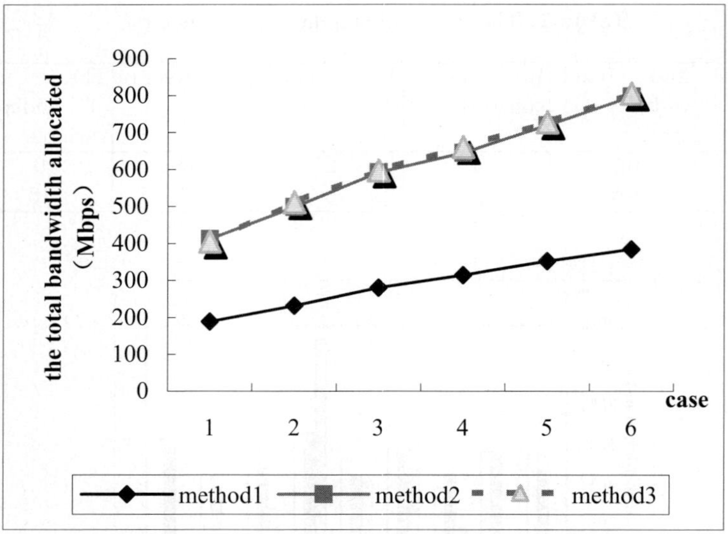

Fig. 5. Total bandwidth to be allocated

Fig. 3 represents the utilization result of the optimization with the fourth data groups after allocating bandwidth for EF and AF services. Fig. 4 and Fig. 5 are standard deviation of link utilization and total bandwidth to be allocated for all instances. From Fig. 3, we know that method 1 will lead to over utilizing of some network resource while other resource is not used, but method 2 and 3 will not. With the increase of load if method 2 is used, a service with higher class will preempt resource belonging to a service with lower class, and may even throttle the service with lower class. If method 3 is used, the above problem can be avoided. From Fig. 4 and Fig. 5, it is known that the performance of method 3 is close to that of method 2 and sometimes its load balance is even better than that of method 2.

6 Conclusion

The hose model is first introduced in this paper. Then the GA is used in the optimization of bandwidth assignment problem and is shown to be suitable and efficient for the problem. GAs are superior to classical optimization techniques since there is no restrictions on the objective or constraints in GAs. The proposed GA to solve the problem of bandwidth assignment in hose-modeled VPN is simple to be implemented. Further more, it is an offline and static method to bandwidth allocation.

Acknowledgements

The research is supported by Chinese National Science Foundation (grant 60472105) and in parts by Jiangsu Provincial Education Bureau (grant

JS2002-10) and Nanjing University of Posts and telecommunications (grant NY2005-002), whose funding support is gratefully acknowledged.

References

1. Blake, S., Black, D., Carlson, M., et al.: An Architecture for Differentiated Services. RFC 2475, December (1998)
2. Rosen, E., Viswanathan, A., Callon, R..: Multiprotocol Label Switching Architecture. RFC 3031, January (2001)
3. N.G. Duffield, Pawan Goyal, et al.: A Flexible Model for Resource Management in Virtual PrivateNetworks. In Proc. ACM Sigcomm Comput. Commun. REV, Vol 29, Oct (1999) 95-108
4. Duffield, N.G., Pawan Goyal, et al.: Resource Management With Hoses:Point-to-Cloud Services for Virtual Private Networks. IEEE/ACM Transactions on Networking,Vol 10, No.5 October (2002)
5. Tequila Consortium.: D3.4, Final System Evaluation -Part B. October (2002)
6. Amit Kumar, Rajeev Rastogi, et al.: Algorithms for Provisioning Virtual Private Networks in the Hose Model. IEEE/ACM Transactions on Networking,Vol 10, No.4 August (2002)
7. Ash., J.: Max Allocation with Reservation Bandwidth Constraints Model for Diffserv-aware MPLS Traffic Engineering & Performance Comparisons RFC4126 June (2005)
8. User's Guide.: Genetic Algorithm and Direct Search Toolbox for Use with MATLAB. The MathWorks (2004)

A Kind of Adaptive Negotiation Mechanism for Flexible Job Shop Scheduling*

Cixing Lv[1,2], Zhongqi Sheng[1], Sufen Li[1], Chaowan Yin[1], and Yunlong Zhu[1]

[1] Shenyang Institute of Automation, Chinese Academy of Sciences 110016 Shenyang, China
{smale, shengzhonqi, lisufen, ycw, ylzhu}@sia.cn

[2] Graduate School of the Chinese Academy of Sciences 110089 Beijing, China

Abstract. Agent-based production scheduling is a promising approach to solve production scheduling problem, especially in a dynamic, uncertain environment. In the system, agents are connected through a network and negotiate with each other to fulfill scheduling. The negotiation mechanism specifies the way in which negotiation should take place. This paper proposes an adaptive negotiation framework and two kinds of negotiation policies to fulfill scheduling and rescheduling in the flexible job shop. The mechanism makes the system more adaptive in dynamic production environments. The computational experiments are given to demonstrate the feasibility and performance of the mechanism.

1 Introduction

In agent-based production scheduling system, agents are used to encapsulate physical, logic and/or function entities in the production system [1-4]. While making autonomous decision, agents in the system interacts and negotiates with each others to fulfill scheduling [4]. In the system, negotiation mechanisms play a key role in managing message passing, the behaviors of agents, reaching closure, and determining the final schedule.

The negotiation policy can be classified into planning type and reactive type. The planning type, such as combinatorial auction [5,6], can get optimal or near-optimal schedule result in distributed framework. But this type of policy lacks of capacity to react to disturbances in dynamic environment. The reactive type allocates tasks or resources in real time manner, such as contract net [7], voting [8], etc. It behaves well in dynamic environment and balances the loads of agents. Therefore it is adopted in production scheduling system widely. However, the agents that adopt this type of negotiation policy make decision only according to local information and current state of the agents. It is hard to predict the performance of the result. The real world manufacturing problems are dynamic and tightly coupled. A slight change may make a previously ideal schedule totally unacceptable. Agents must have an efficient way to select right negotiation policies, related negotiation strategies and negotiation partners under various environment situations [9].

* The research is supported by National Basic Research Program of China (No. 2002CB 312204−03) and National Nature Science Foundation of China (No. 70431003).

D.-S. Huang, K. Li, and G.W. Irwin (Eds.): ICIC 2006, LNAI 4114, pp. 324 – 333, 2006.

In that case, such negotiation mechanisms, which achieve good performance and keep responsive capacity to handle disturbance at the same time, have not hitherto been considered, and so we consider them here. The adaptive negotiation mechanism utilizes an adaptive negotiation framework and two kinds of negotiation policy to fulfill scheduling and rescheduling problem of flexible job shop. The design and description of the negotiation mechanism are presented. In the last part of the paper, a prototype system and two experiments are presented to demonstrate and verify feasibility and performance of the mechanism.

2 The Adaptive Negotiation Mechanism

2.1 Problem Description

The problem considered here is scheduling and rescheduling of flexible job shop in dynamic production environments. The scheduling problem is to schedule N tasks on M resources in order to minimize the total tardiness of the tasks. If there is disturbance in the system, such as emergency task, breakdown of resource or task cancelled, original schedule is not feasible, and rescheduling is needed to keep system running and keep performance of the system in certain extent. Adaptive negotiation mechanism is considered as an approach to increase the adaptability of the system. By adaptive negotiation more intelligence and rationality are integrated into negotiation mechanisms, thus makes the system adaptive in dynamic environments. The negotiation mechanism is presented below.

The symbol used is presented as following:

- Agent types

  Part Agent – PA; Resource Agent – RA; Part Mediate Agent – PMA; Resource Mediate Agent RMA; Job Manage Agent – JMA; Mobile Submit Agent – MSA.
- Variables

  $O(i, j)$ — The jth subtask of the task i; T — The length of the planning horizon; M — The number of resources; t — The index of time slot; h — The index of resource; $\lambda_{h,t}$ — The price for time slot t for resource h; N — The number of tasks; n_i — Number of subtask of task i; $p_{i,j,h}$ — processing time of $O(i, j)$ if it is processed on $h \in H_{i,j}$, otherwise 0; ω_i — Weight of task i; $H_{i,j}$ — Resource set capable processing $O(i, j)$; $I_{i,j}$ — Set of subtasks preceding immediately $O(i, j)$; $TD_{i,t}$ — Cost for task i to complete in time slot t; $X_{i,j,t}$ =1 if $O(i, j)$ is complete at time t, 0 otherwise; $Y_{i,j,h}$ =1 if $O(i, j)$ is processed on resource h, 0 otherwise.
- Logical symbols

  NOT — ~; AND — $\cap$; OR — $\cup$.
- Events and messages

  Resource breakdown — Br; Emergency task — E; Task cancelled — C; Preparation for combinatorial auction negotiation mechanism — $A_{auction}$; Adoption of disturbance handling negotiation mechanism — $A_{dynamic}$; All PA's task lists are empty — P_{empty}; Start auction — Sa; Stop auction — Pa; MSA_i is ready — Mr.

B_i — Bid submitted by MSA_i; PA_i's planning list — P_{li}; Auction result — Ar; M_{list} — MA_j's planning list.

State of scheduling policy: S_{alloc} — Static state; D_{alloc} — Dynamic state.

Value of auction state (AuctionState): Auction is initiated— S_{init}; MSA is dispatched — S_{disp}; A new round auction starts— S_{new_round}; The prices is announced — S_{ann}; Bid is constructed — S_{con_bid}; Bid is submit — S_{sub_bid}; Market is cleared — S_{cl_mar}; Revenue is calculate — S_{cal_rev}; Prices is updated — S_{upd_pri}; Result is notified— S_{result}; Auction is end — S_{end}; MSA returns — S_{return}; Auction is stopped— S_{stop}.

- Basic behavior of agents
  SEND (message1<content1>, message2<content2> ...) TO (agent1, agent2 ...)
  SET_STATE (state1, state2 ...) TO (state_new1, state_new2 ...)
  SET_CONTEXT(context1, context2 ...)
  DISPATCH (mobile_agent) TO (agent)
  (mobile_agent) RETURN TO (agent)
  CREATE (agent)
  DESTROY (agent)
  UNREGISTER (agent)

2.2 The Adaptive Negotiation Framework

To realize adaptive negotiation in the agent-based system, an appropriate framework is important [9]. The negotiation mechanism makes the system adaptive to the dynamic environments by applying different negotiation policy. The adaptive negotiation framework is proposed as a foundation for management of negotiation policies in the system. The framework implements adaptive characteristics of agent negotiation by system architecture, knowledge to select negotiation policy and different negotiation policy. The system architecture has some important characteristics which explicitly support adaptive negotiation among agents. The knowledge is integrated into the agent negotiation mechanism is used by agents in terms of rational decision making. Two kinds of negotiation policy and some selection heuristics have been presented as well. Furthermore, the preprocessing for switch negotiation policy is presented.

2.2.1 The Heuristics to Select Negotiation Protocols

In the adaptive negotiation framework, negotiation policy selecting heuristics play an important role. They are used to select suitable negotiation policy under different situations. For the agent-based production scheduling, some domain specific heuristics are adopted to distinguish the important characteristics of different negotiation policies under different environment conditions.

The selection process is shown in the Fig. 1. While in smooth progress, corresponding agents uses combinatorial auction negotiation policy to allocate tasks. The auction result is global near optimal. If disturbance happens, such as emergency task, task cancelled and resource breakdown, the combinatorial auction would be stopped. And after disturbance preprocessing is done, modified contract net would be initiated to allocate the tasks that are not processed. After that, according to the state of the system, combinatorial auction or modified contract net is used to schedule tasks. The corresponding behaviors of agents and its description are given in the table 1.

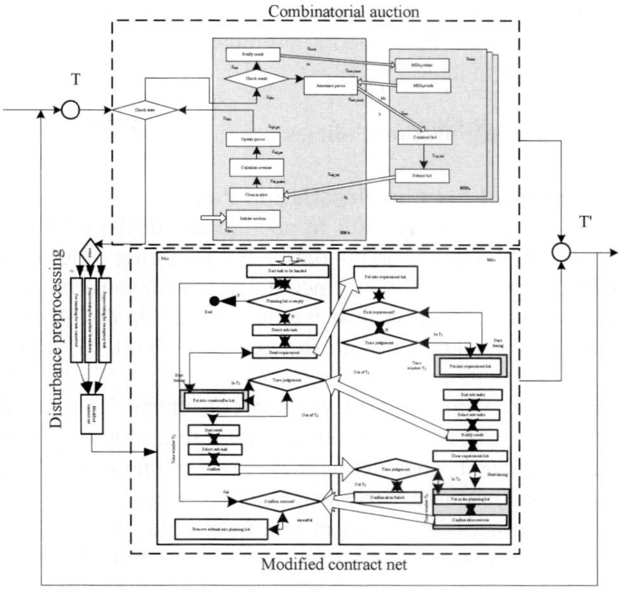

Fig. 1. The process of adaptive negotiation mechanism

Table 1. The switch between different kinds of negotiation mechanism

Behavior	agent	Behavior description
Adopt combinatorial auction mechanism	JMA	Context: P_{empty} Behavior: SET_STATE (T') TO (S_{alloc}); SEND ($A_{auction}$) TO (RMA)
Adopt disturbance handling mechanism	JMA	Context: $Br \cup E \cup C$ Behavior: SET_STATE (T') TO (D_{alloc}); SEND ($A_{dynamic}$) TO (RMA,MAs,PAs,PMA)

2.2.2 The Prepossessing for Switching Different Negotiation Protocols

If disturbance happens, rescheduling is needed to keep system running and keep certain performance of the system. Rescheduling is done in two steps. The disturbance is handled and then tasks left in the Combinatorial Auction Time Window (CATW) are allocated through modified contract net. Preprocessing negotiation mechanism specifies corresponding agents to handle disturbance. The process of preprocessing is shown in Fig. 2. The preprocessing is performed according to the type of disturbance.

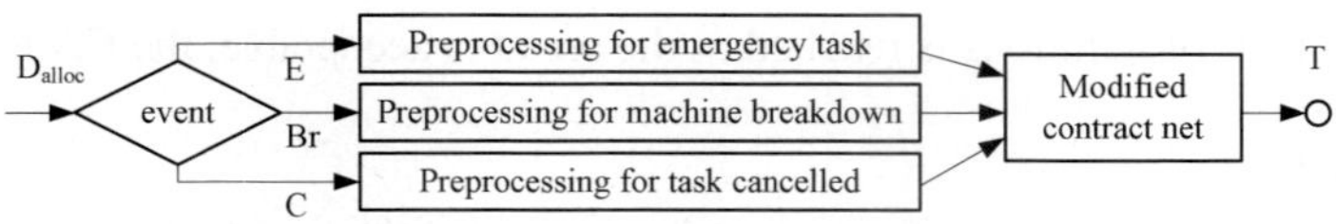

Fig. 2. The process of disturbance preprocessing

The purpose of preprocessing is to recover from disturbance and prepare for task allocation through modified contract net. The preprocessing is done by corresponding agents' behaviors (shown in table 2).

2.3 Description of the Negotiation Policies

2.3.1 The Combinatorial Auction Negotiation Policy

Combinatorial auctions commonly refer to auction mechanisms in which agents are allowed to bid on combinations, or bundles f items. Being able to bid on bundles clearly mitigates the exposure problem, since it gives the agents the option to bid their precise valuations for any collection if items they desire. On the other hand, combinatorial auctions require the market maker, the agents, or both, to solve complex decision problems.

For the scheduling problem, the time window considered for scheduling is divided into T time slots equably. All resources delegate their time slots to a mediator who acts as s-agent, jobs act as b-agents and auction items are the time slots of the resources and defined as a set of pairs (resource, timeslot). Each job competes for time slots with its precedence constraint, process requirement and local utility function. The s-agent adjusts the price of each time slot according to the demand from b-agents to reduce the resource conflicts among the b-agents until result of auction is obtained, and the resource and complete time for all operations in each job are determined. The schedule generated according to auction result is near-optimal [10]. Formally, we have:

Definition 1

The descriptor of a CA is $P_{CA} = \langle G, Buyer, S, \lambda_p, Bid, t_{round} \rangle$, where:

- $G = \{ g_{h,t} \}$ is the goods, time slots on resources, to be auctioned.
- $B = \{ b_1, b_2, \cdots, b_n \}$ is finite set of identifiers of b-agents, where n is the number of b-agents, also, the number of jobs.
- S is the identifiers of seller-agent.
- $Bid = \{ Bid_1, Bid_2, \cdots, Bid_n \}$ is the bids constructed by the b-agents, where $Bid_i = \{ (Bid_{i,1}, Bid_{i,2}, \cdots, Bid_{i,n_i}), p_i \}$ is the bid submitted by the ith b-agents. Here, p_i is the payment for the bid, and triple $Bid_{i,j}(m_{i,j}, t_{i,j}, l_{i,j})$ presents requirement of $O(i,j)$ for timeslots, $m_{i,j}$ presents resource, $t_{i,j}$ presents start index of time slot, $l_{i,j}$ presents the number of time slots which means the processing time on the resource.
- t_{round} is used for defining the condition for terminating the CA, that is, the maximum number of iterations is reached or the result is acceptable, the CA terminates.

Definition 2

A round in a CA is the time period between two successive deals or the period from the beginning of the CA to the time when the first deal takes place. If a round is the

rth ($r \in IN^{+}$) round of the CA, then r is called the round number. A CA consists of multiple rounds.

The following is the formal definition of the valid behaviors of agents during a CA.

Definition 3

The CA protocol with descriptor P_{CA} consists of the following steps:

Each PA dispatches a MSA to the platform in which RMA lies in.

1. MSAs with routing, precedence constraints, utility function and construct bid method are dispatched into the platform which RMA lies in.
2. $r = 1$, $\lambda_{h,t} = 0$.
3. A new round of the CA starts, $r = r + 1$, RMA clears market, updates λ_p and announces new prices to all MSAs.
4. MSAs construct bids to minimize the utility function under current prices and submit them to RMA.
5. If closure is reached goto 3, else goto 6.
6. MSAs bring result including the processing resource and starting time of each subtask to the corresponding PA.

The reason for introducing MSA is to improve the communication efficiency, because the communication cost in same platform is 10 times lower than that in different platform [10]. For the design of combinatorial auction, Lagrangian Relaxation approach is adopted [11]. by In combinatorial auction, the communication cost is $C = O(N \times R \times (M \times T + |n_i|))$ for each round auction, if platform factor (JADE [12], Java Agent Development Framework) is considered, the communication cost is adjusted to $C = O(N^2 \times R \times (M \times T + |n_i|))$ [11].

2.3.2 Modified Contract Net Negotiation Policy

After disturbance preprocessing is done, PAs compete for process time on resource through modified contract net until all tasks left in the CATW are allocated. According to the requirement to allocate tasks, several improvements are proposed to basic contract net protocol. The first improvement is sending offers to a limited number of agents instead of broadcasting them. And subtasks satisfying precedence constraints can send offers in parallel. At last the reactive time of agents is limited. There are three time windows: T_1 for MA to receive offers, T_2 for PA to select subtask and T_3 for MA to confirm. In modified contract net, PAs select subtasks whose precedence subtasks have been allocated and sends offers to corresponding MAs. If MAs receive first requirement and the requirement list is empty, the T_1 time window of the MA starts timing. When the T_1 is out, the MA sorts the offers in the list according to its own objective and selects the first offer and notifies result to the concerned PA. And the T_3 time window starts timing. When the PA receives first notification, the T_2 time window starts timing. And the PA puts the notification into counteroffer list. When the T_2 is out, the PA sorts the notification according to its own objective, selects the first notification and sends confirmation to the MA. If the MA receives confirmation message in the T_3 time window, the MA would put the subtask into its planning list and send re-confirmation to the PA. The process of modified contract net is shown in Fig. 3.

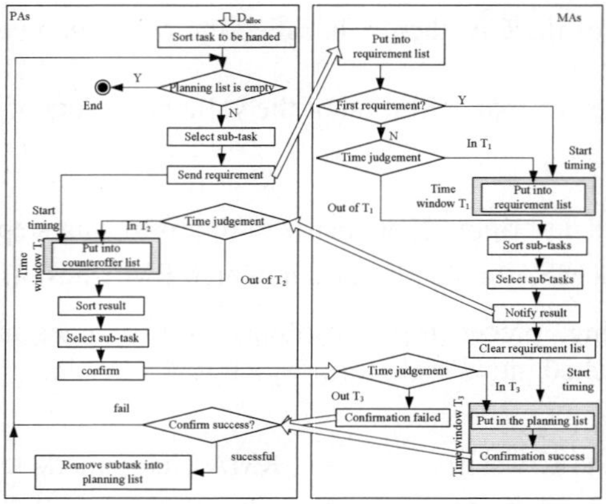

Fig. 3. Negotiation process of the modified contract net

3 Experiments

Based on prototype system, two experiments are used to demonstrate the feasibility and efficiency of negotiation mechanism. Experiment one compares combinatorial auction negotiation mechanism with dispatching rule for tardiness and flowing time. Experiment two shows a rescheduling example after disturbance happens.

Parameters in the experiments are set as following. Because the value of α affects the performance of the system, the value of α is specified for 1.05, 1.1, 1.15, 1.2, 1.25. Also, considering of the dynamic character of the environment, the negotiation mechanism must has the character of "anytime", which means that a feasible solution can be available whenever the negotiation is stopped. In real environment, the cycle times of the auction can't be guaranteed. For the reason, cycle times of 100, 200, 300, 400 and 500 are adopted respectively. Therefore, total 25 times for each experiment were performed and the average value of the experiment was obtained.

3.1 Experiment One

This experiment is designed to compare the performance of the negotiation mechanism with dispatching rules for tardiness and flowing time. Four groups data, including 6×6, 8×8, 10×10, 12×12, are generated randomly. The subtasks number is six in former two groups and eight in latter two groups. The experiment data is generated randomly in the manner as same as reference [13]. The parameters for generating are described as following. The process time of each subtask is an integer chosen randomly from [3,12]. The alternative resource number is chosen randomly from [0,2]. The process time in alternative resource is the process time in original resource multiply a coefficient chosen randomly from [0.5,2]. The weight of each production task is 1.0. The due date of each production task is calculated by $\sum_{i=1}^{N}\left(\min\left\{p_{i,j,h} \mid h \in H_{i,j}\right\}\right)$. The number of direct precedence of subtask is chosen randomly from [0,3]. Using above data, the performance of negotiation mechanism is compared to SPT and EDD dispatching rule.

Table 2. Simulation result of experiment one

problem	method	Total tardiness	Flowing time
6×6	SPT	749	56
	EDD	855	58
	Combinatorial auction	126	45
8×8	SPT	1945	65
	EDD	1706	79
	Combinatorial auction	593	60
10×10	SPT	3804	134
	EDD	2963	177
	Combinatorial auction	818	110
12×12	SPT	4158	174
	EDD	4267	187
	Combinatorial auction	1121	133

Using above data, average value of total tardiness and flow time of all tasks are got. As shown in table 2, combinatorial auction negotiation mechanism gets better performance in total tardiness comparing to SPT and EDD dispatching rules. In addition, the experiment shows that the negotiation mechanism does better in flowing time comparing to dispatching rules.

3.2 Experiment Two – Example of Rescheduling

Take 6×6 experiment data in experiment one to describe rescheduling example after disturbance happens. The disturbances include resource breakdown, emergency task

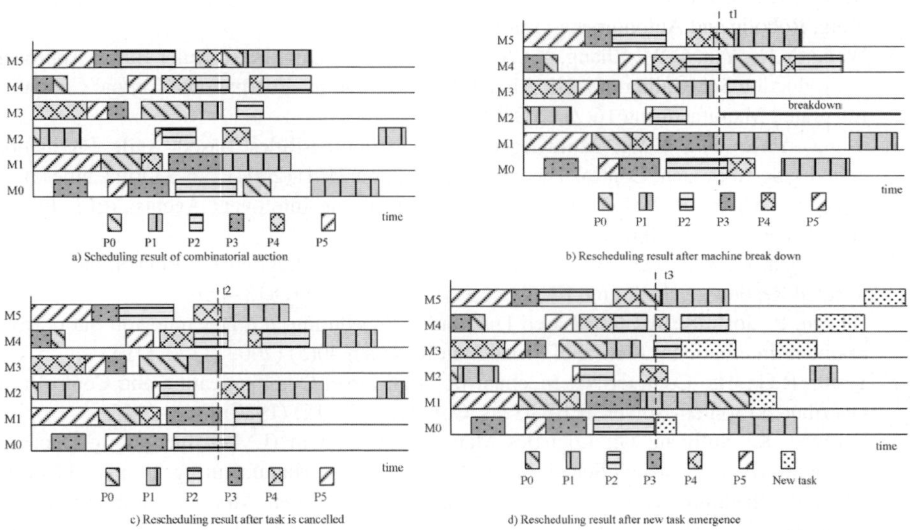

Fig. 4. Example of rescheduling after disturbance

and task cancelled. In the example, MA takes SPT dispatching rule, PA takes EDD dispatching rule, and we suppose the part, which is processing on the resource that is breakdown, need to be processed from beginning. The result of rescheduling is shown in Fig. 4. The example shows that the negotiation mechanism can fulfill rescheduling when disturbance happens in the system. And the negotiation mechanism is adaptive to dynamic environments, whereas the rescheduling is feasible but not optimal now.

4 Conclusions

Based on survey of negotiation mechanism in the agent-based production scheduling, an adaptive negotiation mechanism is proposed in the paper. The adaptive negotiation mechanism includes an adaptive negotiation framework, knowledge to select negotiation policy and two kinds of negotiation policies. The mechanism is designed to schedule production tasks with flexible routing and in-tree precedence constraints in dynamic environment in distributed manner. A prototype system is developed and two experiments are performed based on the mechanism to demonstrate the mechanism to be feasible and effective.

The rescheduling heuristics in the paper is feasible but not optimal. According to specified production environment and production objective, appropriate selection of rules is needed to achieve optimal result. The selection of the rules hitherto mainly depends on experiences. How to transform the experiences into agent's knowledge and help agent to make decision to improve the performance of rescheduling is our future work.

References

1. Rabelo, R.J., Camarinha-matos, L.M., Afsarmanesh, H.: Multi-Agent-Based Agile Scheduling. Robotic and Autonomous System 27 (1999) 15-28
2. Wang, Y.H., Yin, C.W., Zhang, Y.: A Multi-Agent and Distributed Ruler Based Approach to Production Scheduling of Agile Manufacturing Systems. International Journal Computer Integrated Manufacturing 16(2) (2003) 81-92
3. Wang, Y.H., Yin, C.W.: Multi-Agent and Distributed-Rules Based Agile Production Scheduling Approach. Control Theory & Application 21(4) (2004) 526-530(in Chinese)
4. Shen, W.: Distributed Manufacturing Scheduling Using Intelligent Agents. IEEE Intelligent Systems 17(1) (2002) 88-94
5. Kutanoglu, E., Wu, S.D.: On Combinatorial Auction and Lagrangean Relaxation for Distributed Resource Scheduling. IIE Transactions 31(9) (1999) 813 –826
6. Dewan, P., Josh, S.: Auction-Based Distributed Scheduling in a Dynamic Job Shop Environment. International Journal of Production Research 40(5) (2002) 1173-1191
7. Smith, R.G.: The Contract Net Mechanism: High-Level Communication and Control in a Distributed Problem Solver. IEEE Trans. Computers 29(12) (1980) 1104–1113
8. Fordyce, K., Sullivan, G.: Logistics Management System (LMS): Integrating Decision Technologies for Dispatch Scheduling in Semiconductor Manufacturing, Chapter 17 in Intelligent Scheduling, edited by Mark Fox and Monte Zweben, Morgan Kaufman Publishers, (1994) 473-516

9. Wang, C., Shen, W.M., Ghenniwa, H.: An Adaptive Negotiation Framework for Agent Based Dynamic Manufacturing Scheduling. In: IEEE International Conference on Systems, Man and Cybernetics (2003) 1211-1216
10. Cortese, E.: Benchmark on JADE Message Transport System [EB/OL]. http://jade.cselt.it/doc/tutorials/benchmark/JADERTTBenchmark.htm (2003)
11. Lv, C.X., Zhu, Y.L., Yin, C.W.: Resource Allocation Based on Combinatorial Auction in E-Manufacturing Environment. In: The Fifith International Conference on Computer and Information Technology (CIT 2005), Los Alamitos, California: IEEE Computer Society (2005) 983-989
12. Te, S.C., He, T.: Project. Java Agent Development Framework Is an Open Source Platform for Peer-To-Peer Agent Based Applications [EB/OL]. http://jade.cselt.it/ (2004)
13. Chen, H., Chu, C., Proth, J.M.: An Improvement of the Lagrangean Relaxation Approach for Job Shop Scheduling: A Dynamic Programming Method. IEEE transactions cn robotics and automation 14(5) (1998) 786-795
14. Debra, J.H., Peter, B.L., Krishna, R.P.: A Practical Approach to Job-Shop Scheduling Problems. IEEE transactions on robotics and automation 9(1) (1993) 1-13
15. Chen, H.X., Peter, B.L.: An Alternative Framework to Lagrangian Relaxation Approach for Job Shop Scheduling. European Journal of Operational Research 149(3) (2003) 499-512

A Novel Key Management and Access Control Scheme for Mobile Agent

Jen-Yi Pan[1,2,3], Tzer-Long Chen[1], and Tzer-Shyong Chen[4]

[1] Department of Communications Engineering, National Chung Cheng University
[2] Department of Electrical Engineering, National Chung Cheng University
[3] Center for Telecommunication Research, National Chung Cheng University
[4] Department of Information Management, Tung Hai University
jypan@ccu.edu.tw

Abstract. The speed and convenience of the Internet facilitated the development of electronic commerce (e-commerce). E-commerce research and technologies have always drawn the attention of researchers. Among them, the application of mobile agent on e-commerce has drawn much attention in recent years. Mobile agents can roam freely over different execution environments to execute tasks assigned to them. However, a mobile agent may be attacked when it requests services from other servers or when comes in contact with and exchange information with another agents while roaming on the internet. Hence, a mobile agent user may be concerned that his mobile agent could be corrupted or private information tapped and pirated by other agents. To ensure the security of mobile agents in public network environment, this paper proposes a security scheme that is suitable for mobile agents. The scheme includes access control and key management; it is also an improvement on the key management and access control for mobile agent scheme of Volker and Mehrdad. The proposed scheme corrects the drawback in Volker and Mehrdad's scheme which is the need of a large amount of storage for storing the secret keys. Security and performance analysis of our scheme proves the proposed scheme to be more efficient and secure.

1 Introduction

Following the easy availability of the Internet, in order to improve efficiency, complex distributed computing can now be performed online. Simultaneous computing on distributed system can be performed through transmission of bulk information and messages between host servers. However, the bulky data causes overloading of network flow [5].

A mobile agent is a type of program that can move between servers and simultaneously handle distributed computing. Compared to the traditional structure, mobile agent has the following qualities:

1. Reduce network load: Distributed systems are completely dependent on communication mediums for exchange of information, especially when using security protocols. This causes bulk network flow. Mobile agent does not require constant connection with the target server, it packages the instructions

D.-S. Huang, K. Li, and G.W. Irwin (Eds.): ICIC 2006, LNAI 4114, pp. 334 – 345, 2006.

and send it to the target server and can interact on the target server. Mobile agent can also compute large amount of data on remote servers, reducing the network flow and the number of connections between the source server and target server.

2. Overcome network delay: When the control system needs to process large amount of data instantaneously, delays could happen. Therefore, if a mobile agent is used, then messages can be exchanged on remote servers by sending the agent to each of the servers to carry out the task. Thus network delay can be reduced.
3. Packaging protocol: Traditional distributed systems have a fixed protocol for exchanging data. However, varying platforms require each server to create their own protocol, each having its own coding. Therefore, if the protocol needs to be redesigned when met with efficiency or security problems and if one of the servers were not quick enough with its update, then incompatibility or delays may occur. A mobile agent can package the message and request a connection with the remote server when it reaches the same; hence it does not face protocol problems.
4. Non-simultaneous and spontaneous execution: A mobile agent can non-simultaneously and spontaneously execute its task while a server is offline. It reports back when the task is completed.
5. Adapt to dynamic environment: A mobile agent has the ability to assess its environment and make spontaneous adjustment to adapt to the environment.
6. Innate heterogeneity: From the point of view of hardware or software, network computing is basically of diverse nature. Mobile agent is independent from the computer or the network transmission layer; it is related only to the environment.
7. Expandability: Mobile agent allows flexible adjustment or expansion between source and target.

Recently, many mobile agent researchers are exploring ways to apply mobile agent technology to improve business activities [10]. A mobile agent, during its execution, roams about the Internet and may come in contact with other agents and exchange information; consequently it may face some security problems [5, 9]. The security problem of mobile agent happens mostly at unsafe contact. Therefore, this paper has put together four types of security risks [4] a mobile agent may face, as follows.

1. Host server gets accessed by unauthorized personnel: An unauthorized agent accesses data on a host server.
2. Host server is attacked by malicious agent: An agent forges another agent's identification marking to access services or resources, or to evade responsibility and break the trust of the rightful agent.
3. An agent is attacked by another agent: An agent forges another agents ID to trick another agent. The malicious agent constantly sends messages to cause receiving end server to overload and cause computation time on the receiving end server to increase.
4. Agent attacked by a malicious host: A host may impersonate another host to trick agents; or a malicious host may ignore an agent's request. For example, a host deliberately delays an agent's request, or even terminates an agent without

warning causing other agents awaiting response from this agent to enter into a deadlock. In addition, another case is that a malicious host deliberately causes an agent to be unable to carry out his task causing the agent to be live-locked.

The first three security risks listed above can be resolved using present cryptography technology. Since a mobile agent carries along the commissioner's private information while visiting hosts of different security levels to deliver computations carried out by the host, there is a need for codes, secret keys and security schemes that protects the agent and the information it carries. However, since a mobile agent is controlled by an agent host, it is not possible to guard against malicious behavior of a server. Therefore it is very difficult to resolve the fourth security risk; this is also the problem this paper proposes to solve.

Researchers in recent years are focusing their research on the security of mobile agents. Corradi et al. [3] proposed a mobile agent structure, SOMA. This structure included agent, agent server, management system, and security approach. Karnik and Tripathi [9] also proposed a structure, Ajanta; it has the same functions as SOMA. In response to SOMA and Ajanta, Volker and Mehrdad [13] proposed a tree structure; its functions include authorization of mobile agent, key management and access control. This paper examines Volker and Mehrdad's security scheme, amending its drawback and proposes two mobile agent key management and access control schemes based on hierarchical structures [1]. This paper, through systematic and complete mobile agent, and related security technology, proposes to combine present security technologies to design a more suitable mobile agent key management and access control scheme. At the same time, we shall compare and analyze security and efficiency to prove the feasibility and efficiency of the scheme, and its ability to protect the safety of a mobile agent in its work environment; and thus protects user rights.

This paper is divided into six sections. Section 1 introduces mobile agent, its characteristics and security risks in addition to explaining the purpose of this paper. Section 2 examines Volker and Mehrdad's mobile agent key management and access control scheme and points out its drawbacks. Section 3 proposes the new schemes, which is analyzed in section 4. Section 5 compares efficiency between Volker and Mehrdad's scheme and the proposed scheme to prove that the drawback in Volker and Mehrdad's scheme has been effectively amended. A conclusion is finally drawn in section 6.

2 Volker and Mehrdad's Scheme

Volker and Mehrdad [13] proposed a scheme with access control and key management for mobile agents to effectively protect an agent. This section examines the security and drawbacks of the scheme.

2.1 Volker and Mehrdad's Scheme

This security scheme designed a tree as the basic structure; it supports agent authorization, key management and access control. The structure is as shown in fig. 1.

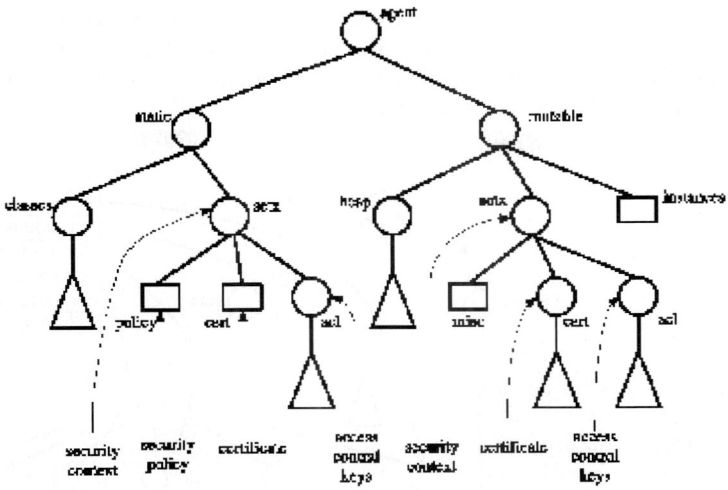

Fig. 1. A tree based mobile agent structure

The whole structure can be divided into two parts: static and dynamic. The static part includes all permanent information, like group classification, security approach, and others, which will not change during the agent's lifetime. In order to prevent information from being tampered, an agent owner can use security technologies (like digital signature) to accomplish data comprehensiveness and authenticable identity. In the static part, the accuracy of a message can be verified by the visited host. Relatively, modified data is stored in the dynamic part, like group, shared storage space and the confidential message. When the agent completes its task on a server, the agent's status and information gathered by the agent could be altered by the same server. In order to maintain comprehensiveness of the message, the last visited host must sign the root node, which also supports the source and all visited hosts' signature [2].

On the other hand, a confidential message whether in static part or dynamic part must maintain confidentiality. To prevent unauthorized personnel from accessing the message, we need a fine access control method. For this purpose, Volker and Mehrdad proposed an access control and key management scheme, which employs the public key cryptosystem and the symmetric encryption system. A summary of their scheme is as follows. Create a folder for each visited node in the static/sctx/acl folder. Each folder includes the decryption key of the same node. A host authorized to a particular file can find its corresponding decryption key in the same folder. The files in the folders are also encrypted.

Use the host's public key to encrypt the folder stored under static/sctx/acl. When the agent reaches a certain host, the same host can find the corresponding folder under static/sctx/acl. Each host can only use its corresponding secret key to decrypt and access the corresponding folder.

Figure 2 [11] explains this scheme's simple access control and key management scheme example. In the diagram, the classes folder contains seven files: agent.zip, application.zip, server.zip, support.zip, picture.zip, control.zip, and route.zip. Except for agent.zip, the rest of the six files are confidential and has been encrypted with the secret keys, SK_1, SK_2, SK_3, SK_4, SK_5 and SK_6. Additionally, SK_1, SK_2, SK_3, SK_4, SK_5 and SK_6 denote six different hosts, thu.edu.tw, pu.edu.tw, fcu.edu.tw, nchu.edu.tw, ncku.edu.tw and nctu.edu.tw, respectively.

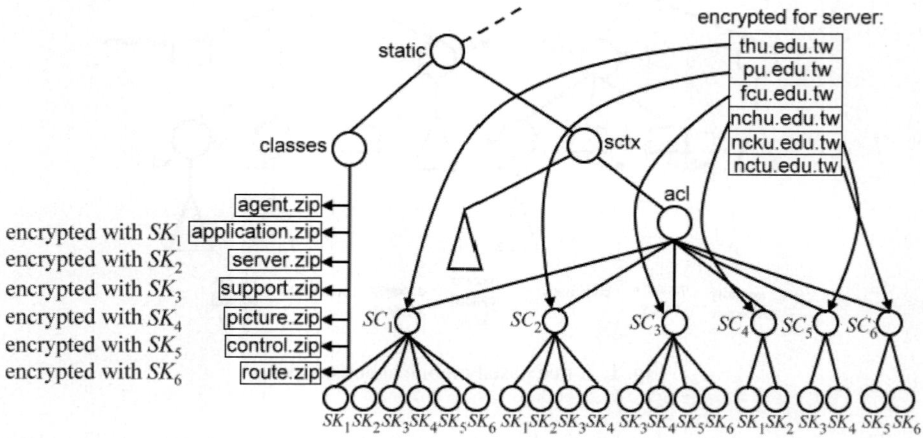

Fig. 2. An example of the Volker and Mehrdad access control and key management scheme

Suppose a host is authorized to a certain file, then the decryption key can be found under the host's folder. For example, Host has six decryption keys: SK1, SK2, SK3, SK4, SK5 and SK6; hence, host SC1 can decrypt the files, application.zip, server.zip, support.zip, picture.zip, control.zip, and route.zip. Host SC2 has four decryption keys: SK1, SK2, SK3, and SK4; hence, host SC2 can decrypt the files, application.zip, server.zip, support.zip, and picture.zip. The same applies to host SC3, SC4, SC5 and SC6. The six folders, static /sctx/acl/SC1, static/sctx/acl/SC2, static/sctx/acl/SC3, static/sctx/acl/SC4, static/sctx/acl/ SC5, and static/sctx/acl/SC6 must each be encrypted with the secret key of their corresponding host, and the secret keys are held only by the authorized host. Hence, confidential files can be protected by adhering to and adopting the access control and key management scheme.

2.2 Drawbacks of Volker and Mehrdad's Scheme

Volker and Mehrdad's scheme is based on the tree structure. This study examined their scheme and discovered the following drawbacks.

(1) Wastage of large amount storage space: From Volker and Mehrdad's security scheme, this study discovered that the decryption key in the scheme is repeatedly stored under different folders. From fig. 2, we can see that secret key SK_1 can be found under the folders of hosts SC_1, SC_2 and SC_4; secret key SK_2, SK_3, SK_4, SK_5 and SK_6 are also repetitively stored. Therefore, we can clearly see that the scheme wastes large amount of storage space on repetitive storage, increasing the size of the mobile agent.

(2) Large amount of public key computations: The decryption key for decrypting confidential files are repeatedly stored under the folder,

static/sctx/acl/. Therefore, a mobile agent owner spends large amount of time computing the public key to maintain the security of the folder.

To allow a mobile agent to move easily through the Internet, the storage space required by an ideal mobile agent as well as the computation cost of its secret key should the lower the better. This study proposes amendments to Volker and Mehrdad's scheme in the next section, explaining the cited concept, describing its process of execution and stating examples.

3 The Proposed Scheme

In 1983, Akl and Taylor [1] proposed an access control scheme based on hierarchical structure. In their proposed method, each user is assigned to a security group, C1, C2, …, Cm. According to the hierarchical structure, user Ci of a higher hierarchy has greater access rights than user Cj of a lower hierarchy. This kind of access relationship can be denoted by Cj<Ci. Akl and Taylor also proposed a superkey concept to handle key management problems. Suppose user Ci has greater access rights than user Cj, then Ci can use his superkey to compute and determine the superkey of user Cj to access data available to Cj. This paper cites the superkey concept of Akl and Taylor's scheme to design two highly efficient access control and key management schemes for mobile agent, to mend the drawback in Volker and Mehrdad's scheme.

Before a mobile agent is sent to work in an internet environment, the source host must first decide which hosts will the mobile agent be visiting and which information can be accessed by the visited hosts. Furthermore, mobile agent owner must also first decide the path the agent shall take as well as the access plan. Afterwards, agent owner uses individual secret key to encrypt each confidential file, and may use symmetric cryptosystems [12] like AES, DES or IDEAL to encrypt the files. Then, according to access plan customize various access rights, and according to the extent of access rights construct access hierarchy. Agent owner will assign a superkey to each host and publish the public parameters of a number of agents. Each host can use its superkey to access data of lower access rights host.

Before describing the proposed scheme, this paper first shall modify the tree structure of Volker and Mehrdad's scheme, turning it into the hierarchical structure of our proposed scheme as shown in fig. 3. Figure 3 is a hierarchy based on fig. 2.

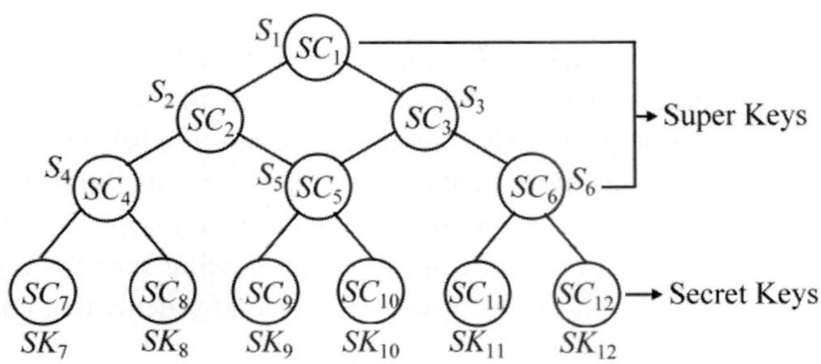

Fig. 3. Hierarchy after modification

The SK_7 of the leaf node in a hierarchy represents the decryption key used to encrypt files; the other internal nodes *SCs* represent the various corresponding hosts; *Ss* represent host superkey. This superkey is used to obtain the decryption key of their successors. In figure 3, root node SC_1 has superkey S_1 and also the right to access all decryption keys. Node SC_2 has superkey S_2 and right to access the decryption key of SK_7, SK_8, SK_9 and SK_{10}.

Scheme one of this paper is a hierarchy based scheme; it uses exponential operations to construct polynomials and also employs the modulus of a large prime number n to encrypt the decryption key of each leaf node. Scheme two adopts the polynomial concept of scheme one; the exponent is replaced by the elliptic curve paired with one way hash function, which not only reduces the length of the polynomial but also strengthens security. The security of the two schemes proposed in this paper is mainly dependent on the difficulty of solving the polynomial by using the congruence of large prime number.Consequently, the proposed scheme ensures that only authorized hosts can access the decryption key to encrypted confidential files.

3.1 Scheme One

Step 1: Agent owner randomly chooses a large prime number $n \doteq 2^{180}$ and a non-repeated parameter $g_j \in Z_n$ for each leaf node. Both n and g_j are public.

Step 2: Agent owner chooses a non-repeated superkey S_i for each host (internal node), and chooses a non-repeated decryption key SK_j for each leaf node. Both S_i and SK_j are private.

Step 3: When host SC_i has access to SC_j, that is, $SC_j < SC_i$, and when $i \neq j$, agent owner calculates all and then uses the same to construct $f_j(x)$; $f_j(x)$ is as shown below:

$$f_j(x) = \prod_{SC_j < SC_i} (x - g_j^{Si}) + SK_j \pmod{n} . \tag{1}$$

Step 4: If a host SC_i wants to access the decryption key SK_j of a successor, then it can use its superkey S_i and public parameter g_j to calculate $f_j(g_j^{S_i})$ to obtain decryption key SK_j.

Compared to Volker and Mehrdad's scheme, scheme one proposed by this paper clearly reduces the number of time a key is stored, thus the storage space needed is greatly reduced, and consequently the mobile agent size is also much smaller. hash function not only compresses stored data into a fixed size, its non-reversible nature strengthens the security of the agent. Also, the ECC reduces storage space and therefore fewer calculations to be performed; the processing speed is also faster and the security stronger. Hence, this paper proposes a second scheme that combines ECC and one way hash function.

3.2 Scheme Two

Step 1: Agent owner randomly chooses a large prime number $n \doteq 2^{180}$, and then define an elliptic curve E with base n, and from E_n select a base point G_j for each leaf node. Both n and G_j are public.

Step 2: Agent owner selects a non-repeated superkey S_i for each host (internal node), and selects a non-repeated decryption key SK_j for each leaf node. Both S_i and SK_j are private.

Step 3: Agent owner employs the algorithm below to calculate the value obtained after encryption with one way hash function h, and uses the same to construct $f_j(x)$ for each leaf node to protect decryption key SK_j.

Begin algorithm:
  For all hosts SC_i with access rights to leaf nodes SC_j
    Generate $S_iG_j=(x_{j,i}, y_{j,i})$ and use one way hash function to calculate the value of $h(x_{j,i} \| y_{j,i})$, $\|$ denotes a successive operator
  End For
End algorithm

Afterwards, use each $h(x_{j,i} \| y_{j,i})$ to construct $f_j(x)$, $f_j(x)$ can be denoted as follows:

$$f_j(x) = \prod_{SC_j < SC_i} (x - h(x_{j,i} \| y_{j,i})) + SK_j \pmod{n} . \tag{2}$$

Step 4: If a host SC_i wants to obtain the decryption key SK_j of its successor, it can use its superkey S_i and public parameter G_j to calculate S_iG_j after one way hash function operation; finally, substitute the result in $f_j(x)$ to obtain decryption key SK_j.

4 Security Analysis

This section analyzes the schemes proposed in this paper to prove their security and feasibility. The analysis is based on the possible forms of attack. Through security analysis, this study can prove that the security of the proposed schemes is very strong.

4.1 Reverse Attack

The first potential attack is, when host SC_j and host SC_i have a $SC_j < SC_i$ relationship or when host SC_j and host SC_i belongs to the same level of a hierarchy, can host SC_j use its superkey and public parameters to derive the super key of host SC_i to access or modify internal information of host SC_i?

In the proposed schemes, host SC_j and host SC_i are independent. When there exists a $SC_j < SC_i$ relationship between the two hosts, host SC_j cannot access internal information on host SC_i. This paper proposes two schemes. Scheme one uses exponential operations and large prime numbers which requires long periods of time to calculate making the result not worth the cost and therefore it is very difficult for the attacker to determine the victim's superkey. Scheme two adopts the non-reversibility of the one way function and the ECC to meet security requirements. Since one way hash function is a method that is incapable of obtaining the input via the output, and the correct base point of the ECC cannot be determined without first solving the elliptic curve discrete logarithmic problem (ECDLP) [14, 15]. Thus, attacker SC_j cannot determine superkey S_i and therefore cannot access confidential information. If host SC_j and host SC_i belonged to the same level of a hierarchy, the attacker will meet with complex exponential computations and large prime numbers, or the challenge of solving the one way hash function and ECC.

4.2 Conspiracy Attack

The second potential attack is, if a host SC_j corresponding to a mobile agent and another host SC_i has a $SC_j < SC_i$ relation, can hosts SC_j, SC_{j+1}, …, SC_{j+k} work together to collect correlated public parameters to derive the superkey of host SC_i? For instance, in figure 3, can host SC_4 and host SC_5 conspire to derive the superkey of host SC_1? Or the access right of host SC_i and host SC_j is greater than equal to that of host SC_k, but SC_i, SC_j and SC_k do not have mutual access relationship, can hosts SC_i and SC_j conspire to derive the superkey of host SC_k? For instance, can hosts SC_2 and SC_4 in figure 3 conspire to derive the superkey of host SC_6?

Generally speaking, the attacker uses known information to determine the desired superkey. The attacker must resolve the barrier created by exponential operation, large prime number application, ECC and one way hash function. This situation has been described in the first form of attack. Although users from the lower levels of a hierarchy conspire by collecting known public parameters and superkeys, the information remains incomplete; therefore this method of attack shall fail.

4.3 External Collective Attack

The third potential attack is an external attack. Can an intruder determine the desired superkey via known public parameters? In scheme one of this paper, an intruder not only need to reverse the public polynomial to its original form, but also find the matching superkey in exponential operations and among the large prime numbers; both of which are extremely difficult to accomplish. Moreover, scheme two employs the one way hash function which is not only irreversible, but also incapable of deriving the inputs via the output; in addition, the use of ECC makes it extremely difficult to determine the superkey. Therefore, the intruder cannot possibly succeed within the valid period. In other words, the proposed schemes are highly secure against intruders.

We shall assess the computation load of the two proposed schemes. The notations are defined as follows:

T_{MUL} : time cost of modulus multiplication operation

T_{EXP} : time cost of modulus operation

T_H : time cost of one way hash function operation

T_{EC_MUL} : time cost of perform elliptic curve multiplication operation

Next, we shall equate the time complexity of multiplication operation of the two proposed schemes to allow comparison of the two below. According to reference [16], in $g^t \bmod p$ operation, t is a 160 bits random integer, p is a 1024 bits prime number, and elliptic curve multiplication is performed to calculate bG, where $G \in E(Z_p)$ and $p \approx 2^{160}$, b is a 160 bits random integer. Combining all of the above, we can derive the following:

Table 1 below is the time complexity of the two proposed scheme composed from the above-mentioned information. From table 1, we can see that in the parameter generation stage, the computation load of scheme one is greater than that of scheme two, and scheme two has one way hash function operation but not scheme one. And the computation load varies according to the adopted one way hash function. In the equation construction stage, since both schemes need to only calculate the leaf nodes, therefore computation load is same.

$$T_{EXP} \doteqdot 240T_{MUL} . \qquad (3)$$

$$T_{EC\_MUL} \doteqdot 29T_{MUL} . \qquad (4)$$

Table 1. Time complexity comparison table

Item		Equation construction stage
Scheme one	Time complexity	$\sum_{r=1}^{n} r(n-r+2)T_{EXP} + \sum_{r=1}^{n} r(n-r+2)T_{MUL} - 2nT_{MUL}$
	Rough estimate	$241\sum_{r=1}^{n} r(n-r+2)T_{MUL} - 2nT_{MUL}$
Scheme two	Time complexity	$\sum_{r=1}^{n} r(n-r+2)T_{EC\_MUL} + \sum_{r=1}^{n} r(n-r+2)T_{MUL}$ $-2nT_{MUL} + \sum_{r=1}^{n} r(n-r+2)T_{H}$
	Rough estimate	$30\sum_{r=1}^{n} r(n-r+2)T_{MUL} - 2nT_{MUL} + \sum_{r=1}^{n} r(n-r+2)T_{H}$

6 Conclusion

Mobile agent is a growing research arena in today's advanced internet environment. Putting internet resources to good use will be a great help to the improvement of efficiency of an organization and the reduction of costs. Mobile agent is also important in e-commerce, and we predict a thriving future for mobile agents. At the same time, mobile agent is also a challenging research subject. Presently, mobile agent is facing an all out execution barrier which stems mainly from security problems. Hence, we need a wholesome mobile agent security system structure.

This study applies existing information security tools along with related security technology to propose a more suitable key management and access control scheme for mobile agent. We have successfully used exponential operation, ECC encryption technology and one way hash function to form a new direction of thinking and solution. The above-mentioned also proved that the proposed schemes are feasible and secure; it not only successfully ensures the security of a mobile agent, but is also more advantageous than Volker and Mehrdad's scheme. The proposed scheme effectively reduced the storage space required by an agent as well as the number of computations, making the mobile agent operate more efficiently.

Acknowledgement

This work was supported partially by National Science Council of Republic of China under Grants NSC 94-2213-E-194-042.

References

1. Akl, S. G., Taylor, P. D..: Cryptographic Solution to a Problem of Access Control in A Hierarchy, ACM Transactions on Computer Systems. Vol. 1, No. 3, August, (1983), 239-248
2. Chess, D., Grosof, B., Harrison, C., Levine, D., Parris, C., Tsudik, G..: Itinerant Agents for Mobile Computing, IEEE Personal Communications, Vol. 2, No. 5, October, (1995), 34-49
3. Corradi, A., Montanari, R., Stefanelli, C..: Security Issues in Mobile Agent Technology, Proceedings of the 7th IEEE Workshop on Future Trends of Distributed Computing Systems, Cape Town, South Africa, (1999), 3-8
4. Hohl, F..: A Model of Attacks Malicious Hosts Against Mobile Agents, Proceedings of the 4th Workshop on Mobile Object Systems: Secure Internet Mobile Computations, Brussels, Belgium, July, 21, (1998), 105-120
5. Karmouch, A..: Mobile Software Agents for Telecommunications, Guest Editorial, IEEE Communications Magazine, Vol. 36, No. 7, July, (1998), 24-25
6. Karnik, N. M., Tripathi, A. R..: A Security Architecture for Mobile Agents in Ajanta, Proceedings of The 20th International Conference on Distributed Computing Systems (ICDCS 2000), Taipei, Taiwan, April, (2000), 402-409
7. Lange, D. B., Oshima, M..: Programming and Deploying Java Mobile Agents with Aglets, Addison-Wesley Press, Massachusetts, USA, (1998)
8. Lin, I. C., Ou, H. H., Hwang, M. S.: Two Secure Transportation Schemes for Mobile Agents, Agent-Based Technologies- Information & Security,International Relations and Security Network ISN, Vol. 8, No. 1, (2002), 87-97
9. Lin, I. C., Ou, H. H., Hwang, M. S.: Efficient Access Control and Key Management Schemes for Mobile Agents, Computer Standards & Interfaces, Vol. 26, No. 5, (2004), 423-433

10. Maes, P., Guttman, R. H., Moukas, A.G..: Agents that Buy and Sell, Communications of the ACM, Vol. 42, No. 3, March, (1999), 81-91
11. Lin, I. C., Ou, H. H., Hwang, M. S..: Efficient Access Control and Key Management Schemes for Mobile Agents, Computer Standards & Interfaces, Vol. 26, No. 5, (2004), 423-433
12. Schneier , B..: Applied Cryptography: Protocols, Algorithms, and Source Code in C, 2nd ed., John Wiley & Sons, New York, (1996)
13. Volker , R., Mehrdad, J. S..: Access Control and Key Management for Mobile Agents, Computer Graphics, Vol. 22, No. 4, (1998), 457-461
14. Miller , V. S..: Uses of Elliptic Curves in Cryptography, Advances in Cryptology-CRYPTO'85, Proceedings, Lecture Notes in Compute Science, New York, NY : Springer-Verlag, No. 218, (1985), 417-426
15. Koblitz.: Elliptic Curve Cryptosystems, Mathematics of Computation, Vol. 48, (1987), 203-209
16. Koblitz , N., Menezes , A., Vanstone , S. A..: The State of Elliptic Curve Cryptography, Designs, Codes and Cryptography, Vol. 19, No. 2-3, March, (2000), 173-193

Analysis on Negotiation in Platform-Level Armored Force Combat Entity Agents System

Xiong Li, Kai Wang, Xianggang Liu, and Jiuting Duo

Department of Command and Administration, Academy of Armored Force Engineering, Beijing 100072, China
lixiong2609@126.com

Abstract. In this paper we present a platform-level simulation architecture for tactical armored force combat entity agents system by setting up mappings from combat entities to respective combat entity agents. In order to solve the problems on negotiation to enhance overall system efficiency, based on qualitative description of its framework, we place particular emphasis on quantitative analysis. Through transforming the system into a series-wound queueing system, we attain a Markov chain of stationary transition probabilities, since its stationary transition process in negotiation is a discrete state Markov process and accords with real military combat behaviors. Solving the stationary transition equations makes us find high-efficiency negotiation according to optimized system configuration. The obtained results show the effectiveness of the proposed approach and model.

1 Introduction

The concept of agency is being now broadly used not only as a model for computer programming units displaying a certain kind of characteristics but also in a more abstract and general way, as a new metaphor for the analysis, specification and implementation of complex software systems. Although, in many cases, agents can act separately to solve a particular problem, it often happens that a complete system made of several different agents has to be designed to cope with a complex problem involving either distributed data, knowledge, or control. A multi-agent system [1]~[3] can therefore be defined as a collection of, possibly heterogeneous, computational entities, having their own problem solving capabilities and which are able to interact among them in order to reach an overall goal.

On information battlefield, tactical armored force has some members including tanks and armored command platforms (information processing vehicles) which have lives and administrative levels. These platforms, or members, have believes, desires, intentions, and may adopt roles or have relationships with each other. Therefore, it may be seen as a system revealing a kind of a synergy that would not be expected from the simple sum of its component agents. This synergy is an emergent property of the system as a whole. In this paper, we view this synergy as a multi-agent-oriented model of armored force on information battlefield to build underlying mechanisms for the advanced concept technology demonstration of land combat action.

D.-S. Huang, K. Li, and G.W. Irwin (Eds.): ICIC 2006, LNAI 4114, pp. 346 – 354, 2006.

In a multi-agent system, a negotiation protocol contains the basic rules for the negotiation process and the communication. Thus it is explicit to point out existing and challenging problems that researchers are facing in designing and implementing this agent-based military combat system, such as

(1) how can we enforce the necessary teamwork, leading to coherent and effective results according to the overall system's goals and making all combat entity agents perform actions and fulfill tasks with higher efficiency?

and (2) how can we design and implement a system in a way that avoids computational overload by means of load balancing strategies so that we can attain higher negotiation efficiency?

However, current research on agent or multi-agents technologies usually concentrates on domain specification, and implementation problems [3]~[8]. There exists deficiency on negotiation efficiency by system organization optimization. The principal aim of this paper is to suggest possible answers to the above questions by using Markov chain model based on system framework description and its series-wound queueing system design.

2 Problem Statement

An agent with human being properties such as autonomy, sociality, adaptability and intelligence can act as a human. Especially multi-agent systems technology considers how a group of intelligent and autonomous agents coordinate their capacities and plan in order to achieve certain (local or global) goals [2], [4]. Agents may be seen as a natural extension of the concept of software objects. Object-oriented programming added abstraction entities, i.e., objects, which have persistent local states to the structured programming paradigm. Similarly, agent-based programming adds abstraction entities, i.e., agents, which have an independent execution thread and pro-activity to the object-oriented paradigm [5]. Thus, compared to an object, an agent is able to act in a goal-directed fashion (e.g., by interacting with other agents, reading sensors, or sending commands to effectors) rather than only passively react to procedure calls, as shown in Fig. 1.

In addition, an agent typically has also one or more of the following abilities: to communicate with other agents, to learn from experience and adapt itself to changes in the environment, to make plans, to reason using logic or game theory, to negotiate with other agents. Also, agents are sometimes programmed, or at least modeled, in terms of "mental states", such as, believes, desires, and intentions. A multi-agent system is a collection of agents co-operating with each other in order to fulfill common and individual goals (in some environments they may also compete). In a multi-agent system different agents often have different roles and individual goals.

According the above analysis, tactical armored force is so alike a multi-agent system in behaviors that we can set up mappings from the internal members of armored force to agents, i.e., tank → tank agent, information processing vehicle → information processing vehicle agent. Thus, we can establish a platform-level tactical armored force combat entity agents system model.

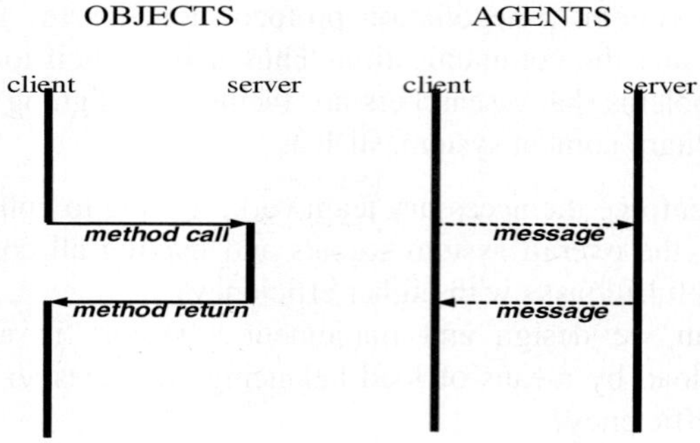

Fig. 1. Multi-threaded agents

Furthermore, we can define these combat entity agents as two multi-agent subsystems as follows:

$MAS_1=A=\{A_i\}$;
$MAS_2=B=\{B_i\}$;

where MAS_1 consists of all tank agents and MAS_2 consists of all information processing vehicle agents. They exchange information by network system (NS). The armored force combat entity agents system can be illustrated as Fig. 2.

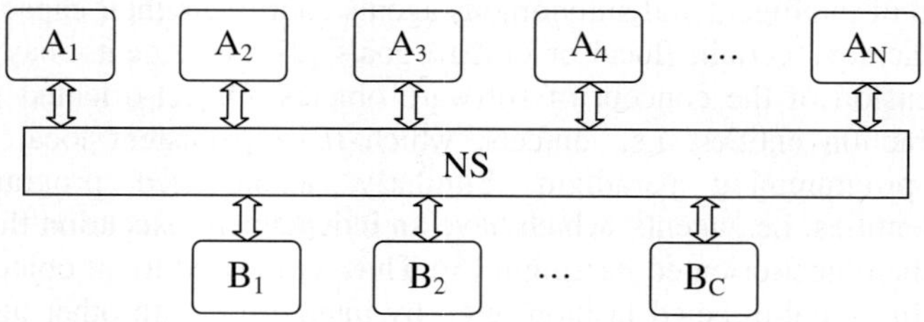

Fig. 2. Organization of combat entity agents system

In our system the distributed negotiation protocol has the following properties:

(1) The negotiation leads to a finite number of states.

(2) The negotiation process does not enter cyclic or infinite sequences but always reaches a terminal state.

The multi-agent negotiation has the following features:

(1) There is a seeding agent who initiates the negotiation.

(2) Each agent can be active or inactive.

(3) Initially all agents are inactive except for a specified seeding agent, which initiates the computation.

(4) An active agent can do local computation, send and receive messages and can spontaneously become inactive.

(5) An inactive agent becomes active, if it receives a message.

(6) Each agent may retain its current belief, revise or update its belief as a result of receiving a new message by performing a local computation. If it modifies its belief, it communicates its new belief to other concerned agents; else it does not modify its belief and remains silent.

Fig. 3 shows the negotiation behaviors process.

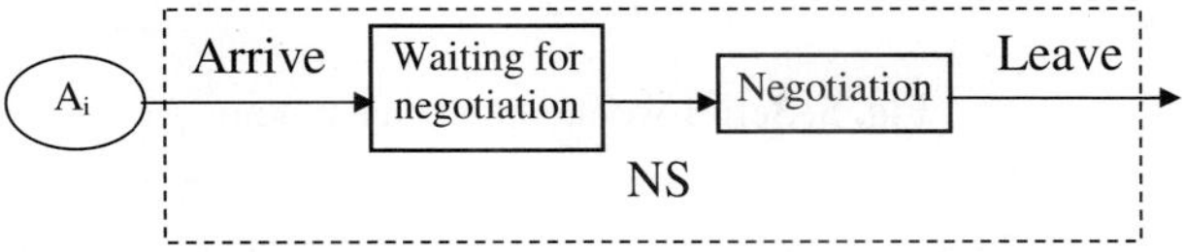

Fig. 3. Negotiation behaviors process

The distribution law of negotiation priority can be illustrated as Fig. 4.

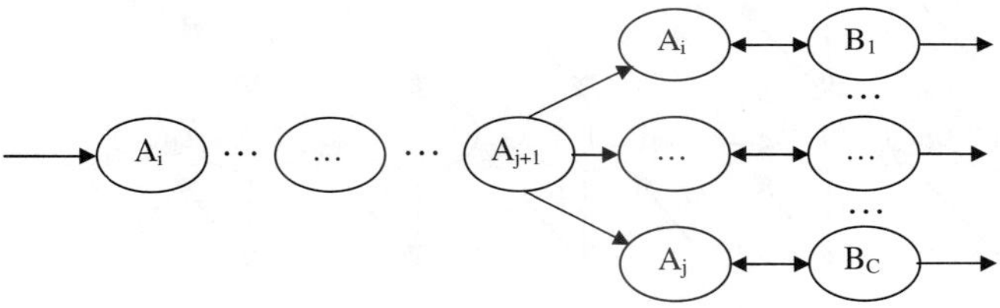

Fig. 4. Distribution law of negotiation priority

3 Problem Analysis

We assume that there are N tank agents (TAs) and C information processing vehicle agents (IPVAs), where

(1) A TA works independently and brings forward randomly requests on combat tasks, and the time T between requests from each TA is an exponential distribution, i.e., $P(t \le T) = e^{-\lambda t}$.

(2) The NS acts as a server and affords functions of control logics and communication service, and the time used in serving a combat task is another exponential distribution, i.e., $P(t \le T) = e^{-\mu_1 t}$.

(3) An IPVA works independently and performs randomly requests on combat tasks and the time T between requests performed from each TA is another exponential distribution, i.e., $P(t \le T) = e^{-\mu_2 t}$.

By military experts' evaluation, these hypotheses are consistent with real tactical armored force combat behaviors, i.e., they reflect battlefield combat rules in some senses. In addition, according to the military experiences on tactical armored force combat process on distributed battlefield, we can think that there is only one combat task produced by an arbitrary TA at any time, i.e., it is impossible for two or more combat tasks to be produced by a TA simultaneity. Of course, it is reasonable to think

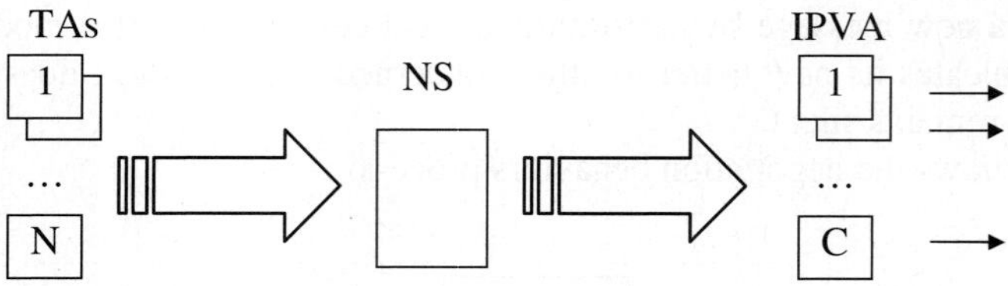

Fig. 5. Series-wound queueing system

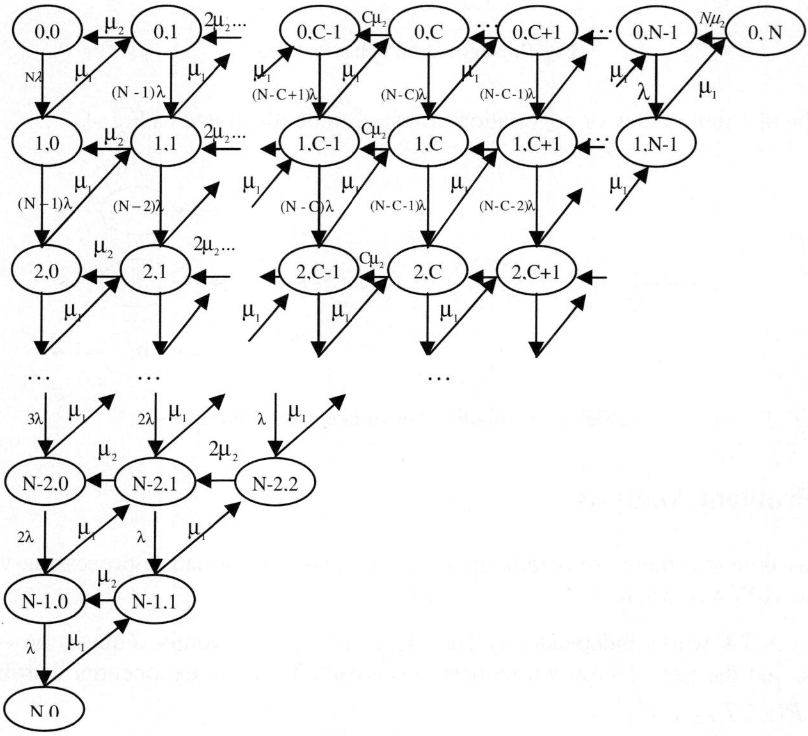

Fig. 6. Stationary transition diagram

that a combat task can be performed by an IPVA. Thus the agent-based platform-level armored force combat entities system can be viewed as a series-wound queueing system shown as Fig. 5.

In a balanceable state, the probability of n_1 requests on combat tasks in NS and n_2 requests on combat tasks in IPVAs is P_{n_1,n_2}. When a new request on combat tasks arrives, n_1 adds 1; when it enters the IPVAs service, n_1 decreases 1 and n_2 adds 1; and when the IPVAs performs a request, n_2 decreases 1.

A Markov chain is a sequence of random values whose probabilities at a time interval depend upon the value of the number at the previous time. The controlling factor in a Markov chain is the transition probability, which is a conditional probability for the system to go to a particular new state, given the current state of the system [9]~[12]. In fact, in our problem the probability P_{n_1,n_2} is only relevant to the previous time, i.e., future evolution of this stochastic process depends only on current state. Therefore the negotiation process is a discrete state Markov process and can be represented by a Markov chain with stationary transition probabilities (See Fig. 6).

According to Fig. 6, we can obtain the stationary transition equations as follows:

$$N\lambda P_{0,0} = \mu_2 P_{0,1}$$
$$(N-n_1)\lambda P_{n_0,0} + \mu_1 P_{n_1,0} = \mu_2 P_{n_1,1} + (N-n+1)\lambda P_{n_1-1,0} (\text{ when } 1 \le n_1 \le N-1)$$
$$\mu_1 P_{N,0} = \lambda P_{N-1,0}$$
$$n_2\mu_2 P_{0,n_2} + (N-n_2)\lambda P_{0,n_2} = (n_2+1)\mu_2 P_{0,n_2+1} + \mu_1 P_{1,n_2-1} (\text{ when } 1 \le n_2 \le C-1)$$
$$C\mu_2 P_{0,n_2} + (N-n_2)\lambda P_{0,n_2} = C\mu_2 P_{0,n_2+1} + \mu_1 P_{1,n_2-1} (\text{ when } C \le n_2 \le N-1)$$
$$C\mu_2 P_{0,N} = \mu_1 P_{1,N-1}$$
$$n_2\mu_2 P_{n_1,n_2} + \mu_1 P_{n_1,n_2} = \lambda P_{n_1-1,n_2} + \mu_1 P_{n_1+1,n_2-1} (\text{ when } 1 \le n_2 \le C-1, n_1+n_2 = N)$$
$$C\mu_2 P_{n_1,n_2} + \mu_1 P_{n_1,n_2} = \lambda P_{n_1-1,n_2} + \mu_1 P_{n_1+1,n_2-1} (\text{ when } C \le n_2 \le N-1, n_1+n_2 = N)$$
$$n_2\mu_2 P_{n_1,n_2} + \mu_1 P_{n_1,n_2} + (N-n_1-n_2)\lambda P_{n_1,n_2} = (N-n_1-n_2+1)\lambda P_{n_1-1,n_2} +$$
$$(n_2+1)\mu_2 P_{n_1,n_2+1} + \mu_1 P_{n_1+1,n_2-1} (\text{ when } 1 \le n_2 \le C-1, 1 \le n_1 \le N-1, n_1+n_2 \le N-1)$$
$$C\mu_2 P_{n_1,n_2} + \mu_1 P_{n_1,n_2} + (N-n_1-n_2)\lambda P_{n_1,n_2} = (N-n_1-n_2+1)\lambda P_{n_1-1,n_2} +$$
$$C\mu_2 P_{n_1,n_2+1} + \mu_1 P_{n_1+1,n_2-1} (\text{ when } C \le n_2 \le N-1, 1 \le n_1 \le N-1, n_1+n_2 \le N-1)$$
$$\sum_{n_1=0}^{N}\sum_{n_2=0}^{N-n_1} P_{n_1,n_2} = 1$$

Thus, we can obtain

$$P_{n_1,n_2} = \begin{cases} \dfrac{1}{Q(N)} \cdot \dfrac{\left[\frac{\lambda}{\mu_1}\right]^{n_1}\left[\frac{\lambda}{\mu_2}\right]^{n_2}}{(N-n_1-n_2)!\cdot n_2!} (\text{ when } 0 \le n_2 \le C-1) \\ \dfrac{1}{Q(N)} \cdot \dfrac{\left[\frac{\lambda}{\mu_1}\right]^{n_1}\left[\frac{\lambda}{\mu_2}\right]^{n_2}}{(N-n_1-n_2)!\cdot C!\cdot C^{n_2-C}} (\text{ when } C \le n_2 \le N) \end{cases}$$

where

$$Q(N) = \sum_{n_2=2}^{C-1}\sum_{n_1=0}^{N-n_2} \frac{\left[\frac{\lambda}{\mu_1}\right]^{n_1}\left[\frac{\lambda}{\mu_2}\right]^{n_2}}{(N-n_1-n_2)!\cdot n_2!} + \sum_{n_2=C+1}^{N}\sum_{n_1=0}^{N-n_2} \frac{\left[\frac{\lambda}{\mu_1}\right]^{n_1}\left[\frac{\lambda}{\mu_2}\right]^{n_2}}{(N-n_1-n_2)!\cdot C!\cdot C^{n_2-C}}$$

Thus we can attain the numbers of TAs which are in state "waiting" in the first and the second queueing systems respectively as follows:

$$L_1 = \sum_{n_1=2}^{N} \sum_{n_2=0}^{N-n_1} (n_1 - 1) P_{n_1,n_2}, L_2 = \sum_{n_1=C+1}^{N} \sum_{n_1=0}^{N-n_2} (N_2 - C) P_{n_1,n_2}$$

The mean utilization rate of IPVAs can be computed as

$$q = \sum_{n_2=0}^{C-1} \sum_{n_1=0}^{N-n_2} n_2 \cdot C^{-1} \cdot P_{n_1,n_2} + \sum_{n_2=C}^{N} \sum_{n_1=0}^{N-n_2} P_{n_1,n_2} = \sum_{n_2=0}^{C-1} \sum_{n_1=0}^{N-n_2} n_2 \cdot C^{-1} \cdot P_{n_1,n_2} + 1 - \sum_{n_2=0}^{C-1} \sum_{n_1=0}^{N-n_2} P_{n_1,n_2}$$

$$= 1 - \sum_{n_2=0}^{C-1} \sum_{n_1=0}^{N-n_2} \frac{C-n_2}{C} P_{n_1,n_2}$$

Fig. 7, Fig. 8 and Fig. 9 present respectively the relations of *N-C-q*, *N-C-*L_1/N and *N-C-*L_2/N in case 1 (λ=0.2/min, μ_1=3/min, μ_2=3/min) and case 2 (λ=0.2/min, μ_1=6/min, μ_2=3/min).

From these relations we can present the analysis results as follows:

(1) In case 1, when $C = 1$ and N augments, i.e., the number of TAs gets larger, the ratio of L_1/N increases, the ratio of L_2/N increases tardily and presents downtrend in the end (at this time approximately $N \geq 25$), and the mean utilization rate of IPVAs q increases a lot and gets reposeful in the end (at this time approximately $N \geq 20$). The fact shows that the jam-up in this system occurs mainly in NS. Once more IPVAs are joined to the military combat system, i.e., C augments, the ratio of L_2/N descends fleetly and the jam-up is resolved well. But meanwhile the ratio of L_1/N increases and q descends. Therefore, under this condition we should pay more attention to NS and enhance its performance.

(2) In case 2 (here μ_1=6/min), when $C = 1$ and N augments, which means only service efficiency of NS is enhanced, the ratio of L_1/N increases tardily and begins to descend (at this time approximately $N \geq 25$), the ratio of L_2/N increases rapidly, and q increases accordingly and gets reposeful in the end (at this time approximately $N \geq 25$); when N augments, the jam-up in this system is resolved dramatically with a linearly increasing q.

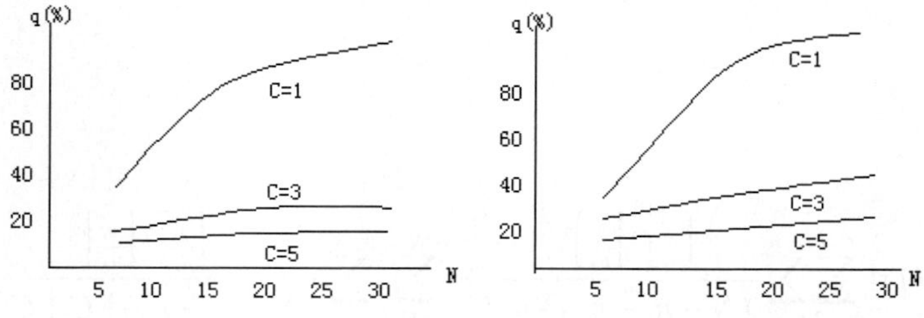

Fig. 7. Contrastive *N-C-Q* relation graph (in case 1 and case 2)

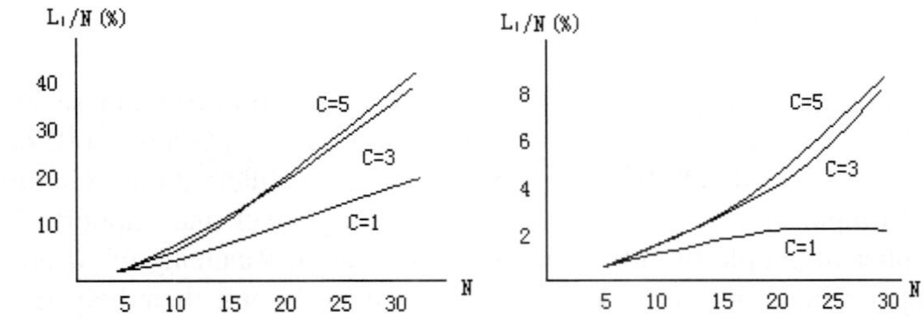

Fig. 8. Contrastive *N*- L_1/N relation graph (in case 1 and case 2)

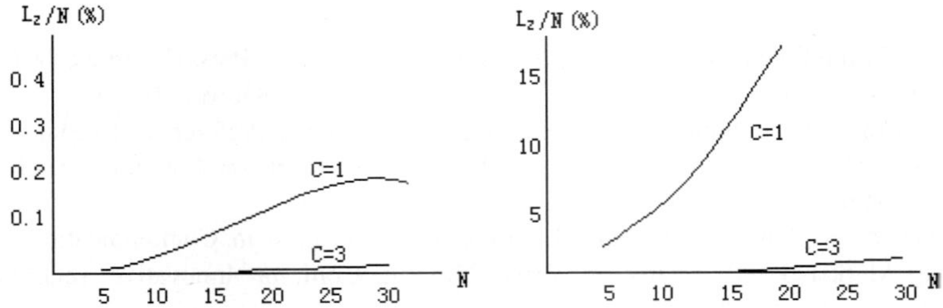

Fig. 9. Contrastive *N*- L_2/N relation graph (in case 1 and case 2)

These computational results are testified by the simulation of our platform-level tactical agent-based armored force combat system where some combat entities are designed to demonstrate combat behavior on dynamic and distributed battlefield and explore some issues, such as the role of speed in combat, how combat strategies might change when more combat platforms are added to a force or force structure is changed, and how distribution of combat power affect overall force effectiveness.

4 Conclusion

Analyzing the configuration and overall efficiency of negotiation in a complex military multi-agent system, especially like a platform-level armored force combat entity agents system, is a problem needing to be studied by researchers interested in this area. Markov chain approach is a useful tool to analyze a discrete state system. In this paper, according to military operational experiences and the system framework, we transformed agent-based armored force combat entities system into a series-wound queueing system, and developed a Markov chain model on the negotiation process, since the stationary transition probabilities of the next state depend only on current state. The feasibility and efficiency of our model are proved by the results. The fact shows that the analyzing technique we proposed has the capability of analyzing the negotiation problems of practical platform-level armored force combat entity agents systems.

Acknowledgments

This work is partially supported by the Strategic Foundation of Chinese PLA Grant #2004ZL19 and by the Equipment Project of Chinese PLA Grant #2005ZB05. The authors would like to thank the professors of the 2006 International Conference on Intelligent Computing for their instruction, encouragement and support. They also thank a number of people from the Faculty of Science of Academy of Armored Force Engineering for their prompt response to their requests and their help in technical direction.

References

1. Shi, Z.Z.: Intelligent Agents and Their Applications. Science Press. Beijing (2001)
2. Lesser, V.: Autonomous Agents and Multi-Agent Systems. Kluwer (1998)
3. Coehoorn, R.M., Jennings, N.R.: Learning an Opponent's Preferences to Make Effective Multi-issue Negotiation Tradeoffs. In: Proc. 6th Int Conf. on E-Commerce, Delft, The Netherlands (2004) 59–68
4. Haque, N. R. Jennings, Moreau, L.: Resource Allocation in Communication Networks Using Market-Based Agents. In: Proc. 24th Int. Conf. on Innovative Techniques and Applications of AI (2004) 187–200
5. Franco Zambonelli, H. Van Dyke Parunak: Signs of a Revolution in Computer Science and Software Engineering. In: Proc. Agent Oriented Software Engineering Workshop at AAMAS 2002 (2002) 68–74
6. Li Xiong, Liu Xiaobin, Hao Na: Multi-agent-oriented Modeling for Intelligence Reconnaissance System. In: Proc. 6th Int. Proc. Conf. on Parallel and Distributed Computing. IEEE, Los Alamitos, California (2005) 563–566
7. Li Xiong, Liu Degang, Cong Hua: Multi-Agent-Based Space Information Interaction Simulation Model. In: Proc. Int. Conf. on Space Information Technology, SPIE Press (2005) 598509-1–598509-5
8. Zhao Huaici, Huang Shabai: Modeling and Simulation of Agent-Oriented Complex System. Chinese Journal of System Simulation. 5(2003) 910–913
9. Barnett G., Kohn R. and Sheather, S.: Bayesian Estimation of an Autoregressive Model Using Markov Chain Monte Carlo. Jorlrnal of Econonietrics, 74 (1996) 237–254
10. Eronen, L., Geerts, F., Toivonen, H.: A Markov Chain Approach to Reconstruction of Long Haplotypes, In: Proc. Pacific Symposium on Biocomputing (2004) 126–139
11. Mahmoud, H. M.: Evolution of Random Search Trees. John Wiley & Sons, Inc., New York (1992)
12. Jacobson, M. T., Matthews, P.: Generating Uniformly Distributed Random Latin Squares. Journal of Combinatorial Design, 4 (1996) 405–437

Conflict Resolution and Preference Learning in Ubiquitous Environment

Md. Kamrul Hasan, Kim Anh, Lenin Mehedy, Young-Koo Lee, and Sungyoung Lee*

Real-Time & MultiMedia Lab, Department of Computer Engineering,
Kyung Hee University, 449-701, Republic of Korea
{kamrul, anhpnk, lenin}oslab.khu.ac.kr, yklee@khu.ac.kr,
sylee@oslab.khu.ac.kr

Abstract. Building intelligent environment is one of crucial challenges for ubiquitous computing developers. To make the environment adapt rationally according to the desire of users, the system should be able to guess users' interest, by learning users' behavior, habit or preference. While learning the user preference, dealing with uncertainty and conflict resolution is of the utmost importance. When many users are involved in a ubiquitous environment, the decisions of one user can be affected by the desires of others. This makes learning and prediction of user preference difficult. To address the issue, we propose an approach of user preference learning which can be used widely in context-aware systems. We use Bayesian RN-Metanetwork, a multilevel Bayesian network to model user preference and priority.

1 Introduction

Ubiquitous computing is mainly about building systems which are useful to users, which "...weave themselves into the fabric of everyday life until they are indistinguishable from it" [1]. Users tend to move around often, doing new things, visiting new places, changing their minds suddenly, and changing their moods, too. Therefore, a helpful system should react according to the changing context of the user.

Absorbing and developing the key ideas of ubiquitous computing as well as context-awareness, a smart environment (e.g. smart office, smart home) contains a large number of invisible sensors and actuators which enable the system to "think and work" based on its own perception of users' context [2]. Let us consider following scenario of a smart office:

"In the morning, secretary comes to the office. When she enters the room, the light is turned on and the curtain is opened. The music player plays the secretary's favorite song. After that, professor arrives. Because the priority of professor is higher than that of secretary, the music is changed to professor's favorite. When a student enters the office and sits down on the chair in front of professor's desk, knowing that professor is having a meeting with his students, the music will be switched off..."

The scenario sounds like it has some intelligence involved. It somehow satisfies the "invisible interface" requirement of a ubiquitous computing system, because the

* Corresponding author.

D.-S. Huang, K. Li, and G.W. Irwin (Eds.): ICIC 2006, LNAI 4114, pp. 355 – 366, 2006.

user does not need to use any explicit interface to interact with the system. However, this is just an automatic system triggered by events. System developer creates the rules and therefore thinks about what the system should do in each situation. The smart system built in this way, will make the same decision, even if the user changes his preference. We argue that, a real smart system should have three capabilities. First, a smart system should be able to do inference. Second, a smart system should be able to learn by itself. User and developers can act like teachers, but the knowledge should be improved incrementally. Finally, a smart system should be able to solve some difficult problems, such as the conflict among the users [3]. Let us add some details to the above scenario to reflect this idea:

"The music playing is stopped. Even though the command is from the remote control on the secretary's desk, it does not totally mean that the secretary herself wants to stop the music. Maybe professor uses that remote control, or maybe the secretary does it because professor tells her to do. Moreover, there are some possible reasons that he or she does not want to listen to music at this time. The data from other sensors should be used to detect the person who wants to stop the music and his/her reason, so that the next time when the same situation happens, the music will be automatically stopped."

The preference of user changes over time or based on situation. It makes *online learning* (or adaptation) a crucial requirement. Sometimes there is uncertainty in user's temporary preference. User does not always select the most weighted choice. Again, when there are many users in the smart environment, the action of one user can affect others' choice [4]. It raises the challenges of *distinguishing* the preference of each user as well as *resolving* the *conflicts* among different user preferences. The introduction of probabilistic model can handle these uncertainty and adaptive prioritization of users. But how the system measures the utility or user satisfaction level? If the system can read the user's expression, and then tell whether the user is sad or happy, or anything else, it makes a very good utility function for the learning process. However, so far this is not realistic. Hence we base the utility function on the user control commands. After the smart system gives a command to an actuator, if the user selects another command, implies he does not agree with the system's decision. If he does nothing, it means he is satisfied. By other words, this is a "Yes/No", or Boolean utility function. Anyway, it is enough for a smart system to learn about the user's preference, at least at the current level. In this paper, we discuss Bayesian RN-Metanetowok [5] for preference learning with conflict resolution scheme. We also discuss the adaptation of the Bayesian model over time span.

To resolve conflicts for Context-aware Media services in smart home environments, GIST [6] applies Naïve Bayes classifier to resolve conflicts among users. The system sums up the preferences of users who are collided with each other and recommends the specific contents ordered by the summed preference. However, this system does not have online learning capability. Reactive Behavioral System (ReBa) resolves conflicts by inferring only the group activities [7], so it is very difficult in ReBa to provide particular services to a specific user when a group of people is present.

In the next section, we point the superiority of our method with an introduction of Bayesian RN-Metanetwork. The subsequent sections describe the modeling of the network for user preference and priority.

2 Bayesian RN-Metanetwork

The smart system should deal with uncertainty, should learn the preference of each user in a multi-user environment, should utilize domain knowledge and user-defined rules and should adapt to the changed user preference. Besides, we see that when combining the preferences of many users, we often base on user priority. Priority can be fixed, but normally it changes over time, or based on situation; for example a sleeping user will be considered more important than others. Hence the context-aware system should be able to learn and adapt to the changes of user's situation-based priority. To address these issues, We propose a Bayesian RN-Metanetwork (RN stands for Relevant Network).

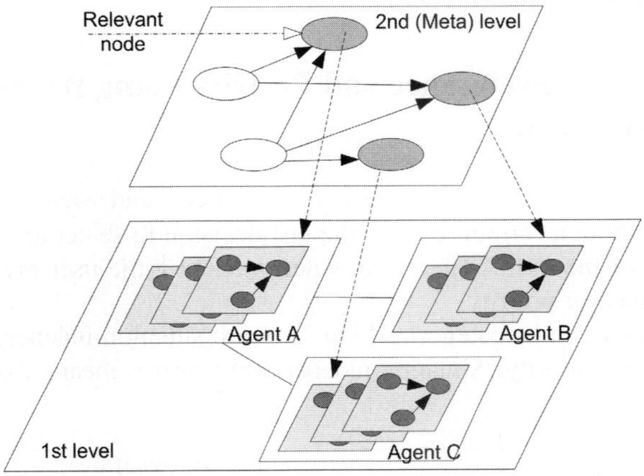

Fig. 1. A Bayesian RN-Metanetwork structure

The Bayesian RN-Metanetwork is a set of Bayesian networks, which are put on two levels in such a way that the distribution of probabilistic networks on first level depends on the local probability distributions associated with the nodes of the second level network. The Bayesian RN-Metanetwork is a triplet:

$$\text{RMBN} = (\text{BN0}, \text{BNS}, \text{R}) \tag{1}$$

where BNS = {BNS1, BNS2, ... BNSn} is a set of sets of Bayesian networks in first layer and BN0 is the second level Bayesian networks; R = {R1 ... Rn} is a set of inter level links. The probability distribution of each Bayesian network is included inside it. Each R_i is a link "vertex – network set" meaning that stochastic values of vertex v_i in the network BN0 correspond to the distribution of one set of Bayesian networks in the first level.

Bayesian RN-Metanetwork supports multi-agent systems. As depicted in Fig. 1, each set of Bayesian networks in the first level is hold by an agent. Each agent uses the distribution of its Bayesian networks to calculate some needed values, and they communicate with other agents through some interfaces. The interfaces consist of common nodes between agents' networks. The mechanism for belief updating in a multi-agent Bayesian network system is described in [8].

We use the Bayesian RN-Metanetwork to learn both user preference and priority at the same time, as well as to resolve the conflict among many user preferences. Our approach is special in the following aspects:

- The Bayesian RN-Metanetwork model is very suitable for multi-agent systems. Especially in ubiquitous environments, due to the complex, diverse and open-ended characteristic of the system, the multi-agent paradigm brings much more advantages than the single-agent paradigm.
- The adaptation algorithm for Bayesian RN-Metanetwork is fully described to adapt the model to the continuously changing preference of users.
- Finally, no matter how many users are there in the environment, the priority and preference of each user is calculated separately. This is very useful for widening the scale of systems, as well as knowledge reuse.

3 Modeling User Preference and Priority Using Bayesian RN-Metanetwork

When many users are present in a smart environment, and each user has his or her own preference about a certain service, the last decision to select the service is related to the priorities of the users. Therefore, when modeling the user preference, we also need to model the user priority.

The user priority can be categorized into 2 types: situation-independent priority and situation-dependent priority. Situation-independent priority means that the priority of

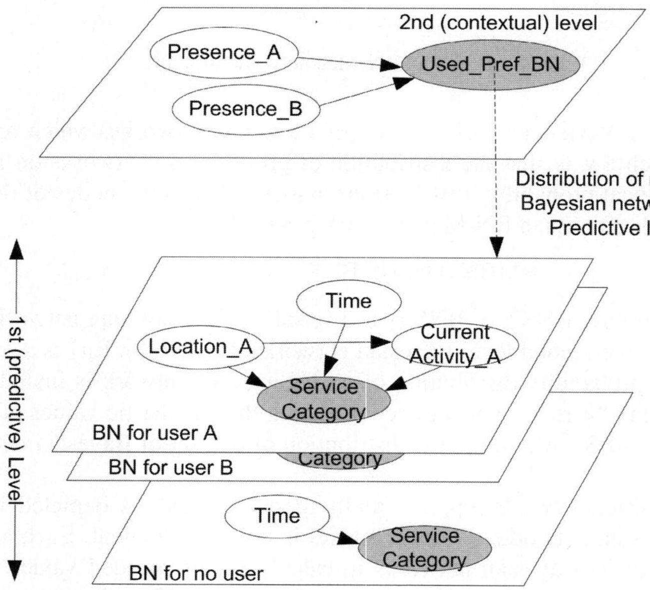

Fig. 2. A Bayesian RN-Metanetwork to learn multimedia service preference of 2 users A, B in case of situation-independent priority

a user does not change when situation changes, i.e. it does not change by time or by place or under any condition. In contrast, situation-dependent priority changes when situation changes, such as when user changes his place or activity.

The user preference in case of situation-independent priority can be modeled using the 2-level Bayesian RN-Metanetwork. Fig. 2 shows the Bayesian RN-Metanetwork for modeling user preference about Multimedia service in a 2-user system.

The model is based on the idea that the priority of one user can be understood as how much that user can contribute into the final decision. In the model, the distribution of relevant Bayesian networks, which model individual user preferences, indicates the proportion of each user preference in the compound preference. Hence the meta-level of this Bayesian RN-Metanetwork also models the user priority. We can see that the user priority in this case depends only on the user presence. Table 1 shows an example of value of the conditional distribution of relevant Bayesian networks (or user priority).

Table 1. Conditional probability of Used_Pref_BN node in 2nd level Bayesian network in Fig.2

Presence_A	Y		N	
Presence_B	Y	N	Y	N
Use_A_pref	0.5	1	0	0
Use_B_pref	0.5	0	1	0
Use_Nouser_pref	0	0	0	1

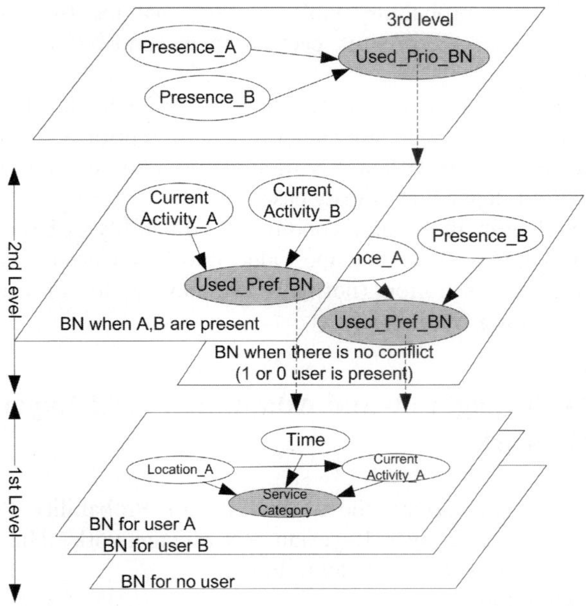

Fig. 3. A Bayesian RN-Metanetwork to learn multimedia service preference of 2 users A, B in case of situation-dependent priority. Priority depends on not only user presence but also user activity.

Table 2. Conditional probability of Used_Prio_BN node in 3rd level Bayesian network in Fig.3

Presence_A	Y		N	
Presence_B	Y	N	Y	N
Use_AB_prio	1	0	0	0
Use_single_prio	0	1	1	1

Table 3. Conditional probability of Used_Pref_BN node when both A and B are present

CurrentActivity_A	Working		Sleeping	
CurrentActivity_B	Working	Sleeping	Working	Sleeping
Use_A_pref	0.5	0.3	0.9	0.5
Use_B_pref	0.5	0.7	0.1	0.5
Use_Nouser_pref	0	0	0	0

Table 4. Conditional probability of Used_Pref_BN node in 2nd level Bayesian network when there is no conflict

Presence_A	Y		N	
Presence_B	Y	N	Y	N
Use_A_pref	-	1	0	0
Use_B_pref	-	0	1	0
Use_Nouser_pref	-	0	0	1

From the conditional probability table, we see that the two users have same priority. When both users are present, each of them contributes 50% into the final preference decision.

In case of situation-dependent priority, the 2nd (or Meta) level is replaced by a metanetwork. In other words, one more level for learning priority based on situation is added. Fig. 3 depicts the Bayesian RN-Metanetwork for the multimedia services preference in situation-dependent priority case.

Tables 2, 3 and 4 show the sample conditional probability of Used_Prio_BN node and Used_Pref_BN nodes. Note that the value range of Current Activity nodes is reduced for easier demonstration (normally we have a lot of activities such as Reading, Walking, Eating, Working, etc.)

4 Probability Propagation and Adaptation for 2-Layer Bayesian RN-Metanetwork

In this session, we will explain the algorithms for Probability Propagation and Adaptation for the basic 2-layer Bayesian RN-Metanetwork. The algorithms are illustrated by computations on the model in Fig. 2.

Notations and Definitions

The Bayesian RN-Metanetwork in Fig. 2 has parameters:

+ 1st level:

- This level has only one set of Bayesian networks: 2 Bayesian networks modeling the preferences of 2 users and one Bayesian network for the case of no user.
- The attributes of the Bayesian networks: Time (denoted T), Location_A/B (denoted Li, i=1, 2 corresponding to A and B), CurrentActivity _A/B (denoted CAi), ServiceCategory (denoted Sx, x=1, 2, 3 for its duplications in 3 networks) and has the values {SV1 ...SVj}.
- The prior probabilities: P(T); P(Li); P(CAi), P(Sx).
- The conditional probability P(Si|T, Li, CAi), i=1, 2 and $P(S_3|T)$.

+ 2nd level:

- The attributes: Presence_A/B (denoted by Pr_i, i=1, 2) represents the Presence of user A/B with the values {yes/no}
- The relevance node: Used_Pref_BN (denoted BN) holds the probability to have each Bayesian model in the predictive level with the values {BN1, ... BN3}.
- The prior probabilities: P(Pr) denotes the probability distribution of the set Pr and $P(Pr_i)$ denotes that of each item in the set.
- The relevance probability: P (BN). The conditional probability P (BN|Pr)

4.1 Probability Propagation

Given the evidence P (Pr), P(BNx) is calculated as:

$$P(BN_x) = P(BN = BN_x \mid \mathrm{Pr}).P(\mathrm{Pr}) \tag{2}$$

Then the probability of the target attribute ServiceCategory can be estimated:

$$P(S) = \sum_{x=1}^{3} P(BN_x).P(S_x) \tag{3}$$

with P(Sx) calculated given the evidence T, Li and CAi

$$P(S_x) = \begin{cases} P(S_x \mid T, L_x, CA_x).P(T).P(L_x).P(CA_x) & x = 1,2 \\ P(S_x \mid T).P(T) & x = 3 \end{cases} \tag{4}$$

In other words, the probability of ServiceCategory preference of each user will be calculated separately, and then combined with the weight coefficients which are the distributed probabilities of the Bayesian networks in Predictive level. The target ServiceCategory SVj with highest P(S=SVj) will be selected.

The Bayesian RN-Metanetwork provides an easy but efficient method for modeling many kinds of user preferences, from multimedia services such as music, television, radio, web page, public information, etc. to the environment parameter such as light, temperature, etc. All we have to do is identify the features which affect the preference of users, build the preference model for each user and finally combine them by a RN-Metanetwork. When the system learns, each preference model is updated separately so that they can be reused in other systems.

4.2 Adaptation

Even though some approaches address learning issue as the initial of the conditional probabilities from example data sets, the true meaning of learning in a ubiquitous system is online learning. When a ubiquitous system starts working, there is no example data but only the domain knowledge and user-defined rules. So, the task of online learning, or adaptation, is crucial.

Each time the system makes a decision about which service category to be selected, it then wait a time interval t_w for the response of users. There are 2 cases of user responses:

Approval: If there is no response, then the system assumes that the users are pleased with the decision. In this case, the decision together with the evidences will be considered a single sample and be used to update the Bayesian networks conditional probabilities.

Denial: If one user gives a control command to the system to change the selected service category, it means that the user may not be satisfied with the decision of the system. This is a serious case, and the system should not make the same wrong prediction again. So the user's selection together with the evidences will be considered N samples (N>>1) and be used to update the Bayesian networks conditional probabilities.

The adaptation algorithm is based on two assumptions:

Assumption 1: The contribution of one user preference in the combined preference is equal to his contribution in making a decision. The assumption means that when the system estimates the preference of many users, it gives each user's preference a weight. On the other hand, whenever a control command is given by a group of user, each user has his contribution in that command. The weight in first case and the contribution in second case are assumed to be equal.

Assumption 2: Every user has the tendency of selecting the option which has highest probability calculated by his preference model. This option is called the most favorite option. The assumption means that given the evidences, calculate the posterior distribution of a preference using the preference model of one single user (one of 2 Bayesian networks for 2 users A and B in the previous example, for instance), the option with highest probability can be considered that user's most favorite, and is most likely to be selected by the user himself. Assumption 2 leads to a definition: *A decision matches user preference if it matches the most favorite option of that user.*

Based on the above assumptions and definition, the adaptation algorithm for RN-Metanetwork is introduced:

Adaptation Algorithm

Step 1: update the meta-layer network

+In Approval case, there is no need to update the meta-layer network (users satisfy with the current priority)

+ In Denial case:

- Find the most favorite option of each user

$$SV*_i = \arg\max(P(S_i)) \tag{5}$$

Where SV*i denotes the most favorite service of user i.

- Count 1 for the value of relevant node related to the user's preference model if the final decision is the same with user's most favorite option. We use the sequential updating introduced in [9]. We perform the following adaptation:

If SV*i = SV* then, $P(BN_i \mid \Pr_e) = \dfrac{P(BN_i).s.q+1}{s}$ (6)

Else, $P(BN_j \mid \Pr_e) = \dfrac{P(BN_j).s.q}{s}$ with $j \neq i$

With SV*: the finally selected services, $\Pr_e$: the set of evidences of the presences of users, q: the fading factor, q ∈ (0, 1), s: the effective sample size which is calculated by:

$$s = \frac{1}{1-q} \tag{7}$$

<u>Step 2: update the preference model of each user based on the contribution of that user into the decision</u>

For each user i: Calculate w_i, the distribution probability of that user's preference model: $w_i = P(BN_i)$. Count w_i for the final selected option and update the user's preference model 1 or N times, in approval or denial case respectively.

$$P(S_i = SV^* \mid T_e, L_{ei}, CA_{ei}) = \frac{P(S_i = SV^* \mid T_e, L_{ei}, CA_{ei}).s.q_i + w_i}{s} \text{ and} \tag{8}$$

$$P(S_i = SV_j \mid T_e, L_{ei}, CA_{ei}) = \frac{P(S_i = SV_j \mid T_e, L_{ei}, CA_{ei}).s.q_i}{s} \text{ with } SV_j \neq SV^*$$

Where T_e, L_{ei}, CA_{ei} denote the evidences of the Time, user location, user current activity of user i, $P(S_i \mid T_e, L_{ei}, CA_{ei})$ denotes the distribution of conditional probabilities in preference model of user i q_i: the fading factor which is calculated separately for each preference model, to maintain the same experience size according to the following equation:

$$q_i = \frac{s - w_i}{s} \tag{9}$$

The probability propagation algorithm and adaptation algorithm which were described above can also be applied for multi-layer Bayesian RN-Metanetwork in a recursive manner.

The probability propagation process for the Bayesian RN-Metanetwork in Fig.3:

Step 1: applying the probability propagation algorithm for the first 2 layers to calculate the marginal of Used_Pref_BN

Step 2: use the marginal of Used_Pref_BN as the distribution for the Bayesian networks in third layer to calculate the marginal for Service_Category.

The adaptation process for the Bayesian RN-Metanetwork in Fig.3:

Step 1: in case of denial, applying the adaptation algorithm for the first 2 levels of the Bayesian RN-Metanetwork.

Step 2: calculate the marginal of Used_Pref_BN and use it to do adaptation for the third level.

5 Evaluation

One can argue that the traditional Bayesian network is still faster than the Bayesian RN-Metanetwork, because for Bayesian RN-Metanetwork we have the overhead of the meta-layer propagation. In fact, the Bayesian RN-Metanetwork is slower just in case the distribution of every Bayesian network in the first layer is not equal to 0, or by other words, when all users are present in the system.

Let estimate the calculation time for the Multimedia preference example above when using the traditional Bayesian network and Bayesian RN-Metanetwork. Analysis in [10] shows the runtime for the brute force method of enumeration is $O(q^m)$, where q is the size of the alphabet (in our example: q = number of values for Service Category i for the preference model, or number of users + 1 in the meta network) and m is the number of unknown variables.

We have seen that Pearl's algorithm [11], for the special case of a polytree, has an efficient runtime of $O(Nq^e)$, where e is the maximum number of parents on a vertex. It can be seen that in the case of the turbo-decoding algorithm [12], the runtime is linear in the size of the network, as evidence is propagated a constant number of times.

Here because both the number of unknown variables and the number of maximum parents will increase when the node number increase, we assume that in general the runtime is $O(q^x)$ with x is proportional to the size of the network. The size, S of the network in traditional case is proportional to the number of user. So with N = number of user and q = number of values for Service Category i for the preference model, the propagation time is $O(q^{\alpha N})$ with α is proportional to the number of node in a single user preference model. From Fig.1, the size S' of each preference network in Bayesian RN-Metanetwork remains the same for every user. S' = S / N. We have the propagation time of each preference network is $O(q^{\alpha})$ and the propagation time of meta network in Fig.1 is O (1) given that we know the location of all the users. Then the numbers of preference model should be propagated, k has the binomial distribution, because this is the distribution of obtaining exactly k (Presence = Yes) out of N trials.

$$P(k \mid N) = \frac{N!}{(N-k)!k!}.p^k (1-p)^{N-k} \tag{10}$$

Where p is the mean probability of one user is presented in the location.

The expected value of k is $E[k] = N.p$. So, expected propagation time is $O(Npq^{\alpha})$. We have $O(Npq^{\alpha}) < O(q^{\alpha N})$. The Bayesian RN-Metanetwork is still more efficient.

In case of situation-dependent priority, the propagation runtime is added with the time for calculating the priority given the evidences about situation. The runtime for each priority model is $O(q^{\alpha N^*})$ with N* is the mean of the binominal distribution of taking k users from N users. We have N* = N.p. Hence the expected propagation runtime for a priority model is $O(q^{\alpha Np})$. So, the total propagation runtime is $O(Npq^{\alpha} + q^{\alpha Np})$. In this case, it is hard to tell whether the Bayesian RN-Metanetwork is faster or slower. However, besides the speed, the advantages of Bayesian RN-Metanetwork come from at least two aspects:

- First, with the division of a large network into small and single-user models, the design of any Bayesian RN-Metanetwork becomes much easier, especially when we have to assign the conditional probabilities for the network.
- Second, we have the separate models for priority and preference. We also have separate models for each user. This dramatically increases the reusability of the models.

6 Conclusion and Future Works

Context-aware computing poses interesting issues for information system researches. Learning user preference in order to adapt the system automatically to the need of user is one of those issues. The challenges in this are due to the uncertain, heterogeneous, distributing characteristic of a context-aware system. Especially when there are many users involve in an intelligent environment, the system has to cope with conflict resolution and distinguishing among the user preferences. A solution for learning user preference in a multi-user context-aware environment which can efficiently resolve the above mentioned problems is the contribution of this paper. We have first presented the Bayesian RN-Metanetwork which can be used to model the user preference as well as user priority for many users, while still maintain separate preference model for each user. The propagation algorithm showed how to calculate the composite preference of all the users in the system and make decision about the service to provide. To actively and continuously adapt the models to the newest preferences and priorities of the users, the adaptation algorithm for Bayesian RN-Metanetwork was described. However, this is just the first step to make the system intelligent. There are still a lot of challenges such as user behavior routine learning, in which the prediction of the future actions of user is the most important task. We leave that as a future work.

Acknowledgement

This work was supported by IITA Professorship for Visiting Faculty Positions in Korea from Ministry of Information and Communications.

References

1. Weiser, M., Scientifc, A.: The Computer for the 21st Century. Reprinted in IEEE Pervasive Computing, (2002) 19-25
2. Meyer, S., Rakotonirainy.: A survey of Research on Context-Aware Home.Proc. of the Australasian information security workshop conference on ACSW frontiers, (2003) 159-168
3. Keith, W., Edwards, R., Grinter, E.: At Home with Ubiquitous Computing: Seven Challenges. LNCS 2201, New York (2001) 256-272
4. Hughes, J., O'Brien, J., Rodden, T.: Understanding Technology in Domestic Environments: Lessons for Cooperative Builds. In Proceedings of the First International Workshop on Cooperative Buildings (CoBuild'98). Darmstadt, Germany, Heidelberg, Germany: Springer-Verlag, Berlin (1998) 246-261
5. Vagan, Y., Terziyan, O.: Vitko.:Bayesian Metanetworks for Modelling User Preferences in Mobile Environment. In proceedings of KI, (2003)
6. Shin, C., Woo, W.: Conflict Management for Media Services by Exploiting Service History and User Preference. UbiPCMM05: 1st International Workshop on Personalized Context Modeling and Management for UbiComp Applications, (2005)
7. Nicholas, H., Ajay, K., Rattapoom, T., Tyler, H.: Building Agent-Based Intelligent Workspaces. In ABA Conference Proceedings, New York (2002)
8. Yang, X.: Probabilistic Reasoning in Multiagent Systems: A Graphical Models Approach. Published by the press syndicate of the University of Cambridge. ISBayesian network 0 521 813085, (2002)
9. Spiegelhalter, D., Lauritzen, S. L.: Sequential Updating of Conditional Probabilities on Directed Graphical Structures. Networks, 20 (1990) 579–605
10. Cooper, G. F.: The Computational Complexity of Probabilistic Inference Using Bayesian Belief networks. Artificial Intelligence, (1990) 393-405
11. MacKay, D. J., McEliece, R. J., Cheng, J. F.: Turbo Decoding as an Instance of Pearl's Belief Propagation Algorithm. IEEE Journal of Selected Areas of Communication, (1998) 140-152
12. Rodemich, E., McEliece, R. J., Cheng, J. F.: The Turbo Decision Algorithm. Proceedings 33rd Allerton Conference on Communications, Control and Computing, Monticello, Illinois (1995) 366-371

Design and Implement of Customer Information Retrieval System Based on Semantic Web

Mi Sug Gu, Jeong Hee Hwang, and Keun Ho Ryu*

Database/BioInformatics Laboratory Chungbuk National University
{gumisug, jhhwang, khryu}@dblab.chungbuk.ac.kr

Abstract. Recently semantic web is an important issue in many areas. Ontology specifies the knowledge in a specific domain and defines the concepts of knowledge and the relationships between concepts. To specify and define the knowledge in a specific domain, it is required to generate the ontology which conceptualizes the knowledge. Accordingly, to search the information of potential customers for home-delivery marketing of post office, we design a specific domain to generate the ontology in this paper. And we propose how to retrieve the information, using the generated ontology. We also implement the data search robot which collects the information based on the generated ontology. Therefore we confirm that the ontology and the search robot perform the information retrieval exactly.

1 Introduction

The current web search engine estimates the similarity of the documents, using the frequency of words, and then gives the grades. Therefore the users waste too much time finding the useful information. To solve this problem, the semantic web is appearing. The semantic web defines the meaning of the information, specifies the relations of the concepts, and gives the information of the meaning to the web documents. And the software agent retrieves and provides the information to the users automatically [1].

The ontology is needed to provide the semantic web based services. It not only specifies the domain of knowledge, but also formalizes the concept of knowledge and the relationships between the concepts. The ontology describes the words in the specific domain by the hierarchical structure, and contains the reasoning rules to expand it. The ontology is used when the different databases use the different words or identifiers about the same concepts. Therefore when we compare and integrate the information of the two different databases, the ontology can help to compare the differences between them. Therefore the ontology is essential and indispensable to the semantic web based information retrieval.

In this paper, the domain of the ontology is arranged to the information for the home delivery service. Home delivery service marketing is one of the strategies for the profit of the home delivery company or post office. Extracting the information of the shopping sites from the existing web, we can do the home delivery service

* Corresponding author.

D.-S. Huang, K. Li, and G.W. Irwin (Eds.): ICIC 2006, LNAI 4114, pp. 367 – 378, 2006.

marketing based on the information. We can use the information such as the items, the areas, the telephone numbers, and e-mail addresses of the company for the home delivery marketing. The potential customer in this paper means these kinds of shopping sites.

Therefore, to retrieve the customer information of the home delivery service, we design the specific domain for generating the semantic web based ontology. And also we propose a technique of the information retrieval using the generated ontology. Accordingly, to retrieve intelligently the information, we implemented the retrieval robot [2] which can collect the information of the internet shopping sites, the items, and the customers on the web. And we describe the method about how to implement the retrieval system based on the ontology.

This paper comprises as follows. Section 2 will describe the technique of the information retrieval based on the ontology. And Section 3 will explain the domain and the design of the ontology to search for the customer information. In Section 4, we will describe the design of the automatic ontology generation for implementing the retrieval system based on the semantic web. And also we will explain the design of the agent and the whole framework of the ontology based information retrieval system. And then Section 5 will describe the implementation of the ontology based retrieval system and the result of the retrieval, and then conclude this paper.

2 Semantic Web Based Customer Information Retrieval

Semantic web is the extended one of the existing web. We give a well defined meaning to the information on the web. It has the paradigm that people can work with the computers co-operatively [1], [2].

2.1 Ontology Based Information Retrieval

As the semantic web gives a well defined meaning to the information on the web, not only people but also computer can interpret and understand the meaning of the documents. Therefore it is proposed to retrieve, interpret, and integrate the information automatically using computer. In general, the semantic web contains the ontology for the definition of the knowledge, RDF and RDFS for describing the web resource, and the agent which is the program used for collecting the information automatically [3], [4].

The ontology is the specification of a conceptualization. That is, it is used to define the concepts of the specific domain and the relationships of the concepts [5], [6]. Conceptualization is the abstract model to determine the concepts related to the phenomenon of the objects. And the specification means that it can specify the type of the concepts and the constrained condition. Formation means the machine can read and understand the meaning of the information. Sharing means that the concepts in the ontology are not individual, but they are based on the knowledge mutually agreed by the members.

To explain what the ontology is useful for, we will compare the search engines such as Google and Yahoo. Basically Google retrieves and provides the web documents by machine, using the key words suggested by the users. It is the calculated results rather depending on the superficial characteristics than representing the intent of the customers. On the other hand, Yahoo used the user defined subject, inheritance relations and the part-whole relations. And it classified the web documents by the subject hierarchically, and defined the relations among them. The hierarchical category of Yahoo is similar to the method of the document classification and the retrieval method based on the ontology defined hierarchically [7].

As the role of the ontology is increasing in the semantic web, the semantic web based retrieval system, searches the important information fast. The ontology based information retrieval system utilizes the concept and the rules defined in the ontology. Because it uses the reasoning rules to develop the exactness of the retrieval, it not only can provide the documents to the user query, but also can query and modify the query and the related information properly according to the relations. [7] suggested the structure of the semantic web based retrieval system. This system has subsystems such as the search engine and the ontology system.

To share the knowledge among people and machines, it is necessary to define the terms which can understand each other. And then the standard model and the formalized language are needed. It is also necessary to design the ontology which contains s specific knowledge about a specific domain. Therefore in this Section we will design the domain of the knowledge in a specific domain which is the base of this system

2.2 Definition and Design of the Ontology Domain

In this paper, we used the Topic Maps to construct the ontology. RDF [8], [9], [10], [11], [12], [13] in W3C usually focuses on the resources on the web, and links among the web page. On the other hand, Topic Map has the characteristics that can represent not only objects such as web page, picture, and electronic documents, but also abstract concepts such as psychology, history, ethics, etc. Topic in a special document consists of words which represent the writer's intention. From now on, I will explain three kinds of topic map models [12], [13].

First, we will explain topic. In this paper, we constructed the ontology to retrieve the information of the customers of the home shopping sites for marketing. Accordingly, the ontology has three topic types. First, the region is the area which the home shopping sites are located on. Second, the items are what the home shopping sites are dealing with. And third, the company information means the basic information about the company which operates the home shopping sites. They are phone numbers, URL, e-mail etc.. The region has a domain that home shopping sites are located on, and it is represented hierarchically. The root of the topic is the region. And the region has sub nodes that represent each region and the name of the city in a hierarchical structure. And the whole item is a root node. And there are also sub nodes which have a hierarchical structure. The hierarchy of the region and the items are classified by the clustering, association rules, and classification rules etc. [14], [15], [16]. And the company information contains the address, the phone number, the items and URL of the home shopping sites. Therefore, we can make up the associations with other topic types such as region and items.

Second, we will talk about occurrence. Each topic is linked to the resources which it refers to. For example, to investigate the company information we can refer to URL which has the information, http://dblab.chungbuk.ac.kr/~information. And we can also refer to the web site, http://dblab.chungbuk.ac.kr/~regions, in case we want to know the address of the home shopping site. The information about linking is called occurrence. There are many kinds of occurrence such as document files, image files, video files, specific records in the database etc.. And then we store the information which occurrence refers to into the database. To indicate the resources about topics in the topic map, HyTime and Xpointer are used.

Third, we are going to tell you the association. The standard spec about Topic Map provides the associations among topics. It defines not the hierarchical structure but the semantic association among topics. There are some examples as follows.

"Home Shopping Site of Computer is located in Seoul."
"Home Shopping Site of Television has the information of the company."

```
<!-- Association Type -->
    <topic id="has">
        <baseName>
            <baseNameString>AT: Has</baseNameString>
        </baseName>
    </topic>
    <!-- Role Spec -->
    <topic id="product_item">
        <baseName>
            <baseNameString>RoleSpec: product_item</baseNameString>
        </baseName>
    </topic>
    <topic id="company_info">
        <baseName>
            <baseNameString>RoleSpec: company_info</baseNameString>
        </baseName>
    </topic>
    <association id="has-information_tv">
        <instanceOf>
            <topicRef xlink:href="#has"/>
        </instanceOf>
        <member>
            <roleSpec>
                <topicRef xlink:href="#product_item"/>
            </roleSpec>
            <topicRef xlink:href="#tv"/>
        </member>
        <member>
            <roleSpec>
                <topicRef xlink:href="#company_info"/>
            </roleSpec>
            <topicRef xlink:href="#information_tv"/>
        </member>
    </association>
```

Fig. 1. XTM of Association Type

In the above example, "Computer" and "Seoul" are topics, and they have the association such as "is located in" each other. Topics in the topic map not only are independent objects, but also have links of special relation. Just as topics are classified into topic types, the associations are classified into association types. That is, in the above example, "is located in" and "has a member of" are the association types. Topic type and association type are important functions of the topic map for representing, classifying, and structuring the knowledge and the information. And "Computer" has "product_item" as "roleSpec". Also "information" which contains the phone number, the address, URL, the company name has "company_info" as a roleSpec. Fig. 1 shows the association which represents the association types, "has" in XTM file.

To retrieve efficiently the information of the company which operates on line shopping mall, we constructed "Shopping Sites Topic Map". Based on it, we just generated the ontology about the shopping sites. In Fig. 2, we design the classes about the topics and the associations as follows.

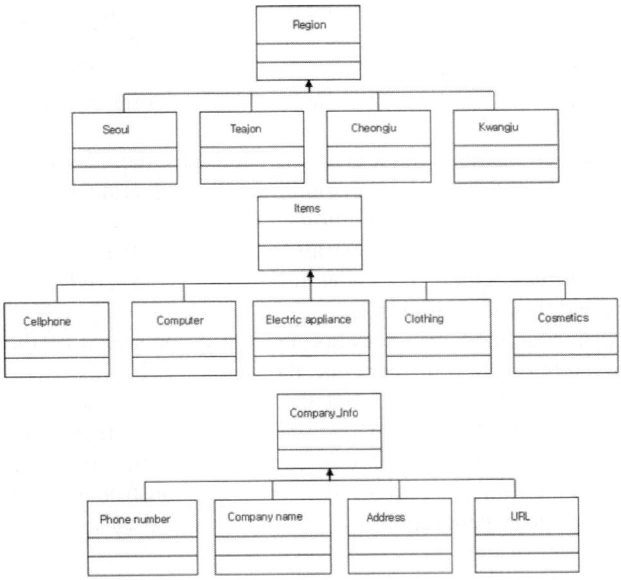

Fig. 2. Class structure about topics

3 Design of the Retrieval System Based on the Ontology

In this chapter we will describe the semantic web based customer information retrieval system. And also we will explain the ontology generation and the retrieval agent.

To generate the ontology, we need to design the ontology about the related domain. The information of the company in shopping sites is classified into the region and the item. Based on it, the topic map can be generated. Fig. 3 shows the knowledge map based on the topic map. This information can provide the exact knowledge while the user buys and retrieves the specific products.

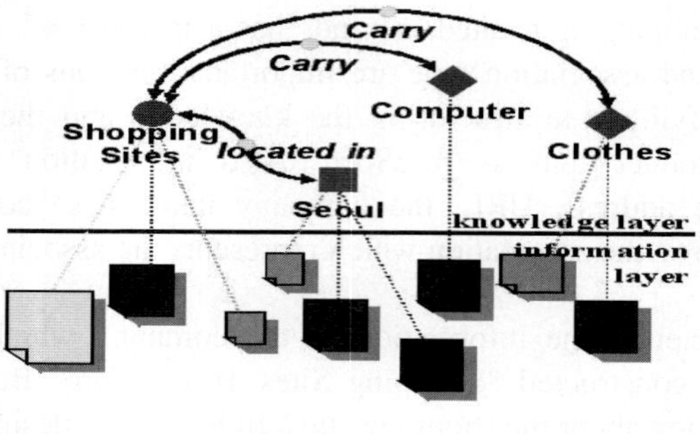

Fig. 3. Knowledge Map of the Shopping Sites

After defining the domain for the ontology construction, we specify the basic elements of the Topic Map such as topic, association, and occurrence. The specification of the topic association was written using the XTM, XML Topic Map. We verified the syntax errors about the source of XTM for the ontology by Omnigator of Ontopia [17].

XTM source which has no syntax errors is parsed by the TM4J [18], open source Topic Map engine. During parsing the source code, to guarantee the integrity of the data we investigate the constraint condition in advance. Accordingly, we refer to the schema of Topic Map to verify the constraint condition of the association cardinality, the kinds of sub topics which the upper topics can have. And also we verify the occurrence type and the association role.

We designed and defined the concepts and the associations of the concepts and then make programming them to generate the ontology. In this paper, we classified the data from the web by the agent, and then construct the ontology with the data. And then we define the knowledge resource information from the web as topic, association, and occurrence. Through this ontology we can retrieve the information. Table 1 shows "bulid.xtm", a part of the ontology constructed. Fig. 4 shows the procedure of the ontology generation.

Table 1. The example of ontology generation

```
<association id="x1jt8jnf72-3b1">
    <instanceOf>
      <topicRef xlink:href="#serves"/>
    </instanceOf>
    <member id="x1jt8jnf72-3b2">
      <roleSpec>
        <topicRef xlink:href="#facility"/>
      </roleSpec>
      <topicRef xlink:href="#children book-enjoy Big - KTmall"/>
    </member>
    <member id="x1jt8jnf72-3b3">
      <roleSpec>
        <topicRef xlink:href="#benificiary"/>
      </roleSpec>
      <topicRef xlink:href="#enjoy Big - KTmall"/>
    </member>
  </association>
    ...
```

Agent means a representative that is a program, which substitutes the work in computer. The information retrieval engine which uses the agent is a web site which supports the information retrieval as on-line database [2]. Therefore the retrieval engine is a database which stores the linking information. The robot agent travels around the web sites, and then collects the information, following the links. And then it classifies, indexes the information and stores it into the database.

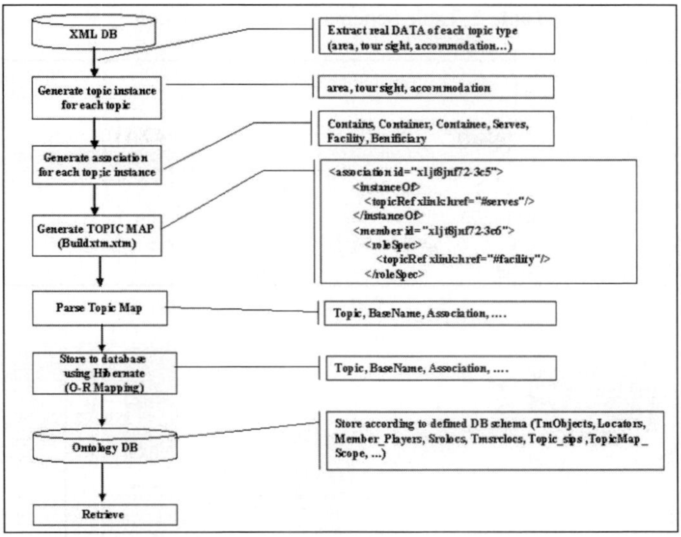

Fig. 4. Ontology generation procedure

It starts retrieving after inputting the address of the web site as an initiative value. To filter the shopping sites, it checks the words or the documents related to "shopping". It examines the words and the documents which contain items, and then it determines whether it is a shopping site or not. From the retrieved shopping sites, it extracts URL of the shopping sites, URL of the linked sites, the titles, the items, the address of the shopping sites, etc.. Fig. 5 shows the structure of the retrieval agent.

Web agent comprises as follows. Retrieving module retrieves the web sites, and the retrieved information is divided into the classifier module and the link module. From the classified information, the suitable information is extracted into the filter module.

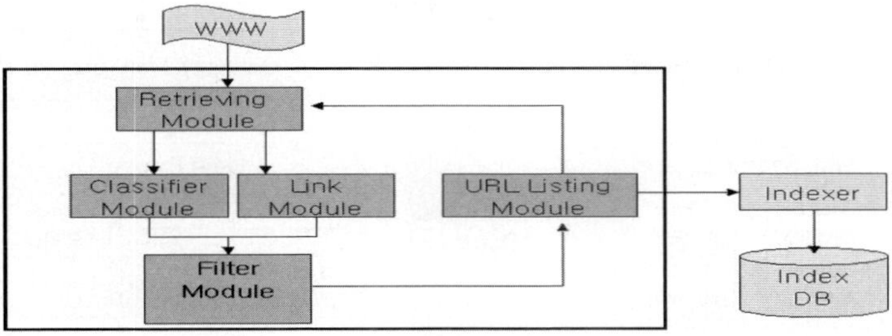

Fig. 5. The structure of Web Search Engine

The retrieved results by the agent are stored into the database. And then four tables are generated. They are the page table for the URL, the item table for the items of the company, the image address table which the address of the company is represented as an image file, the text address table which contains the address and text information, etc.. Table 2 shows a part of them.

Table 2. Table Schema of Site Information

Table Specification						
Table ID	page					
NO	Col ID	Col Nmae	Type	Length	NULL	Key
1	p_no	page num	int			P.K
2	site	site address	varchar2	256		
3	title	site name	varchar2	256		
4	visited	visit	varchar2	1	N.N	

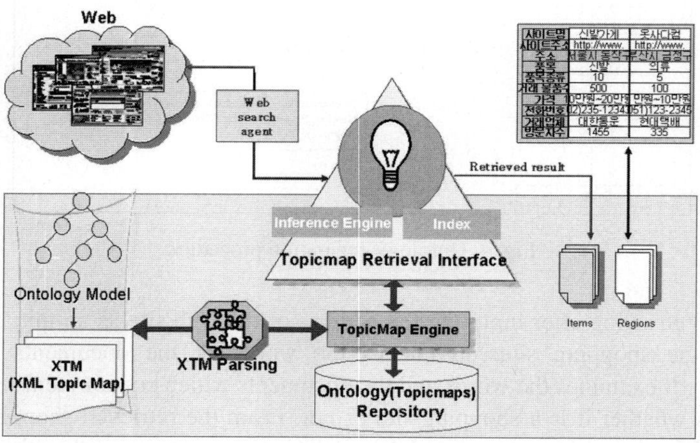

Fig. 6. The Framework of the Retrieval System

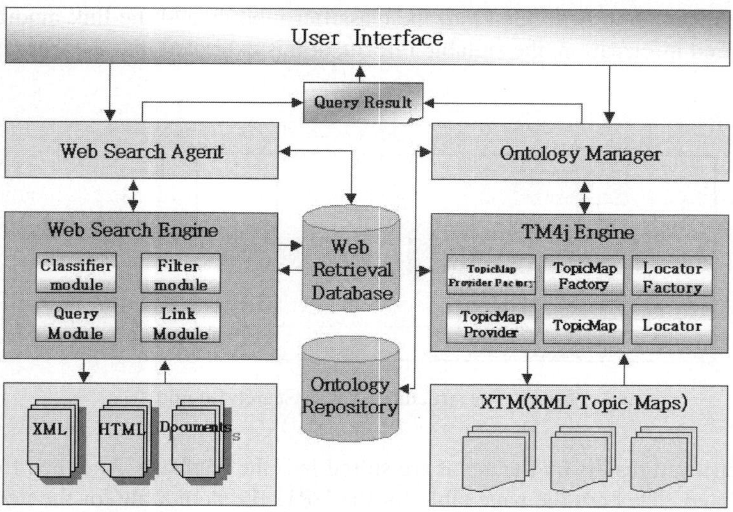

Fig. 7. Structure of the specific module

From now on, we will describe the information retrieval system based on the ontology to extract the information of the shopping sites. Fig. 6 shows the framework of the information retrieval system. This system extracts the information from the web by the agent, and then retrieves the exact information from the extracted information. Fig. 7 shows the specific modules. They are classified into two kinds of modules; the module for the web retrieval agent and the module for generating and managing the ontology.

The ontology based retrieval system is composed of the user interface, the ontology storage, the ontology generation engine, the web server etc.. In this paper we used TM4J to generate and manage Topic Map, and also to generate the ontology.

In this system, the user can query the information which he wants to know through the user interface. Therefore the user can be provided the information from the storage, where the ontology engine already stored the information which extracted by the agent.

4 Implementation of the Information Retrieval System Based on the Semantic Web

In this Section, we will show the ontology construction and the implementation. And we will describe not only the result which stored in the database by the web agent, but also the retrieved result by the ontology according to the result by the agent.

Here we will explain the ontology generation. Topic Map information is stored into the table of the object relational database according to Hibernate of TM4J [19].

Then we will describe the result by the web retrieval agent. To retrieve the shopping sites on the web, we gave fourteen special shopping malls as an initiative value. Fig. 8 is the result of "search. java" which executes the agent. The result is seen in Korean because we experimented the system using Korean web sites.

Here we can see URL of the shopping sites on the right, and the phone number, the title and the items of the special site on the left. If we select a special site on the right, we can see the special information about it. And "INPUT URL" is used to determine the initiatives of the site which the user wants to retrieve. If we input the address of the site directly, the agent travels and searches a lot of sites which are linked to.

Finally we will show the retrieved results using the ontology, after the web search agent stores the information about the shopping. Fig. 9 shows the retrieved results by the region ontology.

Item ontology is composed of the hierarchy of the items which are sold in the shopping mall. If we select the suitable item, we can see the information of the shopping site which sells the item.

To retrieve the information for the home delivery marketing, we generated three ontologies. They are the company information ontology, the region ontology, and the item ontology. And we design and implement the web search agent to implement the retrieval engine using the ontology. And also we show the retrieved results by the ontology.

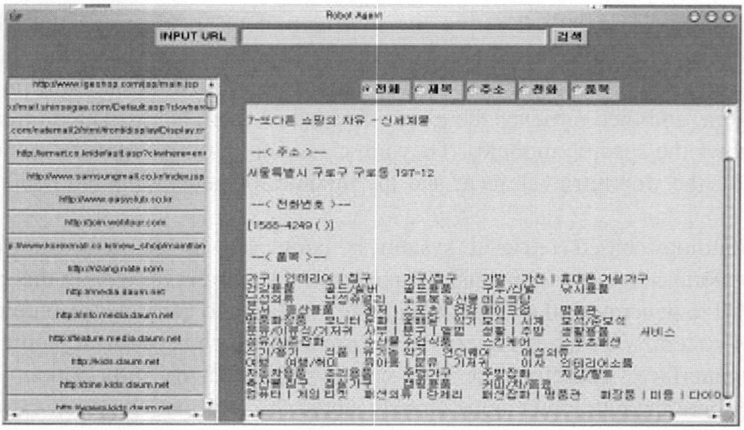

Fig. 8. The Result of the Agent

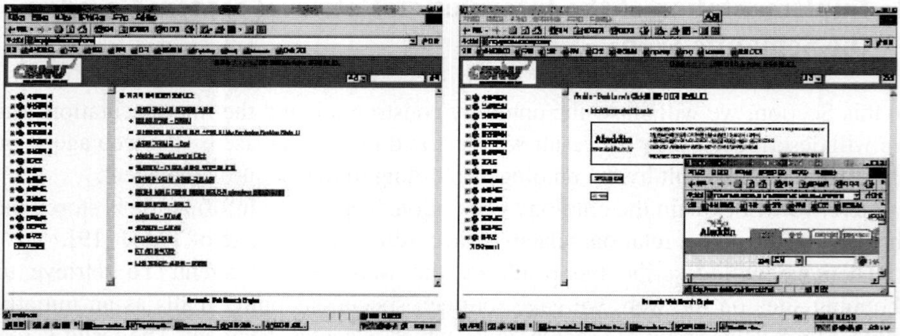

Fig. 9. The result of the retrieval

And item ontology has the hierarchical structure of the items which are sold in the shopping mall. As in the region ontology, if the user clicks the wanted items along the hierarchical structure, the ontology can show the information of the shopping site which sells the item. That is to say, because the relation of concepts is defined and then the ontology is constructed based on it, it can filter out the irrespective information and provide the exact information which the user wants. And from now on, we will compare our system with the existing ontology based retrieval system. The existing ontology system is using the stored data. However, the retrieval system in this paper is using the real time data from the web agent. Therefore, the ontology based retrieval system in this paper has the semantic meaning apart from the existing web retrieval system. And also apart from the existing ontology based retrieval system, this system can perform the real time data.

Because the existing information retrieval system such as Google and Yahoo has the problem of keyword based retrieval system it just displays the various information irrelevant to the users' intents. However, the ontology based retrieval system solves these kinds of problems.

5 Conclusions

In this paper, to retrieve the information of the customer needed for the home delivery marketing based on the semantic web, we generate the ontology for a specific knowledge domain. And also based on the generated ontology, we implemented the web robot to retrieve the information needed for the users from the web.

That is to say, we implemented the ontology to define the knowledge domain and formalize the knowledge for the retrieval of the potential customer. And also we designed and implemented the web agent to extract the information from the web. And we showed that the ontology is generated for the home delivery marketing. Therefore, we described that the information retrieval is performed efficiently using the ontology. The proposed ontology generation method and the retrieval system based on it is the base of the efficient information retrieval. Because the ontology is sharing the knowledge and considering the related domain knowledge, it is also the base for the recommendation, the marketing strategy, and the home delivery service for the efficient shopping. Future work is to develop the procedure of the ontology generation and to research the technique to compare with the existing ontology based system.

Acknowledgements

This work was supported by the Regional Research Centers Program of Ministry of Education & Human Resources Development and by the MIC (Ministry of Information and Communication), Korea, under the ITRC (Information Technology Research Center) support program supervised by the IITA (Institute of Information Technology Assessment).

References

1. Berners-Lee, T., Hendler, J., Lassila, O.: The Semantic Web. Scientific American (2001)
2. Hendler, J.: Agents and the Semantic Web. IEEE Intelligent Systems, Vol. 16 No.2 (2001)
3. Decker, S., Melink, S., van Harmelen, F., Fensel, D., Klein, M., Broekstra, J., Erdmann, M., Horrocks, I.: The Semantic Web; the roles of XML and RDF. IEEE Internet Computing, Vol. 4 No. 5 (2000) 63-73
4. Klein, M.: XML, RDF, and Relatives. IEEE Intelligent System, Vol. 16 No.2 (2001)
5. Gomez-Perez, A., Corcho, O.: Ontology Languages for the Smantic Web. IEEE Intelligent Systems, Vol. 17 No. 1 (2002)
6. Choi H. S., Ok C. Y.: Information Retrieval System and Ontology. KISS Journal Vol. 22 No. 4 (2004)
7. W3C. RDF website. http://www.w3c.org/RDF (2006)
8. W3C. RDFS website. http://www.w3c.org/TR/rdf-schema (2006)
9. International Organization for Standardization, ISO/IEC 13250, Information Technology SGML Applications-Topic Map (ISO,Geneva (2000)
10. Biesunski, M., Bryan, M., Newcomb, S.: ISO/IEC 13250 TopicMaps.
11. Pepper, S., Moore, G.: XML Topic Maps(XTM) 1.0. TopicMpas.org.
12. Pepper, S.: The TAO of Topic Maps. XML Conference & Exposition (2000)

13. Gu, M. S., Hwang, J. H., Ryu, K. H.: Designing the Ontology of XML Documents Semi-Automatically. ICIC(1) (2005) 818-827
14. Hwang, J. H. Ryu, K. H.: Clustering and Retrieval of XML Documents by Structure. ICCSA(2) (2005) 925-935
15. Hwang, J. H., Gu, M. S., Ryu, K. H.: Context-Based Recommendation Service in Ubiquitous Commerce. ICCSA(2) (2005) 966-976
16. http://www.ontopia.net (2006)
17. http://www.tm4j.org (2006)
18. http://www.hibernate.org (2006)

Emerging Hybrid Computational Models

Roman Neruda

Institute of Computer Science, Academy of Sciences of the Czech Republic
Pod vodárenskou věží 2, 18207 Prague 8, Czech Republic
roman@cs.cas.cz

Abstract. In this paper we present an approach where a hybrid computational model is represented as a set of communicating agents composing a multi-agent system. A general concept of representation of connected groups of agents is introduced and utilized for automatic building of schemes to solve a given computational task. We propose a combination of an evolutionary algorithm and a formal logic resolution system which is able to generate and verify new schemes. Furthermore, the adaptive cooperation support of individual computational agents is described, which improves their efficiency in time. These features are implemented within a software system and demonstrated on several examples.

1 Introduction

Hybrid models including combinations of artificial intelligence methods, such as neural networks, genetic algorithms (GA) and fuzzy logic controllers, have shown to be a promising and extensively studied research area [1]. They have demonstrated better performance over individual methods in many real-world tasks. The disadvantages are their bigger complexity and the need to manually set them up and tune various parameters. Also, there are not many software packages that provide a large collection of individual computational methods, as well as the possibility to connect them into hybrid schemes in various ways.

The use of distributed Multi-Agent Systems (MAS) instead of monolithic programs has become a popular topic both in research and application development. Autonomous agents are small self-contained programs that can solve simple problems in a well-defined domain [2]. In order to solve complex problems, agents have to collaborate, forming Multi-Agent Systems (MAS). A key issue in MAS research is how to generate MAS configurations that solve a given problem [3]. In most systems, an intelligent (human) user is required to set up the system configuration. Developing algorithms for automatic configuration of Multi-Agent Systems is one of major challenges for research in computational agents area.

We have designed a distributed multi-agent system [4] called Bang 3 [5] that provides a support for an easy creation of hybrid AI models by means of autonomous software agents [6]. The main goal of our approach is to allow to create new agent classes consisting of several cooperating agents. The *MAS scheme* is a concept for describing the relations within such a set of agents. The basic motivation for schemes is to describe various computational methods. It should be easy to 'connect' a particular computational method (implemented by an agent) into hybrid methods, using schemes

D.-S. Huang, K. Li, and G.W. Irwin (Eds.): ICIC 2006, LNAI 4114, pp. 379–389, 2006.

description. The scheme description should be strong enough to describe all the necessary relations within a set of agents that need to communicate one with another in a general manner.

Bang as a software system has been designed to provide general MAS functionality, optimized for the typical usage area, which is the computational intelligence modeling. Technically, *Bang* consists of the infrastructure layer and agents. The infrastructure is typically a set of programs (called airports) running in a homogeneous networked environment (such as a cluster of workstations), and connected via TCP/IP. The infrastructure provides the basic functionality for agent life cycle, communication via messages, persistence, and migration.

Agents on one machine can either possess individual processes, or share a common process. Since the communication in the computational intelligence area usually employs large volumes of data, the message delivery process has been optimized to employ compression, caching, and usage of shared memory instead of XML streams whenever possible. The whole system has been programmed in C++, mainly in order to seamlessly cooperate with several libraries for scientific computation.

Among agents, there is the main group of computational agents realizing AI methods, such as several neural networks, evolutionary algorithms, and fuzzy logic controllers. There are also more 'traditional' agents such as scheduler, directory services, ontology services, etc. A special set of agents and modules provides the functionality that is described in this paper — the MAS schemes representation and autonomous behavior support. These can be seen as a higher level layer of abstraction, and are by no means necessary for simpler usage of the system. For more detailed overview of the system, cf. [5,7].

In the following we describe the main features of our system supporting cooperation of agents within MASes. We focus on implementation and logical descriptions of computational agents, mechanisms for verifying and proposing MAS schemes, and the decision support architecture for computational agents. The combination of these features is unique and makes *Bang* a valuable prototyping tool for computational intelligence modeling.

2 MAS Formal Description

Bang agents communicate via messages and triggers. Messages are XML documents send by an agent to another agent. Triggers are XML patterns with an associated function. When an agent receives a message matching the XML pattern of one of its triggers, the associated function is executed. In order to identify the receiver of a message, the sending agent needs the message itself and a link to the receiving agent. A conversation between two agents usually consists of a number of messages. For example, when a neural network agent requests training data from a data source agent, it may send the following messages: Open the data source located at XYZ; Randomize the order of the data items; Set the cursor to the first item; Send next item.

These messages belong to a common category: Messages requesting input data from a data source. In order to abstract from the actual messages, we subsume all these messages under a *message type*. The set of message types understood by an agent is called its *interface*. For outgoing messages, each link of an agent is associated with a message type. Via this link, only messages of the given type are sent. We call a link with its associated message type a *gate*.

Now it is easy to define if two agents can be connected: Agent A can be connected to agent B via gate G if the message type of G is in the list of interfaces of agent B. Note that one output gate sends messages of one type only, whereas one agent can receive different types of messages. This is a very natural concept: When an agent sends a message to some other agent via a gate, it assigns a specific role to the other agent, e.g. being a supplier of training data. On the receiving side, the receiving agent usually should understand a number of different types of messages, because it may have different roles for different agents.

class(decision_tree)
type(decision_tree, computational_agent)
has_gate(decision_tree, data_in)
gate_type(data_in, training_data)
interface(decision_tree, control_messages)

Fig. 1. Example agent class

An *agent class* is defined by an interface, a set of message types, a set of gates, and a set of types. An *agent* is an instance of an agent class. It is defined by its name and its class.

Multi-Agent Systems are assembles of agents (for now, only static aspects of agents are modeled). Therefore, a Multi-Agent System can be described by three elements: The set of agents in the MAS, the connections between these agents, and the characteristics of the MAS. The characteristics (constraints) of the MAS are the starting point of logical reasoning: In *MAS checking* the logical reasoner deduces if the MAS fulfills the constraints. In *MAS generation*, it creates a MAS that fulfills the constraints, starting with a partial MAS.

An example agent class description is given in figure 1. It defines the agent class “decision_tree”. This agent class accepts messages of type “control_message”. It has one gate called “data_in” for data agent and emits messages of type “training_data”. The following paragraphs show two examples for logical descriptions of MAS. It should be noted that these MAS types can be combined, i.e. it is possible to query for trusted, computational MAS.

Computational MAS. A computational MAS can be defined as a MAS with a task manager, a computational agent and a data source agent which are connected:

comp_MAS(MAS) $\leftarrow$
 type(CAC, computational_agent)$\wedge$
 instance(CA, CAC)$\wedge$
 has_agent(MAS, CA)$\wedge$
 type(DSC, data_source)$\wedge$
 instance(DS, DSC)$\wedge$

has_agent(MAS, DS)∧
connection(CA, DS, G)∧
type(TMC, task_manager)∧
instance(TMC, TM)∧
has_agent(MAS, TM)∧
connection(TM, CA, GC)∧
connection(TM, GC, GD)

Trusted MAS. A MAS is trusted if all of its agents are trusted. These examples use the Prolog predicate `findall`. `findall` returns a list of all instances of a variable for which a predicate is true. In the definition of predicate `all_trusted` the usual Prolog syntax for recursive definitions is used.

trusted_MAS(MAS) ←
findall(X, has_agent(MAS,X), A))∧
all_trusted(A)
all_trusted([]) ← true
all_trusted([F|R]) ←
instance(F,FC)∧
type(FC, trusted)

3 Evolutionary Algorithm

The proposed evolutionary algorithm operates on schemes definitions in order to find a suitable scheme solving a specified problem. The genetic algorithm has three inputs: First, the number and the types of inputs and outputs of the scheme. Second, the *training set*, which is a set of prototypical inputs and the corresponding desired outputs, it is used to compute the fitness of a particular solution. And third, the list of types of agents available for being used in the scheme. Note that the evolutionary algorithm uses the agents logical description and reasoning component (described above) in order to produce only such schemes that satisfy given constrains.

We supply three operators that would operate on graphs representing schemes: *random scheme creation*, *mutation* and *crossover*. The aim of the first one is to create a random scheme. This operator is used when creating the first (random) generation. The diversity of the schemes that are generated is the most important feature the generated schemes should have. The 'quality' of the scheme (that means whether the scheme computes the desired function or not) is insignificant at that moment, it is a task of other parts of the genetic algorithm to assure this. The algorithm for random scheme creation works incrementally. In each step one building block is added to the scheme being created. In the beginning, the most emphasis is put on the randomness. Later the building blocks are selected more in fashion so it would create the scheme with the desired number and types of gates (so the process converges to the desired type of function).

The goal of the crossover operator is to create offsprings from two parents. The crossover operator proposed for scheme generation creates one offspring. The operator horizontally divides the mother and the father, takes the first part from father's scheme, and the second from mother's one. The crossover is illustrated in Fig. 2. There are two

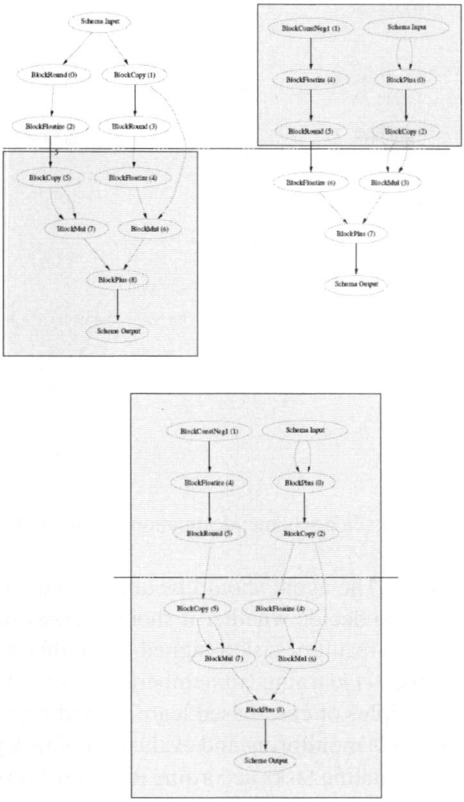

Fig. 2. Crossover of two schemes: both parents are horizontally divided and the offspring becomes a mixture of both

types of mutation, one randomly changes a node in the graph, and the other swaps agent connections. The latter mutation finds two links in the scheme of the same type (at random) and then switches their destinations (cf. Fig. 3).

4 Autonomous Behavior Support

In order to act autonomously, an agent should be able to cope with three different kind of problems [8]: cooperation of agents, a computation processing support, and an optimization of the partner choice.

Cooperation of agents: An intelligent agent should be able to answer the questions about its willingness to participate with particular agent or on a particular task. The following subproblems follow: (1) deciding whether two agents are able to cooperate, (2) evaluating the agents (according to reliability, speed, availability, etc.), (3) reasoning about its own state of affairs (state of an agent, load, etc.), (4) reasoning about tasks (identification of a task, distinguishing task types, etc.).

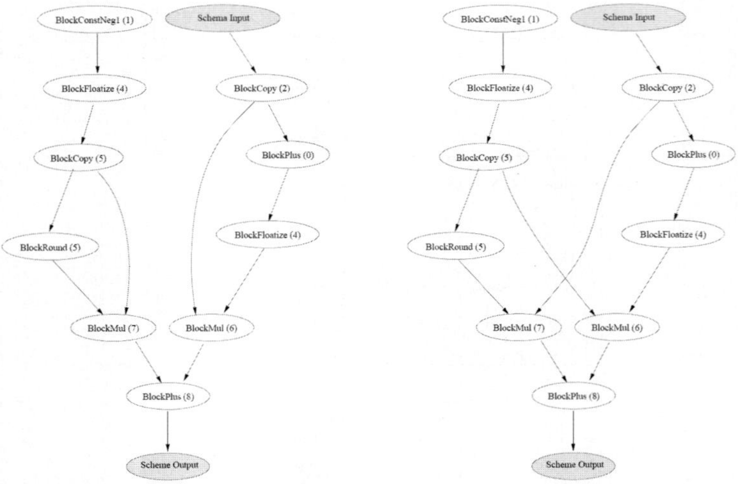

Fig. 3. Mutation of links in a scheme: destinations of two links are switched

Computations processing: The agent should be able to recognize what it can solve and whether it is good at it, to decide whether it should persist in the started task, and whether it should wait for the result of task assigned to another agent. This implies the following new subproblems: (1) learning (remembering) tasks the agent has computed in the past (we use the principles of case-based learning and reasoning — see [9], [10] — to remember task cases), (2) monitoring and evaluation of task parameters (duration, progress, count, etc.), (3) evaluating tasks according to different criteria (duration, error, etc.).

Optimization of the partner choice: An intelligent agent should be able to distinguish good partners from unsuitable ones. The resulting subproblems follow: (1) recognizing a suitable (admissible) partner for a particular task, (2) increasing the quality of an evaluation with growing experience.

So, the architecture must support *reasoning*, *descriptions* of agents and tasks (we use ontologies in descriptions logics — see, e.g., [11]), *monitoring* and *evaluation* of various parameters, and *learning*. The architecture is organized into layers. Its logic is similar to the vertically-layered architecture with one-pass control (see [4, p. 36]). The lowest layer takes perceptual inputs from the environment, while the topmost layer is responsible for the execution of actions.

The architecture consists of four layers (see Figure 4): the *monitors* layer, the *evaluators modeling* layer, the layer for *decision support*, and the *behavior generation* layer. All layers are influenced by global *preferences*. *Global preferences* allow us to model different flavors of an agent's behavior, namely, we can set an agent's pro-activity regime, its cooperation regime and its approach to reconsideration. *The monitors layer* interfaces directly with the environment. It works in a purely reactive way. It consists of rules of the form $condition \longrightarrow action$. *Evaluators modeling layer* is used to model more aggregate concepts on top of already defined concepts (either monitors or other evaluators). *Decision support layer* enables an agent to solve concrete problems. *Behavior generation layer* generates appropriate actions that the agent should perform,

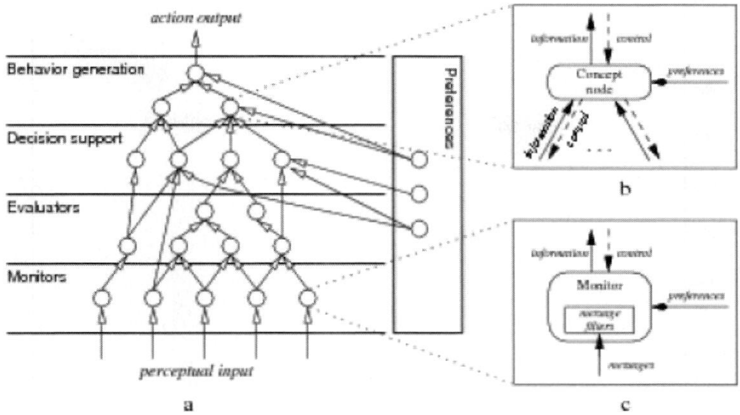

Fig. 4. Architecture — network of concepts (a); Concept node (b); Monitor (c)

and thus controls the agent's behavior. The mechanisms for action generation and selection are provided by the BDI model (see [4, pages 55–61]).

5 Experiments

Here we show two experiments demonstrating the functionality of the above described approach. They illustrate the emergence of hybrid solution to a symbolic regression problem (experiment 1), and the improvement of time complexity of neural network learning with the autonomous behavior support (experiment 2).

The training sets used for the first experiment represented various polynomials. The genetic algorithm was generating the schemes containing the following agents representing arithmetical operations: *Plus* (performs the addition on floats), *Mul* (performs the multiplication on floats), *Copy* (copies the only input (float) to two float outputs), *Round* (rounds the incoming float to the integer) and finally *Floatize* (converts the int input to the float). The computation is relatively time demanding, one generation typically takes several seconds on a 2GHz Linux machine.

The results of the experiments depended on the complexity of the desired functions. The functions, that the genetic algorithm learned well and quite quickly were functions like $x^3 - x$ or x^2y^2. The learning of these functions took from tens to hundred generations, and the result scheme precisely computed the desired function. Also more complicated functions were successfully evolved. The progress of evolving function $x^3 - 2x^2 - 3$ can be seen in the Fig. 5, Fig. 6 and Fig. 7. We can see that the resulting scheme is quite big, and it took 3000 generations to achieve the maximal fitness.

In the second experiment we have adapted two existing computational agents embedding the multi-layer perceptron (MLP) and the radial basis function (RBF) neural network. These agents represent two different computational methods for the solution of similar categories of tasks. Both agents were tested with and without the autonomous behavior support.

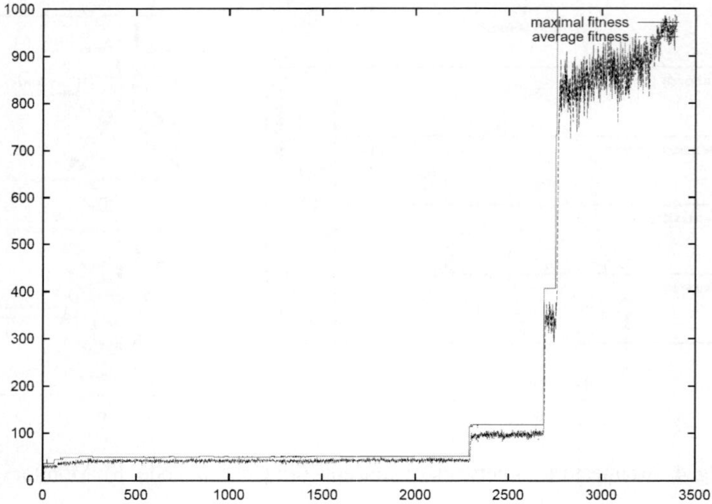

Fig. 5. Approximating function $x^3 - 2x^2 - 3$: the history of the maximal and average fitness

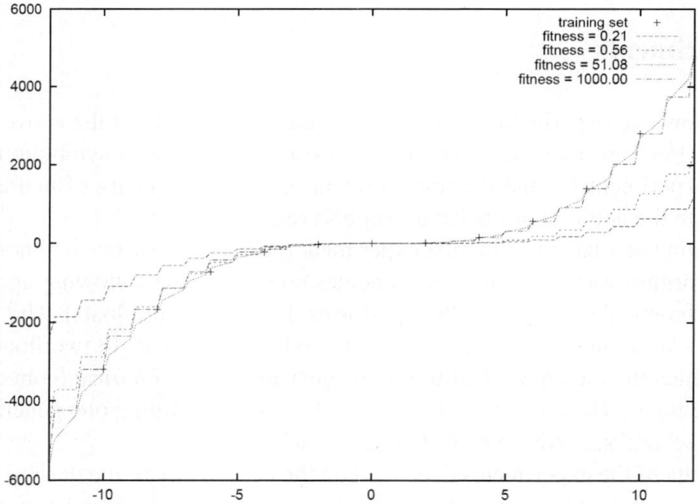

Fig. 6. Approximating function $x^3 - 2x^2 - 3$: the best schemes from generation 0, 5, 200 and 3000

Overheads of the architecture are summarized in Table 1. The creation of the agent takes 2-3 times longer since all the structures must be initialized. The communication overhead is around 30% when dealing with message delivering. However, in real-life scenario of task solving, the overhead is only about 10%.

Table 2 summarizes the measured results of *optimization of the partner choice*. We simulated a usual scenario when an agent needs to assign some tasks to one of

Fig. 7. Approximating function $x^3 - 2x^2 - 3$: the best scheme from generation 3000

admissible partners. This agent uses a collection of different tasks and assigns them to the computational agents successively. The total duration of the computation and the average error of computed tasks were measured. A significant improvement of the efficiency can be seen.

Experiments with *optimization by reusing results* are summarized in Table 3. We have constructed several collections of tasks with different ratios of repeated tasks (quite a usual situation when, e.g., evaluating the population in genetic algorithms). We compared the total computation-times of the whole collection with and without the optimization enabled. We can see that the optimization is advantageous when the ratio of repeated tasks is higher than 20%. When more than 40% are repeated the results are significant.

Table 1. Comparison of the agent with and without the autonomous support architecture

	Without the arch.	With the arch.
Agent creation time	3604 μs	9890 μs
Message delivery time	2056 μs	2672 μs
Total computation time	8994681 μs	9820032 μs

Table 2. Optimization of the partner choice: comparison of choices made by different criteria

	Error	Duration
Random choice	11.70	208710ms
Best speed	1.35	123259ms
Best Accuracy	1.08	274482ms
Best services	1.17	102247ms

Table 3. Optimization by reusing the results of previously-computed tasks (duration in milliseconds)

Repeated tasks	Optimized	Standard
0 %	135777097	121712748
20%	94151838	90964553
40%	50704363	91406591
60%	47682940	90804052

6 Conclusions and Future Work

We have demonstrated that *Bang* is able to help both scientists and end-users with data analysis tasks. The niche for this software has been prototype building and testing various hybrid models so far. However, it is possible to employ it for large scale distributed computations running on a cluster of workstations. The nature of evolution of MAS schemes has brought several issues that are currently being solved. We are building an ontological descriptions of computational agents and data tasks, and we are enhancing the evolution by reasoning component. The resulting hybrid search for MAS solution to a particular problem represented by data should be not only automatic, but also feasible in terms of computational time and resources consumption.

Acknowledgment

This work was supported by the Ministry of Education of the Czech Republic under the project Center of Applied Cybernetics No. 1M684077004 (1M0567). The experiments have been performed partly in the EPCC under the project HPC-EUROPA (RII3-CT-2003-506079) with the support of the European Community — Research Infrastructure Action under the FP6 "Structuring the European Research Area" Programme.

References

1. Bonissone, P.: Soft Computing: the Convergence of Emerging Reasoning Technologies. Soft Computing. 1 (1997) 6–18
2. Nwana, H.S.: Software Agents: an Overview. Knowledge Engineering Review. 11 (2) (1995) 205–244
3. Doran, J.E., Franklin, S., Jennings, N.R., Norman, T.J.: On Cooperation in Multi-agent Systems. The Knowledge Engineering Review. 12 (3) (1997) 309–314
4. Weiss, G., ed.: Multiagents systems. The MIT Press (1999)
5. Neruda, R., Krušina, P., Petrová, Z.: Towards Soft Computing Agents. Neural Network World. 10 (5) (2000) 859–868
6. Franklin, S., Graesser, A.: "Is It an Agent, or just a program?": a Taxonomy for Autonomous Agents. In: Intelligent Agents III, Springer-Verlag (1997) 21–35
7. Neruda R., et al: Bang Project Home Page. http://bang.sf.net
8. Vaculín, R., Neruda, R.: Concept Nodes Architecture Within the Bang3 system. Technical report, Institute of Computer Science, Academy of Science of the Czech Republic (2004)
9. Aha, D.W., Wettschereck, D.: Case-based Learning: Beyond Classification of Feature Vectors. In: European Conference on Machine Learning. (1997) 329–336
10. Aamodt, A., Plaza, E.: Case-based Reasoning: Foundational Issues, Methodological Variations, and System Approaches. AICom — Artificial Intelligence Communications. 7 (1) (1994) 39–59
11. Baader, F., Calvanese, D., McGuinness, D., Nardi, D., Patel-Schneider, P.: The Description Logic Handbook. Cambridge University Press (2003)

Knowledge Base Constructing Based on Intelligence Technology

Jian Zhang, Peng Gao, and Miao Li

Institute of Intelligent of Machines, China Academy of Sciences, Anhui, China
{mli, jzhang}@iim.ac.cn

Abstract. In general, Knowledge base is constructed by domain expert, but in practice, domain expert have no time and energy to do these multifarious tasks. The main objective of a truly user-friendly knowledge base constructing platform is to focus on the decrease of the user's work. This paper describes the design of a knowledge base constructing platform using multi-agent and XML technology, with which we can easily build a knowledge base, get a veracity-enhanced and structured knowledge base. We firstly describe the main framework, and then illuminate the hierarchical knowledge atoms stored by structured XML Document. All agents, will be described separately in the relevant sections, including mainly control agent, inducting agent, and verifying agent.

1 Introduction

Knowledge acquisition plays an important part in the domain knowledge base constructing, including the elicitation, collection, analysis, modelling and validation of knowledge. Experts have vast amounts of knowledge and tacit knowledge, but they don't know what they know and use, tacit knowledge is hard or impossible to describe. nevertheless, experts are very busy and valuable people or not each expert know every aspect of the domain knowledge, so most of the work to constructing the knowledge base must be done by the ordinary user.

The users of our knowledge base constructing system are mainly ordinary technicians, who have mastered the agricultural knowledge, but know little about the programming, especially the expert system description language. Thus during the process of building a knowledge base for an Expert System, the users often make misakes, in spite of the elaborate help documents of the platform, some errors can not be detected easily and immediately, and for the worse, some certain ones can not be detected when the Expert System is in use. The format of knowledge base can be non-structured, half-structured and structured; and it is often stored by a text document [1]. We don't care about the storage format (non-structured or half-structured format) of the knowledge base itself, but from the aspect of knowledge sharing and knowledge reusability, we consider that it is not convenient to exchange and share knowledge.

Agent technology is one of the hottest topic and active field in the study of software intelligence. According to FIFA (Foundation for Intelligent Physical Agents) [2], agent is an entity existing in some certain environment, which can interpret the data of the events happened in the environment, perform certain task for users, and

D.-S. Huang, K. Li, and G.W. Irwin (Eds.): ICIC 2006, LNAI 4114, pp. 390 – 398, 2006.

take some action that can affect the environment. It is working under the task\object-driven mode.

The agent exists in a working environment as the user's assistant, and cooperates with the user closely [3]. The user can deliver a great deal of general repeated work to the agent.

We conclude questions as follows: How to steer the users to build a knowledge base correctly and quickly, What kind of style can we to store the knowledge base as a structured format and How to create inference rules that can be effectively captured and used for automated reasoning in these environments?

In this paper, we designed a framework with multi-agent to help the user reduce the errors and used structured XML Document [4] to standardize the format of knowledge unit. We will demonstrate it in detail in the following

2 Architecture of the System

Our prospective goal is to help users reduce the errors and standardize the format of knowledge unit in the constructing process of the knowledge base of expert system. Therefore, we need to construct an open and convenient system, which can not only make all the agents smoothly work together, but also achieve new tasks which can not be resolve by any single one.

Since the data and resources of this platform are dispersive, every agent should be able to manage its own information or tasks. We use distributed parallel processing-technology and modularization method to divide this complex system into several-comparatively independent agents as follows: control agent, inducting agent, verifying agent, user agent, storing agent and resource agent. Architecture of the constructing platform is shown in figure 1.

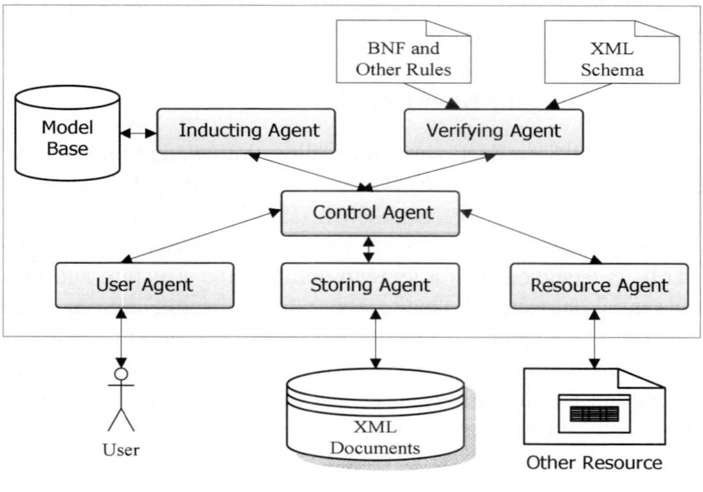

Fig. 1. Architecture of the Knowledge Base Constructing Platform

These agents can cooperate with each other to achieve our expected goals. Respectively, control agent is able to manage other subsystems; inducting agent can lead the user to build a knowledge base, which has integrated a MS cartoon agent and some inducting planning arithmetic; verifying agent should make sure of the validity of the every operation of the user, including the syntax checking, reasoning logic verifying, and giving a response to the user; user agent is in charge of the displaying of the data, and man-machine conversation; resource agent can collect some related resource, add or delete a model to the model base; storing agent translates the knowledge base into XML format. These agents smoothly work together and harmoniously serve each other, in order to accomplish the same task. The conflict among them can be harmonized or solved by their negotiation.

3 Structured Knowledge Based by XML

3.1 The Representation of Hierarchical Knowledge

Here we use hierarchical-knowledge-atom structure to describe the knowledge. A knowledge atom is a knowledge entity that is comparatively independent and can describe and solve a problem according to the knowledge of certain domain. By this approach we can plot out the domain knowledge into knowledge atoms based on the internal architecture of knowledge, and each knowledge atom has its own role to play. If the function of a knowledge atom is too complicated, then we can divide it into smaller atoms. The definition of variables, rule lists, scripts, and computing models are included in the atom. Besides these, every knowledge atom has its own ID and certain I/O interfaces which can receive parameters from other atoms as well as users' inputs. According to their internal relationship, these knowledge atoms compose a digraph and form a knowledge base to store the domain knowledge. This hierarchical knowledge structure is very suitable for the representation of complicated knowledge and capable of adapting for man-machine conversation. And the reasoning network is a digraph, which is more flexible than the structure of a tree.

3.2 Using XML to Store the Knowledge Base

In this section we will introduce something about knowledge base stored in structured XML Document [4] format. XML (Extensible Markup Language) is a simple, very flexible text format derived from SGML (ISO 8879), and is also playing an increasingly important role in the exchange of a wide variety of data on the Web and elsewhere. XML is designed with a view to defining the structure and meanings of a file; and its essential characteristic is the syntax of knowledge representation. With its flexible extensibility, we can use RDF (Resource Description Framework) [5] derived from XML to describe semantic meaning of the knowledge. XML is mainly used to describe the data but not the display format of the data. So, it is very suitable for describing knowledge; and we have designed a XML Schema to standardize the structure knowledge representation, with its benefits demonstrated as follows:

(1) Offering a uniform standard about syntax and storing format.

(2) Structuralizing the data; can exchange knowledge base with other AI systems; and even can be changed for database.

(3) Integrating different information source and forming a standard document.

(4) This XML Schema can be extended for augmenting the ability of knowledge representation.

(5) This structured knowledge can easily be shared or reused merely by a common XML parser, such as DOM and SAX.

3.3 Metadata Modeling

There are two common types of a knowledge atom: frame unit (FU) and rule unit (RU). FU is in charge of describing the relations between knowledge atoms, and controlling the reasoning procedure. RU performs a concretely reasoning, solves a question and responses an answer. Additionally, every knowledge atom has its own properties that have corresponding XML elements. Since XML is a kind of meta language, we can create plenty of metadata to describe the properties of knowledge atom. For example, for a simple IF-THEN rule, we can use metadata to describe it as figure 2.

Then, we will design some XML elements to describe the metadata separately. Every XML element plays different roles in the structured knowledge base. In one group it requires the elements to appear in the specified sequence within the containing element; or allows the elements to appear (or not appear) in any order in the containing element; or allows one and only one of the elements contained to be present within the containing element, which is up to the schema we have designed. And one of the important jobs of verifying agent is to validate the knowledge base according to this schema.

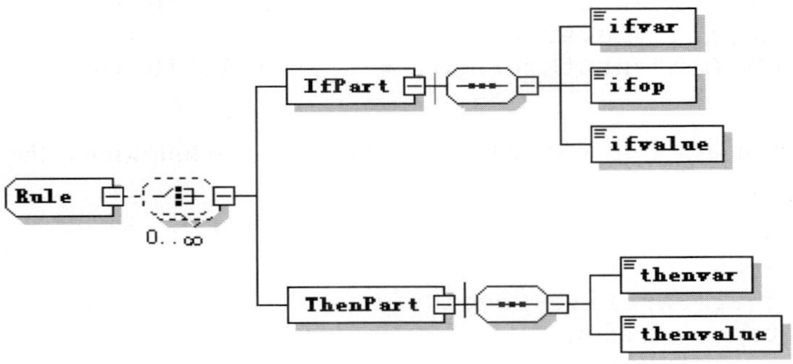

Fig. 2. An Example of metadata

3.4 A Simple Example

We will give a small example to show the approach of knowledge representation. This example comes from an agricultural knowledge base, including four knowledge atoms: content-of-nitrogen, content-of-phosphor in the soil, fertility-calculator and CF value. And the later two are man-machine conversation units that need our real-time inputs during the automated reasoning process. The relationship is showed in figure 3.

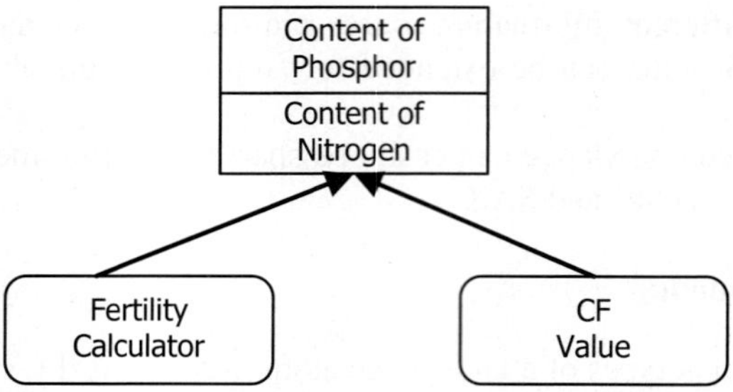

Fig. 3. An example snippet of relationship

These knowledge atoms are composed of variables or rules, which are illuminated as follows:

```
FU fertilizing
{
  ENUM FertilityLevel;FertilityLevel = {"High", "Me-
dium", "Low"};
  REAL CF (MIN: 0, MAX: 1.0);
}
RU Content-of- nitrogen
{
  IF FertilityLevel=="High"
    THEN ContentOfNitrogen = (100*CF+80)*0.15;
  IF FertilityLevel=="Medium”
    THEN ContentOfNitrogen = (60*CF+60)*0.15;
  IF FertilityLevel=="Low"
    THEN ContentOfNitrogen = (30*CF+40)*0.15;
}
```

Then we can use XML to store the knowledge base, the following is the snippet of the code:

```
<Rule>
<IfPart>
  <ifvar>FertilityLevel</ifvar>
  <ifop>==</ifop>
  <ifvalue>High</ifvalue>
</IfPart>
<ThenPart>
  <thenvar>ContentOfNitrogen </thenvar>
  <thenvalue>(100*CF+80)*0.15</thenvalue>
</ThenPart>
</Rule>
```

For this structured knowledge base, we can effectively capture the interface rules and use them for automated reasoning than any non-structured or half-structured knowledge base. After all, parsing a XML document is more and more easy nowadays.

4 Construction and Communication of the Agent Models

Now we will briefly illuminate something about the agents existing in the platform. Firstly, we will introduce the structure and functions of the main three agents. There are three common fundamental parts of them: administration unit (AU), communication unit (CU) and planning unit (PU). AU is in charge of administration of the gent, analyzing messages from other unit in the agent, controlling and coordinating jobs of units. CU is in charge of communication with other agents and performs translation information between KQML [6] and internal representation in agent. PU decomposes and plans the task that it should finish in the process of constructing a knowledge base, and then submit them to CU.

As space is limited, we will only give the inducting agent's structure shown in figure 4.

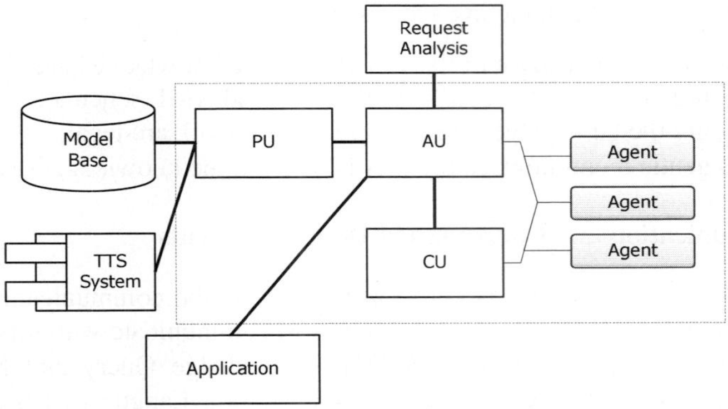

Fig. 4. Structure of Inducting Agent

4.1 Control Agent

Control agent, which is a kernel constituent in the platform, monitors all the other agents, and coordinates their actions. Its main functions are stated as follows:

(1) Create an action list to record all the other agents' status (active or inactive) and services.

(2) The other agent should register on Control Agent when it is to be activated.

(3) Response other agents' requests for service, and return the handle of the relevant agent.

(4) Coordinate all of other agents' actions; make a plan to decompose the task, and send command to the corresponding agent.

4.2 Inducting Agent

Inducting Agent leads the user to build a knowledge base that is in full accords with the BNF and schema we defined. During the leading process, MS agent and TTS (Text-To-Speech) technology play an import part. With the help of audio and animate cartoon agent technology, the user can easily master every step of this process. The developing periods will obviously be shortened. Inducting agent's main tasks are briefly described as follows:

(1) Analyze the user's requests, and then make a decision about the knowledge base's main function.

(2) Collect all the application circumstances and offer one or several models from the model base.

(3) Work with verifying agent to evaluate the knowledge framework repeatedly, including the evaluation and revises of logical integrality, the necessity analysis and revises of computing parameters and other data.

(4) Finish the full knowledge framework according to the user's requests.

4.3 Verifying Agent

When building a knowledge base, the verifying agent is monitoring not only the user's inputs, but also the inducting agent's suggestions:

(1) Check out the namespace of the variables of the knowledge base.
(2) Make sure all the rules accord with the BNF and XML schema.
(3) Make sure the knowledge frame and reasoning work are legal.
(4) Give a gentle mention when the user is revising the knowledge base.

4.4 Communication and Coordination Design of Agents

The capability of the platform is partly influenced by the communication and cooperation among these agents. If any agent wants to communicate with others, the standard language is required. Mainly, KQML (Knowledge Query and Manipulation Language) [6] and FIPA-ACL (Agent Communication Language) [7] are the most two popular agent communication language; and also there are three mechanisms to perform coordination of agents [8] [9]: forwarding broker, handle-driven broker and hybrid broker.

In our platform, the communications between all agents are comparatively simple, the message format is not complex, and the messages are transported only within the platform, so we have designed our agent communication language referred KQML.

We choose hybrid broker mode as a control mechanism that mediates interactions between client agents needing services and server agents capable of providing them.

In the process of building a knowledge base, that has a great deal of data transmitting but does not need global knowledge, we use handle-driven broker approach; while editing and verifying a knowledge base, that needs interoperation of agents, we employ forwarding broker approach and use Control Agent, which has global knowledge, as a mediator of these agents. In this way, by hybrid broker, we avoid shortcoming arises from using single approach of forwarding broker or handle-driven broker.

5 Build a Knowledge Base

Here we give an example of building rules about "How to fertilize"in the knowledge base of cotton planting, with the help of inducting agent and verifying agent. The process is briefly described as follows:

First, inducting agent will ask us "what is the name of the rule?" telling us to create a root node, which is unique in a rule-page of the knowledge base. After we input "How to fertilize?"in the text dialogue, verifying agent will receive a notice to check out the validity of the input. At last, the platform will create a root node named "How to fertilize? ".

Then, inducting agent will give a gentle mention about the composing of how to fertilize, that is to say, what are the children of the root node? We give the answer: Nitrogen Required In Growth, Category Of Nitrogenous Fertilizer and Content Of Nitrogen In Soil; in the same time, verifying agent is analyzing and validating then answer; finally the system will create four nodes has the name accordingly.

Next, inducting system will go on to ask us for the composing of How to fertilize, and lead us to do next operating, until we give a signal of END.

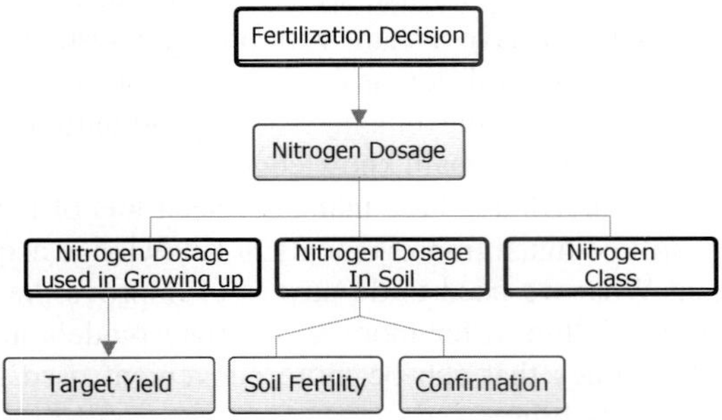

Fig. 5. The Structure of the Tutor Process

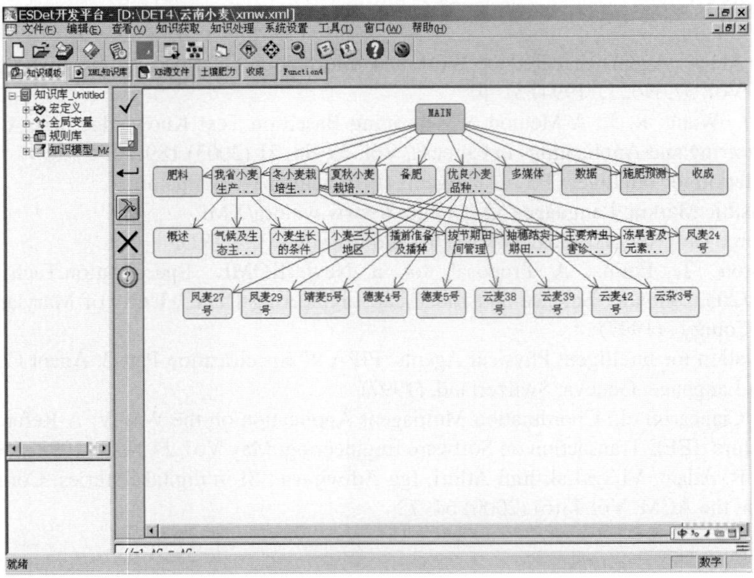

Fig. 6. Interface of Tutor Process

At the end of this process, we can get a structured knowledge base stored by XML documents, which can easily can used for automated reasoning. Additionally, if the knowledge base is verified by storing agent, it can be added to our model base as a new model.

Figure 5 describes the whole constructing process and Figure 6 is one screen picture of the system after the Knowledge base was constructed.

6 Conclusion and Future Work

This paper has described a knowledge base developing platform with multi-agent and XML technology. The user can easily build a knowledge base with the help of inducting agent and other agents, which greatly reduce the user's developing time and work.

And with the structured storing format, we can easily reuse the knowledge developed formerly to redesign it or have a share with other AI systems. This platform has been applied in several agricultural demonstration areas of National 863 Program of China, and has got a very good achievement. And beyond agriculture, we can extend this approach/technique to other domain knowledge.

Constructing very big knowledge base manually need lots of manpower and material resources. There still be much improvements in Knowledge acquisition and representation method, and What we need to do next is to improve the efficiency and the veracity of inducting algorithm, offer more appropriate models in the platform, and create flexible interface rules that can be more convenient used for the knowledge sharing and knowledge reusability.

References

1. Pattie Maes.: Agents that Reduce Work and Information Overload. Communication of the ACM Vol. 37, No. 7, (1994) 31-40
2. Xue, J., Wang, R. J.: A Method of Reasoning Based on Text Knowledge-base. Computer Engineering and Applications in Chinese, Vol. 39 No. 21 (2003) 189-191
3. Foundation for Intelligent Physical Agents (FIFA) http://www.fipa.org
4. Extensible Markup Language (XML). http://www.w3.org/XML
5. Resource Description Framework (RDF). http://www.w3.org/RDF
6. YLabrou, T. Finin.: A Proposal for a New KQML. Specification.Tech. Report CS297203,Computer Science and Electrical Engineering Dept. , Univ. of Maryland, Baltmore County , (1997)
7. Foundation for Intelligent Physical Agents. FIPA 97 Specification Part 2: Agent Communication Language. Geneva, Switzerland, (1997)
8. Paolo Ciancarini el.: Coordination Multiagent Application on the WWW: A Reference Architecture. IEEE Transaction on Software Engineering. May Vo1.24 No.5 (1998) 362-375
9. Nabil R. Adam, VijayaLakshmi Atluri, Igg Adiwijaya.: SI in digital libraries. Communications of the ACM. Vol.43(6) (2000) 64~72

Managing Workflows in Data Environments Using Semantic Technologies

Nada Hashmi[1], Abdullah Al-Malaise[1,2], Suleman Shahid[2], and Muhammad Zubair Afzal[3]

[1] College of Business Administration, Jeddah, Saudi Arabia
{nada, almalaise}@cba.edu.sa
[2] Jeddah Telecommunication and Technical College, Jeddah, Saudi Arabia
[3] NetMedia, Fraunhofer Gesellschaft (FhG-IMK) Schloss Birlinghoven, Germany
{Suleman.shahid, zubair.afzal}@rwth-aachen.de

Abstract. This paper describes a unique, open source and free solution to managing workflows in data intensive environments. The Semantic Web offers languages to create ontologies that can provide better semantic matches and help automate workflows. We create an ontology for essay reviewers in various disciplines and use an automated service to query and find comprehensive matches. In particular, we use a free essay review service as a proof-of-concept for our work.

1 Introduction

"Adam was applying to a variety of universities for graduate school in Computer Science. He submitted his 'statement of purpose' essays, for each school, to a free review service. The review service assigned, for each essay, a point-of-contact who managed the essay review process: confirming the submission with the author, further assigning four reviewers for his essays based on availability and area of expertise and tracking the essays as the reviews came back. Finally, within two weeks from the date of submission by Adam, the point-of-contact successfully sent the reviews back to Adam and closed the review process."

The scenario described above can be managed in a simple way in a fully dedicated office environment with dedicated personnel and resources. However, in a virtual environment where the reviewers are geographically located all over the world, in various time-zones and availability depends on volunteer time allocated, is it possible to create a virtual point-of-contact, an agent per-say, to handle the review process?

It is this question that motivated the authors of this paper to use semantic web technologies to intelligently automate the workflow management. We defined an ontology in the Web Ontology Language (OWL) [1] and a system which consumes this ontology to help automate the selection of reviewers and initiate the essay review process. As proof-of-concept, we initiated contact with and worked closely with The Rahber Foundation [2], a non-profit free essay review service, which has over 2 dozen

D.-S. Huang, K. Li, and G.W. Irwin (Eds.): ICIC 2006, LNAI 4114, pp. 399 – 409, 2006.

volunteer reviewers and receives at an average of 10 essays a month. The service follows a strict 'blind review' process where the reviewers and authors of essays remain anonymous from each other to help eliminate any biases.

Our paper is organized as follows: Section 2 outlines the motivating factors for using semantic web technologies and the implications of a fully automated system. Section 3 describes the architecture and implementation details. That is followed a discussion on related works and we conclude by discussing our future directions and work in progress.

1.1 Background

Automating workflows is not a new concept in the computer science domain. Many artificial intelligence techniques have been developed in the past to enable automation by defining goals which need to be achieved and using AI planning techniques to reach that goal. [3, 4] Medical Decision Support systems first explored various AI planning techniques to help reach conclusions and diagnosis for the patients in the early 80s. [5, 6, 7, 20] But due to the complexities of the domain, these techniques remain theoretical in nature and continue to researched on.

The bioinformatics domain recently took advantage of the semantic web technologies and web services to help automate complex workflows. Taverna[8] used OWL-S [10], a custom workflow engine and a custom definition language to help users define the parameters from which a workflow can be created. [9] Other bioinformatics workflow tools include Pegasys [12], Wildfire [11] and Piper [13]. All these workflows are geared towards the bioinformatics domain and employ input/output matching techniques to link workflows. While these techniques are innovative and useful for the bio-informatics domain, they can not be used for services which are not exposed as web-services. Furthermore, the require user interactive to help compose the workflow. Our system and its needs require the system to compose the workflow on its own with minimal user input.

Nowadays, the competitions are very crucial to the organizations. Timeless business productions and speedy decisions need a very high automated technology such as Workflow technology. The following are the definitions given in the Workflow Management Coalition (WfMC) Glossary [17]:

- **Business Process**—A set of one or more linked procedures or activities that collectively realize a business objective or policy goal, normally within the context of an organizational structure defining functional roles and relationships
- **Workflow**—The automation of a business process, in whole or part, during which documents, information or tasks are passed from one participant to another for action, according to a set of procedural rules
- **Workflow Management System**—A system that defines, creates and manages the execution of workflows through the use of software, running on one or more workflow engines, which is able to interpret the process definition, interact with workflow participants and, where required, invoke appropriate IT tools and applications.

Charles Plesums states the following when using the automated workflow management system [18]:

- Work doesn't get misplaced or stalled—expediters are rarely required to recover from errors or mismanagement of the work.
- The managers can focus on staff and business issues, such as individual performance, optimal procedures, and special cases, rather than the routine assignment of tasks. The army of clerks is no longer required to deliver and track the work.
- The procedures are formally documented and followed exactly, ensuring that the work is performed in the way planned by management, meeting all business and regulatory requirements.
- The best person (or machine) is assigned to do each case, and the most important cases are assigned first. Users don't waste time choosing which item to work on, perhaps procrastinating on important but difficult cases.
- Parallel processing, where two or more tasks are performed concurrently, is far more practical than in a traditional, manual workflow.

2 Motivation

Given the volunteer nature of the service, the following factors prompted the need for a fully automated service:

- *Time:* the Rahber Foundation does not receive any money for its services. It is purely volunteer in nature and hence necessitates a dire need to cut any time expenditure for processing and tracking essays.
- *Resources:* Proprietary packages to help manage workflows could not be used due to monetary constraints. Hence, open source solutions were sought.
- *Usability:* Both the authors and the reviewers needed to be able to process their essays without comprising the ease of usability for the service. An automated process which required additional steps and complicated forms could not be used. Use of email as the primary form of communication for the flows of essays was essential.
- *Research Agenda:* Using traditional methods of databases alone proved inefficient. They did not have the ability to manage intelligence centrally nor the ability to track and administer changes. Developing a virtual point-of-contact required the need to embed 'intelligence' and 'semantics' which could only be captured using ontologies.

3 Implications

The concept of our work can be extended to a variety of areas/disciplines:

Papers are reviewed in various disciplines all the time: for conferences, journals and admission processes. However, the scope of these reviews is limited. Their lifetime starts and ends with each review. With the ability to automate selection of reviewers and the ability to track essays, a central repository where people with similar interests can log in, see examples of past papers and what criterion were used for reviews can be created. Furthermore, interesting analyses can be conducted to find the common reasons for rejection/acceptance, to find common/popular mistakes and to formulate better suggestions for writing papers in that discipline.

Many businesses involve a process for quality assurance (QA). A prime example is Emergency Medical Services which documents each case and initiates a QA process where various personnel provide feedback for how each case was handled. In a situation where the ability to automate the administration and track feedbacks and comments in a seamless manner, the time and resources can then be spent to find ways of improving healthcare and save lives. Findings of the frequency of certain types of cases and the feedbacks for improvement can help focus research on handling of those particular cases.

4 Implementation

This is work in progress. It is hoped through proper exposure and interaction with other experts in the field, the final project will be reflective of a real-life application of the semantic web.

4.1 Current Methodology

The current system relies on the following technologies for processing essays:

- HTML and PHP was used to create static and dynamic web pages. Static web pages were used to display information about the services while dynamic web pages were created dynamically as the result of actions for submitting essays, receiving feedback and posting questions.
- Custom PHP web-based form submission: PHP Forms with basic error checking were created for the submission of essays through the website. The error checks prevented authors from submitting their essays without proper email addresses (checked for '@' present) and forced essays to be submitted in either word or text formats.
- Custom PHP automated email: Upon successful submission, the form with the attached essay was emailed to a group email list.
- Database: MySQL was used to create different databases to maintain the website and store following information:
  - Reviewers
  - Submitted Essays
  - Authors
  - Archive

4.1.1 Workflow Description

The current workflow for each essay is the following:

The author submits from a web-site a form with the following information:

Name
Email Address
Subject or General Area of Interest
Essay, either as an attachment or as part of the text.

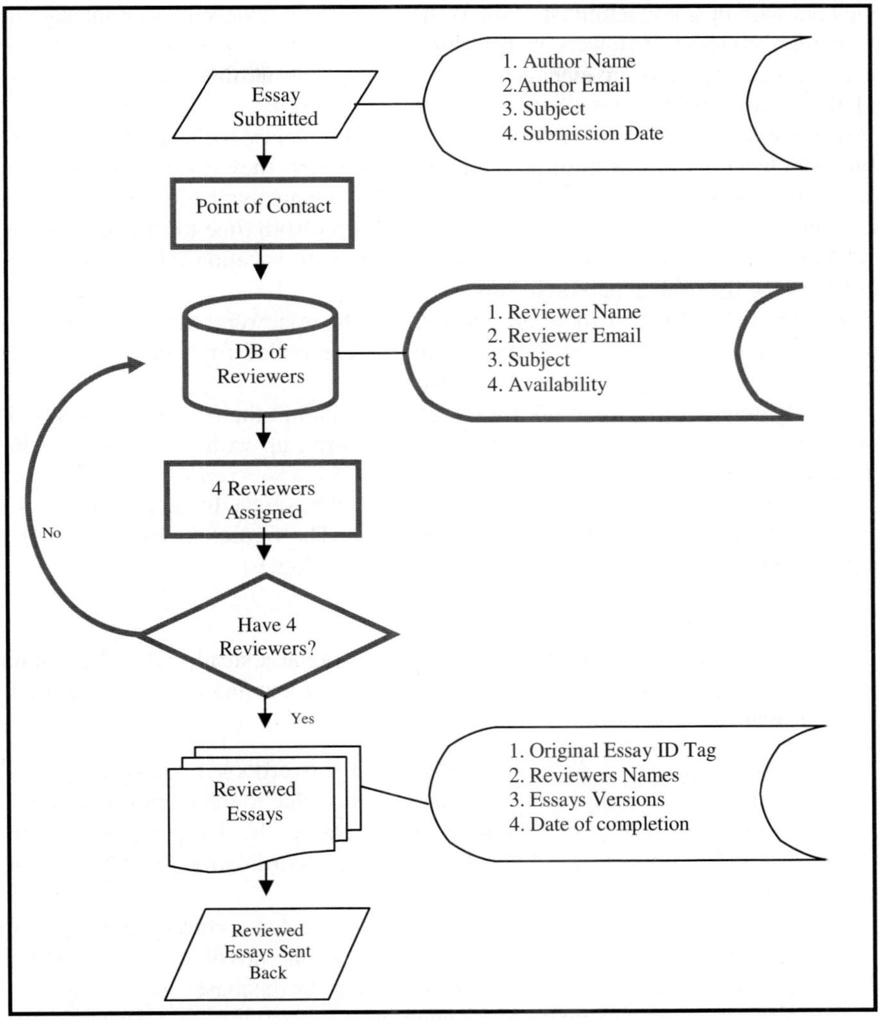

Fig. 1. Current Workflow for each Essay

The form automatically notes the system time and sends the email with the above information to a group list email.

Using a manual round-robin process, a 'point-of-contact' (POC) is assigned from a group of three individuals managing the review service. The POC first checks to make sure it is the correct type of essay (e.g. for admissions and not a research paper review), then sends a template email to the author acknowledging the acceptance or rejection of the submission.

The POC then extracts all the reviewers who match the area of interest for the submitted essay. This process involves having knowledge of the areas of interest and making certain types of judgments. For example, a student interested in obtaining an MBA in Information System can have his essay reviewed by the following reviewers:

reviewers with business administration as their expertise, reviewers with management information systems, reviewers in Information Technology or reviewers with Computer Science expertise in management positions. Furthermore, a list of 'general reviewers' who wish to review any type of essay also exists.

From the list of matching reviewers, the noted frequency for availability is noted. Reviewers have options of limiting the number of essays they review a month, e.g. 2 essays a month. They can also specify times when they are available, e.g. every weekend. Furthermore, they can send updated information from time to time tagging their availability, e.g. not available for the month of June, on vacation. This criterion further filters the list of matched reviewers.

From the filtered list, if there are more than four reviewers, the first four are selected and contacted. Otherwise, the remainders are pulled from the list of general reviewers to complete the number of reviewers.

The POC then allows one week for reviewers to submit their reviewed essays. The POC tracks the responses as they come in and follows up with reviewers who have not submitted their reviews.

After all the responses have been submitted, the POC sends the reviewed essays.

Fig.1 summarizes the workflow for each essay. The figures in **RED/ BOLD** are the processes our work automates with the help of ontologies.

4.1.2 Problems with the Current System

The number of essays submitted a month is increasing at a steady rate. The number of POCs remains at a steady rate of three. Manually processing essays cause the following problems:

- *Over Selection of Reviewers:* POCs often overbook reviewers by asking them to review essays simultaneously. This is due to the inability to 'lock' or tag the 'availability' of reviewers. Furthermore, the demographics and time zone differences creates difficulties in proper coordination for POCs to effectively communicate and lock reviewers.
- *Incomplete Matching of Expertise:* Searching for a correct match requires multiple queries which often do not relay all the possible matches. This results in manually and sequentially searching the databases for a complete list of matches. The example of a student who is applying for a masters in business administration for information systems should theoretically return the results stated previously. However, the current inability to create relations within various disciplines or to define the disciplines prevents comprehensive search capabilities.
- *Tracking Essay Progress:* As one POC is assigned upto three or four essays at a time, tracking each one becomes a tedious task. Currently POCs manage their lists by creating temporary spreadsheets for each essay they manage.

4.2 System Architecture

The system architecture was designed for flexibility and adapting to the ever-changing lists and requirements of the volunteers. Figure 2 displays the proposed system architecture.

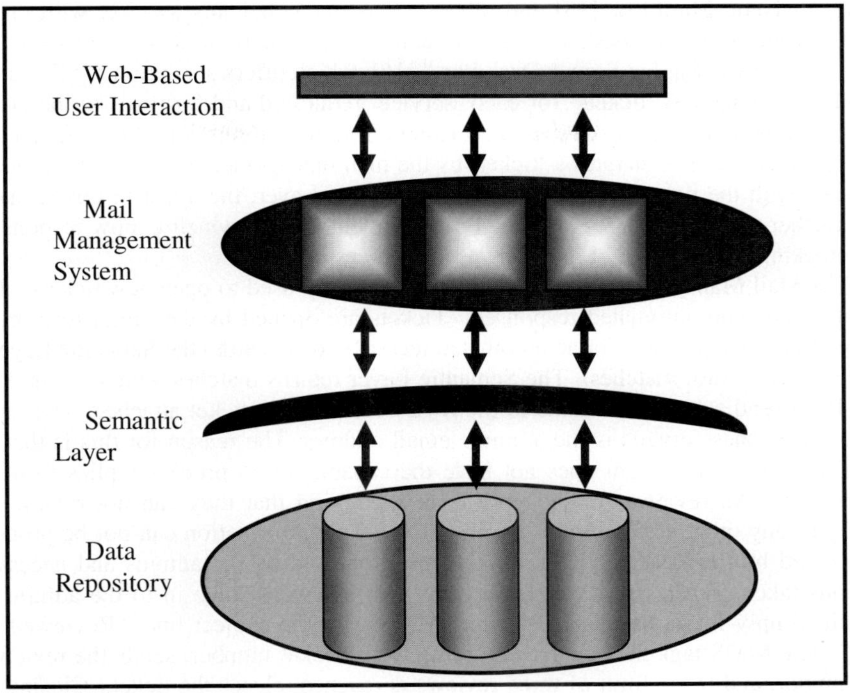

Fig. 2. System Architecture for an automated essay review service

4.2.1 Web-Based User Interaction

This is a simple web-based form which authors enter their information and submit for review. This captures essential information necessary to create instances for the ontology and thereby allow semantic matching of proper expertise.

Information captured in this phase includes:

1. Author Name and Email Address: This is used only for administrative purposes and does not effect the processing in anyway.
2. Subject / Area of Interests: Users can select multiple subject areas to help maximize matches.
3. About yourself: This is free text we are currently capturing for a future research project where we use Natural Language Processing to try and extract certain types of information from this text and compare it to human analysis. It is not being used for this project.
4. The Essay: This can be included as free text in a separate section or attached as a word or text document.

This form, upon submit, is sent to the mail management system which resides on the host site.

4.2.2 Mail Management System

Many proprietary mail management systems exist which offer 'intelligent' responses by assessing the content of the email. Such systems include, Answer by Firepond

[14], VisNetic MailFlow [15] and others. It is our belief any service, with proper customization can be used. For our system, we used a freeware mail management system "ManageEngine ServiceDesk Plus" [16], which offers a solution for IT service request. It generates 'tickets' for each 'service' requested and forwards to the proper agents. For Rahber, a 'service' request results from the submission of the initial essay by the author. This generates a 'ticket' by the mail management service which sends a request with the ticket information to the Semantic Layer, the agent in this scenario, for further processing. It is the mail management service which is now responsible for tracking the life-span of the essay as it is processed.

The Mail Management System (MMS) is primarily used to open new tickets, close tickets and send automated responses. Tickets are opened by the initial form being submitted. This prompts for an automated message to be sent to the Semantic Layer to process and return matches. The Semantic Layer returns matches which prompts the MMS to send automated emails to the reviewers with the ticket attached. The reply-address for these emails is the admin's email address. The reason for this is that the mail management system does not have the capabilities to process replies from the reviewers. An reviewer might reply back specifying that they can not review this essay or any other essay until a specified time. This information can not be properly processed by the system. These replies are processed by the admins and necessary actions taken. When the actual reviews by the reviewers come in to the admin, the admin simply forwards this back to the MMS with the subject line: "Reviewed Essay". The MMS tags the content according to the ticket number, sends the review to the author, and if the limit of three reviews is reached, closes the ticket. Closing the tickets prompts a message to the Semantic Layer which enters the necessary information into the database.

In this service, there were checks placed to ensure abnormalities trigger an email alert to the administrators. Abnormalities include any failure of delivery messages, no match found message from the Semantic Layer or an open ticket that exceeds three weeks time. Such cases require the admins to log in and take control of the ticket to resolve the issues.

4.2.3 Semantic Layer

The semantic layer is primarily responsible for deducing which volunteer reviewer is best suited for the essay. It accomplishes this by extracting and matching information from the ticket against the ontology describing the reviewers (described in the next section). A "match" can be any one of the following, in this order of preference:

1. An exact subject area match.
2. A match against a super-class subject in the ontology. In the ontology, there is a subject area, "Computer Science" which has sub-classes such as "Artificial Intelligence", "Databases", "Distributed Systems", "Natural Language Processing", etc. If the author specifies AI as an interest, but none of the reviewers have specified that as an interest, the Semantic Layer then turns to the parent and finds matches in that category, in this particular case, "Computer Science".
3. A match against relations and associations for the subject area in the ontology. An example of this includes, in the "Business Administration (BA)" a subclass "Management Information Systems (MIS)" exists. If no match can be found for either MIS or BA, then Semantic Layer searches for relationships defined to

those subjects. An existing relation is “Management Information Systems” *involves* “Database” research *which is part of* Computer Science. From this, reviewers from databases and computer science can be pulled as matches. This match better than no match and general match but not as good as the above matches.

4. General match: If the above matches fail, the semantic layer queries for a category of general reviews. Reviewers have also specified they are willing to review any essay for its grammar and structural format but not necessarily for its contents. These reviewers fall into this category and are pulled up as matches.

A match of a review does not necessarily mean the reviewer is available. The semantic layer also queries for the availability based on the frequency as specified by the reviewer, e.g. two essays a month against the history of essays reviewed by the reviewer. Furthermore, reviewers are tagged if they are un-available either because they are currently in the process of reviewing another essay or not available for other reasons. This tag is controlled either by the system or by the admins.

The semantic layer further prompts the mail management system with a list of matches which the mail management system then sends automated email responses requesting reviews.

4.2.4 Data Repository

The data repository includes two types of data information: the ontology which stores a definition of the essay review world and a database which stores the essays processed and who reviewed it and when.

4.2.4.1 Ontology. The ontology is defined in Web Ontology Language (OWL), a standard endorsed by W3C. [1] It allows for powerful descriptions to be specified as well as limited forms of reasoning for finding consistencies and/or classifications to be deduced. [19] Our ontology has the following entities:

- Reviewer
  - Subject Area Interest
  - Frequency of Availability
  - Availability Tag
- Essay
  - Subject Area Interest
  - Author information
  - Reviewed by
- Subject Area
  - Computer Science
  - Business Administration
  - English
  - Physics
  - Medicine
  - Law
  - (Etc)

The subject areas are further expanded to include specific areas of interests and relations between various subjects are specified.

The ontology was created by cooperative efforts of the authors of this paper and using web resources for each subject to find specific areas of interests. It was modeled in a subjective manner to first cover subjects that seem to be most common for the essay review service, e.g. Computer Science. Other subjects were added according to the interests specified by the reviewers and some subjects were added as a result of relations and associations being defined by other subjects (e.g. "Management Information System" was added to Business Administration due to the relationship with Computer Science, a commonly occurring subject).

4.2.4.2 Traditional Relational Database. The role played by the traditional database is to store information for the essay, who reviewed it and its life-span; that is, when it was first submitted and until the ticket for this essay was officially closed. Control of this database is primarily with the Semantic Layer which enters information as new tickets are opened and old tickets are closed.

5 Preliminary Analysis

The use of the semantic web provides excellent ways of automating workflows. Ontologies have the semantic logistics embedded into the descriptive language(s) to allow for representing complex relations. In our case, ontologies provided a better solution than relational databases. However, ontologies come with inherent universal agreement problems that need to be further studied. The ontology is a viewpoint, a description that the author(s) of the ontology agrees with. However, it is not necessarily the universal viewpoint for the domain. Furthermore, if another user disagrees with the description presented, e.g. Management Information Systems essays CANNOT be reviewed by Computer Scientists, this viewpoint creates an alternative and a disagreement that has yet to find a way of being incorporated.

Another drawback to the use of semantic technologies is that better tools need to be available for consuming ontologies. Relational databases have an abundant set of tools, both open-sourced and free, that can be deployed with minimal resources. Tools that consume and use ontologies in OWL are still currently being developed and are limited in their functionalities. More tools need to be developed and made freely available.

6 Conclusion and Future Directions

While the system has been deployed, the next step is to carry out experiments and empirical studies. Representative cases for complex and interesting matches need to be developed for test cases. It is our intention to run empirical tests and run the old system parallel to the current system. The following metrics will be noted:

- *Time Efficiency:* It is hypothesized the automated system will save time. However, it is quite possible as the systems are run parallel, cases not covered will cause problems which will consume more time than the current system.
- *Expertise Match:* Does the automated system infact return a comprehensive list of possible reviewers who are available and capable of reviewing the

essays? If not, is this a problem with the ontology created or a problem with the representation for the data?

- *Analysis with the types of Essays reviewed:* Does the automated system in fact allow interesting research analysis to be conducted on the types of essays reviewed?

Furthermore, we would like to extend our concepts to domains with larger volumes of data to see how the metrics are affected. One such domain is quality assurance process for emergency medical response.

References

1. http://www.w3.org/TR/owl-features/
2. http://www.rahber.org
3. Elliott, C. D.: The Affective Reasoner: A Process Model of Emotions in a Multi-agent System. Ph.D Thesis (TR#32), Northwestern University, (1992)
4. Freedman, N.: The Analysis of Movement Behavior During Clinical Interview. In Studies in Dyadic Communcation, (1972) 153-175
5. Kurgan, L.A., Cios, K.J., Tadeusiewicz, R., Ogiela, M., Goodenday, L.S.: Knowledge Discovery Approach to Automated Cardiac SPECT Diagnosis. Artificial Intelligence in Medicine, 23 (2001) 149-169
6. Slatkin, A.B., Burdick, J.: The Development of a Robotic Endoscope, Proc. 1995 IROS Conf
7. Azuaje, F.: In Silico Approaches to Microarray-based Disease Classification and Gene Function Discovery. Annals of Medicine (2002) Vol.34 299-305
8. http://taverna.sourceforge.net/
9. Oinn, T., Addis, M., Ferris, J., Marvin, D., Greenwood, M., Carver T., Pocock, M., Wipat, A., Li, P.: Taverna: a Tool for The Composition and Enactment of Bioinformatics Workflows. Bioinformatics,16 (2004)
10. http://www.daml.org/services/owl-s/
11. http://web.bii.a-star.edu.sg/~francis/wildfiregel
12. Shah, S.P., He D., Sawkins, J. N., Druce, J., Quon, G., Lett, D., Zheng, G., Xu, T., Quellette, B.: Pegasys: Software for Executing and Integrating Analyses of Biological Sequences. BMC Bioinformatics, (2004) 5-40
13. http://bioinformatics.org/piper/
14. http://www.firepond.com/
15. http://www.deerfield.com/
16. http://manageengine.adventnet.com/products/service-desk/
17. Workflow Management Coalition (WfMC) Glossary: http://www.wfmc.org/standards/docs.htm
18. http://www.e-workflow.org/
19. Haarslev, V., Möller, R.: Racer.: An OWL Reasoning Agent for the Semantic Web. In Proceedings of the International Workshop on Applications, Products and Services of Web-based Support Systems, in conjunction with the 2003 IEEE/WIC International Conference on Web Intelligence,Ê Halifax, Canada, October 13 (2003) 91–95

On Studying P2P Topology Based on Modified Fuzzy Adaptive Resonance Theory*

Yufeng Wang[1] and Wendong Wang[2]

[1] Communications Engineering Department, Nanjing University of Posts and Telecommunications (NUPT), Nanjing 210000, China
[2] State Key Laboratory of Networking & Switching Technology, Beijing University of Posts and Telecommunications (BUPT), Beijing 100876, China
wfwang@njupt.edu.cn

Abstract. Considering vast and miscellaneous contents in P2P system, intelligent P2P network topology is required to route queries to a relevant subset of peers. Based on the incremental clustering capability of Fuzzy Adaptive Resonance Theory (Fuzzy ART), this paper made use of the modified fuzzy ART to provide small-world P2P construction mechanism, which was not only to categorize peers so that all the peers in a cluster were semantically similar, but, more important, to construct the P2P topology into small-world network structure. In detail, the modified fuzzy ART net was used to cluster peer into one or more appropriate categories according to its data interest, and the reverse selection mechanism in modified fuzzy ART was provided to construct semantic long-range edges among clusters. Simulations demonstrated that P2P small-world network emerged, i. e., highly clustered networks with small diameter, and the information retrieval performance was significantly higher than random topology.

1 Introduction

Recently, there have been much research interests in emerging Peer-to-Peer (P2P) overlay networks because they provide a good substrate for creating large-scale data sharing, content distribution etc. Research implies that P2P content sharing has become very popular in the last few years, and is nowadays the biggest consumer of Internet bandwidth [1]. Generally, there exist two classes of P2P overlay networks: unstructured and structured [2]. The technical meaning of structured is that the P2P overlay network topology is tightly controlled and contents are not placed at random peers but at specified locations that will make subsequent queries more efficient. Such structured P2P systems use the Distributed Hash Table (DHT) as a substrate to provide lookup of data based on keys through mathematical functions. Although structured P2P networks can efficiently locate rare items since the key-based routing is scalable, they incur significantly higher overheads than unstructured P2P networks

---

* Research supported by the NSFC Grants 60472067, JiangSu education bureau (5KJB510091) and State Key Laboratory of Networking and Switching Technology, Beijing University of Posts and Telecommunications.

D.-S. Huang, K. Li, and G.W. Irwin (Eds.): ICIC 2006, LNAI 4114, pp. 410–420, 2006.

for popular content, and they do not provide efficient fuzzy keyword based search (semantic-based search), which is more important in large-scale file sharing. P2P systems are unstructured in that the overlay topology is ad hoc and the placement of data is completely independent of the overlay topology. The network uses flooding-like search mechanisms to send queries across the overlay with a limited scope. Flooding based techniques are effective for locating highly replicated items and are resilient to peers joining and leaving the system, but they are poorly suited for locating rare items and not scalable as the load on each peer growing linearly with the total number of queries and the system size. Thus, intelligent network topologies are required to route queries to a relevant subset of peers in unstructured P2P systems.

Many artificial intelligence techniques including neural networks and fuzzy inference methods have recently been proposed to search contents in P2P network. An intelligent P2P content-based document retrieval system, known as iSearch-P2P, was proposed in [3], which incorporated an intelligent technique based on Fuzzy ART neural network to perform document clustering in order to support content-based publishing and retrieval over P2P networks. This approach avoided indexing and query flooding problems of most existing P2P systems, and improved scalability greatly. But in iSearch-P2P, the P2P architecture was static two-level hierarchy, which could not adapt to the high dynamic P2P environment, furthermore, the objects were classified into certain one category, but, in fact, one object may belongs to several categories at the same time. In document clustering, Ref. [4] made use of a modified version of the Fuzzy ART to enable a document to be in multiple clusters, and the number of clusters was determined dynamically.

Semantic Overlay Network (SONs) [5] used static profile to organize P2P networks to improve search in P2P data-sharing networks by clustering peers with semantically similar contents. Each piece of data must be assigned manually to a globally predefined classification hierarchy maintained by some authority, which broke the model of truly decentralized networks. The large size of the P2P system and the great number of contents in high dynamical P2P environment made the static classification unsuitable for large-scale applications. Ref. [6] proposed a model in which peers advertised their expertise in the P2P network. The knowledge about the expertise of other peers formed a semantic topology. Based on the semantic similarity between the subject of a query and the expertise of other peers, a peer could select appropriate peers to forward queries to, instead of broadcasting the query or sending it to a random set of peers.

In many networks found in nature and society, a so-called small world structure has been observed, namely, a small average diameter and a high degree of clustering, which make them effective and efficient in terms of spreading and finding information. Ref. [7] demonstrated how small world of peers can organize themselves in an ontology-based P2P knowledge management system, which provided rewiring strategies to build a network in which peers with similar semantic interest formed clusters. These strategies only relied on the local knowledge of each peer and on the notion of similarity derived from the relationships of entities in ontology. Ref. [8] presented a new algorithm for content-oriented search in P2P networks, in which the P2P architecture was organized into a small world network structure. This structure could then be exploited for implementing an efficient search algorithm: each peer forwarded incoming queries to just one of its neighbors (the one whose document profile best matched the query). Semantic small world (SSW) [9] was proposed to cluster peers into a small world overlay network according to the local data semantic.

The main focus of this paper was to examine the use of fuzzy ART to classify (or organize) peers into clusters corresponding to their data interest, and formed the P2P architecture into semantic small world network. Our paper's contribution lied in combining many of the above ideas in a way that was guided by the concept of fuzzy adaptive resonance theory and small world network model to organize the P2P architecture into connected semantic clusters. Although Fuzzy ART has the name "fuzzy" in the mean that it is used to work with fuzzy data, it categorizes an object into certain one cluster (i.e. it is a hard clustering algorithm), thus it cannot be used for peer clustering effectively, in that a peer many belong to several semantic categories. A modified version of the Fuzzy ART was used to enable a peer to be in multiple semantic clusters, and reverse selection in modified Fuzzy ART was provided to form the connectivity among semantic clusters.

The paper is organized as follows: a brief introduction about Fuzzy ART and small world network model was given in Section 2. In Section 3, we provided the modified fuzzy ART-based peer clustering algorithm and organized the P2P architecture into semantic small world based on reverse selection in soft fuzzy ART. In Section 4, from the measure metrics in small network model (like average clustering coefficient and average shortest path length) and information retrieval (recall ratio), the search performance of our architecture was simulated. Finally, the brief conclusion and future work was given in Section 5.

2 System Architecture

To facilitate to carry out semantic based search in P2P systems, peers usually were represented by a collection of attribute values which could be derived from the share contents in those peers. In our intelligent P2P architecture, considering cooperation and understanding amongst peers, assume there was an ontological definition that defined the semantics of commonly used concepts and terminologies. The ontology could be defined using DAML-OIL (http://www.daml.org/). Each peer could be seen as a point in a multidimensional semantic space. P2P overlay network designed for efficient semantic based search should be constructed in a way such that the peers are organized in accordance with their location in semantic space. But the shared contents in P2P systems are vast and miscellaneous, more important, the peer churn rate (the rate of peer joining/leaving P2P systems) is very high, so it is imperative to study how to cluster peers in those high dynamic systems and adapt to rapid change of P2P architecture. It was shown that a self-organizing ART network is suitable for dynamic partnership seeking, so, in this paper, the Fuzzy ART network was used to conduct the dynamic cluster formation process. ART neural networks were developed to address the problem of stability-plasticity dilemma, which could be proposed as follows: How can a learning system be designed to remain plastic or adaptive and at the same time remain stable to irrelevant events? The ART networks solved this problem through incremental algorithm. In detail, it adapted to new inputs indefinitely, at the same time, it wouldn't let new inputs to change any stored patterns until the input pattern matched the stored pattern within a certain tolerance. That is, new categories could be formed when the environment did not match any of the stored patterns, but the environment couldn't change stored patterns unless they are sufficiently similar. But, basic ART worked only with binary input patterns, which didn't fit the P2P environment. So we used fuzzy ART net model which accepted "fuzzy binary" inputs (i.e. analog numbers between 0 and 1), and incorporated theories from fuzzy logic. The general structure of a fuzzy ART network is shown in Fig.1.

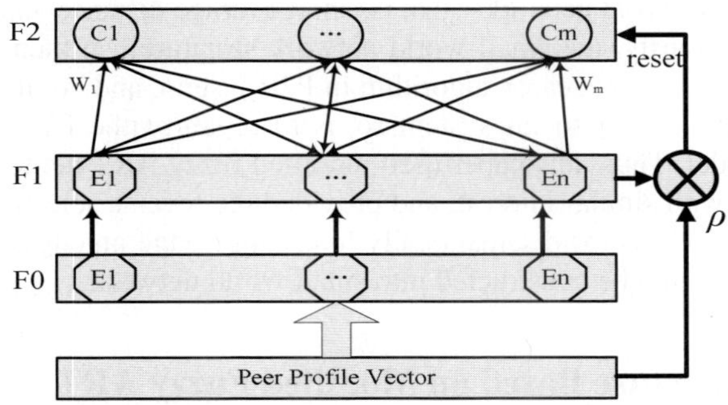

Fig. 1. Fuzzy adaptive resonance theory

A typical ART network includes three-layers. The layers F0, F1 and F2 are input, comparison and recognition layers, respectively. The input layer F0 gets the attributes of peers which are needed to be classified. Each peer advertises its capability in the comparison layer F1 for competence comparison. The nodes in F0 and F1 are composed of the entities of the ontology. The corresponding nodes of layer F0 and F1 are connected together via one-to-one, non-modifiable links. Nodes in recognition layer F2 are candidates of the semantic clusters. There are two sets of distinct connections between the layers: bottom-up (F1 to F2) and top-down (F2 to F1). Then there is a vigilance parameter ρ which defines some kind of "tolerance" for the comparison of vectors. F2 is a competitive layer, which means that only the node with the largest activation becomes active and the other nodes will be inactive (in other words, each node in F2 corresponds to a category). Therefore, every node in F2 has its own, unique top-down weight vector, also called "prototype vector" (it is used to compare the input pattern to the prototypical pattern that is associated with the category for which the node in F2 stands).

But the traditional fuzzy ART mechanism has the following disadvantages: one is that they are slow compared to non-fuzzy algorithms. Fuzzy clustering algorithms tend to be iterative, which require repeatedly calculating the associations between every cluster/peer pair; furthermore, a single peer very often contains multiple themes. For example, the share contents in author's computer are related two fields: basketball, and computer science. The traditional fuzzy ART clustering algorithms mentioned above assign each peer to a single cluster. So, for the problem of constructing P2P topology, this paper used the soft fuzzy architecture to classify peers into several appropriate clusters.

In a social system, people tend to be surrounded mostly by people who are similar to themselves in some sense. On the other hand, if people are related to very similar people only, this will lead to so-called "caveman worlds", i.e. disconnected cliques which are not connected to each other. In practice, however, many people maintain relationships to people from different professions, geographical locations, etc., which are called long-range edges. The topology of the social network graph– where nodes are persons and edges are acquaintances connecting them – is called a "small world". This phenomenon can be found not only in social networks, but also in a great number of other self-organizing systems. Watts and Strogatz [10] describe the basic notions of the clustering coefficient and characteristic path length measures as indicators of small-world networks (that is, short average distance and large clustering coefficient). Obviously, the small-world network structure can then be exploited for implementing an efficient search algorithm in P2P system, and we need algorithms to mimic the behavior of a social system so as to organize the P2P architecture into small-world model. Thus, this paper used modified fuzzy ART net to form the cluster including peers with similar interest, and provided the reverse selection mechanism in modified fuzzy ART to form semantically long-range edge among cluster so that the P2P architecture could be constructed into small world network.

3 P2P Architecture Based on Modified Fuzzy ART

Before describing our small-world P2P architecture based on modified fuzzy ART, we introduce several concepts.

Peer profile: The P2P network consisted of a set of peers. Every peer had a knowledge base that contains the knowledge that it wanted to share. The knowledge was condensed to form peer profile, which consisted of a summarization of the peer's contents. The paper would later explain in detail how profiles could be calculated.
Peer neighbor set: a peer stored the addresses of other peers together with their profile. These sets of neighbors represented the connections between peers and thus define the P2P network topology.
Common Ontology: We assumed that in our P2P architecture, peers operated on knowledge represented in terms of common ontology, which provided a common conceptualization of their domains.

Each peer maintained a modified fuzzy ART neural net to run the intelligent P2P topology construction algorithm which could be broadly divided into three stages: pre-processing, cluster building & small-world network formation and topology adaptation.

3.1 Pre-processing

While there were many traditional clustering algorithms available, peer clustering brought along many distinctive issues to deal with. One such issue is representation. A peer is typically represented as a profile, where each dimension corresponds to a term (word), and the value indicates the importance percentage of corresponding term for the peer. In detail, each peer is represented as a vector $\vec{I} = [\omega_1, \cdots, \omega_n]$, where n is the size of peer profile vector, ω_i is the term frequency that indicates the number of times the term i occurred in the peer. We assume the vector to be normalized according to a sum norm, i.e. $\sum_{i=1}^{n} \omega_i = 1$.

3.2 Clustering Building and Small-World Network Formation

Each peer maintained a personal semantic shortcut index, which defined the virtual topology of P2P architecture. Two strategies were used to create and maintain the semantic shortcut index in high dynamic P2P setting.

① Clustering strategy
Although Fuzzy ART has the name "fuzzy" in the sense that it is used to work with Fuzzy data. But it is a hard clustering algorithm, which categorizes an object into a specific cluster. The basic fuzzy ART model doesn't fit the P2P environment in which peer may belong to several categories. So, a modified version of Fuzzy ART was used for soft peer cluster building. Instead of choosing a maximum similarity category and applying the vigilance test to check if it is close enough to the input pattern, we checked every category in the F2 layer and applied the vigilance test. If the category passed the vigilance test, the peer was put into that particular category. The similarity measure computed in the vigilance test defines a degree of membership of the given input pattern to the current cluster. Each peer maintained a modified fuzzy ART neural net to run the intelligent P2P topology construction algorithm, which takes two input parameters, vigilance parameter ($0 \le \rho \le 1$) and learning rate ($0 \le \lambda \le 1$), and. The detailed steps are given as follows:

Step 1: Initialization: Initialize all the parameters, that is, each peer will calculate its peer profile according to pre-processing.
Step 2: Apply input peer profile: let ***I*** be the input next peer profile vector; Let **P** denote the set of candidate prototype vectors (semantic categories), which represents the features of the known categories for peer. Initially, the set **P** only contain the current peer's own profile, since the current peer has no knowledge about other semantic categories.
Step 3: Vigilance test: each prototype vector undergoes a vigilance test that compares the similarity between the prototype and the current input peer profile, let *sim*[i]=$\left\|\vec{I} \wedge \vec{P_i}\right\| / \left\|\vec{I}\right\|$ where $\vec{I} \wedge \vec{P_i}$ is a vector that its *ith* component is equal to the minimum of $\vec{I}$ and $\vec{P_i}$ and $\|\bullet\|$ is the norm of an vector, which is defined to be the sum of its components. The vector *sim* is used to record similarity between each prototype and the current input peer profile, which is sorted in decrease order. All prototype vectors which pass the vigilance test (that is, *sim*[i]>ρ) will be adapted to the given input peer profile (Step 4). Note that each prototype vector actually represents a specific cluster's semantics. This mechanism makes the updated prototype vector accommodate the features of the new peer, that is, the updated prototype vector represents the features of the whole cluster (the original cluster plus the new peer). If none of them passes the test, a new prototype (cluster) is created. Go to step 2 to continue for the next input peer profile.

Step 4: Matched prototype update: The matched prototype is updated to move closer to the current input peer profile according to the following equation: $\vec{P}_i = \lambda(\vec{I} \wedge \vec{P}_i) + (1-\lambda)\vec{P}_i$, where λ is the learning rate. If λ is 1, it is called fast learning. After the update, all the prototypes are reactivated and the algorithm continues with the next input peer profile (step 2).

Our modified Fuzzy ART has the following advantages: first, it avoid iterative search because every F2 node is checked. This makes it computationally less expensive; another advantage is that by eliminating the category choice step, this method reduces the number of user-defined parameters in the system.

② Inter-cluster strategy

To construct the overlay with small-world network properties, each peer maintains a set of short range contacts pointing to peers in the same semantic cluster and a certain number of long range contacts to other semantic clusters. Inspired by small-world formation mechanism provided by Kleinberg [11], the long range contacts are obtained by choosing peer categories in reverse order in the above modified fuzzy ART algorithm (that is, select new neighbors whose profile is least similar to the current peer). The detailed process is given as follow: In step 3, select several categories from the sorted vector *sim* in bottom-up order (that is, the selected categories are semantically far away from the current peer), and connect the corresponding categories based on the following distribution: $C^*sim[j]^2$, where *sim[j]* represents the similarity between current peer and selected category *j*, and *C* is a normalization constant that brings the total probability to 1. Our approach made use of the above modified fuzzy ART to construct the semantic long-range edge in P2P topology.

3.3 Query Processing and Topology Adaptation

When a peer received a query, the query profile vector was summarized as the similar way of calculation of peer profile. Then the query profile was input into the modified fuzzy ART model to recognize the appropriate cluster matching with query profile. If the query belonged to the semantic cluster where the current peer located (that is, the similarity between query profile and the current peer's cluster exceeded the vigilance test parameter), then the query results was returned from the semantic cluster corresponding the query interest. Otherwise, if query profile belonged to other category which the current peer knows about, the query was forwarded to the semantic cluster corresponding to its interest. In the worst case, if query profile couldn't be classified into any category (for, till now, the modified fuzzy ART has not recognized the new category), the new category was formed. Then, the query was forwarded to several semantic long-range neighbors according to the similarity measure which is defined as a simple scalar product between the query profile vector $\vec{q}$ and the category profile vector $\vec{p}$. Note that, in the processing of query, the fuzzy weights are not be updated.

For the high dynamic P2P environment, this paper made use of gossiping mechanism responsible for propagating and learning change, in which each peer randomly selected other peer to exchange their neighborhood view, and used the modified fuzzy ART net to update the topology structure. Peers also inspected any passing queries that they have not issued themselves. Because storage space is limited, cached files and routing table entries may have to be replaced occasionally, which will be done using a LRU (least recently used) strategy.

Generally, category (and peer) profile attributes are defined in two types: one is defined as a feature vector, in which each element represents the ability of the category (peer); another is defined as the attributes that is assessed by others who have contacted with. So, ideally, a category (peer) attributes are combined by those two types of features. That is, the modified fuzzy ART weights of certain semantic category should be updated according to the evaluation of the peer which contacted with this category in the past, then based on the changed fuzzy ART weights, the semantic small-world network should be updated. The processing of small-world P2P based on modified fuzzy ART is given in Fig.2.

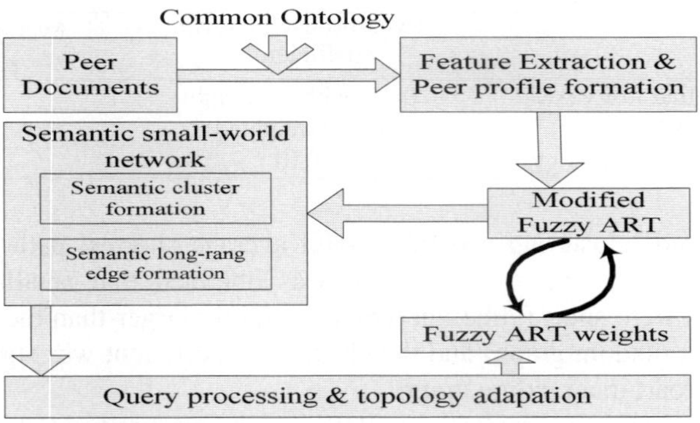

Fig. 2. Architecture of P2P topology construction based on modified ART

4 Simulation Results

In our experiment, some simplifying assumptions had to be made in order to reduce the complexity of the problems. The first simplification concerned peer profile: Instead of working with real peer knowledge base, we assumed peer profile vectors to consist of semantic categories, that is, we presume that each peer can be classified according to the topics it covers and – for our simulation – we assume this classification to be available for all peers. This means that each peer is represented by a category vector $\vec{I} = [\omega_1, \cdots, \omega_n]$, the weight ω_i indicating how important topic i is for this peer. Ref. [12] suggested that the number of files per peer is significantly skewed in typical P2P networks: there are a few peers that hold a large number of documents whereas the majority of the peers share few files. So, we implemented a Zipf distribution for the number of topics per peers: most peer profiles consist of just one category whereas a few peer profiles cover many categories. In our experiments, we used 2000 peers, each of which was allowed to have a routing index of size 20, and keep 14 "inner-cluster" neighbors and 6 "inter-cluster" ones. The query TTL was set to 5; the vigilance parameter is defined in the experiment is 0.7.

We used the free software package PeerSim1.0 to perform the actual simulation. The simulator structure was based on components, which made it easy to reach extreme scalability and to support dynamism. Simulation experiments consisted of the following sequence of operations: We created the peers with their profile according to the peer profile distribution and arranged them in a random network topology, where every peer knew 20 random peers. We did not make any further assumptions about the network topology. This random graph will serve as a benchmark for our modified fuzzy ART-based intelligent P2P topology construction mechanism, that is, we will examine the topology characteristics obtained through our approach and evaluate which of the two graphs allows a better search. Similar with the Ref. [7], this paper used the weighted clustering coefficient and the characteristic path length (average shortest path length) to measure emergence of the P2P small-world network.

Table 1. Characteristics of formed P2P topology

	(weighted)Clustering coefficient	Average shortest path
Modified fuzzy ART-based Topology	0.35 (without weight) 0.21 (weighted)	4.1
Random topology	0.01	3.4

The (weighted) clustering coefficient and average shortest path in the stabilized P2P topology was given in Table 1. It was obtained that small world structure emerged: paths were short (although they are slightly larger than the average shortest path length in a random graph) and the clustering coefficient was significantly higher than its counterpart in a random graph.

To evaluate search performance in P2P system, we used recall measures known from classical information retrieval (this measure indicated, for a given query, how many of the peers that had relevant information were reached), which was defined as follows:

$$\mathrm{Re}\,call_{peer} = \frac{\#\,\text{peers found based on our approach in P2P network}}{\#\,\text{peers in whole P2P network}}$$

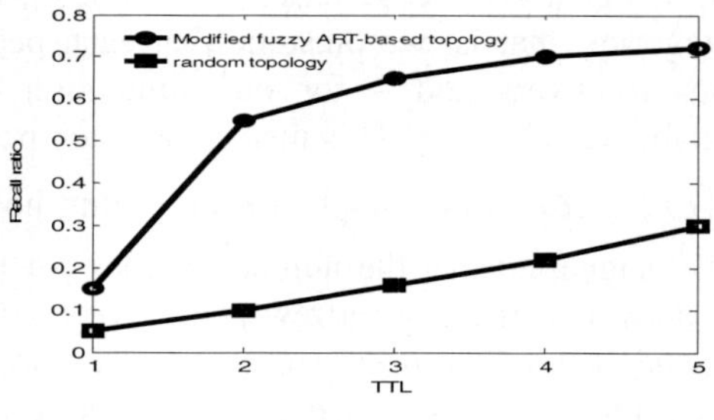

Fig. 3. Recall ratio vs. TTL in two types of network topology

From the Fig. 3, we could obtain the recall in the modified fuzzy ART-based P2P topology was significantly higher than in a random graph. The main reason was that our approach organized the P2P topology into small-world pattern, in which peers with similar contents were clustered in semantic category, and the long-range edges were constructed to maintain the connectivity in P2P systems. So, query could be answered by the category where the querying peer was located, or by other categories that could be reached through few hops in long-rang edges among categories.

Note that the simulation in our experiment was mainly carried on a certain number of cycles, that is, in one cycle, each peer which maintained a modified fuzzy ART neural would run the intelligent P2P topology construction algorithm through gossiping protocol to exchange the view of semantic categories with randomly selected peer. So the communications overhead and computational complexity may be greatly larger than other P2P topology construction mechanisms, which should be further investigated in future work.

5 Conclusion

The traditional unstructured P2P systems randomly selected the peer neighborhood, and used the flood-like search mechanism to forward the query messages, which was not suitable for the features of P2P systems: the large size, vast and miscellaneous contents, and high churn rate etc. Thus, the intelligent network topology is required to route queries to a relevant subset of peers. In this paper we provided small-world P2P construction mechanisms based on modified Fuzzy ART. The most important feature of the Fuzzy ART neural network was its incremental clustering capability that was very effective in dynamic P2P systems. Considering that the traditional fuzzy ART clustering algorithms assigned each peer to single cluster, this paper used the soft fuzzy architecture to classify peers into appropriate clusters (one or more) or form new semantic category. Inspired by the small-world formation methods, the reverse selection mechanism in fuzzy ART was provided to form the long-range edges among semantic clusters. In detail, our intelligent P2P topology construction algorithm was composed of three stages: pre-processing, cluster building & small-world network formation (including clustering strategy to form the semantic cluster, and intra-cluster strategy to form the long-range edges in P2P topology) and topology adaptation using the gossiping mechanism. From the characteristics of small-world model and metric in information retrieval, the simulation results showed that the small-world P2P network emerged, and recall ratio in our approach was significantly higher than in random P2P topology. To our knowledge, it was the first time to use fuzzy ART neural network to construct P2P topology, but our works was very preliminary, which can be improved in the following aspects:

- The approach assumed same ontology used in peer profile and worked only with hypothetical semantic categories, which may not be realistic in existing P2P networks. In real P2P systems, the problems of emergent ontologies, ontology alignment and mapping, would have to be solved.
- The approach only briefly mentioned that: the modified fuzzy ART weights of certain semantic category should be updated according to the evaluation of the peer which contacted with this category in the past, which, in turn, made the semantic small-world network updated. The further research is to realize this idea, and evaluate its effect on P2P topology and search performance.

References

1. Saroiu, S., Gummadi, K. P., Dunn, R., Gribble, S. D., Levy, H. M.: An Analysis of Internet Content Delivery Systems. In Proc. of OSDI'02, (2002)
2. Eng, K. L., Jon, C., Marcelo, P., Ravi, S., Steven, L.: A Survey and Comparison of Peer-to-Peer Overlay Network Schemes. IEEE Communications Survey and Tutorial, (2004)
3. Rodionov, M., Siu, C. H.: Intelligent Content-Based Retrieval for P2P Networks. Proceedings of the 2003 International Conference on Cyberworlds, (2003)
4. Ravikumar, K., Robert, K.: A Modified Fuzzy ART for Soft Document Clustering. International Joint Conference on Neural Networks, World Congress on Computational Intelligence, (2002)
5. Arturo, C., Hector, G.: Semantic overlay Networks for P2P Systems. Available at: http://www-db.stanford.edu/~crespo/publications/op2p.ps
6. Haase, P., Siebes, R., Harmelen, F. V.: Peer Selection in Peer-to-Peer Networks with Semantic Topologies. Proceedings of the International Conference on Semantics in a Networked World (ICNSW'04), LNCS 3226, Berlin Heidleberg New York (2004)
7. Christoph, S.: Self-organization of a Small World by Topic. Proceedings of 1st International Workshop on Peer-to-Peer Knowledge Management, (2005)
8. Witschel, H. F.: Content-oriented Topology Restructuring for Search in P2P Networks. http://www.sempir.informatik.uni-leipzig.de/Veroeffentlichungen-Dateien/simulation.pdf.
9. Li, M., Lee, W.C., Sivasubramaniam: Semantic Small World: An Overlay Network for Peer-to-Peer Search. Proceedings of the 12th IEEE International Conference on Network Protocols (ICNP'04), (2004) 1579-1586
10. Watts, D. J., Strogatz, S.: Collective Dynamics of 'Small-World' Networks. Nature 93 (1998) 440–44
11. Kleinberg, J.: The Small-World Phenomenon: An Algorithmic Perspective. In Proceedings of the 32nd ACM Symposium on Theory of Computing, (2000)
12. Saroiu, S., Gummadi, P., Gribble, S.: A Measurement Study of Peer-to-Peer File Sharing Systems. In Proceedings of Multimedia Computing and Networking, (2002)

A Self-organising Agent Assistant System*

Jun Hu[1] and Ji Gao[2]

[1] College of Computer and Communication,
Hunan University, Changsha 410082, China
[2] Institute of Artificial Intelligence,
Zhejiang University, Hangzhou 310027, Zhejiang, China
hujun_111@126.com

Abstract. To resolve the problem of agent tending to be helpless when performing tasks in the Internet in which is full of uncertain factors, this paper proposes a hierarchy-like agent assistant service framework that provides mediate services in agent society. This assistance services system is divided into three layers: the bottom is a description layer, which describes agent services and domain ontology by self-defined Ontology Based Knowledge Representation Language (OKRL); the middle is a support layer, which provides management mechanism to organize middle agent nodes and information repository of assistant services for upper layer; the top is assistant services layer, which provides services for registration, advisement and matchmaking of agent services. The growth mechanism and joint matchmaking process of middle agents, which realizes self-organising characteristic for agent assistant system, are also discussed in this paper. Finally, this paper gives evaluation and conclusion.

1 Introduction

There are two kinds of services in agent society; one is agent services that provide services according to application requirement, these agents are named application agent; the other is assistant services that provide meta-services for application agent to support agent service, the matchmaking services between services requester and provider is the main function of assistant services, which are provided by middle agent. The agent assistant system in agent society is composed of middle agents.

Efficiency, speediness and extensibility decide the performance of agent assistant system, so, it also decides the performance of agent assistant services. The assistant system should adapt to extension of agent society and could deal with new requirement of assistant services in distributed, dynamic internet environment. This paper presents a hierarchy-like agent assistant service framework which have dynamic, on-demand and self-organising characteristics, it makes application agent to accurately and conveniently gain the services at anytime and anywhere.

---

* This work is supported by the National Basic Research Program of China under Grant No. 2003CB317000 (973 Program). Jun Hu was born in 1971, male, doctor and his research areas are multi-agent system and autonomic computing. Ji Gao was born in 1948, male, professor and doctoral supervisor and his research areas are artificial intelligence and software engineering.

D.-S. Huang, K. Li, and G.W. Irwin (Eds.): ICIC 2006, LNAI 4114, pp. 421 – 430, 2006.

2 Related Work

There are several typical multi-agent systems that use middle agent to achieve assistant services, which are Impact [1], InfoSleuth [2], Retsina/Larks [3] [4] and [5]. Impact [1] describe agent services by pair of verb-name and did not provide services representation language, assistant services is provided by Yellow Pages Servers. InfoSleuth[2] make use of KIF and deducible database language LDL++ and realizes services matching by constraint matchmaking. Obviously, the application range of matchmaking algorithm is very limited (is mainly suited to database system). RETSINA [3,4] realizes matchmaking services by LARKS (Language for Advertisement and Request for Knowledge Sharing), but in which middle agent is single and static. [5] presents a ring-based architectural model for middle agent in agent-based system which can achieves sample cooperative matchmaking among middle agents, but this architecture is static and can not expansive, lacking the flexibility. A self-organising agent assistant system (SOAS), described in this paper, defines a new dynamic hierarchy for middle agents corresponding to ontologies structure, which can realize dynamic extension of assistant system and self-adapt matchmaking process base on it, which make assistant system to adapt to open, evolutional internet environment.

3 The Architecture of Agent Assistant System

The architecture of agent assistant system is divided into three layers which shown in figure 1, including describe layer, support layer and assistant services layer. The bottom layer provides foundation language for agent communication; the middle layer provides manage mechanism and information repository for middle agent nodes; the top layer provide assistant services for application agent. So, SOAS (self-organising agent assistant system) is described with a three-tuple as follows:

SOAS= (ASL, SL, DLL)

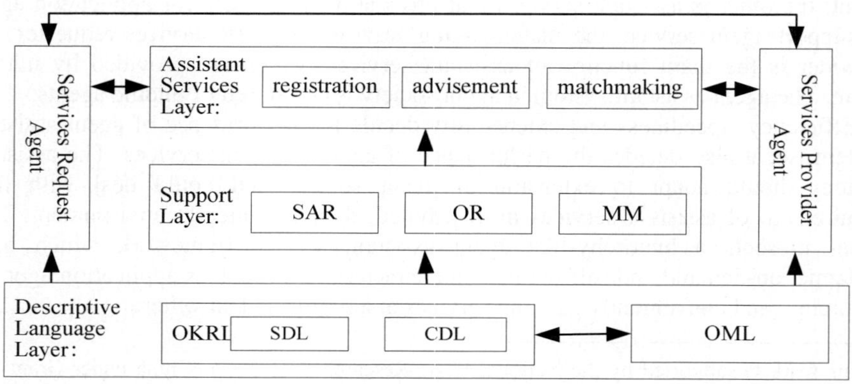

Fig. 1. The architecture of agent assistant system

- ASL----assistant services layer, it provide assistant services for application agent, including registration, advisement, cancellation and matchmaking services. Compatible matchmaking mechanism and joint match method are adopted in this layer.
- SL----support layer, it includes two aspects: the one part is manage mechanism (MM) for middle agent, the other is information repository which include services advisement repository (SAR) and domain ontologies repository (OR) for middle agent.
- DLL----descriptive language layer, which include OKRL (Ontology Based Knowledge Representation Language) [6, 7] and OML (Ontology Based Markup Language), connected with one-to-one mapping mechanism. OKRL is used in inner part of agents, including SDL and CDL, SDL is services descriptive language that describes services of application agent; CDL is concept definition language that describes domain ontologies. OML is used as the communication language among agents.

3.1 The Descriptive Language Layer

The main function of descriptive language layer is to establish the explicitness semantics for information content and support semantic interoperation among agents based on domain ontologies. OKRL represents knowledge needed by middle agent when it launches assistant services, from two aspects: description of services request and provider (SDL) and domain ontology description (CDL). Among them, SDL prescribes general descriptive format of agent services; CDL defines the domain conceptual description, including concept (object class), relationship, property and reasoning rules, and supports to establish domain term sets (concept, relation, property name) and taxonomic system of terms for agent services description. Such, as long as the communication contents are already defined in the ontology and application service, it can effectively realizes semantic interoperation among agents. OML is designed as limitary XML, which contains the descriptive ability of OKRL and could be comprehended and used by third-part agent, and insure the open property of SOAS.

Services Description Language (SDL) establishes the descriptive format for services provider and services requester; its BNF form as follows:

Service::=<Service-Name><General-Information> <Application-Constraints>

<General-Information>::=[<Description>][<General-Classification>][<Domain-Classification>]

<Application-Constraints>::=[App-Input:{<type> <parameter-name>}*][App-Output:{<type><parameter-name>}*][Pre-Condition :< Condition-Expression>]

[Post-Condition:<Condition-Expression>][Resource-Constraint :< Condition-Expression>]

<Condition-Expression>::={<Concept-instance> |<Boolean-function-invoke expression> | <Relation-expression>}*

The Application-Constraints then explains input and output parameters of agent service, input parameter must satisfied with Pre-Condition, output parameter must satisfied with Post-Condition and related resources restriction of agent services, which as gist when services matchmaking inspection.

CDL defines domain ontology, its form of BNF as follows:

Ontology::=<Ontology-Name>[<Version-declaration>][<Ontology-Citation>][<Synonymous-Concepts>][<Synonymous-Properties>][<Property-Definitions>][<Concept-Definitions>][<Type-Definitions>]

<Concept-Definitions>::=Concept<Concept-Name>[Super:{<superclass-name>}*]{<Slot-Name>:{<Aspect-Name><Aspect-Content>,}*;}*[Constraint:<Condition-Expression>]

<Aspect-Name>::=val |type |mode |number |derive |restriction |unit |inverse | superslot

The main part of ontology is concept set. The Super slot of the concept uses for establishing inclusion relation between concepts and composite definition of concept, for supporting to establish the taxonomic system of concepts; the definition of all other slots unites restrict definition of concept. By the value of user-defined slot is defined as another concept, it can establishes random user-defined relationship between concepts.

3.2 The Support Layer

The support layer provides basic knowledge and managing mechanism for upper layer. The former is composed of taxonomy of agent services and structure of domain ontologies; the latter will be discussed in section four.

In order to improve performance and efficacy of assistant service, it is necessary to establish classified system of agent services. Because of various agent services and lack of uniform classified specification, it is unpractical to establish uniform classified system. So, Classified system (CS) is divided into two levels:

$CS = CS_g \cup (CS_{d1} \cup CS_{d2} \ldots \cup CS_{dn})$

- CS_g——the upper level is general classified system and is shared with all middle agents;
- CS^j_{di}——the lower level is sub-classified system of various domain.

The upper level is general classified system according to commerce yellow-page classified specification; the lower level is sub-classified system of various domains. The single classified system of the upper level provide standard code rules, which establish classified code of application services for every services provider and services requester. Every domain has several sub-classified systems according to various application requests.

In order to solve problem caused by ontology diversity, the ideal method is establishing uniform domain ontology. Nevertheless, because of complexity and flexibility of domain, it is unpractical to establish uniform ontology. An eclectic and practical method is to establish uniform term set and taxonomic system of terms as shared basic ontology of domain; structural concept definition, which are easily cause dispute , are included in special ontology. The definition of domain ontology Oa is composed of two parts:

$Oa = Oa_b \cup (Oa_{s1} \vee Oa_{s2} \ldots \vee Oa_{sn})$

- Oa_b----shared basic ontology of domain, it depends on comprehensive common ground and popular specification of domain, which establish the uniform term set and classifying system of terms.
- Oa_{si}----special ontology of domain, each special ontology includes unshared concept definition and even causing dispute structural concept definition, which refer terms from Oa_b when be defined.

So, when describe services, services provider and services requester maybe refer different special ontology, as long as the definition terms refer the same basic ontology, it support services compatible matchmaking through semantic compatibility examination between with terms.

3.3 The Assistant Services Layer

In this layer, middle agent provides assistant services for provider and requester of agent services. The agent services are described with SDL, OKRL sub-language, which was mentioned before, and then change into the form of OML to public on the web. The middle agents collects service advertisement and systematically deposits in the local services advisement repository (SAR). Once middle agent receive request message of services, the middle agent then starts compatible matchmaking mechanism(CMM), searching suited agent services from SAR, offers the agency and recommendation services. When the middle agent that receives this message can not meet the demand, it triggers joint matchmaking mechanism of middle agents and look for suited agent services in whole assistant services system. Through the event-driven mechanism, middle agents deal with registration, quest, update and cancellation of event, triggers the corresponding assistant services. The gridding-distributing of middle agents and middle agent cooperation form the sound and strong assistant services system.

4 The Middle Agent

Middle agent is autonomic element in assistant system, the autonomy of middle agent make assistant system to become an autonomic system having self-organising, self-maintenance and self-configure function. The middle agent node dynamic join and quit assistant system is realized by middle agent with growth mechanism, which make the whole assistant system is flexible and extensible. Self-organising characteristic of agent assistant system can be expressed from four aspects: the organization structure of middle agents, middle agent node growth mechanism, domain ontology extend mechanism and joint matchmaking mechanism of middle agents. The three aspects will be discussed as follows and the last aspect is introduced in section 5.

4.1 The Structure of Middle Agents

The main part of agent assistant system is middle agents which are organized as tree-like structure and shown in figure 2. The whole node tree of middle agents is corresponding to structure of domain ontologies in agent assistant system, grayer

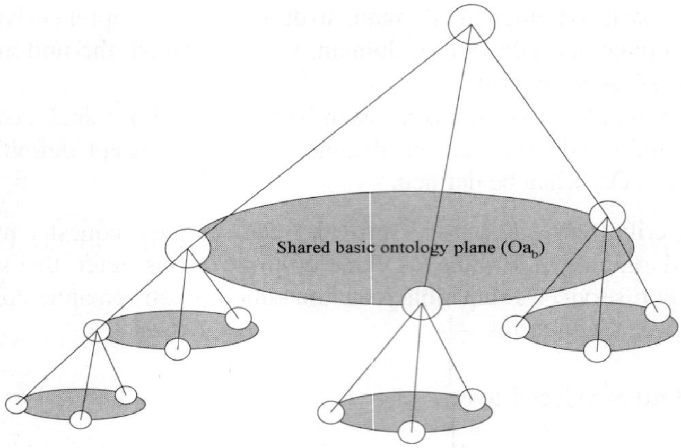

Fig. 2. The organization of middle agents

ellipse denotes domain plane that have shared basic ontology, circle denotes middle agent which manage a special ontology. From root node to leaves nodes, the domain range that middle agent faced is more and more small and refined.

It is a foundation for middle agent to match according to shared ontology. The shared basic ontology and special ontology of domain ontology structure can expand with domain extend. The shared basic ontology is also a tree-like structure; the more the altitude of the tree is high, the more the definition of ontology is refined. Each middle agent which is not leaf node is connected with a shared basic ontology and a special ontology based on shared basic ontology of upper layer; each middle agent that is leaf node is connected with a special ontology based on shared basic ontology of upper layer. The shared basic ontology is the foundation of assistant services for requester and provider of agent services, which is also shared with their son nodes. Namely, middle agents that have the same father node and tree altitude constitute a shared ontology plane. The ontology plane in figure 2 is Oa_b----shared basic ontology of domain, the different middle agent in same basic ontology plane has a corresponding special ontology of domain, MA_i-> Oa_{si}.

The middle agent itself is composed of five components which are the core controller, the communication interface unit, the custom interface layer, the environment perception module and the status unit. As shown in figure 3, the core controller is a centralized control unit of middle agent, which includes the matchmaker and manager. The matchmaker realizes matchmaking services that the core function of middle agent, the manager is responsible for scheduling and controlling of the whole middle agent behavior. The communication interface unit is control module of middle agent to communicate with other agent including services provider agents, services request agents and other middle agents. The customer interface layer is the palace where customer can manually adjust parameters of middle agent, including internal date list of middle agent. The environment perception module includes a brother linked list, a son linked list and a father node pointer, by which middle agent can make sure the location in whole middle agent nodes tree. The status unit includes three repository pointers: a shared basic ontology repository pointer, a services advisement repository pointer and a special ontology repository pointer, they make sure the service range of this middle agent.

The tree-like structure of middle agents is constructed with connection of the environment perception module in different middle agents. In fact, the environment perception module is a data structure having three doubly linked lists, including a father node field where a pointer point at father node, a brother node field which constitute a doubly linked list with all brother nodes, a son field which constitute a doubly linked list with all son nodes. So, all these doubly linked lists contact together, describe the whole tree-like structure of middles agents. Similarly, in middle agent, the status unit including a linear linked list having three pointer fields describes the whole domain ontology structure of agent assistant system.

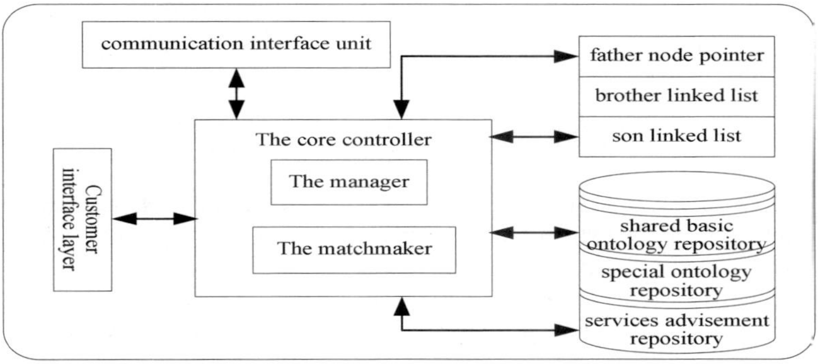

Fig. 3. The internal structure of middle agent

4.2 The Evolutional Mechanism of Middle Agents

Self-organising characteristic of agent assistant system is shown with self-maintenance self-configure and self-organising of middle agents and domain ontology. Middle agents monitor the change of environment by listening connector. When a new middle agent joins in the middle agents system, the environment perception module of this new node only has his father node pointer, he communicate with his father node, the father node know that he is a new middle agent node and pass the son list to this new middle agent node, the new node get this son list of father node which also is his brother list, he update his brother list and connect with his brothers with listening connector, and other middle agent node update his environment perception module, so, the whole middle agent structure is updated. When a middle agent node goes out of assistant system, his son nodes also exit together. When the round nodes can not find this middle agent node by listening connector, they update own environment module and get rid of pointer field of this middle agent and do not send listening message to it. In consideration of the circumstance of the network, administrator can setup the numbers of unsuccessful connection by listening messages, which is consider as disconnect of middle agent, to meet with network communication environment.

The process of the dynamic growth mechanism of middle agent node can be explained as follow: At the beginning, there is one middle agent node with services advertisement repository and initial basic ontologies. Alone with the domain refined, the basic ontologies extend in the first place forming a new shared basic ontology plane where a son node of middle agent come forth, they update their linked links of environment perception module at the same time. With the appearance of new special ontologies, new middle agents are born within the same shared basic ontology and update related linked lists. The growth is realized from two directions: in vertical direction, the shared basic ontology is extended; in horizontal direction, the special ontology is extended. The process of middle agent growth is shown in figure 4.

This self-organising assistant system has flexible, dynamic and extensible characteristics which make it adapt to distributed, heterogeneous and dynamic network environment.

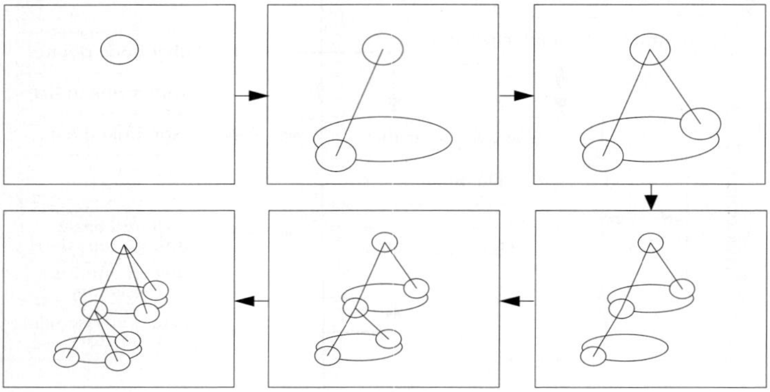

Fig. 4. The growth process of middle agents

5 The Service Matchmaking Mechanism

As mention before, SDL describes agent services from three parts: General-Information; Input and Output parameter; Pre-Condition, Post-Condition and Resource-Constraint. Correspond to these three levels, the assistant services system provided three compatible matchmaking strategies:

- The classifying matching----according to the general classification code and domain classification code, the compatible candidate advertisement (agent services) are selected from services advertisement repository;
- The parameter matching----compatible matches with the input and output parameters of agent services request and provider;
- The constraint matching----compatible matches with the Pre-Condition, Post-Condition and Condition-expression in Resource-Constraint slot of agent services request and provider.

When only all slots are compatible, the compatible matchmaking is just considered as success. The detail of matchmaking process is explained in paper [8].

Joint matchmaking is to find suitable agent services provider by several middle agents cooperation. The match process is shown in figure 5. The request services message can be received by any middle agent, when a middle agent receive this

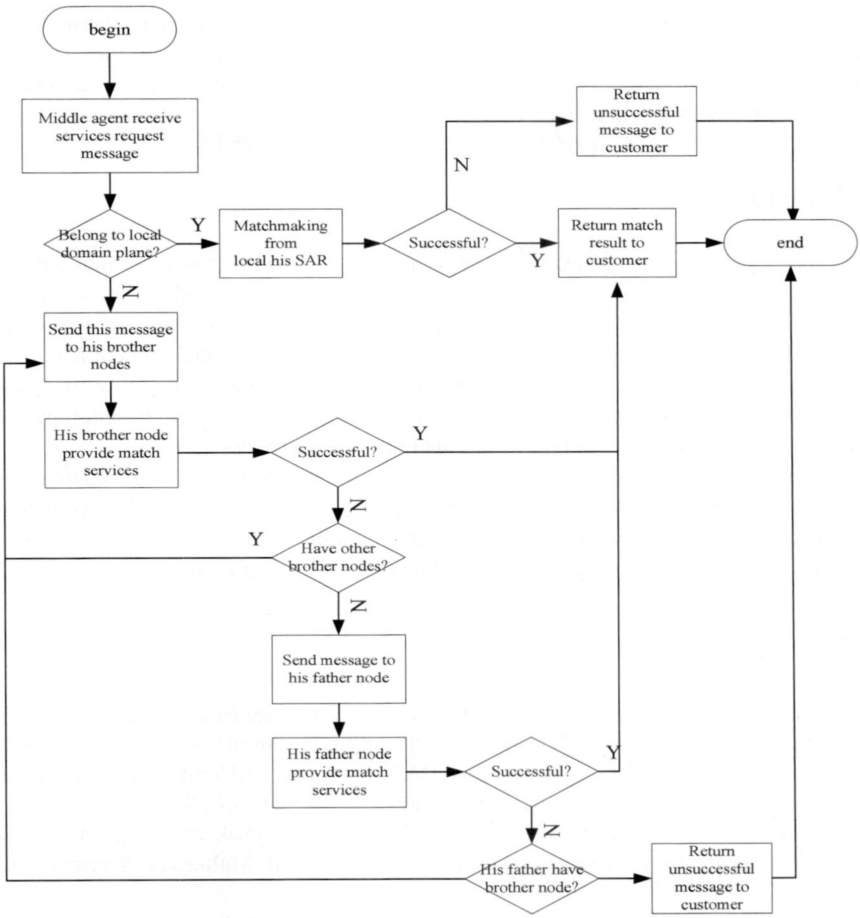

Fig. 5. The match process of middle agents

message, he would check classification code of agent services at first, if classification code shows that this agent services request is belong to the domain where this middle agent work for, the middle agent start matchmaking process directly and find suitable agent services in local services advisement repository.

When request services is out of range of a middle agent work for, then this middle agent ask other middle agents to find suitable agent services by joint matchmaking method. First of all, if a request service is belong to ontology plane of this middle agent, he send out request message to other middle agents according to the order of his brother linked list, and the brother agent fulfill matchmaking process, if match success, the address of services provider is pass to this middle agent, then this middle agent return result to customer. Otherwise, this middle agent send request services message to his father node, the father node judge that whether the range of request services is belonged to his shared ontology plane, if it is, this father node send request message to other middle agents according to the order of his brother linked list, and then get result of matchmaking; if it not, the request message is forwarded to his father node, according this way until to find the suitable services provider, otherwise return unsuccessful message to customer. Through this method, it can expand the range of match services and find suitable services as possible.

6 Conclusion

This paper proposes an integrated agent assistant services system which has self-organising characteristic. The tree-like middle agent organization and middle agent nodes growth mechanism form the self-organising structure of agent assistant services system. The extend mechanism of ontologies from vertical and horizontal direction and joint matchmaking method make agent assistant services system have capability of dynamic extending the domain of match services. Semantics match is realized by ontology based knowledge representation language in this agent assistant services system.

Because of autonomy of this system, it has more intelligence and adaptabilities than other assistant services system. It provides good meta-services for constructing agent grid in open and dynamic network environment. It also gives a new solution of assistant services for multi-agent system extending to wide area network.

References

1. K.Arisha, T.Eiter, S.Kraus ,F.Ozcan, R.Ross, and V.S. Subrahmanian. Impact:Interactive maryland platform for agents collaborating together. IEEE Intelligent Systems, 14(2), (2000)
2. M.Nodine, J.Fowler, T.Ksiezyk, B.Perry, M.Taylor, and A.Unruh. Active information gathering in InfoSleuth Cooperative Information Systems, 9(1/2), (2000)
3. K .Sycara, M.Klusch, S.Wido, and J.Lu Larks Dynamic matchmaking among heterogeneous software agents in cyberspace. Autonomous Agents and Multiagent Systems. March (2001)
4. K.Sycara, J.Lu, M.Klusch, and S.Wido Dynamic service matchmaking among agents in open information environments ACM SIGMOD Record. (1999)
5. Chunsheng Li, Chengqi Zhang, and Zili Zhang. A Ring-Based Architectural Model for Middle Agents in Agent-Based System. Fourth International Conference on Intelligent Data Engineering and Automated Learning (IDEAL'03). LNCS 2690, (2003) 94--98
6. Hu Jun, Gao Ji, Liao Beishui, Chen Jiujun. An Agents Based Grid Infrastructure of Social Intelligence. International Conference on Advanced Workshop on Content Computing. Nov. 15-17, 2004. Zhenjiang, JiangSu, PR China. LNCS (Lecture Notes in Computer Science). Vol. 3309, Springer-Verlag, (2004)33-38
7. Hu Jun, Gao Ji. IMCAG: Infrastructure for Managing and Controlling Agent Grid. The Second International Workshop on Grid and Cooperative Computing. December 7-10, 2003. LNCS (Lecture Notes in Computer Science). Vol. 3033, 161-165, Springer-Verlag, (2004)
8. Hu Jun, Gao Ji, Li Chang-yun. Ontology-based service compatible matchmaking mechanism in multi-agent system. Journal of Computer-aided Design & Computer Graphics. 2006, 18(5) (in Chinese)

Semantic Based Approximate Query Across Multiple Ontologies

Yinglong Ma[1,2] and Beihong Jin[2]

[1] School of Computer Sciences and Technology,
North China Electric Power University, Beijing 102206, P.R. China
m_y_long@otcaix.iscas.ac.cn, epuwkh@126.com
[2] Technology Center of Software Engineering, Institute of Software,
Chinese Academy of Sciences, Beijing 100080, P.R. China
jbh@otcaix.iscas.ac.cn

Abstract. In this paper, we propose an approach for better ontology interoperability using approximation technology of semantic terminology across multiple ontolgies. We use description logic language for describing ontological information and perform approximate query across multiple ontologies. Meanwhile, we discuss system implementation, and provided some experimental results for evaluating the method.

1 Introduction

Within Semantic Web, ontologies play a key role because they can provide and define a shared vocabulary about a definition of the world. Semantic Web will not be realized by agreeing on a single global ontology, but rather by weaving together a large collection of partial ontologies that are distributed across the Web [1]. Web agents based on distributed environments will often use theirselves private ontologies that define terms in different ways making it impossible for the other agent to understand the contents of a message [2]. Because there are seldom exact terminological correspondences between heterogeneous ontologies, it is difficult for ontological engineers to find out exact mappings between terminologies of these distributed ontologies. In order to address non-exact terminology match problem above, we propose a method of terminological approximation. We use description logic [4] for describing ontology because it is regarded as an ideal ontology language candidate [5]. We formally specify the mappings between distributed ontologies. We introduce the concepts of upper bound (UB) and lower bound (LB) for ontological terminology approximation. Through terminological approximation, a query terminology can be replaced by another one that is most approximate to the query terminology.

This paper is organized as follows: In section 2 and 3, we give formal representations of local distributed ontologies and mappings between these ontologies. Section 4 discusses approximation of classes. We use terminological replacements for approximation of classes. In section 5, we discuss system implementation and experimental evaluation of our semantic approximation method. Section 6 and section 7 are related work and conclusion, respectively.

D.-S. Huang, K. Li, and G.W. Irwin (Eds.): ICIC 2006, LNAI 4114, pp. 431–437, 2006.

2 Representations of Local Ontologies

Definition 1. *The set of atomic classes is denoted as* **AC**, *the set of properties is denoted as* **P**, *and the set of complex classes is denoted as* **C**. *Complex classes are constructed by some different class constructors,* **C** *includes some elements as follows:*

— C, *where* $C \in \mathbf{AC}$
— $C \sqcap D$, $C \sqcup D$, $\exists P.C$, $\forall P.C$, $\neg C$, $\geq nP.C$, $\leq nP.C$
where $C, D \in \mathbf{C}$, $P \in \mathbf{P}$

Definition 2. *An ontology* **O** *is a tuple, and* **O**=(**C**, **P**, **A**), *where*

— **C** *is the set of classes in ontology* **O**
— **P** *is the set of properties in ontology* **O**
— **A** *is the set of axioms of the form as follows:*
  — $C \sqsubseteq D$, $P \sqsubseteq R$, $C \sqsubseteq D$, *where* $C, D \in \mathbf{C}$, *and* $P, R \in \mathbf{P}$
  — $C(a), P(a, b)$, *where* $C \in \mathbf{C}$, $P \in \mathbf{P}$, $a, b \in \mathbf{L}$, *where* **L** *is a non-empty set consisting of individual objects and literals.*

Definition 3. *The semantic representation of ontology* **O**=(**C**, **P**, **A**) *is defined based on an interpretation* $\mathcal{I}=\langle \mathbf{L}, \cdot^{\mathcal{I}} \rangle$, *where* **L** *is the non-empty set consisting of individual objects and literal, and* $\cdot^{\mathcal{I}}$ *is the interpretation function. Function* $\cdot^{\mathcal{I}}$ *maps* $C \in \mathbf{C}$ *into a set* $C^{\mathcal{I}} \in \mathbf{L}$, *and* $P \in \mathbf{P}$ *into* $P^{\mathcal{I}} \in \mathbf{L} \times \mathbf{L}$. *The axiom set* **A** *must be ensured to keep consistent.* **A** *is consistent iff there exists a model* $\mathcal{I}$ *of* **A**; $\mathcal{I}$ *is an interpretation of* **A** *iff for every axiom* $R \in \mathbf{A}$, $\mathcal{I} \models R$. $\mathbf{A} \models R$ *iff for every interpretation* $\mathcal{I}$ *of* **A** *such that* $\mathcal{I} \models R$.

3 Mappings Between Local Ontologies

Definition 4. *The mapping specification from ontological* O^i *to ontology* O^j *is expressed as a tuple* $M^{ij}=(O^i, O^j, MA^{ij})$, *where :*

— $O^i=(C^i, P^i, A^i)$ *is the source ontology representation*
— $O^j=(C^j, P^j, A^j)$ *is the target ontology representation*
— MA^{ij} *is the axiom set of the form as follows:*
  — $C^i \sqsubseteq C^j$, $C^i \sqsubseteq \neg C^j$, $C^j \sqsubseteq C^i$, $C^j \sqsubseteq \neg C^i$, $C^i \equiv C^j$, *where* $C^i \in \mathbf{C}^i$, *and* $C^j \in \mathbf{C}^j$
  — $P^i \sqsubseteq P^j$, $P^j \sqsubseteq P^i$, $P^i \equiv P^j$, *where* $P^i \in \mathbf{P}^i$, $P^j \in \mathbf{P}^j$

In MA^{ij}, $A \equiv B$ iff $A \sqsubseteq B$ and $B \sqsubseteq A$. $A \equiv B$ indicates that the terms A and B are exactly matched. The axiom set of MA^{ij} also must be consistent.

Definition 5. *Two local ontologies are* $O^i=(C^i, P^i, A^i)$ *and* $O^j=(C^j, P^j, A^j)$. *Their mapping specification is* $M^{ij}=(O^i, O^j, MA^{ij})$. *Then the shared ontology SharedOnto*=(C_{sh}, P_{sh}, A_{sh}), *where* C_{sh}, P_{sh}, A_{sh} *are the class set, property set, and axioms set of SharedOnto, respectively. And*

— *For any concept* C *in* A_{sh}, $C \in C_{sh}$, *where* $C \in \mathbf{C}^i$ *or* $C \in \mathbf{C}^j$
— *For any* P *in* A_{sh}, $P \in P_{sh}$, *where* $P \in \mathbf{P}^i$ *or* $P \in \mathbf{P}^j$
— $A_{sh}=AS \cup MA^{ij}$, *where* $AS \subseteq A^i \cup A^j$

According to definition 5, we say that the shared ontology *SharedOnto* is called the least shared ontology iff *SharedOnto*=(C_{sh}, P_{sh}, MA_{ij}).

Ontology mappings are used for achieving information sharing and interoperability. Users can obtain the information that they need indeed by performing semantic queries.

Definition 6. *A semantic query is denoted as* Q=$Q_C \wedge Q_P$ *, where*
- Q_C *is a first order expression consisting of* $C(x)$*, where* $C \in \cup_{i\in I}\mathbf{C}^i$*, and* $x \in \cup_{i\in I}\mathbf{C}^i \cup \mathbf{V}$
- Q_P *is a first order expression consisting of* $P(x, y)$*, where* $P \in \cup_{i\in I}\mathbf{P}^i$*, and* $x, y \in \cup_{i\in I}\mathbf{P}^i \cup \mathbf{V}$

where $\mathbf{V}$ *is the set of variables contained in the query* Q*.*

The results of Q are denoted as $ANS(Q)$.
$ANS(Q(v_1, v_2, \cdots, v_n))$=$\{ \ (a_1, a_2, \cdots, a_n) \ \mid \ (a_1, a_2, \cdots, a_n)$=$\delta(v_1, v_2, \cdots, v_n)$ such that $Q(a_1, a_2, \cdots, a_n)$ is true, where the substitution function $\delta : ((\cup \boldsymbol{L}^i) \cup \mathbf{V})^n \rightarrow (\cup \boldsymbol{L}^i)^n$, $1 \leq i \leq n \ \}$.

4 Query Approximation and Replacement

Assume that there are two agents in multi agent system. The shared ontology is constructed according to section 4, denoted *SharedOnto*=(C_{sh}, P_{sh}, MA_{ij}).

Definition 7. *Let* $C \in C_{sh}$*. The concept* $C_{lb} \in C_{sh}$ *is the lower bounds of* C *if 1)* $C_{lb} \sqsubseteq C$ *and 2) there doesn't exist any concept* $C' \in C_{sh}$ *such that* $C' \sqsubseteq C$ *and* $C_{lb} \sqsubseteq C'$*. The concept* $C_{ub} \in C_{sh}$ *is upper bounds of* C *if 1)* $C \sqsubseteq C_{ub}$ *and 2) there doesn't exist the concept* $C' \in C_{sh}$ *such that* $C \sqsubseteq C'$ *and* $C' \sqsubseteq C_{ub}$*.*

Let $lb_{SharedOnto}(C)$ *and* $ub_{SharedOnto}(C)$ *denote the sets of all lower bounds and upper bounds of concept* C *in SharedOnto, respectively.*

Definition 8. *A query concept* C *in SharedOnto can be replaced according to the following rules:*

1) C *is replaced by* $\bigvee_{C' \in lb_{SharedOnto}(C)} C'$.

2) $\neg C$ *is replaced by* $\neg \bigwedge_{C' \in ub_{SharedOnto}(C)} C'$.

Some theoretical properties have been discussed in [11]. From the view of the underlying theory, these properties have ensured that our approximation method is theoretically verified correct. In [11], we also developed a terminology replacement algorithm (*ApproximateTermReplacement*) for approximate terminology replacements. Some specifical examples have been used for representing our formalization. Because of lack of paper space, we will not introduce these properties, its related theoretical proofs and some specific examples. These can refer to [11] in details . In the followings, we will focus on experimental evaluation of the method through a prototype system.

5 Experimental Evaluation

5.1 System Architecture

We developed a prototype system for evaluating the method. Jena Semantic Web toolkit [6]was used for system implementation. Jena can load ontology representation from ontology text (e.g., file described using OWL language[7])and ontology database such as RDFDB [3]. Jena also provides built-in reasoners for ontology reasoner such as RDFS reasoner, OWL reasoner. It can easily implement transform the ontology representations into ontology models which consist of all of possible triples of the form (`subject`, `property`, `object`). After we use Jena API for generating ontology models, we must manually configure semantic mappings between model terminologies. Using these mappings, we can compute all upper bounds and lower bounds of each concept from set of mapping concepts. Then we further use our approximation algorithm to find out a replacement concept most approximate to the queried concept. The system architecture is demonstrated in Figure 1. Its main components include the loader and reasoners from Jena. Ontology mapping manager component maintains a shared ontology model which expresses the mappings between related ontology distributed terminologies. UB and LB resolver component computes upper bounds and lower bounds of concepts. Approximation Terminology Replacement component performs terminology replacement. Each agent has theirselves query interface for semantic queries.

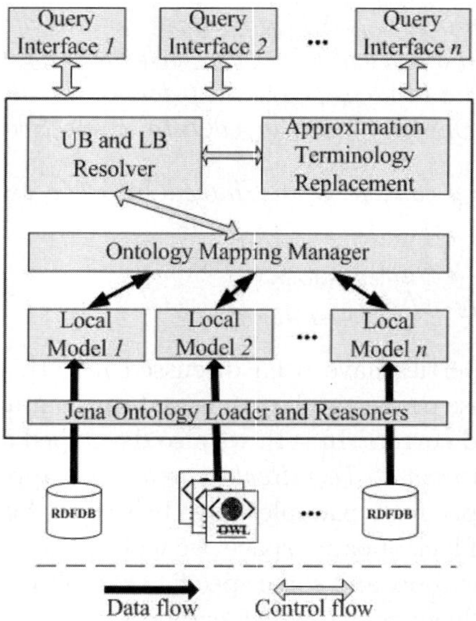

Fig. 1. System Architecture

5.2 Experimental Setup

1. **Evaluation Indexes**. We use the following indexes for evaluating our approximation method in this section.

Precision(P): $\mathbf{P} = \frac{|A \cap B|}{|B|}$; **Recall(R)**: $\mathbf{R} = \frac{|A \cap B|}{|A|}$

Where A is the standard result set. B is the returned result set and represents the cup of matched result sets that all distributed agents return.

2. **Data Sets**.

i) **EPU-IOS 1**. The first data set also covers the courses from IOS and EPU. But they are described by students from IOS and EPU. They probably changed some course labels and describe their courses in different ontology structures. EPU ontology includes 43 concept entities and 143 individuals. IOS course ontology includes 51 concept entities and 151 individuals.

ii) **EPU-IOS 2**. The second data set includes EPU Course ontology and IOS Course ontology, respectively. They are created according to contents of independent websites about Department of Computer Sciences of EPU and Institute of Software. EPU ontology includes 59 concepts and 143 individuals. IOS course ontology includes 63 concepts and 157 individuals.

iii) **ShowPlace**. The third data set includes two ontologies separately describing some showplaces from China. All placename terminologies of the two ontologies are randomly and objectively collected from Websites Baidu[1] and Google[2]. Both ontologies have an extent of about 150 entities. Some relative pictures about these places are also collected as instances of ontologies.

5.3 Experimental Data Analysis

We make evaluation on above three data sets. We consider the semantically overlapped terminologies in each data set. If we find two terminologies X and Y from different ontologies in $Dataset$, and there are semantical mapping relation, then we say they are semantically overlapped terminologies. We use $Overlap(Dataset)$ to represent the number of semantically overlapped terminologies in data set $Dataset$. In fact, *SharedOnto* mentioned in previous sections consists of semantically overlapped terminologies and their mapping axioms. The following graph shows the relations between query precision (Recall) and number of semantically overlapped terminologies from the three data sets.

From Figure 2, we find an interesting fact, i.e, more semantical overlapped terminologies among distributed ontologies are found, more high precision is obtained. This means that when we perform semantic approximation query across multiple ontologies, we should find more concepts that are most approximate to the replaced concept in query. More approximate concepts are found, more exact mappings between local ontologies will be. Therefore query precision will be improved greatly. However, in Figure 3, it seems that our method cannot help improve recall rate greatly. Even we find recall rate is reduced to certain extents. A reasonable interpretation of this problem is that the replacing concepts are

[1] www.baidu.com

[2] www.google.com

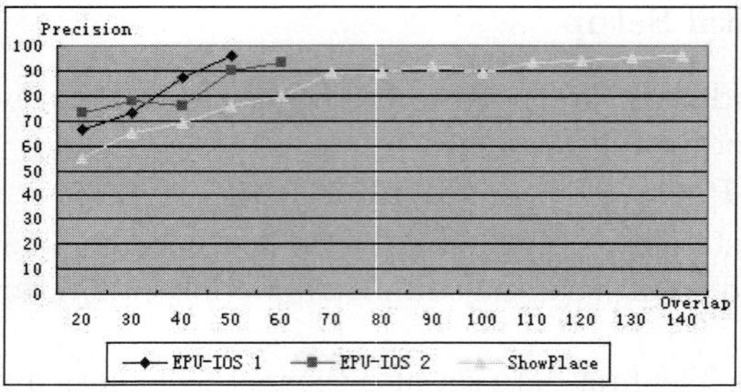

Fig. 2. Precision Evaluation from Three Datasets

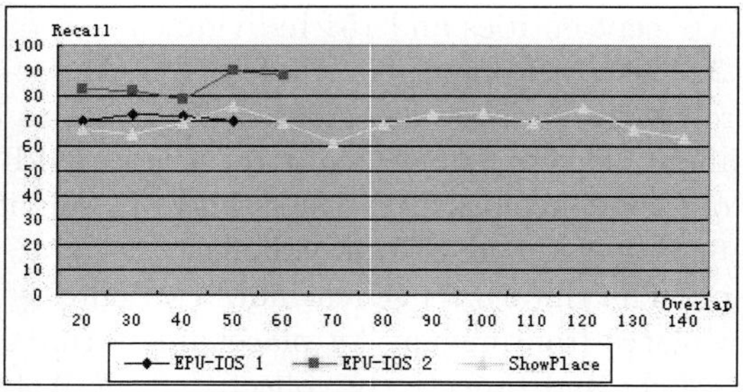

Fig. 3. Recall Evaluation from Three Datasets

strictly smaller than replaced concepts. Consequently, returned results of queries will decrease. Of course, a good method will need more evaluation. Our method also need be further evaluated, especially for a large case system. This will deal with more complex problems such as more reliable ontology storage, access and reasoning, but they are out of the scope of this paper.

6 Related Work

The method proposed in this paper has some obvious advantages: it is operated well and its theory is graceful and simple. The complexity of the main algorithms is $O(n^2)$, which is rather low. Currently, some approximate query methods [2,8,9] based on description logic aim to tackle information integration and maintenance of information repositories. They didn't consider incomplete and non-exact matching of Web information. Schaerf and Cadoli [10] defined a well founded logic and provided a fast algorithm for approximate reasoning. It is difficult to decide which parameters can lead to a good approximation. In this paper, our method is similar to the work of [2], but can differentiate with each other. 1) We combine alignments of ontologies with mappings of ontologies. As mentioned in previous section, we construct a shared ontology of distributed ontologies. It at least contains some information such as terminological mapping axioms and related concepts and properties. 2) from the viewpoint of semantics, our method can strictly ensure correctness of queries and reduce failures of queries. But their work cannot ensure the point, which means that users probably get the results that they don't want indeed.

Our future work also needs to address the problem of automatically constructing approximate mappings of terminologies (concepts) from distributed ontologies. We have concentrated on ontology learning for Semantic Web [12] and applied this method to mine and learn new mapping rules.

7 Conclusion

We proposed an approximate query method for tackling this problem. The terminologies contained in query are replaced by the ones that are semantically most approximate to the query terminologies, which will make the query continue and return the approximate results that users need. At last, we discuss system implementation and experimental evaluation of our semantic approximation method.

Acknowledgements. This work is supported by National Natural Science Fund (No.60573013). We also thank anonymous referees for their valuable comments.

References

1. Hendler, J.: Agents and the Semantic Web. *IEEE Intelligent Systems*, **16** (2001) 30–37
2. Stuckenschimdt, H.: Exploiting Partially Shared Ontologies for Multi-Agent Communication. In: Proceedings of CIA'02, 2002
3. Guha,R. V.: RDFDB:An RDF Database. 2004. http://www.guha.com/rdfdb/
4. Baader, F., et al.: *The Description Logic Handbook*: *Theory, Implementation and Applications*. Cambridge University Press, Cambridge, 2003
5. Baader, F., Horrocks, I. and Sattler, U. Description logics as ontology languages for the semantic web. Mechanizing Mathematical Reasoning: Essays in Honor of Jorg H. Siekmann on the Occasion of His 60th Birthday, Lecture Notes in Artificial Intelligence, **2605** (2005) 228–248
6. HP Lab.: Jena Semantic Web Framework. 2004. http://www.hpl.hp.com/semweb/
7. W3C. OWL Web Ontology Language Reference. 2004. http://www.w3.org/TR/owl-ref/
8. Stuchenschmidt, H.: Approximate information filtering with multiple classification hierarchies. *International Journal of Computational Intelligence and Applications*, **2** (2002) 295–302
9. Akahani, J., et al.: Approximate query reformulateion for ontology integration. In: Proceedings of ICWS2003, 2003
10. Schaerf, M. and Cadoli, M.: Tractable reasoning via approximation. *Artificial Intelligence*, **74** (1995) 249–310
11. Y.-L, Ma., et al.: Approximate Semantic Query Based on Multi-Agent Systems. In: Proceedings of Rough Set and Knowledge Technology 2006, 2006 (to appear)
12. Maedche, A. and Staab, S.: Ontology learning for the semantic web. *IEEE Intelligent Systems*, **16** (2001) 72–79

A Simulation-Based Process Model Learning Approach for Dynamic Enterprise Process Optimization

WenAn Tan

School of Mathematics & Information Sci. and Engineering,
Zhejiang Normal University
JinHua, Zhejiang, China, 321004
{jk76, jk80}@zjnu.cn

Abstract. Dynamic enterprises process optimization (DEPO) is a multi-parametric and multi-objective system optimization problem. This paper proposes a simulation-based process model learning approach for dynamic enterprise process optimization. Some concepts such as *Evolving_region, Evolving_Potential, Degenerate_region* and *Degenerate_limit* are proposed to extend the concept of *Tabu area. Tabu area extension and connection* is successfully presented for realizing rapidly the domain reduction of a candidate set and speeding up global optimization. A distributed parallel optimization environment has been implemented using intelligent agents to validate the proposed approach.

1 Introduction

Dynamic enterprises process optimization (DEPO) supports enterprise process evaluation with spiral life cycle by using process modeling, process simulation and analysis, process optimization, and process enactment within an enterprise cooperative work environment. It can be used to instruct enterprise management and support decision analysis. Process simulation and optimization (PSO) is an essential tool for the design analysis of complex systems that cannot be easily described by analytical or mathematical model. It is useful for calculating utilization statistics, finding bottlenecks, pointing out scheduling errors and even for creating manufacturing schedules. The objectives of using PSO are to create an optimized enterprise model for instructing enterprise operation and management. Using PSO technologies, computer-aided solutions can be obtained economically.

This paper discusses a simulation-based process model evolution approach for supporting dynamic enterprises process optimization (DEPO). In fact, the process optimization algorithm in DEPO is a multi-parametric and multi-objective systematic optimization problem for implement automatic optimization of parameters inside process model. Traditional optimization methods such as the gradient method, Newton method, Fletcher Reeves (FR) method, quasi-Newton method, and Powell method are suitable for the optimization of a single optimal solution [1], *i.e.*, they are just suitable for solving local optimization issues. If there are multi-pole existed, or there are high factorial non-linear issues, the aforementioned methods could not find the

D.-S. Huang, K. Li, and G.W. Irwin (Eds.): ICIC 2006, LNAI 4114, pp. 438 – 449, 2006.

global optimum in the feasible solution space. Prevailing optimization algorithms are Heuristics, such as Genetic algorithms, Tabu Search (TS) method, Simulative anneal arithmetic, and combinatorial algorithm [2-6]. A meta heuristic might be described as an enhanced local search algorithm, where the main improvement lies in the ability to move away from local optima. To use a local search, it is necessary to have a solution to start with. By performing a *change* in this solution, a new solution is obtained. The solutions that can be reached from the initial solution by a certain change are called *neighbors*, and the total set of neighbors is referred to as the *neighborhood*. In a local search, the neighborhood (or a part of it) is explored, and the best neighbor is selected as the improving solution. If no better solution can be found in the neighborhood, the algorithm terminates. These prevailing algorithms could break through the limitation of multi-pole issues by randomly selecting and evaluating a solution in the neighborhood.

The classic reference for TS is Glover [7] in 1986, but today information on the heuristic can be found in many textbooks, e.g., Aarts and Lenstra [8] in 1997. The enhancement built into a TS algorithm, i.e., what separates it from a local search algorithm, is the addition of a *tabu list*. The *tabu list* consists of certain attributes that define if a move from a certain solution to another is allowed. The main purposes are to assure that the algorithm does not stop at a local optimum, and to prevent cycling, i.e., that the same solutions are visited repeatedly. If the *tabu list* consists of the L latest solutions, it is possible to guarantee that cycles shorter than L iterations will not occur. We could not define length of *tabu list* very big, but if we define it shorter, *tabu list* could not save more information of the recently visited solutions, it is not longer possible to guarantee to find out the global optimum. So, for the conventional TS method, it is the limitation that the speed of searching optima will from bad to worse with increasing of *tabu list* size if *tabu list* is a dynamic data structure.

Because of the diversification of parameters in the process model, literatures [9,10] proposed an optimization method, which is called as FR-TS algorithm, and compared with aforementioned algorithms. The proposed method combines FR method and TS method, where FR is used for seeking the local optimal solution, as well as TS for breaking through the limitation of local optimization. These two methods will be alternately iterated many times so as to get the global optimum. *Tabu area* was firstly proposed as one of taboo solution space for next searching optimum, which has addressed FR method's limitation to multi-pole issues as well as it extends tabu domain of *tabu list* in TS method. But if the initial solution is near to the local optimum solution, the area will be very small, and the number of Tabu area also may increase rapidly and consumes more and more memory and influences searching optima.

Aim to address above issues, this paper introduces dialectics into FR-TS method to redefine *Tabo area* and proposes a process model evolution approach. As we known, FR method can be used for searching local optimum from a certain solution, and it also can be used for seeking inferior from there in the reversed directory. If we combine two searching domains as a *Tabu region*, and link all *Tabu regions* connecting each other into a *Tabu area*, the enlarged *Tabu area* will be reasonable and integrated. Based on this idea, this paper introduces some new concepts such as *Evolving_region, Evolving_Potential, Degenerate_region* and *Degenerate_limit* for redefining the concept of *Tabu area*, and develops *Tabu area extension and connection* algorithm for speeding up the process of goal-searching in the process optimizations of multi-dimensional spatial issues. It supports enterprise dynamic optimization and facilitates to BPR (Business Process Reengineering) and ERP management.

2 Process Model Evolution Approach

The basic idea of our proposed process model evolution approach is that: For a set of experience process model data, FR is used for model learning, i.e., approaching the local best solution and the local worst solution. Let a combined space of the two traversal spaces as a *Tabu region*. Following is to use TS to do global random search to discover a new random feasible solution within non-taboo space, and to continue using FR to begin new generational model learning from this new solution. While generating Tabu Area, *Tabu region extension* and *Tabu region connection* algorithms are used for expanding the tabu area and reducing the feasible solution space to facilitate overall optimization.

2.1 The Definitional Extensions of Tabu Area

In order to understand better the new concept of extended Tabu Area, the first thing we need to do is to introduce following concepts:

Definition 1. Let the largest traversal scope of local optimization using FR method from initial solution ${}^{start}x_j$ is the evolution region of ${}^{start}x_j$, signed as *Evolving_region*(${}^{start}x_j$), *i.e.*, from initial solution ${}^{start}x_j$ (${}^{start}x_{j,1},\ldots, {}^{start}x_{j,,i},\ldots, {}^{start}x_{j,n}$) start searching in negative gradient direction to the farthest point ${}^{end-}x_j$ (${}^{end-}x_{j,1},\ldots, {}^{end-}x_{j\,,i},\ldots, {}^{end-}x_{j,\,n}$). The local optimum solution ${}^{best}x$ is called as the evolution potential of ${}^{start}x_j$ in this evolution region, signed as *Evolving_Potential*(${}^{start}x_j$).

Definition 2. Let the largest traversal scope of local inferior using FR method from initial solution ${}^{start}x_j$ is the degenerative region of ${}^{start}x_j$, signed as *Degenerate_region*(${}^{start}x_j$), *i.e.*, from initial solution ${}^{start}x_j$(${}^{start}x_{j,1},\ldots, {}^{start}x_{j\,,i},\ldots, {}^{start}x_{j,\,n}$) begin searching in the reversed direction, i.e., gradient direction, to the farthest point ${}^{end+}x_j$ (${}^{end+}x_{j,1},\ldots, {}^{end+}x_{j\,,i},\ldots, {}^{end+}x_{j,\,n}$). The local most inferior solution ${}^{worst}x$ is called as the degenerative limit of ${}^{start}x_j$ in this degenerative region, signed as *Degenerate_ limit*(${}^{start}x_j$).

On the base of *evoluting_region* and *Degenerate_ region*, we can redefine the concept of *Tabu area* as:

Definition 3. Defining the union of *Evolving_region*(${}^{start}x_j$) and *Degenerate_ region*(${}^{start}x_j$), as a *Tabu region* generated by FR method from initial solution ${}^{start}x_j$, *i.e.*, *Tabu_region*(*j*) = (${}^{end-}x_j$, ${}^{end+}x_j$). We build a list to link all the *Tabu regions* and call it *Tabu Area* of process model evolution.

In order to support *Tabu area extension and connection*, a multi-link data structure of *Tabu Area* can be defined as following node structure:

$({}^{end-}\boldsymbol{x}_j, {}^{end+}\boldsymbol{x}_j)$	*// The scope of jth Tabu_region*
$\{{}^{best}\boldsymbol{x}^{(i)}{}_j, Q({}^{best}\boldsymbol{x}^{(i)}{}_j)\}$	*// Evolutional potential and evaluation value used for Tabu region extension.*
$\{{}^{worst}\boldsymbol{x}^{(i)}{}_j, Q({}^{worst}\boldsymbol{x}^{(i)}{}_j)\}$	*//Degeneration limit and value used for Tabu region connection.*
Flag	*//a flag to label whether tabu region is visited when expanding and connecting*
**Ext1, *Ext2*	*//bi-directional points used for Tabu region extension*

**Link1, *Link2* *// bi-directional points used for Tabu region connection*
**Next* *//a point to the next disconnected Tabu region*

In this multi-link Tabu Area, there are following three key information: $({}^{end-}\boldsymbol{x}_j, {}^{end+}\boldsymbol{x}_j)$ is vector space of the *j*th *Tabu region*, i.e., $<({}^{end-}x_{j,1}, {}^{end+}x_{j,1}), \ldots, ({}^{end-}x_{j,i}, {}^{end+}x_{j,i}), \ldots, ({}^{end-}x_{j,n}, {}^{end+}x_{j,n})>$; $\{{}^{best}\boldsymbol{x}_j, Q({}^{best}\boldsymbol{x}_j)\}$ is the evolutional potential in the *j*th *Tabu region* and its evaluation value; $\{{}^{worst}\boldsymbol{x}_j, Q({}^{worst}\boldsymbol{x}_j)\}$ is the degenerative limit of the *j*th *Tabu region* and its evaluation value. *Tabu Area* is a dynamic link structure expanding with the progress of searching optima. At last, only a *Tabu region* is existed in *Tabu Aera*, and *Tabu Area* includes the domain of whole feasible solutions.

2.2 Tabu Rule

Tabu rule: Let ***TAs*** is the set of Tabu area, if there is a individual $\boldsymbol{x}(x_1,\ldots,x_j,\ldots,x_n)$ and $\boldsymbol{x}$ In *TAs*, *i.e.*, $\exists j \forall i (x_i \in ({}^{end-}x_{j,i}, {}^{end+}x_{j,i}))$, then $\boldsymbol{x}$ is a taboo individual.

In global searching optima, only non-taboo individual $\boldsymbol{x}$ can be used as a feasible solution to begin new generational model learning by FR method to find new evolutional potentials, degeneration limits and new *Tabu regions*. The tabu individuals are abandoned, and a new individual will be regenerated until it is a non-tabu individual. Repeating the whole process, we could get the global optimum solution.

2.3 Candidate Set

Candidate set is an important concept in TS method. In enterprise process optimization, all potential solution space outside of *Tabu area* in domain *D* is called Candidate set defined as follows:

$$Can\_N = D - \bigcup_{i=1}^{m} Tabu\_Aera(i) \tag{1}$$

Each local searching optimum constructs a *Tabu region*. After running *Tabu region extension* and *Tabu region connection*, current candidate set will get smaller. When candidate set becomes null, *i.e.*, *Tabu area* occupies all potential solution space in domain D, the process of searching optima will be ended.

2.4 Evaluation Function

In TS method, evaluation function is used for comparing new individual performance with the global optimum individual selected from candidate sets. We use the integrated enterprise evaluation Q(x) as the evaluation function, which can be calculated as [11]:

$$Q(x)=w_1\times Time_{index}+w_2\times Service_{index}+w_3\times Quality_{index}+w_4\times Speed_{index}+w_5\times Efficiency_{index}+w_6\times Cost_{index} \tag{2}$$

In searching optima, current optimum solution (individual) ${}^{best}x$ is automatically recorded. If $Q({}^{now}x)<Q({}^{best}x)$, then set the solution ${}^{now}x$ as the current optimum solution ${}^{best}x$ by formula ${}^{best}x = {}^{now}x$. After this replacement, current optimum solution is outputted into corresponding file, which can be illustrated by EXCEL in chart of the process optimization track.

2.5 Generation of New Individual

Domain *D* in process model is a virtual set. In resource model we usually predefined available resource usage. Random-number-generator is used to create a new individual grouped by some parameters according to the defined resource usages occupied by the key activities, the distribution characteristics of the key activities' durations (such as Constant, Uniform, Normal, Poisson), and the source products' arrival frequencies defined in process model. These parameters are limited to the predefined information in resource model and process model. Judging according to the aforementioned Tabu rule, if the generated individual is in *Tabu area*, then another new individual need to be generated; else, this individual can be used as a new solution ${}^{new}x$ which is selected from the candidate set for new generation of local optimization.

2.6 Halt Condition

Tabu area extension and connection are effective to control the increase of the memory occupied by *tabu list* in TS method. It enables rapid reduction of candidate set to realize global optimization. There are following rules can be used as the halt conditions for FR-TS algorithm:

- *Fixed step halt.* Setting a big number *Loop_N* as the iterative times, it is easy to implement, but it could not guarantee we can get the global optimum solution. When the iterated times is *Loop_N*, the thread of searching optima will be ended.
- *Frequency halt.* When the *Tabu area* occupies the total domain of *D*, search algorithm terminates. When the times which new individual was continuously in *Tabu area* equals to a specified value, e.g., 10000, the potential solution space *Can_N* can be considered as Null.

We usually use both two rules to control optimization process. Each temporary optimum solution should be recorded for enterprise decision analysis.

3 Algorithm Implementation

After building a new *tabu region*, the first thing we need to do is to analyze whether its *evolution potential* point is the same as some one in the *Tabu area*. If it is true, these two tabu regions can be combined. This operation, firstly searching out that node by scanning *Tabu area* with *Tabu area's* extension link (*Ext1 and *Ext2) and then putting the new *Tabu region* at the end of the tabu region, is named as *Tabu region Extension*. As showed as Figure 1.

If it is not true, we continue to search the *Tabu area* to find whether there is a *Tabu region* whose *degeneration limit* is the same as that of new tabu region. If there is the *Tabu region*, we seek it out by using *Tabu area's* connective link (*Link1 and *Link2) with , and append new tabu region at the end of this region. This operation means that if two tabu regions are jointed in a degeneration limit, these two tabu regions can be connected. This operation is named as *Tabu region Connection.*

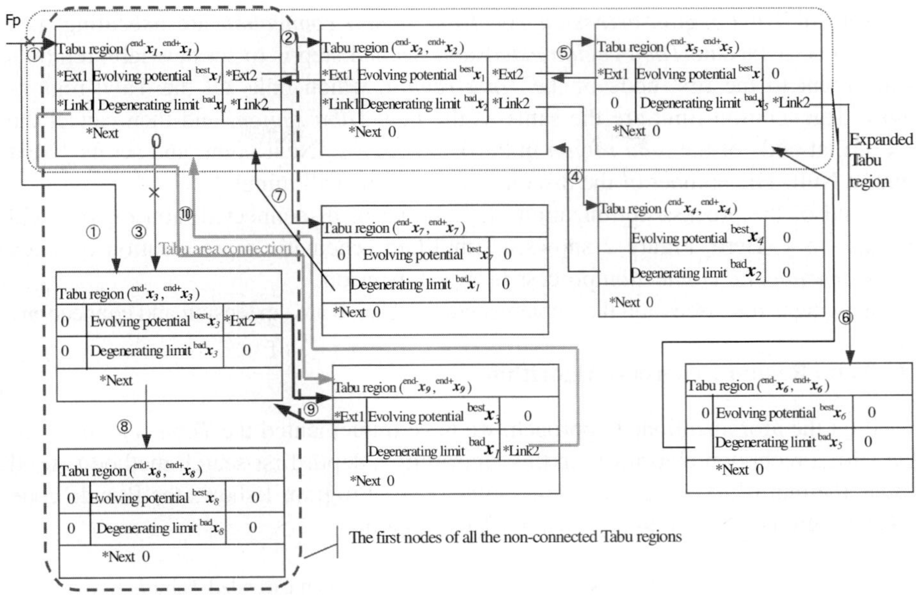

Fig. 1. Schematic representation of Tabu area extension and connection process

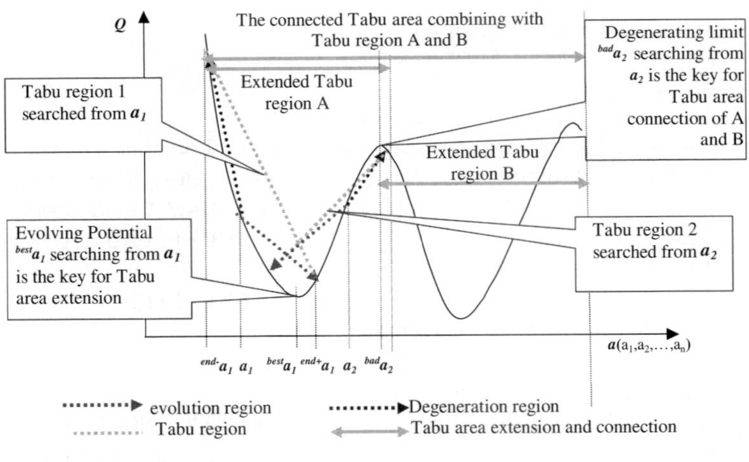

Fig. 2. Schematic representation of Tabu area extension and connection

If there are not any tabu region whose *degeneration limit* nor *degeneration limit* is the same as the relative part of new tabu region, this new tabu region will be appended into the end of the *Tabu area* by point *Next, and the number of disjointed tabu regions plus 1.

If the new tabu region's evolution potential is the same as some one in the *Tabu area* and its *degeneration limit* is the same as other one tabu region in the *Tabu area* too, both of *Tabu region extension* nor *Tabu region connection* are executing, i.e., first step is to execute *Tabu region extension*, Second step is to set new tabu region's Link2 point to the first node of the *Tabu region*, which links all the Tabu regions whose degeneration limit are the same as the new *Tabu region,* and then cancel the link of that node of the *tabu region* in the Tabu Area's *Next point, and set its *Next point to Null. The number of the disconnected regions will minus 1.

At end of the process optimization, the number of disconnected tabu regions will decrease to 1. Here, Figure 2 shows a simplified schematic representation of *Tabu area extension and connection* process in two-dimension.

Following is the discussion the implementation of Tabu area extension and connection.

3.1 Tabu Region Extension Algorithm

Based on the aforementioned approach, we have implemented the *Tabu region extension* with a recursion algorithm. In this algorithm, a depth-first-search method is used to scan the multi-link *Tabu Area* using point *Ext2. Program 1 shows the Pseudo code of Tabu region extension in an extended Tabu region.

Program 1. Pseudo code of Tabu Region Extension in an extended Tabu region

```
Boolean Function Tabu_region_extend(Tabu_Area *fp,
*New_Tabu_region)
{
 Boolean  result = FALSE;
 Tabu_area  *temp, *before;
 temp = fp;
 if (temp->Ext2!= NULL) then
 //traversal fp's expanding area until no more exists
 result=Tabu_region_extend(temp->Ext2,New_Tabu_region);
 if (equal (temp->Evolving_potential, New_Tabu_region-
>Evolving_potential) and (result!=TRUE)) then {
      temp->Ext2 = New_Tabu_region;
      //  add new Tabu region into the link
      New_Tabu_region->Ext1 = temp;
      New_Tabu_region->Ext2 = NULL;
      result = TRUE;
 } if ((result!=TRUE) and (temp->Link2!= NULL)) then
 //judging whether there is a linked Tabu region whose
 //evolving potential is the same as new Tabu region
 result=Tabu_region_extend(temp->Link,New_Tabu_region);
 return result;
}//End of extend
```

Tabu Area usually contains more than one disconnected Tabu regions during process optimization. *Tabu region extension* in the whole Tabu Area is implemented as Program 2.

Program 2. Pseudo code of Tabu Region Extension in the whole Tabu Area

```
Boolean function Tabu_area_extend(Tabu_Area  *fp,
*New_Tabu_region)
{
  Boolean result = FALSE;
  Tabu_Area  *temp= fp;
  While((temp!=NULL)and (result!=TRUE)) Do{
 // Tabu area extension and connection for single
 // Tabu region link
    result= Tabu_region_extend(temp,New_Tabu_region);
    temp = temp->Next; } // End-While
  return result;
 }         //End of Funcation Tabu_area_extend
```

3.2 Tabu Region Connection Algorithm

Similar to *Tabu region extension, Tabu region connection* algorithm scans *Tabu Area* using point *Link2. It tries to find whether there are the nodes whose degeneration limit is the same as the new *Tabu region*. If search algorithm has found the node, it will return TRUE and the found node together with the head-node of the *Tabu region*. Otherwise, the algorithm will continue doing depth-first-seeking along the extension point (*Ext1 and *Ext2) until all tabu regions have visited one time. At last, it returns false. The pseudo code of *Tabu region connection* named *Tabu_area_link* is omitted.

3.3 Implementation of Tabu Area Extension and Connection Algorithm

According to the aforementioned approach, *Tabu Area Extension and Connection* algorithm can be implemented easily based on *Tabu_area_extend* and *Tabu_area_link*.

Program 3. Pseudo code of Tabu area extension and connection algorithm

```
Procedure Tabu_area_ext_link(Tabu_Area *fp,
*New_Tabu_region)
{
Boolean Ext_result=Link_result=FALSE;
Tabu_Area *temp;
Tabu_Area *Head, *temp_Node;
//point to the Head node and the node whose
//degeneration limit is same as new Tabu region
Temp = fp;
Ext_result =Tabu_area_extend(Temp, New_Tabu_region);
// extending Tabu region
Temp_Head= temp_Node =fp;
// Tabu region connecting judgment
Link_result = Tabu_area_link(Temp_Head, temp_Node,
New_Tabu_region);
if ((Ext_result =TURE)and (Link_result =TURE)) then {
// both expanding and connecting is executive
  Temp=Temp_Head->Next;
```

```
    Temp_Head->Next= NULL; // remove the node whose
  //degeneration limit is equivalent
    Temp_Node->Link1= New_Tabu_region;
  // Tabu region connecting
    New_Tabu_region->Link2= Temp_Node;
    New_Tabu_region->Next = Temp;      // form the link
    Temp = fp;
    While(Temp->Next!=Temp_Head) Do Temp=Temp_Next;
    Temp->Next = New_Tabu_region;      // Break link to
  //Temp_Head node in Tabu Aera's next link
   }else if (Link_result =TURE) // If only connecting is
  //executive, Link New_Tabu_region after temp_Node
    then { temp_Node->Link1->link2= New_Tabu_region;
           New_Tabu_region->Link1= temp_Node->Link1;
           New_Tabu_region->Link2 =temp_Node;
           temp_Node->Link1 = New_Tabu_region;
           New_Tabu_region->Next = NULL;
    }elseif ((Link_result !=TRUE) and (Ext_result!=TURE))
  then {// neither expanding nor connecting is executive
        While(Temp->Next!=NULL)do Temp = Temp->Next;
        Temp->Next = New_Tabu_region;
  //no Tabu region's evolution potential is equivalent
  // to new Tabu region, append this new Tabu region
   }// at the end of Tabu area
  }//End of Tabu_Area_ext_link
```

3.4 Distributed Parallel Optimization Environment

Because of the complexity of large-scale enterprise process simulation, it generally costs much time to do process optimization in a single computer. We have implemented the proposed approach using multi-agents in a distributed environment to speed up optimization.

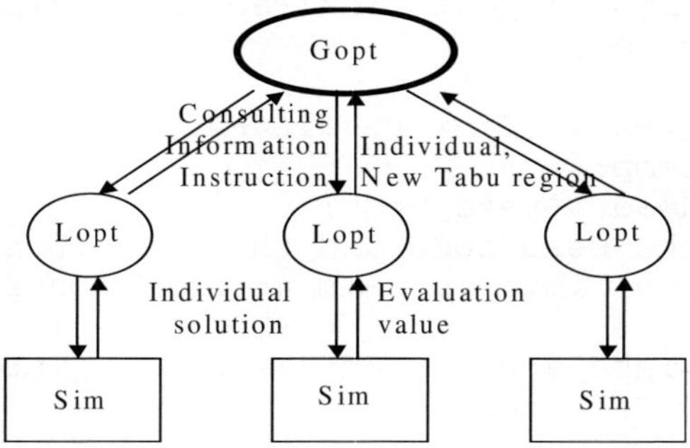

Fig. 3. Distributed parallel optimization environment framework

As illustrated in Figure 3, the distributed parallel optimization environment mainly contains local Optimization agent (*Lopt*), global Optimization agent (*Gopt*) and Simulator agent (*Sim*). Lopt is responsible for the local optimization and constructing a single *Tabu region* to implement process model learning by using FR algorithm and process simulation. In local process optimization, *Lopt* generates a new individual solution (a group of key parameters) to ask *Gopt*, a server, whether this new solution is in *Tabu area*. If yes, *Lopt* will regenerate a new solution again, otherwise, it begins local optimization, and computes its evolution potential and degeneration limit, and then builds a *Tabu region* from this solution. The generated *Tabu region* will be sent to *Gopt* to implement Tabu area extension and connection. *Gopt* is responsible for Tabu area extension and connection and consultation, and controls the process of enterprise process optimization. *Sim* is just responsible for process simulation and providing the evaluation of process model with currently individual solution.

4 Application and Conclusions

We have applied the proposed approach in the design process optimization of an airplane comparing with the *Fletcher-Reeves* (FR) method and *Tabu search* method. The results are illustrated in Figure 4, 5, 6.

Figure 4 illustrates that during process optimization by FR method, the tracking of process model optimization follows the conjugate gradient direction until finding a local optimal solution. X-coordinate is the generations of process optimization iteration, as well as Y-coordinate presents the evaluation function of the individuals. The FR method could not break through the local optimization area, because FR method is a conjugate gradient methods and it is applicable to quadratic functions. If there are multiple optima, FR method can only find an optimum related to the selected initial solution. So, Figure 4 only shows one iteration process of enterprise process evolution. In fact the FR method is applicable to large problems of quadratic functions.

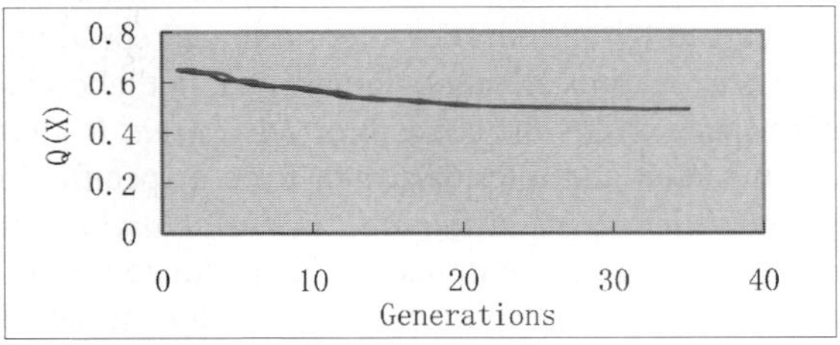

Fig. 4. Q vs Generations by method

Figure 5 shows that tracking process optimization is not available control, and it only records the best solution currently. TS method is a random probing method and could be used to find out the optimization solutions in global domain by seeking the no-tabooed solution space if the Tabu list is enough big. It needs probing all potential solution space in domain D.

Figure 6 illustrates that the FR-TS method can be used to rapidly track the local optimization, and it can apply the advance of TS method, breaking through the restriction of the local optimization to find out a new no-tabooed individual solution, for getting the global optima. The FR-TS method is the combining of FR method and TS method for solving manufacturing process optimization problems.

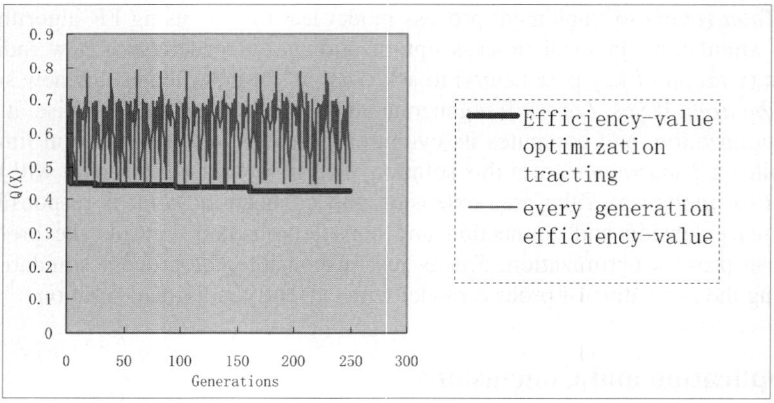

Fig. 5. Q vs Genereations using Tabu Search method

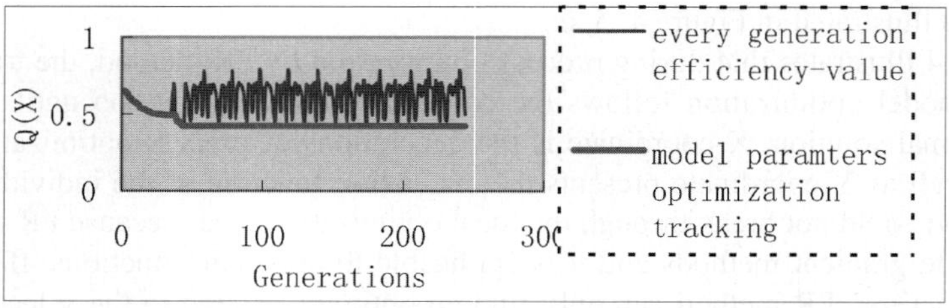

Fig. 6. Q vs Generations using FR-TS method

This case study proves that the proposed approach can effectively avoid rapid increase of memory occupied by optimization algorithm and speed up global optimization because the *tabu area* records all taboo domains but not taboo individuals [8].

In summary, this paper extends the concept of *Tabu area*: If a new solution is not taboo, doing optimum search and inferior search from a specific initial solution can build a large integrated *Tabu region*. *Tabu area extension and connection* is successfully proposed to rapidly decrease the domain of a candidate set and speed up global optimization. A distributed parallel optimization environment has been implemented using intelligent agents to validate the proposed approach. The proposed approach is suitable for solving the optimization of multi-dimensional spatial issues. It is beneficial to enterprise in implementing BPR and ERP management.

Acknowledgement

The majority of the work presented in this paper was done by the first author during his Ph.D studies in BeiHang University, China. Appreciations should be given to Prof. Bosheng Zhou, the Ph.D supervisor and the team members in BeiHang University. This work was partially supported by the National Natural Science Foundation of China (Grant No. 69803003) and the Research Foundation for University Young Academic Leaders of Zhejiang Province of China (Grant No. SD200103).

References

1. Fletcher, R., : Practical Methods of Optimization, John Wiley & Sons, New York, 2004
2. Fontanili, F., Vincent, A., Ponsonnet, R.: Flow Simulation and Genetic Algorithm as Optimization Tools. Int. J. Production Economics 64(2000) 91-100
3. Nowicki, C.S.: A Fast Tabu Search Algorithm for the Job Shop Problem. Management Science, 42(6).(1996) 797-813
4. Liu, G.Q, CHEN, E.H, CAI, Q.S.: A Genetic Algorithm Based Job-Shop Scheduling Problem Solving Method. Journal of Software, 9(2) (1998)139-143
5. Wang H.G.: An Excellent Schemas Self-Learning Genetic Algorithm. ACTA Automatica SINICA, 25(3) (1999) 375-379
6. Felix, P.: Analysis and Modeling of Science Collaboration Networks. Advances in Complex Systems, 4 (2003) 477-485
7. Glover, F.: Future Paths for Integer Programming and Links to Artificial Intelligence. Computers & Operations Research, 5 (1986) 533–549
8. Aarts, E., J. Lenstra, (eds.): Local Search in Combinatorial Optimization. John Wiley & Sons Ltd. (1997)
9. Tan, W.A. Zhou B.S., Li M.S.: Research on a Simulation-Based Auto-Optimization Technique in Enterprise Process Model. Journal of Software, 13(4) (2002) 706-712
10. Tan, W.A.: A Study and Development for Dynamic Optimizing Enterprise Process Technique and Its Supporting Environment. Ph.D. Thesis, BeiHang University, Beijing (2001)
11. Tan, W.A., Zhao, J.M., Shen, W.M.: A Simulation-based Dynamic Evaluation Methodology for Enterprise Process Performance. The 17th IASTED International Conference on Modelling and Simulation, May 24-26, Montreal, Quebec, Canada (2006)

Task Assigning and Optimizing of Genetic-Simulated Annealing Based on MAS

Yong Liu, Shujuan Li, and Yan Li

School of mechanical & instrumental engineering,
Xi'an University of Technology, 710048 Xi'an, PRC
shujuanli@xaut.edu.cn

Abstract. This paper suggests the optimization method of task assigning based on genetic-simulated annealing algorithm focus on the alternative scheme of bidding invitation parameters obtained in the bidding process in MAS. Through reasonable assessing the bidding documents from bid, bidding result determined is obtained, viz. the task assigning scheme. All of the tasks' assigning optimization is carried out by setting the parameters of genetic-simulated annealing algorithm; the algorithm can search steadily the optimal scheme and overcome the flaws of traditional simulated annealing algorithm such as big undulation and poor astringency. It is found via the analysis of experiment data that the algorithm can improve assignment scheme further rationality and feasibility.

1 Introduction

In recent years, the production scheduling in manufacturing industry has become a research focus, particularly with intelligent Agent application applied to scheduling problem for many scholars [1]. The task assignment is an indispensable key link to the production scheduling based on Agent. This key link mainly consists of the management Agents and resource Agents, and is completed through bidding invitation forms. With an aim at some task set, the management Agent can issue the bidding invitation information to the resource Agent; and the resource Agent can supply the bidding documents in terms of its production capacity(the items of the bidding document in this paper refer to the time or duration and cost of task completion), and then, the resource Agent can select the optimal resources to complete some task from all the bidding resources(the shortest possible time and cost for completing the task), and finally, one production scheduling is formed[2],[3]. However, the production scheduling obtained via this tactics can not be the optimal scheduling[4],[5], and particularly in the system without special management Agent, the common resource Agent and management Agent have no overall viewpoint of the complete scheme scheduling problem but can only obtain the local optimization. Accordingly, in the process of bid evaluation, we can not consider the optimal completion of one single task by some bidding resource as the evaluation standard, but take the optimal completion of multi-task effect as the objective [6].

In the process of the bidding invitation using contract net, authors in this paper proposed using the genetic-simulated annealing to calculate the objective function

D.-S. Huang, K. Li, and G.W. Irwin (Eds.): ICIC 2006, LNAI 4114, pp. 450–460, 2006.

value to determine the assigning scheme of tasks. Thus, the method gets a scheme which is not only the best scheme of all tasks, but also a better scheme for single task, and raises the resource using efficiency, reduces makespan of tasks.

2 Multi-agent Tasks Assigning Model

In this multi-agent system, task assigning is completed by cooperation of two type Agents: Management Agent and Resource Agent.

(1) Management Agent

It is usually used to establish the coordination relationship among the general agents or to process some local information; for this reason, it is just like a virtual working operator to some extent [8]. In the study a task assigning Agent (TdAgent) is defined as bidding invitation Agent, according to the format of contact net's bid and bidding incitation. TdAgent collects the tasks from task publisher to make them into bidding documents, and then send to each resource Agent, after that, waits for bidding from resource Agents. Machining time and cost provided by resource Agents are considered as the measurements. Genetic-simulated annealing method is adopted to determine the resource Agent to complete tasks in the process of task assigning. The process bid and bidding invitation among Agents as follow Fig.1.

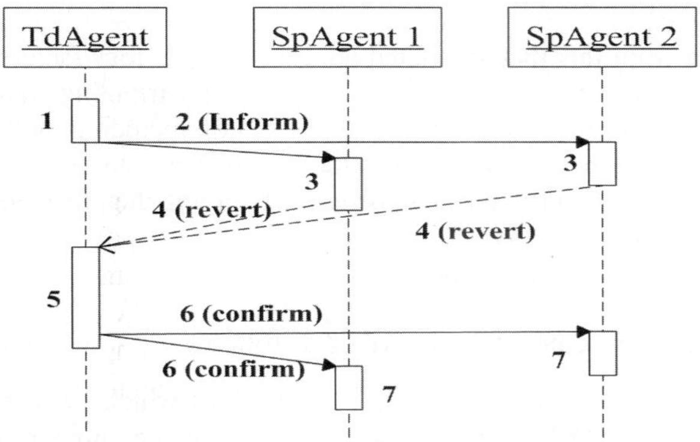

Fig. 1. Schematic drawing of Agents bidding invitation. 1—making bid documents of tasks set; 2—Sending bidding information to workshop Agents; 3—filling in the documents; 4—answering the documents to TdAgent; 5—collecting bid documents, using annealing to evaluate bid documents; 6—sending information to notify bidding success; 7—executing the tasks of bidding success.

(2) Resource Agent

One resource refers to the unit or units' combination which are able to complete one function at least. Therefore, individual machine, tools, fasteners and transporting equipment or installations in the manufacturing system are the basic functional units, which are all the resources. When they are combined with each other to complete one basic operation, they can be considered as one resource. And even in terms of problem needs, one workshop can also be considered as one resource [9]. The workshop Agent (SpAgent) is defined as bid Agent that receives and fills in the task bidding documents, and returns the bid to TdAgent based on machining ability and capability in processing tasks.

3 Application of Simulated Annealing to Task Assigning

Simulated annealing algorithm is earliest found in the articles by S.Kirkpatrick, et al. in IBM Tomas Research Center. After the research on combination optimization, they presented "simulated annealing" in terms of improved iteration thought, the basic thought of which is as follows[10]:

The research objective of this algorithm is to study some disposal determined by one parameter set. In order to be convenient for analyzing the problem, it is necessary to set an objective function *f* based on this disposal. In this way, the optimal process of the disposal can be converted into *f* minimum process. The *f* minimum process can simulate the annealing process in nature, controlled by a gradual cooling temperature *t*. As to every temperature value, a certain minimum step should be tried, and a new disposal scheme is selected at random to calculate *f* function. It is just at this time that if *f* is smaller than the former *f*, the new disposal scheme is selected; if *f* is larger than the former *f*, the probability value $prob=\exp[-\Delta f/(k\cdot t)]$ is calculated, where *k* is Poltzman Constant. And then, the random number *rand* is yielded on (0, 1), if $prob \geq rand$, the new scheme is selected; If $prob < rand$, the existing scheme is remained. These steps can be repeated until this system cooling can no longer produce the better disposals.

It can be seen from this that simulated annealing needs four factors at least: (1) the description of some scheme disposals; (2) the redistributing random producing mechanism; (3) a quantified trade-off objective function including multi-factors; and (4) a cooling mechanism $t=\alpha \cdot t$, α is known as the astringency rate, $0<\alpha<1$. After the above 4 factors are designed properly, they can be used in solving the practical problems.

3.1 Description of Task Assigning

Task assignment can be concretely described as follows:

Definition 1. Task set T=[ts_1 , ts_2 , …, ts_i , … , ts_n], of which ts_i is single task in task set, which is called as a task element, ts_i={c, t, d, s}, *n* is the number of task elements.

c——task code

t——the latest finish time, marked as rt_{ji}.t

d——task description

s——task state

Definition 2. Bidding Agent set A=[A_1, A_2, …, A_j ,…, A_m]^T, of which *m* is the number of bidding Agents.

Definition 3. rt_{ji} is the bidding document of Agent A_j for task element ts_i, then bidding invitation Agent gains bid set *RT* that can be illustrated as formula (1), of which

c——task code

et——executing time, marked as $rt_{ji}.et$

ec——executing cost, marked as $rt_{ji}.ec$

ft——the latest finish time, marked as $rt_{ji}.ft$

$$RT = A \cdot T = [A_1, A_2, \ldots, A_m]^T \cdot [ts_1, ts_2, \ldots, ts_n] = \begin{bmatrix} rt_{11} & rt_{12} & \cdots & rt_{1n} \\ rt_{21} & rt_{22} & \cdots & rt_{2n} \\ \cdots & \cdots & \cdots & \cdots \\ rt_{m1} & rt_{m2} & \cdots & rt_{mn} \end{bmatrix}. \quad (1)$$

Meeting the condition of assigning objective, this study is adopting the genetic-simulated anneal algorithm to find the best assigning scheme *P* in bid set *RT*.

3.2 Algorithm Design

With an aim at different requirements, optimal objectives should also be different. In general, we require that the final scheduling scheme should achieve the effect of lowest cost and the shortest possible time. Such a kind of scheduling scheme can save processing cost, but the fine implementing ability of some operator can frequently lead to task loading far more surpassing the loading of other operators, whereby rendering the maximum flow time (makespan) of the whole task to be prolonged, delaying the task completion time, decreasing the resource use efficiency and causing invisible cost increase. Although this kind of scheduling scheme can satisfy the current requirement of task completion, the completion of the following-up production task will be affected from a long-term point of view. In order to solve the occurrence of the above mentioned problems, we have adopted the following methods to realize the optimal determination of scheduling scheme. In the whole process of optimization, we assume there are *n* task elements and *m* bid Agent, the algorithm is designed as follow:

Step 1: eliminating the redundant information.

Since the participating evaluation elements provided by the bidding Agent are not sure to satisfy task element requirements, which are mainly shown in unsatisfying the time requirement so that the tasks are not completed in the specified time so that this kind of bidding information should be eliminated so as to reduce the redundant degree for reducing the operation time. This operation is mainly to extract *ft* value from rt_{ji} and *t* value from ts_i, to do comparison. If *ft*>*t*, this information of this item can be eliminated.

The concrete operation process is as follows:

```
For i=1; i<=n; i++
{  For j=1; j<=m; j++
   { If( rt_ji.ft > ts_i.t ){ remove(rt_ji) }}
}
```

Step2: setting the initial value.

The set of P_0 and P_n of two storage disposal schemes should be set up to represent the existing scheme and new scheme respectively, $P=\{ rt_{h1}, rt_{k2}, \ldots rt_{ln}\}$, of which *h*, *k*, $l \in [1,m]$. It is necessary to set the initial temperature *tmp*, astringency rate α. The objective function *cost* for evaluating the advantages and disadvantages of disposal scheme is used see Eq.(2).

$$cost = \sum_{i=1}^{n} \left(rt_{ji\bullet}ec + rt_{ji\bullet}et \cdot \beta \right) + \beta \cdot \mathrm{Max}_j \left\{ \sum rt_{ji\bullet}et \right\} . \qquad (2)$$

Where, ①the front part in Eq.(2) indicates the total consumption cost of the disposal scheme, consisting of two parts of the implementing cost and time; ②the latter part indicates the convertible cost of the maximum circulation time of the task set in Agent. The cost and balancing task loading of the scheme should be controlled via the two parts. β is the coefficient of time convertible into cost. The coefficient β is not a fixed value and it can vary in terms of different objective requirements. When the time requirement is high, β value can be larger, and when the cost requirement is high, β value can be smaller so that the corresponding adjustment should be made.

Step 3: producing the initial population of disposal scheme at random.

Assume there are 10 individuals in initial population, the method of each individual produced is as follows: to read a task element ts_i from T set in terms of sequence, and then, to find out the bidding results set $Rt_{i=}[rt_{1i}, rt_{2i}, \ldots, rt_{mi},]$ from the corresponding task element ts_i in RT, from which some Agent bidding information rt_{ji} extracted at random can be served as the disposal scheme for the task element. By so doing, repeating extraction, until all the task elements obtain the disposal scheme, whose extracting process is shown in Fig.2.

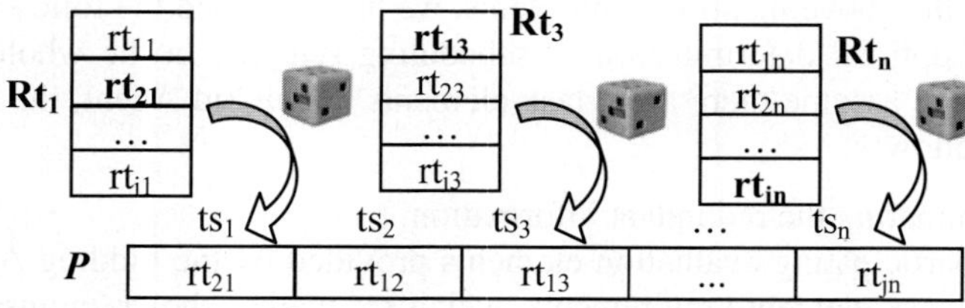

Fig. 2. The principle of stochastic disposition scheme

The computer operation flow is as follow:

```
For k=1; k<=10; k++
{  For i=1; i<=n; i++
  { //Produce a integer between 1 and the amount of
    //Rt_i's elements at random
    j=Random(1,Rt_i.size());
    P_i= rt_ji;}
  Q_k=P;}
```

Finally, the results will be stored in the set Q_k of the disposal scheme. Q=[Q_1, Q_2,…, Q_{10}].

Step 4: evaluating the scheme in population.

Ten assigning schemes from Q are substituted into the objective function (2) equations, compared and evaluated respectively, and search the best scheme P_o.

The process of scheme evaluated as follow:

```
Po=Q1;
For k=2; k<=10; k++
{ Pn=Qk;
  Δcost=costn-costo;
  If(Δcost<0){Po=Pn;}
  If(Δcost≥0){prob=exp[-Δcost/(k·tmp)];
  rand=random(0,1);
  If(prob≥rand) {Po=Pn;}}
}
```

Step 5: producing new assigning scheme population.

(1) Cross-breeding: The two disposal schemes with a certain probability value can be extracted from Q at random to produce a crossover point, and then, the task element disposal results in the rear of the crossover point are exchanged so as to establish two new disposal schemes, which can be served as two individuals in the next generation, as shown in Fig.3.

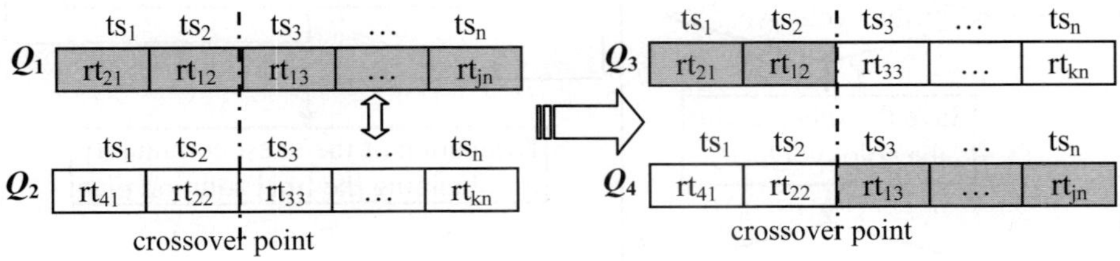

Fig. 3. Diagram of crossover and reproduction

(2) Variating: One disposal scheme with a certain probability value can be extracted from the population at random to carry out the variation, viz. to change the bidder rt_{ji} of some certain task element ts_i, in that disposal scheme. And then a new individual is generated and put into the new population.

(3) Replicating: replicate 4 the best assigning schemes(P_o) in Step 4 and put them into the new population.

(4) Produce new individuals according to the principle of Step 3, and put them into the new population until the number of new individuals in the population reaches 10.

By Implementing above 4 operating steps, the population is reproduced in the new generation, and is guaranteed that it always has the most individuals tending to the most superior disposition.

Step 6: decreasing annealing temperature.

Judge the current temperature, Enable the system to tend to cooling, set $tmp=\alpha \cdot tmp$, if $tmp>1$, go to the Step4; if $tmp<1$, continue.

Step 7: task assigning and determining.

The Final Scheme Evaluation from the population of last generation Q adopting the method of step 4, find out the optimal results P_o which is the assigning scheme to search.

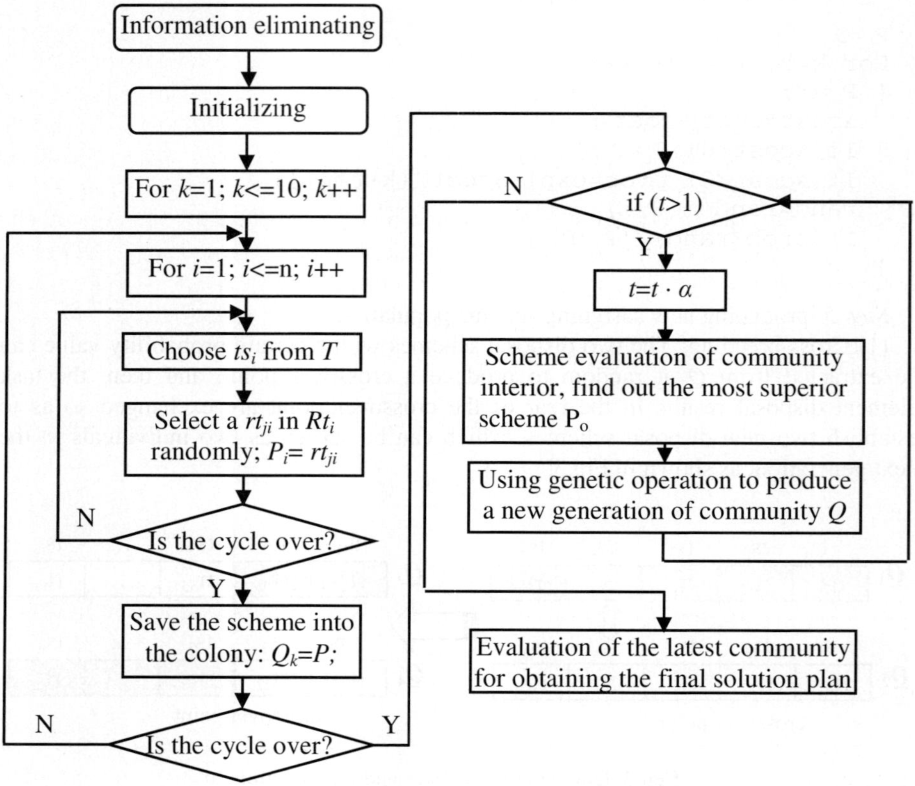

Fig. 4. Flow of evaluating Algorithm

Fig.4 clearly describes the above-mentioned optimal process. It is here that we will make a brief analysis of the effect of *prob* value upon scheme disposal. *k* is the constant. Under the certain temperature when the scheme selection is carried out, *tmp* can also be considered as the constant so that *prob* can only be related to $\Delta cost$ and decreases with an increase in $\Delta cost$. Accordingly, when $\Delta cost$ is smaller, this indicates that although the new scheme is inferior to the existing scheme, it is close to the existing scheme because it is a "better" scheme; just at this time, the larger is the *prob*, the larger the possibility of *prob*>*rand* establishment is, which is easy to be accepted. It can be seen that two kinds of new schemes are selected in the selection processes; one is the new scheme superior to the existing scheme; and the second is that although it is inferior to the existing scheme, the objective function is close to the new scheme of the existing scheme, whereby making the whole level of the new scheme be superior to the existing scheme set.

So far, our task of bid evaluation has been completed, with the optimal disposal scheme P_0 obtained. However, the task assignment Agent will notify or inform the bid winning Agent to implement the scheme.

4 Analysis of Real Examples

In the following, one real example is adopted to illustrate the performance of genetic-simulated annealing in bid evaluation. This is an optimal bid evaluation problem with the 7-Task (Task *i*), and 3-Workshop Agent (SA001, SA002 and SA003) participated. The objective is to obtain the rational task assignment scheme and to determine which workshop will complete each assignment. We have obtained the following set of simulated data through bidding. To be simplified, we assume all the Agents can complete all the tasks in the specified time so that it is only to provide the time (T) for implementing tasks and cost (C) served as examination and evaluation indexes, see Table 1. The parameter initial values of algorithm are set as tmp_0=1000, tmp_∞=1, α=0.9, β=5.

Table 1. Results of bidding

Tasks	Task1	Task 2	Task 3	Task4	Task 5	Task 6	Task 7
SA001(C/T)	20/3	28/5	32/7	25/5	23/2	10/2	19/2
SA002(C/T)	17/4	34/4	33/6	30/4	18/3	15/1	15/3
SA003(C/T)	24/2	31/5	39/4	27/4	20/3	14/1	13/3

4.1 Real Example Analysis

In the algorithm, we incorporate data collection function and carry out the collection of total cost of task completion, total time *ET*, the maximum circulation time Max_j and the optimal scheduling scheme at this time under the different temperature *tmp*. The collection frequency is to collect data once when the temperature drops by every five times, with the results set in Table 2. Also, scheduling results at the temperatures of 656°, 131° and 1° are given. See Fig. 5.

After the completion of the algorithm regulation, we have obtained the bid evaluation results and the corresponding parameters, as shown in Table 3.

Table 2. Objective function value under corresponding temperature

Parameters	Value under different temperature									
tmp	656°	386°	226°	131°	75°	43°	24°	12°	6°	1°
EC	175	151	170	167	158	179	167	174	174	174
ET	22	27	22	23	24	20	22	21	21	21
Max_j	15	12	12	11	9	8	8	7	7	7
cost	360	346	340	337	323	319	317	314	314	314

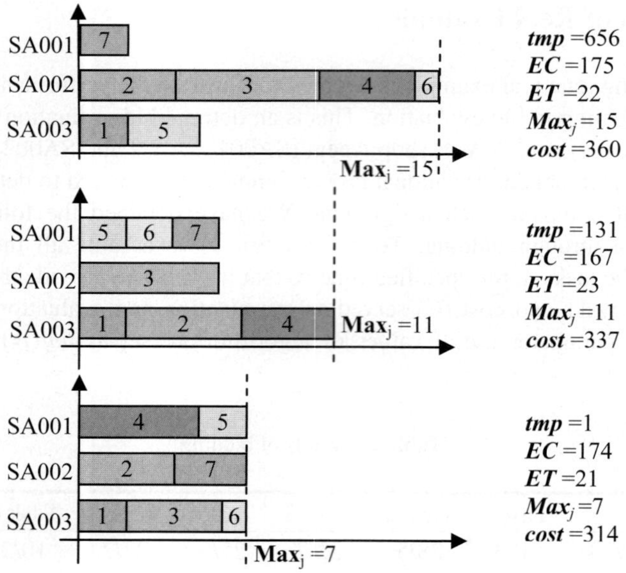

Fig. 5. Schedule results under different temperature. Rectangular strip expression execution time of correspondence task on workshop Agent.

Table 3. The optimization bid evaluation results and corresponding parameters

Task	Task1	Task2	Task3	Task4	Task5	Task6	Task7
Bided Agent	SA003	SA002	SA003	SA001	SA001	SA003	SA002
parameters(C/T)	24/2	34/4	39/4	25/5	23/2	14/1	15/3
EC /ET/ Max$_j$				174 / 21 / 7			
cost				314			

4.2 Results Analysis

We illustrate the superiority of bid evaluation by the application of genetic-simulated annealing through comparisons. Firstly, the principle of setting bid is, in general, based on the comprehensive objectives of the lowest implementation costs and the shortest possible duration or time, and to find out the optimal disposal of each task element and to obtain a scheduling scheme, just as fig. 6(a); and the assigning results using simulated annealing as fig. 6(b), and the assigning results using genetic-simulated annealing as fig. 6 (c).

Three schemes are contrasted in fig. 6, task assigning results can be obtained , that is, the task assigning scheme using genetic-simulated annealing(fig. c) is not only more reasonable and excellent than that one using general method(fig. a), but also than that one using traditional simulated annealing algorithm(fig. b). From this point, the genetic-simulated annealing can achieve task assigning result and then optimize the structure and process of task assigning, thus, reduces on-line time of all tasks

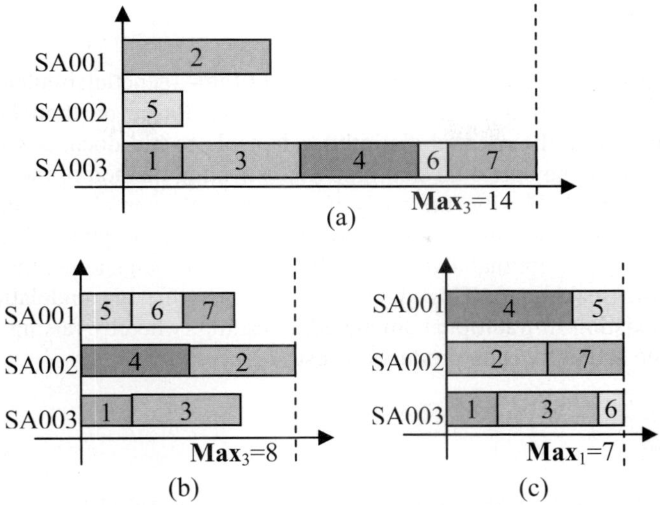

Fig. 6. Comparison of the task assigning schemes obtained by three methods

(makespan), raises the resource utilization rate and decreases the production cost indirect.

The change trend of objective function (*cost*) curve can be obtained as fig. 7. It is clear that genetic-simulated annealing algorithm overcomes traditional simulated annealing algorithm's defects such as big undulation and poor astringency. The results show that this algorithm is effective and feasible in assigning task, and the stability of processing is hold.

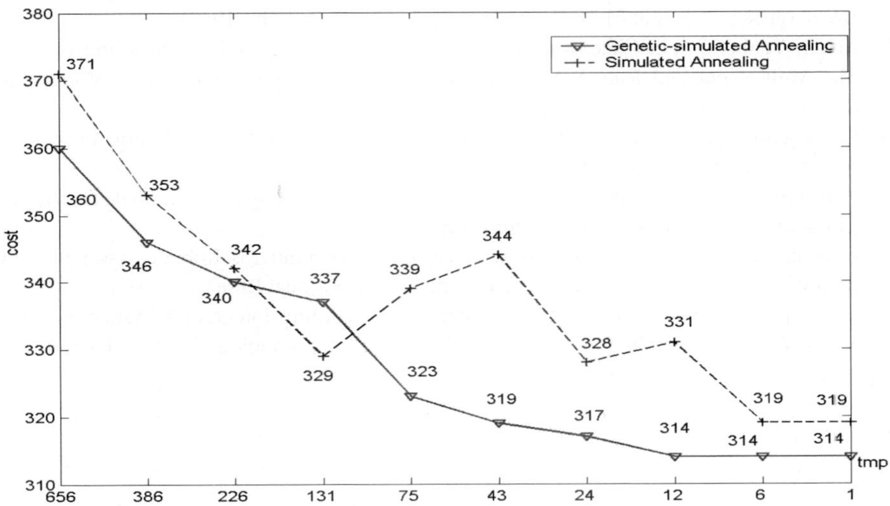

Fig. 7. Tendency of objective function value

5 Conclusions

This study mainly discusses the optimized algorithm—genetic-simulated annealing adopted in bid evaluation of task assignment Agent. Based on thought of genetic-simulated annealing, the optimal algorithm adaptable to bid document evaluation is designed, and also, the operating steps and implementing method of the algorithm are introduced in details. Finally, the analysis via one real example in combining with collected data in the annealing process concludes that the adoption of the feasibility and superiority of the optimal algorithm in bid evaluation can shorten the on-line time of overall task (makespan), This algorithm overcomes the big undulation and poor astringency existing in traditional simulated annealing, whereby raising the resource utilization rate and decreasing production cost.

References

1. Zhao Bo, Fan Yushun: Application of MAS in Production Scheduling Research, Vol.01. Control and Decision (2003) 1–6
2. Lu Taping, Yih Yuehwern: An Agent-based Production Control Framework for Multiple-line Collaborative Manufacturing, No. 10, Vol. 39. Int. J Prod. Res. (2001) 2155–2176
3. Li Shujuan, Li Yan, Liu Yong: Combine NN Model and GA in Estimating Makespan. International Conference on Intelligent Computing. HeFei China (2005) 23–26
4. He Yanxiang: Design & Application of Agent and Multi-Agent System. Wuhan University Publishing House (2001)
5. Jun Bin, et al: Research & Realization of Production Scheduling System Based on Multi-Agent Mechanism. Computer Technology & Automation (2002) 105–108
6. J, Vancza*, A. Markus: An agent Model for Incentive-based Production Scheduling, Computers in Industry(2000) 173–187
7. Gao Zhijun, Yan Guozheng, Ding Guoqing: Task Distribution of Multi-agent Systems Based on Network, Vol.31 No 10. Computer Engineering(2005) 19–21
8. Zhang Yanhong, Yin Chaowan, Zhang Yu: The research of Agile Scheduling Based on The Multi-agent and Rule Scheduling, Vol.6, No.4. Computer Integration Manufacture System CIMS(2000) 45–49
9. Grace Yuh-jiun Lin, James J. Solberg: Integrated Shop Floor Control Using Autonomous Agents. IIE Transactions (1992) 57–71
10. Zhu Fuxi, et al: Scheduling Algorithm Theory and Design in Parallel Distribution Computation. Wuhan University Publishing House (2003)
11. Levitin, Gregory, Rubinovitz, Jacob: A Genetic Algorithm for Robotic Assembly Line Balancing, Vol. 168 Issue 3. European Journal of Operational Research(2006) 811–825
12. Li Shujuan, Li Yan: The CAPP & Production Scheduling Integration System Based on MAS, Vol.20, No.2. The Journal of Xi'an University of Technology (2004) 149–153

A Domain-Based Intelligent Search Engine

Minjuan Zhong[1] and Xingdong Lü[2]

[1] College of Information Management, Jiangxi University of Finance and Economy, Nanchang 330013 P.R. China
[2] College of Electronics, Jiangxi University of Finance and Economy, Nanchang 330013 P.R. China
{lucyzmj, luxingdong0267}@sina.com

Abstract. Nowadays amount of information on Internet is dramatically increasing. The ability of facilitating users to achieve useful information is more and more important for search field. CDSE, a model for the domain-based intelligent search engine is proposed in this paper. The model can help users to retrieve what they need by combining text classification with keywords extraction. Several algorithms that use key technologies are proposed, such as statistics, data mining and agents. Then a new criterion named ranking error is contributed to solve the problem of evaluation ranking inefficiency in traditional performance evaluation methodologies. The experimental results indicate that the proposed model can effectively improve retrieval precision and solve the problem of relevant document ranking behind in current search engine.

1 Introduction

Nowadays much amount of information on Internet is dramatically increasing and totally reaches ten billion static pages. How to dynamically deal with the huge information has become a very important research issue. However, current major search engines have significant limitations — they are often out-of-date, they only index a fraction of the publicly indexable web, they do not index documents with authentication requirements and many relevant documents behind search forms[1,2]. As more of the population goes online, and more tasks are performed on the web, the needs for better search services is becoming increasingly important and meanwhile leads the domain-based intelligent search engine to develop. Justin Boyan[3] proposed a method to optimize search engine by using machine learning. Based on it, McCallum[4] set up a special search engine – cora, which only index the papers in the field of computer science.

Based on previous works, CDSE, a model for the domain-based intelligent search engine, is designed and implemented in this paper. Combining artificial intelligence (especially machine learning and agents technologies) with the structure characters of computer papers, the model can help users to retrieve what they need.

When a user poses a query, our system will be able:

- To improve the recall

When a user asks for documents with a particular keyword, he may also interest in those documents in which have not the submitted keyword. How to guarantee the

D.-S. Huang, K. Li, and G.W. Irwin (Eds.): ICIC 2006, LNAI 4114, pp. 461 – 467, 2006.

relevant documents to be listed as possible is very important. In CDSE model, query expansion is applied, which make some relevant documents to be retrieved in spite of term mismatching between queries and documents.

- To improve high precision

All users wish the returned documents to be relevant. Guaranteeing the accuracy and relevance of the returned documents is also necessary in retrieval system. In our system, the class keywords sets, which reflect the main content of each class of documents, are formed by text classification and information extraction. It combines the technology of machine learning, statistics method and association rule mining, and has the features of high precision and automatic searching.

- To rank the relevant documents in the top list

In general, users only browse the results of initial several pages because it is tempted to believe that documents are always ranked by their relevance probability. In CDSE system, the citation relationship between papers and the location analysis of information are fully used, and the most relevant papers are ranked in the front of the lists.

2 System Model of CDSE

CDSE, a multi-agent system is divided into two layers. One is the interactive layer between user and machine, and another is the information processing.

2.1 Interactive Layer

Users. The roles of users are submitting queries and accepting services of system. The submitted queries are usually keywords, and the system returns the most relevant documents to the users after receiving queries.

Query Agent. A critical problem in information retrieval is that the vocabulary the users select as query terms is not the same as the ones by which the documents have been indexed. The term mismatching between queries and documents greatly affects the effectiveness of retrieval results. Query expansion in IR can deal with this kind of problem in some degree. According to mutual information, the term similarity is calculated by using co-occurrence model[5], then the candidates are obtained to do query expansion, and the final queries are formed.

2.2 Information Processing Layer

Class Selection Agent. The agent calculates similarity between final queries and class keywords sets in classification database, and then finds the most relevant classes whose similarity values are higher than appointed threshold.

Document Classification Agent. The agent can classify each pre-processing papers into categories automatically. The classifier is firstly trained by labeled data of fixed class, and then automatically classifies the large information into the directories of pre-classified content by using machine learning. Therefore, it is very convenient for users to browse the papers and search their needed information through categories. This not only improves the quality of retrieval but also reduces the searching time.

Document Extraction Agent. The agent extracts information from the head of each paper and reference. After that, by performing the keywords extraction algorithm, the keywords set of each paper is obtained and the class keywords set is formed according to the class of the paper.
Selection and Recommendation Agent. According to the former results of class selection agent, the selection and recommendation agent searches information in the most relevant classes in classification database. The searching strategy is separated into two cases. If the document keywords set contains the query, this document is thought to be relevant and similarity value is set as max, otherwise, calculation is completed with n-search method. The document whose similarity value is higher than the appointed threshold is returned to the user in descent.
Task Agent. If the class selection agent fails to find the relevant classes, the task agent searches the relevant information in the term database by using final queries. The search strategy is still n-search algorithm.

3 Implementation of Key Technology in CSDE System

3.1 Algorithm of Keywords Extraction

The keywords extraction algorithm is the most important component of CDSE because the accuracy of the extraction affects the succedent retrieval performance. This algorithm mainly extracts keywords from a single paper. It begins with high frequent words, then finds the associated words or phrases forward and backward respectively, and constitutes a group of keywords. Many former researchers used to extract keywords from the whole document, but in this paper, the head of paper (including title、abstract、key words) rather than whole document is used to extract keywords.

Algorithm description:

Input: the head of a single paper; Output: the keywords set named *keyphraseset;*

(1) Filter the head information using stoplist;

(2) Calculate the frequencies of the rest words, then rank them in descent , put the top *n* words into the set *wordset*

(3) Initialize *keyphraseset*=NUL,*number*=1,*maxwordnum*=m, where m is the maximum number of words in each phrase;

(4) Take out the first element of wordset, w*ord*=first(wordset);

(5) Take the *word* as center, select the words *number* forward and backword to it respectively and place into the *temphrase* set;

(6) Take out the next element of wordset, while the element is not NULL, jump(5);

(7) Adjust the value of *n*, *n=n-number;*

(8) Calculate the frequencies of each element in *temphrase*, then rank them in descent , put the top *n* words into the *wordset* and *keyphraseset* set respectively;

(9) Adjust the value of *number, number=number+1*,while *number* is less than *maxwordnum,* jump(4).

3.2 Calculating Relevant Weights for Keywords of Each Class

The relevant weight of keywords means the similarity between the class and the keywords. The larger weight is, higher the similarity and larger the contribution to the class. Generally, the weight calculation should consider two factors [6], local weight *L(i,j)* and global weight *C(i)*. The two factors indicate the importance of the *i*th phrase in the *j*th class document and the whole collection respectively. *L(i,j)* is the sum of the frequency of the *j*th keyword in the *i*th class, while *C(i)* take inverse document frequency.

3.3 N-Search Algorithm

Terms appearing in different locations of a paper may have different significance in identifying the document. For example, the terms that appear in the title, header, or are emphasized in the text are more important for retrieval than the rest of the terms [7,8,9]. Filippo Menczer [10] reported that citation from document A to B implies that the author of document A thinks document B contains relevant information. Based on them, n_search algorithm firstly matches between the query and the extracted paper title of references, if match successfully, the linked paper is regarded as relevance, (that is to say, the weight is set max value) and the weight of source paper is calculated. Otherwise, the part of paper(such as title、abstract、introduction and so on)is scanned and the weight is also calculated.

Therefore, two cases in the weight computation are considered. In the first case, If matches successfully between the query and the paper title of the references, the method of weight computation adopts the formulas mentioned in the [8], which proposed the algorithm based on the N-level vector model and thought the whole document could be partitioned into N level text paragraphs. So, the weight of source paper can be calculated successfully because the paper title of references is also one of the unattached text paragraphs. The computation equation is as followings,

$$W_{ik} = tf_{ik} / L_i \,. \tag{1}$$

Where W_{ik} is the importance of the *k*th term in *i*th reference (R_i), L_i is the length of R_i and tf_{ik} is the frequency of the term t_k in the R_i. So, a piece of matched reference weight(W_j) is the sum of the W_{ik} $(k=1,2,\ldots,m)$, where m indicates the number of the different terms in query. The weight of paper is the total of the matched reference weight.

In the other case, if fail to match between the query and the paper title of the references, the system scan three parts of the paper-- title、abstract and introduction. Combined the above equations (1), the similarity between the query and ith text paragraph (S_i) is calculated by the following equation:

$$Sim(QS, S_i) = \cos\theta_i = \frac{\sum_{j=1}^{k} W_{ij} * q_j}{\sqrt{\left(\sum_{j=1}^{k} W_{ij}^{\,2}\right) * \left(\sum_{j=1}^{k} q_j^{\,2}\right)}} \quad i \in [1, 2 \ldots N] \text{ N=3.} \tag{2}$$

The weight of paper is calculated by following formula.

$$weight = Sim(QS, d_i) = \sum_{j=1}^{N} Sim(QS, S_{ij}) \Big/ N \quad . \tag{3}$$

4 Performance Analysis of the Algorithms

In this paper, several algorithms are simulated. Table1 is the experimental results of keywords extraction algorithm. The experiment compares the keywords accuracy under the different parameter values according to the size of paper and actual practice. It is shown that the precision can be got best when m=3, n=8. So m=3, n=8 are used in the succedent experiments.

Table 1. Keywords accuracy

n=12 m=2	n=12 m=3	n=10 m=2	n=10 m=3	n=8 m=2	n=8 m=3
0.756	0.734	0.764	0.760	0.780	0.828

Table2 shows the results of the n-search algorithm. From the results, it can be shown that the search time can be reduced while the precision improved if the class is judged correctly. Classification is probably the most important contribution to the improvement, which reduces the retrieval scope and avoids retrieving in the whole collection. At the same time, collection classification can get the topic related documents into together, which seems to take a pre-filtering to the whole collection firstly in some degree and makes the retrieval relative to query scope. Furthermore, the adoption of keywords extraction avoids low precision in traditional search engine. In traditional search engine, the paper that only contains the query term is thought to possible relevant to the query, but the same term has many different meanings in different context, which lead many irrelevant papers to be returned.

Table 2. n-search algorithm results

Items	Correct judgment	Incorrect judgment
Number of test papers	80	800
Search time	1.425s	18.32s
Number of relevant papers in results	36	40
Precision	0.62	0.45

Three measures -- precision, recall and speed are widely used in IR performance. Precision is defined as the ratio of relevant documents to the number of retrieved documents, recall is the proportion of relevant documents retrieved, and speed is the response time measure from system to users. The three measures interplay each other.

Although these measures can correctly reflect the retrieval performance most of time, it performs not well under some special circumstances. For example, some relevant documents are retrieved, but rank in the list far away from the top. Users usually only browse the results of initial several pages because they always think the documents are ranked by their probability of being relevant. Therefore, the document may not be browsed in spite of relevance. In this paper, a new performance evaluation methodology named error ratio for the ranking results is introduced which is specified by:

$$errotio = \frac{\sum_{i=1}^{total} \left|\exp erank_i - realrank_i\right| \Big/ \exp erank_i}{total} \quad (4)$$

Where $experank_i$ is the expected ranking of the ith document, $realrank_i$ is the actual ranking in results, and *total* is the total number of documents returned. The smaller error ratio is, more front the relevant document and well system performance.

Table 3. Error ratio

Algorithms	Error ratio
N-search	0.18
TF*IDF	0.32

In table 3, it is also shown that the error ratio in n-search algorithm is much smaller than in the traditional method – TF*IDF. The main reason is that citation relationship between papers is considered and the keywords extraction is performed. The paper title of reference hints the key content of linked document, and the keywords extraction guarantees the maximum similarity value to those relevant documents firstly, which lead the relevant papers all to be ranked in the top list.

5 Conclusions and Future Work

In this paper, we proposed a model for a domain-based intelligent search engine and introduced the system architecture and design idea. At the same time, the function of three agents and relative algorithms were mentioned and discussed. Through the experiments, we found that the system solved the existing problems of tradition search engine in low precision and some relevant documents behind search form.

We plan to study question answering. We believe that the QA can obtain better performance by the deep combination between the information retrieval and information extraction.

References

1. Steve Lawrence, C.Lee Giles.: Searching the World Wide Web. Science, 280(5360) (1998) 98-100
2. Steve Lawrence, C.Lee Giles.: Accessibility of information on the Web. Nature, 400(6740) (1999) 107-109

3. Boyan J,Freitag D,Joachims T.: A Machine Learning Architecture for Optimizing Web Search Engines. In AAAI Workshop on Internet-based Information Systems. (1996)
4. McCallum A,Nigam K,Rennie J,et al.K.: Building Domain-specific Search Engines with Machine Learning Techniques.Working Notes of the AAAI Spring Symposium on Intelligent Agents in Cyberspace. (1999)
5. He, H. Z., He, P. L., Gao, J. F., Huang, C. N.: Query Expansion for Chinese Information Retrieval by Using Decaying Co-occurrence Model. Transaction of Tianjin University, Vol. 8(3) (2002) 183-186
6. P. Husbands, H. Simon, C.Ding.: On the Use of Singular Value Decomposition for Text Retrieval. http ://www.citeseer.nj.nec.com/540137.html. (2000)
7. Michal Cutler,Yungming Shib,Weiyi Meng.: Using the Structure of HTML Documents to Improve Retrieval 〔C〕USENIX Symposium on Internet Technologies and Systems (NSITS'97). Monterey, 241~251,California, December (1997)
8. Chen, Z. P., Lin, Y. P., Tong, D. S.: An Information-Retrieval Method Based on N-level Vector Model, Journal of Computer Research and Development, 39(10) (2002) 1233~1237
9. Liu, F., Lu, Z. D.: Effectively Retrieve HTML Documents, Mini-Micro System (in Chinese), 21(9) (2000) 986~988
10. Filippo Menczer, Gautam Pant, Padmini Srinivasan.: Evaluating Topic Driven Web Crawlers. Proc. of 24th international ACM SIGIR conference on Research and Development in Information retrieval, (2001) 241~249

A PDA Based Personalized 3D Facial Expression System

Seongah Chin and Jongkyeong Park

Division of Multimedia, Sungkyul University, Anyang-City, Korea
{solideo, danteol}@sungkyul.edu

Abstract. In this paper, we propose a novel method to create a personalized 3D face in PDA devices from two orthogonal images of users. The approach is useful for making a personalized 3D face keeping identical features of the face and efficient. The basic idea is to transform a canonical Korean male face to individualized ones standing for genuine features of the face by linear transforming filters in the PDA device. Moreover 6 universal facial expressions are simply created just by transformation of the contract values of 18 muscles in a PDA mobile device. Each expression is analyzed with respect to displacement of the feature points from those of the neutral face. Experimental results convey the proposed scheme is quite reliable and efficient with respect to similarity between pictures and the generated 3D face and running time.

1 Introduction

Creating a 3D virtual human face has increasingly attracted in computer graphics society and research fields because it can represent themselves in digital contents. In addition, facial expression has been an interesting topic among researchers. By the fact that lots of application areas exist, the popularity becomes getting higher and higher in the areas of game industry, medicine, avatars and even in mobile devices.

Even though the face is a relatively small part of human-beings, the essence of the face however acts a key role in explicit distinction between human-beings as well as a way of communication. Accordingly it is considerably important to create a 3D face and generate expressions keeping characteristics of anatomical approaches of the facial expressions [1-5].

Modeling a human face is the first step to create virtual human face. Several key aspects such as determining geometric descriptions and animation capabilities representing facial expressions should be keeping in modeling procedures. Even though most faces have almost same configuration and feature set, clearly considerable variation between individual faces or different ethnics, enabling us to recognize individual faces. Moreover mobile devices are familiar and pervasive in Ubiquitos environment providing us with various conveniences.

Thus our approach begins with bringing the 3D canonical face of Korean Young male [14] to the PDA device followed by making the personalized 3D virtual face from two orthogonal pictures obtained by a PDA camera in real time. The system presented here is also useful for representing 6 universal facial expressions simply by parameter passing activating 18 muscle vectors. Very few researches relating to

D.-S. Huang, K. Li, and G.W. Irwin (Eds.): ICIC 2006, LNAI 4114, pp. 468 – 475, 2006.

making 3D face in mobile devices have not been founded so far. It might not exist at all in commercial fields.

Similar systems making 3D faces have tradeoffs in cost, accuracy, speed and expertise knowledge. Most of them concern precision and accuracy, which result in the intensive needs for high cost, expertise knowledge and a special environment setting in using them. Thus, those systems have limitations when compared practically to a commercial product such as mobile devices for the input of data for 3D face reconstruction and animation.

In this paper, we have developed the system enabling an easy cloning of the personalized Korean male person.

2 Personalized 3D Face in Mobile

Now some distance-related functions called linear transforming filter between two orthogonal pictures taken from PDA camera should be defined to compute newly generated 3D vertices. From front and side view of the pictures users are asked to locate key feature points on to the positions as shown in Fig. 1. (a) and (b). The positioning is very simple and useful since feature points can be adjusted simply by moving rubber band appearing in Fig. 1. (a) and (b). This enables to obtain distance parameters and shape of the face. The coordinates of newly moved positions obtained PDA screen make it possible to calculate newly created vertices suitable for facial configuration of the user by linear transforming filters. The linear transforming filter is defined by distance ratio parameters between pictures in Fig. 1. (a) and (b) and canonical 3D face as shown in Fig. 1 (c) and (d).

Let p_i' be a point in an input image corresponding to vertex p_i in the canonical model. And let q_i be th vertex for the personalized face model. Now we derive two linear transforming filters ψ_s and ψ_p. ψ_s is the filter for drawing 3D shape of input pictures whereas ψ_p computing vertices of the personalized face mesh for input pictures by converting vertex p_i of the canonical model into vertex q_i for the new face mesh model. Let q_i be a vertex in a new face model. We define vector l_i' consisting of p_i' and p_j' in an input image as shown Fig. 1. (a). The Eq. (1) computes the shape of the personalized 3D face and Eq. (2) calculates x vertex with transforming parameters $\alpha$and β respectively.

$$q_i = \psi_s(p_i) = \begin{bmatrix} \alpha & 0 & 0 & 0 \\ 0 & 1 & 0 & 0 \\ 0 & 0 & 1 & 0 \\ 0 & 0 & 0 & 1 \end{bmatrix} \begin{bmatrix} x_i \\ y_i \\ z_i \\ 1 \end{bmatrix} = \begin{bmatrix} \alpha_j x_i \\ y_i \\ z_i \\ 1 \end{bmatrix}. \tag{1}$$

where $\alpha_j = \frac{w_j' H}{H' w_j}$, w_j' is the width of the input image and H' is the height in Fig. 1. (a) whereas w_j and H are similar in Fig. 1 (c).

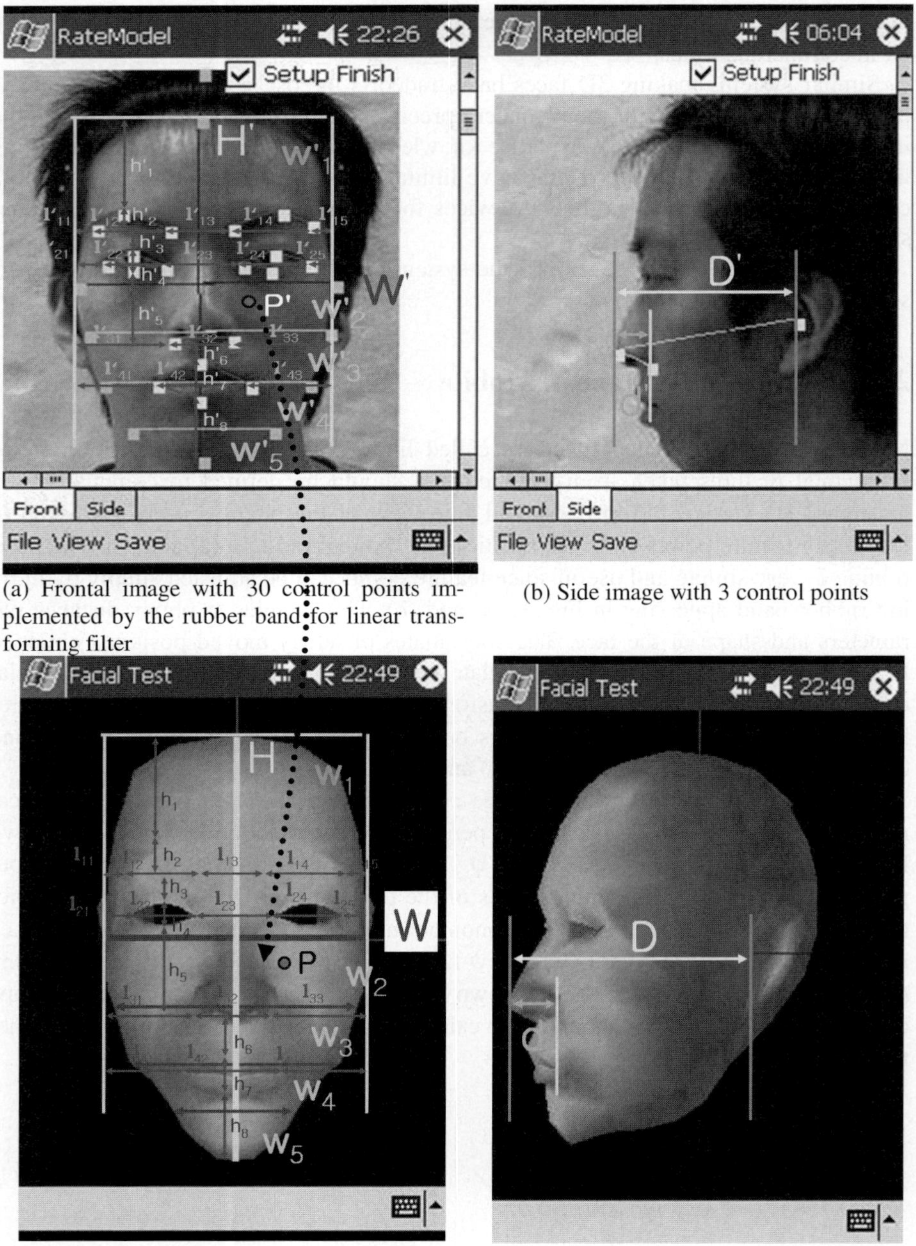

(a) Frontal image with 30 control points implemented by the rubber band for linear transforming filter

(b) Side image with 3 control points

(c) Front view of Canonical Face

(d) Side view of canonical Face

Fig. 1. Linear transforming filter for creating a personalized 3D virtual face

$$q_i = \psi_p(p_i) = \begin{bmatrix} \beta & 0 & 0 & 0 \\ 0 & 1 & 0 & 0 \\ 0 & 0 & 1 & 0 \\ 0 & 0 & 0 & 1 \end{bmatrix} \begin{bmatrix} x_i \\ y_i \\ z_i \\ 1 \end{bmatrix} = \begin{bmatrix} \beta x_i \\ y_i \\ z_i \\ 1 \end{bmatrix}. \tag{2}$$

Every vertex should be accurately transformed by Eq. (2). Y and z coordinates are easily acquired in the same manner.

Where $\beta = \dfrac{l_j' W}{W' l_j}$, W′ and l_j' are in input pictures shown in Fig. 1. (a). W and l_j appear in our canonical face shown in Fig. 1. (c). Finally reconstruction of newly created vertices draws an adaptive 3D personalized face as shown in Fig. 2. (a) and (b).

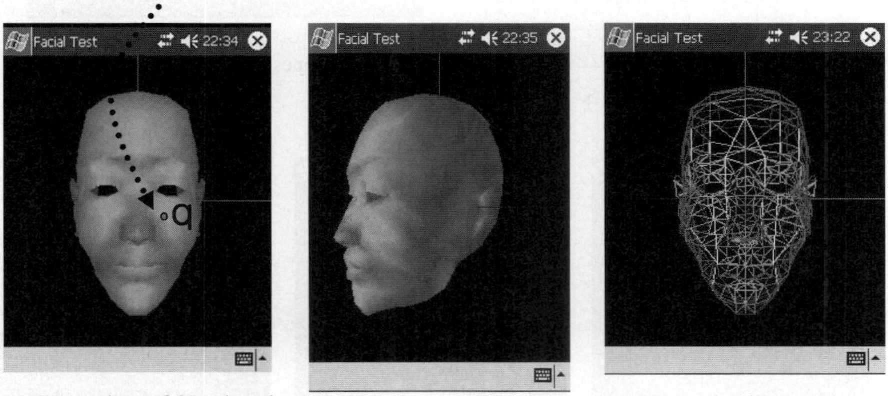

(e) Front view of 3D virtual Face for input image Fig. 1. (a) defined by ψ_p

(f) Side view of 3D virtual Face for input image Fig.3. (b)

(g) 3D mesh with muscle vectors

Fig. 2. Personalized 3D Virtual Face Creation in PDA

3 Facial Expressions in PDA Devices

Muscle-based facial expressions have been adapted here in order to create 6 universal facial expressions because the proposed system is implemented in PDA in real time.

When muscle contraction occurs in adjacent vertices attempt to draw together. The facial movement involves drawing the skin attached to the point of skeletal surface. Muscle movement is thought of as the displacement of surface nodes to transformed locations as well as direction and magnitude in three dimensions [7]. Muscle-based method makes sure that the system generates facial expressions easily and efficiently just by transforming contraction values as shown in Fig. 3. Table 1 shows various contraction values of 18 muscles corresponding to facial expressions appeared in Fig 4. The following equations Eq. (3) and (4) compute transformed vertices with angles, contraction values. In Fig. 3. (a) shows 18 muscle vectors and Fig. 3. (b) illustrates principles to calculate the movement of vertex q' based on angle a_2 and defined vectors (p_1, p_2) and (p_1, q) associating with influence area α and β as well.

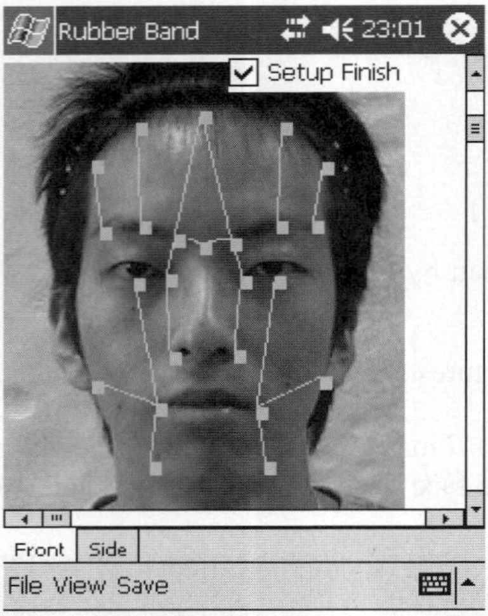

(a) Muscle vectors

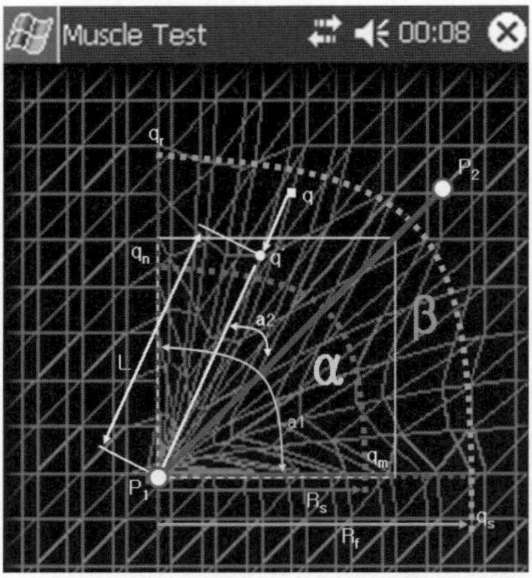

(b) Muscle zones and movement parameters

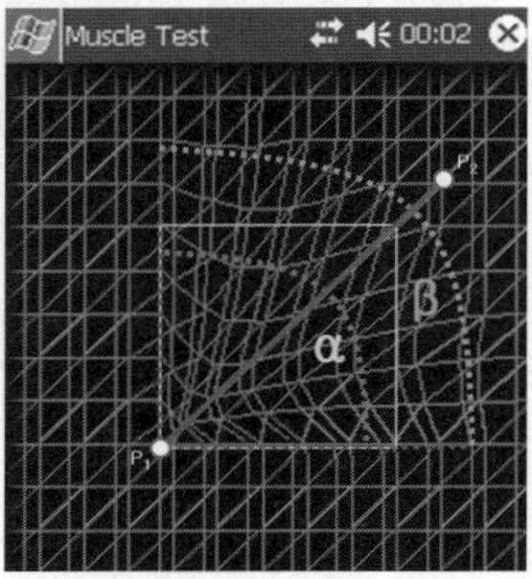

(c) Angle : 45, contraction : +8

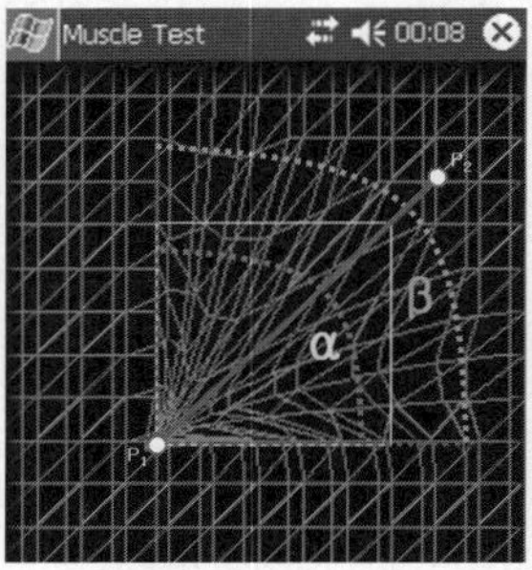

(d) Angle : 45, contraction : +10

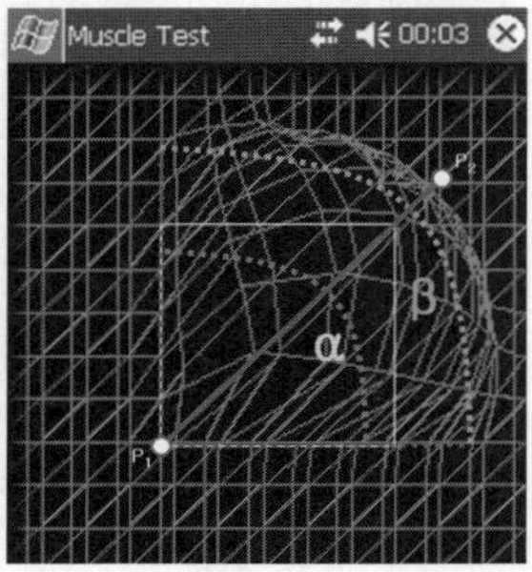

(e) Angle : 45, contraction : -8

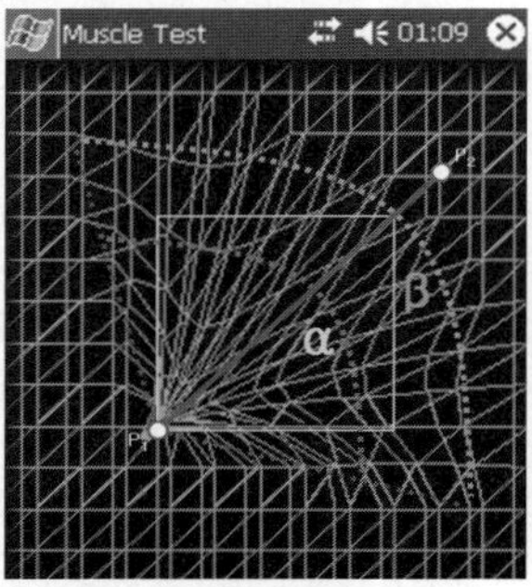

(f) Angle : 60, contraction : +8

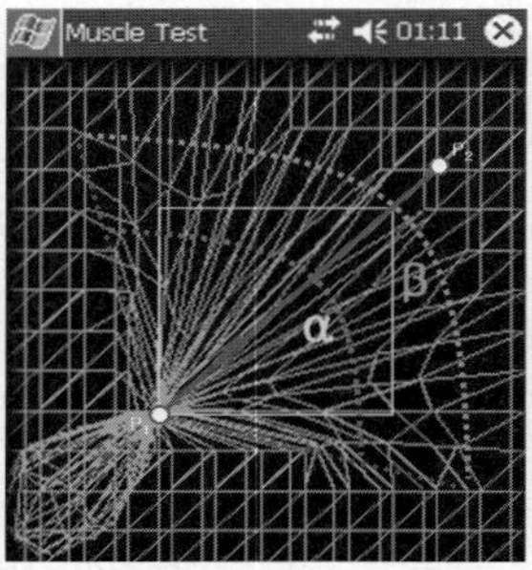

(g) Angle : 60, contraction : +10

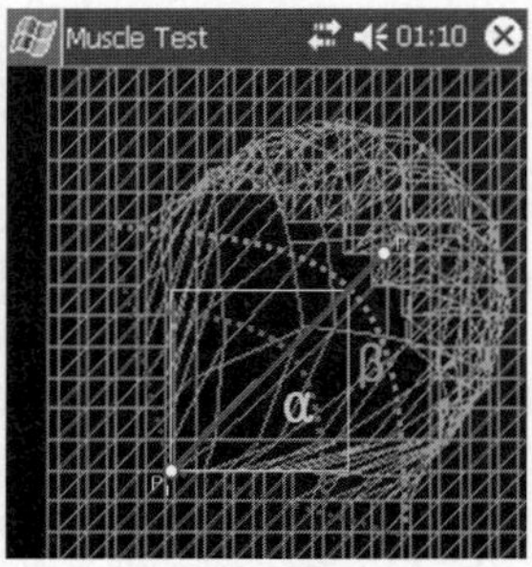

(h) Angle : 60, contraction : +10

Fig. 3. Muscle vectors associating with various angles and contractions

Table 1. Contract valeus of 18 muscle vectors for Fig. 3

Expression	Contract values of 18 muscles
Happiness	3, 3, -5, -5, -1, -1, 2, 2, 0, 0, 4, 4, ,0, 0, 0, 0, 0, 0
Anger	5, 5, 4, 4, 0, 0, 1, 1, 0, 0, 6, 6, 10, 10, 20, 20, 5, 5
Surprised	8, 8, ,2 2, 0, 0, 0, 0, 0, 0, 0, 0, -3, -3, 13, 13, 0, 0
Sadness	3, 3, 7, 7, -2, -2, -2, -2, -0.5, -0.5, 1, 1, 0.5, 0.5, 10, 10, 1, 1
Fear	8, 8, 6, 6, 0, 0, 0, 0, 0, 0, 3, 3, -5, -5, 7, 7, 1, 1
Disgust	-3, -4, 1, 4, -3, -3, -3, -3, -1, -1, 8, 3, 0, 0, 1, 1, -3, -3

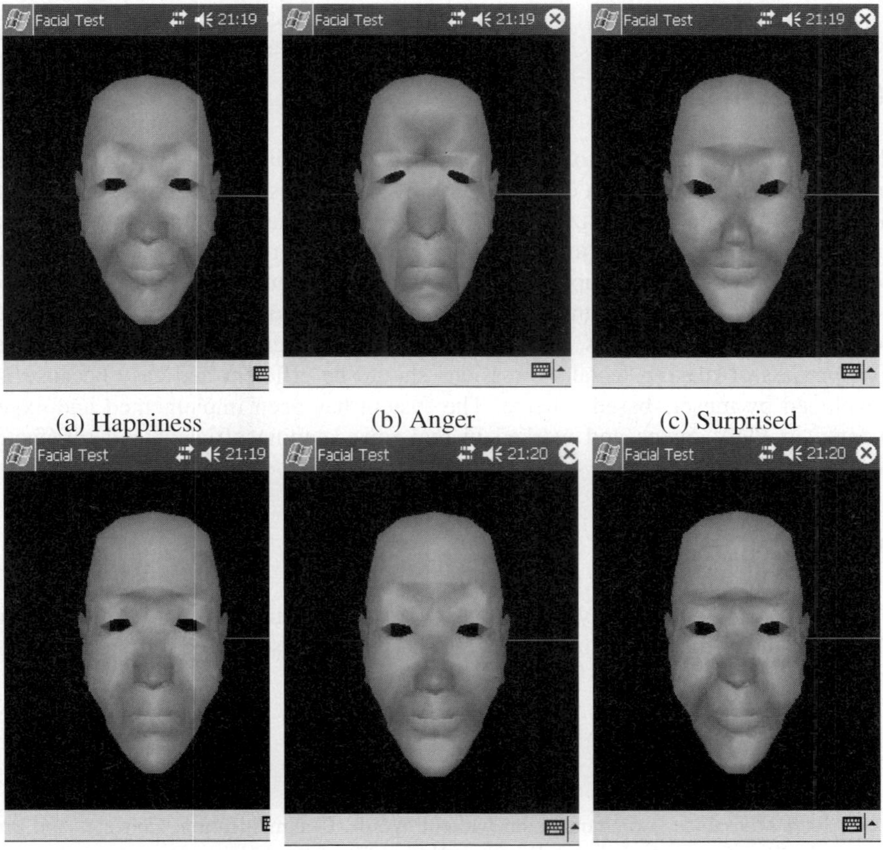

(a) Happiness (b) Anger (c) Surprised

(d) Sadness (e) Fear (f) Disgust

Fig. 4. 18 muscle-based 6 universal facial expressions for input image (a) in Fig. 1

$$q' = q + aer \frac{qp_1}{|qp_1|}. \tag{3}$$

where $a = \cos(a_2)$ and a_2 is the angle between the vectors (p_1, p_2) and (p_1, q), L is $|p_1\text{-}q|$, r a radial displacement argument and e a fixed constant representing the elasticity of skin as shown in Fig. 3. (b). Adjusting the contraction values enable us to create facial expressions.

$$r = \begin{bmatrix} \cos(\frac{(1-L)}{R_s})\ for \quad \alpha\ area \\ \cos(\frac{L-R_s}{R_f - R_s})\ for \quad \beta\ area \end{bmatrix}. \tag{4}$$

4 Conclusion

The work presented here is to create a personalized 3D virtual face from two orthogonal pictures taken from PDA camera. Very few researches have been performed in the area of PDA based personalized 3D virtual face and facial expressions. At first users interact with pictures by adjusting feature points using rubber band. Then distance-related function should be applied to compute newly generated vertices for the personalized 3D face in real time. Moreover the system provides 6 universal facial expressions such as happiness, anger, surprised, fear, disgusted, and sadness as well. The process of making facial expressions should be efficient and easy because it is developed by muscle-based scheme. The system has been implemented and experimented in PDA device and worked in real time keeping efficient and satisfactory results.

Acknowledgments

This work has been partially supported by Korea Industrial Technology Foundation (KOTEF) under the project named “Mobil-based 3D Personalized Virtual Face Modeling System”.

References

1. Albert Mehrabian: Communication without Words, Communication: Concepts and Process (editor: Joseph A. DeVito), Prentice–Hall (1971) 106–114
2. Albert Mehrabian, James A. Russell: An Approach to Environmental Psychology, MIT Press (1974)
3. Ekman, P., Friesen, W. V.: Facial Action Coding System(FACS), Consulting Psychologist Press, Palo Alto. (1978)
4. Ekman, P. , Friesen, W. V.: Emotion in the Human Face System, Cambridge University Press, San Francisco, CA, 2nd Edition (1982)

5. Hara, F., Kobayashi, H.: Use of Face Robot for Human−Computer Communication, IEEE Conference on SMC (1995) 1515−1520
6. Parke, F. I., Keith Waters : Computer Facial Animation, A K Peters Wellesley (1996)
7. P. Ekman, W.V Friesen: Manual for the Facial Action Coding System. Consulting Psychologist Press, Palo Alto. (1978)
8. Moccozet, L., Thalmann, N. M.: Dirichlet Free-form Deformations and Their Application to Hand Simulation. Proc. Computer Animation (1997)
9. Milan Sonka, et. Al.: Image Processing, Analysis, and Machine Vision, PWS Publishing, (1999)
10. Thalmann, N. M., Thalmann, D.: The Direction of Synthetic Actors in the Film Rendezvous a Montreal, IEEE Computer Graphics and Applications, 7(12): (1987) 9-19
11. Fua, P., Leclerc, Y.G.: Taking Advantage of Image-Based and Geometry-Based Constraints to Recover 3-D Surfaces, Computer Vision and Image Understanding, 64(1): (1996) 111-127
12. Lee, W.S., Jin Gu, Thalman, N.M.: Generating Animatable 3D Virtual Humans from Photographs, Eurographics, Paris (2000)
13. Lee, Y., et. Al.: Realistic Modeling for Facial Animation, Computer Graphics (1996) 55-62
14. Chin, S.: A Canonical Face based Virtual Face Modeling, LNCS Vol. 3784 (2005) 179-186

A Skew Free Korean Character Recognition System for PDA Devices

Seongah Chin, Youngmee Choi, and Moonwon Choo

Division of Multimedia, Sungkyul University, Anyang-City, Korea
{solideo, mchoi, mchoo}@sungkyul.edu

Abstract. In this paper, a skew free Korean character recognition system is developed for PDA devices. There is no doubt text information existing on our real life conveys meaningful messages. It is obviously necessary to capture text images in any place and time in pervasive computing in order to recognize and keep text information in digital forms. In this background, a new mobile-based Korean character recognition system is designed and implemented which is capable of capturing text images and recognizing Korean characters under PDA devices. The algorithm begins with taking images from PDA client followed by skew correction and normalization of character blocks for matching. Experimental results show the proposed scheme is quite novel and efficient.

1 Introduction

There is no doubt text information existing on our real life conveys meaningful messages. It is obviously necessary to capture text images in any place and time in pervasive computing in order to recognize and keep text information in digital forms. In addition recently the number of applications and contents on mobile devices has been highly increasing in our daily life providing plenty of convenience as well as the changes of the ways we live [1-3]. Unfortunately very few researches in this issue have been detected to solve Korean character recognition on mobile devices. Thus our approach begins with purifying pre-processing of the text images meaning that we need to reduce running time due to shortcoming of mobile environment. Once capturing images completed in PDA client, PDA client connects to PC server operating main procedures such as skew correction, scaling input image to DB size image, followed by character blocking images. Normalization of character block images is required for matching. In particular cutting space of character block images is useful for making high accuracy in matching.

2 Methodology

The proposed system can be roughly classified into two groups such as the PC Server bound by the dotted rectangle and the PDA Client located in two sides with respect to devices of the use as shown in Fig. 1.

D.-S. Huang, K. Li, and G.W. Irwin (Eds.): ICIC 2006, LNAI 4114, pp. 476 – 483, 2006.

The PDA Client starts to capture input images with an embedded camera in PDA devices showing on the screen. Users are required to mark 4 corner points in order to acquire the area of the text image for OCR.

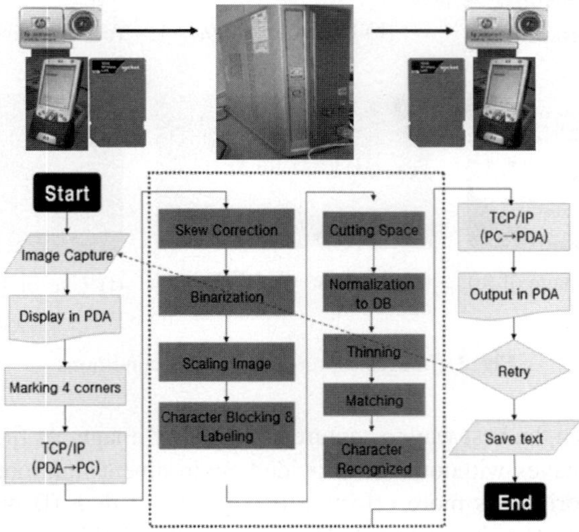

Fig. 1. System Overview

On denoting 4 corner points, the PDA Client sends them to the PC server via way of TCP/IP since OCR is more efficiently performed in the PC Server facilitating fast computation than the PDA Client. Skew correction is obtained by simple bilinear transformations followed by making a binary image that needs to be scaled for the character size of DB.

The system labels on the character blocks after projections performed in two orthogonal ways. Once knowing each character block, the algorithm gets rid of the space of the character block for matching process. Linear transformation is required to adjust the character block to the one in DB followed by thinning and matching. At last it sends recognized characters to the PDA Client.

2.1 Capturing Images

At first we have trouble in capturing high quality of the image using mobile cameras than common digital camera. In addition some limitations of focusing lens have been detected in mobile devices unable to adjust focal distance so that it has difficulty in acquiring clear text images. Very few of them provide automatic focal lens enabling us to capture more apparent than nonuse of them as shown in Fig. 2 (a) and (b). In addition, various lighting conditions definitely affect the quality of images as shown in Fig. 2. (c), (d), (e), and (f).

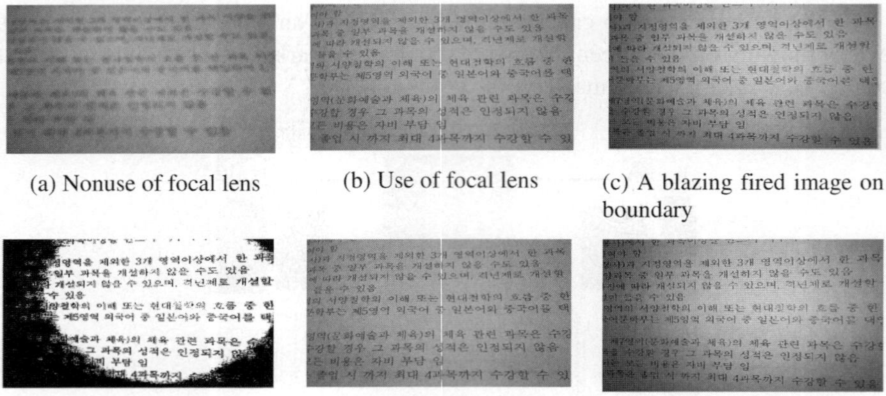

(a) Nonuse of focal lens (b) Use of focal lens (c) A blazing fired image on boundary

(d) The binary image of (c) (e) Nonuse of LED light condition (f) Use of LED light condition

Fig. 2. Images captured in various conditions

At last we reach the best way to capture high quality image. At first we recommend that users take images without flash provided environment light conditions are good enough. The algorithm is more effective on Fig. 2. (e) than (f) due to hardness of making a binary image shown in (d). The adaptive threshold has been applied to obtain a binary image. Furthermore users are demanded to locate text contents not affective by shadow as well as skew.

2.2 Skew Correction

Once obtaining 4 corner positions on the PDA screen, the text image along with 4 corner points is transferred to PC Server via way of TCP/IP provided by wireless LAN card as shown in Fig. 1. In the approach it is useful for users to select the text area marked by 4 corner points needed to be recognized implying reducing computations. Bilinear transformation is applied to rectify skew. Basically it solves coordinate correspondence between the input text image f(s, t) on the left and the transformed image f'(x, y) on the right shown in Fig. 3. The position P in image f(s, t) on PDA client is corresponding to P' in f'(x, y) on PC server using the Eq. (1)-(4) [4].

$$s = s_{01} + (s_{23} - s_{01})\Delta y,\ t = t_{03} + (t_{12} - t_{03})\Delta x\,. \tag{1}$$

$$s_{01} = s_0 + (s_1 - s_0)\Delta x,\ s_{23} = s_3 + (s_2 - s_3)\Delta x\,. \tag{2}$$

$$t_{03} = t_0 + (t_3 - t_0)\Delta y,\ t_{12} = t_1 + (t_2 - t_1)\Delta y\,. \tag{3}$$

$$\Delta x = \frac{x - x_0}{x_1 - x_0},\ \ \Delta y = \frac{y - y_0}{y_3 - y_0}\,. \tag{4}$$

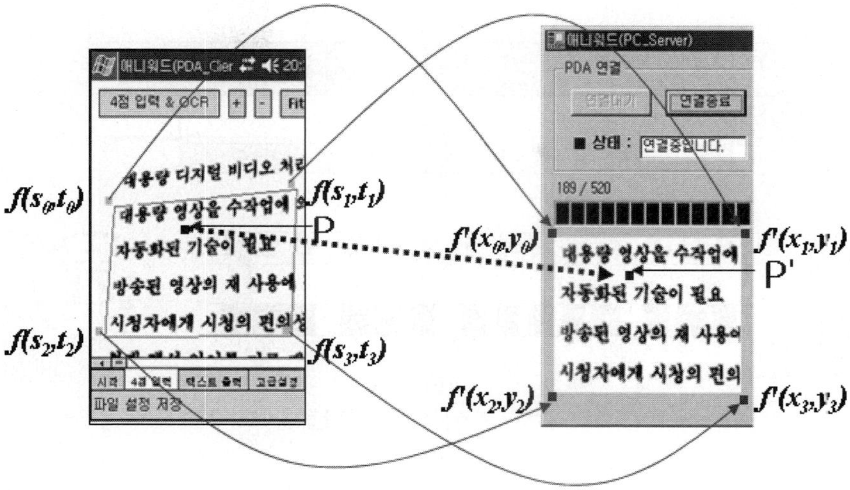

Fig. 3. Skew correction

Then a skew free image needs to be a binary image using adaptive threshold enabling users to select the high quality of binary images.

2.3 Character Blocking

A skew free image obtained in the previous section needs to be somewhat normalized form of images in order to perform matching character images to the ones in DB. The size of input character image is definitely different from the ones in DB whose size is 9 points equivalent to 25 by 25 pixels as shown on the right side denoted by dotted circle in Fig. 4. (b). Thus the prior thing we should do is to separate each row from the text image so that we are capable of knowing scaling constants. Two orthogonal projections are applied to the text images to obtain scaling constants such as h'/h and w'/w as shown in Fig. 4. (a). Scaling transformation works as the Eq. (5) meaning that the position P in the first row in Fig. 4. (a) maps into P' in the second row.

$$p' = \begin{bmatrix} x' \\ y' \\ 1 \end{bmatrix} = \begin{bmatrix} h'/h 0 0 \\ 0 w'/w 0 \\ 0 0 1 \end{bmatrix} p = \begin{bmatrix} xh'/h 0 0 \\ 0 yw'/w 0 \\ 0 0 1 \end{bmatrix}, \text{ where } p = \begin{bmatrix} x \\ y \\ 1 \end{bmatrix}. \tag{5}$$

Finally, character blocks shown in Fig. 4. (c). are registered for next processing accompanying with labels. However we have still problems to overcome since each character is written in slightly different space even in a same character shown in Fig. 5. (a). Thus we have to remove extra space of all character blocks including DB shown in Fig. 5. (b) followed by thinning on that character block image shown in Fig. 5. (c).

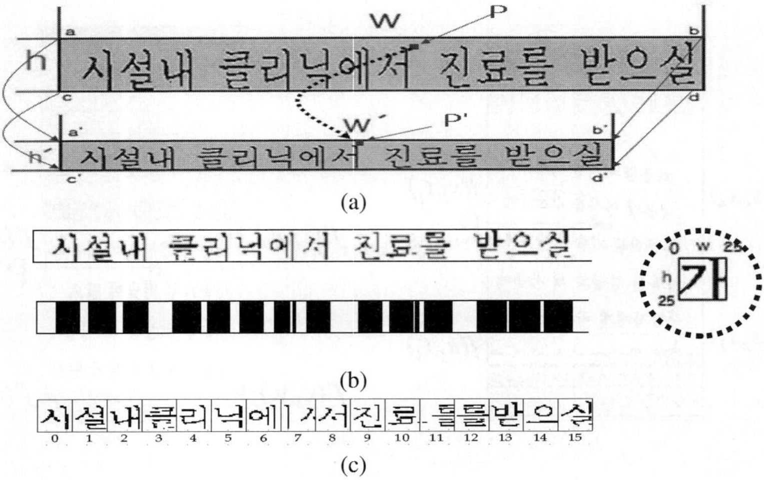

Fig. 4. Scaling transformation and character blocking

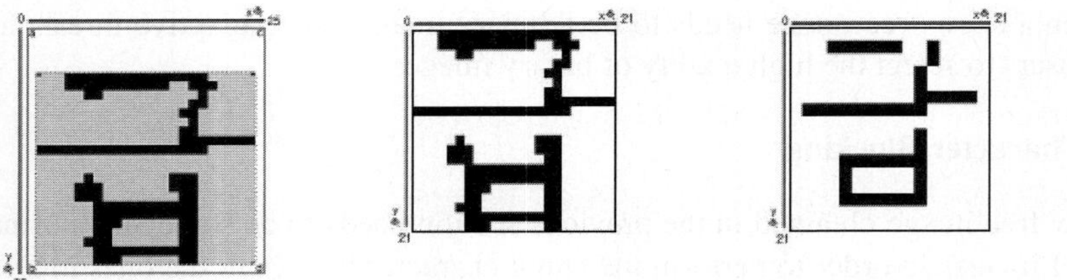

(a) 25*25 pixel character image (b) 21*21 pixel image after cutting space (c) 21*21 pixel image after thinning

Fig. 5. Progress of character blocks for matching

2.4 Fast Matching

The most important thing for matching in the proposed system is to reduce running time due to shortcoming of resources and ubiquitous environment of PDA devices. The system basically works in PC desktop server and PDA client which should keep efficiency with respect to running time. Thus robust and fast matching algorithm is a necessity. The aim of matching is to minimize computations by supporting the quality of pre-processing image. The system uses difference between the character block of thinning images and the ones in DB. The sum of rest dust implies decision factors as shown in Fig. 6. (b). Korean characters consist of combinations of each component. Building our DB is based on 'Korean Information base' implemented by KAIST providing 520 characters as shown in Fig. 6. Thinning has been performed into input character blocks whereas character blocks in DB do not.

(a) Characters in DB

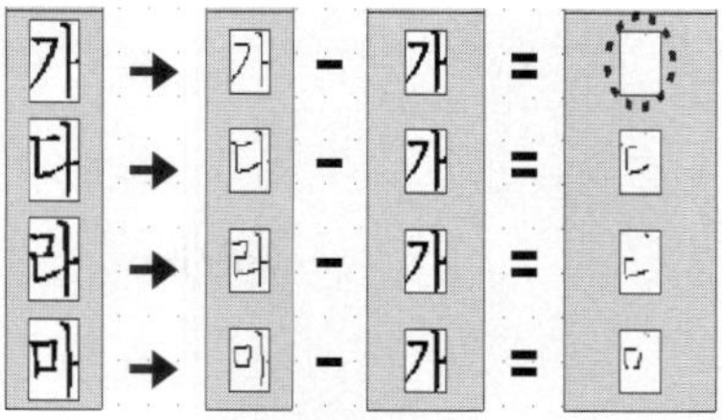

(b) Matching

Fig. 6. Character DB and Matching

3 Experimental Results

The system has been implemented under the various resources such as Visual Studio .Net 2003, .Net Compact Framework, HP iPAQ 2210, HP FA-185 mobile camera, socket SDIO wireless LAN and PC Pentium 4. The algorithms running on PC server,

(a) PC server interface with progress bar on the bottom

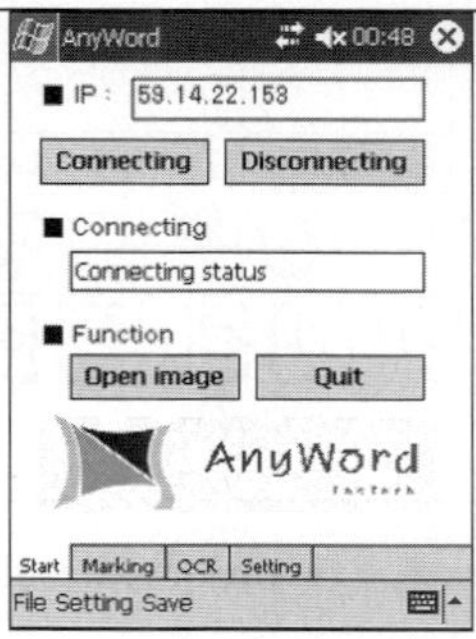

(b) PDA client interface conveying IP of PC server

(c) Image captured surrounded by 4 corner points

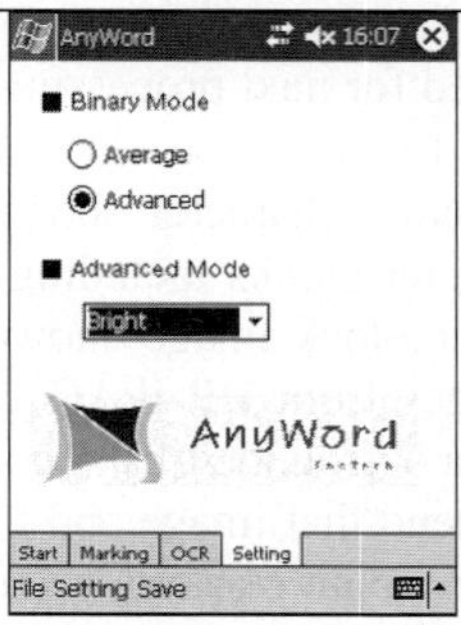

(d) Adaptive binarization along with plentiful menus on the bottom

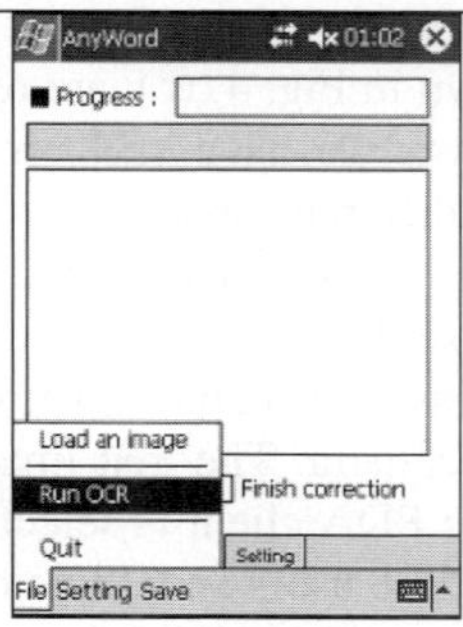

(e) Run OCR

(f) Matching completed

Fig. 7. System procedures

Fig. 8. Experimental Results

PDA client including TCP/IP connections provided by TcpListener and TcpClient are developed using .Net FrameWork C#. User interfaces both PC server and PDA client appear in Fig. 7.

Finally, character blocks shown in Fig. 4. (c). are registered for next processing accompanying with labels. However we have still problems to overcome since each character is written in slightly different space even in a same character shown in Fig. 5. (a). Thus we have to remove extra space of all character blocks including DB shown in Fig. 5. (b) followed by thinning on that character block image shown in Fig. 5. (c). The work flow begins with capturing text images from HP iPAQ 2210 attached by HP FA-185 mobile camera. The text image area surrounded by 4 corner points shown in Fig. 7. (c) on the PDA client is selected to send that image and those points to PC server. In the procedure users should be cautious about marking accurate corner points along with alignment. Once PDA is connected to PC server shown in Fig. 7. (a) and (b) users choose Run OCR menu shown in Fig. 7. (e). Fig. 7. (f) shows matching completed.

Experimental results shown in Fig. 8. (a), (b) and (c) displays input text images surrounded by 4 corner points. Completed results appear in PDA client shown in Fig. 8 (d), (e) and (f) along with recognized characters bound by rectangles.

4 Conclusion

The work presented here is to develop the Korean OCR system in Mobile devices. Very few researches have been conducted in the area of PDA based OCR. Thus we have constructed a new mobile-based Korean character recognition system capable of capturing text images and recognizing Korean characters under PDA devices. We have provided experimental results showing the proposed scheme is quite novel and efficient.

Acknowledgments

This work has been partially supported by Korea Research Foundation Grant reference KRF-2005-081-D00012.

References

1. Farella, E., Brunelli, D., Benini, L., Ricco, B.: Pervasive Computing for Interactive Virtual Heritage,.IEEE Multimedia, 1070-986x/05 2005, July-September (2005) 46–57
2. Kortz, D.: Agent Systems, Mobile Agents, and Applications. Second International Symposium on Agent Systems and Applications and 4th international symposium on mobile Agent, Sep. LNCS Vol. 1882 (2000)
3. Adelstein, F., Gupta, S., Richard, G., Schwiebert, L.: Fundamentals of Mobile and Pervasive Computing,.McGraw-Hill (2005)
4. Sonka, M., Hlavac, V., Boyle, R.: Image Processing, Analysis, and Machine Vision. PSW publishing, (1998)

An Agent-Based Multi-issue Negotiation Model in E-Commerce

Xiao-Xuan Zhang[1], Supratip Ghose[1], and Geun-Sik Jo[2]

[1] Intelligent E-Commerce Systems Laboratory, School of Computer Science & Engineering, Inha University, Incheon, 402-751, South Korea
zhangxiaoxuan@gmail.com, SGresearch@gmail.com
[2] School of Computer Science and Engineering, Inha University, Incheon, 402-751, South Korea
gsjo@inha.ac.kr

Abstract. Our paper proposes an agent-based automated negotiation model. The agents can perform an integrative negotiation with multi-issue in a one-to-many way. The negotiation protocol follows the offer-counteroffer principal, and an adapted mechanism of offer generation strategy. With the utility theory, agent could evaluate the offers and determine the following actions. In order to yield a top-quality deal and shorten the negotiation period, agents propose multiple offers, which consist of a particular combination of issue values and have the identical utility with the given utility. The experiment shows that the model ensures the participants could reach a mutually beneficial agreement in a short time.

1 Introduction

Negotiation means two or more parties bargain with one another in order to reach mutually beneficial agreements on price or other transaction terms. In the research realm of agent-mediated electronic commerce, agent-based negotiation system has shown its attractiveness in recent years because the flexible characteristics of agent - autonomous, reactive, and proactive [1] radically change the style of the traditional electronic commerce. In agent-based negotiation systems, software agents, under consideration of multiple issues, automatically prepare offers for and evaluate offers on behalf of the parties they represent with the aim of obtaining the maximum benefit for their users.

From the agent-based negotiation perspective, many approaches have been proposed. Bartolini [2] proposed a rule-based framework for enforcing specific negotiations. Luo [3] developed a fuzzy constraint-based framework for multi-issue negotiations in competitive trading environments.

This study proposes an agent-based one-to-many parallel negotiation system, which uses software agents to facilitate the multi-issue negotiation. In order to shorten the negotiation period and improve the negotiation efficiency, agents generate multiple offers in each round. With this mechanism, agents could try to make utmost possible effect for meeting opponents' desire. The rest of the paper is structured as

D.-S. Huang, K. Li, and G.W. Irwin (Eds.): ICIC 2006, LNAI 4114, pp. 484 – 489, 2006.

follows. In section 2, we represent the negotiation Model. Section 3 shows the implementation and experiments results. Section 4 concludes our work.

2 Negotiation Model

In the proposed architecture, we define set $A=\{a,b\}$ be a pair of negotiating agents. More specifically, an agent member a ($a \in A$) has issue set J ($J=\{1,...,n\}$) under negotiation in a given encounter. For each issue j ($j \in J$), each agent a has a lower and an upper reservation value, min_j^a and max_j^a respectively, resulting a domain for each particular issue: $D_j^a=[min_j^a, max_j^a]$. A offer (proposal) from agent b to agent a in the rth negotiation round is defined as $p_{b\to a}^r =< pName, S >$, where $pName$ denotes product name; S denotes the issue set, each element in the set is a name-value pair:

$$S =< (issue_1, value_1), (issue_2, value_2), (issue_3, value_3), ..., (issue_s, value_s) > .$$

In addition here, p_j designate the jth issue and $p_{b\to a}[j]$ is the value of the jth issue in the set of S.

2.1 Offer Evaluation

Evaluation of received offers in negotiation systems is very important since it is the basis of determining the following actions for agents. We adopted Multi-Attribute Utility Theory (MAUT) [4] to evaluate offer. MAUT is a tool for making decisions involving multiple objectives based on preference analysis. According to MAUT, evaluation of an offer $p_{b->a}$ involves summing the valuation of each issue in the negotiation subject. The evaluation function of agent a over an issue j is given by V_j^a where $V_j^a : D_j \to [0,1]$. A weight w_j^a is associated by agent a to issue j where the sum of weights of issues is 1. Thus, the utility of agent a over an offer p, consisting of a set of values for all issues, can be defined as:

$$U^a(p) = \sum_{1\le j\le n} w_j^a V_j^a(p_j). \tag{1}$$

The evaluation function over the issues as required by equation 2, is given by the distance to the worst bid acceptable to this agent, relative to its range of acceptable values:

$$V_j^a(p_j) = \begin{cases} \dfrac{distance(p_{b\to a}[j], \min_j^a)}{distance(\max_j^a, \min_j^a)}, & \text{if increasing} \\ \dfrac{distance(\max_j^a, p_{b\to a}[j])}{distance(\max_j^a, \min_j^a)}, & \text{if decreasing} \end{cases} \tag{2}$$

where increasing and decreasing refer to the direction of change in score with increasing value of the issue. If the issue's value is not in D_j^a, the issue's utility is 0.

If the negotiation offer contains an un-negotiable issue, the utility of this issue is $-\infty$. Consequently the offer's utility is $-\infty$, and agent will send a REFUSE message to its opponent. The utility of a valid offer is on the interval [0, 1]. The offer is good if the utility value is close to 1. Conversely, if the utility value is close to 0, the offer is bad.

2.2 Offer Acceptability Criteria

During the negotiation process, a Buyer Agent (BA) on behalf of a buyer, and a number of Seller Agents (SAs) on behalf of available sellers, compare received offers with its expectation and tend towards coming to a mutually beneficial agreement over multiple issues. In each round, both sides propose offers in alternate. Each agent reserves a utility threshold T that represents how keen the agent expects to get received offers. If the received offers' utilities are greater than its expectation, this offer is acceptable. Otherwise, agent will concede to decrease its threshold T according to an adjustment parameter Δ ($T^r = T^{r-1} - \Delta$) and generate multiple offers with the new threshold, and in this manner, the process continues until an agent gets an offer whose utility is greater than or equal to its T.

In any negotiation round, each agent may get multiple offers from its opponent(s). Let S be the received offers set and p ($p \in S$) be one offer and p' be any other offers from the relative complement of $\{p\}$ in S. Accordingly, the acceptability criteria of agent a over p can be described as follows:

$$U^a(p) \geq T$$
$$U^a(p) \geq U^a(p') \tag{3}$$

where $p \in S$ and $p' \in S - \{p\}$

2.3 Offer Generation

The basic negotiation of exchanging a single offer in each round is time-consuming and laborious, especially if both sides are unwilling to concede. The unwillingness to make compromises might result from the fact that the negotiation just does not tend towards the desired direction. This could cause the both sides block the progress of the negotiation, although a compromise would be possible, the utility of the final deal may be much lower. In order to reduce the number of negotiation round and possibly avoid such a deadlock situation, we adopt "multiple offers per round" instead of "one offer per round". The idea is that the generated offers have the same utility while they consist of a particular combination of issue values. Submitting several offers per round could speed up the negotiation process, because the offers with various combinations of issue values provide a wider selection to choose from and thus increase the possibility of the opponent gets a desired offer. The offer generation involves search for offers satisfying following constraints:

$$min_j^a \leq p[j] \leq max_j^a \tag{4}$$
$$U^a(p) = T$$

2.4 Negotiation Protocol

Negotiation protocol determines the flow of messages between the negotiating parties. It is public and open to all parties. The negotiation protocol for this model is given as the state sequence of agents in Figure 1.

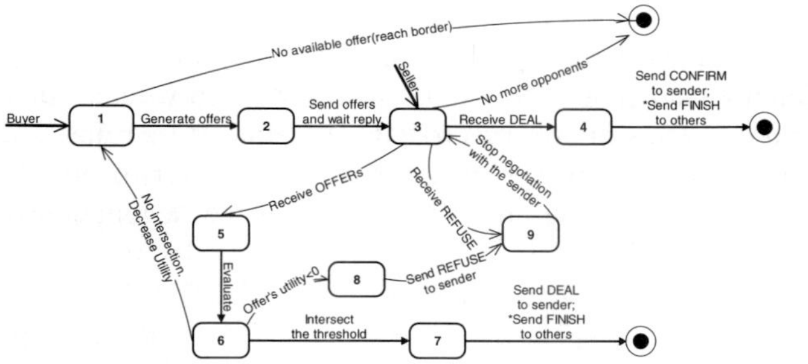

Fig. 1. Protocol shown as the state sequence of agent (*: the individual activity of BA)

Table 1. The issues' weight of each participant

Participant	Price	Delivery	Warranty
Buyer	0.5	0.2	0.3
Seller 1	0.3	0.2	0.5
Seller 2	0.3	0.4	0.3
Seller 3	0.4	0.3	0.3
Seller 4	0.4	0.2	0.4

The experimentation finished in 5 rounds, BA made a deal with SA2 ultimately, and the deal offer is [price: 10300.00, delivery: 12, warranty: 18]. With respect to this offer, BA has utility 0.65, while SA2 has utility 0.52. In Figure 2, (a), (b), (c), and (d) illustrates the detailed negotiation process between BA and SA1, SA2, SA3, and SA4 respectively. From the first round to the fourth round, both sides conceded but still cannot reach an agreement. In the fifth round, BA compromised the threshold to 0.65, a set of offers were generated and sent to four SAs. Meanwhile, SA2's threshold was 0.50, there existed a BA's offer having a higher utility with 0.52. Finally, SA2 made a deal with BA. The negotiation process ended successfully with an agreement.

3 Implementation and Evaluation

We have implemented a prototype system using IBM Aglet Software with JDK1.4.2. Three kinds of agents had been developed for the solution of negotiation problems: BA to interact with sellers and initiate the negotiation, SA to act on behalf of seller, Negotiation Engine Agent (NEA) provides the functionality of evaluating offers and generating offers for both BA and SA. We have analyzed the negotiation data of purchasing a computer server, the issues are price (dollar), delivery day (day), and warranty (month). Without loosing the generality in the experiment, we assumed each participant shares the same value range for each issue. Issue price has a minimum value 10000 and maximum value 15000, issue delivery day's value domain is within {1, 2, 3, …, 12}, issue warranty's value domain is {6, 12, 18, 24}. We deployed a BA on behalf of a buyer and four SAs on behalf on sellers. Each agent has a different preference, which is given in Table 1. Each participant's adjustment value (Δ) is assigned to 0.05.

Since the adjustment parameter determines the step of threshold changed in two continuous rounds, and if it is too small, the generated offers will not have much difference from the offers in previous round. Therefore these offers are unlikely to be accepted by opponent(s). However since it changes the offers gently, it can assist user to get better negotiation results. It will also extend the negotiation round. Figure 3

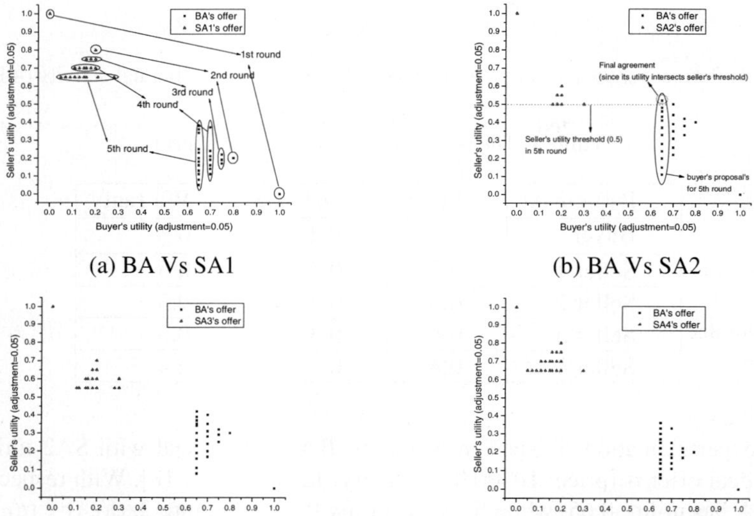

(a) BA Vs SA1

(b) BA Vs SA2

(c) BA Vs SA3

(d) BA Vs SA4

Fig. 2. The negotiation process - split into four individual conversations

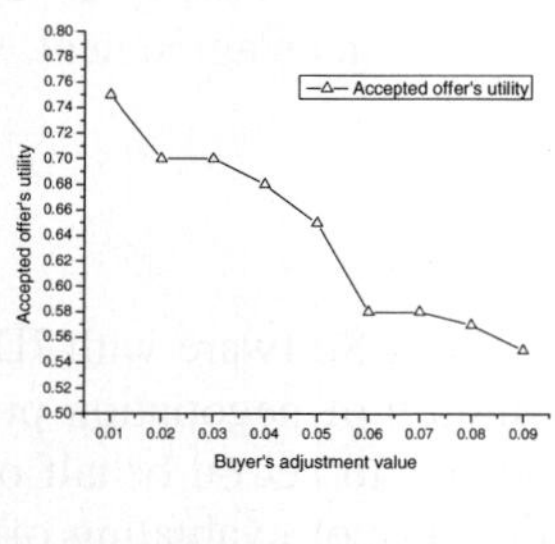

Fig. 3. Comparison of adjustment and deal's utility

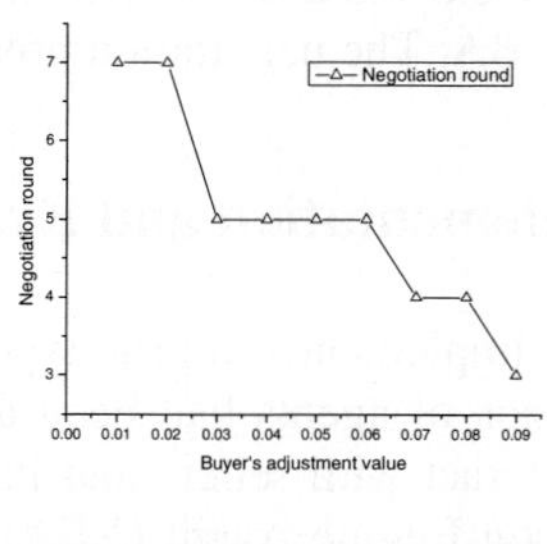

Fig. 4. Comparison of adjustment and negotiation round

illustrates the relation between the adjustment and the final deal's utility from buyer perspective while four SAs' adjustment are kept constant (0.05). Figure 4 shows the relation between the adjustment and the negotiation round while four SAs' adjustment values are kept constant (0.05). The results showed that this model is flexible and sensitive to users' preferences.

4 Conclusion

We have proposed an agent-based negotiation system. Automated software agents deal with a negotiation in a one-to-many way. The agent can perform complex negotiations over multiple issues. The system ensures the agents on behalf on different users could reach a mutually beneficial agreement. The system effectiveness has been evaluated with a prototype system for a real world simulation.

Acknowledgments

This research was supported by the MIC(Ministry of Information and Communication), Korea, under the ITRC(Information Technology Research Center) support program supervised by the IITA(Institute of Information Technology Assessment).

References

1. Wooldridge, M., Jennings, N. R.: Intelligent Agents: Theory and Practice. The Knowledge Engineering Review, 10 (1995) 115-152
2. Bartolini, C., Preist, C., Jennings, N. R.: A Software Framework for Automated Negotiation. In: Proc. SELMAS2004, LNCS 3390, Springer Verlag, New York (2005) 213–235
3. Luo, X., Jennings, N. R., Shadbolt, N., Leung, H .F., Lee, J. H. M.: A Fuzzy Constraint Based Model for Bilateral, Multi-Issue Negotiation in Semi-Competitive Environments. Artificial Intelligence, 148 (2003) 53-102
4. French, S.: Decision Theory. An Introduction to the Mathematics of Rationality. Ellis Hoerwood, New York (1998)

Integrating Extended Attributed Relational Graph and Structured Modeling: Toward Multimedia-Based Decision Support in Virtual Product Design

Oh-Byung Kwon[1], Kyoung-Yun Kim[2], and Hyung-Jeong Yang[3]

[1] School of International Management, Kyunghee University, Yongin, South Korea
obkwon@khu.ac.kr
[2] Department of Industrial and Manufacturing Engineering, Wayne State University, Detroit, MI 48201, USA
kykim@eng.wayne.edu
[3] School of Electronics and Computer Engineering, Chonnam National Univ., South Korea
hjyang@chonnam.ac.kr

Abstract. In this paper, a multimedia-based decision making model is proposed integrating extended attributed relational graph (eARG) and structured modeling (SM). The proposed methodology manages multimedia information with the use of an extended attributed relational graph. SM technique is adopted to graphically integrate the multimedia information with decision models and hence to support 'pervasive and seamless decision on demand': making decision at the time of gazing multimedia objects as if all data and models for decision support are closely at hand.

1 Introduction

Multimedia information has been extensively applied to the disciplines of design and development, resulting in group DSS and organizational DSS with multimedia support [1]. In the majority of past research, the application of multimedia technologies on DSS has focused on individual models of media presentation in DSS, such as voice [2], video conferencing [3], and graphics models [4]. However, little attention has been paid to the integrated model of multimedia information and decision technology although the integrated multimedia presentations are widely used in organizations and decision makers find them useful in decision-making processes.

Moreover, if multimedia information, domain knowledge, decision models and clients are distributed in network-based collaboration, then an integrative view to conjointly use the resources in a seamless and automated manner is highly necessary. As past research in DSS seldom addresses the integration of multimedia information with decision-making models, efficient and seamless ways of managing multimedia information in decision-making processes has been a missing piece in this research paradigm. Hence, this paper aims to integrate the decision-making processes with ad hoc multimedia information for collaborative virtual product design. The proposed methodology manages multimedia information with the use of an extended attributed relational graph. The eARG is introduced to represent product image data and product-related data in a seamless way because the conventional ARG [5] can only represent

D.-S. Huang, K. Li, and G.W. Irwin (Eds.): ICIC 2006, LNAI 4114, pp. 490 – 495, 2006.

images along with corresponding graphical information. SM technique is adopted to graphically integrate the multimedia information with decision models and hence to support 'pervasive and seamless decision on demand': making decision at the time of gazing multimedia objects as if all data and models for decision support are closely at hand.

2 Decision Support with Multimedia Data

2.1 Extended Attributed Relational Graph (eARG) Construction

In a conventional ARG like Fig. 1 images and graphical information are described through object properties and the relationship between the objects. The properties for a node can be size, orientation, and roundness. The relationships between two nodes can be represented by distance and relative position. The key processes to generate an ARG include object extraction and object relation. We use edge-based labeling method to segment each part.

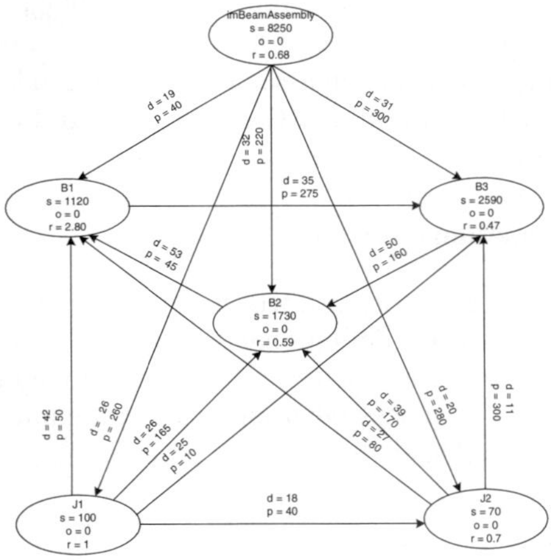

Fig. 1. An example of ARG

The conventional ARG has a critical drawback that inhibits direct use in decision support system because it cannot incorporate information about decision-making models that play a crucial role in decision-making. Hence, we propose an eARG in which decision-making models can be incorporated with specific multimedia information. While binary attributes in ARG represent the relationships between two nodes in terms of visual features such as angle, adjacency or distance, these in eARG illustrate relationships in object levels such as compatibility between two objects. In order to express a procedure for generating an eARG by integrating a conventional ARG and object-relationship model, the following four steps have been proposed

STEP 1: Decompose an object-relationship model O and an ARG A into basic elements $O_1, O_2, \ldots, O_{N(O)}$ and $A_1, A_2, \ldots, A_{N(O)}$, respectively, such that each basic element contains two

nodes and one arc. N(O) and N(A) indicate the number of basic elements generated from O and A, respectively.
STEP 2: Merge the two sets of basic elements into one set $V=\{V_1, V_2, \ldots\ldots, V_{N(O)+N(A)-N(R)}\}$.
STEP 3: Remove identical elements from V. Set index i to 1. Compare (not end of V) V_i and V_j, determine whether or not they are identical (i.e., if two nodes and one arc are exactly the same as each other), remove V_i. Increase j by one. Modify V into $V=\{V_1, V_2, \ldots\ldots, V_{N(O)+N(A)-N(R)}\}$, where N(R) denotes the number of removed basic elements.
STEP 4: Perform an integration on V. Set indices i and k to 1. For all i, set index j to i+1. Compare (not end of V), whether the two elements, V_i and V_j contain only one node that is identical, attempt to generate a compound element CV by attaching an arc to the other identical node. Note that k is the current number of compound elements found. Then remove V and increase j.

An eARG encompasses a unified representation scheme in which information about image and corresponding decision-making models are organized. ARG obtained from an assembly image and an assembly relation model similar to the assembly can be combined and a relevant eARG can be formed. Fig. 2 shows an example eARG for a beam assembly.

2.2 Schema Transformation from eARG to SM

A model schema of SM is primarily defined in terms of genera that organize a set of data elements that are based on definitional similarity. There are six types of data elements. The first is primitive entity (/pe/) that exists in nature. The second is compound entity (/ce/) which references other entities that are already defined and therefore do not require a value. This is followed by attribute (/a/) that associates a certain

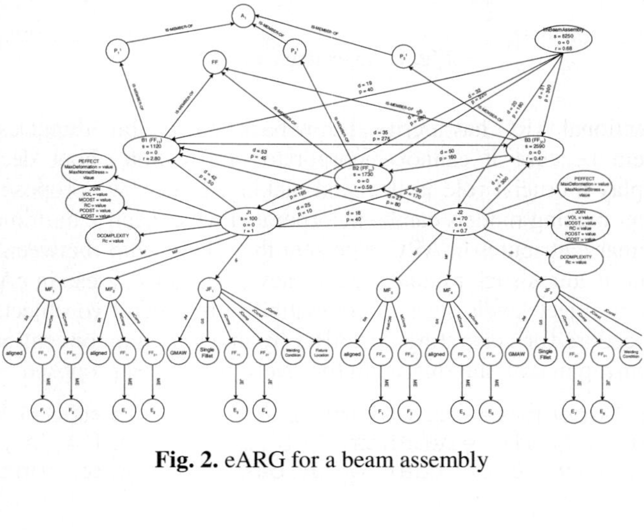

Fig. 2. eARG for a beam assembly

property and value with an entity or compound entity. The variable attribute (/va/) resembles decision variables in an optimization model. Function (/f/) allows its elements to have a value that depends on those of other functions or attributes. Finally, the test (/t/) is a function in which the value is fixed to binary values. In order to incorporate decision-making models with eARGs in a more effective way, the eARG schema and the SM schema must be integrated.

The proposed mapping rules for converting an eARG into SM can be stated more formally as in the following steps.

```
STEP 1. Convert all nodes of the eARG into primitive en-
tities (/pe/) of SM.
STEP 2. Convert all properties in the objects into at-
tributes (/a/), variable attributes (/va/), functions
(/f/), or tests (/t/) of the corresponding primitive en-
tities.
STEP 2.1 If the property is identical to the name of a
test, it is transformed into /t/.Else go to Step 2.2.
STEP 2.2 If the property is identical to the name of a
function, it is transformed into /f/.Else go to Step 3
STEP 3. Convert all arcs of the eARG into compound enti-
ties (/ce/) of the primitive entities.
Naming rule is: one primitive object + "*" + the other
primitive object.
STEP 4. Convert all properties in the arcs of the eARG
into attributes (/a/) of the corresponding compound en-
tities.
```

3 System Implementation

In a collaborative design environment, assembly design and various aspects of decision knowledge need to be integrated remotely and seamlessly. This integration can provide designers information about the behavior/performance of an assembly design. In multimedia-based decision support system, a simulation model can be triggered during the initial assembly design stage in a concurrent manner. Properly capturing the assembly effects and implications will allow designers to make appropriate design decisions in the early stages of assembly design.

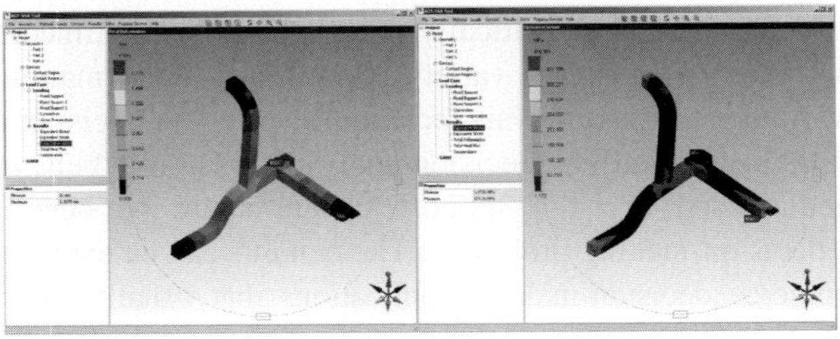

(a) Model I - total deformation (b) Model I - equivalent stress

Fig. 3. Test result of joining effect simulation models

In our model, design decision information can be acquired remotely and transparently. For example, assembly design decision knowledge, including design complexity, joining cost, and joining effects, can be integrated into the e-ARG. Table 1 shows design decision analysis results. Three components of decision analysis knowledge (i.e., design complexity knowledge, joining cost knowledge, and joining effect simulation model) are employed. The design complexity model represents the complexity of the selected design and the joining cost model estimates the cost of the specified joining method. Also, two joining effect simulation models are employed. Joining effect simulation model I measures physical effects from joining, and joining effect simulation model II measures impact on the front bumper area. The maximum deformation and maximum stress can be used to evaluate the structural performance of the design. Fig. 3 illustrates the simulation results (total deformation and equivalent stress) from the joining effect simulation models. To show the feasibility of the idea proposed in this paper, we are extending the application domains such as production scheduling and fault tolerant systems.

Table 1. Design decision analysis results

Decision Knowledge or Models	Material	Joining	Design complexity knowledge	Joining cost knowledge ($)	Joining effect simulation model I		Joining effect Simulation II	
					Max Deformation (mm)	Max Stress (MPa)	Max Deformation (mm)	Max Stress (MPa)
Design A	AA 6063	GMAW	1.5	2.52	1.93	474.36	11.89	4041.00

4 Conclusion

This paper has researched the possibility of an integration of multimedia data with decision-making knowledge in decision support system. To address this issue, we have introduced an eARG and integrated it into SM in order to transform multimedia data into objects. We conclude that the proposed multimedia-based decision support system can provide the following advantages: (1) Mathematical decision-making knowledge can be systematically integrated with multimedia information, such as graphics and images. (2) A variety of multimedia information can be stored and used for various decision analysis techniques. (3) The decision quality can be enhanced with the use of various decision analysis tools. We believe that the proposed multimedia-based decision support system could be beneficial to many organizational decision-making processes. The benefits can be extended to mobile or ubiquitous commerce decision-making applications that usually experience limited workspace but require a large amount of information – ideally, multimedia information.

Acknowledgments

This research is supported by the ubiquitous Autonomic Computing and Network Project, the Ministry of Information and Communication (MIC) 21st Century Frontier R&D Program in Korea (2006-2008).

References

1. Jiang, Zhenhui, Wang, Weiquan, Benbasat, Izak: Multimedia-based Interactive Advising Technology for Online Consumer Decision Support. Communications of the ACM, Volume 48, Issue 9 (2005)
2. Wallace, M. J. D. a. W. A.: The Effects on Decision Task Performance of Computer Synthetic Voice Output. International Journal of Man-Machine Studies 36(1) (1992) 65-80
3. Jones, L. C. a. B.: Impact of Communication Medium and Computer Support on Group Perceptions and Performance: A Comparison of Face-to-Face and Dispersed Meetings. MIS Quarterly 17(4) (1993) 465-491
4. Swink, M., Robinson, E. P.: Complexity Factors and Intuition-based Methods for Facility Network Design. Decision Sciences 28(3) (1997) 583-613
5. Liu, J., Chang, M. M. Y.: Online Chinese Character Recognition using Attributed Relational Graph Matching. IEE Proceedings: Vision, Image & Signal Processing (1996)

Multi-agent Modeling and Simulation for Petroleum Supply Chain

Jiang Tian and Huaglory Tianfield

School of Computing and Mathematical Sciences
Glasgow Caledonian University
Glasgow G4 0BA, UK
ti_ji006@sina.com, h.tianfield@gcal.ac.uk

Abstract. The petroleum supply chain is an old problem with new challenges. Multi-agent system has recognized as an effective methodology for supply chain management. This paper conducts a systematic multi-agent methodology to China petroleum supply chain system, where multi-agent models are constructed, and the multi-agent system is simulated in Zeus agent platform. Particularly, the advantages of multi-agent modeling and simulation in supply chain management are addressed and demonstrated.

1 Introduction

Roughly speaking, computerization of enterprise systems has evolved over three levels, i.e., the basic level – automation of departmental business processes and workshop-wide processes in an enterprise, the middle level – automation of enterprise-wide business processes and workflows, and the high level – inter-enterprise collaborations. Supply chain management (SCM) is one of such strategies through which individual enterprises form partnerships and achieve inter-enterprise collaboration. A supply chain comprises multiple enterprises to collaboratively provide customers with products or services. SCM is the management of relationship across the supply chain [1]. SCM evolves the inter-enterprise collaboration and enhances the adaptation of enterprises in the volatile environment.

Multi-agent system (MAS) has been recognized as a promising technology for the automation of SCM in recent years. An agent is a physical or logical (semi-) autonomous entity, and MAS is an organic and systematic society comprising agents to provide functions [2]. Multi-agent supply chain management (MA-SCM) is a multi-agent paradigm for the computerization of SCM. A supply chain can naturally be viewed as a society of autonomous agents, and a SCM system can be viewed as MAS, where supply chain partners are represented by different agents which provide certain functions of the supply chain system [3, 4]. The distinctive characteristic is that the interaction between agents using an agent communication language enables supply chain partners to be able to negotiate and coordinate in an automated manner with each other more effectively in dynamic management of supply chain.

MA-SCM has been applied in various industries, but so far there is not MAS that systematically addresses China petroleum supply chain management (CP-SCM). The aim of the paper is to conduct MAS methodology for the SCM in petroleum industry

D.-S. Huang, K. Li, and G.W. Irwin (Eds.): ICIC 2006, LNAI 4114, pp. 496 – 501, 2006.

MAS can be used as a natural and powerful tool to model SCM. Multi-agent model consists of a set of agents and a framework for simulating their decisions and interactions. The basic building blocks are the multiple agents modeling the partners in the supply chain [5, 6].

2 Multi-agent Modeling for China Petroleum Supply Chain

China petroleum supply chain is characterized by long chain involving a large number of participating enterprises, geographically scattered business units, complicated technological interdependency, and the semi-monopolized market [7]. The distinctive characteristic of CP-SCM is the semi-monopolized market. For the special requirements, the CP-SCM system should be adaptable, open, and scalable in the competitive environment worldwide.

CP-SCM system can be decomposed into six main subsystems, i.e., customer, products distribution, refining, transportation, exploration and exploitation, imported petroleum subsystem, and development of substitute. The customer subsystem is the terminal in petroleum supply chain and drives the other subsystems. The subsystems of CP-SCM system are represented by agents, respectively, as shown in Fig. 1.

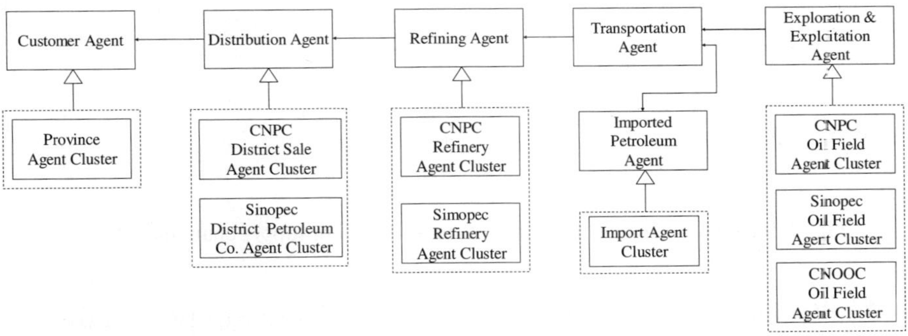

Fig. 1. The multi-agent system of China petroleum supply chain

Moreover, Because three petroleum corporations (CNPC, Sinopec and CNOOC) monopolize the petroleum supply businesses from exploration and exploitation, transportation, refining, to distributions, this MAS is further depicted by instantiation architecture, where the agents at lower level instantiates the attributes of the agents at the higher level. Customer Agent, Refining Agent, Distribution Agent, Exploration and Exploitation Agent, and Imported Petroleum Agent can have their instantiation architectures to carry out their tasks, respectively. The clusters of province agent, sale agent, refinery agent, oil field agent and import agent instantiate customer agent, distribution agent, refining agent, and exploration and exploitation agent, and imported petroleum agent, respectively.

Usually, a supply chain is made of supply chain predecessors and successors [8]. There is consumer-supplier relationship between the predecessors and the successors in supply chain. The predecessor who is the final consumer in the supply chain is the supply chain Head, while the successor who is the final supplier in the supply chain is the supply chain Tail. The partners between supply chain Head and supply chain Tail, who are either suppliers or consumers, are the supply chain Participants. In the MAS of CP-SCM, Customer Agent is the supply chain Head, Exploration and exploitation Agent and Imported Petroleum Agent are the supply chain Tails, and Distribution Agent, Refining Agent and Transportation Agent are the supply chain Participants, which play different roles, as shown in Fig. 2. The speech acts of interactions between the agents are summarized as follows. Speech Act No. 1 represents Call for proposal Published, No. 2 represents Consider Proposal, No. 3 represents Bid Formulated, No. 4 represents Bid Issued, No. 5 represents Bid Consider, No. 6 represents Bid Accepted/Rejected, No. 7 represents Produce, and No. 8 represents Deliver.

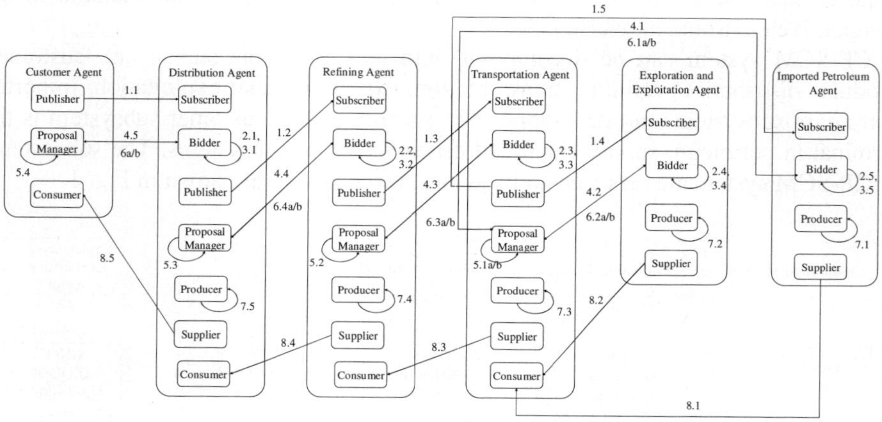

Fig. 2. Interactions between agents in China petroleum supply chain management

3 Multi-agent Simulation for China Petroleum Supply Chain Management

Multi-agent simulation is the execution of a multi-agent model. The MAS for CP-SCM is simulated in Zeus 1.1 Platform, which was developed by British Telecommunications public limited company. Zeus is a dominant agent platform for SCM [8].

In the MAS for CP-SCM, Customer Agent is the kernel of the supply chain and drives the other participants in the supply chain. The realization of the MAS in Zeus includes the following steps, i.e., ontology creation, agent creation, utility agent configuration, task agent configuration, and code generation and agent implementation. These steps translate the specification into agent descriptions and further generate source code for the petroleum supply chain application.

The implementation screenshots are shown in Fig. 3 and 4. Fig. 3 shows the relationship between agents, where the monopolization is represented by subordinate in a petroleum corporation. Fig. 4 shows the interactions between agents such as “subscribe”, “query-ref”, and “inform” etc.

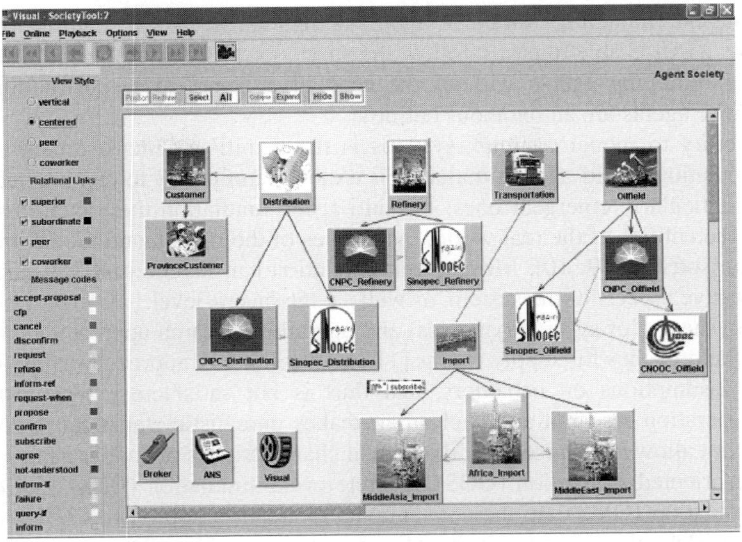

Fig. 3. The screenshot of society of China petroleum supply chain management in Zeus

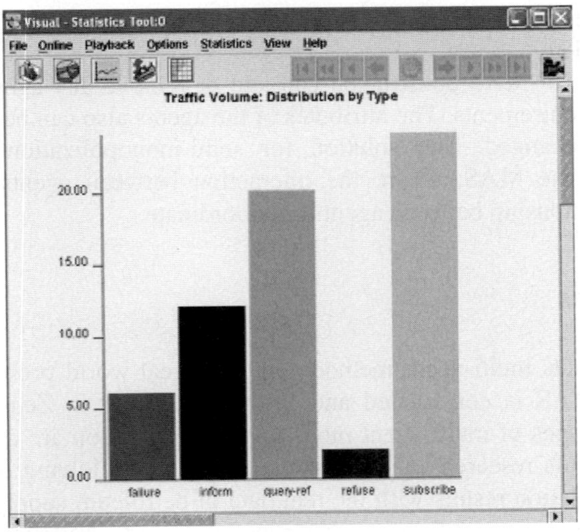

Fig. 4. The screenshot of statistics of China petroleum supply chain management in Zeus

4 Evaluations

Multi-agent modeling and simulation have many advantages in SCM [5]. MAS can easily be set up on legacy information systems without particular disruption on their functioning. The natural ability of MAS to solve problems depends on the cooperation, which better reflects the behaviors of supply chain partners. Agents can be deployed as a real-time decision support software to its modeled supply chain partners.

Multi-agent modeling supports more comprehensive and flexible modeling capability. MAS is able to easily follow the strong evolvablity of the supply chain by adding or removing agents without the need of a complete reconstruction of the system since agents are autonomous entities.

The ability to model complex systems is the significant improvement of multi-agent simulation. Multi-agent simulation is a more natural way to capture behavior in system, particularly emergent ones. In multi-agent simulation there is a close match between the entities of the real world, the entities of the model, and the entities of the simulation software [9, 10]. Multi-agent simulation can handle both the micro-level and dispersive aspects of the system, as well as, the macro-level.

Control theory (or system dynamics) and operation research approach are the main modeling approaches for supply chains [11]. Control theory approach mainly relies on linearity assumptions on behaviors, and thus is not satisfactory for most supply chains. Operation research approach often makes unrealistic statistical assumptions, and does not allow to represent the dynamical characteristics of supply chains.

Object-oriented simulation (OOS), discrete event simulation (DES), and dynamic micro simulation (DMS) are the conventional simulation approaches. They are used to create models of well known parts of a system to deeply analyze a part of a whole system, but are often limited for complex and difficult to predict system [10].

However, one major disadvantage of multi-agent simulation is that no theorems can be established, except through multiple runs covering various initial conditions and parameters [12].

The MAS for CP-MAS constructed can add or remove any agents depending on the application requirements. The attributes of the agents also can be modified as their environment is changed. The solution for semi-monopolization requirements is demonstrated in the MAS, where the interaction between agents is restricted by defining interrelationship between agents as subordinate.

5 Conclusions

This paper conducts multi-agent methodology to a real-world problem domain, i.e., CP-SCM. The MAS is constructed and further simulated in Zeus agent platform, where the advantages of multi-agent modeling and simulation are demonstrated. The future works of this research can be undertaken in the following directions, i.e., to evaluate the simulation results with the real data of petroleum supply chain in China; and to propose a multi-agent framework for modeling and simulating dynamic supply chain in petroleum industry.

References

1. Sauter, J. A.; Parunak, H. V. D., Goic, J.: ANTS in the Supply Chain. Proceedings of Workshop on Agents for Electronic Commerce at Agents'99 (1999)
2. Wooldridge, M.: An Introduction to MultiAgent Systems. John Wiley and Sons Ltd (2002)
3. Barbuceanu, M., Fox, M. S.: Coordinating Multiple Agents in the Supply Chain. Proceedings of Fifth Workshop on Enabling Technologies: Infrastructure for Collaborative Enterprises, Stanford, CA, Jane (1996) 134-142

4. Sauer, J., Appelrath, H.-J.: Scheduling the Supply Chain by Teams of Agents. Published in the Proceedings of the 36th. Hawaii International Conference on System Sciences (HICSS' 03) (2003)
5. Lau, Jason S. K.; Huang, George Q., Mak, K. L.: Impacts of Sharing Production Information on Supply Chain Dynamics: A Multi-agent Simulation Study. Proceedings of 30th International Conference of Computers and Industrial Engineering, 27–30 June 2002, Tinos Island, Aegean Sea, Greece (2002) 527-532
6. Tah, Joseph H. M.: Towards an Agent-based Construction Supply Network Modeling and Simulation Platform. Automation in Construction, 14(3) (2005) 353-359
7. Li, C.B., Wu, X.J.: Elementary Study of Petroleum Industry Supply Chain Management in China (2004) http://www.jctrans.com/xueyuan/topic.asp?id=1519
8. Collis, J., Nudumu, D.: The Zeus Agent Building Toolkit. Intelligent Systems Research Group, BT Labs, Release 1.01 (1999)
9. Hoog, S. V. D.: Social Simulation Some Remarks on Agent Based Simulation. http://www.xs4all.nl/~svdhoog/papers/mabs.pdf
10. Davidsson, P.: Multi Agent Based Simulation: Beyond Social Simulation. Lecture Notes in Computer Science (2000) 97-107
11. Parunak, H. V. D., Savit, R., Riolo, R. L., Clark, S. J.: DASCh-Dynamic Analysis of Supply Chains, Final Report of the DASCh project, Center for Electronic Commerce, ERIM, Inc., Ann Arbor
12. Gopal, K., Pai, R.: CPSC 631 (Spring 2002): Multi-Agent Systems Project Report: Macroeconomic Modeling and Simulation Using Bounded Rational Agents.

Optimize Cooperative Agents with Organization in Distributed Scheduling System

Wei Fan and Fan Xue

Software Technology Research Center, Civil Aviation University of China,
Tianjin 300300, China P.R.
fanxinhui@eyou.com

Abstract. DSAFO (Dynamic Scheduling Agents with Federation Organization) is a novel multi-agent constraint satisfaction algorithm for AGSS problem (a NP-hard scheduling problem). This paper improves on DSAFO by employing a resource requisition strategy, and models this parallel multi-agent algorithm in polyadic π-calculus. The time complexity of the improved DSAFO is $\mathrm{O}(n^3) + \mathrm{O}(n^2) \times t_{\text{trans}}$. Experiments show improved DSAFO performs well in AGSS consumptions optimization of resources and man-days. Though it is unstable, improved DSAFO makes good probability to find better solutions than classical heuristics and its distributed and parallel agents viewpoint is potential to deal with distributed dynamic troubles in real applications.

1 Introduction

Airport ground service is a service process from flight landing to takeoff, including gate assignment, baggage handling, catering, fueling, cleaning, etc. AGSS (Airport ground service scheduling) is to schedule many kinds of dynamic ground resources (baggage trucks, fuel trucks, etc.), to fulfill all constrained service subtasks of flights timely to meet their arrival and departure deadlines [1].

AGSS problem is a NP-hard problem. Moreover, it could be viewed as either a JSSP (Job-Shop Scheduling Problem) [2] $\mathrm{J}_m|r_j, prmp|\Sigma w_j U_j$ [3] or a Dis-CSP [4], because of the ways that real subtasks and resources are organized. In real AGSS, most resources are ample except some prepared for accidents. Consequently the scheduling target $\Sigma w_j U_j = 0$ is not difficult to achieve, however how many resources and man-days consumed are important to airports and airlines. The algorithm in this paper optimizes the resources and man-days consumptions.

DSAFO (Dynamic Scheduling Agents with Federation Organization) [1] is a novel multi-agent algorithm for Dis-CSP (Distributed Constraint Satisfaction Problem), especially for AGSS problem under high constraint. DSAFO employs blackboard mechanism, federation organization, meta-level guided resource borrowing and domain knowledge guided plan backtrack. The principle of DSAFO is coordinating distributed resources with cooperative agents.

The remainder of the paper is structured as follows: Chap. 2 represents the improved DSAFO in form of polyadic π-calculus to precisely describe the parallel essence of improved DSAFO. Chap. 3 analyzes the time complexity. Experiment results appear in Chap. 4 and a brief conclusion is given in Chap. 5.

D.-S. Huang, K. Li, and G.W. Irwin (Eds.): ICIC 2006, LNAI 4114, pp. 502–509, 2006.

2 Improved DSAFO

2.1 Polyadic π-Calculus

The polyadic π-calculus developed by Milner [5] is a very powerful tool to model processes in parallel systems such as multi-agent systems and mobile systems. The most primitive entity in polyadic π-calculus is a *name*. Names, infinitely many, are $x, y, \ldots \in \chi$; they have no structure. The other kind of entity, a *process*, is built from names by syntax

$$P ::= \Sigma_{i \in I} \pi_i . P_i \mid P|Q \mid !P \mid (\nu\, x)P$$

In this paper, we model DSAFO in π-calculus and usually abbreviate name sequences in π-calculus to vector names, e.g. a subtask tuple structure may be abbreviated to "$\overrightarrow{task}$". A name in vector name could be accessed using "$\triangleright$", e.g. the LFT (Latest Finish Time) of a task is $task \triangleright LFT$.

2.2 DSAFO: An Overview

DSAFO is based on several parameters such as *Heartbeat*. And it implements a unique Blackboard, a unique ResAdmin, some Coordinators and more Members.

$$\begin{aligned} \text{DSAFO} \stackrel{\text{def}}{=} & (Schtasks, Agents_t, Resources, Tskinres_r, Heartbeat, Clockzero) \\ & (\nu\, query_t^a, inform_t^a, request_t^a, reply_t^a, cancel_t^a, synbuddy_t^a, ackbuddy_t^a, \\ & borrow_t^a, lend_t^a, refuse_t^a, syndemand_t^a, ackdemand_t^a, reqres_t^a, allot_t^a, \\ & release_t^a)\ (\text{BLACKBOARD}|\text{RESADMIN}|\text{MEMBER}_t^a \\ & |\text{COORDINATOR}_r)\ (t \in Schtasks, a \in Agents_t, r \in Resources) \end{aligned}$$

Channels among agents are organized as Fig. 1.

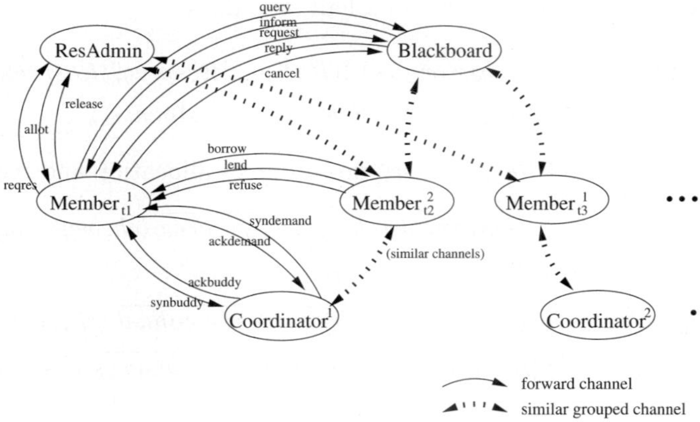

Fig. 1. channel organization of DSAFO

2.3 Blackboard Agent

The unique agent BLACKBOARD perceives information of flights coming in half an hour, decomposes them into subtasks and assigns subtasks with plans from member agents.

$$\begin{aligned} \text{BLACKBOARD} \stackrel{\text{def}}{=} (Flights, Subtasks_f^t) \\ (BbFunc|RespQuery_t^a|RespReq_t^a|RespCancel_t^a) \\ (t \in Schtasks, a \in Agents_t, f \in Flights) \end{aligned}$$

BLACKBOARD has four sorts of behaviors responding messages from members. For example, $RespQuery_t^a$ receives signals from channel $Query_t^a$ and then responses with the top of ready subtasks and the most delayed subtask.

$$\begin{aligned} RespQuery_t^a \equiv\, & !query_t^a.(\nu\, c)(\overline{readytask_t}\langle c\rangle|c(\overrightarrow{tsk}).[\overrightarrow{tsk} \neq nil]\overline{inform_t^a}\langle\overrightarrow{tsk}\rangle) \\ & .(\nu\, uc)(\overline{delaytask_t}\langle uc\rangle|uc(\overrightarrow{utsk}).[\overrightarrow{utsk} \neq nil]\overline{inform_t^a}\langle\overrightarrow{utsk}\rangle) \\ RespReq_t^a \equiv\, & !request_t^a(\overrightarrow{plan}).(\nu\, ch)(\overline{getplan}\langle ch, plan \triangleright fno, plan \triangleright tsk\rangle \\ & |ch(\overrightarrow{myplan}).[\overrightarrow{myplan} = nil](\overline{assign}\langle\overrightarrow{plan}\rangle.\overline{reply_t^a}\langle syn, \overrightarrow{plan}\rangle)) \\ RespCancel_t^a \equiv\, & !cancel_t^a(\overrightarrow{plan}).(\nu\, ch)(\overline{getplan}\langle ch, plan \triangleright fno, plan \triangleright tsk\rangle \\ & |ch(\overrightarrow{myplan}).[\overrightarrow{myplan} = \overrightarrow{plan}]\overline{free}\langle plan \triangleright fno, plan \triangleright tsk\rangle) \end{aligned}$$

2.4 ResAdmin

Agent RESADMIN is a resource administrator. When received resources request, RESADMIN would search free resources and allot one if possible. After half a man-day (4-hour work), the resource would be free again. Additionally, one resource serves no more than one and a half man-days.

$$\begin{aligned} \text{RESADMIN} \stackrel{\text{def}}{=} & (reslist_r, historylist_r)(RaFunc|Respreq_t^a|Resprelease_t^a) \\ & (r \in Resources, t \in Schtasks, a \in Agents_t) \end{aligned}$$

Behaviors $Respreq_t^a$ and $Resprelease_t^a$ do resources allocation and recovery.

$$\begin{aligned} Respreq_t^a \equiv\, & !resreq_t^a(begintm).(\nu\, ch)(\overline{gettopfreeres_t}\langle ch, begintm\rangle|ch(\overrightarrow{res}) \\ & .[\overrightarrow{res} \neq nil]\overline{allot_t^a}\langle res \triangleright name, begintm\rangle) \\ Resprelease_t^a \equiv\, & !release_t^a(resname).(\nu\, ch)(\overline{getresfromhash}\langle ch, resname\rangle \\ & |ch(\overrightarrow{res}).[\overrightarrow{res} \neq nil]\overline{loghistory}\langle\overrightarrow{res}\rangle.\overline{releaseres}\langle\overrightarrow{res}\rangle) \end{aligned}$$

2.5 Member

A member agent MEMBER$_t^a$ is in charge of subtask t. It always has a desire to handle subtasks. After MEMBER$_t^a$ received available subtask goals from

BLACKBOARD, it intends to make suitable plans and request for them. Every member agent always has an open hand when others need help.

$$\begin{aligned}\text{MEMBER}_t^a \stackrel{\text{def}}{=} &(Resource_t^a, Remoteres_t^a)(MbFunc \\ &|ActQry_t^a|MkPlan_t^a|CallBd_t^a|Ackres_t^a|TryLend_t^a|AckLend_t^a) \\ &(t \in Schtasks, a \in Agents_t)\end{aligned}$$

Cyclic behavior $ActQuery_t^a$ is infinite (but finite in practical scheduling). It sends subtask requests to drive the DSAFO and releases expired resources. The behaviors $MakePlan_t^a$ perceives subtask information and try to make plans for them. If the subtask cannot be locally scheduled, $CallBd_t^a$, $TryLend_t^a$ and $AckLend_t^a$ cooperate to perform resource borrowing. After all resources borrowing failed, it would send resource request to RESADMIN, and behavior $Ackres_t^a$ would receive the coming resource.

$$\begin{aligned}
ActQry_t^a \equiv &(\overline{query_t^a}.\overline{block_t^a}\langle Heartbeat\rangle.(\nu\, ch)(\overline{getexpiredres_t^a}\langle ch\rangle|ch(\overrightarrow{reslist}) \\
&.[\overrightarrow{reslist} \neq nil]\overline{releaseall_t^a}\langle\overrightarrow{reslist}\rangle).)^{+\infty} \\
MkPlan_t^a \equiv &!inform_t^a(\overrightarrow{tsk}).(\nu\, ch)(\overline{makenullplan_t}\langle ch, \overrightarrow{tsk}\rangle|ch(\overrightarrow{n})) \\
&.(\nu\, p)(\overline{locallyplan}\langle p, \overrightarrow{n}\rangle|p(\overrightarrow{plan}, res).([res \neq null]\overline{request_t^a}\langle\overrightarrow{plan}\rangle \\
&+[res = null]\overline{synbuddy_t^a}(\overrightarrow{plan}))) \\
CallBd_t^a \equiv &!(ackbuddy_t^a(\overrightarrow{uplan}, \overrightarrow{lst})|refuse_t^a(\overrightarrow{uplan}, \overrightarrow{lst})).(\nu\, c)(\overline{topof}\langle c, \overrightarrow{lst}\rangle \\
&|c(next, \overrightarrow{nlist}).([next \neq null]\overline{next}\langle\overrightarrow{uplan}, \overrightarrow{nlist}, lend_t^a, refuse_t^a\rangle \\
&+[next = null]\overline{reqres}\langle uplan \triangleright EST - 1\rangle)) \\
Ackres_t^a \equiv &!allot_t^a(name, begintm).(\nu\, ch)(\overline{genres_t}\langle ch, name, begintm, 239\rangle \\
&|ch(\overrightarrow{res}).[\overrightarrow{res} \neq nil]\overline{addres2locallist}\langle\overrightarrow{res}\rangle) \\
TryLend_t^a \equiv &!borrow_t^a(\overrightarrow{uplan}, \overrightarrow{lst}, succ, fail).(\nu\, ch)(\overline{locallyplan}\langle ch, \overrightarrow{uplan}\rangle \\
&|ch(\overrightarrow{plan}, res).([res \neq null]\overline{assign_t^a}\langle\overrightarrow{plan}\rangle.\overline{succ}\langle\overrightarrow{plan}\rangle \\
&+[res = null]\overline{fail}\langle\overrightarrow{uplan}, \overrightarrow{lst}\rangle)) \\
AckLend_t^a \equiv &!lend_t^a(\overrightarrow{plan}).\overline{assignremote}\langle\overrightarrow{plan}\rangle.\overline{request_t^a}\langle\overrightarrow{plan}\rangle
\end{aligned}$$

2.6 Coordinator

A coordinator agent COORDINATOR_r coordinates all member agents having resource r. After elimination of plan backup mechanism, it has several behaviors on information synchronization and buddy list making up.

$$\begin{aligned}\text{CORDINATOR}_r \stackrel{\text{def}}{=} &(Metainfo_r, Syncycle)(CooFunc|Synch_r|Store_t^a|RespBd_t^a) \\ &(r \in Resources, t \in TskinRes_r, a \in Agents_t)\end{aligned}$$

$Synch_r$ and $Store^a_t$ cyclically collect meta-level information of member agents which belong to it. Behavior $RespBd^a_t$ tells a member buddy list sorted by meta-level information.

$$Synch_r \equiv (\overline{synall_r}.\overline{block_r}\langle Syncycle \times Heartbeat\rangle.)^{+\infty}$$

$$Store^a_t \equiv !ackdemand^a_t(dm).(\nu\, ch)(\overline{setval}\langle ch, dm\rangle | ch(demands^a_t)$$
$$.\overline{removelist}\langle demands^a_t\rangle.\overline{insertsort}\langle demands^a_t\rangle)$$

$$RespBd^a_t \equiv !synbuddy^a_t.(\nu\, ch)(\overline{genbuddylist_t}\langle ch\rangle | ch(\overrightarrow{blst}).\overline{ackbuddy^a_t}\langle\overrightarrow{blst}\rangle))$$

3 Complexity

First of all, we abbreviate the number of flights $\|Flights\|$ to "n" as well as $24 \times 60 \times Heartbeat$ to "WholeDay".

3.1 Preparation

For any subtask t, there are n jobs to do at most. And there must be a minimal completion time $\mathrm{ct}^{\min}_t$ for t. The resource expectation res^*_t

$$\mathrm{O}(n) = n \times \mathrm{ct}^{\min}_t/\mathrm{WholeDay} \leq res^*_t \leq n = \mathrm{O}(n)$$

Hence, $res^*_t = \mathrm{O}(n) \ \ (t \in Schtasks)$

For each resource r, there is a constant set $Tskinres_r$. By summing it up one by one, we have expectation of each resource $r \in Resources$ is $res^*_r = \mathrm{O}(n)$. In fact, resources to allocate usually approximates the expectations $\mathrm{O}(n)$, so we assume the number of each resource $r \in Resources$ is $res_r = \mathrm{O}(n)$.

Because the agents number affects the complexity, we assume there are O(n) agents to compute the upper bound of complexity.

3.2 Time Complexity

Time complexity of improved DSAFO is mainly from two parts: resource borrowing and demand synchronization. The rest processes are less complex.

Resource Borrowing. In the worst case, there are $\mathrm{O}(n)$ searches and $\mathrm{O}(n)$ borrowing message transmissions to fulfill every subtask. All $\mathrm{O}(n)$ subtasks cost $t_{\mathrm{borrow}} = \mathrm{O}(n^2) \times t_{\mathrm{search}} + \mathrm{O}(n^2) \times t_{\mathrm{trans}} = \mathrm{O}(n^3) + \mathrm{O}(n^2) \times t_{\mathrm{trans}}$.

Demand Synchronization. Demand synchronization is a cyclic action. Each member has only one coordinator in federation organization, therefore, each synchronization transmits $\mathrm{O}(n)$ messages and do $\mathrm{O}(n \times n)$ sorts. The synchronization costs

$$t_{\mathrm{syn}} = \big(\mathrm{O}(n) \times t_{\mathrm{trans}} + \mathrm{O}(n^2)\big) \times \frac{\mathrm{WholeDay}}{Heartbeat \times Syncycle} = \mathrm{O}(n^2) + \mathrm{O}(n) \times t_{\mathrm{trans}}$$

To sum up, the upper bound of complexity $t_{\mathrm{DSAFO}} = \mathrm{O}(n^3) + \mathrm{O}(n^2) \times t_{\mathrm{trans}}$.

4 Experiment Result

We implemented DSAFO in JADE [6], a multi-agent development environment, and implemented the channels on FIPA ACL [7].

In classical JSSP, EDD (Earliest Due Date first) and FCFS (First Come Fist Serve, also well known as ERT, Earliest Ready Time) are two powerful heuristic algorithms for minimal uncompleted jobs scheduling [3]. We tested these algorithms with a 282 transfer flights problem under normal constraint.

As a multi-agent algorithm, DSAFO is an unstable algorithm. Consequently we gave spontaneous 250 runs to get the distribution of the solutions. Figure 2 shows the baggage truck solution distribution for trucks and man-days consumed by DSAFO with 8 baggage truck agents.

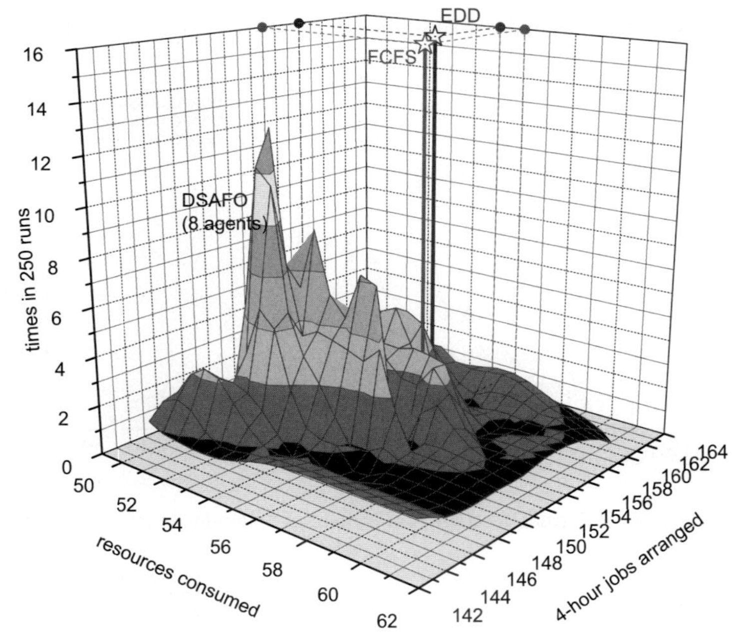

Fig. 2. Distribution of DSAFO (8 agents) solutions for baggage trucks

Furthermore, we tested DSAFO in different quantities of MEMBER agents. The results were accumulated in Fig. 3 and 4. From the marginal distributions in Fig. 3, we can see that 76.8% resource solutions of DSAFO with 8 agents are not worse (59.6% better) than EDD and FCFS, the probabilities are 54% and 32% with 12 agents and 16 agents. But the best solutions of the three are nearly the same. And so is in Fig. 4. It means when the number of agents increases, probabilities of good solutions decrease, but the best solution seems stable.

Figure 5 shows the simultaneous serving resources of solutions done by different optimization algorithms.

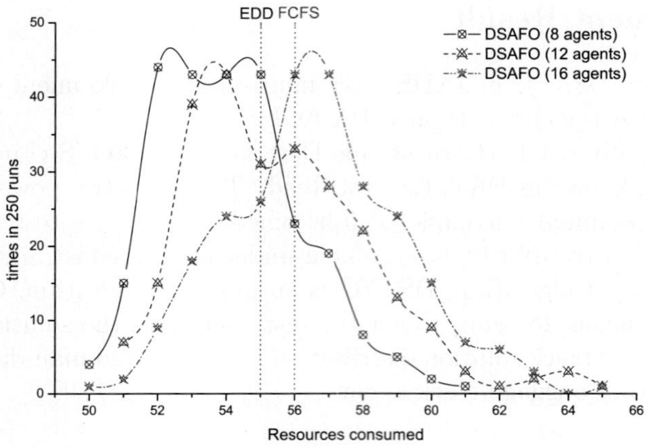

Fig. 3. Marginal distribution of baggage trucks consumed

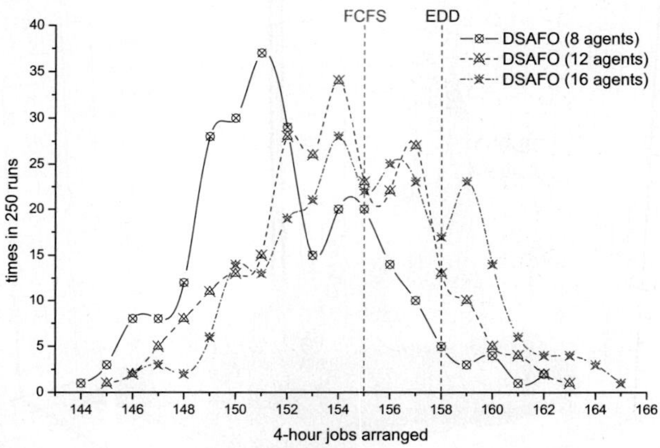

Fig. 4. Marginal distribution of 4-hour baggage truck works

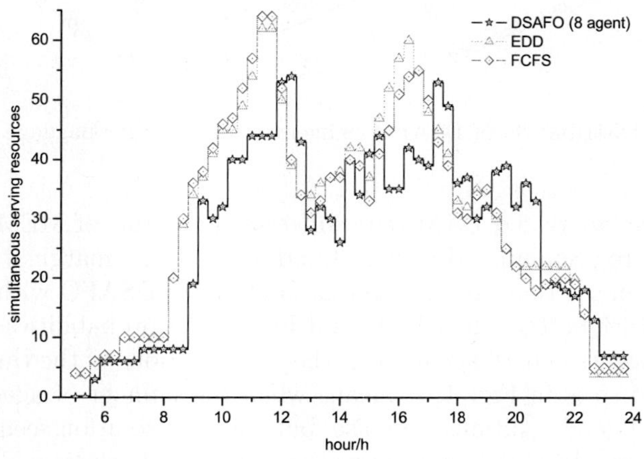

Fig. 5. Simultaneously serving baggage trucks by different optimization algorithms

5 Conclusion

AGSS problem is a typical dynamic distributed scheduling problem. To optimize AGSS consumptions of resources and man-days is difficult, but it is important to economy. DSAFO is a novel multi-agent constraint satisfaction algorithm for AGSS problems.

We improved DSAFO for optimizing consumptions of resources and man-days by incorporating a resource allocation strategy. Experiments show that improved DSAFO performs well in optimization. And when the number of agents increase, probabilities of good solutions would decrease but the best solution would be stable.

Though improved DSAFO is unstable, it makes good probability to find better solutions than classical heuristics, and its construction of distributed and parallel agents is potential to deal with distributed dynamic troubles in real applications. Furthermore, DSAFO may be allied to common dynamic distributed scheduling problems for its low complexity and sound effect.

Acknowledgements. The authors acknowledge the support by National Natural Science Foundation of China (NSFC) under Grant No. 60472123.

References

1. Xing, J., Fan, W., Ji, L.: Design of Airport Ground Service System Based on Multi-agent. Journal of Civil Aviation University of China, 24 (2006) (in Chinese).
2. Modi, P. J.: Distributed Constraint Optimization for Multiagent Systems. Ph.D. Dissertation. University of Southern California, USA (2003)
3. Tang, H., Zhao, L.: Introduction to Scheduling Theory. Chapter 2. Chinese Acdemic press, Beijing (2002) (in Chinese).
4. Yokoo, M.: Distributed Constraint Satisfaction: Foundation of Cooperation of Multi-agent System. Springer Verlag, Heidelberg, Berlin (2001)
5. Milner, R.: The Polyadic π-calculus: A Tutorial. Tech. Report ECS-LFCS-91-180. University of Edinburgh, UK (1991)
6. Bellifemine, Poggi, F., Rimassa, A., Jade, G.: A FIPA2000 Compliant Agent Development Environment. In Proceedings of The Fifth International Conference on Autonomous Agents (AGENT01), Montreal, Canada, ACM Press, New York (2001) 216-217.
7. FIPA: FIPA ACL Message Structure Specification. Document No. 00061, Geneva, FIPA, http://www.fipa.org/specs/fipa00061/SC00061G.pdf (2002)

Phrase-Based Statistical Machine Translation by Using Reordering Search and Additional Features

Miao Li, Peng Gao, Jian Zhang, and Yi Luo

Institute of Intelligent of Machines, China Academy of Sciences, Anhui, China
{mli, jzhang}@iim.ac.cn, lookingforid@gmail.com

Abstract. The state of the art statistical machine translation (SMT) systems are based on phrase (a group of words), which are modeled using log-linear maximum entropy framework. In this paper, we constructed a phrase-based statistical machine translation system with additional feature models. The translation model is combined with four specific additional feature functions. When comparing our system with the baseline system of IWSLT2005, we can conclude that our system improve the SMT system accuracy with the same corpus.

1 Introduction

The development of statistical methods for machine translation has resulted in high quality translations that can be used in real applications with increasing confidence [1],[2]. Our system draws from these advances and implements a number of these techniques including log-linear model combination and minimum error rate training to translate foreign language sentences.

The basic translation training and decoding processes are shown in Figure 1. We first start with a word alignment extracted from a training set. These alignments are expanded and phrases are counted to form the phrase translation model. Language models are then trained from the English side of training set (and possibly with other English texts, if available). Using development bitexts separated from the training set, we then employ a minimum error rate training process to optimize model parameters utilizing a held out development set. These trained parameters and models can then be applied to test data during decoding and rescoring phases of the translation process.

The paper improves the phrase-based translation model by using additional models, and reorders the outcome lists using new reordering strategies with pruning in the process of decoding. It is organizes as follows: Section 2 introduces the basic models and the log-linear combination translation framework, section 3 describes all the feature functions used in our SMT system. Decoding strategies are introduced in section 4 concisely, some experiments of the translation accuracy and efficiency based on our models are reported in section 5 and section 6 concludes and outlines further research.

D.-S. Huang, K. Li, and G.W. Irwin (Eds.): ICIC 2006, LNAI 4114, pp. 510 – 517, 2006.

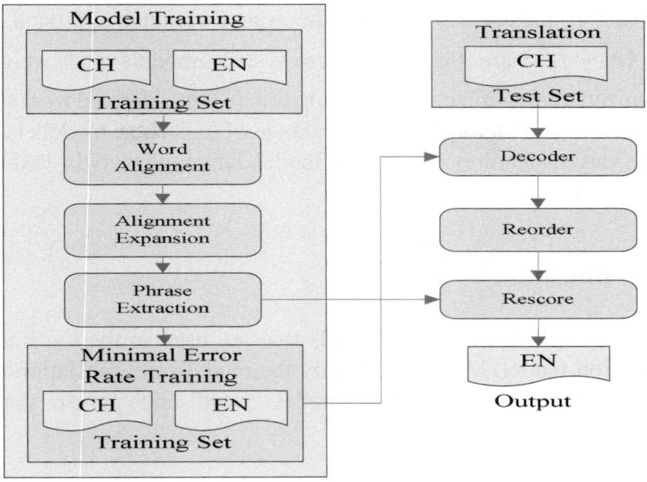

Fig. 1. Basic Statistical Machine Architecture

2 Baseline SMT System

The goal of the translation is to translate source ("foreign language") sentence $f_1^J = f_1, ..., ..., f_J$ into a target ("English") sentence $e_1^I = e_1, ...e_i, ..., e_I$. We choose the sentence with the highest probability as the best translation [3]:

$$\hat{e}_1^I = \arg\max_{e_1^I} \{\Pr(e_1^I \mid f_1^J)\}. \tag{1}$$

We can get the equivalent equation (2) by using Bayes' decision rule.

$$\hat{e}_1^I = \arg\max_{e_1^I} \{\Pr(e_1^I) \cdot \Pr(f_1^J \mid e_1^I)\}. \tag{2}$$

Recently, most SMT systems tend to use sequences of words, commonly called phrases [4], aiming to introducing word context in the translation model. As alternative to the source channel approach the decision rule can be modeled through a log-linear maximum entropy framework, $\Pr(e_1^I \mid f_1^J)$ is the posterior probability:

$$\Pr(e_1^I \mid f_1^J) = P_{\lambda_1^M}(e_1^I \mid f_1^J) = \frac{\exp\left[\sum_{m=1}^{M} \lambda_m h_m(e_1^I, f_1^J)\right]}{\sum_{\tilde{e}_1^I} \left[\sum_{m=1}^{M} \lambda_m h_m(\tilde{e}_1^I \mid f_1^J)\right]}. \tag{3}$$

According equation (1) and (3),we can get:

$$\hat{e}_1^I = \arg\max_{e_1^I} \{\Pr(e_1^I \mid f_1^J)\} = \arg\max_{e_1^I} \left\{\sum_{m=1}^{M} \lambda_m h_m(e_1^I, f_1^J)\right\}. \tag{4}$$

This approach is a generalization of the source-channel approach. The feature functions $h_m(e_1^I \mid f_1^J)$ are the translation system models and weights λ_m are typically optimized to maximize a scoring function [5]. It is derived from the Maximum Entropy approach as shown in [6]. One advantage of log-linear models is the ability to easily combine various features: translation model, language models, lexical reordering models and other models.

3 Feature Functions in SMT

In this section, we will describe the models that are used in the log-linear statistical machine translation model. More specifically the models are translation model, target language model, word-based lexicon model, word and phrase penalty model, reordering model and rescoring models.

3.1 Translation Model

The phrase-based translation model is the main component of our translation system. The hypotheses are generated by concatenating target language phrases [7]. The pairs of source and corresponding target phrases are extracted from the word aligned bilingual training corpus. The phrase extraction algorithm is described in detail in [8]. The main idea is to extract phrase pairs that are consistent with the word alignment. We use relative frequencies to estimate the phrase translation probabilities:

$$P(\tilde{f} \mid \tilde{e}) = \frac{N(\tilde{f}, \tilde{e})}{N(\tilde{e})}. \tag{5}$$

Here, the number of co-occurrences of a phrase pair $(\tilde{f}, \tilde{e})$ that are consistent with the word alignment is denoted as $N(\tilde{f}, \tilde{e})$. If one occurrence of a target phrase $\tilde{e}$ has N > 1 possible translations, each of them contributes to $N(\tilde{f}, \tilde{e})$ with 1/N. The marginal count $N(\tilde{e})$ is the number of occurrences of the target phrase $\tilde{e}$ in the training corpus. The resulting feature function is:

$$h_{Phr}(f_1^J, e_1^I, s_1^K) = \log \prod_{k=1}^{K} p(\tilde{f}_k \mid \tilde{e}_k). \tag{6}$$

To obtain a more symmetric model, we use the phrase-based model in both directions $p(\tilde{f} \mid \tilde{e})$ and $p(\tilde{e} \mid \tilde{f})$.

3.2 Target Language Model

We use the SRI language modeling toolkit [11] to train a standard n-gram language model. The smoothing technique we apply is the modified Kneser-Ney discounting with interpolation. The order of the language model depends on the translation direction. The resulting feature function is:

$$h_{LM}(f_1^J, e_1^I, s_1^K) = \log \prod_{i=1}^{I} p(e_i \mid e_{i-n+1}^{i-1}) . \tag{7}$$

3.3 Word-Based Lexicon Model

We are using relative frequencies to estimate the phrase translation probabilities. The score of a phrase pair is computed similar to the IBM model 1, but here, we are summing only within a phrase pair and not over the whole target language sentence:

$$h_{Lex}(f_1^J, e_1^I, s_1^K) = \log \prod_{k=1}^{K} \prod_{j=b_k}^{j_k} \sum_{i=i_{k-1}+1} P(f_j \mid e_i) . \tag{8}$$

The word translation probabilities p(f|e) are estimated as relative frequencies from the word-aligned training corpus. The word-based lexicon model is also used in both directions p(f|e) and p(e|f).

3.4 Word and Phrase Penalty Model

In addition, we use two simple heuristics, namely word penalty and phrase penalty:

$$h_{wp}(f_1^J, e_1^I, s_1^K) = I \cdot \tag{9}$$

$$h_{pp}(f_1^J, e_1^I, s_1^K) = K . \tag{10}$$

These two models affect the average sentence and phrase lengths. The model scaling factors can be adjusted to prefer longer sentences and longer phrases.

3.5 Reordering Model

We use a very simple reordering model, It assigns costs based on the jump width:

$$h_{RM}(f_1^J, e_1^I, s_1^K) = \sum_{k=1}^{K} \lvert b_k - j_{k-1} - 1 \rvert + J - j_k . \tag{11}$$

3.6 Rescoring Models

IBM model 1 rescoring rates the quality of a sentence by using the probabilities of one of the easiest single-word based translation models:

$$h_{IBM1}(f_1^J, e_1^I) = \log\left(\frac{1}{(I+1)^J} \prod_{j=1}^{J} \sum_{i=0}^{I} p(f_j \mid e_i) \right) . \tag{12}$$

After IBM model 1 rescoring, We use the HMM to compute the log-likelihood of a sentence pair (f_1^J, e_1^I):

$$h_{HMM}(f_1^J, e_1^I = \log \sum_{a_1^J} \prod_{j=1}^{J} (p(a_j \mid a_{j-1}, I) \cdot p(f_j \mid e_{a_j}). \quad (13)$$

4 Decoder

In SMT decoding, to find the optimal path, a beam search algorithm with pruning, offering good possibilities to adjust the trade-off between quality and efficiency is used widespread [9],[10].

The search of decoding is performed by building partial translations (hypotheses), which are stored in one or several lists. These lists are pruned out according to the accumulated probabilities of their hypotheses. Worst hypotheses with minor probabilities are discarded to make the search feasible.

Our decoder is something like Marie [10] utilizing a Viterbi graph search algorithm, where the graph is built from left to right a word at a time. Each node in the search graph contains a list of back pointers to previous nodes, the probabilities for each translation option, the trigram/bigram context needed for node expansion, and the best path so far. When creating new nodes, the number of nodes can be greatly reduced by using bigrams whenever a particular trigram does not exist in the language model.

After all possible phrases are added for each word, both beam pruning and histogram pruning are used to rid the search graph of unlikely candidate nodes based on the best path. This search algorithm offers fast decoding and easy generation of output word lattices by simply traversing the final data structure. In the case of monotone decoding, this search algorithm is capable of real-time decoding one word at a time (as from a speech recognizer). In order to include distortion in the search, additional information needs to be kept for each node including a word coverage vector, the distortion probability, and an estimate of the future cost. Nodes are connected to previous nodes only if the intersection of the word coverage vectors is empty. The future cost estimate is used so that all nodes can be pruned together (A-star search). This limits the search space enough so that unconstrained reordering can be used without running out of memory, but there is a possibility that the search will not be able to select a final path that covers all input words. In the case of a search failure, the search is restarted using improved future cost heuristics from the previous pass.

See [9] for future details.

5 Experiments

5.1 Corpus

Experiments have been carried out using IWSLT 2005 BTEC[1] (Chinese to English).

The BTEC is a small corpus translation task. Table 1 shows the main statistics of the used data, namely number of sentences, words, vocabulary, and means sentence lengths for each language.

[1] www.slt.atr.jp/IWSLT2005

Table 1. BTEC corpus, Chinese to English and Arabic to English Training, Development and Test data sets. The developments data has 16 references.

BTEC	Chinese	Arabic	English
Training Sentences		20,000	
Running Words	176,199	180,075	189,927
Vocabulary	8,687	15,371	6,870
Singletons	4006	8319	2888
IWSLT'04 Sentences		500	
Running Words	3681	3597	3837
IWSLT'05 Sentences		506	
Running Words	3918	3562	3909

5.2 Preprocessing and Training

The training data was preprocessed using standard tools. Chinese Sentences was segmented into separate words using ICTCAS[2], and English ones was tokenized with TokenizeE in the EGYPT1.0[3]. The word alignment has been carried out in both translation directions using GIZA++[4]. Afterwards, five iterations for models IBM1 and HMM, and three iterations for IBM3 and IBM4, were performed for the combination (intersection and union sets) of source-target (s2t) and target-source (t2s) alignments.

Table 2. Vocabulary of phrases for alignment from dual directions

Alignment	sUt	s2t	sAt
Chinese – English	122,912	288,290	294,452
Arabic - English	186,320	421,258	422,240

The vocabulary of tuples was pruned out using different pruning techniques, mainly based on limiting bilingual units to those:

(1) Consisting on the N best translation candidates;
(2) Occurring a minimum number of times in the train set;
(3) Not exceeding a size threshold (number of words on each side of the unit);
(4) Not exceeding a fertility threshold (difference in source-side and target-side number of words).

Once the models were computed, sets of optimal log-linear coefficients were estimated for each translation direction and system configuration according to log-linear maximum entropy framework. For all these optimizations, a development data set of 500 sentences was used. It was independent from both the training data and test data.

In order to evaluate the translation model performance and the additional features' contributions to the translation accuracy and efficient, three different system configurations were considered:

---

2 mtgroup.ict.ac.cn/~zhp/ICTCLAS.htm
3 www.clsp.jhu.edu/ws99/projects/mt/toolkit
4 www.fjoch.com/GIZA++.html

Baseline system: The baseline considers the models and the phrase lengths mentioned in the subsection above.

Full system: all additional models were considered. At the same time, using the reordering and pruning strategies in the course of decoding.

Table 3 Shows the coefficient gotten from our developments data.

Table 3. The different coefficient applied in the three system

System	λ_{LM}	λ_{wp}	λ_{fl}	λ_{bl}
baseline	-	-	-	-
full	0.48	0.28	0.48	0.13

5.3 Results

Finally, the Chinese test sentences were translated into English by using the computed model, additional models and the estimated optimal coefficients for the SMT system.

Table 4 shows the translation results of baseline, reinforced and full system using BTEC corpus.

Table 4. Results for the Chinese to English translation system using different features

Phrase-based		WER(%)	PER(%)	BLEU(%)	NIST
Chinese-	B	45.2	37.5	48.2	8.60
English	B+F	42.8	35.8	50.7	9.21
Arabic-	B	38.2	33.0	50.3	8.92
English	B+F	37.2	32.3	52.7	9.25

6 Conclusions

We described a phrased-based system in this paper. The translation model is set in the log-linear maximum entropy framework using several additional features, what's more, the decoding of the SMT is based on a beam search with reordering and distortion. The use of reordering search and distortion has allowed efficiently perform a search with low cost. Experiments prove that these methods can improve the translation accuracy and efficiency and get better results in Chinese to English while keeping reasonable the number of phrases.

In the future, we will analyze the more complex combination of different features, explore more supplicated reordering search strategies in order to improve the ability of the decoder, and investigating the use of heuristic to better prune out the search space.

References

1. Zens, R., Och, F., Ney, H.: Phrase-based Statistical Machine Translation. Advances in Artificial Intelligence, volume LNAI 2479, Sringer Verlag ,(2002)18-32
2. Zens, R., Och, F., Ney, H.: Improvements in Phrase-based Statistical Machine Translation. Proc. of the Human Language Technology Conference, HLT-NAACL'2004, (2004)257-264

3. Brown, P., Cocke, J., Della Pietra, S. , et al: A Statistical Approach to Machine Translation, Computational Linguistics, vol. 16, no. 2, (1990)79-85
4. Koehn, P., Och, F. , Marcu, D.: Statistical Phrase-based Translation. Proc. of the Human Language Technology Conference, HLT-NAACL'2003 (2003)
5. Och, F., Ney, H.: Discriminative Training and Maximum Entropy Models for Statistical Machine Translation. 40th Annual Meeting of the Association for Computational Linguistics, (2002) 295-302
6. Berger, A., Della Pietra,S. , Della Pietra, V.: A Maximum Entropy Approach to Natural to Natural Language Processing. Computational Linguistics, 22(1): (1996) 39-72
7. Och, F.J., Gildea, D., Khudanpur, S., et.al: A Smorgasbord of Features for Statistical Machine Translation. Proc. of the Human Language Techonology Conference, HLT-NAACl'2004, (2004) 161-168
8. Och, F., Ney, H.: The Alignment Template Approach to Statistical Machine Translation. Computational Linguistics, vol. 30, no. 4, (2004) 417-449
9. Koehn, P.: Pharaoh: A Beam Search Decoder for Phrase-based Statistical Machine Translation Models. Proc. of the 6th Conf. of Association for Machine Translation in the America, (2004) 115-124
10. Grego, J.M., Marino, J., Dispert, A.de: An Ngram-based Statistical Machine Translation Decoder. EUROSPEECH 05(2005)
11. Andreas Stolcke: SRILM - An Extensible Language Modeling Toolkit, in Proc. Intl. Conf. Spoken Language Processing, Denver, Colorado(2002)

Smart E-Learning Using Recommender System

Nuanwan Soonthornphisaj[1], Ekkawut Rojsattarat[2], and Sukanya Yim-ngam[2]

[1] Department of Computer Science, Faculty of Science, Kasetsart University, Bangkok, Thailand
fscinws@ku.ac.th

[2] Department of Computer Science, Faculty of Resource and Environment, Kasetsart University Sri-racha campus, Chonburi, Thailand
ekkawut@src.ku.ac.th, sukanya@src.ku.ac.th

Abstract. We develop an e-learning web application that integrates the materials recommender system to facilitate the learners during the learning process. The system evaluates each learner via the quiz generator by randomly selecting a set of questions that are created by the instructor. Our smart e-learning system helps instructors to create and maintain both compulsory materials and questions. We implemented the system at the faculty of Resource and Environment, Kasetsart University at Sri-racha campus and found that our system got a very good response from the instructors and learners. Furthermore, we propose the global e-learning framework using web service that has an ability to aggregate the recommended materials from other e-learning web sites and predicts more suitable materials to learners.

1 Introduction

Recommender systems use the opinions of a community of users to help individuals in that community more effectively identify content of interest from a potentially overwhelming set of choices [1]. One of the most successful technologies for recommender systems, called *collaborative filtering*, has been developed and improved over the past decade to the point where a wide variety of algorithms exist for generating recommendations. We propose a smart e-learning web application that allows all learners to collaborate their expertise in order to predict the most suitable learning materials to each learner. Our system has two main features which are the quiz generator and the material feeder. The quiz generator creates a set of questions from the warehouse with three difficulty levels (beginner, medium, expert). The material feeder module provides two sets of materials which are the compulsory set and the recommended set. Note that the compulsory materials are learning documents given by an instructor in each subject.

Furthermore, we introduce the recommender system in the context of web service, since we believe that the global e-learning system could bring more benefit from a larger set of co-operative learners which make more predictive power on the recommender system.

D.-S. Huang, K. Li, and G.W. Irwin (Eds.): ICIC 2006, LNAI 4114, pp. 518 – 523, 2006.

The following section presents our smart e-learning framework. Section 3 discusses recommender systems. The recommender web service is introduced in Section 4. Finally, Section 5 presents some concluding remarks.

2 Smart E-Learning Framework

Web-based learning environment plays an important role for today's education. Currently, learners have more options in studying compared to the previous time. Many e-learning applications have been developed such as Virtual-U [2] and Web-CT [3]. In a virtual classroom, the instructor provides an online course which consists of the learning materials, self quiz and learning path. Typical learners study course material and do self quiz in order to evaluate their knowledge. The most important thing for the success learners is related to the quality of the learning materials which are not only depend on the given materials provided by the instructor but also depend on other learners recommendations. Our smart e-learning system applies the collaborative filtering approach that has an ability to predict the most suitable documents to the learner. All learners have the chance to introduce new material by uploading the documents to the server or pointing out the web link from the Internet and rate the currently available materials.

As shown in Figure 1, the instructors are responsible for the course materials preparation and creating a set of questions for the quiz. In order to create the question, our system provides an easy to use tool for the instructor to create the multiple choices and solution. The instructors can indicate the level of difficulty for each question. The quiz generator's function is to randomly select a set of questions based on the difficulty level to generate the quiz for each lesson. The learning path for each learner depends on his/her quiz's score.

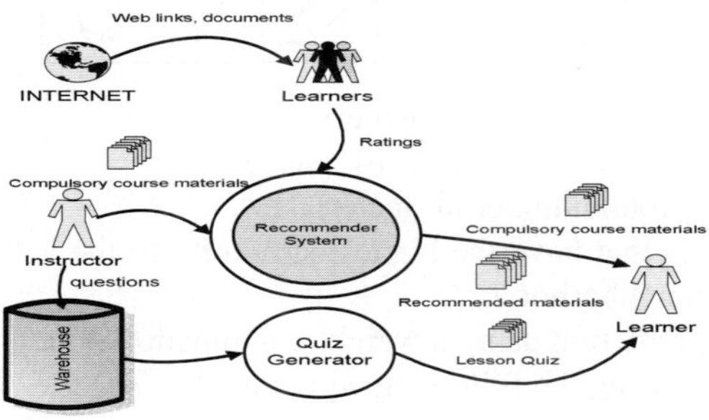

Fig. 1. The smart e-learning framework

3 The Recommender System

The recommender system is a software agent that gathers the rating information from all users in order to predict or recommend the most suitable materials to each user. There are two traditional approaches for constructing recommender systems. The recommender systems were originally defined as ones in which "people provide recommendations as inputs, the system then aggregates and directs to appropriate recipients" [1]. Numerous recommender systems have been built for both research and applications. The algorithms used in these systems can be categorized into 2 categories which are collaborative filtering and content-based filtering. The concept of collaborative filtering is to use "word of mouth" process. It means that each user provides the system with the evaluations of items that may be used to build a profile of her likes or dislikes. The system aggregates all of the evaluations and creates top N lists of most popular items.

Most of the collaborative filtering systems trace their roots to Tapestry [4]. It is an active collaborative filtering system in which a user takes a direct role in the process of deciding whose evaluations are used to provide his recommendations. The system operates the set of email and Usenet news group and allows the user to create rules or queries that indicate their preferences.

Another way to do collaborative filtering called automated collaborative filtering. Its algorithm can automatically handle the process of user personalization. It means that the algorithm forms a set of individualized neighborhood for each user. The neighborhood consists of a subset of users whose opinions are highly correlated with the individual user. There are several systems such as GroupLens project [5, 6] MovieLens [7, 8, 9], Video Recommender [10], Audio CD recommender [11].

Table 1. The algorithm for recommending materials in e-learning system

Algorithm: Neighborhood-based

Step 1: Weight all users with respect to the similarity of the active learner using Pearson correlation between their rating vector (see the following equation)

$$P_{a,u} = \frac{\sum_{i=1}^{m}(r_{a,i} - \bar{r}_a)\times(r_{u,i} - \bar{r}_u)}{\sqrt{\sum_{i=1}^{m}(r_{a,i} - \bar{r}_a)^2 \times \sum_{i=1}^{m}(r_{u,i} - \bar{r}_u)^2}}$$

Where $r_{a,i}$ is the rating given to material i by user a

r_a is the mean rating given by user a

m is the total number of materials

Step 2: Select n users that have the highest similarity to the active learner in order to form the neighborhood.

Step 3: Compute a prediction using a weight combination obtained from the neighborhood using the following equation

$$p_{a,i} = \bar{r}_a + \frac{\sum_{u=1}^{n}(r_{u,i} - \bar{r}_u)\times P_{a,u}}{\sum_{u=1}^{n} P_{a,u}}$$

Where $p_{a,i}$ is the prediction for the active learner a for material i

$p_{a,u}$ is the similarity between the active learner a and u

n is the number of learners in the neighborhood

The problem space of the collaborative filtering can be defined as a matrix of users versus items. Each cell represents user's rating on a specific item. [12]. The objective of the algorithm is to predict the value of the empty cell.

We employ an algorithm called neighborhood-based [8] to do material prediction for each learner. The concept of the algorithm is to select a subset of learner based on their similarity to the active learner. Then do the weight aggregation using all ratings in order to generate the prediction to the active learner. The detail of neighborhood-based algorithm can be found in Table 1.

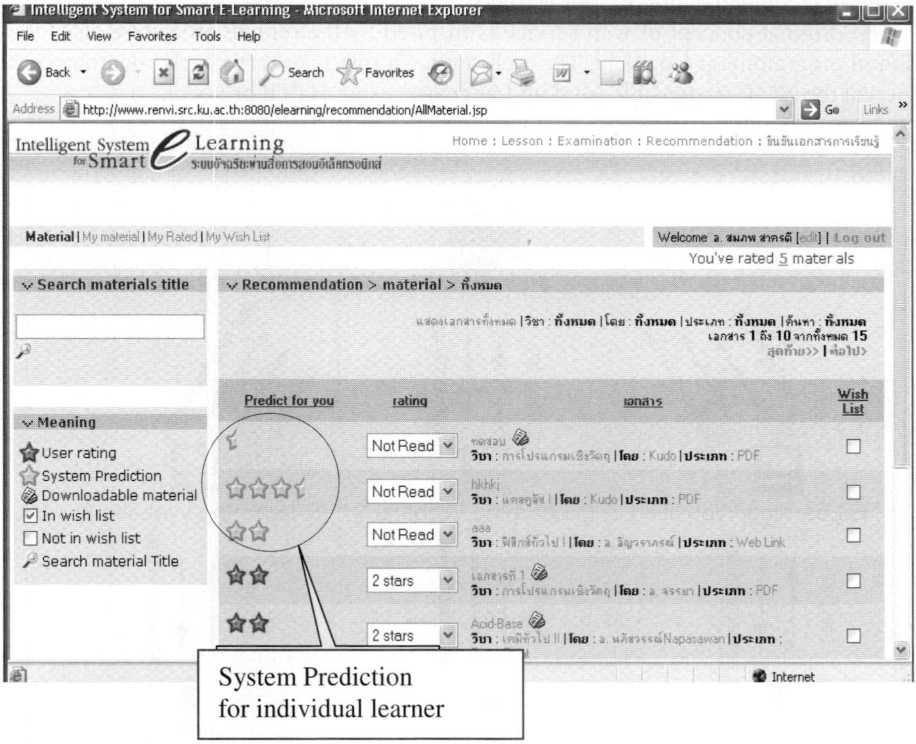

Fig. 2. The smart e-learning Web application

4 Global E-Learning Using Web Service

In order to make the recommender system more practical, we implement the recommender system web service in order to extend the e-learning system from local learners to global learners. As shown in Figure 3, the web service is responsible for cooperate all learners' recommendations from different e-learning websites. First, each e-learning website administrator must register to be the member of the recommender system web service. The web service maintains the database of materials in order to do the collaborative filtering process. The advantage of using web service is to provide more chance to each learner to get better quality of materials. The web service will facilitate all e-learning web sites to get the recommended materials for their learners. These web-sites don't need to implement the collaborative filtering algorithm and maintain any of their learner's ratings. Therefore, it is very convenient for those web-sites.

The global e-learning web service provides a wide variety of items to learners such as the text book recommendation. We investigate the web service performance by connecting our system to the AMAZON web site (www.amazon.com) in order to get the book recommendation for our learners.

The original concept of web service is inspired by the remote procedure call function in programming language. The web service's role is to serve each e-learning web site via the XML (Extensible Markup Language) using HTTP protocol.

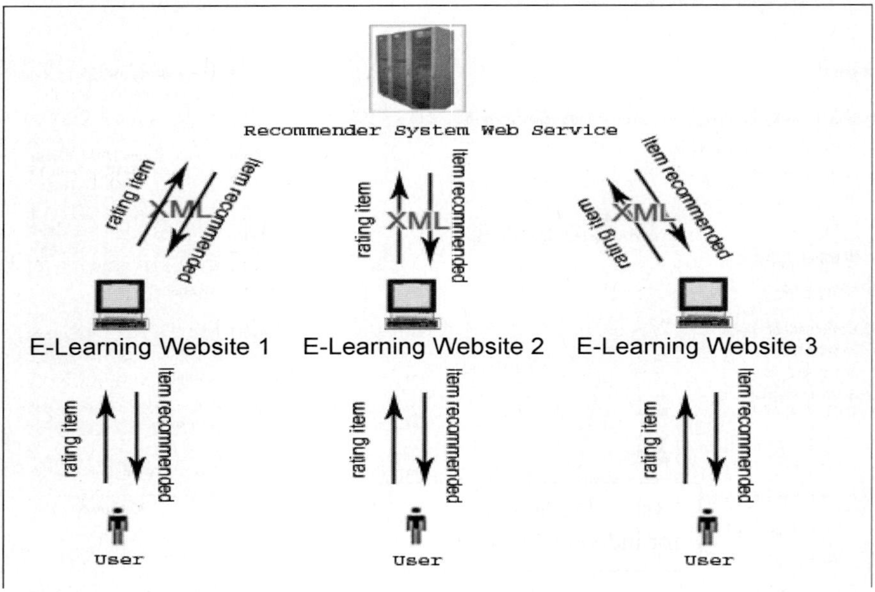

Fig. 3. The recommender system web service architechture

5 Discussion and Future Work

The global smart e-learning system is a new vision for the e-learning. Learners will be benefited from this system. They have more chance to obtain better quality of materials and a wide variety of recommended items. The database of material maintained by the Web service can be used for data mining project that will enhance the performance of all e-learning web site members. We plan to extend our work to the data mining discipline in the near future.

Acknowledgment

This work is supported by Kasetsart University Research and Development Institute (KURDI).

References

1. Resnick, P., Varian, H. R.: Recommender Systems. Communication of ACM 40, (1997) 56–58
2. Groeneboer,T.-C.C., Stockley, D.: Virtual-u: A Collaborative Uodel for Online Learning Environments. Proceeding of the Second International Conference on Computer Support for Collaborative Learning, Toronto, Canada, December (1997)
3. Webct, available on August 2002. http://www.webct.com/
4. Goldberg, D., Nichols, D., Oki, B.M., Terry, D.: Using Collaborative Filtering to Weave an Information Tapestry. Communications of the ACM 35(12): (1992) 61-70
5. Resnick, P., Iacovou, N. Suchak, M., Bergstrom, P., Riedl, J.: GroupLens: An Open Architecture for Collaborative Filtering of Netnews, Proceeding of ACM CSCW' 94 Conference on Computer Supported Cooperative work.(1994) 175-186
6. Konstan, J.A., Miller, B.N., Malz, D., Herlocker, J.L., Gordon, L.R., Riedl, J. GroupLens: Applying Collaborative Filtering to Usenet News. Communications of the ACM (1997)
7. Dahlen, B.J., konstan, J.A., Herlocker, J.L., Good, N., Borchers, A., Riedl, J.: Jump-Starting MovieLens: User Benefits of Starting a Collaborative Filtering System with "Dead Data", University of Minesota, (1998)
8. Herlocker, J.L., Konstan J.A. Borchers, A., Riedl J.: An Algorithmic Framework for Performing Collaborative Filtering. Proceedings of the 22nd Annual International Conference on Research and Development in Information Retrieval. (1999) 230-237
9. Sarwar, B.M., Konstan, J.A., Borchers, A., Herlocker J., Miller B., Redl, J.: Using Filtering Agents to Improve Prediction Quality in the GroupLens Research Collaborative Filtering System. Proceeding of the ACM Conference on Computer Supported Cooperative Work. (1998) 345-354
10. Hill, W., Stead, L., Rosenstein, M., Furnas, G.: Recommending and Evaluation Choices in a Virtual Community of Use, pp. 194-201. Proceeding of the Conference on Human Factors in computing Systems. (1995) 194-201
11. Shardanand, U., Maes, P.: Social Information Filtering: Algorithms for Automating Word of Mouth, pp. 210-217. Proceeding of the 1995 Conference on Human Factors in Computing Systems. (1995) 210-217
12. Breese, J., Heckerman, D., Kadie, C.: Empirical Analysis of Predictive Algorithms for Collaborative Filtering. Proceeding of 14th Conference on uncertainty in Artificial Intelligence. (1998)

Strategic Learning in the Sealed-Bid Bargaining Mechanism by Particle Swarm Optimization Algorithm

Xiaobo Zhu, Qian Yu, and Xianjia Wang

Institute of Systems Engineering, Wuhan University, Wuhan 430072, China
kean78@tom.com

Abstract. The learning behaviours of buyers and sellers in the sealed-bid Bargaining Mechanism were studied under the assumption of bounded rationality. The learning process of the agents is modelled by particle swarm optimization (PSO) algorithm. In the proposed model, there are two populations of buyers and sellers with limited computation ability and they were randomly matched to deal repeatedly. The agent's bidding strategy is assumed to be a linear function of his value of trading item and each agent adjusts his strategy in repeated deals by imitating the most successful member in his population and by own past experience. Such learning pattern by PSO is closer to the behaviours of human beings in real life. Finally, the simulated results show that the bidding strategies of the agents in both populations will converge near the theoretical linear equilibrium solutions (LES).

1 Introduction

Learning by adaptive agents has been one of the hot topics of economic research during past years, the learning or adaptive process of the agents has extensively been found in the laboratory [1, 2] and in human society. A good many arguments have focus on the assumption of rational agents who have enough information and ability to respond optimally to the given information. In many real circumstances the agents are often not capable of satisfying such rigid assumption for rationality.

In this paper, we study the learning behaviors of bounded rational agents in the sealed-bid bargaining mechanism which has been analyzed extensively in vast literatures from a theoretical and an empirical point of view. Chatterjee and Samuelson [3] firstly established a simple model for the bargaining mechanism and derived the Linear Bayesian Equilibrium Solution (LES) and LES has been a criterion for further research. Myerson [4] had proved that LES could produce more profit than other equilibriums. Radner and Schotter [5] found that bids of the participants in the laboratory differ from the LES at the beginning, but their bidding strategies were adjusted over time. Daniel and Seale [6] also conducted similar experiments and simulated by a reinforcement-base model of adaptive learning, they found that the agents learned from own past deals. In [5, 6], each agent mostly learned only from own past experience, however, Dawid [7] proposed a learning model of a two-population genetic algorithm, the agents choose their bidding strategies by imitating successful behavior and adding innovations triggered by random errors.

D.-S. Huang, K. Li, and G.W. Irwin (Eds.): ICIC 2006, LNAI 4114, pp. 524 – 529, 2006.

In real human society, the learning behaviors of the individuals commonly include two aspects: one is individual learning from own past experience, another is learning from population by imitating the successful individual. Therefore, in order to getting better behavior explains for the agents, we will combine these two aspect's learning behaviors. We introduce Particle Swarm Optimization (PSO) algorithm into our strategic learning model. PSO was first proposed by Kennedy and Eberhart [8, 9] in 1995, which was inspired by the swarming behavior as is displayed by a flock of birds, a school of fish, or even human social behavior being influenced by other individuals. According to PSO, the behavior of each individual is affected by either the best local or the best global individual to help it fly through a hyperspace, so PSO is very fit for description of the learning behaviors of human beings.

Furthermore, some have to be mentioned in our model that we deal with a population of buyers and a population of sells rather than single buyer and seller; the trade between buyer and seller is repeated rather than once; the agents adjust their strategies every other some round. We will model and simulate such learning process.

2 The Sealed-Bid Bargaining Mechanism

The 1:1 sealed-bid bargaining mechanism was firstly modeled by Chatterjee and samuelson in 1983. In this model, a seller has a single object that he may sell to a buyer if an acceptable price. Assume that V_b denotes the buyer's private reservation value of the item and V_s denotes the seller's private reservation value of the item. It is assumed that each trade's reservation value is a random variable whose value is uniformly contained in interval of $[0,1]$ and the distributions are common knowledge to both traders. Simultaneously the seller submits ask P_s and the buyer submits bid P_b. Trade occurs with no delay at the price $P = (P_b + P_s)/2$, if $P_b \geq P_s$, otherwise negotiations are broken off.

When assume that the bid of each trader is a linear function of his private reservation value of the item, the Bayesian Nash equilibrium solution (LES) for this sealed-bid mechanism with two-sided incomplete information was obtained as follows: $P_b(\mathrm{v_b}) = 1/12 + 2/3V_b$; $P_s(\mathrm{v_s}) = 1/4 + 2/3V_s$.

3 Our Adaptive Learning Model by PSO Algorithm

PSO algorithm firstly initializes a population of particles randomly in a D-dimensional space, each particle whose position is denoted by $X_i = (X_{i1}, X_{i2}, ..., X_{iD})$ moves in the search space with a velocity vector $V_i = (v_{i1}, v_{i2}, ..., v_{iD})$. Moreover, each particle contains a memory that stores its own best position $P_i = (p_{i1}, p_{i2}, ..., p_{iD})$ and a global best position $P_g = (p_{g1}, p_{g2}, ..., p_{gD})$ which is obtained through its neighbor particles.

Intuitively, the information about good solutions spreads through the swarm, and thus the particles tend to move to good areas in the search space. For each movement, the updates of the velocity and position are determined by following two equations: $v_{id} = w * v_{id} + c_1 * rand() * (p_{id} - x_{id}) + c_2 * rand() * (p_{gd} - x_{id})$ and $x_{id} = x_{id} + v_{id}$ where w is an inertia weight value,ï c_1, c_2 determine the significance of P_i and P_g, and $rand()$ ïare random numbers between 0 and 1. Such learning pattern by PSO is closer to the behaviours of human beings in real life. So it is quite reasonable that PSO algorithm is applied to our learning model which is presented as follows:

1) Setting the Initial Circumstance:

There are two populations of agents called buyers and sellers. Both populations contain the same number denoted by N of agents; Each buyer randomly gets an initial linear bidding strategy which is denoted by $B_i^b = \left(a_i^b,\ b_i^b\right)$, $a_i^b \in [0,1], b_i^b \in [0,1], i \in [1, N]$ and $a_i^b + b_i^b < 1$ (otherwise, the profit of agent maybe negative), similarly the strategy of each seller is denoted by $B_j^s = \left(a_j^s,\ b_j^s\right)$, $a_j^s \in [0,1]$, $b_j^s \in [0,1]$, $j \in [1, N]$; The initial velocity for all agents $V_i^b = (0,0)$, $V_j^s = (0,0)$, and the present best local solution for each agent is defined: $B_{ibest}{}^b = B_i^b$, $B_{jbest}{}^s = B_j^s$.

2) Trading between Buyers and Sellers:

In each round, each agent in the population of buyers is randomly matched to trade with a seller in the population of sellers by the sealed-bid bargaining mechanism, and a period consists of m rounds. Both the buyers' private reservation value of the trading item V_b and the sellers' value V_s are randomly re-produced on the uniform distribution of the interval of $[0,1]$ in each round, and the bid of each buyer P_i^b is calculated by $P_i^b = a_i^b + b_i^b * V^b$, $P_i^b = V^b$ when $P_i^b > V^b$ (otherwise, the profit of agent maybe negative), and the bid of each seller P_j^s is calculated by $P_j^s = a_j^s + b_j^s * V^s$, $P_j^s = V^s$ when $P_j^s < V^s$, and a trade occurs, the profit of the buyer and seller is respectively obtained.

3) Adaptive Learning by PSO:

When the trades of m rounds (a period) have finished, the total profit $A_{ip}{}^b$ of each buyer at $P-th$ period and the total profit $A_{jp}{}^s$ of each seller are calculated, here $A_{ip}{}^b$ and $A_{jp}{}^s$ represent the fitness value. Each agent adjusts his linear bidding strategy for the next period according to the follow algorithm:

(1) Individual learning:

Compare the fitness value (profit) $A_{ibest}{}^b$ of the present best local strategy $B_{ibest}{}^b$ of each buyer with the fitness value $A_{ip}{}^b$ of the present strategy B_i^b, and update the local best strategy $B_{ibest}{}^{b} = B_i^b$ if $A_{ibest}{}^{b} < A_{ip}{}^{b}$; similarly for each seller update the local best strategy $B_{jbest}{}^{s} = B_j^s$ if $A_{jbest}{}^{s} < A_{jp}{}^{s}$.

(2) Learning from population:

We define the global best strategy in the population of buyers $B_g{}^{b} = B_{pbest}{}^{b}$, and the global best strategy for sellers $B_g{}^{s} = B_{pbest}{}^{s}$, where $B_{pbest}{}^{b}$ and $B_{pbest}{}^{s}$ represent separately the strategy of the agent who gains most profit at $P-th$ period rather than in all past period in the population of buyers and sellers. Because we apply PSO algorithm in a game model here, the fitness value of an agent is determined not only by his strategy and bid, but also by his opponent's strategy and bid, the optimal strategy is regarded as the optimal respond to the opponent's current strategy.

(3) Update:

The moving velocity and strategy of the buyer are updated by the equation: $V_i^b = w * V_i^b + c_1 * rand() * (B_{ibest}{}^{b} - B_i^b) + c_2 * rand() * (B_g{}^{b} - B_i^b)$; $B_i^b = B_i^b + V_i^b$.

The moving velocity and strategy of the seller are updated by the equation: $V_j^s = w * V_j^s + c_1 * rand() * (B_{jbest}{}^{s} - B_j^s) + c_2 * rand() * (B_g{}^{s} - B_j^s)$; $B_j^s = B_j^s + V_j^s$.

(4) Termination:

Stop the iteration, if the condition $\underset{i\in[1,N]}{MAX}\left|V_i^b\right| < \lambda, \underset{j\in[1,N]}{MAX}\left|V_j^s\right| < \lambda$ is satisfied which shows the strategy of each agent nearly does not change or iteration number is larger than the maximal iteration number.

4 Simulation Results

We conducted 50 simulation runs under the parameter values: $N = 50$; $m = 50$; $w = 0.2$; $c_1 = c_2 = 2$; $v_{ia}{}^{b}, v_{ib}{}^{b}, v_{ja}{}^{s}, v_{jb}{}^{s} \in [-0.2, 0.2]$, and find that the results of these runs have no marked difference. We present here a series of figures which are produced by the results of a representative experiment and make some interpretations.

Fig.1 shows the initial bidding strategies of all buyers and sellers. Each point in this figure denotes the initial linear strategy B_i^b for buyers and B_j^s for sellers, as mentioned above B_i^b are randomly distributed in the triangle area $X + Y \le 1$, B_j^s are randomly distributed in the rectangle area $\{0 \le X \le 1, 0 \le Y \le 1\}$.

Fig.2 shows the bidding strategies of the agents at the midst of the iteration. From this figure we distinctly find that the beginning scattered points in Fig.1 markedly congregate towards the points of the theoretical equilibrium that is $[1/12, 2/3]$ for buyers and $[1/4, 2/3]$ for sellers, particularly a small portion of all points have assembled near the theoretical equilibrium points.

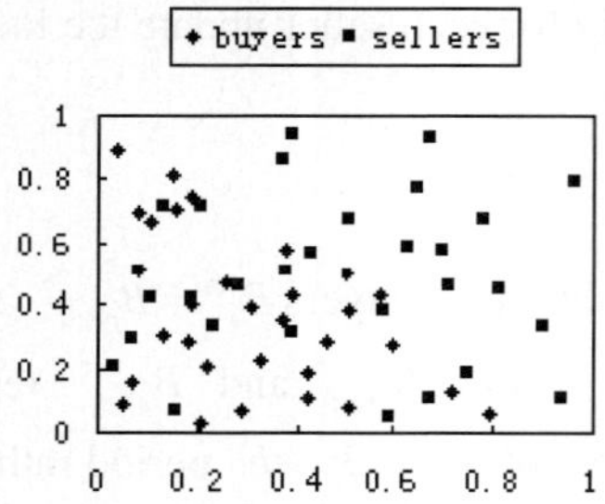

Fig. 1. The Beginning of iteration

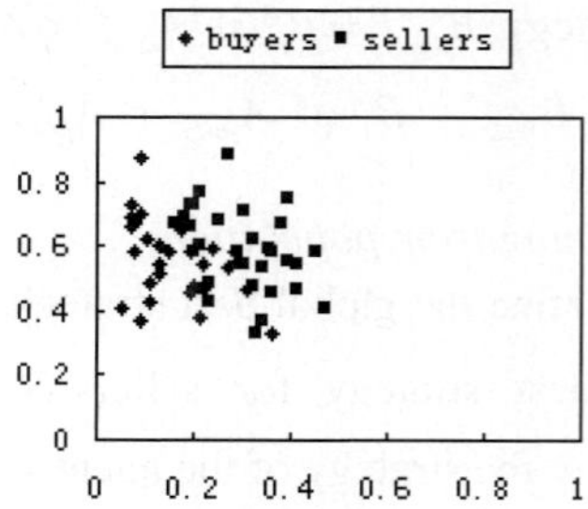

Fig. 2. The midst of iteration

Fig.3 shows the bidding strategies of the agents after the termination of iteration. We can find that the points have almost convergent near the points of the theoretical linear equilibrium. The speed of iteration has some difference in all the 50 simulation runs, and the fastest experiment can accomplish only through 20 periods which consists of 1000 rounds for deal. Furthermore, the equilibrium concept in our learning model is not very rigid, even when the iteration has terminated, the bidding strategy of each agent fluctuates near the equilibrium point. Our interpretation for the fluctuation of the bidding strategy is that the LES is the Bayesian-Nash equilibrium solutions, and the agent using the equilibrium strategy only gains the maximal profit expectably for one game, then the most successful strategy is various at different period, and the existing fluctuation is reasonable.

Fig.4 shows the whole dynamic evolutionary tendency of the bidding strategies in both populations. Each point in this figure denotes the average linear bidding strategy of the agents in the same population at a given period. Firstly, the beginning point of the population of buyers is about $[1/3,1/3]$ which is the center of gravity of the triangle area $X+Y\leq 1$, similarly the beginning point of the population of buyers is about $[1/2,1/2]$ which is the center of gravity of the rectangle area $\{0\leq X\leq 1, 0\leq Y\leq 1\}$. At the sequent periods, the average strategies of both populations move towards the points of the theoretical equilibrium in shape of a

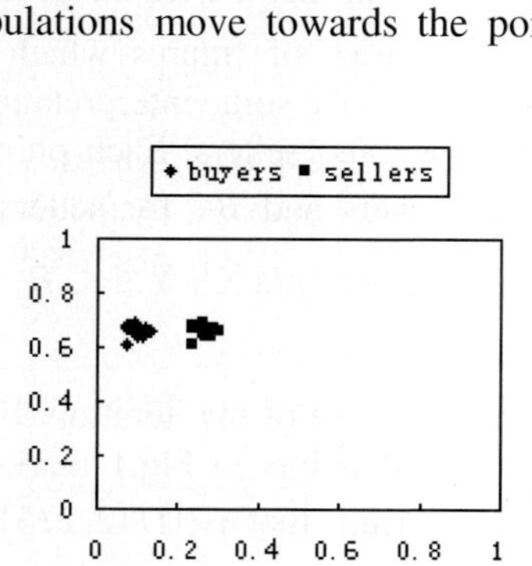

Fig. 3. The termination of iteration

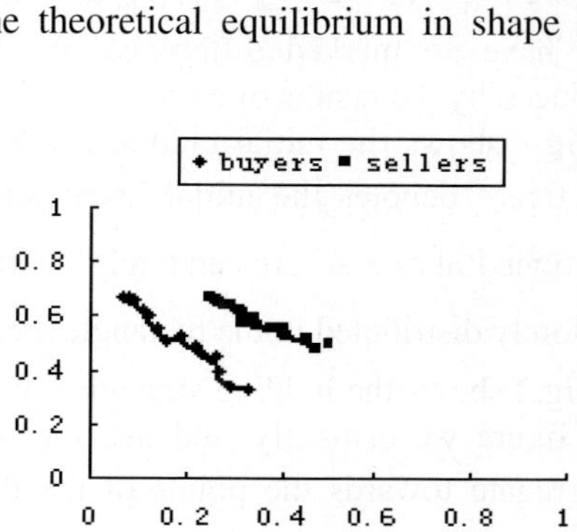

Fig. 4. Evolutionary curve of average strategies

curve. In the earlier periods, the moving curve is more flexural because the most strategies of the agents are scattered very much, and the global best strategy of the imitated agent varies markedly with iteration, then the whole learning direction of population is various, but the moving curve gradually becomes more flat in the late periods as the result of the maturity of the strategies, finally, the average strategies of the agents in both populations respectively converge at LES.

5 Conclusions

In this paper we apply PSO algorithm to simulate the learning behaviors of the buyers and the sellers who are assumed to be bounded rational in the sealed-bid bargaining mechanism. PSO algorithm is not only simple for implement, but more important point is that its idea which combines individual learning from own experience and imitating-learning from population has perfect intelligent presentations for the behaviors of the real life human beings. Our simulated results show that the bidding strategies of the agents in both populations always converge near the theoretical linear equilibrium solutions (LES).

References

1. Huyck, J. V., Battalio, R., Beil, R.: Tacit Coordination Games,Strategic Uncertainty and Coordination Failure. Amer.Econ.Rev. 80(1990) 234–248
2. Huyck, J. V., Battalio, R., Beil, R.: Strategic Uncertainty, Equilibrium Selection Principles and Coordination Failures in Average Opinion Games. Quart.J.Econ.106(1991) 885–910
3. Chaterjee, K., Samuelson, W.: Bargaining under Incomplete Information. Operations Research. 31(1983) 835-851
4. Myerson, R., Chaterjee, K.: Efficient Mechanisms of Bilateral Trading. Journal of Economic Theory. 28(1983) 265-281
5. Radner, R., Schotter, A.: The Sealed-bid Mechanism: An Experimental Study. Journal of Economic Theory. 48(1989) 179-220
6. Daniel, E., Seale, A.: Strategic Play and Adaptive Learning in the Sealed-Bid Bargaining Mechanism. Journal of Mathematical Psychology. 42(1998) 133-166
7. Herbert, D.: On the Convergence of Genetic Learning in a Double Auction Market. Journal of Economic Dynamics & Control. 23(1999) 1545-1567
8. Kennedy, J., Eberhart, R.: Particle Swarm Optimization. Proceedings of the 1995 IEEE International Conference on Neural Networks, Perth, Australia (1995) 1942-1948
9. Eberhart, R., Kennedy, J.: A New Optimizer Using Particle Swarm Theory. Proceedings of the Sixth International Symposium on Micro Machine and Human Science, Nagoya, Japan (1995) 39-44

System on a Chip Implementation of Social Insect Behavior for Adaptive Network Routing

Jin-Ho Ahn[1], Hyunjin Kim[1], Byung In Moon[2], and Sungho Kang[1]

[1] Department of Electrical and Electronic Engineering, Yonsei University,
134 Shinchon-dong, Sodaemun-gu, Seoul, 120-749, Korea
{sominaby, nagicman}@soc.yonsei.ac.kr, shkang@yonsei.ac.kr
[2] School of Electrical Engineering & Computer Science, Kyungpook National University,
1370 Sankyuk-dong, Buk-gu, Daegu, 702-701, Korea
bihmoon@knu.ac.kr

Abstract. In this paper, a new efficient hardware architecture and its implementation for an AntNet-based routing are proposed. This architecture is based on the modified AntNet algorithm, and optimized to the ant packets defined in this paper. The modified AntNet is evaluated by the performance comparisons with the original AntNet algorithm through C-level simulations, and then implemented into RTL design. Consequently, the hardware implementation result of the proposed architecture is described.

1 Introduction

Ant Colony Optimization (ACO) is a kind of artificial model based on social insect behavior, especially ants, to solve optimization problems [1]. Communication network is a major application of ACO. A routing method based on ACO mechanisms has many merits such as adaptability, survivability, and self-organization. Di Caro and Dorigo proposed AntNet applied routing to packet switched data networks [2]. AntNet is an adaptive and distributed routing algorithm using mobile agents, called ants, that mimic the activities of social insects such as communicating with each other by chemical substance called pheromone. According to the simulation results reported in [2], AntNet has shown superior performance with respect to other state-of-the-art algorithms for a wide range of scenarios. However, its efficiency is fully determined by the quality of collected information. An ant's trip time, same as routing time, is the most important factor in determining it. Therefore, it is necessary to minimize and regularize the processing time of an ant packet in each node to get accurate trip time of ants. Also, a rapid routing information update is essential to select the correct routing path of normal data packets to maximize the throughput. According to these requisites, the block to process ants should as much as possible have a hard-wired form like forwarding or classification of packet in a router. In this paper, we present a hardware architecture to realize an AntNet-based routing in practical SoC application. The original AntNet algorithm is simplified and modified for the proposed hardware architecture. To evaluate the efficiency of the modified AntNet algorithm, we compare it with the original algorithm using C-level simulations under the same traffic patterns and topologies.

D.-S. Huang, K. Li, and G.W. Irwin (Eds.): ICIC 2006, LNAI 4114, pp. 530 – 535, 2006.

2 Hardware Implementation

The proposed architecture is mainly based on the AntNet algorithm depicted in [2]. We call the architecture "Stigmergy Engine (SE)" which means a dedicated hardware modeling of ecology. A top block diagram of SE is shown in Fig. 1 (b). The structure is designed only to handle ant packets as defined in Fig. 1 (a) and is optimized to minimize and regulate the processing time of an ant. It consists of 4 major sub-blocks excluding external interface blocks. We developed the SE to fit system on a chip peripheral system based on ARM920T microprocessor and AMBA bus specification ver. 2.0 [3]. The SE is an AMBA master module, and connects to AHB bus. Therefore, all address and data have 32bit width. A user can control all sub-blocks with register configuration using a controller including an APB interface, such as UART. An ant packet is 160byte in size. The organization of an ant packet is as follows:

- *Type* indicates whether the packet is a forward ant or a backward ant.
- *sNode* denotes the address of the start node that an ant is produced.
- *dNode* denotes the address of the end node to which an ant goes.
- *pNodeOdr* indicates the order of the nodes that an ant visits on the way to a destination node. The value starts from zero.
- *tNodeNum* indicates the total number of the nodes that an ant visits.
- *intNode* denotes the address of the nodes that an ant visits.

The time information at all nodes is synchronized by a network time protocol, such as SNTP (Simple Network Time Protocol). We currently use the protocol based on SNTP ver. 4 [4], which configures the time information by 64bit size and 200ps resolution. A probability entry is set to 1byte size for efficient calculations.

Sellink is a unit to select a next node using the probability values of a routing table at a current node. Its detailed functional procedure is depicted in Fig. 1 (c). Sellink uses the probability data of a routing table from external memory.

The reinforcement calculation flow in Setrfm block is shown in Fig. 1 (d). A reinforcement value allows us to speculate the quality of each link, and set the amount of varying probability of a routing table. The equation for a reinforcement value, *r*, is shown in (1) and (2).

$$r' = norm(curCost - bCost) \,. \tag{1}$$

$$r = (255 - r')/C_{res} \,. \tag{2}$$

In Eq. (1), *bCost* means the best trip time experienced by the forward ants traveling the link between a next node, *n*, and a destination node, *d*. *curCost* means the current trip time on the same path. A trip time is obtained by determining the difference between a visiting time of a current node and that of a destination node. *bCost* is the local traffic model data stated in [2]. The difference between *curCost* and *bCost* is normalized to a predefined reinforcement level. However, *r'* only indicates the absolute difference of a trip time regardless of relative quality of trip time. The resolution value, C_{res} in Eq. (2), is induced to weigh *r'* to solve the problem,. If the *bCost* that is used to get *r'* increases, C_{res} decreases simultaneously. As the amount of varying C_{res} in proportion to *bCost* is variable according to practical network conditions, we parameterized it to change easily. If *bCost* is not updated during the given time threshold, it is initialized. This helps to raise the reliability of *bCost*. The limitation of *curCost* by size threshold also provides a reduction of calculation time and hardware size. The probability entries that have the same destination node are updated by the procedure shown in Fig. 1 (e). Topctrl block controls local functional blocks and other glue logics through the results of parsing ant packets. The control flow consists of FSM including five stages and is depicted in Fig. 1 (f).

- *Start*: If the ant function is allowed to activate, a forward ant is generated, and transmitted to a next node.
- *Forwarding*: The forwarding operation happens if a current node is not a starting node. *pNodeOdr* and *tNodeNum* of a current forward ant increase by one. Also, current node address and time, *intNode* and *visTime*, are inserted into the ant. Then the new ant is sent to a next node selected at a Sellink block.
- *Destination*: If a current node is a destination node, a forward ant changes into a backward ant as soon as *pNodeOdr* and *tNodeNum* increase. The backward ant starts to return to a source node with the routing information.
- *Backwarding*: A backward ant traces along the nodes which a forward ant has visited until it arrives at a source node. On the way to the source node, a routing table and local traffic model at the visited nodes are changed to some degree according to the routing information.
- *Source*: If a backward ant reaches a source node, the ant vanishes after updating a routing table and traffic model of the node.

3 Performance Evaluation and Conclusion

The algorithm for hardware implementation is evaluated through the comparison with the original AntNet on topologies having various network conditions. Test topologies presented in Fig. 2 are the same as those used to verify the original AntNet to provide as identical conditions as possible. We assume the network states as follows.

- *Normal*: all traffic is equally distributed among nodes.
- *Biasing*: the trip time of a specific path to destination is shorter than others.
- *Heavy*: all network traffic is uniformly distributed as for the normal state, but the amount of traffic is so heavy that the trip time between nodes takes at least 10 times longer than normal.

The metric used for the comparison is the dynamics of probabilities within a routing table at each node. We primary monitored the variation of routing probabilities at a source node. The update number means the number of changing routing probabilities at the source node. In the simulation, we assumed that the network states changed sequentially to a normal, biasing, and heavy. Ant packets were generated at the source node periodically. The maximum number of ants moving concurrently on the whole topology was 30.

First, we simulated in the case that the source node was node 0, and destination was node 5 on SimpleNet. Simulation results presented the variation of the routing probabilities of the above three paths at node 0.

The network condition started a normal state. If the update number at node 0 reached 500, the state changed into a biasing. Finally the biasing state became a heavy from 1000. In a normal network state, the trip time between nodes is nearly same in

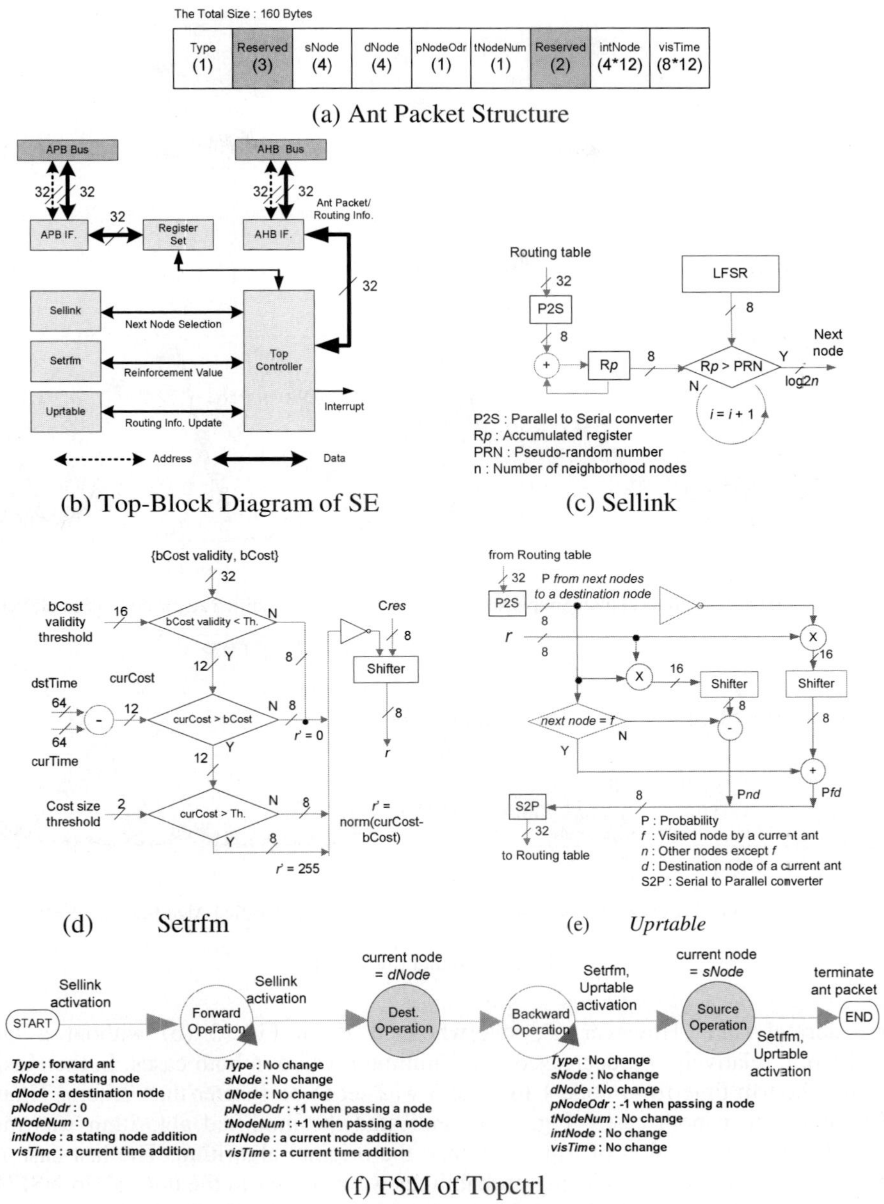

Fig. 1. Hardware Implementation of AntNet

all links. Therefore, there are two paths having the best trip time. One is the path via 0-2-4-5, and the other is via 0-7-6-5. Ants will prefer one of two paths rather than the path via node 1. The oscillation of graph means the competition among paths. If the difference of routing quality among paths decreases, the probabilities will oscillate more. In Fig. 3 (a), P_{25} and P_{75}, having the same trip time, oscillated continuously in

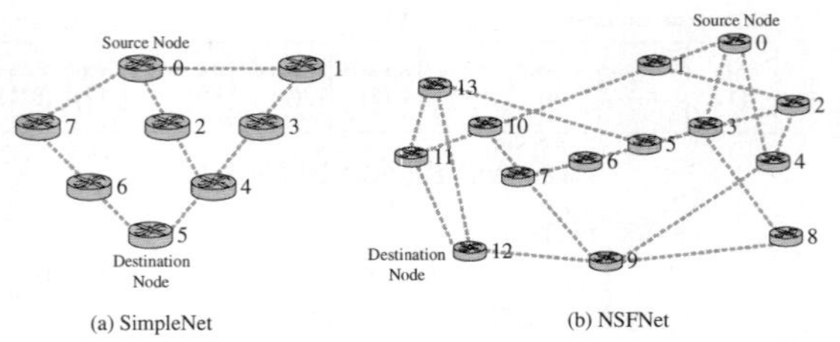

Fig. 2. Test Topology

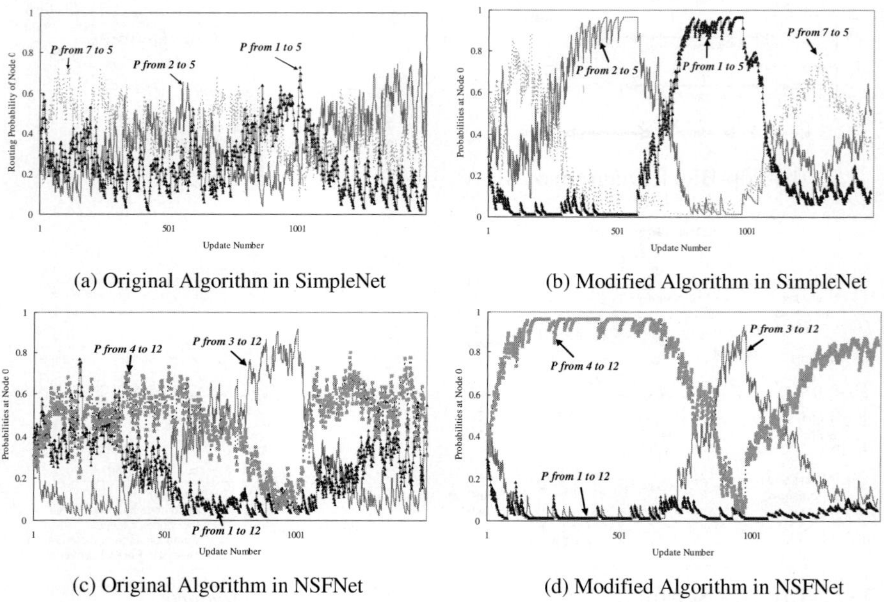

Fig. 3. Simulation Results

the normal state. However, P_{25} overwhelmed P_{75} in Fig. 3 (b) without a large oscillation relatively. P_{15} decreased at its minimum value in both cases. In the biasing mode, the trip time from node 1 to node 5 was set to be shorter than others. Though P_{15} increased in both cases, Fig. 3 (b) indicated the modified algorithm was more sensitive to the variation of trip times than the original algorithm. The last case is a heavy state. The traces of routing probabilities were similar to the normal. In NSFNet, the source node was node 0, and the destination was node 12. The path via 0-4-9-12 has the smallest number of nodes visited to reach the destination node. As expected, both algorithms selected the optimal path clearly in the normal and heavy state. In the biasing mode, we diminished the trip time of the path via 0-3-5-6-7-9-12. The results are shown in Fig. 3 (c) and (d). The RTL design of the modified AntNet was verified by Seamless HW/SW co-verification tool of Mentor Graphics. The results of hardware implementation are summarized in Fig. 4. The overall gate counts of the architecture including register sets were about 85K under 100MHz operating clock and TSMC 0.25μm CMOS technology. The register set consisted of 16 32bit-registers and some glue logics. In Fig. 4, we assumed the time to wait for system bus arbitrations and memory accesses is 0. On the other hand, the architecture has been developed to change easily as the AntNet-based routing algorithms evolve continuously. In summary, the proposed hardware architecture can provide high reliability of routing information by reducing and regularizing the processing time of ants.

- System clock : 100MHz
- m : # of neighborhood nodes
- n : # of destination nodes
- * : Not include interface time with an arbiter and ext. memory
- R : Read, W : Write
- F : Forward ant, B : Backward ant

<table>
<tr><th>Blocks</th><th>Gate Count (m = 16)</th><th>Ant Processing Time* (ns)</th><th>Mem. Size</th></tr>
<tr><td>AHB Interface</td><td>2K</td><td>(R) 50 (W) 60</td><td rowspan="8">m*n+ 4*n Bytes</td></tr>
<tr><td>APB Interface</td><td>0.5K</td><td>-</td></tr>
<tr><td>Register Sets</td><td>15K</td><td>-</td></tr>
<tr><td>Topctrl</td><td>43.5K</td><td>(F)240 (B)260</td></tr>
<tr><td>Sellink</td><td>5K</td><td>m*10 + 40 (max.)</td></tr>
<tr><td>Setrfm</td><td>8K</td><td>80</td></tr>
<tr><td>Uprtable</td><td>11K</td><td>m*10 + 100</td></tr>
<tr><td>Total</td><td>85K</td><td>(F) m*10 + 440
(B) m*10 + 770</td></tr>
</table>

Fig. 4. Summary of Implementation Results

References

1. Bonabeau, E., Dorigo, M., Theraulaz, G.: Inspiration for Optimization from Social Insect Behavior. Nature, Vol. 406 (2000) 39-42
2. Caro, G. D., Dorigo, M.: AntNet: Distributed Stigmergetic Control for Communications Networks. Journal of Artificial Intelligence Research 9 (1998) 317-365
3. ARM IHI 0011A, AMBA (Rev 2) Specification, ARM Limited (1999)
4. RFC-2030 : SNTPv4 for IPv4 and IPv6 and OSI (1996)

Authoritative Server's Impact on Domain Name System's Performance and Security

Yao Wang, Ming-Zeng Hu, Bin Li, and Bo-Ru Yan

Research Center of Computer Network and Information Security Technology, Harbin Institute of Technology, Harbin 150001, Heilongjiang, China
wangyao@hit.edu.cn

Abstract. The Domain Name System (DNS) is the most crucial infrastructure for mapping human-readable host names to the corresponding IP addresses and providing the routing information of Email. Comparing with the top-level domains (TLD) such as the root servers, the local authoritative servers are more vulnerable to device failures and malicious attacks. This paper described the existence condition of authoritative servers and presented a novel domain measurement tool named DNSAuth to collect the information of local authoritative servers automatically. Experiments to the real-life authoritative servers were conducted which highlighting three important aspects: the distribution, the geographic location and their impacts on performance and security. According to five representative attributes, the authoritative servers of China Top100 websites are evaluated and the result shows that only 32% of all the servers act preferably in performance and security.

1 Introduction

The Domain Name System (DNS) is a hierarchical database distributed around the world and its primary function is to translate human-readable domain names to the corresponding IP addresses. As the most successful distributed system on the Internet, A great deal of daily network applications such as emails and web surfing all need DNS work properly. At the same time, many rising network applications ranging from load balancing to service discovery all depend on DNS. If an application fails to receive a reply for its DNS query, it is a denied service; if a forged or malicious reply is received, a DNS hijacking happened. Obviously DNS is one of the most crucial components of Internet infrastructure. According to [1], the number of host records (only one of the record types carried by DNS) has grown from 20,000 in 1987 to 353,284,187 in July 2005. The number of independent zones has skyrocketed from a handful in 1987 to around 83 million in 2005. Despite such phenomenal growth in size, the key role of DNS is not seriously concerned about. There are many configuration errors existed in the enormous global system [2], even in giant computer companies such as Microsoft [3].

As is known to us all, DNS is susceptible to failures mainly owing to its ill-considered design and implementation on integrity and authenticity [4],[5]. Now researchers have realized the significance of reliable communications in DNS, and

D.-S. Huang, K. Li, and G.W. Irwin (Eds.): ICIC 2006, LNAI 4114, pp. 536 – 544, 2006.

plenty of measures have been presented to tolerate device failures (e.g. node and route failures) and to antagonize malicious attackers. These measures are mainly aimed at root servers and focused on the performance impacted by query or implementation errors especially. Danzig et al. performed an extensive study of the DNS traffic on the ISI (Information Sciences Institute) root name server in 1992[6]. They observed a variety of DNS implementation bugs such as recursion loops and poor failure detection algorithms. The finding is such errors incurred unnecessary wide-area DNS traffic by a factor of twenty. In 2001, Brownlee et al. [7] measured passively on the DNS traffic directed toward the F-root server and identified some queries repeated, to private address space or invalid top-level domains (TLDs), they also found some new errors such bogus *A* queries, source port zero and requests trying to update root servers. In a further work, Jung et al. [8] measured the client-perceived performance of DNS, including the latency to receive answers, the performance of the DNS protocol, the prevalence of failures and errors, and the interactions with root/gTLD servers, and studied the effectiveness of caching. They observed that a significant fraction of lookups never receive an answer and furthermore, DNS server implementations continue to be overly persistent in the face of failures. To break the limitation of location numbers in the Internet topology and focus on performance from the perspective of the clients, Liston et al. [9] presented a large scale study of wide-area DNS performance at clients differing across locations in the Internet. They showed that the greatest performance enhancements can be achieved by reducing the response time of servers other than root and gTLD servers. Lee et al. [10] studied the optimal placement of root servers and showed that geographical distribution of root servers can help improve overall performance perceived by clients. They also proposed a methodology to estimate the effects of root servers' relocation.

In spite of suffering from all kinds of attacks such as publicized DDoS attacks, the root servers themselves are well equipped and monitored closely to guard against these compromises, which make exploits towards the top-level servers arduous [11] and cause hackers transfer their attentions to local authoritative servers - the handlers of name information in the corresponding domains. In contrast with root servers, local authoritative servers are lack of enough arms. Despite the best current practice recommending placing authoritative servers in diverse locations for maximum protection against network failures [12], the number and the distribution of authoritative servers are generally irrational due to the less consideration of security or the absence of professional knowledge.

This paper describes the existence of authoritative servers by taking China Top100 websites for instance. By utilizing DNSAuth, a domain measurement tool we design for the automatic collection of authoritative servers, names and IP addresses of these authoritative servers are presented at first. Subsequently, these servers are located and showed in a geographic map to demonstrate potential security issues. At last, taking the number, the distribution and the performance into account, we evaluate the China Top100 websites and give the relevant advice. Compared with passive measurements towards top-level domains, our approach utilizes certain properties from the network infrastructure to discover the pervasive troubles existed in the local authoritative servers and the evaluation will instruct the network operators to improve their deployments and configurations on the corresponding domains.

The rest of this paper is organized as follows: Section 2 provides the data source and describes the domain measurement tool - DNSAuth. Section 3 examines the impact of authoritative server's location and distribution on domain's performance and security. Section 4 evaluates the impact thoroughly and Section 5 summarizes the contribution of our work.

2 Measurement Methodology

In this section, we analyze the data of China Top100 websites with DNSAuth to obtain their corresponding authoritative servers and describe DNSAuth's merits briefly.

2.1 Data Source

The data we study originated from www.alexa.com[13], a famous web navigation service provider. These Top100 websites provide various services including news, recreation, online games, shopping, mailbox, search engine, sports, chat room and forum, therefore the data sample is quite representative.

2.2 DNSAuth

DNSAuth is a DNS authoritative records query tool which can obtain the authoritative servers of specific websites automatically. The input can be a single domain or a file contained the domain set, and the output can be saved in a specific format for further analysis.

Table 1. Sample of experimental results from DNSAuth

Domain	Authoritative Server: IP
www.sina.com.cn	ns1.sina.com.cn: 202.106.184.166
	ns2.sina.com.cn: 61.172.201.254
	ns3.sina.com.cn: 202.108.44.55
www.sohu.com	dns.sohu.com: 61.135.131.86
	ns1.sohu.com: 61.135.131.1
	ns2.sohu.com: 61.135.132.1
…	…
www.cctv.com	ns1.chinacache.net: 61.136.61.253
	ns2.chinacache.net: 61.163.241.5
	ns3.chinacache.net: 211.154.222.123

Table 1 illustrates an example of China Top100 website's authoritative servers we measured with DNSAuth. The domains and the corresponding IP addresses are listed at the same time. This sample shows some problems which can be found at first glance. For example, all the three authoritative servers of sohu.com are in a B prefix and more surprisingly two of them are in a same C prefix. Once a single point of failure occurred, the website's availability of services will be affected badly.

Compared with traditional domain lookup tools such as nslookup or dig, DNSAuth has more competitive features:

a) Support batch work, which providing the option of processing a single domain or a domain set;
b) Possess domain to IP function, which can obtain the authoritative server's domains and the corresponding IP addresses simultaneously.

3 Experiment Results

In this section, we present the measurement results for a real-life DNS workload. Our experiments highlight three important aspects of authoritative servers. First, they show the distribution of authoritative servers among the China Top100 websites. Second, they demonstrate the geographic location of these authoritative servers. Finally, they present the impact of these servers' location on the corresponding websites' security and performance.

3.1 Distribution Status

The amount of authoritative servers has a direct impact on the website's security and performance.

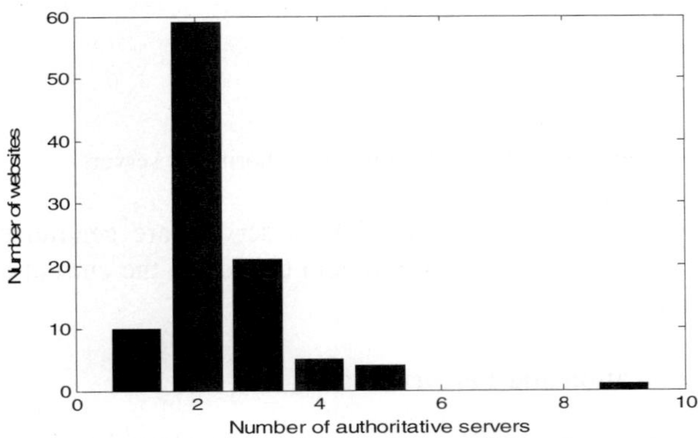

Fig. 1. Distribution of authoritative servers among China Top100 websites

Fig. 1 plots the distribution of the China Top100 websites that have different numbers of authoritative servers. Nearly 60% of the websites are served by just two authoritative servers, and a surprising 10% by only one. It seems that about 90% of all the websites have at least two authoritative servers, which satisfies the minimum requirement of DNS deployment [5], however, the statistics show many authoritative servers are located in same subnets, which highlights that large numbers of websites are vulnerable to network attacks or link failures. These problems are crucial and affect both top-level domains and popular web sites.

Overall, a large portion of the websites can be compromised by infiltrating a small number of gateways or routers.

3.2 Geographic Location and Security

As a distributed cooperative system, the geographic location of authoritative servers is a key factor in the security of infrastructure. Natural disaster, war and burst of virus such as worm propagation all threaten the integrity and availability of DNS. Next we visualize the geographic location of China Top100 websites' authoritative servers with our IP orientation system and demonstrate the impact of geographic location on the network security.

As illustrated in Fig. 2, the location of authoritative servers is very unbalanced and more than 110 servers are deployed in Beijing, the capital of China, accounting for 45% of all the servers. In the same way, there are also 40 servers located in Shanghai, another international metropolis, accounting for 17% of all the servers.

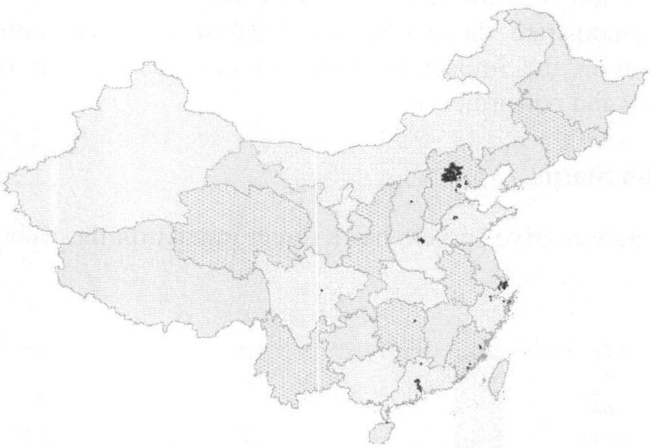

Fig. 2. Geographic location of authoritative servers

Overall, more than 60% of the authoritative servers are centralized in the two cities, and which reflects the prevalent problem existed in the current deployment of authoritative servers.

3.3 Geographic Location and Performance

The geographic distribution of authoritative servers also plays the most important role for the overall performance of infrastructure. Clients usually have lower round-trip time (RTT) to geographically nearby servers and customarily use these servers for lookups, so the more dispersedly the servers are deployed, the better performance of the network is achieved.

Fig. 3 demonstrates the decrease of mean RTT followed by the increase of servers' locations. Table 2 summarizes the results of Fig.3 by providing the mean and the median latency respectively. It shows that the mean RTT of the authoritative servers which have only one location vibrate from 337.2 ms to 1658.8 ms and the average RTT of these latencies is 444.9 ms, whereas the servers that have three locations and above achieve fewer vibrations and lower latencies as the average RTT is about 360.0 ms. These measurements indicate that the location of authoritative servers is a major factor in the performance of DNS query as measured by RTT.

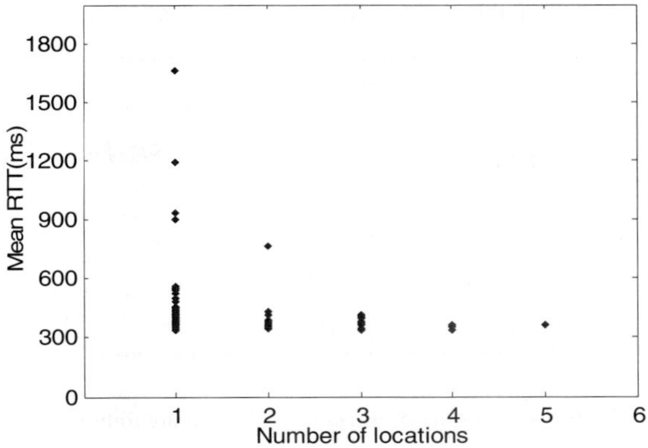

Fig. 3. Location of authoritative servers and the corresponding latency

Table 2. Latency of authoritative servers

Latency	Mean	Median
1	444.9ms	387.2 ms
2	404.8 ms	374.6 ms
3	380.1 ms	380.8 ms
4	352.7 ms	355.8 ms
5	365.2 ms	365.2 ms

4 Evaluation

In this section, we evaluate the authoritative servers of China Top100 websites according to five representative attributes (namely the number of servers, prefix, load balance, geographic location and mean RTT) and calculate the final scores.

4.1 Attributes and Weights

Let A be the attribute set where $a_i \in A$ (i=1,2,…,n) is the value of A, and let W be the set of given weights where each $w_i \in W$ (i=1,2,…,n) is the value of W, so the score are calculated as (1):

$$S = W \times A = \frac{1}{n} \sum_{i=1}^{n} w_i \times a_i \quad . \tag{1}$$

where S denote the evaluated score of authoritative servers.

Table 3 illustrates the checked attributes and Table 4 lists the corresponding weights.

Table 3. Attributes for evaluation

A	Value
a_1	number of servers
a_2	prefix
a_3	load balance
a_4	geographic location
a_5	mean RTT

Table 4. Weights of the corresponding attributes

W	w_1	w_2	w_3	w_4	w_5
Value	0.4	0.4	1	$1/a_1$	$1000/a_5^2$

As mentioned in section 3.1, the amount of authoritative servers is a key factor that impacts the websites' performance and security, and furthermore, many servers are located in the same subnet which degrading the servers' Quality of Service (QoS) dramatically. So the number of servers and the prefix are treated as two independent attributes and checked respectively.

Let the server's total number is N_{total}, and the number of IP that has the same prefix is $N_{(/i)}$ (i=8,16,24), the group number is $G_{(/i)}$ (i=8,16,24), then the attribute a_2 is calculated as (2):

$$a_2 = \begin{cases} N_{total}, & N_{(/i)} = 0 \\ N_{total} - \frac{1}{4}(N_{(/8)} - G_{(/8)}), & N_{(/8)} > 0, N_{(/16)} = N_{(/24)} = 0 \\ N_{total} - \frac{1}{2}(N_{(/16)} - G_{(/16)}), & N_{(/16)} > 0, N_{(/24)} = 0 \\ N_{total} - (N_{(/24)} - G_{(/24)}), & N_{(/24)} > 0 \end{cases} \quad (2)$$

For example, if a website has five authoritative servers and there are no any same prefix, i.e. $N_{(/i)}$=0, then the value of a_2 is 5; if there are two /24 prefix groups and each group has two IP, i.e. $N_{(/24)}$=4 and $G_{(/24)}$=2, then the value of a_2 is 3. So the more same prefixes appeared, the lower evaluation scores calculated, and it also indicates the dispersion of network topology should be considered when deploying authoritative servers.

Similarly, the geographic location of authoritative servers plays an important role as described in section 3.2. In order to study the correlation of the number of servers and the geographic location, we designate the weight of geographic location w_4 as the reciprocal of server's amount, namely $1/a_1$, and then $w_4 \times a_4 = a_4/a_1$. Obviously, this ratio evaluates the geographic impact more accurately.

4.2 Comparison of Attributes

Fig. 4 illustrates the cumulative distribution of the checked attributes according to the order of scores. It shows that the mean RTT still plays the most important role in the evaluation of authoritative servers in this scenario. The curve is quite even from 2 to 4.5 points. Subsequently, it becomes very steep, indicating that the servers which get high scores have better performance indeed. At the same time, the prefix and the location are lower than the number of servers from the start to about 6.7 points and surpass it later, which proves that the authoritative servers with high scores have more rational deployments and better robustness.

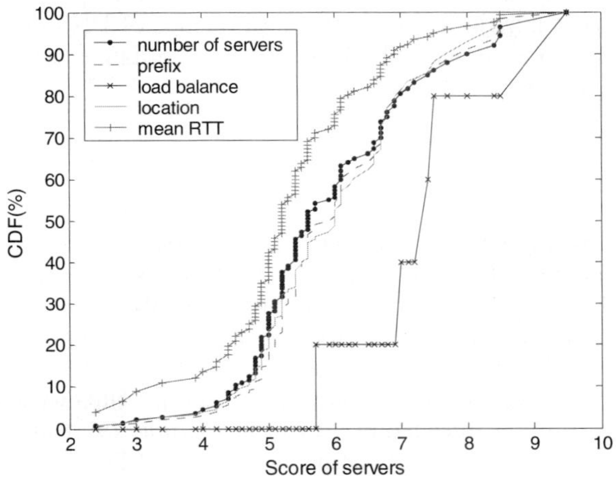

Fig. 4. Cumulative distribution of attributes on the score of servers

Overall, there are only 32% of the authoritative servers which achieving 6 points and above in our evaluation, and this proves our worry towards the status of local authoritative servers' performance and security is necessary.

The network administrators must keep the advices below in mind:

a) Deploy multiple authoritative servers for high availability;
b) Avoid single point of failure at full steam: Do not put all the authoritative servers on a single subnet or behind a single router, namely deploy servers on multiple networks and/or ISPs;
c) Deploy servers in different Autonomous Systems (AS): Analyze the query distribution of clients and optimize the location of authoritative servers in accordance with the current geographic distribution of their clients for high performance and better service.

5 Conclusions

The explosive growth of Internet and the frequent emergence of large-scale distributed attacks highlight the performance and security issues of authoritative servers.

In this paper, we study the existence of authoritative servers by analyzing the data of China Top100 websites provided by Alexa Internet.

By using DNSAuth, a domain measurement tool we design for the collection of authoritative servers, names and IP addresses of these authoritative servers are presented.

The experiments show that the status of authoritative servers' performance and security is discouraging. Nearly 60% of the websites are served by just two authoritative servers, and a surprising 10% by only one.

At the same time, more than 60% of the authoritative servers are centralized in only two cities. All these degrade the availability of DNS confronting with coordinated attacks. The experiments also indicate that the geographic location of authoritative servers is a major factor in the performance of DNS query. Finally, the evaluation results are present and only 32% of the authoritative servers are qualified in the performance and security.

References

1. Internet Domain Survey. http://www.isc.org/ops/ds/, (2005)
2. Pappas, V., Xu, Z.G., Lu, SW., Massey, D., Terzis, A., Zhang LX.: Impact of Configuration Errors on DNS Robustness. SIGCOMM'04: Proceedings of the 2004 conference on Applications, Technologies, Architectures, and Protocols for Computer Communications. ACM Press, New York (2004) 319–330
3. Thurrott, P.: Microsoft Suffers Another DoS Attack. http://www.winnetmag.com/ Windows Security/Article/ArticleID/ 19770/WindowsSecurity 19770.html, (2001)
4. Mockapetris, P.V.: Domain Names: Concepts and Facilities. RFC 1034, (1987)
5. Mockapetris, P.V.: Domain Names: Implementation and Specification. RFC 1035, (1987)
6. Danzig, P.B., Obraczka, K., Kumar, A.: An Analysis of Wide-area Name Server Traffic: A Study of the Domain Name System. Proceeding of ACM SIGCOMM (1992) 281−292
7. Brownlee, N., Claffy, K., Nemeth, E.: DNS Measurements at a Root Server. GlobeCom, San Antonio, TX (2001) 1672−1676
8. Jung, J., Sit, E., Balakrishnan, H., Morris, R.: DNS Performance and the Effectiveness of Caching. In: Proceedings of the First ACM SIGCOMM IMW, ACM Press (2001) 153–167
9. Liston, R., Srinivasan, S., Zegura, E.: Diversity in DNS Performance Measures. Proceedings of the Second ACM SIGCOMM IMW, ACM Press (2002) 19–31
10. Lee, T., Huffaker, B., Fomenkov, M., claffy, kc.: On the Problem of Optimization of DNS Root Servers' Placement. In: Passive Measurement and Analysis Workshop, (2003)
11. CAIDA. Nameserver DoS Attack October 2002. http://www.caida.org/projects/dns-analysis/, (2004)
12. Elz, R., Bush, R., Bradner, S., Patton, M.: Selection and Operation of Secondary DNS Servers. RFC 2182, (1997)
13. Alexa Internet.: China Top100 Sites. http://www.alexa.com/site/ds/top_sites?ts_mode=lang&lang=zh_gb2312

Comparison Model and Algorithm for Distributed Firewall Policy

Weiping Wang, Wenhui Chen, Zhepeng Li, and Huaping Chen

School of Management, University of Science & Technology of China,
230026, China
brucechen@ustc.edu

Abstract. As a traditional technique of information security, distributed firewall has taken very important position, while problems remain. Correct configuration of distributed firewall policies and keeping individual firewall filter decisions compatible to each other are quite inconvenient for administrators. To realize the comparison between firewalls' policies, this paper provide FPT(firewall policy tree) model, and the construction algorithm which can turn a firewall policy into a policy tree, as well as the comparison algorithm. Combination of the two algorithms can be used to perform a comparison between distributed firewalls' policies. By doing this, the paper can obtain the set of data packages on which different firewalls have made inconsistent filter decision, and find out the inconsistency in distributed firewall policies. Besides, this model could be extended to package classification systems for policies comparison.

1 Introduction

In order to achieve the security of enterprise network, avoiding the threats of security breach, independent firewalls in distributed firewall may be purchased from different manufacturer. Difference might exist in their method of configuration, and this would bring inconveniences into configuring these firewalls. On the other hand, although the distributed firewall security policy is unified, this kind of security policy is usually presented in natural language. It might cause inconsistent understanding between different administrators because of obscurity in natural language. Hence the inconsistence policies between independent firewalls would appear when these administrators are configuring firewall policy.

We investigate the firewall policy configuration in distributed environment, and present the model and algorithms for comparing distributed firewalls. By these algorithms, we can compare m independent firewalls in distributed firewall scenario, and find out those data packages on which different firewalls have made different filter decision. This will facilitate the correction of those mis-configurations.

The remainder of this paper is organized as follows: Section 2 is related work; we propose the FPT(firewall policy tree) model in Section 3 as the basis for policies comparison; followed by construction algorithm for FPT in Section 4, which can translate a firewall's policy into policy tree; the comparison algorithm

D.-S. Huang, K. Li, and G.W. Irwin (Eds.): ICIC 2006, LNAI 4114, pp. 545–556, 2006.

for FPT is included in Section 5; simulation experiments are given in Section 6; at the end is the conclusion of our study.

2 Related Work

Firewall always attracts researcher's attention as a classic technique of network security. The conflict detection in firewall field has fruitful achievements.

The contributions of literature [1,2,3,4] concentrate in three area: conflicts classification and detection algorithm between firewall rules, updating algorithm for firewall rule and high-level textual translation for firewall rule. Policy tree is introduced to describe rules in firewall, on which they developed conflicts detection and updating algorithm for firewall rules.

Detection algorithm and solution scheme for rules' correlation conflict is proposed in [5], they adopted a recursive trie method to develop a fast detection algorithm for rules' correlation conflict detection. The authors of [6] improved the previous detection algorithm for package classification conflicts, by altering the semantic meaning of variables and adding more variables, they sped up conflicts detection about 40 times.

Besides, considerable literatures are provided in the field of high-level textual description. A query tool is provided in [7], it can answer some intelligent question like "which port is open in a given server?" [8] suggests a method of making use of expert system to detect the firewall conflicts.

[9,10] made use of a tool called Firewall Decision Diagraph (FDD) to describe firewall. Authors can make sure of the integrity, compactness and consistence of an independent firewall. FDD was introduced to describe firewall and enabled the comparing of firewalls designed by two groups, then find out differences for future analysis and design of firewall accord to enterprise security policy. Based on [10], we will go forward in this paper. We will compare $m(m \geq 2)$ independent firewalls in distributed firewall scenario.

As the basis of comparison model for firewall policy, we introduce the firewall policy tree model in the first place.

3 Firewall Policy Tree Model

On specific requirements of security, every enterprise has its own security policy which is called firewall policy in the area of firewall. Similarly, it is distributed firewall policy for distributed firewalls. In nature, firewall policy is an access control list which can help deciding what operation to do when a package arrives. Specifically, the access control list(ACL) is made up by several items, each denotes a rule (firewall rule). Every rule contains 3 parts: order, filter domain(network domain) and action domain. Order is the sequence of rules in ACL, ensuring the matching sequence of data packages. Filter domain can be composed by many items in which 5 items are frequently quoted: source/destination IP address, source/destination port number and protocol type. Action domain generally has two choices: *accept*, i.e. permit the passing of a data package through the firewall; *deny*, i.e. reject the passing of a package.

When a data package arrives at firewall, it firstly checks the first rule, if the head of the package matches the filter domain of the rule, the firewall will adopt the behavior as the action domain of the rule; if not, then check the second rule, this course will go on until a matching filter domain of a rule, hence the firewall can take corresponding behavior to the rule's action domain.

Given P is firewall policy, which contains n firewall rules, denoted as $R_1, \cdots, R_n$. Supposedly, R is a rule in them, it has *Order*, *Filter* and *Action* domains, denoted as $R[order]$, $R[filter]$ and $R[action]$. $R[order]$ lies in $[1, +\infty)$; $R[action]$ lies in $\{Accept, Deny\}$; $R[filter]$ is d-tuple$(R[F_1], R[F_2], \cdots, R[F_d])$. For $\forall i, 1 \leq i \leq d$, F_i denotes real filter domain, e.g. source IP address domain. $R[F_i]$ is taken from $D(F_i)$, both are finite, nonempty, and nonnegative integer set.

In summary, for a rule R, we can view it as a following standard form:

$$order \quad R[F_1] \wedge R[F_2] \wedge \cdots \wedge R[F_d] \rightarrow (action)$$

3.1 FPT Model

In [9], Alex suggested FDD model which effectively ensure the integrity, compactness and consistence of an independent firewall, and shed some light on our FPT model. Actually, we carried on some modifications on the FDD to get FPT, then use FPT model f to compare firewalls' policies.

Based on filter domain $F_1, F_2, \cdots, F_d$, FPT model should satisfy six qualifications:

1. FPT is a tree model. It has only one root, while several nodes between root and leaves. Nodes are connected by edges.
2. Every node v in f has a label $F(v)$, details can be found in [9]:

$$F(v) \in \begin{cases} \{F_1, \cdots, F_d\} & \text{if } v \text{ is not leaf node} \\ \{accept, deny\} & \text{if } v \text{ is leaf node} \end{cases}$$

3. Every edge e in f has an label $I(e)$, if e is an edge from node v, then[9]:

$$I(e) \subseteq D(F(v))$$

4. In f, it is so called decision path which is a direct path from root to leaf, denoted as $(v_1 e_1 \cdots v_k e_k v_{k+1})$, where v_1 is root, v_{k+1} is leaf node, e_i is an edge from v_i to v_{i+1}, then[9]:

$$F(v_i) \neq F(v_j), \quad \forall i, j \in \{1, \cdots, k\}, i \neq j$$

   i.e. any different nodes on decision path can't have the same label.
5. For any two edges e and e' from v:

$$I(e) \cap I(e') = \emptyset, \quad e \neq e'$$

6. Order, constituted by ordinal nodes and ordinal edges.

(a) Order of nodes. In filter domain $F_1, F_2, \cdots, F_d$, we set up a priority relation $\prec$, let $F_1 \prec F_2 \cdots \prec F_d$, then for any decision path $(v_1 e_1 \cdots v_k e_k v_{k+1})$:

$$F(v_1) \prec F(v_2) \cdots \prec F(v_k)$$

(b) Order of edges. Given S_1 and S_2 are integer set, $S_1 < S_2$ means the largest element of S_1 is smaller than the smallest in S_2. For any node v in policy tree, $e_1 \cdots e_k$ are edges from v, in sequence from left to right:

$$I(e_i) < I(e_j), \quad \forall i, j \in \{1, \cdots, k\}, i < j$$

In fact, decision path $(v_1 e_1 \cdots v_k e_k v_{k+1})$ can be translated into a rule[9]:

$$order \quad R[F_1] \wedge R[F_2] \wedge \cdots \wedge R[F_d] \rightarrow F(v_{k+1})$$

Where, $R[F_i] = \begin{cases} I(e_j) & \exists j \in \{1, \cdots k\}, F(v_j) = F_i \\ D(F_i) & \forall i, F_i \in \{F_1, \cdots, F_d\} - \{F(v_1), \cdots, F(v_k)\} \end{cases}$, because there exists no intersection of rules which are translated from different decision path, the rule's *order* is inessential.

It appears that we can build a FPT f for any given firewall policy P, such that P and f will give identical filter decision for the same data package. An example is shown in Fig. 1 and Fig. 2. We will present the construction algorithm for FPT f in the following study.

Order	F_1	F_2	Action
1	1, 3	4, 6, 7, 8	1
2	1, 2, 3, 5	1, 3, 6	0
3	6, 7	2, 7, 8	0

Fig. 1. A firewall policy P over the fields F_1 and F_2, both are taken from interval $[1, 9]$

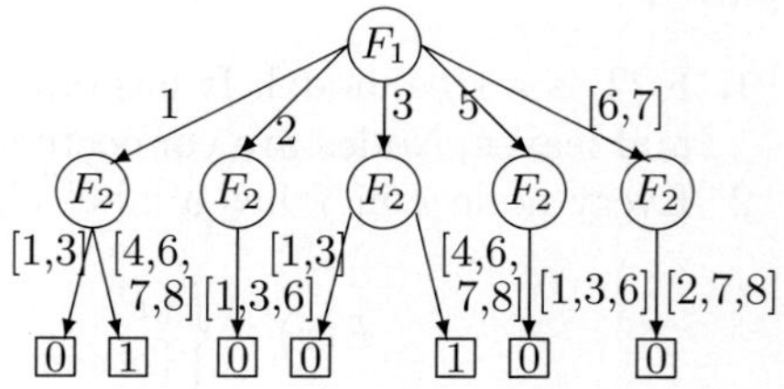

Fig. 2. The FTP f which is equivalent to P shown in Fig.1

4 Construction Algorithm of FPT

A firewall policy P built on $F_1, F_2, \cdots, F_d$ contains n firewall rules: $R_1, R_2, \cdots, R_n$. We need to establish a FPT f, which is equivalent to P, i.e. P and f will give the same filter decision on a given data package p. Without loses of generality, we assume $F_1 \prec \cdots \prec F_d$. According to the order of nodes, f's root is labeled by F_1, nodes in the second hierarchy is $F_2, \cdots$, so is the rest nodes represented in the d-hierarchy policy tree f. The process of constructing FPT is like constructing FDD which Alex had done in [10]. The construction procedures of FPT f as follows.

Let's start with R_1, and establish a decision path $(v_1e_1\cdots v_de_dv_{d+1})$, where:

$$\begin{cases} F(v_i) = F_i, I(e_i) = R_1[F_i], & \forall i \in \{1, \cdots, d\} \\ F(v_{d+1}) = R_1[action] \end{cases}$$

it is equal to R_1. This decision path is the first decision path of f, we add rules $R_2 \cdots R_n$ into the f in turn, and then form the f which is equivalent to P. Supposedly $R_1 \cdots R_j$ have already been added to policy tree f, when v is the root of f, edges from v are $e_1 \cdots e_k$, in sequence from left to right. Now we need to add R_{j+1}, which takes us two steps[10].

Firstly, let $I = R_{j+1}[F_1] - \bigcup_{i=1}^{k} I(e_i)$, $J = R_{j+1}[F_1] - I$, if $I = \emptyset$, means we don't need to append new edges on node v, if $I \neq \emptyset$, means we need to append new edges. Given X, Y are integer sets, denote $l(X,Y) = \{z|z \in X \wedge \{z\} < Y\}$. Comparing edge e_i in order, $1 \leq i \leq k$, while $I \neq \emptyset$ is satisfied and $I(e_i) < I$ is not satisfied, we execute following operations:

- if $l(I(e_i), I) \neq \emptyset$, split edge e_i, construct an edge e, appending e to the left of e_i, let $I(e) = l(I(e_i), I)$, copy the sub-tree that e_i pointing to, let ϵ point to it, let $I(e_i) = I(e_i) - l(I(e_i), I)$;
- if $l(I, I(e_i)) \neq \emptyset$, append an edge e to the left of e_i, let $I(e) = l(I, I(e_i))$, $I = I - l(I, I(e_i))$, construct a decision path and make it equivalent to $R_{j+1}[F_2] \wedge R_{j+1}[F_3] \wedge \cdots \wedge R_{j+1}[F_d] \rightarrow R_{j+1}[action]$, then let new edge e point to it.

For the last, if $I \neq \emptyset$, append an edge e to the right of e_k, let $I(e) = I$, build a decision path and make it equivalent to $R_{j+1}[F_2] \wedge R_{j+1}[F_3] \wedge \cdots \wedge R_{j+1}[F_d] \rightarrow R_{j+1}[action]$, and let new edge e point to it.

So far, we accomplished the first step.

Secondly, if $J \neq \emptyset$, still denote those edges outgoing from v with $e_1 \cdots e_k$, in sequence from left to right. compare J and $I(e_i)$ in order, $1 \leq i \leq k$. There are three results:

1. $J \cap I(e_i) = \emptyset$. The data package p which satisfy edge e_i in domain F_1 is either independent from R_{j+1} or satisfying the newly appended edge at step 1, so it is not required to alter edge e_i.
2. $J \cap I(e_i) = I(e_i)$. A data package p, satisfying edge e_i in domain F_1, probably matches some certain rule in first j rules of policy P, also it could matches R_{j+1}. So, we add $R_{j+1}[F_2] \wedge R_{j+1}[F_3] \wedge \cdots \wedge R_{j+1}[F_d] \rightarrow R_{j+1}[action]$ to the sub-tree which edge e_i is pointing to[10].
3. $J \cap I(e_i) \neq \emptyset \wedge J \cap I(e_i) \neq I(e_i)$. We split e_i into two edges e' and e'', let $I(e') = I(e_i) - J$, $I(e'') = I(e_i) \cap J$, and make two copies of the sub-tree that edge e_i pointing to, let e' and e'' point to them separately, then delete edge e_i and the sub-tree connected to it. If $I(e') < I(e'')$, put e' to the left of e'', if $I(e'') < I(e')$,put e' to the right of e'', both we apply 2 to the edge e''. If both of the previous two conditions are not true, it means $I(e')$ and $I(e'')$

have intersection. We split e' and e'' ensuring the order of policy tree, and copy the corresponding sub-trees at the same time, we apply 2 to all those edges split from e''.

Here we present the pseudo code of construction algorithm:

Construction Algorithm

Input : A firewall policy P with order $F_1 \prec \cdots \prec F_d$
Output: A firewall policy tree f equivalent with P
Steps[10]:
  1. build a decision path with root v from rule R_1;
  2. **for** $j = 2$ **to** n **do** APPEND(v, R_j);
end

---

5 Comparison Algorithm of FPT

Considering m FPT $f_1, f_2, \cdots, f_m$, which are built on filter domain $F_1, F_2, \cdots, F_d$, they fulfill $F_1 \prec \cdots \prec F_d$. We are interested in the data package p, which has different filter decisions from at least two FPT f_i and f_j among m FPT. Two steps of finding out set S of this kind data package p are written subsequently.

First of all, form unification of policy trees.

1. For $\forall i, 1 \leq i \leq m$, v_i denotes the root of f_i, v_i contains $k(i)$ edges: $e_1^i, e_2^i, \cdots, e_{k(i)}^i$ from left to right. Denote $I(e^i) = \bigcup_{j=1}^{k(i)} I(e_j^i)$, where $I(e^i)$ is the judge scope of f_i on domain F_1, i.e. for those packages which exceed $I(e^i)$ on domain F_1, f_i can not make any filter decision. For all m firewall policy trees, $f_1, f_2, \cdots, f_m$, let $I = \bigcap_{i=1}^{m} I(e^i)$, I presents the judge scope they are sharing on domain F_1. Hence, those packages, who take value from $D(F_1) - I$ in domain F_1, can not be judged by at least one policy tree, we put these packages into S.
2. For $\forall v_i, 1 \leq i \leq m$, compare I and edge e_j^i sequentially where $1 \leq j \leq k(i)$, there are two results:
   (a) $I \cap I(e_j^i) = \emptyset$. Because a package p which fulfills edge e_j^i in domain F_1 is inevitably be contained in S, we delete edge e_j^i and the sub-tree connected to it from policy tree f_i.
   (b) $I \cap I(e_j^i) \neq \emptyset$. If $I \cap I(e_j^i) \neq I(e_j^i)$, we change the label of edge e_j^i, let $I(e_j^i) = I \cap I(e_j^i)$, by this way sub-tree is deleted indirectly.
3. For $\forall f_i, 1 \leq i \leq m$, f_i has undertaken some pruning, we still denote those edges from v_i with $e_1^i, e_2^i, \cdots, e_{k(i)}^i$ such that $I(e^i) = I(e^j), 1 \leq i, j \leq m$. Let $J(e_j) = \bigcap_{i=1}^{m} I(e_j^i)$, which indicates the sharing section of all policy tree on the j-th edge. Considering edges $e_1^1, e_1^2, \cdots, e_1^m$, we compare $J(e_1)$ and $I(e_1^i)$ sequentially, where $1 \leq i \leq m$. The comparison will come up with two results:

Function APPEND(v, $R_j[F_m] \wedge \cdots \wedge R_j[F_d] \rightarrow R_j[action]$)

```
/* F(v) = F_m and F_m ≺ ··· ≺ Fd.                                          */
/* {e_1, ···, e_k} is the edge collection and I(e_1) < ··· < I(e_k).       */
/* e.t denotes the (target) node that the edge e points to[10].            */
I = R_j[F_m] − ⋃_{i=1}^{k} I(e_i), J = R_j[F_m] − I;
// Step 1, append new edges.
if I ≠ ∅ then
    for i = 1 to k do
        while I ≠ ∅ ∧ ¬(I(e_i) < I) do
            if l(I(e_i), I) ≠ ∅ then // l(X,Y) = {z|z ∈ X ∧ {z} < Y}.
                (a) construct an edge e with label l(I(e_i), I), put e to the left of e_i;
                (b) make a copy of the sub-tree rooted at e_i.t, and make e points
                    to the root of the copy;
                (c) replace the label of e_i by I(e_i) − l(I(e_i), I);
            if l(I, I(e_i)) ≠ ∅ then
                (a) construct an edge e with label l(I, I(e_i)), put e to the left of e_i;
                (b) build a decision path from rule R_j[F_{m+1}] ∧ ··· ∧ R_j[F_d]
                    → R_j[action] and make e point to it;
                (c) I = I − l(I, I(e_i));
    if I ≠ ∅ then
        (a) construct an edge e with label I, put e to the right of e_k;
        (b) build a decision path from rule R_j[F_{m+1}] ∧ ··· ∧ R_j[F_d]
            → R_j[action] and make e point to it;
// Step 2, compare J with all the outgoing edges of v.
if J ≠ ∅ then
    if m < d then
        for i = 1 to k do // k is the new number of the edge of v.
            if I(e_i) ⊆ J then
                APPEND(e_i.t, R_j[F_{m+1}] ∧ ··· ∧ R_j[F_d] → R_j[action]);
            else if I(e_i) ∩ J ≠ ∅ then
                (a) construct an edge e with label I(e_i) ∩ J;
                (b) make a copy of the sub-tree rooted at e_i.t, and make e points
                    to the root of the copy;
                (c) replace the label of e_i by I(e_i) − J;
                (d) split e and e_i to keep the order of f;
                (e) foreach edge e' spitted by e do
                        APPEND(e'.t, R_j[F_{m+1}] ∧ ··· ∧ R_j[F_d] → R_j[action]);
```

(a) $J(e_1) = I(e_1^i)$. For v_i, the next comparison will start with edge e_2^i.

(b) $J(e_1) \subset I(e_1^i)$. We split edge e_1^i into e and e', e is put on the left side. Let $I(e) = J(e_1)$ and $I(e') = I(e_1^i) - J(e_i)$, while making two copies of the sub-trees connected with e_1^i, let e and e' point to them, and delete edge e_1^i and the sub-trees. The next comparison will start with e'.

It's not hard to tell, *the labels of edges involved in each comparison are started from the same number.* And the comparison can continue until all the nodes reach the most right edge where all labels are the same then.

4. Thus, all the roots of $f_1, f_2, \cdots, f_m$, have k edges, each edge's label in a tree is the same with its counterpart on other trees. We repeat above procedures on their corresponding sub-trees until reach the leaves. Therefore, we obtain m firewall policy trees $f_1, f_2, \cdots, f_m$, they identical formation.

For the second thing, comparison of policy trees. $f_1, f_2, \cdots, f_m$ have identical formation, the only difference might exist on leaves. Let l_j^i denotes the j-th leaf in f_i, where $1 \le i \le m, 1 \le j \le k$, k is number of leaf nodes. For $\forall j, 1 \le j \le k$, we compare all l_j^i, where $1 \le i \le m$, and the comparison results can be classified into two categories:

– $\forall x, y, 1 \le x, y \le m, \quad l_j^x = l_j^y$. If package p satisfies the decision path connected with l_j^1, all firewalls take the same filter decision with it.
– $\exists x, y, 1 \le x, y \le m, \quad l_j^x \ne l_j^y$. If package p satisfies the decision path connected with l_j^1, firewall f_x and f_y take inconsistent filter decision. We will include these p into set S.

The establishment of set S is accomplished, and it contains all the packages we are interested in. An example is shown in Fig. 3 and Fig. 4.

We present the pseudo code of policy tree comparison algorithm as follows.

Comparison Algorithm

Input : firewall policy tree $f_1, f_2, \cdots, f_m$ with order $F_1 \prec \cdots \prec Fd$
Output: Set S, for any element p in it, at least two firewall policy trees will make inconsistent filter decision
Steps:
1. SHAPE($''\ ''$, $v_1, v_2, \cdots, v_m$);
end

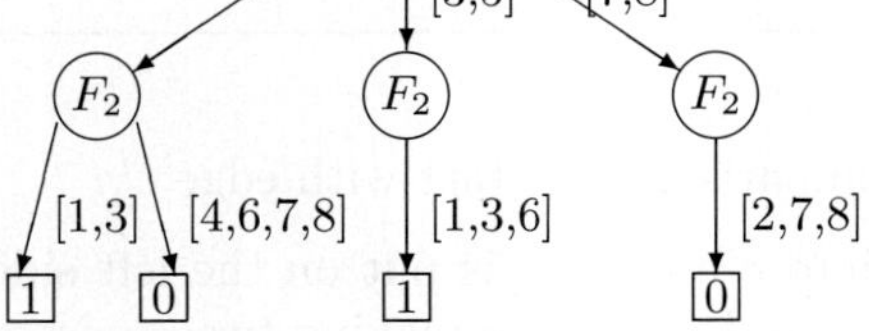

Fig. 3. A FTP f' over the fields F_1 and F_2 as f shown in Fig. 2

Order	F_1	F_2
1	4, 6, 8, 9	1, 2, 3, 4, 5, 6, 7, 8, 9
2	1	2, 5, 9
3	1	1, 3
4	1	4, 6, 7, 8
5	2	2, 4, 5, 7, 8, 9
⋮	⋮	⋮
11	7	1, 3, 4, 5, 6, 9

Fig. 4. The comparison result set S about f and f'

Function SHAPE(Q, $v'_1, v'_2, \cdots, v'_m$)

```
/* v'_i is the root of the sub-tree of f_i.                          */
/* Q save the path from v_1 to v'_1.                                 */
if v'_1 is not a leaf node then
    // Step 1, find the common judge scope on domain F(v'_1).
    for i = 1 to m do
        foreach outgoing edge e of v'_i do
            I(e^i) = I(e^i) ∪ I(e);
    I = ∩_{i=1}^{m} I(e^i);
    if D(F(v'_1)) − I ≠ ∅ then
        put all the packages satisfy Q and D(F(v'_1)) − I to S;
    // Step 2, prune some edges.
    for i = 1 to m do
        foreach outgoing edge e of v'_i do
            if I ∩ I(e) = ∅ then
                cut the edge e and the sub-tree with it;
            else if I ∩ I(e) ≠ I(e) then
                replace the label of e by I ∩ I(e);
    // Step 3, form unification.
    while Σ_{i=1}^{m} (K[i] < k(i)) > 0 do
        // K[i] is a temporary array, all the element is 1 at first.
        // if x is less than y, then (x < y) = 1 and (y < x) = 0.
        // now, k(i) is the new number of the outgoing edges of v'_i
        J = ∩_{i=1}^{m} I(e^i_{K[i]});
        for i = 1 to m do
            if J = I(e^i_{K[i]}) then
                K[i] = K[i] + 1;
            else
                (a) construct an edge e, label e with J, and put e to the left of
                    e^i_{K[i]} ;
                (b) make a copy of the sub-tree rooted at e^i_{K[i]}.t, make e point to
                    the root of the copy;
                (c) I(e^i_{K[i]}) = I(e^i_{K[i]}) − J;
    // Step 4, iterative.
    // Now, k is the number of the outgoing edge of v'_1.
    for i = 1 to k do
        SHAPE(Q + I(e^1_i), e^1_i.t, e^2_i.t, ..., e^m_i.t);
else
    for i = 2 to m do
        if F(v'_i) ≠ F(v'_1) then
            put all the packages satisfy Q to S;
            break;
```

6 Experiments

To examine the correctness and efficiency of the algorithms, we implement suggested algorithm using Visual Basic 6.0, and make use of Microsoft Access to store the firewall policies and policy trees. We also test average time required for building a policy tree with proposed construction algorithm. For the comparison algorithm, we test average time needed to compare m firewall policy trees. We also simulate the total time for comparing m firewall policies, which includes the overall time spending on constructing m corresponding policy trees and the time spending on comparing these m policy trees.

The configuration of our machine is CPU 2GHZ and RAM 1GB, OS is Windows. The results are shown in Fig. 5, Fig. 6 and Fig. 7.

In short of publicized firewall policy data, we simulate firewall policies for the test. Without loses of generality, we build firewall policies with 5 filter domains: source/destination IP address, source/destination port number and protocol type, the values in all of which are randomly generated. We have noticed the practical characteristics of actual firewall in [12], but we haven't applied their method, because we prefer to test execution efficiency in inferior settings.

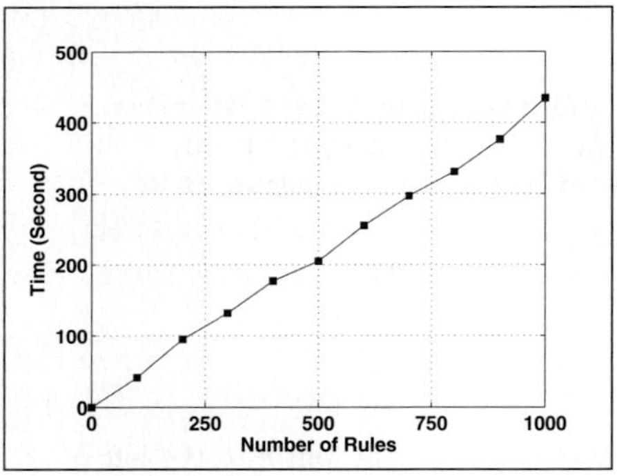

Fig. 5. Construction Algorithm

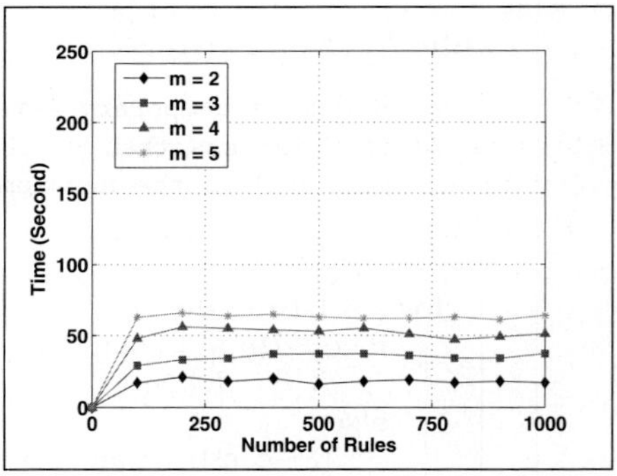

Fig. 6. Comparison Algorithm

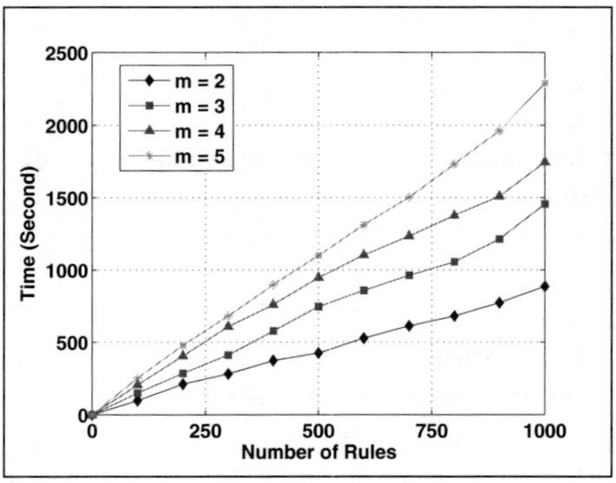

Fig. 7. Total Time

Shown in Fig. 5, it is acceptable for the construction algorithm spends about 7 minutes to establish a policy tree for a firewall policy containing 1,000 rules. In Fig. 6, along with the increasing of firewall policy trees number, the time spending on comparison increases, when $m = 5$, it takes about 1 min which is rather fast. This worth our attention, the time spent by comparison algorithm has no direct correlation with rule number. Figure 7 shows that total time is about 38 minutes when there are 5 firewall policies and 1,000 rules contained in each policy.

In fact, according to actual firewall's characteristics, there are about 4 rules to match in each data package[12], but it will substantially increase for the randomly generated policies. For this reason, it could be more efficient when applying above algorithms to actual firewalls. Besides, we adopt Microsoft Access to store the firewall policies and policy trees, large amount of I/O operation is required, thus more efficient data structure will reduce the execution time greatly.

7 Conclusion

For the consistent filter decision from each independent firewall in distributed firewall, we have proposed the comparison model and algorithm for distributed firewall policy. We presented the FPT(firewall policy tree) model in the first place as the platform for comparison of different firewall policies. Followed by construction algorithm of policy tree, which can translate a firewall policy into equivalent policy tree. And then we have given the comparison algorithm for policy tree, which can give the differences between policy trees.

Experiments are provided for all the algorithms, and it shows the effectivity and efficiency of the algorithms. Furthermore, we have discussed how to improve the algorithm's efficiency.

In fact, our model and corresponding algorithms focus on the comparison of firewall policies, since firewall in nature is a package classification system, our model and algorithms can also be extended to package classification system.

References

1. Al-Shaer,E., Hamed,H. : Management and Translation of Filtering Security Policies. In *IEEE ICC'03*, 1 (May) (2003)256 – 260
2. Al-Shaer,E., Hamed,H. : Firewall Policy Advisor for Anomaly Detection and Rule Editing. In *IEEE/IFIP Integrated Management*, March (2003)17 – 30
3. Al-Shaer,E., Hamed,H. : Discovery of Policy Anomalies in Distributed Firewalls. In *IEEE INFOCOM'04*, 4 (March)(2004) 2605 – 2616
4. Al-Shaer,E., Hamed,H., Boutaba,R., Hasan,M. : Conflict Classification and Analysis of Distributed Firewall Policies. *IEEE journal on Selected Areas in Communications*, 23 (10) (2005)2069 – 2084
5. Hari,B., Suri,S., Parulkar,G . : Detecting and Resolving Packet Filter Conflicts. In *IEEE INFOCOM'2000*, 3 March(2000) 1203 – 1212
6. Baboescu,F., Varghese,G . : Fast and Scalable Conflict Detection for Packet Classifiers. In *Proc. of the 10th IEEE International Conference on Network Protocols*, November(2002) 270 – 279

7. MayerA. , Wool,A., Ziskind,E, Fang: A Firewall Analysis Engine. In *Proc. of IEEE Symposium on Security and Privacy*, May (2000)177 – 187
8. Eronen,P., Zitting,J . : An Expert System for Analyzing Firewall Rules. In *Proc. of 6th Nordic Workshop on Secure IT-Systems*, November (2001)100 – 107
9. Gouda,M.G., Xiang-Yang, Liu,A. : Firewall Design: Consistency, Completeness and Compactness. In *Proc. of the 24th IEEE International Conference on Distributed Computing Systems*, March (2004)320 – 327
10. Liu,A. X., Gouda,M. G. : Diverse Firewall Design. In *Proc. of the International Conference on Dependable Systems and Networks*, June (2004)595 – 604
11. Baboescu,F., Varghese,G. : Scalable Packet Classification. *IEEE/ACM journal on Networking*, 13 Feb(2001)2 – 14
12. Baboescu,F., Singh,S., Varghese,G. : Packet Classification for Core Routers: Is There an Alternative to Cams? In *IEEE INFOCOM'03*, 1 March (2003)53 – 63
13. Ioannidis,S., Keromytis,A. D. , Bellovin,S. M., Smith,J. M. : Implementing a Distributed Firewall. In *ACM Conference on Computer and Communications Security*, November (2000)190 – 199
14. Uribe,T. E., Cheung,S . : Automatic Analysis of Firewall and Network Intrusion Detection System Configurations. In *Proc. of the 2004 ACM workshop on Formal methods in security engineering* (2004)66 – 74

Fourier and Wavelet Transformations for the Fault Detection of Induction Motor with Stator Current

Sang-Hyuk Lee, Seong-Pyo Cheon, Yountae Kim, and Sungshin Kim

School of Electrical and Computer Engineering, Pusan National University
Changjeon-dong, Geumjeong-gu, Busan 609-735, Korea
{leehyuk, buzz74, dream0561, sskim}@pusan.ac.kr

Abstract. In this literature, fault detection of an induction motor is carried out using the information of stator current. After preprocessing actual data, Fourier and Wavelet transforms are applied to detect characteristics under the healthy and various faulted conditions. The most reliable phase current among 3-phase currents is selected by the fuzzy entropy. Data are trained with a neural network system, and the fault detection algorithm is carried out under the unknown data. The results of the proposed approach based on Fourier and Wavelet transformations show that the faults are properly classified into six categories.

1 Introduction

Fault detection techniques of induction motors to deduce maintenance cost down and prevent unscheduled downtimes have been studied by the numerous researchers [1-8]. Faults of an induction machine are classified by bearing fault, coupling and rotor bar faults, air gap, rotor, end ring and stator faults [2,3]. We need various measurements to monitor the status of the motor and to detect the faults. It is well known that it is convenient to decide fault with only current signal because of cost reduction. Fault detection method of induction motor has been studied by the analytic and intelligent approaches [1, 2]. Nandi *et. al* had proposed the frequency extraction method for the air gap fault. This approach requires specification of induction machine; furthermore it is restricted to the limitative fault decision. Fault detection approach via intelligent design has been actively studied [3-9]. Combastel *et. al* and Nejjari *et. al* have applied fuzzy logic to the fault detection. Liu *et. al*, Bo Li *at. al* and Filippetti *et. al* have induced the results using the Neural Network system. The fault detection through the neuro-fuzzy approach is also reported in [8,9]. Recently, rotor bar fault detection has been carried out by Abbaszadeh *et. al* through Wavelet transformation. In this paper, we employ a neural network system to detect various faults with the help of Wavelet and Fourier transformations. To obtain better result fuzzy entropy is used to choose reliable phase current. For the Neural Network design complete bivariate polynomials are used to search for finding their numeric coefficients. We overcome overfitting problem and decreasing numerical time with this structure.

In the next chapter, we introduce various faults of induction motor. Fourier and Wavelet transformations are introduced for the purpose of feature extraction. In Chapter 3, feature extraction procedure via Wavelet transformation is illustrated, and fuzzy

D.-S. Huang, K. Li, and G.W. Irwin (Eds.): ICIC 2006, LNAI 4114, pp. 557–569, 2006.

entropy is also induced to obtain more reliable results. Neural Network system is introduced for the fault detection in Chapter 4. Test results are discussed and shown in Chapter 5. Finally conclusions are followed in Chapter 6.

2 Induction Motor Failures and Feature Extraction

In this chapter, we introduce the failures of induction motors and conventional studies. Fourier transformation and Wavelet transformation for the analysis of stator currents are also illustrated.

A. Various Faults and Conventional Approaches
Various faults have been categorized by outer bearing race defect, inner bearing race defect, ball defect and train defect [1];

$$f = (N/2) f_r [1 - b_d \cos(\beta)/d_p]$$
$$f = (N/2) f_r [1 + b_d \cos(\beta)/d_p]$$
$$f = d_p f_r / b_d [1 - [b_d \cos(\beta)/d_p]^2]$$
$$f = (f_r/2) f_r [1 - b_d \cos(\beta)/d_p]$$

where f_r is the rotational frequency, N is the number of balls, b_d and d_p are the ball diameter and ball pitch diameter respectively, and β is the contact angle of the ball. Stator faults are usually related to insulation failure. Penman et. al analyze the axial flux component of the machine, the frequency components to detect in the axial flux component is given by

$$(k \pm n(1-s)/p) f$$

where p is the number of pole pairs, f is the main frequency, $k = 1,3$ and $n = 1, 2, 3, \cdots, (2p-1)$, s denotes slip. Spectrum analysis of machine line current(MCSA) is used by Kliman, Thomson and Elkasabgy[10-12]. For detecting broken bar faults, side band components are obtained

$$f_b = (1 \pm 2s) f$$

Air-gap eccentricity is finally classified. There are two types of air-gap eccentricity, the static air-gap and the dynamic eccentricity. Static eccentricity may be caused by the ovality of the stator core or by the incorrect positioning of the rotor or stator at the commissioning stage. In the case of dynamic eccentricity, it is caused due to several factors such as a bent rotor shaft, bearing wear or misalignment, ets. Static or dynamic eccentricity can be also detected with MCSA [1].

$$f \left[(kR \pm n_d) \left(\frac{1-s}{p} \right) \pm n_w \right]$$

where f is the fundamental supply frequency, k =1, 2, …, R denotes the number of slots, n_d =0 in the case of static eccentricity, n_d =1, 2, …, in the case of dynamic eccentricity. Also s is slip, p is the number of pole pairs, and n_w is the order of the stator time harmonics. However these methods require the specification of the motor, rotational and current frequencies.

B. Feature Extraction Technique

Fig. 1. illustrates healthy and faulted signals. The classification based on the statistical analysis is difficult. Hence the frequency analysis is employed to extract features

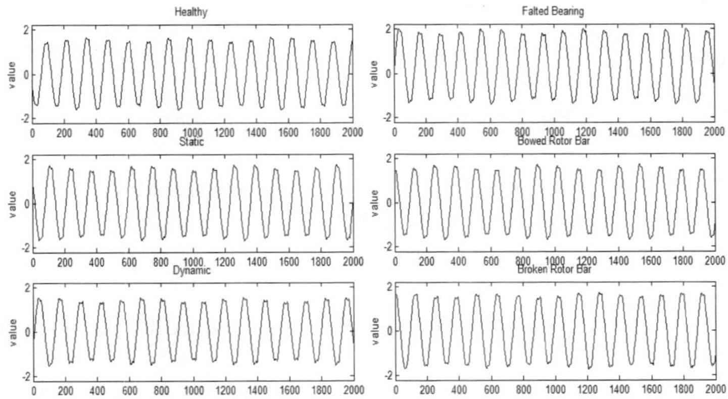

Fig. 1. Measured current signal

– *Fourier transformation*

For discrete signal, discrete Fourier transformation (DFT) is applied [13, 14]. Let T is the sampling time, sample sequences $x(nT) = x(0), x(1), \ldots, x[(N\text{-}1)T]$, are represented. Fourier transformation of $x(nT)$ has the sequences of $\{X(k)\}$. Discrete Fourier transformation satisfies

$$\begin{aligned} X(k+N) &= \sum_{n=0}^{N-1} x(nT)e^{-jk2\pi n/N}e^{-jN2\pi n/N} \\ &= \sum_{n=0}^{N-1} x(nT)e^{-jk2\pi n/N} = X(k) \end{aligned} \quad (1)$$

Hence, DFT represents N periodic function. Fourier transformation of Fig. 1 is illustrated in Fig. 2. In Fig. 2, we can find the distinctive side band of DFT in the case of broken rotor bar. Fourier transformation can be utilized detecting broken rotor bar fault among all possible failures because the other cases didn't show the sideband.

– *Wavelet transformation*

Wavelet transformation is used to analyze continuous or discrete signal [15, 16]. Wavelet transformation overcomes the shortcomings of the window Fourier transformation.

Especially it has the advantage over the nonstationary signal. Difference of information between two approximations at the resolutions 2^{j+1} and 2^{j} is extracted by

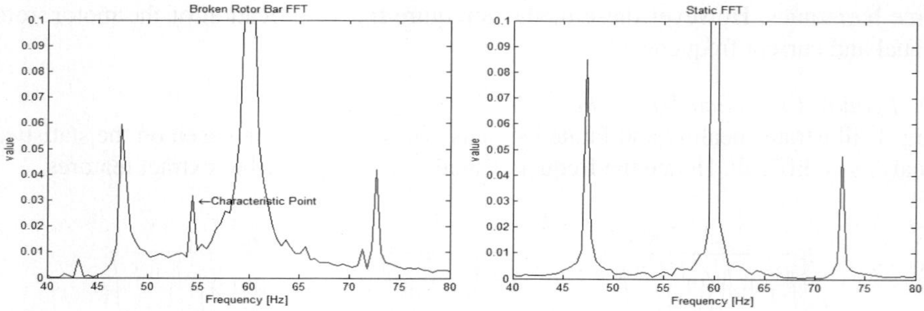

Fig. 2. Current signal via Fourier transform

decomposing the function in a wavelet orthonormal basis. Meyer showed that the family of orthonormal basis of $L^2(R)$ is defined by

$$\{\psi_{j,k}\}_{j,k\in Z} = \{2^{j/2}\psi(2^j x - k)\}. \tag{2}$$

Discrete Wavelat transformation of signal $f(x)$ is obtained by the inner product as follows

$$f(x) = \sum_{j,k} \langle f, \psi_{j,k} \rangle \psi^*_{j,k} . \tag{3}$$

Now we illustrate the procedure of obtaining signal approximation and detail using the multi resolution analysis. For vector space $(V_{2^j})_{j\in Z}$, let $\phi(x)$ be the scale function, then $\sqrt{2^{-j-1}}\phi_{2^{j+1}}(x - 2^{-j-1}k)_{k\in Z}$ is the orthonormal basis for vector space $V_{2^{j+1}}$ [15,16]. It is known that for any $n \in Z$, the function $\phi_{2^j}(x - 2^{-j}n)$ is a member of V_{2^j} which is included in $V_{2^{j+1}}$. The approximation of the signal $f(x)$ at 2^j, $A_{2^j} f(x)$ is characterized by the set of inner products

$$A^d_{2^j} f = (< f(x), \phi_{2^j}(u - 2^{-j}n) >)_{n\in Z} . \tag{4}$$

Eq. (4) is the discrete approximation of signal $f(x)$ at the resolution 2^j [15, 16]. Next, we explain how to extract the difference of information between the approximation of a function $f(x)$ at the resolution 2^j and 2^{j+1}. The difference of information denotes the detail signal at the resolution 2^j. The approximation at the resolution 2^j and 2^{j+1} of a signal is equal to its orthogonal projection on V_{2^j} and $V_{2^{j+1}}$ respectively [16]. Detail signal of $f(x)$ at the resolution 2^j is characterized by the set of inner products:

3 Feature Extraction

In this chapter, we derive data preprocessing feature extraction.

A. Preprocessing

Applying Wavelet transformation, data are not consistent because of phase discrepancy etc. Therefore we need data synchronizing to overcome this trouble. Also unneeded noise can be deleted through this preprocessing. Consider measured current signal.

$$\tilde{f}(t) = f_H(t) + DN(t) + MN(t)\,. \tag{5}$$

where f_H is the healthy signal, $DN(t)$ denotes faulted signal, $MN(t)$ is the measurement noise. $MN(t)$ is considered to the white random noise. White noise has mean zero. However faulted signal $DN(t)$ has its character during period. Average value of measured signal $\tilde{f}(t)$ is obtained as follows

$$\tilde{f}_{peri}(t) = \{\sum_{i=1}^{n}(f_{Hi}(t) + DN_i(t))\}/n\quad. \tag{6}$$

where $i = 1,\ldots,n$, $f_{Hi}(t)$ and $DN_i(t)$ are the functions of each period. We illustrate filtered signal in Fig. 3 when n=64. It is not easy to classify fault in the time domain for a small difference case. Hence we will transform these signals with the Wavelet transformation.

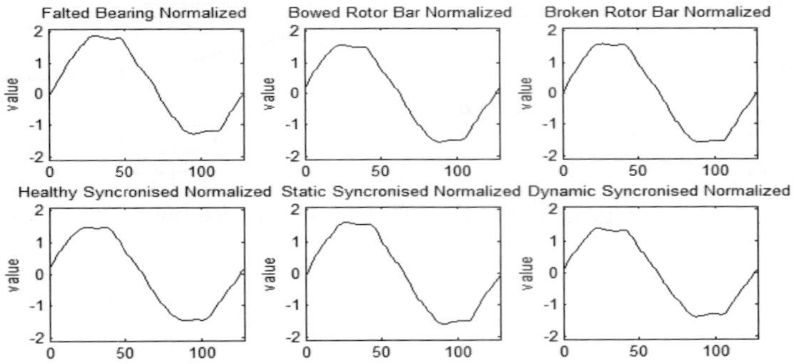

Fig. 3. Filtered signal

B. Feature Extraction

We consider 3-phases induction motor with 220*V*, 3450*rpm*, 0.5*hp*, 34 slots, 4 poles, 24 rotor bars. Stator currents of faulted bearing, bowed rotor, broken rotor bar, static eccentricity, dynamic eccentricity, healthy case are transformed through Fourier and Wavelet transformations. 12 details of the signal are illustrated in Fig. 4. 4th value of the 6th detail has good pattern to classify 6 cases. Front slope and maximum value are shown in Fig. 5 and 6. Static eccentricity and broken rotor bar cases show similar feature, however it can be settled with Fourier transformation results.

With 20 experimental data of 6 cases, we have done Wavelet transformation. Table 1 shows the results of Wavelet transformed data.

– *Fuzzy entropy, distance measure, similarity measure*

Recently, study of the measuring about data set has been focused by numerous researchers. The axiomatic definition of entropy was proposed by Liu [17]. Through out this paper, all notations are followed by Fan, Ma and Xie's [18]. Now we propose

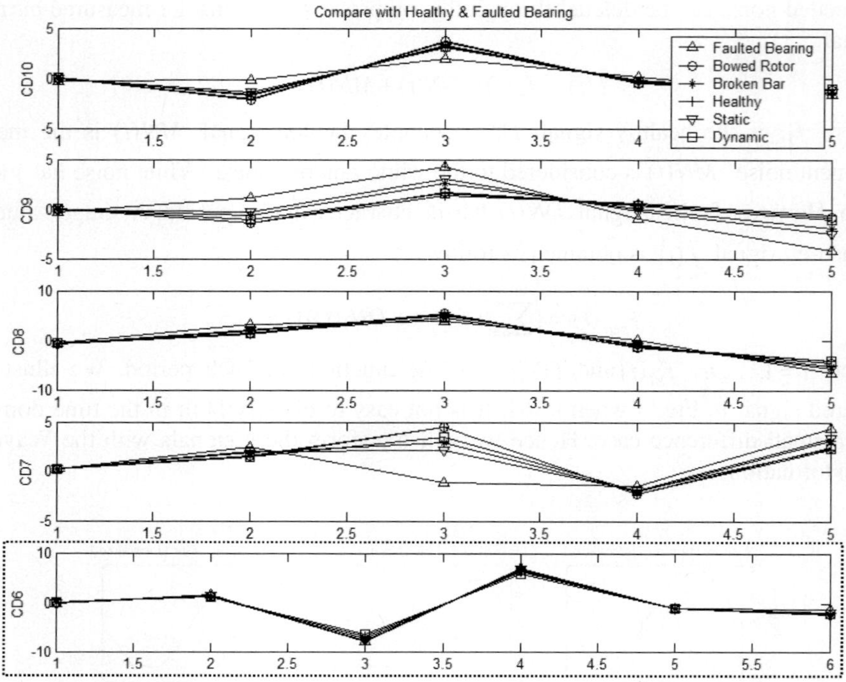

Fig. 4. 6th detail to 10th of Wavelet transform

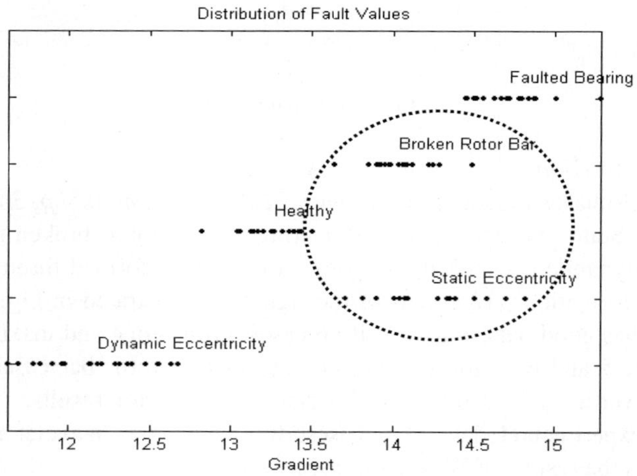

Fig. 5. Characteristic distribution via Wavelet transform (pre-slope)

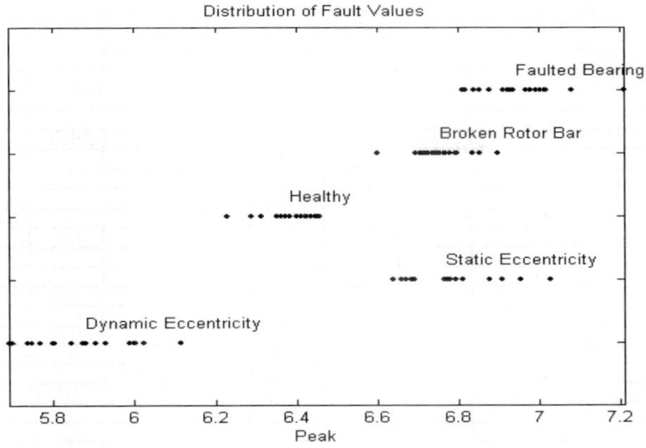

Fig. 6. Characteristic membership function distribution via Wavelet transform (Max. value)

fuzzy entropy function induced by the distance measure. Among the distance measures, Hamming distance is generally used between fuzzy set A and B,

$$d\ (A,B)=\frac{1}{n}\sum_{i=1}^{n}\left|\mu_A(x_i)-\mu_B(x_i)\right|. \tag{7}$$

where, $X=\{x_1, x_2, \cdots, x_n\}$.

In the next Theorem, we propose fuzzy entropy function of A which is induced only crisp set A_{near}.

Theorem 3.1: If distance measure d satisfies $d(A^c,B^c)=d(A,B)$, A, $B\in F(X)$, then

$$e(A)=2d(A\cap A_{near},[1])+2d(A\cup A_{near}),[0])-2. \tag{8}$$

is the fuzzy entropy. Proof can be found in [20].

Theorem 3.1 has the simple structure compare to Fan, Ma and Xie's. We also propose another fuzzy entropy.

Theorem 3.2: If distance measure d satisfies $d(A^c,B^c)=d(A,B)$, A, $B\in F(X)$, then

$$e(A)=2d((A\cap A_{far}),[0])+2d((A\cup A_{far}),[1]). \tag{9}$$

is also fuzzy entropy. Proof can be also found in [20]. Fuzzy entropy function in Theorem 3.1 and 2 are used to select the most reliable phase current. Bearing faulted signals are transformed through Wavelet transformation. We run 50 times of Bootstrap method and 4th values of the 6th detail are obtained from 20 data for each phase [19]. In the literature [20], the first phase ranges 6.866~7.1, the second phase 5.0~7.16, and the third phase 3.5~9.0. With the results of Theorem 3.1 and 2, we calculate entropies of 3-phase currents in Table 2. The results of Theorem 3.1 are same as those of Theorem 3.2 as shown in Table 2. 1st phase current entropy value is the smallest one, hence first current is the most reliable.

Table 1. 4th value of 6th detail of faulted and healthy conditions

No. \ Con.	Fualt Bearing		Bowed Rotor		Broken Rotor Bar		Healthy		Static		Dynamic	
	Gradient	Peak	Gradient	Peak	Gradient	Peak	Gradient	Peak	Gradient	Peak	Gradient	Peak
data 1	14.88	7.0172	13.71	6.5854	14.49	6.8991	13.04	6.2908	14.51	6.878	12.29	5.9028
data 2	14.5	6.8379	13.55	6.5338	14.09	6.7671	13.4	6.4371	14.01	6.6925	11.79	5.7362
data 3	14.84	7.0021	13.27	6.442	13.93	6.7198	13.42	6.4537	14.36	6.811	12.21	5.8725
data 4	14.56	6.879	13.32	6.427	14.09	6.7804	13.36	6.3996	14.36	6.7807	11.69	5.6959
data 5	14.63	6.9143	13.36	6.4479	13.85	6.6965	13.36	6.3996	14.1	6.6862	12.68	6.1149
data 6	15.29	7.2088	12.66	6.2307	13.9	6.7061	13.06	6.3142	14.05	6.6599	12.48	5.9872
data 7	14.8	6.9674	14.23	6.751	13.99	6.7557	13.2	6.3737	14.1	6.6882	12.64	6.0213
data 8	14.87	7.0154	13.9	6.6272	13.95	6.7262	13.14	6.3528	14.82	7.027	12.37	5.9286
data 9	14.46	6.8168	13.34	6.455	14.29	6.8534	13.44	6.4484	14.59	6.9077	11.96	5.7996
data 10	14.7	6.9265	13.6	6.5718	14.29	6.8534	13.51	6.4572	13.82	6.6394	11.98	5.8011
data 11	14.8	6.9789	13.72	6.5766	13.64	6.5992	13.13	6.3512	14.08	6.6932	11.63	5.6883
data 12	14.71	6.9384	13.57	6.5133	13.91	6.7101	13.32	6.4012	14.08	6.686	11.9	5.7664
data 13	14.67	6.9236	13.38	6.4662	14.06	6.7501	13.42	6.4213	14.28	6.7739	12.39	5.998
data 14	15.01	7.0807	12.25	6.0685	14.08	6.7694	13.4	6.4247	14.34	6.7925	12.18	5.8778
data 15	14.52	6.8524	13.85	6.6335	13.98	6.7455	13.26	6.3643	14.34	6.7925	12.32	5.9288
data 16	14.72	6.9335	13.42	6.4734	14.25	6.8368	13.25	6.3611	14.7	6.9562	12.55	6.0009
data 17	14.5	6.8386	14.08	6.6788	14.22	6.7934	13.42	6.4254	13.71	6.6383	12.56	6.0024
data 18	14.45	6.8124	13.23	6.4259	13.91	6.7165	12.82	6.2286	14.39	6.8116	11.83	5.7474
data 19	14.78	6.9692	13.78	6.628	14.12	6.7988	13.17	6.351	13.9	6.6699	12.13	5.8449
data 20	14.8	6.9924	13.8	6.6063	13.99	6.7362	13.39	6.4127	14.28	6.7652	12.14	5.8456
AVRG	14.72	6.9453	13.5	6.5071	14.04	6.7558	13.27	6.3826	14.24	6.7675	12.19	5.878
Variance	0.04	0.0093	0.21	0.0239	0.04	0.0043	0.03	0.0036	0.08	0.0118	0.1	0.0143
Order	6		3		4		2		5		1	
STD	0.205248	0.096671	0.454185	0.154702	3.144738	0.065689	2.972407	0.060165	0.288033	0.108818	0.318167	0.119729

Table 2. 3-Phase entropy

	1st Phase	2nd Phase	3rd Phase
Theorem 3.1	0.62396	0.62504	0.62432
Theorem 3.2	0.62396	0.62504	0.62432

4 DPNN and Experimental Results

In this chapter, we introduce neural network which is derived with the Fourier and Wavelet transformed data.

A. Dynamical Polynomial Neural Networks

Complete bivariate polynomials is designed for modeling method that is originated from Kolmogorov-Gabor polynomials represented according to the GMDH method [21-23]. If two inputs are chosen from four inputs as shown in Fig. 6, then we have ${}_4C_2$ nodes in layer 1. A node can be expressed with the combination of $\{x_1, x_4\}$, then

$$y_1 = f_1(x_1, x_4) = w_{01} + w_{11}x_1 + w_{21}x_4 + w_{31}x_1x_4 + w_{41}x_1^2 + w_{51}x_4^2$$

We collect 5 nodes from 6 nodes in the first layer with the minimum error. The selected 5 nodes are used as inputs in the 2nd layer. In the second layer, 10 (${}_5C_2$) nodes are constructed through input vectors y_1 and y_2 :

$$z = f_3(y_1, y_2) = w_{03} + w_{13}y_1 + w_{23}y_2 + w_{33}y_1y_2 + w_{43}y_1^2 + w_{53}y_2^2 .$$

To determine w_{ij} in DPNN, least square method is required, where $i = 0,1,2,\cdots,n,\ j = 0,1,2,\cdots k$. Obtained w_{ij} minimize error between actual measured output and trained output value. Through Eq. (7), w_{ij} is calculated.

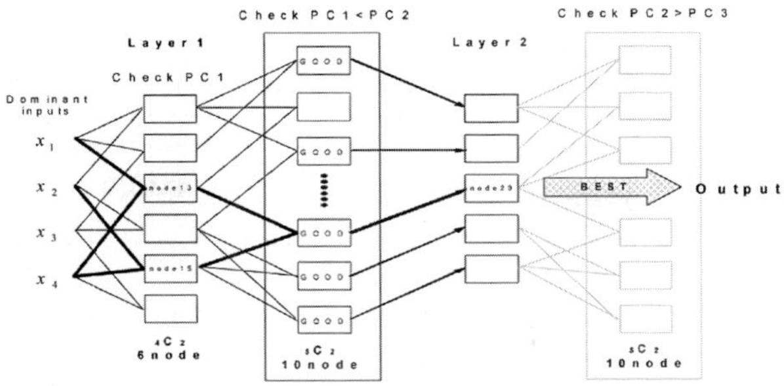

Fig. 7. A simple structure of DPNN

$$J=\sum_{k=1}^{\#ofdata}(z(k)-\hat{z}(k))^2=\| z-\Phi w\|^2 . \tag{10}$$

$$w=(\Phi^T\Phi)^{-1}\Phi^T z . \tag{11}$$

where, $z(k)$ is the actual measured output, $\hat{z}(k)$ is the trained output, w denotes coefficient vector, and Φ is coefficient matrix. Current layer output construct next layer input, and finally reasonable function is obtained by this procedure iteration. Modeling technique with DPNN has the advantage in the simple structure, fast computation time. Furthermore major variable can be detected from the structure of model structure.

B. Model Performance and Choice

– Data classification

DPNN divide total sample data into training and test data by GMDH. Which avoid the preponderance of data by means of using variance. Model structure and coefficients of the each nodes are obtained by the data sets, generally coefficients are obtained from training data and model performance is evaluated through test data. Final model structure is determined by the self organization that is modified through training and test error.

– Model performance

DPNN also takes place overfitting like other neural network. To avoid overfitting DPNN utilizes performance criterion (*PC*). This criterion makes to determine network size to prevent overfitting, costing stability and settlement of training termination. In this paper, we consider *PC* in Eq. (12) that is combined by quadratic form of training error and test error. Eq. (12) evaluates whether the constructed model adapt well for the training data as well as test data which is also applicable to the anew data [24].

$$\begin{aligned} PC &= e_1^2 + e_2^2 + \eta(e_1^2 - e_2^2)^2 \\ e_1^2 &= \sum_{i=1}^{n_A}(y_i^A - f_A(x_i^A))^2 / n_A . \end{aligned} \tag{12}$$

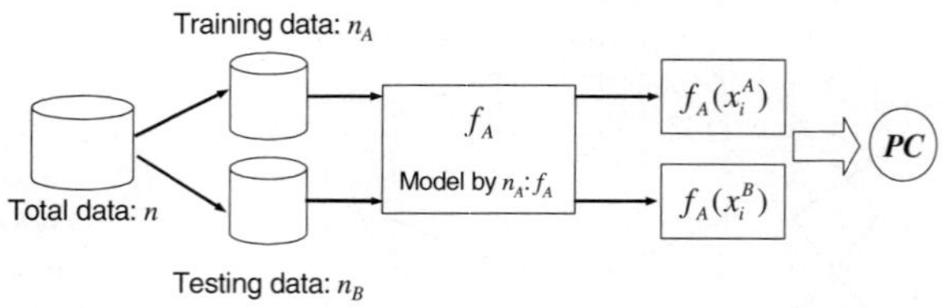

Fig. 8. Data split for model selection

$$e_2^{\,2} = \sum_{i=1}^{n_B} (y_i^{\,B} - f_A(x_i^{\,B}))^2 \,/\, n_B$$

where f_A is the model which is constructed from training data, e_1 denotes training error, e_2 is the test error, n_A is the number of training data, y_i is the measured output, $f_A(x_i^A)$ and $f_A(x_i^B)$ are the training and testing results. The η is the weighting factor between e_1 and e_2.

Optimal model is obtained when minimizing *PC* in Eq. (12). Fig. 9 shows the variations of training error, testing error and *PC* value relative to the layer number. As shown in figure, the layer 3 represents the minimum value of *PC*. Therefore the output of the layer 3 gives the optimal performance.

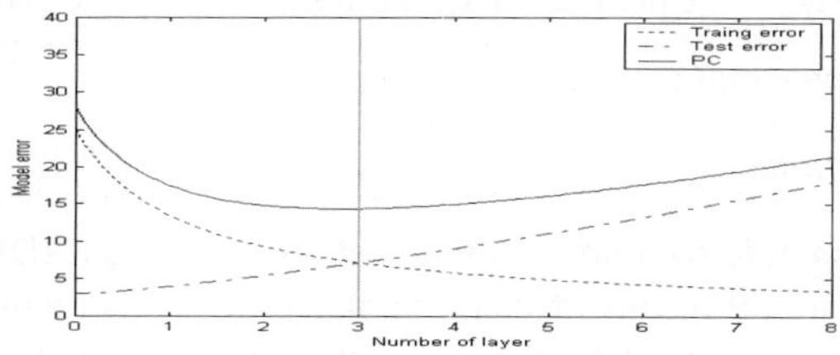

Fig. 9. Variation of *PC* according to the change of layer

5 Illustrative Example

In this paper, input data as features are two Wavelet gradient values and one peak value, and three FFT sidebands. These features are summarized in Table 3.

Table 3. Input dataTable 1

FEATURE INPUT					
Wavelet gradient 1	Wavelet peak	Wavelet gradient 2	FFT side band 1	FFT side band 2	FFT side band 3

20 times of experiments are carried out. Hence 60 input data are allocated to each case. Training data and test data are divided. Output data are corresponded to the target values, and the output cases are allocated by the integer number from 1 to 6. These outputs are shown in Table 4.

Table 4. Output data

No	Motor failure	Target Value
1	Faulted Bearing	1
2	Bowed Rotor	2
3	Broken Rotor Bar	3
4	Healthy	4
5	Static	5
6	Dynamic	6

Table 5. Test results

InputDatas						Output	Target	Targ-Out
W_diff1	W_peak	W_diff2	F_side1	F_side2	Fside3		D *	
14.67341	6.923557	7.917054	25.77623	26.75093	8.050864	1.002311924	1	-0.002311924
15.00554	7.080719	8.121009	25.77623	26.75093	8.050864	1.002311925	1	-0.002311925
14.08417	6.678754	7.690818	26.25063	87.66621	7.258717	1.985566055	2	0.014433945
13.23064	6.425881	7.518335	26.25063	87.66621	7.258717	1.985566054	2	0.014433946
14.22101	6.793435	7.869738	17.52359	315.8903	6.592487	2.949762394	3	0.050237606
13.91303	6.716454	7.83209	17.52359	315.8903	6.592487	2.949762395	3	0.050237605
13.42173	6.425383	7.429609	30.67924	165.8643	7.635858	3.894900943	4	0.105099057
12.82454	6.228617	7.266754	30.67924	165.8643	7.635858	3.894900945	4	0.105099055
13.71187	6.638251	7.71782	25.41188	17.39352	7.798818	4.820981699	5	0.179018301
14.38711	6.811562	7.830917	25.41188	17.39352	7.798818	4.820981701	5	0.179018299
12.56129	6.002426	6.962844	28.42901	80.4102	9.198336	5.728004657	6	0.271995343
11.83004	5.747395	6.738891	28.42901	80.4102	9.198336	5.728004657	6	0.271995343

After training, we get 5.3×10^{-7} training error. Next we test with the remaining data. Total average testing error becomes 0.103. Therefore we could classify the healthy and faulted current signals with the proposed algorithm.

6 Conclusions

In this paper, we carried out induction motor fault detection using Wavelet and Fourier transformations of stator current. Fourier and Wavelet transformations are applied to extract fault characteristics. As shown in Chapter 2, the results of Fourier transformation are insufficient to determine the fault. Hence the complementary cooperation of Wavelet transformation is required. Fourier transformation result shows the sideband in the case of broken rotor bar. The results of Wavelet transformation give the advantageous information to decide the faulted situation. However broken rotor bar and statistic air gap eccentricity illustrate similar results. Hence two transformations are complementary each other. With these fault information, sideband of broken rotor bar from Fourier transformation and 4th coefficients of 6th detail from Wavelet transformation become the input variables of the neural network system to decide the fault case. The neural network system is constructed through polynomial structures which especially has the advantage in short training time and efficient model formulation. With the training and testing results, we verify the usefulness of the neural network. Our results are the specific case of considering motor. If the motor is changed, we need to revisit the Fourier and Wavelet transformations for the target motor. The reliable output could be obtained if the other measurement, vibration, sound, *etc.* be used.

Acknowledgement

This work was supported by "Research Center for Logistics Information Technology (LIT)" hosted by the Ministry of Education & Human Resources Development in Korea.

References

1. Vas, P.: Parameter Estimation, Condition Monitoring, and Diagnosis of Electrical Machines. Clarendron Press, Oxford (1993)
2. Masoud Haji, Hamid, A., Toliyat: Patern Recognition-A Technique for Induction Machines Rotor Fault Detection Eccentricity and Broken Bar Fault. Conference Record of the 2001 IEEE Industry Applications Conference, Vol. 3, 30 Sept.-4 Oct. (2001)1572-1578
3. Nandi, S., Toliyat, H. A.: Cond ition Monitoring and Fault Diagnosis of Electrical Machines – A Review. IEEE Industry Applications Conference, Vol. 1 (1999) 197-204
4. Penman, J., Sedding, H.G., Lloyd, B.A., Fink, W.T.: Detection and Location of Interturn Short Circuits in the Stator Windings of Operating Motors. IEEE Trans. Energy Conv., Vol. 9, No. 4 (1996)
5. Yazici, B., Kliman, G. B.: An Adaptive Statistical Time-Frequency Method for Detection of Broken Bars and Bearing Faults in Motors Using Stator Current. IEEE Trans. On Industry Appl., Vol. 35, No. 2 (1999)
6. Abbaszadeh, K., Milimonfared, J., Haji, M., Toliyat, H. A.: Broken Bar Detection In Induction Motor via Wavelet Transformation. IECON'01: The 27th Annual Conference of the IEEE Industrial Electronics Society (2001)
7. Willsky, A.: A Survey of Design Method for Failure Detection in Dynamic Systems. Automatica, Vol. 12 (1976)
8. Isermann, R.: Fault Diagnosis of Machines via Parameter Estimation and Knowledge Processing – Tutorial Paper. Automatica, Vol .29, No. 4 (1993)
9. Kliman, G. B., Stein, J.: Induction Motor Fault Detection via Passive Current Monitoring. International Conference in Electrical Machines, Cambridge, MA (1990)
10. Kliman, G.B., Koegl, R.A., Stein, J., Endicott, R.D., Madden, M.W.: Noninvasive Detection of Broken Rotor Bars in Operating Induction Motors. IEEE Trans. Energy Conv., Vol. 3, No. 4 (1988)
11. Thomson, W.T., Stewart, I.D.: On-line Current Monitoring for Fault Diagnosis in Inverter Fed Induction Motors. IEE Third international conference on power electronics and drives, London (1988) 432-435
12. Elkasabgy, N.M., Eastham, A.R., Dawson, G. E.: Detection of Broken Bars in the Cage Rotor on an Induction Machine. IEEE Trans. Ind. Appl., Vol. 22, No. 6 (1992) 165-171
13. Bracewell, R.: The Fourier Transform and Its Applications. 3rd ed. New York: McGraw-Hill (1999)
14. Gergkand, G. D.: A Guided Tour of the Fast Fourier Transform. IEEE Spectrum, 6 (1969) 41-52

15. Ingrid Daubechies: Ten Lectures on Wavelets. The Society for Industrial and Applied Mathematics, (1992)
16. Stephane Mallat: A Wavelet Tour of Signal Processing. Academic Press, CA, (1999)
17. Liu Xuecheng: Entropy, Distance Measure and Similarity Measure of Fuzzy Sets and Their Relations. Fuzzy Sets and Systems, 52 (1992) 305-318
18. Fan, J. L., Ma, Y. L., Xie, W. X.: On Some Properties of Distance Measures. Fuzzy Set and Systems, 117 (2001) 355-361
19. Martinez, W. L., Martinez, A.R.: Computational Statistics Handbook with MATLAB. Chapman & Hall/CRC (2002)
20. Development of Fault Detection Algorithm with the Stator Current. POSCON (2003)
21. Ivahnenko, A. G.: Polynomial Theory of Complex System. IEEE trans. Syst. Man and Cybern, Vol. SMC-12 (1971) 364-378
22. Duc Trung Pham, Liu Xing: Neural Networks for Identification. Prediction and control, Springer-Verlag Inc. (1995)
23. Pnadya, A. S., Gilbar, T. C., Kim, K. B.: Neural Network Training Using GMDH Type Algorithm. International Journal of Fuzzy Logic and Intelligent Systems, Vol. 5, No. 1 (2005) 52-58
24. Kim, S. S., Vachtsevanos, G.: Polynomial Fuzzy Neural Network for Identification and Control. NAFIPS'96, North American Fuzzy Information Proc. Society, Berkeley, CA, June 19-22 (1996) 5-9

Prediction of Equipment Maintenance Using Optimized Support Vector Machine

Yi Zeng, Wei Jiang, Changan Zhu, Jianfeng Liu, Weibing Teng, and Yidong Zhang

Department of Precision Machinery and Precision Instrumentation, University of Science and Technology of China,
230026 Hefei, China
zengyi@mail.ustc.edu.cn

Abstract. Failure can be prevented in time by prediction of equipment maintenance so as to promote reliability only if failures can be early predicted. Substantially, it can be boiled down to a pattern recognition problem. Recenty, support vector machine (SVM) becomes a hot technique in this area. When using SVM, how to simultaneously obtain the optimal feature subset and SVM parameters is a crucial problem. This study proposes a method for improving SVM performance in two aspects at one time: feature subset selection and parameter optimization. Fuzzy adaptive particle swarm optimization (FAPSO) is used to optimize both a feature subset and parameters of SVM simultaneously for predictive maintenance. Case analysis shows that this algorithm is scientific and efficient, and adapts to predictive maintenance management for any complicated equipment.

1 Introduction

With the development of computer science, modern engineering systems becomes more and more complicated. Hence, the need for effective equipment maintenance is becoming more significant. It can be approximately divided into three stages for equipment maintenance, post maintenance, regular maintenance and predictive maintenance. Post maintenance disturbs normal produce program, thus enterprises will suffer a great loss with some potential safety problems in addition. Regular maintenance, which demands examination and services in spite of the state of equipment, is a waste of equipment resources, labor force and material resources. Further more, it may lead to superfluous repairs. Shortly, current maintenance modes have much difficulty meeting the need of modernization production. In this circumstance, predictive maintenance with decision function becomes increasingly important[1-3]. According to the daily check record, state monitor and diagnosis information, measures such as data analysis method and expert's knowledge, are taken to determine the category, part and time of maintenance and analyze the degradation degree of the equipment, the trend of malfunctions and hidden troubles, and subsequently to do appropriate services systematically before malfunctions occur. However, it is difficult to choose

D.-S. Huang, K. Li, and G.W. Irwin (Eds.): ICIC 2006, LNAI 4114, pp. 570–579, 2006.

a proper decision-making method for predictive maintenance. At the present time, as a conventional predictive maintenance method, economical major repair model has been applied to predictive maintenance, which determines the lifetime of the equipment by the major repair times. Due to many implicative and intricate factors, it is difficult to analyze a complex equipment system by classical mathematical methods. Although traditional methods have been improved compared to the conventional method, they sometimes fall short of intelligence and lacks of self-learning and adapting abilities. Many AI techniques, such as NN, GA and fuzzy theory have been applied in this area[4-10]. Recently, Support vector machine(SVM) has gained wide acceptance in the applications of intelligent fault diagnosis[11-13].

The paper presents an equipment maintenance prediction methods based on optimized support vector machine, which processes datas with high accuracy, intelligent behavior and super efficiency.

2 Research Background

2.1 Brief Introduction of Pure SVM and PSO

Pure Support vector machines (SVM). The SVM was originally developed by Vapnik[14]. While traditional statistical theory keeps to empirical risk minimization (ERM), SVM satisfies structural risk minimization (SRM) based on statistical learning theory (SLT), whose decision rule could still obtain small error to independent test sampling.SVM mainly has two classes of applications,classification and regression.In this paper,application of classification is discussed.When using SVM, how to simultaneously obtain the optimal feature subset and SVM parameters is a crucial problem. This study proposes fuzzy adaptive particle swarm optimization method for improving SVM performance in two aspects simultaneously: feature subset selection and parameter optimization[15].

Fuzzy Adaptive Particle Swarm Optimization (FAPSO). PSO developed by Kennedy and Eberhart [16] is one of the modern heuristic algorithms under the evolutionary algorithms (EAs) and gained lots of attention in various engineering applications.The pure PSO search process is a nonlinear and complicated process and a linear decreasing inertia weight **w** approach has a linear transition of search ability from global search to local, which does not truly reflect the actual search process required to find the optimum. This is especially true for dynamic optimization problems. But with the appropriate value of **w**, the inertia weight, we can avoid the local search in pure PSO search process to a great extent. We could use FAPSO algorithm to choose the appropriate value of **w**. The experiment mentioned latter will demonstrate using FAPSO could produce a satisfying result[17-19].

3 Hybrid FAPSO-SVM Model

This paper presents a method for improving the performance of SVM in two aspects: feature subset selection and parameter optimization. FAPSO is used to optimize both the feature subset and parameters of SVM simultaneously for maintenance prediction. Fig.1 shows the flow chart of FAPSO-SVM algorithm.

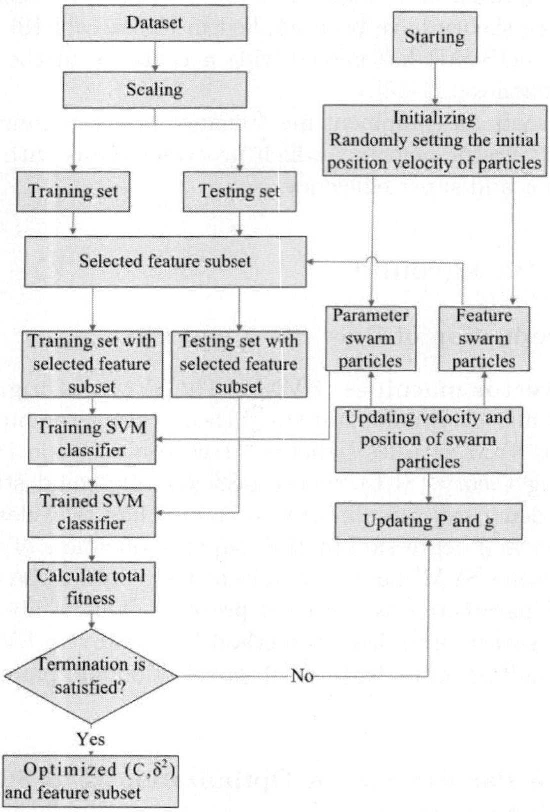

Fig. 1. Flow Chart of FAPSO-SVM

3.1 Optimizing the Feature Subset

Feature subset selection is essentially an optimization problem that involves searching the space for possible features to find one that is optimum or near-optimal with respect to a certain performance measures such as accuracy. In a classification problem, the selection of features is important for many reasons: good generalization performance, running time requirements and constraints imposed by the problem itself.

3.2 Optimizing the Parameters of SVM

One of the big problems in SVM is the selection of the values of parameters. Selecting appropriate values for parameters of SVM plays an important role in the performance of SVM. But it is not known beforehand which values are the best for the problem. Optimizing the parameters of SVM is crucial for the best prediction performance.

This paper proposes FAPSO as the method of optimizing parameters of SVM. In this paper, the radial basis function is used as the kernel function for equipment maintenance prediction. There are two parameters while using RBF kernels: C and δ^2. These two parameters play an important role in the performance of SVM. In this paper, C and δ^2 are encoded as decimal numbers, and optimized by FAPSO.

3.3 Simultaneous Optimization of SVM Using FAPSO

In general, the choice of the feature subset has an influence on the appropriate kernel parameters and vice versa. Therefore the feature subset and parameters of SVM need to be optimized simultaneously for the best prediction performance. Fig.1 shows the flow chart of the proposed model which optimizes both the feature subset and parameters of SVM simultaneously for maintenance prediction. The procedure starts with the randomly selected particles which represent the feature subset and values of parameters of SVM. Each new particle is evaluated by sending it to the SVM model. The SVM model uses the feature subset and values of parameters in order to obtain the performance measure. This performance measure is used as the fitness function and is evolved by FAPSO.

The particles for the feature subset are first encoded as binary strings standing for some subset of the original feature set list. Each bit of the binary strings represents whether the corresponding feature is selected or not. 1 in each bit means the corresponding feature is selected, whereas 0 means unselected. Then convert the binary strings to decimal number within the corresponding boundary. The components of particles for parameters of SVM are randomly generated for C and δ^2. Fig.2 shows examples of generating for FAPSO. Each of the selected feature subsets and parameters is evaluated using SVM. This process is iterated until the best feature subset and values of parameters are found. The data set is divided into a training set and a validation portion. The training set (T)consists of both T_1 and T_2.

FAPSO evolves a number of particles. Each particle consists of sets of features of a given size and the values of parameters. SVM is trained on T_1 using only the features of the individual and the values of parameters of the individual. The fitness is the average prediction accuracy of SVM over T_2.

The fitness function is represented mathematically as follows:

$$Fitness = \frac{\sum_{i=1}^{n} H_i}{n}$$

Table 1. Steps of FAPSO-SVM

Step 1	Define the particles $A(x_1, x_2, x_3)$. x_1: features of SVM are encoded into decimal number. x_2, x_3: parameters of SVM are expressed by decimal numbers.
Step 2	Define population size, the velocity for particle A, acceleration coefficients c_1 and c_2. Use fuzzy adaptive particle swarm optimization to choose the appropriate value of **w**.
Step 3	Generate initial population of particles randomly.
Step 4	While stopping condition is false, do Step 4∼8.
Step 5	Decode jth particle ($j = 1, 2, \ldots, N_{pop}$) to obtain the corresponding feature subset x_{1j} and parameters x_{2j}, x_{3j}.
Step 6	Apply x_{1j} and x_{2j}, x_{3j} to the SVM model to compute the output, O_p.
Step 7	Evaluate fitness, F_j of the jth particle using O_p (fitness function: average predictive accuracy).
Step 8	Calculate total fitness function of particles swarm: $TF = \sum_{i=1}^{N_{pop}} F_1(x_1, x_2, x_3)$.
Step 9	Generate new particle swarm.
Step 10	Stop the iterative step when the terminal condition is reached.

where H_i is 1 if the actual output equals the predicted value of the SVM model, otherwise H_i is zero. The details of the proposed model in an algorithmic form are explained in Table 1.

Particle A(x_1,x_2,x_3)

(a) Feature Subset

1	0	1	. . .	0	1	0
f_1	f_2	f_3	. . .	f_{13}	f_{14}	f_{15}

Feature Subset $=\{f_1, f_3, f_{14}\}$

$x_1 = 12^{14} + 12^3 + 12^1$

(b) Parameters—δ^2 and C

e.g: $x_2 = \delta^2 = 6; x_3 = C = 30$

4 Experimental Design

Out of total 15 main factors, three feature subsets are selected for the experiment. The selected variables and feature subsets are shown Table 2. In Table 2, 15FS represents all main factors. 4FS means 4 main factors which are selected by the independent-sample t-test between each main factor as an input variable, and whether or not to maintenance as the output variable. 12FS and 4FS represent the feature subset selected by logistic regression(LR) stepwise and the simple SVM respectively.

The data set for FAPSO-SVM is separated into two parts: the training set, and the validation set. The ratios are about 0.7 and 0.3. The training data for NN and FAPSO-SVM is divided into two portions again: one is for the training model and the other is for avoiding over fitting. Additionally, to evaluate the effectiveness of the proposed model, we compare two different models with arbitrarily selected values of parameters and a given feature subset. The first model, labeled LR, uses logistic regression. The second model, labeled Pure SVM means SVM.

Table 2. Variables and Feature Subsets

Features	**Feature Subset for model comparision**				**Selected by FAPSO-SVM**
	4FS	8FS	12FS	15FS	
Vibration		√	√	√	√
Oily contamination	√		√	√	
Times of overload		√		√	
Temperature			√	√	√
Pressure	√		√	√	√
Date of last maintenance		√	√	√	
Point inspection		√	√	√	√
Times of maintenance	√			√	
Error rate		√	√	√	
Humidity		√	√	√	√
Cost of maintenance			√	√	√
Precision	√	√		√	
Work eficiency			√	√	
Noise		√	√	√	√
Service age			√	√	√

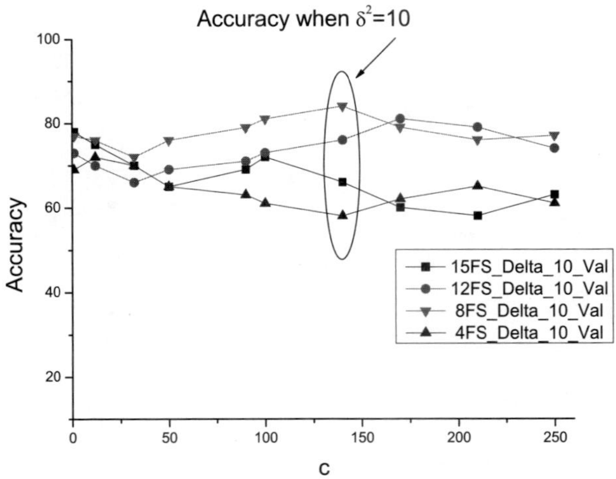

Fig. 2. Accuracy of validation set when $\delta^2 = 10$

5 Experimental Results

5.1 Sensitivity of Pure SVM to Feature Sets and Parameters

Experiments show the classification accuracies of various parameters in SVM using various feature subsets. From the data of the experiments, we can see that, the values of parameters to get the best prediction using 12FS are $\delta^2 = 10$ and

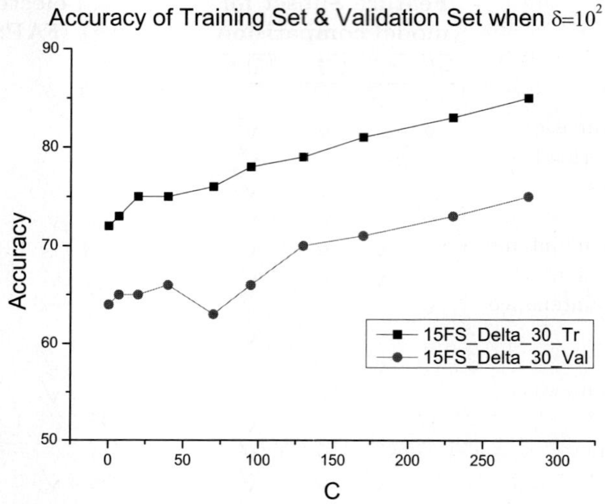

Fig. 3. Accuracy of validation set when $\delta^2 = 10$

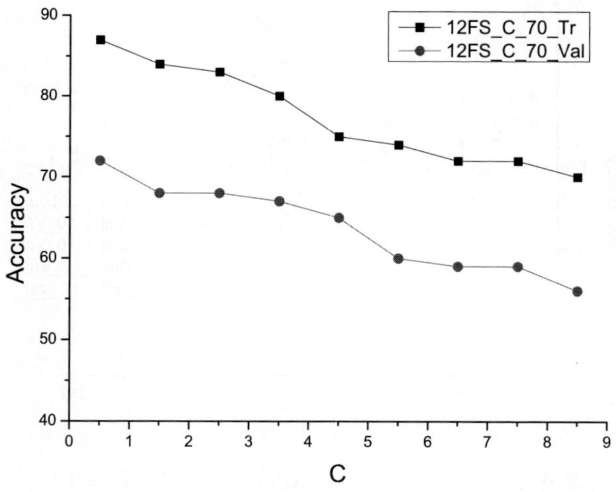

Fig. 4. Accuracy of 12FS's training set (Tr) and validation set (Val) when $C = 70$

C=100. However, with the values of parameters, the prediction using 15FS is poor. Fig.2 shows the sensitivity of SVM to various feature subsets and parameters. The experimental results show that the prediction performance of SVM is sensitive not only to various feature subsets but also to various parameters. Thus, the results show that simultaneous optimization of the feature set and parameters are needed for the best prediction.

Fig.3 shows one of the results of SVM with 15FS where δ^2 is fixed at 55 as C increases. As Tay and Cao[13] mentioned, we can observe that a large value for C would over-fit the training data.

Fig.4 shows the result of SVM with 12FS where C is fixed on 70 and δ^2 increases. We can observe that a small value for δ^2 would over-fit the training data, and δ^2 plays an important role on the generalization performance of SVM.

5.2 Results of FAPSO-SVM

Table 2 shows the feature subset selected by FAPSO. Experiment describes the average prediction accuracy of each model. In Pure SVM, we use the best parameter from the validation set out of the results also from experiment. In Table 3, the proposed model shows better performance than the other models.

Table 3. Average Prediction Accuracy

	LR		Pure SVM		PSO-SVM	
	Training(%)	Validation(%)	Training(%)	Validation(%)	Training(%)	Validation(%)
15FS	76.59%	64.81%	82.35%	78.26%	89.65%	86.31%
12FS	80.20%	71.20%	86.37%	75.20%		
8FS	69.68%	59.96%	80.30%	73.98%		
4FS	73.54%	70.23%	74.29%	70.55%		

6 Discussion and Conclusion

Equipment maintenance prediction is an important and widely studied topic since it has a significant impact on equipment maintenance prediction and reliability. Recently, the SVM has been applied to the problem of intelligent fault diagnosis and maintenance. The SVM-based model has been compared with other methods such as NN and LR, and has shown good results. However, few studies have dealt with integration of FAPSO and SVM although there is a great potential for useful applications in this area. This paper focuses on the improvement of the SVM-based model by means of the integration of FAPSO and SVM. This study presents the methods for improving SVM performance in two aspects simultaneously: feature subset selection and parameter optimization. FAPSO is used to optimize both the feature subset and parameters of SVM simultaneously for maintenance prediction. This paper applies, the proposed FAPSO-SVM model to the maintenance prediction problem using a real data set from a regular examination records of rotation machines in an automobile factory of Anhui province[6]. We evaluated the proposed model using the real data set and compared it with other models. The results showed that the proposed model was effective in finding the optimal feature subset and parameters of SVM, and that it improved the prediction of maintenance. The results also demonstrate that the choice of the feature subset has an influence on the appropriate kernel parameters and vice versa. For future work, we intend to optimize the kernel function, parameters and feature subset simultaneously. We would also like to expand this model to apply to instance selection problems.

Acknowlegement

Thanks to the funds for Chinese Academy of Sciences, special fund for innovative Research of graduate student and special fund for Ph.D candidate of University of Science and Technology of China(USTC) for innovative research.

References

1. Discenzo, F. M., et al.: Motor Diagnostics: Technological Drivers Leading to 21st Century Predictive Diagnostics. In Proceedings of the 1997 of International Conference of Maintenance and Reliability 11∼12
2. Tsang, A. H. C.: Condition-Based Maintenance: Tools and Decision Making. J Quality Maintenance Eng. (1995) 3∼17
3. Wang, J.: Mechanical Fault Diagnosis Technology and Its Applications, Press of North-west Polytechnic University, Xian, China (2001) 77∼120
4. Velarde, S., Santolaria, C.: Development of a Predictive Maintenance System for Centrifugal Pump. J Quality Maintenance Eng 1998(3) 198∼ 211
5. Cheng, L. H., Chieh, J. W.: GA-Based Feature Selection and Parameters Optimization for Support Vector Machines. Expert Systems with Applications (2005) 1∼10
6. Chen, K. X., Li, C. Q.: Techique of State Monitoring and Fault Diagnosis of Equipment. Press of University of Science and Technology of China, Hefei, Anhui, (1991) 420∼421
7. Wang, J. P., Hu, H. T.: Vibration-Based Fault Diagnosis of Pump Using Fuzzy Technique. Measurement 39 (2006) 176∼185
8. Shin, H. J., Eom, D. H.: One-Class Support Vector Machinesan Application in Machine Fault Detection and Classification. Computers Industrial Engineering 48 (2005) 395∼408
9. Hong, D. H., Hwang, C. H.: Support Vector Fuzzy Regression Machines.Fuzzy Sets and Systems 138 (2003) 271∼281
10. Yang, M. S., Shih, H. M.: Cluster Analysis Based on Fuzzy Relations. J. Fuzzy Sets and Systems 120(2) (2001) 197∼212
11. Burges, C.: A Tutorial on Support Vector Machines for Pattern Recognition. Data Mining and Knowledge Discovery 2(2) (1998) 121∼167
12. Toscano, R., Lyonnet, P.: Parameterization of a Fuzzy Classifier for the Diagnosis of an Industrial Process. Reliability Engineering and System Safety 77 (2002) 269∼279

13. Cao, L., Tay, F. E. H.: Financial Forecasting Using Support Vector Machines. Neural Computing & Applications 10 (2001) 184∼192
14. Vapnik, A.N.: The Nature of Statistical Learning Theory. Springer, New York
15. Bradley, P. S.: Feature Selection Via Mathematical Programming. INFORMS Journal on Computing 10 (1998) 209∼217
16. Kennedy, J., Eberhart, R.: Particle Swarm Optimization. In: IEEE Int'l Conf on Neural Networks, Perth, Australia (1995) 1942∼1948
17. Eberhart, R., Kennedy, J.: A New Optimizer Using Particle Swarm Theory. In Proceedings of the Sixth International Symposium on Micro Machine and Human Science, Nagoya, Japan (1995) 39∼43
18. Shi, Y., Eberhart, R.: A Modified Particle Swarm Optimizer. In: IEEE World Congress on Computational Intelligence(1998) 69∼73
19. Shi, Y., Eberhart, R. C.: Fuzzy Adaptive Particle Swarm Optimization. In: Proc Congress on Evolutionary Computation, Seoul, Korea (2001)

The Covariance Constraint Control Method of Fault Detect for Complicated Systems

Darong Huang[1,2], Xiyue Huang[2], Changcheng Xiang[2], Wei Li[3], and Yin Zhang[3]

[1] College of Information and Mathematics, Chongqing Jiaotong University, Chongqing 400074, China
hcx1978@yahoo.com.cn

[2] College of Automation, Chongqing University, Chongqing 400044, China
xyhuang@cqu.edu.cn

[3] College of Coputer Science, Chongqing Jiaotong University, Chongqing 400074, China
Zh_angY_in916@yahoo.com.cn

Abstract. Based on covariance constraint control theory and statistic, the fault predicts problem inner the dynamic complicated system is researched. First of all, according to the important factor to influence the running state by the Multifactor analyze method, we have defined and analyzed the parameter structure of the average and error for state observe values correspondence to the fault point; Simultaneous, the fitting quantitative model and error control threshold of complicated system were presented; secondly, we has given the running principium of integration system to fault detect and designed the network topological structure and the data transfer model; Finally, a simulated example have shown that the technique is effectively and exactly. The theoretical analyze indicated that the presented integration technology of Fault detect has a broad prospect for practical application.

1 Introduction

In the recent years, because all kinds of fatal accidents were continually occurred by reason of fault for key equipment, all national governments, societies and researchers attached importance to the study that the fault diagnosis and forecasting complex systems. Whereas, because nonlinear degree of some complex equipment system is more and more high, problem of Fault Prediction is so complicated and difficult that is need analyzed from different angle. Many scholars [1-2] were promoted to use neural network to study the fault diagnose and prediction of non-linear system from different views and utilized a spot of information to forecast and to diagnose the fault. In [3-5], some scholars studied the fault prediction based on observation data of the fault state. However, above fault prediction model weren't considered enough statistical character of the on-line data and the control threshold judging the fault state may be given subjective, as a result the fault predict isn't quite effectively.

To solve these problems, the scholars tried to use various methods for the fault prediction of complicated systems. And that had provided an application background

D.-S. Huang, K. Li, and G.W. Irwin (Eds.): ICIC 2006, LNAI 4114, pp. 580 – 588, 2006.

for covariance control [6-8] forming and developing since 80's. Their main ideas include: First the appropriate state covariance was selected accord with the different performance index of systems, and then we will design the control algorithms to satisfy the anticipant performance. The idea was shown that the performance object about fault predict technology may be achieved by the covariance constraint control of running state for complicated systems. According to this, some scholars [9-11] had researched the fault predict problems of some complex systems by covariance control theory and achieved some better effect. It is a pity that these investigations were effectively only in oneself special predict target environment. In other words, the different object demand to the different method, and to the large system construction have no a united frame to proceed the fault predict; moreover, owing to uncertain factor, as a result the accurate fault predict is impossible. To solve these problems, the authors studied the fault prediction of complicated systems by hybrid methods of covariance control theory and statistics and presented a new algorithm for Fault Prediction applying in practical Engineering.

The layout of the rest of the paper is as follow: The model of fault predicts was constructed in Section 2.Section 3 describes corresponding the algorithms and designs the network topological of fault predict. Section 4 discusses the simulative results of systems by an example, and Section 5 concludes this paper with final inferences and directions for future work.

2 Construct and Analyses of Model

2.1 Description of Problem

For the complex systems, the stability is the basal condition to ensure the well-balanced running of systems. Therefore, effective real-time control was carried out by continuous detect the fault states and adjust the failures in the running process of systems.

In the running process of complicated systems, the various factors influencing to the running state of systems were called the condition attribute, and the corresponding fault states were called decision attribute. However, not all condition attributes are same importance to the well-balanced running of systems: Some are so no important that it may confound right and wrong, thereby cleaning the redundancy datum from the database to ensure the right decision making. If the information is extracted from these data and analyzed by rational ways, the certain relationship between these conditions attribute and fault occurred can be found, then we can use the data of fault situation to judge fault to take place whether or not. Thus the author extracts the vital factors influencing to fault situation by factor-analyze of statistical, and analyzes information's about running situation; thus gives the fitting quantities model of forecasting decision-making fault, and designs the control threshold model of fault according to covariance control theory.

2.2 Construct of Model

Suppose there are n state variables $X_1, X_2, \cdots, X_n$ interrelated with the fault of systems, and Y notes the fault point. So the state variables set $X = \{X_1, X_2, \cdots, X_n\}$

is the condition attribute and the fault point Y is the decision attribute for whole systems. Owing to that not all condition attributes are same importance to the well-balanced running of systems, the vital factors influencing the running situation may be extracted by factor-analyze method in statistic: First, a percentage of total effect of the vital factors is given by the actual running situation; and then the vital factors were extracted by using the factor-analyze module in the SPSS software package.

If the vital factors which the factor-analyze module extracted were m state variables $X_1, X_2, \cdots, X_m$. Let $X = \{X_1, X_2, \cdots, X_m\}$. Thus, for the fault point Y, the vital factor of fault had different state value of systems at the different moment in historical fault database (for example, the traffic flow magnitude is different at the different moment). For facility, we selected n different states of fault from the historical fault database for every vital factor. Let

$$\begin{array}{c} \quad X_1 \quad X_2 \quad \cdots\cdots \quad X_m \\ \begin{array}{c} 1 \\ 2 \\ \vdots \\ n \end{array} \begin{pmatrix} X_{11} & X_{12} & \cdots & X_{1m} \\ X_{21} & X_{22} & \cdots & X_{2m} \\ \vdots & \vdots & \cdots & \vdots \\ X_{n1} & X_{n2} & \cdots & X_{nm} \end{pmatrix} = \hat{\bar{X}} \end{array} \tag{1}$$

Where every fault observation vector $h_{(i)} = (X_{i1}, X_{i2}, \cdots, X_{im})$ $(i = 1, 2, \cdots, n)$ was regarded as a stochastic vector on account of the data come from the oneself systems and the state indexes of the m influencing factors were not presupposed, thus $\hat{\bar{X}}$ was a stochastic matrix and was regarded a observation matrix or sample database. Thereby, the quantitative model between the running state Y and the influencing factors was gotten by least-square approximation as following.

$$Y = \beta X + \omega \tag{2}$$

Where $\beta = (\beta_1, \beta_2, \cdots, \beta_m)$, $X = \{X_1, X_2, \cdots, X_m\}^T$, ω is fitting error and satisfy that $\omega \sim (0, \sigma^2)$.

Hence the prediction model of running situation of systems was gotten, and we can use the quantitative model to judge fault to take place whether or not. Its main idea includes: first of all, computing the average-value exponent of state data of influencing factors for n faults coming from the fault database. Secondly, the decision average-value $\bar{Y}$ were gotten by the forecasting quantitative model of systems; whereafter, the error which is made between forecasting decision situation Y and the decision average-value $\bar{Y}$, i.e. $\Delta = \left|Y - \bar{Y}\right|$, can be used to judge fault to take place whether or not. If the error threshold $\bar{\Delta}$ can be presented and exists $\left|Y - \bar{Y}\right| \geq \bar{\Delta}$, that may judge that the systems have abnormal phenomenon and need to repair it.

From above analysis know that must establish the error control threshold of abnormal running of systems, and that is very vital problem in research of fault predict technology for complex systems. Follow we will establish the error control threshold model of abnormal running of systems.

2.3 Analysis of Error Control Threshold Model

In the running process of systems, because the dimension of all fault state observations is consistent for every influencing factor, as a result the average-value exponent model of all state observations, which belong to i th influencing factor, were designed as following.

$$\overline{X}_{(i)} \overset{\Delta}{=} \sqrt{\frac{(\max_j x_{ji})^2 + (\frac{1}{n}\sum_{j=1}^{n} X_{ji})^2}{2}} \quad (i=1,2,\cdots,m) \tag{3}$$

So the average-value vector $\overline{X}=(\overline{X}_{(1)},\overline{X}_{(2)},\cdots\overline{X}_{(m)})^T$ was gotten using (3) for i th $(i=1,2,\cdots,m)$ influencing factor of complex systems. And that average-value $\overline{Y}$ of the fault state was computed by formula (2). Simultaneity, we can compute the error between the average-value $\overline{Y}$ and historical fault state $Y_i\,(i=1,2,\cdots,n)$. The computed formula is as following.

$$\Delta_i = \left|\overline{Y} - Y_{(i)}\right| \quad (j=1,2,\cdots,n) \tag{4}$$

Obviously, before an arbitrary on-line fault of systems took place, the corresponding running state observation-value had abnormal change and there exits an error between the factual state-value and the average-value, as a result every fault-state has an abnormal error .For logical forecasting, the paper gave the quantitative index of analyzing fault predict, which were regard as the error average-value exponent model, i.e.

$$\overline{\Delta} \overset{\Delta}{=} \sqrt{\frac{(\max_i \Delta_i)^2 + (\frac{1}{n}\sum_{i=1}^{n} \Delta_i)^2}{2}} \quad (i=1,2,\cdots,m) \tag{5}$$

According to the covariance constraint theory, we can use the error, which is made between running state-value Y and the decision average-value $\overline{Y}$, i.e. $\Delta = \left|Y-\overline{Y}\right|$, to judge fault to take place whether or not. If there exists $\left|Y-\overline{Y}\right| \geq \overline{\Delta}$, that may judge that the systems have abnormal phenomenon and need to adjust the systems. As for the detailed adjustive scheme, the most important point is that weight coefficient of influencing factor in the prediction model when we designed the integrated systems. The bigger the coefficient $\beta_i\,(i=1,2,\cdots,m)$ is, the more influence the i th factor is. First adjust the i th parameter, thus it is to ensure the system normal running to avoid the vital expense on account of fault.

3 Designs and Implementation of Algorithms

In the running process of complicated system, because the whole system character presents entirely in the all data of on-line observation, we should install a software system of fault prediction on-line to ensure the system to run stability in practical and to avoid paralysis of system.

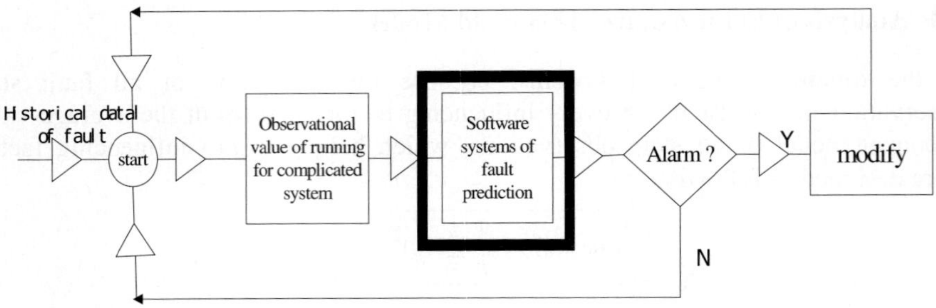

Fig. 1. Design chart of real-time observation for decision-making systems

Once singular phenomenon appears in the complicated system, the embedded software system can give an alarm and warn operator to maintain the complicated system. Its main design is showed as Fig. 1.

Obviously, the black-frame of this design figure is the software system of FP on-line that is embedded into the complicated system .So we should analyze the algorithm and implementation of software for the key part.

In section 2, we presented that control threshold which was used to judge the abnormal phenomenon of the online detect data to take place whether or not. If the abnormal phenomenon existed, thus need repair the systems and restore to the normal situation. Therefore the algorithm is presented as following.

1) Initialization of system. Input the historical fault database, and the vital factors $X = \{X_1, X_2, \cdots, X_m\}$ were extracted by using the factor-analyze module in the SPSS software package, thus we get $\hat{X}$ and pre-storage in the computer.

2) Established the quantitative model between the factors $X = \{X_1, X_2, \cdots, X_m\}$. Simultaneous, computed the historical fault state Y_i and the average-value $\overline{Y}$ by the quantitative model and formula (3).

3) Computing the control threshold $\overline{\Delta}$ of the fault state using (4) and (5), and storage in the computer.

4) Computing the error Δ_j between the running states Y_j and the average-value $\overline{Y}$ for the online detecting systems, then invoking the fault control threshold $\overline{\Delta}$ of the fault state from database and going on next step.

5) Verifying whether $\Delta_j > \overline{\Delta}$ exists or not, if exist, thus adjust the systems and return step 1. Otherwise directly return step1.

6) Printed the analyzing report of system.

The implementation algorithm is shown in the flowing chart as Fig 2.

Fig. 2 shows that the network topological structure was composed of the pattern recognition module, discriminate module, decision module and the invoke module. Where, the pattern module and the discriminate module were elements and the kernel respectively. Thus in the running process of complex systems the control flow of transmitted data is shown in the flowing chart as Fig. 3.

Obviously, all data may be returned to the control center and be real-time controlled, so the effective online detecting of complex systems can be carried out.

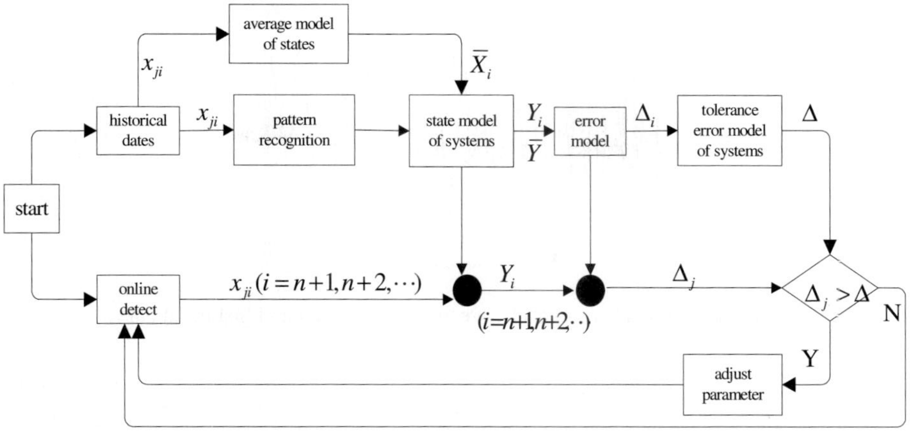

Fig. 2. Network topological structure of Fault detect for complicated systems

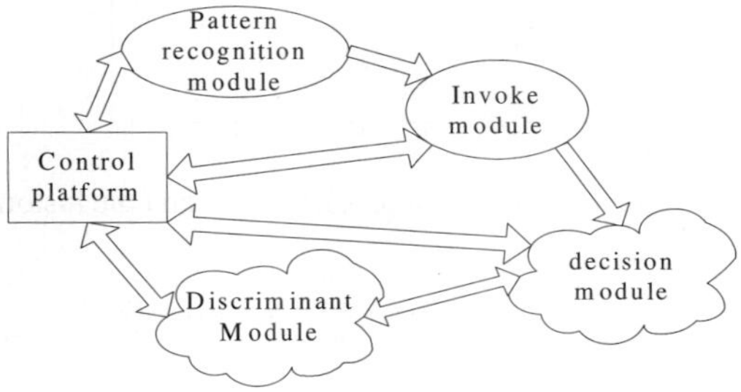

Fig. 3. Control flow of data for complicated systems

4 Simulation Examples

The paper applied the fault detecting integrated technology, which was designed according to the covariance constraint theory and statistic, to the forecasting fault of the excitation device systems of the power equipment. First of all, the important influencing factors, which were extracted by multifactor analyze from the historical data, consist of the PT break-phase, CT signal, volts d.c. and current, synchronous signal, temperature of sensors and the Airborne capacity. Secondly, for the historical fault data, the curve fitting chart between the predicting model and the actual observation-value was gotten by simulation: Fig. 4 displays the total fitting analysis chart and Fig.5 shows the part fitting analysis.

Fig.4 and Fig. 5 indicated that the error between the fitting data and the actual data is very small and the designed systems may achieve the anticipant error threshold 0.003,so that the model of systems is effectively and can be applied to the practical systems. In practical application the designed systems had run almost 1000 epochs and Fig.6 shows the total running performance.

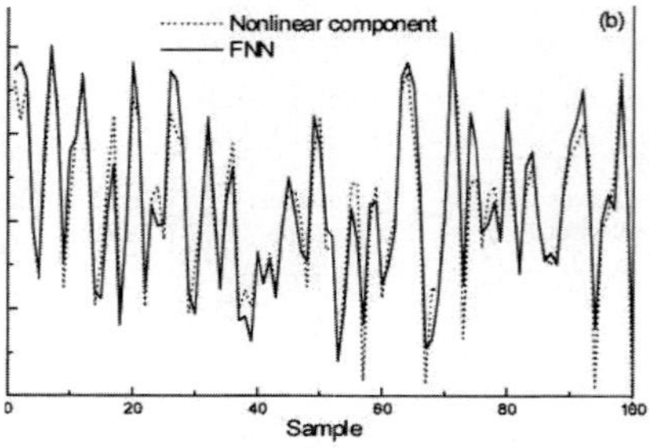

Fig. 4. Fitting analysis chart between predict model and historical data

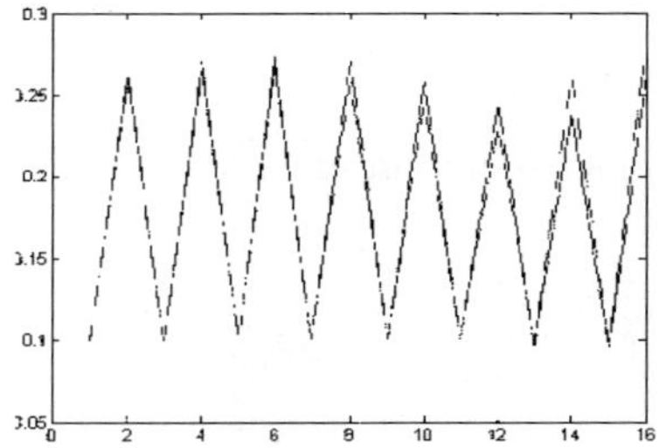

Fig. 5. Part fitting chart between predict model and the historical data

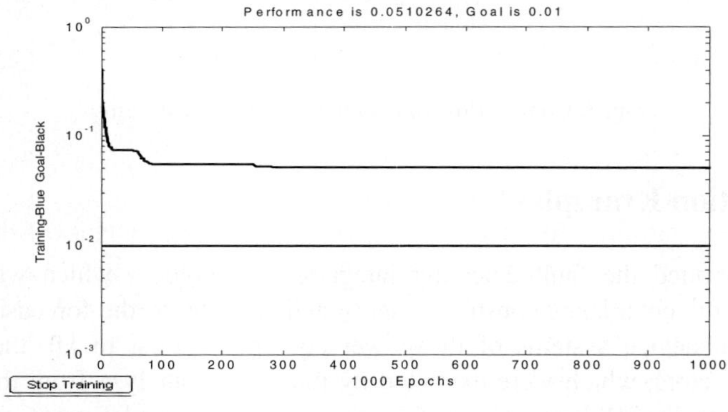

Fig. 6. Total running performance chart of the excitation device systems

The running effect of systems indicated that the abnormal phenomenon of the security alarm took place at 20th second, and then adjusts the parameter of systems to ensure the systems normal running. But the security alarm systems gave an alarm at 60th second and 249th second, and continuously adjust the parameter of the systems to ensure the systems normal running. Fig.6 displays that the abnormal phenomena of the designed systems seem to change wee, and yet the running performance is very instable during the warning. For the sake of detailed analyzing the danger, we take the running performance chart from 0th second to 40th second as Fig. 7.

Fig. 7 displays that the interior change of systems was quite rapidly. It accorded with the practical situation. Simultaneous, there exists a glacis from the initial warning to normal running; as a result the demand time which was used to adjust parameter of the systems was satisfied.

These analyses indicated that the covariance constraint control of fault detecting for complex systems is effectively.

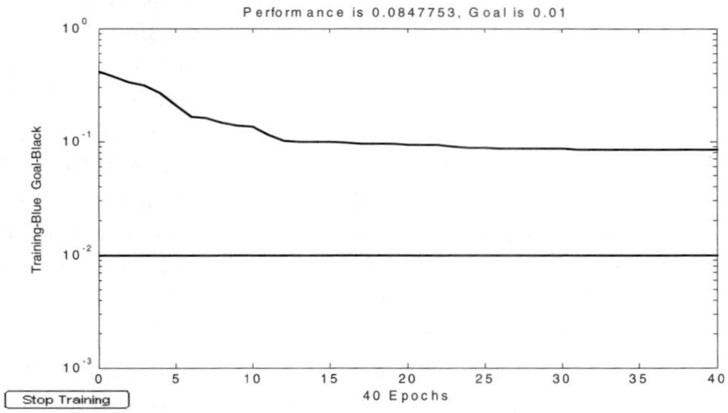

Fig. 7. Part running performance chart of the excitation device systems

5 Conclusions

The paper applied the fault detecting integrated technology, which was designed according to the covariance constraint theory and statistic, to practical engineering. The experiment shows that the fault predicting technology is effectively, and can carry out the intelligent fault-predict. Simultaneous, the structure between all sub-modules is high cohesion and low coupling, and the all data may be returned to the control center for information fusion. Therefore, the disadvantage which data is transmitted by one-way communication was overcome, and then the internal information interchange of the complex systems is possible. And moreover, the integrated systems have well opening and adaptability.

However, owing to that worker manipulated the intelligent systems; the running situation of the systems was influenced. Thereby, investigation about how to logically distribute the information resources of complex systems remains an interesting area for further research.

Acknowledgments

The authors acknowledge the research grants provided by technological project of chongqing education council to Da-rong huang (No.KJ060414) and NSF P.R.China to Xi-yue Huang (No.60443006).

References

1. Zhao, X., Xiao, D.Y.: Fault Diagnosis of Nonlinear Systems Using Multistep Prediction of Time Series Based on Neural Network. Control theory and applications. 6 (2000) 803-808
2. Wu, A.G., Wang, D.Q., Liang, J.: Application of Generalized Predictive Control with Neural Error Correction in Networked Control System. Proceedings of the 5th World Congress on Intelligent Control and Automation, IEEE. 4 (2004) 1386-1390
3. Wu, J.F., Hu, N.S., Hu, S., Zhao, Y.: Application of Some Neural Network in Fault Diagnosis of the Steam Turbine Regenerative System. Proceeding of the First international conference on machine learning and cybernetics, Bejing, IEEE.1 (2002) 184-187
4. Wu, D., Wu, M., An, J.W.: Design of an Expert System Based on Neural Network Ensembles for Missile Fault Diagnosis. Proceedings of the 2003 IEEE international conference on robotics, intelligent systems and signal processing, IEEE. 3 (2003) 903-908
5. Guo, M., Xie, L., Wang, S.Q.: Model Based Multiscale Performance Monitoring for Batch Processes. Theory and practice of system engineering. 1 (2004) 97-102 (In Chinese)
6. Hotz, A.F., Skelton, R.E.: Covariance Control Theory. Int. J. Control. 1 (1987) 13-32
7. Skelton, R.E, Iwasaki, T.: Lyapunov and Controllers. Int. J. Control. 3 (1993) 519-536
8. Iwasaki, T., Skelton, R.E., Corless, M.: A Recursive Construction Algorithm for Covariance Control. IEEE Transactions on Automatic Control. 2 (1998) 268-272
9. Lu, J.B., Skelton, R.E.: Covariance Control Using Closed Loop Modeling for Structures. Proceeding of the 1997 ASCE Structures Congress. (1997) 1-5
10. Abid, S., Fnaiech, F., Tunisia, T., Najim, M.: Evaluation of the Feed-Forward Neural Network Covariance Matrix Error. Neural Networks in Signal Processing, IEEE. 2 (2000) 3482-3485
11. Roger, B.: Stationary Covariance Realization with a Specified Distribution of Amplitudes. Proceeding of the 37th IEEE conference on decision & control. (1998) 3742-3744

A Fault Diagnosis Prototype System Based on Causality Diagram

Xinghua Fan, Feng Hu, and Simon X. Yang

College of Computer Science and Technology,
Chongqing University of Posts and Telecommunications, Chongqing 400065, P.R. China
{fanxh, hufeng}@cqupt.edu.cn, syang@uoguelph.ca

Abstract. There exists a challenge, i.e., to diagnose failures of such a complex system that has the following characters: (1) it has a causality loop structure; (2) system observed variables are discrete, or continuous, or mixed; and (3) system has time lag, i.e., it has delay of fault effect. For the task, this paper proposes a fault diagnosis prototype system based on causality diagram, and describes the key technologies used. The proposed prototype system comprises datum collection subsystem, model design subsystem, fault diagnosis subsystem, and diagnosis result display subsystem. In this system, the fault knowledge related fault diagnosis is represented in a fault influence propagation diagram (FIPD), which results from a causality diagram. The fault knowledge related delay of fault effect is represented in a 2-time-slice causality diagram (2-TSCD), which is a time stochastic model extended from a FIPD. The method of find fault modes in a FIPD or a 2-TSCD is presented. The proposed prototype system has flexible fault knowledge representation, rapid diagnosis process, and well practicability.

1 Introduction

Fault detection and fault diagnosis of complex system on-line become increasingly important for many technical processes, especially for safety related processes like unclear plants and chemical plants. There exist causality relations among the inputs and outputs of complex system. These relations are determined by its structure and have imprecise quantitative or logistic character. So, it does not one to one mapping between its failures and its symptoms. As a result, the fault diagnosis of complex system becomes more complex and difficult. At present, there exists a challenge, i.e., to detect and diagnose the failures of such a complex system that has the following characters: (1) it has a causality loop structure, i.e., there exists causality loop influence among system states or system observed variables; (2) system observed variables are discrete, or continuous, or mixed; and (3) system has time lag, i.e., not all causality relations among system variables occur at the same time, and some causality relation effects have time lag. For example, the flow rate F and the pressure P in an oil tank have differential coefficient relation. This relation brings time lag between F and P, i.e., the flow rate Ft at time t will affect the pressure Pt+1 at time t+1. If employing the existing fault-diagnosis technologies to the task described in

D.-S. Huang, K. Li, and G.W. Irwin (Eds.): ICIC 2006, LNAI 4114, pp. 589 – 595, 2006.

above, it is difficult to get a valid result rapidly. The possible reasons are as follows: some of them are mainly suitable for the diagnosis of single component, some of them are not mature in theory, and some of them have shortcoming in knowledge representation and reasoning. For example, qualitative reasoning method, which is famous in AI community, is not suitable for fault diagnosis of complex system that has continue variable and non-deterministic system dynamics [1]. The reason is that qualitative reasoning method lacks of precise knowledge representation, ant its reasoning has fuzzy and uncertainty.

Causality diagram is a knowledge representation and reasoning model under uncertainty based on probability [2]. Outstanding characteristics of causality diagram are as follows. (1) It is satisfied probability theory absolutely, and has well theory foundation; (2) It can deal with the causality loop. The reason is that causality diagram represents the causality relationship among the domain random variables described by random event's probability. This representation implies a joint probability distribution. So, it has no limitation to the topology structure of diagram, i.e., it does not require a DAG; (3) It exploits direct causality intensity not condition probability to represent knowledge, and this process can avoid the correlativity difficulty among the giving knowledge when domain experts represent knowledge. The reason is that this process is consistent with the knowledge structure in expert's brain; and (4) It has dynamic characteristic, i.e., its structure can be modified according to on-line information received. This is very important for its application such as fault diagnosis, because this process can reduce the scale of causality diagram according to the evidence received and improve the system performance. From the characters of causality diagram, it can be seen that there is a very good mapping between the knowledge representation of causality diagram and the fault character of complex system. So, causality diagram can represent the fault knowledge of complex system effectively, and be suited for fault diagnosis of complex system. The objective of this paper is to propose a fault diagnosis prototype system based on causality diagram, which can deal with the challenge task described in above.

2 Architecture of Fault Diagnosis Prototype System

The fault diagnosis prototype system comprises datum collection subsystem, model design subsystem, fault diagnosis subsystem, and diagnosis result display subsystem. Its architecture is illustrated as Fig.1.

Datum collection subsystem gathers the state information of complex system, which is related to fault diagnosis, from locale equipment, and save these state information to database in term of time sequence. **Model design subsystem** provides graphical interfaces for domain engineers, to acquire and save the causality diagram model, which is needed for fault diagnosis. **Diagnosis result display subsystem** accepts the diagnosis results and all kinds of real-time state information from fault diagnosis subsystem, and then display all kinds of datum and diagnosis results to operator. **Fault diagnosis subsystem** gets the state information from database, and monitor system state. Once find the system' abnormal behavior, fault diagnosis subsystem begins to work, to find the possible failures and sort them according to the probability that failure occurs under giving evidence. This is implemented by using

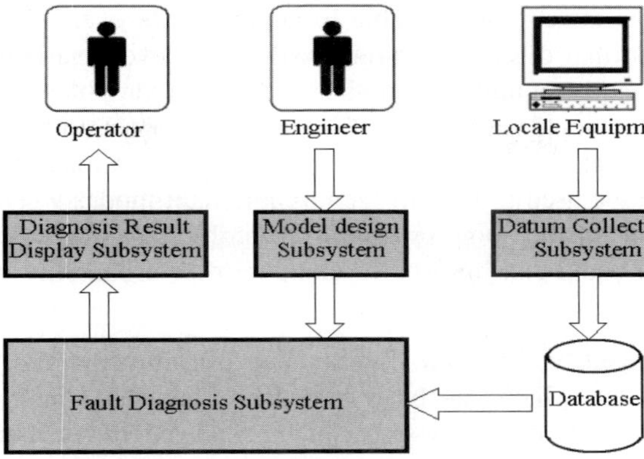

Fig. 1. Architecture of the fault diagnosis prototype system

the causality diagram model and the state information (i.e., evidence received). Finally, it sends the diagnosis result to diagnosis result display subsystem.

The key question of implementing the proposed prototype system is as follows. (1) How to use expert knowledge to construct the causality diagram? (2) How to get fault mode from the causality diagram? (3) How to compute the probability of fault mode under giving evidence. The third question, i.e., the reasoning algorithm of causality diagram, is presented in [3-4]. In this paper, we only concentrate on the former two questions. So, we will discuss the former two questions in the next two sections.

3 Fault Knowledge Representations in Causality Diagram

If the complex system has not time lag, the fault knowledge related fault diagnosis is represented in a multi-value causality diagram; otherwise these knowledge is represented in a 2-time-slice causality diagram.

Fault influence propagation diagram. The multi-value causality diagram is called fault influence propagation diagram (FIPD) when it is used for fault diagnosis. The differences between causality diagram and FIPD are as follows. (1) The node event variable represents a signal of complex system, which can be observed. Every state of node event variable represents an abnormal behavior of the checker, which corresponds to the target signal. The default state of node event variable represents a normal behavior of the checker. For example, if a node event variable represents a signal of stream flow, its state corresponds an abnormal behavior such as stream flow abnormal high or stream flow abnormal low. (2) The basic event variable represents component failure of complex system. Every state of basic event variable represents a component failure state, and its default state represents that the corresponding component is normal. (3) The linkage event variable represents the fault influence propagation relation between the causation variable and result variable. The linkage variable, which points from a basic event variable to another node event variable, represents that component failure of corresponding to the basic event variable cause the signal abnormal of corresponding to node event variable. The linkage variable, which points from a node event variable to another node event variable, represents that the signal abnormal of corresponding to the node event variable cause another signal abnormal of corresponding to another node event variable. The fault influence propagation diagram includes two kind of important information that is useful for the fault diagnosis: One is the fault influence propagation relationship in the causality diagram, which can be used to find all the possible fault modes when the evidence is received. The other is the joint probability distribution, which is implied in all variables of a FIPD, and can be used to compute post-probability of failure modes under giving evidence.

Two-time-slice causality diagram. 2-time-slice causality diagram (2-TSCD) is a time stochastic model, which can be regarded as a extended multi-value causality diagram. Suppose that complex system can be modeled by system variable set z, system variables are divided to two subsets Y and X: subset $Y \subseteq Z$ represents observed variable set, i.e., the value of every variable in sub set Y can be known. And these observed variable in subset Y could be discrete or continuous. The other subset $X \subseteq Z$ represents un-observed variable set, and these variable in subset X must be discrete. The system is modeled as evolvement in discrete time steps, so there exists an instance z(t) for every system variable z at time t. 2-time-slice causality diagram is a directed diagram, which represents the fault influence propagation among system variable at time t+1. The differences between a 2-TSCD and a fault influence propagation diagram are as follows. (1) In **2-TSCD**, every node event variable X has a time tag, which is denoted as superscript (t+1). Variable $X^{(t+1)}$ represents an instance of variable X at time t+1. Anyone variable X that has no time tag represents in default an instance of variable X at time t+1, i.e., its time tag is ignored. Node event variables are divided two parts: one is observed variables, i.e., their values can be known. These variables can be discrete or continuous. The other is un-observed variable, and these variables must be discrete. (2) In 2-TSCD, every basic event variable X has a time tag, which is denoted as superscript (t) or (t+1). Variable X(t) or X(t+1) represents an instance of variable X at time t+1. Anyone variable X that has no time tag represents in default an instance of variable X at time t+1, i.e., its time tag is ignored. Basic event variables are divided two parts: one is component failure, and its time tag is (t+1). These kinds of basic event variable represents failure state of component, every state of variable X represents that the corresponding component fails, and X's default state represents that the corresponding component is normal. The other basic event variables are instances of un-observed variable at time t. And they can affect directly system variable at t+1. So, they can be regarded as failure variable of component, which has no input, at time t+1. All basic event variables must be discrete. (3) In 2-TSCD, every linkage event variable X has a time tag, which is denoted as superscript (t, t+1) or (t+1, t+1). The linkage event variable that has superscript (t, t+1) represents that the instance X(t) of causation event variable X at time t cause the instance Y(t+1) of result event variable Y at time t+1. Anyone variable X that has no time tag represents in default the instance X(t+1) of causation event variable X at time t+1 cause the instance Y(t+1) of result event variable Y at time t+1, i.e., its time tag is ignored. Usually, time tag (t+1, t+1) is ignored. (4) In 2-TSCD, anyone instance X(t) of variable X at time t is introduce as a causation of instance Y(t+1) of variable Y (including such a case: Y is X itself) at time t+1, and instance X(t) is regarded as a basic event variable. So, there exists two cases only: 1) the instance X(t) of variable X at time t cause the instance Y(t+1) of variable Y at time t+1; 2) the instance X(t+1) of variable X at time t+1 cause the instance Y(t+1) of variable Y at time t+1. The former represents the delay of fault effect.

4 Find Failure Modes

Fault diagnosis subsystem does not work when system is at normal state. Once an abnormal signal is received, fault diagnosis subsystem begins to diagnose process. At this moment, the node event variable in fault influence diagram can be divided to two parts: $X_i \in X_F$ and $X_i \notin X_F$. Here, X_F is the set of node event variable that are abnormal, or called evidence E.

Find failure modes in fault influence propagation diagram. The steps of finding failure modes are as follows. (1) Get the level-1 cut set (CSs-1) formula of node event variable $X_i \in X_F$, and simplify it according to **Rule-1**. Here, CSs-1 formula is this kind of cut set formula, in which all event variable (including basic event variable and node event variable) are neighbouring to the target node event variable X_i in a FIPD. At this step, node event variable is treated as a random event. The cut set, in which there exists a node event variable X_i or linkage event P_{ij}, must be removed from CSs-1. **Rule-1**: When evidence E is received, a node event variable X_i, which is at normal state, cannot be a possible causation of causing another node event variable X_j that is at abnormal. (2) Get the final level cut set (CSs-f) formula of node event variable $X_i \in X_F$, and expand it to a state matrix. Here, CSs-f formula is this kind of cut set formula, in which all event variable are basic event variables or linkage event variable, and has none of node event variable. The process steps are as following: to expand the CSs-1 formula of X_i, i.e., for every node event variable in the CSs-1 formula, use its corresponding CSs-1 formula to replace it. This process is going recursively until getting the final level cut set (CSs-f) of formula of X_i. In the expanding process, if a directed loop is encountered, **Rule-Loop-Break** [2] is applied to break down the loop. When a causality loop is encountered, the descendant variable, which is the same as the head variable of the loop, should be treated as a null set and be deleted. In the process of getting the CSs-f, the node event variable is regarded as a random event as a whole. **Rule-Loop-Break**: a node event variable cannot be a possible causation that causes itself at the same time. (3) Get the fault cut set formula (CSs-F) of every $X_i \in X_F$. Here, the fault cut set formula (CSs-F) is evidence cut set formula, which is consisted only of some and other state of basic event variable. Take state cut set formula of $X_i \in X_F$ from its final level cut set (CSs-f) state matrix, and delete all the state event of the linkage event variable. As a result, get the fault cut set formula of every $X_i \in X_F$. (4) Get the fault cut set formula of evidence $E = \{X_i \mid X_i \in X_F\}$. This is implemented by logical AND operation for the entire fault cut set formula of every $X_i \in X_F$. And then to reduce the fault cut set formula of every $X_i \in X_F$ according to **Rule-2**, finally the possible failure modes can be found according to **Rule-3**. **Rule-2**: The mode, which consists of more than one initiating event, should be deleted from fault cut set formula of evidence E. The reason is that the probability of more than one initiating event simultaneous occurrence is high-order infinitesimal. **Rule-3**: The different fault sub-structures are different failure modes, which are mutual exclusive and cannot occur simultaneously.

Find failure modes in 2-time-slice causality diagram. The steps to find failure modes in a 2-TSCD are as follows. (1) Delete those basic event variables that have time tag (t), and delete those linkage event variables that have time tag (t, t+1). In this way, 2-time-slice causality diagram becomes fault influence propagation diagram, which represents the fault influence propagation among system variable at time t+1. (2) Use the method, which is used to find failure modes in fault influence propagation diagram, to find failure modes in 2-time-slice causality diagram.

5 Fault Diagnosis Experiments Based on Causality Diagram

There are many examples of fault diagnosis based on causality diagram. Here only list several examples. Fan [2] took the full-size 950MW nuclear power simulator at Beijing Nuclear Power Simulating Training Central in Tsinghua University as the diagnosis object, and built the fault diagnosis causality diagram of classic failures in the secondary loop. On the causality diagram intelligence fault diagnosis platform developed by him, eight representative failures in the secondary loop, including failure of valve, failure of pump and pipe rupture, have been diagnosed. Experiments show that the diagnosis result coincides with the practice, diagnose rapidity, and the result is well. Wang [5] applied causality diagram model to fault diagnosis of pressure vessels. Experiments show that the fault diagnosis method based on causality is efficient. It can overcome the shortcomings of fault tree diagnosis method, has the superiority of both fuzzy fault diagnosis method and fault tree diagnosis method. So, the method based on causality diagram has better practicability. Liang [6] applied causality diagram model to fault diagnosis of machine equipment in coal mine. Experiments show that the fault diagnosis method based on causality is efficient, and its diagnosis precision is better than that of fault tree diagnosis method.

6 Conclusions

Causality diagram is a knowledge representation and reasoning model under uncertainty based on probability. Its outstanding characteristics show that there is a very good mapping between the knowledge representation of causality diagram and the fault character of complex system, thus causality diagram can represent the fault knowledge of complex system effectively, and be suited for fault diagnosis of complex system. This paper presents a fault diagnosis prototype system based on causality diagram, and describes the key technologies used. Comparing with other fault diagnosis methods, for example the fault diagnosis method of hybrid dynamic Bayesian network [7], the methods used in this paper have the following characteristics. (1) It can deal with causality loop structure, and does not require DGA in Bayesian network. (2) The causality intensity among variables can be given according to real case, and has no limitation such as conditional linear Gaussian used in [7] that is a subset of hybrid dynamic Bayesian network. (3) In some case, the method can avoid the computation difficulty. For example, if the fault mode of finding from a FIPD at time t is one, the post-probability computation does not need, and the diagnosis result can be given directly. So, the proposed prototype system has flexible fault knowledge representation, rapid diagnosis process, and well practicability.

References

1. Hamscher, W., Console, L., Kleer, J.de.: Readings in Model-based Diagnosis. San Mateo: Morgan Kaufmann Publishers (1992) 1-24
2. Fan, X.H.: Causality Diagram Theory Research and Applying It to Fault Diagnosis of Complex System. Ph.D Dissertation of Chongqing University, P.R. China (2002)
3. Fan, X.H., Zhong, X., Zhang, Q., Sun, M.S., Huang, X.Y.: Reasoning Algorithm in Multi-valued Causality Diagram. Chinese Journal of Computers. 26 (2003) 310-322
4. Fan, X.H., Sun, M.S.: A Reasoning Algorithm of Applying Causality Diagram to Fault Diagnosis of Complex Hybrid Systems. In Proceeding of The 5th World Congress on Intelligent Control and Automation. Hangzhou, P.R. China (2004) 1741-1745
5. Wang, H.C.: Fuzzy Causality Diagram and Application in Fault Diagnosis of Pressure Vessels. Computer Engineering. 25 (2005) 199-201
6. Liang, X.Y.: Application of Causality Diagram in Fault Analysis of Machine Equipment in Coal Mine. Computer Engineer. 31 (2005) 204-206
7. Lerner, U., Parr, R., Koller, D., Biswas, G.: Bayesian Fault Detection and Diagnosis in Dynamic Systems. In Proceeding of The Seventeenth National Conference on Artificial Intelligence (AAAI-00). (2000) 531-537

Adaptive Neural Model Based Fault Tolerant Control for Multi-variable Process*

Cuimei Bo[1,2], Jun Li[2], Zhiquan Wang[1], and Jinguo Lin[2]

[1] College of Automation Nanjing University of Sciences and Technology Nanjing, Jiangsu, 210094 China
lj_bcm@163.com

[2] College of Automation Nanjing University of Technology Nanjing, Jiangsu, 210009 China

Abstract. A new FTC scheme based on adaptive radial basis function (RBF) neural network (NN) model for unknown multi-variable dynamic systems is proposed. The scheme designs an adaptive RBF model to built process model and uses extended Kalman filter (EKF) technique to online learn the fault dynamics. Then, a model inversion controller is designed to produce the fault tolerant control (FTC) actions. The proposed scheme is applied to a three-tank process to evaluate the performance of the scheme. The simulation results show that component fault can be quickly compensated so that the system performances are recovered well.

1 Introduction

Fault Tolerant Control (FTC) has received increasing attention recently from the viewpoint of safety as well as reduced manufacturing costs [1]. Recently, adaptive control for nonlinear multi-variables systems has received considerable attention, and many new approaches have been proposed [2]. In this paper, a new FTC approaches for unknown multi-variable dynamic process is proposed. The approach combines adaptive RBF model and the EKF algorithm to update on-line the network weights to learn the system time-varying and fault dynamics. Then an iterative inversion algorithm based on the model is designed to compute an optimal control variable.

The remaining parts are organized as follows: the adaptive RBF model is presented in Section2; Section 3 presents the configuration of adaptive tolerant controller and model iterative inversion algorithm; the online simulation study of the three-tanks is provided in Section 4. Finally conclusions are included in Section 6.

2 The Adaptive Model Based Estimator

In system identification, multi-variable non-linear process with scalar input u and output y affected by additive state noise can be represented by the nonlinear

* This work was supported by National Natural Science Foundation (grant Nos. 60574082).

D.-S. Huang, K. Li, and G.W. Irwin (Eds.): ICIC 2006, LNAI 4114, pp. 596 – 601, 2006.

auto-regressive with exogenous (NARX) input process model, whose dynamic behavior is assumed to be described by

$$y(k) = f(u(k-d-1),\cdots,u(k-d-n_u), y(k-1),\cdots, y(k-n_y)) + w(k) \tag{1}$$

Here, $\{w(k) \in R^p\}$ are distributed random variables. The $f(.)$ is unknown nonlinear function; $u(k) \in R^m$ and $y(k) \in R^p$ are the process input and output respectively, n_u and n_y denote the input order and output order, d is time-delay.

2.1 Reformulated RBF Network

A RBF neural network is trained to perform a mapping of NARX process. The network may be used to approximate the nonlinear function $f(.)$ in Eq.(1). So as to identify the nonlinear system:

$$\hat{y}(k) = \hat{f}(u(k-d-1),\cdots,u(k-d-n_u), y(k-1),\cdots, y(k-n_y)) \tag{2}$$

The RBF network with n inputs, c prototypes, and p outputs, input nodes are $n = m \times n_u + p \times n_y$, input vector $x(k) = [u(k-d-1),\cdots,u(k-d-n_u), y(k-1),\cdots, y(k-n_y)]^T$, c neurons in the hidden layer applies Gaussian function as activation function. A Gaussian functions of the form: $g(v) = \exp(-v/\sigma^2)$ σ is a real constant.

The outputs of the network consist of sums of the weighted hidden layer neurons. The network can be written as follows:

$$\hat{Y} = WH \tag{3}$$

$$\begin{bmatrix} w_{10} & w_{11} & \cdots & w_{1c} \\ w_{20} & w_{21} & \cdots & w_{2c} \\ \vdots & \vdots & \vdots & \vdots \\ w_{p0} & w_{p1} & \cdots & w_{pc} \end{bmatrix} = \begin{bmatrix} w_1^T \\ w_2^T \\ \vdots \\ w_p^T \end{bmatrix} = W \begin{bmatrix} 1 & \cdots & 1 \\ g(\|x_1 - v_1\|^2) & \cdots & g(\|x_n - v_1\|^2) \\ \vdots & \vdots & \vdots \\ g(\|x_1 - v_c\|^2) & \cdots & g(\|x_n - v_c\|^2) \end{bmatrix} = [h_0 \;\; h_1 \;\; \cdots \;\; h_n] = H \tag{4}$$

Here, the RBF model is initialized with the weights trained off-line by the gradient descent algorithm, and then is updated on-line using the following EKF.

2.2 Online Updating the Network Using the EKF Algorithm

The EKF is used for online updating the network weight of the RBF model because its training converges is faster than the back propagation algorithm. We use $y(k)$ denote the target vector for the RBF outputs, and $f(\hat{\theta}_k)$ denote the actual outputs. In order to update online the network weight matrix W and prototypes v_i using the EKF algorithm, we let W and v_i constitute the state of a nonlinear system:

$$\theta = \begin{bmatrix} w_1^T & \cdots & w_p^T & v_1^T & \cdots & v_c^T \end{bmatrix}^T \tag{5}$$

$$\theta(k+1) = \theta(k) + \omega(k), \; y(k) = \hat{f}(\theta(k)) + e(k) \tag{6}$$

Where $\omega(k)$ and $e(k)$ are artificially added white noise. EKF algorithm is used to update the parameter vector θ using the new measurement data.

$$\theta(k) = \theta(k-1) + K(k)[y(k) - \hat{f}(\theta(k-1))] \tag{7}$$

$$K(k) = E(k)H(k)[R + H^T(k)E(k)H(k)]^{-1} \tag{8}$$

$$E(k+1) = (I - K(k)H(k))E(k) + Q \tag{9}$$

K(k) is the Kalman gain; *E(k)* is the covariance matrix of the estimation error; Q , R are the covariance matrices of $\omega(k)$ and $e(k)$ respectively. *H(k)* is the Jacobi matrix.

$$H(k) = \frac{\partial \hat{Y}}{\partial \theta} = \left[\frac{\partial \hat{Y}}{\partial w} \quad \frac{\partial \hat{Y}}{\partial v} \right]^T = [H_w \quad H_v]^T \tag{10}$$

$$H_w = \left[\frac{\partial \hat{Y}}{\partial w} \right] = \begin{bmatrix} H & 0 & \cdots & 0 \\ 0 & H & \cdots & 0 \\ \vdots & \vdots & \vdots & \vdots \\ 0 & \cdots & 0 & H \end{bmatrix}_{c \times (cn)} \tag{11}$$

$$H_v = \left[\frac{\partial \hat{Y}}{\partial v} \right] = \begin{bmatrix} -w_{11}g'_{11}2(x_1 - v_1) & \cdots & -w_{11}g'_{n1}2(x_n - v_1) & \cdots & -w_{p1}g'_{11}2(x_1 - v_1) & \cdots & -w_{p1}g'_{n1}2(x_n - v_1) \\ \vdots & \vdots & \vdots & \vdots & \vdots & \vdots & \vdots \\ -w_{1c}g'_{1c}2(x_1 - v_c) & \cdots & -w_{11}g'_{nc}2(x_n - v_c) & \cdots & -w_{pc}g'_{11}2(x_1 - v_c) & \cdots & -w_{pc}g'_{n1}2(x_n - v_c) \end{bmatrix} \tag{12}$$

Where *H(k)* is an *[n(c + 1) + mc]* × *nM* matrix, *H* is the *(c + 1)* × *M* matrix given in Eq. (4), w_{ij} is the element in the *i*th row and *j*th column of the *W* weight matrix in Eq.(4); $g'_{ij} = g'(\|x_i - v_j\|^2)$ (where *g(•)* is the activation function at the hidden layer); x_i is the *i*th input vector, and v_j is the *j*th prototype vector. H_w is an *n(c + 1)* × *nM* matrix, H_v is an *mc* × *nM* matrix. The procedure of applying the EKF algorithm to learn on-line weight value and prototypes of model is given as follows:

Step (1): At sample time k, use *y(k-i) u(k-d-i)* to form NN model input vector *x(k)*;
Step (2): Obtain the current process output, *y(k)* and use it as the training target;
Step (3): Calculate H_w, H_v to form *H(k)*, then, update *K(k)* $\theta(k)$ by Eq. (8) , Eq.(7);
Step (4): calculate *E(k+1)* using Eq.(11) for use in next sample period.

3 Adaptive Tolerant Controller

3.1 FTC Configuration

When actuator or component faults occur, the adaptive model will learn the change of dynamics caused by the fault so that the degradation of the model will be recovered with the model self-learning. The configuration of the FTC scheme shown in Fig. 1 used combination of an adaptive neural model and model iterative inversion controller.

Along with the model updating, a model iterative inversion algorithm is used to find an optimal control to recover the performance and maintain the stability. A double line in Fig.1 is used to indicate that the weights of the adaptive neural model are shared by the neural estimator and the model inversion controller.

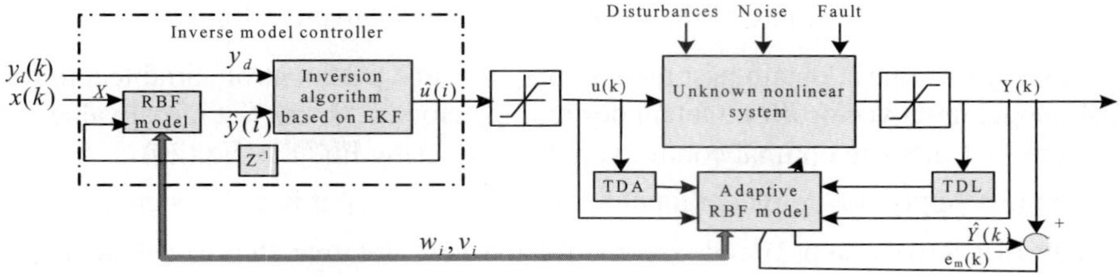

Fig. 1. FTC system structure based on iterative RBF inversion

3.2 Iterative Inversion Algorithms Based on Adaptive Neural Model

The neural network inversion methods used in reference [3] are typically direct inversion and iterative inversion. In the FTC scheme, adaptive neural model-based an iterative inversion is developed using the EKF algorithm.

To separate the control variable *u(k)*, the input vector *X(k)* is defined as:

$$X(k)=[u(k-d-1),\cdots,u(k-d-n_u+1),y(k),\cdots,y(k-n_y+1)]^T \tag{13}$$

Then, the RBF model in the inversion is described as: $\hat{y}(k+1)=\hat{f}[u(k),X(k)]$. The objective of model inversion is to estimate the control variables $u(k)$, which will drive the adaptive model output $\hat{y}(k+1)$ to track the trajectory $y_d(k+1)$. The EKF algorithms again adopted here to estimate the optimal control variable $\hat{u}(k+1)$ to minimize quadratic model tracking error:

$$e_t(k+1)=y_d(k+1)-\hat{y}(k+1)=y_d(k+1)-\hat{f}[\hat{u},X(k)] \tag{14}$$

To avoid confusing with iterative step *i*, the variable at sample time *k* is changed as' $|_k$ ', i.e. $u(k)\rightarrow u|_k$. Use $\hat{u}(i)$ to denote the optimized control at iteration step *i*. For the optimization of *u(k),* we formulate the following equation using EKF algorithm:

$$\hat{u}(i+1)=\hat{u}(i) \tag{15}$$

$$y_d(k+1)=\hat{y}(i)=\hat{f}[\hat{u}(i),X|_k] \tag{16}$$

$$\hat{u}(i)=\hat{u}(k-1)+K_u(i)[y_d|_{k+1}-\hat{y}(i-1)] \tag{17}$$

$$K_u(i)=E_u(i-1)H_u(i)[H_u^T(i)E_u(i)H_u(i)]^{-1} \tag{18}$$

$$E(i+1)=[I-K_u(i)H_u(i)]E_u(i) \tag{19}$$

$$H_u(i)=\begin{bmatrix} w_{11}g'_{11}2(x_1-v_1) & \cdots & w_{11}g'_{n1}2(x_n-v_1) & \cdots & w_{p1}g'_{11}2(x_1-v_1) & \cdots & w_{p1}g'_{n1}2(x_n-v_1) \\ \vdots & \vdots & \vdots & \vdots & \vdots & \vdots & \vdots \\ w_{1c}g'_{1c}2(x_1-v_c) & \cdots & w_{11}g'_{nc}2(x_n-v_c) & \cdots & w_{pc}g'_{11}2(x_1-v_c) & \cdots & w_{pc}g'_{n1}2(x_n-v_c) \end{bmatrix}_{op} \tag{20}$$

The calculation procedure of the iterative inversion is given as follows:

Step (1): At time *k*, obtain past process output, *y* and past control variable *u* to form RBF model input vector *X(k)*. Obtain desired trajectory, $y_d(k+1)$. Set initial value.

Step (2): Calculate optimal control variable $\hat{u}(i)$ using Eq.(17)–Eq.(20).

Step (3): Apply $\hat{u}(i)$ to model input to obtain $\hat{y}(i)$, $\hat{e}_t(i)$ at iteration step *i*.

Step (4): Repeat step(2) and step (3) for the next iterative step to calculate $\hat{u}(i+1)$ until the neural network model tracking error, $\hat{e}_t(i)$ is less than a predefined threshold or assigned maximum iteration step. Set *u*(*k*) equal to $\hat{u}$; then apply it to the process.

4 Applied FTC Scheme to Three-Tank Process

The three-tank process is simulated to evaluate the performance of the proposed FTC scheme. The process is setup up as follows equations [4]:

$$\dot{h}_1 = (-az_1 S_p sign(h_1 - h_3)\sqrt{2g|h_1 - h_3|} + Q_1)/A + \eta_1(t) \tag{21}$$

$$\dot{h}_2 = (-az_3 S_p sign(h_2 - h_3)\sqrt{2g|h_2 - h_3|} - az_2 S_p \sqrt{2gh_2} + Q_2)/A + \eta_2(t) \tag{22}$$

$$\dot{h}_3 = (az_2 S_p sign(h_1 - h_3)\sqrt{2g|h_1 - h_3|} + az_3 S_p sign(h_2 - h_3)\sqrt{2g|h_2 - h_3|})/A + \eta_3(t) \tag{23}$$

Here, h_i is liquid level (h_{max}=62cm); az_i is outflow coefficient (az_1=0.45 az_2=0.61 az_3=0.46); $S_p=0.5cm^2$ is cross section of the connection pipes; Q_i is supplying flow rates ($Q_{1max}=Q_{2max}$=100ml/s); $A=154cm$ is section area of cylindrical; $\eta_i(x,u)$ is modeling uncertainty and noise in measurement. The modeling uncertainty is assumed to Gauss white noise. Here Q_1 and Q_2 are input variables; h_1 and h_2 are output variables.

A adaptive RBF network with 8 inputs, 11 prototypes, and 2 outputs(i.e.8:11:2) is used to serve as the dynamic model of the process. The EKF algorithm is used in the NN model to learn on-line post-fault dynamic. And the model inversion control using the EKF algorithm has been realised in MATLAB and combined with the adaptive RBF model to form the FTC scheme. Fig.2(a) show the process tracking response with the proposed FTC scheme under no fault condition. Fig.2(b) show the corresponding control variable to the process.

Supposed a incipient leakage fault occurred in tank 2 at 250s. Leakage flow rates is is described by the following equations:

$$F_1(k) = -az_2 \pi r_2^2 \sqrt{2gh_2(k)} U(k-250) \quad r_2(k) = 0.2(1 - e^{-0.5(k-250)}) \tag{24}$$

The process tracking responses and the associated control variables are displayed in Fig.2 (c) and (d) respectively. The process tracking result show that the adaptive RBF model can quickly learn the post-fault dynamics so that the model inversion controller can generate a corresponding change in the control variables, supplying flow rates Q_1, Q_2, to compensate the effects of the fault on the process output.

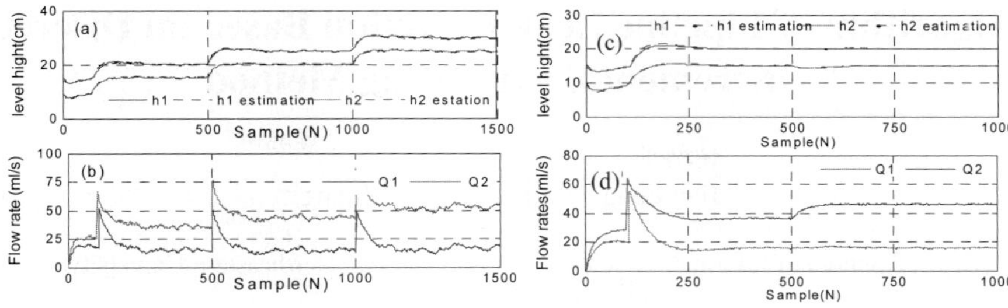

Fig. 2. The level tracking responses and control variables response of proposed FTC scheme

5 Conclusions

A new FTC scheme for unknown non-linear dynamic systems is proposed in this paper. The scheme designs an adaptive RBF model to learn fault dynamics based on EKF filter technique and a model inversion controller to produce the fault tolerant control actions. The proposed scheme is applied to three-tank process to eveluate the performance of the scheme. The simulation results shows that component can be quickly compensated so that the sysetem performance are recovered well.

References

1. Blanke, M: Fault-Tolerant Control Systems in New Trends in Advanced Control. Berlin: Springer. (1999) 171-196
2. Wang, D., Zhou, D.H., Jin, Y.H.: Adaptive Generic Model Control for a Class of Nonlinear Time-Varying Processes with Input Time Delay. Journal of Process Control. 14 (2004) 517-531
3. Yua, D.L., Changa, T.K, Yu, D.W.: Adaptive Neural Model-Based Fault Tolerant Control for Multi-Variable Processes. Engineering Applications of Artificial Intelligence. 18 (2005) 393-411
4. Yen, G., Ho, L.: Fault Tolerant Control: An Intelligent Sliding Mode Control Strategy. In Proc. American Control Conf. (2000) 4204-4208

Algorithm of Pipeline Leak Detection Based on Discrete Incremental Clustering Method

Jian Feng[1,2] and Huaguang Zhang[1,2]

[1] School of Information Science and Engineering, Northeastern University, Shenyang, 110004, P.R. China
fjneu@163.com, hg_zhang@21cn.com
[2] Key Laboratory of Process Industry Automation, Ministry of Education, Northeastern University, Shenyang, 110004, P.R. China
fjneu@163.com, hg_zhang@21cn.com

Abstract. A novel approach for pipeline leak fault detection has been studied, which applies self-organizing fuzzy clustering neural network to identify work status. The proposed method utilized fuzzy neural clustering of DIC method instead of constructing exact mathematical model. After normalizing the sample data, together with prior knowledge, a fuzzy neural network is used to evaluate work status. An adaptive algorithm is developed to diagnose the leak fault. The experiment results have shown the validity and practicability of the method.

1 Introduction

Leak fault detection methods are crucial in acquiring safe and reliable operation in oil transporting pipeline systems. The conventional leak fault detection approaches often have to work with explicit mathematical models. In addition, most of detection methods are deterministic or non-adaptive [1][2]. Therefore, the faults are presumed to appear as parameter or state changes caused by malfunctions of different components of the plant. In many cases, these changes can be successfully determined by using estimation techniques, residual generation methods [3][4]. They usually use relatively exact mathematical to represent the plant in different conditions. This is not always possible in an Industrial environment.

The identification of work status is the basis of the leak fault detection in oil pipelines. In this paper, we propose a leak fault detection method, which is based on Discrete Incremental Clustering (DIC) fuzzy neural network to resolve the problem. The advantages of DIC network are combined with fuzzy clustering to form a novel leak fault detection scheme. In Section 2, the fuzzy clustering neural networks will be described. In Section 3, the DIC method will be detailed. In Section 4, the leak detection scheme and work status identification methods will be discussed. In Section 5, a set of experiments results are given. Finally, Section 6 will conclude the present paper on the whole.

2 Fuzzy Clustering Neural Network

One common approach for fault detection and diagnosis utilizes the learning and recall properties of Fuzzy Neural Network (FNN). The input to the FNN is a set of features

D.-S. Huang, K. Li, and G.W. Irwin (Eds.): ICIC 2006, LNAI 4114, pp. 602–607, 2006.

vector extracted from raw sensor information. The output of the FNN is then provided with fault vectors, which can indicate the normal or faulty running status messages of the plant. The network is a six-layered feed forward network as shown in Fig. 1.

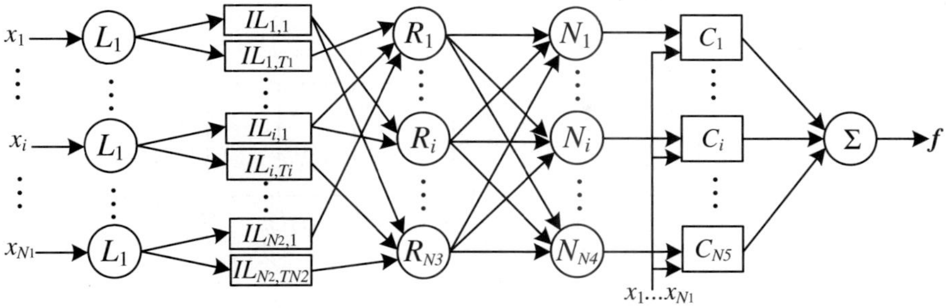

Fig. 1. Overall structure of fuzzy neural network

The layers are characterized by the fuzzy operations they perform. From left to right, the layers are: Layer I (the Input Layer), Layer II (the Condition Layer), Layer III (the Rule-base Layer), Layer IV (the Normalization Layer), and Layer V (the Consequence Layer) and Layer VI (the Output Layer). The rectangular used for layers II and V simply means that its parameter value might be changed.

Each layer has a number of ordered neurons. The number of neurons in layer k is labeled by N_k, where $k \in \{1,2,3,4,5,6\}$. The label $E_{i,j}^k$ denotes a link originating from the *ith* neuron in layer k-1 terminating at the *jth* neuron in layer k, where $k \in \{2,3,4,5,6\}$, $i \in \{1, \dots N_{k-1}\}$ and $j \in \{1, \dots N_k\}$. No links exist between neurons in the same layer. The derivation of fuzzy rules normally consists of two phases: Firstly, a cluster analysis is performed on the input data set to form clusters, and secondly, fuzzy rules are extracted using the clusters obtained in the first phase.

3 Discrete Incremental Clustering Method

We use Discrete Incremental Clustering (DIC) method for clustering [5][6][7], and then to generate Gaussian type membership functions from the clusters obtained. The greatest advantage of this way is that it enables the network to self generate number of membership functions without any predefined number of membership function [8]. The DIC method has four parameters: fuzzy set support parameter *SLOPE*, plasticity parameter β, tendency parameter *TD*, and threshold value *T*.

Each new cluster in DIC begins as a triangular fuzzy set. As training continues, the cluster "grows" to include more points. This triangular fuzzy set expands its center part to become a trapezoidal fuzzy set (see Fig. 2) but maintains the same amount of buffer regions on both sides of the center.

In Fig. 2(a), the triangular fuzzy set is defined by a_1, b_1, and c1. Point b_1` is the middle point of $a_1b_1$. So, *SLOPE* is the length of $a_1b_1$` or b_1`$c_1$. Hence *SLOPE* refers to the projection on the x-axis. In Fig. 2(b), the trapezoidal fuzzy set is defined by $a_2$, $b_2$, $c_2$, and $d_2$. Point e is the middle point of center segment and e` is the middle point of

a_2d_2. Point b_2` and $c_2$` are the projection points of b_2 and c_2 respectively. In this case, *SLOPE* is the length of a_2b_2` or $c_2$`d_2. *SLOPE* does not change when the membership function changes, it is set to a predefined value before clustering.

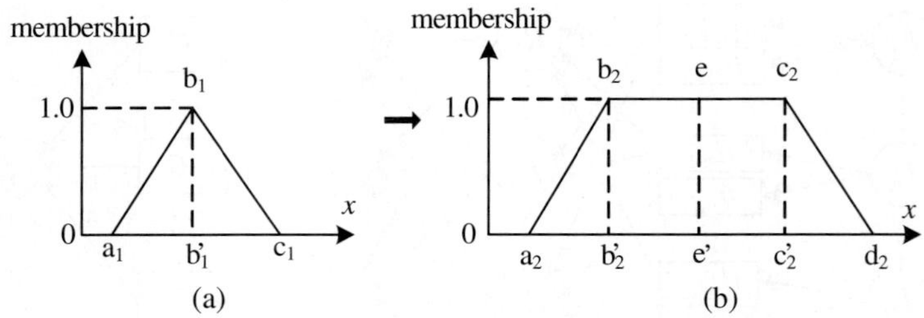

Fig. 2. Illustration of fuzzy sets with their *SLOPE*

A cluster "grows" by expanding its center. The expansion is controlled by the plasticity parameter β. A cluster expands its center when it is the best-fit cluster (has the highest membership value) to a data point and this data point falls outside its center.

The plasticity parameter β governs how much a cluster (fuzzy set) expands its center to include the new data point. To satisfy the stability-plasticity dilemma, the initial value of β is 0.5. The value of β decreases as the cluster expands its center. The first quadrant of a cosine waveform (see Fig. 3) is used to model the change of β in a cluster. The parameter θ is intuitively interpreted as the maximum expansion a cluster can have and it increases from 0 to 1.57 radians. Hence, the amount of expansion a cluster can adopt decreases with the number of expansions.

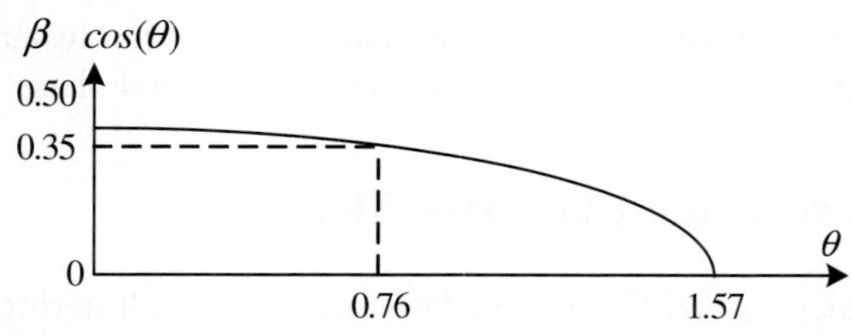

Fig. 3. Modeling of plasticity parameter β

The tendency parameter *TD* is analogous to a cluster's willingness to "grow" when it is the best-fit cluster to a data point that falls outside its center. Parameter *TD* maintains the relevance of a cluster and prevents it from incorporating too many data points that has low "fitness" (membership value) to the cluster. Otherwise, the center of a cluster may become overly large and the semantics of the fuzzy label the cluster represents may become obscure and poorly defined. The initial value of *TD* of a newly created cluster is 0.5 and the cluster stops expanding its center when *TD* reaches zero. The decreasing rate depends on the "fitness" of the data points that the cluster incorporates as shown in equation(1):

$$TD_{i,j}^{new} = TD_{i,j}^{old} + (A - TD_{i,j}^{old}) \times (1 - \mu_{i,j}(x_i))^2 \tag{1}$$

All the notations in the above equation are with respect to node $IL_{i,j}$. $\mu_{i,j}$ is the membership function of the node $IL_{i,j}$, and A is a predefined value. A has to be less than zero, otherwise TD can never be less or equal to 0. This is because the value of $(1-\mu_{i,j}(x_i))^2$ is in the range [0, 1]. Hence, the less fit the data points (with small membership values) a cluster tries to incorporate or absorb, the faster its TD decreases, and vice versa. When TD is less or equal to zero, the cluster stops growing.

TD (willingness of a cluster to grow towards the new data point) and β (degree of a cluster to grow towards the new data point) together maintain the integrity of the input clusters and the fuzzy labels they represent.

The threshold T specifies the minimum "fitness" or membership value a data point must have before it is considered as relevant to any existing cluster or fuzzy set. If the fitness of the data point to the existing best-fit cluster falls below the predefined threshold value T, then a new cluster needs to be created. In addition, T determines the degree of overlapping of two clusters.

Fig. 4(a) corresponds to a high threshold value T=0.85, while Fig. 4(b) corresponds to a median threshold value T=0.5. The larger the value T is, the closer the computed clusters are and hence more number of clusters is created. Great care should be taken in order to prevent excessive overlapping of clusters.

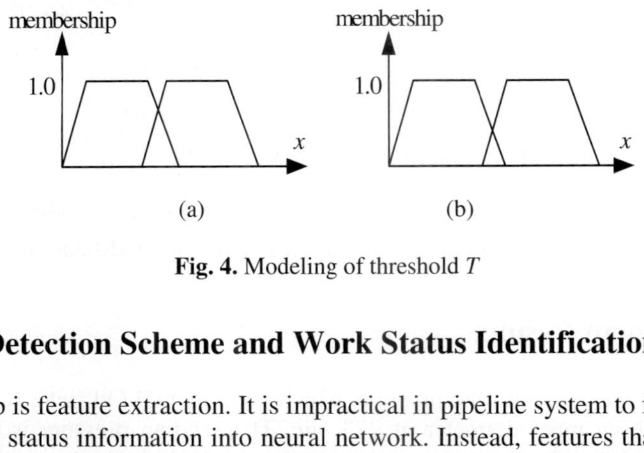

Fig. 4. Modeling of threshold T

4 Leak Detection Scheme and Work Status Identification

The first step is feature extraction. It is impractical in pipeline system to feed all available running status information into neural network. Instead, features that are characteristic of leak faults are first extracted from the raw sensor data. The features that can be easily used to calculate and identify the faults are the ones selected [9].

Using a prior knowledge of running status, a catalogue of running status is generated. For each running status, locale data of the pipeline system is collected in both normal and fault leak operation. When actual data of the system running in a leak fault can be collected, it is used as well. Each simulation or actual running data is preprocessed to produce a feature vector. The set of feature vectors and corresponding all kinds of running status are then used to train the FNN.

Extended sigmoid function (1) is used to normalize the input vectors. x_i is the *ith* variable of feature vector, σ_i is its distribution width, c_i is the statistic center of x_i. The value region of the function is between –1 and 1.

$$sigmoid(x_i,\sigma_i,c_i) = \frac{2}{1+\exp(-\sigma_i(x_i-c_i))} - 1 \tag{1}$$

The familiar running status includes increasing pressure, decreasing pressure, leak fault and normal running. They are all prior knowledge. According to these characteristics, we decide 4 centers of clustering: Status 1 (increasing pressure), Status 2 (decreasing pressure), Status 3 (leak fault) and Status 4 (normal running).

In order to detect on line, the parameters (σ_i and c_i) in (1) must be obtained when system runs normally. Without loss of universality, we assume that x_1, x_2, x_3, x_4 and x_5 all satisfy normal distribution. Their probability density function is

$$f(x_i) = \frac{1}{\sqrt{2\pi}\sigma_i}\exp\left(\frac{-(x_i-c_i)^2}{2\sigma_i^2}\right), \tag{2}$$

where σ_i is the mean of x_i, c_i is the statistic mean squared root error. To avoid noise disturbing, σ_i and c_i is calculated by (3). They are all updated online by (4)-(6).

$$c_i = E(x_i), \sigma_i = D(x_i) = \sqrt{E(x_i^2) - E(x_i)^2}, E(x_i^2) = \frac{1}{m}\sum_{j=1}^{m} x_{ij}^2. \tag{3}$$

$$E(x_i)_{n+1} = \alpha_{n+1}E(x_i)_n + \beta_{n+1}\cdot(x_i)_{n+1}, \tag{4}$$

$$E(x_i^2)_{n+1} = \alpha_{n+1}E(x_i^2)_n + \beta_{n+1}\cdot(x_i^2)_{n+1}, \tag{5}$$

$$(\sigma_i)_{n+1} = D(x_i)_{n+1} = \sqrt{E(x_i^2)_{n+1} - E(x_i^2)_{n+1}}. \tag{6}$$

α_{n+1} and β_{n+1} is weight factors, $\alpha_{n+1} + \beta_{n+1} = 1$. Along with the modifying σ_i and c_i, the lasted weights become smaller gradually. So, dynamic modification is realized.

5 Experiment Results

The approach was tested in the pipeline, which is in Shengli Oil field. It is 14.117 *km* long and with an inner diameter of 273 *mm*. The sending pressure is 0.4 *Mpa*. To obtain pressure and flow signals, we have only installed one high precision pressure sensor and one flow sensor at each terminal of the pipeline, whose position is 30 *m* away from its corresponding terminals. There was a tap located at 6.15 *km* away from the inlet of the pipeline to imitate true leak. The leak amount is about 40 *L/s*.

Leak experiments have been taken 20 times. Work status change experiments have been taken 45 times. All of the leaks could have been detected successfully. The average detection time was about 10*s*. The time of detection fully satisfies the need of engineering on the whole. All the wrong alarms are induced by work status unsteadiness. The results are shown in Table 1.

Table 1. The work status identification results based on fuzzy clustering neural network

Experiment items	Total times	Right	Wrong	Average leak amount(L/s)	Percentage(%)
Status 1 (increasing pressure)	15	14	1	---	93.3
Status 2 (decreasing pressure)	15	14	1	---	93.3
Status 3 (leak fault)	20	20	0	40.8	100
Status 4 (normal running)	15	15	0	---	100

6 Conclusion

This paper studies leak fault detection method by means of Fuzzy Neural Network. Together with prior knowledge, we construct a status evaluator. It can distinguish leak fault from normal running and adjusting pump in pipeline. Experiment results show that the proposed method can effectively detect and diagnose leak fault.

Acknowledgment

This work was supported by the National Natural Science Foundation of China under grant no. 60572070 to Zhang Huaguang. This work is also supported in part by Open Project Foundation of Key Laboratory of Process Industry Automation, Ministry of Education China, and the China Postdoctoral Science Foundation to Feng Jian.

References

1. Willsky, A.S.: A Survey of Design Methods for Failure Detection in Dynamic Systems. Automatica. 2 (1976) 431-434
2. Himmelblau, D.M.: Fault Detection and Diagnosis in Chemical and Petrochemical Processes. Elsevier, Amsterdam (1978)
3. Isermann, R.: Process Fault Detection Based on Modelling and Estimation Methods: A Survey. Automatica. 20 (1984) 387-404
4. Frank, P.M.: Fault Diagnosis in Dynamic Systems Using Analytical and Knowledge-Based Redundancy: A Survey and Some New Results. Automatica. 26 (1990) 459-474
5. Tung, W. L., Quek C.: GenSoFNN: a Generic Self-organizing Fuzzy Neural Network, IEEE Transactions on Neural Networks. 13 (2002) 1075-1086
6. Carpenter, G.A., Grossberg, S., Rosenm, D.B.: Fuzzy ART: Fast Stable Learning and Categorization of Analog Patterns by an Adaptive Resonance System. Neural Networks. 4 (1991) 759-771
7. Kohonen, T.K.: Self-Organized Formation of Topologically Correct Feature Maps. Bio. Cybern. 43 (1982) 59-69
8. Wang, D., Chai, Q., Geok, S.N.: MS-TSKfnn: Novel Takagi-Sugeno-Kang Fuzzy Neural Network Using ART Like Clustering. Proceedings of 2004 International Joint Conference on Neural networks, Budapest, Hungary, July 2004, 2361-2366
9. Jiang, C., Zhou, D.: Fault Detection and Identification for Uncertain Linear. Computers and Chemical Engineering. 30 (2006) 228-242

A BP Neural Network Based Technique for HIF Detection and Location on Distribution Systems with Distributed Generation

Arturo Suman Bretas[1], Luciano Pires[1], Miguel Moreto[2], and Rodrigo Hartstein Salim[1]

[1] Federal University of Rio Grande do Sul
Av. Osvaldo Aranha, 103
Porto Alegre, RS, Brazil
abretas@ece.ufrgs.br, lopires@gmail.com, salim@eletro.ufrgs.br
http://www.ece.ufrgs.br/~gmasp

[2] Federal University of Santa Catarina
CEP 88040-900
Florianópolis, SC, Brazil
moreto@labspot.ufsc.br

Abstract. High Impedance Faults (HIF) are faults of difficult detection and location while using traditional digital relaying. In this article it is presented a new proposal for detection and location of HIF's in distribution systems with distributed generation (DG), based on artificial neural networks. The methodology inputs are the local measured voltage and current phase components, supplying as output the detection, classification and location of the fault, when it occurs. The basic characteristics, the algorithm and comparative tests with other detection and location methodologies are presented in this article. The proposed scheme was tested in a simulation platform of a distribution system with DG. The comparative results of the technique with usual fault detection and location schemes show the high efficiency and robustness of the method.

1 Introduction

The detection and location process of high impedance faults (HIF) in power distribution systems (PDS) are becoming one of the major problems for the protection systems of the electric power distribution companies. Besides presenting characteristics that can be confused with normal operations in the network, its low magnitude fault current inhibits the detection of this kind of failure when overcurrent relays are used.

The HIF's are faults caused by the contact of line cables with trees or ground [1], originating a situation with high danger to the population. Moreover, the fact that these faults are not usually detected puts also in risk the maintenance staff of the distribution companies.

A new difficulty managed by the protection systems of distribution companies nowadays is the new trend on the distribution systems, known as distributed

D.-S. Huang, K. Li, and G.W. Irwin (Eds.): ICIC 2006, LNAI 4114, pp. 608–613, 2006.

generation (DG). DG is defined as the generation of power inside the PDS. But these new sources of power have impacts in the PDS.

The main consequences of the presence of the DG in PDS are the changes in magnitude, direction and duration of the fault currents, making necessary a reformulation of the planning of the PDS protection schemes.

With the intention to reduce the problems caused by the HIF occurrence, several studies were developed, in order to characterize HIF. Among the several characteristics observed, it could be cited: the measure of the imbalance between phases [1], the angle difference between the complex numbers representing the fundamental component of the voltage and the 3rd harmonic of the current [2], [3], and the voltage and current harmonic content analysis [4], [5].

In opposition to the necessity of total reformulation of the distribution systems protection schemes and with the intention to reduce the problems caused by the HIF, the present work proposes a new method to detect and locate high impedance faults in distribution systems with DG. The above-mentioned method is based on artificial neural network (ANN).

2 High Impedance Faults

The HIF are a special case of faults that can occur in power systems. Its low fault current magnitude and the presence of an electric arc make its detection, and also its modeling [6], difficult. The existence of an electric arc in the fault occurrence generates a non-linear characteristic, as can be seen in Figure 1(a).

The non-linear characteristic denotes to this phenomenon a unique harmonic content, as illustrated on Figure 1(b). This particular behavior is used to characterize HIF, according to the studies made and presented in [2], [3], [4], [5]. The modeling process of HIF in this work was based in the model proposed in [7]. This model is shown in Figure 1(c).

3 Distributed Generation Impacts

The addition of new generation units to the PDS has great consequences in the overall operation of these systems. The main change is the loss of the radial

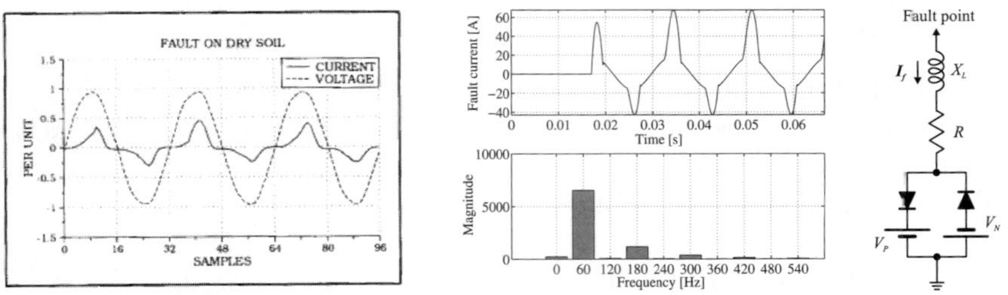

(a) Current and voltage relation. (b) Harmonic content. (c) Model.

Fig. 1. High impedance faults

characteristic of the PDS, changing the original power flow of the system. This makes necessary a modification in the protection systems parameters. In result of these facts, the reliability, the safety and the efficiency of the protection systems are affected by the DG. With this, the system capacity in maintain the electric power supply with minimum interruptions, with quality and without putting the system and the consumer in risk gets compromised, making necessary a new approach for PDS protection that considers the DG.

4 Artificial Neural Networks

As described in [8], mathematical models of the biological neurons and its interconnections were developed aiming to represent its processing properties, such as: learning, generalization, non-linearity, failure tolerance and answer to evidences. The ANN operates in two stages: the training and the test process. The training process trains the ANN so it outputs the correct results of the process. In this stage, different data, covering both faulty and non-faulty states of the system, are presented to the model. This work is done through different optimization algorithms and the one used in the present work is the backpropagation algorithm [8]. The test stage is the process where another data in presented to the trained ANN and the results are verified for the validation of the ANN performance.

5 Proposed Scheme

The proposed model to HIF detection and location in PDS with DG was developed based in ANN, having four different processes, as shown in Figure 2.

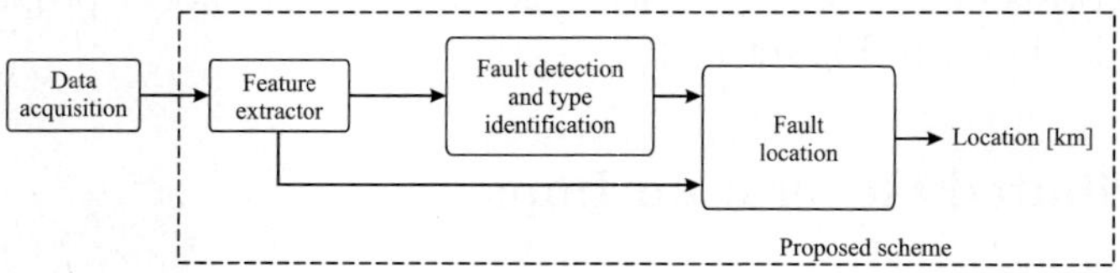

Fig. 2. Proposed scheme

5.1 Data Acquisition

The first part of the scheme consists in the data acquisition for the ANN training and test processes. This data acquisition can be done through a digital fault recorder, a digital relay or even with computer simulations of the system model in which the method will be applied.

5.2 Characteristics Extraction

With the data obtained in the above mentioned process, the characteristics extraction process begins. In this process the filtering of the information obtained in the data acquisition is done. This process was developed with the philosophy of detect and locate HIF.

As described in [2] and [3], the angle difference between the complex numbers representing the fundamental voltage phasor and the 3rd harmonic current phasor is a good track of HIF occurrence. Thus, this relation is used to detect and locate faults in the proposed methodology. The fault type classification, in turn, is done with the symmetrical components unbalance analysis of the current, present in the system.

The subroutine has a Fourier Filter, with the addition of the algorithm proposed and described in [9], for voltage and current data DC component elimination. This filter extracts the 2nd, 3rd and 5th harmonic components that, in addition to the voltage and current fundamental phasors, are the extraction process output data.

5.3 Fault Detection and Identification

The fault detection is based in the 1st, 2nd, 3rd and 5th harmonics of the symmetrical components of the current phasors measured at the local terminal. In one time samples intervals, these components are calculated, using a one-cycle sampling window (fundamental frequency) in the algorithm described on section 5.2, and the fault state is identified, with the output vector of this ANN representing the type of fault and the phases involved. If a fault state is identified for more than 10 consecutive samples, a fault state is detected and the incidence point is determined.

5.4 Fault Location

Once the fault detection and identification process is complete, the fault location process starts. This routine is based in two different ANN: one is trained for phase faults and the other for ground faults. The input vector of these ANN are based in the phases involved in the fault, and contains the fundamental voltage and current components $(|V^{1h}|, |I^{1h}|)$, the angle difference between them $(\Delta\theta^{1h})$ and the angle difference between the complex numbers representing the voltage fundamental phasor and the 3rd harmonic current phasor $(\Delta\theta^{3h})$, as illustrated in Equation 1.

$$X = \left[|V^{1h}|, |I^{1h}|, |I^{3h}|, \Delta\theta^{1h}, \Delta\theta^{3h}\right] \tag{1}$$

6 Tests and Results

The proposed scheme was tested in the modified system from [10]. A 3.2MVA/440V distributed generation facility was added to this system, in order to validate the methodology. The distribution feeder is illustrated on Figure 3.

Different types of faults were simulated: Phase-to-ground, double-phase, double phase-to-ground and three-phase. A total of 67 fault points were simulated for each type of fault, and for each point, high impedance faults, faults with

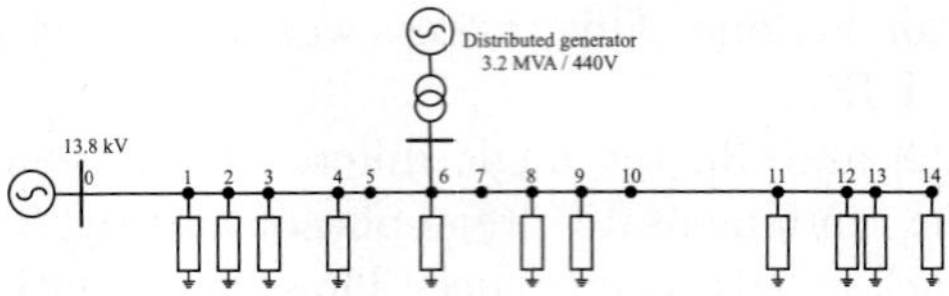

Fig. 3. Distribution feeder model

linear resistance of $R_{fault} = 0, 10, 20, 50, 100\ \Omega$ and even non-fault cases were simulated. The faults were simulated using the ATP/EMTP Software [11].

These data was used for the training and validation processes. After the ANN training, the methodology was tested and the results are shown above.

6.1 Fault Detection Results

The results obtained with the proposed methodology for fault detection are shown on Table 1. The methodology was compared for the same fault cases with an overcurrent relay scheme (set with a detecting current of two times the maximum load current) and achieved 100% of correctness for all fault types and resistances (including HIF) and fault distance, showing its robustness for these parameters.

6.2 Fault Location Results

The methodology performance analysis was accomplished based on the percentage of the fault locating error in respect to the total line length. The methodology was tested and compared with a classical fault location method, presented in [12], for the same fault cases.

The maximum error obtained with the proposed fault location methodology for ground faults and 100% load was approximately 7%. Parameters like fault resistance, fault distance and HIF have few influence in the proposed scheme, not affecting its performance. For the same cases, the classic method obtained results with severe influence of the same parameters. For fault resistances higher than 50 Ω or HIF, the classic algorithm did not converged.

Phase faults have a lower maximum error with the proposed algorithm, around 4%. The same happened for the classic method, but it still suffers great influence from fault distance and its resistance.

Table 1. Correct detection values for Overcurrent Relay and ANN techniques

	R_{fault}	0 Ω	10 Ω	20 Ω	50 Ω	100 Ω	HIF
Ground	OR	47.76%	0%	0%	0%	0%	0%
Faults	ANN	100%	100%	100%	100%	100%	100%
Phase	OR	46.27%	13.43%	0%	0%	0%	0%
Faults	ANN	100%	100%	100%	100%	100%	100%

7 Conclusions

In this article a new HIF detection and location methodology for PDS with DG is proposed. The algorithm and its theoretical basement are also shown in this work. The results had shown the robustness of the scheme for fault parameters such as: fault resistance, fault distance and HIF. The DG does not affect the algorithm performance. Comparing to classic methods, the quality of the results obtained is verified. The results of this work also show that the methodology is worthy of continued research aiming real time applications.

Acknowledgments

The authors would like to thank Companhia Estadual de Energia Elétrica do Rio Grande do Sul (CEEE-RS) for financing this work.

References

1. Cabral, S.L.S., Senger, E.C., Santos, J.C.: Falta de alta impedância - proposta de solução através de sistemas supervisórios. In: Seminário Nacional de Distribuição de Energia Elétrica, Blumenau, SC (1992)
2. Wester, C.G.: High impedance fault detection on distribution systems. In: 42nd Rural Electric Power Conference. (1998) c5–1–5
3. Gómez, J.C., Morcos, M.M.: A practical protective relay for downconductor faults. IEEE Transactions on Power Delivery **6**(2) (1991) 565–574
4. Lien, K., Chen, S., Liao, C., Guo, T., Lin, T., Shen, J.: Energy variance criterion and threshold tuning scheme for high impedance fault detection. IEEE Transactions on Power Delivery **4**(3) (1997) 810–817
5. Benner, C.L., Russel, B.D.: Practical high-impedance fault detection on distribution feeders. IEEE Transactions on Industry Applications **33**(3) (1997) 635–640
6. Moreto, M.: Localização de faltas de alta impedância em sistemas de distribuição de energia: Uma metodologia baseada em redes neurais artificiais. Master's thesis, Universidade Federal do Rio Grande do Sul (UFRGS), Porto Alegre (2005)
7. Emanuel, A.E., et al.: High impedance fault arcing on sandy soil in 15kv distribution feeders: contributions to the evaluation of the low frequency spectrum. IEEE Transactions on Power Delivery **5**(2) (1990) 676–686
8. Haykin, S.: Neural Netowrks: A comprehensive Foundation. 2nd ed. Prentice Hall, NJ, USA (1998)
9. Lin, Y.H., Liu, C.W.: A new dft-based phasor computation algorithm for transmission line digital protection. In: IEEE/PES Transmission and Distribution Conference and Exhibition: Asia Pacific. Volume 3., Yokohama, Japan (2002) 1733–1737
10. Wakileh, J.J., Pahwa, A.: Optimization of distribution system design to accommodate cold load pickup. IEEE Transactions on Power Delivery **12**(1) (1997) 339–345
11. L. Prikler and H. K. Hoidalen USA: ATPDraw Version 3.5 Usert's Manual: preliminary release no. 1.0. (2002)
12. Lee, S.J., et al.: An intelligent and efficient fault location and diagnosis scheme for radial distribution systems. IEEE Transactions on Power Delivery **19**(2) (2004) 524–532

The Application of Grey Relation Close Degree Model in the Fault Diagnosis

Cuifeng Li[1,2] and Wenzhan Dai[2]

[1] Net Center of Zhejiang Business Technology Institute,
315012, Ningbo, Zhejiang
cuicui107@hotmail.com

[2] Electronic Engineering College of Zhejiang Gongshang University,
310035, Hangzhou, Zhejiang
dwzhan@zist.edu.cn

Abstract. According to the theory of grey relation degree and the definition of the distance of two points, a decision method which is named grey relation close degree model is proposed .The model is successfully used in fault diagnosis of oil-sample analysis. The practical application results show the effectiveness of the proposed approach. It is proved that the method is not only concise but reliable and can greatly widen range of application of grey model.

1 Introduction

The grey system theory has been caught great attention by researchers since 1982 and has already been widely used in many fields[1],[2]. Relation analysis is one of grey system analytical methods, which is a quantitative method to describe relevance level among things or factors· It is the premise of systematic qualitative analysis and the basis of systematic quantitative analysis among similar factors[3].

Relation analysis has already been used in analysis of economic development, multivariate correlation and the advantage and disadvantage of comprehensive plan and social system[4]. For recent years, what the relation degree is utilized to diagnose the equipment has been attracted considerable attention[5],[6],[7].

According to the theory of grey relation degree and the definition of the distance of two space points, a decision method which is named grey relation close degree model is proposed. The method is successfully used in fault diagnosis of oil-sample analysis. The practical application results show the effectiveness of the proposed approach. It is proved that the method is not only concise but reliable and can greatly widen range of application of grey model.

2 Grey Relational Close Degree Analysis

2.1 Grey Relation Analysis

Relation degree is an index that signifies similarity between two systems. Suppose $\{x_i(t)\},\{x_j(t)\}$ are two sequences at $t = k$, the definition of relation degree is held as follow.

D.-S. Huang, K. Li, and G.W. Irwin (Eds.): ICIC 2006, LNAI 4114, pp. 614 – 619, 2006.

$$r_{ij} = \frac{1}{N}\sum_{k=1}^{N}\varepsilon_{ij}(k). \tag{1}$$

Where, $\varepsilon_{ij}(k)$ ——relation coefficients.

N —— length of the sequence.

$$\varepsilon_{ij}(k) = (\Delta_{\min} + \rho\Delta_{\max})/[\Delta_{ij}(k) + \rho\Delta_{\max}]. \tag{2}$$

Where $\Delta_{ij}(k)$ —absolute differences of two sequences at time of k .

$$\Delta_{ij}(k) = \left|x_i(k) - x_j(k)\right|. \tag{3}$$

$\Delta_{\max}$ ——the maximum of absolute differences at any time.

$\Delta_{\min}$ ——the minimum of absolute differences at any time.

ρ ——discrimination coefficient.Generally, let ρ be 0.5.

2.2 Grey Relation Close Degree Description

Suppose that the number of fault characteristic vector is m, and the number of each kind of typical fault mode is n, then characteristic vector matrix of the corresponding typical fault mode can be established as follow.

$$\boldsymbol{X}_R = \begin{bmatrix} \boldsymbol{X}_{r1} \\ \boldsymbol{X}_{r2} \\ \vdots \\ \boldsymbol{X}_{rm} \end{bmatrix} = \begin{bmatrix} x_{r1}(1) & x_{r1}(2) & \cdots & x_{r1}(n) \\ x_{r2}(1) & x_{r2}(2) & \cdots & x_{r2}(n) \\ \cdots & \cdots & \cdots & \cdots \\ x_{rm}(1) & x_{rm}(2) & \cdots & x_{rm}(n) \end{bmatrix}. \tag{4}$$

Let the eigenvector of actual detected- signal be denoted by:

$$\boldsymbol{X}_T = \left[x_t(1) \quad x_t(2) \quad \cdots \quad x_t(n)\right]. \tag{5}$$

Every characteristic vector represents a kind of fault modes, then the problem of fault diagnose is how to identify the fault mode from the detected- modes.

In grey diagnosis, the principal diagram of the model identification of the grey diagnosis is as fig.1.

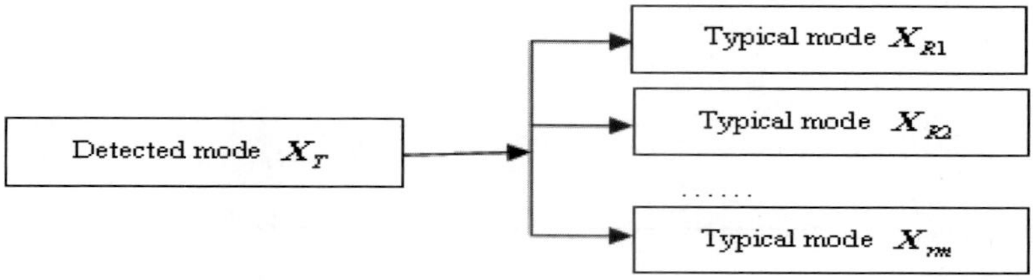

Fig. 1. The diagram of the model identification of the grey diagnosis

The next problem is how to ascertain grey relation close degree between the characteristic vector $\boldsymbol{X}_T$ and $\boldsymbol{X}_{Rj}(j=1,2,...,m)$.

Let $\boldsymbol{X}_T$ be detected-mode vector, then the relation coefficients sequence $\boldsymbol{R}$ is held by calculating relation coefficients between $\boldsymbol{X}_T$ and typical mode vector $\boldsymbol{X}_{Rj}(j=1,2,...,m)$ as follow.

$$\boldsymbol{R}=(\varepsilon_{ij})_{m\times n}=\begin{bmatrix}\varepsilon_{11} & \varepsilon_{12} & \cdots & \varepsilon_{1n}\\ \varepsilon_{21} & \varepsilon_{22} & \cdots & \varepsilon_{2n}\\ \cdots & \cdots & \cdots & \cdots\\ \varepsilon_{m1} & \varepsilon_{m2} & \cdots & \varepsilon_{mn}\end{bmatrix}. \tag{6}$$

Definition 1. The $(m+1)*n$ number of ε is arranged as a matrix $\tilde{\boldsymbol{R}}$ as follow:

$$\tilde{\boldsymbol{R}}=(\varepsilon_{ij})_{(m+1)\times n}=\begin{bmatrix}\varepsilon_{01} & \varepsilon_{02} & \cdots & \varepsilon_{0n}\\ \varepsilon_{11} & \varepsilon_{12} & \cdots & \varepsilon_{1n}\\ \varepsilon_{21} & \varepsilon_{22} & \cdots & \varepsilon_{2n}\\ \cdots & \cdots & \cdots & \cdots\\ \varepsilon_{m1} & \varepsilon_{m2} & \cdots & \varepsilon_{mn}\end{bmatrix}. \tag{7}$$

then $\tilde{\boldsymbol{R}}$ is called as grey relation degree widen matrix.
Where $\varepsilon_{0j}(j=1,2,...,n)$ is defined as self relation coefficient. Obviously, $\varepsilon_{0j}=1,(j=1,2,...,n)$.

Grey relation degree judge matrix can be constructed as above in order to compare the relation degree between the detected -mode and typical fault modes.

Definition 2. If characteristic vectors of every kind typical fault mode and the detected- mode are regarded row vectors, then d_i is called as grey relation close degree between the detected- mode and typical fault mode shown in Fig.2.

According to the definition of the distance of two space points, d_i could be gotten.

$$d_i=\left|\overline{A_0A_i}\right|=\sqrt{\sum_{j=1}^{m}(r_{0j}-r_{ij})^2},(i=1,2,...,n). \tag{8}$$

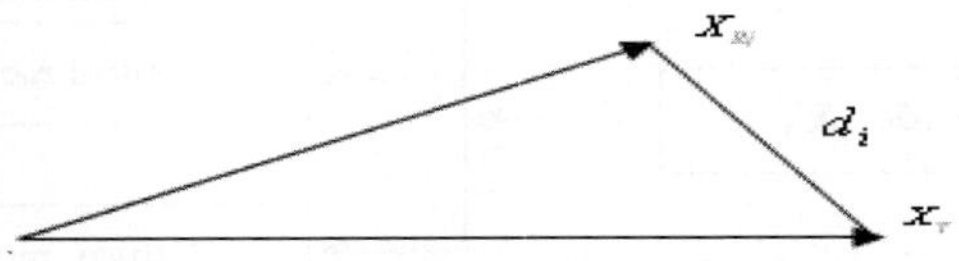

Fig. 2. Grey relation close degree diagram

2.3 Results

According to (8), let $\boldsymbol{X}_T$ be detected- mode vector, the sequence of relation close degree can be obtained by calculating the relation close degree between $\boldsymbol{X}_T$ and typical mode vector $\boldsymbol{X}_{Rj}(j=1,2,...,m)$. Then the grey relation close degree $d_i(i=1,2,...,m)$ can be rearranged from the lowest to the highest. If d_1 is the lowest, then the detected- mode works in the state $\boldsymbol{X}_{Rl}$.

3 Example

There are a lot of quantitative parameters of Fe-spectrum analysis, thus quantitative parameters with representative characteristic are usually selected as follows:

Wear particle concentration:

$$\text{WPC} = (\text{D}l + \text{D}s)/\text{oil - sample output}$$

Where Dl -Large wear particle reading
Ds - Small wear particle reading

Percentage of large wear particle:

$$PLP = (\text{D}l - \text{D}s)/(\text{D}l + Ds)$$

Which indicates the radio of wear severity indices to the total wear particle.

Large wear particle ratio:

$$M = \text{D}l/(\text{D}l + Ds)$$

Which indicates the radio of large wear particles to total wear particle.

Wear severity indices:

$$Es = (\text{D}l + \text{D}s)/(\text{D}l - Ds)$$

Now, let WPC,PL P,M and Es be the reference pattern vectors of different states as table 1, then the state of machine can be judged according to the values of WPC, PLP,M ,Es.

Suppose that X_{R1} is reference pattern vector of normal state, X_{R2} is reference pattern vector of abnormal state, X_{R3} is reference pattern vector of fault state, reference pattern matrix can be obtained as follow:

$$\boldsymbol{X}_R = \begin{bmatrix} 119.8 & 0.32 & 0.64 & 4543.9 \\ 149.8 & 0.40 & 0.80 & 5679.9 \\ 230.3 & 0.50 & 0.90 & 7991.1 \end{bmatrix}$$

Table 1. Reference model of the characteristic condition

states	*WPC*	*PLP*	*M*	Es
Normal state	119.8	0.32	0.64	4543.9
Abnormal state	149.8	0.40	0.80	5679.9
Failure state	230.3	0.50	0.90	7991.1

Now, the value of WPC, PLP, M, Es equals to 203.1, 0.38, 0.76, 7691.3 respectively after measuring some series engine of CAT3400 which have been operating 120 hours. What state of engine can be judged by calculating the relation close degree as follows.

(1) Structure the detected mode

$$\boldsymbol{X}_T = \begin{bmatrix} 230.1 & 0.38 & 0.76 & 7691.3 \end{bmatrix}$$

(2) Data is processed for typical mode and detected mode as follow:

$$\boldsymbol{X}_R = \begin{bmatrix} 1.198 & 0.32 & 0.64 & 4.5439 \\ 1.498 & 0.40 & 0.80 & 5.6799 \\ 2.303 & 0.50 & 0.90 & 7.9911 \end{bmatrix}$$

Namely

$$\begin{aligned} \boldsymbol{X}_T &= \begin{bmatrix} 2.301 & 0.38 & 0.76 & 7.6913 \end{bmatrix} \\ \boldsymbol{X}_{R1} &= \begin{bmatrix} 1.198 & 0.32 & 0.64 & 4.5439 \end{bmatrix} \\ \boldsymbol{X}_{R2} &= \begin{bmatrix} 1.498 & 0.40 & 0.80 & 5.6799 \end{bmatrix} \\ \boldsymbol{X}_{R3} &= \begin{bmatrix} 2.303 & 0.50 & 0.90 & 7.9911 \end{bmatrix} \end{aligned}$$

(3) Calculating relation coefficient matrix

$$\boldsymbol{R} = \begin{bmatrix} 0.680 & 0.975 & 0.941 & 0.338 \\ 0.758 & 1 & 0.988 & 0.445 \\ 0.864 & 0.941 & 0.930 & 0.851 \end{bmatrix}$$

Then grey relation degree judgment widen matrix can be written as follow:

$$\boldsymbol{R} = \begin{bmatrix} 1 & 1 & 1 & 1 \\ 0.680 & 0.975 & 0.941 & 0.338 \\ 0.758 & 1 & 0.988 & 0.445 \\ 0.861 & 0.941 & 0.930 & 0.851 \end{bmatrix}$$

(4) According to (8), grey relation close degree d_i between the detected- mode and typical mode is obtained as follow:

$$d_i = (0.7381 \quad 0.6056 \quad 0.2215)$$

(5) Arrange relation close degree

$$\because 0.2215 < 0.6056 < 0.7381$$

Then the relation close degree between X_T and X_{Rj} can be rearranged from the lowest to the highest as follow:

$$d_3 < d_2 < d_1$$

From above, we can come to conclusion that the diesel engine CAT3400 is in "fault state". Although this conclusion is same to paper's conclusion[8], the results given by this paper have much higher resolution and are more reasonable because the data is measured in the real fault state.

4 Conclusion

According to theory of grey relation degree and the definition of the distance of two space points, a decision method which is named grey relation degree method is established. The method is used in fault diagnosis of oil-sample analysis. It is proved that the method is not only concise but reliable and can greatly widen range of application of grey model.

References

1. Fu Li.:Grey Systematic Theory and Application, Scientific Technical Document Publishing House(1992)
2. Liu Sifeng, Guo Tianbang, Dang Yaoguo.: Grey System Theory and Its Application, Science Press, Oct(1999)
3. Jin Shengcan.: The Application of the Gray Connection Analysis in the Decision, Coal Mine Machinery, Feb(2005)136~137
4. Lv Feng, Cui Xiaohui.: Multi-Criteria Decision Grey Relation Projection Method and Its Application, Systems Engineering theory & Practice, Jan(2002) 103~107
5. Li Erguo,Yu Jinshou.: Gray Cognate Analysis-based Research on Compressor's Fault Diagnosis, Journal of Shanghai Maritime University, Sep(2001)294~297
6. Qu Xiaohui, Qiao Xinyong.: Condition Evaluation for Diesel Engine Based on Grey Relation Analysis, Acta Armamentarii , Jul(2005)557~559
7. Zhang Zhenkun,Xia Hong.: Fault Diagnosis of a Steam Generator based on Gray Cognate Analysis, Applied Science and Technology, Apr(2004) 54~56
8. Gong Wenwei, Shi Guohong.: Application of Gray Correlation Analysis in the Fe-spectrum Analysis Technique, Journal of Jiangsu University of Science and Technology(Natural Science), Jan (2001) 59~61

Embedded Reversible Medical Image Compression Using Integer Wavelet Transform

Li-bao Zhang and Ming-quan Zhou

College of Information Science and Technology, Beijing Normal University,
Beijing, 100875, China
libaozhang@163.com

Abstract. The increasing need for efficient image storage in hospitals imposes heavy requirements on the design of picture archiving and communication systems. Thus new methods are needed to improve the medical image compression performance. In this paper, we propose an efficient coding algorithm called OSS (Optimal Subband Shift) scheme based on the RB-IWT (Reversible Biorthogonal Integer Wavelet Transform). In the new scheme, the original image is first decomposed by the RB-IWT. Then, the image coefficients of every subband are multiplied by the powers of two. Finally, the SPECK coding is applied. Experimental results show that the OSS scheme does not only provide the PSNR performance better than SPECK using the original RB-IWT without the subband shift, but also has the low coding complexity. So this idea is valuable for future research in medical image coding and its applications.

1 Introduction

In recent year, the research for medical image compression is more and more significant because medical imaging produce prohibitive amounts of data. In the literature, several efficient medical image coding methods have been proposed. They include SPIHT (Set Partitioning in Hierarchical Trees) in [1], EBCOT (Embedded Block-based Coding with Optimized Truncation) and SPECK (Set Partitioning Embedded bloCK) in [2], [3]. These algorithms are efficient based on DWT. However, the image coefficients decomposed by the DWT are floating-point numbers, which increases the computational complexity and is not well suited for efficient lossless coding application. To solve the above problems, I. Daubechies and W. Sweldens presented the lifting scheme (LS) [4]. Based on the LS, a kind of new transforms called integer wavelet transforms (IWT) are proposed, which is a low complexity and efficient implementation of the DWT and can support the lossless image coding.

The main drawback of the IWT is that using it instead of the DWT degrades the performances of the lossy coding [5]. In this paper, we propose an improved scheme called OSS (Optimal Subband Shift) for the medical image using the RB-IWT (Reversible Biorthogonal Integer Wavelet Transform). In the new scheme, every subband of the wavelet image is multiplied by the two of power. Experimental results show that the proposed algorithm does not only provide the PSNR performance better than

D.-S. Huang, K. Li, and G.W. Irwin (Eds.): ICIC 2006, LNAI 4114, pp. 620 – 624, 2006.

SPECK using the original RB-IWT without the subband shift, but also has the low coding complexity.

2 Integer Wavelet Transform and Its Main Drawback

The common wavelet transforms as the DWT often result in floating point coefficients and cannot complete the lossless image coding. So I. Daubechies and W. Sweldens presented an integer-to-integer transform model called IWT based on the LS. The LS consists of three steps: the first step split the data into two subsets, even and odd; the second step calculates the wavelet coefficients (high pass) as the failure to predict the odd set based on the even set; and the third step updates the even set using the wavelet coefficients (low pass). The inverse transform can be obtained by reversing the steps of forward transform. The more details can be referred in [4]. The IWT realization based on the LS is shown from formula (1) to formula (3):

$$\begin{cases} s_{j,2l} = even\ (s_j) \\ s_{j,2l+1} = odd\ (s_j) \end{cases} \tag{1}$$

$$d'_{j-1} = s_{j,2l+1} - P(s_{j,2l}) \tag{2}$$

$$s'_{j-1} = s_{j,2l} + U(d'_{j-1}) \tag{3}$$

In these LS-based IWTs, there is a kind of biorthogonal integer transform called RB-IWT. All the transform parameters consist of powers of two. As the RB-IWT has the low computational complexity, it is applied for lossless medical image compression extensively. In table 1, two RB-IWTs are indicated [6].

The most main problem for RB-IWT is that the RB-IWT has the worse lossy compression performance than the DWT. This is due to the fact that the transform is no more unitary, and the information content of each coefficient is no longer directly related to magnitude; this is particularly harmful for encoders with rate allocation based on bitplanes, such as SPIHT [1] and SPECK [3] coding scheme.

Table 1. Two forward transforms of RB-IWTs

Name (x,y)	Forward transform of IWT
5/3	$\begin{cases} d[n]=d_0[n]-\lfloor 1/2(s_0[n+1]+s_0[n])\rfloor \\ s[n]=s_0[n]+\lfloor 1/4(d[n]+d[n-1])+1/2\rfloor \end{cases}$
13/7	$\begin{cases} d[n]=d_0[n]+\lfloor 1/16((s_0[n+2]+s_0[n-1])-9(s_0[n+1]+s_0[n])+1/2)\rfloor \\ s[n]=s_0[n]+\lfloor 1/32(9(d[n]+d[n-1])-(d[n+1]+d[n-2])+1/2\rfloor \end{cases}$

3 Optimal Subband Shift Scheme

Integer wavelet transform has worse energy compaction than common wavelet transform, which is a disadvantage for efficient medical image compression. In this paper, a new scheme called OSS is proposed.

The OSS scheme takes full advantage of the scaling factor K of the RB-IWT. For the reversible biorthogonal transform, K is defined as 1, which can decrease the computational complexity of RB-IWT and is advantageous for the lossless image coding. However, the K value will depress the lossy coding performance of RB-IWT. If we hope to improve the lossy coding performance, the K value must be defined as $\sqrt{2}$, but that destructs the integer transforms.

Fortunately, if we only consider the LS and do not consider the integer operation, the scaling factors in the two-dimension transforms will be rational numbers. For the one level wavelet decomposition, the scaling factor of LL is 2, the scaling factor of LH is 1, the scaling factor of HL is 1, and the scaling factor of HH is 1/2. When the number of the decomposed levels improves, the scaling factors will be powers of two. If we define that the scaling factor of HH is 1, then the scaling factor of every subband will be multiplied by 2.

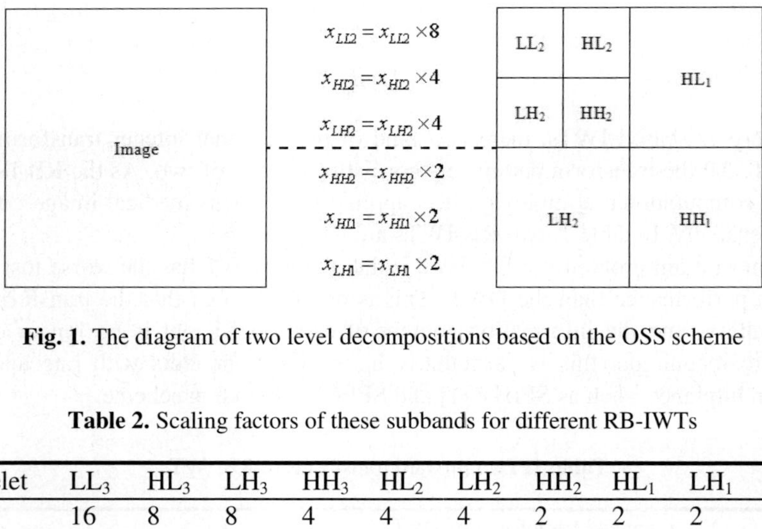

Fig. 1. The diagram of two level decompositions based on the OSS scheme

Table 2. Scaling factors of these subbands for different RB-IWTs

Wavelet	LL_3	HL_3	LH_3	HH_3	HL_2	LH_2	HH_2	HL_1	LH_1	HH_1
5/3	16	8	8	4	4	4	2	2	2	1
6/14	16	8	8	4	4	4	2	2	2	1
13/7	16	8	8	4	4	4	2	2	2	1

For the RB-IWT, if the errors of the integer round operation are ignored, all subbands will be multiplied by powers of two except the HH. Lower the frequency of the subband is, higher the scaling value is. Because the encoder uses powers of two as encoding thresholds, we can utilize the bitplane shift of some subbands instead of the integer round operation. Figure 1 shows the diagram of two level decompositions based on the OSS scheme.

Table 2 gives the scaling factors of different RB-IWTs for two-dimensional wavelet decomposition with OSS scheme.

The basic coding steps based on the OSS scheme can be introduced as follows:

1) The image is first decomposed by the common RB-IWT, and the number of decomposing levels can be decided by the area of the original image;
2) The OSS scheme is applied for the decomposed wavelet image;
3) The SPECK coding algorithm and the arithmetic coding is applied.

According to the basic coding steps, we can obtain the PSNR (Peak Signal Noise Ratio) value of the medical images about 3~6 dB better than that based on the original RB-IWT without the OSS.

4 Experimental Results for Medical Images

In the figure 2, the reconstructed CT1 images using the OSS scheme and using original RB-IWT are presented. The image is a 512×512 gray CT image. The 13/7 filters and the SPECK coding algorithm are selected. The decoding bit-rate is 0.25 bpp.

Table 3 shows the PSNR value comparison of reconstructed CT1 image with different IWT schemes. Figure 3 presents the comparison of compression results with different IWT schemes for the CT2 image at 0.25bpp.

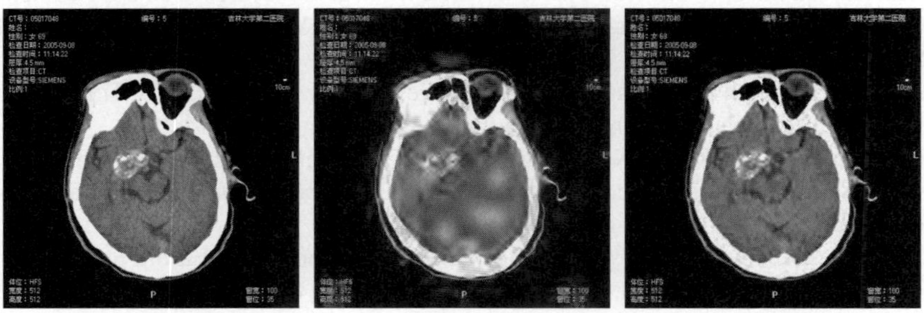

Fig. 2. The comparison of compression results with different IWT schemes for the CT1 image at 0.25bpp. The original image (left); the reconstructed image without the OSS scheme (medium); the reconstructed image with the OSS scheme (right).

Table 3. The PSNR value comparison of reconstructed CT1 with different IWT schemes (PSNR: dB)

bpp	0.125	0.25	0.5	1.0	2.0
13/7 filters with OSS	22.81	27.45	33.89	41.57	47.16
13/7 filters without OSS	16.82	22.09	27.94	37.46	44.59

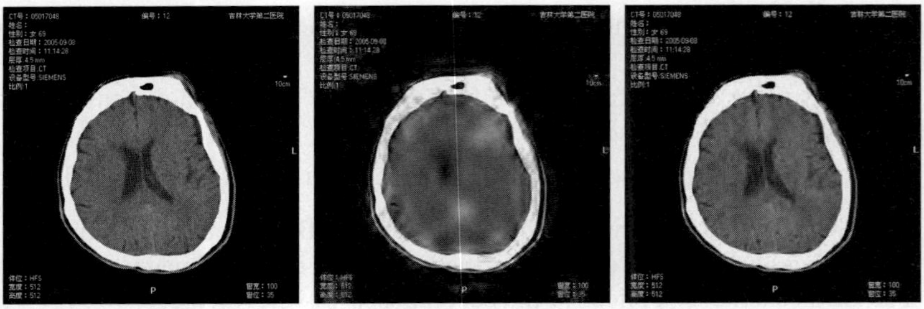

Fig. 3. The comparison of compression results with different IWT schemes for the CT2 image at 0.25bpp. The original image (left); the reconstructed image without the OSS scheme (medium); the reconstructed image with the OSS scheme (right).

5 Conclusions

In this paper, a new subband shift scheme is propose for the RB-IWT. As the OSS is applied for the medical image coding, the new coding method can obtain low computational complexity and high lossy compression performance. So we hope this idea is valuable for future research in medical image coding and its applications.

References

1. Said, A., Pearlman, W.A.: New Fast and Efficient Image Codec Based on Set Partitioning in Hierarchical Trees. IEEE Transaction on Circuit System Video Technology, Vol. 6 (1996) 243-249
2. Taubman, D.: High Performance Scalable Image Compression with EBCOT. Proceeding of IEEE, IEEE International Conference on Image Processing, (1999) 24-28
3. Pearlman, W.A., Islam, A., Nagaraj, N., Said, A.: Efficient, Low-complexity Image Coding with a Set-partitioning Embedded Block Coder. IEEE Transaction on Circuit and Systems for Video Technology, Vol.14 (2004) 1219-1235
4. Daubechies, I., Sweldens, W.: Factoring Wavelet Transforms into Lifting Steps. Journal of Fourier Analysis Application, Vol.4 (1998) 247-269
5. Grangetto, M., Magli, E., Martina, M.: Optimization and Implementation of The Integer Wavelet Transform for Image Coding. IEEE Transaction on Image Processing, Vol.11 (2002) 596-604
6. Calderbank, R.C., Daubechies, I., Sweldens, W.: Lossless Image Compression Using Integer to Integer Wavelet Transforms. IEEE International Conference on Image Processing, vo1.1 (1997) 596-599

Fault Detection Method Based on Artificial Immune System for Complicated Process

Chunliu Xiong, Yuhong Zhao, and Wei Liu

Institute of Industrial Control, Zhejiang University, Hangzhou 310027, China
{clxiong, yhzhao, wliu}@iipc.zju.edu.cn

Abstract. Fault detection is an important problem in process engineering. A new fault detection method based on artificial immune system is developed for complicated process. Real-valued negative selection algorithm with variable–radius detectors is adopted to generate the detectors set which covers the non-self space. In order to decrease the complexity of detector generation, principal component analysis is introduced to reduce the dimension of the process data. The effectiveness of the proposed method is illustrated by the simulation on the Tennessee Eastman process.

1 Introduction

Since it is extremely important for the successful operation of any process to detect process upsets, equipment malfunctions, or other special events as early as possible and then to find and remove the factors causing those events. Online monitoring and fault detection of complex process is receiving more attention from industrial practitioners as well as academic researchers. An abundance of literature has been published in this field [1].

From a modern perspective, process monitoring methods can be classified as being associated with one or more of three approaches, namely data-driven, analytical and knowledge-based [2]. The analytical approach uses dynamic mathematical models often constructed from first principles to generate residuals which indicate faults in the process. Most analytical methods are based on parameter estimation, observer-based design or parity relations. Hence, the analytical approach is of no effect for systems in which detailed mathematic models are not available. The knowledge-based approach uses qualitative models such as causal analysis, expert systems or pattern recognition to develop process monitoring measures. Like the analytical approach, the knowledge-based approach has been limited to relatively small systems because it requires a large amount of effort to construct the fault models for large-scale complex systems. The data-driven approaches have an advantage over the others for complicated processes.

However, most data-driven methods require process data under various fault conditions. It is difficult to make a complete catalog of all the possible and probable anomalous situations in reality. Hence a robust method which should detect any unacceptable (unseen) change rather than looking for specific known activity patterns is required.

D.-S. Huang, K. Li, and G.W. Irwin (Eds.): ICIC 2006, LNAI 4114 , pp. 625 – 630, 2006.

In general, the purpose of the immune system is to protect the body against infection and include a very distributed and adaptive, novel pattern recognition mechanism. The Artificial Immune System (AIS) has been adopted by a growing number of researchers to simulate the interactions between various components or the overall behaviors based on an immunology viewpoint in fault detection [3~5].

The Real-valued Negative Selection Algorithm (RNSA) is proposed to detect a broad spectrum of known and unforeseen faults [4~6]. However, when the RNSA is applied in the complicated process which contains the characteristic of high-dimensionality, the performance was terrible without basic validity. A new fault detection method for complicated process is researched in this paper. Principal Component Analysis (PCA) is introduced to reduce the data dimension so as to decrease the complexity of the detector generation and improve the performance of the detection. Then the real-valued negative selection algorithm with variable-coverage detectors [6] is used on the reduced data to generate detectors set.

In the next section, the basic immunity-based detection algorithm and the method based on artificial immune system and principal component analysis are described. Then the effectiveness of the proposed method is demonstrated by the application on the Tennessee Eastman process. Finally, conclusions are drawn and the further research is indicated.

2 Fault Detection Method Based on AIS and PCA

2.1 Negative Selection Algorithm

Based on the principles of self/non-self discrimination in the immune system, a change detection technique called the Negative Selection Algorithm has been developed. The negative selection algorithm can be summarized as follows:

- Define self as a collection $\boldsymbol{S}$ of elements in a feature space $\boldsymbol{U}$, a collection that needs to be monitored. For instance, if $\boldsymbol{U}$ corresponds to the space of states of a system represented by a list of features, $\boldsymbol{S}$ can represent the subset of states that are considered as normal condition of the system.
- Generate a set $\boldsymbol{F}$ of detectors, each of which fails to match any element in $\boldsymbol{S}$. An approach that mimics the immune system generates random detectors and discards those that match any element in the self set.
- Monitor $\boldsymbol{S}$ for changes by continually matching the detectors in $\boldsymbol{F}$ against $\boldsymbol{S}$. If any detector ever matches, then an abnormality is known to have occurred, because the detectors are designed not to match any representative samples of $\boldsymbol{S}$.

Figure 1 illustrates the concept of self and non-self in a feature space. The process of detectors generating is covering the non-self subspace. And a good detectors set is formed to cover the non-self space maximally.

2.2 Real-Valued Negative Selection Algorithm (RNSA)

Most of the research works on the NS algorithm have been restricted to the binary matching rules like *r*-contiguous. However, the scalability issue has prevented it from being applied more extensively [5].

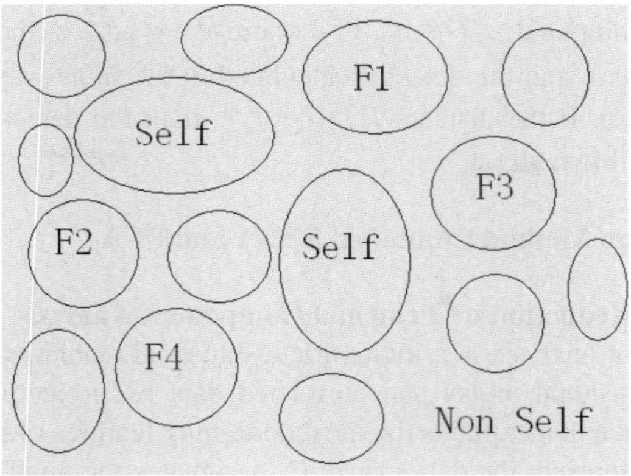

Fig. 1. The figure illustrates the concept of self and non-self in a feature space. Here F1, F2 etc. indicate different fault conditions represented by detectors.

In order to alleviate the limitations mentioned above, a real-valued NS algorithm (RNSA) is proposed by using the structure of the higher-level-representation to speed up the detector generation process. The RNSA applies a heuristic process that changes iteratively the position of the detectors driven by two goals: to maximize the coverage of the non-self subspace and to minimize the coverage of the samples. The RNSA with variable-coverage detectors can be summarized as follows (more detail can be found in [5, 6]):

- The feature space ***U*** is defined as hyper-spherical.
- A detector is defined as $d=(c,r_d)$, where $c=(c_0,c_1,\cdots,c_{m-1})$ is an *m*-dimensional point that corresponds to the center of a unit hyper-sphere with r_d as its radius.
- Generating detectors: detector generation starts with a population of candidate detectors, which are then matured through an iterative process. In particular, the center of each detector is chosen at random and the radius is a variable parameter which determines the size (in *m*-dimensional space) of the detector.
- Using Euclidean distance(*D*) to calculate the detector radius, which is defined as

$$D(x,y)=\left(\sum\left|x_i-y_i\right|^2\right)^{1/2} \tag{1}$$

where $x=\{x_0,x_1,\cdots,x_{m-1}\}$ is a point of the detector, $y=\{y_0,y_1,\cdots,y_{m-1}\}$ is self in the training dataset. If the distance between a candidate detector $d=(c,r_d)$ and its nearest self point in the training dataset is not greater than $(D-r_s)$, where r_s is a threshold value (allowable variation) of a self point, then the detect radius is replaced by $r_d=(D-r_s)$.

- Detection process: The detection process is straightforward. The matured detectors are continually examined with new samples in the test datasets. For example, the distance between a sample pattern $p=(c_p,r_s)$ and a detector

$d = (c, r_d)$ is computed as $D = (c_p, c)$, where $D = (c_p, c)$ is the distance between the sample pattern and the detector calculated in the same way as in the detector generation phase. If the distance $D < (r_s + r_d)$, then the detector d gets activated indicating possible fault.

2.3 Fault Detection Method Combined RNSA and PCA

2.3.1 Dimension Reduction by Principal Component Analysis

Principal component analysis is a multivariate statistical technique that is capable of treating high dimensional, noisy and correlated data by projecting it onto a lower dimensional subspace that explains the most pertaining features of the system.

Let $X \in R^{N\times m}$ represent the data matrix (*N* designates the number of observations, and *m* denotes the number of variables). Due to high degree of correlation among variables, one often finds *k* principal components (*k*<<*m*) suffice to explain most of the relevant information contained in the data matrix ***X***. Algebraically, the ***X*** matrix can be reconstructed by

$$\boldsymbol{X} = \boldsymbol{t}_1\boldsymbol{p}_1^T + \boldsymbol{t}_2\boldsymbol{p}_2^T + \cdots + \boldsymbol{t}_k\boldsymbol{p}_k^T + \boldsymbol{E} = \boldsymbol{T}\boldsymbol{P}^T + \boldsymbol{E} \tag{2}$$

where $\boldsymbol{T} = [\boldsymbol{t}_1, \boldsymbol{t}_2, \cdots, \boldsymbol{t}_k]$ is defined to be the matrix of principal component scores, $\boldsymbol{P} = [\boldsymbol{p}_1, \boldsymbol{p}_2, \cdots, \boldsymbol{p}_k]$ is the matrix of principal component loadings and ***E*** is the residual matrix. Without the residual matrix ***E***, which contains the sole redundant information, Eq. (2) is referred to as the PCA model that encompasses the major variation in the data.

Usually *k* is selected to be capable of explaining a specific minimum percentage of the total variance (mostly 85%). Finally, the low-dimension data should be normalized to make the state-space a unit hyper-sphere.

2.3.2 Detector Generation and Fault Detection

The reduced and normalized normal data is taken as the input of the RNSA to generate the detectors. The aim is to find a small number of detectors (as signature of fault condition) to occupy the non-self space maximally. The detectors are generated through the algorithm described in Section 2.2. However, there are some heuristic methods which can be used for generating detectors. How to generate the detectors set with high efficiency will be investigated in further works.

The matured detectors are examined with the new observations which need to be preprocessed by PCA and mapped to a unit hyper-sphere first. If a detector gets activated with current pattern, an abnormal change is indicated and a fault is detected.

3 Results and Discussion

The proposed approach is tested on the data collected from the process simulation for the Tennessee Eastman process (TEP). The TEP process was created by the Eastman Chemical Company to provide a realistic process for evaluating process control and monitoring methods.

The flowsheet for the industrial plant is depicted as figure 2. A detail description for TEP is available elsewhere [2]. The data sets used in this paper are downloaded from http://brahms.scs.uiuc.edu. The data contains 41 measured and 12 manipulated variables and consists of one normal condition and 21 faulty operating conditions. Each data set contains 480 and 960 observations for training and testing respectively.

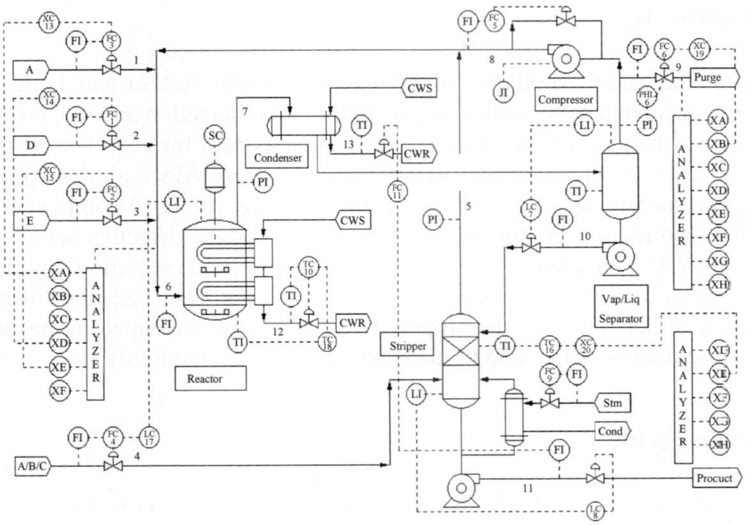

Fig. 2. Process flowsheet for the TEP

The detection results for the normal operating data and the faults 2, 6, 12 data by the proposed method are given in Table 1, where parameter r_s is threshold value(allowable variation) of a self point. As is showed in the table, large r_s provides better performance for the normal data, but the performance for the faulty data is worse. That is, r_s is an important parameter which is a balance between false positive

Table 1. Test results (Number of Detectors: N=500)

Operating State	r_s	Amount of test data	Hits	Detection rate %
Normal	0.1	960	903	94.1
	0.05	960	876	91.2
Fault 2	0.1	960	860	90.0
	0.05	960	893	93.0
Fault 6	0.1	960	802	83.5
	0.05	960	848	88.3
Fault 12	0.1	960	768	80.0
	0.05	960	822	85.6
Overall	0.1	3840	3333	86.8
	0.05	3840	3439	89.6

and false negative. More than 90% of the data from the normal condition are detected correctly. The detection results of the fault states are acceptable because over 85% of the overall state data can be identified correctly. The results show that the immunity based method proposed in this paper can be used effectively in the fault detection of complicated process.

4 Conclusions

Because of the nature similarity of biological immune system and fault detection system, the AIS possesses promising potential in fault detection and diagnosis. A new fault detection method based on artificial immune system for complicated process is presented in this paper. Since the performance of current AIS fault detection method to the high-dimensional process dataset is unsatisfying, principal component analysis is introduced to reduce the dimension of the data. Then the detectors set covering the non-self space is generated through the real-valued negative selection algorithm with variable–radius detectors. The simulation results on the Tennessee Eastman process illustrate the effectiveness of the proposed method. However, much further work still remains to be done to achieve fault diagnosis and algorithm optimized.

Acknowledgements

The project is supported by National Natural Science Foundation of China (No.60503065).

References

1. Venkatasubramanian, V., Rengaswamy, R., Kewen, Y., Kavuri, S. N.: A Review of Process Fault Detection and Diagnosis Part I~III. Computers and Chemical Engineering, Vol. 27 (2003) 293~346
2. Chiang, L. H., Russell, E. L., Braatz, R. D.: Fault Detection and Diagnosis in Industrial Systems. Springer-Verlag, London (2001)
3. Costa Branco, P. J., Dente, J. A., Mendes, R. V.: Using Immunology Principles for Fault Detection. IEEE Trans. Industrial Electronics, Vol. 50 No.2 (2003) 362~373
4. Dasgupta, D., Majumdar, N. S.: Anomaly Detection in Multidimensional Data Using Negative Selection Algorithm (2001)
5. Dasgupta, D., KrishnaKumar, K., Wong, D. et al.: Negative Selection Algorithm for Aircraft Fault Detection. 3rd International Conference on Artificial Immune Systems, Springer-Verlag, 23 (2004) 1~13
6. Ji, Z., Dasgupta, D.: Augmented Negative Selection Algorithm with Variable-Coverage Detectors. Congress on Evolutionary Computation, IEEE (2004) 1081~1088

Induction Machine Rotor Diagnosis Using Support Vector Machines and Rough Set

Ruiming Fang

College of Information Science and Engineering, National Huaqiao University, Quanzhou City, Fujian Province, 362021, China
fangrm@hotmail.com

Abstract. A fault diagnosis system based on integration of rough set theory (RST) and support vector machine (SVM) is developed for induction machine rotor faults detection. The proposed algorithm uses the stator current spectrum as inputs. By RST attribute reduction, redundant attributes are identified and removed. Then the reduction results are used as the input of SVM based classifiers to distinguish different motor conditions. A series of experiments using a three phase 1.5KW induction machine performed in different conditions are used to provide training and test data. The diagnosis results demonstrated that the solution can reduce the cost and raise the efficiency of the diagnosis.

1 Introduction

Induction machines dominate the field of electromechanical energy conversion, so the issue of preventive maintenance and noninvasive diagnosis of the condition of these induction machines is of great importance. However, the measurement noise together with nonlinear behavior of induction machine makes the task of fault diagnosis difficult.

In the author's previous works, we tried to apply the Support vector machine (SVM) method to induction machine fault diagnosis [1]. SVM is a new and promising machine learning technique proposed by Vapnik and his colleagues [2]. It is widely applied to classification and regression problems because of its greater generalization performance. However, there are some drawbacks that it doesn't distinguish the importance of sample attributes, computation rate is slow and takes up more data storage space because of a large number of sample attributes. Moreover, it doesn't effectively deal with vagueness and uncertainty information.

In order to resolve those problems, a kind of SVM fault diagnosis system based on rough set pre-processing is proposed in this paper. Rough set theory is a mathematical tool for dealing with vagueness and uncertainty [3]. By adopting the RS based preprocessing unit, redundant diagnosis information is reduced and the reduction results are handled as inputs of SVM fault classifiers. Therefore, dimensions of input data are decreased and the efficiency and accuracy of the fault diagnosis system is improved.

D.-S. Huang, K. Li, and G.W. Irwin (Eds.): ICIC 2006, LNAI 4114 , pp. 631 – 636, 2006.

2 Spectrum Analysis of Motor Current Under Fault Conditions

When induction machine runs under fault conditions, some special components occur at the stator current. Spectrum analysis of the machine line current show that the sideband components f_b around the fundamentals of the line current spectrum usually appear. For example, when the rotor bar breaks, the feature components in the motor stator line current are [4]:

$$f_b = (1 \pm 2ks) f_1 \qquad (k = 1, 2, 3 \cdots) \tag{1}$$

where f_1 is the supplied frequency, s is the slip.

It is easy to measure the stator currents, and the frequency spectrum can be derived using Fast Fourier Transformation method. Therefore the fault detection can be done by analyzing the sidebands around the fundamental present in the line current.

3 Overview of the Rough Set

Rough set theory deals with information represented by a table called an information system composed of a 4-tuple as following [3]:

$$S = \langle U, A, V, f \rangle \tag{2}$$

where U is the universe, a finite set of N objects. $A = C \bigcup D$, is condition attribute and decision attribute. V is attribute value. $f : U \times A \rightarrow V$, is the total decision function called the information function.

Attribute reduction is one of the most important concepts in RS. Given an information system S, for a given set of condition attributes $P \subseteq (C)$, we can define a positive region $POS_p(D) = \bigcup_{X \in U/D} \underline{P}X$, the positive region $POS_p(D)$ contains all objects in U, which can be classified without error into distinct classes defined by $IND(D)$ based only on information in the $IND(P)$. Another important issue in data analysis is discovering dependencies between attributes. Let D and C be subsets of A. D depends on C in a degree denoted as

$$\gamma_C(D) = |pos_C(D)| / |U| \tag{3}$$

It was shown that the number $\gamma_C(D)$ expresses the degree of dependency between attributes C and D, It may be checked how the coefficient $\gamma_C(D)$ changes when some attribute is removed.

4 Support Vector Machine

The SVM developed by Vapnik implemented the principle of Structural Risk Minimization by constructing an optimal separating hyper plane $\mathrm{W} \bullet \mathrm{X} + b = 0$ [2].

To find the optimal hyper plane, the norm of the vector W needs to be minimized; on the other hand, the margin $1/\|W\|$ should be maximized between two classes.

Given a set of training data $\{x_i, y_i\}, i = 1, 2, \cdots, l.$, where $x_i \in R^n$ is the training data, each point x_i belongs to either of two classes and is given a label $y_i \in \{1, -1\}$. For the nonlinear case, we first mapped the data to some other Euclidean space H, using a mapping, $\phi : R^d \to H$. Then a kernel function K is issued such that $K(x_i, x_j) = \phi(x_i) \bullet \phi(x_j)$. Using a dual problem, the quadratic programming problems can be re-written as

$$Q(\alpha) = \sum_{i=1}^{l} \alpha_i - \frac{1}{2} \sum_{i.j=1}^{l} \alpha_i \alpha_j y_i y_j K(x_i, x_j) \tag{4}$$

$$\text{subject to } 0 \le \alpha_i \le C \quad \sum_{i=1}^{l} \alpha_i y_i = 0$$

with the decision function

$$f(x) = \operatorname{sgn}\left(\sum_{i=1}^{l} y_i \alpha_i K(x, x_i) + b \right) \tag{5}$$

In this paper, the author defines the fault diagnosis problem as a nonlinear problem and uses RBF function as the kernel function to optimize the hyperplane.

$$K(x, y) = \exp\left(\frac{-\|x - y\|^2}{2\sigma^2} \right). \tag{6}$$

5 Rotor Fault Detection System Based on RST and SVM

Integrating the advantages of RS and SVM, a kind of intelligent diagnosis system for rotor fault of induction machine is presented. When given a sample set, we firstly symbolize them, and then use RS method to reduce redundant attributes, finally construct a support vector machine fault diagnosis system. When giving a test set, we reduce the corresponding attributes and then put into SVM classifiers, then acquire the testing results. The flowchart of the RS-SVM fault diagnosis for power transformer is shown in Fig.1whole process is shown as fig. 1.

5.1 Experimental Data Analysis and Data Preparation

The features considered in this work are the amplitude of the sidebands. As there are two sideband harmonics (the left and the right sideband), so the features are listed as Tab.1

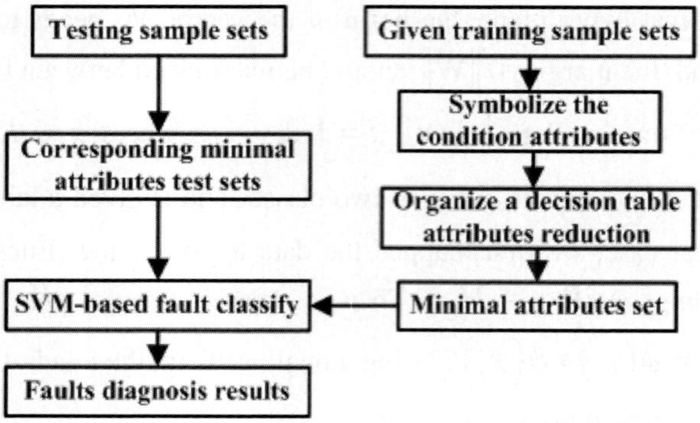

Fig. 1. The RS-SVM based intelligent diagnosis system for rotor fault of induction machine

Table 1. Attributes set

Serial number	Attributes
A1	The left sideband harmonic for rotor broken
A2	The right sideband harmonic for rotor broken
A3	The left sideband harmonic for dynamic eccentricity
A4	The right sideband harmonic for dynamic eccentricity
A5	The left sideband harmonic for static eccentricity
A6	The right sideband harmonic for static eccentricity
A7	Load level of the motor

The rough set is a method based on symbol analyzed, so the above features should be changed into symbol data by taking the values: S (small), M (medium), and L (large).

The decision attributes are listed in Tab.2.

Table 2. Decision attributes

Serial number	Fault type
D1	Health
D2	Broken bar
D3	Dynamic eccentricity
D4	Static eccentricity respectively

5.2 Rough Set Preprocess

A knowledge base reduction technique was used to filter out the redundant information. The algorithm can be represented by the following steps:

Step 1: Eliminate the dispensable attribute.
Step 2: Compute the core of each example.
Step 3: Compose a table with reduce value.
Step 4: Merge possible examples.

5.3 Multi-classification Based on SVM

The SVM based classifier is a two-class classifier in nature. In this work, to deal with multi-classification problem, we use "binary tree classifier" method to decompose the multi-class problem to several 2-class problems [5]. We may combine K classes into 2 classes at first, and so on, different layers at last, we can classify by SVM in each layer. When constructing the sub SVM classifier, we can make use of the advantages of RS in extraction features, in order to improve classification efficiency.

6 Experimental Results

Experimental results were obtained from a 3 phases, 1.5KW, 50Hz cage induction machine with different cage rotors. The experiments were performed at different fault conditions, including health, one bar broke, two bars broke, static eccentricity (2.5%), static eccentricity (5%), dynamic eccentricity (2.5%), and dynamic eccentricity (5%). Each fault was performed at 10 different loads varying 10 to 100% of rated load. Then we got 70 examples. The FFT method was employed to get the frequency spectrum of current signals. And then features described in section 5.1 were calculated. 50 samples of the calculated attributes were used for training the RS-SVM based classifiers. The other 20 samples were used as testing samples. The diagnosis results are shown in Tab.1. To illustrate the performance of the proposed approach, we also gave the results of both ANN approach and SVM approach (without RS based preprocess unit). The results are shown in Tab.3.

Table 3. Comparison of different methods

Methods	TE	Training time (s)	Diagnosis accuracy (%)
RS-SVM	0.01	Less than 1s	100
ANN [6]	0.01	124	80
SVM	0.01	3.5	90

The result in Table 3 shows that the proposed approach has better performances than ANN method and SVM method both in diagnosis accuracy and in training time. It must be pointed out, a wavelet transformation is operated firstly to extract the features and to reduce the dimensions when using neural network. And in [6], only broken-bar fault was considered. When deal with multi fault classification problems, the correct classification of ANN method would be lowered.

7 Conclusion

In this paper, a method of rotor fault intelligent diagnosis system for induction machine based on the integration of rough set and support vector machine is proposed. The data information of fault diagnosis is obtained from the spectrum data of motor line current. By data-analyzed method of rough set, the method can remove large amount of redundancy, and decreased volume of SVM training data. By means of excellent classify ability of SVM; the method classifies the smallest attribute subset that had been reduced by rough set. The experimental results show that this method has a better performance in diagnosis accuracy and less training time than other methods.

References

1. Fang, R. M., Ma, H. Z.: Classification of Induction Machine Rotor Faults Based on Least Square Support Vector Machine. Transactions of China Electrotechnical Society, 21 (2006) 21-28
2. Vapnik, V. N.: Statistical Learning Theory, John Wiley & Sons, New Work (1998)
3. Wang, G. Y.: Rough Set Theory and Knowledge Acquisition. Xi'an Jiaotong University Press, Xi'An, China (2001)
4. Benbouzid, M.: What Stator Current Processing-Based Technique to Use for Induction Motor Rotor Faults Diagnosis. IEEE Trans. On Energy Conversion, 18 (2003) 238–244
5. Mayoraz, E., Alpaydin, E.: Support Vector Machines for Multi-Class Classification. Int. Workshop on Artificial Neural Networks, Libr. 2 (1999) 833-842
6. Hou, X., Xia, L., Wu, Z.: Fault Diagnosis Method for Induction Motor Based on Wavelet Transformation and Neural Network. Journal of Data Acquisition and Processing, 19 (2004) 32-36

Intelligent Process Trend Recognition Fault Diagnosis and Industrial Application

Sien Lu and Biao Huang

Department of Chemical and Materials Engineering,
University of Alberta, Edmonton, Alberta, Canada T6G 2G6

Abstract. An intelligent process monitoring approach, which consists of process trend recognition and fault detection, is presented in this paper. This method incorporates wavelet transform, symbolic representation of data trend, pattern recognition, and Hidden Markov model (HMM) for intelligent reasoning. A simulation example and an industrial case study have shown the value of this approach.

1 Introduction

The traditional fault detection and isolation (FDI) approaches take advantages of a wealthy collection of data processing algorithms such as time series analysis and filtering. However, nuisance alarms are a common problem in its applications in industries. It is not uncommon that a new FDI algorithm is carefully tuned and successfully implemented initially, but it is turned off after a while due to numerous false alarms. What is the fundamental limitation of the traditional approaches? It is often the process and disturbances, usually time varying or nonlinear, that can not be captured well by models used in the traditional approaches. On the other hand, if a human operator monitors a process trend, he/she is often able to correctly identify the problem; however, it is beyond the possibility to have thousands of process variables be watched out by human operators. Why is a human operator able to capture the problem more reliably? Human being is able to learn/accumulate experiences and to view the overall trends (including magnitude, duration, and frequency of occurrence) of process changes rather than a single or a few points of process data. The noises are more or less filtered out by viewing the pattern rather than the isolated data points. Once a trend is picked up, the operator can determine what has happened by comparing the trend with the historical record/memory. Thus, three steps in sequence have been implicitly taken by human operators to effectively pick up a fault: 1) filtering noise, 2) identifying a trend, 3) intelligent reasoning.

With a large scale of process operation being a norm in modern manufactories, there is clearly a need to develop intelligent computation algorithms, to mimic what a human operator does when facing process data, for process trend recognition and subsequent fault detection/diagnosis. One of the most important steps in this process is the trend identification. The series of paper by Stephanopoulos and his coworkers [1, 2, 3] developed a triangular representation to describe qualitative and quantitative information in a process trend. Using this method, every

D.-S. Huang, K. Li, and G.W. Irwin (Eds.): ICIC 2006, LNAI 4114, pp. 637–642, 2006.

episode can be described using a triangle. Wong *et al.* [5, 6] studied the same problem using trend recognition and Hidden Markov Models for reasoning. The work to be presented in this paper is based on the previous work of [1, 2, 3, 5, 6] by developing a compact version of trend recognition and probability reasoning algorithm with emphasis on applications. An industrial application is used to illustrate the effectiveness of the developed algorithm.

2 Methodology

This type of method consists of two parts: representation and classification. In the first part, the process data is filtered by wavelet transform and described by triangular episodes. Therefore, the original process data is converted into qualitative and semi-quantitative information. Then this information is input into one or more hidden Markov models (HMM) for classification (reasoning). Finally, based on the classification results, process faults are determined.

2.1 Wavelet Analysis

In this application, the wavelet analysis is used to extract significant temporal features contained in a record of measured data. There are different type of wavelet families, such as Haar wavelet and Daubechies wavelets. Depending on the application property, we can select appropriate wavelet.

The wavelet is used not only to smooth the raw data, but also detect the extreme and inflexion points. Using wavelet decomposition, we can get approximations and details at different scales. At a lower scale, the detail consists of high frequency noise signal and the approximation keeps the dynamic behavior of data. On the other hand, at a higher scale, the basic trend of data is extracted and the detail shows the low frequency noise. Since the wavelet is used for the noise filtering and the feature extraction in this work, high scale is more suitable. However, if the selected scale is beyond certain level, the most important information contained in a signal, which can help to differentiate it from others, will lost. Therefore, the selection of an appropriate level is the first and the most crucial step of this process monitoring method.

2.2 Approximate Derivative Calculation

Process trend may be represented by a series of triangles shown, as an example, in Fig.1. A triangle shape is determined by three points. These three points are either the extrema or the inflexion of data trends. The extraction of extrema and inflexion points from a trend is based on the calculation of first and second derivative. The simplest way to perform derivative calculation is by numerical differentiation:

$$f'(x_i) = \frac{f(x_i) - f(x_{i-1})}{x_i - x_{i-1}}. \tag{1}$$

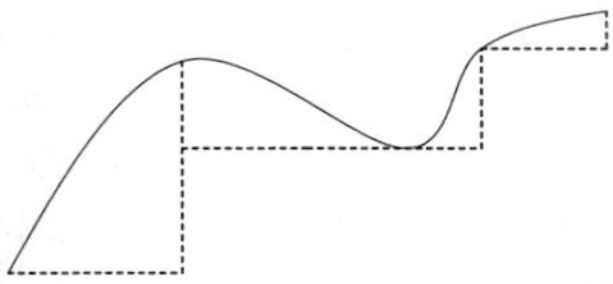

Fig. 1. A process trend represented by three triangulars

For discrete data, the sample intervals usually are even and equal to one, then Equation 1 can be simplified to

$$f'(x_i) = f(x_i) - f(x_{i-1}) \tag{2}$$

Similarly, the second derivative can be calculated as

$$f''(x_i) = f'(x_i) - f'(x_{i-1}). \tag{3}$$

2.3 Representation of Process Trends

In this work, four kinds of triangle: A, B, C and D are adopted to represent process trends shown in the left panel of Figure 2. The type of triangle determines the qualitative information of an episode. In addition to the type, some semi-quantitative information can also be used to characterize and classify an episode, such as duration and magnitude. The duration of a triangle is defined as the time interval between two end points of an episode and the magnitude of a triangle is the magnitude difference between these two end points. There are three kinds of magnitude: large, medium and small. There are three kinds of duration: long, middle and short. Then, for every type of triangle, say, "A", there are nine possible outcomes, as shown in the right panel of Figure 2 (Wong *et al.* 1998) [5]. For example, "lmA" stands for a large magnitude, middle duration, type "A" triangular. The same is for the triangles "B" to "D". Therefore, this triangular representation method not only gives the qualitative but also semi-quantitative characteristics of a trend.

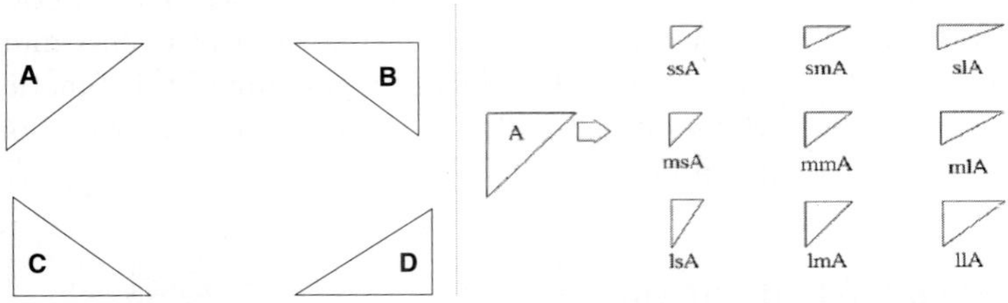

(a) Triangles (b) Example of sub-triangle

Fig. 2. Triangle representation of process trends

Finally, using this triangular representation method, a signal can be converted into a 36 symbolic character alphabet. As Bakshi and Stephanopoulos (1994) [1] pointed out, this method "*is complete, correct and robust, and allows explicit description of the important information of a trend.*" The advantage of this method is that it converts a signal into a symbolic sequence, which captures the most important qualitative and quantitative information contained in the signal. Compared with filtered process data, this symbolic form is convenient as the input of a following classifying system such as HMM.

2.4 Hidden Markov Modeling

Hidden Markov model, like a state space model, represents the sequential evolvements of process state that may not be directly observed. The state needs not to be continuous. The state transitions are represented by conditional probability functions. The state variables are typically hidden but indirectly observed through output equation.

Rabiner (1989) [4] summarized that there are three basic problems of interest for an HMM application: 1) Given the observation sequence and a model, how do we efficiently compute the probability of this observed sequence generated from the model? 2) Given the observation sequence and the model, how do we choose a corresponding state sequence which is optimal in some meaningful sense (filtering)? 3) How do we adjust the model parameters so as to best account for the observed sequence?

For the method proposed in this work, the first and last problems are of interests. The last one is a training problems – given an observation sequence, how do we optimize the model parameters to create the best model? Similar to other model based process monitoring and fault detection methods, this problem is the most difficult and the solution to this problem is crucial. The solution to the first problem is used for classification. Given a model and any observation sequence, how do we compute the probability that the observed sequence was produced by this model? Another case of classification is that, given several models and one sequence of observation, how do we determine the model which best matches this observation?

The HMM-based classification method introduced in this paper is implemented using the Matlab statistics toolbox, which includes five functions designed for HMM analysis. The function *hmmtrain* calculates the maximum likelihood estimate of HMM parameters. The default algorithm of this function uses an iterative algorithm – Baum-Welch method. Detailed information about this algorithm can be found in Rabiner (1989) [4].

3 Industrial Application

The industrial case study is concerned with a real problem arising from an industrial separation process. There are three PID control loops involved in this process, level loop y_L, density loop y_D, and speed control loop y_S. Simply speaking, the control objective is to maintain the level and density of the fluid in a tank around their desired setpoints by manipulating the outlet flow speed. The outlet flow is controlled by manipulating the pump. The problem it is facing is that there is a cycling in the process. Cycling occurs once about every ten minutes.

In order to reduce the cycling, field process control engineers tried to tune the controller parameters. One of the tuning tests is shown in Figure 3. Based on these figures, it appears that the control performance has been improved; however, one may question the result by arguing that these figures have been plotted on different time and magnitude scales. Plotting them in same scales, as shown in Figure 4, it is obvious that this tuning does not change the behaviors of density and level control loops. For the speed control loop however, there is difference in terms of oscillation magnitude and period indeed.

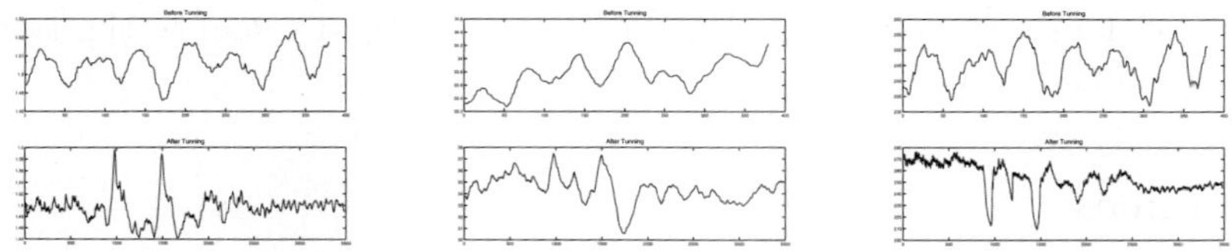

(a) Density response (b) Level response (c) Speed response

Fig. 3. Closed-loop responses before and after tuning

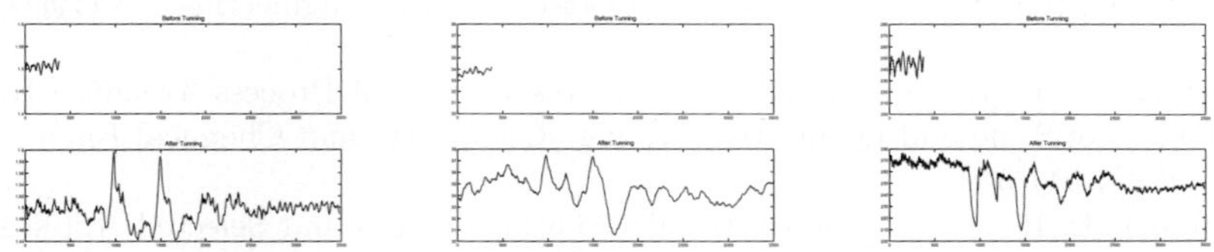

(a) Density response (b) Level response (c) Speed response

Fig. 4. Closed-loop responses before and after tuning plotted in the same scale

Using the data after tuning, three HMMs are trained by applying the approach introduced in this paper for these three control loops, respectively. The probabilities that the data before and after tuning are generated by the model are given in Table 1. From this table we can see that the probabilities of y_D and y_L before and after tuning are quite similar, which means that the behaviors did not really change. The probability of y_S before tuning is zero and 23.9 after tuning (the probability ratio is of interest for the comparison). The interpretation

Table 1. PSV tuning data analysis result

	DC181PV	LC161PV	SC2136PV
Before Tuning	12.3%	35.7%	0%
After Tuning	19.0%	55.1%	23.9%

is that this tuning did change the behavior of this speed control loop. All these conclusions coincide with the observations observed from Figure 4.

4 Conclusions

In this paper, an intelligent process monitoring approach is presented. It consists of wavelet transform, symbolic representation and HMM classification. The proposed method is verified by an industrial application example, which shows that this method can effectively detect the behavior change of the monitored variable. The potential use of this method is also illustrated by industrial case study. The intelligent monitoring algorithm is useful when we are facing a large amount of data and variables, where it is impossible to visualize the trend of each individual variable.

References

[1] Bakshi, B. R., Stephanopoulos, G.: Representation of Process Trends – III. Multiscale Extraction of Trends from Process Data. Computers and Chemical Engineering, 18 (1994) 267-302

[2] Cheung, J. T., Stephanopoulos, G.: Representation of Process Trends – I. A Formal Representation Framework. Computers and Chemical Engineering, 14 (1990) 495-510

[3] Cheung, J. T., Stephanopoulos, G: Representation of Process Trends – II. The Problem of Scale and Qualitative Scaling. Computers and Chemical Engineering, 14 (1990) 511-539

[4] Rabiner, L. R.: A Tutorial on Hidden Markov Models and Selected Applications in Speech Recognition. Proceedings of IEEE, New York, 77 (1989) 257-286

[5] Wong, J. C., McDonald, K. A., Palazoglu, A.: Classification of Process Trends Based on Fuzzified Symbolic Representation and Hidden Markov Models. Journal of Process Control, 8 (1998) 395-408

[6] Wong, J. C., McDonald, K. A., Palazoglu, A.: Classification of Abnormal Plant Operation Using Multiple Process Variable Trends. Journal of Process Control, 11 (2001) 409-418

Multiple Fault Diagnosis Approach for Rotary Machines Based on Matter-Element*

Wen Jin[1,2], Chang-Zheng Chen[1], and Zhi-Hao Jin[2]

[1] College of Mechanical Engineering, Shenyang University of Technology, Shenyang, China, 110023
jin89386217@sina.com
[2] Department of Mechanical Engineering, Shenyang Institute of Chemical Technology, Shenyang, China, 110142
jzh_sict_ln@sina.com

Abstract. An approach was put forward to diagnose the multiple faults of rotary machines according to the characteristic frequency spectrum of vibration. Based on the matter-element of extension theory, a matter-element model was built to describe the fault situation of rotary machines qualitatively. The dependent function and degree of a symptom of the fault were introduced to evaluate the possibility of the fault quantitatively. The diagnosis example was taken to validate the approach. The diagnosed result is consistent with the real result.

1 Introduction

A rotary machine is a complicated machine with many components. In a real rotary machine, the case of multiple faults is quite common, such as the simultaneous presence of an unbalance, a bow, rubbing and a coupling misalignment etc. Many papers are available in the literature about single fault diagnosis in rotary machines[1],[2],[3]. Multiple fault diagnosis is still an actively investigating subject.

Intelligent fault diagnosis technique has been a major research topic in the fault diagnosis of rotary machines for the last decades. There has been much progress, but industrial acceptance has not been high because of the difficulty of acquiring the knowledge, the difficulty to deal with novel faults and the difficulty of the knowledge updating.

Forming a diagnosis matrix between the symptoms and causes of faults, fuzzy diagnosis method has made some progress on overcoming the difficulty in acquirement of knowledge bases[4],[5],[8]. It still has some disadvantage because of the artificial selection of the membership function.

The fault diagnosis method based on neural network obtains the knowledge from the samples and carries out the nonlinear mapping between the symptoms and causes of faults[5],[6],[7]. It gets into good graces of many researchers in mechanical fault diagnosis. For the fault diagnosis method based on neural network, a lot of training

* Supported by the National Natural Science Foundation of China, No.50535010.
Supported by the Chunhui Plan of Ministry of Education of China, No. z2005-1-21007.

D.-S. Huang, K. Li, and G.W. Irwin (Eds.): ICIC 2006, LNAI, pp. 643 – 648, 2006.

samples are needed to get a satisfactory diagnosis. In fact, it is difficult to get so many training samples of a real machine that restricts the application of this method.

Extension set theory analyses problems quantitatively and qualitatively[10],[11],[12]. The extension-set analysis is based on the matter-element analysis. The purpose of this paper is to develop a new method of multiple fault diagnosis based on the matter-element analysis and the extension-set analysis of spectral characteristic parameters, by building the matter-element modals and introducing the dependent functions.

2 Brief Description of Extension Set Theory

Extension set theory is developed on the base of the classical set theory and fuzzy set theory. The classical set theory studies the definiteness of matter and the fuzzy set theory studies the fuzziness of matter while the extension set theory studies the transformability of matter.

A matter-element is the basic element to describe matter or a thing. Supposed that thing N possesses the characteristic $c_1, c_2, c_3, \cdots, c_n$ and the corresponding values of the characteristics are $v_1, v_2, v_3, \cdots, v_n$, the matter-element R of N is defined as

$$R = \begin{bmatrix} N & c_1 & v_1 \\ & c_2 & v_2 \\ & \vdots & \vdots \\ & c_n & v_n \end{bmatrix} = \begin{bmatrix} R_1 \\ R_2 \\ \vdots \\ R_n \end{bmatrix}. \tag{1}$$

Matter-element combines the thing, its characteristics and corresponding values into one set. For a multiple dimension matter-element can describe multiple aspects of a thing, it is possible to build a multiple fault modal which describes the multiple fault situation of a rotary machine by matter-element.

Supposed that x is a point in the real field $X=(-\infty, +\infty)$ and $X_0=\langle a, b\rangle$ is a real interval in the real field $X=(-\infty, +\infty)$, then define the distance on real axis between point x and real interval X_0 as Equation (2) and the position of point x with respect to the real interval X_0 and X as Equation (3). Supposed interval X_0 and X have no superposition point, we define the dependent function as Equation (4).

$$\rho(x, X_0) = \left| x - \frac{a+b}{2} \right| - \frac{b-a}{2}. \tag{2}$$

$$D(x, X_0, X) = \begin{cases} \rho(x, X) - \rho(x, X_0) & \text{when } \; x \notin X_0 \\ -1 & \text{when } \; x \in X_0 \end{cases}. \tag{3}$$

$$K(x) = \frac{\rho(x, X_0)}{D(x, X_0, X)}. \tag{4}$$

The dependent function can express the dependent degree of point x with respect to the intervals X_0 and X. If $K(x) \geqslant 0$, it expresses the level that x belongs to interval X_0. If $K(x) \leqslant -1$, it means that x does not belong to interval X_0. If $-1<K(x)<0$, it means that x has the possibility of belonging to interval X_0 and the bigger $K(x)$ is, the more the possibility is. So the dependent function can be regarded as the tool to describe the qualitative change and quantitative change of things.

When the denominator in equation (4) is zero, the dependent function is defined as $K(x) = -\rho(x, X_0)/\ l_{x0}$, where l_{x0} is the length of X_0.

Usually, X_0 is called classic field, while X is called admittable field.

3 Diagnosis Approach of Rotary Machines

The concept of the multiple dimension matter-element offers a new idea about the multiple fault diagnosis of rotary machine. In fault diagnosis of rotary machines, the faults usually are recognized by the frequency analysis of collected vibration signal[3],[8][9]. The vibration spectral information can be divided into some characteristic spectral bands that can be used as characteristic value of the relevant fault. Then the relations between fault symptoms and characteristic values of faults can be figured out by use of the dependent function.

3.1 Fault Category of Rotary Machines

We will take the fault diagnosis of SK15HE gas turbines as an example to illustrate the fault diagnosis pattern. According to information collected in years' operation of SK15HE[8], the faults commonly found in the gas turbines can be categorized into rotor faults, shafting faults, supporting faults, resonance faults, assembly faults and other faults. The characteristic frequency bands for various faults at different positions are shown in Table 1[8]. The values in Table 1 are the ratios of the fault frequencies to the working frequency of the rotor. C_1, C_2, C_3, C_4, C_5 are the characteristic frequency bands at different positions of the motor, C_6, C_7, C_8 the characteristic frequency bands at different positions of the gear, C_9 the characteristic frequency bands at the vane, C_{10} the characteristic frequency bands at critical situation and C_{11} the characteristic frequency bands at structural resonance.

Table 1. Matrix of classic fields

No. of I	C_1	C_2	C_3	C_4	C_5	C_6	C_7	C_8	C_9	C_{10}	C_{11}
1	<0.4, 0.75>	<0.9, 1.1>	<1.8, 2.2>	<2.8, 3.2>	<3.8, 4.2>	<0.9, 1.1>	<1.9, 2.1>	<0.8, 1.2>	<0.8, 1.2>	<0.8, 1.2>	<0.1, 1.2>
2	<0, 0.1>	<0.9, 1.1>	<1.8, 2.2>	<2.8, 3.2>	<3.8, 4.2>	<0, 0.1>	<1.9, 2.1>	<0, 0.1>	<0.8, 1.2>	<0, 0.1>	<0, 0.1>
3	<0.4, 0.75>	<0, 0.1>	<0, 0.1>	<0, 0.1>	<0, 0.1>	<0, 0.1>	<0, 0.1>	<0, 0.1>	<0, 0.1>	<0, 0.1>	<0, 0.1>
4	<0, 0.1>	<0, 0.1>	<0, 0.1>	<0, 0.1>	<0, 0.1>	<0, 0.1>	<1.9, 2.1>	<0, 0.1>	<0, 0.1>	<0.8, 1.2>	<0.1, 1.2>
5	<0, 0.1>	<0, 0.1>	<0, 0.1>	<2.8, 3.2>	<3.8, 4.2>	<0.9, 1.1>	<1.9, 2.1>	<0.8, 1.2>	<0.8, 1.2>	<0, 0.1>	<0, 0.1>
6	<0, 0.1>	<0.9, 1.1>	<1.8, 2.2>	<0, 0.1>	<0, 0.1>	<0.9, 1.1>	<0, 0.1>	<0, 0.1>	<0.8, 1.2>	<0.8, 1.2>	<0.1, 1.2>
7	<0,0.1>	<0,0.1>	<0,0.1>	<0,0.1>	<0,0.1>	<0,0.1>	<0,0.1>	<0,0.1>	<0,0.1>	<0,0.1>	<0,0.1>

3.2 Matter-Element Model of Faults

Let the I be the set of possible fault types of the gas turbines, C the set of the corresponding symptoms, V_{ij}=<a_{ij}, b_{ij}> the real field of characteristic symptom C_j of the fault I_i, and v_{ti} the value of symptom C_i, (i=1, 2, ··· 11). The matter-element model R_i of the fault I_i, can be expressed in Table 1 and Table 2 respectively.

The matrix in Table 1 is the classic field matrix $V(V_{ij})$, (i=1, 2, ··· 7, j=1, 2, ··· 11). We define the possible field of symptom C_j of the fault I_i as V_{ij}'=<a_{ij}', b_{ij}'>, and call it admittable field. When symptom C_j of the fault I_i is in the area V_{ij}'=<a_{ij}', b_{ij}'>, it means there is some possibility of fault I_i. The admittable field are artificially assumed to be V_{ij}'=<0, 10>, (i=1, 2, ··· 7, j=1, 2, ··· 11) according to their classic field.

3.3 Dependent Function and Dependent Degree

According to Equation (4), the dependent function of the symptom of the fault is

$$K_{ij}\left(v_{ij}\right)=\frac{\rho\left(v_{ij},V_{ij}\right)}{\rho\left(v_{tj},V_{ij}^{'}\right)-\rho\left(v_{ij},V_{ij}\right)}. \tag{6a}$$

When the denominator in Equation (6a) is zero, the dependent function takes the form

$$K_{ij}\left(v_{tj}\right)=-\rho\left(v_{tj},V_{ij}\right)/\,l_{Vij}. \tag{6b}$$

where l_{Vij} is the length of V_{ij}. The dependent degree of the symptom to the fault is

$$\lambda(I_i)=\sum_{j=1}^{11}W_{ij}K_{ij} \quad i=1,2,\cdots,7. \tag{7}$$

where W_{ij} is the weight of symptom C_j in the fault I_i. To conveniently observe the results of dependence, we normalize the Equation (7) as below

$$\lambda'(I_i)=\frac{2\lambda(I_i)-\lambda_{\min}-\lambda_{\max}}{\lambda_{\max}-\lambda_{\min}} \quad i=1,2,\cdots,7. \tag{8}$$

where $\lambda_{\max}=\max\limits_{1\le i\le 7}\{\lambda(I_i)\}$; $\lambda_{\min}=\min\limits_{1\le i\le 7}\{\lambda(I_i)\}$.

3.4 Multiple Fault Diagnosis

The multiple fault diagnosis can be made according to the dependent degree $\lambda(I_i)$ of treating fault, usually according to the normalized dependent degree $\lambda'(I_i)$.

If $\lambda'(I_i)\le 0$, then the fault I_i didn't occur. If $\lambda'(I_i)>0$, then it is possible that the fault I_i may occur. The bigger the $\lambda'(I_i)$ is, the more possibly the fault I_i occurs. Usually we diagnose the symptom with the biggest $\lambda'(I_i)$ as the fault I_i. This rule is called the biggest dependence rule. If there are more than one top normalized dependent degrees whose values are almost the same (the difference is less than the difference field β, 0.05) and the normalized dependent degrees are obviously great than the others (the difference is more than the recognition field γ, 0.1), then it is possible that more than one faults may occur. The difference field β means the nearness degree of different faults and the recognition field γ means the difference degree of different faults. By considering the $\lambda'(I_i)$, β and γ properly, we can make the diagnosis for multiple faults.

4 Diagnosis Examples

In order to validate the diagnosis approach, we diagnose more than 100 symptoms of gas turbine faults collected in recent years. Table 2 shows some of the frequency ratios of treating faults collected. In the table, T.F. means treating fault. The diagnosis can be made by use of the approach introduced above.

Table 2. The symptoms frequency ratios of faults

No.of T.F.	C_1	C_2	C_3	C_4	C_5	C_6	C_7	C_8	C_9	C_{10}	C_{11}
1	0.5	1.0	2.0	3.0	4.0	1.0	2.0	0	1.0	0	0
2	0	1.0	2.0	3.0	4.0	0	2.0	0	1.0	0	0
3	0.5	0	0	0	0	0	0	0	0	0	0
4	0	0	0	0	0	0	2.0	0	0	1.0	1.0
5	0	1.0	0	3.0	4.0	1.0	2.0	0	1.0	0	0
6	0	0	0	3.0	4.0	1.0	2.0	0	1.0	0	0
7	0	1.0	2.0	0	0	1.0	0	0	0	1.0	1.0
8	0	0	0	0	0	0	0	0	0	0	0

Table 3. Results obtained by the extension diagnosis method

No.of T.F.	dependent degrees of symptoms to the faults							diagnosed faults	real faults
	$\lambda'(I_1)$	$\lambda'(I_2)$	$\lambda'(I_3)$	$\lambda'(I_4)$	$\lambda'(I_5)$	$\lambda'(I_6)$	$\lambda'(I_7)$		
1	$\underline{1.00}$	0.59	-0.32	-1.00	0.086	-0.61	-0.54	1	1
2	0.26	$\underline{1.00}$	-0.70	-0.87	-0.18	-1.00	-0.32	2	2
3	-1	-0.91	$\underline{1.00}$	-0.06	-0.91	-0.63	0.80	3	3
4	-1	-0.53	0.29	$\underline{1.00}$	-0.53	0.17	0.53	4	4
5	0.78	$\underline{0.99}$	-0.56	-0.80	$\underline{1.00}$	-1.00	-0.034	2,5	2,5
6	0.26	0.41	-0.10	-0.27	$\underline{1.00}$	-1.00	0.27	5	5
7	-0.69	-0.58	-0.10	0.27	-1.00	$\underline{1.00}$	0.16	6	6
8	-1.00	-0.50	0.75	0.25	-0.50	-0.25	$\underline{1.00}$	7	7

Table 3 shows the results of the diagnosis. Take treating fault 5 as an example to illustrate the quantitive and qualitative diagnosis by means of extension method. As for treating fault 5, it can be judged that fault I_3, I_4, I_6 and I_7 did not occur according to the negative dependent degree $\lambda'(I_3)$, $\lambda'(I_4)$, $\lambda'(I_6)$, and $\lambda'(I_7)$. We can qualitatively determined that the fault I_1, I_2 and I_5 are possible because of the positive $\lambda'(I_1)$, $\lambda'(I_2)$ and $\lambda'(I_5)$. Sorting the positive dependent degree in descending order, $\lambda'(I_5)>\lambda'(I_2)>\lambda'(I_1)$, we can find that the most possible fault is I_5 because of the biggest dependent degree $\lambda'(I_5)$ according to the biggest dependence rule. The value $\lambda'(I_5)$ quantitatively represents the possibility of fault I_5. The difference between $\lambda'(I_5)$ and $\lambda'(I_2)$ is less than the difference field β, 0.05, and the difference between $\lambda'(I_2)$ and $\lambda'(I_1)$ is more than the recognition field γ, 0.1, that means the dependent degree $\lambda'(I_5)$ and $\lambda'(I_2)$ are almost the same and it can be judged that the fault I_5 and I_2 occurred at the same time. In fact, the fault I_5 and I_2 really occurred. The diagnosed result is consistent with the real result.

5 Conclusions

The matter-element model of extension set theory can describe the fault situation s of rotary machines well. The classic fields express the real fields of characteristic symptoms of the faults. The admittable fields express the possible fields of characteristic symptoms of the faults. The dependent function and the dependent degree $\lambda'(I_i)$ of the symptom to the fault are determined by admittable fields, classic fields and the value of symptom, and represent the possibility of the fault and the fault may be judged by the biggest dependence rule. The difference field β expresses the nearness degree of different faults and the recognition field γ denotes the difference degree of different faults. By considering the $\lambda'(I_i)$, β and γ properly, we can make the diagnosis for multiple faults quantitatively and qualitatively.

References

1. Changzheng Chen, Changtao Mo.: A Method for Intelligent Fault Diagnosis of Rotating Machinery. Digital Signal Processing, (2004) 203-217
2. Mingsian Bai, Jiamin Huang, etc.: Fault Diagnosis of Rotating Machinery Using an Intelligent Order Tracking System. Journal of Sound and Vibration, (2005) 699–718
3. Wen Banchun, Wu Xinhua, etc.: Practical Technology of in Situ Diagnosis for Large Rotary Machines. Beijing Science Pub (2004)
4. Dexter, A.L.: Fuzzy Model Based Fault Diagnosis. IEEE Proceeding of Control Theory Appl. Vol.142, No.6(1995)545-550
5. Sheng Zhang, Toshiyuki Asakura, etc.: Fault Diagnosis System for Rotary Machines Based on Fuzzy Neural Networks. Proseedings of the IEEE/ASME International Conference on Advanced Intelligent Mechatronics,199-204
6. William, G. Fenton, T. M. McGinnity, Liam, P. Maguire.: Fault Diagnosis of Electronic Systems Using Intelligent Techniques a Review. IEEE Transactions on Systems, Man, and Cybernetics-Part C: Application and Reviews, Vol.31, No.3, 269-280
7. Kaewkongka, T., Joe Au, Y H., Rakowski, R., Jones, B E.: Continuous Wavelet Transform and Neural Network for Condition Monitoring of Roto-dynamic Machinery, IEEE Instrumentation and Measurement Technology Conference Budapest, Hungary, May (2001)21-23
8. Hu Tao,Lǔ Bingchao,Chen Guangju.:A Rotary Machinery Fault Diagnosis Approach Based on Rough Set Theory. Proceedings of the 3th World Congress on Intelligent Control and Automation, 685-689
9. Bachschmid, N., Pennacchi, P., Vania, A.: Identification of Multiple Faults in Rotor Systems. Journal of Sound and Vibration (2002) 327-366
10. Cai Wen.: Extension Theory and its Application. Chinese Science Bulletin, Vol. 44, No. 17, (1999)1538-1548
11. Qin Jianjun, Li Qiang.: A Model of Intellective Fault Diagnosis on the Basis of Extension. ICNGC2001, Harbin: Harbin Engineering University Press, (2001) 357-360
12. Cai Wen, Yang Chunyan.: Methods of Extension Engineering. Beijing: Science Pub (2000)

Numerical Model and Analysis on Dynamics of Composites for Active Damage Detection

Zhi Wei[1], Minqiao Lu[2], and Jun Zhang[3,4,*]

[1] School of Mechanical Engineering, Hebei University of Technology, China
[2] Xingtai Vocational and Technical College, China
[3] Department of Computer Science, Sun Yat-sen University, China
[4] Guangdong Key Lab of Information Security, China
junzhang@ieee.org

Abstract. This paper presents a study on active detection of internal damage based on numerical analysis of vibration dynamics in composites. Damage-induced variations of dynamic parameters are investigated both numerically and experimentally. Finite element method (FEM) is used to compute the modal parameters of composites with or without damages. Natural frequency, modal displacement, modal strain and strain energy are analyzed for the determination of damage severity and location. Vibration measurements are carried out using piezoelectric patch actuators and sensors for comparison and verification of the FEM model proposed in this study. Energy spectrum for wavelet packets decomposition of structural dynamic responses is used to highlight the features of damaged samples. The mechanism of mode-dependent energy dissipation of composite plates due to delamination is revealed for the first time. Both numerical and experimental findings in this study are significant to the establishment of guideline for damage identification in composite structures.

1 Introduction

The use of composite materials in space vehicles and various machine components has increased considerably over the past decades. Under repeated or impact loads these materials are subjected to various forms of damage, mostly delamination and crack [1-2]. Such damage becomes an obstacle to the more extensive usage of composite materials. Therefore, the monitoring of internal or hidden damage in composite materials is critical in engineering practice [3]. The use of vibration-based techniques as nondestructive testing methods for damage monitoring of laminated composite is a field attracting the interest of many researchers [4]. The basic idea for vibration-based damage detection is that the modal parameters depend on the physical properties of the structure to be inspected. Therefore, changes in physical properties of a structure due to damage can result in detectable variations in its modal parameters, such as natural frequencies, mode shapes and modal damping. A number of studies have been

* Corresponding author. This work was supported in part by NSF of China Project No.60573066; NSF of Guangdong Project No. 5003346 and Guangdong Key Lab of Information Security.

D.-S. Huang, K. Li, and G.W. Irwin (Eds.): ICIC 2006, LNAI 4114, pp. 649 – 654, 2006.

carried out to show the effectiveness of dynamic response measurements for NDT of composites [5,6].

The initial state of any damage in a material or structure is always in a tiny extent. Early detection of initial damage can prevent a catastrophic failure or structural deterioration beyond repair. Therefore, it is important to detect such damage in the early stage for practical composites or structures. The online detection of damage in composites is nowadays an attractive topic for developing the safe, reliable and effective methods to discover initial damage. Numerous researchers have studied various aspects of delamination damage including changes in dynamic response due to delamination. The introduction of damage into a material generally results in an increase of damping, which is related to energy dissipation during dynamic excitation [7].

However, few literatures can be found to feasibly study the structural dynamic responses for various damages in composites based on dynamic model. This paper, therefore, focuses on the correlation of modal parameters and damage in composite plates. The relationship between the modal parameters and damage location and sizes is analyzed. Experiment for measurement of response to selected excitations is carried out to detect the damage in some samples by means of wavelet packets decomposition. For relatively small damage, the damage-induced changes of modal parameters are too slight to be practically detectable, however, by means of analysis on energy spectrum of wavelet packets decomposition even very small damage can be detected according to the measured response signals.

2 Dynamic Model of Composite Plates with Damage

The finite element used for multi-layer composite plates with delamination is an eight-node rectangular thin plate element. For each node, there are three degrees of freedom, i.e., translations along the global coordinate axes of x, y and z, respectively. The element thickness is assigned to be equal to that of the corresponding individual lamina, which may not be the same for all elements. The element coordinate system is arranged with the first axis coincident with the fiber direction. All parameters throughout an element are assumed to be the same.

For an arbitrary laminated plate, to ensure the material continuity, displacements and their variations of each pair of the coincident nodes on the upper and lower adjacent laminae have to be equal in the whole process of computation for the intact plate. When the plate is damaged somewhere, each pair of the coincident nodes just on the upper and lower surfaces within the delamination region will no longer be connected with each other. If a composite plate experiences a harmonic motion the modal parameters such as mode shapes, natural frequencies and modal strains, etc., can be obtained by solving an eigenvalue problem.

Three damage variables θ_1, θ_2, and θ_3 are adopted to represent damages of matrix rupture, crack and delamination, respectively. They can be determined using parameter calculation based on structural damage theory. Then, the elastic matrix for damaged element can be written as

$$[Q]=\begin{bmatrix} Q_{11}^0+C_1\theta_1+C_2\theta_2+C_3\theta_3 & Q_{12}^0+(C_{10}\theta_1+C_{11}\theta_2+C_{12}\theta_3)/2 & C_{13}\theta_1/2 \\ Q_{21}^0+(C_{10}\theta_1+C_{11}\theta_2+C_{12}\theta_3)/2 & Q_{22}^0+C_4\theta_1+C_5\theta_2+C_6\theta_3 & C_{14}\theta_2/2 \\ C_{13}\theta_1/2 & C_{14}\theta_2/2 & Q_{66}^0+(C_7\theta_1+C_8\theta_2+C_9\theta_3) \end{bmatrix} \quad (1)$$

where C_1~C_{14} are material-dependent damage coefficients, which can be determined experimentally using normative composite specimens.

3 Damage Feature Extraction Using Wavelet Packets Decomposition

There is an equivalent relationship between the energy of wavelet transform and that of the original signal. Therefore, it is reasonable to express energy variation in the original signal by energy spectrum of wavelet packets. Hence, the sum of square of the decomposed signal is selected as the feature of energy spectrum within every frequency span. In subspace $V_{2^j i}$ (the ith frequency span of the jth layer) the result of wavelet packets decomposition is expressed by $\{S_i(k), k=1, 2,\ldots, M\}$, and its energy is expressed as

$$U_{2^j i} = \sum_{k=1}^{M} |S_i(k)|^2 \tag{2}$$

where M is the length of samples in the subspace. If $U^0_{2^j i}$ and $U^d_{2^j i}$ represent the energy spectrums of the signals measured from intact and damaged samples, respectively, the dimensionless index

$$\eta_i = \frac{U^d_{2^j i} - U^0_{2^j i}}{U^0_{2^j i}} \tag{3}$$

can demonstrate the damage-induced energy variation of the signal in subspace $V_{2^j i}$.

4 Samples

Fig. 1 shows a sample plate composed of epoxy matrix and glass fiber with 17 layers in 0° and 90° orientations. There is an area of 0.5×1 cm^2 containing a crack in the damaged plate. The relative changes of energy spectrums between the intact plate and damaged plate with a crack of length a_c=5mm and width b_c=0.1mm are shown in Fig. 2. It is seen that this set of data can be taken as the index vector of the crack damage for online damage detection of in-service composite structures.

Further numerical analysis shows that the crack with length 2.3mm and width 0.1mm or length 3mm and width 0.05mm can be well detected. The relationship between the maximum energy variation and the crack size shows that for crack length within 5mm the maximum energy variation increases linearly with crack length.

The other samples are plates of carbon fiber-reinforced epoxy composite. The plate has length 240 mm, width 180 mm and height 2.4 mm, and consists of 16 layers in orientation of $[0°/0°/90°/90°/0°/0°/90°/90°]_s$. Each damaged plate has only one rectangular delamination between the fourth and fifth layers inside the plate at the position with the center. The samples are also in free boundary condition. Damaged samples with delamination sizes of 18×12, 36×24, 54×36 and 72×48 mm^2 are considered and named A, B, C and D, respectively.

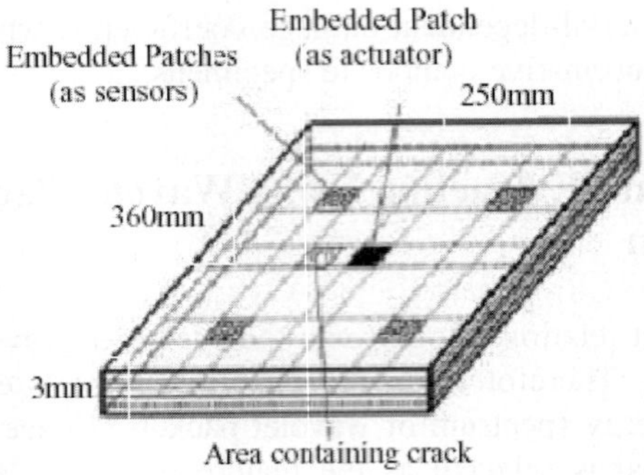

Fig. 1. Sample for active detection of matrix crack in composite plate

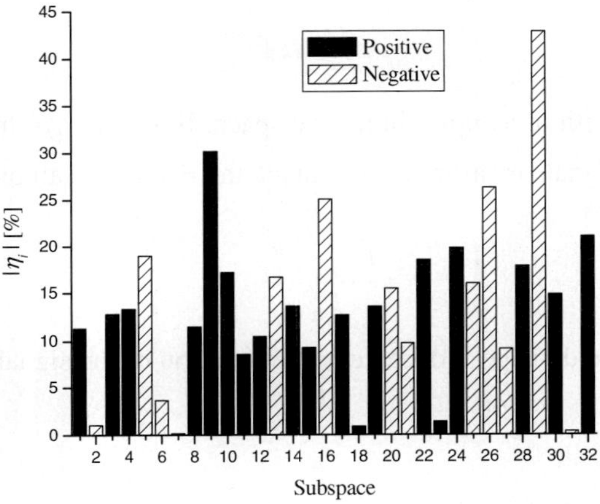

Fig. 2. Crack-induced energy variation in wavelet component of vibration response

Natural frequencies are firstly computed for the first six modes. The results show that with the increase of delamination size, the natural frequency decreases. Fig. 3 shows the percentage changes of natural frequencies with delamination sizes, where the heights of the columns represent the absolute values of the percentage changes of natural frequencies. It is obvious that they increase with the delamination size. It is also seen that the decrease of natural frequency is not the same for different modes. The delamination-induced decreases of natural frequencies are relatively large for modes 2, 4 and 5, and the change of natural frequency in mode 1 can hardly be seen. The largest change occurs in mode 4 for all the plates with free boundary condition. The relatively large changes of natural frequencies occur in modes 4, 5 and 6 in the case of simply supported condition. However, the variation manner of the values is not the same for every plate, e.g., for simply supported plate the maximum change in natural frequency of plate D is in mode 6, while that of plate C is not in mode 6 but in mode 4. The delamination-induced frequency change is insignificant for small delamination.

Natural frequencies are firstly computed for the first six modes. The results show that with the increase of delamination size, the natural frequency decreases. Fig. 3 shows the percentage changes of natural frequencies with delamination sizes, where the heights of the columns represent the absolute values of the percentage changes of natural frequencies. It is obvious that they increase with the delamination size. It is also seen that the decrease of natural frequency is not the same for different modes. The delamination-induced decreases of natural frequencies are relatively large for modes 2, 4 and 5, and the change of natural frequency in mode 1 can hardly be seen. The largest change occurs in mode 4 for all the plates with free boundary condition. The relatively large changes of natural frequencies occur in modes 4, 5 and 6 in the case of simply supported condition. However, the variation manner of the values is not the same for every plate, e.g., for simply supported plate the maximum change in natural frequency of plate D is in mode 6, while that of plate C is not in mode 6 but in mode 4. The delamination-induced frequency change is insignificant for small delamination.

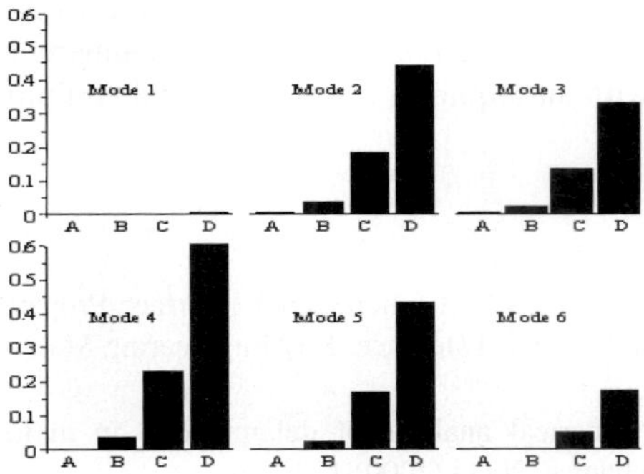

Fig. 3. Percentage changes of natural frequencies for different delamination areas

The above results imply that the delamination region exerts specific effects on the relevant modes. Relative displacements are analyzed for points within the delamination region of plate B. Numerical result shows that obvious penetrations occur in modes 2 and 4, this is indicated by the negative values. As there is no restriction within the delamination region in the FE model, penetration occurs in some modes. However, this is physically impossible, then, it can be deduced that impact exists within the delamination region in modes 2 and 4 during vibration of the plate. Therefore, energy dissipation will be larger in modes 2 and 4 for plate B during vibration. The relative displacements in x and y directions for the above mentioned points are also larger in modes 2 and 4, which implies that, the interactive motion within the delamination region is more serious in these two modes than in others for plate B during vibration. Hence, the effect of delamination on the plate is more significant for modes 2 and 4 than in others for plate B. It is clear that these results are consistent with those as shown in Fig. 3.

Three delaminated plates with constant size at deferent locations have been respectively experimentally analyzed. The result shows that the delamination-induced changes of modal damping are not only mode-dependent but also vary with the location of the delamination. This result and along with other modal parameters such as natural frequency and modal strain energy can be used to predict the location of delamination for each experimental specimen.

5 Conclusions

The results of this study show that the initial crack in composite can be effectively detected using the energy variation of vibration response. The effect of damage location on the variation of mode shapes is consistent with that of natural frequency. There exists intrinsic connection between damage location and the changes of modal parameters.

Numerical analysis provides a good explanation for damage-induced energy dissipation by the tendency of penetration in damaged region. It is convenient and feasible to detect damage using the method proposed in this paper, because experimental modal analysis is till now one of the most practical and reliable methods for structural vibration measurements. This study has attractive application to damage detection of composites, especially for smart structures because of their inherent ability to provide excitation to the structure without requiring much additional equipment.

References

1. Li V. C., Kanda T., Lin Z.: Influence of Fiber/Matrix Interface Properties on Complementary Energy and Composite Damage Tolerance. Key Engineering Materials, 145-149 (1998) 465-471
2. Osset Y., Roudolff F.: Numerical analysis of delamination in multi-layered composite plates. Computational Mechanics, 20(1) (2000) 122-126
3. Gerardi T. G.: Health monitory aircraft. Journal of Intelligent Material System and Structure, 1 (1990) 375-385
4. Abry J. C., Choi Y. K.: A Chateauminois. In-situ monitoring of damage in CFRP laminates by means of AC and DC measurements. Composites Science and Technology, 61(6) (2001) 855-864
5. Tracy J. J., Dimas D. J., Pardoen G. C.: Effect on impact damage on the dynamic properties of laminated composite plates. Proceedings of 5th International Conference on Composite Materials, USA (1985) 111-125
6. Mantena R., Gibson R. F., Place T. A.: Damping capacity measurements of degradation in advanced materials. SAMPE Quarterly, 17(3) (1986) 20-31
7. Birman V., Byrd L. W.: Effect of matrix cracks on damping in unidirectional and cross-ply ceramic matrix composites. Journal of Composite Materials, 36(15) (2002) 1859-1877

SoC Test Scheduling Algorithm Using ACO-Based Rectangle Packing

Jin-Ho Ahn and Sungho Kang

Department of Electrical and Electronic Engineering, Yonsei University,
134 Shinchon-dong, Sodaemun-gu, Seoul, 120-749, Korea
sominaby@soc.yonsei.ac.kr, shkang@yonsei.ac.kr

Abstract. This paper presents a new SoC test scheduling method based on an ant algorithm. The proposed scheduling algorithm formulates the SoC test scheduling problem as a rectangle bin packing problem and uses ACO to cover more solution space to increase the probability of finding optimal solutions. The experimental results conducted using ITC '02 SoC benchmarks show that the proposed idea gives the test application time comparable to earlier researches in less calculation time.

1 Introduction

The general issue of a SoC test includes the design of test wrapper and TAM (Test Access Mechanism), and test scheduling. The test wrapper is the logic added around an embedded core to isolate it from the surrounding logic and to provide test access to the core through TAM. TAM is the physical mechanism connecting cores from test sources or sinks, and it determines how efficiently test stimuli and test results can be transported. A test scheduling is applied to find the test organization that minimizes the overall test time while considering test power and TAM architecture. Several prior researches are related to the SoC test scheduling problems. In [1], the SoC test scheduling problem was formulated as a 2-dimensional bin packing problem, and each core was represented by a rectangle, the width of which was the number of SoC pins allocated and the height of which was the core test time given the number of SoC pins. Rectangle representation for test scheduling has been used in many papers [2]. In [3], RAIN (RAndom INsertion) scheduling algorithm, which used the sequence pair representation and sequential insertion of cores by random selection, was proposed. Though it gave the shortest test application time for most of the benchmarks, it had too much dependence on randomness.

Ant algorithm or Ant Colony Optimization (ACO) is a population-based approach and realizes an adaptive and social behavior of ants of finding the best route to the food source from the nest by indirect communications between ants using a chemical substance called pheromone. In other words, ants leave a pheromone trail behind while moving, other ants can smell this pheromone, and follow it. In ACO, artificial ants stochastically build new solutions using a combination of heuristic information and an artificial pheromone trail. This pheromone trail is reinforced according to the quality of the solutions built by the ants. ACO has been proved to be very effective in terms of solving many NP problems. In this paper, we present the ACO-based test

D.-S. Huang, K. Li, and G.W. Irwin (Eds.): ICIC 2006, LNAI 4114, pp. 655 – 660, 2006.

scheduling algorithm to increase the probability of finding optimal solutions within shorter periods.

2 Wrapper/TAM Width Selection Using ACO

In this section, we describe how an ACO algorithm can be implemented to schedule a SoC test. Testing of a core is represented as a rectangle whose height indicates the TAM width assigned to that core and width denotes the test time of the core for the corresponding value of the TAM width [2]. Taken as a whole, a test scheduler packs all rectangles into a bin having a fixed height and an unlimited width, and aims at minimizing the overall width of the bin without overflowing the bin's height. We now take up the scheduling problem of a SoC based on a rectangle packing modeling. First, we assume that a SoC *N* includes *m* cores and has the TAM width *W*. Also, let w_i be the TAM width assigned to core *i* embedded to *N* and t_i be the test time of core *i* for w_i. If so, all rectangles of core *i*, $\boldsymbol{R}_i$, are represented as a ordered pair such that

$$\boldsymbol{R}_i = (w_i(k), t_i(k)), \quad 1 \le i \le m, \quad 1 \le k \le W. \tag{1}$$

where *k* denotes the size of TAM width assigned to core *i*. Note that $\boldsymbol{R}_i$ is *Pareto-optimal*. The scheduling problem can be summarized as selecting one rectangle r_i from $\boldsymbol{R}_i$, ($1 \le i \le m$), packing the selected rectangles into a bin of height *W* and unbounded width without overlapping between the r_i rectangles and minimizing the width of the bin.

---

w_{prefer} **Calculation Procedure** (*m* : # of embedded cores, *W* : # of TAM widths)

---

1. for (i = 1; $i \le m$; i++) {
    $A_i(k) = w_i(k) * T(w_i(k))$, ($1 \le k \le W$);
    Set $w_{prefer}(i) = w_i(k)$,
    where $w_i(k)$ **is the highest** *Pareto-optimal* **width, such that** $(A_i(k) - A_i(0)) \le (p * A_i(0))$;
    $T_{sum} = T_{sum} + T(w_{prefer}(i))$;
}
2. for (i = 1; $i \le m$; i++) {
    Update $w_{prefer}(i) = w_i(k)$,
    where $w_i(k)$ **is the highest** *Pareto-optimal* **width in** $\boldsymbol{R}_i$, **if** $(T(w_{prefer}(i)) / T_{sum}) \ge q$;
}

Fig. 1. Heuristic TAM Width Calculation

ACO combines the pheromone information with heuristic favorability to find solutions since heuristic parameter can reduce a premature stagnation of the search and help ACO be applicable to various conditions. Search stagnation is the situation where all ants follow the same path and construct the same solution again, such that better solutions cannot be found anymore. In this paper, we utilized a preferred TAM width for core *i*, $w_{prefer}(i)$, as a heuristic favorability. The calculation flow to seek $w_{prefer}(i)$ is presented in Figure 1. Let $T(w_i)$ be the test time of core *i* in case of a TAM width w_i and $A_i(k)$ indicate the result of $w_i(k)\cdot T(w_i(k))$, ($1\leq k\leq W$). In our algorithm, $w_{prefer}(i)$ was set to the highest w_i in $\boldsymbol{R}_i$ such that the difference between $A_i(k)$ and $A_i(0)$ was less than the $p\%$ of $A_i(0)$. Furthermore, we assigned a core the TAM width providing the corresponding core with the best test time if $T(w_{prefer})$ of the core was more than the $q\%$ of the total sum of $T(w_{prefer})$ of all embedded cores. The search space to find the best p and q was selected on an experimental basis. The pheromone trail $\tau_i(k)$ as the favorability of choosing k as the TAM width assigned to core i and the probability $p_i(k)$ that an ant will choose k for core i are given by

$$\tau_i(k)=\sum_{j\in S}\tau(k_i,g_j),\quad 1\leq i,j\leq m,\quad 1\leq k,g\leq W$$

$$p_i(k)=\frac{\tau_i(k)\cdot\beta}{\sum_{k=1}^{W}(\tau_i(k)\cdot\beta)},\quad \begin{matrix} \text{if } w_{prefer}(i)=k, & \beta\geq 1 \\ \text{else} & \beta=1 \end{matrix} \tag{2}$$

where S is the rectangle set of cores already chosen by the current ant, and g_j is the TAM width selected for core j. Consequently, $\tau(k_i, g_j)$ means the favorability of choosing k as the TAM width for core i when the size of TAM width assigned to core j is g. $p_i(k)$ consists of the pheromone trail τ_i and the heuristic value β. β is the parameter which defines the relative importance of $w_{prefer}(i)$ as opposed to τ_i. For reference, all ants choose an initial core and its TAM width randomly. According to the result of scheduling, the pheromone trails are updated by Equation (3).

$$\tau(k_i,g_j)=\rho\cdot\tau(k_i,g_j)+\Delta\tau(k_i,g_j). \tag{3}$$

where ρ is the evaporation parameter, which determines the speed of decay of pheromone, and Δτ means the amount of pheromone deposited by the ant on the basis of the quality of scheduling result. Δτ is defined as

$$\Delta\tau(k_i,g_j)=N_{k_i g_j}\cdot\lambda. \tag{4}$$

where N_{kg} indicates how many times k of core i and g of core j go together in the best scheduling result S^{best}. λ is the constant value to weigh N_{kg}. In order to balance exploration of solution space and exploitation of S^{best}, we implemented the iteration-best ant (S^{ib}), global-best ant (S^{gb}), and the lower limit for the pheromone value (τ^{min}) introduced in [4-5].

3 SoC Test Scheduling Based on Rectangle Packing Algorithm

The general procedure of the proposed test scheduling is shown in Figure 2. Before beginning the scheduling, we designed test wrappers for embedded cores and found $\boldsymbol{R}_i$ (line 1). Although any wrapper design procedure can be applied, we used the One-Element Exchange algorithm [3]. The reason for this is that since the scan chain partitioning derived using the Largest Processing Time (LPT) is not always best-optimized, One-Element Exchange algorithm was used to additionally optimize the partitioning. Next, pheromone table entries were initialized (line 2). And then, an ACO-based test scheduling procedure was advanced (line 3~14). In line 4 and 5, γ indicates the number of updates we wait before we use S^{gb} again and N_{colony} is the number of ants in a colony. From line 5 to 12 the procedure that an ant makes a scheduling is shown. After finding w_i for all cores as described in section 2 (line 6), the scheduler packed them well minimizing the idle space. While many ideas about 2D bin packing had been proposed, we used the packing process presented in [2] for its simplicity and feasibility (line 7~11). In this packing process, cores having w_i chosen in line 6 were firstly scheduled in succession on the basis of their test time (line 8). If there remained room, the scheduler tried to supplement cores to idle room (line 9) or assigned additional TAM widths available to cores scheduled earlier for reducing the overall test time (line 10). In Figure 2, *begin_time*(i) and *end_time*(i) denote the test start and end time of core i, *scheduled*(i) indicates core i has been scheduled and *completed*(i) indicates the testing of core i has been completed respectively. If the scheduling result of the ant was better than the current best result, the scheduler updated the best test time. Unless the condition to terminate simulation was satisfied, the scheduler would search the solution space continuously with new r_i combinations of cores. Currently the termination condition is whether S^{gb} is uniform until γ rotates ten times and the pheromone information is biased sufficiently.

4 Experimental Results and Conclusions

We simulated four ITC'02 benchmark circuits [6] to evaluate the proposed scheduling algorithm. All of our simulations were conducted on a SUN Blade 2000 with 1.2-GHz processors. Since [3] gave the lowest test time results for most of the cases, its results were presented in this section for comparison with our results. In order to compare with results in [3], the unbalanced core wrapper design was used. The unbalanced wrapper design is to assign a different number of wrapper ports to scan-in and scan-out to reduce the length of the longest wrapper scan chain. The final results reported in this paper were based on the ACO parameter values as follows;

- N_{colony} : 10, γ : 10, ρ : 0.95, τ^{min} : 2.0, $\tau(0)$: 20.0, $\beta = 10$, λ : 0.2

where $\tau(0)$ is an initial value of pheromone trail. In order to get parameter values which give good performance, tests using circuits having different sizes and structures are required. The parameter values used in this paper were chosen on the recommendation of [5] and consideration in terms of balancing the test application times with the calculation times.

As shown in Table 1, the ACO-based scheduling algorithm produced a bit lager test times than those of [3] for most cases. We listed in braces the percentage difference in test times compared to the results of [3] in Table 1. However, algorithm run-times could be reduced by up to an order of magnitude as seen in Table 2. Moreover, though the run-times of [3] varied extensively under repetitive runs of scheduling procedures, the run-times of proposed algorithm were nearly uniform. However, the run-times of our method were longer in p34392-32~64TAM cases. The reason for that was because it took some times to satisfy the termination condition of simulation. Thus, it could not help but be compelled to accept to find more optimal solutions in various circuits.

Consequently, though the scheduling results are slightly inferior or almost the same as previous results, the proposed method finds solutions more quickly and consumes the uniform calculation times regardless of the number of executions. Experimental results using some ITC'02 benchmark circuits show that the proposed algorithm is very efficient and feasible on various conditions.

Procedure of SoC Test Scheduling

```
1. Compute R_i from wrapper design of cores;
2. Initialize ptable[W][m][W];
3. Until result is acceptable {
4.    Until N_ib becomes γ {
5.       Until i becomes N_colony {
           Initialize cur_time = 0; next_time = 0, w_avail = W;
6.         Calculate w_prefer(i) AND Select w_i using ptable and w_prefer(i);
7.         Until all cores are tested {
           /* Start of rectangle packing heuristics for a bin */
             If (w_avail ≥ 0) {
8.             If core i can be found, such that (w_i ≤ w_avail AND T(w_i) is maximum) {
                 Rectangle packing process with assigning w_i(k) to cores }
               Else {
                 If core i can be found, such that (scheduled(i) = YES) AND (completed(i) = NO)
                                      AND (end_time(i) > cur_time) AND end_time(i) is minimum {
                   next_time = end_time(i); }
9.               If core i can be found, such that (scheduled(i) = NO) AND
                                      (T(w_avail + cur_time) ≤ next_time AND
                                      (T(w_avail + cur_time) is maximum {
                   replace w_i with a value w, where w is the highest Pareto-optimal width, such that w ≤ w_avail
                   Rectangle packing process with rectangle insertion in idle time }
                 Else {
10.                If core i can be found, such that (scheduled(i) = YES) AND (completed(i) = NO) AND
                                      (begin_time(i) = cur_time) AND (w_i ≤ w_avail) AND
                                      (T(w_i) - T(w_i+w_avail) is maximum {
                     replace w_i with a value w, where w is the highest Pareto-optimal width, such that w ≤ w_i+w_avail
                     Rectangle packing process with increasing TAM widths to fill idle time }
                   Else {
                     set w_avail = 0; } } } }
             Else {
               move to next and update information }
11.        } /* End of rectangle packing heuristics for a bin */
         If max. cur_time is less than current Best_test_time,
12.      Update Best_test_time = cur_time; }
13.   Find S^ib; pheromone_update(S^ib); }
14. Find S^gb; pheromone_update(S^gb); }
```

Fig. 2. Test Scheduling Procedure

Table 1. Test Application Times (Unit: Test Clock Cycle)

SoC Name	Algorithm	Number of TAM Wires						
		16	24	32	40	48	56	64
D695 10cores	ACO-Based	41737	28080	21098	17075	14310	12110	10783
		0.7%	1.3%	0.7%	1.3%	0.9%	0.2%	1.5%
	RAIN [3]	41442	27725	20948	16852	14182	12084	10628
P22810 30cores	ACO-Based	424889	289190	218035	177314	147898	130479	115791
		0.6%	1.6%	1.7%	2.1%	1.5%	3.1%	2.8%
	RAIN [3]	422345	284632	214354	173637	145781	126548	112620
P34392 21cores	ACO-Based	931588	631035	544579	544579	544579	544579	544579
		-0.9%	0.9%	0.0%	0.0%	0.0%	0.0%	0.0%
	RAIN [3]	939855	625543	544579	544579	544579	544579	544579
P93791 32cores	ACO-Based	1747504	1175988	891103	716112	598286	517692	452951
		0.3%	1.6%	2.4%	2.1%	1.8%	3.3%	2.5%
	RAIN [3]	1742995	1157974	870059	701204	587907	500976	441786

Table 2. CPU Run-Times (Unit: Second)

SoC Name	Algorithm	Number of TAM Wires						
		16	24	32	40	48	56	64
D695 10cores	ACO-Based	9	20	11	11	15	14	17
	RAIN [3]	95	226	190	236	262	260	132
P22810 30cores	ACO-Based	56	120	74	120	140	71	72
	RAIN [3]	782	1537	1457	963	82	312	131
P34392 21cores	ACO-Based	32	55	32	34	34	34	35
	RAIN [3]	214	377	19	2	3	2	1
P93791 32cores	ACO-Based	174	268	107	137	189	194	148
	RAIN [3]	177	1077	655	414	288	543	116

References

1. Huang, Y., Cheng, W.-T., Tsai, C.-C., Mukherjee, N., Samman, O., Zaidan Y., Reddy, S. M.: Resource Allocation and Test Scheduling for Concurrent Test of Core-Based SOC Design. Proc. of ATS (2001) 265-270
2. Iyengar, V., Chakrabarty, K., Marinissen, E. J.: On using Rectangle Packing for SOC Wrapper/TAM Co-optimization. Proc. of VTS (2002) 253-258
3. Im, J. B., Chun, S., Kim, G., Ahn, J. H., Kang, S.: RAIN (RAndom INsertion) Scheduling Algorithm for SoC Tes. Proc. of ATS (2004) 242-247
4. Stützle, T., Hoos, H.: MAX-MIN Ant System. Future Generation Computer Systems, Vol. 16, No. 8 (2000) 889-914
5. Levine, J., Ducatelle, F.: Ant Colony Optimisation and Local Search for Bin Packing and Cutting Stock Problems. Journal of the Operational Research Society, Special Issue on Local Search, Vol. 55, No. 7 (2004) 705-716
6. Marinissen, E. J., Iyengar, V., Chakrabarty, K.: ITC'02 SoC Test Benchmarks, http://www.hitech-projects.com/itc02socbenchm

Fault Diagnosis and Accommodation Based on Online Multi-model for Nonlinear Process

Jun Li, Cuimei Bo, Jiugen Zhang, and Jie Du

College of Automation, Nanjing University of Technology
Nanjing, Jiangsu, 210009 China

Abstract. Fault diagnosis and accommodation(FDA) for nonlinear multi-variables system under multi-fault are investigated in the paper. A complete FDA architecture is proposed by incorporating the intelligent fault tolerant control strategy with a cost-effective fault detection and diagnosis (FDD) scheme based on a multiple-model. The schem efficiently handles the accommodation of both the anticipated and unanticipated failures in online situations. The three-tank with multiple sensor fault concurrence is simulated, the simulating result shows that the fault detection and tolerant control strategy has stronger robustness and tolerant fault ability.

1 Introduction

While most research attention has been focused on fault detection and diagnosis (FDD), the less research effort has been devoted to fault accommodation (FA) [1]. Recently, the robust FDA for nonlinear systems has received much more attention for the universal existence of nonlinearities and model uncertainties in practice [2], [3].

Traditional FDA approaches are based on hardware redundancy. Due to higher costs and complexity for hardware redundancy, the approaches based on analytical redundancy have dominated the FDA research. A complete FDA architecture is proposed in the paper, which incorporated the intelligent fault tolerant control strategy and a multi-model based failure diagnosis process. The remaining parts are organized as follows: A problem statement is presented in Section II. A complete FDA architecture based on multi-models is provided in Section III. The online simulation study is provided in Section IV to demonstrate the effectiveness of the FDA scheme. The conclusion is included in Section V.

2 Problem Statement

Consider a general multi-variable non-linear system, which can be described by the following nonlinear auto-regressive moving average (NARMA) model [4]:

$$y(k) = f[u(k-d-1),\cdots,u(k-d-n_u), y(k-1),\cdots, y(k-n_y)] + e(k) \tag{1}$$

Here, The $f(.)$ is a vector-value unknown nonlinear function; $u(k)\in R^m$ and $y(k)\in R^p$ are the sampled process input and output respectively, n_u and n_y denote the input order

D.-S. Huang, K. Li, and G.W. Irwin (Eds.): ICIC 2006, LNAI 4114, pp. 661 – 666, 2006.

and output order, d represents the input time-delay. $\{e(k)\in R^p\}$ denotes the measurement noise. It is possible to develop an acceptable realization to describe the system behavior offline with neural network modeling technique as shown in Eq.(2)

$$\hat{y}(k)=\hat{f}[u(k-d-1),\cdots,u(k-d-n_u),y(k-1),\cdots,y(k-n_y)]+\eta(y,u)) \tag{2}$$

Here $\hat{y}(k)\in R^p$ is the NN model output and $\hat{f}(.)$ is the estimation of the non-linear function $f(.)$.Eq.(1) denotes a healthy system under fault-free situation, while Eq.(2) represent the corresponding nominal model.

Under different component failure, the system dynamic is represented by Eq.(3):

$$y(k)=f[u(k-d-1),\cdots,u(k-d-n_u),y(k-1),\cdots,y(k-n_y)]+\sum_{i=1}^{r}\beta_i(k-T_i)F_i(y,u,k) \tag{3}$$

Where $F_i(.)$ represents the dynamic change caused by the failure. The characteristics of two typical faults (abrupt fault and incipient fault) can be described by the time-varying constant gain $\beta_i(.)$ as Eq.(4):

$$\beta_i(k-T_i)=U(k-T_i)\text{, }\beta_i(k-T_i)=[1-\exp(-\alpha(k-T_i))]U(k-T_i) \tag{4}$$

$\alpha\in R^+$ is an unknown constant, which defines the time profile of the incipient failure mode, and $U(t)$ denotes the unit step function.

3 FDA Based on Multi-model

Due to the unknown dynamic changes caused by the failures, the control law in a close-loop form is not readily available for general online FDA. For the post-failure, the signatures and the corresponding reconfigurable control actions can be developed offline beforehand and pre-stored in a database. The appropriate online FA actions are then suggested by a fault detection and diagnosis scheme that detects and identifies the failure patterns online. This idea has been adopted in many multiple-model-based FDA research works. Therefore, an intelligent FDA framework is proposed as shown in Fig. 1. The architecture is made up of three layers: a bottom layer with the control loop, a second with fault diagnosis and accommodation functions based multi-model and a third with supervisor functionality.

3.1 Level 1: Control

This level comprises a traditional control loop with self-adaptable controller, actuator and sensor interfaces, signal conditioning and filtering. In online situations, the effective control actions may come from one of the three sources: the nominal controller, the FA actions for post-failure and the intelligent control regulator.

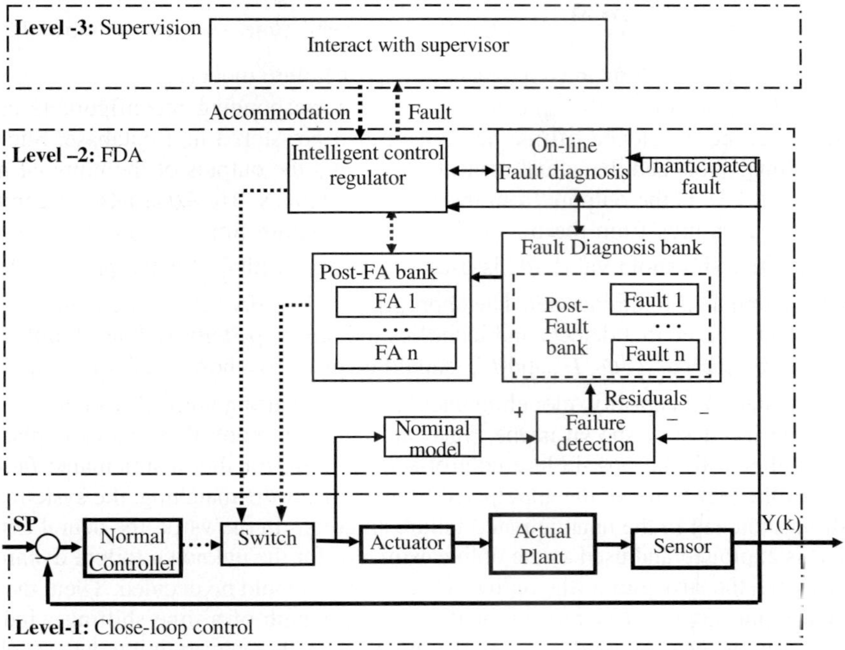

Fig. 1. FDA architecture based on multiple models

3.2 Level 2: Multi-module- Based FDA

The proposed FDA framework incorporates a separate fault detection scheme, a failure diagnosis mechanism, and post-failure control action, and an intelligent control regulator to form a more complete FDA methodology. Under this framework, the system's health is continuously monitored by the fault detection scheme with the nominal system model every certain period of time. Any abnormal behavior will trigger the FDA mechanism to analyze the scenario and further decide which control actions should be taken. Moreover, the failure scenarios can be further categorized into anticipated and unanticipated faults.

A possible cost-effective and conservative fault detection and diagnosis schemes used in the simulation section is shown in (5) and (6), respectively:

$$\bar{r}_f = \frac{1}{L}\sum_{i=k-L+1}^{k} \eta_i (y(i) - \hat{y}(k))^2 \tag{5}$$

$$\bar{r}_{FD} = \frac{1}{L'}\sum_{i=k-L'+1}^{k} (y(i) - \hat{y}(i) - pf_j(i))^2 \tag{6}$$

Where k is the current sampling time; η_i is weight coefficient; $\hat{y}(.)$ is the output from normal model; $y(.)$ is the real actual measurements from plant; L is a certain length of time shifting window. A pre-specified threshold value, λ , is used to compare with $\bar{r}_f$ to examine the system healthiness every time shifting window L. $pf_j(i)$ represent the time –domain signatures of the post-failure model i.

For the post-failure, the signatures and the corresponding reconfigurable control actions can be developed offline beforehand and pre-stored in a database. Supposed the residuals between the actual measurements and the outputs of the nominal model are considered as the outputs from the failure dynamics. The residuals are compared with the signatures from the post-failure models within time shifting window L'. A pre-specified threshold value, φ, is used to compare with $\bar{r}_{FD}$ for the proper selection of the anticipated failure model. The appropriate online FA actions are then suggested by a FDD scheme that detects and identifies the failure patterns online. Some design parameters, such as λ, φ, L, and L', should be properly chosen under considerations of computational capacity, modeling uncertainty, measuring noises, as so on.

In the framework shown in the Fig.1, an intelligent control regulator is placed in the parallel with the post-failure control-actions bank for the unanticipated faults. If none of the signatures of the anticipated failures meets the matching, the system status will be switched to the unanticipated failure situation. In the work, the neural network (NN) is exploited and used as the online estimator for the unknown failure dynamic.

At first, the structure of the online NN estimator should be decided. Then, the most recent input-output measurements within a fixed length of a time shifting window L are chosen as the training data set of the model. The choice of training data set should be decided based on the system computational capability, sampling rate and the performance criteria. And the gradient-descent algorithms are used to train network online. Moreover, the maximum number of the effective control signal searching iterations is another important design parameter in real-time applications.

3.3 Level 3: Supervision

The supervising interface accept higher priority commands from the engineers, such as change of the control objective or design parameters, accommodating measure for unanticipated failure situation and warn the supervisor for emergent shutdown of the system in cases that the unanticipated system failures are catastrophic and the system is actually uncontrollable.

4 Simulation Studies

A well-regarded simulation model, the three-tank process [5] shown in Fig.2, is used to demonstrate feasibility of the proposed FDA architecture in a real application. Use the balance equations to all the three cylinders, the model is setup up as follows:

$$\begin{bmatrix} \dot{h}_1 \\ \dot{h}_2 \\ \dot{h}_3 \end{bmatrix} = \frac{1}{A}\begin{bmatrix} -Q_{13} \\ Q_{32}-Q_{20} \\ Q_{13}-Q_{32} \end{bmatrix} + \frac{1}{A}\begin{bmatrix} 1 & 0 \\ 0 & 1 \\ 0 & 0 \end{bmatrix}\begin{bmatrix} Q_1 \\ Q_2 \end{bmatrix} + \begin{bmatrix} \eta_1(h,Q) \\ \eta_2(h,Q) \\ \eta_3(h,Q) \end{bmatrix} \tag{7}$$

$$\dot{h}_1 = (-az_1 S_p sign(h_1-h_3)\sqrt{2g|h_1-h_3|}+Q_1)/A+\eta_1(t) \tag{8}$$

$$\dot{h}_2 = (-az_3 S_p sign(h_2 - h_3)\sqrt{2g|h_2 - h_3|} - az_2 S_p \sqrt{2gh_2} + Q_2)/A + \eta_2(t) \tag{9}$$

$$\dot{h}_3 = (az_2 S_p sign(h_1 - h_3)\sqrt{2g|h_1 - h_3|} + az_3 S_p sign(h_2 - h_3)\sqrt{2g|h_2 - h_3|})/A + \eta_3(t) \tag{10}$$

Here, h_i is liquid level (h_{max}=62cm); az_i is outflow coefficient (az_1=0.45 az_2=0.61 az_3=0.46); $Sp=0.5cm^2$ is cross section of the connection pipes; $A=154cm$ is section area of cylindrical; Q_i is flow rates from pumps 1 and 2 ($Q_{1max}=Q_{2max}$=100ml/s); Q_{ji} is flow rates; $\eta_i(h,Q)$ is modeling uncertainty; $sign(.)$ denotes the sign function.

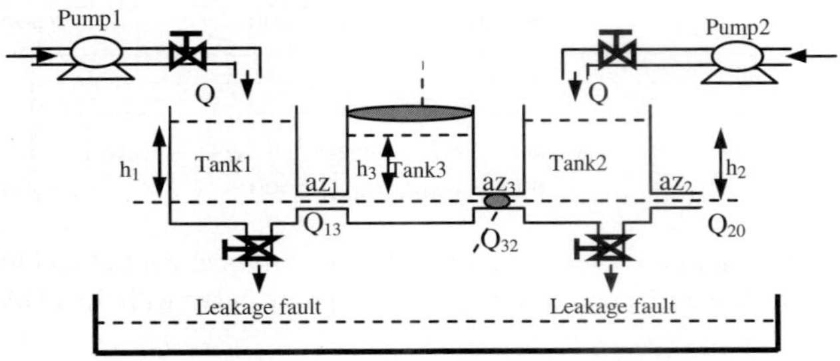

Fig. 2. Configuration chart of three-tank system

The discrete-time model is derived by this forword Euler approximation, sampling period $T=1$ s. The normal models in the form of Eq (2) are found by the neural network modeling technique. Initial liquid level $h_i(0)=0$cm, the control objectives are $h_{1d}(k)=15cm$, $h_{2d}(k)=10cm$ respectively. In the normal instance, the levels of tank 1 and tank 2 need to be controlled respectivly by both PID controllers.

Consider a Precision degradation fault in tank 1 sensor and a bias failure in tank 2 senor. The fault dynamics are reprented Eq(11):

$$h_{1s}(k) = h_1(k) + N(0,\sigma_2^{\ 2})U(k-400) + N(0,\sigma_1^{\ 2}) \tag{11}$$

$$h_{2s}(k) = \begin{cases} h_2(k) + N(0,\sigma_1^{\ 2}) & k < 700 \\ h_2(k) + N(0,\sigma_1^{\ 2}) + 6/100(k-700) & 700 \le k < 800 \\ h_2(k) + N(0,\sigma_1^{\ 2}) + 6 & k > 800 \end{cases}$$

Here, $N(0,\sigma_1^2)$ $N(0,\sigma_2^{\ 2})$ denote measuring noise and precision degradation fault ($\sigma_1 = 0.1, \sigma_2 = 8$);$U(k-T)$ is unit step function.

The sensor failures are detected by the cost-effective method above in section 3.2.1, the threshold value, λ is selected as 0.5. The time shifting window L is selected as 5. Two separate BP neural network models are exploited to restructure the signals of h_{1s} and h_{2s}.The BP model may be described as follow function:

$$\hat{h}_1 = f_{3:7:1}(Q_{13}, Q_1, h_3), \hat{h}_2 = \hat{f}_{(4:7:1)}(Q_{32}, Q_{20}, Q_2, h_3) \tag{12}$$

$\hat{f}_{(3:7:1)}(.)$ is a three layers BP network with 3 inputs, 7 neurons in hidden layer and 1 outputs. $\hat{f}_{(4:7:1)}(.)$ is the one with 4 inputs, 7 neurons in hidden layer and 1 outputs.

Fig.3(a) shows the liquid level respons under the nominal PID control law. As measureing precision in level 1 is declined, the level 1 fluctuate quickly. As the sensor of level 2 occure bias fault, the liquid level 2 drops quickly ,causing a dropping of the level 3. The response curve with the proposed the FDA methods is shown in Fig.3(b). The system performance is improved by the proper the reconfiguration the control law.

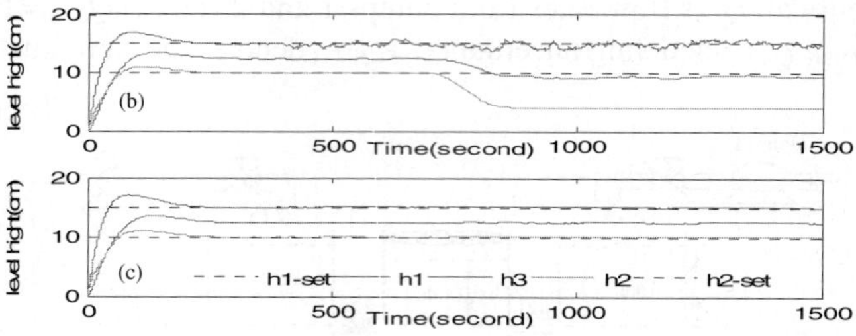

Fig. 3. Comparing the liquid level response between under normal control and under FDA. (a) The level response under the PID controller; (b) The response curve with the FDA methods.

5 Conclusions

This paper has dealt with the online fault-tolerant control for a class of nonlinear multi-variable system. A complete FDT architecture based on multiple models is proposed to efficiently handle the fault diagnosis and the accommodation of multiple sensor failures in online situations. In the three-tank process, multi-faults with Precision degradation fault and incipient complete fault are set to test the fault tolerant control methods proposed in the paper. The simulating result shows that the fault detection and tolerant control strategy has stronger robustness and tolerant fault ability.

References

1. Gary,G.Yen, Liang-Wei Ho: Online Multiple-Model-Based Fault Diagnosis and Accommodation. IEEE transactions on industrial electronics, Vol.50. No.2 .(2003), 296-311
2. Linglai Li, Donghua Zhou: Fast and robust fault diagnosis for a class of nonlinear systems delectability analysis.Computers and Chemical Engineering 28 (2004) 2635-2646
3. Polycarpou, M. M, Trunov, A. B.: Learning approach to nonlinear fault diagnosis: delectability analysis. IEEE Transactions on Automatic Control, 45 (2000) 806-812
4. Yua, D.L., Changa, T.K., Yu, D.W.: Adaptive neural model-based fault tolerant control for multi-variable processes. Engineering Applications of Artificial Intelligence 18 (2005) 393-411
5. Zhang, X., Polycarpou, M., Parisini, T.: Abrupt and incipient fault isolation of nonlinear uncertainty systems. American Control Conf. (2000) 3713 - 3717

A Mongolian Speech Recognition System Based on HMM

Guanglai Gao[1], Biligetu[1], Nabuqing[1], and Shuwu Zhang[2]

[1] College of Computer Science Inner Mongolia University, 010021 Hohhot, China
[2] Institute of Automation Chinese Academy of Sciences, 100080 Beijing, China
csggl@imu.edu.cn

Abstract. Speaker independent large vocabulary continuous speech recognition technique has always been the research focus in the domain of artificial intelligence and pattern recognition. A Mongolian large vocabulary continuous speech recognition system is introduced in this paper. Mongolian is belonged to Altai phylum, and similar with the Western language. According to the characteristics of Mongolian pronunciation, we build the Mongolian acoustic model. We collected a large size corpus to construct the language model. HTK (HMM Toolkit) has been used to construct the system. The experimental results indicated that the design of models related to the Mongolian speech recognition is rational and correct.

1 Introduction

The purpose of speech recognition is to make computers understand human speaking. This includes two aspects. One hand is to convert spoken language literally to written language, i.e. letters; another hand is to react to the commands in the spoken language. A lot of work had been done in Chinese and English speech recognition, which gained plentiful and substantial fruits. Some of the famous examples include speech dictation system ViaVoice by IBM and Chinese speech recognition system by Institute of Automation Chinese Academy of Sciences.

Mongolian is an influential language in the worldwide. And it belongs to Altai phylum. Chahaer dialect is recognized as the standard pronunciation of Mongolian. There are thirty-one characters in Mongolian character, including seven vowels and twenty-four consonants. Moreover, Mongolian is a multi-syllable structure language, which consists of two kinds of syllable; one is vowel, and the other is the combination of vowel and consonant. As a result, a Mongolian sentence is composed by many syllables, and there is strong synergy pronunciation phenomenon within syllable or between syllables. The pronunciation of the vowel or consonant is affected by its adjacent phoneme. Therefore, aiming at the acoustic characteristics and language rules of Mongolian, we use HMM technology to design and build a Mongolian large vocabulary speaker independent continuous speech recognition system.

According to different functions[1], a speech recognition system can be divided into following parts: speech signal pretreatment part, core arithmetic part and elementary database, etc. And how to aim at the Mongolian acoustic characteristics and language rules to build the acoustic model and language model are our main

D.-S. Huang, K. Li, and G.W. Irwin (Eds.): ICIC 2006, LNAI 4114, pp. 667 – 676, 2006.

tasks. So in this paper, we will articulate the preparation of the corpus and recording, the choice of acoustic model and language model.

2 Corpus and Recording

The establishment of the corpus, which includes the text corpus and the speech corpus, is an infrastructure work in the speech recognition system. Through establishing a reasonable text corpus, we could train language model, and begin the recording work to build a speech corpus as well. The quality of corpus strongly influences the performance of the recognition result. So in this part, we would minutely discuss how we establish a corpus which is oriented to Mongolian speech recognition system.

2.1 Corpus

In speech recognition, the selection of corpus for speech training is an extremely important issue. Corpus should cover as much speech phenomenon as possible. Both training of acoustic model and language model, are involved with the problem of how to choice a corpus[2]. Thus, the selected corpus must be representative, possible to cover all speech phenomenon, and not sparse with its training data.

We collected approximately 1.2 million words of Mongolian original corpus, total size of which is about 12M. The main corpus we used in the system is involved with travel-oriented field、 news-oriented field、 daily communications and primary and secondary schools' textbooks, and the ratio of which is: news(70%), primary and secondary schools' textbooks(18%), travel(7%), daily(5%).

According to the characteristics of Mongolian pronunciation, we selected triphone as the basic sub-word speech unit, to assure that the selected corpus could cover all triphones phenomena. There is no uniform standard for Mongolian pronunciation label, however, we labeled to the corpus in three kinds of way: Latin code, original code and phonetic symbol, as shown below:

Original:

Latin : UbUr MONgol on yehe sorgagoli

phonetic: Ober Monggo_l in yeh sOrgu:l

Most Mongolian electronic corpus is labeled with original code, and just few with Latin code. The problem is that adjacent three letters of the original code or Latin code word can not be used to train triphones, because their pronunciation differs with different words. So we can not estimate the number of triphones in the sentences which are labeled with these two kinds of code. The source of the original Mongolian electronic corpus is scarce, so our collection is limited and the sources are quite different. According to the characteristics of original corpus, we use automatic selection, combined with artificial supplement in the following way, to select the training corpus.

(1) Compute the appearance frequency of each word: We found out all words in the corpus whose appearance frequencies are 10 or bigger, and we called them high-frequency words.

(2) The corpus is designed for continuous speech recognition system, so the sentence is treated as a basic unit. Therefore, we selected all the sentences which contain high-frequency words.

(3) Threw off those sentences whose lengths are too long or too short.

(4) Calculate the coefficient of priority = number of high frequency words in the sentence / number of all words in the sentence.

(5) Each sentence was ordered by descend according to its priority.

(6) We chose some higher priority sentences based on the results, and some of the low-priority sentences can be chosen repeatedly.

(7) Many sentences in original corpus were too long, which are not convenient to record. In order to cut these sentences into short ones, we construct a toolkit which could shorten long sentences automatically.

After the selection of corpus, there were still many words whose frequencies are 1. So we created many artificial sentences to improve the coverage. Finally, we selected about 13,800 sentences, 150,000 words, containing more than 10,000 different words. What's more, we established a pronunciation dictionary for these 10,000 words. And we established the corpus with phonetic code based on pronunciation dictionary. So we could calculate the contribution of triphones for each sentence. With the triphone as a basic unit we filtered corpus once again, and obtained the better corpus.

Table 1. Statistic results of the corpus

Item	Most frequency of occurrence	Lest frequency of occurrence	Total number
Words	1425	13	12280
Bi-phones	79	15	868
Triphones	58	12	2018
Sentences	No statistic	No statistic	13800

2.2 Speech Corpus

To establish a standard of Mongolian speech corpus, we organized 200 students from the Xilin Gol League to record, whose pronunciation of Mongolian is most standard in China. During the speech corpus collection, we select recording personnel by following principles as below:

(1) Based on the difference between the characteristics of men voices and women voices, we take the ratio of male and female personnel as 3:2;
(2) Pronunciation must be standard;
(3) Voices are mature, and wave forms are clear;
(4) Ages are between 19 to 40 years old.

Based on the above principles, we collected the accounts of 80 female and 120 male speech data. And the recording information was kept in the form of WAV in speech corpus. Finally, we established successfully a Mongolian speech corpus with a size of 8.93G.

3 Acoustic Model

Acoustic model is the bottom model in a recognition system, and it is the most essential part for a recognition system. The function of acoustic model is to provide an efficient method to calculate the distance between the feature sequence of utterance and the template of utterance. The design of acoustic model is closely related to characteristics of a given language utterance.

3.1 Selection of Mongolian Sub-word Speech Units

Vowels have positive and negative differences. Most of the differences between written Mongolian and spoken Mongolian follow certain rules. And these rules are mainly embodied in the pronunciation altering of vowels, the combination of consonants and harmony of vowels.

Vowels and consonants are the most basic units for swing analysis. But the smallest units in spoken Mongolian are syllables. In Mongolian, syllables are constituted with vowels and consonants, and vowels are the major part of a syllable.

Because the system is a continuous speech recognition system based on Hidden Markov Model[4],[5],[6],[7],[8], the triphone has been used as the basic sub-word speech unit. This is coming from following reasons: Firstly, although syllable is the basic unit for pronunciation, the number of syllables in Mongolian is 1304[3] in total. And if we take influences of adjacent syllables into account, then the number of HMM would become too many. Secondly, each syllable is independent to others, and they share nothing among themselves, which results in the difficulty of training syllables, whose frequencies of occurrence are very low. And using phones as the basic sub-word speech units, the biggest advantage is that the small number of Mongolian phones, just 52 in total, moreover, they are shared by all words. But the problem is that simply using phones as sub-word speech units, the pronunciation of each phone would be heavily influenced by phones around it. And its pronunciation will be altered in different context. What's more, in Mongolian the pronunciation of many phones in accessional components are not sufficient, owing to connecting pronunciation of these phones and neighbor phones. Therefore, only using phones as sub-word speech units is not an optimized method too. In sum, triphones are selected as the basic sub-word speech units. The total number of Mongolian speech units is listed in the following table:

Table 2. Total number of Mongolian speech units

Syllables	Phonemes	Phones.(bi-phones、triphones)
1304	52	Depend on the corpus

3.2 The Decision Tree Based on Triphone Acoustic Modeling

In Mongolian speech recognition, connected pronunciation of the phones with their adjacency phones is a very serious phenomenon, which needs to establish the context-related pronunciation models.

The main problem of triphone modeling is robustness of re-estimated parameters. To solve this problem, we should achieve sharing parameters between different models, thereby reducing the number of model parameters. The decision tree technology is a good solution to share parameters, whose advantages are:

(1) data-driven: it could obtain the optimum balance among the complexity, accuracy and robustness of the model, so that the capability of speech recognition system achieves the best state in condition of limited speech corpus, and it is easy to operate, and easy to optimize as well;

(2) guiding of expert knowledge: combining the knowledge of acoustic, phonetics and linguistics with the process of decision tree generation, we could guide and split the decision tree with expert knowledge, and integrate the clustering process of the expert knowledge and acoustic model organically, to improve the accuracy of acoustic models classification ;

(3) capability of forecasting: It could forecast triphones, which are not in the training data, by searching decision tree to find out most matching models for those triphones, and therefore, improve the accuracy of triphone models, which have no samples or few samples in the training data. Appling decision tree methods on triphone modeling could be extremely effective in resolving the sparsity problem of data, and make good use of knowledge of phonetics. The following are examples of the two key problems of this technology, designing the context-related questions and the generation of the decision tree.

3.3 Design the Context-Related Questions

In the decision tree modeling, the Mongolian knowledge of phonetics and the linguistics is described in question form. Because these knowledge guide the split of decision tree, and designing the context-related questions become an essential problem to establish the decision tree, which is worth to spend much more time and effort on. At the same time, designing the context-related questions is a process of repeated experiments, analysis and revision.

Decision tree is a bi-tree[9],[10], each node tied a question of "Yes/No", all HMM states that allow entering the root nodes should answer the question tied on it, and select the left stick or right stick according to the answer. Finally, based on a set of answers for the node questions each HMM state that enters the root node will enter a leaf node (only). HMM states that enter into the same leaf node will be considered as similar, and parameters will be shared together. Moreover, the context-related questions are used for building the decision tree. When nodes split, the question selected will be tied with this node. Thus, we could determine which state of which basic unit is shared. And the context-related question affects the capability of the triphone model.

In this paper, acoustic modeling unit is triphone, we only consider the left or right modeling unit which influences the middle modeling units. In Mongolian speech recognition, the basic modeling units are vowel and consonant. Designing their own context-related question is based on the vowel and consonant. Notice that for a triphone system, it is necessary to include questions referring to both the right and the left contexts of a phone. Questions should progress from wide, general classifications (such as consonant, vowel, nasal, and diphthong, etc.) to specific instances of each phone. There is no harm in creating extra unnecessary questions, for those determined to be irrelevant to data would be ignored. In the end, the ultimate design is containing 48 questions. Some of the questions are shown below:

(1) According to the pronunciation of consonant
stopper {b,p,d,t,g,k}
  no aspirate stopper {b,d,g}
  aspirate stopper {p,t,k}
  ……
(2) According to the position of consonant pronunciation
lingua tine {z,c,d,t,n,l,r}
  dentinasal lingua tine {z,c}
  gingiva lingua tine {d,t,n}
  behind of gingiva lingua tine {l,r}
……
(3) According to the pronunciation of vowel
close vowel {i,i:,u,u:,U,U:}
……

When the nodes split, it would put forward a series of context-related questions, such as "the left basic unit is quiet?" and "the right basic unit is friction sound?" If it is, it would be assigned to the node of "yes ", else to the node of "no ". All context-related questions designed for this basic unit would be mentioned here. At last one "best question" is selected as the question of this node. And the "best question" means that it is consistent with the guidelines the split principle.

3.4 Generation of the Design Tree

In a general way, firstly put all HMM states which are possible to share into state pool. According to some splitting criterion of splitting the pool, this process is repeated until the stopping criterion is satisfied. And we generate the decision tree in this way.

4 Language Model

Language model consists of rule-based language model and statistical language model. By training language model, we could get the syntax and semantic parsing. Small vocabulary speech recognition systems are used primarily for command-and-control applications where the vocabulary words are essentially acoustic control signals that the system has to respond to. As such, these systems generally do not rely heavily on language models to accomplish their selected tasks. A large vocabulary speech recognition system, however, is generally critically dependent on linguistic knowledge embedded in the input speech. Therefore, for large vocabulary speech recognition, language model is essential. For example, when the classing work is incorrect, especially when a few monophony words need to be confirmed by their context, we could rectify it by studying language model, syntax structure, semantics, and so on.

Presently, the most successful language models are statistical language model and Formula based language model. In this paper, we use the statistical language model, which could study the statistical knowledge between different words and phrases through training a large text corpus. Moreover, statistical language model is one of the most popular task in the natural language processing field. It is widely used in not only the speech recognition research, but also translation machine system, character recognition system, and information detecting and digging system.

4.1 N-Gram Language Model

The most common language model used in speech recognition system is N-gram language model. The N-gram language model primarily predict the perplexity of Nth word based on the former N-1 words. Considering the complexity, we always select N=2, N=3, and N=4, and then call them bigram language model, trigram language model, and 4-gram language model. N-gram language model is established by training the text corpus. However, due to the limited size of corpus, in the training work, the appearance time of most words strings p(Wi,Wi-1,Wi-2)might be 0. And it is entirely possible that these word strings would be used in practice, which is called the 0 perplexity problem. Because of the serious 0 perplexity problem of N-gram language model, in the condition of the limited corpus data, we could not use the simple perplexity counting to get p (Wi|Wi-1Wi-2), we must estimate the bigram perplexity p(Wi|Wi-1Wi-2) by utilizing the bigram perplexity p(Wi|Wi-1) and unigram perplexity p(Wi). The most common methods are Smoothing, Backing-off, Deleting Interpolation and Discounting.

4.2 Trigram Language Model

In this paper, we used the former-discussed corpus as training data, and constructed trigram and inverted trigram language models. We would discuss the problems we met during the establishing work of language model and the corresponding solutions[11].

Firstly, to get the perplexity of all possible word strings $P_r[W_i / W_{i-2}W_{i-1}]$, and assure the statistic precision, we need a large enough and model-oriented corpus, which is composed of large amount of sentences. If there are three words W^a、W^b、W^j in the vocabulary, then we could compute the occurrence of the word string {W^a、W^b、W^j} and each occurrence time of W^a and W^b in the corpus. And if we suppose that the former is C(W^a、W^b、W^j) times, and the latter is C(W^a、W^b) times, then in the condition of $W_{i-2} = W^a, W_{i-1} = W^b$, we could compute the perplexity of $W_i = W^j$ as below:

$$P_r[W_i=W^j/W_{i-2}=W^a,W_{i-1}=W^b]=\frac{C(W^a、W^b、W^j)}{C(W^a、W^b)},j、a、b=1\sim L. \quad (1)$$

Having constructed a language model from a training corpus, one may ask how well the language model will perform in the context of speech recognition. Someone used to take an experiment, using the corpus of 1,500,000 words, which was composed of all kinds of letters in the office. Firstly, all the conditional perplexity of trigram language model was computed. Secondly, he or she selected a test corpus of 30,000 words, which is in the same speech condition with the original training corpus, but not included in. After testing, it is found that, 23% of trigram word strings in the latter corpus were not appeared in the former, which illuminated that the statistical result was somehow not reliable, even with such a large training sample. Although an English-oriented and certain speech condition experiment result, it still has a common instructive signification.

Comparatively, the training result of $P_r[W_i=W^j/W_{i-1}=W^b]$ and $P_r[W_i=W^j]$ is much more reliable. The formulae computing these two perplexities are shown as below:

$$P_r[W_i=W^j/W_{i-1}]=\frac{C(W^b、W^j)}{C(W^b)},j、b=1\sim L. \quad (2)$$

$$P_r[W_i=W^j]=\frac{C(W^j)}{C(W)},j=1\sim L. \quad (3)$$

and, $C(W^b)$ and $C(W^j)$ are the occurrence time of W^b and W^j respectively, and C(W) is the total word number of the corpus. Due to the reason that no matter how large the corpus is, the statistics would not be totally reliable, we use the formula(2) and(3) for the more reliable result to perform smoothing process, which might reduce the predicting ability of the model, but increase the embranchment, however, this is much better than an unreliable statistical parameter. The formula of computing $P_r[W_i=W^j/W_{i-2}=W,^aW_{i-1}=W^b]$ using smoothing method is shown as below:

$$P_r[W_i=W^j/W_{i-2}=W^a,W_{i-1}=W^b]=q_3^{ab}\frac{C(W^a,W^b,W^j)}{C(W^a,W^b)}+q_2^{ab}\frac{C(W^b,W^j)}{C(W^b)}+q_1^{ab}\frac{C(W^j)}{C(W)},$$

$$jab=1\sim L\ . \quad (4)$$

And, $q_1^{ab}+q_2^{ab}+q_3^{ab}=1$.The problem now is that for each $\{W^a、W^b、W^j\}$, we should obtain three weights to use formula(4) , and compute all conditional perplexities of all predictable word W^j (j=1~L) appearing after word string

{ W^a、W^b }. Obviously, different weighs would direct different results. However, methods of obtaining these three weighs would not be discussed in this paper.

5 Training of Mongolian Speech Recognition System

The training work of the Speech Recognition System includes the acoustic model training and language model training. In this paper, we used HTK to train the acoustic model. And after confirming the speech signal sampling ratio, recognition parameter, the size of recognition units, and HMM state frame, training work of the acoustic model could be performed. The training process takes multi-step training method. (1) Given the initial model and training files, each model parameter would be segmented. (2) The initial model would be re-estimated by maximum likelihood estimation method, and we would get better HMM parameters then. (3) Composing multiple-model of sub-word model from training corpus, and nest it into training system, which would be trained again with large data. Through these steps, we could get delicate HMM parameters.

Constructing the language model would also need training a large size corpus. Some new language model is now using maximum entropy estimating method, which has a rather complex algorithm. In this paper, we utilized the CMU (Cam Language Model Toolkit) to construct our language model.

6 Conclusion

The experimental system is a Mongolian large vocabulary continuous speech recognition system that is based on HMM. Through the system, we have taken an instructive attempt aiming at the Mongolian acoustic characteristics and language rules. When building the HMMs, triphones have been used as the basic sub-word speech units, and statistical language model was used for the experiment. Besides building the models and programming, we also accumulated experience in terms of building and optimizing the corpus. And Mongolian Speech Recognition System LVCSR could reach a result of 85.16%.However, due to the deficiency of the training data, the robust of the system is not very well, especially under the conditions of noises. We should research more and solve these problems in the future.

Acknowledgements

This work was supported by National Hi-tech Research Plan under the grant No.2003AA115520.

References

1. Lawrenec, R. Rabiner, Proceedings of The IEEE,Vol. 77, No. 2,Feb (1989)
2. Wu-Hua, Xu-Bo ,Huang-Taiyi.: An Algorithm for Automatic Selection Training Data Based on Triphones, Software transaction,(2000) 271-276

3. Qing gertai, Mongolian Grammer, Hohhot, Inner Mongolia people's press (1995)
4. Deng, L., Adsmanovic, M., Wu C.: Speech Recognition Using Hidden Markov Models with Polynomial Regression Functions as Nonstationary States, IEEE transactions on speech and audio processing, 2(4), Oct (1994)
5. Du Preez,J.A.: Efficient Training of High-order Hidden Markov Models Using First-order Representations, Computer speech & language, 12(1),p.23,Jan (1998)
6. Mari, J., Haton, J., Kriouile, A.: Automatic Word Recognition Based on Second-Order Hidden Markov Models, IEEE transactions on speech and audio processing,5(1), Jan (1997)
7. Jelinek, F. , .Mercer, R.L:Interpolated Estimation of Markov Source Parameters From Sparse Data, Pattern Recognition in Practice, E.S.Gelsema and L.N.Kanal, Eds., North-Holland Pub. Co., Amsterdam(1980)381-397
8. Known, O., Un, C.: Discriminative Weighting of Hmm State-Likelihoods Using the GPD Method, IEEE signal processing letters,3(9),Sep (1996)
9. Jing Li,Fang Zheng,Ji Yong Zhang,WenHu Wu.: Context Dependent Initial/Final Acoustic Modeling for Chinese Continuous Speech Recognition, J Tsinghua Univ (Sci & Tech), Jan. Vol. 24, No. 1 (2004)61-64
10. Sheng Gao.:Acoustic Modeling and Search Method, doctor paper of Institute of Automation Chinese Academy of Sciences, July(2000)

Conditional Random Fields Based Label Sequence and Information Feedback*

Wei Jiang, Yi Guan, and Xiao-Long Wang

School of Computer Science and Technology, Harbin Institute of Technology, 150001, Harbin, P.R. China
{jiangwei, guanyi, wangxl}@insun.hit.edu.cn

Abstract. Part-of-speech (POS) tagging and shallow parsing are sequence modeling problems. While HMM and other generative models are not the most appropriate for the task of labeling sequential data. Compared with HMM, Maximum Entropy Markov models (MEMM) and other discriminative finite-state models can easily fused more features, however they suffer from the label bias problem. This paper presents a method of Chinese POS tagging and shallow parsing based on conditional random fields (CRF), as new discriminative sequential models, which may incorporate many rich features and well avoid the label bias problem. Moreover, we propose the information feedback from syntactical analysis to lexical analysis, since natural language should be a multi-knowledge interaction in nature. Experiments show that CRF approach achieves 0.70% F-score improvement in POS tagging and 0.67% improvement in shallow parsing. And we also confirm the effectiveness of information feedback to some complicated multi-class words.

1 Introduction

Part of Speech (POS) tagging is a process in which syntactic categories are assigned to words, and it is a preprocessing stage to parsing, information retrieval, text to speech systems, Question and Answer System etc. Shallow parsing involves the segmented sentence (usually augmented with POS tags) into none-overlapping phrases, such that syntactically related words are grouped together in the same phrase. POS tagging and shallow parsing can be seemed as labeling the words in a sentence with their corresponding tag ---- part-of-speech tag or syntactical tag respectively.

The two factors determining the tag of a word are its lexical probability and its contextual probability. Some approaches have been adopted, which can mainly fall into rule-based approaches, e.g. Transformation-Based method [1], and Statistical approaches, such as Decision-Tree [2], Hidden Markov model (HMM)[3]. Maximum Entropy (ME)[4] and Support Vector Machines (SVM)[5]. These models are also tried to deal with the shallow parsing task and have achieved a good performance.

* This investigation is supported by the Key Program Projects of National Natural Science Foundation of China (60435020), National Natural Science Foundation of China (60504021), and also supported by Microsoft fund of Chinese Ministry of Education (01307620).

D.-S. Huang, K. Li, and G.W. Irwin (Eds.): ICIC 2006, LNAI 4114, pp. 677 – 689, 2006.

Though HMM is a powerful tool for representing sequential data, there are two problems [6], firstly, the feature independent assumption. HMM is generative model, which defines a joint distribution over label and observation sequences means that all possible observation sequences must be enumerated. As a result, though many tasks would benefit from a richer representation of observations — in particular a representation that describes observations in terms of many overlapping features, rich features are not easily added into the model. Secondly, it is inappropriate to use a generative joint model in order to solve a conditional problem in which the observations are given. Unlike HMM, MEMM is conditional probabilistic model that avoids above shortcomings. Each source state has an exponential model that takes the observation features as input, and output a distribution over possible next states. This lead it suffer from label bias problem [7]: the transitions leaving a given state compete against each other, rather than all the states.

Feature is another important factor. Trigger has been used to solve long distance dependency, which are extracted by average mutual information [8]. And we have also applied Rough Sets to extract feature and fused them into POS Tagging models [9]. In this paper, the improvement in terms of model and features is also be made. Firstly, Conditional Random fields (CRF) model is introduced to perform Chinese POS tagging and shallow parsing task; Secondly, we explore the feedback performance of syntactic information to lexical information. Zipf's law has indicated that it is not avoided to the sparse data problem, which is one reason why to try more advance features. Natural language processing is NP-hard problem, and human also adopts diversiform knowledge in understanding process. So besides some feature extraction and feature selection methods, the advance syntactical features are also essential to improve the lexical analysis performance. This paper also explores the effectiveness of information feedback to the complicated multi-class words, "为"(for), "和"(and), "到"(to). We testify all the improvement with the large-scale corpora.

2 System Construction and Label Bias Problem

2.1 System Construction

Figure 1 exhibits the frame of our system, where the word segmentation and Named Entity Recognition have been reported in the paper [12], and this paper mainly expatiates on the POS tagging and shallow parsing modules.

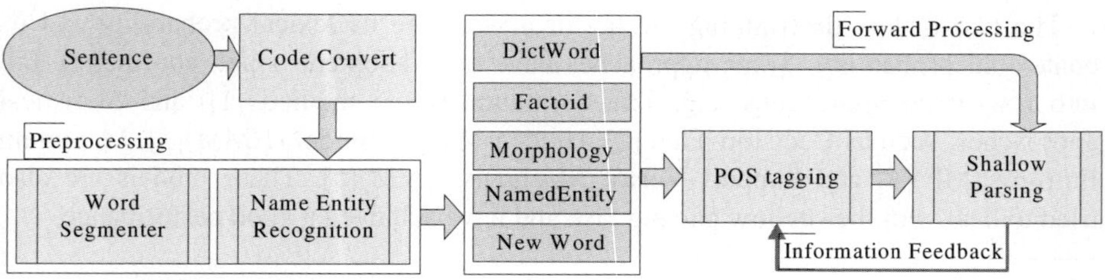

Fig. 1. System construction

There are 15% multi-class words in our vocabulary that includes 121 thousand words, in figure 2(a). While only the part of words would present frequently due to Zipf's law, so the percentage of multi-class words has changed, about 35% in common words[1], as shown in figure 2(b).

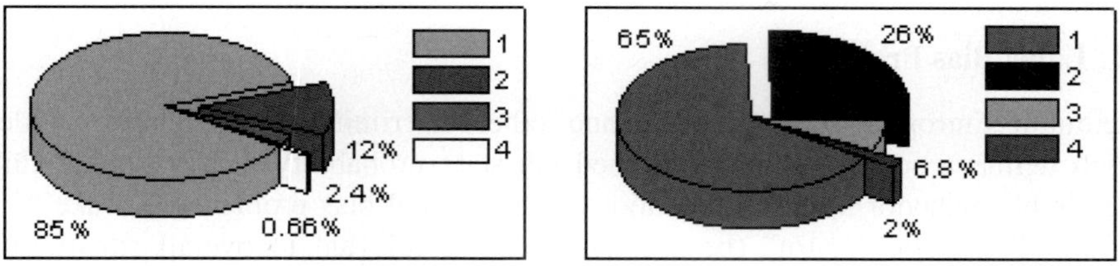

Fig. 2. The proportion of word count according to the number of POS

Figure 2 exhibits the percentage of the multi-class words. To some application, such as Machine Translation, the correct POS tagging is important, e.g. the POS of "和"(and) includes conj. and prep. The sentence "a 和 b 玩" should be translated into "a and b play", we can also say "b 和 a 玩"; while the sentence "a 和 b 请示" should be "a ask for instruction from b", here, we can't say "b 和 a 请示". So to the keyword "和", the former is conj. and the latter is prep. This example shows that it is important to correctly judge the POS of the word "和" to Machine Translation.

However, above judging or POS classification isn't always easily, since the complicated multi-class words almost include the empty words, such as conj. and prep., unlike substantive words, they are usually relevant to the syntax of the whole sentence. In order to solve above problem, we introduce shallow parsing information in this paper. In addition, the features used in existing models are mainly word features, POS features or the other little granularity features, this must be cause sparse data problem. The features to erroneous tagging words are shown in figure 3.

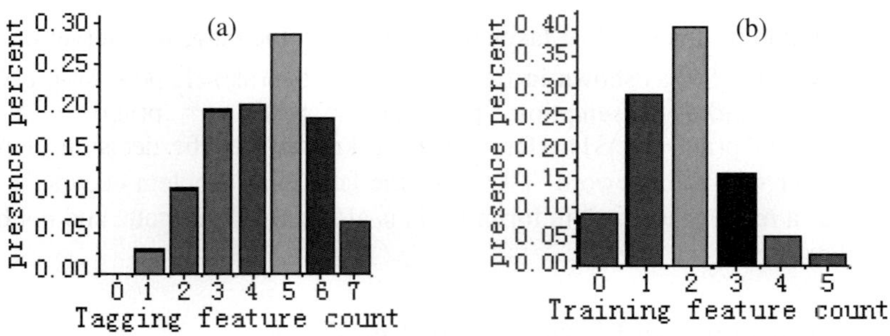

Fig. 3. The present case of the features to erroneous tagging words

[1] The corpora come from the prior six months of Chinese People's Daily in 1998, and we view the words, which presents 5 times or more, as complicated multi-classes words subjectively.

Figure 3(a) seems that when error occurs, there are enough available features, however, the figure 3(b) tell us the truth that the really relevant features are quite a few: it is more than 78% that the feature count presents less or equal 2. This kind of sparse data problem is hard to avoid, while it can be relaxed by improving the feature collection method. In this sense, as advance syntactical features, shallow parsing features are introduce is necessary and meaningful, just like human doing.

2.2 Label Bias Problem

Maximum Entropy Markov models and other discriminative finite-state models, which define a set of separately trained per-state probability distributions, exhibit undesirable behavior in certain situations, termed label bias problem [7]. Take "是/v 因为/p 事/n 关/v 大局/n" (because the thing is relevant to overall situation) as example, all the possible POS for this sentence, are shown in figure 4.

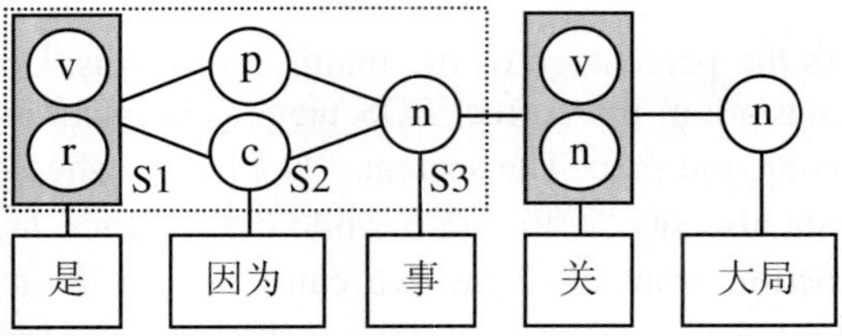

Fig. 4. Label bias problem in POS tagging

The keyword "因为"(because) has two possible POS, i.e. prep. or conj. (thereafter p and c respectively). CRF can correctly label POS tag p, while MEMM mislabels c, due to label bias problem. MEMM defines each state-observation transition function to be a log-linear model:

$$P_s(s'|x) = \frac{1}{Z(s,x)} \exp\left(\sum_k \lambda_k f_k(s',x)\right) \tag{1}$$

where Z(s,x) is a normalization factor, each λ_k are parameters to be estimated and each f_k is a feature function that takes two arguments, the current observation and a potential next state. So, as shown in figure 4, p(n|p)=1, p(n|c)=1, p(p|S1)+p(c|S1)=1, and base the Markov assumption, p(S1,p,n) = p(p|S1) * p(n|p) = p(p|S1), p(S1,c,n)=p(c|S1)*p(n|c)=p(c|S1). Here, we have known that the decision of p or c does not matter with the keyword "因为", so the label bias problem occurs. In other words, it's as a result that Z(s,x) in formula (1) is affected by one state, and not by the whole sentence.

3 Label Sequence and Information Feedback

3.1 Conditional Random Fields

Use $\mathbf{x} = x_1 \ldots x_n$ and $\mathbf{y} = y_1 \ldots y_n$ for the generic input sentence and label sequence respectively. A CRF on (**X**,**Y**) is specified by a vector $\boldsymbol{f}$ of local features and a corresponding weight vector $\boldsymbol{\lambda}$. Each local feature is either a state feature $s(y,\mathbf{x},i)$ or a transition feature $t(y,y',\mathbf{x},i)$, where y, y' are labels, i is an input position. For any state feature s and transition feature t, we rewrite $s(y,y',\mathbf{x},i) = s(y',\mathbf{x},i)$, $s(\mathbf{y},\mathbf{x},i) = s(y_i,\mathbf{x},i)$, if $i = 0$ then $t(\mathbf{y},\mathbf{x},i) = 0$ else $t(y_{i-1},y_i,\mathbf{x},i)$. Thus, the global feature vector is

$$\mathrm{F}(\mathbf{y},\mathbf{x}) = \sum_i f(\mathbf{y},\mathbf{x},i) \tag{2}$$

The conditional probability distribution defined by the CRF is then

$$\mathrm{p}_\lambda(\mathbf{Y} \mid \mathbf{X}) = \frac{\exp \boldsymbol{\lambda} \cdot \mathrm{F}(\mathbf{Y},\mathbf{X})}{\mathrm{Z}_\lambda(\mathbf{X})} \tag{3}$$

normalization factor $\mathrm{Z}_\lambda(\mathbf{X})$ is computed by $\mathrm{Z}_\lambda(\mathbf{x}) = \sum_{\mathbf{y}} \exp \boldsymbol{\lambda} \cdot \mathrm{F}(\mathbf{y},\mathbf{x})$. Under this circumstance, the most probable label sequence $\mathbf{y}^*$ for input sequence $\mathbf{x}$ is

$$\mathbf{y}^* = \underset{\mathbf{y}}{\operatorname{argmax}}\ \mathrm{p}_\lambda(\mathbf{y} \mid \mathbf{x}) = \underset{\mathbf{y}}{\operatorname{argmax}}\ \boldsymbol{\lambda} \cdot \mathrm{F}(\mathbf{y},\mathbf{x}) \tag{4}$$

Since $\mathrm{Z}_\lambda(\mathbf{x})$ does not depend on $\mathbf{y}$, it can be omitted in formula (4). According to formula (2), F($\mathbf{y}$,$\mathbf{x}$) decomposes into a sum of terms for consecutive pairs of labels, so the most likely $\mathbf{y}$ can be found with Viterbi algorithm.

In above algorithm, acquiring weight vector $\boldsymbol{\lambda}$ needs to train CRF by maximizing the log-likelihood. Several methods have been found to train CRF, such as generalized iterative scaling (GIS) algorithms [7], preconditioned conjugate-gradient (CG) and limited-memory quasi-Newton (LBFGS) [10]. The latter can perform comparably on very large problems and acquire faster training speed, so LBFGS is used to train CRF model in this paper.

We compare formula (1) and (3), the former normalizes in one state, while the latter normalizes in the whole sequence, so CRF can well avoid the label bias problem, e.g. in figure 4, according to formula (3), usually, $p(n|p)\neq 1$, $p(n|c)\neq 1$, then $p(S1,p,n)\neq p(p|S1)$, $p(S1,c,n)\neq p(c|S1)$.

3.2 Label Sequence

POS tagging and shallow parsing can be regarded as labeling sequence problem and finding a function g:$\mathbf{x}$->$\mathbf{y}$, where each y_i in $\mathbf{y}$ is POS tag or syntactical tag, as described in section 3.1, since nearly all the observations in $\mathbf{x}$ comply with the local dependency in the natural language. Figure 5 demonstrate HMM, MEMM and chain-structured CRF for solving the sequence problem.

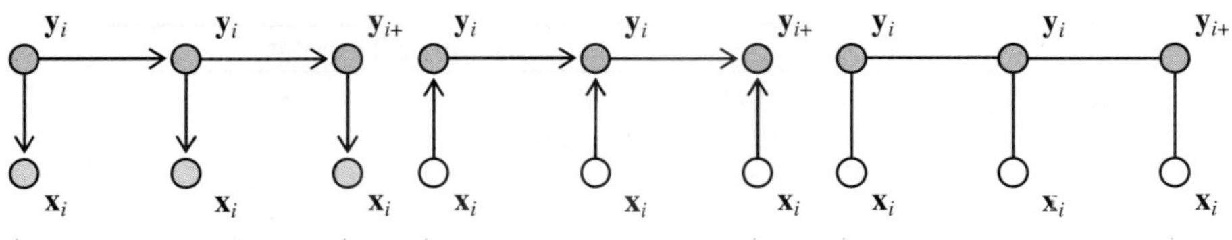

Fig. 5. HMM(left), MEMM(center), CRF(right) for sequence

HMM needs to calculate the transition probability $p(y_i|y_{i-1})$ and the emitting probability $p(x_i|y_i)$, so it can be viewed through the set of stochastic processes that generate an observation sequence. Unlike HMM, according to formula (1), MEMM can use the feature that represents observation x_i to the state y_i. Compared with the prior two graphical models, CRF is undirected graphical models, because it does not care the feature direction, and each feature is regarded as a part of global feature, as shown in formula (2) and formula (3).

The choice of features mainly governed by the knowledge dependency and the computing power. Formula (2) denotes that the global feature can be represented via many local features, since the local dependent phenomenon is nearly fitted all along in natural language. On the other hand, CRF maximizes the log-likelihood of the possible sequence, as shown in formula (3), so a lot of computing time is needed. In our system construction, as shown in figure 1, the word feature is only available, table 1 summarizes the feature set of our the POS tagging features in our system.

Table 1. POS tagging feature template

Type	Feature Template
one order feature	w_{i-2}, w_{i-1}, w_i, w_{i+1}, w_{i+2}
two order feature	$w_{i-1:i}$, $w_{i:i+1}$

From the syntactical point of view, some factoid words have the same function in constructing sentence, for instance, the number 3 and 10 are the same syntactical function in the sentence "我度假 3 天"(I have a holiday for 3 days) and "我度假 10 天" (I have a holiday for 10 days). So, more than 7 kinds of factoid types are divided, including Number, Date, Time, English, website, Email, Phone. Each factoid type is viewed as the same word class. For the same reason, morphological and derived words are divided by their original root words, and Named Entities [12] are divided through their types, such as Person Name, Location Name and Organization Name.

Class-based method can relax the sparse data problem to some extend, improve the tagging performance, since it seems more appropriate that the POS tagging task and the shallow parsing task should be regarded as syntax tagging. Unlike English word, Chinese word is short of morphological feature, such as the suffix -ed, -ing.

Compared with POS tagging task, shallow parsing can also utilize POS feature, as shown in table 2. Here, we are inspired by the F. Sha's method [10].

Table 2. Shallow parsing feature template

Type		Feature Template
Word feature	One order	w_{i-2}, w_{i-1}, w_i, w_{i+1}, w_{i+2}
	Two order	$w_{i-1:i}$, $w_{i:i+1}$
POS feature	One order	t_{i-2}, t_{i-1}, t_i, t_{i+1}, t_{i+2}
	Two order	$t_{i-2:i-1}$, $t_{i-1:i}$, $t_{i:i+1}$, $t_{i:i+2}$
	Three order	$t_{i-2:i-1:i}$, $t_{i-1:i:i+1}$, $t_{i:\ i+1:i+2}$

B-X, I-X or O tag is used to represent the syntactical chunk, e.g. B-NP, I-NP for the NP chunk. Before tagging, POS tagging need to do, then CRF to label the syntactical chunk, for instance, "医院[NN]/B-NP 扩大[VV]/B-VP 药品[NN]/B-NP 和[CC]/I-NP 医疗[NN]/I-NP 仪器[NN]/I-NP 采购[NN]/B-NP 规模[NN]/B-NP".

The features in table 1 or in table 2 are extracted from the local context beside the keyword. The long distance dependency and the complicated feature may also be used, and more detail has been reported in the paper [8][9].

3.3 Information Feedback

It has been explained in section 2.1 that some complicated multi-class words, such as "和"(and), "为"(for), "用"(with), are usually affected by syntactical information, so shallow parsing is introduce here to improve the POS tagging performance. For instance, in two sentences, "这/是/为/人民/服务"(It serves the people) and "他为/[祖国/人民]/服务"(he serves the people in his country), "服务"(serve) is a good hint to judge the POS of "为"(for), however if don't use the chunk [祖国/人民], the model can hardly use this kind of feature effectively.

Maximum Entropy (ME) model is applied to make disambiguation, which is defined over $H \times T$, where H is the set of possible contexts around target word, which will be tagged, and T is the set of POS candidate. Then the model's conditional probability is defined as

$$p(t \mid h) = \frac{p(h,t)}{\sum_{t' \in T} p(h,t')}, \text{ where } p(h,t) = \pi\mu \prod_{j=1}^{k} \alpha_j^{f_j(h,t)}$$

ME model trained on the conditional model can correctly handle the overlapping features. Training of the parameters is performed with Generalized Iterative Scaling (GIS) [4]. Let s(c) is syntactical feature in the current context c, then the corresponding ME feature is defined as

$$f_j(a,b) = \begin{cases} 1 & if((w = KeyWord) and(\mathrm{s}(c) = b)) \\ 0 \end{cases}$$, where eq. $\mathrm{s}(c) = b$ represents that the syntactical feature s(c) can be reconstructed in the current context c. Here, s(c) may be the chunk type feature, the head feature or the relevant features.

Though conditional probability model, such as CRF, ME, or MEMM, relaxes the feature independent assumption, it doesn't say that it is free of this kind of assumption. As an extreme condition, considering the feature set $\{fa, fb, fb\}$, fb are added twice into the event space, obviously, the ME model will more emphasize the importance of the feature fb. In order to relax this problem, we propose applying rough set theory to extract effective feature from the possible constraint candidates [9]. All the syntactical features are fused into the ME model so as to classify the most possible POS of the keyword, and the weight of each feature is assigned by the ME model.

4 Experiment and Analysis

The experimental corpora include Chinese People's Daily Newspaper, CoNLL-2000 standard corpora and the Penn Chinese Treebank 5.0. The precision P = the right count / the model count, the recall rate R = the right count / the corpus count, and the overall F-measure = (2 * P * R) / (P + R).

4.1 POS Tagging Evaluation

The corpora used in this section come from the Chinese People's Daily Newspaper in 1998, which are annotated by Institute of Computational Linguistic of Peking University, include word segmentation, POS tagging and Named Entity information.

Table 3 demonstrates the performance of several language models. In this experiment, the training corpus is the first month Newspaper, which includes about 124 thousand sentences and 1121 thousand words, and the testing corpus is the sixth month Newspaper, including about 137 thousand sentences and 1244 thousand words. In table3, because the all the word should have corresponding tag, the precision, recall rate and F-measure are equal.

Table 3. The performance of several language models

Language model	Precision
HMM1 (1-order)	92.40%
HMM2 (2-order)	92.39%
MEMM	92.50%
SVM	92.89%
CRF	93.59%

The comparing result in table 3 indicates that CRF acquires the best performance, since a lot of richer features can be effectively fused into the model and label bias problem also be avoided. In addition, SVM also achieves the competing result, as a result of his optimized generalization in theory by structrual risk minimization principle. ME or MEMM can prefer to HMM, because they can be easily added features and relax feature independent assumption, which is the limitation of generative model. In above experiment, we don't consider the influence of named entities, so as to well compare the model performance. Figure 6 demonstrates the compared case by POS in terms of F-measure.

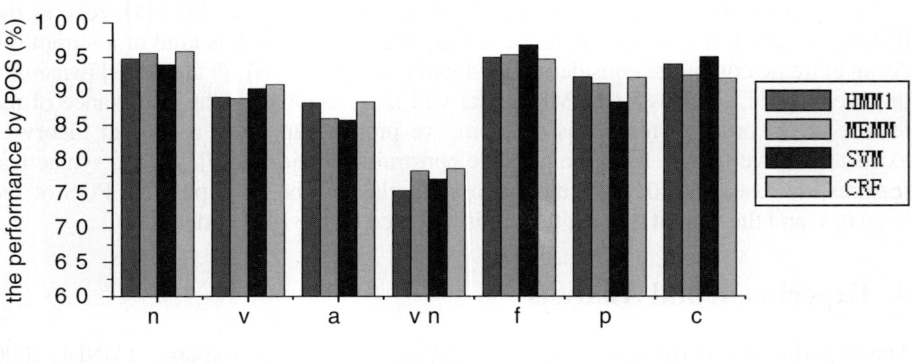

Fig. 6. The compared case by POS in terms of F-measure

The detail evaluation indicates that each model has the different superiority in special POS, especially in POS "c", CRF do not outperform the others'. This seems to be inconsistent with the whole performance presented in table 3, however, CRF is optimized according to the sentence, as shown by formula (3), as a result, it can achieve the best performance in the whole. The POS "c" (conj.) is usually relevant to the syntax of the sentence, while we only use the local context feature, which must affect the perfomance of this specified POS. This kind of problem will be considered in the section 4.3. On the other hand, figure 6 also inspires us to be able to combine or fuse multi-models, such as by voting or stacking method etc[2].

Figure 7 shows the training log-likelihood values, and it also exhibits the maximizing process.

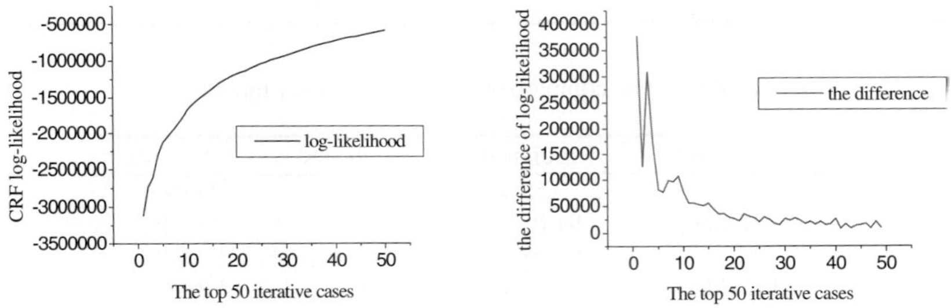

Fig. 7. The log-likelihood of the top 50 CRF iteration in training

The left figure demonstrates that the log-likelihood was increasing, since CRF adopts Maximize Likelihood Estimation method, accordingly the object convex function makes sure the global optimized solution. The right figure exhibits the difference of each iteration, and tells us that the trend of the log-likelihood difference nears zero in whole, so CRF will convergent in finally.

4.2 Shallow Parsing Evaluation

Firstly, several models are evaluated in CoNLL-2000[3] with the standard training corpus and the standard testing corpus. Our result has shown the superiority over the other reported systems.

Table 4 shows that the CRF achieves better performance than MEMM do. And we have compared CRF and MEMM with ME and Memory Based method in CoNLL-2000 shared task, as shown in table 5. The baseline result is obtained by selecting the chunk tag which is most frequently associated with the current part-of-speech tag.

---

[2] In fact, we've done experiment indicated that multi-models combining by voting and stacking can work better.

[3] http://www.cnts.ua.ac.be/conll2000/. The corpora were open and free, and some other systems had been evaluated.

Table 4. The performance of several shallow parsing in CoNLL-2000

chunk type	MEMM Precision	Recall rate	F-measure	CRF Precision	Recall rate	F-measure
NP	92.78%	93.56%	93.17%	93.84%	93.65%	93.74%
VP	92.92%	93.50%	93.20%	93.18%	93.34%	93.26%
PP	95.32%	97.32%	96.31%	96.38%	97.51%	96.94%
ADVP	79.16%	76.33%	77.72%	81.04%	78.98%	80.00%
ADJP	73.22%	68.04%	70.53%	76.88%	69.86%	73.21%
SBAR	85.15%	76.07%	80.36%	87.62%	82.06%	84.75%
PRT	73.53%	70.75%	72.12%	77.78%	72.64%	75.12%
CONJP	33.33%	44.44%	38.10%	57.14%	44.44%	50.00%
INTJ	100.00%	50.00%	66.67%	50.00%	50.00%	50.00%
LST	0.00%	0.00%	0.00%	0.00%	0.00%	0.00%
Overall	92.26%	92.68%	92.47%	93.28%	93.00%	93.14%

Table 5. The comparison of CRF and other models

Language Model	Precision	Recall rate	F-measure
Baseline	72.58%	82.14%	77.07%
Memory-Based	91.05%	92.03%	91.54%
ME	92.08%	91.86%	91.97%
MEMM	92.26%	92.68%	92.47%
CRF	93.28%	93.00%	93.14%

The accuracy of CRF is better than that of ME, MEMM and Memory Based method. CRF chunking model utilizes the sufficient context information that can describe the actual language phenomenon effectively and make the relation of context tags much tight. Compared with MEMM, CRF also avoid the label bias problem. All above reasons make CRF model be more efficient to resolve shallow parsing problem. The overall improvement is 0.67% in F-score.

Another evaluation experiment adopts the Chinese Penn Treebank 5.0 (CPTB5.0) corpora, which contains 507,222 words, 824,983 Hanzi, 18,782 sentences, and 890 data files. in CPTB5.0, there are 114 golden files, which are annotated carefully. These golden files include 63,223 words (12.46% of the corpus), and they are used as testing files, the left files are used as training files.

Table 6. The perfomance in the Chinese Penn Treebank

Language Model	Precision	Recall rate	F-measure
Baseline	68.30%	80.43%	73.87%
MEMM	91.00%	91.46%	91.23%
CRF	91.96%	91.87%	91.92%

Table 6 also exhibits CRF method is better than MEMM method on condition of the same feature template. About NP type, ME is "Precision 87.11%; Recall 87.69%; FB1: 87.40%", while CRF is "Precision: 89.25%; Recall: 87.46%; FB1: 88.34%"。This method is also used in the next section.

4.3 Feedback Information Gain

It is supposed that the POS tagging in the experiment of table 6 is always right. While, it's not possible in fact, so we use our own POS tagging to label the POS of the sentence in CPTB. And this makes the following research more near the fact. Due to the limitation of available corpus at present, we use the Peking POS tagging set to replace the Penn Treebank POS tagging set.

Table 7. The comparison on condition of Ideal POS and of Real POS

Language Model	Precision	Recall rate	F-measure
MEMM + Ideal POS (Penn)	91.00%	91.46%	91.23%
MEMM + Real POS (Peking)	81.83%	82.53%	82.18%

In table 8, syntactical features are used to disambiguate complicated multi-class words. The erroneous count of these words nearly rank the top of the error list, when evaluating the CRF or MEMM model. And we are also easy to find that these words usually contain the POS of empty word, so it's hard to label these words correctly only by using the local features, which has been explained in figure 6, where CRF has the low performance in the POS "c".

Table 8. The disambiguation to the complicated multi-class words

Keyword	Main POS	Baseline(%) *P R F*	Syntax feature(%) *P R F*	F-score error decrease rate
为 (for)	prep.	93.92 93.60 93.76	94.69 94.76 94.73	15.24%
	verb.	91.72 92.17 91.94	93.18 93.13 93.16	
和(and)	prep.	62.05 46.36 53.07	66.33 49.81 56.89	6.73%
	conj.	98.78 99.46 99.12	98.84 99.51 99.17	
到 (to)	prep.	84.14 67.69 75.02	84.10 71.09 77.05	5.99%
	verb.	92.01 96.76 94.33	92.77 96.59 94.64	

Compared with baseline method, "Syntax feature" column is added syntactical features into maximum entropy disambiguation model. the "error descendent" column indicates that syntactical features are effective, since they can achieve the better performance, especially to these complicated multi-class words.

We believe that our method should achieve more exciting result when we have a better corpus in the future, because our own POS tagging set has brought a decreasing performance, as shown in table 7. So we can further improve the result in table 8 by augmenting the training set and using the original POS tagging set. Though our corpus is not perfect, our method has achieved a satisfying performance.

5 Conclusion

POS tagging and shallow parsing are typical sequence labeling problem. We have emphasized the prior knowledge all along in this paper, due to the "No free lunch" theorem and "Ugly duckling" theorem. The good performance of our method contributed to the following main respects:

1) present a new method of Chinese POS tagging and shallow parsing based on conditional random fields, which is conditional probability model, and able to avoid the label bias problem. As a result, our method has achieved better performance than the traditional method, such as HMM, MEMM, in POS tagging task and Shallow parsing task.

2) propose to use the feedback information of syntactical information to lexical processing, and have improved the POS tagging performance.

3) Apply rough sets theory to extract the syntactical features, which make the model be able to utilize the effective features.

The work in the future is concentrated on two respects. One is that we should try to seek more delicate feature templates according to language knowledge, and deal with them by the method proposed in this paper. The other is that we could build data-driven clustering to expand the extracted features, so as to make the model more robust and improve the model performance.

Acknowledgments

This investigation is supported by the Key Program Projects of National Natural Science Foundation of China (60435020), National Natural Science Foundation of China (60504021), and also supported by Microsoft fund of Chinese Ministry of Education (01307620).

References

1. Eric, B.: Some Advances in Transformation-Based Part of Speech Tagging. In Proceedings of the Twelfth National Conference on Artificial Intelligence, (1994) 722-727
2. David, M.M.: Statistical Decision-Tree Models for Parsing. In Proceeding of the 33rd Annual Meeting of the ACL, (1995) 276-283
3. Kupiec, J.: Robust Part-of-speech Tagging using a Hidden Markov Model. Computer Speech and Language, 6 (1992) 225–242
4. Adwait, R.: A Maximum Entropy Model for Part-of-speech Tagging. Proceedings of the Conference on Empirical Methods in Natural Language Processing, (1996)
5. Jesús, G., Lluís, M.: SVMTool: A General POS Tagger Generator Based on Support Vector Machines. Proceedings of the 4th International Conference on Language Resources and Evaluation (LREC'04). Portugal (2004)
6. McCallum, A., Freitag, D., Pereira, F.: Maximum Entropy Markov Models for Information Extraction and Segmentation. In proceedings of ICML, (2000) 591–598
7. Lafferty, J., McCallum, A., Pereira, F.: Conditional Random Fields: Probabilistic Models for Segmenting and Labeling Sequence Data. In International Conference on Machine Learning, (2001) 282–289
8. Zhao, Y., Wang, X.L.: Applying Class Triggers in Chinese POS Tagging Based on Maximum Entropy Model. ICMLC2004. (2004) 1641-1645

9. Wei, J., Wang, X.L.: Applying Rough Sets to Extract Feature in POS Tagging. Chinese High Technology Letters, (2006)
10. Sha, F., Pereira, F.: Shallow Parsing with Conditional Random Fields. In the proceedings of Human Language Technology/North American chapter of the Association for Computational Linguistics annual meeting, (2003) 213-220
11. Yongmei, T., Tianshun, Y., Qing, C.: Applying Conditional Random Fields to Chinese Shallow Parsing. In CICLing 2005, (2005) 167-176
12. Wei, J., Jian, Z.: Chinese Word Segmentation based on Mixing Model. 4th SIGHAN Workshop, (2005) 180-182

Ontology-Based Automatic Classification of Web Documents

MuHee Song[1], SooYeon Lim[1], DongJin Kang[2], and SangJo Lee[1]

[1] Department of Computer Engineering, Kyungpook National University, 702-701 Daegu, Korea
{mhsong, sjlee}@knu.ac.kr, nadalsy@hotmail.com

[2] Information Technology Services, Kyungpook National University, 702-701 Daegu, Korea
djkang@knu.ac.kr

Abstract. The use of an ontology in order to provide a mechanism to enable machine reasoning has continuously increased during the last few years. This paper proposed an automated method for document classification using an ontology, which expresses terminology information and vocabulary contained in Web documents by way of a hierarchical structure. Ontology-based document classification involves determining document features that represent the Web documents most accurately, and classifying them into the most appropriate categories after analyzing their contents by using at least two pre-defined categories per given document features. In this paper, Web documents are classified in real time not with experimental data or a learning process, but by similarity calculations between the terminology information extracted from Web documents and ontology categories. This results in a more accurate document classification since the meanings and relationships unique to each document are determined.

1 Introduction

As the Internet usage rate has rapidly increased, the volume of electronic documents that can be seen on the Web has also substantially increased. Since so many of these electronic texts now exist in terms of their pure numbers and volumes, it is impossible for people to individually classify information contained in millions and millions of Web documents. Thus, there is an increasing need for a tool, which can classify electronic documents into appropriately pre-defined categories.

As a means to resolve the problem of classifying an almost infinite volume of electronic documents accurately and efficiently, an automated document classification method, using the ontology method, is proposed in this paper. Typically, Web documents have the following characteristics: First, they are structured in a Web site with the Web site as a unit, in other words, a Web site normally consists of many Web texts with the same subject or similar topics. Second, each Web document exists as a part of other Web sites. Finally, individuals or organizations that have specific purposes manage typical Web sites.

D.-S. Huang, K. Li, and G.W. Irwin (Eds.): ICIC 2006, LNAI 4114, pp. 690 – 700, 2006.

This paper considers the fact that terminology information can be easily extracted using such Web text characteristics. In our research, Web documents are classified based on similarities determined by the ontology, which expresses the meaning structure of the Web documents' terminology information and vocabulary in a hierarchical manner. Identifying and comparing the meaning content and relationship of each document can perform document classification more accurately and efficiently. The ontology mentioned in this paper is comprised of concepts, concepts features, relations between concepts, and constraints for document classification, all in a hierarchical manner. Also, the ontology's hierarchical structure is applied to the document classification.

Our work is distinguished from others for the following reasons: (1) Rather than using a dictionary or knowledge index, ontology is used for document classification. (2) Our ontology is based on syntax information contained in the Web documents. (3) Mapping between the established ontology and terminology information extracted from Web documents is performed.

We wish our classification system could be used to classify current web documents into proper categories and to generate reports if the web documents belong to unwanted sites.

In the following section of this paper, we will discuss related approaches to our classifier. Section 3 describes the details of our framework how ontology, as proposed in this paper, is applied to document classification, and we show the experiments and evaluation of web documents in Section 4. In conclusion we summarize our results and mention further research issues.

2 Related Work

Document classification involves determining the document features that represent documents most appropriately, and placing the documents into the most related categories after evaluating its contents, by using at least two pre-defined categories based on the already defined document features. This section describes research which has been carried out by people in the area of automatic document classification, and it examines the key difference between our work and other research.

The rule-based model [2] utilizes experts' help based on generally distinguished rules that appear in study texts or applies rules that are extracted by studying the documents. The Bayesian probability model [5,9] applies the probability theory to the document features extracted from the documents. The SVM (Support Vector Machine: SVM)[7] uses the machine learning method. The text which is to be classified from the information retrieval standpoint is queried and similar texts are searched in the k-nearest neighbor model [17]. Although these methods have some degree of accuracy, all of them require some rule learning level and they must have the training data as a reference.

There have been several approaches which focus on ontologies to classify Web documents [10,3,16]. Prabowo et. al. [10] defined ontology as "a single entity which holds conceptual instances of a domain, and differentiates itself from another," and used ontologies for web document classification with respect to the Dewey Decimal Classification(DDC) and Library of Congress Classification(LCC). The weakness of their approach is the fact that it is not adaptive when users require more sophisticated classification, even if the approach follows the standard classifications. However, since our approach builds an adaptive ontology, we provide a flexible classification reflecting requests.

This paper proposes an ontology-based, automated document classification method, which does not require these learning processes and can be performed in real time.

3 Document Classification Using Ontology

3.1 Ontology

An ontology can be defined as specification of a representational vocabulary for a shared domain of discourse which may include definitions of classes, relations, functions and other objects. An ontology includes a selection of specific sets of vocabulary for domain knowledge model construction, and the context of each vocabulary is represented and constrained by the ontology. Therefore, an ontological model can effectively disambiguate meanings of words from free text sentences, overcoming the problem faced in natural language where a word may have multiple meanings depending on the applicable context.

In this paper, an ontology is defined as one independent, collective representation of all standardized concepts for vocabulary and terms in one place. Here, we are not talking about collections of simple words, but we are referring to collection of vocabulary, which have relationships with both simple rules and meanings. Ontology expressions are based not only on the logical relations between term definitions and other meanings, but also on the bottom-out structure where the interpretation starts from primitive terms. We have decided to apply ontology to Web documents classification, because it has the unique, hierarchical structure and characteristic of machine reasoning, starting from very primitive terms.

The advantages of an ontology-based classification approach over the existing ones, such as hierarchical, -[13] and probabilistic – approach [8], are that (1) the nature of the relational structure of an ontology provides a mechanism to enable machine reasoning; (2) the conceptual instances within an ontology are not only a bag of keywords but have inherent semantics, and a close relationship with the class representatives of the classification schemes. Hence, they can be mapped to each other; (3) this is a kind of Web document and class representative. It also enables us to get insights into and observe the way the classifier assigns a class representative to a Web documents by tracking the links between the conceptual instances involved and the associated class representative [10].

The main factors and relationships in this paper's ontology are listed below.

- Main Factors in Ontology
    - Concept: Generally used terms in specific domains
    - Feature: Used to describe an individual item
    - Relation: Defines and connects relationship patterns among concepts
    - Constraint: Required condition to promote each individual item
- Relationships in Ontology
    - Equal (E-R): When meanings between concepts are the same.
    - Succession (is-a): When the class and the instance are the same
    - Part (has-a): When A has B as part of A (has-part, part-of)

3.2 Building Domain Ontology for Classification

Ontology means information used in a specific domain and relationships defined in relation to the information. Concepts and their relational structure are defined through discussion with specialists in the corresponding domain, and based on them is constructed ontology. This study purposes to suggest a method of constructing ontology semi-automatically in the domain of economy. Fig.1. shows four steps of ontology construction processed proposed [14]. Ontology for the 'economy' domain has been developed for experimental purposes of document classification. To configure and develop the ontology, it is first assumed that the vocabulary which frequently appears in document collection is similarly related to other vocabulary. The second point is this frequently appearing vocabulary is used to build the basic network structure. Third, adding vocabulary that has a relationship with those selected words expands the ontology. Then, similarities between the terminology information extracted from Web document, and ontology terminology data are identified and compared in order to start the document classification process.

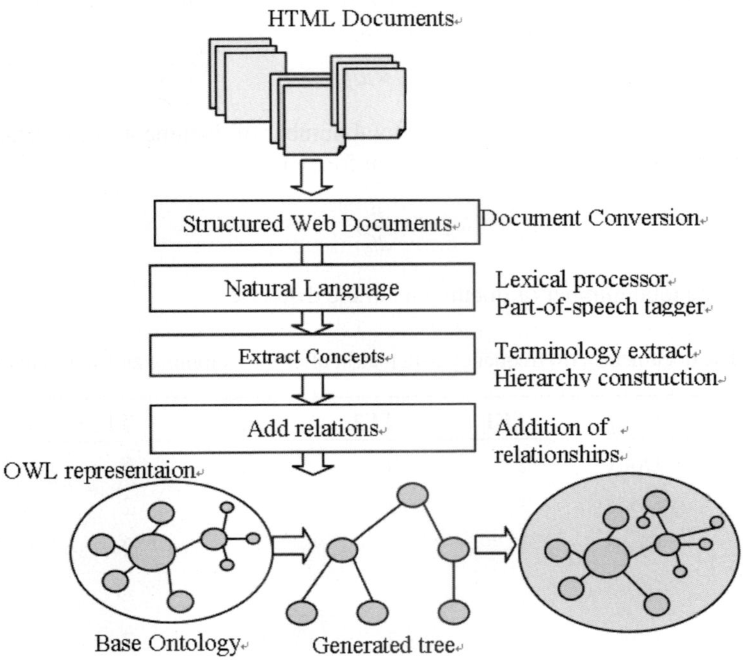

Fig. 1. Ontology construction process

3.3 Document Classification Using Ontology

We model a Web page using an ontology and classify Web pags based upon the ontology, as consisting of a hierarchy of concepts. Each class in the ontology contains a tapestry of representing terms.

The process of Web document classification basically involves two procedures: Finding key vocabulary in the documents and mapping onto a node in the concept hierarchy (ontology) using the extracted words.

As part of the key vocabulary extraction process from documents, the removal of stop words and the stemming of words, both as the pre-classification procedures as well as the application of information retrieval measurement, *tf×idf*(term frequency times inverted document frequency), take place. Stopping is a process of removing the most frequent word that exists in a web document such as 'to', 'and', 'it', etc. Removing these words will save spaces for storing document contents and reduce time taken during the search process. Stemming is a process of extracting each word from a web document by reducing it to a possible root word. For example, the words, 'compares', 'compared', and 'comparing' have similar meaning with the word 'compare'. After the stemming and stopping process of the terms in each document, we will represent them as the document-term frequency matrix ($Doc_j \times TF_{jk}$) as shown in Table 1. Doc_j is referring to each web document that exists in the news database where $j=1,....,n$. Term frequency TF_{jk} is the number of how many times the distinct word wk occurs in document Docj where $k=1,...,m$. The calculation of the terms weight xjk of each word wk is done by using a method that has been used by Salton[1,12] which is given by

$$x_{jk} = TF_{jk} \times idf_k \tag{1}$$

where the document frequency d_{fk} is the total number of document in the database that contains the word w_k. The inverse document frequency

$$idf_k = \log(\frac{n}{df_k}) \tag{2}$$

where n is the total number of documents in the database.

Table 1. The document-term frequency data matrix after the stemming and stopping processes

Docj	TF1	TF2	...	TFm
Doc1	2	4	...	5
Doc2	2	3	...	2
Doc3	2	3	...	2
...	...	...	...	...
Docn	1	3	...	7

tf×idf is a mathematical algorithm which is used to efficiently find key vocabulary that best represents the texts by applying the term frequency and the inverted document frequency together.

tf(i,j) is the term frequency of Term *j* that appears in Document $di \in D^*$, where $i=1,2,3...,N$. *df(j)* is the document frequency of Term *j* and represents how often Term *j* appears in other documents. Then, *tf×idf* for Term *j* is defined as given below [12].

$$tf \times idf(i, j) = tf(i, j) \times \log\left(\frac{N}{df(j)}\right) \tag{3}$$

For vocabulary with a low or rare appearance frequency, the value of *tf×idf* is low, compared to that with a high appearance frequency, thus resulting words successfully classifying the documents. In the term selection process, a list of all terms contained in one document from the text collection is made. Then, the document selection process chooses Term *j* that maximizes *W(j),* which is expressed as a vector for Document d_j as follows. Document d_j includes *tf×idf(i,j),* which is *tf×idf* for the most appropriate term.

$$W(j) = \sum_{i=1}^{N} tf \times idf(i, j) \cdot \tag{4}$$

The similarity calculation for classification is done using the following formula: The document is mapped onto a node with the highest similarity value, and one document is ultimately classified into one class.

$$Sim(Node, d) = \frac{\sum_{i=0}^{N} freq_{i,d} / \max_{i,d}}{N} \times \frac{V_d}{V} \cdot \tag{5}$$

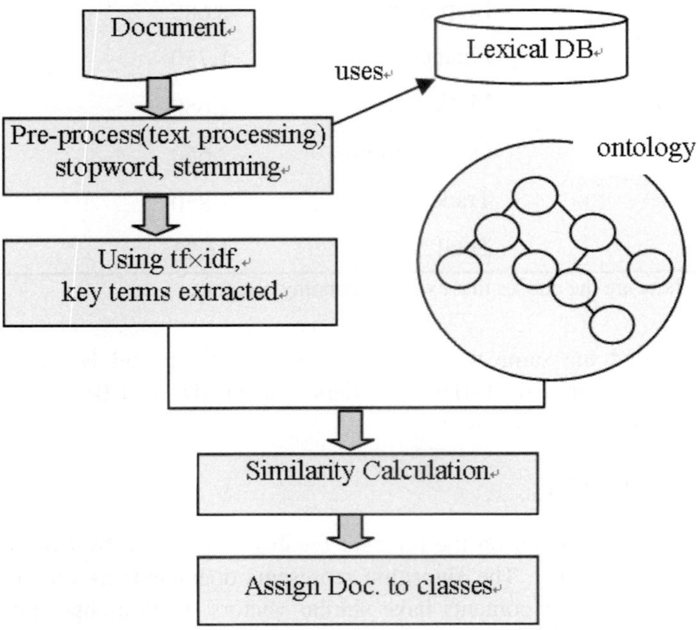

Fig. 2. Web Document Classification Process Using Ontology

N is the feature frequency of a node. $freq_{i,d}$ represents the frequency of feature i that is matched in document d. $max_{i,d}$ is the frequency of the feature that is matched the most in document d. V is the number of constraints, while V_d represents the number of constraints that are satisfied by document d. The document classification takes place only when the use of the relations is "is-a", "has-a", "part-of", or "has-part". When another node is related, it is also included in the classification process to calculate the similarity. Using this approach, a more accurate classification can be performed.

The overall classification process for Web documents is as shown below (Fig. 2.).

4 Experimental Procedures

We have used a web documents dataset from Yahoo Economy news as shown in Table 2. The types of news in the database are Cooperatives, Employment, Finance, Marketing, Organizations and Trade. The total of documents is 13,235.

Table 2. The number of document that are stored in the news database

Class no.	Class name	Number of documents
1	Cooperatives	1,620
2	Employment	2,685
3	Finance	1,750
4	Marketing	2,680
5	Organizations	2,650
6	Trade	1,850
	Total	13,235

* These are the classes that exist in Economy category.

We have used the same test as being done by Yang and Honavar [6], which includes the Bayesian and TF-IDF classifiers. The TF-IDF and Bayesian methods for the tests are described as below.

4.1 TF-IDF Classifier

TF-IDF classifier is based on the relevant feedback algorithm by Rocchio using the vector space model [11]. The algorithm represents documents as vectors so that the documents with similar contents have similar vectors. Each component of a vector corresponds to a term in the document, typically a word. The weight of each component is calculated using the term frequency inverse document frequency weighting scheme (TF-IDF) which tries to reward words that occur many times in a few documents. To classify a new document *Doc'*, the cosines of the prototype vectors with corresponding document vectors are calculated for each class. *Doc'* is assigned to the class whose document vector has the highest cosine. Further description on the TF-IDF measure is described by Joachim [15].

4.2 Bayesian Classifier

For the statistical classification, we have used a standard Bayesian classifier [16]. When using the Bayesian classifier, we have assumed that term's occurrence is independent of other terms. We want to find a class cs that gives the highest conditional probability for given document $Doc'{\cdot}w_k^m = \{w_1, w_2, \cdots, w_m\}$ is the set of words representing the textual content of the document *Doc'* and *k* is the term number where *k=1,…,m* The classification score is measured by

$$J(cs) = \prod_{k=1}^{m} P(w_k \mid cs) P(cs) \tag{6}$$

Where *P(cs)* is the prior probability of class *cs*, and $P(w_k|cs)$ is the likelihood of a word W_k in a class *cs* that is estimated on a labeled training document. A given web document is then classified in a class that maximizes *J(cs)*. If values of *J(cs)* for all the classes in the economy category are less than a given threshold, then the document is considered unclassified.

4.3 Evaluation

Automatic classification of web document is evaluated using the standard information retrieval measures that are precision, recall, and F1 [4]. The F1 measure is a kind of average of precision and recall. They are defined as follows

$$precision = \frac{a}{a+b} \tag{7}$$

$$recall = \frac{a}{a+c} \tag{8}$$

$$F1 = \frac{2}{\frac{1}{precision} + \frac{1}{recall}} \tag{9}$$

Table 3. The definitions of the parameters a, b, and c which are used in Table 4

value	Meaning
a	The system and the expert agree with the assigned category
b	The system disagree with the assigned category but the expert did
c	The expert disagree with the assigned category but the system did
d	The system and the expert disagree with the assigned category

Under this appraisal, the values *a, b, c* is defined on Table 3. The F1 measurement method shows the certain average value in terms of accuracy and rate of repeat. Table 5 shows the result of the classification, using the method proposed by this research paper. And the method proposed by using the F1 measurement is compared with TF-IDF and also with Bayesian method on Table 6 and Figure 4.

In Our the classification results, the precision, recall, and F1 measures are 88.62%, 94.33%, 91.30%, respectively, as shown in Table 5.

A better document selection approach needs to be used for selecting the candidate documents from each class in order to increase the F1 classification results.

Table 4. The decision matrix for calculating the classification accuracies

Expert	**System**	
	Yes	No
Yes	a	b
No	c	d

Table 5. The classification results

Class no.	Precision(%)	Recall(%)	F1(%)
1	76.27	92.64	83.66
2	90.25	93.61	91.90
3	92.62	94.38	93.49
4	89.3	95.15	92.13
5	91.3	96.92	94.03
6	91.97	93.26	92.61
Average	88.62	94.33	91.30

Table 6. The Classification results using the F1 measure

class	**TFIDF(%)**	**Bayesian(%)**	**Proposed method**
Cooperatives	76.15	74.24	83.66
Employment	88.51	80.81	91.9
Finance	86.86	82.56	93.49
Marketing	79.39	78.79	92.13
Organizations	68.03	87.1	94.03
Trade	80.26	91.22	92.61
Average	79.87	82.45	91.30

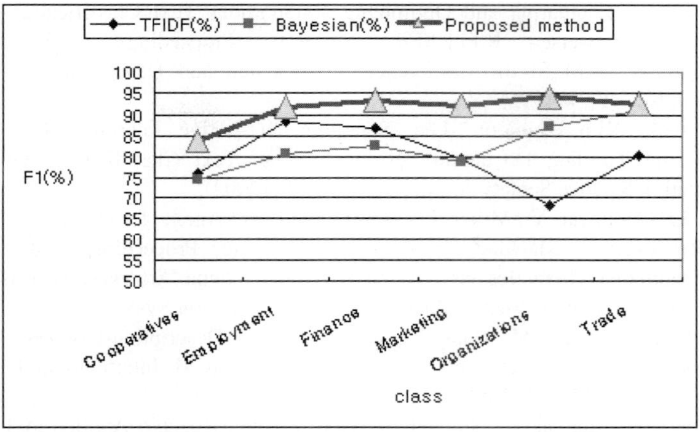

Fig. 4. F1 Comparison

5 Conclusion and Future Research

This paper introduced the use of ontology to conceptually express the meaning of relationships contained in Web documents and proposed an automated document classification method using the ontology. In particular, this paper focused on document classification based on the similarities of documents already categorized by ontology using terminology information extracted from the documents. Our work is distinguished from other studies in the following areas. (1) Rather than using a dictionary or knowledge index, ontology is used for document classification. (2) Our ontology is based on syntax information contained in the Web texts. (3) Mapping between the established ontology and the term information extracted from Web documents is performed. The document classification technique proposed by this paper does not involve any learning processes or experimental data and can be performed in real time.

Further research is required to develop more efficient and accurate ontological expressions and to document classification methods. We plan to conduct further studies on how to improve the efficiency of an information search using the document classification technique proposed in this paper and how to automatically determine the meaning of concepts and relations from Web documents.

References

1. Hotho, A., Maedche, A., Staab, S.: Ontology-Based Text Document Clustering, Http://www.aifb.uni-karlsruhe.de/WBS
2. Apt, C., Damerau, F., Sholom, M.W.: Towards Language Independent Automated Learning Of Text Categorization Models, Proc. of the 17th annual international ACM-SIGIR (1994)
3. Jenkins, C., Jackson, M., Burden, P., Wallis, J.: Automatic RDF Metadata Generation for Resource Discovery, Proc. Of 8th International WWW Conference, Toronto (1999) 11-14

4. Lewis, D.D.: Evaluating and Optimizing Autonomous Text Classification Systems, in: E.A.Fox, P.Ingwersen, R.Fidel(Ed.), SIGIR'95: Proceedings of the 18th Annual International ACM SIGIR Conference on Research and Development in Information Retrival, New York(1995)
5. Kim, Jeuk, Kim, Hanjoon, Lee, Sanggoo: an Active Learning-based Method for Composing Training Document Set In Bayesian Text Classification Systems, Korea Information Science Society Journals, Volume 29 (2002).
6. Yang, J.P., Honavar, V., Miller, L.: Mobile Intelligent Agents for Document Classification and Retrieval: A Machine Learning Approach, in: Proceeding s of the European Symposium on Cybernetics and Systems Research, Vienna, Austria (1998) 707-712.
7. Hearst, M. A.: Support Vector Machines, IEEE Information Systems, 13(4), (1998) 18~28
8. Goevert, N., Lalmas, M., Fuhr, N.: A Probabilistic Description-Oriented Approach for Categorisiong Web Documents, Proc. Of the 8th ACM International Conference on Information and Knowledge Management (1999) 475-482
9. Shapire, R.E., Singhal, Y., Singhal, A.: Boosting and Rocchio Applied to Text Filtering, Proc. Of the 21th annual international ACM-SIGIR (1998)
10. Prabowo, Rudy, Jackson, Mike, Burden, Peter, Knoell, Heinz-Dieter: Ontology-Based Automatic Classification for the Web Documents Design, Implementation and Evaluation, Proc. Of the 3rd International Conference on Web Information Systems Engineering (2002)
11. Korfhage, R.R.: Information Storage and Retrieval, John Wiley and Sons Inc., USA (1997)
12. Salton, M.: Introduction to Modern Information Retrival, New York, Mcgraw-Hill, USA (1983)
13. Dumais, S.T., Chen, H.: Hierarchical Classification of Web Content, Proc of the 23rd Annual International ACM SIGIR, Arthens, Greece (2000)
14. Lim, S.Y., Song, M.H., Lee, S.J.: the Construction of Document Ontology and Its Application to Document Retrival, Proc. of the third Biennial International Conference on Advances in Information Systems (2004)
15. Joachims, T.: Probabilistic Analysis of the Rocchio Algorithm with TFIDF for Text Categorization, Proceedings of International Conference on Machine Learning, Nashvile, TN, USA (1997) 143-151
16. Ng, Y., Tang, J., Goodrich, M.: A Binary Categorization Approach for Classifying Multiplerecord Web Documents Using Application Ontologies and A Probabilistic Model, Proc. Of 7th International Conference on Database Systems for Advances Applications (2001) 58-65
17. Yang, Y.M., Liu, X.: A Re-examination of Text Categorization Methods, Proc. Of the 22th annual International ACM-SIGIR (1999)

Recognition of Emotion with SVMs

Zhi Teng[1], Fuji Ren[1,2], and Shingo Kuroiwa[1]

[1] Faculty of Engineering, The University of Tokushima
2-1 Minamijosanjima, Tokushima, 770-8506, Japan
[2] School of Information Engineering, Beijing University of Posts and Telecommunications, Beijing, 100876, China
{teng, ren, kuroiwa}@is.tokushima-u.ac.jp

Abstract. In recent years, several methods on human emotion recognition have been published. In this paper, we proposed a scheme that applied the emotion classification technique for emotion recognition. The emotion classification model is Support Vector Machines (SVMs). The SVMs have become an increasingly popular tool for machine learning tasks involving classification, regression or novelty detection. The Emotion Recognition System will be recognise emotion from the sentence that was inputted from the keyboard. The training set and testing set were constructed to verify the effect of this model. Experiments showed that this method could achieve better results in practice. The result showed that this method has potential in the emotion recognition field.

1 Introduction

The need to develop emotion recognition systems from human speech has increased as human-computer interaction is increasingly playing a significant role in everyday environment [1] [2]. Recognizing a human's emotional state can be helpful in various contexts. The most promising one is probably the man-machine interaction, e.g. the communication between an assisting robot in the household and its human user [3] [4]. For the robot, emotion recognition and classification is an important step in understanding its environment. But also for patient monitoring, emotion recognition might be helpful. An automatic classification of a patient's emotional expressions reveals much information on his/her pre-sent state. Therefore we executed the emotion recognition system. The theory of emotion recognition is the emotion classification with the SVMs.

Support Vector Machines (SVMs) have recently been successfully applied to a number of applications ranging from particle identification, face identification and text categorization to engine knock detection, bioinformatics and database marketing [5]. The approach is systematic and motivated by statistical learning theory [6] and Bayesian arguments. The training task involves optimization of a con vex costfunction: there are no false local minima to complicate the learning process. The approach has much other benefit, for example, the model constructed has an explicit dependence on the most informative patterns in the data (the support vectors).

D.-S. Huang, K. Li, and G.W. Irwin (Eds.): ICIC 2006, LNAI 4114, pp. 701 – 710, 2006.

Although such efforts have focused on a few basic emotion classes such as anger, sadness, happiness, and other "universal" emotions, the class boundaries between emotion categories are vague or fuzzy because of the linguistic uncertainties in the definition of the emotional classes in everyday use [7]. In this study, we used two broad emotion categories, negative and non-negative, and those emotion classes in turn would cover various emotions; e.g., negative emotion class might include "anger", "frustration", and "boredom", and non-negative class would have "blessedness", "happiness" , "pleasure" and other positive emotions. In prior work, we relied on statistical description of class specific data.

This paper describes an Emotion Recognition System. This system recognizes the emotion from the sentence that be inputted from the keyboard. The theory of emotion recognition is the emotion classification with the SVMs. The tool of the SVMs model is the LIBSVM [8]. The system uses the data which has been rightly classed by us for training the classification model and then uses the classification model to predict the sort of emotion, namely negative or non-negative. In this way, the emotion of sentences which be inputted from the keyboard can be recognised. The result will be showed by face image (if the result is non-negative it can be showed by a laughing face image, and, contrariwise, it can be showed by a non-laughing face image).

The remainder of the paper is organized as follows. Section 2 describes the theory of SVMs. Section 3 describes the Emotion Recognition System. Section 4 describes the Data and Result. Section 5 describes concludes and Section 6 give some directions for future work.

2 SVM

From the perspective of statistical learning theory the motivation for considering binary classifier SVMs comes from theoretical bounds on the generalization error [9]. Though we do not quote the relevant theorem here we note that it has two important features.

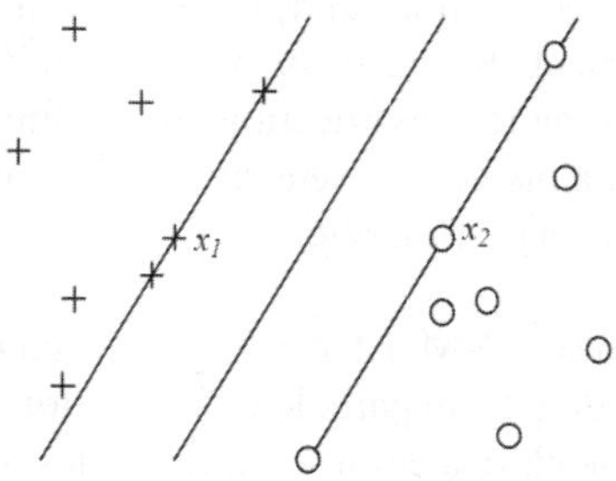

Fig. 1. The margin is the perpendicular distance between the separating hyperplane and a hyperplane through the closest points (the support vectors). x1 and x2 are examples of support vectors of opposite sign. The margin b and is the region between the hyperplanes on both sides of the separating hyperplane.

Firstly, the upper bounds on the generalization error do not depend on the dimension of the space. Secondly, the error bound is minimised by maximising the margin, γ, i.e. the minimal distance between the hyperplane separating the two classes and the closest datapoints to the hyperplane (Figure 1).

Let us consider a binary classification task with datapoints xi (i = 1, …, m) having corresponding labels yi = ±1 and let the decision function be:

$$f(x) = \mathrm{sign}(w \cdot x + b)$$

If the dataset is separable then the data will be correctly classified if yi (w · xi+b) > 0 $\forall i$. Clearly this relation is in variant under a positive rescaling of the argument inside the sign-function, hence we can define a canonical hyperplane such that w · x+b = 1 for the closest points on one side and w · x+b = -1 for the closest on the other. For the separating hyperplane w · x+b = 0 the normal vector is clearly w= ||w||2, and hence the margin is given by the projection of x1-x2 on to this vector (see Figure 1).Since w · x1+b = 1 and w · x2+b = -1 this means the margin is γ= 1/||w||2. To maximise the margin the task is therefore:

$$\text{Minimise} \quad g(\mathbf{w}) = \frac{1}{2} ||\mathbf{w}||_2^2$$

subject to the constraints:

$$y_i (\mathbf{w} \cdot \mathbf{x}_i + b) \geq 1 \qquad \forall i$$

and the learning task can be reduced to minimisation of the primal Lagrangian:

$$L = \frac{1}{2}(\mathbf{w} \cdot \mathbf{w}) - \sum_{i=1}^{m} \alpha_i \left(y_i(\mathbf{w} \cdot \mathbf{x} + b) - 1\right)$$

where αi are Lagrangian multipliers, hence αi ≥0. Taking the derivatives with respect to b and w and resubstituting back in the primal gives the Wolfe dual Lagrangian:

$$W(\alpha) = \sum_{i=1}^{m} \alpha_i - \frac{1}{2} \sum_{i,j=1}^{m} \alpha_i \alpha_j y_i y_j (\mathbf{x}_i \cdot \mathbf{x}_j) \tag{1}$$

which must be maximised with respect to the αi subject to the constraint:

$$\alpha_i \geq 0 \qquad \sum_{i=1}^{m} \alpha_i y_i = 0 \tag{2}$$

In the dual lagrangian (1) we notice that the datapoints, xi; only appear inside an inner product. To get a potentially better representation of the data we can map the datapoints in to an alternative space, generally called feature space (a pre-Hilbert or inner product space) through a replacement:

$$\mathbf{x}_i \cdot \mathbf{x}_j \rightarrow \phi(\mathbf{x}_i) \cdot \phi(\mathbf{x}_j)$$

The functional form of the mapping Ø(xi) does not need to be known since it is implicitly defined by the choice of kernel: K(xi; xj) = Ø (xi) · Ø (xj) or inner product in Hilbert space. With a suitable choice of kernel the data can become separable in feature space despite being non-separable in the original input space. Thus, whereas data for n-parity or the two spirals problem is non-separable by a hyperplane in input space it can be separated in the feature space defined by RBF kernels (giving an RBF-type network):

$$K(\mathbf{x}_i, \mathbf{x}_j) = e^{-||\mathbf{x}_i - \mathbf{x}_j||^2/2\sigma^2} \tag{3}$$

Many other choices for the kernel are possible e.g.:

$$K(\mathbf{x}_i, \mathbf{x}_j) = (\mathbf{x}_i \cdot \mathbf{x}_j + 1)^d$$

$$K(\mathbf{x}_i, \mathbf{x}_j) = \tanh(\beta \mathbf{x}_i \cdot \mathbf{x}_j + b) \tag{4}$$

defining polynomial and feedforward neural network classifiers. Indeed, the class of mathematical objects which can be used as kernels is very general and includes, for example, scores produced by dynamic alignment algorithms [10]. For binary classification with the given choice of kernel the learning task therefore involves maximisation of the Lagrangian:

$$W(\alpha) = \sum_{i=1}^{m} \alpha_i - \frac{1}{2} \sum_{i,j=1}^{m} \alpha_i \alpha_j y_i y_j K(\mathbf{x}_i, \mathbf{x}_j) \tag{5}$$

subject to constraints (2). After the optimal values of αi have been found the decision function is based on the sign of:

$$f(\mathbf{z}) = \sum_{i=1}^{m} y_i \alpha_i K(\mathbf{z}, \mathbf{x}_i) + b \tag{6}$$

Since the bias, b, does not feature in the above dual formulation it is found from the primal constraints:

$$b = -\frac{1}{2}\left[\max_{\{i|y_i=-1\}}\left(\sum_{j\in\{SV\}}^{m} y_j\alpha_j K(\mathbf{x}_i,\mathbf{x}_j)\right) + \min_{\{i|y_i=+1\}}\left(\sum_{j\in\{SV\}}^{m} y_j\alpha_j K(\mathbf{x}_i,\mathbf{x}_j)\right)\right]$$

The confidence of a classification is directly related to the magnitude of f(z) [11].When the maximal margin hyperplane is found in feature space, only those points which lie closest to the hyperplane have αi > 0 and these points are the support vectors. All other points have αi = 0. This means that the representation of hypothesis is solely given by those points which are closest to the hyperplane and they are the most informative patterns in the data. This framework can be elaborated in many ways, for example: The Multiclass Classification, the soft margins and allowing for training errors, the Novelty Detection and the Regression [12].

3 The Emotion Recognition System

The Emotion Recognition System consists of four mostly parts: the keyword extraction, the keyword processing, the predict processing and the result processing. The framework of the recognition engine is presented in Figure 2.

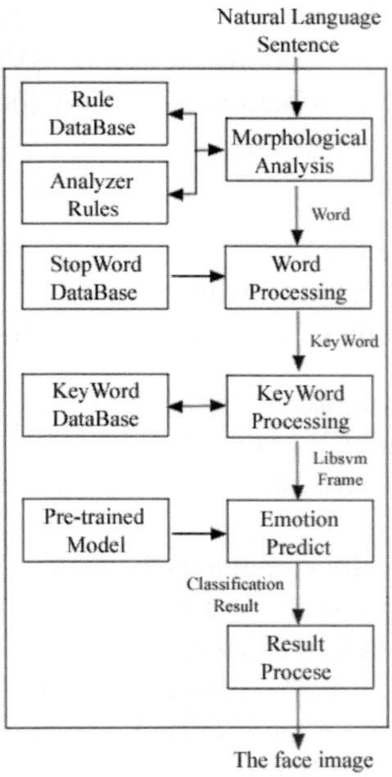

Fig. 2. The framework of Recognition Engine

3.1 The Keyword Extraction

The sentence which be inputted from the keyboard is analyzed by the morphological analysis system through the rule database and analyzer rules. The word will be extracted from the sentence. If there are stopword or stopword-only phrase in the word, it will be eliminated by the stopword processing. In our system, we think that the best important word is the noun, the verb, the adjective and the adverb. So, after the Word Processing we eliminate the word except the noun, the verb, the adjective and the adverb. We think the word that is left is the keyword and the keyword extraction is finished. For instance:

翘首企盼多时的学子们也用欢歌、用笑语表达着他们的喜悦。
The result by the morphological analysis, as below:
翘首/vd 企盼/v 多/m 时/ng 的/u 学子/n 们/k 也/d 用/v 欢歌/v 、/w 用/p 笑语/n 表达/v 着/u 他们/r 的/u 喜悦/an 。/w
The result by the stopword processing, as below:
翘首/vd 企盼/v 时/ng 学子/n 欢歌/v 笑语/n 表达/v 喜悦/an
The result by the keyword extraction, as below:
翘首/vd 企盼/v 时/ng 学子/n 欢歌/v 笑语/n 表达/v 喜悦/an

3.2 The Keyword Processing

In our system we used the tool of SVMs model is the Libsvm. Libsvm is an integrated software for support vector classification, (C-SVC, nu-SVC), regression (epsilon-SVR, nu-SVR) and distribution estimation (one-class SVM). It supports multi-class classification.

The step of use the Libsvm, as:

(1). Prepare data in specified format.
(2). Train the data to create a model with svmtrain.
(3). Predict new input data with svmpredict and get the result.

The input file format of Libsvm, as:
[label] [index1]:[value1] [index2]:[value2] ...

Label: referred to as "class", the class (or set) of your classification. Usually we put integers here.

Index: ordered indexes, usually continuous integers.

Value: the data for training. Usually lots of real (floating point) numbers.

Each line has the structure described above. It means, I have an array (vector) of data (numbers): value1, value2, ... valueN (and the order of the values are specified by the respective index), and the class (or the result) of this array is label.

One record per line, as: +1 1:0.708 2:1 3:1 4:-0.320 5:-0.105 6:-1

The best important question is that how to make the keyword into the specified format of Libsvm. The function of the keyword processing is the solution to this question. Our method is that, first how to process the "label". We define the label value of non-negative is "1", the label value of negative is "-1". In the data of training, the label value was defined by us and in the data of predict, the label value was predicted by Libsvm. Secondly, process the "index". In our system, we constructed the Vector Space Model (VSM) by keyword. The index value of keyword is the place value of it in the Vector Space Model. Finally, process the "value". The value of keyword is the frequency of word. If the frequency of keyword is once in sentence, the value of keyword is "1", the rest may be deduced by analogy. Let's take an example of the keyword processing. The following keywords are processed from the "翘首/vd 企盼/v 时/ng 学子/n 欢歌/v 笑语/n 表达/v 喜悦/an". The specified format of Libsvm, as: 1 747:1 752:1 779:1 780:1 782:1 783:1 784:1 834:1

3.3 The Predict Processing

Use the Libsvm, you must train the data before predict the new data. The svmtrain accepts some specifically format which will be explained below and then generate a "Model" file. You may think of a "Model" as a storage format for the internal data of SVM. This should appear very reasonable after some thought, since training with data is a time-consuming process, so we "train" first and store the result enabling the "predict" operation to go much faster. Then, Output the predicted class of the new input data according to a pre-trained model. Now you can use SVM to do whatever you want! Just write a program to output its data in the correct format, feed the data to SVM for training, then predict and read the output.

In our system, we prepared 1140 sentences that the emotion of sentence has been rightly classed by us. These sentences have been processed, the keywords have been transformed into the specified format of Libsvm and the "Model" file will be generated. The new input data can then only be transformed into the specified format of Libsvm and the new data which be processed will be predicted by "Model" file.

3.4 The Result Processing

The result which will be predicted by Libsvm is the "1" or "-1". Those two emotional categories non-negative and negative are defined in a pragmatic way to follow the need for the given application domain. The meaning of "1" is meaning that the sort of emotion is the non-negative and "-1" is meaning that the sort of emotion is the negative. The function of the result processing is that if the sort of emotion is the non-negative it will be showed by a laughling face image, and, contrariwise, it will be showed by a non-laughling face image. It is presented in Figure 3 and Figure 4.

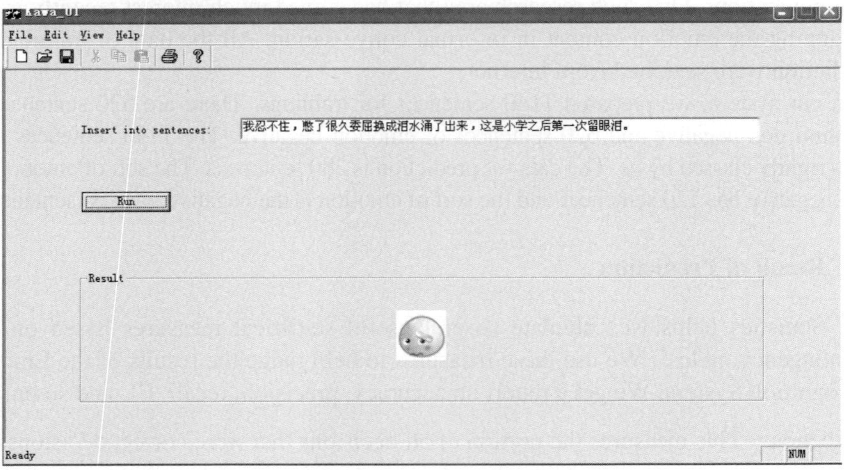

Fig. 3. The sort of emotion is the negative

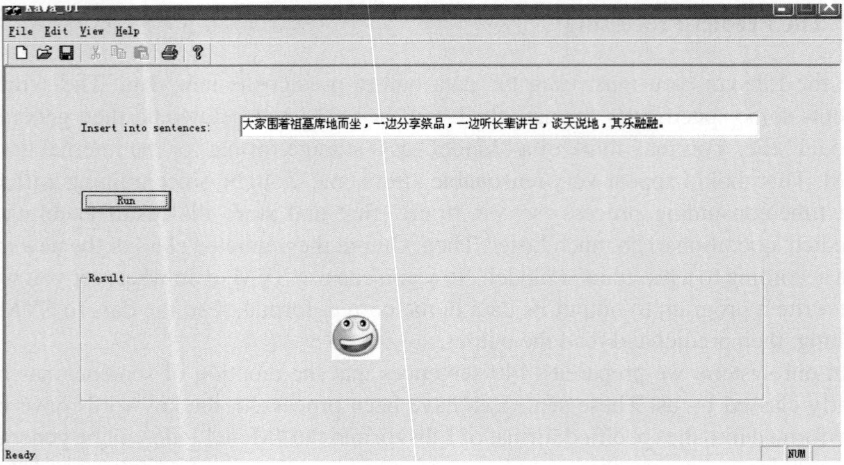

Fig. 4. The sort of emotion is the non-negative

4 Data and Result

4.1 Data of Training and Prediction

With the information revolution well under way, the degree of communication and number of communication methods is growing rapidly. People converse frequently via a number of mediums. One such medium is Internet chat using various instant messaging clients (e.g., AOL Instant Messenger, MSN Messenger, etc). These communications provide an excellent platform to perform research on informal communications. One such research area that has gained much interest recently is that of tagging the emotion content in informal conversation. All the data of training and prediction were searched from internet.

In our system, we prepared 1140 sentences for trainings. There are 520 sentences of emotion non-negative and 620 sentences of emotion negative. The 1140 sentences have been rightly classed by us. The data for prediction is 280 sentences. The sort of emotion for non-negative has 120 sentences and the sort of emotion is the negative has 160 sentences.

4.2 Result of Prediction

The Statistics helps we calculate several useful statistical measures based on 2x2 "contingency tables". We use these measures to help judge the results of the Emotion Recognition System. We get a report on accuracy, precision, recall, F1, and so on.

Accuracy-This measures the portion of all decisions that were correct decisions.
Precision-This measures the portion of the assigned categories that were correct.
Recall-This measures the portion of the correct categories that were assigned.
F1-This measures an even combination of precision and recall. It is defined as 2*p*r/(p+r).

The precision, recall and F1 of non-negative and negative were presented in Table1. The accuracy of non-negative and negative was presented in Table2. Experiments showed that this method could achieve better results in practice.

Table 1. The precision, recall and F1

The sort of emotion	predict data number	rightly predict data number	precision	recall	F1
non-negative	120	109	90.8%	82%	86.2%
negative	160	136	85%	92.5%	88.6%

Table 2. The accuracy

The number of train data	The number of predict data	The number of rightly predict data	accuracy
1140	280	245	87.5%

5 Conclusions

This paper outlines a method that applied the emotion classification technique for using the Support Vector Machines for emotion recognition. The training set and testing set were constructed to verify the effect of this Emotion Recognition System. The result showed that this method has potential in the emotion recognition field.

6 Future Works

Now, in our system the sort of emotion is only non-negative and negative. There's plenty of the emotion classification in fact. for instance ,"anger", "frustration", "boredom", "blessedness", "happiness" , "pleasure" and so on. In the future, we want to construct more emotion classification to recognise the emotions.

We believe that there are many applications that need a system able to recognizing emotions or user attitudes, and this work can help design and develop a real emotion recognition system.

Acknowledgment

This research has been partially supported by the Ministry of Education, Science, Sports and Culture, Grant-in-Aid for Scientific Research (B), 14380166, 17300065, Exploratory Research, 17656128.

References

1. Cowie, R., Douglas ,C.E., Tsapatsoulis , N., Votsis, G., Kollias, S., Fellenz, W., Taylor, W.G. : Emotion Recognition in Human-computer Interaction, IEEE Sig. Proc. Mag. 18 (2001) 32–80
2. Lee, C.M., Narayanan, S., Pieraccini, R.: Recognition of Negative Emotions from the Speech Signal, In Proc. Automatic Speech Recognition and Understanding (2001)
3. Ren, F.J.: Recognizing Human Emotion and Creating Machine Emotion, Information. 8 (2005) 7-20
4. Jiang, P.L., Xiang, H., Ren, F.J., Kuroiwa, S.: An Advanced Mental State Transtion Network and Psychological Experiments, Lecture Notes in Computer Science, Vol. 3824 Springer-Verlag GmbH (2005) 1026-1035
5. http://www.clopinet.com/isabelle/Projects/SVM/applist.html
6. Vapnik, V.: Statistical Learning Thoery. Wiley (1998)
7. Plutchik, R.: The Psychology and Biology of Emotion, HarperCollins College, New York. (1994)
8. Chang, C.C., Lin, C.J.: Libsvm: A Library for Support Vector Machines. Software available at http://www.csie.ntu.edu.tw/~cjlin/libsvm. 2001
9. Cristianini, N., Shaw, E.J.: An Introduction to Support Vector Machines and other Kernel-based Learning Methods, Cambridge University Press. (2000)
10. Haussler ,D.: Convolution Kernels on Discrete Structures, UC Santa Cruz T echnical Report UCS-CRL-99-10 (1999)
11. Shaw, E.J.: Condencestimates of Classification Accuracy on New Examples. In S. Ben-David (ed.), EuroCOLT97, Lecture Notes in Artificial Intelligence.1208 (1997) 260-271
12. Campbell, C.: ESANN2000 Proceedings- European Symposium on Artificial Neural Networks Bruges (Belgium).26-28 April 2000.DFacto. ISBN 2-930307-00-5 27-36

A Proposal for an XML Definition of a Dynamic Spoken Interface for Ambient Intelligence

Germán Montoro[1], Pablo A. Haya[1], Xavier Alamán[1], Ramón López-Cózar[2], and Zoraida Callejas[2]

[1] Dept. of Computer Science and Engineering, Universidad Autónoma de Madrid, Spain
{German.Montoro, Pablo.Haya, Xavier.Alaman}@uam.es
[2] Dept. of Languages and Computer Systems, Universidad de Granada, Spain
{rlopezc, zoraida}@ugr.es

Abstract. Environments based on ambient intelligence require new interfaces that allow a natural interaction. The development of these interfaces has to be done in a standard way, considering the dynamic characteristics of these environments. In this paper we present the results in the development of an intelligent environment and a description language for the automatic generation of a spoken dialogue interface, which adapts to the characteristics of every environment.

1 Introduction

Ambient intelligence and intelligent environments [1] have appeared as a new field of research in the area of user interfaces. One of the aims of the ambient intelligence is to provide a natural interaction between an environment and its inhabitants.

These environments provide new possibilities of interaction [2], offering new challenges to the designers of the interfaces [3]. The environment must help people in their everyday life, offering non-intrusive ways of communication. Therefore classrooms, offices, laboratories and homes should be provided with their own entity and be capable of assisting their occupants in their tasks. Moreover, this interaction must be adapted to the task, the environment, its occupants, and the available devices [4, 5].

Furthermore, considering the heterogeneous and continuously changing characteristics of the intelligent environments, the spoken interface should be created automatically, adapting dynamically to the specific peculiarities of each environment.

In this paper we present the results in the process of definition and implementation of a spoken dialogue interface for intelligent environments that adapts to every domain. Dialogues are automatically constructed and it allows interaction with the environment, controlling the devices by means of a natural language spoken interface.

The generated dialogue system is based on a tree structure, where linguistic parts are represented by nodes. In addition, it contains a set of grammars that are also automatically created and define the possible ways of interaction with the environment. This tree is employed in the processes of comprehension and interaction with the users, that is, to interpret and generate sentences [6].

D.-S. Huang, K. Li, and G.W. Irwin (Eds.): ICIC 2006, LNAI 4114, pp. 711 – 716, 2006.

```
<class name="name" extends="type">
    <property name="propiety_name">
        [set_of_properties, ...]
    </property>
    [, <property name="propiety_name">
        [set_of_properties, ...]
       </property>
    ] ...
</class>
set_of_properties:
<paramSet name="set_name">
    <param name="parameter_name">value</param>
    [, <param name="parameter_name">value</param> ] ...
</paramSet>
```

Fig. 1. Syntax of a Document of Definition of Classes of Entity (DDCE)

The interaction interface is defined by an XML user interface definition language (XML-UIDL). This language has similar characteristics to other UIDLs such as UIML [7] or XIML [8], but provides new functionalities that adapt to the peculiarities of the intelligent environments.

To carry out our research we have built a real intelligent environment. This environment is a laboratory furnished as a living room, provided with several devices. Among them, we can find lights and switches, an electronic lock mechanism, speakers, microphones, a radio tuner, a TV set and RFID cards.

2 Definition of the Entities of an Intelligent Environment

In our system, the possible types of entities that can be found in an intelligent environment are defined in one or several Documents of Definition of Classes of Entities (DDCE). Each class of entity defines the universal characteristics that all the entities of that type must have. Instances of that class of entity inherit the common characteristics and may, if necessary, add new specific characteristics to the instance (see section 3).

Therefore, when a new type of physical device or application is designed, it comes with a DDCE, corresponding to the XML description of the general characteristics of that type of entity.

Each class is defined by its properties (specified by the label *property*) and, optionally, a set of common parameters (represented by the labels *paramSet* and *param*). Parameters can be associated with a specific property or a whole class. Besides, each class inherits the properties of its parent class (using the attribute *extends*). Figure 1 shows the syntax of a DDCE.

There are some universal types of classes, such as, *room, device* or *person*. Every class has to inherit from one of these types or from a class that has inherited from them. The definition of a universal type contains the basic characteristics that can be shared by all the classes of that type.

3 Interface Definition

The definition of the linguistic information associated with the entities is established in a set of documents called Documents of Parameterization of Classes of Entity (DPCE). This information is related to the classes of entity. This way, instances of these types automatically inherit all the defined properties. These instances are described in the Documents of Definition of the Entities of the Environment (DDEE).

The definition of the interface is done in two different steps, which can be carried out by different people at different times:

- Firstly, it is necessary to define the information related to each new class of entity in the DPCE. This is the linguistic information for the interaction, the methods employed for the automation of the system and, optionally, new grammar templates. This information is defined once and shared by all the entities of the same type.
- Secondly, the entities that can be found in the environment and their type are defined in the DDEE. The linguistic information of each entity of the environment is provided by the definition of the classes of entities at the DPCE. This way, in many cases, to create a spoken dialogue interface it is only necessary to define in the DDEE which elements are present in the environment. It is not required to modify or add any kind of additional linguistic information. Even so, the information inherited by each entity can also be parameterized, adapting it to the special characteristics of the environment.

3.1 Definition of the Linguistic Information Associated to the Classes of Entities

As mentioned above, each class of entity has its own linguistic information that establishes all the possible interactions that can be accomplished with the entities of that type. This information is classified in seven possible linguistic parts:

- Verb part (VP). It describes the actions that can be taken with the entity.
- Object part (OP). It establishes the possible names that the entities can take.
- Location part (LP). It describes the physical situation of the entity in the environment.
- Indirect object part (IOP). It specifies who receives the specified action.
- Modal part (MODALP). It describes how the action can be carried out.
- Quantification part (QP). It defines a value or amount that is applied to the action.
- Modifier part (MP). It adds new information to some of the previous parts.

The linguistic information associated with the classes of entities is defined in the DPCE. Later, this information will be shared by all the entities of that type defined in the DDEE. Therefore two entities of the same type inherit the same linguistic information and can be later parameterized depending on the specific characteristics of the entity in the environment.

In order to add the information related to the oral interface it is necessary to attach a set of parameters under a *dialogue* class label. Next, there will be an *action* parameter for every action that can be taken with the entity and, for each of them, one

```
<class name="name">
    <property name="property">
        <paramSet name="dialogue">
            <param name="action1"> action_name </param>
            <param name="skeleton1"> Part Word [, Part Word ]...
            </param>
             [, <param name="skeleton2"> Part Word
                 [, Part Word ]...
                 </param> ] ...
             [, <param name="skeletonm"> Part Word
                 [, Part Word ]...
                 </param> ] ...
        </paramSet>
    </property>
</class>
Part:
VP | OP | LP | IOP | MODALP | QP | MP
```

Fig. 2. Syntax of the linguistic information attached to the DPCE

or several *skeleton* parameters that define the possible skeletons of sentences that can be employed to invoke the action. The syntax is shown in figure 2.

The *action* parameters identify a new action and contain the description of the action that can be realized. The skeletons of sentences are identified by the *skeleton* parameter and hold the keywords employed to build the sentences that will invoke the associated action. Each keyword must be preceded by the linguistic part that it represents (*VP, OP, LP, IOP, MODALP, QP* or *MP*). It is possible to specify synonyms in a linguistic part writing two or more consecutive words. Sentence skeletons can begin with any linguistic part and be repeated as many times as it is necessary.

This document can be edited and modified to adapt to different oral ways of communication. For instance, some synonyms can be added or removed to adapt the interaction to the dialect of different regions. The interaction is easily definable and reconfigurable and can change, grow or adapt to new necessities in a straightforward way. Therefore, it is not necessary to modify the implementation of the dialogue interface, rather it is sufficient to edit and modify the definitions in the DPCE to make the changes available in the new interface.

3.2 Definition of the Instances of Entity

With the definition of the linguistic information associated with the classes of entities, and considering that all the entities of the same type share the same possibilities of interaction, most of the time it is only necessary to define which entities can be found in an environment to automatically obtain a customized speech interface.

This definition of the elements that can be found in an environment is written in the DDEE following the syntax showed in Figure 3.

Nevertheless, sometimes it will be necessary to specify linguistic information related to the specific environment in which the interface is created. This is the case, for instance, of an environment in which there are several entities of the same type, making necessary the addition of new information to differentiate between them.

```
<instances>
    instante_definition
    [, instante_definition ] ...
</instances>

instante_definition:
<entity name="name" type="entity_class"/>
[, <entity name="name" type="entity_class"/> ] ...
```

Fig. 3. Syntax of the Document of Definition of the Entities of the Environment (DDEE)

A similar situation arises with specific characteristics of the entities in a concrete environment, such as color, size, position, etc.

To solve this problem, it is possible to define a Document of Parameterization of the Entities of the Environment (DPEE), which allows the stipulation of new linguistic information related to a specific entity. To do this, it is required to append the parameter *add* to the properties which will receive the new information. Next, the attribute can be followed by a number that points out the number of the sentence skeleton where the new information must be attached. It may also be followed by the word *all.* Tshis specifies that the information should be added to every sentence skeleton in that property. Figure 4 shows the syntax of the linguistic parameterization of a property in an entity.

Once again, this is done to permit the configuration, description, modification and adaptation of the linguistic interactions in a homogeneous and straightforward way.

After the linguistic information associated with the classes of entities is defined in the DPCE, the designer of the environment interface only has to declare which entities are present in the environment, employing the DDEE. This designer or others will be able to modify these definitions, employing the DPEE and adapting the interface to a specific environment.

This information is gathered and merged in the Document of Description of the Environment (DDE), which is employed for the automatic generation of the spoken dialogue interface.

The definition of the linguistic information is carried out in a similar fashion as the definition of the entities, their properties and possible new interfaces. This way, the system provides a homogeneous and standard mechanism for the definition of the environment and its characteristics, including the interfaces.

```
<entity name="name">
    <property name="property">
        <paramSet name="dialogue">

            <param name="add_(1, all)">value</param>
            [ , <param name="add_2">value</param> ] ...

        </paramSet>
    </property>
</entity>
```

Fig. 4. Syntax of the linguistic parameterization in a DPEE

4 Automatic Generation of the Spoken Dialogue Interface

The linguistic information obtained from the DDE allows the automatic creation of a spoken dialogue interface which is adapted to the characteristics of the environment.

The creation process is comprised of two parallel steps. Firstly, the system creates a set of proper grammar for the interaction with the system. Secondly, it builds a linguistic tree employed for the interpretation and generation of sentences.

In order to automatically create the interface, the system reads the information stored in the DDE. For each one of the entities represented in the document (that is, for each of the entities of the environment), it obtains the linguistic information associated to the class of entity and, if necessary, it adds the new specific linguistic information for that entity.

At the same time, the system builds the linguistic tree. This process begins with an empty root node. Each of the parts of the sentence skeletons associated with the entities is transformed into information that is later attached to the tree. This can be done in the form of a new node or adjoining information to an existing one.

When the system finds a part with several synonyms it creates a node for each of them. The following children of that sentence skeleton will hang from each of them.

Acknowledgments

This paper has been funded by the Spanish Ministry of Science and Education, project number TIN2004-03140.

References

1. Remagnino, P., Foresti, G.L., Ellis, T. (Eds.): Ambient Intelligence: A Novel Paradigm. Springer Verlag (2005)
2. Weiser, M.: The World Is Not a Desktop. ACM Interactions. 1 (1994) 7-8
3. Shafer, S., Brumitt, B., Cadiz, J.J.: Interaction Issues in Context-Aware Intelligent Environments. Human-Computer Interaction. 16 (2001) 363-378
4. Paternò, F., Santoro, C.: One Model, Many Interfaces. In Proceedings of CADUI (2002)
5. Rayner, M., Lewin, I., Gorrell, G., Boye, J.: Plug and Play Speech Understanding. 2nd SIGdial Workshop on Discourse and Dialogue (2001)
6. Germán Montoro, Pablo A. Haya, Xavier Alamán.: Context Adaptive Interaction with an Automatically Created Spoken Interface for Intelligent Environments. INTELLCOMM 04. Bangkok, Thailand. November (2004)
7. Ali, M.A., Pérez-Quiñones, M.A., Abrams, M., Shell, E.: Building Multi-Platform User Interfaces with UIML. In Proceedings of CADUI. (2002)
8. Puerta, A., Eisenstein, J.: XIML: A Universal Language for User Interfaces. White paper. Available at http://www.ximl.org/Docs.asp. (2001)

Intelligent Interface for Recognition and Verification of Natural Language Commands

Maciej Majewski and Wojciech Kacalak

Technical University of Koszalin,
Department of Mechanical Engineering
Raclawicka 15-17, 75-620 Koszalin, Poland
{maciej.majewski, wojciech.kacalak}@tu.koszalin.pl

Abstract. New applications of artificial neural networks are capable of recognition and verification of effects and the safety of commands given by the operator of the technological device. In this paper, a review of selected issues is carried out in relation to estimation of results and safety of the operator's commands as well as the supervision of the process. A view is offered of the complexity of effect analysis and safety assessment of commands given by the operator using neural networks. The first part of the paper introduces a new concept of modern supervising systems of the process using a natural language human-machine interface and discusses general topics and issues. The second part is devoted to a discussion of more specific topics of automatic command verification that has led to interesting new approaches and techniques.

1 Intelligent Two-Way Communication by Voice

The advantages of intelligent two-way voice communication between the technological devices and the operator in Fig. 1 include the following [1,3]:

- More resistance from the operator's errors and more efficient supervising of the process with the chosen level of supervision automation.
- Elimination of scarcities of the typical co-operation between the operator and the technological device.
- Achieving a higher level of organization realization of the technological process equipped with the intelligent two-way voice communication system, which is relevant for its efficiency and production humanization.
- No need of an operator being present at the work stand by the technological device (any distance from the technological device) [7].

The intelligent two-way voice communication layer in Fig. 2 is equipped with the following intelligent mechanisms: operator identification, recognition of words and complex commands, command syntax analysis, command result analysis, command safety assessment, technological process supervision, and also operator reaction assessment [2].

D.-S. Huang, K. Li, and G.W. Irwin (Eds.): ICIC 2006, LNAI 4114, pp. 717–723, 2006.

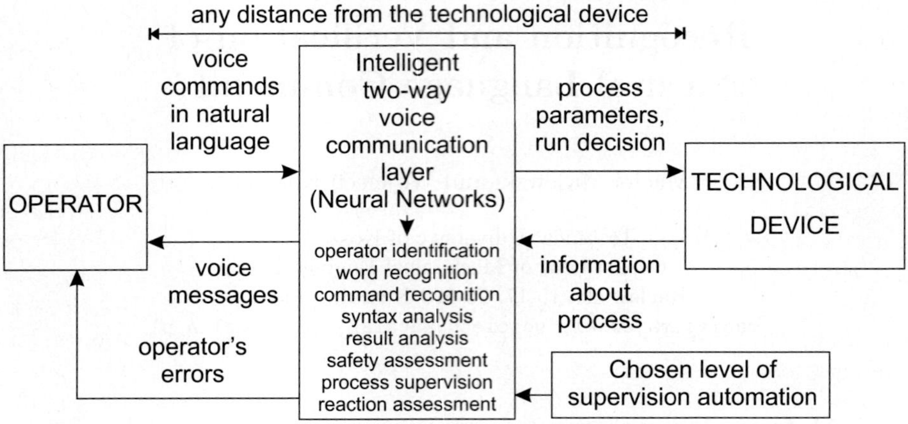

Fig. 1. General scheme of intelligent two-way voice communication between the technological device and the operator

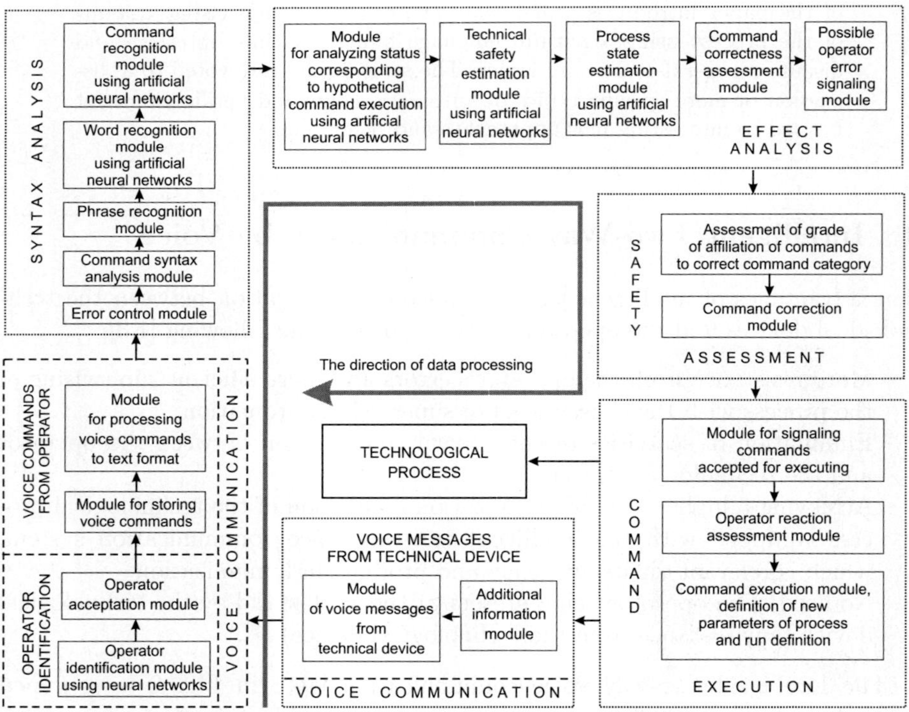

Fig. 2. Scheme of the intelligent layer of two-way voice communication

2 Command Safety Estimation

The effect analysis module, shown in Fig. 3a, makes analysis of the recognised command. The technical safety of the technological device is checked by analysing the state of execution of the commands required to have been done as well as the commands to execute in subsequent decisions. The process parameters to be modified by executing the command are checked and the allowable changes of the parameter values are determined. The analysis of the parameter values is based on the technological process features. The values of the parameter changes are the input signals of the neural network of the process state assessment system. The neurons of the neural network represent solutions to the diagnostics problem. The neural network also makes an estimation of the level of safety of the recognised command. The system for checking the state of the automatic device for grinding small ceramic elements is shown in Fig. 3c, before executing the subsequent commands presented in Fig. 3d. The technological safety assessment system, shown in Fig. 3b, is based on a neural network which is trained with the model of work of the technological device. New values of the process parameters are the input signals of the neural network [6]. As the work result of the system, voice messages from the technological device to the operator about the possibility of executing the command are produced [4,5].

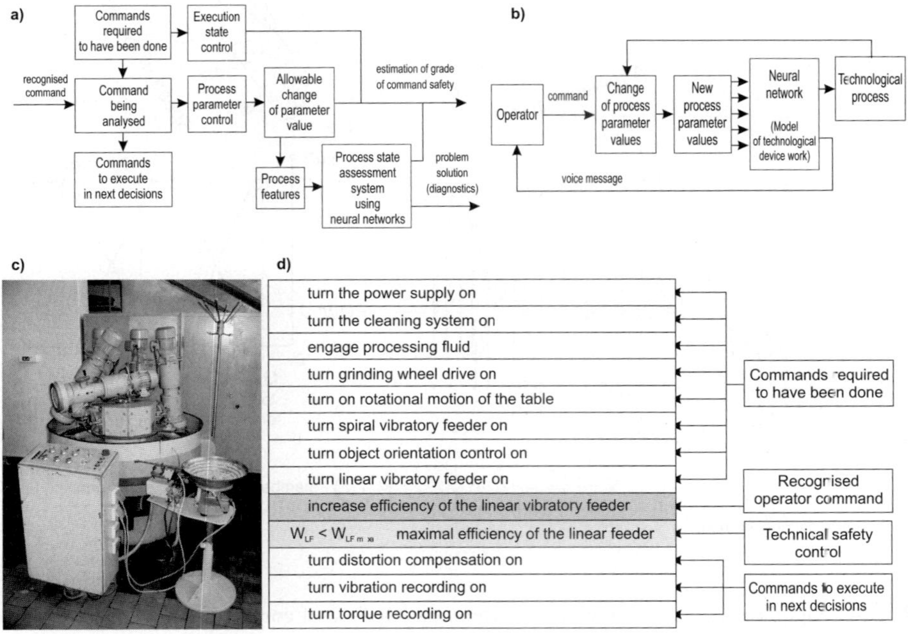

Fig. 3. Scheme of the command effect analysis and safety assessment system

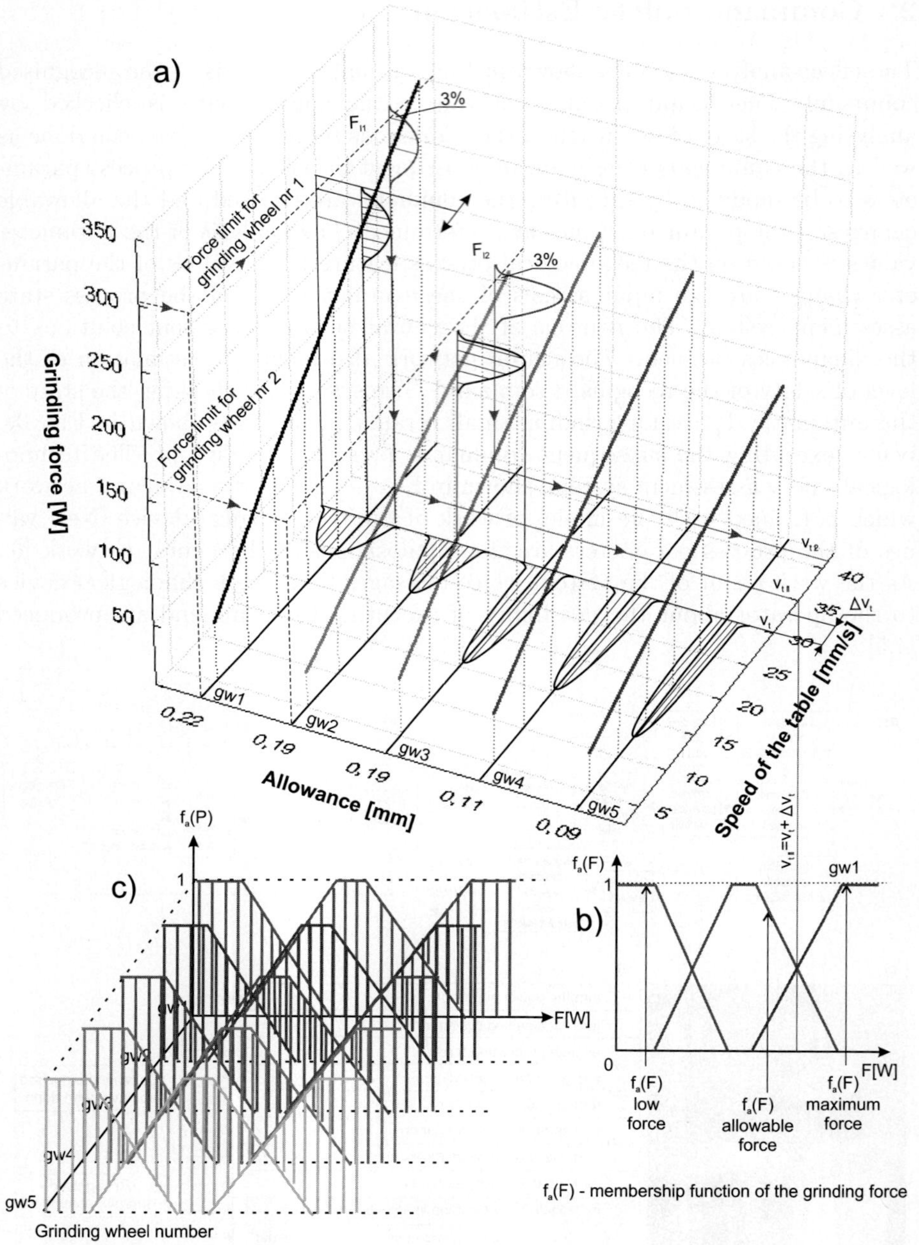

Fig. 4. Algorithm for assessing the technological safety of commands based on the real technological process

An algorithm was created for assessing the technological safety of commands. In Fig. 4, the lines represent force dependence on the grinding process parameters for particular grinding wheels. Based on the specified criteria, the grinding force limit is determined for each grinding wheel. Based on the grinding force limit, the table speed limit is assigned. According to the operator's command, if the increase in speed makes the speed of the table smaller than the smallest speed determined from the force limit for all the grinding wheels, then the command is safe to be executed.

3 Research Results

The simulation set of the technological device diagnostics and the process state assessment, built for creating and training artificial neural networks is shown in Fig. 5a. The neural networks are trained with the model of the technolcgical

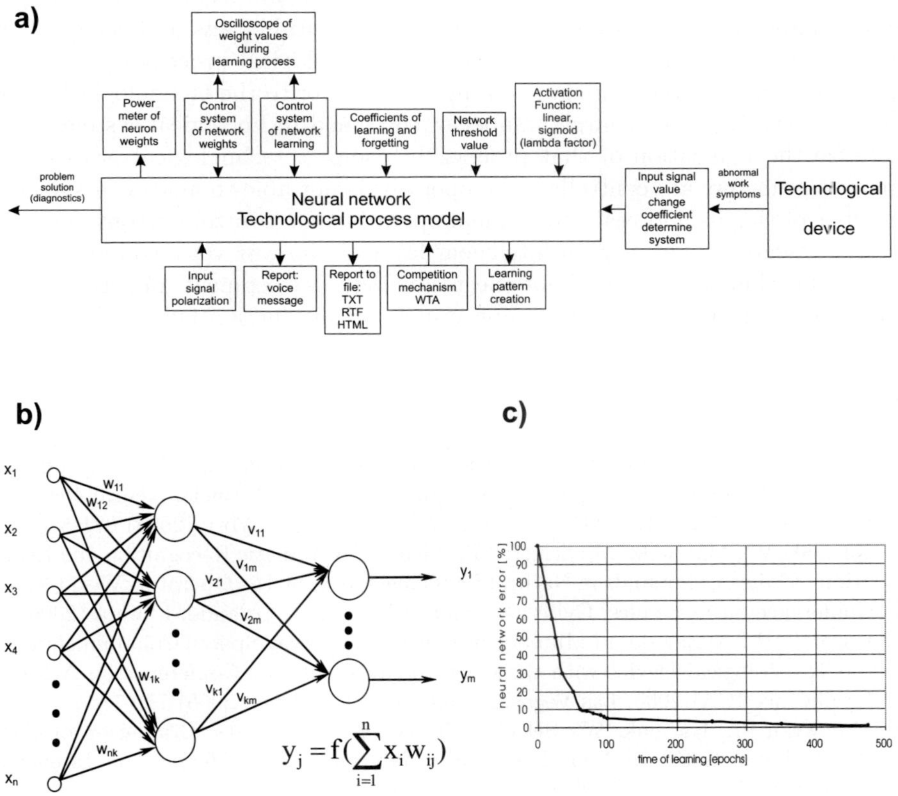

Fig. 5. Neural network simulations of the technological process models, neural network architecture and error rate

process. The applied neural network architecture is presented in Fig. 5b. The networks consist of two layers of neurons with the competitive mechanism.

The ability of the neural network to learn to recognise specific process states depends on the number of learning epochs. The specified time of learning enables the network to minimize the error so that it could work more efficiently. Based on the research, the following conclusion has been reached as shown in Fig. 5c.

Error rate is about 20% at learning time equals 50 epochs and 5% at 100 epochs. The error rate dropped by about 90% after training with 60 series of all patterns.

4 Conclusions and Perspectives

In the automated processes of production, the condition for safe communication between the operator and the technological device is analyzing the state of the technological device and the process before the command is given and using artificial intelligence for assessment of the technological effects and safety of the command. In operations of the automated technological processes, many process states and various commands from the operator to the technological device can be distinguished. A large number of combined technological systems characterize the realization of that process. In complex technological processes, if many parameters are controlled, the operator is not able to analyse a sufficient number of signals and react by manual operations on control buttons. The aim of this research to develop an intelligent layer of two-way voice communication is difficult, but the prognosis of the technology development and its first use shows a significant efficiency in supervision and production humanisation.

References

1. Kacalak, W., Majewski, M.: Recognition and Safety Estimation of Voice Commands in Natural Language Using Artificial Neural Networks. Artificial Neural Networks in Engineering ANNIE 2004 St. Louis. ASME Press New York (2004) 831-836
2. Kacalak, W., Majewski, M.: Selected Problems of Automatic Recognition and Evaluation of Voice Commands in Natural Language Given by the Operator. World Multi-Conference on Systemics, Cybernetics and Informatics, Orlando, Florida (2005)
3. Kacalak, W., Majewski, M.: Intelligent Layer of Two-Way Speech Communication of the Technological Device with the Operator. International Conference on Artificial Intelligence ICAI 2005, Las Vegas, Nevada. CSREA Press (2005) 779-785
4. Majewski, M., Kacalak, W.: Selected Problems of Automatic Evaluation of Commands Using Artificial Neural Networks. International Conference on Intelligent Computing ICIC2005, Hefei Anhui, China (2005) 3605-3614
5. Majewski, M., Kacalak, W., Selected Problems of Automatic Evaluation of Commands Using Artificial Neural Networks. Engineering Mechanics International Journal for Theoretical and Applied Mechanics 12(3) (2005) 185-192

6. Principe, J. C., Euliano, N. R., and Lefebvre, W. C.: Neural and Adaptive Systems: Fundamentals through Simulations. John Wiley and Sons Inc., New York (2000)
7. O'Shaughnessy, D.: Speech Communications: Human and Machine. IEEE Press, New York (2000)

Intrusion Detection Based on Data Mining*

Jian Yin, Fang Mei, and Gang Zhang

Department of Computer Science, Sun Yat-Sen University, Guangzhou 510275, China
issjyin@mail.sysu.edu.cn

Abstract. Many traditional algorithms use single metric generated by multi-events to detect intrusion by comparison with a certain threshold. In this paper we present a metric vector-based algorithm to detect intrusion while introducing the sample distance for both discrete and continuous data in order to improve the algorithm on heterogeneous dataset. Experiments on MIT lab Data show that the proposed algorithm is effective and efficient.

1 Introduction

Recently, data mining methods are widely used in intrusion detection especially in host audit data analysis. There are many famous probabilistic algorithm such as Decision Tree, Hotelling's T2, Chi-Square, first-order and high-order Markov model [1],[2]. These algorithms focus on some data features to mark anomaly state. But these algorithms mostly used single metric generated by multi-events in order to detect intrusion by comparison with a certain threshold. On the other hand, some research have focused on the redefinition of distance function such as Minkowsky, Euclidean and so on, but there is of no effect for both discrete and continuous data.

This paper is focused on the expression of multiple events vector on intrusion detection with a formalized model. First we propose a generating algorithm of multiple events vector and a definition based on the bizarrerie distance function[3], and then generalize the algorithm on heterogeneous dataset, last present the corresponding detection algorithm and compare with the traditional algorithms.

2 Multi Event-Based Vector on Heterogeneous Dataset

For the description of single event, we only need introduce a variable X, which can describe the type of a certain event in a certain moment. If there are n types of events, then there may be n values about this variable. For frequency property of multi events, we use an array of random variables, $(X_1,X_2,,,,,X_n)$, to represent the frequency of n different types of events for a given sequence of events.

* This work is supported by the National Natural Science Foundation of China (60573097), Natural Science Foundation of Guangdong Province (05200302,04300462), Research Foundation of National Science and Technology Plan Project (2004BA721A02), Research Foundation of Science and Technology Plan Project in Guangdong Province (2005B10101032) and Research Foundation of Disciplines Leading to Doctorate degree of Chinese Universities(20050558017).

D.-S. Huang, K. Li, and G.W. Irwin (Eds.): ICIC 2006, LNAI 4114, pp. 724 – 729, 2006.

Many algorithms have a good performance on congeneric dataset, but the effect on heterogeneous dataset is not good. This paper generalizes the traditional algorithm based on the research result of Bernhard Scholkopf[4],[5],[6], combined with the definition of the bizarrerie distance function [6] on heterogeneous dataset which is proposed by D. Randall Wilson. First we give the distance definition on both discrete attributes and continuous attributes of heterogeneous dataset.

Definite 1. Formalized distance: Let x and y be two continuous data on heterogeneous dataset X, and the ath attributes are x_a and y_a, then the Formalized distance of the two points on the ath attribute is: $\text{normalized\_diff}_a(x, y) = \frac{|x - y|}{4\sigma_a}$, where,$\sigma_a$ is the variation of the ath attribute on the dataset.

Definite 2. VDM (Value Difference Metric): Let x and y be two discrete data on heterogeneous dataset X, and the ath attributes are x_a and y_a, then VDM distance of the two points on the ath attribute is: $\text{normalized\_vdm}_a(x, y) = \sum_{c=1}^{C} \left(\left| \frac{N_{a,x,c}}{N_{a,x}} - \frac{N_{a,y,c}}{N_{a,y}} \right| \right)^2$,where, $N_{a,x}$ is the count of the data whose value of the ath attribute is x_a in the whole dataset X, and $N_{a,x},c$ is the count of the data whose value of the ath attribute is x_a and the output type is c. c is the output types of dataset.

3 Mining Intrusion Data

3.1 Multi-event-Based Vector Generation

We use vector X $(X_1,X_2,\ldots.X_n)$ to represent n event types of original hosts audit dataset. In Chi-square multivariate test, the detection value is calculated as below:

$x^2 = \sum_{i=1}^{n} \frac{(xi - Avg(xi))^2}{Avg(xi)}$. In this algorithm, only the mean Vector X is considered. And the detection is made only by the mean shift on one or more of the n variables.

From the formula above we can see that metrics calculated from multiple events in event vector have been summarized to a single value. This will hide details information from individual events. To preserve such details, we provide a new algorithm to calculate a vector to represent per event-based metric. The output of our algorithm is a vector based on the input mean vector. So we expand the summarized procedure to a vector. The calculation of per event-based vector is same as Chi-square algorithm. The vector is represented as below:

$$\left[\frac{x_1 - Avg(x_1)^2}{Avg(x_1)}, \frac{x_2 - Avg(x_2)^2}{Avg(x_2)}, \ldots, \frac{x_n - Avg(x_n)^2}{Avg(x_n)} \right]. \tag{1}$$

Each term in our vector represents a certain event type in host audit dataset. With this vector, we get the character of audit dataset per event instead of just a summarized value.

3.2 The Generalized Vector on Heterogeneous Dataset

The process of heterogeneous data on the sample dataset is always a difficult point on intrusion detection, D. Randal Wilson proposed a more efficient distance function HVDM (Heterogeneous Value difference metric)[6], which could show different impact of detection result for different attributes, and also it can measure the difference effectively between different data.

Given x, y ∈X, then the HVDM distance between x and y is defined as:

$$H(x, y) = \sum_{a=1}^{m} [d_a(x_a, y_a)]^2 ,$$

If the ath attribute is discrete, then $d_a(x, y) = \text{normalized\_diff}_d(x, y)$.

If the ath attribute is continuous, then $d_a(x, y) = \text{normalized\_vdm}_d(x, y)$.

Based on above, we generalize the formula (1) into formula (2) as below:

$$\left[\frac{(H(x_1 - Avg(x_1)))^2}{Avg(x_1)}, \frac{(H(x_2 - Avg(x_2)))^2}{Avg(x_2)}, ..., \frac{(H(x_n - Avg(x_n)))^2}{Avg(x_n)}\right]. \tag{2}$$

In order to compare these terms with a single threshold, a formalized procedure is necessary. We use geometric mean value to formalize this vector. Let: $pAvg = \sqrt[n]{Avg(x_1)Avg(x_{2)}...Avg(x_n)}$, Let vector (2) be $(p_1, p_{2,...}p_n)$, then the formalized vector is formed as following: $\left(\frac{P_1}{pAvg + p_1}, \frac{P_2}{pAvg + p_2}, ..., \frac{P_n}{pAvg + p_n}\right)$.

3.3 Mining Anomaly Status

Here, we use two methods. The first is area comparison method based on the area rounded by formalized vector curve and X- and Y-axis. The second one is curve fitting. For area comparison method, we use integral to calculate the area. We use a curve to describe result vector and calculate the area lapped with X-axis by integral from 0 to n:

$$\int_0^n f(x)dx = \sum_{i=1}^{n}\left(\frac{P_i}{pAvg + P_i} \cdot P_i\right) = \sum_{i=1}^{n}\left[\frac{(P_i)^2}{pAvg + P_i}\right]$$

The result of integral is compared with that of the standard curve (of average mean). A larger result indicates an anomaly status may occur.

For curve fitting method, we do not really calculate the area between standard curves. A discrete point comparison method is used. Only points appeared in the multi-event vector will be used in comparison. If you need, you can email us and ask the detailed C++ codes about this procedure.

4 Experiment Results

4.1 Training and Test Data

We use 1999 DARPA intrusion testing data of the MIT Lincoln Lab as training data. This dataset was obtained from one simulation real network environment, including the normal data and intrusion data. It can be downloaded from the following URL[7],[8]: http://www.ll.mit.edu/IST/ideval/data/1999/1999_data_index.html

This dataset simultaneously provided the training data and the test data. The training dataset includes three week-long trainings data. First week and the third week training data comes from normal behavior, the second week training data contained the attack data. Fourth, the fifth week data is the test data. These test data tested about 201 examples of 56 kinds of intrusions. We provided the primitive BSM model binary output document and the BSM structure document as well as the outer covering original document used in the initialization of BSM audit information [8].

The experimental result was based on the above dataset. First, the training dataset is used to construct the normal frames model. Then, the test data is used to gain the experimental result and provide the ROC curve.

4.2 The Result of Two Kinds of Examine Method

For the area comparison method, we use ROC curve to describe our experiment result. Each point in an ROC curve indicates a pair of the hit rate and the false alarm rate for a signal threshold. By varying the value of the signal threshold, we obtain an ROC curve. The closer the ROC is to the top-left corner of the chart, the better detection performance the intrusion detection algorithm does.

Figure 1 shows the comparison result of Chi-square multivariate test and our multi-event vector area comparison. From the figure we can see that our algorithm is more accurate and more effective than the old one. In this figure, our algorithm uses a formalized process as described in our related work.

Figure 2 shows ROC curve without our formalized process. From the curve we can see that our formalized procedure will increased the accuracy of detection. The reason lies in with our formalized procedure, not only mean shifts but also multi-event counter-relationship have been added to the result vector. Experiment result shows that there may be some internal relationship between events in intrusion detection.

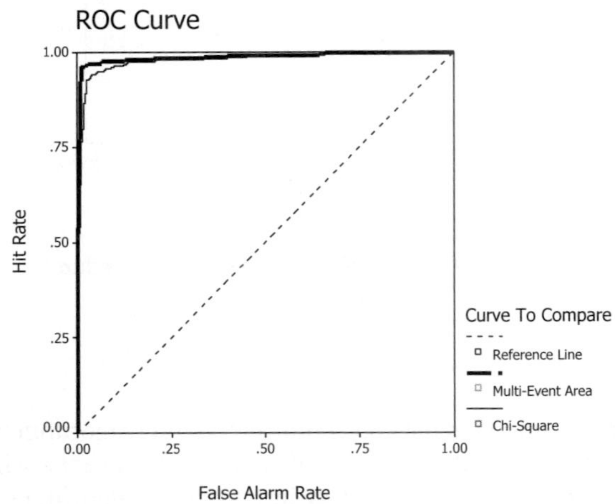

x-axis: false rate   y-axis: hit rate

Fig. 1. Comparison of Chi-Square and Multi-Event Area

For curve fitting method, we observe the related output through the establishment of different threshold value. In between 0% and 100%, find the point leads hit rate that can reach the maximum value. Table 1 listed the hit probability which corresponded under each threshold value.

Comparing the output of the test data with the training data characteristic, we obtained the hit probability which showed in table 1. As can be seen from the table that the best threshold range is between 80% and 90%.

Table 1. The Hit Rate results of different thresholds

Threshold	*Hit Rate*
10%	5.53%
20%	13.81%
30%	23.11%
40%	31.92%
50%	52.00%
60%	61.19%
70%	75.07%
80%	91.12%
90%	80.83%

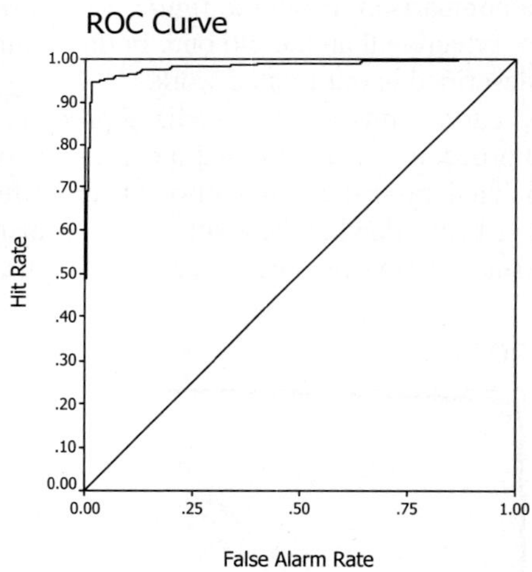

Fig. 2. ROC curve without normalized procedure

5 Conclusion

The paper proposed an intrusion data detection and mining algorithm on heterogeneous dataset. The core idea is based on the use of multi-vector events, which replaced the probability value as the only measurement in traditional algorithms. The concept of distance is introduced and vector dataset is generalized by processing the discrete and continuous attribution distinctively. Experiments show that the measure could describe audit dataset more precisely, the promoted vector on the heterogeneous collection could enhance the accuracy and the validity, while keeping the time and space complexity of original algorithm.

References

1. Ye, N., Li, X. Y., Chen, Q., Syed Masum Emran, Xu, M. M.: Probabilistic Techniques for Intrusion Detection Based on Computer Audit Data. IEEE Transactions on Systems, Man, And Cybernetics—Part A: Systems and Humans, Volume.31, NO.4, (2001)266 – 274
2. Lee, W. K., Stolfo, S.J., Mok, K.W.: A Data Mining Framework for Building Intrusion Detection Models. Security and Privacy, 1999. Proceedings of the 1999 IEEE Symposium , (1999)120 – 132
3. Yoshida, K.: Entropy Based Iintrusion Detection. Communications, Computers and Signal Processing, PACRIM. 2003. IEEE Pacific Rim Conference on, Vol.2, (2003)840 – 843
4. D Randall Wilson, Tony R Martinez: Improved Heterogeneous Distance Functions. Journal of Artificial Intelligence Research, Vol. 6, No.1,(1997) 1-34
5. Bernhard Scholkof, John C Plattz: Estimating the Support of a High-dimensional Distribution. Neurral Computation, Vol.13, No.7, (2001)1443-1472
6. Bernhard Scholkopf: The Kernel Trick for Distance. Microsoft Research, Tech Rep: MSR-TR-2000-51, 2000
7. Bernhard Scholkopf: Statistical Learning and Kernel Methods. Microsoft Research, Tech Rep: MSR-TR-2000-23, 2000
8. Haines, J.W., Rossey, L.M., Lippmann, R.P., Cunningham, R.K.: Extending the DARPA Off-line Intrusion Detection Evaluations. DARPA Information Survivability Conference & Exposition II, DISCEX '01. Proceedings, Vol.1, 12-14 ,(2001)35 – 45
9. http://www.ll.mit.edu/IST/ideval/data/1999/1999_data_index.html
10. Lindqvist, U., Porras, P.A.. eXpert-BSM: A Host-based Intrusion Detection Solution for Sun Solaris. Computer Security Applications Conference, ACSAC 2001. Proceedings 17th Annual, (2001) 240 – 251

Knowledge Representation in a Behavior-Based Natural Language Interface for Human-Robot Communication

Fangju Wang

Department of Computing and Information Science
University of Guelph, Canada
fjwang@cis.uoguelph.ca

Abstract. Service robots are built to help ordinary people in their daily life. The most desirable way for communicating with service robots is through natural language interfaces. In our research, we develop a novel bio-inspired approach, called the *collaborative behavior based approach*, to build a natural language interface between a robot and its human user. In this approach, knowledge about collaborative behaviors of both the robot and its user is applied to solve ambiguity in a natural language. In building a system that is based on knowledge about behaviors, a key issue is representing the knowledge. So far, little research has been done in representing knowledge about behaviors. In this paper, we describe the collaborative behavior based approach, with emphasis on its knowledge representation structures.

1 Introduction

More and more robots have entered ordinary people's homes, offices, stores, etc. to serve people in their daily life. Such robots include those for performing office secretary duties, purchasing goods, guiding visitors in a museum, and delivering meals in a hospital. This kind of robots are usually called *service robots.* According to UNECE, the UN Economic Commission for Europe, the number of service robots will reach about six millions by 2007 to provide a very wide range of services [8].

The users of most service robots are ordinary people like seniors, house wives, office secretaries, shoppers, and tourists. Unlike specially trained operators of industrial robots, users of service robots have less expertise in robotic control and operations. For such users, the most desirable way to control robots is through natural language interfaces, which allow communicating with robots in English, French, Chinese, and so on. A natural language interface translates user instructions into robot control commands.

Work for developing robot natural language interfaces started as early as in 1970s. The early work included [6] and [1]. The more recent work included the projects reported in [7] [2] and [5]. The research efforts have made significant contributions towards creating practical natural language interfaces for robots. However, the techniques are still far from mature. Most of the existing natural

D.-S. Huang, K. Li, and G.W. Irwin (Eds.): ICIC 2006, LNAI 4114, pp. 730–735, 2006.

language interfaces, including those for robots and those for other applications, mainly based on knowledge about the surrounding world. Robot applications were characterized by behaviors and actions. Without knowledge about behaviors and actions, a robot natural language interface can hardly handle problems in practical situations.

One of the most challenging tasks in creating natural language interfaces for robots is handling ambiguity in natural languages. In our research, we develop a novel approach for handling ambiguity in robot natural language interfaces. It is called the *collaborative behavior based approach.* In this approach, knowledge about the behaviors that have happened, that will happen, their temporal relationships, their effects to the surrounding world, etc. is used to solve ambiguity when it occurs. Experiments have showed the initial success of this approach.

A key issue in using knowledge about robot and user behaviors is knowledge representation. The knowledge about historical and future behaviors, as well as their relationships, must be properly represented, so that it can be applied in the process of natural language understanding. Currently, the representation schemes in artificial intelligence and knowledge-based systems were mainly developed for representing knowledge about facts, procedures, events, rules and situations. Little research has been reported that is conducted on representing knowledge about behaviors. In building our behavior-based robot natural language interface, we develop a knowledge representation structure, in which the knowledge about behaviors, the knowledge about the world, and knowledge about parsing, can be integratedly represented. In this paper, we describe the collaborative behavior based approach for building a robot natural language interface, with the emphasis on its knowledge representation structures.

2 Ambiguity in a Robot Natural Language Interface

The task of a robot natural language interface is to transform natural language instructions into robot commands. Ambiguity may occur in every step in natural language processing. Assume we have a service robot working in a kitchen and the user may control the robot using English. The user may tell the robot "Warm the pizza in the microwave oven." After the robot warms the pizza, the user may say "Add some hot pepper". And then the user says "Bring me the pizza with a knife."

Ambiguity may occur in processing all the three instructions. When the first instruction is parsed, phrase "in the microwave oven" may be associated with verb "warm" or noun "pizza", as an adverbial or a noun complement respectively. Two commands may be generated from the two associations: warm the pizza using the microwave oven, or warm the pizza that is in the microwave oven. The other two instructions are ambiguous and vague as well. An objective of this research is to equip the natural language interface with an ability that enables creating the most plausible parse tree when ambiguity exists.

3 Use of Knowledge to Solve Ambiguity

Our approach is characterized by applying a technique of possibility theory to knowledge about the world and behaviors of both the robot and user, in solving ambiguity in user language instructions.

Possibility theory deals with *possibility distributions* of variables that are restricted by fuzzy sets. Let x be a variable taking values in U. x may be restricted by fuzzy set F. We denote such a restriction as $\Re(x, F)$ and call F the *restricting fuzzy set* of x. $\Re(x, F)$ associates a *possibility distribution* with x. The *possibility distribution function*, $\pi_F^x(u)$ denotes the possibility for x to take value u under the restriction of F.

In handling ambiguity in natural language processing, the restricting fuzzy set can be one whose members are parse trees generating sentence S, denoted as $F_S \subset U$, and its membership function μ_{F_S} indicates the plausibility for the members to be parsed from S in terms of both syntax and semantics. The technique of *fuzzy grammar* [4] can be used to associate each parse tree with the plausibility or membership grade in F_S.

A fuzzy grammar can be represented as a quadruple $G = (V_N, V_T, P, s)$ where V_N, V_T, and P are sets of nonterminal symbols, terminal symbols and productions respectively, and s is the starting symbol. Differing from the conventional grammar, a production rule in P is of the form

$$\alpha \xrightarrow{\rho} \beta \ . \tag{1}$$

where α and β are strings in $(V_T \cup V_N)^*$, and $\rho \in [0, 1]$ indicates the plausibility for β to be reduced into α in a reduction action.

When a grammar rule is applied, the plausibility value is decided by using knowledge about the world, and knowledge about the behaviors that happened in the past and will happen in the future. In this section, we discuss how the knowledge is used in solving ambiguity in natural language instructions. For example, the ambiguity in the instruction of "warm the soup in the microwave oven" can be solved by using knowledge about the history: where the robot placed the soup.

For each of the tasks that can be performed by the robot, the natural language interface stores information about historical behaviors and the expected behaviors. By using the information, at any point of time, the interface is able to predict the possible behaviors of both the robot and the user. The knowledge may play decisive roles to solve ambiguity in many situations.

4 Knowledge Representation

4.1 The Knowledge Bases

In the collaborative behavior based approach, we use knowledge about the world, knowledge about history, and knowledge about future behaviors to solve ambiguity in natural language instructions. The knowledge is stored in three knowledge bases. In this section, we describe the data structures of the three knowledge bases. The world knowledge base W is a graph

$$W = \{N, E\} . \tag{2}$$

where N is a set of nodes and E is a set of edges. Every object (instance), including the robot and the user, in the robot world is represented as a node $n \in N$. Each node is associated with its state information. Every $e \in E$ represents a relationship between two objects. For every pair of nodes, there may be one or more edges between them to represent possible relationships. Each $e \in E$ is associated with a pair (l, p), where l denotes the relationship and p is the plausibility value of the relationship between the two objects represented by the two nodes.

The history knowledge base H contains the knowledge about events (including actions) that have happened in the robot world related to operations of the robot. It is also represented as a graph.

$$H = \{N, D\} . \tag{3}$$

where N is the same as in the world knowledge graph, and D is a set of directed edges representing the sequence of events that have happened. When a command has been executed by the robot, an edge is added between the objects that are involved in the execution. Each $d \in D$ is associated with a t value which is the *time stamp* indicating the time the event occurs.

The behavior knowledge base B contains knowledge about behaviors of the robot and user, organized by tasks. That is

$$B = \{V_i\} . \tag{4}$$

where V_i represents the knowledge about how the i'th task is performed. V_i is structured as a graph

$$V_i = \{N_i, B_i\} . \tag{5}$$

where $N_i \subseteq N$ is the set of all the nodes involved in the behavior, including the robot and the user, and B_i is a set of directed edges representing the ordered sequence of behaviors to be performed for providing the i'th task:

$$B_i = \{b_{i,1}, b_{i,2}, ..., b_{i,n}\} . \tag{6}$$

where $b_{i,j}$ $(j = 1, 2, ..., n)$ is an directed edge in the behavior knowledge graph, representing the j'th behavior in the sequence.

For behavior $b_{i,j}$,

$$\{b_{i,j+1}, b_{i,j+2}, ..., b_{i,n}\} . \tag{7}$$

is called the sequence of *predicted behaviors* relative to it.

4.2 Representation of Parsing Structures

The parser of our system is built on a modified Earley dynamic programming algorithm[3]. In parsing a sentence of l words, the Earley algorithm creates a *chart* of $l+1$ entries. A chart entry contains a number of chart *states*. A chart state represents the state of using a certain grammar rule, say $\alpha \rightarrow \beta_1...\beta_n$, to parse a range of words, that is, a sub-sequence. The kth $(0 \leq k \leq l)$ chart entry contains the states of parsing sub-sequences up to the kth word. A state may be "complete" or "incomplete". A complete state implies that the rule has "covered" (i.e. parsed) the sub-sequence, while an incomplete state implies that the rule is being used to parse a sub-sequence. The state of using a rule is decided by the position of a *dot* on the right hand side of the rule. When the dot is to the right end, that is, $\alpha \rightarrow \beta_1...\beta_n\bullet$, the state is complete, otherwise incomplete. The initial position of the dot is to the left end, that is $\alpha \rightarrow \bullet\beta_1...\beta_n$. Each time when a subsequence has been parsed as a syntactical constituent β_i $(1 \leq i \leq n)$, the dot jumps over that β_i towards the right end.

The chart is implemented as a 3-D table Π. The kth layer of the table is the kth entry of the chart. Element $\Pi[a,i,k]$ stores the state of using the ath rule to parse the sub-sequence between the ith and the kth words $(0 \leq i,k \leq l$ and $i \leq k)$. The data structure of table element $\Pi[a,i,k]$ is $(\delta, \rho, \tau_u, \tau_d)$, where δ is the position of the dot, ρ is the plausibility value for applying the ath rule to the sub-sequence between the ith word and the kth word, τ_u is a set of pointers between the element and elements in upper chart entries, and τ_d is a set of pointers between the element and elements in lower chart entries. If $\Pi[a,i,k]$ contains an incomplete state, ρ, τ_u, and τ_d are null values.

When the entire sequence has been parsed, if we can find an a such that $\Pi[a,0,l]$ contains a complete state, we can create a parse tree for the sequence. If we can find more than one such table element, we have multiple parse trees for the same sequence.

5 Selection of the Most Plausible

When we use a bottom-up parsing technique, as we mentioned, at any point of time before the completion of parsing an instruction, the content of the parse stack can be represented as a forest. When the parsing is completed, the forest becomes a single parse tree. Assume we are at a point of the process of parsing an instruction, and the parse stack content can be represented as forest Fr. Also assume there are two different rules that can be applied to the parse stack: $\alpha^1 \stackrel{\rho^1}{\rightarrow} \beta^1$ and $\alpha^2 \stackrel{\rho^2}{\rightarrow} \beta^2$. Usually, different rules may reduce different βs into different αs. Thus, after the two rules are applied, we have two different parse stacks, and contents of them can be represented by two different forests Fr^1 and Fr^2.

To evaluate the plausibility of applying the two rules, we map Fr^1 and Fr^2 into two graphs G^1 and G^2. The node sets of both G^1 and G^2 are subsets of N, the node set of the knowledge bases. The edges in the two graphs represent the relationships between nodes, which have been identified.

In calculating ρ^1 and ρ^2, we can use the knowledge about the future behaviors when possible. First of all, we identify from knowledge base H the task (or service) B_i that the robot is currently perform, and also identify from H the lastest action that has been performed by the robot, denoted as d ($d \in D$ of H). We use a graph matching method to search knowledge base B to locate edge $b_{i,j} \in B_i$ that corresponds to d. Then we find the predicted behavior sequence relative to $b_{i,j}$: $\{b_{i,j+1}, b_{i,j+2}, ..., b_{i,n}\} \in B_i$.

Assume that $e^1 \in G^1$ and $e^2 \in G^2$ correspond to the applications of the two rules. An e may represent an action or static relationship between objects in the robot world. To evaluate the ρ value for applying a rule, we match the resulted edge with the predicted behavior sequence, as well as knowledge base W.

6 Conclusion

We develop a new approach for building robot natural language interfaces. This approach is based on the nature of robot applications, that is, the behaviors of both the robot and user are the center of a robot application. Representing knowledge about behaviors is essential to our approach. In our research, we also address a new topic in developing intelligent systems (or knowledge based systems): representation of knowledge about behaviors. The structure is adequate for the current application of our approach. To better use knowledge about behaviors, we will need a better knowledge representation structure for behaviors, as well as their interactions, their temporal relationships, their effects to the robot and user, their effects to the world, and so on. We will include the development of the knowledge representation structure in our future work.

References

1. Amori, R. D.: A Multiple Cooperating Intelligent Agents Project Progress Repost. Proceedings of the 1988 ACM Sixteenth Annual Conference on Computer science (1988) 454–461
2. Fischer, C., Buss, M., and Schmidt, G.: Human-Robot-Interface for Intelligent Service Robot Assistance. Proceedings of IEEE International Workshop on Robot and Human Communication (1996) 177-180
3. Jurafsky, D., and Martin, J. H.: Speech and Language Processing. Prentice Hall (2000)
4. Lee, E. T., and Zadeh, L. A.: Note on Fuzzy Languages. Information Science Vol.1 (1969) 421-434
5. Perzanowski, D., Schultz, A. C. and Adams, W.: Integrating Natural Language and Gesture in a Robotics Domain. Proceedings of the IEEE ISIC/CIRA/ISAS Joint Conference (1998) 247-252
6. Sondheimer, N. K.: Spatial Reference and Natural Language Machine Control. International Journal of Man-Machine Studies, Vol.8 (1976) 329-336
7. Torrance, M. C.: Natural Communication with Robots. Department of Electrical Engineering and Computer Science, MIT (1994)
8. UNECE: 2004 World Robotics Survey (2004) http://www.unece.org

Method Combining Rule-Based and Corpus-Based Approaches for Oracle-Bone Inscription Information Processing

Huiying Cai[1], Minghu Jiang[1], Beixing Deng[2], and Lin Wang[3]

[1] Lab of Computational Linguistics, School of Humanities and Social Sciences, Tsinghua University, Beijing, 100084, China
[2] Dept. of Electronic Eng., Tsinghua University, Beijing, 100084, China
[3] School of Electronic Eng., Beijing Univ. of Post and Telecom, Beijing, 100876, China
jiang.mh@tsinghua.edu.cn

Abstract. Word segmentation and part of speech (POS) tagging are basis of processing oracle-bone inscription by using computer. It is hard to build a large tagged oracle-bone inscription corpus with grammar information. This is an obstacle if we want to use statistical method. In this paper, we propose to solve both problems with methods combining corpus-based and rule-based approaches. The accuracy of segmentor and tagger are 98.33% and 96.75% respectively. Our experiment result shows that the combining method is quite practical for processing the oracle-bone inscription, especially when the corpus is too sparse. In the end, we briefly discuss how to use the tagged result to complete syntax analysis with rule-based method.

1 Introduction

Oracle-bone inscription is a kind of character of Shang Dynasty, which was called the archives of ancient China, it's helpful for the modern people to learn ancient society.

Several organizations have made important contribution to computerizing oracle-bone data. However, so far no one has tried to study on automatic recognizing and explaining oracle-bone characters with computer, this is a rising issue which can advance the study of oracle-bone inscription, even the whole study of ancient writing.

This paper mainly discusses on how to achieve segmentation and part of speech (POS) tagging of oracle-bone inscription. In the end, we briefly discuss how to use the tagging result to complete syntax analysis with rule-based method.

2 Glossarial Features

The oracle-bone characters are 3,000 years old, its system is relatively perfect in common with modern Chinese character system in several places.

The academe has agreed that most oracle-bone inscription characters and words were identical; the amount of monosyllabic words is much larger than that of polysyllabic words. Most of the polysyllabic words are nouns (especially proper noun), a few of them are numeral, verb, preposition etc.

D.-S. Huang, K. Li, and G.W. Irwin (Eds.): ICIC 2006, LNAI 4114, pp. 736 – 741, 2006.

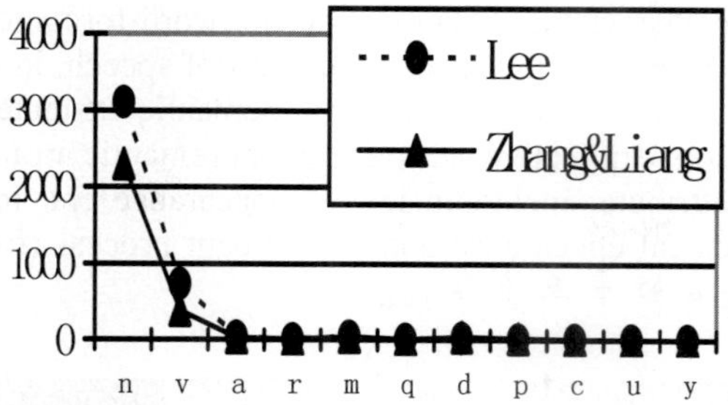

Fig. 1. Distribution of POS

Generally, there are 11 kinds of POS in oracle-bone inscription system. The amount of nouns and verbs is the largest in oracle-bone inscription system, which accounts for 95%, as shown in Fig. 1.

The phenomena of class-ambiguous words in oracle-bone inscription system are much simpler than that in modern Chinese system.

There are chiefly 3 kinds of class-ambiguous words in oracle-bone inscription [3]:

1. Noun & verb:

鱼: a. 不其网鱼? (n.) b. 王鱼?勿鱼? (v.)

2. Verb & adjective:

及: a. 三侯王其令追召方, 及于口? (v.) b. 庚午卜, 贞: 禾 又及雨? (a.)

3. Noun & verb & adjective:

疾: a. 妇好有疾. (n.) b. 妇井疾. (v.) c. 今夕其雨, 疾? (a.)

The first kind is much more familiar than other two. All three kinds of class-ambiguous words include verbs. We checked the 317 verbs listed in [5] word by word, found 78 verbs are class-ambiguous words, 64 of which are both noun and verb.

3 Design and Experimental Results

Word segmentation and POS tagging are the first step for processing oracle-bone inscription with computer. We tried the rule-based method, corpus-based method and method combining rule-based and corpus-based approaches respectively.

3.1 The Construction of Dictionary

First, a segmentation dictionary was constructed. We've set up a dictionary of oracle-bone inscription including 2373 words. The dictionary is built into open form, as shown in Fig. 2 (a). Also, we developed a multiple-information electronic dictionary. It contains four-dimension description: lexical, syntax, semantic and pragmatic words and phrases of oracle-bone inscription.

The lexicon attribute is based on following parts: 1. Basic information: including oracle-bone inscription, modern Chinese characters, Chinese phoneticize spell (*pinyin*), usual fake characters, variant characters, word-formation manner, font style explanation etc; 2. Syntax attribute: including part of speech, in common use arrange in pairs or groups, example paraphrase etc; 3. Semantic attribute: including semantic sort, basic acceptation, explicative acceptation and semantic arrange in pairs or groups etc; 4. Pragmatic attribute: including lexical appearance era, in common use style, serial number of lexical appearance and evolvement process (for example, vehicle's evolving process is 車 車 車 车) etc.

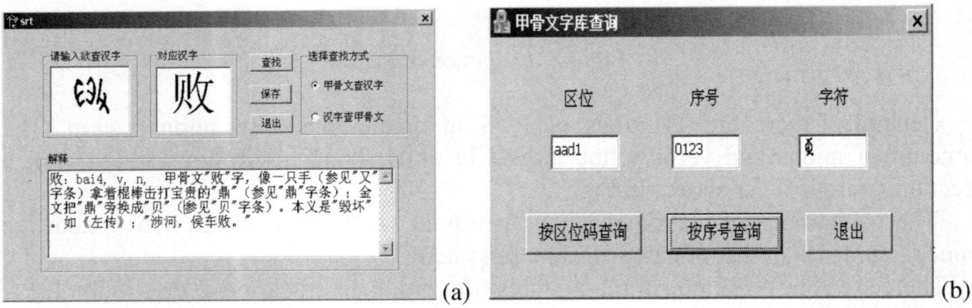

Fig. 2. (a) Dictionary of oracle-bone inscription (b) Oracle-bone inscriptions consulted by section-location code or serial number of lexical appearance

There are more than 2,000 words of oracle-bone inscription which can't be understood till today, these strange characters can be consulted by section-location code or serial number of lexical appearance, as shown in Fig. 2 (b).

3.2 Word Segmentation

We tried three word segmentation techniques:

1. *Rule-based method*: Dictionary-based methods include Maximum Matching, Reverse Maximum Matching and Bi-directional Maximum Matching, etc. These methods segments sentences according to a segmentation dictionary and the "Long Word First" rule; and we can summarize some rules manually or automatically with computer, we use those rules to segment sentences;
2. *Corpus-based method*: using statistical model and decision algorithm;
3. *The combination of rule-based method and corpus-based method*: use the two methods together.

The absolute amount of polysyllabic words is small, but they appear frequently in sentences. According to our experiment results, many sentences can be disambiguated by dictionary-based methods, but there do exist sentences composing ambiguous intersection which dictionary-based methods can not solve:

Example 1: 贞今十三月不其雨.

Segmentation 1: 贞/今/十三/月/不/其/雨.

Segmentation 2: 贞/今/十/三月/不/其/雨.

Thus we'll try corpus-based method and rule-based method:

Suppose the ambiguous intersection is ABC, and the segmented result may be AB/C or A/BC. We can obtain word frequency from the corpus, for example WF(A), WF(BC), WF(AB), WF(C). Set a critical value CV which determined by experience.

(1) If WF(A)*WF(BC)-WF(AB)*WF(C)>CV go (2), else go (4);
(2) If WF(A)*WF(BC)>WF(AB)*WF(C), choose AB/C as final result, else go (3)
(3) Choose A/BC as final result;
(4) Output ABC without processing.

The corpus-based method needs a large tagged oracle-bone inscription corpus with grammar information, so that the word frequency can be close to reality. However, it is hard to collect tagged oracle-bone inscription sentences, thus our corpus data is quite sparse, and we can't use statistical method solely.

We summarized several rules according oracle-bone inscription grammar features. For example, word E follows word D, word F never follows word D etc.

Once there is intersection can't be processed by dictionary-based and corpus-based approaches, we search for any matching rule. Suppose we find a rule, saying A/BC existed and AB/C never appeared, apparently we choose A/BC as the final result.

Summarizing rule is difficult, too. So we try to combine rule-based method and corpus-based method together. The General processing course shows as follows:

(1) Process the sentence with BMM method, if there is no ambiguous intersection, go (4), else go to (2);

(2) Process the ambiguous intersection with corpus-based method mentioned before, if disambiguation succeeds, go to (4), and else go to (3);

(3) Try the rule-based method to disambiguate the intersection, if succeeds, output the result, else leave it without processing.

The experimental results shows as in Fig.3. The segment accuracy of combining method is 98.33%.

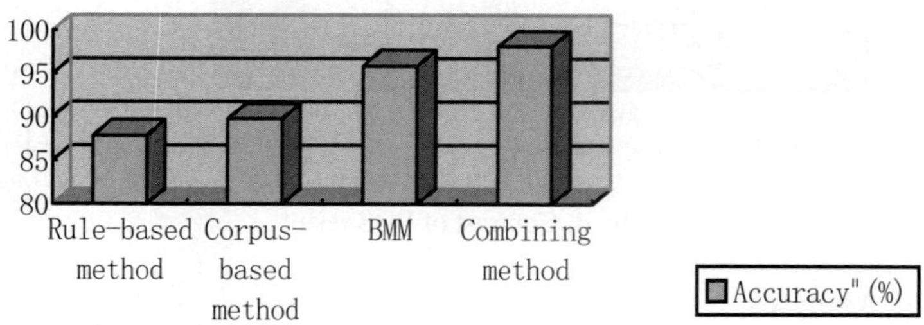

Fig. 3. Contrast of segmentation results

3.3 POS Tagging

POS tagging tries to output POS in one sentence automatically.

Example: 翌日/壬/王/其/田/不/风

Tagged: n. n. n. d. v. d. v.

Assume that V means vocabulary, C means POS, W means word, and T means tag, so $W \in V, T \in C$. $W_s = W_1 W_2 \ldots W_n$ is an input word sequence, and $T_s = T_1 T_2 \ldots T_n$ is the output of a proper tag sequence. We adopted the following methods to disambiguate sentences:

1. *Rule-based method*: Disambiguating sentences by using grammar rules;
2. *Corpus-based method*: An initial corpus is tagged first, after tagging is finished, the neighbor probabilities between words are computed in a large corpus, then the sentences are disambiguated according to the probability knowledge. The latter is much more efficient than the other methods.
3. *Method combining rule-based and corpus-based approaches*: use two approaches together.

Though the class-ambiguous words are few in oracle-bone Inscription, they are used frequently, nearly *20%* in each sentence, we must take it seriously. First, the rule-based method was used to disambiguate. We summarized some combining rules manually, for example, an adverb never follows with noun. There are totally 67 rules we used. When ambiguity appears, search and adopt the matching rules if existed.

It is hard to acquire long-tested rules. So the corpus-based method was used. Assume an input word sequence is W_s, the probability of output tagging sequence T_s is $P(T_s / W_s)$. The transferring probability for the tagging sequence $T_s^{'}$ is:

$$P(T_s^{'} / W_s) = \max_{T_s} P(T_s / W_s) \tag{1}$$

When n=2, i.e., bigram model, a word relate just with the former word and POS.

Fig.4 shows the results, the accuracy of combining method reaches 96.75%.

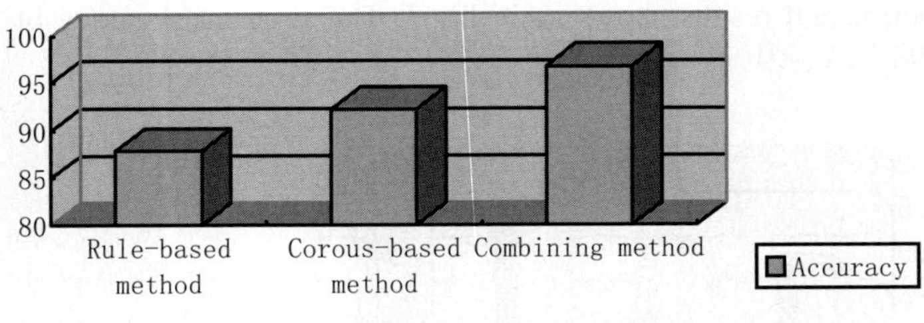

Fig. 4. Contrast of POS result

3.4 Syntax Analyses

Combining POS and multiple-information dictionary of oracle-bone inscription, we can obtain the results of syntax analyses.

For example: 王 其 观 日 出

POS: n adv v n v

According to context syntax rules, there will be several syntax trees, as shown in Fig.5. For the former syntax tree, structure of “观 日 出” (watch sunrise) is verb+object, "日出" (sunrise) is object. In the latter syntax tree, structure of "观日出" is join-verb, "王" first "观日" (watch sun), then "出" (come out), by searching the oracle-bone inscription dictionary, we know "谓宾" (predicate object) attribute of verb "观" is "是" (be), it means that verb "观" (watch) can have a predication structure as object. Therefore, "其" (that) can't modify join-verb structure, the former syntax tree structure is right, the latter syntax tree structure is wrong.

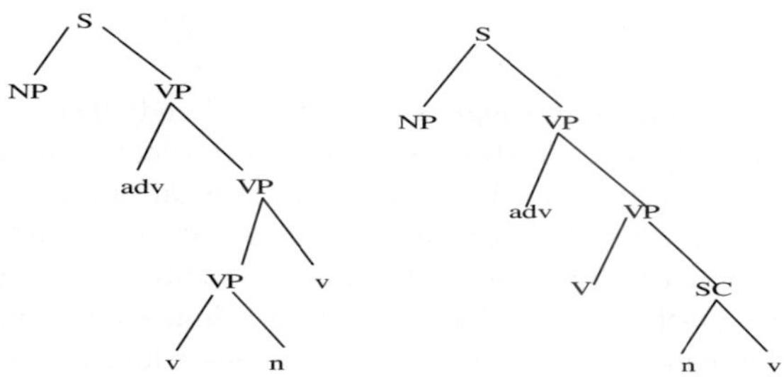

Fig. 5. Two syntax trees for the analysis of 王其观日出

4 Conclusion

Oracle-bone inscription processing is a rather new issue. We propose to solve word segmentation and POS tagging with methods combining corpus-based and rule-based approaches. The accuracy are 98.33% and 96.75% respectively. Our experiment result shows that the combining method is quite practical for processing the oracle-bone inscription, especially when the corpus is sparse.

References

1. Yao, X., Xiao, D.: Collective of Yinxu Oracle-Bone Inscription, Zhonghua Press, Beijing (1988)
2. Jiang, M., Cai, H.: An Application of Natural Language Processing: Oracle-Bone Inscription Information Processing, Issues in Chinese Information Processing, Scientific Press, Beijing. (2003) 415-422
3. Jiang, M., Zhu, X., Gielen, G., et al.: Braille to Print Translations for Chinese. Information and Software Technology, 44 (2002) 91-100
4. Chen, N.: Study on Oracle-Bone Inscription Verbs, Bashu Press, Chengdu. (2001)
5. Shi, Z.: Knowledge Discovery, Tsinghua University Press, Beijing. (2002)
6. Yao, T.: Machine Learing and Natural Language Processing, Issues in Chinese Information Processing, Scientific Press, Beijing. (2003) 246-255
7. Ma, Y.: Study on Estimate-based Automatic Chinese Word Segmentator. In: Special Issues in Language Information Processing, Tsinghua University Press, Guangxi Science and Technology Press. (1992) 2-36
8. Hu, C., Han, Z.: Application Study of Hidden Markov Model Based Part-Of-Speech Tagging, Computer Engineering and Application. 6 (2002) 62-64

Intelligent System for Natural Language Processing

Maciej Majewski and Wojciech Kacalak

Technical University of Koszalin, Department of Mechanical Engineering
Raclawicka 15-17, 75-620 Koszalin, Poland
{maciej.majewski, wojciech.kacalak}@tu.koszalin.pl

Abstract. Nowadays technological devices can already be provided with enough intelligence to understand and act appropriately on voice commands. The voice communication with technological devices becomes a stronger challenge as technology becomes more advanced and complex. In this paper, a natural language interface is presented which consists of the intelligent mechanisms of human identification, speech recognition, word and command recognition, command syntax and result analysis, command safety assessment, technological process supervision as well as human reaction assessment. In this paper, a review is carried out of selected issues with regards to recognition of speech commands in natural language given by the operator of the technological device. A view is offered of the complexity of the recognition process of the operator's words and commands using neural networks made up of a few layers of neurons. The paper presents research results of speech recognition and automatic recognition of commands in natural language using artificial neural networks.

1 Intelligent Two-Way Speech Communication

If the operator is identified and authorized by the natural language interface in Fig. 1, a command produced in continuous speech is recognized by the speech recognition module and processed in to a text format. Then the recognised text is analysed by the syntax analysis subsystem. The processed command is sent to the word and command recognition modules using artificial neural networks to recognise the command, which is sent to the effect analysis subsystem for analysing the status corresponding to the hypothetical command execution, consecutively assessing the command correctness, estimating the process state and the technical safety, and also possibly signalling the error caused by the operator. The command is also sent to the safety assessment subsystem for assessing the grade of affiliation of the command to the correct command category and making corrections. The command execution subsystem signalises commands accepted for executing, assessing reactions of the operator, defining new parameters of the process and run directives [4]. The subsystem for voice communication produces voice commands to the operator [5].

D.-S. Huang, K. Li, and G.W. Irwin (Eds.): ICIC 2006, LNAI 4114, pp. 742–747, 2006.

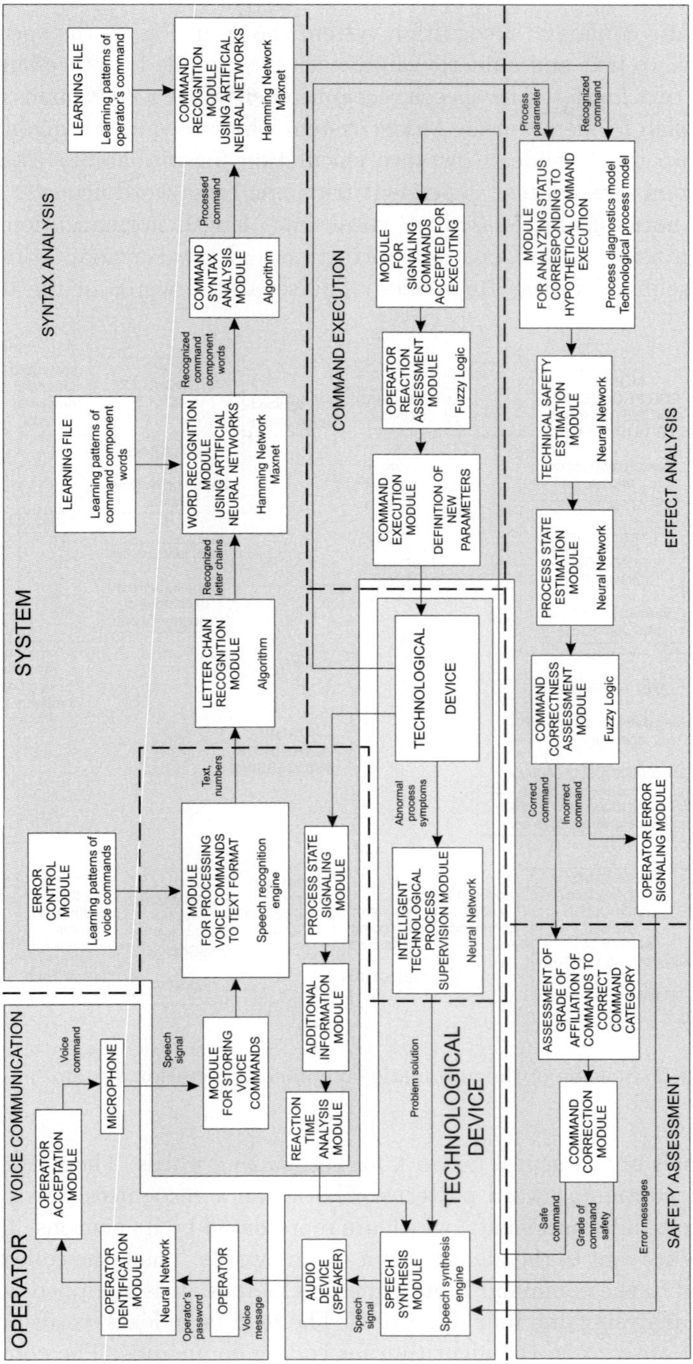

Fig. 1. Architecture of the natural language human-machine interface

2 Recognition of Commands in Natural Language

In the automatic command recognition system shown in Fig. 2, the speech signal is processed to text and numeric values with the module for processing voice commands to text format. The speech recognition engine is a continuous density mixture Gaussian Hidden Markov Model system which uses vector quantization for speeding up the Euclidean distance calculation for probability estimation [1,2]. The system uses context dependent triphonic cross word acoustic models with speaker normalization based on vocal tract length normalization, channel adaptation using mean Cepstral subtraction and speaker adaptation using Maximum Likelihood Linear Regression. The separated words of the text are

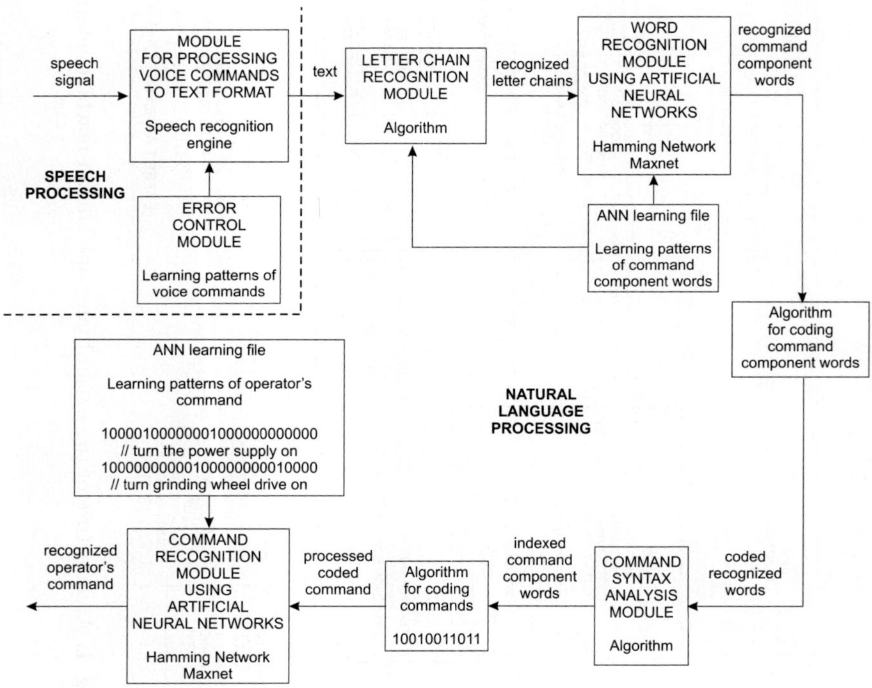

Fig. 2. Scheme of the automatic command recognition system

the input signals of the neural network for recognizing words. The network has a training file containing word patterns. The network recognizes words as the operator's command components, which are represented by its neurons. The recognized words are sent to the algorithm for coding words. Then, the coded words are transferred to the command syntax analysis module. It is equipped with the algorithm for analysing and indexing words. The module indexes words properly and then they are sent to the algorithm for coding commands. The commands are coded as vectors and they are input signals of the command recognition module using neural network. The module uses the 3-layer Hamming neural network in Fig. 3, either to recognize the operator's command or to produce the information that the command is not recognized. The neural network is equipped with a training file containing patterns of possible operator commands [3].

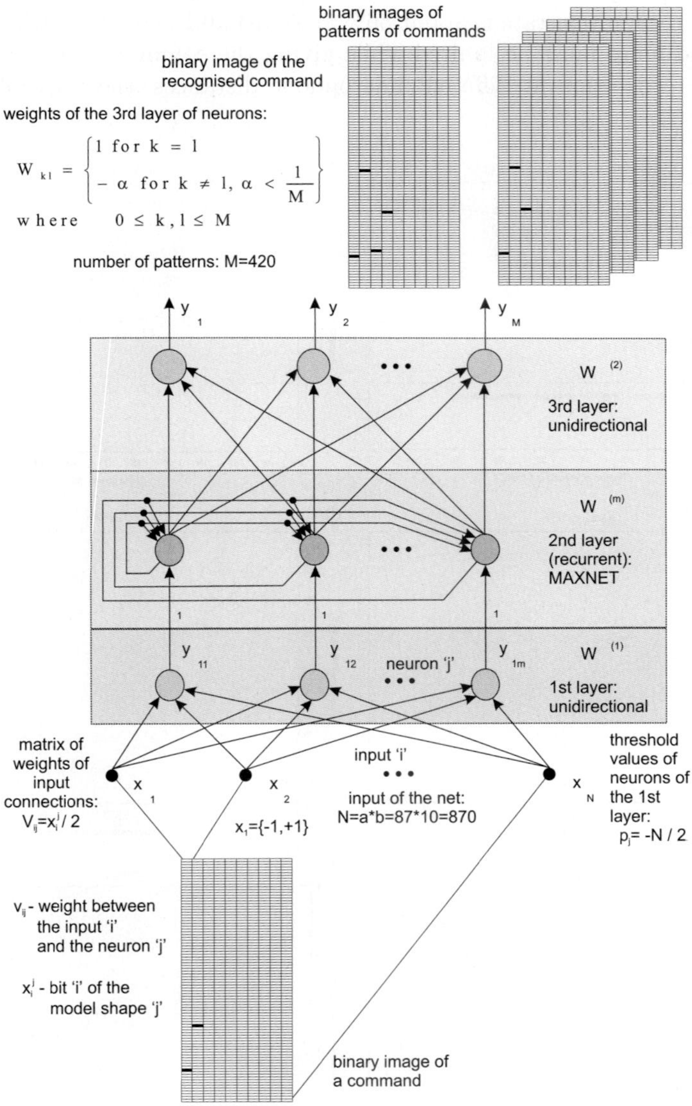

Fig. 3. Scheme of the 3-layer neural network for automatic command recognition

3 Research Results of Automatic Command Recognition

As shown in Fig. 4a, the speech recognition module recognizes 85-90% of the operator's words correctly. As more training of the neural networks is done, accuracy rises to around 95%. For the research on command recognition at different noise power, the microphone used by the operator is the headset microphone. As shown in Fig. 4b, the recognition performance is sensitive to background noise. The recognition rate is about 86% at 70 dB and 71% at 80 dB. Therefore, background noise must be limited while giving the commands. For research on command recognition at different microphone distances, the microphone used

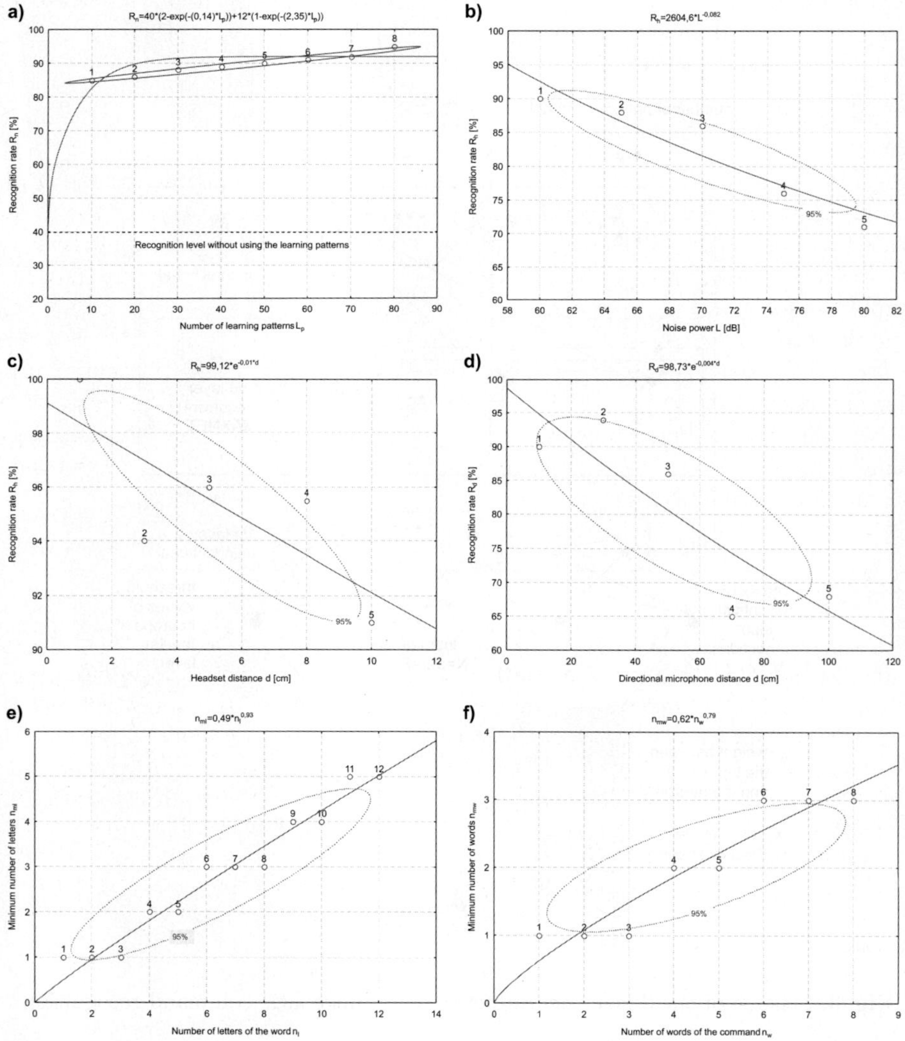

Fig. 4. Speech and command recognition rate

by the operator is the headset microphone. As shown in Fig. 4c, the recognition rate decreases when the headset distance increases. The recognition rate dropped by 9% after the headset distance is changed from 1 to 10 cm. Likewise, the research on command recognition at different microphone distances, the microphone used by the operator is the directional microphone. As shown in Fig. 4d, the recognition rate after 50 cm decreases reaching a rate of about 65%. As shown in Fig. 4e, the ability of the neural network to recognise the word depends on the number of letters. The neural network requires the minimal number of letters of the word being recognized as its input signals. As shown in Fig. 4f, the ability of the neural network to recognise the command depends on the number of command component words. Depending on the number of component words of the command, the neural network requires the minimal number of words of the given command as its input signals.

4 Conclusions and Perspectives

The condition of the effectiveness of the presented system is to equip it with mechanisms of command verification and correctness. In operations of the automated technological processes, many process states and various commands from the operator to the technological device can be distinguished. A large number of combined technological systems characterize the realization of that process. In complex technological processes, if many parameters are controlled, the operator is not able to analyze a sufficient number of signals and react by manual operations on control buttons. The aim of this research to develop an intelligent layer of two-way voice communication is difficult, but the prognosis of the technology development and its first use shows a significant efficiency in supervision and production humanization.

References

1. Kacalak, W., Majewski, M.: Automatic Recognition of Voice Commands in Natural Language Using Artificial Neural Networks. Artificial Neural Networks in Engineering ANNIE 2004 Conference, St. Louis. ASME Press, New York, (2004) 831-836
2. Majewski, M., Kacalak, W.: Intelligent Human-Machine Voice Communication System. Engineering Mechanics International Journal, 12(3) (2005) 193-200
3. Majewski, M., Kacalak, W.: Intelligent Layer of Human-Machine Voice Communication. The 9th International Conference KES2005, Melbourne, Australia (2005), Lecture Notes in Computer Science 3683, Springer-Verlag, New York, (2005) 930-936
4. Majewski, M., Kacalak, W.: Intelligent Human-Machine Speech Communication System. International Conference on Intelligent Computing ICIC2005, Hefei Anhui, China, (2005) 3441-3450
5. O'Shaughnessy, D.: Speech Communications: Human and Machine. IEEE Press, New York, (2000)

Text-Based English-Arabic Sentence Alignment

Mohamed Abdel Fattah[1], Fuji Ren[1,2], and Shingo Kuroiwa[1]

[1] Faculty of Engineering, University of Tokushima
2-1 Minamijosanjima
Tokushima, Japan 770-8506

[2] School of Information Engineering, Beijing University of Posts & Telecommunications
Beijing, 100088, China

{mohafi, ren, kuroiwa}@is.tokushima-u.ac.jp

Abstract. In this paper, we present a new approach to align sentences in bilingual parallel corpora based on the use of the linguistic information of the text pair in Gaussian mixture model (GMM) classifier. A feature parameter vector is extracted from the text pair under consideration. This vector contains text features such as length, punctuation score, cognate score and a bilingual lexicon extracted from the parallel corpus under consideration. A set of manually prepared training data has been assigned to train the Gaussian mixture model. Another set of data was used for testing. Using the Gaussian mixture model approach, we could achieve error reduction of 160% over length based approach when applied on English-Arabic parallel documents. In addition, the results of (GMM) outperform the results of the combined model which exploits length, punctuation, cognate and bilingual lexicon in a dynamic framework.

1 Introduction

Last few years, much work has been reported in sentence alignment using different techniques. Length-based approaches (length as a function of sentence characters [1] or sentence words [2] are based on the fact that longer sentences in one language tend to be translated into longer sentences in the other language, and that shorter sentences tend to be translated into shorter sentences. Cognate's approaches were also proposed and combined with the length-based approach to improve the alignment accuracy [3].

In this paper we present non traditional approaches for sentence alignment problem. In sentence alignment problem, we may have:

1-0 (One English sentence does not match any of the Arabic sentences), similarly, 0-1, 1-1, 1-2, 2-1, 2-2, 1-3 and 3-1 are possible categories. There may be more categories in bitexts, however they are rare, hence we consider only the previous mentioned categories. As illustrated above, we have eight sentence alignment categories. Hence we can consider sentence alignment as a classification problem. This classification problem may be solved by using Gaussian mixture model classifier.

2 English–Arabic Text Features

There are many features that can be extracted from any text pair. The most important feature is text length, since Gale achieved good results using this feature.

D.-S. Huang, K. Li, and G.W. Irwin (Eds.): ICIC 2006, LNAI 4114, pp. 748 – 753, 2006.

The second text feature is punctuation symbols. We can classify punctuation matching into the following categories: A. 1-1 matching type, where one English punctuation mark matches one Arabic punctuation mark, similarly there are: B. 1-0 and C. 0-1 matching types. The probability that a sequence of punctuation marks $AP_i = Ap_1 Ap_2 ...... Ap_i$ in a text of the Arabic language translates to a sequence of punctuation marks $EP_j = Ep_1 Ep_2 ...... Ep_j$ in a text in the English language is $P(AP_i, EP_j)$. The system searches for the punctuation alignment that maximizes the probability overall possible alignments given a pair of punctuation sequences corresponding to a pair of parallel sentences from:

$$\underset{AL}{\arg\max} \; P(AL \mid AP_i, EP_j) \tag{1}$$

Since "*AL*" is a punctuation alignment. Punctuation symbols for 1000 English – Arabic sentence pairs were manually aligned to calculate each punctuation mark pair probability. After specifying the punctuation alignment that maximizes the probability overall possible alignments given a pair of punctuation sequences, the system calculates the punctuation compatibility factor for the text pair under consideration as: $\gamma = \frac{c}{\max(m,n)}$ .Where γ = the punctuation compatibility factor, c = the number of direct punctuation matches, n = the number of Arabic punctuation marks, m = the number of English punctuation marks.

The third text pair feature is cognates. Many UN and scientific Arabic documents contain some English words and expressions. These words may be used as cognates. We define the cognate factor (cog) as the number of common items (translation pairs or cognate words) in the sentence pair divided by the average number of tokens exists in the sentence pair under consideration.

3 The Proposed Sentence Alignment Model

We have two modes of operations:

1- Training mode where features are extracted from 7653 manually aligned English-Arabic sentence pairs and used to train the Gaussian mixture model (GMM).
2- Testing mode where features are extracted from the testing data and go through (GMM) to be aligned.

We have used 18 input unites and 8 output unites for (GMM). Each input unit represents one input feature. The input feature vector X is as follows:

$$X = [\ \frac{L(S1a)}{L(S1e)}, \frac{L(S1a)+L(S2a)}{L(S1e)}, \frac{L(S1a)}{L(S1e)+L(Se2)}, \frac{L(S1a)+L(S2a)}{L(S1e)+L(S2e)},$$
$$\frac{L(S1a)+L(S2a)+L(S3a)}{L(S1e)}, \frac{L(S1a)}{L(S1e)+L(S2e)+L(S3e)}, \gamma(S1a,S1e), \gamma(S1a,S2a,S1e),$$
$$\gamma(S1a,S1e,S2e), \gamma(S1a,S2a,S1e,S2e), \gamma(S1a,S2a,S3a,S1e), \gamma(S1a,S1e,S2e,S3e),$$
$$Cog(S1a,S1e), Cog(S1a,S2a,S1e), Cog(S1a,S1e,S2e), Cog(S1a,S2a,S1e,S2e),$$
$$Cog(S1a,S2a,S3a,S1e), Cog(S1a,S1e,S2e,S3e)\ ]$$

Where:

$L(S1a)$ = character length of the Arabic sentence number 1.

$\gamma(S1a, S1e)$ = the punctuation compatibility factor when matching the first Arabic sentence with the first English sentence.

$Cog(S1a, S1e)$ = the cognate factor when matching the first Arabic sentence with the first English sentence. The rest of the X vector items are similarly defined.

The outputs are 8 categories specified as follows:

The output $S1a \rightarrow 0$ means that the first Arabic sentence has no English match.

Similarly, the rest of the output items are: $S1e \rightarrow 0$, $S1a \rightarrow S1e$, $S1a + S2a \rightarrow S1e$, $S1a \rightarrow S1e + S2e$, $S1a + S2a \rightarrow S1e + S2e$, $S1a \rightarrow S1e + S2e + S3e$ and $S1a + S2a + S3a \rightarrow S1e$ (the first three Arabic sentences are matched with the first English sentence).

The input pattern X is propagated through (GMM) in the following ways:

3.1 Gaussian Mixture Model

The use of Gaussian Mixture models as a classification tool is motivated by the interpretation that the Gaussian components represent some general output dependent features and the capability of Gaussian mixtures to model arbitrary densities [4]. The probability density function for a certain class (category) feature vector X is a weighted sum, or *mixture*, of k class-conditional Gaussian distributions. For a given class model λc , the probability of observing X is given by:

$$p(X \mid \lambda c) = \sum_{k=1}^{K} w_{c,k} N(X; \vec{\mu}_{c,k}, \Sigma_{c,k}) \tag{2}$$

Where $w_{c,k}$, $\vec{\mu}_{c,k}, \Sigma_{c,k}$ are the mixture weight, mean, and covariance matrix, respectively, for the i-th component, which has a Gaussian distribution given by:

$$N(X; \vec{\mu}, \Sigma) = \frac{1}{\sqrt{(2\pi)^n \mid \Sigma \mid}} e^{-\frac{1}{2}(X-\vec{\mu})^{\tau} \Sigma^{-1} (X-\vec{\mu})} \tag{3}$$

Where n is the dimension of X . We used Σ as diagonal covariance matrices. Given a set of training vectors of a certain class, an initial set of means is estimated using the k-means clustering. The mixture weights, means, and covariances are then iteratively trained using the expectation maximization (EM) algorithm.

Using this approach, we constructed class-dependent model for each category. After that we used all models for sentence alignment task using maximum likelihood of each category as follows:

For a given class-dependent reference models ($\lambda 1, \lambda 2, ..., \lambda 8$) and one feature vector sequence $X = \{ x_1, x_2, ..., x_n \}$, the minimum error Bays' decision rule is:

$$arg\ max_{1 \le l \le 8}\ p(\lambda l \mid X) = arg\ max_{1 \le l \le 8} \frac{p(X \mid \lambda l)}{p(X)} p(\lambda l) \tag{4}$$

Assuming equal prior probabilities for all categories, equation (4) will be:

$$arg\ max_{1 \le l \le 8}\ p(X \mid \lambda l) \quad (5)$$

Using formula (5), a certain feature vector sequence X may be classified as one of the eight classes.

4 English-Arabic Corpus

We have used the technique mentioned in [5, 6] to construct the Arabic-English parallel corpus. We have collected 191,623 English sentences and 183,542 Arabic sentences. In order to avoid accumulation of error during sentence alignment procedures, we have specified some anchor points in the English and Arabic texts based on some words or symbols that are appeared at the beginning of some sentences and had to be reasonably frequent.

5 Experimental Results

5.1 Length Based Approach

A dynamic programming framework was constructed to conduct experiments using the length based approach as a baseline experiment in order to compare the results with the proposed system. Table 1 illustrates the results using 1200 English–Arabic sentence pairs as a test set.

Table 1. The results using length based, combined model and GMM approaches

Category	Frequency	Length based % Error	Combined model % Error	GMM approach % Error
1-1	1099	4.9%	3.0%	1.9%
1-0, 0-1	2	100%	50.0%	50.0%
1-2, 2-1	88	15.9%	6.8%	3.4%
2-2	2	50%	50.0%	50%
1-3, 3-1	9	66%	44.4%	33.3%
Total	1200	6.4%	3.7 %	2.4%

5.2 Combined Model Using Length, Punctuation and Cognate in a Dynamic Framework

We employ sentence alignment, which maximizes the probability overall possible alignment, given a pair of parallel texts, according to the following equation:

$$\arg\max_{AL}\ P(AL \mid A, E) \quad (6)$$

Since *AL is the alignment, A* and *E* are the Arabic and English texts. We can use a binomial distribution to approximate the value *P(AL|A,E)* as follows:

$$P(AL|A,E) = \prod_{v=1}^{t} P(match).P(\delta \mid match).\binom{n_v}{r_v} P(Ap_v, Ep_v)^{r_v}.(1-(P(Ap_v, Ep_v))^{n_v - r_v} \quad (7)$$

Since: t = the total number of sentences to be aligned, n_v = the maximum number of punctuation marks plus cognates in either the English text or the Arabic text in the vth sentence to be aligned, r_v = the number of compatible punctuation marks and cognates in ordered comparison; $P(Ap_v,Ep_v)$ = the probability of the existence of a compatible punctuation mark and cognate in both languages; $P(match)$ = the match type probability of aligning English and Arabic text pair. Table 2 gives the possible values of $P(match)$. $P(\delta \mid match)$ is as in [1]. Table 1 shows the results using combined model.

Table 2. The values of *P*(*match*) for each category

Category	Frequency	*P*(*match*)
1-1	915	0.915
1-0, 0-1	1	0.001
1-2, 2-1	75	0.075
2-2	1	0.001
1-3, 3-1	8	0.008

5.3 Gaussian Mixture Model Approach

The system is extracting features from the 7653 manually aligned English-Arabic sentence pairs and uses them to construct Gaussian mixture model for each category (we have 8 categories). Use the 1200 English–Arabic sentence pairs as a testing set. Use equation (5) to align the 1200 English–Arabic sentence pairs.

Table 1 illustrates the results when we applied this approach on the 1200 English – Arabic sentence pairs.

6 Conclusions and Future Work

In this paper, we have investigated the use of Gaussian mixture model on sentence alignment task. We have applied our new approach on a sample of English – Arabic parallel corpus. Our approach results outperform the length base approach and the combined model results. The proposed approach has improved the total system performance in terms of effectiveness. This approach decreased the total error to 2.4%. Our approach has been used the feature extraction criteria which gives researchers opportunity to use many varieties of these features based on the used language pair and the texts type (Hanzi characters in Japanese-Chinese texts may be used for instance). In the future work, we will use the resulted corpus in MT and CLIR.

Acknowledgments

This research was partially supported by the Ministry of Education, Science, Sports and Culture, Grant-in-Aid for Scientific Research (B), 14380166 and 17300065, Exploratory Research 17656128 in 2005, International Communications Foundation (ICF).

References

1. Gale, W.A., Church, K.W.: A Program for Aligning Sentences in Bilingual Corpora. Computational Linguistics. 19 (1993) 75-102
2. Brown, P., Lai, J., Mercer, R.: Aligning Sentences in Parallel Corpora. In Proceedings of the 29th annual meeting of the association for computational linguistics, Berkeley, CA, USA. (1991)
3. Simard, M., Foster, G., Isabelle, P.: Using Cognates to Align Sentences in Bilingual Corpora. Proceedings of TMI92.ontreal, Canada. (1992) 67-81
4. Fattah, M., Ren, F., Kuroiwa, S.: Speaker Recognition for Wire/Wireless Communication Systems. The international Arab Journal of Information Technology "IAJIT". 3 (2006) 28-34
5. Fattah, M., Ren, F., Kuroiwa, S.: Stemming to Improve Translation Lexicon Creation form Bitexts. Information Processing & Management. 42 (2006) 1003 – 1016
6. Resnik, P., Smithy, N. A.: The Web as a Parallel Corpus. University of Maryland technical report UMIACS-TR-2002-61(2003)

The Advantage of Harmonic Asian Options and an Approximation Approach

Xu Chen and Jianping Wan

Huazhong University of Science & Technology, Department of Mathematics,
Wuhan 430074 P.R. China
chenxu981388@yahoo.com.cn

Abstract. We demonstrate that European Asian options with harmonic averaging behave better than Asian options with arithmetic and geometric averaging procedures under some situation. Approximation methods for the valuation of harmonic average options and numerical illustrations are also given.

1 Introduction

Asian options are averaging options where the terminal payoffs depend on some form of averaging of the price of the underlying asset over a part or the whole of the life of the option. Under some situation where traders may be interested to hedge against the average price of a commodity over a period rather than the end-of-period price. Averaging options are particularly useful for business involved in trading on thinly-traded commodities. The use of such financial instruments may avoid the price manipulation near the end of the period. There are two main classes of Asian options, namely, the average value options and the average strike options with terminal payoff functions being $max(A-X,0)$ and $max(S_T-A,0)$, respectively, where S_T is the asset price at expiry, X is the strike price, and A denotes some form of average of the price of underlying asset. The value of A depends on the path followed by the asset price. The common averaging procedures are the discrete arithmetic averaging defined by

$$A_a = \frac{1}{n}\sum_{i=1}^{n} S(t_i)$$

and the discrete geometric averaging defined by

$$A_g = [\prod_{i=1}^{n} S(t_i)]^{\frac{1}{n}}$$

Here, $S(t_i)$ is the asset price at discrete time $t_i, i = 1, 2, \ldots n$, in the limit $n \to \infty$, the discrete sampled averages become the continuous sampled averages.

Under Black-Scholes framework, the general partial differential equation formulations and approximation methods for the valuations of arithmetic and geometric Asian options have been discussed. The comprehensive summaries can

D.-S. Huang, K. Li, and G.W. Irwin (Eds.): ICIC 2006, LNAI 4114, pp. 754–765, 2006.

be found in [6]. Recently, many studies go beyond the traditional Black-Scholes framework by generalizing underlying price dynamics to Lévy Processes such as [1],[4],[10]. In general no explicit analytical expression is available. One can use Monte Carlo simulation techniques to obtain numerical estimates of the prices[7].

In this paper, we shall consider evaluation of the Asian option with harmonic averaging (Actually, we only need consider the average value call options). It's price is according to a risk-neutral measure Q given by

$$AH_0 = e^{-rT} E^Q[(\frac{n}{\sum_{i=1}^{n} \frac{1}{S_i}} - K)^+]. \tag{1}$$

Where $E^Q[.]$ denotes the expectation under Q, r is riskless interest rate, T is the expiration date and S_i is the asset price at time $t_i, 0 \leq t_i \leq T, i = 0, \ldots n$. AH_0 is based on the harmonic averaging procedure $A_h = \frac{n}{\sum_{i=1}^{n} \frac{1}{S_i}}$. Few literatures study this kind of Asian options. One reason of being not widely employed at present is that harmonic average usually is regarded as the transfiguration of arithmetic average; the other reason is the computation of harmonic average is very complex and intractable. But under some situation, harmonic averaging procedure actually behaves better than arithmetic and geometric averaging procedures. We will present this idea in Section 2.

The main difficulty in evaluating (1) is to determine the distribution of A_h. We will discuss a technique of approximation of the distribution, which was first developed for the arithmetic Asian options in Black-Scholes model [9] and later on adapted to arithmetic Asian options in Lévy setting [1]. We amend this approximation approach and apply it to harmonic Asian options in Black-Scholes model and NIG Lévy asset price model.

The organization of this article is as follows.

In Section2, we compare the Asian options with three kinds of averaging procedures and analyze the advantage of harmonic average options. Monte Carlo simulation is adopted.

In Section3, approximation method is introduced. Numerical illustrations of the accuracy of the approximations are given in Black-Scholes model and NIG Lévy asset price model.

Finally, we present our conclusion in Section4.

2 The Advantage of Harmonic Asian Options

2.1 Black-Scholes Model

Assume that asset price dynamics to be given by

$$\frac{dS_t}{S_t} = \mu dt + \sigma dZ_t$$

Where Z_t is the standard Wiener process, μ and σ are the expected rate of return and volatility of the asset price, respectively.

2.2 NIG(Normal Inverse Gaussian) Lévy Asset Price Model

Let now S_t for $t \geq 0$ denote the following dynamics for the stock price process

$$dS_t = S_{t-}(dZ_t + e^{\triangle Z_t} - 1 - \triangle Z_t). \tag{2}$$

where $(Z_t)_{t\geq 0}$ denotes the NIG Lévy motion on some filtered probability space $(\Omega, \mathcal{F}, (\mathcal{F}_t)_{t\geq 0}, P)$, Z_{t-} the left hand limit of the path at time t and $\triangle Z_t = Z_t - Z_{t-}$ the jump at time t. Then, the solution of the stochastic differential equation (2) is given by

$$S_t = S_0 \exp(Z_t)$$

and it follows that the log-returns $\ln(S_t/S_{t-1})$ are indeed NIG-distributed. The density of the $NIG(\alpha, \beta, \delta, \mu)$ distribution is defined by

$$f_{NIG(\alpha,\beta,\delta,\mu)}(x) = \frac{\alpha\delta}{\pi} \exp(\delta\sqrt{\alpha^2 - \beta^2} + \beta(x-\mu)) \frac{K_1(\alpha\sqrt{\delta^2 + (x-\mu)^2})}{\sqrt{\delta^2 + (x-\mu)^2}}. \tag{3}$$

with $0 \leq |\beta| \leq \alpha$, $\delta \geq 0$, $\mu \in R$. Here $K_1(x)$ denotes the modified Bessel function of the third kind of order 1. The moment generating function of (3) is given by

$$M_{NIG}(u) = \exp(\delta(\sqrt{\alpha^2 - \beta^2} - \sqrt{\alpha^2 - (\beta + u)^2}) + \mu u). \tag{4}$$

2.3 Asian Options with Three Kinds of Averaging Procedures

In Figure **1**, we simulate a sample path in Black-Scholes framework with the corresponding parameters taking values to be $\sigma = 0.1$ and $r = 0.1$. Then we give the barcharts of average option prices with three kinds of averaging procedures by generating 1 thousand sample paths in Figure **2**.

In Figure **3**, we simulate a sample path in Black-Scholes framework with the corresponding parameters taking values to be $\sigma = 0.3$ and $r = 0.1$. Then we give the barcharts of average option prices with three kinds of averaging procedures by generating 1 thousand sample paths in Figure **4**.

In Figure **5**, we simulate a sample path in NIG Lévy asset price model with the corresponding parameters taking values to be $\alpha = 81.6, \beta = -3.69, \mu = -0.000123$ and $\delta = 0.0103$. Then we give the barcharts of average option prices with three kinds of averaging procedures by generating 1 thousand sample paths in Figure **6**.

In Figure **7**, we simulate a sample path in NIG Lévy asset price model with the corresponding parameters taking values to be $\alpha = 81.6, \beta = -3.69, \mu = -0.000123$ and $\delta = 0.0001$. Then we give the barcharts of average option prices with three kinds of averaging procedures by generating 1 thousand sample paths in Figure **8**.

In Figures, AA, AG, AH denote the Asian option prices with arithmetic averaging, geometric averaging and harmonic averaging procedures, respectively. We can see when the stock prices fluctuate stably as in Figure **1** and Figure **5** the barcharts of option prices with three kinds of averaging procedures have

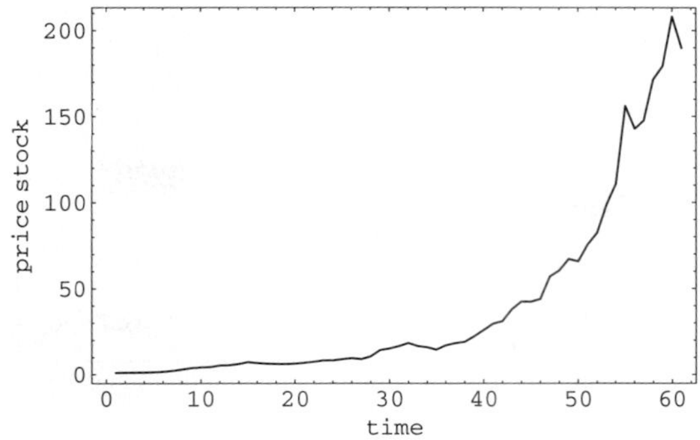

Fig. 1. A sample path of the stock in Black-Scholes model($r = 0.1, \sigma = 0.1$)

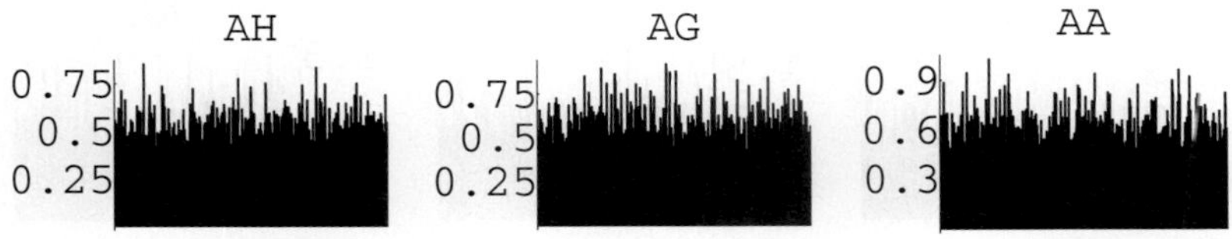

Fig. 2. Barcharts of simulated option prices with different averaging procedures in Black-Scholes model($r = 0.1, \sigma = 0.1$)

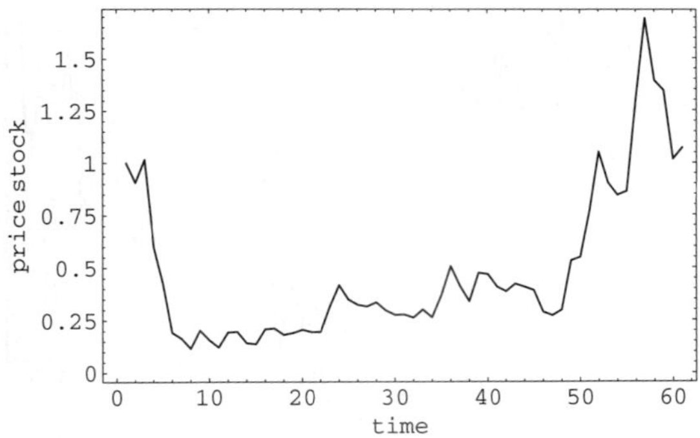

Fig. 3. A sample path of the stock in Black-Scholes model($r = 0.1, \sigma = 0.3$)

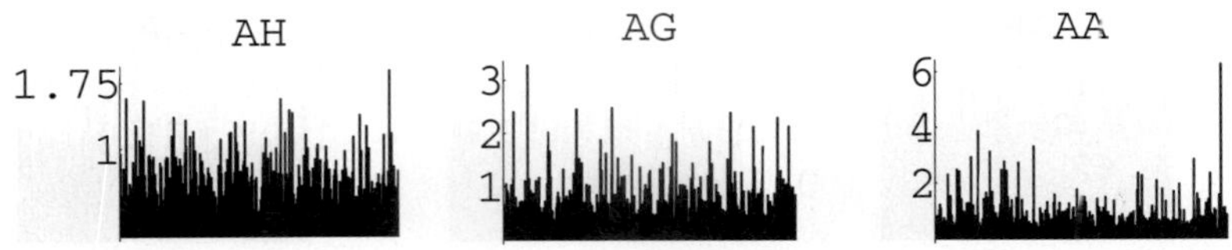

Fig. 4. Barcharts of simulated option prices with different averaging procedures in Black-Scholes model($r = 0.1, \sigma = 0.3$)

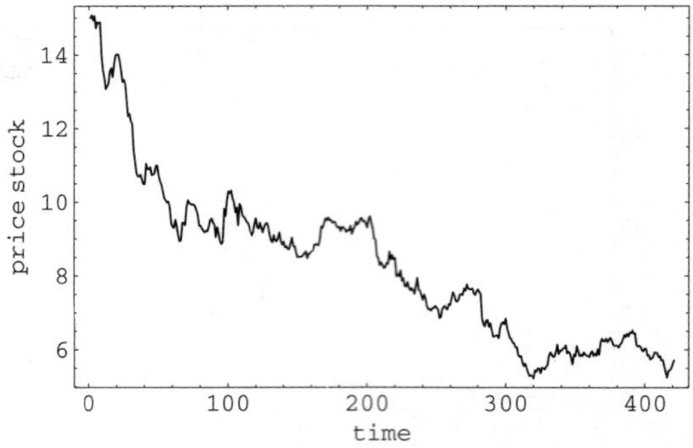

Fig. 5. A sample path of stock in NIG asset price model ($\alpha = 81.6$, $\beta = -3.69$, $\mu = -0.000123$, $\delta = 0.0103$)

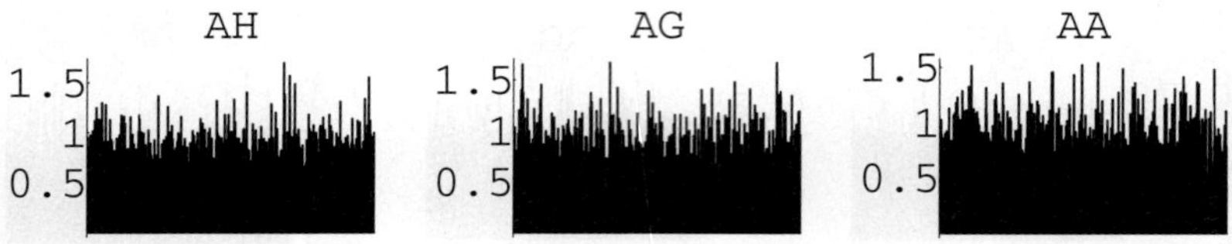

Fig. 6. Barcharts of simulated option prices with different averaging procedures in NIG asset price model($\alpha = 81.6$, $\beta = -3.69$, $\mu = -0.000123$, $\delta = 0.0103$)

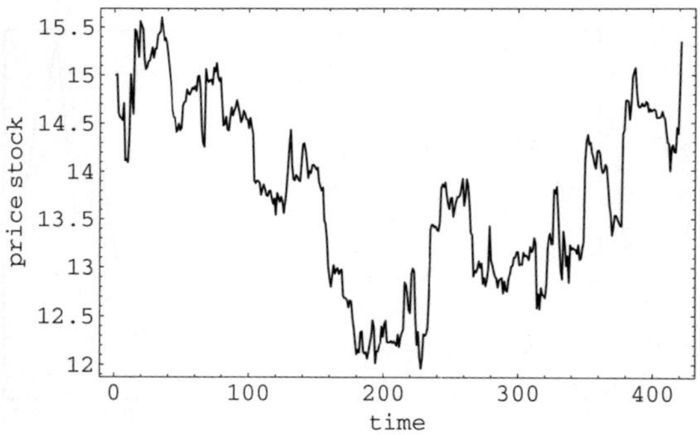

Fig. 7. A sample path of stock in NIG asset price model ($\alpha = 81.6$, $\beta = -3.69$, $\mu = -0.000123$, $\delta = 0.0001$)

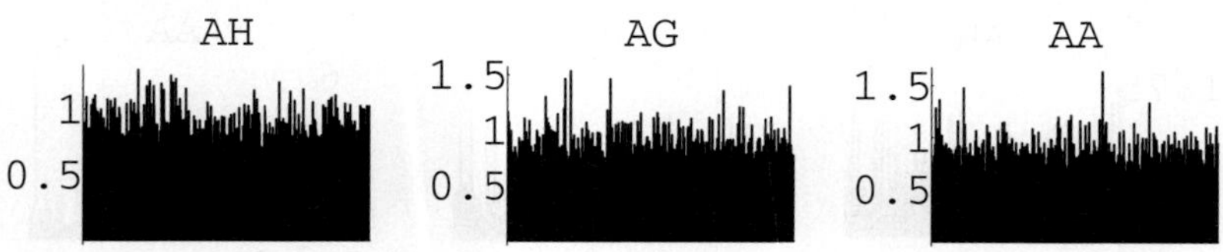

Fig. 8. Barcharts of simulated option prices with different averaging procedures in NIG asset price model ($\alpha = 81.6$, $\beta = -3.69$, $\mu = -0.000123$, $\delta = 0.0001$)

little difference as in Figure **2** and Figure **6**; when the stock prices fluctuate remarkably as in Figure **3** and Figure **7**, the simulated harmonic averaging prices behave more stable than arithmetic and geometric averaging prices as in Figure **4** and Figure **8**. In other words, the harmonic averaging reduces the variance of estimate. The reason is that harmonic averaging eliminates the influence of the stock prices which are not coordinate. So the harmonic averaging can reflect the convergence trend of data and is more suitable for the stock with remarkable fluctuation.

3 Approximations for Discrete Harmonic Asian Options

3.1 Approximations in Black-Scholes Model

The price of harmonic Asian option is according to risk-neutral measure Q given by (1). For notational simplicity we will assume $t_0 = 0$ and $n = T$ i.e the averaging starts at time $t = 1$ and we determine the price at time $t = 0$. The probability distribution of A_h has no available explicit representation. The best approach for deriving approximate analytic price formulas is to approximate the distribution of A_h by an approximate lognormal distribution through the method of generalized Edge Worth Series expansion. Recall that the cumulants of a random variable X with distribution function F are defined by

$$\chi_i(F) = [\frac{\partial^i \ln E[e^{tX}]}{\partial t^i}]_{t=0}, i = 1, 2, \ldots$$

and can also be expressed in terms of moments. For the first four cumulants we have

$$\begin{aligned}
\chi_1(F) &= E[X] \\
\chi_2(F) &= E[(X - E[X])^2] \\
\chi_3(F) &= E[(X - E[X])^3] \\
\chi_4(F) &= E[(X - E[X])^4] - 3\chi_2^2(F)
\end{aligned}$$

In the sequel we will make use of the following classical result:

Lemma 1. *(Jarrow and Rudd[5])Let F and G be two continuous distribution functions with $G \in \epsilon^5$ and $\chi_1(F) = \chi_1(G)$, and assume that the first five moments of both distributions exsist. $f(x)$ and $g(x)$ are the density functions of F and G respectively. Then we can expand the density f(x) in terms of the density g(x) as follows*

$$f(x) = g(x) + \frac{\chi_2(F) - \chi_2(G)}{2}\frac{\partial^2 g}{\partial x^2}(x) - \frac{\chi_3(F) - \chi_3(G)}{3!}\frac{\partial^3 g}{\partial x^3}(x) +$$

$$\frac{\chi_4(F) - \chi_4(G) + 3(\chi_2(F) - \chi_2(G))^2}{4!}\frac{\partial^4 g}{\partial x^4}(x) + \varepsilon(x)$$

where $\varepsilon(x)$ is a residual error term.

We will now approximate the distribution function of $\frac{n}{\sum_{i=1}^{n}\frac{1}{S(t_i)}}$ (which we denote by F) by a lognormal distribution G. The density of the lognormal distribution is given by

$$g(x) = f_{LN}(x) = \frac{1}{\sigma\sqrt{2\pi}x}\exp(-\frac{(\ln x-\mu)^2}{2\sigma^2})\chi_{0,\infty}(x)$$

Let us define

$$R_i = \frac{S_i}{S_{i-1}}, i = 1, \dots, n$$

and

$$\frac{1}{L_n} = 1$$

$$\frac{1}{L_{i-1}} = 1 + \frac{1}{R_i L_i}, i = n, , n-1 \dots, 2$$

Then we have

$$\sum_{k=1}^{n}\frac{1}{S_k} = \frac{1}{S_0}(\frac{1}{R_1} + \frac{1}{R_1}\frac{1}{R_2} + \dots + \frac{1}{R_1}\frac{1}{R_2}\cdots\frac{1}{R_n}) = \frac{1}{S_0 R_1 L_1}$$

Since we can rewrite equation (1) to

$$AH_0 = nS_0 e^{-rT} E^Q[(L_1 R_1 - \frac{K}{nS_0})^+]$$

it remains to determine $E^Q[(L_1R_1)^m]$ for $m = 1,2,3,4$. Because of the independent increments property of a Lévy process, we have $E^Q[(L_1R_1)^m] = E^Q[L_1^m]E^Q[R_1^m]$ and

$$E^Q[\frac{1}{L_{i-1}^m}] = E^Q[(1 + \frac{1}{R_i L_i})^m] = \sum_{k=0}^{m}\binom{m}{k} E^Q[\frac{1}{L_i^k}]E^Q[\frac{1}{R_i^k}]. \tag{5}$$

In order to apply recursion (5), we need to determine the moments $E^Q[R_i^{-k}]$.

Lemma 2. *For all $k \in Z$ we have*

$$E^Q[R_i^k] = \exp\{\frac{k^2\sigma^2}{2} + k(r - \frac{\sigma^2}{2})\}. \tag{6}$$

The moments $E^Q[L_1^{-m}] (m = 1,2,3,4)$ can now be calculated recursively using (5), (6) and the fact that $E^Q[L_n^{-k}] = 1$ for all $k \in \{0,\dots,m\}$. In order to determine the moments $E^Q[L_1^m]$ we approximate the distribution of L_1^{-1} by lognormal distribution. From the numerical illustrations we can see it is a good approximate. The parameters of the approximating lognormal distribution for L_1^{-1} are chosen in such a way:

$$E^Q[L_1^{-m}] = e^{\frac{\sigma_-^2 m^2}{2} + \mu_- m}, m = 1,2$$

Where σ_-^2 and μ_- denote the variance and mean of the approximating lognormal distribution for L_1^{-1}. After we get the values of σ_-^2 and μ_- , the moments $E^Q[L_1^m], m = 1,2,3,4$ and subsequently the cumulants $\chi_i(F)$ can now be calculated. The parameters of the approximating lognormal distribution for F are chosen(a so-called Wilkinson approximation):

$$\widetilde{\mu} = 2\ln(\chi_1(F)) - \frac{1}{2}\ln(\chi_1^2(F) + \chi_2(F))$$

$$\widetilde{\sigma}^2 = \ln(\chi_1^2(F) + \chi_2(F)) - 2\ln(\chi_1(F))$$

In this way we have derived a lognormal approximation pricing formula for a harmonic average option , which we call the Turnbull-Wakeman price AH_C^{TW} at time $t = 0$.

Proposition 1. *The price at time 0 of a European-style harmonic average option with maturity T and strike price K is*

$$AH_0^{TW} = e^{-rT} nS_0 (e^{\widetilde{\mu}+\frac{\widetilde{\sigma}^2}{2}} \Phi(\frac{\widetilde{\mu}+\widetilde{\sigma}^2 - \ln(\frac{K}{nS_0})}{\widetilde{\sigma}}) - \frac{K}{n}\Phi(\frac{\widetilde{\mu} - \ln(\frac{K}{nS_0})}{\widetilde{\sigma}}))$$

$$-e^{-rT} nS_0 (\frac{\chi_3(F) - \chi_3(G)}{3!} \frac{\partial g(\frac{K}{nS_0})}{\partial x} + \frac{\chi_4(F) - \chi_4(G)}{4!} \frac{\partial^2 g(\frac{K}{nS_0})}{\partial x^2}). \tag{7}$$

Where Φ denotes the standard normal distribution function.

If only the first two cumulants are considered, we call the corresponding approcimation the Lévy price AH_0^L given by

$$AH_0^L = e^{-rT} nS_0 (e^{\widetilde{\mu}+\frac{\widetilde{\sigma}^2}{2}} \Phi(\frac{\widetilde{\mu}+\widetilde{\sigma}^2 - \ln(\frac{K}{nS_0})}{\widetilde{\sigma}}) - \frac{K}{n}\Phi(\frac{\widetilde{\mu} - \ln(\frac{K}{nS_0})}{\widetilde{\sigma}})). \tag{8}$$

3.2 Approximations in NIG Lévy Price Model

The approximation approach is same with the case in Black-Scholes model except the values of the moments of R_i.

Lemma 3. *For all $k \in Z$ we have*

$$E^\theta[R_i^k] = \exp(\delta(\sqrt{\alpha^2 - (\beta+\theta)^2} - \sqrt{\alpha^2 - (\beta+\theta+k)^2} + k\mu). \tag{9}$$

Where θ is the (unique) solution of

$$r = \mu + \delta(\sqrt{\alpha^2 - (\beta+\theta)^2} - \sqrt{\alpha^2 - (\beta+\theta+1)^2}). \tag{10}$$

$E^\theta[.]$ denotes the expectation under equivalent probability measure P^θ defined through

$$dP^\theta = \exp\{\theta Z_t - t\log(M_{NIG}(\theta))\}dP$$

Under P^θ the discounted stock price process $(e^{-rt}S_t)_{t\geq 0}$ is a P^θ-martingale.

3.3 Numerical Illustrations

We now give some numerical illustrations of the accuracy of the approximations. We assume $S_0 = 1$ in black-Scholes model.

Table 1. Approximations and Monte Carlo simulated option prices in Black-Scholes model

T	σ	r	K	AH_0^{TW}	AH_0^L	AH_0^{MC}	AA_0^{MC}	AG_0^{MC}
10	0.03	0.06	0.5	0.476652	0.476652	0.478	0.501183	0.488546
			0.6	0.421771	0.4721771	0.42093	0.44666	0.435854
			0.7	0.36689	0.36689	0.367246	0.388192	0.380814
			0.8	0.321009	0.321009	0.311147	0.332817	0.32444
			0.9	0.257128	0.257128	0.256482	0.281612	0.270179
			1.0	0.202247	0.202247	0.205934	0.224207	0.21403
			1.1	0.147363	0.147366	0.148556	0.168945	0.160167
			1.2	0.0924995	0.0925961	0.0943131	0.114575	0.102128
		0.1	0.5	0.42741	0.42741	0.426791	0.479315	0.453353
			0.6	0.390622	0.390622	0.390486	0.44343	0.414235
			0.7	0.353834	0.353834	0.354285	0.406382	0.378317
			0.8	0.317046	0.317046	0.315922	0.369834	0.342639
			0.9	0.280258	0.280258	0.280993	0.330588	0.307457
			1.0	0.24347	0.24347	0.243948	0.296017	0.266986
			1.1	0.206682	0.206682	0.205448	0.260073	0.231946
			1.2	0.169894	0.169894	0.169227	0.224403	0.196551
	0.1	0.1	0.5	0.418778	0.418778	0.417505	0.483967	0.449209
			0.6	0.38199	0.38199	0.380172	0.443089	0.416442
			0.7	0.34521	0.345202	0.353508	0.407292	0.372287
			0.8	0.308506	0.308415	0.307996	0.369344	0.340416
			0.9	0.272077	0.271634	0.261247	0.327221	0.311506
			1.0	0.236029	0.234909	0.22962	0.301581	0.266947
			1.1	0.20003	0.198441	0.196735	0.252667	0.233209
			1.2	0.16388	0.16388	0.163187	0.229049	0.196173

In Table1, we compare the approximation techniques for the harmonic average options with Monte Carlo simulated prices AH^{MC} in Black-Scholes model. The arithmetic average option prices AA_0^{MC} and geometric average option prices AG_0^{MC} are also given. We can see from the results the accuracy of approximations is satisfied and the harmonic average option prices are smaller than arithmetic and geometric average option prices.

In Tables 2-4, we give the average relative percentage error (ARPE) of AH_0^{TW} and AH_0^L with respect to AH_0^{MC}. The results show ARPE increases with σ.

Table 2. The ARPE in Black-Scholes model($T = 20, \sigma = 0.03, r = 0.06$)

T	σ	r	K	AH_0^{TW}	AH_0^L	AH_0^{MC}	$ARPE(AH_0^{TW})$	$ARPE(AH_0^L)$
20	0.03	0.06	0.5	0.380948	0.380948	0.380198		
			0.6	0.350829	0.350829	0.350528		
			0.7	0.320709	0.320709	0.321366		
			0.8	0.29059	0.29059	0.29176		
			0.9	0.26047	0.26047	0.259527		
			1.0	0.230351	0.230351	0.231038		
			1.2	0.170113	0.170112	0.17095	0.292%	0.2913%

Table 3. The ARPE in Black-Scholes model($T = 20, \sigma = 0.1, r = 0.06$)

T	σ	r	K	AH_0^{TW}	AH_0^L	AH_0^{MC}	$ARPE(AH_0^{TW})$	$ARPE(AH_0^L)$
20	0.1	0.06	0.5	0.366836	0.366836	0.359127		
			0.6	0.336717	0.336717	0.337602		
			0.7	0.306599	0.306599	0.301936		
			0.8	0.276495	0.276495	0.272125		
			0.9	0.246455	0.246455	0.240383		
			1.0	0.216629	0.216626	0.217068		
			1.1	0.187325	0.187323	0.185187		
			1.2	0.159031	0.159031	0.161754	1.39%	1.39%

Table 4. The ARPE in Black-Scholes model($T = 20, \sigma = 0.1, r = 0.1$)

T	σ	r	K	AH_0^{TW}	AH_0^L	AH_0^{MC}	$ARPE(AH_0^{TW})$	$ARPE(AH_0^L)$
20	0.1	0.1	0.5	0.25243	0.25243	0.251441		
			0.6	0.238896	0.238896	0.243987		
			0.7	0.225362	0.225362	0.230608		
			0.8	0.211828	0.211829	0.210502		
			0.9	0.198289	0.198295	0.19816		
			1.0	0.184738	0.184762	0.179673		
			1.1	0.171169	0.171231	0.171989		
			1.2	0.15759	0.157708	0.160738	1.125%	1.114%

In Tables 5,6 we compare the approximation techniques for the harmonic average options with Monte Carlo simulated prices AH^{MC} in NIG Lévy asset price model.

From the calculate results we can see the approximate calculate approach developed in our paper do better in Black-Scholes framework than NIG Lévy asset price model.

Table 5. Approximations in NIG Lévy price model ($\alpha = 99.4, \beta = -1.76, \delta = 0.1, \mu = 0.0459$)

T	r	S_0	K	AH_0^{TW}	AH_0^{L}	AH_0^{MC}
20	0.05	45	40	11.7715	11.7708	10.7
			41	11.4042	11.4029	10.375
			42	11.0372	11.0351	10.0199
			43	10.6706	10.6672	9.20368
			44	10.3047	10.2994	9.44471
			45	9.9395	9.93173	9.148
			46	9.57525	9.56413	8.587
			47	9.21209	9.19672	8.1718
			48	8.85072	8.8296	7.75
			49	8.48962	8.46292	7.522
			50	8.13051	8.09688	7.299

Table 6. Approximations in NIG Lévy price model ($\alpha = 99.4, \beta = -1.76, \delta = 0.5, \mu = 0.035$)

T	r	S_0	K	AH_0^{TW}	AH_0^{L}	AH_0^{MC}
20	0.05	80	50	28.6047	28.6047	28.6099
			60	24.9259	24.9259	23.8567
			70	21.2471	21.2475	19.5818
			80	17.5732	17.5744	16.4731
			90	13.9385	13.9402	12.7901
			100	10.454	10.4545	8.56315
			110	7.31896	7.3174	6.64592
			120	4.74428	4.74194	3.81282

4 Conclusion

The Asian option pricing with discrete harmonic averaging is discussed in this paper. Monte Carlo simulated prices show the difference during the three averaging procedures. The difference indicates that the harmonic averaging is more suitable for the stock with remarkable fluctuation. We give an approximation approach of the harmonic averaging and approximation is used twice in our approach. Finally, numerical illustrations are given, the numerical results show the approximation method behaves poor in NIG Lévy asset price model. So better approximation method should be sought for in the further study.

References

1. Albrecher, H., Predota, M.: On Asian Option Pricing for NIG Lévy Processes. Journal of Computational and Applied Mathematics **172** (2004) 153-168
2. Albrecher, H., Predota, M.: Bounds and Approximations for Discrete Asian Options in Variance-gamma Model. Grazer. Math. Ber. **345** (2002) 35-57

3. Boyle, P. P.: New Life Forms on the Option Landscape. Journal of Financial Enginering **2(3)** (1993) 217-252
4. Eberlein, E., Papapantoleon, A.: Equivalence of Floating and Fixed Strike Asian and Lookback Options. Stochastic Processes and their Application **115** (2005) 31-40
5. Jarrow, R., Rudd, A.: Approximate Option Valuation for Arbitrary Stochastic Processes. J.Financial Econom **10** (1982) 347-369
6. Kwok, Y. K. : Mathematical Models of Financial Derivatives. New York, Springer(1998)
7. Kemna, A.G.Z., Vorst, T.C.F.: A Pricing Method for Options Based on Average Asset Values. Journal of Banking and Finance **14** (1990) 113-129
8. Simon, S., Goovaerts, M. J., Dhaene, J.: An Easy Computable Upper Bound for the Price of an Arithmetic Asian Option. Insur. Math. Econom **26** (2000) 175-183
9. Turnbull, S., Wakeman, L.: A Quick Algorithm for Pricing European Average Options. J. Finance Quant.Anal **26** (1991) 377-389
10. Večeř, J., Xu, M. X.: Pricing Asian Options in a Semimartingale Model. Quantitative Finance **4** (2004) 170-175
11. Zhang, P. G.: Flexible Asian Options. Journal of Financial Enginering **3(1)** (1994) 65-83

An Estimation Model of Research Cost Based on Rough Set and Artificial Neural Network*

Yangyi Jiang[1], Hengxi Zhang, Jiang Xie, and Ke Meng

Engineering college, Air Force Engineering University, Xi'an 710038, China
[1]j.yy@163.com

Abstract. The problem of research cost estimation is a typical multi-factors estimation issue, which has not been solved satisfactorily. A method integrating rough sets theory and artificial neural network is presented to estimate cost. In term of the important degree of input influencing factor to output, rough set approach and the conception of information entropy are employed to reduce the parameters of the input parameter set with no changing classification quality of samples. Thus, the number of the input variables and neurons is gotten, and the cost estimation model based on rough set and BP artificial network is set by learning from the original data of typical samples. At last, its application to the cost estimation of missile system is given. It was shown that the approach can reduce the training time, improve the learning efficiency, enhance the predication accuracy, and be feasible and effective.

1 Introduction

The estimation of Materiel research cost can provide reliable guidance for the verification, research and production in acquisition, and also for cutting the defense budget. The factors affecting the research cost are numerous, such as various weapon characteristics, and the relation among factors is complex. It is a typical problem of multi-factors estimation, which has not been solved satisfactorily. There are many classic methods of cost estimation, for instance, parameter method, analogy method, engineering method and so on. But the estimation result is not satisfied because of their disadvantages [1].

Many researches have been done recently on the theory and method of multi-factors estimation. Several methods of multi-factors estimation have been present, for example, time serial analysis methods, regression analysis methods and other approach based on fuzzy mathematics, grey theory or artificial neural networks(ANNs) [2]. Among these methods, ANNs behave excellently on function approximation, leaning , self-organizing and self-adapting. But ANN has two obvious shortcomings when applied to a large number of data [3,4]. The first is that ANN requires a long time to train the huge amount of data of large data-bases. The second is that ANN lacks explanation facilities for their knowledge.

Rough set theory, proposed by Z.Pawlak in 1982, is a mathematic tool to describe and process uncertainty and incompleteness effectively [5]. Rough set (RS) can reduce

* The research was supported by the Doctorate Foundation of the Engineering College, Air Force Engineering University(BC0504).

D.-S. Huang, K. Li, and G.W. Irwin (Eds.): ICIC 2006, LNAI 4114, pp. 766–771, 2006.

the dimension of input data space by mining the relation among data and eliminating redundant data. However, Rough set method is worse at generalization and is sensitive to noise. The result will be bad when applying test data contained noise on the RS model obtained from training data without noise [6]. Fortunately, ANNs has preferable noise suppressant and good generalization ability. The combination of rough sets and neural networks is a natural choice because of their complementary features.

Therefore, a method of integrating RS theory and ANN (RSANN) is presented to solve the problem of multi-factors estimation in the paper. Basic concepts of rough set theory and some relevant techniques are briefly introduced in Section 2.1. The construction of RSANN model is described and the algorithms to reduce the parameters are proposed in Section 2.2. An application of the proposed model to materiel research cost estimation is presented in Section 3, and finally concluding remarks are given in Section 4.

2 RSANN Cost Estimation Model

2.1 Basic Concepts of Rough Sets and ANN

An information system is a 4-tuple $S =< U, A, V, f >$, where U is a finite set of objects, called the universe, A is a finite set of attributes, $V = U_{a \in A}, V_a$ is a domain of attribute a, and $f : U \times A \rightarrow V$ is called an information function such that $f(x, a) \in V_a$, for $\forall a \in A, \forall x \in U$.

In the classification problems, an information system is also seen as a decision table assuming that $A = C \cup D$ and $C \cap D = \emptyset$, where C is a set of condition attributes and D is a set of decision attributes. Let $S =< U, A, V, f >$ be an information system: every $P \subset A$ generates a indiscernibility relation $IND(P)$ on U, which is defined as follows:

$$IND(P) = \{(x, y) \in U \times U : f(x, a) = f(y, a), \forall a \in P\}. \tag{1}$$

Let $P \subseteq A$, $X \subseteq U$. The P-lower approximation of X (denoted by $\underline{P}X$) and the P-upper approximation of X (denoted by $\overline{P}X$) are defined in the following expressions:

$$\underline{P}(X) = \{Y \in U/P : Y \subseteq X\}, \tag{2}$$

$$\overline{P}(X) = \{Y \in U/P : Y \cap X \neq \emptyset\}. \tag{3}$$

$\underline{P}X$ is the set of all objects from U which can be certainly classified as elements of X employing the set of attributes P. $\overline{P}X$ is the set of objects of U which can possibly be elements of X using the set of attributes P. Decision rules derived from a decision table can be used for recommendations concerning new objects.

ANN models the structure of neurons in the human brain, with the network consisting of processing units arranged in layers. The ANN learns by adjusting the values of these weights through a back propagation algorithm that permits error corrections to be fed through the layers. ANN are renowned for their ability to learn and generalize from example data, even when the data is noisy and incomplete. This ability has led to an investigation into the application of ANNs to automated knowledge acquisition. They also help to discern patterns among input data, require few assumptions, and achieve a high degree of prediction accuracy.

2.2 The Construction of RSANN Model

Rough Set decision models must be built firstly in order to reduct the input parameters of RSANN. The character parameters impacting on outputs, $x_1, x_2, \ldots, x_n$, are treated as condition attributes. So the set of condition attribute is $C = \{x_1, x_2, \ldots, x_n\}$. The output parameter y is treated as the decision attribute, and the set of decision attribute is $D = \{y\}$. Every historic input and output data of the system composes an object $u_i = \{x_{i_1}, x_{i_2}, \ldots, x_{i_n}; y_i\}$. The university is $U = \{u_i | i = 1, 2, \ldots, m\}$. Thus, the decision data model $S =< U, C \cup D >$ is obtained.

The combination of rough sets and neural networks is very natural for their complementary features. For example, in [3], a rule set and a neural network are obtained by the data from the same database. In the prediction phase, a new object is first predicted by the rule set, if it does not match any of the rules, it is fed into the neural network to get its result. In [7] Rough set method was also applied to generating rules from trained neural networks. There are also other approaches to integrate rough set and neural networks [8,9].

In this paper, rough set theory is only used to selected input parameters. Let RS be a preset system and ANN be a postposition system. The multi-factors estimation model is set by learning from the original data of reducted parameters. The cost estimation can be made by putting new data into the neural networks trained. The flow chart of RSANN model is shown in Fig.1.

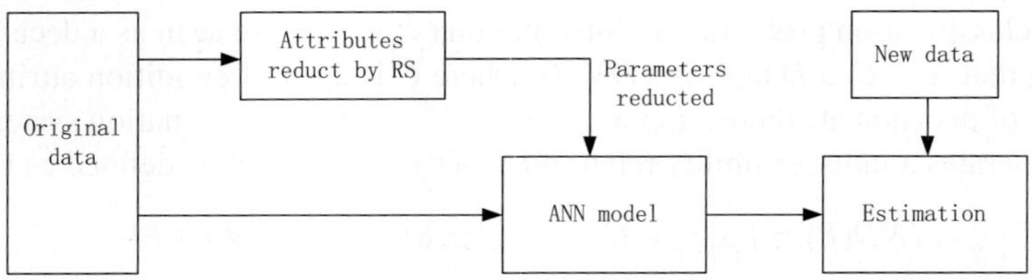

Fig. 1. The flow diagram of RSANN model

Parameter Reduct. For simplification, the discretized decision data model is also $S =< U, C \cup D >$. The signification of attributes is defined by information entropy. Parameters are reducted by the importance of attributes.

Let $A \subseteq C$, the probability distribution of σ algebra composed by subsets on U/A is

$$P(X) = \frac{card(X)}{card(U)}, \qquad X \in U/A, \tag{4}$$

where $card(X)$ is the potential of X. $card(X)$ denotes the number of entries in X when X is a finite set. Let

$$H(A) = -\sum_{X \in U/A} P(X) ln(P(X)), \tag{5}$$

where $H(A)$ is the information entropy of the condition attribute set A. Let

$$H(D|A) = -\sum_{X \in U/A} P(X) \sum_{Y \in U/D} P(Y|X) ln(P(Y|X)) \tag{6}$$

$$P(Y|X) = \frac{card(Y \cap X)}{card(X)}, \tag{7}$$

where $H(D|A)$ is the condition information entropy of decision attributes D corresponding to condition attribute subset A. The parameter $H(D|A)$ provide a reasonable measurement of information dependency of decision attributes D corresponding to condition attribute subset A. The dependency is stronger when $H(D|A)$ is bigger, otherwise weaker. Let $C_j = C - \{x_j\}, j = 1, 2, \ldots, n$, and

$$\lambda(x_j, C, D) = H(D|C_j) - H(D|C), \qquad j = 1, 2, \ldots, n. \tag{8}$$

If $\lambda(x_j, C, D)$ is greater, the effect of output y impacted by the input parameter x_j (condition attribute) is stronger. So the parameter is more importance. If $\lambda(x_j, C, D) = 0$, the parameter x_j is redundant and should be deleted from the set C. Then the input parameter set C is reducted to C_j. The importance of input parameters is computed continually until the importance of all parameters is greater than 0. So the reducted parameter set C^* is obtained. We can supposed $C^* = \{x_1, x_2, \ldots, x_N\}$, where N is the count of reducted parameters.

The Model of Artificial Neural Network. Here we use BP artificial neural network. The typical structure of BP ANN is three layers feed-forward ANN, containing input layer, hidden layer and output layer. In input layer the number of neurons is equal to the count of reducted parameters set C^*. The decision attribute is treated as the output of BP model. The fundamental function of output neurons is logic *sigmoid* function, $f(u) = (1 + e^{-u})^{-1}$. Thus, the multi-factors estimation model based on rough set and ANN is set by learning from the original data of reducted parameters.

3 The Cost Estimation of Equipments Research

Here the RSANN model is applied to the research cost estimation of surface-to-air missiles. The main factors affecting the research cost of missile systems are launch weight $G_0(kg)$, missile length $L(m)$, wingspan $E(m)$, maximum flight speed $M_{max}(m/s)$, top launch height $H_{max}(km)$, maximum diameter $d_{max}(m)$, warhead weight $G_z(kg)$ and maximum rang of missile $R_{max}(lm)$ [10]. The data of eight missiles are treated as training samples, as shown in Table1(the data have been processed and converted to the same finance year and the unit of cost is hundred million).

Firstly, we build the decision data model on the base of Table 1 using threshold method. A threshold is set for each attribute and the value of attribute is converted to 1 if it is greater than the threshold, otherwise 0. So the model is characted and a decision table is obtained, as shown in Table 2.

The importance of input parameters corresponding to research cost can be calculated using equation (6). We can get that the importances of G_0, L, d_{max}, t G_z and R_{max} is 0 corresponding to research cost. So they are redundant and will be delete from parameters set. The three selected parameters are E, M_{max} and H_{max} and they are input to artificial neural network. The ANN model take three layers, with transform function

Table 1. The data of eight missiles and their costs

MISSILE	G_0	L	E	M_{max}	H_{max}	d_{max}	G_z	R_{max}	Cost
Roland	63.5	2.4	0.5	1.6	5.5	0.16	5.9	9.3	3.2
MIM-72F	86.2	2.9	0.64	2.5	2.5	0.12	4.5	5	3.7
AIM-9	78	2.94	0.55	2.3	3	0.16	4	14.5	4.5
AIM-9X	87	2.94	0.54	2.2	4	0.16	14	10	5
MIM–23	630	5.03	1.2	2.5	11	0.36	50	25	7.2
MIM-23B	625	5.03	1.2	2.5	18	0.36	50	40	8.9
SM-2	1360	8.23	1.58	3	24	0.34	61.2	127.9	18
PAC-2	1000	5.3	0.80	6	24	0.41	100	70	18.7

Table 2. Two-dimensional information table

U	C								D
	G_0	L	E	M_{max}	H_{max}	d_{max}	G_z	R_{max}	
1	0	0	0	0	0	0	0	0	0
2	0	0	0	0	0	0	0	0	0
3	0	0	0	0	0	0	0	0	0
4	0	0	0	0	0	0	0	0	1
5	1	1	1	0	0	1	1	1	1
6	1	1	1	0	1	1	1	1	1
7	1	1	1	1	1	1	1	1	1
8	1	1	0	1	1	1	1	1	1

transig, *transig* and *purelin*. The training function is *trainlm* and the number of neurons in hidden layer is 6. The initial rate of learning is 0.06. The momentum constant is set as 0.9 and the goal training error is set as 0.001. When achieving precision request, the test samples are input to test. Here, the average error square is 0.00055519 at the end of network iteration and the error curve is shown as Fig.2.

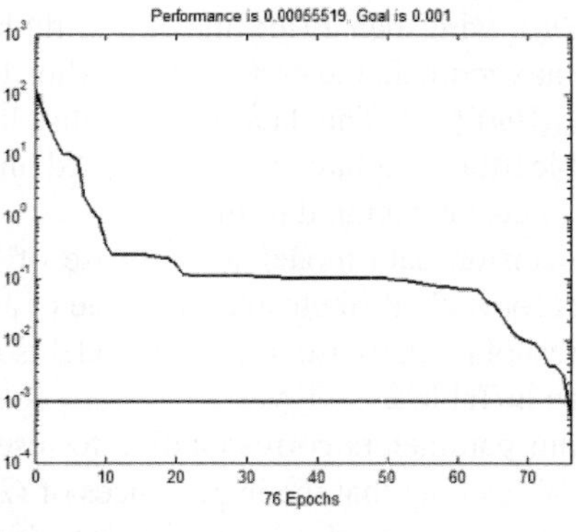

Fig. 2. The error curve

The new data of PAC-1 missile is treated as test data and put into the ANN model trained above. The parameters are $E = 0.87$, $M_{max} = 6$ and $H_{max} = 24$. The real research cost is 19.3 hundred million dollars. The estimation result is 18.6998 hundred million and the relative error is 2.61%. However, the result of regression analysis methods is 17.8 hundred million [10] and the result of pure BP network is 18.2 hundred million. The relative errors are 7.2% and 5.7% respectively. It was shown that the approach can enhance the predication accuracy, and is feasible and effective.

4 Conclusion

Our main contribution is the combination of rough set and artificial neural network to solve the problem of multi-factors estimation. Based on the capability of data analysis and process of Rough Set theory, the input parameters set can be reducted and then the structure of ANN is simplified. The reduct method is based on the concept of information entropy and the importance of input parameters corresponding to output. The RSANN model can reduce the training time, improve the learning efficiency and enhance the predication accuracy. The application of RSANN model to cost estimation of missile research demonstrates its usefulness and effectiveness. It can also be extended to solve other estimation issues.

References

1. Chen, X.C.: Materiel System Engineering. Defense Industry Publishing Press, Beijin,China (1998)
2. Craveirinha, J., Martins, L., Gomes, T., Antunes, C., Clímaco, J.: A new multiple objective dynamic routing method using implied cost. Journal of Telecommunications and Information Technologies **3** (2003) 51–59
3. Ahn, B.S., Cho, S.S., Kim, C.Y.: The integrated methodology of rough set theory and artificial neural network for business failure prediction. Expert Systems with Applications **18** (2000) 65–74
4. Lingras, P.: Comparision of neofuzzy and rough neural networks. In: RSSC'97. Volume 110. (1998) 207–215
5. Pawlak, Z.: Rough sets. International journal of information and computer science **11** (1982) 341–356
6. Stepaniuk, J.L., Kierzkowska, K.: Hybrid classiler based on rough sets and neural networks. Electronic Notes in Theoretical Computer Science **82** (2003) 1–11
7. Yasdi, R.: Combining rough sets learning and neural network learning method to deal with uncertain and imprecise information. Neurocomputing **7** (1995) 61–64
8. Jelonek, J., Krawiec, K., Slowinski, R.: Rough set reduction of attributes and their domains for neural networks. Computational Intelligence **11** (1995) 339–347
9. Swiniarski, R.W., Hargis, L.: Rough set as a front end of neural-networks texture classifiers. Neurocomputing **36** (2001) 85–102
10. Xu, P.G.: Surface-to-Air Missiles System Design. Space Navigation Publishing Press, Beijin,China (1996)

Analyzing Livestock Farm Odour Using a Neuro-fuzzy Approach

Leilei Pan and Simon X. Yang

School of Engineering, University of Guelph, Guelph, ON N1G 2W1, Canada
{lpan, syang}@uoguelph.ca

Abstract. An adaptive neuro-fuzzy based method for analyzing odour generation factors to the perception of livestock farm odour was proposed. In this approach, the parameters associated with a given membership function could be tuned so as to tailor the membership functions to the input/output data in order to account for these types of variations in the data values. A multi-factor livestock farm odour model was developed, and both numeric factors and linguistic factors were considered. The proposed method was tested with a livestock farm odour database. The results demonstrated the effectiveness of the proposed approach in comparison to a typical neural network.

1 Introduction

In the livestock industry, measure and control offensive odours from livestock production facilities are important as the requirement of environmental conditions. Prediction of odour intensity is difficult due to the complexity of livestock farm odour and a limited understanding of the odour itself. [1]. Various factors influence the perception of the odour, such as environment conditions, type of facilities, and farm management practises. However, how and by how much a generation factor would influence livestock farm odour still remain unclear. As a result of a poor understanding of the odour problem, existing odour control technologies are not efficient.

Livestock odour system is a complex, highly non-linear system. Therefore conventional statistical methods is not suitable for analyzing livestock farm odour. Artificial neural networks (ANNs) have been commonly used to predict odour intensity, for their generalization abilities [2], but ANNs are not capable of incorporating non-numeric or subjective human expert knowledge. Fuzzy logic based methods can incorporate human experience and expert knowledge, however they do not have learning ability, so that it is difficult to analyze complex systems without prior knowledge on the system being analyzed.

To overcome the limitations of both neural and fuzzy systems, in this paper, an Adaptive Network-based Fuzzy Inference System (ANFIS) approach is proposed to predict livestock farm odour intensity. Various comparative studies are also presented in this paper.

D.-S. Huang, K. Li, and G.W. Irwin (Eds.): ICIC 2006, LNAI 4114, pp. 772–777, 2006.

2 Methods

2.1 Adaptive Network-Based Fuzzy Inference System (ANFIS)

In common fuzzy logic systems, membership functions are arbitrarily chosen, and only membership functions that have been fixed are considered. Also, fuzzy inference is applied only to modelling systems whose rule structure is essentially predetermined by the user's interpretation of the characteristics of the variables in the model. However, in practice, these approaches may cause errors due to limit knowledge about the system, and incorrect selection of membership parameters.

The proposed ANFIS approach incorporated neuro-adaptive learning techniques into Fuzzy Logics. Instead of arbitrarily choosing the parameters of a given membership function, the parameters could be selected so as to tailor the membership functions to the input/output data in order to account for these types of variations in the data values.

ANFIS represents a Sugeno-type fuzzy system [3][4], where the fuzzy rules take the following form:

$$R_p\text{: If } x_1 \text{ is } A_1^p \text{ and } x_2 \text{ is } A_2^p \text{... and } x_n \text{ is } A_n^p \text{ Then } o_p = a_0^p + a_1^p x_1 + ... + a_n^p x_n \quad (1)$$

where x_i is i-th input linguistic variable in the antecedent part of p-th rule with $i = 1,...,n$ and A_i^p is the linguistic label associated with it in that rule. A_i^p has its associated fuzzy membership function. o_p is the consequent output of the p-th rule and a_i^p is the Sugeno parameters. The structure of ANFIS consists of a five-layer feedforward network.

Layer 1: Fuzzification layer. In this layer, the crisp inputs x_1 and x_2 are fuzzified through mapping into membership functions A_i and B_i of the linguistic variables. The membership functions can be any appropriate parameterized functions. In this paper, all the membership functions are bell functions as

$$\mu_A(x) = \frac{1}{1 + \left|\frac{x-c_i}{a_i}\right|^{2b_i}}, \quad (2)$$

where a_i, b_i and c_i are the parameters.

Layer 2: Rule operation layer. In this layer, each rule node performs a connective operations within the rule antecedent.

Layer 3: Normalization layer. In this layer, the firing strength of the fuzzy rules are normalized. The ratio of the i-th rule's firing strength to the sum of all rules' firing strength is calculated based on

$$O_i = \bar{w}_i = \frac{w_i}{\sum_i w_i}. \quad (3)$$

Layer 4: Consequent layer. In this layer, the values of the consequent are multiplied by normalized firing strengths according to

$$O_i = \bar{w}_i z_i. \quad (4)$$

Layer 5: Aggregation layer. The overall output of this layer as the aggregation of the incoming signals is computed by:

$$O = \sum_i \bar{w}_i z_i = \frac{\sum_i w_i z_i}{w_i}. \quad (5)$$

2.2 Data Sets

The proposed ANFIS approach was tested by a livestock database. Data were collected in the fields downwind from fourteen poultry, dairy and swine facilities in 2004. Outdoor temperature, wind speed, distance to the odour source, and odour Dilution-to-Threshold (D/T) intensity levels were recorded at each site. The detailed measuring procedure is described in paper [5]. There were a total of 264 samples in the data available for the development and testing of models. Approximately 20% of its data points were randomly selected for testing and the remaining 80% were used for training the neural network models.

2.3 Livestock Farm Models

ANFIS1 To estimate the odour intensity, a ANFIS model (ANFIS1) was designed. The model has 3 inputs: temperature, wind speed, and distance to the odour source. All the inputs are numeric data that have to be fuzzified in the fuzzification layer. The output is the odour intensity. The model was trained by a back-propagation (BP) algorithm.

ANFIS2 In order to test the ability of of the proposed approach of incorporating linguistic information, a ANFIS model (ANFIS2) was developed. The model has 3 inputs: temperature, type of facilities, and distance to the odour source. The type of facilities can generally represent such measures as type of animals, farm activity, odour emission rates, and other physical measures that may influence odour intensity. The output is the odour intensity. The model was trained by a BP algorithm.

NN In order to analyze the effectiveness of the proposed approach, a feedforward neural network model (NN) was designed with an input layer, one hidden layer, and an output layer.The model has 3 input neurons, where the inputs are temperature, wind speed, and distance to the odour source. The output is the odour intensity. The neural network was trained by a typical BP algorithm, and the results were compared with the results from ANFIS1 and ANFIS2.

3 Results and Analysis

3.1 Performance of NN

The performances of models were evaluated based on the accuracy of the predicted odour intensities. The predicted odour intensities using NN and perceived odour intensities by human assessors is shown in Figure 1. The correlation

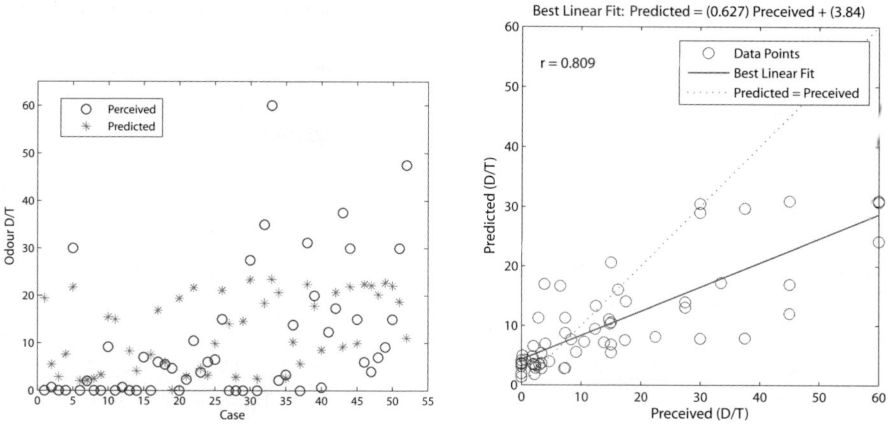

Fig. 1. Comparison of predicted odour intensities using NN with perceived odour intensities by human assessors

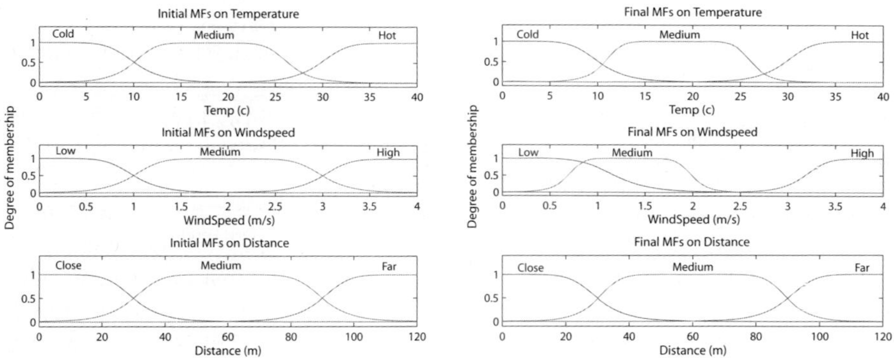

Fig. 2. Comparison of initial membership functions before the learning with final membership functions after learning using ANFIS1

coefficient of the predicted odour intensity and perceived odour intensity was r = 0.809 by using neural network technique alone.

3.2 Performance of ANFIS1

The comparison of predicted odour intensities using ANFIS1 with perceived odour intensities by human assessors is shown in Figure 2. By using the proposed ANFIS approach, the prediction accuracy was significantly improved (r = 93.7). The comparison of initial membership functions before the learning with final membership functions after learning using ANFIS1 is shown in Figure 5. Only the parameters of "Medium" in wind speed was obviously changed during the learning. The results shows that the proposed ANFIS approach is able to

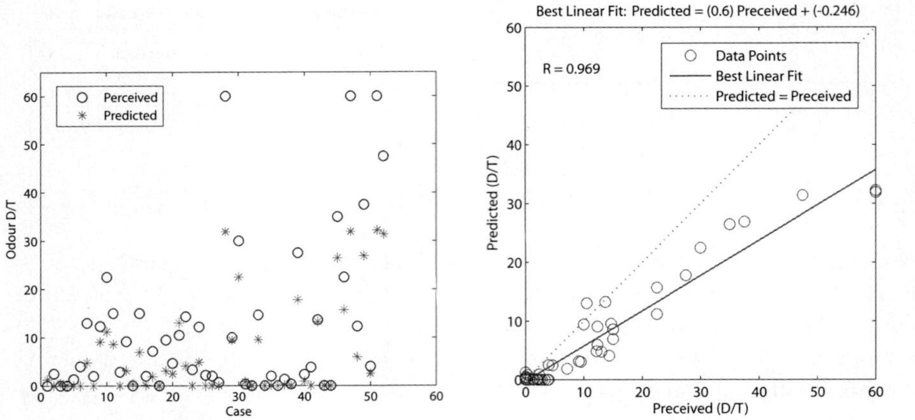

Fig. 3. Comparison of predicted odour intensities using ANFIS2 with perceived odour intensities by human assessors

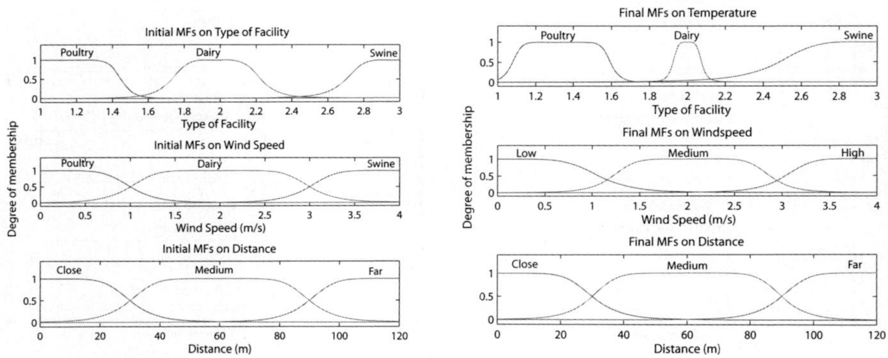

Fig. 4. Comparison of initial membership functions before the learning with final membership functions after learning using ANFIS2

incorporate human experience and knowledge, which allows prior knowledge to be embedded in the model, and thus improve the results of learning.

3.3 Performance of ANFIS2

The comparison of predicted odour intensities using ANFIS2 with perceived odour intensities by human assessors is shown in Figure 3. By incorporating type of facility, the prediction accuracy was improved (r = 96.9) compared to those of NN and ANFIS1.

The comparison of initial membership functions before the learning with final membership functions after learning using ANFIS1 is shown in Figure 4. Only the parameters of "Medium" in temperature was obviously changed during the learning. This result shows that type of facility does affect odour intensity. The proposed ANFIS approach is able to interpret linguistic variables such as type of facility and cloud cover conditions, and therefore increase the accuracy of odour prediction.

4 Conclusion and Discussion

An adaptive neuro-fuzzy based approach which incorporates neuro-adaptive learning techniques into Fuzzy Logics was proposed to analyze livestock farm odour. The proposed approach can to incorporate non-numeric or subjective human expert knowledge, which allows prior knowledge to be embedded in the model. Furthermore, the parameters of membership functions could be tuned during the learning so as to tailor the membership functions to the input/output data in order to account for these types of variations in the data values. A livestock farm database has been used as an example. The results show that the proposed approach is effective and can significantly increase the accuracy of odour prediction, in comparison with a typical feedforward neural network.

References

1. Zahn, J.A., DiSpirito, A.A., Do, Y.S., Brooks, B.: Correlation of Human Olfactory Response to Airbone Intensity of Malodourous Volatile Organic Compounds Emitted From Swine E2uent. Journal of Environmental Quality. 30 (2001) 535-647
2. Haykin, S.: Neural Networks: A Comprehensive Foundation. Prentice Hall, New Jersey, America (1999)
3. Jang, J., Sun, C., Mizutani, E.: Neuro-Fuzzy and Soft Computing: A Computational Approach to Learning and Machine Intelligence. Prentice Hall, New Jersey, America (1997)
4. Karray, F., De Silva, C.: Soft Computing and Tools of Intelligent Systems Design: Theory and Applications. Addison Wesley, New Jersey, America (2005)
5. Pan, L., Yang, S., Debruyn, J.: Measurement and Analysis of Downwind Odours from Livestock and Poultry Farms. In: Proceedings of ASAE International Livestock Engineering Symposium, Beijing, China (2005) 365-373

Credit Risk Assessment in Commercial Banks Based on Multi-layer SVM Classifier

Wei Sun and Chenguang Yang

Department of Economy Management, North China Electric Power University, Baoding 071003, Hebei, China
ycg1125@126.com

Abstract. According to the analysis of credit risk assessment in commercial banks, a set of index system is established. The index system combines financial factors with non-financial factors for credit risk assessment. The credit rating is separated into five classes- normality, attention, sublevel, doubt and loss. To classify the credit risks of five classes, a multi-layer support vector machines (SVM) classifier is established to assess the credit risk. In order to verify the effectiveness of the method, a real case is given and BP neural network is also used to assess the same data. The experiment results show that multi-layer SVM classifier is effective in credit risk assessment and achieves better performance than BP neural network.

1 Introduction

As one of the most important parts of the national finance system, commercial banks play important roles in economy development and stabilizing currency. However commercial banks often encounter a lot of risks. As one of the most hazardous risks, credit risk has great effect on banks management and development. Hence, how to assess credit risk in commercial banks effectively becomes an important topic in the finance field.

The method for credit risk assessment can be classified into two types: statistics method and artificial intelligence method. The common methods for credit risk assessment are KMV, neural networks [1], expert system [2] and etc. As a new method, SVM has been used to assess the credit risk [3], [4]. But the most of literatures which use SVM to assess credit risk have two shortages: index system emphasizes the financial factors while neglects the non-financial factors and credit rating is usually separate into two classes.

According to the research, a set of index system combining financial factors with non-financial factors for credit risk assessment is established, and multi-layer SVM classifier is established to assess the five-class risks. In order to prove the effectiveness of the method, we give an example coming from a commercial bank and the results show that the method can classify the data effectively.

2 Support Vector Machines

SVM is the theory based on statistical learning theory. It realizes the theory of VC dimension and principle of structural risk minimum. The whole theory can be simply

D.-S. Huang, K. Li, and G.W. Irwin (Eds.): ICIC 2006, LNAI 4114, pp. 778 – 785, 2006.

described as follows: searching an optimal hyperplane satisfies the request of classification, then using a certain algorithm to make the margin of the separation beside the optimal hyperplane maximum while ensuring the accuracy of correct classification. According to the theory, we can classify the separable data into two classes effectively. The following is the brief introduction of SVM in two cases: the linear case and the nonlinear case [5], [6], [7], [8], [9].

2.1 The Linear Case

Suppose we are given a set of training data $x_i \in R^n$ ($i = 1,2\cdots,$ n) with the desired output $y_i \in \{+1,-1\}$ corresponding to the two classes. And suppose there exists a separating hyperplane with the target functions $w \cdot x_i + b = 0$ (w represents the weight vector and b the bias).To ensure all training data can be classified, we must make the margin of separation $(2/\|w\|)$ maximum. Then, in the case of linear separation, the linear SVM for optimal separating hyperplane has the following optimization problem,

$$\text{Minimize} \qquad \phi(w) = \frac{1}{2} w^T w \tag{1}$$

$$\text{Subject to} \quad y_i(x_i \cdot w + b) \ge 1,\ i = 1,2\cdots,\ n \tag{2}$$

The solution to above optimization problem can be converted into its dual problem. We can search the nonnegative Lagrange multipliers by solving the following optimization problem,

$$\text{Maximize} \quad Q(\alpha) = \sum_{i=1}^{n} a_i - \frac{1}{2}\sum_{i=1}^{n}\sum_{j=1}^{n} a_i a_j y_i y_j x_i^T x_j \tag{3}$$

$$\text{Subject to} \quad \sum_{i=1}^{n} a_i y_i = 0 \ \ \alpha_i \ge 0 \ \ i = 1,2\cdots,\ n \tag{4}$$

The corresponding training data are the support vectors. Suppose α_i^* are the optimal Lagrange multipliers, the optimal weight vectors are

$$w^* = \sum_{i=1}^{n} \alpha_i^* y_i x_i \tag{5}$$

The optimal biases are

$$b^* = y_j - \sum_{i=1}^{n} y_j \alpha_i^* x_i^T x_j \tag{6}$$

Then, the optimal equation for classification is

$$f(x) = \operatorname{sgn}\{(w^* \cdot x) + b^*\} \tag{7}$$

The above discussion is restricted to the case that the training data is separable. To generalize the problem to the non-separable case, slack variable $\varepsilon_i \geq 0, i = 1, 2 \cdots n$ is introduced under the constraints of (2).The objective equation is

$$\text{Minimize} \quad \phi(w, \varepsilon) = \frac{1}{2} w^T w + C \sum_{i=1}^{n} \varepsilon_i \tag{8}$$

$$\text{Subject to} \quad y_i (w^T x_i + b) \geq 1 - \varepsilon_i \;\; \varepsilon_i \geq 0 \,, \; i = 1,2 \cdots, \; \text{n} \tag{9}$$

C is the nonnegative parameter chosen by users. Solving the problem is similar to the problem of the case of linear separation. But the constraints are changed to be

$$\sum_{i=1}^{n} a_i y_i = 0 \;\; 0 \leq \alpha_i \leq C \,, \; i = 1,2 \cdots, \; \text{n} \tag{10}$$

2.2 The Nonlinear Case

As to the non-linear separable data, the data can be mapped into a high dimensional feature space with a nonlinear mapping in which we can search the optimal hyper-plane. The linear classification after mapping is performed by selecting the appropriate inner-product kernel satisfies the Mercer's condition. Then the problem is converted into searching the nonnegative Lagrange multipliers $\{\alpha_i\}_{i=1}^{n}$ by solving the following optimization problem,

$$\text{Maximize} \quad Q(\alpha) = \sum_{i=1}^{n} \alpha_i - \frac{1}{2} \sum_{i=1}^{n} \sum_{j=1}^{n} \alpha_i \alpha_j y_i y_j K(x_i, x_j) \tag{11}$$

$$\text{Subject to} \quad \sum_{i=1}^{n} a_i y_i = 0 \;\; 0 \leq \alpha_i \leq C \,, \; i = 1,2 \cdots, \; \text{n}. \tag{12}$$

Hence, the final classification function is

$$f(x) = \text{sgn} \left\{ \sum_{i=1}^{n} \alpha_i^* y_i K(x_i, x_j) + b^* \right\} \tag{13}$$

The common used kernel function is RBF kernel function.

$$K(x, x') = \exp\left(-\frac{\|x, x'\|^2}{2\sigma^2}\right) \tag{14}$$

2.3 Multi-layer SVM Classifier

The standard SVM is only used to classify two classes. If the samples have *n* classes, a multi-layer SVM classifier which combines SVM and binary tree is established [10], [11], [12], [13].

For *n* classes training samples, *n*-1 SVMs should be trained. The first SVM use the first-class samples as -1 and the second-class, third-class…*n*th-class samples as +1 and then train SVM1. The *i*th SVM use the *i*th-class samples as -1 and the (*i*+1)th-class, (*i*+2)th-class…*n*th-class samples as +1 and then train SVM*i*. Until SVM (*n*-1) is trained, training samples of *n* classes will be classified.

3 Credit Risk Assessment Based on Multi-layer SVM Classifier

In the actual assessment, credit rating is usually separated into five classes: normality, attention, sublevel, doubt and loss. The process of credit risk assessment based on multi-layer SVM includes the following steps.

(1) Establish the index system;
(2) Establish the model based on multi-layer SVM;
(3) Collect the data which have been classified by experts or commercial banks;
(4) Train the network and classify the testing samples.

3.1 Index System

We use the real data from a commercial bank to assess the debtors' credit risk and judge the credit risk class by using multi-layer SVM. The index system of risk assessment is established according to the situation of the industrial organization [14]. The data of financial indexes can be gotten from the financial reporting, while the data of non-financial indexes can be evaluated by experts in the bank. Each index is used as one input in the model. The index system is shown in Table 1.

Table1. Index system of credit risk assessment

Number	Index
S_1	(Current assets-current liability) /total assets
S_2	Undistributed profit/ total assets
S_3	(Total profit+ interest expense) / total assets
S_4	Equity capital/total liability
S_5	Sales income/ total assets
S_6	Trade risk
S_7	Policy risk
S_8	Credit record
S_9	Development prospect
S_{10}	Level of management

3.2 Network Training

According to the character of credit risk, four SVMs are established to classify the five credit risk classes. The following are the detailed steps [15].

(1) SVM1 is established to train the first layer classification. SVM1 classify the normality class and other four classes (attention, sublevel, doubt and loss). If the class is normality, the output of SVM1 is -1; otherwise the output is +1.
(2) SVM2 is established to train the second layer classification. SVM2 classify the attention class and other three classes (sublevel, doubt and loss). If the class is attention, the output of SVM2 is -1; otherwise the output is +1.

(3) SVM3 is established to train the third layer classification. SVM3 classify the sublevel class and other two classes (doubt and loss). If the class is sublevel, the output of SVM3 is -1; otherwise the output is +1.
(4) SVM4 is established to train the forth layer classification. SVM4 classify the doubt class and loss class. If the class is doubt, the output of SVM4 is -1; otherwise the output is +1.

In the four SVMs, RBF function is used as the basic kernel to train the network. The whole process is` shown in Fig. 1.

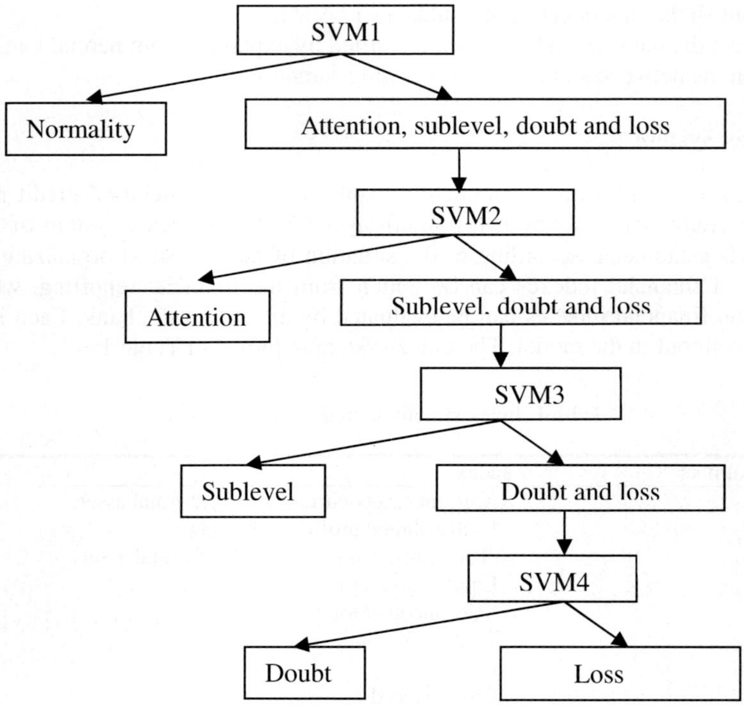

Fig. 1. The process of risk assessment based on multi-layer SVM

3.3 Network Test

The testing samples can be collected from banks. After training the network, the testing samples are inputted into the trained four-layer SVMs (SVM1, SVM2, SVM3 and SVM4). According to the output, the five classes can be classified [16], [17].

According to the output of SVM1, normality class and other classes (attention, sublevel, doubt and loss) can be classified. If the output is the latter, SVM2 is used to classify the attention class and other classes (sublevel, doubt and loss). Finally the five classes can be classified by using SVM3 and SVM4. So the five classes can be classified by a four-layer SVM classifier.

4 Application and Analysis

The credit data of 120 industry firms are obtained in this study. 80 samples of them are used as training samples, which include 17 firms of normality class, 16 firms of attention class, 18 firms of sublevel class, 14 firms of doubt class and 15 firms of loss class. Four-layer SVM classifier is established to train the network, and then SVM1, SVM2, SVM3 and SVM4 are gotten.

The rest 40 samples are used as testing samples. They include 9 samples of normality class, 7 samples of attention class, 8 samples of sublevel class, 7 samples of doubt class and 9 samples of loss class. Then the trained network (SVM1, SVM2, SVM3 and SVM4) is used to classify the testing samples.

4.1 Experiment Results

The results are shown as follows:

Testing samples of SVM1= [9 normality class, 7 attention class, 8 sublevel class, 7 doubt class, 9 loss class]

The output of SVM1= [-1 -1 -1 -1 -1 -1 -1 -1 -1 +1 +1…+1]

According to the output of SVM1, 9 firms of normality class and 31 firms of other classes (attention, sublevel, doubt and loss) are classified. Then 31 samples of other classes are as inputs of SVM2.

Testing samples of SVM2= [7 attention class, 8 sublevel class, 7 doubt class, 9 loss class]

The output of SVM2= [-1 -1 -1 -1 -1 -1 -1 +1 +1…+1]

According to the output of SVM2, 7 firms of attention class and 24 firms of other classes (sublevel, doubt and loss) are classified. Then 24 samples of other classes are as inputs of SVM3.

Testing samples of SVM3= [8 sublevel class, 7 doubt class, 9 loss class]

The output of SVM3= [-1 -1 -1 -1 -1 -1 -1 -1 +1 +1…+1]

According to the output of SVM3, 8 firms of sublevel class and 16 firms of other classes (doubt and loss) are classified. Then 16 samples of other classes are as inputs of SVM4.

Testing samples of SVM4= [7 doubt class, 9 loss class]

The output of SVM4= [-1 -1 -1 -1 -1 -1 -1 +1 +1 +1 -1 +1 +1 -1 +1 +1]

According to the testing results, a four-layer SVM classifier can classify the five credit risk classes. SVM1, SVM2 and SVM3 can correctly classify the samples. But SVM4 mistakes 2 samples of loss class for samples of doubt class.

Because the method of multi-layer SVM classifier is similar with BP neural network classification, BP neural network is also used to train the same training samples and test the same testing samples [18], [19], [20], [21]. The neuron number of input layer, interlayer and output layer is 10, 7and 5. Learning rate is 0.01, target error is 0.001, training time is 5000, and sigmoid function is used as active function. The following matrixes are used as the five classes.

Normality class= [1, 0, 0, 0, 0]

Attention class= [0, 1, 0, 0, 0]

Sublevel class= [0, 0, 1, 0, 0]

Doubt class= [0, 0, 0, 1, 0]
Loss class= [0, 0, 0, 0, 1]

The following table is the comparison of the results by using four-layer SVM classifier and BP neural network.

Table 2. Classification results of four-layer SVM classifier and BP

Class	Original number	Four-layer SVM classifier	B P
Normality	9	9	8
Attention	7	7	7
Sublevel	8	8	6
Doubt	7	7	6
Loss	9	7	6
Accuracy		95%	82.5%

4.2 Analysis

From Table 2, we can see that the four-layer SVM classifier can classify the testing samples of five classes in a high accuracy of classification. The classification correct rate of testing samples is 95%. The testing samples of normality class, attention class, sublevel class and doubt class are correctly classified. Only two samples of loss class are incorrectly classified as doubt class, which is not so important in real world. This means the four-layer SVM classifier shows great effective in credit risk assessment. Four-layer SVM classifier shows great classification capability in credit rating in the condition of similar data between two adjacent classes.

BP algorithm is also used to classify the testing samples. The classification correct rate of testing samples is 82.5%, which means BP algorithm is effective in credit risk assessment. Comparing with multi-layer SVM classifier, the classification correct rate of BP algorithm is less than multi-layer SVM classifier. From Table 2, we can see that only the testing samples of attention class are correctly classified. Some testing samples of normality class, sublevel class, doubt class and loss class are incorrectly classified. This means BP algorithm is not fit for practice.

BP shows lower classification correct accuracy than four-layer SVM classifier, which because the basic theory of BP and SVM is different. SVM is established with principle of structural risk minimum and has not over fitting, while BP algorithm is established with empirical risk minimum which leads to over fitting and lower classification correct accuracy.

5 Conclusions

SVM is a good learning algorithm which can solve the nonlinear, small sample and high dimensional problems. In this paper, a set of index system combining financial factors with non-financial factors for credit risk assessment is established. And then the model of multi-layer SVM classifier is established and studied when we classify the credit rating in commercial banks. In order to prove the effectiveness of the method, a real case is used and the experimental results show that the method is effective and classified the testing samples in a high accuracy. And the method shows higher classification correct rate than BP algorithm. The method shows two merits in the research: high classification accuracy and small sample, which mean it has great use value.

References

1. Xu, J. N., Xi, B.: AHP-ANN Based Credit Risk Assessment for Commercial Banks. Journal harbin univ.sci. & tech. 6 (2002) 94-98
2. Yu, G. A., Xu, H. B.: Design and Implementation of an Expert System of Loan Risk Evaluation. Computer Engineering & Science (2004) 104-106
3. Shin, K. S., Lee, T. S., Kim, H. J.: An Application of Support Vector Machines in Bankruptcy Prediction Model. Expert System with Applications 28 (2005) 127-135
4. Jae, H. M., Lee, Y. C.: Bankruptcy Prediction Using Support Vector Machine with Optimal Choice of Kernel Function. Expert System with Applications 28(2005) 603-614
5. Vladimir, N. V., Zhang, X. G.: Nature of Statistics Theory. Tsinghua university press, Beijing (2000)
6. Haykin, S., Ye, S. W., Shi, Z. Z.: Neural Network: a Comprehensive Foundation. China machine press, Beijing (2004)
7. Deng, N. Y., Tian, Y. J.: A New Method in Data Mining: Support Vector Machines. Science press, Beijing (2004)
8. Zhu, Y. S., Zhang, Y. Y.: The Study on Some Problems of Support Vector Classifier. Computer Engineering and Applications (2003) 66-38
9. Qi, H. N.: Support Vector Machines and Application Research Overview. Computer Engineering (2003) 6-9
10. Rank, Y. S., Zhang, K.: Support Vector Machine Networks for Multi-Class Classification. International Journal of Pattern Recognisition and Artificial Intelligence (2005) 775-786
11. Ayan, M. S., Narenkumar, P.: Minimal Classification Method with Error Correlation Codes for Multiclass Recognization. International Journal of Pattern Recognization and Artificial Intelligence (2005) 663-680
12. arl, G., Peter, S.: Model Selection for Support Vector Machine Classification. Neurcomputting (2005) 221-249
13. Lv, G. Y., Chen, H. Z.: Fault Diagnosis of Power Transformer Based on Multi-Layer SVM Classifier. Proceedings of the CSU EPSA 6 (2005) 19-23
14. An, J. L., Wang, Z. O.: A New SVM Multiclass Classification Method. Information and Control 7(2004) 262-267
15. Lu, B., Yang, J. W.: A Strategy of Multilevel Classification Based on SVM. Computer Engineering 1(2005) 73-76
16. Hou, H. F., Liu, S. H.: Credit Risk Assessment in Commercial Banks Based on SVM. Computer Engineering and Applications (2004) 176-179
17. Liu, Y. T., Wu, C., Wang, M.: The Model of Credit Risk Assessment in Commercial Banks on Support Vector Machine. Forecasting 1 (2005) 52-55
18. Wang, C. F., Wan, H. H.: Credit Risk Assessment in Commercial Banks Using Neural Networks. Theory and Application of System Engineering 9 (1999) 24-32
19. He, Y., Jiang, G. Y., Liu, X. S.: The Credit Assessment Model for Enterprise Based on BP Neural Networks. Mathematic in Economics 1 (2005) 64-71
20. Pang, S. L., Wang, Y. M.: Research of Credit Assessment Model Based on BP Algorithm. Mathematics in Practice and Theory 8 (2003) 48-55
21. Zhang, D. D., Zhang, Q.: Enterprise Credit Rating Model Based on Neural Networks. Transactions of Beijing Institute of Technology 11(2004) 982-985

Poisson Process with Fuzzy Time-Dependent Intensity

Shunqin Li, Wansheng Tang, and Chao Zhang

Institute of Systems Engineering, Tianjin University, Tianjin 300072, China
shunqinli@yahoo.com.cn, tang@tju.edu.cn,
tjuzhangchao@yahoo.com.cn

Abstract. By characterizing the number of events occurred in any time as a Poisson distributed random fuzzy variable, and dealing with the intensity function of Poisson process with time-dependent intensity as a fuzzy variable, the concept of a Poisson process with fuzzy time-dependent intensity is defined. And then, related to the process, several theorems on the expected value of the number of events occurred in any time and average chances of random fuzzy events are respectively discussed.

1 Introduction

Poisson process with time-dependent intensity is an important Poisson process. Conventionally, the intensity function of the process is thought to be a function of time. Doubly stochastic Poisson process introduced by Cox [1] is an extension of Poisson process with time-dependent intensity, where the intensity function related to the process is assumed as a random variable. Some conclusions on doubly stochastic Poisson process can be found in Grandell [2], Serfozo [3,4], Snyder [5]. However, the estimate of the intensity function is often provided by the experiment data with quite small sample sizes. Sometimes, it is more realistic and appropriate to characterize the intensity function as a fuzzy variable rather than a crisp number or a random variable. In such a case, Poisson process with time-dependent intensity is a Poisson process including randomness and fuzziness simultaneously.

Recently, Liu [6] proposed the random fuzzy theory to depict the phenomena that randomness and fuzziness occurred simultaneously. Random fuzzy variable is a natural extension of fuzzy variable, and its realization value is not a real value but random variables under possibilistic uncertainty. Replacing interarrival times with random fuzzy ones, Zhao *et al* [7] discussed a renewal process and established the random fuzzy elementary renewal theorem as well as random fuzzy Blackwell's theorem.

In this paper, by characterizing the number of events occurred in any time as a Poisson distributed random fuzzy variable and the intensity function of the process as a fuzzy variable, respectively, the concept of a Poisson process with fuzzy time-dependent intensity is given.

D.-S. Huang, K. Li, and G.W. Irwin (Eds.): ICIC 2006, LNAI 4114, pp. 786–797, 2006.

2 Fuzzy Variables

Let Θ be a universe, $\mathcal{P}(\Theta)$ the power set of Θ, Pos a possibility measure (see Zadeh [8]), and $(\Theta, \mathcal{P}(\Theta), \text{Pos})$ a possibility space.

Definition 1 (Nahmias [9]). *A fuzzy variable ξ is defined as a function from the possibility space $(\Theta, \mathcal{P}(\Theta), \text{Pos})$ to the real line $\Re$.*

Definition 2 (Liu and Liu [10]). *Let ξ be a fuzzy variable on the possibility space $(\Theta, \mathcal{P}(\Theta), \text{Pos})$, and $\alpha \in (0, 1]$. Then*

$$\xi_\alpha^L = \inf\left\{r \mid \text{Pos}\{\xi \le r\} \ge \alpha\right\} \quad \text{and} \quad \xi_\alpha^U = \sup\left\{r \mid \text{Pos}\{\xi \ge r\} \ge \alpha\right\} \tag{1}$$

are called the α-pessimistic value and the α-optimistic value of ξ, respectively.

Definition 3 (Nahmias [9]). *The fuzzy variables $\xi_1, \xi_2, \cdots, \xi_n$ are independent if and only if*

$$\text{Pos}\{\xi_i \in B_i,\ i = 1, 2, \cdots, n\} = \min_{1 \le i \le n} \text{Pos}\{\xi_i \in B_i\} \tag{2}$$

for any sets $B_1, B_2, \cdots, B_n$ of $\Re$.

Definition 4 (Liu [11]). *The fuzzy variables ξ and η are identically distributed if and only if*

$$\text{Pos}\{\xi \in B\} = \text{Pos}\{\eta \in B\} \tag{3}$$

for any set B of $\Re$.

Proposition 1. *Let ξ and η be two independent fuzzy variables. Then for any $\alpha \in (0, 1]$,*

$$(\xi + \eta)_\alpha^L = \xi_\alpha^L + \eta_\alpha^L, \quad (\xi + \eta)_\alpha^U = \xi_\alpha^U + \eta_\alpha^U. \tag{4}$$

Proposition 2. *If ξ and η are two independently nonnegative fuzzy variables, for any $\alpha \in (0, 1]$,*

$$(\xi \cdot \eta)_\alpha^L = \xi_\alpha^L \cdot \eta_\alpha^L, \quad (\xi \cdot \eta)_\alpha^U = \xi_\alpha^U \cdot \eta_\alpha^U. \tag{5}$$

In order to define the expected value of a fuzzy variable ξ, Liu and Liu [12] introduced the credibility measure Cr as

$$\text{Cr}\{\xi \ge r\} = \frac{1}{2}\left(\text{Pos}\{\xi \ge r\} + 1 - \text{Pos}\{\xi < r\}\right). \tag{6}$$

Definition 5 (Liu and Liu [12]). *The expected value of a fuzzy variable ξ is defined as*

$$E[\xi] = \int_0^{+\infty} \text{Cr}\{\xi \ge r\}\text{d}r - \int_{-\infty}^0 \text{Cr}\{\xi \le r\}\text{d}r \tag{7}$$

provided that at least one of the two integrals is finite. Especially, if ξ is a non-negative fuzzy variable, then $E[\xi] = \int_0^{+\infty} \text{Cr}\{\xi \ge r\}\text{d}r$.

Proposition 3 (Liu and Liu [10]). *Let ξ be a fuzzy variable with the finite expected value $E[\xi]$, then we have*

$$E[\xi] = \frac{1}{2}\int_0^1 \left(\xi_\alpha^L + \xi_\alpha^U\right) \text{d}\alpha. \tag{8}$$

3 Random Fuzzy Variables

Definition 6 (Liu [6]). *A random fuzzy variable is a mapping from the possibility space $(\Theta, \mathcal{P}(\Theta), \mathrm{Pos})$ to the collection of random variables.*

Definition 7. (Poisson Distributed Random Fuzzy Variable) *A random fuzzy variable ξ defined on the possibility space $(\Theta, \mathcal{P}(\Theta), \mathrm{Pos})$ is said to be Poisson distributed if for each θ, $\xi(\theta)$ is a Poisson distributed random variable. That is, for any positive integer k,*

$$\Pr\{\xi(\theta) = k\} = e^{-\lambda(\theta)} \cdot \tfrac{\lambda^k(\theta)}{k!} \tag{9}$$

where λ is a positive fuzzy variable defined on the space $(\Theta, \mathcal{P}(\Theta), \mathrm{Pos})$. A Poisson distributed random fuzzy variable is denoted by $\xi \sim p(k; \lambda)$, and the fuzziness of random fuzzy variable ξ is characterized by the fuzzy variable λ.

Definition 8 (Liu and Liu [10]). *Let ξ be a random fuzzy variable defined on the possibility space $(\Theta, \mathcal{P}(\Theta), \mathrm{Pos})$. Then the expected value $E[\xi]$ of ξ is defined as*

$$E[\xi] = \int_0^{+\infty} \mathrm{Cr}\left\{\theta \in \Theta \mid E[\xi(\theta)] \geq r\right\} \mathrm{d}r - \int_{-\infty}^0 \mathrm{Cr}\left\{\theta \in \Theta \mid E[\xi(\theta)] \leq r\right\} \mathrm{d}r \tag{10}$$

provided that at least one of the two integrals is finite.

Proposition 4. *Let ξ be a random fuzzy variable defined on the possibility space $(\Theta, \mathcal{P}(\Theta), \mathrm{Pos})$, then we have*

$$E[\xi] = \frac{1}{2} \int_0^1 \left(E[\xi(\theta)]_\alpha^L + E[\xi(\theta)]_\alpha^U\right) \mathrm{d}\alpha, \tag{11}$$

where $E[\xi(\theta)]_\alpha^L$ and $E[\xi(\theta)]_\alpha^U$ are the α-pessimistic value and the α-optimistic value of the fuzzy variable $E[\xi(\theta)]$, respectively.

Proposition 5 (Liu [11]). *Let ξ be a random fuzzy variable defined on the possibility space $(\Theta, \mathcal{P}(\Theta), \mathrm{Pos})$. Then, for any $\theta \in \Theta$, we have*

(1) $\Pr\{\xi(\theta) \in B\}$ *is a fuzzy variable for any Borel set B of $\Re$;*
(2) $E[\xi(\theta)]$ *is a fuzzy variable provided that $E[\xi(\theta)]$ is finite for each $\theta \in \Theta$.*

Definition 9 (Liu [11]). *The random fuzzy variables $\xi_1, \xi_2, \cdots, \xi_n$ are iid if and only if*

$$(\Pr\{\xi_i(\theta) \in B_1\}, \Pr\{\xi_i(\theta) \in B_2\}, \cdots, \Pr\{\xi_i(\theta) \in B_m\}), i = 1, 2, \cdots, n \tag{12}$$

are iid fuzzy vectors for any Borel sets $B_1, B_2, \cdots, B_m$ of $\Re$ and any positive integer m.

Definition 10 (Liu and Liu [13]). *Let ξ be a random fuzzy variable defined on $(\Theta, \mathcal{P}(\Theta), \mathrm{Pos})$. Then the average chance* Ch *is defined as*

$$\mathrm{Ch}\{\xi \geq r\} = \int_0^1 \mathrm{Cr}\left\{\theta \in \Theta \mid \Pr\{\xi(\theta) \geq r\} \geq p\right\} \mathrm{d}p. \tag{13}$$

Theorem 1. *Let ξ be a random fuzzy variable defined on $(\Theta, \mathcal{P}(\Theta), \mathrm{Pos})$. Then the average chance* Ch *can be written as*

$$\mathrm{Ch}\{\xi \geq r\} = \frac{1}{2}\int_0^1 \left(\Pr{}_\alpha^L\{\xi(\theta) \geq r\} + \Pr{}_\alpha^U\{\xi(\theta) \geq r\}\right) \mathrm{d}\alpha, \tag{14}$$

where $\Pr_\alpha^L\{\xi(\theta) \geq r\}$ and $\Pr_\alpha^U\{\xi(\theta) \geq r\}$ are the α-pessimistic value and the α-optimistic value of the fuzzy variable $\Pr\{\xi(\theta) \geq r\}$, respectively.

Proof. It follows from Proposition 3 that

$$E\left[\Pr\{\xi(\theta) \geq r\}\right] = \frac{1}{2}\int_0^1 \left(\Pr{}_\alpha^L\{\xi(\theta) \geq r\} + \Pr{}_\alpha^U\{\xi(\theta) \geq r\}\right) \mathrm{d}\alpha.$$

In addition, for any $p \geq 1$, $\mathrm{Cr}\left\{\theta \in \Theta \mid \Pr\{\xi(\theta) \geq r\} \geq p\right\} = 0$, a.e. and consequently $\int_1^{+\infty} \mathrm{Cr}\left\{\theta \in \Theta \mid \Pr\{\xi(\theta) \geq r\} \geq p\right\} \mathrm{d}p = 0$. Therefore,

$$\begin{aligned}
\mathrm{Ch}\{\xi \geq r\} &= \int_0^1 \mathrm{Cr}\left\{\theta \in \Theta \mid \Pr\{\xi(\theta) \geq r\} \geq p\right\} \mathrm{d}p \\
&= \int_0^1 \mathrm{Cr}\left\{\theta \in \Theta \mid \Pr\{\xi(\theta) \geq r\} \geq p\right\} \mathrm{d}p \\
&\quad + \int_1^{+\infty} \mathrm{Cr}\left\{\theta \in \Theta \mid \Pr\{\xi(\theta) \geq r\} \geq p\right\} \mathrm{d}p \\
&= \int_0^{+\infty} \mathrm{Cr}\left\{\theta \in \Theta \mid \Pr\{\xi(\theta) \geq r\} \geq p\right\} \mathrm{d}p \\
&= E\left[\Pr\{\xi(\theta) \geq r\}\right].
\end{aligned} \tag{15}$$

The proof is completed.

Proposition 6 (Liu and Liu [13]). *Let ξ be a random fuzzy variable defined on the possibility space $(\Theta, \mathcal{P}(\Theta), \mathrm{Pos})$. Then the average chance* Ch *is self dual, i.e.,*

$$\mathrm{Ch}\{\xi \geq r\} = 1 - \mathrm{Ch}\{\xi < r\}. \tag{16}$$

4 Poisson Process with Fuzzy Time-Dependent Intensity

Let $N(t)$ be a random fuzzy variable defined on possibility space $(\Theta, \mathcal{P}(\Theta), \mathrm{Pos})$ with $N(t) \sim p\left(k; \int_0^t \lambda(x)\mathrm{d}x\right)$. That is, for each $\theta \in \Theta$,

$$\Pr\{N(t)(\theta) = k\} = e^{-\int_0^t \lambda(x)(\theta)\mathrm{d}x} \cdot \frac{\left(\int_0^t \lambda(x)(\theta)\mathrm{d}x\right)^k}{k!}, \tag{17}$$

where $\lambda(x)$ is a positive fuzzy variable on $(\Theta, \mathcal{P}(\Theta), \text{Pos})$ for fixed $x \geq 0$. In such a case, the counting process $\{N(t), t \geq 0\}$ is called a *Poisson process with fuzzy time-dependent intensity* and $\lambda(x)$ the *intensity function.*

Theorem 2. *Let $\{N(t), t \geq 0\}$ be a Poisson process with fuzzy time-dependent intensity and $\lambda(x)$ the intensity function, then we have*

$$E[N(t)] = E\left[\int_0^t \lambda(x)\mathrm{d}x\right]. \tag{18}$$

Proof. For any fixed $x > 0$, let $\lambda(x)_\alpha^L$ and $\lambda(x)_\alpha^U$ be the α-pessimistic value and the α-optimistic value of fuzzy variable $\lambda(x)$. For the sake of simplicity, assume that the α-level set of fuzzy variable λ is closed and bounded set for any $\alpha \in (0, 1]$. That is, $\{x \mid \mu(x) \geq \alpha\}$ is a closed and bounded set for any $\alpha \in (0, 1]$, where $\mu(\cdot)$ is the membership function of fuzzy variable λ. Furthermore, for any point $\alpha \in (0, 1]$, there exist points $\theta', \theta'' \in \Theta$ with $\text{Pos}\left\{\theta'\right\} \geq \alpha$ and $\text{Pos}\left\{\theta''\right\} \geq \alpha$ such that

$$\lambda(x)\left(\theta'\right) = \lambda(x)_\alpha^L, \quad \lambda(x)\left(\theta''\right) = \lambda(x)_\alpha^U. \tag{19}$$

For any $\theta \in \Theta$ with $\text{Pos}\{\theta\} \geq \alpha$, it follows from Definition 2 that

$$\lambda(x)_\alpha^L \leq \lambda(x)(\theta) \leq \lambda(x)_\alpha^U. \tag{20}$$

Consequently,

$$\int_0^t \lambda(x)_\alpha^L \mathrm{d}x \leq \int_0^t \lambda(x)(\theta)\mathrm{d}x \leq \int_0^t \lambda(x)_\alpha^U \mathrm{d}x. \tag{21}$$

Thus,

$$0 \leq N(t)\left(\theta'\right) \leq_d N(t)(\theta) \leq_d N(t)\left(\theta''\right) \tag{22}$$

(the symbol $\leq_d$, called stochastically smaller, see Stoyan [15]). That is,

$$\Pr\left\{N(t)\left(\theta''\right) \leq r\right\} \leq \Pr\left\{N(t)(\theta) \leq r\right\} \leq \Pr\left\{N(t)\left(\theta'\right) \leq r\right\} \tag{23}$$

for any real number $r \in \Re$. Taking expectations of (22) yields

$$E\left[N(t)\left(\theta'\right)\right] \leq E[N(t)(\theta)] \leq E\left[N(t)\left(\theta''\right)\right]. \tag{24}$$

By Definition 2,

$$E[N(t)(\theta)]_\alpha^L = E\left[N(t)\left(\theta'\right)\right], \quad E[N(t)(\theta)]_\alpha^U = E\left[N(t)\left(\theta''\right)\right]. \tag{25}$$

Furthermore, from the results of a Poisson process with time-dependent intensity,

$$E\left[N(t)\left(\theta'\right)\right] = \int_0^t \lambda(x)\left(\theta'\right)\mathrm{d}x, \quad E\left[N(t)\left(\theta''\right)\right] = \int_0^t \lambda(x)\left(\theta''\right)\mathrm{d}x. \tag{26}$$

That is,

$$E[N(t)(\theta)]_\alpha^L = \int_0^t \lambda(x)_\alpha^L \mathrm{d}x, \quad E[N(t)(\theta)]_\alpha^U = \int_0^t \lambda(x)_\alpha^U \mathrm{d}x. \tag{27}$$

In addition, from (20), (21) and Definition 2,

$$\left(\int_0^t \lambda(x)\mathrm{d}x\right)_\alpha^L = \int_0^t \lambda(x)\left(\theta'\right)\mathrm{d}x = \int_0^t \lambda(x)_\alpha^L \mathrm{d}x, \tag{28}$$

$$\left(\int_0^t \lambda(x)\mathrm{d}x\right)_\alpha^U = \int_0^t \lambda(x)\left(\theta''\right)\mathrm{d}x = \int_0^t \lambda(x)_\alpha^U \mathrm{d}x. \tag{29}$$

Finally, it follows from Proposition 4 that

$$\begin{aligned} E[N(t)] &= \frac{1}{2}\int_0^1 \left(E[N(t)(\theta)]_\alpha^L + E[N(t)(\theta)]_\alpha^U\right)\mathrm{d}\alpha \\ &= \frac{1}{2}\int_0^1 \left(\left(\int_0^t \lambda(x)\mathrm{d}x\right)_\alpha^L + \left(\int_0^t \lambda(x)\mathrm{d}x\right)_\alpha^U\right)\mathrm{d}\alpha = E\left[\int_0^t \lambda(x)\mathrm{d}x\right]. \end{aligned} \tag{30}$$

The proof is finished.

Theorem 3. *Let $\{N(t), t \geq 0\}$ be a Poisson process with fuzzy time-dependent intensity and $\lambda(x)$ the intensity function, then for any $t, a \geq 0$,*

$$E[N(t+a) - N(t)] = E[N(t+a)] - E[N(t)] = E\left[\int_t^{t+a} \lambda(x)\mathrm{d}x\right]. \tag{31}$$

Proof. For any $\theta_1, \theta_2 \in \Theta$ with $\mathrm{Pos}\{\theta_1\} \geq \alpha$ and $\mathrm{Pos}\{\theta_2\} \geq \alpha$, using (22),

$$N(t)\left(\theta'\right) \leq_d N(t)(\theta_1) \leq_d N(t)\left(\theta''\right), \tag{32}$$

$$N(t+a)\left(\theta'\right) \leq_d N(t+a)(\theta_2) \leq_d N(t+a)\left(\theta''\right). \tag{33}$$

Using (21),

$$\begin{aligned} 0 \leq N(t+a)\left(\theta'\right) - N(t)\left(\theta'\right) &\leq_d N(t+a)(\theta_2) - N(t)(\theta_1) \\ &\leq_d N(t+a)\left(\theta''\right) - N(t)\left(\theta''\right). \end{aligned} \tag{34}$$

Taking expectations yields

$$\begin{aligned} E\left[N(t+a)\left(\theta'\right) - N(t)\left(\theta'\right)\right] &\leq E[N(t+a)(\theta_2) - N(t)(\theta_1)] \\ &\leq E\left[N(t+a)\left(\theta''\right) - N(t)\left(\theta''\right)\right]. \end{aligned} \tag{35}$$

By Definition 2, we have

$$E[N(t+a)(\theta)-N(t)(\theta)]_\alpha^L = E\left[N(t+a)\left(\theta'\right)\right] - E\left[N(t)\left(\theta'\right)\right], \tag{36}$$

$$E[N(t+a)(\theta)-N(t)(\theta)]_\alpha^U = E\left[N(t+a)\left(\theta''\right)\right] - E\left[N(t)\left(\theta''\right)\right]. \tag{37}$$

That is, using (25),

$$E[N(t+a)(\theta)-N(t)(\theta)]_\alpha^L = E[N(t+a)(\theta)]_\alpha^L - E[N(t)(\theta)]_\alpha^L, \tag{38}$$

$$E[N(t+a)(\theta)-N(t)(\theta)]_\alpha^U = E[N(t+a)(\theta)]_\alpha^U - E[N(t)(\theta)]_\alpha^U. \tag{39}$$

It follows from Proposition 4 that

$$\begin{aligned}
&E[N(t+a)-N(t)] \\
&= \frac{1}{2}\int_0^1 \left(E[N(t+a)(\theta)-N(t)(\theta)]_\alpha^L + E[N(t+a)(\theta)-N(t)(\theta)]_\alpha^U\right) \mathrm{d}\alpha \\
&= \frac{1}{2}\int_0^1 \left(E[N(t+a)(\theta)]_\alpha^L - E[N(t)(\theta)]_\alpha^L\right) \mathrm{d}\alpha \\
&\quad + \frac{1}{2}\int_0^1 \left(E[N(t+a)(\theta)]_\alpha^U - E[N(t)(\theta)]_\alpha^U\right) \mathrm{d}\alpha \\
&= \frac{1}{2}\int_0^1 \left(E[N(t+a)(\theta)]_\alpha^L + E[N(t+a)(\theta)]_\alpha^U\right) \mathrm{d}\alpha \\
&\quad - \frac{1}{2}\int_0^1 \left(E[N(t)(\theta)]_\alpha^L + E[N(t)(\theta)]_\alpha^U\right) \mathrm{d}\alpha \\
&= E[N(t+a)] - E[N(t)].
\end{aligned} \tag{40}$$

In addition, it is easy to prove

$$\left(\int_t^{t+a} \lambda(x)\mathrm{d}x\right)_\alpha^L = \int_t^{t+a} \lambda(x)_\alpha^L \mathrm{d}x, \quad \left(\int_t^{t+a} \lambda(x)\mathrm{d}x\right)_\alpha^U = \int_t^{t+a} \lambda(x)_\alpha^U \mathrm{d}x. \tag{41}$$

Using Theorem 2,

$$\begin{aligned}
&E[N(t+a)] - E[N(t)] \\
&= \frac{1}{2}\int_0^1 \left(\left(\int_0^{t+a} \lambda(x)\mathrm{d}x\right)_\alpha^L + \left(\int_0^{t+a} \lambda(x)\mathrm{d}x\right)_\alpha^U\right) \mathrm{d}\alpha \\
&\quad - \frac{1}{2}\int_0^1 \left(\left(\int_0^{t} \lambda(x)\mathrm{d}x\right)_\alpha^L - \left(\int_0^{t} \lambda(x)\mathrm{d}x\right)_\alpha^U\right) \mathrm{d}\alpha \\
&= \frac{1}{2}\int_0^1 \left(\left(\int_t^{t+a} \lambda(x)\mathrm{d}x\right)_\alpha^L + \left(\int_t^{t+a} \lambda(x)\mathrm{d}x\right)_\alpha^U\right) \mathrm{d}\alpha \\
&= E\left[\int_t^{t+a} \lambda(x)\mathrm{d}x\right].
\end{aligned} \tag{42}$$

The proof is finished.

Theorem 4. *Let $\{N(t), t \geq 0\}$ be a Poisson process with fuzzy time-dependent intensity and $\lambda(t)$ the intensity function. If, for any $\alpha \in (0,1]$, $\lambda(t)_\alpha^L$ and $\lambda(t)_\alpha^U$ are continuous at x, and $E[\lambda(t)] < +\infty$, then*

$$\lim_{s\to 0} \frac{E[N(t+s) - N(t)]}{s} = \lim_{s\to 0} \frac{E[N(t+s)] - E[N(t)]}{s} = E[\lambda(t)]. \tag{43}$$

Proof. From the results of a Poisson process with time-dependent intensity,

$$\lim_{s\to 0} \frac{E\left[N(t+s)\left(\theta'\right)\right] - E\left[N(t)\left(\theta'\right)\right]}{s} = \lambda(t)\left(\theta'\right), \tag{44}$$

$$\lim_{s\to 0} \frac{E\left[N(t+s)\left(\theta''\right)\right] - E\left[N(t)\left(\theta''\right)\right]}{s} = \lambda(t)\left(\theta''\right). \tag{45}$$

That is, using (19) and (25),

$$\lim_{s\to 0} \frac{E\left[N(t+s)(\theta)\right]_\alpha^L - E\left[N(t)(\theta)\right]_\alpha^L}{s} = \lambda(t)_\alpha^L, \tag{46}$$

$$\lim_{s\to 0} \frac{E\left[N(t+s)(\theta)\right]_\alpha^U - E\left[N(t)(\theta)\right]_\alpha^U}{s} = \lambda(t)_\alpha^U. \tag{47}$$

Since

$$\int_0^1 \left(\lambda(t)_\alpha^L + \lambda(t)_\alpha^U\right) \mathrm{d}\alpha = 2E[\lambda(t)] < +\infty, \tag{48}$$

it follows from Proposition 4 and the dominated convergence theorem that

$$\begin{aligned}
&\lim_{s\to 0} \frac{E[N(t+s)] - E[N(t)]}{s} \\
&= \lim_{s\to 0} \frac{1}{2}\left(\int_0^1 \left(\frac{E\left[N(t+s)(\theta)\right]_\alpha^L}{s} + \frac{E\left[N(t+s)(\theta)\right]_\alpha^U}{s}\right) \mathrm{d}\alpha\right. \\
&\quad \left. - \int_0^1 \left(\frac{E\left[N(t)(\theta)\right]_\alpha^L}{s} + \frac{E\left[N(t)(\theta)\right]_\alpha^U}{s}\right) \mathrm{d}\alpha\right) \\
&= \frac{1}{2}\int_0^1 \left(\lim_{s\to 0} \frac{E\left[N(t+s)(\theta)\right]_\alpha^L - E\left[N(t)(\theta)\right]_\alpha^L}{s}\right) \mathrm{d}\alpha \\
&\quad + \frac{1}{2}\int_0^1 \left(\lim_{s\to 0} \frac{E\left[N(t+s)(\theta)\right]_\alpha^U - E\left[N(t)(\theta)\right]_\alpha^U}{s}\right) \mathrm{d}\alpha \\
&= \frac{1}{2}\int_0^1 \left(\lambda(t)_\alpha^L + \lambda(t)_\alpha^U\right) \mathrm{d}\alpha \\
&= E[\lambda(t)].
\end{aligned} \tag{49}$$

From Theorem 3, the proof is proved.

Theorem 5. *Let $\{N(t), t \geq 0\}$ be a Poisson process with fuzzy time-dependent intensity and $\lambda(t)$ the intensity function, then we have*

$$\mathrm{Ch}\{N(t) = 0\} = E\left[e^{-t\cdot\lambda(t)}\right]. \tag{50}$$

Proof. From the results of a Poisson process with time-dependent intensity,

$$\Pr\left\{N(t)\left(\theta'\right) = 0\right\} = e^{-t\cdot\lambda(t)\left(\theta'\right)}, \quad \Pr\left\{N(t)\left(\theta''\right) = 0\right\} = e^{-t\cdot\lambda(t)\left(\theta''\right)}. \tag{51}$$

That is, using (19),

$$\Pr\left\{N(t)\left(\theta'\right) = 0\right\} = e^{-t\cdot\lambda(t)_\alpha^L}, \quad \Pr\left\{N(t)\left(\theta''\right) = 0\right\} = e^{-t\cdot\lambda(t)_\alpha^U}. \tag{52}$$

In addition, for any $\theta \in \Theta$ with $\mathrm{Pos}\{\theta\} \geq \alpha$,

$$\Pr\{N(t)(\theta) = 0\} = e^{-t\cdot\lambda(t)(\theta)}. \tag{53}$$

Hence, by Definition 2,

$$\Pr_\alpha^L\{N(t)(\theta) = 0\} = \Pr\left\{N(t)\left(\theta''\right) = 0\right\} = e^{-t\cdot\lambda(t)_\alpha^U}, \tag{54}$$

$$\Pr_\alpha^L\{N(t)(\theta) = 0\} = \Pr\left\{N(t)\left(\theta'\right) = 0\right\} = e^{-t\cdot\lambda(t)_\alpha^L}. \tag{55}$$

Thus, it follows from Theorem 1 that

$$\begin{aligned}\mathrm{Ch}\{N(t) = 0\} &= \frac{1}{2}\int_0^1 \left(\Pr_\alpha^L\{N(t)(\theta) = 0\} + \Pr_\alpha^U\{N(t)(\theta) = 0\}\right) \mathrm{d}\alpha \\ &= \frac{1}{2}\int_0^1 \left(e^{-t\cdot\lambda(t)_\alpha^L} + e^{-t\cdot\lambda(t)_\alpha^U}\right) \mathrm{d}\alpha.\end{aligned} \tag{56}$$

Since $e^{-x\cdot t}$ is a decreasing function of x for any fixed t, then

$$\left(e^{-t\cdot\lambda(t)}\right)_\alpha^L = e^{-t\cdot\lambda(t)_\alpha^U}, \quad \left(e^{-t\cdot\lambda(t)}\right)_\alpha^U = e^{-t\cdot\lambda(t)_\alpha^L}. \tag{57}$$

Consequently,

$$E\left[e^{-t\cdot\lambda(t)}\right] = \frac{1}{2}\int_0^1 \left(e^{-t\cdot\lambda(t)_\alpha^L} + e^{-t\cdot\lambda(t)_\alpha^U}\right) \mathrm{d}\alpha, \tag{58}$$

which completes the proof.

Theorem 6. *Let $\{N(t), t \geq 0\}$ be a Poisson process with fuzzy time-dependent intensity and $\lambda(t)$ the intensity function, then*

$$\mathrm{Ch}\{N(t) \geq 1\} = 1 - E\left[e^{-t\cdot\lambda(t)}\right]. \tag{59}$$

Proof. It immediately follows from Proposition 6 and Theorem 5.

Theorem 7. *Let* $\{N(t), t \geq 0\}$ *be a Poisson process with fuzzy time-dependent intensity and* $\lambda(x)$ *the intensity function, then for any positive integer* k, *we have*

$$\mathrm{Ch}\{N(t) \leq k\}$$
$$= \frac{1}{2}\sum_{j=0}^{k}\int_0^1 \left(e^{-\int_0^t \lambda(x)_\alpha^L \mathrm{d}x}\frac{(\int_0^t \lambda(x)_\alpha^L \mathrm{d}x)^j}{j!} + e^{-\int_0^t \lambda(x)_\alpha^U \mathrm{d}x}\frac{(\int_0^t \lambda(x)_\alpha^U \mathrm{d}x)^j}{j!}\right)\mathrm{d}\alpha. \tag{60}$$

Proof. Using (22), we have

$$\Pr\left\{N(t)\left(\theta''\right) \leq k\right\} \leq \Pr\{N(t)(\theta) \leq k\} \leq \Pr\left\{N(t)\left(\theta'\right) \leq k\right\}. \tag{61}$$

From Definition 2,

$$\Pr{}_\alpha^L\{N(t)(\theta) \leq k\} = \Pr\left\{N(t)\left(\theta''\right) \leq k\right\}, \tag{62}$$

$$\Pr{}_\alpha^U\{N(t)(\theta) \leq k\} = \Pr\left\{N(t)\left(\theta'\right) \leq k\right\}. \tag{63}$$

In addition, by the results of a Poisson process with time-dependent intensity,

$$\Pr{}_\alpha^L\{N(t)(\theta) \leq k\} = \sum_{j=0}^{k} e^{-\int_0^t \lambda(x)_\alpha^U \mathrm{d}x} \cdot \frac{(\int_0^t \lambda(x)_\alpha^U \mathrm{d}x)^j}{j!}, \tag{64}$$

$$\Pr{}_\alpha^U\{N(t)(\theta) \leq k\} = \sum_{j=0}^{k} e^{-\int_0^t \lambda(x)_\alpha^L \mathrm{d}x} \cdot \frac{(\int_0^t \lambda(x)_\alpha^L \mathrm{d}x)^j}{j!}. \tag{65}$$

By Theorem 1, the proof is finished.

Theorem 8. *Let* $\{N(t), t \geq 0\}$ *be a Poisson process with fuzzy time-dependent intensity and* $\lambda(t)$ *the intensity function, then for any positive integer* k,

$$\mathrm{Ch}\{N(t) \geq k\} = 1-$$
$$\frac{1}{2}\sum_{j=0}^{k-1}\int_0^1 \left(e^{-\int_0^t \lambda(x)_\alpha^L \mathrm{d}x}\frac{(\int_0^t \lambda(x)_\alpha^L \mathrm{d}x)^j}{j!} + e^{-\int_0^t \lambda(x)_\alpha^U \mathrm{d}x}\frac{(\int_0^t \lambda(x)_\alpha^U \mathrm{d}x)^j}{j!}\right)\mathrm{d}\alpha. \tag{66}$$

Proof. It immediately follows from Proposition 6 and Theorem 7. The proof is finished.

Theorem 9. *Let* $\{N(t), t \geq 0\}$ *be a Poisson process with fuzzy time-dependent intensity and* $\lambda(t)$ *the intensity function, If* $E[\lambda(t)] < +\infty$, *then*

$$\mathrm{Ch}\{N(t+h) - N(t) \geq 1\} = h \cdot E[\lambda(t)] + o(h), \tag{67}$$

where $\lim\limits_{h\to 0} \frac{o(h)}{h} = 0$.

Proof. From the results of a Poisson process with time-dependent intensity,

$$\Pr\left\{N(t+h)\left(\theta^{'}\right)-N(t)\left(\theta^{'}\right)\geq 1\right\}=h\cdot\lambda(t)\left(\theta^{'}\right)+o(h)=h\cdot\lambda(t)_{\alpha}^{L}+o(h), \tag{68}$$

$$\Pr\left\{N(t+h)\left(\theta^{''}\right)-N(t)\left(\theta^{''}\right)\geq 1\right\}=h\cdot\lambda(t)\left(\theta^{''}\right)+o(h)=h\cdot\lambda(t)_{\alpha}^{U}+o(h). \tag{69}$$

For any $\theta_1,\theta_2\in\Theta$ with $\mathrm{Pos}\{\theta_1\}\geq\alpha$ and $\mathrm{Pos}\{\theta_2\}\geq\alpha$, using (34),

$$\begin{aligned}&\Pr\left\{N(t+h)\left(\theta^{'}\right)-N(t)\left(\theta^{'}\right)\geq 1\right\}\leq\Pr\{N(t+h)(\theta_2)-N(h)(\theta_1)\geq 1\}\\&\leq\Pr\left\{N(t+h)\left(\theta^{''}\right)-N(t)\left(\theta^{''}\right)\geq 1\right\}.\end{aligned} \tag{70}$$

From Definition 2, we obtain

$$\begin{aligned}\Pr_{\alpha}^{L}\{N(t+h)(\theta)-N(h)(\theta)\geq 1\}&=\Pr\left\{N(t+h)\left(\theta^{'}\right)-N(t)\left(\theta^{'}\right)\geq 1\right\}\\&=h\cdot\lambda(t)_{\alpha}^{L}+o(h),\end{aligned} \tag{71}$$

$$\begin{aligned}\Pr_{\alpha}^{U}\{N(t+h)(\theta)-N(h)(\theta)\geq 1\}&=\Pr\left\{N(t+h)\left(\theta^{''}\right)-N(t)\left(\theta^{''}\right)\geq 1\right\}\\&=h\cdot\lambda(t)_{\alpha}^{U}+o(h).\end{aligned} \tag{72}$$

That is,

$$\lim_{h\to 0}\frac{\Pr_{\alpha}^{L}\{N(t+h)(\theta)-N(h)(\theta)\geq 1\}}{h}=\lambda(t)_{\alpha}^{L}, \tag{73}$$

$$\lim_{h\to 0}\frac{\Pr_{\alpha}^{U}\{N(t+h)(\theta)-N(h)(\theta)\geq 1\}\}}{h}=\lambda(t)_{\alpha}^{U}. \tag{74}$$

Since

$$\int_0^1\left(\lambda(t)_{\alpha}^{L}+\lambda(t)_{\alpha}^{U}\right)\mathrm{d}\alpha=2E[\lambda(t)]<+\infty, \tag{75}$$

By Theorem 4 and the dominated convergence theorem, we have

$$\begin{aligned}&\lim_{h\to 0}\frac{\mathrm{Ch}\{N(t+h)-N(h)\geq 1\}-h\cdot E[\lambda(t)]}{h}\\&=\frac{1}{2}\int_0^1\left(\lambda(t)_{\alpha}^{L}+\lambda(t)_{\alpha}^{U}\right)\mathrm{d}\alpha-E[\lambda(t)]=0,\end{aligned} \tag{76}$$

which yields $\mathrm{Ch}\{N(t+h)-N(h)\geq 1\}=h\cdot E[\lambda(t)]+o(h)$. The proof is finished.

Theorem 10. *Let $\{N(t),t\geq 0\}$ be a Poisson process with time-dependent intensity and $\lambda(t)$ the intensity function, then*

$$\mathrm{Ch}\{N(t+h)-N(t)\geq 2\}=o(h). \tag{77}$$

Proof. The proof is similar to that of Theorem 9, we omit it.

5 Conclusions

In this paper, we mainly defined a Poisson process with fuzzy time-dependent intensity. Some theorems on the the process were given. All theorems on the expected value of the number of events occurred by any time and average chances of random fuzzy events are extensions of those in a stochastic case.

Acknowledgments

This work was supported by National Science Foundation of China Grant No. 70471049 and China Postdoctoral Science Foundation No. 2004035013.

References

1. Cox, D.R.: Some Statistical Models Connected with Series of Events. J. Roy. Statist. Soc, B. 17 (1955) 129-164
2. Grandell, J.: Doubly Stochastic Poisson Processes. Lecture Notes in Mathematics 529. Springer, New York (1976)
3. Serfozo, R.F.: Conditional Poisson Process. J. Appl. Prob. 9 (1972) 288-302
4. Serfozo, R.F.: Processes with Conditional Stationary Independent Increments. J. Appl. Prob. 9 (1972) 303-315
5. Snyder, D.L., Miller, M.I.: Random Point Processes in Time and Space. Springer-Verlag, New York (1991)
6. Liu, B.: Theory and Practice of Uncertain Programming. Physica-Verlag, Heidelberg (2002)
7. Zhao, R., Tang, W., Yun, H.: Random Fuzzy Renewal Process. European Journal of Operational Research. 169 (2006) 189-201
8. Zadeh, L.A.: Fuzzy Sets as a Basis for a Theory of Possibility. Fuzzy Sets and Systems. 1 (1978) 3-28
9. Nahmias, S.: Fuzzy Variables. Fuzzy Sets and Systems. 1 (1978) 97-110
10. Liu, Y.K., Liu, B.: Expected Value Operator of Random Fuzzy Variable and Random Fuzzy Expected Value Models. International Journal of Uncertainty, Fuzziness and Knowledge-Based Systems. 11 (2003) 195-215
11. Liu, B.: Uncertainty Theory: An Introduction to Its Axiomatic Foundations. Springer-Verlag, Berlin (2004)
12. Liu, B., Liu, Y.K.: Expected Value of Fuzzy Variable and Fuzzy Expected Value Models. IEEE Transactions on Fuzzy Systems. 10 (2002) 445-450
13. Liu, Y.K., Liu, B.: Random Fuzzy Programming with Chance Measures Defined by Fuzzy Integrals. Mathematical and Computer Modelling. 36 (2002) 509-524
14. Zadeh, L.A.: Fuzzy Sets. Information and Control. 8 (1965) 338-353
15. Stoyan, D.: Comparison Methods for Queues and Other Stochastic Models. Wiley-Interscience, New York (1983)

Pricing R&D Option with Combining Randomness and Fuzziness

Jinliang Zhang, Huibin Du, and Wansheng Tang

Institute of Systems Engineering, Tianjin University, Tianjin 300072, China
{ruishifeng, duhuibin1007}@yahoo.com.cn, tang@tju.edu.cn

Abstract. Random fuzzy theory is introduced to evaluate the option value of R&D project in this paper. Based on a new theoretical insight, we develop a random fuzzy jump amplitude model to price R&D option. In classic stochastic jump amplitude model, the value of R&D option depends on the expected number of jumps and the expected size of the jumps. However, in practice, it is so hard to get enough data that the distribution functions of them are difficult to be confirmed accurately. So random fuzzy theory can deal with these problems better. In this paper, the number of jumps and the size of jumps are taken as random fuzzy variables, and investment costs and future cash flows are depicted as fuzzy variables. New research tools for option pricing of R&D project are developed and the capability of dealing with practical problems is enhanced.

1 Introduction

Enterprises increasingly pay more attention to research and development (R&D) activities because it is more and more important for any enterprise's future survivance and development. However, the value created by R&D can't be fully captured with applying traditional valuation tools such as the method of discount cash flow because they can not correctly model the nature of the developing process. Fortunately, with the advent of real options thinking, R&D evaluation is improved remarkably because the growth opportunities and flexible characteristic in R&D are sufficiently depicted under such a new criteria.

The costs of developing new products in uncertain markets are low comparing with the investment costs which are necessary for a global market introduction. Therefore, R&D investments can be thought of as the price of an option on major follow-on investments. In this paper, we consider R&D options as typically European options since market introduction can generally be not executed until successful completion of the R&D stages. Here, considering R&D options as European instead of American will not significantly affect the overall results [1].

Black-Scholes (B-S) formula [2] is a very important tool in option pricing methods. However, there are two critical problems when applying B-S formula to price R&D option. Black and Scholes's formula assumes that the underlying asset follows a geometric Brownian motion, which is highly questionable for the value of innovative research projects. It implies a continuous arrival of information

D.-S. Huang, K. Li, and G.W. Irwin (Eds.): ICIC 2006, LNAI 4114, pp. 798–808, 2006.

that changes the underlying variable. In financial markets, the underlying assets are traded and new information will directly be reflected in the prices of the assets. However, the Information that affects future net cash flows of research projects will arrive at a discrete point in time. So, in real markets managers will not continuously adjust the present value of future cash flows, but will only adjust it when information with strategic impact arrives [1].

The other problem is that the underlying asset of a real option is non-traded which makes it hard to estimate the volatility of the underlying asset. In contrast with financial options, there are no historic time series that enable us to estimate the volatility of the underlying asset. However, it is a well-established fact that the option value is very sensitive to the volatility of the underlying asset. Reasonable estimates of the volatility are therefore required. At Merck, the stock volatility was taken to approximate the volatility of the NPV of future cash flows resulting from pharmaceutical R&D, see Nichols [3]. Unfortunately, no convincing heuristics have been proposed so far. Determining the standard deviation of the underlying value, however, appeared to be arduous in R&D practice. So future use of B-S formula to price R&D option would be limited a certain extent.

A distinct difference between financial option and real option is imbedded in the underlying value of the option. The current value of the underlying asset of financial option is known, while the underlying value of real options is uncertain at present, as it rests with estimates of future profits. Carlsson and Fullér [4] gianed the present value of expected cash flow could not usually be characterized by a single number. However, their experiences with the practical projects showed that managers were able to estimate the present value of expected cash flows by using a trapezoidal fuzzy variable. Different with Carlsson and Fullér, basing on fuzzy simulation, we can employ discretional fuzzy variables including trapezoidal variables to depict future cash flows and costs. Due to the specialties of trapezoidal variable, it is used in our example.

Pennings and Lint [1] presented a new theoretical insight by developing a stochastic jump amplitude model in a real setting, which appeared to be closer to reality. The literatures applying jump process in financial or real assets were partially seen in Merton [5], Baldwin and Meyer [6]. In Pennings and Lint's model, jump process instead of a geometric Brownian motion was used to depict the change of the underlying asset, which was more suitable for describing the movement of the underlying asset of R&D project. To be able to calculate the option value, we need estimate some unknown key parameters such as the parameters related to the number of jumps and the size of the jumps. However, the number of observations for an investment project is not always large, so the parameter estimate may be cumbersome. Zmeškal [7] proposed that in the case of an option methodology the estimation of an option value is determined by input data precision. It seems that applying a random fuzzy methodology to establish a random fuzzy jump model is better. In this paper, basing on random fuzzy theory, we will advance a random fuzzy jump model through extending Pennings and Lint's model to price R&D option.

We assume that the necessary time for completing R&D can be given with reasonable accuracy. In order to focus on uncertainty and the arrival of information over time, we will take no account of dividends.

With real options, however, the underlying asset is non-traded and hence we need the assumption of complete markets in order to use risk neutral valuation [8]. Complete markets are assumed throughout the literature on capital budgeting. Cox and Ross [9] made an important contribution with the method of risk neutral valuation. We apply random fuzzy jump process to depict the motion of underlying assets and prove the expected growth rate of underlying assets equal to the risk free rate in the model. In the risk neutral world, we use random fuzzy simulation based on Monte Carlo simulation to price the option value of R&D project since the risk neutral approach opens the door to a host of option valuation techniques that use Monte Carlo method to model future asset values.

This paper is organized as follows. In section 2, we review some basic concepts and results on fuzzy variables and random fuzzy variables, respectively. In section 4, we develop a random fuzzy jump model to value the options of R&D projects. In section 5, fuzzy simulation arithmetic and random fuzzy arithmetic are provided in order to calculate the option value of R&D project. In section 6, a numerical example is given to price an R&D option.

2 Preliminaries

Let Θ be a nonempty set, $P(\Theta)$ the power set of Θ, and Pos a possibility measure. Then, $(\Theta, P(\Theta), \mathrm{Pos})$ is called a possibility space (for details, see Nahmias [10] and Liu [11]). Based on the possibility measure, necessity and credibility of a fuzzy event are given as $\mathrm{Nec}\{\mathcal{A}\} = 1 - \mathrm{Pos}\{\mathcal{A}^c\}$ and $\mathrm{Cr}\{\mathcal{A}\} = \frac{1}{2}(\mathrm{Pos}\{\mathcal{A}\} + \mathrm{Nec}\{\mathcal{A}\})$, respectively [12].

Definition 1. *A fuzzy variable ξ is defined as a function from the possibility space $(\Theta, P(\Theta), \mathrm{Pos})$ to the set of real numbers, and its membership function is defined by*

$$\mu_\xi(r) = \mathrm{Pos}\{\theta \in \Theta \mid \xi(\theta) = r\}, \quad r \in \Re. \tag{1}$$

Definition 2 (Liu and Liu [12]). *Let ξ be a fuzzy variable on the possibility space $(\Theta, P(\Theta), \mathrm{Pos})$, the expected value $E[\xi]$ is defined by*

$$E[\xi] = \int_0^{+\infty} \mathrm{Cr}\{\xi \geq r\}\mathrm{d}r - \int_{-\infty}^0 \mathrm{Cr}\{\xi \leq r\}\mathrm{d}r, \tag{2}$$

provided that at least one of the two integrals is finite.

Definition 3 (Liu [13]). *A random fuzzy variable is a function from a possibility space $(\Theta, P(\Theta), \mathrm{Pos})$ to a collection of random variables.*

Definition 4 (Liu [13] Random Fuzzy Arithmetic on Different Spaces). *Let $f : \Re^n \to \Re$ be a Borel measurable function, and ξ_i random fuzzy variables on the possibility spaces $(\Theta_i, P_i(\Theta), \mathrm{Pos}_i)$, $i = 1, 2, \cdots, n$, respectively. Then $\xi = f(\xi_1, \xi_2, \cdots, \xi_n)$ is a random fuzzy variable defined on the product possibility space $(\Theta, P(\Theta), \mathrm{Pos})$, defined as*

$$\xi(\theta_1, \theta_2, \ldots, \theta_n) = f(\xi_1(\theta), \xi_2(\theta), \cdots, \xi_n(\theta)) \tag{3}$$

for all $(\theta_1, \theta_2, \ldots, \theta_n) \in \Theta$.

Definition 5 (Liu and Liu [14]). *Let ξ be a random fuzzy variable defined on the possibility space $(\Theta, P(\Theta), \mathrm{Pos})$, the expected value $E[\xi]$ is defined by*

$$E[\xi] = \int_0^{+\infty} \mathrm{Cr}\{\theta \in \Theta | E[\xi(\theta)] \geq r\}\mathrm{d}r - \int_{-\infty}^{0} \mathrm{Cr}\{\theta \in \Theta | E[\xi(\theta)] \leq r\}\mathrm{d}r \tag{4}$$

provided that at least one of the two integrals is finite.

3 A Random Fuzzy Jump Model for Valuing R&D Projects

Uncertainty about the NPV of new product at the moment of industrialisation arises from unforeseen events. A manager will only exercise a real option – market the new product – at the moment of industrialisation (denoted by T) when the expected present value of future net cash flows (denoted by S) exceeds the investment sum (denoted by I). The expected present value of future profits will be adjusted at a series of uncertain times between the present time (denoted by t) and the moment of industrialisation. We assume that the waiting time until new information affecting future cash flow arrives is denoted by w_i. And it is exponentially distributed with parameter λ, denoted by

$$w_i \sim \mathcal{EXP}(\lambda). \tag{5}$$

During the waiting time, no uncertain shocks occur. The exponential distribution also implies that the number of new information arriving follows a homogeneous Poisson process with intensity parameter λ. So, we can know $P\{N(T) - N(t) = N\} = e^{-\lambda(T-t)}\frac{(\lambda(T-t))^N}{N!}, N = 0, 1, 2, \cdots$, where $N(t)$ denotes the number of new information arriving at present time t. Namely, N (the number of new information arriving during the research period $[t, T]$) is Poisson distribution with parameter $\lambda[T - t]$. The parameter λ will typically depend on the kind of business of the research projects. For the lack of historical data, it is often hard to estimate the precise value of λ in practical projects. Under the condition, manager need obtain the data from other investment projects with similar characteristics, which has inevitably subjectivity and randomness. So, in this paper, it is accordant with actual case that λ is assumed as a fuzzy variable defined on a possibility space. And $w_i, i = 1, 2, \ldots$ are random fuzzy variables and specially they are defined on the same possibility space as the one λ is defined on. The reason we define random fuzzy variables $w_i, i = 1, 2, \ldots$ on the same possibility space instead of a series of different spaces, is that $w_i, i = 1, 2, \ldots$ can degenerate into a series of random variables which are independently identically exponentially distributed for any $\theta \in \Theta$. Here, the possibility space is denoted by $(\Theta_1, P_1(\Theta), \mathrm{Pos}_1)$ in order to distinguish conveniently from other possibility spaces. N is also a random fuzzy variable and in addition, N and w_i are defined on the same possibility space due to their correlation. For any $\theta \in \Theta_1$, $\lambda(\theta)$ is a clear real number, $w_i(\theta), i = 1, 2, \ldots$ are random variables with independent identical exponential distributions, and $N(\theta)$ is Poisson distributed with parameter $\lambda(\theta)(T - t)$.

Depending upon all information at present time t denoted by $\Omega(t)$, with $\Omega(t) \subseteq \Omega(r)$ for $t < r \leq T$, the market value of future net cash flows based on industrialisation is equal to

$$S(t) = \sum_{i=0}^{m} \exp(-(T + i - t)\mu) E[CF_{T+i} | \Omega(t)], \tag{6}$$

where μ denotes the firm's cost of capital, CF_{T+i} is the ith year's net cash flow after the irreversible investment and m denotes the lifecycle of the new product.

As be presented in the introduction, here, we apply fuzzy variable to depict the future net cash flow. In this paper, we expand the method using trapezoidal fuzzy variable depicts the future net cash flow in some literatures so that CF_{T+i} can be figured not only by a trapezoidal fuzzy variable but also by a arbitrary fuzzy variable as long as it is fit for describing the future net cash flow. And then we can apply fuzzy simulation method to calculate $E[CF_{T+i}]$. In addition, the investment I, at the industralisation moment T, is also depicted as a fuzzy variable and the expectation is treated as the expected industralisation investment at T moment. We assume that all cash flows have equal risk characteristics and hence that μ is constant for any cash flow. The option value F, at the moment of industriasation is defined as

$$F(S(T)) = \max[0, S(T) - I]. \tag{7}$$

Pennings and Lint[1] pointed out the idea of stochastic jump amplitudes closely matches our perception of manager's decision making process, as the impact of new information is random. From the observation, the value of underlying assets does not change when no new information arrives, and a geometric Brown motion that captures continuous changes in the value of the underlying asset can be disregarded. We develop a random fuzzy jump amplitudes model basing on Pennings and Lint's model. In practice, not only impact of new information is random, but also confirming the parameter of distribution of jump amplitudes has fuzzy character. So adopting random fuzzy jump amplitudes which mix random character and fuzzy character more closely accords with manager's understanding for the jump process.

Here, we must point out that we disregard of the situation the new information affects the cash inflows and cash outflows in the same way, such that their joint impact on the underlying variable will be close to zero since this will seldom occur in practice.

For any $\theta \in \Theta$, a random fuzzy variable degenerates to a random variable. We sometimes need to let a certain random fuzzy variable degenerate to a random variable so that we can illuminate what conditions it has to meet.

In the analysis of Pennings and Lint [1], the jump amplitude is treated as a product of two random variables. One variable describes the direction of the jump while the other one describes the absolute size of the jump. Pennings and Lint point out that the Weibull distribution with shape parameter 2, known as the Rayleigh distribution, seems to fit the absolute jump size best and have also proved the idea. Following the lines of Pennings and Lint, we develop a random fuzzy jump amplitude model through introducing random fuzzy theory. Jump amplitude, Ξ_i, is expressed by

$$\Xi_i = X_i \Gamma_i, \tag{8}$$

where

$$X_i = \begin{cases} 1, & \text{with probability } p \\ -1, & \text{with probability } 1-p, \end{cases} \tag{9}$$

$$\Gamma_i | X_i \sim \mathcal{WEI}(\gamma_{X_i}, 2). \tag{10}$$

It is reasonable that Ξ_i is regarded as random variable. But in practice it is generally hard to make certain the value of parameter γ_{X_i} accurately. So the parameter should be treated as fuzzy variable which more closely matches manager's perception for the jump motion process. According to Definition 3, if γ_{X_i} is a fuzzy variable, Ξ_i is a random fuzzy variable and so is $\Xi_i|X_i$. Similar way of dealing with $w_i, i = 1, 2, \ldots$, we define random fuzzy variable $\Xi_i|X_i, i = 1, 2, \ldots$ on the same possibility space as the one γ_{X_i} is defined on. According to equation (12), γ_1 and γ_{-1} should be defined on the same possibility space. So, we define random fuzzy variable $\Xi_i, i = 1, 2, \ldots$ on the same possibility space which is denoted by $(\Theta_2, P_2(\Theta), \mathrm{Pos}_2)$. We assume that for any $\theta \in \Theta_2$, $\Xi_i(\theta), i = 1, 2, \ldots$ are independent each other.

Merton [5] puts forward a significant idea that if jump components are uncorrelated with the aggregate market, then they belong to dispersible risks which however should not obtain expected return. Jump components in R&D projects will in general be disrelated with the aggregate market [1]. So, according to Merton's thinking, the unconditional mean of stochastic jump amplitude $\Xi_i(\theta)$ should equal to zero. For any $\theta \in \Theta_2$, $\gamma_{X_i}(\theta)$ is a real number, $\Xi_i(\theta)$ is random variable, and furthermore $\Xi_i(\theta)|X_i$ is also a random variable which is $\mathcal{WEI}(\gamma_{X_i}(\theta), 2)$. The mean of $\Xi_i(\theta)|X_i$ is given by

$$E[\Xi_i(\theta)|X_i] = \frac{1}{2}\sqrt{\pi} X_i \gamma_{X_i}(\theta). \tag{11}$$

Hence, the unconditional mean of $\Xi_i(\theta)$ is zero when the following equation holds:

$$p\gamma_1(\theta) = (1-p)\gamma_{-1}(\theta). \tag{12}$$

Underlying asset's value $S(T)$ can be expressed as

$$S(T) = S(t)\prod_{i=0}^{N}[w_i r + \Xi_i + 1], \tag{13}$$

where $\Xi_0 = 0, w_0 = 0$, r is a risk-free interest rate.

$S(T)$ is a random fuzzy variable defined on the product possibility space $(\Theta, P(\Theta), \mathrm{Pos})$ which is the product of $(\Theta_1, P_1(\Theta), \mathrm{Pos}_1)$ and $(\Theta_2, P_2(\Theta), \mathrm{Pos}_2)$. On the product possibility space, for any $\theta \in \Theta$, we assume that $\Xi_i(\theta), i = 1, 2, \ldots$ and $\boldsymbol{w}_i(\theta), i = 1, 2, \ldots$ are independent one to the other. Underlying asset takes a risk-free interest rate as its growth rate during the period of no strategetic information. When strategetic information arrives the value of underlying asset will jump. In the appendix, we have proved $E[S(T)(\theta)] = S(t)e^{r(T-t)}$, which means the expected growth rate of underlying assets equals to the risk free rate from the present time t to the industrialisation moment T under the random condition. So it accords with the assumption of risk-neutral world.

At the moment of industrialisation, the option value of the R&D project will be the expectation of the maximum of zero and the net present value of industrialising the new product. Therefore, the present option value equals

$$F(t) = \exp(-r(T-t))E[\max(0, S(T) - I)], \tag{14}$$

where $\max(0, S(T) - I)$ is a random fuzzy variable defined on the same product possibility space as the one $S(T)$ is defined on, whose expected value can be obtained theoretically. But, it is in general very hard to get $E[\max(0, S(T) - I)]$ applying the analytic method. In practice, random fuzzy simulation is employed to calculate $E[\max(0, S(T) - I)]$, then it is easy to get R&D option value $F(t)$ at present time t.

4 Simulation Arithmetic

Fuzzy simulation was developed by Liu and Iwamura[15]. A fuzzy simulation will be designed to estimate $E[CF_{T+i}]$. Random fuzzy simulation was developed by Liu and Liu[14]. A random fuzzy simulation will be introduced to compute the expected value $E[\max(0, S(T) - I)]$.

4.1 Fuzzy Simulation

Provided that N is sufficiently large, and $E[CF_{T+i}]$ can be estimated by the following procedures.

Step 1. Set $e = 0$.

Step 2. Uniformly generate θ_k from Θ such that $\mathrm{Pos}\{\theta_k\} \geq \varepsilon$, where ε is a sufficiently small number.

Step 3. Set $a = CF_{T+i}(\theta_1)\wedge\cdots\wedge CF_{T+i}(\theta_N), b = CF_{T+i}(\theta_1)\vee\cdots\vee CF_{T+i}(\theta_N)$.

Step 4. Randomly generate r from $[a, b]$.
Step 5. If $r \geq 0$, then $e \leftarrow e + \mathrm{Cr}\{CF_{T+i} \geq r\}$.
Step 6. If $r \leq 0$, then $e \leftarrow e - \mathrm{Cr}\{CF_{T+i} \leq r\}$.
Step 7. Repeat the fourth to sixth steps for N times.
Step 8. $E[CF_{T+i}] = a \vee 0 + b \wedge 0 + e \cdot (b-a)/N$.

4.2 Random Fuzzy Simulation

Provided that N is sufficiently large, and $E[\max(0, S(T) - I)]$ can be estimated by the following procedures, where,$E[\max(0, S(T)(\theta_k) - I)]$, $k = 1, 2, \ldots, N$ may be calculated by Monte Carlo simulation.

Step 1. Set $E = 0$.
Step 2. Uniformly generate θ_k from the product possibility space's Θ such that $\mathrm{Pos}\{\theta_k\} \geq \varepsilon$, $k = 1, 2, \ldots, N$, where ε is a sufficiently small number.
Step 3. Set $a = \min_{1 \leq k \leq N} E[\max(0, S(T)(\theta_k) - I)]$, $b = \max_{1 \leq k \leq N} E[\max(0, S(T)(\theta_k) - I)]$.
Step 4. Randomly generate r from $[a, b]$.
Step 5. If $r \geq 0$, then $E \longleftarrow E + \mathrm{Cr}\{\theta \in \Theta \mid E[\max(0, S(T)(\theta) - I)] \geq r\}$.
Step 6. If $r < 0$, then $E \longleftarrow E - \mathrm{Cr}\{\theta \in \Theta \mid E[\max(0, S(T)(\theta) - I)] \leq r\}$.
Step 7. Repeat the fourth to sixth steps for N times.
Step 8. $E[\max(0, S(T) - I)]] = a \vee 0 + b \wedge 0 + E \cdot (b-a)/N$.

5 Illustrative Example

Now, let us consider a numerical example. Assume a high-tech company is planning to put an R&D project into practice and invest 1.5 million dollars in the phase in order to develop a new product. Here, we assume $T = 3$ years, risk-free rate $r = 7\%$ and cost of capital $\mu = 12\%$. According to the forecast and the judgements, the return of the project is estimated as follows. After completing market introduction, the projet will generate cash flows in future ten years. The annual cash flows return in the future can be depicted by a trapezoidal fuzzy variable. The cash flows return of the first year in the future will take the form of $(3.00, 3.28, 3.68, 3.86)$ million dollars. In the second and third years in the future, every crisp number of the trapezoidal fuzzy variable will increase 0.55 million dollars per year. In the second future three years, the return of future cash flows will remain stable, and in the succedent two years, every crisp number will decrease 0.5 million dollars per year and in the last two years every crisp number will decrease 0.8 million dollars per year. Here, we assume the scrap value is zero at the end of period. Fuzzy simulation of 10000 times yields the NPV of the return of future ten years at the industrialisation moment is 21.426 million dollars, which is 21.564 million dollars calculated by analytical method. So fuzzy simulation has good precision. As declared in the above sections, we can use any fuzzy variable including trapezoidal fuzzy variable to depict future cash flows, and then apply fuzzy simulation to calculate the expected value. According to the estimates, at the industrialisaton moment, the investment $I = 2.26$ million dollars. Applying the NPV method, at the industrialisation moment NPV $= 21.426 - 22.60 = -1.174$ million dollars and the NPV is negative, which indicates the R&D project is not feasible. But the NPV calculation denies the flexibility of not investing at the moment of industrialisation.

Now, let us calculate the option value of the R&D project. According to the forecast and the judgements, the waiting time until new information arrives, w_i, is exponentially distributed with parameter $\lambda = (4.1, 4.3, 4.48)$. Up-side jump $\Xi_i|X_i = 1$ submits to Weibull distribution with shape parameter 2, known as the Rayleigh distribution and size parameter $\gamma_1 = (0.09, 0.11, 0.126)$. The up-side jumps happen with probability $p = 0.7$. Down-side jump $\Xi_i|X_i = -1$ submits to the Rayleigh distribution which size parameter is determined according to the equation (12). Accordingly, the down-side jumps happen with probability $1 - p = 0.3$. Random fuzzy simulation of 5000 times yields an option value of 2.579 million dollars, and Fig. 1 illustrates the relationship between the number of iterations N and the estimated expected values. The result indicates that we can gain the value of 2.579 million dollars only with 1.5 million dollars investment on the R&D project. So, this R&D project is worthy of investing.

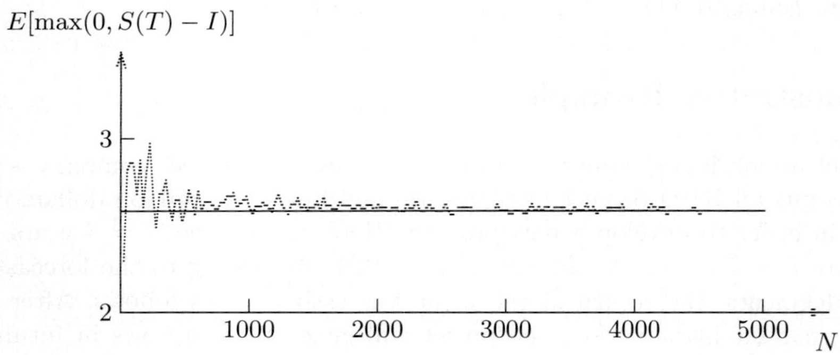

Fig. 1. Variations of the estimated expected values

6 Conclusion

The aim of this paper is to introduce a random fuzzy jump model to price R&D option. In many situations, for the lack of enough data, some important parameters in classical jump model can't always be confirmed accurately, which need generally be determined by the manager's own subjective judgments on the basis of the objective information. Therefore, the random fuzzy theory provides a useful tool to overcome this kind of impreciseness. The advantage of the random fuzzy jump model is that the manager's subjective estimation is incorporated into the jump model.

Acknowledgements

This work was supported by the National Natural Science Foundation of China Grant No. 70471049.

References

1. Pennings, E., Lint, O.: The Option Value of Advanced R&D. European Journal of Operational Research. 103 (1997) 83-94
2. Black, F., Scholes, M.: The Pricing of Options and Corporate Liabilities. Journal of Political Economy. 81 (1973) 637-654
3. Nichols, A.: Scientific Management at Merck. Harvard Business Review. 72 (1994) 89-99
4. Carlsson, C., Fullér, R.: A Fuzzy Approach to Real Option Valuation. Fuzzy Sets and Systems. 139 (2003) 297-312
5. Merton, C.: Option Pricing When Underlying Stock Returns Are Discontinuous. Journal of Financial Economics. 3 (1976) 125-144
6. Baldwin, Y., Meyer, F.: Liquidity Preference under Uncertainty: A Model of Dynamic Investment in Illiquid Opportunities. Journal of Finacial Economics. 7 (1979) 347-374
7. Zmeškal, Z.: Application of the Fuzzy-Stochastic Methodology to Appraising the Firm Value as a European Call Option. European Journal of Operational Research. 135 (2001) 303-310
8. Majd, S., Pindyck, S.: Time to Build, Option Value, and Investment Decisions. Journal of Industrial Economics. 18 (1987) 7-27
9. Cox, C., Ross, A.: The Valuation of Options for Alternative Stochastic Processes. Journal of Financial Economics. 3 (1976) 145-166
10. Nahmias, S.: Fuzzy Variables. Fuzzy Sets and Systems. **1** (1978) 97-110
11. Liu, B.: Uncertainty Theory: An Introduction to Its Axiomatic Foundations. Springer-Verlag, Berlin. (2004)
12. Liu, B., Liu, Y.: Expected Value of Fuzzy Variable and Fuzzy Expected Value Model. IEEE Transactions on Fuzzy Systems. 10 (2002) 445-450
13. Liu, B.: Theory and Practice of Uncertain Programming. Phisica-Verlag, Heidelberg. (2002)
14. Liu, Y., Liu, B.: Expected Value Operator of Random Fuzzy Variable and Random Fuzzy Expected Value Models. International Journal of Uncertainty Fuzziness & Knowledge-Based Systems. 11 (2003) 195-215
15. Liu, B., Iwamura, K.: Chance Constrained Programming with Fuzzy Parameters. Fuzzy Sets and Systems. 94 (1998) 227-237

Appendix

On the product possibility space $(\Theta, P(\Theta), \mathrm{Pos})$, for any $\theta \in \Theta$, random fuzzy variables N, w_i, Ξ_i accordingly degenerate to random variables $N(\theta), w_i(\theta), \Xi_i(\theta)$. It can be proved that $E[S(T)(\theta)] = S(t)e^{r(T-t)}$, which means the expected growth rate of underlying assets equals to the risk free rate from the present time t to the industrialisation moment T under the random condition in our model.

Proof

$$
\begin{aligned}
& E\left[\prod_{i=0}^{N(\theta)}(w_i(\theta)+\Xi_i(\theta)+1)\right] \\
&=\sum_{n=0}^{\infty} E\left[\prod_{i=0}^{n}(w_i(\theta)+\Xi_i(\theta)+1)\right] P[N(\theta)=n] \\
&=\sum_{n=0}^{\infty}\left(\prod_{i=0}^{n} E[w_i(\theta)+\Xi_i(\theta)+1]\right) P[N(\theta)=n] \\
&=\sum_{n=0}^{\infty}\left(\prod_{i=0}^{n}\left(1+\frac{r}{\lambda(\theta)}\right)\right)\frac{(\lambda(\theta)(T-t))^n \exp(-\lambda(\theta)(T-t))}{n!} \\
&=\sum_{n=0}^{\infty}\left(1+\frac{r}{\lambda(\theta)}\right)^n\frac{(\lambda(\theta)(T-t))^n \exp(-\lambda(\theta)(T-t))}{n!} \\
&=\sum_{n=0}^{\infty}\frac{[(T-t)(r+\lambda(\theta))]^n}{n!}\exp(-\lambda(\theta)(T-t)) \\
&=\exp((T-t)(r+\lambda(\theta)))\exp(-\lambda(\theta)(T-t)) \\
&=\exp(r(T-t)).
\end{aligned}
$$

Two-Person Zero-Sum Matrix Game with Fuzzy Random Payoffs

Lin Xu[1], Ruiqing Zhao[1], and Yufu Ning[1,2]

[1] Institute of Systems Engineering, Tianjin University, Tianjin 300072, China
xulin93@163.com, zhao@tju.edu.cn, ning@tju.edu.cn
[2] Department of Computer Science, Dezhou University, Dezhou 253023, China

Abstract. The purpose of this paper is to introduce a two-person zero-sum matrix game in which the payoffs are characterized as fuzzy random variables. Based on fuzzy random expected value operator, a fuzzy random expected minimax equilibrium strategy to the game is defined and the existence of the strategy is proved. Then an iterative algorithm based on fuzzy random simulation is designed to seek the minimax equilibrium strategy. Finally, a numerical example is provided to illustrate the effectiveness of the algorithm.

1 Introduction

Game theory is generally considered to have begun with the publication of von Neumann and Morgenstern's Theory of Games and Economic Behavior [1] in 1944. It is the mathematical study on conflict situations which opens up a wide range of game-like problems in economics, sociology, psychology, and strategic studies to the precise interpretation of mathematical analysis. In game theory, two-person zero-sum matrix game is the fundamental problem. Employing the method of statistical mechanics, Berg and Engel [2], Ein-Dor and Kanter [3] discussed a two-person zero-sum matrix game with random payoffs.

Since most games always take place in uncertain environments, the payoffs cannot be exactly assessed for these games. In these games, the uncertainty is due to inaccuracy of information and fuzzy comprehension of situations by experts. In such situations, it is reasonable to model the problems as games with fuzzy payoffs. The theory of fuzzy sets initiated by Zadeh [4] is an effective way to deal with games with fuzzy payoffs. Two-person zero-sum matrix game with fuzzy payoffs was studied by Campos [5], who employed linear programming models to solve the fuzzy matrix game. As the extension of the idea of Campos [5], Nishizaki and Sakawa [6] discussed multiobjective matrix game with fuzzy payoffs. Furthermore, Bector *et al* [7] introduced a dual for linear programming problems with fuzzy parameters to matrix games with fuzzy payoffs. Vijay [8] provided a solution procedure for solving two-person zero-sum matrix games with fuzzy goals and fuzzy payoffs. Xu *et al* [9] defined three equilibrium strategies to a game with fuzzy payoffs and provided an algorithm for seeking the equilibrium strategies.

When game theory is applied to real world problems, sometimes the payoffs contain both randomness and fuzziness. For example, when a player in a game

D.-S. Huang, K. Li, and G.W. Irwin (Eds.): ICIC 2006, LNAI 4114, pp. 809–818, 2006.

plays a strategy to the other players' actual strategy choices, the payoffs that the player receives will be about 100 dollars with probability p. In such situations, we need to take into account both randomness and fuzziness of payoffs and deal with the payoffs as fuzzy random variables. The notion of fuzzy random variable was first introduced by Kwakernaak [10,11], then this concept was developed by several researchers such as Puri and Ralescu [12], and Kruse and Meyer [13]. Roughly speaking, a fuzzy random variable defined by Kwakernaak [10,11] is a measurable function from a probability space to a collection of fuzzy numbers, and its expected value is described as a fuzzy number. Based on the concept of fuzzy random variable, Yoshida [14] discussed a stopping game for a sequence of fuzzy random variables and gave a saddle point.

Another concept of the fuzzy random variable defined by Liu and Liu [15] is a measurable function from a probability space to a collection of fuzzy variables and its expected value was defined as a scalar value. In this paper, we discuss a two-person zero-sum matrix game with fuzzy random payoffs, in which the notion of fuzzy random variable is proposed by Liu and Liu [15]. A new kind of minimax equilibrium strategy-fuzzy random expected minimax equilibrium strategy is provided, and the existence of the strategy is proved by employing the Kakutani's fixed-point theorem. Since traditional analytical solution methods are not applicable to find the minimax equilibrium strategy, an iterative algorithm based on fuzzy random simulation is designed to find it. Finally, a numerical example is provided to illustrate this idea.

2 Preliminaries

Let Θ be a nonempty set, $\mathcal{P}(\Theta)$ the power set of Θ, and Pos a possibility measure, then the triplet $(\Theta, \mathcal{P}(\Theta), \text{Pos})$ is called a possibility space. Based on the possibility measure Pos, the *credibility* Cr of a fuzzy event was defined.

Definition 1 (Liu and Liu [16]). *Let $(\Theta, \mathcal{P}(\Theta), \text{Pos})$ be a possibility space, and $\mathcal{A}$ a set in $\mathcal{P}(\Theta)$, then the credibility measure of $\mathcal{A}$ is defined by*

$$\text{Cr}\{\mathcal{A}\} = \frac{1}{2}\left(\text{Pos}\{\mathcal{A}\} + 1 - \text{Pos}\{\mathcal{A}^c\}\right), \tag{1}$$

where $\mathcal{A}^c$ is the complement of $\mathcal{A}$.

Definition 2. *A fuzzy variable ξ is a function defined on a possibility space $(\Theta, \mathcal{P}(\Theta), \text{Pos})$ to the set of real numbers, and its membership function is derived from the possibility measure by*

$$\mu(x) = \text{Pos}\left\{\theta \in \Theta \mid \xi(\theta) = x\right\}, \quad x \in \Re. \tag{2}$$

Definition 3 (Liu and Liu [16]). *Let ξ be a fuzzy variable on the possibility space $(\Theta, \mathcal{P}(\Theta), \text{Pos})$, the expected value $E[\xi]$ is defined by*

$$E[\xi] = \int_0^{+\infty} \text{Cr}\{\xi \geq r\}\text{d}r - \int_{-\infty}^0 \text{Cr}\{\xi \leq r\}\text{d}r \tag{3}$$

provided that at least one of the two integrals is finite.

Definition 4. *An n-dimensional fuzzy vector is defined as a function from a probability space* $(\Omega, \mathcal{A}, \Pr)$ *to the set of n−dimensional real vectors.*

Proposition 1 (Liu and Liu [16]). *Let* ξ *be an n-dimensional fuzzy vector,* $f : \Re^n \to \Re$ *and* $g : \Re^n \to \Re$ *measure functions. If functions f and g are comonotonic, then for any nonnegative real numbers a and b, we have*

$$E[af(\xi) + bg(\xi)] = aE[f(\xi)] + bE[g(\xi)]. \tag{4}$$

Definition 5 (Liu and Liu [17]). *The fuzzy variables* $\xi_1, \xi_2, \cdots, \xi_n$ *are said to be independent if and only if*

$$\mathrm{Pos}\{\xi_i \in \mathcal{B}_i \;\; i = 1, 2, \cdots, n\} = \min_{1 \le i \le n} \mathrm{Pos}\{\xi_i \in \mathcal{B}_i\} \tag{5}$$

for any sets $\mathcal{B}_1, \mathcal{B}_2, \cdots, \mathcal{B}_n$ *of* $\Re$.

Definition 6 (Liu and Liu [15]). *A fuzzy random variable is a function* ξ *defined on a probability space* $(\Omega, \mathcal{A}, \Pr)$ *to the set of fuzzy variables such that* $\mathrm{Pos}\{\xi(\omega) \in \mathcal{B}\}$ *is a measurable function of* ω *for any Borel set* $\mathcal{B}$ *of* $\Re$.

Definition 7. *An n−dimensional fuzzy random vector is a function* ξ *from a probability space* $(\Omega, \mathcal{A}, \Pr)$ *to the set of n−dimensional fuzzy vector such that* $\mathrm{Pos}\{\xi(\omega) \in \mathcal{B}\}$ *is a measurable function of* ω *for any Borel set* $\mathcal{B}$ *of* $\Re^n$.

Definition 8 (Liu and Liu [15]). *Let* ξ *be a fuzzy random variable. Then its expected value is defined by*

$$E[\xi] = \int_0^{+\infty} \Pr\left\{\omega \in \Omega \mid E[\xi(\omega)] \ge r\right\} \mathrm{d}r - \int_{-\infty}^{0} \Pr\left\{\omega \in \Omega \mid E[\xi(\omega)] \le r\right\} \mathrm{d}r \tag{6}$$

provided that at least one of the two integrals is finite.

Theorem 1. *Let* ξ *be a fuzzy random vector,* $f : \Re^n \to \Re$ *and* $g : \Re^n \to \Re$ *measure functions. If functions f and g are comonotonic, then for any nonnegative real numbers a and b, we have*

$$E[af(\xi) + bg(\xi)] = aE[f(\xi)] + bE[g(\xi)]. \tag{7}$$

Proof. For each $\omega \in \Omega$, $f(\xi(\omega))$ and $g(\xi(\omega))$ are fuzzy variables. It follows from Proposition 1 that

$$E[af(\xi(\omega)) + bg(\xi(\omega))] = aE[f(\xi(\omega))] + bE[g(\xi(\omega))].$$

Therefore

$$\begin{aligned}
&E\left[af(\xi) + bg(\xi)\right] \\
&= E\left[E\left[af\left(\xi\left(\omega\right)\right) + bg\left(\xi\left(\omega\right)\right)\right]\right] \\
&= E\left[aE\left[f\left(\xi\left(\omega\right)\right)\right] + bE\left[g\left(\xi\left(\omega\right)\right)\right]\right] \\
&= E\left[aE\left[f\left(\xi\left(\omega\right)\right)\right]\right] + E\left[bE\left[g\left(\xi\left(\omega\right)\right)\right]\right] \\
&= aE\left[E\left[f\left(\xi\left(\omega\right)\right)\right]\right] + bE\left[E\left[g\left(\xi\left(\omega\right)\right)\right]\right] \\
&= aE[f(\xi)] + bE[g(\xi)].
\end{aligned}$$

The theorem is proved.

Proposition 2 (Liu and Liu [18]). *Assume that ξ and η are two fuzzy random variables with finite expected values. If for each $\omega \in \Omega$, the fuzzy variables $\xi(\omega)$ and $\eta(\omega)$ are independent, then for any real numbers a and b, we have*

$$E[a\xi + b\eta] = aE[\xi] + bE[\eta]. \tag{8}$$

3 Two-Person Zero-Sum Matrix Game

In this section, we discuss a two-person zero-sum matrix game in which the payoffs are characterized as fuzzy random variables. And then we define a fuzzy random expected minimax equilibrium strategy to the game.

Let $I \triangleq \{1, 2, \cdots, m\}$ denote a set of pure strategies of player I and $J \triangleq \{1, 2, \cdots, n\}$ a set of pure strategies of player II. We denote the strategy spaces of player I and player II by

$$\mathcal{X} = \left\{ \boldsymbol{x} = (x_1, x_2, \cdots, x_m)^T \mid \sum_{i=1}^{m} x_i = 1, x_i \geq 0, i = 1, 2, \cdots, m \right\},$$

and

$$\mathcal{Y} = \left\{ \boldsymbol{y} = (y_1, y_2, \cdots, y_n)^T \mid \sum_{j=1}^{n} y_j = 1, y_i \geq 0, j = 1, 2, \cdots, n \right\}.$$

Let fuzzy random variable ξ_{ij} represent the payoffs that player I receives or player II loses when player I plays the pure strategy i and player II plays the pure strategy j, then a two-person zero-sum game is represented by fuzzy random payoffs matrix

$$\eta = \begin{bmatrix} \xi_{11} & \xi_{12} & \cdots & \xi_{1n} \\ \xi_{21} & \xi_{22} & \cdots & \xi_{2n} \\ \vdots & \vdots & \ddots & \vdots \\ \xi_{m1} & \xi_{m2} & \cdots & \xi_{mn} \end{bmatrix}. \tag{9}$$

When the mixed strategies $\boldsymbol{x}$ and $\boldsymbol{y}$ are chosen by player I and player II, respectively, then the fuzzy random payoffs of player I are

$$\boldsymbol{x}^T \eta \boldsymbol{y} = \sum_{j=1}^{n} \sum_{i=1}^{m} \xi_{ij} x_i y_j, \tag{10}$$

and the fuzzy random payoffs of player II are $-\boldsymbol{x}^T \eta \boldsymbol{y}$.

Since the payoffs are characterized as fuzzy random variables, the player cannot predict how many payoffs will actually be when he chooses a strategy. It is a natural idea for the player to maximize his or minimize the opponent's fuzzy random expected payoffs. The problem for the player is to choose the strategy so that the fuzzy random expected payoffs achieves the optimal values. So based on fuzzy random expected value operator, we give the following minimax equilibrium strategy.

Definition 9. *Let ξ_{ij} $(i = 1, 2, \cdots, m, j = 1, 2, \cdots, n)$ be fuzzy random variables with finite expected values. Then $(\boldsymbol{x}^*, \boldsymbol{y}^*) \in \mathcal{X} \times \mathcal{Y}$ is called a fuzzy random expected minimax equilibrium strategy to the game if*

$$E\left[\boldsymbol{x}^T \eta \boldsymbol{y}^*\right] \leq E\left[\boldsymbol{x}^{*T} \eta \boldsymbol{y}^*\right] \leq E\left[\boldsymbol{x}^{*T} \eta \boldsymbol{y}\right], \tag{11}$$

where η is defined by (9).

Theorem 2. *In a two-person zero-sum game, the payoffs ξ_{ij} $(i=1, 2, \cdots, m, j = 1, 2, \cdots, n)$ are characterize as fuzzy random variables with finite expected values. Then there at least exists a fuzzy random expected minimax equilibrium strategy to the game.*

Proof. For any $\boldsymbol{y} \in \mathcal{Y}$, let

$$Q(\boldsymbol{y}) = \left\{\overline{\boldsymbol{x}} \in \mathcal{X} \mid \mathrm{E}\left[\boldsymbol{x}^T \eta \boldsymbol{y}\right] \leq \mathrm{E}\left[\overline{\boldsymbol{x}}^T \eta \boldsymbol{y}\right],\ \forall \boldsymbol{x} \in \mathcal{X}\right\}, \tag{12}$$

then $Q(\boldsymbol{y}) \subset \mathcal{X}$. For any $\boldsymbol{x} \in \mathcal{X}$, let

$$P(\boldsymbol{x}) = \left\{\overline{\boldsymbol{y}} \in \mathcal{Y} \mid \mathrm{E}\left[\boldsymbol{x}^T \eta \overline{\boldsymbol{y}}\right] \leq \mathrm{E}\left[\boldsymbol{x}^T \eta \boldsymbol{y}\right],\ \forall \boldsymbol{y} \in \mathcal{Y}\right\}, \tag{13}$$

then $P(\boldsymbol{x}) \subset \mathcal{Y}$.

We first prove that $Q(\boldsymbol{y})$ and $P(\boldsymbol{x})$ are both convex sets. For any $\boldsymbol{x}_1, \boldsymbol{x}_2 \in Q(\boldsymbol{y})$, it is clear that $\lambda \boldsymbol{x}_1 + (1 - \lambda)\boldsymbol{x}_2 \in \mathcal{X}$ with any $\lambda \in [0, 1]$. Since the components of $\boldsymbol{x}_1, \boldsymbol{x}_2$ are all nonnegative real numbers, it follows from Theorem 1 that

$$E\left[(\lambda \boldsymbol{x}_1 + (1 - \lambda)\boldsymbol{x}_2)^T \eta \boldsymbol{y}\right] = \lambda E\left[\boldsymbol{x}_1^T \eta \boldsymbol{y}\right] + (1 - \lambda) E\left[\boldsymbol{x}_2^T \eta \boldsymbol{y}\right]. \tag{14}$$

Moreover, it follows from (12) that

$$\begin{cases} \mathrm{E}\left[\boldsymbol{x}_1^T \eta \boldsymbol{y}\right] \geq \mathrm{E}\left[\boldsymbol{x}^T \eta \boldsymbol{y}\right] \\ \mathrm{E}\left[\boldsymbol{x}_2^T \eta \boldsymbol{y}\right] \geq \mathrm{E}\left[\boldsymbol{x}^T \eta \boldsymbol{y}\right] \end{cases} \tag{15}$$

for any $\boldsymbol{x} \in \mathcal{X}$.

Thus for any $\lambda \in [0, 1]$,

$$\begin{cases} \lambda \mathrm{E}\left[\boldsymbol{x}_1^T \eta \boldsymbol{y}\right] \geq \lambda \mathrm{E}\left[\boldsymbol{x}^T \eta \boldsymbol{y}\right] \\ (1 - \lambda)\mathrm{E}\left[\boldsymbol{x}_2^T \eta \boldsymbol{y}\right] \geq (1 - \lambda)\mathrm{E}\left[\boldsymbol{x}^T \eta \boldsymbol{y}\right]. \end{cases} \tag{16}$$

Hence, we have

$$\mathrm{E}\left[(\lambda \boldsymbol{x}_1 + (1 - \lambda)\boldsymbol{x}_2)^T \eta \boldsymbol{y}\right] \geq \mathrm{E}\left[\boldsymbol{x}^T \eta \boldsymbol{y}\right],\ \forall \boldsymbol{x} \in \mathcal{X}. \tag{17}$$

This implies that

$$\lambda \boldsymbol{x}_1 + (1 - \lambda)\boldsymbol{x}_2 \in Q(\boldsymbol{y}). \tag{18}$$

Hence, $Q(\boldsymbol{y})$ is a convex set. Similarly, we can prove that $P(\boldsymbol{x})$ is a convex set.

Let $F : \mathcal{X} \times \mathcal{Y} \to \mathcal{P}(\mathcal{X} \times \mathcal{Y})$ be a set-valued map defined by

$$F(\boldsymbol{z}) = Q(\boldsymbol{y}) \times P(\boldsymbol{x}),\ \forall \boldsymbol{z} = (\boldsymbol{x}^T, \boldsymbol{y}^T)^T \in \mathcal{X} \times \mathcal{Y}, \tag{19}$$

where $\mathcal{P}(\mathcal{X} \times \mathcal{Y})$ is the power set of $\mathcal{X} \times \mathcal{Y}$. Then we have

$$(\boldsymbol{u}, \boldsymbol{v}) \in F(\boldsymbol{z}) \Longleftrightarrow \boldsymbol{u} \in Q(\boldsymbol{y}), \boldsymbol{v} \in P(\boldsymbol{x}). \tag{20}$$

Let $\boldsymbol{z}_n = (\boldsymbol{x}_n^T, \boldsymbol{y}_n^T)^T$ and $(\boldsymbol{u}_n, \boldsymbol{v}_n) \in F(\boldsymbol{z}_n)$, where $\boldsymbol{u}_n \to \boldsymbol{u}_0$, $\boldsymbol{v}_n \to \boldsymbol{v}_0$, $\boldsymbol{x}_n \to \boldsymbol{x}_0$, and $\boldsymbol{y}_n \to y_0$ as $n \to \infty$. Since $\boldsymbol{u}_n \in Q(\boldsymbol{y}_n)$, for any $\boldsymbol{x} \in \mathcal{X}$, we obtain

$$\mathrm{E}\left[\boldsymbol{x}^T \eta \boldsymbol{y}_n\right] \le \mathrm{E}\left[\boldsymbol{u}_n^T \eta \boldsymbol{y}_n\right]. \tag{21}$$

Hence,

$$\lim_{n \to +\infty} \mathrm{E}\left[\boldsymbol{x}^T \eta \boldsymbol{y}_n\right] \le \lim_{n \to +\infty} \mathrm{E}\left[\boldsymbol{u}_n^T \eta \boldsymbol{y}_n\right]. \tag{22}$$

It implies that

$$\mathrm{E}\left[\boldsymbol{x}^T \eta \boldsymbol{y}_0\right] \le \mathrm{E}\left[\boldsymbol{u}_0^T \eta \boldsymbol{y}_0\right]. \tag{23}$$

Thus $\boldsymbol{u}_0 \in Q(\boldsymbol{y}_0)$.

Similarly, since $\boldsymbol{v}_n \in P(\boldsymbol{x}_n)$, for any $\boldsymbol{y} \in \mathcal{Y}$, we have

$$\mathrm{E}\left[\boldsymbol{x}_n^T \eta \boldsymbol{v}_n\right] \le \mathrm{E}\left[\boldsymbol{x}_n^T \eta \boldsymbol{y}\right]. \tag{24}$$

Hence,

$$\lim_{n \to +\infty} \mathrm{E}\left[\boldsymbol{x}_n^T \eta \boldsymbol{v}_n\right] \le \lim_{n \to +\infty} \mathrm{E}\left[\boldsymbol{x}_n^T \eta \boldsymbol{y}\right]. \tag{25}$$

It implies that

$$\mathrm{E}\left[\boldsymbol{x}_0^T \eta \boldsymbol{v}_0\right] \le \mathrm{E}\left[\boldsymbol{x}_0^T \eta \boldsymbol{y}\right]. \tag{26}$$

Thus $\boldsymbol{v}_0 \in P(\boldsymbol{x}_0)$. Hence, $Q(\boldsymbol{y})$ and $P(\boldsymbol{x})$ are both convex closed sets, and the graph of F is convex closed.

What's more, it is clear that the set-valued map F is upper semi-continuous with non-empty, convex, closed values. It follows from Kakutani's fixed-point theorem that there at least exists a point $\boldsymbol{z}^* \in \mathcal{X} \times \mathcal{Y}$ such that $\boldsymbol{z}^* \in F(\boldsymbol{z}^*)$, i.e., there at least exists a point $(\boldsymbol{x}^*, \boldsymbol{y}^*) \in (\mathcal{X}, \mathcal{Y})$, such that

$$\begin{cases} \boldsymbol{x}^* \in Q(\boldsymbol{y}^*) \Rightarrow \mathrm{E}\left[\boldsymbol{x}^T \eta \boldsymbol{y}^*\right] \le \mathrm{E}\left[\boldsymbol{x}^{*T} \eta \boldsymbol{y}^*\right],\ \forall \boldsymbol{x} \in \mathcal{X} \\ \boldsymbol{y}^* \in P(\boldsymbol{x}^*) \Rightarrow \mathrm{E}\left[\boldsymbol{x}^{*T} \eta \boldsymbol{y}^*\right] \le \mathrm{E}\left[\boldsymbol{x}^{*T} \eta \boldsymbol{y}\right],\ \forall \boldsymbol{y} \in \mathcal{Y}. \end{cases} \tag{27}$$

The theorem is proved.

Remark 1. If for each $\omega \in \Omega$, the fuzzy variables $\xi_{ij}(\omega)$ are independent, then for any mixed strategies $\boldsymbol{x}$ and $\boldsymbol{y}$, it follows from Proposition 2 that

$$E\left[\boldsymbol{x}^T \eta \boldsymbol{y}\right] = E\left[\sum_{j=1}^{n} \sum_{i=1}^{m} \xi_{ij} x_i y_j\right] = \sum_{j=1}^{n} \sum_{i=1}^{m} E\left[\xi_{ij}\right] x_i y_j. \tag{28}$$

It is well known that every two-person zero-sum matrix game with crisp payoffs has a minimax equilibrium strategy, then the game with fuzzy random payoffs has a fuzzy random expected minimax equilibrium strategy.

4 Iterative Algorithm Based on Fuzzy Random Simulation

When payoffs are characterized as fuzzy random variables, traditional analytical solution methods are not applicable to find a fuzzy random expected minimax equilibrium strategy. Considering the payoffs are independent in general cases, we propose an algorithm, in which fuzzy random simulation is employed to estimate the expected value, and iterative technique is used to seek the minimax equilibrium strategy.

The fuzzy random simulation technique proposed by [18] is an effective tool to evaluate the expected value of fuzzy random payoffs. Assume that ξ is an $n-$dimensional fuzzy random vector on the probability space $(\Omega, \mathcal{A}, \Pr)$, and $f : \Re^n \to \Re$ a measure function. We generate ω_k from Ω according to the probability measure Pr and produce $\xi(\omega_k)$ for $k = 1, 2, \cdots, N$, then $E[f(\xi(\omega_k))]$ is the expected value of fuzzy variable $f(\xi(\omega_k))$ for each realization ω, respectively. Since $E[f(\xi(\omega))]$ is a random variable, applying the strong law of large numbers, the expected value $E[f(\xi)]$ of fuzzy random variable $f(\xi)$ can be estimated by $\frac{1}{N}\sum_{k=1}^{N} E[f(\xi(\omega_k))]$ provided that N is sufficiently large. Thus, $E[f(\xi)]$ can be estimated by the following procedure.

Step 1. Set L=0.
Step 2. Sample ω from Ω according to the probability measure Pr.
Step 3. Set e=0.
Step 4. Randomly sample θ_k from the universe Θ such that $\text{Pos}\{\theta_k\} \geq \varepsilon$, $k = 1, 2, \cdots, M$, where ε is a sufficiently small number and M is a sufficiently large number.
Step 5. Set $a = \min_{1 \leq k \leq M} f(\xi(\omega)(\theta_k))$ and $b = \max_{1 \leq k \leq M} f(\xi(\omega)(\theta_k))$.
Step 6. Randomly generate r from $[a, b]$.
Step 7. If $r \geq 0$, $e \leftarrow e + \text{Cr}\left\{\theta_k \in \Theta \mid f(\xi(\omega)(\theta_k)) \geq r\right\}$.
Step 8. If $r < 0$, $e \leftarrow e - \text{Cr}\left\{\theta_k \in \Theta \mid f(\xi(\omega)(\theta_k)) \leq r\right\}$.
Step 9. Repeat the sixth to eighth steps for M times.
Step 10. $E[f(\xi(\omega))] = a \vee 0 + b \wedge 0 + e \cdot (b - a)/M$.
Step 11. Set $L \leftarrow L + E[f(\xi(\omega))]$.
Step 12. Repeat the second to eleventh steps for T times, where T is a sufficiently large number.
Step 13. $E[f(\xi)] = L/T$.

Now we embed fuzzy random simulation into an iterative algorithm to find the fuzzy random expected minimax equilibrium strategy. The procedure is summarized as follows:

Step 1. Firstly, let x_{i_1} be a pure strategy selected randomly from the set of pure strategies $\{1, 2, \cdots, m\}$ by player I, and y_{j_1} a pure strategy selected randomly from the set of pure strategies $\{1, 2, \cdots, n\}$ by player II.
Step 2. After the tth game, the pure strategies selected by player I are $x_{i_1}, \cdots, x_{i_t}$ while the pure strategies selected by player II are $y_{j_1}, \cdots, y_{j_t}$. In the

$(t+1)$th game, the pure strategy $x_{i_{t+1}}$ selected by player I should satisfy the condition

$$\sum_{k=1}^{t} E\left[\xi_{i_{t+1}j_k}\right] = \max_{1\leq i\leq m} \sum_{k=1}^{t} E\left[\xi_{ij_k}\right]. \tag{29}$$

The pure strategy $y_{j_{t+1}}$ selected by player II should satisfy the condition

$$\sum_{k=1}^{t} E\left[\xi_{i_k j_{t+1}}\right] = \min_{1\leq j\leq n} \sum_{k=1}^{t} E\left[\xi_{i_k j}\right], \tag{30}$$

where $E\left[\xi_{ij}\right]$ can be estimated by fuzzy random simulation.

Step 3. Return to Step 2 with $t = t + 1$ until the iteration number is N, here N is a predetermined number of iterations.

Step 4. Let $\boldsymbol{x}^* = \{x_1^*, x_2^*, \cdots, x_m^*\}$, where x_i^* is the ratio of times of the pure strategy i selected by player I in the above-mentioned steps to N, $i = 1, 2, \cdots, m$. Let $\boldsymbol{y}^* = \{y_1^*, y_2^*, \cdots, y_n^*\}$, where y_j^* is the ratio of times of the pure strategy j selected by player II in the above-mentioned steps to N, $j = 1, 2, \cdots, n$.

Step 5. Estimate $E\left[\boldsymbol{x}^{*T}\eta\boldsymbol{y}^*\right]$ by fuzzy random simulation, then display the fuzzy random expected minimax equilibrium strategy $(\boldsymbol{x}^*, \boldsymbol{y}^*)$ and $E\left[\boldsymbol{x}^{*T}\eta\boldsymbol{y}^*\right]$.

5 Numerical Example

When the game theory is applied in the fields of economic and management problems, international and national politics, and social policy, sometimes the players should consider the state of uncertainty. In fuzzy stochastic environments, the payoffs are usually the random variable taking fuzzy values. In this section, we give an example of a two-person zero-sum game with fuzzy random payoffs and illustrate the effectiveness of the algorithm provided in Section 4. In order to simplify the game, each of two players is assumed to have two pure strategies. Then the normal form of the game reduces to a matrix

$$\eta = \begin{bmatrix} \xi_{11} & \xi_{12} \\ \xi_{21} & \xi_{22} \end{bmatrix},$$

where fuzzy random variables ξ_{ij} $(i = 1, 2, j = 1, 2)$ are characterized as

$$\mu_{\xi_{11}}(x) = e^{-\frac{(x-\rho_{11})^2}{2}}, \quad \text{with} \quad \rho_{11} \sim N(1, 1),$$

$$\mu_{\xi_{12}}(x) = e^{-\frac{(x-\rho_{12})^2}{2}}, \quad \text{with} \quad \rho_{12} \sim N(3, 2),$$

$$\mu_{\xi_{21}}(x) = e^{-\frac{(x-\rho_{21})^2}{2}}, \quad \text{with} \quad \rho_{21} \sim N(4, 3),$$

$$\mu_{\xi_{22}}(x) = e^{-\frac{(x-\rho_{22})^2}{2}}, \quad \text{with} \quad \rho_{22} \sim N(2, 1).$$

By 100 iterations (2000 sample points in fuzzy random simulation), the fuzzy random expected minimax equilibrium strategy is

$$\left((x_1^*, x_2^*), (y_1^*, y_2^*)\right) = \left((0.4800, 0.5200), (0.2600, 0.7400)\right),$$

with $E\left[\boldsymbol{x}^{*T}\eta\boldsymbol{y}^*\right] = 2.7114$.

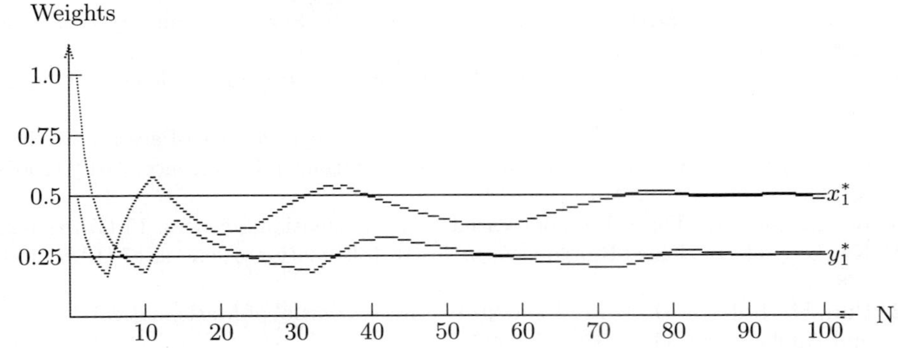

Fig. 1. An interative process based on fuzzy random simulation

The results of iterative algorithm are shown in Fig. 1, in which the two straight lines represent the optimal solutions of x_1^* and y_1^*, respectively, and the curves represent the solutions obtained by different numbers of the iterative numbers.

6 Conclusions

In this paper, a two-person zero-sum matrix game with fuzzy random payoffs is studied. Employing fuzzy random variables to describe the payoffs of the game, we present a fuzzy random expected minimax equilibrium strategy and prove the existence of the strategy. An algorithm based on fuzzy random simulation is designed to seek the minimax equilibrium strategy.

Acknowledgments

This work was supported by the National Natural Science Foundation of China Grant No. 70571056 and China Postdoctoral Science Foundation No. 2004035013.

References

1. von Neumann, J., Morgenstern, O.: Theory of Games and Economic Behavior. New York, Wiley (1944)
2. Berg, J., Engel, A.: Matrix Games, Mixed Strategies, and Statistical Mechanics. Physical Review Letters. 81 (1998) 4999-5002

3. Ein-Dor, L., Kanter, I.: Matrix Games with Nonuniform Payoff Distributions. Physica A. 302 (2001) 80-88
4. Zadeh, L.: Fuzzy Sets. Information and Control. 8 (1965) 338-353
5. Campos, L.: Fuzzy Linear Programming Models to Solve Fuzzy Matrix Games. Fuzzy Sets and Systems. 32 (1989) 275-289
6. Nishizaki, I., Sakawa, M.: Fuzzy and Multiobjective Games for Conflict Resolution. Physica-Verleg, Heidelberg (2001)
7. Bector, C., Chandra, S., Vijay, V.: Duality in Linear Programming with Fuzzy Parameters and Matrix Games with Fuzzy Payoffs. Fuzzy Sets and Systems. 146 (2004) 253-69
8. Vijay, V., Chandra, S., Bector,C.: Matrix Games with Fuzzy Goals and Fuzzy Payoffs. Omega. 33 (2005) 425-429
9. Xu, L., Zhao, R., Shu, T.: Three Equilibrium Strategies for Two-Person Zero-Sum Game with Fuzzy Payoffs. Lecture Notes in Artificial Intelligence. 3613 (2005) 350-354
10. Kwakernaak, H.: Fuzzy Random Variables-I. Information Sciences. 15 (1978) 1-29
11. Kwakernaak, H.: Fuzzy Random Variables-II. Information Sciences. 17 (1979) 153-178
12. Puri, M., Ralescu, D.: Fuzzy Random Variables. Journal of Mathematical Analysis and Applications. 114 (1986) 409-422
13. Kruse, R., Meyer, D.: Statistics with Vague Data. D.Redial Publishing Company, Dordrecht (1987)
14. Yoshida, Y.: A Stopping Game in a Stochastic and Fuzzy Enviroment. Mathematical and Computer Modelling. 30 (1999) 147-158
15. Liu, Y., Liu, B.: Fuzzy Random Variables: A Scalar Expected Value. Fuzzy Optimization and Decision Making. 2 (2003) 143-160
16. Liu, B., Liu, Y.: Expected Value of Fuzzy Variable and Fuzzy Expected Value Model. IEEE Transactions on Fuzzy Systems. 10 (2002) 445-450
17. Liu, B.: Uncertainty Theory: An Introduction to its Axiomatic Foundations. Springer-Verlag, Berlin (2004)
18. Liu, Y., Liu, B.: A Class of Fuzzy Random Optimization: Expected Value Models. Information Sciences. 155 (2003) 89-102

Estimating the Contingency of R&D Project in a Fuzzy Environment

Changsheng Yi, Wansheng Tang, and Ying Liu

Institute of Systems Engineering, Tianjin University, Tianjin 300072, China
yics2004@tom.com, tang@tju.edu.cn,
luckynumber20042003@yahoo.com.cn

Abstract. This paper develops a fuzzy model that considers the uncertain attributes of change orders in a research and development (R&D) project. It is assumed that the arrival times of change orders follow a fuzzy renewal process. The contingency based on the confidence level offered by the decision-maker is estimated by fuzzy simulation. Furthermore, the effect of schedule delays which increase further the project cost and schedule is considered explicitly. Finally, three numerical examples are presented to illustrate the application of the proposed model.

1 Introduction

Cost or schedule overrun has always been one of the most important management problems of R&D project as well as of all other projects. The standard practice of allowing for unexpected cost or delay is to add a percentage figure above the basic cost or schedule estimate. The additional amount of money or time, usually called contingency, intends to contain any unforeseen cost or delay incurring within the project duration. In realistic situations, it is impossible to ensure a total protection by any finite contingency provision, which always reflects a certain level of risk acceptance whether known or not.

There is a number of estimating methods that attempt to identify and assess various categories of uncertainties and risks in order to compute the overall project cost or schedule distributions [1]. For example, the probability that actual cost will not exceed a given cost estimate can be determined [2] [3]. However, in many situations, the probability distribution functions may be unknown or partially known. For budgeting and decision purposes, experts' subjective opinions can be used to provide the estimations of uncertain parameters. These subjective opinions are usually characterized by linguistic terms such as "low", "high", or "fairly high" because of either the lack of evidence or the inability of experts. The classical set theory or probability theory will be useless since it is difficult to assign a crisp value to a subjective judgement. In such a case, the use of fuzzy theory provides an effective way to handle these problems.

The purpose of this paper is to estimate the contingency of R&D project by means of fuzzy theory. Specifically, it is assumed that the interarrival times between uncertain events causing delays and cost adjustments (change orders) are fuzzy variables. Thus the arrival times of these uncertain events follow a

D.-S. Huang, K. Li, and G.W. Irwin (Eds.): ICIC 2006, LNAI 4114, pp. 819–824, 2006.

fuzzy renewal process. Furthermore, the costs and delays caused by uncertain events are regarded as fuzzy variables. Similar to other projects' management, the contingency based on the confidence level which means the possibility of meeting the project budget is estimated by fuzzy simulation.

2 Fuzzy Model for Estimating the Contingency

In an R&D project duration, it is assumed that the arrival times of uncertain events follow a fuzzy process $\{N(t), t \geq 0\}$, where $N(t)$ denotes the number of events in the interval $(0, t]$. Specifically, let T_i be the interarrival times between the $(i-1)$th and the ith events, $i = 1, 2, \ldots$, respectively. $\{T_i, i \geq 1\}$ denotes a sequence of bounded nonnegative fuzzy variables with the same membership function defined on the possibility spaces $(\Theta_i^1, \mathcal{P}(\Theta_i^1), \text{Pos}_i^1)$, $i = 1, 2, \ldots$, respectively. Let S_n denote the arrival time of the nth event,

$$S_n = \sum_{i=1}^{n} T_i, \tag{1}$$

and define $S_0 = 0$, then the process $\{S_n, n \geq 1\}$ becomes a fuzzy renewal process on the product possibility space $(\Theta^1, \mathcal{P}(\Theta^1), \text{Pos}^1)$ of $(\Theta_i^1, \mathcal{P}(\Theta_i^1), \text{Pos}_i^1)$, $i = 1, 2, \ldots$

Let $N(t)$ denote the total number of events during the interval $(0, t]$, then

$$N(t) = \sup\{n : 0 < S_n \leq t\}. \tag{2}$$

Obviously, $N(t)$ is also a fuzzy variable on the possibility space $(\Theta^1, \mathcal{P}(\Theta^1), \text{Pos}^1)$, and

$$\text{Pos}\{N(t) = n\} = \text{Pos}\{S_n \leq t < S_{n+1}\}, \quad n = 0, 1, 2, \ldots \tag{3}$$

Let T be the original estimated project duration. We further assume that each event will affect the R&D project duration and cost. Specifically, the ith event causes the project to be delayed by an interval D_i. It is assumed that all these intervals D_i are bounded nonnegative fuzzy variables with the same membership function and defined on the possibility spaces $(\Theta_i^2, \mathcal{P}(\Theta_i^2), \text{Pos}_i^2)$, $i = 1, 2, \ldots$, respectively. Furthermore, we assume that these delays are non-overlapping. The total delay of change orders can be denoted by

$$D = \sum_{i=1}^{N(T)} D_i. \tag{4}$$

Let C_i denote the cost associated with the ith interarrival time T_i. It is assumed that C_i, $i = 1, 2, \ldots$ are bounded nonnegative fuzzy variables with the same membership function and defined on the possibility spaces $(\Theta_i^3, \mathcal{P}(\Theta_i^3), \text{Pos}_i^3)$, $i = 1, 2, \ldots$, respectively. So the total cost of change orders can be expressed by

$$C = \sum_{i=1}^{N(T)} C_i. \tag{5}$$

2.1 Estimation of Contingency Without Interaction

It is assumed that all costs of change orders are independent and identically distributed (iid) fuzzy variables. The same assumption applies to the delays of change orders. Thus, the expected values of total cost and delay of change orders can be expressed as

$$E[C] = E\left[\sum_{i=1}^{N(T)} C_i\right] = E[N(T) \cdot C_1], \tag{6}$$

$$E[D] = E\left[\sum_{i=1}^{N(T)} D_i\right] = E[N(T) \cdot D_1], \tag{7}$$

respectively (Zhao and Liu [4]).

Now that we have the expressions of cost and schedule overruns, we can specify a desired contingency value. Here, we again assume that costs and delays of change orders are independent with each other. If the decision-maker desires a confidence level α against cost overrun, he or she would get a minimal contingency of $\overline{C}$ such that

$$\text{Pos}\left\{C \le \overline{C}\right\} = \text{Pos}\left\{\sum_{i=1}^{N(T)} C_i \le \overline{C}\right\} \ge \alpha, \tag{8}$$

where $\overline{C}$ is the α-pessimistic value of fuzzy variable C.

The similar approach can be used for contingency of delay. If the decision-maker desires a confidence level β against schedule overrun, he or she would get a minimal contingency of $\overline{D}$ such that

$$\text{Pos}\left\{D \le \overline{D}\right\} = \text{Pos}\left\{\sum_{i=1}^{N(T)} D_i \le \overline{D}\right\} \ge \beta, \tag{9}$$

where $\overline{D}$ is the β-pessimistic value of fuzzy variable D.

2.2 Estimation of Contingency with Interaction

The total cost and delay of change orders mentioned above are estimated on condition that T is the original project duration. However, the number of events will increase correspondingly in the duration increase D. It is assumed that the rate of change remains the same during delay periods. Then the impact on cost can be approximately expressed by

$$\text{Pos}\left\{C \le \overline{C}\right\} = \text{Pos}\left\{\sum_{i=1}^{N(T+E[D])} C_i \le \overline{C}\right\} \ge \alpha. \tag{10}$$

The similar approach can be used for contingency of delay as follows,

$$\text{Pos}\left\{D \le \overline{D}\right\} = \text{Pos}\left\{\sum_{i=1}^{N(T+E[D])} D_i \le \overline{D}\right\} \ge \beta. \tag{11}$$

3 Fuzzy Simulation for Estimating Contingency

In the fuzzy model formulated in Section 2, it is difficult to find an analytic method to calculate the expected values and pessimistic values due to the complexity of fuzzy renewal process in an R&D project. Here, we employ fuzzy simulation techniques proposed by Liu [5] to estimate these values.

3.1 Fuzzy Simulation for Estimating Expected Value

In this section, we design the fuzzy simulation for estimating the expected value of total cost of change orders. The expected value of total delay can be estimated by the same method. For a given R&D project duration T, by the definition of expected value of fuzzy variable presented by Liu and Liu [6] and equation (6), the expected value $E[C]$ can be expressed by

$$E[C] = E\left[N(T)C_1\right] = \int_0^{+\infty} \mathrm{Cr}\left\{N(T)C_1 \geq r\right\} \mathrm{d}r. \tag{12}$$

The procedure for estimating $E[N(T)C_1]$ can be summarized as follows.

Step 1. Set L=0.
Step 2. Randomly sample $\boldsymbol{\theta}_k$ from the universe Θ such that $\mathrm{Pos}\{\boldsymbol{\theta}_k\} \geq \varepsilon$, and denote $\mu_k = \mathrm{Pos}\{\boldsymbol{\theta}_k\}$, $k = 1, 2, \cdots, M$, respectively, where ε is a sufficiently small number and M is a sufficiently large number.
Step 3. Set $a = (N(T)C_1)(\boldsymbol{\theta}_1) \wedge \cdots \wedge (N(T)C_1)(\boldsymbol{\theta}_M)$ and $b = (N(T)C_1)(\boldsymbol{\theta}_1) \vee \cdots \vee (N(T)C_1)(\boldsymbol{\theta}_M)$.
Step 4. Randomly generate r from $[a, b]$.
Step 5. For any real number $r \geq 0$, $\mathrm{Cr}\{N(T)C_1 \geq r\}$ can be estimated by

$$\frac{1}{2}\left(\max_{1\leq k\leq M}\{\mu_k \mid (N(T)C_1)(\boldsymbol{\theta}_k) \geq r\} + 1 - \max_{1\leq k\leq M}\{\mu_k \mid (N(T)C_1)(\boldsymbol{\theta}_k) < r\}\right), \tag{13}$$

and set $L \leftarrow L + \mathrm{Cr}\left\{(N(T)C_1)(\boldsymbol{\theta}_k) \geq r\right\}$.
Step 6. Repeat the fourth and fifth steps for M times.
Step 7. $E[N(T)C_1] = a \vee 0 + b \wedge 0 + L \cdot (b - a)/M$.
Step 8. Return $E[N(T)C_1]$.

3.2 Fuzzy Simulation for Estimating α-Pessimistic Value

Here, we employ the fuzzy simulation for estimating the contingency value of total cost of change orders. The same approach can be applied to the contingency value of total delay of change orders. The procedure for estimating $\overline{C}$ can be summarized as follows.

Step 1. Set $\overline{C} = +\infty$.
Step 2. Randomly generate $\boldsymbol{\theta}$ from the α-level set of fuzzy variable C.
Step 3. If $\overline{C} > C(\boldsymbol{\theta})$, then set $\overline{C} = C(\boldsymbol{\theta})$.
Step 4. Repeat the second and third steps M times, where M is a sufficiently large number.
Step 5. Return the minimal value $\overline{C}$.

4 Numerical Examples

Usually, uncertain events causing delays and cost adjustments are assumed to occur randomly in time. Often their probability distributions can be estimated from historical data. However, collecting enough and effective historical data is usually difficult in an R&D project. Thus, these parameters can be regarded as fuzzy variables. Consider an R&D project in which the interarrival times of change orders are triangular fuzzy variables $T_i = (1.0, 1.5, 2.0)$ months, the delays of change orders are triangular fuzzy variables $D_i = (0.3, 0.5, 0.7)$ months, and the associated costs are triangular fuzzy variables $C_i = (0.8, 1.0, 1.2)$ thousand dollars, $i = 1, 2, \ldots$ In addition, the project duration T is 12 months.

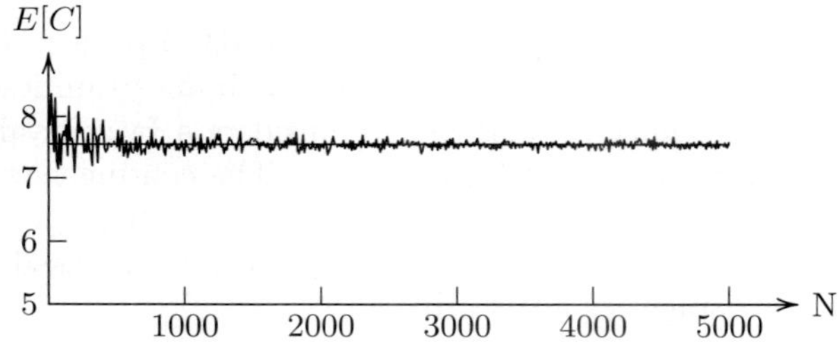

Fig. 1. A simulation process for expected value of total cost

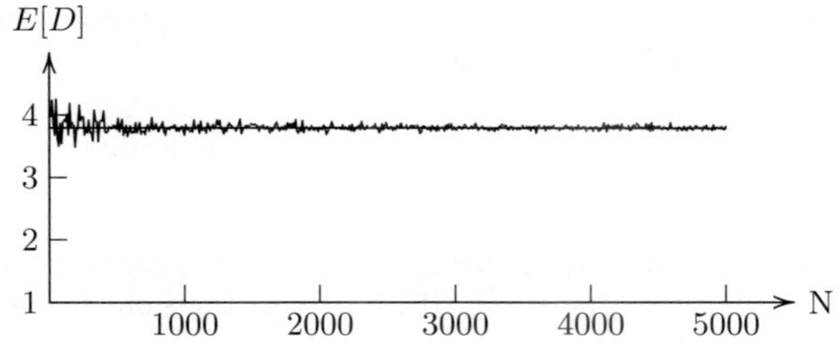

Fig. 2. A simulation process for expected value of total delay

Example 1. According to the expressions (6) and (7), we employ fuzzy simulation to estimate the expected total cost and delay of change orders, respectively. The variations of expected total cost with different numbers of samples are shown in Fig. 1, and the ones of expected total delay are shown in Fig. 2, where N represents the number of samples. The expected value of total cost of change orders is 7.5033 thousand dollars and the expected value of total delay is 3.7695 months when 5000 samples are employed.

Example 2. According to the expressions (8) and (9), we take fuzzy simulation to estimate the contingency values of total cost and delay of change orders. For the total cost of change orders, the confidence level $\alpha = 0.9$. For the total delay of change orders, the confidence level $\beta = 0.85$. The α-pessimistic value $\overline{C}$ is estimated to be 9.2757 thousand dollars with 5000 samples. The β-pessimistic value $\overline{D}$ is estimated to be 5.1146 months with 5000 samples.

Example 3. Here, we consider the estimation of contingency with interaction. The R&D project duration T is replaced by the new value $(T + E[D])$ considering the effects of delays to project duration. The parameters α and β take the same values with Example 2, respectively. By the expressions (10) and (11), we can estimate the contingency values that $\overline{C} = 16.2172$ thousand dollars and $\overline{D} = 8.3149$ months with 5000 samples.

5 Conclusions

Cost and schedule overruns often take place in an R&D project duration. Estimating a reasonable contingency budget to deal with uncertainties is imperative for R&D project management. This paper considers a fuzzy evaluation model for estimating the contingency of R&D project. The contingency based on the confidence level which means the possibility of meeting the project budget is estimated by fuzzy simulation. The proposed approach can be used for budgeting purpose at the early stages of R&D project.

Acknowledgments

This work was supported by the National Natural Science Foundation of China Grant No. 70471049 and No. 70571056.

References

1. Balachandra, R., Friar, J.: Factors for Success in R&D Projects and New Product Innovation: A Contextual Framework. IEEE Transactions on Engineering Management. 44 (1997) 276-287
2. Ranasinghe, M.: Contingency Allocation and Management for Building Projects. Construction Management & Economics. 12 (1994) 233-243
3. Touran, A.: Calculation of Contingency in Construction Projects. IEEE Transactions on Engineering Management. 50 (2003) 135-140
4. Zhao, R., Liu, B.: Renewal Process with Fuzzy Interarrival Times and Rewards. International Journal of Uncertainty, Fuzziness and Knowledge-Based Systems. 11 (2003) 573-586
5. Liu, B.: Theory and Practice of Uncertain Programming. Phisica-Verlag, Heidelberg. (2002)
6. Liu, B., Liu, Y.: Expected Value of Fuzzy Variable and Fuzzy Expected Value Models. IEEE Transactions on Fuzzy Systems. 10 (2002) 445-450

Parallel Combination of Genetic Algorithm and Ant Algorithm Based on Dynamic K-Means Cluster

Jianli Ding[1,2], Wansheng Tang[1], and Liuqing Wang[1]

[1] Institute of Systems Engineering, Tianjin University, Tianjin 300072, China
jianliding@yahoo.com.cn, tang@tju.edu.cn, liuqing5210@sina.com
[2] Tianjin Key Lab for Advanced Signal Processing, Civil Aviation University of China, Tianjin 300300, China

Abstract. Many actual project problems generally belong to large-scale TSP, The large-scale TSP as a famous NP-hard problem will be faced with the dual challenges of the optimization performance and the CPU run-time performance for any single algorithm. In fact, the optimal solution is not pursued overwhelmingly in actual projects, but it needs to meet certain optimization efficiency. This paper reduces the problem's complexity based on the idea of "divide and rule". We use the method of K-Means cluster to divide the nearest neighbor quickly. Then, we employ parallel computing method to all divided areas by using combination of genetic algorithm and ant algorithm (GAAA). Finally, we globally link all the subsets using the method of K centers connect. The results of simulations show that its complexity has been greatly reduced and we can quickly obtain a satisfactory solution to the large-scale problem. It is one effective way to solve the large-scale complex problems.

1 Introduction

In fact, many actual project problems generally belong to large-scale TSP, such as the VLSI chip processing problem (corresponding to 1.2×10^6 cities TSP, Korte, 1988), X-ray (corresponding to 14000 cities TSP, Bland et al, 1989), printed circuit board drilling problem (corresponding to $17,000$ cities TSP, Litke, 1984), and the famous PCB442 problem (corresponding to 442 cities TSP, Grotschel et al. 1991). For many practice problems, due to the structure's complexity, there often exist a lot of local minima in the neighborhood of the optimal solution. Any single algorithm will be faced with the dual challenge of the optimization performance and the CPU run-time performance when dealing with this kind of large-scale problems due to the TSP complexity [1]. For the complex large-scale TSP, scholars pin their hope on great enhancement of the super computer and the parallel computation group's performance; On the other hand, they continue to explore new algorithms.

The spatial decomposition of neighborhood search is based on the idea of "divide and rule", combining mixing optimization strategy, which is one effective way to solve the large-scale complex problems. Its basic idea is as follows: to

D.-S. Huang, K. Li, and G.W. Irwin (Eds.): ICIC 2006, LNAI 4114, pp. 825–830, 2006.

separate the entire problem into certain small scale subsets with a kind of classified method, for each small scale subset, parallel computing with one better optimization algorithm, and then link all subsets by combining a certain linking way, thus we can quickly obtain a satisfactory solution to the large-scale problem. By using this decomposition strategy, we can not only reduce the problem's complexity, but also obtain the higher optimization efficiency and the more satisfactory optimization quality of the large-scale problems. The optimal solution is not pursued overwhelmingly in actual projects, but needs to meet certain optimization efficiency. Therefore, the above solution strategy may be accepted. If $m \times n$ cities are divided into m areas, then spatial capacity will be significantly reduced from $(m \times n)!$ to $m \times n!$ [2]. If we parallel compute m areas, then $m \times n$ cities problem will be a n cities problem, and its complexity will be greatly reduced.

This paper tries to use the method of fast dynamic K-means cluster to divide the neighborhood areas, then comes on the subset parallel optimization computation by using the genetic algorithm-ant algorithm (GAAA) [3]. Finally, we globally link all the subsets using the method of K centers connect to fast obtain the satisfactory solution to the large-scale TSP problems.

2 The Combinative Model of Genetic Algorithm and Ant Algorithm (GAAA)

2.1 Global Frame of GAAA

GAAA defines objective function and fitness-value function based on specific problems first; the genetic algorithm is carried out secondly to bring several optimal solutions; thirdly, based on the distribution of the initial pheromone brought by the optimal solution, ant algorithm is carried out; the output is the best solution finally. The global frame is shown in Fig. 1.

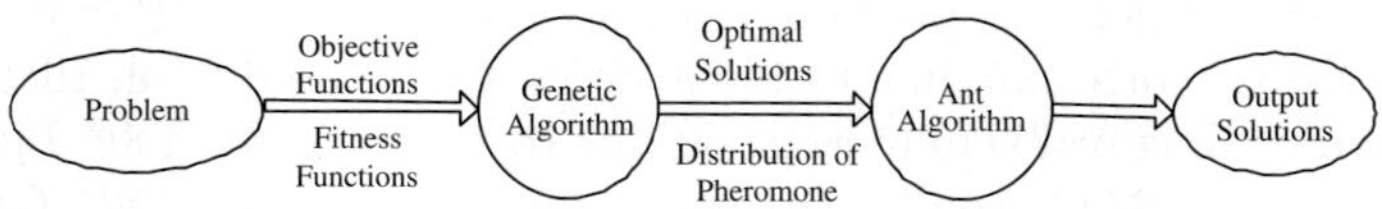

Fig. 1. Global frame of GAAA

2.2 Selection and Connection for the Model of GAAA

The GA in GAAA is based on the theory and definition of elitist selecting GA. Decimal code is used to confirm the fitness function of corresponding object; a dual of mating father chromosomes are selected based on the fitness-value function; Davis sequential-cross method is adopted; the method of reversion mutation is used.

The AA in GAAA is based on the model of ant loop of AS [4,5] and MMAS [6] algorithm, it is improved based on assimilation of the merits, that is: the placement for the initial value of pheromone (the solving result of GA is transformed into the initial value of pheromone), and updating model of pheromone (pheromone is updated by using the model of ant loop).

The key of the connection of the two algorithms is the way to transform the result of genetic algorithm into the pheromone of ant algorithm. MMAS sets the initial values of pheromones in the paths max τ_{max}. Here, it is obtained certain pheromones in the path by GA. Therefore, the initial value of pheromone is set as:

$$\tau_s = \tau_c + \tau_g, \tag{1}$$

where τ_c is a constant of pheromone given by the problem of solving solution, it is equivalent to τ_{min} in algorithm of MMAS, τ_g is the value of pheromone in the result of solving solution in GA.

3 Design of Parallel GAAA Based on Dynamic K-Means Cluster

3.1 Design Idea and the Objective Function

The core of this algorithm is to apply the idea of "divide and rule" to the complicated large-scale problems. It can be concretely described as Fig. 2.

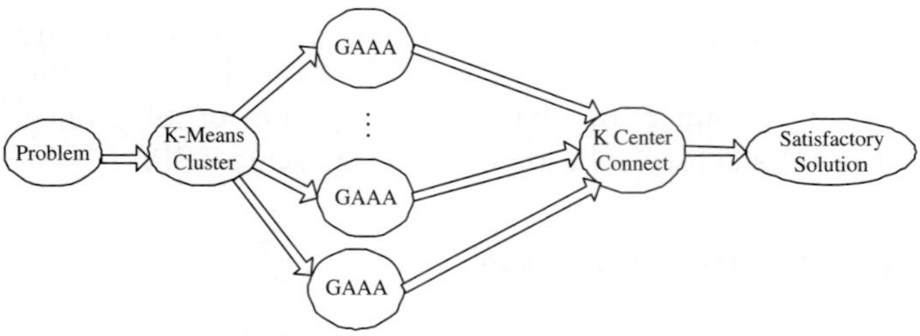

Fig. 2. Parallel GAAA based on dynamic K-Means cluster

The method of the fast nearest neighbor classified using dynamic K-Means cluster can divide the large-scale TSP into K subsets.

For K subsets, carry on parallel computation with network interconnection groups computer or multi-processor computer.

Carry on the global linkage with the method of K centers.

Its objective function is:

$$MinZ = \sum Z_k - \sum S_i + \sum S_j, \tag{2}$$

where Z_k is TSP optimum value of every subset, S_i the disconnection chain for every subset, and S_j the connection chain between the subsets.

3.2 Dynamic K-Means Cluster

For the large data table such as the large-scale TSP, the method of the fast nearest neighbor classified using dynamic K-Means cluster is fast and effective. It can not only divide the problem into K kinds, making the element in every kind aggregate, but also distinguish every kind well. More importantly, this method can not be matched for economization in store space and high speeding in computing, etc. Firstly, let k be the integer value by the scale of TSP divided by 100 and let ε be the algorithm's stop criteria. Then, running K-Means. Finally, calculate and output the distance between K centers, k value of the center, the neighbor point of each K centers and its quantity. The program of the algorithm references [2].

3.3 The Method of K Center Neighbor's Link

The procedure of the method of K center neighbor's link is described as follows.

Step 1 According to K centers and the distance between them, decide the link way of k neighbor areas.
Step 2 In order to keep TSP loop enclosed after linking the whole spatial neighbors, according near to far connect two neighbors in K centers until TSP loop.
Step 3 According to the mid value of the line between the centers of the neighbors; decide the possible link point sets of the neighbor area.
Step 4 According to the subset optimization solved by parallel GAAA, choose the connection chain in the inner neighbor of TSP loop and the disconnection chain between the neighbors at the possible point of two linking neighbors.
Step 5 For each subset, calculate the sum of all the TSP optimum values, the number of all disconnection chains, and the sum of all connection chains, thus get the satisfactory solution of the large-scale TSP.

4 Simulations and Analysis

Now we will apply the method mentioned above to the Grotschel-442 cities TSP problem.

4.1 Divide the Large-Scale TSP by K-Means Dynamic Cluster

According to size of 442 cities, set the number of dividing area K=4, and the stop criteria $\varepsilon = 0.02$. The results are shown in Table 1: the center value (coordinate), distance between them, the number of affiliated cities in its dividing area and the concrete city (coordinate) of K_1, K_2, K_3, and K_4.

4.2 Apply the Parallel GAAA to Solve Each Divided-Area TSP at the Same Time

According to the dynamic cluster divided area mentioned above, we use the multi-processors of network to parallel solve every divided area TSP at the same time. The results reported in Table 2 are obtained after many times of iterations.

Table 1. Cluster's center and the number of affiliated cities

Cluster dividing area	K_1	K_2	K_3	K_4
Number of dividing cluster	112	136	106	88
Center coordinate (X, Y)	(232,121)	(78, 281)	(69,108)	(248,290)
Distance between cluster's centers K_1		223	164	170
K_2	223		173	170
K_3	164	173		255
K_4	170	170	255	
Midpoint coordinate (X, Y) (K_3-K_1-K_4-K_2)	(K_1, K_3)=(150.5,115.5) (K_1, K_4)=(240, 205.5) (K_2, K_4)=(163, 285.5)			

Table 2. The TSP GAAA value and time for every cluster division

	K_1		K_2		K_3		K_4	
	value	time	value	time	value	time	value	time
Iteration 50	1439	36	1558	50	1434	31	1145	9
Iteration 100	1428	60	1530	134	1406	50	1128	16
Iteration 200	1419	136	1522	329	1401	113	1119	40
Iteration 300	1415	246	1506	550	1398	206	1115	82
Iteration 400	1415	378	1498	820	1394	320	1111	135
Iteration 500	1415	529	1491	1156	1394	440	1111	205

4.3 Link the K Centers Globally to Get the Satisfactory Solution of the Large-Scale TSP

According to the coordinates of K centers in Table 1 and the distance between them in Table 2, decide that K_3-K_1-K_4-K_2 makes up one close circle linking globally (Fig. 3). According to the line (mid point coordinate) between centers, decide the possible point sets and the dividing area TSP array. For each divided

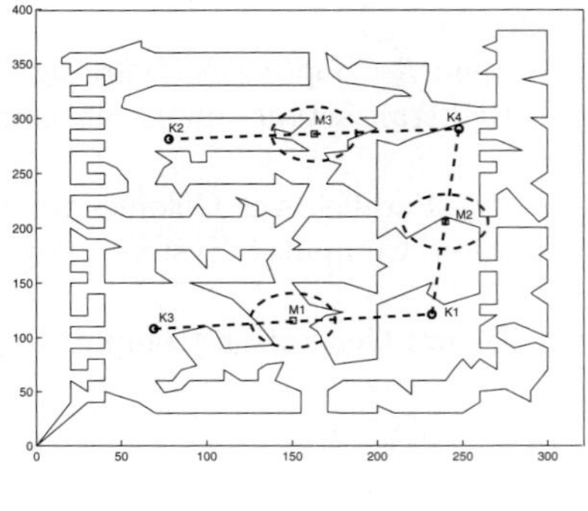

Fig. 3. K_3-K_1-K_4-K_2 makes up one close circle linking globally

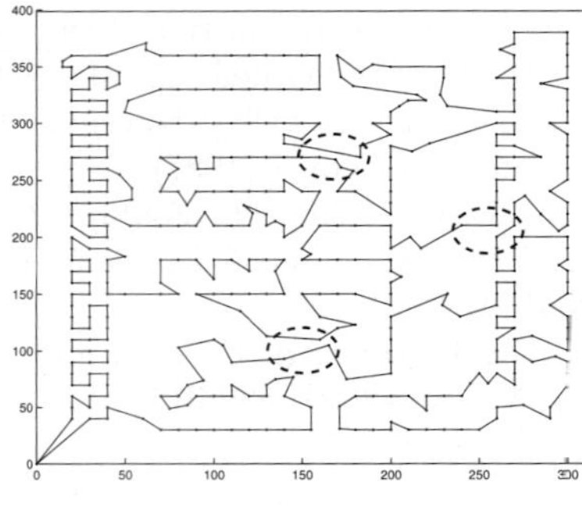

Fig. 4. Grotschel-442 cities TSP global connection circle

area, calculate the sum of the TSP optimum value, the sum of disconnection chain, and the sum of connection chain, thus we can get the satisfactory solution for Grotschel-442 cities TSP. Fig. 4 shows the global connection circle.

5 Conclusion

Through the instance analysis of the large-scale TSP, we can see that the algorithm can obtain a satisfactory result on optimization performance and time performance, thus it has actual project value. K-means dynamic cluster method is very fast; therefore, the algorithm has not increased the burden of extra operation while reducing the difficulty of the large-scale TSP problems. The number of neighbor dividing area (K) and the scale of dividing area are important indices influencing the optimization speed and optimization result. If the number of the dividing area is too big, the quality of the global solution will descend; if the number of the dividing area is very few, the optimization speed of the dividing area will be too slow. We can get the best global solution by setting the scale of the dividing area about 100 cities and iterating 300 times.

Acknowledgments

This work was supported by the National Natural Science Foundation of China Grant No. 60572167 and China Postdoctoral Science Foundation No. 2004036138.

References

1. Wang, L.: Intelligent Optimization Algorithms with Applications (In Chinese). Tsinghua University Press, Beijing (2001)
2. Ding, J., Chen, Z., Yuan, Z.: Parallel Ant Colonies Optimization Algorithm Based on Nearest Neighbor Classify Used to Dynamic K-means Cluster. Systems Engineering-Theory & Practice (In Chinese), Vol. 23 (2003) 105-110
3. Ding, J., Tang, W., Ning, Y.: Model and Convergence for the Combination of Genetic Algorithm and Ant Algorithm. Lecture Notes in Artificial Intelligence, Vol. 3801. Springer-Verlag, Berlin Heidelberg (2005) 230-237
4. Dorigo, M., Gambardella, L. M.: Ant Colony System: A Cooperative Learning Approach to the Traveling Salesman Problem. IEEE Transactions on Evolutionary Computation, Vol. 1 (1997) 53-66
5. Talbi, E. G., Roux, O., Fonlupt, C., Robillard, D.: Parallel Ant Colonies for the Quadratic Assignment Problem. Future Generation Computer System, Vol. 17 (2001) 851-871
6. Stutzle, T., Hoos, H. H.: Max-min Ant System. Future Generation Computer System, Vol. 16 (2000) 889-914

Properties and Relations Between Implication Operators

Jiaxin Han[1], Huacan He[1], and Yingcang Ma[2]

[1] School of Computer Science, Northwestern Polytechnical University, Xi'an, China
[2] College of Science, Xi'an University of Engineering Science and Technology, Xi'an, China
jxhanxa@126.com, hehuac@nwpu.edu.cn, mayingcang@263.net

Abstract. Fourteen properties and their interdependencies contributed to the analysis of six classes implication operators－S-implications, R-implications, QL-implications, Force implication, f-generated implication operator and g- generated implication operator－ are explored in this paper. It is found that all the properties can be inferred from three mutually independent properties. Then , the proven concerning which properties are true , false or satisfied for each of the six classes of implication operators is given. Based on which , the author get the property I(x(n(x)) = n (x) for all x∈[0,1] that does not hold for force implication, f-generated implication operator and g-generated implication operator.

1 Introduction

One of the most important and central problems of fuzzy logic is the proper definition of logical operations(see [1],[5],[10],[14],[15],[17],[19],[21]). At the beginning, the 'min' for the connective And, the 'max' for the connective Or and '1-x' for the connective Not. We can see that they are easy to work but too crisp. Now in fuzzy logic we consider that, connectives And(∧), Or(∨) and Not(¬) are usually modelled by t-norm, i.e., a commutative, associative monotone binary operator $T:[0,1]^2 \rightarrow [0,1]$ with T(1,a)=a for each a x∈[0,1], t-conorm, i.e., a commutative, associative monotone binary operator $S:[0,1]^2 \rightarrow [0,1]$ with S(0,a)=a for each x∈[0,1], and strong negation, i.e., an order-reversing involution negation n:[0,1]→[0,1]. We also know that the implication operator is very important in one logic, but how to define the implication operator in fuzzy logic? There are many definitions about it and which is better is still an open problem.

The paper organized as follows. In section 2 we will introduce six classes of implication operators and some properties in the literature for us to study the implication operator. We also analyze some interdependencies among the properties. In section 3 we will reveal which properties are true, false or satisfied for the six classes of implication operators respectively. As a particular case, We will prove whether they satisfy the property I(x(n(x)) = n(x) for all x∈[0,1]. The final section offers the conclusions.

2 The Analysis of Properties of Implication Operators

Although there are some different views on fuzzy implication operators' definition, fuzzy implication operators are widely studied by many authors in the literature.

D.-S. Huang, K. Li, and G.W. Irwin (Eds.): ICIC 2006, LNAI 4114, pp. 831 – 837, 2006.

Three general classes of implication operator I have been provided in [6], The definitions as follows:

• The S-implication I based on a t-conorm S and a strong negation n is defined as $I(x, y)=S(n(x),y)$, $x, y\in[0,1]$.
• The R-implication I based on a t-norm T is defined as $I(x, y) = \sup\{ z\in[0,1] \mid T(x, y)\leq y\}$, $x, y\in[0,1]$.
• The QL-implication I based on a t-norm T, a t-conorm S and a strong negation n is defined as $I(x, y) = S(n(x),T(x, y))$, $x, y\in[0,1]$.

In [7], the force implication operator has been identified. The definition as follows:
• The force implication operator based on a t-norm T and a distance d is defined as $I(x, y)=T(x,1-d(x, y))$.

In [20], two new classes of implication operators is introduced and the definitions as follows:

• A binary operator $I:[0,1]\to[0,1]$ defined such that $I(x, y)=f^{(-1)}(x\ f(y))$ with the understanding that $0\times\infty=0$, is called an f- generated implication operator.
• A binary operator $I:[0,1]\to[0,1]$ defined such that $I(x, y)=g^{(-1)}(g(y)/x))$ with the understanding that $0\times\infty=0$, , is called an g- generated implication operator.

Of course, there are some implication operators that don't include in the above six classes(see [3,4]). So we can see that the definition of implication operator is more difficult. But which class is better? or how to define the implication operator? In general, a fuzzy implication operator should extend the classical boolean implication. In the literature some other properties are provided , such as the D-P conditions in [6]. We summarize some properties as following(see [2,6,8,9,11-13,16,18]):

P1: $x\leq z$ implies $I(x, y)\geq I(z, y)$ for all $y\in[0,1]$.
P2: $y\leq t$ implies $I(x, y)\leq I(x,t)$ for all $x\in[0,1]$.
P3: $I(0, x) =1$ for all x all $x\in[0,1]$.
P4: $I(x, 1) =1$ for all $x\in[0,1]$.
P5: $I(1 ,0) = 0$.
P6: $I(1,x) = x$ (neutrality of truth).
P7: $I(x, y, z) = I(y, I(x, z))$ (exchange property).
P8: $I(x, y) = 1$, iff $x\leq y$.
P9: $I(x, 0) = n(x)$ is a strong negation
P10: $I(x ,y) \geq y$.
P11: $I(x, x) =1$ (identity).
P12: $I(x, y) = I(n(y),n(x))$ with a strong negation n.
P13: I ia a continuous function (continuity).
P14: $I(0,0) = I(0,1) = I(1,1) =1$.

A implication operator can't satisfy the full properties from P1 to P14, it only satisfies some of them in general. Evidently, the properties P1-P14 aren't independent of one another. For example: P6 $\Rightarrow$ P5; P10 $\Rightarrow$ P4; P8 $\Rightarrow$ P3, P4, P11, P14. The following Lemma 1 can be found in [2].

Lemma 1. *Let $I:[0,1]^2\to[0,1]$.*

1) If I satisfies P1 and P12, then I satisfies P2;
2) If I satisfies P2 and P12, then I satisfies P1;
3) If I satisfies P3 and P12, then I satisfies P4;
4) If I satisfies P4 and P12, then I satisfies P3;
5) If I satisfies P6 and P12, then I satisfies P9;
6) If I satisfies P9 and P12, then I satisfies P6;
7) If I satisfies P2 and P9, then I satisfies P3;
8) If I satisfies P1 and P6, then I satisfies P10;
9) If I satisfies P7 and P9, then I satisfies P12;
10) If I satisfies P1, P6 and P12, then I satisfies P2, P3, P4, P5, P9 and P10;
11) If I satisfies P2, P7 and P8, then I satisfies P1, P3, P4, P5, p6, P10 and P11.

Lemma 2. *Let $I:[0,1]^2\to[0,1]$.*
12) If I satisfies P7 and P8, then I satisfies P1, P3, P4, P5, P10, P11 and P14.

Proof. P3, P4, P11 and P14 are obvious because of P8. Let x, y, z$\in$[0,1],x$\leq$z. Because I satisfies P7 and P8, then I(z, I(z, y),y)) = I(I(z, y), I(z, y)) =1, hence z $\leq$I (I(z,y),y). From our assumption we have also x $\leq$ I(I(z,y),y). It follows 1 = I (x ,I(z , y),y)) = I(I(z, y),I(x, y)). By virtue of P8 it means, I(z, y) $\leq$I(x, y). So I satisfis P1.

Because I(y, I(x, y) = I(x, I (y, y)) = 1, so I(x, y)$\geq$y. So I satisfies P10.

If we assume I(1,0)= a>0, so 1 = I(a,I(1,0)) = I(1,I(a,0)) $\neq$1, it is a contradiction. So we have I(1,0)=0. So I satisfies P5. □

Lemma 3. *See [9], If $I:[0,1]^2\to[0,1]$ satisfies P1, P3, P4, P5 and P14, then the function $n:[0,1]\to[0,1]$ defined by*

$$n(x) = I(x, 0),\ x\in[0,1]. \tag{1}$$

is a negation. If additionally, I satisfies

$$I(I(x, 0),0) = x,\ x\in[0,1]. \tag{2}$$

Then n is a strong negation.

Lemma 4. *See [9] Let a function $I:[0,1]^2\to[0,1]$ satisfies P7 and P8. Then I satisfies (2) iff the function n defined by (1) is continuous.*

Theorem 1. *Let $I:[0,1]^2\to[0,1]$,If I satisfies P7, P8 and P13. Then I satisfies P1-P14.*

Proof. Because I satisfies P7, P8, P13, so I(x,0) is continuous. From Lemma 4, we can get I satisfies (2). Hence from Lemma 2 and Lemma 3, the negation n defined by (1) is a strong negation. So I(n(y) ,(n(y)) = I(I(y,0),I(x,0)) = I(x,I(I(y,0),0)) = I(x,y), x, y$\in$[0,1]. Hence I satisfies P12. From Lemma 1 and Lemma 2, P7,P8 $\Rightarrow$P1, P14; P1, P12$\Rightarrow$P2; P2, P7, P8$\Rightarrow$ P1,P3, P4, P5, P6, P10 , P11; P6, P12$\Rightarrow$P9. □

Theorem 2. *The three properties P7, P8 and P13 are mutually independent.*

Proof. In fact the function I(x,y)=min(max(1/2,min(1-x+y,1)),2-2x+2y) satisfies P8 and P13 , but not satisfies P7. The function I(x ,y) = 1-x + xy satisfies P7 and P13, but not satisfies P8. The function $I(x, y) = \begin{cases} 1, x \le y; \\ b, otherwise \end{cases}$. satisfies P7 and P8, but not satisfies P13. □

3 Study of Six Classes of Implication Operators

In this section we will analyze the properties of six classes implication operators. the following definition is necessary.

Definition1. *For one particular class of implication operator, we say property P (one of P1-P14) is true if any operator in the class satisfies the property P. we say property P (one of P1-P14) is false if any operator in the class doesn't satisfy the property P. we say property P (one of P1-P14) is satisfied if some operators in the class satisfy the property P and also some operators don't satisfy the property P.*

Theorem 3. *For S-implication, we have: 1) the properties P1, P2, P3, P4, P5, P6, P7, P9, P10, P12 and P14 are true;2) the properties P8, P11, P13 are satisfied.*

Proof. From the definitions of S-implication and strong negation, we can see that P1,P1, P2, P3, P4, P5, P6, P7, P9, P10 and P14 are true. I(n(y),n(x)) = S(n(n(y),n(x)) = S(y,n(x)) = S(n(x),y) = I(x,y), x,y∈[0,1], So P12 is true.

We can see the Lukasiewicz implication I(x,y)=min(1,1-x+y) satisfy P8, P11 and P13. But Diene implication I(x,y)=max(1-x,y) does not satisfy P8; it also does not satisfy P11, the Dubois-Prade implication $I(x, y) = \begin{cases} 1 - x, y = 0; \\ y, x = 1; \\ 1, otherwise \end{cases}$. does not satisfy P13. □

Theorem 4. *For R-implication, fixing the t-norm is left continuous t-norm. we have : 1) the properties P1, P2, P3, P4, P5, P6, P7, P8, P10, P11 and P14 are true;2) the properties P9, P12, P13 are satisfied.*

Proof. In this case, left-continuous t-norm and R-implication be an adjoint couple. So P1, P2, P3, P4, P5, P6, P7, P8, P10, P11 and P114 are true.

We can see the Lukasiewicz implication I(x,y)=min(1,1-x+y) satisfy P9, P12 and P13. But Goguen implication $I(x, y) = \begin{cases} \min(1, y / x), x \ne 0; \\ 1, x = 0. \end{cases}$ does not satisfy P9, Godel impliation $I(x, y) = \begin{cases} 1, x \le y; \\ y, otherwise \end{cases}$. does not satisfy P12, it also does not satisfy P13. □

Remark: If R-implication I based on a t-norm T, then I does not satisfy P7 generally. For P8, I only satisfies: if x≤y,I(x,y)=1,.For example the implication $I(x,y)=\begin{cases} y, x=1; \\ 1, otherwise \end{cases}$.

Theorem 5. *For QL-implication. we have:1) the properties P2, P3, P5, P6, P9 and P14 are true;2) P1, P4, P7, P8, P10, P11, P12 and P13 are satisfied.*

Proof. It is easy to prove P2, P3, P5, P6, P9 and P14 are true.
Zadeh implication I(x,y)=max(1-x, min(x,y)) satisfies P13 ,it does not satisfy P1, P4, P7, P8, P10, P11, P12. QL-implication I(x,y)=1-x+xy (in this case, S(x,y) = min(x+y,1),n(x)=1-x, T(x,y)=xy) satisfies P1, P7, P10, P12. Select $s(x,y)=\begin{cases} \max(x,y), \min(x,y)=0; \\ 1, otherwise \end{cases}$ then QL- implication I(x,y)=S(1-x,min(x,y)) satisfies P4, it also does not satisfy P13. Select S(x,y)=min(x+y,1), then QL-implication I(x,y)=S(1-x,min(x, y)) satisfies P8, P11. □

Theorem 6. *For force implication. we have: 1) the properties P5 and P11 are true; 2) the property P3 is false; 3) the properties P1, P2, P4, P6, P7, P8, P9, P10, P12 and P13 don't satisfy generally; 4) I(0,0) = I(0,1) = 0,I(1,1) = 1.*

Proof. I(x,y) = T(x,1-d(x,y)), then I(1,0) = T(1,1-d(1,0)) = 0, I(x,x) = T(1- d(x,x)) = x. So P5 and P11 are true.

I(0,x) = T(0,1-d(0,x)) = 0. then P3 is false.

If select I(x,y)=T(x,1-|x-y|)=x(1-|x-y|), then I does not satisfy P1, P2, P4, P7, P8, P9, P10, P12. If select I(x,y)=T(x,1-(x-y)^2)=x(1-(x-y)^2), then it does not satisfy P6. If select I(x,y)=T(x,1-|x-y|), $T(x,y)=\begin{cases} \min(x,y), \max(x,y)=1; \\ 0, otherwise \end{cases}$,then it does not satisfy P13. So force implications don't satisfy the properties P1, P2, P4, P6. P7, P8, P9, P10, P12 and P13 generally.

It can easily get I(0,0)=I(0,1)=0,I(1,1)=1. □

Theorem 7. *For f- generated implication operator. we have: 1) the properties P1, P2, P3, P4, P5, P6, P7, P10, P13 and P14 are true; 2) the properties P8 and P11 are false; 3) the properties P9 and P12 are satisfied.*

Proof. It can easily prove P1, P2, P3, P4, P5, P6, P7, P10, P13 and P14 are true(also see[20]).

I(x,y)=$f^{(-1)}$(xf(y)), , if I(x,y)=1, then we can get xf(y)=0, we can't get x≤y. So P8 is false. In the same way P11 is also false.

f-generated implication operator I(x,y)=1-x+xy satisfies P9,P12. But f-generated implication operator I(x,y)=y^x does not satisfy P9 and P11. □

Theorem 8. *For g- generated implication operator. we have: 1) the properties P1, P2, P3, P4, P5, P6, P7, P10, P13 and P14 are true; 2) the properties P9 and P12 are false;3) the properties P8 and P11 are satisfied.*

Proof. It can easy prove P1, P2, P3, P4, P5, P6, P7, P10, P13 and P14 are true(also see[20]).

$I(x,y)=g^{(-1)}(g(y)/x))$,$I(x,0)=0$, So P9 is false. In the same way P12 is also false.

g-generated implication operator $I(x, y) = \begin{cases} \min(1, y/x), x \neq 0 \\ 1, x = 0 \end{cases}$ satisfies P8 and P11. g- generated implication operator $I(x, y)=1-(1-b)^{1/a}$ does not satisfy P8 and P11.

In paper [2], S-implication, R- implication and QL- implication whether satisfy the property $I(x, n(x))=n(x)$ for all $x\in[0,1]$,]have been explored. The following theorem tells us whether satisfy the above property for force implication, f-generated implication operator and g- generated implication operator. □

Theorem 9 *Let I be force implication, f-generated implication operator or g-generated implication operator, then $I(x,n(x))=n(x)$ for all $x\in[0,1]$ does not hold.*

Proof. For force implication, $I(x,y) = T(x,1-d(x,y))$, then $I(x,n(x)) =T(x,1-d(x, n(x)))$,so $I(0,n(0)) = T(0, 1-d(0,n(0))) = 0 \neq n(0) = 1$. then $I(x, n(x)) = n(x)$ for all $x\in[0,1]$ does not hold.

For f-generated implication operator, $I(x,y)=f^{(-1)}(x f(y))$ then $I(x,n(x)) = n(x) \Leftrightarrow f^{(-1)}(xf(n(x))) = n(x) \Leftrightarrow xf(n(x))=f(n(x)) \Leftrightarrow f(n(x))\equiv0$.It is a contradiction because of the definition of f. Similar to the above proof, let I be g-generated implication operator, then $I(x, n(x)) = n(x)$ for all $x\in[0,1]$ does not hold. □

4 Conclusion

Logic is art of inference. Inference and implication operators are closely related. So the study of implication operator is very necessary and useful. The class of implication operators is very important in the fuzzy implication operators, so the properties of six classes of implication operators have been investigated in the paper. We also obtain three mutually independent properties P7, P8 and P13 that can infer all the properties P1-P14. For force implication, f-generated implication operator and g-generated implication operator, we prove that the property $I(x, n(x)) = n(x)$ for all $x\in[0,1]$ does not hold. We hope that the results of the present paper will be of some help or practical users of fuzzy logic.

References

1. Alsian, C., Trillas, E., Valverde, L.: On Some Logical Connectives for Fuzzy Sets Theory, Jouranl of Mathematical Analysis and Applications, Vol. 93 (1983) 15-26
2. Bustince, H., Burillo, P., Soria, F.: Automorphisms, Negations and Implication Operators. Fuzzy Sets and Systems, Vol.134 (2003) 267-272
3. Cordón, O., Herrera, F., Peregrín A.: Searching for Basic Properties Obtaining Robust Implication Operators in Fuzzy Control, Fuzzy sets and systems, Vol.111 (2000) 237-251
4. Cordón, O., Herrera F., Peregrín A.: Applicability of the Fuzzy Operators in the Design of Fuzzy Logic Controllers, Fuzzy Sets and Systems, Vol.86 (1997)15-41
5. Dubois, D., Prade, H.: A Theorem on Implication Functions Defined from Triangular Norms, Stochastica, Vol. 8, No. 3 (1985)267-279

6. Dubois, D., Prade, H.: Fuzzy Sets in Approximate Reasoning. Part 1: Inference with Possibility Distributions, Fuzzy Sets and Systems, Vol.40 (1991)143-202
7. Dujet, C., Vincent N., Force Implication: A New Approach to Human Reasoning, Fuzzy Sets and Systems, Vol.69 (1995) 53-63
8. Fodor, J.C.: Contrapositive Symmetry of Fuzzy Implications, Fuzzy Sets and Systems, Vol.69 (1995) 141-156
9. Fodor, J.C., Roubens, M.: Fuzzy Preference Modelling and Multicriteria Decision Support, Kluwer, Dordrecht (1994)
10. Fodor, J.C.:On Fuzzy Implication Operators, Fuzzy Sets and Systems, Vol.42 (1991) 293-300
11. Fodor, J.C.: A New Look at Fuzzy Connectives, Fuzzy Sets and Systems, Vol.57 (1993) 141-148
12. Nola, A.D., Ventre, A.G.S.: On Fuzzy Implication in de Morgan Algebras, Fuzzy Sets and Systems, Vol.33 (1989) 155-164
13. Pei, D.: R0 Implication:Characteristics and Applications, Fuzzy Sets and Systems, Vol.131 (2002) 297-302
14. Smets, P., Magrez, P.: Implication in Fuzzy Logic, International Journal of Approximate Reasoning, Vol.1 (1987) 327-347
15. Trillas, E., Cubillo, S., Castro,J.L.: Conjunction and Disjunction on ([0,1],≤), Fuzzy Sets and Systems, Vol.72 (1995) 155-165
16. Türksen, I.B., Kreinovich, V., Yager, R.R.: A New Class of Fuzzy Implications. Axioms of fuzzy implication revisited, Fuzzy sets and systems, Vol.100 (1998) 209-229
17. Weber, S.: A General Concept of Fuzzy Connectives, Negations and Implications Based on t-norms and t-conorms, Fuzzy Sets and Systems, Vol.11 (1983) 115-134
18. Wu, W.M.: Fuzzy Reasoning and Fuzzy Relational Equations, Fuzzy Sets and Systems, Vol.20 (1986) 67-78
19. Yager, R.R.: On the Implication Operator in Fuzzy Logic, Information Sciences, Vol. 31 (1983)141-164
20. Yager, R.R.: On Some New Classed of Implication Operators and Their Role in Approximate Reasoning, Information Sciences , online (2004)
21. Zadeh, L.A.: Fuzzy Sets. Information and Control (1965) 338-353

Quantum Network Optimization Based on the Use of Relaxing Qubits

Min Jiang[1], Zeng-ke Zhang[1], and Tzyh-Jong Tarn[1,2]

[1] Department of Automation, Tsinghua University, Beijing, 100084, P.R. China
jiangmin03@mails.tsinghua.edu.cn,
zzk@mail.tsinghua.edu.cn

[2] Department of Systems Science and Mathematics, Washington University, St. Louis, MO 63130, USA
tarn@wuauto.wustl.edu

Abstract. Any quantum algorithm has to be implemented by quantum circuit. However, due to the existence of decoherence time and the difficulty of importing ancillae qubits, we introduce a new method which can greatly reduce the operating time steps by making good use of relaxing qubits without new ancillae qubits.This concept presented in this paper can be generalized to the other quantum networks.

1 Introduction

Since the shor's[1] discovery of an efficient algorithm on prime factorization, the field of quantum computing is rapidly evolving[2,3]. However, any quantum algorithm involves evolution of the initial state under a series of unitary operations on arrays of coupled qubits and hence calls for techniques to efficiently implement any given algorithm [4,5]. Analogous to implement classical algorithms using classical electric circuit,quantum algorithms are usually performed on quantum circuits.

However, the interaction with external environment quickly destroys superpositional states. This process is usually called "decoherence"[6].Quantum computation must be done on a time-scale less than the time of decoherence.

By using of the ancillae qubits we can greatly improve the parallelism and reduce the implementation time. However,importing ancilla qubits will increase the difficultly of scalability. In this paper,we will greatly reduce the operational time by the use of the relaxing qubits. The relaxing qubits work as the ancilla qubits before practically implemented that can enhance their work efficiency.

2 Notation

Definition 1. *Qubit involved by the unitary gate is called the working qubit.*

Definition 2. *The qubit which has not been involved by any unitary gate is called relaxing qubit.Here we must point out that if the relaxing qubit once has been involved by a unitary gate then it is no longer the relaxing qubit that means*

D.-S. Huang, K. Li, and G.W. Irwin (Eds.): ICIC 2006, LNAI 4114, pp. 838–843, 2006.

the relaxing qubit must always remain at the same state and in this paper it must keep in the state of $|0\rangle$.

Consider a controlled unitary gate as follows:

$$U = \begin{bmatrix} 1 & & & \\ & 1 & & \\ & & a & b \\ & & c & d \end{bmatrix} \tag{1}$$

The two qubits involved by the controlled unitary gate can be divided into two classes: controlled qubit and target qubit.

Definition 3. *when the controlled unitary gate acts on such qubit, what remains unchanged is called control qubit.However,its state determines how to act on the other qubit.*

Definition 4. *Target qubit is the other qubit involved by the controlled unitary gate. If the state of control qubit is* $|0\rangle$ *,it remains unchanged. If the state of control qubit is* $|1\rangle$ *,then a unitary transform acts on it.*

Definition 5. *Parallelity means to implement several gate operations simultaneously.*

3 Quantum Network Based on the Use of Relaxing Qubits

Let's first to review a shallow parallel circuit. We can fan out one of the inputs into multiple copies. The controlled-cnot gate can be used to copy a qubit onto an ancilla in the pure state $|0\rangle$ by making a non-destructive measurement:

$$(\alpha\,|0\rangle + \beta\,|1\rangle) \otimes |0\rangle \rightarrow \alpha\,|00\rangle + \beta\,|11\rangle \tag{2}$$

Note that the final state is not a tensor product of two independent qubits,since the two qubits are completely entangled.However,the classic 'no cloning'theorem need to disentangle the ancilla by the end of the computation and return them to their initial state $|0\rangle$,which is a non-trivial and important part of such quantum circuit.

Theorem 1. *A series of* n *controlled unitary gates coupling the same input to* n *target can be parallelized to* $O(\log_2 n)$ *time steps[7].*

Proof. The circuit in Fig.1 copies the input onto n-1 ancillae and applies all the controlled unitary gates simultaneously, and uncopies the ancillae back to their original state. Its total depth is $2\log_2 n + 1$.

For the large multiqubit network importing ancillae qubits will reduce the time steps.However,more qubits will accelerate the influence produced by the environment which will degrade the performance of the implementation. We can make

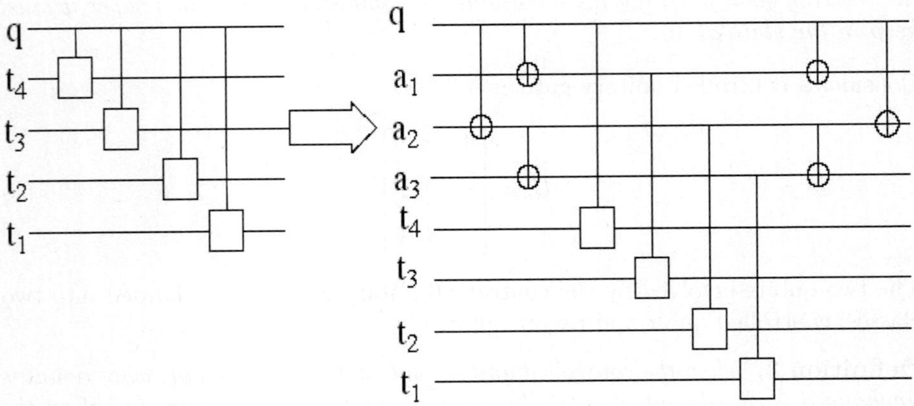

Fig. 1. Parallelizing n controlled gates on a single input qubit q to $O(\log n)$ depth

good use of the relaxing qubits whose states are the $|0\rangle$ state instead of using ancillae qubits to parallelize the circuit similar to the Fig.1 for n controlled unitary gates .

We begin by first checking the quantum Fourier transform .If we want to get the most entanglement state, it is an available approach by the use of quantum Fourier transform beginning from the initial state is $|0,0,\cdots,0\rangle$. This transformation acts as follows on a n-qubit register index $|n-1,n-2,...,1,0\rangle$[5].

$$F_n : |x\rangle \rightarrow \frac{1}{2^{n/2}} \sum_{y=0}^{2^n-1} e^{2\pi i x y} |y\rangle \tag{3}$$

This evolution relies on two logical gates.One is the H gate:

$$H = \frac{1}{\sqrt{2}} \begin{bmatrix} 1 & 1 \\ 1 & -1 \end{bmatrix} \tag{4}$$

Another gate B_{jk} is as follows:

$$B_{jk} = \begin{bmatrix} 1 & 0 & 0 & 0 \\ 0 & 1 & 0 & 0 \\ 0 & 0 & 1 & 0 \\ 0 & 0 & 0 & e^{i\theta_{jk}} \end{bmatrix} \tag{5}$$

with $\theta_{jk} = \pi/2^{k-j}$. We must pay attention to the B_{jk} gate which belongs to the controlled-unitary gates which is the predetermination condition of our method.

The standard circuit for the QFT on n qubits can be carried as the Fig.2[7].

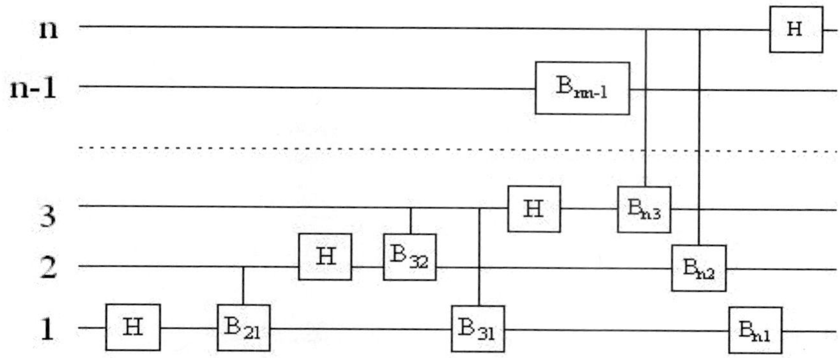

Fig. 2. The standard circuit for the quantum Fourier transform on n qubits

Take an example of a $2k$ qubit QFT network. if we don't make good use of the relaxing qubits,then the total time steps is:

$$n = \sum_{i=1}^{2k} i = (4k^2 + 2k)/2 \tag{6}$$

Then we take measures to parallelize this part of the circuit .The part of $2k$ qubit QFT network which has left more than k relaxing qubits is regarded as the first part of the network while the other part is called the second part.

In the first part we can use these relaxing qubits as ancilla qubits.For example,if the ith qubit works as the the control qubit in the first part ,then there have $i-1$ controlled unitary gates act on $i-1$ qubits which are indexed from the 1th to the $i-1$th. First,we use the controlled-cnot to copy the ith qubit's state $|0\rangle$ into the other $i-1$ relaxing qubits which may need $\lceil \log(i) \rceil$ time steps.Then we can implement the $i-1$ controlled unitary gates simultaneously.After that ,according to the classic 'no cloning'theorem we need to disentangling the ancilla by the end of the computation and returning them to their initial state $|0\rangle$ .We use the reverse circuit to complete the return the relaxing gate to the sate of $|0\rangle$ which also need $\lceil \log(i) \rceil$ time steps.At last,we must plus the time step of H gate.So if the whole process of implementing the $i-1$ controlled unitary gates which take the ith qubit as the target qubit needs $2\lceil \log(i) \rceil + 1 + 1$ time steps.

4 Experiment Results

The total time steps of the first part can be calculated as follows:

$$n = \sum_{i=1}^{k-1} ((2\lceil \log(i) \rceil + 1) + 1) \tag{7}$$

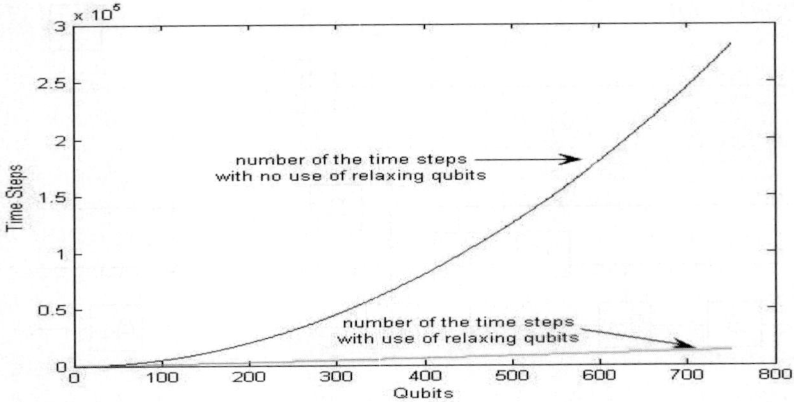

Fig. 3. Comparison for the number of time steps for part of $2k$ qubits QFT network which has left more than k qubits relax

By comparing the two results, from Fig.3 we can find out this method has nearly the same effect as importing ancillae qubits and greatly decrease the time steps of this part of circuit. We can also calculate the total time steps for the whole 2k qubits QFT network is:

$$n = \sum_{i=1}^{k-1} (2\lceil \log(i) \rceil + 2) + \sum_{i=k}^{2k} i \tag{8}$$

From Fig.4 we can find the implementation time for the whole circuit can be greatly decreased correspondingly.

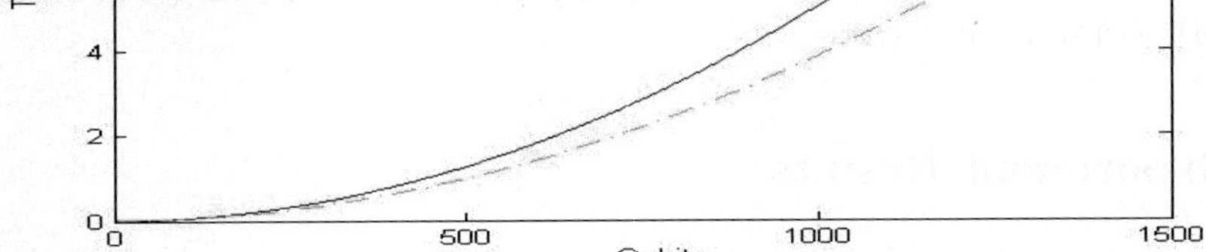

Fig. 4. Comparison for the number of time steps of the whole $2k$ qubits QFT network

5 Conclusion

This paper proposes an efficient method to make full use of the relaxing qubits in order to decrease the implementation time steps since the decoherence aroused by the environment may degrade the performance of the circuit if the computation time exceeds the decoherence time.If we use ancille qubits , the operation time of quantum circuits can be reduced in a large scale. However ,more qubits means the entanglement between the quantum system and environment will be more complicated. Our method has potential significance which can yield the nearly same effects while not importing ancilla qubits.

Similarly ,this method can be generalized to other networks. In fact ,besides the optimization of the first part of the QFT network, we can also further improve the other part of QFT network by the use of relaxing qubit. However, if we further implement the QFT network, there will be less and less relaxing qubits.Therefore it must exist one superior bound for the number of relaxing qubits which can be used most efficiently.Currently,we are working on this problem and we expect a good solution will appear soon.

Acknowledgement

This research was supported by the National Natural Science Foundation of China under Grant Number 60433050 and 60274025. T.J. Tarn would also like to acknowledge partial support from the U.S. Army Research Office under Grant W911NF-04-1-0386.

References

1. Shor, P.W.: Algorithms for Quantum Computation: Discrete Logarithms and Factoring. In: Proceedings of the 35nd Annual Symposium on the Foundations of Computer Science (FOCS), Santa Fe, New Mexico(1994) 124–134
2. Grover, L.K.: Quantum Mechanics Helps in Searching for a Needle in a Haystack, Physical Review Letter. 79 (1997) 325–328
3. Zhang, J., Vala, J., Sastry, S., Whaley, K.B.: Minimum Construction of two- Qubit Quantum Operations, Physical Review Letters. 93 (2004) 020502-1–4
4. Barenco, A., Ekert, A.K.: Dense Coding Based on Quantum Entanglement, J. Mod. Opt. 42 (1995) 1253–1259
5. Blais, A.: Quantum Network Optimization, Physical Review A. 64 (2001) 022312-1–6
6. Chuang, I.L., Laflamme, R., Shor, P.W., Zurek, W.H.: Quantum Computers, Factoring and Decoherence, Science.270 (1995) 1633–1635
7. Moore, C., Nilsson, M.: Parallel Quantum Computation and Quantum Codes, [http://www.arxiv.org.sixxs.org/pdf/quant-ph/9808027] (1998)

Neural Network Based Modeling for Oil Well Pressure Data Compensation System

Jian-long Tang[1], En li[1], Zeng-guang Hou[1], Qi Zuo[2], Zi-ze Liang[1], and Min Tan[1]

[1] Laboratory of Complex System and Intelligence Science, Institute of Automation, Chinese Academy of Science , No.95 Zhongguancun. Road, Beijing, China
{jianlong.tang, en.li}@ia.ac.cn,
{zzl, hou, tan}@compsys.ia.ac.cn

[2] Automation Department Field Bus Tech&Automation Key lab. North China University of Technology, No.5 Jinyuanzhuang Road, Shijingshan District, Beijing China
zuoqi9463@sohu.com

Abstract. This paper mainly focuses on the modeling of oil well pressure data compensation system(OWPCS) based on Neural Networks(NN). Firstly, the operational principle and configuration of OWPCS is described. Then the currently widely used modeling method for OWPCS is given, and its limitations and disadvantages are also illustrated. Secondly, in order to solve the OWPCS modeling problem more reasonably, a new approach based on Neural Network is proposed. Thirdly, the feasibility of using NN to solve this problem is analyzed, and a three-layer BP network is constructed to testify the new modeling method. Fourthly, considering the defect of BP learning algorithm and the special application environment of OWPCS, some improvements are given. Finally, experiment results are presented to show the reasonableness and effectiveness of the new method.

1 Introduction

During the process of oil exploration, the stratum pressure is a fairly important parameter. Because it is the primary foundation of engineers to make evaluations to oil deposit and establish the corresponding exploration project. Additionally, in the process of producing, the dynamical change of oil well pressure also reflects the oil supply capability of the well. According to that, engineers can establish the appropriate producing project, adjust the producing timely and analyze the producing condition of the stratum. So, the acquisition of oil well pressure data plays a fairly important part in oil exploration and producing. The structure of commonly used oil well pressure acquisition system is shown in Fig.1.

In order to facilitate the following discussion, first of all, the operational principle of OWPCS will be briefly introduced. As is shown in Fig.1, The capillary tube is filled with Nitrogen or Helium. In order to provide the driven cubage for the system, the cubage of pressure transferring tube is much larger than that of capillary tube. The structure of the system is in favor of maintaining gas-liquid equilibrium. The basic principle of the system is: pressure change of the pressure tap under the well acts on the air column of pressure transferring tube and is transferred to the mouth of well by

D.-S. Huang, K. Li, and G.W. Irwin (Eds.): ICIC 2006, LNAI 4114, pp. 844 – 854, 2006.

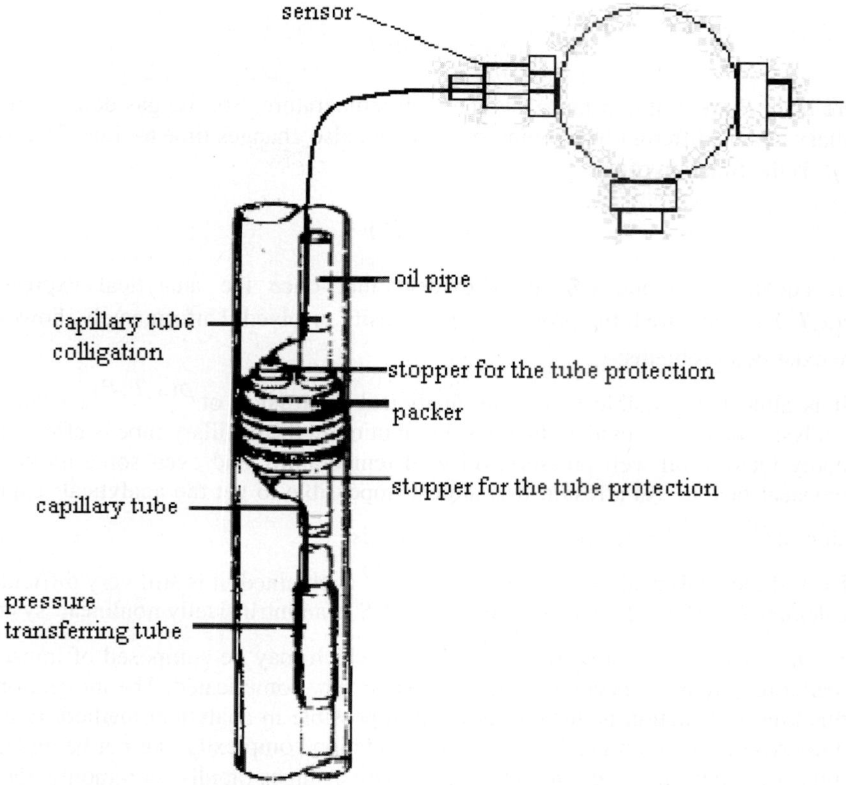

Fig. 1. Oil well pressure data compensation system

gas. So, after collecting the pressure of the capillary tube on the ground side, the sensor signal is transmitted to data collection station, which displays and stores the pressure data. However, the pressure data collected by the sensor isn't the actual pressure of the well according to Fig.1, as a result, the pressure data should be compensated to get the well real pressure data. Assume that the sensor reading is P, and the pressure of air column in the capillary tube is P_g. Then the actual pressure of oil well P_w should be obtained by:

$$P + P_g = P_w . \tag{1}$$

Obviously, in order to get the actual pressure (P_w), according to the sensor readings, the air column pressure (P_g) must be obtained. It is clear that P_g should be calculated by the following equation:

$$p_g = \int_0^h \rho \cdot g dx . \tag{2}$$

where, h is the well depth and $\rho(x)$ is the gas density at point x. The oil well pressure changes according to the equation of state for actual gases:

$$(p+\frac{a}{v^2})(v-b)=nRT \quad . \tag{3}$$

where *a, b, R* are real constant, *T* is the well temperature. So, the gas density in the capillary tube is different from point to point, and also changes time to time. That is to say ρ is the function of x, T, ρ:

$$\rho = \rho(x, T, P) \quad . \tag{4}$$

From equation (2) and (4), it is evident that once the analytical expression of $\rho(x,T,P)$ is acquired, the problem can be easily resolved. Unfortunately, however, there exist two problems:

1) It is almost impossible to get the analytical expression of $\rho(x,T,P)$. From the analysis above, it is evident that gas distribution in the capillary tube is affected by many factors: oil well pressure, oil well temperature, and even some un-known physical factors. As a result, it is almost impossible to get the analytical expression of $\rho(x,T,P)$ through mechanism analysis.
2) Even if the analytical expression of $\rho(x,T,P)$ is obtained, it is still very difficult to calculate equation (2). Theoretically, OWPCS is an intrinsically nonlinear system. So, the analytical expression of $\rho(x,T,P)$, which may be composed of transcendental functions or special functions, must be very complicated. The integration of this kind of function is difficult or even impossible in analytical method. Even if numerical integration is adopted, the computation complexity can not be underestimated. Especially when the oil well pressure changes rapidly (commonly, the oil well pressure should be captured every 1～2 seconds), it is fairly difficult to carry out the numerical integration of equation (2) in an embedded system which cannot provide enough resources. This obviously cannot meet the requirements of real time application.

In fact, equation (2) just provides a theoretical method for the calculation of air column pressure, but it is impractical in engineering.

The pressure data compensation system based on capillary tube can be viewed as an input/output system. The actual pressures of oil well, the temperature of oil well, the depth of oil well are the inputs of the system, while the sensor reading is the output. This is an intrinsically nonlinear system.

This kind of system can often be found in engineering because of the widely existence of nonlinear system in technical application. For the modeling of intrinsically nonlinear system, the commonly used method is global linearization or piecewise linearization. Taking OWPCS as an example, in practice, the actual pressure of the oil well and the sensor reading are usually viewed as linear relationship, thus according to a series of empirical formula, the linearity coefficient can be obtained. Obviously, this method has so many disadvantages. Firstly, the acquirement of empirical formula is inevitably affected by many artificial factors. Furthermore, linearizing an intrinsically nonlinear system to a linear system may cause large errors in some cases.

2 Solutions and Feasibility

There are quite a few methods on how to describe a nonlinear system quantitatively in math. Here, we are trying to study on how to describe a nonlinear system in the point of technical application rather than pure mathematics.

Based on the above analysis, Neural Network is used to approximately describe OWPCS. In the following chapter, firstly, in order to facilitate the discussion, two theorems are given, then, the feasibility of using NN to solve this problem is analyzed.

Theorem 1[13]: The training error and the generalization error of BP net satisfy:

$$V(\theta) - \lambda\sqrt{\frac{d_{vc}}{m}\ln\frac{m}{d_{vc}}} < P(\theta) < V(\theta) + \lambda\sqrt{\frac{d_{vc}}{m}\ln\frac{m}{d_{vc}}} \ . \tag{5}$$

where, $V(\theta)$ is the training error, $P(\theta)$ is the generalization error, m is the sample number, and d_{vc} is the VC dimension of the net.

Theorem 2[13]: If $\sigma(x)$ is a continuous and bounded sigmoid function, then, the functions with the following form:

$$\sum_{i=1}^{N} \alpha_i \sigma(y_i x + \theta_i) \ . \tag{6}$$

is dense in $C(I^n)$. That is to say, to $\forall f \in C(I^n)$ and $\varepsilon > 0$, the following equation is obvious:

$$\left| f(x) - \sum_{i=1}^{N} \alpha_i \sigma(y_i x + \theta_i) \right| < \varepsilon \ . \tag{7}$$

Where, $y_i \in R^n$, $x \in I^n$, $y.x$ is the inner product of y and xα_i and θ_i are real number respectively. $I^n = [0,1]^n$, $C(I^n)$ is a continuous function space in hypercube I^n

Considering the following two facts, it is believed that using Neural Network to solve this problem is feasible.

1) The nonlinear approximation capability of NN. Theorem 2[13] illustrates that a three-layer feedforward network whose hidden layer adopts sigmoid function can approximate any continuous function in $C(I^n)$ with any precision. Based on this fact, it can be deemed that a well trained NN can meet the requirements in practice.
2) The generalization capability of NN. Theorem 1 tells us that the length of region the generalization error in is:

$$L = 2\lambda\sqrt{\frac{d_{vc}}{m}\ln\frac{m}{d_{vc}}} \ . \tag{8}$$

It is worthy of being noticed that $\lim_{m\to\infty} L = 0$, this fact shows that to any positive number ε, there must exist a positive integer M, such that $|P(\theta) - V(\theta)| < \varepsilon$ while m > M. That is to say, if the number of the training data is large enough, the generalization error can always be converged to any defined region.

3 Construction of NN

Based on the analysis above, a three-layer BP network is constructed, which is a feed-forward network with three inputs (well temperature, well depth, sensor reading) and one output (actual pressure of the oil well). That is m=3, according to the Kolmogolov theorem[13], the element number of hidden layer is n = 2m+1. The basic structure of the BP net is shown in Fig.2.

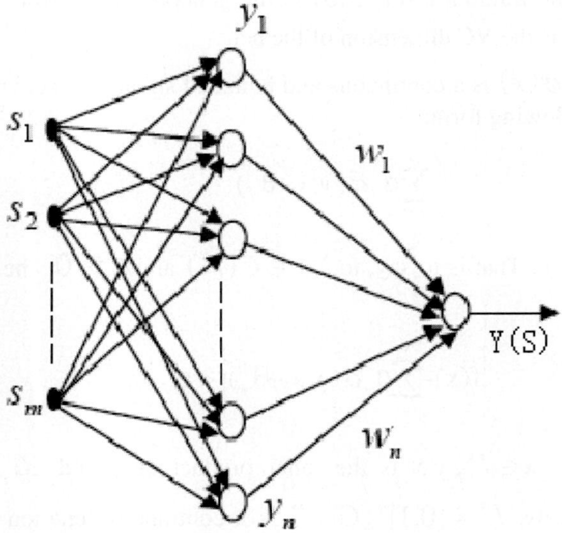

Fig. 2. The structure of BP net

In order to improve the generalization capability of the net, sigmoid function is used as the activation function in the hidden layer, while linear function is adopted in the input and output layer. Suppose $S = \{s_1, s_2, s_3\}$, thus:

$$x_k = \sum_{i=1}^{m} w_{ik} \cdot s_i \quad . \tag{9}$$

$$y_i = \frac{1}{1 + \exp\{-\xi x_i\}} \quad . \tag{10}$$

Where, x_i is the input of the i th neuron in the hidden layer, y_i is the output of the ith hidden layer, ξ is a real constant number. A linear combination function is used as the activation function for the output layer, so:

$$y(s) = \sum_{i=1}^{n} w_i \cdot y_i \quad . \tag{11}$$

First order gradient descent method is used to calculate the weight w_i in classic BP algorithm, meanwhile, in order to resolve the contradictions of the convergence speed and stability. w_i is calculated by[2]:

$$w_{ij}^{l}(k+1) = w_{ij}^{l}(k) - \eta\delta_i^l(k)\cdot\frac{\partial\sigma(x_i^l(k))}{\partial x_i^l(k)}\cdot y_j^{l-1}(k) + \alpha[w_{ij}^{l}(k) - w_{ij}^{l}(k-1)] \; . \tag{12}$$

where, y_i is the output of the ith hidden layer, $\sigma(x)$ is sigmoid function, η is learning rate, and $\delta^l{}_i(t)$ is the backward propagation error of the lth layer to the node of ith layer. $\alpha \in [0, 1)$ is momentum factor. It has been approved that, the learning speed and stability of the net are remarkably improved by appending the momentum term[2].The learning object is to minimize the following function:

$$E_{VA} = \frac{1}{2N}\sum_{j=1}^{N}\sum_{j\in c}(d_j(n) - y_j(n))^2 \tag{13}$$

where, N is the sample size, c is the output set, $d(n)$ is the output of the training data, and $y(n)$ is the actual output. It has already been proved that the network is convergent when $\eta < 2$ [2].

4 Some Improvements of Neural Networks

In the special application of OWPCS, considering the effect of the environment, the pressure data will be inevitably disturbed. So, in order to improve the net generalization, the learning model of the net should be optimized. Additionally, in order to speed up the learning speed and avoid getting into the local minimal value, the classic BP training algorithm should be improved. In this paper, LM algorithm is used to optimize the classic BP algorithm.

4.1 Optimization of the Learning Function

The main disadvantage of the classic BP algorithm is its convergence speed and the possibility of getting into the local minimal value. To a great extent, this restricts the application of BP net. So, in order to resolve this problem, LM algorithm is adopted as the training algorithm.

LM algorithm, which doesn't need to calculate Hessian matrix, is based on numerical optimization techniques. It is suitable for online computation. Firstly, we'll briefly introduce LM algorithm. For the iteration, the variance of the weight is given by[11]:

$$\Delta w(k) = -(J^T(w)J(w) + \mu I)^{-1} J^T(w)e(w) . \tag{14}$$

where, I is an identity matrix, J is the Jocobian matrix, which can be calculated by the following equation:

$$J(w) = \begin{pmatrix} \frac{\partial e_1(w)}{\partial w_1} & \cdots & \frac{\partial e_1(w)}{\partial w_n} \\ \vdots & \ddots & \vdots \\ \frac{\partial e_m(w)}{\partial w_1} & \cdots & \frac{\partial e_m(w)}{\partial w_n} \end{pmatrix} . \tag{15}$$

Where, $e(w) = d(w) - y(w)$, by introducing LM algorithm, equation (12) is optimized as:

$$w_{ij}^l(k+1) = w_{ij}^l(k) - \Delta w_{ij}(k) + \alpha[w_{ij}^l(k) - w_{ij}^l(k-1)] . \tag{16}$$

where, u is the learning rate. When u =0, LM algorithm is Newton algorithm with approximate Hessian matrix; when u is large enough, LM is nearly gradient method with small step length. The operation speed of LM algorithm is prominently higher than that of gradient method. In addition, since $J^T(w)J(w) + \mu I$ is positive, equation (14) has resolution definitely. This is a great advantage compared to Gauss～Newton algorithm, in which $J^T(w)J(w)$ is not always positive. In the actual computation, u is a tentative parameter: if training successfully, reducing u , else increasing u .

4.2 Improvement of the Learning Goal Function

Commonly, equation (13) is used as the goal function of training. In practice, the training data is inevitably disturbed by noises, especially in the special application of OWPCS, the disturbance will be much more serious. This may have bad influence on the net generalization. Even much worse, when optimizing equation (13), over learning happens.

How to improve the generalization capability of Neural Network has been an extensive studied field, for which a wide variety of techniques have been developed. Some research has focused on the use of rough set[4] or the probabilistic description of the network[5], while others have taken different approaches such as introducing simulating assistant sample[6], randomized expanded training sets[7]. A common ground for most of these methods is trying to improve in two aspects: one is the training data optimization, and the other is the improvements of the net structure. In this paper, we mainly confine our attention to the facts that the training data is disturbed by noises. Somebody[5] has done comprehensive research on this issue. A new training error calculation method was proposed as:

$$J_{VA} = \frac{E_{VA}}{2E'_{VA}} + \frac{1}{2}\ln E'_{VA} . \tag{17}$$

where:

$$E_{VA}' = \frac{1}{N}\sum_{i=1}^{N}\left\{[d_i(n) - y_i(n)] - \frac{1}{N}\sum_{j=1}^{N}[d_j(n) - y_j(n)]\right\}^2 \tag{18}$$

where, N is the number of sample data, $d(n)$ is the output of the training data, and $y(n)$ is the actual output of the net. Now, the training goal of the net is to minimize equation (17).

5 Simulation and Experiment

In the experiment, a three multi-layer feedforward Neural Network with an input layer, a hidden layer and an output layer is constructed to validate our method. The input layer has three neurons, corresponding to the sensor reading, well depth, and well temperature, while the hidden layer has seven neurons and the output layer has one neuron. The net parameter u, α, N, J_{VA} are fixed as $u = 10^{-3}$, $\alpha = 0.9$, $N = 300$, $J_{VA} = 0.0001$, while the testing sample number is intend to be 100.

A group of net input is composed of three constituents: sensor reading, well depth and well temperature. Net output is the actual pressure of the oil well. The main tasks of the experiment are to validate two aspects: one is the operation speed of the improved BP training algorithm; the other, which is much more important, is the modeling capability of the improved BP algorithm.

5.1 Operation Speed of the Improved Algorithm

Research results have already pointed out that the convergence speed of BP algorithm is very slow. In this paper, LM algorithm is adopted to optimize the traditional BP algorithm. Experiment result shows that after optimizing, the convergence speed is prominently increased. Fig.3 illustrates the convergence speed of LM optimized BP algorithm:

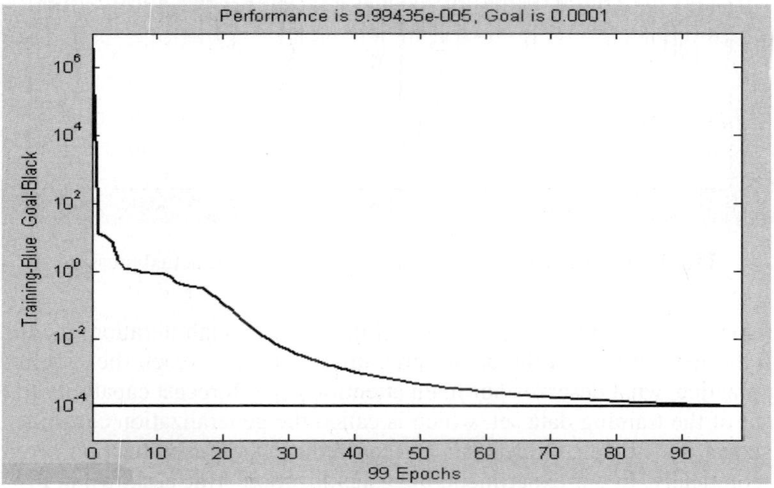

Fig. 3. Convergence of improved BP algorithm

It can be seen that the improved BP algorithm has fairly high convergence speed and can reach very high accuracy. Here, what is worthwhile to be mentioned is that the convergence speed of the net highly depends on the initial weights, learning rate and momentum factor. Especially, the initial weights have great effect on convergence speed. However, generally speaking, there is no universal rule to determine the initial weights. Usually, it is set to be a random number between $(-1,1)$.

5.2 Modeling Capability of NN to OWPCS

The previous analysis has already pointed out that a three-layer feedforward net with one hidden layer can approximate any nonlinear continuous function with any accuracy. In the experiment, the pressure, which is calculated by numerical integration according to the method proposed in section one, is viewed as the actual pressure of the oil well. The main means we adopt to validate our method is to compare the pressure calculated by NN to the actual pressure. If the difference between the two is small enough, then, we can say that NN describes OWPCS perfectly. During the experiment, first of all, 300 groups' data, which is the input of OWPCS, are set artificially. Then, the actual pressure are calculated by equation (1)~(2). The 300 groups' data including the corresponding 300 outputs are used to train the BP net. The difference of BP modeling is shown in Fig.4.

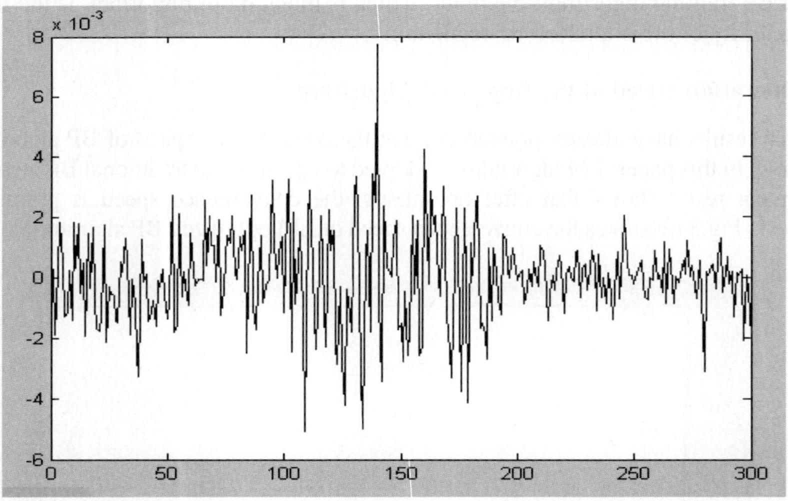

Fig. 4. The difference between the net output and the actual pressure

From the above figures, it can be noticed that after enough iteration, the difference between the net output and the actual pressure can always reach the required precision. In practice, what deserves our main attention is the forecast capability to the data that is out of the training data set, which is called the generalization capability. Theorem 1 shows that a well trained BP net can reduce the generalization error to any value theoretically. In our experiment, the generalization error is shown in Fig.5.

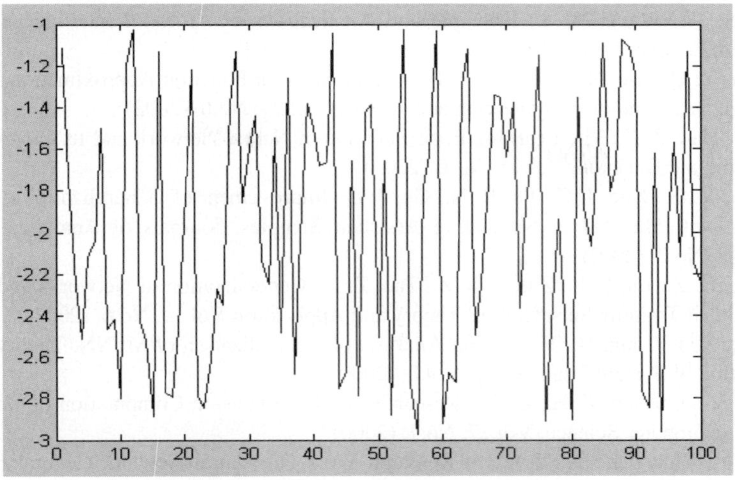

Fig. 5. Generalization error

Fig.5 illustrates that the generalization error of BP net is comparatively small (the actual pressure is higher than 2000, so the modeling precision is lower than 0.001, this can meet the requirements of most engineering applications). This fact validates the correctness of using NN to model OWPCS. Here, it is necessary to be stressed that the generalization error is highly depending on the testing data. If the difference between training data and testing data is two large (an extreme case is that the testing data is entirely out of the training data set), then, BP net almost cannot model any nonlinear function without prior knowledge.

6 Conclusions

In this paper, an approach of using BP net to nearly approximate an intrinsically nonlinear system has been proposed. Great importance has been attached to improve the learning speed and generalization capability of BP net. Based on the idea proposed in this paper, pressure data compensation system based on neural network is implemented. The experiment results show that the ameliorated BP algorithm can operate at fairly high speed and reach the required precision. In the future, we plan to make some improvements in the net input especially well temperature (we use ground temperature to approximately replace well temperature at present) to further improve the modeling capability of NN to OWPCS.

References

1. Sun, Z. Q.: Theory and Technology of Intelligent Control. Beijing: Tsinghua University Press. (2002)
2. Shi, Z. K.: Control Theory Based On Neural Network, Xi'an: Northwestern Polytechnic University Press. (1998)

3. Ye, S. W., Wang, W. J.: Principle and Applications of Artificial Intelligence, Beijing: Posts&Telecom Press. (2004)
4. Zhou, Y. Q., Xie, N. X., Deng, Y. P.: Neural Network Function Approximation Based On Rough Set, Computer engineering and science, Vol.24, No.6, (2002)
5. Li, J., Han, Z. Z.: The Learning Error Function of Neural Network and Its Generalization, Control and Decision, Vol.15, No.1, (2000)
6. Chen, X. G., Xue, J. C., Fu, R. N., Gu, J. L.: Improvement of Generalization of BP Networks with the Aid of Simulating Assistant Samples. Journals of Analytical Science, Vol.18, No.2, (2002)
7. Yang, H. Z., Lu, P. F., Zhang, S. Z., Tao, Z. L.: Generalization of Networks and Random Expanded Training Sets. Control Theory and Application.Vol.19, No.6, (2002)
8. Jiang, X. J., Tang, H. W.: System Analysis of Generalization of MFNN. Theory and Application of System Engineering. Vol.8, (2000)
9. Cui, W. D., Zhou, Z. H., Li, X.: Research of VC-Dimension Computation of Neural Network. Computer Science. Vol.27, No.7, (2000)
10. Wu, Y., Zhang, L.: A Survey of Research Work On Neural Network Generalization and Structure Optimization Algorithm. Research On Computer Application. Vol.6, (2002)
11. Su, C. S.: Advanced engineering thermodynamics, Beijing: Higher Education Press. (1987)
12. Research Center of FEISI Tech: Theory of Neural Network and Implementation in MATLAB7. Beijing: Publishing House of Electronics Industry. (2005)
13. Yan, P. F., Zhang, C. S.: Artificial Neural Network and Simulated Evolutionary Computing. Beijing: Tsinghua University Press. (2000)

Video Object Contour Tracking Using Improved Dual-Front Active Contour

Qihe Li, Yuping Luo, and Deyun Xiao

Department of Automation, Tsinghua University, Beijing, China
[1] lqh02@mails.tsinghua.edu.cn

Abstract. In this paper, we present an approach for moving object contour tracking in video by using an improved dual-front active contour model. Dual-front active contour model is first proposed for medical image segmentation. In order to adapt it to object tracking problem, we make two improvements on the original model. First, region force of the external front is modified by restricting its support region. This modification can speed up the algorithm greatly but may result in the active contour's wrong convergence to the real object boundary when it locates in a large homogeneous region. Then, a new function called quasi-balloon force is brought into the model by modifying its active region construction method. It can not only solve the problem result from the first improvement but also make tracking more flexible. The algorithm does not need an a priori shape so it is fit for deformable object tracking. By adjusting the parameters, it can be used to track fast moving target. Since the level set method is used, the topology change of the object can be controlled automatically. And no static background of the scene is assumed which means the contour can be tracked under the condition that both the camera and the object are moving. Experimental results demonstrate its effectiveness and robustness.

1 Introduction

Moving object contour tracking has a wide variety of applications in computer vision such as video surveillance, medical imaging, motion analysis, action recognition, etc. During the last decade, a lot of approaches have been proposed to tackle this problem.

First proposed by Kass et al. [1], snakes (active contour models) are widely used for deformable object tracking problem. These methods need an initialization step to set an initial contour of the object, and the contour is driven by an energy function to converge on the real edge of the object. Then the result of current frame will be used as the initial contour of the next frame. The contours are usually parametric (e.g. using B-splines) and the solution space is constrained to have an a priori shape [2]. The defect of the model is that it cannot control the contour's topology change automatically. To conquer this difficulty, the geometric flow based models using level set method [3] such as the geodesic active contour [4] are proposed as the alternative. Paragios and Deriche proposed an algorithm for tracking objects using this model [5]. The model uses only the

D.-S. Huang, K. Li, and G.W. Irwin (Eds.): ICIC 2006, LNAI 4114, pp. 855–865, 2006.

boundary information, so it fails to get the correct result if the edge of the object is not distinctive. To tackle this problem, another class of models emerged which use not only the boundary information but the region information such as the geodesic active regions [6], and Paragios and Deriche also proposed a tracking algorithm based on it [7]. Better results are acquired through integrating the region force with the edge force. A drawback of the two algorithms proposed by Paragios and Deriche is that they assume the background is static, so they are not fit for an application with moving background. Recently, an active contour model for tracking distributions was proposed [8]. It integrates the photometric features such as the color distribution or texture with the level set framework. And to some extent, it is also a region based algorithm. But it may not get good result if the photometric distribution is nonuniform. Another problem should be noted is that all the above methods need the application to meet an overlap constraint, that is, the overlapped part of the corresponding object in consecutive frames should be large enough which means the object's velocity of movement cannot be very high.

In [9], Xu and Ahuja used a two-front model named graph cuts based active contour (GCBAC) [10] for tracking. This model combines active contour and the optimization tool of graph cuts. The drawback is the time consumption of the construction of the graph. And it also cannot control the topology change automatically. Li et al. proposed a similar model called dual-front active contour model for the application of medical image segmentation [11,12]. It is implemented by using level set method, thus, some of the drawbacks of GCBAC are conquered. Though robust and fast, the dual-front active contour model is not fit for the tracking problem directly.

In this paper, we propose a tracking algorithm based on an improved dual-front active contour model which has the following desirable properties:

1. It can be used in the scenes whether the background is static or not, namely, the object contour can be tracked even both the object and the camera are moving;
2. It is fit for deformable object tracking since no a priori shape is set;
3. It has the ability of tracking fast moving object and dealing with abrupt motion changes;
4. It is topology change adaptive;

Though we have not combined the function of tracking distributions as proposed in [8], we will focus on it in the future. And since the two models are both under the level set framework, such function will be integrated with our model easily.

The rest of the paper is organized as follow: In Sect. 2 we describe the improved dual-front active contour model after a brief introduction on the original model, and then interpret how to tackle the tracking problem by using this model. Section 3 shows the experimental results. Finally, Sect. 4 gives the conclusion and future work.

2 Improved Dual-Front Active Contour

For the destination of video object tracking, the original dual-front active contour is improved. Before we interpret our improvements, we give a brief introduction of the original model.

2.1 Background

The original model is described here briefly, and for more details please refer to [11,12]. In fact, this model is an iterative procedure of dual-front evolution. So, we will describe the evolution first, and then the dual-front active contour model.

Dual-front Evolution is based on the minimal path theory proposed by Cohen and Kimmel [14]. The path of minimal action map $U_0(p)$ (also known as minimal geodesic) is defined as the minimal energy integrated along a path between a starting point p_0 and any other point p [12], as shown by the following equation: $U_0(p) = \inf_{\mathcal{C}(L)=p}(\int_{\mathcal{C}} \tilde{P}\,\mathrm{d}s) = \inf_{A_{p_0,p}} E(\mathcal{C})$, where $A_{p_0,p}$ is the space of all curves connecting p_0 and p. $\mathcal{C}$ denotes a curve. $E(\mathcal{C})$ represents the energy along the curve, and $\tilde{P}$ is the integral potential. Given the minimal action surfaces U_0 to p_0 and U_1 to p_1, the minimal geodesic between p_0 and p_1 is the set of points p_g that satisfy $U_0(p_g) + U_1(p_g) = \inf_{p\in\mathbb{R}^2}\{U_0(p) + U_1(p)\}$.

According to [14], the minimal path between p_0 and p in the image can be calculated from the action map U by solving the Eikonal Equation:

$$\|\nabla U\| = \tilde{P} \quad \text{or} \quad \|\nabla U\|F = 1 \quad \text{with} \quad U(p_0) = 0. \tag{1}$$

The front starting from p_0 will first meets the front starting from p_1 at the points satisfying $U_0(p) = U_1(p)$ who are the global minimum energy points between p_0 and p_1. Generalize the two points to two regions, we can find the region boundary by finding the points satisfying $U_0(p) = U_1(p)$. It is a global way for extracting the global minimum.

Based on above analysis, the dual-front evolution is to find the potential weighted minimum partition of a defined narrow region (named active region). Figure 1 shows the evolution. The narrow light gray region R_n is active region, and has two boundaries denoted by C_{in} and C_{out}. The propagation of C_{in} and C_{out} can be calculated by solving (1). The speed term F (inverse of $\tilde{P}$) is shown as:

$$F_{in} = 1/(m_{in} \times E^r_{in} + n_{in} \times E^e_{in}) \tag{2a}$$

$$F_{out} = 1/(m_{out} \times E^r_{out} + n_{out} \times E^e_{out}) \tag{2b}$$

Where E^r_{in} and E^r_{out} represent the terms calculated from the region inside the internal front (R_i) and the region outside the external front (R_o) respectively. E^e_{in} and E^e_{out} denote the edge features (usually the function of gradient). m and n are the corresponding coefficients. The discrete Eikonal equation can be solved by the fast marching method which has a complexity of $\mathcal{O}(n \log n)$ [15].

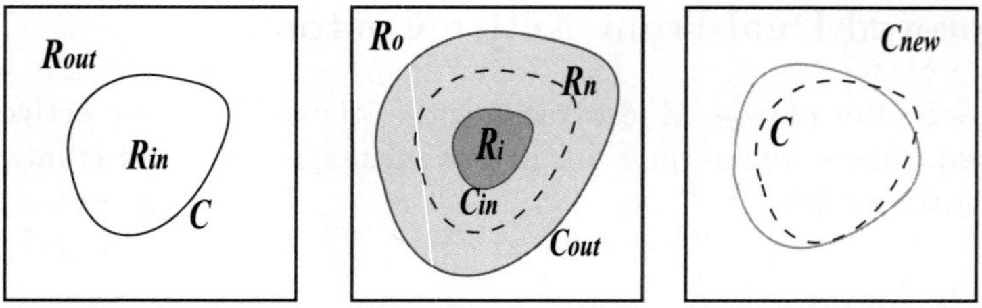

(a) (b) (c)

Fig. 1. Dual front evolution. (a): initial curve C, who separates the whole region into R_{in} and R_{out}; (b): active region R_n is formed by dilating curve C, and it has two boundaries C_{in} and C_{out}; (c): after the propagation of C_{in} and C_{out}, the new minimal partition curve C_{new} is formed which will be used to replace C for the next iteration.

The fast sweeping method proposed by Zhao [16] whose complexity is $O(N)$ is another good choice, so we adopt the fast sweeping method. The algorithm is implemented by labeling the two boundaries with different labels, then evolving the curves with different speed F_{in} (2a) and F_{out} (2b) to the unlabeled region until each point inside R_n is assigned a unique label. Thus, the minimal partition curve C_{new} within the active region is formed.

Dual-front Active Contour is an iterative procedure based on dual-front evolution. After the initial curve C is placed, active region is formed by dilation, then a new curve C_{new} can be acquired by the aforementioned evolution. Replacing C by the C_{new}, we can repeat the evolution iteratively until the difference between the new and old curves is less than a threshold.

The completed algorithm is presented below:

1. Set the intial curve C;
2. Construct the active region by dilation;
3. Get C_{new} by dual-front evolution;
4. Comparing C_{new} with the old curve, if the difference is larger than a threshold, then replace the old curve by C_{new} and goto step 2, else step 5;
5. Stop

2.2 Support Region Restriction

Here, we define *support region* as the region used for calculating the region term of speed F, i.e., the region inside the internal front (support region of internal front, denoted by R_i) and the region outside the external front (support region of external front, denoted by R_o).

Though the original model is robust, topology adaptive and fast (fast sweep method used), it is not fit for the tracking problem. The original model uses the region force similar to Chan and Vese used in [13] to deal with medical images which are usually two-phase, i.e., the support region R_o they use is all the region out of the external front in the image. Since the region force should be re-calculated every iteration, the computation load becomes higher and higher as the times of iteration for each frame increasing, especially when multiple curves are evolving simultaneously for multi-object tracking. Furthermore, real video images are usually multi-phase, multiple objects with different features in the image may result in the inappropriation of calculating the region term from a large region.

To adapt the model for the tracking problem, we restrict the support region of the external front (R_o) in a small range based on the truth that the object of interest is always small enough comparing with the whole image, namely, only a small region should be used as R_o. Usually, the support region selected is a bit larger than the external front. This modification makes the model much faster than the original one. The constraint is that the part of the object of interest which inside the initial curve should be the dominant part of region R_{in}.

Though this simple modification makes the model be more adaptive for tracking, it brings another problem to be solved. When the curve is contained in a homogeneous region, the model will not be able to converge at the correct boundary. Our solution is to introduce a function named quasi-balloon force.

2.3 Quasi-balloon Force

To solve the problem of wrong convergence of the primitive snakes model based on only edge information when the initial curve is far from the correct boundary, balloon force was proposed by Cohen [17]. It can force the curve to inflate or shrink to the object boundary by choosing appropriate parameters. The geodesic active contours [4] which base on level set method also integrate the balloon term.

Apparently, balloon force is a good choice for solving the problem introduced by *support region restriction* of the dual-front active contour model. We can add the balloon term to the model as it in the geodesic active contours. Considering the speed term (2) of the evolution model, by adding a positive number term to the external speed term (2b), the inflation force is acquired. Similarly, a positive number added to (2a) will result in a shrinkage force. Though such balloon force can overcome the difficulty, it is not convenient for practical use. How to determine the magnitude of the positive number is a problem. It should be adapted to the image features where the active region localizes and cannot be adjusted direct viewing. Here, we proposed a quasi-balloon force which is very flexible for practical use by some modifications on the original dual-front active contours algorithm.

The quasi-balloon force which not only is convenient for parameters choosing but also can enable the tracking more flexible is acquired by modifying the measure that the active region is formed . In [11,12], the active region is formed by morphological dilation, and the structure element used is symmetrical. But how about the effect when asymmetrical structure element is used? For easy implementation, we use a binary morphological dilation and erosion to get the two boundaries as shown in the following equations:

$$C_{out} = edge((C \cup R_{in}) \oplus A) \tag{3a}$$
$$C_{in} = edge((C \cup R_{in}) \ominus B) \tag{3b}$$

where $edge(x)$ is a function of extracting the edge of a region, A and B are square structure elements of size $a \times a$ and $b \times b$ respectively. Thus, by setting $a \neq b$, we can get the asymmetrical result. We will use the phrase $a \times b$ to denote the size of two structure elements used simultaneously, for example, 9×5 means the region will be dilated by a 9×9 structure element and eroded by a 5×5 one.

In this study, we find different structure-element pairs will give different evolution modes. When the symmetrical pair is used ($a = b$, as the original model) in a homogeneous region, the model behaves like the original snakes [1] that will shrink slowly. If a is two-pixel larger than b, the evolution will achieve a balance, that is, the curve's change stopped. The curve will inflate just like the inflation force acts on it when $a - b \geq 4$. In a word, $a - b = 2$ is the balance, the larger a is, the more the trend of the curve inflation is, and the larger b is, the more it tends to shrink. For example, 9×7 is a balance; 9×5 will inflate the curve, and 9×11 shrink. The reason is that the speeds are the same for both fronts in a homogeneous region, and the larger the distance, the more the time is needed for propagation, so C_{new} will transfer more close to the boundary formed by the larger structure element. Thus, we can adjust the magnitude of the balloon force easily by adjusting a and b no matter what kind of image is being processed.

Another merit of this quasi-balloon force is for the tracking of fast moving object. In such case, the overlapped region of the same object between two consecutive frames maybe very small or even none, and sometimes the two corresponding regions may be far away from each other. By some a priori knowledge about the velocity of the object, we can use an appropriate large a to evolve for some times firstly, then use a smaller a to get the precise contour. Such policy is also applicable for tracking object with severe deformation.

2.4 Object Contour Tracking

When the snakes model is used for tracking, we usually set the result of the previous frame as the initial curve of the current frame. First, the curve should be enlarged to enclose the whole object [5] or at least a part of it [7]. Then the curve is evolved according to the edge or region information. But how much the curve should be enlarged depends on the velocity of the object, the degree of its deformation, and the image information (intensity, color, etc.). The parameter setting is a non-trivial task even for an experienced user. By using the quasi-balloon force, the parameter setting is simplified since less information should be considered.

Before tracking, the speed term F and the size $a \times b$ will be determined by some a priori information about the probable speed and deformation degree of the object.

In general, following speed is used for tracking:

$$F = 1/(m \times |I(x, y) - I'_{mean}| + n \times (1 + \nabla I)) \tag{4}$$

where I is the intensity of the image, and ∇I denotes its gradient. When the first frame is considered, I'_{mean} denotes the mean of I in the support region, but in subsequent frames, I'_{mean} denotes the mean of the region in last frame enclosed by C_{new} of last frame.

Usually, two or three structure-element pairs are suggested to be used. The first is a dilation pair that make the curve approach to the object quickly. By some a priori knowledge about the velocity and characteristic of the object, we can choose appropriate a and b. When the moving speed of the object is fast or the deformation is severe, a larger a should be used. Other wise, a smaller a is prefer. Then a shrinkage pair is used for fast convergence on the contour. If necessary, one pair with force between the first two could be used for contour refinement.

3 Experimental Results

To test the performance of the algorithm, four experiments are performed and the results are shown here. The experiments were done on a Pentium IV 1.8G computer, and the algorithm was implemented using C++.

The first experiment was done for testing the degree of improvement of support region restriction by segmenting a static image. The first frame of the *hand sequence* with size 360×240 was used. The same initial curve (a 22×14 rectangle at the same location) was used and iterated for 30 times. The segmentation results are shown in Fig. 2. The results of time consumption are shown in Table 1. We can see that the segmentation results are almost the same (see Fig. 2(b) and 2(c)), but the speed of the improved model is much faster than the orginal one. The results show the obvious improvement of our algorithm.

Table 1. Comparison of time consumption between the original and improved model

iteration time	1	4	7	11	15	20	25	27	30	average
time consumption of original model (ms)	46.41	43.35	38.98	39.37	39.71	37.31	38.40	40.24	41.89	39.40
time consumption of improved model (ms)	13.85	14.91	16.94	16.30	15.97	18.30	16.01	16.43	15.95	16.20

Figure 3 shows the result of the test on fast moving object tracking. The *ping-pong sequence* is used and the ball is the object being tracked. The velocity of the ball varies severely in different time. The distance between its corresponding regions in two consecutive frames can be even larger than the diameter of ball when it is near its lowest point of the trajectory, and can be so small that the two regions are almost the same when it achieves the highest point of the trajectory. The speed used is $F = 1/(0.6 \times |I(x, y) - I'_{mean}| + 0.4 \times (1 + \nabla I))$. Three structure-element pairs are used. For each frame, a 33×3 one is used for the first two iterations, thus at least part of the ball can be captured even the

(a) the original image and the initial curve (b) the result of the original model after 30 iterations (c) the result of the improved model after 30 iterations

Fig. 2. comparison between the original model and the improved model

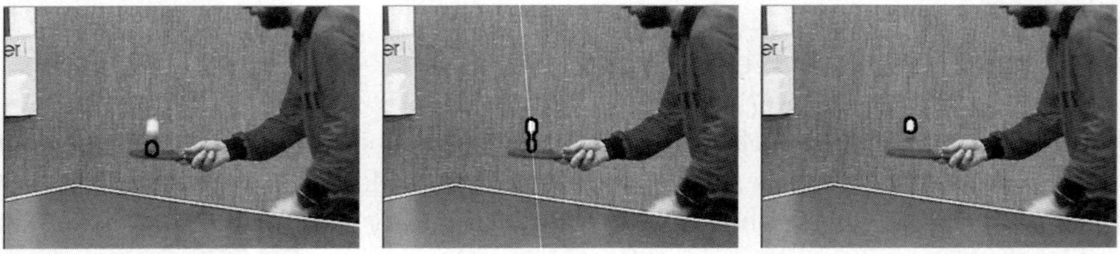

(a) the beginning of the 40th frame (b) the intermediate result of tracking (c) the final result of the 40th frame

Fig. 3. tracking of the fast moving ball

ball in the new frame is far from its location in last frame. Then a 9×7 one is used for fast convergence. At last, a 9×5 one is used to make the contour more precise. Experiment shows the ball can be tracked steadily in all the 54 frames until the ball is held by the man's hand.

The third experiment shows the model's ability about tracking the severe deformation object in scenes with moving backgrounds. As shown in Fig. 4(a)-4(c), both the hand and the camera are moving. Since the moving speed of the hand is not high which means the overlapped region is not small between consecutive frames, in order to test the model's ability of dealing with the fast change of the shape, we also tracked the hand in the 178th frame by using the result of the 153rd frame as the initial curve and the result is shown in Fig. 4(d)-4(f). Since the moving speed of the hand is not very high, only two structure-element pairs were used. The first is a 9×5 pair for tracking and the other is a 9×7 one for contour refinement. Except for replacing the intensity of gray scale by C_b component of YC_bC_r color space, the speed and other parameters are the same as the second experiment's. In all the 350 frames, the hand was tracked correctly.

The last experiment shows that the model can control the contour's topology change automatically. As shown in Fig. 5, the contour can naturally split or merge when the two hands separate or encounter. The speed and structure-element pairs used are the same as those the third experiment used.

(a) the 1st frame (b) the 102nd frame (c) the 135th frame

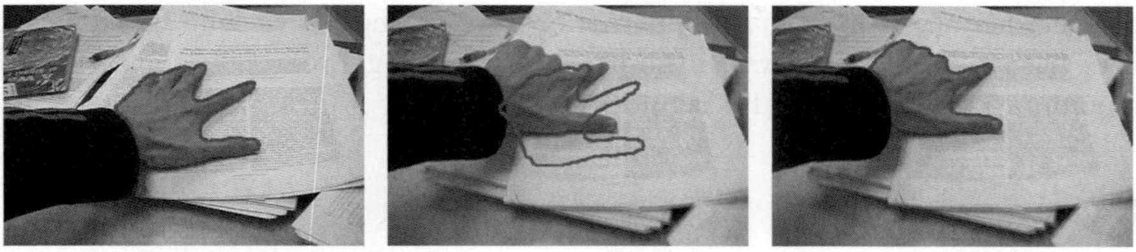

(d) result of the 153rd frame (e) initial curve of the 178th frame (f) result of the 178th frame

Fig. 4. Tracking of the deformation object

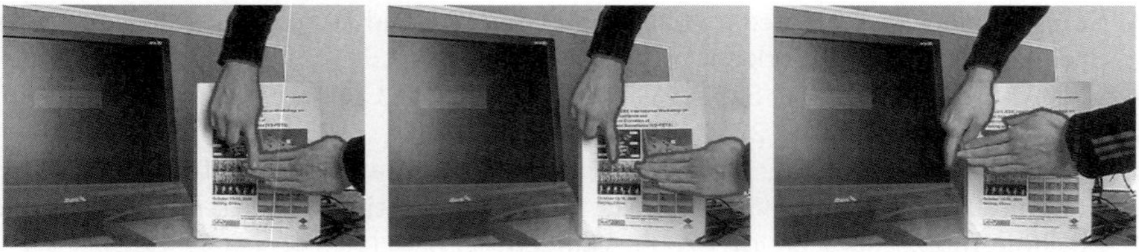

(a) the 9th frame (b) the 22nd frame (c) the 56th frame

Fig. 5. Topology change adaptive

4 Conclusion and Future Work

A new tracking algorithm based on improved dual-front active contour model has been presented. By restricting the support region and introducing the quasi-balloon force to the dual-front active contour model, we improved it to be fit for object contour tracking. Experiments show that the method is robust and effective. It is applicable for tracking fast moving object and deformable objects, and no static background is assumed. In addition, the model can control the topology change automatically for its implementation by using level set method. And since the fast sweeping method whose complexity is $O(N)$ is used, it is fast comparing with other level set based algorithms.

A defect of the model is that it can only cope with patially occlusion instance and will be failed when full occlusion exist, that is, when the object disappears completely for some frames and appears again, the contour cannot be maintained. For example, when the object is full ocludded or moves out of the scene, its contour will disappear at the same time, and when the object come back, the contour cannot be recovered. This problem cannot be solved by the dual-front active contours model algorithm itself. It may be tackled by integrating the idea of object permanence as [18].

In the future, we will try to integrate more measures to the model to make it adapt to more different classes of video sequence. For example, combining the function of tracking distributions as the method proposed in [8] is a good choice. It will enable the model to track objects with more complex appearance (e.g. the object with texture). Motion information is another feature should be considered, since it may enable the model to track the object who has different parts with different colours. In addition, integrating prediction tools such as Kalman or particle filters [19] is another direction.

References

1. Kass, M., Witkin, A., Terzopoulos, D.: Snakes: Active Contour Models. International Journal of Computer Vision, 1 (4) (1988) 321-331
2. Blake, A., Isard, M.: Active Contours: the Application of Techniques from Graphics, Vision, Control Theory and Statistics to Visual Tracking of Shapes in Motion. Springer-Verlag, London (1998)
3. Stanley Osher, Ronald Fedkiw: Level Set Methods and Dynamic Implicit Surfaces. Springer-Verlag New York Inc. (2003)
4. Caselles, V., Kimmel, R., Sapiro, G.: Geodesic Active Contours. International Journal of Computer Vision, 22 (3) (1997) 61-79
5. Paragios, N., Deriche, R.: Geodesic Active Contours and Level Sets for the Detection and Tracking of Moving Objects. IEEE Transaction on Pattern Analysis and Machine Intellegence, 22 (3) (2000) 266-280
6. Paragios, N., Deriche, R.: Geodesic Active Regions: A New Framework to Deal with Frame Partition Problems in Computer Vision. Journal of Visual Communication and Image Representation, 13 (2002) 249-268
7. Paragios, N., Deriche, R.: Geodesic Active Regions and Level Set Methods for Motion Estimation and Tracking. Computer Vision and Image Understanding, 97 (2005) 259-282
8. Freedman D., Zhang T.: Active Contours for Tracking Distributions. IEEE Transaction on Image Processing, 13 (4) (2004) 518–526
9. Xu N., Ahuja, N.: Object Contour Tracking Using Graph Cuts Based Active Contours. Proceedings of IEEE International Conference on Image Processing (ICIP), New York, USA (2002) 277-280
10. Xu, N., Bansal, R., Ahuja, N.: Object Segmentation Using Graph Cuts Based Active Contours. Proceedings of IEEE CS Conf. Computer Vision and Pattern Recognition (CVPR), Madison, Wisconsin, USA (2003) 46-53
11. Li, H., Abderrahim, E., Jala, F., Su R.: A Multi-label Front Propagation Approach for Object Segmentation. Proceedings of IEEE International Conference on Pattern Recognition (ICPR), Cam- bridge, UK (2004) 600-603
12. Li, H., Anthony, Y.: Local or Global Minima: Flexible Dual-Front Active Contours. Proceedings of International Conference on Computer Vision (ICCV) Workshop CVBIA, Beijing, China (2005) 356-366
13. Chan T. F., Vese, L. A.: Active Contours Without Edges. IEEE Transaction on Image Processing, **10** (2) (2001) 266-277

14. Laurent, D. Cohen, Ron, K.: Global Minimum for Active Contour Models: A Minimal Path Approach. International Journal of Computer Vision, 24 (1) (1997) 57-78
15. Sethian, J. A.: A Fast Marching Level Set Method for Monotonically Advancing Fronts . Applied Mathematics, 93 (4) (1996) 1591-1593
16. Zhao, H. K.: Fast Sweeping Method for Eikonal Equations. Mathematics of Computation, 74 (2005) 603-627
17. Laurent, D. C.: On Active Contour Models and Balloons. CVGIP: Image Understanding, **53** (2) (1991) 211-218
18. Huang, Y. Irfan, E.: Tracking Multiple Objects Through Occlusions. Proc. IEEE CS Conf. Computer Vision and Pattern Recognition (CVPR), San Diego, CA, USA (2005) 1051-1058
19. Hue, C., Cadre, J. L., Perez, P. : Sequential Monte Carlo Methods for Multiple Target Tracking and Data Fusion. IEEE Transaction on Signal Processing, **50** (2) (2002) 309-325

Motion Deblurring for a Power Transmission Line Inspection Robot

Siyao Fu[1], Yunchu Zhang[1,2], Xiaoguang Zhao[1], Zize Liang[1], Zengguang Hou[1], Anmin Zou[1], Min Tan[1], Wenbo Ye[3], and Lian Bo[3]

[1] Key Laboratory of Complex Systems and Intelligence Science, Institute of Automation, The Chinese Academy of Sciences, P.O. Box 2728, Beijing 100080, China

[2] School of Information and Electric Engineering,Shandong University of Architecture and Engineering, Jinan 250014, China

[3] Zunyi Power Supply Bureau, Guizhou Power Grid Corporation, Zunyi, 563000, China

{siyao.fu, yunchu.zhang, zengguang.hou}@ia.ac.cn

Abstract. Inspection robot must detect the obstacles from the complex background according to their types when it is crawling along the power transmission line in order to negotiate reliably. In ideal cases, robot's vision system can give satisfactory results, however, motion blur due to camera motion caused by wind or other unknown causes can significantly degrade the quality of the image acquired. It is an undesired effect. In this paper, a complete motion deblurring procedure for obstacle images has been proposed, we try to analyze the running environment of the robot to develop the model of the motion blur. The acquired motion blur information is used to identify the point spread function (PSF) as well as restore the blurred image at the same time. Experiments on real blurred images on power transmission line prove the feasibility and reliability of this algorithm.

1 Introduction

Autonomous high-voltage power line inspection robot can perform various surveillance and monitoring tasks on the power transmission line by replacing human workers for dangerous and highly specialized operations, it can do self-navigation to detect the obstacles or send the desired images to the ground center. Most inspection robot fulfill the task with its vision system in order to negotiate autonomously and reliably on the power line. In the ideal situation, still image captured by the imaging sensors can provide satisfactory outputs for obstacle recognition, unfortunately, in most cases, due to the vibration of the power transmission line or swing motion caused by the wind force, there will be a relative motion between the camera and the object during the integration time of the image, named motion blur, which is considered to be an effect that can significantly degrade image quality, sometimes makes the image useless. Therefore, how to estimate the true image from the motion degraded image characteristics is a challenging problem. Generally speaking, motion deblur can be restored by the image deconvolution, provided that the motion is shift-invariant, and that the the blur function that caused the blur is known, or at least can be[1]. However, in real-world applications, the PSF is not usually known in prior, this makes motion deblurring hard to solve.

Though in many practices, the relative motion between object and camera is ambiguous, the situation in the power line inspection robot is different. As matter of fact, one

D.-S. Huang, K. Li, and G.W. Irwin (Eds.): ICIC 2006, LNAI 4114, pp. 866–871, 2006.

Fig. 1. Different camera motions lead to different motion blurs. Here, in top right corner and bottom left corner, the unblurred still image (top left corner) is blurred by linear vertical and horizontal motions, respectively. In bottom right corner, the image is blurred due to motion blur with a angle.

can find that the robot's swing motion on the power transmission line can be modeled as a pendulous swing motion with small swing angle. It is well recognized that this case can be approximated by a linear motion with the small angle. Thus, we can estimated the motion model (PSF model), usually this is done by using the traditional iterative methods such as blind image deconvolution, which contains two steps: identify the blur model's parameters first, then deblur the image. Although these methods are effective in some cases, the assumption of the simple motion models does not hold in many practical situations. In addition, deblurring methods which use deconvolution require very accurate PSFs that are usually hard to obtain. Thus, they are often fail to satisfy the real time requirements. In this paper, we present a novel approach to motion deblurring of an image acquired by the line inspection robot. Our method estimates the unknown PSF parameter from the raw data first, a search technique or optimization method is used to find the parameter, which minimizes the square prediction error. The result is chosen to be the image and PSF model parameter estimates. During the model parameter's identification procedure, restoration method is required to solve the problem as well.

This paper is organized as follows: Section 2 presents the image restoration problem and the blur model is formulated, then we propose the PSF estimation algorithm and related image restoration algorithm proposed. Real world experiment of the robot negotiating obstacles are shown in Section 3. Then conclusions follow.

2 Degradation Models and Parameter Estimation

2.1 Problem Formulation and Motion Model Definition

The image degradation process related in this paper can be approximated by a linear blur with an additive noise term. The standard observation model is expressed as follows [7]:

$$g(x, y) = h(x, y) * f(x, y) + \eta(x, y). \tag{1}$$

where $g(x, y)$ is the observed degraded image, $f(x, y)$ is the original image we wish to estimate; $\eta(x, y)$ is the additive noise term; $h(x, y)$ is convolution operator representing the degradation function. In spatial domain, $h(x, y)$ is referred as *point spread function*, a term that aries from letting $h(x,y)$ operate on a point of light to obtain the characteristics of the degradation for any type of input. The image restoration problem is to inverse the direct model of equation (1). In most cases, We try to recover the original image $f(x,y)$ by deconvoluting the motion blur operator $h(x,y)$ from the degraded observation $g(x,y)$. This classical problem is called blind image deconvolution and has been well studied and can be solved by several well-known techniques such as Wiener filtering, recursive Kalman filtering, and iterative deconvolution methods ([3],[7]). Fig. 2 (a)

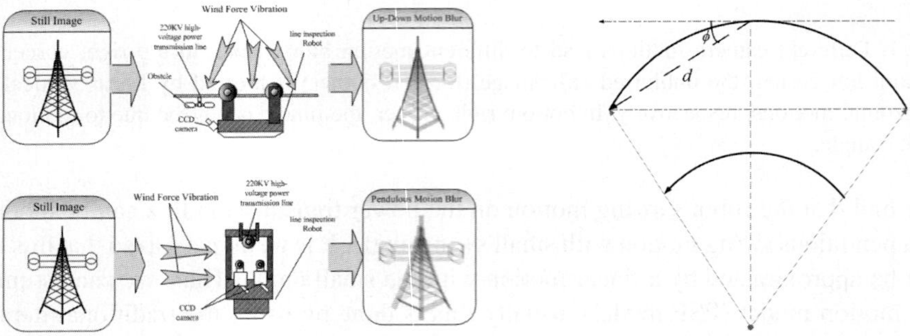

(a) Proposed inspection robot camera motion blur model.

(b) Approximation of the blur.

Fig. 2. Approximation of the motion blur from the angle-view of the camera

presents the principe of blurring caused by motion in real world situation. As we can see clearly, the motion blur on the power transmission line can be divided into two major types:

1) Up-Down vibration due to the upper wind force and the robot's movement.
2) Pendulous motion caused by the wind force from the side of the robot's body.

Generally speaking, the first one is the typical vertical camera motion which can be completely identified as follows
1) Vertical camera motion blur of length L

$$h_{\Theta_M}(x,y) = \begin{cases} 0 & \text{if } x \neq 0, -\infty \leq y \leq \infty. \\ \frac{1}{2L} & \text{if } x = 0, \quad -L \leq y \leq L. \end{cases} \tag{2}$$

For the second one, in most cases, one can approximate the pendulous motion as linear motion with a small angle which is illustrated in Fig. 2 (b). This is possible since we assume that the swing angle is relatively small and the arms of our robot are long enough to be seen as the swing arms. Thus, the model is as follows
2) Pendulous motion blur of length L and angle ϕ

$$h_{\Theta_M}(x,y) = \begin{cases} \frac{1}{L} & \text{if } \sqrt{x^2+y^2} \leq L. \\ 0 & \text{otherwise.} \end{cases} \tag{3}$$

$$\tan(\phi) = \frac{x}{y}. \tag{4}$$

where $\Theta_M^T = (L, \phi) \in S_M$. In this paper we only consider the second case. it is worth to note that the first case can be seen as the special case of the second one with no swing angle ($\phi = 0$). Note that in our experiments, as we shall see, these models can give us the sufficient information needed to deblur images. In the following section, we will describe our parameterized blur estimation approach in detail.

2.2 The Blur Parameters Estimation and Image Restoration

Motion Angle Estimation. As mentioned above, an image blurred due to motion is usually represented by a linear system of a convolution $g(x, y) = f(x, y) * h(x, y)$ with $h(x, y)$, the convolution kernel which causes the motion blur. The motion blue kernel, as matter of fact, is a low-pass distortion operator which low-passes the image in the direction of the blur. If we take the spectrum of the blurred image, we can see that most of the energy is in the direction, perpendicular to the motion direction. This can be seen as a line in binary spectrum. Here Hough Transform is used to detect the orientation of this line in the spectrum, which corresponds to the blurred direction.

Motion Length Estimation. The identification of blur length requires the knowledge of blur direction (angle). In this paper we try to use the error-parameter validation approach [2] to identify the blur function and restore the blurred image as well. The key principle of the approach is to give a error-parameter curve, and by which can we identify the parameter of the PSF. The detailed steps are as follows:

Step 1. Definitions: x is the restored image, y is the observation, h is the PSF. α is the parameter which is the blur length here. α is the initialization value. $\Delta\alpha$ is the search step, and K is the number of iteration. E_{cx} is the estimation error.
Step 2. Initialization ($K = 0$). Set initial values using a priori information about the PSF or true image, or by inspection of the blurred image. Choose the parameter searching range.
Step 3. Iteration:
for $i = 1 : k$
$\alpha = \alpha_0 + (i - 1)\Delta\alpha$
Identify the blur function h by the parameter α;
Then the image restoration method is carried out by the information of the PSF h and blurred image y to obtain the restored image x.
Compute the restoration error $E_x = \|y - x * h\|^2$.
end.
Step 4. Plot the $E - \alpha$ curve, decide the real value of the α for the blur function, get the real blur function. If α is a good estimate, then should be selected as the good approximation of the PSF's parameter.

Image Restoration. Now, for every step of estimation for the blur function parameters, we need to deblur the image by any restoration methods. The results reported in this paper are produced using the classic Richardson-Lucy iterative deconvolution algorithm [7]. This method maximizes a Poisson-statistics image model likelihood function, yielding the following iteration:

$$\hat{f}_{k+1}(x,y) = \hat{f}_k(x,y)\left[h(-x,-y) * \frac{g(x,y)}{h(x,y) * \hat{f}_k(x,y)}\right]. \tag{5}$$

where $g(x,y)$ is the measured image, $\hat{f}_k(x,y)$ is the kth estimation of the result, $\hat{f}_0(x,y) = I$. $h(x,y)$ is the convolution kernel (the PSF).

3 Experiments and Discussions

This section present some experiments to verify the proposed technique. Fig. 3 (c) and (d) show the original still insulator strings image and degraded one caused by motion blurring, respectively. As we can see clearly, the latter one can not be used for mobile robot to negotiate the obstacles.

In order to restore the degraded image, we need to estimate the blur function parameters. The estimation of the blur angle (direction) is carried out in the first step of our proposed approach and the results are given in Fig. 3 (e). And then the blur length follows. Fig. 3 (f) gives the error-parameter curves for the estimation of blur length. The Abscissa is our estimated length d, and the programme gives it a variation range, the real value of d is unknown, but it should contains in this range. The y-axis shows the computation error. We hope to identify the real value of d by the error-parameter curve. For

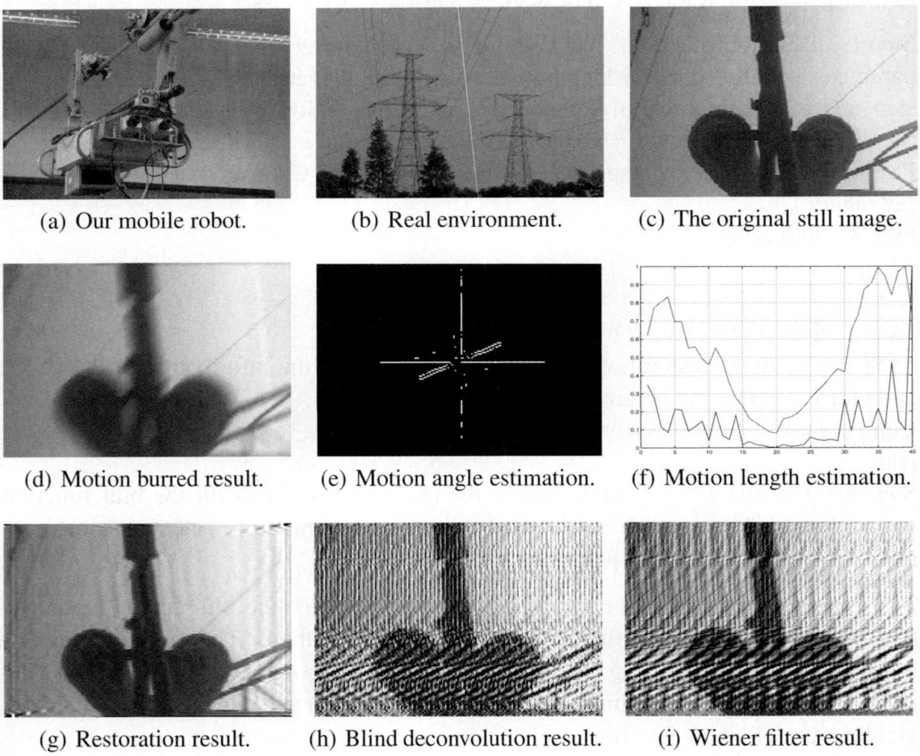

(a) Our mobile robot. (b) Real environment. (c) The original still image.

(d) Motion burred result. (e) Motion angle estimation. (f) Motion length estimation.

(g) Restoration result. (h) Blind deconvolution result. (i) Wiener filter result.

Fig. 3. Whole image motion deblur procedure

comparison, we also plot another curve for the high frequency term $E_{cx} = \|C \cdot X\|^2$, which is actually smoothness constraint term, where C is the second order differential operator. As we can see clearly, our error criterion $E_x = \|y - x * h\|^2$ curve (blue one) can acquire the minimum error at the length of 20. It seems that the curve corresponding to the E_{cx} (red one) has the same relation to the real value but with a slightly higher error, one can find that the variation rate of error curve will decreased remarkably. One may find that there lies a flat area in the true value nearby, which may causes the uncertainty of the d. So we take the middle value of this flat area as the identified value of length d. Fig. 3 (g) shows our final restoration result by L-R method. For comparison, we also give the results using the traditional Wiener approach and blind image deconvolution method shown in and Fig. 3 (h) and (i) respectively. It is clear that the strong deconvolution artifacts in the figures are the result of incorrect PSF parameter estimation, whereas our method can offer better restoration results.

4 Conclusions

In this paper, we have presented a method for motion deblurring which aims at solving the obstacle detection problem in an autonomous high voltage power transmission line inspection robot. We first propose the motion blur models based on the knowledge about the degradation situation which inspection robot will encounter. Then we use this information to estimate the PSF that causes the blur. Finally, we use Lucy-Richardson restoration method to restore the blurred image. Simulation and real test results show that our methods can effectively restore the degraded images.

Acknowledgment

This research has been supported by the Hi-Tech R&D Program (863) of China (grant 2005AA420060), and the Filed Bus Tech & Automation Key Lab of Beijing. The authors also wish to acknowledge the help and suggestions from Prof. GongpingWu, with the College of Power and Mechanical Engineering,Wuhan University.

The authors would also like to specially thank Prateek Garg, Wilson Picardo & Akshata Gangolli, for their great helps to this work.

References

1. Zera, M. Ben , Nayar, S. K. .: Motion-Based Motion Deblurring, IEEE Trans on Pattern Analysis and Machine Intelligence. vol 26. June. (2004) 689 - 698
2. Zou, M. Y.: Deconvolution and Signal Recovery, Defence Industrial Press, (2001)
3. Andrews, H. C., Hunt, B. R.: Digital Image Restoration, Prentice-Hall,Inc. (1977)
4. Jiang, B., Mamishev, A. V.: Mobile Monitoring and Maintenance of Power Systems *On Press*, Dec. (2001)
5. Kundur, D., Hatzinakos, D.: Blind Image Restoration, IEEE Signal Processing Mag, May. (1996) 43 - 64, New York: IEEE and Wiley, (2004)
6. Chardon, S., Vozel, B., Chehdi, K.: A Comparative Study Between Parametric Blur Estimation Methods, Proc. Int. Conf. Acoustic, Speech, Signal Processing, (1999)
7. Gonzales, R. C., Woods, R. E.: Digital Image Processing. Second Edition, (2003)

Viewpoint-Invariant Face Recognition Based on View-Based Representation

Jinyun Chung, Juho Lee, Hyun Jin Park, and Hyun Seung Yang

Korea Advanced Institute of Science and Technology, 373-1, Guseong-dong, Yuseong-gu, Daejeon, 305-701, Republic of Korea
{mage, jhlee, hjpark, hsyang}@paradise.kaist.ac.kr

Abstract. In this paper, we suggest a viewpoint-invariant face recognition model based on view-based representation. The suggested model has four stages: view-based representation, viewpoint classification, frontal face estimation and face recognition. For view-based representation, we obtained the feature space by using independent subspace analysis, the bases of which are grouped like the neurons in the brain's visual area. The viewpoint of a facial image can be easily classified by a single-layer perceptron due to view-dependent activation characteristic of the feature space. To estimate the independent subspace analysis representation of frontal face, a radial basis neural network learns to generalize the relation of the bases between two viewpoints. Face recognition relies on a normalized correlation for selecting the most similar frontal faces in a gallery. Through our face recognition experiment on XM2VTS [9], we obtained a face recognition rate of 89.33%.

1 Introduction

Face recognition has been an active research area due to its importance in surveillance systems. There have been great technological advances and nowadays some researchers try to develop commercial products with face recognition technology. In most face recognition methods, however, environmental variations such as variations in the viewpoint and illumination cause significant degradation of performance. As a result, many researchers now concentrate on developing face recognition algorithms that overcome those problems. We focus here on ways of overcoming the viewpoint variation problem.

A trivial solution to the viewpoint variation problem is to remember the facial images of every viewpoint, though facial images of every viewpoint are generally not available. We therefore need to develop a face recognition algorithm that relies on a limited number of facial images.

To develop a face recognition algorithm that achieves this purpose, other researchers have used a 3-D facial model to get view-invariant facial features or they have tried to develop a computational transformation model between the facial images of two different viewpoints. However, these approaches assume that the surface of the face is a Lambertian surface [1] or that the face is a plane [2]. To compute 3-D facial model parameters or transformation parameters, we should find the corresponding

D.-S. Huang, K. Li, and G.W. Irwin (Eds.): ICIC 2006, LNAI 4114, pp. 872 – 878, 2006.

points between two images of different viewpoints but this task is vulnerable to illumination variation.

To solve the viewpoint variation problem from another viewpoint, we examine the characteristics of the human visual system, which is robust to viewpoint variation.

Neurophysiological study of the brain reveals that neurons in the inferior temporal area respond to the facial image of a certain viewpoint [3]. Such specialization of neurons progresses as a result of unsupervised learning, and we deduce that this characteristic of neurons will be useful for classifying the viewpoint of an observed facial image and for learning the relation between the responses of neurons. Hence, we focuse on this characteristic of the human brain and suggested a viewpoint-invariant face recognition model. To simulate unsupervised learning of view-specific neurons, we use independent subspace analysis (ISA). A facial image is represented in a subspace obtained through ISA and this representation shows a view-specific activation characteristic.

After using the ISA subspace to produce representations of the facial images, then their viewpoints are classified with the aid of a single-layer perceptron (SLP). According to the results of the viewpoint classification, a neural network is selected to estimate the ISA representation of a frontal face image from that viewpoint. The neural network that we use to estimate the representation of the frontal face image was a radial basis function neural network (RBF-NN), which is trained with the aid of support vector regression (SVR). The recognition is performed by comparing the normalized correlation between the estimated facial image and the gallery of facial images with a frontal viewpoint.

The proposed model needs no manually constructed model because unsupervised learning is used to obtain the view-based representation. Other face recognition methods need facial models whose feature points are selected manually [1, 2]. Furthermore, although the eigensignature method estimates the facial representation of an unfamiliar view in an eigenspace [4], we do so in view-specific subspaces. In view-based representation, the relation between bases is simpler. Moreover, it is advantageous to classify viewpoints and to regress the relation between two facial images of different viewpoints.

2 A Viewpoint-Invariant Face Recognition Model Based on View-Dependent Representation

The proposed face recognition model has four stages: view-dependent representation on an ISA subspace, viewpoint classification, estimation of frontal face representation, and face recognition with a normalized correlation. In this section, we describe each stage.

2.1 Unsupervised Learning for View-Based Representation

Neurons in the visual area of the brain are responsive to specific facial viewpoints, such as frontal or profile views. The neurons that respond to similar viewpoints are spatially proximate to each other. The neural networks of the cerebral visual cortex tend to organize themselves in the direction of increasing independency of the neural coding [5]. We can apply this unsupervised learning principle to learn view-based representation in a manner that is similar to the brain's view-tuned neural coding scheme [6].

The ISA computational algorithm is adequate for unsupervised learning of view-based representation [7]. Through ISA, independent subspaces, groups of bases, can be obtained, although independent bases can be obtained through independent component analysis. By maximizing the following equation, we can find the linear transformation, **W**, which maximizes the independency between groups of output variables:

$$\log P(\mathbf{X} \mid \mathbf{W}) = \sum_{t=1}^{T} \sum_{j=1}^{J} G(\sum_{i \in S_j} \mathbf{w}_i^T \mathbf{x}(t)) + T \log |\det \mathbf{W}|, \quad (1)$$

where **x** is a feature vector of a sensory signal, **w** is the basis of an ISA subspace, G is a non-Gaussian function, T is the number of samples, J is the number of subspaces, and S_j is a jth subspace.

A facial image can be projected to an ISA subspace and we can get its view-dependent representation. As shown in Fig. 1, when the bases are grouped according to their viewpoints, the projection norm to a certain group of bases that represent the same viewpoint of a given facial image is higher than the projection norm to other groups. This characteristic is very useful for classifying the viewpoint and for obtaining the relation of bases.

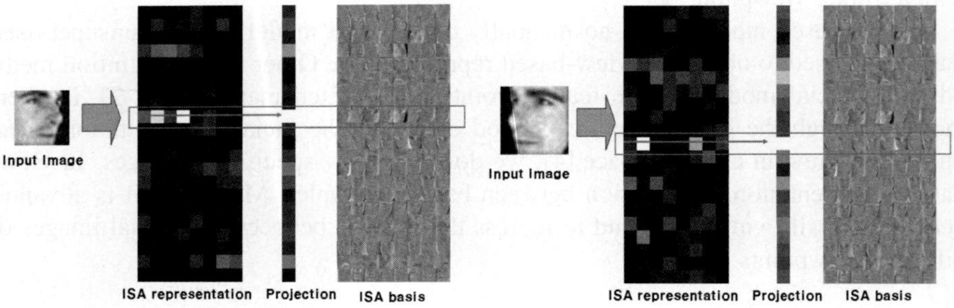

Fig. 1. View-specific activation of an ISA representation. Two facial images with a different viewpoint show high activation values in different groups of ISA bases.

2.2 Viewpoint Classification from View-Based Representation

When we use ISA, the proposed view-based representation shows a view-dependent activation characteristic. Hence, we thought the viewpoint could be easily classified with the aid of an SLP. The SLP can learn which bases are related to a certain viewpoint and which bases are not. We therefore quantized the viewpoint of a horizontal rotation from -45° to +45° and a vertical rotation from -15° to +15° to 21 units at intervals of 15°. The input layer of the SLP is an ISA representation of an observed facial image and the output layer consists of 21 neurons. To determine the viewpoint of a given image, we selected the maximum output neuron with the highest activation value.

2.3 Estimation of the Representation of a Frontal Face Image

The human brain can learn an association of viewpoints by remembering representative examples. If a person's facial image and a remembered representative face from frontal viewpoint resemble each other, his or her facial image and the remembered representative face from profile viewpoint may also resemble each other. Hence, as shown in Fig. 2, we simulated a neural association between the facial images of two other viewpoints as an RBF-NN. The hidden layer of the RBF-NN has representative examples and the output layer shows the estimated representation of the frontal face.

The RBF-NN could be effectively trained with the aid of SVR [8]. When SVR is performed with an RBF kernel, the SVR result is the same as that of an RBF-NN in which the nodes of the hidden layer are representative examples. However, because SVR has only a single output unit, we had to repeat SVR for each basis. In our experiment, there were 168 ISA bases; hence, we obtained 168 SVR results for a single RBF-NN.

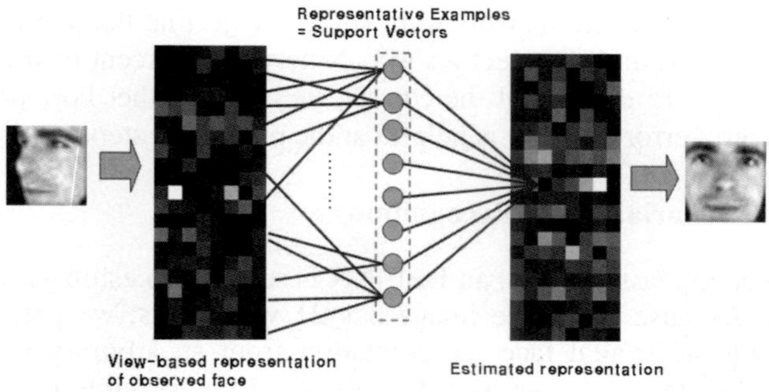

Fig. 2. Estimation of a front face representation by using an RBF-NN trained by SVR

2.4 Face Recognition with a Normalized Correlation

Face recognition results are obtained by comparing the estimated representation of an observed facial image with the representations of gallery images, all of which have a frontal viewpoint. For the comparison, we computed the degree of similarity by using the normalized correlation of the following equation:

$$similarity = \left(\frac{\mathbf{x}_i^{\mathrm{T}} \mathbf{x}}{|\mathbf{x}_i| |\mathbf{x}|} \right), \tag{2}$$

where **x** is the estimated representation of an observed faical image and x_i is the representation of a gallery image.

We obtained the recognition result by selecting the gallery representation with the highest degree of similarity.

3 Experimental Results

To validate our model, we performed experiments on viewpoint classification and face recognition from unknown viewpoints. By way of preparation, we trained the view-based representation, view-classification network, and a view-prediction network.

First, we rendered the face images by means of a rendering textured 3-D mesh model in the virtual reality markup language included in XM2VTS DB [9]. We generated 21 viewpoint images for each of the 291 face models, resulting in 5061 gray-scale images. The dimensions of the gray-scale images were 32×32 pixels.

View-based representation was learned as explained in section 2.1. After using principal component analysis to reduce the dimensions of the facial images to 168 dimensions, we maximized Eq. (1) by using a gradient descent and we obtained 168 bases. There were 21 groups and eight bases in each group. The detailed ISA procedures are explained in [7].

3.1 Viewpoint Classification

For a viewpoint-classification network, we divided the face images into roughly 3000 as a training set and 2000 as a test set. We then used the standard perceptron rule to train the network. The network subsequently took the basis activation as the input and gave one out of 21 quantized viewpoints. The pure test recognition rate was 90.2%, though the major classification errors were small, suggesting that the classified viewpoints were not far from the correct answer. Ninety-five percent of the false classifications were within 15 degrees of the correct viewpoint, either horizontally or vertically. This graceful error property is helpful at the prediction step.

3.2 Viewpoint-Invariant Face Recognition

After the viewpoint classification, an RBF-NN is selected to estimate the frontal face representation. Because each face image has 21 viewpoints, we prepared 20 RBF-NNs to estimate the frontal face representation from an arbitrary non-frontal face representation. For the SVR, we used Gunn's SVM open source [8]. Moreover, we used the face data of 241 people for the training, and we used the face data of 50 people for the face recognition testing.

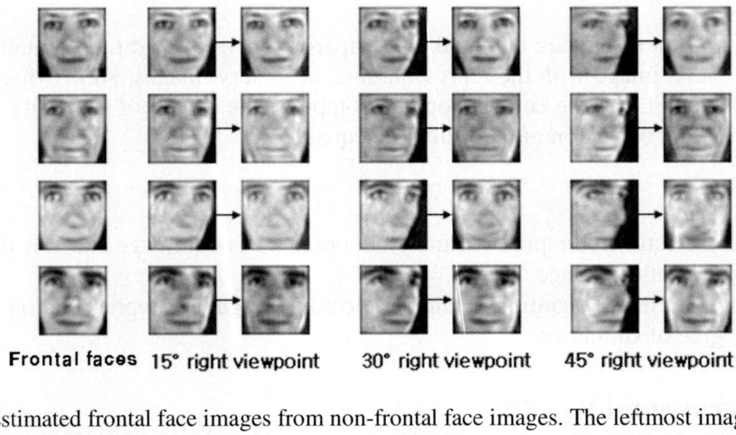

Fig. 3. Estimated frontal face images from non-frontal face images. The leftmost images are the original frontal face images. The images on the right are various viewpoint images and their estimation results.

Use of the selected RBF-NN enabled the frontal face representation to be estimated from the representation of the observed non-frontal facial image. The estimation result is shown in the gray image of Fig. 3. The estimated frontal face images look similar to the original frontal images. However, when the viewpoint difference is large, the estimated frontal face images have some artifacts. This phenomenon means that the relation between two widely different viewpoints is more complex than that of two narrowly different viewpoints. For a more accurate estimation, either more examples are needed for the training of the RBF-NN or the facial features should be simplified.

Table 1 shows the face recognition results of 50 people. The face recognition method, which is explained in section 2.4, obtained an overall face recognition rate of 89.33%. The face recognition rate dropped when the viewpoint was rotated horizontally by ±45° and also when the viewpoint was rotated vertically.

Table 1. Recognition rate of viewpoint-invariant face recognition

	-45 (L)	-30	-15	0	15	30	45 (R)
Up 15	84%	94%	92%	98%	94%	88%	74%
Front	90%	96%	96%	100%	100%	94%	74%
Down 15	70%	86%	96%	100%	94%	90%	66%

4 Conclusion

Inspired by the biology of human vision, we proposed viewpoint-invariant face recognition model based on view-based representation. We used ISA to simulate view-based representation and we showed that this type of representation has view-dependent characteristics. Thanks to these view-dependent characteristics, our model uses an SLP to easily classify each viewpoint. Furthermore, the association between different viewpoints can be learned by using an RBF-NN that has been trained with SVR. When given a non-frontal face image, the model uses the viewpoint classification to select an RBF-NN for the estimation of the frontal face representation. The RBF-NN successfully estimates the representation of frontal face images from the representation of non-frontal face images. The overall recognition rate was 89.33%.

The results highlight the potential of our biologically inspired model, though the recognition rate dropped for widely different viewpoints. For better results, we plan to find a simpler feature space where associations between viewpoints can be learned more easily. Furthermore, because our experiments were performed with synthesized facial images under ideal illumination conditions, we plan try to gather and experiment on real images.

Acknowledgments

This research was supported by the Brain Neuroinformatics Research Program, which is sponsored by the Ministry of Commerce, Industry and Energy, and by the Ubiquitous Autonomic Computing and Network Project of the 21st Century Frontier R&D Program, which is sponsored by the Ministry of Information and Communication.

References

1. Georghiades, A.S., Belhumeur, P. N., Kriegman, D. J.: Illumination-Based Image Synthesis: Creating Novel Images of Human Faces Under Differing Pose and Lighting. IEEE Workshop on Multi-View Modeling and Analysis of Visual Scenes Fort Collins, Colorado (1999) 47-54
2. Okada, K., Steffans, J., Maurer, T., Hong, H., Elagin, E., Neven, H., et al.: The Bochum/USC Face Recognition System and How it Fared in the FERET Phase III Test. Face Recognition: From Theory to Applications, Springer-Verlag (1998) 186-205
3. Desimone, R., Albright, T.D., Gross, C.G., Bruce, C.: Stimulus-Selective Properties of Inferior Temporal Neurons in the Macaque. Journal of Neuroscience, 4(8), (1984) 2051-2062.
4. Graham, D., Allinson, N.: Face Recognition from Unfamiliar Views: Subspace Methods and Pose Dependency. In 3rd Int. conf. on automatic face and gesture recognition (1998) 348-353
5. Hinton, G. E., Sejnowski, T. J.: Unsupervised Learning. Bradford Book (1998)
6. Li, S., Lu, X., Zhang, H.: Unsupervised Learning of View-Subspaces and View-based Clustering of Appearance. MS Research Technical Report, MSR-TR-2001-08 (2001)
7. Hyvärinen, A., Hoyer, P. O.: Emergence of Phase and Shift Invariant Features by Decomposition of Natural Images into Independent Feature Subspaces. Neural Computation,12(7): (2000) 1705-1720,
8. Gunn, S. R.: Support Vector Machines for Classification and Regression. Technical Report ISIS-1-98, Department of Electronics and Computer Science, University of Southampton (1998)
9. Messer, K., Matas, J., Kittler, J., Luettin, J., Maitre, G.: XM2VTS DB: The Extended XMVTS Database. Int. conf. on Audio and Video-based Biometric Person Authentication, Washington D.C. (1999)

Visual Information Representation Using Embedded Block with Significance Selecting Model

Wentong Xue, Jianshe Song, Lihai Yuan, and Tao Shen

Xi'an Research Institute of Hi-Tech, Hongqing town, P.R. China
xwt_sea@163.com

Abstract. In this paper, we propose a new scheme based on contourlet to represent the visual information from the aspect of magnitude and orientation. Based on the detail statistics analysis of the individual, joint behaviors and correlations of contourlet coefficients of natural images across scales, positions and directions, it reveals strong local dependencies and clustering when the coefficients are at low amplitude. According to these fundamental findings, a novel embedded block with significance selecting model is developed to present the transformed coefficients. Experimental results demonstrate that our proposed representation is efficient .It is comparable to the wavelet coder in terms of the PSNR metric, and visually superior to the wavelet coder for the images with detailed texture, which is more fit for the Human Visual System.

1 Introduction

The wavelet transform is proved to be powerful in many signal and image processing applications. The success of wavelets is mainly due to the good performance for piecewise smooth functions in one dimension. Unfortunately, such is not the case in two dimensions. In essence, wavelets are good at catching zero-dimensional or point singularities, but two-dimensional piecewise smooth signals resembling images have one-dimensional singularities. When dealing with images characterized by one-dimensional discontinuities, classical two-dimensional wavelets can no longer claim to be sparse. Numerous methods have been proposed independently to overcome the problem. These different directional multiresolution image analysis techniques are classified as: Radon-based, filter bank based and adaptive. The ridgelet transform [1] was developed over several years in an attempt to overcome the weakness of wavelets in higher dimensions. A basic model for calculating ridgelet coefficients is to use the Radon transform to map a line singularity to a point singularity and uses the wavelet transform to deal with the point singularity effectively. However, in image processing, edges are typically curved rather than straight and ridgelets alone cannot yield efficient representation. As a consequence, the curvelet transform [2] has been introduced. For discrete images, sampled on a rectangular grid, the discrete implementation of the curvelet transform is very challenging. To overcome this problem, a new image representation method was introduced: the Pyramidal Directional Filter Bank (PDFB) also known as the contourlet transform [3]. This approach overcomes the block based approach of the curvelet by using a directional filter bank. Adaptive techniques are techniques where the directional component of an

D.-S. Huang, K. Li, and G.W. Irwin (Eds.): ICIC 2006, LNAI 4114, pp. 879 – 886, 2006.

image is adaptively estimated and the transform is steered based on the estimate. For example, the bandelet transform [4] links the significant wavelet coefficients along a discontinuity and represents it as a smooth 1-D curve.

2 Structure Definitions of Coefficient Relationships and Corresponding Statistics

2.1 Structure Definitions of Coefficient Relationships

The contourlet coefficient relationships are defined, and the wavelet coefficient relationships which are well known are taken for an example, as depicted in Fig.1. For a given contourlet coefficient X, two kinds of relationships are defined. Firstly, the coefficient in the same spatial location in the immediately coarser scale is defined as its parent (PX), while those in the same spatial location in the immediately finer scale are its children. Secondly, the adjacent coefficients around it in the same subband are defined as its neighbors (NX), and there are eight neighbors around. Those at the same scale and spatial location but in different directions are defined as cousins (CX) of each other. The major difference between the wavelet and contourlet is that there are more directions in the contourlet representation. While wavelet coefficients are always separated into only three directions, contourlet coefficients can have an arbitrary power of two's number of directions.

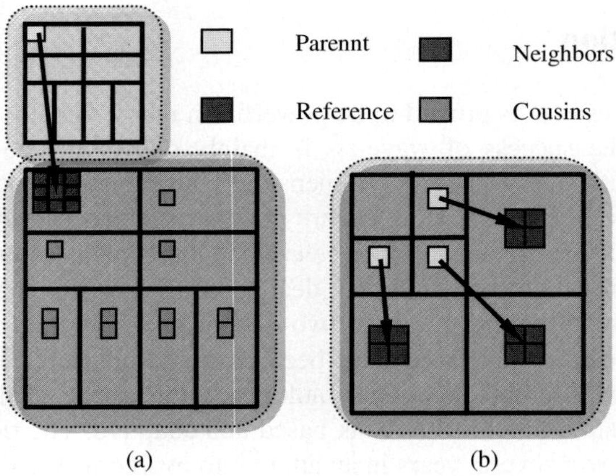

Fig. 1. (a) shows contourlet coefficient relationships, (b) shows wavelet coefficient relationships. Note that the arrow points from the parents to the children, and the same color shows the coefficients in different directions of the same scale.

2.2 Contourlet Statistics

For the statistical studies, the highly textured image "Barbara" is adopted. As for the contourlet transform, in the multiscale decomposition stage the 5-3 biorthogonal filters (referred to as 5-3 filters) are used, and the McClellan transformed directional filters of the 5-3 filters for the directional decomposition stage. We partition the finest and second finest scales into eight directional subbands, and the two next coarser scales into four directional subbands. We describe comprehensive studies on individual behaviors of each coefficient and the dependencies between coefficients across scales, space, and directions in the contourlet domain using the marginal statistics and mutual information separately.

To study the individual behaviors of each coefficient, we first study the marginal statistics of the contourlet coefficients. Table 1 shows the kutorsis of contourlet coefficients histogram of "Barbara". It is important to note that the kurtosis of this six distributions range form 8.34 to 13.53, which are much higher than the kurtosis of 3 for Gaussian distributions. Thus, we can conclude that, firstly, the contourlet transform representing is sparse, and secondly, the subband marginal distributions of the test image in the contourlet domain are highly non-Gaussian.

Table 1. Kurtosis of histograms in different position

Position	Kurtosis			
Level-1	8.90	11.92	12.24	7.58
Level-2	11.61	11.74	8.34	14.67
Level-3	13.53	22.98	44.86	15.44

Joint statistics are particularly important because in the wavelet case, image processing algorithms exploiting joint statistics of coefficients, such as EZW [10], SPIHT [11] and others, show significant improvements in performance over those that exploit marginal statistics alone. As the contourlet transform is similar to the wavelet transform, it is natural to extend this assumption to the contourlet case as well. In order to characterize these statistics, we consider several kinds of coefficients relationships conditioned on its parents(*X-PX*), neighbors(*X-NX*) and cousins(*X-CX*) respectively. Fig.2(a) shows the conditional scatter graphs, using the image "Barbara". From Fig.2(a), we can draw the following conclusion. First, all these three scatter graphs exhibit a phenomenon of clustering around a point near zero amplitude, where we can find heavy dependencies on the reference coefficients and their parents, cousins and neighbors at low amplitude coefficients. Second, comparing with the strong dependencies between lower amplitude coefficients, little dependencies conditioned on their parents, cousins and neighbors can be found when the coefficients are at higher amplitude. This indicates that the dependencies in these three kinds of conditional distributions are local, especially when the contourlet transformed coefficients, including the reference and its parents, cousins and neighbors are small.

In order to qualitative study the joint statistics of contourlet coefficients, we use the mutual information as a measure of dependencies. Our goal is to compare the dependencies across scales, space, and directions in the contourlet domain.

The mutual information results for the contourlet transform are presented in Fig.2(b) To explore the factors affecting the mutual information, different multiscale filters and directional filters, such as the famous filters 9-7, 5-3, PKVA [9] and Haar, are used to the experimental image. In each subset of Fig.2(b), the axis coordinate “1” shows the mutual information in case of the contourlet transform using the PKVA as the directional filter; “2” shows results using 9-7 as the directional filter; and “3” shows the results using 5-3 as the directional filter.

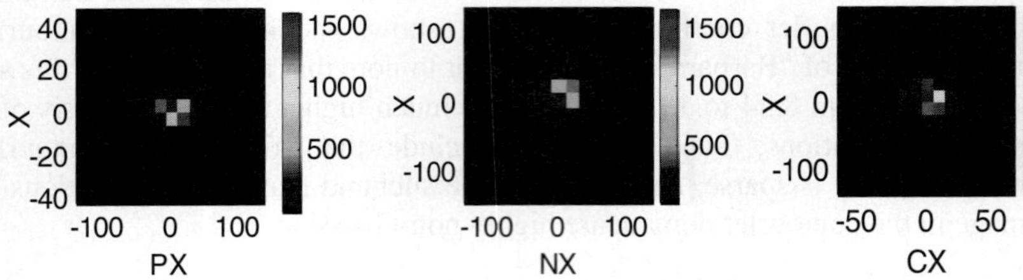

(a)

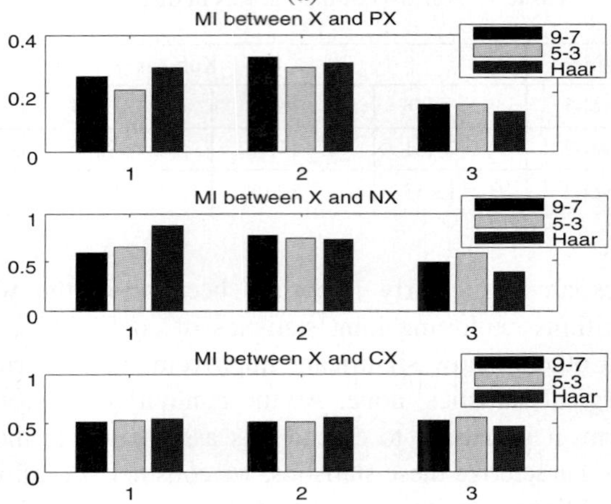

(b)

Fig. 2. Contourlet statistics: (a) Joint scatter graphs, conditioned on parent P(X|PX), neighbors P(X|NX) and cousins P(X|CX) (b) Mutual information(MI) between the contourlet sets X and its parents PX, its neighbors NX and its cousins CX

3 Contourlet Represention Using Embedded Block with Significance Selecting Model

The good performance of wavelets in the state-of-the-art image compression algorithms relies on the use of embedded trees that effectively point to significant or insignificant coefficients in the transform domain [7]. The PDFB has a pyramid structure like the wavelet; some coding scheme used in wavelet domain can be adopted to the contourlet domain [8].

3.1 Model Fundamentals

In the case of the contourlet transform, we find the fact that first, the lowest subband contains most of energy, and directional subbands in different scales tend to have different energy, that is to say, for the image the visual information in different directions is not the same; second, the previous coefficients have heavy correlation with its neighbors and this kind of correlation depends on some factors such as multiscale filters and directional filters.

So, our proposed contourlet representation using Embedded Block with Significance Selecting Model (EBSSM) is consisted of two parts as follow: the directional subbands significance decision model and embedded block representation model.

The Directional Subbands Significance Decision Model (DSSDM) aims to decide the importance order of different directional subbands, according to the energy in those directional subbands. It bases on the facts that the visual information in different directions is not the same. The decision criterion is to compare the energy of each directional subband and the directional subband with higher energy is decided as the most important directional subband. That means there is more visual information in this direction than those in other directions.

Embedded Block Representation Model (EBRM) aims to represent the coefficients in each subband. From the statistics study on contourlet coefficients, we know that there are heavy correlations between the previous coefficients with its neighbors. Thus can be the direct evidence for us to use the block-based model to represent the coefficients in same subband.

3.2 Model Diagram

First, the contourlet transform is applied on the image to get the multiscale and multidirectional subbands. Second, those subbands lie at the lowest resolutions are selected as the most significant subbands. Third, in each resolution level, the directional significance decision model is used to decide which the most important

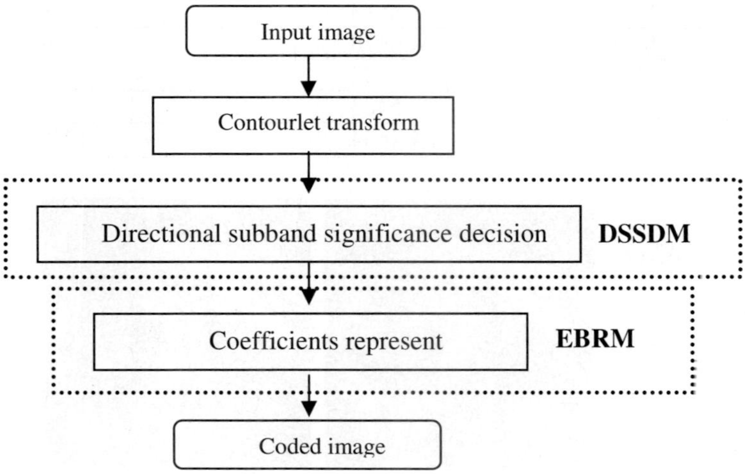

Fig. 3. Diagram of contourlet representation using embedded block with directional significance selecting decision model

directional subband is, and those more important directional subbands has higher superiorities in the process. After that, in each subband, the most significant bit of the significant coefficients are coded firstly with the technology of bit plane to ensure higher reconstruction performance and the good feature of progressive transmission with the embedded block representation model. See fig.3.

4 Experimental Results

We tested the proposed coding scheme in contourlet domain as well as the original wavelet SPECK coder on several images, each having a size of 512×512. An arithmetic encoder is used to entropy-code the resulting bit streams. Table 2 shows the Peak Signal Noise Ratio (PSNR) obtained for the proposed EBSSM and wavelet SPECK coder. From these figures, we can see that there are some differences in their PSNR values. The wavelet coder shows better performance in terms of PSNR values up to 0.4 to 0.5 dB, except at the bit rate of 0.2 where contourlet gains 0.6 dB than wavelet. Fig.4 and Fig.5 show respectively the coded results of the Barbara image at 0.2 bpp. The experiments indicated that the proposed contourlet EBSSM is superior in preserving textures and details in the coded images than the wavelet SPECK does, for detail, see the zoomed area. This observation is not effectively demonstrated by the PSNR metric. As can be seen, more textures in the coded image by the contourlet EBSSM are retained. These figures clearly show the capability of the contourlet EBSSM for images consisting of mainly textures and oscillatory patterns.

Table 2. PSNR comparisons between contourlet EBSSM and wavelet SPECK

Bit/Pixel	Contourlet EBSSM	Wavelet SPECK
0.125	23.8613	24.1955
0.15	24.0178	24.2148
0.2	25.3102	24.6796
0.5	29.5483	29.9896
1.0	34.4654	34.8750

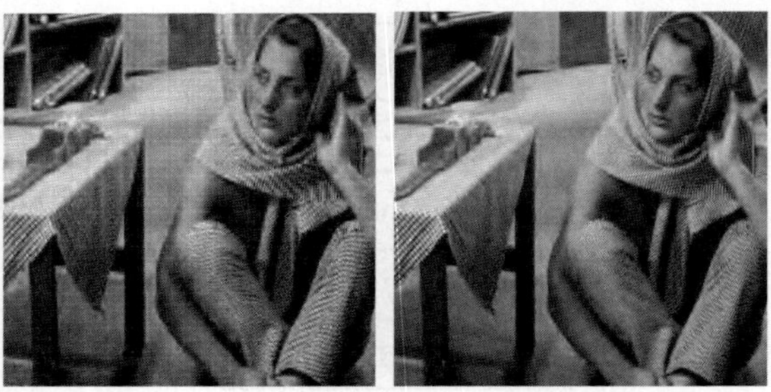

Fig. 4. Comparison at 0.2 bpp. Left: contourlet EBSSM; Right: wavelet SPECK.

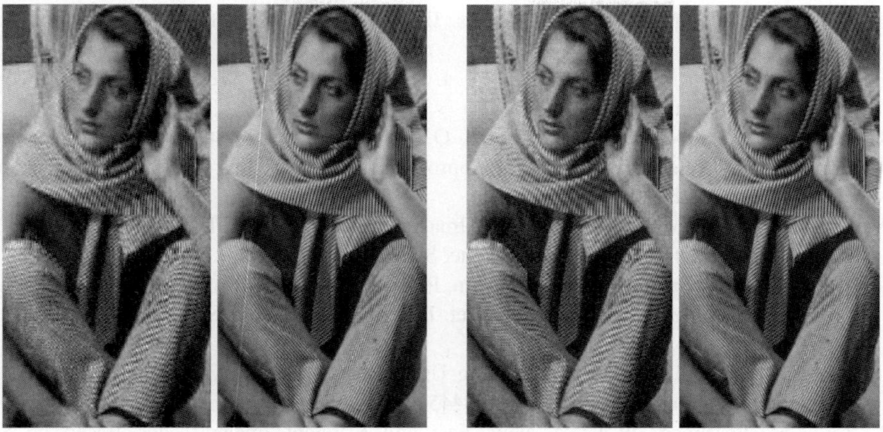

(a) (b)

Fig. 5. Zoomed parts of the Barbara image coded at 0.2 bpp in (a) and 0.5 in (b).Left: contourlet EBSSM; Right: wavelet SPECK

5 Conclusion

We propose a new scheme based on contourlet to represent the visual information from the aspect of magnitude and orientation. According to the fundamental findings on contourlet transformed domain, we proposed a novel visual information representation –Embedded Block with Significance Selecting Model, which bases on the following facts: first, the lowest subband contains most of energy, and directional subbands in different scales tend to have different energy, that is to say, for the image the visual information in different directions is not the same; second, the previous coefficients have heavy correlation with its neighbors. The simulation results indicated that the contourlet EBSSM is visually superior to the wavelet SPECK codec in preserving details and textures in the coded images. Because of the redundancy of 33%, it is a drawback for contourlet for the application of image coding, which needs to be improved in the near future.

References

1. Candes, E. J., Donoho, D. L.: Ridgelets: A Key to Higher-Dimensional Intermittency. Phil. Trans. R. Soc. Lond. A. (1999) 2495-2509
2. Candes, E.J., Donoho, D.L.: Curvelets - A Surprisingliy Effective Non-Adaptive Representation for Objects with Edges. In Curve and Surface Fitting, A. Cohen, C. Rabut, and L.L. Schumaker, Eds. Saint Malo: Vanderbilt University (1999)
3. Do, M.N., Vetterli, M.: The Contourlet Transform: An Efficient Directional Multiresolution Image Representation. IEEE Trans. on Image Processing, 14 (2005) 2091 – 2106
4. PENNEC, E. L., MALLAT, S.: Image Compression with Geometric Wavlets. Proc. IEEE International Conference on Image Processing (2000)

5. Do, M., Vetterli, M.: Framing Pyramids. IEEE Trans. On Signal Processing 51 (2003) 2329-2342
6. Do, M., Vetterli, M.: Contourlets. in: J. Stoeckler, G. V. Welland (Eds.), Beyond Wavelets, Academic Press, (2002) 1-27
7. Cohen, A., Daubechies, I., Guleryuz, O.G., Orchard, M.T.: On the Importance of Combining Wavelet-based Nonlinear Approximation with Coding Strategies. IEEE Trans. on Info. Theory. 48 (2002) 1895-1921
8. Do, M.N.: Directional Multiresolution Image Representations. Ph.D. dissertation, Swiss Federal Institute of Technology, Lausanne, Switzerland (2001)
9. Phoong, S.-M., Kim, C.W., Vaidyanathan, P. P., Ansari, R.: A New Class of Two-Channel Biorthogonal Filter Banks and Wavelet Bases. IEEE Trans. Signal Proc. 43 (1995) 649–665
10. Shapiro, J.M.: Embedded Image Coding Using Zerotress of Wavelet Coefficients. IEEE Trans. on Signal Processing. 41 (1993) 3445–3462
11. Said, A., Pearlman, W.A.: A New, Fast and Efficient Image Codec Based on Set Partitioning in Hierarchical Trees. IEEE Trans. Circuits and Systems for Video Technology. 6 (1996) 243–250
12. Islam, A., Pearlman, W.A.: An Embedded and Efficient Low-Complexity Hierarchical Image Coder. Visual Communications and Image Processing '99, Proceedings of SPIE. 3653 (1999) 294–305
13. Duncan, D.-Y. Po, Minh, N.D.: Directional Multiscale Statistical Modeling of Images. Proceedings of the SPIE. 5207 (2003) 69-79

Visual Navigation for a Power Transmission Line Inspection Robot

Yunchu Zhang[1,2], Siyao Fu[1], Xiaoguang Zhao[1], Zize Liang[1], Min Tan[1], and Yongqian Zhang[1]

[1] Laboratory of Complex Systems and Intelligence Science, Institute of Automation, Chinese Academy of Sciences, P.O. Box 2728, Beijing 100080, China
{yunchu.zhang, siyao.fu, min.tan}@ia.ac.cn
[2] School of Information and Electric Engineering, Shandong University of Architecture and Engineering, Jinan 250101, China

Abstract. Inspection robot must plan its behavior to negotiate obstacles according to their types when it is crawling along the power transmission line. For this purpose, a visual navigation system is designed to recognize the obstacles and locate their positions by stereovision.We propose a structure-constrained obstacle recognition algorithm based on improved circle detection methods to recognize obstacles from complex background robustly. After the obstacle is recognized, a region based stereo matching algorithm is used to search the correspondence points in the stereo images, and the position of the obstacle relative to the robot is calculated by 3D reconstruction. Experiments with simulation and real transmission line show its effectiveness.

1 Introduction

A mobile robot that can crawl along the transmission line to perform part of power line inspection tasks is developed. The inspection robot is wheel-driven, when it crawls along the power transmission line, the line subsidiary equipments will act as obstacles to block its way. A navigation system is needed to recognize and locate the obstacles with its sensors; then the control system of inspection robot will plan its motions according to the obstacle information to negotiate these obstacles autonomously. Sawada[1] developed an inspection robot which was equipped with ultrasonic sensor and contacting sensor to detect tower and its subsidiary equipments. Peungsungwal[2] used a camera to recognize the obstacle and navigate their inspection robot to avoid the collision against the obstacle. Peters[3] equipped an inspection robot with up to 34 proximity sensors, and applied a rough neuro-computing approach to design an obstacle classifier to recognize obstacles according to the information acquired by these sensors.

In this paper, we design a visual navigation system to recognize the obstacles and locate their positions by stereovision.The obstacle recognition algorithm is designed based on an improved circle detection method. After the obstacle is recognized, a region-based stereo matching algorithm is used to search the correspondence points in the stereo images, and the distance of the obstacle relative to the robot is calculated

D.-S. Huang, K. Li, and G.W. Irwin (Eds.): ICIC 2006, LNAI 4114, pp. 887–892, 2006.

by 3D reconstruction. To improve the matching speed, the epipolar constraint and a dynamic search window is applied.

The rest of the paper is organized as follows. In Section 2, a brief introduction of our inspection robot and the structure of the 220KV transmission line is given. Section 3 describes the obstacle recognition algorithm. Section 4 presents the algorithm of obstacle locating. The results of experiments with simulation and real transmission line are shown In Section 5. Then conclusions follow.

2 Power Transmission Line Inspection Robot and Its Navigation Problem

There are three typical obstacles attached to the 220KV power transmission line and power tower, as shown in Fig.1. The first type of obstacle is called counterweight, the second type of obstacle is strain clamp, and the third type of obstacle is called suspension clamp. Each type of obstacle has different spatial structure, the inspection robot should plan its motion sequence according to the type of the obstacle.

The robot is equipped with two CCD cameras in the front of the robot's body (see in Fig.1), note that the angle between the camera's optical axis and the robot's moving direction is about 30°, this configuration ensures the most part of the background is sky, thus reduce complexity of the background.

Obstacle recognition is the key problem of the navigation system. It is not easy to recognize the clamps themselves because there aren't effective features to be used for recognition. But the isolator strings, from which the suspension clamp or strain clamp is suspended, consist of disks; and their projections on the camera's image plane are circular or elliptic geometric patterns under the camera's configuration in Fig.1. So we select these simple geometric patterns as the key clues of the obstacles existence.

3 Obstacle Recognition

Under the camera configuration in Fig.1, the projection of the isolator string's bottom, from which the suspension clamp is suspended, is an ellipse; and the projection of the

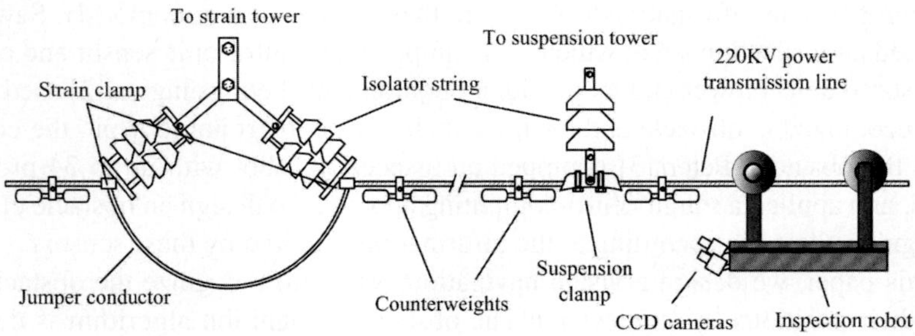

Fig. 1. Obstacles on power transmission line

two isolator strings' bottoms, from which the strain clamp is suspended, is two circles situated on each side of the power line. So we select the circular or elliptic pattern, and their relationship with the power line to model the obstacles. Then the obstacle detection problem can be converted into the problem of detect the circles or ellipses in the image.

3.1 Circle Detection

We propose an effective algorithm for detecting approximate circles in an edge image based on existence probability map, this algorithm is an improvement of the circle-finding concept sketched by Duda and Hart[4]. Duda uses a three-dimensional array of accumulators to detect circular objects in an image, but the method needs massive storage requirement and high cost of computation. Our proposed algorithm only needs two two-dimensional arrays and a one-dimensional array of accumulator.

Let $f(x, y)$ denotes the edge image extracted by Canny edge detector; $\{P(x, y)\}$ denotes a two-dimensional array which is used to save circle's existence probability; $\{R(x, y)\}$ denotes a two-dimensional array which is used to save candidate circle's radius; and $\{A(k)\}$ denotes a one-dimensional array of accumulator.

The general equation of a circle in an image is defined by $(x - a)^2 + (y - b)^2 = r^2$,where (a, b) is the circle' center, and r is the circle's radius. Assume there exists a circle centered at (u, v), and then the hypothetical circle's radius r can be calculated by using a Hough Transform-like scheme. Since we only need to vote on the radius r, one-dimensional accumulator array $\{A(k)\}$ is enough.

For each edge point (x_i, y_i) in $f(x, y)$, the distance between (x_i, y_i) and $(u. v)$ can be calculate by the equation:$r_i = \sqrt{(x_i - u)^2 + (y_i - v)^2}$.

If r_i is greater than the required least distance, increase the cell $A(r_i)$ by 1. After all the edge points are computed for this hypothetical circle, their distances from the hypothetical circle center are accumulated in a one-dimensional accumulator array. Then find the maximum element in the accumulator array; let $A(r_m)$ represents this maximum value, which is the number of concyclic points centered around point (u, v). The index r_m of the cell correspond to the hypothetical circle's radius.

Let P_e represents the existence probability of a hypothetical circle, whose center and radius is (u, v) and r_m respectively. Define P_e as follows:

$$P_e = A(r_m)/2\pi r_m \tag{1}$$

Then save P_e in the cell $P(u, v)$ of the array $\{P(x, y)\}$, and r_m in the cell $R(u, v)$ of the array $\{R(x, y)\}$.

For every point (u, v) in $f(x, y)$, suppose there exist a circle whose center is (u, v); calculate its existence probability P_e and the radius r_m according above procedure, and save them in the correspondence cell of $\{P(x, y)\}$ and $\{R(x, y)\}$. We call $\{P(x, y)\}$ the existence probability map, which is the mapping of configuration information of concyclic edge points in the image space to the circle's parameter space. Each peak of $\{P(x, y)\}$ suggests that there exists a circle in the original image; the predicted circles' center is the peak's 2-d index (u_p, v_p), its radius is $R(u_p, v_p)$; and the existence probability of this predicted circles is given by $P(u_p, v_p)$. The greater $P(u_p, v_p)$ is, the more possible the prediction is.

3.2 Isolator Recognition

As mentioned above, we select the ellipse and circle in the image as the key clues of the existence of obstacles, that is, an ellipse and its relationship with the power line in the image suggests that there exist an isolator string from which the suspension clamp is suspended; two circles and its relationship with the power line in the image suggests that there exist two isolator strings from which a strain clamp is suspended. First we use the circle detection method discussed in Section 3.1 and ellipse detection method given by[5]to find circles and ellipse in the image, and then check its relationship with the power line to determine if it is an obstacle or a false target. The isolator recognition procedure is given as follows.

Step 1: Search the edge image to find whether there is an ellipse in the edge image.
Step 2: If there is an ellipse, and its parameters are (x_0, y_0), a, b; where (x_0, y_0) is the ellipse's center coordinates; a, b is the half-length of major and minor axes respectively. Then check its relationship with the power line. If the perpendicular distance from the ellipse's center (x_0, y_0) to the power line is less than a given threshold, then the ellipse is considered as the existence proof of the suspension clamp.
Step 3: If any ellipse is not found, then search the edge image for two circles.
Step 4: If there are two circles found, and their parameters are (a_1, b_1), r_1, (a_2, b_2), r_2; and then check its relationship with the power line. If they are situated at each side of the power line, then the two circles is considered as the existence proof of the strain clamp.

4 Obstacle Locating

After the obstacle is recognized, the next task of visual navigation system is to locate the obstacle's spatial position. The left camera is the principal camera whose image is used to recognize the obstacles; together with the right camera, obstacle locating can be achieved by stereovision. We select the center of the ellipse or the leftmost circle to represent the obstacle and let P denotes it, then the spatial position of point P relative to the left camera can be estimated as follows.

$$Z_{c1}\begin{bmatrix} u_1 \\ v_1 \\ 1 \end{bmatrix} = \begin{bmatrix} \alpha_1 & 0 & u_{01} & 0 \\ 0 & \beta_1 & v_{01} & 0 \\ 0 & 0 & 1 & 0 \end{bmatrix} \begin{bmatrix} X_{c1} \\ Y_{c1} \\ Z_{c1} \\ 1 \end{bmatrix}, Z_{c2}\begin{bmatrix} u_2 \\ v_2 \\ 1 \end{bmatrix} = \begin{bmatrix} \alpha_2 & 0 & u_{02} & 0 \\ 0 & \beta_2 & v_{02} & 0 \\ 0 & 0 & 1 & 0 \end{bmatrix} \begin{bmatrix} X_{c2} \\ Y_{c2} \\ Z_{c2} \\ 1 \end{bmatrix} \tag{2}$$

$$\begin{bmatrix} X_{c2} \\ Y_{c2} \\ Z_{c2} \\ 1 \end{bmatrix} = \begin{bmatrix} \mathbf{R} & \mathbf{t} \\ \mathbf{0}^t & 1 \end{bmatrix} \begin{bmatrix} X_{c1} \\ Y_{c1} \\ Z_{c1} \\ 1 \end{bmatrix} = \begin{bmatrix} r_{11} & r_{12} & r_{13} & t_1 \\ r_{21} & r_{22} & r_{23} & t_2 \\ r_{31} & r_{32} & r_{33} & t_3 \\ 0 & 0 & 0 & 1 \end{bmatrix} \tag{3}$$

Combining these three equations and eliminate(X_{c2}, Y_{c2}, Z_{c2}), the solution (X_{c1}, Y_{c1}, Z_{c1}) can be obtained by *LS* (least square method).

Where (X_{c1}, Y_{c1}, Z_{c1}), (X_{c2}, Y_{c2}, Z_{c2}) is the spatial coordinates of P in the left-camera and right-camera coordinate system respectively; (u_1, v_1) and (u_2, v_2) are the projected points of P on the left and right image respectively. α_1, β_1, u_{01}, v_{01} are the pinhole model parameters of the left camera; α_2,β_2, u_{02},v_{02} are the pinhole model parameters of the right camera; **R** is the rotation matrix and **t** is the translation vector.

But how to identify the projected points of P on the left and right image, i.e. p_1, p_2, has been an extremely challenging research problem known as the stereo matching problem. We use the SSD [6,7] (Sum of Squared Differences) based stereo matching method with an adaptive window to search the correspondence points p_1 and p_2. Let point p_1 with the coordinates (u_1, v_1) in the left image f_1 denote the center of the ellipse, we assume p_2 with the coordinates (u, v) in the right image f_2 be p_1's potential matching point. We compute the sum of squared differences between a small searching window of pixels centered around p_1 in the left image and a similar window centered around every potential matching point p_2 in the right image. The point in the right image with the lowest sum of squared differences is considered as the match. In order to reduce the searching time, only those points that satisfy the epipolar constraint are considered for matching. The size of the searching window is $(2m+1)(2n+1)$, which is adaptive to the size of the detected ellipse or circle. Then we get

$$SSD(u, v) = \Sigma_{i=-m}^{m} \Sigma_{j=-n}^{n} \left[f_1(u_1 + i, v_1 + j) - f_2(u + i, v + j) \right]^2 \qquad (4)$$

$$(u_2, v_2) = \arg \min_{(u,v)} \{SSD(u, v)\}. \qquad (5)$$

5 Experimental Results

The visual navigation system is tested on indoor simulation power transmission line and outdoor real power transmission line. In spite of the scene background is cluttered, the obstacles can be recognized correctly (see Fig.2). The distances from the obstacle to the left camera are measured as the Table 1. The accuracy of the distance measurement

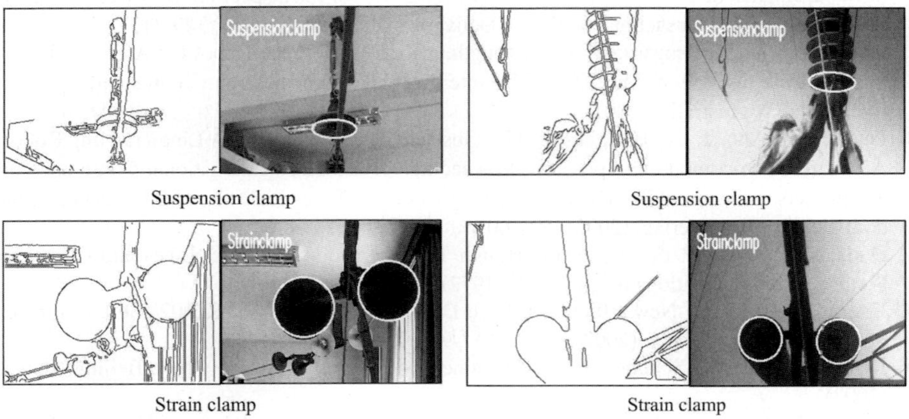

(a) Simulation power transmission line (b) Real power transmission line

Fig. 2. Obstacle recognition experimental results

Table 1. Comparison between the actual and measured distance

Measured Distance (cm)	161	223	275	281
Actual Distance (cm)	152	210	257	271
Error Percent	6%	6.2%	7%	7.3%

result is depended on the cameras model and stereo matching result. Though the measuring errors are approximate 7%, it could be accepted for our application.

6 Conclusions

This paper has presented a visual navigation system for an inspection robot to detect and locate the typical obstacles on the power line. It utilizes the notion that the structure elements of all the obstacles in the power transmission line are circular or elliptic and that the structure elements of the background objects like tower or transmission lines are straight line, then the problem of detecting obstacle from complex image is formulated into a circle/ellipse detection problem. The improved circle detection algorithm reduces significantly the memory space and computation required. Experiments with simulation and real transmission line show promising results.

Acknowledgment

This research has been supported by the Hi-Tech R&D Program (863) of China (grant 2005AA420060), and the Filed Bus Tech & Automation Key Lab of Beijing. The authors also wish to acknowledge the help and suggestions from Prof. Gongping Wu, with the College of Power and Mechanical Engineering, Wuhan University.

References

1. Sawada, J., Kusumoto, K., Munakata, T.: A Mobile Robot for Inspection of Power Transmission Lines, IEEE Transactions on Power Delivery, (1991),vol. 6, no. 1, 309-315
2. Peungsungwal, S., Pungsiri, B., Chamnongthai, K.: Autonomous Robot for A Power Transmission Line Inspection, The 2001 IEEE International Symposium on Circuits and Systems, Sydney, NSW Australia, (2001), 121-124
3. Peters, J. F., Ahn, T. C. , Borkowskii, M. : Obstacle Classification by A Line-crawling Robot: A Rough Neurocomputing Approach, Proceedings of the Third International Conference on Rough Sets and Current Trends in Computing - Lecture Notes in Artificial Intelligence, London, UK, Springer-Verlag, (2002), 594-601
4. Duda, R. O., Hart, P. E.: Use of the Hough Transformation to Detect Lines and Curves in Pictures, Communications of the ACM, (1972), vol. 15, no. 1, 11-15
5. Xie, Y. H., Ji, Q.: A New Efficient Ellipse Detection Method," ICPR2002,IEEE Computer Society, Quebec, Canada, (2002), vol. 2, 957-960
6. Jain, R., Kasturi, R., Schunck, B. G.: Machine Vision, China Machine Press, Beijing, China, (2003)
7. Kanade, T., Okutomi, M.: A Stereo Matching Algorithm with An Adaptive Window: Theory and Experiment, IEEE Transactions on Pattern Analysis and Machine Intelligence, , (1994), vol. 16, no. 9, 920-932

A Semantic Analyzer for Aiding Emotion Recognition in Chinese

Jiajun Yan[1], David B. Bracewell[1], Fuji Ren[1,2], and Shingo Kuroiwa[1]

[1] Department of Information Science and Intelligent Systems
Faculty of Engineering, The University of Tokushima
Minami-Josanjima-Cho Tokushima-shi 770-8506, Japan
[2] School of Information Engineering, Beijing University of Posts and Telecommunications Beijing 100876, China
{yanjj, davidb, ren, kuroiwa}@is.tokushima-u.ac.jp

Abstract. In this paper we present a semantic analyzer for aiding emotion recognition in Chinese. The analyzer uses a decision tree to assign semantic dependency relations between headwords and modifiers. It is able to achieve an accuracy of 83.5%. The semantic information is combined with rules for Chinese verbs containing emotion to describe the emotion of the people in the sentence. The rules give information on how to assign emotion to agents, receivers, etc. depending on the verb in the sentence.

1 Introduction

In recent years the chances for human-computer interaction have risen greatly. From ATM to mobile phones, people are interacting and communicating with computers more and more. As such, the field of Affective Computing has been steadily growing and much research has been done on classifying and mimicking human emotion.

One of the fundamental sources of emotion is language. However, to fully understand emotion in language a full understanding of the sentence is needed. To understand the sentence, semantic analysis must be done. Semantic analysis helps to understand the roles and relations between objects, humans, etc. in the sentence.

In this paper, we propose a system for understanding emotion in Chinese verbs. The system uses semantic analysis and emotion predicates. In this way, the emotion "felt toward" and "felt by" can be known.

The paper will continue as follows, in section 2 semantic analysis is examined. Then, in section 3 the SEEN system for semantic analysis is described. Next, in section 4 the emotion predicates and how they were created are shown. In section 5 the experimental results are examined. Finally, in section 6 concluding remarks are made and future work is discussed.

2 Semantic Analysis

A dependency grammar (DG) is a grammar describing the dependency structure among words or constituents of a sentence. A dependency tree is a parse tree

D.-S. Huang, K. Li, and G.W. Irwin (Eds.): ICIC 2006, LNAI 4114, pp. 893–901, 2006.

for a dependency grammar showing the dependency structure of a sentence. [1] formulates four axioms to govern the well-formedness of dependency structures, shown below.

1. One and only one element is independent
2. All others depend directly on some element
3. No element depends directly on more than one other
4. If A depends directly on B and some element C intervenes between them (in linear order of the string), then C depends directly on A or B or some other intervening element

Generally, semantic dependency analysis builds a dependency tree with the optimal semantic relationship for the parent node (headword) and child node (dependent) between which there is a dependency link according to DG. In semantic dependency grammar, the word that is able to best represent the meaning of the headword-dependent pair is chosen as the headword. The headword of a sentence represents the main meaning of the entire sentence and the headword of a headword-dependent pair represents the main meaning of the pair. In a compound constituent the headword inherits the headword of the head sub-headword-dependent pair and headwords of other sub-headword-dependent pairs are dependent on that headword.

Normally, in the phrase structure, the sentence is broken down into its component parts of speech with an explanation of the form, function, and syntactical relationship of each part. Even though we can know the logical structure in the sentence, it is difficult to know the potential sense. Figure 1 gives the phrase structure for a Chinese sentence from the Penn Chinese Treebank [2].

Figure 2 gives an example of an annotated sentence with dependency structure and semantic relationships. The dependency structure is a tree with directed arrows as the dependency link and the main verb as the headword. The set of labeled arrows represent dependency relations from headwords to dependents. Such text annotated with semantic dependency structure can make implicit knowledge in sentences and documents more explicit, allowing a deeper understanding that can aid knowledge extraction and information retrieval. It is easy to explain agreement, or any semantic relations between words or constituents according to such word-to-word dependency links.

Figure 3 shows another representation of a semantic dependency analysis tree which preserves the phrase structure from the Penn Chinese Treebank. In this tree the bold lines denote headwords.

3 SEEN

Determining the semantic structure of sentences is strongly desired. If the semantic structure can be determined then machine translation, question and answering, etc. can be improved as they would have a greater insight on the meaning of the sentence. There has been much research on determining semantic structure

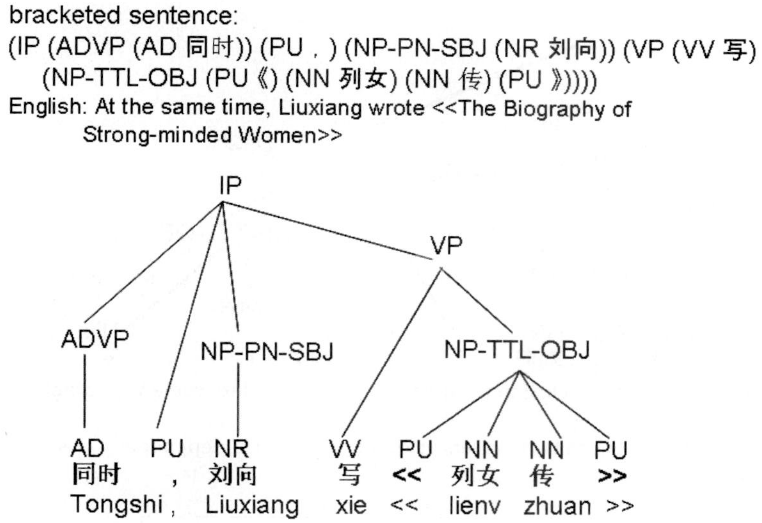

Fig. 1. Phrase structure for Chinese sentences from the Penn Chinese Treebank

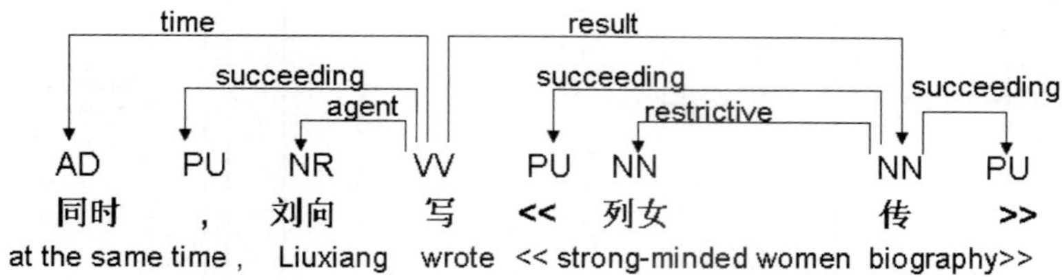

Fig. 2. Manually annotated sentence with dependency structure and semantic relationships

in English, [3] and [4] are examples. Also there are freely available corpora with semantic annotation such as [5].

There has, however, been much less research done for Chinese. The most prominent research done is by You and Chen [6]. However, in their research they used the Sinica corpus [7], which uses Taiwanese Chinese. Our focus is on Mandarin Chinese. The two forms of Chinese are different enough that a system for one may not be effective for the other. Also, since the Sinica corpus already has semantic information tagged they used that tag set. With the growing popularity of HowNet [1] among the Chinese NLP community and the incredible amount of knowledge that can be obtained by using it, a semantic analyzer for Mandarin should use HowNet's semantic tag set.

The SEEN (Semantic dEpendency parsEr for chiNese) system is broken into 3 main modules, as seen in Figure 4. The first module is syntactic analysis. This module takes care of morphological analysis and parsing. The second module is

[1] www.keenage.com

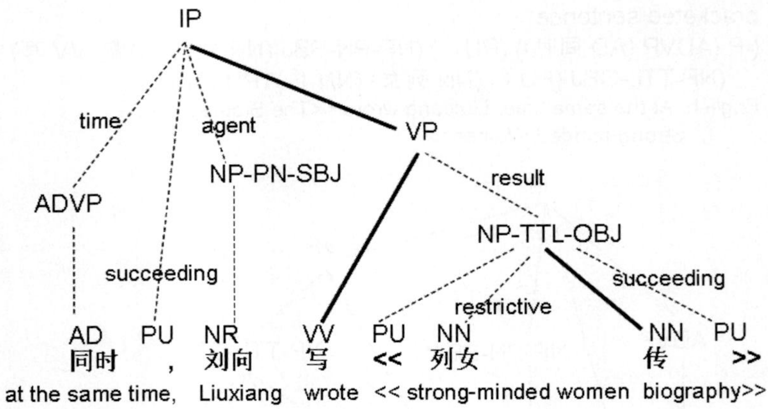

Fig. 3. Another representation of a semantic dependency tree

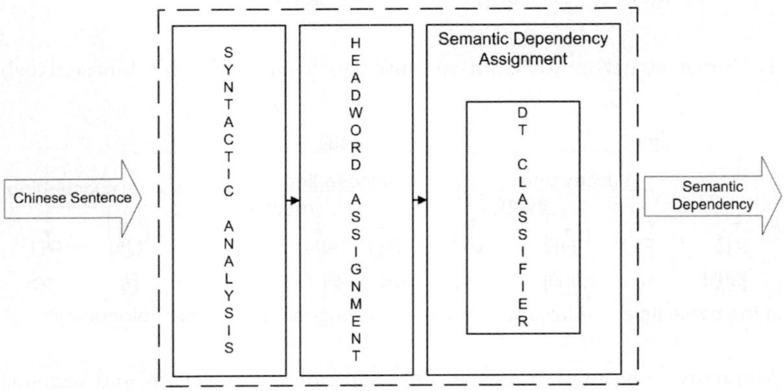

Fig. 4. The SEEN System

headword assignment. This module assigns headwords to sentences and phrases. The final module is semantic dependency assignment. Each of the modules will be described in more detail in the following subsections.

3.1 Syntactic Analysis

The syntactic analysis module is made up of morphological analysis and parsing. While not as far along as English, Chinese programs do exist and are rapidly improving. In the following subsections Chinese morphological analysis and parsing will be briefly discussed.

Morphological Analysis. Morphological analysis consists of word segmentation and part-of-speech tagging. It is a widely researched topic and many languages have these tools available including Chinese. ICTCLAS 2.0 [8], based on

Hidden Markov Models, is a free a morphological analyzer that has a precision of 97.58% for segmentation and 87.32% for part-of-speech tagging. In SEEN, this morphological analyzer will be used.

Chinese Parsing. There has been a lot of research done in Chinese Parsing. Some of the notable research is [9], which reported that their statistics-based Chinese parser had 86% precision and 86% recall. Levy and Manning [10] developed a factored-model statistical parser and used on the Penn Chinese Treebank. Because the parser was used on the Penn Chinese Treebank, and it is freely available, it was chosen as the parser for the SEEN system.

3.2 Headword Assignment

In this module, headwords are assigned to each chunk (phrase). In a semantic dependency grammar, headwords are the constituent that can represent the main meaning of the chunks. Headwords are assigned using a set of handcrafted rules that were created from observations made from the Penn Chinese Treebank. The handcrafted rules were designed to look at the syntactic head of a chunk and the other constituents. It was found that the different syntactic heads followed certain patterns that could easily be defined in rules. Figure 5 shows some example rules. For example, in Figure 3, there is a chunk with the POSes of "PU NN NN PU". According to the handcrafted headword assignment rules, the last tag which is neither "PU" nor "PRN" will become the headword of the chunk.

```
ADJP    the last ADJP or JJ will become headword.
ADVP    the last ADVP or AD will become headword.
DNP     the last DEG or DEC will become headword.
DVP     the last DEV will become headword.
LCP     the last LC will become headword.
QP      the last QP or CLP will become headword.
PP      the last P or PP will become headword.
CP      the last tag that is neither PU nor SP will become headword.
NP      the last tag which is neither PU nor PRN will become headword.
VRD     the first tag that is neither PU nor SP will become headword.
```

Fig. 5. Sample Headword Assignment Rules

3.3 Semantic Dependency Assignment

The semantic dependency assignment module uses a Decision Tree classifier [11] to assign semantic relations between a headword and dependent. The classifier achieves accuracy of just under 84% in relation assignment using a set of four features, listed below.

- Phrase Type
- Headword & Dependent
- Headword & Dependent Part-of-Speech
- Context

高兴 (glad, happy)
Emotion: *joy* + Agent (joy)

(a)

表扬(praise)
Emotion: *joy* + Agent (Respect) + Patient (joy)

(b)

讨厌(hate, dislike)
Emotion: *hate* + Agent (*hate*) + Relevant (sorrow)

(c)

爱上(fall in love with)
Emotion: *love* + Agent (love) + Patient (happy)

(d)

苦恼(worry about)
Emotion: *anxiety* + Agent (anxiety)

(e)

尊敬(have respect for)
Emotion: *respect* + Agent (respect) + Patient (joy)

(f)

嘲笑(laugh at)
Emotion: *joy* + Agent (joy) + Patient (sorrow)

(g)

喜爱(like)
Emotion: *love* + Agent (love) + Patient (happy)

(h)

Fig. 6. Emotion Predicates

4 Chinese Emotion Predicates

A predicate is one of the two main constituents of a sentence, which shows what is being predicated of the subject of a proposition. Its role is to tell something about the subject. In NLP, various research has been done that examines the uses of predicates, such as semantic interpretation [4].

In this research, emotion predicates are used to describe the emotion of the actor(s) in relation to the emotion. The semantic roles assigned to the predicate are a subset of the roles used in the semantic analyzer described previously. The roles in the predicate that undergo emotion are used and as such the roles are restricted to agent, relevant, etc.

We have defined eight predicates that cover five emotions; joy, love, hate, anxiety, and respect. The eight emotion predicates can be seen in Figure 6. Currently, only the emotion is looked and not modifiers to the emotion that would change the degree of emotion or even the emotion itself.

Each predicate has an emotion assigned to the verb and to the semantic roles. In some predicates, like "laugh at" of Figure 6(g), the emotion for the semantic roles does not match the emotion of the verb. This is because often times the person who is doing the verb and the person who is receiving or experiencing the verb have different emotions.

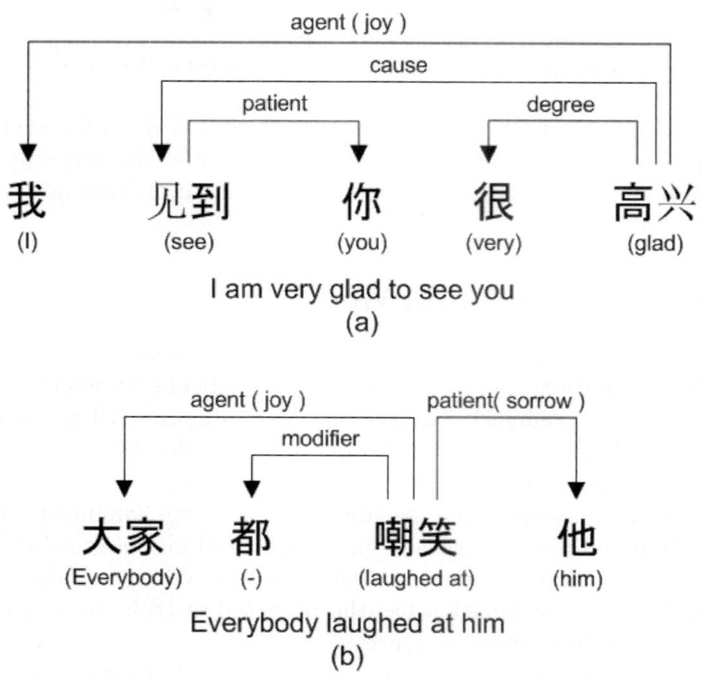

Fig. 7. Example Sentences

5 Experimentation

For experimentation, 80 sentences (10 sentences per predicate) were collected and examined. Currently, negated emotions, such as "do not love" in English, are not looked at. To see the effectiveness of the predicates, the semantic dependency was manually given. The accuracy was 100%. The results show that semantic analysis and predicate based emotion classification for semantic roles is extremely effective. Figures 7(a) and 7(b), show two examples of successful emotion assignment.

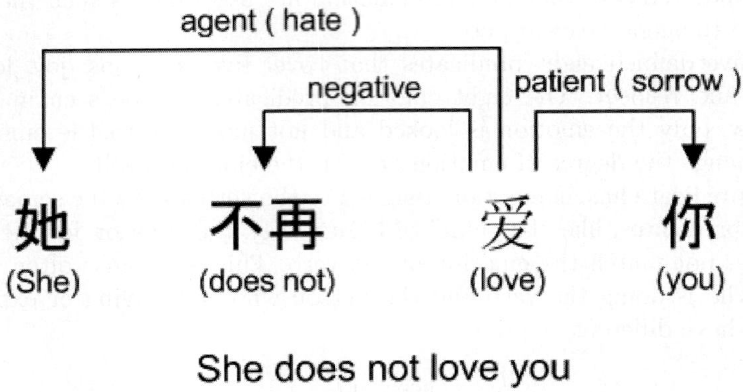

Fig. 8. Example of a Currently Unclassifiable Sentence

While an accuracy of 100% was achieved there is still room for improvement. For example, currently, the sentence in Figure 8 cannot be correctly handled, because emotion modifiers are not examined. It is a simple task however to add this in the future.

6 Conclusion and Future Work

In this paper we presented a system to semantically analyze Chinese sentences and use this information combined with emotion predicates to determine emotion in Chinese sentences. Semantic analysis was done using the SEEN system, which uses a Decision Tree classifier to determine semantic dependency relations and achieves an accuracy just under 84%.

For determining emotion the semantic analysis was combined with hand-crafted emotion predicates. This combination allowed for determination of emotion felt toward people, events, etc. and felt by actors. We showed through experimentation that this combination has the potential of truly gaining knowledge about the emotion in Chinese sentences.

In the future, we hope to semi-automatically build the emotion predicates from tagged corpora. This should eliminate the only drawback of the system, predicate creation. In addition we hope to add information about modifiers that change the degree of the emotion or negate the emotion.

Acknowledgement

This research has been partially supported by the Ministry of Education, Culture, Sports, Science and Technology of Japan under Grant-in-Aid for Scientific Research (B), 14380166, 17300065, Exploratory Research, 17656128, and the Outstanding Overseas Chinese Scholars Fund of the Chinese Academy of Sciences No. 2004-1-1.

References

1. Robinson, J.J.: Dependency structures and transformation rules. **46** (1970) 259–285
2. Xia, F., Palmer, M., Xue, N., Okurowski, M.E., Kovarik, J., Chiou, F.D., Huang, S., Kroch, T., Marcus, M.: Developing guidelines and ensuring consistency for chinese text annotation. In: Proceedings of the 2nd International Conference on Language Resources and Evaluation (LREC-2000), Athens, Greece (2000)
3. Gildea, D., Jurafsky, D.: Automatic labeling of semantic roles. Computational Linguistic **28** (2002) 496–530
4. Gomez, F.: An algorithm for aspects of semantic interpretation using an enhanced wordnet. In: Proceedings of the 2nd Meeting of the North American Chapter of the Association for Computational Linguistics, NAACL-2001. (2001)
5. Gomez, F.: Automatic semantic annotation of texts. Technical report, University of Central Florida (2004)
6. You, J.M., Chen, K.J.: Automatic semantic role assignment for a tree structure. In: Proceedings of the 3rd SigHAN Workshop on Chinese Language Processing. (2004) 109–115
7. Chen, F.Y., Tsai, P.F., Chen, K.J., Hunag, C.R.: The construction of sinica treebank. Computational Linguistics and Chinese Language Processing **4** (1999) 87–104
8. Zhang, H., Yu, H., Xiong, D., Liu, Q.: Hhmm-based chinese lexical analyzer ictclas. In: the Second SIGHAN workshop affiliated with 41st ACL. (2003)
9. Zhou, Q.: A statistics-based chinese parser. In: Proceedings of the Fifth Workshop on Very Large Corpora. (1997)
10. Levy, R., Manning, C.D.: Is it harder to parse chinese, or the chinese treebank? In: Proceedings of the Association of Computational Linguistics 2003. (2003)
11. Berger, A., Pietra, S.D., Pietra, V.D.: A maximum entropy approach to natural language processing. Computational Linguistics **22** (1996)

Emotion Estimation System Based on Emotion Occurrence Sentence Pattern

Kazuyuki Matsumoto[1], Ren Fuji[1,2], and Shingo Kuroiwa[1]

[1] Department of Information Science and Intelligent Systems
Faculty of Engineering, The University of Tokushima
Minami-Josanjima-Cho Tokushima-shi 770-8506, Japan
[2] School of Information Engineering, Beijing University of Posts and Telecommunications Beijing, 100876, China
{matumoto, ren, kuroiwa}@is.tokushima-u.ac.jp

Abstract. The approach of emotion estimation from the conventional text was for estimating superficial emotion expression mainly. However emotions may be included in human's utterance even if emotion expressions are not in it. In this paper, we proposed an emotion estimation algorithm for conversation sentence. We gave the rules of emotion occurrence to 1616 sentence patterns. In addition, we developed a dictionary which consisted of emotional words and emotional idioms. The proposed method can estimate emotions in a sentence by matching the sentence pattern of emotion occurrence and the rule. Furthermore, we can get two or more emotions included in the sentence by calculating emotion parameter. We constructed the experiment system based on the proposed method for evaluation. We analyzed weblog data including 253 sentences by the system, and conducted the experiment to evaluate emotion estimation accuracy. As a result, we obtained the estimation accuracy of about 60 %.

1 Introduction

Recently, there have been some attempts to simulate human sensibility using computers in the research field of affective information processing. One aim is to realize an affective computer which can behave as a human. The human aspects of AIBO [1] and Ifbot [2] are the results of similar attempts. This research tries to make artificial behavior of robots more acceptable to people by copying animal behavior or human facial expressions. These robots focus on representing human emotions rather than understanding them. The emotional state of one party in a conversation is also an important condition for eliciting emotional responses from another party. For example, we might sympathize for unhappiness of an intimate friend as if we experience the same unhappiness. In such empathy, the other party's emotional state affects the occurrence of our emotion. In other words, the emotion recognition and the emotion expression have interacting relations. This paper proposes an emotion estimation method designed primarily more for conversations. Interactive relation between one party's emotions and another party's emotions combine with traditional methods which mainly focus on extracting emotional meaning of words and sentences.

D.-S. Huang, K. Li, and G.W. Irwin (Eds.): ICIC 2006, LNAI 4114, pp. 902–911, 2006.

2 Algorithm for Estimating Human Emotions

This Section proposes an emotion estimation algorithm and describes the estimation flow produced by the algorithm. By inputting conversations, an "emotion dictionary," "image value database," and "favor value database" are identified and "emotion attribute," "attribute image value" and "likability" are decided for each word in the conversations. Next, the "modifier dictionary" enlarges or reduces an emotion attribute for each noun or verb. The sentence pattern is searched for in the "emotion occurrence phenomenon dictionary." When the same pattern is found in the dictionary, the emotion attribute value is set for the sentence according to the emotion occurrence rule. The emotion parameter is calculated and one emotion out of 12 emotions (Table 1) is judged.

Table 1. 12 Emotions

Joy	Pleasure	Anticipation
Reception	Adoration	Surprise
Sadness	Disgust	Anger
Fear	Regret	Anxiety

3 Emotion Dictionary

Section 3 explains the emotion dictionary constructed in our research. Emotional evaluation (emotion attribute) for each semantic attribute of words included in the "Japanese Lexicon"[3] was used to construct the emotion dictionary. Table 2 shows 19 emotion attributes. Table 3 shows the total number of emotion word and emotion idiom.

3.1 Emotion Attributes of Words

The semantic attributes of general nouns defined in the "Japanese Lexicon"[3] are classified as "Emotion," "Personal Emotion," "Interpersonal Emotion," "Sentiment," "Mood," etc. Extracted general nouns from the "Japanese Lexicon" were 1) nouns belonging to the subordinate semantic attributes from the category of "emotion" and 2) nouns belonging to the semantic attributes expressing emotions from the categories: "facial expression" and "disposition." There was

Table 2. Emotion Attributes

Joy	Anger	Sadness	Fear
Shame	Like	Dislike	Excitement
Relief	Surprise	Approbation	Appreciation
Reception	Regret	Boast (Pride)	Respect
Contempt	Hope	Equilibrium	

Table 3. The Total Number of Emotion Word and Emotion Idiom

Noun	Verb	Adjective
1438	937	1834
Adverb	Interjection	Idiom
4890	81	582

further extraction of words which express emotions by themselves. Emotion attributes consist of the 10 kinds of emotions identified in the "Emotion Expression Dictionary" plus "Equilibrium," "Approbation," "Appreciation," "Reception," "Regret," "Boast," "Respect," "Hope," and "Contempt." These attribute values have three steps from 1 to 3 according to their expression levels. Words with added emotion attribute values are put in the emotion dictionary. Except for emotion attributed words, attribute image values, which give images of positive/negative to semantic attributes with emotional evaluation functions, are created. In the emotion attributes, words with positive attribute image values belong to "Like" and words with negative attribute image values belong to "Dislike." The attribute image values are registered in the image value database independently from the emotion dictionary. The emotion attribute values and the attribute image values are used to calculate the emotion parameter which will be described in Section 4. Image value of adjectives other than nouns are adopted as attribute image values [4]. Image values are emotional evaluations that are independent from context and have 7 levels from -3 to +3. Image values, emotion attribute values are set for each adjective and registered in the "modifier dictionary".

3.2 Change Emotion Attribute Using Modifier Database

When the modifier modifies the emotion word, emotion attributes are changed. The modifiers are classified into the following four types. (i) direct modification type, (ii) dependence modification type, (iii) no modification type, and (iv) level expression type. The modifier of type (i) compulsorily changes the emotion attribute of the modificand to the emotion attribute of the modifier.

4 Emotion Estimation Method Based on Sentence Pattern of Emotion Occurrence Events and Emotion Parameter

Section 4 discusses the emotion estimation method based on emotion occurrence events. The "Japanese Lexicon" [3] introduces sentence patterns for each word. In the example of "Crying", the sentence patterns are:

- N1 *ga* N2 *ni/de Naku* (N1 cries over N2)

Table 4. Emotion Occurrence Rule

Sentence pattern(S_p)			Sbj	FV of Noun	EA
English	Case Pattern	Predicate			
N1 cries over N2	N1[3]-*ga* , N2[*]-*ni/de*	*Naku*	N1	$f_{N2} <= 0$	Sadness
				$f_{N2} > 0$	Joy
N1 is angry at N2	N1[4]-*ga* , N2[*]-*ni*	*Okoru*	N1	N/A	Anger
N1 laughs at N2	N1[4]-*ga*, N2[*]-*wo*	*Warau*	N1	$f_{N2} >= 0$	Joy
				$f_{N2} < 0$	Contempt
N1 worries about N2	N1[3]-*ga*, N2[*]-*wo*	*Ureeru*	N1	N/A	Anxiety
N1 is flustered by N2	N1[4]-*ga*, N2[1000]-*de*, *Ochitsuki – wo*	*Ushinau*	N1	N/A	Surprise
N1 subdues N2fs pride	N1[4]-*ga*, N2[4]-*no*, *Hana – wo*	*Oru*	N2	N/A	Shame
N1 discommodes N2	N1[3]-*ga*, N2[4]-*ni*, *Meiwaku – wo*	*Kakeru*	N2	N/A	Disgust
N2 is filled with N1	N1[1253]-*ga*, N2[4,41,238]-*ni*	*Komiageru*	N2	N/A	N1fs EA

N1 and N2 are nouns. The emotion expressed by the sentence can differ depending on the noun applicable to N1 and N2. Referring to the example sentence: "*Jiro* cries over his debt," "debt" generally has a negative image. However, the emotion generated in this sentence can be affected by the speaker's attitude to "*Jiro*." Table 4 shows rules for each sentence pattern of declinable words which can generate emotions. The abbreviations in table 4 are as follows.

- $Rule_a$: Restriction condition of semantic attribute
- S_p : Sentence Pattern
- Sbj : Subject which experience the emotion
- FV of Noun: Favor Value of noun
- EA : Occurrence emotion attribute

These rules are registered in the "emotion occurrence event dictionary" and used for emotion estimations, considering the emotional meaning of the sentence.

4.1 Calculation of Emotion Parameter

This section explains a method of calculating Emotion Parameters. The Emotion Parameters "EP" are calculated as follows: The $(x + 1)$ kinds of emotion attribute values, which are included in the predicates, are indicated as $ea_{j,p}$ ($j = 0, 1, 2, ..., x$). The emotion attribute values of other case slot elements are indicated as $ea_{j,ni}$ ($j = 0, 1, 2, ..., x, i = 1, 2, 3, 4, ...$) .

The emotion attribute matrix (EAM) is shown as the formula (1). "W" is a weight matrix whose weight changes according to the element (predicate or N1 – Ni) of the sentence patterns valued most for emotion estimations The weight matrix is shown as the formula (2). "w_i" shows the weight to each case element and "w_p" shows the weight to predicate. The predicate is valued when the sentence pattern is registered in the emotion occurrence event dictionary. Next, the weight is decreased by multiplying 0.5 when the predicate has past modality or unconfirmed modality. However, when the predicate has past modality, the weight for the emotion attribute value "Regret" is not decreased and when the predicate has unconfirmed modality, the weight for the emotion attribute values

"Anticipation," and "Anxiety" and "Fear" are not decreased, either. Finally, the speaker's emotion can be judged from the emotion attribute with the maximum value. The calculation of "EA" (Emotion Attribute Value Vector) is shown in the formula (3). "EA_c" shows the emotion attribute value vector of current sentence. Next, the Emotion Parameter "EP" of each kind of emotion is calculated. The strength of emotion would be decreased as time goes by. The attenuation of the strength of emotion is expressed by the approximate expression of forgetting curve [5] propounded by Ebbinghaus. The calculation of "EP" is shown in the formula (4). "EP_x" shows the Emotion Parameter when time $t = x$.

$$EAM = \begin{bmatrix} ea_{0,p} & ea_{0,n1} & \cdots & ea_{0,ni} \\ ea_{1,p} & ea_{1,n1} & \cdots & ea_{1,ni} \\ \vdots & \vdots & \ddots & \vdots \\ ea_{x,p} & ea_{x,n1} & \cdots & ea_{x,ni} \end{bmatrix} * W \tag{1}$$

$$W = \begin{bmatrix} w_0 & w_1 & w_2 & \ldots & w_n & w_p \end{bmatrix} \tag{2}$$

$$EA_c = \sum_{i=0}^{n-1} ea_i * w_i + ea_p * w_p \tag{3}$$

$$EP_x = EA_x + \sum_{t=0}^{x-1} \frac{1}{(x - t + \frac{1}{x})^{(x-1)}} * EA_t. \tag{4}$$

5 Structuring the Emotion Estimation System

Section 5 suggests an emotion estimation system based on the proposed methods in the previous sections. Fig.1 shows a structure of Emotion Estimation System, and Fig.2 shows a screenshot of the system interface. By showing Fig.1 , we will explain the module 'A' (analyze sentences), the module 'B'(set emotion attributes), the module 'C'(match sentence patterns), the module 'D'(judge wordings), the module 'E' (calculate emotion parameters), the module 'F' (estimate emotions). The process flow of the emotion estimation system is as follows. First, in module 'A', on inputted sentence is converted to surface frame expression using the parsing result. Second, in module 'B', words included in the sentence are emotion attribute value is set by using the Emotion Dictionary. Third, in module 'C', the result of sentence analysis is matched with a sentence pattern in the Emotion Occurrence Event Dictionary. Forth, module 'D', judges the aspect and the wording of the sentence by using the Aspect and Wording Dictionary. Fifth, in module 'E', the emotion parameter is calculated by using the Personal Pronoun DB and the Intimacy DB. Finally, in module 'F', the emotion is estimated by using emotion estimation rules.

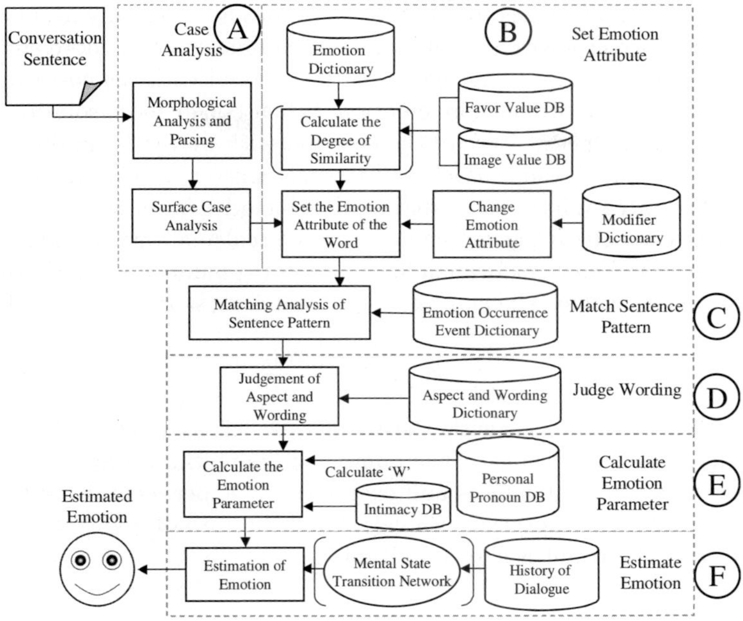

Fig. 1. Structure of Emotion Estimation System

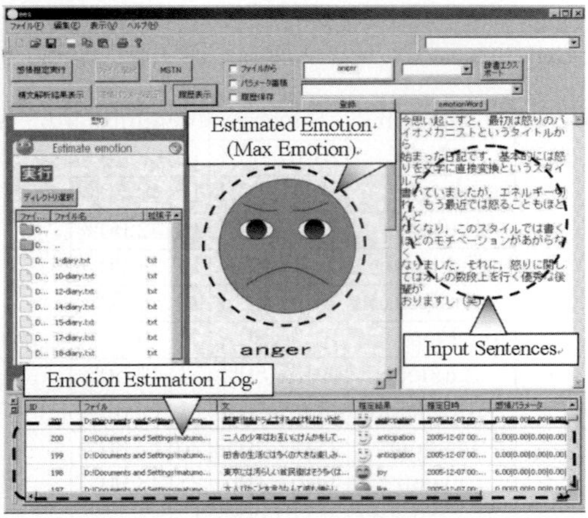

Fig. 2. Interface of Emotion Estimation System

6 Experimentation

To confirm the effectiveness of the method, the prototype system was run on 253 sentences from weblogs. The evaluation method is as follows:

(1) The speaker' emotions towards the sentences are manually decided, which are set as the correct answers. (One sentence can have two or more emotions.)

(2) The output results of the system are compared with the correct answers. Many sentences show two or more emotion. When two or more solutions are obtained by the system, we evaluate the emotion with over 0.5 emotion attribute value. If the estimated result matches the correct answer, we give 1.0 as matching score. On the contrary, if the estimated result is included in the same class with the correct answer, we give 0.5 as matching score. The calculation of evaluation figure for each sentence is shown in formula (5). C shows the number of emotion attribute which has over 0.5 value. The val_n shows the matching score(0 or 0.5 or 1.0).

$$Score = \frac{\sum_{n=0}^{c-1} val_n}{c} \tag{5}$$

We defined the sentence with the score over 0.5 as success. The result of experiment is shown in Table 5. The numbers in parenthesis represents unkown. The following section introduces and examines the experimental results of both success and failure. In addition, we calculated the rate of a correct answer for each emotion. The result is shown in Table 6.

Table 5. Result of the Experimentation

Success	Failure
160(63.2%)	93 (36.8%)

Table 6. The Rate of Correct Answer for Every Kind of Emotion

Emotion	Success		Failure	
Joy	25	67.60%	12	32.40%
Anger	22	59.50%	15	40.50%
Sadness	12	48.00%	13	52.00%
Surprise	28	71.80%	11	28.20%
Anticipation	46	61.30%	29	38.70%
Fear	10	90.90%	1	9.10%
Anxiety	69	57.50%	51	42.50%
Adoration	7	87.50%	1	12.50%
Disgust	27	57.40%	20	42.60%
Pleasure	44	61.10%	28	38.90%
Reception	35	72.90%	13	27.10%
Regret	5	83.30%	1	16.70%

6.1 Example of Success

Successful results were obtained in the following sentences.

[1] " There were varieties of vegetables other than this. All the vegetables had a profound feeling and were really good. I felt I had a good deal for the first time in a long period."

- Estimated result (correct answer): "Joy"

Example[1] has the phrase corresponding to the emotion occurrence event "N1 is good" therefore the emotion "Joy" was obtained successfully.

6.2 Example of Failure

The failure example is shown as follows.

[2] "When I went out from the office for home, it was rather tepid and smelled bloody outside, making me feel uplifted. Spring comes soon. I'm floating on air ⋆ ."

- (Estimated result) : "Disgust"
- (Correct answer) : "Anticipation" or "Pleasure"

[3] "Today is my darling's bonus-day. Because for our family, at the beginning of fiscal year 2005 the amount of bonus amount was decided as a result of the spring offensive, we don't have a feeling that it will be 'high (∗/ ▽ /∗) ' or low (/◇ ≤) .' Anyway, we are glad on this day."

- (Estimated result) : "Equilibrium"
- (Correct answer) : "Joy"

Example[2] failed in collating to the emotion attribute "dislike" which is a negative emotion of "Disgust" with the adjective " lukewarm" and " bloody". The " ⋆ " signs in the sentence show the happy or pleasurable state of mind of the speaker (writer). Example[3] failed because the expression "as was expected + happy" suggests that positive phrase should immediately follow the expression. The combination expression of adverb and adjective are not registered in the emotion dictionary. Additionally, one of the reasons for extraction failure is the system cannot handle for emoticons such as (∗/▽/∗) or (/◇ ≤). The meanings of these emoticons are very simple.However, we don't develop the estimation method for emoticon yet. It is because the emotional meaning of a emoticon may change depending on the co-occurrence with emotions which a sentence expresses.

6.3 Discussion

More successful results are obtained from sentences having words corresponding to the vocabulary in the emotion dictionary than words corresponding to the sentence patterns of the occurrence events. The main reasons of the failure results are: (1) not so many sentences matching the sentence patterns of the emotion occurrence events, (2) some symbols such as emoticon is not extracted, (3) emotion expression phrases are not considered. Contrasting conjunction special character sets such as emoticons, onomatopoeias, mimetic words and adverbs might be important elements describing emotions. Therefore, it is necessary to extract these features from a large amount of weblogs and conversational sentences in order to build new rules for emotion estimations. We would like to propose the extraction method of emoticon which express emotions. The proposed method considers interpersonal relationships between the speakers (writers), but, the experiment was conducted on weblogs. Therefore, we plan to construct the prototype system which recognizes emotions with the emotion vocabulary and the emotion expression phrase are collected by using the conversation sentence of the chat system etc. , and the interpersonal relationship registered beforehand. In future research, we would like to conduct an experiment on e-mail sentences in order to confirm the effectiveness of the emotion estimation rules based on interpersonal relationships.

7 Conclusion

This paper, reports on an emotion estimation system (as basic research) constructed to create an affective robot which can recognize emotion based on language information obtained from utterances and can behave more like humans. In future studies, the sentence patterns of the emotion occurrence event should be expanded and the emotion vocabulary in the emotion dictionary should be better arranged. To estimate emotion varieties generated from a pattern, requires occurrence conditions such as information of conjunctions, adverbs and contexts, the element of emotion continuity in addition to the case slot information. We would like to construct an emotion estimation method more similar to human emotional state based on the concepts of time and mental state transitions in order to estimate. In addition, it is necessary to add adverbs, onomatopoeias and mimetic words to the emotion dictionary in order to consider the emotional meanings of these words. By using intimacy degree between speakers, we can make an emotion estimation system which estimate empathy, too. Moreover, we plan to construct the emotion recognition mobile-phone system as applied application of proposed method.

Acknowledgement

This research has been partially supported by the Ministry of Education, Culture, Sports, Science and Technology of Japan under Grant-in-Aid for Scientific Research (B), 14380166, 17300065, Exploratory Research, 17656128.

References

1. AIBO Offcial Site: http://www.jp.aibo.com/
2. M. Kanoh, S. Iwata, S. Kato and H. Itoh : Emotive Facial Expressions of Sensitivity Communication Robot "Ifbot", Kansei Engineering International, Vol.5, No.3 (2005) 35-42
3. Satoru, I., Masahiro, M., Satoshi, S., et al.: A Japanese Lexicon, Iwanami Shoten (1999)

4. Yoshifumi, H., Hideko, A.: Adjective Usage Dictionary, Tokyodo (1991)
5. Gray, P.: Psychology NY, Worth publishers, (1991)
6. Fuji, R.: Recognizing Human Emotion and Creating Machine Emotion, INFORMATION, Vol.8, No.1, ISSN , January (2005)1343-4500
7. Kazuyuki, M., Fuji, R., Shingo, K.: An Algorithm for Measuring Human Emotions based on Context and Sentence Pattern, Proceedings of the third International Conference on Information (2004) 215-218
8. Kazuyuki, M., Junko, M., Fuji, R., Shingo, K.: Estimating Human Emotion Using Wording and Sentence Pattern, IEEE International Conference on Information Acquisition, Hong Kong and Macau (2005) 421-426

Acoustic and Physiological Feature Analysis of Affective Speech

Dandan Cui and Lianhong Cai

Key Laboratory of Pervasive Computing (Tsinghua University), Ministry of Education
Beijing 100084, P.R. China
cuidd02@mails.tsinghua.edu.cn,
clh-dcs@tsinghua.edu.cn

Abstract. The paper presents our recent work on the acoustic and physiological feature analysis of affective speech. An affective speech corpus is first built up. It contains passages read in neutral state and ten typical emotional states selected in Pleasure Arousal Dominance (PAD) space. Physiological data, including electrocardiogram, respiration, electro dermal data, and finger pulse, are also collected synchronized with speech. Then, based on the corpus, the relationship between emotional categories\dimensions and acoustic\physiological features is analyzed in three methods: average, correlation and co-clustering. The analysis results show that most acoustic features and physiological features are significantly correlated with the arousal dimension, whereas respiration features are more correlated with the pleasure dimension.

1 Introduction

Affective computing refers to computing that relates to, arises from, or deliberately influences emotions [1]. It is very appealing if the computer can recognize emotions in speech signal or synthesis affective speech in human-computer interaction. To reach these goals, the emotionally correlated features in speech signal should be first analyzed. Most previous works focused on analyzing features of basic categories of emotion [1] [2] [3], and the analyses of more emotions were often qualitative [1] [2]. Usually analyzed emotionally correlated features include prosodic features (F0, duration, and energy) and spectral features [2] [3]. However, the basic emotional categories are not sufficient to reflect the subtle changes of human emotions, and studies have demonstrated that physiological features are also important in analyzing emotions besides prosodic and spectral features [6].

In our work of affective speech analysis, emotions are described by the Pleasure, Arousal, and Dominance (PAD) emotion space [4]. Corpus containing 11 emotions which covers the PAD space is first built up. The emotional data are collected by asking the subjects read pre-designed passages with the desired emotion. Physiological data, including electrocardiogram, respiration, electro dermal data, and finger pulse, are also recorded synchronized with speech to give more information about the emotional states [1]. Then, to find the correlates of emotions, 16 features including 7 acoustic and 9 physiological ones are extracted. Unlike previous qualitative analysis, the speech and emotions are analyzed quantitatively in 3 methods. First, to compare

D.-S. Huang, K. Li, and G.W. Irwin (Eds.): ICIC 2006, LNAI 4114, pp. 912–917, 2006.

the emotionally distinctive abilities of features, their averages in each of the emotions are calculated separately. Secondly, to see their correlations with PAD dimensions more clearly, correlation coefficients between the features and PAD coordinates are calculated. Co-clustering is a fairly new method which can group features and samples simultaneously [7]. Then thirdly, a co-clustering analysis is made to grouping both the samples and features to investigate the correlations among features.

The rest of this paper is organized as follows: Section 2 introduces the corpus we built to support the analysis. Then in section 3, we extract the acoustic and physiological features; and section 4 makes analysis. Finally, conclusions are drawn with discussions in section 5.

2 Corpus

First, a corpus is built according to the needs of our analysis.

2.1 Describing the Emotional States

Emotion can be described with categories or dimensions [1]. Categories are typically too rough to represent the subtle differences between emotions. While only two continuous dimensions are traditionally agreed on: "arousal", and "valence". In this research, we use the PAD space [4] to represent emotions.

PAD Emotion Model is a 3D emotion model getting increasing applications in human-computer interaction. It has three nearly independent dimensions: Pleasure-Displeasure (P), Arousal-Nonarousal (A), and Dominance-Submissiveness (D). We take it as the base of our descript system because: the D dimension can be really helpful, e.g. in dialog systems; it is a quantified model so that it can distinguish all emotional states as points in the 3D space; furthermore, reliable and valid measure method is offered, and its Chinese Version is also developed.

Besides the neutral, we select ten typical emotions that are typical and can cover all the octants of PAD space. They are: exuberant, relaxed, docile, disdainful, disgusted, angry, fearful, anxious, surprised, and sad.

2.2 Script Design

As our analysis requires the speech to be under strict control, the modality is designed as reading/reciting of passages under certain situation. 10 passages are designed for each category, and each passage contains 100 syllables or so. For situation selection, we refer to a previous work of Dr. Mehrabian, the author of PAD [5]. In every passage, we embedded a sentence that is emotionally unbiased. Here is an example:

Situation：[今天，你被升职了。你迫不及待地要告诉你的爱人，你们终于可以拥有一起向往已久的房子了！]

Script：把准备好的放着新家钥匙的盒子轻轻放在她手上，在看到她打开盒子眼睛里绽放出喜悦光彩的那一瞬间，我雀跃了，紧紧地握着她的手，就像紧紧握着幸福一样，每一个细胞都仿佛呼吸着一种叫做喜悦的情绪，我不由得说：“啊，我们有自己的家了！将来我们的孩子在那里长大，然后结婚，生子，你和我就天天哄孙子~”

Sentence across emotions:每一个细胞都仿佛呼吸着一种叫做　的情绪，我不由得说：“啊，

2.3 Data Collection and Processing

Speaker Selection: The current 20 speakers, including 10 boys and 10 girls, are selected from more than 100 chief subjects in a previous experiment. The age ranges from 18 to 25.
Recording: The speaker reads or recites the script, imaging himself in the situation. Besides speech, physiological data is also collected. It includes electrocardiogram, respiration, electro dermal data, and finger pulse.
Data Processing: Boundaries of prosodic constituents are annotated, and the F0 contours as well. Besides the emotional categories, PAD values are also scored.

Finally, we got a data set of 2200 passages from 20 speakers and accordingly 2200 samples of emotionally unbiased sentence. Passage segmenting and prosodic boundary marking are finished. F0 value annotation for male speech is ready. And PAD scoring is in process.

3 Feature Extraction

We extract 16 features from all the emotionally unbiased sentences, 7 from speech data and 9 from physiological data. Physiological features are a bit more because we are not sure about which of them are significant for affective computing.

3.1 Acoustic Features

In researches on affective speech, prosodic features such as F0 and duration are used most often [2]. Jiang found several spectral ones valuable [3]. Then, we selected 7.

(1), (2): F0 and its first order difference (dF0).
(3): Duration (Dur) of syllable.
(4): Short term energy (Ene).
(5): Spectral Centroid (SC). It reflects the high frequency content in spectrum.
(6): Spectral Flux (SF). It reflects the intensity of spectral flux.
(7): Band Periodicity (BP). It reflects the intensity of the periodicity in spectrum.

3.2 Physiological Features

Physiological data changes following an affective stimulus, and several valuable parameters are agreed on [6]. Considering both significance and reliability, we choose the following 9 features out of electrocardiogram and respiration data.

(1), (2): The peak value of R wave in electrocardiogram (PRH) and its first order difference (dPRH) which may reflect the intensity of heart beat and its variance.

(3), (4): Interval of R wave peak represented in the unit of ms, i.e. heart period (HP), and its first order difference (dHP) which may reflect heart rate and its variance.

(5), (6): The min (minR) and max (maxR) value in respiration data which may reflect the range of respiration.

(7), (8): The mean (meaR) and median (medR) value in respiration data which may reflect the volume of respiration.

(9): The first order difference of value in respiration data (dR).

4 Feature Analysis

Given the features, to find and compare their relations with PAD dimensions and furthermore the correlations among them, we make three analyses as follows.

4.1 Averages

First, averages are calculated within each utterance, then within each emotion.

As Table 1 shows, the features vary significantly with emotional categories. Being consistent with the results of previous researches [3, 6], F0 rises when peoples are surprised, exuberant, disgusted, fearful, anxious, or angry and so does the speech rate and heart rate; DF0 is highest when fearful; energy is high in anxiety and anger and so on. Surprise and Exuberance are emotions that can not be well distinguished from each other in speech, but their dHP and respirational features are quite different.

Table 1. Everages of features within each emotion.

	Neutral	Relaxed	Docile	Surprised	Exuberant	Disdainful	Disgusted	Fearful	Sad	Anxious	Angry
F0	127.1	144.2	141.86	218	230.75	178.45	207.92	259.62	174.51	249.59	230.52
DF0	2.209	2.873	2.764	4.542	4.6340	2.923	3.831	5.08	3.170	4.883	4.762
Dur	0.138	0.123	0.121	0.094	0.103	0.113	0.102	0.088	0.129	0.096	0.078
Ene	39.315	34.113	33.917	43.836	43.925	40.725	41.891	42.924	40.162	45.616	45.357
SC	2274.7	2362.5	2346.4	2715.9	2774.8	2571.7	2877.1	3090.3	2484.9	3045.4	3155.4
SF	0.265	0.276	0.316	0.640	0.646	0.433	0.585	0.716	0.435	0.678	0.797
BP	0.684	0.777	0.701	0.630	0.644	0.706	0.631	0.644	0.714	0.643	0.662
PRH	0.963	0.974	0.945	0.959	0.959	0.957	0.959	0.955	0.937	0.937	0.918
dPRH	0.075	0.0823	0.0812	0.126	0.117	0.0914	0.110	0.128	0.092	0.115	0.114
HP	687.49	674.29	682.91	640.08	621.57	676.29	625.78	596.08	646.71	609.73	606.34
dHP	12.614	12.359	14.78	13.445	9.5273	12.813	11.108	9.3339	13.463	9.709	9.4175
minR	-0.5	2.8182	4.7273	-0.727	1.25	0.7	2.4167	4.2857	-2.636	5.75	5.3
maxR	6.7	7.2727	7.5455	7.5455	7.5833	7.7	7.8333	8	7.9091	8	8
meaR	5.386	6.3049	6.8825	5.9828	6.9499	6.5249	7.1031	7.7514	6.2398	7.8595	7.8301
medR	5.695	6.4243	6.8923	6.5794	7.4335	7.0652	7.4383	7.942	7.0098	7.9741	7.9599
10^3 dR	2.087	1.451	9.98	2.896	1.884	1.792	1.614	1.222	2.27	0.994	1.042

4.2 Correlation Coefficients Between Features and PAD Coordinates

Features seem to relate to different emotional aspects. We calculated the correlation coefficients between each feature and its PAD coordinates to see more clearly.

As it shows in table 2, most of the features have high correlation coefficients with the dimension A, within which BP has the highest. For the dimension P, SC, PRH, maxR and medR have correlation coefficients above 0.5. It may implicate that respirational features are more correlative with the intensity of pleasure in emotion. The dimension D is almost unrelated with any of the features.

4.3 Co-cluster

Then, co-clustering is utilized. It is a fairly new method. Not like the traditional clustering, it can group the features and samples simultaneously [7]. Thus, not only the sample clustering is optimized, but the features' correlations are also mined out.

Table 2. The correlation coefficient between features and their PAD coordinates

	P	A	D
F0	-0.38306	0.80821	-0.11271
DF0	-0.22349	0.83314	-0.13742
Dur	0.27241	-0.76929	-0.055276
Ene	-0.47356	0.82093	-0.011013
SC	-0.52391	0.80376	0.018542
SF	-0.38452	0.83607	-0.025527
BP	0.23345	-0.88642	0.19527
PRH	0.50317	-0.18226	0.21604
dPRH	-0.20754	0.84108	-0.14404
HP	0.43712	-0.81251	0.086374
dHP	0.39947	-0.74481	-0.28249
minR	-0.12943	0.3115	0.03945
maxR	-0.57247	0.32324	-0.15557
meaR	-0.45274	0.49517	-0.00038422
medR	-0.53809	0.52052	-0.010612
dR*	0.27194	-0.02983	-0.098619

Both the result of speech sample and feature are satisfying, especially the later.

Speech Clustering Result: Co-clustering using the acoustic features gets a pretty good precision of 83.9%. Co-clustering with all the 16 features raises the precision to 87.2%. The physiological features really help, but more features are still needed.

Feature Grouping Result: We tried to change the min group number from 2 to 3, and the max from 3 to 8, while the grouping result of features keeps unchanged. It is:

Table 3. Feature groups in the co-clustering result

Group ID	Features
1	F0, DF0, SF, dHP, minR
2	Dur, BP, PRH, HP, dPRH, dR
3	Ene, SC, maxR, meaR, medR

As it shows in table 3, the grouping result is similar with previous, but not the same. All the features in group 1 have high correlation coefficients with the dimension A, except for minR. While BP is in group 2, which contains most heart activity features. The third group contains most respirational features. In short, the grouping result shows correlation with PAD dimensions, but may not simply.

5 Conclusion and Discussion

In this study, we build up an affective corpus containing 11 typical emotional categories which covers the PAD space. Both speech data and physiological data are collected. Then, to find the correlates of emotions in the data, 16 features including 7 acoustic and 9 physiological ones are extracted. To compare the emotionally distinctive abilities of features, their averages in each emotion are calculated separately and compared; then, to see their correlations with PAD dimensions more clearly, correlation coefficients between the features and PAD coordinates are calculated and compared; thirdly, a co-clustering analysis is made to grouping both the samples and features to find the correlations among features. The analysis results showed that:

(1) Different features tend to be correlated with different aspects of emotion.
(2) Features are correlated to PAD dimensions but their relations may not be linear correlation or there exist coupling variables.
(3) Features in respect to respiration may have special contributions, particularly to the Pleasure-Displeasure dimension.

It could be further improved by finding new features such as hierarchy of prosody taking breath group and break interval into account.

Acknowledgements

We thank Professor Mehrabian for authorizing us to use the PAD model and the PAD Emotion Scales in our research and giving valuable comments. The work in this paper is supported by National Science Foundation of China (60433030).

References

1. Rosalind, W. P.: Affective Computing. Cambridge, Mass. MIT Press (1997)
2. Cowie, R., Douglas-Cowie, E., Tsapatsoulis, N., *et al.*: Emotion recognition in human-computer interaction. IEEE Signal Processing Magazine, Vol. 18(1) (2001) 32-80
3. Jiang, D.: Acoustic Feature Analysis and Modeling of Emotion Speech. PhD dissertation, Tsinghua University, China (2005)
4. Mehrabian, A.: Pleasure-arousal-dominance: A general framework for describing and measuring individual differences in temperament. Current Psychology: Developmental, Learning, Personality, Social, Vol. 14 (1996) 261-292.
5. Mehrabian, A.: Emotional Correlates of Preferences for Situation-Activity Combinations in Everyday Life. In: Genetic, Social, and General Psychology Monographs, Vol. I23 (4) (1997).
6. Hugdahl, K.: Psychophsiology: the mind-body perspective. Cambridge, Mass., Harvard University Press (1995)
7. Dhillon, I.S., Mallela, S. and Modha, D.S.: Information Theoretic Co-clustering. In: Proc. of the 9th ACM SIGKDD International Conference on Knowledge Discovery and Data Mining, Washington. DC, USA (2003) 89-98

Determining the Emotion of News Articles

David B. Bracewell[1], Junko Minato[1], Fuji Ren[1,2], and Shingo Kuroiwa[1]

[1] Department of Information Science and Intelligent Systems
Faculty of Engineering, The University of Tokushima
Minami-Josanjima-Cho Tokushima-shi 770-8506, Japna
{davidb, j_minato, ren, kuroiwa}@is.tokushima-u.ac.jp
[2] School of Information Engineering
Beijing University of Posts and Telecommunications
Beijing 100876, China

Abstract. Authors of news stories through their choice in words and phrasing inject an underlying emotion into their stories. A story about the same event or person can have radically different emotions depending on the author, newspaper, and nationality. In this paper we propose a system to judge the emotion of a news article based on emotion word, idiom and modifier dictionaries. This type of system allows one to judge the world opinion on varying topics by looking at the emotion used within news articles about the topic.

1 Introduction

We exist in a world of emotion and opinion. These feelings are brought out in the manner and depth that events are covered in the news. Determining the emotion in news leads to a better understanding of world opinion on an event or topic.

Even within a country, different news sources and different parts of the country will have varying opinions and emotions toward a topic. For example, drilling for oil in Alaska is more likely to have a stronger negative emotion in Alaska than in Florida. Politics have always been entwined in news and major media [1]. By understanding the emotion toward certain topics found in news, the political climate for a region can be roughly determined. Whether used for judging the views of a people or by politicians to get a rough idea on their standing in an area, this research has wide-spread uses.

Recently a good deal of research has been done on emotion classification and prediction. Alm et al. look at emotion prediction in children's fairy tales [2]. [3] presents an emotion classification system that was tested and trained on marriage counseling data. [4] describe emotion classification for text in internet chat. Despite the interest and research done on emotion classification there has been no work on classifying emotion in news.

As such, we present an initial look at identifying the emotion of news articles. The emotion is narrowed down to three types; positive, negative and neutral. This paper looks at the creation of an emotion dictionary and a simple word-based algorithm for classification.

D.-S. Huang, K. Li, and G.W. Irwin (Eds.): ICIC 2006, LNAI 4114, pp. 918–923, 2006.

This paper will continue as follows, in section 2 the creation of the emotion dictionary is discussed. In section 3, the classification algorithm is given. Then, in section 4 the experimental results are shown. Finally, in section 5 concluding remarks are made and future research discussed.

2 Emotion Dictionary

The dictionary was semi-automatically created using WordNet [5] and a standard English thesaurus. The creation process is shown in figure 1. The first step is to enter a word and whether it is a positive (+) or negative (-) emotion word. The word is then looked up in WordNet and any senses that are hyponyms or have related forms that are hyponyms of emotion or emotional-state are gathered. For each of those senses all the hyponyms under it are extracted.

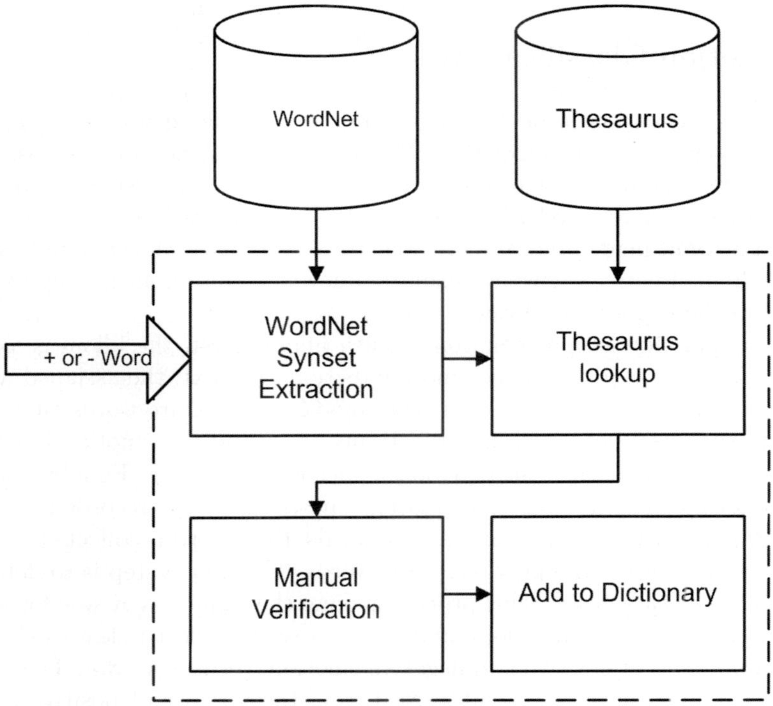

Fig. 1. Dictionary Creation Overview

After a set of words are gathered in WordNet they are looked up in the thesaurus. The synonyms as well as alls the antonyms are collected. The antonyms get assigned an emotion opposite the inputed emotion, i.e. if the inputted word was positive emotion then the antonyms would have negative emotion. Once collection of words from the thesaurus is done the proposed additions to the dictionary are sent for user verification. This is to ensure that the emotion dictionary is kept accurate.

In addition to the WordNet and thesaurus based creation, news articles were mined for possible emotion causing words. Certain words, such as "war" and "fight" have an emotion attached to them, but are not themselves emotion words. A set of articles that were manually tagged with emotion were mined and the most frequent words were examined by humans. Phrases and idioms were also gathered and examined by humans. Those words and phrases that were judged to be useful were added to the dictionary.

The last thing to be collected was common modifiers that would negate the emotion. In English, these include words such as "not" and they often appear a short distance before the emotion word. In the end, three dictionaries were collected; word, idiom (phrase) and modifier. In total about 1,000 emotion words, 100 emotion idioms and 10 emotion modifiers were extracted.

3 Emotion Classification

Emotion classification is done using a simple word-based approach. Figure 2 shows an overview of the algorithm. The algorithm is done in five steps.

In the first step, emotion idioms are searched for and extracted from the article. In their place "NULL" place holders are inserted. In addition to the idiom, a window made up of the previous three words are collected and assigned to the idiom. Figure3 shows an example in which the idiom is "'flying like a kite"' and the window is "'I really am."'

The second step assigns emotion to each idiom. First, the idiom is assigned the emotion that is given in the emotion dictionary. Next, the assigned window is searched for modifier words. For now, modifier words are words that negate emotion, such as "'not"' or "'never."' If any are found the emotion is negated, meaning for example a positive emotion becomes negative. Finally, the total numbers of positive and negative emotions are counted and recorded.

The third step is to search for emotion words. Each word is collected as well as a window made up of the previous three words. The fourth step is to determine the emotion of each word. This process is done the same way it was for idioms.

After the emotion of the idioms and words present in the article are calculated, the total number of positive and negative emotion words is known. The number of negative emotion words is subtracted from the number of positive emotion words to give an emotion score, see equation 1. To determine the article's emotion the emotion score is thresholded.

The threshold is a range of numbers. Articles with a score that fall below the threshold are assigned negative emotion. Articles with a score that are above the threshold are assigned positive emotion. The articles whose score are in between the threshold are assigned neutral emotion. Through testing the best threshold was discovered to be -4 to 4.

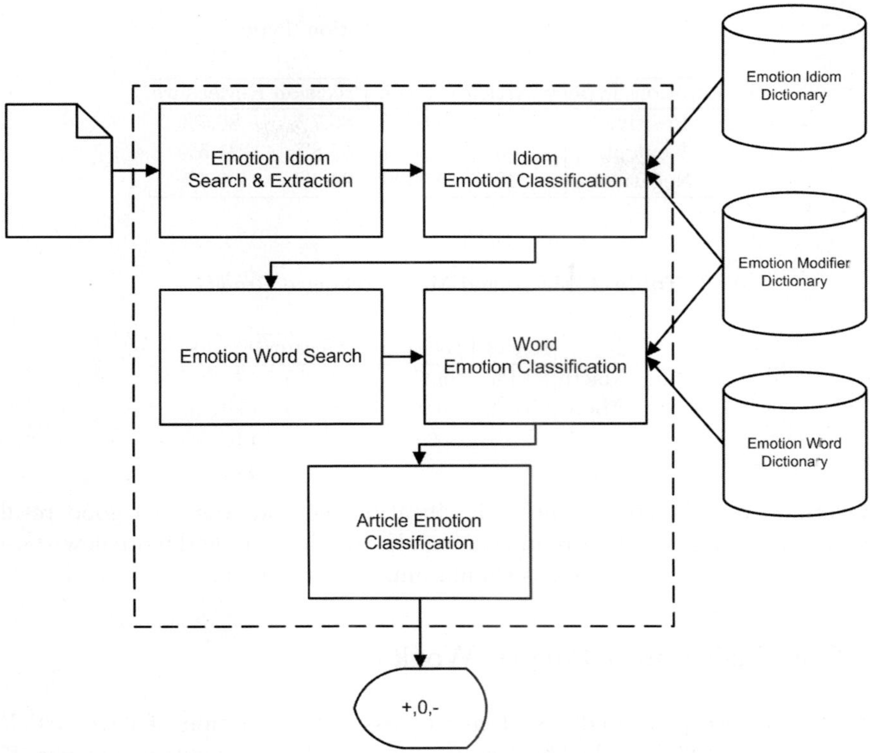

Fig. 2. Classification Overview

[I really am] flying like a kite today.

Fig. 3. Window Example

$$EmotionScore = Total\#ofPositive - Total\#ofNegative \tag{1}$$

4 Experimentation

For experimentation, 100 random news articles were acquired from Yahoo! News[1] and had their emotion manually assigned. Out of the 100 documents, 15 were assigned positive emotion, 45 with neutral emotion, and 40 with negative emotion.

Table 1 shows the recall, precision and f-measure per emotion type. What can be seen from the results is that all emotion types had a recall of at least 85% and precision greater than 86%. Table 2 shows the macro and micro averaged results. It can be seen that both have about a 90% f-measure.

[1] http://news.yahoo.com

Table 1. Results per Emotion Type

Emotion Type	# Articles	Recall	Precision	F-Measure
Positive	15	86.7%	86.7%	86.7%
Neutral	45	95.6%	87.8%	91.5%
Negative	40	85.0%	94.4%	89.5%

Table 2. Macro and Micro Averaged Results

	Recall	Precision	F-Measure
Macro	89.1%	89.6%	89.2%
Micro	90.0%	90.0%	90.0%

Overall, even though a simple classification method was used good results were obtained. With further refinements in the dictionaries and more news-based emotion words added the results should improve even more.

5 Conclusion and Future Work

In this paper we presented a system to classify the emotion of news articles. The articles were classified as having positive, negative, or neutral emotion. The system was able to achieve a macro and micro averaged precision and recall of about 90%. We also found that 85% of the 100 randomly selected articles fell into the negative or neutral emotion category.

We also presented a semi-automatic way of building an emotion dictionary. Using WordNet and an English thesaurus, an initial emotion dictionary was built. Then using a small set of pre-classified articles, common words were extracted and hand verified on whether they should be used to convey emotion or not. A small emotion dictionary of about 1,000 words, 100 idioms, and 10 modifiers was built.

In the future we hope to expand the dictionary to be much larger. We also want to look at using sentence structure to determine emotion. In addition, we hope to build a larger set of experimental data and test machine learning algorithms using the emotion words and sentence structure as features.

Acknowledgement

This research has been partially supported by the Ministry of Education, Culture, Sports, Science and Technology of Japan under Grant-in-Aid for Scientific Research (B), 14380166, 17300065, Exploratory Research, 17656128.

References

1. Cook, T.E.: Governing With the News: The News Media as a Political Institution. University of Chicago Press (1998)
2. Alm, C., Roth, D., Sproat, R.: Emotions from Text: Machine Learning for Text-based Emotion Prediction. In: Proceedings of HLT/EMNLP 2005. (2005)
3. Chambers, N., Tetreault, J., Allen, J.: Approaches for Automatically Tagging Affect. In: Proceedings AAAI Symposium of Exploring Affect and Attitude in Text. (2004)
4. Holzman, L.E., Pottenger, W.M.: Classification of Emotions in Internet Chat: An Application of Machine Learning Using Speech Phonemes. Technical report, Lehigh University (2003)
5. Miller, G.: Wordnet: A Lexical Database for English. Communications of the ACM 38 (1995) 39–41

Statistical Analysis of a Japanese Emotion Corpus for Natural Language Processing

Junko Minato[1], David B. Bracewell[1], Fuji Ren[1,2], and Shingo Kuroiwa[1]

[1] Department of Information Science and Intelligent Systems
Faculty of Engineering, The University of Tokushima
Minami-Josanjima-Cho Tokushima-shi 770-8506, Japan
[2] School of Information Engineering, Beijing University of Posts and Telecommunications, Beijing 100876, China
j_minato@is.tokushima-u.ac.jp

Abstract. In this paper, we build a Japanese emotion corpus and perform statistical analysis on it. We manually entered in about 1,200 example dialogue sentences. We collected statistical information from the corpus to analyze the way emotion is expressed in Japanese dialogue. Such statistics should prove useful for dealing with emotion in natural language. We believe the collected statistics accurately describe emotion in Japanese dialogue.

1 Introduction

A fact of human life is emotion, whether it is happiness, sadness, etc., at some point all humans undergo emotion. Because of this, emotion has become entwined with natural language. As such, to understand natural language and the intention of a speaker we must understand the underlying emotion.

Recently, various research has been done concerning emotion in natural language processing. Some examples are for internet chat [1], machine translation [2] and human-robot interaction [3]. As the importance of dealing with emotion grows, emotion corpora and statistical analysis of emotion is necessary.

In this paper we build a Japanese emotion corpus. The corpus is made up of about 1,200 sentences taken from [4]. Then we manually tagged the words for emotion using 8 categories of emotion. From the tagged corpus we collected statistics to describe emotion in Japanese dialogue and to help deal with emotion in natural language processing (NLP).

This paper will proceed as follows, in section 2 we introduce affective computing and its uses to NLP. In section 3, the annotation of the corpus is described. In section 4 , the collected statistics are examined in detail. Finally, in section 5, we discuss future work and make concluding remarks.

2 Affective Computing and Natural Language Processing

Affective computing is an area of artificial intelligence that focuses on emotion understanding. The development of information technology increased the

D.-S. Huang, K. Li, and G.W. Irwin (Eds.): ICIC 2006, LNAI 4114, pp. 924–929, 2006.

chances of human-computer interaction. Affective computing hopes to improve such interactions, opening the door to many new possibilities.

With the increased use of network computing and personal computers, more information is documented and exchanged through the internet and e-mail. By analyzing the texts and obtaining not only semantic, but also emotional information, the computer can deal with more interpersonal matters such as understanding the relationships between the people or can reuse the information for future decisions. NLP techniques are essential for affective computing when it deals with emotion expressed in language. However, affective computing can also be useful for NLP.

Saeki et.al, suggested the application to machine translation by focusing on emotional adverbs and their sentence structures in Japanese and English to find the translation tendency among both languages [2]. Ma et.al, try to create an internet chat system which can asses the emotion in the textual messages and present the emotion through an avatar in order to realize natural and social communication between distant communication partners [1]. Holzman and Pottenger, also attempt to detect the emotional attributes in chat data for homeland security purposes [5]. In [3], the idea of a welfare robot to assist the elderly using emotion and NLP was discussed.

In order to obtain knowledge and information from emotion text it is necessary to have a reliable tagged emotion corpus. As the study of affective computing combined with natural language processing is rather new, it is still difficult to obtain a tagged emotion corpus. For that reason there is also research underway to create a reliable tagged emotion corpus [6][7].

3 Corpus Annotation

Using [4], Japanese-English sentences were entered to create the untagged corpus. For now only the Japanese sentences have been tagged. The words and idioms from the Japanese sentences had their emotion were manually tagged. Eight basic emotions were decided on; Joy, Hate, Love, Sorrow, Anxiety, Surprise, Anger, and Respect. Single word emotions were tagged with an 'S' meaning "single." Words in an idiom were tagged with 'B,' 'I,' and 'E' for beginning, intermediate, and end. This tagging scheme was taken from [8].

In addition to annotating emotion, emotion modifiers were annotated. An emotion modifier is a word or word phrase that changes the degree of or the type of emotion a word has within in the context of the sentence. A simple example would be "not," which would negate the emotion within in the sentence. Four types of modifiers were chosen (plus, minus, neutral and negative) and they were tagged in the same manner as emotion words and idioms. In the end the corpus included just under 1,200 sentences. From those sentences there were 1,160 single word emotions and 275 emotion idioms.

Table 1. Corpus Statistics

Description	Frequency/Percentage
Total # of Words	14,195
Total # of Unique Words	2,338
Total # of Unique Emotion Words	653
Average # of times an emotion word did not carry emotion	0.22

4 Statistical Analysis

In this section some statistics from the created corpus will be discussed. The first set of statistics can be seen in table 1. The corpus was made up of 1,191 sentences, 14,195 words of which 2,338 were unique. There were 1,160 single word emotions and 275 emotion idioms. 653 unique words were used to describe emotion in the corpus. On average, in single word emotion words, a word that was marked as an emotion was used as a non-emotion only 0.22 times.

Figure 1, shows the frequency of emotion in the corpus. The interesting result was that the four most frequent emotions contain two sets of converse emotions; love and hate, joy and sorrow.

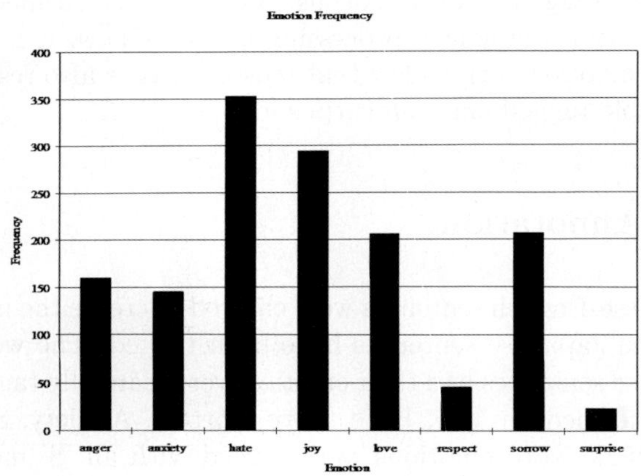

Fig. 1. Emotion Frequency

Figure 2, shows the part-of-speech frequency for the emotion words. It can be seen that nouns and verbs tend to carry emotion in Japanese. Together they account for 75% of all the emotion words.

Figure 3, shows a break down of part-of-speech per emotion. For the most part, the part-of-speech are evenly distributed among the different emotion categories, i.e. the noun frequency is similar across all emotions.

Finally, in figure 4, the distribution of emotion along the sentence can be seen. It was found that emotion often takes place right after the middle of the sentence.

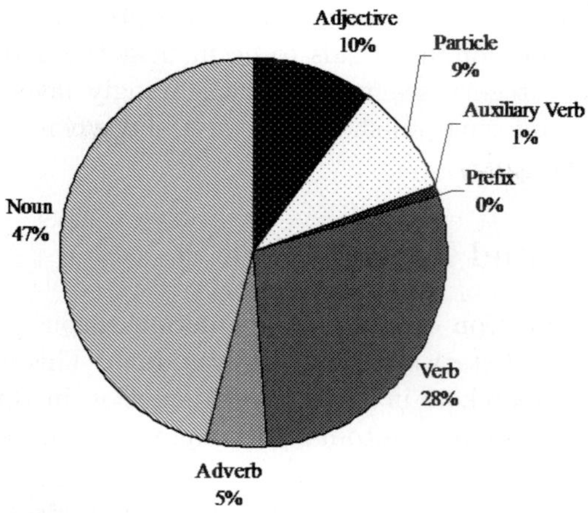

Fig. 2. Part-of-Speech Frequency for Emotion Words

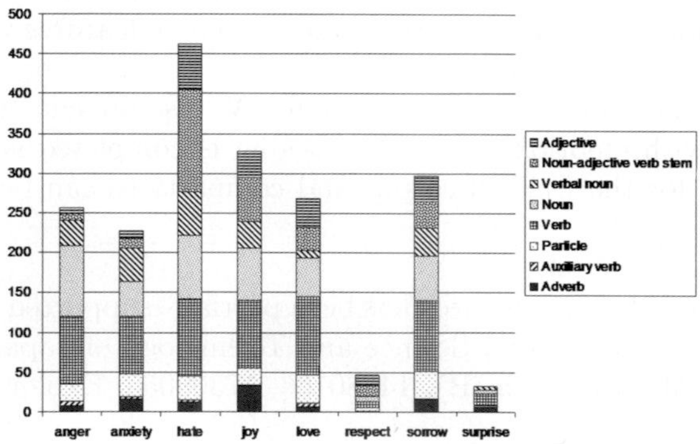

Fig. 3. Part-of-Speech per Emotion Frequency

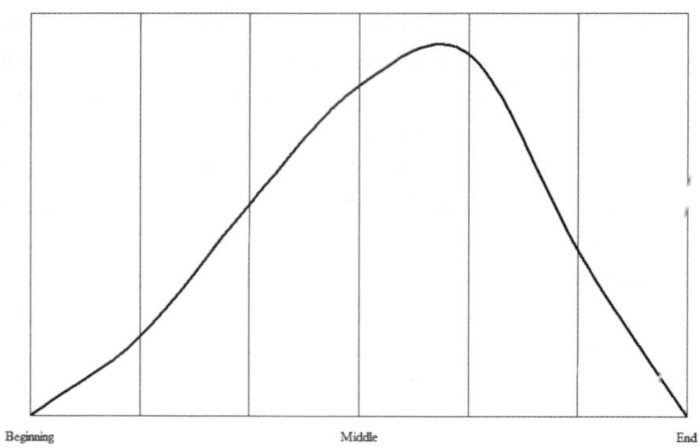

Fig. 4. Distribution of Emotion in a Sentence

The statistics show that emotion in Japanese is predominately described using nouns and verbs. Emotion also tends to occur near the middle of the sentence. Also, no emotion category seems to overwhelmingly favor one part-of-speech over another. This information should prove useful when dealing with emotion in Japanese sentences.

5 Conclusion and Future Work

In this paper the creation of a Japanese emotion corpus was discussed. From the corpus a thorough statistical analysis was done. This analysis, we believe, can benefit NLP researchers in dealing with emotion in text. In addition, the outline for a future system to automatically tag words and idioms with emotion was given.

We found that Japanese tends to use nouns and verbs to describe emotion. Typically emotion is described in only one word and in a sentence emotion tends to occur near the middle. The different emotion categories do not have a bias toward one part-of-speech or another. Finally, we found that for single emotion words, the word usually always carries emotion. These features will suggest how to recognize the emotion from sentences.

In the future, we hope to finish the system. We also are currently tagging the English words with emotion. After the tagging is completed statistical analysis will be done for the English corpus and comparisons can be made between Japanese and English.

Acknowledgement. This research has been partially supported by the Ministry of Education, Culture, Sports, Science and Technology of Japan under Grant-in-Aid for Scientific Research (B), 14380166, 17300065, Exploratory Research, 17656128.

References

1. Ma, C., Osherenko, A., Prendinger, H., Ishizuka, M.: A chat system based on emotion estimation from text and embodied conversational messengers. In: proceedings of the International Conference on Entertainment Computing. (2005) 535–538
2. Saeki, M., Tokuhisa, M., Murakami, J., Ikehara, S.: Comparative analysis of japanese-english adverb focused on emotion expression (in japanese). In: Proceeding of the 11th Language Processing Annual Conference. (2005) 33–36
3. Matsumoto, K., Minato, J., Ren, F., Kuroiwa, S.: Estimating human emotions using wording and sentence patterns. In: Proceedigns of the IEEE International Conference on Information Acquisition. (2005) 421–426
4. Hiejima, I.: Japanese-English Emotion Dictionary. Tokyodo Shuppan (1995)
5. Holzman, L.E., Pottenger, W.M.: Classification of emotions in internet chat: An application of machine learning using speech phonemes. Technical report, Lehigh Tech Report 03-002 (2003)
6. Koshino, T., Tokuhisa, M., Murakami, J., Ikehara, S.: Error analysis of emotion annotated dialogue corpus. In: Proceedings of the 18th Annual Conference of the Japanese Society for Artificial Intelligence. (2004)

7. Tokuhisa, R., Inui, K., Tokuhisa, M., Okada, N.: Two complementary case studies for emotion tagging in text corpora. In: Proceedings of the Japanese Society for Artificial Intelligence SIG-SLUD. (2001)
8. Tanaka, Y., Takamura, H., Okumura, M.: Research concerning facemarks in text based communication (in japanese). In: Proceedings of the 10th Annual Natural Language Processing Conference. (2004)

Treatment of Quantifiers in Chinese-Japanese Machine Translation

Dapeng Yin[1], Min Shao[1], Peilin Jiang[1], Fuji Ren[1,2], and Shingo Kuroiwa[1]

[1] Department of Information Science and Intelligent Systems Faculty of Engineering, The University of Tokushima, Minami-Josanjima-Chou,Tokushima-shi 770-8506, Japan
[2] School of Information Engineering, Beijing University of Posts and Telecommunications, Beijing 100876, China
{yin, shaomin, Jiang, ren, kuroiwa}@is.tokushima-u.ac.jp

Abstract. Quantifiers and numerals often cause mistakes in Chinese-Japanese machine translation. In this paper, an approach is proposed based on the syntactic features after classification. Using the difference in type and position of quantifiers between Chinese and Japanese, quantifier translation rules were acquired. Evaluation was conducted using the acquired translation rules. Finally, the adaptability of the experimental data was verified and the methods achieved the accuracy of 90.75%, which showed that they were effective in processing quantifiers and numerals.

1 Introduction

A lot of practical machine translation systems have rapidly developed during these past years [1]. However, there are several unsolved problems that need to be further explored for Chinese-Japanese machine translation. This paper presents a method for processing quantifier. There are many various quantifiers in Chinese because of the corresponding relationship between modifiers and the modified words in Chinese. On the other hand, there are few quantifiers in Japanese.

To generate translation with correct expressions, this paper puts forward a processing method for translation between Chinese quantifiers and Japanese quantifiers. We have collected a large number of aligned Chinese-Japanese sentences and a lot of articles about the quantifier grammar from variant researches. We also have collected about 5000 aligned sentence pairs that include quantifiers. Then, we parse the Chinese and Japanese sentences [2], compare the results and count position information in the sentences. Then translation rules of corresponding quantifiers for Chinese and Japanese can be obtained. We applied these rules to develop an experiment system in Chinese-Japanese machine translation and have achieved an improved result.

2 Quantifier Translation Model

2.1 Chinese Quantifier Translation Model

A Chinese sentence is morphologically analyzed and checked against which pattern of translation (“One + quantifier”, “The number except 1 + quantifier”, “Indefinite

D.-S. Huang, K. Li, and G.W. Irwin (Eds.): ICIC 2006, LNAI 4114, pp. 930 – 935, 2006.

quantifier") it belongs to, and also confirmed the location information of the quantifiers and their semantic classifications [3][4][5]. Figure 1 shows model of the Chinese-Japanese machine translation system for quantifiers.

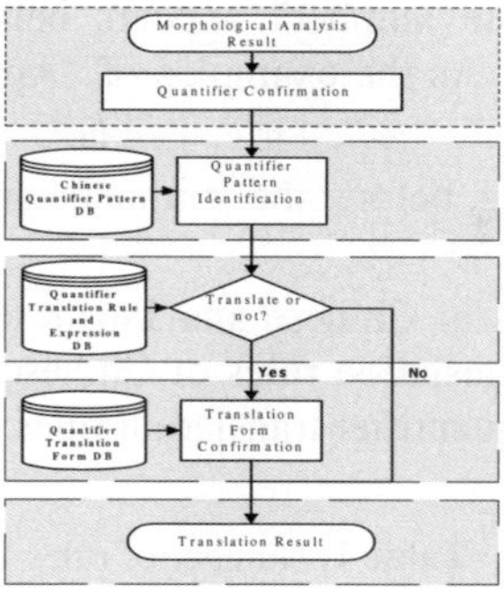

Fig. 1. Model of the Chinese-Japanese machine translation system for quantifiers

2.2 Classification of Chinese Quantifier

Even the same quantifiers have different features depending on where they appear in the sentence. For example, quantifiers are always translated when the quantifiers emphasizes the subjects that appear in the sentence beginning. We further divide the quantifiers into three kinds by the positions on in the sentence as follows (1. Appear at the beginning of the sentence, 2. Appear in the middle of the sentence, 3. Appear in the end of the sentence).

3 Translation Rule of Quantifier Expression and Confirmation of Translation Form

3.1 Translation Rules of Quantifier Expression

Quantifiers are divided into 3 kinds: "One + quantifier", "The number except 1 + quantifier" and "Indefinite quantifier" The "One + quantifier" is divided into two kinds based on the Chinese grammatical characteristics ("Noun quantifiers" and "Verb quantifiers"). "Noun quantifiers" are divided into three kinds (Individual quantifier, aggregate quantifier, measure/time quantifier). When "One + quantifier" appears in front of the sentence, it must be translated. When "One + quantifier" appears in the middle of the sentence, there are three kinds of cases (translation, no translation, and selected translation). When "One + quantifier" appears in the end of the sentence, the quantifiers are either to be translated or no translated. There is no example where the "Verb quantifier" comes in front of the sentence. When "Verb quantifier" appears in the middle of the sentence, it is not translated. When "Verb quantifier" appears in the end of the sentence, it is not translated.

"The number except 1 + quantifier" means all numbers except one and quantifier. Regardless of the position it is always translated.

"Indefinite quantifier" is an important component of quantifiers too; covering; about 9% of the all quantifiers. (Ex. "几个", "几条' etc.) The structure of "Indefinite quantifier" is comparatively complex. "Indefinite quantifier" is divided into two kinds as shown below. One is "Approximate number +quantifier"; and the other is "Indefinite quantifier". "Approximate number" appears before or after the number and means the uncertain quantity. As the examples of "Approximate number" appearing after the numbers mainly "来", "多", "把", "左右", "上下."Etc. There are "Approximate number" appearing before the numbers are such as "成", "上", "近", "约."Etc.

We considered the features of Chinese and Japanese, analyzed collected bilingual corpuses, and collected the translation rules of Chinese-Japanese quantifiers. Table 2 shows the distribution of the quantifier translation rules.

Table 1. Number of rules

	Beginning of Sentence	Middle of Sentence	End of sentence
One + Quantifier	4	20	6
The number except one + Quantifier	1	8	1
Indefinite + Quantifier	2	2	2
Total		46	

3.2 Selection of Japanese Translation Form

There are about 150 common Chinese quantifiers. On the other hand, the Japanese quantifiers are about 50. To solve this problem of translation in Chinese-Japanese quantifiers the quantifiers were analyzed using a large corpus. As the result it has been understood that the quantifiers are limited to the modified noun. Next, analyzed the features of nouns, and created translation rules for 150 Chinese quantifiers for Chinese-Japanese machine translation. Actually, because there are numbers of Chinese nouns, it is impossible to register all nouns into the translation table. "Semantic Similarity"[6] is used to solve this problem that is based on. It calculates by the semantic similarity of "HowNet"[7]. The higher the similarity is, the more often the same quantifiers will be used. Table 2 shows the samples of "Chinese-Japanese quantifier translation table". Next we explain the semantic similarity computational method in detail through one concrete example.

Table 2. Chinese-Japanese quantifier translation table

Chinese quantifier	Type of Translation	Chinese noun set N1	Japanese noun set T1	…	Japanese noun set Tn
条	4	毛巾	Q+枚	…	Q＋隻
只	12	鸟	Q+羽	…	Q＋匹
件	2	衣服	Q+着		
…	…	…	…	…	…

Similarity is calculated by distance between nodes in the thesaurus as expression (1) shows.

$$D=Dis(W1,W2)\ . \tag{1}$$

In expression (1), W1 and W2 represent two nodes respectively. A similarity of two words is represented by the distance between two nodes. A similarity of the words is converted to a similarity of the sememe. Similarity $Sim_1(S_1,S_2)$ of the sememe is decided depending on the distance d in the sememe thesaurus. It shows in expression (2).

$$Sim_1(S_1,S_2)=\frac{a}{d+a}\ . \tag{2}$$

The definition of a word consists of four parts of sememes, basic sememe (BS), other basic sememes (OS), related sememes (RS), and related sign sememes (RSG). Summation of similarities $Sim_j(S_1,S_2)$ of the four parts of sememe becomes similarity of word W1 and W2 as. shown in (3).

The accuracy deciding the entire similarity decreases from sim1 to sim4 as expressed (3) while calculating a similarity. $\beta_i\,(1\le i\le 4)$ is one parameter here that can be adjusted.

$$\begin{aligned}&Sim(W_1,W_2)=\sum_{i=1}^{4}\beta_i\prod_{j=1}^{i}Sim_j(S_1,S_2)\\&(\beta_1+\beta_2+\beta_3+\beta_4=1,\\&\beta_1\ge\beta_2\ge\beta_3\ge\beta_4)\end{aligned}\ . \tag{3}$$

Moreover, in $\beta_1+\beta_2+\beta_3+\beta_4=1,\beta_1\ge\beta_2\ge\beta_3\ge\beta_4$. a basic sememe accomplishes the decision action. β_1 is adjusted to 0.5 or more. When Sim1 is small, and Sim3 or Sim4 is comparatively large, an equation similarity increases, too. It quotes Π to make sure that such an irrational thing will not happen. The value of each parameter was set as $\alpha=1.6,\beta_1=0.5,\beta_2=0.2,\beta_3=0.17,\beta_4=0.13\,\delta=0.2$.

4 Experiments and Evaluation

4.1 Evaluation Experiment and Experimental Result

In this chapter we conducted experiments to evaluate the machine translation of the quantifiers based on our translation rules. The Chinese-Japanese bilingual corpus which we used for the experiment consists of four pieces: "坊ちゃん", "鼻", "斜陽" and"家". 5000 sentences including quantifiers are extracted from them. We used the 5000 sentences, and tested the translation system that we developed. Only the number representation was assumed to be a criterion by the above-mentioned evaluation experiment, and the result in Table 3 was obtained. As the result, the 4365 sentences were successfully translated and the 635 sentences failed. The 190 sentences failed in the Chinese sentence morphological analysis in the failing sentence. The results are shown in Table 3.

Table 3. Experimental results

Sentence	Success	Fail
4810(50000-190)	4365	445(635-190)
	90.75%	9.25%

The open test evaluation experiment was done by using 3000 sentences other than the corpus. Table 4 shows the result.

Table 4. Experimental results

Sentence	Success	Fail
3000	2560	440
	(85.33%)	(14.67%)

4.2 Evaluation and Consideration

Here considered the cause of failing. The translation is as follows while failing.

Firstly, there are two modified nouns. It is necessary to judge the subject that the quantifier modifies when there are two nouns that the quantifier modifies. Such an example has 130 sentences.

The second is vagueness in the modified noun. It can have a different meaning depending on the context even in the same word in Chinese. Even though there is the same noun and the same quantifier, the translation is different when translating into Japanese. Examples of the failure are 54 sentences according to this cause.

5 Conclusions

In this paper, we proposed a technique for translating Chinese amount expression into Japanese, and the quantifiers were classified into three kinds. Moreover, whether to be translated was examined by the appearance position in the sentence, and the translation rule and the Japanese translation form were brought together. The proposed technique is confirmed to be effective in the processing of the quantifiers in the Chinese-Japanese machine translation by the experimental results. According to the experiment, if the semantic features of the noun that a quantifier modifies can be identified, the accuracy of the quantifier processing can be improved.

Acknowledgment

This research has been partially supported by the Ministry of Education, Culture, Sports, Science and Technology of Japan under Grant-in-Aid for Scientific Research (B), 14380166, 17300065, Exploratory Research, 17656128, 2005 and the Outstanding Overseas Chinese Scholars Fund of the Chinese Academy of Sciences (No.2003-1-1).

References

1. Eiji Aramaki, Sadao Kurohashi, Hideki Kashioka, Naoto Kato:Probabilistic Model for Example-based Machine Translation. Proc. of MT Summit X,(2005)219-226
2. Zhang, H. P., Yu, H. K., Xiong, D. Y., Liu, Q.: HHMM-based Chinese Lexical Analyzer ICTCLAS. proceedings of 2nd SigHan Workshop,(2003)184-187
3. Zhu ,X.F., Yu, S.W., Wang, H.: The Development of Contemporary Chinese Grammatical Knowledge Base and it's Applications. Communications of COLIPS 5,(1995)1-2
4. Liu, Y. H., Pan, W. Y., Gu, W.: The Contemporary Chinese Grammatical Compendium. Kuroshio Pub, (1988)
5. Asako IIDA: A Descriptive Study of Japanese Major Classifiers. Ph.D. Thesis ,(1999)
6. Liu, Q., Li, S. J.: Word Similarity Computing Base on HowNet. Computational Linguistics and Chinese Language Processing, Vol.7, No.2, (2002)59-76
7. Dong, Z. D., Dong, Q.: Hownet: http://www. keenage. com/

A Pruning Based Incremental Construction of Horizontal Partitioned Concept Lattice

Lihua Hu[1,*], Jifu Zhang[1,2], and Sulan Zhang[1]

[1] School of Computer Science and Technology, Tai-Yuan University of Science and Technology, Tai-Yuan 030024, P.R. China
hulihua198204151@sohu.com

[2] National Laboratory of Pattern Recognition, Institute of Automation, Chinese Academy of Sciences, Beijing 100080, P.R. China

Abstract. Since the completeness of the concept lattice, its construction efficiency is a key of restricting the application. For the inevitable redundant information occurred in the construction process of partitioned concept lattice, an improved incremental construction algorithm PHCL of horizontal partitioned concept lattice, called the pruning based incremental algorithm is proposed, which uses a pruning process to eliminate redundant information during the construction, to improve the construction efficiency of horizontal partitioned concept lattice. In the end, the experiment results prove the correctness and validity of the pruning based algorithm PHCL by taking the star spectra from the LAMOST project as the formal context.

1 Introduction

From a philosophical point of view, a concept is a unit of thoughts consisting of two parts, the extension and the intension. Based on the philosophical understanding of concept, the formal concept analysis [1] was introduced by Wille in 1982, and later used to detect, sort and display of concepts. Based on the formal concept analysis, the extension covers all objects belonging to this concept and the intension comprises all attributes valid for all those objects, by which the philosophical understanding of concept was realized. By nature, concept lattice describes the relationship between objects and attributes, indicates the relationship of generation and specialization between concepts. Besides, its Hasse diagram is an effective tool of data visualization. Thanks to its straightness, simplicity and completeness of knowledge expressing, the concept lattice has been widely applied in software engineer, knowledge engineering, knowledge discovery and so on [2], [3].

At present, broadly speaking, there are two kinds of concept lattice construction algorithms: The incremental algorithm [4-6] and the patch algorithm [8]. Lots of experiments show that the incremental construction algorithm is a promising one, and the Godin algorithm is a typical incremental construction algorithm.

* Corresponding author: Lihua Hu, "This paper is supported by the National Natural Science Foundation of P. R.China" (60573075).

D.-S. Huang, K. Li, and G.W. Irwin (Eds.): ICIC 2006, LNAI 4114, pp. 936 – 945, 2006.

Due to the completeness of concept lattice, its construction efficiency is always a key problem. The above patch algorithms and incremental algorithms aim at the case of single formal context constructing single concept lattice. With the sharp increasing of the data to deal with, above construction algorithms have the low updating efficiency if the newly added objects have one million or more during the incremental construction of concept lattice. In order to improve the construction efficiency of concept lattice, the construction process can be divided into many pieces, namely one partitioned method. In other words, the newly added objects can be regarded as a new formal context that can construct a new concept lattice, and then the original concept lattice can be united with the new concept lattice. About the union algorithm of concept lattice, a union algorithm of multiple concept lattices [11] and horizontal union algorithm of multiple concept lattices [12] have been proposed.

In the union process of concept lattice, the intension of original concept lattice nodes must be compared with the intension of new concept lattice nodes one by one. As a result, with more concept lattice nodes, the union construction efficiency of multiple concept lattices becomes worse. In fact, much redundant information is generated during the union process, which unnecessarily increases the comparing times of concept lattice intension and has no effect on the structure of concept lattice. Hence how to eliminate or reduce the redundant information in the concept lattice union process is a key issue to increase its construction efficiency. To this end, we propose a technique, coined as "pruning", to eliminate possible redundant information in this work, and propose algorithm PHCL (pruning based incremental construction of horizontal partitioned concept lattice), which decreases comparing times of concept lattice intension, and thus improves the construction efficiency of concept lattice.

2 Concept Lattice and Its Construction

2.1 General Concept Lattice and Its Construction [4, 5]

Definition 1. A formal context is defined as a triplet K=(O, D R), where O is a set of objects, D is a set of attributes and R is a binary order set between O and D, which describes the inherent lattice structure and defines the natural groupings and relationships between the objects and their attributes. This structure is known as a concept lattice or Galois lattice L.

Definition 2. Given a concept lattice L constructed from formal context K, each one of its nodes is a couple, denoted as C (A, B), where $A \in P(O)$ is called the concept lattice extension, $B \in P(D)$ called the concept lattice intension.

Definition 3. Concept lattice L must be a complete couple with respect to R, which means following two conditions are both satisfied for each node C (A, B):

$$(1)\ A=B'=\{a \in O \mid \forall b \in B,\ a\, R\, b\}$$

$$(2)\ B=A'=\{b \in D \mid \forall a \in A,\ a\, R\, b\}$$

Definition 4. In the concept lattice L, if a node $C_i(A_i, B_i)$satisfies the following condition, it is defined as the supermum of this node, denoted as $Sup(C_i)$. (J is the alphabetical order set of concept lattice L)

$$\underset{i\in J}{\vee}(A_i, B_i) = \left(\left(\bigcap_{i\in J} B_i\right)', \bigcap_{i\in J} B_i\right) \tag{1}$$

Definition 5. If $C_1=(A_1, B_1)$ and $C_2=(A_2, B_2)$ are two different nodes, then $C_1<C_2 \Leftrightarrow A_1\subset A_2 \Leftrightarrow B_2\subset B_1$. If there does not exist other node $C_3=(A_3,B_3)$ in the lattice such that $C_1<C_3<C_2$, we say C_1 is the sub(child) concept of C_2 , denoted as C_1=child(C_2); C_2 is the super (parent) concept of C_1, denoted as C_2=father (C_1).

The basic idea of Godin algorithm is that while a new object is added during the incremental construction of concept lattice, its attributes must be compared with the intension of original concept lattice nodes one by one, then adopted different suitable operations based on the intersection difference between the attributes of a newly added object with the intension of the original concept lattice nodes. According to the different intersection, concept lattice nodes can be classified into three cases: old node, modified node and newly added node, and then modified original concept lattice nodes.

2.2 Partitioned Concept Lattice and Its Construction

Definition 6 [11]. Given formal context K_1= (O_1, D_1, R_1) and formal context K_2= (O_2, D_2, R_2), if $D_1=D_2$ and $O_1\cap O_2=\phi$, we can call K_1 and K_2 horizontal partition of formal context. If $O_1=O_2$ and $D_1\neq D_2$,we can call K_1 and K_2 vertical partition of formal context .

Definition 7 [11]. Given K_1 and K_2 are the horizontal partitions of formal context, concept lattice L_1 constructed from formal context K_1, and concept lattice L_2 constructed from formal context K_2, the concept lattice which union L_1 and L_2 is called as horizontal partitioned concept lattice; Given K_1 and K_2 are the vertical partitions of formal context, concept lattice L_1 constructed from formal context K_1, concept lattice L_2 constructed from formal context K_2, the concept lattice which union L_1 and L_2 is called as vertical partitioned concept lattice.

Based on the different intersection between the intension of the new concept lattice nodes with the intension of the original concept lattice nodes, concept lattice nodes can be classified into three cases as follows:

Definition 8 [11]. Let C (A, B) be a node of concept lattice L_1 constructed from formal context K_1, and D (O, S) be a node of concept lattice L_2 constructed from formal context K_2, if the B is a true subset of S (S is a true subset of B), i.e., $B\subset S$ ($S\subset B$), the concept C is called the up-concept of the concept D (the concept C is called the down-concept of the concept D).

Definition 9 [11]. Let C (A, B) be a node of concept lattice L_1 constructed from formal context K_1, and D (O, S) be a node of concept lattice L_2 constructed from formal context K_2. If B=S, the concept C is equal to the concept D.

Definition 10 [11]. Let C (A, B) be a node of concept lattice L_1 constructed from formal context K_1, and D (O, S) be a node of concept lattice L_2 constructed from formal context K_2. If the intersection between B and S, $H=B\cap S$, is not NULL, denoted as $H\neq\Phi$, and additionally satisfy the following two conditions:

(1) H is not equal to the intension of concept lattice L_1 and L_2 nodes
(2) The intersection of H with the intension of concept lattice L_1 and L_2 nodes is not equal to H.

then C is called a newly added concept.

Definition 11 [11]. Let C (A, B) be a node of concept lattice L_1 constructed from formal context K_1, the number of the objects contained in A is called the support of extension of concept C, denoted as $|A|$. The number of the attributes contained in B is called the support of intension of concept C, denoted as $|B|$.

Literature [11] proposed a union algorithm of multiple concept lattices, the basic idea of the algorithm is to compare the intension of concept lattice nodes constructed from new formal context with the intension of original concept lattice nodes one by one. According to the different intersection between nodes, concept nodes can be classified into three kinds: larger concept, equal concept, less concept. Based on the basic idea of Godin algorithm, the nodes of concept lattice adopt different operation.

Taking the formal context that is parted by K_1 and K_2 for example, the time complexity of horizontal partitioned of concept lattice is analyzed as follows: Let the number of concept lattice L_1 nodes constructed from formal context K_1 is U_1, let the number of concept lattice L_2 nodes constructed from formal context K_2 is U_2. In the union process of L_2 and L_1, if the node D (O, S) of L_2 inserts into concept lattice L_1, the most number of added nodes is 2^S. So the time complexity is $O(2^S \times |U_1|)$, and correspondingly the time complexity of the entire nodes of L_2 inserting into L_1 is $0(2^S \times |U_1| \times |U_2|)$.

3 Pruning Based Incremental Construction of Concept Lattice

In the incremental construction process of horizontal partitioned concept lattice, much repeated comparative procedure is existed, which only increases comparing times of concept lattice intension and has no effects on the structure of concept lattice. Hence by eliminating or avoiding such unnecessary comparisons, the construction efficiency could be improved.

Definition 12. Let C (A, B) be a node of concept lattice L_1 constructed from formal context K_1, and D (O, S) be a node of concept lattice L_2 constructed from formal context K_2. If node C is a down-concept of node D during the union process, and node D is modified as node C_1 (A_1, B_1), where $A \subset A_1$ and $B_1=B$, then node C_1 (A_1, B_1) is called the redundant information in the construction process of horizontal partitioned concept lattice.

Theorem 1. Let C (A, B) be a node of concept lattice L_1 constructed from formal context K_1, and D (O, S) be a node of concept lattice L_2 constructed from formal context K_2. In the formation of horizontal partitioned concept lattice, if node C is a down-concept of node D that can be modified as node C_1 (A_1, B_1), and B is not the supermum of S, then C_1 (A_1, B_1) must be redundant information.

Proof: Since B is not the supermum of S, there must be node C_2 (A_2, B_2) such that $B_2 \subset B$, $A \subset A_2$ in the concept lattice L_1. Since node C is a down-concept of node D, there must exist B⊂S, and then B_2⊂S is acquired. In the construction process of horizontal partitioned concept lattice, node C_1 (A ∪ {O}, S) could be generated from node C and node D, and node C_3 (A_2 ∪ {O}, S) could be generated from node C and node C_2. By definition 12, C_1 is redundant information.

Definition 13. In the incremental construction process of horizontal partitioned concept lattice, the operations of eliminating redundant information is called as the pruning of horizontal partitioned concept lattice.

Theorem 2. The pruning process does not disrupt the structure of horizontal partitioned concept lattice.

Proof: Let redundant information C_1 (A_1, B_1) be generated during the construction process of concept lattice L_1. From theorem 1, node C_1 (A ∪ {O}, S) and node C_3 (A_2 ∪ {O}, S) could be generated during the process of generating redundant information. In the construction process of horizontal partitioned concept lattice, node C_1 (A ∪ {O}, S) could be generated at first, and then modified as node C_3 (A_2 ∪ {O}, S). After the pruning process, redundant information has been eliminated, C_3 (A_2 ∪ {O}, S) could be generated from C and C_2 directly, therefore, the pruning process of horizontal partitioned concept lattice only decreases the comparative time and not affects the structure of horizontal partitioned concept lattice. So the pruning of horizontal partitioned concept lattice does not disrupt the structure of horizontal partitioned concept lattice.

If the node of L_2 is the up-concept of the node of L_1, the node of L_2 do not need to compare with other nodes of L_1 in the union process of horizontal partitioned concept lattice. From the above description, the basic idea of the pruning based incremental construction of horizontal partitioned concept lattice is given(formal context is parted into K_1 and K_2): Two concept lattices L_1 and L_2 are constructed firstly, and the nodes of two concept lattices are sorted in the decreasing order of their support of intensions, then the nodes of concept lattice L_1 constructed from formal context K_1 should be compared with the nodes of concept lattice L_2 constructed from formal context K_2 one by one. If the node of L_2 is the up-concept of the node of L_1, according to the theorem 2, we can know that the nodes of L_2 do not need to compare with other nodes of L_1. So the redundant information during the construction process is eliminated, the comparative time of the concept lattice intension is decreased, so the construction efficiency is improved.

4 Pruning Based Incremental Construction Algorithm of Horizontal Partitioned Concept Lattice

4.1 Algorithm Description

According to above idea, a pseudo-code of our pruning based incremental construction algorithm of horizontal partitioned concept lattice (PHCL in short) could be described as:

```
Algorithm PHCL(pruning of horizontal partitioned concept
lattice)
input : Original concept lattice L1, L2, the nodes of con-
cept lattice L1, L2 are sorted in the deceasing order of
their support of intensions
output : New concept lattice
   (1) Input concept lattice L2
   (2) Search the node of concept lattice L1 from top to
         down, and compare with the node of concept lattice
         of L2 one by one.
   (3) FOR J=now1 to 1
   (4)  For I=now to 1
   (5)   determine the relationship of new and inte
   (6)      call procedure "judge"(new, inte) ;
   (7)  next I
   (8) next J
   (9) end PHCL;
    judge (new, inte)
   (1)  if  new⊂inte then
   (2)     fetch newfahter
   (3)        if I∉newfather then
   (4)          add edge I->new
   (5)          code=exte∪code
   (6)          father=father∪code
   (7)      newchild=newchild∪code
   (8)          end if
   (9)        exit for
   (10)  elseif inte⊂new then
   (11)       fetch newchild
   (12)       if I∉newchild then
   (13)     add edge new->I
   (14)         newfather=I∪newfather
   (15)         exte=exte∪code
   (16)         child=child∪code
   (17)       end if
   (18)  elseif inte=new then
   (19)   fetch the extension of the super node of I exte
   (20)       exte=exte∪code
   (21)       delete new
   (22)       exit for
   (23)  elseif  inte∩new≠Φ then
   (24)       add a new concept lattice node newjoin, the
        intersection intension is join
```

```
     for j=1 to now1  /*compared with the nodes of concept lattice 1*/
          if  j≠now1 then
            if  join=inte  then
               update j
       delete newjoin
            end if
          end if
  next j
     for j=1 to now  /* compared with the nodes of concept lattice 2*/
          if  j≠now then
            if  join=inte  then
       update j
               delete newjoin
            end if
          end if
     next j
    if not exist equal then
      njexte=code∪exte
      njinte=join
      njchild=code∪I
  determine the superconcept relationship between newjoin and other concept
      if ∃newjoin's super node  then
        repeat the above modifying operations of the super node
      end if
    end if
  end if;
end judge;
```

4.2 Algorithm Analysis

Let the number of the concept lattice L_1 nodes be U_1, and the number of the concept lattice L_2 nodes be U_2. From above analysis, as for the general union algorithm of multiple concept lattices[11] ,the time complexity of general horizontal partitioned concept lattice is $0(2^S \times |U_1| \times |U_2|)$.

For the PHCL, the redundant information has been eliminated by the pruning process, which can decreases comparing times of concept lattice intension, and thus improves the construction efficiency of concept lattice. In other words, it decreases comparing times of U_1, and the time complexity of PHCL algorithm is no larger than $0(2^S \times |U_1| \times |U_2|)$.

5 Experiment Analysis

Now a large telescope called LAMOST (Large Sky Area Multi-Object Fiber Spectroscopic Telescope) is under construction in the National Observatory in Beijing, China. After its scheduled completion in 2006, it is expected to collect more than 40,000 spectrums in a single observation night [13]. Such voluminous data demand automatic spectrum processing and data mining. In this section, we will report some of our experiments on the concept lattice construction from the observed celestial spectrums. The star spectra are treated by the following steps, then used as the formal context:

1) For each star spectrum, choose 200 wave-lengths from 3510 A to 8330 A at a step of 20 A as its attributes set.

2) At the above each chosen wave length, the corresponding flux, peak width and shape information of the spectrum are quantified respectively into one of the 13 different intervals in total.

The experiment setup is: PentiumIII-1.0G CPU, 256M memory, Windows 2000 operating system and ORACLE 9i DBMS. Both the PCL algorithm and the Godin algorithm are coded in Visual Basic 6.0. Table1 are the results of the horizontal partitioned concept lattice construction, where 125 wave-lengths are used as the attribute set, 400, 800, 1200, 1600, 2000, 2404 B-type star spectra are used as the data objects.

Table 1. Experimental Comparison of Various Object Sets

The number of objects	The number of nodes	Godin(s)	HUM CL_P2(s)	HUMC L_P4(s)	PHCL_ P2(s)	PHCL_ P4(s)
400	208	28	20	8	13	4
800	501	104	30	24	25	15
1200	677	134	37	30	33	24
1600	748	228	46	39	38	30
2000	804	536	145	100	130	80
2400	1108	1385	1020	256	890	198

According to the Table1, it can be concluded as follow:

1. The algorithm Godin, algorithm HUMCL and algorithm PHCL can form the same concept lattice. In other words, the number of the constructed nodes, the corresponding intension, extension, and father-son relationships are the same for both the two algorithms. This proves the correctness of the PHCL algorithm;

2. With the increase of objects, the construction time of PHCL algorithm is less than HUMCL and Godin algorithms. In other words, redundant information exists in the construction process of the Godin and HUMCL algorithms.

3. From the above experiment results, we can know that the construction time of

four-partitioned concept lattice (formal context is parted by four parts-P2) is less than two-partitioned concept lattice (formal context is parted by two parts-P4). So the construction efficiency of concept lattice is related to the number of partitioned formal context.

4. The efficiency of algorithm PHCL is affected by the redundant information in the constructing concept lattice. For the different the formal context, redundant information is different, so the elevated percent of algorithm PHCL is different.

6 Conclusion

In the paper, an improved algorithm PHCL for the union of multiple concept lattices is proposed. The key novelty of our proposed algorithm is that during the construction process of concept lattice, a pruning process is activated to detect and eliminate possible generated redundant information, by which the number of the comparisons of concept lattice intensions is largely reduced, and the construction efficiency is consequently increased. In addition, a pruning based horizontal partitioned incremental construction algorithm is experimented using the star spectra from the LAMOST project as the formal context. Finally, as the performance of a pruning based horizontal partitioned algorithm depends crucially on the formal context, and our currently used attributes of spectra are rather simple, our future work will focus on how to divide formal context more appropriate to further boost the construction efficiency in the star spectra mining for the LAMOST project.

References

1. Wille R.: Restructuring Lattice Theory: An Approach Based on Hierarchies of Concepts: Rival ed. Ordered Sets, Dordrecht: Reide, l (1982) 415-470
2. Wille, R.: Knowledge Acquisition by Methods of Formal Concept Analysis. Data Analysis, Learning Symbolic and Numeric Knowledge (Diday E ed.). Nova Science Publisher, New York (1989) 365-380
3. Belen, D. A., Pddro, A., Gonzalez, C.: Formal Concept Analysis as a Support Technique for CBR. Knowledge-based Systems, 14 (2001) 163-171
4. Godin, R., Missaoue, R.: An Incremental Concept Formation Approach for Learning from Database: Theoretical computer science, 133 (1994) 387-419
5. Godin, R, Missaoue, R, Alaui, H.: Incremental Concept Formation Algorithms Based on Galois(concept) Lattice. Computational Intelligence, 11 (1995) 246-267
6. Nourine, L, Raynaud, O.: A FastAlgorithm for Building Lattices. Wordshop on Computational Graph Theory and Combinatories, Victoria, Canada (1999) 1-12
7. Han, J., Kambr, M.: Data Mining Concepts and Techniques. Morgan Kaufmann Publishers, USA (2000)
8. Hu, K. Y., Lu, Y. C., Shi, C. Y.: Advances in Concept Lattice and Its Application. J. Tsinghua University (Sci & Tech), 40 (2000) 77-81
9. Xie, Z. P., Tian, L. Z.: A Fast Incremental Algorithm for Building Concept Lattice. Chinese Journal of Computers, 25 (2002) 490-496
10. Wang, Z. H., Hu, K. Y., Hu, X. G.: General And Incremental Algorithms of Rule Extraction Based On Concept Lattice. Chinese Journal of Computers, 22 (1999) 66-70

11. Liu, Z. G., Li, L. S.: Research on A Union Algorithm of Multiple Concept Lattices: RSFDGrC 2003, LNAI 2639, Berlin, Springer-Veriag, Berlin Herdellberg (2003) 533-540
12. Yun, L., Liu, Z. T.: Horizontal Union Algorithm of Multiple Concept Lattices. Chinese Journal of Electronics, 11 (2004) 1849-1854
13. Mei, Q. D.: Studies on Automated Spectral Recognition of Celestial Objects. Institute of Automation, Chinese Academy of Sciences, Beijing (2003)

Research on Spatial Data Mining Based on Knowledge Discovery

Zhong Qu and Lian Wang

College of Computer Science and Technology,
Chongqing University of Posts and Telecommunications,
400065 Chongqing, China
{quzhong, wanglian}@cqupt.edu.cn

Abstract. This paper proposes spatial outliers detection method of studying multiple non-spatial attributes based on special objects. The spatial outliers detection algorithm based on the Mahalanobis distance is proposed in this paper. The simulated experiment results demonstrate this method is feasible and effective, simultaneously the time complexity of center algorithm is analysed. Except the research type mentioned, spatial outliers detection still includes time-order data and time-space data outliers detections, which are related to the attribute values of other neighbors.

1 Introduction

Outliers have been informally defined as observations in a data set which appear to be inconsistent with the remainder of that set of spatial data, or which deviate so much from other observations so as to arouse suspicions that they were generated by a different mechanism[1]. Spatial outlier detection is becoming popular in the GIS and spatial database, such as communication, ecology, public safety, public sanitation analysis, earthquake and tsunami predication and so on.

Spatial data sets are usually spatial reference objects such as models of street, building and city. The attributes of spatial object can be grouped into two categories: spatial attribute and non-spatial attribute[2]-[7]. Spatial attribute includes position, shape and other geographical topology relationships. Non-spatial attribute normally includes length, height, construction time and name. The neighborhood relationships of spatial objects are spatial data sets based on spatial relationships (such as distance and connection relationships). This paper proposes spatial outliers detection method of studying multiple non-spatial attributes based on special objects.

2 Related Study Summary

Spatial outliers detection methods at early stage is based on statistics technique, and can be divided into 2 groups: methods based on distribution and methods based on depth[6]-[8].

With the upcoming of spatial data mining, Shekhar presented a graph element sets used for spatial outliers detection. This method compares the average attribute value

D.-S. Huang, K. Li, and G.W. Irwin (Eds.): ICIC 2006, LNAI 4114, pp. 946 – 951, 2006.

of neighborhood points with the attribute value of target point to determine whether this point is outliers. There are several spatial outliers detection methods based on statistics technique so far, which can be divided into two groups: graph theory method and quantitative testing method. The graph theory method is based on visualized spatial data, which can spatial outliers obviously. The quantitative testing method detects spatial outliers by computation. Scatterplot and Moran Scatterplot are two types of standard algorithms. The main reason that the traditional methods can't be used for multiple attributes spatial outliers detection is that high dimensional sparse spatial database can't be used. In high dimensional sparse spatial database every point can be treated as outlier, or no point is outlier because all data values are very close.

A novel algorithm detecting spatial outliers is proposed in the paper, which employs Mahalanobis distance to detect outliers. Computation time complexity is analyzed. The simulated experiments demonstrate that our approach can effectively identify local abnormality in large spatial data sets. In fact, the characteristics of spatial outliers can't be reflected because the traditional Euclidean distance uses the average value of all points. It is necessary to point out there are two research directions currently: dimension reduction technique, and redesign distance function.

All of multiple attributes spatial outliers detection methods are pointed to non-spatial attributes. But spatial outliers detection includes two types of dimensions: spatial dimension and non-spatial dimension, which should be considered separately. Spatial dimension determines neighborhood relations, and no-spatial dimension is used to define distance function. The algorithm in this paper treats the spatial dimension and non-spatial dimension separately.

3 Detection Algorithms

3.1 Problem Description

Assume spatial object X is composed with m variable attributes $(y_1, y_2, ..., y_m)$ $(m \geq 1)$, represented as $y = (y_1, y_2, ..., y_m)^T$. For a given spatial data set $X = (X_1, X_2, ..., X_p)$, $(p \geq 1)$, attribute function f is defined as map from X to R^m (m dimensional Euclidean space), and let the function $f(X)$ of every point X equal to attribute vector. For convenience reason, let

$$\begin{aligned} Y_i &= f(X_i) \\ &= (f_1(X_i), f_2(X_i), ..., f_m(X_i))^T \\ &= (y_{i1}, y_{i2}, ..., y_{im})^T, \end{aligned}$$

$i = 1,2,..., p$, let $A = (y_1, y_2, ... y_p)$.

For a given integer *k*, let $NN_k(X_i)$ as the kth nearest neighbor of X_i, ($i = 1,2,..., p$). Neighborhood function g is defined as a map from X to R^m, let j component of $g(X)$ (expressed as $g_j(X)$) as general statistics for attribute value y_i of all the spatial points in $NN_k(X)$.

In order to detect spatial outliers all components of Y neighboring to X are compared. The sum of comparison function h is function of f and g. Its definition domain is X, variable range is R^r ($r \le m$). If $h = f - g$, it represents a map from X to R^m ($r = m$). Let $h(X_i)$ as h_i.

For given attribute function *f*, neighborhood function g and comparison function *h*, if h_i is changing obvious point of array($h_1, h_2, ..., h_n$), then point X_i corresponding to h_i is called spatial outlier. The definition of spatial outlier implies that its determination depends on the selection of function g and *h*. The standardization of spatial outlier detection algorithm is shown in the following.

A given spatial data set: $X = (X_1, X_2, ..., X_n)$;
Neighborhood relationship: $NN_k(X_1)$, $NN_k(X_2)$, ..., $NN_k(X_1)$;
Attribute function f: $X \rightarrow R^m$;
Neighborhood function g: $X \rightarrow R^m$;
Comparison function h: $X \rightarrow R^r$;

3.2 Algorithms for Spatial Outlier Detection

The following introduces multiple attribute spatial outlier algorithm–mean value algorithm. Different g and *h* may results different outlier detection. The selection standard is to detect most of meaningful outliers. For example, resulting reason can be used to determine if the detected outlier satisfies requirement.

By computing Mahalanobis distance of mean *h* value between $h(X)$ and its neighbor *X*, the difference between *f* and g can be found out, which is $h = f - g$. Then the special attribute vector can be detected by considering the expectation, variance and covariance of attribute values. In order to describe this method, the following need be considered.

Under special condition, it can assume that $h(X)$ satisfies multidimensional normal distribution:

If the distribution function of $h(X)$ is $N_m(\mu, \Sigma)$, meaning *m* dimensional vector $h(X)$ satisfies one expectation μ. The difference of variance matrix and covariance matrix is multidimensional normal distribution of Σ. Then $(h(X) - \mu)^T \Sigma^{-1} (h(X) - \mu)$ satisfies χ_m^2 distribution and here χ_m^2 distribution is χ^2 distribution with *m*. Therefore the statistics for $h(X)$ satisfying $(h(X) - \mu)^T \Sigma^{-1} (h(X) - \mu) > \chi_p^2(\alpha)$ is α.

Now assume that there are *n* spatial object $X_1, X_2, \cdots, X_n$ and sample $h(X_1), h(X_2), \cdots, h(X_n)$, sample mean value is $\mu_s = \frac{1}{n} \sum_{i=1}^{n} h(X_i)$, sample variance matrix – sample covariance matrix is $\Sigma_s = \frac{1}{n} \sum_{i=1}^{n} [h(X_i) - \mu_s][h(X_i) - \mu_s]^T$. Then expect that the statistics for $h(X)$ satisfying $(h(X) - \mu)^T \Sigma^{-1} (h(X) - \mu) > \chi_p^2(\alpha)$ is α.

Assume that $d^2(X)=(h(X)-\mu_s)\sum_s^{-1}(h(X)-\mu_s)$, for any given X, if $d^2(X_i)$ is big enough, X will be treated as spatial outlier. Or in other words: if $d^2(X_i)>\theta$, then X is a spatial outlier. Of course if the given value is not spatial outlier detection threshold value but the spatial outlier number t of testing, then only need to pick the first t values from $d^2(X_i)$ in descending order.

Many algorithms for detecting spatial outlier can be derived from the discussion above. The following algorithm can be obtained by choosing g as the center of attribute vector. The reason to use vector center is the sample center is a relatively good and robust observation value and this algorithm is called center algorithm.

(1) Define spatial data set $X=(X_1,X_2,...,X_n)$, threshold θ, attribute function f and the nearest neighbor number k;

(2) For each given j($1\le j\le m$), normalize attribute function f_j, or $f_j=(f_j(X_i)-\mu_{f_j})/\sigma_{f_j}$, ($i=1,2,...,n$);

(3) For each spatial point X_i, calculate the nearest neighbor array $NN_k(X_i)$ for k;

(4) For each spatial point X_i, calculate neighbor function g and let g_j equal to the center value of $f_j(X)$, here $f_j(X)=\{f_j(X)\mid f_j(X),X\in NN_k(X_i)\}$, comparison function $h(X_i)=f(X_i)-g(X_i)$;

(5) Calculate $d^2(X)=(h(X)-\mu_s)\sum_s^{-1}(h(X)-\mu_s)\bullet$ if $d^2(X_i)>\theta$, then X_i is spatial outlier.

3.3 Analysis of Complexity

Step (2) of center algorithm needs standard distribution function, and the time complexity is $O(mn)$. Step (3) of center algorithm needs to calculate the k nearest neighborhoods (KNN) of each spatial point. The time complexity here is up to the KNN enquiry manner, if gridding method is adopted and gridding directory can be saved to main memory, the time complexity is $O(n)$. If index structure (e.g. R-tree) is used, the time complexity is $O(\log n)$. In step (4), the time complexity to calculate neighborhood function and comparison function is $O(mkn)$. In step (5), the time complexity to calculate Mahalanobis distance is $O(nm^2)$. In conclusion, if the gridding structure is adopted, the time complexity of center algorithm is $O(mn)+O(n)+O(mkn)+O(nm)^2$; If index structure is used, the time complexity is $O(mn)+O(n\log n)+O(mkn)+O(nm^2)$; In case of $n>>k$ and $n>>d$, the total time complexity of center algorithm is $O(n)$ if gridding is adopted, otherwise is $O(n\log n)$ if index structure is adopted. The time complexity lies on the KNN enquiry strategy adopted.

4 Simulation and Experiment Analysis

(1) n=293, three-dimensional data adopted.

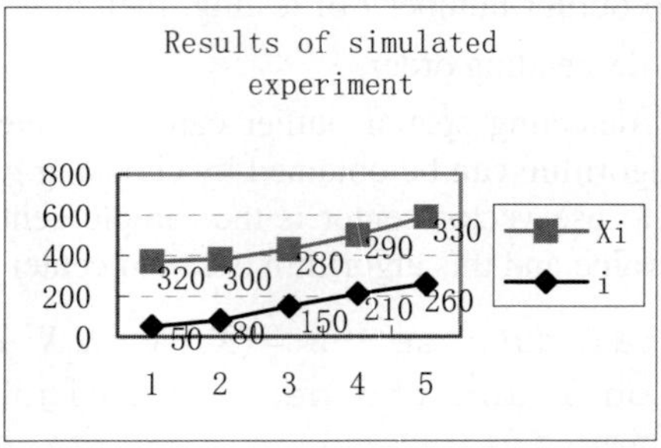

Fig. 1. Diagram of simulated experiment

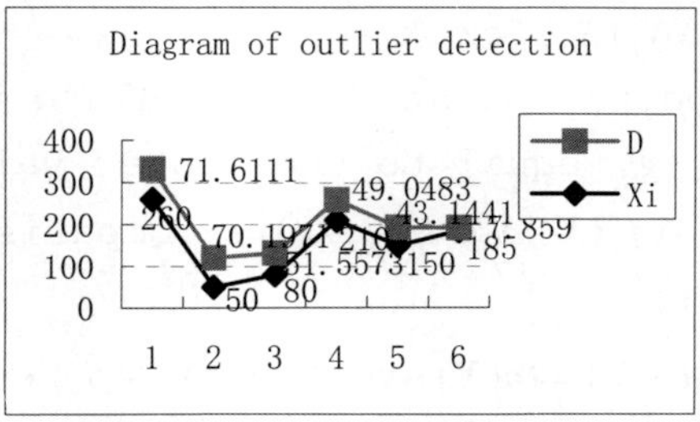

Fig. 2. Diagram of outlier detection

(2) m=1, namely each spatial data point has unique attribute value. Except the 5 outliers intentionally set, the attribute value of each data point meets the normal distribution of mean 50, standard deviation 5. The 5 outliers are 50th, 80th, 150th, 210th and 260th spatial point, the attribute value distributions among the outliers and the others are apparently different. In algorithm implementation, the algorithm to calculate k nearest neighbors is based on the spatial point Euclidean distance, the other is according to the algorithm described above.

5 Conclusion

The experiment results demonstrate this method is feasible and effective, simultaneously the time complexity of center algorithm is analysed. Except the research type mentioned above, spatial outliers detection still includes time-order data and time-space data outliers detections, which are related to the attribute values of other neighbors.

References

1. Ordonez, C., Omiecinski, E.: Discovery Association Rules Based on Image Content. in Proceedings of the 1999 IEEE Forum on Research and Technology Advances in Digital Libraries, Baltimore, MD (1999) 38-49
2. Koperski, K., Han, J.: 1995. Discovery of Spatial Association Rules in Geographic Information Databases. In Adv. in Spatial Databases: Proc. of the 41h International Symp. on Large Spatial Databases, Portland, Maine, Springer (1995) 47-66
3. Bloch, I.: Fuzzy Relative Position Between Objects in Image Processing: A Mrphological Aproach. IEEE Transactions on Patten Analysis and Machine Intelligence, (21)7 (1999) 657-664
4. Shekhar, S., Huang, Y., Wu, W., Lu, C. T., Chawla, S.: What's Spatial About Spatial Data Mining: Three Case Studies. in Data Mining for Scientific Engineering Applications, V. Kumar, R. Grossman, C. Kamath, K. Nambaru, Eds. Kluwer Academic (2001)
5. Peuquet, D. J., Duan, N.: An Event-Based Spatiotemporal Data Model ESTDM for Temporal Analysis of Geographical Data. International Journal of Geographical Information Systems, 9 (1995)7–24
6. Han, J., Koperski, K., Stefanovic, N. G.: A System Prototype for Spatial Data Mining[C].In.Proc ACM SIGMOD Conference on the Management of Data Tucson Arizona, (1997) 553-556
7. Pokajac, D., Obradovic, Z.: Improved Spatial-Temporal Forecasting through Modeling of Spatial Residuals in Recent History. In.Proc First SIAM Int'I Conf on Data Mining SDM 2001.Chicago.USA, (2001) 225–272
8. Roddick, J. F., Hornsby. K., Spiliopoulou, M.: An Updated Temporal Soatial and Spatio-Temporal Data Mining and Knowledge Discovery Research Bibliography. In.Post-Workshop Proceedings of the International Workshop on Temporal. Spatial and Spatio-Temporal Data Mining TSDM2000 Springer Lecture Notes in Artificial Intelligence, (2001)

Similarity Measure Construction Using Fuzzy Entropy and Distance Measure

Sang-Hyuk Lee, Jang-Mok Kim, and Young-Kiu Choi

School of Electrical and Computer Engineering, Pusan National University
Changjeon-dong, Geumjeong-gu, Busan 609-735, Korea
{leehyuk, jmok, ykichoi}@pusan.ac.kr

Abstract. The similarity measure is derived using fuzzy entropy and distance measure. By the relations of fuzzy entropy, distance measure, and similarity measure, we first obtain the fuzzy entropy. And with both fuzzy entropy and distance measure, similarity measure is obtained. We verify that the proposed measure become the similarity measure.

1 Introduction

Similarity between two sets can be applied to the pattern classification or reliability field *etc*.. Similarity measure has been known as the complementary meaning of the distance measure, *i.e.*, $s+d=1$, where d and s are distance and similarity measure respectively. In the above, 1 means the sum of similarity and dissimilarity. In the previous literatures, fuzzy entropy of a fuzzy set represents a measure of fuzziness of the fuzzy set [1-7]. Furthermore, well-defined distance measure represents the fuzzy entropy. By the summing relation, we can notice that the similarity measure can be constructed through distance measure or fuzzy entropy function. Well known-Hamming distance is usually used to construct fuzzy entropy, so we compose the fuzzy entropy function through Hamming distance measure. Using the relation of distance measure and similarity measure, we construct the similarity measure with fuzzy entropy, and similarity measure is also constructed through distance measure. In the next section, the axiomatic definitions of entropy, distance measure and similarity measure of fuzzy sets are introduced and fuzzy entropy is constructed through distance measure. In Section 3, similarity measures are constructed and proved through fuzzy entropy and the distance measure. Used distance measure is proposed by considering support average. Conclusions are followed in Section 4.

Throughout this paper, terminologies are used in the reference of Fan and Xie[6].

2 Preliminary

In this section, we introduce and discuss some preliminary results. Liu suggested three axiomatic definitions of fuzzy entropy, distance measure and similarity measure as follows [4].

D.-S. Huang, K. Li, and G.W. Irwin (Eds.): ICIC 2006, LNAI 4114, pp. 952–958, 2006.

Definition 2.1 (Liu, 1992). A real function $e: F(X) \rightarrow R^+$ or $e: P(X) \rightarrow R^+$ is called entropy on $F(X)$, or $P(X)$ if has the following properties:

(E1) $e(D) = 0,\ \forall D \in P(X)$
(E2) $e([1/2]) = max_{A \in F(X)} e(A)$
(E3) $e(A^*) \le e(A)$, for any sharpening A^* of A
(E4) $e(A) = e(A^C),\ \forall A \in F(X)$.

Where $[1/2]$ is the fuzzy set in which the value of the membership function is $1/2$.

Definition 2.2 (Liu, 1992). A real function $d: F^2 \rightarrow R^+$ is called a distance measure on $F(X)$, or $P(X)$ if d satisfies the following properties:

(D1) $d(A,B) = d(B,A)$, $\forall A,B \in F(X)$
(D2) $d(A,A) = 0$, $\forall A \in F(X)$
(D3) $d(D,D^C) = max_{A,B \in F} d(A,B)$, $\forall A,B \in F(X)$, $\forall D \in P(X)$
(D4) $\forall A,B,C \in F(X)$, if $A \subset B \subset C$, then $d(A,B) \le d(A,C)$ and $d(B,C) \le d(A,C)$.

Definition 2.3 (Liu, 1992). A real function $s: F^2 \rightarrow R^+$ or $P^2 \rightarrow R^+$ is called a similarity measure, if s has the following properties:

(S1) $s(A,B) = s(B,A)$, $\forall A,B \in F(X)$
(S2) $s(A,A^C) = 0$, $\forall A \in F(X)$
(S3) $s(D,D) = max_{A,B \in F} s(A,B)$, $\forall A,B \in F(X)$, $\forall D \in P(X)$
(S4) $\forall A,B,C \in F(X)$, if $A \subset B \subset C$, then $s(A,B) \ge s(A,C)$ and $s(B,C) \ge s(A,C)$.

Liu also pointed out that there is an one-to-one relation between all distance measures and all similarity measures, $d + s = 1$. Fuzzy normal similarity measure on F is also obtained by the division of $max_{C,D \in F} s(C,D)$. If we divide universal set X into two parts D and D^C in $P(X)$, then the fuzziness of fuzzy set A be the sum of the fuzziness of $A \cap D$ and $A \cap D^C$. By this idea, following definition is followed.

Definition 2.4. (Fan and Xie, 1999). Let e be an entropy on $F(X)$. Then for any $A \in F(X)$,

$$e(A) = e(A \cap D) + e(A \cap D^C).$$

is σ-entropy on $F(X)$.

Definition 2.5. (Fan and Xie, 1999). Let d be a distance measure on $F(X)$. Then for any $A,B \in F(X)$, and $D \in P(X)$,

$$d(A,B) = d(A \cap D, B \cap D) + d(A \cap D^C, B \cap D^C).$$

be the σ-distance measure on $F(X)$.

Definition 2.6. (Fan and Xie). Let s be a similarity measure on $F(X)$. Then for any $A, B \in F(X)$, and $D \in P(X)$,

$$s(A,B) = s(A \cap D, B \cup D^C) + s(A \cap D^C, B \cup D).$$

be the σ-similarity measure on $F(X)$.

From definition 2.4-6, we can focus interesting area of universal set and extend the theory of entropy, distance measure and similarity measure of fuzzy sets. Fan and Xie derived new entropy via defined entropy, which is introduces by $e' = e/(2-e)$, where is an entropy on $F(X)$.

Now we propose another fuzzy entropy induced by distance measure which is different from Fan, Ma and Xie's [7]. Proposed entropy needs only A_{near} or A_{far} crisp set, and it has the advantage in computation of entropy.

Theorem 2.2. Let d be a σ-distance measure on $F(X)$, and if d satisfies $d(A^C, B^C) = d(A,B)$, $A, B \in F(X)$, then

$$e(A) = 2d((A \cap A_{near}),[1]) + 2d((A \cup A_{near}),[0]) - 2. \qquad (1)$$

is a fuzzy entropy.

Theorem 2.3. Let d be a σ-distance measure on $F(X)$; if d satisfies $d(A^C, B^C) = d(A,B)$, $A, B \in F(X)$, then

$$e(A) = 2d((A \cap A_{far}),[0]) + 2d((A \cup A_{far}),[1]). \qquad (2)$$

is a fuzzy entropy.

Proofs of theorem 2.2 and 2.3 are found in [9].

Proposed entropies Theorem 2.2 and 2.3 have some advantages over Fan, Ma and Xie's. They need simple assumption compare to the previous one. Furthermore, (1) and (2) use only one crisp sets A_{near} and A_{far}, respectively.

3 Derivation of Similarity Measure

We obtain the fuzzy entropy with the distance measure in previous section. Generally, fuzzy entropy is expressed through distance measure, *i.e.,* $e(A) = e(d(A))$. Hence, by the result of Liu's,

$$d(A) + s(A) = 1. \qquad (3)$$

We modify the similarity measure as $s(A)=1-e(A)$, that means fuzzy set A matches to the crisp set A_{near} nearly as $s(A)$ approaches to 0. We illustrate the similarity measure with the entropy function in subsection 3.1 and the similarity measure construction using the distance measure in the subsection 3.2.

3.1 Similarity Measure Using the Entropy Function

We propose the similarity measure in the following theorems.

Theorem 3.1 For fuzzy set $A \in F(X)$, if d satisfies distance measure, then

$$s(A, A_{near}) = 4 - 2d((A \cap A_{near}), [1]) - 2d((A \cup A_{near}), [0]) . \tag{4}$$

is the similarity measure between fuzzy set A and crisp set A_{near} .

Proof. We prove that the eq. (4) satisfies the Definition 2.3. (S1) means the commutativity of set A and A_{near} , hence it is clear from (4) itself. From (S2), $s(A, A^C) = 0$ is shown as

$$\begin{aligned} s(A, A^C) &= 4 - 2d((A \cap A^C), [1]) - 2d((A \cup A^C), [0]) \\ &= 4 - 2d([0], [1]) - 2d([1], [0]) \\ &= 4 - 2\cdot 1 - 2\cdot 1 = 0. \end{aligned}$$

For all $A, B \in F(X)$, inequality of (S3) is proved by

$$\begin{aligned} s(A, B) &= 4 - 2d((A \cap B), [1]) - 2d((A \cup B), [0]) \\ &\le 4 - 2d((D \cap D), [1]) - 2d((D \cup D), [0]) \\ &= s(D, D). \end{aligned}$$

Inequality is satisfied from $d((A \cap B), [1]) \ge d((D \cap D), [1])$ and $d((A \cup B), [0]) \ge d((D \cup D), [0])$.

Finally, (S4) is $\forall A, B, C \in F(X)$, $A \subset B \subset C$,

$$\begin{aligned} s(A, B) &= 4 - 2d((A \cap B), [1]) - 2d((A \cup B), [0]) \\ &= 4 - 2d(A, [1]) - 2d(B, [0]) \\ &\ge 4 - 2d(A, [1]) - 2d(C, [0]) \\ &= s(A, C) \end{aligned}$$

also,

$$\begin{aligned} s(B, C) &= 4 - 2d((B \cap C), [1]) - 2d((B \cup C), [0]) \\ &= 4 - 2d(B, [1]) - 2d(C, [0]) \\ &\ge 4 - 2d(A, [1]) - 2d(C, [0]) \\ &= s(A, C) \end{aligned}$$

is satisfied.

Inequality is also satisfied with $d(B,[0]) \le d(C,[0])$ and $d(B,[1]) \le d(A,[1])$.

Therefore proposed similarity measure (4) satisfies Definition 2.3. Similarly, we propose another similarity measure in the following theorem.

Theorem 3.2. For fuzzy set $A \in F(X)$ and distance measure d,

$$s(A, A_{near}) = 2 - 2d((A \cap A_{near}^C),[0]) - 2d((A \cap A_{near}^C),[1]) . \quad (5)$$

is the similarity measure of fuzzy set A and crisp set A_{near}.

Proof. Proofs are shown similarly as Theorem 3.1.

We have proposed the similarity measures that are induced from fuzzy entropy. These fuzzy entropies are also induced from distance measure. Hence to obtain more implicit result, we consider distance measure directly. In the following subsection, we suggest similarity measure which is constructed using distance measure.

3.2 Similarity Measure Using Distance Measure

We have represented the relation $s(A) = 1 - d(A)$ in (3), that means the sum of similarity measure and distance measure is constant. Hence, we solve the similarity measure directly from distance measure in this subsection. To obtain the similarity, proper distance measure is needed. First, we consider the Hamming distance $d(A,B) = \frac{1}{n}\sum_{i=1}^{n} \left| \mu_A(x_i) - \mu_B(x_i) \right|$. By the relation of (3),

$$s(A,B) = 1 - d(A,B) = 1 - \frac{1}{n}\sum_{i=1}^{n} \left| \mu_A(x_i) - \mu_B(x_i) \right| . \quad (6)$$

Is the similarity measure? We check the definition (S1) to (S4). (S1) is clear from the eq. (6). (S2) and (S3) are also obtained from (D3) and (D2) of definition 2.2. Finally, (S4) is proved with the help of (D4). Naturally we conclude that if the distance measure is constructed properly, then the similarity measure can be obtained. Now we consider the membership functions type1 and 2 in Fig. 1 and 2. In the Fig. 1 and 2, area between μ_A and μ_B are the same, value of Hamming distance of Fig. 1 and 2 are same. Then which case is more similar?

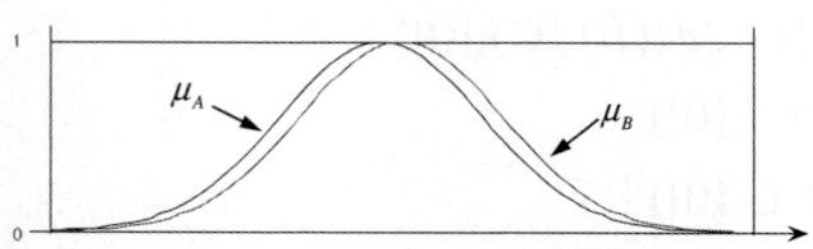

Fig. 1. Membership functions type 1

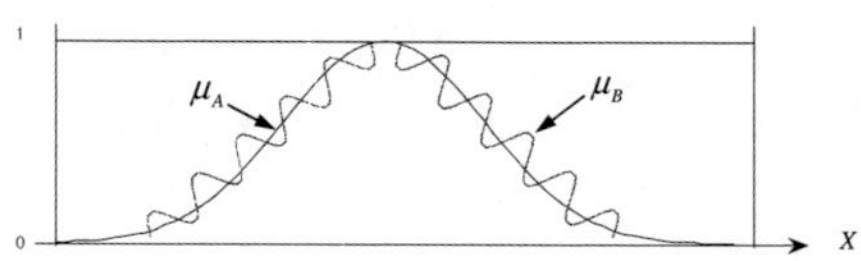

Fig. 2. Membership functions type 2

Consider the function

$$d(A,B)=\frac{1}{n}\sum_{i=1}^{n}|\mu_A(x_i)-\mu_B(x_i)|+|support_A(x_i)-support_B(x_i)|. \quad (7)$$

where $support_A(x_i)=\frac{1}{n}\sum_{i=1}^{n}|x_i|, x_i\in A$ and $support_B(x_i)=\frac{1}{n}\sum_{i=1}^{n}|x_i|, x_i\in B$ are the average values of support. In this case, the first part of (7) is the Hamming distance, hence the value of Fig. 1 and Fig. 2 are the same. However the last part of (7) represents the difference of average support. Now, we check whether the eq. (7) satisfy the distance measure definition or not. For (D1), commutativity is clear from (7). $d(A,A)=0$ is also clear, and the first part of distance between D and D^C represents the sum 1. (D4) is clear because Fig. 2 has similar average value compare to Fig. 1. Eq. (9) is the distance measure, thus we can propose similarity measure as

$$s(A,B)=1-\frac{1}{n}\sum_{i=1}^{n}|\mu_A(x_i)-\mu_B(x_i)|-|support_A(x_i)-support_B(x_i)|. \quad (8)$$

proof of (8). Proof is similar to theorem 3.1 and 2, commutativity of (S1) is proved by (8). (S2) is also proved by $support_A(x_i)=support_B(x_i)$. Also $d(D,D)=0$, hence $s(D,D)=1$ is proved. (S4) is finally proved by the (D4). Proof verify that eq. (8) represent similarity measure.

4 Conclusions

We introduce the distance measure, similarity measure and fuzzy entropy, fuzzy entropy can be represented by the function of distance measure. By the one to one correspondence of distance measure and similarity measure, we construct the similarity measure using distance measure. As we noted before, fuzzy entropy is the function of distance measure. Hence similarity measure is constructed through the fuzzy entropy, and we prove. And similarity measure is also induced through distance measure. We verify that the proposed measure is the similarity measure.

Acknowledgement

This paper was supported by "Research Institute of Computer, Information and Communication (PNU)".

References

1. Bhandari, D., Pal, N. R.: Some New Information Measure of Fuzzy Sets. Inform. Sci. 67, (1993) 209-228
2. Ghosh, A.: Use of Fuzziness Measure in Layered Networks for Object Extraction: a Generalization. Fuzzy Sets and Systems, 72 (1995) 331-348
3. Kosko, B.: Neural Networks and Fuzzy Systems, Prentice-Hall, Englewood Cliffs. NJ, 1992

4. Liu Xuecheng, : Entropy, Distance Measure and Similarity Measure of Fuzzy Sets and Their Relations. Fuzzy Sets and Systems, 52 (1992)305-318
5. Pal, N.R., Pal, S.K.: Object-background Segmentation using New Definitions of Entropy. IEEE Proc. 36 (1989)284-295
6. Fan, J. L., Xie, W. X.: Distance Measure and Induced Fuzzy Entropy. Fuzzy Set and Systems, 104 (1999) 96~105
7. Fan, J. L., Ma, Y. L., Xie, W. X.: On Some Properties of Distance Measures. Fuzzy Set and Systems, 117 (2001) 355-361
8. Aksoy, S., Haralick, R.M.: Feature Normalization and Likelihood-based Similarity Measures for Image Retrieval. Pattern Recognition Letters, 22 (2001) 563-582
9. Lee, S.H., Kang, K.B., Kim, S.S.: Measure of Fuzziness with Fuzzy Entropy Function. Journal of Fuzzy Logic and Intelligent Systems, vol. 14, no. 5 (2004) 642-647

Software Metrics Data Clustering for Quality Prediction

Bingbing Yang, Xin Zheng, and Ping Guo*

Image Processing and Pattern Recognition Laboratory,
Beijing Normal University, 100875, China
chris@mail.bnu.edu.cn, pguo@ieee.org

Abstract. Software metrics are collected at various phases of the software development process. These metrics contain the information of software and can be used to predict software quality in the early stage of software life cycle. Intelligent computing techniques such as data mining can be applied in the study of software quality by analyzing software metrics. Clustering analysis, which is one of data mining techniques, is adopted to build the software quality prediction models in early period of software testing. In this paper, three clustering methods, k-means, fuzzy c-means and Gaussian mixture model, are investigated for the analysis of two real-world software metric datasets. The experiment results show that the best method in predicting software quality is dependent on practical dataset, and clustering analysis technique has advantages in software quality prediction since it can be used in the case having little *prior* knowledge.

1 Introduction

Software reliability engineering is one of the most important aspects of software quality [1]. Recent studies show that software metrics can be used in software module fault-proneness prediction [2]. A software module has a series of metrics, some of which are related to the module's fault-proneness. Norman E. Fenton [2] presented software metrics introduction and the direction. Many research work about the software quality prediction using the relationship between software metrics and software module's fault-proneness have been done in the last decades [3, 4, 7].

There are several techniques that are proposed to classify the modules for identifying fault-prone modules. From learning point of view, these techniques can be divided into two categories: supervised learning and unsupervised learning. Supervised learning method is based on the prior knowledge, that means enough samples must be provided to train the prediction model. On the other side, unsupervised learning methods do not need prior knowledge. Clustering analysis, which can groups the software modules by software metrics, is one of the unsupervised learning methods.

In this paper, three clustering methods are used in predicting two software project qualities, these clustering methods include k-means, fuzzy c-means and Gaussian mixture model with EM algorithm. The purpose is to perform comparative studies for these clustering methods with new datasets in order to obtain the most suitable technique to build the prediction model. In Section 2, the datasets are introduced and

* Corresponding author.

D.-S. Huang, K. Li, and G.W. Irwin (Eds.): ICIC 2006, LNAI 4114, pp. 959 – 964, 2006.

the metrics chosen are illustrated. In Section 3, the three clustering methods are reviewed. In Section 4, the empirical study results are presented and analyzed. Finally, the discussion and, conclusion are given in Section 5.

2 Datasets and Metrics Description

In this section, we introduce the metrics datasets extracted from two real-world software project. These metrics are extracted by Krakatau Professional tool, which can extract more than twenty metrics of projects, files and functions. In the experiment, we choose some common ones from extracted metrics.

2.1 Celestial Spectrum Analysis System

Celestial Spectrum Analysis System (CSAS) is a subsystem of a Large Sky Area Multi-Object Spectroscopic Telescope (LAMOST) national key project of China. CASS is developed by more than 20 students of two college and graduate school with standard C program language, and it is well tested based on the function of the project. One function is considered as one module, CASS includes 70 modules each of which has a risky level obtained by software testing.We select 12 metrics from the software source code to anlyze.

2.2 Redundant Strapped-Down Inertial Measurement Unit project

The Redundant Strapped-Down Inertial Measurement Unit (RSDIMU) project involved more than one hundred students. RSDIMU has 34 versions each of which is developed independently, it is also developed by standard C. The reliability properties of the software were analyzed by Cai and Lyu [8] . The details of the project and development procedures are discussed in [5]. In this paper, we used all the modules of every version counted 223 each of which has its faults number. RSDIMU's module is based on files, which is different from CSAS. Each file is counted as one module. We select 11 metrics from the source code to analyze.

3 Modeling Methodology

In this section, we review the three modeling methods mentioned above. These methods we choose to compare are the classical clustering methods.

3.1 *K*-Means Clustering

K-means is one of the typical clustering methods. It has been widely used in many fields. *K*-means classify the objects into *k* clusters and make the objects be high similar in the same cluster. The squared-error convergent criterion is defined as

$$E = \sum_{i=1}^{k} \sum_{p \in C_i} \left| p - m_i \right|^2 \tag{1}$$

Where E is the sum of square-error for all objects in the database, p is the point in space representing a given object, and m_i is the mean of cluster C_i. The algorithm attempts to determine k partitions that minimize the squared-error function.

3.2 Fuzzy *C*-Means Clustering

Fuzzy clustering is different from other clustering methods. For example, k-means clustering give a result with affirmed partition index, while fuzzy clustering's result give the probability result. That means an object is either a member of one particular subset, or it is not a member of that subset using traditional clustering methods. But fuzzy clustering permit one object partly belongs to more than one subset by a degree indicated by the membership value for that point in that cluster, so long as the sum of that object's membership values is 1.

Fuzzy *c*-means clustering is an iterative algorithm which attempts to cluster through minimizing the cost function

$$L(f) = \sum_{x \in X} \sum_{k \in K} f^m(x)(k) \cdot d^2(x,k) \tag{2}$$

where f is a fuzzy partition, $f(x)(k)$ is the membership of pattern x in cluster k, m is the *fuzzifier* exponent, and $d(x;\ k)$ is the distance between pattern x and the prototype (centroid) of the kth cluster. More detail introduction can be found in reference [6].

3.3 Gaussian Mixture Model with EM Algorithm

Gaussian mixture model is based on Gaussian probability distribution. To explain the method we assume that there are k partitions in a data set, then there will be k Gaussian models forming a mixture with joint probability density:

$$p(x,\Theta) = \sum_{i=1}^{k} \alpha_i G(x, m_i, \Sigma_i) \text{ with } \alpha_i \geq 0 \text{, and } \sum_{i=1}^{k} \alpha_i = 1 \tag{3}$$

$$G(x, m_i, \Sigma_i) = \frac{\exp[-\frac{1}{2}(x - m_i)^T \Sigma_i^{-1} (x - m_i)]}{(2\pi)^{d/2} |\Sigma_i|^{1/2}} \tag{4}$$

Here G is multivariate Gaussian density function, x denotes random vector (which integrates a variety of software metrics), d is the dimension of x, and parameter $\mathbf{\Theta}=\{\alpha_i, \mathrm{m}_i, \mathbf{\Sigma}_i\}$ is a set of finite mixture model parameter vectors. Here α_i is the mixing weight, m_i is the mean vector, and $\mathbf{\Sigma}_i$ is the covariance matrix of the ith component [7].

To estimate the mixture model parameters, we use the maximum likelihood learning (ML) with EM algorithm which is described in [7] in details.

4 Experiments and Analysis

Clustering method can group the software modules into any amount of cluster. In the experiment, we choose the cluster number to be 2 or 3 in order to compare the methods' performance. This partition method is meaningful because if number of module group is greater than 3, it can not give the testing manager useful information to plan how to do the test.

In practice, not only the entire classification accuracy is important, but also the pureness of fault-prone cluster. That is because if the pureness of fault-prone cluster is low, it means many fault-prone modules are not predicted accurately. They may not be tested well in testing phrase so that the software product's quality will be low. So in our experiment, we also consider the fault-prone cluster's pureness as an important point.

4.1 Experiment with CASS

Every CASS's module is tested and has a risky level. The lower risky level is, the more non-fault-prone module is. At the situation of 2 objective clusters, we choose the non-fault-prone cluster with the risky level 0 and fault-prone cluster's risky level greater than 0. At the situation of 3 objective clusters, we choose the non-fault-prone cluster with the risky level 0, the mean of fault-prone cluster with the risky level is in 0 to 1 and the fault-prone cluster greater than 1.

Table 1 shows the result of 2 clusters instance, and table 2 shows the result of 3.

Table 1. Result of CASS with 2 objective clusters. Row-caption presents the methods and Col-caption presents the entire accuracy and each objective cluster's pureness.

	Entire	High-risky	Low-risky
K-means	68.60%	76.80%	64.30%
Fuzzy *c*-means	61.40%	72.40%	8.30%
Mixture model	55.70%	69.20%	38.70%

Table 2. Result of CASS with 3 objective clusters. Row-caption presents the methods and Col-caption presents the entire accuracy and each objective cluster's pureness.

	Entire	High-risky	Mean-risky	Low-risky
K-means	75.70%	91.70%	46.20%	66.70%
Fuzzy *c*-means	58.60%	46.70%	33.30%	80%
Mixture model	57.10%	70.20%	33.30%	30%

From the result, we know that *k*-means shows the best effect of these three methods. In 2-clusters instance, k-means gives the highest entire accuracy 68.60% and fault-prone pureness 76.80%. In 3-clusters instance, *k*-means also gives the highest entire accuracy 75.70% and fault-prone pureness 91.70%. We also see that except fuzzy c-means the clustering effect of 3-clusters is better than 2-clusters. But the accuracy of fuzzy c-means in 3-clusters instance is only a little lower than that in 2-clusters instance. So the effect of 3-clusters is better than that of 2-clusters.

4.2 Experiment of RSDIMU

RSDIMU's modules are different from CASS's, they are based on files but not on functions. So the metrics used in the experiment are not the same as CASS. Another difference is that RSDIMU's modules do not have the risky level, but have the number of faults. At the situation of 2 objective clusters, we choose the non-fault-prone cluster with the fault number 0 and fault-prone cluster's fault number greater than 0. At the situation of 3 objective clusters, we choose the non-fault-prone cluster with the fault number 0, the mean of fault-prone cluster with the fault number is in 1 to 2 and the fault-prone cluster greater than 2.

Table 3 shows the result of 2 clusters instance, and table 4 shows the result of 3.

Table 3. Result of RSDIMU with 2 objective clusters. Row-caption presents the methods and Col-caption presents the entire accuracy and each objective cluster's pureness.

	Entire	High-risky	Low-risky
K-means	55.60%	48.40%	64.90%
Fuzzy *c*-means	55.60%	48.40%	64.90%
Mixture model	72.20%	81.90%	64.10%

Table 4. Result of RSDIMU with 3 objective clusters. Row-caption presents the methods and Col-caption presents the entire accuracy and each objective cluster's pureness.

	Entire	High-risky	Mean-risky	Low-risky
K-means	52%	58.70%	19.60%	63.90%
Fuzzy *c*-means	50.20%	66.70%	21.60%	64%
Mixture model	55.30%	78.70%	52.90%	35%

From the result, we see that the result is quite opposite to the CASS. Mixture model with EM shows the best effect of these three methods. In 2-clusters instance, Mixture model with EM gives the highest entire accuracy 72.20% and fault-prone pureness 81.90%. In 3-clusters instance, Mixture model with EM gives also gives the highest entire accuracy 55.30% and fault-prone pureness 78.70%. We also see that all the three clustering methods' effects of 2-clusters are better than 3-clusters. So the effect of 2-clusters is better than that of 3-clusters.

5 Conclusions and Future Work

By analyzing the experiment results, we can conclude that one clustering method which does well in a dataset may not also be good at another practice dataset. Besides that, different numbers of objective clusters also affect the prediction precision. What we also find is that clustering analysis is an effective method to predict the software quality in the early software development stage.

A proper clustering method will be effective to help software manager predict the software quality. It does not need any software fault measurement which must be prepared at the beginning of the test phrase. But how to select the proper method and what number of objective clusters are challenges. In our future work, we will focus on how to choose the method automatically based on new algorithms, and possible solution is to analyze the distribution of modules combining with cluster number selection criteria [9] to determine the suitable number of objective clusters.

References

1. Lyu, M.R.: Handbook of software Reliability Engineering. IEEE Computer Society Press. McGraw Hill (1996)
2. Fenton, N.E., Neil, M.: Software metrics: successes, failures and new directions. The Journal of Systems and Software 47 (1999) 149-157
3. Gyimothy, T., Ferenc, R., Siket, I.: Empirical Validation of Object-Oriented Metrics on Open Source Software for Fault Prediction. IEEE Transactions on Software Engineering, Vol. 31, No. 10 (2005)
4. Lanning, D.L., Khoshgoftaar, T., Pandya, A.S.: A comparative study of pattern recognition techniques for quality evaluation of telecommunications software. IEEE J. Selected Areas in Communication, Vol. 12, No. 2 (1994) 279–291
5. Lyu, M.R., Huang, Z., Sze, K.S., Cai, X.: An empirical study on testing and fault tolerance for software reliability engineering. In Proceedings 14th IEEE International Symposium on Software Reliability Engineering (ISSRE'2003). Denver, Colorado (2003) 119-130
6. Dick, S., Meeks, A., Last, M., Bunked, H., Kandel, A.: Data mining in software metrics databases. Fuzzy Sets and Systems 145 (2004) 81–110
7. Guo, P., Lyu, M.R.: Software Quality Prediction Using Mixture Models with EM Algorithm. Proceedings of the First Asia-Pacific Conference on Quality Software (APAQS 2000), ed. by TSE & CHEN. Hong Kong. (2000) 69-78
8. Cai, X., Lyu, M.R.: An Empirical Study on Reliability Modeling for Diverse Software Systems. Proceedings of the 15th International Symposium on Software Reliability Engineering (2004)
9. Guo, P., Chen, C.L.P., Lyu, M.R.: Cluster Number Selection for a Small Set of Samples Using the Bayesian Ying-Yang Model. IEEE trans. Neural Network, Vol.13, No.3 (2002) 757-763

A Hybrid Intelligent Algorithm for Vehicle Routing Models with Fuzzy Travel Times

Jin Peng, Gang Shang, and Huanbin Liu

College of Mathematics and Information Sciences
Huanggang Normal University, Hubei 438000, China
pengjin01@tsinghua.org.cn

Abstract. Vehicle routing problems (VRP) arise in many real-life applications within transportation and logistics. This paper considers vehicle routing models with fuzzy travel times and its hybrid intelligent algorithm. Two new types of credibility programming models including fuzzy chance-constrained programming and fuzzy chance-constrained goal programming are presented to model fuzzy VRP. A hybrid intelligent algorithm based on fuzzy simulation and genetic algorithm is designed to solve the proposed fuzzy VRP models. Moreover, some numerical experiments are provided to demonstrate the applications of the models and the computational efficiency of the proposed approach.

Keywords: vehicle routing problem, fuzzy travel times, fuzzy programming, hybrid intelligent algorithm.

1 Introduction

Vehicle routing problems(VRP) are concerned with finding efficient routes, beginning and ending at a central depot, for a fleet of vehicles to serve a number of customers with demands for some commodity. VRP arise in many real-life applications in the area of transportation and logistics and appear widely in the literature. Surveys on exact algorithms and heuristic algorithms for solving VRP may be found in Bodin et al. [6], Solomon and Desrosiers [30], Laporte [17], Liu and Shen [26], Lau et al. [19], and Irnich et al. [15].

Practically, there are uncertain factors within VRP. Waters [34] listed various potential uncertainties, such as demands of customers, travel times between customers, customers to be visited, locations of customers, capacities of vehicles, and number of vehicles available. This provides motivation to study uncertain VRP. Bertsimas and Simchi-Levi [5] surveyed the new developments in the research area of VRP under uncertainty. Gendreau et al. [12] provided a detailed summary of the scientific literature on stochastic VRP. Golden and Yee [13] presented a chance-constrained programming(CCP) model for VRP with stochastic demands and provided some analytic results. Stewart and Golden [31] extended and generalized the work of Golden and Yee [13], and gave some computational results. Dror and Trudreau [8] presented a Clarke-Wright heuristic for a CCP model of VRP with stochastic demand. Dror et al. [9] modelled stochastic VRP

D.-S. Huang, K. Li, and G.W. Irwin (Eds.): ICIC 2006, LNAI 4114, pp. 965–976, 2006.

by CCP and expected value model, and discussed some mathematical properties. Bastian and Rinnooy Kan [2] presented CCP models for various situations in stochastic VRP. Dror [10] presented a multistage stochastic model and a Markov decision model for stochastic VRP, and discussed some mathematical properties of solutions. Laporte et al. [18] introduced a CCP model for VRP with stochastic travel times. Liu and Lai [25] presented some multiobjective models for VRP with stochastic demands and travel times, and designed a GA for solving the stochastic VRP models.

Although stochastic programming has been successfully applied in VRP, many problems require subjective judgment either due to the lack of data or due to the extreme complexity of VRP. This fact motives us to apply fuzzy programming to VRP in which the uncertainty is treated as fuzzy variables. Teodorovic and Kikuchi [32] introduced a VRP model which treats all the travel times between customers are fuzzy numbers, and the proposed model followed the principles of the classical Clarke-Wright algorithm to develop a set of vehicle routes. Teodorovic and Pavkovic [33] considered the VRP in which the demands of customers are fuzzy, and developed a model based on the heuristic 'sweeping' algorithm. Kagaya et al. [16] presented a technique of grouping trips on the basis of their similarity in the vehicle routing and scheduling problem. The proposed approach treats the similarity of two trips as a fuzzy relation.

This paper will present some fuzzy VRP models and its hybrid intelligent algorithm (HIA). There is no traditional algorithm to solve the proposed model due to its complexity. Thus we design an effective HIA to solve them. Some numerical experiments are provided to demonstrate the applications of the models and the computational efficiency of the proposed approach.

2 Assumptions and Notations

In fuzzy VRP, we assume that: (a) each vehicle has a container with a physical capacity limitation and the total loading of each vehicle cannot exceed its capacity; (b) a vehicle will be assigned for only one route on which there may be more than one customer; (c) a customer will be visited by one and only one vehicle; (d) each route begins and ends at the company site (depot); (e) each customer specifies its time window within which the delivery is permitted or preferred to start; and (f) the travel times between customers are assumed to be fuzzy variables.

Let us first introduce the following indices, model parameters and decision variables.

$i = 0$: depot;

$i = 1, 2, \cdots, n$: customers;

$k = 1, 2, \cdots, m$: vehicles.

q_i: the demand of customer i, $i = 1, 2, \cdots, n$;

Q_k: the physical capacity of vehicle k, $k = 1, 2, \cdots, m$;

D_{ij}: the distance between customers i and j, $i, j = 0, 1, 2, \cdots, n$;

T_{ij}: the fuzzy travel time between customers i and j, $i, j = 0, 1, 2, \cdots, n$;

S_i: the unloading time at customer i, $i = 1, 2, \cdots, n$;

$[a_i, b_i]$: the time window of customer i, where a_i and b_i are the beginning and end of the time window, $i = 1, 2, \cdots, n$, respectively.

To describe the operational plan, three decision variables $\boldsymbol{x}$, $\boldsymbol{y}$ and $\boldsymbol{t}$ are introduced as follows.

$\boldsymbol{x} = (x_1, x_2, \cdots, x_n)$: integer decision variables representing n customers with $1 \le x_i \le n$ and $x_i \ne x_j$ for all $i \ne j$, $i, j = 1, 2, \cdots, n$. In other words, the sequence $\{x_1, x_2, \cdots, x_n\}$ is a rearrangement of $\{1, 2, \cdots, n\}$;

$\boldsymbol{y} = (y_1, y_2, \cdots, y_{m-1})$: integer decision variables with $y_0 \equiv 0 \le y_1 \le y_2 \le \cdots \le y_{m-1} \le n \equiv y_m$;

$\boldsymbol{t} = (t_1, t_2, \cdots, t_m)$: each t_k represents the starting time of vehicle k at the depot, $k = 1, 2, \cdots, m$.

It should be noted that the operational plan can be fully determined by the distinctive decision variables $\boldsymbol{x}$, $\boldsymbol{y}$ and $\boldsymbol{t}$ in the following way. For each k $(1 \le k \le m)$, vehicle k is not used if $y_k = y_{k-1}$; vehicle k is used (and dispatched from the depot at time t_k) if $y_k > y_{k-1}$. And the tour of vehicle k is

$$0 \to x_{y_{k-1}+1} \to x_{y_{k-1}+2} \to \cdots \to x_{y_k} \to 0. \tag{1}$$

In this way, the above decision variables $\boldsymbol{x}$, $\boldsymbol{y}$ and $\boldsymbol{t}$ ensure that: (a) each vehicle will be used at most one time; (b) all tours begin and end at the depot; (c) each customer will be visited by one and only one vehicle; and (d) there is no subtour.

Let $f_i(\boldsymbol{x}, \boldsymbol{y}, \boldsymbol{t})$ be the arrival time function of some vehicle at customer i, $i = 1, 2, \cdots, n$. It will be seen that $f_i(\boldsymbol{x}, \boldsymbol{y}, \boldsymbol{t})(i = 1, 2, \cdots, n)$ are determined by the decision variables $\boldsymbol{x}$, $\boldsymbol{y}$ and $\boldsymbol{t}$, and are related to fuzzy travel times T_{ij}, $i, j = 0, 1, 2, \cdots, n$. Since unloading can start either immediately, or later, when a vehicle arrives at a customer, the calculation of $f_i(\boldsymbol{x}, \boldsymbol{y}, \boldsymbol{t})$ is heavily dependent on the operational strategy. Here we assume that the customer does not permit a delivery earlier than the time window. That is, the vehicle will wait to unload until the beginning of the time window if it arrives before the time window starts. If a vehicle arrives at a customer after the beginning of the time window, unloading will start immediately. For each k with $1 \le k \le m$, if vehicle k is used (i.e., $y_k > y_{k-1}$), then we have

$$f_{x_{y_{k-1}+1}}(\boldsymbol{x}, \boldsymbol{y}, \boldsymbol{t}) = t_k + T_{0 x_{y_{k-1}+1}} \tag{2}$$

and

$$f_{x_{y_{k-1}+j}}(\boldsymbol{x}, \boldsymbol{y}, \boldsymbol{t}) = f_{x_{y_{k-1}+j-1}}(\boldsymbol{x}, \boldsymbol{y}, \boldsymbol{t}) \vee a_{x_{y_{k-1}+j-1}} + S_{x_{y_{k-1}+j-1}} + T_{x_{y_{k-1}+j-1} x_{y_{k-1}+j}} \tag{3}$$

for $2 \le j \le y_k - y_{k-1}$, where $\vee$ denotes the maximum operator. It follows from the fuzziness of travel times T_{ij}'s that the arrival times $f_i(\boldsymbol{x}, \boldsymbol{y}, \boldsymbol{t})$, $i = 1, 2, \cdots, n$ are fuzzy variables fully determined by (2) and (3).

Let $g(\boldsymbol{x}, \boldsymbol{y})$ be the total distance travelled of all vehicles, then we have

$$g(\boldsymbol{x}, \boldsymbol{y}) = \sum_{k=1}^{m} g_k(\boldsymbol{x}, \boldsymbol{y}) \tag{4}$$

where

$$g_k(\boldsymbol{x}, \boldsymbol{y}) = \begin{cases} D_{0x_{y_{k-1}+1}} + \sum_{j=y_{k-1}+1}^{y_k-1} D_{x_j x_{j+1}} + D_{x_{y_k}0}, & \text{if } y_k > y_{k-1} \\ 0, & \text{if } y_k = y_{k-1} \end{cases} \tag{5}$$

for $k = 1, 2, \cdots, m$.

3 Fuzzy CCP and CCGP Models

CCP was developed by Charnes and Cooper [7] as a powerful means of handling randomness by specifying a confidence level at which it is desired that the stochastic constraint holds. Liu [22], and Liu and Iwamura [20][21] proposed a series of fuzzy CCP models. In this section, we employ fuzzy CCP to VRP. The CCP models presume that the decision makers will be allowed to consider the fuzzy objectives and constraints in terms of their attainment of the possibility measure in a fuzzy environment.

In fuzzy VRP, we hope that the total amount of demands in a route cannot exceed the capacity of the associated vehicle. Thus we have a capacity constraint,

$$\sum_{j=y_{k-1}+1}^{y_k} q_{x_j} \le Q_k, \quad k = 1, 2, \cdots, m. \tag{6}$$

For each i, we also hope that each customer i is visited within its time window $[a_i, b_i]$ with a confidence level β_i. Then we have the following chance constraints,

$$\text{Cr}\{a_i \le f_i(\boldsymbol{x}, \boldsymbol{y}, \boldsymbol{t}) \le b_i\} \ge \beta_i, \quad i = 1, 2, \cdots, n \tag{7}$$

where $\text{Cr}\{a_i \le f_i(\boldsymbol{x}, \boldsymbol{y}, \boldsymbol{t}) \le b_i\}$ represents the credibility measure ([23][24][28]) to what degree the ith customer is visited by some vehicle within the given time window. Note that $f_i(\boldsymbol{x}, \boldsymbol{y}, \boldsymbol{t})$ defined in (2) and (3) are fuzzy variables for $i = 1, 2, \cdots, n$.

If we want to minimize the total distance travelled of all vehicles subject to constraints (6) and (7), then we have the following CCP model,

$$\begin{cases} \min g(\boldsymbol{x}, \boldsymbol{y}) \\ \text{subject to:} \\ \qquad \text{Cr}\{a_i \le f_i(\boldsymbol{x}, \boldsymbol{y}, \boldsymbol{t}) \le b_i\} \ge \beta_i, \quad i = 1, 2, \cdots, n \\ \qquad 1 \le x_i \le n, \quad i = 1, 2, \cdots, n \\ \qquad x_i \ne x_j, \quad i \ne j, \ i, j = 1, 2, \cdots, n \\ \qquad 0 \le y_1 \le y_2 \le \cdots \le y_{m-1} \le n \\ \qquad \sum_{j=y_{k-1}+1}^{y_k} q_{x_j} \le Q_k, \quad k = 1, 2, \cdots, m \\ \qquad x_i, y_j, \quad i = 1, 2, \cdots, n, \quad j = 1, 2, \cdots, m-1, \quad \text{integers.} \end{cases} \tag{8}$$

Sometimes, management goals have the following priority structure set by the decision-maker:

Priority 1: Each customer i should be visited within its time window $[a_i, b_i]$ with a confidence level β_i. We thus have the following goal constraints,

$$\begin{array}{l} \text{Cr}\left\{f_i(\boldsymbol{x},\boldsymbol{y},\boldsymbol{t}) - b_i \le d_i^+\right\} \ge \beta_i,\ i = 1,2,\cdots,n \\ \text{Cr}\left\{a_i - f_i(\boldsymbol{x},\boldsymbol{y},\boldsymbol{t}) \le d_i^-\right\} \ge \beta_i,\ i = 1,2,\cdots,n \end{array} \tag{9}$$

in which $\sum_{i=1}^{n}\left(d_i^+ + d_i^-\right)$ should be minimized.

Priority 2: We should minimize the total distance travelled of all vehicles, so that we have

$$g(\boldsymbol{x},\boldsymbol{y}) + d_{n+1}^- - d_{n+1}^+ = 0 \tag{10}$$

in which d_{n+1}^+ will be minimized.

We thus have the following chance-constrained goal programming (CCGP) model for fuzzy VRP,

$$\left\{\begin{array}{l} \text{lexmin}\left\{\sum\limits_{i=1}^{n}(d_i^+ + d_i^-), d_{n+1}^+\right\} \\ \text{subject to:} \\ \qquad \text{Cr}\left\{f_i(\boldsymbol{x},\boldsymbol{y},\boldsymbol{t}) - b_i \le d_i^+\right\} \ge \beta_i, \quad i = 1,2,\cdots,n \\ \qquad \text{Cr}\left\{a_i - f_i(\boldsymbol{x},\boldsymbol{y},\boldsymbol{t}) \le d_i^-\right\} \ge \beta_i, \quad i = 1,2,\cdots,n \\ \qquad g(\boldsymbol{x},\boldsymbol{y}) + d_{n+1}^- - d_{n+1}^+ = 0 \\ \qquad 1 \le x_i \le n, \quad i = 1,2,\cdots,n \\ \qquad x_i \ne x_j, \quad i \ne j,\ i,j = 1,2,\cdots,n \\ \qquad 0 \le y_1 \le y_2 \le \cdots \le y_{m-1} \le n \\ \qquad \sum\limits_{j=y_{k-1}+1}^{y_k} q_{x_j} \le Q_k, \quad k = 1,2,\cdots,m \\ \qquad x_i, y_j, \quad i = 1,2,\cdots,n, \quad j = 1,2,\cdots,m-1, \quad \text{integers} \end{array}\right. \tag{11}$$

where lexmin represents lexicographically minimizing the objective vector.

4 A Hybrid Intelligent Algorithm

Intelligent algorithm (IA) have demonstrated considerable success in providing good solutions to many complex optimization problems. They have received growing attention over the past three decades, have been well documented in the literature, such as GA in Michalewicz [27], and have been applied to a wide variety of optimization problems. In particular, the readers may consult Liu [23] in which numerous GAs have been suggested for use in solving uncertain programming models. Potvin [29] presented a competitive neural network model and a GA to improve the initialization and construction phase of a parallel insertion heuristic for the VRP with time windows. Filipec [11] proposed a GA in conjunction with handy heuristic techniques to solve the non-fixed destination multiple depot capacitated VRP. Liu and Lai [25] designed a GA to solve the VRP with stochastic demands and travel times. Baker and Ayechew [1] considers the application of a GA to the basic VRP, in which customers of known demand are supplied from a single depot. Bell [3] applies the meta-heuristic method of ant colony optimization (ACO) to an established set of VRP. Ho and Haugland [14] propose a solution method based on tabu search for solving the VRP with time windows and split deliveries without imposing any restrictions on the split delivery options.

In this section we design a HIA based on GA and fuzzy simulation (FS) to solve the fuzzy VRP as follows.

Representation Structure: We represent an operational plan by the chromosome $V = (\boldsymbol{x}, \boldsymbol{y}, \boldsymbol{t})$, where the genes $\boldsymbol{x}, \boldsymbol{y}, \boldsymbol{t}$ are the same as the decision variables. Without loss of generality, we also assume that the time window at the depot is $[a, b]$. This means that the gene $\boldsymbol{t}$ will be restricted in the hypercube $[a, b]^m$.

Recall that there exists one to one correspondence between a distinctive decision variable or chromosome $(\boldsymbol{x}, \boldsymbol{y}, \boldsymbol{t})$ and the real operational plan in the way mentioned in Section 2. In the following genetic operations, the crossover operation of two chromosomes means that two new operational plans (offsprings) are produced from the two old operational plans (parents). Similarly, the mutation operation of one chromosome means that a new operational plan (offspring) is produced from the old operational plan (parent). Keeping these in mind, we can understand the genetic operations much more visually and describe a simple and convenient GA.

Initialization: Initialize *pop_size* chromosomes in which fuzzy simulations may be employed to check the feasibility. We define an integer *pop_size* as the number of chromosomes and initialize *pop_size* chromosomes randomly. For gene $\boldsymbol{x}$, we define a sequence $\{x_1, x_2, \cdots, x_n\}$ of n customers with $x_i = i$, $i = 1, 2, \cdots, n$. We repeat the following process from $j = 1$ to n: generating a random position n' between j and n, and exchanging the values of x_j and $x_{n'}$. It is clear that $\{x_1, x_2, \cdots, x_n\}$ is just a random rearrangement of $\{1, 2, \cdots, n\}$. Then we obtain a gene $\boldsymbol{x} = (x_1, x_2, \cdots, x_n)$. For each i with $1 \leq i \leq m-1$, we set y_i as a random integer between 0 and n. Then we rearrange the sequence $\{y_1, y_2, \cdots, y_{m-1}\}$ from small to large. We thus have a gene $\boldsymbol{y} = (y_1, y_2, \cdots, y_{m-1})$. Finally, for each i with $1 \leq i \leq m$, we set t_i as a random number on the time window $[a, b]$. Then we get a gene $\boldsymbol{t} = (t_1, t_2, \cdots, t_m)$. If the generated chromosome $V = (\boldsymbol{x}, \boldsymbol{y}, \boldsymbol{t})$ is proven to be feasible by fuzzy simulation (please consult the book [23]), then it is accepted as a chromosome; otherwise we repeat the above process until a feasible chromosome is obtained. We may generate *pop_size* initial chromosomes $V_1, V_2, \cdots, V_{pop\_size}$ by repeating the above process *pop_size* times.

Crossover Operation: Let us illustrate the crossover operator on each pair of two old operational plans by (V_1', V_2'). We denote $V_i' = (\boldsymbol{x}_i, \boldsymbol{y}_i, \boldsymbol{t}_i)$ with $i = 1, 2$, respectively. First, we generate a random number c from the open interval $(0, 1)$ and define

$$\boldsymbol{t}_1' = c \cdot \boldsymbol{t}_1 + (1 - c) \cdot \boldsymbol{t}_2, \qquad \boldsymbol{t}_2' = (1 - c) \cdot \boldsymbol{t}_1 + c \cdot \boldsymbol{t}_2.$$

The two children V_1'' and V_2'' are produced by the crossover operation as follows: $V_1'' = (\boldsymbol{x}_1, \boldsymbol{y}_2, \boldsymbol{t}_1')$ and $V_2'' = (\boldsymbol{x}_2, \boldsymbol{y}_1, \boldsymbol{t}_2')$. We note that the two children are not necessarily feasible, thus we must check the feasibility of each child (here fuzzy simulation may be used) and can replace the parents only with feasible children.

Mutation Operation: For each selected parent, denoted by $V = (\boldsymbol{x}, \boldsymbol{y}, \boldsymbol{t})$, it is mutated in the following way. For the gene $\boldsymbol{x}$, we randomly generate two mutation positions n_1 and n_2 between 1 and n, and rearrange the sequence $\{x_{n_1}, x_{n_1+1}, \cdots, x_{n_2}\}$ at random to form a new sequence $\{x'_{n_1}, x'_{n_1+1}, \cdots, x'_{n_2}\}$; thus we obtain a new gene

$$\boldsymbol{x}' = (x_1, \cdots, x_{n_1-1}, x'_{n_1}, x'_{n_1+1}, \cdots, x'_{n_2}, x_{n_2+1}, \cdots, x_n).$$

Similarly, for gene $\boldsymbol{y}$, we generate two random mutation positions n_1 and n_2 between 1 and $m-1$, and set y_i as a random integer number y'_i between 0 and n for $i = n_1, n_1+1, \cdots, n_2$. We then rearrange the sequence

$$\{y_1, \cdots, y_{n_1-1}, y'_{n_1}, y'_{n_1+1}, \cdots, y'_{n_2}, y_{n_2+1}, \cdots, y_{m-1}\}$$

from small to large and obtain a new gene $\boldsymbol{y}'$. For the gene $\boldsymbol{t}$, we choose a mutation direction $\boldsymbol{d}$ in $\Re^m$ randomly, if $\boldsymbol{t} + M \cdot \boldsymbol{d}$ is not in the time window $[a, b]^m$, then we set M as a random number between 0 and M until it is in $[a, b]^m$, where M is a predetermined step length. If the above process cannot yield a gene $\boldsymbol{t}$ in $[a, b]^m$ in a predetermined number of iterations, then we set $M = 0$. We replace the parent gene $\boldsymbol{t}$ with its child $\boldsymbol{t}' = \boldsymbol{t} + M \cdot \boldsymbol{d}$. Finally, we replace the parent V with the offspring $V' = (\boldsymbol{x}', \boldsymbol{y}', \boldsymbol{t}')$ if it is proven to be feasible by fuzzy simulation. If it is not feasible, then we repeat the above process.

Computation of Objective Values: Calculate the objective values for all chromosomes using fuzzy simulations.

Evaluation Function: According to the calculated objective values for all chromosomes $V_1, V_2, \cdots, V_{pop\_size}$ by fuzzy simulations, we rearrange these chromosomes from good to bad. Here, we adopt the following rank-based evaluation function,

$$Eval(V_i) = a(1-a)^{i-1}, \qquad i = 1, 2, \cdots, pop\_size \tag{12}$$

where parameter $a \in (0, 1)$, $i = 1$ means the best individual, and $i = pop\_size$ the worst individual.

Selection Process: The selection method is based on spinning the roulette wheel *pop_size* times. We select a single chromosome for a new population each time until *pop_size* copies of chromosomes are finally obtained.

GA Procedure: Following crossover, mutation, evaluation, and selection, the new population is ready for its next evaluation. The GA will terminate after a given number of cyclic repetitions of the above steps and output the best chromosome as the optimal operational plan of vehicles.

With the techniques mentioned as above, the designed HIA for solving fuzzy VRP can be stated as follows.

Step 1. Input the GA parameters: population size *pop_size*, crossover probability P_c, mutation probability P_m, the parameter in the rank-based evaluation function a.

Step 2. Initialize *pop_size* chromosomes (operational plans), and check their feasibility by fuzzy simulations.
Step 3. Update the chromosomes by crossover and mutation operations, where the feasibility of the offspring must be calculated by *fuzzy simulations*.
Step 4. Compute the objective values for all chromosomes by fuzzy simulations.
Step 5. Calculate the fitness of each chromosomes according to the objective values.
Step 6. Select the chromosomes by spinning the roulette wheel.
Step 7. Repeat the third to sixth steps for a given number of cycles.
Step 8. Report the best chromosome as the optimal operational plan.

5 Application and Computational Experiment

The computer code for the HIA to the fuzzy chance-constrained programming model of the fuzzy VRP has been written in C language. In order to illustrate the effectiveness of the HIA, we now give a numerical example performed on a personal computer with the following parameters: the population size is 200, the probability of crossover P_c is 0.3, the probability of mutation P_m is 0.6, the parameter a in the rank-based evaluation function is 0.05. GAs are often criticized because of the setting of these parameters. Fortunately, GAs are very robust in the setting of parameters.

Example: Now we consider a VRP in which there are 20 customers labelled "$1, 2, \cdots, 20$" in a company and one depot labelled "0". We assume that the travel times between customers are all triangular fuzzy numbers. The time windows and demands of customers are shown in Table 1. The travel time and distance matrixes for the depot and customers are listed in Tables 2 and 3, respectively.

We also assume that the unloading times ($S_i, i = 1, 2, \cdots, 20$) at the 20 locations are 20, 10, 15, 10, 13, 18, 20, 12, 15, 16, 18, 20, 15, 16, 20, 15, 12, 14, 10, 18, and the capacities ($Q_k, k = 1, 2, 3, 4$) of the four vehicles are 800, 850, 900, 1000, respectively.

If we assign a confidence level of 0.9 at which all customers are visited within their time windows, and want to minimize the total distance travelled of all vehicles, then we have the following CCP model,

$$\begin{cases} \min g(\boldsymbol{x}, \boldsymbol{y}) \\ \text{subject to:} \\ \qquad \mathrm{Cr}\left\{a_i \le f_i(\boldsymbol{x}, \boldsymbol{y}, \boldsymbol{t}) \le b_i, i = 1, 2, \cdots, 20\right\} \ge 0.90 \\ \qquad 1 \le x_i \le 20, \quad i = 1, 2, \cdots, 20 \\ \qquad x_i \ne x_j, \quad i \ne j, \ i, j = 1, 2, \cdots, 20 \\ \qquad 0 \le y_1 \le y_2 \le y_3 \le 20 \\ \qquad \sum_{j=y_{k-1}+1}^{y_k} q_{x_j} \le Q_k, k = 1, 2, 3, 4 \\ \qquad x_i, y_j, \quad i = 1, 2, \cdots, 20, \quad j = 1, 2, 3, \quad \text{integers} \end{cases}$$

Table 1. Time Windows and Demands

Customers	Time Windows $[a, b]$	Demands
1	$[08:00, 15:20]$	200
2	$[08:20, 14:30]$	100
3	$[08:40, 14:40]$	140
4	$[08:20, 14:30]$	160
5	$[08:00, 15:20]$	200
6	$[08:00, 14:20]$	60
7	$[08:30, 14:00]$	200
8	$[08:00, 15:30]$	135
9	$[08:00, 15:50]$	160
10	$[08:30, 14:20]$	165
11	$[08:40, 13:20]$	140
12	$[08:10, 14:20]$	100
13	$[08:00, 15:20]$	200
14	$[08:20, 15:30]$	80
15	$[08:20, 15:00]$	60
16	$[08:20, 14:30]$	200
17	$[08:00, 14:10]$	90
18	$[08:00, 15:20]$	200
19	$[08:30, 15:00]$	90
20	$[08:30, 15:20]$	100

Table 2. Travel Time Matrix

LCTs	0	1	2	3	4	5	6	7	8	9
1	(25,50,75)									
2	(5,10,15)	(20,40,60)								
3	(25,50,75)	(5,10,15)	(20,40,60)							
4	(7,15,23)	(25,50,75)	(7,15,23)	(22,45,68)						
5	(25,50,75)	(17,35,53)	(17,35,53)	(15,30,45)	(17,35,53)					
6	(25,50,75)	(7,15,23)	(20,40,60)	(2,5,8)	(22,45,68)	(15,30,45)				
7	(12,25,38)	(20,40,60)	(15,30,45)	(17,35,53)	(7,15,23)	(12,25,38)	(17,35,53)			
8	(7,15,23)	(20,40,60)	(5,10,15)	(22,45,68)	(10,20,30)	(17,35,53)	(20,40,60)	(17,35,53)		
9	(25,50,75)	(7,15,23)	(22,45,68)	(5,10,15)	(22,45,68)	(15,30,45)	(5,10,15)	(20,40,60)	(20,40,60)	
10	(10,20,30)	(22,45,68)	(12,25,38)	(22,45,68)	(7,15,23)	(15,30,45)	(20,40,60)	(5,10,15)	(12,25,38)	(22,45,68)
11	(25,50,75)	(5,10,15)	(17,35,53)	(15,30,45)	(17,35,53)	(5,10,15)	(15,30,45)	(5,10,15)	(17,35,53)	(17,35,53)
12	(27,55,83)	(17,35,53)	(17,35,53)	(15,30,45)	(17,35,53)	(2,5,8)	(15,30,45)	(7,15,23)	(17,35,53)	(17,35,53)
13	(5,10,15)	(20,40,60)	(5,10,15)	(20,40,60)	(7,15,23)	(15,30,45)	(17,35,53)	(17,35,53)	(5,10,15)	(20,40,60)
14	(25,50,75)	(5,10,15)	(20,40,60)	(2,5,8)	(22,45,68)	(15,30,45)	(2,5,8)	(17,35,53)	(17,35,53)	(5,10,15)
15	(22,45,68)	(5,10,15)	(20,40,60)	(5,10,15)	(22,45,68)	(15,30,45)	(5,10,15)	(17,35,53)	(17,35,53)	(2,5,8)
16	(7,15,23)	(22,45,68)	(7,15,23)	(22,45,68)	(10,20,30)	(15,30,45)	(22,45,68)	(17,35,53)	(10,20,30)	(22,45,68)
17	(15,30,45)	(20,40,60)	(12,25,38)	(20,40,60)	(10,20,30)	(12,25,38)	(17,35,53)	(2,5,8)	(12,25,38)	(20,40,60)
18	(25,50,75)	(5,10,15)	(22,45,68)	(5,10,15)	(25,50,75)	(15,30,45)	(7,15,23)	(17,35,53)	(20,40,60)	(7,15,23)
19	(15,30,45)	(20,40,60)	(12,25,38)	(20,40,60)	(10,20,30)	(12,25,38)	(17,35,53)	(2,5,8)	(12,25,38)	(20,40,60)
20	(12,25,38)	(20,40,60)	(12,25,38)	(22,45,68)	(10,20,30)	(15,30,45)	(20,40,60)	(5,10,15)	(12,25,38)	(22,45,68)

LCTs	10	11	12	13	14	15	16	17	18	19
11	(15,30,45)									
12	(12,25,38)	(7,15,23)								
13	(20,40,60)	(17,35,53)	(17,35,53)							
14	(20,40,60)	(15,30,45)	(15,30,45)	(20,40,60)						
15	(20,40,60)	(15,30,45)	(20,40,60)	(20,40,60)	(2,5,8)					
16	(15,30,45)	(17,35,53)	(7,15,23)	(7,15,23)	(22,45,68)	(22,45,68)				
17	(5,10,15)	(12,25,38)	(12,25,38)	(12,25,38)	(17,35,53)	(17,35,53)	(12,25,38)			
18	(20,40,60)	(15,30,45)	(20,40,60)	(20,40,60)	(7,15,23)	(7,15,23)	(20,40,60)	(20,40,60)		
19	(5,10,15)	(12,25,38)	(12,25,38)	(12,25,38)	(17,35,53)	(17,35,53)	(12,25,38)	(2,5,8)	(20,40,60)	
20	(5,10,15)	(15,30,45)	(10,20,30)	(10,20,30)	(20,40,60)	(20,40,60)	(20,40,60)	(5,10,15)	(22,45,68)	(5,10,15)

A run of the proposed algorithm (5000 cycles in fuzzy simulation, 1000 generations in GA) shows that the best operational plan is:

Vehicle 1: depot$\rightarrow$ 9 $\rightarrow$ 15 $\rightarrow$ 14 $\rightarrow$ 6 $\rightarrow$ 18 $\rightarrow$ 3 $\rightarrow$depot, starting time: 8:01;

Vehicle 2: depot$\rightarrow$ 1 $\rightarrow$ 11 $\rightarrow$ 5 $\rightarrow$ 12 $\rightarrow$ 16 $\rightarrow$depot, starting time: 8:12;

Vehicle 3: depot$\rightarrow$ 2 $\rightarrow$ 8 $\rightarrow$ 13 $\rightarrow$ 4 $\rightarrow$depot, starting time: 8:22;

Vehicle 4: depot$\rightarrow$ 7 $\rightarrow$ 17 $\rightarrow$ 19 $\rightarrow$ 20 $\rightarrow$ 10 $\rightarrow$depot, starting time: 8:18.

The total distance travelled by the four vehicles is 720. Furthermore, when the obtained operational plan is performed, we have

Table 3. Travel Distance Matrix

Locations	0	1	2	3	4	5	6	7	8	9	10	11	12	13	14	15	16	17	18	19
1	90																			
2	20	70																		
3	80	30	60																	
4	30	90	25	75																
5	85	65	55	70	75															
6	95	25	70	15	85	60														
7	45	70	65	75	35	45	65													
8	35	80	20	85	40	65	70	65												
9	80	35	85	20	75	60	20	90	70											
10	45	85	45	85	25	60	80	20	35	85										
11	90	20	65	60	65	20	65	20	75	75	60									
12	95	65	65	70	55	15	60	25	65	65	45	35								
13	20	80	20	80	25	60	75	75	20	80	80	75	75							
14	95	20	80	15	85	60	15	75	75	20	80	60	60	80						
15	85	20	80	20	85	60	20	65	75	10	80	60	80	80	15					
16	25	85	25	85	40	60	75	75	40	85	60	65	30	25	85	85				
17	60	80	55	80	40	45	65	15	45	80	20	45	45	45	65	65	45			
18	90	20	85	20	95	60	25	75	80	25	80	60	80	80	25	25	80	80		
19	60	70	45	80	40	55	65	15	45	80	20	45	45	45	65	75	45	15	80	
20	55	80	45	85	40	60	80	20	45	85	20	60	40	40	80	80	80	20	85	20

$$\text{Cr}\left\{a_i \le f_i(\boldsymbol{x}^*, \boldsymbol{y}^*, \boldsymbol{t}^*) \le b_i, i = 1, 2, \cdots, 20\right\} = 0.90.$$

The time complexity of this type of problem is the sum of the time spent for the fuzzy simulation and the time spent for the GA, where the computation time for the fuzzy simulation is exactly proportional to the number of sampling points of fuzzy VRP.

6 Conclusion

In this paper we contributed to the VRP research area in the following three aspects: (*i*) we presented two new types of fuzzy vehicle routing models; (*ii*) we designed an effective HIA for solving the fuzzy vehicle routing models; and (*iii*) numerical example is provided to illustrated the HIA application to VRP with fuzzy travel times. We also note that the proposed modelling idea is applicable to the case of fuzzy demands, fuzzy locations and fuzzy capacities. The applied strategies of fuzzy VRP are helpful to deal with more complicated vehicle routing problems in uncertain environment. The cross combination of fuzzy VRP and stochastic VRP can be considered in the future.

Acknowledgments

This work was supported by the Natural Science Foundation No.2006ABA185 of Hubei Province, the Significant Project No.Z200527001 of Hubei Provincial Department of Education, and the Scientific and Technological Innovative Group Project of Hubei Provincial Institutions of Higher Education, China.

References

1. Baker, B. M. and Ayechew, M. A.: A Genetic Algorithm for the Vehicle Routing Problem. Computers & Operations Research **30** (2003) 787–800
2. Bastian, C. and Rinnooy Kan A.H.G.: The Stochastic Vehicle Routing Problem Revisited. European Journal of Operational Research **56** (1992) 407–412

3. Bell, J.E. and McMullen, P. R.: Ant Colony Optimization Techniques for the Vehicle Routing Problem. Advanced Engineering Informatics **18** (2004) 41–48
4. Bertsimas, D.J.: A Vehicle Routing Problem with Stochastic Demand. Operations Research **40** (1992) 574–585
5. Bertsimas, D.J. and Simchi-Levi, D.: A New Generation of Vehicle Routing Research: Robust Algorithms, Addressing Uncertainty. Operations Research **44** (1996) 286–304
6. Bodin, L., Golden, B.L., Assad, A.A., and Ball, M.: Routing and Scheduling of Vehicles and Crews: The State of the Art. Computers & Operations Research **10** (1983) 63–211
7. Charnes, A. and Cooper, W.W.: Chance-constrained Programming. Management Science **6** (1959) 73–79
8. Dror, M. and Trudreau, P.: Stochastic Vehicle Routing with Modified Savings Algorithm. European Journal of Operational Research **23** (1986) 228–235
9. Dror, M., Laporte, G., and Trudreau P.: Vehicle Routing with Stochastic Demands: Properties and Solution Frameworks. Transportation Science **23** (1989) 166–176
10. Dror, M.: Modeling Vehicle Routing with Uncertain Demands as a Stochastic Programming: Properties of the Corresponding Solution. European Journal of Operational Research **64** (1993) 432–441
11. Filipec, M., Skrlec, D., and Krajcar, S.: Genetic Algorithm Approach for Multiple Depot Capacitated Vehicle Routing Problem Solving with Heuristic Improvements. International Journal of Modelling and Simulation **20** (2000) 320–328
12. Gendreau, M., Laporte, G., and Séguin, R.: Stochastic Vehicle Routing. European Journal of Operational Research **88** (1996) 3–12
13. Golden, B.L. and Yee, J.R.: A Framework for Probabilistic Vehicle Routing. AIIE Transactions **11** (1979) 109–112
14. Ho, S. C. and Haugland, D.: A Tabu Search Heuristic for the Vehicle Routing Problem with Time Windows and Split Deliveries. Computers & Operations Research **31** (2004) 1947–1964
15. Irnich, S., Funke, B., and Grünert, T.: Sequential Search and its Application to Vehicle-routing Problems. Computers & Operations Research **33** (2006) 2405–2429
16. Kagaya, S., Kikuchi, S., and Donnelly, R.A.: Use of A Fuzzy Theory Technique for Grouping of Trips in the Vehicle Routing and Scheduling Problem. European Journal of Operational Research **76** (1994) 143–154
17. Laporte, G.: The Vehicle Routing Problem: An Overview of Exact and Approximate Algorithms. European Journal of Operational Research **59** (1992) 345–358
18. Laporte, G., Louveaux, F.V., and Mercure, H.: The Vehicle Routing Problem with Stochastic Travel Times. Transportation Science **26** (1992) 161–170
19. Lau, H.C., Sim, M., and Teo, K.M.: Vehicle Routing Problem with Time Windows and a Limited Number of Vehicles. European Journal of Operational Research **148** (2003) 559–569
20. Liu, B. and Iwamura, K.: Chance-constrained Programming with Fuzzy Parameters. Fuzzy Sets and Systems **94** (1998) 227–237
21. Liu, B. and Iwamura, K.: A Note on Chance-constrained Programming with Fuzzy Coefficients. Fuzzy Sets and Systems **100** (1998) 229–233
22. Liu, B.: Minimax Chance-constrained Programming Models for Fuzzy Decision Systems. Information Sciences **112** (1998) 25–38
23. Liu, B.: Theory and Practice of Uncertain Programming. Physica-Verlag, Heidelberg (2002)
24. Liu, B.: Uncertainty Theory: An Introduction to its Axiomatic Foundations. Springer-Verlag, Heidelberg (2004)

25. Liu, B. and Lai, K.K.: Stochastic Programming Models for Vehicle Routing Problems. Asian Information-Science-Life **1** (2002) 13–18
26. Liu, F. F. and Shen, S.: An Overview of a Heuristic for Vehicle Routing Problem with Time Windows. Computers & Industrial Engineering **37** (1999) 331–334
27. Michalewicz, Z.: Genetic Algorithms + Data Structures = Evolution Programs (3rd ed.). Springer-Verlag, New York (1996)
28. Peng, J., Mok, H. M.K., Tse, W.-M.: Fuzzy Dominance Based on Credibility Distributions. Lecture Notes in Artificial Intelligent (LNAI 3613) (2005) 295–303
29. Potvin, J.-Y., Dube, D., and Robillard, C.: Hybrid Approach to Vehicle Routing Using Neural Networks and Genetic Algorithms. Applied Intelligence **6** (1996) 241–252
30. Solomon, M.M. and Desrosiers, J.: Time Window Constrained Routing and Scheduling Problems. Transportation Science **22** (1988) 1–13
31. Stewart, W.R.Jr. and Golden, B.L.: Stochastic Vehicle Routing: A Comprehensive Approach. European Journal of Operational Research **14** (1983) 371–385
32. Teodorovic, D. and Kikuchi, S.: Application of Fuzzy Sets Theory to the Saving Based Vehicle Routing Algorithm. Civil Engineering Systems **8** (1991) 87–93
33. Teodorovic, D. and Pavkovic, G.: Fuzzy Set Theory Approach to the Vehicle Routing Problem When Demand at Nodes Is Uncertain. Fuzzy Sets and Systems **82** (1996) 307–317
34. Waters, C.D.J.: Vehicle-Scheduling Problems with Uncertainty and Omitted Customers. Journal of the Operational Research Society **40** (1989) 1099–1108

Solving Fuzzy Chance-Constrained Programming with Ant Colony Optimization-Based Algorithms and Application to Fuzzy Inventory Model

Yuanguo Zhu

Department of Applied Mathematics, Nanjing University of Science and Technology Nanjing, Jiangsu 210094, China
ygzhu@mail.njust.edu.cn

Abstract. An ant colony optimization algorithm is designed to solve continuous optimization models. Based on this algorithm, a hybrid intelligent algorithm combined with fuzzy simulation and neural network is introduced for solving fuzzy chance constrained models. Several numerical examples are given to show the algorithms effective. As an application, a fuzzy inventory model is established and solved with the hybrid intelligent algorithm.

1 Introduction

Dorigo [1] started the study and applications of ant colony optimization algorithm (ACOA) in the early nineties last century. In ACOA, the computational resources are allocated to a set of relatively simple agents (artificial ants) that exploit pheromone communication. ACOA and its improved versions have demonstrated considerable success in providing optimal solutions to many complex optimization problems and received more and more attentions during the past decade such as [2] [3] [4].

As we have seen, heuristic approaches are effective in finding solutions of uncertain programming. Liu and Iwamura [5] and Liu [6] integrated fuzzy simulation, neural network(NN), and genetic algorithm(GA) to produce a hybrid intelligent algorithm for solving many kinds of uncertain programming including fuzzy chance constrained programming. In this paper, we design an ant colony optimization algorithm for solving continuous optimization problems. Based on this algorithm, we present a hybrid intelligent algorithm combined fuzzy simulation and neural network for solving fuzzy chance constrained models.

2 Ant Colony Optimization Algorithm

Consider the following optimization problem

$$\begin{cases} \min f(x_1, x_2, \cdots, x_n) \\ \text{subject to:} \\ \qquad g(x_1, x_2, \cdots, x_n) \le 0 \end{cases} \tag{1}$$

D.-S. Huang, K. Li, and G.W. Irwin (Eds.): ICIC 2006, LNAI 4114, pp. 977–983, 2006.

where $x_1, x_2, \cdots, x_n$ are decision variables which are in the feasible set of constraints $\Omega = \{(x_1, x_2, \cdots, x_n) \in \mathbb{R}^n \mid g(x_1, x_2, \cdots, x_n) \leq 0\}$. Without loss of generality, we let Ω is included in a hypercube $L = \{(x_1, x_2, \cdots, x_n) \in \mathbb{R}^n \mid a_i \leq b_i,\ i = 1, 2, \cdots, n\}$. Suppose that the intervals $[a_i, b_i]$ are averagely divided into r_i subintervals, where r_i are positive integers, $i = 1, 2, \cdots, n$. These subintervals are associated to pheromone trails τ.

Given a fixed point $a \in \mathbb{R}$ (called start point) not in L, set $a_0 = b_0 = a$, $r_0 = 1$. Connect a with all subintervals of $[a_1, b_1]$, and connect each subinterval of $[a_i, b_i]$ with all subintervals of $[a_{i+1}, b_{i+1}]$, $i = 1, 2, \cdots, n-1$. Artificial ants build candidate solutions by movement on these connections. The procedures are described as follows.

(1) *Initialization Process*: Randomly generate a feasible solution s' and set $\hat{s} = s'$. For each ant, set $\tau_{i,j}(0) = \tau_0$, $j = 1, 2, \cdots, r_i$, $i = 1, 2, \cdots, n$, where τ_0 is a parameter, and $0 < \tau_{\min} \leq \tau_0 < +\infty$ for some fixed parameter $\tau_{\min}$.

(2) *Ant Movement*: At each step i after building the sequence $\langle x_1, x_2, \cdots, x_{i-1}\rangle$, select the next subinterval of $[a_i, b_i]$ in probability following

$$p_{i,j} = \frac{\tau_{i,j}(t)}{\sum_{k=1}^{r_i} \tau_{i,k}(t)}\,. \tag{2}$$

Randomly produce a point v from the chosen subinterval, and mutate this point to x_i so that it is still in the interval $[a_i, b_i]$. The mutation is made as follows: given a number $M > 0$, randomly produce a direction γ; choose $M' < M$ such that $x_i = v + \gamma M' \in [a_i, b_i]$. If the new sequence is infeasible, then the ant is dropped and its movement is terminated.

(3) *Pheromone Update*: At each moment t, let $\hat{s} = (x_1, x_2, \cdots, x_n)$ be the best feasible solution found so far. Reinforce the pheromone trails on subintervals in which corresponding coordinates of $\hat{s}$ are, and evaporate the pheromone trails on others:

$$\tau_{ij}(t) = \begin{cases} (1-\rho)\tau_{i,j}(t-1) + \rho g(\hat{s}), & \text{if } x_i \text{ is in the } j\text{th subinterval} \\ & \quad \text{of } [a_i, b_i], \\ (1-\rho)\tau_{i,j}(t-1), & \text{otherwise,} \end{cases} \tag{3}$$

where ρ, $0 < \rho < 1$ is the evaporation rate, and $g(s)$, $0 < g(s) < +\infty$ is a function with that $g(s) \geq g(s')$ if $f(s) < f(s')$.

3 Fuzzy Chance-Constrained Programming

We first recall some concepts in fuzzy environment [6]. Let Θ be a nonempty set, and $\mathcal{P}(\Theta)$ the power set of Θ. A function $\text{Pos} : \mathcal{P}(\Theta) \to \mathbb{R}$ is called a possibility measure if (i) $\text{Pos}\{\Theta\} = 1$, (ii) $\text{Pos}\{\emptyset\} = 0$, (iii) $\text{Pos}\{\cup_i A_i\} = \sup_i \text{Pos}\{A_i\}$ for any collection $\{A_i\}$ in $\mathcal{P}(\Theta)$. Then the triplet $(\Theta, \mathcal{P}(\Theta), \text{Pos})$ is called a possibility space. The credibility measure (Liu and Liu [7]) of an element A in

$\mathcal{P}(\Theta)$ is defined by $\mathrm{Cr}\{A\} = \frac{1}{2}(\mathrm{Pos}\{A\} + 1 - \mathrm{Pos}\{A^c\})$. A fuzzy variable ξ is defined as a function from a possibility space $(\Theta, \mathcal{P}(\Theta), \mathrm{Pos})$ to the set of real numbers $\mathbb{R}$. The membership function of a fuzzy variable ξ is derived from the possibility measure Pos by $\mu(x) = \mathrm{Pos}\{\theta \in \Theta \mid \xi(\theta) = x\}, \quad \text{for } x \in \mathbb{R}$.

Fuzzy Chance-Constrained Programming(CCP) are studied such as in Liu and Iwamura [5] and Liu [6]. When the optimistic return is maximized, a general single-objective fuzzy CCP may be formulated as

$$\begin{cases} \max \overline{f} \\ \text{subject to:} \\ \qquad \mathrm{Cr}\{f(x,\xi) \geq \overline{f}\} \geq \beta \\ \qquad \mathrm{Cr}\{g_j(x,\xi) \leq 0, \quad j = 1, 2, \cdots, p\} \geq \alpha \end{cases} \tag{4}$$

where α and β are the predetermined confidence levels, x is a decision vector, ξ is a fuzzy vector, $f(x,\xi)$ is the return function, and $g_j(x,\xi)$ are fuzzy constraint functions for $j = 1, 2, \cdots, p$. Liu and Iwamura [5] and Liu [6] integrated fuzzy simulation, neural network(NN), and genetic algorithm(GA) to produce a hybrid intelligent algorithm for solving fuzzy CCP, which was illustrated to be effective with several numerical examples.

Now, we will present an ant colony optimization-based hybrid intelligent algorithm for solving fuzzy CCP, which are introduced as following section.

4 Hybrid Intelligent Algorithm

In order to solve the fuzzy CCP (4), we embed the fuzzy simulation and neural network(NN), which would be referred to [6] for detail, into ant colony optimization algorithm to form a hybrid intelligent algorithm.

Algorithm: (Hybrid Intelligent Algorithm)

Step 1. Generate training input-output data for uncertain functions like

$$U_1 : x \to \max\{\overline{f} \mid \mathrm{Cr}\{f(x,\xi) \geq \overline{f}\} \geq \beta\} \tag{5}$$

$$U_2 : x \to \mathrm{Cr}\{g_j(x,\xi) \leq 0, j = 1, 2, \cdots, p\} \tag{6}$$

by fuzzy simulations.

Step 2. Train a neural network to approximate the uncertain functions by the generated training data.

Step 3. Partition the region which contains the optimal solution.

Step 4. Initialize all pheromone trails with the same amount of pheromone and randomly generate a solution whose feasibility may be checked by the trained neural network.

Step 5. Ant movement according to the pheromone trails to produce solution whose feasibility may be checked by the trained neural network.

Step 6. Repeat the fifth step for a given number of ants.

Step 7. Pheromone update according to the best feasible solution in the current algorithm iteration.

Step 8. Repeat the fifth to seventh steps for a given number of cycles or a terminate criterion.

Step 9. Report the best solution as the optimal solution.

5 Numerical Examples

In the following examples, the evaporation rate ρ and the probability of mutation p_m are chosen by several experiments.

Example 1. Consider the following fuzzy CCP,

$$\begin{cases} \max \overline{f} \\ \text{subject to:} \\ \qquad \text{Cr}\{\ln|x_1+\xi_1| + \ln|x_2+\xi_2| + \ln|x_3+\xi_3| \geq \overline{f}\} \geq 0.95 \\ \qquad \text{Cr}\{(x_1-\xi_1)^2 + (x_2-\xi_2)^2 + (x_3-\xi_3)^2 \leq 25\} \geq 0.90 \\ \qquad 0 \leq x_1, x_2, x_3 \leq 6 \end{cases} \tag{7}$$

where ξ_1, ξ_2, and ξ_3 are triangular fuzzy variables $(-1, 0, 2)$, $(0, 1.5, 2.5)$, and $(1, 2, 3)$, respectively. Let us first generate input-output data for the uncertain functions

$$U_1 : x \to \max\{\overline{f} \mid \text{Cr}\{\ln|x_1+\xi_1| + \ln|x_2+\xi_2| + \ln|x_3+\xi_3| \geq \overline{f}\} \geq 0.95\} \tag{8}$$

$$U_2 : x \to \text{Cr}\{(x_1-\xi_1)^2 + (x_2-\xi_2)^2 + (x_3-\xi_3)^2 \leq 25\} \tag{9}$$

by fuzzy simulations. Then we train an NN (3 input neurons, 15 hidden neurons, 2 output neurons) to approximate the functions $U_1(x), U_2(x)$. We averagely divide the interval $[0, 6]$ to 10 subintervals. Now the hybrid intelligent algorithm (6000 cycles in simulation, 2000 data in NN, 50 ants, 200 generations) is employed with the evaporation rate $\rho = 0.6$ and the probability of mutation $p_m = 0.4$ to show that the optimal solution is $x^* = (3.4634, 2.6106, 3.1366)$, whose objective value is 3.6542.

Table 1 shows that parameters ρ and p_m less effect the objective value but generation numbers.

Example 2. Consider the following fuzzy chance-constrained goal programming,

$$\begin{cases} \text{lexmin}\{d_1^-, d_2^-, d_3^-\} \\ \text{subject to:} \\ \qquad \text{Cr}\{0.7 - |\sin(\xi_1 - x_1)| \leq d_1^-\} \geq 0.90 \\ \qquad \text{Cr}\{0.6 - |\sin(\xi_1 + \xi_2 - x_1 - x_2)| \leq d_2^-\} \geq 0.85 \\ \qquad \text{Cr}\{0.75 - |\sin(\xi_2 + \xi_3 - x_2 - x_3)| \leq d_3^-\} \geq 0.80 \\ \qquad x_1^2 + x_2^2 + x_3^2 \leq 25 \\ \qquad x_1, x_2, x_3, d_1^-, d_2^-, d_3^- \geq 0 \end{cases} \tag{10}$$

Table 1. Several experiment results

ρ	p_m	generation numbers	objective values
0.2	0.8	1308	3.6517
0.2	0.7	1287	3.6535
0.3	0.6	959	3.6535
0.5	0.6	959	3.6535
0.5	0.5	703	3.6533
0.6	0.4	182	3.6542
0.8	0.2	299	3.6417
0.2	0.3	602	3.6534
0.5	0.3	602	3.6534
0.5	0.2	1324	3.6534

where ξ_1, ξ_2 and ξ_3 are triangular fuzzy variables $(0,1,2), (-2,-1,0)$, and $(1,2,3)$, respectively. The d_i^- is the optimistic negative deviation from the target of goal i, defined as

$$d_1^- = \min\{d \vee 0 \mid \mathrm{Cr}\{0.7 - |\sin(\xi_1 - x_1)| \le d\} \ge 0.90\}, \quad (11)$$

$$d_2^- = \min\{d \vee 0 \mid \mathrm{Cr}\{0.6 - |\sin(\xi_1 + \xi_2 - x_1 - x_2)| \le d\} \ge 0.85\}, \quad (12)$$

$$d_3^- = \min\{d \vee 0 \mid \mathrm{Cr}\{0.75 - |\sin(\xi_2 + \xi_3 - x_2 - x_3)| \le d\} \ge 0.80\} . \quad (13)$$

It is easy to know that the feasible set is contained in the following hypercube $L = \{(x_1, x_2, x_3) \mid 0 \le x_1 \le 5,\ 0 \le x_2 \le 5,\ 0 \le x_3 \le 5\}$. Let us first generate input-output data for the uncertain functions

$$U_1 : x \to \max\{d \mid \mathrm{Cr}\{|\sin(\xi_1 - x_1)| \ge d\} \ge 0.90\}, \quad (14)$$

$$U_2 : x \to \max\{d \mid \mathrm{Cr}\{|\sin(\xi_1 + \xi_2 - x_1 - x_2)| \ge d\} \ge 0.85\}, \quad (15)$$

$$U_3 : x \to \max\{d \mid \mathrm{Cr}\{|\sin(\xi_2 + \xi_3 - x_2 - x_3)| \ge d\} \ge 0.80\} \quad (16)$$

by fuzzy simulations. Then we train an NN (3 input neurons, 15 hidden neurons, 3 output neurons) to approximate the functions $U_1(x), U_2(x), U_3(x)$. Note that

$$d_1^- = [0.7 - U_1(x)] \vee 0,\ d_2^- = [0.6 - U_2(x)] \vee 0,\ d_3^- = [0.75 - U_3(x)] \vee 0 . \quad (17)$$

We averagely divide the interval $[0, 5]$ to 10 subintervals. Now the hybrid intelligent algorithm (6000 cycles in simulation, 2000 data in NN, 50 ants, 400 generations) is employed with the evaporation rate $\rho = 0.2$ and the probability of mutation $p_m = 0.2$ to show that the optimal solution is $x^* = (0.0088, 2.3504, 0.7164)$, which satisfies the first two goals, but the third objective value is 0.0447.

6 Inventory Model with Fuzzy Demands

Inventory problem is classic in management. Due to the complexity of social society, many factors in management behave uncertainty such as fuzzy variables. Researchers then presented some fuzzy inventory models, for example, inventory models with fuzzy demands [8], fuzzy production quantity [9], fuzzy holding cost [10], and so on.

We in this section establish a new fuzzy inventory model. First present some parameters as follows: x represents order quantity per block; y represents reorder point; ξ represents fuzzy demands per year; η represents fuzzy demands per day at a cycle; ζ represents fuzzy time between order and delivery (unite: day); c_1 represents order cost per block; c_2 represents holding cost per item at a year; c_3 represents penalty cost per item out of stock per day; T represents total inventory cost per year.

Total inventory cost per year is the sum of yearly order cost, yearly holding cost, and yearly penalty cost. Then $T = c_1\frac{\xi}{x} + c_2 Q_1 + c_3\frac{\xi}{x}Q_2$, where $Q_1 = y + \frac{x}{2} - \eta\zeta$, and $Q_2 = \eta\zeta - y$ if $y < \eta\zeta$, 0 if $y \geq \eta\zeta$. We will consider the following fuzzy CCP model if we want to minimize the α-pessimistic cost

$$\begin{cases} \min \overline{T} \\ \text{subject to:} \\ \qquad \text{Cr}\{T \leq \overline{T}\} \geq \alpha \\ \qquad x > 0, y > 0 \end{cases} \tag{18}$$

where $\overline{T}$ is the α-pessimistic cost.

Suppose that $c_1 = 100$, $c_2 = 150$, $c_3 = 30$, $\alpha = 0.90$ and ξ, η, ζ are trapezoidal fuzzy variable $(440, 450, 470, 480)$, trapezoidal fuzzy variable $(1, 1.5, 2, 3)$, triangle fuzzy variable $(9, 10, 11)$, respectively.

We can let the feasible set be contained in the hypercube $L = \{(x, y) \mid 0 < x \leq 100,\ 0 < y \leq 50\}$. Let us first approximate the uncertain function $U : (x, y) \rightarrow \min\{\overline{T} \mid \text{Cr}\{T \leq \overline{T}\} \geq 0.90\}$ by fuzzy simulation. Then the solution of problem (18) can be approximated by the following problem

$$\begin{cases} \min U(x, y) \\ \text{subject to:} \\ \qquad 0 < x \leq 100,\ 0 < y \leq 50\ . \end{cases} \tag{19}$$

Divide averagely the interval $[0, 100]$ to 10 subintervals, and $[0, 50]$ to 5 subintervals. Now the ant colony optimization algorithm (50 ants, 500 generations) is employed with the evaporation rate $\rho = 0.2$ and the probability of mutation $p_m = 0.3$ to show that the optimal solution is $x = 31.4673$, $y = 23.4291$, whose objective value is 5792.43. This means that when the amount of inventory items is 23.4291, it is required to order items 31.4673 so that yearly total cost is minimum.

7 Conclusions

Based on ant colony optimization algorithm, we designed a hybrid intelligent algorithm mixed fuzzy simulation and neural network for solving fuzzy chance constrained programming. Then we gave some numerical examples to illustrate the efficiency of the algorithms. Several experiments showed that the algorithm is stable with regard to main parameters. As an application, finally we established a fuzzy inventory model and solved it with the hybrid intelligent algorithm.

References

1. Dorigo, M.: Optimization, Learning and Natural Algorithm. Ph.D. dissertain (in Italian). Department of Electronics, Politecnico di Milano, Italy(1992)
2. Bullnheimer, B., Hartl, R.F., Strauss, C.: A New Rank-based Version of the Ant System: A Computational Study. Central European Journal for Operations Research and Economics. **7** (1999) 25-38
3. Parpinelli, R.S., Lopes, H.S., Freitas, A.A.: Data Mining with an Ant Colony Optimization Algorithm. IEEE Transactions on Evolutionary Computing. **6** (2002) 321-332
4. Stützle, T., Dorigo, M.: A Short Convergence Proof for a Class of Ant Colony Optimization Algorithm. IEEE Transactions on Evolutionary Computation. **6** (2002) 358-365
5. Liu, B., Iwamura, K.: Chance Constrained Programming with Fuzzy Parameters. Fuzzy Sets and Systems. **94** (1998) 227-237
6. Liu, B.: Theory and Practice of Uncertain Programming. Physica-Verlag, Heidelberg(2002)
7. Liu, B., Liu, Y.-K.: Expeccted Value of Fuzzy Variable and Fuzzy Expected Value Models. IEEE Transactions on Fuzzy Systems. **10** (2002) 445-450
8. Chen, S., Hsieh, C.H.: Optimization of Fuzzy Simple Inventory Models. IEEE International Fuzzy System Conference Proceedings. **1** (1999) 240-244
9. Hsieh, C.H.: Optimization of Fuzzy Production Inventory Models. Information Science. **146**(2002) 29-40
10. Park, K.S.: Fuzzy Set Theoretic Interpetation of Economic Order Quantity. IEEE Transactions on Systems, Man, and Cybernetics SMC. **17** (1987) 1082-1084
11. Liu, B.: Uncertainty Theory: An Introduction to its Axiomatic Foundations. Springer-Verlag, Berlin(2004)

The Infinite Dimensional Product Possibility Space and Its Applications

Yan-Kui Liu[1], Baoding Liu[2], and Yanju Chen[1]

[1] College of Mathematics and Computer Science, Hebei University, Baoding 071002, Hebei, China
yliu@mail.hbu.cn

[2] Department of Mathematical Sciences, Tsinghua University, Beijing 100084, China
liu@tsinghua.edu.cn

Abstract. This paper is devoted to the construction of infinite dimensional product possibility space as well as its applications in theory of fuzzy processes. First, the countably infinite dimensional product ample field, and the extension of countably many product possibility measures based on a continuous triangular norm are discussed. Then the results are generalized to the case of uncountably many factors. Finally, the obtained results about the product possibility space is applied to the construction of a fuzzy vector, a sequence of fuzzy variables and a fuzzy process.

1 Introduction

Since the pioneering work of Zadeh [17], possibility theory has been studied by a number of researchers such as Dubois and Prade [1], Klir [3], Janssen *et al.* [12], Nahmias [13], Wang [14], Wang and Klir [15], and Yager [16]. It is based on two nonadditive set functions, possibility and necessity measures, and may be characterized in terms of either of two measures. Although possibility and necessity measures have been widely used, the two set functions are inherently possessed of some shortcomings as they are employed to measure a fuzzy event. For instance, a fuzzy event may fail to occur even through its possibility is 1, and occur even through its necessity is 0. In addition, the two set functions have no self-duality property. However, a self-dual measure is required in both theory and practice. For this purpose, Liu and Liu [8] presented the concept of credibility measure via possibility and necessity measures. Moreover, an axiomatic approach based on credibility measure, called credibility theory, was developed [6]. In credibility theory, four axioms are required to define the possibility, the first three were given by Nahmias [13] to define a possibility measure, while the fourth one was given by Liu [4] to define the product possibility measure. Credibility theory provides the theoretical foundation for optimization under possibilistic uncertainty [5,9]. The reader who is interested in the recent development of credibility theory and its various applications may refer to [7,10]. The objective of this paper is to discuss the construction of the infinite dimensional product possibility space in credibility theory, and deal with its applications in theory

D.-S. Huang, K. Li, and G.W. Irwin (Eds.): ICIC 2006, LNAI 4114, pp. 984–989, 2006.

of fuzzy processes. The obtained results in this paper can be regarded as a generalization of the fourth axiom [4] in the case of the infinite dimensional product possibility space.

2 Possibility Spaces

Given a universe Γ, an ample field [14] $\mathcal{A}$ on Γ is a class of subsets of Γ that is closed under the formation of arbitrary unions, arbitrary intersections, and complement. The pair $(\Gamma, \mathcal{A})$ is called an *ample space* [14], whose counterpart in nonadditive measure theory [11,15] is a *measurable space.*

Let $\mathcal{C}$ be a subclass of $\mathcal{P}(\Gamma)$. Then the smallest ample field generated by $\mathcal{C}$ is denoted by $\mathcal{A}(\mathcal{C}) = \cap\{\mathcal{A} \mid \mathcal{C} \subset \mathcal{A} \text{ (ample field)}\}$. An *atom* $[\gamma]_{\mathcal{A}}$ of $\mathcal{A}$ containing the element γ of Γ is defined by $[\gamma]_{\mathcal{A}} = \cap\{A \mid \gamma \in A, A \in \mathcal{A}\}$.

Let $(\Gamma, \mathcal{A})$ be an ample space. A set function Pos defined on $\mathcal{A}$ is called a possibility measure [1,3] if it satisfies the following conditions:

P1) $\text{Pos}(\emptyset) = 0$, $\text{Pos}(\Gamma) = 1$, and
P2) $\text{Pos}(\cup_{i\in I} A_i) = \sup_{i\in I} \text{Pos}(A_i)$ for any subclass $\{A_i \mid i \in I\}$ of $\mathcal{A}$.

The triplet $(\Gamma, \mathcal{A}, \text{Pos})$ is called a *possibility space*, which was called a *pattern space* by Nahmias [13]. A function $\xi : \Gamma \to \Re$ is called a fuzzy variable if for any $t \in \Re$, $\{\gamma \mid \xi(\gamma) \le t\} \in \mathcal{A}$. The possibility distribution of the fuzzy variable ξ is defined as $\mu_\xi(t) = \text{Pos}\{\gamma \mid \xi(\gamma) = t\}$ for any $t \in \Re$.

3 Product Possibility Spaces

3.1 Countably Infinite Dimension

Suppose $\Gamma_n, n = 1, 2, \cdots$, is a sequence of nonempty sets, the product of the sequence of sets is denoted by $\prod_{n=1}^{\infty} \Gamma_n = \{(\gamma_1, \gamma_2, \cdots) \mid \gamma_n \in \Gamma_n, n = 1, 2, \cdots\}$.

Let $\{(\Gamma_n, \mathcal{A}_n), n = 1, 2, \cdots\}$ be a sequence of ample spaces. For each positive integer n, denote by $\mathcal{D}_{[n]} = \{A \times \prod_{k=n+1}^{\infty} \Gamma_k, A \in \mathcal{D}_{(n)}\}$, where $\mathcal{D}_{(n)} = \{\prod_{k=1}^{n} A_k \mid \mathcal{A}_k \ni A_k \text{ atoms}, k = 1, \cdots, n\}$.

The sets in the class $\mathcal{D} = \bigcup_{n=1}^{\infty} \mathcal{D}_{[n]}$ are called *measurable atom-cylinders* determined by the ample fields $\{\mathcal{A}_n, n = 1, 2, \cdots\}$. The ample field $\prod_{n=1}^{\infty} \mathcal{A}_n = \mathcal{A}(\mathcal{D})$ generated by $\mathcal{D}$ is called the product ample field of $\{\mathcal{A}_n, n = 1, 2, \cdots\}$, and $(\prod_{n=1}^{\infty} \Gamma_n, \prod_{n=1}^{\infty} \mathcal{A}_n)$ is called the product ample space of $\{(\Gamma_n, \mathcal{A}_n), n = 1, 2, \cdots\}$.

Particularly, the product of a sequence of same ample space $(\Gamma, \mathcal{A})$ is denoted by $(\Gamma^\infty, \mathcal{A}^\infty)$.

For each n, the map $p_n(\gamma_1, \gamma_2, \cdots) = \gamma_n$ is called the projection from the product space $\prod_{n=1}^{\infty} \Gamma_n$ to the space Γ_n, while the map $p_{(n)}(\gamma_1, \gamma_2, \cdots) = (\gamma_1, \cdots, \gamma_n)$ is called the projection from the product space $\prod_{n=1}^{\infty} \Gamma_n$ to the space $\prod_{k=1}^{n} \Gamma_k$.

Proposition 1. *Let $\{(\Gamma_n, \mathcal{A}_n), n = 1, 2, \cdots\}$ be a sequence of ample spaces. Then*

(1) *For each* $n = 1, 2, \cdots$, *the projection* p_n *is a measurable map from the product ample space* $(\prod_{n=1}^{\infty} \Gamma_n, \prod_{n=1}^{\infty} \mathcal{A}_n)$ *to the space* $(\Gamma_n, \mathcal{A}_n)$;

(2) $\prod_{n=1}^{\infty} \mathcal{A}_n$ *is the smallest ample field such that* $p_1, p_2, \cdots$ *are all measurable, i.e.,* $\prod_{n=1}^{\infty} \mathcal{A}_n = \mathcal{A}(\bigcup_{n=1}^{\infty} p_n^{-1} \mathcal{A}_n)$.

Proof. For any $n = 1, 2, \cdots$, and any $A_n \in \mathcal{A}_n$, if A_n is an atom of $\mathcal{A}_n$, then one has

$$p_n^{-1} A_n = \bigcup_{\gamma_i \in \Gamma_i, i \le n-1} \prod_{i=1}^{n-1} [\gamma_i]_{\mathcal{A}_i} \times A_n \times \prod_{i=n+1}^{\infty} \Gamma_i \in \mathcal{A}(\mathcal{D}) = \prod_{n=1}^{\infty} \mathcal{A}_n.$$

If A_n is not an atom, then it can be expressed as the union of atoms, i.e., $A_n = \bigcup_{\gamma_n \in A_n} [\gamma_n]_{\mathcal{A}_n}$, and it follows that $p_n^{-1} A_n = \bigcup_{\gamma_n \in A_n} p_n^{-1} [\gamma_n]_{\mathcal{A}_n} \in \prod_{n=1}^{\infty} \mathcal{A}_n$, which implies that p_n is measurable, the first assertion is proved. Moreover, $\bigcup_{n=1}^{\infty} p_n^{-1} \mathcal{A}_n \subset \prod_{n=1}^{\infty} \mathcal{A}_n$, it follows that $\mathcal{A}(\bigcup_{n=1}^{\infty} p_n^{-1} \mathcal{A}_n) \subset \prod_{n=1}^{\infty} \mathcal{A}_n$.

On the other hand, for any $D \in \mathcal{D} = \bigcup_{n=1}^{\infty} \mathcal{D}_{[n]}$, there exists a positive integer n such that $D \in \mathcal{D}_{[n]}$. As a consequence, there exists $A = \prod_{k=1}^{n} A_k \in \mathcal{D}_{(n)}$ such that

$$D = A \times \prod_{k=n+1}^{\infty} \Gamma_k = \bigcap_{i=1}^{n} p_i^{-1} A_i \in \mathcal{A}\left(\bigcup_{n=1}^{\infty} p_n^{-1} \mathcal{A}_n \right),$$

which implies $\prod_{n=1}^{\infty} \mathcal{A}_n = \mathcal{A}(\mathcal{D}) \subset \mathcal{A}(\bigcup_{n=1}^{\infty} p_n^{-1} \mathcal{A}_n)$. The assertion (2) is verified.

Proposition 2. *Let* $(\Gamma, \mathcal{A})$ *be an ample space,* $\{(Y_n, \mathcal{F}_n), n = 1, 2, \cdots\}$ *a sequence of ample spaces, and* $\xi = (\xi_1, \xi_2, \cdots)$ *a map from* Γ *to* $\prod_{n=1}^{\infty} Y_n$. *Then* ξ *is a measurable map from the ample space* $(\Gamma, \mathcal{A})$ *to the product ample space* $(\prod_{n=1}^{\infty} Y_n, \prod_{n=1}^{\infty} \mathcal{F}_n)$ *iff* $\xi_n, n = 1, 2, \cdots$, *are measurable maps from the ample space* $(\Gamma, \mathcal{A})$ *to* $(Y_n, \mathcal{F}_n)$.

Proof. Since

$$\begin{aligned}\xi^{-1} \prod_{n=1}^{\infty} \mathcal{F}_n &= \xi^{-1} \mathcal{A}\left(\bigcup_{n=1}^{\infty} p_n^{-1} \mathcal{F}_n \right) = \mathcal{A}\left(\xi^{-1} \left(\bigcup_{n=1}^{\infty} p_n^{-1} \mathcal{F}_n \right) \right) \\ &= \mathcal{A}\left(\bigcup_{n=1}^{\infty} \xi^{-1} \left(p_n^{-1} \mathcal{F}_n \right) \right) = \mathcal{A}\left(\bigcup_{n=1}^{\infty} (p_n \circ \xi)^{-1} \mathcal{F}_n \right) = \mathcal{A}\left(\bigcup_{n=1}^{\infty} \xi_n^{-1} \mathcal{F}_n \right),\end{aligned}$$

it follows that the desired assertion is valid.

We now discuss the product possibility space of a sequence of possibility spaces $(\Gamma_n, \mathcal{A}_n, \text{Pos}_n), n = 1, 2, \cdots$. For each $D = A \times \prod_{k=n+1}^{\infty} \Gamma_k \in \mathcal{D}$, we define a set function Π as follows

$$\Pi(D) = T_{k=1}^{n} \text{Pos}_k(A_k) \tag{1}$$

where $A = \prod_{k=1}^{n} A_k \in \mathcal{D}_{(n)}$, and T is a continuous triangular norm [2].

Theorem 1. *The set function* Π *defined by Eq. (1) can be uniquely extended to a possibility measure* Pos *on the product ample field* $\prod_{n=1}^{\infty} \mathcal{A}_n$.

Proof. For each $E \in \prod_{n=1}^{\infty} \mathcal{A}_n$, define

$$\mathrm{Pos}(E) = \sup_{\gamma \in E} \inf_{D | \gamma \in D \in \mathcal{D}} \Pi(D).$$

Noting that $\pi(\gamma) = \inf_{D|\gamma \in D \in \mathcal{D}} \Pi(D)$ is a map from $\prod_{n=1}^{\infty} \Gamma_n$ to [0,1], it is easy to check that Pos is a possibility measure on $\prod_{n=1}^{\infty} \mathcal{A}_n$.

Suppose $E \in \mathcal{D}$, then we have $\mathrm{Pos}(E) = \Pi(E)$. In fact, for E, there exist some positive n and $A = \prod_{k=1}^{n} A_k \in \mathcal{D}_{(n)}$ such that $E = A \times \prod_{k=n+1}^{\infty} \Gamma_k$. Letting $\gamma_k \in A_k, k = 1, \cdots, n$, then $[\gamma_k]_{\mathcal{A}_k} = A_k, k = 1, \cdots, n$. Hence

$$\begin{aligned}\mathrm{Pos}(E) &= \sup_{\gamma \in E} \inf_{D|\gamma \in D \in \mathcal{D}} \Pi(D) = \sup_{\gamma \in E} T_{m=1}^{\infty} \mathrm{Pos}_m([\gamma_m]_{\mathcal{A}_m}) \\ &= \sup_{\gamma \in E} T\left(T_{k=1}^{n} \mathrm{Pos}_k([\gamma_k]_{\mathcal{A}_k}), T_{k=n+1}^{\infty} \mathrm{Pos}_k([\gamma_k]_{\mathcal{A}_k})\right) \\ &= T_{k=1}^{n} \mathrm{Pos}_k([\gamma_k]_{\mathcal{A}_k}) = \Pi(E).\end{aligned}$$

We now discuss the uniqueness of the extension. Suppose A has the following two expressions $A = \bigcup_{\theta \in \Theta} A_\theta = \bigcup_{s \in S} A_s$. Then, for any A_θ, there is $\gamma \in A_\theta$ such that $[\gamma]_{\prod_{n=1}^{\infty} \mathcal{A}_n} = A_\theta$. Since $\gamma \in \bigcup_{s \in S} A_s$, there is s' such that $\gamma \in A_{s'}$, which implies $A_\theta = A_{s'}$. Therefore, $\mathrm{Pos}(A_\theta) = \mathrm{Pos}(A_{s'}) \le \sup_{s \in S} \mathrm{Pos}(A_s)$, it follows that $\sup_{\theta \in \Theta} \mathrm{Pos}(A_\theta) \le \sup_{s \in S} \mathrm{Pos}(A_s)$ by the arbitrary of θ. The converse inequality can be proved similarly. The proof is complete.

3.2 Uncountably Infinite Dimension

We now discuss the generalization of product space theory to uncountably many factors. For this purpose, let I be an arbitrary index set, and $\{\Gamma_i, i \in I\}$ a family of nonempty sets. Then the set

$$\prod_{i \in I} \Gamma_i = \{\gamma = \{\gamma_i, i \in I\} \mid \gamma_i \in \Gamma_i, \forall i \in I\}$$

is called the arbitrarily infinite dimensional product space of sets $\{\Gamma_i, i \in I\}$.

For each $i \in I$, the map $p_i\{\gamma_i, i \in I\} = \gamma_i$ is called the projection from the product space $\prod_{i \in I} \Gamma_i$ to the space Γ_i, and the map $p_J\{\gamma_i, i \in I\} = \{\gamma_j. j \in J\}$ is called the projection from the product space $\prod_{i \in I} \Gamma_i$ to the space $\prod_{j \in J} \Gamma_j$, where J is a subset of I, and $\{\gamma_j, j \in J\}$ is an element of $\prod_{j \in J} \Gamma_j$.

Let

$$\mathcal{J} = \{J \mid J = \{j_1, \cdots, j_n\}, j_k \in I (k \le n), n \in N\}.$$

Then the sets in the class $\mathcal{D} = \bigcup_{J \in \mathcal{J}} \{p_J^{-1} \prod_{j \in J} A_j \mid \mathcal{A}_j \ni A_j \text{ atoms}, \forall j \in J\}$ are called *measurable atom-cylinders* determined by the ample fields $\{\mathcal{A}_i, i \in I\}$. The ample field $\prod_{i \in I} \mathcal{A}_i = \mathcal{A}(\mathcal{D})$ generated by $\mathcal{D}$ is called the product ample field of $\{\mathcal{A}_i, i \in I\}$, and $(\prod_{i \in I} \Gamma_i, \prod_{i \in I} \mathcal{A}_i)$ is called the product ample space of $\{(\Gamma_i, \mathcal{A}), i \in I\}$.

Particularly, the product of a family of same ample space $(\Gamma, \mathcal{A})$ is denoted by $(\Gamma^I, \mathcal{A}^I)$.

Proposition 3. *Let $\{(\Gamma_i, \mathcal{A}_i), i \in I\}$ be a family of ample spaces. Then*

(1) *For each $i \in I$, the projection p_i is a measurable map from the product ample space $(\prod_{i\in I} \Gamma_i, \prod_{i\in I} \mathcal{A}_i)$ to the space $(\Gamma_i, \mathcal{A}_i)$;*
(2) *$\prod_{i\in I} \mathcal{A}_i$ is the smallest ample field such that $p_i, i \in I$, are all measurable, i.e., $\prod_{i\in I} \mathcal{A}_i = \mathcal{A}(\bigcup_{i\in I} p_i^{-1}\mathcal{A}_i)$.*

Proposition 4. *Let $(\Gamma, \mathcal{A})$ be an ample space, $\{(Y_i, \mathcal{F}_i), i \in I\}$ a family of ample spaces, and $\xi = \{\xi_i, i \in I\}$ a map from Γ to $\prod_{i\in I} Y_i$. Then ξ is a measurable map from the ample space $(\Gamma, \mathcal{A})$ to the product ample space $(\prod_{i\in I} Y_i, \prod_{i\in I} \mathcal{F}_i)$ iff $\xi_i, i \in I$, are measurable maps from the ample space $(\Gamma, \mathcal{A})$ to $(Y_i, \mathcal{F}_i)$.*

We now discuss the product possibility space of $\{(\Gamma_i, \mathcal{A}_i, \mathrm{Pos}_i), i \in I\}$. For each $D = p_J^{-1} \prod_{j\in J} A_j \in \mathcal{D}$, we define a set function Π as follows

$$\Pi(D) = T_{j\in J} \mathrm{Pos}_j(A_j), \tag{2}$$

where T is a continuous triangular norm. Then we have

Theorem 2. *The set function Π defined by Eq. (2) can be uniquely extended to a possibility measure* Pos *on the product ample field $\prod_{i\in I} \mathcal{A}_i$.*

4 Applications in Theory of Fuzzy Processes

Theorem 3. *Let $\pi_k, k = 1, 2, \cdots, n$, be $[0, 1]$-valued functions defined on $\Re$ and T a continuous triangular norm. If for each k, $\sup_{t_k\in\Re} \pi_k(t_k) = 1$, then there exist some possibility space $(\Gamma, \mathcal{A}, \mathrm{Pos})$ and a fuzzy vector $\xi = (\xi_1, \xi_2, \cdots, \xi_n)$ defined on the space such that the possibility distribution of ξ is $T_{k=1}^n \pi_k$.*

Theorem 4. *Let $\pi_n, n = 1, 2, \cdots$, be a sequence of $[0, 1]$-valued functions defined on $\Re$ and T a continuous triangular norm. If for each n, $\sup_{t_n\in\Re} \pi_n(t_n) = 1$, then there exist some possibility space $(\Gamma, \mathcal{A}, \mathrm{Pos})$ and a sequence of fuzzy variables $\xi = (\xi_1, \xi_2, \cdots)$ defined on the space such that for any positive integer n, the joint possibility distribution of $\xi_k, k = 1, 2, \cdots, n$, is $T_{k=1}^n \pi_k$.*

Theorem 5. *Let $\pi_i, i \in I$, be a family of $[0, 1]$-valued functions defined on $\Re$ and T a continuous triangular norm. If for each i, $\sup_{t_i\in\Re} \pi_i(t_i) = 1$, then there exist some possibility space $(\Gamma, \mathcal{A}, \mathrm{Pos})$ and a fuzzy process $\xi = \{\xi_i, i \in I\}$ defined on the space such that for any finite index set $J = \{j_1, j_2, \cdots, j_n\}$, the joint possibility distribution of $\xi_j, j \in J$, is $T_{j\in J}\pi_j$.*

5 Conclusion

In this paper, the issue of infinite dimensional product possibility space was examined, and its applications were also considered. First, the countably many product ample field, and countably many product possibility measure based on a continuous triangular norm were constructed so that a triangular norm-based countably infinite dimensional product possibility space was well-defined in credibility theory. Second, the results about the countably infinite dimensional product possibility space were generalized to the case of triangular norm-based arbitrarily many infinite dimensional product possibility space. Finally, the product possibility theory was applied to the construction of a fuzzy vector, a sequence of fuzzy variables and a fuzzy process.

Acknowledgments

This work was supported by the National Natural Science Foundation of China under Grant No.70571021, and the Natural Science Foundation of Hebei Province under Grant No.A2005000087.

References

1. Dubois, D., Prade, H.: Possibility Theory. Plenum, New York (1988)
2. Klement, E.P., Mesiar, R., Pap, E.: Triangular Norms. Kluwer Academic Publishers (2000)
3. Klir, G.J.: On Fuzzy-Set Interpretation of Possibility Theory. Fuzzy Sets Syst. **108** (1999) 263–273
4. Liu, B.: Toward Fuzzy Optimization without Mathematical Ambiguity. Fuzzy Optimization and Decision Making **1** (2002) 43–64
5. Liu, B.: Theory and Practice of Uncertain Programming. Physica-Verlag, Heidelberg (2002)
6. Liu, B.: Uncertainty Theory: An Introduction to Its Axiomatic Foundations. Springer-Verlag, Berlin Heidelberg New York (2004)
7. Liu, B.: A Survey of Credibility Theory. Fuzzy Optimization and Decision Making (to appear)
8. Liu, B., Liu, Y.K.: Expected Value of Fuzzy Variable and Fuzzy Expected Value Models. IEEE Trans. Fuzzy Syst. **10** (2002) 445–450
9. Liu, Y.K.: Fuzzy Programming with Recourse. Int. J. Uncertainty Fuzziness Knowl.-Based Syst. **13** (2005) 381-413
10. Liu, Y.K.: Convergent Results About the Use of Fuzzy Simulation in Fuzzy Optimization Problems. IEEE Trans. Fuzzy Syst. **14** (2006) 295-304
11. Liu, Y.K.: The Completion of a Fuzzy Measure and Its Applications. Fuzzy Sets Syst. **123** (2001) 137-145
12. Janssen, H.J., de Cooman, G., and Kerre, E.E.: Ample Fields as a Basis for Possibilistic Processes. Fuzzy Sets Syst. **120** (2001) 445–458
13. Nahmias, S.: Fuzzy Variables. Fuzzy Sets Syst. **1** (1978) 97–101
14. Wang, P.: Fuzzy Contactability and Fuzzy Variables. Fuzzy Sets Syst. **8** (1982) 81–92
15. Wang, Z., Klir, G.J.: Fuzzy Measure Theory. Plenum, New York (1992)
16. Yager, R.R.: Determining Equivalent Values for Possibilistic Variables. IEEE Trans. Syst., Man, Cybern. B **31** (2001) 19–31
17. Zadeh, L.A.: Fuzzy Sets as a Basis for a Theory of Possibility. Fuzzy Sets Syst. **1** (1978) 3–28

A New Sensor Fault Diagnosis Technique Based Upon Subspace Identification and Residual Filtering

Srinivasan Rajaraman[1,2], Uwe Kruger[3], M. Sam Mannan[1], and Juergen Hahn[2,⋆]

[1] Department of Chemical Engineering, Texas A&M University, College Station, TX 77843-3122, U.S.A.
s0r2637@chemail.tamu.edu, hahn@tamu.edu
[2] Mary Kay O' Connor Process Safety Center,Texas A&M University, College Station, TX 77843-3122, U.S.A.
mannan@tamu.edu
[3] Intelligent Systems and Control Group, Queen's University Belfast, BT9 5AH, U.K.
uwe.kruger@ee.qub.ac.uk

Abstract. This paper presents a new methodology for designing a detection, isolation, and identification scheme for sensor faults in linear time-varying systems. Practically important is that the proposed methodology is constructed on the basis of historical data and does not require *a priori* information to isolate and identify sensor faults. This is achieved by identifying a state space model and designing a fault isolation and identification filter. To address time-varying process behavior, the state space model and fault reconstruction filter are updated using a two-time-scale approach. Fault identification takes place at a higher frequency than the adaptation of the monitoring scheme. To demonstrate the utility of the new scheme, the paper evaluates its performance using simulations of a LTI system and a chemical process with time-varying parameters and industrial data from a debutanizer and a melter process.

1 Introduction

The development of first principles models for monitoring complex process systems is expensive in terms of the associated cost and time [1]. Therefore, the presented paper extends the fault diagnosis technique proposed in [2] by identifying the model using subspace model identification (SMI) [3].

In contrast to some of the existing process monitoring techniques [4,5,6,7], this new scheme performs fault detection, isolation, and identification of sensor faults in linear time-varying systems. To isolate and identify sensor faults, a residual filter is applied, which is updated together with the state space model at predefined intervals.

⋆ Corresponding author: hahn@tamu.edu, Tel.: +(979)845-3568, Fax: (979)845-6446.

D.-S. Huang, K. Li, and G.W. Irwin (Eds.): ICIC 2006, LNAI 4114, pp. 990–998, 2006.

The structure of the paper is as follows: A detailed presentation of the new dynamic sensor fault diagnosis methodology is followed by the presentation of two application studies. Section IV presents the conclusions for this paper.

2 A New Model-Based Fault Diagnosis Scheme

This section details the development of the new model-based methodology for diagnosing sensor faults. Subsection 2.1 presents a technique for combining empirical state space models with a model-based fault diagnosis scheme. Subsection 2.2 then discusses how to detect faulty sensors, followed by how to isolate and identify the sensor faults in Subsections 2.3 and 2.4. Finally, Subsection 2.5 outlines how to update the monitoring model using a two-time-scale approach.

2.1 Residual Generation Using State Space Models

The model structure for multivariate discrete LTI systems that is used in this work is given by:

$$\begin{aligned} \mathbf{x}(k+1) &= \mathbf{A}\mathbf{x}(k) + \mathbf{B}\mathbf{u}(k) + \mathbf{w}(k) \\ \mathbf{y}(k) &= \mathbf{C}\mathbf{x}(k) + \mathbf{D}\mathbf{u}(k) + \mathbf{v}(k) \end{aligned} \tag{1}$$

where $\mathbf{w}(k) \in \mathcal{N}(\mathbf{0}, \boldsymbol{\Sigma}_w)$ represents process noise and $\mathbf{v}(k) \in \mathcal{N}(\mathbf{0}, \boldsymbol{\Sigma}_v)$ represents sensor noise, which are normally distributed white noise sequences of zero mean with covariance matrices $\boldsymbol{\Sigma}_w$ and $\boldsymbol{\Sigma}_v$. Prior to the application of the N4SID algorithm, the recorded measurements of the input and output variables are mean centered and scaled to unit variance:

$$\widetilde{\mathbf{u}}(k) = \mathbf{S}_u^{-\frac{1}{2}} \left(\mathbf{u}(k) - \bar{\mathbf{u}}\right) \qquad \widetilde{\mathbf{y}}(k) = \mathbf{S}_y^{-\frac{1}{2}} \left(\mathbf{y}(k) - \bar{\mathbf{y}}\right), \tag{2}$$

where $\mathbf{S}_u$ and $\mathbf{S}_y$ are diagonal matrices storing the standard deviation of the input and output variables and $\bar{\mathbf{u}}$ and $\bar{\mathbf{y}}$ are vectors storing the mean values of the input and output variables, respectively. Using estimations of the state sequences, $\widehat{\mathbf{x}}(k+1)$ and $\widehat{\mathbf{x}}(k)$, sequences of the process and sensor noise, $\widehat{\mathbf{w}}(k)$ and $\widehat{\mathbf{v}}(k)$, and the state space matrices, $\widehat{\mathbf{A}}$, $\widehat{\mathbf{B}}$, $\widehat{\mathbf{C}}$ and $\widehat{\mathbf{D}}$, Equation (1) becomes:

$$\begin{aligned} \widehat{\mathbf{x}}(k+1) &= \widehat{\mathbf{A}}\widehat{\mathbf{x}}(k) + \widehat{\mathbf{B}}\widetilde{\mathbf{u}}(k) + \widehat{\mathbf{w}}(k) \\ \widetilde{\mathbf{y}}(k) &= \widehat{\mathbf{C}}\widehat{\mathbf{x}}(k) + \widehat{\mathbf{D}}\widetilde{\mathbf{u}}(k) + \widehat{\mathbf{v}}(k). \end{aligned} \tag{3}$$

It is assumed that the above state-space model captures the scaled input-output response of the actual system, described in Equation (1), accurately. In the presence of a sensor fault, characterized by the fault vector $\mathbf{f}_s(k)$, Equation (1) can be reformulated as follows:

$$\begin{aligned} \mathbf{x}(k+1) &= \mathbf{A}\mathbf{x}(k) + \mathbf{B}\mathbf{u}(k) + \mathbf{w}(k) \\ \mathbf{y}^f(k) &= \mathbf{C}\mathbf{x}(k) + \mathbf{D}\mathbf{u}(k) + \mathbf{v}(k) + \mathbf{f}_s(k) \end{aligned} \tag{4}$$

Here, $\mathbf{y}^f(k)$ represents the faulty sensor measurement. It should be noted that actuator faults are not considered in this work. Although this is an equally important problem, the application of the above technique for actuator faults is proposed for future research. To use the fault detection, isolation and identification algorithm, the input and output measurements of the system, given by Equation (4), are scaled according to Equation (2). This provides a common metric to compare the predicted and actual system measurements, where:

$$\widetilde{\mathbf{y}}^f(k) = \widetilde{\mathbf{y}}(k) + \widetilde{\mathbf{f}}_s, \quad \widetilde{\mathbf{f}}_s = \mathbf{S}_y^{-\frac{1}{2}}\mathbf{f}_s \tag{5}$$

A closed-loop observer is developed using the identified state space model to estimate the actual process outputs. Although the state sequences may alternatively be obtained by using Equation (8), it has been shown in reference [8] that utilizing a closed-loop state estimator increases the rate of decay of the prediction error and reduces the effect of plant-model mismatch and measurement noise on the estimated outputs. The estimation of the state sequences is given by the following equation:

$$\begin{aligned} \widehat{\mathbf{x}}(k+1) &= \widehat{\mathbf{A}}\widehat{\mathbf{x}}(k) + \mathbf{L}\left(\widetilde{\mathbf{y}}^f(k) - \widehat{\widetilde{\mathbf{y}}}(k)\right) + \widehat{\mathbf{B}}\widetilde{\mathbf{u}}(k) \\ \widehat{\widetilde{\mathbf{y}}}(k) &= \widehat{\mathbf{C}}\widehat{\mathbf{x}}_k + \widehat{\mathbf{D}}\widetilde{\mathbf{u}}(k) \end{aligned} \tag{6}$$

where, $\widehat{\mathbf{x}}(k) \in \mathbb{R}^n$ and $\widehat{\widetilde{\mathbf{y}}}(k) \in \mathbb{R}^m$ are the estimates of $\mathbf{x}(k)$ and $\widetilde{\mathbf{y}}(k)$ respectively. Finally, the filtered residual vector $\widetilde{\mathbf{r}}(k)$ is given by:

$$\widetilde{\mathbf{r}}(k) = \sum_{\tau=1}^{k} \mathbf{Q}(k-\tau)\left(\widetilde{\mathbf{y}}^f(\tau) - \widehat{\widetilde{\mathbf{y}}}(\tau)\right), \tag{7}$$

Next, it is discussed how a sensor fault can be detected, isolated and identified.

2.2 Fault Detection

The main purpose of fault detection is to determine whether there are faulty sensor readings. It can be seen from Equation (15) that:

$$\begin{aligned} &(1)\ \widetilde{\mathbf{r}}(k) = \mathbf{0} \quad \text{if} \quad \widetilde{\mathbf{f}}_s = 0 \quad \text{since } \mathbf{S}_y^{-\frac{1}{2}} \text{ is an invertible matrix} \quad \Rightarrow \quad \mathbf{f}_s = \mathbf{0} \\ &(2)\ \widetilde{\mathbf{r}}(k) \neq 0 \quad \text{if} \quad \widetilde{\mathbf{f}}_s \neq \mathbf{0} \quad \Rightarrow \quad \mathbf{f}_s \neq \mathbf{0}, \end{aligned}$$

which indicates that the value of $\widetilde{\mathbf{r}}(k)$ offers a boolean decision as to whether or not any faulty sensor readings are present.

2.3 Fault Isolation

To perform fault isolation, the state-space system given by Equation (11) is assumed to be observable through each of the outputs $\mathbf{y}$. It was shown that this requirement is mandatory for the existence of a fault isolation filter [9]. However, the application of subspace identification to produce a state space process model guarantees that this requirement is fulfilled [3].

To achieve fault isolation as well as identification, the proposed approach uses a series of dedicated observers. More precisely, the residuals of each output variables are filtered through an individual filter leading to the following isolation decision:

(3) $\widetilde{r}_i(k) = 0 \quad \text{if} \quad \widetilde{f}_{s_i} = 0$
(4) $\widetilde{r}_i(k) \neq 0 \quad \text{if} \quad \widetilde{f}_{s_i} \neq 0 \quad i = 1, 2, 3, \ldots, m,$

2.4 Fault Identification

Fault identification entails the reconstruction of the shape and size of the fault signal. To estimate the shape and size of the fault, the residuals have to meet the following objective [9]:

(5) $\lim_{k \to \infty} \left(r_i(k) - \widetilde{f}_{s_i} \right) = 0 \quad i = 1, 2, 3, \ldots, m$

In other words, residuals should asymptotically converge to the actual fault signal. Since a dedicated observer scheme is utilized in the proposed approach, it remains to choose a suitable filter $\mathbf{Q}(k)$ to meet all the conditions for fault detection, isolation, and identification. The following diagonal elements of the filter matrix $\mathbf{Q}(z)$ satisfies the requirement for fault detection, isolation, and identification:

$$q_{ii}(z) = 1 + \widehat{\mathbf{c}}_i^T \left[z\mathbf{I} - \widehat{\mathbf{A}} \right]^{-1} \mathbf{l}_i, \quad i = 1, 2, \ldots, m, \tag{8}$$

where $\widehat{\mathbf{c}}_i^T$ is the ith row of $\widehat{\mathbf{C}}$. Note that the non-diagonal matrix elements of $\mathbf{Q}(z)$ are equal to zero. Finally, the unscaled fault is reconstructed through $\mathbf{f}_s = \mathbf{S}_y^{\frac{1}{2}} \widetilde{\mathbf{f}}_s$

2.5 Adaptation of the Monitoring Model

The model structure detailed above is linear and time-invariant. On the basis of the work in reference [2], an adaptation of the state space model and consequently the filter is considered to address time-varying process behavior. This is also of significant practical importance, since the performance deterioration of process units, e.g. heat exchanger and valves, are common. Figure 1 illustrates that the adaptation of the monitoring model is carried out using a two-time-scale approach. In the above figure, stage 1 represents the initial state when the introduced monitoring scheme is identified and implemented. This stage entails the identification of an initial state space model and filter. Stages 2 and 3, are repeated alternatingly throughout the operation, where the time between the start of each stage is decided by the nature of the process. It should be noted that the stage where the state space model and the filter are adapted, i.e. stage 3, only represent a "short period" to record reference data of the process. In contrast, stage 2 represents a "long period", where the monitoring technique is applied on-line. This period depends on the time-varying nature of the process and may last up to 6 month [10] in industrial practice.

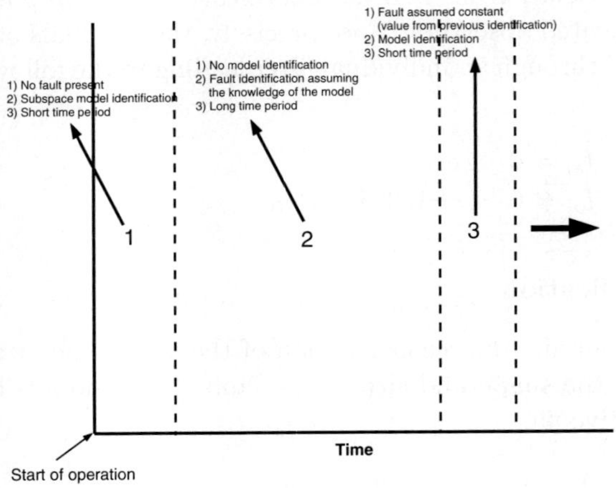

Fig. 1. Schematic fault identification for systems with time-varying parameters

3 Application Studies

In this section, the performance of the subspace model-based fault diagnosis methodology is evaluated using simulations and data from processes found in industry.

3.1 Application to an Industrial Distillation Process

This case study summarizes the application of the linear subspace model-based fault methodology to industrial data from a debutanizer process, which is designed to purify Butane from a fresh feed comprising of a mixture of hydrocarbons, mainly Butane and Hexane and impurities of Propane. This process has

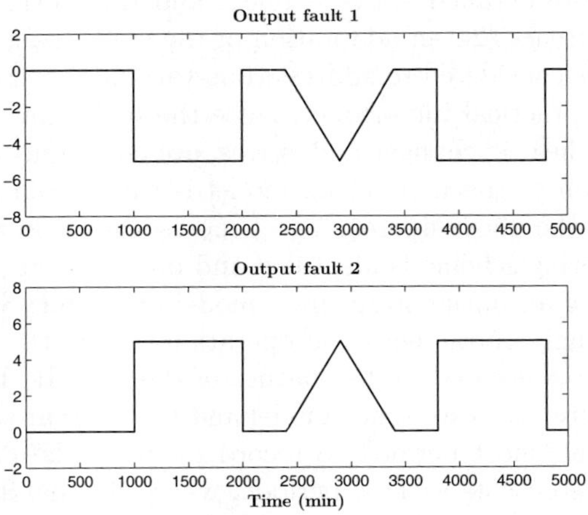

Fig. 2. True output fault signals

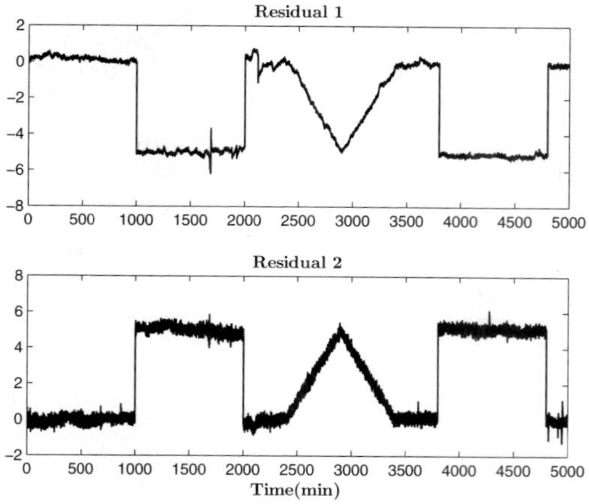

Fig. 3. Output residuals through the proposed scheme

twelve outputs and four inputs [11]. The distillation tower includes 33 trays with which the separation is achieved. A purified Butane stream leaves the distillation process as the top product and consequently, Hexane and impurities leave the distillation process with the bottom draw. From this process, two data sets, sampled at an interval of 30 seconds, were available. The first data set was used as reference data set to identify the new monitoring scheme, whilst the second data set served as testing data to detect sensor faults that were superimposed on two output variables.

Figure 2 shows the signature of the augmented sensor faults which were imposed on the data collected from plant operation. The residuals that the determined observer produced for both "faulty" sensors are given in Figure 3 By comparing Figures 2 and 3, it can be seen that the new monitoring methodology was capable of estimating the signature of fault conditions with sufficient accuracy for this industrial example.

3.2 Application to an Industrial Melter Process

The melter process is part of a disposal procedure. Waste material is preprocessed by evaporation treatment to produce a powder that is then clad by glass. The melter vessel is continuously filled with powder and raw glass is discretely introduced in the form of glass frit. This binary composition is heated by four induction coils, which are positioned around the vessel. Because of the heating procedure, the glass becomes molten homogeneously. The process of filling and heating continues until the desired height of the liquid column is reached. Then, the molten mixture is poured out through an exit funnel. After the content of the vessel is emptied to the height of the nozzle, the next cycle of filling and heating is carried out.

Measurements of 8 temperatures, the power in the 4 induction coils and voltage were recorded every five minutes. The filling and emptying cycles represented a dynamic relationship between the temperatures (process output variables),

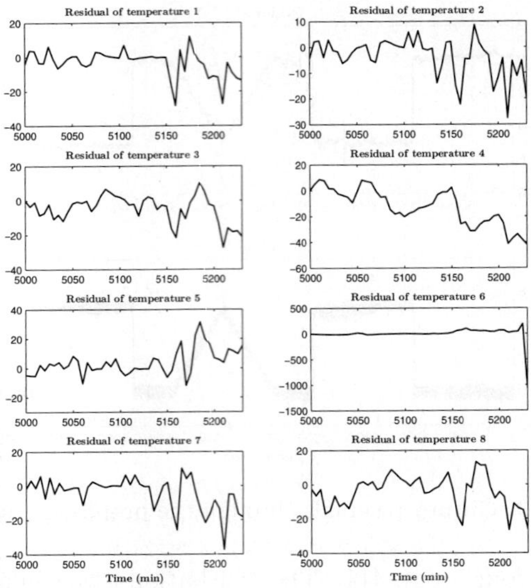

Fig. 4. Output residuals for melter data through the proposed scheme

power in the induction coils and voltage (process input variables). The variable set therefore comprised $m = 8$ output and $q = 5$ input variables [12]. Two data sets formed the basis of the analysis. A reference data set containing 1000 samples and a second data set of 50 samples describing a sensor fault were recorded at a sampling interval of 5 minutes. The sensor fault resulted from a crack in the melter vessel and influenced the variation of other sensor readings through controller feedback.

The state space models for describing the relationship between inputs and each output variable was identified using the first 1000 observations. The results of applying the monitoring scheme to the second data set are summarized in Figure 4, which shows the generated residuals of the output variables. From this figure, it can be concluded that the predicted sequence of temperature sensor #6 departed from the recorded sequence after 5150 minutes of the combined data set. The "increase" in temperature produced controller feedback to reduce the power of induction coil #1 and voltage. This, in turn, resulted in a reduction in temperature, noticeable by temperature sensor #4, which is in the vicinity of sensor #6. Towards the end of the recording period, sensor #6 failed. This is correctly represented in Figure 4 where a sharp drop of the residual can be seen. It should be noted that the temperature within the glass melter is in the region of 1100 to 1150 °C and the temperature variation, which result from the filling procedure, are around 200°C. Furthermore, the thermocouples have a resolution of 7°C, which implies that the identified state space model can predict the temperature variables with sufficient accuracy up until 5150min. The larger variations after 5150min are caused by the measurement failure and feedback control based upon the incorrect sensor reading.

4 Conclusions

This paper studied a recently proposed methodology for detecting and diagnosing sensor faults in linear and time-varying process systems. As the core contributions of this work, the paper discussed the practically important aspect of casting a subspace model identification technique into a model-based fault detection, isolation and identification methodology. The practical benefits of this data-driven scheme is that (i) the expensive and time consuming development of a complex mechanistic first principle model is circumvented, (ii) a generic state space model which includes process input and output variables is used, and (iii) no a priori knowledge of any sensor fault is required.

In this work, the state space models are identified using the N4SID algorithm on the basis of scaled input and output variables. The construction of the fault isolation and identification filter to diagnose a sensor fault relates to the identified state space model. In order to address the issue of time-varying process behavior, the linear state space model together with the fault identification and isolation filter are updated on a predefined schedule. During these updates, the methodology is applied to diagnose sensor faults.

The utility of the new sensor fault methodology was demonstrated using two simulation studies and recorded data of two industrial processes. The simulations related to a LTI system and a CSTR with a time-varying parameter, whilst the industrial examples involved recorded data from an debutanizer process and a glass-melter. Using the new scheme, the injected sensor faults in both simulation examples were correctly estimated. The data of the debutanizer process were augmented by superimposing sequences that represented a sensor fault on two of the output variables, which were also accurately estimated. Finally, a recorded sensor fault of the melter process was identified and correctly diagnosed.

References

1. Russell, E.L., Chiang, L.H., Braatz, R.: Data-Driven Techniques for Fault Detection and Diagnosis in Chemical Processes. Springer-Verlag, New York (2000)
2. Rajaraman, S., Hahn, J., Mannan, M.S.: A methodology for fault detection, isolation and identification for nonlinear processes with parametric uncertainties. Industrial & Engineering Chemistry Research **43**(21) (2004) 6774–6786
3. van Overschee, P.V., de Moor, B.D.: Subspace Identification For Linear Systems - Theory, Implementation and Applications. Kluwer Academic Publishers (1996)
4. Qin, S.J., Li, W.: Detection, identification, and reconstruction of faulty sensors wiht maximized sensitivity. AIChE Journal **45** (1999) 1963
5. Qin, S.J., Li, W.: Detection, identification of faulty sensors in dynamic processes. AIChE Journal **47** (2001) 1581–1593
6. Li, W., Raghavan, H., Shah, S.: Subspace identification of continuous time models for process fault detection and isolation. Journal of Process Control **13** (2003) 407–421
7. Treasure, R.J., Kruger, U., Cooper, J.E.: Dynamic multivariate statistical process control using subspace identification. Journal of Process Control **14** (2004) 279–292

8. Chen, J., Patton, R.: Robust Model Based Fault Diagnosis For Dynamic Systems. Kluwer Academic Publishers (1999)
9. Ding, X., Frank, P.M.: Fault detection via factorization approach. Systems & Control Letters **14** (1990) 431
10. Dudzic, M.S., Vaculik, V.: On-line industrial implementation of process monitoring and control applications using multivariate statistical technologies: Challenges and opportunities. In: CD Proceedings of the 7th International Conference on Dynamics and Control of Process Systems (DYCOPS-7), Cambridge,Massachussets, U.S.A. (2004)
11. Wang, X., Kruger, U., Lennox, B.: Recursive partial least squares algorithms for monitoring complex industrial processes. Control Engineering Practice **11** (2003) 603–632
12. Chen, Q., Wyne, R., Goulding, P.R., Sandoz, D.J.: The application of principal component analysis and kernel density estimation to enhance process monitoring. Control Engineering Practice **8**(5) (2000) 531–543

Particle Swarm Optimization for Open Vehicle Routing Problem

Wanliang Wang[1], Bin Wu[1], Yanwei Zhao[2], and Dingzhong Feng[2]

[1] College of Information Engineering, Zhejiang University of Technology, 310032, Hangzhou, China
wwl@zjut.edu.cn

[2] College of Mechanical Engineering, Zhejiang University of Technology, 310032, Hangzhou, China
zyw@zjut.edu.cn

Abstract. The Open Vehicle Routing Problem was brought forward several decades ago, but it has still received little attention from researchers for a satisfactory solution. In this paper, a novel real number encoding method of Particle Swarm Optimization (PSO) for Open Vehicle Routing Problem is proposed. The vehicle is mapped into the integer part of the real number; and the sequence of customers in the vehicle is mapped into the decimal fraction of the real number. After decoding, several heurist methods are applied into the post-optimization procedure, such as Nearest Insertion algorithm, GENI algorithm, and 2-Opt. They are used to optimize the inner or outer routes and modify illegal solutions. In the experiments, a number of numerical examples are carried out for testing and verification. The performance of the proposed post-optimization algorithm is analyzed and the particle swarm optimization algorithm is compared with other heuristic methods for the same problem.

1 Introduction

The Open Vehicle Routing Problem (OVRP) consists of defining the routes for a fleet of vehicles that must service a set of customers with a given demand and known geographical location. Each route is a sequence of customers that starts at the depot and finishes at one of the customers. The major difference between the OVRP and the well-known Vehicle Routing Problem (VRP) is that in the OVRP each route is a Hamiltonian path, instead of a Hamiltonian cycle in the VRP. This difference is due to the fact that the vehicles do not return to the starting depot or, if they do so, they make exactly the same trip in the opposite order for the collection of goods from the customers. OVRP is encountered in many fields, such as the third part logistics companies, the newspaper home delivery, and the school bus. These companies subcontract a driver who has its own car, thus, he needn't back to the depot when he finishes the delivery.

The constraints considered in this problem are the following: all the vehicles have the same capacity; the traveling time of each vehicle should not exceed a given threshold, which is defined by the drivers' legal traveling time; the total demand of all the customers on a route must not exceed the capacity of the vehicle; each customer is

D.-S. Huang, K. Li, and G.W. Irwin (Eds.): ICIC 2006, LNAI 4114, pp. 999 – 1007, 2006.

visited just once by one of the vehicles, and its requirements must be completely fulfilled. The objective is to minimize the number of the vehicles, and for a given number of vehicles, to minimize the total distance (or time) traveled by the vehicles.

The VRP has attracted considerable research attention and a number of algorithms have been proposed for its solution, such as tabu search algorithm, simulated annealing algorithm, ant colony optimization, and genetic algorithm. Contrary to the VRP, the OVRP has only been studied by very few people. So far as we know, the first author to mention the OVRP was Schrage [1] in an article dedicated to the description of realistic routing problems, bringing attention to some of its applications. Sariklis and Powell [2] use the "Cluster First, Route Second" method, in the second phase, they generate open routes by solving a minimum spanning tree problem. Their method is rapid, but doesn't get so good solution. Brandao et al. [3] apply the hybrid tabu Search algorithm for the problem. They generate the initial solution using a variety of methods including nearest neighbor heuristic and K-tree method. In the tabu search algorithm, they only use two types of simple trial moves, an insertion move and a swap move. Fu et al. [4] also use the tabu search algorithm. They develop a farthest first heuristic to generate an initial solution, and they develop four types of moves.

There are two problems existed in solution for OVRP. First, the applied methods are singleness. Many algorithms have not been attempted, such as particle swarm optimization, ant colony optimization and genetic algorithm. Second, the model of OVRP is simple. Some constraints in the practice have not considered in the model. In the paper, we develop a particle swarm optimization algorithm for OVRP in order to exploit the research method. Particle swarm optimization is an evolutionary algorithm that simulates the social behavior of bird flocking to a desired place. Similar to metaheuristic methods, PSO starts with initial solutions and updates them from iteration to iteration. Updating of particle-represented solution is achieved through formulated equations that are able to exploit the searching experience of one particle itself or the best of all the particles. In addition to the advantages the metaheuristc methods have, including computational feasibility and effectiveness, PSO shows its uniqueness such as easy implantation and consistency in performance.

2 Particle Swarm Optimization for OVRP

2.1 Fundamental Principle of PSO

The Particle Swarm Optimization (PSO) algorithm is an adaptive algorithm based on a social-psychological metaphor. It was originally proposed by J.Kennedy [5].A population of individuals adapts by returning stochastically toward previously successful regions in the search space, which is influenced by the successes of their topological neighbors. PSO is related with Artificial Life, and specifically to swarming theories, and also with Genetic Algorithms (GA). PSO can be easily implemented and it is computationally inexpensive. Moreover, it does not require gradient information of the objective function under consideration, but only its values, and it uses only primitive mathematical operators. PSO has been proved to be an efficient method for many optimization problems, such as Design Combinational Logic Circuits, Evolving Artificial Neural Networks, Multiple Object Problems, and TSP.

Two versions of the PSO algorithm have been developed, one with a global neighborhood, and the other with a local neighborhood. The global version was used in the paper. Each particle moves towards its best previous position and towards the best particle in the whole swarm. On the other hand, according to the local version, each particle moves towards its best previous position and towards the best particle in its restricted neighborhood. The global version PSO algorithm can be described as follows: Suppose that the search space is D-dimensional, then the i-th particle of the swarm in the t-th iteration can be represented by a D-dimensional vector, $Xi_t = (x_{i1t}, x_{i2t}, \ldots x_{iDt})$. The velocity of this particle can be represented by another D-dimensional vector. $Vi_t = (v_{i1t}, v_{i2t}, \ldots v_{iDt})$. The best previously visited position of the i-th particle in t-th iteration is denoted as $P_{i,t}$. The global best particle in t-th iteration denoted as $P_{g,t}$. Then the swarm is manipulated according to the following two equations:

$$Vi_{t+1} = c_1 Vi_t + c_2 * r_1 * \left(P_{i,t} - Xi_t\right) + c_3 * r_2 * \left(P_{g,t} - Xi_t\right) \tag{1}$$

$$Xi_{t+1} = Xi_t + Vi_{t+1} \tag{2}$$

Where i=1, 2…P, and P is the total number of particles in the swarm, i.e. the population size; t=1, 2…T, and T is the iteration limited; c_1 is an inertia weight which is employed to control the impact of the previous history of velocities on the current one. Accordingly, the parameter c_1 regulates the trade-off between the global (wide-ranging) and local (nearby) exploration abilities of the swarm. r_1, r_2 are random numbers, uniformly distributed in [0, 1]; c_2, c_3 are two positive constants, called cognitive and social parameter respectively. That proper fine-tuning these two parameters may result in faster convergence and alleviation of local minima. The details of tuning the parameters of PSO were discussed in [6]. Formula (1) is used to calculate a particle's new velocity according to its previous velocity and the distance from its current position to its local best and the global best. Formula (2) is used to calculate a particle's new position by utilizing its experience (i.e., local best) and the best experience of all particles (i.e., global best). Formulas (1) and (2) also reflect the information-sharing mechanism of PSO.

2.2 Real Number Encoding Method

In general, there are three encoding methods, i.e. real number encoding, integer encoding, and binary bit encoding. For the combination optimization problem, Clerc [7] presented the integer encoding PSO for Traveling Salesman Problem (TSP) firstly. Each particle's position was represented a permutation of integer and the velocity was different from continuous problem. Clerc defined a so-called "exchange number" to represent the velocity of particles. "Exchange number" $(i_k, j_k), i_k, j_k \in \{1,2,..n\}$ represented that the two numbers i_k, j_k did the 2-Opt. As described above, Clerc also defined the operation rules about the velocity, such as addition and subtraction. The advantages of integer encoding method are decoding and computing fitness conveniently. This encoding method, however, has not well used the advantages of PSO.

Ayed Salmen et al. [8] used the real number encoding of PSO for task assignment problem. They mapped an M-task assignment instance into corresponding M-coordinate particle position. Since values in a particle are processor numbers, a real value is meaningless. Therefore, in the decoding algorithm, they rounded these numbers to the closest processor number by dropping the sign and the fractional part. Li Ning et al. [9] applied PSO for Vehicle Routing Problem (VRP). They presented that each particle was encoded as a vector X with $2L$ dimensions, which represented L customers VRP. The one L dimensions X_v represented the vehicles of the customers; the other X_r represented the sequence of customers visited in the vehicle. Higher dimension is presented in the encoding method, and every dimension should be rounded the number closest integer and sorted. It operates difficult and consumes much CPU time. Meanwhile, if the position presents the infeasible solution, it is very difficult to be adjusted.

The paper presents a novel real number encoding method of PSO for OVRP. In the method, the dimension size of the particle's position equals to the number of customers. When the particle position is decoded, it only does once round the number to the closest integer and sort. Meanwhile, it is convenient for readjusting the particle position when updated. For L customers, each particle is encoded as a real number vector with L dimensions. The integer part of each dimension or element in the vector represents the vehicle. Thus, the same integer part represents the customer in the same vehicle. The fractional part represents the sequence of the customer in the vehicle.

Definition:
[X] represents the integer part of X.
{X} represents the fractional part of X.
The decoding procedure is:
(1) Each dimension of the particle's position gets the [X].
(2) Form different groupings according to the values of [X].
(3) Each particle gets {X} in the team.
(4) Build the sequence of the visited customer according to the values of {X}.

For example, if there are 7 customers and 3 vehicles in an OVRP instance, according to the encoding method, we can present encoding like:

Customer serial number:	1	2	3	4	5	6	7
Particle's position X :	4.1	1.86	1.53	1.12	1.24	3.29	3.05

Based on the decoding rules as above described, first, we round X to the closest integer by dropping the fractional part. The X_i, which is the same integer part, is assigned into the same team. We can get the three teams: (4.1), (1.86, 1.53, 1.12, 1.24), (3.29, 3.05). Second, X_i is arranged from small to big according to the fractional part in the same team. We can get the result as: (4.1), (1.12, 1.24, 1.53, 1.86), (3.05, 3.29) Finally the above position is mapped into the corresponding customer, and then, we can get the result of delivery plan which the position represents.

First route: 0-1
Second route: 0-4-5-3-2
Third route: 0-7-6

2.3 Post-optimization Procedures

In order to improve the quality of solution, many researchers studied the algorithms for the post-optimization procedure. Gendreau et al. [10] applied tabu search algorithm for VRP, they used 2-Opt, 3-Opt, GENIUS as the post-optimization procedure, and then got the best result as we knew now. Brandao applied tabu search algorithm with Nearest Neighbor and US for OVRP. In the paper, we use many insert algorithms and exchange algorithms as the post-optimization procedure. The insertion algorithms are: Nearest Insert (NI), Farthest Insert (FI), Cheapest Insert (CI), GENI (Generalized Insertion Procedure, GENI), etc. The exchange algorithms are: 2-Opt, 3-Opt, US. In the post-optimization procedure, an insertion algorithm is used first to adjust the customer's inner or outer routes and then an exchange algorithm is used to improve the above solution.

3 Framework of PSO for OVRP

Fig.1 shows the flowchart of the PSO procedure when the real number encoding representation and the post-optimization procedures are adopted. The initial particle positions were produced randomly. Firstly, customers' permutation was randomly generated and then every customer was assigned to the vehicles. Secondly, the delivery plan was mapped to the particle's position according to the encoding rules. Repeat the procedure until it produced the initial population. The initial particle velocities were also generated randomly and they were subject to the limit [-*Vmax*, *Vmax*].

4 Computational Experiments

The algorithms presented in article were implemented in JAVA language on a Pentium 2.8G, 512 MB machine running in Windows environment. The testing problems were taken from Christofides, Mingozzi and Toth' instance lib. In the experiments, the parameters were set as following: the iterations number $N = 1000$, $c_1 = 1$, $c_2 = c_3 = 0.5$, The population size *P* is usually taken as the one close to the number of the customers in the problem, considering that more particles may increase searching success but similarly require more evaluation runs. The objective of the computational experiments is to evaluate the performance of the PSO in terms of quality of the solution and to determine the influence of insertion and exchange operator in that performance. Another aim is to compare the performance of the PSO with other algorithms, which is done in the end of this section.

Since the total number of combinations of insertion and exchange operator with PSO is large, it is necessary to conduct the experiments in a systematic way, in order to guarantee that the good combinations of algorithms are selected. We firstly compute the small instance E-n51-k5. Each algorithm runs 10 times. The average result is illustrated in Fig2. The horizontal coordinate represents the post-optimization algorithms. We use insertion operator name plus exchange operator name to present the

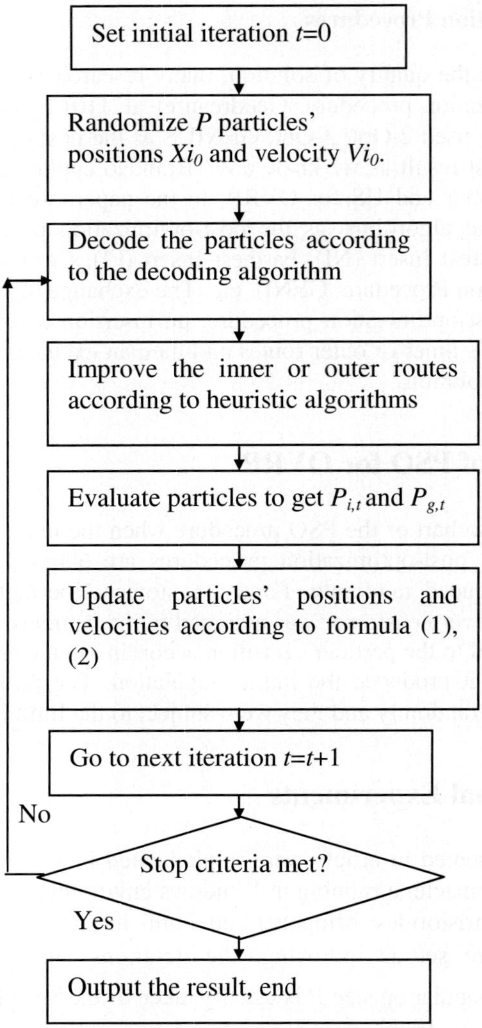

Fig. 1. Procedure of PSO for OVRP

algorithms name. For example, 2NI represents Nearest Insertion algorithm hybrid 2-Opt. Other algorithms obey the same rules. The ordinate coordinate represents total length of the routes. Fig2 shows GENI hybrid 2-Opt has the best performance, and Farthest Insertion hybrid 3-Opt, Nearest Insertion hybrid 3-Opt and Nearest Insertion hybrid 2-Opt also have the better performances. Fig3 illustrates the optimal results of every algorithm. It shows about the same trend with Fig2. Nearest Insertion algorithm hybrid 2-Opt gets the best result. GENI hybrid US also has the better performance, but its computation time is 16 times longer than the Nearest Insertion algorithm hybrid 2-Opt. In order to select the best algorithm, we classify the algorithm according to the exchange operator and insertion operator. Fig4 illustrates the average result of the algorithms, which are classified by the exchange operator. It shows that 3-Opt has a little better performance than 2-Opt, but the computation time is 3 times longer than 2-Opt. Us Operator has the lower efficiency. Fig5 illustrates the average results of the algorithms classified by the five insertion operators. It shows the GENI has the better performance than others, but its computational time is much longer than others. Other insertion operators only have little difference in the result and computational time. In the following experiment, the solution quality and computational time of the algorithms was taken into count, and then Nearest Insertion and GENI were used as the insertion operator and 2-Opt was used as the exchange operator in the post-optimization procedure.

The PSO-based method is compared with other approaches, including the heurist which was presented by Sariklis.D.,Powell and the Tabu Search with Nearest Neighbor Heurist which was presented by Brandao.J et al. We obtain the result in the Table 1, where the first column to the left gives the instance. E-n51-k5, presents a problem with 51 customers and 5 vehicles. According to Table 1, TSA-NNH produces

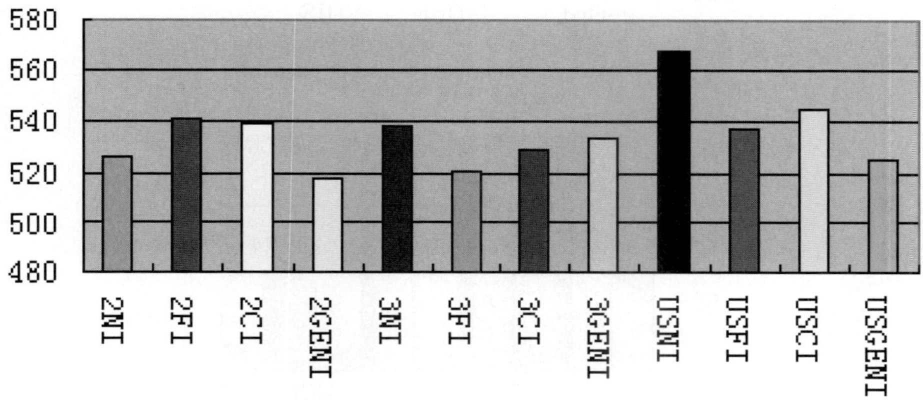

Fig. 2. Average results of the algorithms

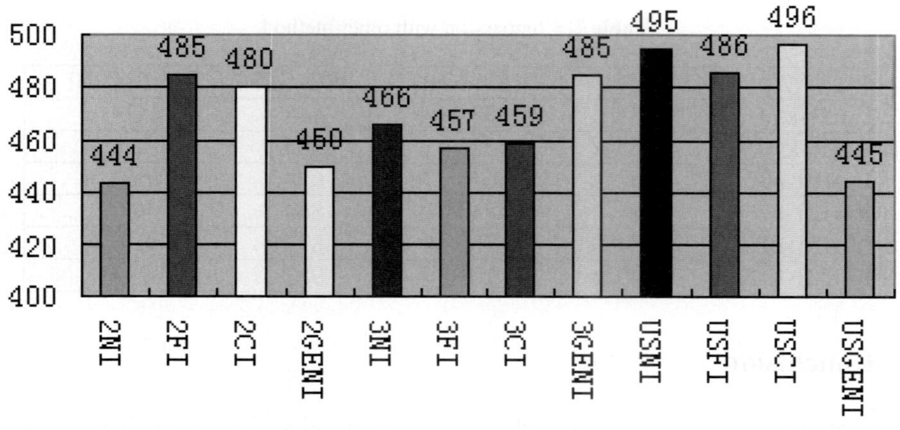

Fig. 3. Optimization result of the algorithms

the best results in terms of solution quality of algorithms. PSO-based method is performaned better than Sariklis,D.and Powell's algorithm. In additional to the fact that PSO-NI outperforms PSO-GENI method (except E-n201-k17) as shown above, PSO-NI has close performance as the TSA-NNH. But in problem E-n121-k7, the PSO-based is much inferior to TSA-NNH.

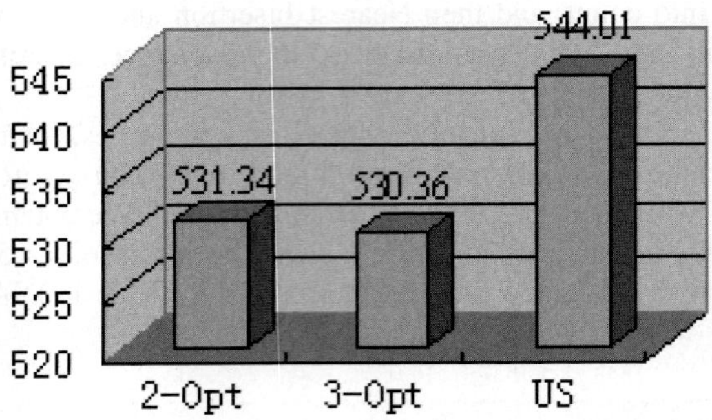

Fig. 4. Average result of the exchange operator

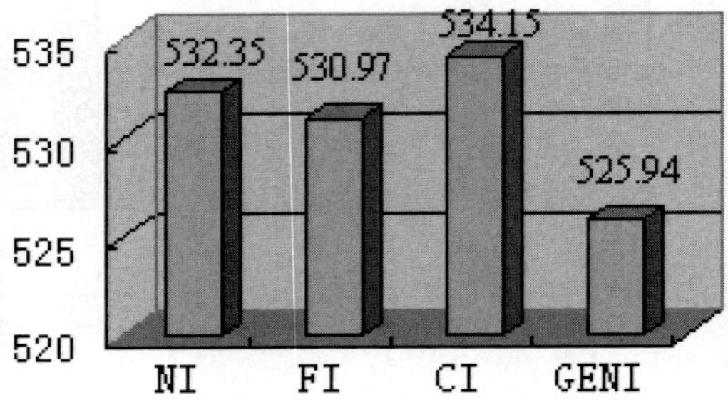

Fig. 5. Average result of the insertion operator

Table 1. Comparsion with other method

	SarP	TSA-NNH	PSO-GENI	PSO-NI
E-n51-k5	488	438	445	438
E-n76-k10	795	585	603	598
E-n101-n8	815	643	674	667
E-n121-k7	828	713	864	860
E-n151-k12	1034	767	837	836
E-n201-k17	1349	1010	982	993

5 Conclusion

Although Open Vehicle Routing Problem has been developed for more than two decades, there are only a few incomplete solutions available. In the paper, based on PSO principle, a new solution-solving scheme for OVRP is proposed. In consideration of a real number encoding method of PSO, the decoding rules of PSOs for OVRP are developed. In order to improve the solution quality, several heurist methods are applied into the post-optimization procedure, such as Nearest Insertion algorithm, and GENI algorithm, which can optimize the inner or outer routes and modify the illegal solution. The performance of PSO algorithm is evaluated in comparison with some other heurists. The results showed that the PSO algorithm is efficient for OVRP. The investigation not only provides a new metaheurist method for OVRP, but also solves other NP problems, such as TSP, and BPP, through changing decoding rules.

Acknowledgement

This project is supported by the National Natural Science Foundation of China (Grant No. 60374056), the Zhejiang Province Science and Technology Tackle Key Problem (Grant No.2003C11033), the Plan of Zhejiang Province Science and Technology (Grant No. 2004C33084).

References

1. Schrage,L.: Formulation and Structure of More Complex/realistic Routing and Scheduling Problems. Networks, 11 (1981) 229-232
2. Sariklis,D., Powell, S.: A Heuristic Method for the Open Vehicle Routing Problem. Journal of the Operational Research Society, 51(5) (2000) 564-573
3. Brandao,J.: A Tabu Search Algorithm for the Open Vehicle Routing Problem. European Journal of Operational Research, 157(8) (2004) 552-564
4. Zhuo, F.: Research for Open Vehicle Routing Problem and its Application. Doctor Dissertation of Central South University (2003)11
5. Kennedy, J., Eberhart, R. C.: Particle Swarm Optimization. Proceedings of IEEE International Conference on Neural Networks, Piscataway, NJ. (1995) 1942-1948
6. Shi, Y., Eberhart, R. C.: Parameter Selection in Particle Swarm Optimization. Evolutionary Programming VII: Proceedings of the Seventh Annual Conference on Evolutionary Programming, New York. (1998) 591-600
7. Clerc, M.: Discrete Particle Swarm Optimization Illustrated by the Traveling Salesman Problem. (2000) http://www.mauriceclerc.net
8. Ayed S., Imtiza, A., Sabah, Al-M.: Particle Swarm Optimization for Task Assignment Problem. Microprocessor and Microsystems, 26(8) (2002) 363-37
9. Li N., Zou,T., De-bao, S.: Particle Swarm Optimization for Vehicle Routing Problem. Journal of Systems Engineering, 19(6) (2004) 596-600
10. Gendreau, M., Hertz, A., Laporte.G.: New Insertion and Postoptimization Procedures for the Traveling Salesman problem. Operations Research, 40(8) (1992) 1086-1093

A Genetic Algorithm Approach on a Facility Layout Design Problem with Aisles

Gengui Zhou[1], Mujing Ye[2], Zhenyu Cao[1], and Feng Ye[1,⋆]

[1] College of Business Administration, Zhejiang University of Technology, Hangzhou, P.R. China
ggzhou@zjut.edu.cn

[2] Department of Industrial and Manufacturing Engineering, The Pennsylvania State University, U.S.A.

Abstract. Facility layout problems concerning space layout optimization have been investigated in depth by researchers in many engineering fields. In this paper, a particular facility layout problem with aisles and two objectives at minimizing total cost of material handling and maximizing adjacent requirement between resources is discussed and formulated as an nonlinear mixed-integer programming. To solve the NP-hard problem, a multiple objective genetic algorithm approach with local search method is developed. The application on a practical FLP case and numerical analysis show the effectiveness and efficiency of the proposed method on FLPs.

1 Introduction

Facility layout problems (FLPs) involve the arrangement of a given number of facilities or resources on the factory floor of a manufacturing system, which is a common industrial problem of allocating facilities to minimize the total cost of transporting materials [1] or to maximize adjacency requirement [2] or to both minimize the cost of transporting materials and minimize adjacency requirement between the facilities [3].

Based on the Gómez et at.'s research work [4], In this paper, we present a particular facility layout problem with aisles but involving the explicit consideration of fixed lengthways and transverse passageways between sections, together with two objectives: total cost of material handling and adjacent requirement between resources. It is formulated as a bi-criteria nonlinear mixed-integer programming model. An improved approach of a multiple objective genetic algorithm (MOGA) with local search is developed to obtain its optimal or near *Pareto* solutions. A practical case of layout design on a hydraulic pressure manufactory and further numerical experiments of different problem sizes demonstrate the effectiveness and efficiency of the proposed method for the FLPs.

⋆ This research work was partially supported by grant No. Y104171 from Zhejiang Provincial Nature Science Foundation.

D.-S. Huang, K. Li, and G.W. Irwin (Eds.): ICIC 2006, LNAI 4114, pp. 1008–1013, 2006.

2 Problem Description

The FLP studied in this paper is to find the best allocating scheme for rescurces in a given plant that fixes some aisles probably due to the position of gate or the need of transporting routing for AGVs, aiming at minimizing total cost of material handling and maximizing adjacent requirement between resources. Without the loss of generality, it is assumed that each resource is located at the central line of each column and can be laid into any working-space (defined as block parts) except aisles in the given plant.

The above-described FLP can be mathematically formulated as the following bi-criteria nonlinear mixed-integer programming:

$$Min \quad F_1 = \sum_{i=1}^{n-1} \sum_{j=i+1}^{n} C_{ij} f_{ij} d_{ij} \tag{1}$$

$$Min \quad F_2 = \sum_{i=1}^{n-1} \sum_{j=i+1}^{n} (M - R_{ij} b_{ij}) \tag{2}$$

$$s.t. \quad x_k = \sum_{n=1}^{p_k - 1} W_n^F + \sum_{n=1}^{p_k} W_n^L + \frac{1}{2} W_{p_k}^F \tag{3}$$

$$(y_i^t - y_j^b)(y_j^t - y_i^b) Z_{irl} Z_{jrl} \leq 0 \tag{4}$$

$$(y_k^t - y_s^{Pb})(y_s^t - y_k^{Pb}) \leq 0 \tag{5}$$

$$\sum_{k=1}^{n} a_k - A_{available} \leq 0 \tag{6}$$

$$\sum_{l=1}^{L} \sum_{r=1}^{R} Z_{irl} = 1, \sum_{l=1}^{L} \sum_{r=1}^{R} Z_{jrl} = 1 \tag{7}$$

$$P_k = \sum_{r=1}^{R} \sum_{l=1}^{L} l \bullet Z_{krl} \tag{8}$$

$$i, j, k = 1, 2, \cdots, N; s = 1, 2, \cdots, R$$

f_{ij} material flow frequency between resources i and j

c_{ij} material handling cost per unit between resources i and j

d_{ij} distance between center points of resources i and j

b_{ij} adjacency factor between resources i and j

R_{ij} adjacency value (0-5)between resources i and j

P_k ordinal of column for resource k

y_i^t ,y_i^b y-coordinates of the top and bottom boundaries of resource i (so is y_j^t, y_k^t)

y_s^{Pt}, y_s^{Pb} y-coordinates of the top and bottom boundaries of passage way s

Z_{irl} Z_{irl} is equal to 1 if resource i located at column r and row l, otherwise 0

$A_{available}$ R, L, N total sum of available areas, rows, column, resource number respectively
M maximum adjacency rating (=5)

In the above formulation, objective function (1) minimizes the total cost of material handling, while objective function (2) in form of minimal function is designed to maximize the total adjacency requirement. Constraint (3) assures that the x-coordinate of every resource is located at the center of any column. Constraint (4) assures that there is no overlap between resources in direction of y-axis in the same column. Constraint (5) assures that interference between resources and passage ways is not allowed in direction of y-axis. Constraint (6) assures that the total area of resource should be less than the total sum of available areas. Constraint (7) assures every resource should be uniquely distributed in any column and any row.

Moreover, the quantifiable value for R_{ij} can be determined as proposed by Lee [5] and the adjacency factor b_{ij}, which represents the adjacency ratio between resources i and j, can be determined from distance d_{ij} between resources i and j. Here, we adopt the quantifiable value for b_{ij} as Lee did [6], where d_{max} is the maximum value of d_{ij}.

3 MOGA with Local Search Approach

The overall pseudo-code procedure for this FLP is outlined as follows:

```
Main ()
 { t = 0;
   initialize the population of Parents P(0);                //N_pop
   determine the tentative set of Pareto optimal Solutions PS(0);
   while (not termination condition) do
   { Reproduce P(t) to generate offspring C(t);              //N_pop − N_e
     select elite individuals E(t) from PS(t);               //N_e
     local search for E(t) + C(t) to generate P(t + 1);      //N_pop
     update PS(t) from P(t + 1);
     t = t + 1;}
 }
```

In order to raise the effectiveness of the proposed MOGA, we design a local neighborhood searching procedure and hybrid it with the MOGA in the evolutionary process.

The pseudo-code of local search procedure is outlined as follows:

```
Local_search(CurrentSolution)
 do {NewSolution: swap two genes of CurrentSolution;
     if (NewSolution ominated CurrentSolution)
        CurrentSolution = NewSolution;
```

}while (non-swapped genes $\neq \varnothing$);
return CurrentSolution;

4 Application and Numerical Analysis

For solving the FLP problem discussed in this paper, we first use the systematic layout planning (SLP) [7] method to analysis the relationship on material flows to get the corresponding parameters. Table 1 shows a practical case on a manufactory of hydraulic pressure redirectors for the setting up of 11 resources on a plant with areas of $160000m^2(200 \times 800m^2)$.

Table 1. Resources and their areas

No.	Resources	Areas (m^2)
1	Raw material warehouse	20×30
2	Casting department	12×24
3	Heat-treat department	12×12
4	Mechanical department	18×36
5	Precision department	12×36
6	In-process product warehouse	12×24
7	Assembly department	12×36
8	Performance testing department	12×12
9	Final product warehouse	12×12
10	Maintenance department	12×24
11	Officeservice houses	80×60

After analyzed by the SLP method, we can obtain the initial input date as shown in Table 2.

Table 2. The initial input data

$$[c_{ij}]=\begin{bmatrix} 0&3&1&1&2&3&1&3&1&2&2\\ &0&3&5&1&4&5&5&1&1&1\\ &&0&1&2&1&1&3&4&1&2\\ &&&0&2&5&2&1&1&3&2\\ &&&&0&4&4&2&2&2&4\\ &&&&&0&2&1&3&3&2\\ &&&&&&0&4&4&2&1\\ &&&&&&&0&3&3&3\\ &&&&&&&&0&1&2\\ &&&&&&&&&0&1\\ &&&&&&&&&&0 \end{bmatrix}$$

(4-1)

$$[f_{ij}]=\begin{bmatrix} 0&123&23&25&0&0&0&0&0&0&0\\ &0&0&75&0&0&0&0&0&0&0\\ &&0&34&15&0&0&0&0&0&0\\ &&&0&53&11&0&0&0&0&0\\ &&&&0&63&0&0&0&0&0\\ &&&&&0&76&0&0&0&0\\ &&&&&&0&76&0&0&0\\ &&&&&&&0&76&0&0\\ &&&&&&&&0&0&0\\ &&&&&&&&&0&0\\ &&&&&&&&&&0 \end{bmatrix}$$

(4-2)

$$[R_{ij}]=\begin{bmatrix} I&O&E&U&E&U&U&U&U&U\\ &U&I&U&U&U&U&U&I&X\\ &&A&X&U&U&U&U&O&X\\ &&&X&O&U&O&U&I&I\\ &&&&I&U&U&U&I&O\\ &&&&&E&U&U&U&U\\ &&&&&&E&U&O&E\\ &&&&&&&A&I&O\\ &&&&&&&&O&O\\ &&&&&&&&&O \end{bmatrix}$$

(4-3)

It is assumed that resource 11 is fixed at the south most due to its large area and serving requirement. Because of environmental reasons there is at least a 10m distance spared between resource 11 and others. The constants of this problem are set as $W^R = 15$m, $W^F = 20$m, $W^L = 10$, $M = 100$. Parameters

Table 3. *Pareto* optimal solutions

No.	Value of F_1	Value of F_2	Solutions (in order)
1	86814	43.8	10 4 6 7 3 2 5 8 9 1 11
2	89358	42.6	4 5 8 9 3 2 10 6 7 1 11
3	94602	42.4	4 7 6 3 2 10 9 8 5 1 11
4	96198	41.8	4 5 8 9 2 3 10 6 7 1 11
5	107233	41.6	2 1 7 6 10 4 9 8 5 3 11
6	117362	41.4	10 4 6 7 3 2 9 8 5 1 11
7	118597	41	2 1 6 7 10 4 9 8 5 3 11
8	121831	40.8	1 2 6 7 3 4 9 8 5 10 11
9	157902	40.8	2 10 8 6 5 3 4 9 7 1 11

of MOGA are set as population size = 100, maximum number of generations = 500, crossover rate = 0.2, mutation rate = 0.7. In all different random trials run by the proposed MOGA approach, we obtain the same results as summarized in Table 3. Figure 1 shows one of its *Pareto* optimal solutions by visualization.

In order to further test the effectiveness of the proposed MOGA approach, nine FLP problems with a little larger scale are tested on a PC-type computer (P4 1.7G, RAM 128M). All parameters are set as follows: population size = 300; maximum number of generations = 500; crossover rate = 0.2 and mutation rate = 0.7. Each test is repeated 20 times and the average results are summarized in Table 4.

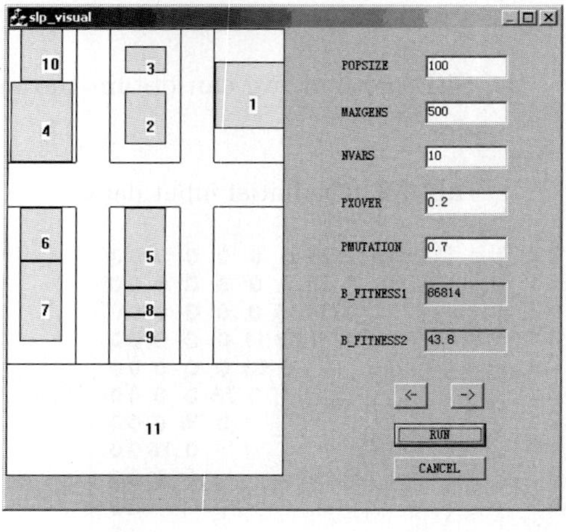

Fig. 1. Illustration of a *Pareto* optimal solution

From Table 4, it can be concluded that the MOGA with local search could obtain good solutions for the FLPs of moderate scale within acceptable running time, whereas it produces the same results for the FLPs of problem scale of less than 14 and get the satisfying results for the FLPs of problem scale of less than 19.

Table 4. Numerical experiments

Problem Scale	*All Solutions (A)*	*Pareto Solutions (B)*	Ratio B/A	*CPU time(s)*
11	140	140	100%	462
12	300	300	100%	566
13	216	216	100%	897
14	456	420	92%	1190
15	586	544	93%	1514
16	456	392	86%	2029
17	456	384	84%	2906
18	508	406	80%	3261
19	458	336	73%	3881

5 Conclusion

In this paper, a bi-criteria facility layout problem with fixed aisles is discussed aiming at minimizing total cost of material handling and maximizing adjacent requirement between resources. Given the successful application of the method on a practical FLP with moderate scale, the numerical analysis showed the effectiveness to obtain most optimal *Pareto* solutions of the FLPs with scale ranging from 11 resources to 19 resources within acceptable CPU times. The research work would be a powerful support for the facility layout design problems in the field of engineering design and optimization.

References

1. Seppanen, J., Moore, J.M.: Facilities Planning And Graph Theory. International Journal of Management Science, vol. 17(1970) 242-253
2. Koopmans, T.C., Beckmann, M.: Assignment Problems And The Location Of Economic Activities. Econometrica, vol. 25(1)(1957) 53-76
3. Meller, R-D., Gau, K.Y.: Facility Layout Objective Functions And Robust Layouts. International Journal of Production Research, vol. 34(10)(1996) 2727-2742
4. Gome,z A., Fernandex, Q.I., Farcia, D. F., Farcia, P.J.: Using Genetic Algorithms to Resolve Layout Problems in Facilities where There are Aisles, International Journal of Production Economics, vol. 84(3)(2003) 271-282
5. Lee, H.J.: Heuristic Graph-Theoretic Approach In Facility Layout Problem: The Development Of A Decision Support System: Arlington, USA: University of Texas, (1988)
6. Lee, K.Y, Roh, M.I., Jeong, H.S.: An Improved Genetic Algorithm For Multi-Floor Facility Layout Problems Having Inner Structure Walls And Passages. Computers & Operations Research, vol. 30(1) (2003) 117-138
7. Muther, R.: Systematic Layout Planning. Von Nostrand Reinhould, New York, (1961)

A Novel Game-Theory-Based Analysis Approach for Running a Supply Chain Project

Ding-zhong Feng, Lei-lei Chen, and Mei-xian Jiang

The MOE Key Laboratory of Mechanical Manufacture and Automation, Zhejiang University of Technology, Hangzhou, 310032, P.R. China
fdz@zjut.edu.cn

Abstract. As one of the most important management strategies, supply chain management (SCM) is increasingly being emphasized. And, an increasing focus is placed on the integration of overall supply chain resources. In running the strategy, one of key problems is how to judge the suitability that a project is managed by SCM paradigm. For this reason, a novel feasibility analysis approach based on game theory is presented for running a supply chain project. First of all, some basic conditions for judging the feasibility of a SCM project are discussed both on individual rationality and group rationality. Then, a viable bargain price range of candidate partners is proposed by using Bayes-Nash equilibrium, and a numerical example is given to illustrate its application. Finally, we discuss the relationship between the bargain price range and the competitive index in a SCM project.

1 Introduction

With the globalization of economic markets, the competitive relationship among enterprises increasingly becomes both competitive and cooperative [1-5]. Thus, the applications of game theory in SCM field attracted much attention of lots of researchers [6-7]. Main works in this research domain could be summarized into three aspects. First, some researchers [8] applied game theory to make decisions, such as whether to join a supply chain or not, and whether to share their information to other members in supply chain or not. Second, some research work [9-10] was conducted on the coordination game process between enterprises. Third, profits allocation and risk control were paid a lot of attention. Some researchers [11] proposed profits allocation model based on game theory, and discussed how to optimize allocation strategies.

This paper aims to present a novel analysis approach for judging whether or not a project is suitable for constructing a supply chain alliance. First of all, two basic conditions for judging the feasibility of a SCM project are discussed in section 2. Then, a bargain price range of cooperative partners is proposed in section 3 by using Bayes-Nash equilibrium, and its application is illustrated by a numerical example in section 4. Finally, some discussions are made on the relationship between the bargain price range and the competitive index in section 5. And our conclusions are given in the final section.

D.-S. Huang, K. Li, and G.W. Irwin (Eds.): ICIC 2006, LNAI 4114, pp. 1014 – 1019, 2006.

2 Supply Chain Project's Feasibility

Generally speaking, a core enterprise and its potential cooperative partners usually have the ability to judge whether a possible alliance will result in more profits. Apparently, a SCM project must make sure that every member can gain more profits than does business independently, and the total profits of the project must be not less than the sum of all members' profit expectation. Thus we can get the following two basic conditions for analyzing the feasibility of a supply chain project:

(1) Individual rationality

$$\begin{cases} E(V_i) \geq E(\overline{V}_i) \\ E(V_0) \geq E(\overline{V}_0) \end{cases} . \tag{1}$$

where i denotes supply chain member, V_i denotes the income of member i by joining a supply chain, $\overline{V}_i$ denotes the income of member i by doing business himself, V_0 denotes the income of core enterprise in this project, and $E(\bullet)$ denotes an expectation for one issue.

(2) Group rationality

$$E(V) \geq \sum_{i=1}^{n} E(V_i) + E(V_0) . \tag{2}$$

where V denotes the whole income of a supply chain project and n the number of supply chain members.

The average income in the industry a partner belongs to can be taken as the estimated value of the partner income expectation, when a core enterprise makes its feasibility analysis for a supply chain project. Then, we have

$$E(V) \geq \sum_{i=1}^{n} \tilde{E}(V_i) + E(V_0) . \tag{3}$$

$$E(V) \geq \sum_{i=1}^{n} I_i(1+\alpha_i) + E(V_0) . \tag{4}$$

where $\tilde{E}(V_i)$ denotes the estimated value of income expectation of member i, I_i denotes the input of member i, and α_i denotes the average industry profit rate of member i. It shows that, according to group rationality, a productive supply chain project must make sure that its members gain much more profits than their own industry average profits.

3 Game-Theory-Based Analysis Approach

After making sure that a supply chain project is productive, a core enterprise has to analyze the scope of feasible potential partners. Due to the fact of nonsymmetrical distribution of information between core enterprise and its potential partners, the Bayes-Nash game model is applied to analyze the relationship between both of them.

Supposed that **A** is a core enterprise and **B** is one of potential partners. Partners' type set is their attitude information {"arduous", "ordinary", "lazy"}, denoted as $\{\theta_1, \theta_2, \theta_3\}$, respectively. And their relative probability is denoted by P_1, P_2 and P_3, respectively. The total input of a supply chain project is signed as I, and its total income is signed as V. Income functions are $f_1(I)$, $f_2(I)$, and $f_3(I)$ (generally, $f_1(I) > f_2(I) > f_3(I)$), respectively. Competitive index between **A** and **B** is signed as β ($0 \le \beta \le 1$). And industrial average profit rate is α ($0 \le \alpha \le 1$). λ_A and λ_B ($0 \le \lambda_A, \lambda_B \le 1$) is an input/allocation proportion in total input/allocation for **A** and **B**, respectively, and meets $\lambda_A + \lambda_B = 1$ (usually $\lambda_A \ge \lambda_B$).

According to the above information, a payoff matrix can be obtained, as shown in Table 1.

Table 1. Payoff Matrix

		B					
		θ_1		θ_2		θ_3	
		Yes	No	Yes	No	Yes	No
A	Yes	V_A, V_B	$-\lambda_A I$, $\alpha I \lambda_B$	$V_A^{'}, V_A^{'}$	$-\lambda_A I$, $\alpha I \lambda_B$	$V_A^{''}$, $V_B^{''}$	$-\lambda_A I$, $\alpha I \lambda_B$
	No	$\alpha \lambda_A I$, $-\lambda_B I$	$\alpha \lambda_A I$, $\alpha I \lambda_B$	$\alpha \lambda_A I$, $-\lambda_B I$	$\alpha \lambda_A I$, $\alpha I \lambda_B$	$\alpha \lambda_A I$, $-\lambda_B I$	$\alpha \lambda_A I$, $\alpha I \lambda_B$

For **A**: "Yes" means forming the supply chain and "No" means not forming the supply chain.
For **B**: "Yes" means joining the supply chain and "No" means not joining the supply chain.

Table 1 gives all possible situations, where $V_A = f_1(I) - \lambda_A \cdot I$, $V_{\mathbf{B}} = f_1(I) - \lambda_B \cdot I$; $V_A^{'} = f_2(I) - \lambda_A \cdot I$, $V_{\mathbf{B}}^{'} = f_2(I) - \lambda_B \cdot I$; $V_A^{''} = f_3(I) - \lambda_A \cdot I$, $V_B^{''} = f_3(I) - \lambda_B \cdot I$.

In this game model, the attitude type information for **B** is nonsymmetrical, and it is uncertain for **A**. Thus **A** applies the expectation value of the total income instead of the real total income when it makes its decision on forming a supply chain. Then,

$$E(V) = P_1 \cdot f_1(I) + P_2 \cdot f_2(I) + P_3 \cdot f_3(I) . \tag{5}$$

According to Eq.(1), **A** forms a supply chain under the following condition.

$$E(V) \cdot \lambda_A - I \cdot \lambda_A + \beta \cdot (\lambda_A - \lambda_B) \cdot E(V) \ge \alpha \cdot \lambda_A \cdot I . \tag{6}$$

For **B**, its attitude type information becomes fully known. We can obtain its condition of joining a supply chain, just as Eq.(6) for **A**. Then, to meet $\lambda_A + \lambda_B = 1$, we have:

$$\lambda_A \ge \frac{\beta \cdot E(V)}{E(V) \cdot (1 + 2\beta) - I(1 + \alpha)} . \tag{7}$$

$$\text{For } \theta_1 : \ \lambda_B \ge \frac{\beta \cdot f_1(I)}{f_1(I) \cdot (1 + 2\beta) - I(1 + \alpha)} . \tag{8}$$

$$\text{For } \theta_2: \ \lambda_B \geq \frac{\beta \cdot f_2(I)}{f_2(I)\cdot(1+2\beta)-I(1+\alpha)}. \tag{9}$$

$$\text{For } \theta_3: \ \lambda_B \geq \frac{\beta \cdot f_3(I)}{f_3(I)\cdot(1+2\beta)-I(1+\alpha)}. \tag{10}$$

Further,

$$\frac{\beta \cdot f_3(I)}{f_3(I)\cdot(1+2\beta)-I(1+\alpha)} \geq \frac{\beta \cdot E(V)}{E(V)\cdot(1+2\beta)-I(1+\alpha)} \geq \frac{\beta \cdot f_1(I)}{f_1(I)\cdot(1+2\beta)-I(1+\alpha)}.$$

Assumed that there is a maximum value (λ), which is supposed to meet:

$$\begin{cases} \lambda_A \geq \lambda \\ \lambda_B \geq \lambda \end{cases}.$$

Then, the bargain price scope of a suitable potential partner can be expressed as

$$[\, E(V)\cdot\lambda \,, E(V)\cdot(1-\lambda)\,]\,. \tag{11}$$

where the value of λ depends on the risk-level of the core enterprise. For a risk-medium supply chain organizer,

$$\lambda = \frac{\beta \cdot E(V)}{E(V)\cdot(1+2\beta)-I(1+\alpha)}.$$

4 Numerical Example

There is a cosmetic manufacturer (**A**) which was to form a supply chain for its new product. Supplier **B** was considered as one of potential partners since it could provide a specific kind of raw materials and services. The value of input is estimated as one million dollar, and income functions listed as $f_1(I) = 2I$, $f_2(I) = 1.5I$ and $f_3(I) = 1.3I$. The relative probability of attitude status $\{\theta_1, \theta_2, \theta_3\}$ for **B** is 0.4, 0.2 and 0.4, respectively. In addition, $\beta = 0.2$ and $\alpha = 0.2$.

Some relative parameters could be calculated from Eqs.(6-10), and their results are shown in Table 2.

Table 2. Income Value and Allocation Proportion

$E(V)$	$f_1(I)$	$f_2(I)$	$f_3(I)$	λ_A	$\theta_1 : \lambda_B$	$\theta_2 : \lambda_B$	$\theta_3 : \lambda_B$
1.62	2.00	1.50	1.30	≥ 0.303	≥ 0.25	≥ 0.333	≥ 0.419

For a risk-medium manufacturer, we can conclude from Eq.(11) that suitable potential partners are the ones with their bargain price scope [49, 113]. Apparently, different risk levels will result in different scopes. If **A** is a pessimistic decision-maker who considers **B** to be lazy and irredeemable, the scope will be narrowed to [68, 94]. Different scopes show the feasibility performance of the supply chain project, and also show the bargain space for supply chain organizer and potential cooperative members.

Relatively, the scope is also a rational price range for potential partners (e.g. supplier **B**).

5 Discussions

It can be obtained from Eq.(11) that the length of suitable bargain price range:

$$d = E(V)\cdot(1-2\lambda) = E(V)\cdot\left(\frac{E(V)-(1+\alpha)\cdot I}{E(V)(1+2\beta)-I\cdot(1+\alpha)}\right). \tag{12}$$

Since $0 \le \beta \le 1$, equation (12) can be expressed into:

$$d = \begin{cases} E(V) & for \quad \beta = 0 \\ E(V)\cdot\left[\frac{E(V)-I\cdot(1+\alpha)}{E(V)\cdot(1+2\beta)-I\cdot(1+\alpha)}\right] & for \quad 0<\beta<1 \\ E(V)\cdot\left[1-\frac{2E(V)}{3E(V)-I\cdot(1+\alpha)}\right. & for \quad \beta = 1 \end{cases}. \tag{13}$$

According to Eq.(13), we can make further analysis of the relationship between the bargain price scope and the competitive index.

(1) If there are no competitions ($\beta = 0$) between a core enterprise and its potential partners, then $d = E(V)$. This means the length of the range (d) will not change with the change of parameter λ. And the range in this case is widest among all any other cases ($0<\beta\le 1$).

(2) If $0<\beta<1$, then d decreases when β increases, and decreases when α increases. This means, the enterprises with less competitiveness and relatively low industrial profit rate are more possible to become the suitable potential partners.

(3) If competitive index $\beta = 1$ (that is, these two enterprises compete each other drastically), then the range becomes very narrow. And when $E(V) = I(1+\alpha)$, $d = 0$, which means there is no possibility to form the supply chain alliance.

6 Concluding Remarks

Supply chain management is considered as one of most popular and effective management strategies. The analysis approach presented in this paper provides an important tool, from the viewpoint of game theory, for judging whether a project is feasible to a supply chain alliance, and also for evaluating and finding suitable potential partners. It is worthy of noting that some settings of parameters mentioned in the game analysis approach may be modified and adjusted according to practical situations. And it should be point out that this approach emphasizes the feasibility analysis of a supply chain project from the viewpoint of economics in an ideal market competition environment.

Future research will pay more attention to develop an n-person game model for the feasibility analysis of a supply chain project. Also, more non-economic factors will be considered, such as, credit, brand, and so on.

Acknowledgment

This work was supported by Zhejiang Provincial Nature Science Foundation (grant No.Y605451) and Zhejiang Provincial Key Disciplines: Advanced Manufacturing Technology & Equipment.

References

1. Ma, S.H., Shen, L.: Time Competition-Based Operational Mode for Push & Pull in Supply Chains. Chinese Journal of Management, Vol.2 (2005) 347-352
2. Feng, D.Z., Yamashiro, M.: A Pragmatic Approach for Optimal Selection of Plant-specific Process Plans in a Virtual Enterprise. Production Planning & Control, Vol.14 (2003) 562-570
3. Feng, D.Z., Yamashiro, M., Chen, L.L.: A Novel Approach for Vendor Combination Selection in Supply Chain Management. Lecture Notes in Computer Science, Vol.3809 (2005) 1331-1334
4. Feng, D.Z., Chen L.L., Jiang, M.X.: Evaluation and Selection of Vendor Combination in Global Supply Chain System. Proceedings of 2005 ICMA2005 (IEEE Press), Vol.2 (2005) 1129-1133
5. Feng, D.Z., Zhang, L.B.: Optimal Production Policy for a Volume-Flexibility Supply-Chain System. Lecture Notes on Computer Science, Vol.3645 (2005) 900-909
6. Min, H., Zhou, G.G.: Supply Chain Modeling: Past, Present and Future. Computer & Industrial Engineering, 43 (2002) 231-249
7. Chen, F., Federgruen, A., Zheng, Y.: Near-optimal Pricing Replenishment Strategies for a Retail/Distribution System. Operations Research, Vol.49 (2001) 839-853
8. Cao, J., Du, Y.P., P X.: Game Analysis on Supply Chain Information Share. Journal of Information, 1(2005) 75-79
9. Cachon, G., Zipkin, P.: Competitive and Cooperative Inventory Policies in a Two-stage Supply Chain. Management Science, Vol.45 (1999) 936-953
10. Li, Y., Zhang, Y.: Cooperative R&D Game Models of Manufacturer-Supplier in Supply Chain. Journal of Systems Engineering, Vol.20 (2005) 12-18
11. Wu, Y.H., Zhao, Q., Wang, C.: The Study of the Distribution of Inventory Cost Saving in Supply Chain Based on N-Person Cooperation Theory. Chinese Journal of Management Science, Vol.10 (2002) 44-47

The Dynamics Mechanism Study on Interactive Development of Industry Clusters and Urbanization*

Weixiang Xu, Ye Jiang, Bin Yu, and Gennian Tang

College of Business Administration, Zhejiang University of Technology,
Hangzhou, 310014, P.R. China
xwq@zjut.edu.cn

Abstract. Industry clusters with urbanization interactive development is a multi-factor complex system. In this research, we present a system dynamics methodology to construct an industrial clustering and urbanization interactive dynamics model, and further to make its simulation computation and analysis. The simulation results show that the development of industrial clusters stimulates the rise of urbanization level, and the level of urbanization and the growth of industrial clusters promote the development of industrial clusters. Also, a case study for Yiwu City, P.R.China is conducted. It shows that the urbanization of Yiwu City is a fairly advanced virtuous circle.

1 The Dynamics Mechanism Construction of the Interactive Development of Industry Clusters and Urbanization

The system dynamics introduced by Professor Forrester (Jay Forrester W) is a quantitative method based on feedback control theory with computer simulation technology. It is usually used to research complex socio-economic system. The issue considering interactive development of industry clusters with urbanization involves many factors [1-2]. The interaction among the factors, and between the factors and the entire system creates a big complex of dynamic feedback with multi-variables and multi-levels, and being nonlinear [3-4]. In order to correctly catch the development trend, we must adopt the thinking of system analysis. Combining the actual situation of several medium and small cities, we have chosen 11 flow variables required for the system. The correlation between variables is as followed.

To further describe the interrelationship of the system variables, industry clusters with urbanization interactive system is divided into four subsystems: clustering subsystems, economic structure subsystems, energy and infrastructure security subsystems and urbanization subsystems.

(1) In the clustering subsystem (Fig. 2), we describe the interactions between clustering output and other variables, such as, land, labor, technical information, availability of electricity and industry competition (cluster size : enterprises quantity in the

* This paper is sponsored by Natural Science Foundation of China (Project NO. 70373037), and sponsored by Foundation of Art & Social Science Research and Plan, Ministry of Education (Project NO. 05JA790072).

D.-S. Huang, K. Li, and G.W. Irwin (Eds.): ICIC 2006, LNAI 4114, pp. 1020 – 1025, 2006.

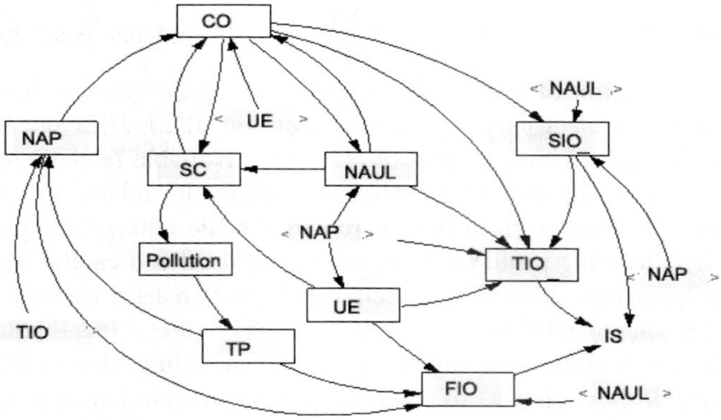

CO= clustering output
SC= scales of cluster
NAUL= non-agricultural using land
P= pollution
TP= total population
IS= industrial structure
PNAP= Proportion of non-agricultural population
NAP= non-agricultural population
UE= usable electricity
SIO= the second industrial output
TIO= the tertiary industrial output
FIO= the first industrial output
TP=Total Population

Fig. 1. Industry clusters with urbanization interactive development system variables

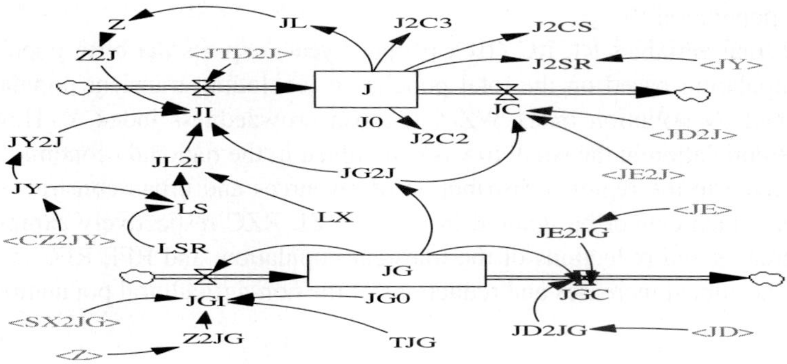

Fig. 2. Cluster sub-system flowchart

clusters). Taking clustering output J (t) (100 mn) and clustering scale JG (t) (a) as flow variables, and J0 and JG0 were initial data of clustering output and number of enterprises in certain scale quantity within the clusters respectively in year 0.

JI (100 mn per year) is said as expectation of incremental clustering output value based on the actual production capability. JI is affected by employment JY, capital input Z, scale enterprises quantity JG, labour quality in clusters LS and information sharing degrees JX. JY2J, JZ2J, JG2J and JL2J are said respectively as effective factors of employment, capital inputs, scale enterprises quantity and the labour quality and information to the incremental clustering output. Among them, labour quality LS (no dimension) is defined as value of high-ranking technicians LSR (10 k persons) to employment LY (10 k persons) $LS = \dfrac{LSR}{LY}$. JC (100 mn per year) is defined as the bias from expectation of incremental clustering output value which is affected by land, availability of electricity and peer competition. JD2J, JE2J and JG2J are respectively expressed as effective factors of clustering available land JD, clustering availability of electricity JE and scale enterprise quantity JG related to clustering output. JGI (a/year) is known as clustering incremental scale enterprises quantity, and it is controlled by clustering profit (JL), the market demand and capital input. SX2JG and Z2JG are respectively defined as effective factors of market demand and capital inputs related to incremental enterprises quantity. JGC (unit / year) indicates peer competition, the constraints of available resources, including electricity, land, and the reduction size of these clusters of enterprises. This subsystem requires input variables of JD2J, JD2JG and JE2J, JE2JG, and the effective factor CZ2JY of urban population related to employment. The effective factor J2SR of clustering output to disposable income of urban population per capita, and the effective factor J2CS clustering output to infrastructure as outputting variables that link to other subsystems.

(2) The economic structure subsystem (Fig. 3), the output value (all in RMB) in the first industry C1 (t) (100 mn), output of secondary industry C2 (t) (100 mn) and the output tertiary industry C3 (t) (100 mn) as spaces variables analyze I, II, III industrial linkages. which is not discussed in details.

(3) In the urbanization subsystem (Fig. 4), there are three population flow-variables, i.e. transient population RZ (t), the total population of R (t), the non-farming population RF (t).

Flow rate variables RI, RC (10 k people / year) express the birth population and death population based on the total population (excluding transient population), are constrained by pollution index WZ and urban crowdedness index Y. However the transient population in the small towns is involved in the regional economic activities, and involved in the regional distribution of resources and urban construction, it is a big force which cannot be ignored in towns. RZI, RZC respectively express the annual increases and reductions of the transient population, and RFI, RFC respectively express the annual increases and reductions of the non-agricultural population.

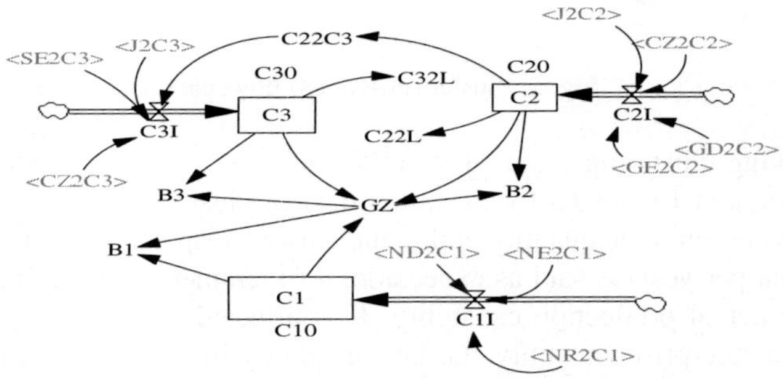

Fig. 3. The economic structure subsystem

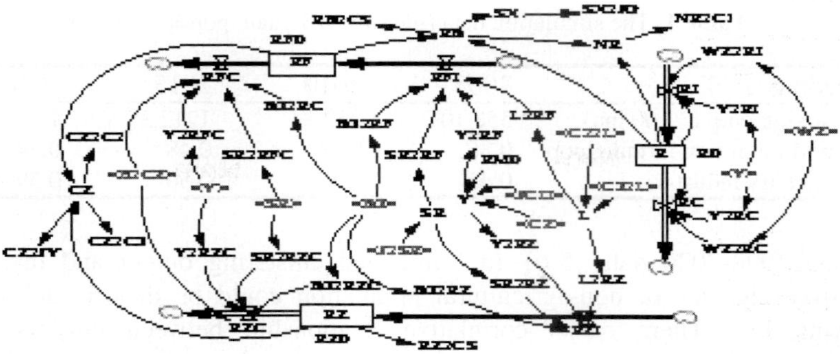

Fig. 4. The urbanization subsystem

Y defined as urban crowdedness index: $Y = (\frac{CZ}{JD}) / RM0$. Among them, J.D. is construction area; RM0 is the initial urban population density. CZ by the effective factors CZ2JY, CZ2C1 and CZ2C2 CZ controls cluster employment, secondary and tertiary industry output value, to make urbanization subsystems and industrial clustering subsystems, economic structure linked together. SR is (10k yuan / person) disposable income per capita of urban population, and L expresses demand for labours in the second and tertiary industries. SR, L and the proportion of the tertiary industry B3 restricts the annual increase and reduction of non-agricultural population and the transient population. In the system, agricultural population (10 k people) as a supplementary variable, is constrained by the ratio of non-farming population to the total population RM as well as total population R, at the same time it controls the fluctuations of first industrial output, and also indicates the link of population and the economic structure system. RB and the transient population RZ together constrain infrastructure through RB2CS and RZ2CS, so it indicates the link of urbanization subsystems and energy and infrastructure protection subsystems. The market demand SX (100 mn yuan, total retail sales of consumer goods) is controlled by RB, and restricts the annual growth of number enterprises with certain scale within the cluster. Energy and infrastructure security subsystem, and the close relationship and interaction among these 4 subsystems are not discussed in details because of the paper limitation.

2 Analysis of Yiwu City Models of Industrial Clusters Development and Result of Interactive Dynamics Simulation

The study on inherent mechanism of interaction between industrial cluster and urbanization of Yiwu City, Zhejiang provides a good reference on the industrial development of China's medium and small cities. A series calculation results could be gained by setting up the interaction dynamics between industry cluster and urbanization, and conducting the simulation calculation based on relevant programs. Table 1 is the simulation data of clustering output, the proportion of non farming population (rural), and the proportion of tertiary industry output.

Table 1. The simulation data (mn in RMB yuan, pop=population)

Heading level	2005	2010	2015	2020
Clustering output (100 mn)	558.10	862.24	1212.35	1410.78
Proportion of non farming pop	0.36	0.44	0.48	0.54
The tertiary industry	0.45	0.48	0.56	0.59

Using 1998-2020 data [5-6], the simulated clustering output and the trend of proportion changes of non-agricultural population could be drawn, and shown as following Fig. There exists correlative relationship between clusters of non-agricultural output and proportion of the non-agricultural population.

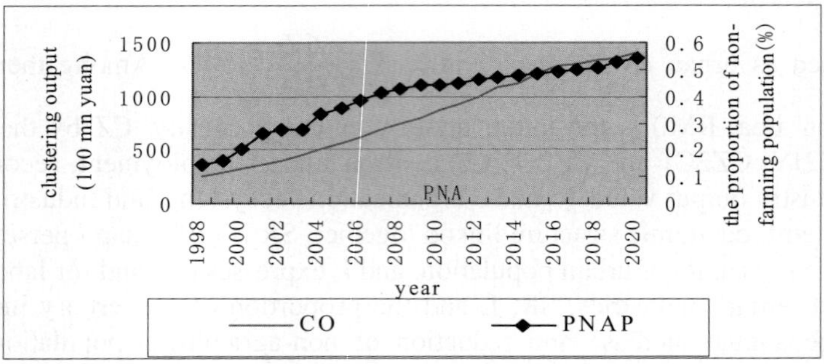

Fig. 5. The Transformation Trend of Clustering Output and the Proportion of Non farming Population

Based on the Pairwise Granger Causality Tests and simulation data from 1998 to 2020, the causal relationship between the cluster output and proportion of non-agricultural population is examed. In the tests with lag=3, the result is shown in following table.

With the lag=3, correlative relationship between both is existing. In order to ensure the validity of the test results, the same test was conducted with variable number of lags, the results were similar. It might be proven that interaction between urbanization and industrial clusters exists.

Industrial clusters, as shown in Fig. 5, are kinds of carrier of the agricultural population moving toward cities. The increase of the cluster output between 1998 and 2010 will drive the increase of the proportion of non-agricultural population. And the non-agricultural population is the main labour source in industrial clusters, supports

Table 2. Pairwise Granger Causality

Tests Sample: 1998 2020 Lags: 3			
Null Hypothesis:	Obs	F-Statistic	Probability
the proportion of non-farming population does not Granger Cause Clustering output	20	2.097	0.1507
Clustering output does not Granger Cause the proportion of non-farming population		1.231	0.3387

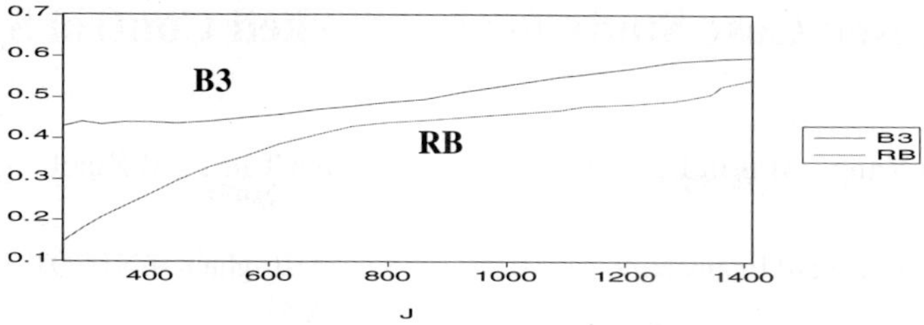

Fig. 6. The Relation between C- O J and B3, Prop of Non-farming Pop RB (urban rate)

the development of industrial clusters. After 2010, as the increase rate of non-agricultural population will be slow down, it leads to a growth of cluster output (C-O=cluster output).

As shown in Fig. 6, in the early stage of cluster development the increase of non-agricultural population is promoted, however, the growth of proportion of the non-agricultural population is getting slower while clustering output reaching 80 billion yuan. In Yiwu City, most of clusters consist of labor-intensive industries. The output growth needs substantial mass labor support, and it stimulates the increase of non-agricultural population. Simultaneously, due to the increase of cluster output, the income of urban population is increasing. The income increase of the urban population will attract the agricultural population moving toward to non-agricultural sector. Since cluster development is restricted by available land, electricity supply and industry competition, increase rate of the cluster output is getting down, and leads to less demand of labor. The proportion change of non-agricultural population is getting smaller.

By using the simulated results we can further analyze the cluster output, non-agricultural population and the proportion of the second and third industries, availability of electricity and correlative degree of land use for the transportation to out of the clusters.

In other words, in Yiwu, the industry cluster development and urbanization are both positively functioning in the healthy manner and forming a sound circulation.

References

1. Wu, Q.T.: The Coupled Mechanisms Analysis of Industry Clusters and Regional Economic Development. Management of the World (2004)
2. Li, T. L., Li, C.G.: The Responding and Feedback Mechanisms of Regional Industrial Structure Evolved in to Urbanization. Urban Issues (2003)
3. Jia, R.N., Ding, R.H.: Edited: The Feedback Dynamic Complex Analysis of System Dynamics. Higher Education Press (2002)
4. The Policy Research Center of CPC Zhejiang Provincial Committee: The Study on Increasing Zhejiang Regional Massive Economic Competitiveness. Internal Reference (2002)
5. China Statistical Yearbook
6. Yiwu City Statistical Yearbook

A Proposed Case Study for Networked Control System

Taicheng Yang[1], Minrui Fei[2], Dingyu Xue[3], Yuemei Tan[2], and Xiaobing Zhou[2]

[1] Department of Engineering, University of Sussex, Brighton BN1 9QT, UK
taiyang@sussex.ac.uk
[2] School of Mechatronical Engineering and Automation,
Shanghai University, Shanghai 200072, China
{mrfei, tanya}@staff.shu.edu.cn, zxb7058@263.net
[3] Faculty of Information Science and Engineering,
Northeastern University, Shenyang 110004, China
xuedingyu@ise.neu.edu.cn

Abstract. Numerical examples and some simple systems, for instance an inverted pendulum on a cart, are often used in the analytical and simulation study of Networked Control Systems (NCSs). In this paper, we propose to use a system of "Two inverted pendulums Coupled by a Spring" to extend the existing study to investigate: (1) asynchronised multi-rate sampling in a NCS, (2) random, distributed and discrete time delay in networked signal-transfer with possible loss of signals, (3) NCS for nonlinear systems, (4) Robust control of NCS with plant uncertainties and external disturbances, and (5) using NCS to implement controller structure beyond the limit of decentralised control. This system has been used, in the context of point-to-point connections, to study a number of control problems including a study on robust stabilisation of nonlinear systems via decentralised control. Therefore the performances of the system having a NCS structure can be compared with those having a traditional structure of fixed connections. The detailed model, some simulation results of the system under both of a traditional structure and a NCS structure, and proposed further studies are presented in the paper.

1 Introduction

An application example of "Two inverted pendulums Coupled by a Spring" (TCS, see Figure 1) was used in decentralised control literature to demonstrate "optimality and robustness of linear quadratic control for nonlinear systems" in a paper in *Automatica* [1]; "decentrally optimal systems" in a well-known book on decentralised control [2]; and "robust stabilisation of nonlinear systems via linear state feedback" in another control research book [3]. In [3], robust stabilisation of nonlinear systems is achieved by decentralised control, which is a particularly challenging problem. In this paper, we propose to use this TCS system as an example to investigate feedback control system under a Networked Control System (NCS) structure.

D.-S. Huang, K. Li, and G.W. Irwin (Eds.): ICIC 2006, LNAI 4114, pp. 1026 – 1036, 2006.

2 Modelling and Simulation

The variables of the system (Figure 1) are:

θ_i : angular displacement of pendulum i (i = 1, 2)
τ_i : torque input generated by the actuator for pendulum i (i = 1, 2)
F : spring force
l_s : spring length
ϕ : angle of the spring to the earth

and the constants are:
l_i : length of pendulum i (i = 1, 2)
m_i : mass of pendulum i (i = 1, 2)
L : distance of two pendulums
κ : spring constant

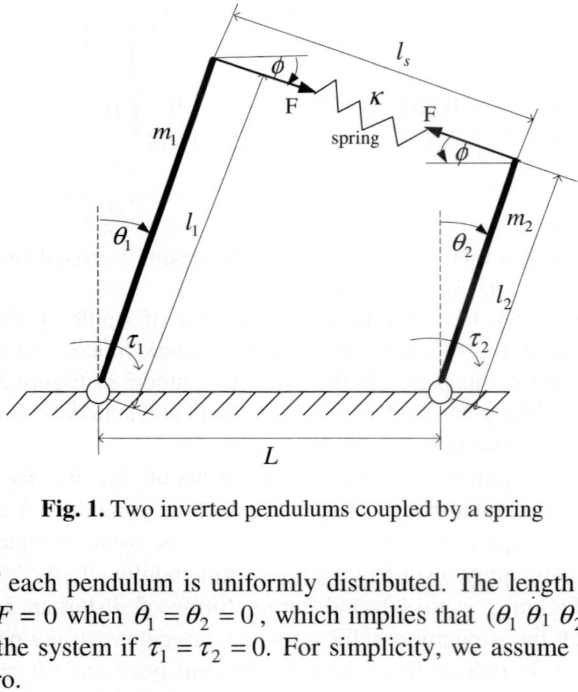

Fig. 1. Two inverted pendulums coupled by a spring

The mass of each pendulum is uniformly distributed. The length of the spring is chosen so that F = 0 when $\theta_1 = \theta_2 = 0$, which implies that $(\theta_1\ \dot{\theta}_1\ \theta_2\ \dot{\theta}_2)^T = 0$ is an equilibrium of the system if $\tau_1 = \tau_2 = 0$. For simplicity, we assume that the mass of the spring is zero.

The equations of motion of the coupled pendulums are written as

$$\begin{aligned} [m_1(l_1)^2/3]\ddot{\theta}_1 &= \tau_1 + m_1 g(l_1/2)\sin\theta_1 + l_1 F\cos(\theta_1 - \phi) \\ [m_2(l_2)^2/3]\ddot{\theta}_2 &= \tau_2 + m_2 g(l_2/2)\sin\theta_2 - l_2 F\cos(\theta_2 - \phi) \end{aligned} \quad (1)$$

where $g = 9.8\text{m/sec}^2$ is the constant of gravity, and

$$F = \kappa(l_s - [L^2 + (l_1 - l_2)^2]^{1/2})$$
$$l_s = [(L + l_2 \sin\theta_2 - l_1 \sin\theta_1)^2 + (l_2 \cos\theta_2 - l_1 \cos\theta_1)^2]^{1/2} \tag{2}$$
$$\phi = \tan^{-1} \frac{l_1 \cos\theta_1 - l_2 \cos\theta_2}{L + l_2 \sin\theta_2 - l_1 \sin\theta_1}$$

The following plant numerical values are used in [3]:

$l_1 = 1m \quad l_2 = 0.8m \quad m_1 = 1kg \quad m_2 = 0.8kg$
$L = 1.2m \quad \kappa = 4N/m$

The initial conditions of the two pendulums are noted as: $\theta_1(0) = x01 \quad \theta_2(0) = x02$.

In [3], the movements of the two pendulums are assumed no more than 30 degree (0.53 radian) from their equilibrium positions ($\theta_1 = \theta_2 = 0$). A decentralised state feedback control law:

$$\begin{bmatrix} \tau_1 \\ \tau_2 \end{bmatrix} = -\begin{bmatrix} 10.957 & 3.485 & 0 & 0 \\ 0 & 0 & 7.500 & 2.375 \end{bmatrix} \begin{bmatrix} \theta_1 \\ \dot{\theta}_1 \\ \theta_2 \\ \dot{\theta}_2 \end{bmatrix} \tag{3}$$

is designed to stabilise this unstable system. The design is based on a few theorems and corollaries proved in [3].

Although the system has been used in a number of studies [1-3], no simulation result is presented in the literature. A Matlab/Simulink model and some simulation results are presented in this paper. In the simulation model of Figure 2, subsystem 1 is for the dynamics of the plant, and associated sensors and actuators. Subsystem 2 is for the dynamics of the controller, i.e., the above equation.

Subsystem 1 has 4 outputs, i.e., the measurements of θ_1, $\dot{\theta}_1$, θ_2 and $\dot{\theta}_2$. It has four inputs, i.e., two disturbance torques applied to pendulum 1 and 2; and two feedback control torques τ_1 and τ_2 . Since there is some symmetry of the two pendulums, we only apply disturbance torques to pendulum 1. A "Multiport Switch" on the left of Figure 2 is to select different forms of disturbance signals. In our simulation model, the simulation will stop if the movement of any pendulum is more than 60 degree (1.05 radian) from their equilibrium positions ($\theta_1 = \theta_2 = 0$). If this happens, the system is considered unstable.

Typical simulation results are presented in Figures 3-6. In Figure 3, there is no external disturbance torque (In Figure 2, the switching option number is 1; and disturbance torque is a constant with a value of zero) and the system responses to a non-zero initial condition: $\theta_1(0) = x01 = 0.5; \quad \theta_2(0) = x02 = 0$. In Figure 4, with a zero initial condition, a step function with a magnitude of 7.5 N·m is applied to the system at *t* = *0.1* sec. Although the position of pendulum 1 moves beyond the assumed upper value of 0.52 radian in the design, the system is still stable. This is due to the conditions

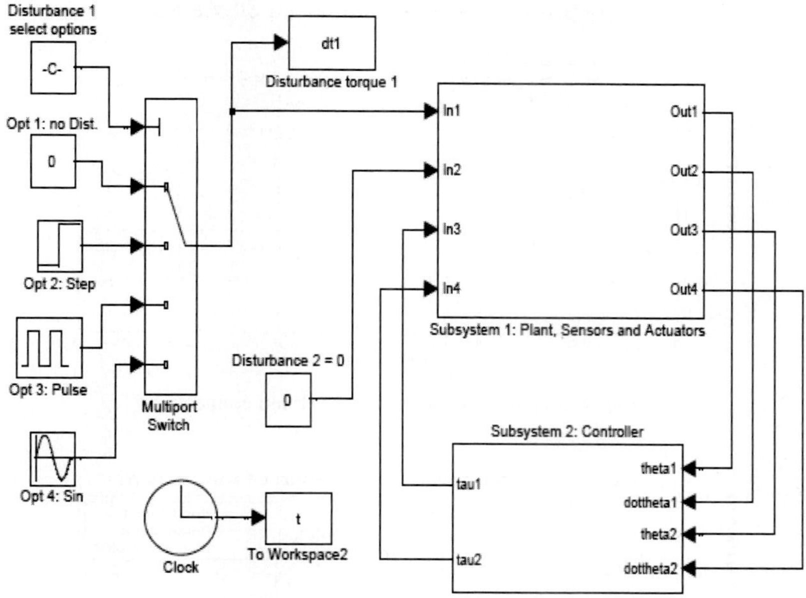

Fig. 2. A Matlab/Simulink model

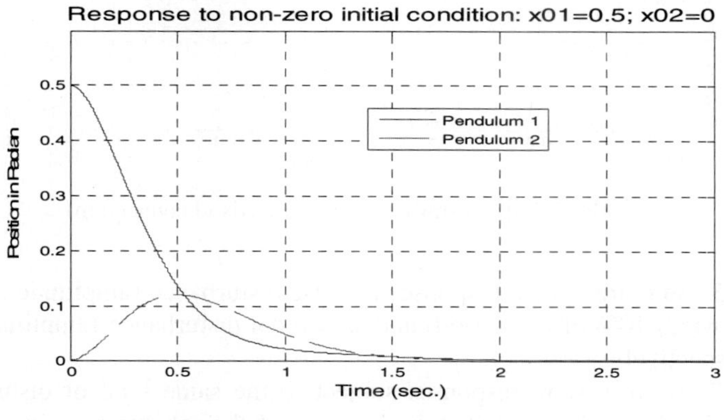

Fig. 3. Initial condition response (fixed connection)

used in the design [3] are sufficient conditions. At the final steady-state, on pendulum 1 the toque due to the spring force F, the feedback control torque τ_1, and the disturbance torque result a net zero torque. Similarly, at the steady-state, on pendulum 2 the feedback control torque τ_2 is equal to the toque due to the spring force F in magnitude but in opposite directions. These steady-state values are:

$$[\theta_1 \ \theta_2 \ \tau_1 \ \tau_2] = [1.0268 \ \ 0.3202 \ \ -11.3455 \ \ -2.3832]$$

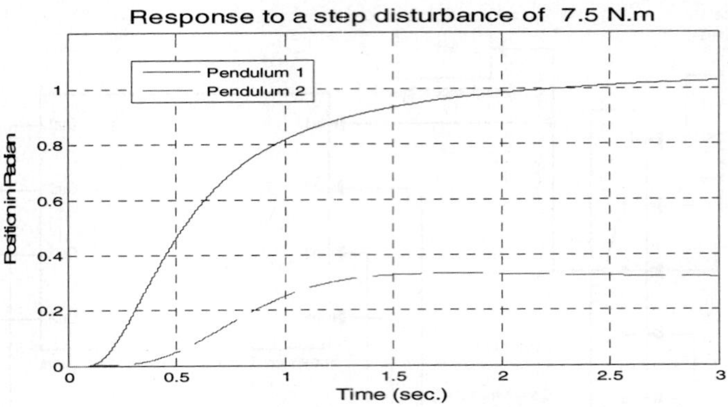

Fig. 4. Step disturbance response (fixed connection)

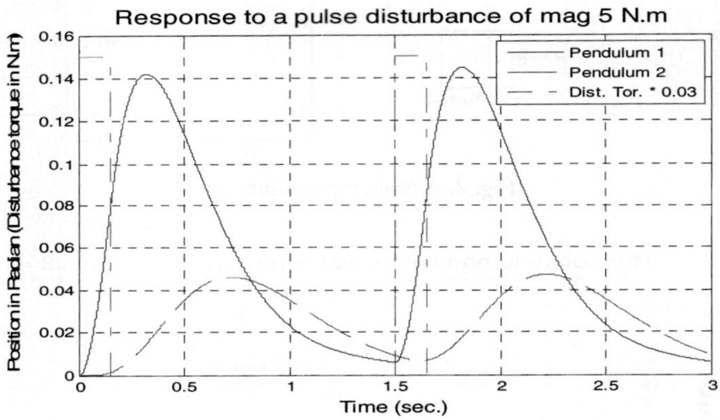

Fig. 5. Pulse disturbance response (fixed connection)

Figures 5 and 6 are system responses to pulse disturbance (amplitude 5; period 1.5 sec.; pulse width 10% of the period) and sinusoidal disturbance (amplitude 8; period 1.5 sec.) respectively.

Figures 7-10 are system responses subject to the same kind of disturbances but under a NCS scheme. The detailed descriptions of the scheme are given in the next section. Notice that (1) in order to have “stable” outputs, signal magnitudes of disturbances are reduced (see titles of the figures for detail), and (2) plotting scales used in Figures 7-10 are different from those used in Figures 3-6. The description of simulation package used for the NCS case, which is still under further development, can be found from http://www.sussex.ac.uk/Users/taiyang/ under “selected presentations”.

Remark. From the simulation results presented in Figures 3-10, where the cases simulated under NCS are very limited, one can see that, as can be predicted, the system responses deteriorate when the point-to-point connections between sensors and the controller are replaced by network communications.

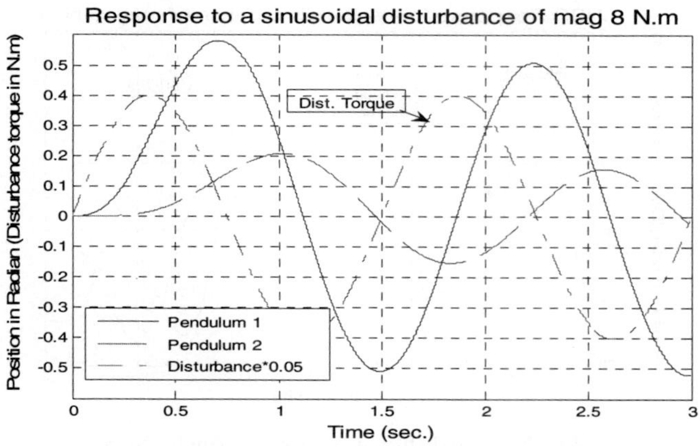

Fig. 6. Sinusoidal disturbance response (fixed connection)

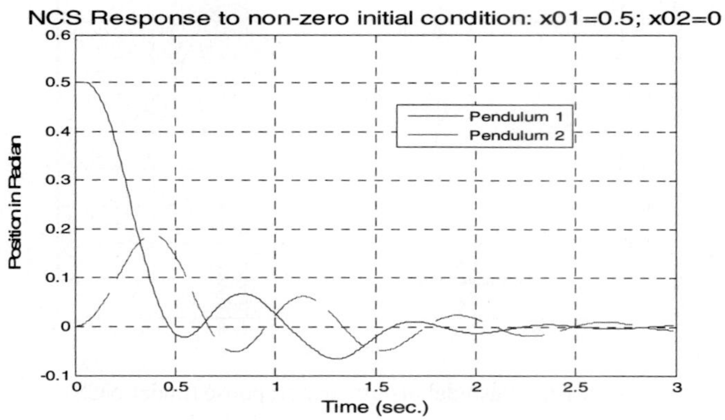

Fig. 7. Initial condition response (under NCS)

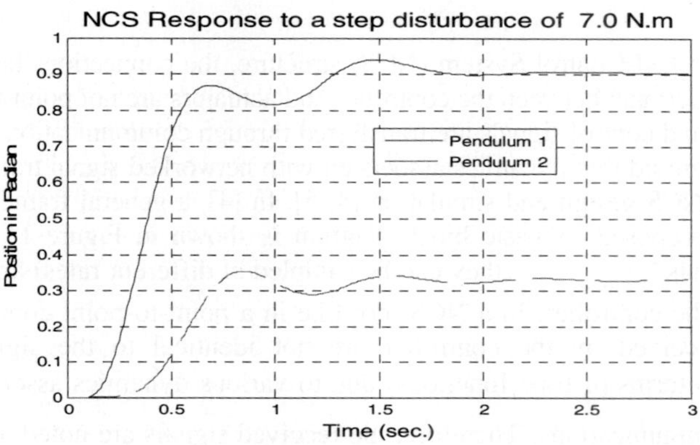

Fig. 8. Step disturbance response (under NCS)

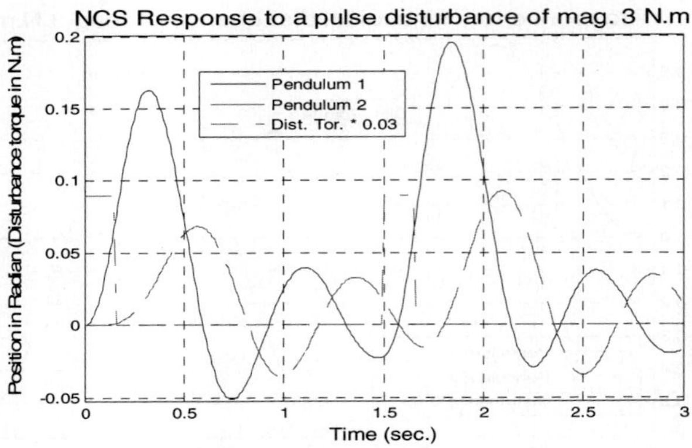

Fig. 9. Pulse disturbance response (under NCS)

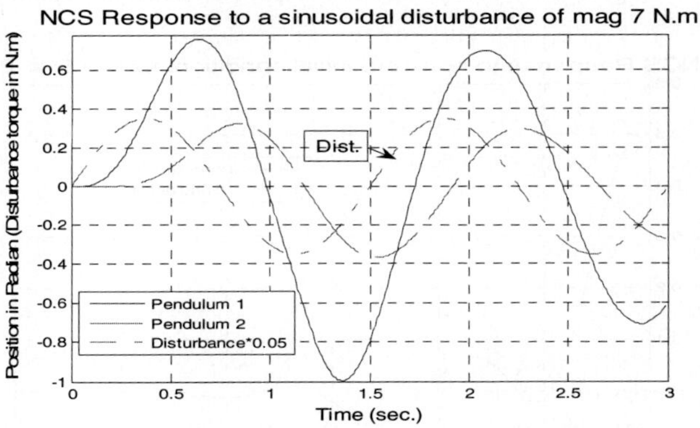

Fig. 10. Sinusoidal disturbance response (under NCS)

3 Analytical and Simulation Study of the System Under a NCS Structure

Under a Networked Control System (NCS) structure, the connections between sensors and the controller; and between the controller and actuators are not point-to-point wired. Measurement and control signals are transferred through communication networks. It is generally recognised that dynamics associated with networked signal transfer should be considered in NCS design and simulation [4, 5]. In [4], a general framework for NCS simulation is proposed. A basic block diagram is shown in Figure 11, where the N measured signals y^1 ...... y^N (they can be sampled at different rates) are sent through a network to the controller. In a NCS, not like in a point-to-point connected system, the signals received by the controller are not identical to the signals sent out: y^1 ...... y^N (in terms of time functions) due to various dynamics associated with the networked communications. Therefore, the received signals are noted as w^1 ...... w^N .

Similarly, the plant actuator signals u^1 ...... u^m are not identical to the controller output signals: v^1 ...... v^m .

Figure 12 is a typical timing diagram for signal transfer in a NCS. For our example system, we can assume that the measurements of angular position and the speed of pendulum 1: θ_1 $\dot{\theta}_1$ (or y^1 y^2 in Figure 11), as data source 1, are sampled at a rate with a period of T_1 . They are put into a data packet D^{s1} with a sequence of D_1^{s1}, D_2^{s1}, ..., where the subscript of D^{s1} is the sampling sequence. The packets arrived at the controller (the receiving end) are noted as D_1^{r1}, D_2^{r1}, ... (not shown in the figure). The signals used for controller input are noted as w^1 w^2 before. Similarly, the measurements of θ_2 $\dot{\theta}_2$ (or y^3 y^4 in Figure 11), as data source 2, are sampled at a rate with a period of T_2. They are put into a data packet D^{s2} with a sequence of D_1^{s2}, D_2^{s2}, ... to send through the network to reach at the controller, noted as D_1^{r2}, D_2^{r2}, ... as shown in the figure. The controller itself has an updating (sampling) rate with a period of T. With the given data, we propose to set $T_1 = 0.05$sec.; $T_2 = 0.04$sec. and $T = 0.04$sec. From this timing diagram, one can observe that:

(1) Sources 1 and 2 have different sampling rates.
(2) Although the sampling rate of source 2 is the same as that of the receiving end, there is a “time skew” γ between the sampling instances of the two. This and (1) are to reflect asynchronised multi-rate sampling in a typical NCS.
(3) The time-delay between sending a packet and receiving it is random.
(4) There is a possibility of packet loss. In Figure 12, data packet D_3^{s2} is lost in the transmission.
(5) There is a possibility of packets arriving in a wrong order. This is due to the randomness of the time-delay in packet transmission. In Figure 12, a newly received packet D_k^{r2} is not a packet with newly sampled signals at the source.

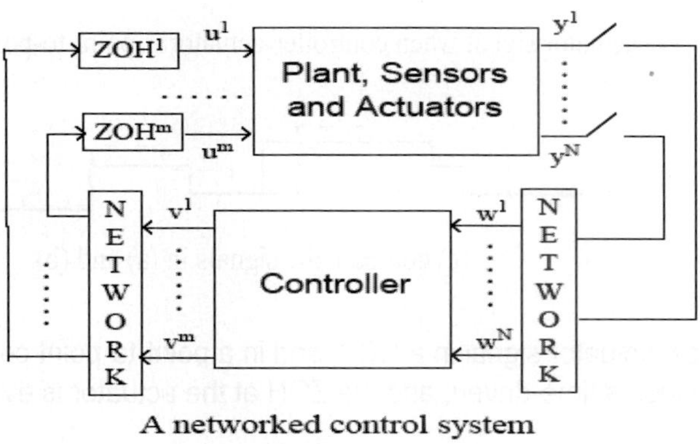

Fig. 11. Networked control

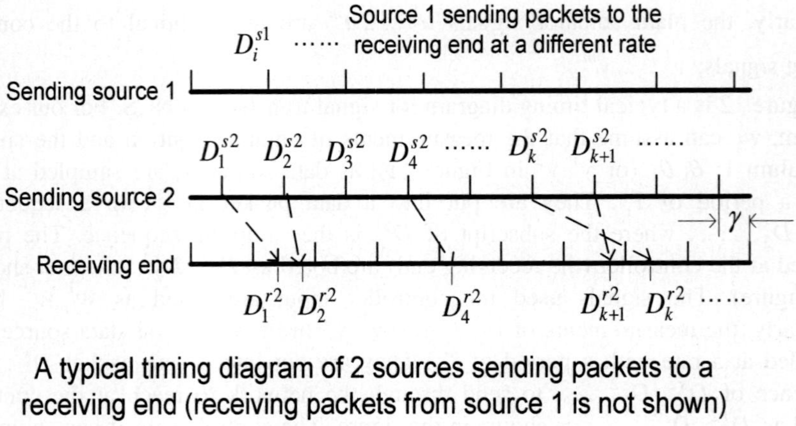

Fig. 12. Typical timing diagram of a NCS

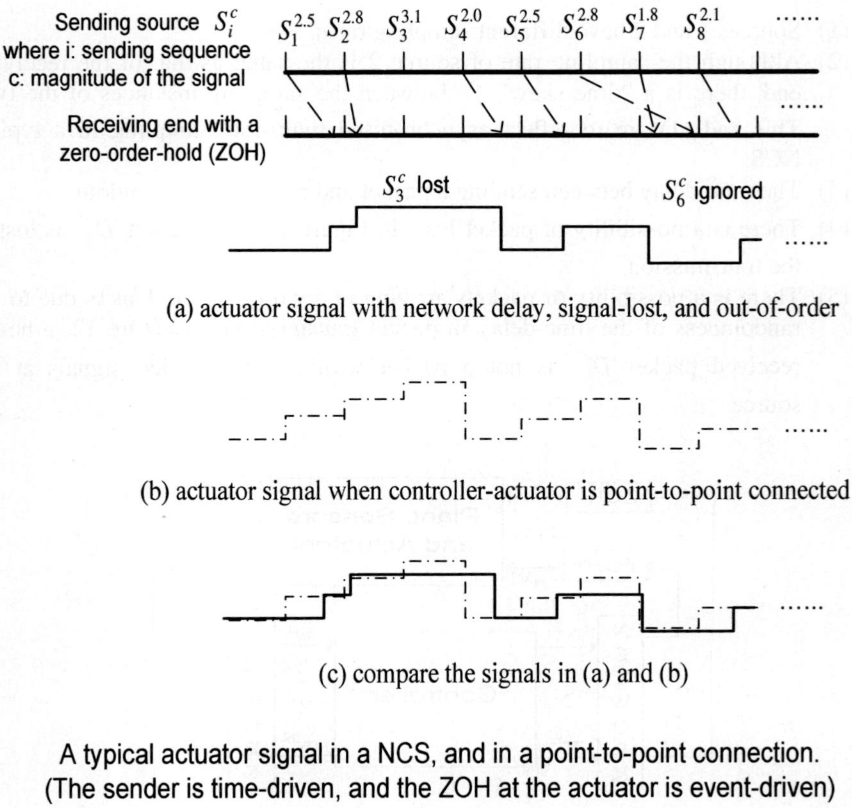

Fig. 13. Compare signals under fixed connection and NCS

The above is to show some typical characteristics of sensor-controller signal transfer in a NCS. Similarly, some typical characteristics of controller-actuator signal transfer can be shown in Figure 13. It is interesting to compare the actuator signals in a NCS, Figure 13 (a), and actuator signals in a traditional point-to-point connection, Figure 13 (b).

(a) In the previous analytical studies [1-3], the design is within the framework of a linear-system with structured uncertainties to count for the actual nonlinearity of the plant model; and is based on traditional point-to-point connections. To make the design problem even more challenging, in addition to the dynamics associated with the network communications in a NCS system, we can make some additional assumptions, for example: The dynamics of the actuators, torque motors, is to be included in the plant model.
(b) There are some uncertainties in the inertias of the moment of the two pendulums.
(c) There are some uncertain friction forces to rotational movements.
(d) There are measurement errors (within certain percentage bounds).

This system can also be used to investigate a NCS implementation of controller structures beyond the limit of decentralised control. Details of possible non-decentralised control structures to be considered can be found in [6]. In general, a discussion about the impact of NCS on large-scale system control methodology can be found in [7].

4 Conclusion

A system which was previously used in three design studies under the traditional point-to-point connection structure is proposed as a benchmark for the analytical and simulation studies of networked control systems. The detailed modelling and some simulation results are presented. These limited simulation results show that, the system responses deteriorate when the point-to-point connections between sensors and the controller are replaced by network communications.

Acknowledgments

This work is sponsored by Doctoral Program Foundation of Science & Technology Special Project in University under grant 20040280017, Program for New Century Excellent Talents in University under grant NCET-04-0433, Shanghai Leading Academic Disciplines under grant T0103, and Shanghai Key Laboratory of Power Station Automation Technology.

References

1. Ikeda M., Siljak D. D.: Optimality and Robustness of Linear Quadratic Control for Nonlinear System. Automatica, Vol. 26, No. 3 (1990) 499-511
2. Siljak D. D.: Decentralized Control of Complex Systems. Academic Press, Boston, MA, (1991)

3. Ikeda M., Siljak D. D.: Robust Stabilisation of Nonlinear Systems via Linear State Feedback in Control and Dynamic Systems. Vol.51, Edited by C. T. Leondes, Academic Press (1992)
4. Yang, T.C.: Networked Control System: A Brief Survey. To be Published in IEE Proceedings: Control Theory and Applications, Available from: http://www.sussex.ac.uk/Users/taiyang/publications/2006paper1.pdf
5. Yang, T. C., Yu H., Fei, M. R., Li, L X: Networked Control Systems: A Historical Review and Current Research Topics. Measurement and Control, Vol.38, No.1 (2005) 12-17
6. Šiljak, D. D., Zečević, A. I.: Control of Large-Scale Systems: Beyond Decentralized Feedback. Opening Plenary Talk, The 10th IFAC Symposium on Large Scale Systems, Osaka, Japan, July (2004) 26-28
7. Yang T.C.: Some Issues in the Study of Networked Control System. available from: http://www.sussex.ac.uk/Users/taiyang/publications/2006paper2.pdf

Adaptive Control Systems with Network Closed Identification Loop

Lixiong Li, Minrui Fei, and Xianya Xie

School of Mechatronical Engineering & Automation, Shanghai University, 200072 Shanghai, P.R. China
lxli@staff.shu.edu.cn

Abstract. In this paper, a class of adaptive control systems is to be studied, in which the identification loop is closed over communication networks. The network-induced delays caused by the communication network are then inevitable and randomly time-varying in general. And these delays between controller and identifier can make a mess of the transmitted packet sequences which may deteriorate the control performance even destabilize the system. Obviously, the randomly time-varying delay is a key problem in networked adaptive control systems, and a strategy using the concept of fixed maximum delay is presented to avoid this problem. The adaptive system is proven to be convergent if such strategy is to be used. After that, with a view to further improve the performance, another modified strategy is proposed and the simulation results verify its validity and practicability.

1 Introduction

The basic idea of adaptive control system is that the controller can automatically adapt itself to retain control performance as the controlled plant is under changes. An ARMA model of the plant is formed by online parameter estimation, on which the control law is based, using the principle of certainty equivalence. Hence the controller changes in accordance with the plant. The adaptive control systems have a two-loop structure to respectively implement parameter estimation and control law. The inner loop is a control loop composed of the plant and the controller. The outer loop is an online identification loop, where the identifier estimates the parameters of the plant and the estimates are provided to the controller to implement the control law.

It is well known that the adaptive control routine for linear time-invariant systems was well established in the latter decades of the last century [1]. The self-tuning regulator was presented by K.J. Åström and Wittenmark in 1973. Since then many excellent researches on adaptive control systems have been done and reported [2-4].

In recent years, on the other hand, the rapid growth of communication networks provides many opportunities for control systems, and a large amount of interests have been focused on the control systems over networks [5]. Hence, the concept of networked control systems (NCSs) [6-8], whose control loop is closed over a communication network, is emerging.

Within this paper, we intend to study a class of adaptive systems whose identification loop is closed over communication networks, while the inner loop is not. We shall

D.-S. Huang, K. Li, and G.W. Irwin (Eds.): ICIC 2006, LNAI 4114, pp. 1037 – 1048, 2006.

use the term *Networked Adaptive Control Systems* to describe it for simplicity. Fig. 1 illustrates a typical setup and the information flows of a networked adaptive control system. Obviously, the controller is developed with the ability to communicate to remote identifier through networks. Thus, the identifier can handle very complex tasks such as online parameter estimation for the controller while the local controller can be simple and cheap enough to only do limited work [9].

Building an adaptive control system over communication networks offers a lot of advantages. However, the communication networks inevitably introduce some network-induced delays. In NCSs, it is well known that the network-induced delay existing in the control loop introduces an additional phase lag in frequency domain, tending to degrade the control quality and even to destabilize the system [6, 7].

Our main purpose in this paper is to study the effects on system performance caused by network-induced delays, which exists in the identification loop of the networked adaptive control systems. To the best of our knowledge, adaptive control systems with outer loop closed over communication networks has not been presented yet so far. Furthermore we believe that most of the results presented in this paper will be useful in or can be extended to analysis and design of the *Network Learning Based Control Systems* [9]. As a matter of fact, the latter is the aim of our recent researches.

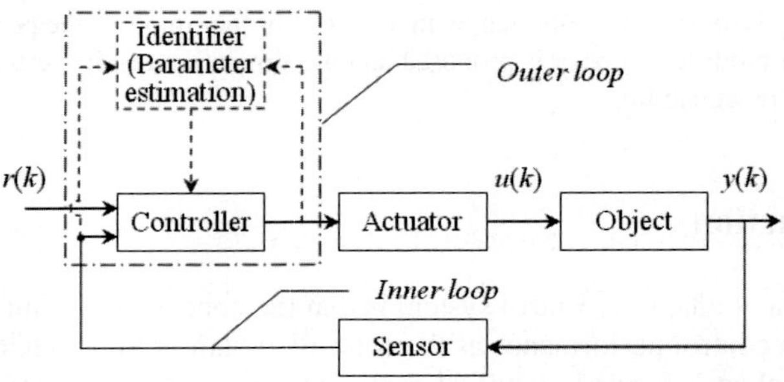

Fig. 1. Adaptive control systems over communication networks. The inner loop (control loop) is connected locally (solid line). The outer loop (identification loop) is connected over communication network (dashed). A local controller and a remote identifier can be found in this setup. The real-time control is implemented by local controller. Parameter estimation is performed by remote identifier.

2 Problem Description

We consider a plant described as DARMA model

$$A(q^{-1})y(k) = q^{-d}B(q^{-1})u(k) \ . \tag{1}$$

where $\{u(k)\}$ and $\{y(k)\}$ denote the input and output sequences respectively. $A(q^{-1}) = 1 + a_1 q^{-1} + \cdots + a_n q^{-n}$ and $B(q^{-1}) = b_0 + b_1 q^{-1} + \cdots + b_m q^{-m}$ are polynomials of the unit delay operator q^{-1}. d is the plant delay between its input and output. $k = 0, 1, \cdots$ implies the real time t=kh where h represents the sampling period.

Equation (1) can be expressed in predictor form as

$$y(k+d)=\varphi^{T}(k)\theta_{0} \tag{2}$$

where $\varphi(k)$ denotes the information vector and θ_0 denotes the parameter vector. And

$$\varphi^{T}(k)=\left[y(k),\cdots,y(k-n+1);u(k),\cdots,u(k-m-d+1)\right].$$

$$\theta_{0}^{T}=\left[\alpha_{0},\cdots,\alpha_{n-1};\beta_{0},\cdots,\beta_{m+d-1}\right],\ \beta_{0}\neq 0.$$

Since the parameter vector θ_0 is unknown, recursive least squares (RLS) algorithm can be used to compute the parameter estimates by measured plant input/output data ($y(k)$,$u(k-d)$). In general cases, the controller and identifier exist in the same processor, and the online estimation scheme [3] can be expressed as

$$\hat{\theta}(k)=\hat{\theta}(k-1)+\frac{P(k-d-1)\varphi(k-d)}{1+\varphi^{T}(k-d)P(k-d-1)\varphi(k-d)}\left(y(k)-\varphi^{T}(k-d)\hat{\theta}(k-1)\right). \tag{3}$$

$$P(k-d)=P(k-d-1)-\frac{P(k-d-1)\varphi(k-d)\varphi^{T}(k-d)P(k-d-1)}{1+\varphi^{T}(k-d)P(k-d-1)\varphi(k-d)}. \tag{4}$$

with the given initial estimate $\hat{\theta}(0)$ and $P(-d-1)$ is a pre-selected positive definite matrix, where $\hat{\theta}(k)$ denotes the parameter estimate at time $t=kh$. And then the control signal at $t=kh$ is chosen to satisfy

$$y^{*}(k+d)=\varphi^{T}(k)\hat{\theta}(k). \tag{5}$$

where $y^{*}(k+d)$ is the given reference signal at $(k+d)$th sampling instant.

If the identification loop is closed over communication networks, however, the controller and identifier are distributed geographically. The controller periodically sends ($y(k)$,$u(k-d)$) to identifier through network. But the identifier can not receive them immediately for the existence of the network-induced delay. Hence the parameter estimate $\hat{\theta}(k)$ can not be computed by (3) and (4) at time $t=kh$. Furthermore the new estimate $\hat{\theta}(k)$ can not be transmitted back to the controller immediately for the same reason. So in (5) $\hat{\theta}(k)$ is not available at the input port of the controller at time $t=kh$. As a result, the existence of network in identification loop will impede both the real-time computation of parameter estimation and control signal.

We assume in the rest of this paper that the packet size is large enough so that data do not need to be broken into multiple packets for transmission. And we also assume that the round-trip delay for the data transmission from controller to identifier and from identifier back to controller may be longer than one sampling period.

3 Effect of Network-Induced Delays on Control Performance

The network-induced delays play an important role in the networked adaptive control systems. Normally, this control systems will experience two distinct network-induced delays: one delay $\tau_{ci}(t)$ from the controller to the identifier, and another delay $\tau_{ic}(t)$ from the identifier to the controller (see Fig.2). For the sake of completeness, the computational delay $\tau_c(t)$ of the identifier should also be considered. And the following assumptions about these delays should be made for simplicity.

Assumption 1. The controller is clock-driven, and the identifier is event-driven.

Assumption 2. $\tau_{ci}(t)$ and $\tau_{ic}(t)$ are bounded, and the maximum values of them are known as $\tau_{ci}^{\max}$ and $\tau_{ic}^{\max}$ respectively.

Assumption 3. The computational delay of the identifier can be regarded as a fixed delay $\tau_c(t)= \tau_c$, while the computational delay of the controller is negligible.

And, temporarily, *Assumption 4* is also made. No packet loss happens during delivery and this problem will be discussed later.

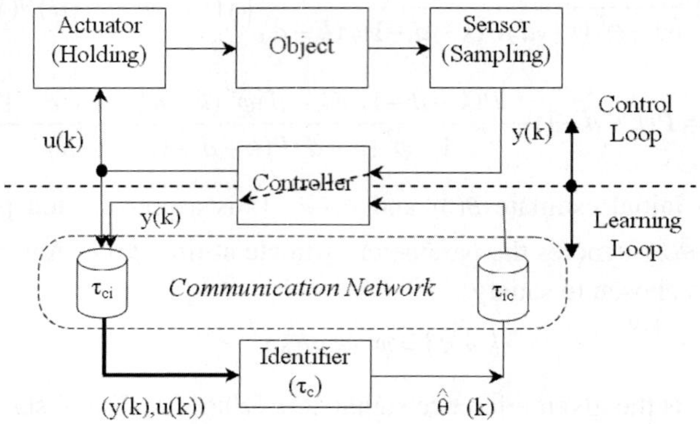

Fig. 2. Block diagram of networked adaptive control systems. Network induced delays $\tau_{ci}(t)$ and $\tau_{ic}(t)$ are explicitly illustrated instead of communication networks.

3.1 Analysis on Time Delays

In real applications, the network-induced delays τ_{ci} and τ_{ic} caused by communication networks can vary in a random fashion. In addition $\tau_{ci}(t)$ and $\tau_{ic}(t)$ are independent of each other and are dependent on the link [10-12]. Furthermore, these delays are strongly related to controller and identifier respectively.

3.2 Analysis on Out-of-Order Arrival of Packets

In practice, not only the network-induced delays are randomly time-varying but also the packets may be delivered in a way that may occur the phenomenon of out-of-order arrival of packets in some cases, implying that a packet may arrive at the receiver later than some of those packets which were sent later than it by the same transmitter.

3.3 System Performance Degradation Caused by Network-Induced Delays

Although the network-induced delays and computational delay are inevitable, the RLS algorithm (3)-(4) can also be used to implement the estimation scheme if neither packet loss happens during delivery from controller to identifier nor the out-of-order arrival of packets occurs at the input of the identifier. Otherwise, the RLS algorithm can not proceed correctly because of the misuse of estimation algorithm, which may deteriorate control performance and even destabilize the system.

Example 1. Consider a DARMA plant model

$$y(k+1)=1.2y(k)-0.7y(k-1)+0.5u(k)+0.1u(k-1) \ . \tag{6}$$

Then Equation (6) can be expressed in the form of (2), where

$$\varphi^T(k)=\big(y(k),y(k-1),u(k),u(k-1)\big),\ \theta_0^T=\begin{bmatrix}1.2 & -0.7 & 0.5 & 0.1\end{bmatrix}.$$

Select the sampling period h=5*ms*. And the reference signal is $r(k)=3.25\text{-}3\cdot\text{square}(2\pi\text{k}/110)$, where $\text{square}(\cdot)$ is a square function. When the identification loop is closed over a network, the excessive delays discussed above become inevitable. In this example, τ_{ci} and τ_{ic} are random delays, and $\tau_{ci}^{\max}=3.708h$, $\tau_{ic}^{\max}=3.432h$. Moreover we assume the computational delay of identifier τ_c=5*ms*. The simulation results indicate that the packet re-ordering at the input of the identifier will lead to the misuse of RLS algorithm, which destabilize the system.

4 Strategy I - Fixed Maximum Delay

4.1 Making Compensation of All Delays to Their Maximum

Our intention is to provide strategies to solve the packet re-ordering problem and improve overall control performance. We know that both the network-induced delays $\tau_{ci}(kh)$ and $\tau_{ic}(t)$ are bounded because of *Assumption 2*. And it is always possible to reduce the problem of time-varying delay to a time-invariant one by introducing suitable additional delay such that the sum of the delays experienced by a signal on the communication links is always constant [13].

This policy can be implemented by introducing suitable buffers at both the input of controller and identifier. And timestamps are used to indicate the "age" of the data packet [6]. Therefore, plant input/output packet becomes $(y(k),u(k-d),k)$ and parameter estimate packet becomes $(\hat{\theta}(k),k)$. If the delivery delays are bounded, we can compensate the controller-to-identifier delay to be $\tau_{ci}^{\max}$ and the identifier-to-controller delay to be $\tau_{ic}^{\max}$ using buffers. Now the round-trip delay is

$$\tau^{\max}=ceil\left(\frac{\tau_{ci}^{\max}+\tau_c+\tau_{ic}^{\max}}{h}\right)\times h\ ,\ \Delta^{\max}=\frac{\tau^{\max}}{h}=ceil\left(\frac{\tau_{ci}^{\max}+\tau_c+\tau_{ic}^{\max}}{h}\right), \tag{7}$$

where $\Delta^{\max}$ is this delay in terms of the number of sampling period. Obviously, $\Delta^{\max}\in N$ and there is not any out-of-order arrival of packets at the inputs of both identifier and controller.

Example 2. In *Example 1*, the system is unstable when out-of-order arrival of packets occurs at the input of identifier. Now *Strategy I* is to be used to continue that example. From (7) the maximum round-trip sampling interval becomes $\Delta^{\max} = 8$. The simulation results shown in Fig. 3 indicate that parameter estimates is approaching to their true values and the plant output asymptotically tracks the reference signal.

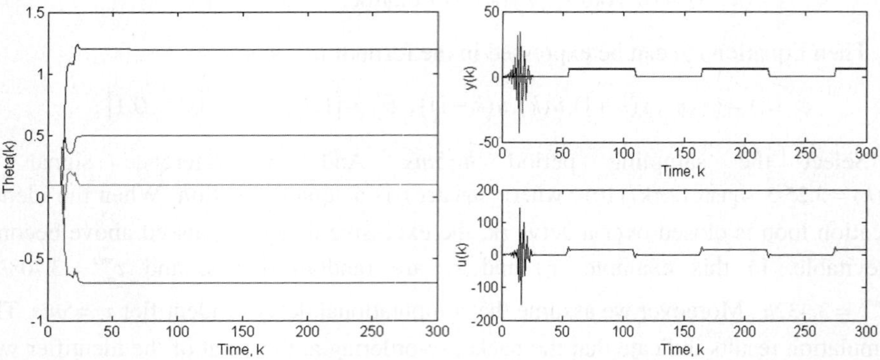

(a) Parameter Estimates (b) Plant output and control signal

Fig. 3. Simulation results as *Strategy I* being used in *Example 3*. (a) shows the parameter estimates for the plant (6). (b) shows the plant output and control signal.

4.2 Convergence Analysis

The simulation results in *Example 3* indicate that plant output can asymptotically track the reference signal if *Strategy I* is used. Now the convergence is to be analyzed theoretically, and the following assumption on the plant should be made [3].

Assumption 5 (Plant):

- The time delay d is known, here assuming d=1 for simplicity.
- An upper bound for the orders of the polynomials in (2) is known.

(i) All modes of the inverse of the model (2) [the zeros of the polynomial $B(q^{-1})$] lie inside or on the closed unit disk.

(ii) All controllable modes of the inverse of the model (2) [the zeros of the transfer function $B(q^{-1})/A(q^{-1})$] lie strictly inside the unit circle.

(iii) Any modes of the inverse of the model (2) on the unit circle have a Jordan block size of 1.

We begin the analysis with the adaptive control system without network connection, which is the base for the analysis of the networked case. For d=1 (2)-(5) can be rewritten as

$$y(k+1) = \varphi^T(k)\theta_0 , \tag{8}$$

$$\hat{\theta}(k) = \hat{\theta}(k-1) + \frac{P(k-2)\varphi(k-1)}{1+\varphi^T(k-1)P(k-2)\varphi(k-1)}\left(y(k) - \varphi^T(k-1)\hat{\theta}(k-1)\right) , \tag{9}$$

$$P(k-1) = P(k-2) - \frac{P(k-2)\varphi(k-1)\varphi^T(k-1)P(k-2)}{1+\varphi^T(k-1)P(k-2)\varphi(k-1)} , \tag{10}$$

$$\varphi^T(k)\hat{\theta}(k) = y^*(k+1) . \tag{11}$$

Convergence can be guaranteed under above conditions for adaptive control systems without network connection [3]. We now assume temporarily for simplicity that no packet loss occurs (the problem of packet loss will be discussed later). Using *Strategy I*, all the random delays are replaced by the fixed maximum delays and no packet re-ordering will occur. The estimation algorithm (9)-(10) can still work while the parameter estimate $\hat{\theta}(k-\Delta^{\max})$ is definitely available to construct the control signal at kth sampling instant, so the control law should be so chosen that

$$y^*(k+d) = \varphi^T(k)\hat{\theta}(k-\Delta^{\max}) . \tag{12}$$

Compared with (11), the difference is that $u(k)$ is not constructed by $\hat{\theta}(k)$ but rather by $\hat{\theta}(k-\Delta^{\max})$, $0 \le \Delta^{\max} < \infty$. The stability results can be summarized in the following theorem.

Theorem 1. Given the networked adaptive control systems with the plant given by (8) which satisfies *Assumption 5* and with the communication network satisfying *Assumption 1-4*, and using *Strategy I* the control law (12) with estimation algorithm (9)-(10) will ensure that

- $\{y(k)\}$ and $\{u(k)\}$ are bounded;
- $\lim_{k\to\infty}\left(y(k) - y^*(k)\right) = 0$

Proof: Redefine the tracking error as

$$\begin{aligned} e(k) &= y(k) - y^*(k) = \varphi^T(k-1)\left(\theta_0 - \hat{\theta}(k-\Delta^{\max}-1)\right) \\ &= \varphi^T(k-1)\left(\left(\hat{\theta}(k-1) - \hat{\theta}(k-\Delta^{\max}-1)\right) - \tilde{\theta}(k-1)\right) \end{aligned} . \tag{13}$$

Now examine

$$\begin{aligned} &\lim_{k\to\infty}\frac{e(k)}{\sqrt{1+k_2\varphi^T(k-1)\varphi(k-1)}} \\ &= \lim_{k\to\infty}\frac{\varphi^T(k-1)\left(\hat{\theta}(k-1) - \hat{\theta}(k-\Delta^{\max}-1)\right)}{\sqrt{1+k_2\varphi^T(k-1)\varphi(k-1)}} - \lim_{k\to\infty}\frac{\varphi^T(k-1)\tilde{\theta}(k-1)}{\sqrt{1+k_2\varphi^T(k-1)\varphi(t-1)}} \end{aligned} . \tag{14}$$

From *Lemma 3.3.6* in literature [3], we have

$$\lim_{k\to\infty}\left(\hat{\theta}(k-1)-\hat{\theta}(k-\Delta^{\max}-1)\right)=0\ ,\ 0\le\Delta^{\max}<\infty\ ,$$

then the first term on the right-hand side of (14) is equal to zero. Using *Lemma 3.3.6* in literature [3] again, we have

$$\lim_{k\to\infty}\frac{\varphi^T(k-1)\tilde{\theta}(k-1)}{\sqrt{1+k_2\varphi^T(k-1)\varphi(t-1)}}=\lim_{k\to\infty}\frac{\varepsilon(k)}{\sqrt{1+k_2\varphi^T(k-1)\varphi(t-1)}}=0 \tag{15}$$

thus the second term on the right-hand side of (14) is also equal to zero. So we have

$$\lim_{t\to\infty}\frac{e^2(k)}{1+k_2\varphi^T(k-1)\varphi(k-1)}=0 \tag{16}$$

Now using *Lemma 6.2.1* (The Key Technical Lemma) in literature [3], we have $\lim_{t\to\infty}e(k)=0$, that is $\lim_{k\to\infty}\left(y(k)-y^*(k)\right)=0$, and $\{\varphi(k)\}$ is bounded.

5 Strategy II – Dropping Over-Delayed Packets

Strategy I is designed to avoid the happening of packet re-ordering so that convergence can be guaranteed. However the way of maximum delay is far from the best solution because all delays for packets are artificially complemented to maximum value. Furthermore, we assumed in *Strategy I* that no packet loss happens (*Assumption 4*). But packet loss is one of the inevitable features on networks when there are node failures or message collisions. The presence of packet loss can be regarded as the special case of infinite network-induced delay. In this way, *Assumption 2*, which gives bounded delay, is unfeasible. Therefore, *Strategy I* is no longer suitable at the identifier. To address this problem, we devise a new strategy.

5.1 Dropping Strategy at the Identifier

Reducing waiting-time for packets in the input buffer at the identifier. Once the expected *k*th packet $(y(k),u(k-d),k)$ is available in the buffer input at the identifier, it will then be immediately sent to the identifier and does not need to stay in buffer for some time. Thus, the waiting time for packet will generally be shorter than $\tau_{ci}^{\max}$.

Dropping Strategy: Given a time threshold T_{ci}^{hold}, after this time has expired, if the currently expected *k*th packet $(y(k),u(k-d),k)$ is still unavailable, the identifier need not wait for it anymore. And the identifier will restart the parameter estimation algorithm if the (*k*+1)th or a newer packet becomes available. Hence the *k*th packet is regarded as being lost no matter whether or not that packet will be coming later.

However, information loss is inevitable due to dropping over-delayed packets. Furthermore, packet dropping also leads to the misuse of estimation algorithm. So the estimation scheme should be modified slightly to accommodate the information losses.

- If packet $(y(k),u(k-d),k)$ is available at time $t \le kh+T_{ci}^{hold}$, recursive parameter estimation scheme (3)-(4) can be adopted without any modification.
- If packet $(y(k),u(k-d),k)$ is unavailable at time $t > kh+T_{ci}^{hold}$ and next packet $(y(k+1),u(k-d+1),k+1)$ or even newer packet is available, the recursive algorithm (3)-(4) should be restarted.

5.2 At the Controller

Reducing waiting time for parameter packets in the input buffer at the controller: When controller receives an estimate with timestamp from the identifier, the timestamp will tell the controller how old the new received estimate is. This information can then be used by the controller in the control signal calculation as follows.

- If the stamp shows that this new arrived estimate is 'older' than the previously received estimates, this packet will be discarded immediately. The previous used estimate will be used again for computing the control signal in this case.
- If the stamp shows that this new arrived estimate is 'younger' than all of the estimates, which have already arrived at the controller, the youngest packet will be used to construct the control signal, because that in general the youngest estimate is more close to the true value θ_0 under the condition that the plant is time-invariant.

Example 3. Strategy II is used to solve the packet loss problem. Suppose that 6 packets are lost due to the congestion during the transmission from the controller to identifier(at *k*=5, 55, 105, 155, 205 and 255). The simulation results shown in Fig. 4 indicate that *Strategy II* still work well in the presence of packet losses.

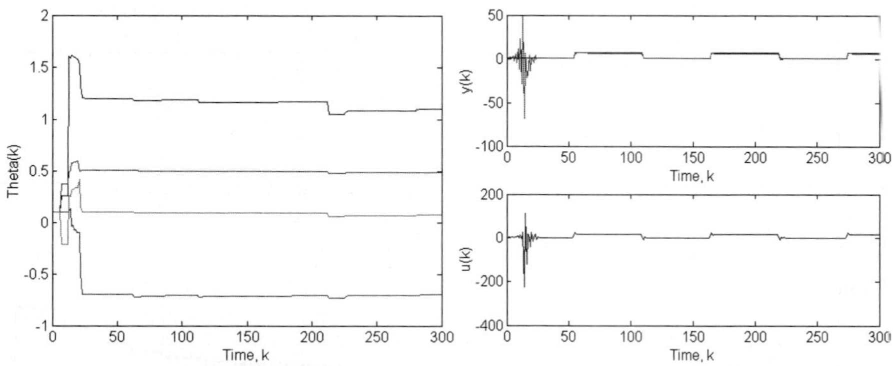

(a) Parameter Estimates (b) Plant output and control signal

Fig. 4. Packet losses and simulation results as *Strategy II* being used. We select $T_{ci}^{hold} = 5h$ as the threshold for packet dropping. (a) shows the parameter estimates for the plant (6). (b) shows the plant output and control signals.

5.3 Performance Analysis in the Presence of Packet Dropping

There is no doubt that packet dropping policy makes the networked adaptive control systems applicable in practice. However packet losses also make the information incomplete, resulting in extra uncertainties in the parameter estimate as well as in control signal. Hence, packet loss probability is needed to be considered. From the perspective of communication engineering, packet loss probability is defined as the fraction of packets that are lost due to the aggregate traffic being greater than the communication network capacity. But the packet loss here is not only due to the above reason but also because of the fact that the packet will be regarded as a lost one if its arrival at the identifier is too late, that is the delay with it is larger than the given threshold T_{ci}^{hold}. Therefore the packet loss probability P_{ci}^{l} should be defined as follows,

$$P_{ci}^{l} = 1 - P_{ci}^{r}(\tau_{ci} \le T_{ci}^{hold}) = \int_{T_{ci}^{hold}}^{\infty} f_d(\tau) d\tau \tag{17}$$

where $f_d(\cdot)$ is the probability density function of the random network induced delay from controller to identifier.

Obviously, the choice of the threshold T_{ci}^{hold} is important. There is a fundamental tradeoff as follows. The packet loss probability becomes small when T_{ci}^{hold} is large, and the identifier can receive more plant input and output information. Hence, more knowledge about the plant and better control performance should be expected. However the round-trip delay, which is dependent on T_{ci}^{hold}, will be large, resulting in deterioration of system performance.

Example 4: Select different thresholds to continue *Example 3*. T_{ci}^{hold} is chosen as $T_{ci}^{hold} = (2 \sim 12)h$. And Fig. 5 indicates the existence of an optimal T_{ci}^{hold} in this example. Therefore, proper choice of the T_{ci}^{hold} is needed. All those discussed above is also suitable to the adaptive control for slowly time-varying plant.

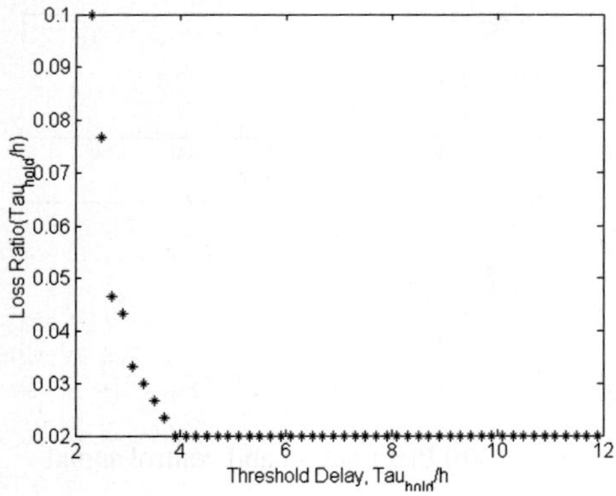

(a) T_{ci}^{hold}/h vs. P_{ci}^{l}

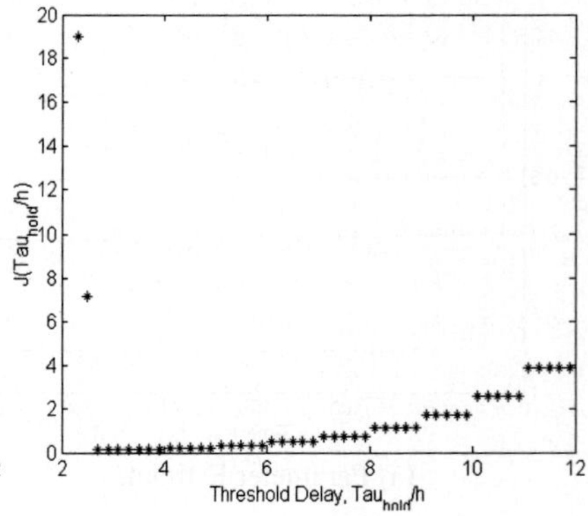

(b) T_{ci}^{hold}/h vs. J

Fig. 5. Packet loss probability and performance comparison under different T_{ci}^{hold}/h -using *Strategy II*. (a) shows T_{ci}^{hold}/h vs. P_{ci}^{l}. (b) shows T_{ci}^{hold}/h vs. J (performance index). At (2.9, 0.1705) we can obtain the minimum *J*.

Control systems and communication networks are designed using very different principles. Traditional adaptive control theory requires the information about the controlled plant to be as accurate as possible. Conversely, random delay and packet loss are generally acceptable in communication network design. From a higher level there is a tradeoff between control performance and communication performance. In a word, it is necessary for designer to have a good knowledge of network features before designing and implementing the networked adaptive control systems.

6 Conclusions and Future Work

In this paper, the networked adaptive control system whose outer loop is closed over communication networks is proposed and studied. The excessive delays caused by communication networks will degrade the control performance even destabilize the system. As a result, a preliminary approach (*Strategy I*) using maximum delay policy is proposed to solve this problem. The system using *Strategy I* is proven to be convergent with bounded delays. Furthermore, *Strategy II* with the concept of delay threshold is presented to deal with the existence of packet loss, and an optimal delay threshold is presented. The simulation results show that the output can asymptotically track the reference signal.

This paper provides approaches for communication networks to be applicable in adaptive control applications with a focus on meeting the requirement of stability and dynamic performance. With the rapid development of network techniques, the possibility of online parameter adjustment for the controller by remote devices is emerging. Hence closing the learning loop over communication networks may be a good way, thus delivering a more scalable architecture for building future control systems. Although only the adaptive control is investigated in this paper, the results are possible to be extended to other control systems. It is our conjecture as well as our future work that the control systems with an identification or learning loop closed over communication networks be applicable for practical applications as long as some effective measures are taken.

Acknowledgements

This work was supported by National Natural Science Foundation of China (under Grant No. 60274031), Program for New Century Excellent Talents in University (under Grant No. NCET-04-0433), Research Project for Doctoral Disciplines in University (under Grant No. 20040280017), Shanghai Leading Academic Disciplines (under Grant No. T0103) and Shanghai Key Laboratory of Power Station Automation Technology.

References

1. Åström, K.J., Wittenmark, B.: Adaptive Control. Addison-Wesley Longman Publishing Co., Boston, MA (1994)
2. Goodwin, G.C., Ramadge, P.J., Caines, P.E.: Discrete-Time Multivariable Adaptive-Control. Vol.25, Issue 3, IEEE Transactions on Automatic Control (1980) 449 - 456

3. Goodwin, G.C., Kwai, Sang Sin: Adaptive Filtering, Prediction and Control. Prentice Hall, Englewood Cliffs, NJ (1984)
4. Wang, L.X.: Combining Mathematical Model and Heuristics into Controllers: An Adaptive Fuzzy Control Approach. Fuzzy Sets and Systems, Vol. 89, Issue 2 (1997) 151 - 156
5. Murray, R.M., Åström, K.J., Boyd, S.P., Brockett, R.W., Stein, G.: Future Directions in Control in an Information-Rich World. IEEE Control Systems Magazine, Vol. 23, Issue 2 (2003) 20 - 33
6. Nilsson, J.: Real-Time Control Systems with Delays. PhD thesis, Dept. Automatic Control, Lund Institute of Technology, Lund Sweden (1998)
7. Zhang, W., Branicky, M.S., and Phillips, S.M.: Stability of Networked Control Systems. IEEE Control Systems Magazine, Vol. 21, Issue 1 (2001) 84 - 99
8. Montestruque, L.A., Antsaklis, P.: Stability of Model-Based Networked Control Systems with Time-Varying Transmission Times. IEEE Transactions on Automatic Control, Vol. 49, Issue 9 (2004) 1562 - 1572
9. Fei, M.R., Li, L.X.: Network Learning based Control Systems. Proceedings of Conference on Artificial Intelligent Control 2003, Hong Kong China, (2003)184 - 190 (in Chinese)
10. Bauer, P., Sichitiu M., Premaratne K.: On the Nature of the Time-Variant Communication Delays. Proceedings of IASTED Conference Modeling, Identification and Control, Innbruck, Austria (2001) 792 - 797
11. Lian, Feng-Li, Moyne, J.R., Tilbury, D.M.: Performance Evaluation of Control Networks: Ethernet, ControlNet, and DeviceNet. IEEE Control Systems Magazine, Vol. 21, Issue 1 (2001) 66 – 83
12. Li, L.X., Fei, M.R., Zhou, X.B.: Analysis on Network-Induced Delays in Networked Learning based Control Systems. Lecture Notes in Computer Science, Vol. 3314, Springer-Verlag, Berlin Heidelberg New York (2004) 310 - 315
13. Luck, R., Ray, A.: An Observer-Based Compensator for Distributed Delays. Automatica, Vol. 26, Issue 5 (1990) 903 - 908

An Initial Study of Gain-Scheduling Controller Design for NCS Using Delay Statistical Model

Minrui Fei[1], Xiaobing Zhou[1], T.C. Yang[2], Yuemei Tan[1], and Heshou Wang[1]

[1] Shanghai Key Laboratory of Power Station Automation Technology
School of Mechatronical Engineering and Automation, Shanghai University
Shanghai 200072, China
mrfei@staff.shu.edu.cn, zxb7058@263.net
[2] The Department of Engineering, University of Sussex, Brighton BN1 9QT, UK
taiyang@sussex.ac.uk

Abstract. In this paper, the statistical model of communication network delay based on the data measured from a network in operation is studied. In our study, it is found that modeling the round trip time (RTT) in our network by a single statistical model is not adequate. Therefore two combined statistical distributions, Pareto distribution and generalized exponential distribution, are used to develop our model. This approach is verified by the standard Chi-square test widely used by statisticians. Based on the model developed, a gain-scheduling algorithm to adjust controller gain to compensate time delay in a networked control system (NCS) is developed. This paper presents the results of our initial study. In addition, further research based on the design methodology pioneered in this paper is also proposed.

1 Introduction

Control loops that are closed over a communication network have become more and more common as the hardware devices for networks and network nodes have become cheaper. Networked Control Systems (NCSs) have many advantages, for example, modularity, decentralization of control, integrated diagnostics, quick and easy maintenance, and low cost. Due to this, in addition to many newly-designed controllers, many existing controllers are also upgraded to NCS configurations. However, it is known that time-delay due to networked signal transfer in a NCS causes stability and performance problems. Currently there is a great research interest in this area [1]. One particular challenge in this area is that when existing controllers are upgraded into a NCS configuration, is any simple method to modify the existing controllers so that the time-delay in the NCS can be compensated? From the application point view, a simple and workable method is preferred. For any existing controllers, from an advanced H-infinite based robust controller to a relatively simple PID controller, one can always extracts a gain factor. An intuitive thought is therefore to adjust this gain factor, increase or decrease, according to the information of network delay. For example, if the transfer function for an existing controller is $G_e(s)$, it can always be rewritten as

$$G_e(s) = K_{ncs} \cdot G_{ncs}(s) \tag{1}$$

D.-S. Huang, K. Li, and G.W. Irwin (Eds.): ICIC 2006, LNAI 4114, pp. 1049 – 1060, 2006.

where k_{ncs} is an extracted gain factor and to be changed on-line according to the information of network delay.

The above can be applied to any $G_e(s)$. In this paper, we present our initial study to explore this design idea, which can be represented by Fig.1. It can be seen that the design idea presented here can also be applied to new NCS controller design. First, one designs a $G_e(s)$ disregarding network delay, then followed by the design of an appropriated gain-scheduling algorithm to adjust k_{ncs} to compensate the network delay.

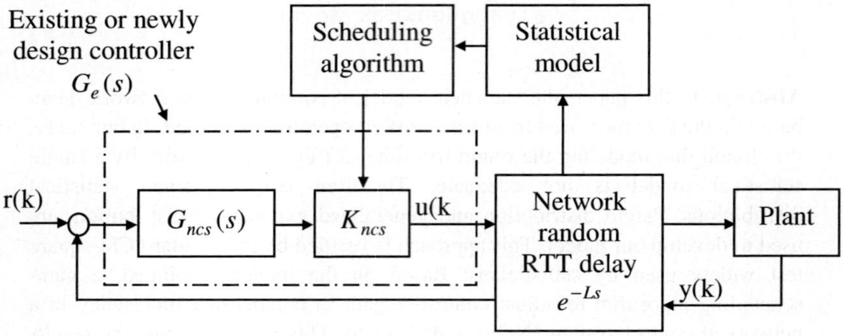

Fig. 1. The networked control system used in this paper

It is known that, if a NCS is based on shared network communications (a typical example of this is internet-based control system), due to uncertainties in the volume of network traffic and many other factors, communication delay in the NCS is random. Therefore, a statistical model has to be used for the delay information. Before a statistical model is to be built, one needs to decide a quantity to specify the delay. In this paper RRT (Round Trip Time) is used for this purpose. RRT is an important time specification in communication networks, in particular, for those running under the TCP/IP protocol. In Section 2, we investigate the statistical model for network delay and the measurement of our campus RRT data is used in the study. In Section 3, we propose a gain-scheduling algorithm to adjust k_{ncs}. As an initial study, in this paper we only consider simple PI controller for $G_e(s)$ and the plant to be controlled is a simple two-time-constant model.

2 Statistics Model of RTT Delay over Campus Net

2.1 Measurements and Modeling of the RTT Delay

Campus net is an example of shared communication network, and most of them adopt TCP/IP protocol. In order to investigate the statistics of the RTT delays over such net, the delay needs to be measured. Fig.2 describes the measurement system of delay based on our campus net.

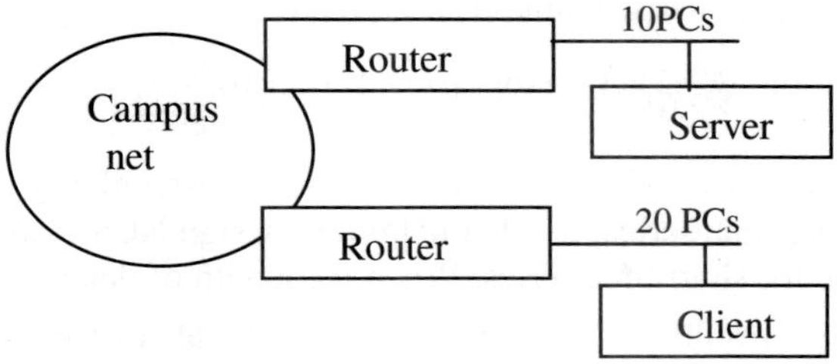

Fig. 2. The architecture adopted of RTT delay measurement

In this system, RTT delay is measured using two networked computer, client and server. Assuming τ_{cp} is the delay from client to server, and τ_{pc} is the delay from server to plant, the RTT delay can be denoted as $L = \tau_{cp} + \tau_{pc}$. These two computers are connected to Ethernet via 100Mbps network card, respectively. TCP/IP protocol are adopted. Visual C++ software is used to program the measurement codes. The client sends a new data packet every 0.01s, and records the current time into the packet before sending. The sever will return the packets once it receives. When the client receives this packet, it calculates the RTT delay. Two precise time function, QueryPerformanceFrequency() and QueryPerformanceCounter(), are used to obtain precise RTT delay L. Fig.3 gives a delay data set of the RTT delay L.

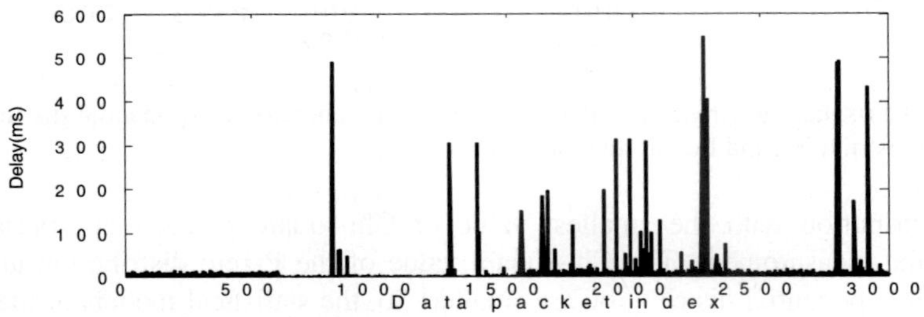

Fig. 3. Delays measurement data over campus net

Many studies of Internet delays measurement have revealed that delays in IP networks exhibits self-similarity [2-4]. We analyzed the experiment data, and the results show the same characteristic [5]. Furthermore, the probability distribution function of RTT delay can be well approximated by Pareto distribution for long delay series in all candidate distributions. These candidates are exponential distribution, lognormal distribution, shift-gamma distribution and generalized exponential distribution. The Pareto distribution and Generalized exponential distribution are given as following.

The Pareto distribution is

$$F(x) = 1 - \left(\frac{k}{x}\right)^{\alpha} \quad (x \geq k) \tag{2}$$

Generalized exponential distribution is described as

$$F(x) = 1 - \exp(-\frac{x-\eta}{\theta}) \quad (\theta > 0) \tag{3}$$

Pareto distribution is a self-similar model. But self-similarity is the statistical characteristic of long time series; it is not helpful to design NCS. Pareto distribution is not always suitable for short time series. When the length of delay series is 100, Fig.4 gives the χ^2 -test results of generalized exponential distribution, exponential distribution, log normal distribution and Pareto distribution for a measurement.

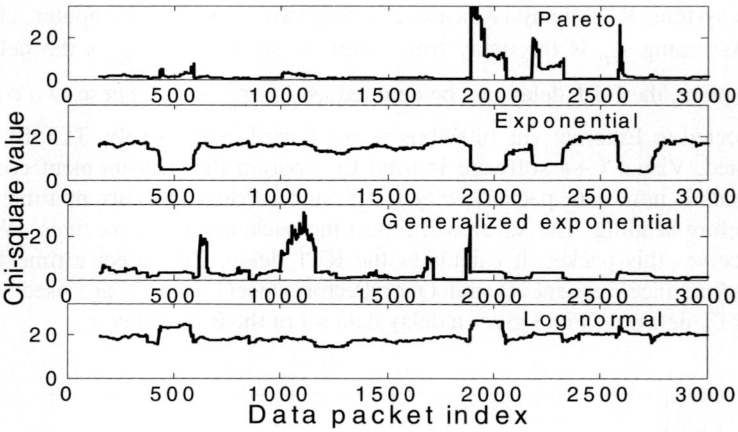

Fig. 4. The Chi-square test results of Pareto distribution, generalized exponential distribution, exponential distribution and Log normal distribution

The distribution with the smallest value of Chi-square is most appropriate to represent the measurement. The Chi-square value of the Pareto distribution and the generalized exponential distribution are smaller. So, the statistical models of the RTT delay over campus net can be described by the Pareto distribution and the generalized exponential distribution. Through analyzing the delay data, the k of the Pareto distribution can range from 1.4 to 1.6, and the α is from 1 to 16. The η of the generalized exponential distribution equals to k, and the θ can range from 0.1 to 11.

2.2 Support Vector Classification (SVC) for Suitable Distribution Model

The Chi-square test is used to test if a sample of data came from a population with a specific distribution. However, the values of the Chi-square test statistic are dependent on how the data is binned. Another disadvantage of the Chi-square test is that it requires a sufficient sample size in order for the Chi-square test approximation to be valid. Thus, the support vector machine classifier is applied to pick the suitable distribution from the Pareto distribution and the generalized exponential distribution. The detail about support vector machine classifier can be found in [6].

Consider the problem of separating the set of training vectors belonging to two separate classes,

$$D = \{(x^1, y^1), \quad \cdots, \quad (x^l, y^l)\}, \; x \in R^n, y \in \{-1, \; 1\} \tag{4}$$

with a hyperplane $< w, x > +b = 0$.

The function of support vector classifier is to determine the optimal hyperplane so that the set of vectors is separated without error and the distance between the closest vector and the hyperplane is maximal.

In order to find out the optimal hyperplane, SVC solves the following optimization problem.

$$\min_x \frac{1}{2}\alpha^T H\alpha + c^T \alpha \tag{5}$$

with constraints

$$\alpha^T Y = 0, 0 \le \alpha_i \le C, i = 1, \cdots, l$$

where $H = ZZ^T$, Z is a $l \times l$ nonnegative definite matrix, $Z_{ij} = y_i y_j K(x_i, x_j)$, $c^T = (-1, \cdots, -1)$, $K(x_i, x_j) = \Phi^T(x_i)\Phi(x_j)$ is kernel function performing the non-linear mapping into a high dimensional feature space. $Y = (y_1, \cdots, y_l)^T$, C is upper bound.

Assuming that α^0 is the solution, the classification function is

$$f(x) = sign(\sum_{i=1}^{l} y_i \alpha_i^0 K(x_i, x) + b) \tag{6}$$

In order to find out the appropriate delay distribution model, 40 vectors are chosen to train the SVC from measured delay data set. In these vectors, there are 20 vectors that can be commendably fitted by Pareto distribution, and the others are modeled by generalized exponential distribution. The size of the vector is 100.

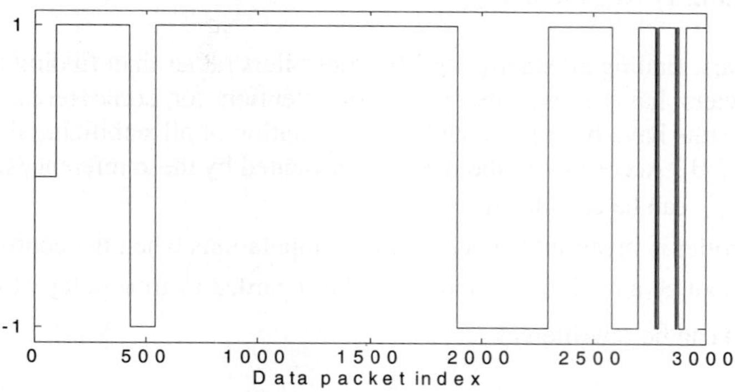

Fig. 5. The result of the support vector machine classification, 1 denotes that the delay can be well approximated by Pareto distribution, and –1 denotes that the generalized exponential distribution is better

The Gaussian radial basis kernel function is adopted to perform the non-linear. The function is described as

$$K(x,x^{'}) = \exp\left(-\frac{\left\|x-x^{'}\right\|^2}{2\sigma^2}\right) \tag{7}$$

Let $\sigma = 1.1$ and $C = 100$, and the classification result of a measured delay data set is illustrated by Fig.5. To compare Fig.5 with Fig.4, the result generally coincide with the Chi-square test.

3 The Scheduling Algorithm for Adjust k_{ncs}

In order to explore how to use the statistical model of RTT delay to compensate an existing controller disregarding network delay, we only consider simple PI controller as Eq. (8) for $G_e(s)$ and the plant to be controlled is a simple two-time-constant model as Eq. (9).

$$G_e(s) = K_p s + K_i \tag{8}$$

$$G_p(s) = \frac{k}{(T_1 s+1)(T_2 s+1)} \tag{9}$$

According to Eq.1, Eq.8 can be rewritten as

$$G_e(s) = K_{ncs}(K_p^0 + K_i^0 / s) \tag{10}$$

where $G_{ncs}(s) = K_p^0 + K_i^0 / s$.

In order to adjust k_{ncs}, the stability region of it needs to be investigated.

3.1 The Stability Region of K_{ncs}

In recent years, finding all stabilizing PID controllers rather than finding a good set of PID parameters has become the center of attention for some researchers. Many important results have been presented on computation of all stabilizing P, PI, and PID controllers [7-9]. According to the methods presented by these references, the stability region of K_{ncs} can be calculated.

The controller is invariant between twice computations when the controller is event driven. τ_{pc} can be added to τ_{cp} and L can be regarded as time delay of plant. So the plant Eq. (9) can be rewritten as

$$G(s) = \frac{k}{(T_1 s+1)(T_2 s+1)} e^{-Ls} \tag{11}$$

This is a second process with time delay, and is controlled by a PI controller described as Eq.8. Substituting $s = jw$, $w \in (0,+\infty)$, and let $\alpha = Lw$, According to the method presented by (7), the stability region of K_p can be obtained as

$$-1/k < K_p < \left[(T_1T_2\alpha^2 - L^2)\cos\alpha + (T_1+T_2)\alpha L\sin\alpha\right] / KL^2 \tag{12}$$

where α is the solution of the equation

$$\tan\alpha = \frac{(T_1+T_2)\alpha L}{T_1T_2\alpha^2 - L^2} \tag{13}$$

where $\alpha \in (0,\frac{\pi}{2})$, for $L<\frac{\pi}{2}\sqrt{T_1T_2}$; $\alpha \in (\frac{\pi}{2},\pi)$, for $L>\frac{\pi}{2}\sqrt{T_1T_2}$; $\alpha = \frac{\pi}{2}$, for $L=\frac{\pi}{2}\sqrt{T_1T_2}$.

To compare Eq. (8) and Eq. (10), let $K_p = K_{ncs}K_p^0$ and $K_i = K_{ncs}K_i^0$.

The stability region of K_{ncs} is obtained as

$$0 < K_{ncs} < \left[(T_1T_2\alpha_1^2 - L^2)\cos\alpha_1 + (T_1+T_2)\alpha_1 L\sin\alpha_1\right] / kK_p^0L^2 \tag{14}$$

where α is the solution of the equation

$$\tan(\alpha) = \frac{aL\alpha_1^2 + L^3}{b\alpha_1^3 + c\alpha_1 L^2},\ \alpha_1 \in (0,\alpha) \tag{15}$$

where $a = r(T_1+T_2) - T_1T_2$, $b = rT_1T_2$, $c = T_1+T_2-r$, $r = \dfrac{K_p^0}{K_i^0}$.

3.2 Off-Line Optimizing K_{ncs} with Actual Delay

The optimal k_{ncs} is determined by genetic algorithm (GA) [10] for the plant as Eq. (11). The optimizing approach is described as follows.

Step(1) Using the inverses of the Pareto distribution and the generalized exponential distribution functions to design random variant generators. The parameters of these two generators are determined by actual parameters variations. The generators can produce random variants for optimizing. To find the maximum of these random variants as L, the stability region of k_{ncs} can be computed by Eq. (14) and Eq. (15). The optimal k_{ncs} in this region can be computed by genetic algorithm.

Step(2) Selecting the evaluation function of genetic algorithm. This evaluation function is called from the GA to determine the fitness of each solution string generated during the search. The function that we adopted is described as $J = w_1J_1 + w_2J_2 + w_3J_3$

where

$$J_1 = \begin{cases} (MSE - MSE_0)^2 & MSE > MSE_0 \\ 0 & MSE \le MSE_0 \end{cases}, \quad J_2 = \begin{cases} (P.O. - P.O._0)^2 & P.O. > P.O._0 \\ 0 & P.O. \le P.O._0 \end{cases}, \text{ and}$$

$$J_3 = \begin{cases} (t_r - t_{r0})^2 & t_r > t_{r0} \\ 0 & t_r \le t_{r0} \end{cases}.$$

where $MSE = \frac{1}{N}\sum_{k=0}^{N} e^2(k)$ is the mean-squared error, N is the total amount of the plant outputs that the controller has received. $e(k) = r(k) - y(k)$, $y(k)$ is the k-th plant output that the controller has received, and $r(k)$ is reference input at this moment. MSE_0 is the nominal mean-squared error, $P.O._0$ is the nominal percentage overshoot, and tr_0 is the nominal rise time. w_1, w_2 and w_3 are the weights.

Step(3) Initializing of the population. The amount of the starting population is 50 individuals, and these individuals are randomly created. The binary digits are applied to represent the individual.

Step(4) Selecting individuals to produce successive generations. The roulette wheel selection approach is adopted to select better individuals.

Step(5) Using genetic operators, crossover and mutation, to produce successive generations.

Step(6) Estimating the termination condition. The criterion is maximum number of generations.

3.3 On-Line k_{ncs} Scheduling Algorithm

The following algorithm is applied to schedule k_{ncs} under the variable delay condition. The algorithm can be realized in software.

Step(1) The scheduling software initializes the packet index as $i = 0$. Let $n = 0$, $M = 100$, $K_{ncs} = 1$, and $y(1) = 0$.

Step(2) The controller calculates $e(i) = r(i) - y(i)$, and computes $u(i+1)$ according to Eq. (10). Controller sends it out to scheduling software, and the software puts $u(i+1)$ and current time $t_s(i)$ in one TCP packet. The software sends the packet out to the plant if the network is available and increases the packet index by $i = i+1$, otherwise, this packet has to wait for sending at the instant that the network is ready.

Step(3) The plant is event driven. Once it receives $u(i)$, it return the output $y(i+1)$, i, and $t_s(i)$, as a packet back to the scheduling software.

Step(4) When the scheduling software receives a packet containing $y(i+1)$, i, and $t_s(i)$, it will record the arrival time $T_r(i)$. The RTT delay can be computed as $RTT(i)=t_r(i)-t_s(i)$, and $n=n+1$.

Step(5) Once $n=M$, the scheduling software uses the 100 RTT delays to determine the fittest distribution model by the support vector classifier. Then, the parameters of this distribution will be evaluated and the optimal k_{ncs} can be determined from the off-line optimizing results.

Step(6) Let $n=N-1$, and $RTT(i)=RTT(i+1)$ for $i=0,\cdots,N-1$. Then let $i=n$. Steps 1-6 will be repeated for the next iteration.

4 Simulation Study

A dc motor transfer function with network-induced delay is used to illustrate the method. The transfer function is described by

$$G(s)=\frac{2029.826}{(s+26.29)(s+2.296)}e^{LS} \tag{17}$$

The parameters of the motor are from [11], [12]. Let (K_p^0, K_i^0)=(0.1701,0.378). The left figure of Fig.6 describes the stability region of K_p, K_i and k_{ncs} in the (K_p, K_i) plane ($L=0.03s$). The upper bound for K_{ncs} is point of intersection of the boundary locus $l(K_p, K_i, w)$ and line $K_i = K_p / r$, w is the frequency. For stable system, k_{ncs} can range from 0 to the upper bound. The upper bound relies on the values of delay L. The right figure of Fig.6 shows that the upper bound for k_{ncs} given in Eq. (14) is a monotonically decreasing function of the time delay L.

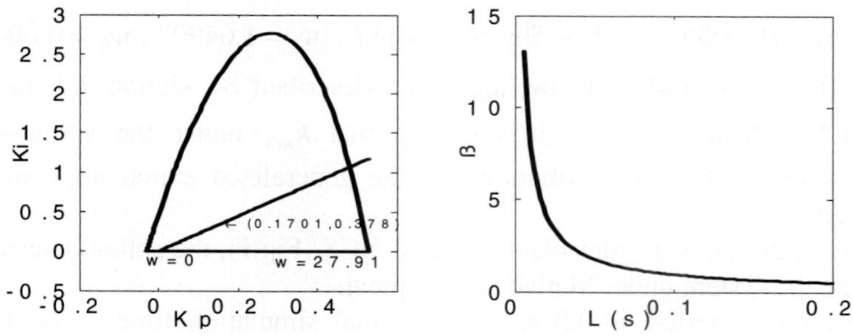

Fig. 6. The left figure shows the stability regions of k_{ncs}, k_p, and k_i of the PI controller for plant (17)($L=0.03s$). The right one gives the upper bound of the k_{ncs} under different delay.

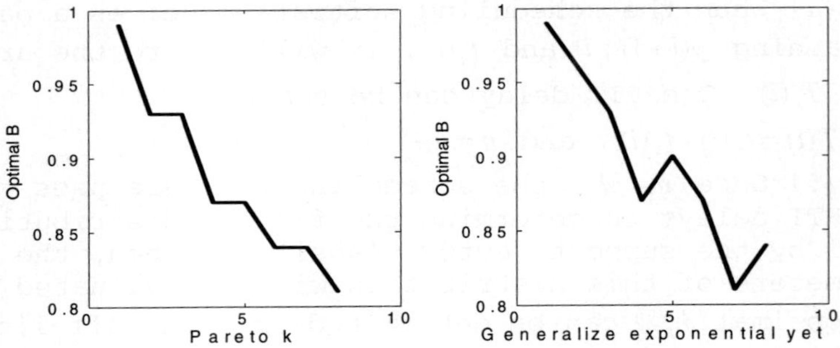

Fig. 7. The left figure gives the optimal K_{ncs} under different k of the Pareto distribution ($\alpha = 1$). The right figure gives the optimal k_{ncs} under different η of the generalized exponential distribution ($\theta = 1$).

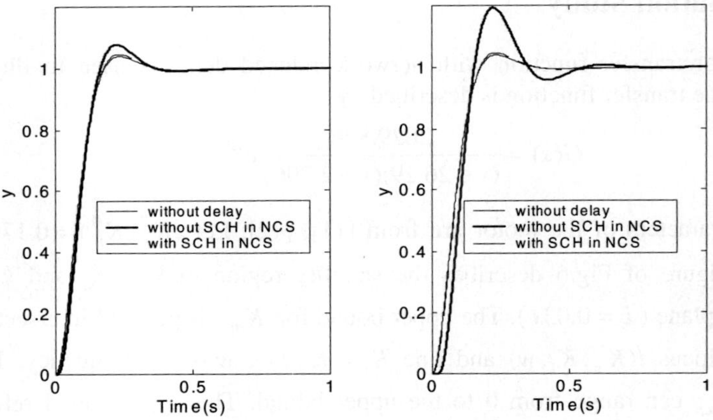

Fig. 8. The left figure describes the step responses of the plant (17) using a RTT delay data set which mean is 0.004s, and the right figure describe the step responses of the plant (17) using a RTT delay data set which mean is 0.03s

Let MSE_0 =0.00595, $P.O._0$=5%, $tr_0 = 0.117$, $w_1 = 1.64902$, $w_2 = 0.00833$, and $w_3 = 10.01395$. According to the algorithm described by section 3.2, the optimal k_{ncs} can be obtained. Fig.7 gives the optimal k_{ncs} under the variation of the parameters of the Pareto distribution and the generalized exponential distribution, respectively.

Aiming at the second order plant (17) and NCS (Fig.1), the actual delays are used to simulate the system under Matlab environment.

The Sampling period is 0.01s, and the final simulation time is 1s. Using the algorithm described as section 3.3, the left figure of Fig.8 shows the step responses from a measured delay set with mean 0.004s. The values of their evaluation functions described as Eq.(16) are 8.38e-5 (with gain scheduling algorithm) and 1.00e-4 (without gain scheduling algorithm). Because the delays are smaller, the effect of control can't be distinctly observed. The right figure of Fig.8 gives the step responses with the larger delay set with mean 0.03s. The values of their evaluation functions are 0.04645 (with gain scheduling algorithm) and 0.6506 (without gain scheduling algorithm).

The networked PI controllers with gain scheduling have lower evaluation function value, and exhibit better performances than the PI controller without gain scheduling algorithm.

5 Conclusion

In this paper, it is found that the round trip time (RTT) delay can not be described by only one statistical model. Therefore two distributions, Pareto distribution and generalized exponential distribution, are used to model the RTT delay. An initial study of gain-scheduling controller design for NCS using the delay statistical model is presented. Further study based on the design idea presented in this paper is planned in two directions. One direction is to consider complicated plant model to be controlled and the other direction is to consider more advanced controllers.

Acknowledgments

This work is sponsored by National Natural Science Foundation of China under grant 60274031, Doctoral Program Foundation of Science & Technology Special Project in University under grant 20040280017, Program for New Century Excellent Talents in University under grant NCET-04-0433, and Shanghai Leading Academic Disciplines under grant T0103.

References

1. Yang, T.C.: Networked Control System: A Brief Survey. To be published in IEE Proceedings: Control Theory and Applications, http://www.sussex.ac.uk/Users/taiyang/ publications/ 200 6 paper1.pdf
2. Li, Q, Mills, D L: On the Long-range Dependence of Packet Round Trip Delays in Internet. Proceedings of the IEEE International Conference on Communications, Piscataway, NJ, USA: IEEE Press (1998) 1185-1191
3. Michael, S. B.: On Estimating Long Range Dependence of Network Delay. International Journal of Chaos Theory and Applications, 6(4) (2001) 1-20
4. Fujimoto, K, Ata, S., Murata, M.: Statistical Analysis of Packet Delays in the Internet and its Application to Playout Control for Streaming Applications. IEICE Transactions on Communications E84-B(6) (2001) 1504-1512
5. Zhou, Xiaobing, Fei, Minrui, Li, Lixiong: Measurement and Statistical Analysis of Ethernet Network Induced Delay Based on Application Layer. Information and Control, 34 (6) (2005) 641-646
6. Cortes, V. Vapnik: Support Vector Networks. Machine Learning, 20 (1995) 273-297
7. Guillermo J. Silva, Aniruddha Datt, S. P. Bhattacharyya: New Results on the Synthesis of PID Controllers. IEEE Transactions on Automatic Control, 47(2) (2002) 241-252

8. Guillermo, J. Silva, Aniruddha, Datt, S. P. Bhattacharyya: Robust Control Design Using the PID Controller. Proceeding of the 41st IEEE Conference on Decision and Control, Las Vegas, Nevada USA, December (2002) 1313-1318
9. Li, Yinya, Sheng, Andong, Wang, Yuangang: Robust Control Design for Time-delay Systems with Parameter Uncertainties Using the PID Controller. Control and Decision, 19(10) (2004) 1178-1182
10. Chris, Houck, Jeff, Joines, Mike, Kay: A Genetic Algorithm for Function Optimization: A Matlab Implementation. NCSU-IE TR (1995) 95-09
11. N. B. Almutairi, M.-Y. Chow: Stabilization of Networked PI Control System Using Fuzzy Logic Modulation. Proceedings of the American Control Conference, Denver, Colorado, JUNE (2003) 975-980
12. Y. Tipsuwan, M.-Y. Chow: On the Gain Scheduling for Networked PI Controller Over IP Network. IEEE/ASME Transactions On Mechatronics, 9(3) (2004) 491-498

An Overview of Wireless Networks in Control and Monitoring

George W. Irwin, Jeremy Colandairaj, and William G. Scanlon

School of Electronics, Electrical Engineering and Computer Science
Queen's University Belfast, Belfast BT9 5AH, UK

Abstract. This paper provides an overview of the current field in wireless networks for monitoring and control. Alternative wireless technologies are introduced, together with current typical industrial applications. The focus then shifts to wireless Ethernet and the specialised requirements for wireless networked control systems (WNCS) are discussed. This is followed by a brief look at some current WNCS research, including reduced communication control.

1 Introduction

The field of control has seen huge advances over the past 50 years, leveraging technological improvements in sensing and computation with breakthroughs in the underlying principles and mathematics. Nowadays embedded processors, sensors, and networking hardware are becoming increasingly cheap and pervasive, enabling the development of increasingly complex, intelligent and autonomous systems for monitoring and control. In networked control systems, for example, strong interest in wireless solutions is driving the development of this technology as a potential replacement for the current generation of wired industrial networks.

Wireless technologies are attracting considerable attention from industrialist [1]. Firstly, with the increasing installation costs of network cabling, there are sound economic reasons for considering wireless links in industrial locations. Mobility and the ability to operate in harsh or ultra-clean environments provide further motivation. In addition, as competition drives shorter concept-to-design development times and reduced time-to-market cycles, flexibility in plant floor architectures is needed to respond to changing market conditions. Information on the state of the control systems must be both readily accessible and transparent; whether from human to machine (e.g. a maintenance engineer observing from a handheld device) or from machine to machine (e.g. communication between field devices for supervisory control and/or data acquisition). The overall objective is the scalable enterprise incorporating ease of expansion with minimal implementation and maintenance costs. Wireless based control and monitoring is seen as having an important role in enabling this goal.

However, there are crucial underlying technical issues that have yet to be addressed, notably reliability of the wireless link [2] and despite the efforts of its proponents [3], wireless control is currently a niche technology in industrial

D.-S. Huang, K. Li, and G.W. Irwin (Eds.): ICIC 2006, LNAI 4114, pp. 1061–1072, 2006.

applications, seldom applied to critical systems and often relegated to monitoring duties. Other concerns include security as well as logistical problems such as power delivery. More fundamental work is therefore needed to fully research the potential and to properly quantify the domain for wireless networked control systems (WNCS).

The aim of this paper is to broadly review the current state of wireless networked control systems, covering both an industrial perspective and some of the latest pertinent research. Although different technologies will be discussed, particular attention will be paid to the IEEE 802.11 standard, the so-called wireless Ethernet. The requirements of wireless control networks will be contrasted with those for regular data communications and, in the context of existing technology, the suitability of wireless Ethernet will be examined. This provides the necessary context for discussing selected research themes in WNCS research. The paper to follow is organised as follows. Section 2 briefly looks at the application of wireless networks in industry, with a particular focus on a hierarchical distributed process control architecture. The commercial-off-the-shelf (COTS) wireless technologies currently available are detailed in section 3, with a view to highlighting their different characteristics and capabilities. Section 4 deals with the latest advances in academic research while section 5 contains concluding remarks.

2 Wireless Networks for Industry

In general wireless is increasingly being employed for industrial data communications. Typical application scenarios include: (i) human-machine communication with fixed stations and mobile machines (automated guided vehicles, mono-rail systems, conveyor belts, warehouse transportation systems), often using a handheld device, (ii) communication in time-limited configurations (quick-changing factory layouts, experimental test set-ups, commissioning and servicing) (iii) communication with difficult-to-reach nodes requiring costly cabling installations (bridging streets, buildings, railway lines and waterways), hazardous nodes (radioactive or corrosive environments) or clean room situations (in the semiconductor and pharmaceutical fields).

While it would appear that most current industrial applications of wireless networks are information related, with limited usage for feedback control, the likelihood of considerable future growth is predicted. To illustrate this, consider the potential for distributed process control as found in the petrochemical, chemical manufacturing, pharmaceutical and man-made fibres sectors [4]. The common architecture used for distributed control falls into three levels. Each is now considered in turn in terms of replacing the current wired network with commercial-off-the -shelf (COTS) wireless networking.

The *Bottom Level* where smart devices and controllers are networked. As the process is effectively run at this layer, there is a tight real-time requirement of high predictability and reliability, typically based on network protocols like Fieldbus. This layer needs reliable short-range transmission of measurement/control data packages which are small, usually below 100 bytes. There is much debate around which wireless technology could be used here, as all work well at short range. One solution clearly is to define new wireless standards, for Fieldbus for example.

The *Middle Level* which networks the controllers at the Bottom Level to workstations. The function of this level is to support user interaction, including configuration, control and monitoring and the network protocol could be either proprietary, or industry standard like Ethernet. The timing requirements are less strict than at the Bottom Level, but good reliability is still required. Middle Level networks have longer transmission ranges, bigger data packet sizes and stricter requirements than COTS technologies. Satellite and Wi-Max supports long-range transmission, while microwave and radio can be used for shorter distances.

The *Top Level* networks the workstations at the Middle Level to management and to the outside world. This provides a gateway for the control system to corporate systems like accounting, inventory and management decision support systems. Conventional data networks are deployed at this level and there are no special implications for process control in using COTS wireless technologies.

Replacing a wired network by wireless at the Middle Level, while minimising possible change to the existing control system was also discussed in [4]. This paper argued that the use of a common protocol, such as TCP/IP, enables COTS technology to be applied, with seamless replacement of the existing wired network. However, middleware is needed to sit on top of the wireless network to handle communication of the process control data. Interestingly, rather than having wireless communications between all nodes in the Bottom and Top Levels, wireless communication is restricted to two dedicated remote nodes, which then act as a gateway for all the local nodes. Further, since wireless is less reliable, the solution is to only transfer pass only essential data through the wireless link. For example, diagnostic information is retrieved on demand and non-time critical data is passed across between production phases.

The proposed strategy has been successfully applied to an oil extractor control system which removes oil from a well, which is metered and pumped to a storage tank. The system employs radio wireless communication to a master site, which in turn uses cellular communications to remote operators. The overall wireless network offers remote commands to the extractor, local operation with a hand-held unit, the detection of abnormalities like leaks, auto-calibration and metering, and the upload of measurements and events.

The focus of this paper is the Bottom Level and the potential advantages and limitations inherent in WNCS.

3 Current COTS Technologies

Cost considerations and the availability of agreed standards to support plug-and-play, has generated considerable interest in the use of the commercial-off-the-shelf (COTS) wireless solutions, notably Wi-Fi, Bluetooth and ZigBee. However, these were all developed for the office, IT and domestic markets and the requirements for industrial networks are markedly different, as indicated in Table 1.

Table 1. Contrasting Requirements of Commercial/Domestic and Industrial Wireless Networks

Office/Consumer Requirements	Industry Requirements
Wireless traffic can be prioritised but not predicted	Predictable communication cycle for deterministic data transfer
No monitoring of the link	Cyclical monitoring of a wireless link and quick warning to the process
Interruption of the link can only be corrected manually	Redundancy: automatic switchover
Wireless channel is a 'shared medium' - everyone has access	Data reservation for selected clients (e.g. PLC) guarantees access to the wireless network

Table 2. Comparison of Wireless Communication Networks

	PCS	WMAN	WLAN	WPAN
Maximum Distance	km(worldwide)	km (city)	hundreds of meters (area)	tens of meters (building)
Data Rates	9.6 kbps - 2.4 Mbps	0.5 - 2.0 Mbps	1 - 108 Mbps	0.2 - 300 Mbps
Technologies	GSM, GPRS, 3G, UMTS	WiMax, MBWA	Wi-Fi	Bluetooth, ZigBee, UWB
Standards		IEEE 802.16/802.20	IEEE 802.11	IEEE 802.15
Application	Voice & data messaging	Broadband access	Voice & data	Serial/USB replacement

Industrial networks generally, and the newly emerging wireless networks in particular, must offer real-time operation, reliability, redundancy, and determinism.

Table 2 compares worldwide personal communications service (PCS), wireless metropolitan area networks (WMAN), wireless local area networks (WLAN) and wireless personal area networks (WPAN) in terms of coverage, typical data rates, the technology used, the communication standard employed and typical data applications.

In Table 2, IEEE 802.11 refers to an agreed set of standards for wireless LANs as follows:

– 801.11a : 5 GHz band, 52-subcarrier orthogonal frequency-division multiplexing (OFDM) , maximum raw data rate of 54 Mbit/s
– 802.11b : 2.4 GHz band, Direct-sequence spread spectrum (DSSS), maximum raw data rate of 11 Mbit/s

- 802.11e : Quality of Service (QoS) extensions
- 802.11g : 2.4 GHz band, orthogonal frequency-division multiplexing (OFDM), maximum raw data rate of 54 Mbit/s
- 802.11i : Enhanced Security

It is worth noting that 802.11b is at the same frequency as Bluetooth and ZigBee, which has implications for interference in practical monitoring and control, as will be seen later. With 802.11b networks, as indeed with all wireless communications, signal propagation effects such as multipath fading and partition shadowing can have a very significant impact on both the achievable distance and data rate available for monitoring and control purposes. This is reflected in the comparative performance figures listed in Table 3.

Table 3. Achievable Data Rates and Ranges for 802.11 Networks

	1 Mbps	2 Mbps	5.5 Mbps	11 Mbps
Open Environment	550 m	400 m	270 m	160 m
Semi-Open Environment	115 m	90 m	70 m	60 m
Closed Environment	50 m	40 m	35 m	25 m

In a factory or other indoor environment, direct and reflected wireless transmissions (multipath) arrive and combine with different time delays and amplitudes. In the worst case the received signal can be completely cancelled. The solution adopted by the 802.11 standard is data-rate scaling, whereby the bandwidth is reduced under poor transmission conditions. An emerging 802.11 standard will use multiple antennas at both transmitter and receiver MIMO to increase throughput but the increased spatial diversity will also serve to mitigate the effects of multipath fading. Good design of the antenna/receiver hardware is another solution to improving any wireless link as is the transmitted power since higher level transmissions are less susceptible to interference and noise.

Ethernet has emerged as the 'de facto' standard for industrial communications. However, despite its advantages, both the cost and distance limitations remain a major issue on sprawling factory floors and large industrial settings. Further, running cable to new or relocated equipment can interrupt production. Wireless Ethernet, which refers to any over-the-air connection between Ethernet network nodes or devices, is one solution. As Wi-Fi networks are of primary interest in this paper, this technology is discussed more fully in the next subsection.

3.1 Wireless Ethernet-Based NCS

Unfortunately, as yet there is no single agreed standard but two classes have emerged: IEEE 802.11, and those based on proprietary protocols. The ability of IEEE 802.11 to address the unique challenges and requirements of industrial communications is examined first.

Multipath fading and RF interference immunity: The 802.11b standard only employs direct sequence spread spectrum (DSSS) and does not offer the better frequency hopping spread spectrum (FHSS) [3]. The ability to overcome signal fade and interference is said to be relatively weak. Also, the effect of channel contention and channel error are particularly detrimental since both greatly increase the time delay around the feedback loop. As the number of devices transmitting on the network increases, so does the chance of collisions occurring. In this event, all transmitted signals are corrupted and become unintelligible which requires the signal to be transmitted again, governed by the retransmission mechanism within 802.11b. The same situation applies in the presence of frame loss. The 2.4 Ghz GSM band is free of charge and not subject to registration. Bluetooth devices, smoke and movement detectors all use this band and can interfere with 802.11b/g traffic, introducing unwanted delays for control and monitoring data communications, as shown in figure 1.

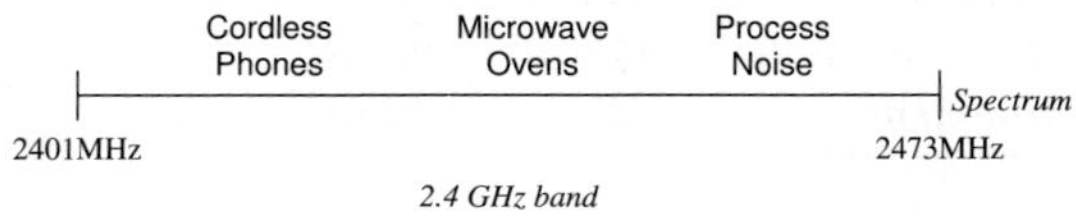

Fig. 1. Interference in the WiFi, Bluetooth and ZigBee Band

One solution is to introduce a redundant wireless connection in the 2.4 and 5 Ghz bands with both signals transmitted simultaneously to guarantee an interference-free wireless connection. Such redundancy increases the availability of a wireless link and reduces the susceptibility to interference at an increased equipment cost.

To reduce the probability of collisions, the Carrier Sense Multiple Access with Collision Avoidance (CSMA/CA) mechanism introduces a backoff procedure before transmitting. When the channel becomes idle, the node keeps sensing for an additional random duration called DCF Interframe Space (DIFS) after which it transmits following a further random time period. The latter are multiples of a slot time (T_{slot}) and each node keeps a different Contention Window (CW), used to determine the number of slot times it has to wait before transmission. For each successful packet reception, an acknowledgment (ACK) packet is sent. If an ACK is not received within a Short Interframe Space (SIFS) period, transmission failure is assumed and the node performs a backoff with double the CW size. The CW is doubled for every retransmission attempt i.e. failed attempts to transmit due to collisions or erroneous channel conditions are retransmitted with an enlarged CW of $2^j CW_{min}$, where j is the number of retransmission attempts. In addition to waiting until the next moment the channel is free, the enlarged CW size increases the delay substantially with the increase in number of retransmissions.

Data Throughput Capacity and Latency Tolerance: Throughput is the amount of data delivered per unit time. Latency is the maximum acceptable delay between data transmission and reception. While longer packets may lead to reduced overheads, this comes at the expense of higher latency, as other devices in the network have to wait while long packets are transferred. A maximum over-the-air data rate of 11 Mbps (for 802.11b) is seldom possible, especially in industrial settings. Low signal strength or quality (resulting from interference or fade) may cause throttle back until wireless links operate at just 10% of their theoretical capability, again introducing transmission delays. One of the reasons for this is bandwidth limitation as generally wireless networks are slower than their wired counterparts. While physical transmission rates are limited to 11 Mbps on 802.11b and 54 Mbps on 802.11g networks, wired Ethernet transmits at much greater rates of 100 Mbps up to 1 Gbps. This restriction naturally increases the time to physically transmit the control-measurement frames through the wireless medium. It also limits the bandwidth of the channel, which effectively determines the maximum sampling rate and the number of control systems transmitting simultaneously.

Network Architecture Flexibility: A star configuration is usual, involving an access point connected to a wired network and one (point-to-point) or more (point-to-multi-point) remote devices. As multiple wireless links are employed in a single location, the ability of the wireless device to operate in the presence of others must be considered. But 802.11b devices have just three non-overlapping channels and thus only three separate links can be employed at the same location while maintaining a reasonable throughput.

Node and Antenna Placements: Directional antennas generally provide better performance than omni-directional ones, in respect of backside rejection of multipath cancellation - however, this is only relevant where mobility is not required.

Operational Range: This is the most difficult parameter to ensure in indoor environments due to multipath effects. The typical range of 100 m with the 802.11b standard falls far short of this on the typical factory floor. Extending the range requires the use of repeaters and extra base stations, adding expense, unnecessary complexity, and extra cabling. Industrial wired Ethernet links, by contrast, provide operational range of the order of miles without additional equipment.

Device Power: The electrical power for wireless devices is an important practical consideration for WNCS. Table 4 provides some comparative figures for the peak and average power, assuming usage frequency of 10Hz. Device power is clearly an issue in mobile devices for example where batteries are needed.

Table 4. Power Comparisons of Wireless Technologies for Monitoring and Control

	Average Power	Peak Power	Usage Frequency
IEEE 802.11b (WiFi)	20 mW	1000 mW	10 Hz
IEEE 802.15.1 (Bluetooth)	11 mW	405 mW	10 Hz
IEEE 802.15.4 (ZigBee)	3 mW	30 mW	10 Hz

In conclusion, while 802.11b-based wireless Ethernet offers excellent connectivity, the performance alters significantly when deployed in industrial and factory settings. To deliver industry grade data communications with the needed speed and reliability, an enhanced wireless Ethernet solution is needed.

3.2 Proprietary Wireless Ethernet

To meet this demand, the major suppliers of industrial networking hardware and software platforms are tending to offer proprietary solutions via wireless extensions to their existing wired networks.

One example of this trend is PROFINET, the automation product from Siemens, which has evolved from vertical integration of wireless Ethernet and PROFIBUS. Applications of such wireless technology to a bottle filling machine, to AGVs for transporting building elements, to a high-crane steel warehouse, to a monorail system and to cranes, conveyor belts, robots, underground trains, lifts, theatre stages have all been reported [1].

Cirronet Inc (Norcross, Georgia, USA) networking technology is another example [5]. Applications mentioned include SCADA, medical telemetry, mining vehicle control, fleet management, remote overhead crane, factory automation and nuclear power plant radiation monitoring.

4 Current NCS Related Research

Much of the research in WNCS exists only in computer-based simulations and therefore accurate modelling is required to satisfy the following criteria: - (i) simultaneous simulation of the control system and computer network, both communicating and affecting each other at the same time (i.e. co-simulation) with the time delays and frame loss based on real-time traffic load and channel conditions, and (ii) accurately models the behaviour of the networking protocol. Although numerous co-simulation tools for NCS exist, only two extend support to wireless networks. Queen's University Belfast introduced the first wireless NCS simulator that was aimed at closed-loop control using industry-standard IEEE 802.11b (Wi-Fi) wireless networks (figure 2) [6]. By implementing it as a C MEX S-function for seamless integration with Simulink, this tool makes interfacing between the network and control system relatively straightforward and allows them to be run simultaneously. It also supports different traffic types (e.g. control system data, regular data) running on the same network to analyse mixed-traffic networks. In addition, a frame-level correlated channel model complements the simulator. This realistically reproduces the effects of non-line-of-sight (Rayleigh) multipath fading often experienced in built-up indoor environments. Using this model, the fading statistics of a wireless channel as well as physical-layer models are retained but at much reduced complexity. The other available simulator is TrueTime, which is fast becoming the standard co-simulation tool for NCS [7]. The newest version provides support for 802.11b/g ad-hoc WLAN and 802.15.4 ZigBee wireless networks. One notable feature is the facility for modelling power consumption of batteries in mobile devices. This is useful for simulating the

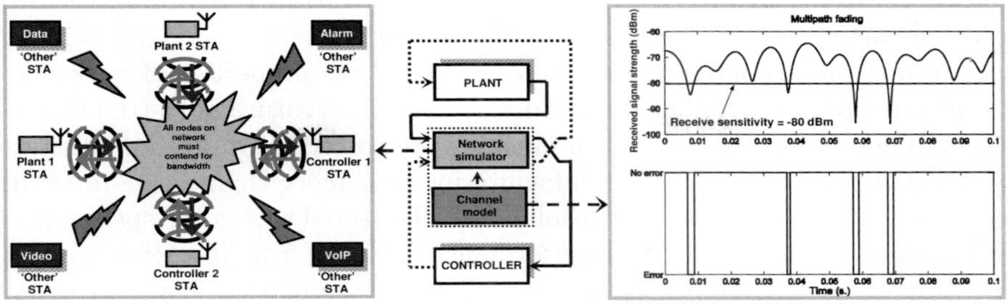

Fig. 2. Representation of the simulator within Simulink (*centre*): the network simulator emulates multiple field devices in an NCS contending for bandwidth on the channel in the presence of 'other' traffic (*left*), while the channel model uses an error-trace to decide when a frame is in error (*right*)

performance of portable or mobile control systems, as well as for determining a sensor lifetime in wireless sensor networks.

Many different approaches have been taken in an attempt to better understand the effects of using wireless communication for closed-loop control, either mathematically or from simulation. The first critical analysis on the use of wireless control was performed by [8]. It explores a wide spectrum of issues relating to the affect of the wireless medium and protocol on control performance - from the networking layer (e.g. the routing problem in multi-hop networks) up to the physical layer (e.g. the power control problem in choosing the power level to transmit). While addressing certain issues, it also called for further exploration of the impact of the wireless protocol. This was answered in part in [9] which highlighted the cross-layer design problem (the interconnectivity between all the different communication layers) and revealed how variations in data rate, error correction coding and different maximum bounds in the number of retransmissions can affect control performance. Later work in [10] examined various MAC layer mechanisms, including CSMA/CA which forms part of 802.11. The 802.11b MAC layer was also studied in great detail in [11,12], which investigated the properties of the WNCS under heavy contention from control-only and mixed-traffic data, as well as its performance under less-than-perfect channel conditions.

Experimental work has also been done to determine the practicality of WNCS under realistic operating conditions. Experiments were performed on an 802.11b wirelessly networked inverted pendulum mounted on a rotating base [13], with UDP communication and a timing scheme that uses clock driven sensing with event driven control. These (experiments) were performed on the first and ground floors of the Mechanical Engineering Lab at the University of Illinois at Urbana Champaign. LQR state feedback control was applied successfully, for both swing-up control and stabilisation, using a 1.47Ghz PC running Windows 2000 under a MATLAB and Simulink control environment. It was found that the system maintained stability over a wide range of network conditions and sample rates, with robustness to changing network conditions being further improved by varying the measurement sampling interval. Furthermore, the setup was extended to multiple controller-plant systems which performed satisfactorily, even with the increased contention for bandwidth on the network.

In an attempt to better understand the statistical properties of packet loss and bit-error patterns for the design and simulation of future industrial wireless local area network protocols, measurements were performed in Produktionstechnisches Zentrum (PTZ), a research facility for machinery engineering in Berlin, Germany [14]. Several important results were discovered within the span of these investigations including the poor performance obtained from 5.5 MBit/s and 11 MBit/s modulation schemes and the variability of the wireless link over several timescales due to frequently changing environmental conditions (e.g. moving people, portal crane activity, moving parts of machines) and common characteristics of such environments (e.g. strong motors, metal sufaces, and machines switching on- and off). Although the quantitative results (e.g mean bit error rate) may not be valid for other scenarios, the qualitative results (on time-varying behaviour, burstiness behaviour and the order of magnitude of packet losses, high variability of error bursts) are generally useful. Other experimental work of note concerned the study of the retention of frames and long periods of disconnection from the 802.11b network attributed to the re-association procedure that the wireless card executes in order to find the access point with the strongest signal [15].

Possible approaches to the issues of frame loss and round-trip delays around the feedback have adopted broadly similar solutions to those found in wired networks; either neglecting the network characteristics and modifying the controller design appropriately [15] or else developing protocols that assign priority to control or measurement type data and reduce transmission delay so that existing standard control techniques can be implemented [16,17].

However, due to the limited bandwidth and susceptibility to varying channel conditions in wireless networks, another form of compensation which optimises both network and control performance simultaneously is gaining new ground in the area of WNCS research. Known collectively as 'reduced communication control', the general basis is to underutilise the bandwidth of the channel (by down-sampling) during periods where it is blocked either from sudden bursts of traffic or from long periods of poor channel conditions. Such a strategy has the following benefits:- (i) the network is prevented from becoming saturated, which ensures sufficient bandwidth is always available for transmission of measurement-control signals as well as allowing for retransmission of frames which have been dropped, (ii) queues are prevented from building up at the transmitter end - only the most up-to-date measurement-control signal is transmitted rather than previous blocked frames, and (iii) the control and network performances are optimised simultaneously without the use of complex control and/or prediction algorithms. The experimental work by [14] showed that while faster sampling extended the range of stability with respect to packet loss, higher sampling rates in turn produce higher rates of data loss for a given signal-to-noise ratio. Motivated by the goal of maintaining low levels of data loss, while keeping to the highest possible rate of sampling and control, positive results were obtained by dynamically adjusting the sampling interval to reflect changing network conditions using a PI controller which maintained the mean data loss consistently at 5%. Later work included a two-state Markov model to estimate the evolution of frame loss over time using a moving window that allows detection of network disturbances and prediction of how the system should operate in terms of stability and disturbance rejection [18]. In [19], an optimisation algorithm called the primal-dual algorithm, often used for congestion control schemes in communication networks, was used to obtain the optimal bandwidth allocation scheme based on an estimation error utility function. Another technique involves adapting the sampling interval based on a QoS measurement of the round-trip delay. Here stability in the mean square sense was proved using Markov Jump Linear System (MJLS) theory [20].

5 Conclusions

Wireless Ethernet or 802.11b is widely used for monitoring and control, with Bluetooth and ZigBee rapidly emerging. While the majority of reported applications are for monitoring, the anticipated market for wireless control is expected to grow. Research progress has been made on co-simulation and on analysing the effects of wireless communication on control performance, with reduced communication control looking promising.

References

1. IEE, ed.: IEE Seminar on Industrial Networking and Wireless Communications in Control, Warwick, United Kingdom (2006)
2. Strothman, J.: Wireless Control? Ok, if 'Slow' and not Critical... World Bus Journal (2002) 9–10
3. Thorner, C.: Industrial Interfaces can Be Wireless, and Reliable. IEE Computing and Control Engineering **15**(4) (2004) 34–35
4. Nixon, M., Shepard, R., Bennett, B., Chen, D., Mok, A.K.: A Framework to Transmit Process Control Data over Commercial Wireless Networks. In: Technical Conference and Emerging Technologies Conference, Houston, TX, US (2004)
5. Cirronet: Wireless Communications for Industrial Applications. White Paper (2002)
6. Colandairaj, J., Scanlon, W.G., Irwin, G.W.: Understanding Wireless Networked Control Systems Through Simulation. IEE Computing and Control Engineering (2005) 26–31
7. Andersson, M., Cervin, A., Årzén, K.E.: Simulation of Wireless Networked Control Systems. In: Proceedings of the IEEE Conference on Decision and Control and European Control Conference, Seville, Spain (2005)
8. Kumar, P.: New Technological Vistas for Systems and Control: The Example of Wireless Networks. IEEE Control Systems Magazine **21**(1) (2001) 24–37
9. Liu, X., Goldsmith, A.: Wireless Communication Tradeoffs in Distributed Control. In: Proceedings of the IEEE Conference on Decision and Control, Maui, HI, U.S. (2003) 688–694
10. Liu, X., Goldsmith, A.: Wireless Medium Access Control in Networked Control Systems. In: Proceedings of the American Control Conference, Boston, US (2004) 3605–3610

11. Colandairaj, J., Irwin, G.W., Scanlon, W.G.: Analysis and Co-simulation of an IEEE 802.11b Wireless Networked Control System. In: Proceedings of the IFAC World Congress, Prague, Czech Republic (2005)
12. Colandairaj, J., Irwin, G.W., Scanlon, W.G.: Analysis of an IEEE 802.11b Wireless Networked Control System. In: Proceedings of the First Networked Control Systems and Fault Tolerant Control (NeCST) Workshop, Ajaccio, France (2005) 19–25
13. Ploplys, N.J., Kawka, P.A., Alleyne, A.G.: Closed-loop Control over Wireless Networks. IEEE Control Systems Magazine **24** (2004) 58–71
14. Willig, A., Kubisch, M., Hoene, C., Wolisz, A.: Measurements of a Wireless Link in an Industrial Environment Using an IEEE 802.11-compliant PHY Layer. IEEE Transactions on Industrial Electronics **49**(6) (2002) 1265–1282
15. Sandoval-Rodriguez, R.and Abdallah, C., Jerez, H., Byrne, R.: Experimental Results on the Effects of 802.11b WLAN on Networked Control System. In: IEEE International Symposium on Intelligent Control and 13th Mediterranean Conference on Control and Automation, Limassol, Cyprus (2005) 1119–1124
16. Ye, H., Walsh, G., Bushnell, L.: Real-time Mixed-traffic Wireless Networks. IEEE Transactions on Industrial Electronics **48**(5) (2001) 883–890
17. Sheu, J.P., Liu, C.H., Wu, S.L., Tseng, Y.C.: A Priority MAC Protocol to Support Real-time Traffic in ad Hoc Networks. Wireless Networks **10**(1) (2004) 61–69
18. Kawka, P., Alleyne, A.: Stability and Feedback Control of Wireless Networked Systems. In: Proceedings of the American Control Conference, Portland, OR, US (2005) 2953–2959
19. Xiao, L., Johannsson, M., Hindi, H., Boyd, S., Goldsmith, A.: Joint Optimization of Wireless Communication and Networked Control Systems. Lecture Notes in Computer Science **3355** (2005) 248–272
20. Colandairaj, J., Irwin, G., Scanlon, W.: Wireless Networked Control Systems with QoS-based Sampling. IEE Proceedings in Control Theory and Applications (Under review) (2006)

An Improved Deadline-Based Message Scheduling Algorithm for Real-Time Control Network

Qingyu Yang[1], Lincang Ju[2], Sibo Ge[1], and Ren Shi[1]

[1] Dept. of Automation, Xi'an Jiaotong University,
710049 Xi'an, P.R.C.
yangqingyu@mail.xjtu.edu.cn
[2] Dept. of Power & Control Engineering, Xi'an Jiaotong University,
710049 Xi'an, P.R.C.
lincang@mail.xjtu.edu.cn

Abstract. A good message scheduling algorithm could give timeliness guarantee to real-time control network. Based on DM algorithm, this paper presents an improved deadline-based algorithm, Deadline Monotonic with Urgent Message Considered (DMUMC), for FF control network message scheduling. The main idea of DMUMC is that deadline of urgent aperiodic message, such as alarms, was taken into account when establishing BAT. The simulation results show that DMUMC algorithm significantly reduces response time of urgent aperiodic message by adjusting service time of low priority periodic message with large deadline, and improves timeliness and message schedulability of FF control network, compared with traditional methods that didn't consider the issue of aperiodic message.

1 Introduction

Foundation Fieldbus (FF) is a popular control network in industrial automation. Real-time message scheduling is an important research field for FF, especially establishing of bus arbitrator table (BAT) for periodic message. Recent works in this area mainly include establishing BAT and scheduling of aperiodic message. Periodic and aperiodic message is managed by Link Active Scheduler (LAS) in FF[1-4]. Accordingly, the bandwidth of FF is divided into periodic message window and aperiodic message window in a microcycle time. Only the remainder time after periodic message scheduled can be used by aperiodic message. Therefore timeliness and schedulability of aperiodic message are affected by periodic message greatly. However, the traditional methods haven't thought over aperiodic message when establishing BAT, which may lose schedulability for some urgent alarm message.

So the authors' work attempts to improve timeliness and schedulability of both periodic and aperiodic message, especially urgent aperiodic message. When establishing BAT, if the deadline of some periodic message is larger than that of aperiodic message, priority inversing is forbidden. Using this algorithm, which is called Deadline Monotonic with Urgent Message Considered (DMUMC) in this paper, the aperiodic message with smaller deadline is scheduled firstly. The purpose is to improve timeliness and schedulability of urgent message, by adjusting service time of the low priority periodic message with large deadline reasonably.

D.-S. Huang, K. Li, and G.W. Irwin (Eds.): ICIC 2006, LNAI 4114, pp. 1073–1078, 2006.

The paper is organized as follows. Section 2 briefly introduces DM algorithm and traditional methods of establishing BAT for FF. Section 3 describes DMUMC algorithm in detail, and section 4 is an analysis of simulation results using DMUMC. A short conclusion is drawn in section 5.

2 DM Algorithm and Establishment of BAT

Fig.1 is the bandwidth assignment chart of FF control network. As mention before, the most importance is how to establish BAT for FF.

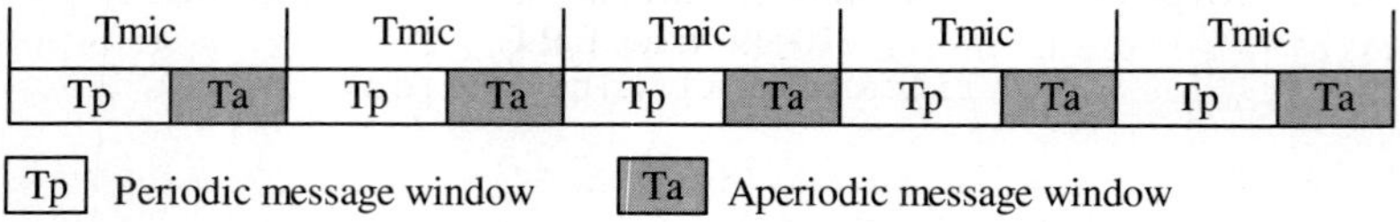

Fig. 1. Bandwidth assignment of FF control network

Before discussing DM algorithm, we give message model of FF firstly. We know that numbers of periodic message are independent of the stations because periodic message is managed by LAS uniformly. Suppose the number of periodic message on FF is *np*, and deadline is equal to its periodicity, then the ith periodic message Mp_i can be described as

$$Mp_i = (Cp_i, Tp_i, Dp_i, P_i), \quad \forall i = 1,2,...,np \tag{1}$$

Where Cp_i, Tp_i, Dp_i and P_i are respectively longest computation time, periodicity, deadline and priority of Mp_i.

In FF control network, the aperiodic message is scheduled when the station get PT (Post Token), so numbers of aperiodic message depends on the stations. Suppose the number of aperiodic message on k^{th} station is na^k for a segment including n stations, the mth aperiodic message Ma_m^k on the kth station is described as

$$Ma_m^k = (Ca_m^k, Ta_m^k, Da_m^k, P_m^k), \quad \forall m \in [1, na^k], k \in [1, n] \tag{2}$$

Where Ca_m^k, Ta_m^k, Da_m^k and P_m^k are respectively longest computation time, smallest release time, deadline and priority of Ma_m^k.

In a real-time system, priority of a task can be assigned according to its relative deadline. The famous assignment method is: the smaller the relative deadline, the higher the priority. That is, $Di < Dj \Rightarrow Pi > Pj$. Where Di is the deadline of a task, and Pi is its priority. This kind of priority assignment is known as the Deadline Monotonic (DM) algorithm[5]. The traditional methods is Highest Common Factor/Lowest Common Multiple (i.e. HCF/LCM) when establishing BAT[6]. For the message described by equation (1) we have: $Tmic = \underset{i=1,...,np}{HCF}(Tp_i)$, and $Tmac = \underset{i=1,...,np}{LCM}(Tp_i)$. Where $Tmic$ and $Tmac$ denote microcycle and macrocycle respectively.

However, the traditional methods when establishing BAT do not consider urgent aperiodic message, such as alarms message. The urgent aperiodic message with highest priority could lose their deadline, and become unscheduled when there are some periodic messages with larger deadline. We know that the control message is very important in a control system, but an alarm message could hurt to people or device. So we must give timeliness guarantee to the urgent aperiodic message.

ALGORITHM: Establishing BAT using DMUMC

Step1 Scheduling Start: calculate HCF and LCM of all periodic messages, get the microcycle $Tmic$ and macrocycle $Tmac$.

Step2 Deadline Compared: deadline of urgent aperiodic message and periodic message are compared, if deadline of some urgent aperiodic message is less than periodic message, and their computation time is equality nearly, then go to Step4, or else go to Step3. That is to say, if $Da_m^k < Dp_i \cap Ca_m^k \le Cp_i$, then $P_m^k > P_i$.

Step3 Preemptive: during $Tmac$, reset the time used in every microcycle, then start the cycle from the periodic message Mp_1 with smallest periodicity:

The periodic message Mp_i would be scheduled if the remainder time in n^{th} microcycle is not less than the computation time of Mp_i, then update the time used $Tused(n)$, otherwise to the next microcycle until finding a microcycle that can deal with Mp_i. If Dp_i is reached, there is not appropriate microcycle, we can get the conclusion that Mp_i can not be scheduled. Scheduling of Mp_i, Then go to the next microcycle that Mp_i releases, and transact Mp_i repeatedly until end of macrocycle. Then to the next periodic message Mp_{i+1}. After all periodic messages are scheduled, go to Step5, start scheduling of aperiodic message and calculate response time.

Step4 Non-Preemptive: during the time $Tmac$, reset the time used in every microcycle, then start the cycle from the first microcycle:

Calculate $Need_{i,n}$ (Where, i denotes service needed or not, 1 and 0 denote that the message is scheduled or not respectively) of all periodic message. For every microcycle n, for any Mp_i with $Need_{i,n} = 1$, beginning with highest priority message, if the remainder time in current microcycle is not less than the computation time of Mp_i, schedule it and update the time used $Tused(n)$, or else to the next microcycle without scheduling lower priority message. Then to next message with lower priority until the end of a macrocycle, go to Step5, start scheduling of aperiodic message and calculate response time.

Step5 Scheduling Aperiodic Message: from the first microcycle, check the remainder time after scheduling periodic message. The aperiodic message Ma_m^k would be scheduled if the remainder time in n^{th} microcycle is not less than the computation time of Ma_m^k, and update $Tused(n)$. Calculate the response time Ra_m^k of Ma_m^k, according to $Ra_m^k = Tmic \times (n-1) + Tused(n)$. Judge next aperiodic message Ma_{m+1}^k, and check all microcycle until end of macrocycle.

Fig. 2. Main step of DMUMC scheduling algorithm

3 DMUMC Algorithm

The purpose of DMUMC is to overcome the shortcomings of traditional methods. Its main idea is that the urgent aperiodic messages with smallest deadline are taken into account when establishing BAT. If the deadline of some aperiodic messages is less than that of periodic, and the computation time of theirs are equality approximately, the urgent aperiodic message is scheduled firstly, and the periodic message be delayed to the next microcycle. DMUMC algorithm can be described as Fig.2.

4 Experiments and Discussion

Consider a FF control network including three stations, with the following set of periodic and aperiodic message described as Tab.1.

Table 1. Set of periodic and aperiodic message

No.	Identifier	Periodicity (ms)	Deadline (ms)	Computation times(ms)
1	Mp_1	10	10	3.5
2	Mp_2	20	20	3.5
3	Mp_3	20	20	2
4	Mp_4	40	40	3.5
5	Mp_5	40	40	2.5
6	Mp_6	40	40	1
7	Ma_1^1		20	1
8	Ma_1^2		50	2
9	Ma_1^3		60	3

Where, the number of periodic message is six, and every station has an aperiodic message. For the message set of Tab.1, we can get BAT using traditional DM method and DMUMC. Tab.2 is the result of establishing BAT using traditional DM, and Tab.3 is the result using DMUMC. Where, 1 and 0 denote that the message was scheduled or not respectively, and * denote the message was delayed to the next microcycle. The remainder time is used to scheduling aperiodic message in corresponding microcycle.

Tab.2 shows there was no time left to schedule aperiodic message in the first microcycle. That is to say, the aperiodic message Ma_1^1 with the highest priority may lose its deadline. The bandwidth assignment is shown in Fig.3 and Fig.4.

As shown in Fig.4, when using DMUMC algorithm, periodic message Mp_6 with lower priority was preempted by urgent aperiodic message Ma_1^1 with smaller deadline during the remainder time after periodic messages Mp_1 to Mp_3 were scheduled. Using the DMUMC, the response times of all aperiodic messages Ma_1^1 to Ma_1^3 were 10ms, 35.5ms and 38.5ms respectively, which are all less than their deadline, i.e., they are schedulability.

Table 2. BAT using traditional DM methods

Microcycle	Mp_1	Mp_2	Mp_3	Mp_4	Mp_5	Mp_6	Remainder time (ms)
1	1	1	1	*	*	1	0
2	1	0	0	1	1	0	0.5
3	1	1	1	0	0	0	1
4	1	0	0	0	0	0	6.5

Table 3. BAT using DMUMC algorithm

Microcycle	Mp_1	Mp_2	Mp_3	Mp_4	Mp_5	Mp_6	Remainder time (ms)
1	1	1	1	*	*	*	1
2	1	0	0	1	1	*	0.5
3	1	1	1	0	0	1	0
4	1	0	0	0	0	0	6.5

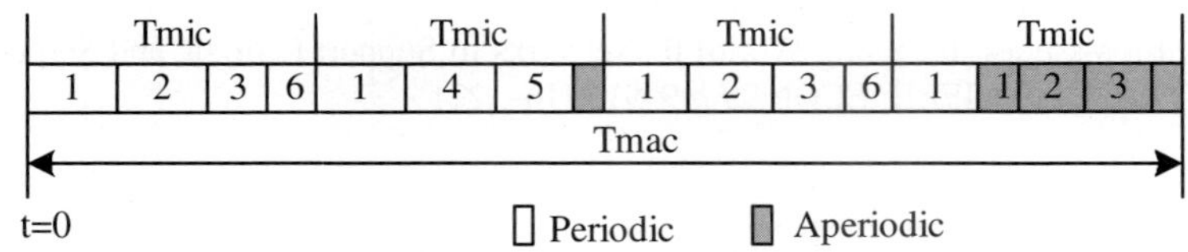

Fig. 3. Results of traditional DM message scheduling algorithm

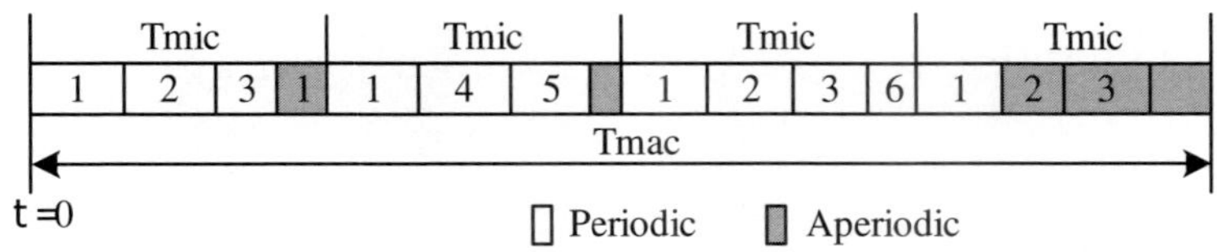

Fig. 4. Results of DMUMC algorithm

Contrarily, using traditional DM message scheduling algorithm, all aperiodic message were relayed to the forth microcycle in Fig.3. In this situation, the response times of all aperiodic messages Ma_1^1 to Ma_1^3 were 34.5ms, 36.5ms and 39.5ms respectively. The aperiodic Ma_1^1 lose its deadline, and could not be scheduled. If Ma_1^1 was urgent alarm, the serious results may be produced.

5 Conclusion

Considering urgent aperiodic message, this paper explores a novel deadline-base scheduling algorithm - Deadline Monotonic with Urgent Message Considered (DMUMC) - to establish BAT of FF control network. DMUMC takes into account urgent aperiodic message with smaller deadline when establishing BAT of FF, and shorten the response time of urgent aperiodic message by adjusting the service time of some periodic message with large deadline.

Compared with the traditional DM method, DMUMC strengthens the timeliness of urgent message and the schedulability of all message of FF control network. Especially some alarm and interlock message can be scheduled correctly, and the safety of control system and people is guaranteed. This algorithm can be extended to other real-time control networks.

References

1. Yang, X.H.: Fieldbus and Its Application. Tsinghua University Press, Beijing (1999)
2. David, A. G.: Foundation Fieldbus Technical Overview. Fieldbus Foundation (1998)
3. ANSI/ISA-50.2: Fieldbus Standard for Use in Industrial Control Systems Part 3-Data Link Service Definitions. 2nd Edn. Instrument Society of America (1997)
4. ANSI/ISA-50.2: Fieldbus Standard for Use in Industrial Control Systems-Part 4-Data Link Protocol Specifications. 2nd Edn. Instrument Society of America (1997)
5. Leung, J., Whitehead, J.: On the Complexity of Fixed-Priority Scheduling of Periodic Real-Time Tasks. Performance Evaluation (1982) 237–250
6. Tovar, E., Vasques, F.: Using WorldFIP Networks to Support Periodic and Sporadic Real-Time Traffic. Proc. IEEE IECON'99 (1999) 1216–1221

Study on Inter-operability Unit for an Automobile Network

Sungyun Jung, Sung-oh Yang, and Kwang-Ryul Baek

Deptartment of Electronics Engineering, Pusan National University,
Busan, Korea
{syjung, kalkiny, krbaek}@pusan.ac.kr

Abstract. Communication in an automobile is coming to be important and complex little by little, because of hundreds of circuits, sensors, and many other electrical components. For example, some high-end luxury cars contain more than three miles and nearly 200 pounds of wiring. Therefore, the difficulty in connecting these components is gradually important issue for the automotive industries. As a solution to this affair, networking provides a more efficient method for today's complex in-vehicle communications. And then, many automotive buses have emerged in last years. Especially, to connect multimedia devices(eg, audio, GPS navigation system, DVD player, PC), the MOST(media oriented systems transport) is proposed to automotive industries as multimedia network in an automobile. To follow the tendency of network integration, we try to connect CAN(controller area network) to MOST. Indeed, it is that we use MOST as control network instead of CAN. To do this, we explain the characteristic of MOST and CAN. Secondly, the inter-operability unit is analyzed by queueing model. Thirdly, we substitute the real CAN traffic for queueing model.

1 Introduction

In today's in-vehicle communications, the electrical smart components have complicated network connections although these are very succinct as compared with point-to-point connections. To make matter worse, many exclusive standards have confused car-makers and venders of components.

However, CAN network have consolidated its disposition in European in-vehicle communications especially as a control network. Furthermore, the modern automobiles have to be equipped variety of multimedia peripherals(eg, audio, GPS navigation system, DVD player, PC). To solve their connections, MOST was proposed as multimedia network in automobiles.

This new standard would have given a additional confusions to venders. But, if CAN that is practically verified for control networks, is connected MOST, network in automobiles is very simpler than the existence of some autonomous networks.

D.-S. Huang, K. Li, and G.W. Irwin (Eds.): ICIC 2006, LNAI 4114, pp. 1079–1084, 2006.

2 MOST and CAN

2.1 MOST

As mentioned above, MOST have advantages what can connect multimedia components, reduce cables and unify the methods of interface[1]. Because it substitutes heavier copper cables, the fuel efficiency is eventually increased. Table.1 is the prominent characteristic of MOST. Especially, a transmission type is various from synchronous to sporadic transmission. Moreover, a synchronous data type

Table 1. The prominent characteristic of MOST

speed	up max. 40MBits/s
node	max. 64 nodes
type	synchronous, asynchronous, sporadic
media	fiber optic, twisted pair(suggested)
method	master/slave, token ring
layer	physical, link, network, transport,application

can transmit audio stream because it is consisted with 60 bytes. And a asynchronous data type can transmit video stream with length of 48 to 1024 bytes. Lastly, control data type is transmitted through CSMA with 19 bytes. The structure of each frame is well defined at Fig. 1. A block contains 16 frame that is consisted with 3 data types mentioned above. And the length of all data type is real data size besides redundancy with speed of 20MBits/s. We use MOST with this transmission speed.

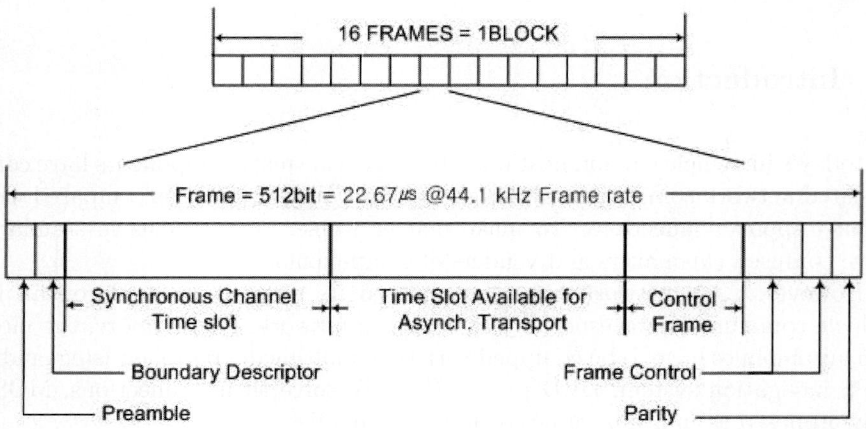

Fig. 1. Structure of blocks and frames on the MOST

2.2 CAN

CAN is widely adopted to in-vehicle network by many car-maker in Europe. Today, CAN has no doubt in its performance and confidence although many other network standards are newly emerged. The transmission speed of CAN has 1Mbits/s and the packet is consisted of between 1 and 8 bytes through CSMA transmission topology [2].

Because of using CSMA methods, CAN is analyzed by worst-case latency time or discrete event simulations [4]. Both of maximum latency time and simulations gives boundary of using CAN to system designer. And also, both methods are well adopted to Class C application and real applications of a car [4].

Fig. 2 is the time-delay model of CAN [3].

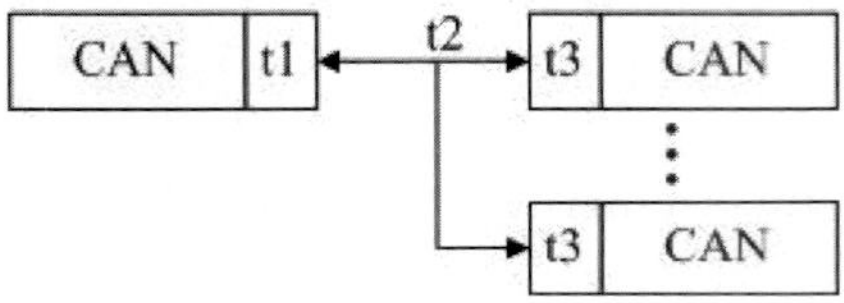

Fig. 2. A communication system of CAN

The main delay term is physically measured and followed.

t1 source system processing time(0.8ms)
t2 CAN data sending time(4ms)
t3 destination system processing time(0.8ms)

CAN communication system is adopted to M/D/1 queueing model. The total service time is,

$$E[\tau_1] = t1 + t2 + t3 = 5.6ms. \tag{1}$$

And, the expectation of waiting time of M/D/1 is zero. The followed equation is satisfied.

$$E[W_{M/D/1}] = \frac{\rho_1}{2(1-\rho_1)} E[\tau_1]. \tag{2}$$

Where, ρ_1 = arrival rate/service rate at M/D/1.

2.3 Inter-operability Unit(IU)

Although MOST is used for multimedia data, it should be afford to delivery the control data transmitted through CAN. Modern car network will be developed to be converged and inter-operated. And then, we suggest following Fig. 3.

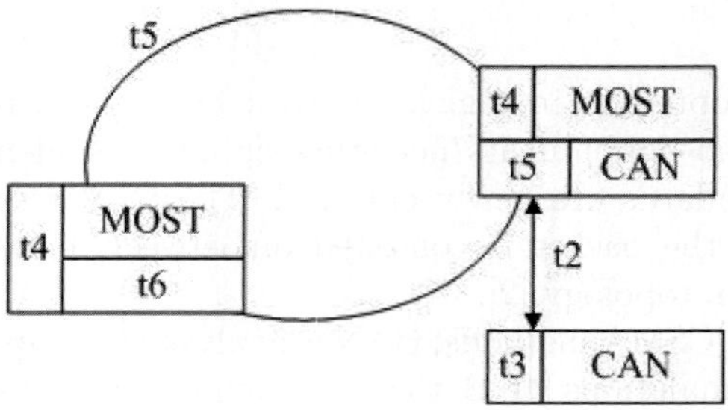

Fig. 3. The whole network of MOST and CAN

The time delay term is physically measured and followed.

t4 MOST data sending time(4ms)
t5 MOST,CAN converting time(0.1ms)
t6 MOST data frame time(uniform R.V.)

Mentioned above, what CAN and MOST would be emerged to one system is the IU. MOST communication is well adopted M/G/1 queuing model. The total service time is

$$E[\tau_2] = E[\tau_1] + t4 + t5 + E[t6] = 5.724ms. \tag{3}$$

And, the expectation of waiting time of M/G/1 is zero. The followed equation is satisfied.

$$E[W_{M/G/1}] = \frac{\lambda(\sigma_{\tau_2}^2 + E[\tau_2]^2)}{2(1-\rho_2)}. \tag{4}$$

Where, ρ_2 = arrival rate/service rate at M/G/1.

3 Comparison of Performance

The waiting time of two systems is simulated by Matlab 7.1 to Fig. 4. The waiting time is increased because arrival time rate is large. Actually, the arrival rate of CAN data is Fig. 5, if all transmitting data is synchronized [4]. And also, Fig. 5 is used for benchmark data for the in-vehicle network.

The arrival rate of data don't overcome max. 0.05. This result is adopted to Fig. 4, the two system have equally same waiting time. This means control frame of MOST can afford to the bandwidth of CAN. The IU of MOST to CAN is realized very well at the in-vehicle network through SAE benchmark test. We implemented MOST2CAN module physically in Fig. 6.

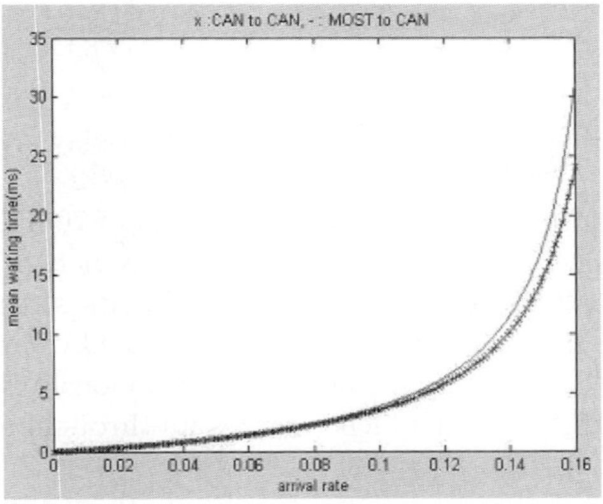

Fig. 4. The comparison of MOST2CAN, CAN2CAN system with arrival rate

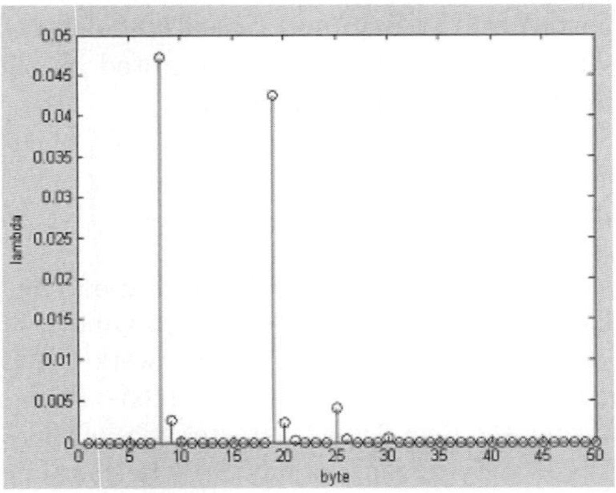

Fig. 5. The arrival rate of CAN data in a vehicle

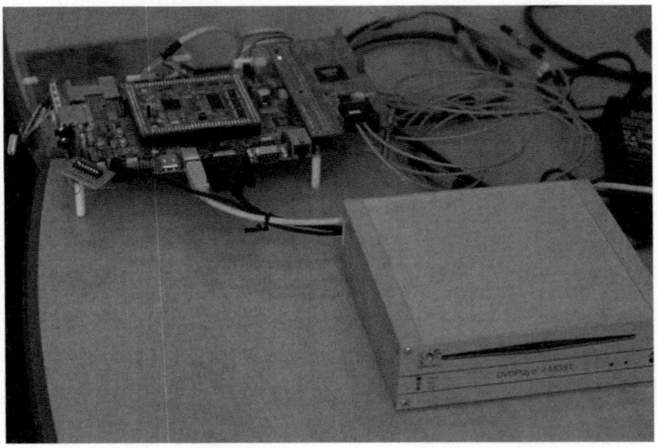

Fig. 6. Structure of blocks and frames on the MOST

4 Conclusion

We investigate inter-operability with in-vehicle network i.e. MOST and CAN. And also, CAN to MOST converter is analyzed by delay scheme and queueing model.

The control data frame is transmitted with speed of 706KBit/s, but its transmission method(token-ring) is well adopted to CAN network. Moreover, if the bit rate of MOST will be eventually up to 150MBits/s, the control frame of MOST can afford to inter-operate and substitute for CAN network.

Practically, MOST specification has been continuously improved, and then this paper suggests the method which enlarges its throughput for a control network.

Acknowledgements

This work was supported by the Regional Research Centers Program(Research Center for Logistics Information Technology), granted by the Korean Ministry of Education & Human Resources Development.

References

1. MOST: MOST Specification Rev. 2.3. MOST corporation (2004)
2. Bosch: CAN Specification Version 2.0. Robert Bosch GmbH, Stuttgart (1991)
3. Tindel, K., et al.: Calculating Controller Area Network(CAN) Message Response Times. Control Engineering Practice, 3(8) (1995) 1163–1169
4. BhargavP, U.: Analyzing the Real-Time Characteristics of Class C Communications in CAN Through Discrete Event Simulations. SAE technical paper SP-1012 (1994) 25–34
5. Leon-Garcia, A.: Probability and Random Processes for Electrical Engineering. Addison Wesley, Newyork (1994) 526–529

The Networked Control Systems Based on Predictive Functional Control

Jianguo Wu[1,2] and Minrui Fei[2]

[1] School of Electric Engineering, Nantong University, Jiangsu Province 226007, China
wu.jg@ntu.edu.cn
[2] School of Mechatronical Engineering and Automation, Shanghai University, Shanghai 200072, China
mrfei@staff.shu.edu.cn

Abstract. Owing to the fact that the networked control system is featured by uncertain delays, the stochastic time delay can be transformed into a deterministic delay by placing a special mount of buffers at the nodes in the networked control system, thus transform the stochastic networked control system into a deterministic delay system. A controller applying the predictive functional control is hence designed, for the purpose of improving the control capability through realizing the presumption of mould matching and multi-step prognosis. The results of both the simulation based on MATLAB and the experiment based on distributed control system (DCS) show that the method put forward in this paper are not only correct but also effective.

1 Introduction

With the fast development of network technique and computer, the traditional control systems can no longer satisfy the requirement to control the system in complicated engineering systems. The node to node control system is being replaced by the one based on the network. The system using network to form a closed loop one is called networked control system (NCS), whose major advantages include the share of resources, high diagnosis ability, simple to install and maintenance, and the improvement of flexibility and reliability of the system [1-3].

The introduction of the communication network into the control system makes it very difficult to do the control system analysis and system design. The information transfer among the modules of NCS via the network inevitably causes the inductive time delay of the network, including the sensor-controller time delay and the controller-actuator time delay, which lowers the system function and even brings about unsteadiness of the system. Therefore, the functions of the controller which was designed before the entering of network should be verified again. Since the network inductive time delay changes with the random time, the NCS is a random system, and such random system can be controlled through the random control method [4,5]. However, the use of the random control method requires that the network inductive time delay should obey a certain distribution. If the network inductive time delay does not obey this distribution, the above mentioned method becomes inapplicable [6,7].

D.-S. Huang, K. Li, and G.W. Irwin (Eds.): ICIC 2006, LNAI 4114, pp. 1085 – 1092, 2006.

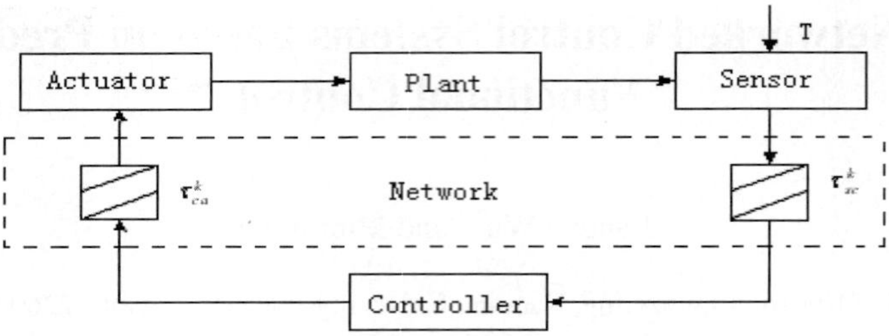

Fig. 1. NCS structure sketch map

Literature [8][9] puts forward a method to install a buffer area with certain length at the controller and actuator receiving ends, which transforms the NCS random time delay into a deterministic one, and in this way changes the random close-loop system into a deterministic close-loop one. This method has been accepted by many scholars, and they have started to make relevant researches and experiments to have it verified. Based on this method, the paper puts forwards the idea of an equivalent value system for the deterministic networked control system, and the design of a controller based on the predictive functional control.

2 The Problem Description

Fig.1 is the sketch map of NCS. τ_{sc} indicates the time delay between the sensor and the controller, while τ_{ca} indicates the time delay between the controller and the actuator. Because τ_{sc} and τ_{ca} are all random variables, NCS is a random system, which makes the system control very difficult. Literature [8][9] puts forward the method to install a buffer area with certain length at the receiving end of the controller and actuator, which transforms NCS random time delay into a deterministic time delay, thus transforms the random system into a deterministic one.

Fig. 2 shows the structure of NCS with deterministic time delay. Because both the network inductive time delay (sensor-controller and controller-actuator) are constants, the positions of time delay (sensor-controller and controller-actuator) can be exchanged with the controller [10]. Therefore, as a closed loop system, the systems shown in Fig. 1 and in Fig.2 are equivalent in value. Obviously, the system in Fig. 2 belongs to the type of pure time delay systems. For systems of this type, satisfactory control can be acquired by applying the advanced method like predictive functional control.

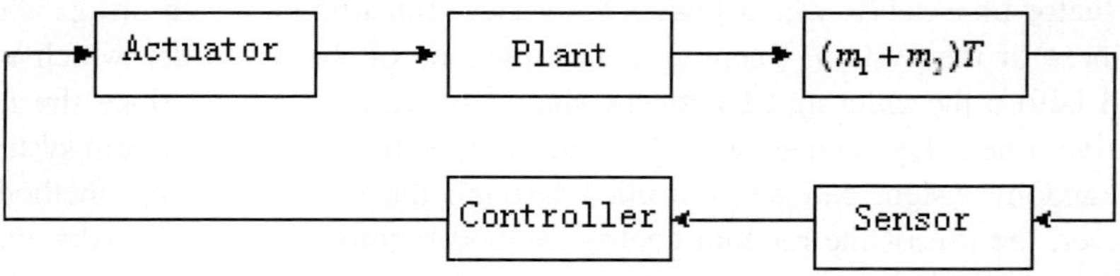

Fig. 2. Sketch map of the deterministic NCS with the equivalent value system

3 The Basic Principle of Predictive Functional Control

The control of PFC applies a linear combination of several known basic functions f_n $(n = 1,\cdots,N)$.

$$u(k+i) = \sum_{n=1}^{N} \mu_n f_n(i) \quad i = 0,1\cdots P-1 \tag{1}$$

where, $f_n(i)$ is the value representing f_n at samples time iT_s ,and P is the optimized time length, while μ is the coefficient of linear combination.

The output of predictive model in PFC consists of two sections:

$$y_m(k) = y_1(k) + y_f(k) \tag{2}$$

Among them, $y_1(k)$ is the free response to the predictive model, which only depends on the controlled volume and output in a past period, and has nothing to do with the present and the future controlled volume. $y_f(k)$ is the controlled output of the model, which is the newly added model response after the present applying of the control function. This response represents itself as the piling up of the different basis function response $g_n(i)$. Since $g_n(i)$ can be calculated off line, $y_f(k)$ can be expressed as :

$$y_f(k+i) = \sum_{n=1}^{N} \mu_n g_n(i) \tag{3}$$

Owing to the disturbances of model unfitness and noise, there often exist some differences between the model output and the process output. The future difference is calculated by using following formula:

$$e(k+i) = y(k) - y_m(k) \tag{4}$$

During the predicative functional control, the purpose of rolling optimization is to look for a group of coefficients $\mu_1,\mu_2,\cdots,\mu_N$, so as to make the predictive output as close to the reference locus as possible. The reference locus often varies. For a stable system, the form of one stage exponential is usually used.

$$y_r(k+i) = c(k+i) - \beta^i(c(k) - y(k)) \tag{5}$$

Here, $c(k)$ is the given value for tracking. $\beta = e^{(-T_S/T_r)}$, T_s is the sample cycle, while T_r is the response time for 95% of the reference loci.

The standard formula for minimization is as follows:

$$\min J = \sum_{i=P_1}^{P_2} (y_r(k+i) - y_1(k+i) - \sum_{n=1}^{N} \mu_n g_n(i) - e(k+i))^2 \tag{6}$$

Through optimization, μ_n can be acquired, and subsequently the acquisition of the control value $u(k)$.

It can be seen that, by adopting the basis function's linear combination to acquire the control function, and a series methods like the predictive model, the feedback rectification, the rolling optimization, PFC reduces by a large volume the on-line calculation, and lowers the demand on the model precision at the same time.

4 Application of the Predictive Functional Control in the Network System

For the network system shown in Fig.2, if in its broad sense the mathematical models of the plant and the controller are $W(S)$ and $D(S)$ respectively, then the network system can be expressed in Fig.3.

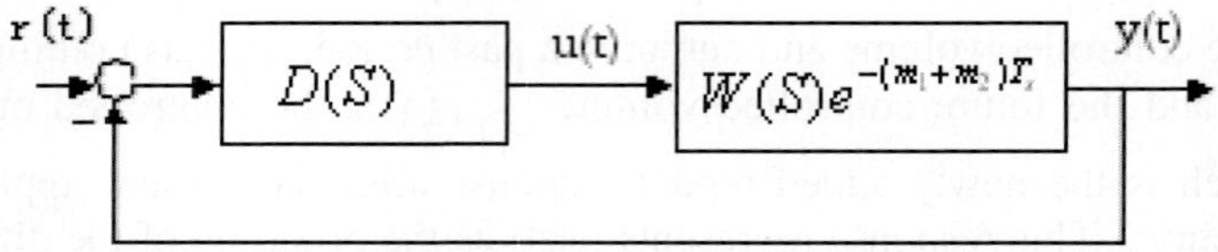

Fig. 3. The diagram of equivalent value network systems

Because of the complexity of the network system, the predictive functional control can be applied to make up for the unmatchedness between the predictive model and the actual plant resulted from the pure time delay and the change of the model.

Since each plant, in its broad sense, can be looked approximately as one order plant, we take the predictive model of the predictive functional control as:

$$W_m(s) = \frac{K_m}{T_m S + 1} e^{-T_{dm} S} \tag{7}$$

Here, the pure time delay $T_{dm} = (m_1 + m_2)T + \tau$. τ is the pure time delay of the plant.

In PFC, the controlled accuracy mainly depends on the selection of the basis functions. According to literature [13], when the set value is less than or equal to one threshold value θ in the controlled area, step function can be used for the control input. This condition can be met in our system. So the control input is:

$$u(k+i) = u(k) \quad i = 1,2,\cdots,P-1 \tag{8}$$

Let us first suppose $T_{dm} = 0$, which means there is no pure time delay. After having it distributed by adding a zero order hold, the following differential equation can be acquired:

$$y_m(k+1) = \alpha_m y_m(k) + K_m(1-\alpha_m)u(k) \tag{9}$$

where $\alpha_m = e^{(-T_s/T_m)}$

Through mathematic induction, we get:

$$y_m(k+P) = \alpha_m^{\ P} y_m(k) + K_m(1-\alpha_m^{\ P})u(k) \tag{10}$$

In order to get the control input, we make $\frac{\partial J}{\partial u(k)} = 0$. From formulae (4), (5), (6) and (9), the following control input at the moment of k can be got:

$$u(k) = \frac{c(k+P) - \beta^P c(k) - (1-\beta^P)y(k)}{K_m(1-\alpha_m^{\ P})} + \frac{y_m(k)}{K_m} \tag{11}$$

When $T_{dm} \neq 0$, according to Smith's predictive control, PFC still uses the mould $T_{dm} = 0$, while making correction to the plant output at the same time. Let $D=T_{dm}/T_s$, $y_{pav}(k)$ is the corrected output:

$$y_{pav}(k) = y(k) + y_m(k) - y_m(k-D) \tag{12}$$

$$e(k+p) = y_{pav}(k) - y_m(k) \tag{13}$$

Then putting into the time delay, the PFC output is as follows:

$$u(k) = \frac{c(k+P) - \beta^P c(k) - (1-\beta^P)y_{pav}(k)}{K_m(1-\alpha_m^{\ P})} + \frac{y_m(k)}{K_m} \tag{14}$$

In actual application, in order to increase the robustness of the system, the combined form of PFC with PID is used.

5 Examples of Simulink and Imitative Experiment

In order to verify the accuracy of PFC method put forward in this paper, we first proceeded to do the imitation research. The transfer function of the plant is illustrated in Fig.3. It may be seen that it belongs to the big pure time delay plant, which is hard to control effectively in the traditional way. Even if the Smith predicative estimation control is applied, the system tends to become unsteady once the model unmatchedness occurs. However, PFC can resolve all these problems satisfactorily, as is shown in the Simulink curves of Fig.4, among which a) is the model matched and b) is the model unmatched (the pure time delay has changed by 10%).

$$W(s) = \frac{220}{900S+1} e^{-1000s} \tag{15}$$

As to the networked control system, we may use the process control system to simulate and verify. We proceeded with the experiment by using the DCS (JX-300X) and industrial experiment devices that made up the big pure time delay system. In this system, the plant is made up together by an electricity heating boiler and the big time delay fitting. The hot water output from the boiler goes into the entrance connector of the time delay fitting. The water temperature at the time delay fitting output is a controlled variable (please refer to Fig.5). The temperature sensor applies PT100, and the measured signal is sent to the DCS input card directly.

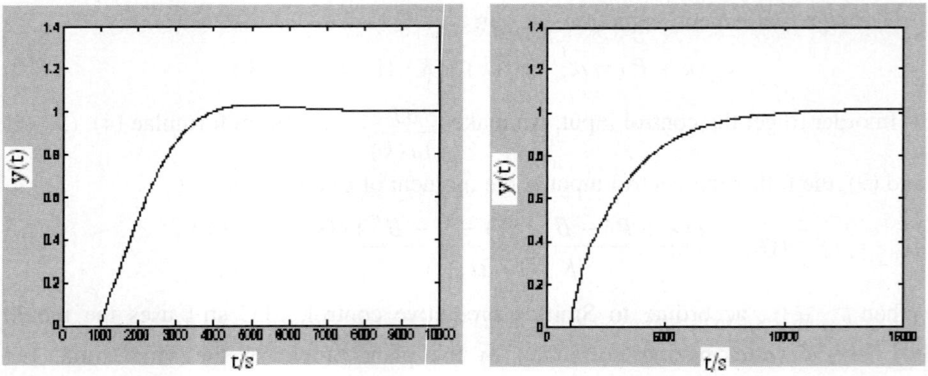

a) b)

Fig. 4. The simulation curves by Matlab. a) is the model matched and b) is the model unmatched (the pure time delay has changed by 10%).

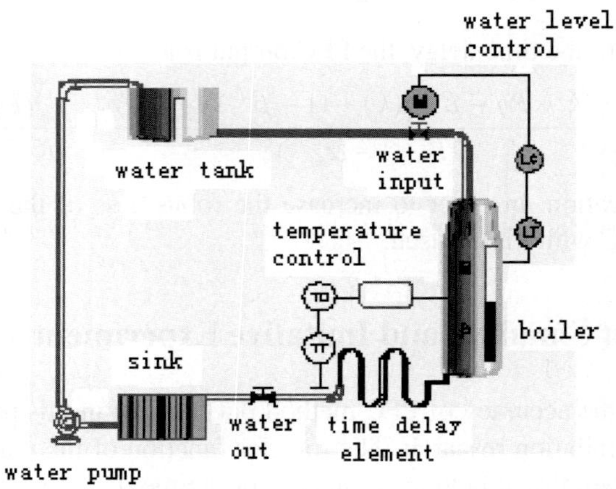

Fig. 5. The diagram of the imitation system

The actuator is the heater whose input signal is 4~20mA, which is delivered directly to the DCS analogy output card. The working principle of the system is that the water pump sends the water from the sink out up to the water tank, then the water in water tank flows into the boiler passing through the regulation valve. The water in the boiler is heated by the electricity heating device, and then returns to the sink after flowing through the big pure time delay fitting.

During the whole process, the output regulation valve is set at the hand operating mode with the opening fixed, and the water level is controlled by the input regulation valve. It can be seen that the temperature control of the pure time delay plant is realized by maintaining the dynamic balance of the liquid level.

Through setting up the engineering mould, the mathematical model of the plant obtained is as follows:

$$W(s) = \frac{0.45e^{-12s}}{598S+1} \bullet e^{-315s} = \frac{0.45}{598S+1} e^{-327S} \tag{16}$$

The control procedure is written in SCX language. Experiment curve is shown in Fig.6, with SV being the setting value for temperature, whose variety scope ranges between 30℃ and 55℃ in this experiment, and PV is the temperature value at the output of the big time delay fitting. As is shown in the diagram, the static state difference may be controlled within 3%, the overshoot is about 11%, and the whole system may be operated steadily.

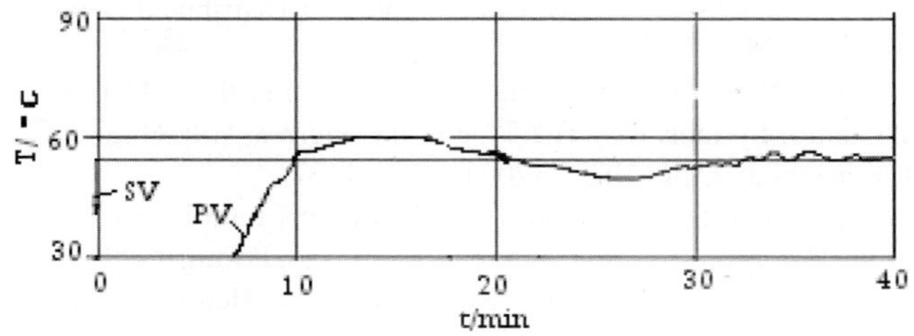

Fig. 6. The actual running curve

6 Conclusion

This paper puts forward the system equivalent value of the definite NCS and design of the controller for the plant based on predictive functional control. The results of Simulink and imitation experiment verify the accuracy and effectiveness of this method. When using the nonlinear predictive model or the predicative model based on the characteristic model of the controlled plant, this method may also be applied in the nonlinear system.

Acknowledgement

This project was supported by the Program for New Century Excellent Talents in University (NCET-04-0433) , the Doctoral Program Foundation of Science & Technology Special Project in University (20040280017) and the National Natural Science Fund(60474076) .

References

1. Hu Shousong, Zhu Qixin: Stochastic Optimal Control and Analysis of Stability of Networked Control Systems with Long Delay [J]. Automatica, 39(11) (2003) 1877–1884
2. Wei Z., Michael S.B., Philips S.M.: Stability of Networked Control Systems [J]. IEEE Control Systems Magazine, 121(1) (2001) 84–99
3. Walsh G. C., Beldiman O., Bushnell L.G.: Asymptotic Behavior of Nonlinear Networked Control Systems [J]. IEEE Trans. Automat. Cont, 146(4) (2001) 1093–1097

4. Nilsson J., Bernhardsson B., Wittenmark B.: Stochastic Analysis and Control of Real–time Systems with Random Time Delays [J], Automatica, 34(1) (1998) 57–64
5. Chan H., Ozguner U.: Closed-loop Control of Systems over A Communication Network with Queues [J]. Int. J. Control, 62(3). (1995) 493–510
6. Liou L-W., Ray A.: A Stochastic Regulator for Integrated Communication and Control Systems: Part I–Formulation of Control Law [J], Transactions of the ASME, 113(4) (1991)604–611
7. Liou L-W., Ray A.: A Stochastic Regulator for Integrated Communication and Control Systems: Part II- Numerical Analysis and Simulation [J].Transactions of the ASME, 113(4) (1991)612–619
8. Luck R., Ray A.: An Observer-based Compensator for Distributed Delays [J]. Automatica, 26(5) (1990) 903–908
9. Wu Jianguo, Zhu Qixin, Hu Shousong: The Output Feedback Control of Deterministic Networked Control Systems [A]. The 5th World Congress on Intelligent Control and Automation[C], Hangzhou , China, IEEE (2004) 1134–1137
10. Marti P., Villa R., Fuertes J.M, et al.:, On Real-time Control Tasks Schedulability, Proceedings of the European Control Conference[C], Porto, Portugal (2001)2227–2232
11. Richalet J., Rault A., Testud J. L.,et al.: Model Predictive Heuristic Control: Application to industrial processes[J].Automatics, 14(5) (1978) 413–428
12. Richalet J., Doss S. A. A. , Arber C,et al.: Predictive functional control: applications to fast and accurate robots[A]. Automatic Control 10th Triennial World Congress of IFAC[C],Oxford: Pergamon Press.(1988) 251–258
13. Wu Jianguo, Zhang Peijian: PVC Polymerization Kettle Temperature System Based on Double Model Predictive Functional Control[J]. Journal of Nanjing University of Science and Technology, 29(4) (2005)441–445

A Modified Fuzzy C-Means Algorithm for Association Rules Clustering*

Dechang Pi[1], Xiaolin Qin[2], and Peisen Yuan[3]

College of Information Science and Technology, Nanjing University of Aeronautics and Astronautics, Yudao Street 29, Nanjing, Jiangsu, 210016, China
[1] dechang_pi@hotmail.com
[2] qinxcs@nuaa.edu.cn
[3] nuaacs@126.com

Abstract. The Fuzzy C-Means (FCM) algorithm is commonly used for clustering. It is one of the problems in association rules mining that a great number of rules generated from the dataset makes it difficult to analyze and use. From the angle of knowledge management, a modified FCM algorithm is proposed and applied to association rules clustering, which partitions these rules into the given classes by the attribute's weight based on information gain for evaluating the attribute's importance. Experiment with the UCI dataset shows that this algorithm can efficiently cluster the association rules for a user to understand.

1 Introduction

Data mining, or the efficient discovery of interesting patterns from large collections of data, has been recognized as an important area of database research. The most commonly sought patterns are association rules. Intuitively, an association rule identifies a frequently occuring pattern of information in a database. When mining association rules from this type of nontransactional data, hundreds or thousands of rules corresponding to specific attribute values are discovered [1]. Rule is one manifestation of knowledge. We will classify these rules for the point of view of knowledge management for a user to understand. The cluster is formed by similar, "adjacent" association rules.

In practice it is very important that rules mined from a given database are understandable and useful to the user. Clustered association rules are helpful in reducing the large number of association rules that are typically computed by existing algorithms, thereby rendering the clustered rules much easier to interpret and visualize. A practical use of these clusters is to perform segmentation on large customer oriented databases. Brian Lent et al. [2] proposed a geometric algorithm for locating clusters in a two-dimensional grid, and their algorithm only clusters two-dimensional association rules. Literature [3] gives an overview of cluster analysis techniques from a data-mining point of view.

---

* This research is supported by the Aeronautical Science Foundation of China under Grant No. 02F52033 and the Hi-Tech Research Project of Jiangsu province under Grant No. BG2004005.

D.-S. Huang, K. Li, and G.W. Irwin (Eds.): ICIC 2006, LNAI 4114, pp. 1093 – 1103, 2006.

Fuzzy set has been applied to many fields including data mining. The clustering groups a sample set of vectors into K clusters via an appropriate similarity (or dissimilarity) criterion, such as distance from the center of the cluster.

Fuzzy clustering method is more precise in dealing with data simulation, and the results are easier to be understood and used. Therefore, research into fuzzy clustering method for knowledge is significant not only to theory, but also to application. Many fuzzy clustering methods have already been proposed and used in data mining. Fuzzy clustering with squared Minkowski distances was proposed in [4]. Fuzzy c-means method has been used in dynamic data mining [5]. Clustering algorithm based on self-similarity of the dataset can cluster transactional data with the standard definition of mathematical distance used in the K-means algorithm to represent dissimilarity among transactions [6]. Relative proximity was used to cluster a numerical dataset [7]. Clustering method can be used to detect anomalous behavior in audit data, and to select some "representative" rules but not a large number of rules for a user to understand [8, 9]. Clustering rules are necessary in merging multi-sources, which may contain conflicting knowledge. Otherwise the conflicting knowledge can make us illusive [10]. To the best of our knowledge, we have not found similar reports to cluster association rules based on FCM with attribute's weight for a user to expediently understand.

The rest of the paper is organized as follows. In section 2, we provide a brief description of association rule, and the relative researches on fuzzy clustering. In section 3, we propose a modified fuzzy C means algorithm, which we call FCM+. In section 4, we discuss the design of our experiment and the results returned; finally, in section 5, we present our conclusion and the further work.

2 Background

Association rules are used to discover the relationships, and potential associations, of items or attributes among huge amounts of data. These rules can be effective in uncovering the unknown relationships, providing results that can be the basis of forecast and decision. They have proven to be very useful. The application and development about association rules is a popular topic in data mining.

2.1 Review of Association Rules and the Classical Mining Algorithm

The early data mining method for association rules use the support-confidence framework established by Agrawal et al. [1]. They proposed a model to discover meaningful itemsets and construct association rules for market analysis.

Let I={i_1, i_2, i_3,…,i_N} be a set of N distinct literals, called items. In general, a set of items is called an itemset. The number of items in an itemset is the length of an itemset. Itemset of length k is referred to as a k-itemset. Let D be a set of variable length transactions, where each transaction T is a set of items such that T⊆I. Associated with each transaction is a unique identifier, which shall be referred to as its TID. |D| is the cardinality of database D. A transaction T is said to support an itemset X, where $X \subseteq$I, if it contains all items of X, i.e. X⊆T. The fraction of the transactions in D that support X is called the support of X, denoted Support(X). An itemset is large if its support is above some user-specified minimum support threshold, denoted MinSup. An association rule is an implication of the form r: $X \Rightarrow Y$, where $X \subset I$, $Y \subset I$, and $X \cap Y = \varnothing$. The support for rule r is defined as Support($X \cup Y$). A confidence factor defined as support($X \cup Y$)/support(X), is used to evaluate the strength of such association rules.

The process of Apriori mining association rule algorithm makes multiple passes over the database D to build candidate itemsets, and then create large itemsets. In the kth level, the algorithm finds all large k-itemsets. Denoting L_k is the set of all large k-itemsets, and C_k is the set of candidate k-itemsets by obtaining from L_{k-1}, that is, potentially large k-itemsets. For each transaction in D, the candidates in C_k also contained in the transaction are determined and their support is increased by $1/|D|$. At the end of scanning, if their supports are greater than, or equal to, the user-specified minimum support (MinSup), the candidate k-itemsets immediately become the large k-itemsets. Meanwhile, it will generate a large number of the candidate itemsets that need to be contrasted with the whole database level by level in the process of mining the association rules. Therefore, performance is dramatically affected, as the database is repeatedly scanned. The most time-consuming part of the algorithm is to discover large itemsets while the generation of association rules given the large itemsets is straightforward enough. Many researchers have tried to improve its efficiency from different angles, and decreased the number of database scans and the number of candidate itemsets. [18].

A common problem in association rule mining is that a large number of rules are generated from the datasets, which makes it difficult for users to analyze and make use of the rules. Solutions have been proposed to overcome this problem, which include constraint-based data mining, post-pruning rules, grouping rules [11], dynamic pruning [12] and unexpected patterns based on user's beliefs [13].

2.2 Related Research on Fuzzy Clustering

Currently, most of the commercial clustering systems are based on the boolean logic model. They assume that a user's requirements can precisely be characterized by the terms. However, this assumption is inappropriate due to the fact that the user's requirements may contain fuzziness. The reason for the fuzziness contained in the user's requirements is that the user may not know much about the subject he/she is clustering or may not be familiar with the clustering system. Since fuzzy set technology can be used to describe imprecise or fuzzy information, many researchers have applied the fuzzy set technology to many systems including clustering [11,14].

The objective of fuzzy clustering methods is to divide a given dataset into a set of clusters based on similarity [9]. In classical cluster analysis each datum must be assigned to exactly one cluster. Fuzzy cluster analysis relaxes this requirement by allowing membership degrees, thus offering the opportunity to deal with data that belong to more than one cluster at the same time. Most fuzzy clustering algorithms are objective function based: they determine an optimal classification by minimizing an objective function. In objective function based clustering usually each cluster is represented by a cluster prototype. This prototype consists of a cluster center and maybe some additional information about the size and the shape of the cluster. The cluster center is an instantiation of the attributes used to describe the domain, just as the data points in the dataset to divide. However, the cluster center is computed by the clustering algorithm and may or may not appear in the dataset. The size and shape parameters determine the extension of the cluster in different directions of the underlying domain.

The degrees of membership to which a given data point belongs to the different clusters are computed from the distances of the data point to the cluster centers. The closer a data point lies to the center of a cluster, the higher is its degree of membership to this cluster. Hence, the problem to divide a dataset X={ x_1, …, x_n } into c clusters can be stated as the task to minimize the distances of the data points to the cluster centers.

3 An Improved Fuzzy C Means Clustering Algorithm

3.1 The FCM Algorithm

Clustering is the process of grouping some vectors into classes. Let $\{x^{(m)}$: m = 1,…,M} be a set of M vectors. Each vector $x^{(m)} = (x_1^{(m)}, \ldots, x_N^{(m)})$ has N components. The process of clustering is to assign the M vectors into K clusters $\{c^{(k)}$: k = 1, …, K} usually by the minimum distance principle, such as Euclid distance, Minkowski distance and Hamming distance.

The K-means algorithm assigns vectors to clusters by the minimum distance assignment principle, which assigns a new vector $x^{(m)}$ to the cluster $c^{(k)}$ such that the distance from $x^{(m)}$ to the center of $c^{(k)}$ is the minimum over all K clusters. The basic K-means algorithm is as follows [9,11]:

(1) Randomly select the initial centers.
(2) Each object is assigned to the cluster where the distance from its center to the object is minimum.
(3) Re-calculate the centers.
(4) Repeat steps 2 and 3 until there is not change in the centers.

The advantages of the method are its simplicity, efficiency, and self-organization. It is used as initial process in many other algorithms. The disadvantage of this algorithm is that k must be provided and this algorithm is linearly separating and maybe resulting in inconsistent clustering and local minima.

The FCM algorithm is an iterative clustering method that used to partition a data set and it has successfully been applied to a wide variety of clustering problems [15]. The objective of FCM segmentation is to compute the cluster centers and generate the class membership matrix [16]. Let $X = \{x_1, x_2, \ldots x_N\}$ be a set of *N* objects. Let $d(x_j, x_i)$ be the distance or dissimilarity between objects x_i and x_j. Let $V = \{v_1, v_2, \ldots, v_K\}$, each v_c be the mean of the *c-th* cluster. Let $d(v_c, x_i)$ be the distance or dissimilarity between the object x_i and the mean of the cluster that it belongs to.

The fuzzy clustering partitions these objects into K overlapped clusters based on a computed minimizer of the fuzzy within-group least squares functional:

$$J_m(U,V)=\sum_{c=1}^{K}\sum_{i=1}^{N}U^m(v_c,x_i)d(v_c,x_i) \tag{1}$$

Minimization is performed over all $v_c \in V$. $U(v_c,x_i)$ is the membership function for object x_i belonging to cluster v_c. To optimize (1), one can alternate between optimization of $\bar{J}_m(U \mid V^*)$ over U with V^* fixed and $\bar{J}_m(V \mid U^*)$ over V with U^* fixed, producing a sequence $\{U^{(p)},V^{(p)}\}$. Specifically, the p+1st value of $V=\{v_1,v_2,...,v_K\}$ is computed using the p-th value of U in the right-hand side of:

$$v_c^{(p+1)}=\frac{\sum_{i=1}^{N}x_i*[U^{(p)}(v_c^{(p)},x_i)]^m}{\sum_{i=1}^{N}[U^{(p)}(v_c^{(p)},x_i)]^m} \tag{2}$$

The updated p+1st value of V is then used to calculate the p+1st value of U via:

$$U^{(p+1)}(v_k^{(p+1)},x_i)=\frac{d(x_i,v_k^{(p+1)})^{-1/(m-1)}}{\sum_{c=1}^{K}d(x_i,v_c^{(p+1)})^{-1/(m-1)}} \tag{3}$$

$m\in(1,+\infty)$ is the so-called "fuzzifier".

Two often used dissimilarity measures between two objects (x_j,x_i), as well as between an object and the mean (v_c,x_i) are the LP norm distance:

$$d(v_c,x_i)=\left(\sum_{j=1}^{N}|x_{i,j}-v_{c,j}|^p\right)^{1/p} \tag{4}$$

where $p\in[1,+\infty)$ ($p=2$ and $p=1$ lead to the Euclidean and Manhattan distances respectively); and cosine-based dissimilarity: $d(v_c,x_i)=e^{-Sim(v_c,x_i)}$ where $Sim(v_c,x_i)$ is defined as:

$$Sim(v_c,x_i)=\frac{\sum_{j=1}^{S}x_{i,j}*v_{c,j}}{\sqrt{\sum_{j=1}^{S}x_{i,j}^2\sum_{j=1}^{S}v_{c,j}^2}} \tag{5}$$

The "K-center" method is used for initialization. The first candidate is picked up as the mean over all the items in X, and each successive one is selected in such a way that each one is most dissimilar to all the means that have already been picked.

3.2 Attribute's Importance Analysis Based on Information Gain

A validation method based on information gain (IG) is devised for assessing the qualities of the clustering results. It is widely used in the classification problem [17]. Explicitly, ID3 and C4.5 used IG measurement to select the test attribute. The higher the information gain value of an attribute, to improve the quality of a clustering a higher weight or emphases should be placed on the corresponding attribute when constructing the distance metric used in the clustering.

Let *D* be a set of training samples, where the class label of each sample is known. Let *D* contains s_i samples of each class C_i, for i=1,…,m. An arbitrary sample belongs to class C_i with a probability s_i/s, where s is the cardinality of *D*. An attribute *A* with values $\{a_1, a_2,..,a_v\}$ can be used to partition *D* into the subsets $\{s_1, s_2,\ldots,s_v\}$, where s_j contains those samples in *D* that have value a_j of *A*. The expected information based on this partitioning by *A* is known as the entropy of *A*. It is the weighted average:

$$E(A)=\sum_{j=1}^{v}\frac{s_{1j}+\ldots+s_{mj}}{s}I(s_{1j},\ldots,s_{mj}) \tag{6}$$

where

$$I(s_{1j},\ldots,s_{mj})= -\sum_{i=1}^{m}\frac{s_i}{s}\log_2\frac{s_i}{s} \tag{7}$$

The information gain obtained by this partitioning on *A* is defined by

$$Gain(A)=I(s_{1j},\ldots,s_{mj})- E(A) \tag{8}$$

We can compute the information gain for each of the attributes defining the sample in *D*. The attribute with the highest IG is considered the most discriminating attribute of the given set. The larger an information gain value, the better the clustering quality is. By computing the IG for each attribute, we can obtain a ranking of the attributes. The ranking can be used for importance analysis to set attributes weights in the relevant IG order. The weight w_i for attribute A_i is set by

$$w_i = IG_i \Big/ \sum_{i=1}^{M} IG_i \tag{9}$$

where M is the number of attributes. Obviously these weights meet the restriction

$$\sum_{i=1}^{M} w_i = 1 \tag{10}$$

3.3 The Modified FCM Algorithm

The initial matrix of FCM algorithm depicts the degrees of membership to which a given object belongs to the different clusters. So this algorithm cannot cluster association rules for it does not consider the "importance" of the attributes.

Let $X=\{X_1, \ldots, X_k, \ldots, X_n\}$, and each X_k has *m* attributes, $X_k=\{x_{k1}, \ldots, x_{km}\}$. Then $X_{n\times m} = (x_{kj})_{n\times m}$.

Step 1: Transform the eigenvalue of $x_{ij}\in X_i$ into [0, 1], where $1\le i\le n$, $1\le j\le m$
Step 2: Assign a weight *w* to each attribute, where w_i denotes importance of the corresponding attribute. Each weight *w* can be obtained by the method related in section 3.2.

$$W=(w_1, w_2, \ldots, w_m)' \tag{11}$$

Step 3: Let Y=X

$$.W=(Y_1, Y_2, \ldots, Y_n)' \tag{12}$$

Now the relative importance of the samples has been gotten.

Step 4: Set the distribution for Y based on the practical needs.

For example, suppose Y meets the even-distribution.

(1) Let max=MAX(Y_i), min=MIN(Y_i) where i∈[1, n]

(2) Equably part the whole of min to max into c small sections, and the median for each section is

$$a_j = \text{min}+(\text{max-min})/c\times(j\text{-}0.5),\ j\in[1,\ c] \tag{13}$$

Step 5: Set the distribution for each clustering center based on the practical needs. Assume that each section satisfies the normal distribution with the centroid being a_i, i∈[1, c].

$$A(x) = e^{(-k\times(x-a_i))^2} \tag{14}$$

Where *e* is the exponential function, and k=1 or 2.

Now the initial membership degree matrix is obtained with the following code.

```
for ( i=1 ;  i<=N; i++)
    //Compute the membership degree with the cluster
    //center being aj for each sample
    for ( j=1; j<=C; j++)
       u0[i,j]=exp(-1*( Yi - aj ))^2  //where  k=1
```

Some explications,

(1) Step 4 assumes that the samples meet the even-distribution. But some idiographic instances may not satisfy the requirement. In this case some appropriate distribution function must be selected for meeting the practical needs.

(2) Step 5 assumes that the samples of each section meet the normal distribution. This presumption must be reconsidered based on the fact.

The initial partition matrix u_0 has gotten after the above five steps are carried out. The rest is just like the FCM algorithm and will not be related any more.

4 Experiment

As C++ STL is powerful, this fuzzy clustering algorithm is implemented with C++ STL, compiled with Microsoft Visual C++ 6.0. We use Apriori algorithm to mine association rules from the postoperative-patient-dataset with different support and confidence. This dataset can be obtained from UCI Machine Learning Database Repository at http://www.ics.uci.edu/~mlearn/ MLRepository.html, and it contains 90 instances and 9 attributes (The last one is the decision attribute). The decision attributes can take on values *I*, *S*, or *A*. There are 2 instances in class *I*, 24 instances in class *S* and 64 instances in class *A*.

The classification task of this database is to determine where patients in a postoperative recovery area should be sent to next. Because hypothermia is a significant concern after surgery, the attributes correspond roughly to body temperature measurements. Table 1 shows the numbers of association rules generated from the dataset with different support and confidence.

Table 1. Numbers of association rules mined from the postoperative-patient-dataset

MinConf \ MinSup	0.6	0.5	0.4	0.3
0.9	2	3	8	7
0.8	2	3	8	7
0.7	4	11	23	26
0.6	4	11	35	37
0.5	4	12	38	45

Table 2. Information gain and the relative weight for of each attribute

Order	Attribute Name	IG	Weight
1	L-CORE	0.010802	0.0538662
2	L-SURF	0.0293591	0.146404
3	L-O2	0.0114602	0.0571484
4	L-BP	0.0300606	0.149903
5	SURF-STBL	0.0118933	0.0593081
6	CORE-STBL	0.0416893	0.207891
7	BP-STBL	0.0325222	0.162178
8	COMFORT	0.0327474	0.163301

If the thresholds for support and confidence are 0.4 and 0.5 respectively, 38 rules are found. The following four rules are examples, and obviously they should be clustered into one class.

1. *if* COMFORT = 10 *then* L-BP is mid AND CORE-STBL is stable
   support = 0.411111 confidence = 0.569231
2. *if* COMFORT = 10 *then* CORE-STBL is stable
   support = 0.677778 confidence = 0.938462

3. *if* COMFORT = 10 *then* CORE-STBL is stable AND decision ADM-DECS=A
support = 0.511111 confidence = 0.707692
4. *if* COMFORT = 10 AND decision ADM-DECS = A *then* CORE-STBL is stable
support = 0.511111 confidence = 0.958333

The training dataset is selected randomly with a ratio about 20% from each class *S*, *A* and *I* in the postoperative-patient-dataset. It includes 5 instances of class *S*, 14 instances of class *A* and one instance of class *I*. The weight w_i for attribute A_i is set by

$$w_i = IG_i \Big/ \sum_{i=1}^{8} IG_i \quad (15)$$

Table 2 depicts the IG and relative weights for each attribute.

We use this algorithm to cluster the above 16 rule-sets as shown in Table 1 and get the clustering results as shown in Fig. 1. For example, with the thresholds of support and confidence being 0.4 and 0.9, the numbers of the association rules clustering is 4.

5 Conclusions and Further Work

Usually the number of association rules found by data mining algorithms is large. Although these rules have high supports and confidences, they are often pertained to some aspects and have higher similarity. From the angle of knowledge management, an improved FCM algorithm is proposed to cluster the association rules. Using this method we can categorize the association rules; hence they can be easily understood and used.

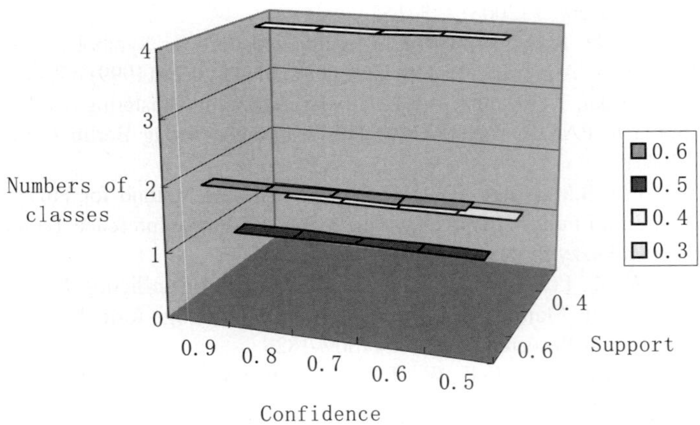

Fig. 1. He association rules discovered from the postoperative-patient-dataset

We use Apriori algorithm to mine association rules from the postoperative-patient-data provided by the UCI, and employ our algorithm to cluster these found rules. Experiment shows that this algorithm is efficient in clustering the association rules.

What we need to explain is the differences between FCM+ and FCM. Firstly, The angles of consideration for these two algorithms are different. FCM+ mainly considers the relative importance of attributes in the association rules, and it can cluster the rules based on the weight set by the validation model based on information gain to assess the importance of the attributes in the tested dataset. But FCM offers the membership degree to deal with samples that belong to more than one cluster at the same time, and it cannot cluster the association rules. Secondly, FCM+ is more maneuverable than old FCM. New algorithm needs little parameters compared *m* weights for the attributes with a $C \times N$ membership degree matrix needed by FCM.

We occasionally find an interesting topic during the experiments. If the weights are not offered by the information gain but are set randomly by the user, we find that the clustering results are error. This is a new question that needs to be further considered.

References

1. Agrawal, R., Srikant, R.: Fast Algorithm for Mining Association Rules in Large Databases. Proceedings of 1994 International Conference on VLDB, (1994) 487–499
2. Brian, L., Arun, N., Jennifer, W.: Clustering Association Rules. Proceedings of the Thirteenth International Conference on Data Engineering, (1997) 220-231
3. Grabmeler, J., Rudolph, R.: Techniques of Cluster Algorithms in Data Mining. Data Mining and Knowledge Discovery, 6 (2002) 303–360
4. Groenen, P. J.F., Jajuga, K.: Fuzzy Clustering with Squared Minkowski Distances. Fuzzy Sets and Systems, 120 (2001) 227-237
5. Fernando, C., Richard, W.: A Methodology for Dynamic Data Mining Based On Fuzzy Clustering. Fuzzy Sets and Systems 150 (2005) 267–284
6. Daniel, B., Chen, P.: Using Self-Similarity to Cluster Large Data Sets. Data Mining and Knowledge Discovery, 7 (2003) 123–152
7. Ravi, T.V., Gowda, K.C.: An FCM Clustering Procedure for Symbolic Objects using A Distributed Genetic Algorithm. Pattern Recognition Letters, 20 (1999) 659-666
8. Hirano, S., Shusaku, T.: Dealing with Relative Similarity in Clustering: An Indiscernibility Based Approach. PAKDD 2003, LNAI 2637, Springer-Verlag Berlin Heidelberg 2003, (2003) 513–518
9. Horng, Y., Chen, S.M., Chang, Y.C., Lee, C.H.: A New Method for Fuzzy Information Retrieval Based on Fuzzy Hierarchical Clustering and Fuzzy Inference Techniques. IEEE Transactions on Fuzzy Systems, 13 (2005) 216-227
10. Christopher, W. Z., Loren, P. R.: Automated Merging of Conflicting Knowledge Bases, using A Consistent, Majority-rule Approach with Knowledge-form Maintenance. Computers & Operations Research, 32 (2005) 1809–1829
11. Bezdek, J.C., Ehrlich, R., Full, W.: FCM: The Fuzzy C-means Clustering Algorithm. Computers and Geosciences, 10 (1984) 191-203
12. Pi, D.C., Qin, X.L. Gu, W.F., Cheng, R.: STBAR: A More Efficient Algorithm for Association Rule Mining. The Fourth International Conference on Machine Learning and Cybernetics, (2005) 1529-1533
13. Padmanabhan, B., Alexander, T.: Unexpectedness as a Measure of Interestingness in Knowledge Discovery. Decision Support Systems, 27, (1999) 303–318
14. Du, X.Y., Sachiko, S., Naohiro, I.: A Distance-Based Clustering and Selection of Association Rules on Numeric Attributes. RSFDGrC'99, LNAI 1711, Springer-Verlag Berlin Heidelberg 1999, (1999) 423–433

15. Cao, G.H., Song, D.W., Peter, B.: Fuzzy K-Means Clustering on a High Dimensional Semantic Space. APWeb 2004, LNCS 3007 (2004) 907–911
16. Nikhil, R.P., James, C.B.: On Cluster Validity for the Fuzzy c-Means Mode. IEEE Transactions on Fuzzy Systems, 3 (1995) 370-379
17. Han, J., Micheline, K.: Data Mining Concepts and Techniques. Morgan Kaufmman Publishers.2000
18. Tsay, Y.J., Chiang, J.Y.: CBAR: An Efficient Method for Mining Association Rules. Knowledge-Based Systems 18 (2005) 99–105

Adaptive Fuzzy Control of Lateral Semi-active Suspension for High-Speed Railway Vehicle

Jianwei Yang, Jie Li, and Yanping Du

School of Machine-electricity Engineering, Taiyuan University of Science and Technology
Taiyuan Shanxi Province 030024, China
railyjw@163.com

Abstract. In order to meet the require of high speed and comfort and low producing cost, semi-active suspension for high-speed railway vehicle is adopted to control the vibration of car body. But accurate mathematic model of vehicle dynamics system is difficult to establish for the particularity of wheel-rail interaction and non-linear of system, and sky damper control needs the absolute speed of car body that its exact value is difficult to obtain. So adaptive fuzzy control method based on the acceleration feedback is put forward in the paper. The method which can modify automatically the scaling factor and control rules according to the acceleration and its change rate of car body is simulated by using ADAMS and MATLAB software. The simulation results show that the method can attenuate the vibration of car body and improve the comfort and stationarity effectively.

1 Introduction

Increasing the speed of train is an effective way to improving railway transportation competition. But when the speed is increased, the passenger will feel less comfortable than before. In order to increase the speed and comfort simultaneously, the control technology of car body vibration should be adopted. Among all vibration control technology, the semi-active suspension is a compromise between the passive and the active suspension, and it is an ideal way for performance improvements and simplicity of design implementations. The semi-active damper is time-varying, controllable, and adjustable. However, the semi-active damper is considered a passive component because it can only dissipate energy (excepting a small valve actuating force). So the semi-active suspension system can be an effective countermeasure to improve the vehicle vibration and riding comfort. To the vehicle, the accurate mathematics model is difficult to establish because of the uncertainty of wheel-rail interactions and strong non-linear and time-varying parameter of vehicle in a given area, which have limited the application of modern control theory in the practical vehicle suspension system[1~4].

Sky damper control decreases the vibration acceleration of car body by the control force which is proportion to the absolute velocity, but the absolute velocity is difficult to measure, and it is achieved by integrated the acceleration tested by velocity sensor generally. So the sensor error and system noise can generate the error of absolute velocity then effect the damping performance.

D.-S. Huang, K. Li, and G.W. Irwin (Eds.): ICIC 2006, LNAI 4114, pp. 1104 – 1115, 2006.

To solve the above problem, adaptive fuzzy control method based on the acceleration feedback is put forward in the paper. The dynamic model established by ADAMS/RAIL software is used to simulate the dynamic performance. Then the simulation results transmit to MATLAB software, and the adaptive fuzzy control algorithm developed by MATLAB software will work out the control force real-time and send the force value to the vehicle model. The method combines the MATLAB software and ADAMS/RAIL software to simulate, and it can modify automatically the scaling factor and control rules according to the acceleration and its change rate of car body, and make the fuzzy controller have the self-adaptive ability to the variable of vehicle running condition.

2 Semi-active Suspension Systems

2.1 Semi-active Suspension Dynamics Model

Vibration response of vehicle running in line includes vertical vibration and lateral vibration, which is produced by track irregularity. To lateral vibration, wheel set is excited by direction irregularity and level irregularity. 300km/h vehicle dynamics model to control the lateral vibration of 17-freedom motor vehicle is established in the paper, which is shown in Fig.1. The 17-freedom of the vehicle is:

Lateral and yawing of wheel set: $(Y_{wi}, \psi_{wi}), i=1,2,3,4,$

Lateral, rolling and yawing of bogie frame: $(Y_{tj}, \phi_{tj}, \psi_{tj}), j=1,2$,

Lateral, rolling and yawing of car body: (Y_c, ϕ_c, ψ_c).

In the above model, secondary lateral damper is controlled damper, and the change of damp is expressed by the change of control force. Vibration differential equation contained control item is:

$$[M]\{\ddot{q}\}+[C_0]\{\dot{q}\}+[K]\{q\}+[B']\{u\}=\{G\{w,\dot{w}\}\} \quad . \tag{1}$$

Where, $[M],[C_0],[K]$ is mass matrix, basic damping matrix and stiffness matrix separately. $[B']$ is control input matrix. $\{q\}$ is freedom vector. $\{G\{w,\dot{w}\}\}$ is exciting vector. w is track irregularity input vector. $\{u\}$ is control input vector.

And

$$\{q\}=\left[Y_{wi}, \psi_{wi}, Y_{tj}, \phi_{tj}, \psi_{tj}, Y_c, \phi_c, \psi_c\right], i=1,2,3,4; j=1,2 \,. \tag{2}$$

$$\{u\}=[F_1, F_2]^T \,. \tag{3}$$

$$[B']=\begin{bmatrix} 0 & \cdots & 1 & 0 & -h_5 & 0 & 0 & 0 & -1 & -h_2 & -l \\ 0 & \cdots & 0 & 1 & 0 & -h_5 & 0 & 0 & -1 & -h_2 & l \end{bmatrix}_{2\times 17}^{T} \,. \tag{4}$$

In the above formula, F_1, F_2 is the attenuation force provided by controllable damper between front and rear bogie and car body. h_5 is height between controllable damper (centre) and bogie mass-centre, h_2 is height between controllable damper(centre) and car body mass-centre, l is a half distance between bogie centres.

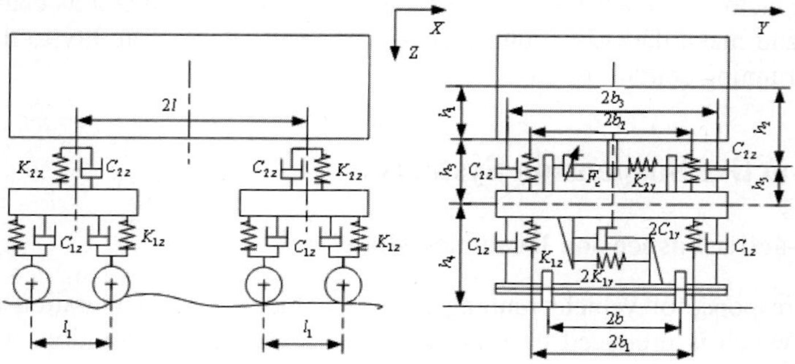

Fig. 1. Lateral vehicle dynamics model based on semi-active suspension

K_{1z} ,vertical stiffness of axle spring, K_{1y} effective stiffness of yaw damper, C_{1z} Vertical damping coefficient of axle damper, C_{1y} damping coefficient of yaw damper, K_{2z} vertical stiffness of air spring, K_{2y} Horizontal stiffness of air spring, C_{2z} vertical damping coefficient of secondary damper, C_{2y} Horizontal damping coefficient of secondary damper, l_1 Rigid wheel base of bogie, b_1 distance between bogie mass-center and axle spring, b_2 distance between mass-center and air spring 、 b_3 distance between car body mass-center and secondary vertical damper 、 b rolling distance between right wheel and left wheel, h_1 height between air spring(top)and car body mass-center, h_4 height of bogie mass-center, h_3 height between air spring(top)and bogie mass-center

2.2 Control System of Semi-active Suspension

Control system of semi-active suspension can be divided into signal collection part, signal process and decision part and execute part, its concrete structure is shown in Fig.2. DSP technology possesses good real-time quality, rapid operation speed, so the control board has been developed to meet the real-time quality of the test and control system of semi-active suspension based on DSP technology. The execute part is high-speed on-off valve damper, its structural design can be shown in reference [5, 6].

Control board is composed of signal collection part (except sensor) and signal process and decision part. Signal process and decision part is the system hardcore in the whole system, and it is the base for constructing the system. Decision part is adaptive fuzzy controller.

Concrete physics realizing process of semi-active suspension is described as follows. Firstly, Measure the yawing and rolling acceleration by acceleration sensor. Secondly, Process the data through the signal collection part of control board (including signal

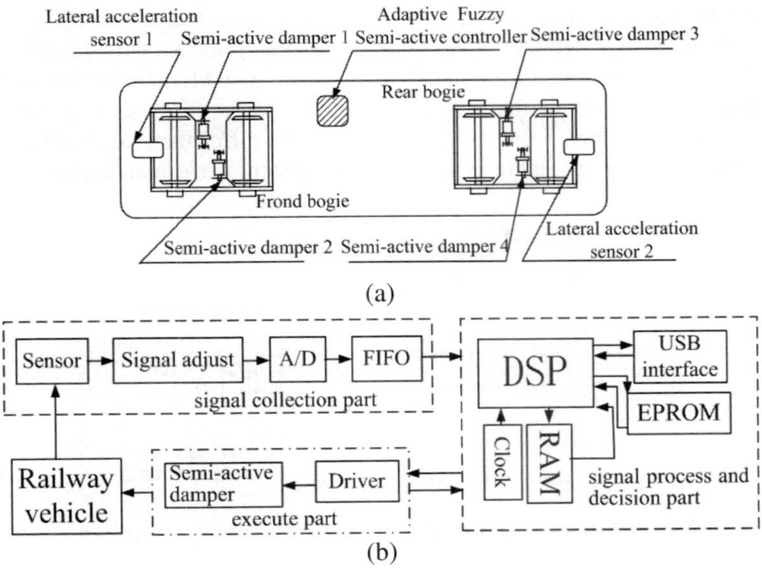

Fig. 2. system of semi-active suspension

filtration and data), then deliver to signal process and decision part. Thirdly, calculate the controlled quantity by self-adapting algorithm to decide the state of damper, which is to attenuate the lateral vibration of vehicle by changing the damp value of damper[7].

3 Design of Control System

The variable of vibration acceleration of car body is owed to the change of track spectrum of vehicle running line and the change of velocity and the car body mass at the same track spectrum. So the input universe of normal fuzzy controller is difficult to define exactly, and it is defined approximately by the regular change range. But the oversize or little size universe will affect the control purpose seriously. The information shows that the acceleration input of fuzzy controller will be gone beyond the range of input universe when the vibration improves for the change of velocity if the fixed scaling factor is adopted at the same line, in this condition, only the single rule excited by PB or NB may act in the fuzzy input set, which makes the suspension damp too little or too large so that the control effect may be baddish.

To conquer the disadvantage, a fuzzy controller that can adapt the self parameter or control rule according to the motion performance is hoped to design to improve the system capacity and adapt the change environment and ensure the control effect. This controller is named as adaptive fuzzy controller. The adaptive fuzzy control method based on the acceleration feedback is put forward in the paper. The controller diagram is shown in Fig.2. Seen from the figure, comparing with general fuzzy controller, the controller has added three functions module: (1) Module to measure system performance, it can calculate the data to characterize the system performance according to lateral acceleration of car body. (2) Module to adjust the scaling factor and scale factor, it can adjust on-line the scaling factor and scale factor according to lateral acceleration and its change rate of car body, which can improve the dynamic response index of system to eliminate the steady-state error. (3) Module to find optimizing control rule, it can improve the adaptive capacity of control system by adapting the weight number of the error and its change rate in the differ interval to obtain a group of optimum parameter and achieve the minimum system performance index.

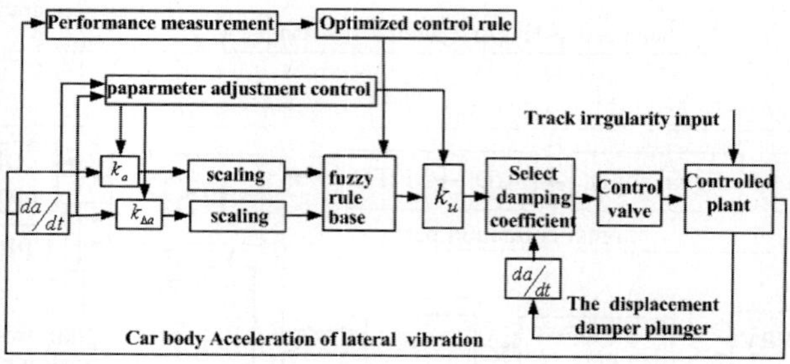

Fig. 3. Adaptive fuzzy controller based on acceleration feedback

The input of fuzzy controller is the lateral acceleration signal of car body and its change rate, and then the needed control force is computed to improve the vibration performance of vehicle. The rule of fuzzy control is defined by the stationarity rule control to assure the root-mean-square value of accelerate is a less value. Generally, the rule of fuzzy control is inference rule got by experience and they are two-dimension. The fuzzy set of input and output language variable can be divided to seven grade, they are NB、NM、NS、ZO、PS、PM、PB separately, and there are 49 control rules.

Table 1. Fuzzy control rule

a	det a						
	NB	NM	NS	ZE	PS	PM	PB
NB	NM	NS	NS	NS	ZE	PS	PM
NM	NM	NM	NM	NS	PS	PM	PM
NS	NB	NM	NM	NS	PM	PB	PB
ZE	NB	NB	NM	ZE	PM	PB	PB
PS	NB	NB	NM	PS	PM	PM	PB
PM	NM	NM	NS	PS	PM	PM	PM
PB	NM	NS	ZE	PS	PS	PS	PM

Using the language variable, control rule R_i can be described as

$$R_i : \text{if } \alpha_1 \text{ is } A_{i1} \text{ and } \alpha_2 \text{ is } A_{i2} \text{ then } \beta \text{ is } B_i, i = 1 \sim N. \tag{5}$$

α_1 、α_2 and β are input variable and output variable separately, and correspond universe are [-4 4]、[-4 4] and [-3 3], and A_{i1} , A_{i2} and B_i are fuzzy set of input variable and output variable. The membership grade function of input variable and output variable are $\mu_{Ai1}(\alpha)$ 、 $\mu_{Ai2}(\alpha)$ and $\mu_{Bi}(\beta)$, the appropriate membership grade function is needed (triangle membership grade function is adopted in the paper).

$$\alpha_1 = ak_a, \alpha_2 = \Delta ak_{\Delta a}, \Delta a = {\left[a(n)-a(n-1)\right]}\Big/{\Delta t}. \tag{6}$$

Where, k_a and $k_{\Delta a}$ are scaling factor, Δt is sampling time interval. k_a and $k_{\Delta a}$ are computed by the maximal value of acceleration (a)and the maximal value of acceleration change rate (Δa) in the differ speed state of passive suspension. When the work station is changed in the running process, the scaling factor should be adjusted on-line according to the lateral vibration acceleration of car body and its change rate. If α_1^0 , α_2^0 are given, the relevance weights of each rule can be solved,

$$\varpi_i = \mu_{Ai_1}(\alpha_1^0) \wedge \mu_{Ai_2}(\alpha_2^0) \qquad i = 1 \sim n. \tag{7}$$

Then the output membership grade function is

$$\mu_B(\beta) = \varpi_1\mu_{B1}(\beta) \vee \varpi_2\mu_{B2}(\beta) \vee \ldots \vee \varpi_N\mu_{BN}(\beta). \tag{8}$$

Output value β of fuzzy controller is

$$\beta = c\alpha_1 + (1-c)\alpha_2. \tag{9}$$

Where, α_1 and α_2 are separately the input of fuzzy controller, they signify lateral vibration acceleration and its difference of car body. c is weight number, which is real number between 0 and 1, its size directly signify weighting between lateral vibration acceleration and its difference. In course of actual control, the weighting requirement between lateral vibration acceleration and its difference of control rule is different. In order to improve control performance and meet the different request for adjusting weight number in different controlling state, the new fuzzy controller is designed by modifying control rule, and the modified control rule is [8]

$$\beta = \begin{cases} c_0\alpha_1 + (1-c_0)\alpha_2 & \alpha_1 = 0 \\ c_1\alpha_1 + (1-c_1)\alpha_2 & \alpha_1 = \pm 1 \\ c_2\alpha_1 + (1-c_2)\alpha_2 & \alpha_1 = \pm 2 \end{cases}. \tag{10}$$

Where, weight number $c_0, c_1, c_2 \in [0，1]$, and $c_0 < c_1 < c_2$.

In order to change the c_0, c_1, c_2 more scientifically, a Self-optimizing fuzzy controller is adopted, which can search the optimum value of c_i ($i = 1,2,3$) automatically to realize the self-organizing and self-consummating of controlling rules.

ITAE integral performance index is adopted in the paper to Self-optimizing the weighting factor.

$$J(ITAE) = \int_0^\infty t\left|\alpha_1\right| dt = \min. \tag{11}$$

$J(\bullet)$ is the object function, which expresses the integral area after weighting time of acceleration function. According to the value of object function, c_0 is corrected continuously until the control performance meets the request. The performance index shown as formula is the object function, and the weighting factors are corrected continuously in the optimum-searching process to obtain the minimum value of object function step by step, then achieve a set of optimal weighting factors: $c_0 = 0.79$, $c_1 = 0.68$, $c_1 = 0.45$.

The defuzzified value β^0 can be acquired by the centre of gravity of $\mu_B(\beta)$ as

$$\beta^0 = \int \beta \mu_B(\beta) d\beta \Big/ \int \mu_B(\beta) d\beta . \tag{12}$$

When the defuzzified value is expressed as $\beta^0(n)$ at n-th sampling interval, the output semi-active control force $u(n)$ at the sampling instant is

$$u(n) = k_u \beta^0(n) . \tag{13}$$

Where: $u(n)$ is the output proportional factor, which can gain according to the size of output universe of fuzzy set and controllable damping forcer. According to fuzzy controller, control forcer F_1 and F_2 that act separately frond and rear bogie of railway vehicle is

$$F_1 = k_{u1}\beta^0(n), F_2 = k_{u2}\beta^0(n) . \tag{14}$$

The semi-active suspension attenuate car body vibration with varying damping coefficient, the formula of adjust damping coefficient under SOF semi-active control are

$$C_1(t) = C_0 + k_{u1}\beta^0(n) \Big/ v_{fcr} , C_2(t) = C_0 + k_{u2}\beta^0(n) \Big/ v_{rcr} . \tag{15}$$

Where v_{fcr} is relative speed between center-mass of frond bogie and center-mass of car body, v_{rcr} is relative speed between center-mass of rear bogie and center-mass of car body, k_{u1} and k_{u2} are separately the output proportional factor of SOF fuzzy control in frond and rear bogie.

Three points are considered to accord with actual system in the simulation process.

①Input delay-time of control system is set 10ms in the paper in order to deal with lag time of varying damping coefficient.

②In fact, varivation range of damping coefficient is limited. So, when adopting SOF fuzzy control, the varivation range realized in the engineer is defined as follows:

$$0.5C_{opt} \le C(t) \le 4C_{opt} . \tag{16}$$

Where, C_{opt} is optimal damping coefficient of lateral passive suspension.

③Actual executing part in the semi-active control is controlling damper, and attenuation force of damper to the vibration of car body is direct proportional to relative speed of car body and bogie. When the force requested by SOF control is opposite to the relative speed, the damp is instructed to minimum, otherwise, the damp can be calculated according to formula (15), but if the damp exceeds $4C_{opt}$, the damp is defined as $4C_{opt}$,which can be expressed as follows:

$$C(t)=\begin{cases} 4C_{opt} & 4C_{opt} \le k_u\beta^0(n) \Big/ \dot{x}_2-\dot{x}_1 \\ 0.5C_{opt}+\dfrac{k_u\beta^0(n)}{\dot{x}_2-\dot{x}_1} & 0 \le \dfrac{k_u\beta^0(n)}{\dot{x}_2-\dot{x}_1} \le 4C_{opt} \\ 0.5C_{opt} & k_u\beta^0(n) \Big/ \dot{x}_2-\dot{x}_1 \le 0.5C_{opt} \end{cases} \quad . \tag{17}$$

4 Simulation Result

To verify the effectivity of the method, the combined simulation method of ADAMS and MATLAB is designed in the paper to study the system dynamics of vehicle suspension. Aimed at the high speed vehicle, the ADAMS simulation model is established, which is shown as Fig.4. The mass character parameters of the high speed dynamic model are displayed in the Table 2, and the parameter of suspension system and the size of the structure can refer to literature [9]. Then the result simulated by the model should be transferred to MATLAB and computed to find the real-time damp coefficient based on the fuzzy control theory of MATLAB6.1/Smulink. When the damp coefficient is transferred to ADAMS model, the dynamic performance will be simulated over again according to the new dynamics circumstance, and the simulating results will be transferred to the MATLAB again. By doing the above step several, the inter-transfer of ADAMS and MATLAB is realized to implement the semi-active control strategy.

The simulating results running in the straight track for the vehicle model are shown in Fig.5 and Fig.6. The input of track irregularity adopts ORE high-disturb track spectrum, and the speed is 306km/h. Seen from Fig.4, comparing with the active control, the semi-active control based on the fuzzy control strategy can reduce the lateral vibration amplitude of car body centre up frond bogie, and the adaptive fuzzy semi-active control is superior to the general fuzzy semi-active control for the lateral damping of car body. Seen from Fig.5, when the frequency is 0.8~20Hz, the damper vibration energy in the semi-active control is less than that in the passive control, especially in the frequency of 2~4Hz, in which the riding comfort of lateral vibration is affected obviously[10].

The dynamic performance of the model based on ADAMS is simulated to study on adaptive fuzzy semi-active control validity when the model based on ADAMS run in the difference of speed grade. Track irregularity adopts ORE high-disturb track spectrum. The performance of adaptive fuzzy semi-active control is estimate by three evaluating indicators, and the results are shown as figure 7~8.

Table 2. Mass parameters of the vehicle mode

name	number	units
Wheel load	1.75	t
Roll inertia of wheel-axle set	1.4	$t{\cdot}m^2$
Pitch inertia of wheel-axle set	0.150	$t{\cdot}m^2$
Yaw inertia of wheel-axle set	1.4	$t{\cdot}m^2$
Wheel rolling diameter	915	mm
rolling distance of wheel-axle set	1493	mm
Bogie mass	3.296	t
Bogie roll inertia	1.9	$t{\cdot}m^2$
Bogie pitch inertia	3.7	$t{\cdot}m^2$
Bogie yaw inertia	2.1	$t{\cdot}m^2$
height of bogie mass-center	702.5	mm
Car-body mass	32	t
Car-body roll inertia	75	$t{\cdot}m^2$
Car-body pitch inertia	2240	$t{\cdot}m^2$
Car-body yaw inertia	2240	$t{\cdot}m^2$
height of car-body mass-center	1700	mm
Bogie wheel base	2500	mm
Bogie centers	18000	mm

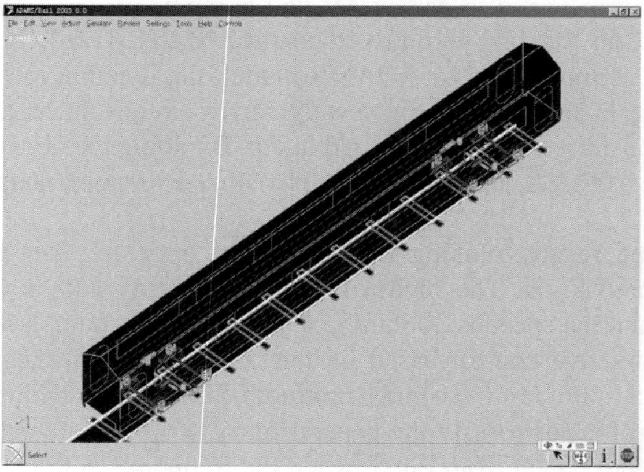

Fig. 4. Vehicle dynamics model based on ADAMS

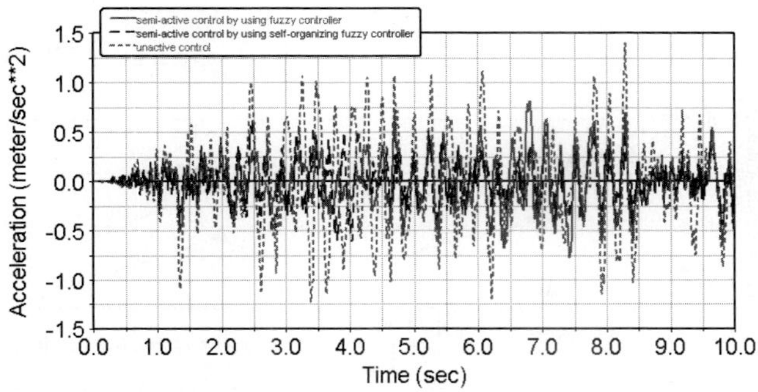

Fig. 5. The comparison of lateral acceleration on frond truck center

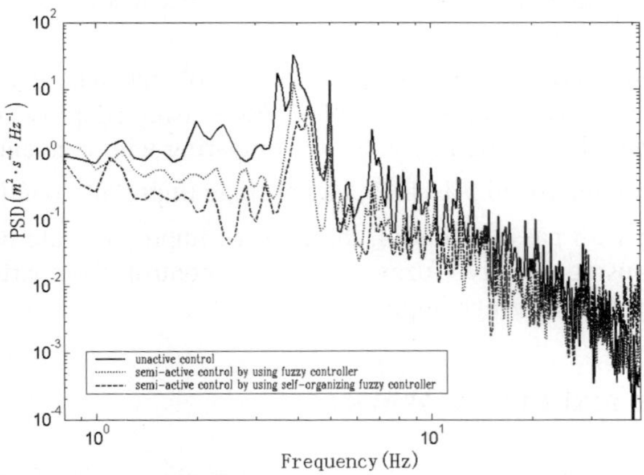

Fig. 6. Lateral aocceleration PSD of frond truck center

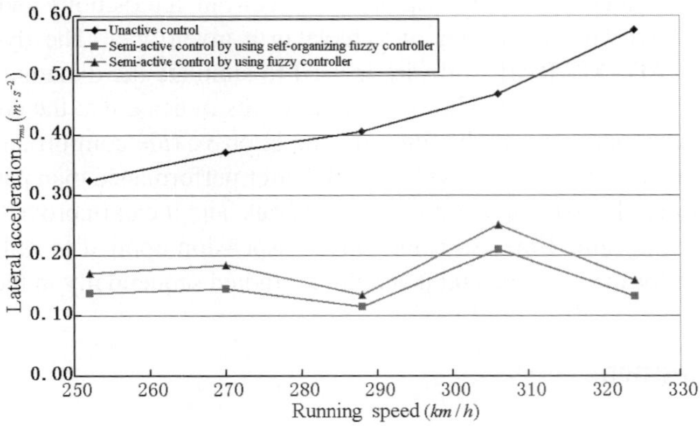

Fig. 7. The comparison of lateral acceleration mean-square A_{rms}

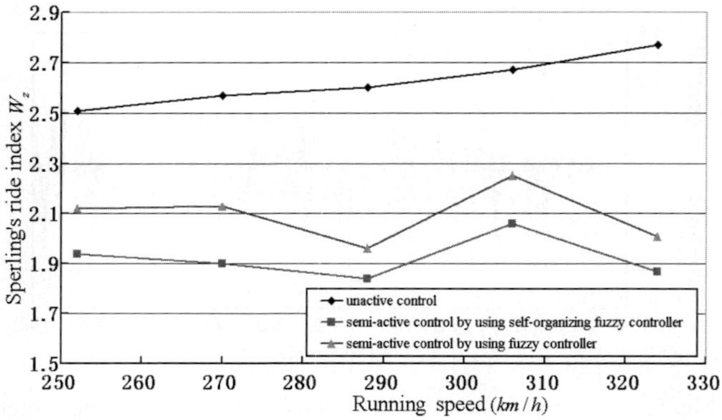

Fig. 8. The comparison of Sperling's ride index W_Z

Seen from Fig.7, comparing with passive control, the lateral acceleration root-mean-square of car body is decreased 55%~77% by using adaptive fuzzy semi-active control, the average decreasing rate is 65%. Comparing with conventional fuzzy control, A_{rms} has been improved 5%~11%, and average improving rate is 8%. Seen from Fig.8, comparing with passive control, the average improving-rate of Sperling's ride index is 27% by using adaptive fuzzy semi-active control. Comparing with conventional fuzzy control, the average improving rate is 7%.

5 Conclusion and Future Works

Adaptive fuzzy control method based on the acceleration feedback is put forward for the lateral secondary semi-active suspension system of high speed railway vehicle. The method can solve semi-active control question of railway vehicle suspension system that is limited by the uncertainty of wheel-rail interactions and strong non-linear and time-varying parameter of vehicle in a given area. The dynamic model established by ADAMS/RAIL software is used to simulate the dynamic performance with adaptive fuzzy controller. The simulation results indicate that the control method can effectively attenuate car body vibration and improve ride comfort and stationarity of railway vehicle, which also provides much better performance than passive suspension system when the vehicle operating mode varies, and it can improve the speed and ride quality at the same time. So semi-active suspension applied to railway vehicles has researched for many years, and it should be studied sequentially in the future.

Acknowledgment

This paper is support by the opening project of national power traction laboratory (No: TPL0406).

References

1. Kimiaki, S.: Improving Lateral Ride Comfort of High-speed Trains Applying Semi-active Suspension System to High-speed Train. Journal of the China Railway Society, 2 (2004) 105-115
2. Goodall, R.: Active Railway Suspensions: Implement Status and Technological Trends. Vehicle System Dynamics, 2 (1997) 87-117
3. Wu, X. J., Yang, S. J.: Computer Control and Measure System Applied to the Active vibration Control System. China Measurement Technology, 11 (2004) 60-62
4. Stribersky A., Kienberger A., Wagner G.: Design and Evaluation of a Semi-active Damping System for Rail Vehicles. Vehicle System Dynamics, 8 (1998) 669-681
5. Sasaki, K., Kamoshit, S., Simomura, T.: Development and Filed Result of Semi-active Suspension for High Speed Train. RTRI Report. 5 (1996) 25-30
6. Nakasato, M., Gao, K. Y.: Development of the Semi-active Dampers for Railway Cars. FOREIGN ROLLING STOCK. 4 (2003) 33-38
7. Yang J. W., Du, Y. P.: Study on Dynamic Test Method of Fit Clearance of Spherical Pair. Proceedings of 6th International Symposium on Test and Measurement, 13 (2005) 256-259
8. Wang, H. J.: The Simulation and Test Research on Semi-active Air Spring Suspension Based on Fuzzy Control. Jilin University, Jilin, China (2005)
9. Dong, X. Q.: Research on Lateral Semi-active Suspension of High Speed Railway Vehicle. Beijing Jiaotong University, Beijing, China (2003)
10. ISO2631-1, 2. Evaluation of Human Exposure to Whole-body Vibration, (1997)

Car Plate Localization Using Modified PCNN in Complicated Environment

Xin Yuan, Lei Wang, and Miaoliang Zhu

College of Computer Science, Zhejiang University, Hangzhou, P.R. China, 310027
yxxinyuan@zju.edu.cn

Abstract. Car plate Localization, which remains a difficult problem under complicated environment, is the key problem in many traffic related applications. In this paper we describe a new method based on modified Pulse Coupled Neural Network (PCNN) with adaptive threshold, which can capture relatively complete objects in human perception. After inverse filtering, PCNN processing is applied to produce a firing time sequence image. Then car plates' position and rotated angle can be extracted from the firing image. Experiment results show that the correct car plate locating rate reaches 98%, which is higher than other Localization methods on the same image database.

1 Introduction

Car plate recognition is the key problem in many traffic related applications such as traffic control, automatic payment of tolls on highways or bridges, parking system, Intelligent Transport System (ITS) and general vehicle security systems. Generally, it consists of three procedures: Localization of car plate regions, segmentation of characters from the plate regions and recognition of each character [1]. So the first step, Localization of car plate regions, is very important for the whole system.

In the past years, a large number of efforts have been made to localize car plate regions from the images. These efforts have led to the development of several classical methods, such as gradient information [2], morphological operators [3], generalized symmetry transform [4], neural network [5] [6] and horizontal and vertical projections [7]. Recent studies by Yang suggested a mixed method, which utilized the color collocation of the plate's background and characters combined with the plate's structure and texture to localize the vehicle license plate and reached the recognition rate 95% [8]. Chacon gave another new method based on Pulse Coupled Neural Network (PCNN) [9]. He applied PCNN to the original image to generate candidate regions and obtained 85% precision.

In spite of extensive research, reliable car plate Localization is still not an easy problem especially in outdoor scenes. In an outdoor environment, not only illumination changes greatly because of different whether, but also images captured by cameras may contain multiple licenses or no license plate at all. Moreover, when they do appear in an image, car plates may have arbitrary sizes, orientations and positions. These factors pose considerable challenge during car plate Localization.

D.-S. Huang, K. Li, and G.W. Irwin (Eds.): ICIC 2006, LNAI 4114, pp. 1116–1124, 2006.

The methods mentioned above do not work well in outdoor environment because they can not capture complete car plate regions or even miss the whole plates. We propose a new method based on PCNN since it can capture relatively complete objects in human perception. If we use original image processing pulse coupled neuron model mentioned in Ranganath's paper [10], it is difficult to choose suitable PCNN parameters automatically because of varying illumination in outdoor scenes. So we modified the model so that it could be adaptive to select suitable parameters.

In this paper, inverse filtering is applied to original image firstly. Then a firing time sequence image is produced by our adaptive threshold PCNN. Finally, we localize the car plate on this firing image.

2 Methodology

In our detection scheme, car plate Localization is split into three stages: preprocessing using inverse filtering, PCNN processing to form a firing time sequence image, and Localization of the car plate.

2.1 Preprocessing

Since varying illumination causes images degradation to various pixel distribution, we use inverse filtering to enhance images. The choice of a suitable degradation function depends on specified problem. We choose a two dimensional Poisson distribution function as point-spread function because we can obtain the best result experimentally. The comparison of final results with and without inverse filtering is illustrated at the end of the article.

2.2 PCNN Processing

Pulse Coupled Neural Network (PCNN) is a new kind of artificial neural network model, which emulates the behavior of cortical neurons observed in visual cortices of cats [11]. It has proven to be highly effective when used in image processing, such as segmentation [12], smoothing [10], fusion [13], noise propagation reduction[14], etc.

Pulse Coupled Neuron Model. Original pulse coupled neuron model, which was given by Eckhorn [11] in 1990, had several practical limitations [12]. In 1995, Ranganath developed a simple model [10], which has been applied to most image processing applications. This model also has a defect. Since it uses a fixed threshold in captured firing, a big gradient area may be segmented to several regions though it belongs to one region in human perception. So we modify the pulse coupled neuron model based on Ranganath with adaptive threshold so that it could select suitable parameters automatically and yield better segmentation results.

Modified Pulse Coupled Neuron Model. Fig. 1 illustrates the pulse coupled neuron model with adaptive threshold. When neuron's internal activity U_j is higher than its threshold θ_j, the neuron *fires* and emits a pulse. A neuron that fires due to the influence of the feeding input alone is said to be *firing naturally.* If it fires due to the influence of not only the feeding input, but also the linking input, it is said to be *captured* by other neurons. If we define that the neurons that have the highest feeding input fire at T_{max} moment and the lowest ones fire at T_{min}, $[T_{max}, T_{min}]$ is called an *interval.*

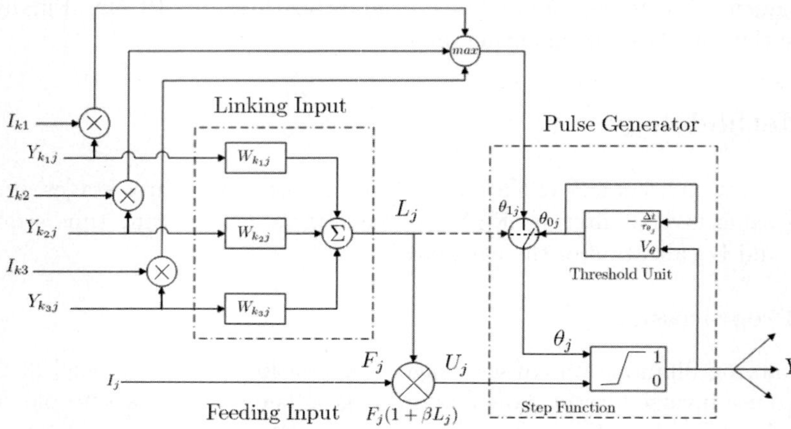

Fig. 1. Pulse coupled neuron model with adaptive threshold

Ranganath's model can be described using following equations. The feeding input of the neuron model can be defined as follows,

$$F_j(t) = I_j \ , \tag{1}$$

where F_j is the feeding input of the jth neuron, I_j is the intensity of the pixel, and t is the time. The linking input can be described as

$$L_j(t) = \sum_k Y_{kj}(t-1)W_{kj} \ , \tag{2}$$

where L_j is the linking input of the jth neuron, W_{kj} is the synaptic connection weight between k^{th} neuron's output and j^{th} neuron's linking input, and Y_{kj} is the jth neuron's linking input that gain from the kth neuron's output. The internal activity of the neuron depends on the linking and feeding activities denoted as

$$U_j(t) = F_j(t)(1 + \beta L_j(t)) \ , \tag{3}$$

where U_j is the jth neuron's internal activity, and β is the linking strength, which decides the linking input portion in U_j. The threshold of the neuron is implemented by

$$\theta_j(t) = \begin{cases} V_\theta & \text{if } U_j(t-1) > \theta_j(t-1) \\ e^{-\frac{\Delta t}{\tau_{\theta_j}}}\theta_j(t-1) & \text{otherwise} \end{cases} , \tag{4}$$

where θ_j is the current threshold of the jth neuron, V_θ is a fixed high value to make sure that each neuron pulses exactly once during an interval, Δt is the time interval, and τ is the time constant of the leaky integrators. The final output of the neuron is defined by

$$Y_j(t) = \begin{cases} 1 & \text{if } U_j(t) > \theta_j(t) \\ 0 & \text{otherwise} \end{cases} , \tag{5}$$

where Y_j is the output of the the jth neuron.

In Ranganath's model, at t moment, the feeding input range of naturally firing neurons is $[\theta_j(t), \theta_j(t-1)]$ and the one of the captured firing neurons is $[\theta_j(t) - \beta I_j L_j(t), \theta_j(t)]$. If neurons' feeding input is lower than $\theta_j(t) - \beta I_j L_j(t)$, they have no chance to be captured though they may belong to the naturally firing neurons in human perception. To solve this problem, we introduce a captured firing threshold θ_{1j}, which is defined as

$$\theta_{1j}(t) = \max(I_k(t-1) Y_{kj}(t-1)) , \tag{6}$$

where I_k is the neighborhood feeding inputs of the neuron. Denote θ_j in equation (4) as θ_{0j}, and the adaptive threshold of the neuron is implemented by

$$\theta_j(t) = \begin{cases} \theta_{0j}(t) & \text{if } L_j(t) = 0 \\ \theta_{1j}(t) & \text{otherwise} \end{cases} . \tag{7}$$

In our model, the feeding input range of captured firing neurons expands to $[0, \theta_j(t)]$. So the neurons with any feeding input can be captured as long as the difference between capturing neuron's feeding input (equals to θ_{1j}) and captured neuron's one (equals to I_j) is less than $\beta I_j L_j(t)$. Fig. 2 illustrates the difference of feeding input ranges between Ranganath's model and ours.

PCNN Processing Algorithm. The pulse coupled neural network is a single layer two-dimensional array of laterally linked pulse coupled neurons. Each pixel in the image is associated with a unique neuron and vice versa. The feeding input (F_j) is the intensity of its corresponding pixel which is scaled between 0 and 1. Each neuron receives a linking input from its four neighbors. The algorithm can be described as follow:

1. At the beginning, because threshold θ of each neuron is zero, all neurons fire together at $t = 0$. The outputs of all the threshold units are charged to V_θ and start to decay exponentially according to the time constant τ_θ.
2. The neurons corresponding to the highest intensity pixels fire first naturally at $t = T_{max}$ moment and capture all the neighbor neurons as long as the difference of their feeding inputs is less than $\beta I_j L_j(t)$. Then the captured neurons will capture their neighbor neurons, too. This behavior continues

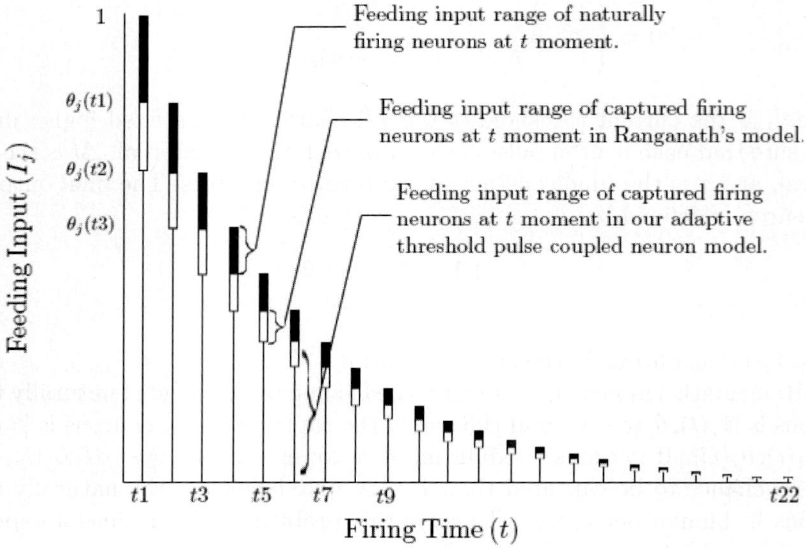

Fig. 2. Difference of feeding input ranges between Kuntimad's model and our model

(a) (b) (c)

Fig. 3. Firing time sequence image. (a) Original image. (b) Result image by Ranganath's model. (c) Result image by our model.

until all the neurons that satisfy the condition are captured. All the fired neurons will not fire again, no matter naturally or captured, in the interval $[T_{max}, T_{min}]$ because of their high threshold which has been set to V_θ at firing time.

3. As the threshold θ decay exponentially, at next time $t+1$, the neurons corresponding to the lower intensity pixels fire naturally and capture other neurons within their capture ranges. The procedure repeats until $t = T_{min}$. All the neurons fire once and exactly once in the interval $[T_{max}, T_{min}]$.
4. We record the firing time of each neuron and form a firing time sequence image. Fig. 3 compares two firing time sequence images formed by Ranganath's model and ours.

2.3 Localization of Car Plate

At first, adaptive thresholding is applied on the firing time sequence image. Then several features are extracted from each 4-adjacency connectivity region, such as the ratio of the area to the perimeter, to obtain several candidate character regions. After that, we use a window to slide through the image to get the car plate Localization, which contains maximum number of candidate character regions. Finally, rotated angle of the car plate can be obtained through calculating top pixel coordinates of each character region.

3 Experimental Results

Car plate Localization algorithm mentioned above was tested with an image database of 100 images acquired with a camera installed in a entrance of parking. The size of images is 528 × 384. All of them are obtained under outdoor scenes. So the brightness of the images, the positions and the sizes of the car plates are different.

At first, we preprocessed the original image using inverse filtering with a 3 × 3 Poisson distribution template, which is illustrated in Tab. 1. Then our adaptive threshold PCNN were applied on the image to form a firing time sequence image. Tab. 2 gives the PCNN parameters. After PCNN processing we applied adaptive thresholding to each 40 × 40 region of the firing time sequence image. Finally, we used a search window to localize the car plate. The height and the width of the search window are 80 and 180 separately. Fig. 4 illustrates the final results on one image with complicated illumination and another with low contrast. Both of them are very difficult to be localized using other methods. Fig. 5 compares the results with and without inverse filtering on one image. It is easy to see that the final result with inverse filtering is better than that without inverse filtering.

Table 1. 3 × 3 Poisson distribution template

0.13534	0.099574	0.08242
0.099574	0.073263	0.060642
0.08242	0.060642	0.050195

Table 2. Parameters for PCNN

Parameters	β	W_{kj}	V_θ	Δt	τ_θ
Values	0.04	1.0	10.0	1.0	50.0

Tab. 3 compares the precision and average algorithm speed of several methods, which contain our algorithm and others mentioned in previous works, on the same image database. Obviously, the precision of our algorithm, which is above 98%, is much higher than others'. The total process of our algorithm needs 4 seconds when running in P4 machine with 2.0G CPU speed and windows platform.

Table 3. Comparison of several license plate Localization methods on the same image database

Methods	Precision	Average Algorithm Speed
Our algorithm	98.5%	3814ms
Gradient information[2]	82.4%	1203ms
Morphological operator[3]	83.8%	441ms
Neural network[5][6]	88.8%	466ms
Projection[7]	87.1%	385ms
Chacon's PCNN[9]	85.3%	4349ms

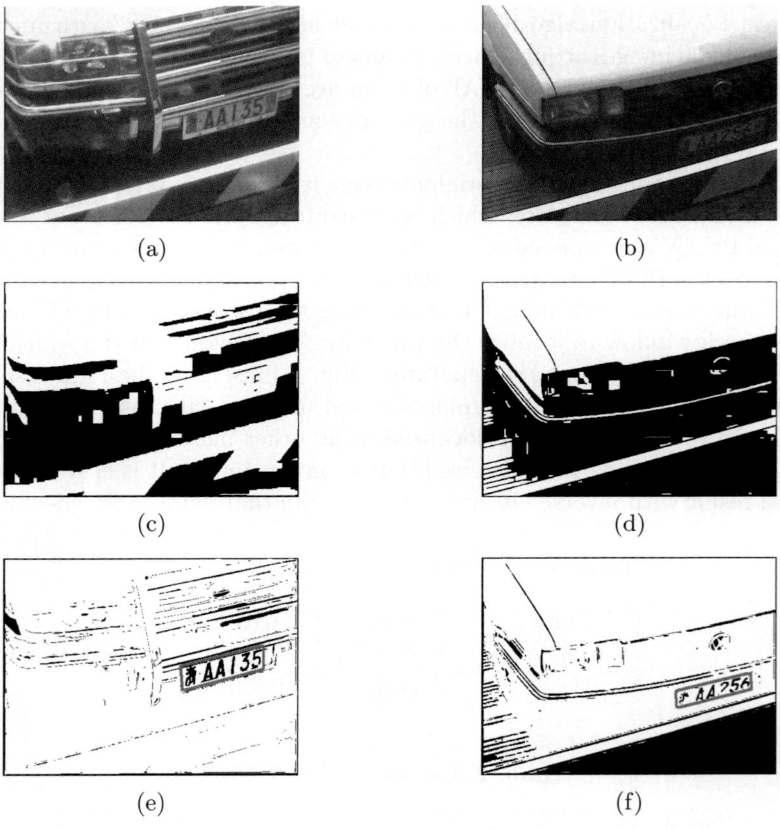

Fig. 4. Comparison of the results by Ranganath's model and our model. (a) Original image with complicated illumination. (b) Original image with low contrast. (c) Result of image (a) by Ranganth's model. (d) Result of image (b) by Ranganth's model. (e) Result of image (a) by our adaptive threshold model. (f) Result of image (b) by our adaptive threshold model.

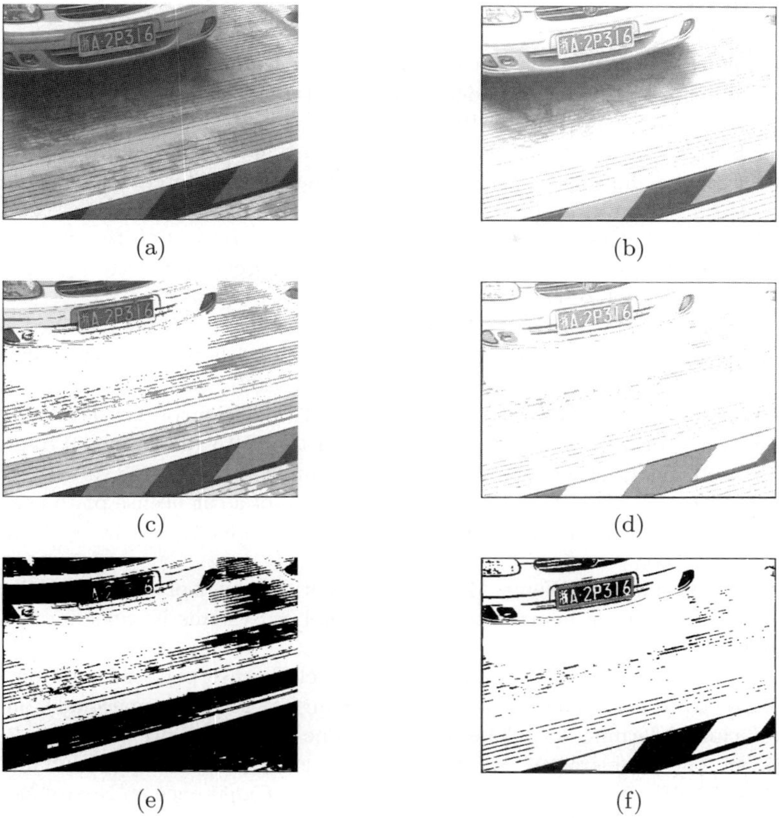

Fig. 5. Comparison of the results with and without inverse filtering. (a) Original image. (b) Image after inverse filtering. (c) Firing time sequence image without inverse filtering. (d) Firing time sequence image with inverse filtering. (e) Result image without inverse filtering. (f) Result image with inverse filtering.

4 Conclusion

In this paper, we proposed a new method based on adaptive threshold pulse coupled neuron model to detect license plate in images. The advantage of this algorithm is that it is robust under complicated illumination. Furthermore, it can get rotated angle of car plate directly while detecting car plate position. Experiments on our images acquired from outdoor scenes produce the correct-locating rate of 98%, showing that our approaches are promising. The further work includes development of the high speed algorithm of PCNN and precision improvement of car plate Localization.

References

1. Takashi, N., Toshihiko, T., Keichi, Y., et al.: Robust license-plate recognition method for passing vehicles under outside environment. IEEE Trans. on Vehicular Technology **49** (2000) 2309–2319
2. Kim, S., Kim, D., Ryu, Y., Kim, G.: A robust license-plate extraction method under complex image conditions. In: Proceedings of 16th International Conference on Pattern Recognition. (2002) 216–219
3. Hsieh, J., Yu, S., Chen, Y.: Morphology-based license plate detection from complex scenes. In: Proceedings of 16th International Conference on Pattern Recognition. Volume 3. (2002) 176–179
4. Kim, D., Chien, S.: Automatic car license plate extraction using modified generalized symmetry transform and image warping. In: IEEE International Symposium on Industrial Electronics. Volume 3. (2001) 2022–2027
5. Sirithinaphong, T., Chamnongthai, K.: The recognition of car license plate for automatic parking system. In: Proceedings of the Fifth International Symposium on Signal Processing and Its Applications. Volume 1. (1999) 455–457
6. Lee, E., Kim, P., Kim, H.: Automatic recognition of a car license plate using color image processing. In: Proceeding of International Conference on Image Processing. (1994) 301–305
7. Wei, W., Huang, X., Wang, M.: An automatic system of vehicle number-plate recognition based on neural networks. Journal of Systems Engineering and Electronics **12** (2001) 63–72
8. Yang, Y., Bai, J., Tian, R., Liu, N.: A vehicle license plate recognition system based on fixed color collocation. In: Proceedings of 2005 International Conference on Machine Learning and Cybernetics. Volume 9. (2005) 5394–5397
9. Chacon, M., Zimmerman, A.: License plate location based on a dynamic pcnn scheme. In: Proceedings of the International Joint Conference on Neural Networks. Volume 2. (2003) 1195–1200
10. Ranganath, H., Kuntimad, G., Johnson, J.: Pulse coupled neural networks for image processing. IEEE Proceedings on Southeastcon: Visualize the Future (1995) 37–43
11. Eckhorn, R., Reitboeck, H., Arndt, M., Dicke, P.: Feature linking via synchronization among distributed assemblies:simulations of results from cat visual cortex. Neural Comput. **2** (1990) 293–307
12. Kuntimad, G., Ranganath, H.: Perfect image segmentation using pulse coupled neural networks. In: IEEE Transactions on Neural Networks. Volume 10. (1999)
13. Broussard, R., Rogers, S., Oxley, M., Tarr, G.: Physiologically motivated image fusion for object detection using a pulse coupled neural network. IEEE Transactions on Neural Networks **10** (1999) 554–563
14. Clark, N., Banish, M., Ranganath, H.: Smart adaptive optic systems using spatial light modulators. IEEE Transactions on Neural Networks **10** (1999) 599–603

Enhancing Contrast for Image Using Discrete Stationary Wavelet Transform and Non-linear Gain Operator

Changjiang Zhang, Xiaodong Wang, and Haoran Zhang

College of Information Science and Engineering, Zhejiang Normal University, Postcode 321004 Jinhua, China
{zcj74922, wxd, hylt}@zjnu.cn

Abstract. Having implemented discrete stationary wavelet transform (DSWT) to an image, combining generalized cross validation (GCV), noise is reduced directly in the high frequency sub-bands which are at the better resolution levels and local contrast is enhanced by combining de-noising method with non-linear gain operator (NGO) in the high frequency sub-bands which are at the worse resolution levels. In order to enhance the global contrast for the image, the low frequency sub-band image is also enhanced employing in-complete Beta transform (IBT) and simulated annealing algorithm (SA). IBT is used to obtain non-linear gray transform curve. Transform parameters are determined by SA so as to obtain optimal non-linear gray transform parameters. In order to avoid the expensive time for traditional contrast enhancement algorithms, which search optimal gray transform parameters in the whole gray transform parameters space, a new criterion is proposed with gray level histogram. Contrast type for original image is determined employing the new criterion. Gray transform parameters space is given respectively according to different contrast types, which shrinks gray transform parameters space greatly. Finally, the quality of enhanced image is evaluated by a total cost criterion. Experimental results show that the new algorithm can improve greatly the global and local contrast for an image while reducing efficiently gauss white noise (GWN) in the image. The new algorithm is more excellent in performance than histogram equalization, un-sharpened mask algorithm, WYQ algorithm and GWP algorithm.

1 Introduction

Traditional image contrast enhancement algorithms include: point operators, space operators, transform operators and pseu-color contrast enhancement [1]. Recently, some new algorithms for image enhancement have been proposed. Such as Ramar and Shang-ming Zhou gave two kinds of algorithms for contrast enhancement based on fuzzy operators respectively [2],[3]. However, the algorithm, which was proposed by Shang-ming Zhou, cannot be sure to be convergent. Ming Tang gave a kind of adaptive enhancement algorithm far infrared image sequences [4]. Performance of the algorithm is affected greatly by mathematic model. Lots of improved histogram equalization algorithms were proposed to enhance contrast for kinds of images[5-9]. algorithms have been proposed [5],[6],[7],[8],[9], however, the visual quality cannot be improved greatly with above algorithms. Tubbs gave a simple gray transform

D.-S. Huang, K. Li, and G.W. Irwin (Eds.): ICIC 2006, LNAI 4114, pp. 1125 – 1135, 2006.

algorithm to enhance contrast for images [10]. However, the computation burden of the algorithm was large. Based on Tubbs algorithm, Zhou Ji-liu gave a new kind of genetic algorithm to optimize non-linear transform parameters [11]. Although the algorithm can enhance contrast for image well, the computation burden is larger. Many existing enhancement algorithms' intelligence and adaptability are worse and much artificial interference is required, which restricts their wide applications. Most of them only enhance either the global or the local contrast for image.

To solve above problems, a new algorithm employing incomplete Beta transform (IBT), DSWT and SA is proposed. To improve optimization speed and intelligence of algorithm, a new criterion is proposed based on gray level histogram. Contrast type for original image is determined employing the new criterion. Contrast for original images are classified into seven types: particular dark (PD), medium dark (MD), medium dark slightly (MDS), medium bright slightly (MBS), medium bright (MB), particular bright (PB) and good gray level distribution (GGLD). The new algorithm is still a kind of gray transform method. IBT operator transforms original image to a new space. A certain criterion or objective function is used to optimize non-linear transform parameters. SA, which was given by William, is used to determine the optimal non-linear transform parameters. Having made DSWT to the original image, the global contrast is enhanced directly employing IBT in the low frequency sub-band image. The local contrast is enhanced employing de-nosing algorithm combining IBT, which was proposed by Tubbs in 1997 [10]. We expand the IBT to SWT domain so as to extrude the detail in the original image. Noise is reduced directly at the better resolution levels by the de-noising algorithm. The de-noising asymptotic thresholds can be obtained employing GCV without the accurate statistic information of the noise. Local enhancement is enhanced combining de-noising algorithm with IBT. In order to evaluate the quality of the enhanced image, a new total cost criterion is proposed. Experimental results show that the new algorithm can enhance efficiently the global and local contrast for the image while the gauss white noise in the image can be reduced well. The total performance of the new algorithm is more excellent than the HIS, USH, GWP algorithm in [11] and WYQ algorithm in [12].

2 IBT

Usually, an image has three kinds of contrast types: particular bright, particular dark and all gray levels are centralized on the middle certain region in gray levels histogram. Different transform functions are used to enhance contrast according to different contrast types. Figure 1(a)-(c) shows gray transform curve corresponding to particular dark type, particular bright type and all gray levels are centralized on the middle certain region type respectively.

Tubbs employed unitary incomplete Beta function to approximate above three non-linear functions [10]. Parameter α and β control the shape of non-linear transform curve. The incomplete Beta function can be written as following:

$$F(u) = B^{-1}(\alpha, \beta) \times \int_0^u t^{\alpha-1}(1-t)^{\beta-1} dt, \quad 0 < \alpha, \beta < 10. \tag{1}$$

In generally, $\alpha < \beta$ when the image is particular dark. $\alpha > \beta$ when the image is particular bright. $\alpha = \beta$ when the image is all gray levels are centralized on the middle certain region type. All the gray levels of original image have to be unitary before implementing IBT. All the gray levels of enhanced image have to be inverse-unitary after implementing IBT. Let x shows gray level of original image, g indicates unitary gray level. We have:

$$g = \frac{x - \min(x)}{\max(x) - \min(x)}. \tag{2}$$

Where $\min(x)$ and $\max(x)$ shows the minimum gray level and the maximum one in original image respectively. g is mapped to g':

$$g' = IB(a, b, g). \tag{3}$$

Let x' shows gray level of enhanced image, we have:

$$x' = [\max(x) - \min(x)]\, g' + \min(x). \tag{4}$$

Objective function in Ref. [1] is employed to evaluate the quality of enhanced image. The function can be written as following:

$$C_{contrast} = \frac{1}{MN}\sum_{i=1}^{M}\sum_{j=1}^{N} g'^2(i,j) - \left[\frac{1}{MN}\sum_{i=1}^{M}\sum_{j=1}^{N} g'(i,j)\right]^2. \tag{5}$$

Where M, N show width and height of original image. $g'(i,j)$ Shows gray level at (i,j) in enhanced image. More $C_{contrast}$ is, more well proportioned the distribution of image gray level is.

3 Contrast Classification for Image Based on Histogram

Based on gray level histogram, contrast classification criterion can be described in Fig.1:

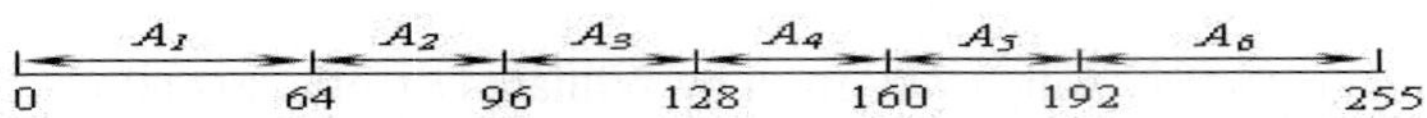

Fig. 1. Image classification sketch map based on gray level histogram

Given that original image has 255 gray levels, the whole gray level space is divided into six sub-spaces: $A_1, A_2, A_3, A_4, A_5, A_6$ .Where A_i (i=1, 2, ⋯, 6) is the number of all pixels which distribute in the ith sub-space. Let,

$$M = \max_{i=1}^{6} A_i, \quad B_1 = \sum_{k=2}^{6} A_i, \quad B_2 = \sum_{k=2}^{5} A_i, \quad B_3 = \sum_{k=1}^{5} A_i,$$

$$B_4 = A_1 + A_6, \quad B_5 = A_2 + A_3, \quad B_6 = A_4 + A_5,$$

Following classification criterion can be obtained:

$if\ (M = A_1)\ \&\ (A_1 > B_1)$

Image is PB;

$elseif\ (B_2 > B_4)\ \&\ (B_5 > B_6)\ \&$

$(B_5 > A_1)\ \&\ (B_5 > A_6)\ \&\ (A_2 > A_3)$

Image is MD;

$elseif\ (B_2 > B_4)\ \&\ (B_5 > B_6)\ \&$

$(B_5 > A_1)\ \&\ (B_5 > A_6)\ \&\ (A_2 < A_3)$

Image is MDS;

$elseif\ (B_2 > B_4)\ \&\ (B_5 < B_6)$

$\&\ (A_1 < B_6)\ \&\ (A_6 < B_6)\ \&\ (A_4 > A_5)$

Image is MBS;

$elseif\ (B_2 > B_4)\ \&\ (B_5 < B_6)\ \&$

$(A_1 < B_6)\ \&\ (A_6 < B_6)\ \&\ (A_4 < A_5)$

Image is MB;

$elseif\ (M = A_6)\ \&\ (A_6 > B_3)$

Image is PB;

else

Image is GGLD;

end

Where symbol $\&$ represents logic "and" operator.

4 Transform Parameters Optimization with SA

We will employ the SA, which was given by William L. Goffe, to optimize transform parameters [5]. If the algorithm is used directly to enhance image contrast, it will result in large computation cost and worse robust to initial points. The range of α and β can be determined by Tab.1 so as to solve above problems.

Let $\mathbf{x} = (\alpha, \beta)$, $F(\mathbf{x})$ is function to be minimized, corresponding to (4). Where $a_i < \alpha, \beta < b_i$ ($i = 1,2$), a_i and b_i ($i = 1,2$) can be determined by Tab.1.

Table 1. Range of α and β

Parameter	PD	MD	MDS	MBS	MB	PB
α	[1 , 2]	[1 , 2]	[1, 1.5]	[1.5 , 2]	[2 , 3]	[3 , 4]
β	[3 , 4]	[2 , 3]	[1.5 , 2]	[1, 1.5]	[1 , 2]	[1 , 2]

Having made lots of experiments and tests, a satisfactory result will be obtained to all contrast types of images when parameters above are determined as follows: $N_S = 20$, $N_T = 100$, $c_i = 2$, $i = 1,2$, $T_0 = 5$, $r_T = 0.95$. Detail steps on SA can be found in [5].

5 Global Contrast Enhancement Based on SWT and IBT

SWT has been independently discovered several times, for different purpose and under different names, e.g. shift/translation invariant wavelet transform, redundant wavelet transform and un-decimated wavelet transform [14]. The transform matrix exists a left inverse and its computation complexity is $O(N \log N)$. Classical orthonormal wavelet transform is a kind of non-redundant wavelet transform, so it is proper to deal with un-correlative problems. For discrete SWT, it is proper to deal with correlative problems because it is a kind of redundant wavelet transform. Because the correlation between gray levels in infrared image is greater, discrete SWT is proper to enhance the contrast of infrared image. Later experimental results also certify this point. Detail information on discrete SWT can be found in reference [14].

Next, based on discrete stationary wavelet transform, IBT is employed to enhance the global and local contrast for image. Having made DSWT to the original image, the low frequency sub-band image is enhanced employing IBT. According to section 2, section 3 and section 4, proper non-linear gray transform parameter α and β are selected to enhance the global contrast for the image.

6 Local Contrast Enhancement Based on SWT and NGO

6.1 De-noising Principle

Wavelet transform of the correlated noise is non-stationary. De-noising effect is worse if employing traditional "global threshold" to reduce noise in the image. Fortunately, *I. M. Johnstone* has proved that wavelet transform of the correlated noise is still stationary at all scales of every resolution level [15]. Thus de-noising thresholds at all scales of every resolution level are calculated respectively so as to reduce noise in the image effectively. We consider discrete image model as follows:

$$g[i, j] = f[i, j] + \varepsilon[i, j],\ i = 1,\cdots,M,\ j = 1,\cdots,N. \tag{6}$$

Above equation can be written matrix as follows:

$$\mathbf{g} = \mathbf{f} + \boldsymbol{\varepsilon}. \tag{7}$$

Where, $\mathbf{g} = \{g[i, j]\}_{i,j}$ shows observation signal, $\mathrm{f} = \{f[i, j]\}_{i,j}$ indicates uncorrupted original image, $\boldsymbol{\varepsilon} = \{\varepsilon[i, j]\}_{i,j}$, $i = 1,\cdots,M; j = 1,\ldots,N$ is stationary signal.

DSWT is implemented to Equation (7):

$$\mathbf{X} = \mathbf{S}\mathbf{f}. \tag{8}$$

$$\mathbf{V} = \mathbf{S}\boldsymbol{\varepsilon}. \tag{9}$$

$$\mathbf{Y} = \mathbf{S}\mathbf{g}. \tag{10}$$

$$\mathbf{Y} = \mathbf{X} + \mathbf{V}. \tag{11}$$

Where $\mathbf{S}$ shows two-dimension stationary wavelet transform operator. "Soft-threshold" function, which was proposed by *Donoho*, is employed to reduce the noise in the image:

$$\mathbf{Y}_{\boldsymbol{\delta}} = \mathbf{T}_{\boldsymbol{\delta}} \circ \mathbf{Y}. \tag{12}$$

$$\mathbf{T}_{\boldsymbol{\delta}} = diag\{t[m,m]\},$$

$$t[m,m] = \begin{cases} 0, & |\mathbf{Y}[i, j]| < \delta \\ 1 - \frac{\delta}{|\mathbf{Y}[i,j]|}, & |\mathbf{Y}[i, j]| \ge \delta \end{cases}$$

Where, $i = 1,\cdots,M$, $j = 1,\cdots,N$, $m = 1,\cdots,MN$. Similarly, we have

$$\mathbf{X}_{\boldsymbol{\delta}} = \mathbf{T}_{\boldsymbol{\delta}} \circ \mathbf{X}. \tag{13}$$

According to Equation (10) and (12), inverse transformation for input signal is written as:

$$\mathbf{g}_{\boldsymbol{\delta}} = \mathbf{S}^{-1} \circ \mathbf{Y}_{\boldsymbol{\delta}}. \tag{14}$$

The total operator can be expressed as:

$$\mathbf{g}_{\boldsymbol{\delta}} = \mathbf{Z}_{\boldsymbol{\delta}} \circ \mathbf{g}. \tag{15}$$

$$\mathbf{Z}_{\boldsymbol{\delta}} = \mathbf{S}^{-1} \circ \mathbf{T}_{\boldsymbol{\delta}} \circ \mathbf{S}. \tag{16}$$

Where $\mathbf{T}_{\boldsymbol{\delta}}$ is correlated to threshold δ and input signal $\mathbf{g}$.

If the statistic properties of the noise are employed to approximate the optimal threshold δ, standard variance σ will be used [15]. This will be almost impossible in practice according to above discussion. Generalized cross validation principle is employed to solve the problem [16].

6.2 De-noising Threshold

Let the original signal $f[i,j]$ can be expressed employing the linear combination of its neighbor elements. Consider $\tilde{g}[i,j]$ is a linear combination of $g[k,l]$, thus special noise can be reduced. Because they can be replaced by weight average values of their neighbor elements, and the noise in the image will be smoothed in the procedure, cleaner signal can be obtained.

Revised signal $\tilde{\mathbf{g}}$ is employed to calculate the de-nosing threshold. $g[i,j]$, which is the $[i,j]$ element of $\mathbf{g}$, is replaced by $\tilde{g}[i,j]$:

$$\tilde{\mathbf{g}} = \mathbf{Z} \cdot (g[1,1],\ldots,\tilde{g}[i,j],\ldots,g[M,N])^T . \tag{17}$$

We consider the ability that $\tilde{g}_\delta[i,j]$ "predicts" $g[i,j]$ as the standard to determine the optimal threshold.

If the threshold δ is too small, main component of $g[i,j] - \tilde{g}_\delta[i,j]$ is noise. If the threshold δ is too big, much useful signal will be reduced. The same processing is repeated to all the components and proper thresholds can be obtained employing following equation:

$$OCV(\delta) = \frac{1}{MN}\sum_{i=1}^{M}\sum_{j=1}^{N}(g[i,j] - \tilde{g}_\delta[i,j])^2 . \tag{18}$$

The forms of $\tilde{g}[i,j]$ are many kinds, here let $\tilde{g}_\delta[i,j] = \tilde{g}[i,j]$, we have:

$$g[i,j] - \tilde{g}_\delta[i,j] = \frac{g[i,j] - g_\delta[i,j]}{1 - \tilde{z}[i,j]} . \tag{19}$$

Where, $\tilde{z}[i,j] = \dfrac{g_\delta[i,j] - \tilde{g}_\delta[i,j]}{g[i,j] - \tilde{g}_\delta[i,j]} \approx z'[m,n] = \dfrac{\partial g_\delta[i,j]}{\partial g[k,l]}$

Where, $m,n = 1,\cdots,MN$; $i,k = 1,\cdots,M$; $j,l = 1,\cdots,N$. However, in Equation (19), $z'[m,m]$ is either zero or 1. This will result in Equation (19) not to be able to be calculated in practice. Thus "generalized cross validation" formula in the wavelet domain will be given as follows:

$$SGCV(\delta) = \frac{\frac{1}{MN}\cdot\|\mathbf{Y} - \mathbf{Y}_\delta\|^2}{\left[\frac{trace(\mathbf{I} - \mathbf{Z}'_\delta)}{MN}\right]^2} . \tag{20}$$

Where $trace$ shows the trace of a matrix, $\|\cdot\|$ indicates Euclidean norm based on inner product, $\mathbf{I}$ shows unit matrix $M \times N$, meaning of other signs is the same as the front. Let $\delta^* = \arg\min MSE(\delta)$, $\tilde{\delta} = \arg\min GCV(\delta)$, M. Jansen has proved that $\tilde{\delta}$, which is obtained by "generalized cross validation", is an asymptotic optimal solution [17].

6.3 Non-linear Gain Operator

Next, based on DSWT, a non-linear enhancement operator, which was proposed by A. Laine in 1994, is employed to enhance the local contrast for image [18]. For convenience, let us define following transform function to enhance the high frequency sub-band images in each decomposition level respectively:

$$g[i, j] = MAG\{f[i, j]\}. \tag{21}$$

Where $g[i, j]$ is sub-band image enhanced, $f[i, j]$ is original sub-band image to be enhanced, MAG is non-linear enhancement operator, M, N is width and height of image respectively.

Let $f_s^r[i, j]$ is the gray values of pixels in the $\mathbf{r}th$ sub-band in the $\mathbf{s}th$ decomposition level, where $s = 1,2,\cdots,L$; $r = 1,2,3$. $maxf_s^r$ is the maximum of gray value of all pixels in $f_s^r[i, j]$. $f_s^r[i, j]$ can be mapped from $[-maxf_s^r, maxf_s^r]$ to $[-1, 1]$. Thus the dynamic range of a,b,c can be set respectively. The contrast enhancement approach can be described by:

$$g_s^r[i, j] = \begin{cases} f_s^r[i, j], & |f_s^r[i, j]| < T_s^r \\ a \cdot \max f_s^r\{\mathrm{sigm}[c(y_s^r[i, j] - b)] - \\ \mathrm{sigm}[-c(y_s^r[i, j] + b)]\}, & |f_s^r[i, j]| \ge T_s^r \end{cases}. \tag{22}$$

$$y_s^r[i, j] = f_s^r[i, j] / maxf_s^r. \tag{23}$$

7 Evaluation Criterion for Enhanced Image

According to the new algorithm, our propose is that the global and the local contrast for the image is enhanced greatly while the gauss white noise in the image can be reduced efficiently. We wish that ratio of signal-to-noise is bigger and contrast is better for enhanced image. A new criterion for evaluating the quality for enhanced image is proposed to solve above problem. The quality for enhanced image is evaluated employing the Equation (5). Combining the ratio of signal-to-noise, a total evaluation criterion is propose as follows:

$$C_{total} = \frac{C_{contrast} * C_{snr}}{\beta}. \tag{24}$$

Where C_{snr} shows the ratio of signal-to-noise for enhanced image, $C_{contrast}$ can be calculated by the Equation (5), and β is a constant. It is obvious that more the value of Equation (24) is, better the total visual quality is.

8 Experimental Results

Daubechies wavelet with two vanishing moments is used to make DSWT to an image in the experiment. Global enhanced image is decomposed into three levels. Fig.2 shows non-linear enhancing curve, where b=0.15, c=30. Fig.3 shows non-linear gray transform curve, where $\alpha = 1.7846$, $\beta = 1.4974$. The non-linear transform curve is employed to enhance the global and the local contrast of Fig.4 (a). Fig.4 (a) is a Lena image, which is corrupted by GWN ($\sigma = 8.8316$).

In order to extrude excellent performance of the new algorithm, two traditional contrast enhancement algorithms are compared with the new algorithm. They are histogram equalization (HE) and unsharpened mask algorithm (USM) respectively. Fig.4 (b)-Fig.4 (f) show enhanced images by HE, USM, the new algorithm, GWP and WYQ algorithm respectively.

Based on one-dimension gray level histogram in the section 3, the contrast type of Fig.4 (a) is “MBS”. From the experimental results above, the noise in the image is enhanced greatly when USM and HIS enhance the image, which is obvious in Fig.4 (b)-(c). Noise reduction is also considered in Ref.[11] and Ref.[12]. The total contrast is better employing GWP algorithm, however, it is not efficient to reduce the noise in the image. From Fig.4 (e), it is obvious that the noise in the image is enhanced greatly and the background clutter is also enlarged. This is very obvious in Fig.4 (e). Although WYQ algorithm can reduce the noise in the image well, the whole brightness of the image is too high so that some detail in the image lost. Lots of burr is produced in Fig.4 (f), such as the hat of Lena. Compared with the above four algorithms, the new algorithm can reduce efficiently GWN in the image while enhance the contrast for the image well. It is obvious that the new algorithm is more excellent in the total performance than USM, HIS, GWP and WYQ.

In order to explain further the efficiency of the new algorithm, Equation (25) is used to evaluate the quality of enhanced images. The total evaluation values of enhanced images by HIS, USH, SWT, GWP and WYQ in Fig.4 are 27.0131, -95.5358, 72.1523, 8.7313 and –2.9249 respectively. This can draw the same conclusion with the above analysis to enhanced images.

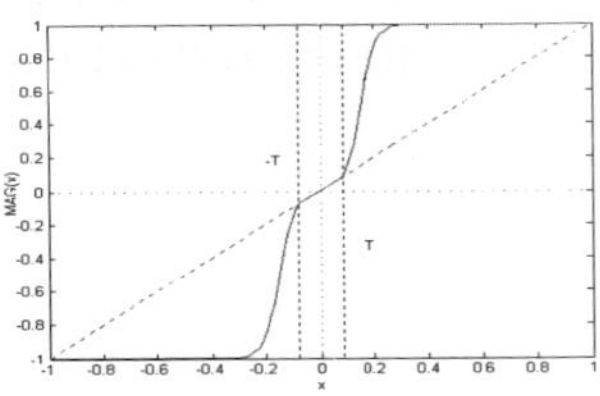

Fig. 2. Non-linear gain curve

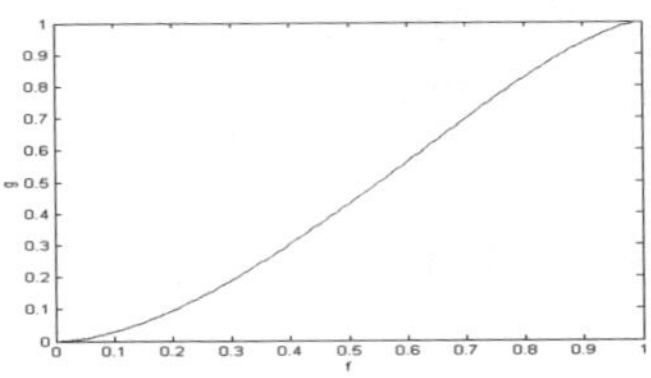

Fig. 3. Gray levels transform curve

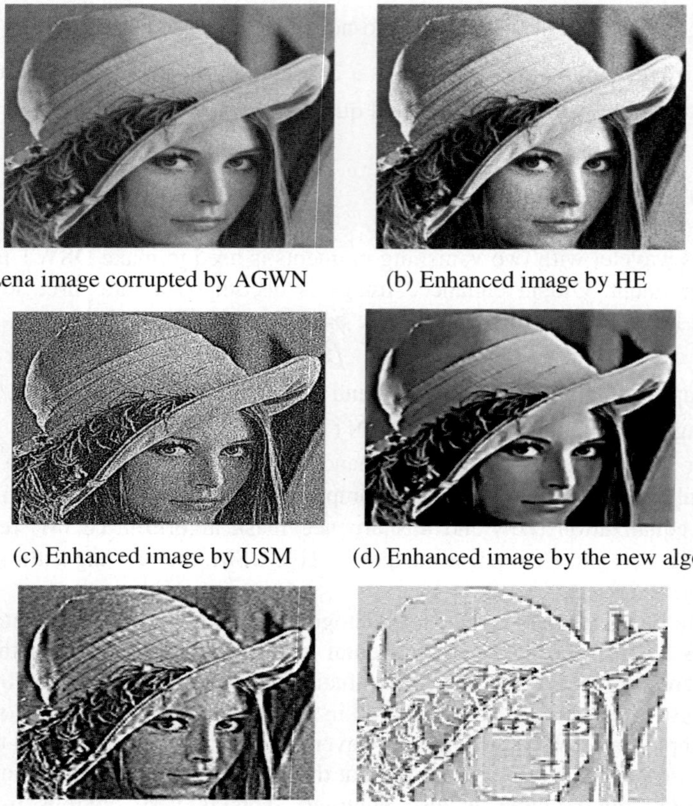

(a) Lena image corrupted by AGWN (b) Enhanced image by HE

(c) Enhanced image by USM (d) Enhanced image by the new algorithm

(e) Enhanced image by GWP (f) Enhanced image by the WYQ

Fig. 4. Enhanced images by five algorithms

9 Conclusion

Employing GCV, the asymptotic optimal de-noising threshold can be obtained when the accurate statistic properties are not prior-known. The global contrast of the image is enhanced directly combining IBT and SA. The local contrast of the image is enhanced combining de-nosing algorithm and non-linear gain operator. Experimental results show that the new algorithm can enhance adaptively the global and local contrast for image effectively while keeping detail information in the original image well. The total performance of the new algorithm is more excellent than HE, USM, GWP and WYQ algorithm.

Acknowledgements

The work described in this paper was supported by grants from the Zhejiang Province Educational Office foundation of China (No. 20050292).

References

1. Azriel Rosenfield, Avinash, C. K.: Digital Picture Processing. New York: Academic Press(1982)
2. Ramar, K., Arumugam, S., Sivanandam, S. N.: Enhancement of Noisy and Blurred Images: A Fuzzy Operator Approach. Advances in Modeling and Analysis, 42 (1992) 49-60
3. Shang-Ming Zhou, Qiang Gan.: A New Fuzzy Relaxation Algorithm for Image Contrast Enhancement. Proceedings of the 3rd International Symposium on Image and Signal Processing and Analysis, 1 (2003) 11-16
4. Ming Tang, SongDe Ma, Jing Xiao.: Model-based Adaptive Enhancement of Far Infrared Image Sequences. Pattern Recognition, 30 (2000) 827-835
5. Stark, J.A.: Adaptive Image Contrast Enhancement Using Generalizations of Histogram Equalization. IEEE Transactions on Image Processing, 9 (2000) 889-896
6. Joung-Youn Kim, Lee-Sup Kim.: An Advanced Contrast Enhancement Using Partially Overlapped Sub-block Histogram Equalization. IEEE Transactions on Circuits and Systems for Video Technology, 11 (2001) 475-484
7. Seungjoon Yang, Jae Hwan Oh, Yungjun Park.: Contrast Enhancement Using Histogram Equalization with Bin Underflow and Overflow. Image Processing, 2003. Proceedings. 2003 International Conference on, **1** (2003) 881-884
8. Soong-Der Chen, Ramli, A.R.: Contrast Enhancement Using Recursive Mean-separate Histogram Equalization for Scalable Brightness Preservation. IEEE Transactions on Consumer Electronics, 49 (2003) 1301-1309
9. Soong-Der Chen, Ramli, A.R.: Minimum Mean Brightness Error Bi-histogram Equalization in Contrast Enhancement. IEEE Transactions on Consumer Electronics, 48 (2003) 1201-1207
10. Tubbs, J. D.: A Note on Parametric Image Enhancement. Pattern Recognition, 30 (1997) 616-621
11. GONG Wu-Peng, WANG Yong-Zhong.: Contrast Enhancement of Infrared Image via Wavelet Transforms. Chinese Journal of National University of Defense Technology, 22 (2000) 117-119
12. WU Ying-Qian, SHI Peng-Fei.: Approach on Image Contrast Enhancement based on Wavelet Transform. Chinese J. Infrared and Laser Engineering, 32 (2003) 4-7
13. William, L., Goffe, Gary, D., Ferrier, John Rogers.: Global Optimization of Statistical Functions with Simulated Annealing. Journal of Econometrics, 60 (1994) 65-99
14. Lang, M., Guo, H., odegend, J.E., Burrus, C.S., , Wells,Jr, R.O.:Nonlinear Processing of a Shift-invariant DWT for Noise Reduction. In SPIE Conference on wavelet applications, 2491 (1995)
15. Johnstone, I.M., Silverman, B.W.: Wavelet Threshold Estimators for Data with Correlated Noise. Journal of the Royal Statistical Society, Series B, 59 (1997) 319-351
16. Hall, P., Koch, I.:On the Feasibility of Cross-validation in Image Analysis. SIAM J.Appl. Math, 52 (1992) 292-313
17. Maarten Jansen, Geert Uytterhoeven, Adhemar Bultheel.: Image De-nosing by Integer Wavelet Transforms and Generalized cross Validation. Technical Report TW264, Department of Computer Science, Katholieke Universiteit, Leuven, Belguim, August(1997)
18. Laine, A., Schuler, S.: Hexagonal Wavelet Processing of Digital Mammography. In Medical Imaging 1993, Part of SPIE's Thematic Applied Science and Engineering Series(1993) 1345-1348

Graph-Based Ant System for Optimal Sizing of Standalone Hybrid Wind/PV Power Systems

Daming Xu, Longyun Kang, and Binggang Cao

Department of Mechatronics, Xi'an Jiaotong University, Xi'an 710049, PR China
xu_daming@hotmail.com, {kang, inte-cao}@mail.xjtu.edu.cn

Abstract. In the design of standalone hybrid wind/photovoltaic power systems, the optimal sizing is an important and challenging task. The coordination among renewable energy resources, generators, energy storages and loads is very complicated. The size of wind turbine generators (WTGs), the size of photovoltaic (PV) panels and the capacity of batteries must be optimized when sizing a standalone hybrid wind/PV power system, which is formulated as a nonlinear integer programming problem. Our objective is selected as minimizing the total capital cost, subject to the constraint of the Loss of Power Supply Probability (LPSP) calculated by simulation. We propose a specific Graph-based Ant System to solve the concerned problem intuitively and easily. The death penalty method is used to deal with the constraint. Simulations have shown that the proposed Graph-based Ant System is efficient with respect to the quality of solutions and computing time.

1 Introduction

Global environmental concerns and the ever-increasing need for energy, coupled with a steady progress in renewable energy technologies are opening up new opportunities for utilization of renewable energy resources. Hybrid wind/photovoltaic (PV) power systems are one important type of standalone renewable energy power systems. The hybrid combination of PV panels and wind turbine generators (WTGs) improves overall energy output and reduces energy storage requirements [1].

In the design of standalone renewable energy power systems, the optimal sizing is an important and challenging task, as the coordination among renewable energy resources, generators, energy storages and loads is very complicated. Generally the objective of the optimization design is cost, subjected to power reliability evaluated by simulation, and the decision variables are the capacities of generators and storages. This can be formulated as a nonlinear integer programming problem.

For standalone hybrid wind/PV power systems, a typical method, the tangent method, is to fix the size of WTGs and optimize the size of PV panels and the capacity of batteries [2,3]. There isn't an optimization method that the parameters such as the size of WTGs, the size of PV panels and the capacity of batteries can be taken as decision variables collectively [1-7]. Recently a genetic algorithm for the concerned problem has been proposed by Xu *et al.* [8], which can take the size of WTGs, the size of PV panels and the capacity of batteries as decision variables.

D.-S. Huang, K. Li, and G.W. Irwin (Eds.): ICIC 2006, LNAI 4114, pp. 1136 – 1146, 2006.

Although this method has better performance in comparison to the old methods, we hope to find a method with higher computational efficiency.

Ant Colony Optimization (ACO) algorithms for the heuristic solution of combinatorial optimization problems enjoy a rapidly growing popularity (see, e.g., the survey article by Dorigo and Blum [9]). Formulating the approach explicitly as a metaheuristic, the so-called ACO metaheuristic, Dorigo and Di Caro [10] have emphasized its broad range of applicability. The starting point for ACO algorithms is a biological metaphor: Natural ant colonies are able to find shortest paths between anthill and food by a specific type of reinforcement learning, using local pheromone trails for information exchange. In [11,12], Dorigo, Maniezzo and Colorni have transferred this principle to the algorithmic solution of optimization problems. In the last decade, it has been recognized that not only routing problems as the famous traveling salesperson problem (TSP), but also any other type of combinatorial optimization problems can be encoded as "best path" problems and solved using the ant colony metaphor.

Intuitively, the basic idea of ACO is the following: In order to solve a best-path problem in a graph, random walks of a fixed number of "ants" through the graph are simulated. The transition probabilities of each ant are governed by two types of parameters assigned to the edges of the graph:

(i) *pheromone* values representing, in some sense, the "common memory" of the ant colony (the "past" perspective), and
(ii) *visibility* values computed by heuristic pre-evaluations of how promising a transition along each edge appears (the "future" perspective).

The pheromone values are updated by a combination of two mechanisms: *evaporation*, a global reduction of the pheromone vectors by a certain factor per time unit simulating the process that in a natural environment, pheromone trails diminish in course of time, and *reinforcement* of pheromone on paths recognized as "good".

In [13,14], nonlinear 0-1 programming problems were solved with ant algorithms. Gutjahr presented an ACO variant called Graph-based Ant System (GABS) [15]. Inspired by GABS, we have an idea that whether we can describe the nonlinear integer programming problem using a graph and let artificial ants find the shortest path on the graph with high computational efficiency. In this paper, we will propose a specific Graph-based Ant System to deal with the nonlinear integer programming problem.

2 Calculation of Loss of Power Supply Probability

The configuration of standalone hybrid wind/PV power systems is shown in Figure 1. In this paper, we investigated the case that a system has only one type of WTGs.

The Loss of Power Supply Probability (LPSP) [2], which is defined in terms of the battery state of charge (SOC), is the power reliability index of a system. The LPSP can be defined as the long-term average fraction of the load that is not supplied by the standalone power system. In terms of the SOC, the LPSP can be defined as:

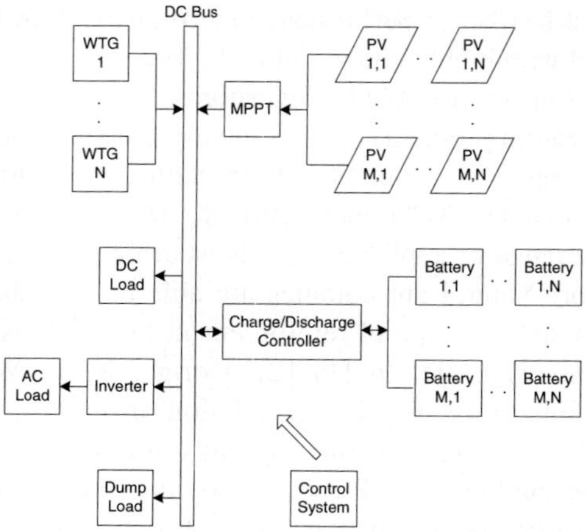

Fig. 1. Schematic of standalone hybrid wind/PV power systems

$$\mathrm{LPSP} = \Pr\left\{E_{\mathrm{B},t} \le E_{\mathrm{B\,min}},\ t \in T\right\} \tag{1}$$

where $E_{\mathrm{B,t}}$ is energy stored in batteries at any time step t, E_{Bmin} is battery minimum allowable energy level and T is the operation period that can be divided into many time steps.

An operation simulation of the hybrid wind/PV power system must be performed in order to compute the LPSP. The load, wind energy and solar energy are assumed to be constant during a time step. For each time step, when the energy generated from the PV array and WTGs exceeds that of the load demand, the batteries will be charged with the round-trip efficiency. When the load demand is greater than the available energy generated, the batteries will be discharged by the amount that is needed to cover the deficit. When the available energy generated and stored in batteries is insufficient to satisfy the load demand $E_{\mathrm{L,t}}$ for time step t, that deficit is called Loss of Power Supply (LPS_t). The LPSP for a considered operation period T is the ratio of all LPS_t values for that period to the sum of the load demand, as defined by:

$$\mathrm{LPSP} = \sum_{t \in T} \mathrm{LPS}_t \Big/ \sum_{t \in T} E_{\mathrm{L},t} \tag{2}$$

In this paper, the operation period is 1 year and the time step is 1 hour.

The operation simulation follows the rule of energy balance that the sum of all energy sources must equal the sum of all sinks in a time step. This assures that energy is conserved throughout the entire simulation. The procedure of compute the LPS_t for a time step is as follows:

1. Compute the wind speed to a particular hub height according to the measured wind data; compute the solar radiation incident on a tilted solar panel surface according to the total radiation on a horizontal surface.
2. Compute the output power of WTGs and PV panels.
3. Compute the LPS_t.

The wind speed to a particular hub height is computed by the well-known power law equation. The Hay-Davies-Klucher-Reindl (HDKR) anisotropic model described by Duffie and Beckman [16] is employed to compute the incident radiation on the tilted PV panel surface.

The power curve, which is used in computing the output power of a WTG, is represented by a piecewise cubic spline interpolation. The output power from a PV panel can be computed by an analytical model given by France Lasnier and Tony Gan Ang [17], in which a maximum power point tracker (MPPT) is considered.

Lead acid batteries are main energy storage devices in standalone power systems. The battery charging efficiency is set equal to the round-trip efficiency, and the discharge efficiency is set equal to 1. The maximum battery life can be obtained if the depth of discharge (DOD) is set equal to 30%~50%.

The MPPT, battery controller, inverter and distribution lines are assumed to have constant efficiencies. Assume the efficiencies of the MPPT, battery controller and distribution lines as 1 and that of the inverter as 0.9.

3 Nonlinear Integer Programming Using GBAS

3.1 Problem Description

Minimization of cost for a given demand of power reliability is the objective of sizing standalone hybrid wind/PV power systems. The cost index is C_{WPB}, which is the total capital cost of WTGs, PV panels and batteries [8]. Let C_{WPB} as the objective, the LPSP as the constraint, then the problem is described as follows:

$$\begin{cases} \min\ C_{\mathrm{WPB}} = C_{\mathrm{WTG}} N_{\mathrm{WTG}} + C_{\mathrm{PV}} N_{\mathrm{PV}} + C_{\mathrm{bat}} N_{\mathrm{bat}} \\ s.t.\quad \mathrm{LPSP} \le \mathrm{LPSP}_{\mathrm{set}} \\ \qquad N_{\mathrm{WTG}} = 0,1,2,\cdots \\ \qquad N_{\mathrm{PV}} = N_{\mathrm{PV\_s}} N_{\mathrm{PV\_p}},\ N_{\mathrm{PV\_p}} = 0,1,2,\cdots \\ \qquad N_{\mathrm{bat}} = N_{\mathrm{bat\_s}} N_{\mathrm{bat\_p}},\ N_{\mathrm{bat\_p}} = 0,1,2,\cdots \end{cases} \tag{3}$$

where:

C_{bat}	cost of the battery,
C_{PV}	cost of the PV panel,
C_{WTG}	cost of the WTG,
$\mathrm{LPSP}_{\mathrm{set}}$	LPSP set according to the load characteristics,
N_{bat}	number of the batteries,
$N_{\mathrm{bat\_p}}$	number of the batteries in parallel,
$N_{\mathrm{bat\_s}}$	number of the batteries in series,
N_{PV}	number of the PV panels,

N_{PV_p} number of the PV panels in parallel,

N_{PV_s} number of the PV panels in series,

N_{WTG} number of the WTGs.

In the optimization model, the tilt angle is a variable of the HDKR model that is used in computing LPSP. The fixed tilt angle θ is set equal to the site latitude value.

3.2 The Specific Graph Based Ant System

Defination 3.1. Let an instance of a nonlinear integer programming problem be given. By a *construction graph* for this instance, we understand a directed graph $C = (V, A)$ together with a function Φ with the following properties [15]:

1. In C, a unique node is marked as the so-called *start node*.
2. Let W be the set of (directed) paths w in C satisfying the following conditions:
   (i) w starts at the start node of C;
   (ii) w contains each node of C at most once;
   (iii) the last node on w has no successor node in C that is not already contained in w (i.e., w cannot be prolonged without violating (ii)).

Then Φ maps the set W onto the set of solutions of the given problem instance. In other words: To each path w in W, there corresponds (via Φ) a solution, and to each solution, there corresponds (via Φ^{-1}) at least one path in W.

The specific Graph-based Ant System for the nonlinear integer programming problem contains the following components:

1. A construction graph (C, Φ) according to Defination 3.1. Except the start node, each node represents a decision variable. For a node, each arriving arc represents an integer value of the node and the range of the decision variable consists of these arcs. As it can be seen from the definition, a construction graph (C, Φ) specifies a particular encoding of the solutions, which are feasible or infeasible, as "walks". The objective function value of the walk is set equal to the objective function value of the corresponding solution of the original problem.
2. Initially, K ants are placed on start node, from which they start their tours. An ant stochastically selects the next node and chooses an arc with a transition probability (see component 3) to get to the node. If its walk fulfills the constraint it can stop in advance. If its walk does not fulfill the constraint although it has visited all the nodes, it is called infeasible. A time period in which each performs a walk (consisting of several single moves) through the construction graph will be called an *iteration*. An application of the Graph-based Ant System consists of several iterations 1, …, N_{max}, and n is the iteration counter.
3. *Transition probabilities* for the move of the ants before each node. The probabilistic choice of an arc arriving the selected node is biased by the pheromone trail $\tau_{i,j}(n)$ and by heuristic information $\eta_{i,j}$, where i is node number,

j is arc number of the node. Let $\eta_{i,j} = 1/(Cost_i \cdot Value_j)$, where $Cost_i$ is cost of the equipment ith node represents and $Value_j$ is numerical value jth arc represents. Let u denote the set of nodes ant k has already traversed. For the Graph-based Ant System, ant k stochastically selects node i and then chooses its arc j with a probability:

$$p_{i,j}^k(n) = \frac{[\tau_{i,j}(n)]^\alpha [\eta_{i,j}]^\beta}{\sum_{s \in F_i} [\tau_{i,s}(n)]^\alpha [\eta_{i,s}]^\beta} \quad \text{if } i \notin u \tag{4}$$

where α and β are two parameters which determine the relative importance of the pheromone trail and the heuristic information, F_i is the value range of ith variable.

4. An array of *pheromone values* $\tau_{i,j}$, where $\tau_{i,j}$ is assigned to arc (i, j) in the construction graph. The pheromone update follows the strategy of Ant System (*ant-cycle*) [18]. After all ants have completed the tour construction, the pheromone values are updated. First, to deal with the constraint, the death penalty method is introduced, by which all the infeasible solutions are refused. That means if a path walked by an ant is infeasible, the ant cannot be considered in pheromone update. Second, for the feasible ants, the update follows this rule:

$$\tau_{i,j}(n+1) = \rho \tau_{i,j}(n) + \sum_{k \in Feas(n)} \Delta \tau_{i,j}^k(n) \tag{5}$$

where the parameter ρ (with $0 \le \rho < 1$) is the trail persistence (thus, $1-\rho$ models the evaporation), $\Delta \tau_{i,j}^k(n)$ is the amount of pheromone ant k puts on arc (i, j) if it has passed arc (i, j) and $Feas(n)$ is the set of all feasible ants passing arc (i, j) in this iteration. The evaporation mechanism helps to avoid unlimited accumulation of the pheromone trail. While an arc is not chosen by the ants, its associated pheromone trail decreases exponentially; this enables the algorithm to "forget" bad choices over time. In the Graph-based Ant System, $\Delta \tau_{i,j}^k(n)$ is defined as:

$$\Delta \tau_{i,j}^k(n) = \begin{cases} 1/C_{\text{WPB}}^k(n) & \text{if arc}(i, j) \text{ is used by feasible ant } k \text{ in iteration } n, \\ 0 & \text{otherwise} \end{cases} \tag{6}$$

where $C_{\text{WPB}}^k(n)$ is C_{WPB} according to the walk of ant k in iteration n. By Eq. (6), the better the ant's tour is, the more pheromone is received by the arcs belonging to this tour.

4 Application Example

The location of Boston, Massachusetts with Latitude 42°22′N is chosen. The load curve of a typical house [2] is shown in Figure 2. The typical meteorological year data sets (TMY2s) contain hourly values of solar radiation and meteorological elements for a one-year period [19]. The data of extraterrestrial horizontal radiation, global horizontal radiation, diffuse horizontal radiation, temperature and wind speed of station Boston are utilized. Generally, the ground reflectance is 0.2.

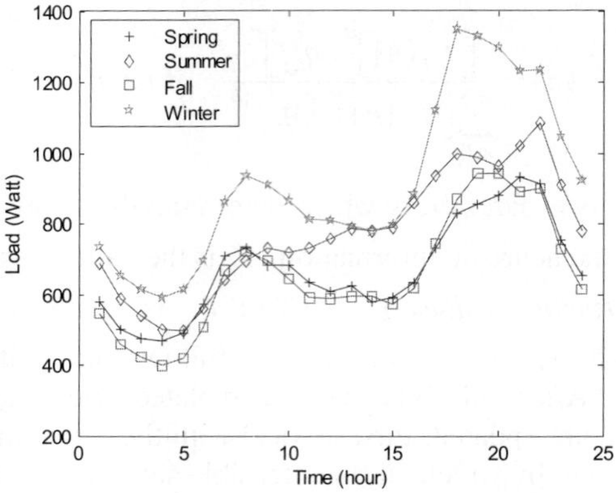

Fig. 2. A typical load profile in Boston

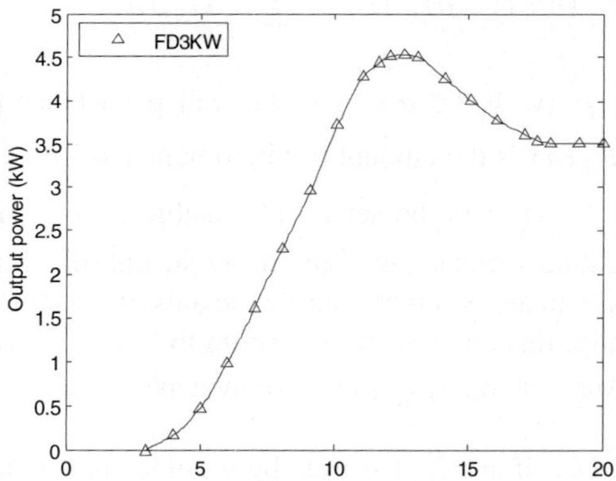

Fig. 3. The power curve of the FD3KW WTG (The symbols represent data sampled from the power curve graphs given by the manufacturer)

The FD3KW WTG with rated power of 3kW made by Tianfeng Green Energy Company of China are considered. The power curves of the WTG is shown in Fig. 3. A 50W$_{peak}$ PV panel made by Yunnan Semiconductor Device Factory in China is used for this simulation study. The capacity of a single battery used is 200Ah. That battery has a round-trip efficiency of 0.7 and DOD=50%.

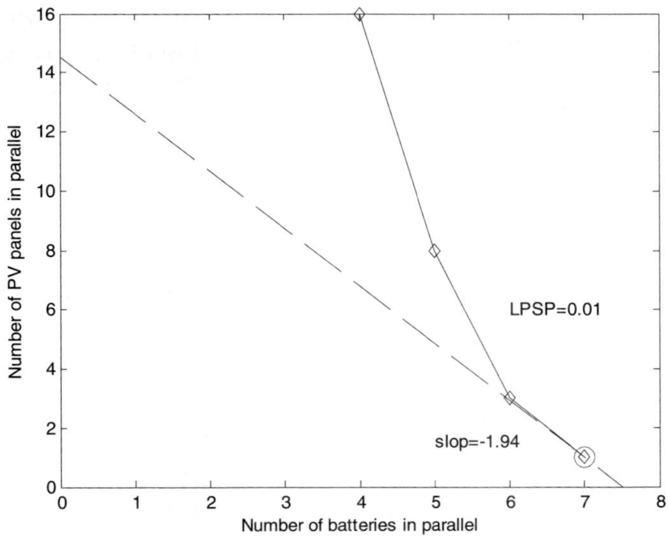

Fig. 4. The optimal configuration of N_{PV_p}=1 and N_{bat_p}=7 for the given conditions as N_{WTG}=3, $\theta = 42^\circ$, LPSP$_{set}$=0.01

For the parameters of the power system, according to the voltage, let N_{PV_s}=3 and N_{bat_s}=24. Let LPSP$_{set}$=0.01 and $\theta = 42^\circ$. The LPSP of every solution is computed by simulation of 8760 hours in a year. Let the integer variables $N_{WTG} \in [0,15]$, $N_{PV\_p} \in [0,15]$, $N_{bat\_p} \in [0,15]$.

For the parameters of the ant algorithm, let [node1 node2 node3]=[N_{WTG} N_{PV_p} N_{bat_p}], and let ant number K=50, maximum number of iteration N_{max}=200, $\alpha = 1$, $\beta = 5$, $\rho = 0.8$ and $\tau_0 = 10^{-8}$ be default setting.

In order to verify the solutions, we use the tangent method [2,3]. The procedure is:

```
for every N_WTG do;
  find the optimal N_PV_p and N_bat_p;
end for.
```

We take a solution [N_{WTG} N_{PV_p} N_{bat_p}]=[3 1 7], LPSP=0.0086, C_{WPB} =179310 (Yuan) for example. Let N_{WTG}=3, we get N_{PV_p}=1 and N_{bat_p}=7, as shown in Figure 4. The minimum cost is at the tangent point of the cost line and the curve that represents the relationship between the size of PV panels and capacity of batteries. The slope of the cost line is:

$$-\frac{C_{bat} N_{bat\_s}}{C_{PV} N_{PV\_s}} = -\frac{520\ (\text{Yuan}) \times 24}{2150\ (\text{Yuan}) \times 3} = -1.94 \tag{7}$$

Enumerate the cases of N_{WTG}, we get the optimal configuration [N_{WTG} N_{PV_p} N_{bat_p}]=[3 1 7], C_{WPB} =179310 (Yuan) for LPSP$_{set}$=0.01. So [N_{WTG} N_{PV_p} N_{bat_p}]=[3 1 7] is the optimal solution given LPSP$_{set}$=0.01.

The influence of the parameter ρ on the proposed algorithm performance is evaluated. In this paper, every result of the Graph-based Ant System is the average of 25 runs. The effect of parameter ρ is represented graphically in Figure 5. The tests show that ρ should be set as 0.8.

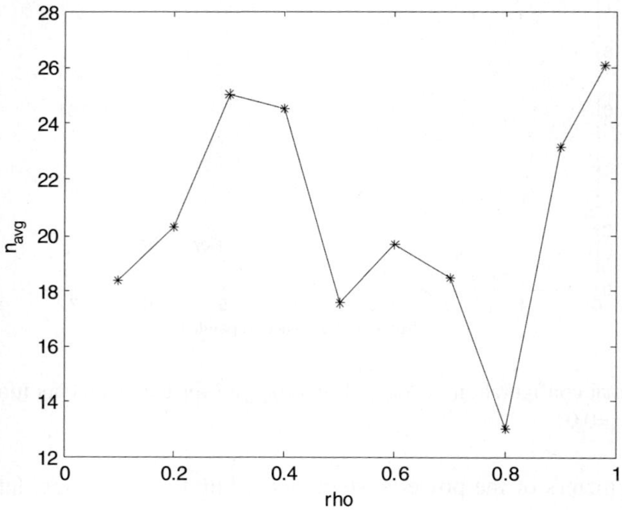

Fig. 5. Influence of coefficient ρ on the performance of the proposed algorithm ($\alpha = 1$, $\beta = 5$). Y-axis represents the average number of iteration n_{avg} to find the best solution in a run. Averages are taken over 25 trails.

As the efficiency of the tangent method is much lower than the genetic algorithm [8], we only make comparison between the specific Graph-based Ant System and the genetic algorithm. The genetic algorithm is standard genetic algorithm with elitist strategy. Its number of individual is 50 and maximum number of iteration is 200. The computational results are presented in Table 1. The results have shown that the proposed Graph-based Ant System is efficient with respect to the quality of solutions and computing time compared to the genetic algorithm.

Table 1. Experiment results of the specific Graph-based Ant System and the genetic algorithm

Algorithm	Best	Average	Worst	n_{avg}	$time_{avg}$ (s)
GBAS	179310	179310	179310	19.08	2.458
GA	179310	179355	179730	96.75	11.746

[a] Given are the algorithm used, the best solution, the average solution, the worst solution, the average number of iteration n_{avg} and average time $time_{avg}$ to find the best solution in a run. Averages are taken over 25 trails.

5 Conclusions

This paper deals with sizing of standalone hybrid wind/PV power systems, which is formulated as a nonlinear integer programming problem. Inspired by Graph-based Ant System we proposed a heuristic approach. A construction graph specifies a particular encoding of the solutions as walks. On the construction graph, a node represents a decision variable. For a node, each arriving arc represents an integer value of the node and the number of these arcs is determined by the range of the decision variable. The constraint must be computed by simulation. To deal with the constraint, the death penalty method is introduced, by which infeasible ant cannot be considered in pheromone update. The specific Graph-based Ant System converges very well and this can be verified using the tangent method. The experimental results reveal that the proposed algorithm is effective and efficient for sizing of standalone hybrid wind/PV power systems.

References

1. Habib M. A., Said S. A. M., El-Hadidy M. A., Zaharna, A. I.: Optimization Procedure of Hybrid Photovoltaic Wind Energy System. Energy, 24 (11) (1999) 919-929
2. Borowy, B. S., Salameh, Z .M.: Methodology for Optimally Sizing the Combination of a Battery Bank and PV Array in a Wind/PV Hybrid System. IEEE Trans. On Energy Conversion, 11 (2) (1996) 367-375
3. Willis, H. L., Scott W.G.: Distributed Power Generation: Planning and Evaluation. Marcel Dekker, New York (2000)
4. Kaldellis, J. K.: Parametric Investigation Concerning Dimensions of a Stand-alone Wind-Power System. Applied Energy, 77 (1) 2004 35-50
5. Ai, B., Yang, H., Shen, H., Liao, X.: Computer-aided Design of PV/wind Hybrid System. Renewable Energy, 28 (2003) 1491-1512
6. Elhadidy, M. A., Shaahid, S. M.: Optimal Sizing of Battery Storage for Hybrid (wind+diesel) Power Systems. Renewable Energy. 18 (1) (1999) 77-86
7. Al-Ashwal, A. M., Moghram, I. S.: Proportion Assessment of Combined PV-Wind Generating Systems. Renewable Energy, 10 (1) (1997) 43-51
8. Xu, D., Kang L., Cao, B.: Optimal Sizing of Standalone Hybrid Wind/PV Power Systems Using Genetic Algorithms. Proc. of IEEE Canadian Conference on Electrical and Computer Engineering. Sascatoon, Canada, (2005) 1705-1708
9. Dorigo, M., Blum, C.: Ant Colony Optimization Theory: A Survey. Theoretical Computer Science, 344 (2005) 243-278
10. Dorigo, M., Di., Caro, G.: The Ant Colony Optimization Metaheuristic. New Ideas in Optimization. McGraw-Hill, New York (1999)
11. Dorigo, M., Maniezzo, V., Colorni, A.: The Ant System: An Autocatalytic Optimization Process. Technical Report 91-016, Dept. of Electronics, Politecnico di Milano, Italy (1991)
12. Dorig,o. M.: Optimization Learning and Natural Algorithms. PhD Thesis, Dept. of Electronics, Politecnico Di Milano, Italy (1992)
13. Solimanpur, M., Vrat, P., Shankar, R.: An Ant Algorithm for the Single rRow Layout Problem in Flexible Manufacturing Systems. Computers & Operations Research. 32 (2005) 583-598

14. Nahas, N., Nourelfath, M.: Ant System for Reliability Optimization of A Series System with Multiple-choice and Budget Constraints. Reliability Engineering and System Safety. 87 (2005) 1-12
15. Gutjahr, W. J.: ACO Algorithms with Guaranteed Convergence to the Optimal Solution. Information Processing Leters. 82 (2002) 145-153
16. Duffie, J. A., Beckman, W. A.: Solar Engineering of Thermal Processes. 2rd edn. Wiley, New York (1991)
17. Lasnier, F., Ang, T.G.: Photovoltaic Engineering Handbook. Hilger, Bristol (1990)
18. Dorigo, M., Maniezzo, V., Colorni, A.: The Ant System: Optimization by a Colony of Cooperating Agents. IEEE Trans on Systems, Man, and Cybernetics–Part B, 26 (1) (1996) 1-13
19. Marion, W., Urban, K.: User's Manual for TMY2s. National Renewable Energy Laboratory, (1995)

Maximizing Dual Function by Genetic Algorithm – A New Approach for Optimal Manpower Planning

Xiaoqiang Cai[1,3], Yongjian Li[2,⋆], and Fengsheng Tu[3]

[1] Department of System Engineering & Engineering Management
The Chinese University of HongKong, Shatin N. T., Hong Kong, China
[2] Business School, Nankai University, Tianjin 300071, China
liyongjian@nankai.edu.cn
[3] College of Information Technical Science
Nankai University, Tianjin 300071, China

Abstract. We propose a new approach to tackle the manpower planning problem with multiple types of jobs in a long planning horizon, where dynamic demands for manpower must be fulfilled by allocating enough number of employees with qualified skills. We first apply Lagrangean relaxation to decompose the problem into a number of subproblems, each corresponding to one skill type, and then develop a coordination scheme based on a Genetic algorithm, which updates the Lagrangean multipliers to maximize the dual objective function. We report computational results, which demonstrate the effectiveness of our approach.

1 Introduction

The manpower planning problem is to determine the optimal decisions on recruiting, dismissing, and assignment of the right employees to meet the demands for manpower in an organization over a given planning horizon. This is a problem of prominent importance for any organization, in particular those that are labor intensive. As such, this problem has received considerable attentions in the literature; see, e.g.,[1]-[3]. Considering the dynamic fluctuations of manpower demands, it is natural for an organization to determine the optimal size of its workforce by making proper and dynamic decisions on recruitment and dismissal over different periods of time. Such models, however, have not received much attention in the literature, due to properly the inherent complexity in deriving the optimal dynamic solutions, especially, for the problem with more than one type of job. Li, *et al.* [4], [5] have studied a manpower planning problem with single employee type. Cai, *et al.* [6] have studied the problem with two types of jobs, and proposed an optimization approach. However, the approach in this paper is problem-specific, which cannot be extended to problems with more than two-employee-types.

⋆ Corresponding author.

D.-S. Huang, K. Li, and G.W. Irwin (Eds.): ICIC 2006, LNAI 4114, pp. 1147–1157, 2006.

The manpower planning optimization models can be applied in many areas. Verbeek [7] has suggested a framework for a pilot planning decision support system and described some of the complexities of such a system. Yu *et al.* [8] have provided an advanced optimization model and solution techniques to solve complex, large-scale pilot staffing and training problems, and so on.

In this paper, we investigate a manpower planning problem where different types of workers are needed to meet the manpower demands that fluctuate dynamically. We consider the situation where an employee of a higher skill can be assigned to do the job of a lower-skill worker, but not *vice versa*. Our model seeks to determine an optimal solution for the problem by treating the decisions on recruitment, dismissal, and substitution in an integrated manner.

Our main contribution is the development of a novel approach to derive the solution of the manpower planning problem. Our approach first decomposes the overall problem into a number of subproblems, each corresponding to a single-skill job. It then updates the Lagrangean multipliers by a genetic procedure, performed through a specifically designed genetic algorithm to maximize the dual objective function. We describe the optimal solution approach for the subproblems, and our designs of the genetic algorithm for the dual problem. Numerical results are also reported, to evaluate the effectiveness of the approach.

2 Problem Description

We consider the situation where an organization has to maintain sufficient staff to meet the demands for manpower to perform two types of jobs; one can be performed only by a group of workers of a higher skill, whereas the other can be performed either by workers of the lower skill or by workers of the higher skill. We will show later (Section 7) that the approach we are going to develop in this paper can be generalized directly to problems with a higher-level job and r lower-level jobs, where $r \geq 2$.

Specifically, we assume that the two types of jobs require manpower resources D_{1t}, D_{2t} respectively during period t ($t = 1, 2, \cdots, T$), where T is the planning horizon. For simplicity, we let the initial demands $D_{i0} = 0, i = 1, 2$. A problem with nonzero initial demands can be tackled similarly. Two types of employees are to be maintained in the organization. Type-1 employees have skill 1 and can be assigned to type-1 job, while type-2 employees have a higher skill, and can be assigned not only to type-2 job, but also to type-1 job.

The costs for using different types of employees are different, and usually type-2 employees are more expensive. The problem is to find optimal decisions on when and how many type-i (i=1,2) employees should be recruited, dismissed, or assigned to do a lower-level job, so that the total manpower-related cost, including salary, recruitment cost and dismissal cost, is minimized.

Let

$f_i(x)$ The cost for maintaining x type-i employees in one time period, $i = 1, 2$.
β_i^+ The recruiting cost per type-i employee, $i = 1, 2$.

β_i^- The dismissal cost per type-i employee, $i = 1, 2$.
$X_i[t]$ The number of type-i employees available during period t, $i = 1, 2$
$u_i[t]$ The number of type-i employees recruited ($u_i[t]>0$) or dismissed ($u_i[t]<0$) at the end of period t, $i = 1, 2$.

The basic constraint in the manpower planning problem is that the total available employees in the system must be able to cover the demands for performing each type of jobs. In period t, only $X_2[t]$ type-2 employees can be assigned to do type-2 job. Hence, for type-2 job, the following inequalities must be satisfied.

$$X_2[t] \geq D_{2t}, \quad t = 1, 2, \cdots, T \tag{1}$$

If there are, however, unassigned type-2 employees at any time period t, they can be used to perform type-1 job. Thus, to satisfy the demand for type-1 job, we have

$$X_1[t] + X_2[t] \geq D_{1t} + D_{2t}, \quad t = 1, 2, \cdots, T \tag{2}$$

At the end of each period t, we should decide whether to recruit new employees or dismiss existing employees so that the total cost of the system is minimized. For simplicity, we assume no employees are dismissed/recruited at the end of the final period T (A problem with other terminal conditions can be treated similarly). Therefore,

$$X_i[t+1] = X_i[t] + u_i[t], \quad i = 1, 2;\ t = 0, 1, \cdots, T-1 \tag{3}$$

To summarize, the problem (denoted as Problem **P2**) can be formulated as follows

$$\min_{u_1[t], u_2[t]} J = \sum_{i=1}^{2} \left\{ \sum_{t=1}^{T} f_i(X_i[t]) + \sum_{t=0}^{T-1} \left[\beta_i^+ u_i^+[t] + \beta_i^- u_i^-[t]\right] \right\} \tag{4}$$

s. t.

$$X_i[t+1] = X_i[t] + u_i[t], \quad i = 1, 2; t = 0, 1, \cdots, T-1 \tag{5}$$

$$X_1[t] + X_2[t] \geq D_{1t} + D_{2t},\ t = 1, 2, \cdots, T \tag{6}$$

$$X_2[t] \geq D_{2t}, \quad t = 1, 2, \cdots, T \tag{7}$$

$$X_i[0] = X_i^0, \quad i = 1, 2 \tag{8}$$

where $u_i^+[t] = \max\{u_i[t], 0\}$, $u_i^-[t] = \max\{-u_i[t], 0\}$, and X_i^0 (i=1,2) are given constants. We assume that $f_i(x)$ is a convex function of x (This represents many practical situations, including the case of linear functions). Moreover, we assume that $arg \min_x\{f_i(x)\} \leq \max\{D_{it}, 1 \leq t \leq T\}$ for $i = 1, 2$. Otherwise, $X_i[t] = arg \min_x\{f_i(x)\}$ are optimal solutions for $t = 1, 2, \cdots, T$ and $i = 1, 2$.

Further, we assume that $\alpha_1 \leq \alpha_2, \beta_1^+ \leq \beta_2^+$ and $\beta_1^- \leq \beta_2^-$. Otherwise, an optimal solution can be easily found by solving the problem **P2** with only type-2 employees and demands $D_t = D_{1t} + D_{2t}$, $t = 1, 2, \cdots, T$.

3 Decomposition

In this Section we will decompose the problem P2 into two subproblems by Langrangean relaxation. The optimal solutions for the subproblems will be derived in Section 4. The coordination of the solutions for the subproblems will be performed by a Genetic algorithm, which will be described in Section 5.

We see that, in problem P2, the couple that links the two types of employees together is the constraint $X_1[t] + X_2[t] \geq D_{1t} + D_{2t}$. To decompose the problem into decoupled subproblems, we apply duality theory, by incorporating this constraint into the objective function with nonnegative Lagrangean multipliers, which results in the problem as follows.

RP2

$$\min_{u_1[t],u_2[t]} \sum_{i=1}^{2} \left\{ \sum_{t=1}^{T} \left[f_i(X_i[t]) - \lambda_t X_i[t] + \lambda_t D_{it} \right] + \sum_{t=0}^{T-1} \left[\beta_i^+ u_i^+[t] + \beta_i^- u_i^-[t] \right] \right\} \tag{9}$$

subject to (5), (7) and (8).

The objective function (9) is now composed of two terms. The first term $f_i(X_i[t]) - \lambda_t X_i[t] + \beta_i^+ u_i^+[t] + \beta_i^- u_i^-[t]$ is a weighted sum over all $X_i[t]$ and $u_i[t]$, whereas the second one $\lambda_t D_{it}$ is independent of all variables and can be neglected in terms of finding the optimal $\{u_i(t)\}$ and $\{X_i(t)\}$. On the other hand, the constraints of RP2, namely (5), (7) and (8), can be decomposed into two independent sets, each of which corresponds to exactly one employee type. Consequently, RP2 can be decomposed into two independent subproblems when the Lagrangean multipliers $\lambda = [\lambda_1, \lambda_2, \cdots, \lambda_T]$ are taken as known constants, which are labelled by **SP**i and are given below, respectively:

SP1

$$\min_{u_1[t]} J_1(\lambda) = \sum_{t=1}^{T} \left\{ f_1(X_1[t]) - \lambda_t X_1[t] \right\} + \sum_{t=0}^{T-1} \left\{ \beta_1^+ u_1^+[t] + \beta_1^- u_1^-[t] \right\} \tag{10}$$

s. t.

$$\begin{cases} X_1[t+1] = X_1[t] + u_1[t], \ t = 0, 1, \cdots, T-1 \\ 0 \leq X_1[t] \leq \mathrm{maxD}_1, \quad t = 1, 2, \cdots, T \\ X_1[0] = X_1^0 \end{cases}$$

SP2

$$\min_{u_2[t]} J_2(\lambda) = \sum_{t=1}^{T} \left\{ f_2(X_2[t]) - \lambda_t X_2[t] \right\} + \sum_{t=0}^{T-1} \left\{ \beta_2^+ u_2^+[t], 0 \right\} + \beta_2^- u_2^-[t] \} \tag{11}$$

s. t.

$$\begin{cases} X_2[t+1] = X_2[t] + u_2[t], t = 0, 1, \cdots, T-1 \\ D_{2t} \leq X_2[t] \leq \mathrm{maxD}_2, \quad t = 1, 2, \cdots, T \\ X_2[0] = X_2^0 \end{cases}$$

where $u_1^+[t] = \max\{u_1[t], 0\}$, $u_1^-[t] = \max\{-u_1[t], 0\}$, and $\text{maxD}_i = \max_t D_i(t)$, $i = 1, 2$. We can show that the constraint $X_1[t] \leq \text{maxD}_1$ in subproblem SP1 and the constraint $X_2[t] \leq \text{maxD}_2$ in subproblem SP2 do not affect the optimality of the problem RP2 under the assumption that $arg \min_x\{f_i(x)\} \leq \max\{D_{it}, 1 \leq t \leq T\}$ for $i = 1, 2$. However, they limit the range of feasible solutions for the subproblems and therefore enable the subproblems to be solved more efficiently.

The dual problem of the original problem P2, denoted by **DP2**, is given below.

$$Z(\lambda^*) = \max_{\lambda \geq 0} \left\{ \sum_{t=1}^{T} \lambda_t (D_{1t} + D_{2t}) + \sum_{i=1}^{2} \min_{u_i[t]} J_i(\lambda) \right\}. \tag{12}$$

4 Solving the Subproblems

First we present an optimization approach for the following problem, which involves only a single employee type.

P1:

$$\min_{u[t]} J = \sum_{t=1}^{T} f(X[t]) + \sum_{t=0}^{T-1} \left(\beta^+ u^+[t] + \beta^- u^-[t]\right) \tag{13}$$

s. t.

$$X[t+1] = X[t] + u[t], t = 0, 1, 2, \cdots, T-1 \tag{14}$$

$$X[t] \geq D_t^{(1)}, t = 1, 2, \cdots, T \tag{15}$$

$$X[0] = X^0 \tag{16}$$

A direct approach for solving the problem P1 is dynamic program. We can show that such a dynamic program will have a time complexity of $O(T\text{maxD}^2)$. This is not an efficient approach, particularly when the maximal demand maxD is large. In the following, we will present a method by analyzing the intrinsic nature of the problem, whose computational complexity is $O(T)$ in the worst case. Let $X_{min} = arg \min_x f(x)$. (Due to limit of space, we omit the proofs for all results in this paper, which are available upon request.)

Property 4.1. *The optimal states of the problem P1 satisfy*

$$X[t] \geq \max\{D_t, X_{min}\}.$$

Property 4.1 implies that the optimal states $X[t]$ obtained based on the demands $\overline{D}_t$ are also optimal with respect to the demands D_t, where $\overline{D}_t = \max\{D_t, X_{min}\}$.

Property 4.2. *If $X[t] \leq \overline{D}_{t+1}$, then $u[t] = \overline{D}_{t+1} - X[t]$.*

Let $d(x) = \lceil \frac{\beta^+ + \beta^-}{f(x) - f(x-1)} \rceil$ and $L(x) = t_R(x) - t_L(x) - 1$, where x ($x \geq \overline{D}_t$) is a state in period t, $t_R(x)$ is the nearest period to the period t that satisfies

$\overline{D}_{t_R(x)-1} \leq \overline{D}_t < \overline{D}_{t_R(x)}$, and $t_L(x)$ is the nearest period to the period t that satisfies $\overline{D}_{t_L(x)+1} \leq \overline{D}_t < \overline{D}_{t_L(x)}$. Then we get the following results.

Property 4.3. *The function $d(x)$ is decreasing monotonically with respect to x and $L(x[t]) = t_R(X[t]) - t_L(X[t]) - 1$ is increasing monotonically with respect to $X[t]$.*

Property 4.4. *If $X[t] > \overline{D}_{t+1}$ and $L(\overline{D}_{t+1}) \geq d(\overline{D}_{t+1})$, then $u[t] = \overline{D}_{t+1} - X[t]$.*

Property 4.5. *If $X[t] > \overline{D}_{t+1}$ and $L(\overline{D}_{t+1}) < d(\overline{D}_{t+1})$, then there exists a constant x^* satisfying $\overline{D}_{t+1} < x^* < \overline{D}_t$ and $d(x^*) < L(x^*) \leq d(x^* - 1)$, such that $u[t] = x^* - X[t]$.*

Based on the properties above, we now propose the algorithm to solve the problem P1.

Algorithm OC1

Step 1. Compute $X_{min} = arg\min_x f(x)$ and $d(x) = \lceil \frac{\beta^+ + \beta^-}{f(x) - f(x-1)} \rceil$ for $x = X_{min}, X_{min} + 1, \cdots, maxD$.
Step 2. For $t = 1, 2, \cdots, T$, perform Steps 3-6.
Step 3. If $X[t] \leq \overline{D}_{t+1}$, then $u[t] = \overline{D}_{t+1} - X[t]$.
Step 4. If $X[t] > \overline{D}_{t+1}$, then compute $L(\overline{D}_{t+1})$.
Step 5. If $X[t] > \overline{D}_{t+1}$ and $L(\overline{D}_{t+1}) \geq d(\overline{D}_{t+1})$, then $u[t] = \overline{D}_{t+1} - X[t]$.
Step 6. If $X[t] > \overline{D}_{t+1}$ and $L(\overline{D}_{t+1}) < d(\overline{D}_{t+1})$, then we search the optimal value x^* within $\overline{D}_{t+1} < x^* < \overline{D}_t$ and $d(x^*) < L(x^*) \leq d(x^* - 1)$, and let $u[t] = x^* - X[t]$.
Step 7. For $t = 0, 1, 2, \cdots, T-1$, compute $X[t+1] = X[t] + u[t]$.

Property 4.6. *The time requirement of the algorithm OC1 is bounded above by $O(T)$.*

We now consider Subproblem SP1. Let $f_1'(x) = f_1(x) - \lambda_t x$. Then it is clear that $f_1'(x)$ is also a convex function of x because $f_1(x)$ is convex and λ_t is a nonnegative number. Suppose $X_{min}' = arg\min_x f_1'(x)$. Then obviously, $X_{min}' \leq X_{min}$. Thus the optimal solution for the subproblem SP1 is specified below.

Property 4.7. *The optimal states for the subproblem SP1 are given by $X_1[t] = \max\{X_{min}', maxD_1\}$ for $t = 1, 2, \cdots, T$.*

For the subproblem SP2, we also let $f_2'(x) = f_2(x) - \lambda_t x$. Similarly, it is clear that $f_2'(x)$ is also a convex function of x, since $f_2(x)$ is convex. One can see that SP2 falls in exactly the formulation of the problem P1. Therefore we can solve it using the algorithm OC1.

5 Coordination by a Genetic Procedure

We now describe our approach to coordinate the solutions to the two subproblems so as to generate an integrated solution for the original problem. Basically, this concerns the update of the Lagrangean multipliers λ_t, namely, the solution for the dual problem DP2. Our idea is to solve the dual problem by using a Genetic Algorithm (GA).

Recall our dual problem DP2 (see (12)), which is to maximize $Z(\lambda)$ with respect to the Lagrangean multipliers $\lambda \geq 0$, where

$$Z(\lambda) = \left\{ \sum_{t=1}^{T} \lambda_t (D_{1t} + D_{2t}) + \sum_{i=1}^{2} \min_{u_i[t]} J_i(\lambda) \right\}. \tag{17}$$

We design a genetic algorithm to solve the problem of maximizing $Z(\lambda)$ with respect to λ. The specifics of our genetic algorithm, including its coding scheme, parent selection, crossover, and mutation, etc, are described in the sequel of this section.

- **Coding scheme.** The Lagrangean multipliers $\lambda = [\lambda_1, \lambda_2, \cdots, \lambda_T]$ are the decision variables. Let $x_i = \lambda_i / \sum_{t=1}^{T} \lambda_t$, $i = 1, 2, \cdots, T$, then $x_i \in [0, 1]$ and we obtain a normalized vector $x = [x_1, x_2, \cdots, x_T]$. A vector x is a chromosome (or individual) in a population of our GA. Each gene x_i in a chromosome corresponds to a Lagrangean multiplier.

- **Fitness.** For any x, we get a corresponding Lagrangean multiplier vector λ, and then find the optimal solution to the dual problem DP2. Since DP2 is to maximize the objective function $Z(\lambda)$, we use the value of $-Z(\lambda)$ to represent the fitness value of the individual x.

More specifically, when an individual x is to be evaluated in terms of its fitness, we first get the vector λ by computing $\lambda_t = x_t(\sum_{t=1}^{T} \lambda_t)$ for $t = 1, 2, \cdots, T$, and then evaluate $Z(\lambda)$ through (17) (which requires solutions for the subproblems SP1 and SP2 for the corresponding λ).

- **Parent selection**

- **Crossover**

We use arithmetic crossover. Suppose $x_i^{(k)}$ and $x_j^{(k)}$ are two parents in the population k, then two offsprings are generated by a crossover operation as follows.

$$\begin{cases} x_i^{(k+1)} = a x_j^{(k)} + (1-a) x_i^{(k)} \\ x_j^{(k+1)} = a x_i^{(k)} + (1-a) x_j^{(k)} \end{cases} \tag{18}$$

where a is a random number selected uniformly in interval [0, 1].

- **Mutation**

We adopt a uniform mutation method. First we choose randomly an individual from the current population, and then apply a mutation operation to it. Specifically, suppose $x = [x_1, x_2, \cdots, x_k, \cdots, x_T]$, if x_k is the gene to be mutated, then the mutation operation will change it to

$$x_k{}' = U_{min}^{(k)} + r(U_{max}^{(k)} - U_{min}^{(k)}) \tag{19}$$

where r is a random number selected uniformly in interval [0, 1]. In our design, we select $U_{min}^{(k)} = 0$ and $U_{max}^{(k)} = 1$ for all $1 \leq k \leq T$, and so $x_k{}' = r$.

- **Stopping criteria**

The genetic procedure terminates when one of the following criteria is met. One criterion is that the number of generations reaches a pre-specified upper limit. The second one is that differences between mean fitness values in the preceding N generations are not more than a threshold value ϵ_1. And the third one is that variance of all individuals is not more than a threshold value ϵ_2.

6 Numerical Results

We have studied the effectiveness of our proposed approach by computational experiments. First, a set of small-size problem instances were solved, by our approach and also by a dynamic program (DP). The DP was used to generate the optimal solutions for comparison with the solutions generated by our approach. By some proper design (which is omitted here due to space limit), we can show that DP can find an optimal solution, at the cost of excessive computing time.

The GA parameters we used in the computational experiments are as follows. The crossover rate and the mutation rate were chosen to be 80% and 0.8%, respectively. The population size was set to be $m = 30$. Other parameters include $N = 10$, $\epsilon_1 = 1$ and $\epsilon_2 = 0.05$. The computations are implemented on the Matlab platform.

Computational results obtained for the two of these instances are illustrated in Fig. 1 and Fig. 2, where the demand trajectories are shown. The cost coefficients used in the problem instances were $f_1(x) = 800((x-10)^2+5)$, $f_2(x) = 1000((x-8)^2 + 20$, $\beta_1^+ = 1000$, $\beta_2^+ = 1100$, $\beta_1^- = 1500$ and $\beta_2^- = 1600$.

The results show that generally the state trajectories obtained by the two approaches follow the same trend. For the example in Fig. 1, in most periods the state trajectories obtained by the two approaches are identical, whereas in some periods they have some small difference. For the example in Fig. 2, there is a big difference between state trajectories obtained by our approach and by the dynamic program in some periods. However, the gap, represented by $\frac{Z_{GA}-Z_{DP}}{Z_{DP}}$, is not more than 1%, where Z_{GA} and Z_{DP} are objective values obtained by the two approaches respectively. This observation indicates that our proposed approach could effectively find optimal or near optimal solutions.

Furthermore, we compared the performance of our approach against the classical Lagrangean relaxation (LR) approach. The demand data were generated stochastically through a uniform distribution in [100, 300]. Planning horizons with $T = 20, 25, 30, \cdots, 50$ were considered respectively. All other parameters are same as the above examples. The final results have been summarized on Table 1. From these results one can see that the solutions obtained by our approach are much better than those obtained by the classical LR approach, although the computation time of our approach is a bit larger than that of the classical LR approach.

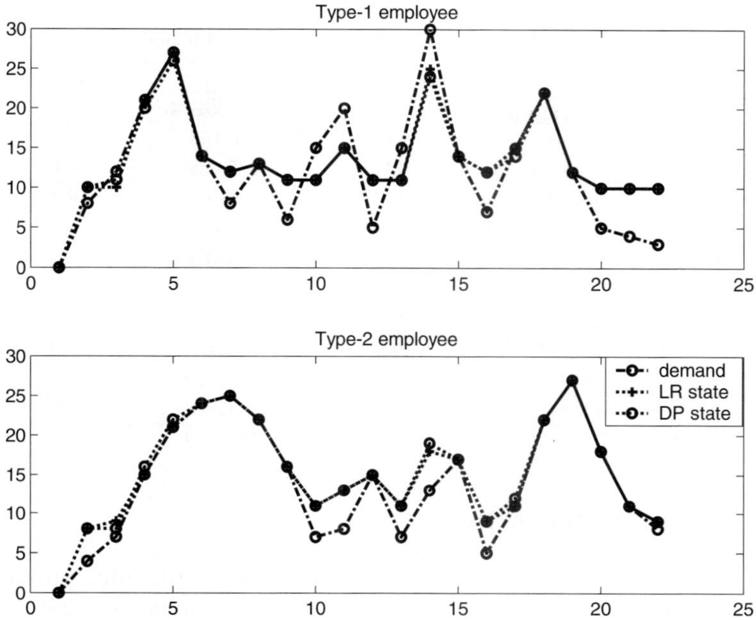

Fig. 1. Problem 1

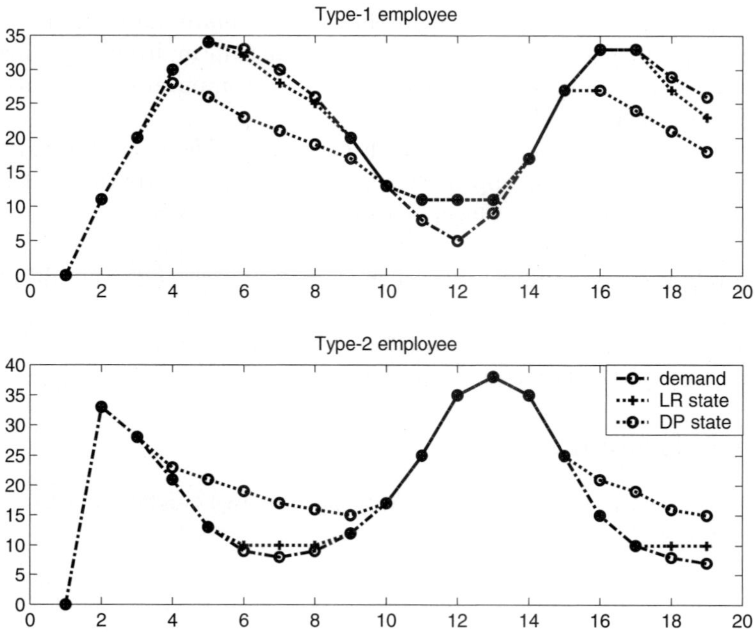

Fig. 2. Problem 2

Table 1. Comparing approach with the classical LR appraoch

Time horizon	Our approach		LR approach	
	Cost	Computation time(s)	Cost	Computation time(m)
20	4.12+E8	6.5	4.18+E8	5.4
25	5.84+E8	7.1	5.91+E8	6.1
30	6.48+E8	10.1	6.56+E8	8.9
35	7.97+E8	12.5	8.12+E8	10.2
40	9.42+E8	16.4	9.56+E8	12.3
45	1.079+E9	17.5	1.211+E9	15.8
50	1.203+E9	19.1	1.356+E9	18.2
55	1.428+E9	19.5	1.562+E9	17.3
60	1.669+E9	20.5	1.897+E9	18.6
65	1.855+E9	21.6	1.982+E9	19.7
70	2.101+E9	22.7	2.368+E9	20.7

7 Concluding Remarks

We have developed a new approach to tackle a manpower planning problem with two types of jobs in a long planning horizon, where dynamic demands for manpower must be satisfied by allocating enough number of employees of qualified skills. We first apply Lagrangean relaxation to decompose the problem into two subproblems, each corresponding to one skill type and can therefore be solved efficiently. We then design a genetic algorithm to coordinate the solutions obtained from the subproblems, which updates the Lagrangean multipliers to maximize the dual objective function. We have also reported computational results, which show the effectiveness of our approach.

Although we deal with a problem with two types of jobs only, our GA based decomposition-coordination approach can be extended directly to problems with multiple types of jobs of a two-level hierarchic structure, where staff for the top-level job can be assigned to do any jobs at the lower-level, but not *vice-versa.* The extension requires no modifications on the GA approach. The only difference is that a number of subproblems, each corresponding to one lever-level job, must be solved in order to obtain the value of the dual function $Z(\lambda)$ when the fitness of an individual in the GA is to be updated.

Acknowledgements

This work was partly supported by the National Science Foundation of China under Grant No. 60074018 and 70501014.

References

1. Bartholomew, D.J., Forbes, A.F., Mclean, S.I.: Statistical techniques for manpower planning (2nd). Wiley, New York, (1991)
2. Bowey, A. M.: Coorporate manpower planning. Manage. Decis. **15** 421-469,(1977)

3. Alfares, H.K.: Survey, Categorization, and Comparison of Recent Tour Scheduling Literature. Ann. Opers. Res., **127** 145-175,(2004)
4. Li, X.D., Tu, F.S., Li, Y.J., *et. al.*: Optimal Manpower Recruitment and Dismissal Decision For Single-Type Job, J. of Sys. Sci. & Infor. **2** 545-555,(2004)
5. Li, Y.J., Chen, J., Cai, X.: Optimal Manpower Planning With Temporal Labor And Contract Period Constraint. Lecture Notes in Computer Science (No. 3521) , 350-359, Springer-Verlag, (2005)
6. Cai, X., Li, Y.J., Tu, F.S., *et. al.*: Optimal Manpower Planning with Two Types of Jobs through dynamic programming approach. Working paper, Dept. of Sys. Eng. & Eng. Manage., The Chinese University of HongKong, HONG KONG,(2003)
7. Verbeek, P.: Decision Support Systems-An application in strategic manpower planning of airline pilots. Eur. J. of Oper. Res. **55** 368-381,(1991)
8. Yu, G., Pachon, J., Thengvall, B.: Optimization-based Integrated Manpower Management for Airlines. Operations Research in Space & Air, edited by Tito A. Ciriani, Kluwer Academic Publishers, Boston,(2003)
9. Sevaux, M., Dauz, S.,ère-Pérès.: Genetic algorithms to minimize the weighted number of late jobs on a single machine, *European Journal of Operational Research*, 151: 296-306,(2003)

Solving Multi-period Financial Planning Problem Via Quantum-Behaved Particle Swarm Algorithm

Jun Sun, Wenbo Xu, and Wei Fang

Center of Intelligent and High Performance Computing,
School of Information Technology, Southern Yangtze University,
No. 1800, Lihudadao Road, Wuxi,
214122 Jiangsu, China
{sunjun_wx, xwb_sytu, wxfangwei}@hotmail.com

Abstract. A multistage stochastic financial optimization manages portfolio in constantly changing financial markets by periodically rebalancing the asset portfolio to achieve return maximization and/or risk minimization. In this paper, we present a decision-making process that uses our proposed Quantum-behaved Particle Swarm Optimization (QPSO) Algorithm to solve multi-stage portfolio optimization problem. The objective function is classical return-variance function. The performance of our algorithm is demonstrated by optimizing the allocation of cash and various stocks in S&P 100 index. Experiments are conducted to compare performance of the portfolios optimized by different objective functions with Particle Swarm Optimization (PSO) algorithm and Genetic Algorithm (GA) in terms of efficient frontiers.

1 Introduction

Financial optimization involves asset allocation and risk management. A multi-stage stochastic financial optimization is a quantitative model that integrates asset allocation strategies and saving strategies in a comprehensive fashion. It manages portfolio in constantly changing financial markets by periodically rebalancing the asset portfolio to achieve return maximization and risk minimization. Stochastic optimization of portfolio is NP-hard and is non-linear with many local optima.

A number of different algorithmic approaches have been proposed for solving stochastic optimization problems. To solve the asset allocation problem, one may employ linear programming solvers such as CPLEX and OSL by piecewise linearizing the nonlinear objective function [2]. The interior-point algorithms are another type of methods well suited to the scenario structure of multi-stage stochastic programs. Searching the global solution by these methods, however, is computationally expensive and ineffectively. Since time is a constraint for financial problems, a trade-off should be made between the performance and the computational time. Heuristic methods, such as Tabu Search [1] and GA [3] provide some appropriate ways to find optimal asset allocation.

Particle Swarm Optimization (PSO) was originally proposed by J. Kennedy as a simulation of social behavior of bird flock, and was initially introduced as a heuristic optimization method in 1995 [7]. More recently, a new version of PSO, called

D.-S. Huang, K. Li, and G.W. Irwin (Eds.): ICIC 2006, LNAI 4114, pp. 1158 – 1169, 2006.

Quantum-behaved Particle Swarm Optimization (QPSO), has been proposed in order to improve the global search performance of the original PSO [12], [13], [14]. The QPSO is a global convergent and has fewer parameters to control, which makes it easier to implement.

In this paper, we explore the practicability of QPSO in multi-stage financial optimization problem. To do so, we used S&P 100 Index and the prices of its component stocks as the training samples. The PSO and GA were also tested on the sample data for performance comparison. The rest of the paper is organized as follows. In next section, the multi-stage portfolio optimization model is described. In Section 3 and Section 4, we describe the PSO and QPSO in detail. Section 5 is the presentation of experiment results and the paper is concluded in Section 6.

2 Multi-stage Portfolio Optimization Model

Single period portfolio optimization model possesses several drawbacks. For examples, the risk is inconsistent over time. The multi-stage stochastic programming model proposed by Mulvey *et al* [8], [9] captures dynamic aspects of asset allocation problem. It manages portfolio in constantly changing financial markets by periodically rebalancing the asset portfolio to achieve return maximization and/or risk minimization, leading to optimal portfolio.

To define the model, we divide the entire planning horizon T into two discrete intervals T_1 and T_2, where $T_1 = 0,1,\cdots,\tau$ and $T_2 = \tau+1,\cdots,T$. The former corresponds to periods in which investment decisions are made. Period τ defines the date of planning horizon; we focus on the investor's position at the beginning of period τ. Decisions occur at the beginning of each time stage. T_2 handles the horizon at time τ by calculating economic and other factors beyond period τ up to period T. The investor cannot render any active decisions after the end of period τ.

Asset investment categories are defined by set $A = 1,2,\cdots,I$, with category 1 representing cash. The remaining categories can include broad investment groupings such as stocks, bonds, and real estate. Ideally, the co-movements between pairs of asset returns would be relatively low so that diversification can be done across the asset categories. In the model, uncertainty is modeled through a large but finite number S of scenarios. Each scenario represents a possible realization of all uncertain parameters in the mode. To be specific, let ω_t represent the vector of random parameters whose values are revealed in period t. Then the set of all scenarios is the set of all realizations $(\omega_1^s,\omega_2^s,\cdots,\omega_\tau^s), s \in S := \{1,2,\cdots,S\}$, of $(\omega_1,\omega_2,\cdots,\omega_\tau)$. Each scenario s has a probability π_s, where $\pi_s > 0$ and $\sum_{s=1}^{S}\pi_s = 1$. Since in a dynamic model information on actual value of the uncertain parameters is revealed in stages, a suitable representation of scenarios is given by a scenarios tree, such as in Figure 1. In this case τ=3 and S=8. Each path form t=0 to t=τ represents one scenario. Any node of the tree, corresponding to time t, symbolizes a possible state of the world at time t, represented by the observed values of $\omega_1,\omega_2,\cdots,\omega_t$. The branches directly to the right of it symbolize the various values of ω_{t+1} (and their corresponding conditional probabilities) given the realization of $\omega_1, \omega_2, \cdots, \omega_t$. Obviously, all scenarios passing this node have the same history in periods $1, 2, \cdots, t$. The status of decision variables is related to the scenario tree, too. Basically, a decision at time t may depend on the observed part of the scenario at that time, but not on unknown values of future periods. That is, for each possible history (i.e. for each node at time t in the scenario tree) there is precisely one vector of decision variables representing the decisions at hand.

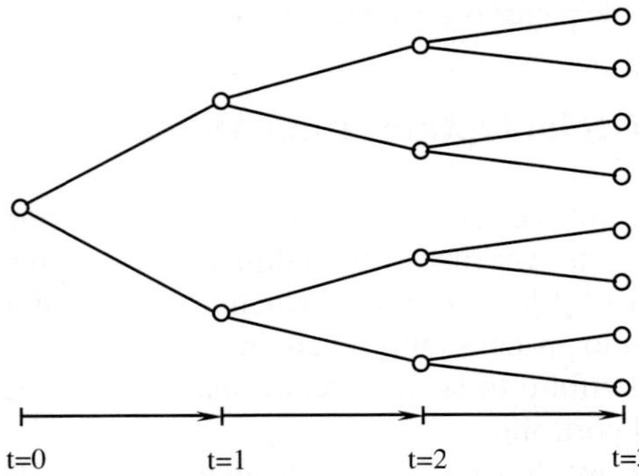

Fig. 1. A scenario tree with two scenarios and three time periods

We assume that the portfolio is rebalanced at the beginning of each period. Alternatively, we could simply make no transaction except reinvest any dividend and interest – a buy and hold strategy. For convenience, we also assume that the cash flows are reinvested in the generating asset category and all the borrowing is done on a single period basis. For each $i \in A, t \in T_1$, and $s \in S$, we define the following parameters and decision variables.

Parameters

$r_{i,t}^s = 1 + \rho_{i,t}^s$, where $\rho_{i,t}^s$ is the return percentage of asset *i*, time period *t* under scenario *s* (projected by the stochastic scenario generator, for example, see [10]).

π_s Probability that scenario *s* occurs, thus $\sum_s^S \pi_s = 1$.

w_0 Wealth in the beginning of time period 0.

$\sigma_{s,t}$ Transaction costs incurred in rebalancing asset *i* at the beginning of time period t (symmetric transaction costs are assumed, i.e., cost of selling equals cost of buying)

β_t^s Borrowing rate in period t under scenario *s*.

Decision variables

$x_{i,t}^s$ Amount of money for asset category *i*, in time period *t*, under scenario *s*, after rebalancing.

$v_{i,t}^s$ Amount of money in asset category i, in the beginning of time period t, under scenario s, before rebalancing.

w_t^s Wealth at the beginning of time period t, under scenario s.

$p_{i,t}^s$ Amount of asset i purchased for rebalancing at time t under scenario s.

$d_{i,t}^s$ Amount of asset i sold for rebalancing in time period t, under scenario s.

b_t^s Amount of money borrowed in period t, under scenario s.

Given these definitions, we outline the general stochastic programming model in financial optimization.

Model SP

$$\text{Max} \quad Z = \sum_{s=1}^{S} \pi_s f(w_\tau^s) \tag{1}$$

s.t.

$$\sum_i x_{i,0}^s = w_0 \qquad \forall s \in S, \tag{2}$$

$$\sum_i x_{i,t}^s = w_t^s \qquad \forall s \in S, \quad t = 1,2,\cdots \tau, \tag{3}$$

$$v_{i,t}^s = r_{i,t-1}^s x_{i,t-1}^{st} \qquad \forall s \in S, \quad t = 1,2\cdots,\tau, i \in A, \tag{4}$$

$$x_{i,t}^s = v_{i,t}^s + p_{i,t}^s(1-\sigma_{i,t}) - d_{i,t}^s \qquad \forall s \in S, \quad t = 1,2,\cdots,\tau, \quad i \neq 1 \tag{5}$$

$$x_{1,t}^s = v_{1,t}^s + \sum_{i \neq 1} d_{i,t}^s(1-\sigma_{i,t}) - \sum_{i \neq 1} p_{i,t}^s - b_{t-1}^s(1+\beta_{t-1}^s) + b_t^s$$
$$\forall s \in S, \quad t = 1,2,\cdots,\tau, \tag{6}$$

$$x_{i,t}^s = x_{i,t}^{s'} \text{ for all scenarios } s \text{ and } s' \text{ with identical past up to time } t \tag{7}$$

As with the single-period models, the nonlinear objective function (1) can take several different forms. If the classical return-risk function is employed, then (1) becomes $\text{Max} \quad Z = \eta \cdot \text{Mean}(w_\tau) - (1-\eta) \cdot \text{Var}(w_\tau)$, where $\text{Mean}(w_\tau)$ is the average total wealth and $\text{Var}(w_\tau)$ is the variance of the total wealth across the scenarios at the end of period τ. Parameter η indicates the relative importance of variance as compared with the expected value. This objective leads to an efficient frontier of wealth at period τ.

Constraint (2) guarantees that the total initial investment equals the initial wealth. Constraint (3) states the wealth accumulated at the end of t-th period under scenario s before rebalancing in asset i. This constraint can be modified to include assets, liabilities, and investment goals. Constraint (4) depicts the wealth $v_{i,t}^{s}$ accumulated at the beginning of period t before rebalancing in asset *i*. The flow balance constraint for all assets except cash for all periods is given by constraint (5). This constraint guarantees that the amount invested in period t equals the net wealth for asset. Constraint (6) represents flow balancing constraint for cash. Non-anticipativity constraint is represented by (7). These constraints ensure that the scenarios with the same past will have identical decisions up to that period.

3 Particle Swarm Optimization

In a Particle Swarm Optimization (PSO) system, individuals representing the candidate solutions to the problem at hand fly through a multidimensional search space to find out the optima or sub-optima. In PSO with M individuals, each individual is treated as a volume-less particle in the *D*-dimensional space, with the position vector and velocity vector of particle *i* at *k*th iteration represented as $X_i(k)=(X_{i1}(k),X_{i2}(k),\cdots,X_{iD}(k))$ and $V_i(t)=(V_{i1}(k),V_{i2}(k),\cdots,V_{iD}(k))$. The particles move according to the following equations:

$$V_{ij}(k+1)=w\cdot V_{ij}(k)+c_1\cdot r_1\cdot(P_{ij}(k)-X_{ij}(k))+c_2\cdot r_2\cdot(P_{gj}(k)X_{ij}(k)) \tag{8}$$

$$X_{ij}(k+1)=X_{ij}(k)+V_{ij}(k+1) \tag{9}$$

for $i=1,2,\cdots M; j=1,2\cdots,D$. Parameters c_1 and c_2 are called acceleration coefficient. Vector $P_i=(P_{i1},P_{i2},\cdots,P_{iD})$ is the best previous position (the position giving the best fitness value) of particle *i* called *personal best position*, and vector $P_g=(P_{g1},P_{g2},\cdots,P_{gD})$ is the position of the best particle among all the particles in the population and called global best position. The parameters r_1 and r_2 are random numbers distributed uniformly in (0,1). Generally, the value of V_{id} is restricted in the interval $[-V_{\max},V_{\max}]$. The inertia weight *w* in equation (8) was introduced by Shi and Eberhart [13]. The addition of the inertia weight results in faster convergence.

4 Quantum-Behaved Particle Swarm Optimization

Trajectory analyses in [5] demonstrated the fact that convergence of the PSO algorithm may be achieved if each particle converges to its local attractor. Let the local attractor $p_i=(p_{i1},p_{i2},\cdots p_{iD})$ of particle *i* be defined at the coordinates

$$p_{ij}(k)=\varphi\cdot P_{ij}(k)+(1-\varphi)\cdot P_{gj}(k), \qquad where \quad \varphi=c_1r_1/(c_1r_1+c_2r_2) \tag{10}$$

with regard to the random numbers r_1 and r_2 in equation (8). It can be seen that the local attractor is a stochastic attractor of particle *i* that lies in a hyper-rectangle with P_i and P_g being two ends of its diagonal and moves following P_i and P_g.

Assume that there is one-dimensional Delta potential well on each dimension at its local attractor p and each particle has quantum behavior. For simplicity, we consider a particle in one-dimensional space, with point p the center of potential. Solving the *Schrödinger equation*, we can get the normalized the following probability density function Q and distribution function D

$$Q(x) = \frac{1}{L} e^{-2|p-x|/L} \text{ and } D(x) = e^{-2|p-x|/L} \tag{11}$$

where L determines search scope of each particle like standard deviation in Gaussian distribution. Using Monte Carlo method, we can obtain the position of the particle

$$x = P \pm \frac{L}{2} \ln(1/u) \qquad u = rand\,(0,1) \tag{12}$$

where u is a random number uniformly distributed in (0, 1).

A global point called Mainstream Thought or Mean Best Position of the population is introduced into PSO for the evaluation of L. The global point, denoted as C, is defined as the mean of the *personal best* positions among all particles. That is

$$C(k) = (C_1(k), C_2(k), \cdots, C_D(k)) = \left(\frac{1}{M} \sum_{i=1}^{M} P_{i1}(k), \quad \frac{1}{M} \sum_{i=1}^{M} P_{i2}(k), \quad \cdots, \quad \frac{1}{M} \sum_{i=1}^{M} P_{iD}(k) \right), \tag{13}$$

where M is the population size and P_i is the personal best position of particle i. Thus the value of L and the position are evaluated as $L = 2\alpha \cdot |C_j(k) - X_j(k)|$

$$X_{ij}(k+1) = p_{ij} \pm \alpha \cdot |C_{ij}(k) - X_{ij}(k)| \cdot \ln(1/u) \tag{14}$$

where α is Expansion-Constraction Coefficient (CE), which can be tuned to control the convergence speed of the algorithm. The PSO with equation (14) is called Quantum-behaved Particle Swarm Optimization (QPSO) described as follows.

```
QPSO Algorithm

Initialize particles with random position Xi=X[i][:]
and velocities Vi=V[i][:];
Let personal best position Pi=Xi;
while termination criterion is not met do
  Compute the mean best position C[:] by equation (13);
  for i=1 to swarm size M
    if f(Xi)<f(Pi) then Pi=Xi; endif
      Find the Pg=P[g][:]across the swarm;
      for j=1 to D
        fi=rand(0,1); u=rand(0,1);
        p=fi*P[i][j]+(1-fi)*P[g][j];
        if (rand(0,1)>0.5
          X[i][j]=p+α*abs(C[j]-X[i][j])*ln(1/u);
        else
          X[i][j]=p-α*abs(C[j]-X[i][j])*ln(1/u);
        endif
      endfor
```

```
      endif
    endfor
  endwhile
```

Generally, the value of α no more than 1.0 can lead to a good performance if it is fixed over the running of QPSO. But in most cases, α decrease linearly from α_0 to α_1.

5 Numerical Experiments

In order to evaluate the performance of QPSO on multistage financial optimization, experiments were carried out. Weekly closing prices of S&P 100 Index and its component stocks from 1 January 2000 to 31 December 2004 were collected. Cash and stocks of ten corporations that belong to different industries were selected to be optimized. The planning horizon interval T_1 was divided into three periods.

In our approach, the economic parameter that determines scenarios is the mark index and therefore each scenario represents a possible realization of market index. We set the market index two possible realization:(1) the market index has been raised and (2) the market index has been dropped. Denoting rise with 1 and drop with 0, we can obtain the scenario tree as Figure 1 with 8 scenarios: (0,0,0), (0,0,1), (0,1,0), (0,1,1), (1,0,0), (1,0,1), (1,1,0) and (1,1,1). Each edge in the scenario tree corresponds to a realization of market index's raise and drop as well as a set of percentage returns of all assets in time period t under a certain scenario. We worked out π_s of each scenario and $\rho_{i,t}^s$ of each stock according to closing price of the index and stocks. For the percentage return of cash, we set a fixed annual interest rate 6%, and therefore the weekly percentage return is 0.12% across the whole period of planning.

Using π_s and $\rho_{i,t}^s$ as parameters, we tested three optimizers: QPSO, PSO and GA, to search the optimal $x_{i,t}^s$ to maximize the objective function (1). To implement the algorithms, we adopted $a_{i,t}^s$, allocation proportion of the selected assets after rebalancing under different scenarios over the planning horizon as our decision variables. Therefore, $x_{i,t}^s$ is determined by $x_{i,t}^s = a_{i,t}^s \cdot w_t^s$.

There are 15 nodes in the scenario tree with each node containing the allocation proportions of 11 assets under the corresponding scenario. For each scenario s at time *t*, the total asset allocation proportion must be equal to 100%. Hence, each of asset allocation proportion $a_{i,t}^s$ under scenario is normalized by $a_{i,t}^{s\,\prime} = a_{i,t}^s \Big/ \sum_{i=1}^{A} a_{i,t}^s$, after the optimization algorithm has run for an iteration, where $a_{i,t}^{s\,\prime}$ is the normalized asset allocation proportion. Moreover, in our numerical experiment, we don't take borrowing and transaction costs into account. The values of $\sigma_{s,t}$, β_t^s and b_t^s in constraint (5), (6) are zeros consequently.

We employed the classical return-risk function as the objective function. Therefore the purpose of our experiment was to generate an efficient frontier of wealth at period τ. In order to generate the entire efficient frontier, we adopt a series of different values of η in interval [0,1]. Some of these values of η are listed in the first column of Table 4. Each objective function corresponding to a particular η was maximized to generate a couple of Expected Return and Variance at period τ. Thus, a series Expected Return-Variance can be obtained to yield a curve of the efficient frontier.

Three groups of experiments were implemented with each group running an optimization algorithm. The configurations of the three algorithms are as follows. For the QPSO, the CE Coefficient was varying linearly from 1.0 to 0.5 over 500 iterations for a running of the algorithm. The objective function corresponding to each vale of η was maximized for 10 runs by the QPSO. For the experiment performed by the PSO, the acceleration coefficients c_1 and c_2 in are set to be 2 keeping constant and the inertia weight w was decreasing from 0.9 to 0.4 over 500 iterations for a running as adopted in most existing literatures. Also each objective function was optimized for 10 runs. Sixty particles were used in both the QPSO and PSO. For the GA, 100 individuals were employed. Each objective function was also maximized for 10 runs with each run executed for 500 iterations too. The experiments of GA were performed using real-valued encoding, binary tournament selection. Probability of mutating a genome is $p_m = 0.2$, and probability of crossover is $p_c = 0.9$. The algorithm use a arithmetic crossover with one weight for each variable. All weights exept one are randomly assigned to either to 0 or 1. The other ones are set to a random number between 0 and 1. This crossover operator is hybrid between uniform and arithmetic crossover and showed a better performance than traditional uniform and arithmetic crossover [15]. The mutation operator used here is standard Gaussian mutation with zero mean and variance $\sigma^2 = 1/\sqrt{k+1}$, where k is iteration number.The search scope for every decision variable is [0,1] for all experiments. At an iteration during executing the algorithm, if the allocation proportions of all assets at time t under scenario s were all be zeros, the allcotion proportion of cash would be set to 1 to satisfy the normalization ceriterion.

We depicted the efficent frontiers generated by the three algorithms and presented in Figure 2. The curves in (a) are the efficient frontiers traced out by the Expected Return-Variance values with the best optimized objective function value (or say best fitness value) out of the results of 10 runs. It is shown that the efficient frontier generated by the QPSO is the best, because all points on the curve are left to those on the curves by PSO and GA. The efficient frontier generated by GA is the worst in this case. In (b), the three curve is depicted by the Expected Return-Variance values corresponding to the worst optimized objective function value out of the resutls of 10 runs. The efficient frontier by the QPSO is also the best, while the curve by the PSO is the worst now. The efficient frontiers in (c) is tranced out by the average Expected Return-Variance values of 10 results corresponding to 10 runs for each objective function. The QPSO also generated the best curve. Concludingly, the QPSO can search out the optimal solution and generate the optimal efficient frontier more frequently than other two optimizers, while the PSO always trapped in local optimal algough it can

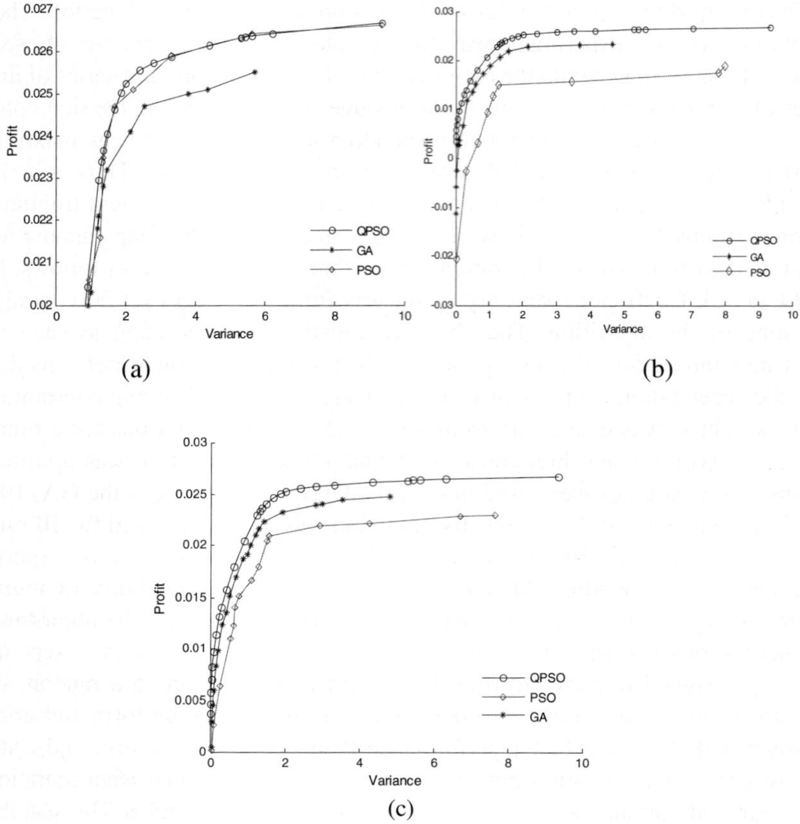

Fig. 2. (a) Efficient frontiers generated by the best solutions out of 10 runs. (b). Efficient frontiers generated by the worst solutions out of 10 runs. (c) Those generated by mean of solutions.

Table 1. Numerical results with some different values of η

	QPSO			GA			PSO		
η	Max.	Mean	St. Dev.	Max.	Mean	St.Dev	Max.	Mean	St.Dev.
0.01	1.0037	1.0037	0.00007	0.9839	0.9803	0.0018	1.0036	0.8864	0.1336
0.2	20.1199	20.1198	0.00003	20.0635	20.0332	0.024	20.11	19.9772	0.1366
0.4	40.3817	40.3817	0.00006	40.3237	40.298	0.0172	40.3538	40.1117	0.2095
0.6	60.8801	60.88	0.00016	60.8199	60.7798	0.0317	60.7852	60.5629	0.1985
0.8	81.6346	81.6346	0.00000	81.5505	81.4797	0.0427	81.6346	81.3659	0.2004
1.0	102.664	102.664	0.00000	102.552	102.479	0.0372	102.664	102.299	0.3996

find out the global opima occasionally. The fact that the performance of the GA is inferior to that of the QPSO is due to its slow convergence rate, which can be seen in the following part of the paper.

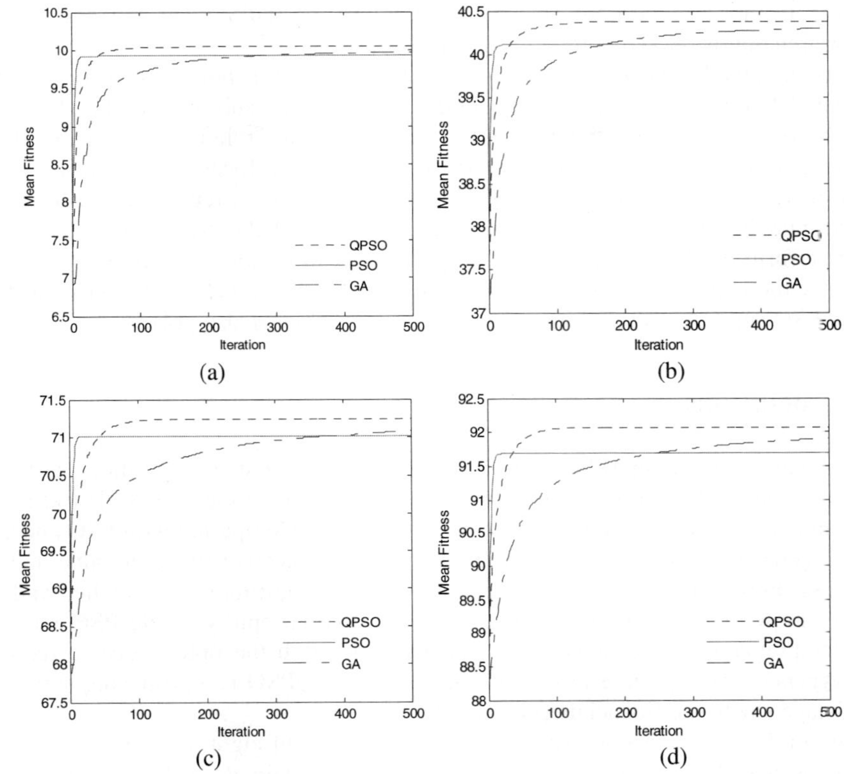

Fig. 3. Convergence process of three algorithms, when (a) η=0.1, (b) η=0.4, (c) η=0.7, (d) η=1.0

We also list in Table the Table 1 the mean, maximum and minimum of the best objective values of 10 runs for the objective functions with η=0.01, 0.2, 0.4 0.6 0.8 1.0. It can be seen that at each particular η, the QPSO yielded the best objective function values with lowest standard deviation. For example, when η=0.01, the mean of the 10 objective function values (best fitness values) yielded by the QPSO is 1.0037, while those yielded by the GA and PSO is 0.9803 and 0.8864 respectively. But the standard deviation of the QPSO is only 0.00007, which means that the QPSO is a robust and stable algorithm. That does explain why the QPSO always generates better efficient frontier than either of the GA and PSO.

To visualize and compare convergence rates of the three algorithms on the asset allocation problem, we depict the searching process of the algorithms averaged over 10 runs for each η. We present those of cases when η=0.1,0.4, 0.7, 0.9 in Figure 4. It is shown that the PSO converge most rapidly in early stage of the running, but may encounter premature convergence and therefore only find out sub-optima. The GA has the slowest convergence rate than the QPSO and PSO, but it encounters premature convergence less frequently than the PSO. The GA's slow convergence rate may cause the population to not converge to a point in the search space when the running is over. Comparing with the other two algorithms, the QPSO can converge rapidly and search out the global optima most frequently.

Although the PSO is invented to solve GO problems, it is not a global convergence guaranteed algorithm. If the particles in the PSO trap into sub-optima, they have less possibility to skip out, particularly in the late stage of the running. The GA is global convergent, but its convergence rate are so slow that its local search ability in late stage of running is weakened. The QPSO not only possess, rapid convergence rate, the strongpoint of the PSO, but it is guaranteed to be global convergent, which makes it outperform the PSO and GA in our tested portfolio optimization problem. In fact, not only the portfolio optimization problem is the QPSO excellent in, but it superior to the PSO and GA in other function optimization problems also [14].

6 Conclusions

In this paper, QPSO algorithm is used to optimize a multi-stage portfolio. The objective function used is classical expected return-variance function with S&P 100 index, cash and 10 selected component stock been optimized. Comparing with PSO and GA, QPSO generate better efficient frontiers with better objective function value and robustness. Furthermore, the convergence rates of the algorithms was studied and the results show that QPSO could converge to the optima rapidly, while PSO may encounter premature convergence and GA may not reach the optima due to its slow convergence rate. By these tests, it is suggested that QPSO is a promising solver for multistage stochastic financial optimization problems.

The problem test in our experiment has 3 stages and eight scenarios. Many real problems may have more large scale. QPSO may obtain the solutions efficiently. However, computation of objective functions is time consuming. Since saving computational time is very important in financial planning, a resolvent for this issue is parallelization.

References

1. Berger, A.J., Glover, F., Mulvey, J.M.: Solving Global Optimization Problems in Long-Term Financial Planning. Statistics and Operations Research Technical Report. Princeton University (1995)
2. Carino, D.R., Ziemba, W.T.: Formulation of the Russell-Yasuda Kasai Financial Planning Model. Frank Russell Company, Tacoma, WA (1995)
3. Chan, M.-C., Wong, C.-C., Cheung, B.K.-S.: Genetic Algorithms in Multi-Stage Asset Allocation System. Proc. 2002 IEEE International Conference on Systems, Man and Cybernetics, Vol. 3. Piscataway, NJ (2002) 316-321
4. Clerc, M.: The Swarm and Queen: Towards a Deterministic and Adaptive Particle Swarm Optimization. Proc. 1999 Congress on Evolutionary Computation. Piscataway, NJ (1999) 1951-1957
5. Clerc, M., Kennedy, J.: The Particle Swarm: Explosion, Stability, and Convergence in a Multi-dimensional Complex Space. IEEE Transactions on Evolutionary Computation, Vol. 6, No. 1. Piscataway, NJ (2002) 58-73

6. Danzig, G., Infanger, G.: Multi-stage Stochastic Linear Programs for Portfolio Optimization. Annals of Operation Research, Vol. 45, No. 1. Springer Netherlands (1993) 59-76
7. Kennedy, J., Eberhart, R.C.: Particle Swarm Optimization. Proc. 1995 IEEE International Conference on Neural Networks. Piscataway, NJ (1995) 1942-1948
8. Mulvey, J.M., Vladimirou, H.: Stochastic Network Optimization Models for Investment Planning. Annals of Operation Research, Vol. 20, Issue 1-4, J. C. Baltzer AG, Science Publishers, Red Bank, NJ (1998) 187-217
9. Mulvey, J.M., Rosenbaum, D.P., Shetty, B.: Strategic Financial Risk Management and Operations Research. European Journal of Operational Research, Vol. 97, No. 1. Elsevier Science, Amsterdam (1997) 1- 16
10. Mulvey, J.M., Rosenbaum, D.P., Shetty, B.: Parameter Estimation in Stochastic Scenario Generation System. European Journal of Operations Research, Vol. 118, No.3. Elsevier Science, Amsterdam (1999) 563-577
11. Shi, Y., Eberhart, R.C.: A Modified Particle Swarm. Proc. 1998 IEEE International Conference on Evolutionary Computation. Piscataway, NJ (1998) 1945-1950
12. Sun, J., Feng, B., Xu, W.-B.: Particle Swarm Optimization with Particles Having Quantum Behavior. Proc. 2004 Congress on Evolutionary Computation. Piscataway, NJ (2004) 325-331
13. Sun, J., Xu, W.-B., Feng, B.: A Global Search Strategy of Quantum-behaved Particle Swarm Optimization. Proc. 2004 IEEE Conference on Cybernetics and Intelligent Systems. Singapore (2004) 111-115
14. Sun, J., Xu, W.-B., Feng, B.: Adaptive Parameter Control for Quantum-behaved Particle Swarm Optimization on Individual Level. Proc. 2005 IEEE International Conference on Systems, Man and Cybernetics. Piscataway NJ (2005) 3049-3054
15. Ursem, K.: Models for Evolutionary Algorithms and Their Applications in System Identification and Control Optimization. PhD Dissertation. Department of Computer Science, University of Aarhus, Denmark (2002)

A Boosting Approach for Utterance Verification

Chengyu Dong[1], Yuan Dong[1,2], Dezhi Huang[2], Jun Guo[1], and Haila Wang[2]

[1] School of Information Engineering
Beijing University of Posts and Telecommunications, 100876, P.R. China
dongcy@gmail.com, {yuandong, guojun}@bupt.edu.cn
[2] France Telecom R&D Beijing Co, Ltd.,
2 Science Institute South Road,Haidian District, Beijing, 100080, P.R. China
{dezhi.huang, haila.wang}@francetelecom.com

Abstract. Utterance verification is a process, in which a spoken utterance is verified against the given keyword. This process is used to make a decision on acceptance or rejection. In this paper, we propose a new approach to the utterance verification, using a boosting classifier with ten confidence measures. This classifier combines a set of 'weak' learners into a 'strong' one. The experimental results present that it can remarkably improve the verification performance. Compared with a single confidence measure, the equal error rate is reduced by up to 23%. The results also show that the boosting classifier is better than the SVM and MLP classifiers, in term of the equal error rate.

1 Introduction

Recently, hidden Markov modeling has successfully migrate from the laboratory to many applications in speech recognition, such as information services, name dialing and other consumer products. As the technology develops, many powerful pattern recognition methods are proposed to further reduce the recognition error rate.

When the speech input is recognized reliably, we have to verify the speaker's input against the given transcription. One approach for this task is two-pass Utterance Verification (UV) which consists of two stages[1][2]. First the input utterance is processed through Viterbi segmentation. Then the confidence measures for the hypothesis phones are computed using phone boundaries and corresponding acoustic models. The final decision is made in the utterance level verification stage.

Therefore the aim of this paper is to determine whether we have to 'accept' or 'reject' the input utterance. We investigate the several confidence measures and their combinations to an effective classifier.

The literature contains many techniques for UV. In [3], on-line garbage model is proposed as a confidence measure which computes the local garbage scores for each time frame as the average of the N best local scores of phone models. Other techniques used include multi-level confidence measures [1], discriminative UV [4], anti-models which is commonly used in verbal information verification [5], [6].

D.-S. Huang, K. Li, and G.W. Irwin (Eds.): ICIC 2006, LNAI 4114, pp. 1170–1176, 2006.

It is possible to combine several confidence measures using various classification methods. Some researchers try to use different features using the hybrid model. The experiments show that hybrid models perform better than those single ones [1]. Other pattern recognition approaches, such as Support Vector Machines (SVM) [7] and Multiple Layer Perceptions (MLP) are often used in combining different confidences.

In this paper, we explore boosting techniques [8] to combine confidence measures for UV. Boosting is a learning algorithm which combines many "weak" classifiers into a "strong" one with a weighted majority vote. By applying boosting techniques, the accuracy of any given learning algorithm can be improved. In [8], boosting is successfully used in image recognition. However, in speech recognition area, boosting approach is also proposed for combining confidence scores in audio indexing [9].

Based on the confidence features mentioned above, we perform UV on the complete keyword and produce confidence scores for that keyword. After combining these scores by applying boosting technology, we can produce the final rejection or acceptance decision.

2 Utterance Verification

A block diagram of typical UV is shown in Fig.1. There are three modules, utterance segmentation by forced-alignment, subword level verification and utterance level verification. The speech signal is processed in two steps. First the input utterance is segmented by forced alignment in which the Viterbi algorithm is applied to maximize the likelihood of the subword sequence. Then the observed speech segments between the phone boundaries are processed in the second pass stage. Based on the lexical representation and acoustic models, each hypothesis test represents a subword level verification test. An utterance level verification test combines the results of subword level verification to make the final accept/reject decision.

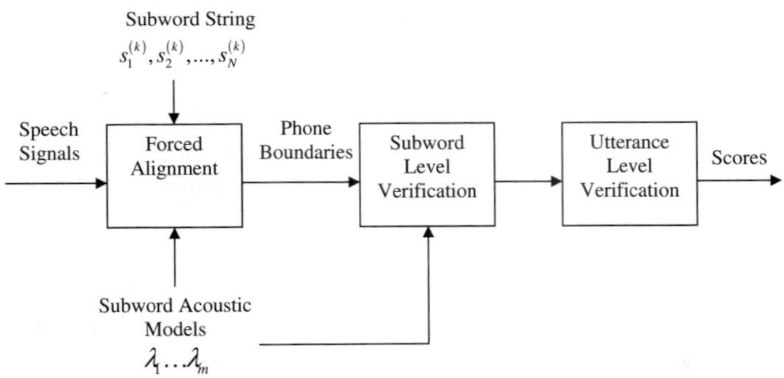

Fig. 1. Utterance verification block diagram

2.1 Hypothesis Testing

Given a subword string $S_1^{(k)}, S_2^{(k)}, \cdots, S_N^{(k)}$, which represents a corresponding keyword $S^{(k)}$, where N is the total number of $S^{(k)}$. We need a decision rule to minimize the classification errors. Under the assumption of the Neyman-Pearson hypothesis testing, the likelihood ratio can be written as Eqn.1.

$$LR(O_{ti-1}^{t_i}; S_i^{(k)}) = \frac{P(O_{ti-1}^{t_i}|H_0)}{P(O_{ti-1}^{t_i}|H_1)} = \frac{P(O_{ti-1}^{t_i}|S_i^{(k)})}{P(O_{ti-1}^{t_i}|\bar{S}_i^{(k)})} \tag{1}$$

where H_0 is the hypothesis that the segment $O_{ti-1}^{t_i}$ is belonging to the actual subword $S^{(k)}$, and H_1 is the alternative hypothesis that $O_{ti-1}^{t_i}$ is belonging to the alternative subwords.

2.2 Confidence Measures

For the UV, we have to mainly estimate the likelihood ratio of the exact probability density corresponding to $P(O_{ti-1}^{t_i}|H_0)$ and $P(O_{ti-1}^{t_i}|H_1)$. There are various ways to use these measures. The scores exhibit different levels of confidence in speech recognition. In this paper, we show two level confidence measures (CMs) based on likelihood ratio. The first one is a frame-level CM. The second one is a phone-level CM in which the confidence score is calculated at the end of each phone. To sum up, our confidence measures are listed in Table.1.

Table 1. Confidence measures for UV

No.	Confidence Measures
1	Phone-level LR (HMM)
2	Frame-level LR (HMM)
3	Phone rank (HMM)
4	Phone-level LR (GMM)
5	Frame-level LR (GMM)
6	Phone rank (GMM)
7	Cohort anti-model (GMM)
8	World anti-model (GMM)
9	Phone-level forced-alignment score
10	Frame-level force-alignment score

One of novel features is rank information of phoneme according to the acoustic likelihood of each phone. Rank information is used for UV due to its relatively good performance. Then to alleviate the problem of alternative hypothesis $P(O_{ti-1}^{t_i}|H_1)$ of each phone,one dominant approach is anti-model, including cohort anti-models and world anti-models [5] which are applied in speaker verification. In our system, these two anti-models are involved in the confidence measures.

To construct subword models, we proposed to use both HMM-based acoustic models and GMM-based ones. The GMM model can be considered as a special case of HMM which has only one effective state. In the two-pass UV GMM is more appropriate for modeling data to classify various classes.

Unlike the anti-models, another alternative hypothesis can be estimated using on-line garbage models which refer to the normalization of the probability of the best decoding hypothesis by the average probability of the N-Best decoding hypotheses [3]. This process can be used in both frame-level and phone-level with HMM and GMM approach. Therefore, features 1,2,4,5 are derived on this assumption.

In addition to these basic confidences, we include the forced-alignment acoustic scores subtracted by the best decoding scores. Then two levels normalization is used by the duration penalties.

2.3 Utterance Level Verification

There are several ways to analyze the phone level scores and derive an utterance level score. Prominent functions for this task are the arithmetic mean and geometric mean [1]. The geometric mean is well fitted for small value of confidence scores than arithmetic mean. However, some weighted mean using discriminative training is provided for the combination of subword level scores [10]. Considering the complexity and robustness of the system, we have used the geometric mean as the final verification function which can make the utterance rejection/acceptance decision by comparing $V(O;W_k)$ to a predefined threshold.

As the result, the utterance-level likelihood ratio can be written as the geometric mean of subword-level likelihood ratios on the assumption of independence as Eqn..

$$V(O;W_k) = (\prod_{i=1}^{N} V(O_{t_{i-1}}^{t_i}; S_i^{(k)}))^{1/N} \tag{2}$$

where N is the total number of subwords in W_k.

We note that silence models are used in the forced-alignment for phoneme segmentation but only nonsilence subwords are used in computing the confidence measures. For each confidence measure, we will produce a confidence score of the utterance level. Therefore, total 10 confidence scores are used to construct the feature vector for the given keyword as the concatenation of confidence feature set.

3 Boosting Classifier

Boosting is a learning algorithm which can combine some 'weak' classifiers into a single strong one by applying a classification procedure iteratively with a weighted majority vote. The basic algorithm was introduced by Schapire and Freund [8].

The classifier computes in a particular way: at each iteration t, called a 'weak' classifier, the example weights for next iteration $t+1$ are adjusted due to the

Input: N training examples $\{(x_1, y_1), \cdots, (x_N, y_N)\}$, where x_i for confidence scores vectors, and $y_i \in \{0,1\}$ for target and imposter examples respectively.

Initialize the weight vector: $\omega_{t,i} = \frac{1}{2m}, \frac{1}{2n}$ $(i = 1, \ldots, N)$ for $y_i \in \{0,1\}$, where m and n are the number of targets and imposters respectively. T specifying number of iterations.

Do for $t = 1, 2, \ldots, T$

1. Set $P_{t,i} = \frac{\omega_{t,i}}{\sum_{j=1}^{N} \omega_{t,j}}$
2. Providing with the distribution $P_{t,i}$; for each confidence measure j, train a classifier h_j using neural networks.
3. Calculate the error of $h_{t,j}$: $\varepsilon_{t,j} = \sum_{i=1}^{N} \omega_{t,i} |h_j(x_i) - y_i|$.
4. Set $\beta_{t,j} = \frac{\varepsilon_{t,j}}{1 - \varepsilon_{t,j}}$, Choose the optimal classifier h_t corresponding to the lowest error $\varepsilon_{t,j}$.
5. Update the weights: $\omega_{t+1,i} = \omega_{t,i} \cdot \beta_t^{1-e_i}$

where $e_i = 0$ if the classifier hypothesis $h(x_i) = y_i$ is correct, $e_i = 1$, otherwise.

Ouput: the final hypothesis is:

$$h_f(x) = \arg\max \sum_{t=1}^{T} \left(\log \frac{1}{\beta_t} \right) \cdot e_t$$

where $e_t = 0$ if the example x_t is classified correctly, $e_i = 1$, otherwise.

Fig. 2. The boosting algorithm

training errors. If the 'weak' classifier can always find a hypothesis with the error below 1/2, then boosting approach will consider this vote given to the correct class. Finally boosting tends to increase the performance of classifier and the test set error continues to decrease. Fig.2 gives a description of boosting algorithm.

Freund and Schapire prove that the training error ε of the strong classifier is a form of the Chernoff bound [8] as Eqn.3.

$$\varepsilon \leq exp(-2T\gamma^2) \tag{3}$$

where $\gamma = \frac{1-2\varepsilon}{1-\varepsilon}$; T is the number of weak learners. In practice, we use AdaBoost [8] algorithm which is closely related to Bayesian analysis. Some experiments using AdaBoost on real-world problems indicate that AdaBoost tends not to over-fit, after hundreds rounds of boosting, the generalization error continues to drop, or at least does to increase.

4 Experimental Results

4.1 Speech Database

The speech database used for training consists of 70 speakers (35 female speakers and 35 male speakers). The total amount of training set's time duration has been estimated as about 49.6 hours.

For testing, we used 100 Chinese names (2 or 3 Chinese characters) as the fixed phrase for each speaker to read. 13 speakers (6 males and 7 females) were required to speak each name for 4 sessions. The first session of speaker's own recordings were used as the testing data while the other 3 sessions were further used for adaptation. The testing data used for UV is microphone based which was separately designed. Total 1300 utterances made the set of clients, and 7800 utterances which were partly selected from the other 99 Chinese names were test of imposters.

4.2 Experimental Results

In our experiment, the acoustic features are composed of 12 PLP coefficients and the energy. By including the first and second derivatives of the parameters, 39-dimension feature vectors were finally used.

We use a set of context-independent (CI) phone units as a universal phone set. There are 59 (21 Initials and 38 Finals) CI phonemes models. The experiment is carried out to achieve an overall good verification performance. The optimal number of mixtures is determined empirically. Finally 8 mixtures per state are used for HMM-based confidence measures and 128 mixtures per state for GMM-based confidence measures.

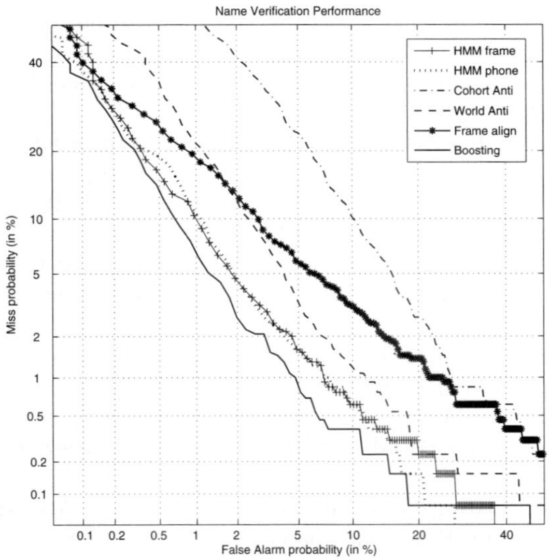

Fig. 3. Comparison of performance on various features and boosting algorithm

Fig.3 shows the Detection Error Tradeoff (DET) curves [11] for the evaluation of UV. With the single confidence measure, the lowest Equal Error Rate (EER) is 2.96% which is achieved by HMM on-line garbage model. Applying boosting approach, we reduced the EER to 2.27%, a relative improvement of 23.3%. We also experiment with the conventional classifier of Multiple Layer Perceptions (MLP) and Support Vector Machines (SVM). The MLP and SVM produce the EER of 2.38% and 2.59% respectively.

5 Conclusion

We have investigated a boosting approach for the utterance verification. In this work, we combine several confidence measures together with boosting classifier. The experiments show that it can remarkably improve the verification performance of the system. Compared with the best confidence measure, the EER is reduced from 2.96% to 2.27% (-23% relative). Additionally, we found the boosting approach is better than SVM and MLP classifiers, in term of the EER.

References

1. Koo, M. W., Lee, C. H., Juang, B. H.: Speech Recognition and Utterance Verification Based on a Generalized Confidence Score. IEEE Trans. on Speech Audio Proc, **9** (2001) 821-832
2. Li, Q., Juang, B. H., et al.: Automatic Verbal Information Verification for User Authentication. IEEE Trans. on Speech Audio Proc, **8** (2000) 585-596
3. Bourlard, H., D'hoore, B., Boite, J.: Optimizing Recognition and Rejection Performance in Word-Spotting Systems. In Proc. ICASSP, **1** (1994) 373-376
4. Sukkar, R., Lee, C.: Vocabulary Independent Discriminative Utterance Verification for Non-Keyword in Subword Based Speech Recognition. IEEE Trans. on Speech Audio Proc, **4** (1996) 420-429
5. Qin, C., Lee, T., Meng, H.: On Anti-Model Design for Cantonese Verbal Information Verification. In: Proc NCMMSC, (2005) 375-378
6. Li, X., Chen. K.: Mandarin Verbal Information Verification. In: Proc. ICASSP, (2002)
7. Burges, C.: A Tutorial on Support Vector Machines for Pattern Recognition. Data Mining and Knowledge Discovery, **2** (1998) 121-167
8. Freund, Y., Schapire, R. E.: A Decision-Theoretic Generalization of On-Line Learning and an Application to Boosting. Journal of Computer and System Sciences, **55** (1997) 119-139
9. Moreno, P., Logan, B., Raj, B.: A Boosting Approach for Confidence Scoring. In: Proc. Eurospeech (2001) 2109-2112
10. Abdou, S., Scordilis, M. S.: Beam Search Pruning in Speech Recognition Using a Posterior Probability-Based Confidence Measure. Speech Communication, **42** (2004) 409-428
11. Martin, A., Doddington, G., et al: The DET Curve in Assessment of Detection Task Performance. In: Proc. Eurospeech (1997) 1895-1898

A Comparative Study on Computerised Diagnostic Performance of Hepatitis Disease Using ANNs

Revna Acar Vural, Lale Özyılmaz, and Tülay Yıldırım

Department of Electronics & Communications Eng.,
Yıldız Technical University, İstanbul 34349, Turkey
{racar, ozyilmaz, tulay}@yildiz.edu.tr

Abstract. Artificial Neural Networks (ANNs) have been studied intensively in the field of computer science in recent years and have been shown to be a powerful tool for a variety of data-classification and pattern-recognition tasks. In this work, computerised diagnostic performance of hepatitis disease was investigated by various ANNs. Multilayer Perceptron, Radial Basis Function Neural Network, Conic Section Function Neural Network, Probabilistic Neural Network, and General Regression Neural Network structures have been used for this purpose. To determine diagnostic performance of networks for hepatitis disease, cross validation method and ROC analysis were applied.

1 Introduction

Artificial Neural Networks (ANNs) have been studied intensively in the field of computer science in recent years and have been shown to be a powerful tool for a variety of data-classification and pattern-recognition tasks.

There are many types of hepatitis disease. Causes include viruses, toxic chemicals, alcohol consumption, parasites and bacteria, and certain drugs. Symptoms of hepatitis are nausea, fever, weakness, loss of appetite, sudden distaste for tobacco smoking, and jaundice. A number of viruses can cause acute viral hepatitis. Five have been identified and named hepatitis A through E. At least ten other viruses are under study. Hepatitis can be incurred as a complication of several other disorders in addition to viral infection, among them amebic dysentery, cirrhosis of the liver, and mononucleosis. [1,2]

In the following section, an overview is given about applied neural networks for classification. In the third section, the methods used for showing the performance of neural networks have been explained. Data set and obtained results have been given in the fourth section. Finally, the results have been interpreted in the last section.

2 Overview of Applied Artificial Neural Network Structures

Five different neural network structures have been used and compared in this work. These are Multilayer Perceptron (MLP), Radial Basis Function Neural Network (RBF), Conic Section Function Neural Network (CSFNN), Probabilistic Neural Network (PNN), and General Regression Neural Network (GRNN).

D.-S. Huang, K. Li, and G.W. Irwin (Eds.): ICIC 2006, LNAI 4114, pp. 1177 – 1182, 2006.

2.1 Multilayer Perceptrons (MLPs)

Multilayer Perceptrons have been applied successfully to solve some difficult and diverse problems by training them in a supervised manner with a highly popular algorithm known as the error back-propagation algorithm. This algorithm is based on the error-correction learning rule. The activation of a hidden unit (neuron *j*) is a function f_j of the weighted inputs plus a bias, as given in Eq.1.

$$x_{pj} = f_j\left(\sum_i w_{ji} x_{pi} + \theta_j \right) = f_j(y_{pj}) \tag{1}$$

where w_{ji} is the weight of input i to neuron j, x_{pi} is input i, that is, output i from the previous layer, for input pattern p and θ_j is the threshold value. The output of the hidden units is distributed over the next layer of $x_{h,2}$ hidden units until the last layer of hidden units, of which the outputs are fed into a layer of x_o output units. [3,4]

2.2 Radial Basis Function Neural Network (RBFNN)

Radial Basis Function Neural Network is curve fitting approximation in multi-dimensional space. Generalization of RBFNN is equivalent to usage of multi-dimensional surface found during training phase. Hidden layer function is usually a Gaussian function which takes the exponential of standard Euclidean distance as shown in Eq(2) .

$$\varphi_k(\|x - c_k\|) = e^{\left(\frac{1}{2\sigma^2}\|x-c_k\|\right)} \tag{2}$$

Each RBF neuron corresponds to a region of the n-dimensional input space centered at location c. The activation of a RBF neuron in response to an input x is a function of the distance from x to its center. Activation ranges from 0 for distant inputs to 1 for inputs coincident with basis center. [3,4]

2.3 Conic Section Function Neural Network (CSFNN)

Conic Section Function Neural Network is a unified framework based on hyperplanar and hyperspherical decision regions as special cases of conic sections. These are decision regions of MLP and RBF networks, respectively. The idea of CSFNN is to generalise unit function that contains all decision regions by providing a relationship between RBF and MLP units. Activation for CSFNN can be given in a general form as

$$y_j = \sum_{i=1}^{n+1} (x_i - c_{ij}) w_{ij} - \cos \omega_j \sqrt{\sum_{i=1}^{n+1} (x_i - c_{ij})^2} \tag{3}$$

$$x_{n+1} \equiv 0$$

where i and j are the indices referring to the units in the input and hidden layer, y is the output of network. This equation consists of two major parts analogous to the MLP and RBF networks. w_{ij} refers to the weights for MLP network and c_{ij} refers to the centre coordinates in an RBF network. ω_j is the opening angle of a cone to provide transition from RBF to MLP.[5]

2.4 Probabilistic Neural Network (PNN)

The PNN is a normalized RBF network in which there is a hidden unit centered at every training case. These RBF units are called "kernels" and are usually probability density functions such as the Gaussian. Each pattern neuron computes a distance measure between the input and the training case represented by that neuron as given in Eq(4). The output neuron is a threshold discriminator that decides which of its inputs from the summation units is the maximum. [6]

$$d(x) = \frac{1}{(2\pi)^{\frac{r}{2}} \sigma^r n} \sum_{i=1}^{n} e^{\frac{-|x - x_i|^2}{2\sigma^2}} \tag{4}$$

2.5 General Regression Neural Network (GRNN)

General Regression Neural Network was proposed by Specht [7] as an alternative to iterative training of feedforward networks. Unlike MLP, GRNN requires only a one-pass training process. Due to such a property, the training time of GRNN is incomparably short. GRNN is a statistical solution to system identification and modeling [7] problems, however, it exhibits a parallel structure that can be implemented as a feed forward neural network.

3 Diagnostic Performance

Cross validation method and receiver operating characteristic analysis were used to show diagnostic performance for hepatitis disease.

3.1 Cross Validation (CV) Method

Cross validation is a model evaluation method that is better than residuals. The problem with residuals is that they do not give an indication of how well the learner will do when it is asked to make new predictions for data it has not already seen. One way to overcome this problem is to remove some of the data before training begins. When training is done, the data that was removed can be used to test the performance of the learned model on "new" data. This is the basic idea for cross validation.

In cross validation, a portion of the data is set aside as training data leaving the remainder as testing data. For k-fold cross validation is the data set is divided into *k* subsets, and the holdout method is repeated *k* times. Each time, one of the *k* subsets is used as the test set and the other *k-1* subsets are put together to form a training set. Then the average error across all *k* trials is computed. The variance of the resulting estimate is reduced as *k* is increased. The disadvantage of this method is that the training algorithm has to be rerun from scratch *k* times. [8]

3.2 Receiver Operating Characteristic (ROC) Analysis

ROC analysis is related to cost/benefit analysis of diagnostic decision making. Widely used in medicine, it has been introduced recently in machine learning .

ROC methodology is appropriate in situations where there are two possible "truth states" (i.e., diseased/normal, event/non-event, or some other binary outcome), "truth" is known for each case, and "truth" is determined independently of the diagnostic tests / predictor variables / etc. under study.

In ROC analysis, there are two important measures: sensitivity and specificity.

$$sensitivity = \frac{number\ of\ true\ positives}{number\ of\ true\ positives + number\ of\ false\ negatives}$$

$$specificity = \frac{number\ of\ true\ negatives}{number\ of\ true\ negatives + number\ of\ false\ positives}$$

where #true positives and #false negatives are the number of disease case correctly classified and incorrectly classified as normal case, respectively. Similarly, #true negatives and #false positives are the number of normal case correctly classified and incorrectly classified as disease case. [9]

4 Data Set, Methods and Simulation Results

Hepatitis database [10] used in this work contains 155 samples in total with 75 of them having missing attributes. There are two classes in the hepatitis disease: death (disease case) and life (normal case). First class has 13 instances and second class has 67 instances. All samples have 19 attributes [10,11].

Table 1. Overall classification accuracies of ANNs for 5-fold CV

Structures	train set (%)	test set (%)	average
MLP-bfg	96.91	83	89.96
MLP-cgb	95.31	84	89.66
MLP-cgf	89.81	81.25	85.53
MLP-cgp	95.29	83.5	89.40
MLP-gdm	78.38	74	76.19
MLP-gda	83.69	77.75	80.72
MLP-gdx	83.88	79.13	81.51
MLP-oss	91.91	81.25	86.58
MLP-scg	93.66	80.25	86.96
MLP-br	92.44	79	85.72
MLP-gd	79.47	76.88	78.18
MLP-lm	100	83.88	91.94
MLP-rp	99.56	83	91.28
RBF-rb	100	67.5	84
RBF-rbe	100	82.5	91.3
CSFNN	95.62	90	92.81
PNN	100	88.75	94.5
GRNN	100	83.8	92

5-fold cross validation method was used to demonstrate the generalization ability of the networks. Five neural network structures; MLP with various learning algorithms, RBF trained by Orthogonal Least Squares algorithm (RBF-rb) and fixed centres (RBF-rbe), CSFNN, PNN, and GRNN have been trained and tested with the appropriate data. Classification accuracies of the networks for both train and test sets were given in Table 1. Average results can also be seen from Table 1.

The levels of sensitivity and specificity are very important to evaluate real performances of the networks. Therefore, ROC analysis was applied to all networks. It can be seen from the Table 1, LM backpropagation and resilient backpropagation algorithms gave the best two results. For this reason, these two algorithms were chosen for MLP in ROC analysis. The comparative sensitivity and specificity values of the networks for train and test sets were given in Table 2.

Table 2. Results of ROC analysis

Networks	Train		Test	
	Sensitivity	Specificity	Sensitivity	Specificity
MLP-lm	1	1	0.38	0.94
MLP-rp	0.99	1	0.53	0.91
RBF-rb	1	1	0.85	0.57
RBF-rbe	1	1	0.99	0.27
CSFNN	0.98	0.84	0.94	0.7
PNN	1	1	0.97	0.47
GRNN	1	1	0.97	0.53

5 Conclusions and Discussion

In this paper, the computerised diagnostic performances of MLP, RBF, CSFNN, PNN, and GRNN structures were evaluated for hepatitis disease. The networks were 5-fold cross-validated to show the performances on unknown cases.

In the previous work [11], only gradient descent with momentum and adaptive learning backpropagation for MLP, RBF trained by Orthogonal Least Squares algorithm and CSFNN have been used. In this work, to show the performances of different neural networks and training algorithms, 13 MLP and 2 RBF algorithms were used and PNN and GRNN have been also investigated.

In terms of accuracy, PNN gave the best result with 94.5% in average. CSFNN has the second best accuracy with 92.81%; however, CSFNN is better than all the other networks over the test set with an accuracy of 90%. On the other hand, high classification accuracy is less important than the high sensitivity and/or specificity of a classifier system for many medical problems. As ROC analysis allows quantifying the accuracy of diagnostic tests, sensitivity and specificity values of all ANNs have been considered for both train and test sets separately to show real performances.

After ROC analysis applied to training set, it was seen that all sensitivity and specificity values were 1 for MLP-lm, RBF, PNN, and GRNN networks since they classified all training samples correctly. However, for test set, in terms of both sensitivity and specificity values, the performance of CSFNN was the best, by matching with the classification accuracy.

MLP-lm produced the worst result for the test set with respect to determination of diseased cases. RBF-rbe was observed that the worst network regarding to specificity for the test set although it has the best value for sensitivity. As a result, it was seen that the CSFNN can be successfully used in computerised diagnosing of hepatitis since it has the best results in terms of both accuracy and ROC analysis in the test set.

Acknowledgements

This research has been supported by Yıldız Technical University Scientific Projects Coordination Department. Project Number : 24-04-02-02.

References

1. Cheung, N.: Machine Learning Techniques for Medical Analysis, Bs.C. Thesis, University of Queensland, Australia (2001)
2. The Columbia Electronic Encyclopedia, Sixth Edition, Columbia University Press. Licensed from Columbia University Press, USA (2003)
3. Schalkoff, R. J.: Artificial Neural Networks, McGraw-Hill Inc., Singapore (1997)
4. Haykin, S.: Neural Networks: A Comprehensive Foundation, Macmillan College Publishing, New York (1994)
5. Dorffner, G.: Unified Framework for MLPs and RBFNs: Introducing Conic Section Function Networks, Cybernetics and Systems, 25 (1994)511-554
6. Specht, D. F.: Probabilistic Neural Networks, Neural Networks, 3 (1990) 109-118
7. Specht, D. F.: A General Regression Neural Network, IEEE Trans. Neural Networks, 2 (6) (1991) 568-576
8. Sarle, W.: What Are Cross-validation and Bootstrapping?, Available at http://www.faqs.org/faqs/ai-faq/neural-nets/part3/section-12.html, (2005)
9. Sboner, A.: A Multiple Classifier System for Early Melanoma Diagnosis. AI in Medicine, 27(2003) 29-44
10. Blake, C. L., Merz, C. J., UCI Repository of Machine Learning Databases [http://www.ics.uci.edu/~mlearn/MLRepository.html]. Irvine, CA: University of California, Department of Information and Computer Science, (1998)
11. Özyılmaz, L., Yıldırım, T.: Artificial Neural Networks for Diagnosis of Hepatitis Disease, International Joint Conference on Neural Networks. IEEE publication, New York (2003) 586-589

A Two-View CoTraining Rule Induction System for Information Extraction

Jing Xiao

Department of Computer Science, SUN Yat-Sen University, Guangzhou, China, 510275
xiaoj2@mail.sysu.edu.cn

Abstract. Information extraction is becoming an important task due to the vast growth of the online texts. Pattern rule induction is one kind of main methods to do information extraction. Manually constructing pattern rules is tedious and error prone. In this paper, we present GRID_CoTrain, a weakly supervised paradigm by bootstrapping GRID (a supervised rule induction system) with co-training and active learning. We also utilize external knowledge resource such as WordNet and existing ontology knowledge to optimize the learned pattern rules.

1 Introduction

Due to the huge amount of online texts from the web, Information Extraction (IE) is becoming an essential tool for intelligent text processing. Among several popular machine learning technologies for information extraction, pattern rule induction plays an important role [1]. Since it is time-consuming and error prone to manually annotate training data for supervised systems, there are many research efforts in recent years that focus on bootstrapping an IE system using a small set of annotated data and plentiful un-annotated data to implement weakly supervised learning [2, 3, 4]. Co-training is one such bootstrapping strategy. Co-training begins with a small number of labeled data and a large number of unlabelled data. It trains more than one classifier from the labeled data, uses the classifiers to label some unlabelled data, trains again the new classifiers from all the labeled data, and repeats the above process. Co-training with multiple views learners reduce the need for labeled data by exploiting disjoint subsets of features (views) such as contextual and content views, each of which is sufficient for learning. Initial studies of co-training focused on the applicability of co-training on clarifying the assumptions needed to ensure its effectiveness. [4] presented a PAC-style analysis of co-training and made two important conclusions: first, each view of the data should itself be sufficient for learning the classification task; and second, the views should be conditionally independent of each other. More formally, given that X is the training feature set and Y is the classification, we assume that $X=X_1 \times X_2$, where there exist functions $g_1: X_1 \rightarrow Y$ and $g_2: X_2 \rightarrow Y$ such that $f(X) = g_1(X_1) = g_2(X_2)$ for all $X=X_1|X_2$. In the real world domain, this ideal assumption is not fully satisfied as there are some ambiguities in the classes of noun phrases [5]. For example, the noun phrase "*Columbia*" could be a "*location*" (in the context of "*headquartered in Columbia*") or

D.-S. Huang, K. Li, and G.W. Irwin (Eds.): ICIC 2006, LNAI 4114, pp. 1183 – 1190, 2006.

an "*organization*" (in the context of "*Columbia published* ..."). Although the tight constraints are not fully satisfied in most information extraction tasks, researchers found that co-training with separate feature sets still performed better than the ones which do not split the feature sets [6]. [5] showed that combination of active learning and bootstrapping (using CoEM algorithm) made the information extractor robust although the ambiguities of noun phrase classes exist. One of the problems when applying co-training algorithms for natural learning from large datasets is the scalability problem. Degradation in the quality of the bootstrapped data arises as an obstacle to further improvement [7] in the learning process. In this paper, we combine co-training with active learning to overcome this problem. Active learning methods attempt to select only the most informative examples for annotation and training and therefore are potentially very useful in natural language applications. In the experiments, we include a human to annotate some instances after a few iterations in an active learning framework. We investigate several active learning strategies in the co-training model to determine which instances should be annotated by the human. The strategies considered include: uniform random selection, density selection, committee-based sampling and confidence-based sampling. On the other hand, during the course of bootstrapping, the quality of the learned pattern rules is crucial for the effectiveness of the final learner. We use WordNet as a general dictionary source to optimize the learned rules.

In this paper, we describe a bootstrapping pattern rule-based IE system, called GRID_CoTrain, which co-trains the context and content views with active learning using an existing pattern rule learner GRID [8]. In Section 2, we describe some related research of bootstrapping for IE tasks. Section 3 briefly introduces the supervised rule learning system, GRID. Section 4 describes the bootstrapping algorithm, GRID_CoTrain in detail and the strategies of rule optimization using the general WordNet plus the domain ontology knowledge. Section 5 presents our experimental results on the terrorism domain. Finally, we conclude this paper in Section 6.

2 Related Bootstrapping Systems for IE Tasks

In recent years, many researchers have used bootstrapping technology for various information extraction tasks. The *Snowball* system [2] introduced the strategies for generating patterns and extracting tuples from plain-text documents that require only a handful of training examples from users. They use a simple relation which is "organization-location" (where is the organization located) for evaluation. Multi-level bootstrapping is used in [9] for generating both the semantic lexicon and extraction patterns simultaneously. To alleviate the deterioration in performance due to non-category words entering the semantic lexicon, the outer bootstrapping mechanism compiles the results from the inner bootstrapping process and identifies the most reliable lexicon entries. As input, it requires only un-annotated training texts and a handful of seed words for a category. [3] described two bootstrapping algorithms, DL_CoTrain (DL stands for decision list) and AdaBoost for named entity classification. In [7], the authors pointed out that there are some limitations to co-training for natural language learning from large datasets. They proposed a "correct co-training" to solve the scalability problem during the course of bootstrapping and suggested the combination of weakly supervised learning (such as co-training) with active learning. [10] described an active learning model with a strong view and a weak view, Aggressive Co-Testing, for wrapper induction. A strong view consists of features that are adequate for learning the target concept (such as contextual view); in contrast, in a weak view, one can only learn a concept that is more general or specific than the target concept (such as the content view). Take for an example, to extract the telephone number from a webpage, a strong view rule could be "* Phone: (number)" which indicates "skip any token until "phone" appears followed by numbers". This strong view rule is sufficient to extract the telephone numbers from structured web pages. A weak view rule, such as "(number) – number number", is not sufficient to identify whether it's a fax number or a telephone number. Aggressive Co-Testing exploits both strong and weak views and uses the weak views both for detecting the most informative examples in the domain and for improving the accuracy of the predictions. [11] introduced competition among several scenarios simultaneously. This provides natural stopping criteria for the unsupervised learners, while maintaining good precision levels at termination. In GRID_CoTrain, we plan to combine co-training with active learning. Co-training is performed by training content rules and contextual rules. After several iterations, a human being is in charge of labeling several instances that are selected by several active learning strategies. We will investigate the performances of various active learning methods in the experimental evaluation section.

3 A Brief Introduction to GRID

GRID (Global Rule Induction for online Documents) [8] is a supervised covering pattern rule induction system. It examines all training instances for one class at the representation levels of lexical, syntactic and semantic simultaneously. GRID adopts chunks (noun or verb phrase) information provided by a shallow parser as units to determine the context of the pattern rules. As chunk is of higher syntactic level than word or token, it provides a more appropriate unit to model context. Also GRID incorporates named entity recognition to provide semantic constraints for pattern rule induction and uses a novel statistics based lexical chaining method to generalize pattern rules. GRID obtained good IE performance in semi-structured webpages and free texts and can be applied successfully in definitional question answering and video story segmentation tasks [12]. We list some of the typical pattern rules learned by GRID as follows (in MUC-4 terrorism domain):

"murder/killing" followed by "of" followed by any noun phrase → noun phrase is "victim"
any noun phrase followed by a passive verb phrase with "kill" → noun phrase is "victim"
any noun phrase followed by a passive verb phrase with "kidnap" → noun phrase is "victim"

4 Bootstrapping Algorithm GRID_CoTrain

We use GRID as the base learner in the bootstrapping scheme. The bootstrapping scheme is co-trained by two views, one is the content view and the other is the contextual view.

4.1 Bootstrapping GRID Using Co-Training with Two Views

Co-Training with multiple views is a weakly supervised paradigm for learning a classification task from a small set of labeled data and a large set of unlabeled data, using separate, but redundant, views of the data. The main task of information extraction is to extract specific semantic entities from the text documents and to determine their relationship in filling in a template. The extraction of semantic entities requires the use of context, which can be expressed in the general form as:

$$<c_{-k}>\ldots<c_{-2}><c_{-1}> <c_0> (sem\_entity) <c_{+1}><c_{+2}>\ldots<c_{+k}> . \quad (1)$$

where $<c_i>$ $\{i = -k \text{ to } +k;\ i \neq 0\}$ refers to the context token at position *i* of the semantic entity, and *k* is the number of context tokens considered. $<c_0>$ represents the central semantic entity itself.

We consider the $<c_0>$ *(sem_entity)* as the content view X_1; the left and right context information (*i.e.* $<c_i>$ $\{i = -k \text{ to } +k;\ i \neq 0\}$) are considered as contextual view X_2. Figure 1 indicates the basic procedure of GRID_CoTrain with two views.

Given instance space: X
Distribution D over X: $D = \{(x_i, y_i)\}_{i=1}^{m}$ *; Y is the classifications.*
$X = X_1 \times X_2$ *(two views: content view* X_1 *and contextual view* X_2*)*
GRID (G) is the base learner;
Apply G to the two views, $X_1(G)$, $X_2(G)$ *to create two classifiers:* g_1, g_2;
Combine co-training (two classifiers g_1 *and* g_2*) with active learning*
to get mapping $F: X \rightarrow Y$

Fig. 1. Overall paradigm of GRID_CoTrain

We present the detailed algorithm of GRID_CoTrain as following:

(a) Initialization: We define two pools in this algorithm. One is *lexicon pool* which contains list of words/phrases for content view for each category. The other is *pattern pool* which contains list of patterns for contextual view derived so far for different category. Initially, we set the *lexicon pool* to the set of user selected seed words for each category. The initial set of content rules equal to the set of "*seed*" words for each type. For example, "*FMLN*" is one of the seed words for the category of "*perpetrator*" in the MUC-4 corpus. The corresponding content rule is "*full string = FMLN → FMLN is a perpetrator*". The *pattern pool* is initially set to null.
(b) Label the training set using the current set of content rules. Instances where no rule can be applied are left unlabeled.
(c) Use the labeled examples to induce the pattern rules by employing the GRID algorithm. In the weakly supervised learning model of GRID_CoTrain, we do not have enough positive and negative examples to evaluate the pattern rules in which it is different from what we do in the supervised model of GRID. Instead of using the *Laplacian* measure in the supervised version, we use an *RlogF* metric [9] to score each pattern rule. The score for each pattern is computed as:

$$R\log F(pattern_i) = \left(F_i / N_i\right) * \log_2(F_i) \ . \quad (2)$$

where F_i is the number of category members extracted by $pattern_i$ and N_i is the total number of noun phrases extracted by $pattern_i$.

We select the top n=3 extraction patterns for each category and put them in the *pattern pool* accordingly. Intuitively, the *RlogF* measure is a weighted conditional probability; a pattern receives a high score if a high percentage of its extractions are category members.

(d) Label the training set using the current set of pattern rules in the pattern pools for each category. Examples where no rule applies are left unlabeled. For each extracted noun phrase or word, we use the average logarithm metric used in [13] to score it. The score for each phrase or word is computed as:

$$AvgLog(phrase_i) = \sum_{j=1}^{P_i} \log_2(F_j + 1) \Big/ P_i \tag{3}$$

where P_i is the number of patterns that extract $phrase_i$ and F_j is the number of distinct category members extracted by $pattern_j$.

We select the top 3 phrases or words for each category and put them in the *lexicon pool* accordingly. Generate the content rules for the noun phrases or words added to the lexicon pools as in step (a). Set the content rules to be the seed set plus the words or the noun phrases added to the lexicon pools and go to step (b). The algorithm can be stopped when it runs a fixed number of iterations or when there is no new entries added to the lexicon pools and pattern pools.

4.2 Active Learning Strategies in GRID_CoTrain

As discussed in Section 1, one problem in co-training paradigm is the degradation in quality of automatically bootstrapped data which presents an obstacle to further improvement in performance. In GRID_CoTrain, we combine the active learning strategies with co-training to tackle this problem. Active learning is to determine which unlabeled instances to label next in order to maximize the learning objective with least labeling effort. We restrict our study to selective sampling of active learning here. Sample frequency is usually used in selective sampling strategies. Given a training example of "$<c_{-k}>\ldots<c_{-2}><c_{-1}>$ $<c_0>$ *(sem_entity)* $<c_{+1}><c_{+2}>\ldots<c_{+k}>$", we consider the frequency of the $<c_0>$ *(sem_entity)* as our criteria for selective sampling. Some researchers used the frequency of occurrences of context information as the criteria for selective sampling [5]. We investigate several active learning strategies for GRID_CoTrain.

The active learning strategies we investigate are as following:

(a) Uniform random selection: It selects the *<sem_entity>* that appear in the training examples at least once randomly with equal probability. The actual sample frequency is ignored. This sampling selection could be considered as baseline among the various strategies.

(b) Density selection: This sampling selection considers the actual sample frequency. The most frequent *<sem_entity>* in the unlabeled examples set is selected for annotation first. This method is based on the assumption that labeling frequent occurring samples would be beneficial for the learner.

(c) Certainty-based selection [14]: This sampling selection selects samples with lowest certainties and presents them to the user for annotation. We use the Equation (3) as the certainty metric.
(d) Committee-based selection [15]: In this paradigm, we regard the committee-based sampling as feature set disagreement. Since we learn two classifiers based on content view and context view, one way is to select samples where a human can provide useful information to identify samples where these two classifiers disagree. If there are such instances, we present them to the human annotator.

We trust the classification of the samples annotated by the human annotator. So the samples that are labeled by the human are considered as correctly labeled training samples and the tagged noun phrases are put into their according lexicon pools. The labeled samples are put into the labeled training pool for the base learner in the later iterations. In Section 6, we will present the performances of different active learning strategies in the terrorism domain. In our study, after every 5 iterations, we ask a human user to annotate up to 20 samples selected by the active learning strategies.

4.3 Rule Optimization Using External Dictionary

At the end of the rule induction learning, we extract a set of satisfied pattern extraction rules. In general, the rule set obtained is not optimal as it did not consider the lexical and semantic relationships between features used in different rules. For example, for the <victim> slot in the terrorism attack domain, we may generate similar rules but with one different slot element, such as the "*murder of <victim>*" and "*assassination of <victim>*". As these rules share similar semantic meaning, they should be merged into a more general rule where the root noun is of the semantic class *{murder, assassination}*. The generalized rule's score is re-computed according to Equation (2).To achieve this, we aim to perform lexical chaining on those rules that contain feature representations of verb phrases or noun phrases. We employ a lexical chaining algorithm as described in [16] to determine if the root verbs or head nouns can be replaced by their semantic groups. The process uses synsets in WordNet along with corpus statistics to find the common semantic group of different lexical tokens. At the end of lexical chaining process, we obtain a set of semantic groups, each containing a cluster of related words. These semantic groups are used as the basis to generalize some features related to nouns and verbs.

5 Experimental Evaluation

To evaluate the active learning and rule generalization strategies in GRID_CoTrain, we perform experiments on terrorism news articles from the MUC-4 corpus. For training, we use the training corpus and the TST1 and TST2 documents. Altogether, there are 1500 documents of the terrorism texts of which 50% are relevant to terrorism attacks. The TST3 and TST4 documents are used for testing the learned rules. We compare our bootstrapping algorithm of GRID_CoTrain with the supervised results of GRID. We run the two algorithms on three semantic categories (perpetrator, victim, and target). We used a list of seed words to start the bootstrapping experiments. First, we evaluate the different active learning strategies discussed in Section 4.2. Each extracted item is assigned to one of the five categories of: *correct, missed, mislabeled, duplicate,* or *spurious*. We compute the F_1-measure as following: Recall(R) = *correct* / (*correct* + *missing*); Precision (P) = (*correct* + *duplicate*) / (*correct* + *duplicate* + *mislabeled* + *spurious*); $F_1 = 2 \times P \times R / (P + R)$

We run GRID_CoTrain algorithm 100 times and ask a human to annotate up to 20 samples manually after every 5 iterations where the samples are selected using different strategies of active learning. The learned rule sets are re-evaluated every 10 iterations. From our experimental findings we can draw the following conclusions:

(a) Bootstrapping with co-training by content view and context view without active learning performs well in the first 50 iterations. However, as the automatically annotated samples become larger, the performance decreases. This is partly due to the errors accumulated by automatically labeled samples.
(b) The use of the active learning helps GRID_CoTrain to improve its performance steadily as we perform more bootstrapping iterations, as compared to the non-active learning system. Among the active learning strategies, we found the certainty-based and committee-based strategies to be the most effective.
(c) GRID_CoTrain performs almost comparable to the supervised learning by using the active learning strategies. Thus the human-involved active learning maintains the quality of the learned rules, and yet the effort on the part of human annotator remains small (needs only about 20% in our experiments) in proportion to the amount of labeled data needed for training the fully supervised version of GRID.

To evaluate the effect of specific ontology knowledge on rule generalization, we perform further experiment to compare rule generalization using WordNet. We use the committee-based active learning strategy (averaged F_1 for the three concept slots) as the experimental setting for evaluating the rule generalization method with WordNet. The result shows that WordNet can improve the performance of IE by 1.5%.

6 Conclusion

Based on our previous pattern rule induction algorithm, GRID, this paper describes a bootstrapping pattern induction algorithm, GRID_CoTrain, which combines co-training with two contextual and content views and several active learning strategies. GRID_CoTrain required about 20% human annotation instances through the use of active learning strategy during the bootstrapping process to achieve comparable performance of the fully supervised learner of GRID. It shows that the weakly supervised algorithm we proposed is effective and alleviates some manual labor work.

References

1. Muslea, I.: Extraction Patterns for Information Extraction Tasks: A Survey. The AAAI-99 Workshop on Machine Learning for Information Extraction (1999)
2. Agichtein, E., Gravano, L.: Snowball: Extracting Relations from Large Plain Text Collections. Proceedings of the 5th ACM International Conference on Digital Libraries (2000)

3. Collins, M., Singer, Y.: Unsupervised Models for Named Entity Classification. Proceedings of the Joint SIGDAT Conference on Empirical Methods in Natural Language Proceedings and Very Large Corpora (1999)
4. Blum, A., Mitchell, T.: Combining Labeled and Unlabeled Data with Co-Training. Proceedings of the 11th Annual Conference on Computational Learning Theory (1998)
5. Jones, R., Ghani, R., Mitchell, T., Riloff, E.: Active Learning for Information Extraction with Multiple View Feature Sets. Proceedings of European Conference on Machine Learning Workshop on Adaptive Text Extraction and Mining (2003)
6. Nigam, K., Ghani, R.: Analyzing the Effectiveness and Applicability of Co-Training. Proceedings of Information and Knowledge Management (2000)
7. Pierce, D., Cardie, C.: Limitations of Co-Training for Natural Language Learning from Large Datasets. Proceedings of the 2001 Conference on Empirical Methods in Natural Language Processing (2001)
8. Xiao, J., Chua, T. S., Liu, J.: Global Rule Induction for Information Extraction. International Journal on Artificial Intelligence Tools. Vol. 13, No. 4 (2004)
9. Riloff, E., Jones, R.: Learning Dictionaries for Information Extraction by Multi-Level Bootstrapping. Proceedings of the 16th National Conference on Artificial Intelligence (1999)
10. Muslea, I., Minton, S., Knoblock, C.: Active Learning with Strong and Weak Views: a Case Study on Wrapper Induction. Proceedings of the 18th International Joint Conference on Artificial Intelligence (2003)
11. Yangarber, R.: Counter-Training in Discovery of Semantic Patterns. Proceedings of the 41st Annual Meeting of the Association for Computational Linguistics (2003)
12. Xiao, J.: Global Rule Induction for Information Extraction. Ph.D thesis, National University of Singapore (2004)
13. Thelen, M., Riloff, E.: A Bootstrapping Method for Learning Semantic Lexicons using Extraction Pattern Contexts. Proceedings of the 2002 Conference on Empirical Methods in Natural Language Processing (2002)
14. Lewis, D. D., Catlett, J.: Heterogeneous Uncertainty Sampling for Supervised Learning. Proceedings of the 11th International Conference on Machine Learning (1994)
15. Freund, Y., Seung, H. S., Shamir, E., Tishby, N.: Selective Sampling using the Query by Committee Algorithm. Machine Learning, 28 (1997)
16. Chua, T. S., Liu, J.: Learning Pattern Rules for Chinese Named Entity Extraction. Proceedings of the 18th National Conference on Artificial Intelligence (2002)

A Ubiquitous Healthcare Service System for Benign Prostatic Hyperplasia Patients

Keon Myung Lee[1], WonSeob Yang[1], Kyung Mi Lee[1], Wun-Jae Kim[2], and Seok Jung Yoon[2]

[1] School of Electrical and Computer Engineering, RICIC, Chungbuk National University, Korea*
[2] College of Medicine, Chungbuk National University, Korea
kmlee@cbnu.ac.kr

Abstract. This paper presents a benign prostatic hyperplasia management system which allows patients to cut down the number of hospital visits by using mobile devices like PDA phones or using Web applications and some information management techniques for patient care.

1 Introduction

According to the Korea National Statistical Office, Korea has already entered into the aging society with more than 3.35 million aged people in 2000.[1] The aging of population leads various social problems such as social dynamics drop, increase in social security cost, reduction in the economically productive population, and so on. In the perspective of disease statistics, it is expected that more and more aged people would be suffering from chronic diseases like cerebrovascular diseases, urinary diseases, and so on. Especially, the urinary chronic diseases such as benign prostatic hyperplasia (BPH) and urinary incontinence are typical one which lots of aged people come to have as they get older.

In the case of benign prostatic hyperplasia, usually it does not threaten the life, but degrades the quality of life. The patients with this disease need to see doctors on a regular basis, e.g. once or twice a month depending on their disease severity, in order to check up and treat the disease over their aged life. Therefore, this kind of urinary diseases cost lots of time and money. As the society gets older, the disease will be more aged people affected by the disease.

This paper presents a medical care service system which has been developed to provide medical health care service for BHP patients using mobile communication and information management techniques. The number of patients' hospital visits could be reduced by making them enter self-observed symptoms into the system and then by causing the system to inform them of whether they seem to be good to see their doctor on the scheduled date.

* The work was supported by Korea Institute of Industrial Technology Evaluation & Planning as the Regional Industry Priority Technology Development Program (Health-Medical Care IH-3-41) in 2004-2006.

D.-S. Huang, K. Li, and G.W. Irwin (Eds.): ICIC 2006, LNAI 4114, pp. 1191–1197, 2006.

2 BPH Patient Care

In order to follow up the BPH patients' disease state, the physicians in urology department usually ask them to fill out the well-specified symptom questionnaire on a periodic basis. When they see a physician, they bring the answer sheets and the physician writes the prescription based on the sheets, his/her diagnosis, and the medical lab test results, if necessary. As the typical questionnaires, there are International Prostatic Symptom Score (IPSS)[5] and NIH-Chronic Prostatitis Symptom Index(NIH-CPSI)[6]. The questionnaires ask several questions such as the frequency to feel unease on urination, the frequency of night urination, the interruption during urination, average flow rate, and so on, and makes the patients score their symptoms. This kind of patients' questionnaire answers are considered as important information when a physician diagnoses patients. Due to inherent characteristics of BPH, the patients need to visit hospital regularly to control their disease.

In order to reduce the number of hospital visits and to provide better medical care services for the BPH patients, we have designed and developed a prototype system with which the BPH patients are cared. In the developed system, the BPH patient care service is practiced as follows: At the first visit of a BPH patient to a hospital, the physician registers him into the system and records all pieces of information about patients including basic lab tests and observation results like prostate size, prostate specific antigen, digital rectal examination, urine analysis, Bun, maximum/average flow rate, blood pressure, waist circumference, weight, and so on. According to the diagnosis results, the physician issues a prescription for the patient and sets for the patient the next hospital visit date which is somewhat farther than in the conventional treatment which does not use such developed system. At home, the patient observes his symptoms by himself and enters them into the system using a mobile device like a PDA phone on a regular basis (e.g., once a week). Each time the system receives a patient's input about his symptoms, it decides his disease state using the diagnosis knowledge constructed by the BPH specialists and determines whether it is good for him to visit the hospital on the scheduled date. Depending on the decision, the system sends the patients a message about hospital visit schedule. If the diagnosis tells that his disease state gets worse, the system informs him of urgent visit. With the system, the BPH patients can lessen the number of hospital visits but they receive still the quality care for themselves.

3 The BPH Patient Care Service System

3.1 The System Architecture

Figure 1 shows the architecture of the developed system which provides the health care services for the BPH patients. The system consists of several distributed servers and modules as follows: Patient Data Communication Software, Patient Web Interface Physician side Patient Information Retrieval Software, Patient EMR DB Server, SMS Server, Patient Disease State Decision Server, and

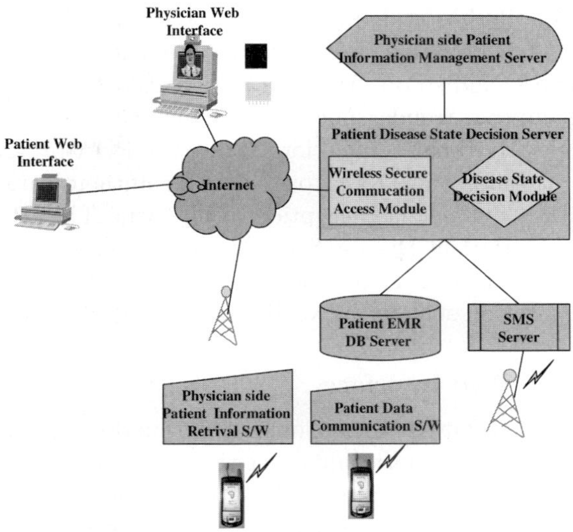

Fig. 1. The BPH Patient Care Service System

Physician side Patient Information Management Server. The following sections describe the constituents of the system in more detail.

3.2 The Patient Data Communication Software

The BPH patient care service system is developed to reduce the number of hospital visits and to provide quality patient care service for BPH outpatients. In order to follow up their disease state, the BPH patients need to report their symptoms to the hospital or their physician on a regular basis while they stay home. It would be desirable for them to report their symptoms in a computerized way regardless of time and place. Therefore, as one of data terminals for patients, we chose to use PDA phones which have the computing capability as well as wireless communication capability. We have developed a PDA program which helps the BPH patients to answer the questionnaire about their symptoms and sends the answers to the Patient Disease State Decision Server. Despite the PDA phones are an excellent platform to run such software and to make data communication over the wireless Internet, they are still unfriendly especially to the aged people. Hence, we have paid special attention to the user interface design of the PDA program. The program was developed to allow the patients to answer the questions by their finger on the touch screen of PDA phones without using a tiny stylus pen. In addition, to make the patients feel easy in using the program, it plays recorded voices to read the questions at each question page. The audio guidance was recorded by a physician who sees the BPH patients in Chungbuk National University Hospital, Korea. Although a patient has a slight sight problem, he can answer the questions by choosing a button corresponding to the answer. At the end of the question-answering sequence, the program asks the patient whether he wants to send the answers to the Patient Disease State

Decision Server in the hospital. In the meanwhile, the Patient PDA program allows the user to retrieve his past history data like history of IPSS scores, waist circumferences, and so on, from the Patient EMR DB server and thus he can survey his symptom trends. The PDA phone accesses the hospital servers through the wireless Internet connection. When the PDA program accesses the hospital servers, it sends his ID and password for authentication and encrypts the messages with a symmetric encryption mechanism. The IP address and the port number for the Patient Disease State Decision Server are set up by default when the program is installed. On the PDA phones, the users are allowed to change the configuration such as server IP address and port number.

3.3 The Patient Web Interface

The PDA phone-based Patient Data Communication devices are excellent in the perspective of mobility and portability, yet they have some restrictions such as device costs, small screen size, wireless Internet access cost, and so on. Hence, the developed BPH patient care system additionally provides the patients with a web-based interface which has the same functionality as the PDA phone-based program. The Patient Web Interface accesses the hospital servers through the web browsers like MS Internet Explorer over the wired Internet and also provides the audio guidance along with some additional information about BPH management. For the consistent interface, the Patient Web Interface has been designed with the same style as that of the PDA phone-based program.

3.4 The Physician-Side Patient Information Management Server

The Physician-side Patient Information Management Server takes charge of registering new patients, adding/deleting/updating the records of patients, and retrieving relevant records according to the physicians' requests. When a new patient decides to employ the BPH patient care service, his physician creates a new account for the patient. All pieces of information about the BPH including the basic personal information and lab test results, diagnosis results, prescription, and next hospital visit date come to be stored in the EMR DB server through the Physician side Patient Information Manager Server. Each time the patients see a physician, the physician adds a new record about his/her diagnosis, and some factors such as prostate size, maximum/average flow rate, IPSS score, quality of life score, and so on.

When a physician sees a patient, the physician may refer to the patient's past clinical history data with the help of the Patient Information Management Server. In order to make it convenient for the physicians to use the server, the Web-based interface has been implemented and thus they can use the server through a Web browser from any computer over the Internet.

3.5 The Patient EMR DB Server

The BPH Patient EMR(Electronic Medical Record) database(DB) is the repository for all pieces of information about the BPH patients served by the BPH

Patient Care Service System. For each patient, it keeps the basic personal information, the clinical history data about the lab test results, symptoms submitted by the patients through their PDA phones or Patient Web Interface, and the diagnoses and treatments. In BPH treatments, it is important to trace the trends of the changes of symptoms and disease states in order to figure out the patient's disease progress. Therefore, the database server maintains the historical data for the patients and allows to retrieve such information. The server provides the DB access interface for the other servers like Physician side Patient Information Management System, Patient Disease State Decision Server, and SMS Server.

3.6 The Patient Disease State Decision Server

The major goal of the developed service is to reduce the number of hospital visits while maintaining the disease control quality level. If a patient seems to remain in same disease state as that of the previous hospital visit or to be improving, the BPH Patient Care system is expected to inform him he could pay a visit to the hospital on the scheduled date or to recommend him to change the amount of medicine to take within the allowance range of his physician's prescription. If a patient is suspected to get the disease state worse, the system is expected to recommend him to see doctor immediately or earlier than the scheduled date. In order to make such decision, the service system makes use of medical diagnosis knowledge provided by the BPH medical specialists. When the service system has been developed, the BPH specialists have participated in building the diagnosis knowledge. The knowledge acquired from the specialists had some incomplete or conflict aspects and thus such knowledge was engineered to cover all possible cases and to resolve the conflicts in the knowledge with the help of BPH specialists. Table 1 shows a piece of BPH disease state decision knowledge used in the developed system. In the developed system, the Patient Disease State Decision Server also plays the role of the access point for the Patient Data Communication programs and it authenticates the patients with their ID and password.

Table 1. A piece of BPH state decision knowledge

The situation that $8 \leq IPSS \leq 19$ and $Q_{max} < 15$ and $Prostate\ size \geq 30$

	$\Delta F \leq -3$	$\Delta F < \lvert 3 \rvert$	$\Delta F = 3$	$3 < \Delta F < 4$	$\Delta F \geq 4$
$\Delta I \leq -3$	next visit in 1 mth	next visit in 1 mth	prostate checkup	prostate checkup	prostate checkup
$-3 < \Delta I < 0$	next visit in 1 mth	next visit in 1 mth	next visit in 1 mth	next visit in 1 mth	next visit in 1 mth
$\Delta I = 0$	next visit in 1 mth	next visit in 1 mth	next visit in 1 mth	next visit in 1 mth	next visit in 1 mth
$0 < \Delta I < 3$	next visit in 2 mths	next visit in 1 mth	next visit in 2 mths	next visit in 2 mths	next visit in 2 mths
$3 \leq \Delta I < 4$	next visit in 2 mths	next visit in 1 mth	next visit in 2 mths	next visit in 2 mths	next visit in 2 mths
$\Delta I \geq 4$	next visit in 2 mths	next visit in 1 mth	next visit in 2 mths	next visit in 2 mths	next visit in 2 mths

ΔF : the change of average flow rate, ΔI : the change of $IPSS$

3.7 The SMS Server

After a patient sends his symptoms to the Patient Disease State Decision server, the server makes decision about the hospital visit date and how to control the dose of the prescribed medicine with reference to the diagnosis knowledge base. During the decision process, it accesses the patient EMR database and thus takes some time until to inform the patient of the decision. Therefore, instead of notifying its decision during the current Internet access session, the service system sends its decision to the patient by a SMS(Short Message Send) message. The SMS server sends messages to the patients about both the recommended hospital visit date and the dose control information based on the symptom data provided by the patients, and it also plays a role of providing alarm services like notifying the schedule to observe and send their symptoms to the service system, and so on.

3.8 The Physician-Side Patient Information Retrieval Software

With this service system, the physicians would provide better medical care services for the BPH patients and thus they are willing to provide advice for their patients when they seek for some advice about their disease. To understand the patient's state, the physicians need to look up the patient's medical records. If the Internet is available around them, they could access the Physician side Patient Information Management server with the Web browsers and get the necessary information. Sometimes, they could not access the Internet even if they want to look at the patient's records. To handle this kind of situations, the Physician side Patient Information Retrieval Software has been developed which runs on a PDA phone and allows the physicians to retrieve patients' records on their PDA phone. With this PDA phone accessibility, the patients could provide necessary advice for their patients at any time, at any place.

4 Conclusions

The number of BPH patients is expected to grow as the population gets older. As the ubiquitous computing infrastructure goes well established, various kinds of ubiquitous health care services would be available. The BPH patient care system has been developed to reduce the number of patients' hospital visits, yet provides quality medical services. The system has been developed to apply the service to the BPH patient care from the Urology Department, Chungbuk National University, Korea. The distant medical services could cause some legal problems according to the Korea operative legal system. Due to this reason, the information provided to the patients was carefully chosen. The system does not tell whether the patient states is getting better or worse. Instead of that, the system informs patients of the next hospital visit date chosen within the pre-specified visit schedule. As we accumulate sufficient experience on experimental services for a limited volunteer group of BPH patients, the service is expected to be stabilized into a mature service in near future.

References

1. Korea National Statistical Office: Korea Population Census/The Aged People. http://www.nso.go.kr. (2000)
2. Jung, T.K., Jung, J.S., Jung, M.S., Ahn, H.J.: An epidemiologic study for Benign Prostatic Hyperplasia in Jeong-eup Area in Korea. Journal of the Korea Urology Society. 40(1) (1999) 52-58
3. Giarratano, J., Riley, G: Expert Systems Principles and Programming. 2nd edn. PWS. (1994).
4. Duda, R., Hart, P., Stork, D.: Pattern Classification. 2nd edn. John Wiley. (2001)
5. International Prostate Symptom Score. http://www.urologix.com/
6. NIH-Chronic Prostatitis Symptom Index. http://www.niddk.nih.gov/fund/divisions/kuh/useful-tools/english-nih-cpsi.pdf.
7. Blobel, B., Gell, G., Hidlebrand, C., Engelbrecht R. : Contribution of Medical Informatics to Health: Integrated Clinical Data and Knowledge to Support Primary, Secondary, Tertiary Home Care. In Proc. of European Federation for Medical Informatics Special Topics Conference. (Muunich, Germany) (2004)

An ANN-Based Classification System for Automobile Parts with Different Shapes

Jihong Liu, GuangLu Zhao, and Lingbo Kong

College of Information Science and Engineering, Northeastern University,
Shenyang 110004, Liaoning, China
liujihong@ise.neu.edu.cn, cyber810623@yahoo.com.cn

Abstract. In this paper, a system based on Artificial Neural Network (ANN) for classifying automobile parts with different shapes is presented. The system gets the original information from an image sensor, classifies two sorts of automobile parts with different shapes after processing these images. The classifier designed in this paper adopts the ANN with an improved BP algorithm. The perimeter, acreage and the degree of the decentralization of the automobile parts in the intensity image are taken as the input feature vectors. For the No.1 part and No.2 part, the experimental result indicates that the recognition accuracy rate can reach up to 99% in this system and the productivity will be improved obviously comparing with the checking result in the off-line system manually.

1 Introduction

Along with the continuous development of the computer vision technology in industrial producing, it is possible to carry on the on-line test to the products on the assembly line with the image processing [1]. In other words, the on-line processing automatically and the quality monitoring can be real.

Generally humanity recognizes the different objects by their contours, such as the airplane, the industrial components and so on. Since the object shapes can be understood by their contour lines or object on the outside surface, the shape description can be transformed to the outline or the superficial description. There are mainly two kinds of methods in shape recognition. One is based on the region shape recognition methods, which describes the region and starts from the image content. Another is based on the outline, which extracts the edge of the image to produce a continual contour line, and then describes this outline [2].

The following aspects are requested: (1) Withdrawing the revolution invariability, the position invariability and the size invariability of the shape. (2)Strong robust if the input image is noisy or damaged. (3) High running speed for the real-time application system. For the good robust and the association memory function, ANN can be utilized to optimize system parameter and enhance the recognition effect.

D.-S. Huang, K. Li, and G.W. Irwin (Eds.): ICIC 2006, LNAI 4114, pp. 1198 – 1203, 2006.

The system presented in this paper meets the above requirement with acceptable correct rate.

2 Systemic Design

Classifying the industrial parts according to their shapes is a kind of pattern recognition problems. It is one of the high-tech researches and can be used in many application domains. The typical pattern recognition system consists of five processes: Acquiring Information, Image Preprocessing, Feature Extraction and Selecting, Design of the Classifier and Classifying Realization.

The pattern recognition methods can be approximately divided into five sorts [1]: statistical decision-making, structure pattern recognition, fuzzy pattern recognition, ANN pattern recognition and Support Vector Machine (SVM) pattern recognition. The first two methods are developed early, so the theory is mature. For the fuzzy pattern recognition is more logical and the ANN methods have stronger ability to solve the complex pattern recognition problems, researchers pay more attention on them gradually. SVM was developed quickly in the research on pattern recognition in the recent years, which with high learning capability. Compared with ANN, SVM can overcome efficiency problems, such as partial minimum, dimension disaster and so on. However, with the information processing parallelism, self-organizing and self-adapting abilities, strong learning capability and the high fault-tolerant performance, ANN has shown its unique superiority in solving complex pattern recognition problems [2, 3, 4].

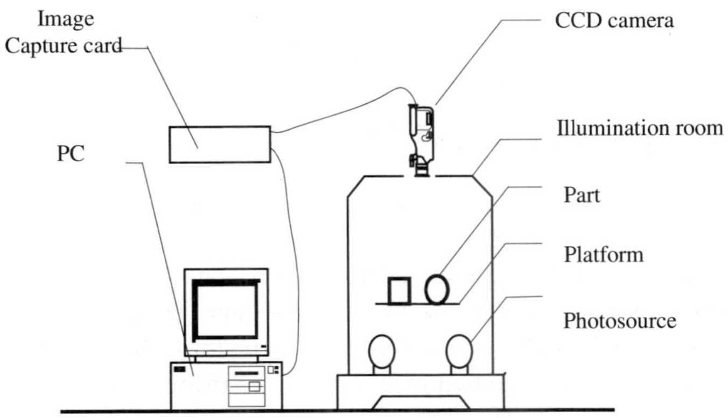

Fig. 1. The classifying system of industrial parts

In this paper, the ANN-based classification system mainly consists of five parts. It is shown in Fig. 1. In this system, the input variables express the sample's features. In training stage, the classifier adjusts the weights by a study algorithm according to the feedback from the classifier's output layer after get the correct result

When the following test sample is extremely similar to the sample using in training, the classifier can make the correct response. It endues the system better modularization, transplantation and transparency to adopt the optimized BP ANN. Fig.2. show the procedure. This classifier is realized by Visual C++. Input sample set and the corresponding training objective set are saved in hard disk in order to guarantee the data reliability.

According to the sample's construction and the object set, the training module decides the construction of the network and initializes the weight value and trains the network. The entire transformation module is transparent to the users.

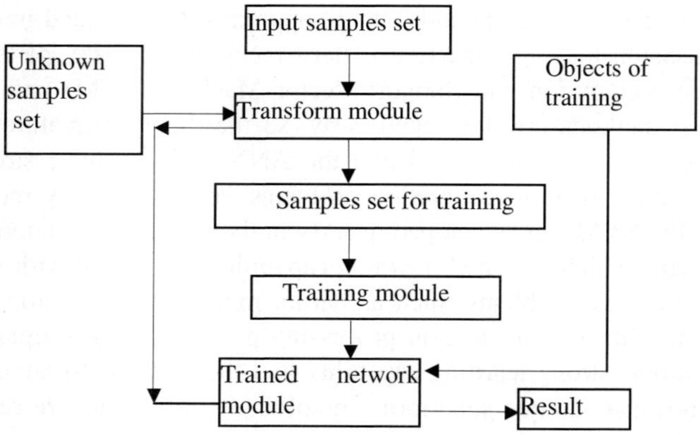

Fig. 2. Flowchart of the neural network classifier

3 Realization of Classifying Algorithm

3.1 Procedure of the Whole System

The system presented in this paper is used to classify two sorts of parts with different shapes automatically. The parts are shown in Fig. 3.The system gains the images through the image gathering system, and then carries out the image preprocess- ing, which including the image enhancement, the smoothing, the edge withdraws and so on. After image preprocessing, it recognizes the parts through the feature extraction, with ANN-based pattern recognition methods. The software design diagram is shown in Fig.4.

3.2 ANN-Based Recognition Module Realization

Feature vector obtaining. In this system, the perimeter, acreage and the degree of the decentralization are taken as the input feature vectors. The detailed extracting methods are as follows.

(a)Part No.1 (b)Part No.2

Fig. 3. Two sorts of parts

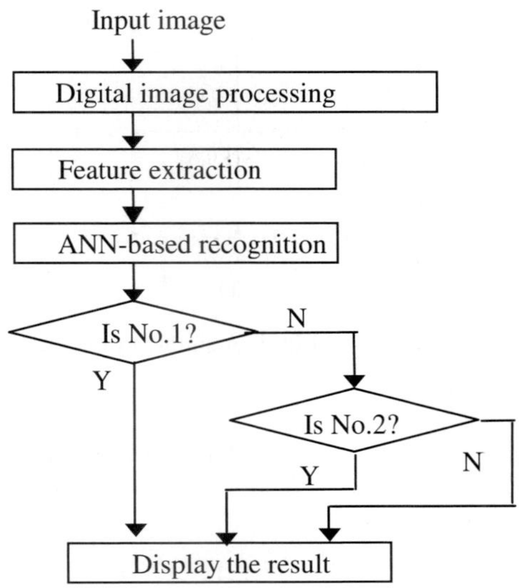

Fig. 4. The diagram of the system software

Usually there are 3 similar definitions of perimeter:(a) If each pixel in the image is regarded as a square with unit area, the region S and background are all composed by small squares. The perimeter of the region S may be defined as the length of the boundary. (b) If each pixel is regarded as one spot, the perimeter may be defined as the length of the 8-connected chain codes of the region boundary. (c) The perimeter is expressed as the area that covers the boundary, i.e. the sum of the boundary points. In this paper, as shown in Fig.5, the boundary length, i.e. perimeter is expressed using 8-connected chain code.The Freeman chain code is a compact way to represent a contour of an object. The chain code is an ordered sequence of N links $\{c_i, i = 1, 2, 3, \cdots, N\}$, where c_i is a vector connecting neighboring contour pixels. The directions of c_i are coded with integer values k=0,1,...,K-1 in a counterclockwise sense starting from the direction of the positive x-axis. The number of directions K takes integer values $2^{(m+1)}$, where M is a positive integer. The chain codes where K>8 are called generalized chain codes. Fig. 5(a) is the directions of an eight connected chain code. Fig. 5 (b) is a sample object, a square with 6×6 pixels. The starting point for the chain coding is marked with a black point, and the direction is clockwise.Its 8-connected chain codeis c_i={0,0,0,0,0,7,6,6,6,6,6,5,4,4,4,4,4,3,2,2,2,2,2,1}. Its perimeter can be calculated by equation (1). The object's acreage in the two-valued image is defined as the pixels' number that the object covers, i.e. the total number of the pixels which are surrounded by the boundary of the area. The size of image $f(x, y)$ is $M \times N$, and the object value in $f(x, y)$ is 1, while background value in $f(x, y)$ is 0, so the acreage A is as equation (3).

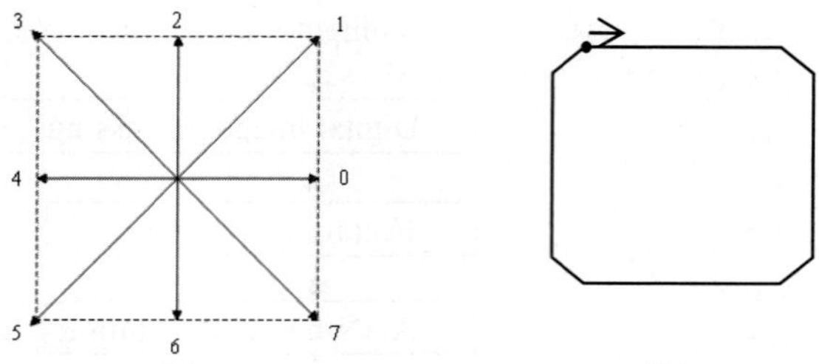

Fig. 5. A simple example of 8-connected chain code

$$Perimeter = \sum_{i=0}^{N} n_i \cdot \quad (1)$$

where

$$n_i = \begin{cases} 1, & if \quad c_i \bmod 2 = 0 \\ \sqrt{2}, & if \quad c_i \bmod 2 = 1 \end{cases} . \quad (2)$$

$$A = \sum_{x=0}^{M-1} \sum_{y=0}^{N-1} f(x, y) \cdot \quad (3)$$

The degree of decentralization is a measurement of the area shape. If the subset of the image is S, the acreage is A, i.e. there are A pixels and the perimeter is P, then the degree of decentralization of S is P^2/A .For the objects with the different geometry shape and the same acreage, the shorter the perimeter is, the tighter the degree of concentrated is. As for the circle shape, $P^2/A = 4\pi$, therefore the figure is the tightest in the degree of decentralization. As for the other shapes, $P^2/A > 4\pi$. The more complex the geometry shape is, the greater the value of degree of decentralization is.

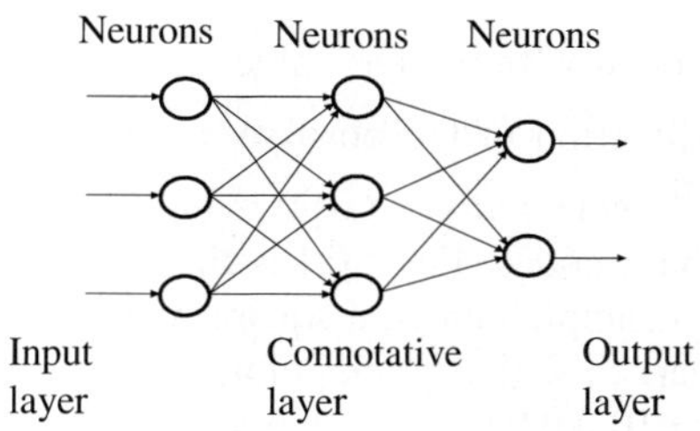

Fig. 6. The structure of BP network

ANN-based classifier. As shown in Fig. 6, the classifier is designed by the improved BP algorithm. After training, we can get the final network architecture: there are 3 input layer node. The input eigenvector has 3 parameters, i.e. perimeter, acreage and the degree of decentralization. The amount of output layer nodes is 2(circular and quadrate parts). The training sample set includes 32 samples (16 No.1 parts and. 16 No.2 parts). The testing sample set includes 100 samples.

3.3 Results

Using the ANN-based classifier presented to recognize the 2 sorts of parts (No.1 and No.2 parts), the experimental results are shown in table 1. The recognizing rate is up to 99%. If choosing the stable auxiliary photo source, the effect will be better.

Table 1. The experimental results

Type of parts	Number of modes	Exactly recognized	Recognition rate
No.1	50	49	98%
No.2	50	50	100%
Total	100	99	99%

4 Conclusion

Classifying manually causes the high production cost and the heavy labor's intensity. So, an ANN-based system for classifying automobile parts with different shapes is presented in this paper. The system gets the original information from an image sensor, classifies two sorts of automobile parts after processing these images. The classifier adopts the ANN with an improved BP algorithm. The perimeter, acreage and the degree of the decentralization of the automobile parts in the intensity image are taken as the input feature vectors. For the No.1 part and No.2 part, the experimental result indicates that the recognition accuracy rate can reach up to 99% in this system and the productivity will be improved obviously comparing with the offline system. After adjusting the algorithm in future, it can be used in classifying more complex parts.

References

1. Zhang, Xinfeng., Shen, Lansun.: Pattern Recognition and Its Application in Image Processing. Measure and Control Technology, 23 (5) (2004) 28-32
2. Huang, Deshuang.: Neural Network Pattern Recognition System Theory. Beijing: Publishing House of Electronic Industry, (1996)
3. Zhao, Guanglu.: Research on Classifying of Industrial Parts with Different Shapes [D]. Shenyang: Northeastern University, (2005)

An Indirect and Efficient Approach for Solving Uncorrelated Optimal Discriminant Vectors

Quan-Sen Sun[1], Zhong Jin[1], Pheng-Ann Heng[2], and De-Shen Xia[1]

[1] Department of Computer Science, Nanjing University of Science &Technology, Nanjing 210094, China
qssun@126.com, zhongjin@mail.njust.edu.cn, deshen_x@263.net

[2] Department of Computer Science and Engineering, The Chinese University of Hong Kong, Hong Kong
pheng@cse.cuhk.edu.hk

Abstract. An approach for solving uncorrelated optimal discriminant vectors (UODV), called indirect uncorrelated linear discriminant analysis(IULDA), is proposed. This is done by establishing a relation between canonical correlation analysis (CCA) and Fisher linear discriminant analysis(FLDA). The advantages of our method for solving the UODV over the two existing methods are analyzed theoretically. Experimental result based on the Concordia University CENPARMI handwritten character database has shown that our algorithm can increase the recognition rate and the speed of feature extraction.

1 Introduction

Fisher discriminant analysis(FLDA) is a very important method for feature extraction, which has been widely used in the areas of pattern recognition[1]. Based on the Fisher discriminant criterion, uncorrelated optimal discriminant vectors(UODV), namely uncorrelated linear discriminant analysis(ULDA), which was put forward by Z. Jin[2], has been successfully applied to image recognition. Based on the generalized Fisher discriminant criterion, two improved UODV algorithms were proposed respectively[3,4]. All methods for solving UODV are based on the Fisher discriminant criterion of the original feature space directly. However, the dimension of the original feature vectors is usually very large, it is time consuming in feature extracting.

A new approach for solving UODV, called indirect ULDA(IULDA), is proposed in this paper. We establish a relation between the canonical correlation analysis (CCA)[5] and FLDA, and obtain UODV indirectly by solving a low dimensional canonical projection vector. Experimental result based on Concordia University CENPARMI handwritten character database has shown that this is efficient.

2 Fisher Discriminant Analysis

2.1 LDA

Suppose there are c known pattern classes. Let a pattern sample $x \in \mathrm{R}^p$, S_b, S_w and S_t denote the between-class scatter matrix, the within-class scatter matrix

D.-S. Huang, K. Li, and G.W. Irwin (Eds.): ICIC 2006, LNAI 4114, pp. 1204 – 1209, 2006.

and the total scatter matrix respectively. The Fisher discriminant criterion function is defined by

$$J(\varphi)=\frac{\varphi^{\mathrm{T}}S_b\varphi}{\varphi^{\mathrm{T}}S_w\varphi},\ \varphi\in \mathrm{R}^p(\neq 0) \tag{1}$$

The generalized Fisher discriminant criterion function is defined by

$$J(\varphi)=\frac{\varphi^{\mathrm{T}}S_b\varphi}{\varphi^{\mathrm{T}}S_t\varphi},\ \varphi\in \mathrm{R}^p(\neq 0) \tag{2}$$

Generally, we choose eigenvectors of the first d maximum eigenvalues of generalized eigenequation (3) or (4) as the optimal discriminant vectors (ODV) based on criterion (1) or (2). ODV compose the transformation matrix W. Therefore we can extract the optimal discriminant features with $\eta = W^{\mathrm{T}}x$ to classify the samples. For the generalized eigenequation (3) or (4) has no more than c-1 nonzero eigenvalues, the number of ODV satisfies $d \le c-1$.

$$S_b\varphi=\mu S_w\varphi \tag{3}$$

$$S_b\varphi=\mu S_t\varphi \tag{4}$$

2.2 ULDA

The first d eigenvectors of the generalized eigenequation (3) or (4) do not always make the projected features uncorrelated. So Z. Jin[2] proposed a kind of ULDA whose basic principle is as follows:

The first optimal discriminant direction is the vector φ_1 corresponding to the maximization Fisher discriminant criterion (1). Suppose $k\ (k\ge 1)$ ODV $\varphi_1,\varphi_2,\ldots,\varphi_k$ are obtained, we can calculate the $(k+1)^{\mathrm{th}}$ vector φ_{k+1} which maximizes Fisher discriminant criterion (1) under the constraint: $\varphi_{k+1}^{\mathrm{T}}S_t\varphi_i=0(i=1,2,\cdots,k)$.These vectors $\{\varphi_k\}$ are called UODV since for any $i\neq j$, $\varphi_i^{\mathrm{T}}x$ and $\varphi_j^{\mathrm{T}}x$ are uncorrelated. Z. Jin gives the algorithm of UODV as follows:

The $(k+1)$th UODV φ_{k+1} is the eigenvector corresponding to the maximum eigenvalue of the generalized eigenequation $P_{k+1}S_b\varphi_{k+1}=\lambda_{k+1}S_w\varphi_{k+1}$. Where $P_1=I$,

$$P_{k+1}=I-S_tD_{k+1}^{\mathrm{T}}(D_{k+1}S_tS_w^{-1}S_tD_{k+1}^{\mathrm{T}})^{-1}D_{k+1}S_tS_w^{-1}(k\ge 1),\ I=diag\{1,\cdots,1\},\ D_{k+1}=[\varphi_1\cdots\varphi_k]^{\mathrm{T}}.$$

J. Yang[3] has presented an improved algorithm based on the ULDA theory. Under the Fisher discriminant criterion (2), UODV $\varphi_1,\cdots,\varphi_d$ ($d\le c-1$) can be the S_t-orthogonal eigenvectors corresponding to the first d maximal eigenvalues of the generalized eigenequation(4). UODV $\varphi_1,\cdots,\varphi_d$ is obtained in this way: Suppose S_t can be decomposed orthogonally into $U^{\mathrm{T}}S_tU=\Lambda=diag(a_1,\cdots,a_n)$. Let $C=U\Lambda^{-\frac{1}{2}}$, the eigenvectors corresponding to the first d maximal eigenvalues of the eigenequation $(C^{\mathrm{T}}S_bC)\varphi=\lambda\,\varphi$ can be used as UODV.

3 Feature Extraction Based on CCA

Considering two zero-mean random vectors $x \in \mathrm{R}^p$ and $y \in \mathrm{R}^q$, CCA finds pairs of directions α and β that maximize the correlation between the projections $x^* = \alpha^{\mathrm{T}} x$ and $y^* = \beta^{\mathrm{T}} y$. In general, the projective directions α and β are obtained by maximizing the criterion function as follows:

$$J(\alpha,\beta) = \frac{\alpha^{\mathrm{T}} S_{xy} \beta}{(\alpha^{\mathrm{T}} S_{xx} \alpha \cdot \beta^{\mathrm{T}} S_{yy} \beta)^{1/2}} \tag{5}$$

Where S_{xx} and S_{yy} are the covariance matrices of x and y respectively, while S_{xy} denote their between-set covariance matrix, and S_{xx} and S_{yy} are positive definite, and $S_{xy}^{\mathrm{T}} = S_{yx}$, $r = rank(S_{xy})$.

The projective vectors $\{\alpha_i\}$ and $\{\beta_i\}$ that maximizes criterion function $J(\alpha,\beta)$ are called *CPV*. In Ref.[6], we have discussed how to solve CPV and its properties, the basic process is as follows:

Solving CPV with criterion function (5) is equivalent to the two generalized eigenequations:

$$S_{xy} S_{yy}^{-1} S_{yx} \alpha = \lambda^2 S_{xx} \alpha \tag{6}$$

$$S_{yx} S_{xx}^{-1} S_{xy} \beta = \lambda^2 S_{yy} \beta \tag{7}$$

Let $H = S_{xx}^{-1/2} S_{xy} S_{yy}^{-1/2}$, we employ the singular value decomposition theorem: $H = \sum_{i=1}^{r} \lambda_i u_i v_i^{\mathrm{T}}$, where $\lambda_1^2 \geq \lambda_2^2 \geq \cdots \geq \lambda_r^2$ are the nonzero eigenvalues of the matrices $G_1 = H^{\mathrm{T}} H$ and $G_2 = H H^{\mathrm{T}}$. u_i and v_i are the unit orthogonal eigenvectors of G_1 and G_2 corresponding to the nonzero eigenvalue λ_i^2, where $i = 1,2,\cdots,r$. Then we can get two important theorems[6]:

Theorem 1. Given $\beta_i = S_{yy}^{-1/2} v_i$, $\alpha_i = \lambda_i^{-1} S_{xx}^{-1} S_{xy} \beta_i$, $i = 1,\cdots,r$, then

(1) α_i and β_i are the eigenvectors of generalized eigenequation (6) and (7) corresponding to λ_i^2;

(2) $\alpha_i^{\mathrm{T}} S_{xx} \alpha_j = \beta_i^{\mathrm{T}} S_{yy} \beta_j = \delta_{ij}, \alpha_i^{\mathrm{T}} S_{xy} \beta_j = \lambda_i \delta_{ij} (i,j = 1,2,\cdots,r)$. (8)

Theorem 2. Under criterion (5), the number of the efficient CPV satisfying the constraint (8) is r pairs at most, where $r = rank(S_{xy})$, and $d (\leq r)$ pairs of CPV are composed of the eigenvectors corresponding to the first d maximal eigenvalues of two generalized eigenequations (6) and (7).

4 Indirect ULDA(IULDA)

Supposing the pattern sample $x \in \mathrm{R}^p$ has c classes and $n = n_1 + \cdots + n_c$ training samples, while n_i denotes the i th training sample number. The data matrix

$X = (X_1\ X_2 \cdots X_c) \in \mathrm{R}^{p \times n}$, where X_i $(1,2,\cdots,c)$ denotes the matrix composed of all i th training samples. S_b, S_w and S_t denote the between-class scatter matrix, the within-class scatter matrix and the total scatter matrix of the training sample set, respectively, then $S_b = \sum_{i=1}^{c} n_i(\overline{x}_i - \overline{x})(\overline{x}_i - \overline{x})^{\mathrm{T}}, S_t = XHX^{\mathrm{T}}, S_w = S_t - S_b$ .where $\overline{x}_i$ is the mean of the i th training samples, and $\overline{x}$ is the mean of all training samples. $H = I - \frac{1}{n}J$ is a center matrix, where I is a n-rank unit matrix, and J is a n-rank matrix of which the elements are equal to 1 ($J = (1)_{n \times n}$).

In order to explore the relationship between CCA and FLDA, we hope to construct a class matrix which has same class information with the data matrix X. The purpose of CCA is to find the weight vector α_k such that

$$\alpha_k = \arg \max_{\substack{\alpha^{\mathrm{T}} S_{xx} \alpha = 1 \\ \beta^{\mathrm{T}} S_{yy} \beta = 1}} J(\alpha, \beta) \ \forall k = 1,2,\cdots,d \ (d \le rank(S_{xy}))$$

subject to the orthogonality constraint $\alpha_k^{\mathrm{T}} S_{xx} \alpha_j = 0$ for all $1 \le j < k$.

In other words, considering the generalized eigenequation (6), can we convert it into the generalized eigenequation (4): $S_b \varphi = \mu S_t \varphi$? And what condition should data matrix Y satisfy if so? Fortunately, the conversion can be done, and the eigenvector y has a very simple form. The detailed discussion is as follows:

Let $Y = (Y_1\ Y_2 \cdots Y_c)$, as a column (sample) class marker of matrix X , also called the class marker matrix of matrix X , where

$$\begin{cases} Y_i = (e_i, e_i, \cdots, e_i) \in \mathrm{R}^{(c-1) \times n_i} & i = 1, \cdots, c-1 \\ Y_i = 0 \in \mathrm{R}^{(c-1) \times n_i} & i = c \end{cases}$$

The vector e_i denotes ($c-1$)dimensional column vector whose ith component is 1, and the others are 0.

In this instance, the covariance matrix and the co-covariance matrix of the two sample sets can be estimated as: $S_{xx} = \frac{1}{n} S_t = \frac{1}{n} XHX^{\mathrm{T}}, S_{yy} = \frac{1}{n} YHY^{\mathrm{T}}, S_{xy} = \frac{1}{n} XHY^{\mathrm{T}}$ .We can prove that S_{yy} is a c-1 rank positive definite matrix, and $r = rank(S_{xy}) \le c-1$.

Under the above supposition, we can infer

$$(XHY^{\mathrm{T}})\,(YHY^{\mathrm{T}})^{-1}\,(YHX^{\mathrm{T}}) = S_b \tag{9}$$

So the generalized eigenequation (6) can be written as

$$S_b \alpha = \lambda^2 S_t \alpha \tag{10}$$

Compare the generalized eigenequation (4) with Eq.(10), we will find that they have the same eigenvectors. We can obtain the following theorem:

Theorem 3. Under the class marker matrix Y, CPV $\alpha_1, \alpha_2, \cdots, \alpha_d$ $(d \le r \le c-1)$ determined by Theorem 1 and Theorem 2 is namely the d UODV based on the Fisher discriminant criterion (4). The extracted d dimensional discriminant features based on the linear transformation $X^* = W_x^{\mathrm{T}} x$ are uncorrelated. Where $W_x = (\alpha_1, \alpha_2, \cdots \alpha_d)$.

Now we have established the relation between CCA and LDA, where LDA can be seen as a particular case of CCA, so problems of LDA can be solved by CCA. The algorithm above is a new approach for solving UODV. The dimension of the extracted uncorrelated optimal discriminant features is no more than $c-1$, which is consistent with K.Fukunaga's dimensional Theorem[1].

5 Experiment

In this experiment, we use the Concordia University CENPARMI handwritten numeral database[7]. This database contains 6,000 samples of 10 numeral classes (each class has 600 samples). Here, our experiment is performed based on 256-dimensional Gabor transformation features[8], which turned out to be effective for handwritten digit classification.

In our experiments, 400 samples are chosen from each class for training, while the remaining 200 samples are used for testing. Thus, the training sample set size is 4,000 and the testing sample set size is 2,000.

Computing through the arithmetic mentioned in Section 4, the UODV can be solved and the uncorrelated optimal discriminant features can be extracted. Table 1 and Table 2 shows the classification results by minimum distance classifier and the quadratic Bayesian classifier, respectively, in which the quadratic Bayesian function is defined as[1]:

$$g_i(x) = \frac{1}{2} \ln \left| \Sigma_l \right| + \frac{1}{2} (x - \mu_l)^{\mathrm{T}} \Sigma_l^{-1} ((x - \mu_l)$$

where μ_l and Σ_l are the ith mean vector and co-covariance matrix respectively. The classifying decision-making based on the discriminant function will be $x \in \omega_k$ if sample x satisfies $g_k(x) = \min_l g_l(x)$.

In addition, we extract the uncorrelated optimal discriminant vector sets with methods of Z. Jin and J. Yang, and then classify the samples in the minimum distance classifier and the quadratic Bayesian classifier respectively. The classification results are shown in Table 1 and Table 2 as well.

Table 1. Classification error rates of our algorithm and Jin Zhong's algorithm in minimum distance classifier

Dimension	*1*	*2*	*3*	*4*	*5*	*6*	*7*	*8*	*9*
Z.Jin[2]	0.674	0.489	0.340	0.277	0.262	0.207	0.191	0.190	***0.183***
Ours	0.618	0.394	0.301	0.259	0.239	0.194	***0.179***	0.191	0.195

Table 2. Classification error rates of our algorithm and J. Yang's algorithm in quadratic Bayesian classifier

Dimension	*1*	*2*	*3*	*4*	*5*	*6*	*7*	*8*	*9*
J.Yang[3]	0.660	0.576	0.330	0.246	0.199	0.166	0.157	***0.153***	0.153
Ours	0.613	0.387	0.294	0.233	0.206	0.160	0.150	0.152	***0.149***

As shown in Table 1 and Table 2, in minimum distance classifier, the classification error rates of our algorithm (IULDA) are lower than those of Z. Jin. Considering the feature extracting speed, 256-rank matrices'eigenvalues and eigenvectors must be calculated with Z. Jin's algorithm. While using our method, only a calculation involving a 9-rank matrix is needed to obtain the ODV indirectly. At the meantime, in this sense a lot of repeated calculations can be avoided when compared with Z. Jin's algorithm. In quadratic Bayesian classifier, the classification error rates of our algorithm are lower than those of J. Yang. The descending speed of classification error rates of our algorithm is faster than that of J. Yang's.

6 Conclusion

In this paper, the relation between CCA and LDA is presented, the framework of solving LDA with CCA is established, and a new method for solving the UODV is proposed within the framework. Compared with existing methods, our method can increase both the recognition rate and the speed of feature extraction. The significance of our research is that a new approach of discrimiant analysis is presented, and algorithms based on Fisher discriminant criterion can be transformed into relevant canonical correlation analysis methods.

References

1. Fukunaga, K.: Introduction to Statistical Pattern Recognition. New York: Academic (1990)
2. Jin, Z.: Research on Feature Extraction of Face Images and Feature Dimensionality. Ph D Dissertation, Nanjing University of Science and Technology (1999)
3. Yang, J., Yang, J.Y., Jin, Z.: A Feature Extraction Approach Using of Optimal Discriminant Transform and Image Recognition. Journal of Computer Research and Develoment (in Chinese), 38(11) (2001)1331-1336
4. Jin, X. Y., Zhang, D., Jin, Z.: UODV: Improved Algorithm and Generalized Theory. Pattern Recognition, 36(11) (2003) 2593-2602
5. Zhang, X. T., Fang, K. T.: Multivariate Statistical Introduction. Beijing: Sciences Press (1999)
6. Sun, Q.S., Zeng, S.G., Liu, Y., Heng, P.A., Xia, D.S.: A New Method of Feature Fusion and its Application in Image Recognition. Pattern Recognition, 38(12) (2005) 2437-2448
7. Lou, Z., Liu, K., Yang, J.Y., Suen, C.Y.: Rejection Criteria and Pairwise Discrimination of Handwritten Numerals Based on Structural Features. Pattern Analysis and Applications, 2(1) (1992) 228-238
8. Hamamoto, Y., Uchimura, S., Watanabe, M., Yasuda, T., Tomita, S.: Recognition of Handwritten Numerals Using Gabor Features. Proc. 13th Int'l Conf. Pattern Recognition, (1996) 250-253

Constructing Full Matrix Through Naïve Bayesian for Collaborative Filtering

Kyung-Yong Jung[1], Hee-Joung Hwang[2], and Un-Gu Kang[2]

[1] School of Computer Information Engineering, Sangji University, Korea
kyjung@sangji.ac.kr
[2] Department of Information Technology Engineering,
Gachon University of Medicine and Science, Korea

Abstract. Collaborative filtering systems based on a matrix are effective in recommending items to users. However, these systems suffer from the fact that they decrease the accuracy of recommendations, recognized specifically as the sparsity and the first rater problems. This paper proposes the constructing full matrix through Naïve Bayesian, to solve the problems of collaborative filtering. The proposed approach uses Naïve Bayesian, in order to convert the sparse ratings matrix into a full ratings matrix; subsequently using collaborative filtering, to provide recommendations. The proposed method is evaluated in the EachMovie dataset and the approach is demonstrated to perform better than both collaborative filtering and content-based filtering.

1 Introduction

Nowadays, Users spend much time and effort in finding the best suitable items since more and more information is placed in ubiquitous recommendation systems. To save their time and effort in searching the items they want, a personalized ubiquitous recommendation system is required. The ubiquitous recommendation system utilizes in general an information filtering technique called collaborative filtering [2][13]. However, collaborative filtering suffers from the first rater problem, because an item cannot be recommended unless another user has rated it previously. This problem applies to new items and also obscure items, being particularly detrimental to users with eclectic tastes. Most users do not rate items and hence the matrix is typically very sparse. Therefore the probability of finding a set of users with similar ratings is usually low. This is often the case when systems have a very high ratio [8]. The other reason of sparsity for a matrix in collaborative filtering, is a result of the missing value, caused from partial rating on items [1][3][5]. This problem is very significant when the system is in the initial stage of usage. In this paper, the sparsity of the matrix, the first rater problem, and missing values are solved by reconstructing the user preferences, which are elements of a full matrix, based on the preferences through Naïve Bayesian. Naïve Bayesian is used to classify items and lower the dimensions of the matrix. Therefore, it is possible to predict items for new users. The proposed method was tested using the EachMovie dataset, which consisted of user rated preferences on items, proving its effectiveness, compared with existent methods.

D.-S. Huang, K. Li, and G.W. Irwin (Eds.): ICIC 2006, LNAI 4114, pp. 1210–1215, 2006.

2 Collaborative Filtering

The main idea of collaborative filtering is to recommend new items of interest for a particular user based on other users' ratings. A variety of collaborative filtering algorithms have been reported and their performance has been evaluated empirically [10]. Collaborative filtering considers every user as an expert for his taste, therefore, recommendations can be provided based on the expertise of taste-related users. Usually the task is to predict the rating of a particular $user_i$ for an $item_j$. The system compares the $user_i$'s rating with the ratings of all other users, who have rated the considered $item_j$. Then a weighted average of the other users rating is used as a prediction. If I_u is a set of items that a $user_i$ has rated then the mean rating of a $user_i$ can be defined by Equation (1).

$$\overline{r_u} = \frac{1}{|I_u|}\sum_{i\in I_u} r_{i,j} \tag{1}$$

Collaborative filtering algorithm predicts rating based on the rating of similar users. When the *Pearson correlation coefficient* is used, the similarity is determined from the correlation of the rating vectors of a $user_u$ and the other $user_a$ by Equation (2).

$$w(u,a) = \frac{\sum_{i\in I_u\cap I_a}(r_{u,i}-\overline{r_u})(r_{a,i}-\overline{r_a})}{\sqrt{\sum_{i\in I_u\cap I_a}(r_{u,i}-\overline{r_u})^2 \bullet \sum_{i\in I_u\cap I_a}(r_{a,i}-\overline{r_a})^2}} \tag{2}$$

It can be noted that $w\in[-1,+1]$. The value of w measures the similarity between the two users' rating vectors. A high absolute value signifies high similarity and low absolute value dissimilarity. The general predict formula is based in the assumption that the prediction is a weighed average of other users' ratings [12].

$$p^{collab}(u,i) = \overline{r_u} + \{1/\sum_{a\in U_i} w(u,a)\}\cdot\sum_{a\in U_i} w(u,a)(r_{a,i}-\overline{r_a}) \tag{3}$$

The weights refer to the amount of similarity between the user and the other users, presented in Equation (3). U_i is a set of users who rated items.

3 Constructing Full Matrix Through Naïve Bayesian

3.1 The Similarity Weight Through Naïve Bayesian

The Naïve Bayesian is one of the most successful algorithms on many classification domains. Despite of its simplicity, it is shown to be competitive with other complex approaches especially in text categorization and content-based filtering. The Naïve Bayesian classifies items in two phases, viz. the learning phase and the classification phase [9][10]. The learning phase assigns a probability to an item from the training set, which consists of data collected through the genre item. Equation (4) is used to accord a probability to an $item_j$. In this case, n is the total number of items in the training set with a target value, n_k is the frequency of an $item_j$, and $|TotItem|$ is the total number of items. $r_{a,j}$ represents the preferences that the active $user_a$ accords to an $item_j$.

$$\beta_{a,j} = \frac{n_k + 1}{n + |TotItem|} \times r_{a,j} \tag{4}$$

The similarity weight is applied differently to the preference of the items which users evaluate as an object to the genre estimated value. For this process, as the user applies the learning set which the estimated value granted to the item rating the preference. In applying the *Pearson correlation coefficient* [10][11] based on Equation (4), the user similarity weight between a $user_a$ and a $user_i$ is defined by Equation (5).

$$\beta(a,i) = \frac{Cov(a,i)}{\delta_a \cdot \delta_i} = \frac{\sum_j (\beta_{a,j} - \overline{\beta_a})(\beta_{i,j} - \overline{\beta_i})}{\sqrt{\sum_j (\beta_{a,j} - \overline{\beta_a})^2 \sum_j (\beta_{i,j} - \overline{\beta_i})^2}} \tag{5}$$

Where $\beta_{a,j}$ refers to the preference granted to the estimated value between a $user_a$ and an $item_j$, $\overline{\beta_a}$ refers to the average value assigned to the weight of an item for which user a has already input the preference, j refers to the item for which a $user_a$ and a $user_i$ have input the preference in common.

3.2 Constructing Full Matrix Through Preference Revaluation Process

The matrix for revaluating the preference is changed using the Naïve Bayesian. The preference through the preference revaluation is defined as $r_{i,j}'$. The preferences of a matrix should be expressed in six degrees ranging from 0-1 [5][6]. However, the preferences in a matrix revaluated by the preference revaluation process have a value ranging from, 0-1, therefore, the preference revaluation process should be redefined as Table 1. The preference $r_{i,j}'$ that is revaluated in a matrix through the preference revaluation process, should be redefined as Table 1.

Table 1. Revaluated preference expressed in one of 6 levels

Revaluated preference	*Preference for matrix*	*Revaluated preference*	*Preference for matrix*
$0 \le r_{i,j}' < 0.1$	$r_{i,j} = 0.0$	$0.5 \le r_{i,j}' < 0.7$	$r_{i,j} = 0.6$
$0.1 \le r_{i,j}' < 0.3$	$r_{i,j} = 0.2$	$0.7 \le r_{i,j}' < 0.9$	$r_{i,j} = 0.8$
$0.3 \le r_{i,j}' < 0.5$	$r_{i,j} = 0.4$	$0.9 \le r_{i,j}' < 1.0$	$r_{i,j} = 1.0$

4 Evaluation

For the evaluation, the EachMovie dataset of the Compaq Computer Corporation [7] was processed for a total of 20,864 users, such that each user rated at least 80 movies and 1,612 kinds of items through data integrity. This constituted the training set for the Naïve Bayesian learning phase. The schema was followed in the EachMovie for the 10 genres classification. The EachMovie also provides the matrix; which is a matrix of users vs. items, where each cell is the rating given by a user for an item. The matrix is very sparse, as most items are not rated by many users [8]. The training set is constructed from the items for which the preferences are determined, based on the user's representative attribute [5][6]. The item of the training set is learned, in order to

Table 2. Changed full matrix given to Bayesain estimated value

	$item_5$	$item_{10}$	$item_{18}$	$item_{21}$		$item_5$	$item_{10}$	$item_{18}$	$item_{21}$
$user_1$	0.25	0.98	0.35	0.97		0.2	1.0	0.4	1.0
$user_{19}$	0.42	0.24	0.18	0.75		0.4	0.2	0.2	0.8
$user_{21}$	? → 0.20	0.34	? →0.43	0.37	►	0.2	0.4	0.4	0.4
$user_{35}$	0.78	0.86	0.19	? →0.26		0.8	0.8	0.2	0.2
$user_{45}$	0.12	0.17	0.66	0.47		0.2	0.2	0.6	0.4
$user_{49}$	? →0.34	0.67	0.49	0.94		0.4	0.6	0.4	1.0

grant the estimated value by means of the Naïve Bayesian. Table 2 presents a changed full matrix revaluated by the preference given to Bayesian estimated value.

Table 2 demonstrates that the problem of the missing value of "?" is solved and information regarding the missing values, for which the weight of the preference for a particular item is assigned differently, depending on the classified genre. The shaded boxes represent the predictive preference obtained by granting the Bayesian estimated values to the missing values. Since a full matrix is used, the sparsity and first rater problems are solved. The full matrix contains ratings for all items. Therefore, all users are considered potential neighbors. This increases the chances of finding similar users. In collaborative filtering, for the new user, a prediction cannot be made for an item, unless other users have rated the item previously. However, such a prediction can be made using a full matrix.

To verify this hypothesis the following experiments were conducted. The computer for the experiment consisted of a PentiumIV, 2-way CPU, 3.0GHz, 512 MB RAM PC. The algorithms used MS-Visual Studio C++ 6.0, and MS-SQL Server 2000. Sets of 3,500 users were selected for the systematic sample from the preprocessed EachMovie dataset. 1,500 of these users were treated as test users, producing predictions on 40% of the items rated [8]. This paper uses the following methods: The proposed constructing full matrix through Naïve Bayesian (FM_NB), the former memory based methods used the *Pearson correlation coefficient* (P_Corr), the recommendation method only used content-based filtering (Content). Predictions were computed for the items using each of the different predictors. The quality of the various prediction algorithms was measured by comparing the predicted values for the ratings to the actual ratings. Various methods were used to compare performance by changing the number of clustering users.

Fig. 1 demonstrates the MAE [3][4][12] of the number of users. The performance of the FM_NB, and the P_Corr also increases, whereas the Content shows no notable change in performance. In terms of prediction accuracy, it is evident that the FM_NB, which uses collaborative filtering with a full matrix through Naïve Bayesian, is superior to the P_Corr method. Fig. 2 presents the sparsity change of a full matrix according to process time (sec). 100% sparsity means that a matrix is very sparse and most items have not been rated. 24 seconds were taken, to construct a full matrix from the preprocessed EachMovie. Fig. 3 presents the prediction accuracy by varying the sparsity of a full matrix. The MAE of the different predictors by varying the sparsity of a full matrix, was compared. Fig. 3 confirms the hypothesis, that the FM_NB is more stable than the P_Corr with respect to the sparsity. In fact, when the sparsity

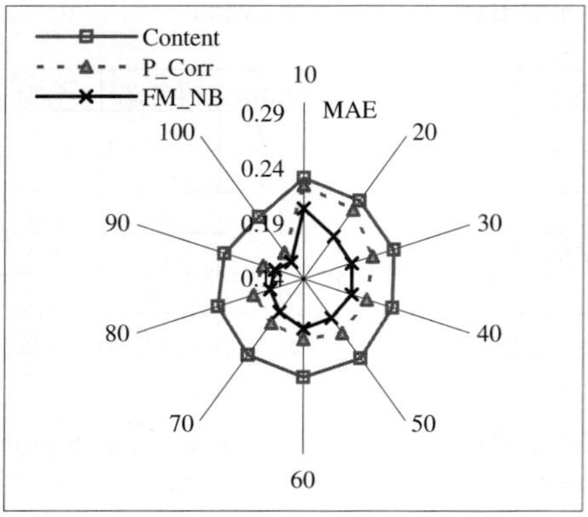

Fig. 1. MAE at varying the number of users

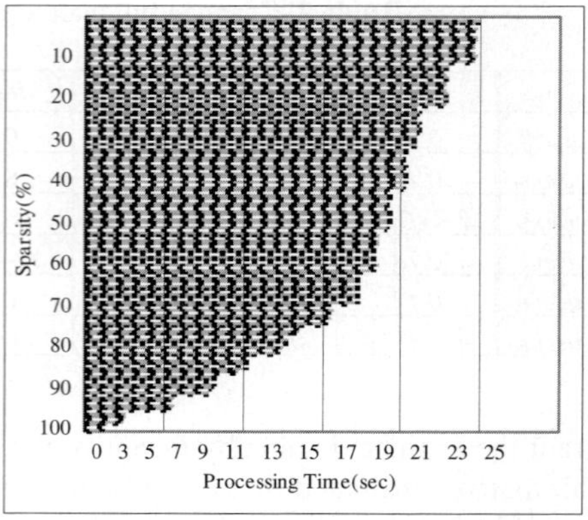

Fig. 2. The sparsity at process time

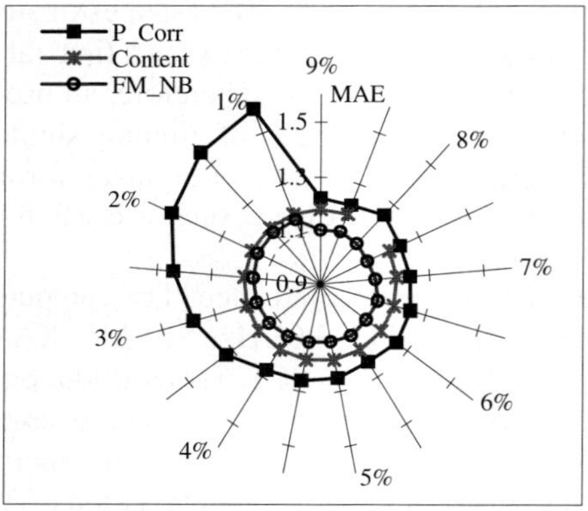

Fig. 3. The sparsity on prediction accuracy

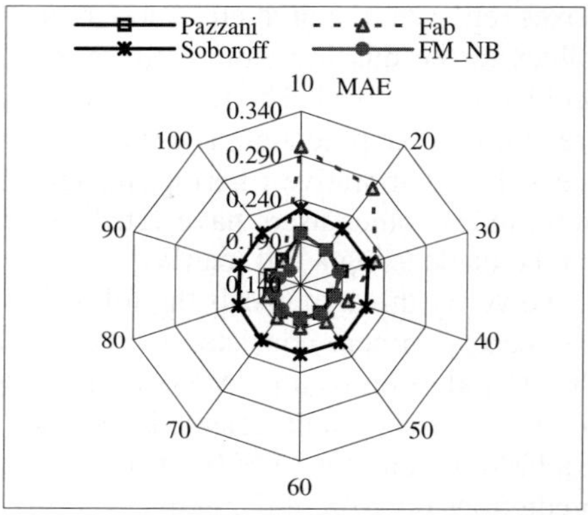

Fig. 4. MAE of *n*th rating number

exceeds 4%, the performance of the P_Corr drops precipitously, while the FM_NB is relatively unaffected. As a result, the proposed method using a full matrix through Naïve Bayesian will converge to collaborative filtering.

The proposed collaborative filtering is considered using a full matrix through Naïve Bayesian (FM_NB) and hypothesized that it would outperform collaborative filtering and content-based filtering. In comparing the FM_NB and those proposed by Soboroff [11], Pazzani [10], and Fab [1], analysis of the predictive accuracy values, such as the MAE, can be achieved. Fig. 4 demonstrates the MAE as the frequency with which the user evaluates the *n*th rating number is increased. Fig. 4 demonstrates the system proposed by Soboroff [11], that solves the first rater problem by decreasing the dimension of matrix, exhibiting lower performance when the number of evaluations is lower. It is important to note, that the method does not solve the first rater problem. The other methods demonstrate higher performance than that of Soboroff. As a result, the method developed by Pazzani and the FM_NB solving both the sparsity problem and first rater problem present the highest accuracy rates.

5 Conclusion

Collaborative filtering systems based on a matrix, which recommend items to users based on the judgment of other users, is the personalized recommendation system used much for the latest recommendations. However, they suffer from the sparsity problem and first rater problem that they decrease the accuracy of recommendations. In this paper, the constructing full matrix through Naïve Bayesian, which generates the user preferences, is proposed, in order to solve the problem of collaborative filtering. The weight of the preferences is calculated using the Bayesian estimated value differently. Therefore, reflecting the information with the statistical value. The proposed method is compared with combining collaborative filtering and content-based filtering. As a result, the proposed method demonstrates higher performance than the existing method in both comparisons.

References

1. Balabanovic, M., Shoham, Y.: Fab: Content-based, Collaborative Recommendation. Communications of the Association of Computing Machinery. (1997) 66-72
2. Basu, C., Hirsh, H., Cohen, W.: Recommendation as Classification: Using Social and Content-based Information in Recommendation. Proc. of the 15th Conf. on AI. (1998) 714-720
3. Herlocker, J. L., Konstan, J. A., Terveen, L. G., Riedl, J. T.: Evaluating Collaborative Filtering Recommender Systems. ACM Transactions on Information Systems (TOIS) archive, Vol. 22, No. 1 (2004) 5-53
4. Kim, H. G., Kim J. T., Herlocker, J. L.: Feature-Based Prediction of Unknown Preferences for Nearest-Neighbor Collaborative Filtering. Proc. of the 4th IEEE Int. Conf. on Data Mining. (2004) 435-438
5. Jung, K. Y., Lee, J. H.: User Preference Mining through Hybrid Collaborative Filtering and Content-based Filtering in Recommendation System. IEICE Trans. on Inf. and Systems, Vol. E87-D, No. 12. (2004) 2781-2790
6. Ko, S. J., Lee, J. H.: Feature Selection using Association Word Mining for Classification. Proc. of the Int. Conf. on DEXA. (2001) 211-220
7. MovieLens Collaborative Filtering Data Set: http://www.cs.umn.edu/research/GroupLens/. Grouplens Research Project. (2000)
8. Melville, P., Mooney, R. J., Nagarajan, R.: Content-Boosted Collaborative Filtering. Proc of the SIGIR-2001 Workshop on Recommender Systems. (2001)
9. Michael, T., *Maching Learning*, McGraq-Hill. (1997) 154-200
10. Miyahara, K., Pazzani, M. J.: Collaborative Filtering with the Simple Bayesian Classifier. Proc. of the 6th Pacific Rim Int. Conf. on Artificial Intelligence, (2000) 679-689
11. Soboroff, I., Nicholas, C. K.: Related, but not Relevant: Content-Based Collaborative Filtering in TREC-8. Information Retrieval, Vol. 5, No. 2-3. (2002) 189-208
12. Wang, J., de Vries, A. P., Reinders, M. J.T.: A User-Item Relevance Model for Log-based Collaborative Filtering. Proc. of the European Conference on Information Retrieval. (2006) 37-48
13. Kim, T. H., Yang, S. B.: An Improved Neighbor Selection Algorithm in Collaborative Filtering. IEICE Trans. on Inf. and Systems, Vol. E88-D, No. 5 (2005) 1072-1076

Enhancing Particle Swarm Optimization Based Particle Filter Tracker

Qicong Wang, Li Xie, Jilin Liu, and Zhiyu Xiang

Departmant of Information and Electronics Engineering, Zhejiang University, Hangzhou, Zhejiang 310013, P.R. China
{wang_qi_cong, xiehan, liujl, xiangzy}@zju.edu.cn

Abstract. A novel particle filter, enhancing particle swarm optimization based particle filter (EPSOPF), is proposed for visual tracking. Particle filter (PF) is sequential Monte Carlo simulation based on particle set representations of probability densities, which can be applied to visual tracking. However, PF has the impoverishment phenomenon which limits its application. To improve the performance of PF, particle swarm optimization with mutation operator is introduced to form new filtering, in which mutation operator maintain multiple modes of particle set and optimization-seeking procedure drives particles to their neighboring maximum of the posterior. When applied to visual tracking, the proposed approach can realize more efficient function than PF.

1 Introduction

Visual tracking is required by many vision applications, but especially in video technology [1]. Particle filters are sequential Monte Carlo methods based on point mass representations of probability densities, which can be applied to any state-space model and has proven very successful for solving non-linear and non-Gaussian state estimation problems [4]. So PF is widely applied in visual tracking. In general, uniform re-sampling is employed in particle filtering, which produces the particle impoverishment problem. To tackle this problem, a large number of particles are used in the filtering at the cost of extra computational costs.

Some algorithms employ complex sampling strategies or specific prior knowledge about the objects to reduce the impoverishment, such as partitioned sampling [5], layered sampling [6], and annealed importance sampling [7]. In [9], kernel particle filter uses an inherent re-sampling approach and broader kernel to improve the performance.

In the paper we introduce a particle swarm optimization (PSO) procedure into particle filtering. PSO is similar to the Genetic Algorithm (GA) in the sense that these two evolutionary heuristics are population-based search methods, but PSO is more computationally efficient than the GA [8]. We combine PSO with mutation operator, which can guarantee enhancing particle swarm optimization (EPSO) to obtain local optima. In EPSOPF, the iterative optimization procedure of EPSO can redistribute particles to their close local modes of the posterior, and mutation operator in EPSO

D.-S. Huang, K. Li, and G.W. Irwin (Eds.): ICIC 2006, LNAI 4114, pp. 1216 – 1221, 2006.

ameliorates implicitly the diversity of particle set to alleviate the impoverishment phenomenon greatly at the same time. Moreover, we use color distributions [1] to evaluate similarity measurement of the object and a candidate for visual tracking.

2 Particle Filter

PF solves non-linear and non-Gaussian state estimation problems in Monte Carlo simulation using importance sampling, in which the posterior density is approximated by the relative density of particles in a neighborhood of state space. In [2], particle filter solves tracking problem based on the system model

$$\mathbf{x}_t = f(\mathbf{x}_{t-1}, \mathbf{w}_t) \tag{1}$$

and on the observation model

$$\mathbf{y}_t = h(\mathbf{x}_t, \mathbf{v}_t) \tag{2}$$

where $\mathbf{w}_t$ and $\mathbf{v}_t$ are only supposed to be independent white noises. $\mathbf{y}_{0:t}$ is defined as the history sequence of the random variables. Our problem consists in computing the posterior density $p(\mathbf{x}_t \mid \mathbf{y}_{0:t})$ of the state $\mathbf{x}_t$ at each time t, which can be obtained through prediction and update recursively. By Eq. (1), we realize prediction according to the following equation

$$p(\mathbf{x}_t \mid \mathbf{y}_{0:t\text{-}1}) = \int p(\mathbf{x}_t \mid \mathbf{x}_{t\text{-}1}) p(\mathbf{x}_{t-1} \mid \mathbf{y}_{0:t-1})\, d\mathbf{x} \tag{3}$$

To obtain the posterior density, we update this prediction with the observation $\mathbf{y}_t$ in terms of the Bayes rule.

In Monte Carlo methods, the posterior is approximated by the set of particles. For particle set $\left\{\left(\mathbf{s}_t^{(n)}, q_t^{(n)}\right)_{n=1,2,\ldots,N}\right\}$, where $\mathbf{s}_t$ is the particle state and q_t is the weight associated to the particle, we approximate the posterior with the following weighted sum on the discrete grids.

$$p(\mathbf{x}_t \mid \mathbf{y}_{0:t}) \approx \sum_{n=1}^{N} q_t^{(n)} \delta\left(\mathbf{x}_t - \mathbf{s}_t^{(n)}\right) \tag{4}$$

where $\delta(\bullet)$ is Dirac's delta function. And the weight q_t can be calculated through the importance density function.

The re-sampling step is crucial in the implementation of particle filtering because without it, the variance of the particle weights quickly increases [12]. In PF, uniform re-sampling is used, which is difficulty in maintain multiple modes of particle set after several updates and can result in the particle impoverishment problem.

3 Enhancing Particle Swarm Optimization

Particle swarm optimization is a parallel evolutionary algorithm developed by Kennedy and Eberhart based on social behavior [10]. Each particle in PSO has an associated fitness value and velocity $v^{(n)}$ and is iteratively moved through problem space R^d. The fitness value is the current solution to the object being optimized based on the position in the problem space. The velocities drive the particles to move through the problem space, as it follows the current optimum particles. The algorithm then searches for optima through a series of iterations. During each iteration, the fitness of each particle is evaluated. If the particle obtains the best fitness value, we define the position $p^{(n)}$ of that value as particle best $pb^{(n)}$. The global best $gb^{(n)}$ describes the position of the best fitness value achieved by any particle during any iteration. PSO can change a certain velocity of each particle moving towards its $pb^{(n)}$ and $gb^{(n)}$ positions which is calculated by the following formulation:

$$v_i^{(n)} = wv_{i-1}^{(n)} + c_1 rand_{i-1}\left(pb_{i-1}^{(n)} - p_{i-1}^{(n)}\right) + c_2 rand_{i-1}\left(gb_{i-1}^{(n)} - p_{i-1}^{(n)}\right) \tag{5}$$

$$p_i^{(n)} = p_{i-1}^{(n)} + v_i^{(n)} \tag{6}$$

where the subscript denotes the iteration number, and superscript n is particle number; w is inertia weight; c_1 and c_2 are positive learning constant; $rand$ are random numbers.

To improve searching ability of PSO and maintain the multiple modes of the population, mutation operator is introduced into PSO [13]. After initializing a population of particles with random positions and velocities, we perform the cyclic procedure of EPSO as following several steps [11]. For each particle, evaluate its fitness value. Compare the fitness value of each particle with its pb. If current value is better than pb, set the current position as pb. Compare pb of each particle with gb of population. If current value is better than gb, reset pb as gb. Refresh the velocity and position of each particle using equations (5) and (6), respectively. For all dimensions of each particle, reinitialize their position and velocity randomly according to mutation probability.

4 The Improved Particle Filter

At the beginning of each update of EPSOPF, all particles are taken as the initial population of EPSO. Then EPSO can realize two functions in filtering. One is an iterative seeking procedure and the other is the implicitly re-sampling using mutation operator. The iterative optimization-seeking procedure can redistribute particles to the local maxima of the posterior density, which produces the proper local representation of the posterior density. During implicitly re-sampling, we use mutation operator which can ameliorate the diversity of particles to maintain multiple modes of particle set. If the iteration number and mutation probability are set properly, the consequential particles set will not include too many repeated points, so the impoverishment problem is efficiently overcome. Moreover, the proposed algorithm requires fewer particles to maintain multiple modes, because particles can be redistributed to their close local maxima actively after several iterations.

We can divide the proposed approach in three main steps. The first step generates particles using Eq. (1) and then these particles are taken as the initial population of EPSO. The second step applies EPSO to all particles until they reach their close local maxima, in which the fitness of particles is recomputed by using the observation model. The third step calculates the weighted average to obtain the best state. We can better explain the second step of the algorithm through defining $\mathbf{EPSO}: R^d \rightarrow R^d$, where d is the state space dimension. Now we can rewrite Eq. (4) as

$$p\left(\mathbf{x}_t \mid \mathbf{y}_{0:t}\right) \approx \sum_{n=1}^{N} q_t^{(n)} k\left(\Sigma_t^{(n)}\left(\mathbf{x}_t - \mathbf{EPSO}\left(\mathbf{s}_t\right)\right)\right) \tag{7}$$

where $\mathbf{EPSO}\left(\mathbf{s}_t\right)$ iterates several times.

5 Experiment

The algorithms are applied to track moving human head whose motions include horizontal acceleration, changes of direction, and self-occlusion and moving face whose motion is rapid. The test sequences of moving human head are downloaded from [3]. The real video of moving face with noises is obtained through SCC-B2005P camera. The object is modeled by a rectangle region with color distribution and the system model is a random walk model.

frame #1 frame #54 frame #102

Fig. 1. Some frames of tracking result for slow motion

The weights associated to particles which represent the fitness of particles can be approximated using a Gaussian distribution of the Bhattacharyya distance. The output state of the tracked object is the expectation of all particles.

In Fig.1 and Fig.2, we show some tracking results using PF and EPSOPF with color distribution, respectively. In Fig. 1, some frames illustrate the performance of different algorithms in slow motion including self-occlusions and changes of direction, and the white rectangles represent the mean states; the tracking results of PF with 250 particles are shown in the top row; the tracking results of EPSOPF 36 particles and 4 iterations are shown in the bottom row. Fig. 2 shows some frames of tracking rapid motion using PF and EPSOPF respectively; the red rectangles represent the mean states; the first row is the tracking results using PF with 250 particles; the second row is the tracking results using EPSOPF with 36 particles and 4 iterations.

From our experiments, we can see that PF does not produce the robust tracking for both slow motion and rapid motion; however, EPSOPF in tracking can obtain better tracking results while effectively dealing with acceleration and self-occlusion motion with fewer particles than PF.

frame #19 frame #23 frame #27

Fig. 2. Some frames of tracking results for rapid motion

6 Conclusion

Utilizing swarm intelligence, we introduce an enhancing particle swarm optimization into particle filtering for visual tracking. It incorporates mutation operator into particle swarm optimization. Optimization-seeking procedure of EPSO can shift particles to the local maxima of the posterior density and reduce implicitly the particle impoverishment problem at the same time. The experimental results on both head tracking and face tracking with noises demonstrate that compared to the conventional particle filter, the proposed algorithm can produce more robust tracking and has smaller computation cost.

Acknowledgements

This work is supported by Grant No.60534070 from the National Science Foundation of China.

References

1. Nummiaro, K., Koller-Meier, E., Gool, L.V.: Object Tracking with an Adaptive Color-Based Particle Filter. DAGM-Symposium, (2002) 353-360
2. Isard, M., Blake, A.: CONDENSATION--Conditional Density Propagation for Visual Tracking. International Journal on Computer Vision, 29 (1998) 5-28
3. http://groups.inf.ed.ac.uk/vision/CAVIAR/CAVIARDATA
4. Arulampalam, M. S., Maskell, S., Gordon, N., Clapp, T.: A Tutorial on Particle Filters for Online Nonlinear/Non-gaussian Bayesian Tracking. IEEE Transactions on Signal Processing, 50 (2002) 174-188
5. MacCormick, J., Blake, A.: Partitioned Sampling, Articulated Objects and Interface-quality Hand Tracking. Lecture Notes in Computer Science, 1843 (2000) 3-19
6. MacCormick, J., Blake, A.: A Probabilistic Exclusion Principle for Tracking Multiple Objects. In: Proceedings of International Conference on Computer Vision. (1999) 572-578
7. Deutscher, J., Blake, A., Reid, I.: Articulated Body Motion Capture by Annealed Particle Filtering. In: Proceedings of Computer Vision and Pattern Recognition. (2000) 126-133
8. Hassan, R., Cohanim, B., Weck, O. de: A Comparison of Particle Swarm Optimization and the Genetic Algorithm. 1st AIAA Multidisciplinary Design Optimization Specialist Conference, (2005)
9. Lehn-Schioler, T., Erdogmus, D., Principe, J. C.: Parzen Particle Filters. In: Proceedings of International Conference on Acoustics, Speech, and Signal Processing. (2004) 781-784
10. Kennedy, J., Eberhart, R. C., Shi, Y.: Swarm Intelligence. Morgan Kaufmann Publishers, (2001)
11. Krohling, R.A., Hoffmann, F., Coelho, Ld. S.: Co-evolutionary Particle Swarm Optimization for Min-Max Problems using Gaussian Distribution. In: Proceedings of the IEEE Conference on Evolutionary Computation. (2004) 959-964
12. Bolic, M., Djuric, P.M., Hong, S.: Resampling Algorithms and Architectures for Distributed Particle Filters. IEEE Transactions on Signal Processing, (2005) 2442-2450
13. Li, N., Liu, F., Sun, D.: A Study on the Particle Swarm Optimization with Mutation Operator Constrained Layout Optimization. Chinese Journal of Computer, (2004) 897-903

Moving Target Tracking Via Adaptive One Step Ahead Neuro-Fuzzy Estimator

Cihan Karakuzu[1] and Gökalp Gürbüzer[2]

[1] Kocaeli University, Electronics and Telecommunication Engineering Department, Eski Gölcük Yolu Veziroğlu Yerleşkesi, 41040, İzmit, Kocaeli, Turkey
cihankk@kou.edu.tr

[2] Kocaeli University, Computer Engineering Department, Eski Gölcük Yolu Veziroğlu Yerleşkesi, 41040, İzmit, Kocaeli, Turkey
dsatanovic@yahoo.com

Abstract. This paper intends to cope with single target tracking nonlinear filtering problem with an Adaptive Neuro-Fuzzy Inference System (ANFIS). ANFIS provides faster adaptation, adequate convergence and easy using over other standard filters. The ANFIS used in this study is trained on-line while the target is moving to estimate the next position of target at the end of the training. The proposed system calculates the speed and the acceleration rate of the object and estimates the next absolute position of the target between two position measurements interval. Estimation performance of the presented system has been tested using few predetermined position data. The test results show that the proposed ANFIS position estimator system has been successively estimated the next position of the moving target and can be used in real target tracking systems.

1 Introduction

Target tracking is estimating the next position of a moving object, given with the momentary positional coordinates. Observations consist of data from radar and infrared sensors, and prior knowledge of the initial location of the target; observation noise comes from background noise sources such as clutter, or internal thermal noise in the sensor. Purposely, "x, y" and "z" coordinates of the target object's position are read from an external device. As this data is considered to have been distorted with an additive noise, the solution system must somehow achieve estimating the correct next position of the target through this false positional data.

The goal of the system being designed is minimizing the error of estimation described below:

$$e = x_r(n+1) - x_e(n+1) \tag{1}$$

Where $x_r(n+1)$ is the "x" coordinate of the next real position, and $x_e(n+1)$ is estimated next real position's "x" coordinate.

Since target's position consists of three components (x, y and z), the system should estimate these components separately, but using the same method. On the other hand, active positional data would not be sufficient for next positional estimation.

D.-S. Huang, K. Li, and G.W. Irwin (Eds.): ICIC 2006, LNAI 4114, pp. 1222 – 1227, 2006.

Consequently, target's velocity (V), and preferably acceleration (a), is required to be read from the same external source or, as this paper proposes, be calculated accurately and quickly. Velocity and acceleration rate of the target on x-coordinate can be calculated as:

$$\left.\begin{aligned} V(n) &= \dot{x}(n) = x(n) - x(n-1) \\ a(n) &= \ddot{x}(n) = x(n) - 2x(n-1) + x(n-2) \end{aligned}\right\} \tag{2}$$

The strategy formulated in Eq. 2 significantly limits the complexity of the solution and serves keeping the error rate at a considerable minimum.

In this study, the object being tracked is considered to be in a cube with all its axes in range [-1, 1], which is also the range of positional data; velocity and acceleration alike. It is consider using an ANFIS for estimating the target's next position. ANFIS should suppress the noise interfered from the positional data and estimate the correct next position. Implicated ANFIS is to get the positional data every "n"th moment, and calculate the approximated velocity and acceleration, decide how the data is corrupted, and accordingly estimate the next positional component. Then, compare this output with the very next data to further converge to the real position. In other words, the ANFIS is to be trained throughout the tracking process.

2 System Structure

Fuzzy reasoning has been used in many different studies such as [1], [2]. Sugeno fuzzy inference system was used with weighted average output form in this study. "Adaptivity" of the structure is due to its capable of training. Output of ANFIS with two rule nodes is defined in Eq. (3) and Eq. (4) [3].

$$f = \frac{w_1}{w_1 + w_2} f_1 + \frac{w_2}{w_1 + w_2} f_2 \tag{3}$$

$$f = \bar{w}_1(p_1x + q_1y + r_1) + \bar{w}_2(p_2x + q_2y + r_2) = (\bar{w}_1x)p_1 + (\bar{w}_1y)q_1 + (\bar{w}_1)r_1 + (\bar{w}_2x)p_2 + (\bar{w}_2y)q_2 + (\bar{w}_2)r_2 \tag{4}$$

Eq. (4) show that output, f, is linear over parameters pi, qi and ri parameters which are also called "consequent parameters". Parameters belonging to membership functions (MFs) of the fuzzy system are called "premise parameters". MFs of the each input variable are defined as homogeny distributed form in predetermined changing interval.

2.1 Training Structure of ANFIS

Training process is achieved in two stage: The first stage is "forward pass" which consists of calculating the outputs of all layers up to 4th and updating consequent parameters using (least square) LS method. The second part named "backward pass" is completed only when premise parameters are updated using gradient descent method. This training method is called "hybrid learning".

LS method is used when a system defined as in Eq. (5). θi parameters in Eq. (5) are the consequent parameters of layer 4 in the ANFIS. These parameters need to be solved with minimal error. LS method solves this problem with matrix arithmetic as $A\theta = y$. An exact solution cannot be found since the matrix θ is non-square. To help the solution, an error parameter is added to Eq. (5), and a column vector, which will minimize the error's square, is calculated [4].

$$\left.\begin{array}{l} f_1(u_1)\theta_1 + f_2(u_1)\theta_2 + \ldots + f_n(u_1)\theta_n = y_1 \\ f_1(u_2)\theta_1 + f_2(u_2)\theta_2 + \ldots + f_n(u_2)\theta_n = y_2 \\ \vdots \\ f_1(u_m)\theta_1 + f_2(u_m)\theta_2 + \ldots + f_n(u_m)\theta_n = y_m \end{array}\right\} \tag{5}$$

Employing a simple analysis given in Eq.(6), consequent parameters of the ANFIS are determined using Eq. (7) at each forward pass.

$$\left.\begin{array}{l} A\theta + e = y,\ e = y - A\theta, \\ E(\theta) = \frac{1}{2}e^T e = \frac{1}{2}(y - A\theta)^T (y - A\theta), \\ \frac{\partial E}{\partial \theta} = \frac{1}{2}\left[-A^T(y - A\theta) - A^T(y - A\theta)\right] = -A^T(y - A\theta) = -A^T y - A^T A\theta = 0, \end{array}\right\} \tag{6}$$

$$\hat{\theta} = \left(A^T A\right)^{-1} A^T y \tag{7}$$

When the ANFIS is trained, A is a matrix consisting of x_i and y_i values, and θ is a vector whose element values are p_i, q_i and r_i. After the consequent parameters updated at the last of forward computing stage, premise parameters are updated via backward pass.

In the second stage, gradient descent which is frequently used method in training artificial neural networks is employed to update premise parameters on backward pass [5][6]. This is can be summarized as following Eq.'s.

$$\left. e = y_d - f,\ E = \frac{1}{2}e^2,\ \alpha_{k+1} = \alpha_k - \eta\frac{\partial E}{\partial \alpha_k} \right\} \tag{8}$$

Where α is any of the premise parameters of ANFIS and η is learning rate. As a result, when the Eq. (8) is processed for each membership function, the error will be reduced in the next training iteration.

2.2 ANFIS Properties Used for Solution of the Problem

As stated in previous sections, ANFIS uses position, velocity and acceleration as inputs and determines the next estimated position. Consequently, a three input-one output first order Sugeno system is designed to be trained in ANFIS. The reason for choosing first order Sugeno system is the linear equation below:

$$x(t+1) = x(t) + V(t) \tag{9}$$

ANFIS designed has 3 inputs, 11 1st layer nodes, 15 PI, N nodes and 4th layer nodes and 1 output node. ANFIS has 3 for position, 5 for velocity and 3 for acceleration gauss membership functions (with z-shaped functions for the left ends and s-shaped functions for the right ends).

Rules are defined to act like a low pass filter. For instance, if velocity is high but acceleration is very low, the next estimated position is calculated with a higher coefficient of acceleration and a lower coefficient of velocity. On the other hand, if the velocity is low and acceleration is high, acceleration and velocity are considered to be equally effective on the next position, with a thought of "object is speeding up". Table 1 states ANFIS rules and output functions related for initial and last condition of the first data set.

Table 1. Initial and updated rule table after the last estimation for the first data set

Velocity (V)	Accel. (a)	Rules with initial parameters	Rules with the last parameters
NB	N	$x+0.1\cdot V+a$	$0.009543x+0.009543V+0.00126a-0.01019$
NB	Z	$x+V+0.5\cdot a$	$0.3673\cdot x+0.3673\cdot V+0.04849\cdot a-0.3923$
NB	P	$x+0.7\cdot V+0.1\cdot a$	0
NS	N	$x+V+0.1\cdot a$	$1.029\cdot x+1.21\cdot V-4.772\cdot a-1.742$
NS	Z	$x+V+0.5\cdot a$	$0.8839\cdot x-0.7138\cdot V-0.48\cdot a+0.07241$
NS	P	$x+0.7\cdot V+0.1\cdot a$	$1.364\cdot x-28.8\cdot V+14.16\cdot a+0.07505$
Z	N	$x+V$	$0.8127\cdot x+4.381\cdot V-5.884\cdot \mathrm{a}-2.881$
Z	Z	$x+V$	$1.032\cdot x-1.033\cdot \mathrm{V}-1.896\cdot \mathrm{a}-0.2344$
Z	P	$x+V$	$1.522\cdot x+17.55\cdot V-48.7\cdot \mathrm{a}+7.979$
PS	N	$x+0.7\cdot V+0.1\cdot a$	$1.135x+2.716V-3.625a+26.$
PS	Z	$x+V+0.5\cdot a$	$1.025\cdot x-1.472\cdot V+7.406\cdot a+0.03733$
PS	P	$x+V+0.1\cdot a$	$0.9282\cdot x+0.6692\cdot V+7.171\cdot a-5.307$
PB	N	$x+0.7\cdot V+0.1\cdot a$	0
PB	Z	$x+V+0.5\cdot a$	0
PB	P	$x+0.1\cdot V+a$	0

3 Simulation Results and Conclusion

The ANFIS should be designed not only to minimize the estimation error, but also to reduce the complexity of the solution, due to the continual movement of the target. This is the reason why ANFIS should be trained for a significantly less number of epochs to speed up the output. This may seem to be a disadvantage at the first glance, but considering that the training will continue during the next measurement interval, this disadvantage may be compensated. Consequently, the more number of positional data received, ANFIS is expected to make the more accurate estimations.

The proposed tracking structure is tested for different position data. Fig. 1 summarizes the simulation results practiced in MATLAB. Input vector for one coordinate has been given as a tangent sigmoid function (first data set) as it may be similar to the altitude of an aircraft in this test. As seen on Fig. 1, ANFIS promises a good estimation of the next values of an unknown function, with an average square error rate of $9,5\ 10^{-7}$ for the test. Table 1 shows ANFIS's updated rule table after the last estimation. One should note that these rules cannot be used for another target, because ANFIS is trained to estimate only this test target function. For the test, changing membership functions of an input is shown by Fig. 2. As can be seen in the figure, the system trains itself during each estimation interval according to previous status.

Another target is most rightfully expected to have a different graph of movement. Fig. 3 (a) shows the estimation results with accuracy of 0.0058 for a target which moves with a sinc trail (the second position data set). Fig. 3 (b) shows the estimation results with accuracy of $2,910^{-4}$ for a $\cos(x) - \sin(x^2)$ target function (the third position data set).

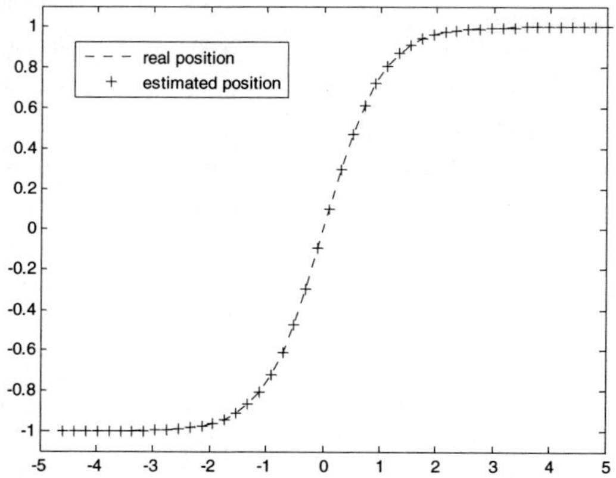

Fig. 1. Tracking performance of the systems for the first data set

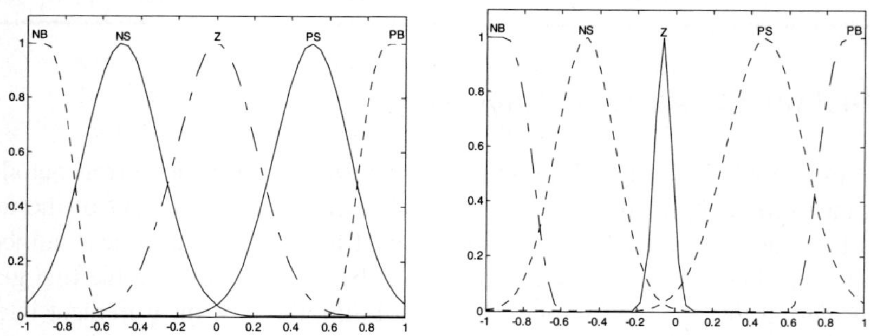

(a) (b)

Fig. 2. (a) Initial membership functions for velocity input and (b) status of these membership functions at the 20th estimation interval

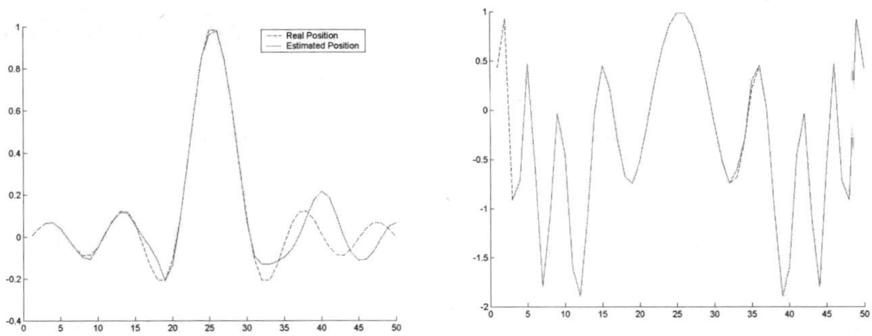

(a) (b)

Fig. 3. Tracking performance of the systems for the second position data set (a), and the third position data set (b)

As can be seen from the results illustrated in figures, the proposed system adequately estimates the next absolute position of the target between two position measurements interval. Estimation performance of the proposed ANFIS in this paper is successive for the used test positional data sets. This performance shows that the proposed system can be used in real target tracking systems.

References

1. Karakuzu C., Öztürk S., Türker M.: Design and Simulation of a Fuzzy Substrate Feeding Controller for an Industrial Scale Fed-Batch Baker Yeast Fermentor. LNAI, Vol.2715 (2003) 458-465
2. Karakuzu C., Türker M., Öztürk S.: Modelling, On-line State Estimation and Fuzzy Control of Production Scale Fed-batch Baker's Yeast Fermentation. Control Engineering Practice, 14 (2006) 959–974
3. Jang, J.-S. R., Sun, C.-T., Mizutani, E.: Neuro-Fuzzy and Soft Computing: A Computational Approach to Learning and Machine Intelligence. Prentice Hall, Upper Saddle River, NJ 07458 (1997)
4. Becerikli, Y.: Optimal Estimation Theory. Lecture Notes (2005)
5. Karakuzu, C.: Introduction to Artificial Neural Networks. Lecture Notes, (2005)
6. Kecman, V.: Learning and Soft Computing: Support Vector Machines. Neural Networks and Fuzzy Logic Models, MIT Press (2001)

Optimization of Special Vehicle Routing Problem Based on Ant Colony System

Xia Liu[1,2], Huan Qi[1], and Yingchun Chen[1]

[1] Dept. of Control Science & Engineering, Huazhong University of Science & Technology, Wuhan 430074, China
lx_hust@163.com, qihuan@hust.edu.cn, chyc@21cn.com

[2] School of Physics and Information Engineering, Jianghan University, Wuhan 430056, China

Abstract. In emergent airdropping, there are some special requirements for the vehicle routing problem. The airdropping personnel and equipment, geographically scattered, should be delivered simultaneously to an assigned place by a fleet of vehicles as soon as possible. In this case the objective is not to minimize the total distance traveled or the number of vehicles as usual, but to minimize the time of all personnel and equipment delivered with a given vehicle number. Ant colony system with maximum-minimum limit is adopted to solve these problems. The distance of each route is computed and the route with maximum distance is chosen. The objective is to minimize the maximum distance. The algorithm is implemented and tested on some instances. The results demonstrate the effectiveness of the method.

1 Introduction

Vehicle Routing Problem (VRP) has been largely studied because of its application in logistic and supply chains management. In classical VRP, customers with known demands are visited by a homogeneous fleet of vehicles with limited capacities, which are initially located at a central depot. Routes are assumed to start and end at the depot. The objective is often to minimize the total distance traveled by all vehicles under the condition that each customer is served exactly once and total load on any vehicle cannot exceed vehicle capacity. The VRP is known to be NP-hard, many researchers have used heuristic algorithms to solve them [1-3].

Recently, a few models of natural swarm-intelligence are presented and transformed into useful artificial swarm-intelligent systems such as Ant Colony System (ACS). Those systems are inspired by the collective behaviors of social insect colonies and other animal societies. They have many features that make them particularly appealing and promising in solving NP-hard problems. Furthermore, swarm intelligence systems are more appealing for distributed optimization, where the problem can be explicitly formulated in terms of computational agents. A number of algorithms inspired by the foraging behaviors of ant colonies have recently been applied successfully to solve many NP-hard combinatorial optimization problems, and it has shown that the improvement attained by these algorithms can make them competitive to other meta-heuristic techniques. ACS has been applied to solve VRP in [4,5]. It is found that the size of the candidate lists used within the algorithm is a significant factor in finding

D.-S. Huang, K. Li, and G.W. Irwin (Eds.): ICIC 2006, LNAI 4114, pp. 1228 – 1233, 2006.

improved solutions and the computational time for the algorithm compares favorably with other solution methods. A hybrid dynamic programming - ant colony optimization technique is introduced in [6] to solve the problem, which is expressed as a bi-criterion optimization with the mutually exclusive aims of minimizing both the total mean transit time and the total variance in transit time.

In emergent airdropping, there are some special requirements for VRP. The airdropping personnel and equipment, which are geographically scattered, must be delivered to an assigned place simultaneously by a fleet of vehicles as soon as possible. Otherwise it is of no use for the personnel without equipment, or for the equipment without personnel to operate. Anyhow, a soldier cannot make something out of nothing. In this case, the objective is to minimize the time of all the personnel and equipment delivered to the assigned place with a given vehicle number. ACS with maximum-minimum limit is used to solve these problems. The rest of the paper is organized as follows. A mathematical formulation for the special VRP is given in Section 2. ACS and its application are elaborated in Section 3. Section 4 gives computation results of an illustrative example, followed with conclusion in Section 5.

2 Problem Description

Consider the case that n customers (i.e., the above-mentioned places with landed personnel and equipment) have a certain amount of goods (i.e., the above-mentioned personnel and equipment) to be collected and delivered to a given depot by m homogeneous vehicles. Each vehicle leaves the depot to collect goods from a subset of the customers, and finally returns to the depot. The quantity of goods collected by a vehicle cannot exceed its capacity. To solve this special VRP, appropriate vehicles are chosen for specific customers first and then their orders to collect goods are determined such that all customer demands are met and no constraints are violated. The object is to minimize the time between the moment of the vehicles leaving the depot and the moment of the last vehicle returning to the depot.

The vehicles are numbered from 1 to m, customers from 1 to n, and the nodes of routes from 0,1,..,n, where 0 is the node for the depot. The mathematical formulation of this VRP is given as follows.

Minimize

$$\max\left(\sum_{i=0}^{n}\sum_{j=0}^{n} d_{ij} x_{ij}^{k}\right), \ k = 1,\ldots,m \ . \tag{1}$$

Subject to

$$\sum_{i=0}^{n}\sum_{k=1}^{m} x_{ij}^{k} = 1, \ j = 0,\ldots,n \ , \tag{2}$$

$$\sum_{j=0}^{n}\sum_{k=1}^{m} x_{ij}^{k} = 1, \ i = 0,\ldots,n \ , \tag{3}$$

$$\sum_{i=0}^{n} x_{ip}^{k} - \sum_{j=0}^{n} x_{pj}^{k} = 0, \ k = 1,\ldots,m, \ p = 1,\ldots,n \ , \tag{4}$$

$$\sum_{i=0}^{n}\sum_{j=0}^{n} g_i x_{ij}^k \le C,\ k = 1,\ldots,m\ . \tag{5}$$

where

m = Number of vehicles,
n = Number of customers,
d_{ij} = Distance from node i to node j,

$$x_{ij}^k = \begin{cases} 1, & \text{if vehicle } k \text{ travels from node } i \text{ to node } j \\ 0, & \text{otherwise} \end{cases},$$

g_i = Quantity of goods of node i,
C = Capacity of a vehicle.

Assuming all vehicles have the same velocity, the objective can be expressed by (1), minimizing the maximum distance of m routes. Constraints (2) and (3) ensure that each customer is served exactly once. Route continuity is enforced by constraint (4). It means that as soon as a vehicle arrives at a delivery place to collect goods, it should leave that place at once. Constraint (5) is the vehicle capacity constraint. Each route should not serve more than the capacity of a vehicle.

3 Ant Colony System for Special VRP

ACS is based on the way that real ant colonies behave in order to find the shortest path between their nest and food sources. Ants leave an aromatic essence, called pheromone, on the path they walk, and other ants can sense the existence of pheromone and choose their way according to the level of pheromone. Paths with more pheromone are to be chosen by ants with a high probability. The amount of pheromone laid on a path is based on the length of the path and the quality of the food source, and it will increase when the number of ants following that path increases. In some time all ants are expected to follow the shortest path. The ACS simulates the described behavior of real ants to solve combinatorial optimization problems with artificial ants. It mainly consists of five steps as follows:

Step1: Set parameters and initialize the pheromone trails.

Step2: Each ant builds routes by the state transition rule and performs local pheromone update according to the solution.

Step3: Apply a local search to improve the ant's solution.

Step4: Update global pheromone based on the best routes after all ants find their solutions.

Step5: Repeat step2 to step4 until the termination condition is met.

3.1 Route Construction

In our ACS an individual ant simulates m vehicles and parallel designs the routes for all vehicles. Initially, each vehicle starts at the depot and the set of customers included in each vehicle's tour is empty. Then the ant continuously selects the next customer to visit from the list of feasible customers for each vehicle. The vehicle returns to the depot when its capacity constraint is met or all customers are visited. By this means the ant constructs *m* routes at the same time.

The quality of the solution is greatly dependent on the selection algorithm from one node to another. In the ACS, the ant moves from current node *i* to next node *v* by using the following probabilistic formula (6).

$$v = \arg\max_{j \notin Tabu} [\tau(i,j)]^{\alpha} [\eta(i,j)]^{\beta} \quad if \quad q \le q_0 \cdot \tag{6}$$

where *Tabu* is the set of the customers visited by the current ant, $\tau(i,j)$ denotes the amount of pheromone on the arc connecting node *i* and *j*. $\eta(i,j)$ is equal to the inverse of the distance of the arc (i,j). The parameter α, β are user-defined constants determining the relative influence of pheromone versus distance. The value q is a random uniform variable within range [0,1] and the value q_0 is a predefined parameter ($0 \le q_0 \le 1$). If q is less than q_0, the arc with the highest value from (6) is chosen. Otherwise the ant selects the next customer to visit based on the probability distribution given in equation (7).

$$p(i,j) = \begin{cases} \dfrac{[\tau(i,j)]^{\alpha} [\eta(i,j)]^{\beta}}{\sum_{j \notin Tabu} [\tau(i,j)]^{\alpha} [\eta(i,j)]^{\beta}} & j \notin Tabu \\ 0 & j \in Tabu \end{cases} . \tag{7}$$

3.2 Pheromone Updating

Local updating is conducted each time an ant moves from node *i* to node *j* to reduce the amount of pheromone of the arc (i,j), in order to diversify solutions obtained by the ants. The local updating rule is shown as follows.

$$\tau(i,j) = \varphi \tau(i,j) + (1 - \varphi) \Delta \tau(i,j) \cdot \tag{8}$$

where φ is a coefficient representing the level of pheromone persistence and $\Delta\tau(i,j)$ represents the contribution of an ant choosing the arc (i,j) in its solution. $\Delta\tau(i,j)$ is equal to a predefined parameter Q varied with different problems.

Global updating is performed to add pheromone to all of the arcs in the best solution after a predetermined number of ants have completed all routes. The global updating rule is given by equation (9).

$$\tau(i,j) = \sigma \tau(i,j) + (1 - \sigma) \Delta \tau^{*}(i,j) \cdot \tag{9}$$

where σ is a coefficient representing the level of pheromone persistence and $\Delta\tau^{*}(i,j)$ is the inverse of the objective of the best tour. Global updating increases the probability of future routes using the arcs contained in the best solution.

If most ants choose the same arcs, the pheromone of the arcs will accumulate quickly. The probability of other customers to be chosen is very small, so the solution cannot attain global optimum. In the paper pheromone trail $\tau(i,j)$ is limited in $[\tau_{min}, \tau_{max}]$ to improve the opportunity of selecting arcs with few pheromone trails and avoid local optimization.

3.3 Local Search

Local search is applied to all routes built by the ants. In the paper we use the common 2-opt heuristic algorithm.

4 Computational Results

Our methods are applied to the data sets from [7], as is shown in Table 1. There are a fleet of 6 vehicles in the depot and a vehicle capacity of 8. The unit of x-coordinate and y-coordinate is km. The unit of supply is ton.

Table 1. The coordinate and supply of the customers

Customer no.	Coordinate	Supply	Customer no.	Coordinate	Supply
0	(52,4)	0			
1	(15,49)	1.64	11	(24,89)	2.35
2	(0,61)	1.31	12	(19,25)	2.60
3	(51,15)	0.43	13	(20,99)	1.00
4	(25,71)	3.38	14	(73,91)	0.65
5	(38,62)	1.13	15	(100,95)	0.85
6	(35,45)	3.77	16	(7,73)	2.56
7	(100,4)	3.84	17	(69,86)	1.27
8	(10,52)	0.39	18	(24,3)	2.69
9	(26,79)	0.24	19	(66,14)	3.26
10	(87,7)	1.03	20	(9,30)	2.97

Based on some preliminary tests, we have found suitable values for parameters. The number of ants is 21, the initial pheromone trail τ_0 0.001, the maximum and minimum pheromone trail, i.e., τ_{max} and τ_{min} 0.001 and 0.00024 respectively, the probability of choosing next node q_0 0.06, coefficients α and β 0.9 and 1 respectively, the parameter in global and local trail updating, i.e., φ, σ, Q 0.02, 0.4 and 0.00024 respectively. The optimal 6 routes are respectively 0-3-14-17-6-0, 0-18-10-7-0, 0-4-13-11-9-0, 0-1-8-20-12-0, 0-19-15-0 and 0-5-16-2-0. The objective is 207.934537. The routes are shown in Fig.1.

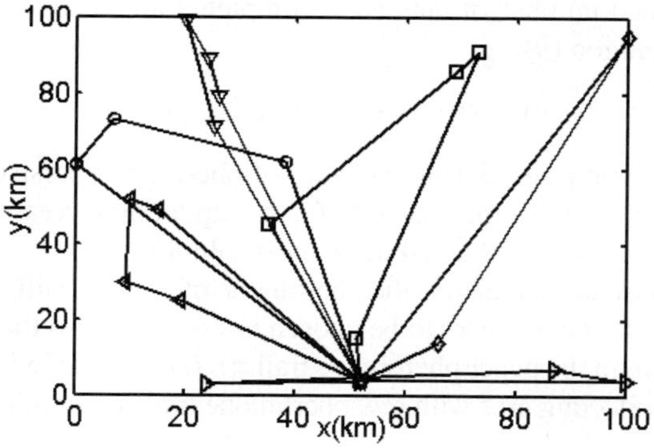

Fig. 1. Six routes resulted from ACS

5 Conclusions

The ACS is adopted to minimize the time of all personnel and equipment delivered to an assigned place with a given vehicle number in emergent airdropping. Some instances are tested and the results demonstrate the effectiveness of the method.

Future work includes the improvement of ACS in order to find better solutions for problems of large scale with less time. The combination of other algorithms with ACS will also be considered.

References

1. Li, Jun, Guo, Yao huang: Logistics Distribution Theory and Method of Vehicle Scheduling Problem, China Logistics Publishing House (2001)
2. Campos, V., Mota, E.: Heuristic Procedures for The Capacitated Vehicle Routing Problem. Computational Optimization and Applications, Vol. 16, No. 3 (2000) 265-277
3. Berger, J., Barkaoui, M.: A New Hybrid Genetic Algorithm for the Capacitated Vehicle Routing Problem. Journal of the Operational Research Society, Vol. 54, No.12 (2003) 1254-1262
4. Bell, J. E., McMullen, P. R.: Ant Colony Optimization Techniques for the Vehicle Routing Problem. Advanced Engineering Informatics, Vol.18, No.1 (2004) 41-48
5. Mazzeo, S., Loiseau, I.: An Ant Colony Algorithm for the Capacitated Vehicle Routing. Electronic Notes in Discrete Mathematics, Vol.18 (2004) 181-186
6. Chitty, D. M., Hernandez, M. L.: A Hybrid Ant Colony Optimization Technique for Dynamic Vehicle Routing. Proceedings of Genetic and Evolutionary Computation Conference (2004) 48-59
7. Yuan, Xia: Research on the Vehicle Routing Problems in Logistics Distribution. PhD thesis, Southeast University (2004)

Pattern Finding Algorithm Based on Cloud Models

Yingjun Weng and Laide Shi

School of Economics & Management, Tongji University, Shanghai 200092, P.R. China
stephen_weng@sjtu.org

Abstract. With the rapid growth in application of series data mining, one important issue is discovering character patterns in larger data sets. Two limitations of previous works were the weak efficiency and rigid partition. In this paper, we introduce a novel pattern searching algorithm that using cloud models to implement concept hierarchies and data reduction. The reduction in this algorithm is based on symbolic mapping which uses cloud transformation method. Compared with other works, we make use of linguistic atoms to describe series character both specifically and holistically. Furthermore, being the fuzzy and probabilistic of cloud models, soft partition to continuous numeric attributes and the capability to data noise were realized. Normal segmentation method was done as comparison to show the performance of cloud models based algorithm. The efficiency is improved obviously. Moreover, noise-adding experiment was implemented to show that algorithm has robustness to the noise.

1 Introduction

There is growing recognition in business community about the importance of knowledge as a critical resource for organizations. It is necessary and interesting to research how to capture knowledge from huge amounts of data. Furthermore, it is sometimes desirable to automatically generate concept hierarchies or adjust some given hierarchies for particular learning tasks [1]. Concept hierarchies reduces the data by collecting and replacing low level concepts (such as numeric values for the attribute age) by higher level concepts (such as young, middle-aged, or senior).There exists a vast body of works on efficiently generating of concept hierarchies such as binning, histogram analysis, clustering analysis, entropy-based discretization and segmentation by natural partitioning, etc. [2]. Discretization reduces the number of values for a given continuous attribute by dividing the range of the attribute into intervals. Interval labels can then be used to replace actual data values. However, these methods generate concept hierarchy by discretizing rigidly universe of discourse that used equal-distance or equal-frequency. Theses hard partition can not reflect exactly the distribution of data and the fuzzy and uncertainty of the qualitative concept and multi-compatibility among different hierarchies.

In this paper, we introduce a method of representing numerical concept using cloud model. Continuous-values attributes are represented by three digital parameters of cloud models: expected valued, entropy and hyper-entropy. Cloud transformation is also realized to automatically produce the basic numerical concepts as the leaf nodes in concept tree. Based on the concept tree model, concept climbing-up and jumping-up

D.-S. Huang, K. Li, and G.W. Irwin (Eds.): ICIC 2006, LNAI 4114, pp. 1234 – 1239, 2006.

along the tree is realized, which can be used as a tools of discovering knowledge in different levels.

We use probabilistic project method and the concept tree to implement robust searching of pattern matching. The probabilistic project is to project the data objects onto lower dimensional subspaces, and randomly chosen subset of the objects features. Compared with other algorithms, symbolic representation using cloud models allows for linguistic symbol expression of numeric attributes, which avoids rigid segmentation between data universes.

The rest of paper is organized as follows. In Section 2, we describe the cloud model and its characteristics. In Section 3, we detailed presented the concept tree generating algorithm based on the cloud models. Finally, we perform two experiments that verify the performance and robustness to the data noise of algorithm.

2 Cloud Model

***Definition* 1:** *Cloud* is:

$$C_T(x): U \rightarrow [0,1] \qquad (1)$$
$$\forall \quad x \in U \qquad x \rightarrow C_T(x)$$

where $U=\{u\}$ is the universe of discourse. Assume that T is a linguistic term associated with U. The compatibility degree of u in U to the linguistic term T is labeled as $C_T(x)$, which is a random number with a stable tendency and takes the values in[0,1] .

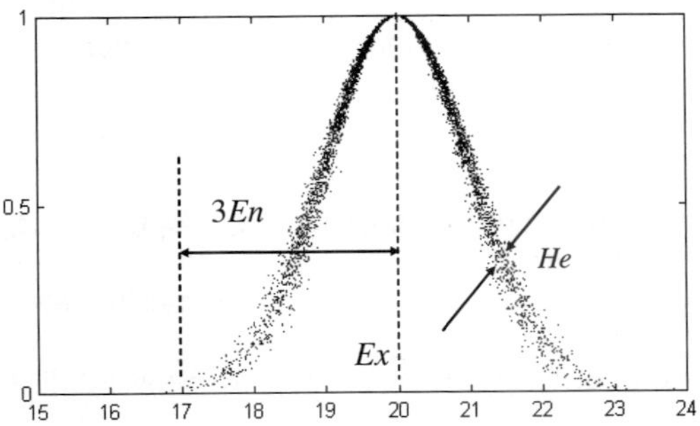

Fig. 1. Cloud models and its digital characteristic

The concept of clouds is often pictured as two dimensional graphs with the universe of discourse represented as one dimensional. There are various ways to interpret it. From the x-axis perspective, it illustrates the role of a compatibility cloud for a linguistic term T in a universe of discourse U. The compatibility degree at each u is all random numbers showing the deviation but obeying certain probability distribution. The thickness of cloud is uneven: near the top and bottom of the cloud, the standard errors are smaller than those near the waist part. In the other way, from the y-axis perspective, it shows that the left and right limits at one degree gives the scope of linguistic term, and the width of this degree is related to the coverage of linguistic term in the universe of discourse. But the width itself becomes random showing the deviation which obeys a certain probability distribution. The geometry of clouds is a great aid understanding the uncertainty and defining the cloud concept related to linguistic terms. Visualizing this geometry may, by itself, be the most powerful argument for fuzziness and randomness.

The bell shape of clouds called normal clouds are based on normal distributions, which have been supported by results in every branch of both social science and natural science. Cloud models use three feature parameters to characterize the qualitative meaning of linguistic atom, which is the *Ex* (Expected Value), *En* (Entropy) and *He* (Hyper Entropy) [3].The three parameters integrate with fuzzy for numeric attributes and randomness of membership. It consists of the mapping between qualitative and quantities, as the basis of the knowledge representation.

3 Concept Tree Generating

Mentioned in literature [4], the slope of series reflects the series tendency. It is obviously that representation of the slope ratio becomes an essential and fundamental issue. Cloud models offer a flexible path to integrate qualitative and quantitative knowledge because linguistic variables use a few 'words' to represent the character of series tendency which both data reduction and soft partition to interval come true [5]. We use the cloud models to construct a concept tree whose nodes are linguistic variables describing segments' trend. These linguistic variables are consisted of a set of linguistic atoms $A=\{A_1(Ex_1,En_1,He_1),\cdots\cdots,A_m(Ex_m,En_m,He_m)\}$.

According to the cloud generator algorithm, we can produce many drops of cloud corresponding to different slope breakpoints. Figure 2 shows the transformation steps. The CG box is an *X* condition cloud models generator which calculates the slope and transforms into corresponding concepts.

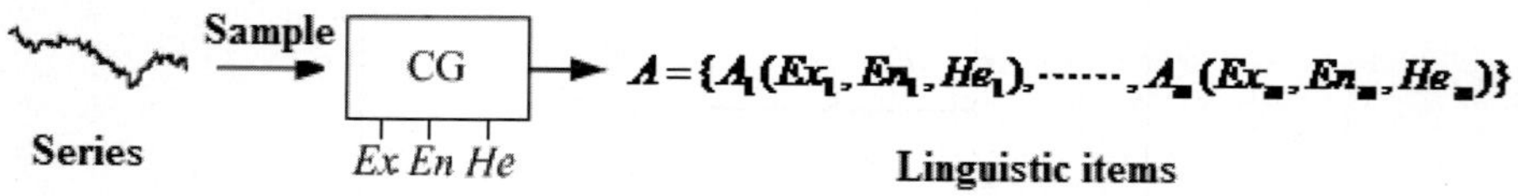

Fig. 2. Symbolic representation of subsequence shape

Being the concept hierarchies transfer high dimension data into lower, the mining efficiency is improved, and also the knowledge can discover at different abstraction levels. In this paper, cloud transform is used to generate the multi-concept hierarchies, which can automatically produce the basic concepts items as the leaf nodes in pan-concept tree. Based on the cloud transformation, we can get a set of leaf nodes of concept tree that consist of linguistic atoms. The automatically generation of concept tree is the leveraging of concept step by step, which based on these nodes.

***Definition* 2:** *Soft-OR operator* Suppose $U=\{u\}$, $A_1(Ex_1,En_1,He_1)$ and $A_2(Ex_2,En_2,He_2)$ are two adjoining basic cloud models on *U*. If $Ex_1 \le Ex_2$, then

$$A_3 = A_1 \cup A_2 \Leftrightarrow \quad (2)$$

$$Ex_{A_3} = \frac{1}{2}(Ex_{A_1} - 3En_{A_1} + Ex_{A_2} + 3En_{A_2})$$
$$En_{A_3} = En_{A_1} + En_{A_2}$$
$$He_{A_3} = \max(He_{A_1}, He_{A_2})$$

This A_3 can be defined as the result of "soft or" value from A_1 and A_2. The operation shows that two adjoining basic concept can be leveraged to a higher level concept by "soft or" operator. The following is the algorithm for concept tree generating.

```
Input:   leaf nodes A;
          Concept numbers for every hierarchy
         {num_n,...num_0}, m > num_{i+1} > num_i, and num_0 = 1
Output: pan-concept-tree{level_{n+1}, level_n, ... level_1, level_0}
BEGIN
        level_{n+1} = A;
        FOR  i = n -> 0, step -1, DO
        {
          level_i = level_{i+1};
         WHERE  (|level_i| > num_i)
          {
        (B,C) = select_min_dis(level_i);  //two nearest cloud model
        level_i = del(level_i, {B,C});
        D = soft_or(B,C);                 //Soft-OR calculation
        level_i = add(level_i, {D});
          }
        }
END
```

4 Experiments

In order to verify the efficiency and robustness of concept tree generating algorithm based on cloud models, we adopted the method of probabilistic projection, presented by Bill and others, to searching matching patterns in database [6].

To verify the efficiency, we implemented the searching using linear scanning and concept-based index searching. The average CPU time ratio was calculated as $T_{concep-based} / T_{linear}$. The results showed concept-based algorithm has good performance.

Table 1. Average CPU time ratio to linear scanning

Data Size (10^6)	0.001	0.005	0.009	0.012	0.035	0.070
CPU time ratio	0.50	0.28	0.20	0.15	0.07	0.05

The concept tree generated by cloud-models-based algorithm was used to implement data reduction. The fluctuation was labeled as 'words' Sharp-Down, Mid-Down, Gentle-Down, Normal, Gentle-Up, Mid-Up and Sharp-UP. The Fig. 3 shows the partial of concept tree.

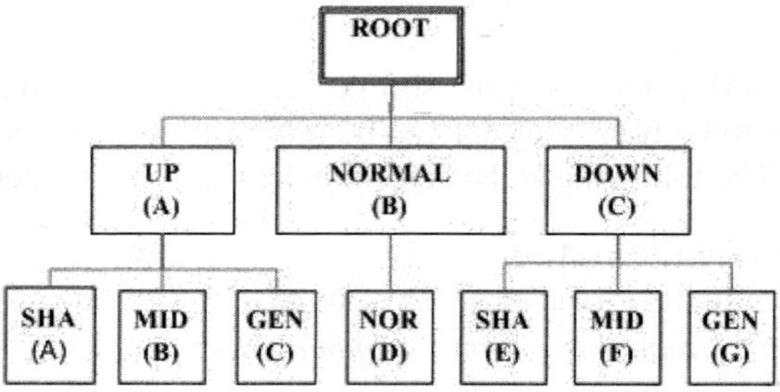

Fig. 3. Concept tree for slope representation

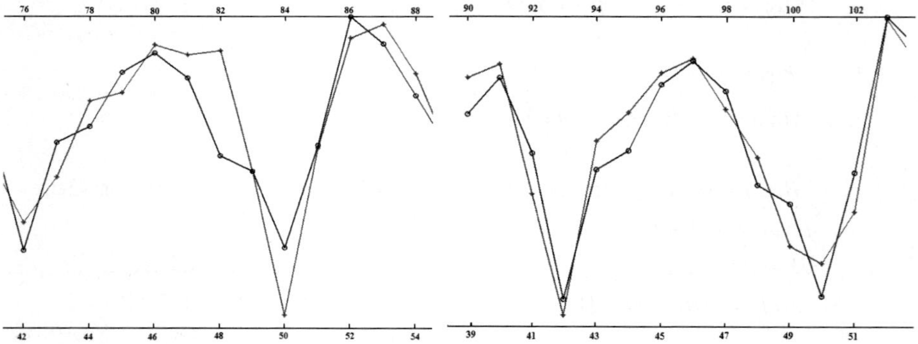

Fig. 4. Patterns discovered using segmentation method and cloud models

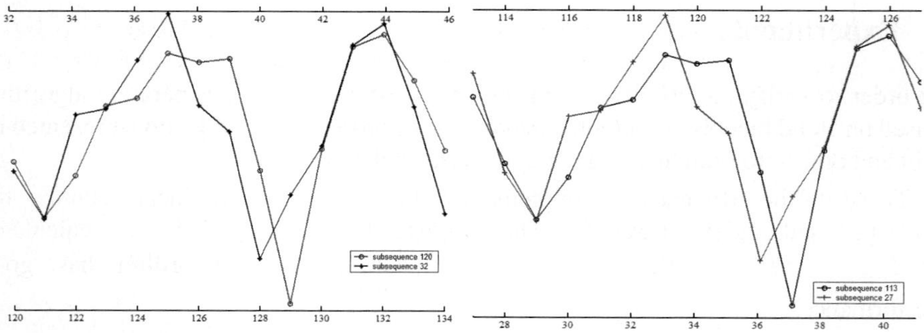

Fig. 5. Pattern discovered using data with/without noise added

We took the dataset of monthly-closings of the Dow-Jones industrial index, Aug. 1968 - Aug. 1981 as test data. First, experiment of cloud models based algorithm was implemented in contrast with segmentation method. The results (Fig.4) showed more accurate matching patterns founded by cloud models based algorithm.

Second, we used normal random noise added to original data. Fig.5 showed that although a typical amount of noise added to raw data, it still can be tolerated by our algorithm. The experiment carried respectively by two conditions with or without noise, and the patterns are founded as shown in figure 5, which is acceptable because the difference between these two segments are within the tiny error.

5 Conclusions

Concept hierarchy plays a fundamentally important role in data mining. Through automatically generating the concept hierarchies, the mining efficiency is improved, and the knowledge is discovered at different abstraction levels. In this paper, the Boolean calculation of cloud models is used to generate the concept tree, that is, cloud transformation is realized to automatically produce discrete concept items as the leaf nodes of the tree. Furthermore, series trend is expressed in concept symbols that hold fuzziness and randomness that avoids rigid segmentation. Not only dimension reduction, but robustness to the data noise is achieved.

It may be interesting to extend our work to the application in clustering, classification and associate rule discovering.

References

1. Han, J., Fu, Y.: Dynamic Generation and Refinement of Concept Hierarchies for Knowledge Discovery in Databases. Proceeding of the KDD'94, Seattle, WA (1994) 157-168
2. Cheung, D., Fu, Y., Han, J.: Knowledge Discovery in Database: a Rule-based Attribute-oriented Approach. Proceedings of the International Symposium on Methodologies for Intelligent Systems, Charlotte, NC (1994) 164-173
3. Li ,D., Cheung, D., Shi, X.: Uncertainty Reasoning Based on Cloud Models in Controllers. Computer Math. Applic, Vol. 3 (1998) 99-123
4. Keogh, E., Lin, J., Fu, A.: HOT SAX: Efficiently Finding the Most Unusual Time Series Subsequence. Proceedings of the 5th IEEE International Conference on Data Mining, Texas (2005) 226-233
5. Jiang, R., Li, D., Fan, J.: Automation Generation of Pan-Concept-Tree on Numerical Data. Chinese J. Computer, Vol. 5 (2000) 470-476
6. Chiu, B., Keogh, E., Lonardi, S.: Probabilistic Discovery of Time Series Motifs. 9th ACM SIGKDD International Conference on Knowledge Discovery and Data Mining. Washington, DC (2003) 493-498

POCS Super-Resolution Sequence Image Reconstruction Based on Image Registration Excluded Aliased Frequency Domain

Chong Fan[1,2], Jianya Gong[2], Jianjun Zhu[1], and Lihua Zhang[2,3]

[1] Department of Surveying and Land Information Engineering, Central South University, Changsha, Hunan, 410083, China

[2] State Key Laboratory of Information Engineering in Surveying, Mapping and Remote Sensing, Wuhan University, Wuhan, Hubei, 430079, China

[3] Dept. of Hydrography and Cartography, Dalian Naval Academy, 667, Jiefang Road, Dalian, Liaoning, 116018, China

Abstract. This paper introduces the theory of super-resolution image reconstruction and degraded model in brief, and presents a new super-resolution image reconstruction algorithm .The algorithm bases on the new image registration excluded aliased frequency domain and the Projection Onto Convex Set (POCS) method. The algorithm can precisely estimate the image registration parameter by excluding aliased frequency domain of the low-resolution images and killing the center part of the magnitude spectrum. In order to compute the shifts and the rotation angle, we set up the polar coordinates in the center of the image. By computing the frequency function of the rotation angle by integrating over radial lines, the algorithm converts the two-dimension correlation to one-dimension correlation. And then, the POCS method is used to reconstruct high-resolution image from these aliased image sequences. As a result, we find that the reconstruction algorithm has the same precision of image registration as the spatial image registration and good effect of super-resolution image reconstruction.

1 Introduction

In 1984, Tsai and Huang [1] introduced the idea of super-resolution based on sequence images firstly. They used the frequency domain approach to demonstrate the ability to reconstruct one improved resolution image from several blurred, down sampled and noisy images. The different approach method of the super-resolution reconstruction is iterative back projection (IBP) method, which was adopted from computer-aided topography (CAT) by Peleg [2]. This method starts with an initial guess of the output image, projects the temporary result to the measurements (simulating them), and updates the temporary guess according to this simulation error. Another approach of the super-resolution reconstruction is presented by Schultz and Stevenson [3]. Their approach uses MAP estimator, with the Huber-Markov Random Field (HMRF) prior. This choice of prior causes the entire problem to be nonquadratic, thus complicating the resulting minimization problem. Set theoretic approach to the super-resolution reconstruction was also presented. The method defines convex sets that

D.-S. Huang, K. Li, and G.W. Irwin (Eds.): ICIC 2006, LNAI 4114, pp. 1240 – 1245, 2006.

represent tight constraints on the required image. Having such constraints, it is straightforward to apply the POCS method [4]. Therefore, through these super-resolution reconstruction methods, image details can be retrieved so much that the restored image is greatly close to the original object.

Most super-resolution methods are composed of two main steps. Firstly, all the images are aligned in the same coordinate system in the registration step, and then a high-resolution image is reconstructed from the irregular set of samples. In the first step, we present an image registration algorithm using a new frequency domain method that is as good as the spatial domain method if the images have some directionality. In this second step, to reconstruct the high-resolution image, we apply POCS method on a high-resolution grid. The super-resolution algorithm we propose reconstructs an image with almost double resolution in both dimensions from four aliased images. At last, we compare our approach in a simulation to the image magnified by linear interpolation.

2 Image Registration

We use a frequency-domain algorithm to estimate the motion parameters between the reference image and each of the other images. Only planar motion parallel to the image plane is allowed. The motion can be described as a function of three parameters: horizontal and vertical shifts Δx and Δy and a planar rotation angle ϕ. A frequency domain approach allows us to estimate the horizontal and vertical shift and the (planar) rotation separately. Assume we have a reference signal $f_1(X)$ and it's shifted and rotated version $f_2(X)$:

$$f_2(X) = f_1(R(X + \Delta X)) \ . \tag{1}$$

where $X = [x \quad y]^T$, $\Delta X = [\Delta x \quad \Delta y]^T$, $R = [\cos\phi \quad -\sin\phi; \ \sin\phi \quad \cos\phi]^T$. In Fourier domain it can be translated as:

$$F_2(u) = e^{i2\pi u^T \Delta X} F_1(u) \ . \tag{2}$$

$$|F_2(u)| = \left| e^{i2\pi u^T \Delta X} \iint_{\infty} f_1(RX')e^{-i2\pi u^T X'} dx' \right| = |F_1(Ru)| \ . \tag{3}$$

Where $X' = X + \Delta X$. As a result, we can conclude that $|F_2(u)|$ and $|F_1(Ru)|$ do not depend on the shift values Δx and Δy, because the spatial domain shifts only affect the phase values of the Fourier transforms. For example, we perfect Fourier transform in an image and its rotated image respectively. We can find that the magnitude rotate the same angle (Fig. 1(a)). It is well known that the shift parameters Δx and Δy can thus be computed as the slope of the phase difference and the rotation angle can be computed as the rotation of the magnitude.

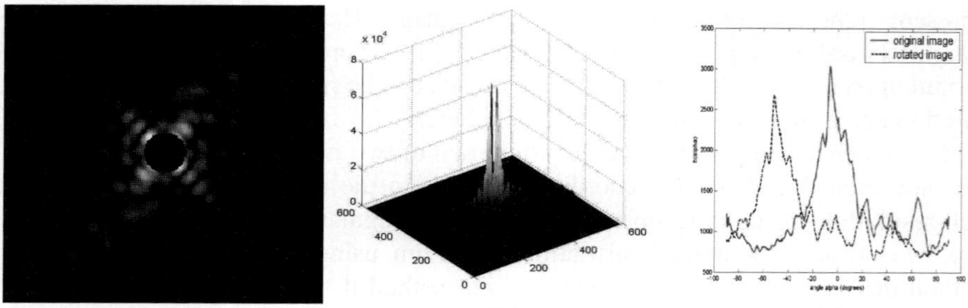

(a) (b) (c)

Fig. 1. (a) The magnitude of the original image. (b) The magnitude of and the rotated image in view of three dimensions. (c)The $h(\alpha)$ of the original image and the rotated image.

Unfortunately, owing to the affection of downsampling, the low-resolution images are aliased .The methods described earlier do not result in precise registration anymore [5]. In this case, (1) and (2) no longer hold. Instead of (2), a shift is now expressed as:

$$F_2(u) = \sum_{-\infty}^{+\infty} e^{i2\pi(u-ku_s)^T \Delta x} F_1(u - ku_s) \; . \tag{4}$$

In order to compute the shifts and the rotation angle, we should cut off the aliased zone. So we can apply the formula (2) and (3). To computer the rotation angle, we present a new method. First of all, we set up the polar coordinates in the center of the image, and compute the frequency content h as a function of the angle α by integrating over radial lines:

$$h(\alpha) = \sum | F(r,\theta) | ; \alpha - \Delta\alpha/2 \le \theta \le \alpha + \Delta\alpha/2 \; . \tag{5}$$

Where $\Delta\alpha$ is the calculating precise of the rotated angle. As the values for low frequencies are very large compared to the other values (Fig. 1(b)) and are very coarsely sampled as a function of the angle, we discard the values for which $r < \varepsilon\rho$ (where ρ is the image radius, or half the image size) with $\varepsilon = 0.1$. Thus, $h(\alpha)$ is computed as the average of the frequency values on a discrete grid with $\alpha - \Delta\alpha/2 \le \theta \le \alpha + \Delta\alpha/2$ and $\varepsilon\rho < r < \rho$. This results in a function $h(\alpha)$ for both $|F_2(u)|$ and $|F_2(r,\theta)|$ (Fig.1 (c)). The exact rotation angle can be computed as the value for which their correlation reaches a maximum.

3 POCS Super-Resolution Sequence Image Reconstruction

In the POCS super-resolution reconstruction approach, the unknown signal $f(x, y)$ is assumed to be an element of an appropriate Hilbert space. Each a priori information or constraint restricts the solution to a closed convex set in H. Thus, for m pieces of information, there are m corresponding closed convex sets $C_i \in H$,i = 1,2,…m and $f \in C_0 = \bigcap_{i=1}^{m} C_i$,provided that the intersection C_0 is nonempty. Given the constraint sets C, and their respective projection operators P_i , the sequence generated by [6]

$$f_{k+1} = P_m P_{m-1} \ldots P_1 f_k \ . \tag{6}$$

Where $T_i = (1-\lambda_i)I + \lambda_i P_i, 0 < \lambda_i < 2$ is the relaxed projection operator, converges weakly to a feasible solution in the intersection C_0 of the constraint sets. Indeed, any solution in the intersection set is consistent with the a priori constraints, and therefore, it is a feasible solution. Note that $T_i^{'}s$ reduce to $P_i^{'}s$ for unity relaxation parameters, i.e., $\lambda_i = 1$. The initialization f_0 can be arbitrarily chosen from H.

Translating the above description to an analytical model, we get:

$$f_{k+1} = P\left[f_k + \sum_{i=1}^{p} \lambda_k \omega_i P(g_i - H_i f_k) \right] . \tag{7}$$

Where P represents band-limited operator of image, g_i represents the ith measured low resolution image, λ_k represents the relaxed operator, H_i represents a blurring operator determined by the PSF, downsampling and transformation of the ith measured low resolution image, ω_i represents the weights.

4 Experiment and Discussions

The super-resolution algorithm described above is tested in simulations experiments. A simulation gives complete control over the setup and gives exact knowledge of the registration parameters. In the first step, we compare our registration method with the keren iterative registration algorithm [7], which is a very popular spatial registration method in image super-resolution reconstruction. It enables us to test the performance of the registration and the reconstruction algorithms separately. In the simulation, we start from a high-resolution image Lena, which was considered as the equivalent for continuous space (Fig. 2(a)). This image was then multiplied by a Tukey window to make the image circularly symmetric and thus avoiding all boundary effects. Then, three shifted and rotated copies are created from this high-resolution image. Then, the four images are blurred by the simulative Point Spread Function, downsampled by a factor two and added Guassian noise .The first of these images will be magnified by linear interpolation (Fig. 2(b)). And finally, the four images are used as input for the POCS super-resolution algorithm .As a result, we find that our registration algorithm has the same precise as keren spatial registration algorithm (Table .1). And our reconstruction image is better than the image, which is magnified by linear interpolation (Fig. 2(c)).

Table 1. The results of keren iterative registration algorithm and registration algorithm excluded aliased frequency domain. Δx , Δy and ϕ is the shift value and rotated angle. μ_x , μ_y and μ_ϕ are the registration absolute error of them the unit of Δx , Δy , μ_x and μ_y is pixel, and the unit of ϕ and μ_ϕ is degree.

Δx	Δy	ϕ	Keren Iterative Registration Algorithm			Our Registration Algorithm		
			μ_x	μ_y	μ_ϕ	μ_x	μ_y	μ_ϕ
3.125	-1.875	15	-0.0750	-0.1421	0.3893	0.0645	0.0897	0.3761
0.875	2.250	-3	-0.0160	0.0813	-0.2560	0.0026	0.0654	0.2641
-1.500	0.500	2	0.0084	-0.0691	0.2728	0.0223	0.0137	0.2460

(a) (b) (c)

Fig. 2. (a) The original high resolution lena image added Tukey window. (b)the linear interpolation image. (c)the POCS super-resolution reconstruction image based on the registration algorithm excluded aliased frequency domain.

5 Conclusion

We presented a new Image Registration method by excluding aliased frequency domain of a set of low resolution, aliased images. The planar rotation and shift parameters can be precisely estimated based on the low frequency, aliasing-free part of the images. In this correspondence, we reconstructed a double resolution image (in each dimension) from the set of aliased images by POCS algorithm .Our experimental results show that the proposed super- resolution algorithm performs effective reconstruction.

Acknowledgments

This work is supported by program of National Natural Science Foundation Of China (No.40574003).

References

1. Tsai R Y., Huang T S.: Multiframe Image Restoration and Registration. Advances in Computer Vision and Image Processing, Vol 1 (1984) 101-106
2. Irani M., Peleg S.: Improving Resolution By Image Registration. CVGIP: Graphical Models and Image Processing,Vol 53 (1991) 231-239
3. Schultz R R., Meng L., Stevenson R. L.: Subpixel Motion Estimation For Super-Resolution Image Sequence Enhancement. Journal of Visual Communication and Image Representation, Vol 9 (1998) 38-51
4. Patti A J., Sezan M I., Tekalp A M.: Superresolution Video Reconstruction With Arbitrary Sampling Lattices And Nonzero Aperture Time. IEEE Transactions on Image Processing, Vol 6 (1997) 1064-1076
5. Vandewalle P., Susstrunk S., Vetterli M.: Super Resolution Images Reconstructed From Aliased Images. Visual Communication and Image Processing Conference in SPIE/IS&T, vol. 5150 (2003) 1398-1405
6. Stark H., OskouI P.: High Resolution Image Recovery From Image Plane Arrays Using Convex Projections. Journal of the Optical Society of American, Vol 6(11) (1989) 1715-1726
7. Keren D., Peleg S., Brada R.: Image Sequence Enhancement Using Sub-Pixel Displacement. Proceedings IEEE Conference on Computer Vision and Pattern Recognition, (1988) 742-746

The Cooperative Optimization Metaheuristic: Inspiration from Nature and Applications

Xiaofei Huang

Coding Research
Foster City, CA 94404, U.S.A.
huangxiaofei@ieee.org

Abstract. The cooperative optimization is a newly discovered metaheuristic for solving difficult combinatorial optimization problems. It is inspired by the cooperation principle in social systems where individuals in a system often work together in a cooperative way to solve hard problems of a complexity beyond the capability of any individual in the system. Unlike any existing metaheuristics, it has a number of global optimality conditions so that the cooperative optimization algorithms know where to find global optima and when to stop searching. Furthermore, a cooperative optimization algorithm has a unique equilibrium and converges to it with an exponential rate regardless of initial conditions and perturbations. In solving real-world optimization problems, the cooperative optimization algorithms have often significantly outperformed state-of-the-art algorithms.

1 Introduction

A metaheuristic is a general, problem independent heuristic method for finding approximate solutions for optimization problems. Unlike problem-specific heuristics, metaheuristic methods are applicable to a wide range of optimization problems. Popular metaheuristics [1] include simulated annealing, branch-and-bound, tabu search, ant colony optimization [2], genetic algorithms, and particle swarm intelligence [3]. They have been proven very useful in solving many interesting optimization problems.

The lack of general global optimality conditions for identifying global optima is the most critical, unsolved problem of classic (meta-)heuristic methods. Without any global optimality condition, they do not know where to find global optima and whether a solution they found is a global optimum. Because of that, they do not know how to organize their optimization processes effectively and when to terminate the processes efficiently. Any global optimality condition is of both practical interests and theoretical importance.

The recently found cooperative optimization metaheuristic [4,5,6,7,8] solves this important problem by offering a number of global optimality conditions. It also provides a general framework for designing optimization algorithms to attack different optimization problems. The cooperative optimization algorithms have many excellent computational properties, most of them are not possessed by any classical optimization methods. This paper describes more about the

D.-S. Huang, K. Li, and G.W. Irwin (Eds.): ICIC 2006, LNAI 4114, pp. 1246–1251, 2006.

intuitions behind the nature-inspired metaheuristic. The successful applications of cooperative optimization are also reported at solving two real-world, NP-hard optimization problems. One of them is the stereo-matching problem from computer vision and the another is the LDPC decoding problem from data communications.

2 Cooperative Optimization as a Metaheuristic

2.1 Basic Ideas

Competition and cooperation are common social behaviors for individuals in a society. Through competition and cooperation among individuals, nature has evolved a number of relatively simple but powerful methods for solving very complex problems. In many cases, those problems can be understood as optimization problems formulated as the minimization or maximization of certain objective functions.

Usually, competition or cooperation alone can hardly lead to good solutions either for a society or for the individuals in the society. Without competition, individuals in a society may lose motivation to pursue better solutions. Without cooperation, they might directly conflict with each other and poor solutions might be reached both for the society and themselves. Often times, through properly balanced competition and cooperation individuals in a society can find the best solutions for the society and possibly good solutions for themselves at the same time.

In a cooperative system, each individual has its own objective. The collection of all individual's objectives form the objective of the system. The objectives of individuals may not be always aligned with each other. The individuals in a cooperative system work together by finding solutions to achieve their own objectives (competition) and compromising their own solutions with their neighbors' solutions at the same time (cooperation). Such a process is iterative and self-organized and each individual in the system is autonomous.

A cooperative system can have many interesting behaviors emerging from simple local interactions of the individuals in the system. Despite of their simplicity, cooperative systems can attack many very challenging optimization problems through competition and cooperation among the individuals in a system. Also, the computations of cooperative systems are inherently distributed and parallel, making the entire system highly scalable and less vulnerable to perturbations and disruptions on individuals than a centralized system.

2.2 Cooperative Optimization in a General Form

Assume that the objective of each individual in a cooperative system is to minimize a local objective function $E_i(x)$ associated with the individual. The summation of the local objective functions is the objective function of the system, called the global objective function, i.e., $E(x) = \sum_i E_i(x)$.

The objective of the system is to minimize the global objective function $E(x)$. Assume further that each individual controls the assignment of one variable, one individual for each variable in $E(x)$. The individual i, for instance, controls the assignment for the variable x_i. The variable x_i is said to be the controlled variable of the individual i. The preferences for assigning the variable x_i with different values by the individual i are stored in a real-valued function, denoted as $\Psi_i(x_i)$, called the soft assignment function. It is the solution of the individual i for assigning variable x_i.

Assume that x_i is in a finite domain D_i. Let the set of the variables contained in the local objective function $E_i(x)$ be X_i. Let $X_i \setminus x_i$ denote the set X_i without the element x_i. The value of the local objective function $E_i(x)$ depends on the assignments for the variables in X_i. The individual i only controls the assignment for the variable x_i. The variables in the set $X_i \setminus x_i$ are controlled by other individuals. They are called the dependent variables of the individual i.

During initialization, the solution searching is achieved by minimizing the local objective functions $E_i(x)$,

$$\Psi_i^{(0)}(x_i) = \min_{X_i \setminus x_i} E_i(x), \quad \text{for each } x_i \in D_i \ .$$

Here the minimization stands for minimizing $E_i(x)$ with respect to all variables in $X_i \setminus x_i$, for each value of x_i. The solution of the individual i is stored as the soft assignment function $\Psi_i^{(0)}(x_i)$, where the superscript stands for the iteration step.

Let the neighbors of the individual i be $\mathcal{N}(i)$. During each iteration k, each individual modifies its local objective function by the linear combination of its own local objective function $E_i(x)$ and the solutions $\Psi_j^{(k-1)}(x_j)$ from its neighbors as follows,

$$\tilde{E}_i^{(k)}(x) = (1 - \lambda_k) E_i(x) + \lambda_k \sum_{j \in \mathcal{N}(i)} w_{ij} \Psi_j^{(k-1)}(x_j) \ , \tag{1}$$

where $\tilde{E}_i^{(k)}(x)$ is the modified local objective function for the individual i at the iteration k. Parameter w_{ij} is a coefficient of the combination determining the weight on the solution of the individual j, $\Psi_j^{(k-1)}(x_j)$, at the previous iteration $k-1$, where the individual j is a neighbor of the individual i. w_{ij} is non-negative and $(w_{ij})_{n \times n}$ forms a $n \times n$ square matrix with non-negative elements, called the propagation matrix. Parameter λ_k is also a coefficient of the combination controlling the level of the cooperation among individuals at the iteration k. It is called the cooperation strength, satisfying $0 \leq \lambda_k < 1$. A higher value for λ_k will weigh the solutions $\Psi_j^{(k-1)}(x_j)$ from an individual's neighbors more than its own local objective function $E_i(x)$. In other words, the solution of each individual will compromise more with the solutions of other individuals in the system. As a consequence, a higher level of cooperation in the optimization is thus reached.

Putting the local objective function modification and minimization together, a cooperative optimization algorithm can be simply defined as the following set of difference equations:

$$\Psi_i^{(k)}(x_i) = \min_{x_j \in X_i \setminus x_i} \left((1-\lambda_k)\, E_i + \lambda_k \sum_j w_{ij} \Psi_j^{(k-1)}(x_j) \right), \tag{2}$$

$$\text{for each } x_i \in D_i \text{ and } 1 \leq i \leq n.$$

The candidate assignment for the variable x_i at the iteration k is $\arg\min_{x_i} \Psi_i^{(k)}(x_i)$. All candidate assignments form the candidate solution at the iteration, simply denoted as $(\arg\min_{x_i} \Psi_i^{(k)}(x_i))$.

The pseudo code of the algorithm is in Fig. 1.

Procedure Cooperative Optimization Algorithm
Initialize the soft assignment functions $(\Psi_i^{(0)}(x_i))$;
for $k := 1$ to *max_iteration* **do**
  for each i **do**
    for each $x_i \in D_i$ **do**
      $\Psi_i^{(k)}(x_i) := \min_{X_i \setminus x_i} (1-\lambda_k) E_i(x) + \lambda_k \sum_j w_{ij} \Psi_i^{(k-1)}(x_i)$;
  $x := (\arg\min_{x_i} \Psi_i^{(k)}(x_i))$; /* update candidate solution */
  if x is a global optimal solution (see [6]) **return** x; /* as an optimal solution */
return x; /* as an approximate solution */

Fig. 1. A cooperative optimization algorithm for minimizing the function $\sum_{i=1}^{n} E_i(x)$

3 Solving Real-World NP-Hard Problems

It has been found in our experiments [6,7,9] that cooperative optimization has achieved unprecedent performance at solving real-world NP-hard problems with the number of variables ranging from thousands to hundreds of thousands. The problems span a wide range of areas, proving its generality and power.

Stereo matching [7,6], is one of the most active research areas in computer vision.The goal of stereo matching is to recover the depth image of a scene from a pair of 2-D images of the same scene taken from two different locations. Like many other problems from computer vision, it can be formulated as the optimization of multivariate energy functions, which is NP-hard in computational complexity. Using a common framework[10] for evaluating different optimization algorithms, cooperative optimization is significantly better both in speed and solution quality than simulated annealing, a classic metaheuristic method offered by the framework as a reference. Figure 2 shows the result of cooperative optimization and simulated annealing for a test optimization problem with $110,592$ variables.

LDPC codes represent recent progress in channel coding for the next generation communication systems (HDTV,3G,HD-DVD, WLAN). Decoding LDPC codes is another real-world NP-hard problem. Because only the global optima are acceptable for this problem, no one has ever reported any success at applying classic metaheuristic methods for solving this very challenging optimization problem. The belief propagation [11,12] is the state-of-the-art algorithm for

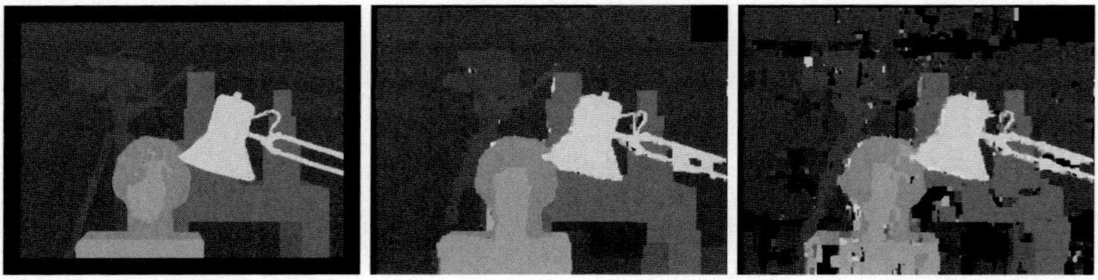

Fig. 2. The ground truth (left). Our algorithm (middle). Simulated annealing (right).

Fig. 3. A sample image corrupted by the additive white Gaussian noise channel of the signal-to-noise rate $Eb/No = 1.8\ dB$ (left). Belief propagation (middle). Cooperative optimization (right).

solving this problem. It is based on empirical rules without much theoretical understandings. We found in our experiments that the cooperative optimization algorithms have often outperformed the belief propagation algorithm both in speed and performance by several orders of magnitude. Figure 3 shows the result of the belief propagation algorithm and our cooperative optimization algorithm at decoding a sample noisy image where the associated optimization problems have $6,500$ to $7,500$ variables.

4 Conclusions and Future Research

The cooperative optimization is a newly discovered, nature inspired metaheuristic for solving hard optimization problems. In real-world applications, it has demonstrated outstanding performance comparable with the state-of-the-art algorithms or significantly better by several orders of magnitude. It has a number of global optimality conditions for identifying global optima, a critical computational property missing in existing optimization methods.

Optimization has a profound impact in every aspects of science and our life. The great challenge in the area of optimization is to discover a general principle for finding global optima because none has ever being found so far. Could cooperative optimization be the one to serve that purpose?

To create life and intelligence, nature demands global optimization processes so that proteins can fold into their designated structures to create life (Levinthal's Paradox) and perception systems of living beings can correctly understand their environments to survive. Could the cooperative optimization theory help us understand deep principles of nature?

It has also been found in our experiments that cooperative optimization has demonstrated asymptotic behaviors at solving the NP-hard problem, LDPC decoding, when problem instances are generated under Shannon channel capacity. Could Shannon channel capacity define a new dimension to measure the complexity of NP-hard problems and could cooperative optimization offer us a promising direction to attack NP-hard problems along that new dimension? These are interesting questions worth pursuing with future research.

References

1. Pardalos, P., Resende, M.: Handbook of Applied Optimization. Oxford University Press, Inc. (2002)
2. Dorigo, M., Stützle, T.: Ant Colony Optimization. The MIT Press, Cambridge, Massachusetts, London, England (2004)
3. Eberhart, R.C., Shi, Y., Kennedy, J.: Swarm Intelligence. Morgan Kaufmann (2001)
4. Huang, X.: A polynomial-time Algorithm for Solving Np-hard Problems in Practice. SIGACT Newsletter **34** (2003) 101–108
5. Huang, X.: A General Framework for Constructing Cooperative Global Optimization Algorithms. In: Frontiers in Global Optimization. Nonconvex Optimization and Its Applications. Kluwer Academic Publishers (2004) 179–221
6. Huang, X.: Cooperative Optimization for Solving Large Scale Combinatorial Problems. In: Theory and Algorithms for Cooperative Systems. Series on Computers and Operations Research. World Scientific (2004) 117–156
7. Huang, X.: Cooperative Optimization for Energy Minimization in Computer Vision: A case study of stereo matching. In: Pattern Recognition, 26th DAGM Symposium, Springer-Verlag, LNCS 3175 (2004) 302–309
8. Huang, X.: A General Extension of Constraint Propagation for Constraint Optimization. In Wallace, M., ed.: Principles of Practice of Constraint Programming - CP 2004, Springer-Verlag, LNCS 3258 (2004) 737–741
9. Huang, X.: Near Perfect Decoding of Ldpc Codes. In: Proceedings of IEEE International Symposium on Information Theory (ISIT). (2005) 302–306
10. Scharstein, D., Szeliski, R.: A taxonomy and evaluation of dense two-frame stereo correspondence algorithms. IJCV **47** (2002) 7–42
11. Pearl, J.: Probabilistic Reasoning in Intelligent Systems: Networks of Plausible Inference. Morgan Kaufmann (1988)
12. Kschischang, F.R., Frey, B.J., andrea Loeliger, H.: Factor Graphs and the Sum-product Algorithm. IEEE Transactions on Information Theory **47** (2001) 498–519
13. Axelrod, R.: The Evolution of Cooperation. Basic Books (1984)

Use APEX Neural Networks to Extract the PN Sequence in Lower SNR DS-SS Signals

Tianqi Zhang[1], Zengshan Tian[1], Qianbin Chen[1], Xiaokang Lin[2], and Zhengzhong Zhou[3]

[1] School of Communication and Information Engineering / Research Centre for Optical Internet and Wireless Information Networks (COIWIN), Chongqing University of Posts and Telecommunications (CQUPT), Chongqing, 400065, China
zhangtianqi@tsinghua.org.cn
[2] Graduate School at Shenzhen of Tsinghua University, Shenzhen 518055, China
[3] School of Communication and Information Engineering, University of Electronic Science and Technology of China (UESTC), Chengdu 610054, China

Abstract. This paper introduces an unsupervised adaptive principal components analysis (APEX) neural network (NN) for blind pseudo noise (PN) sequence extraction of lower signal to noise ratios (SNR) direct sequence spread spectrum (DS-SS) signals. The proposed method is based on eigen-analysis of DS-SS signals. As the eigen-analysis method is based on the decomposition of autocorrelation matrix of signals, it has computational defects when the signal vectors became longer, etc. So, we introduce the APEX NN to extract the PN sequence blindly. We also make complexity analysis of the proposed method and comparison with the other methods. Theoretical analysis and computer simulations verify the effectiveness of the method.

1 Introduction

Since the direct sequence spread spectrum (DS-SS, DS) signals have the distinguished capability of anti-jamming and lower probability interception, the DS signals have used broadly in communication and radar etc for a long time. Usually, the spread spectrum receiver has to perform synchronization before it can start the despreading operation. For the case of DS, this entails establishing complete knowledge of the pseudo noise (PN) sequence and the timing. Synchronization is performed in two stages. The first stage of coarse synchronization is known as PN acquisition and the final stage of maintaining the fine synchronization is called PN tracking. While PN tracking forms an important part of DS synchronization, PN acquisition is a more challenging problem.

Conventional acquisition techniques **[1]** rely on the knowledge of the internal algebraic structure of the PN sequence to establish synchronization. But they tend to break down in environments with high levels of noise and interference because of a high false alarm rate. Besides, reliable algebraic techniques for synchronization have yet to be developed for nonlinear codes, or codes with unknown code structure etc.

A method of cyclic autocorrelation was proposed to de-spread the DS signal [2]. It can operate in the presence of arbitrary delay and for arbitrary PN codes. Because some

D.-S. Huang, K. Li, and G.W. Irwin (Eds.): ICIC 2006, LNAI 4114, pp. 1252 – 1257, 2006.

spectral correlation computations are required, it is difficult to carry out in real-time. Furthermore, it does only de-spread the DS signal without the PN sequence, but it doesn't utilize or analyze any signal structure information. DS packet radio and military systems often require frequent, fast and robust synchronization. Blind estimation of the PN sequence without the a priori knowledge of its structure and timing is useful in achieving these objectives. The signal subspace analysis technique, introduced in [3], is precisely such a technique. But this method belongs to a batch method, when the number of samples in a period of observation window or the length of PN sequence becomes larger, the computation of matrix decomposition may not be feasible in practice.

In this paper, we first prove that the PN sequence can be estimated blindly by eigen-analysis. Furthermore, we implement the estimation via an unsupervised adaptive principal components analysis (APEX) neural network (NN) through principal components extraction of DS signals. We overcome difficulties about computational memory size and speed of the eigen-analysis method in case of longer received signal vectors. We assume that the signal is the same as [2,3].

2 Signal Model

The base band DS signal $x(t)$ corrupted by the additive white Gaussian noise (AWGN) $n(t)$ with the zero mean and σ_n^2 variance can be expressed as [1,3]

$$x(t) = s(t - T_x) + n(t), \tag{1}$$

where $s(t) = d(t)p(t)$ is the DS signal, $p(t) = \sum_{j=-\infty}^{\infty} p_j q(t - jT_c)$, $p_j \in \{\pm 1\}$ is the PN sequence, $d(t) = \sum_{k=-\infty}^{\infty} m_k q(t - kT_0)$, $m_k \in \{\pm 1\}$ is uniformly distributed with $E[m_k m_l] = \delta(k-l)$, $\delta(\cdot)$ is the Dirac function, $q(t)$ denotes a pulse chip with period of T (T may be T_0 or T_c here). Where $T_0 = NT_c$, N is the length of PN sequence, T_0 is its period, T_c is the chip duration, T_x is the random time delay and uniformly distributed on the $[0, T_0]$.

In general, the PN sequence and synchronization are required to de-spread the DS signals. But we only have the knowledge of T_0, T_c and the received DS signals.

3 Eigen-Analysis Method to PN Sequence Blind Estimation

The received DS signal is sampled and divided into non-overlapping temporal windows, the duration of which is T_0. Then one of the received signal vector is

$$\mathbf{X}(k) = \mathbf{s}(k) + \mathbf{n}(k), \quad k = 1, 2, 3, \cdots, \tag{2}$$

where $\mathbf{s}(k)$ is the k-th useful signal vector, $\mathbf{n}(k)$ is the AWGN vector, $\mathbf{X}(k) \in \mathbf{R}^N$. When $0 \le T_x < T_0$, $\mathbf{s}(k)$ may contain two consecutive symbol bits, each modulated by a period of PN sequence: $\mathbf{s}(k) = m_k \mathbf{p}_1 + m_{k+1} \mathbf{p}_2$, where m_k and m_{k+1} are the two consecutive symbol bits. $\mathbf{p}_1$ ($\mathbf{p}_2$) is the right (left) part of the PN sequence waveform.

According to eigen-analysis theory, we definite the $\mathbf{u}_i$ by $\mathbf{u}_i = \mathbf{p}_i / \|\mathbf{p}_i\|$, so $\mathbf{u}_i^T \mathbf{u}_j = \delta(i-j), i, j = 1,2$, $\mathbf{u}_1$ and $\mathbf{u}_2$ are ortho-normal vectors. We have

$$\mathbf{X}(k) = m_k \|\mathbf{p}_1\| \mathbf{u}_1 + m_{k+1} \|\mathbf{p}_2\| \mathbf{u}_2 + \mathbf{n}(k). \tag{3}$$

The autocorrelation matrix of $\mathbf{X}(k)$ may be estimated by

$$\hat{\mathbf{R}}_X(M) = (1/M) \sum_{i=1}^{M} \mathbf{X}(i) \mathbf{X}^T(i). \tag{4}$$

When $M \to \infty$, there exist

$$\mathbf{R}_X = E\left[\mathbf{X}\mathbf{X}^T\right] = \lim_{M \to \infty} \hat{\mathbf{R}}_X(M) = \bar{\mathbf{U}}_s \Lambda_s \bar{\mathbf{U}}_s + \bar{\mathbf{U}}_n \Lambda_n \bar{\mathbf{U}}_n, \tag{5}$$

where M represents the sampling number of signal vectors, $E[\cdot]$ denotes expectation, $\bar{\mathbf{U}}_s = [\bar{\mathbf{u}}_1, \cdots, \bar{\mathbf{u}}_K]$ and $\Lambda_s = diag[\lambda_1, \cdots, \lambda_K]$ denote the estimated eigen-structure of signal, $\bar{\mathbf{U}}_n = [\bar{\mathbf{u}}_{K+1}, \cdots, \bar{\mathbf{u}}_N]$ and $\Lambda_n = \sigma_n^2 \mathbf{I}$ denotes the estimated noise. It is shown in [4] that the estimated principal eigenvectors have the following behavior: $\|\bar{\mathbf{u}}_i - \mathbf{u}_i\| = O\left(\sqrt{\log\log M / M}\right)$, $i = 1, 2, \cdots, K$. Therefore, $M \to \infty$, there always exists $\bar{\mathbf{u}}_i = \mathbf{u}_i$, $i = 1, 2, \cdots, K$.

Assume $\mathbf{s}(k)$, $\mathbf{n}(k)$ are mutually independent, substitute Eq.(3) into Eq.(5)

$$\hat{\mathbf{R}}_X = \bar{\mathbf{U}}_s \Lambda_s \bar{\mathbf{U}}_s^T + \bar{\mathbf{U}}_n \Lambda_n \bar{\mathbf{U}}_n^T = \sigma_n^2 \left\{ \left[\eta \cdot (T_0 - T_x)/T_c\right] \cdot \bar{\mathbf{u}}_1 \bar{\mathbf{u}}_1^T + (\eta \cdot T_x / T_c) \cdot \bar{\mathbf{u}}_2 \bar{\mathbf{u}}_2^T + \mathbf{I} \right\} \tag{6}$$

where $\mathbf{I}$ is an identity matrix of dimension $N \times N$, the expectation of m_k is zero. The variance of m_k is σ_m^2, the symbol is uncorrelated from each other. The energy of PN sequence is $E_p \approx T_c \|\mathbf{p}\|^2$, the variance of $\mathbf{s}(k)$ is $\sigma_s^2 = \sigma_m^2 E_p / T_0$, $\eta = \sigma_s^2 / \sigma_n^2$. In the end, we can recover a period PN sequence from $\bar{\mathbf{p}} = \text{sign}(\bar{\mathbf{u}}_2) + \text{sign}(\bar{\mathbf{u}}_1)$, when $T_x \neq 0$; or $\bar{\mathbf{p}}_1 = \text{sign}(\bar{\mathbf{u}}_1)$, when $T_x = 0$.

Because the estimation of $\hat{\mathbf{R}}_X$ by Eq.(4) is a de-noise process, we can estimate the PN sequence by decomposition of $\hat{\mathbf{R}}_X$ even when the signal to noise ratios is very low. However, the memory size and computational speed will become problems when N becomes bigger.

4 Implementation of the APEX Neural Networks

According to the theory results of section 3, in a general way ($T_x \neq 0$), we have to extract the first and second principal eigen-vectors before realizing a whole PN

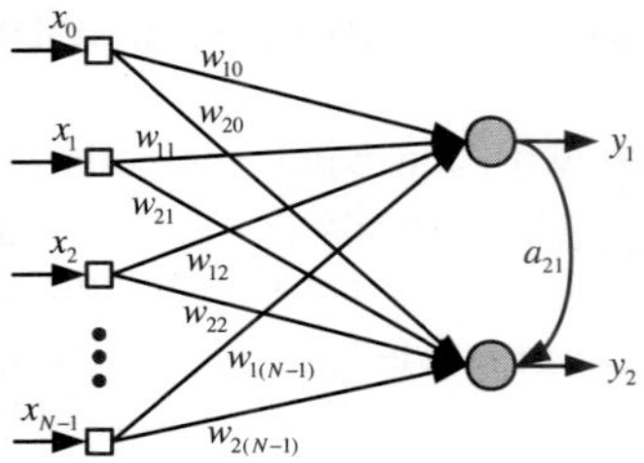

Fig. 1. Neural Networks

sequence blind estimation, so we use the following APEX NN (Fig.1) to perform estimation task. The number of input neurons is given by $N = T_0 / T_c$.

Assume the input signal vector is the same as Eq.(2):

$$\mathbf{X}(t) = \mathbf{X}(k) = \{x(t), x(t-T_c), \cdots, x[t-(N-1)T_c]\}^T = [x_0(t), x_1(t), \cdots, x_{N-1}(t)]^T \tag{7}$$

The feed-forward synaptic weight vector is $\mathbf{w}_j(t) = \left[w_{j0}(t), w_{j1}(t), \cdots, w_{j(N-1)}(t)\right]^T$, $j = 1,2$, where the sign of { $w_{ji}(t)$, $i = 0,1,\cdots,N-1$, $j = 1,2$ } denotes the *j*-th principal eigenvector *i*-th bit of estimated PN sequence.

The lateral synaptic weight vector is $\mathbf{a}_2(t) = [a_{21}(t)]^T$. The output layer of NN have two neurons, its output are

$$y_1(t) = \sum_{i=0}^{N-1} w_{1i}(t) x_i(t) = \mathbf{w}_1^T(t)\mathbf{X}(t) , \tag{8}$$

$$y_2(t) = \sum_{i=0}^{N-1} w_{2i}(t) x_i(t) + a_2(t) y_1(t) = \mathbf{w}_2^T(t)\mathbf{X}(t) + a_{21}(t) y_1(t) . \tag{9}$$

The update equations for the feed-forward weight vector $\mathbf{w}_j(t)$ and the feedback weight vector $\mathbf{a}_j(t)$ for neuron *j* are defined as, respectively,

$$\mathbf{w}_j(t+1) = \mathbf{w}_j(t) + \beta_j \left[y_j(t)\mathbf{x}(t) - y_j^2(t)\mathbf{w}_j(t)\right]^T, \quad j = 1,2, \tag{10}$$

$$\mathbf{a}_j(t+1) = \mathbf{a}_j(t) - \beta_j \left[y_j(t)\mathbf{y}_{j-1}(t) + y_j^2(t)\mathbf{a}_j(t)\right]^T, \quad j = 2, \tag{11}$$

where $\mathbf{y}_{j-1}(t) = \mathbf{y}_1(t) = [y_1(t)]^T$, $\mathbf{a}_j(t) = \mathbf{a}_2(t) = [a_{21}(t)]^T$, $j = 2$. β_j is a positive step-size parameter, it can be fixed or time-varied. In order to achieve good convergence performance, we modify β_j to

$$\beta_j = 1/d_{j(t+1)}, \quad d_{j(t+1)} = B_j d_{jt} + y_j^2(t), \quad j = 1,2 . \tag{12}$$

Eq. (10) represents Hebbian-learning, and Eq. (11) represents anti-Hebbian learning. The stability analysis of the NN of Fig.1 is detailed in [5,6]. For large t, we have $\mathbf{w}_j(t) \to \mathbf{u}_j$, $j = 1,2$, so we can recover a period PN sequence.

5 Complexity Analysis and Comparison with Other Methods

Comparison of NN methods with the batch methods described in section 3 is not straightforward because they approach the problem using different assumptions. The batch methods use the pre-calculated autocorrelation matrix $\mathbf{R}_X$, while adaptive methods don't have this a priori knowledge. Hence NN methods can essentially solve some more difficult problems. In above APEX method of blind PN sequence extraction Eq.(8) to Eq.(12), the computational complexity for a set of 2 patterns of input dimension N requires $8(N+1)$ multiplications and $6N+2$ additions per sweep, which is actually less than the total complexity of the batch methods (e.g. SVD or EVD, has complexity $O(6N^3)$), and in addition, all batch methods implicitly require an initial step for the computation of $\mathbf{R}_X$ which has $O(MN^2)$ complexity. When N becomes bigger, the batch methods may not be feasible actually. And in addition, the NN methods are very promising candidates for parallel VLSI implementation. This is an advantage over some classical batch methods.

The APEX method of blind PN sequence extraction has advantages over the other NN methods is as follows [6]: a) Allows recursive computation of new components as opposed to some other models. It also overcomes the problem Oja's model in being capable of computing the rest of the components (apart from the first). b) The numerical study regarding the best learning rate gives a powerful estimate of the optimal β, which results into impressive convergence speeds. Such numerical analysis is lacking from the other models. c) The method is even more general in that it can be used for extracting the constraint principal components of a random process -- a useful notion for certain applications.

6 Simulations and Conclusions

Simulations: Simulations were carried out to determine the performance of the proposed extractor. The prime measure of performance is the time taken for the extractor to make a perfect estimate of the spreading sequence. From the simulations, we get performance curves when T_x/T_0=2/5.

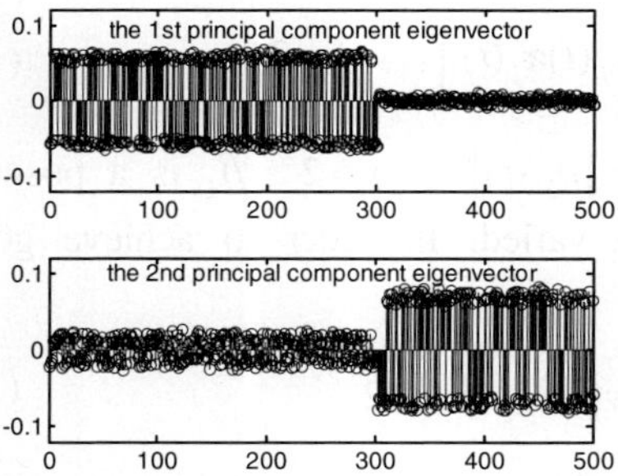

Fig. 2. 1st and 2nd principal component vectors

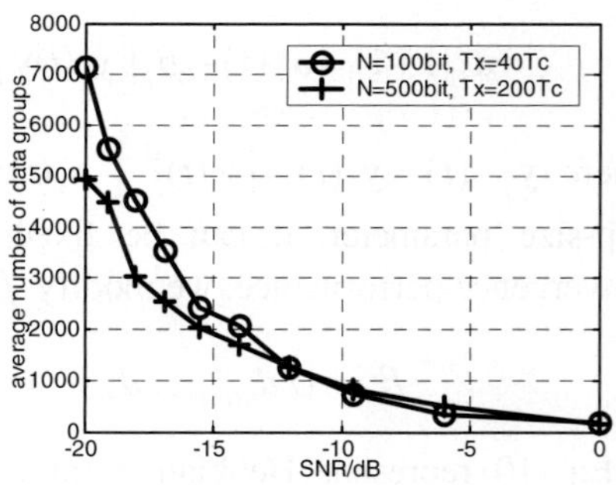

Fig. 3. Performance curves

Fig.2 denote the 1st and 2nd principal eigenvector with $N=500bit$ at $T_x/T_0=2/5$ respectively. Fig.3 shows the time taken for the extractor to perfectly extract the PN sequence for code lengths $N=100$ and $N=500$ at $T_x/T_0=2/5$. Perfect estimation is achieved when the signs of NN synaptic weights are the desired PN sequence or its logical complements. It is shown that under the same conditions, the longer of the PN sequence is, the better the performance is.

Conclusions: Under common circumstances, if we have known PN sequence, we can obtain -20dB～-30dB of *SNR* threshold when we de-spread the received DS signals. In [2] Gardner used the method of "blind de-spreading" to achieve –15dB of the *SNR* threshold, but on the same condition, we can realize threshold of $SNR = -20.0dB$ easily, hence the performance of the methods in this paper is better. Besides this, the NN has higher speed than the matrix decomposition method; it can solve the difficult problem of longer PN sequence blind extraction perfectly. In addition the method requires no a priori knowledge other than knowledge of the code length.

Acknowledgments

This work is supported by the Natural Science Foundation of Chongqing University of Posts and Telecommunications (CQUPT) (No. A2006-04), and the Natural Science Foundation of Chongqing Education Committee (No. KJ060509).

References

1. Simon M.K., Omura J.K., Scholtz R.A., Levitt B.K.: Spread Spectrum Communications Handbook. New York, McGraw-Hill (1994)
2. French, C.A., Gardner, W.A.: Spread-Spectrum Despreading without the Code. IEEE Trans. on Communications.34 (1986) 404-407
3. Zhang, T.Q., Lin, X.K., Zhou, Z.Z.: Blind Estimation of the PN Sequence in Lower SNR DS/SS Signals. IEICE Transaction On Communications, E88-B. (2005) 3087-3089
4. Anderson, T.W.: Asymptotic Theory for Principal Component Analysis. Ann. Math. Statist. 35 (1963) 1296-1303
5. Haykin, S.: Neural Networks-A Comprehensive Foundation. Prentice Hall PTR, Upper Saddle River, NJ, USA (1999)
6. Kung, S.Y., Diamantaras, K.I., Taur, J.S.: Adaptive Principal Component Extraction (APEX) and Applications. IEEE Trans. on Signal Processing. 42 (1994) 1202-1216

A New Chain-Based Data Gathering Protocol for Wireless Sensor Transportation Monitoring Network*

Lingyun Yuan[1,2], Sufen Li[1], and Yunlong Zhu[1]

[1] Shenyang Institute of Automation, Chinese Academy of Sciences, Shenyang
[2] Graduate school of the Chinese Academy of Sciences, Beijing
{wxcyly, lisufen, ylzhu}@sia.cn

Abstract. Data gathering is one of the most important processes in wireless sensor networks (WSN). The sensor nodes gather information and send it to a base station, which consumes significant amounts of power. Due to the limited battery life, energy efficiency is becoming a major challenging problem in WSN. Some energy- efficient data gathering protocols are proposed for WSN such as LEACH, PEGASIS, and PEDAP. But these protocols still have some disadvantages and are not fit for our application, wireless sensor transportation monitoring network (WSTMN). So we present a new chain-based data gathering protocol, CBDGP. The minimum total energy algorithm (MTEA) is used to construct the chain. Moreover, the layered minimum total energy chain construction algorithm with delay reducing is presented for CBDGP. The results show that CBDGP works for WSTMN better than LEACH and PEGASIS. It prolongs the lifetime and reduces the delay of WSTMN.

1 Introduction

The recent advances in micro-sensor, MEMS and low-power wireless communication, have promoted the development of wireless sensor networks (WSN). Wireless sensor networks are consisted of hundreds of inexpensive nodes, which can be readily deployed in physical environments to collect useful information such as seismic, acoustic, medical and surveillance data in a robust and autonomous manner, and then transmit to the base station. WSN has been applied to many areas from military field to commerce and industry, such as environment monitoring, weather monitoring, tactical surveillance, and intelligent transportation monitoring. We mainly focus on intelligent transportation monitoring system based on wireless sensor network, namely, wireless sensor transportation monitoring network (WSTMN).

Wireless sensor networks are consisted of thousands of nodes which are static in general. At the same time, the wireless bandwidth and energy are restricted. Especially, those sensors are deployed in highway, which are unattended. And the power in sensor nodes can be exhausted simply by computations and transmissions. Furthermore it is infeasible to replace thousands of nodes in highway. Therefore, conserving energy so as to prolong the network lifetime is becoming one of the key

* This work is supported by the National Natural Science Foundation, China (No. 70431003) and the National Basic Research Program, China (2002CB312204).

D.-S. Huang, K. Li, and G.W. Irwin (Eds.): ICIC 2006, LNAI 4114, pp. 1258 – 1267, 2006.

challenges for such power-constrained network. Sensing environment and gathering data are the main functions in WSN. So some efficient and energy-aware data gathering protocols are proposed such as LEACH [1], PEGASIS [2], PEDAP [3] and DEEG [4], which sometimes aim at some certain applications and are not fit for WSTMN. Some conditions must be considered in wireless sensor transportation monitoring network: (a) Monitored targets (vehicles). Vehicles in highway are dynamic and move with high speed. (b) System cost. (c) Communication range. According to the above all mentioned factors, a new chain-based data gathering protocol for WSTMN is presented, namely CBDGP. CBDGP considers not only energy, but also network delay. There has a good tradeoff between the two aspects.

The paper is organized as follows. Section 2 reviews some related works. Section 3 describes the wireless sensor transportation monitoring network model and the radio model. Section 4 presents a new chain-based data gathering protocol, which is implemented in section 5. The conclusions are drawn in section 6.

2 Related Work

Several efficient data gathering routing protocols have been proposed in recent years. We can divide them into three categories approximately: cluster-based routing, chain-based routing, and tree-based routing.

LEACH is a cluster-based distributed routing protocol. In LEACH, each node elects itself as cluster-head with some probability. The remaining nodes join a cluster that requires minimum communication energy. In the data gathering process, each cluster-head collects data from sensors in its cluster, fuses the data, and then transmits the result to the base station. LEACH utilizes the randomized rotation of cluster-heads to evenly distribute the energy load among sensors in the network. Simulation results show that LEACH achieves as much as a factor of 8 reduction in energy dissipation comparing with direct transmission. As an improved version to LEACH, LEACH-C [5] uses a centralized clustering algorithm to produce better clusters, thus achieves better performance.

In PEGASIS, sensors are formed by chain. Each sensor communicates only with a close neighbor, and takes turns transmitting to the base station to prevent the failure of network. Only one node is designated to communicate with the base station, consequently the energy dissipation is significantly reduced. PEGASIS achieves better lifetime than LEACH about 100 to 200%.

Tan et al. proposed two tree-based protocols, PEDAP [3] and PEDAP-PA [6]. They tried to compute a minimum spanning tree over the sensor network. In PEDAP, the weights of tree edges are the transmission cost between two connected sensors. In PEDAP-PA, the weight of tree edges is the ratio of the transmission cost between two connected sensor nodes to the remaining energy of the sending node. The basic idea is to minimize the total energy expended in a round of communication while balance the energy consumption among sensors. PEDAP prolongs the lifetime of the last node death while PEDAP-PA provides a good lifetime for the first node death. Simulation results show that these two algorithms perform better than LEACH and PEGASIS both in systems that the base station is far away from and inside the field.

Kemei Du et al. proposed a multiple-chain scheme [7] to decrease the total transmission distance for all-to-all broadcasting in order to prolong the lifetime of a network. The main idea is to divide the whole sensing area into four regions centered at the node that is closest to the center of the sensing area, and the linear sub-chains in each region are constructed.

3 WSTMN Network Model

3.1 Network Model

According to the characteristics of highway, regular deployment is adopted in WSTMN. We assume the monitored highway is *A*, the length is *L*, and the width is *W*. The *N* sensors are deployed in $L \times W$. The WSTMN has the following characteristics:

1. The sensor nodes are static, and they will never move when deployed.
2. There is only one base station in WSTMN. The base station can be deployed in the center of network or somewhere out of A, which depends on the material demand of WSTMN. The experimental results indicate it's more efficient when the base station is deployed in an immobile location out of A.
3. The WSTMN is unattended.
4. The WSTMN nodes are homogeneous, and all sensor nodes have similar processing and communicating capabilities.

3.2 The Radio Model

Low-power and wireless communication are studied in recent years widely. We use the same radio model as used in LEACH, PEGAIS, which is the first order radio model. In this model, a radio dissipates $E_{elec} = 50nJ/bit$ to run the transmitter or receiver circuitry and $\varepsilon_{amp} = 100pJ/bit/m^2$ for the transmitter amplifier. The radios have power control and can expend the minimum required energy to reach the intended recipients. The radios can be turned off to avoid receiving unintended transmissions. This radio model defines a distance threshold d_0. It is a constant and its value depends on the applications. When the distance between transmitting node and receiving node is below on d_0, the energy consumption of the transmitting node is in inverse proportion to d^2, otherwise it' s in inverse proportion to d^4, namely free space model and multi-path fading model. According to the distance between the transmitting nodes and the receiving nodes, the transmitting nodes can use different energy consumption model to calculate the needful energy for transmitting data.

The equations used to calculate transmission costs and receiving costs for a *k-bit* message and a distance *d* are shown below:

Transmitting:

$$E_{Tx}(k,d) = E_{Tx-elec}(k) + \varepsilon_{Tx-amp}(k,d) \tag{1}$$

$$E_{Tx}(k,d) = E_{elec} \times k + \varepsilon_{amp} \times k \times d^2 \tag{2}$$

$$E_{Tx}(k,d) = E_{elec} \times k + \varepsilon_{amp} \times k \times d^4 \tag{3}$$

Receiving:

$$E_{Tx}(k,d) = E_{Tx-elec}(k) \tag{4}$$

$$E_{Rx}(k) = E_{elec} \times k \tag{5}$$

Receiving data is also a high cost operation, therefore, the number of receptions and transmissions should be minimal to reduce the energy cost of an application. With the radio parameters, when k=2,000 and d^2 is 500, the energy spent in the amplifier part equals the energy spent in the electronics part and, therefore, the cost to transmit a packet will be twice as that to receive. Data fusion is used to decrease energy consumption in CBDGP. Data fusion can be used to combine one or more packets to produce a same-size resultant packet, which will be $NK=K$ .In this paper, it is assumed that the radio channel is symmetric so that the energy required to transmit a message from node i to node j is the same as the energy required to transmit a message from node j to node i for a given signal-to-noise ratio. For the comparative evaluation purposes, we assume that there are no packet losses in the network. It is not difficult to model errors and losses in terms of increased energy cost per transmission. With known channel error characteristics and error coding, this cost can be modeled by suitably adjusting the constants in the above equations.

4 CBDGP Description

One of the most important goals is to minimizing the energy consumption and maximizing the lifetime in CBDGP. One good approach in conserving energy is to construct an efficient chain in a chain-based data gathering protocol. The minimum total energy chain-construction algorithm [7] is fit for our applications. On the other hand, the network performance is also affected by delay, which must be considered. So layered-chain construction algorithm is presented to reduce delay. In this paper, we construct a layered minimum total energy chain connecting all nodes to save energy consumption with low delay in each round of data collection.

Similar to PEGASIS, CBDGP is a chain-based data gathering protocol. The nodes are connected to form the layered chain by using the layered minimum total energy chain construction algorithm. And only one node transmits the data to the base station in each round. The details are described in the following sections.

4.1 The Minimum Total Energy Chain Construction Algorithm

To utilize the chain efficiently can conserve energy in a chain-based data gathering protocol. When a packet travels along a chain, the total energy dissipation of the network contains two parts: the transmitting and receiving energy consumption at each node. According to the radio model that is used in our network model, the receiving energy lies on the length of packet. The total energy consumption that is used to receive data packets is $(n-1) \times E_{elec} \times k$. The energy cost of transmitting depends on the distance between the two nodes along a chain（∞d^n）（n=2,4）. So minimizing the total average distance increasing（$\min(\sum d^n)$） chain construction algorithm is presented and utilized, where d is the distance between two nodes along the chain.

The first stage in this algorithm is the same as that in the closest neighbor algorithm [2], which is to find the farthest node from BS as one end of the chain. Then each round selects a new node which is not in the chain. The selection criteria is that $\sum d^n$ of the current chain with this *new* node increases to the minimum possible extent compared to the old chain (here, *new* is just regarded as a variable). There exist two cases depending on insertion position j. In this algorithm, C_j represents the node at location j in the chain. If C_j is already the end of the current chain, we simply append the *new* to the chain, the same as the closest neighbor algorithm. Otherwise we insert *new* between C_j and C_{j+1}. The new transmission path form C_j to C_{j+1} through node C_j increases minimum energy cost to the chain compared to if other nodes or other insertion locations were selected. The algorithm is described in Fig.1.

1. HEAD<- the farthest node from BS; N'<- N-{HEAD};
CHAIN<-{HEAD};
2. while $\{N' \neq \emptyset\}$
3. for each $i \in N'$
4. do key[i, C_j]<- $\min\{d^n(C_j,i)+ d^n(i,C_{j+1})\}- d^n(C_j,C_{j+1})\}$ for all C_j in the CHAIN
5. NEW<-EXTRACT-MIN(N') //select a node with the minimum key
6. INSERT(CHAIN, C_j, NEW) //insert NEW between C_j and C_{j+1}

Fig. 1. The minimum total energy chain-construction algorithm

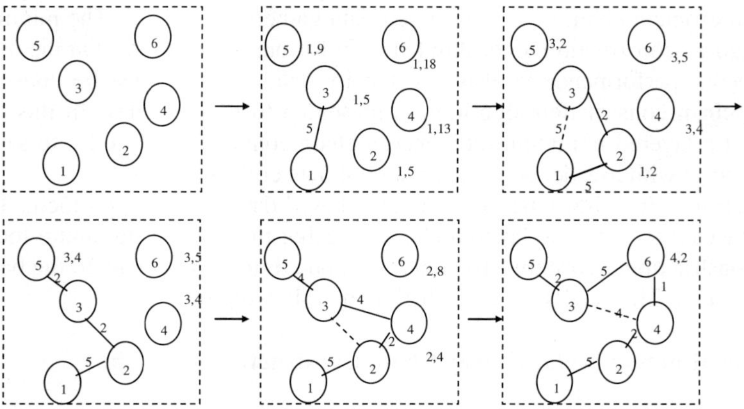

Fig. 2. The minimum total energy chain-construction example

We demonstrate an example as in Fig.2 using the minimum total energy chain-construction algorithm. The chain starts at node 1 and connects node 3 at round 1. The minimum incremental energy is 2 for both node 5 and node 2. Assume node2 is selected and inserted between node1 and node 3. The link between node 1 and node 3 is discarded. The similar procedure continues until the chain 1-2-4-6-3-5 links all nodes at round 5.

4.2 The Layered Minimum Total Energy Chain Construction with Delay Reducing

In the data gathering application, energy consumption is firstly considered, and another factor is the average delay in each round. It is assumed that data gathering rounds are far apart and the only traffic in the network is due to sensor data. So data transmissions in each round can be completely scheduled to avoid delays in channel access and collisions. If there has no queue delay, and the broadcasting delay is ignored compared to the transmission time, the transmitting delay of each packet mainly depends on transmission time. In direct communication, nodes communicate with the base station directly. If the network has *N* nodes, the delay will be *N* time units. In order to reduce delay, parallel transmission is also used. We present the layered minimum total energy chain construction algorithm with delay reducing (LMTEC) for our protocol.

We start with the linear chain among all the nodes and divide them into *G* groups, with each group having *N/G* successive nodes of the chain. Therefore, we will have *G* groups of *N/G* nodes. One node from each group will be active in the second layer, and thus, there will be G nodes. These G nodes in the second layer are divided into *G1* groups of successive nodes. Within each group, we use the minimum total energy chain construction, namely, local minimum total energy chain construction to form local chains. The leader of each local chain will be regarded as the active node in this group. For instance, the node 5 is the active node in the example in Fig.2. For a 100m × 100m network, we define the number of layers is 3, so the *G1* will be set to 2. The 10 successive nodes will be divided into 2 groups, in which local minimum total

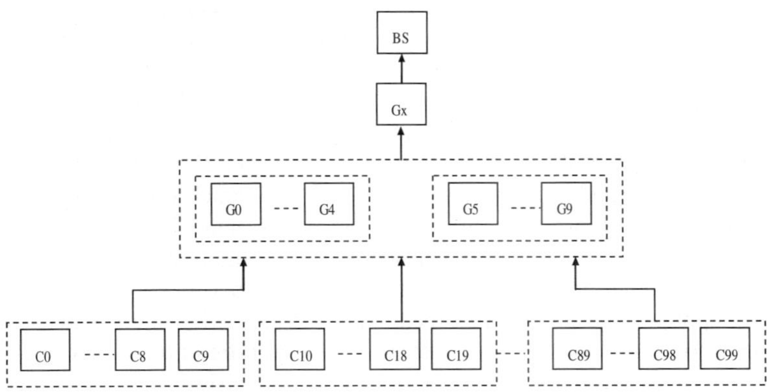

Fig. 3. The minimum total energy layered chain construction algorithm

energy chain construction algorithm is also used. And in the third layer, only one node transmits the data to the base station, which will be the leader of per round. We found that when *G* is equal to 10, we get the best balance for energy and delay. In a 100-node network, only 10 simultaneous transmissions take place at the same time and data fusion takes place at each node. The Fig.3 shows the procedure of the layered minimum total energy chain construction.

5 Experimental Results and Analysis

To evaluate the performances of CBDGP, we simulated CBDGP, PEGASIS and LEACH using the scenes and parameters in Table 1, which is run in NS2. The location of base station can vary at (500,150), (500,250) and (500,300) in the scene 1 and at (1000, 150), (1000, 250) and (1000, 300) in the scene2.

Table 1. Experiment parameters

Parameters	Scene 1	Scene2
The size of area	(0,0) to (1000,100)	(0,0) to (2000,100)
The number of nodes	50	100
The location of base station	(500,250)	(1000,250)
The initial energy	2J	2J
The length of data packet	512bytes	512bytes
$E_{threshold}$	0.01J	0.01J
E_{elec}	50nJ	50nJ
E_{amp}	100pJ/bit/m^2	100pJ/bit/m^2
d_o	100m	100m

5.1 Network Lifetime

CBDGP mainly focuses on prolonging network lifetime and reducing delay. For this experiment, the number of rounds of communication is achieved when 1%, 25%, 50%, 75% and 100% of the nodes die using LEACH, PEGASIS and CBDGP. It is assumed that each node has the same initial energy level of 2J. Once a node dies due to the battery power consumption, it is not recharged for the rest of the simulation.

Fig.4 and Fig.5 show the number of rounds until 1%, 25%, 50%, 75% and 100% nodes die for a 1000m×100m (scene1) and 2000m×100m (scene2) network. PEGASIS and CBDGP are three times or more better than LEACH in all cases. The improvements mainly come from fewer nodes transmitting data to the base station in each round compared to LEACH. Moreover, the experimental results show that CBDGP is approximately two times better than PEGASIS, which is because of the improvement of chain construction algorithm. The minimum total energy chain construction algorithm calculated the minimum total increasing distance, which avoids the long distance communication between two nodes globally. With this approach, the node energy is saved.

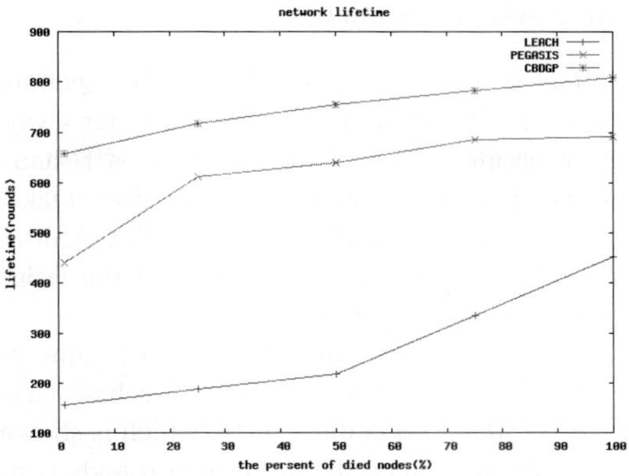

Fig. 4. Network lifetime in the scene 1

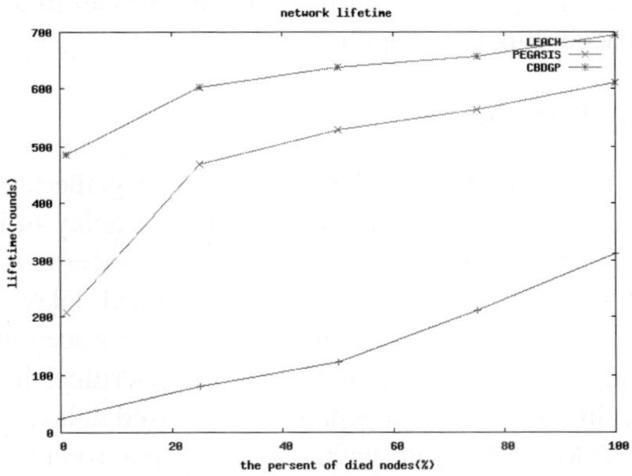

Fig. 5. Network lifetime in the scene 2

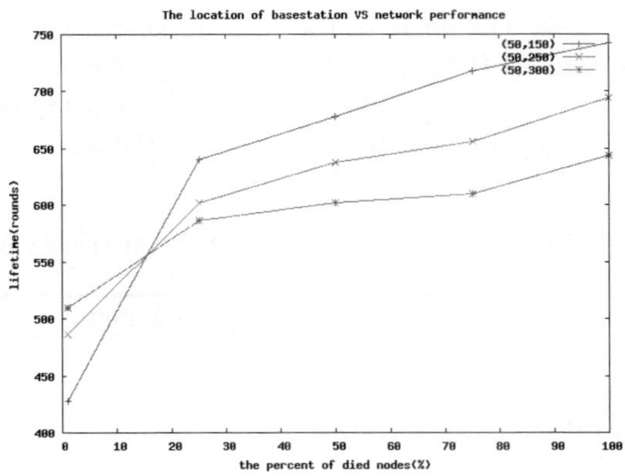

Fig. 6. The effect of base station location for lifetime

5.2 The Effect of Base Station Location

We investigate the effect of base station location in this section. PEDAP-PA performs both well in systems in which the base station is far away form the field and the base station is in the center of the field, which LEACH and PEGASIS perform poor when the base station is inside the field since they do not take the cost of sending data to base station into account. CBDGP is similar to PEGASIS. The performance is not very well when the base station is in the center of the field. We examined the effect of base station location on our algorithm.

Fig.6 shows the number of rounds completed for the same percentages of node deaths with different locations of the base station. The base station locations are at (500,150), (500,250), and (500, 300) in the scene1 (which is shown in above Table 1). Under the same scene and parameters, the number of rounds is more when the location of base station is more far away from the field when the percentage of dead nodes is below 25%. The situation is just adverse after 25% nodes die. CBDGP has an optimal lifetime when a larger percentage of node die. So we can find an optimal location for the base station according to the applications.

5.3 Network Delay Reducing

Another important factor to be considered in the data gathering application is the average delay per round. Clearly, minimizing energy or delay in isolation has drawbacks. For battery -based sensors, longevity is a major concern when energy reserves become depleted. Energy efficiency often brings additional delay along with it. Minimizing delay is not always practical in sensor network applications. Maximizing the throughput is not always the best strategy for energy-critical links too. Generally, increased energy savings come with a penalty of increased delay. We can set limits on our application, WSTMN. The data gathering delay per round may have a bound. Therefore, a tradeoff between energy spent per packet and delay have to be found. The layered minimum total energy chain construction algorithm in our protocol performs well in terms of delay reducing. The experiment results are shown in Table 2 for a 100-nodes network. The delay is 100 units in Direct and PEGASIS, and it is reduced to 27 units in LEACH because of its clustering. While the layered chain construction algorithm make the delay reduce to 15 units in our protocol. Comparing to PEGASIS, the delay has a more than 6 reductions in CBDGP.

Table 2. Delay Cost for Direct, PEGASIS, LEACH and CBDGP

Protocol	Delay (time units)
Direct	100
LEACH	27
PEGASIS	100
CBDGP	15

6 Conclusions

In this paper, we proposed a new chain-based data gathering protocol, CBDGP, which is distributing and power-aware for the wireless sensor transportation monitoring network. The minimum total energy algorithm is used to construct the chain for CBDGP. Moreover, we consider the delay in the chain-construction algorithm, and present a layered chain-construction algorithm to balance the energy consumption and delay reducing. The simulation results show that CBDGP performs better than PEGASIS when 1%, 20%, 50%, and 100% of nodes die for different network sizes and topologies. And CBDGP has an even better performance for the long-distance communication.

The simulations done in NS2 show that CBDGP outperforms other data gathering protocols obviously. In the future work, we will apply it to the real WSTMN environment to verify the results and extend its performance.

References

1. Heinzelman, W., Chandrakasan, A., Balakrishnan, H.: Energy-Efficient Communication Protocol for Wireless Microsensor Networks. In: Proc. of the 33rd Annual Hawaii Int'l Conf. on System Sciences. Maui.: IEEE Computer Society (2000) 3005–3014
2. Lindsey, S., Raghavendra, C. S.: PEGASIS: Power-Efficient Gathering in Sensor Information System. In: Proc. Of the IEEE Aerospace Conf. (2002) 1-6
3. Tan, H.O.: Power Efficient Data Gathering and Aggregation in Wireless Sensor Networks. SIGMOD Record (2003) 66-71
4. Liu, M., Gong, H.G., Mao, Y.C., Chen, L.J., Xie, L.: A Distributed Energy-Efficient Data Gathering and Aggregation Protocol for Wireless Sensor Networks. Journal of Software 16(12) (2005) 2106–2116
5. Heinzelman, W., Chandrakasan, A., Balakrishnan, H.: An Application-Specific Protocol Architecture for Wireless Microsensor Networks. IEEE Trans. on Wireless Communications 1(4) (2002) 660–670
6. Tan, H.O., Korpeoglu, I.: Power Efficient Data Gathering and Aggregation in Wireless Sensor Networks. SIGMOD Record 32(4) (2003) 66–71
7. Du, K.M., Wu, J., Zhou, D.: Chain-Based Protocols for Data Broadcasting and Gathering in the Sensor Networks. In: Proceedings of the International Parallel and Distributed Processing Symposium (PDPS'03), Nice, France, (2003) 260-267
8. Lindsey, S., Raghavendra, C.S., Sivalingam, K.: Data Gathering in Sensor Networks Using the Energy*Delay Metric. In: Proceeding of the IPDPS Workshop on Issues in Wireless Sensor Networks and Mobile Computing. San Francisco (2001) 2001-2008
9. Yang, Y., Bhaskar, K., Viktor, K.P.: Energy-Delay Tradeoffs for Data Gathering in Wireless Sensor Networks. IEEE INFOCOM'04 (2004) 9-11
10. Kalpakis, K., Dasgupta, K., Namjoshi, P.: Maximum Lifetime Data Gathering and Aggregation in Wireless Sensor Networks. Computer Network (2002) 697-716
11. Ravi, M., Jorge, A.C.: Hierarchical-Battery Aware Routing in Sensor Networks. In: IEEE Vehicular Technology Conference (VTC), Dallas (2005) 2311-2315
12. Tilak, S., Abu-Ghazaleh, N.B., Heinzelman, W.: In: Infrastructure Tradeoffs for Sensor Network *WSNA02*, Atlanta (2002) 49-58

Distributed Computing Paradigm for Target Classification in Sensor Networks

Peng Zeng[1], Yan Huang[1,2], and Haibin Yu[1]

[1] Shenyang Institute of Automation, Chinese Academy of Sciences, Shenyang 110016, China
[2] Graduate School of the Chinese Academy of Sciences, Beijing 100049, China
{zp, huangy, yhb}@sia.cn

Abstract. In this paper, we develop an energy and bandwidth efficient approach for target classification in sensor networks. Instead of adopting decision fusion to reduce network traffic as some recent research, we try to realize energy efficient target classification from a computational point of view. Our contribution is we propose a novel tree construction algorithm that autonomously organizes the distributed computation resources to execute the trained BP-network (BPN) in parallel manner. We evaluate the performance of our parallel computing paradigm compared to the traditional client/server-based computing paradigm from perspectives of energy consumption and communication traffic through analytical study. Finally, we take a target classification experiment to show the effectiveness of the proposed computing paradigm.

1 Introduction

Wireless sensor networks promise an unprecedented opportunity to monitor the physical world via cheap wireless nodes that can sense the environment in multiple modalities, including acoustic, seismic, and infrared [1], [2]. Distributed decision making is an important application of sensor networks; for example, the detection and classification of objects in the sensor field. Due to a variety of factors, such as measurement noise and statistical variability in target signals, collaborative processing of multiple node measurements is necessary for reliable decision making.

The key challenges in such distributed decision making are: (i) energy challenge: sensor nodes have limited and unreplenishable power resources. The inappropriate energy usage will largely reduce the system lifetime; and (ii) bandwidth challenge: sensor nodes have limited communication capability. Large amount of data transmission may exceed available bandwidth, resulting in poor performance of the system.

The focus of this paper is target classification in sensor networks which is to extract effective features in sensor measurements (seismic sensors) and classify a target through these features. Figure 1 depicts the flow chart of a widely used target detection and classification algorithm.

D.-S. Huang, K. Li, and G.W. Irwin (Eds.): ICIC 2006, LNAI 4114, pp. 1268 – 1278, 2006.

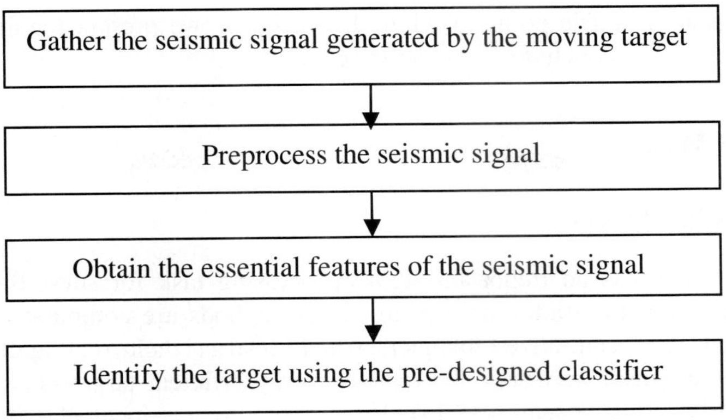

Fig. 1. Flow chart of the target detection and classification algorithm

In this algorithm, when a sensor receives a sensing task, it begins collecting samples. The gathered information is preprocessed on the sensor, which provides the optimal signal for further feature extraction. The computation in the first three steps is relative simple and can be executed on individual sensor that has limited computation capability.

The final step is to identify the target, viz. pattern recognition. The BP networks (BPN) is a suitable candidate for classifier for its simple structure, stable work state, and easy realization by hardware [2]. However, its computation requirement can not be satisfied on a single sensor node. The traditional way is to send the feature sets to a server where a trained BPN algorithm is centrally executed to classify targets. Although widely used, the main disadvantage of this client/server-based computing model is that large amount of data gathered by the sensor nodes have to be moved from the clients to the server, which will consume a lot of energy and largely reduce the lifetime of the system. With the aim of energy efficient target classification, we propose a distributed computing paradigm in this paper, which uses an aggregation tree like structure to organize the distributed computation resources in sensor networks. Under this paradigm, the BPN algorithm will be executed in a parallel manner in the aggregator nodes on the tree. So we also call it parallel computing paradigm. This proposed computing paradigm has many advantages over the traditional centralized paradigm:

(1) Energy efficiency: Since the total amount of data transmission is reduced, the energy usage can also be reduced, as most of the energy consumed goes to radio transmission [3]. The system lifetime is prolonged.

(2) Bandwidth efficiency: Network bandwidth requirement is reduced for the parallel computing. Instead of passing large amount of data over the network through multi-hop trips, computation is distributed over the network, only obtained result is sent to the base station.

The outline of this paper is as follows: In section 2, we briefly discuss related work, and describe the parallel computing paradigm for sensor networks in section 3. Section 4 uses analytical analysis to evaluate the performance of client/server-based computing paradigm and our parallel computing paradigm from energy consumption and communication traffic points of view. In section 5, we present the experimental results and finally we conclude the paper in section 6.

2 Related Work

2.1 Target Classification

Target classification is an important signal processing task for surveillance sensor networks. However, the traditional classification methods are computation intensive and processed in a centralized manner, which restrict their real applications in resource-limited sensor networks. To realize energy efficient target classification in sensor networks, some researchers [4], [5] propose to use local classification and global decision fusion. The main idea is that a local pattern classifier at each sensor node will first make a local decision based on its own feature vector, then encode and transmit the results together with the estimated probability of being a correct decision efficiently via the wireless channel to a local fusion center for decision fusion. Simulation results show the classification rate of this decision fusion is acceptable in some conditions. T. Clouqueur gives an in-depth analysis on the performance of traditional value fusion and decision fusion in [6]. He concludes if fault-tolerance is not required, value fusion performs much better than decision fusion when the SNR is low. Based on this conclusion, in this paper, we try to solve the problem from a computational point of view. We still use the value fusion and propose a new parallel processing model to take the place of the traditional centralized model.

2.2 Computing Paradigm

In the context of sensor networks, computing paradigm refers to the information processing model deployed at the application layer of the protocol stack. Data aggregation model has been widely discussed such as in [7], [8], most of which are focus on eliminating redundant data transmission. Until recently, some distributed computing paradigms [9], [10] are proposed to do some simple computation by utilizing the computing resources in each sensor. The representative is the mobile-agent based computing paradigm proposed by Hairong Qi [10]. In this paradigm, instead of each sensor node sending raw data or pre-processed data to the processing center, the processing code is moved to the data locations through mobile agents. The mobile agent is a special kind of "software". Once dispatched, it can migrate from node to node performing data processing autonomously. The structure of a mobile agent has four attributes: identification, itinerary, data, and processing code. Identification uniquely identifies each mobile agent. Data is the agent's data buffer which carries a partially integrated result. Itinerary is the route of migration. Processing code carries out the integration whenever the mobile agent arrives at a local sensor node. Simulation results show the mobile-agent based computing paradigm performs significantly better than client/server based computing paradigm from perspectives of energy consumption and execution time. However, the mobile-agent based computing paradigm can only be used to solve quadratic optimization problems. Quadratic optimization problems are very special since their solutions are linear functions of data, in which case a simple accumulation process leads to a solution. More complex problems like target classification do not share this simple feature, can not be solved using the mobile-agent based computing paradigm.

3 Parallel Computing Paradigm for Sensor Network

In this section, we propose a parallel computing paradigm which uses an aggregation tree like structure to organize the distributed computation resources in sensor networks to implement an m-layer trained BPN.

3.1 BPN Algorithm

One of the key features of BPN is those neurons' outputs are fed forward to next layers. In a BPN, the output of the j th neuron at the n th layer A_j^n, is

$$A_j^n = f(net_j^n) \quad , \tag{1}$$

and

$$net_j^n = \sum_i W_{ij} A_j^{n-1} - \theta_j \quad . \tag{2}$$

is the active function, where θ_j is the threshold for the j th neuron and W_{ij} are network weights. The function f is a transform function, which is used to map the active function to be the output of a neuron. Investigating the equation (2), it is obviously that each node in a hidden layer can be run in parallel.

3.2 The Sensor Network Model

Consider a network of n sensor nodes and a base station node distributed over a region. All sensor nodes are stationary and have similar capabilities (processing/ communication). For the sensor network is deployed in a big region, it needs to use multi-hop forwarding. We assume that all nodes transmit at the same constant power which implies all sensor nodes have the same radio transmission range. Based on the radio transmission range, we partition the set of all sensor nodes V into subsets $S_0, S_1, \ldots, S_n$, satisfying $V = S_0 \cup S_1 \cup \ldots \cup S_n$, $S_i \cap S_j = \phi$ for all $i \neq j$ and no S_i is empty. S_i is the set of nodes that can be reached from the base station node B in i hops ($S_0 = \{B\}$), but not less than i hops. We call S_i the sphere of radius i around B.

3.3 Aggregation Tree Based Partitioning Scheme

The main idea of our parallel computing paradigm is to form a tree like structure to organize the distributed computation resources in sensor networks, and assign processes to aggregator node on the tree in each intervening sphere by using the following equation,

$$A_{ij} = \left\lfloor \frac{h_j}{p_j} \right\rfloor, i = 0,\ldots, p_j - 1, \tag{3}$$

and

$$A_{ij} = A_{ij} + 1 \;\; if \;\; i < (h_j \bmod p_j) . \tag{4}$$

where A_{ij} stands for the number of assigned neurons at hidden layer j to aggregator node i , h_j is the number of hidden neurons at hidden layer j , and p_j is the number of aggregator nodes in the corresponding sphere S_{n-j} , which is determined based on the computation capability of each sensor node.

The key challenge in such parallel computing paradigm is to form the aggregation trees according to the BPN structure and assign computation tasks to aggregator nodes dynamically and autonomously.

3.4 Reactive Tree Construction Algorithm

For most of recently developed sensors, the transmission range is at least twice the sensing range [11]. So, it is most likely the sensors that detect the target are all located in the same sphere. In this paper, we assume k sensors in sphere S_f detect the target simultaneously, which act as data sources and are used as the input of BPN. We further assume each node in the network stores the structure of the BPN to be implemented. Different from most existing algorithms that derive trees proactively, our tree construction algorithm works in a reactive manner. That is the tree construction is event-driven, and needs no maintenance after data fusion. The algorithm consists of the following three steps:

1) Neighbor beacon exchange

Every node in network periodically broadcasts a beacon packet to its neighbors. This periodic beaconing is only used for link quality estimation. For the parallel computing paradigm is fault sensitive, any packet lost will seriously influence the accuracy of results, this beacon exchange helps each node to setup a neighbor table which consists of its neighbors with good bidirectional links. We argue that the beaconing rate can be low for the sensor network is stationary. Moreover, piggybacking methods can also be exploited to reduce this beacon overhead.

In addition to periodic beaconing, the algorithm uses a type of event-driven beacon in the next root selection step, namely a detection beacon, to quickly identify the data sources.

2) Root selection

When a sensor detects the target, it broadcast a detection beacon packet containing its residual energy level information and the detecting timestamp information. This beacon exchange will confirm the data sources that act as input of BPN. The data source with the highest residual energy level then notify the mth intervening node (resides in S_{f-m}, denoted by T_m) on its shortest path to the base station node to be the root of the tree.

The shortest paths from every sensor node to the base station should be set up using Dijkstra like algorithm at network initialization.

3) Aggregator nodes selection

The final step is to dynamically choose the aggregator nodes between S_f and S_{f-m}. This process is initiated by T_m. It does this by sending a request message piggybacked with the hidden layer number $m-1$ to its neighbors in S_{f-m+1}. Upon receiving the request message, the neighbor node checks to see whether it has enough capabilities to accomplish the computation task of BPN at hidden layer $m-1$. If not, it ignores the request message, else, it responds by sending a reply message to join the tree. T_m confirms the first p_{m-1} replying neighbors to be the aggregator nodes in S_{f-m+1} by sending confirm messages. This request-reply-confirm process repeats sphere by sphere until it reaches S_f. In the situation when there is more than one requestor, for example, in sphere S_{f-j}, there are p_j requestors, the candidates in S_{f-j+1} make response only after receiving all the p_j request messages and join the tree after receiving all the p_j confirm messages. The algorithm completes when all data sources join the tree as leaves. The computation tasks of BPN are distributed to aggregator nodes when they determine their roles in the tree.

Let the network graph G consist of all the nodes in the sensor network. If the sub-graph G' of G induced by the set of k data sources is connected, the aggregation tree can be formed in polynomial time. For more details and the formal proofs, see [8].

4 Performance Evaluation

We choose to use two metrics, the energy consumption and the communications traffic, to evaluate the performance of the client/server-based computing paradigm and our parallel computing paradigm in target classification.

4.1 The Communications Traffic

The communications traffic is the total amount of data transmission, in terms of number of bytes. For the bandwidth is strictly constrained in sensor networks, the communications traffic has a strong impact on the performance of the system. For the shortest paths are needed for both paradigm, we choose to neglect the overhead caused by the shortest paths set-up in this section.

Let b be the size of the feature obtained by FFT executed in all k data sources. The distance (in terms of number of hops) of the shortest path from data sources in sphere S_f to the base station is f. So, the communications traffic generated by the client/server-based computing paradigm in this case (call it CT_{CS}) is

$$CT_{CS} = k \cdot f \cdot b\,. \tag{5}$$

Let the communications traffic required for our parallel computing paradigm be CT_{nb}. CT_{nb} consists of the traffic generated by the tree construction (call it CT_{tree}) and the traffic generated by the parallel computation (call it CT_{comp}). According to our algorithm, to construct an m-layer tree:

$$CT_{tree} \le l \cdot d^{m}\,, \tag{6}$$

where d is the node degree, l is an constant.

In the process of computation, each intervening layer j has P_j aggregator nodes. We assume that the output of each aggregator in the j th layer has the same size w_j. The output of BPN is a one byte result which is transmitted along the shortest path from T_m to the base station. So,

$$CT_{comp} = k \cdot b + p_1 \cdot w_1 + p_2 \cdot w_2 + \ldots + p_{m-1} \cdot w_{m-1} + f - m\,, \tag{7}$$

where $f-m$ is the distance (in terms of number of hops) of the shortest path from T_m to the base station.

According to the structure of the aggregation tree, we have $p_{m-1} \le \cdots \le p_1 \le k$. The communications traffic CT_{nb} satisfies the following bounds:

$$CT_{nb} \le l \cdot d^{m} + m \cdot k \cdot b + f - m\,. \tag{8}$$

Assume d , b , m and k are fixed, then as f tends to infinity (i.e. as the base station is farther and farther away from the sources):

$$\lim_{f \to \infty} \frac{CT_{nb}}{CT_{CS}} = \frac{1}{k \cdot b}\,. \tag{9}$$

4.2 The Energy Consumption

Sensor nodes are normally composed of four basic units: a sensing unit, a processing unit, a communication unit, and a power unit. Among these units, communication and sensing consume most of the energy. However, since the energy consumed in sensing is the same for both computing paradigms we choose to neglect this factor.

The energy consumption for the two computing paradigms depends on two components, energy consumed in data transfer (E_{tran}) and data processing (E_{proc}). Since no matter where the data processing is taken place, be it at the local sensor node or the processing center, the energy consumed for the entire sensor network is the same for both computing paradigms, we choose to neglect E_{proc}.

In our model, we assume that all nodes transmit at the same constant power. So each node has the same energy consumption in transmitting or receiving one bit data. Let r *be* the energy consumption for receiving one bit and t be the energy required to transmit one packet. We calculate the energy consumption for client/server-based computing paradigm as,

$$E_{CS} = CT_{CS} \cdot (r+t)\,. \tag{10}$$

Correspondingly, the energy consumption for the parallel computing paradigm can be calculated as

$$E_{nb} = CT_{nb} \cdot (r+t)\,, \tag{11}$$

as f tends to infinity:

$$\lim_{f \to \infty} \frac{E_{nb}}{E_{CS}} = \frac{1}{k \cdot b}\,. \tag{12}$$

We assume that each sensor has a battery with finite, unreplenishable energy E. Let the lifetime of the sensor network be T. Clearly, it demands that the total energy consumed (call it E_{all}) be no greater than the total energy available at the start,

$$T \times E_{all} \le \sum_{i=1}^{n} E\,, \tag{13}$$

which reduces to,

$$T \le \frac{n \cdot E}{E_{all}}\,. \tag{14}$$

We can calculate the lifetime for both computing paradigm using Eq.(10), Eq.(11) and Eq.(14). It is obvious that the lifetime of the parallel computing paradigm is $k \cdot b$ times longer than that of the client/server-based computing paradigm.

5 Experiments

We implemented both computing paradigms on the "mote" sensor platform [12]. Each node has a 4MHz Atmel microprocessor with 4 KB RAM, 128 KB code space and 512KB external EEPROM. Motes use TinyOS which provides a MAC layer with a simple CSMA/collision avoidance protocol running on a 433MHz RFM radio transceiver at 40kbps. Nodes are placed along two straight lines with inter-node distance of 2.5 meters, as shown in Figure 2. Each node has a degree of 5. Given only a limited number of nodes, our intention is to stress test our approach with the largest network diameter as much as possible. In our experiments, we study three different sensor fields, ranging from 12 to 36 nodes in increments of 12 nodes. So the network diameter ranges from 6 to 18 hops (spheres) in increments of 6 hops.

There are two possible target classes: mobile robot and walking man. The accelerometer sensor (ADXL202JE) is used to measure shock waves generated by the moving target, which has a limited sensing range about 1 meter. We use the data set pre-obtained to train a two-layer BPN, as shown in Figure 3. The size of the features (calculated by FFT) sent by each sensor is 160 bytes. The size of the output of each aggregator node is 20 bytes. To demonstrate how the two computing paradigms behave when the network diameter change, we make targets only pass the outermost sphere, that is, only the four sensor nodes in the outermost sphere can detect the target each time. So, $k = 4$, $b = 160$, f ranges from 6 to 18.

Fig. 2. The topology of sensor network

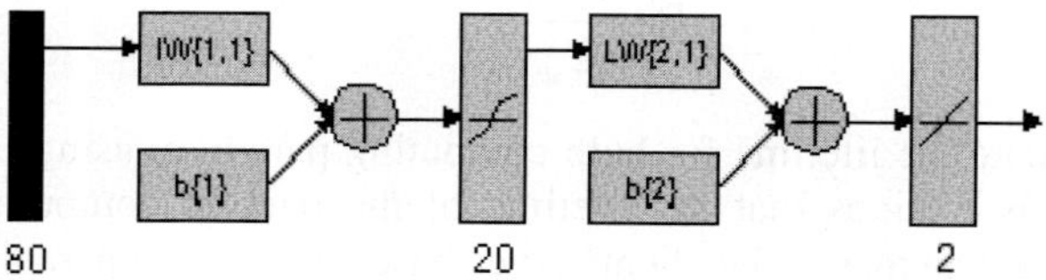

Fig. 3. Architecture of the BPN

Figure 4 shows the communications traffic observed as a function of network diameter. As we analysis in section 4, when the network diameter increases, there is a dramatic increase of the traffic of client/server-based computing paradigm, while the traffic of parallel computing paradigm keeps stable but low growth. We further analysis the constitution of the traffic of parallel computing paradigm. Figure 5 shows the traffic generated by tree construction changes a little with increase of network diameter. It because that the tree construction algorithm is localized and independent of the network size.

In our reactive tree construction algorithm, the two factors that significantly impact aggregator nodes selection are packet loss and node degree. In this experiment, we measure packet loss for each link every minute for an hour. A link is defined as a good link if its average packet loss $p \leq 10\%$. Links between a pair of nodes are defined as symmetric if both are good links. Results show the symmetric link is about 75% of the total links. Under this packet loss condition, we vary node degree by varying the transmit power. For each setting, we run the experiments twenty times and take the success rate of tree construction. Figure 6 shows the success rate increase

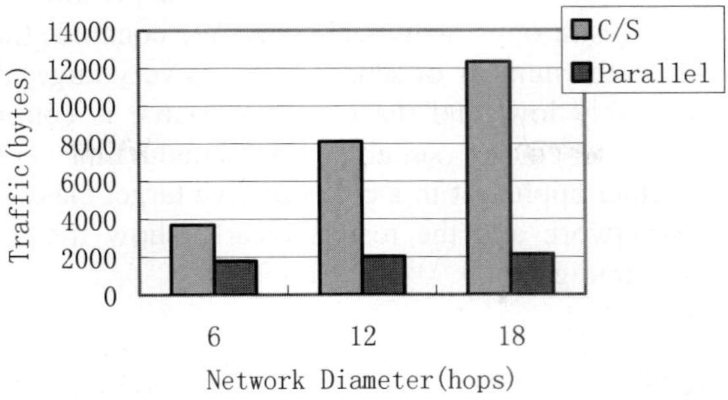

Fig. 4. Communications traffic comparison

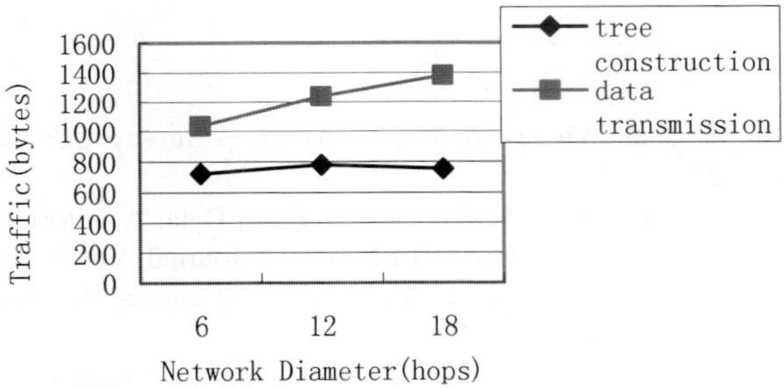

Fig. 5. Traffic constitution of parallel computing paradigm

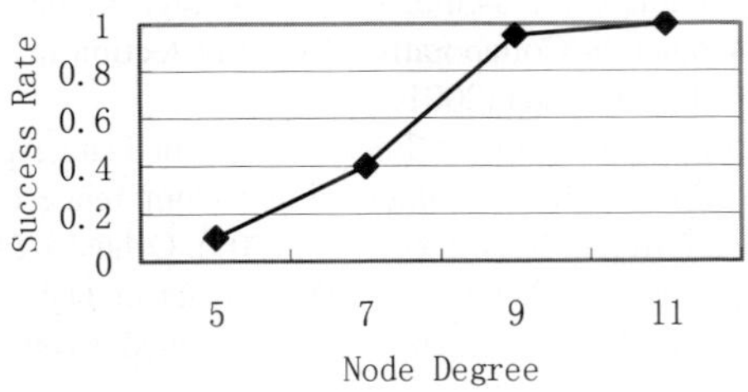

Fig. 6. Successful rate of tree construction

with the increase of node degree. To guarantee the success classification, each node has at least 9 neighbors.

6 Conclusions

In this paper, we presented a parallel computing paradigm for target classification in sensor networks. We compared the performance of our computing paradigm with the classic client/server based paradigm from the communication traffic and energy consumption perspectives through analytical study. We conclude that in the context of sensor networks where the number of sensor nodes is very large, the communication bandwidth is considerably low, and the energy resource is contingent, the parallel computing paradigm is more suitable for conducting collaborative target classification. We further applied it in a collaborative target classification experiment in a ground sensor network and the results clearly show the effectiveness of the proposed computing paradigm.

Acknowledgment

This work is supported by National Natural Science Foundation of China (No. 60374072, 60434030).

References

1. Akyildiz, I, Su, W, et al: Wireless Sensor Networks: A Survey. Computer Networks, Vol. 38. (2002) 393-422
2. Matteo, Pardo, Giorgio, Sberveglieri: Learning From Data: A Tutorial With Emphasis on Modern Pattern Recognition Methods. IEEE Sensors Journal, Vol. 2. (2002) 203-217
3. Estrin, D., Sayeed, A., Srivastava, M.: Mobicom 2002 tutorial: wireless sensor networks. Atlanta, Georgia, USA (2002)
4. Duarte, Marco, Hu, Yu-Hen: Vehicle Classification in Distributed Sensor Networks. Journal of Parallel and Distributed Computing, Vol. 64. (2004) 826-838
5. Duarte, Marco, Hu, Yu-Hen: Optimal Decision Fusion With Applications to Target Detection in Wireless Ad Hoc Sensor Networks. Proceedings of The IEEE International Workshop on Multimedia Signal Processing. Siena, Italy (2004) 319-322
6. Clouqueur, T., Ramanathan, P., Saluja, KK, K. Wang: Value-Fusion Versus Decision-Fusion for Fault-Tolerance in Collaborative Target Detection in Sensor Networks. Fusion 2001 Conference. Quebec, Canada (2001)
7. Chen, Y. P., Liestman, A. L., Liu, J.: Energy-Efficient Data Aggregation Hierarchy for Wireless Sensor Networks. The 2nd International Conference on Quality of Service in Heterogeneous Wired/Wireless Networks (QShine'05). Orlando, FL, USA (2005)
8. Krishnamachari, B., Estrin, D., Wicker, S.: The Impact of Data Aggregation in Wireless Sensor Networks. International Workshop on Distributed Event-Based Systems, (DEBS '02). Vienna, Austria (2002)
9. Zhao, Jerry, Govindan, R., Estrin, D.: Computing Aggregates for Monitoring Wireless Sensor Networks. Proceedings of the International Workshop on Sensor Net Protocols and Applications. Piscataway: IEEE Press (2003) 37-48
10. Qi, Hairong, Xu, Yingyue, Wang, Xiaoling: Mobile-agent-based Collaborative Signal and Information Processing in Sensor Networks. Proceedings of the IEEE, Vol. 91. (2003) 1172-83
11. Zhang, H., Hou, J. C.: Maintaining Sensing Coverage and Connectivity in Large Sensor Networks. In International Workshop on Theoretical and Algorithmic Aspects of Sensor, Ad hoc Wireless and Peer-to-Peer Networks. CRC Press (2004)
12. Hill, Jason l, Culler, David: Mica: A Wireless Platform for Deeply Embedded Networks. IEEE Micro, Vol. 22. (2002) 12-24

QoS Multicast Routing Algorithm in MANET: An Entropy-Based GA

Hua Chen[1], Baolin Sun[1,2], and Yue Zeng[3]

[1] Department of Mathematics and Physics,
Wuhan University of Science and Engineering, Wuhan, 430073, P.R. China
qiuchen_1022@163.com

[2] School of Computer Science and Technology, Wuhan University of Technology,
Wuhan, 430063, P.R. China
blsun@163.com

[3] Department of Computer, Jiangxi Vocational College of Finance and Economics,
Jiujiang, Jiangxi 332000, P.R. China

Abstract. A mobile ad hoc network (MANET) is an autonomous system of mobile nodes connected by wireless links. There is no static infrastructure such as base station in cell mobile communication. Due to the dynamic nature of the network topology and restricted resources, quality of service (QoS) and multicast routing in MANET is a challenging task. Finding and maintaining QoS multicast routing in the data is still more challenging. In this paper, we present an entropy-based genetic algorithm (GA) to support QoS multicast routing in mobile ad hoc networks (EQMGA). The key idea of EQMGA algorithm is to construct the new metric-entropy and select the long-life path with the help of entropy metric to reduce the number of route reconstruction so as to provide QoS guarantee in the ad hoc network. The simulation results demonstrate that the proposed approach and parameters provide an accurate and efficient method to estimate and evaluate the route stability in dynamic mobile networks.

1 Introduction

A mobile ad hoc network (MANET) is an autonomous system of mobile nodes connected by wireless links. There is no static infrastructure such as base station as that was in cell mobile communication [1-7,11]. Due to the dynamic nature of the network topology and restricted resources, quality of service (QoS) and multicast routing in MANET is a challenging task. Finding and maintaining the QoS multicast routing the data is still more challenging [1-7].

Quality of service (QoS) support for multimedia applications is closely related to resource allocation, the objective of which is to decide how to reserve resources such that QoS requirements of all the applications can be satisfied. In [1] presents a QoS multicast routing model and algorithm based on GA. In [2], we propose a methodology to chose optimized fuzzy controller parameters using the GA.

The use of multicasting with the network has many benefits. Multicasting reduces the communication cost for applications that sending the same data to many

D.-S. Huang, K. Li, and G.W. Irwin (Eds.): ICIC 2006, LNAI 4114, pp. 1279–1289, 2006.

recipients [1,3-7]. Instead of sending via multiple unicast, multicast reduces the channel bandwidth, sender and router processing and delivery delay. In addition multicast gives robust communication whereby the receiver address is unknown or modifiable without the knowledge of the source within the wireless environment. In [3], we presents an entropy-based stability QoS multicast routing protocol in ad hoc network. Multicast ad hoc on-demand distance-vector (MAODV) [6] routing protocol provides fast and efficient route establishment between mobile nodes that need to communicate with each other. Since MAODV has been specifically designed for ad hoc wireless networks, it has minimal control overhead and route acquisition latency. In addition to unicast routing, MAODV supports multicast and broadcast as well. The ODMRP [7] protocol is a mesh based rather than a conventional tree based scheme and uses a forwarding group concept.

Entropy [8,9] presents the uncertanity and a measure of the disorder in a system. There are some common characteristics among self-organization, entropy, and the location uncertainty in mobile ad hoc wireless networks. These common characteristics have motivated our work in developing an analytical modeling framework using entropy concepts and utilizing mobility information as the corresponding variable features, in order to support route stability in self-organizing mobile ad hoc wireless networks. The corresponding methodology, results and observations can be used by the routing protocols to select the most stable route between a source and a destination, in an environment where multiple paths are available, as well as to create a convenient performance measure to be used for the evaluation of the stability and connectivity in mobile ad hoc networks.

In this paper, we present an entropy-based model to support QoS multicast routing genetic algorithm in mobile ad hoc networks (EQMGA). The key idea of EQMGA algorithm is to construct the new metric-entropy and select the long-life path with the help of entropy metric to reduce the number of route reconstruction so as to provide QoS guarantee in the ad hoc network whose topology changes continuously.

The rest of the paper is organized as follows. Section 2 introduces the ad hoc network model and routing issues. Section 3 describes EQMGA. Section 4 gives the complexity analysis of the algorithm. Some simulation results are provided in section 5. Finally, the paper concludes in section 6.

2 Network Model and Routing Issues

A network is usually represented as a weighted digraph $G = (N, E)$, where N denotes the set of nodes and E denotes the set of communication links connecting the nodes. $|N|$ and $|E|$ denote the number of nodes and links in the network respectively. In $G(N, E)$, considering a QoS constrained multicast routing problem from a source node to multi-destination nodes, namely given a non-empty set M=$\{s, u_1, u_2, \ldots, u_m\}$, $M \subseteq N, s$ is source node, U=$\{u_1, u_2, \ldots, u_m\}$ be a set of destination nodes. In multicast tree T=(N_T, E_T), where $N_T \subseteq N$, $E_T \subseteq E$. if $C(T)$ is the cost of T, $P_T(s, u)$ is the path from source node s to destination $u \in U$ in T, $B_T(s, u)$ is usable bandwidth of $P_T(s, u)$.

Definition 1: The cost of multicast tree T is:

$$C(T_e) = \sum_{e \in E_T} C(e),\ e \in E_T.$$

Definition 2: The bandwidth of multicast tree T is the minimum value of link bandwidth in the path from source node s to each destination node $u \in U$. i.e.

$$B_T(s,u) = \min(B(e),\ e \in E_T).$$

Definition 3: Assume the minimum bandwidth constraint of multicast tree is B, given a multicast demand R, then, the problem of bandwidth constrained multicast routing is to find a multicast tree T, satisfying:

Bandwidth constraint: $B_T(s,u) \geq B,\ u \in U$.

Suppose $S(R)$ is the set, $S(R)$ satisfies the conditions above, then, the multicast tree T which we find is:

$$C(T) = \min\ (C(T_s),\ T_s \in S(R)).$$

3 EQMGA

Genetic algorithms are based on the mechanics of natural evolution. Throughout their artificial evolution, successive generations each consisting of a population of possible solutions, called individuals (or chromosomes, or vectors of genes), search for beneficial adaptations to solve the given problem.

3.1 Encoding Representation

The chromosomes of genetic algorithms is composed of a series of integral queuing and the encoding method based on routing representation, which the most natural and simplest representing method. Given a source node s and destination nodes set U=$\{u_1, u_2, \ldots, u_m\}$, a chromosome can be represented by a string of integers with length m. The chromosome of genetic algorithms is composed of a series of integral queuing with length m, the gene of genetic algorithms is the path in path set $\{P_i^1, \ldots, P_i^j, \ldots, P_i^l\}$ [4] between s and u_i, where, P_i^j is the j-th path of destination node u_i, l denotes the path number between s and u_i. Each chromosome in population denotes a multicast tree. Now for each destination node $u_i \in U$, by the k-th the shortest route algorithm, the encoding space can be improved by finding out all routes that satisfy bandwidth constraint from source node s to destination node $u_i \in U$ and composing routes set as candidate routes set of genetic algorithm encoding space. Assume that U_i is the set of destination node u_i which satisfies bandwidth constrained, then

$$U_i = \{P_i^1, \ldots, P_i^j, \ldots, P_i^k\},\ k \leq l$$

where, P_i^j denotes the j-th route which satisfies bandwidth constraint of destination node u_i. Choose arbitrarily a route from each route set U_i respectively, and compose the initial population of chromosomes.

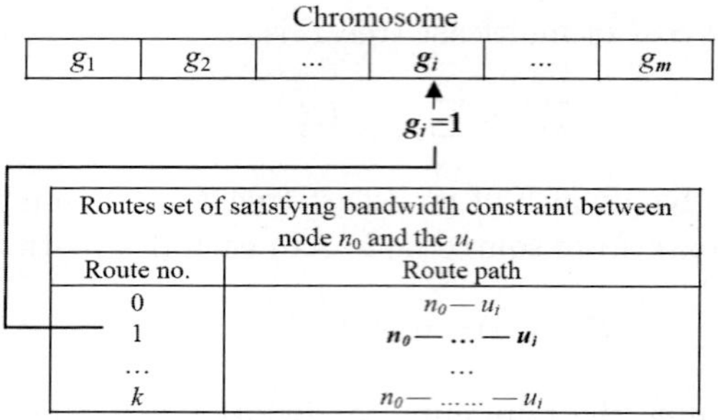

Fig. 1. Representation of chromosomes

3.2 Fitness Sharing Function (Entropy Metric)

The individual with good performance has high fitness level, and the individual with bad performance has low fitness level.

We also associate each node m with a set of variable features denoted by $a_{m,n}$ where node n is a neighbor of node m. In this paper, two nodes are considered neighbors if they can reach each other in one hop (e.g. direct communication). These variable features $a_{m,n}$ represent a measure of the relative speed among two nodes and are defined rigorously later in this section. Any change of the system can be described as a change of variable values $a_{m,n}$ in the course of time t such as $a_{m,n}(t) \rightarrow a_{m,n}(t + \Delta_t)$. Let us also denote by $v(m,t)$ the velocity vector of node m and by $v(n,t)$ the velocity vector of node n at time t. Please note that velocity vectors $v(m,t)$ and $v(n,t)$ have two parameters, namely speed and direction. The relative velocity $v(m,n,t)$ between nodes m and n at time t is defined as:

$$v(m,n,t) = v(m,t) - v(n,t)$$

Let us also denote by $p(m,t)$ the position vector of node m and by $p(n,t)$ the position vector of node n at time t. Please note that position vectors $p(m,t)$ and $p(n,t)$ have two parameters, namely position. The relative position $p(m,n,t)$ between nodes m and n at time t is defined as:

$$p(m,n,t) = p(m,t) - p(n,t)$$

Then, the relative mobility between any pair (m,n) of nodes during some time interval is defined as their absolute relative speed and position averaged over time. Therefore, we have:

$$a_{m,n} = \frac{1}{N} \sum_{i=1}^{N} \frac{|p(m,n,t_i) + v(m,n,t_i) \times \Delta_{t_i}| - |p(m,n,t_{i+1})|}{R}$$

where N is the number of discrete times t_i that velocity information can be calculated and disseminated to other neighboring nodes within time interval Δ_t. R is radio range of nodes. Based on this, we can define the entropy $H_m(t, \Delta_t)$

at mobile during time interval Δ_t. The entropy can be defined either within the whole neighboring range of node (e.g., within set S_m), or for any subset of neighboring nodes of interest. In general the entropy $H_m(t, \Delta_t)$ at mobile is calculated as follows [8,9]:

$$H_m(t, \Delta_t) = \frac{-\sum_{k \in F_m} P_k(t, \Delta_t) \log P_k(t, \Delta_t)}{\log C(F_m)}$$

where $P_k(t,\ \Delta_t) = (a_{m,k}\ /\ \sum_{i \in F_m} a_{m,i}\ )$.

In this relation by F_m we denote the set (or any subset) of the neighboring nodes of node m, and by $C(F_m)$ the cardinality (degree) of set F_m. As can be observed from the previous relation the entropy $H_m(t,\ \Delta_t)$ is normalized so that $0 \leq H_m(t,\ \Delta_t) \leq 1$. It should be noted that the entropy, as defined here, is small when the change of the variable values in the given region is severe and large when the change of the values is small [8,9]. Let us present the route stability between two nodes s and $u \in U$ during some interval Δ_t as route stability. We also define and evaluate two different measures to estimate and quantify end to end route stability, denoted by $F^{'}(s,u)$ and $F(s,u)$ and defined as follows respectively:

$$F^{'}(s,u) = \prod_{i=1}^{N_r} H_i(t, \Delta_t)$$

where N_r denotes the number of intermediate mobile nodes over a route between the two end nodes (s,u).

$$F(s,u) = -\ln F^{'}(s,u) = -\sum_{i=1}^{N_r} \ln H_i(t, \Delta_t)$$

3.3 Selection Operations

Selection operation is used to certain or crossover individuals, and selected individual can produce many sub-individuals. Selection operation has two procedures: firstly, computing fitness value; secondly, queuing it from the smallest to the biggest, namely, $F(s,u_1') \leq F(s,\ u_2') \leq \ldots \leq F(s,\ u_m')$ $(\{u_1',\ u_2',\ \ldots,\ u_m'\} \subset \{u_1,\ u_2,\ \ldots,\ u_m\})$, then, the min fitness value is the best individual, selecting the best individual as father-individual, the selection probability of each individual is proportional to its fitness value, the selected probability is higher when the individual fitness value is bigger. If the same chromosomes have been got, only one chromosome exists. The rest chromosomes can be canceled.

3.4 Crossover and Mutation Operations

In the proposed scheme, two chromosomes chosen for crossover should have at least one common gene (node), but there is no requirement that they be located at the same locus. That is to say, the crossover does not depend on the position of nodes in routing paths [1,4]. Fig. 2 shows an example of the crossover procedure.

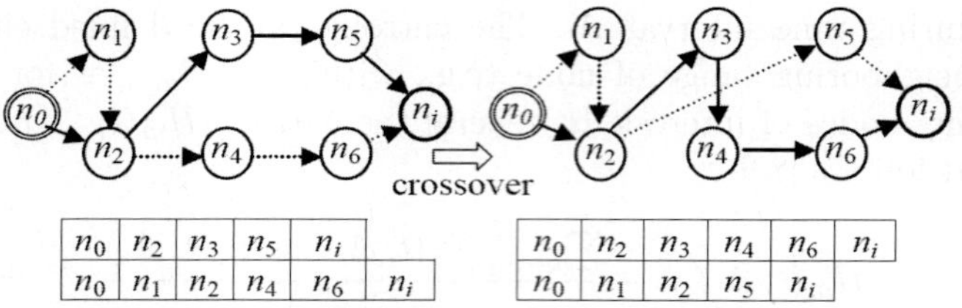

Fig. 2. Overall procedure of the crossover

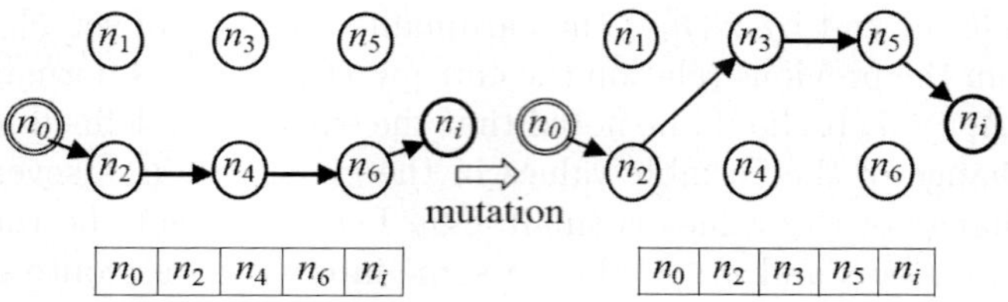

Fig. 3. Overall procedure of the mutation

The population undergoes mutation by an actual change or flipping of one of the genes of the candidate chromosomes, which keeping away from local optima [1,4]. Fig. 3 shows the overall procedure of the mutation operation.

4 Complexity of the Algorithm

The genetic operators crossover and mutation requires $O(n)$ time, where n is the total number of network nodes. Since, the genetic operations are performed on every string in the population, the complexity of a single iteration of the algorithm will be: $O(P \times n)$, where P is the population size. Finally, since, the algorithm is executed for g generations, the total complexity of the algorithm becomes $O(g \times P \times n)$. The simulation experiments in Section 5 makes it clear that in most of the cases, only a few generations will give a near-optimal result. It is true that the number of iterations g varies with the population size P. A poor guess of choosing the initial population might increase the number of iterations leading to a relatively slower solution. However, such penalty is often tolerated while solving such a NP-hard problem.

5 Simulation Experiments

5.1 Random Graph Generation

In generating random graphs, we have adopted the method used in [11], where vertices are placed randomly in a rectangular coordinate grid by generating uniformly distributed values for their x and y coordinates. The graphs connectivity is ensured by first constructing a random spanning tree. This tree is generated by iteratively considering a random edge between nodes and accepting those edges that connect distinct components. The remaining edges of the graph are chosen by examining each possible edge (u,v) and generating a random number $0 \leq r < 1$. If r is the less than a probability function $P(u,v)$ based on the edge distance between u and v, then the edge is included in the graph. The distance for each edge is the Euclidean distance (denoted as $d(u,v)$ between the nodes that form the end-points of the edge. We used the probability

$$P(u,v) = \beta \exp(-\frac{d(u,v)}{\alpha L})$$

where α and β are tunable parameters and L is the number of nodes in the graph. Increasing an increase the number of connections between far off nodes and increasing β increases the degree of each node.

5.2 Simulation Model

To conduct the simulation studies, we have used randomly generated networks on which the algorithms were executed. This ensures that the simulation results are independent of the characteristics of any particular network topology. Using randomly generated network topologies also provides the necessary flexibility to tune various network parameters such as average degree, number of nodes, and number of edges, and to study the effect of these parameters on the performance of the algorithms.

Our simulation modeled a network of mobile nodes placed randomly within 1km × 1km area. Radio propagation range for each node was 250 meters and channel capacity of 2 Mbps is chosen. There were no network partitions throughout the simulation. Each simulation is executed for 600 seconds of simulation time. Multiple runs with different seed values were conducted for each scenario and collected data was averaged over those runs. Table 1 lists the simulation parameters which are used as default values unless otherwise specified. A free space propagation model was used in our experiments. A traffic generator was developed to simulate CBR sources. The size of the data payload is 512 bytes. Data sessions with randomly selected sources and destinations were simulated. Each source transmits data packets at a minimum rate of 4 packets/sec. and maximum rate of 10 packets/sec.

During the experiment, we research EQMGA mainly from cost to control information, the success rate to find the path and the feature of data transmission, the average cost to control information, the success rate to find the path [1,3-7] and the feature of data transmission are decided by following formula:

The cost to control information =

$$\frac{\text{Total number of routed information controls}}{\text{Total number of connection request}}$$

The success rate =

$$\frac{\text{Total number of routed connection requests}}{\text{Total number of connection request}}$$

Table 1. Simulation parameters

Number of nodes	100	Number of multicast receivers	5-30
Terrain range	1km × 1km	Channel bandwidth	2 Mbps
Speed	0-20 m/s	Transmission range	250 m
Mobility model	Random way point	Simulation time	600 seconds
Traffic type	CBR	Node pause time	0-20 seconds
Data payload	512 bytes/packet	Examined routing protocol	MAODV

The data transmission rate =

$$\frac{\text{Total number of data transferred to destination}}{\text{Total number of data sent by the source node}}$$

5.3 Simulation Results

In order to evaluate the performances of our EQMGA, we simulate the proposed mechanisms using NS-2 [12] extended by a complete implementation of IEEE 802.11.

Fig. 4 depicts a comparison of cost to control information MAODV and EQMGA. We can see that comes out with a smaller cost and an increased scale of network in comparison with MAODV [6], with the extend QoS constraints into MAODV, the cost to control information also increased; but for EQMGA, with its feasible path and QoS restrictive diffuse scheme, the growth of cost to control information is lower, so EQMGA will not incur the flooding storm. Due to the scarcity of wireless ad hoc network resource, EQMGA has apparent advantages, in solving ad hoc network multicast routing problems.

Fig. 5 depicts a comparison of number of route reconstructions against mobility between MAODV and EQMGA. Whenever path error occurs, it needs to reconstruct, and route number of reconstructions characterize the route's stability to some extent. From Fig. 5 we can see that the times of route reconstructions for EQMGA is superior and more stable.

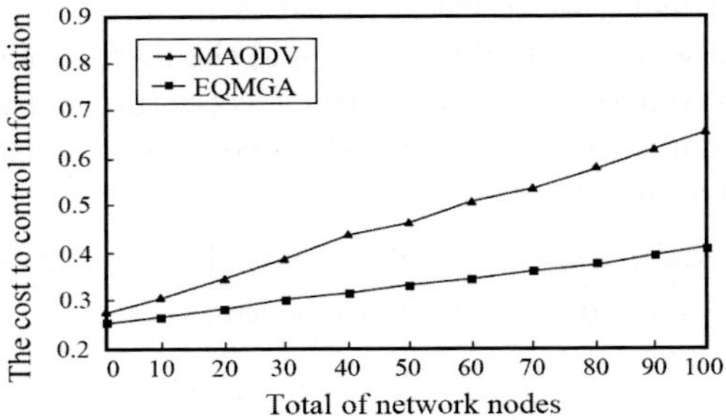

Fig. 4. Cost-comparison with control information

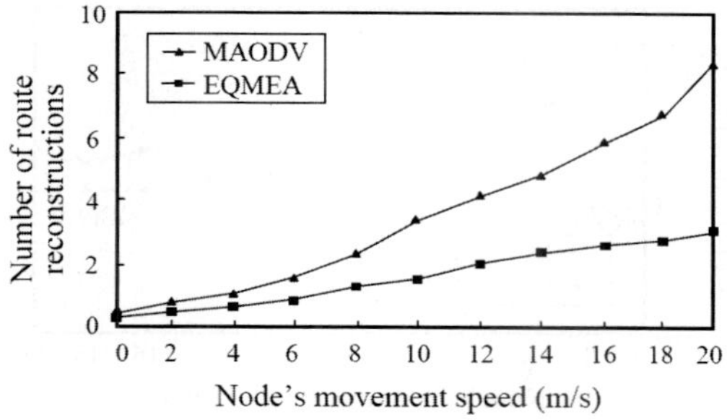

Fig. 5. Number of route reconstructions against mobility

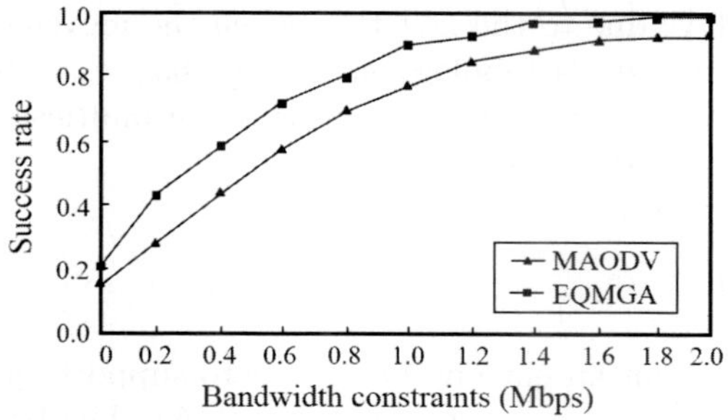

Fig. 6. Comparison of success rate to find the path

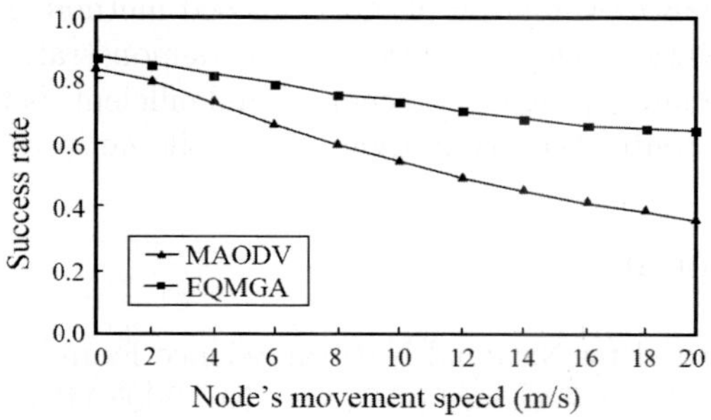

Fig. 7. Comparison of success rate to find the path

Fig. 6 depicts a comparison among success rate to find the path through MAODV and EQMGA. With the relaxation of Bandwidth constraints, the success rate becomes larger for MAODV and EQMGA. EQMGA's success rate is still higher than that of MAODV, which mean EQMGA is more suitable for the routing choosing under timely data transmission application and dynamic network structure.

Fig. 7 and Fig. 8 depicts the comparison of success rate to find the path and data transmission rate under nodes' changing movement speed for MAODV and EQMGA. From Fig. 7 and Fig. 8 we can see that when the movement speed of the node increase, EQMGA success rate and data transmission rate is still higher

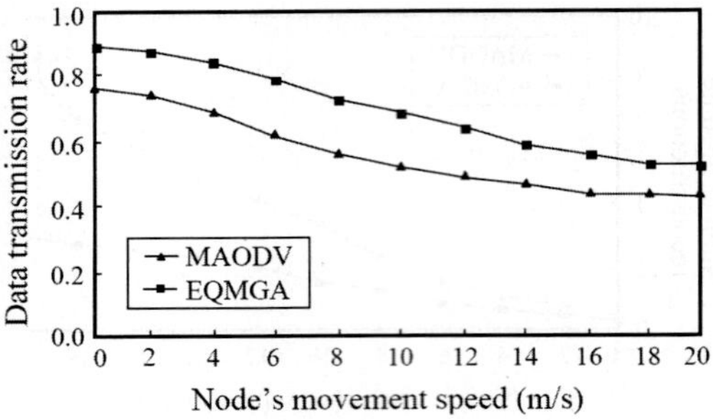

Fig. 8. Comparison of data transmission rate

than that of MAODV, due to the fact that when the movement speed increase for the nodes, the network's topology structure changes faster. The reason is that QoS multicast tree can select the most stable multicast routing between source node and destination node.

6 Conclusion

In this paper, we present an entropy-based GA to support QoS multicast routing algorithm in mobile ad hoc networks (EQMGA). The basic motivations of the proposed modeling approach stem from the commonality observed in the location uncertainty in mobile ad hoc wireless networks and the concept of entropy. The performance evaluation of our proposed method is accomplished via modeling and simulation. The simulation results demonstrate that the proposed approach and parameters provide an accurate and efficient method of estimating and evaluating the route stability in dynamic mobile networks.

Acknowledgement

This work is supported by National Natural Science Foundation of China (No. 90304018), NSF of Hubei Province of China (No. 2005ABA231), and Key Scientific Research Project of Hubei Education Department (No. D200617001).

References

1. Sun, B. L., Li, L. Y.: A QoS Multicast Routing Optimization Algorithms Based on Genetic Algorithm. Journal of Communications and Networks, Vol. 8, No. 1, (2006) 116-122
2. Sun, B. L., Yang, Q., Ma, J., Chen, H.: Fuzzy QoS Controllers in Diff-Serv Scheduler using Genetic Algorithms. Computational Intelligence and Security (CIS2005), LNAI 3801, Springer-Verlag Berlin Heidelberg, (2005) 101-106
3. Sun, B. L., Li, L. Y., Yang, Q., Xiang, Y.: An Entropy-Based Stability QoS Multicast Routing Protocol in Ad Hoc Network. Advances in Grid and Pervasive Computing (GPC 2006), LNCS 3947, Springer Verlag Berlin Heidelberg, (2006) 216-225

4. Wu, K., Harms, J.: QoS Support in Mobile Ad Hoc Networks. Crossing Boundaries-the GSA Journal of University of Alberta, Vol. 1, No. 1, (2001) 92-106
5. Cordeiro, C. M., Gossain, H., Agrawal, D. P.: Multicast over Wireless Mobile Ad Hoc Networks: Present and Future Directions. IEEE Network, Vol. 17, No. 1, (2003) 52-59
6. Royer, E. M., Perkins, C. E.: Multicast Ad Hoc On-Demand Distance Vector (MAODV) Routing. IETF MANET WG Internet Draft, work in progress, July 2000
7. Lee, S. J., Su, W., Hsu, J., Gerla, M.: On-Demand Multicast Routing Protocol (ODMRP) for Ad Hoc Networks. ACM/Kluwer Mobile Networks and Applications, Vol. 7, No. 6, (2002) 441-453
8. An, B., Papavassiliou, S.: An Entropy-Based Model for Supporting and Evaluating Route Stability in Mobile Ad hoc Wireless Networks. IEEE Communications Letters, Vol. 6, No. 8, (2002) 328-330
9. Shiozaki, A.: Edge Extraction Using Entropy Operator. Computer Vision Graphics and Image Processing, Vol. 36, No. 1, (1986) 1-9
10. Sun, Q., Li, L. Y.: An Efficient Distributed Broadcasting Algorithm for Ad Hoc Networks. Advanced Parallel Processing Technologies (APPT 2005), LNCS 3756, Springer Verlag Berlin Heidelberg, (2005) 363-372
11. Waxman, B.: Routing of Multipoint Connections. IEEE Journal on Selected Areas in Communications, Vol. 6, No. 9, (1988) 1617-1622
12. The Network Simulator - NS-2: http://www.isi.edu/nsnam/ns/, (2004)

Simulating an Intelligence Fault Tolerance System for Situation-Aware Ubiquitous Computing

Eung Nam Ko

Department of Information & Communication, Baekseok University
115, Anseo-Dong, Cheonan, ChungNam, 330-704, Korea
ssken@bu.ac.kr

Abstract. The focus of situation-aware ubiquitous computing has increased lately. An example of situation-aware applications is a multimedia education system. The development of multimedia computers and communication techniques has made it possible for a mind to be transmitted from a teacher to a student in distance environment. This paper proposes an Adaptive Fault Tolerance (AFT) algorithm in situation-aware middleware framework and presents its simulation model of AFT-based agents. FTE(Fault Tolerance Environment) provide several functions and features capable of developing multimedia distant education system among students and teachers during lecture. AFT is a system that is suitable for detecting and recovering software error based on distributed multimedia education environment as FTE by using software techniques. This method detects an error by using process database. When an error occurs, FTA(Fault Tolerance Agent) inspects it by using API(Application Program Interface) function for process database. If an error is found, FTA decides whether it is hardware error or software error. In case of software error, it can be recoverable. The purpose of AFT system is to maintain and recover for FTE session automatically. This paper proposes an Adaptive Fault Tolerance (AFT) algorithm in situation-aware middleware framework and presents its simulation model of AFT-based agents.

1 Introduction

In a ubiquitous computing environment, *computing anytime, anywhere, any devices,* the concept of situation-aware middleware has played very important roles in matching user needs with available computing resources in transparent manner in dynamic environments [1,2]. An example of situation-aware applications is a multimedia education system. Education system for distributed multimedia holds the promise of greatly improving all forms of remote education and training[3]. However, since this new education system must be developed in a way that combines various field of technologies, including group communication and distributed multimedia processing which are the basis of packet based videoconferencing systems, integrated service functions such as middle ware are required to support it[4,5,6]. Although the situation-aware middleware provides powerful analysis of dynamically changing situations in the ubiquitous computing environment by synthesizing multiple contexts and users' actions, which need to be analyzed over a period of time, it is difficult to detect errors and recover them for seamless services and avoid a single point of

D.-S. Huang, K. Li, and G.W. Irwin (Eds.): ICIC 2006, LNAI 4114, pp. 1290 – 1299, 2006.

failure. Thus, there is a great need for fault-tolerance algorithm in situation-aware middleware to provide dependable services in ubiquitous computing. QoS guarantees must be met in the application, system and network to get the acceptance of the users of multimedia communication system. There are several constraints which must be satisfied to provide guarantees during multimedia transmission. They are time, space ,device, frequency, and reliability constraints[7]. We propose a method and simulation for increasing reliability through an Adaptive Fault-Tolerance (AFT) model for situation-aware ubiquitous computing. The model aims at simulating it after detecting, classifying, and recovering errors automatically. Section 2 describes related works as fault tolerance and Reconfigurable Context-Sensitive Middleware (RCSM). Section 3 denotes the AFT architecture and algorithm. Section 4 describes simulation results of our proposed AFT model. Section 5 presents conclusion.

2 Related Works

In this section, we describe fault tolerance system and Reconfigurable Context-Sensitive Middleware(RCSM).

2.1 Fault Tolerance System

Fault tolerance is the ability of the system to continue to function in the presence of hardware or software failures. Fault tolerance designed to increase reliability in real-time systems can be classified in two varieties, spatial and temporal. Spatial fault tolerance includes methods involving redundant hardware or software, whereas temporal fault tolerance involves techniques that allow for tolerating missed deadlines. Two different techniques for achieving fault-tolerance in software have been discussed in the recent literature: the recovery block and N-version programming. In the latter a number(N>=2) of independently coded programs for a given function are run simultaneously(or nearly so) on loosely coupled computers, the results are compared, and in case of disagreement a preferred result is identified by majority vote(for N > 2) or a predetermined strategy. This approach had been suggested in a general way by Elmendorf and has more recently been developed into a practical form by Avizienis & Chen who report results on the use of this technique on a classroom problem. A specific constraint on N-version programming is the requirement for N computers that are hardware independent yet able to communicate very efficiently so that rapid comparisons of results can be achieved These N computers must all be operating at the same time, and a hardware failure in any one of them will at best force the system into a different operating mode and may, in minimal configurations, cause loss of the fault-tolerance provisions[8-11]. The recovery block technique can be applied to a more general spectrum of computer configurations, including a single computer(which may also include hardware fault-tolerance). The simplest structure of the recovery block is:

```
Ensure T
        By P
        Else by Q
         Else    Error
```

Where T is the acceptance test condition that is expected to be met by successful execution of either the primary routine P or the alternative routine Q. The internal control structure of the recovery block will transfer to Q when the test conditions are not met by executing P. Techniques have been described for purging data altered during processing by P when Q is called[8-11]. In the DRB scheme, a recovery block is replicated into multiple nodes, forming a DRB computing station for parallel redundant processing. In most cases a recovery block containing just two try blocks is designed and then assigned to a pair of nodes. A try not completed within the maximum execution time allowed for each try block due to hardware faults or excessive looping is treated as a failure. Therefore, the acceptance test can be viewed as a combination of both logic and time acceptance tests[12].

2.2 Reconfigurable Context-Sensitive Middleware(RCSM)

A conceptual architecture of situation-aware middleware based on Reconfigurable Context-Sensitive Middleware (RCSM) is proposed in [2].

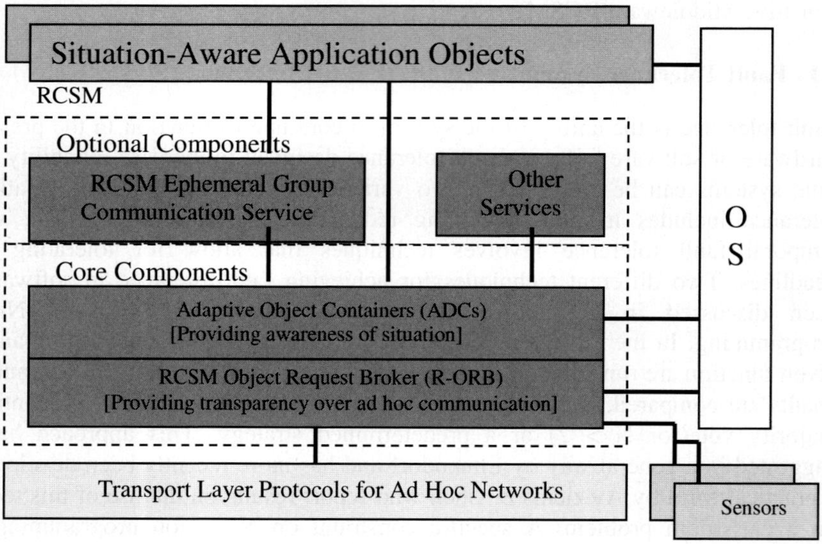

Fig. 1. Overview of Situation-Aware Middleware

Ubiquitous applications require use of various contexts to adaptively communicate with each other across multiple network environments, such as mobile ad hoc networks, Internet, and mobile phone networks. However, existing context-aware techniques often become inadequate in these applications where combinations of multiple contexts and users' actions need to be analyzed over a period of time. All of RCSM's components are layered inside a device, as shown in Figure 1. The Object Request Broker of RCSM (R-ORB) assumes the availability of reliable transport protocols; one R-ORB per device is sufficient. The number of ADaptive object

Containers (ADC)s depends on the number of context-sensitive objects in the device. ADCs periodically collect the necessary "raw context data" through the R-ORB, which in turn collects the data from sensors and the operating system. Initially, each ADC registers with the R-ORB to express its needs for contexts and to publish the corresponding context-sensitive interface. RCSM is called reconfigurable because it allows addition or deletion of individual ADCs during runtime (to manage new or existing context-sensitive application objects) without affecting other runtime operations inside RCSM.

However, it did not include fault-tolerance support in the architecture. In this paper, we propose a new fault-tolerance capability, called "Adaptive Fault-Tolerance (AFT)", in situation-aware middleware.

3 Adaptive Fault-Tolerance (AFT): Our Proposed Approach

In this section, we present an Adaptive Fault-Tolerance (AFT) model for situation-aware ubiquitous computing. The AFT architecture is presented in Section 3.1 and its algorithm in Section 3.2.

3.1 The AFT Architecture

Our proposed AFT model aims at supporting fault –tolerance requirements by detecting errors and recovering them in order to provide seamless services and avoid a single point of failure. An example of situation-aware applications is a multimedia education system. The development of multimedia computers and communication techniques has made it possible for a mind to be transmitted from a teacher to a student in distance environment. As shown in Figure 2, other services have many agents. AFT is one of agent which included in other services. FTE(Fault Tolerance Environment) provide several functions and features capable of developing multimedia distant education system among students and teachers during lecture.

AFT consists of Fault Tolerance Agent (FTA), User Interface Agent (UIA) and Session Management Agent (SMA), as shown in Figure 2 and Figure 3. UIA is an agent which plays a role as an interface to interact between the user and FTA. SMA is an agent which plays a role in connection of UIA and FTA as management for the whole information. AMA consists of various subclass modules. It includes creation/deletion of shared video window and creation/deletion of shared window. ACA controls the person who can talk, and the one who can change the information. MCA support convenient application using situation-aware ubiquitous computing. Supplied services are the creation and deletion of the service object for media use, and media share between the remote users. This agent limits the services by hardware constraint.

If there are some error resource due to resource reliability, AFT performs to keep changing as the applications change. AFT is a system that is suitable for detecting and recovering software error based on distributed multimedia education environment as FTE by using software techniques. This method detects an error by using process database. The purpose of this research is to return to a healthy state or at least an acceptable state for FTE session. It is to recover application software or media running on situation-aware ubiquitous computing automatically.

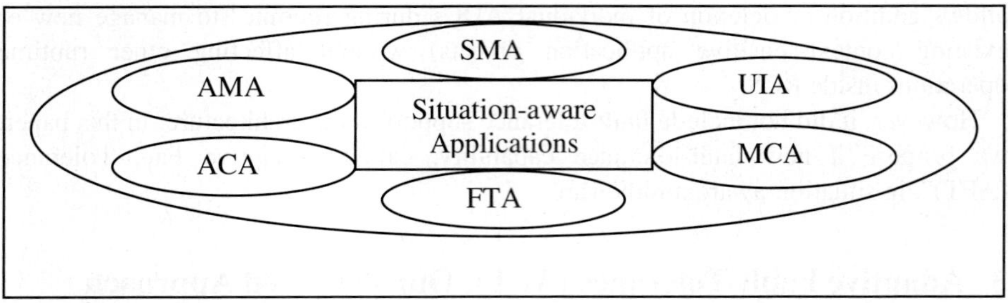

Fig. 2. The Fault-Tolerance Environment (FTE) in Situation-Aware Applications

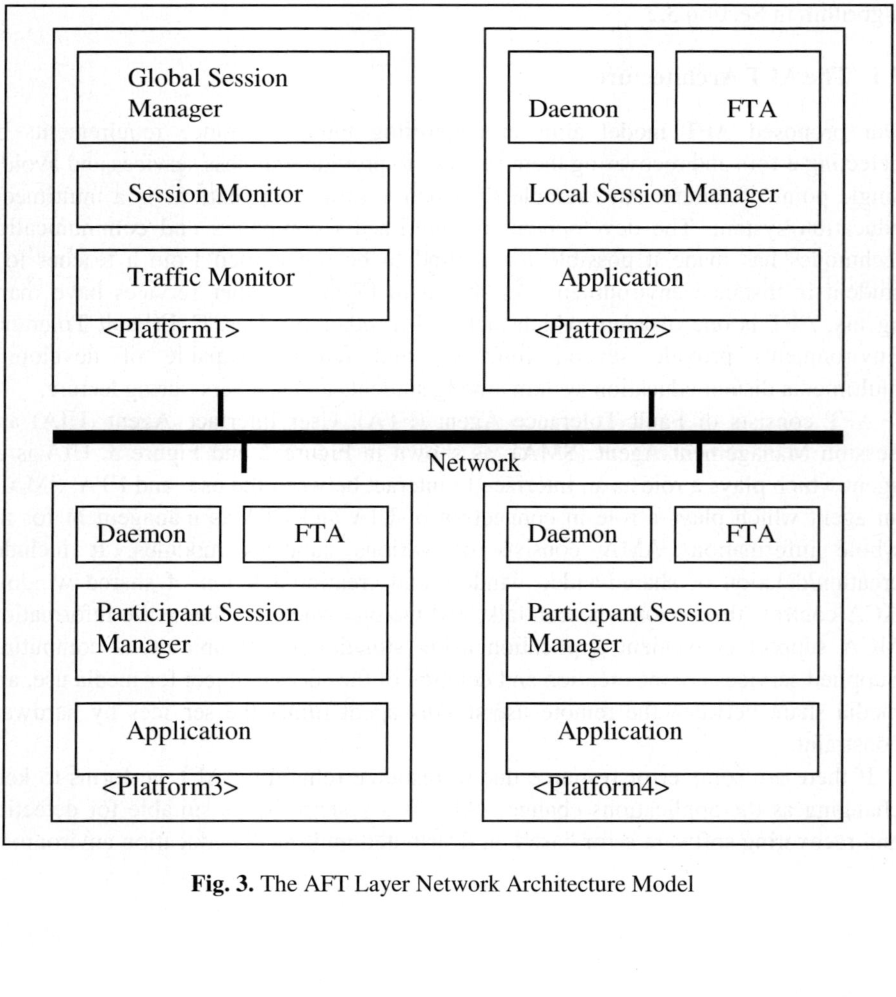

Fig. 3. The AFT Layer Network Architecture Model

SMA monitors the access to the session and controls the session. It has an object with a various information for each session and it also supports multitasking with this information. SMA consists of Global Session Manager (GSM), Daemon, Local Session Manager (LSM), Participant Session Manager (PSM), Session Monitor ,and Traffic Monitor. GSM has the function of controlling whole session when a number of sessions are open simultaneously. LSM manages only own session. For example, LSM is a lecture class in distributed multimedia environment. GSM can manage multiple LSM. Daemon is an object with services to create session. As shown in Figure 3, you can see the single session relationship among a FTA, GSM, LSM, PSM and the application software on LAN. Platform 1 consists of GSM, Session Monitor, and Traffic Monitor. The other platform consists of Daemon, Local Session Manager, Participant Session Manager and FTA. Each platform except platform1 has a FTA. FTA is an agent that plays a role in detecting an error and recovering it. FTA informs SMA of the results of detected errors. Also, FTA activates an error in application software automatically. It informs SMA of the result again.

To ensure required reliability for situation-aware ubiquitous computing automatically, FTA consists of 3 steps that are an error detection, an error classification, and an error recovery. As shown in Figure 4, you can see the organization of FTA. FTA consists of FDA(Fault Detection Agent), FCA(Fault Classification Agent), and FRA(Fault Recovery Agent). That is, FTA becomes aware of an error occurrence after it receives requirement of UIA. FDA has a function of error detection. FCA has a function of error classification. FRA has a function of error recovery. FCA consists of frontend, backend, analyzer, coordinator, filter, and learner. Frontend has a function of playing a role in receiving error detection information from FDA. Backend has a function of playing a role in receiving error recovery information from FRA. Coordinator informs SMA of the result. Analyzer has a function of classifying error's information that is received from frontend. Learner has a function of classifying the type of errors by using learning rules with consideration of information from analyzer. Filter has a function of storing an error's history information in KB from error information that is classified by learner.

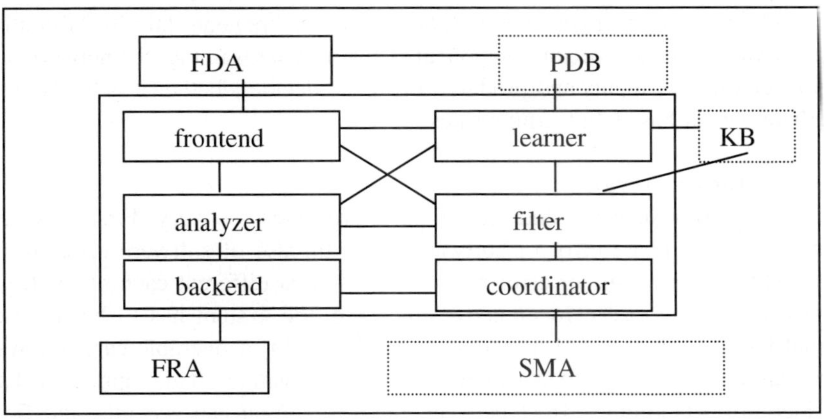

Fig. 4. The organization of FTA

3.2 The Algorithm of AFT

To ensure required reliability of multimedia communication systems, FTA consists of 3 steps that are an error detection, an error classification, and an error recovery.

Step1. (Error detection)
We are first in need of a method to detect an error for session's recovery. One of the methods to detect an error for session's recovery inspects Process Database (PDB) periodically. However, this method has a weak point of inspecting all processes without regard to FTE session. Therefore, we propose an AFT model. This method detects an error by polling periodically the process with relation to FTE session. Windows 95/98//XP creates a process database to represent the process. Process database include a list of threads, a list of loaded modules, the heap handle of the default process heap, a pointer to the process handle table, and a pointer to the memory context that the process runs in. A process handle is essentially the same thing as a file handle. GetExitCodeProcess() function retrieves the termination status of the process specified by the Process handle passed in. While a process is still actively running, its exit code is 0x103(0x: hexadecimal code).

Step2. (Error classification)
FCA is an agent that plays a role as an interface to interact between FDA for detection and FRA for recovery. FCA has a function which classifies the type of errors by using learning rules. FCA deals with learning in reactive multi-agent systems. Generally learning rules may be classified as supervised or unsupervised or reinforcement learning. Reinforcement learning is similar to supervised learning, except it, instead of being provided with the concept output for each network input, the algorithm is only given a grade. The grade (or score) is a measure of the network performance over some sequence of inputs[13]. This paper deals with Q-learning that is one of the reinforcement learning. Because FCA has not knowledge of error classification, it receives an acknowledgement information which is necessary for fault diagnosis from Process Data Base (PDB). Hence the training set consists of a set of input vectors, each with its desired target vector. Input vector components take on a continuous range of values. Target vector components valued. After training, the network accepts a set of continuous inputs and produces FCA can decide whether it is hardware error or software error based on learning rules.

Step3. (Error recovery)
After a system is detected and classified, it processes recovery. First it is decided whether it is hardware error or software error. In case of software error, it can be recoverable. The scheme of error recovery method is different each other. It can be classified as many cases. In unrecoverable case, the system has to be restarted by manual when error occurred in hardware resources. In recoverable case, recoverable case classified as state insensitive and state sensitive. This approach has no consideration of domino effect between processes. You can see message flows in FTE. It consists of Daemon, Session Manager and FTA. After a system is detected

and classified, it processes recovery. First it is decided whether it is hardware error or software error. In case of software error, it can be recoverable.

4 Simulating AFT

The AFT simulation model has been implemented by using VISUAL C++. To evaluate the performance of the proposed system, an error detection method was used to compare the performance of the proposed model against the conventional model by using DEVS(Discrete Event System Specification) formalism. The DEVS formalism introduced by Bernard P. Zeigler provides a means of specifying a mathematical object called a system. Conventional simulation system adequately support only a single level at which change occurs in the model, that of changes in the model descriptive variable, viz. its behavior. The DEVS formalism is a theoretical, well grounded means of expressing hierarchical, modular discrete event models. In DEVS, a system has a time base, inputs, states, outputs based on the current states and inputs. DEVS is a formalism of being developed by Bernard P. Zeigler. The structure of atomic model is as follows [14-16]:

$$M = < X, S, Y, \delta_{int}, \delta_{ext}, \lambda, t_a >$$

X: a set of input events, S: a set of sequential states,
Y: a set of output events, δ_{int} : internal transition function,
δ_{ext} : external transition function, λ : output function, and
t_a : time advance function.

Before system analysis, the variable that is used in this system is as follows. The letter Poll-int stands for "polling interval". The letter App-cnt stands for "The number of application program with relation to FTE session". The letter App_cnt2 stands for "The number of application program without relation to FTE session". The letter Sm-t-a stands for " The accumulated time to register information in SM".

(Simulation 1)
The atomic models are EF, RA1, UA1, and ED1. The combination of atomic models makes a new coupled model. First, it receives input event, i.e., polling interval. The value is an input value in RA1 and UA1 respectively. An output value is determined by the time related simulation process RA1 and UA1 respectively. The output value can be an input value in ED1. An output value is determined by the time related simulation process ED1. We can observe the result value through transducer.

(Simulation 2)
The atomic models are EF, RA2, and ED2. The combination of atomic models makes a new coupled model. First, it receives input event, i.e., polling interval. The value is an input value in RA2. An output value is determined by the time related simulation process RA2. The output value can be an input value in ED2. An output value is determined by the time related simulation process ED2. We can observe the result value through transducer. The error detected time interval is as follows.

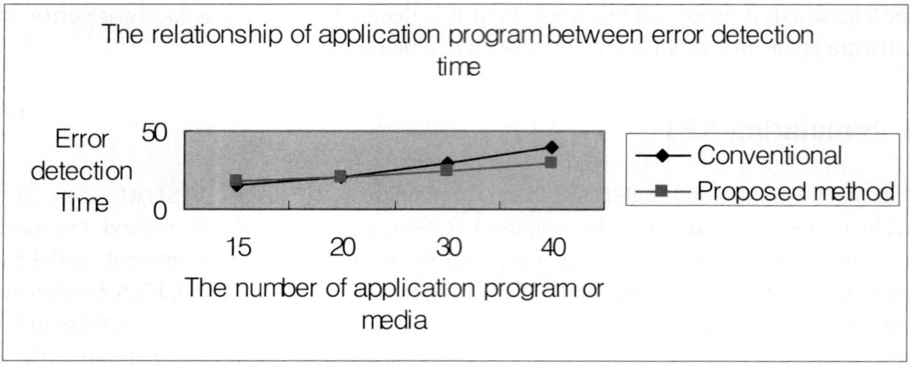

Fig. 5. The relationship of application program and error detection time

Conventional method: Poll_int*(App_cnt + App_cnt2)
Proposed method: Poll_int*(App_cnt) + Sm_t_a
Therefore, in case of App-cnt2 > App-cnt,

Poll_int*(App_cnt + App_cnt2) > Poll_int*(App_cnt) + Sm_t_a

That is, proposed method is more efficient than conventional method in error detected method in case of App-cnt2 > App-cnt. We have compared the performance of the proposed method with conventional method.

5 Conclusion

The focus of situation-aware ubiquitous computing has increased lately. An example of situation-aware applications is a multimedia education system. The development of multimedia computers and communication techniques has made it possible for a mind to be transmitted from a teacher to a student in distance environment. This paper proposes an Adaptive Fault Tolerance (AFT) algorithm in situation-aware middleware framework and presents its simulation model of AFT-based agents. FTE provide several functions and features capable of developing multimedia distant education system among students and teachers during lecture. AFT is a system that is suitable for detecting and recovering software error based on distributed multimedia education environment as FTE by using software techniques. This method detects an error by using process database. The purpose of this research is to return to a healthy state or at least an acceptable state for FTE session. It is to recover application software running on situation-aware ubiquitous computing automatically. When an error occurs, FTA inspects it by using API function for process database. If an error is found, FTA decides whether it is hardware error or software error. In case of software error, it can be recoverable. FTA informs Daemon and Session Manager of the fact. As they receive the information from the FTA, Daemon and Session Manager recovers from the error. The purpose of AFT system is to maintain and recover for FTE session automatically. In the future work, fault-tolerance system will be generalized to be used in any environment, and we will progress the study of domino effect for distributed multimedia environment as an example of situation-aware applications.

References

1. Michael G.M., Kearsley, G.: DISTANCE EDUCATION A System View. An International Thomson Publishing Company (1996)
2. Ahn, J. Y., Lee, G. M., Park, G. C., Hwang, D. J.: An Implementation of Multimedia Distance Education System Based on Advanced Multi-point Communication Service Infrastructure: DOORAE. In proceedings of the IASTED International Conference Parallel and Distributed Computing and Systems, Chicago, Illinois, USA (1996)
3. Agnew, P. W., Kellerman, Anne S.: Distributed Multimedia, ACM Press (1996)
4. Ahn, J. Y., Lee, G. M., Park, G. C., Hwang, D. J.: An implementation of Multimedia Distance Education System Based on Advanced Multi-point Communication Service Infrastructure: DOORAE. In proceedings of the IASTED International Conference Parallel and Distributed Computing and Systems, Chicago, Illinois, USA (1996)
5. ITU-T Recommendation T.122 Multipoint Communication Service for Audiographics and Audiovisual Conferencing Service Definition, ITU-T SG8 Interim Meeting 18th Oct, 1994, mertlesham, issued 14th (1995)
6. Ko, E. N., Hwang, D. J., Kim, J. H.: Implementation of an Error Detection-Recovery System based on Multimedia Collaboration Works: EDRSMCW. MIC'99 IASTED International Conference, Innsbruck Austria (1999)
7. Steinmetz, R., Nahrstedt, Klara.: Multimedia: computing, communications & Applications. Prentice Hall P T R (1996)
8. Pradhan, Dhiraj K.: Fault-Tolerant Computer System Design, Prentice Hall Ptr (1996)
9. Scarlatos, Lori L.: Designing Interactive Multimedia. Proceedings of the Fifth International Multimedia Conference, Seattle, Washington, USA (1997)
10. Nelson, Victor P., Carroll, Bill D.: Fault-Tolerant Computing: Chapter 1 Introduction to Fault-Tolerant Computing. IEEE Computer Society Order Number 677, Library of Congress Number 86-46205, IEEE Catalog Number EH0254-3, ISBN 0-8186-0677-0
11. Nelson, Victor P., Carroll, Bill D.: Fault-Tolerant Computing: Chapter 5: Software Fault Tolerance. IEEE Computer Society Order Number 677, Library of Congress Number 86-46205, IEEE Catalog Number EH0254-3, ISBN 0-8186-0677-0
12. Son, Sang H.: Advances in Real-Time Systems, Prentice Hall, Englewood Cliffs, NJ 07632 (1995) 425-427
13. Hagan, Martin T., Demuth, Howard B., Beale, M.: Neural Network Design. PWS Publishing Company (1996) 3-4
14. Zeigler, B.P.: Object-Oriented Simulation with Hierarchical. Modular Models, San Diego, CA, USA: Academic Press (1990)
15. Cho, T.H., Zeigler, B.P.: Simulation of Intelligent Hierarchical Flexible Manufacturing: Batch Job Routing in Operation Overlapping. IEEE Trans. Syst. Man, Cybern. A, Vol.27 (1997) 116-126
16. Zeigler, B.P., Cho, T.H., Rozenblit, J.W.: A Knowledge-based Environment for Hierarchical Modeling of Flexible Manufacturing System. IEEE Trans. Syst. Man,Cybern. A, Vol.26 (1996) 81-90

An Access Control Mechanism Based on Situation-Aware Ubiquitous Computing for Seamless Multimedia View Sharing

Eung Nam Ko

Department of Information & Communication, Baekseok University
115, Anseo-Dong, Cheonan, ChungNam, 330-704, Korea
ssken@bu.ac.kr

Abstract. This paper proposes a new model of access control by analyzing the window and attributes of the object, and based on this, a mechanism that offers a seamless multimedia view without interfering with access control is also suggested. There are two approaches to software architecture on which applications for multimedia distance education environment in situation-aware middleware are based. Those include CACV(Centralized-Abstraction and Centralized-View) and RARV(Replicated-Abstraction and Replicated-View).To win over such dilemma for centralized or replicated architecture, a combined approach, CARV(the Centralized Abstraction and Replicated View) architecture is used to realize the application sharing agent.

1 Introduction

Context awareness (or context sensitivity) is an application software system's ability to sense and analyze context from various sources; it lets application software take different actions adaptively in different contexts [1]. With the rapid development of multimedia and network technology, more and more digital media is generated[2-4]. Although the situation-aware middleware provides powerful analysis of dynamically changing situations in the ubiquitous computing environment by synthesizing multiple contexts and users' actions, which need to be analyzed over a period of time, access control in using multimedia shared object causes a problem of the seam in the ubiquitous computing environment. It is difficult to avoid a problem of the seam in the ubiquitous computing environment for seamless services. Thus, there is a great need for access control algorithm in situation-aware middleware to provide dependable services in ubiquitous computing. This paper proposes a new model of dynamic window binding by analyzing the window and attributes of the object, and based on this, a mechanism that offers a seamless multimedia view without interfering with access control is also suggested. Section 2 describes situation-aware middleware. Section 3 denotes access control algorithm. Section 4 describes simulation results of our proposed algorithm. Section 5 present conclusions.

2 Background: Situation-Aware Middleware

Ubiquitous applications require use of various contexts to adaptively communicate with each other across multiple network environments, such as mobile ad hoc

D.-S. Huang, K. Li, and G.W. Irwin (Eds.): ICIC 2006, LNAI 4114, pp. 1300 – 1305, 2006.

networks, Internet, and mobile phone networks. However, existing context-aware techniques often become inadequate in these applications where combinations of multiple contexts and users' actions need to be analyzed over a period of time. Situation-awareness in application software is considered as a desirable property to overcome this limitation. In addition to being context-sensitive, situation-aware applications can respond to both current and historical relationships of specific contexts and device-actions. An example of situation-aware applications is a multimedia distance education system. The development of multimedia computers and communication techniques has made it possible for a mind to be transmitted from a teacher to a student in distance environment. However, it did not include access control support in the architecture of situation-aware middleware. In this paper, we propose a new access control mechanism in situation-aware middleware.

3 Access Control Mechanism: Our Proposed Approach

In this section, we present an access control mechanism for situation-aware ubiquitous computing. The environment of access control is presented in Section 3.1, and its algorithm in Section 3.2.

3.1 The Environment for Access Control

A conceptual architecture of situation-aware middleware based on Reconfigurable Context-Sensitive Middleware (RCSM) is proposed in [2]. All of RCSM's components are layered inside a device. The Object Request Broker of RCSM (R-ORB) assumes the availability of reliable transport protocols; one R-ORB per device is sufficient. The number of ADaptive object Containers (ADC)s depends on the number of context-sensitive objects in the device. ADCs periodically collect the necessary "raw context data" through the R-ORB, which in turn collects the data from sensors and the operating system. Initially, each ADC registers with the R-ORB to express its needs for contexts and to publish the corresponding context-sensitive interface. RCSM is called reconfigurable because it allows addition or deletion of individual ADCs during runtime (to manage new or existing context-sensitive application objects) without affecting other runtime operations inside RCSM.

Other services have many agents. They consist of AMA(Application Management Agent), MCA(Media Control Agent), FTA(Fault Tolerance Agent), SA-UIA(Situation-Aware User Interface Agent), SA-SMA(Situation-Aware Session Management Agent), and SA-ACCA(Situation-Aware Access and Concurrency Control Agent), as shown in Figure 1. AMA consists of various subclass modules. It includes creation/deletion of shared video window and creation/deletion of shared window. MCA supports convenient applications using situation-aware ubiquitous computing. Supplied services are the creation and deletion of the service object for media use, and media share between the remote users.

This agent limits the services by hardware constraint. FTA is an agent that plays a role in detecting an error and recovering it in situation-aware ubiquitous environment. SA-UIA is a user interface agent to adapt user interfaces based on situations.

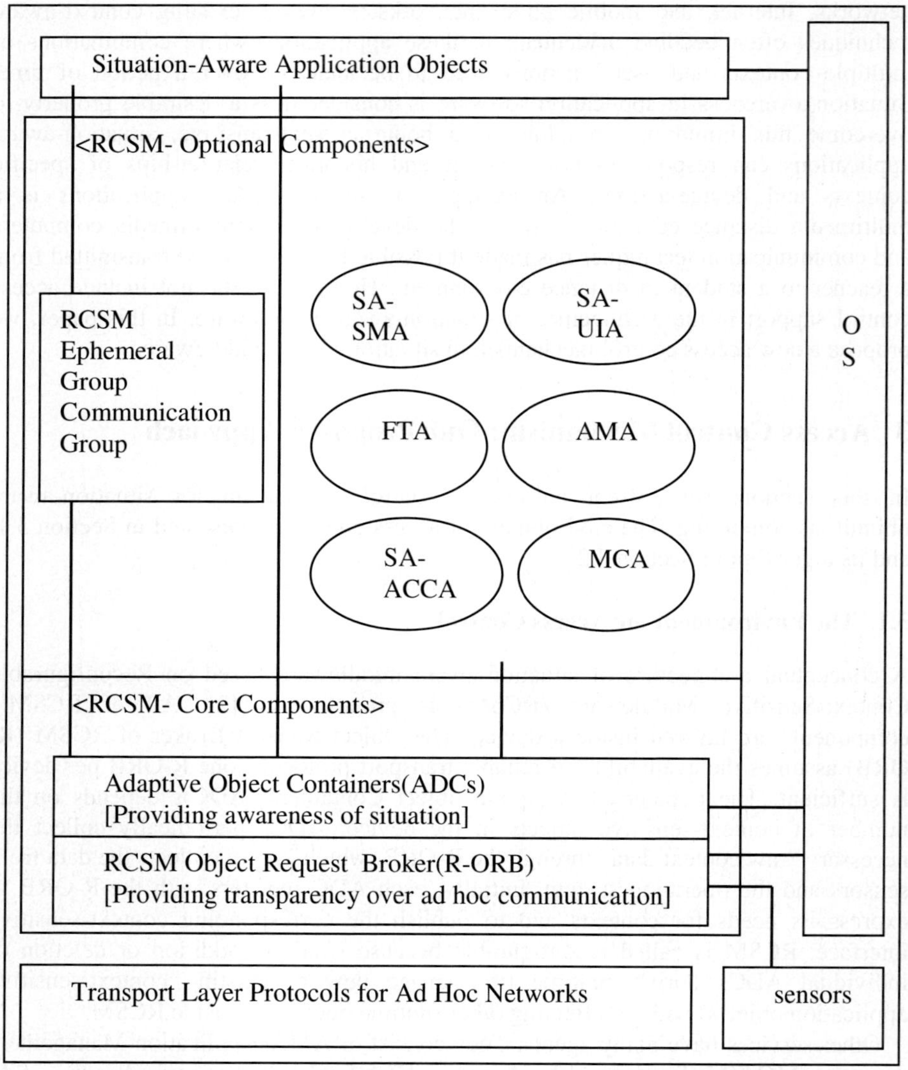

Fig. 1. Other Services in Situation-Aware Ubiquitous Computing

SASMA is an agent which plays a role in connection of SA-UIA and FTA as situation-aware management for the whole information. SA-ACCA controls the person who can talk, and the one who can change the information for access. Our proposed model aims at supporting access control requirements by using dynamic window binding mechanism in order to provide ubiquitous, seamless services.

3.2 The Algorithm for Access Control

There are two approaches to software architecture on which applications for multimedia distance education environment in situation-aware middleware are based.

Those include CACV(Centralized-Abstraction and Centralized-View) and RARV (Replicated-Abstraction and Replicated-View). The environment of access control is based on a hybrid software architecture which is adopting the advantage of CACV and RARV. Access control agent decides who has right to speak and manages distribution of resources along with user status when there is a request for resources. Figure 2 shows the relationship between initiator and participant of an access control for multimedia distance education system.

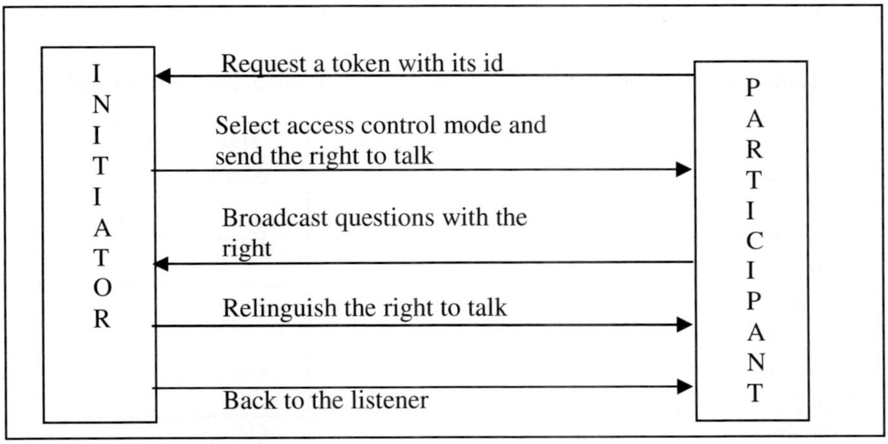

Fig. 2. Access Control in Situation-Aware Ubiquitous Computing

FTA consists of EDA(Error Detection Agent), ECA(Error Classification Agent), and ERA(Error Recovery Agent). ECA consists of ES(Error Sharing) and EC(Error Classification). EDA detects an error by using hooking methods in MS-Windows API(Application Program Interface). When an error occurs, A hook is a point in the Microsoft Windows message-handling mechanism where an application can install a subroutine to monitor the message traffic in the system and process certain types of messages before they reach the target window procedure. Windows contains many different types of hook. The roles of ES(error and application program sharing) are divided into two main parts; Abstraction and sharing of view generation. Error and application program sharing must take different from each other according to number of replicated application program and an event command. This proposed structure is distributed architecture but for error and application program sharing, centralization architecture is used. Error and application program sharing windows perform process communication of message form. In the middle of this process, there are couple ways of snatching message by error and application sharing agent. ESA informs SM of the results of detected errors. Also, ESA activates a failure application software automatically. It informs SM of the result again. That is, ESA becomes aware of an error occurrence after it receives requirement of UIA and transmit it.

4 Simulation Results

As shown in Table 1, you can see the characteristic function of each system function for multimedia distance education. To evaluate the performance of the proposed system, it was used to compare the performance of the proposed model against the conventional model by using DEVS formalism. In DEVS, a system has a time base, inputs, states, outputs based on the current states and inputs. DEVS(Discrete Event System Specification) is a formalism of being developed by Bernard P. Zeigler. The structure of atomic model is as follows [5-10].

Table 1. Comparison for Software Architecture in situation-aware environment

	Centralized	Replicated	Hybrid(Proposed)
Set initial State	Easy	hard	Medium
Allow Late Comer	Easy	hard	Easy
Command Serialization	Easy	hard	Easy
Communication Overhead	High	low	Low
Probability	good	bad	Good
Performance	bad	good	Good
Application Copy	one	more than one	More than one
Control Complexity	Low	high	High

5 Conclusions

The focus of situation-aware ubiquitous computing has increased lately. An example of situation-aware applications is a multimedia education system. The development of multimedia computers and communication techniques has made it possible for a mind to be transmitted from a teacher to a student in distance environment. This paper proposed a new model of access control by analyzing the window and attributes of the attributes of the object, and based on this, a mechanism that offers a seamless view without interfering with access control is also suggested. There are two approaches to software architecture on which applications for multimedia distance education environment in situation-aware middleware are based. Those include CACV(Centralized-Abstraction and Centralized-View) and RARV(Replicated-Abstraction and Replicated-View). The environment of access control is based on a hybrid software architecture which is adopting the advantage of CACV and RARV. The simulation results clearly showed that the access control mechanism proposed in this paper is worth implementation and effective when a large scale of collaboration is required. In the future work, access and fault-tolerance system will be generalized to be used in any environment, and we will progress the study of access and domino effect for distributed multimedia environment as an example of situation-aware applications.

References

1. Yau, S., et al.: Reconfigurable Context-Sensitive Middleware for Pervasive Computing. In IEEEE Pervasive Computing, (2002) 33 - 40
2. Zhang, T., Kuo, C.-C, J.: Hierarchical Classification of Audio Data for Archiving and Retrieval. ICASSP'1999, Vol. 6 (1999) 3001-3004
3. Wold, E., Blum, T., Keislar, D., Wheaton, J.: Content-Based Classification, Search, and Retrieval of Audio. IEEE Multimedia, Vol.3, No.3 (1996) 27-36
4. Zhang, H., Kankanhalli, A., Smoliar, S.: Automatic Partitioning of Full-motion Video, A Guided Tour of Multimedia Systems and Applications. IEEE Computing Society Press, (1995)
5. Zeigler, B. P., Cho, T. H., Rozenblit, J. W.: A Knowledge-Based Simulation Environment for Hierarchical Flexible Manufacturing. IEEE Transaction on Systems, Man, and Cybernetics-Part A: System and Humans, Vol. 26, No.1 (1996) 81-90
6. Cho, T. H., Zeigler, B. P.: Simulation of Intelligent Hierarchical Flexible Manufacturing: Batch Job Routing in Operation Overlapping. IEEE Transaction on Systems, Man, and Cybernetics-Part A: System and Humans, Vol. 27, No.1 (1997) 116-126
7. Zeigler, B. P.: Object-Oriented Simulation with Hierarchical, Modular Models. Academic Press, (1990)
8. Zeigler, B. P.: Multifacetted Modeling and Discrete Event Simulation. Orlando, FL: Academic (1984)
9. Zeigler, B. P.: Theory of Modeling and Simulation. John Wiley, NY, USA (1976), reissued by Krieger, Malabar, FL, USA (1985)
10. Conception, A.I., Zeigler, B. P.: The DEVS formalism: Hierarchical Model Development. IEEE Trans. Software Eng., Vol.14, No.2 (1988) 228-241

Clustering Algorithm Using Bayes' Rule in Mobile Wireless Sensor Networks

Young-Bae Kong, Kyung-Bae Chang, and Gwi-Tae Park

ISRL, College of Science, Korea University. Anam-dong 5-ga Seongbuk-gu, Seoul, Korea
{ybkong, lslove, gtpark}@korea.ac.kr

Abstract. Wireless Sensor Network is an advanced technology that has a variety of applications such as environmental monitoring, battlefield, medical system, and crop precision. Minimizing power consumption of node is important in these networks. Transmit power control and clustering can reduce the energy consumption efficiently when nodes are non-homogeneously dispersed in space. This paper presents the clustering algorithm in wireless sensor networks. The clustering algorithm is based on the optimization of transmit power level by using the soft computing approaches. This solution determines the node transmit power level statistically and achieves energy savings efficiently.

1 Introduction

Wireless Sensor Network is an advanced technology that has a variety of applications such as environmental monitoring, battlefield, medical system, and crop precision. Such a network is composed of a large number of distributed nodes to perform a common task of physical sensing. Each node has a sensor, embedded processor, small memory, and low-power radio and is normally battery operated. It is almost neither changeable nor rechargeable because it is normally in the special or dangerous region. Therefore sensor nodes have limited battery power and network lifetime is a critical problem for theses sensor networks [1, 2].

Transmit power control in wireless sensor networks is a critical problem because it can affect on battery lifetime and traffic carrying capacity [3]. For example, in Fig.1 when N1 tries to transmit a packet to N2, it doesn't need to transmit the packet at 30mW since N1 is located within range at 1mW. Thus N1 saves on battery power. Next, consider N3 tries to broadcast to node N4 at 1mW. If N1 simultaneously tries to broadcast to N2 with 1mW, a transmission from node N3 and N4 can be successfully transmitted. And transmission from N1 to N2 is also successfully achieved since neither is N2 in the range of its interfere N1. However if N1 broadcasts at 30mW, that will interfere with transmission between N3 and N4. Thus, transmit power control can achieve the traffic carrying capacity.

But it is not always true in wireless sensor networks. When nodes are homogeneously distributed in space, as in Fig.1 (a), it is possible to resolve problems with the minimum transmit power level as noted above. However, when nodes are non-homogeneously distributed as in Fig.1 (b), then the minimum power level for network

D.-S. Huang, K. Li, and G.W. Irwin (Eds.): ICIC 2006, LNAI 4114, pp. 1306–1310, 2006.

connectivity is not suitable for the nodes which are far from others [4]. This problem can be effectively resolved by grouping nearly located nodes into clusters with several clusters at different power levels. Therefore the transmission power level of each cluster should be adaptively determined.

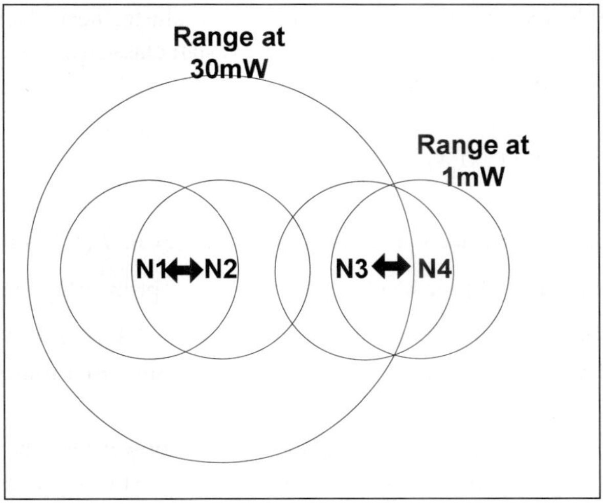

Fig. 1. The need of Transmit Power Control

In this paper, we propose a method of determining the transmit power level adaptively by using bayes' rule. This method can resolve the problems occurred in case of non-homogeneously distributed nodes. Another advantage of our method is that the method can effectively control the clustering size and thus prolongs the network lifetime.

The rest of the paper is organized as follows. Our method is described in detail in Section 2. Next, in Section 3 we present our simulation results. Finally, we conclude the paper and present future research directions in Section 4.

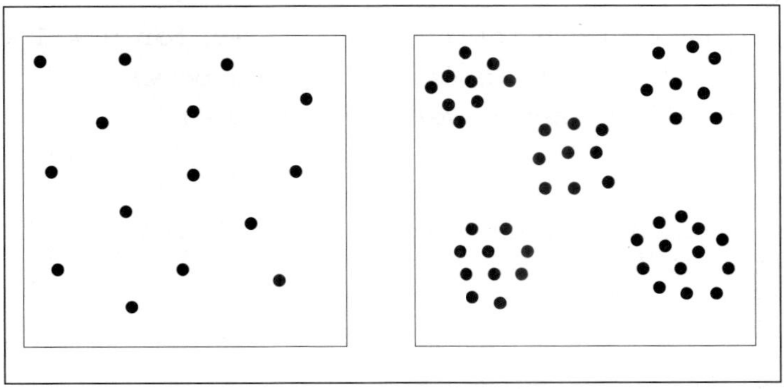

Fig. 2. (a) Homogeneous spatial dispersion of nodes (b) Non-homogeneously dispersed node

2 Clustering Algorithm Details

The transmission power for clustering is determined by bayes' rule. This method is applied to calculate the probability for an arbitrary node to belong to a specific transmission power level, and to select the highest probability. This method is as follows: First each node decides whether or not to become a cluster-head. Next, each cluster-head compute the transmit power level using Bayesian classification based on Priority probability [5]. The probability is set as:

$$P(c_j \mid x_i) = \frac{p(c_j)\,p(x_i \mid c_j)}{P(x_i)} \tag{1}$$

where x_i is each cluster-head, c_i is a transmit power level, $P(x_i)$ is a probability that an arbitrarily extracted cluster-head is x_i, $P(c_j)$ is a probability that an arbitrarily extracted node belong to transmit power level c_j, and $P(x_i \mid c_j)$ is a probability that an arbitrarily extracted node from cluster-head set belongs to a transmit power level c_j is x_i.

Bayesian classification is to determine the transmit power level having the highest possibility to the power level by calculating $P(x_i \mid c_1), P(x_i \mid c_2), P(x_i \mid c_3)$, and $P(x_i \mid c_k)$ for a given node x_j. The classification is represented as:

$$C_{best} = ArgMax\left[\frac{p(x_i \mid c_j)\,p(c_j)}{P(x_i)}\right] \tag{2}$$

By using (2), each cluster-head attains an optimized transmit power level C_{best}. This procedure is repeated whenever clusters are created. The proposed method is described as following:

```
N: cluster-head number
K: transmit power level number

// Initialize transmission power level for n = 1 to N
 n = c_1            // set node to minimum power
P(c_j | x_1) = 1/k  // set power level probability
endfor

// assign each cluster-head to power level
for n = 1 to N
   1. select not clustered node n
   2. calculate c_best of n using (2)
    3. switch (c_best of n)
```

case 1 : apply n to c_1
case 2 : apply n to c_2
...
case k-1 : apply n to c_{k-1}
case k : apply n to c_k
default : apply n to previous c_j
endswitch
endfor

3 Simulation Results

We simulated transmission of data from every node to the base station using MATLAB. Our simulation is involving 100 node placed non-uniformly on a 50m x 100m area and the base station is located at (x=25, y=100). We assume that the node can control the transmit power level and there are only a few discrete power levels available.

Such a topology for clustering with fixed transmit power is illustrated in Fig. 3 (a). When the same simulation is repeated with the constraint that the power level can be chosen only from the different power levels, then the graph in Fig. 3 (b) is obtained. This figure has properties different from the one in Fig. 3 (a). First, as in Fig. 3(b) the connectivity is not overlapped by others. Second, there are no redundant cluster-head, thus can reduce energy consumption for needless local broadcasting. Third, it is well-structured in that the load balance is well better than fixed power and cluster-head overload is smaller than fixed power clustering.

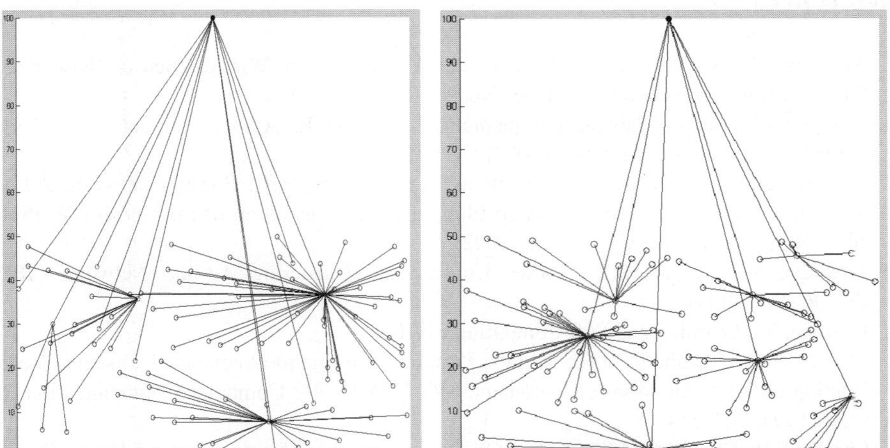

Fig. 3. (a) Topology Control for Fixed Transmit Power Clustering (b) Topology Control for Adative Transmit Power Clustering using Bayes' Rule

Clustering for transmission power control has the following characteristics.

- Since the proposed method is only to select the optimized transmit power lev el, it is simple and provides a distributed clustering. Thus it can give a simple and efficient method for clustering in wireless sensor networks.
- Our method can be applied to all kinds of proactive and reactive routing prot ocols. In case of proactive routing protocols such as DSDV, routing tables ho lding different power levels are maintained by HELLO packets to construct t he clustering [5]. On the other hand, reactive routing protocols like AODV, c an be transmitted to every power level applicable to be used by Discovery Re quest [6].
- Our method can be also efficient in the network which is dynamically change d by node mobility. Moreover, it is possible to select the power level without any network resources and excessive computation. Therefore, our method is an efficient for mobile wireless sensor network.

4 Conclusion

We discuss the transmit power level control method using the bayes' rule. Minimizing power consumption is important in wireless sensor networks. This paper proposes a solution of efficient clustering and transmits power control in non-homogeneously dispersed network. Our proposed method shows an efficient way of clustering by using different transmit power. Moreover, efficient traffic transmission can be realized, transmission routes considering transmission power are possible provided and the method is able to minimize collisions occurring in MAC by using the proposed method.

References

1. Akyildiz, I.F., Su, W., Sankarasubramaniam, Y., Cayirci, E.: Wireless Sensor Networks, A Survey. Computer Networks, Vol. 38, No. 4 (2002) 393-422
2. Akyildiz, I.F., Su, W., Sankarasubramaniam, Y., Cayirci, E.: A Survey on Sensor Networks. IEEE Communication Magazine (2002)
3. Narayaswamy, S., Kawada, V., Sreenivas, R.S., Kumar, P.R.: Power Control in Ad-hoc Networks: Theory. Architecture, Algorithm, and Implementation of the COMPOW Protocol. European Wireless Conference (2002)
4. Kawadia, V., Kumar, P.R.: Power Control and Clustering Ad-hoc Networks. IEEE INFOCOM (2003)
5. Kecman, V.: Learning and Soft Computing 61-103
6. Charles E.P., Elizabeth M.R.: Highly Dynamic Destination-Sequenced Distance-Vector Routing (DSDV) for Mobile Computers. SIG-COMM '94: Computer Communication Review (1994) 234-244
7. Charles E.P., Elizabeth M.R.: Ad hoc On-Demand Distance Vector Routing. Proceedings of the 2nd IEEE Workshop on Mobile Computing Systems and Applications (1999) 90–100

Dynamic Control of Packet Transmission Rate Using Fuzzy Logic for Ad Hoc Networks

Kyung-Bae Chang, Tae-Hwan Son, and Gwi-Tae Park

ISRL, College of Science, Korea University. Anam-dong 5-ga Seongbuk-gu, Seoul, Korea
{lslove, chlilla, gtpark}@korea.ac.kr

Abstract. In this paper, a method of controlling packet transmission rate between nodes on an Ad-hoc network is proposed considering the characteristics of IEEE 802.11 possessing different transmission efficiencies by different transmission distances. There have been a lot of researches about algorithms for efficient routing and power saving using static power sources in the field of mobile Ad-hoc networks up until now. However, those researches have been conducted only on the assumption of ideal experimental cases. This paper considers the way of finding adequate transmission rate for the transmission distances between nodes on a mobile Ad-hoc networks so that a more realizable method is presented. In this research, a controlling algorithm for transmission data rates by the distances between mobile nodes is realized using Fuzzy logic, possibly available to be applied to Ad-hoc network routing.

1 Introduction

Wireless Ad Hoc networks services are in progress to become ubiquitous networks. In addition, the need of expanding multimedia services over whole wireless networks is rapidly increasing. Wireless equipments are being popularized since they can be in operation in areas which cannot be covered by wired networks and they have faster communication speed than wired network in areas where installing wired networks are inefficient. An Ad Hoc network connects its mobile hosts as needed, and it has a temporary network structure which is possible without a previously organized network structure or a central supervisor. The mobility of nodes varies the topology of an Ad Hoc network. This characteristic of Ad Hoc network demands its own application solutions and the way of developing applications should be differently considered from the case of static networks. Ad Hoc networks in currently use has the following characteristics.

- Every node has its mobility,
- Each node functions as both of the end system and the relay system (simultaneously functions as the host and the router),
- The topology of network dynamically varies,
- The limitation in power supply due to the mobility of nodes,
- Band limitation in wireless network and variety channel quality.

D.-S. Huang, K. Li, and G.W. Irwin (Eds.): ICIC 2006, LNAI 4114, pp. 1311 – 1316, 2006.

Researches on routing algorithms show the results under the ideal circumstances with fixed data transmission rate. However, in a real environment which the distances between Ad Hoc nodes are not fixed in, data losses and delays are not avoidable due to the data traffic in a network. Therefore, a more intelligent method for network control is in need. Currently WLANs provide a variety of transmission rate modulation methods such as DBPSK, DQPSK, CCK(1, 2, 5.5, and 11 Mb/s) [1]. In Wireless LANs with providing a multiple transmission rate, data transmission rate is determined by the distances between host nodes so that the transmission rate cannot be guaranteed to be the maximum. The maximum transmission rate is only realized under the condition of host nodes within the transmission range. For instance, the transmission rates of 1/2Mb/s, 5.5 Mb/s, 11 Mb/s are ideal at the distances of 100m, 60m, 30m, respectively. Appropriate data transmission rates for transmission distances between mobile nodes should be considered for more realistic Ad Hoc network routing method as well as researches on developing various mobile routing methods [2]. In this research, Fuzzy logic is suggested for the logical transmission rate selection as the method of controlling transmission rate between nodes in Ad Hoc network, considering the characteristics of IEEE 802.11 which possesses different transmission efficiency by transmission distances. A method of controlling packet transmission rate by distances is realized, which is possibly applied to a generic Ad Hoc network routing.

2 Ad Hoc Routing Algorithm

A mobile Ad Hoc network frequently varies in its topology by the connectivity, transmission state, traffic and its moving pattern and it makes the network organization and maintenance difficult. Therefore, a wide range of consideration from the bottom layer to the upper layer is needed in applying the Ad Hoc network communication. An Ad Hoc network should be stable and efficient while operation with a cooperative routing function between mobile terminals in a multiple hop phase environment composed with fast and arbitrarily varying band limited mobile links. In addition, an Ad Hoc network should be possible to share information by connecting to outside of the network such as internet, with the aid of routing function.

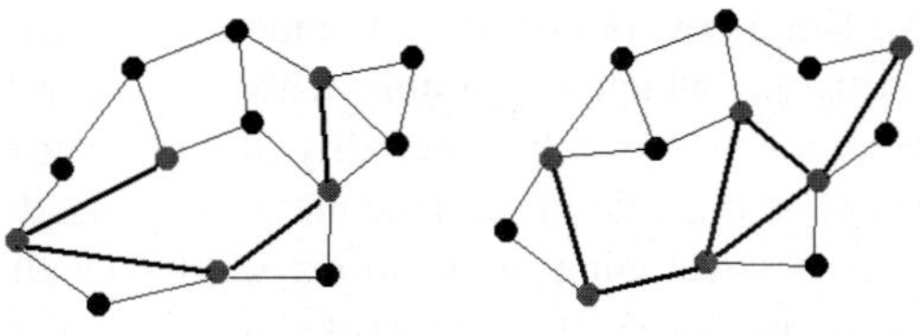

Fig. 1. An Example of temporary topology

There are two mainstreams of researches in developing routing algorithms for Ad Hoc networks. First off, methods of routing for energy saving of mobile nodes are being researched [2]. Nodes in an Ad Hoc network critically depend on batteries since they are remotely operated using only batteries. Therefore, a network structuring optimization problem is very important for minimum power consumption with providing satisfactory communication. At present, researches on using a periodic sleeping and a clustering of nodes are lively being conducted to span the lifetime of batteries by distributing the energy consumption to the whole network. Fig. 1 shows an example of network phase transition derived by a periodic sleeping. It is a method for maintaining equal energy distribution by structuring networks different in phase in a network with the same node distribution. Secondly, there are a number of researches on realizing the shortest distance adapted to the dynamic node changes [3] [4]. In a mobile Ad Hoc network, the phase of the network continuously varies due to the mobility of nodes. The network phase is possible to be rapidly and arbitrarily changed since it is a multiple hops. At this point the existence of a multiple links might bring on the unpredicted bad influences to the protocol performance and the application on the upper layer. Therefore an enhanced routing method resolving this problem should be importantly considered. There are a couple of significant results of researches on DSR, AODV, SPAN and GPSR. However, those researches only use a fixed transmission rate not relevant to distances between nodes in the simulations. In a real system, the distance between nodes certainly affects the network such as signal intensity, transmission delay and packet loss by distances. Therefore, such distance different are considered in this research for the realization of better routing.

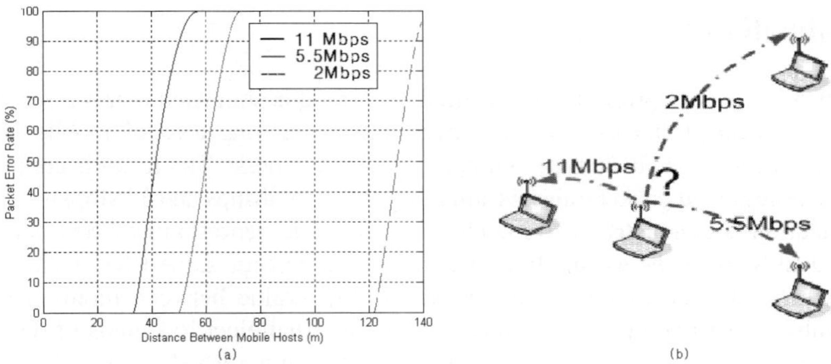

Fig. 2. Transmission Rate Evaluation at Different Distances

3 Transmission Characteristic of 802.11b

IEEE 802.11b shows different transmission characteristics in accordance with distances of mobile nodes. The transmission rate is possible up to 11Mbps. However, it varies by transmission distances and performances of links. In general, receiving signal intensity is illustrated by RSSI (Received Signal Strength Indication) value. Transmission rate of 1 or 2 Mbps, 5.5Mbps and 11Mbps are ideal at distances of 100m, 60m and 30m, respectively [1]. The relation between distances and transmission rates in IEEE 802.11b is depicted in Fig. 2 (a). Fig. 2 (a) indicates the different error rates as the packet transmission rates at over a certain distance. A high data transmission rate possesses a high throughput, and on the other hand a low data transmission rate enables a long distance data transmission. Hence, the most appropriate transmission rate should be selected at a certain mobile distance as shown in Fig. 2 (b).

4 Fuzzy Logic Control and Max-Min Algorithm

In Fuzzy logic theory, a value is represented as a degree of truth similar to be represented in probabilistic theory on the contrary to the conventional logic representing a value with binary logic (0 or 1, black or white, yes or no).

$$R_1 \circ R_2(x,z) = \vee_{y \in Y} (R_1(x,y) \wedge R_2(y,z))$$
$$= \left\{ \left[(x,z), \max_y \{ \min \{ \mu_{R1}(x,y) , \mu_{R2}(y,z) \} \} x \in X, y \in Y, \in z \right. \right\} \tag{1}$$

Fuzzy logic enables a medium value between 0 and 1. In this paper, a Fuzzy logic controller for data transmission rate decision is constructed using 2 inputs, RSSI values and packet delays in Ad Hoc network. MAX-MIN composition is used as the method for combining input values. MAX-MIN method is shown in (1).

5 Simulation

A Fuzzy logic control proposed in the simplest method is simulated in this research. The amount of packet transmission with increasing the moving area of mobile nodes is measured between one host node and one other mobile node. The result is compared to the cases using fixed packet transmission rate (2Mbis, 5.5Mbps and 11Mbps).

Simulation is conducted with membership functions representing RSSI values and packet delays under the assumption that every node has the same RSSI values. Fig. 3 (a) illustrates the membership function about RSSI value between mobile nodes. A RSSI value is a value derived from calculating internal electric signals of devices so that it is possible for membership functions representing a RSSI value to have different values by different calculating formulas and devices. The membership function for packet delay between mobile nodes is shown in Fig. 3 (b).

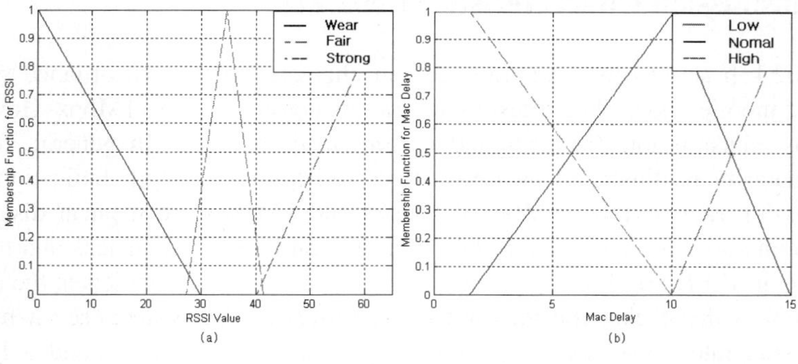

Fig. 3. Membership Function for RSSI Value and Membership Function for Packet Delay

A Fuzzy control logic shown in Table 1 is constructed with those two membership functions. The constructed controller controls transmission rate in three ways of increasing, sustaining and decreasing.

Table 1. Logic Table

RSSI	PD	Control
Strong	High	Zero
Strong	Normal	Up
Strong	Low	Up
Fair	High	Down
Fair	Normal	Zero
Fair	Low	Up
Weak	High	Down
Weak	Normal	Down
Weak	Low	Zero

The Fig. 4 shows the comparison between the amount of packet transmissions in accordance with increasing moving area of mobile nodes. A transmission rate of 2Mbps is stable throughout the whole region but it shows a relatively insufficient transmission amount to other transmission modes. In the case of 5.5Mbps, the transmission rate decreases through the whole region but it doesn't show a large difference. This mode can be concluded as stable and not worse in performance considering other modes. The transmission mode of 11Mbps shown an abrupt decrease in transmission rate as it approaches 30m of distance. So it is said to be sensitive to distances. The modes using Fuzzy logic control shows the highest transmission rate in all cases and it has similar decreasing transmission amount with other modes. This shows that the mode controlled by Fuzzy logic is the most efficient and stable mode in all cases.

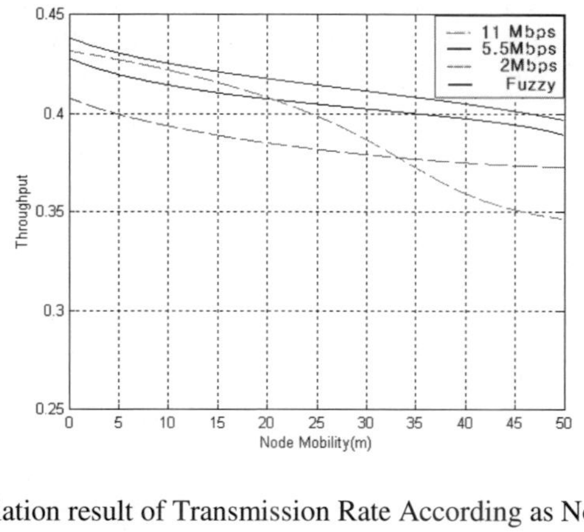

Fig. 4. Simulation result of Transmission Rate According as Node Distances

6 Conclusion

In this paper, Fuzzy logic algorithm is used as a dynamic control method for transmission rate according as varying distances between two mobile nodes. The simulation shows the proposed Fuzzy logic controller possesses better performances than networks using fixed transmission rates. Expanding the result of this research to apply to a multi hop routing algorithm might enable a more stable and faster network. The result shows only the cases of simple comparison in transmission rates. Considerations about transmission data loss and transmission delay are remained as the further research. In addition, a more specific realization is planned using the proposed method with currently researched multi hop routing algorithm.

References

1. Andren, C., Webster, M.: CCK Modulation Delivers 11 Mbps for High Rate 802.11 Extension. Proc. Wireless Symposium/Portable by Design Conference (1999)
2. Chen, B., Jamieson, K., Balakrishnan, H., Morris, R.: SPAN: An Energy-Efficient Coordination Algorithm for Topology Maintenance in Ad Hoc Wireless Networks. Wireless Networks 8 (2002) 481-494
3. Perkins, C.E., Royer, E.M.: Ad Hoc On-Demand Distance Vector Routing. Proc. 2nd IEEE Workshop on Mobile Computer Systems and Applications (WMCSA'99) (1999) 90–100
4. Broch, J., Johnson, D., Maltz, D.: The Dynamic Source Routing Protocol for Mobile Ad Hoc Networks. Internet Draft, IETF Mobile Ad Hoc Networking Working Group (1998)

ESTS: An Error Statistic Based Time Synchronization Protocol for Wireless Sensor Networks*

Limin Sun[1], Haidong Wang[1], Tingxin Yan[1], and Jingjing Liu[2]

[1] Institute of Software, Chinese Academy of Sciences P.O.Box 8718, Beijing 100080, Beijing, P.R. China
{sunlimin, haidong03, tingxin03}@ios.cn
[2] Grade 04 Finance Department of College of Economy, Centre University for Nationalities Beijing 100081, Beijing, P.R. China
liujj0019@sina.com

Abstract. Time synchronization in wireless sensor networks is critical for providing accurate timing service to many applications. This paper presents an Error Statistic based Time Synchronization protocol (ESTS) for wireless sensor networks. ESTS uses a flooding mechanism for basic global time synchronization and delay measurement, and achieves a fine grained synchronization through compensating per hop delay to all the nodes. It is a light weight mechanism for its simplicity in both computation and communication. Experiments show that ESTS obtains a better performance in energy efficiency than most in-situ time synchronization protocols in the same precision level.

1 Introduction

Wireless sensor network (WSN) has emerged as an important and growing research area in recent years [1]. A WSN usually consists of a large number of tiny devices that acquire information from interested areas and work collaboratively to process and forward the sensing data. Time synchronization [2,3] is one of the important functions of wireless sensor network. For many applications, it is required that a common view of time is available to all the nodes. A global clock and a right chronology of events are vital to most applications.

In this paper, we present Error Statistic based time Synchronization Protocol (ESTS) for WSN. ESTS first achieves global time synchronization through a flooding of synchronization command message, in which message transfer delay of each hop accumulates. This delay continues to accumulate within a back-to-root delay reporting process. Then time synchronization error is calculated and compensated by another message flooding process. ESTS achieves a synchronization precision of 10 μs with low cost in complexity and low consumption in energy. ESTS has been implemented and applied in our parking lot management system, in which it is a critical part for parking lot status reporting [8].

* This work is supported by National Natural Science foundation of China under grants No.60272078 and No.60373049.

D.-S. Huang, K. Li, and G.W. Irwin (Eds.): ICIC 2006, LNAI 4114, pp. 1317–1323, 2006.

The rest of this paper is organized as follows. Section2 is related works in time synchronization of WSN. Section 3 introduces our time ESTS synchronization mechanism in detail. Section 4 gives experiment result and analysis, and in section 5 the conclusion is given.

2 Related Works

Timing-Sync Protocol for Sensor Networks (TPSN) [4] first creates a hierarchical topology and then every node exchanges time stamps with its parent in a similar manner to the Simple Network Time Protocol (SNTP) [5]. TPSN calculates the average transfer delay of message which improves the precision but increases the communication overhead considerably.

Delay Measurement Time Synchronization (DMTS) [6] estimates all the delays involved in synchronization process. Message transferring is required only once to synchronize all nodes in a single hop. DMTS can be applied only to low resolution, low frequency clocks as synchronization accuracy is sacrificed for low computational complexity and energy efficiency.

Flooding Time-Synchronization Protocol (FTSP) [7] reaches the unique high precision performance by utilizing comprehensive error compensation. The disadvantages of FTSP are that nodes periodically send synchronization messages, and have complex computation. It takes long time for FTSP to achieve global network time synchronization.

Most in-situ time synchronization algorithms which provide a high precision often suffer from high energy consumption, while some energy efficient protocols cannot offer a satisfying precision [9,10]. In this paper, we propose ESTS to achieve a better compromise in which a fine grained synchronization is achieved while energy consumption is still kept low.

3 Error Statistic Based Synchronization Protocol

ESTS algorithm consists of three phases: time synchronization, delay computing and error compensation. In the first phase, all other nodes are synchronized with the root through a synchronization command flooding, and a hierarchy structure is also built for later use. In the last two phases, per hop delay error is calculated and compensated so that a higher precision of global time synchronization can be achieved through another flooding.

3.1 Time Synchronization Phase

Root starts up this phase by broadcasting a time synchronization command (SYNC command). The format of SYNC command is shown in Fig.1. The hop field represents the hop count from the node which sends the command to root. The nodeId field records the ID of the node which sends the command. The sendTimeStamp field

hop	nodeId	sendTimeStamp	delay

Fig. 1. Format of SYNC command

records the local time when a certain byte of the command is sent. The delay field denotes the accumulated delay during the command transfer from root to current node and is initialized to zero by root. Sender sets sendTimeStamp field at the instant when certain byte is actually transmitted at the MAC layer.

The neighboring node of root records the local time when it receives the corresponding byte of SYNC command as receiveTimeStamp.and synchronizes itself to root by adjusting its local time according to equation (1):

$$T_{revised} = T_{current} + (SendTimeStamp\ -\ receiveTimeStamp) \qquad (1)$$

Every neighboring node records root's ID as its up level node and sets its hop count as that of root plus one. The neighboring node forwards the SYNC command by setting the hop field and nodeId field to its own values. The sendTimeStamp field is set to the local time when certain byte of the command is transmitted. Other nodes deal with the SYNC command in the same way. Only the first SYNC command received is handled. The global time synchronization to the root is achieved when all the nodes have received the command. A level from root and an up level node (parent node) are assigned to every node during this process.

3.2 Delay Calculating Phase

Non-deterministic transfer delay in WSN is critical to the precision of time synchronization. Therefore, the non-deterministic delay needs to be carefully analyzed and compensated for. We use the following decomposition of the message transfer delays as shown in Fig.2 [5].

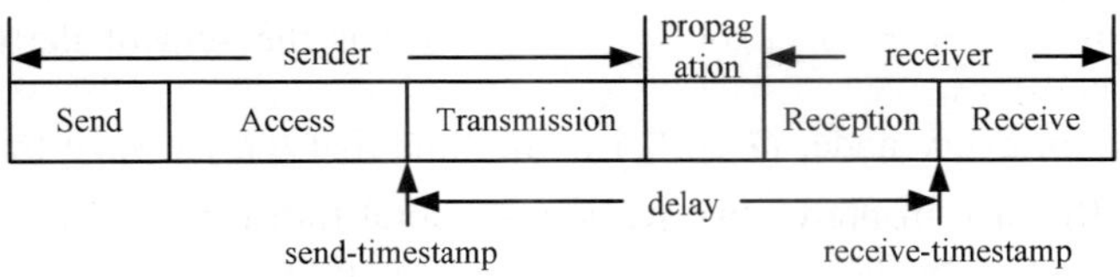

Fig. 2. Decomposition of message delay over a wireless link

In the above synchronization phase, the synchronization error caused by transfer delay during Send Time, Access Time and Receive Time has been completely eliminated by utilizing MAC-layer time stamping. But the error caused by the transfer delay during transmission, propagation and reception time still exists. In addition, the time delay between the node and root usually increases with the hops between them. The following method is used to calculate the per-hop delay error and compensate it in all nodes to increase the synchronization accuracy.

3.2.1 Error Measurement Algorithm

As is shown in Fig 3, there are $n+1$ nodes which build up an n-hop path in the network. Root and node N_0 respectively locate at each end of the n-hop path. At time T_{rs}, root sends a message following path root→N_1→N_2→….. →N_{n-1}→N_0. When node N_0 receives the message, it sends the message back to root along the reversed path. The message is received by root at time T'_{rr}.

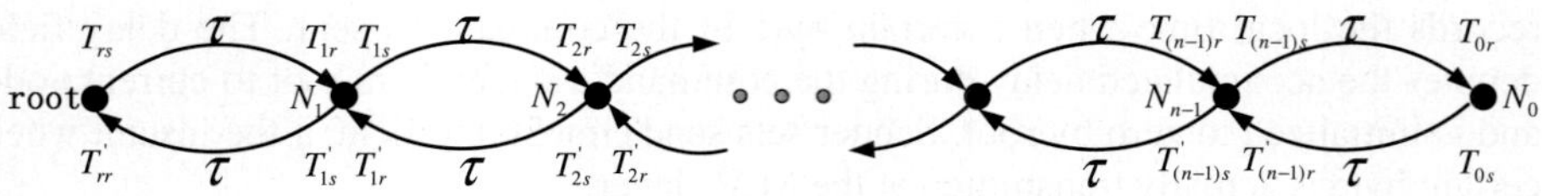

Fig. 3. Delay error measurement process

Lets us suppose that $\Delta t_i = T_{is} - T_{ir}$ *(i=0,1,2...,n-1)* denotes the difference between time T_{ir} when node N_i receives the message and time T_{is} when N_i sends the message to the next node . It's is the same with $\Delta t'_i = T'_{is} - T'_{ir}$ *(i=1,2,3...n-1)* for nodes in the reversed path. T_{rs} ,T'_{rr}, T_{is}, T_{ir}, T'_{is} and T'_{ir}*(i=01,2,3...)* are timestamps recorded by MAC layer at every node. τ is the average transfer delay between adjacent nodes. τ is not considered in the first synchronization phase and results in that the time of left node is slower about τ than that of right node in Fig.3. According to round trip time of a message, τ can be computed as equation (2) and (3):

$$\begin{aligned} T'_{rr} &= T_{rs} + \tau + \Delta t_1 + \tau + \Delta t_2 + \cdots + \tau + \Delta t_0 + \tau + \cdots + \Delta t'_2 + \tau + \Delta t'_1 + \tau \\ &= T_{rs} + 2n\tau + (\sum_{i=1}^{n-1} \Delta t_i + \Delta t_0 + \sum_{i=1}^{n-1} \Delta t'_i) \end{aligned} \tag{2}$$

$$\tau = \frac{(T'_{rr} - T_{rs}) - [\sum_{i=1}^{n-1}(T_{is} - T_{ir}) + (T_{0s} - T_{0r}) + \sum_{i=1}^{n-1}(T'_{is} - T'_{ir})]}{2n} \tag{3}$$

In equation (3), $[\sum_{i=1}^{n-1}(T_{is} - T_{ir}) + (T_{0s} - T_{0r}) + \sum_{i=1}^{n-1}(T'_{is} - T'_{ir})]$ is the sum of the time that the message stays in every node. $(T'_{rr} - T_{rs})$ is the time that the message transfers in the path. The difference of above two parts is the total transfer delay in the path. The total delay divided by hops gets the per-hop delay τ which is the delay error compensated for all nodes in the third phase.

3.2.2 The Selection of Node N_0

The standard for the selection of nodes N_0 must reflect the average transfer delay of the whole network. It requires that the N_0 should distribute evenly on the edge of the network, and the number of N_0 should be small. In the first phase, the time SYNC command is transferred from root to the edge of the network in flooding manner. The message stops when it reaches the edge of network. In the network, there must be some nodes which last transfer SYNC command in their neighbor area. These nodes are marked with N_0. If the number of N_0 are too large in a large scale network, N_0 is to be selected with certain probability P (P<1, determined by network scale).

3.2.3 Error Statistic Process

Root initiates the delay field with zero while it broadcasts the SYNC command. When node N_1 receives the message, it first synchronizes itself to root and then calculates $\Delta T_1 = T_{1r} - T_{rs}$. The result is added to the delay field and the message is transferred as described in 3.1. Other nodes calculate delay field in the same way. When node N_0 receives the message, N_0 synchronizes itself with root and calculates the delay field. It then transfers the message with different type back to root along reversed path. Other fields of the message are same with SYNC command. In this back process, a node will not synchronize itself again. Only the field of delay is calculated and then transferred to its up level node. When root receives the message, it can compute τ according to equation (3).

3.3 Error Compensation Phase

When root receives a certain number of messages, it calculates the average per hop delay error by statistic method. Then the root broadcasts a compensation message which contains the per hop error. When a node receives this message, it will correct its clock by adding the value that is the per hop error multiplied by its count of hops to root. The node only handles the first compensation packet and simply broadcasts the message without modification.

4 Experiment and Analysis

In our experiments, 70 mica2 motes are evenly deployed in an indoor environment with transmission power set to -20dBm. The root is placed at the edge of the network. The network is of 7 hops. All the motes are physically same and run the time synchronization algorithm under TinyOS. In the experiments, the correctness of ESTS algorithm is testified, and the comparison to TPSN, DMTS, FTSP is carried out in aspects of precision and energy efficiency.

4.1 Time Synchronization Precision

Every algorithm is run for an hour, and the average synchronization error among all nodes compared to the root is calculated in an interval of 5 minutes. From Fig.4, we can conclude that the time synchronization error of ESTS is in 10 μs level, which is close to FTPS and TSPN, and much better than DMTS. DMTS uses one flooding

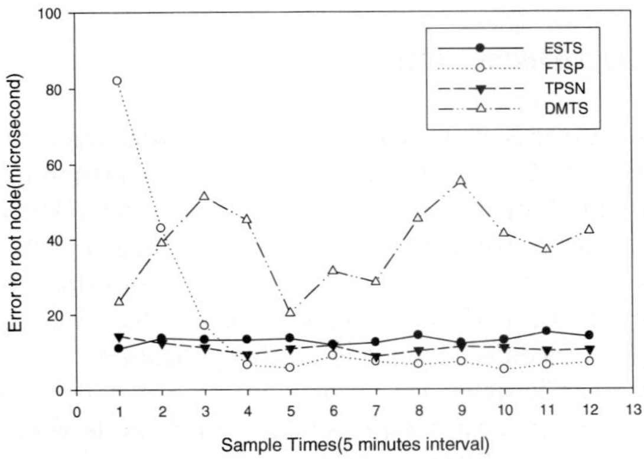

Fig. 4. Time error in one hour experiment

process for synchronization, but it only estimates transfer delay so its precision is much lower than that of other three mechanisms. From Fig 4, we can see that ESTS can achieve synchronization much faster than FTSP as FTSP needs a linear regression process.

4. 2 Energy Consumption

Another critical aspect in WSN is energy efficiency. In WSN, the wireless communication module takes the most part of energy consumption, so we count the amount of message transmitted as the measurement of energy consumption. From Fig 5, we can conclude that ESTS achieves higher energy efficiency than FTPS and TPSN in the time synchronization process. In ESTS, there are two times of flooding and one time of data transfer process to root, which is approximately twice as the energy consumption of the mechanism as DMTS. In FTPS, many times of restricted flooding are needed to reach a reasonable precision and the energy consumption is considerably high. In TPSN, nodes need to communicate with their upper level node, which also increases the energy consumption.

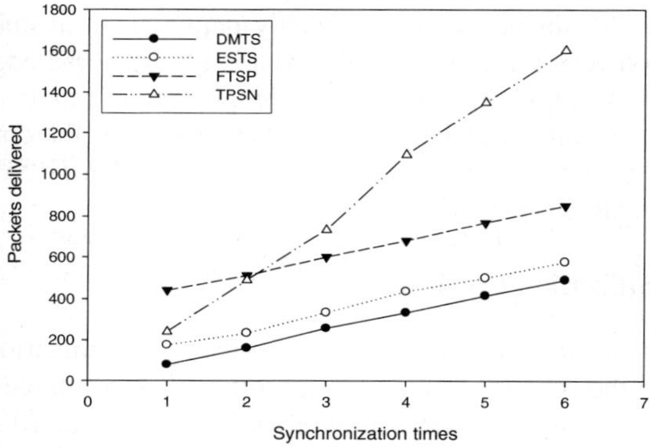

Fig. 5. Energy consumption

5 Conclusion and Discussion

We have introduced Error Statistic based Time Synchronization protocol for WSN. ESTS uses a flooding process to achieve a global synchronization to the root and then refines it through delay error measurement and compensation. The energy efficiency is high in ESTS as only two times of flooding is needed. ESTS can provide a precision of 10μs after the compensation process. Compared with in-situ time synchronization protocols, ESTS is a better compromise between precision and energy efficiency. It has been used in a real-world application.

ESTS utilizes round trip delay values of multi-messages to compute average per hop delay error, and makes error compensation in every node with the average error multiplied by its hop count. ESTS is fit to the wireless sensor networks in which nodes have little difference in communication modules, i.e., in homogeneous networks. For heterogonous nodes, more consideration on nodes' characters is needed to provide a satisfying precision.

References

1. Akyildiz, I.F., Su, W., Sankarasubramanian, Y., Cayirci, E.: A Survey on Sensor Networks. IEEE Communications Magazine, 40(8) (2002) 102–114
2. Bharath Sundararaman, Ugo Buy, Ajay D. Kshemkalyani.: Clock Synchronization for Wireless Sensor Networks: A Survey. Ad Hoc Networks 3(3) (2005) 281-323
3. Sivrikaya F, Yener B.: Time Synchronization in Sensor Networks: A Survey IEEE Network, 18(4) (2004) 45-50
4. Goneriwol, S., Kumor, R., Srivartava, M.: Timing Sync Protocol for Sensor Networks. ACM SenSyr, Los Angeles, CA, Nov. (2003)
5. Simple Network Time Protocol, (SNTP) Version 4.IETF RFC 2030
6. Su P.: Delay Measurement Time Synchronization for Wireless. Sensor Networks. IRB-TR-03-013 (2003)
7. Miklós Maróti, Branislav Kusy, Gyula Simon, Ákos Lédeczi.: The Flooding Time Synchronization Protocol. SynSys (2004) 39-49
8. Bi, Y. Z., Sun, L. M., Zhu, H. S., Yan, T. X., Luo, Z. J.: A Parking Management System Based on Wireless Sensor Network. International Workshop on Sensor Networks and Applications (SNA05), Beijing, China (2005) 20~22
9. Dai, H., Han, R. TSync.: A Lightweight Bidirectional Time Synchronization Service for Wireless Sensor Networks. Mobile Computing and Communications Review 8(1) (2004) 125-139
10. Chang, K. H., Chu, H. H., Huang, P., Lin, T. H., Tian, J. B., Tseng, H. W., Yang, C. L.: A Performance Comparison of Clock vs. Event Synchronization Protocols, Technical Report, National Taiwan University (2005)

Extending the Lifetime of Ad Hoc Wireless Networks*

R.I. da Silva[1], J.C.B. Leite[2], and M.P. Fernandez[3]

[1] Fac. de Tecnologia e Ciências de Conselheiro Lafaiete, Univ. Prof. Antônio Carlos
Conselheiro Lafaiete, MG, Brazil
roneilidio@bol.com.br

[2] Instituto de Computação, Universidade Federal Fluminense
Niterói, RJ, Brazil
julius@ic.uff.br

[3] Lab. de Redes de Comunicação e Segurança, Universidade Estadual do Ceará
Fortaleza, CE, Brazil
marcial@larces.uece.br

Abstract. This paper presents a new algorithm, Extra, for extending the lifetime of ad hoc wireless networks. Extra tries to conserve energy by identifying and switching off nodes that are momentarily redundant for message routing in the network. Extra is independent of the underlying routing protocol and uses exclusively information that is collected locally. Simulation studies conducted have shown promising results.

1 Introduction

Ad hoc wireless networks are computer networks without a predefined topology, whose nodes can move and communicate through radio channels, and cooperate to allow message routing. Several routing protocols for ad hoc networks were proposed in the literature, e.g., DSR [1] and AODV [2] . There are many applications for those networks, like support to rescue teams in disaster areas.

An important characteristic of the mobile devices in an ad hoc network is the energy consumption, because they usually depend on batteries. In that way, besides the traditional metrics to evaluate a protocol, like packet delay and drop rate, lifetime of the network is important. The nodes in an ad hoc network consume energy not only when they are transmitting or receiving messages, but also when they are ready to listen for any data (idle state). That happens because the electronics of the radio has to be energized to maintain the capacity of receiving messages. Several studies indicate that the power for transmission, reception and listening is, typically, in the order of 1.40W, 1.00W and 0.83W, respectively [3] . However, this study also shows that, if the radio is put in sleeping state, the consumption falls to 0.13W. Those values indicate that to have an effective decrease in energy consumption, the radio should be put in a sleeping state during certain periods of the operation of the network.

* This work was partially supported by Capes, CNPq and FAPERJ.

D.-S. Huang, K. Li, and G.W. Irwin (Eds.): ICIC 2006, LNAI 4114, pp. 1324–1331, 2006.

In this work, an algorithm, Extra, is presented to deal with the problem of coordination of node transition to a sleeping state in ad hoc networks. This algorithm allows each node in the network to make decisions in an autonomous way, based only on local information. Additionally, it can work together with any ad hoc routing protocol.

This paper is organized as follows. Section 2 presents some related work. A detailed description of the Extra algorithm follows in Section 3. Section 4 presents the evaluation scenario we set for our simulations, and Section 5 the simulation results. Finally, in Section 6 we draw our conclusions and make suggestions for further work.

2 Related Work

The idea of shutting down the radio to conserve energy in ad hoc networks was already explored by other authors. In the BECA algorithm [4] , the decision to put a node to sleep is taken based on local informations. If the node does not have a message to transmit or if it does not listen any message it goes to the sleeping state. After a certain period it wakes up and listen to messages. If no messages are heard, it goes back to sleep. In the AFECA algorithm [4], each node uses an estimation of the number of neighbor nodes to increase/decrease the time it will stay in the sleeping state. With a increase in node density, more energy can be saved.

GAF [5] uses geographical position information (e.g., produced by a GPS) to support energy conservation. Like AFECA and BECA, GAF is independent of the underlying routing protocol. In this algorithm, the area where the network is active is divided in a virtual mesh, composed by fixed squares. The nodes in each square change between the sleeping and active states, but guaranteeing that one of them is active, in order to maintain the network connectivity. The choice of which node will be active is made in a distributed way. In CEC [6] the authors try to avoid the dependence that GAF has on location information (a GPS does not work inside buildings). Experiments accomplished by the authors demonstrate that CEC has a better performance than GAF for low mobility scenarios.

3 The Extra Algorithm

Our energy saving procedure is based on putting nodes in the sleeping state. The main characteristics of this energy saving mechanism, that makes it different from other proposals, are the the moment a node decides going to sleep and the duration of sleeping state. Because the decision is taken in a distributed way, some nodes enter in the sleeping state for a known period, while others will stay active. In highly populated networks, there is a greater chance that few nodes stay active, maintaining network connectivity, while other nodes save energy. When the density decreases, some cautions are taken to reduce the disconnection probability.

3.1 Algorithm Operation

A node can be in one of three states: *Active*, *Listening* or *Sleeping*, as indicated in Figure 1. Each node starts operation sending a *hello* message, reporting to its neighbors that it is active. In this state a node has its radio on and will stay active for Ta seconds. If during this period it receives a message or a route response, the timer is restarted. After Ta seconds without a message being received, the node runs the decision procedure that will determine, with probability P, whether it will go to sleep or it will stay active.

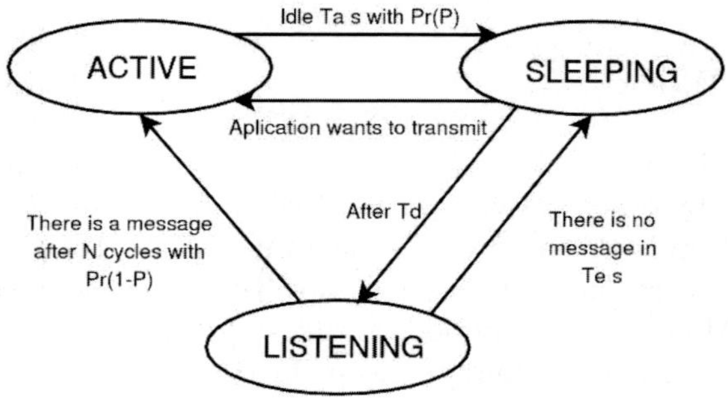

Fig. 1. Node state transition in Extra

If the decision is to stay active, another cycle of Ta seconds is started; otherwise, the node starts the energy saving procedure, sending to its neighbors a message informing that it will move to the *Sleeping* state. This allows each node to estimate its number of neighbors and how many are in the *Active* state.

A node stays in the *Sleeping* state for Td seconds. After that, it changes to the *Listening* state. In this situation, the node listens to verify if either there is a message for him, or a broadcast message. If this is true, the node should go to the *Active* state. In case there are no messages during Te seconds, the node goes back to the *Sleeping* state. This cycle is repeated N times (see Figure 2) and then the decision procedure is again executed. At any moment, if an application running in a node needs to send a message, this node should become active.

When an active node needs to route a message to a neighbor the transmission should be made only when this neighbor is in the *Listening* or *Active* states. If the neighbor is in the *Sleeping* state the transmission should be delayed until it changes state. In order to control the neighbors' state, each node has a cache mechanism, updated when a message is received. A new neighbor is included in the cache when the node receives a route request or a *hello* message. The information on all neighboring nodes are always saved with a time stamp. If, after a time interval, no new message is received from a certain neighbor, its cache entry is considered obsolete.

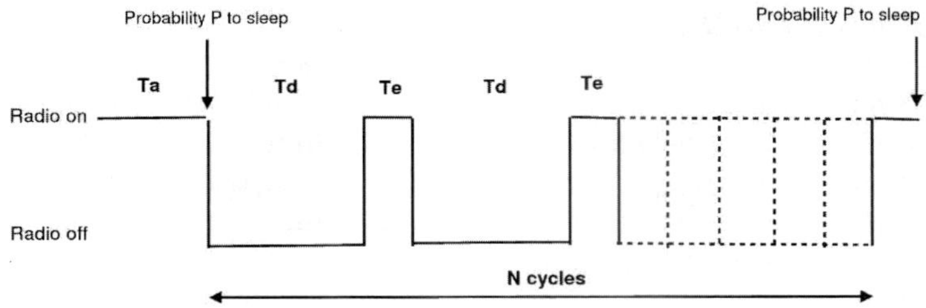

Fig. 2. Example of temporal evolution

3.2 Obtaining Probability P

A node starts an energy saving period with probability P, and this value can change during run time. This is done to adjust the energy saving mechanism to the network conditions. In our implementation, only information regarding the connectivity and energy levels are considered. Simply put, P should be high when the energy level is low and also when the number of neighbors is high. Based on this statement, some heuristics were developed.

Heuristic 1 ($h1$): its characteristic is to try to preserve network connectivity, despite the energy level of the battery. Thus, a greater P is attributed to the nodes in high density areas. P is defined by the product of the number of neighbors by a factor K. However, to avoid that all the nodes in a very populated region go asleep at the same time, P is limited by a constant L:

$P(h1) = K * neighbors\_number()$
if $P(h1) > L$ **then**
  $P(h1) = L$
end if

where $neighbors\_number()$ returns the amount of neighbors of a node. In our simulations K and L were set to 0.1 and 0.9, respectively.

Heuristic 2 ($h2$): its characteristic is also to try to preserve network connectivity. In this case, P will be the relation of the active neighbors to the total number of neighbors.

Heuristic 3 ($h3$): the main objective of this heuristics is to save energy when battery is at a low level, in spite of the connectivity:

$P(h3) = 1 - current\_energy()/initial\_energy()$

where $current\_energy()$ is returns the remaining energy of the battery and $initial\_energy()$ returns its initial value.

Heuristics 4 ($h4$): this heuristics is a combination of the heuristics 1 and 3. It tries to save energy balancing network connectivity and energy conservation at the node:

if $(P(h1) \geq ref)$ and $(P(h3) \geq ref)$ **then**

$P(h4) = max(P(h1), P(h3))$
else if $(P(h1) \geq ref)$ *and* $(P(h3) < ref)$ **then**
$P(h4) = P(h1)$
else if $(P(h1) < ref)$ *and* $(P(h3) \geq ref)$ **then**
$P(h4) = P(h3)$
else if $(P(h1) < ref) and (P(h3) < ref)$ **then**
$P(h4) = min(P(h1), P(h3))$
end if

where $P(h1)$ and $P(h3)$ are the values of P returned by the heuristics 1, and 3, respectively, and ref is an adjustable parameter, whose value in the simulations was set to 0.5.

Heuristics 5 ($h5$): has a similar objective to heuristics 4. It is the combination of the heuristics 2 and 3. It tries to save energy when it is at a low level, yet trying to maintain network connectivity:
if $(P(h2) \geq ref)$ *and* $(P(h3) \geq ref)$ **then**
$P(h5) = max(P(h2), P(h3))$
else if $(P(h2) \geq ref)$ *and* $(P(h3) < ref)$ **then**
$P(h5) = P(h2)$
else if $(P(h2) < ref)$ *and* $(P(h3) \geq ref)$ **then**
$P(h5) = P(h3)$
else if $(P(h2) < ref)$ *and* $(P(h3) < ref)$ **then**
$P(h5) = min(P(h2), P(h3))$
end if

4 Evaluation Scenario

The Extra algorithm was evaluated through simulation. To assess its performance, it was compared to AODV, as the reference protocol, and to GAF running over AODV. To validate the simulation model, each metric was measured in 10 different scenarios, and the average value is presented with a 95% confidence interval. The simulator used in the tests was the Network Simulator - ns-2, version 2.26 [7]. To create the simulation scenario it was used the BonnMotion software, version 1.1 [8].

In all simulations the values attributed to N, Ta, Te and Td were, respectively, 15, 4s, 0.05s and 0.5s. The simulation scenario assumed 60 nodes, moving randomly (random way-point model) in a 1200m by 600m area. The nodes speeds were set to 0m/s (a static network used as reference), 1m/s (a person walking), and 10m/s (a vehicle in an urban environment). Also, four static nodes were placed near the edges of the referred area, two acting as source and two as sink of traffic. The reason for that was to evaluate the message delay and drop rates in a more coherent way, since intermediate nodes will serve exclusively for message routing.

The simulation time was 900 seconds, to permit a comparison with measures done for the GAF algorithm in [5]. In all scenarios, we used pause times of 0,

30, 60, 120, 300, 600 and 900 seconds. The radio range was set to 250m, and the propagation model was the two-ray-ground. For the traffic model we choose two sources and two sinks implemented in fixed nodes, with CBR traffic over UDP transport. The transmission rates were 1pkt/s, 10pkts/s and 20 pkts/s, producing an aggregate of 2, 20 and 40pkts/s, respectively. Message size was set to 512 bytes.

The energy model chosen is based on the measures from [9] of the WaveLAN 2 Mb/s board, that is 1.6W for transmission, 1.2W for reception, 1.0W in idle mode and 0.025W in the sleeping state. To allow for a comparison, those values are the same used for GAF evaluation in [5]. As the energy consumption in the sleeping state is much smaller than in the other cases, and to simplify the algorithm implementation in ns-2, we considered that when a node is sleeping it is shutdown. This simplification was done for all algorithms.

The initial energy attributed to each node was 500J, enough to maintain the network working for about 450s with the AODV protocol. In this case, since the energy consumption in the idle state is important, we could observe that almost all nodes will run out of energy by that time, independently of the traffic forwarded. Given the simulation time is set to 900s, we can thus observe the behavior of our energy saving mechanism. As it is not interesting to evaluate the network behavior when a source/sink shut down by lack of energy, we set an infinite energy level for those nodes, guaranteeing that they will always transmit during the simulation period.

5 Simulation Results

The first experiment shows the extension of network lifetime obtained by Extra, when compared to GAF and AODV (see Figure 3). In this experiment it was assumed a pause time of 0s, maximum node speeds of 1m/s and a rate of 10 pkts/s was maintained for each data source. In this figure we can clearly see the benefit obtained by our algorithm.

Given Extra has a probabilistic basis, we analysed the risk of network disconnection due to all surviving nodes deciding to sleep simultaneously. Figure 4 shows, for heuristics 4, the percentage of operative nodes, that is, nodes either active or listening, considering at any moment just the surviving nodes. In this experiment, pause time, transmission rate and node speed were equal to 0s, 1pkt/s and 1m/s, respectively. As it can be seen, roughly half of the surviving nodes are active or listening during the whole period. This shows that the probability of complete disconnection is negligible.

Figures 5 and 6 show the effect of GAF and Extra on network lifetime, for several transmission rate and node speed values. These graphics present the percentage of surviving nodes at 900s. For lack of space, in all those cases the results are shown just for heuristics 4. In each figure, pause time is equal to 0s and, when not used as a control parameter, transmission rate and node speed were kept constant and equal to 1pkt/s and 1m/s, respectively. For the full range of transmission rates experimented, Extra overcomes GAF. In particular, Extra

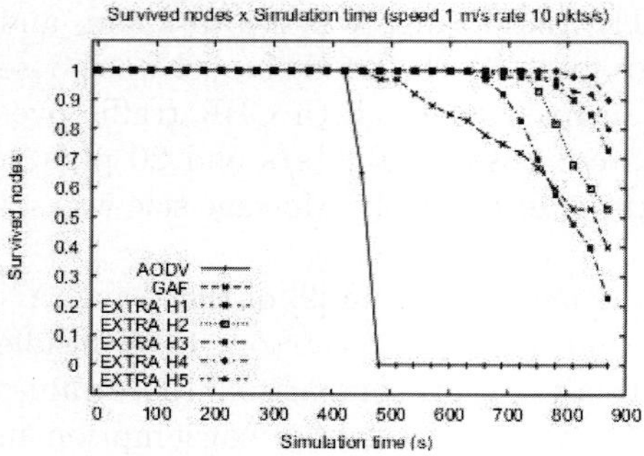

Fig. 3. Lifetime: AODV, GAF and Extra

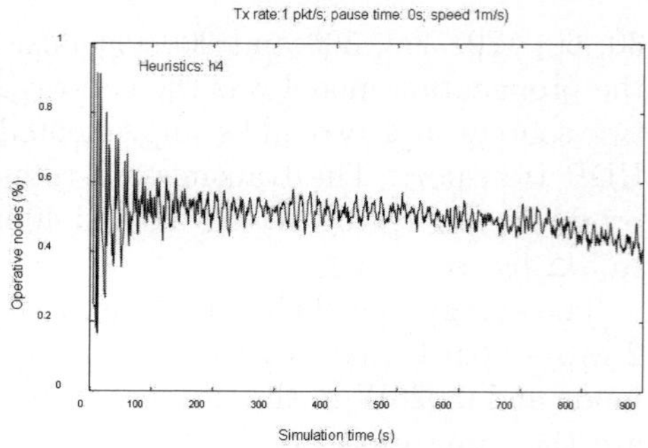

Fig. 4. Percentage of operative nodes

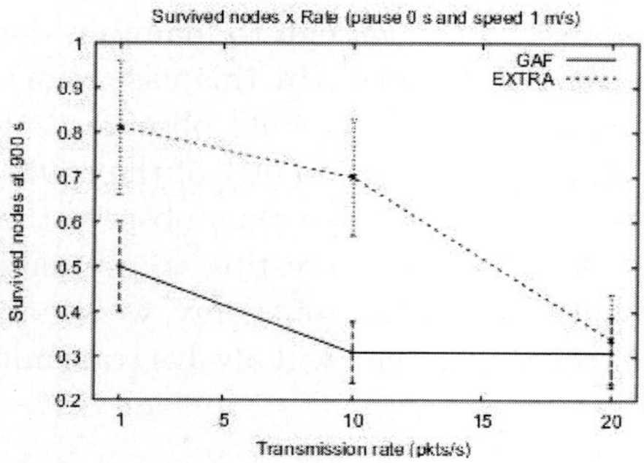

Fig. 5. Surviving nodes *versus* trans. rate

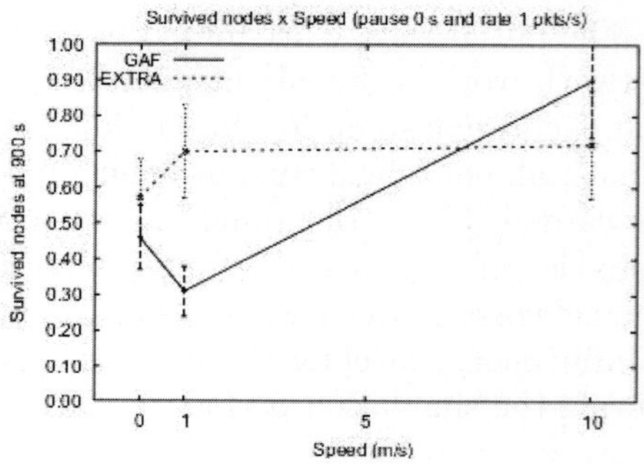

Fig. 6. Surviving nodes *versus* speed

shows a far better performance for low rates (less than10pkts/s). For the class of applications we proposed Extra (i.e., low mobility, as in the case of rescue teams), our algorithm shows better performance and an almost steady behavior as speed is varied. We also studied the loss of packets (drop rate) using the same control parameters as in the previous experiment. In all three cases Extra and GAF produced close results, with a slight advantage for GAF.

6 Conclusions and Future Works

This work presents a new algorithm, Extra, for energy conservation in ad hoc wireless networks. As well as in several other algorithms, its objective is to maximize the lifetime of the network, but yet trying to maintain the network connectivity. Its operation is controlled by a function that defines when the node should enter in a sleeping state. The sleeping time is constant, and the entrance in this state happens with a certain probability. This probability is calculated during execution time through an heuristic method. Five different heuristics were tested, all of them with very simple structure.

As stated, all heuristics use only information obtained locally. As a proposal for a future works, solutions where the neighboring nodes exchange information about their current energy level and neighbors' density could be explored. Obviously, this would cause an increase in the number of control messages, and implies in additional energy consumption. However, it is possible that this negative effect will not be enough to degrade the performance.

Based on the simulation results, we believe that the selection of a small number of parameters and the choice of simple heuristics could produce an important impact on the extension of ad hoc networks lifetime, after all *entia non sunt multiplicanda praeter necessitatem.*

References

[1] Johnson, D. B., Maltz, D. A.: Dynamic Source Routing in Ad Hoc Wireless Networks. Mobile Computing,Kluwer Academic Publishers, 8 (1996) 153-181

[2] Perkins, C. E., Royer, E. M.: Ad Hoc On-Demand Distance Vector Routing. IEEE Workshop on Mobile Computing Systems and Applications, New Orleans, USA, LA (1999) 90-100

[3] Chen, B., Jamieson, K., Balakrishnan, H., Morris, R.: Span: An Energy-efficient Coordination Algorithm for Topology Maintenance in Ad Hoc Wireless Networks. Wireless Networks, 8 (2002) 481-494

[4] Xu, Y., Heidemann, J., Estrin, D.: Adaptive Energy-conserving Routing for Multihop Ad Hoc Networks. Technical Report 527, USC/ISI, Los Angeles, USA (2000)

[5] Xu, Y., Heidemann, J., Estrin, D.: Geography-informed Energy Conservation for Ad Hoc Routing. In ACM/IEEE Int. Conf. on Mobile Computing and Networking, Rome, Italy, (2001) 70-84

[6] Xu, Y., Heidemann, J., Estrin, D.: Topology control protocols to conserve energy in wireless ad hoc networks. Technical Report 6, Center for Embedded Networked Sensing, Los Angeles, USA, 527 (2003)

[7] ns−2: The Network Simulator ns−2. http://www.isi.edu/nsnam/ns (2003)

[8] BonnMotion: A Mobility Scenario Generation and Analysis Tool. University of Bonn. http://www.informatik.uni-bonn.de/IV/BonnMotion (2003)

[9] Stemm, M., Katz, R. H.,: Measuring and Reducing Energy Consumption of Network Interfaces in Hand-held Devices. IEICE Transactions on Communications, E80−B (1997) 1125-1131

about their current energy level and neighbors [illegible] the energy [illegible]. This would naturally increase the number of control messages and imply an additional energy consumption. However, it is possible that [illegible] with [illegible] will not be enough to deplete the [illegible].

Based on the simulation results we believe that [illegible] small number of parameters and the choice of simple heuristics could have a big impact on [illegible] lifetime of the extension of ad hoc networks [illegible] routing [illegible].

References

1. [illegible], D. S.: Dynamic Source Routing in Ad Hoc Wireless Networks. Mobile Computing, Kluwer Academic Publishers (1996) 153-181.
2. Perkins, C. E., Royer, E. M.: Ad Hoc On-Demand Distance Vector Routing. IEEE Workshop on Mobile Computing Systems and Applications, New Orleans, USA (1999) 90-100.
3. Chen, B., Jamieson, K., Balakrishnan, H., [illegible]: Span: An Energy-Efficient Coordination Algorithm for Topology Maintenance in Ad Hoc Wireless Networks. Wireless Networks, 8 (2002) 481-494.
4. Xu, Y., Heidemann, J., Estrin, D.: [illegible] for Multihop Ad Hoc Networks. [illegible] (2001)
5. [illegible] Ad Hoc Routing. In: [illegible] IEEE Int. Conf. on [illegible] Computing and Networking, [illegible] (2001) 70-84
6. [illegible] Technical Report 6, Center for Embedded Networked Sensing, Los Angeles, USA (2003)
7. ns-2: The Network Simulator ns-2. http://www.isi.edu/nsnam/ns (2003)
8. BonnMotion: A Mobility Scenario Generation and Analysis Tool. University of Bonn. http://www.informatik.uni-bonn.de/IV/BonnMotion (2003)
9. Stemm, M., Katz, R. H.: Measuring and Reducing Energy Consumption of Network Interfaces in Hand-held Devices. IEICE Transactions on Communications, E80-B (1997) 1125-1131.

Author Index

Lecture Notes in Artificial Intelligence (LNAI)

Vol. 4114: D.-S. Huang, K. Li, G.W. Irwin (Eds.), Computational Intelligence, Part II. XXVII, 1337 pages. 2006.

Vol. 4108: J.M. Borwein, W.M. Farmer (Eds.), Mathematical Knowledge Management. VIII, 295 pages. 2006.

Vol. 4106: T.R. Roth-Berghofer, M.H. Göker, H. A. Güvenir (Eds.), Advances in Case-Based Reasoning. XIV, 566 pages. 2006.

Vol. 4099: Q. Yang, G. Webb (Eds.), PRICAI 2006: Trends in Artificial Intelligence. XXVIII, 1263 pages. 2006.

Vol. 4093: X. Li, O.R. Zaiane, Z. Li (Eds.), Advanced Data Mining and Applications. XXI, 1110 pages. 2006.

Vol. 4092: J. Lang, F. Lin, J. Wang (Eds.), Knowledge Science, Engineering and Management. XV, 664 pages. 2006.

Vol. 4088: Z.-Z. Shi, R. Sadananda (Eds.), Agent Computing and Multi-Agent Systems. XVII, 827 pages. 2006.

Vol. 4068: H. Schärfe, P. Hitzler, P. Øhrstrøm (Eds.), Conceptual Structures: Inspiration and Application. XI, 455 pages. 2006.

Vol. 4065: P. Perner (Ed.), Advances in Data Mining. XI, 592 pages. 2006.

Vol. 4062: G. Wang, J.F. Peters, A. Skowron, Y. Yao (Eds.), Rough Sets and Knowledge Technology. XX, 810 pages. 2006.

Vol. 4049: S. Parsons, N. Maudet, P. Moraitis, I. Rahwan (Eds.), Argumentation in Multi-Agent Systems. XIV, 313 pages. 2006.

Vol. 4048: L. Goble, J.-J.C.. Meyer (Eds.), Deontic Logic and Artificial Normative Systems. X, 273 pages. 2006.

Vol. 4045: D. Barker-Plummer, R. Cox, N. Swoboda (Eds.), Diagrammatic Representation and Inference. XII, 301 pages. 2006.

Vol. 4031: M. Ali, R. Dapoigny (Eds.), Advances in Applied Artificial Intelligence. XXIII, 1353 pages. 2006.

Vol. 4029: L. Rutkowski, R. Tadeusiewicz, L.A. Zadeh, J. Zurada (Eds.), Artificial Intelligence and Soft Computing – ICAISC 2006. XXI, 1235 pages. 2006.

Vol. 4027: H.L. Larsen, G. Pasi, D. Ortiz-Arroyo, T. Andreasen, H. Christiansen (Eds.), Flexible Query Answering Systems. XVIII, 714 pages. 2006.

Vol. 4021: E. André, L. Dybkjær, W. Minker, H. Neumann, M. Weber (Eds.), Perception and Interactive Technologies. XI, 217 pages. 2006.

Vol. 4020: A. Bredenfeld, A. Jacoff, I. Noda, Y. Takahashi (Eds.), RoboCup 2005: Robot Soccer World Cup IX. XVII, 727 pages. 2006.

Vol. 4013: L. Lamontagne, M. Marchand (Eds.), Advances in Artificial Intelligence. XIII, 564 pages. 2006.

Vol. 4012: T. Washio, A. Sakurai, K. Nakajima, H. Takeda, S. Tojo, M. Yokoo (Eds.), New Frontiers in Artificial Intelligence. XIII, 484 pages. 2006.

Vol. 4008: J.C. Augusto, C.D. Nugent (Eds.), Designing Smart Homes. XI, 183 pages. 2006.

Vol. 4005: G. Lugosi, H.U. Simon (Eds.), Learning Theory. XI, 656 pages. 2006.

Vol. 3978: B. Hnich, M. Carlsson, F. Fages, F. Rossi (Eds.), Recent Advances in Constraints. VIII, 179 pages. 2006.

Vol. 3963: O. Dikenelli, M.-P. Gleizes, A. Ricci (Eds.), Engineering Societies in the Agents World VI. XII, 303 pages. 2006.

Vol. 3960: R. Vieira, P. Quaresma, M.d.G.V. Nunes, N.J. Mamede, C. Oliveira, M.C. Dias (Eds.), Computational Processing of the Portuguese Language. XII, 274 pages. 2006.

Vol. 3955: G. Antoniou, G. Potamias, C. Spyropoulos, D. Plexousakis (Eds.), Advances in Artificial Intelligence. XVII, 611 pages. 2006.

Vol. 3949: F. A. Savacı (Ed.), Artificial Intelligence and Neural Networks. IX, 227 pages. 2006.

Vol. 3946: T.R. Roth-Berghofer, S. Schulz, D.B. Leake (Eds.), Modeling and Retrieval of Context. XI, 149 pages. 2006.

Vol. 3944: J. Quiñonero-Candela, I. Dagan, B. Magnini, F. d'Alché-Buc (Eds.), Machine Learning Challenges. XIII, 462 pages. 2006.

Vol. 3930: D.S. Yeung, Z.-Q. Liu, X.-Z. Wang, H. Yan (Eds.), Advances in Machine Learning and Cybernetics. XXI, 1110 pages. 2006.

Vol. 3918: W.K. Ng, M. Kitsuregawa, J. Li, K. Chang (Eds.), Advances in Knowledge Discovery and Data Mining. XXIV, 879 pages. 2006.

Vol. 3913: O. Boissier, J. Padget, V. Dignum, G. Lindemann, E. Matson, S. Ossowski, J.S. Sichman, J. Vázquez-Salceda (Eds.), Coordination, Organizations, Institutions, and Norms in Multi-Agent Systems. XII, 259 pages. 2006.

Vol. 3910: S.A. Brueckner, G.D.M. Serugendo, D. Hales, F. Zambonelli (Eds.), Engineering Self-Organising Systems. XII, 245 pages. 2006.

Vol. 3904: M. Baldoni, U. Endriss, A. Omicini, P. Torroni (Eds.), Declarative Agent Languages and Technologies III. XII, 245 pages. 2006.

Vol. 3900: F. Toni, P. Torroni (Eds.), Computational Logic in Multi-Agent Systems. XVII, 427 pages. 2006.

Vol. 3899: S. Frintrop, VOCUS: A Visual Attention System for Object Detection and Goal-Directed Search. XIV, 216 pages. 2006.

Vol. 3898: K. Tuyls, P.J. 't Hoen, K. Verbeeck, S. Sen (Eds.), Learning and Adaption in Multi-Agent Systems. X, 217 pages. 2006.

Vol. 3891: J.S. Sichman, L. Antunes (Eds.), Multi-Agent-Based Simulation VI. X, 191 pages. 2006.

Vol. 3890: S.G. Thompson, R. Ghanea-Hercock (Eds.), Defence Applications of Multi-Agent Systems. XII, 141 pages. 2006.

Vol. 3885: V. Torra, Y. Narukawa, A. Valls, J. Domingo-Ferrer (Eds.), Modeling Decisions for Artificial Intelligence. XII, 374 pages. 2006.

Vol. 3881: S. Gibet, N. Courty, J.-F. Kamp (Eds.), Gesture in Human-Computer Interaction and Simulation. XIII, 344 pages. 2006.

Vol. 3874: R. Missaoui, J. Schmidt (Eds.), Formal Concept Analysis. X, 309 pages. 2006.

Vol. 3873: L. Maicher, J. Park (Eds.), Charting the Topic Maps Research and Applications Landscape. VIII, 281 pages. 2006.

Vol. 3863: M. Kohlhase (Ed.), Mathematical Knowledge Management. XI, 405 pages. 2006.

Vol. 3862: R.H. Bordini, M. Dastani, J. Dix, A.E.F. Seghrouchni (Eds.), Programming Multi-Agent Systems. XIV, 267 pages. 2006.

Vol. 3849: I. Bloch, A. Petrosino, A.G.B. Tettamanzi (Eds.), Fuzzy Logic and Applications. XIV, 438 pages. 2006.

Vol. 3848: J.-F. Boulicaut, L. De Raedt, H. Mannila (Eds.), Constraint-Based Mining and Inductive Databases. X, 401 pages. 2006.

Vol. 3847: K.P. Jantke, A. Lunzer, N. Spyratos, Y. Tanaka (Eds.), Federation over the Web. X, 215 pages. 2006.

Vol. 3835: G. Sutcliffe, A. Voronkov (Eds.), Logic for Programming, Artificial Intelligence, and Reasoning. XIV, 744 pages. 2005.

Vol. 3830: D. Weyns, H. V.D. Parunak, F. Michel (Eds.), Environments for Multi-Agent Systems II. VIII, 291 pages. 2006.

Vol. 3817: M. Faundez-Zanuy, L. Janer, A. Esposito, A. Satue-Villar, J. Roure, V. Espinosa-Duro (Eds.), Nonlinear Analyses and Algorithms for Speech Processing. XII, 380 pages. 2006.

Vol. 3814: M. Maybury, O. Stock, W. Wahlster (Eds.), Intelligent Technologies for Interactive Entertainment. XV, 342 pages. 2005.

Vol. 3809: S. Zhang, R. Jarvis (Eds.), AI 2005: Advances in Artificial Intelligence. XXVII, 1344 pages. 2005.

Vol. 3808: C. Bento, A. Cardoso, G. Dias (Eds.), Progress in Artificial Intelligence. XVIII, 704 pages. 2005.

Vol. 3802: Y. Hao, J. Liu, Y.-P. Wang, Y.-m. Cheung, H. Yin, L. Jiao, J. Ma, Y.-C. Jiao (Eds.), Computational Intelligence and Security, Part II. XLII, 1166 pages. 2005.

Vol. 3801: Y. Hao, J. Liu, Y.-P. Wang, Y.-m. Cheung, H. Yin, L. Jiao, J. Ma, Y.-C. Jiao (Eds.), Computational Intelligence and Security, Part I. XLI, 1122 pages. 2005.

Vol. 3789: A. Gelbukh, Á. de Albornoz, H. Terashima-Marín (Eds.), MICAI 2005: Advances in Artificial Intelligence. XXVI, 1198 pages. 2005.

Vol. 3782: K.-D. Althoff, A. Dengel, R. Bergmann, M. Nick, T.R. Roth-Berghofer (Eds.), Professional Knowledge Management. XXIII, 739 pages. 2005.

Vol. 3763: H. Hong, D. Wang (Eds.), Automated Deduction in Geometry. X, 213 pages. 2006.

Vol. 3755: G.J. Williams, S.J. Simoff (Eds.), Data Mining. XI, 331 pages. 2006.

Vol. 3735: A. Hoffmann, H. Motoda, T. Scheffer (Eds.), Discovery Science. XVI, 400 pages. 2005.

Vol. 3734: S. Jain, H.U. Simon, E. Tomita (Eds.), Algorithmic Learning Theory. XII, 490 pages. 2005.

Vol. 3721: A.M. Jorge, L. Torgo, P.B. Brazdil, R. Camacho, J. Gama (Eds.), Knowledge Discovery in Databases: PKDD 2005. XXIII, 719 pages. 2005.

Vol. 3720: J. Gama, R. Camacho, P.B. Brazdil, A.M. Jorge, L. Torgo (Eds.), Machine Learning: ECML 2005. XXIII, 769 pages. 2005.

Vol. 3717: B. Gramlich (Ed.), Frontiers of Combining Systems. X, 321 pages. 2005.

Vol. 3702: B. Beckert (Ed.), Automated Reasoning with Analytic Tableaux and Related Methods. XIII, 343 pages. 2005.

Vol. 3698: U. Furbach (Ed.), KI 2005: Advances in Artificial Intelligence. XIII, 409 pages. 2005.

Vol. 3690: M. Pěchouček, P. Petta, L.Z. Varga (Eds.), Multi-Agent Systems and Applications IV. XVII, 667 pages. 2005.

Vol. 3684: R. Khosla, R.J. Howlett, L.C. Jain (Eds.), Knowledge-Based Intelligent Information and Engineering Systems, Part IV. LXXIX, 933 pages. 2005.

Vol. 3683: R. Khosla, R.J. Howlett, L.C. Jain (Eds.), Knowledge-Based Intelligent Information and Engineering Systems, Part III. LXXX, 1397 pages. 2005.

Vol. 3682: R. Khosla, R.J. Howlett, L.C. Jain (Eds.), Knowledge-Based Intelligent Information and Engineering Systems, Part II. LXXIX, 1371 pages. 2005.

Vol. 3681: R. Khosla, R.J. Howlett, L.C. Jain (Eds.), Knowledge-Based Intelligent Information and Engineering Systems, Part I. LXXX, 1319 pages. 2005.

Vol. 3673: S. Bandini, S. Manzoni (Eds.), AI*IA 2005: Advances in Artificial Intelligence. XIV, 614 pages. 2005.

Vol. 3662: C. Baral, G. Greco, N. Leone, G. Terracina (Eds.), Logic Programming and Nonmonotonic Reasoning. XIII, 454 pages. 2005.

Vol. 3661: T. Panayiotopoulos, J. Gratch, R. Aylett, D. Ballin, P. Olivier, T. Rist (Eds.), Intelligent Virtual Agents. XIII, 506 pages. 2005.

Vol. 3658: V. Matoušek, P. Mautner, T. Pavelka (Eds.), Text, Speech and Dialogue. XV, 460 pages. 2005.

Vol. 3651: R. Dale, K.-F. Wong, J. Su, O.Y. Kwong (Eds.), Natural Language Processing – IJCNLP 2005. XXI, 1031 pages. 2005.